Economic Indicators Handbook

Sixth Edition

Economic Indicators Handbook

TIME SERIES • CONVERSIONS • DOCUMENTATION

Sixth Edition

Compiled and Edited by
Arsen J. Darnay

GALE GROUP

THOMSON LEARNING

Detroit • New York • San Diego • San Francisco
Boston • New Haven, Conn. • Waterville, Maine
London • Munich

Arsen J. Darnay, *Editor*

Editorial Code & Data Inc. Staff

Sherae R. Carroll, *Data Entry*

Gale Group Staff

Chris Lopez, *Assistant Editor and Project Coordinator*
Mary Beth Trimper, *Composition Manager*
Evi Seoud, *Assistant Production Manager*
Nekita McKee, *Buyer*

Gale Group
27500 Drake Road
Farmington Hills, MI 48331-3535
ISBN 0-7876-3557-X
Printed in the United States of America

TABLE OF CONTENTS

INTRODUCTION

SUMMARY

Economic Indicators Handbook (EIH) is now in its sixth edition. It presents a wide range of statistical series commonly used for measuring the economy of the United States. Featured are national income and product accounts, including Gross National Product (GNP) and Gross Domestic Product (GDP); the composite indexes of leading, lagging, and coincident indicators and their subcomponents; other cyclic indicators; selected economic series; a comprehensive presentation of the Consumer Price Index (CPI) in the aggregate and for 26 cities; a substantial selection from Producer Price Index (PPI); and selected stock market indexes. *EIH* covers 266 series in this edition; most are shown with detailed subdivisions or in constant and actual dollars so that, in total, 801 tables are presented.

In all cases, where data are available, at least 50 years' worth of data are presented, typically from 1951 to 2001. In many instances, data from the beginning of the series are presented. GNP is shown from 1869, the earliest date for data in *EIH*. GDP is presented from 1929 to 1958 in 1992 dollars, and in detail from 1959 forward. The CPI series begin in 1913. Other series are presented from onset if later than 1951 or from 1951.

EIH features descriptive text; each major category is introduced and brief explanations, including an indication of significance, are provided for each series. Texts and tables are thoroughly indexed.

SIXTH EDITION REVISONS

Data in *EIH* are now updated throughout to show information for 2001. All series have been completely updated. In those instances where the sources have done retrospective revisions, the datasets have been completely replaced. Typically, two years of new data have been added to series that reach back to historical beginnings. All texts have been updated, to the extent necessary, to reflect changes in the series shown.

SCOPE

EIH presents statistical series grouped by major categories.

GNP and GDP. The fundamental measure of the U.S. economy—at least until the fall of 1991—has been GNP. For that reason, *EIH* still begins with a presentation of aggregate GNP beginning with data for the 1869-1928 period and ending with data for 2001. This section is followed by a comprehensive presentation of GDP and all of its components, from 1929 to 1958 at the aggregate level and from 1959 through 2001 at the detailed level.

1999 was the year for one of the government's comprehensive benchmark revisions of the National Income and Product Accounts (NIPA) and thus of the GDP and its components. The revision was completed in 2000. This edition reflects the latest changes and presents summaries of what has changed in this Introduction and in chapter texts.

Constant dollar data are shown in chained dollars for the national accounts. A complete explanation of chained dollars is provided below.

Business Cycle Indicators. The federal government attempts to predict business cycles—recurring brief periods of decline in GDP followed by recovery and periods of growth—by using a number of economic series that lead the economy, coincide with it, or lag it (see Chapter 3). The composite indexes of leading, coincident, and lagging indicators are presented from 1959 to 2001; the series were obtained by special arrangement with The Conference Board, a not-for-profit business research organization. The Conference Board assumed the task of preparing these indicators under a contract with the U.S. Department of Commerce some years ago.

Cyclic Indicators. Not all series classified as cyclic in behavior are included in the leading, coincident, and lagging indexes. A selection of others is presented under headings of Employment; Production and Income; Consumption, Trade, Orders, and Deliveries; Fixed Capital Investment; Inventories and Inventory Investment; Prices, Costs, and Profits; and Money and Credit. The selection was based in part on a review of series normally published in the business press (hence indicating usage by the public) and editorial judgment.

Economic Series. Many statistical measures of the economy are not classified as cyclic in nature and are not used to *predict* but to *measure* economic activity. The series included in *EIH* were, again, selected because they are commonly reported in the press or, in the editor's opinion, provide interesting insight into the functioning of the economy.

Prices. Chapters 6 and 7 present consumer and producer price indexes in considerable detail. The CPI is shown for both "all urban consumers" and the "urban wage earners" categories. Furthermore, major subcomponents categories (food, apparel, housing, etc.) are shown. Data for 26 cities/metro areas are then presented in the same detail. All CPI data are shown back to the earliest year for which they were collected or estimated by the Department of Labor.

The Producer Price Index is presented in Chapter 7 for 120 major categories and subcategories in monthly format; annual average data are also shown.

Selected Stock Market Indexes. The final chapter shows selected index data from the American Stock Exchange, NASDAQ (National Association of Securities Dealers Automated Quotation system), and the New York Stock Exchange. Another stock index series, the Standard & Poor's 500 index—which is used by The Conference Board as a leading indicator—is presented in Chapter 3.

SOURCES

The information included in *EIH* came from the U.S. Department of Commerce, the U.S. Department of Labor, the American Stock Exchange, the National Association of Securities Dealers, and the New York Stock Exchange, and The Conference Board. Data were typically obtained from these organizations in electronic formats.

Most federal data series, of course, are built from multiple sources, public and private. The majority rely on surveys, some of which are voluntary and some of which, such as the censuses of business conducted every five years, are mandated by law. GNP and GDP data; the indicator series built into the leading, coincident, and lagging indexes; and the CPI and PPI all require substantial statistical work by the federal agencies or private organizations that prepare them. They are, in a very real sense, statistical "products" of the agencies (or consortia of agencies): they are built from a diverse number of statistical "raw materials" and the methods of constructing the final series are continuously being refined.

ORGANIZATION AND PRESENTATION

EIH is organized into eight chapters as follows:

Chapter 1 - Gross National Product   Chapter 5 - Economic Series
Chapter 2 - Gross Domestic Product   Chapter 6 - Consumer Price Index
Chapter 3 - Business Cycle Indicators   Chapter 7 - Producer Price Index
Chapter 4 - Cyclic Indicators   Chapter 8 - Stock Market Indexes

A keyword index holds references to text and table contents.

Each chapter begins with an introductory text. The subject to be covered in the chapter is outlined in general terms. A bibliography is provided. Chapters 1, 3, 4, and 5 are further subdivided. Each subdivision is separately introduced. Each series covered is separately discussed under its own heading in the chapter or section introductions.

STATISTICAL CONVENTIONS

Many statistical series presented in *EIH* make use of conventions which may be unfamiliar to the casual user. While most of these are discussed in context in the chapter and section notes, a general discussion of *Indexing, Base Periods, Constant and Current Dollars, Chained Dollars, Annualized Rates*, and *Seasonal Adjustments* is presented here.

Indexing. Statistical information in *EIH* is presented in the form of raw information (dollars, hours, weeks, etc.) or in the form of indexes. Index numbers are used to present information relative to data obtained for a specific period. A typical example is an index defined to have the value of 100 for the average outcome of a series in the year 1992. The following example illustrates the method used.

Year	Raw Value in Dollar	Index Value
1990	345	83.7
1991	356	86.4
1992	412	100.0
1993	436	105.8
1994	489	118.7

In the illustration above, 1992 is "the base period," discussed further below. It is assigned an arbitrary index value. In this case the value is 100, but it can be any number. Indexes of 10 or 50 are also commonly used, but 100 is the usual index base. The index for any year is calculated by the following formula:

(Current Year Raw Data / Base Year Raw Data) x 100.

Changes from one period to another may be calculated in index points or as a percent change. In the example above, the index point change between 1993 and 1994 is 12.9. The percentage change is 12.2, obtained by the formula:

((Current Index / Previous Index) - 1) x 100.

Measuring the percentage change between two index values produces the same result as measuring the percentage change in the raw data for the same periods.

Base Periods. Statistical series expressed as indexes or in constant dollars (see below) have base periods. A base period can be a day, a month, a year, or a range of years. The Consumer Price Index, for instance, is based on the 1982-1984 period; the average prices for these years are defined as 100.

The government periodically changes the base periods of indexes. The year chosen is typically the year of one of the five-year business censuses. The most recent such census was held in 1997. Many series are still expressed with a base of 1987 or 1992. Rebasing of a series (shifting to a more recent base period) is usually associated with a significant reworking of the statistical machinery which produces the numbers; hence there tends to be a time delay between the most recent business census and the base period in use.

Constant and Current Dollars. The measurement of dollar-denominated values from one period to the next can produce inaccurate results, for some purposes, if changes due *only* to increasing or dropping prices are not taken into account. For this reason, many series are reported both in current dollars (also called "actual" dollars) and in constant dollars (also called "real" dollars). Constant dollars are current dollars that have been adjusted for the effects of inflation relative to a base period. Because a base period is used, people sometimes use phrases like "1982 dollars" or "1987 dollars." They mean constant dollars with a 1982 or a 1987 base year. The purchasing power of the dollar in the base year is arbitrarily defined as "real." And today's dollars are adjusted to that value by using series such as the Consumer Price Index and the Producer's Price Index. These indexes record changes in prices by surveying the actual prices charged for identical products and services two periods apart. If the same loaf of bread costs 89 cents in 1991 and 92 cents in 1992, inflation accounts for 3 cents: it took 3 cents more to get the same loaf in the second period. Constant dollar calculations, of course, use a wide range of representative products and services measured in a systematic manner across the nation.

Chained Dollars. A relatively new measurement of national accounts involves the calculation of chain-type indexes. An explanation of what these are and how they work is presented in this chapter under the next heading. In essence, chained dollar indexes work by averaging price changes in the prices of two adjacent periods and using the resulting change from one period to the next as the current dollar deflator. Chain-type indexes are widely used because they deal more accurately with growth and decline. They are used by the majority of other countries for national accounting. They have now been adopted by the Bureau of Economic Analysis for the same purpose. They may eventually be used by the Bureau of Labor Statistics as well in calculating the CPI and the PPI price indexes.

Annualized Rates. National production and income data—as well as some other series—report some figures quarterly at "annualized rates." This means that data developed for the quarter are multiplied by four to show what the year would be like if results in this quarter continued. The data, typically, are seasonally adjusted (see below) before they are expressed at annualized rates.

Seasonal Adjustments. Economic activity is by nature seasonal. More heating oil will be used in the winter, more people seek employment in the summer as college students come home. Retailers sell proportionally more goods in December than in other months. Many series are seasonally adjusted to take such fluctuations into account. Other series are shown as "not seasonally adjusted." Seasonal adjustments are made by statisticians in and out of government by using experience factors developed over time. Data are recalculated using these experience factors so that, for instance, heavy fuel oil sales in the fall and winter are "distributed" evenly across the entire year.

Fixed Year and Chained Dollar Indexing

Statistical data in this book are presented in both fixed year "constant" dollars as well as in "chained" dollars. Each type of indexing is briefly described in this section. Both types of dollars are attempts to make comparisons between two periods accurate (removing the effect of price inflation or deflation). The newer method, based on "chained" dollars, is preferred today becasue it accounts better for "substitution bias," a term that is explained below.

Fixed-Year Indexes

Calculating Fixed-Year Constant Dollars. Why does the government report GDP in both current (actual) dollars and in constant ("real") dollars? The answer is that Americans want to know whether or not GDP has grown or declined; we want to know the "real" change in the "quantity" of the GDP in order to know how the economy is doing. Current dollar measurements do not tell us the *real* change between two periods. The GDP may have grown in dollars, but how much of that is the result of inflation? How much the result of real growth — an increase in the output of goods and services? To see the "real" changes in the economy, we need to remove that portion of the change due only to changes in prices.

A simple way of doing this is to select one year as the base year for measurement and then to apply the prices that prevailed in the base year to the quantities produced in the current year:

Base year price per unit	95.00	1
Current year price per unit	135.00	2
Units produced in current year	15	3
Current dollar results (135 x 15)	2,025	4
Constant dollar results (95 x 15)	1,425	5

In the example above, current dollars of $2,025 are deflated to $1,425 in constant dollars by using *base year prices* and applying them to *current year quantities*.

For large aggregates like the GDP or its components, quantity measures (line 3 above) cannot be obtained conveniently. Instead, as the smallest subcomponents of GDP are added to GDP, price indexes are used to deflate current to constant dollars at the point where the characteristics of the component are still clearly visible, e.g., indexes are applied to Food Consumption Expenditures before the totals are added to Personal Consumption Expenditures.

Price indexes measure change in prices *only*, from one period to the next. Examples are the Consumer Price Index and the Producer Price Index, each of which is built up of many detailed categories. In the example above, the price index for the current year for our unnamed commodity is the current price per unit divided by the base year price per unit:

Price index in current year (135 / 95)	1.421	6
Constant dollar result (2,025 / 1.421)	1,425	7

The constant dollar result can be calculated by dividing current dollars by the index. Notice that line 5 and line 7 produce identical "deflated" values—one by using a price-quantity multiplication, the other by dividing current dollars by a price index.

The actual construction of GDP deflators must, of course, correctly blend many price indexes into a single number. This is done by applying weights to individual indexes. What percentage of total consumption is food? If that percentage is 5.5, the food index contributes only 5.5 percent to the deflator. Weights needed to create accurate deflators are obtained by surveys.

Pros and Cons of the Fixed-Year Measure. The fixed-year constant dollar measure is simple to calculate and is well understood by the public.

The chief disadvantage of the measure is that it distorts results the farther we move from the base year. Another way to put this is that moving the base period forward causes a lower growth rate when the new constant dollar GDP is calculated: "We thought we were growing at 3.5 percent a year; now they tell us it was only 3.3 percent."

This well-known effect, known as the "substitution bias," is due to the natural tendency of the price structure to change. On the whole, products and services that grow most are those with prices that grow least. The inverse is also true. Using the higher "old" prices and applying them to the larger "new" quantities artificially overstates real growth. When the base year is moved forward, the old high prices are replaced by the new low prices; these are applied to the lower old quantities. Now growth between the periods is artificially understated. The following example makes the point arithmetically:

	YEAR 1					YEAR 2				
	Total in Year 1 Dollars D x E	Total in Year 2 Dollars D x J	Total in Current Dollars D x E	Quantity	Price	Total in Year 1 Dollars I x E	Total in Year 2 Dollars I x J	Total in Current Dollars I x J	Quantity	Price
Apples	3.00	6.00	3.00	30	.10	2.00	4.00	4.00	20	.20
Oranges	2.00	2.50	2.00	10	.20	4.00	5.00	5.00	20	.25
Fruit	5.00	8.50	5.00			6.00	9.00	9.00		
Growth						1.20	1.06	1.80		
	A	**B**	**C**	**D**	**E**	**F**	**G**	**H**	**I**	**J**

In the above table, change between Years 1 and 2 in Year 1 dollars is 1.20 and in Year 2 dollars 1.06. These results are due to the shift in the price structure of this mini-economy.

Using either Year 1 or Year 2 dollars is legitimate, despite the obvious distortions. Neither index is more correct than the other. The only "real" measure is in current dollars—because, in reality, price-quantity relationships (including inflationary effects) are inseparable. Constant dollar measures are analytical attempts at isolating quantitative change and are always correct if calculated correctly.

But what if we took the two results above and averaged them? Would that get us closer to a more accurate, less biased measure? The answer is Yes. And that introduces the topic of chained indexes.

Chain-Type Indexes

Chain-type indexes are created by obtaining the geometrical mean of two growth calculations. The first growth value is obtained using Period 1 dollars for both Period 1 and Period 2. The second is obtained using Period 2 dollars in both periods. These are the rates shown in Columns F and G above. The periods must be adjacent (adjacent years, quarters, months). Using the example above, the calculation is:

chained growth value = square root of (1.20 x 1.06)
chained growth value = 1.13

In the example above, growth between Year 1 and Year 2 in chained dollars would be 13 percent (rather than 20 or 6 percent using one valuation period only). Year 2 results in chained dollars would be $5.56 (Year 1 result of $5 times the 1.13 calculated rate).

In more technical terminology, the annual change in real GDP is calculated using the Fisher Ideal Index formula, defined as the geometric mean of a Laspeyres and a Paasche index. Year 2 values in Year 1 prices (Column F) are the Laspeyres index; Year 2 values in Year 2 prices (Column G) are the Paasche index.

How a Chained Index is Created. To create a hypothetical chain-type index, growth rates for each period are calculated using the Fisher Ideal Index formula, as shown above. For a series of GDP (or component) measurements, this will produce individual growth rates of "real" GDP based on the price weights of the year and the year before, as shown below. Note, please, that the growth rates shown are not those between the current dollar values shown but between constant dollar expressions of these values. The actual step of moving from line 2 values to line 3 values is not illustrated. That step requires both unit quantities and prices for each year, as shown in the earlier table for apples and oranges.

	1989	1990	1991	1992	1993	1994	
Assumed Current $ Values	555	580	719	741	778	708	2
Fisher Ideal growth rates (%)	-	13.0	21.1	5.0	4.0	-7.3	3

The percentages in line 3 are next expressed as multipliers by dividing the cells of line 3 by 100 and adding one (the result is shown in line 4 below). Next, the multipliers are "chained," i.e., multiplied together—hence the name of this type of index. Column A is multiplied by Column B, and the result is placed back in Column B. Column B is then multiplied by Column C and the result placed back in Column C. And so on. Results are shown in line 5 below:

	A	B	C	D	E	F	
Expressed as multipliers	1.000	1.130	1.210	1.050	1.040	.927	4
Chained into Index	1.000	1.130	1.367	1.436	1.493	1.384	5

The chained values of line 5 can now be converted into an index of any desired base year. The method is to divide each cell's value by the base year value and to multiply the result by 100. In what follows, two indexes are created with base 1989 (line 6) and 1992 (line 7). Then the dollar values from line 2, above, will be translated into chained dollars of the base year (lines 8 and 9).

Index with 1989 Base	100.0	113.0	136.7	143.6	149.3	138.4	6
Index with 1992 Base	69.7	78.7	95.2	100.0	104.0	96.4	7
Chained (1989) Dollars	555	627	759	797	829	829	8
Chained (1992) Dollars	516	583	705	741	770	714	9

The chained dollar conversions are done by dividing the index with the appropriate base by 100 and multiplying the base year value (line 1 above) by the result. Thus the value of 516 for 1989, in chained (1992) dollars, is obtained by multiplying 741, the 1992 base value, by 0.697, the chained index value for the 1992 base (line 7).

Notice that the dollar magnitudes are different when expressed in different base year dollars. The growth relationships between the dollars, however, remain the same. The base year can be moved at will without affecting the growth relationships. Thus the growth from 1989 to 1990 in either 1989 or 1992 chained dollars is 13 percent. Note, also, that as in the "old days," when fixed year constant dollars were used, so in chained dollar series, the base year's "current" dollars and "chained" dollars are identical.

In preparing this exposition, the author drew heavily on the wisdom presented in two papers in the *Survey of Current Business*. The first of these, by Allan H. Young, is titled "Alternative Measures of Change in Real Output and Prices," Volume 72, Number 4, April 1992, pp. 32-48. The second is by J. Steven Landefeld and Robert P. Parker, titled "Preview of the Comprehensive Revision of the National Income and Product Accounts: BEA's New Featured Measures of Output and Prices," Volume 75, Number 7, July 1995, pp. 31-38. Particularly useful was a note, appended to this article, written by Jack E. Triplett, titled "Note on Calculating Output and Price Indexes." Whatever merits this presentation has are due largely to these experts. Whatever it lacks is due to the author's failure of grasp.

Most Recent NIPA Revisions

This edition of *EIH* reflects the last comprehensive (benchmark) changes in the National Income and Product Accounts (NIPA) in 1999 by the U.S. Department of Commerce. NIPA underlies the GNP and GDP. The 1999 changes were the 11th comprehensive revision of the accounts. Changes were presented in fine detail in the August, September, and October 1999 issues of *Survey of Current Business*. A brief summary of changes is presented below.

The base year for chained dollar estimates was changed form 1992 to 1996. Due to this change, most "constant dollar" series are only available from 1987 forward. Current dollar series, of course, go father back.

Business and government spending on software was reclassified in this revision. Software, treated as an intermediate input before 1999, is now treated as a fixed investment, with a life of 3 to 5 years depending on the type of software involved. This change caused an increase in GDP of around $115 billion (1996).

Other changes, with minor or no effect on GDP as a whole, included the following. Government employee retirement plans are now treated similarly to private pension plans. Profits of private noninsured pension plans are treated in a new manner. Capital transfers (such as grants for highway construction) are treated in conformity with international guidelines. Changes were made to the manner in which mutual fund divided distributions and services are treated. Also changed was the treatment of Federal Insurance Contribution Act refunds, certain payments of Federal direct loan housing programs, and corporate director's fees.

Statistical changes, other than constant dollar rebasing to 1996, involved the use of the 1992 input/output accounts and their 1996 update and a number of improvements and adjustments to inputs and methodologies of deriving GDP or its components.

ACKNOWLEDGMENTS

Economic Indicators Handbook is based on the hard work and intellectual rigor of many individuals in government, academia, associations, and industry. Some of them took of their valuable time to help in the preparation of this book by providing data and patient explanations of sometimes very difficult concepts. In particular, the editor is indebted to the staff of The Conference Board; the staff of the Bureau of Economic Analysis, U.S. Department of Commerce; and staff of the Bureau of Labor Statistics, U.S. Department of Labor. The continuing cooperation of the Media Relations staff of the American Stock Exchange, the research staff of the New York Stock Exchange, and of the computer support folks at National Association of Securities Dealers Automated Quotation System (NASDAQ) is much appreciated.

COMMENTS AND SUGGESTIONS

Comments on *EIH* or suggestion for its improvement are always welcome. Although every effort is made to maintain accuracy, errors may occasionally occur; the editor will be grateful if these are called to his attention. For technical matters, contact the editor directly at (248) 356-6990. For all other matters, please contact:

> Editor
> Economic Indicators Handbook
> Gale Group
> 27500 Drake Road
> Farmington Hills, MI 48331-3535
> Phone: (248) 699-4253

CHAPTER 1

GROSS NATIONAL PRODUCT

GROSS NATIONAL PRODUCT

The Gross National Product (GNP) is the sum of all purchases of goods and services by individuals and government; the value of gross domestic investment, including changes in business inventories; and exports less imports (net exports). GNP is thus a measure of the productivity of the nation. GNP can be summarized by the following formula:

$$GNP = Consumption + Investment + Government + Exports - Imports.$$

Only final purchases are measured to avoid double counting. The value of unfinished goods purchased by companies and not resold as finished product is reflected in changed business inventories.

GNP measures goods and services *produced by labor and property supplied by U.S. residents*. The labor and property may be located *in* the U.S. or abroad. Conversely, goods and services produced by foreign labor and property are excluded, even if located on U.S. soil. The next chapter covers Gross Domestic Product (GDP) which measures goods and services *produced by labor and property located in the U.S.* GDP has been selected by the U.S. Department of Commerce as the new measure of U.S. production, displacing GNP. However, since GNP accounting had been the dominant method until November 1991, GNP tables are provided here for retrospective reference.

Modern GNP reporting began in 1929 and is the product of a comprehensive statistical system (the National Income and Product Accounts, NIPA) managed by the Department of Commerce, Bureau of Economic Analysis (BEA). GNP estimates were extended back to 1909 based on limited statistical sources by the government; and estimates based on even less information have been made back to colonial times. Data in *EIH* are reported from 1929 forward when possible or from whatever year the Bureau of Economic Analysis, Department of Commerce, makes available. In this edition, for instance, data in the revised formats (1999 revisions) are presented back to 1959 only. *EIH* presents those data and also the earlier GNP series back to 1929.

GNP data are *estimates* based on a large number of surveys conducted by the federal government for other purposes or obtained from private industry or association sources. Precise measurement of economic activity on a scale such as that of the United States is virtually impossible; hence partial data, estimates, and statistical methods are necessary to approximate actual economic activity. During the years of the economic censuses, which recur at 5-year intervals, detailed data are collected for many GNP components which serve as "benchmarks" for estimates.

Presentation of Data

The first table is a summary of GNP for the period 1869-1928. Data were obtained, courtesy of the Bureau of Economic Analysis, for aggregate GNP for this period, in actual and in constant (1982) dollars.

The next table presents annual GNP data for the period 1929 through 1958 in current as well as chained 1992 dollars. This table is presented to provide continuity between the historical series and the officially published, complete GNP series which begins in 1959.

Two tables for the GNP by quarters, for the 1959-2001 period follow. The first is in current dollars, the second in chained 1996 dollars. Detailed component tables are not included because the government has now completely shifted emphasis to Gross Domestic Product (GDP), and all data have been restated using GDP definitions.

Historical Data. The historical data are presented in decade averages for the 1869-1878 and the 1879-1888 periods and then annually thereafter to 1928. Data are shown in actual and in constant dollars, permitting the calculation of growth and decline rates year to year. The implicit price deflator, shown in the table, displays the relationship of prices, in a given year, as they compare to those of a base year—in this case 1982. The deflator is calculated by the formula:

(Actual Dollar Value / Constant Dollar Value) x 100.

With the implicit price deflator known, constant dollar value can be calculated, if unknown, by the formula:

(Current Dollar Value x 100) / Implicit Price Deflator.

And current value, if unknown, can be calculated from constant dollar value by the formula:

(Constant Dollar Value / 100) x Implicit Price Deflator.

Annual Data, 1929 through 1958. Not all of the GNP/GDP series are available in 1992 chained dollars back to 1929. Annual data are released by the Bureau of Economic Analysis in electronic format. Chained 1992 data for these early years are called "unpublished" by the BEA because components of the major series are of lower quality than aggregate series. For this reason, only annual totals are shown here. The data are presented here so that a continuous series from historical times to the present is available to the analyst.

Quarterly Data. Data for quarters, when available, represent seasonally adjusted, annualized quarterly estimates. This means that the results for the quarter are projected for the entire year; for example, if 2 million cars were sold in the quarter, the annual rate would be 8 million cars; therefore, the production value of 8 million cars is reflected in that quarter's estimate. Seasonal adjustments are made to reflect conditions that are due to well known, recurring, seasonal phenomena. For example, fuel oil consumption is known to be much higher in winter than in summer; fuel consumption, therefore, is increased in summer quarters and decreased in winter quarters to "smooth" the data. Each quarter, in other words, shows what GNP would be for the entire year if the conditions in that quarter, as adjusted, were to continue for the balance of the year.

Growth or decline between any two quarters is also annualized, showing a compounded growth rate reached by the formula:

(This Quarter / Last Quarter)^4 *- 1 x 100 = percent growth rate of GNP.*

If this quarter is $4,118.9 billion and last quarter was $4,124.1 billion, the formula results in -0.503 percent because the quarterly growth rate was compounded and annualized—rather than a rate of -0.12 percent, which is the simple percentile difference between the two numbers.

Annual Data. Annual figures show final estimates for GNP. Since GNP estimates are revised as better and better data become available, data for recent years are subject to revision and results for the most recent year tend to be preliminary estimates. Annual growth or decline figures show simple percentile changes between the two years reached by the formula:

(This Year / Last Year) - 1 x 100.

If this year is $4,157.3 billion and last year was $4,117.7 billion, the growth is 0.96 percent.

GNP in Constant Dollars. Constant dollars (also referred to as "real" dollars) are used to measure GNP in order to account for inflationary or deflationary price changes; inflation is believed to come about because prices are raised in response to unusually high demand; deflation (a much rarer phenomenon) results when prices drop because demand is soft; in both cases, products or services sold remain unchanged; only prices change; constant dollar expression of GNP permits direct comparison of one period with another. In the entire 1959 to 2000 period, for instance, GNP showed positive growth in every year in actual dollars; measured in constant dollars, the years 1974-75, 1980, 1982, and 1991 showed negative growth.

GNP in Chained (1996) Dollars. Beginning in 1999, the BEA has adopted an indexing method in chained dollar values—values that remove the effect of inflation. Tables using this method of "normalization" are shown in "chained (1996) dollars." A full explanation of this method is presented in the Introduction. In essence, the "chained dollar" measure is a more sensitive indicator of changes in the quantities of dollars reported. For purposes of analysis, they are essentially equivalent to the "constant dollar" indexing methods of the recent past. Thus values expressed in chained (1996) dollars normalize today's ("current") dollars in terms of 1996 purchasing power—but with greater accuracy.

GNP Revisions

Changes in GNP methodologies and allocation of items to national accounts are continuous. These changes typically involve (1) changes in the classification of certain items from one GNP account to another; for example, in 1985, railroad track replacement costs were shifted from business expenditures to investment; (2) the inclusion or exclusion of areas (e.g., Puerto Rico and U.S. territories were excluded from GNP in 1985); and (3) changes in methodology, especially for estimating categories not fully covered by surveys; for example, in 1985, improved adjustments were made for misreporting on tax returns, the so-called "underground economy adjustments." Major changes in recent decades were introduced in 1976, 1980, 1985, 1991, and 1995.

For a full discussion of the 1999 revisions, please consult the August, September, and October 1999 issues of *Survey of Current Business* (reference 4 below). The major 1999 revision was released in December of that year. For a summary of the changes, please consult the Introduction. The changes described there produce *increases* in current-dollar GNP—so that data for earlier years, in revised format, are higher. In other words, the comprehensive revisions of the national income accounts can, in effect, *revise financial history*.

For a bibliography of major and annual changes, see p. 23-30, reference 3, below, and Fall issues of the *Survey of Current Business* (reference 4).

Bibliography

1. Carnes, W. Stansbury and Stephen D. Slifer, *The Atlas of Economic Indicators*. Harper Collins, 1991.

2. U.S. Department of Commerce, Bureau of Economic Analysis. *GNP: An Overview of Source Data and Estimating Methods*. Methodology Paper Series MP-4. Washington, DC: U.S. Government Printing Office, September 1987.

3. U.S. Department of Commerce, Bureau of Economic Analysis. *An Introduction to National Economic Accounting*. Methodology Paper Series MP-1. Washington, DC: U.S. Government Printing Office, March 1985.

4. U.S. Department of Commerce, Bureau of Economic Analysis. *Survey of Current Business*. Superintendent of Documents, U.S. Government Printing Office, Washington, DC 20302.

Historical Gross National Product
1869-1928

Historial GNP estimates, 1869-1928, shown in billions of actual and constant 1982 dollars. 1869-78 and 1879-88 values are decade averages.

Year	Current Dollars (Billions)	Change from Previous Year - %	Constant 82 Dol. (Billions)	Change from Previous Year - %	Implicit Price Deflator 82=100	Year	Current Dollars (Billions)	Change from Previous Year - %	Constant 82 Dol. (Billions)	Change from Previous Year - %	Implicit Price Deflator 82=100
1869-78	7.7	-	84.6	-	9.102	1908	29.0	-8.8	366.4	-8.3	7.915
1879-88	11.7	-	154.5	-	7.573	1909	33.7	16.2	411.3	12.3	8.194
1889	13.1	-	179.5	-	7.298	1910	35.7	5.9	423.3	2.9	8.434
1890	13.7	4.6	192.8	7.4	7.106	1911	36.1	1.1	436.3	3.1	8.274
1891	14.1	2.9	201.6	4.6	6.994	1912	39.7	10.0	457.2	4.8	8.683
1892	15.0	6.4	220.7	9.5	6.797	1913	39.9	0.5	462.4	1.1	8.629
1893	14.4	-4.0	210.4	-4.7	6.844	1914	38.9	-2.5	444.4	-3.9	8.753
1894	13.2	-8.3	204.5	-2.8	6.455	1915	40.3	3.6	439.6	-1.1	9.167
1895	14.5	9.8	228.8	11.9	6.337	1916	48.6	20.6	472.8	7.6	10.279
1896	13.9	-4.1	223.7	-2.2	6.214	1917	60.7	24.9	481.7	1.9	12.601
1897	15.3	10.1	245.0	9.5	6.245	1918	76.8	26.5	570.0	18.3	13.474
1898	16.1	5.2	250.9	2.4	6.417	1919	84.7	10.3	528.3	-7.3	16.033
1899	18.2	13.0	273.7	9.1	6.650	1920	92.2	8.9	487.1	-7.8	18.928
1900	19.6	7.7	281.1	2.7	6.973	1921	70.2	-23.9	452.8	-7.0	15.504
1901	21.7	10.7	313.4	11.5	6.924	1922	74.8	6.6	519.6	14.8	14.396
1902	22.6	4.1	316.4	1.0	7.143	1923	85.9	14.8	576.9	11.0	14.890
1903	24.0	6.2	331.8	4.9	7.233	1924	85.5	-0.5	582.7	1.0	14.673
1904	24.0	0.0	328.2	-1.1	7.313	1925	94.0	9.9	625.0	7.3	15.040
1905	26.3	9.6	352.4	7.4	7.463	1926	97.9	4.1	662.3	6.0	14.782
1906	30.0	14.1	392.9	11.5	7.636	1927	95.8	-2.1	661.2	-0.2	14.489
1907	31.8	6.0	399.5	1.7	7.960	1928	97.7	2.0	667.7	1.0	14.632

Sources: National Bureau of Economic Research and U.S. Department of Commerce. Obtained as handwritten communication from Bureau of Economic Analysis.

Gross National Product - 1929-1958
(Billions of Current and Chained 1992 Dollars)

Annual GNP estimates, 1929-1958, in billions of current and in chained 1992 dollars. Changes from year to year are percentage changes.

Year	Current dollars	% Change	Chained 1992 dollars	% Change
1929	103.8	-	790.9	-
1930	91.1	-12.2	719.7	-9.0
1931	76.4	-16.1	674.0	-6.3
1932	58.6	-23.3	584.3	-13.3
1933	56.2	-4.1	577.3	-1.2
1934	65.9	17.3	641.1	11.1
1935	73.1	10.9	698.4	8.9
1936	83.6	14.4	790.0	13.1
1937	91.8	9.8	831.5	5.3
1938	85.9	-6.4	801.2	-3.6
1939	91.9	7.0	866.5	8.2
1940	101.2	10.1	941.2	8.6
1941	126.7	25.2	1,101.8	17.1
1942	161.6	27.5	1,308.9	18.8
1943	198.3	22.7	1,523.0	16.4
1944	219.7	10.8	1,644.7	8.0
1945	223.2	1.6	1,626.7	-1.1
1946	222.6	-0.3	1,447.7	-11.0
1947	244.6	9.9	1,430.7	-1.2
1948	269.7	10.3	1,491.0	4.2
1949	267.8	-0.7	1,479.8	-0.8
1950	294.6	10.0	1,611.3	8.9
1951	339.7	15.3	1,734.0	7.6
1952	358.6	5.6	1,798.7	3.7
1953	379.7	5.9	1,881.4	4.6
1954	381.3	0.4	1,868.2	-0.7
1955	415.1	8.9	2,001.1	7.1
1956	438.0	5.5	2,040.2	2.0
1957	461.0	5.3	2,078.5	1.9
1958	467.3	1.4	2,057.5	-1.0

Source: "National Income and Product Account Tables: Selected NIPA Tables," *Survey of Current Business*, November 1997, U.S. Department of Commerce, Bureau of Economic Analysis, National Income and Wealth Division. *Notes*: This table includes some series available only in electronic format. A dash (-) indicates no change.

Gross National Product - Actual Dollars

In billions of actual dollars and percent. Quarterly data are seasonally adjusted and annualized. Growth rates for quarters are compound annual growth rates; changes from year to year are percentage changes.

Year	1st Quarter	% Change	2nd Quarter	% Change	3rd Quarter	% Change	4th Quarter	% Change	TOTAL	% Change
1959	498.8	-	512.0	11.0	513.1	0.9	517.3	3.3	510.3	-
1960	530.9	10.9	530.2	-0.5	533.2	2.3	528.1	-3.8	530.6	4.0
1961	532.6	3.5	543.4	8.4	553.9	8.0	567.1	9.9	549.3	3.5
1962	580.5	9.8	588.0	5.3	595.2	5.0	599.2	2.7	590.7	7.5
1963	608.0	6.0	616.5	5.7	629.4	8.6	639.0	6.2	623.2	5.5
1964	655.5	10.7	664.6	5.7	676.3	7.2	681.1	2.9	669.4	7.4
1965	702.0	12.9	714.8	7.5	731.6	9.7	753.6	12.6	725.5	8.4
1966	777.4	13.2	786.7	4.9	799.9	6.9	813.9	7.2	794.5	9.5
1967	824.6	5.4	829.1	2.2	844.4	7.6	860.0	7.6	839.5	5.7
1968	887.3	13.3	911.8	11.5	927.2	6.9	944.1	7.5	917.6	9.3
1969	968.2	10.6	983.2	6.3	1,003.1	8.3	1,011.3	3.3	991.5	8.1
1970	1,024.5	5.3	1,041.0	6.6	1,058.5	6.9	1,060.3	0.7	1,046.1	5.5
1971	1,107.4	19.0	1,128.6	7.9	1,148.1	7.1	1,160.9	4.5	1,136.2	8.6
1972	1,200.8	14.5	1,235.8	12.2	1,261.0	8.4	1,298.8	12.5	1,249.1	9.9
1973	1,349.2	16.4	1,386.1	11.4	1,408.0	6.5	1,449.7	12.4	1,398.2	11.9
1974	1,467.2	4.9	1,504.2	10.5	1,530.3	7.1	1,565.2	9.4	1,516.7	8.5
1975	1,578.8	3.5	1,615.0	9.5	1,673.1	15.2	1,726.7	13.4	1,648.4	8.7
1976	1,786.3	14.5	1,820.0	7.8	1,854.4	7.8	1,903.5	11.0	1,841.0	11.7
1977	1,960.2	12.5	2,027.8	14.5	2,088.7	12.6	2,131.5	8.5	2,052.1	11.5
1978	2,172.9	8.0	2,295.8	24.6	2,360.0	11.7	2,443.3	14.9	2,318.0	13.0
1979	2,497.5	9.2	2,559.8	10.4	2,638.6	12.9	2,701.3	9.8	2,599.3	12.1
1980	2,771.7	10.8	2,773.7	0.3	2,829.2	8.2	2,948.7	18.0	2,830.8	8.9
1981	3,086.0	20.0	3,118.3	4.3	3,217.9	13.4	3,242.0	3.0	3,166.1	11.8
1982	3,230.2	-1.4	3,289.8	7.6	3,313.3	2.9	3,349.2	4.4	3,295.7	4.1
1983	3,412.5	7.8	3,526.2	14.0	3,620.5	11.1	3,728.0	12.4	3,571.8	8.4
1984	3,849.6	13.7	3,945.9	10.4	4,011.0	6.8	4,065.8	5.6	3,968.1	11.1
1985	4,135.4	7.0	4,197.8	6.2	4,275.5	7.6	4,344.8	6.6	4,238.4	6.8
1986	4,397.0	4.9	4,429.6	3.0	4,499.7	6.5	4,547.1	4.3	4,468.3	5.4
1987	4,623.5	6.9	4,710.3	7.7	4,784.0	6.4	4,906.8	10.7	4,756.2	6.4
1988	4,977.8	5.9	5,085.1	8.9	5,167.5	6.6	5,276.6	8.7	5,126.8	7.8
1989	5,397.2	9.5	5,479.1	6.2	5,547.3	3.1	5,614.1	4.9	5,509.4	7.3
1990	5,745.5	9.7	5,825.8	5.7	5,866.1	2.8	5,891.5	1.7	5,832.2	5.9
1991	5,919.1	1.9	5,983.6	4.4	6,034.0	3.4	6,106.8	4.9	6,010.9	3.1
1992	6,208.6	6.8	6,301.1	6.1	6,367.3	4.3	6,492.4	8.1	6,342.3	5.5
1993	6,552.0	3.7	6,620.6	4.3	6,685.1	4.0	6,809.1	7.6	6,666.7	5.1
1994	6,908.5	6.0	7,032.4	7.4	7,111.1	4.6	7,232.6	7.0	7,071.1	6.1
1995	7,318.9	4.9	7,367.9	2.7	7,444.1	4.2	7,552.7	6.0	7,420.9	4.9
1996	7,656.5	5.6	7,800.3	7.7	7,870.5	3.6	7,997.7	6.6	7,831.2	5.5
1997	8,131.8	6.9	8,291.8	8.1	8,397.7	5.2	8,480.4	4.0	8,325.4	6.3
1998	8,634.5	7.5	8,700.3	3.1	8,802.1	4.8	8,975.4	8.1	8,778.1	5.4
1999	9,089.5	5.2	9,157.0	3.0	9,283.8	5.7	9,517.0	10.4	9,261.8	5.5
2000	9,650.7	5.7	9,841.0	8.1	9,919.4	3.2	10,032.1	4.6	9,860.8	6.5
2001	10,131.3	4.0	10,190.9	2.4	10,213.8	0.9	-	-	-	-

Source: The National Income and Product Accounts of the United States, 1959-01. Published on-line, January 2002, Bureau of Economic Analysis, U.S. Department of Commerce, Washington, D.C. - indicates that data are unavailable or zero.

Gross National Product - Chained (1996) Dollars

In billions of chained (1996) dollars and percent. Quarterly data are seasonally adjusted and annualized. Growth rates for quarters are compound annual growth rates; changes from year to year are percentage changes.

Year	1st Quarter	% Change	2nd Quarter	% Change	3rd Quarter	% Change	4th Quarter	% Change	TOTAL	% Change
1959	2,286.2	-	2,345.5	10.8	2,345.5	-	2,354.1	1.5	2,332.8	-
1960	2,405.4	9.0	2,393.9	-1.9	2,398.9	0.8	2,369.3	-4.8	2,391.9	2.5
1961	2,383.7	2.5	2,427.1	7.5	2,467.2	6.8	2,517.5	8.4	2,448.8	2.4
1962	2,561.0	7.1	2,590.3	4.7	2,615.7	4.0	2,625.1	1.4	2,598.0	6.1
1963	2,654.8	4.6	2,688.2	5.1	2,739.8	7.9	2,760.3	3.0	2,710.8	4.3
1964	2,823.2	9.4	2,855.7	4.7	2,894.7	5.6	2,900.5	0.8	2,868.5	5.8
1965	2,974.0	10.5	3,014.6	5.6	3,073.6	8.1	3,144.5	9.6	3,051.7	6.4
1966	3,222.6	10.3	3,234.8	1.5	3,254.7	2.5	3,283.7	3.6	3,248.9	6.5
1967	3,313.4	3.7	3,310.7	-0.3	3,336.6	3.2	3,360.8	2.9	3,330.4	2.5
1968	3,429.2	8.4	3,488.3	7.1	3,513.4	2.9	3,528.1	1.7	3,489.8	4.8
1969	3,582.2	6.3	3,590.6	0.9	3,610.3	2.2	3,593.3	-1.9	3,594.1	3.0
1970	3,589.1	-0.5	3,597.4	0.9	3,628.3	3.5	3,587.6	-4.4	3,600.6	0.2
1971	3,691.3	12.1	3,712.8	2.4	3,738.4	2.8	3,749.2	1.2	3,722.9	3.4
1972	3,823.4	8.2	3,910.0	9.4	3,950.7	4.2	4,018.7	7.1	3,925.7	5.4
1973	4,125.0	11.0	4,168.3	4.3	4,158.0	-1.0	4,192.5	3.4	4,161.0	6.0
1974	4,168.1	-2.3	4,176.5	0.8	4,126.5	-4.7	4,098.0	-2.7	4,142.3	-0.4
1975	4,040.1	-5.5	4,075.6	3.6	4,148.4	7.3	4,206.7	5.7	4,117.7	-0.6
1976	4,304.2	9.6	4,341.2	3.5	4,362.0	1.9	4,398.4	3.4	4,351.4	5.7
1977	4,457.6	5.5	4,535.9	7.2	4,616.4	7.3	4,616.6	0.0	4,556.6	4.7
1978	4,636.0	1.7	4,804.8	15.4	4,854.6	4.2	4,925.8	6.0	4,805.3	5.5
1979	4,939.6	1.1	4,949.3	0.8	4,995.6	3.8	5,011.4	1.3	4,973.9	3.5
1980	5,028.8	1.4	4,922.5	-8.2	4,911.3	-0.9	4,986.3	6.2	4,962.3	-0.2
1981	5,086.4	8.3	5,048.1	-3.0	5,110.5	5.0	5,056.8	-4.1	5,075.4	2.3
1982	4,969.4	-6.7	4,996.9	2.2	4,963.4	-2.7	4,964.8	0.1	4,973.6	-2.0
1983	5,021.5	4.6	5,142.2	10.0	5,233.9	7.3	5,342.0	8.5	5,184.9	4.2
1984	5,452.6	8.5	5,544.3	6.9	5,591.1	3.4	5,627.1	2.6	5,553.8	7.1
1985	5,664.3	2.7	5,710.9	3.3	5,788.6	5.6	5,839.6	3.6	5,750.9	3.5
1986	5,887.3	3.3	5,901.9	1.0	5,959.0	3.9	5,981.7	1.5	5,932.5	3.2
1987	6,027.6	3.1	6,095.8	4.6	6,145.8	3.3	6,254.1	7.2	6,130.8	3.3
1988	6,302.0	3.1	6,372.8	4.6	6,402.0	1.8	6,487.4	5.4	6,391.1	4.2
1989	6,565.6	4.9	6,599.7	2.1	6,633.4	2.1	6,663.4	1.8	6,615.5	3.5
1990	6,743.6	4.9	6,760.8	1.0	6,742.6	-1.1	6,713.3	-1.7	6,740.0	1.9
1991	6,667.4	-2.7	6,692.1	1.5	6,704.7	0.8	6,749.4	2.7	6,703.4	-0.5
1992	6,811.1	3.7	6,873.8	3.7	6,923.3	2.9	7,015.1	5.4	6,905.8	3.0
1993	7,020.9	0.3	7,056.0	2.0	7,092.4	2.1	7,182.1	5.2	7,087.8	2.6
1994	7,249.8	3.8	7,346.3	5.4	7,385.1	2.1	7,476.0	5.0	7,364.3	3.9
1995	7,510.2	1.8	7,528.6	1.0	7,572.3	2.3	7,645.2	3.9	7,564.0	2.7
1996	7,703.1	3.1	7,820.4	6.2	7,853.5	1.7	7,947.9	4.9	7,831.2	3.5
1997	8,025.1	3.9	8,145.6	6.1	8,225.1	4.0	8,276.9	2.5	8,168.1	4.3
1998	8,405.4	6.4	8,448.7	2.1	8,517.6	3.3	8,662.0	7.0	8,508.4	4.2
1999	8,732.9	3.3	8,769.7	1.7	8,861.5	4.3	9,047.9	8.7	8,853.0	4.1
2000	9,089.1	1.8	9,217.7	5.8	9,247.2	1.3	9,311.7	2.8	9,216.4	4.1
2001	9,329.1	0.7	9,335.5	0.3	9,304.9	-1.3	-	-	-	-

Source: The National Income and Product Accounts of the United States, 1959-01. Published on-line, January 2002, Bureau of Economic Analysis, U.S. Department of Commerce, Washington, D.C. - indicates that data are unavailable or zero.

CHAPTER 2

GROSS DOMESTIC PRODUCT

GROSS DOMESTIC PRODUCT

In December 1999, the U.S. Department of Commerce's Bureau of Economic Analysis (BEA) introduced comprehensive revisions to the National Income and Product Accounts (NIPA) as further discussed below. The net effect of the 1999 NIPA revisions was that GDP was *increased* retrospectively and the accuracy of the GDP improved by shifting from 1992 to 1996 chained dollars to index quantitative changes in GDP and its components.

GDP versus GNP

The GDP and GNP differ in the following manner:

GNP measures goods and services produced by labor and property *supplied* by U.S. residents—wherever the goods and services are produced.

GDP measures goods and services produced by labor and property *located* in the U.S.—regardless of the nationality of the persons supplying the labor and property.

The difference between the two measures is *net factor income*; this is income produced by U.S. residents abroad less income produced by foreign residents in the United States. GNP is a better measure of *income* available to U.S. citizens by reason of their contribution to production. Savings are naturally expressed in relation to GNP; and estimating the availability of total resources (e.g., for education) is more appropriately made by looking at GNP.

GDP is a better measurement of *production* within the borders of the United States.

BEA's reasons for the shift may be summarized as follows:

1. GDP is the "appropriate measure for much of the short-term monitoring and analysis of the U.S. economy." It is "consistent in coverage with indicators such as employment, productivity, industry output, and investment in equipment and structures."

2. GDP is the measuring unit used by other countries; hence country-to-country comparisons are easier. The U.S., in fact, was late in adopting the international System of National Accounts, the set of international guidelines for economic accounting.

3. The GDP measure makes quarterly estimates more accurate because BEA need not estimate factor income (which is received late and requires many adjustments for exchange rates, inflation, etc.) to obtain measures of the economy.

The 1999 Benchmark Revision

In 1999, BEA undertook its 11th comprehensive, benchmark revision of the National Income and Product Accounts. The changes are fully documented in the August, September, and November issues of the *Survey of Current Business* (reference 3, below). What followis is a brief highlighting of the changes:

The base year for the constant dollar estimates has been changed from 1992 to 1996.

Business and government expenditures on software have been reclassified as fixed investment. This caused GDP to rise slightly.

Changes have been made in the treatment of government retirement plans, private pension plan profits, capital transfers, mutual fund distributions of dividends, Federal Insurance Contribution Act refunds, certain payments of Federal direct loan housing programs, and corporate directors' fees.

The 1992 Input-Output table, as revised in 1996, has been incorporated, replacing the 1987 Input-Output table.

Numerous other statistical changes and improvements have been implemented.

Presentation of Data

BEA has issued its revised GDP data from 1959 to 2001. The complete GDP series are shown for this period only. Annual data from 1929 through 1958 are also shown in this edition.

The chapter consists of the 1929-1958 annual totals for GDP in actual and chained (1992) dollars and data for GDP and 24 series in actual and chained (1996) dollars for 1959-2001. In the chained series, many data series begin in 1987. Explanatory texts are provided for subsections on Personal Consumption Expenditures, Gross Private Domestic Investment, Net Exports of Goods and Services, and Government Purchases.

Uses of GDP

Since 1991, the GDP is used as the instrument for measuring the output of the U.S. economy as a whole (its magnitude, growth, or decline) and to determine the economic processes or mechanisms which accounts for the national product (what proportion of it is accounted for by government spending, investment in structures and capital goods, by personal consumption expenditures—and subcategories of these such as durable goods, nondurable goods, services, etc.).

GDP, Business Cycles, and Markets. The best-known use of GDP is as an indicator of economic growth or decline. A sustained period of decline in real GDP is defined as a recession. A sustained period of growth is called an expansion. The period from the trough of a recession to the peak of an expansion is a business cycle. Various economic indicators, covered in this part of *EIH*, have in the past proved capable of predicting the onset of recessions and recoveries.

Since recession invariably means increased unemployment, dropping demand, and slowing production . . . and rapid expansions can result in shortages and inflation, GDP is closely watched by government and private sector alike. Stock and bond market behavior is closely correlated with GDP's behavior as well: the stock market tends to rise and decline with GDP; the bond market behaves "counter cyclically," meaning that it rises when GDP drops and drops when GDP rises.

Bibliography

1. U.S. Department of Commerce. Bureau of Economic Analysis. *An Introduction to National Economic Accounting*. Methodology Paper Series MP-1. Washington, DC: U.S. Government Printing Office, March 1985.

2. U.S. Department of Commerce. Bureau of Economic Analysis. *GNP: An Overview of Source Data and Estimating Methods*. Methodology Paper Series MP-4. Washington, DC: U.S. Government Printing Office, September 1987.

3. U.S. Department of Commerce. Bureau of Economic Analysis. *Survey of Current Business*. Superintendent of Documents, U.S. Government Printing Office, Washington, DC 20302.

Gross Domestic Product - 1929-1958
(Billions of Current and Chained 1992 Dollars)

Annual GDP estimates, 1929-1958, in billions of current and in chained 1992 dollars. Changes from year to year are percentage changes.

Year	Current dollars	% Change	Chained 1992 dollars	% Change
1929	104.6	-	796.8	-
1930	91.8	-12.2	725.4	-9.0
1931	76.9	-16.2	678.5	-6.5
1932	58.9	-23.4	588.0	-13.3
1933	56.5	-4.1	580.3	-1.3
1934	66.1	17.0	643.7	10.9
1935	73.5	11.2	701.4	9.0
1936	83.9	14.1	792.4	13.0
1937	92.2	9.9	835.0	5.4
1938	86.3	-6.4	804.9	-3.6
1939	92.3	7.0	870.3	8.1
1940	101.6	10.1	944.2	8.5
1941	127.2	25.2	1,105.9	17.1
1942	162.1	27.4	1,312.7	18.7
1943	198.7	22.6	1,526.3	16.3
1944	220.2	10.8	1,648.2	8.0
1945	223.5	1.5	1,629.3	-1.1
1946	223.3	-0.1	1,452.0	-10.9
1947	245.8	10.1	1,437.0	-1.0
1948	271.2	10.3	1,498.8	4.3
1949	269.1	-0.8	1,486.8	-0.8
1950	296.1	10.0	1,619.1	8.9
1951	341.7	15.4	1,743.7	7.7
1952	360.7	5.6	1,809.0	3.7
1953	381.7	5.8	1,891.0	4.5
1954	383.4	0.4	1,878.6	-0.7
1955	417.7	8.9	2,012.9	7.1
1956	440.9	5.6	2,053.2	2.0
1957	464.2	5.3	2,092.4	1.9
1958	470.1	1.3	2,069.2	-1.1

Source: "National Income and Product Account Tables: Selected NIPA Tables," *Survey of Current Business*, November 1997, U.S. Department of Commerce, Bureau of Economic Analysis, National Income and Wealth Division. *Notes*: This table includes some series available only in electronic format. A dash (-) indicates no change.

Gross Domestic Product - Actual Dollars

In billions of actual dollars and percent. Quarterly data are seasonally adjusted and annualized. Growth rates for quarters are compound annual growth rates; changes from year to year are percentage changes.

Year	1st Quarter	% Change	2nd Quarter	% Change	3rd Quarter	% Change	4th Quarter	% Change	TOTAL	% Change
1959	496.1	-	509.2	11.0	510.2	0.8	514.2	3.2	507.4	-
1960	527.9	11.1	527.1	-0.6	529.9	2.1	524.6	-3.9	527.4	3.9
1961	528.9	3.3	539.9	8.6	550.3	7.9	563.4	9.9	545.7	3.5
1962	576.8	9.9	583.9	5.0	591.0	5.0	594.4	2.3	586.5	7.5
1963	603.4	6.2	612.1	5.9	624.9	8.6	634.3	6.2	618.7	5.5
1964	650.4	10.5	659.6	5.8	671.2	7.2	676.3	3.1	664.4	7.4
1965	696.5	12.5	709.0	7.4	726.2	10.1	748.7	13.0	720.1	8.4
1966	772.3	13.2	781.5	4.9	794.8	7.0	808.6	7.1	789.3	9.6
1967	819.3	5.4	823.9	2.3	838.7	7.4	854.4	7.7	834.1	5.7
1968	881.4	13.3	905.7	11.5	920.9	6.9	937.8	7.5	911.5	9.3
1969	961.9	10.7	977.0	6.4	997.2	8.5	1,005.3	3.3	985.3	8.1
1970	1,018.2	5.2	1,034.4	6.5	1,051.9	6.9	1,054.2	0.9	1,039.7	5.5
1971	1,099.9	18.5	1,120.6	7.7	1,140.8	7.4	1,153.1	4.4	1,128.6	8.6
1972	1,192.5	14.4	1,227.5	12.3	1,252.0	8.2	1,289.7	12.6	1,240.4	9.9
1973	1,338.4	16.0	1,374.4	11.2	1,394.1	5.9	1,435.3	12.4	1,385.5	11.7
1974	1,450.0	4.2	1,487.6	10.8	1,514.8	7.5	1,551.6	10.1	1,501.0	8.3
1975	1,567.2	4.1	1,603.1	9.5	1,659.9	14.9	1,710.5	12.8	1,635.2	8.9
1976	1,770.3	14.7	1,803.1	7.6	1,837.0	7.7	1,885.3	10.9	1,823.9	11.5
1977	1,939.1	11.9	2,006.6	14.7	2,067.5	12.7	2,112.4	9.0	2,031.4	11.4
1978	2,150.4	7.4	2,276.6	25.6	2,338.5	11.3	2,418.0	14.3	2,295.9	13.0
1979	2,470.9	9.0	2,529.3	9.8	2,601.5	11.9	2,663.8	9.9	2,566.4	11.8
1980	2,732.9	10.8	2,736.9	0.6	2,793.6	8.5	2,918.8	19.2	2,795.6	8.9
1981	3,052.6	19.6	3,086.2	4.5	3,183.5	13.2	3,203.1	2.5	3,131.3	12.0
1982	3,193.8	-1.2	3,248.9	7.1	3,278.6	3.7	3,315.6	4.6	3,259.2	4.1
1983	3,378.5	7.8	3,489.6	13.8	3,582.9	11.1	3,688.8	12.4	3,534.9	8.5
1984	3,813.4	14.2	3,909.4	10.5	3,974.7	6.9	4,033.5	6.1	3,932.7	11.3
1985	4,109.7	7.8	4,170.1	6.0	4,252.9	8.2	4,319.3	6.4	4,213.0	7.1
1986	4,375.3	5.3	4,415.2	3.7	4,483.4	6.3	4,537.5	4.9	4,452.9	5.7
1987	4,612.3	6.8	4,695.8	7.4	4,770.2	6.5	4,891.6	10.6	4,742.5	6.5
1988	4,957.0	5.5	5,066.5	9.1	5,151.5	6.9	5,258.3	8.6	5,108.3	7.7
1989	5,379.0	9.5	5,461.7	6.3	5,527.5	4.9	5,588.0	4.5	5,489.1	7.5
1990	5,720.8	9.9	5,800.0	5.7	5,844.9	3.1	5,847.3	0.2	5,803.2	5.7
1991	5,886.3	2.7	5,962.0	5.2	6,015.9	3.7	6,080.7	4.4	5,986.2	3.2
1992	6,183.6	6.9	6,276.6	6.2	6,345.8	4.5	6,469.8	8.0	6,318.9	5.6
1993	6,521.6	3.2	6,596.7	4.7	6,655.5	3.6	6,795.5	8.7	6,642.3	5.1
1994	6,887.8	5.5	7,015.7	7.6	7,096.0	4.7	7,217.7	7.0	7,054.3	6.2
1995	7,297.5	4.5	7,342.6	2.5	7,432.8	5.0	7,529.3	5.3	7,400.5	4.9
1996	7,629.6	5.4	7,782.7	8.3	7,859.0	4.0	7,981.4	6.4	7,813.2	5.6
1997	8,124.2	7.4	8,279.8	7.9	8,390.9	5.5	8,478.6	4.2	8,318.4	6.5
1998	8,627.8	7.2	8,697.3	3.3	8,816.5	5.6	8,984.5	7.8	8,781.5	5.6
1999	9,093.1	4.9	9,161.4	3.0	9,297.4	6.1	9,522.5	10.0	9,268.6	5.5
2000	9,668.7	6.3	9,857.6	8.0	9,937.5	3.3	10,027.9	3.7	9,872.9	6.5
2001	10,141.7	4.6	10,202.6	2.4	10,224.9	0.9	-	-	-	-

Source: "National Income and Product Account Tables: Selected NIPA Tables," *Survey of Current Business*, January 2002, U.S. Department of Commerce, Bureau of Economic Analysis, National Income and Wealth Division. Data downloaded from www.stat.usa.gov. A dash (-) indicates that no data are available.

Gross Domestic Product - Chained (1996) Dollars

In billions of chained (1996) dollars and percent. Quarterly data are seasonally adjusted and annualized. Growth rates for quarters are compound annual growth rates; changes from year to year are percentage changes.

Year	1st Quarter	% Change	2nd Quarter	% Change	3rd Quarter	% Change	4th Quarter	% Change	TOTAL	% Change
1959	2,273.0	-	2,332.4	10.9	2,331.4	-0.2	2,339.1	1.3	2,319.0	-
1960	2,391.0	9.2	2,379.2	-2.0	2,383.6	0.7	2,352.9	-5.1	2,376.7	2.5
1961	2,366.5	2.3	2,410.8	7.7	2,450.4	6.7	2,500.4	8.4	2,432.0	2.3
1962	2,544.0	7.2	2,571.5	4.4	2,596.8	4.0	2,603.3	1.0	2,578.9	6.0
1963	2,634.1	4.8	2,668.4	5.3	2,719.6	7.9	2,739.4	2.9	2,690.4	4.3
1964	2,800.5	9.2	2,833.8	4.8	2,872.0	5.5	2,879.5	1.0	2,846.5	5.8
1965	2,950.1	10.2	2,989.9	5.5	3,050.7	8.4	3,123.6	9.9	3,028.5	6.4
1966	3,201.1	10.3	3,213.2	1.5	3,233.6	2.6	3,261.8	3.5	3,227.5	6.6
1967	3,291.8	3.7	3,289.7	-0.3	3,313.5	2.9	3,338.3	3.0	3,308.3	2.5
1968	3,406.2	8.4	3,464.8	7.1	3,489.2	2.8	3,504.1	1.7	3,466.1	4.8
1969	3,558.3	6.3	3,567.6	1.0	3,588.3	2.3	3,571.4	-1.9	3,571.4	3.0
1970	3,566.5	-0.5	3,573.9	0.8	3,605.2	3.5	3,566.5	-4.2	3,578.0	0.2
1971	3,666.1	11.6	3,686.2	2.2	3,714.5	3.1	3,723.8	1.0	3,697.7	3.3
1972	3,796.9	8.1	3,883.8	9.5	3,922.3	4.0	3,990.5	7.1	3,898.4	5.4
1973	4,092.3	10.6	4,133.3	4.1	4,117.0	-1.6	4,151.1	3.4	4,123.4	5.8
1974	4,119.3	-3.0	4,130.4	1.1	4,084.5	-4.4	4,062.0	-2.2	4,099.0	-0.6
1975	4,010.0	-5.0	4,045.2	3.6	4,115.4	7.1	4,167.2	5.1	4,084.4	-0.4
1976	4,266.1	9.8	4,301.5	3.4	4,321.9	1.9	4,357.4	3.3	4,311.7	5.6
1977	4,410.5	5.0	4,489.8	7.4	4,570.6	7.4	4,576.1	0.5	4,511.8	4.6
1978	4,588.9	1.1	4,765.7	16.3	4,811.7	3.9	4,876.0	5.5	4,760.6	5.5
1979	4,888.3	1.0	4,891.4	0.3	4,926.2	2.9	4,942.6	1.3	4,912.1	3.2
1980	4,958.9	1.3	4,857.8	-7.9	4,850.3	-0.6	4,936.6	7.3	4,900.9	-0.2
1981	5,032.5	8.0	4,997.3	-2.8	5,056.8	4.8	4,997.1	-4.6	5,021.0	2.5
1982	4,914.3	-6.5	4,935.5	1.7	4,912.1	-1.9	4,915.6	0.3	4,919.3	-2.0
1983	4,972.4	4.7	5,089.8	9.8	5,180.4	7.3	5,286.8	8.5	5,132.3	4.3
1984	5,402.3	9.0	5,493.8	6.9	5,541.3	3.5	5,583.1	3.1	5,505.2	7.3
1985	5,629.7	3.4	5,673.8	3.2	5,758.6	6.1	5,806.0	3.3	5,717.1	3.8
1986	5,858.9	3.7	5,883.3	1.7	5,937.9	3.8	5,969.5	2.1	5,912.4	3.4
1987	6,013.3	3.0	6,077.2	4.3	6,128.1	3.4	6,234.4	7.1	6,113.3	3.4
1988	6,275.9	2.7	6,349.8	4.8	6,382.3	2.1	6,465.2	5.3	6,368.4	4.2
1989	6,543.8	5.0	6,579.4	2.2	6,610.6	1.9	6,633.5	1.4	6,591.8	3.5
1990	6,716.3	5.1	6,731.7	0.9	6,719.4	-0.7	6,664.2	-3.2	6,707.9	1.8
1991	6,631.4	-2.0	6,668.5	2.3	6,684.9	1.0	6,720.9	2.2	6,676.4	-0.5
1992	6,783.3	3.8	6,846.8	3.8	6,899.7	3.1	6,990.6	5.4	6,880.0	3.0
1993	6,988.7	-0.1	7,031.2	2.5	7,062.0	1.8	7,168.7	6.2	7,062.6	2.7
1994	7,229.4	3.4	7,330.2	5.7	7,370.2	2.2	7,461.1	5.0	7,347.7	4.0
1995	7,488.7	1.5	7,503.3	0.8	7,561.4	3.1	7,621.9	3.2	7,543.8	2.7
1996	7,676.4	2.9	7,802.9	6.8	7,841.9	2.0	7,931.3	4.6	7,813.2	3.6
1997	8,016.4	4.4	8,131.9	5.9	8,216.6	4.2	8,272.9	2.8	8,159.5	4.4
1998	8,396.3	6.1	8,442.9	2.2	8,528.5	4.1	8,667.9	6.7	8,508.9	4.3
1999	8,733.5	3.1	8,771.2	1.7	8,871.5	4.7	9,049.9	8.3	8,856.5	4.1
2000	9,102.5	2.3	9,229.4	5.7	9,260.1	1.3	9,303.9	1.9	9,224.0	4.1
2001	9,334.5	1.3	9,341.7	0.3	9,310.4	-1.3	-	-	-	-

Source: "National Income and Product Account Tables: Selected NIPA Tables," *Survey of Current Business*, January 2002, U.S. Department of Commerce, Bureau of Economic Analysis, National Income and Wealth Division. Data downloaded from www.stat.usa.gov. A dash (-) indicates that no data are available.

PERSONAL CONSUMPTION EXPENDITURES
Component of Gross Domestic Product

Personal Consumption Expenditures is the largest component of Gross Domestic Product (GDP). In 2000, it accounted for 67.8 percent of real GDP. The measure includes all expenditures by individuals on goods and services; goods are divided into durable and nondurable goods; services are reported as a single category.

The category is labeled "personal" consumption because it reflects all purchases by individuals. The category also incorporates goods and services that the private sector purchases in order to make final products. Paper clips purchased by an automobile producers, for instance, are accounted for in the ultimate price of cars sold to consumers. The measure excludes government purchases of goods and services and private purchases of goods (such as tooling) which are considered to be capital investments.

Note that Personal Consumption Expenditures do *not* include imported goods; these are measured as a separate category in the national accounts.

Sources for the data included in Personal Consumption Expenditures are many and varied. Typically, different sources are used for "benchmark" years (the years of the economic censuses), for other years, and for the most recent period in order to obtain the best and most accurate information. Where partial data only are available, estimates are made using a variety of procedures, including judgement based on trends.

All explanations are provided in this section, followed by tables showing Personal Consumption Expenditure totals and tables showing the subcomponents of the measure. Each item is shown in actual and in chained (1996) dollars.

Durable and Nondurable Goods

The Bureau of Economic Affairs bases its estimates on six distinct categories, each handled in a different way (reference 1). Most goods are based on census surveys in benchmark years and on annual and monthly retail surveys conducted in other years by the Census Bureau. Other distinct categories, using distinct estimating methodologies, are new trucks, new and used autos, gasoline and oil, and food furnished employees (including the military).

In 2000, durable goods accounted for 9.7 percent and nondurable goods for 20.1 percent of real GDP. Durable goods are products expected to last three years or longer; nondurables for a lesser time period.

Services

The category (38.2 percent of GDP in 2000) measures expenditures on services by individuals. The grouping of categories includes (1) rent paid for housing; (2) medical services; (3) expenditures on education from whatever sources; (4) financial, banking, brokerage services; (5) insurance, hospital expenses, religious activities, cable TV, utilities, and local transportation; (6) water and sanitary services; lotteries, (7) foreign travel by U.S. citizens less foreign visitors' spending in the U.S., and (8) a variety of other services, including repairs, tools, club memberships, etc. Estimating methods differ for each of these groupings.

The Services category of Personal Consumption Expenditures should not be viewed as equivalent to the "services" sector of the economy. The category includes rentals, insurance, banking, and financial services, which are classified elsewhere in the Standard Industrial Classification (SIC) system or the North American Industry Classification System (NAICS). The category also excludes services purchased by corporations and by government; services purchased by the private sector are "hidden" in the price of goods sold or services rendered; those purchased by government appear under the governmental category.

Presentation of Data

Data are shown from 1959 to 2001 in quarterly and in annual increments. Changes from one period to the next are shown. Changes from quarter to quarter are annualized, compounded growth rates as explained in the previous section on Gross National Product. Changes from year to year are simple percentile changes.

Analytical Uses

Personal consumption expenditures measure the allocation of individual resources between consumable products (food, clothing, etc.), durable goods (automobiles, appliances, etc.), and services (medical, entertainment, etc.) over time. As in all GDP series, significance appears when results for different periods are compared. Nondurable goods are the most essential; durable goods purchases can be deferred. Growth in one and decline in the other can thus signal a lack of consumer confidence. Strong growth in durables output, conversely, shows confidence in the future. The shift of expenditures from goods to services or from services to goods indicates, over time, changes in economic structure.

Gross Domestic Product

Personal consumption expenditures: Total - Actual Dollars

In billions of actual dollars and percent. Quarterly data are seasonally adjusted and annualized. Growth rates for quarters are compound annual growth rates; changes from year to year are percentage changes.

Year	1st Quarter	% Change	2nd Quarter	% Change	3rd Quarter	% Change	4th Quarter	% Change	TOTAL	% Change
1959	310.4	-	316.5	8.1	321.7	6.7	323.9	2.8	318.1	-
1960	327.4	4.4	333.3	7.4	333.3	-	335.2	2.3	332.3	4.5
1961	335.7	0.6	340.6	6.0	343.5	3.4	350.8	8.8	342.7	3.1
1962	356.0	6.1	361.6	6.4	365.6	4.5	371.8	7.0	363.8	6.2
1963	375.4	3.9	379.5	4.4	386.5	7.6	391.1	4.8	383.1	5.3
1964	400.7	10.2	408.6	8.1	417.5	9.0	420.1	2.5	411.7	7.5
1965	430.9	10.7	437.9	6.7	447.2	8.8	461.3	13.2	444.3	7.9
1966	471.8	9.4	477.0	4.5	486.2	7.9	492.0	4.9	481.8	8.4
1967	496.3	3.5	505.5	7.6	512.7	5.8	520.3	6.1	508.7	5.6
1968	538.1	14.4	551.9	10.7	568.0	12.2	576.9	6.4	558.7	9.8
1969	588.9	8.6	600.2	7.9	610.5	7.0	622.5	8.1	605.5	8.4
1970	633.7	7.4	643.8	6.5	655.8	7.7	662.5	4.1	648.9	7.2
1971	681.7	12.1	695.7	8.5	708.0	7.3	724.3	9.5	702.4	8.2
1972	741.7	10.0	759.9	10.2	778.2	10.0	803.1	13.4	770.7	9.7
1973	827.9	12.9	843.1	7.5	861.9	9.2	877.2	7.3	852.5	10.6
1974	895.4	8.6	923.6	13.2	951.4	12.6	959.2	3.3	932.4	9.4
1975	984.4	10.9	1,013.7	12.4	1,047.2	13.9	1,076.0	11.5	1,030.3	10.5
1976	1,111.1	13.7	1,131.1	7.4	1,160.8	10.9	1,196.1	12.7	1,149.8	11.6
1977	1,231.6	12.4	1,260.3	9.7	1,291.9	10.4	1,329.9	12.3	1,278.4	11.2
1978	1,359.8	9.3	1,419.0	18.6	1,452.1	9.7	1,490.6	11.0	1,430.4	11.9
1979	1,531.5	11.4	1,566.9	9.6	1,620.1	14.3	1,666.5	12.0	1,596.3	11.6
1980	1,716.0	12.4	1,719.3	0.8	1,777.1	14.1	1,839.2	14.7	1,762.9	10.4
1981	1,893.1	12.2	1,926.7	7.3	1,970.5	9.4	1,986.4	3.3	1,944.2	10.3
1982	2,023.0	7.6	2,048.8	5.2	2,093.7	9.1	2,151.7	11.5	2,079.3	6.9
1983	2,188.4	7.0	2,260.0	13.7	2,319.4	10.9	2,377.9	10.5	2,286.4	10.0
1984	2,427.1	8.5	2,481.4	9.3	2,517.1	5.9	2,568.0	8.3	2,498.4	9.3
1985	2,632.9	10.5	2,682.1	7.7	2,749.8	10.5	2,785.6	5.3	2,712.6	8.6
1986	2,825.1	5.8	2,857.0	4.6	2,928.6	10.4	2,970.0	5.8	2,895.2	6.7
1987	3,011.4	5.7	3,081.5	9.6	3,145.5	8.6	3,182.9	4.8	3,105.3	7.3
1988	3,259.8	10.0	3,319.5	7.5	3,387.0	8.4	3,460.1	8.9	3,356.6	8.1
1989	3,511.8	6.1	3,572.9	7.1	3,626.9	6.2	3,675.1	5.4	3,596.7	7.2
1990	3,754.8	9.0	3,806.2	5.6	3,871.6	7.1	3,893.4	2.3	3,831.5	6.5
1991	3,904.6	1.2	3,958.6	5.6	3,998.2	4.1	4,023.6	2.6	3,971.2	3.6
1992	4,123.1	10.3	4,171.5	4.8	4,225.7	5.3	4,318.3	9.1	4,209.7	6.0
1993	4,350.6	3.0	4,421.3	6.7	4,488.2	6.2	4,558.7	6.4	4,454.7	5.8
1994	4,613.8	4.9	4,677.5	5.6	4,753.0	6.6	4,821.3	5.9	4,716.4	5.9
1995	4,868.6	4.0	4,943.7	6.3	5,005.2	5.1	5,058.4	4.3	4,969.0	5.4
1996	5,130.5	5.8	5,218.0	7.0	5,263.7	3.5	5,337.9	5.8	5,237.5	5.4
1997	5,429.9	7.1	5,470.8	3.0	5,575.9	7.9	5,640.6	4.7	5,529.3	5.6
1998	5,719.9	5.7	5,820.0	7.2	5,895.1	5.3	5,989.1	6.5	5,856.0	5.9
1999	6,080.7	6.3	6,197.1	7.9	6,298.4	6.7	6,424.7	8.3	6,250.2	6.7
2000	6,581.9	10.2	6,674.9	5.8	6,785.5	6.8	6,871.4	5.2	6,728.4	7.7
2001	6,977.6	6.3	7,044.6	3.9	7,057.6	0.7	-	-	-	-

Source: "National Income and Product Account Tables: Selected NIPA Tables," *Survey of Current Business*, January 2002, U.S. Department of Commerce, Bureau of Economic Analysis, National Income and Wealth Division. Data downloaded from www.stat.usa.gov. A dash (-) indicates that no data are available.

Gross Domestic Product

Personal consumption expenditures: Total - Chained (1996) Dollars

In billions of chained (1996) dollars and percent. Quarterly data are seasonally adjusted and annualized. Growth rates for quarters are compound annual growth rates; changes from year to year are percentage changes.

Year	1st Quarter	% Change	2nd Quarter	% Change	3rd Quarter	% Change	4th Quarter	% Change	TOTAL	% Change
1959	1,445.2	-	1,468.2	6.5	1,483.8	4.3	1,485.6	0.5	1,470.7	-
1960	1,499.2	3.7	1,518.1	5.1	1,512.1	-1.6	1,513.5	0.4	1,510.8	2.7
1961	1,512.8	-0.2	1,535.2	6.1	1,542.9	2.0	1,574.2	8.4	1,541.2	2.0
1962	1,590.6	4.2	1,609.9	4.9	1,622.9	3.3	1,645.9	5.8	1,617.3	4.9
1963	1,657.1	2.7	1,673.0	3.9	1,695.7	5.5	1,710.0	3.4	1,684.0	4.1
1964	1,743.8	8.1	1,775.0	7.4	1,807.8	7.6	1,812.8	1.1	1,784.8	6.0
1965	1,852.5	9.1	1,873.2	4.5	1,905.3	7.0	1,959.3	11.8	1,897.6	6.3
1966	1,988.6	6.1	1,994.0	1.1	2,016.6	4.6	2,025.1	1.7	2,006.1	5.7
1967	2,037.3	2.4	2,064.6	5.5	2,075.2	2.1	2,087.9	2.5	2,066.2	3.0
1968	2,136.2	9.6	2,169.6	6.4	2,210.7	7.8	2,220.4	1.8	2,184.2	5.7
1969	2,244.8	4.5	2,258.8	2.5	2,269.0	1.8	2,286.5	3.1	2,264.8	3.7
1970	2,300.8	2.5	2,312.0	2.0	2,332.2	3.5	2,324.9	-1.2	2,317.5	2.3
1971	2,369.8	8.0	2,391.4	3.7	2,409.8	3.1	2,449.8	6.8	2,405.2	3.8
1972	2,482.2	5.4	2,527.5	7.5	2,565.9	6.2	2,626.3	9.8	2,550.5	6.0
1973	2,674.2	7.5	2,671.4	-0.4	2,682.5	1.7	2,675.6	-1.0	2,675.9	4.9
1974	2,652.4	-3.4	2,662.0	1.5	2,672.2	1.5	2,628.4	-6.4	2,653.7	-0.8
1975	2,648.8	3.1	2,695.4	7.2	2,734.7	6.0	2,764.6	4.4	2,710.9	2.2
1976	2,824.7	9.0	2,850.9	3.8	2,880.3	4.2	2,919.6	5.6	2,868.9	5.8
1977	2,954.7	4.9	2,970.5	2.2	2,999.1	3.9	3,044.0	6.1	2,992.1	4.3
1978	3,060.8	2.2	3,127.0	8.9	3,143.1	2.1	3,167.8	3.2	3,124.7	4.4
1979	3,188.6	2.7	3,184.3	-0.5	3,213.9	3.8	3,225.7	1.5	3,203.2	2.5
1980	3,222.4	-0.4	3,149.2	-8.8	3,181.2	4.1	3,219.4	4.9	3,193.0	-0.3
1981	3,233.1	1.7	3,235.5	0.3	3,250.5	1.9	3,225.0	-3.1	3,236.0	1.3
1982	3,244.3	2.4	3,253.4	1.1	3,274.6	2.6	3,329.6	6.9	3,275.5	1.2
1983	3,360.1	3.7	3,430.1	8.6	3,484.7	6.5	3,542.2	6.8	3,454.3	5.5
1984	3,579.7	4.3	3,628.3	5.5	3,653.5	2.8	3,700.9	5.3	3,640.6	5.4
1985	3,756.8	6.2	3,791.5	3.7	3,860.9	7.5	3,874.2	1.4	3,820.9	5.0
1986	3,907.9	3.5	3,950.4	4.4	4,019.7	7.2	4,046.8	2.7	3,981.2	4.2
1987	4,049.7	0.3	4,101.5	5.2	4,147.0	4.5	4,155.3	0.8	4,113.4	3.3
1988	4,228.0	7.2	4,256.8	2.8	4,291.6	3.3	4,341.4	4.7	4,279.5	4.0
1989	4,357.1	1.5	4,374.8	1.6	4,413.4	3.6	4,429.4	1.5	4,393.7	2.7
1990	4,466.0	3.3	4,478.8	1.2	4,495.6	1.5	4,457.7	-3.3	4,474.5	1.8
1991	4,437.5	-1.8	4,469.9	3.0	4,484.3	1.3	4,474.8	-0.8	4,466.6	-0.2
1992	4,544.8	6.4	4,566.7	1.9	4,600.5	3.0	4,665.9	5.8	4,594.5	2.9
1993	4,674.9	0.8	4,721.5	4.0	4,776.9	4.8	4,822.3	3.9	4,748.9	3.4
1994	4,866.6	3.7	4,907.9	3.4	4,944.5	3.0	4,993.6	4.0	4,928.1	3.8
1995	5,011.6	1.4	5,059.6	3.9	5,099.2	3.2	5,132.1	2.6	5,075.6	3.0
1996	5,174.3	3.3	5,229.5	4.3	5,254.3	1.9	5,291.9	2.9	5,237.5	3.2
1997	5,350.7	4.5	5,375.7	1.9	5,462.1	6.6	5,507.1	3.3	5,423.9	3.6
1998	5,576.3	5.1	5,660.2	6.2	5,713.7	3.8	5,784.7	5.1	5,683.7	4.8
1999	5,854.0	4.9	5,936.1	5.7	6,000.0	4.4	6,083.6	5.7	5,968.4	5.0
2000	6,171.7	5.9	6,226.3	3.6	6,292.1	4.3	6,341.1	3.2	6,257.8	4.8
2001	6,388.5	3.0	6,428.4	2.5	6,443.9	1.0	-	-	-	-

Source: "National Income and Product Account Tables: Selected NIPA Tables," *Survey of Current Business*, January 2002, U.S. Department of Commerce, Bureau of Economic Analysis, National Income and Wealth Division. Data downloaded from www.stat.usa.gov. A dash (-) indicates that no data are available.

Gross Domestic Product
Personal consumption expenditures
Durable goods - Actual Dollars

In billions of actual dollars and percent. Quarterly data are seasonally adjusted and annualized. Growth rates for quarters are compound annual growth rates; changes from year to year are percentage changes.

Year	1st Quarter	% Change	2nd Quarter	% Change	3rd Quarter	% Change	4th Quarter	% Change	TOTAL	% Change
1959	41.5	-	43.2	17.4	44.1	8.6	41.8	-19.3	42.7	-
1960	43.2	14.1	44.1	8.6	43.6	-4.5	42.4	-10.6	43.3	1.4
1961	39.9	-21.6	40.9	10.4	42.1	12.3	44.2	21.5	41.8	-3.5
1962	45.2	9.4	46.4	11.0	46.9	4.4	48.9	18.2	46.9	12.2
1963	50.0	9.3	51.3	10.8	52.0	5.6	53.1	8.7	51.6	10.0
1964	55.2	16.8	56.6	10.5	58.4	13.3	56.4	-13.0	56.7	9.9
1965	61.9	45.1	61.7	-1.3	63.6	12.9	65.9	15.3	63.3	11.6
1966	68.9	19.5	66.3	-14.3	68.8	16.0	69.1	1.8	68.3	7.9
1967	67.6	-8.4	71.0	21.7	71.1	0.6	72.0	5.2	70.4	3.1
1968	77.1	31.5	79.1	10.8	83.3	23.0	83.6	1.4	80.8	14.8
1969	85.5	9.4	85.9	1.9	86.1	0.9	86.2	0.5	85.9	6.3
1970	84.9	-5.9	86.0	5.3	86.9	4.3	82.1	-20.3	85.0	-1.0
1971	92.7	62.5	95.5	12.6	97.8	10.0	101.5	16.0	96.9	14.0
1972	104.9	14.1	108.1	12.8	111.4	12.8	117.0	21.7	110.4	13.9
1973	125.2	31.1	124.1	-3.5	123.8	-1.0	121.1	-8.4	123.5	11.9
1974	118.9	-7.1	123.0	14.5	128.8	20.2	118.6	-28.1	122.3	-1.0
1975	123.2	16.4	128.3	17.6	138.0	33.8	144.4	19.9	133.5	9.2
1976	154.1	29.7	156.3	5.8	159.6	8.7	165.3	15.1	158.9	19.0
1977	173.7	21.9	178.8	12.3	183.2	10.2	189.2	13.8	181.2	14.0
1978	187.0	-4.6	204.7	43.6	205.0	0.6	210.2	10.5	201.7	11.3
1979	211.5	2.5	210.3	-2.3	218.9	17.4	216.9	-3.6	214.4	6.3
1980	220.0	5.8	199.8	-32.0	213.1	29.4	223.8	21.6	214.2	-0.1
1981	233.5	18.5	228.3	-8.6	239.2	20.5	224.3	-22.7	231.3	8.0
1982	234.0	18.5	236.6	4.5	239.1	4.3	251.2	21.8	240.2	3.8
1983	255.7	7.4	276.0	35.7	288.3	19.1	304.9	25.1	281.2	17.1
1984	316.7	16.4	326.1	12.4	326.7	0.7	338.0	14.6	326.9	16.3
1985	351.8	17.4	356.6	5.6	379.1	27.7	365.6	-13.5	363.3	11.1
1986	372.7	8.0	387.3	16.6	424.7	44.6	420.5	-3.9	401.3	10.5
1987	397.3	-20.3	417.2	21.6	437.8	21.3	426.5	-9.9	419.7	4.6
1988	446.5	20.1	448.5	1.8	445.3	-2.8	460.5	14.4	450.2	7.3
1989	460.5	-	467.5	6.2	478.7	9.9	464.3	-11.5	467.8	3.9
1990	486.4	20.4	469.2	-13.4	463.7	-4.6	451.0	-10.5	467.6	-0.0
1991	439.4	-9.9	441.4	1.8	448.9	7.0	442.5	-5.6	443.0	-5.3
1992	459.0	15.8	463.3	3.8	474.2	9.7	486.6	10.9	470.8	6.3
1993	487.6	0.8	507.5	17.4	520.8	10.9	537.9	13.8	513.4	9.0
1994	546.2	6.3	553.6	5.5	563.2	7.1	580.0	12.5	560.8	9.2
1995	578.2	-1.2	584.4	4.4	596.2	8.3	600.0	2.6	589.7	5.2
1996	606.4	4.3	621.3	10.2	616.7	-2.9	621.5	3.1	616.5	4.5
1997	635.1	9.0	624.4	-6.6	652.4	19.2	658.3	3.7	642.5	4.2
1998	666.8	5.3	689.3	14.2	691.7	1.4	725.1	20.8	693.2	7.9
1999	731.6	3.6	754.9	13.4	767.9	7.1	789.4	11.7	760.9	9.8
2000	820.7	16.8	813.8	-3.3	825.4	5.8	818.7	-3.2	819.6	7.7
2001	838.1	9.8	844.7	3.2	840.6	-1.9	-	-	-	-

Source: "National Income and Product Account Tables: Selected NIPA Tables," *Survey of Current Business*, January 2002, U.S. Department of Commerce, Bureau of Economic Analysis, National Income and Wealth Division. Data downloaded from www.stat.usa.gov. A dash (-) indicates that no data are available.

Gross Domestic Product
Personal consumption expenditures
Durable goods - Chained (1996) Dollars

In billions of chained (1996) dollars and percent. Quarterly data are seasonally adjusted and annualized. Growth rates for quarters are compound annual growth rates; changes from year to year are percentage changes.

Year	1st Quarter	% Change	2nd Quarter	% Change	3rd Quarter	% Change	4th Quarter	% Change	TOTAL	% Change
1987	435.2	-	453.8	18.2	472.8	17.8	459.0	-11.2	455.2	-
1988	481.7	21.3	481.5	-0.2	474.9	-5.4	488.1	11.6	481.5	5.8
1989	485.6	-2.0	492.5	5.8	502.7	8.5	486.0	-12.6	491.7	2.1
1990	506.7	18.2	489.3	-13.0	483.5	-4.7	468.8	-11.6	487.1	-0.9
1991	452.6	-13.1	454.0	1.2	460.2	5.6	452.8	-6.3	454.9	-6.6
1992	468.7	14.8	471.4	2.3	482.1	9.4	493.8	10.1	479.0	5.3
1993	495.4	1.3	513.3	15.3	524.7	9.2	539.9	12.1	518.3	8.2
1994	546.9	5.3	551.7	3.6	557.7	4.4	574.3	12.4	557.7	7.6
1995	570.4	-2.7	577.4	5.0	590.7	9.5	595.7	3.4	583.5	4.6
1996	601.7	4.1	620.4	13.0	618.1	-1.5	625.7	5.0	616.5	5.7
1997	641.5	10.5	636.5	-3.1	670.5	23.1	680.9	6.4	657.3	6.6
1998	692.5	7.0	719.7	16.7	727.1	4.2	767.3	24.0	726.7	10.6
1999	780.5	7.1	809.5	15.7	827.2	9.0	854.2	13.7	817.8	12.5
2000	892.1	19.0	886.5	-2.5	904.1	8.2	899.4	-2.1	895.5	9.5
2001	922.4	10.6	938.1	7.0	940.2	0.9	-	-	-	-

Source: "National Income and Product Account Tables: Selected NIPA Tables," *Survey of Current Business*, January 2002, U.S. Department of Commerce, Bureau of Economic Analysis, National Income and Wealth Division. Data downloaded from www.stat.usa.gov. A dash (-) indicates that no data are available.

Gross Domestic Product
Personal consumption expenditures
Nondurable goods - Actual Dollars

In billions of actual dollars and percent. Quarterly data are seasonally adjusted and annualized. Growth rates for quarters are compound annual growth rates; changes from year to year are percentage changes.

Year	1st Quarter	% Change	2nd Quarter	% Change	3rd Quarter	% Change	4th Quarter	% Change	TOTAL	% Change
1959	146.1	-	147.7	4.5	149.3	4.4	150.9	4.4	148.5	-
1960	150.8	-0.3	153.6	7.6	153.0	-1.6	153.9	2.4	152.9	3.0
1961	155.2	3.4	156.0	2.1	156.5	1.3	158.6	5.5	156.6	2.4
1962	160.6	5.1	161.9	3.3	163.4	3.8	165.3	4.7	162.8	4.0
1963	166.3	2.4	167.0	1.7	169.4	5.9	169.9	1.2	168.2	3.3
1964	174.1	10.3	177.3	7.6	181.0	8.6	182.3	2.9	178.7	6.2
1965	185.0	6.1	188.7	8.2	192.6	8.5	200.0	16.3	191.6	7.2
1966	204.3	8.9	208.0	7.4	211.0	5.9	211.7	1.3	208.8	9.0
1967	213.9	4.2	215.6	3.2	218.0	4.5	220.9	5.4	217.1	4.0
1968	228.1	13.7	233.3	9.4	239.4	10.9	242.0	4.4	235.7	8.6
1969	246.4	7.5	251.1	7.9	255.2	6.7	259.9	7.6	253.2	7.4
1970	266.2	10.1	269.8	5.5	273.7	5.9	278.4	7.0	272.0	7.4
1971	280.3	2.8	284.1	5.5	286.7	3.7	291.0	6.1	285.5	5.0
1972	295.9	6.9	304.3	11.8	311.5	9.8	320.5	12.1	308.0	7.9
1973	330.4	12.9	337.0	8.2	347.6	13.2	357.4	11.8	343.1	11.4
1974	369.1	13.8	380.4	12.8	391.7	12.4	396.8	5.3	384.5	12.1
1975	404.5	8.0	415.6	11.4	427.8	12.3	435.1	7.0	420.7	9.4
1976	445.4	9.8	452.7	6.7	462.6	9.0	472.6	8.9	458.3	8.9
1977	483.9	9.9	492.2	7.0	498.7	5.4	513.8	12.7	497.2	8.5
1978	524.4	8.5	542.9	14.9	558.5	12.0	575.2	12.5	550.2	10.7
1979	593.9	13.7	610.5	11.7	635.8	17.6	657.6	14.4	624.4	13.5
1980	679.7	14.1	686.6	4.1	699.5	7.7	718.5	11.3	696.1	11.5
1981	745.8	16.1	756.2	5.7	763.2	3.8	770.2	3.7	758.9	9.0
1982	776.2	3.2	778.6	1.2	793.0	7.6	802.7	5.0	787.6	3.8
1983	806.2	1.8	824.0	9.1	842.4	9.2	852.1	4.7	831.2	5.5
1984	866.4	6.9	883.8	8.3	889.7	2.7	898.7	4.1	884.7	6.4
1985	910.5	5.4	924.2	6.2	932.8	3.8	947.5	6.5	928.8	5.0
1986	957.3	4.2	950.6	-2.8	956.9	2.7	969.1	5.2	958.5	3.2
1987	994.4	10.9	1,011.9	7.2	1,022.0	4.1	1,033.1	4.4	1,015.3	5.9
1988	1,049.4	6.5	1,070.3	8.2	1,095.2	9.6	1,116.5	8.0	1,082.9	6.7
1989	1,134.3	6.5	1,161.3	9.9	1,174.0	4.4	1,191.9	6.2	1,165.4	7.6
1990	1,221.7	10.4	1,233.2	3.8	1,258.5	8.5	1,270.9	4.0	1,246.1	6.9
1991	1,267.8	-1.0	1,281.0	4.2	1,284.9	1.2	1,281.5	-1.1	1,278.8	2.6
1992	1,305.2	7.6	1,309.2	1.2	1,326.0	5.2	1,351.4	7.9	1,322.9	3.4
1993	1,355.7	1.3	1,370.4	4.4	1,379.6	2.7	1,395.0	4.5	1,375.2	4.0
1994	1,409.7	4.3	1,425.1	4.4	1,449.9	7.1	1,467.2	4.9	1,438.0	4.6
1995	1,475.8	2.4	1,492.2	4.5	1,502.6	2.8	1,518.5	4.3	1,497.3	4.1
1996	1,539.6	5.7	1,569.4	8.0	1,578.8	2.4	1,608.4	7.7	1,574.1	5.1
1997	1,626.8	4.7	1,627.3	0.1	1,653.1	6.5	1,659.0	1.4	1,641.6	4.3
1998	1,675.8	4.1	1,697.2	5.2	1,716.7	4.7	1,744.4	6.6	1,708.5	4.1
1999	1,776.4	7.5	1,814.7	8.9	1,841.4	6.0	1,892.9	11.7	1,831.3	7.2
2000	1,942.5	10.9	1,978.3	7.6	2,012.4	7.1	2,025.1	2.5	1,989.6	8.6
2001	2,047.1	4.4	2,062.3	3.0	2,057.5	-0.9	-	-	-	-

Source: "National Income and Product Account Tables: Selected NIPA Tables," *Survey of Current Business*, January 2002, U.S. Department of Commerce, Bureau of Economic Analysis, National Income and Wealth Division. Data downloaded from www.stat.usa.gov. A dash (-) indicates that no data are available.

Gross Domestic Product

Personal consumption expenditures
Nondurable goods - Chained (1996) Dollars

In billions of chained (1996) dollars and percent. Quarterly data are seasonally adjusted and annualized. Growth rates for quarters are compound annual growth rates; changes from year to year are percentage changes.

Year	1st Quarter	% Change	2nd Quarter	% Change	3rd Quarter	% Change	4th Quarter	% Change	TOTAL	% Change
1987	1,266.0	-	1,275.0	2.9	1,276.0	0.3	1,281.0	1.6	1,274.5	-
1988	1,295.8	4.7	1,307.4	3.6	1,321.4	4.4	1,336.0	4.5	1,315.1	3.2
1989	1,341.0	1.5	1,341.8	0.2	1,354.7	3.9	1,366.4	3.5	1,351.0	2.7
1990	1,370.2	1.1	1,372.6	0.7	1,375.9	1.0	1,359.8	-4.6	1,369.6	1.4
1991	1,358.9	-0.3	1,368.7	2.9	1,369.4	0.2	1,358.9	-3.0	1,364.0	-0.4
1992	1,381.2	6.7	1,379.1	-0.6	1,388.1	2.6	1,410.3	6.6	1,389.7	1.9
1993	1,410.2	-0.0	1,425.5	4.4	1,438.1	3.6	1,447.4	2.6	1,430.3	2.9
1994	1,465.3	5.0	1,477.6	3.4	1,490.9	3.6	1,506.5	4.3	1,485.1	3.8
1995	1,514.3	2.1	1,525.3	2.9	1,531.7	1.7	1,544.6	3.4	1,529.0	3.0
1996	1,553.9	2.4	1,569.9	4.2	1,578.6	2.2	1,593.9	3.9	1,574.1	2.9
1997	1,605.6	3.0	1,608.2	0.6	1,631.7	6.0	1,634.1	0.6	1,619.9	2.9
1998	1,656.3	5.5	1,680.5	6.0	1,693.6	3.2	1,715.3	5.2	1,686.4	4.1
1999	1,738.8	5.6	1,757.2	4.3	1,768.6	2.6	1,801.1	7.6	1,766.4	4.7
2000	1,823.8	5.1	1,844.9	4.7	1,864.1	4.2	1,866.8	0.6	1,849.9	4.7
2001	1,878.0	2.4	1,879.4	0.3	1,882.0	0.6	-	-	-	-

Source: "National Income and Product Account Tables: Selected NIPA Tables," *Survey of Current Business*, January 2002, U.S. Department of Commerce, Bureau of Economic Analysis, National Income and Wealth Division. Data downloaded from www.stat.usa.gov. A dash (-) indicates that no data are available.

Gross Domestic Product
Personal consumption expenditures
Services - Actual Dollars

In billions of actual dollars and percent. Quarterly data are seasonally adjusted and annualized. Growth rates for quarters are compound annual growth rates; changes from year to year are percentage changes.

Year	1st Quarter	% Change	2nd Quarter	% Change	3rd Quarter	% Change	4th Quarter	% Change	TOTAL	% Change
1959	122.9	-	125.6	9.1	128.4	9.2	131.2	9.0	127.0	-
1960	133.4	6.9	135.6	6.8	136.6	3.0	138.9	6.9	136.1	7.2
1961	140.6	5.0	143.7	9.1	144.9	3.4	148.0	8.8	144.3	6.0
1962	150.2	6.1	153.3	8.5	155.2	5.1	157.6	6.3	154.1	6.8
1963	159.1	3.9	161.3	5.6	165.0	9.5	168.1	7.7	163.4	6.0
1964	171.4	8.1	174.7	7.9	178.1	8.0	181.5	7.9	176.4	8.0
1965	184.0	5.6	187.5	7.8	191.0	7.7	195.4	9.5	189.5	7.4
1966	198.6	6.7	202.8	8.7	206.3	7.1	211.2	9.8	204.7	8.0
1967	214.9	7.2	218.8	7.5	223.6	9.1	227.4	7.0	221.2	8.1
1968	232.9	10.0	239.6	12.0	245.3	9.9	251.3	10.1	242.3	9.5
1969	257.0	9.4	263.2	10.0	269.2	9.4	276.3	11.0	266.4	9.9
1970	282.7	9.6	287.9	7.6	295.2	10.5	302.0	9.5	292.0	9.6
1971	308.7	9.2	316.1	9.9	323.5	9.7	331.8	10.7	320.0	9.6
1972	340.9	11.4	347.5	8.0	355.3	9.3	365.6	12.1	352.3	10.1
1973	372.3	7.5	381.9	10.7	390.5	9.3	398.7	8.7	385.9	9.5
1974	407.3	8.9	420.2	13.3	430.9	10.6	443.7	12.4	425.5	10.3
1975	456.7	12.2	469.8	12.0	481.5	10.3	496.5	13.1	476.1	11.9
1976	511.5	12.6	522.1	8.6	538.6	13.3	558.2	15.4	532.6	11.9
1977	574.1	11.9	589.3	11.0	610.0	14.8	626.9	11.6	600.0	12.7
1978	648.5	14.5	671.4	14.9	688.6	10.6	705.2	10.0	678.4	13.1
1979	726.2	12.5	746.0	11.4	765.5	10.9	792.0	14.6	757.4	11.6
1980	816.3	12.8	832.9	8.4	864.5	16.1	897.0	15.9	852.7	12.6
1981	913.8	7.7	942.2	13.0	968.1	11.5	991.8	10.2	954.0	11.9
1982	1,012.8	8.7	1,033.6	8.5	1,061.6	11.3	1,097.8	14.4	1,051.5	10.2
1983	1,126.4	10.8	1,160.0	12.5	1,188.8	10.3	1,220.9	11.2	1,174.0	11.7
1984	1,244.1	7.8	1,271.4	9.1	1,300.7	9.5	1,331.4	9.8	1,286.9	9.6
1985	1,370.6	12.3	1,401.3	9.3	1,437.9	10.9	1,472.5	10.0	1,420.6	10.4
1986	1,495.1	6.3	1,519.1	6.6	1,547.0	7.6	1,580.4	8.9	1,535.4	8.1
1987	1,619.7	10.3	1,652.5	8.3	1,685.7	8.3	1,723.3	9.2	1,670.3	8.8
1988	1,763.8	9.7	1,800.7	8.6	1,846.5	10.6	1,883.0	8.1	1,823.5	9.2
1989	1,917.0	7.4	1,944.1	5.8	1,974.2	6.3	2,018.8	9.3	1,963.5	7.7
1990	2,046.7	5.6	2,103.8	11.6	2,149.3	8.9	2,171.6	4.2	2,117.8	7.9
1991	2,197.4	4.8	2,236.2	7.3	2,264.4	5.1	2,299.5	6.3	2,249.4	6.2
1992	2,358.9	10.7	2,399.1	7.0	2,425.4	4.5	2,480.3	9.4	2,415.9	7.4
1993	2,507.3	4.4	2,543.4	5.9	2,587.8	7.2	2,625.8	6.0	2,566.1	6.2
1994	2,657.9	5.0	2,698.8	6.3	2,739.8	6.2	2,774.0	5.1	2,717.6	5.9
1995	2,814.7	6.0	2,867.1	7.7	2,906.3	5.6	2,939.9	4.7	2,882.0	6.0
1996	2,984.4	6.2	3,027.4	5.9	3,068.2	5.5	3,107.9	5.3	3,047.0	5.7
1997	3,168.0	8.0	3,219.1	6.6	3,270.4	6.5	3,323.3	6.6	3,245.2	6.5
1998	3,377.3	6.7	3,433.5	6.8	3,486.7	6.3	3,519.6	3.8	3,454.3	6.4
1999	3,572.8	6.2	3,627.5	6.3	3,689.1	7.0	3,742.4	5.9	3,658.0	5.9
2000	3,818.7	8.4	3,882.8	6.9	3,947.7	6.9	4,027.5	8.3	3,919.2	7.1
2001	4,092.4	6.6	4,137.6	4.5	4,159.4	2.1	-	-	-	-

Source: "National Income and Product Account Tables: Selected NIPA Tables," *Survey of Current Business*, January 2002, U.S. Department of Commerce, Bureau of Economic Analysis, National Income and Wealth Division. Data downloaded from www.stat.usa.gov. A dash (-) indicates that no data are available.

Gross Domestic Product
Personal consumption expenditures
Services - Chained (1996) Dollars

In billions of chained (1996) dollars and percent. Quarterly data are seasonally adjusted and annualized. Growth rates for quarters are compound annual growth rates; changes from year to year are percentage changes.

Year	1st Quarter	% Change	2nd Quarter	% Change	3rd Quarter	% Change	4th Quarter	% Change	TOTAL	% Change
1987	2,346.8	-	2,367.8	3.6	2,390.6	3.9	2,411.9	3.6	2,379.3	-
1988	2,443.7	5.4	2,461.7	3.0	2,491.6	4.9	2,511.8	3.3	2,477.2	4.1
1989	2,525.8	2.2	2,535.1	1.5	2,549.2	2.2	2,573.6	3.9	2,546.0	2.8
1990	2,583.0	1.5	2,614.9	5.0	2,635.9	3.3	2,631.1	-0.7	2,616.2	2.8
1991	2,629.6	-0.2	2,651.1	3.3	2,658.3	1.1	2,668.3	1.5	2,651.8	1.4
1992	2,698.9	4.7	2,720.9	3.3	2,734.1	2.0	2,765.0	4.6	2,729.7	2.9
1993	2,772.7	1.1	2,784.9	1.8	2,816.0	4.5	2,836.4	2.9	2,802.5	2.7
1994	2,855.4	2.7	2,879.6	3.4	2,896.8	2.4	2,912.9	2.2	2,886.2	3.0
1995	2,927.3	2.0	2,957.4	4.2	2,977.0	2.7	2,992.0	2.0	2,963.4	2.7
1996	3,018.8	3.6	3,039.2	2.7	3,057.7	2.5	3,072.2	1.9	3,047.0	2.8
1997	3,103.7	4.2	3,130.6	3.5	3,160.6	3.9	3,193.0	4.2	3,147.0	3.3
1998	3,228.4	4.5	3,262.3	4.3	3,295.2	4.1	3,307.6	1.5	3,273.4	4.0
1999	3,340.8	4.1	3,377.8	4.5	3,413.7	4.3	3,440.5	3.2	3,393.2	3.7
2000	3,472.2	3.7	3,509.6	4.4	3,540.2	3.5	3,588.8	5.6	3,527.7	4.0
2001	3,605.1	1.8	3,629.8	2.8	3,640.4	1.2	-	-	-	-

Source: "National Income and Product Account Tables: Selected NIPA Tables," *Survey of Current Business*, January 2002, U.S. Department of Commerce, Bureau of Economic Analysis, National Income and Wealth Division. Data downloaded from www.stat.usa.gov. A dash (-) indicates that no data are available.

GROSS PRIVATE DOMESTIC INVESTMENT
Component of Gross Domestic Product

Gross Private Domestic Investment (GPDI) accounts for all expenditures on building and structures by corporations and individuals, all durable equipment ("capital goods") used in the production of goods and services (e.g., tooling, refineries, power plants, transmission lines, etc.), and change in business inventories. Excluded from this category are investments made by government (accounted for under *Government Purchases of Goods and Services*) and capital goods exports less imports (accounted for under *Net Exports of Goods and Services*).

The category is subdivided into Fixed Investment and Change in Business Inventories as follows:

> *Fixed Investment*
>   Nonresidential
>   Structures
>   Equipment and software
>   Residential
> *Change in business inventories*

GPDI represented 19.2 percent of real GDP in 2000, up a point from 1998.

Fixed Investment

Nonresidential. Nonresidential fixed investment represents expenditures on permanent production facilities and equipment used by the private sector—the engine of economic activity. The category includes farm structures and farm machinery but excludes all investments made by government at all level, e.g., highways and bridges or government owned and operated production facilities. BEA estimates for the category are obtained under the headings of nonfarm buildings, public utilities, mining, other nonfarm structures, farm buildings, equipment except autos, and new and used autos; autos included in this category are used for business purposes; trucks are included under "equipment except autos." Beginning with the 1999 benchmark revisions, but restated retrospectively as well, this category also includes software purchased by business and government entities. This has caused a renaming of the previous "producers' durable equipment" category as "equipment and software." Each category has different sources of data and methods for obtaining estimates.

Residential. Residential fixed investments include permanent-site single-family housing units; multifamily housing units; mobile homes; and additions, alterations, and major replacements. Brokers commissions are also included under this category, as are purchases of capital equipment, used in production in a residential environment (e.g. a small printing press, apartment laundromat equipment, etc.).

Change in Business Inventories

Inventories are universally treated as capital investment—although not as fixed investment. Inventories "turn," meaning that stocks are withdrawn for use or sale while new stocks are added from purchases or production. For this reason, inventories, viewed as investments, are measured by comparing inventory levels at two points in time and measuring the change. The value can well be (1) negative if inventory levels have dropped from the first to the second period, (2) zero if no change took place, or (3) positive if inventory level has increased. Inventories may include finished goods (an automobile), work in process (an engine block), and raw materials in various stages (sheet steel, ingots). They may also be commodities like oil or gasoline stocks, grains or potatoes, or livestock.

The BEA subdivides the category into manufacturing and trade, other nonfarm industries, and farm; for each, different sources and estimating methods are used to arrive at quarterly and annual GDP estimates.

Presentation of Data

Data are shown from 1959 to 2001 in quarterly and in annual increments. Changes from one period to the next are shown for each category except Change in Business Inventories, which is already a change from one period to another. Changes from quarter to quarter are annualized, compounded growth rates as explained in the section on Gross National Product. Changes from year to year are simple percentile changes.

Analytical Uses

At the highest level of abstraction, GPDI is a measure, over time, of the relative proportion of national income that is reinvested to provide future productivity. A long-term decline in GPDI as a percentage of GDP indicates erosion of the nation's productive tooling and private infrastructure. A long-term growth in this measure may herald strong investment with benefits to be reaped in the future. The measure's chief limitation, for such analysis, is that it excludes public investment in infrastructure. Bad roads, unsafe harbors, and crowded airports can counteract the benefits of private investment.

Change in business inventories can be used to evaluate the confidence of producers (signaled by inventory build-ups) or their vulnerability (unusually high inventories as the economy begins to decline). The measure will also reflect the likelihood of economic overheating (when inventories are low and demand is showing strong, sustained growth).

Gross Domestic Product

Gross private domestic investment: Total - Actual Dollars

In billions of actual dollars and percent. Quarterly data are seasonally adjusted and annualized. Growth rates for quarters are compound annual growth rates; changes from year to year are percentage changes.

Year	1st Quarter	% Change	2nd Quarter	% Change	3rd Quarter	% Change	4th Quarter	% Change	TOTAL	% Change
1959	76.2	-	82.2	35.4	76.5	-25.0	79.3	15.5	78.5	-
1960	89.1	59.4	79.7	-36.0	78.7	-4.9	68.1	-43.9	78.9	0.5
1961	70.3	13.6	75.8	35.2	82.3	39.0	84.2	9.6	78.2	-0.9
1962	89.4	27.1	87.9	-6.5	89.3	6.5	86.0	-14.0	88.1	12.7
1963	90.5	22.6	92.2	7.7	95.0	12.7	97.4	10.5	93.8	6.5
1964	100.7	14.3	100.6	-0.4	102.5	7.8	104.5	8.0	102.1	8.8
1965	115.7	50.3	115.8	0.3	119.6	13.8	121.8	7.6	118.2	15.8
1966	131.8	37.1	130.7	-3.3	130.2	-1.5	132.6	7.6	131.3	11.1
1967	129.3	-9.6	123.7	-16.2	128.5	16.4	132.9	14.4	128.6	-2.1
1968	137.2	13.6	143.4	19.3	139.7	-9.9	144.4	14.2	141.2	9.8
1969	155.7	35.2	155.7	-	160.3	12.4	154.1	-14.6	156.4	10.8
1970	150.6	-8.8	153.9	9.1	156.0	5.6	148.9	-17.0	152.4	-2.6
1971	171.3	75.2	178.9	19.0	183.4	10.4	179.1	-9.1	178.2	16.9
1972	193.1	35.1	206.5	30.8	212.4	11.9	218.5	12.0	207.6	16.5
1973	232.6	28.4	246.1	25.3	241.8	-6.8	257.6	28.8	244.5	17.8
1974	244.1	-19.4	252.3	14.1	245.5	-10.4	255.9	18.1	249.4	2.0
1975	218.7	-46.7	216.8	-3.4	237.7	44.5	247.7	17.9	230.2	-7.7
1976	274.8	51.5	291.5	26.6	296.6	7.2	305.0	11.8	292.0	26.8
1977	326.7	31.6	355.1	39.6	378.2	28.7	385.4	7.8	361.3	23.7
1978	396.2	11.7	429.3	37.8	448.8	19.4	469.7	20.0	436.0	20.7
1979	478.5	7.7	490.9	10.8	495.9	4.1	497.3	1.1	490.6	12.5
1980	504.3	5.8	468.2	-25.7	441.7	-20.8	497.2	60.6	477.9	-2.6
1981	562.4	63.7	549.4	-8.9	590.7	33.6	580.7	-6.6	570.8	19.4
1982	525.2	-33.1	529.2	3.1	526.3	-2.2	483.5	-28.8	516.1	-9.6
1983	495.7	10.5	543.7	44.7	578.0	27.7	639.5	49.8	564.2	9.3
1984	709.3	51.3	736.0	15.9	753.2	9.7	743.6	-5.0	735.5	30.4
1985	721.1	-11.6	734.2	7.5	727.7	-3.5	762.3	20.4	736.3	0.1
1986	764.0	0.9	754.2	-5.0	733.6	-10.5	737.1	1.9	747.2	1.5
1987	762.6	14.6	766.4	2.0	765.3	-0.6	831.6	39.4	781.5	4.6
1988	797.7	-15.3	819.2	11.2	825.7	3.2	842.0	8.1	821.1	5.1
1989	881.2	20.0	875.4	-2.6	868.3	-3.2	866.7	-0.7	872.9	6.3
1990	881.6	7.1	883.0	0.6	869.4	-6.0	812.8	-23.6	861.7	-1.3
1991	786.5	-12.3	780.5	-3.0	801.5	11.2	832.1	16.2	800.2	-7.1
1992	810.9	-9.8	867.2	30.8	878.7	5.4	909.8	14.9	866.6	8.3
1993	938.0	13.0	943.6	2.4	943.0	-0.3	995.8	24.3	955.1	10.2
1994	1,042.0	19.9	1,106.4	27.1	1,094.0	-4.4	1,146.1	20.5	1,097.1	14.9
1995	1,162.8	6.0	1,133.1	-9.8	1,123.5	-3.3	1,155.6	11.9	1,143.8	4.3
1996	1,172.4	5.9	1,231.5	21.7	1,282.6	17.7	1,284.3	0.5	1,242.7	8.6
1997	1,324.2	13.0	1,397.7	24.1	1,405.7	2.3	1,434.5	8.5	1,390.5	11.9
1998	1,528.7	29.0	1,498.4	-7.7	1,538.6	11.2	1,589.3	13.8	1,538.7	10.7
1999	1,621.3	8.3	1,595.7	-6.2	1,631.7	9.3	1,698.1	17.3	1,636.7	6.4
2000	1,709.0	2.6	1,792.4	21.0	1,788.4	-0.9	1,780.3	-1.8	1,767.5	8.0
2001	1,722.8	-12.3	1,669.9	-11.7	1,624.8	-10.4	-	-	-	-

Source: "National Income and Product Account Tables: Selected NIPA Tables," *Survey of Current Business*, January 2002, U.S. Department of Commerce, Bureau of Economic Analysis, National Income and Wealth Division. Data downloaded from www.stat.usa.gov. A dash (-) indicates that no data are available.

Gross Domestic Product

Gross private domestic investment: Total - Chained (1996) Dollars

In billions of chained (1996) dollars and percent. Quarterly data are seasonally adjusted and annualized. Growth rates for quarters are compound annual growth rates; changes from year to year are percentage changes.

Year	1st Quarter	% Change	2nd Quarter	% Change	3rd Quarter	% Change	4th Quarter	% Change	TOTAL	% Change
1959	263.0	-	286.2	40.2	266.6	-24.7	275.6	14.2	272.9	-
1960	305.3	50.6	274.0	-35.1	272.4	-2.3	239.5	-40.2	272.8	-0.0
1961	245.0	9.5	263.3	33.4	285.5	38.2	290.2	6.7	271.0	-0.7
1962	307.3	25.7	304.5	-3.6	310.0	7.4	299.5	-12.9	305.3	12.7
1963	315.4	23.0	320.8	7.0	331.5	14.0	335.2	4.5	325.7	6.7
1964	348.9	17.4	347.5	-1.6	355.7	9.8	358.3	3.0	352.6	8.3
1965	394.9	47.6	394.6	-0.3	408.4	14.7	410.1	1.7	402.0	14.0
1966	444.1	37.5	436.5	-6.7	432.7	-3.4	435.8	2.9	437.3	8.8
1967	424.9	-9.6	405.0	-17.5	415.2	10.5	423.6	8.3	417.2	-4.6
1968	433.8	10.0	451.8	17.7	437.3	-12.2	442.2	4.6	441.3	5.8
1969	470.8	28.5	467.1	-3.1	477.2	8.9	452.6	-19.1	466.9	5.8
1970	438.0	-12.3	439.4	1.3	446.5	6.6	421.0	-21.0	436.2	-6.6
1971	475.9	63.3	490.2	12.6	496.5	5.2	480.6	-12.2	485.8	11.4
1972	513.6	30.4	544.9	26.7	554.1	6.9	559.4	3.9	543.0	11.8
1973	595.2	28.2	618.2	16.4	597.5	-12.7	615.3	12.5	606.5	11.7
1974	579.2	-21.5	577.3	-1.3	543.4	-21.5	547.0	2.7	561.7	-7.4
1975	450.8	-53.9	436.4	-12.2	474.9	40.2	486.8	10.4	462.2	-17.7
1976	535.1	46.0	559.8	19.8	561.1	0.9	565.9	3.5	555.5	20.2
1977	595.5	22.6	635.0	29.3	670.7	24.5	656.4	-8.3	639.4	15.1
1978	667.2	6.7	709.7	28.0	728.8	11.2	746.3	10.0	713.0	11.5
1979	746.0	-0.2	745.7	-0.2	732.1	-7.1	717.8	-7.6	735.4	3.1
1980	711.7	-3.4	647.4	-31.5	599.8	-26.3	662.2	48.6	655.3	-10.9
1981	726.3	44.7	693.4	-16.9	733.9	25.5	708.8	-13.0	715.6	9.2
1982	634.8	-35.7	631.6	-2.0	623.5	-5.0	571.1	-29.6	615.2	-14.0
1983	590.7	14.5	650.7	47.3	691.4	27.5	762.2	47.7	673.7	9.5
1984	845.0	51.1	873.2	14.0	890.7	8.3	876.9	-6.1	871.5	29.4
1985	848.9	-12.2	862.8	6.7	854.1	-4.0	887.8	16.7	863.4	-0.9
1986	886.2	-0.7	868.3	-7.8	838.0	-13.2	838.2	0.1	857.7	-0.7
1987	863.4	12.6	863.9	0.2	860.5	-1.6	929.3	36.0	879.3	2.5
1988	884.6	-17.9	902.5	8.3	907.5	2.2	916.7	4.1	902.8	2.7
1989	952.7	16.7	941.1	-4.8	929.3	-4.9	922.9	-2.7	936.5	3.7
1990	934.0	4.9	933.0	-0.4	912.6	-8.5	849.6	-24.9	907.3	-3.1
1991	815.1	-15.3	808.8	-3.1	829.8	10.8	864.2	17.6	829.5	-8.6
1992	843.8	-9.1	901.8	30.5	912.1	4.6	941.6	13.6	899.8	8.5
1993	961.8	10.2	967.0	0.0	964.1	-1.2	1,015.6	23.1	977.9	8.7
1994	1,057.3	17.5	1,118.5	25.2	1,101.8	-5.8	1,150.5	18.9	1,107.0	13.2
1995	1,162.4	4.2	1,128.5	-11.2	1,119.1	-3.3	1,152.4	12.4	1,140.6	3.0
1996	1,172.3	7.1	1,233.4	22.5	1,281.4	16.5	1,283.7	0.7	1,242.7	9.0
1997	1,325.4	13.6	1,400.6	24.7	1,408.6	2.3	1,438.5	8.8	1,393.3	12.1
1998	1,543.3	32.5	1,516.8	-6.7	1,559.7	11.8	1,612.1	14.1	1,558.0	11.8
1999	1,641.8	7.6	1,617.4	-5.8	1,655.8	9.8	1,725.4	17.9	1,660.1	6.6
2000	1,722.9	-0.6	1,801.6	19.6	1,788.8	-2.8	1,778.3	-2.3	1,772.9	6.8
2001	1,721.0	-12.3	1,666.2	-12.1	1,620.5	-10.5	-	-	-	-

Source: "National Income and Product Account Tables: Selected NIPA Tables," *Survey of Current Business*, January 2002, U.S. Department of Commerce, Bureau of Economic Analysis, National Income and Wealth Division. Data downloaded from www.stat.usa.gov. A dash (-) indicates that no data are available.

Gross Domestic Product
Gross private domestic investment
Fixed investment - Actual Dollars

In billions of actual dollars and percent. Quarterly data are seasonally adjusted and annualized. Growth rates for quarters are compound annual growth rates; changes from year to year are percentage changes.

Year	1st Quarter	% Change	2nd Quarter	% Change	3rd Quarter	% Change	4th Quarter	% Change	TOTAL	% Change
1959	72.3	-	74.9	15.2	76.1	6.6	75.2	-4.6	74.6	-
1960	77.9	15.2	76.4	-7.5	74.4	-10.1	73.9	-2.7	75.7	1.5
1961	72.9	-5.3	74.0	6.2	75.7	9.5	78.2	13.9	75.2	-0.7
1962	80.0	9.5	82.4	12.6	83.1	3.4	82.6	-2.4	82.0	9.0
1963	83.6	4.9	87.3	18.9	89.3	9.5	92.3	14.1	88.1	7.4
1964	95.6	15.1	96.1	2.1	97.8	7.3	99.5	7.1	97.2	10.3
1965	104.1	19.8	107.3	12.9	110.4	12.1	114.2	14.5	109.0	12.1
1966	117.9	13.6	118.4	1.7	118.3	-0.3	116.1	-7.2	117.7	8.0
1967	113.8	-7.7	117.4	13.3	119.3	6.6	124.5	18.6	118.7	0.8
1968	128.8	14.5	129.3	1.6	132.0	8.6	138.4	20.9	132.1	11.3
1969	144.2	17.8	146.4	6.2	150.2	10.8	148.3	-5.0	147.3	11.5
1970	148.8	1.4	148.8	-	151.0	6.0	152.9	5.1	150.4	2.1
1971	159.1	17.2	168.0	24.3	173.2	13.0	179.4	15.1	169.9	13.0
1972	189.9	25.5	194.5	10.0	198.7	8.9	211.0	27.2	198.5	16.8
1973	222.0	22.5	227.8	10.9	232.0	7.6	232.6	1.0	228.6	15.2
1974	231.5	-1.9	234.9	6.0	239.9	8.8	235.4	-7.3	235.4	3.0
1975	228.7	-10.9	230.7	3.5	239.1	15.4	247.3	14.4	236.5	0.5
1976	260.1	22.4	269.1	14.6	275.8	10.3	294.5	30.0	274.8	16.2
1977	311.9	25.8	335.6	34.0	347.3	14.7	361.3	17.1	339.0	23.4
1978	370.8	10.9	405.0	42.3	423.9	20.0	441.2	17.4	410.2	21.0
1979	454.6	12.7	463.5	8.1	483.8	18.7	488.7	4.1	472.7	15.2
1980	494.4	4.7	460.5	-24.7	475.5	13.7	506.4	28.6	484.2	2.4
1981	523.7	14.4	537.7	11.1	546.8	6.9	555.9	6.8	541.0	11.7
1982	546.7	-6.5	533.4	-9.4	520.5	-9.3	523.3	2.2	531.0	-1.8
1983	530.8	5.9	551.4	16.5	582.2	24.3	615.6	25.0	570.0	7.3
1984	636.3	14.1	666.6	20.5	681.9	9.5	695.7	8.3	670.1	17.6
1985	704.9	5.4	712.6	4.4	711.4	-0.7	729.2	10.4	714.5	6.6
1986	733.6	2.4	738.5	2.7	740.6	1.1	749.8	5.1	740.7	3.7
1987	734.6	-7.9	749.9	8.6	764.3	7.9	768.5	2.2	754.3	1.8
1988	780.7	6.5	799.5	10.0	807.5	4.1	822.9	7.8	802.7	6.4
1989	833.0	5.0	839.4	3.1	858.4	9.4	850.1	-3.8	845.2	5.3
1990	867.7	8.5	849.3	-8.2	847.6	-0.8	824.2	-10.6	847.2	0.2
1991	801.8	-10.4	798.3	-1.7	800.5	1.1	801.1	0.3	800.4	-5.5
1992	811.8	5.5	845.4	17.6	859.6	6.9	889.6	14.7	851.6	6.4
1993	901.9	5.6	919.3	7.9	936.1	7.5	978.8	19.5	934.0	9.7
1994	998.1	8.1	1,026.6	11.9	1,042.0	6.1	1,071.6	11.9	1,034.6	10.8
1995	1,100.1	11.1	1,097.2	-1.1	1,110.1	4.8	1,135.4	9.4	1,110.7	7.4
1996	1,165.6	11.1	1,201.7	13.0	1,232.6	10.7	1,250.9	6.1	1,212.7	9.2
1997	1,275.5	8.1	1,310.0	11.3	1,355.8	14.7	1,369.3	4.0	1,327.7	9.5
1998	1,422.0	16.3	1,457.5	10.4	1,469.1	3.2	1,513.9	12.8	1,465.6	10.4
1999	1,541.1	7.4	1,565.7	6.5	1,592.7	7.1	1,613.2	5.2	1,578.2	7.7
2000	1,678.1	17.1	1,717.0	9.6	1,735.9	4.5	1,741.6	1.3	1,718.1	8.9
2001	1,748.3	1.5	1,706.5	-9.2	1,682.6	-5.5	-	-	-	-

Source: "National Income and Product Account Tables: Selected NIPA Tables," *Survey of Current Business*, January 2002, U.S. Department of Commerce, Bureau of Economic Analysis, National Income and Wealth Division. Data downloaded from www.stat.usa.gov. A dash (-) indicates that no data are available.

Gross Domestic Product

Gross private domestic investment
Fixed investment - Chained (1996) Dollars

In billions of chained (1996) dollars and percent. Quarterly data are seasonally adjusted and annualized. Growth rates for quarters are compound annual growth rates; changes from year to year are percentage changes.

Year	1st Quarter	% Change	2nd Quarter	% Change	3rd Quarter	% Change	4th Quarter	% Change	TOTAL	% Change
1987	837.2	-	853.1	7.8	868.0	7.2	865.6	-1.1	856.0	-
1988	871.5	2.8	886.7	7.2	891.2	2.0	899.2	3.6	887.1	3.6
1989	905.5	2.8	906.7	0.5	923.3	7.5	909.3	-5.9	911.2	2.7
1990	922.8	6.1	900.3	-9.4	892.7	-3.3	862.7	-12.8	894.6	-1.8
1991	833.1	-13.0	829.5	-1.7	832.1	1.3	835.4	1.6	832.5	-6.9
1992	847.4	5.9	881.4	17.0	894.4	6.0	922.8	13.3	886.5	6.5
1993	929.9	3.1	944.3	6.3	958.7	6.2	1,000.6	18.7	958.4	8.1
1994	1,014.9	5.8	1,039.9	10.2	1,050.9	4.3	1,078.0	10.7	1,045.9	9.1
1995	1,101.9	9.2	1,095.0	-2.5	1,107.1	4.5	1,132.7	9.6	1,109.2	6.1
1996	1,165.2	12.0	1,203.7	13.9	1,231.6	9.6	1,250.2	6.2	1,212.7	9.3
1997	1,275.4	8.3	1,311.1	11.7	1,356.7	14.7	1,371.3	4.4	1,328.6	9.6
1998	1,431.4	18.7	1,471.4	11.7	1,485.4	3.9	1,531.7	13.1	1,480.0	11.4
1999	1,558.2	7.1	1,582.8	6.5	1,610.8	7.3	1,629.7	4.8	1,595.4	7.8
2000	1,683.4	13.8	1,719.2	8.8	1,730.1	2.6	1,732.1	0.5	1,716.2	7.6
2001	1,740.3	1.9	1,696.4	-9.7	1,671.6	-5.7	-	-	-	-

Source: "National Income and Product Account Tables: Selected NIPA Tables," *Survey of Current Business*, January 2002, U.S. Department of Commerce, Bureau of Economic Analysis, National Income and Wealth Division. Data downloaded from www.stat.usa.gov. A dash (-) indicates that no data are available.

Gross Domestic Product
Gross private domestic investment
Fixed investment - Nonresidential - Actual Dollars

In billions of actual dollars and percent. Quarterly data are seasonally adjusted and annualized. Growth rates for quarters are compound annual growth rates; changes from year to year are percentage changes.

Year	1st Quarter	% Change	2nd Quarter	% Change	3rd Quarter	% Change	4th Quarter	% Change	TOTAL	% Change
1959	44.5	-	46.1	15.2	47.8	15.6	47.7	-0.8	46.5	-
1960	49.5	16.0	50.3	6.6	49.0	-9.9	48.6	-3.2	49.4	6.2
1961	47.5	-8.8	48.5	8.7	48.7	1.7	50.4	14.7	48.8	-1.2
1962	51.6	9.9	53.2	13.0	53.9	5.4	53.5	-2.9	53.1	8.8
1963	53.4	-0.7	55.1	13.4	56.8	12.9	58.7	14.1	56.0	5.5
1964	60.1	9.9	62.0	13.3	64.1	14.3	65.7	10.4	63.0	12.5
1965	70.2	30.3	73.1	17.6	76.1	17.5	79.7	20.3	74.8	18.7
1966	83.1	18.2	85.2	10.5	86.4	5.8	86.9	2.3	85.4	14.2
1967	85.5	-6.3	85.7	0.9	85.9	0.9	88.4	12.2	86.4	1.2
1968	91.9	16.8	91.2	-3.0	93.1	8.6	97.5	20.3	93.4	8.1
1969	101.0	15.2	103.0	8.2	106.9	16.0	107.6	2.6	104.7	12.1
1970	108.1	1.9	109.4	4.9	110.6	4.5	107.9	-9.4	109.0	4.1
1971	110.5	10.0	113.4	10.9	114.8	5.0	117.9	11.2	114.1	4.7
1972	123.3	19.6	126.3	10.1	129.1	9.2	136.7	25.7	128.8	12.9
1973	144.2	23.8	152.1	23.8	157.0	13.5	159.8	7.3	153.3	19.0
1974	162.6	7.2	167.4	12.3	172.5	12.8	175.4	6.9	169.5	10.6
1975	171.1	-9.5	170.8	-0.7	174.5	9.0	178.6	9.7	173.7	2.5
1976	183.9	12.4	188.4	10.2	195.1	15.0	202.0	14.9	192.4	10.8
1977	214.3	26.7	224.0	19.4	232.3	15.7	244.3	22.3	228.7	18.9
1978	249.7	9.1	274.5	46.0	288.1	21.3	302.1	20.9	278.6	21.8
1979	316.0	19.7	322.6	8.6	340.3	23.8	347.5	8.7	331.6	19.0
1980	359.8	14.9	349.3	-11.2	359.6	12.3	375.0	18.3	360.9	8.8
1981	391.7	19.0	408.9	18.8	426.6	18.5	446.3	19.8	418.4	15.9
1982	441.9	-3.9	430.6	-9.8	418.2	-11.0	410.5	-7.2	425.3	1.6
1983	399.9	-9.9	403.2	3.3	419.6	17.3	447.0	28.8	417.4	-1.9
1984	460.7	12.8	485.2	23.0	501.1	13.8	514.3	11.0	490.3	17.5
1985	521.5	5.7	529.8	6.5	523.8	-4.5	535.3	9.1	527.6	7.6
1986	529.1	-4.6	520.2	-6.6	516.6	-2.7	524.3	6.1	522.5	-1.0
1987	509.3	-11.0	520.7	9.3	536.9	13.0	540.1	2.4	526.7	0.8
1988	551.1	8.4	566.3	11.5	571.8	3.9	584.5	9.2	568.4	7.9
1989	596.0	8.1	607.1	7.7	628.1	14.6	622.3	-3.6	613.4	7.9
1990	633.6	7.5	625.1	-5.3	635.4	6.8	627.2	-5.1	630.3	2.8
1991	616.8	-6.5	611.7	-3.3	605.9	-3.7	601.1	-3.1	608.9	-3.4
1992	600.1	-0.7	621.5	15.0	633.0	7.6	649.9	11.1	626.1	2.8
1993	659.3	5.9	675.2	10.0	683.2	4.8	711.4	17.6	682.2	9.0
1994	721.7	5.9	738.2	9.5	752.7	8.1	781.8	16.4	748.6	9.7
1995	812.5	16.7	820.3	3.9	825.2	2.4	842.3	8.6	825.1	10.2
1996	865.1	11.3	885.4	9.7	913.6	13.4	933.7	9.1	899.4	9.0
1997	955.5	9.7	984.3	12.6	1,026.0	18.1	1,031.8	2.3	999.4	11.1
1998	1,074.8	17.7	1,099.9	9.7	1,098.6	-0.5	1,131.7	12.6	1,101.2	10.2
1999	1,145.3	4.9	1,163.1	6.4	1,187.2	8.5	1,202.9	5.4	1,174.6	6.7
2000	1,250.9	16.9	1,288.3	12.5	1,314.9	8.5	1,318.2	1.0	1,293.1	10.1
2001	1,311.2	-2.1	1,260.2	-14.7	1,231.0	-9.0	-	-	-	-

Source: "National Income and Product Account Tables: Selected NIPA Tables," *Survey of Current Business*, January 2002, U.S. Department of Commerce, Bureau of Economic Analysis, National Income and Wealth Division. Data downloaded from www.stat.usa.gov. A dash (-) indicates that no data are available.

Gross Domestic Product

Gross private domestic investment

Fixed investment - Nonresidential - Chained (1996) Dollars

In billions of chained (1996) dollars and percent. Quarterly data are seasonally adjusted and annualized. Growth rates for quarters are compound annual growth rates; changes from year to year are percentage changes.

Year	1st Quarter	% Change	2nd Quarter	% Change	3rd Quarter	% Change	4th Quarter	% Change	TOTAL	% Change
1987	554.0	-	566.8	9.6	585.1	13.6	584.0	-0.7	572.5	-
1988	590.5	4.5	603.4	9.0	606.7	2.2	613.8	4.8	603.6	5.4
1989	623.1	6.2	632.2	6.0	651.1	12.5	641.6	-5.7	637.0	5.5
1990	650.0	5.3	639.4	-6.4	645.4	3.8	632.1	-8.0	641.7	0.7
1991	616.2	-9.7	611.9	-2.8	607.7	-2.7	604.6	-2.0	610.1	-4.9
1992	603.6	-0.7	626.1	15.8	637.6	7.6	655.0	11.4	630.6	3.4
1993	661.7	4.2	676.6	9.3	684.2	4.6	711.8	17.1	683.6	8.4
1994	720.0	4.7	734.1	8.1	747.2	7.3	777.1	17.0	744.6	8.9
1995	806.4	16.0	811.4	2.5	816.7	2.6	835.5	9.5	817.5	9.8
1996	861.6	13.1	885.6	11.6	914.3	13.6	936.2	9.9	899.4	10.0
1997	960.8	10.9	992.7	14.0	1,037.0	19.1	1,047.0	3.9	1,009.3	12.2
1998	1,099.5	21.6	1,132.3	12.5	1,136.6	1.5	1,175.4	14.4	1,135.9	12.5
1999	1,192.6	6.0	1,214.9	7.7	1,244.6	10.1	1,262.4	5.8	1,228.6	8.2
2000	1,309.4	15.7	1,347.7	12.2	1,371.1	7.1	1,374.5	1.0	1,350.7	9.9
2001	1,373.9	-0.2	1,320.9	-14.6	1,292.0	-8.5	-	-	-	-

Source: "National Income and Product Account Tables: Selected NIPA Tables," *Survey of Current Business*, January 2002, U.S. Department of Commerce, Bureau of Economic Analysis, National Income and Wealth Division. Data downloaded from www.stat.usa.gov. A dash (-) indicates that no data are available.

Gross Domestic Product
Gross private domestic investment
Fixed investment - Nonresidential - Structures - Actual Dollars

In billions of actual dollars and percent. Quarterly data are seasonally adjusted and annualized. Growth rates for quarters are compound annual growth rates; changes from year to year are percentage changes.

Year	1st Quarter	% Change	2nd Quarter	% Change	3rd Quarter	% Change	4th Quarter	% Change	TOTAL	% Change
1959	17.4	-	18.0	14.5	18.6	14.0	18.5	-2.1	18.1	-
1960	19.4	20.9	19.5	2.1	19.4	-2.0	20.0	13.0	19.6	8.3
1961	19.9	-2.0	19.6	-5.9	19.7	2.1	19.6	-2.0	19.7	0.5
1962	20.0	8.4	20.8	17.0	21.4	12.0	20.9	-9.0	20.8	5.6
1963	20.2	-12.7	21.2	21.3	21.4	3.8	21.9	9.7	21.2	1.9
1964	22.4	9.4	23.4	19.1	24.3	16.3	24.8	8.5	23.7	11.8
1965	26.1	22.7	28.2	36.3	28.5	4.3	30.4	29.5	28.3	19.4
1966	31.1	9.5	31.2	1.3	31.9	9.3	31.2	-8.5	31.3	10.6
1967	31.7	6.6	30.9	-9.7	31.5	8.0	32.0	6.5	31.5	0.6
1968	33.1	14.5	33.2	1.2	33.2	-	34.8	20.7	33.6	6.7
1969	35.8	12.0	36.7	10.4	38.9	26.2	39.4	5.2	37.7	12.2
1970	39.5	1.0	40.3	8.4	40.6	3.0	40.8	2.0	40.3	6.9
1971	41.5	7.0	42.3	7.9	43.1	7.8	43.8	6.7	42.7	6.0
1972	45.8	19.6	46.6	7.2	47.3	6.1	49.0	15.2	47.2	10.5
1973	51.3	20.1	54.1	23.7	56.8	21.5	57.7	6.5	55.0	16.5
1974	59.0	9.3	61.3	16.5	61.4	0.7	63.2	12.3	61.2	11.3
1975	61.7	-9.2	60.4	-8.2	61.3	6.1	62.0	4.6	61.4	0.3
1976	64.1	14.3	65.1	6.4	66.7	10.2	67.8	6.8	65.9	7.3
1977	69.7	11.7	73.6	24.3	76.4	16.1	78.5	11.5	74.6	13.2
1978	79.2	3.6	88.6	56.6	95.8	36.7	102.0	28.5	91.4	22.5
1979	104.8	11.4	110.0	21.4	119.1	37.4	125.7	24.1	114.9	25.7
1980	130.3	15.5	129.8	-1.5	133.6	12.2	141.9	27.3	133.9	16.5
1981	147.5	16.7	158.3	32.7	166.8	23.3	185.7	53.6	164.6	22.9
1982	183.8	-4.0	179.6	-8.8	170.4	-19.0	166.2	-9.5	175.0	6.3
1983	156.7	-21.0	147.8	-20.9	151.0	8.9	155.5	12.5	152.7	-12.7
1984	164.5	25.2	174.4	26.3	181.0	16.0	184.2	7.3	176.0	15.3
1985	193.5	21.8	194.1	1.2	191.0	-6.2	194.6	7.8	193.3	9.8
1986	190.9	-7.4	173.9	-31.1	168.3	-12.3	170.1	4.3	175.8	-9.1
1987	165.4	-10.6	167.3	4.7	175.3	20.5	180.3	11.9	172.1	-2.1
1988	177.5	-6.1	182.8	12.5	182.3	-1.1	184.0	3.8	181.6	5.5
1989	189.0	11.3	189.0	-	197.6	19.5	197.9	0.6	193.4	6.5
1990	203.7	12.2	204.2	1.0	205.2	2.0	197.0	-15.1	202.5	4.7
1991	194.5	-5.0	189.7	-9.5	177.6	-23.2	172.0	-12.0	183.4	-9.4
1992	170.2	-4.1	170.7	1.2	172.6	4.5	175.4	6.6	172.2	-6.1
1993	176.7	3.0	177.5	1.8	179.2	3.9	184.2	11.6	179.4	4.2
1994	178.0	-12.8	188.2	25.0	189.9	3.7	193.9	8.7	187.5	4.5
1995	200.5	14.3	204.8	8.9	206.2	2.8	207.0	1.6	204.6	9.1
1996	213.4	13.0	220.0	13.0	226.3	12.0	240.3	27.1	225.0	10.0
1997	246.9	11.4	247.7	1.3	260.6	22.5	267.9	11.7	255.8	13.7
1998	273.2	8.2	284.9	18.3	283.9	-1.4	287.5	5.2	282.4	10.4
1999	284.8	-3.7	283.4	-2.0	280.3	-4.3	285.6	7.8	283.5	0.4
2000	295.8	15.1	306.4	15.1	321.1	20.6	330.9	12.8	313.6	10.6
2001	345.8	19.3	338.6	-8.1	334.3	-5.0	-	-	-	-

Source: "National Income and Product Account Tables: Selected NIPA Tables," *Survey of Current Business*, January 2002, U.S. Department of Commerce, Bureau of Economic Analysis, National Income and Wealth Division. Data downloaded from www.stat.usa.gov. A dash (-) indicates that no data are available.

Gross Domestic Product

Gross private domestic investment

Fixed investment - Nonresidential - Structures - Chained (1996) Dollars

In billions of chained (1996) dollars and percent. Quarterly data are seasonally adjusted and annualized. Growth rates for quarters are compound annual growth rates; changes from year to year are percentage changes.

Year	1st Quarter	% Change	2nd Quarter	% Change	3rd Quarter	% Change	4th Quarter	% Change	TOTAL	% Change
1987	217.3	-	219.0	3.2	228.3	18.1	232.5	7.6	224.3	-
1988	225.4	-11.7	229.6	7.7	226.9	-4.6	226.6	-0.5	227.1	1.2
1989	230.8	7.6	228.0	-4.8	236.7	16.2	235.2	-2.5	232.7	2.5
1990	240.0	8.4	238.9	-1.8	238.2	-1.2	227.3	-17.1	236.1	1.5
1991	222.3	-8.5	216.6	-9.9	202.9	-23.0	198.5	-8.4	210.1	-11.0
1992	196.5	-4.0	196.2	-0.6	197.5	2.7	199.1	3.3	197.3	-6.1
1993	198.6	-1.0	197.6	-2.0	197.8	0.4	201.5	7.7	198.9	0.8
1994	193.2	-15.5	202.9	21.6	202.3	-1.2	203.8	3.0	200.5	0.8
1995	208.1	8.7	211.0	5.7	210.9	-0.2	210.4	-0.9	210.1	4.8
1996	215.9	10.9	221.3	10.4	225.4	7.6	237.3	22.9	225.0	7.1
1997	241.1	6.6	239.3	-3.0	248.5	16.3	252.7	6.9	245.4	9.1
1998	255.7	4.8	264.8	15.0	263.0	-2.7	265.1	3.2	262.2	6.8
1999	260.7	-6.5	257.9	-4.2	253.2	-7.1	255.7	4.0	256.9	-2.0
2000	261.1	8.7	268.5	11.8	278.2	15.3	283.3	7.5	272.8	6.2
2001	291.7	12.4	282.3	-12.3	276.8	-7.6	-	-	-	-

Source: "National Income and Product Account Tables: Selected NIPA Tables," *Survey of Current Business*, January 2002, U.S. Department of Commerce, Bureau of Economic Analysis, National Income and Wealth Division. Data downloaded from www.stat.usa.gov. A dash (-) indicates that no data are available.

Gross Domestic Product

Gross private domestic investment

Fixed investment - Nonresidential - Equipment and software - Actual Dollars

In billions of actual dollars and percent. Quarterly data are seasonally adjusted and annualized. Growth rates for quarters are compound annual growth rates; changes from year to year are percentage changes.

Year	1st Quarter	% Change	2nd Quarter	% Change	3rd Quarter	% Change	4th Quarter	% Change	TOTAL	% Change
1959	27.1	-	28.1	15.6	29.2	16.6	29.2	-	28.4	-
1960	30.2	14.4	30.8	8.2	29.6	-14.7	28.6	-12.8	29.8	4.9
1961	27.6	-13.3	28.8	18.6	29.1	4.2	30.8	25.5	29.1	-2.3
1962	31.6	10.8	32.4	10.5	32.5	1.2	32.6	1.2	32.3	11.0
1963	33.2	7.6	33.9	8.7	35.4	18.9	36.8	16.8	34.8	7.7
1964	37.7	10.1	38.5	8.8	39.8	14.2	40.9	11.5	39.2	12.6
1965	44.1	35.2	44.9	7.5	47.5	25.3	49.3	16.0	46.5	18.6
1966	52.0	23.8	54.0	16.3	54.5	3.8	55.7	9.1	54.0	16.1
1967	53.8	-13.0	54.8	7.6	54.4	-2.9	56.5	16.4	54.9	1.7
1968	58.8	17.3	58.0	-5.3	59.9	13.8	62.7	20.1	59.9	9.1
1969	65.2	16.9	66.4	7.6	68.0	10.0	68.3	1.8	67.0	11.9
1970	68.6	1.8	69.1	2.9	70.0	5.3	67.2	-15.1	68.7	2.5
1971	69.0	11.2	71.1	12.7	71.7	3.4	74.1	14.1	71.5	4.1
1972	77.5	19.7	79.7	11.8	81.8	11.0	87.7	32.1	81.7	14.3
1973	92.8	25.4	98.0	24.4	100.1	8.9	102.1	8.2	98.3	20.3
1974	103.6	6.0	106.0	9.6	111.1	20.7	112.2	4.0	108.2	10.1
1975	109.4	-9.6	110.4	3.7	113.2	10.5	116.6	12.6	112.4	3.9
1976	119.8	11.4	123.4	12.6	128.5	17.6	134.1	18.6	126.4	12.5
1977	144.6	35.2	150.3	16.7	155.9	15.8	165.8	27.9	154.1	21.9
1978	170.5	11.8	185.9	41.3	192.3	14.5	200.2	17.5	187.2	21.5
1979	211.3	24.1	212.7	2.7	221.1	16.8	221.8	1.3	216.7	15.8
1980	229.5	14.6	219.5	-16.3	226.0	12.4	233.2	13.4	227.0	4.8
1981	244.2	20.2	250.6	10.9	259.8	15.5	260.6	1.2	253.8	11.8
1982	258.1	-3.8	251.0	-10.6	247.8	-5.0	244.3	-5.5	250.3	-1.4
1983	243.2	-1.8	255.3	21.4	268.6	22.5	291.6	38.9	264.7	5.8
1984	296.2	6.5	310.8	21.2	320.1	12.5	330.2	13.2	314.3	18.7
1985	328.0	-2.6	335.7	9.7	332.8	-3.4	340.7	9.8	334.3	6.4
1986	338.2	-2.9	346.3	9.9	348.3	2.3	354.2	6.9	346.8	3.7
1987	343.9	-11.1	353.3	11.4	361.6	9.7	359.8	-2.0	354.7	2.3
1988	373.6	16.2	383.5	11.0	389.5	6.4	400.5	11.8	386.8	9.0
1989	406.9	6.5	418.1	11.5	430.6	12.5	424.4	-5.6	420.0	8.6
1990	429.9	5.3	420.9	-8.1	430.2	9.1	430.2	-	427.8	1.9
1991	422.3	-7.1	421.9	-0.4	428.4	6.3	429.1	0.7	425.4	-0.6
1992	429.8	0.7	450.7	20.9	460.4	8.9	474.5	12.8	453.9	6.7
1993	482.6	7.0	497.7	13.1	503.9	5.1	527.3	19.9	502.8	10.8
1994	543.7	13.0	550.0	4.7	562.8	9.6	587.9	19.1	561.1	11.6
1995	612.0	17.4	615.5	2.3	619.0	2.3	635.3	11.0	620.5	10.6
1996	651.7	10.7	665.4	8.7	687.3	13.8	693.4	3.6	674.4	8.7
1997	708.6	9.1	736.6	16.8	765.4	16.6	764.0	-0.7	743.6	10.3
1998	801.6	21.2	815.0	6.9	814.7	-0.1	844.2	15.3	818.9	10.1
1999	860.6	8.0	879.7	9.2	906.9	13.0	917.3	4.7	891.1	8.8
2000	955.1	17.5	981.8	11.7	993.8	5.0	987.3	-2.6	979.5	9.9
2001	965.4	-8.6	921.7	-16.9	896.8	-10.4	-	-	-	-

Source: "National Income and Product Account Tables: Selected NIPA Tables," *Survey of Current Business*, January 2002, U.S. Department of Commerce, Bureau of Economic Analysis, National Income and Wealth Division. Data downloaded from www.stat.usa.gov. A dash (-) indicates that no data are available.

Gross Domestic Product

Gross private domestic investment

Fixed investment - Nonresidential - Equipment and software - Chained (1996) Dollars

In billions of chained (1996) dollars and percent. Quarterly data are seasonally adjusted and annualized. Growth rates for quarters are compound annual growth rates; changes from year to year are percentage changes.

Year	1st Quarter	% Change	2nd Quarter	% Change	3rd Quarter	% Change	4th Quarter	% Change	TOTAL	% Change
1987	348.1	-	358.8	12.9	368.7	11.5	364.3	-4.7	360.0	-
1988	376.0	13.5	384.7	9.6	390.1	5.7	397.0	7.3	386.9	7.5
1989	402.4	5.6	413.2	11.2	424.1	11.0	416.3	-7.2	414.0	7.0
1990	420.3	3.9	411.1	-8.5	417.4	6.3	413.9	-3.3	415.7	0.4
1991	402.8	-10.3	403.4	0.6	410.9	7.6	411.7	0.8	407.2	-2.0
1992	412.3	0.6	434.1	22.9	444.1	9.5	459.4	14.5	437.5	7.4
1993	466.3	6.1	481.4	13.6	488.5	6.0	512.2	20.9	487.1	11.3
1994	527.4	12.4	532.6	4.0	545.7	10.2	573.7	22.2	544.9	11.9
1995	598.5	18.4	600.7	1.5	606.0	3.6	625.0	13.1	607.6	11.5
1996	645.8	14.0	664.3	12.0	688.9	15.7	698.8	5.9	674.4	11.0
1997	719.6	12.4	753.7	20.3	788.9	20.0	794.5	2.9	764.2	13.3
1998	845.0	28.0	868.6	11.6	875.1	3.0	912.9	18.4	875.4	14.6
1999	936.0	10.5	962.6	11.9	999.5	16.2	1,015.2	6.4	978.3	11.8
2000	1,058.3	18.1	1,089.6	12.4	1,102.3	4.7	1,099.3	-1.1	1,087.4	11.2
2001	1,087.7	-4.2	1,043.2	-15.4	1,019.4	-8.8	-	-	-	-

Source: "National Income and Product Account Tables: Selected NIPA Tables," *Survey of Current Business*, January 2002, U.S. Department of Commerce, Bureau of Economic Analysis, National Income and Wealth Division. Data downloaded from www.stat.usa.gov. A dash (-) indicates that no data are available.

Gross Domestic Product
Gross private domestic investment
Fixed investment - Residential - Actual Dollars

In billions of actual dollars and percent. Quarterly data are seasonally adjusted and annualized. Growth rates for quarters are compound annual growth rates; changes from year to year are percentage changes.

Year	1st Quarter	% Change	2nd Quarter	% Change	3rd Quarter	% Change	4th Quarter	% Change	TOTAL	% Change
1959	27.8	-	28.8	15.2	28.3	-6.8	27.5	-10.8	28.1	-
1960	28.4	13.7	26.1	-28.7	25.3	-11.7	25.3	-	26.3	-6.4
1961	25.3	-	25.5	3.2	26.9	23.8	27.8	14.1	26.4	0.4
1962	28.4	8.9	29.2	11.8	29.2	-	29.1	-1.4	29.0	9.8
1963	30.2	16.0	32.2	29.2	32.5	3.8	33.7	15.6	32.1	10.7
1964	35.4	21.8	34.2	-12.9	33.7	-5.7	33.8	1.2	34.3	6.9
1965	33.9	1.2	34.2	3.6	34.3	1.2	34.5	2.4	34.2	-0.3
1966	34.8	3.5	33.2	-17.2	31.9	-14.8	29.2	-29.8	32.3	-5.6
1967	28.3	-11.8	31.6	55.5	33.4	24.8	36.0	35.0	32.4	0.3
1968	36.9	10.4	38.2	14.9	38.9	7.5	40.9	22.2	38.7	19.4
1969	43.2	24.5	43.4	1.9	43.2	-1.8	40.7	-21.2	42.6	10.1
1970	40.7	-	39.4	-12.2	40.4	10.5	45.0	53.9	41.4	-2.8
1971	48.6	36.0	54.6	59.3	58.3	30.0	61.5	23.8	55.8	34.8
1972	66.6	37.5	68.2	10.0	69.6	8.5	74.3	29.9	69.7	24.9
1973	77.9	20.8	75.8	-10.4	75.0	-4.2	72.7	-11.7	75.3	8.0
1974	69.0	-18.9	67.5	-8.4	67.4	-0.6	60.0	-37.2	66.0	-12.4
1975	57.7	-14.5	59.9	16.1	64.6	35.3	68.7	27.9	62.7	-5.0
1976	76.2	51.4	80.7	25.8	80.6	-0.5	92.5	73.5	82.5	31.6
1977	97.6	23.9	111.7	71.6	115.0	12.4	116.9	6.8	110.3	33.7
1978	121.1	15.2	130.5	34.9	135.8	17.3	139.1	10.1	131.6	19.3
1979	138.6	-1.4	140.9	6.8	143.5	7.6	141.2	-6.3	141.0	7.1
1980	134.5	-17.7	111.2	-53.3	115.9	18.0	131.3	64.7	123.2	-12.6
1981	132.0	2.1	128.9	-9.1	120.2	-24.4	109.6	-30.9	122.6	-0.5
1982	104.8	-16.4	102.8	-7.4	102.3	-1.9	112.8	47.8	105.7	-13.8
1983	130.9	81.4	148.2	64.3	162.6	44.9	168.5	15.3	152.5	44.3
1984	175.6	18.0	181.4	13.9	180.8	-1.3	181.3	1.1	179.8	17.9
1985	183.4	4.7	182.8	-1.3	187.7	11.2	193.9	13.9	186.9	3.9
1986	204.5	23.7	218.3	29.8	224.1	11.1	225.6	2.7	218.1	16.7
1987	225.3	-0.5	229.2	7.1	227.4	-3.1	228.4	1.8	227.6	4.4
1988	229.6	2.1	233.3	6.6	235.7	4.2	238.4	4.7	234.2	2.9
1989	237.0	-2.3	232.3	-7.7	230.2	-3.6	227.8	-4.1	231.8	-1.0
1990	234.1	11.5	224.2	-15.9	212.1	-19.9	196.9	-25.7	216.8	-6.5
1991	185.0	-22.1	186.6	3.5	194.5	18.0	200.0	11.8	191.5	-11.7
1992	211.8	25.8	223.9	24.9	226.6	4.9	239.7	25.2	225.5	17.8
1993	242.7	5.1	244.1	2.3	252.9	15.2	267.3	24.8	251.8	11.7
1994	276.4	14.3	288.4	18.5	289.3	1.3	289.8	0.7	286.0	13.6
1995	287.6	-3.0	276.9	-14.1	284.9	12.1	293.1	12.0	285.6	-0.1
1996	300.5	10.5	316.3	22.7	319.0	3.5	317.2	-2.2	313.3	9.7
1997	320.0	3.6	325.7	7.3	329.8	5.1	337.5	9.7	328.2	4.8
1998	347.2	12.0	357.6	12.5	370.5	15.2	382.2	13.2	364.4	11.0
1999	395.8	15.0	402.6	7.1	405.5	2.9	410.3	4.8	403.5	10.7
2000	427.1	17.4	428.7	1.5	421.0	-7.0	423.4	2.3	425.1	5.4
2001	437.0	13.5	446.2	8.7	451.6	4.9	-	-	-	-

Source: "National Income and Product Account Tables: Selected NIPA Tables," *Survey of Current Business*, January 2002, U.S. Department of Commerce, Bureau of Economic Analysis, National Income and Wealth Division. Data downloaded from www.stat.usa.gov. A dash (-) indicates that no data are available.

Gross Domestic Product
Gross private domestic investment
Fixed investment - Residential - Chained (1996) Dollars

In billions of chained (1996) dollars and percent. Quarterly data are seasonally adjusted and annualized. Growth rates for quarters are compound annual growth rates; changes from year to year are percentage changes.

Year	1st Quarter	% Change	2nd Quarter	% Change	3rd Quarter	% Change	4th Quarter	% Change	TOTAL	% Change
1987	291.3	-	294.1	3.9	289.3	-6.4	288.0	-1.8	290.7	-
1988	287.0	-1.4	289.0	2.8	290.2	1.7	290.8	0.8	289.2	-0.5
1989	287.0	-5.1	277.9	-12.1	274.5	-4.8	269.9	-6.5	277.3	-4.1
1990	275.2	8.1	262.5	-17.2	247.2	-21.4	229.2	-26.1	253.5	-8.6
1991	214.7	-23.0	215.6	1.7	223.4	15.3	230.6	13.5	221.1	-12.8
1992	245.0	27.4	256.6	20.3	257.9	2.0	269.2	18.7	257.2	16.3
1993	269.5	0.4	268.6	-1.3	275.7	11.0	290.1	22.6	276.0	7.3
1994	296.5	9.1	307.5	15.7	305.2	-3.0	301.8	-4.4	302.7	9.7
1995	295.8	-7.7	283.5	-15.6	290.4	10.1	297.3	9.8	291.7	-3.6
1996	303.6	8.7	318.1	20.5	317.3	-1.0	314.0	-4.1	313.3	7.4
1997	314.7	0.9	318.7	5.2	320.3	2.0	324.9	5.9	319.7	2.0
1998	333.0	10.4	340.5	9.3	349.5	11.0	357.4	9.4	345.1	7.9
1999	366.3	10.3	368.9	2.9	368.2	-0.8	369.7	1.6	368.3	6.7
2000	377.3	8.5	376.5	-0.8	366.3	-10.4	365.3	-1.1	371.4	0.8
2001	372.9	8.6	378.3	5.9	380.5	2.3	-	-	-	-

Source: "National Income and Product Account Tables: Selected NIPA Tables," *Survey of Current Business*, January 2002, U.S. Department of Commerce, Bureau of Economic Analysis, National Income and Wealth Division. Data downloaded from www.stat.usa.gov. A dash (-) indicates that no data are available.

Gross Domestic Product

Gross private domestic investment
Change in business inventories - Actual Dollars

In billions of actual dollars. Quarterly data are seasonally adjusted and annualized.

Year	1st Quarter	2nd Quarter	3rd Quarter	4th Quarter	TOTAL
1959	3.9	7.3	0.4	4.1	3.9
1960	11.2	3.2	4.3	-5.8	3.2
1961	-2.5	1.8	6.7	6.0	3.0
1962	9.4	5.4	6.2	3.4	6.1
1963	6.9	4.8	5.7	5.1	5.6
1964	5.1	4.5	4.7	5.0	4.8
1965	11.5	8.6	9.3	7.6	9.2
1966	13.9	12.3	11.9	16.5	13.6
1967	15.4	6.3	9.3	8.4	9.9
1968	8.4	14.1	7.7	6.0	9.1
1969	11.5	9.2	10.2	5.8	9.2
1970	1.8	5.1	5.1	-4.0	2.0
1971	12.3	10.9	10.2	-0.3	8.3
1972	3.2	12.0	13.7	7.5	9.1
1973	10.6	18.2	9.8	25.0	15.9
1974	12.5	17.4	5.6	20.4	14.0
1975	-10.0	-14.0	-1.4	0.3	-6.3
1976	14.7	22.5	20.8	10.5	17.1
1977	14.8	19.5	30.9	24.1	22.3
1978	25.5	24.3	25.0	28.5	25.8
1979	23.9	27.4	12.1	8.6	18.0
1980	9.9	7.8	-33.9	-9.1	-6.3
1981	38.8	11.7	44.0	24.8	29.8
1982	-21.5	-4.2	5.8	-39.8	-14.9
1983	-35.1	-7.7	-4.2	23.9	-5.8
1984	73.0	69.3	71.3	48.0	65.4
1985	16.2	21.7	16.3	33.1	21.8
1986	30.3	15.7	-7.0	-12.7	6.6
1987	28.0	16.5	1.0	63.1	27.1
1988	17.0	19.7	18.2	19.1	18.5
1989	48.2	36.0	10.0	16.6	27.7
1990	13.9	33.7	21.9	-11.3	14.5
1991	-15.3	-17.7	1.0	31.1	-0.2
1992	-1.0	21.8	19.1	20.2	15.0
1993	36.1	24.3	7.0	17.0	21.1
1994	43.8	79.8	52.0	74.6	62.6
1995	62.7	35.8	13.4	20.2	33.0
1996	6.8	29.8	50.0	33.5	30.0
1997	48.8	87.7	49.9	65.1	62.9
1998	106.7	40.9	69.5	75.4	73.1
1999	80.2	30.0	39.1	84.9	58.6
2000	30.9	75.4	52.5	38.7	49.4
2001	-25.5	-36.6	-57.8	-	-

Source: "National Income and Product Account Tables: Selected NIPA Tables," *Survey of Current Business*, January 2002, U.S. Department of Commerce, Bureau of Economic Analysis, National Income and Wealth Division. Data downloaded from www.stat.usa.gov. A dash (-) indicates that no data are available.

Gross Domestic Product
Gross private domestic investment
Change in business inventories - Chained (1996) Dollars

In billions of chained 1996 dollars. Quarterly data are seasonally adjusted and annualized.

Year	1st Quarter	2nd Quarter	3rd Quarter	4th Quarter	TOTAL
1987	33.9	17.3	-2.1	69.3	29.6
1988	17.2	18.9	18.5	18.9	18.4
1989	51.5	38.9	10.2	17.9	29.6
1990	15.7	36.3	24.1	-9.9	16.5
1991	-15.5	-19.6	-1.3	32.4	-1.0
1992	-	24.9	21.4	22.0	17.1
1993	36.2	23.4	4.7	15.7	20.0
1994	47.8	85.8	56.3	77.4	66.8
1995	62.2	32.5	9.0	18.0	30.4
1996	5.6	30.3	51.2	32.9	30.0
1997	49.3	88.3	51.3	66.1	63.8
1998	113.1	42.0	71.8	80.0	76.7
1999	83.4	32.7	39.6	92.7	62.1
2000	28.9	78.9	51.7	42.8	50.6
2001	-27.1	-38.3	-61.9	-	-

Source: "National Income and Product Account Tables: Selected NIPA Tables," *Survey of Current Business*, January 2002, U.S. Department of Commerce, Bureau of Economic Analysis, National Income and Wealth Division. Data downloaded from www.stat.usa.gov. A dash (-) indicates that no data are available.

NET EXPORTS OF GOODS AND SERVICES
Component of Gross Domestic Product

Net exports of goods and services—the trade balance—account for the United States' trade with the rest of the world. This measure presents exports less imports of all goods and services; hence it can be a negative value. The category is subdivided into Exports and Imports. BEA estimates are developed from three categories: (1) merchandise exports and imports, (2) receipts from abroad and payments made abroad, including investment earnings, and (3) receipts and payments for other services; federal purchases and sales abroad are included in this category.

Presentation of Data

Data are shown from 1959 to 2001 in quarterly and in annual increments. Changes from one period to the next are shown for Exports and Imports but not for Net Exports, which can exhibit negative values. Changes from quarter to quarter are annualized, compounded growth rates as explained in the section on Gross National Product. Changes from year to year are simple percentile changes.

Analytical Uses

Net exports are, generally, an indicator of the national vigor in trading with the rest of the world. The category measures the U.S. trade balance directly; the trade balance, in turn, has a direct impact on GDP. Indirectly, net exports reflect (1) the strength of the dollar, (2) U.S. vulnerability in commodity categories, and (3) U.S. competitiveness in manufacturing and services.

A positive net exports figure adds to GDP; a negative figure subtracts from GDP and, consequently, can contribute to or even cause negative GDP growth rate. In national product accounting, exports, manufactured domestically, are part of GDP; imports, manufactured elsewhere, and therefore in another nation's GDP, are taken from GDP.

The trade balance is significantly influenced by the strength of the dollar as measured against other currencies. When the dollar is strong relative to other currencies, it can buy more abroad; at the same time, dollar-denominated goods are more expensive abroad and discourage sales. The value of the dollar, however, is controlled in part by national and international policies and the relative performance of other economies rather than by pure market forces. A negative trade balance, therefore, does not invariably signal economic weakness.

The trade balance has been negative since 1977. As an indicator of economic prospects, the fact that net exports are negative is not as meaningful as the trend: is the trade deficit growing or decreasing. A growing deficit may signal problems; a shrinking deficit may signal a stronger economy because the ratio of exports to imports is changing favorably. The deficit has grown sharply beginning in 1997.

Net exports indicate, indirectly, U.S. dependence on important commodities, e.g. petroleum. An artificial increase in the price of crude oil can produce large trade deficits and also increase prices domestically. Similarly, net exports are influenced by the competitiveness of other economies in selling their goods to us. In recent years attention has focused on Japan and China, for instance.

Gross Domestic Product
Net exports of goods and services - Actual Dollars

In billions of actual dollars. Quarterly data are seasonally adjusted and annualized.

Year	1st Quarter	2nd Quarter	3rd Quarter	4th Quarter	TOTAL
1959	-1.7	-2.5	-1.1	-1.4	-1.7
1960	0.9	1.7	3.0	4.0	2.4
1961	4.4	3.3	2.8	2.9	3.4
1962	2.3	3.2	2.9	1.5	2.4
1963	2.0	3.7	3.1	4.4	3.3
1964	5.9	4.9	5.4	5.7	5.5
1965	3.0	4.7	3.7	4.1	3.9
1966	3.2	2.0	0.8	1.5	1.9
1967	2.3	2.1	1.1	0.2	1.4
1968	-1.2	-0.6	-1.3	-1.9	-1.3
1969	-1.9	-1.8	-1.3	0.1	-1.2
1970	1.1	2.4	0.9	0.4	1.2
1971	0.8	-3.8	-3.1	-6.0	-3.0
1972	-8.6	-8.3	-7.9	-7.1	-8.0
1973	-4.4	-1.1	3.2	4.7	0.6
1974	4.3	-5.6	-9.1	-2.2	-3.1
1975	13.1	16.6	11.6	12.9	13.6
1976	4.2	-1.1	-5.0	-7.2	-2.3
1977	-21.6	-21.7	-21.1	-30.3	-23.7
1978	-39.3	-23.3	-24.6	-17.3	-26.1
1979	-19.2	-23.4	-24.4	-29.0	-24.0
1980	-37.2	-16.7	3.3	-8.9	-14.9
1981	-17.0	-16.4	-10.2	-16.3	-15.0
1982	-17.2	-5.0	-30.3	-29.7	-20.5
1983	-24.6	-45.5	-65.2	-71.3	-51.7
1984	-94.3	-103.5	-103.1	-107.1	-102.0
1985	-91.4	-114.7	-117.2	-133.6	-114.2
1986	-127.1	-129.2	-138.5	-132.8	-131.9
1987	-139.4	-144.7	-142.8	-142.2	-142.3
1988	-121.0	-103.4	-96.3	-104.4	-106.3
1989	-84.2	-81.4	-79.6	-77.6	-80.7
1990	-74.2	-60.7	-78.8	-72.1	-71.4
1991	-33.4	-12.6	-22.3	-14.5	-20.7
1992	-7.7	-27.1	-36.4	-40.1	-27.9
1993	-46.5	-57.3	-72.0	-66.2	-60.5
1994	-71.3	-84.2	-99.1	-93.8	-87.1
1995	-94.5	-109.0	-74.2	-59.3	-84.3
1996	-75.8	-89.8	-110.6	-79.7	-89.0
1997	-89.2	-75.0	-88.6	-104.6	-89.3
1998	-122.6	-154.9	-165.3	-164.1	-151.7
1999	-199.7	-241.1	-273.9	-288.7	-250.9
2000	-333.9	-350.8	-380.6	-390.6	-364.0
2001	-363.8	-347.4	-294.4	-	-

Source: "National Income and Product Account Tables: Selected NIPA Tables," *Survey of Current Business*, January 2002, U.S. Department of Commerce, Bureau of Economic Analysis, National Income and Wealth Division. Data downloaded from www.stat.usa.gov. A dash (-) indicates that no data are available.

Gross Domestic Product

Net exports of goods and services - Chained (1996) Dollars

In billions of chained 1996 dollars. Quarterly data are seasonally adjusted and annualized.

Year	1st Quarter	2nd Quarter	3rd Quarter	4th Quarter	TOTAL
1987	-161.3	-159.5	-153.2	-150.8	-156.2
1988	-124.2	-104.4	-108.8	-111.2	-112.1
1989	-85.2	-76.2	-81.5	-74.7	-79.4
1990	-62.3	-61.7	-67.6	-34.6	-56.5
1991	-18.2	-10.7	-23.9	-10.4	-15.8
1992	-6.7	-23.0	-22.0	-27.3	-19.8
1993	-44.4	-51.7	-72.3	-67.9	-59.1
1994	-80.1	-86.2	-92.2	-87.7	-86.5
1995	-92.5	-97.5	-67.3	-56.4	-78.4
1996	-75.0	-90.4	-115.9	-74.6	-89.0
1997	-94.0	-100.6	-119.6	-139.2	-113.3
1998	-180.8	-223.1	-241.2	-239.2	-221.1
1999	-283.0	-313.4	-333.3	-337.8	-316.9
2000	-371.1	-392.8	-411.2	-421.1	-399.1
2001	-404.5	-406.7	-411.0	-	

Source: "National Income and Product Account Tables: Selected NIPA Tables," *Survey of Current Business*, January 2002, U.S. Department of Commerce, Bureau of Economic Analysis, National Income and Wealth Division. Data downloaded from www.stat.usa.gov. A dash (-) indicates that no data are available.

Gross Domestic Product
Net exports of goods and services
Exports: Total - Actual Dollars

In billions of actual dollars. Quarterly data are seasonally adjusted and annualized.

Year	1st Quarter	2nd Quarter	3rd Quarter	4th Quarter	TOTAL
1959	19.7	20.0	21.8	21.1	20.6
1960	24.2	25.2	25.9	25.8	25.3
1961	26.1	25.2	26.1	26.8	26.0
1962	26.6	28.1	28.0	27.0	27.4
1963	27.2	29.6	29.8	31.1	29.4
1964	32.9	32.6	33.9	35.0	33.6
1965	31.5	36.3	35.7	38.0	35.4
1966	38.2	38.2	39.0	40.4	38.9
1967	41.7	41.1	40.7	41.9	41.4
1968	43.2	44.8	47.0	46.2	45.3
1969	41.9	50.9	51.0	53.2	49.3
1970	54.7	57.6	57.3	58.3	57.0
1971	59.5	59.5	62.4	56.0	59.3
1972	63.5	63.1	66.2	72.1	66.2
1973	81.0	88.3	94.3	103.4	91.8
1974	114.6	123.8	124.5	134.4	124.3
1975	138.0	131.8	133.7	141.7	136.3
1976	143.1	146.0	150.9	155.4	148.9
1977	154.8	161.3	161.8	157.1	158.8
1978	164.0	185.6	190.5	204.5	186.1
1979	210.7	219.7	232.9	251.5	228.7
1980	267.1	275.9	282.5	290.3	278.9
1981	302.8	305.5	299.7	303.2	302.8
1982	292.3	294.2	279.0	265.1	282.6
1983	270.6	272.5	278.2	286.7	277.0
1984	293.7	303.0	306.5	309.2	303.1
1985	305.9	303.9	297.0	305.3	303.0
1986	312.0	314.2	320.1	334.9	320.3
1987	337.5	356.8	373.7	394.5	365.6
1988	421.0	441.9	455.8	469.0	446.9
1989	492.0	512.5	509.4	522.0	509.0
1990	541.6	554.6	555.3	577.1	557.2
1991	577.1	602.5	602.3	624.5	601.6
1992	629.5	633.4	637.2	647.0	636.8
1993	646.4	660.6	646.1	678.8	659.0
1994	683.8	714.5	736.1	765.8	725.1
1995	787.7	802.5	834.1	850.0	818.6
1996	853.3	864.7	865.6	913.1	874.2
1997	927.8	966.8	988.7	982.4	966.4
1998	974.1	959.2	946.7	979.7	964.9
1999	960.2	971.3	996.6	1,031.0	989.8
2000	1,059.7	1,099.7	1,131.1	1,121.0	1,102.9
2001	1,117.4	1,079.6	1,020.6	-	-

Source: "National Income and Product Account Tables: Selected NIPA Tables," *Survey of Current Business*, January 2002, U.S. Department of Commerce, Bureau of Economic Analysis, National Income and Wealth Division. Data downloaded from www.stat.usa.gov. A dash (-) indicates that no data are available.

Gross Domestic Product
Net exports of goods and services
Exports: Total - Chained (1996) Dollars

In billions of chained 1996 dollars. Quarterly data are seasonally adjusted and annualized.

Year	1st Quarter	2nd Quarter	3rd Quarter	4th Quarter	TOTAL
1959	69.1	70.6	76.4	73.5	72.4
1960	83.8	87.3	89.3	89.3	87.5
1961	89.9	85.7	89.2	90.8	88.9
1962	90.1	96.1	95.9	92.5	93.7
1963	92.8	101.3	102.1	106.7	100.7
1964	112.6	111.7	115.0	117.4	114.2
1965	103.2	119.6	117.5	125.6	116.5
1966	124.0	123.1	123.9	126.1	124.3
1967	127.9	126.6	125.3	128.3	127.0
1968	131.3	133.5	141.8	138.7	136.3
1969	124.1	150.5	148.8	151.4	143.7
1970	155.0	160.1	159.9	162.1	159.3
1971	160.7	160.6	169.4	151.0	160.4
1972	168.8	166.4	173.8	184.9	173.5
1973	201.8	210.5	212.4	221.1	211.4
1974	228.6	238.4	226.7	232.6	231.6
1975	232.2	222.7	226.5	238.7	230.0
1976	237.9	240.1	246.8	249.7	243.6
1977	245.9	252.5	254.5	246.0	249.7
1978	251.8	278.2	281.1	292.3	275.9
1979	292.3	292.9	303.1	321.2	302.4
1980	331.3	337.5	336.2	334.3	334.8
1981	340.2	342.0	334.8	337.5	338.6
1982	323.8	326.0	311.3	297.5	314.6
1983	302.4	303.4	307.9	314.1	306.9
1984	321.4	329.4	336.5	343.1	332.6
1985	342.8	341.3	336.2	346.2	341.6
1986	355.9	360.0	368.6	382.6	366.8
1987	383.6	399.3	416.7	432.2	408.0
1988	456.1	468.8	477.3	491.8	473.5
1989	510.5	530.8	530.8	545.5	529.4
1990	565.8	577.6	572.8	586.5	575.7
1991	584.5	613.3	616.9	638.3	613.2
1992	643.9	647.1	650.8	662.2	651.0
1993	661.4	674.4	660.8	694.3	672.7
1994	696.7	725.1	742.4	767.1	732.8
1995	780.6	788.9	821.9	841.4	808.2
1996	846.1	860.1	867.0	923.5	874.2
1997	940.3	979.2	1,004.2	1,002.1	981.5
1998	1,003.4	993.1	987.6	1,025.6	1,002.4
1999	1,007.6	1,018.0	1,041.8	1,072.1	1,034.9
2000	1,095.5	1,130.6	1,159.3	1,147.5	1,133.2
2001	1,144.1	1,108.3	1,052.2	-	-

Source: "National Income and Product Account Tables: Selected NIPA Tables," *Survey of Current Business*, January 2002, U.S. Department of Commerce, Bureau of Economic Analysis, National Income and Wealth Division. Data downloaded from www.stat.usa.gov. A dash (-) indicates that no data are available.

49

Gross Domestic Product
Net exports of goods and services
Exports - Goods - Actual Dollars

In billions of actual dollars. Quarterly data are seasonally adjusted and annualized.

Year	1st Quarter	2nd Quarter	3rd Quarter	4th Quarter	TOTAL
1959	15.6	15.9	17.5	16.9	16.5
1960	19.5	20.5	20.9	20.9	20.5
1961	21.2	20.1	21.0	21.5	20.9
1962	21.2	22.3	22.3	21.1	21.7
1963	21.3	23.4	23.8	24.9	23.3
1964	26.1	26.0	26.9	27.8	26.7
1965	24.4	28.8	27.9	30.1	27.8
1966	30.4	30.1	30.6	31.9	30.7
1967	32.5	32.3	31.6	32.3	32.2
1968	33.6	34.9	36.6	35.9	35.3
1969	31.6	39.9	39.5	42.0	38.3
1970	43.0	45.0	44.8	45.4	44.5
1971	45.9	45.7	48.4	42.2	45.6
1972	49.7	48.9	51.8	56.8	51.8
1973	64.4	70.9	75.6	84.8	73.9
1974	93.1	100.6	101.2	109.0	101.0
1975	112.0	105.9	107.1	113.4	109.6
1976	113.5	116.3	119.0	122.3	117.8
1977	121.3	126.2	126.1	121.0	123.7
1978	125.0	146.1	149.3	161.2	145.4
1979	167.0	175.7	188.0	205.4	184.0
1980	217.8	224.2	226.9	234.2	225.8
1981	242.2	242.0	234.2	238.0	239.1
1982	224.9	226.0	211.6	197.6	215.0
1983	200.7	202.8	207.4	218.3	207.3
1984	218.3	224.6	228.4	231.2	225.6
1985	225.7	223.5	217.4	222.4	222.2
1986	220.5	223.0	224.5	235.9	226.0
1987	234.3	248.7	264.2	283.0	257.5
1988	304.6	321.4	331.6	345.5	325.8
1989	359.3	377.8	370.2	379.4	371.7
1990	391.6	399.8	394.6	408.2	398.5
1991	414.8	428.8	423.9	438.1	426.4
1992	442.1	445.9	447.7	459.0	448.7
1993	451.2	462.2	447.9	477.7	459.7
1994	475.8	499.5	518.8	544.3	509.6
1995	563.6	574.3	593.0	604.4	583.8
1996	607.8	611.4	615.4	639.0	618.4
1997	658.2	688.5	706.7	702.3	688.9
1998	693.6	673.0	666.7	692.0	681.3
1999	675.1	681.4	703.8	732.7	698.3
2000	750.0	779.3	813.4	799.7	785.6
2001	794.2	754.4	710.7	-	-

Source: "National Income and Product Account Tables: Selected NIPA Tables," *Survey of Current Business*, January 2002, U.S. Department of Commerce, Bureau of Economic Analysis, National Income and Wealth Division. Data downloaded from www.stat.usa.gov. A dash (-) indicates that no data are available.

Gross Domestic Product
Net exports of goods and services
Exports - Goods - Chained (1996) Dollars

In billions of chained 1996 dollars. Quarterly data are seasonally adjusted and annualized.

Year	1st Quarter	2nd Quarter	3rd Quarter	4th Quarter	TOTAL
1987	252.1	262.8	278.6	292.1	271.4
1988	309.9	318.5	323.4	338.4	322.6
1989	348.7	366.8	362.9	374.5	363.2
1990	388.3	396.0	389.3	399.2	393.2
1991	405.2	421.5	421.8	435.8	421.1
1992	441.5	445.9	449.3	462.4	449.8
1993	454.5	464.9	451.4	482.7	463.4
1994	478.0	500.0	516.8	538.0	508.2
1995	549.8	556.5	576.7	592.0	568.8
1996	599.2	605.5	617.2	651.7	618.4
1997	672.8	705.8	726.8	727.1	708.1
1998	726.7	710.6	711.5	742.8	722.9
1999	727.3	735.2	758.1	784.6	751.3
2000	800.8	829.2	864.8	849.5	836.1
2001	844.4	805.2	762.9	-	-

Source: "National Income and Product Account Tables: Selected NIPA Tables," *Survey of Current Business*, January 2002, U.S. Department of Commerce, Bureau of Economic Analysis, National Income and Wealth Division. Data downloaded from www.stat.usa.gov. A dash (-) indicates that no data are available.

Gross Domestic Product

Net exports of goods and services
Exports - Services - Actual Dollars

In billions of actual dollars and percent. Quarterly data are seasonally adjusted and annualized. Growth rates for quarters are compound annual growth rates; changes from year to year are percentage changes.

Year	1st Quarter	% Change	2nd Quarter	% Change	3rd Quarter	% Change	4th Quarter	% Change	TOTAL	% Change
1959	4.1	-	4.1	-	4.3	21.0	4.3	-	4.2	-
1960	4.7	42.7	4.7	-	4.9	18.1	4.9	-	4.8	14.3
1961	4.9	-	5.1	17.4	5.2	8.1	5.2	-	5.1	6.2
1962	5.4	16.3	5.8	33.1	5.7	-6.7	5.9	14.8	5.7	11.8
1963	5.9	-	6.2	21.9	6.0	-12.3	6.3	21.6	6.1	7.0
1964	6.8	35.7	6.6	-11.3	6.9	19.5	7.1	12.1	6.9	13.1
1965	7.1	-	7.5	24.5	7.8	17.0	8.0	10.7	7.6	10.1
1966	7.8	-9.6	8.1	16.3	8.4	15.7	8.5	4.8	8.2	7.9
1967	9.2	37.2	8.9	-12.4	9.0	4.6	9.6	29.5	9.2	12.2
1968	9.6	-	9.9	13.1	10.3	17.2	10.3	-	10.0	8.7
1969	10.3	-	11.0	30.1	11.5	19.5	11.2	-10.0	11.0	10.0
1970	11.6	15.1	12.6	39.2	12.6	-	12.9	9.9	12.4	12.7
1971	13.6	23.5	13.8	6.0	13.9	2.9	13.8	-2.8	13.8	11.3
1972	13.8	-	14.2	12.1	14.3	2.8	15.3	31.0	14.4	4.3
1973	16.6	38.6	17.4	20.7	18.7	33.4	18.6	-2.1	17.8	23.6
1974	21.6	81.9	23.1	30.8	23.2	1.7	25.4	43.7	23.3	30.9
1975	26.0	9.8	25.9	-1.5	26.5	9.6	28.3	30.1	26.7	14.6
1976	29.6	19.7	29.7	1.4	31.9	33.1	33.1	15.9	31.1	16.5
1977	33.5	4.9	35.2	21.9	35.7	5.8	36.1	4.6	35.1	12.9
1978	38.9	34.8	39.5	6.3	41.2	18.4	43.3	22.0	40.7	16.0
1979	43.7	3.7	44.0	2.8	44.9	8.4	46.1	11.1	44.7	9.8
1980	49.3	30.8	51.7	20.9	55.6	33.8	56.1	3.6	53.2	19.0
1981	60.6	36.2	63.5	20.6	65.5	13.2	65.1	-2.4	63.7	19.7
1982	67.5	15.6	68.2	4.2	67.4	-4.6	67.5	0.6	67.6	6.1
1983	69.9	15.0	69.7	-1.1	70.8	6.5	68.4	-12.9	69.7	3.1
1984	75.4	47.7	78.4	16.9	78.1	-1.5	78.0	-0.5	77.5	11.2
1985	80.2	11.8	80.4	1.0	79.6	-3.9	82.9	17.6	80.8	4.3
1986	91.5	48.4	91.1	-1.7	95.6	21.3	99.0	15.0	94.3	16.7
1987	103.2	18.1	108.1	20.4	109.5	5.3	111.4	7.1	108.1	14.6
1988	116.4	19.2	120.5	14.9	124.1	12.5	123.6	-1.6	121.1	12.0
1989	132.7	32.9	134.7	6.2	139.3	14.4	142.6	9.8	137.3	13.4
1990	150.0	22.4	154.9	13.7	160.7	15.8	168.9	22.0	158.6	15.5
1991	162.3	-14.7	173.7	31.2	178.4	11.3	186.4	19.2	175.2	10.5
1992	187.5	2.4	187.5	-	189.5	4.3	188.0	-3.1	188.1	7.4
1993	195.2	16.2	198.4	6.7	198.5	0.2	201.1	5.3	198.3	5.4
1994	208.0	14.4	215.0	14.2	217.3	4.3	221.5	8.0	215.5	8.7
1995	224.1	4.8	228.2	7.5	241.1	24.6	245.6	7.7	234.7	8.9
1996	245.5	-0.2	253.3	13.3	250.1	-5.0	274.0	44.1	255.8	9.0
1997	269.6	-6.3	278.2	13.4	282.0	5.6	280.1	-2.7	277.5	8.5
1998	280.4	0.4	286.2	8.5	280.0	-8.4	287.7	11.5	283.6	2.2
1999	285.1	-3.6	289.9	6.9	292.7	3.9	298.3	7.9	291.5	2.8
2000	309.7	16.2	320.4	14.6	317.7	-3.3	321.3	4.6	317.3	8.9
2001	323.2	2.4	325.2	2.5	309.8	-17.6	-	-	-	-

Source: "National Income and Product Account Tables: Selected NIPA Tables," *Survey of Current Business*, January 2002, U.S. Department of Commerce, Bureau of Economic Analysis, National Income and Wealth Division. Data downloaded from www.stat.usa.gov. A dash (-) indicates that no data are available.

Gross Domestic Product
Net exports of goods and services
Exports - Services - Chained (1996) Dollars

In billions of chained (1996) dollars and percent. Quarterly data are seasonally adjusted and annualized. Growth rates for quarters are compound annual growth rates; changes from year to year are percentage changes.

Year	1st Quarter	% Change	2nd Quarter	% Change	3rd Quarter	% Change	4th Quarter	% Change	TOTAL	% Change
1987	134.5	-	139.6	16.1	140.4	2.3	141.7	3.8	139.1	-
1988	147.5	17.4	151.6	11.6	155.4	10.4	153.6	-4.6	152.0	9.3
1989	162.8	26.2	163.8	2.5	168.8	12.8	171.5	6.6	166.7	9.7
1990	178.1	16.3	182.3	9.8	184.8	5.6	188.6	8.5	183.5	10.1
1991	179.5	-17.9	192.4	32.0	196.0	7.7	203.4	16.0	192.9	5.1
1992	203.1	-0.6	201.7	-2.7	202.0	0.6	199.9	-4.1	201.7	4.6
1993	207.5	16.1	210.0	4.9	210.1	0.2	211.9	3.5	209.9	4.1
1994	219.4	14.9	225.6	11.8	226.0	0.7	229.3	6.0	225.1	7.2
1995	230.8	2.6	232.5	3.0	245.3	23.9	249.5	7.0	239.5	6.4
1996	247.0	-3.9	254.6	12.9	249.8	-7.3	271.6	39.7	255.8	6.8
1997	267.6	-5.8	273.7	9.4	277.7	6.0	275.4	-3.3	273.6	7.0
1998	277.0	2.3	282.4	8.0	276.3	-8.4	283.3	10.5	279.8	2.3
1999	280.5	-3.9	283.2	3.9	284.6	2.0	288.7	5.9	284.2	1.6
2000	295.9	10.4	302.9	9.8	297.8	-6.6	300.5	3.7	299.3	5.3
2001	301.8	1.7	303.6	2.4	289.6	-17.2	-	-	-	-

Source: "National Income and Product Account Tables: Selected NIPA Tables," *Survey of Current Business*, January 2002, U.S. Department of Commerce, Bureau of Economic Analysis, National Income and Wealth Division. Data downloaded from www.stat.usa.gov. A dash (-) indicates that no data are available.

Gross Domestic Product
Net exports of goods and services
Imports: Total - Actual Dollars

In billions of actual dollars and percent. Quarterly data are seasonally adjusted and annualized. Growth rates for quarters are compound annual growth rates; changes from year to year are percentage changes.

Year	1st Quarter	% Change	2nd Quarter	% Change	3rd Quarter	% Change	4th Quarter	% Change	TOTAL	% Change
1959	21.4	-	22.5	22.2	22.9	7.3	22.5	-6.8	22.3	-
1960	23.3	15.0	23.5	3.5	22.9	-9.8	21.7	-19.4	22.8	2.2
1961	21.7	-	21.9	3.7	23.3	28.1	23.9	10.7	22.7	-0.4
1962	24.3	6.9	24.9	10.2	25.1	3.3	25.6	8.2	25.0	10.1
1963	25.2	-6.1	25.9	11.6	26.7	12.9	26.8	1.5	26.1	4.4
1964	27.0	3.0	27.7	10.8	28.4	10.5	29.3	13.3	28.1	7.7
1965	28.5	-10.5	31.7	53.1	32.0	3.8	33.9	26.0	31.5	12.1
1966	35.0	13.6	36.2	14.4	38.2	24.0	38.8	6.4	37.1	17.8
1967	39.4	6.3	39.0	-4.0	39.5	5.2	41.7	24.2	39.9	7.5
1968	44.4	28.5	45.4	9.3	48.2	27.0	48.2	-	46.6	16.8
1969	43.8	-31.8	52.7	109.6	52.4	-2.3	53.1	5.5	50.5	8.4
1970	53.5	3.0	55.2	13.3	56.4	9.0	57.9	11.1	55.8	10.5
1971	58.7	5.6	63.3	35.2	65.5	14.6	61.9	-20.2	62.3	11.6
1972	72.2	85.1	71.4	-4.4	74.1	16.0	79.2	30.5	74.2	19.1
1973	85.4	35.2	89.5	20.6	91.1	7.3	98.7	37.8	91.2	22.9
1974	110.3	56.0	129.4	89.4	133.6	13.6	136.6	9.3	127.5	39.8
1975	124.9	-30.1	115.2	-27.6	122.1	26.2	128.7	23.4	122.7	-3.8
1976	138.9	35.7	147.1	25.8	155.8	25.8	162.7	18.9	151.1	23.1
1977	176.4	38.2	183.0	15.8	182.9	-0.2	187.4	10.2	182.4	20.7
1978	203.3	38.5	208.8	11.3	215.1	12.6	221.8	13.1	212.3	16.4
1979	229.8	15.2	243.1	25.2	257.3	25.5	280.5	41.2	252.7	19.0
1980	304.3	38.5	292.6	-14.5	279.2	-17.1	299.2	31.9	293.8	16.3
1981	319.7	30.4	322.0	2.9	309.9	-14.2	319.4	12.8	317.8	8.2
1982	309.5	-11.8	299.1	-12.8	309.3	14.4	294.9	-17.4	303.2	-4.6
1983	295.3	0.5	318.0	34.5	343.4	36.0	358.0	18.1	328.6	8.4
1984	388.0	38.0	406.5	20.5	409.6	3.1	416.4	6.8	405.1	23.3
1985	397.3	-17.1	418.6	23.2	414.2	-4.1	438.9	26.1	417.2	3.0
1986	439.0	0.1	443.4	4.1	458.6	14.4	467.7	8.2	452.2	8.4
1987	476.8	8.0	501.5	22.4	516.5	12.5	536.7	16.6	507.9	12.3
1988	542.0	4.0	545.3	2.5	552.1	5.1	573.5	16.4	553.2	8.9
1989	576.2	1.9	594.0	12.9	589.0	-3.3	599.6	7.4	589.7	6.6
1990	615.8	11.3	615.3	-0.3	634.1	12.8	649.2	9.9	628.6	6.6
1991	610.5	-21.8	615.1	3.0	624.5	6.3	639.0	9.6	622.3	-1.0
1992	637.3	-1.1	660.5	15.4	673.6	8.2	687.1	8.3	664.6	6.8
1993	692.9	3.4	717.9	15.2	718.3	0.2	744.9	15.7	718.5	8.1
1994	755.1	5.6	798.7	25.2	835.2	19.6	859.6	12.2	812.1	13.0
1995	882.2	10.9	911.5	14.0	908.3	-1.4	909.3	0.4	902.8	11.2
1996	929.1	9.0	954.5	11.4	976.1	9.4	992.8	7.0	963.1	6.7
1997	1,017.1	10.2	1,041.7	10.0	1,077.3	14.4	1,087.0	3.7	1,055.8	9.6
1998	1,096.7	3.6	1,114.1	6.5	1,112.0	-0.8	1,143.8	11.9	1,116.7	5.8
1999	1,160.0	5.8	1,212.4	19.3	1,270.5	20.6	1,319.7	16.4	1,240.6	11.1
2000	1,393.6	24.4	1,450.4	17.3	1,511.8	18.0	1,511.6	-0.1	1,466.9	18.2
2001	1,481.2	-7.8	1,427.0	-13.9	1,315.0	-27.9	-	-	-	-

Source: "National Income and Product Account Tables: Selected NIPA Tables," *Survey of Current Business*, January 2002, U.S. Department of Commerce, Bureau of Economic Analysis, National Income and Wealth Division. Data downloaded from www.stat.usa.gov. A dash (-) indicates that no data are available.

Gross Domestic Product
Net exports of goods and services
Imports: Total - Chained (1996) Dollars

In billions of chained (1996) dollars and percent. Quarterly data are seasonally adjusted and annualized. Growth rates for quarters are compound annual growth rates; changes from year to year are percentage changes.

Year	1st Quarter	% Change	2nd Quarter	% Change	3rd Quarter	% Change	4th Quarter	% Change	TOTAL	% Change
1959	102.3	-	108.0	24.2	109.4	5.3	106.7	-9.5	106.6	-
1960	110.5	15.0	111.1	2.2	107.8	-11.4	102.7	-17.6	108.0	1.3
1961	102.2	-1.9	103.5	5.2	110.4	29.5	113.0	9.8	107.3	-0.6
1962	116.4	12.6	119.0	9.2	120.5	5.1	122.0	5.1	119.5	11.4
1963	119.1	-9.2	121.9	9.7	125.0	10.6	124.6	-1.3	122.7	2.7
1964	124.5	-0.3	127.3	9.3	130.7	11.1	134.3	11.5	129.2	5.3
1965	129.4	-13.8	144.7	56.4	145.3	1.7	152.4	21.0	142.9	10.6
1966	156.3	10.6	160.2	10.4	169.2	24.4	171.1	4.6	164.2	14.9
1967	173.5	5.7	172.4	-2.5	174.7	5.4	184.0	23.1	176.2	7.3
1968	194.7	25.4	197.7	6.3	209.5	26.1	207.7	-3.4	202.4	14.9
1969	188.2	-32.6	225.3	105.4	222.4	-5.1	219.9	-4.4	213.9	5.7
1970	219.2	-1.3	223.5	8.1	223.0	-0.9	226.5	6.4	223.1	4.3
1971	223.8	-4.7	240.7	33.8	246.0	9.1	229.3	-24.5	235.0	5.3
1972	262.8	72.5	253.4	-13.6	258.7	8.6	270.3	19.2	261.3	11.2
1973	282.8	19.8	274.7	-11.0	267.1	-10.6	269.1	3.0	273.4	4.6
1974	260.0	-12.9	273.8	23.0	269.0	-6.8	266.3	-4.0	267.2	-2.3
1975	239.6	-34.5	220.4	-28.4	238.7	37.6	251.5	23.2	237.5	-11.1
1976	267.2	27.4	278.8	18.5	290.2	17.4	299.8	13.9	284.0	19.6
1977	313.9	20.2	316.8	3.7	312.4	-5.4	316.8	5.8	315.0	10.9
1978	338.0	29.6	339.1	1.3	343.6	5.4	348.3	5.6	342.3	8.7
1979	347.3	-1.1	349.2	2.2	343.9	-5.9	351.3	8.9	347.9	1.6
1980	351.7	0.5	326.1	-26.1	302.6	-25.9	318.9	23.4	324.8	-6.6
1981	332.5	18.2	333.0	0.6	329.3	-4.4	338.7	11.9	333.4	2.6
1982	329.1	-10.9	323.7	-6.4	338.7	19.9	325.4	-14.8	329.2	-1.3
1983	332.8	9.4	358.4	34.5	386.3	35.0	405.3	21.2	370.7	12.6
1984	437.8	36.1	456.2	17.9	468.0	10.8	481.8	12.3	461.0	24.4
1985	471.1	-8.6	494.2	21.1	489.3	-3.9	508.3	16.5	490.7	6.4
1986	507.3	-0.8	528.8	18.1	543.6	11.7	548.1	3.4	531.9	8.4
1987	544.9	-2.3	558.9	10.7	569.9	8.1	583.0	9.5	564.2	6.1
1988	580.3	-1.8	573.2	-4.8	586.1	9.3	603.0	12.0	585.6	3.8
1989	595.7	-4.8	606.9	7.7	612.3	3.6	620.2	5.3	608.8	4.0
1990	628.1	5.2	639.3	7.3	640.4	0.7	621.0	-11.6	632.2	3.8
1991	602.7	-11.3	623.9	14.8	640.8	11.3	648.7	5.0	629.0	-0.5
1992	650.6	1.2	670.1	12.5	672.9	1.7	689.5	10.2	670.8	6.6
1993	705.8	9.8	726.1	12.0	733.1	3.9	762.2	16.8	731.8	9.1
1994	776.8	7.9	811.3	19.0	834.6	12.0	854.8	10.0	819.4	12.0
1995	873.1	8.8	886.4	6.2	889.1	1.2	897.8	4.0	886.6	8.2
1996	921.1	10.8	950.4	13.3	982.9	14.4	998.1	6.3	963.1	8.6
1997	1,034.3	15.3	1,079.8	18.8	1,123.8	17.3	1,141.2	6.3	1,094.8	13.7
1998	1,184.2	15.9	1,216.2	11.3	1,228.9	4.2	1,264.8	12.2	1,223.5	11.8
1999	1,290.6	8.4	1,331.4	13.3	1,375.1	13.8	1,409.8	10.5	1,351.7	10.5
2000	1,466.6	17.1	1,523.4	16.4	1,570.6	13.0	1,568.5	-0.5	1,532.3	13.4
2001	1,548.6	-5.0	1,515.0	-8.4	1,463.2	-13.0	-	-	-	-

Source: "National Income and Product Account Tables: Selected NIPA Tables," *Survey of Current Business*, January 2002, U.S. Department of Commerce, Bureau of Economic Analysis, National Income and Wealth Division. Data downloaded from www.stat.usa.gov. A dash (-) indicates that no data are available.

Gross Domestic Product
Net exports of goods and services
Imports - Goods - Actual Dollars

In billions of actual dollars and percent. Quarterly data are seasonally adjusted and annualized. Growth rates for quarters are compound annual growth rates; changes from year to year are percentage changes.

Year	1st Quarter	% Change	2nd Quarter	% Change	3rd Quarter	% Change	4th Quarter	% Change	TOTAL	% Change
1959	14.5	-	15.5	30.6	15.8	8.0	15.4	-9.7	15.3	-
1960	15.7	8.0	15.9	5.2	15.1	-18.7	14.2	-21.8	15.2	-0.7
1961	14.1	-2.8	14.3	5.8	15.8	49.0	16.1	7.8	15.1	-0.7
1962	16.4	7.7	16.9	12.8	17.1	4.8	17.0	-2.3	16.9	11.9
1963	16.9	-2.3	17.6	17.6	18.2	14.3	18.2	-	17.7	4.7
1964	18.3	2.2	19.1	18.7	19.7	13.2	20.4	15.0	19.4	9.6
1965	19.6	-14.8	22.4	70.6	22.8	7.3	24.2	26.9	22.2	14.4
1966	24.9	12.1	25.6	11.7	27.2	27.4	27.7	7.6	26.3	18.5
1967	27.7	-	26.8	-12.4	27.0	3.0	29.5	42.5	27.8	5.7
1968	32.1	40.2	33.2	14.4	35.4	29.3	35.1	-3.3	33.9	21.9
1969	30.8	-40.7	39.1	159.7	38.5	-6.0	38.8	3.2	36.8	8.6
1970	39.3	5.3	40.1	8.4	41.2	11.4	42.8	16.5	40.9	11.1
1971	43.4	5.7	47.4	42.3	49.6	19.9	45.7	-27.9	46.6	13.9
1972	55.1	111.3	54.1	-7.1	57.3	25.8	61.3	31.0	56.9	22.1
1973	66.5	38.5	70.0	22.8	72.1	12.6	78.8	42.7	71.8	26.2
1974	88.8	61.3	106.4	106.1	110.6	16.7	112.3	6.3	104.5	45.5
1975	100.9	-34.8	92.3	-30.0	98.8	31.3	104.0	22.8	99.0	-5.3
1976	113.5	41.9	121.3	30.5	128.9	27.5	134.7	19.3	124.6	25.9
1977	147.6	44.2	153.2	16.1	153.2	-	156.6	9.2	152.6	22.5
1978	170.3	39.9	175.1	11.8	179.4	10.2	184.8	12.6	177.4	16.3
1979	192.2	17.0	204.1	27.2	216.8	27.3	238.1	45.5	212.8	20.0
1980	259.7	41.5	248.5	-16.2	234.1	-21.2	252.0	34.3	248.6	16.8
1981	270.2	32.2	271.8	2.4	260.5	-15.6	268.8	13.4	267.8	7.7
1982	257.6	-15.7	245.8	-17.1	257.2	19.9	241.5	-22.3	250.5	-6.5
1983	242.5	1.7	262.8	37.9	285.9	40.1	299.6	20.6	272.7	8.9
1984	322.5	34.3	337.9	20.5	339.9	2.4	345.0	6.1	336.3	23.3
1985	325.4	-20.9	344.4	25.5	340.5	-4.5	362.8	28.9	343.3	2.1
1986	357.7	-5.5	365.1	8.5	374.8	11.1	382.5	8.5	370.0	7.8
1987	389.5	7.5	409.1	21.7	422.8	14.1	437.7	14.9	414.8	12.1
1988	441.5	3.5	445.7	3.9	451.1	4.9	470.2	18.0	452.1	9.0
1989	473.0	2.4	490.3	15.5	483.1	-5.7	491.5	7.1	484.5	7.2
1990	500.4	7.4	497.4	-2.4	511.3	11.7	522.9	9.4	508.0	4.9
1991	488.3	-24.0	493.5	4.3	504.6	9.3	516.5	9.8	500.7	-1.4
1992	516.8	0.2	541.0	20.1	557.2	12.5	564.4	5.3	544.9	8.8
1993	570.8	4.6	593.2	16.6	592.8	-0.3	614.4	15.4	592.8	8.8
1994	622.0	5.0	664.6	30.3	698.2	21.8	722.0	14.3	676.7	14.2
1995	740.4	10.6	766.9	15.1	761.9	-2.6	761.5	-0.2	757.6	12.0
1996	778.6	9.3	801.9	12.5	818.6	8.6	834.3	7.9	808.3	6.7
1997	852.3	8.9	874.5	10.8	903.1	13.7	910.3	3.2	885.1	9.5
1998	915.5	2.3	928.4	5.8	923.2	-2.2	952.8	13.5	930.0	5.1
1999	973.7	9.1	1,022.0	21.4	1,074.1	22.0	1,117.8	17.3	1,046.9	12.6
2000	1,180.7	24.5	1,232.1	18.6	1,283.0	17.6	1,284.0	0.3	1,244.9	18.9
2001	1,248.7	-10.6	1,197.8	-15.3	1,145.6	-16.3	-	-	-	-

Source: "National Income and Product Account Tables: Selected NIPA Tables," *Survey of Current Business*, January 2002, U.S. Department of Commerce, Bureau of Economic Analysis, National Income and Wealth Division. Data downloaded from www.stat.usa.gov. A dash (-) indicates that no data are available.

Gross Domestic Product
Net exports of goods and services
Imports - Goods - Chained (1996) Dollars

In billions of chained (1996) dollars and percent. Quarterly data are seasonally adjusted and annualized. Growth rates for quarters are compound annual growth rates; changes from year to year are percentage changes.

Year	1st Quarter	% Change	2nd Quarter	% Change	3rd Quarter	% Change	4th Quarter	% Change	TOTAL	% Change
1987	431.9	-	440.7	8.4	451.3	10.0	459.3	7.3	445.8	-
1988	458.0	-1.1	453.3	-4.0	464.5	10.3	479.7	13.7	463.9	4.1
1989	472.2	-6.1	482.8	9.3	485.9	2.6	492.6	5.6	483.4	4.2
1990	495.2	2.1	504.8	8.0	504.5	-0.2	487.2	-13.0	497.9	3.0
1991	472.8	-11.3	491.1	16.4	510.1	16.4	516.5	5.1	497.6	-0.1
1992	520.9	3.5	542.4	17.6	551.7	7.0	559.9	6.1	543.7	9.3
1993	576.1	12.1	594.5	13.4	599.4	3.3	623.8	17.3	598.4	10.1
1994	636.1	8.1	669.5	22.7	692.8	14.7	713.3	12.4	677.9	13.3
1995	725.5	7.0	740.3	8.4	742.1	1.0	748.4	3.4	739.1	9.0
1996	769.7	11.9	797.4	15.2	825.6	14.9	840.7	7.5	808.3	9.4
1997	869.6	14.5	913.0	21.5	948.0	16.2	961.9	6.0	923.1	14.2
1998	995.9	14.9	1,024.9	12.2	1,034.2	3.7	1,070.6	14.8	1,031.4	11.7
1999	1,101.2	11.9	1,141.7	15.5	1,182.1	14.9	1,211.6	10.4	1,159.2	12.4
2000	1,258.8	16.5	1,309.6	17.1	1,348.0	12.3	1,345.9	-0.6	1,315.6	13.5
2001	1,322.8	-6.7	1,290.1	-9.5	1,256.6	-10.0	-	-	-	-

Source: "National Income and Product Account Tables: Selected NIPA Tables," *Survey of Current Business*, January 2002, U.S. Department of Commerce, Bureau of Economic Analysis, National Income and Wealth Division. Data downloaded from www.stat.usa.gov. A dash (-) indicates that no data are available.

Gross Domestic Product
Net exports of goods and services
Imports - Services - Actual Dollars

In billions of actual dollars and percent. Quarterly data are seasonally adjusted and annualized. Growth rates for quarters are compound annual growth rates; changes from year to year are percentage changes.

Year	1st Quarter	% Change	2nd Quarter	% Change	3rd Quarter	% Change	4th Quarter	% Change	TOTAL	% Change
1959	6.9	-	7.0	5.9	7.1	5.8	7.1	-	7.0	-
1960	7.6	31.3	7.6	-	7.8	10.9	7.5	-14.5	7.6	8.6
1961	7.6	5.4	7.6	-	7.6	-	7.7	5.4	7.6	-
1962	7.9	10.8	8.0	5.2	8.0	-	8.5	27.4	8.1	6.6
1963	8.3	-9.1	8.3	-	8.6	15.3	8.5	-4.6	8.4	3.7
1964	8.6	4.8	8.6	-	8.7	4.7	8.9	9.5	8.7	3.6
1965	8.9	-	9.2	14.2	9.2	-	9.8	28.8	9.3	6.9
1966	10.1	12.8	10.6	21.3	11.0	16.0	11.1	3.7	10.7	15.1
1967	11.7	23.4	12.2	18.2	12.5	10.2	12.1	-12.2	12.2	14.0
1968	12.3	6.8	12.3	-	12.8	17.3	13.1	9.7	12.6	3.3
1969	13.0	-3.0	13.6	19.8	13.8	6.0	14.3	15.3	13.7	8.7
1970	14.2	-2.8	15.1	27.9	15.3	5.4	15.1	-5.1	14.9	8.8
1971	15.3	5.4	15.9	16.6	15.8	-2.5	16.2	10.5	15.8	6.0
1972	17.1	24.1	17.3	4.8	16.8	-11.1	17.9	28.9	17.3	9.5
1973	18.9	24.3	19.4	11.0	19.0	-8.0	19.9	20.3	19.3	11.6
1974	21.5	36.3	23.0	31.0	23.0	-	24.3	24.6	22.9	18.7
1975	24.0	-4.8	23.0	-15.7	23.3	5.3	24.7	26.3	23.7	3.5
1976	25.4	11.8	25.8	6.4	26.9	18.2	27.9	15.7	26.5	11.8
1977	28.8	13.5	29.9	16.2	29.7	-2.6	30.8	15.7	29.8	12.5
1978	32.9	30.2	33.7	10.1	35.7	25.9	37.1	16.6	34.8	16.8
1979	37.6	5.5	39.0	15.7	40.5	16.3	42.4	20.1	39.9	14.7
1980	44.7	23.5	44.1	-5.3	45.1	9.4	47.2	20.0	45.3	13.5
1981	49.5	21.0	50.2	5.8	49.4	-6.2	50.6	10.1	49.9	10.2
1982	51.9	10.7	53.3	11.2	52.1	-8.7	53.4	10.4	52.6	5.4
1983	52.7	-5.1	55.2	20.4	57.5	17.7	58.4	6.4	56.0	6.5
1984	65.5	58.2	68.6	20.3	69.7	6.6	71.3	9.5	68.8	22.9
1985	71.9	3.4	74.1	12.8	73.6	-2.7	76.0	13.7	73.9	7.4
1986	81.3	31.0	78.3	-14.0	83.9	31.8	85.3	6.8	82.2	11.2
1987	87.3	9.7	92.4	25.5	93.7	5.7	99.0	24.6	93.1	13.3
1988	100.5	6.2	99.7	-3.1	100.9	4.9	103.3	9.9	101.1	8.6
1989	103.2	-0.4	103.7	2.0	106.0	9.2	108.1	8.2	105.2	4.1
1990	115.4	29.9	117.9	9.0	122.7	17.3	126.3	12.3	120.6	14.6
1991	122.2	-12.4	121.7	-1.6	120.0	-5.5	122.5	8.6	121.6	0.8
1992	120.5	-6.4	119.5	-3.3	116.4	-10.0	122.7	23.5	119.8	-1.5
1993	122.1	-1.9	124.7	8.8	125.6	2.9	130.5	16.5	125.7	4.9
1994	133.0	7.9	134.1	3.3	137.0	8.9	137.6	1.8	135.4	7.7
1995	141.8	12.8	144.6	8.1	146.4	5.1	147.8	3.9	145.2	7.2
1996	150.5	7.5	152.6	5.7	157.5	13.5	158.5	2.6	154.8	6.6
1997	164.8	16.9	167.2	6.0	174.1	17.6	176.6	5.9	170.7	10.3
1998	181.2	10.8	185.7	10.3	188.9	7.1	191.0	4.5	186.7	9.4
1999	186.3	-9.5	190.4	9.1	196.4	13.2	201.8	11.5	193.7	3.7
2000	212.9	23.9	218.4	10.7	228.7	20.2	227.7	-1.7	221.9	14.6
2001	232.5	8.7	229.2	-5.6	169.4	-70.2	-		-	-

Source: "National Income and Product Account Tables: Selected NIPA Tables," *Survey of Current Business*, January 2002, U.S. Department of Commerce, Bureau of Economic Analysis, National Income and Wealth Division. Data downloaded from www.stat.usa.gov. A dash (-) indicates that no data are available.

Gross Domestic Product
Net exports of goods and services
Imports - Services - Chained (1996) Dollars

In billions of chained (1996) dollars and percent. Quarterly data are seasonally adjusted and annualized. Growth rates for quarters are compound annual growth rates; changes from year to year are percentage changes.

Year	1st Quarter	% Change	2nd Quarter	% Change	3rd Quarter	% Change	4th Quarter	% Change	TOTAL	% Change
1987	114.4	-	120.1	21.5	120.2	0.3	125.9	20.4	120.2	-
1988	124.3	-5.0	121.6	-8.4	123.2	5.4	124.6	4.6	123.4	2.7
1989	125.1	1.6	125.5	1.3	128.0	8.2	129.0	3.2	126.9	2.8
1990	135.1	20.3	136.6	4.5	138.2	4.8	136.4	-5.1	136.6	7.6
1991	132.3	-11.5	135.0	8.4	132.3	-7.8	133.9	4.9	133.4	-2.3
1992	131.2	-7.8	128.7	-7.4	121.7	-20.0	130.4	31.8	128.0	-4.0
1993	130.4	-	132.2	5.6	134.4	6.8	139.1	14.7	134.0	4.7
1994	141.4	6.8	142.3	2.6	142.1	-0.6	141.6	-1.4	141.9	5.9
1995	147.9	19.0	146.2	-4.5	147.1	2.5	149.4	6.4	147.7	4.1
1996	151.5	5.7	153.0	4.0	157.3	11.7	157.3	-	154.8	4.8
1997	164.7	20.2	166.9	5.5	175.9	23.4	179.4	8.2	171.7	10.9
1998	188.2	21.1	191.3	6.8	194.6	7.1	194.6	-	192.2	11.9
1999	190.5	-8.2	191.3	1.7	195.0	8.0	200.1	10.9	194.3	1.1
2000	209.7	20.6	215.9	12.4	224.6	17.1	224.7	0.2	218.7	12.6
2001	227.4	4.9	226.2	-2.1	207.6	-29.1	-	-	-	-

Source: "National Income and Product Account Tables: Selected NIPA Tables," *Survey of Current Business*, January 2002, U.S. Department of Commerce, Bureau of Economic Analysis, National Income and Wealth Division. Data downloaded from www.stat.usa.gov. A dash (-) indicates that no data are available.

GOVERNMENT CONSUMPTION EXPENDITURES AND GROSS INVESTMENT
Component of Gross Domestic Product

Government—federal, state, and local—represented 17.0 percent of real GDP in 2000, down from 17.4 percent in 1998. The category includes purchases of durable and nondurable goods, expenditures on structures (such as highways and bridges), purchases of services, and compensation of government employees. This category *excludes* transfer payments such as entitlements, transactions in land, grants-in-aid, and financial transactions. The effect of these excluded budgetary items are accounted for in purchases made by those who receive the money. In constant dollars, state and local purchases account for nearlty two-thirds of the total (65.3 percent and growing), the federal government for the rest.

The category is divided as follows:

> *Federal*
>> National defense
>> Nondefense
> *State and local*

Estimates are prepared by BEA under four categories: (1) federal expenditures, derived from the *Budget of the United States* and other sources, with categories such as transfer payments removed; (2) state and local compensation, (3) state and local expenditures for structures, and (4) state and local purchases other than compensation and structures. Each category is governed by its own estimating procedures and analytical methodologies.

Presentation of Data

Data are shown from 1959 to 2001 in quarterly and in annual increments. Changes from one period to the next are shown for each category covered. Changes from quarter to quarter are annualized, compounded growth rates as explained in the section on Gross National Product. Changes from year to year are simple percentile changes.

Analytical Uses

The total category best depicts the importance of government as a customer and employer—in that it includes what governmental bodies purchase and what they pay. It is not a good measure of total governmental activity because it excludes money the government collects for redistribution in transfer payments. Government activity has shown sharp rise during periods of war, but data available at print time did not yet show the consequences of 9/11.

Gross Domestic Product

Government consumption expenditures and gross investment: Total - Actual Dollars

In billions of actual dollars and percent. Quarterly data are seasonally adjusted and annualized. Growth rates for quarters are compound annual growth rates; changes from year to year are percentage changes.

Year	1st Quarter	% Change	2nd Quarter	% Change	3rd Quarter	% Change	4th Quarter	% Change	TOTAL	% Change
1959	111.3	-	113.1	6.6	113.1	-	112.4	-2.5	112.5	-
1960	110.5	-6.6	112.4	7.1	115.0	9.6	117.3	8.2	113.8	1.2
1961	118.5	4.2	120.3	6.2	121.7	4.7	125.5	13.1	121.5	6.8
1962	129.2	12.3	131.2	6.3	133.3	6.6	135.1	5.5	132.2	8.8
1963	135.5	1.2	136.7	3.6	140.3	11.0	141.4	3.2	138.5	4.8
1964	143.1	4.9	145.5	6.9	145.8	0.8	146.0	0.5	145.1	4.8
1965	146.9	2.5	150.6	10.5	155.7	14.2	161.6	16.0	153.7	5.9
1966	165.5	10.0	171.8	16.1	177.7	14.5	182.4	11.0	174.3	13.4
1967	191.4	21.2	192.7	2.7	196.3	7.7	201.0	9.9	195.3	12.0
1968	207.4	13.4	211.0	7.1	214.4	6.6	218.5	7.9	212.8	9.0
1969	219.1	1.1	222.9	7.1	227.6	8.7	228.7	1.9	224.6	5.5
1970	232.7	7.2	234.2	2.6	239.2	8.8	242.4	5.5	237.1	5.6
1971	246.1	6.2	249.8	6.2	252.5	4.4	255.7	5.2	251.0	5.9
1972	266.3	17.6	269.5	4.9	269.4	-0.1	275.1	8.7	270.1	7.6
1973	282.4	11.0	286.4	5.8	287.2	1.1	295.7	12.4	287.9	6.6
1974	306.2	15.0	317.4	15.5	327.0	12.7	338.8	15.2	322.4	12.0
1975	350.9	15.1	356.1	6.1	363.3	8.3	373.9	12.2	361.1	12.0
1976	380.3	7.0	381.5	1.3	384.6	3.3	391.5	7.4	384.5	6.5
1977	402.4	11.6	413.0	11.0	418.5	5.4	427.4	8.8	415.3	8.0
1978	433.7	6.0	451.6	17.6	462.1	9.6	475.0	11.6	455.6	9.7
1979	480.1	4.4	494.9	12.9	509.9	12.7	529.0	15.8	503.5	10.5
1980	549.8	16.7	566.2	12.5	571.6	3.9	591.3	14.5	569.7	13.1
1981	614.1	16.3	626.5	8.3	632.5	3.9	652.3	13.1	631.4	10.8
1982	662.7	6.5	675.8	8.1	688.9	8.0	710.1	12.9	684.4	8.4
1983	719.1	5.2	731.3	7.0	750.7	11.0	742.7	-4.2	735.9	7.5
1984	771.2	16.3	795.5	13.2	807.5	6.2	829.0	11.1	800.8	8.8
1985	847.1	9.0	868.4	10.4	892.5	11.6	905.1	5.8	878.3	9.7
1986	913.2	3.6	933.2	9.1	959.7	11.9	963.2	1.5	942.3	7.3
1987	977.6	6.1	992.6	6.3	1,002.2	3.9	1,019.3	7.0	997.9	5.9
1988	1,020.5	0.5	1,031.2	4.3	1,035.1	1.5	1,060.7	10.3	1,036.9	3.9
1989	1,070.3	3.7	1,094.8	9.5	1,111.9	6.4	1,123.9	4.4	1,100.2	6.1
1990	1,158.5	12.9	1,171.4	4.5	1,182.7	3.9	1,213.1	10.7	1,181.4	7.4
1991	1,228.6	5.2	1,235.5	2.3	1,238.4	0.9	1,239.5	0.4	1,235.5	4.6
1992	1,257.3	5.9	1,265.1	2.5	1,277.8	4.1	1,281.8	1.3	1,270.5	2.8
1993	1,279.5	-0.7	1,289.1	3.0	1,296.2	2.2	1,307.1	3.4	1,293.0	1.8
1994	1,303.3	-1.2	1,316.1	4.0	1,348.1	10.1	1,344.0	-1.2	1,327.9	2.7
1995	1,360.6	5.0	1,374.9	4.3	1,378.3	1.0	1,374.5	-1.1	1,372.0	3.3
1996	1,402.6	8.4	1,423.0	5.9	1,423.4	0.1	1,438.9	4.4	1,421.9	3.6
1997	1,459.2	5.8	1,486.3	7.6	1,498.0	3.2	1,508.2	2.8	1,487.9	4.6
1998	1,501.8	-1.7	1,533.8	8.8	1,548.1	3.8	1,570.3	5.9	1,538.5	3.4
1999	1,590.9	5.4	1,609.6	4.8	1,641.2	8.1	1,688.3	12.0	1,632.5	6.1
2000	1,711.8	5.7	1,741.1	7.0	1,744.2	0.7	1,766.8	5.3	1,741.0	6.6
2001	1,805.2	9.0	1,835.4	6.9	1,836.9	0.3	-	-	-	-

Source: "National Income and Product Account Tables: Selected NIPA Tables," *Survey of Current Business*, January 2002, U.S. Department of Commerce, Bureau of Economic Analysis, National Income and Wealth Division. Data downloaded from www.stat.usa.gov. A dash (-) indicates that no data are available.

Gross Domestic Product

Government consumption expenditures and gross investment: Total - Chained (1996) Dollars

In billions of chained (1996) dollars and percent. Quarterly data are seasonally adjusted and annualized. Growth rates for quarters are compound annual growth rates; changes from year to year are percentage changes.

Year	1st Quarter	% Change	2nd Quarter	% Change	3rd Quarter	% Change	4th Quarter	% Change	TOTAL	% Change
1959	651.5	-	663.9	7.8	668.1	2.6	662.2	-3.5	661.4	-
1960	648.8	-7.9	657.4	5.4	665.9	5.3	673.1	4.4	661.3	-0.0
1961	680.4	4.4	687.2	4.1	694.0	4.0	711.1	10.2	693.2	4.8
1962	723.4	7.1	731.7	4.7	740.8	5.1	744.2	1.8	735.0	6.0
1963	740.0	-2.2	744.3	2.3	765.9	12.1	759.2	-3.5	752.4	2.4
1964	763.1	2.1	772.9	5.2	766.4	-3.3	766.1	-0.2	767.1	2.0
1965	765.5	-0.3	781.3	8.5	800.3	10.1	817.2	8.7	791.1	3.1
1966	832.5	7.7	857.8	12.7	870.1	5.9	888.0	8.5	862.1	9.0
1967	925.6	18.0	921.3	-1.8	926.8	2.4	934.8	3.5	927.1	7.5
1968	951.4	7.3	956.0	1.9	958.3	1.0	960.5	0.9	956.6	3.2
1969	956.9	-1.5	956.0	-0.4	954.1	-0.8	943.1	-4.5	952.5	-0.4
1970	936.2	-2.9	927.3	-3.7	930.9	1.6	929.9	-0.4	931.1	-2.2
1971	918.6	-4.8	915.2	-1.5	911.9	-1.4	909.4	-1.1	913.8	-1.9
1972	920.8	5.1	921.9	0.5	907.6	-6.1	909.1	0.7	914.9	0.1
1973	914.5	2.4	911.5	-1.3	898.5	-5.6	908.4	4.5	908.3	-0.7
1974	920.0	5.2	927.8	3.4	924.2	-1.5	927.4	1.4	924.8	1.8
1975	940.8	5.9	938.3	-1.1	941.8	1.5	949.1	3.1	942.5	1.9
1976	952.5	1.4	943.3	-3.8	938.9	-1.9	938.6	-0.1	943.3	0.1
1977	945.3	2.9	955.1	4.2	956.0	0.4	954.5	-0.6	952.7	1.0
1978	956.7	0.9	982.1	11.1	990.3	3.4	999.6	3.8	982.2	3.1
1979	990.6	-3.6	1,000.5	4.1	1,002.4	0.8	1,010.8	3.4	1,001.1	1.9
1980	1,025.6	6.0	1,028.7	1.2	1,015.4	-5.1	1,013.9	-0.6	1,020.9	2.0
1981	1,027.5	5.5	1,030.1	1.0	1,027.8	-0.9	1,034.8	2.8	1,030.0	0.9
1982	1,033.6	-0.5	1,039.5	2.3	1,046.8	2.8	1,064.0	6.7	1,046.0	1.6
1983	1,069.8	2.2	1,078.2	3.2	1,097.0	7.2	1,078.8	-6.5	1,081.0	3.3
1984	1,091.0	4.6	1,115.2	9.2	1,123.1	2.9	1,144.2	7.7	1,118.4	3.5
1985	1,157.6	4.8	1,180.5	8.2	1,209.2	10.1	1,214.7	1.8	1,190.5	6.4
1986	1,224.0	3.1	1,248.0	8.1	1,277.4	9.8	1,271.5	-1.8	1,255.2	5.4
1987	1,278.4	2.2	1,289.1	3.4	1,292.4	1.0	1,310.0	5.6	1,292.5	3.0
1988	1,300.1	-3.0	1,302.4	0.7	1,300.3	-0.6	1,327.2	8.5	1,307.5	1.2
1989	1,319.3	-2.4	1,340.6	6.6	1,353.5	3.9	1,360.4	2.1	1,343.5	2.8
1990	1,381.2	6.3	1,384.7	1.0	1,384.8	0.0	1,398.6	4.0	1,387.3	3.3
1991	1,404.7	1.8	1,408.9	1.2	1,403.0	-1.7	1,397.0	-1.7	1,403.4	1.2
1992	1,407.6	3.1	1,405.7	-0.5	1,413.1	2.1	1,413.7	0.2	1,410.0	0.5
1993	1,396.4	-4.8	1,398.0	0.5	1,398.4	0.1	1,402.2	1.1	1,398.8	-0.8
1994	1,388.0	-4.0	1,390.4	0.7	1,417.5	8.0	1,404.5	-3.6	1,400.1	0.1
1995	1,407.3	0.8	1,414.0	1.9	1,410.8	-0.9	1,393.5	-4.8	1,406.4	0.4
1996	1,404.8	3.3	1,430.4	7.5	1,422.0	-2.3	1,430.6	2.4	1,421.9	1.1
1997	1,434.6	1.1	1,457.0	6.4	1,464.8	2.2	1,465.3	0.1	1,455.4	2.4
1998	1,456.1	-2.5	1,482.6	7.5	1,489.9	2.0	1,504.8	4.1	1,483.3	1.9
1999	1,512.3	2.0	1,516.8	1.2	1,533.2	4.4	1,564.8	8.5	1,531.8	3.3
2000	1,560.4	-1.1	1,577.2	4.4	1,570.0	-1.8	1,582.8	3.3	1,572.6	2.7
2001	1,603.4	5.3	1,623.0	5.0	1,624.1	0.3	-	-	-	-

Source: "National Income and Product Account Tables: Selected NIPA Tables," *Survey of Current Business*, January 2002, U.S. Department of Commerce, Bureau of Economic Analysis, National Income and Wealth Division. Data downloaded from www.stat.usa.gov. A dash (-) indicates that no data are available.

Gross Domestic Product

Government consumption expenditures and gross investment
Federal: Total - Actual Dollars

In billions of actual dollars and percent. Quarterly data are seasonally adjusted and annualized. Growth rates for quarters are compound annual growth rates; changes from year to year are percentage changes.

Year	1st Quarter	% Change	2nd Quarter	% Change	3rd Quarter	% Change	4th Quarter	% Change	TOTAL	% Change
1959	66.4	-	67.9	9.3	67.9	-	67.4	-2.9	67.4	-
1960	64.2	-17.7	64.8	3.8	66.5	10.9	68.0	9.3	65.9	-2.2
1961	67.4	-3.5	69.1	10.5	69.7	3.5	71.7	12.0	69.5	5.5
1962	75.0	19.7	76.4	7.7	77.7	7.0	78.5	4.2	76.9	10.6
1963	77.4	-5.5	77.7	1.6	79.6	10.1	79.4	-1.0	78.5	2.1
1964	79.9	2.5	80.5	3.0	79.8	-3.4	79.0	-4.0	79.8	1.7
1965	78.6	-2.0	80.2	8.4	82.7	13.1	86.9	21.9	82.1	2.9
1966	88.8	9.0	93.2	21.3	97.0	17.3	98.7	7.2	94.4	15.0
1967	105.3	29.6	105.2	-0.4	107.3	8.2	109.4	8.1	106.8	13.1
1968	112.6	12.2	113.3	2.5	114.4	3.9	115.8	5.0	114.0	6.7
1969	114.3	-5.1	115.2	3.2	117.8	9.3	117.1	-2.4	116.1	1.8
1970	117.5	1.4	115.9	-5.3	115.9	-	116.3	1.4	116.4	0.3
1971	116.6	1.0	117.3	2.4	118.0	2.4	118.3	1.0	117.6	1.0
1972	125.7	27.5	127.6	6.2	124.0	-10.8	125.3	4.3	125.6	6.8
1973	128.2	9.6	128.8	1.9	125.5	-9.9	128.9	11.3	127.8	1.8
1974	132.5	11.6	135.6	9.7	139.2	11.0	145.5	19.4	138.2	8.1
1975	148.1	7.3	150.6	6.9	152.4	4.9	157.2	13.2	152.1	10.1
1976	157.1	-0.3	158.6	3.9	160.9	5.9	165.6	12.2	160.6	5.6
1977	170.3	11.8	175.4	12.5	177.1	3.9	181.4	10.1	176.0	9.6
1978	184.0	5.9	190.0	13.7	193.4	7.4	200.0	14.4	191.9	9.0
1979	203.0	6.1	208.7	11.7	212.7	7.9	222.2	19.1	211.6	10.3
1980	232.8	20.5	244.4	21.5	245.5	1.8	258.4	22.7	245.3	15.9
1981	268.2	16.1	280.5	19.6	283.3	4.1	295.3	18.1	281.8	14.9
1982	300.6	7.4	307.0	8.8	314.7	10.4	328.9	19.3	312.8	11.0
1983	334.2	6.6	343.4	11.5	355.8	15.2	344.4	-12.2	344.4	10.1
1984	361.5	21.4	376.2	17.3	377.2	1.1	390.6	15.0	376.4	9.3
1985	399.3	9.2	408.2	9.2	421.0	13.1	425.1	4.0	413.4	9.8
1986	421.8	-3.1	434.8	12.9	452.0	16.8	446.1	-5.1	438.7	6.1
1987	452.1	5.5	459.7	6.9	461.5	1.6	468.5	6.2	460.4	4.9
1988	461.2	-6.1	460.0	-1.0	457.2	-2.4	472.2	13.8	462.6	0.5
1989	470.4	-1.5	482.6	10.8	490.0	6.3	487.2	-2.3	482.6	4.3
1990	502.0	12.7	506.9	4.0	505.8	-0.9	519.1	10.9	508.4	5.3
1991	530.3	8.9	532.2	1.4	526.9	-3.9	520.1	-5.1	527.4	3.7
1992	527.1	5.5	530.5	2.6	540.6	7.8	539.9	-0.5	534.5	1.3
1993	528.9	-7.9	525.3	-2.7	526.9	1.2	528.0	0.8	527.3	-1.3
1994	515.8	-8.9	515.9	0.1	532.5	13.5	520.0	-9.1	521.1	-1.2
1995	523.4	2.6	525.5	1.6	525.0	-0.4	512.3	-9.3	521.5	0.1
1996	530.6	15.1	537.2	5.1	529.1	-5.9	529.4	0.2	531.6	1.9
1997	529.2	-0.2	543.4	11.2	541.3	-1.5	538.9	-1.8	538.2	1.2
1998	526.1	-9.2	542.9	13.4	539.5	-2.5	548.4	6.8	539.2	0.2
1999	549.8	1.0	553.1	2.4	565.6	9.4	587.6	16.5	564.0	4.6
2000	578.5	-6.1	601.0	16.5	587.0	-9.0	594.2	5.0	590.2	4.6
2001	605.3	7.7	609.9	3.1	615.7	3.9	-	-	-	-

Source: "National Income and Product Account Tables: Selected NIPA Tables," *Survey of Current Business*, January 2002, U.S. Department of Commerce, Bureau of Economic Analysis, National Income and Wealth Division. Data downloaded from www.stat.usa.gov. A dash (-) indicates that no data are available.

Gross Domestic Product
Government consumption expenditures and gross investment
Federal: Total - Chained (1996) Dollars

In billions of chained (1996) dollars and percent. Quarterly data are seasonally adjusted and annualized. Growth rates for quarters are compound annual growth rates; changes from year to year are percentage changes.

Year	1st Quarter	% Change	2nd Quarter	% Change	3rd Quarter	% Change	4th Quarter	% Change	TOTAL	% Change
1987	588.6	-	597.3	6.0	598.2	0.6	607.0	6.0	597.8	-
1988	589.6	-11.0	583.2	-4.3	578.3	-3.3	596.5	13.2	586.9	-1.8
1989	583.0	-8.8	596.0	9.2	601.7	3.9	598.3	-2.2	594.7	1.3
1990	607.8	6.5	608.7	0.6	603.1	-3.6	607.8	3.2	606.8	2.0
1991	612.6	3.2	613.4	0.5	602.7	-6.8	591.0	-7.5	604.9	-0.3
1992	591.8	0.5	591.1	-0.5	598.3	5.0	599.1	0.5	595.1	-1.6
1993	579.6	-12.4	572.2	-5.0	568.9	-2.3	567.3	-1.1	572.0	-3.9
1994	550.9	-11.1	545.2	-4.1	563.2	13.9	546.1	-11.6	551.3	-3.6
1995	544.1	-1.5	544.3	0.1	540.4	-2.8	517.1	-16.2	536.5	-2.7
1996	529.1	9.6	540.2	8.7	529.5	-7.7	527.6	-1.4	531.6	-0.9
1997	521.7	-4.4	534.8	10.4	533.4	-1.0	528.4	-3.7	529.6	-0.4
1998	515.0	-9.8	530.1	12.3	524.9	-3.9	531.7	5.3	525.4	-0.8
1999	526.7	-3.7	527.7	0.8	537.0	7.2	555.5	14.5	536.7	2.2
2000	536.8	-12.8	556.9	15.8	541.8	-10.4	547.9	4.6	545.9	1.7
2001	552.2	3.2	554.7	1.8	559.6	3.6	-	-	-	-

Source: "National Income and Product Account Tables: Selected NIPA Tables," *Survey of Current Business*, January 2002, U.S. Department of Commerce, Bureau of Economic Analysis, National Income and Wealth Division. Data downloaded from www.stat.usa.gov. A dash (-) indicates that no data are available.

Gross Domestic Product
Government consumption expenditures and gross investment
Federal - National defense - Actual Dollars

In billions of actual dollars and percent. Quarterly data are seasonally adjusted and annualized. Growth rates for quarters are compound annual growth rates; changes from year to year are percentage changes.

Year	1st Quarter	% Change	2nd Quarter	% Change	3rd Quarter	% Change	4th Quarter	% Change	TOTAL	% Change
1959	56.4	-	55.8	-4.2	56.0	1.4	55.7	-2.1	56.0	-
1960	54.5	-8.3	54.5	-	55.6	8.3	56.2	4.4	55.2	-1.4
1961	57.0	5.8	57.7	5.0	58.0	2.1	59.8	13.0	58.1	5.3
1962	62.4	18.6	62.8	2.6	62.9	0.6	63.0	0.6	62.8	8.1
1963	62.5	-3.1	62.8	1.9	62.7	-0.6	62.8	0.6	62.7	-0.2
1964	62.5	-1.9	62.2	-1.9	61.6	-3.8	60.7	-5.7	61.8	-1.4
1965	59.9	-5.2	61.1	8.3	62.4	8.8	66.3	27.4	62.4	1.0
1966	68.3	12.6	71.8	22.1	76.2	26.9	78.8	14.4	73.8	18.3
1967	83.4	25.5	84.6	5.9	86.9	11.3	88.2	6.1	85.8	16.3
1968	91.2	14.3	92.3	4.9	92.2	-0.4	93.1	4.0	92.2	7.5
1969	91.3	-7.5	91.8	2.2	93.6	8.1	93.7	0.4	92.6	0.4
1970	92.8	-3.8	90.1	-11.1	90.3	0.9	90.5	0.9	90.9	-1.8
1971	90.3	-0.9	88.7	-6.9	87.8	-4.0	88.9	5.1	89.0	-2.1
1972	94.2	26.1	95.3	4.8	91.7	-14.3	92.6	4.0	93.5	5.1
1973	94.5	8.5	95.1	2.6	91.5	-14.3	94.6	14.3	93.9	0.4
1974	96.1	6.5	99.9	16.8	99.7	-0.8	103.3	15.2	99.7	6.2
1975	105.6	9.2	106.9	5.0	108.1	4.6	111.0	11.2	107.9	8.2
1976	110.7	-1.1	112.1	5.2	113.9	6.6	116.2	8.3	113.2	4.9
1977	119.6	12.2	122.9	11.5	123.3	1.3	124.5	4.0	122.6	8.3
1978	126.9	7.9	130.9	13.2	133.2	7.2	137.0	11.9	132.0	7.7
1979	139.5	7.5	144.6	15.4	147.4	8.0	155.1	22.6	146.7	11.1
1980	161.9	18.7	166.6	12.1	169.8	7.9	180.3	27.1	169.6	15.6
1981	186.4	14.2	195.5	21.0	199.6	8.7	209.7	21.8	197.8	16.6
1982	216.0	12.6	225.0	17.7	231.4	11.9	240.9	17.5	228.3	15.4
1983	243.1	3.7	250.5	12.7	254.3	6.2	262.1	12.8	252.5	10.6
1984	276.1	23.1	281.5	8.1	282.1	0.9	294.5	18.8	283.5	12.3
1985	299.7	7.3	307.1	10.2	319.1	16.6	323.9	6.2	312.4	10.2
1986	319.9	-4.8	330.7	14.2	343.7	16.7	334.6	-10.2	332.2	6.3
1987	341.9	9.0	350.6	10.6	356.5	6.9	355.6	-1.0	351.2	5.7
1988	355.7	0.1	354.9	-0.9	351.9	-3.3	361.1	10.9	355.9	1.3
1989	355.1	-6.5	363.3	9.6	369.8	7.4	364.8	-5.3	363.2	2.1
1990	372.1	8.2	373.4	1.4	370.4	-3.2	383.5	14.9	374.9	3.2
1991	390.7	7.7	389.7	-1.0	383.5	-6.2	374.1	-9.4	384.5	2.6
1992	373.8	-0.3	376.9	3.4	384.8	8.7	378.5	-6.4	378.5	-1.6
1993	367.4	-11.2	364.3	-3.3	363.9	-0.4	364.1	0.2	364.9	-3.6
1994	349.4	-15.2	353.9	5.3	366.9	15.5	350.4	-16.8	355.1	-2.7
1995	352.2	2.1	353.9	1.9	352.7	-1.3	343.6	-9.9	350.6	-1.3
1996	356.1	15.4	361.3	6.0	355.6	-6.2	355.0	-0.7	357.0	1.8
1997	346.4	-9.3	355.0	10.3	354.7	-0.3	354.4	-0.3	352.6	-1.2
1998	338.4	-16.9	348.8	12.9	354.7	6.9	354.7	-	349.1	-1.0
1999	356.1	1.6	354.2	-2.1	366.7	14.9	381.1	16.7	364.5	4.4
2000	366.6	-14.4	380.4	15.9	372.1	-8.4	382.4	11.5	375.4	3.0
2001	392.9	11.4	396.1	3.3	399.6	3.6	-	-	-	-

Source: "National Income and Product Account Tables: Selected NIPA Tables," *Survey of Current Business*, January 2002, U.S. Department of Commerce, Bureau of Economic Analysis, National Income and Wealth Division. Data downloaded from www.stat.usa.gov. A dash (-) indicates that no data are available.

Gross Domestic Product

Government consumption expenditures and gross investment
Federal - National defense - Chained (1996) Dollars

In billions of chained (1996) dollars and percent. Quarterly data are seasonally adjusted and annualized. Growth rates for quarters are compound annual growth rates; changes from year to year are percentage changes.

Year	1st Quarter	% Change	2nd Quarter	% Change	3rd Quarter	% Change	4th Quarter	% Change	TOTAL	% Change
1987	439.0	-	449.8	10.2	456.4	6.0	455.6	-0.7	450.2	-
1988	449.9	-4.9	445.6	-3.8	440.8	-4.2	450.9	9.5	446.8	-0.8
1989	435.0	-13.4	444.2	8.7	449.5	4.9	444.6	-4.3	443.3	-0.8
1990	446.0	1.3	444.9	-1.0	437.3	-6.7	444.7	6.9	443.2	-0.0
1991	449.2	4.1	447.1	-1.9	436.0	-9.6	421.2	-12.9	438.4	-1.1
1992	414.9	-5.9	414.9	-	420.9	5.9	417.6	-3.1	417.1	-4.9
1993	400.7	-15.2	395.0	-5.6	392.3	-2.7	391.0	-1.3	394.7	-5.4
1994	373.3	-16.9	374.5	1.3	387.8	15.0	367.8	-19.1	375.9	-4.8
1995	366.9	-1.0	367.0	0.1	363.3	-4.0	350.4	-13.5	361.9	-3.7
1996	356.4	7.0	363.0	7.6	355.4	-8.1	353.3	-2.3	357.0	-1.4
1997	341.6	-12.6	350.3	10.6	350.4	0.1	348.5	-2.2	347.7	-2.6
1998	332.0	-17.6	342.0	12.6	346.5	5.4	345.8	-0.8	341.6	-1.8
1999	342.7	-3.5	339.7	-3.5	350.0	12.7	361.9	14.3	348.6	2.0
2000	342.3	-20.0	354.8	15.4	345.1	-10.5	353.8	10.5	349.0	0.1
2001	360.3	7.6	362.4	2.4	365.3	3.2	-	-	-	-

Source: "National Income and Product Account Tables: Selected NIPA Tables," *Survey of Current Business*, January 2002, U.S. Department of Commerce, Bureau of Economic Analysis, National Income and Wealth Division. Data downloaded from www.stat.usa.gov. A dash (-) indicates that no data are available.

Gross Domestic Product

Government consumption expenditures and gross investment
Federal - Nondefense - Actual Dollars

In billions of actual dollars and percent. Quarterly data are seasonally adjusted and annualized. Growth rates for quarters are compound annual growth rates; changes from year to year are percentage changes.

Year	1st Quarter	% Change	2nd Quarter	% Change	3rd Quarter	% Change	4th Quarter	% Change	TOTAL	% Change
1959	10.0	-	12.1	114.4	12.0	-3.3	11.7	-9.6	11.4	-
1960	9.7	-52.8	10.3	27.1	10.9	25.4	11.8	37.3	10.7	-6.1
1961	10.4	-39.7	11.3	39.4	11.7	14.9	11.9	7.0	11.3	5.6
1962	12.6	25.7	13.5	31.8	14.8	44.4	15.5	20.3	14.1	24.8
1963	14.9	-14.6	14.9	-	17.0	69.5	16.6	-9.1	15.8	12.1
1964	17.4	20.7	18.3	22.4	18.2	-2.2	18.3	2.2	18.0	13.9
1965	18.7	9.0	19.1	8.8	20.3	27.6	20.6	6.0	19.7	9.4
1966	20.5	-1.9	21.5	21.0	20.8	-12.4	19.9	-16.2	20.7	5.1
1967	22.0	49.4	20.6	-23.1	20.3	-5.7	21.2	18.9	21.0	1.4
1968	21.5	5.8	21.0	-9.0	22.2	24.9	22.7	9.3	21.8	3.8
1969	23.0	5.4	23.4	7.1	24.3	16.3	23.4	-14.0	23.5	7.8
1970	24.7	24.1	25.8	19.0	25.6	-3.1	25.8	3.2	25.5	8.5
1971	26.3	8.0	28.6	39.8	30.2	24.3	29.3	-11.4	28.6	12.2
1972	31.5	33.6	32.3	10.6	32.3	-	32.6	3.8	32.2	12.6
1973	33.7	14.2	33.6	-1.2	34.0	4.8	34.3	3.6	33.9	5.3
1974	36.4	26.8	35.7	-7.5	39.5	49.9	42.3	31.5	38.5	13.6
1975	42.5	1.9	43.7	11.8	44.3	5.6	46.2	18.3	44.2	14.8
1976	46.5	2.6	46.6	0.9	47.0	3.5	49.4	22.0	47.4	7.2
1977	50.7	10.9	52.5	15.0	53.8	10.3	56.9	25.1	53.5	12.9
1978	57.0	0.7	59.1	15.6	60.2	7.7	63.0	19.9	59.8	11.8
1979	63.4	2.6	64.0	3.8	65.3	8.4	67.2	12.2	65.0	8.7
1980	70.9	23.9	77.8	45.0	75.8	-9.9	78.1	12.7	75.6	16.3
1981	81.8	20.3	85.0	16.6	83.7	-6.0	85.6	9.4	84.0	11.1
1982	84.6	-4.6	82.0	-11.7	83.3	6.5	88.0	24.6	84.5	0.6
1983	91.1	14.9	92.9	8.1	101.5	42.5	82.3	-56.8	92.0	8.9
1984	85.4	15.9	94.7	51.2	95.2	2.1	96.0	3.4	92.8	0.9
1985	99.6	15.9	101.2	6.6	101.9	2.8	101.2	-2.7	101.0	8.8
1986	101.9	2.8	104.1	8.9	108.3	17.1	111.5	12.4	106.5	5.4
1987	110.2	-4.6	109.1	-3.9	105.0	-14.2	112.9	33.7	109.3	2.6
1988	105.6	-23.5	105.1	-1.9	105.2	0.4	111.1	24.4	106.8	-2.3
1989	115.3	16.0	119.4	15.0	120.2	2.7	122.4	7.5	119.3	11.7
1990	129.9	26.9	133.5	11.6	135.4	5.8	135.6	0.6	133.6	12.0
1991	139.6	12.3	142.5	8.6	143.4	2.6	146.0	7.5	142.9	7.0
1992	153.4	21.9	153.6	0.5	155.7	5.6	161.4	15.5	156.0	9.2
1993	161.5	0.2	161.0	-1.2	163.0	5.1	164.0	2.5	162.4	4.1
1994	166.3	5.7	162.0	-9.9	165.6	9.2	169.7	10.3	165.9	2.2
1995	171.2	3.6	171.6	0.9	172.3	1.6	168.7	-8.1	170.9	3.0
1996	174.5	14.5	175.9	3.2	173.5	-5.3	174.5	2.3	174.6	2.2
1997	182.8	20.4	188.4	12.8	186.6	-3.8	184.5	-4.4	185.6	6.3
1998	187.7	7.1	194.2	14.6	184.8	-18.0	193.7	20.7	190.1	2.4
1999	193.6	-0.2	198.9	11.4	199.0	0.2	206.5	15.9	199.5	4.9
2000	211.9	10.9	220.6	17.5	214.9	-9.9	211.8	-5.6	214.8	7.7
2001	212.4	1.1	213.8	2.7	216.1	4.4	-	-	-	-

Source: "National Income and Product Account Tables: Selected NIPA Tables," *Survey of Current Business*, January 2002, U.S. Department of Commerce, Bureau of Economic Analysis, National Income and Wealth Division. Data downloaded from www.stat.usa.gov. A dash (-) indicates that no data are available.

Gross Domestic Product
Government consumption expenditures and gross investment
Federal - Nondefense - Chained (1996) Dollars

In billions of chained (1996) dollars and percent. Quarterly data are seasonally adjusted and annualized. Growth rates for quarters are compound annual growth rates; changes from year to year are percentage changes.

Year	1st Quarter	% Change	2nd Quarter	% Change	3rd Quarter	% Change	4th Quarter	% Change	TOTAL	% Change
1987	148.8	-	146.5	-6.0	140.5	-15.4	150.3	31.0	146.5	-
1988	138.4	-28.1	136.3	-5.9	136.3	-	144.5	26.3	138.9	-5.2
1989	147.1	7.4	150.9	10.7	151.2	0.8	152.8	4.3	150.5	8.4
1990	161.2	23.9	163.1	4.8	165.3	5.5	162.4	-6.8	163.0	8.3
1991	162.7	0.7	165.7	7.6	166.2	1.2	169.5	8.2	166.0	1.8
1992	176.8	18.4	176.1	-1.6	177.2	2.5	181.4	9.8	177.9	7.2
1993	179.0	-5.2	177.2	-4.0	176.6	-1.3	176.3	-0.7	177.3	-0.3
1994	177.5	2.8	170.7	-14.5	175.4	11.5	178.3	6.8	175.5	-1.0
1995	177.2	-2.4	177.3	0.2	177.1	-0.5	166.8	-21.3	174.6	-0.5
1996	172.7	14.9	177.2	10.8	174.1	-6.8	174.4	0.7	174.6	-
1997	180.1	13.7	184.5	10.1	182.9	-3.4	179.8	-6.6	181.8	4.1
1998	183.0	7.3	188.0	11.4	178.4	-18.9	185.8	17.7	183.8	1.1
1999	183.9	-4.0	188.0	9.2	187.0	-2.1	193.6	14.9	188.1	2.3
2000	194.4	1.7	202.0	16.6	196.5	-10.5	194.0	-5.0	196.7	4.6
2001	191.8	-4.5	192.3	1.0	194.3	4.2	-	-	-	-

Source: "National Income and Product Account Tables: Selected NIPA Tables," *Survey of Current Business*, January 2002, U.S. Department of Commerce, Bureau of Economic Analysis, National Income and Wealth Division. Data downloaded from www.stat.usa.gov. A dash (-) indicates that no data are available.

Gross Domestic Product
Government consumption expenditures and gross investment
State and local - Actual Dollars

In billions of actual dollars and percent. Quarterly data are seasonally adjusted and annualized. Growth rates for quarters are compound annual growth rates; changes from year to year are percentage changes.

Year	1st Quarter	% Change	2nd Quarter	% Change	3rd Quarter	% Change	4th Quarter	% Change	TOTAL	% Change
1959	44.9	-	45.1	1.8	45.2	0.9	45.0	-1.8	45.1	-
1960	46.3	12.1	47.6	11.7	48.5	7.8	49.2	5.9	47.9	6.2
1961	51.1	16.4	51.2	0.8	52.0	6.4	53.9	15.4	52.0	8.6
1962	54.2	2.2	54.8	4.5	55.6	6.0	56.6	7.4	55.3	6.3
1963	58.1	11.0	59.0	6.3	60.7	12.0	62.0	8.8	59.9	8.3
1964	63.2	8.0	65.0	11.9	66.0	6.3	67.0	6.2	65.3	9.0
1965	68.3	8.0	70.4	12.9	73.0	15.6	74.7	9.6	71.6	9.6
1966	76.7	11.1	78.6	10.3	80.6	10.6	83.7	16.3	79.9	11.6
1967	86.1	12.0	87.5	6.7	89.0	7.0	91.6	12.2	88.6	10.9
1968	94.7	14.2	97.7	13.3	100.0	9.8	102.7	11.2	98.8	11.5
1969	104.8	8.4	107.7	11.5	109.8	8.0	111.6	6.7	108.5	9.8
1970	115.2	13.5	118.4	11.6	123.2	17.2	126.1	9.8	120.7	11.2
1971	129.4	10.9	132.5	9.9	134.5	6.2	137.4	8.9	133.5	10.6
1972	140.6	9.6	141.9	3.8	145.4	10.2	149.9	13.0	144.4	8.2
1973	154.2	12.0	157.6	9.1	161.7	10.8	166.8	13.2	160.1	10.9
1974	173.7	17.6	181.8	20.0	187.9	14.1	193.2	11.8	184.2	15.1
1975	202.8	21.4	205.5	5.4	210.9	10.9	216.7	11.5	209.0	13.5
1976	223.2	12.5	222.9	-0.5	223.7	1.4	225.9	4.0	223.9	7.1
1977	232.1	11.4	237.6	9.8	241.4	6.6	246.0	7.8	239.3	6.9
1978	249.7	6.2	261.6	20.5	268.7	11.3	275.0	9.7	263.8	10.2
1979	277.1	3.1	286.3	14.0	297.2	16.1	306.8	13.6	291.8	10.6
1980	317.0	14.0	321.8	6.2	326.0	5.3	332.9	8.7	324.4	11.2
1981	345.9	16.6	346.0	0.1	349.3	3.9	357.1	9.2	349.6	7.8
1982	362.1	5.7	368.8	7.6	374.2	6.0	381.3	7.8	371.6	6.3
1983	384.9	3.8	387.9	3.2	394.9	7.4	398.3	3.5	391.5	5.4
1984	409.8	12.1	419.3	9.6	430.2	10.8	438.4	7.8	424.4	8.4
1985	447.9	9.0	460.2	11.4	471.5	10.2	480.0	7.4	464.9	9.5
1986	491.4	9.8	498.4	5.8	507.7	7.7	517.1	7.6	503.6	8.3
1987	525.5	6.7	532.9	5.8	540.7	6.0	550.8	7.7	537.5	6.7
1988	559.3	6.3	571.2	8.8	578.0	4.8	588.5	7.5	574.3	6.8
1989	599.8	7.9	612.2	8.5	621.9	6.5	636.8	9.9	617.7	7.6
1990	656.5	13.0	664.6	5.0	676.9	7.6	694.0	10.5	673.0	9.0
1991	698.3	2.5	703.3	2.9	711.5	4.7	719.4	4.5	708.1	5.2
1992	730.2	6.1	734.5	2.4	737.2	1.5	741.9	2.6	736.0	3.9
1993	750.5	4.7	763.9	7.3	769.3	2.9	779.1	5.2	765.7	4.0
1994	787.5	4.4	800.2	6.6	815.6	7.9	824.0	4.2	806.8	5.4
1995	837.1	6.5	849.4	6.0	853.3	1.8	862.2	4.2	850.5	5.4
1996	872.0	4.6	885.7	6.4	894.3	3.9	909.4	6.9	890.4	4.7
1997	930.0	9.4	942.9	5.7	956.6	5.9	969.3	5.4	949.7	6.7
1998	975.8	2.7	990.9	6.3	1,008.6	7.3	1,021.9	5.4	999.3	5.2
1999	1,041.1	7.7	1,056.5	6.0	1,075.6	7.4	1,100.7	9.7	1,068.5	6.9
2000	1,133.2	12.3	1,140.1	2.5	1,157.2	6.1	1,172.6	5.4	1,150.8	7.7
2001	1,199.8	9.6	1,225.5	8.8	1,221.2	-1.4	-	-	-	-

Source: "National Income and Product Account Tables: Selected NIPA Tables," *Survey of Current Business*, January 2002, U.S. Department of Commerce, Bureau of Economic Analysis, National Income and Wealth Division. Data downloaded from www.stat.usa.gov. A dash (-) indicates that no data are available.

Gross Domestic Product
Government consumption expenditures and gross investment
State and local - Chained (1996) Dollars

In billions of chained (1996) dollars and percent. Quarterly data are seasonally adjusted and annualized. Growth rates for quarters are compound annual growth rates; changes from year to year are percentage changes.

Year	1st Quarter	% Change	2nd Quarter	% Change	3rd Quarter	% Change	4th Quarter	% Change	TOTAL	% Change
1987	690.7	-	692.8	1.2	695.1	1.3	704.0	5.2	695.6	-
1988	711.3	4.2	720.0	5.0	722.8	1.6	731.5	4.9	721.4	3.7
1989	737.1	3.1	745.3	4.5	752.7	4.0	762.9	5.5	749.5	3.9
1990	774.1	6.0	776.7	1.4	782.2	2.9	791.3	4.7	781.1	4.2
1991	792.6	0.7	796.0	1.7	800.6	2.3	806.3	2.9	798.9	2.3
1992	816.1	5.0	814.9	-0.6	815.1	0.1	814.9	-0.1	815.3	2.1
1993	817.1	1.1	826.1	4.5	829.7	1.8	835.1	2.6	827.0	1.4
1994	837.3	1.1	845.4	3.9	854.4	4.3	858.5	1.9	848.9	2.6
1995	863.3	2.3	869.7	3.0	870.4	0.3	876.4	2.8	869.9	2.5
1996	875.7	-0.3	890.2	6.8	892.5	1.0	903.0	4.8	890.4	2.4
1997	912.8	4.4	922.2	4.2	931.4	4.1	936.8	2.3	925.8	4.0
1998	940.8	1.7	952.4	5.0	964.7	5.3	972.8	3.4	957.7	3.4
1999	985.2	5.2	988.6	1.4	995.8	2.9	1,009.1	5.5	994.7	3.9
2000	1,023.0	5.6	1,020.1	-1.1	1,027.6	3.0	1,034.3	2.6	1,026.3	3.2
2001	1,050.5	6.4	1,067.4	6.6	1,063.8	-1.3	-	-	-	-

Source: "National Income and Product Account Tables: Selected NIPA Tables," *Survey of Current Business*, January 2002, U.S. Department of Commerce, Bureau of Economic Analysis, National Income and Wealth Division. Data downloaded from www.stat.usa.gov. A dash (-) indicates that no data are available.

CHAPTER 3

BUSINESS CYCLE INDICATORS

BUSINESS CYCLE INDICATORS

The indexes of economic indicators, also called business cycle indicators, are used by government, industry, and other institutions to forecast tendencies in the national economy. They are composites of several statistical series which tend to signal *changes* in the economy's general direction. They are "business cycle indicators" because they can predict the beginnings and ends of periods of sustained growth; each such period is a single business cycle; each ends when economic growth stops, as measured by Gross Domestic Product (GDP), or shows negative growth.

Arthur F. Burns and Wesley C. Mitchell have described business cycles as follows:

> Business cycles are a type of fluctuation found in the aggregate economic activity of nations that organize their work mainly in business enterprises; a cycle consists of expansions occurring at about the same time in many economic activities, followed by similarly general recessions, contractions, and revivals which merge into the expansion phase of the next cycle; this sequence of changes is recurrent but not periodic; in duration business cycles vary from more than one year to ten or twelve years; they are not divisible into shorter cycles of similar character with amplitudes approximating their own. (Reference 2.)

History

Business cycle indicators were developed by the National Bureau of Economic Research, Inc. (NBER). The first list of cyclic indicators was published by Burns and Mitchell in 1938. Publication of the NBER's indicators by the U.S. Department of Commerce began in 1961. Commerce began to publish composite indexes of leading, coincident, and lagging indicators in 1968. Late in 1995, preparation of the series was transferred to The Conference Board, a New York-based, independent, not-for-profit business research organization. The current series are available from 1959 to the present time. The series are revised at regular intervals, usually to move the base year forward.

Characteristics of the Indexes

Three composite indexes are used to predict the peaks and troughs of business cycles—the highest points of growth and the bottoms of periods of decline. The composite index of *Leading Indicators* tends to signal a change (downturn or upturn) before the economy actually turns down or resumes growth. The composite index of *Coincident Indicators* tends to turn up or down at the same time as the economy. And the composite index of *Lagging Indicators* shows changes after they have already become visible.

A graphic presentation following this introductory text illustrates the relationships between the indicator series and Gross Domestic Product (GDP) for the period 1979-2001. The vertical rectangular areas indicate periods of recession as commonly defined.

Each composite index combines several component indexes which behave in the appropriate manner. For example, the composite index of leading indicators is formed of several other leading indicators. A composite of selected leading, coincident, or lagging indicators is used because, over time, it has been found that the composite index predicts more accurately than any one of the components taken alone. Revisions of the business cycle indicators have typically taken the form of removing and adding components and changing the relative weight assigned to each component in calculating the composite index. Components will be discussed in separate sections.

Presentation

Data for each of the composite indexes are presented in sequence. Each section begins with a discussion of the composite index and its components. Tables with the indexes follow. The composite indexes are shown in two formats: the actual index and change from previous month.

Format and Calculation

Data are presented, in most cases, for the years 1959 to 2001 and for each month of the year.

The composite indexes relate to a base year. The base year at present (2002) is 1996, with the value of 100. All other data points are calibrated to 1996. The 1996 base value, in turn, is produced by averaging the 1996 monthly values; for this reason, monthly values in 1996 will be very near 100. The significance of the composite indexes lies in month-to-month changes rather than in absolute value. A change is signalled when the index increases or decreases over a period of three or more months.

Values for the component indexes are shown in various formats (hours, weeks, dollars, percentages, index values). The formats are noted at the top of each component table. All data are shown from 1951 to 2001 unless the series is only available from a later year.

Month-to-month percentage changes in the component series are used to construct the composite index. Calculation of each component's contribution is made by applying mathematical methods to minimize the tendency of volatile series to dominate the average and to standardize each series. These technical methods are described in the references. At present, each component contributes differentially to the composite index; that is to say, weighting factors are used. For example, the average weekly hours in manufacturing contributes 18.4 percent to the leading index. The index of consumer expectations contributes 1.8 percent. For details, see Reference 4.

Bibliography

1. Hertzberg, Marie P. and Barry A. Beckman, "Business Cycle Indicators: Revised Composite Indexes." U.S. Department of Commerce, Bureau of Economic Analysis. *Survey of Current Business*. January 1989, Superintendent of Documents, U.S. Government Printing Office, Washington, DC 20302.

2. *Measuring Business Cycles*. National Bureau of Economic Research, Inc., 1946.

3. U.S. Department of Commerce, Bureau of Economic Analysis. "Composite Indexes of Leading, Coincident, and Lagging Indicators," *Survey of Current Business*. November 1987, Superintendent of Documents, U.S. Government Printing Office, Washington, DC 20302.

4. *Leading Economic Indicators*. The Conference Board, 845 Third Avenue, New York, NY 10022-6679.

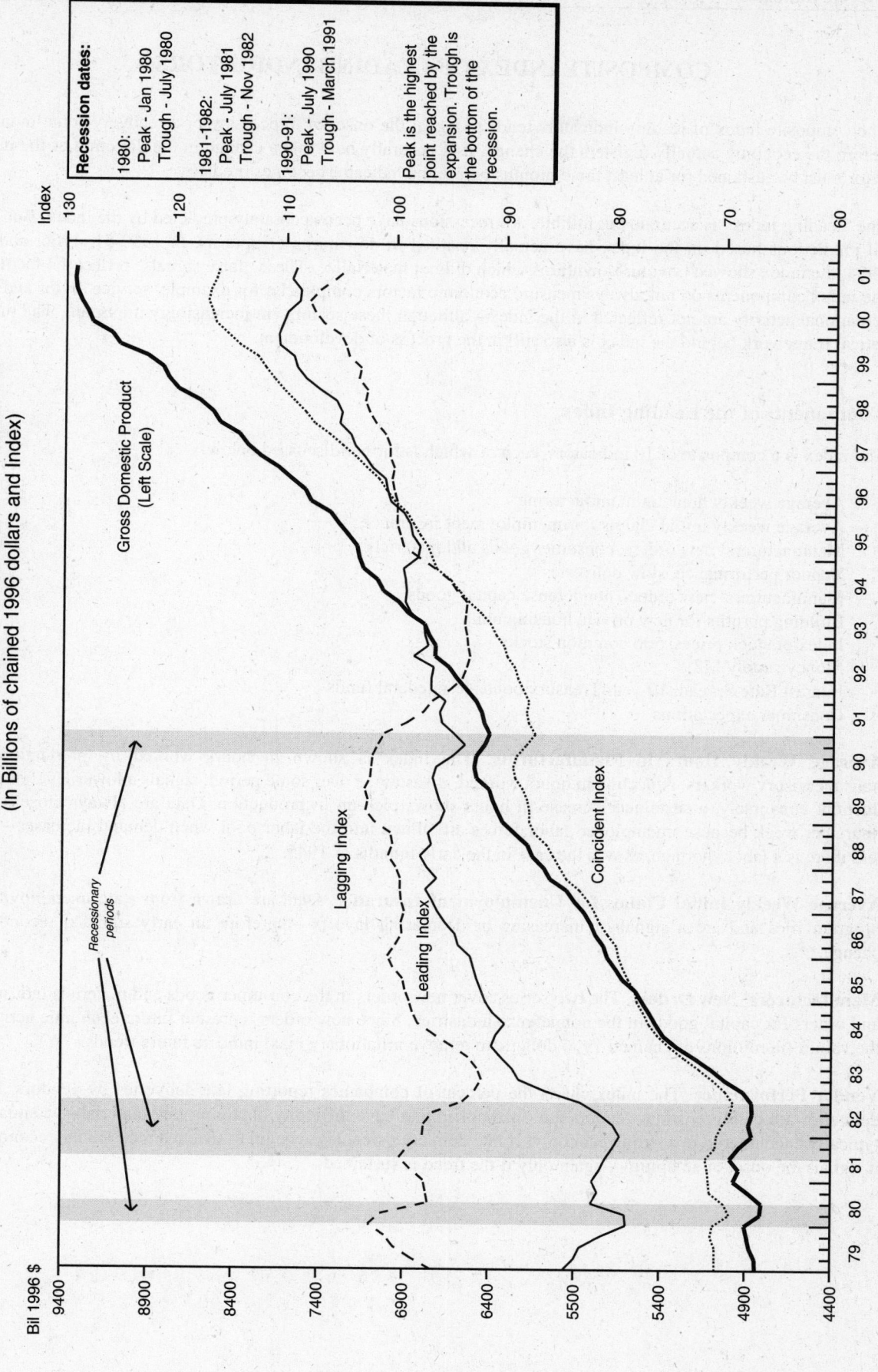

GDP and Economic Indicators: 1980-2001
(In Billions of chained 1996 dollars and Index)

Gross Domestic Product
(Left Scale)

Lagging Index

Leading Index

Coincident Index

Recessionary
periods

Recession dates:

1980:
 Peak - Jan 1980
 Trough - July 1980

1981-1982:
 Peak - July 1981
 Trough - Nov 1982

1990-91:
 Peak - July 1990
 Trough - March 1991

Peak is the highest
point reached by the
expansion. Trough is
the bottom of the
recession.

Index

130

120

110

100

90

80

70

60

Bil 1996 $

9400

8900

8400

7400

6900

6400

5500

5400

4900

4400

79 80 81 82 83 84 85 86 87 88 89 90 91 92 93 94 95 96 97 98 99 00 01

COMPOSITE INDEX OF LEADING INDICATORS

The composite index of leading indicators tends to signal the onset of a recession or a recovery some months before the economy actually registers the change. It is generally held that a change in the direction of the indicator must be sustained for at least three months before the indicator becomes predictive.

The "leading index" is accurate but fallible. All recessions have been accurately predicted by the index. But not all predictions based on the index have actually resulted in downturns or upturns. In 1950-51, 1966, and in 1984, the index showed obvious downturns which did not materialize. These "false signals" reflect the fact that the index components do not always measure economic factors completely; for example, service sector and international activity are not reflected in the index—although these sectors are increasingly important. The theoretical framework behind the index is also still in the process of development.

Components of the Leading Index

The index is a composite of 10 indicators, each of which is further discussed below:

> Average weekly hours in manufacturing
> Average weekly initial claims for unemployment insurance
> Manufacturers' new orders, consumer goods and materials
> Vendor performance, slow deliveries
> Manufacturers' new orders, nondefense capital goods
> Building permits for new private housing units
> Index of stock prices, 500 common stocks
> Money supply M2
> Interest Rate Spread, 10-year Treasury bonds less federal funds
> Consumer expectations

Average Weekly Hours in Manufacturing. The index is shown in hours worked by production or nonsupervisory workers. A decline in hours worked, if sustained over some period, signals a lower level of production; conversely, a sustained increase in hours shows pick-up in production. Data are always close to 40 hours per week because unemployed labor forces are drawn into the labor pool when demand increases—unless there is a labor shortage, as was the case in the early months of 1945.

Average Weekly Initial Claims for Unemployment Insurance. Data are drawn from state unemployment program files and are a signal of increasing or decreasing layoffs—therefore an early signal of economic change.

Manufacturers' New Orders. The two series cover new orders in the consumer goods and materials industries and orders for capital goods in the nondefense industries. Since new orders represent future economic activity, the values (in millions of chained 1996 dollars, to remove inflationary bias) indicate future trends.

Vendor Performance. The index charts the percent of companies reporting late deliveries by vendors. Late deliveries are common when vendors are overbooked and have difficulty obtaining raw materials—a situation typically encountered in a strong economy. If late delivery percentages begin to rise in a recessionary economy, it signals the onset of an upturn—again only if the trend is sustained.

Building Permits for New Private Housing Units. The data are based on local building permits issued. Since permits must be obtained before building begins, this series predicts future housing starts and is thus a leading indicator. Increases in this index imply confidence that the economy will be strong, that money will be available for construction financing and house purchases.

Index of Stock Prices, 500 Common Stocks. This indicator is the Standard & Poor's 500 stock average index; it is an index to the 1941-1943 period, the average of which is expressed as 10. The index reflects stock price averages and is an indirect measure of investor confidence.

Money Supply M2. M2 is one of four monetary aggregates used by the Federal Reserve System to measure money supply. M1 is all currency, checking accounts, and other types of checkable deposits that can be turned into cash easily. M2 includes M1 and adds other liquid assets in the economy, including money market funds, money market deposit accounts, savings accounts, and small time deposits. M3 includes M2 plus large time deposits, institutional money market funds, and other less liquid assets. The fourth measure, labeled L (because it is *Least* under Federal Reserve control and *Least* liquid) includes M3 plus short-term Treasury securities, commercial paper, savings bonds, and bankers' acceptances. M2 is thus a measure of the money supply which includes some funds that are typically held for investment but not assets that are difficult to "liquefy."

M2 is used as a leading indicator because it tends to reach low points in its cycle approximately 12 months before Gross Domestic Product (GDP) reaches the bottom of its cycle. M2 thus serves as an early indicator of future GNP behavior.

Money supply, generally, affects the economy by influencing interest rates; these, in turn, can stimulate housing purchases and investments in capital goods. An increase in money supply usually results in low interest rates: there is more money to lend; a decline in money supply pushes interest rates up. In periods of high inflation, however, interest rates may not respond as just stated because lenders anticipate an inflationary devaluation of their funds and hence compensate by keeping interest rates high.

Interest Rate Spread, 10-year Treasury Bonds. The interest rate spread is the difference between the coupon rate of a bond (fixed interest) and the yield of the bond as traded in secondary markets. In effect this means that if bond prices are bid up, the yield is lowered—more is being paid for a fixed interest yield; conversely, if bond prices fall, yields increase. A positive spread implies confidence in the future; a negative spread implies lack of confidence. Bond prices thus fall in anticipation of expansionary periods and rise in expectation of deflationary periods.

Consumer Expectations. The index, based on surveys conducted by the University of Michigan, Survey Research Center, was added to the leading index in 1989. It is based on a monthly telephone survey of approximately 500 people in 48 states and the District of Columbia and combines the respondents' answers to questions about their expectations for the economy. The index is pegged to the first quarter of 1966, which is expressed as 100. The indicator, of course, measures consumer confidence. The index values, in themselves—while showing how attitudes have changed since 1966—are less valuable than changes month to month indicating a trend in consumer attitudes.

Sources and Revisions

Sources for the component series are largely drawn from federal sources, including the U.S. Department of Commerce, Bureau of Economic Analysis and Bureau of the Census; and U.S. Department of Labor, Bureau of Labor Statistics and Employment and Training Administration. Other sources are Standard & Poor's Corporation (Stock Index), McGraw-Hill Information Systems Company (contributor to Contracts and Orders for Plant and Equipment), National Association of Purchasing Management and Purchasing Management Association of Chicago (Vendor Performance), University of Michigan (Consumer Expectations), and others.

The composite index itself is constructed by The Conference Board, 845 Third Avenue, New York, NY 19922-6678. The Conference Board, a worldwide research and business membership group, took over the preparation of the each index (leading, coincident, lagging) from the Bureau of Economic Analysis of the U.S. Department of Commerce in December 1995.

In the process of index preparation, mathematical operations are performed on the component data series to ensure that volatile series do not dominate the index. A volatile series may be one that fluctuates wildly month to month but shows less volatility when averaged over several months. Other smoothing and standardization methods are used as well.

The index was revised in December 1996, 1997, and in 2001.

Bibliography

1. Frumkin, Norman. *Guide to Economic Indicators*. M.E. Sharpe, Inc., 1990.

2. Green, George R. and Barry A. Beckman. "Business Cycle Indicators: Upcoming Revision of the Composite Indexes." U.S. Department of Commerce, Bureau of Economic Analysis. *Survey of Current Business*, October 1993. Superintendent of Documents, U.S. Government Printing Office, Washington, DC 20302.

3. Hertzberg, Marie P. and Barry A. Beckman. "Business Cycle Indicators: Revised Composite Indexes." U.S. Department of Commerce, Bureau of Economic Analysis. *Survey of Current Business*, January 1989. Superintendent of Documents, U.S. Government Printing Office, Washington, DC 20302.

4. U.S. Department of Commerce, Bureau of Economic Analysis. "Composite Indexes of Leading, Coincident, and Lagging Indicators." In *Survey of Current Business*, November 1987. Superintendent of Documents, U.S. Government Printing Office, Washington, DC 20302.

5. U.S. Department of Commerce, Bureau of Economic Analysis. *Survey of Current Business*. Superintendent of Documents, U.S. Government Printing Office, Washington, DC 20302.

6. *Leading Economic Indicators*. The Confenrence Board, 845 Third Avenue, New York, NY 10022-6679.

Composite Index of 10 Leading Indicators
(1996=100)

Year	Jan	Feb	Mar	Apr	May	Jun	Jul	Aug	Sep	Oct	Nov	Dec
1959	59.3	60.0	60.6	60.5	60.7	60.6	60.4	60.1	60.0	59.6	59.1	60.2
1960	59.9	59.3	58.7	58.8	58.9	59.1	59.0	59.2	59.1	59.0	58.8	58.9
1961	59.3	59.3	60.1	60.7	61.0	61.6	61.6	62.3	61.9	62.4	62.9	63.3
1962	63.3	63.7	63.6	63.6	63.2	62.7	63.1	63.2	63.4	63.5	64.1	64.2
1963	64.6	64.9	65.3	65.7	66.0	66.0	66.0	66.0	66.6	66.8	66.9	67.0
1964	67.4	67.7	67.9	68.2	68.6	68.7	69.1	69.4	69.7	69.7	70.0	70.2
1965	70.7	70.7	71.2	71.1	71.4	71.4	71.6	71.6	71.8	72.5	73.1	73.5
1966	73.4	73.5	74.1	73.9	73.3	72.9	72.7	72.3	72.1	71.8	71.6	71.5
1967	71.8	71.5	71.6	71.9	72.4	73.0	73.4	74.2	74.2	74.3	74.6	75.0
1968	74.9	75.3	75.6	74.9	75.0	75.3	75.8	75.3	76.0	76.8	76.9	76.9
1969	77.2	77.3	77.1	77.3	76.7	76.3	75.9	75.9	76.1	75.6	75.2	74.8
1970	74.2	73.4	73.1	72.4	72.9	73.2	73.1	73.4	73.3	73.0	73.1	74.4
1971	75.1	75.8	76.2	76.5	76.9	77.1	77.1	77.2	77.4	77.7	78.1	79.3
1972	79.9	80.6	80.8	80.9	81.0	81.1	81.7	82.6	83.3	83.6	84.0	84.4
1973	84.6	84.7	84.1	83.6	83.4	83.1	82.6	82.1	82.0	82.1	82.0	80.7
1974	80.5	79.9	80.2	79.3	79.1	78.4	77.8	76.8	75.4	74.8	73.7	72.5
1975	72.2	72.2	72.7	74.5	75.3	75.8	76.8	77.2	77.7	78.1	78.5	78.7
1976	80.2	81.1	81.2	81.1	81.3	81.1	81.6	81.8	82.1	82.2	82.7	83.6
1977	83.4	83.8	84.3	84.3	84.3	84.7	84.6	84.6	84.7	84.6	84.7	84.8
1978	84.0	84.3	84.5	85.3	85.1	85.1	84.8	85.0	85.2	85.4	84.5	84.1
1979	83.9	84.0	84.3	83.1	83.7	83.3	82.5	82.6	82.8	81.7	81.3	80.9
1980	81.2	81.4	78.6	76.8	77.0	78.7	79.9	80.9	81.8	82.3	82.3	81.2
1981	81.0	81.0	81.7	82.5	81.9	81.0	80.8	81.1	80.5	79.8	79.5	79.8
1982	79.5	79.7	79.2	79.8	80.0	79.8	80.4	80.2	81.1	81.5	82.0	82.8
1983	84.2	85.0	86.0	86.7	87.6	88.4	88.8	88.7	89.0	89.7	89.9	90.0
1984	90.8	91.0	90.9	90.8	91.1	90.5	90.5	89.9	89.7	89.8	90.3	90.8
1985	91.4	91.3	91.5	91.2	91.5	91.9	91.9	92.1	92.3	92.2	92.0	92.6
1986	92.7	92.7	92.9	93.3	93.6	94.0	94.0	94.1	94.3	94.8	94.7	95.2
1987	95.1	95.8	95.9	96.0	96.0	96.4	96.8	96.8	97.0	96.8	96.2	96.0
1988	95.9	96.6	96.9	96.7	96.9	97.5	96.7	96.8	96.5	96.6	96.6	96.8
1989	96.9	96.4	95.7	96.1	95.4	95.3	95.3	95.6	95.8	95.5	95.8	96.1
1990	96.5	95.9	96.4	96.0	96.1	96.1	95.9	95.2	94.6	93.9	93.4	93.5
1991	93.2	93.9	94.5	94.9	95.3	95.6	96.4	95.8	95.8	95.8	95.7	95.3
1992	95.8	96.3	96.6	96.5	96.7	96.6	96.4	96.5	96.4	96.7	97.3	98.2
1993	97.7	97.7	96.9	97.2	96.9	97.2	96.8	97.1	97.3	97.4	97.8	98.5
1994	98.6	98.2	99.0	98.8	99.0	98.9	98.5	98.9	99.0	99.1	99.2	99.2
1995	99.1	98.5	97.9	97.6	97.5	97.7	97.9	98.4	98.4	98.2	98.2	98.6
1996	97.8	99.0	99.2	99.5	100.0	100.4	100.5	100.5	100.7	100.7	100.9	100.9
1997	101.4	102.1	102.1	102.1	102.6	102.8	103.4	103.5	103.7	104.1	104.2	104.1
1998	104.3	104.9	105.1	105.3	105.3	104.9	105.4	105.5	105.4	105.7	106.6	106.9
1999	107.5	108.0	108.2	107.9	108.5	109.0	109.5	109.4	109.3	109.4	110.0	110.6
2000	110.8	110.4	110.7	110.5	110.5	110.3	110.2	109.9	109.9	109.4	110.0	108.8
2001	108.8	108.9	108.7	108.7	109.3	109.5	109.8	109.7	109.9	109.1	109.2	109.7	-

Source: The Conference Board. © 2002 The Conference Board. All Rights Reserved. No claim to original U.S. Government works pursuant to U.S. Contract No. 52-SABA-5-00128. Primary source(s): The Conference Board, Inc., Economics Group, 845 Third Avenue, New York, NY 10022. A dash (-) indicates that data are not available or zero.

Composite Index of 10 Leading Indicators
Change in Index from Previous Month

Year	Jan	Feb	Mar	Apr	May	Jun	Jul	Aug	Sep	Oct	Nov	Dec
1959	-	+0.7	+0.6	-0.1	+0.2	-0.1	-0.2	-0.3	-0.1	-0.4	-0.5	+1.1
1960	-0.3	-0.6	-0.6	+0.1	+0.1	+0.2	-0.1	+0.2	-0.1	-0.1	-0.2	+0.1
1961	+0.4	-	+0.8	+0.6	+0.3	+0.6	-	+0.7	-0.4	+0.5	+0.5	+0.4
1962	-	+0.4	-0.1	-	-0.4	-0.5	+0.4	+0.1	+0.2	+0.1	+0.6	+0.1
1963	+0.4	+0.3	+0.4	+0.4	+0.3	-	-	-	+0.6	+0.2	+0.1	+0.1
1964	+0.4	+0.3	+0.2	+0.3	+0.4	+0.1	+0.4	+0.3	+0.3	-	+0.3	+0.2
1965	+0.5	-	+0.5	-0.1	+0.3	-	+0.2	-	+0.2	+0.7	+0.6	+0.4
1966	-0.1	+0.1	+0.6	-0.2	-0.6	-0.4	-0.2	-0.4	-0.2	-0.3	-0.2	-0.1
1967	+0.3	-0.3	+0.1	+0.3	+0.5	+0.6	+0.4	+0.8	-	+0.1	+0.3	+0.4
1968	-0.1	+0.4	+0.3	-0.7	+0.1	+0.3	+0.5	-0.5	+0.7	+0.8	+0.1	-
1969	+0.3	+0.1	-0.2	+0.2	-0.6	-0.4	-0.4	-	+0.2	-0.5	-0.4	-0.4
1970	-0.6	-0.8	-0.3	-0.7	+0.5	+0.3	-0.1	+0.3	-0.1	-0.3	+0.1	+1.3
1971	+0.7	+0.7	+0.4	+0.3	+0.4	+0.2	-	+0.1	+0.2	+0.3	+0.4	+1.2
1972	+0.6	+0.7	+0.2	+0.1	+0.1	+0.1	+0.6	+0.9	+0.7	+0.3	+0.4	+0.4
1973	+0.2	+0.1	-0.6	-0.5	-0.2	-0.3	-0.5	-0.5	-0.1	+0.1	-0.1	-1.3
1974	-0.2	-0.6	+0.3	-0.9	-0.2	-0.7	-0.6	-1.0	-1.4	-0.6	-1.1	-1.2
1975	-0.3	-	+0.5	+1.8	+0.8	+0.5	+1.0	+0.4	+0.5	+0.4	+0.4	+0.2
1976	+1.5	+0.9	+0.1	-0.1	+0.2	-0.2	+0.5	+0.2	+0.3	+0.1	+0.5	+0.9
1977	-0.2	+0.4	+0.5	-	-	+0.4	-0.1	-	+0.1	-0.1	+0.1	+0.1
1978	-0.8	+0.3	+0.2	+0.8	-0.2	-	-	-0.3	+0.2	+0.2	-0.9	-0.4
1979	-0.2	+0.1	+0.3	-1.2	+0.6	-0.4	-0.8	+0.1	+0.2	-1.1	-0.4	-0.4
1980	+0.3	+0.2	-2.8	-1.8	+0.2	+1.7	+1.2	+1.0	+0.9	+0.5	-	-1.1
1981	-0.2	-	+0.7	+0.8	-0.6	-0.9	-0.2	+0.3	-0.6	-0.7	-0.3	+0.3
1982	-0.3	+0.2	-0.5	+0.6	+0.2	-0.2	+0.6	-0.2	+0.9	+0.4	+0.5	+0.8
1983	+1.4	+0.8	+1.0	+0.7	+0.9	+0.8	+0.4	-0.1	+0.3	+0.7	+0.5	+0.1
1984	+0.8	+0.2	-0.1	-0.1	+0.3	-0.6	-	-0.6	-0.2	+0.1	+0.5	+0.5
1985	+0.6	-0.1	+0.2	-0.3	+0.3	+0.4	-	+0.2	+0.2	-0.1	-0.2	+0.6
1986	+0.1	-	+0.2	+0.4	+0.3	+0.4	-	+0.1	+0.2	+0.5	-0.1	+0.5
1987	-0.1	+0.7	+0.1	+0.1	-	+0.4	+0.4	-	+0.2	-0.2	-0.6	-0.2
1988	-0.1	+0.7	+0.3	-0.2	+0.2	+0.6	-0.8	+0.1	-0.3	+0.1	-	+0.2
1989	+0.1	-0.5	-0.7	+0.4	-0.7	-0.1	-	+0.3	+0.2	-0.3	+0.3	+0.3
1990	+0.4	-0.6	+0.5	-0.4	+0.1	-	-0.2	-0.7	-0.6	-0.7	-0.5	+0.1
1991	-0.3	+0.7	+0.6	+0.4	+0.4	+0.3	+0.8	-0.6	-	-	-0.1	-0.4
1992	+0.5	+0.5	+0.3	-0.1	+0.2	-0.1	-0.2	+0.1	-0.1	+0.3	+0.6	+0.9
1993	-0.5	-	-0.8	+0.3	-0.3	+0.3	-0.4	+0.3	+0.2	+0.1	+0.4	+0.7
1994	+0.1	-0.4	+0.8	-0.2	+0.2	-0.1	-0.4	+0.4	+0.1	+0.1	+0.1	-
1995	-0.1	-0.6	-0.6	-0.3	-0.1	+0.2	+0.2	+0.5	-	-0.2	-	+0.4
1996	-0.8	+1.2	+0.2	+0.3	+0.5	+0.4	+0.1	-	+0.2	-	+0.2	-
1997	+0.5	+0.7	-	-	+0.5	+0.2	+0.6	+0.1	+0.2	+0.4	+0.1	-0.1
1998	+0.2	+0.6	+0.2	+0.2	-	-0.4	+0.5	+0.1	-0.1	+0.3	+0.9	+0.3
1999	+0.6	+0.5	+0.2	-0.3	+0.6	+0.5	+0.5	-0.1	-0.1	+0.1	+0.6	+0.6
2000	+0.2	-0.4	+0.3	-0.2	-	-0.2	-0.1	-0.3	-	-0.4	-0.3	-0.4
2001	-	+0.1	-0.2	-	+0.6	+0.2	+0.3	-0.1	-0.6	+0.1	+0.5	-

Source: The Conference Board. © 2002 The Conference Board. All Rights Reserved. No claim to original U.S. Government works pursuant to U.S. Contract No. 52-SABA-5-00128. Primary source(s): The Conference Board, Inc., Economics Group, 845 Third Avenue, New York, NY 10022. A dash (-) indicates that data are not available or zero.

Average Weekly Hours, Manufacturing
(hours)

Year	Jan	Feb	Mar	Apr	May	Jun	Jul	Aug	Sep	Oct	Nov	Dec
1951	40.8	40.8	41.0	41.2	40.9	40.7	40.5	40.2	40.4	40.2	40.3	40.6
1952	40.7	40.7	40.6	40.1	40.4	40.5	40.1	40.5	41.0	41.1	41.0	41.1
1953	41.0	41.0	41.1	41.1	40.9	40.7	40.6	40.4	39.8	40.0	39.8	39.6
1954	39.5	39.7	39.5	39.4	39.5	39.6	39.6	39.7	39.5	39.6	40.1	40.0
1955	40.3	40.5	40.7	40.6	40.9	40.6	40.6	40.6	40.7	40.9	41.0	40.8
1956	40.8	40.6	40.4	40.6	40.2	40.1	40.2	40.2	40.4	40.5	40.4	40.5
1957	40.3	40.4	40.2	40.1	39.8	39.9	39.9	39.8	39.7	39.3	39.2	39.0
1958	38.8	38.6	38.7	38.6	38.8	39.0	39.2	39.4	39.6	39.5	39.8	39.8
1959	40.1	40.2	40.4	40.5	40.6	40.5	40.2	40.3	40.1	40.1	39.8	40.2
1960	40.5	40.1	39.9	39.7	40.0	39.8	39.8	39.7	39.4	39.6	39.2	38.4
1961	39.2	39.3	39.4	39.6	39.6	39.9	40.0	40.1	39.5	40.2	40.5	40.3
1962	40.0	40.3	40.5	40.7	40.5	40.4	40.4	40.3	40.5	40.2	40.3	40.2
1963	40.4	40.3	40.4	40.2	40.5	40.6	40.5	40.4	40.6	40.6	40.5	40.6
1964	40.1	40.6	40.6	40.8	40.7	40.7	40.8	40.9	40.5	40.6	40.8	41.1
1965	41.2	41.2	41.4	41.0	41.2	41.1	41.1	41.0	40.8	41.2	41.3	41.4
1966	41.4	41.6	41.5	41.5	41.4	41.4	41.2	41.4	41.3	41.3	41.2	40.9
1967	41.0	40.4	40.4	40.5	40.4	40.4	40.5	40.6	40.7	40.6	40.6	40.7
1968	40.3	40.9	40.7	40.0	40.9	40.9	40.8	40.7	40.9	40.9	40.8	40.7
1969	40.7	40.4	40.8	40.7	40.7	40.7	40.6	40.6	40.7	40.6	40.4	40.5
1970	40.4	40.2	40.1	39.9	39.8	39.9	40.0	39.8	39.3	39.5	39.5	39.5
1971	39.9	39.7	39.8	39.7	39.9	40.0	39.9	39.8	39.4	39.9	40.0	40.2
1972	40.2	40.4	40.4	40.7	40.5	40.6	40.5	40.6	40.6	40.7	40.8	40.5
1973	40.4	40.9	40.8	40.9	40.7	40.6	40.7	40.5	40.7	40.6	40.7	40.6
1974	40.5	40.4	40.4	39.3	40.3	40.2	40.2	40.2	40.0	40.0	39.5	39.3
1975	39.2	38.9	38.8	39.2	39.0	39.2	39.4	39.7	39.9	39.8	39.9	40.2
1976	40.5	40.3	40.2	39.6	40.3	40.2	40.3	40.1	39.8	40.0	40.1	40.0
1977	39.7	40.3	40.2	40.4	40.4	40.5	40.3	40.4	40.4	40.5	40.4	40.4
1978	39.6	39.9	40.5	40.8	40.4	40.5	40.6	40.5	40.6	40.5	40.6	40.6
1979	40.5	40.5	40.6	39.2	40.2	40.2	40.2	40.1	40.2	40.2	40.1	40.2
1980	40.0	40.1	39.8	39.5	39.3	39.2	39.1	39.4	39.6	39.8	40.0	40.3
1981	40.1	40.0	40.0	40.1	40.1	39.9	39.9	39.9	39.7	39.7	39.5	39.4
1982	38.0	39.6	39.1	38.9	39.0	39.1	39.2	39.0	39.0	38.9	39.1	39.1
1983	39.4	39.3	39.6	39.8	40.0	40.1	40.3	40.3	40.6	40.7	40.7	40.6
1984	40.7	41.1	40.7	40.9	40.7	40.7	40.6	40.5	40.5	40.5	40.5	40.6
1985	40.4	40.1	40.5	40.3	40.4	40.5	40.4	40.6	40.6	40.7	40.7	41.0
1986	40.8	40.6	40.8	40.6	40.7	40.6	40.6	40.8	40.7	40.6	40.8	40.9
1987	40.9	41.2	41.0	40.9	41.0	41.0	41.0	41.0	40.9	41.1	41.1	41.1
1988	41.1	41.0	41.0	40.8	41.0	41.0	41.0	40.9	40.9	41.0	41.1	41.0
1989	41.1	41.2	41.1	41.3	40.9	40.9	40.9	40.9	40.8	40.7	40.8	40.6
1990	40.7	40.8	40.9	40.8	40.9	40.9	40.9	40.8	40.8	40.7	40.5	40.6
1991	40.4	40.3	40.3	40.4	40.4	40.8	40.7	40.9	40.9	40.9	41.0	41.0
1992	40.9	41.1	41.0	41.1	41.2	41.1	41.1	41.1	41.0	41.1	41.2	41.2
1993	41.4	41.4	41.1	41.6	41.3	41.3	41.4	41.5	41.7	41.6	41.6	41.7
1994	41.7	41.2	42.1	41.9	42.0	42.0	42.1	42.0	41.9	42.1	42.1	42.1
1995	42.2	42.0	41.8	41.6	41.4	41.5	41.4	41.5	41.5	41.5	41.5	41.2
1996	39.9	41.6	41.4	41.5	41.7	41.8	41.7	41.8	41.9	41.7	41.7	41.9
1997	41.8	41.9	42.1	42.2	42.0	41.9	41.9	41.9	41.9	42.1	42.1	42.2
1998	42.2	42.0	41.9	41.7	41.8	41.7	41.7	41.7	41.6	41.7	41.7	41.8
1999	41.6	41.6	41.6	41.6	41.7	41.7	41.8	41.8	41.8	41.7	41.7	41.7
2000	41.7	41.9	41.8	42.1	41.6	41.7	41.8	41.4	41.4	41.4	41.2	40.6
2001	41.0	40.9	41.0	41.0	40.7	40.7	40.8	40.7	40.6	40.5	40.3	40.7

Average Weekly Initial Claims, Unemployment Insurance
(Thousands)

Year	Jan	Feb	Mar	Apr	May	Jun	Jul	Aug	Sep	Oct	Nov	Dec
1951	175.3	182.8	167.3	200.7	200.2	210.3	238.0	255.6	243.7	235.2	211.8	215.0
1952	222.8	202.2	210.8	220.3	214.3	243.5	317.2	208.1	169.4	175.9	170.5	191.9
1953	176.3	178.5	189.8	180.5	199.5	196.1	208.1	230.2	240.2	252.4	300.1	281.7
1954	305.4	320.7	321.9	315.5	315.6	316.1	295.7	321.1	324.3	316.8	277.7	254.6
1955	258.0	241.3	229.6	229.6	224.0	223.8	224.2	235.0	205.2	225.8	216.9	215.7
1956	219.1	227.8	222.5	224.5	237.7	229.1	246.9	225.5	238.0	215.6	224.9	231.3
1957	244.0	226.3	221.1	241.1	245.6	247.6	268.8	236.5	307.5	303.7	322.8	357.7
1958	356.5	409.6	439.1	441.1	403.1	412.8	352.2	365.9	340.4	316.7	313.6	322.5
1959	294.1	286.2	259.7	246.1	248.0	259.4	265.5	293.5	273.0	313.1	353.6	277.2
1960	282.6	272.6	305.3	296.0	318.1	323.8	337.7	366.1	353.8	375.7	387.6	383.9
1961	396.0	432.6	381.5	383.8	360.5	336.2	350.9	318.0	331.8	306.4	306.8	298.5
1962	302.9	297.4	289.3	285.2	302.8	306.2	305.2	307.3	302.4	306.5	301.3	312.0
1963	311.9	303.1	289.6	295.5	289.7	285.7	283.9	291.9	287.2	284.4	278.3	303.4
1964	285.3	271.8	279.1	266.8	264.4	258.4	261.4	245.8	247.3	251.0	264.1	252.9
1965	244.7	249.9	239.0	239.2	225.2	226.0	232.4	249.7	219.9	210.3	214.0	208.0
1966	223.4	220.1	183.2	179.9	193.0	195.6	200.3	196.0	198.9	204.0	209.7	220.9
1967	208.7	252.0	247.6	263.6	234.7	221.7	232.1	211.6	215.3	216.6	199.4	214.7
1968	215.5	196.8	196.1	198.8	195.9	191.8	195.8	197.2	190.1	184.4	183.8	199.4
1969	194.2	194.7	185.3	182.3	181.6	191.1	200.3	198.6	194.0	199.5	206.8	219.5
1970	250.9	258.3	267.5	340.3	304.2	296.5	281.8	291.0	324.5	329.1	324.8	304.1
1971	297.5	283.5	293.3	284.4	292.2	290.0	296.8	324.7	304.4	296.7	286.6	267.6
1972	268.9	263.4	262.3	263.7	267.0	293.9	283.6	255.0	255.2	250.4	243.1	246.3
1973	228.3	220.5	227.2	238.5	235.5	240.0	242.3	254.1	247.4	241.3	255.7	290.5
1974	313.3	317.9	313.7	292.4	294.9	311.9	309.0	342.4	360.2	404.7	470.2	523.7
1975	560.6	541.0	546.3	516.4	496.3	495.0	449.0	451.1	444.9	417.6	396.8	373.9
1976	373.1	348.0	360.2	371.3	392.7	396.3	389.8	388.1	403.3	408.7	389.3	368.0
1977	407.1	450.3	356.9	371.3	379.6	357.4	364.1	366.7	361.5	361.5	353.0	357.4
1978	350.6	381.5	342.9	323.7	326.3	333.3	350.6	335.3	324.3	327.8	344.9	349.7
1979	357.2	359.8	358.6	415.2	343.3	365.0	379.1	387.3	384.8	401.7	417.9	430.8
1980	416.6	419.0	439.5	556.3	626.4	606.2	556.6	517.4	482.0	426.5	410.6	409.6
1981	413.7	428.3	407.2	408.8	416.8	432.4	434.5	443.5	476.9	493.3	511.3	534.8
1982	545.2	533.7	556.5	586.7	585.8	596.9	569.7	629.6	671.7	641.8	594.4	517.9
1983	492.8	488.7	479.3	497.0	468.1	435.1	404.3	435.9	409.1	399.5	385.1	369.8
1984	350.9	340.5	345.5	369.4	357.7	362.9	360.3	390.1	398.0	419.3	401.3	381.7
1985	374.9	388.7	382.6	398.2	393.5	392.4	378.1	403.6	408.2	404.2	392.3	385.1
1986	368.9	372.1	380.6	389.6	384.9	373.4	373.1	402.6	391.8	374.9	362.7	357.0
1987	351.4	348.7	333.3	336.2	331.1	322.0	324.8	320.2	305.8	299.9	306.9	319.2
1988	340.1	319.4	301.8	306.1	309.9	299.5	328.7	324.0	308.4	298.6	302.2	307.1
1989	291.1	314.4	317.8	301.3	317.9	328.1	335.0	335.0	341.8	367.0	344.2	370.8
1990	361.4	358.9	344.9	356.5	352.3	351.0	362.4	392.5	399.8	429.6	457.3	468.8
1991	454.1	492.7	505.8	464.3	436.8	417.7	406.7	431.8	430.5	433.0	447.8	463.2
1992	434.0	444.9	432.5	420.3	411.1	411.4	438.0	403.3	417.6	374.0	361.8	334.5
1993	340.8	337.9	353.0	349.5	344.5	338.6	348.7	342.3	343.4	355.7	341.6	322.6
1994	359.8	348.7	336.5	349.0	365.5	342.0	342.8	339.7	334.8	338.8	329.2	324.4
1995	327.0	337.9	338.7	355.3	374.0	369.1	370.7	356.3	365.5	371.6	375.4	361.6
1996	365.5	370.0	389.3	360.0	348.2	348.6	332.9	330.9	342.6	340.1	338.1	353.3
1997	326.9	311.6	314.7	334.8	322.7	333.7	306.1	330.8	314.8	312.3	318.4	314.5
1998	314.1	310.3	308.4	311.6	316.5	348.1	315.7	306.8	299.8	314.1	319.3	322.7
1999	315.6	292.1	294.7	308.2	305.9	300.4	294.4	289.0	295.4	288.9	286.1	283.2
2000	279.8	284.0	263.1	277.6	287.3	300.4	295.3	316.2	306.6	310.0	345.9	355.4
2001	325.9	356.4	377.8	405.6	414.8	408.6	395.6	399.5	455.0	496.2	461.9	-

Source: The Conference Board. © 2002 The Conference Board. All Rights Reserved. No claim to original U.S. Government works pursuant to U.S. Contract No. 52-SABA-5-00128. Primary source(s): U.S. Department of Labor, Employment and Training Administration, Unemployment Insurance Services, Division of Actuarial Services, Washington, DC 20210. A dash (-) indicates that data are not available or zero.

Manufacturers' New Orders, Consumer Goods and Materials
(Millions of chained 1996 $)

Year	Jan	Feb	Mar	Apr	May	Jun	Jul	Aug	Sep	Oct	Nov	Dec
1959	60,704	65,002	66,086	64,872	63,061	63,214	61,567	58,637	58,352	58,197	56,901	61,748
1960	60,215	58,996	57,822	58,324	58,179	58,703	58,367	60,095	59,768	58,419	57,574	56,953
1961	54,677	54,115	58,129	60,084	61,389	62,964	60,573	64,159	63,371	63,466	66,285	68,115
1962	67,280	66,382	65,795	63,510	65,089	64,101	66,101	66,658	66,982	67,940	67,737	66,392
1963	68,095	70,204	70,960	73,381	71,503	70,282	73,142	69,075	70,599	73,346	73,340	73,462
1964	75,672	74,507	74,510	77,953	76,596	77,002	79,812	76,769	81,449	76,926	79,084	82,399
1965	83,360	83,471	84,615	84,486	84,089	84,814	87,286	87,520	81,805	85,646	88,789	90,634
1966	89,868	91,405	95,025	92,758	91,649	92,260	90,143	89,927	91,675	92,068	89,560	88,498
1967	87,854	86,769	85,859	87,058	88,421	89,329	88,643	93,174	89,680	88,174	91,394	97,777
1968	95,519	93,853	93,869	92,821	94,750	95,358	94,122	89,261	98,691	100,095	100,908	98,658
1969	99,313	99,243	98,984	98,910	98,770	98,709	99,599	99,827	101,627	100,894	96,855	96,907
1970	92,407	91,190	90,727	90,536	91,480	93,757	91,310	91,284	90,934	84,885	85,218	93,615
1971	95,718	95,723	96,192	93,484	93,127	92,457	93,642	96,772	95,132	95,566	97,981	100,705
1972	101,779	104,016	103,016	103,645	104,295	106,146	103,598	109,641	112,881	112,394	114,994	118,611
1973	121,865	124,111	124,608	119,876	121,206	119,039	119,089	117,778	116,958	119,261	121,243	116,922
1974	118,938	117,682	116,048	116,101	119,697	116,467	113,613	112,800	107,676	104,136	100,199	90,900
1975	89,022	88,114	83,980	87,096	87,817	88,515	92,909	95,098	95,623	96,440	95,780	97,144
1976	99,825	102,333	104,541	103,323	104,719	104,742	104,808	105,506	104,992	102,335	106,916	110,926
1977	110,999	111,754	116,815	112,934	113,856	114,920	115,002	116,213	116,155	115,532	118,292	118,980
1978	113,792	116,685	119,095	124,362	123,540	123,978	121,610	123,159	121,686	123,572	125,012	128,058
1979	125,145	122,451	125,609	120,652	121,812	121,815	117,861	114,680	115,948	114,187	112,415	111,343
1980	112,606	114,704	106,493	97,740	93,385	95,080	98,089	100,878	106,566	110,856	109,757	110,323
1981	103,805	108,830	108,308	110,529	111,650	111,336	109,709	106,093	103,775	100,215	98,048	96,953
1982	95,377	96,224	99,321	97,990	99,824	98,864	99,565	96,419	98,267	93,417	93,720	94,030
1983	99,597	101,377	101,427	103,023	106,231	109,474	111,026	112,801	112,722	116,969	118,030	119,820
1984	121,705	121,697	119,173	119,019	118,137	115,773	119,431	118,792	113,662	116,056	116,598	117,279
1985	119,355	116,593	116,780	116,791	119,017	118,113	118,020	119,398	119,823	119,587	119,531	118,856
1986	122,940	120,869	117,754	121,072	118,133	121,181	119,767	120,320	123,187	122,343	119,317	124,673
1987	120,283	127,613	128,199	126,649	125,771	128,250	130,108	126,448	129,080	130,237	129,643	129,568
1988	127,491	130,138	130,623	130,496	132,230	133,197	132,493	130,802	133,049	132,643	133,991	139,169
1989	137,968	136,476	131,918	134,561	131,447	131,470	125,274	131,132	131,980	128,103	130,793	129,730
1990	124,527	130,640	133,336	130,163	133,652	132,550	130,497	131,868	128,605	128,398	123,323	119,025
1991	120,358	120,226	116,306	123,486	125,960	123,236	130,314	128,308	130,098	128,566	129,143	124,468
1992	125,118	127,439	128,288	131,295	129,827	133,415	132,518	130,997	130,951	133,087	134,209	139,054
1993	136,809	138,863	136,353	135,607	133,879	135,945	134,269	133,848	137,518	138,805	140,866	142,475
1994	143,814	143,940	149,250	146,016	148,876	148,776	146,204	151,719	150,266	149,513	154,409	156,811
1995	157,892	155,748	155,152	151,002	151,366	151,054	150,134	153,343	151,482	152,665	152,421	152,315
1996	151,669	151,041	148,137	155,173	157,837	156,744	158,883	158,131	158,341	158,651	159,343	154,961
1997	162,545	166,635	162,040	166,036	168,166	167,127	168,578	171,500	171,173	172,093	171,978	172,400
1998	168,783	171,340	170,348	172,174	170,253	164,215	167,571	169,891	171,741	176,032	174,630	178,128
1999	179,709	178,342	178,477	179,885	178,656	179,534	184,834	188,159	184,556	181,300	186,584	189,271
2000	184,837	183,973	193,606	178,472	193,444	185,804	182,562	179,745	184,763	177,434	176,506	176,613
2001	163,062	169,071	168,649	162,347	170,169	166,347	166,274	167,191	156,306	162,050	163,930	-

Vendor Performance, Slower Deliveries Diffusion Index
(Percent)

Year	Jan	Feb	Mar	Apr	May	Jun	Jul	Aug	Sep	Oct	Nov	Dec
1951	88.7	93.3	85.1	65.7	45.0	36.7	32.2	32.0	46.4	47.2	34.9	33.6
1952	31.3	24.9	18.8	19.4	22.4	33.0	47.4	41.2	42.7	43.3	45.0	43.5
1953	41.5	41.8	41.8	38.6	35.1	33.3	28.5	26.5	23.2	20.7	20.2	21.8
1954	23.6	26.9	28.0	30.3	34.3	35.8	38.1	36.4	43.6	49.5	51.9	54.5
1955	60.6	67.2	68.5	71.9	68.7	65.7	67.0	64.3	66.3	66.5	64.9	61.4
1956	53.5	51.3	51.0	51.0	38.6	41.0	53.9	46.8	42.8	40.1	44.6	39.5
1957	36.3	31.2	26.3	28.9	30.0	30.0	36.8	30.8	28.8	32.6	27.8	27.3
1958	30.3	31.0	34.0	35.5	38.5	39.2	43.0	44.7	51.1	52.4	55.8	56.4
1959	61.8	67.3	66.3	64.8	63.0	63.7	59.1	57.4	57.5	58.5	54.6	53.7
1960	46.2	31.7	28.8	28.9	32.3	34.8	35.8	38.0	37.3	36.2	37.6	40.4
1961	39.2	41.1	42.1	47.5	47.9	49.3	49.4	50.6	50.7	52.4	51.1	55.8
1962	57.1	56.2	57.0	47.4	45.2	43.3	45.1	43.7	45.1	46.7	48.7	50.1
1963	50.4	51.0	54.9	58.2	56.4	56.3	43.6	48.5	49.7	47.4	48.7	47.6
1964	55.3	51.9	60.3	57.7	61.4	57.6	61.8	66.2	71.9	71.2	70.3	67.8
1965	68.5	68.1	65.9	69.4	68.9	69.3	65.1	65.4	61.2	59.1	65.1	73.5
1966	74.9	80.1	86.4	79.3	74.6	71.6	73.1	74.3	72.4	68.7	62.6	57.9
1967	48.2	49.9	38.0	36.9	34.4	36.5	40.9	44.8	46.5	51.1	51.4	49.9
1968	50.6	53.9	54.0	49.0	49.4	49.9	55.9	47.8	48.4	53.3	61.0	58.3
1969	63.6	60.1	60.5	63.9	64.9	67.0	65.7	70.3	68.9	66.8	64.1	66.8
1970	57.9	57.7	49.3	48.7	67.2	66.1	49.8	46.1	46.5	39.0	37.8	37.5
1971	39.8	44.2	45.0	48.9	49.4	47.9	47.4	49.7	48.9	50.9	50.9	53.3
1972	55.2	52.6	57.1	55.0	56.1	57.7	61.7	62.9	65.5	73.0	74.5	80.7
1973	83.7	85.2	87.5	86.7	86.6	85.6	85.2	86.7	90.1	88.7	96.8	92.8
1974	91.8	88.8	88.9	82.1	74.5	73.1	69.2	66.3	51.8	45.3	34.0	23.2
1975	19.5	15.9	17.3	21.7	22.7	24.9	28.7	35.1	43.8	44.8	46.8	41.2
1976	54.0	56.1	56.7	57.3	58.3	58.6	54.0	55.2	52.6	49.0	47.2	53.3
1977	55.3	65.1	49.6	54.6	55.4	53.3	58.3	53.5	56.7	53.6	56.3	57.1
1978	55.6	63.4	58.9	57.1	57.4	61.1	59.4	60.6	60.0	64.7	64.5	63.5
1979	66.4	64.0	66.7	75.6	63.7	61.4	57.4	52.9	50.7	46.9	46.8	42.2
1980	42.1	46.0	39.1	36.9	29.8	32.4	36.3	40.1	41.2	46.5	46.8	50.1
1981	49.7	48.5	48.7	51.2	50.2	47.9	44.9	49.6	45.9	37.7	40.5	41.2
1982	40.1	40.8	36.4	38.2	42.1	45.2	45.8	45.3	45.9	46.5	46.9	48.6
1983	46.7	49.9	50.8	52.7	51.9	56.8	58.9	60.2	60.7	62.8	67.5	62.1
1984	64.4	61.5	65.5	64.6	62.5	56.2	59.1	55.2	52.8	49.3	48.1	48.8
1985	50.4	48.6	46.7	46.1	48.0	47.1	45.7	46.6	49.5	50.0	48.5	49.3
1986	50.1	49.8	50.5	50.7	50.2	49.9	49.9	50.8	49.6	51.3	52.0	52.8
1987	51.5	51.2	51.9	52.8	54.0	56.8	58.9	60.3	61.5	62.2	64.9	62.7
1988	62.0	61.2	57.3	58.6	56.9	65.6	58.4	57.4	55.2	54.8	52.1	53.0
1989	53.9	54.0	52.5	52.2	49.1	46.5	46.1	44.0	43.9	43.3	42.5	43.5
1990	48.2	44.4	47.2	47.2	48.2	49.8	46.4	50.1	48.9	48.1	48.6	47.2
1991	44.4	44.7	43.9	45.0	46.0	47.1	49.6	48.3	48.8	50.2	50.1	49.4
1992	48.7	49.3	50.3	47.4	50.0	50.8	52.5	50.3	51.2	48.6	51.3	51.5
1993	52.3	51.7	52.7	52.8	51.5	50.4	51.0	51.8	51.3	50.7	50.9	51.5
1994	54.4	57.0	55.4	57.2	60.2	60.3	58.1	61.6	62.5	64.9	64.7	64.8
1995	62.7	60.7	56.9	56.3	53.3	51.8	51.3	49.1	50.0	48.4	45.3	47.5
1996	47.8	49.5	49.6	49.4	49.9	52.8	50.8	51.9	50.0	50.9	51.2	52.0
1997	49.7	52.2	53.1	53.4	55.0	54.8	54.8	55.2	54.8	54.8	55.0	53.8
1998	53.1	53.0	53.0	52.4	51.6	51.1	50.3	50.2	50.7	49.8	50.1	48.2
1999	51.2	51.1	52.4	49.5	52.1	53.1	54.3	51.2	55.5	56.1	56.1	56.1
2000	55.4	55.3	54.4	55.4	55.1	55.1	54.3	53.3	49.0	51.1	49.3	52.1
2001	50.3	51.3	48.3	47.4	45.7	48.0	47.4	46.5	46.5	49.2	47.3	48.0

Manufacturers' New Orders, Nondefense Capital Goods

(Millions of chained 1996 $)

Year	Jan	Feb	Mar	Apr	May	Jun	Jul	Aug	Sep	Oct	Nov	Dec
1959	8,817	10,544	11,947	10,860	11,375	11,657	11,796	10,873	11,848	11,402	10,658	11,473
1960	10,570	10,930	10,762	11,190	11,176	11,135	10,764	10,768	10,652	10,447	10,120	11,117
1961	10,630	10,684	10,692	10,603	10,346	10,942	11,446	11,983	11,315	11,433	11,823	11,213
1962	11,906	12,717	11,357	12,442	11,752	11,575	11,668	11,649	11,925	12,113	12,981	12,267
1963	12,479	12,834	13,028	13,060	13,619	12,962	13,084	13,541	13,773	13,821	13,470	14,084
1964	15,353	13,693	14,673	14,453	16,007	16,442	15,144	15,314	15,222	15,592	15,776	16,106
1965	16,036	15,763	17,072	16,877	16,427	16,973	17,255	16,763	17,355	17,870	18,225	19,502
1966	18,482	20,203	19,889	20,481	20,613	20,312	21,256	19,803	20,838	20,412	19,600	19,721
1967	16,780	17,724	17,868	18,055	18,415	18,940	19,302	19,689	18,749	18,947	19,143	20,066
1968	24,851	23,364	28,773	24,583	19,276	19,203	24,323	23,793	20,758	26,049	21,914	23,416
1969	25,286	28,267	24,790	30,276	25,048	24,556	24,833	25,529	28,038	23,661	24,395	22,101
1970	24,890	23,281	20,887	19,667	20,579	19,426	20,925	20,639	20,027	19,163	20,371	22,353
1971	21,620	22,928	22,242	21,792	21,171	24,439	19,714	22,280	23,854	21,353	22,419	23,422
1972	21,983	24,018	24,801	24,002	26,592	23,001	26,630	25,399	27,577	26,488	27,127	27,700
1973	27,882	29,646	30,302	31,427	30,722	29,933	31,386	31,736	31,503	34,052	34,284	33,281
1974	34,170	34,620	35,013	33,962	31,313	30,474	35,461	33,413	31,932	28,482	27,411	26,902
1975	27,597	24,767	22,600	25,133	23,108	22,739	25,349	24,948	23,906	24,322	24,234	23,034
1976	24,416	25,396	24,925	26,901	25,925	25,858	29,988	27,227	28,580	29,870	26,844	29,559
1977	28,832	28,063	28,111	28,839	28,907	31,569	29,409	29,876	32,326	32,264	30,844	32,726
1978	31,624	34,044	33,170	34,131	34,144	32,821	32,642	34,056	35,175	38,695	35,987	32,288
1979	35,711	39,239	41,998	34,883	35,286	35,666	34,549	34,467	34,645	35,172	33,000	32,820
1980	34,877	30,038	29,284	29,221	25,627	26,967	29,310	26,125	27,591	28,646	26,072	28,854
1981	31,165	26,717	30,091	31,160	28,555	29,007	29,776	29,587	28,177	28,041	27,370	24,229
1982	27,980	27,267	27,663	27,191	23,429	23,611	24,895	22,739	23,892	25,605	23,037	23,317
1983	24,554	20,544	22,608	24,242	23,911	25,686	23,757	24,939	27,262	28,989	26,000	25,889
1984	29,582	29,355	29,670	28,635	31,706	29,872	30,722	28,993	28,538	29,437	29,235	27,836
1985	28,833	32,522	30,811	28,094	28,521	30,442	29,204	30,208	31,853	31,524	28,094	33,085
1986	29,744	30,959	29,662	28,215	28,318	28,623	28,058	27,698	28,790	29,830	29,019	30,592
1987	29,560	29,087	28,207	29,977	32,245	32,092	33,802	30,377	30,367	31,817	32,070	34,728
1988	36,823	35,958	33,700	34,880	32,587	35,680	37,213	39,933	36,673	35,095	36,197	39,813
1989	39,732	37,220	36,775	38,471	35,869	38,320	40,295	33,705	33,382	33,004	36,366	42,168
1990	37,378	34,539	39,342	35,328	34,405	34,374	38,925	33,758	36,854	39,821	32,516	40,939
1991	35,718	35,452	33,371	30,297	29,593	29,373	39,192	32,263	31,405	31,967	36,091	28,875
1992	33,397	32,817	35,411	33,759	34,014	33,632	32,859	30,961	33,849	33,741	29,421	35,351
1993	30,464	34,852	31,333	33,146	32,207	34,907	30,797	32,775	31,323	33,178	35,002	35,296
1994	37,346	35,820	35,772	35,174	34,473	37,641	35,726	36,902	37,252	37,084	39,603	36,762
1995	39,974	40,121	40,201	38,097	41,545	39,781	37,171	39,179	43,782	40,964	44,030	46,981
1996	46,116	44,629	46,203	40,480	45,154	42,718	45,205	41,239	47,066	47,312	44,232	44,012
1997	45,764	47,914	47,528	48,287	46,986	50,379	51,696	51,244	51,180	53,439	60,839	49,427
1998	52,249	52,431	51,636	54,033	53,064	53,574	51,912	54,007	52,580	51,752	52,931	50,277
1999	53,895	52,169	53,226	52,826	53,763	52,569	56,549	56,345	56,689	56,116	56,534	61,653
2000	62,948	57,165	61,657	62,778	62,002	69,437	63,380	63,994	66,882	61,104	64,828	67,689
2001	58,902	59,121	59,457	56,259	55,530	53,441	51,823	51,411	44,800	47,471	49,880	-

Source: The Conference Board. © 2002 The Conference Board. All Rights Reserved. No claim to original U.S. Government works pursuant to U.S. Contract No. 52-SABA-5-00128. Primary source(s): U.S. Department of Commerce, Bureau of the Census, Manufacturing and Construction Division, Manufacturers' Shipments, Inventories, and Orders Branch, Washington, DC 20233. F.W. Dodge; McGraw-Hill, Inc., Market Analysis Group, 24 Hartwell Avenue, Lexington, MA 02173. Deflators calculated by The Conference Board. A dash (-) indicates that data are not available or zero.

Building Permits for New Private Housing Units
(Thousands)

Year	Jan	Feb	Mar	Apr	May	Jun	Jul	Aug	Sep	Oct	Nov	Dec
1954	1,314	1,294	1,364	1,378	1,403	1,507	1,545	1,533	1,572	1,626	1,752	1,702
1955	1,759	1,946	1,667	1,713	1,723	1,626	1,632	1,576	1,552	1,519	1,386	1,380
1956	1,416	1,376	1,416	1,411	1,314	1,290	1,281	1,251	1,218	1,201	1,208	1,197
1957	1,115	1,172	1,182	1,117	1,167	1,192	1,111	1,187	1,191	1,175	1,141	1,150
1958	1,180	1,015	1,125	1,185	1,240	1,324	1,442	1,440	1,476	1,523	1,729	1,494
1959	1,478	1,542	1,611	1,539	1,513	1,490	1,452	1,465	1,411	1,358	1,298	1,394
1960	1,325	1,319	1,158	1,232	1,276	1,161	1,211	1,205	1,194	1,179	1,187	1,151
1961	1,176	1,166	1,212	1,214	1,246	1,297	1,313	1,405	1,331	1,361	1,396	1,408
1962	1,360	1,447	1,375	1,498	1,384	1,398	1,442	1,455	1,481	1,432	1,499	1,499
1963	1,457	1,415	1,468	1,504	1,576	1,571	1,542	1,529	1,650	1,652	1,585	1,661
1964	1,513	1,684	1,532	1,475	1,516	1,494	1,522	1,525	1,476	1,437	1,463	1,358
1965	1,475	1,383	1,414	1,356	1,409	1,448	1,444	1,458	1,432	1,493	1,525	1,535
1966	1,546	1,353	1,441	1,337	1,259	1,116	1,089	1,024	905	862	859	867
1967	1,125	1,025	1,078	1,171	1,215	1,321	1,330	1,389	1,445	1,446	1,465	1,486
1968	1,332	1,516	1,547	1,454	1,465	1,469	1,519	1,533	1,655	1,606	1,622	1,571
1969	1,649	1,689	1,624	1,627	1,502	1,525	1,444	1,489	1,427	1,374	1,346	1,306
1970	1,200	1,263	1,279	1,383	1,502	1,494	1,497	1,576	1,611	1,768	1,697	1,996
1971	1,857	1,794	1,988	1,973	2,229	2,151	2,338	2,265	2,255	2,289	2,349	2,410
1972	2,487	2,410	2,339	2,377	2,297	2,425	2,438	2,514	2,658	2,616	2,483	2,688
1973	2,523	2,473	2,291	2,120	2,145	2,278	2,021	2,010	1,894	1,569	1,557	1,431
1974	1,478	1,511	1,600	1,393	1,264	1,207	1,113	1,019	933	915	870	965
1975	807	810	788	962	1,016	1,051	1,133	1,105	1,182	1,217	1,233	1,212
1976	1,328	1,323	1,293	1,258	1,327	1,320	1,383	1,455	1,646	1,583	1,701	1,679
1977	1,607	1,734	1,844	1,844	1,853	1,946	1,874	1,978	1,860	1,953	1,969	1,949
1978	1,812	1,808	1,873	2,028	1,839	2,065	1,860	1,761	1,824	1,855	1,869	1,894
1979	1,521	1,553	1,791	1,663	1,754	1,708	1,598	1,657	1,705	1,542	1,329	1,306
1980	1,333	1,249	1,029	842	896	1,165	1,311	1,424	1,545	1,423	1,440	1,300
1981	1,272	1,249	1,232	1,239	1,221	1,017	974	926	882	762	779	829
1982	827	842	928	925	992	951	1,088	964	1,086	1,197	1,280	1,407
1983	1,485	1,532	1,536	1,630	1,738	1,842	1,869	1,784	1,651	1,787	1,737	1,694
1984	1,867	2,043	1,773	1,826	1,790	1,865	1,650	1,573	1,566	1,532	1,689	1,672
1985	1,706	1,709	1,775	1,711	1,757	1,764	1,745	1,859	1,970	1,792	1,739	1,844
1986	1,899	1,816	1,830	1,910	1,847	1,840	1,830	1,774	1,733	1,722	1,690	1,956
1987	1,737	1,736	1,752	1,646	1,542	1,565	1,558	1,553	1,556	1,488	1,498	1,383
1988	1,279	1,478	1,568	1,469	1,484	1,527	1,479	1,501	1,476	1,558	1,550	1,543
1989	1,507	1,422	1,248	1,415	1,420	1,359	1,319	1,371	1,351	1,403	1,382	1,462
1990	1,797	1,366	1,281	1,168	1,097	1,139	1,108	1,099	1,003	951	967	885
1991	808	877	937	942	1,019	991	1,000	970	1,001	1,019	1,012	1,091
1992	1,107	1,178	1,112	1,084	1,086	1,087	1,119	1,105	1,145	1,164	1,149	1,209
1993	1,210	1,180	1,086	1,135	1,143	1,162	1,207	1,264	1,286	1,323	1,395	1,502
1994	1,390	1,269	1,342	1,392	1,396	1,357	1,335	1,377	1,412	1,397	1,340	1,396
1995	1,282	1,254	1,226	1,259	1,271	1,305	1,354	1,386	1,421	1,400	1,430	1,442
1996	1,387	1,420	1,437	1,463	1,457	1,429	1,450	1,413	1,392	1,358	1,412	1,411
1997	1,382	1,445	1,436	1,421	1,414	1,402	1,440	1,449	1,494	1,499	1,469	1,456
1998	1,555	1,647	1,605	1,547	1,554	1,551	1,610	1,654	1,577	1,719	1,672	1,742
1999	1,732	1,720	1,665	1,600	1,640	1,702	1,682	1,671	1,551	1,649	1,672	1,683
2000	1,780	1,736	1,656	1,595	1,540	1,566	1,534	1,544	1,549	1,562	1,614	1,553
2001	1,724	1,663	1,627	1,587	1,621	1,587	1,571	1,571	1,528	1,485	1,595	-

Source: The Conference Board. © 2002 The Conference Board. All Rights Reserved. No claim to original U.S. Government works pursuant to U.S. Contract No. 52-SABA-5-00128. Primary source(s): U.S. Department of Commerce, Bureau of the Census, Manufacturing and Construction Division, Building Permits Branch, Washington, DC 20233. A dash (-) indicates that data are not available or zero.

Index of Stock Prices, 500 Common Stocks
Not seasonally adjusted
(1941-43=10)

Year	Jan	Feb	Mar	Apr	May	Jun	Jul	Aug	Sep	Oct	Nov	Dec
1951	21.21	22.00	21.63	21.92	21.93	21.55	21.93	22.89	23.48	23.36	22.71	23.41
1952	24.19	23.75	23.81	23.74	23.73	24.38	25.08	25.18	24.78	24.26	25.03	26.04
1953	26.18	25.86	25.99	24.71	24.84	23.95	24.29	24.39	23.27	23.97	24.50	24.83
1954	25.46	26.02	26.57	27.63	28.73	28.96	30.13	30.73	31.45	32.18	33.44	34.97
1955	35.60	36.79	36.50	37.76	37.60	39.78	42.69	42.43	44.34	42.11	44.95	45.37
1956	44.15	44.43	47.49	48.05	46.54	46.27	48.78	48.49	46.84	46.24	45.76	46.44
1957	45.43	43.47	44.03	45.05	46.78	47.55	48.51	45.84	43.98	41.24	40.35	40.33
1958	41.12	41.26	42.11	42.34	43.70	44.75	45.98	47.70	48.96	50.95	52.50	53.49
1959	55.62	54.77	56.15	57.10	57.96	57.46	59.74	59.40	57.05	57.00	57.23	59.06
1960	58.03	55.78	55.02	55.73	55.22	57.26	55.84	56.51	54.81	53.73	55.47	56.80
1961	59.72	62.17	64.12	65.83	66.50	65.62	65.44	67.79	67.26	68.00	71.08	71.74
1962	69.07	70.22	70.29	68.05	62.99	55.63	56.97	58.52	58.00	56.17	60.04	62.64
1963	65.06	65.92	65.67	68.76	70.14	70.11	69.07	70.98	72.85	73.03	72.62	74.17
1964	76.45	77.39	78.80	79.94	80.72	80.24	83.22	82.00	83.41	84.85	85.44	83.96
1965	86.12	86.75	86.83	87.97	89.28	85.04	84.91	86.49	89.38	91.39	92.15	91.73
1966	93.32	92.69	88.88	91.60	86.78	86.06	85.84	80.65	77.81	77.13	80.99	81.33
1967	84.45	87.36	89.42	90.96	92.59	91.43	93.01	94.49	95.81	95.66	92.66	95.30
1968	95.04	90.75	89.09	95.67	97.87	100.53	100.30	98.11	101.34	103.76	105.40	106.48
1969	102.04	101.46	99.30	101.26	104.62	99.14	94.71	94.18	94.51	95.52	96.21	91.11
1970	90.31	87.16	88.65	85.95	76.06	75.59	75.72	77.92	82.58	84.37	84.28	90.05
1971	93.49	97.11	99.60	103.04	101.64	99.72	99.00	97.24	99.40	97.29	92.78	99.17
1972	103.30	105.24	107.69	108.81	107.65	108.01	107.21	111.01	109.39	109.56	115.05	117.50
1973	118.42	114.16	112.42	110.27	107.22	104.75	105.83	103.80	105.61	109.84	102.03	94.78
1974	96.11	93.45	97.44	92.46	89.67	89.79	82.82	76.03	68.12	69.44	71.74	67.07
1975	72.56	80.10	83.78	84.72	90.10	92.40	92.49	85.71	84.67	88.57	90.07	88.70
1976	96.86	100.64	101.08	101.93	101.16	101.77	104.20	103.29	105.45	101.89	101.19	104.66
1977	103.81	100.96	100.57	99.05	98.76	99.29	100.18	97.75	96.23	93.74	94.28	93.82
1978	90.25	88.98	88.82	92.71	97.41	97.66	97.19	103.92	103.86	100.58	94.71	96.11
1979	99.71	98.23	100.11	102.07	99.73	101.73	102.71	107.36	108.60	104.47	103.66	107.78
1980	110.87	115.34	104.69	102.97	107.69	114.55	119.83	123.50	126.51	130.22	135.65	133.48
1981	132.97	128.40	133.19	134.43	131.73	132.28	129.13	129.63	118.27	119.80	122.92	123.79
1982	117.28	114.50	110.84	116.31	116.35	109.70	109.38	109.65	122.43	132.66	138.10	139.37
1983	144.27	146.80	151.88	157.71	164.10	166.39	166.96	162.42	167.16	167.65	165.23	164.36
1984	166.39	157.25	157.44	157.60	156.55	153.12	151.08	164.42	166.11	164.82	166.27	164.48
1985	171.61	180.88	179.42	180.62	184.90	188.89	192.54	188.31	184.06	186.18	197.45	207.26
1986	208.19	219.37	232.33	237.98	238.46	245.30	240.18	245.00	238.27	237.36	245.09	248.61
1987	264.51	280.93	292.47	289.32	289.12	301.38	310.09	329.36	318.66	280.16	245.01	240.96
1988	250.48	258.13	265.74	262.61	256.12	270.68	269.05	263.73	267.97	277.40	271.02	276.51
1989	285.41	294.01	292.71	302.25	313.93	323.73	331.93	346.61	347.33	347.40	340.22	348.57
1990	339.97	330.45	338.47	338.18	350.25	360.39	360.03	330.75	315.41	307.12	315.29	328.75
1991	325.49	362.26	372.28	379.68	377.99	378.29	380.23	389.40	387.20	386.88	385.92	388.51
1992	416.08	412.56	407.36	407.41	414.81	408.27	415.05	417.93	418.48	412.50	422.84	435.64
1993	435.23	441.70	450.16	443.08	445.25	448.06	447.29	454.13	459.24	463.90	462.89	465.95
1994	472.99	471.58	463.81	447.23	450.90	454.83	451.40	464.24	466.96	463.81	461.01	455.19
1995	465.25	481.92	493.15	507.91	523.81	539.35	557.37	559.11	578.77	582.92	595.53	614.57
1996	614.42	649.54	647.07	647.17	661.23	668.50	644.07	662.68	674.88	701.45	735.67	743.25
1997	766.22	798.39	792.16	763.93	833.09	876.29	925.29	927.74	937.02	951.16	938.92	962.37
1998	963.36	1,023.74	1,076.83	1,112.20	1,108.42	1,108.39	1,156.58	1,074.63	1,020.64	1,032.47	1,144.43	1,190.05
1999	1,248.77	1,246.58	1,281.66	1,334.76	1,332.07	1,322.55	1,380.99	1,327.49	1,318.17	1,300.01	1,391.00	1,428.68
2000	1,425.59	1,388.87	1,442.21	1,461.36	1,418.48	1,461.96	1,473.00	1,485.46	1,468.05	1,390.14	1,375.04	1,330.93
2001	1,335.63	1,305.75	1,185.85	1,189.84	1,270.37	1,238.71	1,204.45	1,178.50	1,044.64	1,076.59	1,129.68	1,144.93

Source: The Conference Board. © 2002 The Conference Board. All Rights Reserved. No claim to original U.S. Government works pursuant to U.S. Contract No. 52-SABA-5-00128. Primary source(s): Standard & Poor's Corporation, 25 Broadway, New York, NY 10004. A dash (-) indicates that data are not available or zero.

Money Supply M2
(Billions of chained 1996 $)

Year	Jan	Feb	Mar	Apr	May	Jun	Jul	Aug	Sep	Oct	Nov	Dec
1959	1,335.0	1,339.1	1,345.6	1,347.3	1,356.5	1,361.6	1,363.8	1,367.5	1,365.5	1,361.2	1,362.9	1,364.4
1960	1,366.8	1,366.7	1,369.8	1,368.1	1,370.3	1,375.9	1,381.6	1,392.0	1,397.6	1,400.9	1,402.3	1,408.7
1961	1,416.0	1,425.7	1,434.6	1,442.7	1,452.1	1,460.9	1,463.8	1,471.5	1,478.3	1,485.8	1,496.1	1,505.0
1962	1,511.2	1,518.9	1,530.1	1,538.8	1,546.7	1,554.2	1,561.6	1,568.0	1,569.6	1,581.5	1,592.0	1,605.4
1963	1,612.6	1,622.8	1,636.6	1,648.3	1,658.2	1,664.8	1,673.4	1,682.2	1,692.8	1,699.9	1,711.3	1,717.0
1964	1,721.9	1,729.9	1,738.4	1,745.7	1,756.5	1,766.6	1,777.6	1,790.3	1,802.7	1,811.0	1,821.3	1,829.7
1965	1,839.4	1,850.9	1,860.3	1,867.0	1,870.1	1,877.6	1,887.8	1,899.2	1,914.3	1,926.9	1,936.8	1,944.6
1966	1,954.1	1,956.8	1,962.9	1,965.1	1,965.8	1,965.5	1,960.1	1,959.8	1,965.2	1,961.2	1,964.7	1,972.6
1967	1,978.7	1,990.8	2,008.3	2,014.7	2,031.7	2,044.6	2,055.3	2,067.3	2,076.8	2,085.1	2,090.1	2,101.2
1968	2,101.3	2,104.6	2,109.2	2,112.9	2,117.7	2,125.8	2,131.0	2,137.5	2,146.3	2,152.3	2,163.5	2,175.6
1969	2,177.1	2,181.3	2,180.6	2,176.0	2,169.8	2,166.8	2,160.7	2,157.1	2,154.9	2,152.4	2,150.3	2,149.8
1970	2,148.4	2,127.2	2,125.5	2,118.9	2,123.3	2,131.9	2,138.2	2,153.0	2,165.1	2,172.3	2,179.5	2,188.3
1971	2,206.3	2,228.3	2,251.6	2,272.2	2,291.9	2,303.4	2,319.4	2,332.7	2,352.7	2,368.2	2,384.2	2,393.5
1972	2,408.7	2,425.8	2,448.2	2,460.1	2,471.4	2,489.1	2,513.6	2,536.4	2,556.3	2,580.8	2,595.8	2,614.1
1973	2,632.2	2,631.1	2,615.8	2,610.2	2,620.5	2,626.5	2,628.4	2,605.0	2,595.9	2,591.3	2,588.8	2,587.7
1974	2,576.3	2,560.0	2,548.1	2,539.0	2,520.0	2,509.1	2,502.3	2,483.9	2,469.6	2,466.4	2,462.4	2,452.7
1975	2,448.7	2,456.8	2,478.6	2,496.5	2,521.6	2,547.2	2,558.2	2,568.3	2,576.8	2,578.2	2,585.5	2,594.6
1976	2,612.6	2,643.5	2,664.3	2,685.2	2,700.7	2,703.4	2,712.3	2,727.1	2,740.9	2,759.8	2,778.4	2,795.9
1977	2,813.4	2,821.4	2,833.4	2,842.3	2,848.8	2,854.0	2,860.8	2,872.5	2,882.2	2,885.7	2,887.2	2,890.8
1978	2,894.1	2,893.7	2,890.2	2,885.5	2,886.1	2,884.7	2,882.4	2,888.0	2,895.3	2,888.3	2,887.2	2,886.4
1979	2,874.1	2,868.1	2,867.6	2,873.2	2,864.3	2,868.2	2,870.8	2,871.9	2,860.9	2,848.6	2,838.3	2,828.4
1980	2,814.0	2,806.9	2,783.9	2,771.6	2,767.8	2,782.2	2,791.4	2,797.3	2,794.8	2,793.2	2,791.3	2,782.1
1981	2,769.1	2,761.1	2,771.8	2,798.7	2,794.1	2,793.0	2,795.2	2,796.9	2,795.4	2,808.4	2,815.6	2,838.7
1982	2,846.6	2,843.8	2,856.9	2,882.2	2,883.5	2,880.2	2,877.5	2,894.0	2,907.1	2,907.5	2,919.7	2,949.0
1983	3,017.6	3,071.3	3,092.9	3,094.3	3,104.7	3,110.8	3,118.0	3,122.0	3,124.5	3,138.8	3,148.6	3,160.5
1984	3,169.0	3,184.8	3,201.7	3,213.3	3,228.1	3,238.5	3,242.7	3,243.1	3,255.8	3,266.2	3,293.0	3,322.0
1985	3,346.1	3,362.0	3,365.2	3,371.1	3,383.5	3,406.5	3,426.3	3,439.6	3,447.1	3,450.2	3,449.8	3,458.5
1986	3,461.1	3,477.2	3,513.0	3,551.3	3,581.1	3,594.4	3,622.0	3,642.7	3,657.7	3,677.5	3,685.6	3,713.3
1987	3,708.7	3,698.0	3,694.5	3,700.2	3,698.2	3,685.8	3,686.7	3,683.0	3,683.7	3,688.9	3,685.1	3,688.0
1988	3,705.4	3,731.3	3,745.1	3,751.1	3,760.1	3,760.0	3,756.6	3,753.1	3,740.6	3,738.6	3,747.5	3,745.2
1989	3,730.3	3,720.1	3,715.6	3,698.8	3,692.8	3,705.2	3,728.1	3,754.0	3,764.3	3,772.2	3,784.6	3,794.6
1990	3,789.3	3,788.5	3,784.7	3,787.2	3,774.6	3,773.1	3,775.5	3,772.8	3,762.8	3,745.1	3,742.4	3,745.5
1991	3,746.7	3,761.2	3,778.5	3,781.2	3,779.0	3,783.5	3,782.8	3,772.5	3,758.1	3,755.0	3,749.4	3,743.0
1992	3,744.7	3,753.7	3,746.8	3,733.9	3,726.6	3,715.1	3,704.4	3,718.7	3,710.0	3,712.9	3,709.2	3,701.5
1993	3,687.9	3,677.4	3,667.6	3,656.8	3,674.9	3,681.4	3,678.3	3,676.7	3,681.0	3,670.8	3,677.7	3,681.9
1994	3,684.6	3,676.8	3,674.2	3,674.3	3,678.0	3,656.9	3,648.3	3,636.3	3,631.2	3,625.2	3,621.5	3,617.8
1995	3,612.0	3,601.9	3,597.6	3,595.7	3,615.6	3,639.1	3,653.2	3,667.3	3,676.1	3,679.0	3,686.2	3,688.4
1996	3,697.3	3,703.6	3,719.4	3,719.5	3,725.6	3,739.0	3,746.9	3,751.7	3,753.3	3,754.0	3,760.5	3,773.0
1997	3,779.4	3,780.5	3,791.6	3,802.9	3,817.0	3,831.6	3,846.4	3,871.7	3,881.8	3,894.9	3,913.6	3,933.8
1998	3,950.8	3,982.7	4,008.2	4,022.2	4,040.9	4,067.2	4,079.7	4,099.0	4,139.1	4,168.1	4,205.7	4,231.8
1999	4,240.7	4,267.1	4,278.2	4,279.9	4,304.1	4,324.9	4,338.1	4,346.8	4,346.2	4,358.3	4,379.0	4,396.8
2000	4,400.9	4,398.6	4,406.4	4,441.6	4,447.7	4,450.1	4,460.5	4,488.8	4,502.0	4,511.8	4,520.4	4,550.6
2001	4,567.7	4,594.9	4,647.1	4,677.8	4,694.4	4,726.3	4,763.0	4,795.6	4,926.6	4,888.7	4,931.2	-

Source: The Conference Board. © 2002 The Conference Board. All Rights Reserved. No claim to original U.S. Government works pursuant to U.S. Contract No. 52-SABA-5-00128. Primary source(s): Board of Governors of the Federal Reserve System (money supply), Division of Monetary Affairs, Money and Reserve Projections Section, Stop 59, Washington, DC 20551. Deflators are calculated by The Conference Board. A dash (-) indicates that data are not available or zero.

Interest Rate Spread, 10-Year Treasury Bonds Less Federal Funds

Year	Jan	Feb	Mar	Apr	May	Jun	Jul	Aug	Sep	Oct	Nov	Dec
1954	-	-	-	-	-	-	1.50	1.14	1.32	1.58	1.65	1.23
1955	1.22	1.36	1.33	1.32	1.33	1.14	1.22	1.01	0.79	0.64	0.54	0.48
1956	0.45	0.34	0.46	0.56	0.32	0.29	0.36	0.60	0.43	0.38	0.61	0.65
1957	0.62	0.34	0.45	0.48	0.60	0.80	0.94	0.69	0.45	0.47	0.44	0.23
1958	0.37	1.38	1.78	1.62	2.29	2.04	2.52	2.01	2.00	2.00	1.47	1.44
1959	1.54	1.53	1.19	1.16	1.41	0.95	0.93	0.93	0.92	0.55	0.53	0.70
1960	0.73	0.52	0.41	0.36	0.50	0.83	0.67	0.82	1.20	1.42	1.49	1.86
1961	2.39	1.24	1.72	2.29	1.73	2.15	2.75	2.04	2.10	1.66	1.33	1.73
1962	1.93	1.67	1.08	1.06	1.51	1.23	1.30	1.05	1.08	1.03	0.98	0.93
1963	0.91	0.92	0.95	1.07	0.93	1.00	1.00	0.51	0.60	0.61	0.64	0.75
1964	0.69	0.67	0.79	0.76	0.70	0.67	0.77	0.69	0.75	0.83	0.63	0.33
1965	0.29	0.23	0.17	0.11	0.11	0.17	0.11	0.13	0.28	0.27	0.35	0.30
1966	0.19	0.23	0.22	0.08	-0.12	-0.36	-0.28	-0.31	-0.22	-0.52	-0.60	-0.56
1967	-0.36	-0.37	0.01	0.54	0.91	1.04	1.37	1.38	1.31	1.60	1.62	1.19
1968	0.93	0.85	0.69	-0.12	-0.24	-0.35	-0.52	-0.61	-0.32	-0.33	-0.12	0.01
1969	-0.26	-0.42	-0.49	-1.24	-2.35	-2.33	-1.89	-2.50	-1.99	-1.90	-1.71	-1.32
1970	-1.19	-1.74	-0.69	-0.71	-0.03	0.24	0.25	0.92	1.10	1.13	1.24	1.49
1971	2.10	2.39	1.99	1.68	1.76	1.61	1.42	1.02	0.59	0.73	0.90	1.79
1972	2.45	2.79	2.24	2.02	1.86	1.65	1.56	1.41	1.68	1.44	1.22	1.03
1973	0.52	0.06	-0.38	-0.45	-0.99	-1.59	-3.27	-3.10	-3.69	-3.22	-3.30	-3.21
1974	-2.66	-2.01	-2.14	-3.00	-3.73	-4.39	-5.11	-3.97	-3.30	-2.16	-1.77	-1.10
1975	0.37	1.15	2.19	2.74	2.84	2.31	1.96	2.26	2.19	2.32	2.83	2.80
1976	2.87	3.02	2.89	2.74	2.61	2.38	2.52	2.48	2.34	2.39	2.34	2.22
1977	2.60	2.71	2.77	2.64	2.11	1.89	1.91	1.50	1.20	1.05	1.07	1.13
1978	1.26	1.25	1.25	1.26	0.99	0.86	0.83	0.37	-0.03	-0.32	-0.95	-1.02
1979	-0.97	-0.96	-0.97	-0.83	-0.99	-1.38	-1.52	-1.91	-2.10	-3.47	-2.53	-3.39
1980	-3.02	-1.72	-4.44	-6.14	-0.80	0.31	1.22	1.49	0.64	-1.06	-3.17	-6.06
1981	-6.51	-2.74	-1.58	-2.04	-4.42	-5.63	-4.76	-2.88	-0.55	0.07	0.08	1.35
1982	1.37	-0.35	-0.82	-1.07	-0.83	0.15	1.36	2.94	2.03	1.20	1.35	1.59
1983	1.78	2.21	1.74	1.60	1.75	1.87	2.01	2.29	2.20	2.06	2.35	2.36
1984	2.11	2.25	2.41	2.34	3.09	2.50	2.13	1.08	1.22	2.17	2.14	3.12
1985	3.03	3.01	3.28	3.16	2.88	2.63	2.43	2.43	2.45	2.25	1.73	0.99
1986	1.05	0.84	0.30	0.31	0.86	0.88	0.74	1.00	1.56	1.58	1.21	0.20
1987	0.65	1.15	1.12	1.65	1.76	1.67	1.87	2.03	2.20	2.23	2.17	2.22
1988	1.84	1.63	1.79	1.85	2.00	1.41	1.31	1.25	0.79	0.50	0.61	0.35
1989	-0.03	-0.19	-0.49	-0.66	-0.95	-1.25	-1.22	-0.88	-0.83	-0.83	-0.68	-0.61
1990	-0.02	0.23	0.31	0.53	0.58	0.19	0.32	0.62	0.69	0.61	0.58	0.77
1991	1.18	1.60	1.99	2.13	2.29	2.38	2.45	2.24	2.20	2.32	2.61	2.66
1992	3.00	3.28	3.56	3.75	3.57	3.50	3.59	3.29	3.20	3.49	3.78	3.85
1993	3.58	3.23	2.91	3.01	3.04	2.92	2.75	2.65	2.27	2.34	2.70	2.81
1994	2.70	2.72	3.14	3.41	3.17	2.85	3.04	2.77	2.73	2.98	2.67	2.36
1995	2.25	1.55	1.22	1.01	0.62	0.17	0.43	0.75	0.40	0.28	0.13	0.11
1996	0.09	0.59	0.96	1.29	1.50	1.64	1.47	1.42	1.53	1.29	0.89	1.01
1997	1.33	1.23	1.30	1.38	1.21	0.93	0.70	0.76	0.67	0.53	0.36	0.31
1998	-0.02	0.06	0.16	0.19	0.16	-0.06	-0.08	-0.21	-0.70	-0.54	-	-0.03
1999	0.09	0.24	0.42	0.44	0.80	1.14	0.80	0.87	0.70	0.91	0.61	0.98
2000	1.21	0.79	0.41	-0.03	0.17	-0.43	-0.49	-0.67	-0.72	-0.77	-0.79	-1.16
2001	-0.82	-0.39	-0.42	0.34	1.18	1.31	1.47	1.32	1.66	2.08	2.56	3.27

Consumer Expectations

Not seasonally adjusted

(1966:I=100)

Year	Jan	Feb	Mar	Apr	May	Jun	Jul	Aug	Sep	Oct	Nov	Dec
1952	-	-	-	-	-	-	-	-	-	-	92.4	93.4
1953	94.5	95.5	94.2	92.9	91.6	90.3	89.1	87.8	86.5	85.2	83.9	84.4
1954	84.8	85.3	85.6	85.8	86.1	86.7	87.3	87.9	88.5	89.1	89.7	91.4
1955	93.1	94.8	96.5	98.2	99.9	100.6	101.2	101.9	102.5	103.2	103.8	103.7
1956	103.6	103.6	103.5	103.4	103.3	103.9	104.6	105.2	105.2	105.2	105.2	103.7
1957	102.2	100.7	99.2	97.7	96.2	94.6	92.9	91.3	89.6	88.0	86.3	85.7
1958	85.2	84.6	84.0	83.5	82.9	84.8	86.6	88.5	90.4	92.2	94.1	94.7
1959	95.2	95.8	96.4	96.9	97.5	97.2	96.9	96.7	96.4	96.1	95.8	98.7
1960	101.7	104.6	102.6	100.6	98.6	98.2	97.9	97.5	96.1	94.8	93.4	93.9
1961	94.4	94.9	96.0	97.0	98.1	98.2	98.4	98.5	97.9	97.4	96.8	99.0
1962	101.2	103.4	101.1	98.8	96.5	95.5	94.4	93.4	95.3	97.3	99.2	99.4
1963	99.7	99.9	98.0	96.0	94.1	95.1	96.0	97.0	97.0	97.0	97.0	97.8
1964	98.6	99.4	98.7	97.9	97.2	97.8	98.5	99.1	99.8	100.4	101.1	101.7
1965	102.4	103.0	103.2	103.4	103.7	103.9	104.1	104.3	105.3	106.3	107.3	104.9
1966	102.4	100.0	98.7	97.3	96.0	94.2	92.5	90.7	90.5	90.4	90.2	92.3
1967	94.3	96.4	95.7	95.0	94.3	94.7	95.1	95.5	94.0	92.6	91.1	92.2
1968	93.2	94.3	92.8	91.4	89.9	89.8	89.7	89.6	90.3	90.9	91.6	93.7
1969	95.9	98.0	95.7	93.4	91.1	89.6	88.1	86.6	84.3	81.9	79.6	78.3
1970	77.1	75.8	74.3	72.7	71.2	72.7	74.2	75.7	74.2	72.8	71.3	72.8
1971	74.4	75.9	75.9	75.9	75.9	76.7	77.6	78.4	78.0	77.6	77.2	81.8
1972	86.3	90.9	88.0	85.1	82.2	85.2	88.3	91.3	90.1	89.0	87.8	83.0
1973	78.1	73.3	71.3	69.3	67.3	65.9	64.4	63.0	64.4	65.7	67.1	61.2
1974	55.3	49.4	54.2	59.1	63.9	61.8	59.7	57.6	55.5	53.3	51.2	50.8
1975	50.4	50.0	56.6	63.2	69.8	70.1	70.4	70.7	70.4	70.2	69.9	73.7
1976	77.4	81.2	80.6	80.1	79.5	81.5	83.5	85.5	85.6	85.8	85.9	85.3
1977	84.8	84.2	84.0	83.8	83.6	82.9	82.2	81.5	79.6	77.8	75.9	75.8
1978	75.7	77.2	69.5	71.1	73.0	68.1	72.0	67.0	69.8	71.7	62.8	53.8
1979	58.4	62.2	53.7	53.3	54.9	51.4	44.2	49.3	53.6	49.5	52.0	51.5
1980	54.1	54.9	44.3	44.4	45.3	53.0	53.4	59.6	67.2	68.9	76.2	59.7
1981	67.2	61.4	61.4	68.1	72.9	70.5	66.4	70.1	68.3	61.5	55.6	56.8
1982	62.9	58.7	53.1	61.1	62.0	60.1	57.6	60.9	66.9	70.4	71.0	67.9
1983	65.2	71.2	80.9	86.9	93.4	89.2	91.1	88.2	85.8	86.1	87.9	91.0
1984	97.0	93.2	97.7	91.4	90.6	89.8	91.9	93.7	96.4	91.6	91.5	87.9
1985	90.3	86.5	87.3	87.0	84.2	91.1	87.4	86.3	84.2	80.8	84.5	88.1
1986	85.3	87.8	86.9	88.5	87.5	90.3	88.5	85.9	81.3	87.1	81.6	78.3
1987	80.9	81.6	83.3	84.7	80.6	80.8	83.3	85.8	84.2	80.4	72.7	76.7
1988	80.9	81.9	85.2	82.4	87.3	85.7	82.3	88.8	89.5	87.0	86.3	85.5
1989	89.9	88.8	87.6	83.2	80.1	82.0	85.5	80.3	88.6	87.2	84.3	85.5
1990	83.4	81.3	81.3	83.9	79.3	76.6	77.3	62.9	58.8	50.9	52.8	53.7
1991	55.2	62.0	84.5	74.7	71.5	75.9	74.4	75.3	76.4	70.5	61.9	61.5
1992	59.1	61.8	70.3	70.5	71.2	70.7	67.6	69.5	67.4	67.5	78.2	89.5
1993	83.4	80.6	75.8	76.4	68.5	70.4	64.7	65.8	66.8	72.5	70.3	78.8
1994	86.4	83.5	85.1	82.6	84.2	82.7	78.5	80.8	83.5	85.1	84.8	88.8
1995	88.4	85.9	79.8	83.8	80.1	84.1	87.4	86.1	78.8	80.8	79.7	83.7
1996	78.7	77.8	86.2	83.0	79.2	84.0	86.5	87.3	90.1	89.9	93.9	91.8
1997	91.3	94.9	93.6	92.5	96.6	98.9	102.6	100.3	100.7	102.8	102.3	96.1
1998	102.2	104.2	101.9	104.3	101.7	99.3	100.0	98.3	93.9	87.5	94.3	91.9
1999	95.7	103.6	99.0	97.4	97.6	99.8	99.2	98.4	101.5	97.1	101.0	101.1
2000	108.6	107.8	101.7	103.7	104.8	100.8	104.5	104.0	103.4	100.7	101.6	90.7
2001	86.4	80.8	83.9	82.2	85.4	86.9	88.4	85.2	73.5	75.5	76.6	82.3

Source: The Conference Board. © 2002 The Conference Board. All Rights Reserved. No claim to original U.S. Government works pursuant to U.S. Contract No. 52-SABA-5-00128. Primary source(s): University of Michigan, Surveys of Consumers, P.O. Box 1248, Ann Arbor, MI 48106-1248. Used by permission. A dash (-) indicates that data are not available or zero.

COMPOSITE INDEX OF COINCIDENT INDICATORS

The composite index of coincident indicators tends to *confirm* what the composite index of leading indicators has foreshadowed. In other words, the "coincident index" tends to decline just as the economy does (rather than before) and turns up as the economy turns up. As with the other composite indicators, a tendency signaled by this index must be sustained for at least three months before the indicator "confirms" a change in the economy's direction of growth or decline.

The coincident index is a fairly reliable indicator. In the 1948 to 1988 period, for instance, more than half of the turning points in the economy were marked exactly by the coincident index. With the exception of the 1957 peak, which the index showed six months too early, the rest of the turning points were indicated within three months of the actual turn.

Components of the Coincident Index

The index is a composite of 4 indicators, each of which is further discussed below:

> Employees on nonagricultural payrolls
> Personal income less transfer payments
> Index of industrial production
> Manufacturing and trade sales

Employees on Nonagricultural Payrolls. The index is shown in thousands of employees. Employment tends to drop during recessionary periods and increase with expansions. Before a recession or upturn takes place, producers tend to decrease or increase hours worked (hence Average Weekly Hours is part of the leading index). As the trend is confirmed, layoffs or hirings are reflected in actual employment totals. Total employment, of course, tends to grow over time. The significance of the index lies in month-to-month changes that show a pattern.

Personal Income Less Transfer Payments. Expressed in billions of chained 1996 dollars, this index measures all income except that derived from such sources as welfare, unemployment benefits, social security, medicaid, and the like, which are transfer payments. It includes dividends, rents, interest, and wages (the bulk). It is thus a good indicator of money now available to individuals from economic activities—which tends to shrink in recessions (while transfer payments may increase) and grow in periods of economic expansion.

Index of Industrial Production. This indicator, expressed as an index with 1992 as its base (1992 = 100), measures changes in the physical goods and power (rather than dollar sales) produced in mining, manufacturing, and utilities. Other sectors of the economy (construction, services, communications, trade, government, etc.) are, of course, indirectly reflected in this measure. Components of this index are measured and indexed; next, these indexes are weighted by their relative importance to the economy as measured by value added—the amount of value added to raw materials purchased by an industry through its own efforts. Industrial production reflects actual output; it does not signal future intent; therefore it serves well as a coincident indicator.

Manufacturing and Trade Sales. The index is reported in millions of chained 1996 dollars. It represents sales at all levels—production, wholesale, and retail. New orders signal future sales and are therefore indicators of future activity. The actual sales, as they are made, are an indicator of current activity; they drop or increase in cycle with the economy.

Sources and Revisions

The component series are drawn from federal sources, including the U.S. Department of Commerce, Bureau of Economic Analysis and Bureau of the Census; the U.S. Department of Labor, Bureau of Labor Statistics; and the Federal Reserve System.

The composite index itself is constructed by The Conference Board. In the process, mathematical operations are performed on the component data series to ensure that volatile series do not dominate the index. A volatile series may be one that fluctuates wildly month to month but shows less volatility when averaged over several months. Other smoothing and standardization methods are used as well.

The coincident index was last revised late in 2001. See Reference 6 for details.

Bibliography

1. Frumkin, Norman. *Guide to Economic Indicators*. M.E. Sharpe, Inc., 1990.

2. Green, George R. and Barry A. Beckman. "Business Cycle Indicators: Upcoming Revision of the Composite Indexes." U.S. Department of Commerce, Bureau of Economic Analysis. *Survey of Current Business*, October 1993. Superintendent of Documents, U.S. Government Printing Office, Washington, DC 20302.

3. Hertzberg, Marie P. and Barry A. Beckman. "Business Cycle Indicators: Revised Composite Indexes." U.S. Department of Commerce, Bureau of Economic Analysis. *Survey of Current Business*, January 1989. Superintendent of Documents, U.S. Government Printing Office, Washington, DC 20302.

4. U.S. Department of Commerce, Bureau of Economic Analysis. "Composite Indexes of Leading, Coincident, and Lagging Indicators." In *Survey of Current Business*, November 1987. Superintendent of Documents, U.S. Government Printing Office, Washington, DC 20302.

5. U.S. Department of Commerce, Bureau of Economic Analysis. *Survey of Current Business*. Superintendent of Documents, U.S. Government Printing Office, Washington, DC 20302.

6. *Leading Economic Indicators*. The Confenrence Board, 845 Third Avenue, New York, NY 10022-6679.

Composite Index of 4 Coincident Indicators
(1996=100)

Year	Jan	Feb	Mar	Apr	May	Jun	Jul	Aug	Sep	Oct	Nov	Dec
1959	35.5	35.8	36.1	36.4	36.7	36.8	36.7	36.2	36.2	36.2	36.4	37.1
1960	37.4	37.4	37.3	37.4	37.2	37.2	37.1	37.1	37.0	37.0	36.8	36.5
1961	36.5	36.5	36.7	36.8	37.0	37.3	37.4	37.7	37.7	38.0	38.3	38.5
1962	38.4	38.6	38.8	39.0	39.1	39.1	39.2	39.3	39.4	39.5	39.6	39.6
1963	39.6	39.8	40.0	40.2	40.3	40.4	40.5	40.6	40.8	41.0	41.0	41.2
1964	41.3	41.6	41.6	41.9	42.1	42.2	42.4	42.6	42.8	42.7	43.1	43.5
1965	43.6	43.8	44.1	44.3	44.4	44.6	44.9	45.1	45.2	45.6	45.9	46.2
1966	46.4	46.6	47.0	47.1	47.2	47.5	47.6	47.8	47.9	48.1	48.2	48.3
1967	48.5	48.4	48.5	48.6	48.6	48.7	48.8	49.1	49.2	49.2	49.7	50.1
1968	49.9	50.2	50.4	50.5	50.8	51.0	51.2	51.3	51.5	51.7	52.0	52.1
1969	52.2	52.4	52.6	52.7	52.8	53.1	53.2	53.5	53.5	53.7	53.5	53.6
1970	53.3	53.4	53.4	53.4	53.3	53.3	53.4	53.3	53.3	52.8	52.6	53.1
1971	53.4	53.4	53.5	53.7	53.9	54.0	53.9	54.0	54.3	54.4	54.7	55.0
1972	55.5	55.6	56.0	56.3	56.5	56.6	56.8	57.3	57.6	58.2	58.7	59.1
1973	59.2	59.6	59.6	59.7	59.9	60.1	60.3	60.2	60.5	61.0	61.3	61.1
1974	60.8	60.7	60.6	60.5	60.7	60.8	60.8	60.6	60.6	60.5	59.9	59.0
1975	58.6	58.1	57.7	57.8	57.9	58.0	58.2	58.7	59.0	59.2	59.4	59.6
1976	60.1	60.5	60.7	61.0	61.2	61.3	61.5	61.7	61.9	61.8	62.4	62.7
1977	62.8	63.1	63.5	63.8	64.1	64.4	64.7	64.8	65.2	65.5	65.8	66.1
1978	65.8	66.2	66.7	67.7	67.8	68.2	68.4	68.7	68.8	69.2	69.5	69.8
1979	69.8	70.0	70.5	70.0	70.4	70.5	70.5	70.5	70.5	70.7	70.8	70.9
1980	71.0	70.9	70.7	70.1	69.5	69.2	69.1	69.4	69.7	70.3	70.7	71.0
1981	71.1	71.0	71.1	70.9	71.0	71.2	71.6	71.6	71.4	71.1	70.9	70.5
1982	70.1	70.5	70.4	70.3	70.3	69.9	69.6	69.4	69.2	69.0	68.9	68.9
1983	69.3	69.2	69.6	69.8	70.2	70.7	71.2	71.1	72.0	72.5	72.8	73.4
1984	73.9	74.3	74.7	75.1	75.4	75.8	76.1	76.3	76.6	76.6	76.9	77.1
1985	77.2	77.4	77.7	77.8	78.0	77.9	78.0	78.3	78.5	78.6	78.7	79.0
1986	79.2	79.2	79.4	79.7	79.7	79.6	79.9	80.1	80.4	80.4	80.6	81.1
1987	80.8	81.4	81.6	81.7	82.0	82.2	82.6	82.8	83.0	83.5	83.7	84.2
1988	84.1	84.5	84.8	85.0	85.1	85.4	85.7	85.8	86.0	86.3	86.6	87.1
1989	87.5	87.4	87.6	87.7	87.6	87.6	87.5	87.8	87.8	87.7	88.1	88.2
1990	88.3	88.7	88.9	88.9	89.0	89.1	89.1	89.0	88.8	88.4	88.1	87.9
1991	87.4	87.3	87.1	87.3	87.4	87.7	87.7	87.7	87.9	87.8	87.8	87.7
1992	87.9	88.1	88.2	88.5	88.6	88.7	88.9	88.7	89.0	89.3	89.6	89.7
1993	90.0	90.2	90.0	90.3	90.5	90.7	90.7	90.9	91.2	91.5	91.7	92.1
1994	92.1	92.6	93.2	93.4	93.8	94.1	94.2	94.7	94.9	95.4	95.7	96.2
1995	96.5	96.5	96.6	96.6	96.7	97.0	96.9	97.5	97.7	97.8	98.1	98.3
1996	98.1	98.7	98.9	99.2	99.7	100.0	100.2	100.6	100.8	101.0	101.4	101.5
1997	101.7	102.3	102.6	102.9	103.1	103.6	104.1	104.3	104.8	105.2	105.6	106.0
1998	106.5	106.9	107.4	107.7	108.0	108.2	108.2	108.9	109.2	109.6	109.8	110.2
1999	110.2	110.8	111.1	111.1	111.6	111.9	112.3	112.7	112.6	113.1	113.7	114.2
2000	114.7	114.6	115.3	115.7	116.1	116.4	116.3	116.6	116.7	116.8	116.9	117.1
2001	116.8	116.9	116.9	116.7	116.8	116.4	116.7	116.7	116.1	115.7	115.5	-

Source: The Conference Board. © 2002 The Conference Board. All Rights Reserved. No claim to original U.S. Government works pursuant to U.S. Contract No. 52-SABA-5-00128. Primary source(s): The Conference Board, Inc., Economics Group, 845 Third Avenue, New York, NY 10022. A dash (-) indicates that data are not available or zero.

Composite Index of 4 Coincident Indicators
Change in Index from Previous Month

Year	Jan	Feb	Mar	Apr	May	Jun	Jul	Aug	Sep	Oct	Nov	Dec
1959	-	+0.3	+0.3	+0.3	+0.3	+0.1	-0.1	-0.5	-	-	+0.2	+0.7
1960	+0.3	-	-0.1	+0.1	-0.2	-	-0.1	-	-0.1	-	-0.2	-0.3
1961	-	-	+0.2	+0.1	+0.2	+0.3	+0.1	+0.3	-	+0.3	+0.3	+0.2
1962	-0.1	+0.2	+0.2	+0.2	+0.1	-	+0.1	+0.1	+0.1	+0.1	+0.1	-
1963	-	+0.2	+0.2	+0.2	+0.1	+0.1	+0.1	+0.1	+0.2	+0.2	-	+0.2
1964	+0.1	+0.3	-	+0.3	+0.2	+0.1	+0.2	+0.2	+0.2	-0.1	+0.4	+0.4
1965	+0.1	+0.2	+0.3	+0.2	+0.1	+0.2	+0.3	+0.2	+0.1	+0.4	+0.3	+0.3
1966	+0.2	+0.2	+0.4	+0.1	+0.1	+0.3	+0.1	+0.2	+0.1	+0.2	+0.1	+0.1
1967	+0.2	-0.1	+0.1	+0.1	-	+0.1	+0.1	+0.3	+0.1	-	+0.5	+0.4
1968	-0.2	+0.3	+0.2	+0.1	+0.3	+0.2	+0.2	+0.1	+0.2	+0.2	+0.3	+0.1
1969	+0.1	+0.2	+0.2	+0.1	+0.1	+0.3	+0.1	+0.3	-	+0.2	-0.2	+0.1
1970	-0.3	+0.1	-	-	-0.1	-	+0.1	-0.1	-	-0.5	-0.2	+0.5
1971	+0.3	-	+0.1	+0.2	+0.2	+0.1	-0.1	+0.1	+0.3	+0.1	+0.3	+0.3
1972	+0.5	+0.1	+0.4	+0.3	+0.2	+0.1	+0.2	+0.5	+0.3	+0.6	+0.5	+0.4
1973	+0.1	+0.4	-	+0.1	+0.2	+0.2	+0.2	-0.1	+0.3	+0.5	+0.3	-0.2
1974	-0.3	-0.1	-0.1	-0.1	+0.2	+0.1	-	-0.2	-	-0.1	-0.6	-0.9
1975	-0.4	-0.5	-0.4	+0.1	+0.1	+0.1	+0.2	+0.5	+0.3	+0.2	+0.2	+0.2
1976	+0.5	+0.4	+0.2	+0.3	+0.2	+0.1	+0.2	+0.2	+0.2	-0.1	+0.6	+0.3
1977	+0.1	+0.3	+0.4	+0.3	+0.3	+0.3	+0.3	+0.1	+0.4	+0.3	+0.3	+0.3
1978	-0.3	+0.4	+0.5	+1.0	+0.1	+0.4	+0.2	+0.3	+0.1	+0.4	+0.3	+0.3
1979	-	+0.2	+0.5	-0.5	+0.4	+0.1	-	-	-	+0.2	+0.1	+0.1
1980	+0.1	-0.1	-0.2	-0.6	-0.6	-0.3	-0.1	+0.3	+0.3	+0.6	+0.4	+0.3
1981	+0.1	-0.1	+0.1	-0.2	+0.1	+0.2	+0.4	-	-0.2	-0.3	-0.2	-0.4
1982	-0.4	+0.4	-0.1	-0.1	-	-0.4	-0.3	-0.2	-0.2	-0.2	-0.1	-
1983	+0.4	-0.1	+0.4	+0.2	+0.4	+0.5	+0.5	-0.1	+0.9	+0.5	+0.3	+0.6
1984	+0.5	+0.4	+0.4	+0.4	+0.3	+0.4	+0.3	+0.2	+0.3	-	+0.3	+0.2
1985	+0.1	+0.2	+0.3	+0.1	+0.2	-0.1	+0.1	+0.3	+0.2	+0.1	+0.1	+0.3
1986	+0.2	-	+0.2	+0.3	-	-0.1	+0.3	+0.2	+0.3	-	+0.2	+0.5
1987	-0.3	+0.6	+0.2	+0.1	+0.3	+0.2	+0.4	+0.2	+0.2	+0.5	+0.2	+0.5
1988	-0.1	+0.4	+0.3	+0.2	+0.1	+0.3	+0.3	+0.1	+0.2	+0.3	+0.3	+0.5
1989	+0.4	-0.1	+0.2	+0.1	-0.1	-	-0.1	+0.3	-	-0.1	+0.4	+0.1
1990	+0.1	+0.4	+0.2	-	+0.1	+0.1	-	-0.1	-0.2	-0.4	-0.3	-0.2
1991	-0.5	-0.1	-0.2	+0.2	+0.1	+0.3	-	-	+0.2	-0.1	-	-0.1
1992	+0.2	+0.2	+0.1	+0.3	+0.1	+0.1	+0.2	-0.2	+0.3	+0.3	+0.3	+0.1
1993	+0.3	+0.2	-0.2	+0.3	+0.2	+0.2	-	+0.2	+0.3	+0.3	+0.2	+0.4
1994	-	+0.5	+0.6	+0.2	+0.4	+0.3	+0.1	+0.5	+0.2	+0.5	+0.3	+0.5
1995	+0.3	-	+0.1	-	+0.1	+0.3	-0.1	+0.6	+0.2	+0.1	+0.3	+0.2
1996	-0.2	+0.6	+0.2	+0.3	+0.5	+0.3	+0.2	+0.4	+0.2	+0.2	+0.4	+0.1
1997	+0.2	+0.6	+0.3	+0.3	+0.2	+0.5	+0.5	+0.2	+0.5	+0.4	+0.4	+0.4
1998	+0.5	+0.4	+0.5	+0.3	+0.3	+0.2	-	+0.7	+0.3	+0.4	+0.2	+0.4
1999	-	+0.6	+0.3	-	+0.5	+0.3	+0.4	+0.4	-0.1	+0.5	+0.6	+0.5
2000	+0.5	-0.1	+0.7	+0.4	+0.4	+0.3	-0.1	+0.3	+0.1	+0.1	+0.1	+0.2
2001	-0.3	+0.1	-	-0.2	+0.1	-0.4	+0.3	-	-0.6	-0.4	-0.2	-

Employees on Nonagricultural Payrolls
(Thousands)

Year	Jan	Feb	Mar	Apr	May	Jun	Jul	Aug	Sep	Oct	Nov	Dec
1951	47,230	47,531	47,794	47,760	47,805	47,913	47,925	47,794	47,748	47,825	48,027	48,122
1952	48,227	48,493	48,416	48,509	48,474	48,125	47,999	48,686	49,085	49,434	49,719	49,937
1953	50,045	50,273	50,382	50,314	50,358	50,389	50,382	50,271	50,226	50,108	49,825	49,625
1954	49,341	49,276	49,046	49,039	48,852	48,791	48,689	48,643	48,765	48,828	49,103	49,234
1955	49,354	49,523	49,851	50,104	50,404	50,693	50,811	50,929	51,103	51,323	51,507	51,714
1956	51,863	52,093	52,228	52,232	52,365	52,433	51,746	52,382	52,439	52,674	52,752	52,908
1957	52,808	53,003	53,062	53,053	52,996	52,941	52,972	52,913	52,816	52,663	52,482	52,307
1958	52,003	51,441	51,142	50,807	50,770	50,801	50,911	51,113	51,355	51,378	51,814	51,986
1959	52,408	52,568	52,883	53,132	53,422	53,584	53,663	53,220	53,257	53,196	53,509	54,040
1960	54,185	54,414	54,287	54,634	54,362	54,276	54,214	54,198	54,063	53,982	53,845	53,577
1961	53,534	53,380	53,510	53,462	53,677	53,916	54,027	54,222	54,285	54,376	54,622	54,744
1962	54,709	55,018	55,107	55,459	55,514	55,561	55,643	55,778	55,849	55,912	55,936	55,918
1963	55,935	56,055	56,153	56,454	56,513	56,563	56,688	56,823	56,962	57,152	57,126	57,252
1964	57,269	57,603	57,732	57,784	57,975	58,121	58,311	58,510	58,798	58,691	59,114	59,335
1965	59,398	59,683	59,864	60,124	60,363	60,595	60,860	61,085	61,367	61,578	61,882	62,230
1966	62,386	62,720	63,087	63,317	63,560	63,978	64,185	64,344	64,433	64,655	64,854	65,076
1967	65,215	65,208	65,338	65,323	65,478	65,654	65,831	65,964	66,089	66,111	66,591	66,776
1968	66,606	67,029	67,132	67,417	67,495	67,783	68,003	68,219	68,365	68,603	68,855	69,161
1969	69,272	69,542	69,791	69,948	70,180	70,498	70,668	70,799	70,833	70,993	70,941	71,127
1970	71,018	71,165	71,347	71,251	70,993	70,905	70,969	70,789	70,857	70,416	70,296	70,666
1971	70,718	70,657	70,746	70,936	71,129	71,163	71,219	71,220	71,527	71,532	71,734	71,996
1972	72,303	72,525	72,808	73,061	73,341	73,643	73,636	73,929	74,115	74,527	74,881	75,235
1973	75,474	75,908	76,137	76,312	76,516	76,738	76,758	77,018	77,164	77,502	77,833	77,992
1974	77,953	78,177	78,177	78,261	78,407	78,434	78,517	78,478	78,498	78,569	78,238	77,565
1975	77,145	76,742	76,419	76,298	76,459	76,388	76,626	76,980	77,188	77,499	77,619	77,915
1976	78,326	78,606	78,819	79,134	79,192	79,258	79,485	79,581	79,842	79,842	80,141	80,338
1977	80,517	80,794	81,221	81,610	81,977	82,381	82,760	82,974	83,431	83,661	84,031	84,271
1978	84,464	84,808	85,338	86,083	86,404	86,811	87,037	87,324	87,434	87,797	88,249	88,559
1979	88,728	88,985	89,426	89,363	89,681	89,955	90,019	90,159	90,149	90,360	90,466	90,617
1980	90,729	90,876	90,995	90,780	90,316	89,974	89,676	89,964	90,046	90,334	90,550	90,774
1981	91,003	91,095	91,206	91,219	91,142	91,285	91,410	91,320	91,191	91,216	91,014	90,831
1982	90,448	90,474	90,337	90,031	89,965	89,703	89,380	89,177	88,995	88,787	88,649	88,675
1983	88,826	88,758	88,946	89,211	89,497	89,886	90,313	89,973	91,088	91,408	91,727	92,110
1984	92,524	93,043	93,312	93,650	93,952	94,325	94,647	94,885	95,186	95,499	95,829	95,997
1985	96,249	96,397	96,734	96,896	97,163	97,280	97,465	97,696	97,878	98,098	98,286	98,500
1986	98,599	98,718	98,796	98,974	99,096	98,973	99,276	99,435	99,747	99,980	100,145	100,394
1987	100,543	100,772	101,005	101,367	101,564	101,713	102,047	102,266	102,430	102,980	103,200	103,544
1988	103,623	104,046	104,311	104,537	104,811	105,132	105,400	105,599	105,814	106,091	106,368	106,691
1989	106,993	107,244	107,438	107,637	107,738	107,838	107,933	108,048	108,178	108,290	108,571	108,692
1990	108,946	109,263	109,461	109,499	109,790	109,869	109,707	109,543	109,457	109,274	109,074	108,965
1991	108,759	108,500	108,330	108,145	108,107	108,200	108,131	108,215	108,223	108,209	108,115	108,121
1992	108,084	108,077	108,119	108,301	108,495	108,541	108,595	108,741	108,807	108,941	109,119	109,266
1993	109,502	109,816	109,749	110,055	110,398	110,539	110,744	110,957	111,204	111,525	111,780	112,034
1994	112,302	112,532	112,982	113,350	113,697	113,980	114,333	114,673	114,980	115,235	115,641	115,918
1995	116,235	116,523	116,679	116,864	116,830	117,024	117,138	117,444	117,664	117,789	117,946	118,118
1996	118,031	118,501	118,767	118,925	119,269	119,546	119,754	120,041	120,172	120,439	120,711	120,916
1997	121,108	121,423	121,749	122,025	122,288	122,540	122,844	122,924	123,323	123,668	123,952	124,271
1998	124,535	124,743	124,912	125,180	125,548	125,768	125,836	126,237	126,453	126,696	126,940	127,286
1999	127,431	127,864	128,031	128,292	128,476	128,740	129,018	129,224	129,410	129,863	130,093	130,365
2000	130,668	130,843	131,441	131,683	131,909	131,969	131,899	131,837	132,046	132,145	132,279	132,367
2001	132,428	132,595	132,654	132,489	132,530	132,431	132,449	132,395	132,230	131,782	131,411	131,287

Source: The Conference Board. © 2002 The Conference Board. All Rights Reserved. No claim to original U.S. Government works pursuant to U.S. Contract No. 52-SABA-5-00128. Primary source(s): U.S. Department of Labor, Bureau of Labor Statistics, Office of Employment and Unemployment Statistics, Division of Monthly Industry Employment Statistics, Washington, DC 20212. A dash (-) indicates that data are not available or zero.

Personal Income Less Transfer Payments
(Annual Rate, Billions of chained 1996 $)

Year	Jan	Feb	Mar	Apr	May	Jun	Jul	Aug	Sep	Oct	Nov	Dec
1959	1,669.0	1,677.9	1,692.5	1,704.6	1,718.1	1,724.0	1,720.8	1,711.6	1,711.4	1,713.8	1,725.7	1,744.6
1960	1,753.6	1,754.3	1,755.3	1,761.0	1,765.1	1,763.6	1,764.5	1,761.8	1,762.7	1,768.6	1,757.7	1,745.7
1961	1,760.4	1,760.3	1,768.3	1,774.2	1,783.9	1,799.6	1,804.1	1,812.1	1,816.6	1,836.4	1,854.3	1,863.2
1962	1,857.0	1,866.7	1,879.4	1,891.5	1,894.9	1,900.8	1,909.9	1,911.8	1,914.2	1,917.9	1,928.8	1,937.9
1963	1,931.2	1,935.8	1,944.5	1,951.2	1,959.4	1,971.7	1,972.6	1,980.8	1,994.2	2,006.5	2,010.0	2,025.0
1964	2,025.6	2,043.0	2,052.1	2,064.2	2,077.4	2,086.8	2,096.8	2,113.3	2,122.6	2,125.5	2,139.2	2,159.3
1965	2,160.3	2,170.9	2,180.9	2,190.8	2,204.9	2,211.7	2,225.9	2,237.7	2,255.9	2,280.0	2,297.0	2,308.8
1966	2,312.8	2,322.6	2,333.2	2,333.9	2,341.8	2,356.6	2,368.3	2,375.5	2,381.4	2,392.9	2,401.7	2,397.8
1967	2,419.0	2,417.5	2,426.6	2,427.1	2,430.8	2,440.3	2,452.1	2,462.1	2,464.4	2,461.0	2,475.3	2,499.7
1968	2,502.4	2,522.5	2,535.2	2,544.9	2,560.1	2,572.0	2,588.6	2,597.5	2,609.3	2,613.3	2,624.1	2,633.4
1969	2,634.2	2,643.9	2,656.2	2,665.3	2,674.8	2,683.9	2,698.0	2,715.7	2,720.7	2,726.6	2,726.8	2,729.9
1970	2,725.6	2,727.1	2,733.9	2,739.1	2,741.0	2,735.5	2,749.5	2,756.1	2,755.3	2,732.4	2,729.0	2,733.7
1971	2,762.4	2,762.2	2,771.8	2,779.5	2,789.8	2,788.2	2,789.9	2,805.4	2,808.1	2,817.5	2,832.2	2,855.4
1972	2,873.2	2,887.7	2,903.1	2,924.4	2,936.4	2,910.4	2,957.5	2,988.4	3,001.9	3,044.5	3,068.5	3,088.9
1973	3,083.2	3,100.6	3,103.1	3,106.0	3,127.3	3,139.2	3,153.2	3,142.0	3,163.8	3,194.2	3,204.9	3,198.2
1974	3,164.7	3,143.3	3,120.9	3,102.4	3,110.8	3,114.7	3,125.5	3,109.8	3,103.6	3,108.1	3,080.1	3,063.1
1975	3,045.8	3,027.1	3,024.9	3,022.3	3,038.4	3,044.6	3,047.6	3,075.7	3,088.0	3,103.3	3,114.3	3,117.4
1976	3,143.8	3,168.1	3,185.2	3,205.5	3,218.3	3,218.8	3,234.2	3,246.7	3,252.9	3,255.0	3,284.6	3,295.7
1977	3,294.9	3,307.1	3,322.2	3,328.6	3,347.0	3,355.8	3,372.1	3,382.2	3,408.5	3,441.6	3,462.9	3,479.6
1978	3,470.4	3,491.0	3,518.7	3,551.0	3,555.3	3,576.3	3,588.7	3,606.5	3,621.6	3,640.2	3,652.5	3,675.5
1979	3,680.1	3,694.9	3,711.6	3,681.8	3,686.3	3,697.0	3,699.2	3,705.8	3,703.9	3,724.0	3,739.1	3,752.4
1980	3,751.6	3,737.8	3,719.6	3,688.2	3,664.5	3,665.9	3,648.8	3,657.1	3,668.1	3,720.9	3,749.3	3,772.2
1981	3,774.3	3,761.0	3,766.4	3,751.1	3,759.2	3,781.5	3,825.0	3,844.2	3,840.0	3,830.3	3,826.9	3,817.3
1982	3,801.4	3,810.3	3,811.9	3,830.9	3,835.5	3,812.8	3,797.0	3,795.8	3,786.1	3,781.0	3,781.9	3,794.6
1983	3,792.9	3,792.5	3,806.6	3,809.5	3,833.7	3,845.3	3,879.1	3,872.3	3,912.6	3,953.6	3,974.8	4,013.9
1984	4,040.9	4,079.7	4,109.1	4,143.5	4,157.2	4,195.3	4,224.2	4,256.2	4,295.7	4,262.9	4,292.2	4,318.0
1985	4,320.4	4,322.9	4,337.5	4,335.0	4,338.1	4,351.4	4,348.0	4,361.0	4,364.8	4,397.7	4,391.0	4,427.5
1986	4,410.8	4,435.6	4,478.2	4,481.2	4,482.4	4,483.5	4,492.8	4,508.1	4,512.8	4,509.1	4,515.7	4,538.3
1987	4,540.2	4,557.5	4,575.4	4,567.8	4,593.6	4,600.5	4,621.6	4,651.3	4,657.1	4,689.9	4,711.1	4,762.9
1988	4,735.4	4,759.1	4,767.5	4,778.3	4,784.1	4,800.1	4,820.1	4,825.9	4,835.2	4,863.7	4,870.1	4,910.0
1989	4,944.6	4,949.4	4,963.1	4,955.6	4,934.4	4,947.6	4,954.1	4,959.1	4,952.8	4,962.2	4,986.8	4,995.9
1990	5,004.8	5,029.6	5,031.3	5,055.9	5,045.7	5,054.1	5,075.2	5,050.0	5,044.6	4,997.6	4,995.3	5,001.2
1991	4,946.3	4,945.2	4,950.4	4,960.8	4,958.2	4,986.7	4,971.1	4,971.5	4,981.3	4,958.9	4,969.6	4,993.9
1992	4,991.6	5,018.8	5,019.4	5,028.1	5,044.3	5,048.2	5,039.0	5,035.6	5,049.6	5,079.8	5,100.2	5,088.5
1993	5,112.1	5,111.6	5,088.4	5,115.5	5,135.7	5,125.7	5,124.4	5,145.2	5,140.4	5,149.4	5,164.5	5,190.8
1994	5,166.2	5,224.0	5,246.9	5,260.3	5,292.9	5,286.3	5,288.6	5,298.7	5,328.3	5,374.1	5,373.7	5,394.9
1995	5,410.4	5,408.6	5,410.1	5,418.8	5,412.8	5,433.4	5,440.7	5,446.4	5,467.2	5,478.4	5,504.1	5,516.5
1996	5,500.5	5,546.5	5,563.1	5,568.5	5,594.3	5,633.6	5,633.5	5,659.8	5,682.2	5,673.7	5,691.0	5,715.8
1997	5,723.1	5,747.8	5,773.5	5,786.4	5,813.8	5,836.3	5,856.5	5,893.5	5,912.8	5,945.4	5,987.6	6,015.7
1998	6,070.0	6,117.3	6,160.9	6,186.7	6,224.1	6,257.2	6,277.6	6,309.2	6,327.2	6,339.2	6,368.3	6,376.1
1999	6,364.2	6,380.9	6,392.0	6,394.7	6,423.1	6,459.2	6,471.9	6,493.5	6,471.4	6,515.9	6,545.0	6,576.6
2000	6,601.8	6,613.7	6,641.5	6,693.7	6,717.3	6,745.2	6,755.6	6,780.5	6,792.2	6,825.9	6,855.5	6,883.0
2001	6,863.6	6,876.9	6,904.5	6,908.0	6,907.9	6,920.6	6,936.2	6,944.3	6,970.9	6,909.2	6,909.0	-

Source: The Conference Board. © 2002 The Conference Board. All Rights Reserved. No claim to original U.S. Government works pursuant to U.S. Contract No. 52-SABA-5-00128. Primary source(s): U.S. Department of Commerce, Bureau of Economic Analysis, National Income and Wealth Division, BE-54, Washington, DC 20230. A dash (-) indicates that data are not available or zero.

Index of Industrial Production
(1992=100)

Year	Jan	Feb	Mar	Apr	May	Jun	Jul	Aug	Sep	Oct	Nov	Dec
1951	26.887	27.056	27.182	27.225	27.140	27.014	26.592	26.340	26.508	26.466	26.677	26.845
1952	27.140	27.309	27.393	27.140	26.887	26.634	26.213	27.899	28.910	29.205	29.795	29.964
1953	30.048	30.217	30.470	30.596	30.765	30.638	31.017	30.849	30.217	29.964	29.247	28.531
1954	28.320	28.405	28.236	28.067	28.236	28.320	28.362	28.320	28.362	28.700	29.163	29.542
1955	30.217	30.596	31.312	31.692	32.197	32.240	32.492	32.450	32.661	33.209	33.293	33.420
1956	33.630	33.335	33.335	33.588	33.293	32.998	31.987	33.293	34.052	34.347	34.052	34.557
1957	34.431	34.768	34.726	34.262	34.136	34.220	34.431	34.431	34.136	33.630	32.830	32.197
1958	31.607	30.933	30.554	30.048	30.343	31.144	31.607	32.240	32.535	32.914	33.883	33.925
1959	34.431	35.105	35.611	36.370	36.917	36.960	36.075	34.852	34.810	34.557	34.768	36.917
1960	37.887	37.550	37.212	36.917	36.875	36.412	36.285	36.243	35.864	35.822	35.316	34.642
1961	34.684	34.642	34.852	35.569	36.117	36.622	37.044	37.381	37.339	38.055	38.645	38.982
1962	38.645	39.277	39.488	39.572	39.530	39.446	39.825	39.867	40.120	40.162	40.331	40.331
1963	40.626	41.090	41.343	41.722	42.228	42.354	42.185	42.270	42.691	42.986	43.197	43.112
1964	43.492	43.787	43.787	44.503	44.756	44.883	45.178	45.473	45.641	45.009	46.400	46.948
1965	47.453	47.748	48.380	48.591	48.970	49.350	49.813	50.024	50.150	50.656	50.867	51.499
1966	52.005	52.342	53.058	53.143	53.648	53.901	54.196	54.238	54.744	55.123	54.744	54.870
1967	55.129	54.504	54.197	54.708	54.231	54.224	54.100	55.137	55.047	55.496	56.289	56.896
1968	56.834	57.038	57.216	57.299	57.942	58.154	58.065	58.227	58.448	58.564	59.321	59.509
1969	59.869	60.252	60.724	60.501	60.272	60.861	61.182	61.323	61.309	61.327	60.749	60.586
1970	59.464	59.425	59.348	59.195	59.126	58.935	59.080	58.974	58.568	57.396	57.049	58.359
1971	58.808	58.696	58.632	58.961	59.260	59.509	59.336	58.992	59.951	60.399	60.656	61.356
1972	62.719	63.150	63.670	64.689	64.537	64.745	64.648	65.529	66.248	67.199	68.003	68.649
1973	68.703	69.653	69.634	69.889	70.185	70.722	71.161	71.120	71.666	71.933	71.959	70.823
1974	69.843	69.569	69.887	69.757	70.573	70.792	70.465	70.219	70.511	69.999	67.991	65.164
1975	63.470	62.453	61.343	61.911	61.718	62.522	62.889	64.009	64.674	64.991	65.602	66.133
1976	66.848	68.036	67.869	68.133	68.911	68.957	69.363	69.760	69.987	70.226	71.396	71.965
1977	72.362	72.415	73.256	74.295	75.037	75.604	75.642	75.932	76.330	76.170	76.213	75.915
1978	75.660	75.669	76.430	79.030	79.072	79.945	80.180	80.379	80.777	81.186	81.651	81.953
1979	81.566	82.181	82.409	81.637	82.580	82.600	82.001	81.670	81.730	82.070	81.663	81.491
1980	81.870	81.933	81.908	80.311	78.322	77.329	76.833	77.734	78.885	79.453	80.735	81.135
1981	80.436	80.821	81.187	80.644	81.320	81.830	82.554	82.184	81.519	80.897	79.765	78.870
1982	77.601	79.274	78.720	77.977	77.380	77.121	76.488	76.084	75.526	74.900	74.701	74.086
1983	75.666	75.490	76.242	77.197	78.128	78.568	79.961	81.035	82.418	83.068	82.986	83.410
1984	85.144	85.010	85.948	86.405	86.902	87.294	87.470	87.458	87.337	86.928	86.999	86.610
1985	86.914	87.662	87.883	88.026	88.227	88.010	87.627	88.151	88.682	87.916	88.419	89.034
1986	89.612	88.972	88.076	88.749	88.551	88.247	88.534	88.783	88.700	89.499	89.942	90.772
1987	90.196	91.240	91.583	91.958	92.361	93.159	93.721	93.828	93.743	95.014	95.290	95.855
1988	95.926	96.243	96.259	96.816	96.891	96.960	97.593	98.117	97.766	98.035	98.771	99.275
1989	99.827	99.038	99.968	100.213	99.583	99.407	98.424	98.824	98.623	98.171	98.560	99.032
1990	98.572	99.081	99.559	98.959	99.350	99.330	99.284	99.477	99.613	99.064	97.748	97.171
1991	96.693	95.929	95.046	95.379	96.120	97.244	97.321	97.445	98.375	98.280	98.143	97.510
1992	97.507	98.033	98.869	99.582	99.855	99.713	100.627	100.290	100.677	101.224	101.793	101.830
1993	102.183	102.603	102.769	103.112	102.692	102.911	103.154	102.967	103.955	104.397	104.897	105.708
1994	105.946	106.261	107.160	107.751	108.485	109.069	109.429	109.904	110.145	110.976	111.686	112.863
1995	113.397	113.417	113.536	113.298	113.623	114.086	113.536	115.013	115.491	115.385	115.764	115.970
1996	115.634	117.051	116.892	118.059	118.873	119.759	120.020	120.746	121.408	121.423	122.609	123.306
1997	123.745	125.136	125.318	126.067	126.488	127.163	127.780	129.093	129.997	130.875	131.685	131.986
1998	132.740	132.844	133.295	134.017	134.390	133.627	133.301	135.900	135.609	136.421	135.936	135.973
1999	136.900	137.224	137.803	137.943	138.542	138.787	139.555	140.249	140.277	141.335	141.895	142.856
2000	143.173	144.043	144.882	145.636	146.617	147.188	146.532	146.700	146.826	146.266	145.789	145.135
2001	143.934	143.509	142.928	142.007	141.595	140.326	140.402	139.954	138.821	137.551	137.139	-

Source: The Conference Board. © 2002 The Conference Board. All Rights Reserved. No claim to original U.S. Government works pursuant to U.S. Contract No. 52-SABA-5-00128. Primary source(s): Board of Governors of the Federal Reserve System, Division of Research and Statistics, Industrial Output Section, Stop 82, Washington, DC 20551. A dash (-) indicates that data are not available or zero.

Manufacturing and Trade Sales
(Millions of chained 1996 $)

Year	Jan	Feb	Mar	Apr	May	Jun	Jul	Aug	Sep	Oct	Nov	Dec
1959	208,096	211,037	213,685	216,266	219,204	219,908	218,391	213,742	213,261	213,431	213,178	219,879
1960	222,747	221,322	219,359	220,796	216,691	217,116	215,763	215,823	217,833	216,412	215,038	214,392
1961	208,995	210,197	213,518	213,113	215,618	219,597	217,915	222,896	224,417	226,539	229,691	230,859
1962	230,804	230,443	233,980	234,209	234,597	234,181	234,435	235,555	236,167	237,736	241,304	237,272
1963	238,737	243,203	244,085	246,581	244,740	247,666	250,509	247,739	248,722	251,942	250,112	254,128
1964	256,664	257,396	255,743	259,700	262,674	261,992	264,513	263,902	267,737	263,253	265,805	274,134
1965	274,522	273,760	279,945	280,876	279,032	278,768	283,154	283,437	279,733	287,210	291,338	293,238
1966	296,481	296,138	301,542	299,421	296,521	300,802	297,076	298,976	300,599	302,266	300,215	302,811
1967	303,255	302,091	304,279	304,080	303,831	306,088	304,110	308,195	309,283	307,137	315,410	322,423
1968	319,189	318,183	320,551	319,915	322,157	324,435	327,531	321,947	326,453	330,874	333,727	330,632
1969	330,640	331,155	332,373	333,810	333,580	333,389	333,483	337,101	338,728	342,646	337,902	337,279
1970	333,028	333,324	329,429	327,764	331,324	332,651	333,006	332,852	332,274	328,817	323,298	333,558
1971	336,826	338,707	340,112	341,962	343,632	348,351	344,339	346,503	349,623	349,865	355,780	359,102
1972	362,898	358,981	365,632	368,116	370,383	371,999	369,689	378,551	385,061	390,376	397,844	403,150
1973	408,285	408,923	407,290	405,605	404,305	403,498	408,997	400,545	403,310	413,655	420,346	414,720
1974	415,094	413,057	414,454	411,433	413,244	411,802	410,860	406,875	403,428	396,520	392,277	380,778
1975	379,822	377,367	366,032	369,699	369,614	372,937	374,789	379,186	380,094	380,558	380,000	384,025
1976	393,533	395,261	398,249	400,154	399,712	404,625	404,907	406,306	407,482	402,674	409,369	419,974
1977	417,235	422,908	428,024	427,506	427,776	431,635	432,810	433,525	435,117	438,376	440,379	446,215
1978	432,554	442,474	446,917	460,457	460,019	462,569	458,758	464,741	463,680	467,817	469,844	472,359
1979	467,192	464,984	478,440	465,532	475,838	470,980	470,384	471,201	468,541	467,141	467,318	465,953
1980	469,898	465,478	454,879	445,141	439,442	438,177	443,706	446,904	456,317	465,847	466,157	467,308
1981	470,153	468,215	463,378	463,637	460,358	459,143	460,199	458,356	455,203	449,017	445,546	439,778
1982	437,464	444,447	444,802	445,304	447,596	441,250	439,549	435,519	436,360	431,869	433,045	431,855
1983	440,096	438,242	445,592	445,551	452,475	464,100	463,853	463,095	470,182	475,334	480,212	489,106
1984	492,267	492,002	492,423	495,151	499,063	503,502	500,813	500,687	500,070	502,168	506,626	507,232
1985	505,965	507,688	512,132	511,607	517,534	508,974	509,951	519,219	520,612	515,812	519,587	516,811
1986	524,579	521,595	522,104	532,617	527,509	530,893	534,030	534,789	547,476	539,744	538,090	549,355
1987	532,012	551,202	551,731	550,147	549,229	551,970	556,757	554,302	560,411	559,765	558,214	562,944
1988	561,659	568,007	577,105	574,010	575,812	581,457	579,099	579,434	581,726	586,242	588,505	596,176
1989	596,857	590,334	586,820	592,172	589,532	587,714	581,686	596,452	592,273	586,555	591,801	593,757
1990	589,119	597,872	601,356	594,426	599,256	600,805	597,586	603,597	592,499	589,958	582,984	576,916
1991	573,114	576,506	573,173	584,467	589,261	586,622	594,279	591,775	594,306	594,906	592,980	585,431
1992	596,771	598,272	600,680	604,683	599,422	605,741	613,853	604,088	612,487	614,966	616,014	625,603
1993	627,170	626,366	622,406	625,622	626,613	632,406	629,346	632,571	638,204	640,930	644,218	646,255
1994	646,991	652,909	663,780	660,284	661,882	667,958	665,030	680,734	677,787	682,960	688,977	694,151
1995	697,218	693,295	693,050	687,864	692,929	699,608	691,337	705,342	704,480	704,848	710,618	713,986
1996	706,859	713,246	713,601	719,986	725,464	722,044	727,746	730,244	732,477	738,211	743,672	738,316
1997	715,601	725,226	724,004	729,129	726,443	733,928	745,467	739,273	746,450	746,289	749,785	753,905
1998	757,031	764,366	769,521	769,382	768,609	769,376	767,056	771,925	779,009	786,093	789,056	798,879
1999	795,076	806,435	810,186	806,173	815,092	816,862	821,626	827,509	822,904	827,808	839,259	847,549
2000	854,291	844,396	854,938	853,618	857,758	859,468	857,657	860,389	857,751	856,748	853,255	859,045
2001	854,960	855,289	852,185	845,838	851,040	840,153	850,447	851,886	824,986	857,561	-	-

Source: The Conference Board. © 2002 The Conference Board. All Rights Reserved. No claim to original U.S. Government works pursuant to U.S. Contract No. 52-SABA-5-00128. Primary source(s): U.S. Department of Commerce (manufacturing and wholesalers sales; retail sales, deflator), Bureau of Economic Analysis, National Income and Wealth Division, BE-54, Washington, DC 20230 and U.S. Department of Commerce, Bureau of the Census, Services Division, Current Retail Inventories and Sales Branch, Washington, DC 20233. A dash (-) indicates that data are not available or zero.

COMPOSITE INDEX OF LAGGING INDICATORS

The composite index of lagging indicators turns down about 10 months after the economy turns down and turns up about six months after the economy has turned up. Thus it lags behind the economy. It is made up of components that have inertial tendencies—they change more slowly than the economy. The "lagging index," of course, also confirms the cyclical behaviour of the economy by moving in tandem with the leading and coincident indicators—at a lag in time.

The lagging index is also a somewhat uncertain indicator. At business cycle peaks, the lags range from 2 to 13 months; at business cycle troughs, the range is 4 to 15 months.

Components of the Lagging Index

The index is a composite of 7 indicators, each of which is further discussed below:

> Average duration of unemployment in weeks
> Ratio, manufacturing and trade inventories to sales
> Change in index of labor cost per unit of output in manufacturing
> Average prime rate charged by banks
> Commercial and industrial loans outstanding
> Ratio, consumer installment credit outstanding to personal income
> Change in consumer price index for services

Average Duration of Unemployment. The indicator is shown as number of weeks of unemployment. A recession is a sustained downturn in production after a sustained period of growth. The average duration of unemployment, therefore, will tend to be low at the start of a recession. The shrinking of the economy will cause this average to grow. As the economy turns up again, the average will be high; time has to pass until laid-off people are employed again and the average duration of unemployment drops. In this case, also, the indicator grows as the economy shrinks and declines as the economy grows.

Ratio, Manufacturing and Trade Inventories to Sales. The indicator is expressed as a ratio based on inventory and sales measures expressed in chained 1996 dollars. A ratio of 1.0 means that inventories and sales are identical. A high ratio indicates high inventories relative to sales. A low indicator tends to mean that inventories are depleted. A dropping ratio means that inventories are "selling out" while a climbing ratio means that sales are slowing. Manufacturers and merchants caught at the beginning of a recession with high inventories will be unable to sell them; therefore, the ratio will increase as the economy slumps. Conversely, in an expansionary period, the ratio will be dropping because producers cannot keep up with demand. In both cases, the indicator tends to move in the opposite direction of the economy—or in the same direction, but with a lag in time.

Change in Index of Labor Cost per Unit of Output in Manufacturing. The indicator is expressed in percent. Labor cost in manufacturing is in part a reflection of longer-term contractual arrangements between manufacturers and labor unions which are not subject to rapid adjustment as the economy changes. Even the compensation of non-union labor forces tends to lag behind economic events: managements avoid downward adjustments in wages to maintain morale and productivity and resist demands for increased pay in periods of growth. For these reasons, the index lags economic events. Recessionary forces cause the cost of labor to decline—slowly. In periods of upturn, labor cost rises slowly as well. Thus it is normal to have high wages at the start and during recessions and relatively low wages as the economy begins climbing to a new peak.

Average Prime Rate Charged by Banks. The indicator is shown as a percent of interest charged by major banks to their largest customers. Historically, the prime rate has tended to increase during recessions and to decrease during periods of expansion. At the onset of an economic downturn, the rate reflects the conditions of the previous expansion; as the recession deepens and demand for money slackens, the prime rate drops. The prime rate is strongly influenced by actions of the Federal Reserve System. The Federal Reserve's discount rate (interest charged to member banks for short-term borrowings) has an immediate effect on the prime rate; therefore, the behavior of this indicator is indirectly subject to alteration by government action.

Commercial and Industrial Loans Outstanding. The indicator is shown in millions of chained 1996 dollars. Business and industry assume debt in periods of growth and minimize debt in periods of decline. The total debt outstanding, however, reflects the business cycle at a lag in time; borrowers pay off debt over time and may be late in paying during economic turn-downs; they also contract new obligations later than the economy's upturn because both lenders and borrowers are more cautious after a recessionary period.

Ratio, Consumer Installment Credit Outstanding to Personal Income. The indicator is expressed as a percent. A high percentage indicates that consumer debt relative to income is high. A decline in personal income or an increase in consumer debt will cause the indicator to rise and, of course, an increase in personal income or decrease in debt will cause the ratio to decline. At the start of a recession, personal income tends to drop more rapidly than debt outstanding; this indicator, therefore, will increase as the economy decreases. Later, as debt is paid off and less is borrowed (because times are uncertain), the ratio will decrease just as the economy begins to expand again—the signature of a lagging indicator.

Change in Consumer Price Index for Services. The index is expressed as a percent; the data are "smoothed," meaning that data are arithmetically transformed to remove irregular short-term movements. Prices for services are less volatile than prices for food, fuel, and products. Hence this series is a good lagging indicator: it changes more slowly than the economy. More detailed presentations of the Consumer Price Index are provided later in this book.

Sources and Revisions

The component series are drawn from federal sources, including the U.S. Department of Commerce, Bureau of Economic Analysis and Bureau of the Census; the U.S. Department of Labor, Bureau of Labor Statistics; the Federal Reserve System; and the Federal Reserve Bank of New York.

The composite index itself is constructed by The Conference Board. In the process, mathematical operations are performed on the component data series to ensure that volatile series do not dominate the index. A volatile series may be one that fluctuates wildly month to month but shows less volatility when averaged over several months. Other smoothing and standardization methods are used as well.

The lagging index was last revised in 2001. See Reference 6 for details.

Bibliography

1. Frumkin, Norman. *Guide to Economic Indicators*. M.E. Sharpe, Inc., 1990.

2. Green, George R. and Barry A. Beckman. "Business Cycle Indicators: Upcoming Revision of the Composite Indexes." U.S. Department of Commerce, Bureau of Economic Analysis. *Survey of Current Business*, October 1993. Superintendent of Documents, U.S. Government Printing Office, Washington, DC 20302.

3. Hertzberg, Marie P. and Barry A. Beckman. "Business Cycle Indicators: Revised Composite Indexes." U.S. Department of Commerce, Bureau of Economic Analysis. *Survey of Current Business*, January 1989. Superintendent of Documents, U.S. Government Printing Office, Washington, DC 20302.

4. U.S. Department of Commerce, Bureau of Economic Analysis. "Composite Indexes of Leading, Coincident, and Lagging Indicators." In *Survey of Current Business*, November 1987. Superintendent of Documents, U.S. Government Printing Office, Washington, DC 20302.

5. U.S. Department of Commerce, Bureau of Economic Analysis. *Survey of Current Business*. Superintendent of Documents, U.S. Government Printing Office, Washington, DC 20302.

6. *Leading Economic Indicators*. The Confenrence Board, 845 Third Avenue, New York, NY 10022-6679.

Composite Index of 7 Lagging Indicators
(1996=100)

Year	Jan	Feb	Mar	Apr	May	Jun	Jul	Aug	Sep	Oct	Nov	Dec
1959	76.7	77.0	77.0	77.3	77.7	78.0	78.5	79.4	79.9	80.5	80.3	80.1
1960	79.6	80.0	80.5	80.5	81.2	81.7	81.9	81.7	81.4	81.3	81.4	81.7
1961	81.7	81.5	81.0	80.6	80.1	79.6	79.1	79.1	79.3	79.3	79.1	79.5
1962	80.0	79.7	80.1	80.2	80.5	80.8	80.9	81.2	81.2	81.2	81.4	81.5
1963	81.5	81.5	81.6	81.7	81.8	82.0	82.1	82.6	82.7	82.8	83.4	83.5
1964	83.3	83.5	83.7	84.1	83.8	83.8	83.8	84.3	84.6	84.9	84.6	84.7
1965	85.3	85.8	86.0	86.4	86.8	87.0	87.0	87.2	87.4	87.6	87.9	88.0
1966	88.3	88.8	88.9	89.4	89.9	90.4	90.9	91.1	91.0	90.7	91.4	91.3
1967	91.5	91.7	91.8	91.9	91.6	92.1	92.1	91.6	91.7	91.8	91.5	91.5
1968	91.4	91.8	91.9	92.2	92.5	92.6	92.5	93.0	92.9	93.0	93.2	93.5
1969	93.9	94.1	94.5	94.8	95.3	95.5	95.5	95.8	95.8	95.8	95.8	96.1
1970	96.6	96.5	96.6	96.2	95.9	96.0	95.4	95.6	95.1	95.1	94.8	93.9
1971	93.6	93.5	93.2	92.8	92.6	92.1	92.4	92.9	92.9	92.5	92.4	92.2
1972	90.8	90.6	90.9	91.1	91.4	91.7	91.8	91.5	91.3	91.4	91.3	91.3
1973	92.1	92.9	93.4	94.0	94.3	95.0	95.3	95.9	96.0	95.9	96.2	96.8
1974	97.4	97.4	97.4	98.0	98.4	98.5	98.9	99.4	99.8	99.9	100.1	100.4
1975	99.9	99.0	98.5	97.2	96.2	93.7	93.5	92.9	92.6	92.6	92.2	92.2
1976	92.1	91.9	91.7	91.6	91.3	91.1	91.0	91.0	91.0	91.2	91.2	91.0
1977	90.9	91.0	91.0	91.3	91.3	91.8	92.0	92.1	92.2	92.5	92.7	92.6
1978	93.2	93.4	93.7	93.3	93.8	94.2	94.6	94.7	95.0	95.2	95.9	96.1
1979	96.5	96.7	96.3	97.5	97.4	98.1	98.5	98.9	99.7	100.0	100.3	100.5
1980	100.6	100.9	102.0	102.7	102.0	100.9	98.9	97.7	96.6	96.1	96.1	96.8
1981	97.1	97.2	97.0	97.1	98.1	98.2	98.1	98.5	99.2	98.9	98.8	98.4
1982	98.7	97.7	97.1	97.3	97.0	97.0	96.7	96.5	96.2	95.5	94.5	93.5
1983	92.8	92.7	92.4	92.2	91.6	91.8	91.8	92.3	92.2	92.1	92.6	93.0
1984	93.0	93.9	94.5	94.9	95.5	96.1	96.8	97.3	97.6	98.0	97.9	98.1
1985	98.2	98.2	98.4	98.4	98.7	98.8	99.1	99.2	99.0	99.8	99.7	99.9
1986	99.8	100.0	100.4	99.6	99.9	99.7	99.8	99.7	99.1	99.9	99.7	99.2
1987	99.9	99.1	98.9	99.0	99.1	99.2	99.0	99.1	99.3	99.5	99.4	99.3
1988	99.8	99.6	99.7	100.1	100.0	100.4	100.1	100.2	100.0	100.3	100.4	100.2
1989	100.7	101.4	101.7	101.3	102.2	102.5	102.8	102.4	102.3	102.7	102.5	102.6
1990	102.1	101.9	102.1	102.0	101.9	102.0	102.0	101.8	101.9	101.8	101.8	101.4
1991	101.6	100.9	100.8	100.0	99.5	98.8	98.3	97.9	97.3	97.0	96.8	96.5
1992	95.6	95.1	94.9	94.5	94.2	93.8	93.5	93.8	93.4	93.1	93.4	93.1
1993	93.1	93.2	93.3	93.4	93.4	93.4	93.6	93.5	93.6	93.4	93.4	93.5
1994	93.7	93.4	93.4	93.6	93.8	94.3	94.4	94.6	95.0	95.3	96.0	96.3
1995	96.8	97.4	97.8	98.3	98.6	99.2	99.4	99.3	99.5	99.7	99.7	99.8
1996	99.9	99.8	99.8	99.8	99.9	99.8	100.2	100.0	100.1	100.1	100.1	100.3
1997	100.3	100.1	100.1	100.2	100.5	100.5	100.1	100.3	100.5	100.7	101.0	100.9
1998	101.1	101.4	101.8	101.5	101.7	102.4	102.5	102.7	102.8	102.8	102.8	102.6
1999	103.2	103.2	103.4	103.6	103.5	103.2	103.8	103.8	104.3	104.2	104.4	104.6
2000	104.7	105.5	105.1	105.6	105.8	106.6	106.8	107.1	107.4	107.7	108.2	107.9
2001	107.7	107.4	107.0	106.9	106.4	105.6	104.4	104.0	104.4	103.8	103.1	-

Composite Index of 7 Lagging Indicators
Change in Index from Previous Month

Year	Jan	Feb	Mar	Apr	May	Jun	Jul	Aug	Sep	Oct	Nov	Dec
1959	-	+0.3	-	+0.3	+0.4	+0.3	+0.5	+0.9	+0.5	+0.6	-0.2	-0.2
1960	-0.5	+0.4	+0.5	-	+0.7	+0.5	+0.2	-0.2	-0.3	-0.1	+0.1	+0.3
1961	-	-0.2	-0.5	-0.4	-0.5	-0.5	-0.5	-	+0.2	-	-0.2	+0.4
1962	+0.5	-0.3	+0.4	+0.1	+0.3	+0.3	+0.1	+0.3	-	-	+0.2	+0.1
1963	-	-	+0.1	+0.1	+0.1	+0.2	+0.1	+0.5	+0.1	+0.1	+0.6	+0.1
1964	-0.2	+0.2	+0.2	+0.4	-0.3	-	-	+0.5	+0.3	+0.3	-0.3	+0.1
1965	+0.6	+0.5	+0.2	+0.4	+0.4	+0.2	-	+0.2	+0.2	+0.2	+0.3	+0.1
1966	+0.3	+0.5	+0.1	+0.5	+0.5	+0.5	+0.5	+0.2	-0.1	-0.3	+0.7	-0.1
1967	+0.2	+0.2	+0.1	+0.1	-0.3	+0.5	-	-0.5	+0.1	+0.1	-0.3	-
1968	-0.1	+0.4	+0.1	+0.3	+0.3	+0.1	-0.1	+0.5	-0.1	+0.1	+0.2	+0.3
1969	+0.4	+0.2	+0.4	+0.3	+0.5	+0.2	-	+0.3	-	-	-	+0.3
1970	+0.5	-0.1	+0.1	-0.4	-0.3	+0.1	-0.6	+0.2	-0.5	-	-0.3	-0.9
1971	-0.3	-0.1	-0.3	-0.4	-0.2	-0.5	+0.3	+0.5	-	-0.4	-0.1	-0.2
1972	-1.4	-0.2	+0.3	+0.2	+0.3	+0.3	+0.1	-0.3	-0.2	+0.1	-0.1	-
1973	+0.8	+0.8	+0.5	+0.6	+0.3	+0.7	+0.3	+0.6	+0.1	-0.1	+0.3	+0.6
1974	+0.6	-	-	+0.6	+0.4	+0.1	+0.4	+0.5	+0.4	+0.1	+0.2	+0.3
1975	-0.5	-0.9	-0.5	-1.3	-1.0	-2.5	-0.2	-0.6	-0.3	-	-0.4	-
1976	-0.1	-0.2	-0.2	-0.1	-0.3	-0.2	-0.1	-	-	+0.2	-	-0.2
1977	-0.1	+0.1	-	+0.3	-	+0.5	+0.2	+0.1	+0.1	+0.3	+0.2	-0.1
1978	+0.6	+0.2	+0.3	-0.4	+0.5	+0.4	+0.4	+0.1	+0.3	+0.2	+0.7	+0.2
1979	+0.4	+0.2	-0.4	+1.2	-0.1	+0.7	+0.4	+0.4	+0.8	+0.3	+0.3	+0.2
1980	+0.1	+0.3	+1.1	+0.7	-0.7	-1.1	-2.0	-1.2	-1.1	-0.5	-	+0.7
1981	+0.3	+0.1	-0.2	+0.1	+1.0	+0.1	-0.1	+0.4	+0.7	-0.3	-0.1	-0.4
1982	+0.3	-1.0	-0.6	+0.2	-0.3	-	-0.3	-0.2	-0.3	-0.7	-1.0	-1.0
1983	-0.7	-0.1	-0.3	-0.2	-0.6	+0.2	-	+0.5	-0.1	-0.1	+0.5	+0.4
1984	-	+0.9	+0.6	+0.4	+0.6	+0.6	+0.7	+0.5	+0.3	+0.4	-0.1	+0.2
1985	+0.1	-	+0.2	-	+0.3	+0.1	+0.3	+0.1	-0.2	+0.8	-0.1	+0.2
1986	-0.1	+0.2	+0.4	-0.8	+0.3	-0.2	+0.1	-0.1	-0.6	+0.8	-0.2	-0.5
1987	+0.7	-0.8	-0.2	+0.1	+0.1	+0.1	-0.2	+0.1	+0.2	+0.2	-0.1	-0.1
1988	+0.5	-0.2	+0.1	+0.4	-0.1	+0.4	-0.3	+0.1	-0.2	+0.3	+0.1	-0.2
1989	+0.5	+0.7	+0.3	-0.4	+0.9	+0.3	+0.3	-0.4	-0.1	+0.4	-0.2	+0.1
1990	-0.5	-0.2	+0.2	-0.1	-0.1	+0.1	-	-0.2	+0.1	-0.1	-	-0.4
1991	+0.2	-0.7	-0.1	-0.8	-0.5	-0.7	-0.5	-0.4	-0.6	-0.3	-0.2	-0.3
1992	-0.9	-0.5	-0.2	-0.4	-0.3	-0.4	-0.3	+0.3	-0.4	-0.3	+0.3	-0.3
1993	-	+0.1	+0.1	+0.1	-	-	+0.2	-0.1	+0.1	-0.2	-	+0.1
1994	+0.2	-0.3	-	+0.2	+0.2	+0.5	+0.1	+0.2	+0.4	+0.3	+0.7	+0.3
1995	+0.5	+0.6	+0.4	+0.5	+0.3	+0.6	+0.2	-0.1	+0.2	+0.2	-	+0.1
1996	+0.1	-0.1	-	-	+0.1	-0.1	+0.4	-0.2	+0.1	-	-	+0.2
1997	-	-0.2	-	+0.1	+0.3	-	-0.4	+0.2	+0.2	+0.2	+0.3	-0.1
1998	+0.2	+0.3	+0.4	-0.3	+0.2	+0.7	+0.1	+0.2	+0.1	-	-	-0.2
1999	+0.6	-	+0.2	+0.2	-0.1	-0.3	+0.6	-	+0.5	-0.1	+0.2	+0.2
2000	+0.1	+0.8	-0.4	+0.5	+0.2	+0.8	+0.2	+0.3	+0.3	+0.3	+0.5	-0.3
2001	-0.2	-0.3	-0.4	-0.1	-0.5	-0.8	-1.2	-0.4	+0.4	-0.6	-0.7	-

Average Duration of Unemployment in Weeks
(Weeks)

Year	Jan	Feb	Mar	Apr	May	Jun	Jul	Aug	Sep	Oct	Nov	Dec
1951	10.6	10.8	10.1	10.6	9.9	8.7	9.2	9.1	9.1	8.9	9.7	9.3
1952	9.3	8.8	8.4	9.0	7.8	7.3	7.5	7.6	8.1	9.1	9.5	8.8
1953	9.3	8.4	8.5	7.8	7.9	8.2	7.9	8.0	7.1	7.2	7.9	8.0
1954	8.7	9.5	10.6	10.9	11.6	12.3	12.5	12.8	12.9	13.3	13.2	13.4
1955	13.4	14.2	13.4	14.3	14.4	13.4	13.8	12.3	11.7	11.5	11.3	12.0
1956	11.7	12.5	11.6	11.0	10.4	10.1	10.5	12.0	11.8	11.6	10.9	11.4
1957	10.4	10.7	10.8	10.6	10.4	10.2	10.1	10.5	9.8	11.1	10.4	10.4
1958	10.5	11.0	11.2	12.1	13.1	14.4	14.6	15.7	16.5	16.5	16.4	15.7
1959	16.3	15.5	15.3	14.9	14.7	14.9	14.3	13.7	13.7	12.9	13.1	13.1
1960	13.5	13.1	13.0	12.6	11.9	11.9	12.6	12.2	12.9	13.5	13.9	12.4
1961	13.7	13.6	14.1	15.5	15.6	16.2	17.3	17.0	16.1	15.9	17.0	15.8
1962	15.3	16.0	15.0	14.9	15.5	15.1	14.6	14.5	14.1	14.1	13.3	13.6
1963	13.8	14.1	14.5	14.5	14.5	14.0	14.0	13.9	14.2	13.9	13.3	13.3
1964	13.5	13.2	13.5	12.4	13.6	13.6	14.7	13.0	12.7	12.6	14.0	12.7
1965	12.2	12.6	12.0	11.4	11.1	11.6	11.6	11.9	11.9	12.1	11.7	11.4
1966	11.9	11.2	11.1	10.8	10.2	9.7	9.7	9.8	10.1	10.3	9.7	9.5
1967	9.3	9.2	8.9	8.8	8.7	8.3	8.3	8.9	8.4	8.7	8.9	8.6
1968	9.4	8.7	8.5	8.7	8.2	7.9	8.4	8.3	8.2	8.4	8.1	8.2
1969	8.1	7.9	7.9	7.9	7.9	7.7	7.8	7.9	8.0	7.6	8.0	8.0
1970	7.9	8.0	8.3	8.2	8.6	8.6	8.9	8.8	8.9	8.7	9.3	9.8
1971	10.5	10.4	10.6	10.9	11.2	11.6	11.5	11.5	11.9	12.6	12.0	11.5
1972	12.1	12.4	12.3	12.4	12.3	12.4	11.8	11.8	12.1	11.7	11.4	11.4
1973	11.0	10.5	10.6	10.0	10.1	9.6	9.6	9.8	9.4	10.2	9.9	9.5
1974	9.5	9.6	9.7	9.8	9.6	9.7	9.9	9.8	9.6	9.9	9.6	10.1
1975	10.7	11.7	11.8	12.9	13.4	15.3	15.0	15.6	16.1	15.4	16.6	16.5
1976	16.6	16.3	16.5	15.9	15.0	16.9	15.7	15.6	15.2	15.2	15.3	15.1
1977	15.2	14.7	14.5	14.4	14.9	14.4	14.3	13.9	14.0	13.7	13.6	13.6
1978	12.9	12.5	12.4	12.3	12.1	12.1	12.0	11.4	11.4	11.7	11.1	10.6
1979	11.1	11.2	11.7	11.0	11.1	10.4	10.3	10.6	10.5	10.5	10.6	10.8
1980	10.4	10.6	11.0	11.4	10.9	11.3	11.8	12.4	12.9	13.1	13.6	13.7
1981	14.3	14.1	14.0	13.9	13.6	13.7	13.8	14.4	13.6	13.5	13.1	13.1
1982	13.4	14.1	14.1	14.5	14.9	15.7	15.4	16.2	16.6	17.2	17.1	18.1
1983	19.4	19.2	19.4	19.5	20.5	20.8	21.2	20.0	20.2	20.2	19.7	19.2
1984	20.4	19.0	19.1	18.9	18.8	18.1	18.0	17.3	17.0	16.7	17.0	16.8
1985	15.9	15.9	16.1	16.4	15.3	15.5	15.5	15.3	15.3	15.3	15.7	15.1
1986	14.8	15.2	14.6	14.7	14.7	15.2	15.2	15.5	15.4	15.2	15.0	15.0
1987	14.9	14.7	14.9	14.8	14.9	14.9	14.2	14.4	14.2	14.0	14.0	14.2
1988	14.2	14.4	13.7	13.3	13.8	13.1	13.4	13.6	13.6	13.4	12.6	12.9
1989	12.6	12.4	12.3	12.5	12.0	11.1	11.8	11.4	11.5	11.9	11.7	11.6
1990	11.8	11.6	11.7	11.8	11.7	11.6	11.9	12.2	12.4	12.2	12.4	12.5
1991	12.2	12.7	12.9	13.5	12.9	13.7	13.8	13.9	14.0	14.4	14.8	15.4
1992	16.1	16.7	17.1	17.4	17.8	18.2	18.1	18.0	18.1	18.9	17.9	19.0
1993	18.3	18.2	17.6	17.6	17.5	17.8	17.7	18.0	18.1	18.1	18.6	18.3
1994	18.6	19.0	19.0	19.0	19.5	18.8	19.0	18.8	18.7	19.3	18.0	17.8
1995	17.1	17.0	17.3	17.6	17.0	15.9	16.5	16.2	16.2	16.0	16.4	16.3
1996	16.1	16.4	17.3	17.6	17.0	17.6	16.7	17.3	16.8	16.3	15.9	15.6
1997	16.0	15.8	15.5	15.6	15.4	15.5	16.4	16.0	15.9	16.1	15.4	15.9
1998	15.5	15.3	14.5	14.7	14.8	14.1	14.2	13.7	14.5	14.1	14.4	13.9
1999	13.4	13.8	13.5	13.3	13.5	14.4	13.5	13.1	13.2	13.3	12.9	12.8
2000	12.9	12.5	12.6	12.6	12.7	12.4	13.3	12.9	12.2	12.5	12.3	12.5
2001	12.6	12.8	12.8	12.6	12.4	12.9	12.7	13.2	13.3	13.0	14.4	14.5

Source: The Conference Board. © 2002 The Conference Board. All Rights Reserved. No claim to original U.S. Government works pursuant to U.S. Contract No. 52-SABA-5-00128. Primary source(s): U.S. Department of Labor, Bureau of Labor Statistics, Office of Employment and Unemployment Statistics, Division of Labor Force Statistics, Washington, DC 20212. A dash (-) indicates that data are not available or zero.

Ratio, Manufacturing and Trade Inventories to Sales
(Chained 1996 $)

Year	Jan	Feb	Mar	Apr	May	Jun	Jul	Aug	Sep	Oct	Nov	Dec
1959	1.154	1.143	1.139	1.143	1.132	1.136	1.151	1.183	1.181	1.183	1.183	1.164
1960	1.164	1.182	1.204	1.194	1.223	1.222	1.233	1.235	1.230	1.234	1.242	1.230
1961	1.258	1.246	1.221	1.224	1.212	1.189	1.199	1.182	1.181	1.171	1.163	1.160
1962	1.171	1.179	1.171	1.170	1.177	1.185	1.188	1.191	1.195	1.192	1.176	1.199
1963	1.198	1.179	1.179	1.169	1.182	1.174	1.167	1.189	1.188	1.179	1.192	1.173
1964	1.171	1.171	1.182	1.171	1.162	1.169	1.161	1.170	1.162	1.180	1.177	1.150
1965	1.161	1.169	1.157	1.159	1.172	1.180	1.173	1.184	1.198	1.170	1.161	1.160
1966	1.158	1.171	1.163	1.178	1.204	1.200	1.225	1.233	1.232	1.240	1.262	1.262
1967	1.277	1.289	1.286	1.292	1.297	1.286	1.299	1.296	1.290	1.300	1.276	1.256
1968	1.277	1.283	1.275	1.286	1.287	1.281	1.274	1.311	1.289	1.284	1.277	1.290
1969	1.296	1.302	1.303	1.303	1.310	1.314	1.322	1.319	1.316	1.309	1.330	1.338
1970	1.351	1.353	1.370	1.386	1.368	1.367	1.375	1.384	1.383	1.396	1.422	1.374
1971	1.369	1.364	1.367	1.365	1.363	1.347	1.368	1.369	1.359	1.360	1.334	1.326
1972	1.317	1.330	1.308	1.306	1.306	1.302	1.311	1.293	1.279	1.267	1.251	1.235
1973	1.231	1.236	1.245	1.257	1.266	1.276	1.267	1.292	1.287	1.263	1.254	1.281
1974	1.285	1.293	1.299	1.313	1.316	1.328	1.334	1.343	1.362	1.395	1.417	1.474
1975	1.476	1.477	1.510	1.493	1.482	1.460	1.450	1.432	1.428	1.431	1.427	1.408
1976	1.378	1.379	1.374	1.375	1.383	1.378	1.384	1.383	1.390	1.413	1.394	1.364
1977	1.378	1.363	1.350	1.358	1.362	1.354	1.356	1.362	1.367	1.358	1.358	1.347
1978	1.396	1.370	1.369	1.341	1.347	1.345	1.359	1.347	1.354	1.349	1.352	1.354
1979	1.377	1.390	1.352	1.398	1.372	1.391	1.405	1.401	1.403	1.412	1.411	1.417
1980	1.412	1.427	1.462	1.505	1.523	1.524	1.504	1.488	1.454	1.422	1.420	1.418
1981	1.415	1.428	1.446	1.440	1.454	1.463	1.465	1.473	1.488	1.509	1.531	1.545
1982	1.544	1.507	1.507	1.510	1.489	1.516	1.526	1.536	1.532	1.544	1.526	1.523
1983	1.483	1.488	1.455	1.456	1.436	1.402	1.406	1.416	1.402	1.391	1.386	1.370
1984	1.368	1.385	1.400	1.407	1.412	1.405	1.423	1.442	1.449	1.454	1.448	1.451
1985	1.453	1.454	1.440	1.445	1.428	1.457	1.459	1.437	1.429	1.449	1.443	1.454
1986	1.433	1.449	1.454	1.431	1.443	1.436	1.431	1.429	1.391	1.414	1.420	1.382
1987	1.434	1.388	1.395	1.404	1.413	1.409	1.396	1.401	1.391	1.404	1.417	1.415
1988	1.419	1.410	1.391	1.402	1.400	1.396	1.403	1.410	1.410	1.400	1.399	1.392
1989	1.399	1.421	1.434	1.425	1.438	1.449	1.470	1.434	1.444	1.463	1.458	1.452
1990	1.460	1.439	1.437	1.459	1.457	1.454	1.468	1.453	1.484	1.491	1.513	1.522
1991	1.537	1.526	1.524	1.493	1.475	1.480	1.460	1.465	1.465	1.467	1.474	1.498
1992	1.465	1.459	1.455	1.448	1.458	1.448	1.432	1.459	1.438	1.432	1.432	1.415
1993	1.415	1.423	1.441	1.438	1.437	1.428	1.434	1.428	1.422	1.416	1.414	1.410
1994	1.411	1.404	1.382	1.391	1.402	1.396	1.409	1.383	1.392	1.389	1.383	1.381
1995	1.386	1.398	1.406	1.423	1.416	1.408	1.430	1.403	1.409	1.415	1.404	1.396
1996	1.416	1.403	1.397	1.392	1.381	1.387	1.382	1.380	1.378	1.374	1.367	1.377
1997	1.397	1.384	1.386	1.387	1.399	1.392	1.375	1.387	1.381	1.389	1.388	1.384
1998	1.386	1.385	1.388	1.395	1.399	1.400	1.408	1.407	1.402	1.395	1.399	1.385
1999	1.399	1.385	1.385	1.391	1.381	1.381	1.380	1.372	1.385	1.383	1.373	1.370
2000	1.361	1.380	1.366	1.372	1.371	1.379	1.386	1.388	1.394	1.401	1.411	1.404
2001	1.410	1.405	1.405	1.413	1.402	1.412	1.386	1.382	1.421	1.349	-	-

Source: The Conference Board. © 2002 The Conference Board. All Rights Reserved. No claim to original U.S. Government works pursuant to U.S. Contract No. 52-SABA-5-00128. Primary source(s): U.S. Department of Commerce (manufacturing and trade sales and inventories; retail sales deflator), Bureau of Economic Analysis, National Income and Wealth Division, BE-54, Washington, DC 20230 and U.S. Department of Commerce, Bureau of the Census, Services Division, Current Retail Inventories and Sales Branch, Washington, DC 20233. A dash (-) indicates that data are not available or zero.

Change in Index of Labor Cost per Unit of Output, Manufacturing
(6-Month percent, Annual Rate)

Year	Jan	Feb	Mar	Apr	May	Jun	Jul	Aug	Sep	Oct	Nov	Dec
1959	-	-	-	-	-	-	2.6	6.2	6.7	10.0	10.0	1.0
1960	-4.0	-4.4	-2.4	-2.9	-1.5	6.7	7.8	5.1	2.5	2.5	3.0	2.0
1961	4.0	5.0	3.5	-	-2.9	-3.4	-6.2	-8.0	-7.6	-4.9	-4.4	-4.9
1962	-0.5	-0.5	0.5	2.5	3.6	5.7	1.0	2.0	1.5	-0.5	-1.5	-2.5
1963	-1.5	-2.5	-3.0	-4.9	-4.9	-4.0	-2.5	-2.0	-1.0	-	1.0	2.1
1964	-1.5	0.5	1.0	0.5	-	-1.5	0.5	0.5	0.5	1.0	-1.0	-2.0
1965	-2.5	-4.0	-6.0	-6.0	-4.1	-3.6	-4.1	-3.1	-1.0	0.5	1.6	-
1966	2.1	3.7	2.6	3.7	2.1	4.8	4.2	4.2	3.7	1.5	4.7	2.6
1967	3.6	2.0	4.1	3.6	2.0	4.1	4.6	3.5	1.5	1.0	-0.5	-1.0
1968	-0.5	2.0	3.0	6.1	6.1	6.6	6.0	3.4	4.9	4.4	3.4	3.9
1969	2.4	1.9	1.4	2.4	5.3	4.3	4.8	7.3	7.2	5.7	5.6	7.1
1970	10.9	8.4	8.4	7.4	5.5	5.0	0.9	2.2	0.4	1.3	2.2	-
1971	0.4	0.4	1.8	0.9	0.9	1.8	0.9	2.6	-1.7	-3.0	-3.4	-1.7
1972	-3.9	-3.8	0.4	0.4	2.2	0.9	3.6	0.9	0.4	1.8	-	-0.4
1973	1.7	3.5	4.4	6.2	6.6	6.6	5.2	3.9	3.0	3.0	4.7	9.9
1974	12.1	13.9	13.9	14.7	12.8	9.0	8.5	8.4	9.2	10.0	13.2	19.8
1975	20.4	20.2	23.8	18.6	16.7	7.2	3.5	2.8	-1.0	1.0	-0.3	2.1
1976	4.5	1.7	4.5	4.8	3.8	4.1	2.4	5.8	3.0	2.0	3.3	1.7
1977	1.3	3.0	2.6	2.6	3.3	5.0	6.7	3.6	5.6	7.9	7.5	7.8
1978	7.4	10.1	10.0	4.4	4.7	2.8	3.1	0.9	0.3	5.3	5.5	7.7
1979	8.9	8.9	9.5	10.4	8.7	8.4	8.6	10.4	10.9	8.7	10.7	12.1
1980	9.9	8.7	9.2	12.0	15.6	15.4	16.2	15.6	11.8	10.0	4.6	4.2
1981	5.2	3.2	6.0	6.7	7.2	6.4	3.6	8.6	8.0	8.9	10.9	11.8
1982	17.4	8.5	7.7	5.7	4.8	2.5	-0.9	4.3	3.6	3.6	2.4	4.0
1983	-1.1	-1.5	-3.2	-4.5	-5.5	-7.2	-4.1	-5.0	-4.6	-3.3	-1.1	0.9
1984	-1.1	0.7	2.0	2.0	0.4	-1.3	2.0	2.5	3.6	3.4	4.3	6.1
1985	6.1	2.9	4.9	0.9	-0.2	-0.6	-0.2	0.9	-2.6	4.6	2.9	2.8
1986	-1.1	0.4	5.1	-3.4	-0.6	-1.5	1.1	0.2	-3.8	1.3	-1.3	-3.2
1987	-0.4	-2.6	-1.1	-4.1	-1.7	-2.0	-4.7	-0.7	-0.9	-0.2	-0.7	0.4
1988	2.9	1.5	3.8	2.7	3.8	5.8	3.1	2.0	-0.4	5.5	1.7	-0.4
1989	-0.6	2.8	2.6	-2.9	0.4	1.5	4.6	1.3	0.9	7.0	4.3	3.9
1990	1.3	2.6	2.8	2.3	2.7	4.2	4.7	3.0	2.9	1.0	2.9	3.7
1991	4.6	5.7	6.9	5.8	5.0	1.4	0.8	1.2	-2.0	-1.4	-0.4	2.6
1992	1.4	1.0	1.2	0.6	0.2	-0.8	-1.0	-0.6	0.6	-	-0.6	-0.6
1993	-0.2	-0.4	-1.2	0.4	0.8	0.4	1.4	2.2	2.6	1.0	1.0	0.4
1994	0.8	-1.0	-0.6	-1.6	-2.4	-1.8	-2.8	-2.6	-2.4	-1.6	-1.6	-3.0
1995	-3.8	-3.2	-3.8	-1.8	-2.4	-2.0	1.2	-1.6	-2.2	-3.6	-2.6	-2.7
1996	-6.6	-4.1	-3.5	-3.7	-4.3	-4.3	-3.1	-3.7	-4.2	-3.8	-4.0	-3.2
1997	-2.8	-3.4	-3.8	-4.7	-4.3	-5.3	-5.3	-5.4	-5.0	-3.3	-2.4	-0.9
1998	-1.1	0.9	2.3	0.2	0.4	1.1	0.9	-2.0	-0.9	-1.6	-1.3	-2.2
1999	-2.7	-0.7	-2.0	-	-0.7	-0.4	1.4	0.5	1.6	-0.2	-0.9	-1.8
2000	-1.8	-0.9	-3.1	-0.5	-1.6	0.2	2.5	3.0	4.4	6.2	10.6	10.7
2001	9.1	9.8	10.5	9.7	6.0	5.7	3.7	2.8	2.6	0.4	0.4	-

Average Prime Rate Charged by Banks
Not seasonally adjusted
(Percent)

Year	Jan	Feb	Mar	Apr	May	Jun	Jul	Aug	Sep	Oct	Nov	Dec
1951	2.4	2.5	2.5	2.5	2.5	2.5	2.5	2.5	2.5	2.6	2.8	2.8
1952	3.0	3.0	3.0	3.0	3.0	3.0	3.0	3.0	3.0	3.0	3.0	3.0
1953	3.0	3.0	3.0	3.0	3.3	3.3	3.3	3.3	3.3	3.3	3.3	3.3
1954	3.3	3.3	3.1	3.0	3.0	3.0	3.0	3.0	3.0	3.0	3.0	3.0
1955	3.0	3.0	3.0	3.0	3.0	3.0	3.0	3.2	3.3	3.4	3.5	3.5
1956	3.5	3.5	3.5	3.7	3.8	3.8	3.8	3.8	4.0	4.0	4.0	4.0
1957	4.0	4.0	4.0	4.0	4.0	4.0	4.0	4.4	4.5	4.5	4.5	4.5
1958	4.3	4.0	4.0	3.8	3.5	3.5	3.5	3.5	3.8	4.0	4.0	4.0
1959	4.0	4.0	4.0	4.0	4.2	4.5	4.5	4.5	5.0	5.0	5.0	5.0
1960	5.0	5.0	5.0	5.0	5.0	5.0	5.0	4.8	4.5	4.5	4.5	4.5
1961	4.5	4.5	4.5	4.5	4.5	4.5	4.5	4.5	4.5	4.5	4.5	4.5
1962	4.5	4.5	4.5	4.5	4.5	4.5	4.5	4.5	4.5	4.5	4.5	4.5
1963	4.5	4.5	4.5	4.5	4.5	4.5	4.5	4.5	4.5	4.5	4.5	4.5
1964	4.5	4.5	4.5	4.5	4.5	4.5	4.5	4.5	4.5	4.5	4.5	4.5
1965	4.5	4.5	4.5	4.5	4.5	4.5	4.5	4.5	4.5	4.5	4.5	4.9
1966	5.0	5.0	5.3	5.5	5.5	5.5	5.8	5.9	6.0	6.0	6.0	6.0
1967	6.0	5.8	5.7	5.5	5.5	5.5	5.5	5.5	5.5	5.5	5.7	6.0
1968	6.0	6.0	6.0	6.2	6.5	6.5	6.5	6.5	6.4	6.3	6.3	6.6
1969	6.9	7.0	7.2	7.5	7.5	8.2	8.5	8.5	8.5	8.5	8.5	8.5
1970	8.5	8.5	8.4	8.0	8.0	8.0	8.0	8.0	7.8	7.5	7.3	6.9
1971	6.3	5.9	5.4	5.3	5.5	5.5	5.9	6.0	6.0	5.9	5.5	5.5
1972	5.2	4.8	4.8	5.0	5.0	5.0	5.3	5.3	5.5	5.7	5.8	5.8
1973	6.0	6.0	6.3	6.6	7.0	7.5	8.3	9.2	9.9	9.9	9.8	9.8
1974	9.7	9.2	8.9	10.0	11.3	11.5	12.0	12.0	12.0	11.7	10.8	10.5
1975	10.1	9.0	7.9	7.5	7.4	7.1	7.2	7.7	7.9	8.0	7.5	7.3
1976	7.0	6.8	6.8	6.8	6.8	7.2	7.3	7.0	7.0	6.8	6.5	6.3
1977	6.3	6.3	6.3	6.3	6.4	6.8	6.8	6.8	7.1	7.5	7.8	7.8
1978	7.9	8.0	8.0	8.0	8.3	8.6	9.0	9.0	9.4	9.9	10.9	11.6
1979	11.7	11.7	11.7	11.7	11.7	11.6	11.5	11.9	12.9	14.4	15.6	15.3
1980	15.2	15.6	18.3	19.8	16.6	12.6	11.5	11.1	12.2	13.8	16.1	20.3
1981	20.2	19.4	18.0	17.2	19.6	20.0	20.4	20.5	20.1	18.5	16.8	15.8
1982	15.8	16.6	16.5	16.5	16.5	16.5	16.3	14.4	13.5	12.5	11.9	11.5
1983	11.2	11.0	10.5	10.5	10.5	10.5	10.5	10.9	11.0	11.0	11.0	11.0
1984	11.0	11.0	11.2	11.9	12.4	12.6	13.0	13.0	13.0	12.6	11.8	11.1
1985	10.6	10.5	10.5	10.5	10.3	9.8	9.5	9.5	9.5	9.5	9.5	9.5
1986	9.5	9.5	9.1	8.8	8.5	8.5	8.2	7.9	7.5	7.5	7.5	7.5
1987	7.5	7.5	7.5	7.8	8.1	8.3	8.3	8.3	8.7	9.1	8.8	8.8
1988	8.8	8.5	8.5	8.5	8.8	9.0	9.3	9.8	10.0	10.0	10.1	10.5
1989	10.5	10.9	11.5	11.5	11.5	11.1	11.0	10.5	10.5	10.5	10.5	10.5
1990	10.1	10.0	10.0	10.0	10.0	10.0	10.0	10.0	10.0	10.0	10.0	10.0
1991	9.5	9.1	9.0	9.0	8.5	8.5	8.5	8.5	8.2	8.0	7.6	7.2
1992	6.5	6.5	6.5	6.5	6.5	6.5	6.0	6.0	6.0	6.0	6.0	6.0
1993	6.0	6.0	6.0	6.0	6.0	6.0	6.0	6.0	6.0	6.0	6.0	6.0
1994	6.0	6.0	6.1	6.4	7.0	7.3	7.3	7.5	7.8	7.8	8.1	8.5
1995	8.5	9.0	9.0	9.0	9.0	9.0	8.8	8.8	8.8	8.8	8.8	8.6
1996	8.5	8.3	8.3	8.3	8.3	8.3	8.3	8.3	8.3	8.3	8.3	8.3
1997	8.3	8.3	8.3	8.5	8.5	8.5	8.5	8.5	8.5	8.5	8.5	8.5
1998	8.5	8.5	8.5	8.5	8.5	8.5	8.5	8.5	8.5	8.1	7.9	7.8
1999	7.8	7.8	7.8	7.8	7.8	7.8	8.0	8.1	8.3	8.3	8.4	8.5
2000	8.5	8.7	8.8	9.0	9.2	9.5	9.5	9.5	9.5	9.5	9.5	9.5
2001	9.1	8.5	8.3	7.8	7.2	7.0	6.8	6.7	6.3	5.5	5.1	4.8

Source: The Conference Board. © 2002 The Conference Board. All Rights Reserved. No claim to original U.S. Government works pursuant to U.S. Contract No. 52-SABA-5-00128. Primary source(s): Board of Governors of the Federal Reserve System, Division of Monetary Affairs, Banking and Money Market Statistics Section, Stop 81, Washington, DC 20551. A dash (-) indicates that data are not available or zero.

Commercial and Industrial Loans Outstanding
(Millions of chained 1996 $)

Year	Jan	Feb	Mar	Apr	May	Jun	Jul	Aug	Sep	Oct	Nov	Dec
1959	133,068	133,043	134,096	135,111	137,293	139,083	138,720	140,519	141,037	141,923	142,557	143,345
1960	144,076	145,918	146,832	147,221	148,418	150,248	149,900	148,948	149,352	149,350	149,382	148,891
1961	148,765	148,495	149,229	149,179	148,819	148,459	148,409	148,816	149,015	149,053	149,338	149,960
1962	150,369	150,560	151,215	151,973	152,530	153,544	154,647	155,724	156,198	157,775	159,022	159,286
1963	159,134	159,356	160,049	160,984	161,483	161,637	161,904	162,465	163,762	165,577	168,629	170,495
1964	169,627	170,532	170,454	171,892	173,310	174,175	175,233	176,861	179,097	179,868	181,515	184,124
1965	187,436	191,881	195,667	198,118	201,981	203,575	204,902	209,343	213,539	216,323	219,526	221,479
1966	224,993	227,734	230,263	231,878	234,754	238,709	242,353	246,154	247,819	249,744	251,268	251,949
1967	254,226	256,100	258,776	260,370	261,515	263,438	264,200	262,504	262,902	264,140	265,313	268,530
1968	267,955	267,499	267,927	271,661	271,404	272,666	274,554	277,629	280,378	282,368	286,109	288,462
1969	294,639	296,907	300,258	306,656	309,673	312,765	312,860	316,603	319,861	322,295	323,501	325,663
1970	322,551	326,679	330,279	328,950	329,817	331,056	329,788	331,158	330,931	323,090	319,664	318,145
1971	317,088	318,563	318,459	313,720	315,109	310,403	306,864	311,656	317,392	313,536	312,366	309,384
1972	283,559	285,036	287,729	291,033	292,280	293,025	292,540	292,886	290,908	296,815	298,914	300,192
1973	306,300	316,872	321,281	324,102	326,721	331,440	334,729	336,857	335,409	337,220	338,215	338,136
1974	341,607	344,617	344,838	357,392	360,519	361,607	370,913	374,355	382,161	381,987	382,990	380,389
1975	380,099	375,292	370,262	364,667	355,841	347,446	342,719	338,344	332,976	328,120	323,911	322,399
1976	319,060	319,629	313,442	305,841	305,037	306,047	302,737	300,380	297,748	298,690	301,074	301,568
1977	300,568	301,534	300,892	300,806	301,046	302,247	300,324	302,177	302,532	304,163	304,880	305,884
1978	305,767	305,440	309,931	312,121	315,035	318,386	319,644	319,889	320,147	321,425	323,976	323,117
1979	326,930	329,678	331,367	339,823	341,741	345,847	350,591	355,207	361,478	359,663	355,167	357,932
1980	366,520	370,605	372,066	370,175	363,815	368,272	362,667	361,184	361,072	360,803	366,102	367,070
1981	367,168	364,080	358,584	363,696	371,567	377,033	381,476	387,424	391,257	393,680	397,145	400,927
1982	409,639	416,661	417,998	426,176	430,522	430,359	428,251	427,807	428,737	426,259	417,906	408,726
1983	412,879	412,404	412,887	404,520	396,676	396,339	394,345	394,885	393,387	390,883	391,770	397,449
1984	406,756	411,695	422,441	430,877	439,448	452,475	457,492	460,499	465,433	470,114	473,618	473,837
1985	472,426	474,190	475,431	475,112	477,959	474,747	477,540	478,446	475,616	479,919	482,486	483,519
1986	485,127	482,993	481,966	475,251	477,336	476,547	478,074	483,289	480,274	481,839	481,221	487,666
1987	494,742	490,532	487,018	484,928	482,941	482,378	480,005	474,450	477,048	478,823	476,090	478,668
1988	561,699	566,962	568,050	572,345	570,876	571,682	571,357	569,460	566,482	568,845	572,719	579,351
1989	582,239	590,538	590,431	590,689	600,813	601,457	603,552	609,422	606,877	606,156	607,689	608,213
1990	606,626	607,701	615,476	614,211	610,069	608,193	608,058	606,344	608,334	602,732	594,248	592,715
1991	590,128	580,839	581,909	574,524	566,239	562,192	558,179	545,970	537,732	532,095	529,290	521,366
1992	516,117	514,613	513,318	509,446	506,342	502,581	498,112	500,292	494,540	498,741	503,042	499,174
1993	498,459	497,469	491,798	492,668	496,425	497,578	499,398	497,392	495,423	491,828	490,441	491,457
1994	495,189	490,274	489,562	489,297	493,728	497,608	500,432	503,697	509,320	518,686	521,645	528,930
1995	535,649	544,636	549,238	558,685	560,255	565,076	567,211	570,268	571,408	574,699	570,672	578,316
1996	578,604	576,623	582,098	583,473	582,789	582,853	582,164	582,563	584,771	577,671	576,921	579,192
1997	583,557	583,987	587,181	587,303	592,459	601,088	605,455	609,761	616,729	621,495	630,533	630,735
1998	644,723	657,233	662,348	653,647	667,017	683,659	686,230	701,777	714,476	718,125	723,030	717,985
1999	725,503	734,535	740,604	742,661	747,915	746,364	754,746	760,925	767,108	775,279	780,235	794,934
2000	801,807	814,130	814,622	829,530	839,504	856,473	865,126	875,593	867,076	868,885	870,094	863,441
2001	837,715	822,381	799,424	788,110	777,746	741,805	721,206	715,042	713,417	698,263	686,248	-

Source: The Conference Board. © 2002 The Conference Board. All Rights Reserved. No claim to original U.S. Government works pursuant to U.S. Contract No. 52-SABA-5-00128. Primary source(s): Board of Governors of the Federal Reserve System, Division of Monetary Affairs, Banking and Money Market Statistics Section, Stop 84, Washington, DC 20551 and Board of Governors of the Federal Reserve System, Capital Markets, Banking and Money Market Statistics Section, Stop 84, Washington, DC 20551. A dash (-) indicates that data are not available or zero.

Ratio, Consumer Installment Credit to Personal Income
(Percent)

Year	Jan	Feb	Mar	Apr	May	Jun	Jul	Aug	Sep	Oct	Nov	Dec
1959	12.81	12.88	12.90	12.91	12.95	13.04	13.21	13.43	13.55	13.67	13.66	13.81
1960	13.76	13.82	13.92	14.03	14.04	14.13	14.19	14.22	14.29	14.29	14.36	14.48
1961	14.50	14.35	14.34	14.23	14.14	14.03	13.97	14.00	14.02	13.95	13.95	13.99
1962	14.01	13.99	13.98	14.05	14.18	14.24	14.26	14.34	14.34	14.43	14.49	14.54
1963	14.54	14.76	14.85	14.96	14.99	14.98	15.12	15.22	15.25	15.32	15.37	15.43
1964	15.51	15.61	15.70	15.74	15.82	15.85	15.92	15.92	16.01	16.10	16.06	16.07
1965	16.19	16.37	16.41	16.51	16.54	16.61	16.64	16.67	16.38	16.58	16.53	16.48
1966	16.61	16.59	16.59	16.60	16.61	16.56	16.49	16.43	16.29	16.22	16.18	16.21
1967	16.13	16.13	16.08	16.09	16.07	16.05	15.96	15.94	15.96	15.96	15.94	15.85
1968	15.73	15.72	15.64	15.64	15.62	15.60	15.60	15.57	15.58	15.68	15.69	15.77
1969	15.80	15.86	15.85	15.87	15.88	15.86	15.79	15.73	15.72	15.71	15.71	15.69
1970	15.73	15.69	15.62	15.28	15.36	15.42	15.36	15.31	15.29	15.33	15.26	15.24
1971	15.36	15.39	15.37	15.41	15.39	15.15	15.43	15.46	15.56	15.62	15.68	15.64
1972	15.57	15.53	15.61	15.67	15.77	16.07	15.89	15.86	15.89	15.71	15.68	15.76
1973	16.02	16.07	16.15	16.20	16.22	16.29	16.35	16.38	16.31	16.25	16.23	16.20
1974	16.27	16.28	16.28	16.29	16.20	16.14	16.04	16.03	15.93	15.77	15.74	15.63
1975	15.59	15.57	15.49	15.38	15.23	14.67	14.81	14.68	14.65	14.56	14.53	14.60
1976	14.53	14.50	14.53	14.58	14.54	14.59	14.54	14.50	14.54	14.61	14.53	14.59
1977	14.53	14.53	14.63	14.72	14.81	14.92	14.93	14.98	15.00	15.07	15.06	15.03
1978	15.10	15.12	15.17	15.17	15.31	15.46	15.47	15.53	15.58	15.53	15.59	15.60
1979	15.63	15.67	15.66	15.81	15.87	15.88	15.83	15.86	15.91	15.87	15.84	15.74
1980	15.61	15.63	15.54	15.47	15.30	15.10	14.90	14.78	14.62	14.41	14.24	14.14
1981	14.05	14.01	13.97	14.06	14.04	13.96	13.72	13.59	13.67	13.68	13.65	13.62
1982	13.74	13.69	13.67	13.63	13.60	13.62	13.55	13.53	13.55	13.49	13.47	13.51
1983	13.56	13.56	13.59	13.61	13.53	13.64	13.68	13.82	13.80	13.84	13.92	14.01
1984	14.04	14.18	14.20	14.21	14.46	14.57	14.63	14.69	14.67	14.90	14.94	15.00
1985	15.13	15.29	15.45	15.64	15.77	15.83	15.97	16.07	16.26	16.27	16.39	16.36
1986	16.50	16.55	16.50	16.67	16.77	16.80	16.86	16.90	17.01	17.19	17.12	17.03
1987	16.87	16.72	16.57	16.67	16.57	16.61	16.62	16.58	16.60	16.55	16.53	16.37
1988	16.50	16.51	16.49	16.52	16.55	16.50	16.42	16.48	16.40	16.33	16.34	16.22
1989	16.37	16.39	16.41	16.44	16.54	16.54	16.53	16.55	16.57	16.53	16.50	16.51
1990	16.40	16.27	16.19	16.07	16.07	16.02	16.00	16.00	15.93	15.99	15.97	15.78
1991	15.78	15.75	15.72	15.63	15.56	15.41	15.39	15.30	15.19	15.15	15.08	14.91
1992	14.84	14.72	14.66	14.55	14.47	14.42	14.40	14.45	14.34	14.20	14.20	14.25
1993	14.19	14.25	14.25	14.26	14.17	14.25	14.33	14.33	14.44	14.49	14.58	14.65
1994	14.80	14.76	14.85	14.96	15.06	15.22	15.27	15.43	15.54	15.57	15.75	15.83
1995	15.92	16.00	16.20	16.30	16.49	16.61	16.68	16.81	17.00	17.02	17.22	17.26
1996	17.35	17.36	17.41	17.49	17.54	17.57	17.69	17.71	17.66	17.68	17.71	17.64
1997	17.68	17.67	17.59	17.67	17.67	17.62	17.62	17.56	17.54	17.51	17.41	17.42
1998	17.27	17.20	17.19	17.27	17.20	17.25	17.24	17.23	17.31	17.33	17.31	17.32
1999	17.47	17.55	17.61	17.56	17.61	17.60	17.63	17.64	17.66	17.59	17.66	17.69
2000	17.75	17.78	17.77	17.72	17.76	17.86	17.91	18.01	18.01	18.09	18.21	18.19
2001	18.31	18.40	18.42	18.52	18.57	18.50	18.41	18.44	18.49	18.64	18.87	-

Source: The Conference Board. © 2002 The Conference Board. All Rights Reserved. No claim to original U.S. Government works pursuant to U.S. Contract No. 52-SABA-5-00128. Primary source(s): Board of Governors of the Federal Reserve System (consumer installment credit), Publication Services, Stop 127, Washington, DC 20551 and U.S. Department of Commerce (personal income), Bureau of Economic Analysis, National Income and Wealth Division, BE-54, Washington, DC 20230. A dash (-) indicates that data are not available or zero.

Change in CPI for Services
(6-Month percent, Annual Rate)

Year	Jan	Feb	Mar	Apr	May	Jun	Jul	Aug	Sep	Oct	Nov	Dec
1956	-	-	-	-	-	-	1.9	2.9	3.9	2.9	3.9	3.9
1957	4.8	3.8	4.8	4.8	4.8	4.7	3.8	4.7	3.7	4.7	4.7	3.7
1958	4.6	4.6	3.7	3.7	3.6	3.6	3.6	2.7	3.6	2.7	1.8	1.8
1959	1.8	2.7	1.8	2.6	3.5	3.5	3.5	3.5	4.4	4.4	3.5	4.4
1960	3.5	3.4	3.4	2.6	3.4	2.5	3.4	2.5	2.5	2.5	2.5	2.5
1961	2.5	2.5	1.7	2.5	1.7	1.7	0.8	1.6	1.6	1.6	1.6	2.5
1962	2.5	1.6	2.5	1.6	2.4	1.6	2.4	2.4	1.6	1.6	1.6	1.6
1963	1.6	1.6	1.6	2.4	1.6	2.4	1.6	2.4	2.4	1.6	2.4	2.4
1964	2.4	1.6	1.6	2.4	1.6	1.6	1.6	1.6	1.6	1.6	2.3	1.5
1965	2.3	3.1	3.1	3.1	2.3	2.3	2.3	1.5	2.3	2.3	3.0	3.0
1966	3.0	3.0	3.0	3.8	3.8	4.5	5.3	5.3	6.0	5.2	5.9	5.2
1967	4.4	5.1	4.3	4.3	2.9	4.3	3.6	3.6	3.5	4.2	4.2	4.2
1968	4.9	4.9	5.6	4.9	5.6	5.5	6.2	6.9	6.1	6.8	6.8	6.7
1969	6.7	6.0	7.3	7.2	7.9	7.2	7.1	7.8	7.7	7.0	6.9	7.6
1970	8.2	8.1	8.7	9.3	9.2	9.2	8.5	8.4	7.1	7.1	7.0	7.0
1971	6.9	6.3	5.1	4.5	3.9	4.5	3.9	4.4	5.0	5.0	5.0	3.8
1972	4.4	3.8	3.8	3.8	3.8	3.7	3.2	3.2	3.2	3.2	3.2	3.1
1973	3.1	3.1	3.7	3.6	3.6	4.1	4.1	5.2	5.7	7.7	8.8	8.7
1974	9.8	9.2	9.6	8.0	8.9	9.9	10.8	12.3	12.6	13.6	12.9	12.8
1975	11.7	11.1	9.1	8.5	7.6	7.0	6.6	6.1	7.4	7.3	9.0	9.0
1976	10.7	10.6	10.1	9.6	7.4	7.3	6.4	6.4	6.8	7.1	7.9	7.9
1977	7.8	7.8	7.7	8.1	7.6	8.0	8.3	8.3	7.8	7.4	8.1	7.7
1978	7.2	7.6	7.9	8.6	8.5	9.2	9.5	9.8	10.4	10.3	10.6	9.5
1979	9.4	9.7	9.2	9.5	10.1	11.4	12.3	13.1	13.7	14.5	15.4	16.2
1980	16.9	17.0	18.7	19.4	19.1	20.4	15.3	12.2	9.8	9.1	9.2	8.3
1981	11.8	13.7	14.1	13.7	13.5	13.3	14.7	15.4	16.8	15.6	14.6	13.0
1982	10.6	9.1	6.2	7.1	7.0	7.7	7.6	8.0	7.8	6.4	4.2	0.8
1983	1.0	0.6	1.0	1.6	2.5	4.8	4.4	3.9	4.3	4.1	4.9	4.9
1984	5.1	5.7	5.7	5.6	5.2	5.2	5.6	5.5	5.7	5.5	5.5	5.6
1985	4.8	4.8	4.8	4.6	5.1	5.1	5.5	5.3	4.9	5.2	5.0	5.0
1986	5.1	5.1	5.7	5.6	4.9	5.4	4.7	4.6	4.3	4.1	4.2	3.5
1987	3.8	3.8	3.6	4.0	4.1	4.3	4.1	4.4	4.8	4.4	4.4	4.4
1988	4.7	4.3	4.2	4.5	4.5	4.8	4.4	4.8	5.1	4.9	5.0	4.8
1989	5.0	4.8	4.8	4.8	4.9	4.9	5.3	5.3	4.8	5.1	4.9	5.1
1990	4.9	4.9	5.8	5.6	5.4	6.0	6.1	6.9	6.4	6.2	6.3	5.5
1991	6.1	5.5	5.2	4.7	4.7	4.5	3.8	3.6	3.9	4.3	4.3	4.6
1992	4.4	4.1	4.0	4.0	3.8	3.5	3.4	3.5	3.2	3.6	3.9	3.9
1993	4.1	4.1	4.2	3.9	3.9	4.0	3.8	3.8	3.9	3.6	3.5	3.5
1994	3.3	3.7	3.8	3.5	3.1	2.9	2.9	2.9	2.6	2.7	3.2	3.1
1995	3.7	3.4	3.7	3.9	3.7	4.0	3.4	3.3	3.1	3.2	3.1	2.7
1996	3.1	3.3	3.1	3.0	3.3	3.4	3.5	3.3	3.5	3.4	3.4	3.5
1997	3.2	3.2	3.1	3.1	2.7	2.8	2.7	2.5	2.6	2.8	3.0	2.8
1998	2.7	2.8	2.7	2.6	2.4	2.4	2.4	2.6	2.5	2.3	2.5	2.6
1999	2.5	2.3	2.5	2.7	2.3	2.2	2.5	2.6	2.5	2.4	3.0	3.0
2000	3.3	3.3	3.6	3.6	3.4	4.0	3.9	4.2	4.0	4.2	4.2	3.9
2001	5.0	4.7	4.8	4.6	4.8	5.0	3.4	3.7	2.9	2.7	2.8	-

Source: The Conference Board. © 2002 The Conference Board. All Rights Reserved. No claim to original U.S. Government works pursuant to U.S. Contract No. 52-SABA-5-00128. Primary source(s): U.S. Department of Labor, Bureau of Labor Statistics, Office of Prices and Living Conditions, Division of Consumer Prices and Price Indexes, Washington, DC 20212. A dash (-) indicates that data are not available or zero.

RATIO, COINCIDENT TO LAGGING INDEX

The composite indexes of coincident and the lagging indicators are used to create what is sometimes referred to as the "second" or the "best" leading indicator—the ratio of the coincident to the lagging index. The "coincident to lagging ratio" tends to signal changes in the economy's turning points (especially downturns) *sooner* than the leading index.

For example, in the 1970 recession the leading index signaled the downturn 8 months ahead of time, the ratio 13 months earlier. In other recessionary periods, similar results were noted: 1974-75, leading was 8, the ratio 11 months in advance of actual events; in 1980, leading was 15, the ratio 21; in 1982, leading was 2, the ratio was 9.

The ratio has been less predictive of turn-arounds. In 1970 it turned up as the economy turned up (acting as a coincident indicator), whereas the leading index gave a one-month warning; in 1974-1975, this pattern repeated; in 1980 and 1982, both the leading index and the ratio turned up 10 months ahead of the economy's actual turn-around.

The coincident to lagging ratio tends to work because of the manner in which its components—the coincident and the lagging indexes—behave. The lagging index tends to reflect the *past* of a business cycle, the coincident index its *present*. As the coincident index reaches a turning point, its rate of change tends to be smaller than that of the lagging indicator. If, for example, the economy is approaching a peak, monthly growth reflected in the coincident indicator will be small; meanwhile, the lagging indicator, which reflects events a few months back, will still be growing rapidly. The ratio between the two will, therefore, turn down, signaling a future decline in the economy as the peak is reached and passed. The process works in the same manner as a trough is reached: the composite index will decline less than the lagging index (which is still mirroring the earlier period of the recession); the consequence is an upturn in the ratio promising the start of an expansion soon.

Components of the Ratio

The ratio is expressed as an index with a 1996 base (1996 = 100) and is constructed by dividing the composite index value for a month by the lagging index value for the same month.

Bibliography

1. Carnes, W. Stansbury and Stephen D. Slifer. *The Atlas of Economic Indicators*. HarperCollins, 1991.

2. Frumkin, Norman. *Guide to Economic Indicators*. M.E. Sharpe, Inc., 1990.

3. *Leading Economic Indicators*. The Confenrence Board, 845 Third Avenue, New York, NY 10022-6679.

Ratio, Coincident Index to Lagging Index
(1996=100)

Year	Jan	Feb	Mar	Apr	May	Jun	Jul	Aug	Sep	Oct	Nov	Dec
1959	46.3	46.5	46.9	47.1	47.2	47.2	46.8	45.6	45.3	45.0	45.3	46.3
1960	47.0	46.8	46.3	46.5	45.8	45.5	45.3	45.4	45.5	45.5	45.2	44.7
1961	44.7	44.8	45.3	45.7	46.2	46.9	47.3	47.7	47.5	47.9	48.4	48.4
1962	48.0	48.4	48.4	48.6	48.6	48.4	48.5	48.4	48.5	48.6	48.6	48.6
1963	48.6	48.8	49.0	49.2	49.3	49.3	49.3	49.2	49.3	49.5	49.2	49.3
1964	49.6	49.8	49.7	49.8	50.2	50.4	50.6	50.5	50.6	50.3	50.9	51.4
1965	51.1	51.0	51.3	51.3	51.2	51.3	51.6	51.7	51.7	52.1	52.2	52.5
1966	52.5	52.5	52.9	52.7	52.5	52.5	52.4	52.5	52.6	53.0	52.7	52.9
1967	53.0	52.8	52.8	52.9	53.1	52.9	53.0	53.6	53.7	53.6	54.3	54.8
1968	54.6	54.7	54.8	54.8	54.9	55.1	55.4	55.2	55.4	55.6	55.8	55.7
1969	55.6	55.7	55.7	55.6	55.4	55.6	55.7	55.8	55.8	56.1	55.8	55.8
1970	55.2	55.3	55.3	55.5	55.6	55.5	56.0	55.8	56.0	55.5	55.5	56.5
1971	57.1	57.1	57.4	57.9	58.2	58.6	58.3	58.1	58.4	58.8	59.2	59.7
1972	61.1	61.4	61.6	61.8	61.8	61.7	61.9	62.6	63.1	63.7	64.3	64.7
1973	64.3	64.2	63.8	63.5	63.5	63.3	63.3	62.8	63.0	63.6	63.7	63.1
1974	62.4	62.3	62.2	61.7	61.7	61.7	61.5	61.0	60.7	60.6	59.8	58.8
1975	58.7	58.7	58.6	59.5	60.2	61.9	62.2	63.2	63.7	63.9	64.4	64.6
1976	65.3	65.8	66.2	66.6	67.0	67.3	67.6	67.8	68.0	67.8	68.4	68.9
1977	69.1	69.3	69.8	69.9	70.2	70.2	70.3	70.4	70.7	70.8	71.0	71.4
1978	70.6	70.9	71.2	72.6	72.3	72.4	72.3	72.5	72.4	72.7	72.5	72.6
1979	72.3	72.4	73.2	71.8	72.3	71.9	71.6	71.3	70.7	70.7	70.6	70.5
1980	70.6	70.3	69.3	68.3	68.1	68.6	69.9	71.0	72.2	73.2	73.6	73.3
1981	73.2	73.0	73.3	73.0	72.4	72.5	73.0	72.7	72.0	71.9	71.8	71.6
1982	71.0	72.2	72.5	72.3	72.5	72.1	72.0	71.9	71.9	72.3	72.9	73.7
1983	74.7	74.6	75.3	75.7	76.6	77.0	77.6	77.0	78.1	78.7	78.6	78.9
1984	79.5	79.1	79.0	79.1	79.0	78.9	78.6	78.4	78.5	78.2	78.5	78.6
1985	78.6	78.8	79.0	79.1	79.0	78.8	78.7	78.9	79.3	78.8	78.9	79.1
1986	79.4	79.2	79.1	80.0	79.8	79.8	80.1	80.3	81.1	80.5	80.8	81.8
1987	80.9	82.1	82.5	82.5	82.7	82.9	83.4	83.6	83.6	83.9	84.2	84.8
1988	84.3	84.8	85.1	84.9	85.1	85.1	85.6	85.6	86.0	86.0	86.3	86.9
1989	86.9	86.2	86.1	86.6	85.7	85.5	85.1	85.7	85.8	85.4	86.0	86.0
1990	86.5	87.0	87.1	87.2	87.3	87.4	87.4	87.4	87.1	86.8	86.5	86.7
1991	86.0	86.5	86.4	87.3	87.8	88.8	89.2	89.6	90.3	90.5	90.7	90.9
1992	91.9	92.6	92.9	93.7	94.1	94.6	95.1	94.6	95.3	95.9	95.9	96.3
1993	96.7	96.8	96.5	96.7	96.9	97.1	96.9	97.2	97.4	98.0	98.2	98.5
1994	98.3	99.1	99.8	99.8	100.0	99.8	99.8	100.1	99.9	100.1	99.7	99.9
1995	99.7	99.1	98.8	98.3	98.1	97.8	97.5	98.2	98.2	98.1	98.4	98.5
1996	98.2	98.9	99.1	99.4	99.8	100.2	100.0	100.6	100.7	100.9	101.3	101.2
1997	101.4	102.2	102.5	102.7	102.6	103.1	104.0	104.0	104.3	104.5	104.6	105.1
1998	105.3	105.4	105.5	106.1	106.2	105.7	105.6	106.0	106.2	106.6	106.8	107.4
1999	106.8	107.4	107.4	107.2	107.8	108.4	108.2	108.6	108.0	108.5	108.9	109.2
2000	109.6	108.6	109.7	109.6	109.7	109.2	108.9	108.9	108.7	108.4	108.0	108.5
2001	108.4	108.8	109.3	109.2	109.8	110.2	111.8	112.2	111.2	111.5	112.0	-

Source: The Conference Board. © 2002 The Conference Board. All Rights Reserved. No claim to original U.S. Government works pursuant to U.S. Contract No. 52-SABA-5-00128. Primary source(s): The Conference Board, Inc., Economics Group, 845 Third Avenue, New York, NY 10022. A dash (-) indicates that data are not available or zero.

CHAPTER 4

CYCLIC INDICATORS

CYCLIC INDICATORS

The Business Cycle Indicators include, all told, 21 economic series which have been found, over time, to work well as indicators of cyclic change in the economy. In this section are presented 28 other economic series which are also considered cyclic indicators but are not part of the composite indexes of leading, coincident, and lagging indicators. They are grouped under seven headings:

Employment
Production and Income
Consumption, Trade, Orders, and Deliveries
Fixed Capital Investment
Inventories and Inventory Investment
Prices, Costs, and Profits
Money and Credit

A brief introduction to each of these sections provides a description of each series covered, the principal analytical uses of each series, and a listing of related series which are included under the Business Cycle Indicators heading. All series are shown from 1951 to 2001, unless the series are only available from a later year.

Bibliography

1. Fischer, Stanley, Rudiger Dornbusch, and Richard Schmalensee. *Introduction to Macroeconomics*. McGraw-Hill Book Company, New York, 1988.

2. Fitch, Thomas P. *Dictionary of Banking Terms*. Barron's, New York, 1990.

3. Siegel, Barry N. *Money, Banking, and the Economy*. Academic Press, New York, 1982.

3. U.S. Department of Commerce, Bureau of Economic Analysis. *Survey of Current Business*. Superintendent of Documents, U.S. Government Printing Office, Washington, DC 20302.

INDICATORS OF EMPLOYMENT

In modern industrial economies, employment is the single most important indicator of economic well-being—and decline in employment a signal of economic woes. This section presents two series:

   Unemployment rate
   Number of persons unemployed

Related series, reported under Business Cycle Indicators, are:

   Average weekly hours in manufacturing (Leading Index)
   Average weekly initial claims for unemployment insurance (Leading Index)
   Employment on nonagricultural payrolls (Coincident Index)
   Average duration of unemployment in weeks (Lagging Index)

Unemployment Rate. Data are presented for persons unemployed 15 weeks and over as a percent of the work force. The series behaves as a lagging indicator but is not part of the composite index of lagging indicators.

Number of Persons Unemployed. Data show total number of people unemployed in thousands. The series is classified as a leading indicator at business cycle peaks, as a lagging indicator of business cycle troughs, and is unclassified overall.

Unemployment Rate, 15 Weeks and Over
(Percent)

Year	Jan	Feb	Mar	Apr	May	Jun	Jul	Aug	Sep	Oct	Nov	Dec
1951	0.7	0.6	0.6	0.5	0.4	0.4	0.4	0.4	0.4	0.4	0.5	0.4
1952	0.5	0.4	0.4	0.4	0.4	0.3	0.3	0.3	0.4	0.4	0.3	0.4
1953	0.4	0.3	0.3	0.3	0.3	0.3	0.3	0.3	0.3	0.3	0.4	0.5
1954	0.6	0.8	1.2	1.2	1.4	1.4	1.5	1.6	1.6	1.6	1.5	1.3
1955	1.4	1.3	1.3	1.3	1.1	1.0	1.0	0.8	0.9	0.9	0.9	0.9
1956	0.8	0.8	0.8	0.7	0.8	0.8	0.8	0.8	0.9	0.8	0.9	0.9
1957	0.8	0.8	0.8	0.8	0.8	0.8	0.8	0.8	0.8	1.0	1.0	1.1
1958	1.3	1.5	1.7	2.1	2.2	2.5	2.6	2.8	2.6	2.5	2.3	2.2
1959	2.1	1.9	1.8	1.5	1.4	1.4	1.3	1.3	1.3	1.3	1.4	1.3
1960	1.3	1.2	1.4	1.3	1.1	1.2	1.3	1.3	1.4	1.7	1.7	1.6
1961	1.9	2.0	2.1	2.3	2.4	2.3	2.6	2.3	2.2	2.1	2.0	1.9
1962	1.8	1.8	1.7	1.6	1.6	1.5	1.5	1.5	1.5	1.4	1.5	1.5
1963	1.6	1.6	1.5	1.5	1.6	1.5	1.5	1.6	1.5	1.5	1.5	1.4
1964	1.5	1.4	1.4	1.3	1.3	1.4	1.4	1.3	1.3	1.2	1.3	1.2
1965	1.1	1.2	1.1	1.1	1.0	1.1	0.9	1.0	1.0	0.9	0.9	0.9
1966	0.8	0.8	0.8	0.8	0.7	0.6	0.6	0.6	0.6	0.6	0.6	0.6
1967	0.6	0.6	0.6	0.6	0.5	0.5	0.5	0.6	0.6	0.6	0.6	0.6
1968	0.6	0.6	0.6	0.5	0.5	0.5	0.5	0.5	0.5	0.5	0.5	0.4
1969	0.4	0.4	0.4	0.5	0.5	0.5	0.5	0.5	0.5	0.5	0.5	0.5
1970	0.5	0.6	0.6	0.7	0.7	0.8	0.8	0.9	0.9	0.9	1.0	1.3
1971	1.3	1.3	1.3	1.4	1.4	1.4	1.5	1.5	1.5	1.5	1.5	1.5
1972	1.5	1.5	1.4	1.4	1.3	1.3	1.3	1.3	1.3	1.3	1.2	1.1
1973	1.1	1.0	1.0	0.9	0.9	0.9	0.8	0.9	0.9	0.9	0.9	0.8
1974	0.9	0.9	0.9	1.0	1.0	1.0	1.0	1.0	1.1	1.2	1.2	1.4
1975	1.7	2.0	2.2	2.6	2.8	3.0	3.1	3.0	3.1	2.9	3.0	3.0
1976	2.9	2.7	2.6	2.3	2.2	2.4	2.4	2.5	2.4	2.4	2.4	2.4
1977	2.3	2.2	2.1	2.0	2.0	1.9	1.9	1.8	1.9	1.8	1.8	1.7
1978	1.6	1.6	1.5	1.5	1.4	1.3	1.3	1.2	1.3	1.3	1.2	1.2
1979	1.2	1.2	1.3	1.2	1.2	1.1	1.1	1.1	1.1	1.2	1.2	1.2
1980	1.3	1.3	1.4	1.6	1.6	1.6	1.9	2.0	2.2	2.1	2.2	2.2
1981	2.2	2.2	2.1	2.0	2.0	2.1	2.0	2.1	2.1	2.1	2.1	2.2
1982	2.2	2.5	2.7	2.8	3.0	3.1	3.2	3.3	3.5	3.8	4.0	4.2
1983	4.2	4.2	4.2	3.9	4.1	4.0	3.9	3.6	3.4	3.3	3.1	3.0
1984	2.9	2.7	2.6	2.5	2.5	2.3	2.3	2.3	2.2	2.2	2.1	2.1
1985	2.0	2.1	2.1	2.1	2.0	2.0	2.0	2.0	1.9	2.0	1.9	1.9
1986	1.8	2.0	1.9	1.8	1.9	2.0	1.9	1.9	2.0	1.8	1.9	1.8
1987	1.8	1.8	1.7	1.8	1.8	1.7	1.6	1.6	1.6	1.5	1.5	1.5
1988	1.4	1.4	1.4	1.3	1.4	1.3	1.3	1.3	1.3	1.3	1.2	1.2
1989	1.2	1.1	1.1	1.1	1.1	1.0	1.2	1.0	1.1	1.1	1.1	1.1
1990	1.1	1.1	1.1	1.1	1.1	1.1	1.2	1.3	1.3	1.3	1.5	1.4
1991	1.5	1.6	1.7	1.7	1.8	2.0	1.9	2.0	2.0	2.1	2.1	2.3
1992	2.4	2.5	2.5	2.4	2.7	2.9	2.8	2.8	2.7	2.7	2.6	2.8
1993	2.6	2.5	2.4	2.3	2.4	2.4	2.4	2.3	2.4	2.3	2.3	2.3
1994	2.3	2.4	2.3	2.2	2.2	2.1	2.2	2.1	2.1	2.2	2.0	1.9
1995	1.8	1.8	1.7	1.9	2.0	1.7	1.7	1.8	1.7	1.7	1.8	1.8
1996	1.8	1.7	1.8	1.8	1.8	1.8	1.7	1.7	1.7	1.7	1.6	1.6
1997	1.6	1.6	1.6	1.6	1.6	1.5	1.6	1.5	1.5	1.4	1.3	1.4
1998	1.3	1.3	1.3	1.1	1.1	1.2	1.2	1.2	1.2	1.1	1.1	1.1
1999	1.1	1.1	1.1	1.1	1.1	1.2	1.1	1.0	1.0	1.0	1.0	1.0
2000	1.0	0.9	0.9	0.9	1.0	0.9	1.0	1.0	0.9	0.9	0.9	0.9
2001	1.0	1.0	1.1	1.1	1.1	1.1	1.2	1.3	1.3	1.4	1.6	1.7

Source: The Conference Board. © 2002 The Conference Board. All Rights Reserved. No claim to original U.S. Government works pursuant to U.S. Contract No. 52-SABA-5-00128. Primary source(s): U.S. Department of Labor, Bureau of Labor Statistics, Office of Employment and Unemployment Statistics, Division of Labor Force Statistics, Washington, DC 20212. A dash (-) indicates that data are not available or zero.

Number of Persons Unemployed

(Thousands)

Year	Jan	Feb	Mar	Apr	May	Jun	Jul	Aug	Sep	Oct	Nov	Dec
1951	2,305	2,117	2,125	1,919	1,856	1,995	1,950	1,933	2,067	2,194	2,178	1,960
1952	1,972	1,957	1,813	1,811	1,863	1,884	1,991	2,087	1,936	1,839	1,743	1,667
1953	1,839	1,636	1,647	1,723	1,596	1,607	1,660	1,665	1,821	1,974	2,211	2,818
1954	3,077	3,331	3,607	3,749	3,767	3,551	3,659	3,854	3,927	3,666	3,402	3,196
1955	3,157	2,969	2,918	3,049	2,747	2,701	2,632	2,784	2,678	2,830	2,780	2,761
1956	2,666	2,606	2,764	2,650	2,861	2,882	2,952	2,701	2,635	2,571	2,861	2,790
1957	2,796	2,622	2,509	2,600	2,710	2,856	2,796	2,747	2,943	3,020	3,454	3,476
1958	3,875	4,303	4,492	5,016	5,021	4,944	5,079	5,025	4,821	4,570	4,188	4,191
1959	4,068	3,965	3,801	3,571	3,479	3,429	3,528	3,588	3,775	3,910	4,003	3,653
1960	3,615	3,329	3,726	3,620	3,569	3,766	3,836	3,946	3,884	4,252	4,330	4,617
1961	4,671	4,832	4,853	4,893	5,003	4,885	4,928	4,682	4,676	4,573	4,295	4,177
1962	4,081	3,871	3,921	3,906	3,863	3,844	3,819	4,013	3,961	3,803	4,024	3,907
1963	4,074	4,238	4,072	4,055	4,217	3,977	4,051	3,878	3,957	3,987	4,151	3,975
1964	4,029	3,932	3,950	3,918	3,764	3,814	3,608	3,655	3,712	3,726	3,551	3,651
1965	3,572	3,730	3,510	3,595	3,432	3,387	3,301	3,254	3,216	3,143	3,073	3,031
1966	2,988	2,820	2,887	2,828	2,950	2,872	2,876	2,900	2,798	2,798	2,770	2,912
1967	2,968	2,915	2,889	2,895	2,929	2,992	2,944	2,945	2,958	3,143	3,066	3,018
1968	2,878	3,001	2,877	2,709	2,740	2,938	2,883	2,768	2,686	2,689	2,715	2,685
1969	2,718	2,692	2,712	2,758	2,713	2,816	2,868	2,856	3,040	3,049	2,856	2,884
1970	3,201	3,453	3,635	3,797	3,919	4,071	4,175	4,256	4,456	4,591	4,898	5,076
1971	4,986	4,903	4,987	4,959	4,996	4,949	5,035	5,134	5,042	4,954	5,161	5,154
1972	5,019	4,928	5,038	4,959	4,922	4,923	4,913	4,939	4,849	4,875	4,602	4,543
1973	4,326	4,452	4,394	4,459	4,329	4,363	4,305	4,305	4,350	4,144	4,396	4,489
1974	4,644	4,731	4,634	4,618	4,705	4,927	5,063	5,022	5,437	5,523	6,140	6,636
1975	7,501	7,520	7,978	8,210	8,433	8,220	8,127	7,928	7,923	7,897	7,794	7,744
1976	7,534	7,326	7,230	7,330	7,053	7,322	7,490	7,518	7,380	7,430	7,620	7,545
1977	7,280	7,443	7,307	7,059	6,911	7,134	6,829	6,925	6,751	6,763	6,815	6,386
1978	6,489	6,318	6,337	6,180	6,127	6,028	6,309	6,080	6,125	5,947	6,077	6,228
1979	6,109	6,173	6,109	6,069	5,840	5,959	5,996	6,320	6,190	6,296	6,238	6,325
1980	6,683	6,702	6,729	7,358	7,984	8,098	8,363	8,281	8,021	8,088	8,023	7,718
1981	8,071	8,051	7,982	7,869	8,174	8,098	7,863	8,036	8,230	8,646	9,029	9,267
1982	9,397	9,705	9,895	10,244	10,335	10,538	10,849	10,881	11,217	11,529	11,938	12,051
1983	11,534	11,545	11,408	11,268	11,154	11,246	10,548	10,623	10,282	9,887	9,499	9,331
1984	9,008	8,791	8,746	8,762	8,456	8,226	8,537	8,519	8,367	8,381	8,198	8,358
1985	8,423	8,321	8,339	8,395	8,302	8,460	8,513	8,196	8,248	8,298	8,128	8,138
1986	7,795	8,402	8,383	8,364	8,439	8,508	8,319	8,135	8,310	8,243	8,159	7,883
1987	7,892	7,865	7,862	7,542	7,574	7,398	7,268	7,261	7,102	7,227	7,035	6,936
1988	6,953	6,929	6,876	6,601	6,779	6,546	6,605	6,843	6,604	6,568	6,537	6,518
1989	6,682	6,359	6,205	6,468	6,375	6,577	6,495	6,511	6,590	6,630	6,725	6,667
1990	6,752	6,651	6,598	6,797	6,742	6,590	6,922	7,188	7,368	7,459	7,764	7,901
1991	8,015	8,265	8,586	8,439	8,736	8,692	8,586	8,666	8,722	8,842	8,931	9,198
1992	9,283	9,454	9,460	9,415	9,744	10,040	9,850	9,787	9,781	9,398	9,565	9,557
1993	9,325	9,183	9,056	9,110	9,149	9,121	8,930	8,763	8,714	8,750	8,542	8,477
1994	8,630	8,583	8,470	8,331	7,915	7,927	7,946	7,933	7,734	7,632	7,375	7,230
1995	7,375	7,187	7,153	7,645	7,430	7,427	7,527	7,484	7,478	7,328	7,426	7,423
1996	7,491	7,313	7,318	7,415	7,423	7,095	7,337	6,882	6,979	7,031	7,236	7,253
1997	7,158	7,102	7,000	6,873	6,655	6,799	6,655	6,608	6,656	6,454	6,308	6,476
1998	6,364	6,288	6,433	5,984	6,029	6,216	6,272	6,185	6,284	6,273	6,094	6,047
1999	5,953	6,024	5,780	6,054	5,809	5,943	6,032	5,839	5,906	5,793	5,739	5,700
2000	5,619	5,701	5,663	5,531	5,761	5,602	5,730	5,815	5,585	5,528	5,642	5,656
2001	5,887	5,888	6,061	6,310	6,210	6,465	6,545	6,972	7,064	7,665	8,026	8,259

INDICATORS OF PRODUCTION AND INCOME

Production and personal income are indicators of overall economic performance. They are cyclic indicators which tend to be coincident: they turn up or down as the economy does. This section presents four series:

    Personal income
    Wages and salaries
    Industrial Production in the U.S.
    Capacity utilization rate, all industry
    Capacity utilization rate, manufacturing

Related series, reported under Business Cycle Indicators, are:

    Index of industrial production (Coincident Index)
    Personal income less transfer payments (Coincident Index)

Personal Income. Data are reported in billions of dollars and billions of chained 1996 dollars. Monthly data are annualized, meaning that monthly survey results are multiplied by 12 months. Although not part of any composite index of economic indicators, personal income is viewed as a coincident cyclic indicator. The category includes all income received by individuals from any source, including dividends, rents, and transfer payments (welfare, social security, unemployment benefits, medicaid, etc.).

Wages and Salaries. Data are for wages and salaries in mining, manufacturing, and construction and are reported in billions of chained 1996 dollars. Monthly data are annualized, showing what would be annual results if the month's results were applied to the year as a whole. The series behaves as a coincident indicator overall but is not a component of a composite index.

Industrial Production in the U.S. The index of production is based on the year 1990 (1990=100). This data series is frequently used to compare U.S. to international production data.

Capacity Utilization Rate, All Industry. Data are shown as percent of total capacity. The series can be used as a cyclic indicator (it is leading at the peak of the business cycle and coincident at the trough) and as an indicator of inflation. High rates of capacity utilization signal high rates of production and hence upward pressure on prices.

Capacity Utilization Rate, Manufacturing. Data are in percent. The series is a leading indicator at the peak and a coincident indicator at the trough of a cycle.

Personal Income
(Annual Rate, Billions of $)

Year	Jan	Feb	Mar	Apr	May	Jun	Jul	Aug	Sep	Oct	Nov	Dec
1959	382.1	384.5	387.7	391.0	393.9	396.3	396.5	395.0	396.2	397.8	401.2	405.7
1960	407.0	407.7	408.6	411.3	412.8	413.1	414.0	414.5	415.4	417.2	416.8	414.6
1961	418.3	420.3	421.6	422.2	425.6	430.1	432.3	432.9	434.1	438.4	442.6	445.1
1962	444.6	447.8	451.6	454.6	455.7	457.3	459.3	460.7	463.2	464.5	466.9	468.7
1963	472.3	470.1	471.8	473.2	476.0	479.7	480.8	483.4	486.5	490.4	491.9	496.4
1964	499.5	502.0	504.6	507.8	510.9	513.7	516.9	521.1	524.1	525.1	529.0	534.9
1965	538.4	538.6	541.8	545.3	549.5	552.8	556.9	559.5	574.5	571.8	577.2	582.3
1966	584.3	589.2	593.4	595.3	598.0	602.7	606.7	612.3	617.8	622.3	627.0	627.9
1967	633.6	634.7	638.9	639.4	641.8	646.4	652.1	656.9	659.1	660.7	666.8	674.1
1968	678.8	686.7	694.9	700.6	706.7	712.1	718.9	724.8	730.3	734.9	740.4	744.6
1969	748.1	753.3	760.0	765.8	771.7	777.7	785.3	792.4	797.3	802.1	805.7	810.7
1970	812.7	817.2	821.5	840.2	836.9	837.7	845.5	850.4	855.7	855.1	857.1	863.4
1971	873.2	876.6	882.9	888.8	895.6	916.2	906.7	913.9	917.8	921.3	928.8	939.2
1972	948.1	959.2	965.6	972.0	978.1	971.9	989.8	1,002.4	1,010.5	1,032.6	1,046.5	1,054.4
1973	1,056.7	1,067.6	1,076.9	1,085.0	1,098.0	1,107.3	1,114.9	1,125.0	1,136.7	1,153.5	1,166.6	1,173.3
1974	1,175.9	1,182.3	1,187.8	1,194.3	1,209.0	1,220.1	1,236.5	1,243.3	1,253.4	1,265.6	1,266.0	1,273.0
1975	1,276.8	1,281.2	1,285.2	1,291.8	1,304.6	1,336.1	1,333.8	1,350.2	1,361.3	1,376.4	1,386.3	1,396.9
1976	1,414.2	1,426.0	1,433.5	1,443.8	1,453.8	1,462.0	1,480.7	1,493.6	1,504.0	1,511.8	1,533.5	1,547.3
1977	1,553.0	1,570.6	1,585.4	1,597.8	1,611.1	1,622.2	1,641.6	1,655.6	1,671.7	1,691.6	1,714.9	1,730.0
1978	1,736.4	1,753.4	1,777.2	1,803.2	1,820.3	1,839.4	1,861.9	1,880.3	1,896.1	1,918.9	1,935.8	1,956.4
1979	1,977.1	1,994.9	2,018.6	2,022.6	2,041.5	2,059.4	2,090.0	2,109.7	2,125.9	2,154.5	2,178.5	2,205.3
1980	2,234.8	2,248.8	2,260.7	2,258.4	2,265.4	2,282.5	2,314.9	2,336.2	2,366.1	2,409.8	2,439.6	2,470.0
1981	2,491.7	2,508.7	2,531.4	2,530.0	2,547.1	2,571.4	2,629.0	2,656.7	2,671.3	2,675.1	2,689.3	2,690.9
1982	2,695.4	2,712.8	2,720.0	2,739.5	2,758.0	2,764.6	2,780.2	2,786.9	2,792.1	2,807.6	2,825.4	2,838.1
1983	2,843.7	2,849.2	2,867.9	2,884.7	2,914.5	3,266.0	2,955.0	2,958.4	2,992.4	3,026.1	3,055.4	3,087.3
1984	3,116.9	3,155.2	3,184.0	3,220.4	3,233.4	3,506.2	3,294.4	3,328.1	3,360.3	3,350.1	3,377.3	3,411.7
1985	3,426.6	3,444.9	3,470.2	3,475.3	3,486.5	3,703.7	3,515.9	3,527.4	3,540.9	3,576.8	3,585.8	3,623.6
1986	3,630.1	3,647.7	3,674.8	3,674.3	3,686.6	3,937.2	3,721.3	3,734.6	3,752.0	3,756.6	3,770.6	3,797.0
1987	3,823.8	3,854.0	3,878.7	3,886.7	3,922.0	4,253.6	3,961.6	3,998.9	4,016.6	4,057.6	4,082.4	4,130.4
1988	4,132.5	4,155.3	4,182.6	4,206.5	4,223.1	4,589.2	4,288.6	4,305.4	4,332.2	4,368.6	4,385.2	4,431.4
1989	4,493.2	4,511.8	4,547.7	4,566.3	4,564.9	4,903.1	4,607.1	4,616.5	4,628.6	4,659.2	4,695.7	4,717.1
1990	4,766.4	4,807.4	4,828.7	4,865.1	4,869.6	4,903.1	4,935.0	4,943.9	4,975.4	4,967.8	4,977.3	4,999.3
1991	4,987.9	4,999.4	5,012.3	5,038.6	5,059.0	5,094.6	5,089.8	5,105.3	5,135.3	5,135.4	5,156.5	5,210.2
1992	5,241.1	5,284.5	5,304.8	5,330.0	5,355.3	5,371.3	5,383.5	5,373.4	5,415.2	5,464.0	5,484.3	5,677.1
1993	5,461.7	5,470.9	5,464.8	5,575.0	5,607.5	5,603.2	5,609.2	5,640.1	5,641.6	5,669.0	5,693.2	5,883.4
1994	5,656.4	5,725.4	5,759.4	5,832.1	5,870.6	5,879.5	5,904.8	5,932.2	5,968.7	6,026.8	6,034.9	6,065.5
1995	6,095.0	6,109.6	6,125.1	6,148.4	6,157.8	6,183.6	6,203.7	6,223.4	6,250.7	6,278.2	6,304.4	6,331.3
1996	6,352.5	6,413.2	6,449.7	6,472.0	6,506.8	6,549.5	6,563.5	6,595.9	6,631.9	6,643.4	6,676.4	6,713.8
1997	6,754.8	6,792.1	6,830.4	6,850.2	6,877.5	6,909.5	6,937.4	6,982.4	7,016.0	7,058.0	7,103.1	7,132.7
1998	7,199.8	7,256.2	7,308.4	7,340.8	7,385.7	7,421.9	7,456.7	7,497.0	7,518.3	7,548.7	7,581.5	7,597.2
1999	7,612.6	7,631.9	7,649.7	7,683.8	7,717.6	7,757.5	7,789.2	7,831.1	7,835.8	7,898.9	7,934.6	7,984.4
2000	8,053.6	8,097.3	8,162.3	8,223.1	8,272.2	8,317.9	8,344.2	8,377.4	8,423.0	8,478.7	8,513.5	8,566.7
2001	8,604.0	8,640.2	8,676.2	8,697.0	8,709.3	8,737.6	8,768.5	8,775.9	8,771.0	8,761.6	8,756.0	-

Source: The Conference Board. © 2002 The Conference Board. All Rights Reserved. No claim to original U.S. Government works pursuant to U.S. Contract No. 52-SABA-5-00128. Primary source(s): U.S. Department of Commerce, Bureau of Economic Analysis, National Income and Wealth Division, BE-54, Washington, DC 20230. A dash (-) indicates that data are not available or zero.

Personal Income
(Annual Rate, Billions of chained 1996 $)

Year	Jan	Feb	Mar	Apr	May	Jun	Jul	Aug	Sep	Oct	Nov	Dec
1959	1,780.0	1,789.9	1,803.8	1,815.7	1,828.5	1,834.9	1,832.0	1,822.3	1,823.6	1,826.3	1,840.6	1,858.5
1960	1,865.3	1,866.6	1,869.5	1,875.2	1,879.7	1,880.1	1,881.0	1,879.8	1,882.6	1,888.6	1,879.8	1,869.6
1961	1,885.8	1,893.0	1,900.1	1,903.9	1,918.0	1,937.4	1,943.3	1,944.5	1,947.8	1,967.4	1,985.9	1,996.5
1962	1,991.0	2,000.1	2,014.1	2,024.5	2,028.2	2,034.5	2,044.4	2,047.4	2,048.4	2,056.7	2,065.8	2,074.5
1963	2,085.5	2,073.6	2,082.8	2,089.7	2,098.5	2,110.5	2,111.4	2,119.9	2,133.8	2,146.9	2,150.1	2,167.6
1964	2,176.4	2,184.2	2,194.0	2,206.9	2,220.3	2,229.4	2,240.3	2,256.6	2,266.3	2,269.0	2,282.4	2,304.5
1965	2,316.5	2,316.3	2,326.6	2,338.3	2,351.1	2,358.4	2,373.5	2,383.4	2,446.6	2,434.2	2,453.4	2,466.0
1966	2,471.4	2,481.8	2,493.0	2,492.5	2,500.7	2,514.2	2,525.5	2,539.0	2,553.9	2,565.7	2,580.8	2,579.3
1967	2,603.0	2,604.6	2,620.2	2,617.8	2,622.5	2,632.8	2,647.0	2,658.7	2,659.4	2,658.5	2,674.0	2,699.2
1968	2,704.4	2,724.7	2,748.7	2,763.2	2,777.2	2,789.7	2,807.7	2,820.0	2,831.5	2,836.6	2,848.1	2,858.3
1969	2,861.0	2,873.1	2,885.3	2,894.6	2,904.4	2,912.8	2,927.9	2,946.6	2,951.7	2,959.2	2,959.6	2,964.4
1970	2,961.2	2,965.5	2,973.6	3,026.2	3,004.6	2,999.9	3,016.6	3,025.7	3,030.8	3,013.5	3,008.1	3,016.2
1971	3,044.6	3,047.7	3,059.4	3,067.9	3,078.8	3,135.4	3,093.0	3,108.6	3,117.6	3,124.1	3,143.3	3,165.5
1972	3,182.3	3,206.6	3,223.3	3,238.8	3,252.3	3,226.5	3,274.4	3,306.2	3,318.0	3,386.4	3,422.2	3,436.3
1973	3,433.0	3,450.8	3,455.7	3,455.4	3,480.4	3,489.7	3,501.4	3,492.5	3,515.2	3,546.9	3,558.4	3,549.8
1974	3,524.6	3,502.6	3,479.0	3,474.3	3,483.8	3,486.6	3,508.9	3,491.6	3,485.5	3,494.4	3,469.8	3,462.0
1975	3,450.4	3,444.1	3,444.5	3,449.6	3,470.9	3,533.0	3,497.0	3,525.6	3,537.3	3,556.0	3,560.1	3,567.4
1976	3,599.7	3,624.4	3,638.6	3,655.9	3,663.0	3,667.1	3,694.6	3,705.3	3,709.9	3,708.3	3,744.1	3,756.3
1977	3,750.9	3,763.9	3,780.6	3,786.7	3,797.0	3,801.2	3,825.9	3,842.0	3,865.2	3,892.7	3,923.0	3,938.3
1978	3,928.2	3,947.8	3,976.0	4,002.3	4,009.4	4,023.8	4,050.3	4,069.8	4,080.4	4,098.2	4,112.8	4,135.2
1979	4,144.1	4,153.5	4,171.8	4,145.7	4,147.2	4,149.9	4,179.4	4,186.2	4,181.3	4,202.2	4,219.0	4,233.8
1980	4,242.6	4,224.3	4,197.1	4,167.8	4,146.7	4,152.0	4,178.6	4,182.7	4,199.8	4,246.9	4,268.2	4,296.7
1981	4,294.8	4,280.3	4,288.3	4,268.3	4,277.1	4,299.0	4,366.8	4,383.4	4,375.8	4,363.0	4,362.5	4,352.9
1982	4,335.2	4,348.5	4,350.7	4,377.8	4,381.1	4,359.8	4,358.7	4,358.6	4,354.9	4,354.2	4,369.3	4,382.4
1983	4,372.0	4,374.9	4,394.6	4,393.5	4,421.6	4,428.3	4,452.7	4,444.0	4,480.2	4,517.6	4,548.1	4,589.3
1984	4,614.1	4,649.8	4,680.6	4,716.1	4,728.1	4,766.5	4,794.1	4,828.7	4,865.6	4,836.3	4,867.5	4,906.8
1985	4,910.5	4,914.2	4,929.8	4,926.5	4,928.6	4,941.2	4,947.2	4,953.0	4,959.1	4,992.1	4,985.4	5,022.3
1986	5,015.8	5,042.6	5,091.2	5,096.3	5,099.9	5,101.4	5,120.1	5,128.5	5,133.8	5,131.1	5,136.5	5,161.0
1987	5,162.0	5,180.4	5,197.5	5,189.1	5,222.0	5,221.0	5,243.3	5,270.4	5,274.9	5,308.3	5,327.5	5,381.0
1988	5,369.3	5,393.0	5,410.1	5,412.5	5,417.3	5,432.3	5,451.5	5,458.6	5,466.6	5,495.4	5,503.1	5,543.2
1989	5,592.6	5,598.7	5,621.9	5,608.3	5,586.4	5,603.8	5,612.4	5,622.5	5,620.2	5,631.2	5,660.6	5,668.0
1990	5,693.3	5,718.2	5,718.6	5,744.7	5,733.8	5,746.1	5,767.6	5,740.4	5,741.0	5,698.0	5,698.6	5,713.6
1991	5,674.9	5,680.3	5,691.6	5,708.4	5,707.6	5,738.3	5,724.7	5,728.4	5,740.5	5,728.7	5,735.4	5,775.6
1992	5,794.3	5,823.8	5,830.2	5,844.4	5,863.4	5,868.7	5,861.0	5,864.7	5,879.3	5,912.5	5,924.4	6,124.9
1993	5,878.9	5,878.3	5,861.2	5,964.1	5,982.4	5,978.1	5,977.6	6,001.5	5,997.1	6,004.3	6,019.0	6,217.9
1994	5,979.9	6,038.5	6,060.6	6,131.0	6,161.8	6,154.1	6,156.4	6,168.2	6,197.5	6,249.6	6,248.8	6,275.3
1995	6,286.7	6,287.4	6,292.6	6,300.6	6,301.0	6,320.8	6,330.3	6,337.3	6,360.2	6,374.5	6,398.7	6,415.4
1996	6,421.4	6,468.9	6,488.2	6,493.0	6,517.7	6,559.5	6,559.8	6,586.7	6,608.7	6,598.8	6,617.8	6,643.3
1997	6,669.5	6,689.1	6,720.3	6,732.6	6,760.5	6,784.7	6,803.8	6,842.3	6,861.5	6,892.3	6,934.5	6,962.5
1998	7,017.3	7,072.3	7,123.2	7,140.9	7,177.6	7,212.7	7,232.5	7,264.5	7,285.2	7,293.4	7,325.1	7,333.2
1999	7,326.9	7,345.4	7,362.6	7,360.0	7,392.3	7,430.6	7,439.5	7,465.3	7,441.4	7,487.1	7,513.8	7,546.7
2000	7,583.4	7,596.0	7,621.2	7,678.0	7,723.8	7,737.6	7,747.6	7,778.5	7,791.9	7,828.9	7,853.8	7,895.6
2001	7,886.3	7,903.6	7,939.4	7,943.9	7,948.6	7,962.8	7,992.4	7,999.2	8,034.3	7,973.8	7,976.7	-

Source: The Conference Board. © 2002 The Conference Board. All Rights Reserved. No claim to original U.S. Government works pursuant to U.S. Contract No. 52-SABA-5-00128. Primary source(s): U.S. Department of Commerce, Bureau of Economic Analysis, National Income and Wealth Division, BE-54, Washington, DC 20230. A dash (-) indicates that data are not available or zero.

Wages & Salaries in Mining, Manufacturing, Construction

(Annual Rate, Billions of chained 1996 $)

Year	Jan	Feb	Mar	Apr	May	Jun	Jul	Aug	Sep	Oct	Nov	Dec
1959	482.33	485.17	492.84	498.34	504.43	506.94	504.44	490.38	489.25	486.10	491.23	505.95
1960	512.75	513.60	510.66	508.72	510.10	506.10	503.12	499.28	495.55	495.99	489.21	480.18
1961	484.71	482.86	485.58	489.23	493.98	500.50	501.43	504.45	499.06	508.53	516.26	519.11
1962	515.79	520.33	524.98	531.36	529.59	529.88	532.54	531.44	532.91	531.73	533.96	534.61
1963	535.71	535.11	537.06	539.52	543.94	546.26	546.93	547.05	551.02	552.36	553.48	558.27
1964	553.40	562.52	566.01	569.81	571.68	573.78	576.98	581.76	585.52	577.42	586.35	595.74
1965	596.54	601.67	603.12	600.41	605.80	608.22	609.40	612.71	615.37	622.68	628.43	633.87
1966	636.36	643.68	648.40	653.75	655.74	661.90	662.40	666.52	667.59	669.55	669.95	668.16
1967	673.81	667.30	668.42	667.87	665.97	668.23	670.55	676.52	672.19	670.45	680.54	686.80
1968	685.99	695.67	696.40	699.29	704.60	705.25	706.82	706.53	711.28	715.19	719.88	722.50
1969	723.58	723.87	731.15	731.95	734.35	736.78	738.55	742.11	742.76	742.97	738.09	738.90
1970	732.69	730.71	733.19	724.21	716.06	717.66	718.97	715.36	703.40	689.52	684.91	696.68
1971	700.93	698.97	698.97	700.69	705.68	703.00	701.12	699.46	700.75	702.27	704.00	713.53
1972	719.05	725.84	732.24	735.77	737.66	738.98	735.07	743.18	747.68	757.20	762.91	766.59
1973	775.61	784.42	782.37	783.79	785.49	788.04	793.55	785.88	790.65	794.42	797.66	796.50
1974	789.82	786.30	778.80	776.12	779.58	778.80	774.88	774.61	771.12	768.88	745.40	735.38
1975	726.29	709.55	705.49	701.57	705.35	705.22	702.48	713.09	718.56	721.55	723.80	730.55
1976	742.85	746.72	750.68	754.31	756.41	754.12	757.98	761.07	759.65	757.54	767.07	768.33
1977	762.70	770.33	778.29	784.88	791.12	798.52	799.67	799.97	807.14	810.64	811.89	808.03
1978	802.94	809.72	821.85	838.69	837.87	843.34	847.16	848.35	853.03	857.13	865.30	870.88
1979	868.47	870.93	878.03	869.08	874.69	875.98	875.69	870.52	872.32	868.88	866.20	871.04
1980	863.24	860.82	854.86	844.27	832.68	826.91	815.90	826.41	830.13	837.34	845.29	851.32
1981	849.30	837.50	841.53	842.82	843.36	848.85	850.07	851.13	843.71	843.56	836.41	828.97
1982	823.94	824.18	819.69	813.09	810.78	802.41	794.15	787.93	780.44	770.57	765.23	766.13
1983	769.69	766.28	766.81	768.54	771.57	776.43	782.28	784.96	795.14	802.08	807.70	813.01
1984	819.69	825.98	828.17	834.53	837.13	844.35	846.13	849.37	849.33	848.86	853.15	857.58
1985	859.15	854.24	868.05	856.60	857.95	858.93	858.00	861.25	861.39	867.24	863.12	866.75
1986	864.23	861.25	871.61	866.74	865.26	860.11	860.85	864.24	860.60	868.81	862.79	864.62
1987	861.33	860.48	866.47	856.91	860.26	858.74	859.57	863.33	865.19	867.23	869.81	870.11
1988	875.86	880.51	891.85	887.35	887.63	890.07	890.64	887.17	889.28	900.08	893.61	891.45
1989	892.27	889.44	895.60	883.04	877.52	876.17	876.96	879.78	876.82	883.57	878.87	875.79
1990	870.44	880.38	881.20	880.72	876.53	876.38	873.52	865.19	862.67	853.19	843.85	844.88
1991	835.75	830.16	826.00	825.35	824.23	827.55	827.72	828.22	827.69	824.53	820.90	821.58
1992	815.98	817.02	819.51	820.51	822.96	822.36	820.10	823.15	817.34	817.06	818.49	866.90
1993	792.42	795.37	789.46	821.21	819.25	817.82	821.08	822.00	827.17	826.39	829.39	868.84
1994	825.50	825.04	831.61	844.58	848.57	849.24	851.03	851.81	856.45	860.76	864.19	867.25
1995	864.35	864.65	864.64	867.13	862.34	865.59	869.73	869.26	873.19	873.62	875.63	872.18
1996	866.87	880.98	878.89	886.03	889.90	896.48	898.23	902.34	904.34	903.23	907.19	912.16
1997	918.41	922.08	928.27	929.86	934.05	935.90	939.29	946.54	948.96	957.72	965.65	972.93
1998	976.12	980.21	983.43	985.31	989.41	989.99	985.45	997.29	1,001.36	1,001.45	1,004.93	1,009.85
1999	1,003.75	1,009.43	1,011.65	1,012.74	1,019.44	1,024.23	1,029.32	1,028.69	1,033.43	1,034.12	1,037.31	1,040.83
2000	1,045.67	1,046.81	1,051.73	1,058.64	1,054.90	1,062.05	1,070.75	1,072.52	1,073.64	1,083.01	1,089.48	1,089.12
2001	1,086.16	1,087.54	1,091.78	1,087.32	1,082.05	1,078.65	1,078.39	1,074.38	1,076.49	1,060.70	1,056.85	-

Source: The Conference Board. © 2002 The Conference Board. All Rights Reserved. No claim to original U.S. Government works pursuant to U.S. Contract No. 52-SABA-5-00128. Primary source(s): U.S. Department of Commerce (wages and salaries), Bureau of Economic Analysis, National Income and Wealth Division, BE-54, Washington, DC 20230 and U.S. Department of Labor, Bureau of Labor Statistics, Office of Prices and Living Conditions, Division of Consumer Prices and Price Indexes, Washington, DC 20212. A dash (-) indicates that data are not available or zero.

Industrial Production in The U.S.

(1990=100)

Year	Jan	Feb	Mar	Apr	May	Jun	Jul	Aug	Sep	Oct	Nov	Dec
1951	27.2	27.3	27.5	27.5	27.4	27.3	26.9	26.6	26.8	26.8	27.0	27.1
1952	27.4	27.6	27.7	27.4	27.2	26.9	26.5	28.2	29.2	29.5	30.1	30.3
1953	30.4	30.5	30.8	30.9	31.1	31.0	31.4	31.2	30.5	30.3	29.6	28.8
1954	28.6	28.7	28.5	28.4	28.5	28.6	28.7	28.6	28.7	29.0	29.5	29.9
1955	30.5	30.9	31.6	32.0	32.5	32.6	32.8	32.8	33.0	33.6	33.7	33.8
1956	34.0	33.7	33.7	33.9	33.7	33.4	32.3	33.7	34.4	34.7	34.4	34.9
1957	34.8	35.1	35.1	34.6	34.5	34.6	34.8	34.8	34.5	34.0	33.2	32.5
1958	31.9	31.3	30.9	30.4	30.7	31.5	31.9	32.6	32.9	33.3	34.2	34.3
1959	34.8	35.5	36.0	36.8	37.3	37.4	36.5	35.2	35.2	34.9	35.1	37.3
1960	38.3	38.0	37.6	37.3	37.3	36.8	36.7	36.6	36.3	36.2	35.7	35.0
1961	35.1	35.0	35.2	36.0	36.5	37.0	37.4	37.8	37.7	38.5	39.1	39.4
1962	39.1	39.7	39.9	40.0	40.0	39.9	40.3	40.3	40.6	40.6	40.8	40.8
1963	41.1	41.5	41.8	42.2	42.7	42.8	42.6	42.7	43.2	43.4	43.7	43.6
1964	44.0	44.3	44.3	45.0	45.2	45.4	45.7	46.0	46.1	45.5	46.9	47.5
1965	48.0	48.3	48.9	49.1	49.5	49.9	50.3	50.6	50.7	51.2	51.4	52.1
1966	52.6	52.9	53.6	53.7	54.2	54.5	54.8	54.8	55.3	55.7	55.3	55.5
1967	55.7	55.1	54.8	55.3	54.8	54.8	54.7	55.7	55.6	56.1	56.9	57.5
1968	57.4	57.7	57.8	57.9	58.6	58.8	58.7	58.9	59.1	59.2	60.0	60.2
1969	60.5	60.9	61.4	61.2	60.9	61.5	61.8	62.0	62.0	62.0	61.4	61.2
1970	60.1	60.1	60.0	59.8	59.8	59.6	59.7	59.6	59.2	58.0	57.7	59.0
1971	59.4	59.3	59.3	59.6	59.9	60.2	60.0	59.6	60.6	61.0	61.3	62.0
1972	63.4	63.8	64.4	65.4	65.2	65.4	65.3	66.2	67.0	67.9	68.7	69.4
1973	69.4	70.4	70.4	70.6	70.9	71.5	71.9	71.9	72.4	72.7	72.7	71.6
1974	70.6	70.3	70.6	70.5	71.3	71.6	71.2	71.0	71.3	70.8	68.7	65.9
1975	64.2	63.1	62.0	62.6	62.4	63.2	63.6	64.7	65.4	65.7	66.3	66.8
1976	67.6	68.8	68.6	68.9	69.7	69.7	70.1	70.5	70.7	71.0	72.2	72.7
1977	73.1	73.2	74.0	75.1	75.8	76.4	76.5	76.8	77.2	77.0	77.0	76.7
1978	76.5	76.5	77.3	79.9	79.9	80.8	81.0	81.2	81.6	82.1	82.5	82.8
1979	82.4	83.1	83.3	82.5	83.5	83.5	82.9	82.5	82.6	83.0	82.5	82.4
1980	82.8	82.8	82.8	81.2	79.2	78.2	77.7	78.6	79.7	80.3	81.6	82.0
1981	81.3	81.7	82.1	81.5	82.2	82.7	83.4	83.1	82.4	81.8	80.6	79.7
1982	78.4	80.1	79.6	78.8	78.2	78.0	77.3	76.9	76.3	75.7	75.5	74.9
1983	76.5	76.3	77.1	78.0	79.0	79.4	80.8	81.9	83.3	84.0	83.9	84.3
1984	86.1	85.9	86.9	87.3	87.8	88.2	88.4	88.4	88.3	87.9	87.9	87.5
1985	87.9	88.6	88.8	89.0	89.2	89.0	88.6	89.1	89.6	88.9	89.4	90.0
1986	90.6	89.9	89.0	89.7	89.5	89.2	89.5	89.7	89.7	90.5	90.9	91.8
1987	91.2	92.2	92.6	92.9	93.4	94.2	94.7	94.8	94.8	96.0	96.3	96.9
1988	97.0	97.3	97.3	97.9	97.9	98.0	98.6	99.2	98.8	99.1	99.8	100.3
1989	100.9	100.1	101.0	101.3	100.7	100.5	99.5	99.9	99.7	99.2	99.6	100.1
1990	99.6	100.1	100.6	100.0	100.4	100.4	100.4	100.5	100.7	100.1	98.8	98.2
1991	97.7	97.0	96.1	96.4	97.2	98.3	98.4	98.5	99.4	99.3	99.2	98.6
1992	98.6	99.2	100.0	100.7	101.0	100.8	101.6	101.3	101.8	102.3	102.9	102.8
1993	103.2	103.7	103.9	104.3	103.8	104.1	104.2	104.0	105.1	105.6	106.0	106.8
1994	107.0	107.2	108.1	108.7	109.7	110.3	110.7	111.3	111.5	112.1	112.8	113.9
1995	114.6	114.4	114.7	114.5	115.0	115.5	115.0	116.4	116.9	116.7	117.0	117.1
1996	116.8	118.2	117.9	119.2	120.3	121.1	121.2	122.0	122.6	122.5	123.4	123.7
1997	124.3	125.4	125.8	126.6	127.1	127.9	128.5	129.4	130.2	131.0	131.6	132.0
1998	134.2	134.3	134.7	135.5	135.8	135.1	134.7	137.4	137.1	137.9	137.4	137.4
1999	138.4	138.7	139.3	139.4	140.0	140.3	141.1	141.8	141.8	142.9	143.4	144.4
2000	144.7	145.6	146.4	147.2	148.2	148.8	148.1	148.3	148.4	147.8	147.4	146.7
2001	145.5	145.1	144.5	143.5	143.1	141.8	141.9	141.5	140.3	139.0	138.6	-

Source: The Conference Board. © 2002 The Conference Board. All Rights Reserved. No claim to original U.S. Government works pursuant to U.S. Contract No. 52-SABA-5-00128. Primary source(s): U.S. Department of Commerce, International Trade Administration, Office of Trade and Economic Analysis, Stop 2814B, Washington, DC 20230. A dash (-) indicates that data are not available or zero.

Capacity Utilization Rate, Total Industry

(Percent)

Year	Jan	Feb	Mar	Apr	May	Jun	Jul	Aug	Sep	Oct	Nov	Dec
1967	89.390	87.975	87.083	87.509	86.357	85.960	85.383	86.634	86.112	86.432	87.286	87.842
1968	87.380	87.341	87.262	87.040	87.666	87.640	87.160	87.059	87.047	86.879	87.661	87.597
1969	87.795	88.035	88.403	87.758	87.110	87.644	87.791	87.678	87.345	87.060	85.934	85.401
1970	83.538	83.218	82.846	82.371	82.015	81.493	81.436	81.036	80.227	78.377	77.661	79.199
1971	79.580	79.223	78.931	79.169	79.365	79.492	79.058	78.397	79.467	79.858	79.992	80.710
1972	82.287	82.631	83.087	84.192	83.770	83.815	83.473	84.393	85.101	86.101	86.908	87.511
1973	87.348	88.313	88.047	88.128	88.261	88.695	89.004	88.712	89.152	89.244	89.038	87.398
1974	85.946	85.357	85.494	85.085	85.829	85.844	85.200	84.657	84.763	83.905	81.264	77.661
1975	75.454	74.086	72.614	73.131	72.748	73.539	73.814	74.970	75.590	75.800	76.353	76.809
1976	77.471	78.668	78.298	78.425	79.142	79.017	79.304	79.579	79.659	79.754	80.902	81.366
1977	81.647	81.523	82.282	83.258	83.894	84.328	84.191	84.329	84.581	84.210	84.060	83.530
1978	83.038	82.826	83.433	86.036	85.844	86.550	86.572	86.553	86.745	86.947	87.206	87.288
1979	86.656	87.108	87.148	86.132	86.927	86.749	85.937	85.410	85.294	85.470	84.871	84.518
1980	84.733	84.615	84.407	82.583	80.365	79.175	78.510	79.273	80.285	80.699	81.834	82.069
1981	81.201	81.434	81.643	80.934	81.443	81.778	82.326	81.776	80.928	80.121	78.807	77.728
1982	76.303	77.787	77.081	76.189	75.440	75.021	74.247	73.694	72.993	72.229	71.875	71.122
1983	72.513	72.260	72.893	73.717	74.514	74.839	76.077	77.005	78.224	78.743	78.567	78.868
1984	80.368	80.065	80.770	81.019	81.305	81.491	81.482	81.300	81.016	80.464	80.357	79.824
1985	79.920	80.412	80.416	80.344	80.320	79.912	79.353	79.611	79.868	78.955	79.179	79.500
1986	79.842	79.157	78.247	78.732	78.447	78.071	78.222	78.343	78.173	78.784	79.083	79.723
1987	79.139	79.979	80.204	80.458	80.734	81.354	81.765	81.777	81.619	82.638	82.788	83.187
1988	83.163	83.361	83.295	83.696	83.675	83.648	84.107	84.470	84.076	84.214	84.750	85.085
1989	85.440	84.622	85.272	85.336	84.656	84.364	83.394	83.598	83.293	82.778	82.972	83.235
1990	82.720	83.027	83.306	82.681	82.883	82.739	82.576	82.607	82.590	82.003	80.782	80.173
1991	79.646	78.910	78.078	78.244	78.743	79.555	79.513	79.510	80.165	79.983	79.769	79.154
1992	79.016	79.307	79.842	80.274	80.345	80.079	80.680	80.273	80.441	80.734	81.043	80.929
1993	81.065	81.253	81.239	81.365	80.888	80.912	80.951	80.650	81.260	81.435	81.646	82.087
1994	82.072	82.106	82.578	82.801	83.119	83.306	83.311	83.392	83.286	83.614	83.839	84.404
1995	84.478	84.162	83.914	83.399	83.294	83.282	82.531	83.247	83.233	82.795	82.702	82.484
1996	81.880	82.514	82.035	82.486	82.686	82.934	82.749	82.885	82.972	82.614	83.047	83.139
1997	83.052	83.592	83.313	83.403	83.262	83.273	83.234	83.631	83.748	83.835	83.867	83.570
1998	83.560	83.142	82.948	82.932	82.710	81.808	81.201	82.389	81.840	81.974	81.348	81.056
1999	81.312	81.225	81.303	81.136	81.246	81.152	81.364	81.528	81.300	81.659	81.722	82.007
2000	81.915	82.131	82.321	82.458	82.721	82.755	82.107	81.933	81.749	81.199	80.714	80.151
2001	79.309	78.918	78.464	77.846	77.524	76.746	76.715	76.403	75.720	74.963	74.671	-

Capacity Utilization Rate, Manufacturing
(Percent)

Year	Jan	Feb	Mar	Apr	May	Jun	Jul	Aug	Sep	Oct	Nov	Dec
1951	88.330	88.292	88.383	88.203	87.353	86.642	84.869	83.641	83.746	83.058	83.559	83.907
1952	84.384	84.596	84.660	83.560	83.113	81.899	79.801	85.097	87.691	88.751	90.181	90.490
1953	90.548	91.104	91.426	91.498	91.694	90.659	90.979	90.564	88.326	87.195	84.741	82.308
1954	81.331	80.840	80.238	79.401	79.756	79.873	79.398	78.809	79.162	79.747	80.910	81.798
1955	83.491	84.133	85.769	86.705	87.862	87.646	87.659	87.332	87.458	88.367	88.265	89.026
1956	88.231	87.442	86.963	87.800	86.343	85.332	81.522	84.949	85.991	86.491	85.819	86.779
1957	86.151	86.998	86.414	84.997	84.214	84.577	84.317	84.162	83.186	81.395	79.411	77.549
1958	75.698	73.756	72.743	71.333	71.939	73.946	74.342	75.733	76.222	76.410	79.069	79.043
1959	80.197	81.443	82.477	83.992	84.916	84.769	82.980	79.468	79.049	78.154	78.505	83.568
1960	85.562	84.611	83.242	82.259	81.471	80.224	79.727	79.050	77.919	77.529	75.772	74.256
1961	74.109	73.512	73.864	75.383	76.356	77.324	78.109	78.978	78.156	79.553	80.766	81.604
1962	80.241	81.427	81.891	81.743	81.335	80.929	81.476	81.417	81.787	81.385	81.839	81.679
1963	81.945	82.378	82.624	83.458	83.951	83.940	83.345	83.501	83.823	84.307	84.295	84.009
1964	84.462	84.667	84.357	85.587	85.598	85.449	85.861	86.110	86.199	84.625	86.848	88.002
1965	88.599	88.723	89.277	89.287	89.449	89.458	90.297	89.851	89.559	89.789	89.648	90.514
1966	90.859	90.911	91.588	91.542	91.638	91.521	91.405	91.080	91.246	91.618	90.129	90.025
1967	89.842	88.395	87.516	87.656	86.611	86.069	85.307	86.492	86.064	86.370	87.535	88.004
1968	87.408	87.406	87.160	86.863	87.577	87.381	86.739	86.791	86.466	86.638	87.496	87.133
1969	87.304	87.671	88.001	87.298	86.616	86.812	87.112	86.904	86.460	86.224	85.008	84.239
1970	82.116	81.919	81.427	80.881	80.439	79.945	79.943	79.152	78.242	76.257	75.557	77.309
1971	77.743	77.581	77.222	77.429	77.753	77.750	77.685	76.571	77.924	78.884	78.976	79.510
1972	81.182	81.520	81.968	83.091	82.689	82.740	82.524	83.387	83.943	85.039	85.909	86.652
1973	86.607	87.567	87.502	87.493	87.576	87.921	88.146	87.994	88.243	88.524	88.469	86.573
1974	85.320	84.715	84.808	84.224	84.996	85.053	84.338	84.066	83.928	82.956	80.436	76.345
1975	73.895	72.262	70.516	71.126	70.836	71.726	72.280	73.336	74.098	74.475	74.917	75.512
1976	76.162	77.714	77.182	77.248	78.070	77.794	78.336	78.499	78.563	78.686	79.592	80.175
1977	80.588	80.552	81.384	82.344	82.903	83.296	83.151	83.639	83.512	83.225	83.218	83.359
1978	82.874	82.637	82.961	85.189	84.978	85.785	85.826	85.942	86.182	86.346	86.784	86.946
1979	86.393	86.739	86.855	85.332	86.374	86.256	85.558	84.528	84.290	84.476	83.632	83.337
1980	83.258	83.259	82.720	80.782	78.057	76.691	75.928	76.985	77.920	78.561	79.670	79.669
1981	78.976	79.241	79.269	79.252	79.629	79.333	79.631	78.837	78.033	76.982	75.617	74.242
1982	72.578	74.578	73.928	73.125	72.693	72.566	71.846	71.389	70.876	69.927	69.577	68.980
1983	70.611	70.833	71.750	72.459	73.368	73.868	74.845	75.587	77.160	77.554	77.682	77.529
1984	79.272	79.497	79.832	79.991	80.056	80.348	80.363	80.210	79.836	79.635	79.487	79.039
1985	78.869	79.077	79.344	79.227	79.375	78.893	78.333	78.766	78.800	77.920	78.521	78.194
1986	79.149	78.599	77.777	78.731	78.489	78.132	78.211	78.557	78.429	78.913	79.087	79.879
1987	79.123	80.228	80.266	80.553	80.664	81.366	81.788	81.526	81.526	82.487	82.755	83.149
1988	82.878	83.094	82.932	83.671	83.484	83.377	83.846	83.962	84.021	84.092	84.766	85.120
1989	85.724	84.543	85.043	84.953	84.214	84.062	82.980	83.101	82.696	82.073	82.200	82.143
1990	81.832	82.451	82.578	81.798	82.007	81.771	81.617	81.685	81.502	80.866	79.678	79.041
1991	78.224	77.536	76.606	76.757	77.149	78.112	78.183	78.234	79.007	78.853	78.562	78.060
1992	78.025	78.403	79.018	79.357	79.526	79.391	79.992	79.630	79.696	79.906	80.225	79.973
1993	80.387	80.368	80.359	80.624	80.236	80.043	80.071	79.671	80.386	80.505	80.738	81.219
1994	81.063	81.133	81.750	82.167	82.533	82.462	82.606	82.777	82.732	83.125	83.449	83.987
1995	84.121	83.673	83.465	82.876	82.607	82.643	81.666	82.279	82.489	82.073	81.772	81.475
1996	80.856	81.380	80.773	81.321	81.525	81.833	81.889	81.985	82.093	81.673	82.074	82.237
1997	82.142	82.729	82.542	82.531	82.392	82.531	82.393	82.962	82.964	82.972	83.036	82.744
1998	82.954	82.444	82.119	82.158	81.789	80.774	80.134	81.517	80.916	81.152	80.611	80.390
1999	80.527	80.552	80.437	80.311	80.498	80.315	80.338	80.698	80.451	80.769	80.963	81.130
2000	81.021	81.131	81.506	81.446	81.643	81.690	81.037	80.659	80.476	79.842	79.175	78.387
2001	77.554	77.163	76.733	76.034	75.784	74.982	75.051	74.598	73.901	73.206	73.000	-

Source: The Conference Board. © 2002 The Conference Board. All Rights Reserved. No claim to original U.S. Government works pursuant to U.S. Contract No. 52-SABA-5-00128. Primary source(s): Board of Governors of the Federal Reserve System, Division of Research and Statistics, Industrial Output Section, Stop 82, Washington, DC 20551. A dash (-) indicates that data are not available or zero.

INDICATORS OF CONSUMPTION, TRADE, ORDERS, AND DELIVERIES

Consumption, trade, orders, and deliveries are indicators of the economy's general performance. They tend, on the whole, to be leading indicators. Included are two series:

> Manufacturers' new orders, durable goods
> Sales of retail stores

Related series, reported under Business Cycle Indicators, are:

> Manufacturers' new orders, consumer goods and materials (Leading Index)
> Vendor performance (Leading Index)
> Consumer expectations (Leading Index)
> Manufacturing and trade sales (Coincident Index)

Manufacturers' New Orders, Durable Goods. Orders are reported in billions of chained 1996 dollars. New orders for consumer goods and materials are part of the leading index. This series is also considered to be a leading indicator overall but is not part of the composite index of leading indicators—most likely because orders for durable goods are less predictive than those for consumer goods and materials.

Sales of Retail Stores. The series shows data in millions of chained 1996 dollars. Retail sales are classified as leading indicators of the trough of business cycles but produce uncertain results at the peak of cycles. In other words, retail sales tend to grow somewhat earlier than the economy as a whole.

Manufacturers' New Orders, Durable Goods Industries
(Billions of chained 1996 $)

Year	Jan	Feb	Mar	Apr	May	Jun	Jul	Aug	Sep	Oct	Nov	Dec
1959	51,876	54,197	55,381	55,870	53,458	55,896	51,574	49,082	50,420	51,373	48,488	52,932
1960	50,907	50,791	50,284	49,745	50,292	51,255	49,564	52,638	52,384	48,589	48,792	49,476
1961	46,773	48,044	48,200	51,064	51,576	52,652	51,871	54,998	54,208	54,653	56,519	58,332
1962	58,174	58,575	56,925	56,157	56,391	56,054	56,841	56,564	59,130	60,370	58,907	62,042
1963	61,730	62,624	63,953	63,537	64,212	61,653	63,854	61,899	63,627	64,691	63,515	62,319
1964	69,337	66,742	66,204	68,783	68,713	69,127	72,168	66,321	70,476	69,412	68,856	72,391
1965	74,731	73,949	75,683	76,734	74,579	75,552	77,896	78,505	76,173	80,018	80,857	82,711
1966	85,226	84,769	88,246	86,269	84,953	87,015	84,875	82,948	89,122	86,213	83,140	82,631
1967	80,501	79,762	78,394	78,884	83,335	84,805	81,759	83,309	81,638	82,896	83,687	90,980
1968	85,549	85,709	89,173	85,341	83,662	84,685	84,195	83,667	88,443	92,360	88,608	87,774
1969	89,606	91,564	89,812	94,323	88,595	87,097	87,420	89,279	92,376	89,586	87,086	85,700
1970	81,848	81,003	78,676	76,697	78,754	80,022	78,950	78,300	78,396	71,887	72,782	80,689
1971	83,025	84,346	82,319	79,888	78,638	80,472	79,282	83,358	83,300	81,474	84,046	86,001
1972	87,491	89,011	88,709	89,237	90,671	90,969	88,965	93,434	98,826	96,862	99,050	103,477
1973	106,044	108,430	110,882	108,226	108,059	107,388	107,670	107,515	106,334	110,311	113,049	107,014
1974	111,534	110,432	107,813	107,739	111,121	108,080	108,855	110,815	102,827	95,401	92,945	84,284
1975	82,641	80,705	75,428	79,367	77,659	77,557	84,723	85,068	84,717	82,966	83,320	83,734
1976	86,600	90,380	93,593	92,879	92,529	93,739	96,385	95,389	95,560	95,057	97,280	102,183
1977	99,327	99,820	104,762	103,278	103,365	106,580	105,389	106,275	108,337	109,984	108,586	112,549
1978	105,194	108,770	113,505	116,673	117,118	117,894	114,956	118,001	120,007	123,589	122,917	120,953
1979	120,586	123,287	127,142	116,783	118,195	117,856	114,673	111,316	114,599	112,808	109,595	109,871
1980	114,576	113,656	108,441	100,848	92,468	95,487	103,020	100,759	109,280	111,673	107,320	111,006
1981	105,807	105,568	107,617	109,818	109,058	108,543	107,981	104,805	103,066	98,095	96,012	91,985
1982	96,112	95,904	99,034	96,704	93,261	92,926	94,133	89,716	91,967	90,566	87,448	94,075
1983	98,220	91,771	95,154	98,168	97,941	104,772	103,652	103,959	108,494	113,922	113,880	114,486
1984	116,721	117,961	122,935	113,367	116,081	112,351	116,934	115,901	111,986	112,653	117,918	114,316
1985	119,496	115,482	114,323	113,374	116,815	120,354	117,130	119,998	120,283	118,706	114,159	119,942
1986	122,838	120,428	119,233	116,857	115,480	116,238	118,117	114,292	120,003	117,162	117,087	121,199
1987	115,634	120,452	123,929	125,245	126,015	127,574	130,111	124,054	126,103	128,622	128,557	129,492
1988	131,203	132,259	131,006	130,961	132,441	135,591	134,534	135,498	134,980	136,109	134,524	147,131
1989	142,297	137,491	136,830	137,818	130,761	133,930	131,268	129,648	132,718	127,755	135,964	139,037
1990	128,463	131,941	140,003	132,236	136,337	133,412	136,012	132,022	132,817	134,983	122,318	127,353
1991	123,534	124,151	116,571	121,506	124,626	120,610	137,351	129,838	126,414	127,630	129,735	121,116
1992	126,270	126,440	129,190	131,804	129,787	132,830	129,711	128,117	130,135	133,027	130,503	139,958
1993	134,258	138,631	133,907	134,647	131,396	135,546	132,507	133,602	134,803	137,589	141,220	141,901
1994	147,416	144,406	147,214	145,702	147,819	150,726	146,925	151,441	152,369	151,358	157,068	160,411
1995	161,206	160,468	161,360	153,201	157,716	155,263	153,086	160,761	164,710	161,747	163,141	168,202
1996	167,361	163,402	167,137	163,319	171,326	169,821	171,337	167,236	173,847	174,737	174,690	170,558
1997	177,876	185,439	179,891	185,707	184,736	189,728	192,280	194,506	192,519	195,455	205,340	189,797
1998	192,689	196,985	193,534	200,756	193,997	190,037	191,908	196,462	196,727	199,561	199,411	199,790
1999	206,650	202,477	206,044	205,006	204,983	202,225	215,219	214,715	210,451	211,570	212,315	225,427
2000	224,383	213,177	227,227	215,012	227,070	256,138	220,101	220,399	227,368	214,490	221,143	220,902
2001	197,360	205,405	209,556	197,747	203,215	198,136	196,219	195,215	177,323	199,777	190,404	-

Source: The Conference Board. © 2002 The Conference Board. All Rights Reserved. No claim to original U.S. Government works pursuant to U.S. Contract No. 52-SABA-5-00128. Primary source(s): U.S. Department of Commerce, Bureau of the Census, Manufacturing and Construction Division, Manufacturers' Shipments, Inventories, and Orders Branch, Washington, DC 20233. F.W. Dodge; McGraw-Hill, Inc., Market Analysis Group, 24 Hartwell Avenue, Lexington, MA 02173. Deflators calculated by The Conference Board. A dash (-) indicates that data are not available or zero.

Sales of Retail Stores
(Millions of chained 1996 $)

Year	Jan	Feb	Mar	Apr	May	Jun	Jul	Aug	Sep	Oct	Nov	Dec
1959	60,729	61,146	61,588	60,893	61,876	62,368	61,942	62,426	62,291	62,161	60,455	60,903
1960	62,287	62,031	62,294	63,992	62,334	62,749	62,106	62,112	62,245	62,446	62,031	61,358
1961	60,826	60,782	61,336	60,960	61,282	61,460	61,754	62,209	62,846	62,720	63,895	64,224
1962	64,244	64,133	65,507	65,226	66,062	65,445	66,110	66,046	66,876	67,012	67,551	67,628
1963	68,145	67,333	68,012	68,406	67,513	68,731	68,736	68,657	67,813	69,079	68,957	69,433
1964	69,226	70,737	70,614	70,919	72,352	72,135	72,336	73,952	74,734	71,985	71,848	75,747
1965	76,100	76,158	75,307	76,462	77,150	76,124	77,431	77,470	77,011	80,955	80,809	82,008
1966	81,542	81,494	82,356	81,561	79,382	80,713	81,346	81,316	80,886	81,657	81,254	82,204
1967	81,820	81,158	82,008	82,288	81,814	83,973	83,179	82,919	85,179	83,643	85,360	87,716
1968	85,631	86,457	88,308	87,906	88,087	89,431	90,307	91,111	88,756	90,825	92,733	91,271
1969	91,863	92,276	91,054	91,229	91,946	91,002	90,858	91,697	92,639	93,303	92,829	93,443
1970	93,229	93,364	92,455	93,093	94,164	94,712	95,315	95,068	94,968	95,368	92,833	95,160
1971	97,162	97,937	97,800	99,353	98,530	99,928	100,098	100,566	102,546	103,627	104,731	104,204
1972	103,713	104,185	106,824	106,997	108,030	108,692	108,880	109,601	111,022	112,632	113,065	115,066
1973	116,443	117,267	117,081	115,200	114,468	114,859	114,736	113,349	114,688	114,472	114,199	110,292
1974	110,582	109,820	110,003	110,657	110,729	110,229	111,323	113,098	109,256	107,377	106,116	103,918
1975	107,405	108,507	105,688	106,901	111,367	110,464	111,002	111,631	111,675	111,832	111,869	112,982
1976	115,693	114,937	115,661	117,653	116,159	118,270	118,626	117,540	116,878	117,972	118,289	121,285
1977	119,594	121,493	122,026	123,370	122,325	122,513	123,595	123,184	123,586	125,397	125,692	125,509
1978	122,496	124,976	127,357	129,523	129,228	130,510	128,887	129,866	129,840	131,118	132,241	133,216
1979	131,433	131,260	132,643	130,902	130,976	130,355	128,598	132,438	132,687	130,965	131,808	130,980
1980	132,031	129,684	126,175	123,693	123,103	124,176	125,874	125,974	125,214	127,403	127,471	126,829
1981	128,673	128,839	128,734	127,449	126,031	126,748	127,047	128,411	127,283	125,205	124,606	124,794
1982	122,850	125,861	124,720	125,603	126,258	123,223	124,969	124,401	126,055	127,207	129,073	129,162
1983	128,913	129,289	132,466	132,084	133,838	136,591	136,991	134,631	136,911	138,735	140,365	140,955
1984	143,606	143,125	141,794	144,088	145,019	146,925	144,399	143,280	144,928	145,271	147,851	147,086
1985	147,744	148,585	148,786	150,410	151,439	150,403	150,515	152,593	156,685	151,743	151,935	153,178
1986	154,271	153,668	154,476	156,661	158,453	158,093	158,844	160,225	169,055	162,153	161,104	167,705
1987	155,259	162,163	162,898	163,794	163,529	165,116	165,828	168,312	165,664	164,845	165,179	167,257
1988	167,578	168,832	171,267	169,695	170,899	171,258	170,862	171,625	170,366	173,524	174,651	175,418
1989	175,663	172,682	173,052	174,492	174,922	174,778	175,440	178,733	178,318	175,560	176,819	177,057
1990	180,503	178,252	178,331	177,522	177,009	177,767	178,453	177,918	177,186	175,895	175,949	173,063
1991	169,857	172,827	174,485	174,695	175,213	174,970	175,696	174,334	174,907	173,635	173,331	173,688
1992	177,767	178,737	177,005	177,562	178,093	178,364	179,074	179,487	181,206	183,446	183,079	184,541
1993	185,627	184,078	181,646	186,000	187,318	187,947	189,803	189,940	190,668	192,309	193,810	195,381
1994	193,865	197,230	199,893	199,721	198,860	200,125	199,668	202,323	203,127	205,802	205,712	205,452
1995	206,608	203,035	204,475	204,622	206,822	208,749	208,321	210,143	210,115	209,733	212,471	213,685
1996	212,390	215,440	216,266	217,144	218,584	218,027	218,486	219,045	220,691	222,159	221,641	222,225
1997	213,178	214,829	215,660	215,123	213,122	217,105	219,791	221,125	221,523	221,462	223,492	223,979
1998	224,862	225,824	228,443	230,933	232,948	235,440	233,427	232,942	236,150	239,706	241,957	243,951
1999	245,296	248,579	250,409	249,743	253,022	253,884	255,345	257,981	257,571	258,354	262,522	266,648
2000	266,910	270,041	271,280	268,709	270,460	270,295	271,911	273,406	274,378	274,380	272,840	273,198
2001	276,891	276,910	276,677	280,566	280,582	280,801	283,559	285,706	278,221	299,521	-	-

Source: The Conference Board. © 2002 The Conference Board. All Rights Reserved. No claim to original U.S. Government works pursuant to U.S. Contract No. 52-SABA-5-00128. Primary source(s): U.S. Department of Commerce, Bureau of the Census, Services Division, Current Retail Inventories and Sales Branch, Washington, DC 20233 and U.S. Department of Commerce (deflator), Bureau of Economic Analysis, National Income and Wealth Division, BE-54, Washington, DC 20230. A dash (-) indicates that data are not available or zero.

INDICATORS OF FIXED CAPITAL INVESTMENT

Indicators of fixed capital investment cover business formations as well as expenditures on tooling and equipment and on buildings and housing. In the context of business cycles, the series reflect relative confidence in the future and hence tend to be leading indicators. Three series are presented:

> New business incorporations
> Contracts and orders for plant and equipment, current dollars
> New private housing units started

Related series, reported under Business Cycle Indicators, are:

> Manufacturers' new orders, nondefense capital goods (Leading Index)
> Building permits, new private housing units (Leading Index)

New Business Incorporations. New businesses are formed when entrepreneurs anticipate a strong economy and can obtain financing. The series, therefore, is classified as a leading indicator—although not included in the composite index of leading indicators.

Contracts and Orders for Plant and Equipment. Data are shown in billions of current dollars. The series shows commitments to spend money on capital goods in the future—because payment will be made at a later date. The series, therefore, tends to predict future economic activity.

New Private Housing Units Started. Data are in thousands of units, by month. The composite index of leading indicators measures building permits issued—the first step in a cycle of construction. This series measures actual starts. Both series are leading indicators. Since the construction sector tends to be the first to slump and the first to revive, "housing starts" is a closely watched indicator series.

Number of New Business Incorporations
(number)

Year	Jan	Feb	Mar	Apr	May	Jun	Jul	Aug	Sep	Oct	Nov	Dec
1951	7,214	7,016	6,937	7,082	6,848	6,759	6,796	6,880	6,952	6,995	7,119	7,181
1952	7,080	7,214	7,348	7,499	7,441	7,700	7,683	8,065	8,259	8,341	8,265	8,096
1953	8,304	8,351	8,634	8,534	8,785	8,605	8,757	8,515	8,185	8,698	8,556	8,696
1954	8,638	8,937	9,155	9,276	9,158	9,436	9,772	9,882	10,085	10,730	11,212	11,604
1955	11,902	11,843	11,679	11,215	11,521	12,072	11,655	11,572	11,968	11,668	11,761	11,560
1956	11,620	12,449	11,591	11,888	12,245	11,999	11,851	11,707	11,193	11,925	11,186	11,139
1957	11,250	11,359	11,367	11,507	11,109	11,739	11,686	11,593	11,318	11,251	10,788	10,791
1958	11,042	11,049	11,042	10,636	11,752	12,032	12,504	13,644	13,933	13,669	14,599	15,577
1959	16,346	16,255	16,548	16,604	16,296	15,204	15,658	15,813	15,728	15,383	15,695	15,959
1960	16,561	15,274	15,233	15,280	15,176	15,630	15,828	15,114	15,112	15,035	14,264	14,097
1961	13,607	14,570	14,658	15,327	15,298	15,431	15,492	15,277	15,402	16,035	16,149	15,881
1962	15,599	15,758	15,670	15,372	15,245	14,947	15,171	15,056	15,249	14,892	14,951	14,985
1963	14,924	15,390	15,563	15,305	15,682	15,536	15,431	16,093	15,689	16,275	15,759	15,867
1964	15,993	16,326	15,917	16,132	16,473	16,282	16,550	15,692	16,948	16,728	16,804	17,021
1965	16,784	16,854	17,131	16,664	16,580	17,017	16,844	16,901	17,136	16,994	17,606	17,625
1966	18,087	17,451	17,266	17,057	16,644	16,577	16,074	16,343	15,764	16,233	16,206	16,583
1967	16,703	15,987	16,244	16,760	17,627	17,799	16,300	17,674	17,818	17,654	17,958	18,238
1968	18,061	18,041	18,538	18,663	18,723	18,839	19,407	19,947	20,582	21,093	20,890	20,619
1969	21,364	22,105	22,083	23,262	23,118	23,439	23,366	22,871	22,594	24,263	23,125	22,404
1970	22,196	22,968	21,346	21,829	21,874	21,796	21,614	21,796	22,181	21,712	22,217	22,272
1971	22,563	21,034	22,883	22,814	23,960	24,481	24,677	25,012	23,623	25,356	25,510	25,634
1972	25,270	25,084	26,231	26,630	26,270	26,175	26,789	26,365	27,168	27,529	26,234	27,699
1973	27,796	28,752	28,964	28,522	28,286	27,999	27,477	26,689	26,240	26,809	26,718	24,881
1974	26,511	27,056	26,458	29,071	27,562	25,785	27,790	26,495	26,313	25,404	25,555	25,003
1975	24,809	24,931	25,076	26,708	26,632	26,307	28,655	27,810	28,359	29,079	28,634	29,282
1976	29,613	29,772	31,000	30,808	28,784	31,420	31,037	31,301	31,921	32,160	33,183	33,124
1977	34,311	33,844	35,018	34,529	35,256	36,694	36,874	38,180	37,271	38,213	38,308	38,900
1978	36,414	39,434	37,847	39,585	39,059	39,860	40,152	41,007	41,553	41,437	41,423	42,179
1979	42,043	42,014	43,299	43,401	44,317	43,504	44,513	43,634	44,173	45,295	44,540	43,563
1980	44,230	44,175	43,359	42,240	42,710	40,648	43,621	44,255	45,746	45,945	46,750	47,840
1981	46,039	48,588	47,972	49,413	48,866	49,172	49,038	48,631	48,450	47,947	49,413	47,556
1982	43,330	47,234	46,899	46,876	46,995	45,936	44,525	46,981	45,552	45,530	48,474	57,507
1983	49,999	48,296	48,032	48,903	50,211	50,992	48,601	52,828	50,445	50,441	51,642	51,557
1984	52,674	53,535	53,075	53,298	50,736	53,884	53,211	52,025	52,646	52,587	53,838	53,558
1985	53,674	53,479	55,335	55,133	55,545	55,339	54,507	56,159	56,662	58,307	57,308	58,074
1986	57,636	59,114	58,870	59,156	57,747	57,446	57,717	56,299	57,942	57,120	56,652	65,691
1987	55,348	58,495	60,248	57,537	56,178	57,612	57,330	57,650	57,568	55,504	56,681	55,226
1988	56,108	56,475	60,655	54,670	58,046	55,620	56,915	59,730	55,915	56,529	54,553	58,592
1989	58,253	58,560	57,383	57,631	57,326	56,950	54,948	55,500	55,390	54,651	55,116	56,945
1990	59,141	56,325	56,172	55,000	53,616	53,784	52,142	52,958	52,176	51,899	51,429	52,060
1991	51,991	50,384	51,536	52,235	52,327	52,071	52,767	53,313	52,284	53,892	54,163	52,923
1992	58,141	55,092	57,449	54,474	48,688	58,730	56,942	51,245	59,179	52,492	55,392	61,695
1993	55,625	59,691	61,002	59,648	51,765	60,422	58,387	58,209	63,758	55,291	61,739	61,873
1994	61,978	60,680	64,058	58,992	58,528	63,097	56,380	64,844	64,564	67,909	64,542	62,908
1995	66,293	64,755	65,292	57,839	65,422	63,439	59,946	69,337	61,982	67,587	67,042	61,297
1996	69,438	69,709	60,556	67,180	68,186	61,513	73,060	62,164	62,515	69,898	60,665	66,542
1997	72,992	69,265	63,587	67,556	67,530	62,756	72,707	60,465	66,819	69,975	58,307	68,915
1998	66,415	66,178	63,408	64,585	59,452	63,983	70,724	58,827	61,446	-	-	-

Contracts and Orders for Plant and Equipment
(Billions of $)

Year	Jan	Feb	Mar	Apr	May	Jun	Jul	Aug	Sep	Oct	Nov	Dec
1959	2,729	3,188	3,733	3,353	3,459	3,537	3,610	3,224	3,634	3,502	3,295	3,493
1960	3,270	3,353	3,266	3,518	3,509	3,408	3,412	3,405	3,436	3,337	3,202	3,486
1961	3,485	3,403	3,246	3,274	3,223	3,408	3,487	3,667	3,429	3,506	3,719	3,429
1962	3,622	3,939	3,652	3,848	3,679	3,609	3,654	3,661	3,644	3,727	3,996	4,075
1963	3,795	3,909	3,880	3,975	4,361	3,991	3,958	4,074	4,196	4,275	4,497	4,565
1964	4,701	4,238	4,430	4,462	4,825	4,953	4,641	4,693	4,747	4,792	5,097	5,166
1965	4,890	4,927	5,216	5,247	5,178	5,097	5,267	5,082	5,492	5,510	5,450	5,823
1966	5,815	6,280	6,145	6,406	6,337	6,209	6,637	6,216	6,789	6,201	6,139	6,136
1967	5,299	5,688	5,815	5,701	5,879	6,106	6,053	6,264	6,091	6,194	6,216	6,398
1968	7,744	7,484	9,018	7,350	6,433	6,469	7,849	8,137	6,988	8,660	7,189	7,843
1969	8,992	8,999	7,962	9,245	8,510	8,050	8,243	8,364	9,240	8,239	8,058	8,011
1970	9,076	8,401	7,568	7,347	7,199	7,039	7,534	7,355	7,161	6,446	7,297	8,007
1971	7,800	8,414	8,280	8,188	7,771	8,879	7,237	8,463	8,561	7,662	8,246	8,460
1972	8,094	8,433	9,060	8,876	9,722	8,433	9,685	9,153	10,195	9,779	9,966	10,167
1973	10,349	11,061	10,995	11,135	11,532	11,686	12,061	12,528	11,957	13,291	13,281	12,576
1974	12,817	13,193	13,394	12,947	13,880	12,926	15,660	14,450	14,489	14,003	12,391	13,708
1975	12,423	11,572	10,890	12,825	12,913	12,828	12,206	13,735	11,460	11,399	11,261	10,835
1976	13,379	13,140	13,648	13,706	12,094	14,417	15,837	14,085	15,372	15,800	14,401	15,057
1977	14,975	15,124	14,569	15,874	17,444	17,412	15,548	17,498	18,955	16,753	16,732	19,095
1978	18,167	20,579	18,713	18,898	23,460	19,781	20,805	22,261	23,183	26,369	22,173	19,823
1979	23,312	25,629	27,667	25,423	23,676	23,800	24,747	23,648	24,367	25,045	24,561	24,382
1980	26,142	23,841	24,297	24,147	21,483	22,710	25,033	23,872	24,437	25,542	23,859	25,634
1981	27,464	23,800	26,768	28,625	25,204	26,705	26,737	25,252	24,986	25,534	24,274	24,156
1982	26,459	26,789	25,523	24,523	20,865	21,910	22,742	21,267	22,402	22,659	21,330	24,160
1983	22,056	20,252	21,511	23,243	23,797	24,197	22,265	23,926	25,349	26,503	24,597	24,007
1984	27,514	27,376	27,962	26,921	30,203	28,189	29,355	27,636	27,192	28,222	28,023	26,909
1985	27,897	30,618	29,924	27,748	28,161	29,154	28,852	29,144	31,020	31,063	27,834	31,395
1986	28,837	30,157	28,550	27,953	27,621	28,054	27,642	27,444	28,467	29,132	28,890	30,368
1987	29,268	28,696	28,524	29,755	31,168	32,217	33,473	30,661	30,543	31,945	31,947	34,682
1988	35,460	35,808	33,333	33,968	32,527	35,178	36,587	39,834	35,963	34,238	36,049	39,021
1989	40,760	37,340	37,463	39,394	36,625	39,149	41,030	35,530	36,246	35,077	37,800	44,511
1990	39,269	35,998	40,506	36,931	36,729	36,263	40,056	35,037	38,206	41,195	35,765	41,463
1991	36,800	36,977	34,859	33,643	31,773	30,444	40,494	34,293	33,067	33,962	36,951	30,682
1992	35,363	35,239	37,223	37,899	36,085	35,695	35,374	33,638	36,185	36,699	32,366	38,722
1993	33,358	36,680	34,491	36,085	34,574	38,158	34,154	35,844	34,429	36,738	38,662	38,407
1994	40,899	39,682	39,548	38,331	38,041	41,183	39,509	41,819	41,561	40,850	43,696	41,915
1995	44,909	44,845	45,229	43,119	47,070	45,303	42,479	44,499	49,199	45,959	49,735	51,681
1996	51,705	49,094	52,214	47,621	50,974	48,401	51,182	47,473	53,106	52,668	50,994	50,910
1997	51,543	53,035	51,027	51,573	51,797	54,166	54,599	54,207	56,272	58,283	65,295	54,429
1998	59,678	57,854	58,171	58,940	58,427	58,905	58,951	64,142	61,722	58,582	58,497	60,183
1999	66,903	61,559	62,244	60,639	62,715	59,125	63,071	64,519	64,636	64,260	63,045	69,957
2000	70,012	66,691	70,763	70,122	69,321	80,143	70,683	73,727	77,223	68,480	73,604	81,259
2001	72,570	67,154	69,149	-	-	-	-	-	-	-	-	-

Source: The Conference Board. © 2002 The Conference Board. All Rights Reserved. No claim to original U.S. Government works pursuant to U.S. Contract No. 52-SABA-5-00128. Primary source(s): U.S. Department of Commerce, Bureau of the Census, Manufacturing and Construction Division, Manufacturers' Shipments, Inventories, and Orders Branch, Washington, DC 20233. F.W. Dodge; McGraw-Hill, Inc., Market Analysis Group, 24 Hartwell Avenue, Lexington, MA 02173. Deflators calculated by The Conference Board. A dash (-) indicates that data are not available or zero.

New Private Housing Units Started

(Annual Rate, Thousands)

Year	Jan	Feb	Mar	Apr	May	Jun	Jul	Aug	Sep	Oct	Nov	Dec
1951	1,928	1,638	1,481	1,352	1,359	1,419	1,257	1,334	1,456	1,386	1,324	1,330
1952	1,388	1,516	1,483	1,412	1,408	1,353	1,438	1,443	1,483	1,513	1,475	1,476
1953	1,484	1,460	1,506	1,498	1,425	1,380	1,346	1,324	1,348	1,342	1,383	1,343
1954	1,358	1,417	1,411	1,433	1,412	1,498	1,559	1,563	1,618	1,610	1,730	1,807
1955	1,757	1,664	1,684	1,708	1,730	1,704	1,632	1,625	1,580	1,490	1,434	1,431
1956	1,441	1,444	1,401	1,408	1,375	1,325	1,289	1,313	1,234	1,266	1,212	1,184
1957	1,151	1,168	1,173	1,147	1,174	1,175	1,191	1,193	1,191	1,204	1,162	1,146
1958	1,170	1,107	1,108	1,154	1,191	1,236	1,337	1,374	1,451	1,472	1,593	1,598
1959	1,657	1,667	1,620	1,590	1,498	1,503	1,547	1,430	1,540	1,355	1,416	1,601
1960	1,460	1,503	1,109	1,289	1,271	1,247	1,197	1,344	1,097	1,246	1,246	1,063
1961	1,183	1,226	1,312	1,166	1,228	1,382	1,335	1,312	1,429	1,415	1,385	1,365
1962	1,361	1,278	1,443	1,524	1,483	1,404	1,450	1,517	1,324	1,533	1,622	1,564
1963	1,244	1,456	1,534	1,689	1,641	1,588	1,614	1,639	1,763	1,779	1,622	1,491
1964	1,603	1,820	1,517	1,448	1,467	1,550	1,562	1,569	1,455	1,524	1,486	1,484
1965	1,361	1,433	1,423	1,438	1,478	1,488	1,529	1,432	1,482	1,452	1,460	1,656
1966	1,370	1,378	1,394	1,352	1,265	1,194	1,086	1,119	1,046	843	961	990
1967	1,067	1,123	1,056	1,091	1,304	1,248	1,364	1,407	1,421	1,491	1,538	1,308
1968	1,380	1,520	1,466	1,554	1,408	1,405	1,512	1,495	1,556	1,569	1,630	1,548
1969	1,769	1,705	1,561	1,524	1,583	1,528	1,368	1,358	1,507	1,381	1,229	1,327
1970	1,085	1,305	1,319	1,264	1,290	1,385	1,517	1,399	1,534	1,580	1,647	1,893
1971	1,828	1,741	1,910	1,986	2,049	2,026	2,083	2,158	2,041	2,128	2,182	2,295
1972	2,494	2,390	2,334	2,249	2,221	2,254	2,252	2,382	2,481	2,485	2,421	2,366
1973	2,481	2,289	2,365	2,084	2,266	2,067	2,123	2,051	1,874	1,677	1,724	1,526
1974	1,451	1,752	1,555	1,607	1,426	1,513	1,316	1,142	1,150	1,070	1,026	975
1975	1,032	904	993	1,005	1,121	1,087	1,226	1,260	1,264	1,344	1,360	1,321
1976	1,367	1,538	1,421	1,395	1,459	1,495	1,401	1,550	1,720	1,629	1,641	1,804
1977	1,527	1,943	2,063	1,892	1,971	1,893	2,058	2,020	1,949	2,042	2,042	2,142
1978	1,718	1,738	2,032	2,197	2,075	2,070	2,092	1,996	1,970	1,981	2,094	2,044
1979	1,630	1,520	1,847	1,748	1,876	1,913	1,760	1,778	1,832	1,681	1,524	1,498
1980	1,341	1,350	1,047	1,051	927	1,196	1,269	1,436	1,471	1,523	1,510	1,482
1981	1,547	1,246	1,306	1,360	1,140	1,045	1,041	940	911	873	837	910
1982	843	866	931	917	1,025	902	1,166	1,046	1,144	1,173	1,372	1,303
1983	1,586	1,699	1,606	1,472	1,776	1,733	1,785	1,910	1,710	1,715	1,785	1,688
1984	1,897	2,260	1,663	1,851	1,774	1,843	1,732	1,586	1,698	1,590	1,689	1,612
1985	1,711	1,632	1,800	1,821	1,680	1,676	1,684	1,743	1,676	1,834	1,698	1,942
1986	1,972	1,848	1,876	1,933	1,854	1,847	1,782	1,807	1,687	1,681	1,623	1,833
1987	1,774	1,784	1,726	1,614	1,628	1,594	1,575	1,605	1,695	1,515	1,656	1,400
1988	1,271	1,473	1,532	1,573	1,421	1,478	1,467	1,493	1,492	1,522	1,569	1,563
1989	1,621	1,425	1,422	1,339	1,331	1,397	1,427	1,332	1,279	1,410	1,351	1,251
1990	1,551	1,437	1,289	1,248	1,212	1,177	1,171	1,115	1,110	1,014	1,145	969
1991	798	965	921	1,001	996	1,036	1,063	1,049	1,015	1,079	1,103	1,079
1992	1,176	1,250	1,297	1,099	1,214	1,145	1,139	1,226	1,186	1,244	1,214	1,227
1993	1,210	1,210	1,083	1,258	1,260	1,280	1,254	1,300	1,343	1,392	1,376	1,533
1994	1,272	1,337	1,564	1,465	1,526	1,409	1,439	1,450	1,474	1,450	1,511	1,455
1995	1,407	1,316	1,249	1,267	1,314	1,281	1,461	1,416	1,369	1,369	1,452	1,431
1996	1,467	1,491	1,424	1,516	1,504	1,467	1,472	1,557	1,475	1,392	1,489	1,370
1997	1,355	1,486	1,457	1,492	1,442	1,494	1,437	1,390	1,546	1,520	1,510	1,566
1998	1,525	1,584	1,567	1,540	1,536	1,641	1,698	1,614	1,582	1,715	1,660	1,792
1999	1,748	1,670	1,710	1,553	1,611	1,559	1,669	1,648	1,635	1,608	1,648	1,708
2000	1,677	1,745	1,583	1,626	1,573	1,560	1,477	1,531	1,508	1,527	1,559	1,532
2001	1,666	1,623	1,592	1,626	1,610	1,634	1,660	1,559	1,585	1,521	1,645	-

Source: The Conference Board. © 2002 The Conference Board. All Rights Reserved. No claim to original U.S. Government works pursuant to U.S. Contract No. 52-SABA-5-00128. Primary source(s): U.S. Department of Commerce, Bureau of the Census, Manufacturing and Construction Division, Construction Starts Branch, Washington, DC 20233. A dash (-) indicates that data are not available or zero.

INDICATORS OF INVENTORIES AND INVENTORY INVESTMENT

Inventory levels tend to be leading indicators of economic activity. Inventories are built up in anticipation of sales; they stay high when sales do not materialize; they are depleted when the economy is growing rapidly, signaling overheating and the potential for inflation; they are "worked down" in anticipation of recession and built up in expectation of turn-arounds. Two series are shown:

Change in business inventories
Manufacturing trade inventories

Change in Business Inventories. The changes are reported quarterly in billions of chained 1996 dollars. The series is considered a leading indicator but is excluded from the composite index. See also the same category, stated in chained (1996) dollars as a component of GDP.

Manufacturing Trade Inventories. This series is presented in billions of chained 1996 dollars.

Change in Business Inventories

(Annual Rate, Billions of chained 1996 $)

Year	1st Quarter	2nd Quarter	3rd Quarter	4th Quarter
1982	-22.3	-2.2	8.9	-46.9
1983	-42.0	-9.7	-9.9	22.9
1984	84.3	80.5	83.2	56.3
1985	20.2	26.2	22.2	39.9
1986	37.5	19.7	-6.8	-12.1
1987	33.9	17.3	-2.1	69.3
1988	17.2	18.9	18.5	18.9
1989	51.5	38.9	10.2	17.9
1990	15.7	36.3	24.1	-9.9
1991	-15.5	-19.6	-1.3	32.4
1992	-	24.9	21.4	22.0
1993	36.2	23.4	4.7	15.7
1994	47.8	85.8	56.3	77.4
1995	62.2	32.5	9.0	18.0
1996	5.6	30.3	51.2	32.9
1997	49.3	88.3	51.3	66.1
1998	113.1	42.0	71.8	80.0
1999	83.4	32.7	39.6	92.7
2000	28.9	78.9	51.7	42.8
2001	-27.1	-38.3	-61.9	-

Manufacturing and Trade Inventories
(Billions of chained 1996 $)

Year	Jan	Feb	Mar	Apr	May	Jun	Jul	Aug	Sep	Oct	Nov	Dec
1959	240.00	241.16	243.44	247.22	248.05	249.83	251.27	252.80	252.00	252.53	252.26	255.86
1960	259.11	261.69	264.07	263.54	264.93	265.21	265.83	266.38	267.76	266.95	267.04	263.54
1961	263.01	262.03	260.72	260.72	261.17	261.10	261.33	263.48	265.09	265.29	266.99	267.71
1962	270.25	271.75	273.78	273.88	276.12	277.46	278.47	280.65	282.14	283.36	283.75	284.40
1963	285.93	286.87	287.80	288.11	289.32	290.79	292.18	294.50	295.48	297.03	298.17	298.25
1964	300.64	301.52	302.42	304.11	305.05	306.20	306.92	308.66	310.86	310.61	312.85	315.20
1965	318.46	319.73	323.78	325.36	327.10	329.07	332.23	335.73	335.15	335.78	337.96	339.94
1966	343.15	347.01	350.41	352.90	356.83	360.91	363.90	368.57	370.05	374.51	378.95	382.02
1967	387.23	389.28	391.41	392.99	394.04	393.53	394.92	399.39	398.93	399.15	402.43	404.83
1968	407.69	408.29	408.56	411.46	414.71	415.63	417.31	421.94	420.70	424.96	426.17	426.60
1969	428.60	431.08	433.16	434.92	436.98	438.05	440.91	444.56	445.75	448.54	449.29	451.13
1970	450.08	451.12	451.42	454.30	453.13	454.68	457.81	460.82	459.52	459.05	459.73	458.45
1971	461.13	462.01	464.89	466.65	468.45	469.15	470.93	474.28	475.04	475.65	474.47	476.13
1972	477.97	477.28	478.29	480.68	483.79	484.41	484.74	489.31	492.41	494.73	497.53	498.09
1973	502.64	505.39	507.25	509.66	511.70	515.01	518.08	517.34	519.02	522.38	527.07	531.43
1974	533.24	534.21	538.19	540.01	543.92	547.03	547.91	546.34	549.28	553.04	556.01	561.43
1975	560.78	557.28	552.83	551.90	547.79	544.58	543.54	543.00	542.74	544.40	542.19	540.70
1976	542.35	545.23	547.24	550.07	552.84	557.46	560.54	561.80	566.24	568.92	570.82	572.87
1977	574.96	576.40	578.00	580.70	582.60	584.39	586.74	590.50	594.60	595.26	598.18	601.08
1978	603.83	606.27	611.82	617.41	619.86	621.94	623.34	626.10	627.63	631.10	635.15	639.40
1979	643.41	646.25	646.98	650.78	653.05	655.35	660.86	660.31	657.30	659.68	659.38	660.09
1980	663.61	664.21	665.16	669.74	669.45	667.83	667.16	664.83	663.42	662.28	661.94	662.84
1981	665.37	668.76	669.82	667.72	669.49	671.52	674.18	675.22	677.50	677.51	682.11	679.34
1982	675.34	669.56	670.27	672.37	666.25	668.83	670.84	669.09	668.44	666.75	660.87	657.51
1983	652.73	651.95	648.26	648.77	649.78	650.60	651.98	655.95	659.38	660.98	665.34	670.02
1984	673.51	681.43	689.58	696.91	704.67	707.42	712.85	721.87	724.81	730.33	733.68	736.13
1985	735.21	738.20	737.44	739.39	739.25	741.60	744.09	745.89	744.01	747.21	749.95	751.53
1986	751.69	755.54	758.94	762.29	761.34	762.59	764.34	764.05	761.54	763.13	763.87	759.23
1987	762.92	765.00	769.56	772.40	776.11	777.86	777.23	776.47	779.53	785.93	790.80	796.49
1988	796.80	800.75	802.69	805.01	806.39	811.70	812.31	816.97	820.14	820.83	823.56	830.00
1989	834.88	838.98	841.55	843.61	847.65	851.45	855.07	855.50	855.04	858.09	862.85	862.42
1990	860.04	860.46	864.42	867.37	873.22	873.33	877.43	877.30	879.33	879.75	882.01	878.15
1991	881.03	879.90	873.75	872.89	868.95	868.24	867.55	866.96	870.93	872.78	873.77	876.73
1992	874.31	872.85	873.76	875.51	873.71	877.36	879.13	881.27	880.69	880.59	882.36	885.35
1993	887.61	891.29	896.95	899.41	900.27	902.91	902.72	903.25	907.73	907.34	911.08	911.07
1994	912.69	916.44	917.22	918.77	928.08	932.68	936.79	941.38	943.31	948.94	953.00	958.75
1995	966.32	969.11	974.24	978.88	981.09	985.31	988.32	989.78	992.68	997.51	997.89	996.43
1996	1,000.89	1,000.57	997.13	1,002.42	1,002.19	1,001.72	1,006.05	1,007.99	1,009.36	1,013.93	1,016.54	1,016.36
1997	999.79	1,004.04	1,003.66	1,011.22	1,016.54	1,021.70	1,025.29	1,025.43	1,030.61	1,036.47	1,040.47	1,043.76
1998	1,049.32	1,058.64	1,067.82	1,073.17	1,075.63	1,077.27	1,080.34	1,085.99	1,092.24	1,096.80	1,103.56	1,106.26
1999	1,111.96	1,117.15	1,122.23	1,121.14	1,125.95	1,128.19	1,133.94	1,135.50	1,139.91	1,144.98	1,152.42	1,161.42
2000	1,162.73	1,165.54	1,167.69	1,171.34	1,176.05	1,184.86	1,188.55	1,194.19	1,195.50	1,200.69	1,203.97	1,205.83
2001	1,205.89	1,201.93	1,197.53	1,194.80	1,192.86	1,186.07	1,178.34	1,177.65	1,172.40	1,156.82	-	-

INDICATORS OF PRICES, COSTS, AND PROFITS

Prices, profits, and certain kinds of costs tend to react rapidly to changes in the economy—or anticipated changes. They tend, therefore, to be leading indicators. Some costs, however, most notably wages, are lagging indicators because institutional factors work against rapid response to changing circumstances. Three series are presented:

> Index of sensitive materials prices
> Corporate profits after tax
> Index of unit labor costs, all persons, business

Three related series, reported under Business Cycle Indicators, are:

> Index of stock prices (Leading Index)
> Index of labor cost per unit of output, manufacturing (Lagging Index)
> Consumer price index for services (Lagging Index)

Index of Sensitive Materials Prices. The index is based on 1992 (1992 = 100). "Sensitive materials" are those most vital to a modern economy: metals, fibers, and minerals. Being raw materials (rather than finished components), they are purchased early in the production cycle and therefore can predict future economic behavior. A series showing *changes* in these prices is included in the composite index of leading indicators.

Corporate Profits after Tax. Data are available in billions of current dollars and in billions of chainged 1996 dollars, on a quarterly, annualized basis. The series is classified as a leading indicator. The leading character of this series is explained by the fact that corporate profits tend to decline even as the economy is still reaching for a peak; the *rate* of economic growth slows before the economy turns around. Similarly, the rate of decline slows before a turn-around, with the consequence that profits improve before the economy as a whole reflects the shift.

Index of Unit Labor Costs, All Persons, Business. This lagging indicator is available in quarterly increments; it is based on 1992 (1992 = 100). A similar index, for manufacturing only, is included in the composite index of lagging indicators. The lagging character of the index is explained by the fact that wage costs respond more slowly to economic cycles than do prices.

Index of Sensitive Materials Prices
(1992=100)

Year	Jan	Feb	Mar	Apr	May	Jun	Jul	Aug	Sep	Oct	Nov	Dec
1959	30.60	30.79	31.36	31.67	32.02	32.31	32.18	32.34	32.58	32.73	32.63	32.93
1960	32.95	32.75	32.36	32.46	32.41	32.08	31.76	31.73	31.55	31.28	30.98	30.77
1961	30.68	31.00	31.50	31.70	31.71	31.17	31.23	31.48	31.42	31.18	30.55	31.08
1962	31.34	31.12	30.94	30.57	30.68	30.32	30.12	30.00	29.99	30.08	30.21	30.09
1963	30.18	30.01	29.97	29.80	29.94	30.19	30.55	30.52	30.29	30.64	31.02	31.15
1964	31.25	31.31	31.51	32.10	31.66	31.99	32.19	32.83	33.43	34.29	34.47	34.64
1965	34.00	34.00	34.18	34.73	35.29	35.25	35.31	35.67	35.68	35.64	35.58	35.78
1966	36.14	36.43	36.67	36.71	36.42	36.30	36.17	34.93	34.50	33.88	33.71	33.41
1967	33.39	32.91	32.33	31.74	31.70	32.06	31.93	31.71	31.86	31.71	31.75	32.08
1968	31.75	31.69	32.20	31.72	31.41	31.69	31.71	31.80	32.17	32.84	33.49	33.99
1969	34.69	35.32	35.64	35.92	35.92	36.14	36.39	37.17	37.81	37.58	37.86	38.06
1970	37.77	37.05	36.65	36.40	36.35	35.95	35.30	35.24	34.89	35.04	34.95	34.31
1971	33.91	33.94	34.34	34.94	34.25	34.17	34.44	34.77	35.17	35.21	35.37	35.54
1972	36.30	36.28	37.46	37.80	39.58	39.95	40.45	40.75	41.26	42.41	43.88	44.91
1973	46.32	48.44	50.19	51.84	52.35	54.48	56.14	58.78	58.82	59.91	61.82	66.86
1974	68.40	69.71	72.21	72.47	70.58	70.33	70.67	69.73	68.71	65.53	63.54	60.21
1975	58.49	57.41	56.63	57.17	57.82	55.83	55.53	57.27	59.86	59.57	59.55	60.45
1976	60.92	60.56	60.82	62.39	63.47	64.61	67.60	67.24	67.86	67.11	67.25	67.99
1977	68.52	69.26	71.40	70.82	70.57	68.95	69.36	70.20	70.20	70.41	70.13	71.63
1978	72.26	72.45	71.95	72.37	72.67	75.51	76.29	78.05	79.52	81.66	83.22	82.75
1979	83.84	86.17	89.24	92.31	94.06	95.50	96.77	95.88	95.22	98.50	100.12	100.99
1980	102.85	104.84	105.20	99.83	95.22	94.54	95.65	98.17	99.54	100.83	102.13	101.03
1981	98.77	96.05	96.80	97.97	98.23	98.07	98.71	98.91	95.89	94.39	92.43	91.06
1982	90.17	88.93	86.88	84.33	83.46	81.75	82.20	80.94	81.22	80.26	78.96	78.71
1983	79.93	82.55	83.27	83.74	84.83	86.31	87.46	89.93	90.91	92.54	94.63	95.98
1984	96.37	96.93	98.64	98.70	97.62	98.05	96.64	94.33	93.70	91.02	91.58	91.07
1985	89.25	88.10	87.69	87.22	86.47	84.77	83.96	83.13	82.33	81.93	81.26	81.32
1986	81.67	81.13	79.18	78.17	78.74	79.84	80.73	78.06	79.69	83.14	85.61	86.31
1987	87.55	86.69	86.92	88.83	92.18	93.30	95.23	97.13	98.24	99.50	98.30	99.78
1988	100.72	101.15	103.03	103.94	104.68	106.30	106.50	106.92	106.06	106.02	110.60	113.45
1989	115.56	118.04	119.48	117.80	116.75	115.62	114.39	113.18	113.49	114.26	111.97	109.06
1990	107.42	106.13	107.63	108.66	108.66	108.60	108.68	109.25	109.62	109.10	106.67	105.88
1991	105.02	102.81	100.98	99.99	99.52	99.02	99.11	97.83	96.43	96.45	97.10	97.39
1992	96.66	97.39	99.60	101.09	101.85	101.91	101.68	101.70	102.11	100.07	97.67	98.26
1993	99.25	99.07	97.51	95.73	94.71	94.53	94.45	94.27	93.96	95.18	96.15	97.87
1994	99.35	101.66	102.71	103.42	104.98	106.98	109.38	110.99	114.28	117.20	121.41	123.32
1995	125.74	123.65	123.77	125.08	125.08	125.19	124.27	122.17	121.01	120.87	120.87	118.60
1996	117.62	116.41	116.41	116.71	118.01	117.45	116.84	118.61	119.73	118.29	117.37	118.39
1997	120.28	121.01	120.81	119.10	120.59	120.90	120.73	122.09	122.20	121.74	119.92	116.90
1998	113.97	112.23	111.52	110.60	110.04	108.16	107.02	105.28	102.88	102.37	100.95	100.58
1999	101.17	101.13	99.13	99.27	99.62	100.27	101.21	101.79	103.89	101.91	104.30	104.39
2000	105.25	104.66	104.29	104.07	103.69	103.26	102.18	101.96	102.71	101.97	101.59	102.39
2001	101.96	101.82	102.62	101.98	100.81	101.07	99.69	97.39	95.45	93.21	93.57	-

Source: The Conference Board. © 2002 The Conference Board. All Rights Reserved. No claim to original U.S. Government works pursuant to U.S. Contract No. 52-SABA-5-00128. Primary source(s): U.S. Department of Labor, Bureau of Labor Statistics, Office of Prices and Living Conditions, Division of Industrial Prices and Price Indexes, Washington, DC 20212 and Knight-Ridder Financial, 30 South Wacker Drive, Suite 1810, Chicago, IL 60606. A dash (-) indicates that data are not available or zero.

Corporate Profits After Tax
(Annual Rate, Billions of $)

Year	1st Quarter	2nd Quarter	3rd Quarter	4th Quarter
1959	29.8	32.5	29.2	28.6
1960	31.5	29.2	27.9	26.9
1961	26.2	27.7	29.3	31.6
1962	32.2	32.2	33.2	34.0
1963	33.6	35.5	36.4	37.4
1964	40.6	40.5	41.6	41.1
1965	46.8	48.5	49.1	51.9
1966	53.1	53.3	52.9	51.9
1967	49.6	49.6	50.6	52.9
1968	51.5	52.6	52.8	54.3
1969	53.7	52.0	50.4	49.4
1970	46.8	46.6	47.2	44.3
1971	51.0	53.0	56.6	58.2
1972	62.0	62.9	65.6	71.4
1973	82.3	84.4	84.6	88.3
1974	92.8	95.1	101.2	90.9
1975	80.0	85.3	102.3	108.1
1976	113.5	114.1	114.8	115.3
1977	126.8	135.4	140.9	140.9
1978	144.3	161.0	165.2	175.3
1979	176.4	182.5	186.6	182.8
1980	184.0	154.2	162.2	166.0
1981	170.0	155.1	159.1	154.8
1982	133.3	134.6	132.8	128.9
1983	131.2	151.5	164.1	169.7
1984	178.0	178.0	165.7	166.2
1985	153.7	156.6	160.4	164.1
1986	133.2	133.8	136.2	144.4
1987	164.6	187.3	195.6	202.6
1988	225.4	244.1	249.1	260.5
1989	249.3	235.5	223.4	232.8
1990	250.7	261.8	264.7	266.5
1991	281.1	277.9	280.9	290.3
1992	314.2	320.9	281.9	316.8
1993	325.6	340.8	343.5	370.1
1994	349.4	379.8	401.0	416.6
1995	440.1	456.6	464.8	468.5
1996	493.5	501.0	500.9	515.4
1997	530.7	549.4	573.8	566.9
1998	491.8	485.0	480.1	472.2
1999	509.2	511.2	515.1	557.7
2000	567.8	581.6	583.4	563.0
2001	518.9	510.3	475.6	-

Source: The Conference Board. © 2002 The Conference Board. All Rights Reserved. No claim to original U.S. Government works pursuant to U.S. Contract No. 52-SABA-5-00128. Primary source(s): U.S. Department of Commerce, Bureau of Economic Analysis, National Income and Wealth Division, BE-54, Washington, DC 20230. A dash (-) indicates that data are not available or zero.

Corporate Profits After Tax
(Annual Rate, Billions of 1996 $)

Year	1st Quarter	2nd Quarter	3rd Quarter	4th Quarter
1959	111.4	119.6	109.3	107.4
1960	116.5	109.0	105.5	102.1
1961	100.0	104.6	110.0	117.7
1962	119.6	119.6	123.0	125.7
1963	124.4	130.7	133.5	136.7
1964	147.4	147.4	150.7	149.0
1965	166.7	171.8	174.0	182.7
1966	186.0	184.3	181.9	176.7
1967	170.2	170.0	172.2	176.3
1968	172.1	174.6	174.1	176.3
1969	173.1	166.6	160.3	156.3
1970	147.7	144.5	145.2	135.8
1971	151.8	155.0	162.3	165.1
1972	173.5	174.6	180.8	193.4
1973	217.5	219.7	217.7	223.6
1974	229.2	227.9	232.8	204.3
1975	177.3	183.6	212.0	219.7
1976	229.1	228.9	228.3	227.0
1977	242.6	253.7	259.5	256.3
1978	258.8	280.4	283.4	294.7
1979	291.3	294.4	294.2	283.6
1980	279.2	235.1	240.3	240.6
1981	240.6	219.9	222.4	214.3
1982	186.7	185.4	181.6	177.1
1983	180.2	202.6	216.8	223.1
1984	231.9	231.0	216.1	216.2
1985	201.4	204.0	207.4	210.2
1986	176.1	177.3	178.8	186.6
1987	206.9	230.6	238.9	245.3
1988	269.0	287.5	291.6	301.8
1989	289.2	273.2	260.0	268.4
1990	284.3	293.3	293.1	291.1
1991	304.6	300.9	303.2	311.3
1992	333.3	338.9	299.1	333.6
1993	340.5	354.6	356.9	382.7
1994	361.2	390.4	409.6	424.5
1995	495.0	501.7	500.5	513.3
1996	495.0	501.7	500.5	513.3
1997	527.1	545.9	569.3	561.8
1998	486.2	579.5	473.8	465.3
1999	503.3	504.5	507.2	549.5
2000	554.9	566.1	563.9	539.3
2001	490.2	478.9	441.9	-

Unit Labor Cost, All Persons, Business Sector
(1992=100)

Year	1st Quarter	2nd Quarter	3rd Quarter	4th Quarter
1958	27.6	27.3	27.3	27.2
1959	27.3	27.1	27.4	27.7
1960	27.6	28.1	28.0	28.4
1961	28.4	28.1	28.0	28.0
1962	28.0	28.2	28.0	28.1
1963	28.1	28.0	27.9	28.1
1964	27.9	28.0	28.1	28.6
1965	28.3	28.4	28.1	28.0
1966	28.2	28.8	29.2	29.5
1967	29.4	29.8	30.1	30.4
1968	30.6	30.9	31.4	32.1
1969	32.1	33.0	33.6	34.4
1970	34.9	35.0	35.0	35.7
1971	35.3	35.7	35.9	36.5
1972	36.9	36.5	36.8	37.2
1973	37.6	38.1	39.4	40.0
1974	41.3	42.5	44.2	45.0
1975	45.7	45.8	45.9	46.9
1976	47.3	47.9	48.8	49.6
1977	50.2	51.0	51.4	52.8
1978	54.6	54.5	55.4	56.6
1979	58.5	60.0	61.3	62.9
1980	64.5	67.0	68.6	69.6
1981	70.1	72.1	72.7	74.8
1982	77.1	77.7	78.9	79.0
1983	79.0	78.1	78.4	78.9
1984	79.0	79.3	80.1	80.8
1985	81.5	82.0	82.0	83.0
1986	83.1	83.3	83.7	85.3
1987	85.9	86.3	87.1	87.5
1988	88.2	89.5	90.4	90.8
1989	90.5	90.8	91.5	92.5
1990	93.2	94.6	95.9	97.4
1991	97.9	98.3	99.0	99.4
1992	99.6	99.6	100.9	99.9
1993	101.4	102.2	102.5	101.6
1994	102.7	102.3	102.7	102.7
1995	103.5	104.0	104.5	104.4
1996	104.0	103.9	104.8	105.3
1997	105.4	104.7	104.9	106.4
1998	106.9	108.3	108.9	108.8
1999	109.2	110.7	111.3	110.4
2000	112.2	112.5	114.0	115.8
2001	117.3	118.1	118.8	-

Source: The Conference Board. © 2002 The Conference Board. All Rights Reserved. No claim to original U.S. Government works pursuant to U.S. Contract No. 52-SABA-5-00128. Primary source(s): U.S. Department of Labor, Bureau of Labor Statistics, Office of Productivity and Technology, Division of Productivity Research, Washington, DC 20212. A dash (-) indicates that data are not available or zero.

INDICATORS OF MONEY AND CREDIT

This section presents 9 series commonly used to measure the relationships between the economy and money, expressed in measures of money supply, interest and other yields on investments, and credit. These indicators are leading, coincident, or lagging depending on the nature of the series. The series presented are:

> Free reserves
> Member bank borrowings from the Federal Reserve
> Federal funds rate
> Discount rate on new issues of 91-day Treasury bills
> Yield on new high-grade corporate bonds
> Yield on long-term Treasury bonds
> Yield on municipal bonds, 20-bond average
> Secondary market yields on FHA mortgages
> Commercial and industrial loans outstanding, current dollars

Three related series, reported under Business Cycle Indicators, are:

> Money supply M2 (Leading Index)
> Commercial and industrial loans (Lagging Index)
> Average prime rate charged by banks (Lagging Index)

Free Reserves. Data are in millions of dollars; data are not seasonally adjusted. Free reserves are funds held by banks that may be loaned out. Banks are required by the Federal Reserve System to hold reserves in a fixed ratio to their total deposits (the "reserve ratio"). Deposits in excess of the required reserve less borrowings from the Federal Reserve System, are "free" to be lent.

The series is a leading indicator at business cycle peaks. It is an "inverted" indicator: for cyclical analysis, changes from period to period are inverted; a growth is depicted as negative growth, a decline as a growth. A pattern of decreasing free reserves signals an increasing demand for money for purchases, that is, increasing economic activity; a pattern of increasing free reserves indicates the opposite—no demand for money. Thus by "inverting the sign" of this indicator, the right message is obtained. The series is undefined at cycle troughs and overall.

Member Bank Borrowings from the Federal Reserve. To some extent this series is the inverse of the previous series. Both are shown in millions of current dollars. Members of the Federal Reserve System may borrow from the Fed for short-term purposes paying the prevailing "discount rate" charged by each Federal Reserve bank. Banks borrow to satisfy immediate needs for cash, to maintain required reserve ratios, and to meet contingencies (such as, for instance, sudden withdrawals which exceed the bank's cash reserves). Member borrowings and free reserves move in tandem. With high free reserves on hand, banks borrow less.

The series is classified as a leading indicator of cycle peaks and as a lagging indicator of troughs. Before a business cycle peaks, growth will tend to slow and member borrowings therefore fall before the economy stops growing. On a resumption of growth, member borrowings will tend to lag because members have high levels of free reserves.

Federal Funds Rate. Shown as a percent. This is the interest rate charged in the interbank market for bank purchases of excess reserve balances. Excess reserves are bank money holdings that exceed minimum deposit requirements; excess reserves minus loans outstanding to the Fed are "free reserves" (see above). Therefore excess reserves are free reserves plus obligations outstanding to the Fed. These assets may be bought and sold in the federal funds market at an interest rate called the federal funds rate. Unlike the discount rate, the funds rate changes with each transaction.

The series is a leading indicator of cycle peaks and a lagging indicator of troughs; slowing demand for reserves as a business cycle draws to its close causes a drop in the funds rate; as the economy turns around, some time passes before bank demand for reserves causes the funds rate to rise again.

Discount Rate on New Issues of 91-Day Treasury Bills. Data are shown as a percent. Treasury bills are short-term securities issued by the Treasury; 91-day Treasury bills have the shortest maturities. The bills are purchased at prices below the face value (minimum $10,000); the difference between face value and purchase price is the discount rate. The bills are sold at auction; hence the discount rate is set by market forces. The Federal Reserve usually buys or sells treasury bills to carry out its open market operations; purchases act to decrease money supply; sales act to increase money supply. The series acts as a coincident indicator of the peak of business cycles and as a lagging indicator of troughs.

Yield on New Issues of High-Grade Corporate Bonds. Data are shown as percent. Bonds are long-term debt instruments issued by corporations; high-grade "corporates" are bonds with high ratings for security based on the financial strength of the issuer. The yield percentage will tend to decline *after* a recessionary trend is well established and turn up *after* a recovery is clearly under way; hence the series is regarded as a lagging indicator of the business cycle.

Yield on Long-Term Treasury Bonds. Data are shown in percent. Long-term Treasury bonds are debt instruments sold by the U.S. Treasury with maturities of 10 years or more in denominations of $1,000. The series is a coincident indicator of business cycle peaks and a lagging indictor of troughs.

Yield on Municipal Bonds, 20-Bond Average. These instruments are governmental debt instruments sold by municipalities. Data are shown in percent. The series is classified as a lagging indicator of the trough of business cycles; it is unclassified at the peak, indicating behavior that does not follow any discernible pattern. Since most municipal bond yields ("public purpose bonds") are tax exempt, yields will tend to rise in an expanding economy where tax shelters are more valuable than in a declining economy.

Secondary Market Yields on FHA Mortgages. Data are shown in percent from 1949 to 2001. The primary market for Federal Housing Administration (FHA) or other mortgages is that defined by the home buyer and the original mortgage lender. The lender can then sell the loan—at a discount, of course—to investors. This second transaction is the secondary market for mortgages. The original lender receives cash for lending (increases his/her liquidity); the investor obtains an asset. Government agencies buy the original mortgages, assemble them into mortgage pools, and sell them as collateralized mortgage obligations.

The series is a lagging indicator. Before mortgages can be resold, people have to buy homes and take out mortgages. The secondary market, therefore, will tend to "soften" after a downturn in the economy; although housing starts tend to lead an expansion, housing purchases come later and secondary mortgage operations even later than that—explaining the lagging character of this series.

Commercial and Industrial Loans Outstanding, Current Dollars. This series is shown for 1947 through 2001 in millions of current dollars. The same series, in chained 1996 dollars, is a lagging indicator—as is this series. Business and industry assume debt in periods of growth and minimize debt in periods of decline. The total debt outstanding, however, reflects the business cycle at a lag in time; borrowers pay off debt over time and may be late in paying during economic turn-downs; they also contract new obligations later than the economy's upturn because both lenders and borrowers are more cautious after a recessionary period.

Free Reserves

Not seasonally adjusted

(Millions of $)

Year	Jan	Feb	Mar	Apr	May	Jun	Jul	Aug	Sep	Oct	Nov	Dec
1959	-54	-51	-139	-261	-320	-523	-545	-542	-484	-466	-415	-435
1960	-373	-356	-218	-180	-51	46	122	246	412	495	610	669
1961	706	516	476	559	461	527	562	514	542	461	493	451
1962	536	434	383	420	456	371	442	405	409	414	437	312
1963	359	295	286	327	220	158	156	116	109	77	92	158
1964	166	111	108	141	94	107	113	106	86	77	8	142
1965	115	7	-45	-130	-161	-175	-175	-151	-144	-130	-80	-21
1966	-41	-135	-218	-282	-346	-351	-363	-368	-398	-401	-222	-193
1967	-7	5	214	204	276	246	303	284	253	206	226	147
1968	141	13	-322	-350	-381	-366	-176	-236	-143	-198	-237	-320
1969	-490	-581	-683	-836	-1,119	-1,081	-1,027	-982	-805	-987	-974	-833
1970	-785	-872	-735	-693	-811	-691	-1,194	-663	-356	-258	-181	-83
1971	-130	-78	-124	15	-65	-291	-639	-613	-306	-194	-147	56
1972	185	119	92	38	28	103	-45	-200	-329	-344	-254	-766
1973	-902	-1,396	-1,615	-1,488	-1,704	-1,626	-1,638	-1,968	-1,595	-1,208	-1,168	-994
1974	-886	-1,007	-1,180	-1,554	-1,772	-1,582	-1,709	-1,611	-1,472	-1,208	-887	-322
1975	-115	100	131	59	93	-10	-93	-4	-192	28	228	148
1976	173	147	172	111	95	87	101	107	139	125	185	221
1977	198	126	112	119	2	-115	-48	-861	-417	-1,096	-611	-379
1978	-217	-165	-129	-409	-993	-916	-1,120	-972	-867	-1,115	-481	-636
1979	-789	-764	-833	-742	-1,624	-1,197	-960	-863	-1,149	-1,750	-1,661	-1,031
1980	-990	-1,444	-2,538	-1,706	-97	131	142	-115	-964	-1,104	-1,539	-1,173
1981	-951	-933	-705	-1,161	-1,960	-1,692	-1,336	-1,048	-741	-465	-154	-169
1982	-902	-1,253	-886	-1,050	-582	-793	-327	-109	-430	68	-31	52
1983	176	132	-42	-128	10	-198	-368	-609	-428	-83	-370	-211
1984	-98	344	-257	-717	-2,382	-668	-286	-294	-134	-342	-82	253
1985	397	364	141	281	-47	382	240	331	64	186	-293	244
1986	809	622	640	513	586	647	510	333	252	373	567	649
1987	715	920	658	134	320	731	382	536	253	595	709	725
1988	542	947	671	516	576	366	-11	382	237	535	635	589
1989	541	717	439	231	519	335	394	258	274	506	620	696
1990	628	87	707	665	497	252	391	76	295	448	723	1,361
1991	1,635	1,587	996	881	818	661	342	623	588	806	785	798
1992	759	978	936	1,039	848	694	691	689	725	918	938	1,031
1993	1,097	1,047	1,141	1,031	875	710	823	600	655	793	1,028	988
1994	1,384	1,076	926	1,015	666	781	653	534	558	411	738	950
1995	1,207	902	746	642	724	711	733	722	691	840	750	1,033
1996	1,426	821	1,118	1,032	779	723	650	624	679	720	838	1,261
1997	1,179	989	1,009	748	1,020	947	807	657	863	1,145	1,516	1,361
1998	1,583	1,475	1,310	1,316	1,120	1,364	1,113	1,260	1,444	1,398	1,536	1,397
1999	1,280	1,080	1,204	994	1,095	1,150	815	816	872	869	1,094	977
2000	1,646	1,004	1,030	853	610	638	574	425	642	729	918	1,115
2001	1,180	1,381	1,327	1,226	806	1,131	1,124	1,051	15,652	-	-	-

Source: The Conference Board. © 2002 The Conference Board. All Rights Reserved. No claim to original U.S. Government works pursuant to U.S. Contract No. 52-SABA-5-00128. Primary source(s): Board of Governors of the Federal Reserve System, Division of Monetary Affairs, Money and Reserve Projections Section, Stop 59, Washington, DC 20551. A dash (-) indicates that data are not available or zero.

Member Bank Borrowings From Federal Reserve
Not seasonally adjusted
(Millions of $)

Year	Jan	Feb	Mar	Apr	May	Jun	Jul	Aug	Sep	Oct	Nov	Dec
1951	212	330	242	161	438	170	194	292	338	95	340	657
1952	210	365	307	367	563	579	1,077	1,032	683	1,048	1,532	1,593
1953	1,347	1,310	1,202	1,166	944	423	418	651	468	362	486	441
1954	100	293	189	139	155	146	65	115	67	82	164	246
1955	313	354	463	495	368	401	527	765	849	884	1,016	839
1956	807	799	993	1,060	971	769	738	898	792	715	744	688
1957	406	640	834	1,011	909	1,005	917	1,005	988	811	804	710
1958	451	242	138	130	119	142	109	252	476	425	486	557
1959	552	505	599	692	741	930	961	990	927	907	859	941
1960	887	810	641	606	496	434	379	296	215	167	133	74
1961	66	133	70	57	95	63	54	65	38	71	98	133
1962	87	68	89	72	61	102	92	125	81	63	120	260
1963	146	166	148	130	210	259	298	329	319	320	349	332
1964	274	286	278	211	260	268	263	315	345	321	400	264
1965	300	405	411	471	495	537	528	547	554	488	432	444
1966	420	482	560	637	687	707	741	735	769	734	607	532
1967	410	364	200	146	89	106	115	81	89	129	132	228
1968	246	373	659	685	741	694	527	565	504	443	545	746
1969	736	835	902	1,003	1,374	1,385	1,252	1,219	1,079	1,150	1,203	1,119
1970	959	1,080	898	845	968	881	1,360	837	600	463	415	332
1971	364	332	319	153	284	492	823	809	495	357	384	126
1972	21	33	98	118	111	100	238	388	541	555	608	1,050
1973	1,160	1,593	1,824	1,711	1,843	1,851	1,953	2,165	1,852	1,476	1,393	1,298
1974	1,051	1,191	1,314	1,736	2,590	3,006	3,301	3,336	3,282	1,813	1,252	727
1975	398	147	106	110	66	227	301	211	397	190	60	130
1976	78	81	54	44	115	127	133	100	62	94	72	53
1977	68	72	103	73	206	262	323	1,061	626	1,306	862	569
1978	484	406	328	557	1,212	1,094	1,317	1,140	1,060	1,277	703	868
1979	1,003	973	991	918	1,765	1,418	1,171	1,085	1,340	2,022	1,906	1,473
1980	1,241	1,655	2,823	2,455	1,018	379	395	658	1,311	1,310	2,060	1,690
1981	1,395	1,304	1,000	1,338	2,223	2,037	1,679	1,420	1,456	1,181	663	636
1982	1,517	1,789	1,555	1,568	1,117	1,205	691	515	933	477	621	634
1983	529	582	792	1,009	952	1,636	1,453	1,546	1,441	844	905	774
1984	715	567	952	1,234	2,988	3,300	5,924	8,017	7,242	6,017	4,617	3,186
1985	1,395	1,289	1,593	1,323	1,334	1,205	1,107	1,073	1,289	1,187	1,741	1,318
1986	770	884	761	893	876	803	741	872	1,008	841	752	827
1987	580	556	527	993	1,035	776	672	647	940	943	625	777
1988	1,082	396	1,752	2,993	2,578	3,083	3,440	3,241	2,839	2,299	2,861	1,716
1989	1,649	1,487	1,813	2,289	1,720	1,490	694	675	693	555	349	265
1990	440	1,448	2,124	1,609	1,332	881	757	927	624	410	230	326
1991	534	252	241	231	303	340	607	764	645	261	108	192
1992	233	77	91	90	155	229	284	250	287	143	104	124
1993	166	45	91	73	121	181	244	352	428	285	89	82
1994	73	70	55	124	200	333	458	469	487	380	249	209
1995	136	59	69	111	150	272	371	282	278	245	204	257
1996	38	35	21	91	127	386	368	334	368	287	214	155
1997	45	42	156	261	243	367	409	598	438	270	153	324
1998	210	58	41	72	153	251	258	271	251	174	83	117
1999	206	116	65	166	127	145	309	344	338	281	236	320
2000	374	108	179	304	362	479	570	579	477	418	283	210
2001	73	51	58	51	213	229	283	183	3,385	127	-	-

Source: The Conference Board. © 2002 The Conference Board. All Rights Reserved. No claim to original U.S. Government works pursuant to U.S. Contract No. 52-SABA-5-00128. Primary source(s): Board of Governors of the Federal Reserve System, Division of Monetary Affairs, Money and Reserve Projections Section, Stop 59, Washington, DC 20551. A dash (-) indicates that data are not available or zero.

Federal Funds Rate

Not seasonally adjusted

(Percent)

Year	Jan	Feb	Mar	Apr	May	Jun	Jul	Aug	Sep	Oct	Nov	Dec
1954	-	-	-	-	-	-	0.80	1.22	1.06	0.85	0.83	1.28
1955	1.39	1.29	1.35	1.43	1.43	1.64	1.68	1.96	2.18	2.24	2.35	2.48
1956	2.45	2.50	2.50	2.62	2.75	2.71	2.75	2.73	2.95	2.96	2.88	2.94
1957	2.84	3.00	2.96	3.00	3.00	3.00	2.99	3.24	3.47	3.50	3.28	2.98
1958	2.72	1.67	1.20	1.26	0.63	0.93	0.68	1.53	1.76	1.80	2.27	2.42
1959	2.48	2.43	2.80	2.96	2.90	3.39	3.47	3.50	3.76	3.98	4.00	3.99
1960	3.99	3.97	3.84	3.92	3.85	3.32	3.23	2.98	2.60	2.47	2.44	1.98
1961	1.45	2.54	2.02	1.49	1.98	1.73	1.17	2.00	1.88	2.26	2.61	2.33
1962	2.15	2.37	2.85	2.78	2.36	2.68	2.71	2.93	2.90	2.90	2.94	2.93
1963	2.92	3.00	2.98	2.90	3.00	2.99	3.02	3.49	3.48	3.50	3.48	3.38
1964	3.48	3.48	3.43	3.47	3.50	3.50	3.42	3.50	3.45	3.36	3.52	3.85
1965	3.90	3.98	4.04	4.09	4.10	4.04	4.09	4.12	4.01	4.08	4.10	4.32
1966	4.42	4.60	4.65	4.67	4.90	5.17	5.30	5.53	5.40	5.53	5.76	5.40
1967	4.94	5.00	4.53	4.05	3.94	3.98	3.79	3.90	3.99	3.88	4.13	4.51
1968	4.60	4.71	5.05	5.76	6.11	6.07	6.02	6.03	5.78	5.91	5.82	6.02
1969	6.30	6.61	6.79	7.41	8.67	8.90	8.61	9.19	9.15	9.00	8.85	8.97
1970	8.98	8.98	7.76	8.10	7.94	7.60	7.21	6.61	6.29	6.20	5.60	4.90
1971	4.14	3.72	3.71	4.15	4.63	4.91	5.31	5.56	5.55	5.20	4.91	4.14
1972	3.50	3.29	3.83	4.17	4.27	4.46	4.55	4.80	4.87	5.04	5.06	5.33
1973	5.94	6.58	7.09	7.12	7.84	8.49	10.40	10.50	10.78	10.01	10.03	9.95
1974	9.65	8.97	9.35	10.51	11.31	11.93	12.92	12.01	11.34	10.06	9.45	8.53
1975	7.13	6.24	5.54	5.49	5.22	5.55	6.10	6.14	6.24	5.82	5.22	5.20
1976	4.87	4.77	4.84	4.82	5.29	5.48	5.31	5.29	5.25	5.02	4.95	4.65
1977	4.61	4.68	4.69	4.73	5.35	5.39	5.42	5.90	6.14	6.47	6.51	6.56
1978	6.70	6.78	6.79	6.89	7.36	7.60	7.81	8.04	8.45	8.96	9.76	10.03
1979	10.07	10.06	10.09	10.01	10.24	10.29	10.47	10.94	11.43	13.77	13.18	13.78
1980	13.82	14.13	17.19	17.61	10.98	9.47	9.03	9.61	10.87	12.81	15.85	18.90
1981	19.08	15.93	14.70	15.72	18.52	19.10	19.04	17.82	15.87	15.08	13.31	12.37
1982	13.22	14.78	14.68	14.94	14.45	14.15	12.59	10.12	10.31	9.71	9.20	8.95
1983	8.68	8.51	8.77	8.80	8.63	8.98	9.37	9.56	9.45	9.48	9.34	9.47
1984	9.56	9.59	9.91	10.29	10.32	11.06	11.23	11.64	11.30	9.99	9.43	8.38
1985	8.35	8.50	8.58	8.27	7.97	7.53	7.88	7.90	7.92	7.99	8.05	8.27
1986	8.14	7.86	7.48	6.99	6.85	6.92	6.56	6.17	5.89	5.85	6.04	6.91
1987	6.43	6.10	6.13	6.37	6.85	6.73	6.58	6.73	7.22	7.29	6.69	6.77
1988	6.83	6.58	6.58	6.87	7.09	7.51	7.75	8.01	8.19	8.30	8.35	8.76
1989	9.12	9.36	9.85	9.84	9.81	9.53	9.24	8.99	9.02	8.84	8.55	8.45
1990	8.23	8.24	8.28	8.26	8.18	8.29	8.15	8.13	8.20	8.11	7.81	7.31
1991	6.91	6.25	6.12	5.91	5.78	5.90	5.82	5.66	5.45	5.21	4.81	4.43
1992	4.03	4.06	3.98	3.73	3.82	3.76	3.25	3.30	3.22	3.10	3.09	2.92
1993	3.02	3.03	3.07	2.96	3.00	3.04	3.06	3.03	3.09	2.99	3.02	2.96
1994	3.05	3.25	3.34	3.56	4.01	4.25	4.26	4.47	4.73	4.76	5.29	5.45
1995	5.53	5.92	5.98	6.05	6.01	6.00	5.85	5.74	5.80	5.76	5.80	5.60
1996	5.56	5.22	5.31	5.22	5.24	5.27	5.40	5.22	5.30	5.24	5.31	5.29
1997	5.25	5.19	5.39	5.51	5.50	5.56	5.52	5.54	5.54	5.50	5.52	5.50
1998	5.56	5.51	5.49	5.45	5.49	5.56	5.54	5.55	5.51	5.07	4.83	4.68
1999	4.63	4.76	4.81	4.74	4.74	4.76	4.99	5.07	5.22	5.20	5.42	5.30
2000	5.45	5.73	5.85	6.02	6.27	6.53	6.54	6.50	6.52	6.51	6.51	6.40
2001	5.98	5.49	5.31	4.80	4.21	3.97	3.77	3.65	3.07	2.49	2.09	1.82

Discount Rate on New 91-Day Treasury Bills
Not seasonally adjusted
(Percent)

Year	Jan	Feb	Mar	Apr	May	Jun	Jul	Aug	Sep	Oct	Nov	Dec
1951	1.39	1.39	1.42	1.52	1.58	1.50	1.59	1.64	1.65	1.61	1.61	1.73
1952	1.69	1.57	1.66	1.62	1.71	1.70	1.82	1.88	1.79	1.78	1.86	2.13
1953	2.04	2.02	2.08	2.18	2.20	2.23	2.10	2.09	1.88	1.40	1.43	1.63
1954	1.21	0.98	1.05	1.01	0.78	0.65	0.71	0.89	1.01	0.99	0.95	1.17
1955	1.26	1.18	1.34	1.62	1.49	1.43	1.62	1.88	2.09	2.26	2.23	2.56
1956	2.46	2.37	2.31	2.61	2.65	2.53	2.33	2.61	2.85	2.96	3.00	3.23
1957	3.21	3.17	3.14	3.11	3.04	3.32	3.17	3.40	3.58	3.59	3.34	3.10
1958	2.60	1.56	1.35	1.13	1.05	0.88	0.96	1.69	2.48	2.79	2.76	2.81
1959	2.84	2.71	2.85	2.96	2.85	3.25	3.24	3.36	4.00	4.12	4.21	4.57
1960	4.44	3.95	3.44	3.24	3.39	2.64	2.40	2.29	2.49	2.43	2.38	2.27
1961	2.30	2.41	2.42	2.33	2.29	2.36	2.27	2.40	2.30	2.35	2.46	2.62
1962	2.75	2.75	2.72	2.73	2.69	2.72	2.94	2.84	2.79	2.75	2.80	2.86
1963	2.91	2.92	2.90	2.91	2.92	2.99	3.14	3.32	3.38	3.45	3.52	3.52
1964	3.53	3.53	3.55	3.48	3.48	3.48	3.48	3.51	3.53	3.58	3.62	3.86
1965	3.83	3.93	3.94	3.93	3.89	3.81	3.83	3.84	3.91	4.03	4.08	4.36
1966	4.60	4.67	4.63	4.61	4.64	4.54	4.86	4.93	5.36	5.39	5.34	5.01
1967	4.76	4.55	4.29	3.85	3.64	3.48	4.31	4.27	4.45	4.59	4.76	5.01
1968	5.08	4.97	5.14	5.36	5.62	5.54	5.38	5.09	5.20	5.33	5.49	5.92
1969	6.18	6.16	6.08	6.15	6.08	6.49	7.00	7.01	7.13	7.04	7.19	7.72
1970	7.91	7.16	6.71	6.48	7.03	6.74	6.47	6.41	6.24	5.93	5.29	4.86
1971	4.49	3.77	3.32	3.78	4.14	4.70	5.40	5.08	4.67	4.49	4.19	4.02
1972	3.40	3.18	3.72	3.72	3.65	3.87	4.06	4.01	4.65	4.72	4.77	5.06
1973	5.31	5.56	6.05	6.29	6.35	7.19	8.01	8.67	8.48	7.15	7.87	7.36
1974	7.76	7.06	7.99	8.23	8.43	8.14	7.75	8.74	8.36	7.24	7.58	7.18
1975	6.49	5.58	5.54	5.69	5.32	5.19	6.16	6.46	6.38	6.08	5.47	5.50
1976	4.96	4.85	5.05	4.88	5.18	5.44	5.28	5.15	5.08	4.93	4.81	4.35
1977	4.60	4.66	4.61	4.54	4.94	5.00	5.15	5.50	5.77	6.19	6.16	6.06
1978	6.45	6.46	6.32	6.31	6.43	6.71	7.07	7.04	7.84	8.13	8.79	9.12
1979	9.35	9.26	9.46	9.49	9.58	9.05	9.26	9.45	10.18	11.47	11.87	12.07
1980	12.04	12.81	15.53	14.00	9.15	7.00	8.13	9.26	10.32	11.58	13.89	15.66
1981	14.72	14.91	13.48	13.63	16.29	14.56	14.70	15.61	14.95	13.87	11.27	10.93
1982	12.41	13.78	12.49	12.82	12.15	12.11	11.91	9.01	8.20	7.75	8.04	8.01
1983	7.81	8.13	8.30	8.25	8.18	8.82	9.12	9.38	9.05	8.71	8.71	8.96
1984	8.93	9.03	9.44	9.69	9.90	9.94	10.13	10.49	10.41	9.97	8.79	8.16
1985	7.76	8.22	8.56	7.99	7.56	7.01	7.05	7.18	7.08	7.17	7.20	7.07
1986	7.04	7.03	6.59	6.06	6.12	6.21	5.84	5.57	5.19	5.18	5.35	5.49
1987	5.45	5.59	5.56	5.76	5.75	5.69	5.78	6.00	6.32	6.40	5.81	5.80
1988	5.90	5.69	5.69	5.92	6.27	6.50	6.73	7.02	7.23	7.34	7.68	8.09
1989	8.29	8.48	8.83	8.70	8.40	8.22	7.92	7.91	7.72	7.59	7.65	7.64
1990	7.64	7.76	7.87	7.78	7.78	7.74	7.66	7.44	7.38	7.19	7.07	6.81
1991	6.30	5.95	5.91	5.67	5.51	5.60	5.58	5.39	5.25	5.03	4.60	4.12
1992	3.84	3.84	4.05	3.81	3.66	3.70	3.28	3.14	2.97	2.84	3.14	3.25
1993	3.06	2.95	2.97	2.89	2.96	3.10	3.05	3.05	2.96	3.04	3.12	3.08
1994	3.02	3.21	3.52	3.74	4.19	4.18	4.39	4.50	4.64	4.96	5.25	5.64
1995	5.81	5.80	5.73	5.67	5.70	5.50	5.47	5.41	5.26	5.30	5.35	5.16
1996	5.02	4.87	4.96	4.99	5.02	5.11	5.17	5.09	5.15	5.01	5.03	4.87
1997	5.05	5.00	5.14	5.17	5.13	4.92	5.07	5.13	4.97	4.95	5.15	5.16
1998	5.09	5.11	5.03	5.00	5.03	4.99	4.96	4.94	4.74	4.08	4.44	4.42
1999	4.34	4.45	4.48	4.28	4.51	4.59	4.60	4.76	4.73	4.88	5.07	5.23
2000	5.34	5.57	5.72	5.67	5.92	5.74	5.96	6.11	5.99	6.11	6.19	5.83
2001	5.21	4.86	4.45	3.91	3.61	3.48	3.53	3.37	2.87	-	-	-

Source: The Conference Board. © 2002 The Conference Board. All Rights Reserved. No claim to original U.S. Government works pursuant to U.S. Contract No. 52-SABA-5-00128. Primary source(s): Board of Governors of the Federal Reserve System, Division of Monetary Affairs, Banking and Money Market Statistics Section, Stop 81, Washington, DC 20551. A dash (-) indicates that data are not available or zero.

Yield on New High-Grade Corporate Bonds
Not seasonally adjusted
(Percent)

Year	Jan	Feb	Mar	Apr	May	Jun	Jul	Aug	Sep	Oct	Nov	Dec
1951	2.74	2.78	2.90	3.06	2.98	3.24	3.20	3.01	2.91	3.09	3.36	3.22
1952	3.08	2.94	3.14	3.09	3.25	3.09	3.11	3.08	3.14	3.16	3.07	3.04
1953	3.17	3.26	3.41	3.53	3.80	3.82	3.59	3.46	3.60	3.09	3.13	3.23
1954	3.00	2.88	2.74	2.88	2.90	2.91	2.94	2.94	3.01	2.84	2.94	2.87
1955	2.99	3.09	3.14	3.11	3.15	3.11	3.14	3.41	3.27	3.15	3.17	3.27
1956	3.20	3.07	3.25	3.55	3.48	3.56	3.56	4.02	3.96	3.94	4.29	4.26
1957	4.28	4.13	4.18	4.23	4.41	4.81	4.59	4.78	4.68	4.71	4.56	4.04
1958	3.62	3.73	3.88	3.67	3.66	3.61	3.85	4.39	4.56	4.48	4.35	4.44
1959	4.58	4.60	4.53	4.60	4.92	5.00	4.95	4.90	5.28	5.37	5.14	5.27
1960	5.34	5.24	4.98	4.97	4.95	4.91	4.79	4.65	4.64	4.75	4.82	4.94
1961	4.63	4.43	4.37	4.57	4.67	4.82	4.81	4.79	4.72	4.60	4.52	4.58
1962	4.56	4.53	4.41	4.37	4.32	4.30	4.41	4.39	4.28	4.26	4.23	4.28
1963	4.22	4.25	4.28	4.35	4.36	4.32	4.34	4.34	4.40	4.37	4.42	4.49
1964	4.50	4.39	4.45	4.48	4.48	4.50	4.44	4.44	4.49	4.49	4.48	4.49
1965	4.45	4.45	4.49	4.48	4.52	4.57	4.57	4.66	4.71	4.70	4.75	4.92
1966	4.93	5.09	5.33	5.38	5.55	5.67	5.81	6.04	6.14	6.04	6.11	5.98
1967	5.53	5.35	5.55	5.59	5.90	6.06	6.06	6.30	6.33	6.53	6.87	6.93
1968	6.57	6.57	6.80	6.79	7.00	7.02	6.91	6.54	6.69	6.88	7.00	7.28
1969	7.29	7.33	7.76	7.54	7.62	8.04	8.06	8.05	8.36	8.46	8.94	9.22
1970	9.00	8.84	9.00	9.09	9.53	9.70	9.09	9.08	9.00	9.14	8.97	8.13
1971	7.63	7.54	7.62	7.76	8.25	8.15	8.24	8.14	7.90	7.72	7.67	7.54
1972	7.36	7.57	7.53	7.77	7.61	7.63	7.72	7.59	7.72	7.66	7.46	7.50
1973	7.61	7.67	7.75	7.70	7.69	7.73	7.97	8.45	8.10	7.97	7.95	8.09
1974	8.32	8.21	8.60	9.04	9.39	9.59	10.18	10.30	10.44	10.29	9.22	9.47
1975	9.17	8.84	9.48	9.81	9.76	9.27	9.56	9.71	9.89	9.54	9.48	9.59
1976	8.97	8.71	8.73	8.68	9.00	8.90	8.76	8.59	8.37	8.25	8.17	7.90
1977	7.96	8.18	8.33	8.30	8.38	8.08	8.12	8.06	8.11	8.21	8.26	8.39
1978	8.70	8.70	8.70	8.88	9.00	9.15	9.27	8.83	8.78	9.14	9.30	9.30
1979	9.47	9.52	9.65	9.69	9.82	9.51	9.47	9.57	9.87	11.17	11.52	11.30
1980	11.65	13.23	14.08	13.36	11.61	11.12	11.48	12.31	12.74	13.17	14.10	14.38
1981	14.01	14.60	14.49	15.00	15.68	14.97	15.67	16.34	16.97	16.96	15.53	15.55
1982	16.34	16.35	15.72	15.62	15.37	15.96	15.75	14.64	13.78	12.63	11.89	12.15
1983	12.04	12.11	11.81	11.58	11.24	11.90	12.46	12.89	12.68	12.54	12.86	12.87
1984	12.65	12.80	13.36	13.64	14.41	14.49	14.25	13.54	13.37	13.02	12.40	12.47
1985	12.46	12.39	12.85	12.45	11.85	11.33	11.28	11.61	11.66	11.51	11.19	10.42
1986	10.33	9.76	8.95	8.71	9.09	9.39	9.11	9.03	9.28	9.29	8.99	8.87
1987	8.59	8.58	8.68	9.36	9.95	9.64	9.70	10.09	10.63	10.80	10.09	10.22
1988	9.81	9.43	9.68	9.92	10.25	10.08	10.12	10.27	10.03	9.86	9.98	10.05
1989	9.92	10.11	10.33	10.11	9.82	9.24	9.20	9.09	9.29	9.04	9.20	9.23
1990	9.56	9.68	9.79	10.02	9.97	9.69	9.72	10.05	10.17	10.09	9.79	9.55
1991	9.60	9.14	9.14	9.07	9.13	9.37	9.38	8.88	8.79	8.81	8.72	8.55
1992	8.36	8.63	8.62	8.59	8.57	8.45	8.19	7.96	7.99	8.17	8.25	8.12
1993	7.91	7.73	7.39	7.48	7.52	7.48	7.35	7.04	6.88	6.88	7.17	7.22
1994	7.16	7.27	7.64	7.95	8.17	8.16	8.30	8.25	8.48	8.76	8.89	8.66
1995	8.59	8.39	8.23	8.10	7.68	7.42	7.54	7.75	7.42	7.29	7.20	7.02
1996	7.00	7.14	7.57	7.81	7.87	8.00	7.97	7.68	7.84	7.69	7.43	7.45
1997	7.62	7.54	7.85	8.04	7.90	7.71	7.44	7.30	7.04	6.90	6.79	6.68
1998	6.62	6.66	6.63	6.59	6.63	6.43	6.35	6.34	6.27	6.21	6.42	6.13
1999	6.14	6.33	6.52	6.58	6.86	7.21	7.20	7.36	7.38	7.51	7.35	7.55
2000	7.83	7.59	7.54	7.49	7.85	7.75	7.66	7.47	7.50	7.50	7.41	7.21
2001	7.15	7.08	6.87	7.09	7.19	7.11	7.02	6.85	6.83	6.72	6.51	6.80

Source: The Conference Board. © 2002 The Conference Board. All Rights Reserved. No claim to original U.S. Government works pursuant to U.S. Contract No. 52-SABA-5-00128. Primary source(s): U.S. Department of the Treasury, Office of Market Finance, Domestic Finance Division, Washington, DC 20220. A dash (-) indicates that data are not available or zero.

Yield on Long-Term Treasury Bonds
Not seasonally adjusted
(Percent)

Year	Jan	Feb	Mar	Apr	May	Jun	Jul	Aug	Sep	Oct	Nov	Dec
1951	2.39	2.40	2.47	2.56	2.63	2.65	2.63	2.57	2.56	2.61	2.66	2.70
1952	2.74	2.71	2.70	2.64	2.57	2.61	2.61	2.70	2.71	2.74	2.71	2.75
1953	2.80	2.83	2.89	2.97	3.12	3.13	3.04	3.05	3.01	2.87	2.86	2.79
1954	2.69	2.62	2.53	2.48	2.54	2.55	2.47	2.48	2.52	2.54	2.57	2.59
1955	2.68	2.77	2.78	2.82	2.81	2.82	2.91	2.95	2.92	2.87	2.89	2.91
1956	2.88	2.85	2.93	3.07	2.97	2.93	3.00	3.17	3.21	3.20	3.30	3.40
1957	3.34	3.22	3.26	3.32	3.40	3.58	3.60	3.63	3.66	3.73	3.57	3.30
1958	3.24	3.26	3.25	3.12	3.14	3.19	3.36	3.60	3.75	3.76	3.70	3.80
1959	3.90	3.92	3.92	4.01	4.08	4.09	4.11	4.10	4.26	4.11	4.12	4.27
1960	4.37	4.22	4.08	4.17	4.16	3.99	3.86	3.79	3.82	3.91	3.93	3.88
1961	3.89	3.81	3.78	3.80	3.73	3.88	3.90	4.00	4.02	3.98	3.98	4.06
1962	4.08	4.09	4.01	3.89	3.88	3.90	4.02	3.97	3.94	3.89	3.87	3.87
1963	3.88	3.92	3.93	3.97	3.97	4.00	4.01	3.99	4.04	4.07	4.10	4.14
1964	4.15	4.14	4.18	4.20	4.16	4.13	4.13	4.14	4.16	4.16	4.12	4.14
1965	4.14	4.16	4.15	4.15	4.14	4.14	4.15	4.19	4.25	4.27	4.34	4.43
1966	4.43	4.61	4.63	4.55	4.57	4.63	4.74	4.80	4.79	4.70	4.74	4.65
1967	4.40	4.47	4.45	4.51	4.76	4.86	4.86	4.95	4.99	5.18	5.44	5.36
1968	5.18	5.16	5.39	5.28	5.40	5.23	5.09	5.04	5.09	5.24	5.36	5.65
1969	5.74	5.86	6.05	5.84	5.85	6.06	6.07	6.02	6.32	6.27	6.51	6.81
1970	6.86	6.44	6.39	6.53	6.94	6.99	6.57	6.75	6.63	6.59	6.24	5.97
1971	5.91	5.84	5.71	5.75	5.96	5.94	5.91	5.78	5.56	5.46	5.44	5.62
1972	5.62	5.67	5.66	5.74	5.64	5.59	5.57	5.54	5.70	5.69	5.50	5.63
1973	5.94	6.14	6.20	6.11	6.22	6.32	6.53	6.81	6.42	6.26	6.31	6.35
1974	6.56	6.54	6.81	7.04	7.07	7.03	7.18	7.33	7.30	7.22	6.93	6.78
1975	6.68	6.61	6.73	7.03	6.99	6.86	6.89	7.06	7.29	7.29	7.21	7.17
1976	6.94	6.92	6.87	6.73	6.99	6.92	6.85	6.79	6.70	6.65	6.62	6.39
1977	6.68	7.15	7.20	7.13	7.17	6.99	6.97	7.00	6.94	7.08	7.14	7.23
1978	7.50	7.60	7.63	7.74	7.87	7.94	8.09	7.87	7.82	8.07	8.16	8.35
1979	8.43	8.43	8.45	8.44	8.55	8.32	8.35	8.42	8.68	9.44	9.80	9.59
1980	10.03	11.55	11.87	10.83	9.82	9.40	9.83	10.53	10.94	11.20	11.83	11.89
1981	11.65	12.23	12.15	12.62	12.96	12.39	13.05	13.78	14.14	14.13	12.68	12.88
1982	13.73	13.63	12.98	12.84	12.67	13.32	12.97	12.15	11.48	10.51	10.18	10.33
1983	10.37	10.60	10.34	10.19	10.21	10.64	11.10	11.42	11.26	11.21	11.32	11.44
1984	11.29	11.44	11.90	12.17	12.89	13.04	12.82	12.23	11.97	11.66	11.25	11.21
1985	11.15	11.35	11.78	11.42	10.96	10.36	10.51	10.59	10.67	10.56	10.08	9.59
1986	9.51	9.07	8.13	7.59	8.02	8.23	7.86	7.72	8.08	8.04	7.81	7.67
1987	7.60	7.69	7.62	8.31	8.79	8.63	8.70	8.97	9.58	9.61	8.99	9.12
1988	8.82	8.41	8.61	8.91	9.24	9.04	9.20	9.33	9.06	8.89	9.07	9.13
1989	9.07	9.16	9.33	9.18	8.95	8.40	8.19	8.26	8.31	8.15	8.03	8.02
1990	8.39	8.66	8.74	8.92	8.90	8.62	8.64	8.97	9.11	8.93	8.60	8.31
1991	8.33	8.12	8.38	8.29	8.33	8.54	8.50	8.17	7.96	7.88	7.83	7.58
1992	7.48	7.78	7.93	7.88	7.80	7.72	7.40	7.19	7.08	7.26	7.43	7.30
1993	7.17	6.89	6.65	6.64	6.68	6.55	6.34	6.18	5.94	5.90	6.25	6.27
1994	6.24	6.44	6.90	7.32	7.47	7.43	7.61	7.55	7.81	8.02	8.16	7.97
1995	7.93	7.69	7.52	7.41	6.99	6.59	6.71	6.90	6.63	6.43	6.31	6.11
1996	6.07	6.28	6.72	6.94	7.08	7.20	7.13	6.94	7.13	6.87	6.55	6.63
1997	6.89	6.76	7.03	7.18	7.00	6.82	6.55	6.64	6.54	6.37	6.18	6.06
1998	5.87	5.94	6.00	5.98	5.99	5.78	5.76	5.64	5.34	5.24	5.43	5.29
1999	5.39	5.60	5.81	5.77	6.04	6.31	6.22	6.37	6.43	6.60	6.42	6.63
2000	6.81	6.49	6.33	6.14	6.49	6.23	-	-	-	-	-	-

Source: The Conference Board. © 2002 The Conference Board. All Rights Reserved. No claim to original U.S. Government works pursuant to U.S. Contract No. 52-SABA-5-00128. Primary source(s): Board of Governors of the Federal Reserve System, Division of Monetary Affairs, Banking and Money Market Statistics Section, Stop 81, Washington, DC 20551. A dash (-) indicates that data are not available or zero.

           Economic Indicators Handbook, 6th Edition

Yield on Municipal Bonds, 20-Bond Average
Not seasonally adjusted
(Percent)

Year	Jan	Feb	Mar	Apr	May	Jun	Jul	Aug	Sep	Oct	Nov	Dec
1951	1.61	1.58	1.74	1.94	2.00	2.19	2.15	2.02	2.01	2.06	2.05	2.09
1952	2.09	2.07	2.08	2.04	2.06	2.13	2.15	2.24	2.30	2.38	2.38	2.38
1953	2.43	2.55	2.65	2.65	2.78	2.99	2.98	2.90	2.90	2.75	2.62	2.60
1954	2.50	2.42	2.40	2.47	2.50	2.48	2.32	2.26	2.31	2.34	2.32	2.36
1955	2.40	2.44	2.44	2.41	2.38	2.41	2.54	2.60	2.58	2.51	2.46	2.57
1956	2.50	2.44	2.57	2.70	2.68	2.54	2.65	2.80	2.94	2.95	3.16	3.22
1957	3.18	3.00	3.10	3.13	3.27	3.41	3.40	3.54	3.54	3.42	3.37	3.04
1958	2.91	3.02	3.06	2.96	2.92	2.97	3.09	3.36	3.54	3.45	3.32	3.34
1959	3.42	3.36	3.30	3.39	3.58	3.72	3.71	3.58	3.78	3.62	3.55	3.68
1960	3.72	3.60	3.56	3.56	3.60	3.55	3.50	3.34	3.42	3.53	3.40	3.40
1961	3.40	3.31	3.45	3.50	3.43	3.52	3.52	3.52	3.53	3.43	3.41	3.47
1962	3.34	3.21	3.14	3.06	3.11	3.26	3.28	3.23	3.11	3.02	3.05	3.07
1963	3.10	3.15	3.05	3.10	3.11	3.21	3.21	3.13	3.20	3.20	3.30	3.28
1964	3.22	3.14	3.29	3.28	3.21	3.20	3.19	3.19	3.24	3.26	3.18	3.14
1965	3.07	3.09	3.18	3.16	3.17	3.25	3.28	3.24	3.35	3.40	3.46	3.54
1966	3.52	3.65	3.72	3.56	3.65	3.77	3.95	4.12	4.12	3.93	3.87	3.86
1967	3.55	3.52	3.55	3.60	3.89	3.96	4.02	3.99	4.12	4.30	4.34	4.43
1968	4.29	4.31	4.54	4.34	4.54	4.50	4.33	4.21	4.38	4.49	4.60	4.82
1969	4.85	4.98	5.26	5.19	5.33	5.76	5.75	6.00	6.26	6.09	6.31	6.82
1970	6.65	6.36	6.03	6.49	7.00	6.96	6.53	6.20	6.25	6.39	5.93	5.46
1971	5.36	5.23	5.17	5.37	5.91	5.95	6.06	5.82	5.37	5.06	5.20	5.21
1972	5.12	5.29	5.31	5.43	5.31	5.34	5.41	5.30	5.36	5.19	5.02	5.05
1973	5.05	5.13	5.29	5.15	5.15	5.18	5.40	5.48	5.10	5.05	5.18	5.12
1974	5.22	5.20	5.41	5.73	6.02	6.13	6.68	6.71	6.76	6.57	6.61	7.05
1975	6.82	6.39	6.74	6.95	6.97	6.95	7.07	7.17	7.44	7.39	7.43	7.31
1976	7.07	6.94	6.92	6.60	6.87	6.87	6.79	6.61	6.51	6.30	6.29	5.94
1977	5.87	5.89	5.89	5.73	5.75	5.62	5.63	5.62	5.51	5.64	5.49	5.57
1978	5.71	5.62	5.61	5.80	6.03	6.22	6.28	6.12	6.09	6.13	6.19	6.51
1979	6.47	6.31	6.33	6.29	6.25	6.13	6.13	6.20	6.52	7.08	7.30	7.22
1980	7.35	8.16	9.17	8.63	7.59	7.63	8.13	8.67	8.94	9.11	9.56	10.11
1981	9.66	10.10	10.16	10.62	10.78	10.67	11.14	12.26	12.92	12.83	11.89	12.90
1982	13.28	12.97	12.82	12.59	11.95	12.45	12.28	11.23	10.66	9.69	10.06	9.96
1983	9.50	9.58	9.20	9.05	9.11	9.52	9.53	9.72	9.58	9.66	9.75	9.89
1984	9.63	9.64	9.94	9.96	10.49	10.67	10.42	9.99	10.10	10.25	10.17	9.95
1985	9.51	9.65	9.77	9.42	9.01	8.69	8.81	9.08	9.27	9.08	8.54	8.43
1986	8.08	7.44	7.08	7.20	7.54	7.87	7.51	7.21	7.11	7.08	6.85	6.86
1987	6.61	6.61	6.66	7.55	8.00	7.79	7.72	7.81	8.26	8.70	7.95	7.96
1988	7.70	7.49	7.74	7.81	7.90	7.78	7.76	7.79	7.66	7.47	7.46	7.61
1989	7.35	7.44	7.59	7.49	7.25	7.02	6.96	7.06	7.26	7.22	7.14	6.98
1990	7.10	7.22	7.29	7.39	7.35	7.24	7.19	7.32	7.53	7.49	7.18	7.09
1991	7.08	6.91	7.10	7.02	6.95	7.13	7.05	6.90	6.80	6.68	6.73	6.69
1992	6.54	6.74	6.76	6.67	6.57	6.49	6.13	6.16	6.25	6.41	6.36	6.22
1993	6.16	5.86	5.85	5.76	5.73	5.63	5.57	5.45	5.29	5.25	5.47	5.35
1994	5.31	5.40	5.91	6.23	6.19	6.11	6.23	6.21	6.28	6.52	6.97	6.80
1995	6.53	6.22	6.10	6.02	5.95	5.84	5.92	6.06	5.91	5.80	5.64	5.45
1996	5.43	5.43	5.79	5.94	5.98	6.02	5.92	5.76	5.87	5.72	5.59	5.64
1997	5.72	5.63	5.76	5.88	5.70	5.53	5.35	5.41	5.39	5.38	5.33	5.19
1998	5.06	5.10	5.21	5.23	5.20	5.12	5.14	5.10	4.99	4.93	5.03	4.98
1999	5.02	5.03	5.10	5.08	5.18	5.37	5.36	5.58	5.69	5.92	5.86	5.95
2000	6.08	6.00	5.83	5.75	6.00	5.80	5.63	5.51	5.56	5.59	5.54	5.22
2001	5.10	5.18	5.13	5.27	5.29	5.20	5.20	5.03	5.09	5.05	5.04	5.25

Source: The Conference Board. © 2002 The Conference Board. All Rights Reserved. No claim to original U.S. Government works pursuant to U.S. Contract No. 52-SABA-5-00128. Primary source(s): Board of Governors of the Federal Reserve System, Division of Monetary Affairs, Banking and Money Market Statistics Section, Stop 81, Washington, DC 20551. A dash (-) indicates that data are not available or zero.

Secondary Market Yields on FHA Mortgages
Not seasonally adjusted
(Percent)

Year	Jan	Feb	Mar	Apr	May	Jun	Jul	Aug	Sep	Oct	Nov	Dec
1951	4.07	4.07	4.12	4.19	4.27	4.29	4.31	4.31	4.30	4.27	4.27	4.26
1952	4.26	4.27	4.29	4.29	4.29	4.30	4.30	4.30	4.30	4.31	4.32	4.32
1953	4.34	4.34	4.34	-	-	4.67	4.74	4.82	4.86	4.82	4.81	4.78
1954	4.75	4.69	4.64	4.62	4.59	4.57	4.56	4.56	4.56	4.56	4.56	4.56
1955	4.56	4.56	4.59	4.60	4.63	4.63	4.64	4.67	4.70	4.73	4.75	4.73
1956	4.73	4.70	4.68	4.71	4.78	4.81	4.81	4.87	4.92	4.95	-	-
1957	-	5.36	5.35	5.35	5.32	5.35	5.38	-	-	5.63	5.63	5.62
1958	5.59	5.57	5.51	5.44	5.39	5.37	5.35	5.37	5.50	5.58	5.60	5.60
1959	5.60	5.59	5.58	5.59	5.64	5.71	5.75	5.81	-	-	6.23	6.23
1960	6.25	6.23	6.22	6.21	6.20	6.19	6.17	6.14	6.11	6.09	6.07	6.04
1961	6.02	5.86	5.80	5.77	-	-	5.68	5.68	5.69	5.70	5.70	5.69
1962	5.69	5.68	5.65	5.64	5.60	5.59	5.58	5.57	5.56	5.55	5.54	5.53
1963	5.52	5.48	5.47	5.46	5.45	5.45	5.45	5.45	5.45	5.45	5.45	5.45
1964	5.45	5.45	5.45	5.45	5.45	5.45	5.45	5.45	5.45	5.45	5.45	5.45
1965	5.45	5.45	5.45	5.45	5.45	5.44	5.46	5.46	5.46	5.49	5.51	5.62
1966	5.70	-	6.00	-	6.32	6.45	6.51	6.58	6.63	-	6.81	6.77
1967	6.62	6.46	6.35	6.29	6.44	6.51	6.53	6.60	6.63	6.65	6.77	6.81
1968	6.81	6.78	6.83	6.94	-	7.52	7.42	7.35	7.28	7.29	7.36	7.50
1969	-	7.99	8.05	8.06	8.06	8.35	8.36	8.36	8.40	8.48	8.48	8.62
1970	-	9.29	9.20	9.10	9.11	9.16	9.11	9.07	9.01	8.97	8.90	8.40
1971	-	-	7.32	7.37	7.75	7.89	7.97	7.92	7.84	7.75	7.62	7.59
1972	7.49	7.46	7.45	7.50	7.53	7.54	7.54	7.55	7.56	7.57	7.57	7.56
1973	7.55	7.56	7.63	7.73	7.79	7.89	8.19	-	9.18	8.97	8.86	8.78
1974	-	8.54	8.66	9.17	9.46	9.46	9.85	10.30	10.38	10.13	-	9.51
1975	8.99	8.84	8.69	-	9.16	9.06	9.13	9.32	9.74	9.53	9.41	9.32
1976	9.06	9.04	-	8.82	9.03	9.05	8.99	8.93	8.82	8.55	8.45	8.28
1977	8.45	8.55	8.65	8.64	-	8.77	8.77	8.77	8.74	8.81	8.81	8.96
1978	9.18	-	9.35	9.44	9.74	-	9.96	9.81	9.81	9.98	10.04	10.23
1979	10.24	10.24	10.26	-	10.61	10.49	10.46	10.58	11.37	-	12.41	12.24
1980	12.60	-	14.63	13.45	11.99	11.85	12.39	13.54	14.26	14.38	14.47	14.08
1981	14.23	14.79	15.04	15.91	16.33	16.31	16.76	17.96	18.55	17.43	15.98	16.43
1982	17.38	17.10	16.41	16.31	16.19	16.73	16.29	14.61	14.03	12.99	12.82	12.80
1983	12.87	12.65	12.68	12.50	12.41	12.96	14.23	13.78	13.55	13.23	13.23	13.25
1984	13.08	13.20	13.68	13.80	15.01	14.91	14.58	14.21	13.99	13.43	12.90	12.99
1985	13.01	13.27	13.43	12.97	12.28	11.89	12.12	11.99	12.04	11.87	11.28	10.70
1986	10.78	10.59	9.77	9.80	10.07	9.98	10.01	9.80	9.90	9.80	9.26	9.21
1987	8.79	8.81	8.94	10.02	10.61	10.33	10.38	10.55	11.22	10.90	10.76	10.63
1988	10.17	9.86	10.28	10.46	10.84	10.65	10.66	10.74	10.58	10.23	10.63	10.81
1989	10.69	10.88	11.16	10.88	10.55	10.08	9.61	9.95	9.94	9.73	9.69	9.72
1990	10.01	10.22	10.30	10.75	10.23	10.18	10.11	10.28	10.24	10.23	9.81	9.66
1991	9.58	9.57	9.61	9.61	9.62	9.71	9.59	9.14	9.06	8.71	8.69	8.10
1992	8.72	8.74	8.85	8.79	8.66	8.56	8.12	8.08	8.06	8.29	8.54	8.12
1993	8.04	7.55	7.57	7.56	7.59	7.52	7.51	7.02	7.03	7.08	7.51	7.52
1994	7.05	7.59	8.57	8.63	8.63	9.03	8.65	8.66	9.10	9.23	9.53	9.54
1995	9.10	9.05	8.60	8.56	8.03	8.00	8.09	8.03	8.03	7.61	7.51	7.52
1996	7.11	7.57	8.09	8.52	8.57	8.55	8.56	8.58	8.56	8.00	8.14	8.06
1997	8.06	8.08	8.55	8.56	8.05	8.02	7.61	8.02	7.52	7.53	7.51	7.17
1998	7.08	7.06	7.09	7.37	7.07	7.07	7.05	7.03	6.53	7.07	7.02	7.06
1999	7.08	7.10	7.07	7.08	7.58	8.13	8.00	8.10	8.05	8.02	8.06	8.55
2000	8.56	8.53	8.35	8.33	8.58	-	-	-	-	-	-	-

Source: The Conference Board. © 2002 The Conference Board. All Rights Reserved. No claim to original U.S. Government works pursuant to U.S. Contract No. 52-SABA-5-00128. Primary source(s): U.S. Department of Housing and Urban Development, Office of Housing-FHA Comptroller, Program Evaluation Division, Washington, DC 20410. A dash (-) indicates that data are not available or zero.

Commercial and Industrial Loans Outstanding

(Millions of $)

Year	Jan	Feb	Mar	Apr	May	Jun	Jul	Aug	Sep	Oct	Nov	Dec
1951	16,503	17,116	17,579	18,079	18,453	18,646	18,757	18,865	18,968	19,111	19,194	19,411
1952	19,632	19,641	19,761	19,742	19,809	19,969	20,141	20,190	20,381	20,650	21,031	21,133
1953	21,227	21,277	21,430	21,675	21,816	21,747	21,778	21,934	21,819	21,640	21,451	21,058
1954	21,000	21,064	21,036	20,967	20,811	20,650	20,651	19,804	19,753	19,718	19,955	20,314
1955	20,529	20,692	20,916	21,049	21,416	21,796	22,244	22,664	22,977	23,421	23,771	24,110
1956	24,515	24,686	25,414	25,932	26,448	26,799	27,145	27,418	27,778	27,858	28,199	28,395
1957	28,695	28,720	29,182	29,503	29,650	30,033	30,245	30,285	30,374	29,969	29,573	29,517
1958	29,171	28,835	28,728	28,554	28,168	28,079	28,039	27,941	28,122	28,215	28,342	28,496
1959	28,567	28,583	28,820	29,092	29,573	30,042	30,026	30,456	30,646	30,915	31,076	31,288
1960	31,433	31,870	32,093	32,293	32,591	33,011	32,993	32,840	32,956	32,996	33,118	33,018
1961	32,999	32,966	33,111	33,079	33,020	32,955	33,012	33,131	33,214	33,215	33,280	33,429
1962	33,582	33,712	33,907	34,121	34,269	34,509	34,740	35,038	35,318	35,635	35,939	35,986
1963	36,039	36,126	36,251	36,458	36,626	36,740	36,872	37,047	37,341	37,821	38,579	39,045
1964	38,931	39,195	39,201	39,554	39,882	40,137	40,428	40,839	41,418	41,625	42,068	42,737
1965	43,562	44,618	45,563	46,203	47,209	47,718	48,072	49,139	50,141	50,812	51,650	52,300
1966	53,195	54,071	54,805	55,377	56,139	57,228	58,223	59,360	59,950	60,578	61,043	61,332
1967	61,876	62,404	63,100	63,598	63,998	64,682	65,083	64,862	65,155	65,644	66,161	67,068
1968	67,254	67,415	67,732	68,877	69,067	69,598	70,294	71,359	72,318	73,153	74,374	75,150
1969	77,048	77,843	79,091	81,132	82,277	83,502	83,909	85,141	86,404	87,358	88,070	89,059
1970	88,521	90,023	91,243	91,333	91,864	92,444	92,433	93,072	93,435	91,680	91,082	91,069
1971	90,944	91,625	91,904	90,891	91,662	90,706	89,951	91,627	93,437	92,465	92,301	91,788
1972	84,478	85,260	86,195	87,342	87,906	88,268	88,429	88,800	88,593	90,502	91,408	92,111
1973	94,279	98,034	100,124	101,768	103,074	105,166	106,581	108,505	108,458	109,664	110,877	111,764
1974	113,967	116,322	117,738	122,857	125,111	126,537	130,706	133,304	137,429	138,352	139,734	139,873
1975	140,652	139,605	138,152	136,564	133,750	131,397	130,713	129,579	128,146	126,999	126,131	126,245
1976	125,349	125,758	123,490	120,789	121,069	122,018	121,328	121,083	120,710	121,770	123,317	124,225
1977	124,450	125,824	126,179	126,925	127,740	128,990	128,860	130,214	130,848	132,174	133,272	134,372
1978	135,158	135,658	138,536	140,620	143,029	145,547	146,937	147,792	148,769	150,501	152,486	152,870
1979	155,975	158,341	160,335	165,793	168,229	171,623	175,320	179,017	183,790	184,399	183,394	186,443
1980	193,068	197,288	200,406	200,583	198,756	202,454	200,910	201,732	203,417	204,727	209,253	211,014
1981	213,016	213,391	211,676	215,581	221,279	225,515	229,664	234,814	238,847	241,377	244,824	247,853
1982	254,693	259,934	261,328	266,688	271,022	272,899	273,160	273,540	274,885	274,856	270,235	264,699
1983	268,553	268,582	269,450	265,604	261,465	262,099	261,703	262,875	262,747	261,829	263,187	267,368
1984	274,768	279,364	287,370	294,220	300,525	310,036	314,375	317,394	321,437	325,648	328,615	329,459
1985	329,668	332,412	334,670	335,158	338,108	336,876	339,378	340,740	339,599	343,857	347,028	348,859
1986	351,101	349,392	347,888	342,642	345,052	345,978	347,464	351,931	351,008	352,769	353,255	358,781
1987	366,490	364,936	363,447	363,216	362,718	363,766	362,668	359,989	363,258	366,003	364,818	367,421
1988	432,317	436,844	439,171	444,815	445,032	447,644	449,481	449,156	448,931	452,209	456,371	463,156
1989	467,777	475,897	477,617	480,945	490,948	492,563	495,444	500,384	499,806	501,527	504,102	506,179
1990	507,861	510,900	519,702	520,169	518,119	518,971	520,285	522,214	527,207	525,486	519,028	518,614
1991	518,681	511,220	512,452	507,109	501,897	499,125	496,277	486,585	481,039	476,981	475,869	470,330
1992	466,843	466,960	467,057	464,605	462,468	459,982	457,526	458,388	455,506	460,906	465,671	462,675
1993	463,088	462,984	458,538	460,526	465,319	466,375	468,626	467,444	466,054	464,365	463,894	465,016
1994	468,405	464,858	465,231	465,444	470,399	475,405	479,984	484,431	490,521	500,195	503,789	511,248
1995	519,312	529,239	534,617	545,187	547,526	552,814	555,861	560,020	561,574	566,021	562,254	570,734
1996	572,401	571,658	578,640	581,582	581,810	581,967	582,496	583,379	586,824	581,570	582,033	585,343
1997	591,020	592,981	596,805	597,563	602,715	612,148	617,340	622,249	630,618	636,436	645,868	646,156
1998	661,486	674,321	679,569	671,949	686,360	703,485	707,504	724,234	737,339	743,259	748,336	743,832
1999	753,798	763,182	769,487	775,338	780,823	779,204	790,219	798,210	807,765	817,920	823,928	841,040
2000	851,519	867,863	872,460	888,426	899,109	920,709	931,741	943,013	937,309	941,003	943,182	936,833
2001	913,947	899,027	873,611	862,823	852,176	813,983	791,235	784,473	778,837	767,251	753,294	-

Source: The Conference Board. © 2002 The Conference Board. All Rights Reserved. No claim to original U.S. Government works pursuant to U.S. Contract No. 52-SABA-5-00128. Primary source(s): Board of Governors of the Federal Reserve System, Division of Monetary Affairs, Banking and Money Market Statistics Section, Stop 84, Washington, DC 20551 and Board of Governors of the Federal Reserve System, Capital Markets, Banking and Money Market Statistics Section, Stop 84, Washington, DC 20551. A dash (-) indicates that data are not available or zero.

CHAPTER 5

ECONOMIC SERIES

ECONOMIC SERIES

The 21 series in this chapter are classified as "important economic measures" by the Department of Commerce. They are not cyclic indicators but measure other aspects of the economy. The series are grouped under four headings:

Savings
Producer Prices, Wages, and Productivity
Implicit Price Deflators for Gross Domestic Product Sectors
Labor and Employment
International Transactions

The section on implicit price deflators for GDP is a feature introduced in the 4th edition and still carried in the 6th; it is aimed at providing better data to the user for calculating inflationary pressures on personal or institutional income.

A brief introduction to each of these sections provides a description of each series covered and some discussion of the analytical uses of each series. Data are presented from 1959 to 2001.

Bibliography

1. Fischer, Stanley, Rudiger Dornbusch, and Richard Schmalensee. *Introduction to Macroeconomics*. McGraw-Hill Book Company, New York, 1988.

2. Fitch, Thomas P. *Dictionary of Banking Terms*. Barron's, New York, 1990.

3. Siegel, Barry N. *Money, Banking, and the Economy*. Academic Press, New York, 1982.

3. U.S. Department of Commerce, Bureau of Economic Analysis. *Survey of Current Business*. Superintendent of Documents, U.S. Government Printing Office, Washington, DC 20302.

INDICATORS OF SAVINGS

This section presents 5 series used to measure the nation's savings rate. The series presented are:

    Gross saving
    Business saving
    Personal saving
    Personal saving rate
    Government surplus or deficit

In the aggregate, savings taken as a total are an indirect indicator of the nation's capacity to invest in future productive facilities. Business and personal savings create the pool of capital available for new housing, infrastructure, tooling, factories, etc.—investment. These private sources of savings are diminished by government deficits and increased by foreign investment in the United States.

Gross Saving. Data are shown on a quarterly, annualized basis in billions of current dollars. The series is made up of personal savings plus business savings less government deficits at the federal, state, and local levels. If governments are in surplus, the surplus is added.

Business Saving. Presented as billions of current dollars in quarterly, annualized values, business savings is a complex category made up of the following components:

    Undistributed corporate profits
    Corporate capital consumption allowances
    Noncorporate capital consumption allowances
    Wage accruals less disbursements

Corporate profits are adjusted for inventory valuation changes and capital consumption adjustments. Noncorporate capital consumption allowances are also adjusted. The sum of these values combines into savings carried by the business sector from one period into another.

Personal Saving and **Personal Saving Rate**. Data for Personal saving are presented in the same format as Gross and Business saving; Personal saving rate is shown in percent. Personal saving is derived by deducting taxes from personal income, yielding disposable personal income (DPI); personal expenditures are deducted from DPI to obtain personal saving. Personal saving as a percent of DPI is the Personal saving rate. In the third quarter of 2001, this value was 3.8 percent//a significant jump as recession loomed and the 9/11 disaster struck; the highest rate shown in the data was the fourth quarter of 1981 (11.9%), after the onset of a recession. The lowest level was recorded for the first and third quarters of 2000 (0.8%). The saving rate rarely reaches double digits in the United States; in Japan and some European countries, a high double-digit saving rate is the rule rather than the exception.

Government Surplus or Deficit. Data show quarterly values. In the early 1990s, the government ran large deficits; since deficits are financed from savings, deficits reduce total resources available for investment; the government competes with private users of capital for funds. However, if government deficits were erased by higher taxes, the net result would be largely the same: personal and business savings are income *net* of taxes; therefore higher taxes would also reduce gross savings.

Gross Saving

(Annual Rate, Billions of $)

Year	1st Quarter	2nd Quarter	3rd Quarter	4th Quarter
1959	104.8	110.8	102.5	105.2
1960	117.7	110.3	110.6	105.1
1961	107.7	109.7	116.7	121.6
1962	123.6	123.5	125.7	125.6
1963	127.9	132.7	133.3	137.5
1964	139.5	139.5	143.3	149.9
1965	156.4	158.2	158.4	159.4
1966	167.2	167.9	167.6	173.8
1967	168.7	165.1	172.3	178.5
1968	177.2	182.9	183.5	189.6
1969	197.0	197.8	204.2	199.9
1970	193.0	196.2	197.1	190.8
1971	205.6	209.4	212.9	217.6
1972	226.7	233.1	243.5	263.1
1973	276.6	285.9	298.0	318.0
1974	309.4	301.8	300.5	304.4
1975	282.7	282.3	308.7	320.1
1976	337.7	343.2	344.6	345.2
1977	360.3	393.5	418.0	421.1
1978	435.2	475.7	494.6	520.9
1979	535.4	542.7	547.7	553.7
1980	557.7	537.0	537.7	589.7
1981	634.1	628.5	687.0	676.3
1982	638.8	664.6	629.0	570.5
1983	584.0	588.1	605.3	654.7
1984	727.5	763.4	797.3	789.3
1985	787.6	780.5	757.7	764.3
1986	777.8	746.6	708.1	711.3
1987	762.8	786.0	822.5	870.4
1988	888.5	929.6	952.3	974.5
1989	1,002.3	963.4	953.8	950.8
1990	959.9	996.9	976.8	976.9
1991	1,056.3	1,005.5	989.7	1,011.7
1992	1,018.1	1,025.8	1,002.2	983.3
1993	1,029.6	1,047.6	1,022.0	1,058.5
1994	1,122.4	1,145.7	1,151.1	1,204.6
1995	1,238.0	1,233.1	1,260.1	1,298.5
1996	1,295.6	1,328.2	1,372.8	1,400.5
1997	1,422.1	1,492.9	1,528.4	1,565.8
1998	1,610.0	1,617.2	1,681.7	1,679.8
1999	1,730.6	1,693.3	1,694.4	1,711.2
2000	1,736.2	1,799.4	1,807.4	1,799.7
2001	1,754.0	1,750.5	1,751.9	-

Business Saving
(Annual Rate, Billions of $)

Year	1st Quarter	2nd Quarter	3rd Quarter	4th Quarter
1959	71.2	74.0	71.5	72.6
1960	74.4	73.0	73.1	72.4
1961	71.9	75.1	76.2	78.0
1962	82.6	82.2	83.4	86.1
1963	86.4	88.6	89.4	90.6
1964	94.6	94.8	95.8	95.9
1965	103.1	104.8	106.0	108.9
1966	112.0	113.2	113.6	117.8
1967	116.3	116.4	118.7	122.8
1968	120.2	124.1	125.4	128.2
1969	129.8	130.0	130.5	128.0
1970	129.6	131.7	133.7	133.2
1971	145.1	148.6	153.9	159.9
1972	162.5	172.3	172.6	180.7
1973	184.1	184.9	189.5	191.9
1974	190.2	192.3	190.3	202.3
1975	218.9	234.0	249.2	258.5
1976	264.6	263.8	266.7	270.5
1977	281.3	302.4	318.5	317.0
1978	321.5	341.7	351.7	363.8
1979	363.8	373.3	383.3	388.4
1980	385.5	384.2	395.2	414.4
1981	437.9	449.4	473.3	475.4
1982	476.9	499.5	506.4	510.5
1983	527.1	543.0	558.2	567.2
1984	586.2	603.7	613.3	626.2
1985	627.2	637.2	659.5	654.2
1986	643.0	639.3	638.3	637.7
1987	662.8	688.0	705.5	717.1
1988	744.7	760.7	767.3	789.9
1989	761.8	764.7	790.3	789.0
1990	798.8	824.7	804.0	827.3
1991	869.0	862.1	860.7	877.0
1992	904.9	904.2	930.7	844.9
1993	1,002.8	945.0	963.5	933.5
1994	1,084.9	1,009.9	1,029.9	1,051.9
1995	1,084.4	1,116.1	1,154.3	1,172.2
1996	1,172.8	1,184.8	1,194.5	1,217.8
1997	1,236.9	1,264.2	1,290.6	1,295.3
1998	1,245.8	1,243.1	1,269.1	1,286.8
1999	1,366.2	1,365.5	1,383.4	1,426.0
2000	1,436.7	1,467.5	1,488.2	1,473.8
2001	1,447.7	1,461.0	1,478.4	-

Source: The Conference Board. © 2002 The Conference Board. All Rights Reserved. No claim to original U.S. Government works pursuant to U.S. Contract No. 52-SABA-5-00128. Primary source(s): U.S. Department of Commerce, Bureau of Economic Analysis, National Income and Wealth Division, BE-54, Washington, DC 20230. A dash (-) indicates that data are not available or zero.

Personal Saving
(Annual Rate, Billions of $)

Year	1st Quarter	2nd Quarter	3rd Quarter	4th Quarter
1959	26.9	28.4	24.3	26.5
1960	27.4	25.2	26.7	26.3
1961	29.5	30.0	33.7	34.4
1962	33.9	34.3	33.9	31.8
1963	32.1	32.5	32.1	35.8
1964	36.7	41.2	39.9	44.4
1965	39.6	40.3	46.5	44.5
1966	42.3	42.4	44.3	49.0
1967	53.8	51.2	54.7	56.1
1968	54.8	57.1	48.3	50.4
1969	45.0	47.8	58.6	59.2
1970	59.6	69.5	74.3	74.6
1971	77.4	83.3	81.4	78.4
1972	74.1	68.0	75.1	90.3
1973	88.3	99.1	103.4	119.3
1974	116.6	107.6	109.9	123.2
1975	110.4	148.1	119.7	122.8
1976	121.4	122.5	124.7	120.0
1977	116.0	119.8	130.1	136.4
1978	144.2	137.1	147.1	153.3
1979	164.1	163.0	162.2	174.0
1980	192.3	202.2	203.8	224.2
1981	224.1	215.5	258.1	277.2
1982	263.8	274.2	269.9	240.9
1983	238.6	211.9	222.7	238.0
1984	276.0	297.0	332.9	320.0
1985	283.6	317.8	253.5	275.6
1986	290.5	291.0	255.4	234.2
1987	276.8	207.9	241.9	284.5
1988	280.1	288.6	299.3	301.3
1989	328.9	305.3	282.4	290.7
1990	325.9	339.4	333.1	339.0
1991	363.2	367.1	368.3	388.1
1992	406.7	421.9	396.5	429.6
1993	340.0	373.7	331.5	358.2
1994	274.3	319.5	324.1	344.2
1995	346.0	291.5	285.9	286.3
1996	282.2	253.1	286.1	267.1
1997	248.1	270.1	236.0	257.3
1998	307.9	309.1	311.4	277.6
1999	230.4	175.2	140.8	97.2
2000	53.5	88.1	54.5	74.7
2001	78.8	81.5	285.3	-

Source: The Conference Board. © 2002 The Conference Board. All Rights Reserved. No claim to original U.S. Government works pursuant to U.S. Contract No. 52-SABA-5-00128. Primary source(s): U.S. Department of Commerce, Bureau of Economic Analysis, National Income and Wealth Division, BE-54, Washington, DC 20230. A dash (-) indicates that data are not available or zero.

Personal Saving Rate
(Percent)

Year	1st Quarter	2nd Quarter	3rd Quarter	4th Quarter
1959	7.8	8.1	6.9	7.4
1960	7.6	6.9	7.3	7.1
1961	7.9	7.9	8.7	8.8
1962	8.5	8.5	8.3	7.7
1963	7.7	7.7	7.5	8.2
1964	8.2	8.9	8.5	9.3
1965	8.2	8.2	9.2	8.6
1966	8.0	8.0	8.2	8.8
1967	9.6	9.0	9.4	9.5
1968	9.0	9.2	7.7	7.8
1969	6.9	7.2	8.5	8.5
1970	8.4	9.5	9.9	9.9
1971	10.0	10.4	10.1	9.5
1972	8.9	8.0	8.6	9.9
1973	9.4	10.3	10.5	11.7
1974	11.2	10.2	10.1	11.1
1975	9.9	12.5	10.0	10.0
1976	9.6	9.6	9.5	8.9
1977	8.4	8.5	8.9	9.1
1978	9.4	8.6	9.0	9.1
1979	9.4	9.2	8.9	9.2
1980	9.8	10.3	10.0	10.6
1981	10.3	9.8	11.3	11.9
1982	11.2	11.5	11.1	9.8
1983	9.6	8.3	8.5	8.8
1984	9.9	10.4	11.3	10.8
1985	9.4	10.3	8.2	8.7
1986	9.0	9.0	7.8	7.1
1987	8.2	6.1	6.9	8.0
1988	7.7	7.8	7.9	7.8
1989	8.3	7.6	7.0	7.1
1990	7.8	7.9	7.7	7.8
1991	8.3	8.2	8.2	8.5
1992	8.7	8.9	8.3	8.8
1993	7.1	7.6	6.7	7.1
1994	5.5	6.2	6.2	6.5
1995	6.5	5.4	5.3	5.2
1996	5.1	4.5	5.0	4.6
1997	4.2	4.6	3.9	4.2
1998	4.9	4.9	4.9	4.3
1999	3.5	2.7	2.1	1.4
2000	0.8	1.3	0.8	1.0
2001	1.1	1.1	3.8	-

Source: The Conference Board. © 2002 The Conference Board. All Rights Reserved. No claim to original U.S. Government works pursuant to U.S. Contract No. 52-SABA-5-00128. Primary source(s): U.S. Department of Commerce, Bureau of Economic Analysis, National Income and Wealth Division, BE-54, Washington, DC 20230. A dash (-) indicates that data are not available or zero.

Government Surplus or Deficit
(Annual Rate, Billions of $)

Year	1st Quarter	2nd Quarter	3rd Quarter	4th Quarter
1959	6.7	8.5	6.7	6.1
1960	15.8	12.3	10.8	6.5
1961	6.4	4.6	6.9	9.1
1962	7.2	7.0	8.5	7.7
1963	9.3	11.7	11.7	10.9
1964	8.2	3.6	7.6	9.5
1965	13.6	13.1	5.9	6.1
1966	13.0	12.3	9.6	7.0
1967	-1.4	-2.5	-1.1	-0.5
1968	2.3	1.6	9.8	11.0
1969	22.3	20.0	15.1	12.8
1970	6.3	-7.0	-11.4	-17.0
1971	-16.8	-22.5	-22.1	-20.1
1972	-10.3	-7.4	-4.3	-5.7
1973	4.2	1.8	5.1	6.8
1974	2.6	1.3	-1.1	-21.0
1975	-46.5	-99.8	-60.1	-61.0
1976	-48.2	-42.8	-46.7	-45.1
1977	-36.8	-28.7	-30.5	-32.1
1978	-30.4	-3.0	-3.7	4.3
1979	7.5	5.5	2.0	-8.5
1980	-20.2	-49.3	-61.3	-48.9
1981	-27.9	-36.3	-44.1	-76.3
1982	-102.0	-109.1	-147.3	-181.0
1983	-181.7	-168.0	-175.9	-150.5
1984	-134.5	-137.0	-149.1	-156.2
1985	-123.1	-175.5	-155.5	-165.4
1986	-155.7	-183.7	-185.6	-160.6
1987	-176.8	-109.8	-124.7	-131.5
1988	-136.3	-119.8	-114.3	-116.7
1989	-88.4	-106.6	-118.8	-128.9
1990	-164.8	-167.1	-160.3	-189.1
1991	-175.7	-224.1	-239.3	-253.5
1992	-293.4	-300.3	-325.0	-291.2
1993	-313.2	-271.2	-273.1	-233.2
1994	-236.9	-183.6	-202.8	-191.6
1995	-192.4	-174.3	-180.1	-159.9
1996	-159.5	-109.8	-107.8	-84.4
1997	-63.0	-41.4	1.8	13.3
1998	56.3	65.0	101.3	115.4
1999	134.1	152.7	170.3	188.0
2000	246.0	243.8	264.7	251.1
2001	227.6	208.0	-11.7	-

INDICATORS OF PRODUCER PRICES, WAGES, AND PRODUCTIVITY

This section presents 9 series used to measure the nation's inflation rate, prices, and output. The series presented are:

  Producer Price Index, crude materials
  Producer Price Index, intermediate materials
  Producer Price Index, capital equipment
  Producer Price Index, finished consumer goods
  Producer Price Index, finished goods
  Producer Price Index, crude nonfood less energy
  Producer Price Index, petroleum products
  Index of output per hour, business sector
  Index of output per hour, nonfarm business sector

Conspicuous by absence, perhaps, is the *Consumer Price Index*. It is presented in the next chapter in considerable detail. Similarly, much more detailed statistics are presented on the *Producer Price Index*, a summary of which is presented later in this section.

Producer Price Index Series. All seven tables are indexes based on 1982 (1982 = 100). Detailed PPI tables are presented in the next chapter. The tables included in this section are summary series showing broad categories. Production processes refine crude raw materials (ores, logs, crude oil) into intermediate products (steel, pulp, engine blocks); intermediate products are transformed into finished products (autos, writing paper, gasoline). The tables included follow price trends at each of these levels. The data are used in a variety of ways in macroeconomic analysis and in business planning. For example, note that the inflation rate shown by the PPI for crude and intermediate materials is substantially less than it is for finished goods; at lower levels of refinement and product differentiation, competitive forces are greater (the "stuff" handled is more of a commodity); as raw materials are formed into products, differentiation increases and opportunities for aggressive pricing are greater.

Indices of Output Per Hour. Data are shown in quarterly increments as an index based on 1992 (1992 = 100). These are indicators of national productivity. Output per hour reflects all inputs to the production process, including tooling, fuels, improved raw materials, degree of capacity utilization . . . *and* human effort, measured in time. The indicators, therefore, are influenced by the personal productivity of employees but also, more importantly in today's environment, by technology and therefore by the level of investment. Rising productivity means that more is produced, in absolute terms, by one hour of labor. It does not mean that employment is increasing; it may be decreasing as better machines take over human tasks. Rising productivity may also mean that the capital required per workplace is on the increase. The series, therefore, yield best results when viewed in concert with other series on wages, employment, capacity utilization, and investment.

Producer Price Index, Crude Materials
(1982=100)

Year	Jan	Feb	Mar	Apr	May	Jun	Jul	Aug	Sep	Oct	Nov	Dec
1951	38.2	39.6	39.1	39.1	38.4	38.1	36.8	36.2	35.9	36.7	36.4	36.6
1952	35.8	35.5	35.0	34.9	34.8	34.6	34.6	34.7	33.8	33.8	33.7	32.9
1953	32.5	32.4	32.4	31.6	31.8	31.4	32.3	31.8	32.0	31.4	31.2	31.7
1954	32.0	32.0	32.1	32.2	32.1	31.5	31.4	31.3	31.5	31.2	31.4	30.8
1955	31.1	31.0	30.7	31.0	30.2	30.7	30.4	30.1	30.4	30.4	29.4	29.5
1956	29.4	29.9	29.8	30.3	30.7	30.5	30.5	31.0	31.0	31.0	31.1	31.7
1957	31.3	31.0	30.9	30.8	30.7	31.5	32.0	32.0	31.2	31.0	31.1	31.5
1958	31.4	31.9	32.3	31.8	32.4	32.0	32.1	31.9	31.6	31.9	32.1	31.6
1959	31.6	31.4	31.5	31.7	31.5	31.3	31.0	30.7	30.9	30.7	30.5	30.3
1960	30.4	30.4	30.7	30.8	30.8	30.4	30.4	29.8	30.0	30.2	30.2	30.3
1961	30.4	30.5	30.3	30.2	29.9	29.5	29.7	30.5	30.3	30.3	30.2	30.6
1962	30.6	30.5	30.5	30.1	30.1	29.9	30.2	30.5	31.2	30.8	31.0	30.6
1963	30.3	30.0	29.6	29.8	29.6	29.9	30.0	29.9	29.8	29.9	30.2	29.4
1964	29.8	29.4	29.5	29.5	29.4	29.0	29.2	29.4	30.1	29.8	29.9	29.8
1965	29.5	29.9	30.0	30.4	30.8	31.6	31.2	31.5	31.4	31.8	32.1	32.7
1966	33.1	33.7	33.5	33.3	33.0	33.0	33.4	33.5	33.4	32.9	32.3	32.1
1967	32.2	31.5	31.1	30.7	31.1	31.4	31.3	31.3	31.2	31.3	31.1	31.5
1968	31.4	31.5	31.6	31.7	31.5	31.3	31.6	31.7	31.9	32.1	32.8	32.4
1969	32.6	32.3	32.7	33.1	34.0	34.5	34.1	34.4	34.4	34.8	35.2	35.1
1970	35.1	35.2	35.6	35.5	35.0	35.0	35.1	34.7	35.5	35.5	35.1	34.5
1971	34.8	35.9	35.4	36.0	36.0	36.2	35.9	35.8	35.7	36.4	37.0	37.2
1972	37.8	38.1	38.1	38.7	39.3	39.4	40.0	40.3	40.5	40.9	42.0	43.8
1973	45.0	47.1	49.3	50.1	52.5	55.0	52.5	64.1	60.9	58.5	59.0	59.1
1974	63.3	64.3	62.3	60.6	58.3	55.4	59.8	62.9	60.9	63.2	64.2	61.5
1975	59.6	57.9	57.1	59.5	61.2	61.5	62.4	63.0	64.5	65.1	64.4	64.0
1976	63.0	62.1	61.5	63.9	63.6	65.2	64.8	63.6	63.4	63.0	63.4	64.5
1977	64.3	65.7	66.6	68.3	67.6	65.5	64.7	63.9	63.7	64.0	65.4	66.4
1978	67.3	68.4	69.8	72.1	72.8	74.6	74.2	73.7	75.1	77.0	77.4	78.0
1979	80.1	82.1	83.8	84.4	84.7	85.6	86.5	85.5	87.9	88.8	90.0	91.2
1980	90.9	92.6	90.8	88.3	89.5	90.1	94.6	99.0	100.4	102.2	103.5	102.7
1981	103.4	104.2	103.8	104.2	103.8	104.9	105.0	104.0	102.7	101.2	99.7	98.8
1982	99.7	100.0	99.7	100.2	101.9	101.8	100.7	99.8	99.2	98.7	99.2	98.8
1983	98.8	100.0	100.5	101.2	100.9	100.5	99.5	102.2	103.3	103.2	102.3	103.5
1984	104.6	103.8	105.7	105.2	104.5	103.3	104.0	103.3	102.8	101.5	101.9	101.4
1985	99.9	99.4	97.6	96.7	95.8	95.2	94.9	92.9	91.8	94.1	95.7	95.5
1986	94.2	90.5	88.2	85.6	86.5	86.2	86.4	86.7	86.6	87.4	87.6	86.9
1987	89.3	90.2	90.5	92.5	93.8	94.5	95.6	96.5	96.0	95.8	95.1	94.9
1988	94.2	95.2	94.1	95.4	95.8	97.0	96.7	97.0	97.0	96.6	95.2	98.1
1989	102.0	101.7	102.9	104.1	104.5	103.2	103.5	101.2	102.5	102.7	103.5	105.1
1990	106.7	106.8	105.1	102.7	103.1	100.6	101.0	110.5	115.8	125.8	117.8	110.8
1991	113.3	104.1	100.5	100.2	100.9	99.2	99.4	99.1	98.4	100.8	100.7	98.2
1992	97.2	98.6	97.1	98.1	100.3	101.6	101.6	100.7	102.8	102.8	102.5	101.3
1993	101.7	101.2	101.7	103.2	105.6	103.8	101.6	100.8	101.2	103.7	103.0	101.7
1994	103.8	102.1	103.8	103.8	102.2	102.7	101.7	101.6	99.7	98.6	99.8	101.1
1995	102.1	102.9	102.3	103.7	102.4	103.0	101.6	99.7	102.0	101.9	104.1	106.5
1996	109.8	111.6	109.8	114.2	114.6	112.2	114.6	115.3	112.7	111.9	115.7	122.5
1997	127.6	116.8	107.5	107.8	109.2	106.2	106.2	106.7	108.4	113.3	115.5	108.7
1998	102.8	100.6	99.3	100.3	99.4	96.8	97.4	93.6	91.9	94.4	93.9	90.4
1999	91.1	88.7	89.0	91.0	96.4	96.7	97.3	102.5	107.2	104.5	109.8	104.3
2000	106.9	110.9	112.9	111.2	114.7	124.5	122.0	117.6	126.0	130.8	129.1	141.1
2001	165.8	141.8	132.3	133.0	130.1	119.6	113.1	112.3	108.1	98.3	105.5	95.5

Producer Price Index, Intermediate Materials
(1982=100)

Year	Jan	Feb	Mar	Apr	May	Jun	Jul	Aug	Sep	Oct	Nov	Dec
1951	28.5	28.7	28.8	28.8	28.8	28.7	28.4	28.0	28.0	27.9	27.9	27.8
1952	27.8	27.7	27.6	27.5	27.5	27.6	27.5	27.6	27.6	27.5	27.4	27.3
1953	27.4	27.4	27.5	27.5	27.6	27.7	28.0	27.9	27.9	27.9	27.8	27.8
1954	27.9	27.9	27.9	27.9	27.9	27.8	27.9	27.9	27.8	27.8	27.9	27.9
1955	27.9	28.0	28.0	28.1	28.1	28.2	28.4	28.5	28.8	28.9	28.9	29.0
1956	29.1	29.2	29.4	29.5	29.6	29.6	29.4	29.7	29.8	30.0	30.0	30.1
1957	30.3	30.3	30.3	30.2	30.2	30.3	30.3	30.4	30.4	30.3	30.4	30.4
1958	30.4	30.3	30.3	30.2	30.3	30.3	30.3	30.4	30.4	30.4	30.5	30.6
1959	30.6	30.7	30.7	30.7	30.9	30.9	30.8	30.8	30.8	30.8	30.9	30.9
1960	30.8	30.9	30.9	30.8	30.8	30.9	30.8	30.8	30.8	30.8	30.7	30.7
1961	30.6	30.7	30.8	30.7	30.6	30.5	30.5	30.5	30.5	30.4	30.5	30.6
1962	30.5	30.6	30.6	32.2	30.6	30.6	30.6	30.6	30.6	30.5	30.5	30.5
1963	30.5	30.5	30.5	30.5	30.7	30.7	30.7	30.7	30.7	30.8	30.8	30.8
1964	30.8	30.8	30.8	30.8	30.7	30.6	30.7	30.6	30.7	30.8	30.8	30.9
1965	30.9	30.9	31.0	31.1	31.1	31.2	31.2	31.3	31.3	31.3	31.4	31.4
1966	31.4	31.6	31.7	31.8	32.0	32.0	32.2	32.3	32.2	32.1	32.2	32.2
1967	32.2	32.1	32.1	32.1	32.1	32.2	32.2	32.2	32.3	32.3	32.4	32.6
1968	32.6	32.7	32.8	32.8	32.8	32.9	33.0	33.0	33.1	33.2	33.2	33.4
1969	33.6	33.7	33.9	33.8	33.9	34.0	34.0	34.2	34.2	34.4	34.6	34.7
1970	35.0	35.0	34.9	35.1	35.2	35.3	35.5	35.5	35.6	35.8	35.9	35.9
1971	36.0	36.1	36.3	36.3	36.5	36.7	36.9	37.2	37.2	37.1	37.2	37.4
1972	37.5	37.7	37.8	37.9	38.0	38.0	38.1	38.2	38.5	38.7	39.0	39.6
1973	39.8	40.4	41.1	41.3	42.2	43.0	42.3	43.5	43.0	43.4	43.8	44.8
1974	45.9	46.8	48.1	49.0	50.6	51.5	53.4	55.8	55.9	57.2	57.8	57.8
1975	58.0	57.8	57.4	57.5	57.3	57.3	57.5	58.0	58.2	58.8	59.0	59.2
1976	59.4	59.6	59.8	60.0	60.3	60.8	61.1	61.3	61.9	62.0	62.4	62.8
1977	63.0	63.3	63.9	64.4	64.9	64.9	65.1	65.4	65.7	65.8	66.3	66.6
1978	66.9	67.4	67.8	68.1	68.7	69.2	69.4	69.9	70.5	71.3	71.9	72.4
1979	73.1	73.7	74.6	75.7	76.6	77.5	78.7	79.8	81.1	82.4	83.2	84.0
1980	86.0	87.6	88.2	88.5	89.0	89.8	90.5	91.5	91.9	92.8	93.5	94.4
1981	95.6	96.1	97.1	98.3	98.7	99.0	99.2	99.7	99.7	99.8	99.9	100.0
1982	100.4	100.3	99.9	99.7	99.7	99.8	100.0	99.9	100.0	99.9	100.1	100.1
1983	99.8	100.0	99.7	99.5	99.8	100.2	100.5	100.9	101.6	101.7	101.8	101.9
1984	102.1	102.5	103.0	103.2	103.4	103.6	103.4	103.2	103.1	103.2	103.3	103.2
1985	103.1	102.8	102.7	102.9	103.2	102.6	102.3	102.3	102.2	102.3	102.5	102.9
1986	102.4	101.2	99.9	98.9	98.7	98.6	98.0	98.0	98.5	98.3	98.3	98.5
1987	99.0	99.8	99.9	100.3	100.8	101.4	101.9	102.4	102.6	103.1	103.5	103.8
1988	104.1	104.4	104.8	105.5	106.2	107.4	108.3	108.5	108.7	108.6	108.8	109.4
1989	110.8	111.3	111.9	112.5	112.6	112.5	112.2	111.8	112.1	112.2	112.0	112.2
1990	113.7	112.8	112.9	113.1	113.1	112.9	112.8	114.0	115.8	117.4	117.7	116.9
1991	116.9	115.9	114.7	114.2	114.1	113.9	113.6	113.8	114.0	114.0	114.1	114.0
1992	113.4	113.8	113.9	114.1	114.5	115.1	115.2	115.1	115.3	115.3	115.1	115.1
1993	115.4	115.9	116.3	116.6	116.3	116.3	116.3	116.2	116.3	116.4	116.5	116.2
1994	116.5	116.9	117.1	117.1	117.2	117.8	118.3	119.1	119.6	120.1	121.0	121.5
1995	122.8	123.7	124.3	125.0	125.2	125.5	125.6	125.6	125.5	125.4	125.2	125.4
1996	125.5	125.0	125.3	125.7	126.2	125.8	125.5	125.6	126.1	126.0	125.8	126.4
1997	126.6	126.4	126.0	125.6	125.4	125.4	125.1	125.3	125.5	125.4	125.6	125.3
1998	124.5	124.1	123.7	123.7	123.6	123.2	123.1	122.8	122.4	122.2	121.9	121.2
1999	121.1	120.7	121.1	121.9	122.3	122.7	123.4	124.1	124.7	124.9	125.3	125.7
2000	126.2	127.2	128.5	128.4	128.4	129.5	129.8	129.4	130.4	130.6	130.4	130.9
2001	132.0	131.7	131.3	131.2	131.3	131.1	129.5	129.1	129.4	127.4	126.8	125.7

Producer Price Index, Capital Equipment
(1982=100)

Year	Jan	Feb	Mar	Apr	May	Jun	Jul	Aug	Sep	Oct	Nov	Dec
1951	25.1	25.2	25.3	25.5	25.5	25.5	25.6	25.5	25.6	25.7	25.6	25.7
1952	25.7	25.9	25.9	25.9	26.0	26.0	26.0	26.0	25.9	25.9	25.8	25.9
1953	25.9	25.9	26.1	26.1	26.3	26.4	26.5	26.6	26.6	26.6	26.5	26.5
1954	26.5	26.5	26.6	26.6	26.7	26.7	26.7	26.7	26.6	26.7	26.5	26.5
1955	26.8	26.8	26.9	27.0	27.2	27.3	27.3	27.6	27.8	28.1	28.2	28.3
1956	28.4	28.6	28.8	29.0	29.3	29.4	29.4	29.7	30.1	30.3	30.6	30.6
1957	30.7	30.9	31.0	31.0	31.2	31.2	31.4	31.5	31.6	31.7	31.9	32.0
1958	32.0	32.1	32.0	32.1	32.1	32.1	32.1	32.0	32.1	32.1	31.9	32.0
1959	32.4	32.5	32.6	32.7	32.7	32.9	32.8	32.8	32.9	32.8	32.7	32.7
1960	32.8	32.9	32.9	32.8	32.7	32.8	32.8	32.9	32.6	32.8	32.8	32.8
1961	32.9	32.9	32.9	32.9	32.9	32.9	32.9	32.9	32.9	32.6	32.8	32.8
1962	33.0	33.0	33.0	33.0	33.0	33.0	33.0	33.0	33.0	33.0	32.9	32.9
1963	33.0	33.0	33.0	33.0	33.0	33.0	33.0	33.0	33.0	33.0	33.0	33.0
1964	33.2	33.2	33.3	33.3	33.5	33.4	33.5	33.5	33.1	33.1	33.2	33.2
1965	33.6	33.7	33.7	33.8	33.8	33.8	33.8	33.8	33.5	33.5	33.5	33.5
1966	34.0	34.2	34.2	34.3	34.5	34.6	34.7	34.8	34.9	35.0	35.2	35.3
1967	35.4	35.5	35.5	35.6	35.7	35.7	35.8	35.9	35.9	36.1	36.2	36.4
1968	36.5	36.6	36.6	36.8	37.0	37.0	37.1	37.2	37.3	37.4	37.5	37.5
1969	37.6	37.7	37.8	37.9	38.0	38.1	38.3	38.4	38.5	38.7	39.0	39.2
1970	39.3	39.4	39.6	39.7	39.8	39.9	40.0	40.2	40.3	40.8	41.0	41.1
1971	41.3	41.4	41.5	41.6	41.7	41.7	41.9	42.0	41.9	41.8	41.8	42.1
1972	42.3	42.5	42.6	42.7	42.8	42.8	42.9	42.9	43.0	42.8	42.9	43.0
1973	43.0	43.3	43.6	43.8	44.1	44.2	44.3	44.4	44.6	44.7	44.9	45.3
1974	45.8	46.2	46.8	47.4	48.7	49.7	50.7	52.1	53.1	54.2	55.0	55.5
1975	56.2	56.7	57.2	57.5	57.8	58.0	58.4	58.5	58.9	59.3	59.7	60.0
1976	60.4	60.7	61.1	61.3	61.5	61.8	62.1	62.5	62.9	63.1	63.4	64.0
1977	64.0	64.3	64.7	65.0	65.3	65.7	66.0	66.6	67.0	67.6	68.1	68.6
1978	68.8	69.1	69.6	69.9	70.5	71.0	71.5	72.0	72.6	72.8	73.5	74.0
1979	74.5	75.2	75.7	76.4	76.8	77.3	77.8	77.8	78.7	79.2	79.8	80.6
1980	81.7	82.3	83.1	84.4	84.6	85.1	86.2	87.0	87.5	88.8	89.3	89.7
1981	90.8	91.7	92.4	93.1	93.8	94.4	95.0	95.4	96.1	96.9	97.5	98.1
1982	98.6	98.2	98.7	99.0	99.5	100.0	100.3	100.7	101.0	101.1	101.3	101.9
1983	101.8	102.1	102.2	102.3	102.5	102.6	102.8	103.1	103.3	103.4	103.5	103.8
1984	104.1	104.5	104.6	105.3	105.1	105.2	105.5	105.6	105.9	105.6	105.8	105.6
1985	106.3	106.9	107.1	107.1	107.4	107.6	107.7	107.9	107.2	108.3	108.5	108.6
1986	108.6	108.7	108.9	109.2	109.3	109.6	109.7	109.8	109.7	110.6	110.8	110.9
1987	111.3	111.1	111.1	111.6	111.6	111.5	111.7	112.0	112.0	112.0	112.1	112.2
1988	112.8	113.0	113.2	113.5	113.8	114.0	114.4	114.9	115.2	115.5	115.7	116.1
1989	116.9	117.3	117.5	117.6	118.3	118.9	118.9	119.3	119.7	120.0	120.4	120.6
1990	121.0	121.4	121.8	122.1	122.1	122.5	122.9	123.3	123.8	124.1	124.5	124.8
1991	125.6	125.8	126.0	126.1	126.5	126.6	126.7	126.8	127.2	127.6	127.8	128.0
1992	128.2	128.3	128.6	129.0	129.0	129.0	129.1	129.4	129.4	129.7	129.9	130.1
1993	130.4	130.7	130.9	131.1	131.2	131.1	131.5	131.6	131.7	131.8	132.2	132.4
1994	132.9	133.1	133.3	133.7	134.1	134.3	134.4	134.6	134.9	134.4	134.5	134.9
1995	135.6	135.8	135.9	136.2	136.5	136.6	136.9	137.0	136.8	137.6	138.0	138.0
1996	138.0	138.1	138.1	138.2	138.3	138.4	138.4	138.6	138.4	138.5	138.3	138.4
1997	138.7	138.6	138.5	138.4	138.2	138.3	138.2	138.2	138.2	138.0	137.8	137.7
1998	137.7	137.7	137.7	137.6	137.4	137.4	137.5	137.3	137.5	137.7	137.7	137.6
1999	137.6	137.7	137.6	137.6	137.6	137.5	137.4	137.4	137.5	138.0	137.8	138.0
2000	138.1	138.2	138.3	138.4	138.6	138.8	139.0	139.1	139.4	139.3	139.4	139.5
2001	139.8	139.3	139.5	139.8	139.5	139.7	140.1	140.2	140.3	139.3	139.5	139.3

Source: The Conference Board. © 2002 The Conference Board. All Rights Reserved. No claim to original U.S. Government works pursuant to U.S. Contract No. 52-SABA-5-00128. Primary source(s): U.S. Department of Labor, Bureau of Labor Statistics, Office of Prices and Living Conditions, Division of Industrial Prices and Price Indexes, Washington, DC 20212. A dash (-) indicates that data are not available or zero.

Producer Price Index, Finished Consumer Goods
(1982=100)

Year	Jan	Feb	Mar	Apr	May	Jun	Jul	Aug	Sep	Oct	Nov	Dec
1951	32.3	32.8	32.8	32.9	33.0	32.8	32.5	32.4	32.4	32.6	32.6	32.6
1952	32.4	32.5	32.5	32.3	32.3	32.3	32.4	32.3	32.2	32.2	32.0	31.7
1953	31.8	31.7	31.7	31.6	31.7	31.7	31.8	31.8	31.9	31.8	31.6	31.7
1954	31.9	31.6	31.7	31.9	31.9	31.7	31.8	31.8	31.6	31.5	31.5	31.5
1955	31.6	31.6	31.5	31.6	31.4	31.6	31.3	31.4	31.5	31.4	31.5	31.5
1956	31.5	31.5	31.7	31.7	32.0	32.1	32.0	32.0	32.2	32.3	32.4	32.5
1957	32.5	32.6	32.6	32.7	32.7	32.9	32.9	33.0	32.9	33.1	33.2	33.4
1958	33.5	33.5	33.8	33.7	33.7	33.7	33.7	33.5	33.6	33.5	33.5	33.5
1959	33.4	33.4	33.3	33.4	33.3	33.4	33.3	33.1	33.6	33.2	33.1	33.1
1960	33.2	33.2	33.6	33.6	33.6	33.6	33.7	33.6	33.7	34.0	34.0	33.8
1961	33.8	34.0	33.8	33.6	33.4	33.4	33.5	33.5	33.5	33.4	33.5	33.6
1962	33.7	33.8	33.7	33.6	33.5	33.5	33.4	33.6	34.0	33.7	33.8	33.6
1963	33.6	33.6	33.3	33.3	33.5	33.6	33.6	33.5	33.5	33.6	33.5	33.5
1964	33.7	33.4	33.5	33.4	33.4	33.5	33.6	33.6	33.6	33.7	33.6	33.5
1965	33.7	33.7	33.7	34.0	34.1	34.3	34.3	34.3	34.3	34.5	34.7	34.9
1966	35.0	35.3	35.3	35.3	35.2	35.1	35.2	35.6	35.7	35.7	35.6	35.4
1967	35.4	35.3	35.2	35.3	35.4	35.7	35.6	35.7	35.8	35.8	35.9	35.9
1968	35.9	36.1	36.2	36.4	36.4	36.5	36.6	36.7	36.9	37.0	37.0	37.0
1969	37.2	37.1	37.3	37.5	37.8	38.0	38.0	38.1	38.2	38.5	38.8	38.8
1970	39.0	38.9	39.0	39.0	38.9	39.0	39.0	39.0	39.4	39.3	39.5	39.4
1971	39.5	39.7	39.8	40.0	40.1	40.3	40.1	40.4	40.3	40.4	40.6	40.9
1972	40.7	40.9	40.9	40.9	41.1	41.4	41.6	41.7	42.0	41.9	42.1	42.6
1973	43.0	43.5	44.7	45.0	45.3	45.9	45.7	47.7	47.5	47.4	47.9	48.3
1974	49.6	50.7	51.1	51.5	52.0	51.8	53.2	54.1	54.6	55.6	56.7	56.6
1975	56.8	56.6	56.4	56.9	57.3	57.8	58.4	59.0	59.4	59.9	60.1	60.1
1976	59.9	59.6	59.6	60.0	60.0	60.1	60.3	60.4	60.5	60.9	61.4	61.9
1977	62.1	62.8	63.4	63.7	64.2	64.2	64.5	64.8	65.0	65.3	65.8	66.1
1978	66.4	66.9	67.3	68.2	68.6	69.3	69.9	69.9	70.6	71.0	71.5	72.5
1979	73.3	74.2	74.8	75.6	75.9	76.4	77.3	78.3	79.8	80.6	81.8	82.6
1980	83.9	85.2	86.1	86.7	87.1	87.9	89.4	90.5	90.8	91.3	92.0	92.4
1981	93.3	94.1	95.3	96.4	96.6	97.0	97.1	97.1	97.5	97.8	98.0	98.4
1982	99.0	99.0	98.8	98.9	98.8	99.8	100.1	100.5	100.7	101.0	101.4	101.7
1983	100.8	100.8	100.7	100.7	101.0	101.3	101.3	101.6	101.8	101.9	101.5	101.9
1984	102.7	103.1	103.6	103.5	103.5	103.4	103.6	103.3	103.2	103.1	103.4	103.5
1985	103.4	103.4	103.3	103.9	104.2	103.8	103.8	103.6	102.9	103.9	104.6	105.3
1986	104.6	102.8	101.0	100.3	101.0	101.2	100.2	100.7	100.9	101.5	101.4	101.5
1987	102.1	102.5	102.6	103.3	103.4	103.8	104.0	104.2	104.5	104.4	104.3	104.1
1988	104.6	104.4	104.7	105.2	105.4	105.7	106.6	107.1	107.3	107.5	107.9	108.3
1989	109.5	110.5	110.9	111.9	112.9	112.7	112.4	111.7	112.5	113.1	113.2	114.1
1990	116.9	116.7	116.3	116.1	116.3	116.3	116.6	118.2	120.0	121.5	122.3	121.4
1991	122.0	120.8	120.2	120.2	120.4	120.1	119.6	119.9	120.1	120.5	121.0	120.8
1992	120.4	120.8	120.8	120.9	121.4	121.9	121.9	121.9	122.3	122.8	122.6	122.7
1993	122.9	123.2	123.4	124.3	124.4	123.7	123.4	121.9	122.1	122.3	122.3	122.3
1994	122.6	122.9	122.9	122.9	122.7	122.8	123.4	124.0	123.5	123.1	123.9	124.4
1995	124.6	124.9	125.1	125.4	125.5	125.5	125.6	125.5	125.8	126.0	126.2	127.0
1996	127.6	127.5	128.6	129.0	129.1	129.5	129.4	129.9	130.0	130.9	131.1	131.6
1997	131.6	131.1	131.1	130.2	129.7	129.6	129.2	129.8	130.1	130.4	130.1	129.8
1998	128.8	128.6	128.7	128.9	128.8	128.7	129.0	128.8	128.7	129.4	129.0	129.6
1999	130.2	129.4	130.1	130.9	131.0	131.3	131.6	132.8	134.0	134.0	134.2	134.8
2000	134.5	136.2	137.6	137.1	137.1	138.6	138.4	138.1	139.4	140.2	140.4	140.6
2001	142.7	143.0	142.7	143.5	143.8	143.0	140.6	141.3	142.2	139.5	138.4	137.2

Producer Price Index, Finished Goods
(1982=100)

Year	Jan	Feb	Mar	Apr	May	Jun	Jul	Aug	Sep	Oct	Nov	Dec
1951	30.5	30.8	30.9	30.9	31.1	31.0	30.8	30.7	30.6	30.8	30.9	30.9
1952	30.8	30.7	30.9	30.7	30.7	30.7	30.8	30.7	30.6	30.5	30.4	30.2
1953	30.3	30.2	30.3	30.2	30.3	30.4	30.5	30.4	30.4	30.4	30.3	30.4
1954	30.5	30.4	30.4	30.6	30.6	30.4	30.5	30.4	30.3	30.2	30.3	30.3
1955	30.4	30.5	30.3	30.4	30.4	30.5	30.4	30.4	30.5	30.6	30.6	30.7
1956	30.7	30.8	30.9	31.0	31.2	31.4	31.3	31.4	31.6	31.8	31.9	31.9
1957	32.1	32.2	32.1	32.3	32.3	32.5	32.6	32.6	32.6	32.7	32.9	33.0
1958	33.2	33.2	33.4	33.2	33.2	33.3	33.2	33.2	33.2	33.2	32.9	33.0
1959	33.1	33.2	33.2	33.2	33.3	33.2	33.1	33.0	33.4	33.1	33.0	33.1
1960	33.1	33.1	33.4	33.4	33.4	33.4	33.5	33.4	33.4	33.7	33.7	33.6
1961	33.6	33.7	33.6	33.4	33.3	33.3	33.3	33.4	33.3	33.3	33.4	33.4
1962	33.5	33.6	33.5	33.5	33.4	33.4	33.4	33.5	33.8	33.6	33.6	33.5
1963	33.4	33.4	33.3	33.3	33.4	33.5	33.4	33.4	33.4	33.5	33.5	33.4
1964	33.5	33.5	33.4	33.5	33.5	33.5	33.5	33.6	33.6	33.6	33.5	33.6
1965	33.6	33.7	33.7	34.0	34.1	34.2	34.1	34.2	34.3	34.4	34.5	34.7
1966	34.7	35.0	35.0	35.1	35.1	34.9	35.1	35.4	35.6	35.5	35.5	35.4
1967	35.4	35.3	35.3	35.3	35.4	35.7	35.7	35.8	35.8	35.9	35.9	36.0
1968	36.1	36.2	36.3	36.5	36.5	36.6	36.7	36.8	37.0	37.0	37.1	37.1
1969	37.2	37.2	37.4	37.6	37.8	38.0	38.1	38.2	38.3	38.5	38.8	38.9
1970	39.1	39.0	39.1	39.1	39.1	39.2	39.2	39.2	39.6	39.6	39.8	39.8
1971	39.9	40.1	40.2	40.3	40.5	40.6	40.4	40.7	40.7	40.7	40.8	41.1
1972	41.0	41.3	41.3	41.3	41.5	41.7	41.8	42.0	42.2	42.0	42.3	42.7
1973	43.0	43.5	44.4	44.7	45.0	45.5	45.4	47.0	46.9	46.8	47.2	47.6
1974	48.8	49.7	50.2	50.7	51.3	51.3	52.7	53.7	54.3	55.3	56.4	56.4
1975	56.7	56.6	56.6	57.1	57.4	57.9	58.4	58.9	59.3	59.8	60.0	60.1
1976	60.0	59.9	60.0	60.3	60.4	60.5	60.7	60.9	61.1	61.4	61.9	62.4
1977	62.5	63.2	63.7	64.0	64.4	64.6	64.8	65.2	65.5	65.9	66.4	66.7
1978	67.0	67.5	67.8	68.6	69.1	69.7	70.3	70.4	71.1	71.4	72.0	72.8
1979	73.7	74.4	75.0	75.8	76.2	76.6	77.4	78.2	79.5	80.4	81.4	82.2
1980	83.4	84.6	85.5	86.2	86.6	87.3	88.7	89.7	90.1	90.8	91.4	91.8
1981	92.8	93.6	94.7	95.7	96.0	96.5	96.7	96.8	97.2	97.6	97.9	98.3
1982	98.9	98.8	98.8	99.0	99.0	99.8	100.2	100.6	100.7	101.0	101.4	101.8
1983	101.0	101.1	101.0	101.1	101.4	101.6	101.6	101.9	102.2	102.2	102.0	102.3
1984	103.0	103.4	103.8	103.9	103.8	103.8	104.0	103.8	103.8	103.6	104.0	104.0
1985	104.0	104.1	104.1	104.6	104.9	104.6	104.7	104.5	103.8	104.9	105.5	106.0
1986	105.5	104.1	102.8	102.3	102.8	103.1	102.3	102.7	102.9	103.5	103.4	103.6
1987	104.1	104.4	104.5	105.1	105.2	105.5	105.7	105.9	106.2	106.0	106.0	105.8
1988	106.4	106.3	106.6	107.0	107.2	107.5	108.4	108.8	109.0	109.2	109.6	110.0
1989	111.1	111.9	112.3	113.1	114.0	114.0	113.8	113.4	114.0	114.6	114.8	115.5
1990	117.7	117.6	117.5	117.4	117.5	117.6	117.9	119.2	120.7	121.9	122.6	122.0
1991	122.6	121.8	121.3	121.3	121.6	121.4	121.1	121.3	121.5	121.9	122.4	122.3
1992	122.0	122.3	122.4	122.5	122.9	123.4	123.3	123.4	123.7	124.2	124.1	124.2
1993	124.4	124.7	125.0	125.7	125.7	125.2	125.1	123.9	124.1	124.2	124.4	124.4
1994	124.8	125.0	125.1	125.1	125.1	125.2	125.7	126.2	125.9	125.5	126.1	126.6
1995	126.9	127.2	127.4	127.7	127.8	127.8	128.0	127.9	128.1	128.4	128.7	129.3
1996	129.7	129.7	130.5	130.9	130.9	131.3	131.2	131.6	131.7	132.4	132.5	132.9
1997	133.0	132.6	132.6	131.8	131.4	131.3	131.0	131.5	131.7	131.9	131.6	131.3
1998	130.6	130.4	130.5	130.7	130.5	130.5	130.7	130.5	130.5	131.0	130.8	131.2
1999	131.7	131.0	131.5	132.2	132.3	132.4	132.7	133.6	134.5	134.6	134.7	135.2
2000	135.1	136.3	137.5	137.1	137.1	138.3	138.2	138.0	139.0	139.6	139.8	140.0
2001	141.6	141.7	141.6	142.3	142.4	141.9	140.2	140.7	141.4	139.1	138.3	137.4

Producer Price Index, Crude Nonfood Less Energy
(1982=100)

Year	Jan	Feb	Mar	Apr	May	Jun	Jul	Aug	Sep	Oct	Nov	Dec
1974	86.3	86.5	88.3	89.7	83.8	82.9	84.2	85.5	82.5	80.6	77.6	71.6
1975	69.8	69.2	68.2	67.7	68.8	66.5	66.5	67.7	71.2	71.5	71.9	73.1
1976	72.4	73.8	74.5	78.1	80.6	82.8	87.3	84.1	84.4	82.2	81.8	81.1
1977	78.7	79.7	81.5	82.1	82.5	79.7	78.8	79.2	79.2	78.5	78.4	80.1
1978	80.3	80.6	80.3	82.2	84.6	87.4	89.6	90.4	92.3	94.7	96.3	96.8
1979	96.4	99.6	104.2	105.1	106.7	111.6	109.4	106.4	106.5	108.9	111.3	111.3
1980	112.6	115.3	111.7	109.9	107.2	106.1	109.6	112.4	116.2	118.2	119.8	119.3
1981	113.3	106.2	108.9	111.9	113.7	115.5	116.4	115.5	112.6	110.8	107.5	106.0
1982	101.2	100.7	100.0	101.1	102.2	101.0	101.4	100.0	98.9	97.7	96.3	95.9
1983	97.3	99.8	102.2	102.1	103.4	104.8	106.2	108.4	109.0	109.1	109.9	111.2
1984	111.5	113.8	114.8	115.1	115.7	114.1	112.0	109.6	110.5	108.5	107.7	107.3
1985	107.4	107.2	107.0	107.4	105.3	103.6	104.3	103.6	103.3	103.7	103.0	102.4
1986	103.6	103.5	103.8	103.9	104.1	104.7	105.3	99.7	100.3	102.0	102.8	104.1
1987	105.4	106.2	106.5	107.5	110.0	113.2	115.9	119.1	122.8	126.6	127.5	127.9
1988	129.4	131.7	133.0	132.1	130.7	131.1	133.2	134.3	133.3	133.6	136.0	137.6
1989	140.6	140.3	140.6	140.3	139.8	137.9	135.9	136.8	137.5	137.9	134.9	132.8
1990	132.7	131.6	133.9	137.0	138.0	137.3	138.0	140.1	139.9	138.4	135.7	133.8
1991	134.2	133.7	131.8	131.7	130.4	126.1	125.4	125.8	125.7	125.4	124.4	123.4
1992	123.4	125.2	127.7	128.4	129.1	128.8	129.6	130.4	130.4	128.9	128.2	130.5
1993	135.0	136.8	137.0	138.4	140.3	140.3	142.1	140.4	140.7	142.6	144.1	145.3
1994	148.3	151.0	151.5	150.7	149.7	151.2	155.5	158.8	160.5	161.3	166.6	169.9
1995	174.5	176.5	177.8	180.2	179.6	179.5	176.4	173.4	170.9	166.6	163.6	162.3
1996	162.6	162.1	158.2	156.7	157.6	154.6	152.2	152.5	153.5	153.3	153.0	153.6
1997	157.1	158.7	158.7	155.9	157.4	156.8	155.3	156.9	155.8	155.8	155.4	153.7
1998	151.2	150.6	148.5	147.3	146.8	146.0	143.4	139.3	137.6	133.6	130.9	129.2
1999	129.5	130.8	129.4	129.0	130.9	131.7	133.7	136.1	138.6	142.1	143.3	147.4
2000	150.7	151.3	150.5	149.5	148.4	145.8	143.6	141.3	142.5	141.4	138.5	139.1
2001	139.1	136.6	135.2	132.0	131.2	129.8	130.8	128.4	128.3	126.1	125.1	125.2

Source: The Conference Board. © 2002 The Conference Board. All Rights Reserved. No claim to original U.S. Government works pursuant to U.S. Contract No. 52-SABA-5-00128. Primary source(s): U.S. Department of Labor, Bureau of Labor Statistics, Office of Prices and Living Conditions, Division of Industrial Prices and Price Indexes, Washington, DC 20212. A dash (-) indicates that data are not available or zero.

Producer Price Index, Petroleum Products
(1982=100)

Year	Jan	Feb	Mar	Apr	May	Jun	Jul	Aug	Sep	Oct	Nov	Dec
1967	13.1	13.2	13.2	13.1	13.2	13.1	13.1	13.4	13.3	13.1	13.0	12.9
1968	12.9	12.9	12.8	12.9	12.8	13.1	13.0	12.9	12.9	12.9	12.9	12.8
1969	12.9	12.9	13.1	13.1	13.0	13.1	13.1	13.1	13.0	13.2	13.2	13.2
1970	13.1	13.1	13.0	13.0	13.2	13.0	13.0	13.2	13.3	13.5	13.7	14.3
1971	14.3	14.1	13.9	13.7	14.0	13.9	14.0	14.1	14.2	14.3	14.3	14.2
1972	13.9	13.8	13.9	14.0	14.0	14.1	14.2	14.4	14.7	14.8	14.9	14.9
1973	14.8	15.6	15.8	16.0	16.3	16.6	16.9	16.9	17.2	17.7	18.7	20.2
1974	22.0	24.6	26.9	28.1	29.2	30.2	31.1	31.7	31.9	32.3	31.8	31.9
1975	32.0	31.6	31.7	31.8	32.1	32.9	33.6	34.9	35.6	36.1	36.7	36.6
1976	36.2	35.9	35.5	35.2	35.1	35.4	36.0	36.4	36.9	37.3	37.8	38.0
1977	38.5	39.2	40.1	40.7	41.0	41.0	40.8	40.5	40.5	40.9	41.3	41.5
1978	41.7	41.4	40.9	41.0	41.3	41.7	41.9	42.0	42.4	43.2	44.0	44.8
1979	45.8	46.3	47.2	49.6	52.4	55.5	58.6	62.8	67.1	70.3	72.3	73.6
1980	77.4	82.0	86.5	90.1	89.4	89.4	90.4	90.5	90.8	90.5	92.1	94.5
1981	97.6	101.6	108.0	112.1	110.1	108.8	106.3	105.5	105.2	105.0	104.9	105.0
1982	106.1	104.4	100.8	98.3	94.5	97.2	101.1	101.3	99.4	98.4	98.9	98.8
1983	95.4	91.7	87.4	87.0	87.7	90.1	89.6	90.0	90.7	90.6	89.2	88.7
1984	87.6	88.8	89.4	90.1	90.5	89.6	87.4	84.7	84.2	85.2	85.6	85.3
1985	84.0	81.6	81.5	86.0	87.9	82.6	81.3	80.5	80.7	81.5	83.0	85.7
1986	81.7	71.0	58.7	52.1	52.0	52.2	43.8	43.4	48.1	45.4	45.0	46.8
1987	52.4	55.7	54.4	54.8	54.2	56.3	58.3	61.4	58.7	59.4	59.1	57.5
1988	55.2	54.9	53.9	54.1	54.8	54.4	54.5	55.0	52.4	50.7	53.1	53.6
1989	56.0	57.5	59.3	65.2	65.9	65.0	61.8	57.1	60.4	61.8	60.9	63.2
1990	74.3	67.2	65.4	65.9	63.8	63.7	61.1	73.5	84.2	93.4	94.4	89.0
1991	81.4	74.6	66.0	64.6	65.2	65.0	62.1	65.6	65.3	64.1	66.8	65.5
1992	60.0	62.6	61.8	62.0	63.9	68.4	67.7	66.4	66.3	66.4	67.3	62.9
1993	63.0	64.2	65.9	65.4	65.0	63.3	61.5	58.8	58.8	60.7	57.9	53.3
1994	54.2	57.7	56.9	55.9	54.9	56.9	60.7	64.4	60.6	58.3	59.6	58.9
1995	59.3	59.6	60.4	61.8	62.7	62.6	60.1	59.6	58.7	57.6	56.0	60.5
1996	64.2	62.4	66.9	71.9	71.5	67.9	67.6	67.9	68.8	71.9	72.0	75.6
1997	75.5	74.3	71.7	67.3	64.7	64.6	63.0	66.2	65.2	65.6	64.0	63.3
1998	58.3	55.3	52.3	52.3	52.4	51.8	50.8	47.7	46.8	49.3	47.1	43.0
1999	45.9	43.2	48.1	58.5	57.1	57.3	61.8	66.7	68.2	67.0	69.2	75.3
2000	76.8	85.1	93.5	84.6	83.7	94.9	90.2	88.2	96.0	95.4	95.8	93.6
2001	93.3	91.5	89.5	94.1	96.5	92.6	79.9	83.0	89.0	72.1	66.5	60.1

Source: The Conference Board. © 2002 The Conference Board. All Rights Reserved. No claim to original U.S. Government works pursuant to U.S. Contract No. 52-SABA-5-00128. Primary source(s): U.S. Department of Labor, Bureau of Labor Statistics, Office of Prices and Living Conditions, Division of Industrial Prices and Price Indexes, Washington, DC 20212. A dash (-) indicates that data are not available or zero.

Output per Hour, Business Sector
(1992=100)

Year	1st Quarter	2nd Quarter	3rd Quarter	4th Quarter
1958	45.0	45.6	46.4	46.9
1959	47.4	47.7	48.1	48.2
1960	49.5	48.5	48.7	48.4
1961	48.9	50.6	51.1	51.7
1962	52.2	52.5	53.2	53.7
1963	54.1	54.5	55.6	55.8
1964	57.2	57.3	57.9	57.5
1965	58.6	58.7	60.1	60.9
1966	62.0	61.8	61.8	62.4
1967	63.1	63.5	63.4	63.5
1968	64.9	65.6	65.5	65.4
1969	65.7	65.6	65.7	65.6
1970	65.9	66.6	68.0	67.5
1971	69.6	69.7	70.6	69.8
1972	70.7	72.2	72.5	73.4
1973	74.9	74.9	74.0	74.2
1974	73.3	73.7	72.9	73.2
1975	74.4	75.7	76.5	76.6
1976	77.9	78.5	78.6	79.0
1977	79.5	79.5	80.5	79.8
1978	79.3	80.8	81.1	81.4
1979	80.8	80.7	80.6	80.5
1980	80.8	80.0	80.1	80.7
1981	82.0	81.6	82.7	81.6
1982	80.8	81.6	81.7	82.4
1983	83.2	84.7	84.9	85.6
1984	86.3	87.1	87.2	87.5
1985	87.6	88.1	89.5	89.8
1986	90.8	91.4	91.8	91.6
1987	91.2	91.8	91.7	92.7
1988	92.7	92.9	93.0	93.2
1989	93.7	93.9	93.8	94.3
1990	95.0	95.4	95.6	94.8
1991	95.1	96.2	96.4	97.3
1992	99.2	99.7	99.7	101.4
1993	100.2	100.2	100.2	101.4
1994	101.6	101.9	101.6	102.3
1995	102.0	102.3	102.5	103.4
1996	104.4	105.6	105.6	106.0
1997	106.4	107.5	108.5	108.7
1998	110.0	110.0	110.7	111.9
1999	112.7	112.4	113.3	115.3
2000	115.3	117.5	117.8	118.7
2001	118.6	119.3	119.6	-

Source: The Conference Board. © 2002 The Conference Board. All Rights Reserved. No claim to original U.S. Government works pursuant to U.S. Contract No. 52-SABA-5-00128. Primary source(s): U.S. Department of Labor, Bureau of Labor Statistics, Office of Productivity and Technology, Division of Productivity Research, Washington, DC 20212. A dash (-) indicates that data are not available or zero.

Output per Hour, Nonfarm Business Sector
(1992=100)

Year	1st Quarter	2nd Quarter	3rd Quarter	4th Quarter
1958	48.0	48.9	49.8	50.5
1959	50.7	51.4	51.5	51.4
1960	52.6	51.8	52.0	51.4
1961	52.1	53.6	54.2	54.8
1962	55.8	55.6	56.3	56.7
1963	57.1	57.6	58.8	58.8
1964	60.2	60.6	61.1	60.3
1965	61.3	61.7	62.8	63.9
1966	64.8	64.5	64.4	64.8
1967	65.5	65.7	65.9	66.0
1968	67.5	68.1	67.9	67.8
1969	68.4	67.9	67.8	67.5
1970	67.7	68.7	70.0	69.3
1971	71.5	71.7	72.4	71.6
1972	72.9	74.2	74.7	75.2
1973	77.0	77.0	76.4	75.8
1974	75.7	75.7	74.7	75.3
1975	76.0	77.3	78.1	78.1
1976	79.6	80.4	80.5	80.7
1977	81.1	81.5	82.3	81.2
1978	81.2	82.7	82.9	83.4
1979	82.5	82.3	82.1	82.1
1980	82.3	81.5	81.8	82.4
1981	83.5	82.6	83.5	82.5
1982	81.7	82.4	82.7	83.3
1983	84.3	86.3	87.0	87.3
1984	87.5	88.2	88.3	88.4
1985	88.4	88.7	89.8	90.2
1986	91.3	92.1	92.4	92.2
1987	91.7	92.4	92.1	93.1
1988	93.0	93.4	93.5	94.1
1989	94.0	94.1	94.2	94.6
1990	95.1	95.5	95.6	94.9
1991	95.3	96.4	96.7	97.4
1992	99.2	99.7	99.6	101.5
1993	100.2	100.1	100.4	101.3
1994	101.5	101.8	101.6	102.4
1995	102.2	102.6	102.8	103.6
1996	104.5	105.6	105.5	105.9
1997	106.2	107.3	108.2	108.4
1998	109.6	109.8	110.3	111.5
1999	112.2	111.8	112.7	114.8
2000	114.8	116.7	117.2	117.8
2001	117.8	118.4	118.9	-

PRICE INDEXES FOR GROSS DOMESTIC PRODUCT

The 12 series in this section show the functioning of inflation in the U.S. economy from 1959 through 2001.

Price indexes are presented for:

> Gross domestic product as a whole
> Busines sector
> Nonfarm business sector
>   Nonfarm less housing
>   Housing sector only
> Farms
> Households and institutions
> Private households
> Nonprofit institutions
> General government
>   Federal government
>   State and local government

Price Index versus Implicit Price Deflator

Before the 1995 revisions of the national income accounts, a special price index, known as the implicit price deflator (IPD), was used to derive GDP (or its components) in real dollars. The IPD reflects *both* changes in pricing and changes in the composition of GDP from one period to another. For this reason, the IPD was a superior tool for measuring inflation. That is now changing.

With the shift from constant dollar indexes to the chain-type price indexes, IPDs and chain-type price indexes are identical except for the most recent estimates (see Introduction for a full discussion). Both measures use the same weights to aggregate the detailed prices.

For these reasons, chain-type price indexes continue to be used in this edition of *EIH*.

Using the Indexes

The simplest explanation for these indexes is that they shows how inflation or deflation influence Gross Domestic Product and its major sectors. Using artificially simple numbers, if GDP in actual, current dollars was $1,000 in 1992 and $2,000 in 1994 and *no inflation in prices* had taken place in the 1992-1994 period, the chained price index for GDP in 1994 would be 100.0, i.e. the *same* as in the reference year. Therefore, the change between 1992 and 1994 was *real growth*.

Assume, however, that cumulative inflation in the period was 30%; this would mean that, in 1994, a person would have to spend $1.30 to have the same purchasing power as in 1992. The chained (1992) dollar value of the $2,000 GDP in 1994 would therefore be $1,538.46 (2000 / 1.30). The price index would be calculated as follows:

(2000 / 1538.46) x 100

This would produce an index of 130.0. The index, in other words, can be read as an indicator of inflation relative to the reference year—in this case 1992. The difference between any two years is the increase or decrease in prices between those years. In the example above, the *real growth* between 1992 and 1994 is only $538.46 rather than the apparent $1,000.

The price index for GDP is an indicator of *overall* inflation or deflation. Indexes are also provided for major sectors of GDP. Thus the user who wishes to calculate how she or he is doing relative to inflation would consult the table for private households; the business owner would consult the table for busines or for nonfarm business less housing.

An example showing the use of the Private Household table is presented below.

An Example. A person who got a job in March 1995 paying $49,500 a year would like to calculate how he is doing in March 2001. The person now makes $61,500 a year, an increase of $12,000. Has this person gained or lost purchasing power?

The price index for the Private Households sector of GDP was 96.48 in the first quarter of 1995; it was 116.95 in the first quarter of 2001. The following formula provides the percent increase in prices between 1995 and 2001 in the index:

((Current Index / Previous Index) - 1) x 100.

The result is 21 percent. Multiplying the 1995 salary by 1.21 produces $59,895. Therefore the person has kept up with inflation. His effective gain in purchasing power, however, was only $1,615, not $12,000; the rest was equivalent to inflationary adjustments.

Price Indexes for Gross Domestic Product
Based on chained 1996 $

Year	1st Quarter	2nd Quarter	3rd Quarter	4th Quarter
1959	21.79	21.84	21.90	21.99
1960	22.04	22.14	22.23	22.33
1961	22.36	22.40	22.45	22.51
1962	22.64	22.71	22.77	22.84
1963	22.93	22.95	22.98	23.12
1964	23.20	23.27	23.39	23.49
1965	23.60	23.71	23.81	23.97
1966	24.11	24.33	24.57	24.79
1967	24.90	25.06	25.29	25.57
1968	25.86	26.15	26.39	26.76
1969	27.02	27.39	27.79	28.15
1970	28.54	28.94	29.17	29.55
1971	30.00	30.40	30.71	30.96
1972	31.42	31.61	31.92	32.30
1973	32.73	33.27	33.90	34.48
1974	35.18	35.97	37.07	38.20
1975	39.08	39.63	40.35	41.05
1976	41.49	41.93	42.51	43.25
1977	43.97	44.69	45.32	46.08
1978	46.86	47.79	48.64	49.62
1979	50.58	51.73	52.79	53.86
1980	55.08	56.35	57.62	59.16
1981	60.67	61.75	62.95	64.10
1982	65.00	65.84	66.75	67.44
1983	67.98	68.59	69.17	69.75
1984	70.59	71.18	71.74	72.24
1985	73.01	73.49	73.88	74.40
1986	74.69	75.04	75.51	76.05
1987	76.73	77.27	77.83	78.46
1988	78.99	79.79	80.73	81.36
1989	82.20	83.02	83.62	84.24
1990	85.19	86.17	87.00	87.76
1991	88.78	89.41	89.99	90.47
1992	91.16	91.68	91.98	92.56
1993	93.33	93.83	94.26	94.79
1994	95.28	95.72	96.29	96.74
1995	97.45	97.86	98.31	98.79
1996	99.40	99.74	100.23	100.63
1997	101.36	101.82	102.12	102.49
1998	102.76	103.02	103.38	103.66
1999	104.10	104.45	104.81	105.28
2000	106.25	106.81	107.31	107.78
2001	108.65	109.22	109.83	-

Source: U.S. Department of Commerce, Bureau of Economic Analysis, National Income and Wealth Division. A dash (-) indicates that data are not available or zero.

Price Indexes for GDP
Business Sector
Based on chained 1996 $

Year	1st Quarter	2nd Quarter	3rd Quarter	4th Quarter
1959	24.33	24.37	24.43	24.53
1960	24.56	24.66	24.72	24.82
1961	24.84	24.86	24.91	24.95
1962	25.06	25.13	25.18	25.21
1963	25.27	25.27	25.30	25.41
1964	25.46	25.53	25.62	25.73
1965	25.85	25.95	26.02	26.14
1966	26.27	26.51	26.74	26.97
1967	27.07	27.20	27.44	27.66
1968	27.95	28.26	28.45	28.83
1969	29.11	29.49	29.82	30.18
1970	30.46	30.85	31.03	31.44
1971	31.78	32.17	32.49	32.70
1972	33.03	33.20	33.48	33.79
1973	34.19	34.75	35.43	36.02
1974	36.79	37.63	38.85	40.04
1975	41.00	41.52	42.28	42.94
1976	43.34	43.75	44.37	45.10
1977	45.85	46.60	47.24	47.94
1978	48.76	49.79	50.70	51.73
1979	52.73	53.99	55.06	56.12
1980	57.43	58.74	60.07	61.54
1981	63.13	64.26	65.60	66.68
1982	67.54	68.37	69.28	69.87
1983	70.38	70.94	71.47	72.03
1984	72.57	73.10	73.62	74.09
1985	74.78	75.28	75.66	76.12
1986	76.36	76.64	77.00	77.63
1987	78.08	78.69	79.28	79.76
1988	80.26	81.06	82.06	82.72
1989	83.49	84.35	84.92	85.53
1990	86.37	87.32	88.14	88.89
1991	89.83	90.40	90.93	91.34
1992	91.92	92.27	92.55	93.15
1993	93.83	94.33	94.70	95.22
1994	95.61	95.99	96.62	97.04
1995	97.72	98.13	98.55	98.89
1996	99.34	99.80	100.24	100.62
1997	101.28	101.77	102.06	102.38
1998	102.57	102.75	103.05	103.24
1999	103.56	103.83	104.10	104.50
2000	105.33	105.86	106.31	106.77
2001	107.56	108.06	108.62	-

Source: U.S. Department of Commerce, Bureau of Economic Analysis, National Income and Wealth Division. A dash (-) indicates that data are not available or zero.

Price Indexes for GDP

Business Sector - Nonfarm
Based on chained 1996 $

Year	1st Quarter	2nd Quarter	3rd Quarter	4th Quarter
1959	23.95	23.98	24.02	24.14
1960	24.19	24.26	24.34	24.43
1961	24.46	24.51	24.53	24.53
1962	24.65	24.74	24.79	24.80
1963	24.88	24.90	24.90	25.05
1964	25.09	25.18	25.28	25.38
1965	25.49	25.51	25.61	25.70
1966	25.77	26.04	26.25	26.54
1967	26.68	26.83	27.06	27.29
1968	27.57	27.86	28.04	28.41
1969	28.72	29.05	29.36	29.67
1970	29.99	30.42	30.58	31.03
1971	31.36	31.74	32.06	32.21
1972	32.53	32.67	32.89	33.10
1973	33.32	33.69	34.10	34.86
1974	35.56	36.79	37.87	38.98
1975	40.24	40.84	41.49	42.10
1976	42.55	43.01	43.65	44.46
1977	45.16	45.93	46.59	47.41
1978	48.01	48.91	49.86	50.83
1979	51.71	53.03	54.17	55.30
1980	56.75	58.35	59.32	60.55
1981	62.35	63.63	65.07	66.35
1982	67.21	68.04	68.93	69.67
1983	70.02	70.47	70.99	71.53
1984	71.98	72.58	73.19	73.70
1985	74.47	75.11	75.65	76.03
1986	76.37	76.59	76.86	77.45
1987	77.97	78.60	79.22	79.70
1988	80.19	80.97	81.80	82.48
1989	83.24	84.16	84.76	85.34
1990	86.17	87.15	88.01	88.86
1991	89.88	90.41	91.03	91.42
1992	92.00	92.39	92.66	93.28
1993	94.00	94.44	94.80	95.30
1994	95.67	96.14	96.89	97.28
1995	97.95	98.38	98.71	98.96
1996	99.37	99.77	100.16	100.70
1997	101.45	101.99	102.36	102.67
1998	102.89	103.05	103.40	103.59
1999	104.00	104.33	104.62	105.01
2000	105.94	106.41	106.91	107.36
2001	108.11	108.57	109.07	-

Source: U.S. Department of Commerce, Bureau of Economic Analysis, National Income and Wealth Division. A dash (-) indicates that data are not available or zero.

Price Indexes for GDP
Business Sector - Nonfarm Less Housing
Based on chained 1996 $

Year	1st Quarter	2nd Quarter	3rd Quarter	4th Quarter
1959	24.31	24.33	24.37	24.49
1960	24.54	24.61	24.69	24.78
1961	24.81	24.85	24.87	24.87
1962	24.99	25.08	25.12	25.14
1963	25.22	25.23	25.23	25.38
1964	25.43	25.52	25.63	25.73
1965	25.84	25.87	25.97	26.06
1966	26.13	26.41	26.64	26.95
1967	27.10	27.25	27.50	27.75
1968	28.03	28.33	28.52	28.92
1969	29.24	29.58	29.90	30.22
1970	30.54	31.00	31.15	31.61
1971	31.94	32.33	32.65	32.80
1972	33.12	33.26	33.47	33.68
1973	33.88	34.25	34.69	35.49
1974	36.26	37.61	38.78	39.96
1975	41.29	41.90	42.57	43.19
1976	43.63	44.09	44.74	45.56
1977	46.24	47.01	47.67	48.53
1978	49.13	50.09	51.08	52.09
1979	53.00	54.40	55.54	56.66
1980	58.20	59.90	60.84	62.05
1981	63.94	65.23	66.68	67.94
1982	68.77	69.61	70.45	71.15
1983	71.46	71.85	72.36	72.91
1984	73.32	73.86	74.43	74.90
1985	75.65	76.23	76.70	77.00
1986	77.26	77.36	77.58	78.14
1987	78.63	79.22	79.85	80.26
1988	80.68	81.49	82.31	82.97
1989	83.75	84.68	85.25	85.76
1990	86.59	87.55	88.35	89.25
1991	90.34	90.88	91.53	91.86
1992	92.40	92.77	93.03	93.65
1993	94.37	94.79	95.15	95.63
1994	95.96	96.41	97.18	97.53
1995	98.19	98.58	98.86	99.03
1996	99.40	99.78	100.15	100.67
1997	101.43	101.95	102.28	102.54
1998	102.68	102.77	103.06	103.18
1999	103.57	103.87	104.14	104.49
2000	105.40	105.84	106.31	106.71
2001	107.42	107.80	108.22	-

Source: U.S. Department of Commerce, Bureau of Economic Analysis, National Income and Wealth Division. A dash (-) indicates that data are not available or zero.

Price Indexes for GDP
Business Sector - Nonfarm Housing
Based on chained 1996 $

Year	1st Quarter	2nd Quarter	3rd Quarter	4th Quarter
1959	21.09	21.21	21.26	21.38
1960	21.44	21.50	21.60	21.67
1961	21.70	21.81	21.87	21.87
1962	21.99	22.02	22.11	22.13
1963	22.22	22.29	22.31	22.40
1964	22.44	22.48	22.55	22.59
1965	22.65	22.72	22.76	22.83
1966	22.94	23.04	23.07	23.22
1967	23.34	23.41	23.50	23.63
1968	23.80	23.98	24.13	24.32
1969	24.50	24.69	24.95	25.20
1970	25.45	25.72	25.99	26.31
1971	26.65	26.99	27.27	27.46
1972	27.70	27.89	28.14	28.36
1973	28.79	29.09	29.40	29.72
1974	29.89	30.07	30.41	30.93
1975	31.63	32.10	32.58	33.17
1976	33.72	34.17	34.75	35.44
1977	36.28	37.04	37.72	38.31
1978	38.79	39.28	39.81	40.56
1979	41.15	41.83	42.85	44.12
1980	44.86	45.69	46.85	48.29
1981	49.33	50.46	51.81	53.22
1982	54.31	55.10	56.26	57.32
1983	58.02	58.88	59.47	59.96
1984	60.73	61.81	62.76	63.53
1985	64.44	65.59	66.75	67.75
1986	68.76	69.99	70.69	71.50
1987	72.24	73.25	73.79	74.88
1988	75.93	76.52	77.35	78.16
1989	78.87	79.66	80.55	81.67
1990	82.51	83.68	85.04	85.50
1991	85.90	86.30	86.70	87.56
1992	88.51	89.08	89.39	90.07
1993	90.79	91.39	91.75	92.35
1994	93.14	93.80	94.31	95.03
1995	95.89	96.63	97.40	98.31
1996	99.09	99.65	100.30	100.96
1997	101.61	102.32	103.11	103.86
1998	104.80	105.65	106.62	107.52
1999	108.11	108.67	109.23	110.00
2000	111.17	111.87	112.71	113.69
2001	114.83	116.05	117.35	-

Source: U.S. Department of Commerce, Bureau of Economic Analysis, National Income and Wealth Division. A dash (-) indicates that data are not available or zero.

Price Indexes for GDP

Business Sector - Farms
Based on chained 1996 $

Year	1st Quarter	2nd Quarter	3rd Quarter	4th Quarter
1959	46.15	47.03	47.89	46.91
1960	45.91	47.63	46.63	47.53
1961	47.24	45.92	46.92	48.70
1962	48.69	47.63	48.20	49.05
1963	47.74	47.21	48.41	46.72
1964	46.80	46.25	45.94	46.86
1965	47.23	51.16	49.92	51.76
1966	55.28	53.68	55.27	51.57
1967	49.52	48.67	49.43	49.23
1968	50.14	51.54	52.83	53.25
1969	51.59	55.70	57.05	59.74
1970	57.82	55.82	57.42	55.09
1971	56.63	57.44	57.16	60.95
1972	62.74	63.91	68.46	74.84
1973	86.74	100.41	119.07	107.69
1974	113.16	87.20	97.67	104.83
1975	85.81	82.76	89.94	93.23
1976	90.16	87.91	87.46	83.12
1977	87.38	86.09	85.74	78.23
1978	94.15	103.36	101.19	105.81
1979	115.76	112.35	108.83	104.97
1980	96.25	77.29	103.67	120.29
1981	107.10	98.87	93.93	85.26
1982	86.28	86.85	89.21	81.67
1983	90.60	98.44	99.92	100.67
1984	108.21	103.76	98.31	96.31
1985	92.39	84.24	75.40	80.66
1986	74.86	78.22	84.15	87.79
1987	83.96	83.41	81.07	81.97
1988	83.06	84.76	98.57	96.90
1989	98.38	94.97	93.91	96.44
1990	97.56	96.91	94.62	89.14
1991	85.43	88.65	83.11	84.84
1992	85.34	83.75	84.19	83.22
1993	81.58	85.92	86.93	88.62
1994	89.93	84.97	78.26	80.27
1995	80.82	80.18	87.16	94.42
1996	97.05	102.23	105.44	95.28
1997	89.55	86.53	81.93	82.80
1998	81.30	82.35	78.67	79.09
1999	73.21	69.49	68.22	69.36
2000	63.28	67.91	64.80	66.21
2001	69.60	73.02	77.36	-

Source: U.S. Department of Commerce, Bureau of Economic Analysis, National Income and Wealth Division. A dash (-) indicates that data are not available or zero.

Price Indexes for GDP
Households and Institutions
Based on chained 1996 $

Year	1st Quarter	2nd Quarter	3rd Quarter	4th Quarter
1959	10.51	10.56	10.78	11.06
1960	11.01	11.18	11.37	11.45
1961	11.49	11.58	11.65	11.77
1962	11.97	12.08	12.13	12.29
1963	12.48	12.60	12.63	12.72
1964	12.98	13.02	13.26	13.35
1965	13.24	13.58	13.84	14.20
1966	14.09	14.42	14.74	15.00
1967	15.19	15.39	15.58	15.87
1968	16.47	16.60	16.83	17.28
1969	17.68	18.08	18.54	19.26
1970	19.62	20.16	20.80	21.04
1971	21.46	21.81	21.99	22.46
1972	22.89	23.21	23.30	23.92
1973	24.48	24.90	25.34	25.97
1974	26.43	27.12	27.62	28.35
1975	28.68	28.89	29.29	30.09
1976	30.94	31.54	31.86	32.56
1977	32.58	33.27	34.04	34.93
1978	35.87	36.47	37.54	38.11
1979	38.93	39.60	40.56	41.51
1980	42.41	43.55	44.40	45.50
1981	46.58	47.72	48.79	49.64
1982	50.55	51.29	52.43	53.48
1983	54.35	55.25	56.51	57.70
1984	58.63	59.77	60.80	61.27
1985	61.81	62.27	63.06	63.53
1986	63.73	65.00	67.21	64.59
1987	69.46	68.40	68.77	73.18
1988	72.64	73.18	73.77	74.40
1989	75.35	76.11	77.13	78.25
1990	79.82	81.30	82.72	82.67
1991	83.73	85.35	86.07	87.24
1992	88.24	90.79	91.33	92.00
1993	92.38	92.76	93.08	93.40
1994	94.08	94.35	94.82	95.47
1995	95.83	96.38	96.91	97.80
1996	99.08	99.68	100.25	100.99
1997	100.74	100.56	100.64	101.05
1998	101.72	102.85	103.73	104.47
1999	105.12	105.87	106.83	107.79
2000	109.29	110.55	111.83	112.90
2001	114.50	115.80	117.21	-

Source: U.S. Department of Commerce, Bureau of Economic Analysis, National Income and Wealth Division. A dash (-) indicates that data are not available or zero.

Price Indexes for GDP
Private Households
Based on chained 1996 $

Year	1st Quarter	2nd Quarter	3rd Quarter	4th Quarter
1959	15.25	15.27	16.01	16.37
1960	16.49	16.71	16.75	16.79
1961	16.84	16.88	16.88	17.00
1962	17.17	17.26	17.43	17.58
1963	17.64	17.71	17.70	17.75
1964	17.94	18.24	18.41	18.55
1965	18.72	19.00	19.32	19.58
1966	19.82	20.00	20.31	20.73
1967	20.67	20.75	20.87	21.36
1968	22.32	22.94	23.13	23.69
1969	24.15	24.41	24.71	25.36
1970	25.94	26.45	26.91	27.51
1971	27.84	28.11	28.46	28.70
1972	29.24	29.58	29.77	30.16
1973	31.03	31.69	31.90	32.48
1974	32.56	34.33	36.76	37.01
1975	37.14	37.00	37.60	38.89
1976	41.00	42.39	43.04	44.41
1977	45.60	45.96	46.26	46.31
1978	47.20	48.59	50.14	51.34
1979	52.61	53.69	54.77	55.78
1980	56.90	58.15	59.15	60.13
1981	61.40	63.26	64.39	65.81
1982	66.64	67.22	67.56	67.77
1983	68.06	68.48	68.81	69.29
1984	69.97	70.19	70.59	70.97
1985	71.70	72.42	72.90	73.33
1986	73.70	73.93	74.32	74.67
1987	75.07	75.56	75.85	76.08
1988	76.31	78.30	78.73	79.10
1989	79.88	80.14	80.38	80.67
1990	81.21	81.74	82.62	83.67
1991	85.63	86.87	87.33	88.03
1992	88.42	89.26	90.36	91.03
1993	91.16	91.75	92.45	93.02
1994	93.24	93.58	94.12	94.40
1995	96.48	96.80	97.34	98.06
1996	98.67	99.46	100.58	101.36
1997	101.29	102.19	103.01	103.72
1998	104.14	104.97	105.95	106.68
1999	107.28	108.19	108.77	109.85
2000	111.30	112.96	114.07	114.94
2001	116.95	116.84	117.83	-

Source: U.S. Department of Commerce, Bureau of Economic Analysis, National Income and Wealth Division. A dash (-) indicates that data are not available or zero.

Price Indexes for GDP
Nonprofit Institutions
Based on chained 1996 $

Year	1st Quarter	2nd Quarter	3rd Quarter	4th Quarter
1959	10.11	10.17	10.27	10.56
1960	10.46	10.63	10.87	10.96
1961	11.01	11.12	11.21	11.32
1962	11.55	11.67	11.70	11.87
1963	12.10	12.24	12.28	12.38
1964	12.67	12.65	12.92	13.01
1965	12.84	13.20	13.47	13.86
1966	13.69	14.05	14.39	14.63
1967	14.86	15.09	15.30	15.58
1968	16.14	16.19	16.45	16.89
1969	17.30	17.72	18.22	18.96
1970	19.31	19.86	20.54	20.74
1971	21.18	21.55	21.71	22.22
1972	22.65	22.97	23.05	23.70
1973	24.24	24.64	25.11	25.76
1974	26.27	26.87	27.22	27.99
1975	28.34	28.57	28.96	29.73
1976	30.50	31.04	31.34	32.00
1977	31.93	32.65	33.46	34.42
1978	35.39	35.93	36.98	37.50
1979	38.30	38.95	39.90	40.86
1980	41.75	42.89	43.74	44.84
1981	45.92	47.02	48.09	48.92
1982	49.83	50.57	51.75	52.84
1983	53.74	54.66	55.97	57.19
1984	58.12	59.31	60.37	60.86
1985	61.39	61.84	62.64	63.11
1986	63.31	64.62	66.92	64.16
1987	69.23	68.10	68.48	73.06
1988	72.49	72.97	73.57	74.21
1989	75.17	75.94	77.00	78.16
1990	79.77	81.28	82.72	82.64
1991	83.66	85.29	86.02	87.22
1992	88.24	90.84	91.36	92.03
1993	92.43	92.79	93.10	93.42
1994	94.11	94.38	94.84	95.51
1995	95.80	96.37	96.90	97.79
1996	99.10	99.69	100.24	100.98
1997	100.72	100.51	100.55	100.96
1998	101.64	102.77	103.65	104.40
1999	105.05	105.79	106.76	107.71
2000	109.22	110.47	111.75	112.83
2001	114.41	115.76	117.19	-

Source: U.S. Department of Commerce, Bureau of Economic Analysis, National Income and Wealth Division. A dash (-) indicates that data are not available or zero.

Price Indexes for GDP
General Government
Based on chained 1996 $

Year	1st Quarter	2nd Quarter	3rd Quarter	4th Quarter
1959	12.63	12.68	12.72	12.75
1960	12.89	12.92	13.14	13.22
1961	13.27	13.37	13.44	13.53
1962	13.70	13.74	13.81	14.04
1963	14.20	14.27	14.29	14.58
1964	14.73	14.81	14.96	15.04
1965	15.18	15.25	15.44	15.70
1966	15.91	16.07	16.31	16.43
1967	16.59	16.83	17.04	17.48
1968	17.71	17.93	18.36	18.63
1969	18.78	19.03	19.68	19.96
1970	20.77	21.17	21.49	21.79
1971	22.60	23.04	23.36	23.73
1972	24.69	24.99	25.45	26.05
1973	26.57	27.04	27.48	28.01
1974	28.37	28.88	29.55	30.42
1975	31.07	31.79	32.41	33.22
1976	33.75	34.28	34.69	35.43
1977	36.17	36.79	37.29	38.32
1978	38.77	39.27	39.76	40.53
1979	41.33	42.00	43.03	44.13
1980	44.98	46.01	47.05	49.10
1981	50.21	51.01	51.50	53.04
1982	54.17	55.05	55.87	56.99
1983	57.61	58.41	59.00	59.59
1984	62.08	62.79	63.51	64.16
1985	65.44	65.87	66.18	67.05
1986	67.63	68.20	68.85	69.75
1987	70.55	71.15	71.64	72.02
1988	73.01	73.89	74.53	75.01
1989	76.28	76.85	77.47	78.01
1990	79.43	80.44	81.13	82.22
1991	83.72	84.37	85.20	85.92
1992	87.18	88.02	88.39	88.83
1993	90.28	90.87	91.65	92.38
1994	93.44	94.29	94.54	95.14
1995	96.19	96.51	97.11	98.46
1996	99.95	99.33	100.14	100.59
1997	102.19	102.72	103.16	103.87
1998	104.59	105.11	105.77	106.50
1999	107.81	108.66	109.51	110.31
2000	112.21	112.81	113.38	113.71
2001	114.88	115.69	116.37	-

Source: U.S. Department of Commerce, Bureau of Economic Analysis, National Income and Wealth Division. A dash (-) indicates that data are not available or zero.

Price Indexes for GDP

Federal Government
Based on chained 1996 $

Year	1st Quarter	2nd Quarter	3rd Quarter	4th Quarter
1959	12.72	12.76	12.79	12.79
1960	12.85	12.81	13.13	13.20
1961	13.21	13.24	13.24	13.26
1962	13.36	13.37	13.47	13.80
1963	13.95	13.98	13.98	14.38
1964	14.60	14.66	14.84	14.95
1965	15.02	15.09	15.32	15.73
1966	15.82	15.89	16.08	16.05
1967	15.99	16.18	16.31	16.94
1968	17.13	17.29	17.87	18.08
1969	18.11	18.20	19.11	19.27
1970	20.41	20.73	20.98	21.25
1971	22.40	22.91	23.27	23.90
1972	25.40	25.59	26.04	26.91
1973	27.25	27.61	28.11	28.89
1974	29.09	29.48	30.15	31.39
1975	32.12	32.60	33.13	34.31
1976	34.62	35.01	35.42	36.69
1977	37.56	38.04	38.20	39.81
1978	40.03	40.28	40.68	42.03
1979	42.49	43.03	43.56	45.60
1980	46.20	46.95	47.59	51.02
1981	51.70	52.36	52.71	55.35
1982	56.44	57.13	57.52	58.72
1983	58.89	59.55	59.88	60.14
1984	64.76	65.23	65.74	65.98
1985	67.71	67.60	67.18	68.30
1986	68.53	68.91	69.16	69.50
1987	70.49	70.60	70.58	70.70
1988	72.26	73.29	73.77	73.86
1989	75.82	76.08	76.28	75.94
1990	77.31	78.17	78.30	79.73
1991	81.77	82.30	83.20	83.77
1992	85.96	86.90	87.22	86.64
1993	88.80	89.24	90.26	90.83
1994	92.03	93.12	92.57	93.34
1995	94.66	94.76	95.56	98.58
1996	100.29	99.41	99.90	100.40
1997	102.34	102.53	102.50	103.08
1998	103.58	103.92	104.56	105.17
1999	107.13	107.64	108.09	108.32
2000	111.63	111.57	111.78	111.51
2001	113.70	114.22	114.23	-

Source: U.S. Department of Commerce, Bureau of Economic Analysis, National Income and Wealth Division. A dash (-) indicates that data are not available or zero.

Price Indexes for GDP
State and Local Government
Based on chained 1996 $

Year	1st Quarter	2nd Quarter	3rd Quarter	4th Quarter
1959	12.44	12.51	12.56	12.63
1960	12.87	12.98	13.07	13.17
1961	13.26	13.45	13.60	13.77
1962	14.01	14.08	14.11	14.23
1963	14.41	14.50	14.55	14.72
1964	14.81	14.91	15.01	15.08
1965	15.28	15.34	15.49	15.62
1966	15.92	16.18	16.46	16.73
1967	17.13	17.41	17.70	17.95
1968	18.21	18.49	18.77	19.11
1969	19.37	19.76	20.18	20.57
1970	21.09	21.55	21.93	22.26
1971	22.78	23.17	23.47	23.63
1972	24.19	24.57	25.04	25.46
1973	26.09	26.63	27.04	27.40
1974	27.86	28.46	29.12	29.76
1975	30.36	31.22	31.89	32.48
1976	33.14	33.76	34.16	34.58
1977	35.24	35.94	36.64	37.33
1978	37.92	38.56	39.11	39.52
1979	40.52	41.27	42.58	43.14
1980	44.13	45.32	46.58	47.82
1981	49.19	50.06	50.64	51.53
1982	52.67	53.66	54.74	55.81
1983	56.70	57.58	58.33	59.13
1984	60.28	61.15	62.00	62.90
1985	63.89	64.66	65.43	66.14
1986	66.93	67.62	68.51	69.75
1987	70.43	71.33	72.14	72.68
1988	73.31	74.10	74.84	75.55
1989	76.42	77.16	78.04	79.09
1990	80.54	81.63	82.65	83.53
1991	84.72	85.44	86.23	87.04
1992	87.76	88.55	88.95	89.95
1993	91.00	91.68	92.33	93.15
1994	94.12	94.84	95.52	96.03
1995	96.93	97.36	97.86	98.40
1996	99.78	99.29	100.26	100.68
1997	102.13	102.81	103.47	104.24
1998	105.06	105.66	106.32	107.11
1999	108.13	109.12	110.16	111.21
2000	112.49	113.37	114.10	114.69
2001	115.43	116.36	117.32	-

Source: U.S. Department of Commerce, Bureau of Economic Analysis, National Income and Wealth Division. A dash (-) indicates that data are not available or zero.

INDICATORS OF LABOR AND EMPLOYMENT

This section presents 3 indicators of employment and labor:

    Civilian labor force
    Civilian employment
    Civilian labor force participation
      Males, 20 years and over
      Females, 20 years and over
      Both sexes, 16 to 19 years of age

Civilian Labor Force and **Civilian Employment**. The series shows values in thousands. The two series are the source of unemployment data (number and rate) shown in the section on Other Cyclic Indicators. The labor force is defined as individuals working or actively seeking work. Civilian employment is that portion of the labor force which is now employed. The unemployment rate is calculated by the following formula:

(1-(Civilian Employment / Civilian Labor Force)) x 100

For January 1995, the labor force was 132,038,000 and employment was 124,663,000, indicating unemployment of 7,375,000. This number represents 5.6 percent of the labor force.

A certain level of unemployment is a "natural" phenomenon in a healthy economy. Some economists equate 3-4 percent unemployment with "full employment," on the basis that a certain small fraction of the labor force is, of necessity, in transition between jobs. At the peak of the 1961-1969 expansion (12/69), unemployment was at 3.5 percent; at the peak of the 1971-1973 expansion (10/73), unemployment stood at 4.6 percent. By contrast, at the trough of the 1970 recession (12/70), unemployment stood at 6.1 percent; during the 1974-1975 recession, unemployment reached nearly 9 percent (5/75).

Civilian Labor Force Participation. The three tables showing labor force participation extend from 1951 to 2001 and show participation in percent. In January 1991, for instance, 77.9 percent of males 20 years or older participated in the labor force. Base data—the number of people of the gender and age group overall—are derived from the censuses of population and estimates based on them. The participation values are based on estimates of the total labor force.

The values show interesting general patterns. Labor force participation for males has declined gradually from nearly 90 percent in the early 1950s to around 77 percent in recent times. Female labor force participation, however, which was just over 30 percent in the 1950s passed 60 percent in 1996. The participation of young people (16 to 19 years of age) has remained virtually unchanged since the 1950s—although it dipped somewhat in the 1960s.

Underlying the labor participation numbers are complex economic and demographic forces, including efforts to maintain family income levels, the rise in the skill level demanded in the work place, the reduced role of manufacturing and the corresponding rise in the services sectors of the economy, and others.

Civilian Labor Force
(Thousands)

Year	Jan	Feb	Mar	Apr	May	Jun	Jul	Aug	Sep	Oct	Nov	Dec
1951	61,941	61,778	62,526	61,808	62,044	61,615	62,106	61,927	61,780	62,204	62,014	62,457
1952	62,432	62,419	61,721	61,720	62,058	62,103	61,962	61,877	62,457	61,971	62,491	62,621
1953	63,439	63,520	63,657	63,167	62,615	63,063	63,057	62,816	62,727	62,867	62,949	62,795
1954	63,101	63,994	63,793	63,934	63,675	63,343	63,302	63,707	64,209	63,936	63,759	63,312
1955	63,910	63,696	63,882	64,564	64,381	64,482	65,145	65,581	65,628	65,821	66,037	66,445
1956	66,419	66,124	66,175	66,264	66,722	66,702	66,752	66,673	66,714	66,546	66,657	66,700
1957	66,428	66,879	66,913	66,647	66,695	67,052	67,336	66,706	67,064	67,066	67,123	67,398
1958	67,095	67,201	67,223	67,647	67,895	67,674	67,824	68,037	68,002	68,045	67,658	67,740
1959	67,936	67,649	68,068	68,339	68,178	68,278	68,539	68,432	68,545	68,821	68,533	68,994
1960	68,962	68,949	68,399	69,579	69,626	69,934	69,745	69,841	70,151	69,884	70,439	70,395
1961	70,447	70,420	70,703	70,267	70,452	70,878	70,536	70,534	70,217	70,492	70,376	70,077
1962	70,189	70,409	70,414	70,278	70,551	70,514	70,302	70,981	71,153	70,917	70,871	70,854
1963	71,146	71,262	71,423	71,697	71,832	71,626	71,956	71,786	72,131	72,281	72,418	72,188
1964	72,356	72,683	72,713	73,274	73,395	73,032	73,007	73,118	73,290	73,308	73,286	73,465
1965	73,569	73,857	73,949	74,228	74,466	74,412	74,761	74,616	74,502	74,838	74,797	75,093
1966	75,186	74,954	75,075	75,338	75,447	75,647	75,736	76,046	76,056	76,199	76,610	76,641
1967	76,639	76,521	76,328	76,777	76,773	77,270	77,464	77,712	77,812	78,194	78,191	78,491
1968	77,578	78,230	78,256	78,270	78,847	79,120	78,970	78,811	78,858	78,913	79,209	79,463
1969	79,523	80,019	80,079	80,281	80,125	80,696	80,827	81,106	81,290	81,494	81,397	81,624
1970	81,981	82,151	82,498	82,727	82,483	82,484	82,901	82,880	82,954	83,276	83,548	83,670
1971	83,850	83,603	83,575	83,946	84,135	83,706	84,340	84,673	84,731	84,872	85,458	85,625
1972	85,978	86,036	86,611	86,614	86,809	87,006	87,143	87,517	87,392	87,491	87,592	87,943
1973	87,487	88,364	88,846	89,018	88,977	89,548	89,604	89,509	89,838	90,131	90,716	90,890
1974	91,199	91,485	91,453	91,287	91,596	91,868	92,212	92,059	92,488	92,518	92,766	92,780
1975	93,128	92,776	93,165	93,399	93,884	93,575	94,021	94,162	94,202	94,267	94,250	94,409
1976	94,934	94,998	95,215	95,746	95,847	95,885	96,583	96,741	96,553	96,704	97,254	97,348
1977	97,208	97,785	98,115	98,330	98,665	99,093	98,913	99,366	99,453	99,815	100,576	100,491
1978	100,873	100,837	101,092	101,574	101,896	102,371	102,399	102,511	102,795	103,080	103,562	103,809
1979	104,057	104,502	104,589	104,172	104,171	104,638	105,002	105,096	105,530	105,700	105,812	106,258
1980	106,562	106,697	106,442	106,591	106,929	106,780	107,159	107,105	107,098	107,405	107,568	107,352
1981	108,026	108,242	108,553	108,925	109,222	108,396	108,556	108,725	108,294	109,024	109,236	108,912
1982	109,089	109,467	109,567	109,820	110,451	110,081	110,342	110,514	110,721	110,744	111,050	111,083
1983	110,695	110,634	110,587	110,828	110,796	111,879	111,756	112,231	112,298	111,926	112,228	112,327
1984	112,209	112,615	112,713	113,098	113,649	113,817	113,972	113,682	113,857	114,019	114,170	114,581
1985	114,725	114,876	115,328	115,331	115,234	114,965	115,320	115,291	115,905	116,145	116,135	116,354
1986	116,682	116,882	117,220	117,316	117,528	118,084	118,129	118,150	118,395	118,516	118,634	118,611
1987	118,845	119,122	119,270	119,336	120,008	119,644	119,902	120,318	120,011	120,509	120,540	120,729
1988	120,969	121,156	120,913	121,251	121,071	121,473	121,665	122,125	121,960	122,206	122,637	122,622
1989	123,390	123,135	123,227	123,565	123,474	123,995	123,967	124,166	123,944	124,211	124,637	124,497
1990	125,833	125,710	125,801	125,649	125,893	125,573	125,732	125,990	125,892	125,995	126,070	126,142
1991	125,955	126,020	126,238	126,548	126,176	126,331	126,154	126,150	126,650	126,642	126,701	126,664
1992	127,261	127,207	127,604	127,841	128,119	128,459	128,563	128,613	128,501	128,026	128,441	128,554
1993	128,400	128,458	128,598	128,584	129,264	129,411	129,397	129,619	129,268	129,573	129,711	129,941
1994	130,596	130,669	130,400	130,621	130,779	130,561	130,652	131,275	131,421	131,744	131,891	131,951
1995	132,038	132,115	132,108	132,590	131,851	131,949	132,343	132,336	132,611	132,716	132,614	132,511
1996	132,616	132,952	133,180	133,409	133,667	133,697	134,284	134,054	134,515	134,921	135,007	135,113
1997	135,456	135,400	135,891	136,016	136,119	136,211	136,477	136,618	136,675	136,633	136,961	137,155
1998	137,016	137,092	137,240	137,161	137,434	137,453	137,565	137,606	138,249	138,309	138,387	138,624
1999	138,912	138,869	138,679	138,982	139,180	139,358	139,466	139,455	139,600	139,858	140,038	140,213
2000	140,500	140,750	140,718	141,080	140,715	140,837	140,507	140,831	140,752	141,013	141,215	141,544
2001	141,757	141,622	141,869	141,734	141,445	141,468	141,651	141,380	142,068	142,280	142,279	142,314

Civilian Employment
(Thousands)

Year	Jan	Feb	Mar	Apr	May	Jun	Jul	Aug	Sep	Oct	Nov	Dec
1951	59,636	59,661	60,401	59,889	60,188	59,620	60,156	59,994	59,713	60,010	59,836	60,497
1952	60,460	60,462	59,908	59,909	60,195	60,219	59,971	59,790	60,521	60,132	60,748	60,954
1953	61,600	61,884	62,010	61,444	61,019	61,456	61,397	61,151	60,906	60,893	60,738	59,977
1954	60,024	60,663	60,186	60,185	59,908	59,792	59,643	59,853	60,282	60,270	60,357	60,116
1955	60,753	60,727	60,964	61,515	61,634	61,781	62,513	62,797	62,950	62,991	63,257	63,684
1956	63,753	63,518	63,411	63,614	63,861	63,820	63,800	63,972	64,079	63,975	63,796	63,910
1957	63,632	64,257	64,404	64,047	63,985	64,196	64,540	63,959	64,121	64,046	63,669	63,922
1958	63,220	62,898	62,731	62,631	62,874	62,730	62,745	63,012	63,181	63,475	63,470	63,549
1959	63,868	63,684	64,267	64,768	64,699	64,849	65,011	64,844	64,770	64,911	64,530	65,341
1960	65,347	65,620	64,673	65,959	66,057	66,168	65,909	65,895	66,267	65,632	66,109	65,778
1961	65,776	65,588	65,850	65,374	65,449	65,993	65,608	65,852	65,541	65,919	66,081	65,900
1962	66,108	66,538	66,493	66,372	66,688	66,670	66,483	66,968	67,192	67,114	66,847	66,947
1963	67,072	67,024	67,351	67,642	67,615	67,649	67,905	67,908	68,174	68,294	68,267	68,213
1964	68,327	68,751	68,763	69,356	69,631	69,218	69,399	69,463	69,578	69,582	69,735	69,814
1965	69,997	70,127	70,439	70,633	71,034	71,025	71,460	71,362	71,286	71,695	71,724	72,062
1966	72,198	72,134	72,188	72,510	72,497	72,775	72,860	73,146	73,258	73,401	73,840	73,729
1967	73,671	73,606	73,439	73,882	73,844	74,278	74,520	74,767	74,854	75,051	75,125	75,473
1968	74,700	75,229	75,379	75,561	76,107	76,182	76,087	76,043	76,172	76,224	76,494	76,778
1969	76,805	77,327	77,367	77,523	77,412	77,880	77,959	78,250	78,250	78,445	78,541	78,740
1970	78,780	78,698	78,863	78,930	78,564	78,413	78,726	78,624	78,498	78,685	78,650	78,594
1971	78,864	78,700	78,588	78,987	79,139	78,757	79,305	79,539	79,689	79,918	80,297	80,471
1972	80,959	81,108	81,573	81,655	81,887	82,083	82,230	82,578	82,543	82,616	82,990	83,400
1973	83,161	83,912	84,452	84,559	84,648	85,185	85,299	85,204	85,488	85,987	86,320	86,401
1974	86,555	86,754	86,819	86,669	86,891	86,941	87,149	87,037	87,051	86,995	86,626	86,144
1975	85,627	85,256	85,187	85,189	85,451	85,355	85,894	86,234	86,279	86,370	86,456	86,665
1976	87,400	87,672	87,985	88,416	88,794	88,563	89,093	89,223	89,173	89,274	89,634	89,803
1977	89,928	90,342	90,808	91,271	91,754	91,959	92,084	92,441	92,702	93,052	93,761	94,105
1978	94,384	94,519	94,755	95,394	95,769	96,343	96,090	96,431	96,670	97,133	97,485	97,581
1979	97,948	98,329	98,480	98,103	98,331	98,679	99,006	98,776	99,340	99,404	99,574	99,933
1980	99,879	99,995	99,713	99,233	98,945	98,682	98,796	98,824	99,077	99,317	99,545	99,634
1981	99,955	100,191	100,571	101,056	101,048	100,298	100,693	100,689	100,064	100,378	100,207	99,645
1982	99,692	99,762	99,672	99,576	100,116	99,543	99,493	99,633	99,504	99,215	99,112	99,032
1983	99,161	99,089	99,179	99,560	99,642	100,633	101,208	101,608	102,016	102,039	102,729	102,996
1984	103,201	103,824	103,967	104,336	105,193	105,591	105,435	105,163	105,490	105,638	105,972	106,223
1985	106,302	106,555	106,989	106,936	106,932	106,505	106,807	107,095	107,657	107,847	108,007	108,216
1986	108,887	108,480	108,837	108,952	109,089	109,576	109,810	110,015	110,085	110,273	110,475	110,728
1987	110,953	111,257	111,408	111,794	112,434	112,246	112,634	113,057	112,909	113,282	113,505	113,793
1988	114,016	114,227	114,037	114,650	114,292	114,927	115,060	115,282	115,356	115,638	116,100	116,104
1989	116,708	116,776	117,022	117,097	117,099	117,418	117,472	117,655	117,354	117,581	117,912	117,830
1990	119,081	119,059	119,203	118,852	119,151	118,983	118,810	118,802	118,524	118,536	118,306	118,241
1991	117,940	117,755	117,652	118,109	117,440	117,639	117,568	117,484	117,928	117,800	117,770	117,466
1992	117,978	117,753	118,144	118,426	118,375	118,419	118,713	118,826	118,720	118,628	118,876	118,997
1993	119,075	119,275	119,542	119,474	120,115	120,290	120,467	120,856	120,554	120,823	121,169	121,464
1994	121,966	122,086	121,930	122,290	122,864	122,634	122,706	123,342	123,687	124,112	124,516	124,721
1995	124,663	124,928	124,955	124,945	124,421	124,522	124,816	124,852	125,133	125,388	125,188	125,088
1996	125,125	125,639	125,862	125,994	126,244	126,602	126,947	127,172	127,536	127,890	127,771	127,860
1997	128,317	128,298	128,891	129,143	129,464	129,412	129,822	130,010	130,019	130,179	130,653	130,679
1998	130,652	130,804	130,807	131,177	131,405	131,237	131,293	131,421	131,965	132,036	132,293	132,577
1999	132,959	132,845	132,899	132,928	133,371	133,415	133,434	133,616	133,694	134,065	134,299	134,513
2000	134,881	135,049	135,055	135,549	134,954	135,235	134,777	135,016	135,167	135,485	135,573	135,888
2001	135,870	135,734	135,808	135,424	135,235	135,003	135,106	134,408	135,004	134,615	134,253	134,055

Source: The Conference Board. © 2002 The Conference Board. All Rights Reserved. No claim to original U.S. Government works pursuant to U.S. Contract No. 52-SABA-5-00128. Primary source(s): U.S. Department of Labor, Bureau of Labor Statistics, Office of Employment and Unemployment Statistics, Division of Labor Force Statistics, Washington, DC 20212. A dash (-) indicates that data are not available or zero.

Labor Force Participation Rate, Males 20 and Over
(Percent)

Year	Jan	Feb	Mar	Apr	May	Jun	Jul	Aug	Sep	Oct	Nov	Dec
1951	88.0	88.4	88.8	88.3	88.4	88.4	88.2	88.4	88.2	88.6	88.4	88.7
1952	88.8	89.0	88.6	88.5	88.4	88.4	88.3	88.0	88.0	87.6	87.6	88.5
1953	88.3	88.6	88.7	88.2	88.0	88.0	88.1	87.9	87.6	87.6	88.0	87.8
1954	87.8	88.1	87.7	88.2	87.9	87.8	87.7	88.2	88.4	88.0	87.6	87.3
1955	87.4	87.2	87.4	87.5	87.4	87.2	87.6	87.6	87.6	87.6	87.7	87.8
1956	88.1	87.9	87.9	87.8	87.6	87.6	87.5	87.5	87.3	87.2	87.3	87.3
1957	87.0	87.2	87.2	87.1	87.0	87.3	87.1	86.7	86.9	86.6	86.5	86.6
1958	86.4	86.2	86.2	86.6	86.9	86.8	87.0	87.1	87.1	87.0	86.5	86.6
1959	86.2	86.0	86.3	86.4	86.2	86.1	86.6	86.3	86.5	86.4	86.3	86.3
1960	86.2	86.0	85.6	86.1	86.0	85.9	85.9	86.0	86.2	86.1	86.3	86.3
1961	86.1	85.8	85.9	85.8	85.9	85.8	85.6	85.6	85.5	85.5	85.5	85.3
1962	85.1	85.3	85.3	84.7	85.0	84.8	84.4	84.9	84.8	84.6	84.6	84.4
1963	84.3	84.3	84.4	84.4	84.3	84.3	84.5	84.3	84.3	84.2	84.3	84.2
1964	84.2	84.1	84.0	84.5	84.0	84.3	84.1	84.2	84.2	84.0	83.9	83.9
1965	84.1	84.1	84.1	84.1	84.3	83.8	83.9	83.8	83.6	83.6	83.5	83.6
1966	83.6	83.5	83.6	83.7	83.6	83.6	83.4	83.5	83.5	83.4	83.5	83.6
1967	83.7	83.5	83.3	83.5	83.4	83.5	83.5	83.4	83.2	83.4	83.3	83.4
1968	83.1	83.1	83.0	83.1	83.2	83.4	83.3	83.2	83.0	82.9	82.9	83.1
1969	82.9	83.1	83.0	82.8	82.7	82.7	82.7	82.9	82.9	82.8	82.5	82.6
1970	82.8	82.8	82.9	83.0	82.9	82.6	82.6	82.5	82.5	82.4	82.5	82.5
1971	82.3	82.0	81.9	82.2	82.3	82.0	82.1	82.1	82.0	81.7	81.9	81.9
1972	81.6	81.5	81.8	81.7	81.6	81.7	81.7	81.6	81.6	81.4	81.4	81.5
1973	81.2	81.4	81.6	81.4	81.2	81.2	81.3	81.1	81.0	81.1	81.3	81.4
1974	81.8	81.7	81.3	81.0	81.1	80.9	80.7	80.9	80.8	80.8	80.9	80.7
1975	80.6	80.4	80.4	80.5	80.7	80.2	80.4	80.4	80.2	80.0	79.9	79.6
1976	79.7	79.6	79.6	79.9	79.8	79.7	79.9	79.9	79.9	79.8	80.0	79.8
1977	79.6	79.8	79.7	79.6	79.6	79.8	79.6	79.7	79.4	79.8	79.9	80.0
1978	79.9	79.8	79.7	79.8	79.8	79.8	79.7	79.6	79.5	79.6	80.0	80.0
1979	80.1	80.3	79.9	79.8	79.5	79.7	79.8	79.7	79.8	79.6	80.0	80.0
1980	79.7	79.9	79.4	79.5	79.6	79.3	79.4	79.4	79.3	79.2	79.2	79.0
1981	79.1	79.1	79.3	79.3	79.5	78.9	78.9	78.9	78.7	78.7	78.7	78.6
1982	78.6	78.7	78.7	78.8	78.9	78.8	78.8	78.7	78.9	78.8	78.8	78.7
1983	78.2	78.2	78.2	78.3	78.3	78.7	78.7	78.7	78.6	78.4	78.5	78.3
1984	78.3	78.3	78.2	78.3	78.3	78.4	78.4	78.3	78.4	78.3	78.3	78.3
1985	78.1	78.0	78.1	78.2	78.1	78.0	77.9	78.0	78.2	78.3	78.1	78.0
1986	78.3	78.1	78.1	78.0	78.0	78.1	78.1	78.0	78.1	78.0	78.2	78.4
1987	78.2	78.1	78.1	78.0	78.2	78.0	78.0	78.0	77.9	78.0	78.0	77.8
1988	77.9	78.0	77.8	78.1	78.0	77.8	77.9	78.1	77.8	77.9	77.9	77.8
1989	78.1	78.1	78.1	78.2	77.9	78.2	78.1	78.0	77.8	78.0	78.0	78.0
1990	78.6	78.4	78.4	78.1	78.2	78.1	78.1	78.2	78.0	78.0	78.2	78.1
1991	77.9	77.8	78.0	78.1	77.7	77.8	77.7	77.6	77.7	77.4	77.5	77.3
1992	77.5	77.4	77.7	77.8	78.0	78.0	77.9	77.8	77.7	77.4	77.4	77.3
1993	77.3	77.2	77.3	77.2	77.4	77.5	77.5	77.5	77.1	77.2	77.0	76.9
1994	77.0	76.8	76.7	76.6	76.6	76.5	76.6	76.7	76.8	76.9	77.0	77.1
1995	77.1	77.0	77.0	77.0	76.6	76.6	76.5	76.4	76.7	76.5	76.4	76.3
1996	76.4	76.7	76.7	76.7	76.8	76.9	77.0	76.8	76.9	77.0	76.9	76.8
1997	76.9	76.8	77.0	77.0	76.9	77.0	77.0	77.0	76.9	76.9	77.0	76.9
1998	76.8	76.7	76.7	76.9	76.9	76.8	76.9	76.5	76.8	76.8	76.9	76.8
1999	76.9	76.8	76.6	76.6	76.7	76.7	76.7	76.6	76.6	76.6	76.6	76.7
2000	76.8	77.0	76.8	76.6	76.6	76.6	76.4	76.6	76.4	76.5	76.5	76.6
2001	76.6	76.5	76.4	76.6	76.4	76.3	76.3	76.2	76.5	76.5	76.5	76.5

Source: The Conference Board. © 2002 The Conference Board. All Rights Reserved. No claim to original U.S. Government works pursuant to U.S. Contract No. 52-SABA-5-00128. Primary source(s): U.S. Department of Labor, Bureau of Labor Statistics, Office of Employment and Unemployment Statistics, Division of Labor Force Statistics, Washington, DC 20212. A dash (-) indicates that data are not available or zero.

Labor Force Participation Rate, Females 20 and Over

(Percent)

Year	Jan	Feb	Mar	Apr	May	Jun	Jul	Aug	Sep	Oct	Nov	Dec
1951	33.7	33.6	34.3	33.8	34.1	33.6	34.5	33.9	33.8	34.2	34.1	34.5
1952	34.4	34.3	33.5	33.6	34.0	33.8	33.7	33.9	34.9	34.2	34.8	34.2
1953	34.6	34.2	34.5	34.0	33.4	34.1	34.1	33.7	33.7	34.0	33.6	33.2
1954	33.4	34.5	34.5	34.4	34.3	34.1	33.8	33.9	34.5	34.4	34.4	34.0
1955	34.5	34.4	34.3	35.1	34.7	35.0	35.5	36.0	35.9	36.0	36.0	36.4
1956	36.3	36.0	36.0	36.2	36.7	36.4	36.6	36.6	36.8	36.6	36.4	36.4
1957	36.2	36.7	36.5	36.2	36.3	36.4	36.9	36.4	36.5	36.6	36.6	36.9
1958	36.7	36.8	36.8	37.1	37.0	37.0	37.0	37.2	36.8	36.8	36.6	36.7
1959	37.0	36.7	37.0	37.1	37.1	37.2	37.1	36.9	36.9	37.3	37.0	37.2
1960	36.9	36.9	36.3	37.6	37.7	37.9	37.9	37.9	38.1	37.6	38.2	38.2
1961	38.1	38.4	38.5	37.9	38.1	38.4	38.0	37.7	37.5	37.9	37.6	37.5
1962	37.9	38.0	37.7	37.6	37.6	37.5	37.6	38.1	38.3	37.9	37.8	37.8
1963	38.0	38.2	38.2	38.4	38.4	38.2	38.3	38.1	38.4	38.6	38.7	38.5
1964	38.5	38.8	38.8	39.5	39.3	39.0	38.7	38.9	38.6	38.8	38.7	38.9
1965	39.0	39.2	39.2	39.2	39.2	39.7	39.7	39.6	39.3	39.4	39.5	39.6
1966	39.8	39.6	39.6	39.8	40.0	39.9	40.0	40.3	40.6	40.6	40.9	40.8
1967	40.7	40.5	40.4	40.8	40.8	40.9	41.0	41.1	41.4	41.7	41.6	41.8
1968	40.9	41.3	41.4	41.4	42.0	41.9	41.7	41.3	41.6	41.6	41.9	41.9
1969	42.0	42.4	42.4	42.6	42.5	42.8	42.7	42.8	42.8	42.9	42.8	42.9
1970	43.1	43.1	43.4	43.5	43.0	43.2	43.5	43.3	43.0	43.4	43.4	43.4
1971	43.6	43.3	43.2	43.2	43.2	43.0	43.0	43.2	43.4	43.5	43.8	43.8
1972	43.6	43.4	43.7	43.6	43.8	43.6	43.7	43.8	43.7	43.7	43.6	43.7
1973	43.6	44.0	44.1	44.3	44.3	44.5	44.5	44.5	44.6	44.6	44.9	44.8
1974	44.7	45.0	45.1	45.1	45.1	45.3	45.8	45.5	45.5	45.3	45.5	45.6
1975	45.9	45.6	45.9	46.0	46.0	46.0	46.1	46.2	46.1	46.3	46.2	46.3
1976	46.6	46.6	46.7	46.8	46.8	47.0	47.3	47.3	47.1	47.1	47.5	47.6
1977	47.4	47.6	47.9	48.0	48.2	48.1	48.0	48.1	48.5	48.3	48.8	48.7
1978	48.9	48.9	49.1	49.4	49.4	49.6	49.6	49.5	49.9	50.0	50.1	50.2
1979	50.1	50.3	50.5	50.2	50.2	50.3	50.6	50.8	50.8	50.9	51.0	51.2
1980	51.3	51.3	51.2	51.4	51.3	51.2	51.3	51.4	51.2	51.4	51.6	51.4
1981	51.8	51.9	52.1	52.2	52.4	52.2	52.2	52.1	51.7	52.3	52.4	52.2
1982	52.2	52.4	52.5	52.5	52.8	52.9	52.9	52.9	52.9	52.7	52.9	53.1
1983	53.0	53.0	52.9	52.8	52.8	53.1	53.0	53.3	53.5	53.2	53.3	53.3
1984	53.0	53.3	53.4	53.6	54.1	53.8	54.0	53.8	53.6	53.9	53.9	54.1
1985	54.3	54.5	54.8	54.7	54.5	54.5	54.4	54.5	54.8	54.8	54.9	55.1
1986	54.9	55.0	55.1	55.2	55.4	55.7	55.7	55.8	55.8	55.8	55.8	55.6
1987	55.7	55.8	56.0	56.0	56.2	56.2	56.3	56.4	56.3	56.5	56.5	56.6
1988	56.6	56.7	56.7	56.7	56.4	56.5	56.6	56.8	56.8	57.1	57.5	57.4
1989	57.7	57.5	57.5	57.6	57.6	57.5	57.7	57.6	57.7	57.6	58.0	57.8
1990	58.1	58.1	58.0	58.0	58.1	57.9	57.9	58.1	58.1	58.0	57.9	57.9
1991	57.8	57.9	57.8	58.1	58.0	58.0	57.8	57.8	58.0	58.1	58.0	58.0
1992	58.3	58.3	58.4	58.6	58.5	58.6	58.7	58.6	58.5	58.3	58.4	58.5
1993	58.3	58.2	58.2	58.3	58.6	58.7	58.5	58.6	58.5	58.6	58.7	59.0
1994	59.2	59.4	59.2	59.2	59.5	59.2	59.2	59.4	59.6	59.5	59.5	59.2
1995	59.3	59.3	59.2	59.7	59.3	59.1	59.6	59.5	59.5	59.7	59.7	59.4
1996	59.4	59.5	59.6	59.7	59.7	59.7	60.0	59.9	60.0	60.2	60.3	60.4
1997	60.2	60.2	60.4	60.4	60.4	60.5	60.6	60.6	60.7	60.6	60.5	60.8
1998	60.4	60.5	60.5	60.3	60.3	60.3	60.3	60.4	60.5	60.6	60.6	60.7
1999	60.7	60.7	60.6	60.8	60.6	60.9	60.8	60.8	60.7	60.8	60.9	60.8
2000	61.1	61.0	61.1	61.3	61.0	61.0	60.9	60.6	60.7	60.7	60.7	60.9
2001	61.1	61.1	61.2	61.0	60.9	60.7	60.8	60.8	60.8	60.8	60.8	61.0

Source: The Conference Board. © 2002 The Conference Board. All Rights Reserved. No claim to original U.S. Government works pursuant to U.S. Contract No. 52-SABA-5-00128. Primary source(s): U.S. Department of Labor, Bureau of Labor Statistics, Office of Employment and Unemployment Statistics, Division of Labor Force Statistics, Washington, DC 20212. A dash (-) indicates that data are not available or zero.

Labor Force Participation Rate, 16-19 Years of Age
(Percent)

Year	Jan	Feb	Mar	Apr	May	Jun	Jul	Aug	Sep	Oct	Nov	Dec
1951	51.4	51.0	53.3	50.9	52.6	51.3	52.6	53.0	52.7	52.4	51.9	52.9
1952	52.2	51.8	50.9	50.7	52.3	52.8	51.2	50.0	50.5	50.2	51.4	51.1
1953	52.4	54.0	53.1	51.8	49.5	50.9	49.5	49.6	49.1	48.2	48.9	49.2
1954	50.9	51.4	51.7	50.1	48.6	46.3	47.1	48.0	48.5	47.3	46.3	44.6
1955	46.8	45.4	46.3	47.3	47.6	46.7	48.4	49.6	50.5	51.1	52.7	53.4
1956	51.4	50.5	50.0	49.4	52.1	52.5	51.7	50.6	50.3	49.7	50.4	50.3
1957	49.5	49.8	50.6	49.5	49.4	50.2	50.2	48.4	49.3	49.3	49.4	49.3
1958	47.4	48.0	47.5	48.1	48.9	46.5	46.8	47.1	47.9	47.9	49.4	47.1
1959	47.5	46.7	46.7	47.7	46.2	46.0	46.3	46.6	46.9	46.6	46.3	47.4
1960	47.2	47.4	46.7	48.5	48.1	49.7	47.3	46.9	47.4	47.3	47.4	46.5
1961	47.4	46.7	47.6	46.0	45.8	47.8	47.1	48.0	46.4	46.4	47.4	45.6
1962	45.6	45.9	46.8	46.5	47.4	47.8	46.5	46.4	45.8	45.3	44.9	44.8
1963	45.4	45.1	44.8	45.3	46.2	44.6	45.0	44.8	45.7	45.8	44.8	43.9
1964	44.4	45.3	45.0	44.0	44.8	44.4	44.0	44.2	45.5	44.1	44.1	44.3
1965	43.0	43.7	44.1	45.3	45.6	44.0	46.3	45.5	46.5	47.8	47.1	48.1
1966	48.0	46.7	46.9	47.4	46.9	48.5	49.1	49.3	47.5	48.2	49.1	49.3
1967	48.3	48.2	47.5	47.6	47.2	48.8	49.0	49.5	48.3	48.7	48.3	48.3
1968	46.6	48.5	48.2	47.9	48.2	49.3	49.1	49.0	47.9	48.0	47.7	47.8
1969	47.7	47.8	48.3	48.7	47.5	49.6	50.0	50.0	50.5	50.9	50.9	50.4
1970	50.4	50.3	50.4	49.9	49.7	49.0	49.4	49.7	50.4	50.1	50.1	49.8
1971	50.0	49.9	49.3	49.7	49.4	47.5	50.5	50.5	49.3	49.7	50.5	50.6
1972	51.1	51.4	51.9	51.8	51.5	51.9	51.6	52.9	51.6	51.9	52.4	52.8
1973	50.8	52.9	53.5	53.7	53.2	54.5	53.3	53.2	54.3	54.8	55.1	55.1
1974	55.1	55.2	55.0	53.8	54.3	55.3	54.9	53.8	55.7	55.5	55.1	54.4
1975	54.9	54.1	54.1	53.6	54.7	53.8	54.1	53.8	54.1	53.5	53.2	53.8
1976	54.2	54.2	54.4	55.2	55.1	53.8	55.3	55.1	53.9	54.4	54.4	54.1
1977	54.2	55.2	55.5	55.7	55.6	57.0	56.1	57.2	55.9	56.5	57.2	56.3
1978	56.7	56.6	56.5	57.0	57.9	58.5	58.4	59.3	58.1	58.3	58.2	58.2
1979	58.5	58.6	58.4	57.9	57.3	58.0	57.7	56.8	57.8	57.5	57.7	58.3
1980	57.7	57.2	57.2	55.9	57.0	57.0	57.3	55.9	56.3	56.6	56.2	55.9
1981	56.7	56.6	56.4	57.0	56.3	54.0	54.5	55.2	54.8	55.0	55.2	53.8
1982	54.4	54.7	53.8	54.3	55.3	52.5	53.2	54.2	54.0	54.4	54.7	53.9
1983	53.7	52.7	52.5	52.6	52.2	55.2	53.8	55.1	53.8	53.0	53.6	53.8
1984	53.2	53.3	53.3	53.9	53.8	55.2	54.8	53.3	54.4	53.9	53.8	54.5
1985	55.0	54.9	55.3	54.7	55.0	53.0	55.5	53.4	54.1	54.5	54.3	54.1
1986	53.3	54.6	55.1	55.6	55.2	55.4	54.7	54.6	54.8	54.9	54.2	53.4
1987	54.0	54.8	54.4	54.4	55.3	53.7	54.1	56.2	54.3	55.1	54.6	55.4
1988	55.6	55.0	53.8	54.4	54.2	56.4	56.4	56.6	56.1	55.1	54.8	55.1
1989	55.6	54.8	54.5	55.5	55.5	57.0	56.1	57.4	55.6	56.3	56.5	55.8
1990	54.9	54.3	55.0	54.6	54.2	53.5	53.5	53.5	52.6	52.7	52.4	52.6
1991	52.6	52.2	52.5	52.0	51.7	51.4	50.8	50.6	50.8	51.5	51.4	51.2
1992	51.6	51.3	50.5	49.8	50.8	51.6	51.2	52.0	52.1	50.4	51.7	51.9
1993	51.2	51.9	51.7	51.2	52.2	51.0	51.7	51.8	51.3	51.1	51.5	51.1
1994	53.2	52.8	52.4	53.4	52.6	53.0	52.2	53.5	51.5	52.9	52.1	53.2
1995	53.6	53.6	54.0	54.0	53.0	54.1	53.7	54.3	53.4	53.0	52.6	52.8
1996	52.6	52.2	52.0	52.5	52.9	52.0	52.5	51.4	52.5	52.7	52.1	52.1
1997	51.8	52.1	52.1	52.1	52.1	51.2	51.9	51.5	51.1	50.9	52.0	51.3
1998	52.9	52.6	53.1	51.8	52.6	52.9	52.6	53.1	53.8	52.8	52.3	52.6
1999	52.3	52.5	52.1	51.9	52.6	51.0	52.0	51.5	51.7	52.1	51.9	52.0
2000	51.9	52.0	51.8	52.9	52.5	52.4	51.4	53.0	51.9	52.0	52.0	52.2
2001	51.7	50.9	51.1	50.4	49.3	50.2	49.8	47.7	49.7	49.8	49.4	48.2

Source: The Conference Board. © 2002 The Conference Board. All Rights Reserved. No claim to original U.S. Government works pursuant to U.S. Contract No. 52-SABA-5-00128. Primary source(s): U.S. Department of Labor, Bureau of Labor Statistics, Office of Employment and Unemployment Statistics, Division of Labor Force Statistics, Washington, DC 20212. A dash (-) indicates that data are not available or zero.

INDICATORS OF INTERNATIONAL TRANSACTIONS

International trade has been a subject of concern and debate since the mid-1970s, when the U.S. trade balance turned negative and has continued negative since. As a percent of GDP, foreign trade has also grown. And with the rise of new industrial economies on the Asian rim of the Pacific, a world-wide competition for trade has intensified concerns. Negative trade balances have a direct impact on GDP; they are also, indirectly, a measure of U.S. competitiveness in world markets. The three tables included in this section present the basic facts about this phenomenon as seen from the U.S. vantage point. The tables are:

> Merchandise exports, adjusted annual rate, excluding military
> Merchandise imports, adjusted annual rate, excluding military
> Balance on merchandise trade

Merchandise Exports, Excluding Military. Data are in billions of current dollars. Data for each quarter are annualized; the sum of the four quarters, divided by 4, produces the annual value. Data exclude Department of Defense sales contracts (exports) and military grants. Military aid shipments and exports are excluded because, arising from government policy, such shipments would distort the market-based nature of the overall export business.

Merchandise Imports, Excluding Military. Data are also shown in billions of current dollars, annualized. Data exclude Department of Defense purchases (imports).

Balance on Merchandise Trade. Data are in billions of current dollars. The values shown are merchandise exports less merchandise imports from the earlier tables, indicating to what extent the U.S. enjoyed a trade surplus (positive numbers) or a deficit (negative values).

Surplus or deficit in foreign trade has always played an important role in international relations. In pre-modern times, when gold was the standard of exchange, a trade deficit meant that a country lost some of its gold stock to another country; a surplus meant a gain in gold; for this reason, countries tried to maintain surpluses or, failing that, a balance between imports and exports. International trade has become much more complex since, but underlying concepts remain in force. Thus the purchasing power of the dollar has a direct influence on the trade deficit. A strong dollar (meaning a dollar expensive relative to other currencies) acts to diminish exports—because dollar-denominated goods are expensive elsewhere; importers are aided because their goods are relatively cheap in the U.S. market. Conversely, a weak dollar helps exports and impedes imports. The strong and weak dollar have other consequences as well: a strong dollar tends to reduce production but curbs inflation; a weak dollar is associated with high production but also with inflation. Needless to say, the weakening of foreign currencies, e.g., the Korea and Indonesian problems in 1997, also caused the dollar's value to increase.

A strong dollar in the 1985-to-current period was one of the causes of dramatically increasing trade deficits. The value of the dollar, in turn, reflects the strength of an economy relative to other economies and *perceptions* of this strength; perceptions are translated into policy and trading actions by others—which cause the value of the dollar to rise or fall. Public policy can influence—but cannot set—the value of the dollar.

The trade deficit has a negative impact on GDP growth because trade balance is part of GDP. The change from period to period is more important, in this context, than the absolute magnitude of the trade balance or its arithmetic sign. A shrinking deficit or a growing surplus will both translate into a positive signal for GDP.

Exports, imports, and the trade balance are subject to trade policies followed in the U.S. and in foreign countries. Therefore, ultimately, foreign trade data reflect pure market forces only indirectly.

Merchandise Exports
Adjusted Annual Rate, excluding military
(Billions of $)

Year	1st Quarter	2nd Quarter	3rd Quarter	4th Quarter
1960	18.7	19.7	20.1	20.1
1961	20.4	19.2	20.2	20.7
1962	20.3	21.3	21.3	20.1
1963	20.3	22.4	22.7	23.8
1964	25.0	24.8	25.7	26.5
1965	23.1	27.5	26.6	28.7
1966	29.0	28.7	29.2	30.4
1967	31.0	30.8	30.1	30.8
1968	32.0	33.3	35.0	34.2
1969	29.9	38.1	37.6	40.0
1970	41.0	43.0	42.7	43.2
1971	43.7	43.5	46.2	39.9
1972	47.3	46.5	49.4	54.3
1973	61.9	68.4	73.1	82.2
1974	90.5	98.0	98.5	106.3
1975	109.9	103.5	104.4	110.5
1976	110.3	113.0	116.2	119.4
1977	118.7	123.4	123.0	118.2
1978	121.9	142.7	146.1	157.6
1979	165.9	175.5	188.4	207.9
1980	216.9	223.9	223.3	232.9
1981	241.3	240.6	232.1	234.2
1982	220.7	221.4	208.4	194.2
1983	196.8	197.4	201.3	211.7
1984	212.0	218.5	223.6	225.7
1985	219.5	216.6	211.3	216.2
1986	214.1	227.3	222.6	229.3
1987	226.8	240.8	256.9	276.4
1988	302.6	318.2	323.8	336.4
1989	349.7	368.8	360.7	369.3
1990	381.2	390.3	385.4	400.4
1991	405.4	418.1	414.9	429.2
1992	433.4	436.1	438.4	453.6
1993	447.4	456.7	445.7	477.4
1994	473.5	492.1	510.5	533.4
1995	556.1	568.4	583.6	595.3
1996	601.8	610.4	608.0	628.1
1997	650.7	682.5	695.8	689.8
1998	682.4	664.2	657.5	677.1
1999	655.8	665.8	695.5	720.3
2000	740.6	766.2	797.1	784.9
2001	779.8	743.4	-	-

Merchandise Imports
Adjusted Annual Rate, excluding military
(Billions of $)

Year	1st Quarter	2nd Quarter	3rd Quarter	4th Quarter
1960	15.2	15.4	14.6	13.8
1961	13.6	13.8	15.2	15.6
1962	15.9	16.3	16.5	16.4
1963	16.3	16.9	17.5	17.5
1964	17.7	18.4	19.0	19.7
1965	18.8	21.7	22.1	23.4
1966	24.0	24.8	26.3	26.8
1967	26.8	25.9	26.1	28.6
1968	31.2	32.2	34.4	34.1
1969	29.8	38.1	37.5	37.8
1970	38.3	39.1	40.2	41.9
1971	42.4	46.5	48.7	44.8
1972	54.0	53.0	56.1	60.1
1973	65.1	68.7	70.7	77.5
1974	87.8	105.4	109.5	112.6
1975	99.9	91.3	97.9	103.5
1976	112.7	120.7	128.9	134.6
1977	146.3	152.3	152.0	157.0
1978	169.9	173.7	177.7	182.7
1979	190.3	203.1	216.0	238.6
1980	263.3	249.1	236.0	250.6
1981	268.0	268.7	257.6	265.9
1982	254.0	242.3	254.8	239.5
1983	239.0	259.1	281.5	296.0
1984	319.0	335.2	335.7	339.8
1985	321.3	338.3	335.6	357.2
1986	356.9	367.0	371.2	378.6
1987	384.1	402.6	417.6	434.7
1988	439.9	443.3	443.6	462.0
1989	465.9	483.6	475.5	484.4
1990	489.8	488.7	501.6	513.3
1991	480.6	482.8	493.9	506.6
1992	505.1	533.1	547.5	560.0
1993	564.3	590.3	591.7	611.5
1994	620.0	655.4	687.9	711.0
1995	732.4	762.2	752.3	751.5
1996	772.2	803.1	812.8	825.3
1997	848.6	871.5	888.5	896.9
1998	901.0	914.7	915.8	937.2
1999	947.9	1,001.7	1,064.8	1,105.3
2000	1,170.2	1,212.9	1,255.5	1,259.0
2001	1,229.8	1,174.6	-	-

Balance on Merchandise Trade
Adjusted Annual Rate
(Billions of $)

Year	1st Quarter	2nd Quarter	3rd Quarter	4th Quarter
1960	3.5	4.2	5.5	6.3
1961	6.8	5.5	4.9	5.1
1962	4.4	5.0	4.9	3.8
1963	4.0	5.5	5.2	6.2
1964	7.3	6.4	6.7	6.8
1965	4.2	5.8	4.5	5.3
1966	4.9	3.9	2.9	3.6
1967	4.2	4.9	4.0	2.1
1968	0.8	1.1	0.5	0.1
1969	0.1	-	0.1	2.2
1970	2.7	3.9	2.5	1.4
1971	1.3	-2.9	-2.5	-4.9
1972	-6.7	-6.5	-6.7	-5.8
1973	-3.2	-0.2	2.4	4.8
1974	2.6	-7.4	-11.0	-6.3
1975	10.0	12.1	6.5	7.0
1976	-2.4	-7.7	-12.6	-15.2
1977	-27.7	-28.8	-29.0	-38.8
1978	-48.1	-31.0	-31.6	-25.1
1979	-24.4	-27.6	-27.6	-30.7
1980	-46.3	-25.2	-12.7	-17.7
1981	-26.7	-28.2	-25.5	-31.7
1982	-33.4	-20.9	-46.4	-45.2
1983	-42.2	-61.8	-80.2	-84.2
1984	-107.0	-116.7	-112.1	-114.2
1985	-101.8	-121.6	-124.3	-140.9
1986	-142.7	-139.7	-148.6	-149.3
1987	-157.3	-161.8	-160.8	-158.4
1988	-137.2	-125.2	-119.8	-125.6
1989	-116.2	-114.8	-114.8	-115.1
1990	-108.6	-98.4	-116.2	-113.0
1991	-75.2	-64.7	-79.0	-77.4
1992	-71.8	-97.0	-109.2	-106.5
1993	-116.8	-133.5	-146.0	-134.1
1994	-146.5	-163.3	-177.4	-177.6
1995	-176.3	-193.7	-168.7	-156.2
1996	-170.4	-192.6	-204.8	-197.3
1997	-197.9	-189.1	-192.6	-207.0
1998	-218.6	-250.5	-258.3	-260.1
1999	-292.1	-335.9	-369.3	-384.9
2000	-429.6	-446.7	-458.4	-474.1
2001	-450.1	-431.2	-	-

CHAPTER 6

CONSUMER PRICE INDEX

CONSUMER PRICE INDEX

The Consumer Price Index (CPI) is the primary system for measuring price change in the United States in a consistent manner. The CPI, therefore, is the chief measure of inflation and the source of data for converting "current dollar" measurements and estimates into "constant" or "real dollar" values used in National Income and Product Accounts and in cyclic indicators of the economy. It is produced by the U.S. Department of Labor, Bureau of Labor Statistics (BLS), Division of Consumer Prices and Price Indexes.

General Concept

The CPI is based on obtaining the price of an *identical* "basket" of goods at two different points in time and measuring the difference. By way of illustration, consider the following simple case:

A basket of goods is purchased in January 1995 containing a loaf of bread, a quart of milk, a pound of potatoes, a package of bacon, five pounds of flour and of sugar. The price is noted. It is $35.00.

A year later, exactly the same items are purchased. This time the price is $42.00.

In this situation, inflation has been $7.00. Only the price has changed. It has increased by 20%.

Rather than dealing with actual dollar figures, we can express these relationships as an index. If 1995 is chosen as the base year and set to a value of 100, the 1996 value would be 120—showing a 20% inflation rate.

The system works in the same way if prices decrease. Assume that in 1997 the same basket of goods cost $28.00. This price is 20% lower than the price in the base year. The new 1997 index, therefore, would be 80. The change between 1996 and 1997 would be a 33.3% decrease:

$$((80 / 120) - 1) \times 100 = -33.3$$

These concepts underlie the CPI. The index measures the price of a "fixed market basket of goods and services" at monthly intervals. This is a hypothetical basket because it includes not only items one ordinarily buys in a store but also the costs of fuel, housing, transportation, and other services. A base period is selected; currently (in 2000) it is the average of 1982-1984 for most items. The price index is shown with reference to the base period, which is defined as 100.

Implementation of the Concept

In order to implement this concept in a useful manner, it is necessary, first, to determine the make-up of the "fixed market basket": what proportion of a family's budget is devoted to food, clothing, housing, etc. Since consumption patterns differ somewhat from region to region, it is also necessary to know how the market basket's contents change from place to place; fuel costs, typically, will be a lesser proportion of budgets in mild climates, for instance. BLS conducts surveys at regular intervals in selected urban areas to answer these questions. Consumer surveys are then used to change how the index is constructed and what weight or importance to give to each major component in the basket. From the beginning of the CPI, surveys of spending patterns have been followed by comprehensive revisions of the index.

The modern index, specifically the index resulting from the 1998 revisions of the CPI, is built by pricing goods and services in 186 item strata in 87 geographical areas. Sampling areas are selected using population census data to arrive at a representative sampling.

Raw data collected from sampling units are processed into geographical indexes and into a U.S. City average. Major components (food, apparel, housing, etc.) are combined by applying appropriate weights to produce a final consumer price index.

History and Revisions

The CPI was initiated during World War I as a tool for calculating cost-of-living adjustments in wages. The first surveys of consumption patterns were carried out by the Department of Labor from 1917-1919; periodic collection of prices began in 1919 by the Department's Bureau of Labor Statistics. Regular publication began in 1921, with indexes estimated back to 1913. The cycle of surveys and revisions began in 1934-36 (survey) and 1940 (index revision). Thereafter, major changes were introduced as follows:

> 1951 - adjustments to reflect immediate postwar changes
> 1953 - comprehensive postwar revisions, statistical overhaul
> 1964 - new expenditure weights reflecting single persons as well as families
> 1978 - changes in sample, data collection, inclusion of all urban consumers
> 1983 - changes in home ownership cost calculations for all urban consumers
> 1985 - changes in home ownership cost calculations for urban wage earners
> 1987 - improvements of sampling, data collection, processing, and estimation
> 1998 - comprehensive changes in market basket, geography, and methods

The CPI was originally designed to measure the cost of living of urban wage earners and clerical workers (usually called CPI-W). A more encompassing category including all urban families (CPI-U) was introduced in 1978; CPI-U includes, in addition to CPI-W, professional and salaried workers, part-time workers, the self-employed, the unemployed, and retired people.

Sampling, Components, and Methods

Sampling Universe. CPI pricing data are collected in 87 urban areas; 22,500 retail and service establishments are sampled; these include supermarkets, department stores, filling stations, hospitals, and other establishments. Housing costs are collected from 40,000 tenants and on 20,000 owner-occupied housing units.

Product/Service Categories. Items/services to be priced are subdivided into 8 major product groups: food and beverages, fuels and utilities, housing, apparel, transportation, medical care, recreation, education and communication, and other goods and services. Recreation includes the former Entertainment category, with additions. Education and Communication is brand new and is built of elements hitherto in Other Goods and Services. These major groupings are made up of 70 expenditure classes (e.g. furniture and bedding) which, in turn, are divided into 211 item strata (bedroom furniture). Of these 211, 186 strata are actually sampled; 25 are priced by using estimation methods. Item strata, in turn, are divided into several hundred "entry level items," e.g., mattresses and springs. Pricing on approximately 80,000 individual entry level items is conducted for the CPI on a regular basis.

Sampling Frequency. Food, fuel, and selected other items are priced monthly in all of the sample geographies.

Most other goods and services are surveyed monthly in the largest urban areas and bimonthly or semiannually in all the others.

Coverage of Cities. Metro area coverage is reduced from 27 to 26 cities/metro areas. Buffalo, NY was dropped and Tampa, FL was added. Washington and Baltimore, heretofore reported separately, are reported as a single metro area after the 1998 changes.

Basing Years. BLS provides data calculated with a base of 1982-1984—in which the 1982-1984 averages represent 100. A rebasing of the CPI was announced by the BLS in December 1996 for the 1998 revisions. The new base was to have been 1993-1995 = 100. BLS later decided to retain the 1982-1984 basing scheme. Application of the new scheme was rejected because it made historical values for the CPI less accurate. Values in early years become substantially smaller, and rounding produces a less accurate index.

For two Major Groups, Recreation and Education and Communication, new series were created with a base of December 1997 = 100. This is required because the new categories cannot be restated retrospectively. In the tables in this book, these items are footnoted, where appropriate, to indicate the new base.

((Current Index / Previous Index) - 1) x 100.

This formula can be used to calculate, for example, how the cost of living has changed between January 1990 and January 1991 without reference to the base year of the series. The U.S. average data for base 1982-1984 were as follows:

    January 1990 - 127.4
    January 1991 - 134.6

By applying the formula to these values, we get a percent change of 5.7.

The data for the same series but with a 1967 base are:

    January 1990 - 381.5
    January 1991 - 403.1

These values *also* produce a 5.7% change.

The meaning of the change for a person with a fixed income of $40,000 a year would be that his or her income in 1991 was 5.7% less than in 1990 due to inflation. The purchasing power of the income would be $47,150 in 1991.

Uses of the CPI

The CPI is the most widely used measure of inflation; consequently, it plays a role in economic measurement and in the setting of monetary and fiscal policy and is used widely as an indicator in all manner of institutions, public and private, for a range of activities, including wage settlements.

The CPI is used as a deflator of other economic series. Throughout *Economic Indicators Handbook*, references are made to current dollar and constant dollar presentations of data; the latter are also referred to as "real" dollars, meaning that inflation has been removed by use of a deflator. In the example above, the person with a fixed income of $50,000 had an income in 1991 of $50,000 in *current* dollars but only an income of $47,150 in *constant* or "real" dollars (in this case 1990 dollars).

The CPI is used for income adjustments. Around 4 million union workers are covered by contracts tied to CPI. The income of more than 80 million other people is affected by changes in CPI, including 44 million Social Security recipients, 5 million military and federal retirees and survivors, and about 27 million people receiving food stamps. Federal income tax indexing uses the CPI. There are also many uses of the CPI by the private sector.

Presentation and Limitations of Data

In the following tables, data are presented as follows:

U.S. City Average Data. These data are the overall CPI, calculated for all cities. *EIH* presents the following subsets of the data:

    Annual Averages for all items and 8 subcategories
      For all urban consumers
      For urban wage earners and clerical workers

    U.S. City Average for all items, monthly
      All urban consumers
      Urban wage earners and clerical workers

    U.S. City Average for each of 8 subcategories of expenditure
      Monthly for all urban consumers
      Monthly for urban wage earners and clerical workers

Index values are shown from 1913 to 1999 as available. Percent change from one period to the next is precalculated and shown. In tables of annual averages, the comparison is between two rows in the same column; in monthly tables, the comparison is between two columns of the same row.

Limitations of the U.S. City Average Data. The CPI measures cost changes in urban areas and should not be applied to situations in other contexts. The index is based on a sample of consumer purchases rather than all consumer purchases; hence sampling errors are inherent in the series. The CPI cannot be used for demographic subgroups of the population, such as the elderly.

City/Urban Area Data. Following the U.S. City Average tables, data are presented for 26 cities/urban areas. The cities are ordered alphabetically. For each city, the following tables are presented:

    Annual averages for all items and 8 subcategories
      For all urban consumers
      For urban wage earners and clerical workers

All items, monthly
    All urban consumers
    Urban wage earners and clerical workers

Eight tables of subcategories
    Monthly for all urban consumers
    Monthly for urban wage earners and clerical workers

Years and months of coverage for cities varies. For some, categories data are available back to 1913. In other cases, data start at a later date and are shown for the months in which data were collected. The tables, in fact, show how the frequency and timing of collections have changed over time.

Limitations of City/Urban Area Data. Is it more expensive to live in New York than in Los Angeles? *The CPI cannot be used to answer this question.* Cost of living comparisons *between* cities are not a legitimate use of the index. The CPI, in other words, cannot be used to determine "relative" cost of living. The index measures only changes in the cost of living *in* one urban area. The CPI is suitable for determining whether or not prices are rising faster in one city than in another; they do not measure absolute price levels between cities.

Bibliography

1. U.S. Department of Labor, Bureau of Labor Statistics. *BLS Handbook of Methods*, Bulletin 2285, 1987. Washington, DC.

2. U.S. Department of Labor, Bureau of Labor Statistics, *Monthly Labor Review*, December 1996. Washington, DC.

3. U.S. Department of Labor, Bureau of Labor Statistics, at web site http://www.bls.gov.

U.S. CITY AVERAGE
Consumer Price Index - All Urban Consumers
Base 1982-1984 = 100
Annual Averages

For 1913-2001. Columns headed % show percentile change in the index from the previous period for which an index is available.

Year	All Items		Food & Beverage		Housing		Apparel		Trans-portation		Medical Care		Recrea-tion*		Education & Communic.*		Other Goods & Services	
	Index	%	Index	%	Index	%	Index	%	Index	%	Index	%	Index	%	Index	%	Index	%
1913	9.9	-	-	-	-	-	14.9	-	-		-		-		-		-	
1914	10.0	1.0	-	-	-	-	15.0	0.7	-		-		-		-		-	
1915	10.1	1.0	-	-	-	-	15.3	2.0	-		-		-		-		-	
1916	10.9	7.9	-	-	-	-	16.8	9.8	-		-		-		-		-	
1917	12.8	17.4	-	-	-	-	20.2	20.2	-		-		-		-		-	
1918	15.1	18.0	-	-	-	-	27.3	35.1	-		-		-		-		-	
1919	17.3	14.6	-	-	-	-	36.2	32.6	-		-		-		-		-	
1920	20.0	15.6	-	-	-	-	43.1	19.1	-		-		-		-		-	
1921	17.9	-10.5	-	-	-	-	33.2	-23.0	-		-		-		-		-	
1922	16.8	-6.1	-	-	-	-	27.0	-18.7	-		-		-		-		-	
1923	17.1	1.8	-	-	-	-	27.1	0.4	-		-		-		-		-	
1924	17.1	0.0	-	-	-	-	26.8	-1.1	-		-		-		-		-	
1925	17.5	2.3	-	-	-	-	26.3	-1.9	-		-		-		-		-	
1926	17.7	1.1	-	-	-	-	25.9	-1.5	-		-		-		-		-	
1927	17.4	-1.7	-	-	-	-	25.3	-2.3	-		-		-		-		-	
1928	17.1	-1.7	-	-	-	-	25.0	-1.2	-		-		-		-		-	
1929	17.1	0.0	-	-	-	-	24.7	-1.2	-		-		-		-		-	
1930	16.7	-2.3	-	-	-	-	24.2	-2.0	-		-		-		-		-	
1931	15.2	-9.0	-	-	-	-	22.0	-9.1	-		-		-		-		-	
1932	13.7	-9.9	-	-	-	-	19.5	-11.4	-		-		-		-		-	
1933	13.0	-5.1	-	-	-	-	18.8	-3.6	-		-		-		-		-	
1934	13.4	3.1	-	-	-	-	20.6	9.6	-		-		-		-		-	
1935	13.7	2.2	-	-	-	-	20.8	1.0	14.2	-	10.2	-	-		-		-	
1936	13.9	1.5	-	-	-	-	21.0	1.0	14.3	0.7	10.2	0.0	-		-		-	
1937	14.4	3.6	-	-	-	-	22.0	4.8	14.5	1.4	10.3	1.0	-		-		-	
1938	14.1	-2.1	-	-	-	-	21.9	-0.5	14.6	0.7	10.3	0.0	-		-		-	
1939	13.9	-1.4	-	-	-	-	21.6	-1.4	14.3	-2.1	10.3	0.0	-		-		-	
1940	14.0	0.7	-	-	-	-	21.8	0.9	14.2	-0.7	10.4	1.0	-		-		-	
1941	14.7	5.0	-	-	-	-	22.8	4.6	14.7	3.5	10.4	0.0	-		-		-	
1942	16.3	10.9	-	-	-	-	26.7	17.1	16.0	8.8	10.7	2.9	-		-		-	
1943	17.3	6.1	-	-	-	-	27.8	4.1	15.9	-0.6	11.2	4.7	-		-		-	
1944	17.6	1.7	-	-	-	-	29.8	7.2	15.9	0.0	11.6	3.6	-		-		-	
1945	18.0	2.3	-	-	-	-	31.4	5.4	15.9	0.0	11.9	2.6	-		-		-	
1946	19.5	8.3	-	-	-	-	34.4	9.6	16.7	5.0	12.5	5.0	-		-		-	
1947	22.3	14.4	-	-	-	-	39.9	16.0	18.5	10.8	13.5	8.0	-		-		-	
1948	24.1	8.1	-	-	-	-	42.5	6.5	20.6	11.4	14.4	6.7	-		-		-	
1949	23.8	-1.2	-	-	-	-	40.8	-4.0	22.1	7.3	14.8	2.8	-		-		-	
1950	24.1	1.3	-	-	-	-	40.3	-1.2	22.7	2.7	15.1	2.0	-		-		-	
1951	26.0	7.9	-	-	-	-	43.9	8.9	24.1	6.2	15.9	5.3	-		-		-	
1952	26.5	1.9	-	-	-	-	43.5	-0.9	25.7	6.6	16.7	5.0	-		-		-	
1953	26.7	0.8	-	-	-	-	43.1	-0.9	26.5	3.1	17.3	3.6	-		-		-	
1954	26.9	0.7	-	-	-	-	43.1	0.0	26.1	-1.5	17.8	2.9	-		-		-	
1955	26.8	-0.4	-	-	-	-	42.9	-0.5	25.8	-1.1	18.2	2.2	-		-		-	
1956	27.2	1.5	-	-	-	-	43.7	1.9	26.2	1.6	18.9	3.8	-		-		-	
1957	28.1	3.3	-	-	-	-	44.5	1.8	27.7	5.7	19.7	4.2	-		-		-	

[Continued]

U.S. City Average
Consumer Price Index - All Urban Consumers
Base 1982-1984 = 100
Annual Averages
[Continued]

For 1913-2001. Columns headed % show percentile change in the index from the previous period for which an index is available.

Year	All Items		Food & Beverage		Housing		Apparel		Trans- portation		Medical Care		Recrea- tion*		Education & Communic.*		Other Goods & Services	
	Index	%	Index	%	Index	%	Index	%	Index	%	Index	%	Index	%	Index	%	Index	%
1958	28.9	2.8	-	-	-	-	44.6	0.2	28.6	3.2	20.6	4.6	-	-	-	-	-	-
1959	29.1	0.7	-	-	-	-	45.0	0.9	29.8	4.2	21.5	4.4	-	-	-	-	-	-
1960	29.6	1.7	-	-	-	-	45.7	1.6	29.8	0.0	22.3	3.7	-	-	-	-	-	-
1961	29.9	1.0	-	-	-	-	46.1	0.9	30.1	1.0	22.9	2.7	-	-	-	-	-	-
1962	30.2	1.0	-	-	-	-	46.3	0.4	30.8	2.3	23.5	2.6					-	-
1963	30.6	1.3	-	-	-	-	46.9	1.3	30.9	0.3	24.1	2.6	-	-	-	-	-	-
1964	31.0	1.3	-	-	-	-	47.3	0.9	31.4	1.6	24.6	2.1	-	-	-	-	-	-
1965	31.5	1.6	-	-	-	-	47.8	1.1	31.9	1.6	25.2	2.4	-	-	-	-	-	-
1966	32.4	2.9	-	-	-	-	49.0	2.5	32.3	1.3	26.3	4.4	-	-	-	-	-	-
1967	33.4	3.1	35.0	-	30.8	-	51.0	4.1	33.3	3.1	28.2	7.2	-	-	-	-		
1968	34.8	4.2	36.2	3.4	32.0	3.9	53.7	5.3	34.3	3.0	29.9	6.0	-	-	-	-	35.1	-
1969	36.7	5.5	38.1	5.2	34.0	6.3	56.8	5.8	35.7	4.1	31.9	6.7	-	-	-	-	36.9	5.1
1970	38.8	5.7	40.1	5.2	36.4	7.1	59.2	4.2	37.5	5.0	34.0	6.6	-	-	-	-	38.7	4.9
1971	40.5	4.4	41.4	3.2	38.0	4.4	61.1	3.2	39.5	5.3	36.1	6.2	-	-	-	-	40.9	5.7
1972	41.8	3.2	43.1	4.1	39.4	3.7	62.3	2.0	39.9	1.0	37.3	3.3	-	-	-	-	42.9	4.9
1973	44.4	6.2	48.8	13.2	41.2	4.6	64.6	3.7	41.2	3.3	38.8	4.0	-	-	-	-	44.7	4.2
1974	49.3	11.0	55.5	13.7	45.8	11.2	69.4	7.4	45.8	11.2	42.4	9.3	-	-	-	-	46.4	3.8
1975	53.8	9.1	60.2	8.5	50.7	10.7	72.5	4.5	50.1	9.4	47.5	12.0	-	-	-	-	49.8	7.3
1976	56.9	5.8	62.1	3.2	53.8	6.1	75.2	3.7	55.1	10.0	52.0	9.5	-	-	-	-	53.9	8.2
1977	60.6	6.5	65.8	6.0	57.4	6.7	78.6	4.5	59.0	7.1	57.0	9.6	-	-	-	-	57.0	5.8
1978	65.2	7.6	72.2	9.7	62.4	8.7	81.4	3.6	61.7	4.6	61.8	8.4	-	-	-	-	60.4	6.0
1979	72.6	11.3	79.9	10.7	70.1	12.3	84.9	4.3	70.5	14.3	67.5	9.2	-	-	-	-	64.3	6.5
1980	82.4	13.5	86.7	8.5	81.1	15.7	90.9	7.1	83.1	17.9	74.9	11.0	-	-	-	-	68.9	7.2
1981	90.9	10.3	93.5	7.8	90.4	11.5	95.3	4.8	93.2	12.2	82.9	10.7	-	-	-	-	75.2	9.1
1982	96.5	6.2	97.3	4.1	96.9	7.2	97.8	2.6	97.0	4.1	92.5	11.6	-	-	-	-	82.6	9.8
1983	99.6	3.2	99.5	2.3	99.5	2.7	100.2	2.5	99.3	2.4	100.6	8.8	-	-	-	-	91.1	10.3
1984	103.9	4.3	103.2	3.7	103.6	4.1	102.1	1.9	103.7	4.4	106.8	6.2	-	-	-	-	101.1	11.0
1985	107.6	3.6	105.6	2.3	107.7	4.0	105.0	2.8	106.4	2.6	113.5	6.3	-	-	-	-	107.9	6.7
1986	109.6	1.9	109.1	3.3	110.9	3.0	105.9	0.9	102.3	-3.9	122.0	7.5	-	-	-	-	114.5	6.1
1987	113.6	3.6	113.5	4.0	114.2	3.0	110.6	4.4	105.4	3.0	130.1	6.6	-	-	-	-	121.4	6.0
1988	118.3	4.1	118.2	4.1	118.5	3.8	115.4	4.3	108.7	3.1	138.6	6.5	-	-	-	-	128.5	5.8
1989	124.0	4.8	124.9	5.7	123.0	3.8	118.6	2.8	114.1	5.0	149.3	7.7	-	-	-	-	137.0	6.6
1990	130.7	5.4	132.1	5.8	128.5	4.5	124.1	4.6	120.5	5.6	162.8	9.0	-	-	-	-	147.7	7.8
1991	136.2	4.2	136.8	3.6	133.6	4.0	128.7	3.7	123.8	2.7	177.0	8.7	-	-	-	-	159.0	7.7
1992	140.3	3.0	138.7	1.4	137.5	2.9	131.9	2.5	126.5	2.2	190.1	7.4	-	-	-	-	171.6	7.9
1993	144.5	3.0	141.6	2.1	141.2	2.7	133.7	1.4	130.4	3.1	201.4	5.9	90.7	-	85.5	-	183.3	6.8
1994	148.2	2.6	144.9	2.3	144.8	2.5	133.4	-0.2	134.3	3.0	211.0	4.8	92.7	2.2	88.8	3.9	192.9	5.2
1995	152.4	2.8	148.9	2.8	148.5	2.6	132.0	-1.0	139.1	3.6	220.5	4.5	94.5	1.9	92.2	3.8	198.5	2.9
1996	156.9	3.0	153.7	3.2	152.8	2.9	131.7	-0.2	143.0	2.8	228.2	3.5	97.4	3.1	95.3	3.4	206.9	4.2
1997	160.5	2.3	157.7	2.6	156.8	2.6	132.9	0.9	144.3	0.9	234.6	2.8	99.6	2.3	98.4	3.3	215.4	4.1
1998	163.0	1.6	161.1	2.2	160.4	2.3	133.0	0.1	141.6	-1.9	242.1	3.2	101.1	1.5	100.3	1.9	224.8	4.4
1999	166.6	2.2	164.6	2.2	163.9	2.2	131.3	-1.3	144.4	2.0	250.6	3.5	102.0	0.9	101.2	0.9	237.7	5.7
2000	172.2	3.4	168.4	2.3	169.6	3.5	129.6	-1.3	153.3	6.2	260.8	4.1	103.3	1.3	102.5	1.3	258.3	8.7
2001	177.1	2.8	173.6	3.1	176.4	4.0	127.3	-1.8	154.3	0.7	272.8	4.6	104.9	1.5	105.2	2.6	271.1	5.0
																	282.6	4.2

Source: U.S. Department of Labor, Bureau of Labor Statistics, Division of Consumer Prices and Price Indexes. *Base of index is December 1997 = 100.

U.S. CITY AVERAGE
Consumer Price Index - Urban Wage Earners
Base 1982-1984 = 100
Annual Averages

For 1913-2001. Columns headed % show percentile change in the index from the previous period for which an index is available.

Year	All Items Index	%	Food & Beverage Index	%	Housing Index	%	Apparel Index	%	Transportation Index	%	Medical Care Index	%	Recreation* Index	%	Education & Communic.* Index	%	Other Goods & Services Index	%
1913	10.0	-	-	-	-	-	15.0	-	-	-	-	-	-	-	-	-	-	-
1914	10.1	1.0	-	-	-	-	15.1	0.7	-	-	-	-	-	-	-	-	-	-
1915	10.2	1.0	-	-	-	-	15.4	2.0	-	-	-	-	-	-	-	-	-	-
1916	11.0	7.8	-	-	-	-	16.9	9.7	-	-	-	-	-	-	-	-	-	-
1917	12.9	17.3	-	-	-	-	20.3	20.1	-	-	-	-	-	-	-	-	-	-
1918	15.1	17.1	-	-	-	-	27.5	35.5	-	-	-	-	-	-	-	-	-	-
1919	17.4	15.2	-	-	-	-	36.4	32.4	-	-	-	-	-	-	-	-	-	-
1920	20.1	15.5	-	-	-	-	43.3	19.0	-	-	-	-	-	-	-	-	-	-
1921	18.0	-10.4	-	-	-	-	33.4	-22.9	-	-	-	-	-	-	-	-	-	-
1922	16.9	-6.1	-	-	-	-	27.2	-18.6	-	-	-	-	-	-	-	-	-	-
1923	17.2	1.8	-	-	-	-	27.2	0.0	-	-	-	-	-	-	-	-	-	-
1924	17.2	0.0	-	-	-	-	26.9	-1.1	-	-	-	-	-	-	-	-	-	-
1925	17.6	2.3	-	-	-	-	26.4	-1.9	-	-	-	-	-	-	-	-	-	-
1926	17.8	1.1	-	-	-	-	26.0	-1.5	-	-	-	-	-	-	-	-	-	-
1927	17.5	-1.7	-	-	-	-	25.5	-1.9	-	-	-	-	-	-	-	-	-	-
1928	17.2	-1.7	-	-	-	-	25.1	-1.6	-	-	-	-	-	-	-	-	-	-
1929	17.2	0.0	-	-	-	-	24.8	-1.2	-	-	-	-	-	-	-	-	-	-
1930	16.8	-2.3	-	-	-	-	24.3	-2.0	-	-	-	-	-	-	-	-	-	-
1931	15.3	-8.9	-	-	-	-	22.1	-9.1	-	-	-	-	-	-	-	-	-	-
1932	13.7	-10.5	-	-	-	-	19.6	-11.3	-	-	-	-	-	-	-	-	-	-
1933	13.0	-5.1	-	-	-	-	18.9	-3.6	-	-	-	-	-	-	-	-	-	-
1934	13.5	3.8	-	-	-	-	20.7	9.5	-	-	-	-	-	-	-	-	-	-
1935	13.8	2.2	-	-	-	-	20.9	1.0	14.1	-	10.2	-	-	-	-	-	-	-
1936	13.9	0.7	-	-	-	-	21.1	1.0	14.2	0.7	10.3	1.0	-	-	-	-	-	-
1937	14.4	3.6	-	-	-	-	22.1	4.7	14.5	2.1	10.4	1.0	-	-	-	-	-	-
1938	14.2	-1.4	-	-	-	-	22.0	-0.5	14.6	0.7	10.4	0.0	-	-	-	-	-	-
1939	14.0	-1.4	-	-	-	-	21.7	-1.4	14.2	-2.7	10.4	0.0	-	-	-	-	-	-
1940	14.1	0.7	-	-	-	-	21.9	0.9	14.1	-0.7	10.4	0.0	-	-	-	-	-	-
1941	14.8	5.0	-	-	-	-	23.0	5.0	14.6	3.5	10.5	1.0	-	-	-	-	-	-
1942	16.4	10.8	-	-	-	-	26.8	16.5	15.9	8.9	10.8	2.9	-	-	-	-	-	-
1943	17.4	6.1	-	-	-	-	28.0	4.5	15.8	-0.6	11.3	4.6	-	-	-	-	-	-
1944	17.7	1.7	-	-	-	-	30.0	7.1	15.8	0.0	11.6	2.7	-	-	-	-	-	-
1945	18.1	2.3	-	-	-	-	31.5	5.0	15.8	0.0	11.9	2.6	-	-	-	-	-	-
1946	19.6	8.3	-	-	-	-	34.6	9.8	16.6	5.1	12.6	5.9	-	-	-	-	-	-
1947	22.5	14.8	-	-	-	-	40.1	15.9	18.4	10.8	13.6	7.9	-	-	-	-	-	-
1948	24.2	7.6	-	-	-	-	42.7	6.5	20.4	10.9	14.5	6.6	-	-	-	-	-	-
1949	24.0	-0.8	-	-	-	-	41.0	-4.0	22.0	7.8	14.9	2.8	-	-	-	-	-	-
1950	24.2	0.8	-	-	-	-	40.5	-1.2	22.6	2.7	15.2	2.0	-	-	-	-	-	-
1951	26.1	7.9	-	-	-	-	44.1	8.9	24.0	6.2	15.9	4.6	-	-	-	-	-	-
1952	26.7	2.3	-	-	-	-	43.7	-0.9	25.6	6.7	16.8	5.7	-	-	-	-	-	-
1953	26.9	0.7	-	-	-	-	43.3	-0.9	26.3	2.7	17.4	3.6	-	-	-	-	-	-
1954	27.0	0.4	-	-	-	-	43.3	0.0	25.9	-1.5	17.9	2.9	-	-	-	-	-	-
1955	26.9	-0.4	-	-	-	-	43.1	-0.5	25.6	-1.2	18.3	2.2	-	-	-	-	-	-
1956	27.3	1.5	-	-	-	-	44.0	2.1	26.1	2.0	19.0	3.8	-	-	-	-	-	-
1957	28.3	3.7	-	-	-	-	44.7	1.6	27.6	5.7	19.8	4.2	-	-	-	-	-	-

[Continued]

206

U.S. City Average
Consumer Price Index - Urban Wage Earners
Base 1982-1984 = 100
Annual Averages
[Continued]

For 1913-2001. Columns headed % show percentile change in the index from the previous period for which an index is available.

Year	All Items		Food & Beverage		Housing		Apparel		Transportation		Medical Care		Recreation*		Education & Communic.*		Other Goods & Services	
	Index	%	Index	%	Index	%	Index	%	Index	%	Index	%	Index	%	Index	%	Index	%
1958	29.1	2.8	-	-	-	-	44.8	0.2	28.4	2.9	20.7	4.5	-	-	-	-	-	-
1959	29.3	0.7	-	-	-	-	45.2	0.9	29.6	4.2	21.6	4.3	-	-	-	-	-	-
1960	29.8	1.7	-	-	-	-	45.9	1.5	29.6	0.0	22.4	3.7	-	-	-	-	-	-
1961	30.1	1.0	-	-	-	-	46.3	0.9	30.0	1.4	23.0	2.7	-	-	-	-	-	-
1962	30.4	1.0	-	-	-	-	46.6	0.6	30.6	2.0	23.6	2.6	-	-	-	-	-	-
1963	30.8	1.3	-	-	-	-	47.1	1.1	30.8	0.7	24.2	2.5	-	-	-	-	-	-
1964	31.2	1.3	-	-	-	-	47.5	0.8	31.2	1.3	24.7	2.1	-	-	-	-	-	-
1965	31.7	1.6	-	-	-	-	48.0	1.1	31.7	1.6	25.3	2.4	-	-	-	-	-	-
1966	32.6	2.8	-	-	-	-	49.2	2.5	32.2	1.6	26.4	4.3	-	-	-	-	-	-
1967	33.6	3.1	35.0	-	31.1	-	51.2	4.1	33.1	2.8	28.3	7.2	-	-	-	-	35.4	-
1968	35.0	4.2	36.2	3.4	32.3	3.9	54.0	5.5	34.1	3.0	30.0	6.0	-	-	-	-	37.2	5.1
1969	36.9	5.4	38.0	5.0	34.3	6.2	57.1	5.7	35.5	4.1	32.1	7.0	-	-	-	-	39.1	5.1
1970	39.0	5.7	40.1	5.5	36.7	7.0	59.5	4.2	37.3	5.1	34.1	6.2	-	-	-	-	41.3	5.6
1971	40.7	4.4	41.3	3.0	38.3	4.4	61.4	3.2	39.2	5.1	36.3	6.5	-	-	-	-	43.3	4.8
1972	42.1	3.4	43.1	4.4	39.8	3.9	62.7	2.1	39.7	1.3	37.5	3.3	-	-	-	-	45.1	4.2
1973	44.7	6.2	48.8	13.2	41.5	4.3	65.0	3.7	41.0	3.3	39.0	4.0	-	-	-	-	46.9	4.0
1974	49.6	11.0	55.5	13.7	46.2	11.3	69.8	7.4	45.5	11.0	42.6	9.2	-	-	-	-	50.2	7.0
1975	54.1	9.1	60.2	8.5	51.1	10.6	72.9	4.4	49.8	9.5	47.7	12.0	-	-	-	-	54.4	8.4
1976	57.2	5.7	62.0	3.0	54.2	6.1	75.6	3.7	54.7	9.8	52.3	9.6	-	-	-	-	57.6	5.9
1977	60.9	6.5	65.7	6.0	57.9	6.8	79.0	4.5	58.6	7.1	57.3	9.6	-	-	-	-	60.9	5.7
1978	65.6	7.7	72.1	9.7	62.9	8.6	81.7	3.4	61.5	4.9	62.1	8.4	-	-	-	-	64.8	6.4
1979	73.1	11.4	79.9	10.8	70.7	12.4	85.2	4.3	70.4	14.5	68.0	9.5	-	-	-	-	69.4	7.1
1980	82.9	13.4	86.9	8.8	81.7	15.6	90.9	6.7	82.9	17.8	75.6	11.2	-	-	-	-	75.6	8.9
1981	91.4	10.3	93.6	7.7	91.1	11.5	95.6	5.2	93.0	12.2	83.5	10.4	-	-	-	-	82.5	9.1
1982	96.9	6.0	97.3	4.0	97.7	7.2	97.8	2.3	97.0	4.3	92.5	10.8	-	-	-	-	90.9	10.2
1983	99.8	3.0	99.5	2.3	100.0	2.4	100.2	2.5	99.2	2.3	100.5	8.6	-	-	-	-	101.3	11.4
1984	103.3	3.5	103.2	3.7	102.2	2.2	102.0	1.8	103.8	4.6	106.9	6.4	-	-	-	-	107.9	6.5
1985	106.9	3.5	105.5	2.2	106.6	4.3	105.0	2.9	106.4	2.5	113.6	6.3	-	-	-	-	114.2	5.8
1986	108.6	1.6	108.9	3.2	109.7	2.9	105.8	0.8	101.7	-4.4	122.0	7.4	-	-	-	-	120.9	5.9
1987	112.5	3.6	113.3	4.0	112.8	2.8	110.4	4.3	105.1	3.3	130.2	6.7	-	-	-	-	127.8	5.7
1988	117.0	4.0	117.9	4.1	116.8	3.5	114.9	4.1	108.3	3.0	139.0	6.8	-	-	-	-	136.5	6.8
1989	122.6	4.8	124.6	5.7	121.2	3.8	117.9	2.6	113.9	5.2	149.6	7.6	-	-	-	-	147.4	8.0
1990	129.0	5.2	131.8	5.8	126.4	4.3	123.1	4.4	120.1	5.4	162.7	8.8	-	-	-	-	158.9	7.8
1991	134.3	4.1	136.5	3.6	131.2	3.8	127.4	3.5	123.1	2.5	176.5	8.5	-	-	-	-	171.7	8.1
1992	138.2	2.9	138.3	1.3	135.0	2.9	130.7	2.6	125.8	2.2	189.6	7.4	-	-	-	-	183.3	6.8
1993	142.1	2.8	141.2	2.1	138.5	2.6	132.4	1.3	129.4	2.9	200.9	6.0	91.2	-	86.0	-	192.2	4.9
1994	145.6	2.5	144.4	2.3	142.0	2.5	132.2	-0.2	133.4	3.1	210.4	4.7	93.0	2.0	89.1	3.6	196.4	2.2
1995	149.8	2.9	148.3	2.7	145.4	2.4	130.9	-1.0	138.8	4.0	219.8	4.5	94.7	1.8	92.3	3.6	204.2	4.0
1996	154.1	2.9	153.2	3.3	149.6	2.9	130.9	0.0	142.8	2.9	227.6	3.5	97.5	3.0	95.4	3.4	212.2	3.9
1997	157.6	2.3	157.2	2.6	153.4	2.5	132.1	0.9	143.6	0.6	234.0	2.8	99.7	2.3	98.5	3.2	221.6	4.4
1998	159.7	1.3	160.4	2.0	156.7	2.2	131.6	-0.4	140.5	-2.2	241.4	3.2	100.9	1.2	100.4	1.9	236.1	6.5
1999	163.2	2.2	163.8	2.1	160.0	2.1	130.1	-1.1	143.4	2.1	249.7	3.4	101.3	0.4	101.5	1.1	261.9	10.9
2000	168.9	3.5	167.7	2.4	165.4	3.4	128.3	-1.4	152.8	6.6	259.9	4.1	102.4	1.1	102.7	1.2	276.5	5.6
2001	173.5	2.7	173.0	3.2	172.1	4.1	126.1	-1.7	153.6	0.5	271.8	4.6	103.6	1.2	105.3	2.5	289.5	4.7

Source: U.S. Department of Labor, Bureau of Labor Statistics, Division of Consumer Prices and Price Indexes. *Base of index is December 1997 = 100.

Economic Indicators Handbook, 6th Edition

U.S. CITY AVERAGE
Consumer Price Index - All Urban Consumers
Base 1982-1984 = 100
All Items

For 1913-2001. Columns headed % show percentile change in the index from the previous period for which an index is available.

Year	Jan Index	%	Feb Index	%	Mar Index	%	Apr Index	%	May Index	%	Jun Index	%	Jul Index	%	Aug Index	%	Sep Index	%	Oct Index	%	Nov Index	%	Dec Index	%
1913	9.8	-	9.8	0.0	9.8	0.0	9.8	0.0	9.7	-1.0	9.8	1.0	9.9	1.0	9.9	0.0	10.0	1.0	10.0	0.0	10.1	1.0	10.0	-1.0
1914	10.0	0.0	9.9	-1.0	9.9	0.0	9.8	-1.0	9.9	1.0	9.9	0.0	10.0	1.0	10.2	2.0	10.2	0.0	10.1	-1.0	10.2	1.0	10.1	-1.0
1915	10.1	0.0	10.0	-1.0	9.9	-1.0	10.0	1.0	10.1	1.0	10.1	0.0	10.1	0.0	10.1	0.0	10.1	0.0	10.2	1.0	10.3	1.0	10.3	0.0
1916	10.4	1.0	10.4	0.0	10.5	1.0	10.6	1.0	10.7	0.9	10.8	0.9	10.8	0.0	10.9	0.9	11.1	1.8	11.3	1.8	11.5	1.8	11.6	0.9
1917	11.7	0.9	12.0	2.6	12.0	0.0	12.6	5.0	12.8	1.6	13.0	1.6	12.8	-1.5	13.0	1.6	13.3	2.3	13.5	1.5	13.5	0.0	13.7	1.5
1918	14.0	2.2	14.1	0.7	14.0	-0.7	14.2	1.4	14.5	2.1	14.7	1.4	15.1	2.7	15.4	2.0	15.7	1.9	16.0	1.9	16.3	1.9	16.5	1.2
1919	16.5	0.0	16.2	-1.8	16.4	1.2	16.7	1.8	16.9	1.2	16.9	0.0	17.4	3.0	17.7	1.7	17.8	0.6	18.1	1.7	18.5	2.2	18.9	2.2
1920	19.3	2.1	19.5	1.0	19.7	1.0	20.3	3.0	20.6	1.5	20.9	1.5	20.8	-0.5	20.3	-2.4	20.0	-1.5	19.9	-0.5	19.8	-0.5	19.4	-2.0
1921	19.0	-2.1	18.4	-3.2	18.3	-0.5	18.1	-1.1	17.7	-2.2	17.6	-0.6	17.7	0.6	17.7	0.0	17.5	-1.1	17.5	0.0	17.4	-0.6	17.3	-0.6
1922	16.9	-2.3	16.9	0.0	16.7	-1.2	16.7	0.0	16.7	0.0	16.7	0.0	16.8	0.6	16.6	-1.2	16.6	0.0	16.7	0.6	16.8	0.6	16.9	0.6
1923	16.8	-0.6	16.8	0.0	16.8	0.0	16.9	0.6	16.9	0.0	17.0	0.6	17.2	1.2	17.1	-0.6	17.2	0.6	17.3	0.6	17.3	0.0	17.3	0.0
1924	17.3	0.0	17.2	-0.6	17.1	-0.6	17.0	-0.6	17.0	0.0	17.0	0.0	17.1	0.6	17.0	-0.6	17.1	0.6	17.2	0.6	17.2	0.0	17.3	0.6
1925	17.3	0.0	17.2	-0.6	17.3	0.6	17.2	-0.6	17.3	0.6	17.5	1.2	17.7	1.1	17.7	0.0	17.7	0.0	17.7	0.0	18.0	1.7	17.9	-0.6
1926	17.9	0.0	17.9	0.0	17.8	-0.6	17.9	0.6	17.8	-0.6	17.7	-0.6	17.5	-1.1	17.4	-0.6	17.5	0.6	17.6	0.6	17.7	0.6	17.7	0.0
1927	17.5	-1.1	17.4	-0.6	17.3	-0.6	17.3	0.0	17.4	0.6	17.6	1.1	17.3	-1.7	17.2	-0.6	17.3	0.6	17.4	0.6	17.3	-0.6	17.3	0.0
1928	17.3	0.0	17.1	-1.2	17.1	0.0	17.1	0.0	17.2	0.6	17.1	-0.6	17.1	0.0	17.1	0.0	17.3	1.2	17.2	-0.6	17.2	0.0	17.1	-0.6
1929	17.1	0.0	17.1	0.0	17.0	-0.6	16.9	-0.6	17.0	0.6	17.1	0.6	17.3	1.2	17.3	0.0	17.3	0.0	17.3	0.0	17.3	0.0	17.2	-0.6
1930	17.1	-0.6	17.0	-0.6	16.9	-0.6	17.0	0.6	16.9	-0.6	16.8	-0.6	16.6	-1.2	16.5	-0.6	16.6	0.6	16.5	-0.6	16.4	-0.6	16.1	-1.8
1931	15.9	-1.2	15.7	-1.3	15.6	-0.6	15.5	-0.6	15.3	-1.3	15.1	-1.3	15.1	0.0	15.1	0.0	15.0	-0.7	14.9	-0.7	14.7	-1.3	14.6	-0.7
1932	14.3	-2.1	14.1	-1.4	14.0	-0.7	13.9	-0.7	13.7	-1.4	13.6	-0.7	13.6	0.0	13.5	-0.7	13.4	-0.7	13.3	-0.7	13.2	-0.8	13.1	-0.8
1933	12.9	-1.5	12.7	-1.6	12.6	-0.8	12.6	0.0	12.6	0.0	12.7	0.8	13.1	3.1	13.2	0.8	13.2	0.0	13.2	0.0	13.2	0.0	13.2	0.0
1934	13.2	0.0	13.3	0.8	13.3	0.0	13.3	0.0	13.3	0.0	13.4	0.8	13.4	0.0	13.4	0.0	13.6	1.5	13.5	-0.7	13.5	0.0	13.4	-0.7
1935	13.6	1.5	13.7	0.7	13.7	0.0	13.8	0.7	13.8	0.0	13.7	-0.7	13.7	0.0	13.7	0.0	13.7	0.0	13.7	0.0	13.8	0.7	13.8	0.0
1936	13.8	0.0	13.8	0.0	13.7	-0.7	13.7	0.0	13.7	0.0	13.8	0.7	13.9	0.7	14.0	0.7	14.0	0.0	14.0	0.0	14.0	0.0	14.0	0.0
1937	14.1	0.7	14.1	0.0	14.2	0.7	14.3	0.7	14.4	0.7	14.4	0.0	14.5	0.7	14.5	0.0	14.6	0.7	14.6	0.0	14.5	-0.7	14.4	-0.7
1938	14.2	-1.4	14.1	-0.7	14.1	0.0	14.2	0.7	14.1	-0.7	14.1	0.0	14.1	0.0	14.1	0.0	14.1	0.0	14.0	-0.7	14.0	0.0	14.0	0.0
1939	14.0	0.0	13.9	-0.7	13.9	0.0	13.8	-0.7	13.8	0.0	13.8	0.0	13.8	0.0	13.8	0.0	14.1	2.2	14.0	-0.7	14.0	0.0	14.0	0.0
1940	13.9	-0.7	14.0	0.7	14.0	0.0	14.0	0.0	14.0	0.0	14.1	0.7	14.0	-0.7	14.0	0.0	14.0	0.0	14.0	0.0	14.0	0.0	14.1	0.7
1941	14.1	0.0	14.1	0.0	14.2	0.7	14.3	0.7	14.4	0.7	14.7	2.1	14.7	0.0	14.9	1.4	15.1	1.3	15.3	1.3	15.4	0.7	15.5	0.6
1942	15.7	1.3	15.8	0.6	16.0	1.3	16.1	0.6	16.3	1.2	16.3	0.0	16.4	0.6	16.5	0.6	16.5	0.0	16.7	1.2	16.8	0.6	16.9	0.6
1943	16.9	0.0	16.9	0.0	17.2	1.8	17.4	1.2	17.5	0.6	17.5	0.0	17.4	-0.6	17.3	-0.6	17.4	0.6	17.4	0.0	17.4	0.0	17.4	0.0
1944	17.4	0.0	17.4	0.0	17.4	0.0	17.5	0.6	17.5	0.0	17.6	0.6	17.7	0.6	17.7	0.0	17.7	0.0	17.7	0.0	17.7	0.0	17.8	0.6
1945	17.8	0.0	17.8	0.0	17.8	0.0	17.8	0.0	17.9	0.6	18.1	1.1	18.1	0.0	18.1	0.0	18.1	0.0	18.1	0.0	18.1	0.0	18.2	0.6
1946	18.2	0.0	18.1	-0.5	18.3	1.1	18.4	0.5	18.5	0.5	18.7	1.1	19.8	5.9	20.2	2.0	20.4	1.0	20.8	2.0	21.3	2.4	21.5	0.9
1947	21.5	0.0	21.5	0.0	21.9	1.9	21.9	0.0	21.9	0.0	22.0	0.5	22.2	0.9	22.5	1.4	23.0	2.2	23.0	0.0	23.1	0.4	23.4	1.3
1948	23.7	1.3	23.5	-0.8	23.4	-0.4	23.8	1.7	23.9	0.4	24.1	0.8	24.4	1.2	24.5	0.4	24.5	0.0	24.4	-0.4	24.2	-0.8	24.1	-0.4
1949	24.0	-0.4	23.8	-0.8	23.8	0.0	23.9	0.4	23.8	-0.4	23.9	0.4	23.7	-0.8	23.8	0.4	23.9	0.4	23.7	-0.8	23.8	0.4	23.6	-0.8
1950	23.5	-0.4	23.5	0.0	23.6	0.4	23.6	0.0	23.7	0.4	23.8	0.4	24.1	1.3	24.3	0.8	24.4	0.4	24.6	0.8	24.7	0.4	25.0	1.2
1951	25.4	1.6	25.7	1.2	25.8	0.4	25.8	0.0	25.9	0.4	25.9	0.0	25.9	0.0	25.9	0.0	26.1	0.8	26.2	0.4	26.4	0.8	26.5	0.4
1952	26.5	0.0	26.3	-0.8	26.3	0.0	26.4	0.4	26.4	0.0	26.5	0.4	26.7	0.8	26.7	0.0	26.7	0.0	26.7	0.0	26.7	0.0	26.7	0.0
1953	26.6	-0.4	26.5	-0.4	26.6	0.4	26.6	0.0	26.7	0.4	26.8	0.4	26.8	0.0	26.9	0.4	26.9	0.0	27.0	0.4	26.9	-0.4	26.9	0.0
1954	26.9	0.0	26.9	0.0	26.9	0.0	26.8	-0.4	26.9	0.4	26.9	0.0	26.9	0.0	26.9	0.0	26.8	-0.4	26.8	0.0	26.8	0.0	26.7	-0.4
1955	26.7	0.0	26.7	0.0	26.7	0.0	26.7	0.0	26.7	0.0	26.7	0.0	26.8	0.4	26.8	0.0	26.9	0.4	26.9	0.0	26.9	0.0	26.8	-0.4
1956	26.8	0.0	26.8	0.0	26.8	0.0	26.9	0.4	27.0	0.4	27.2	0.7	27.4	0.7	27.3	-0.4	27.4	0.4	27.5	0.4	27.5	0.0	27.6	0.4
1957	27.6	0.0	27.7	0.4	27.8	0.4	27.9	0.4	28.0	0.4	28.1	0.4	28.3	0.7	28.3	0.0	28.3	0.0	28.3	0.0	28.4	0.4	28.4	0.0
1958	28.6	0.7	28.6	0.0	28.8	0.7	28.9	0.3	28.9	0.0	28.9	0.0	29.0	0.3	28.9	-0.3	28.9	0.0	28.9	0.0	29.0	0.3	28.9	-0.3

[Continued]

U.S. City Average
Consumer Price Index - All Urban Consumers
Base 1982-1984 = 100
All Items
[Continued]

For 1913-2001. Columns headed % show percentile change in the index from the previous period for which an index is available.

Year	Jan Index	%	Feb Index	%	Mar Index	%	Apr Index	%	May Index	%	Jun Index	%	Jul Index	%	Aug Index	%	Sep Index	%	Oct Index	%	Nov Index	%	Dec Index	%
1959	29.0	0.3	28.9	-0.3	28.9	0.0	29.0	0.3	29.0	0.0	29.1	0.3	29.2	0.3	29.2	0.0	29.3	0.3	29.4	0.3	29.4	0.0	29.4	0.0
1960	29.3	-0.3	29.4	0.3	29.4	0.0	29.5	0.3	29.5	0.0	29.6	0.3	29.6	0.0	29.6	0.0	29.6	0.0	29.8	0.7	29.8	0.0	29.8	0.0
1961	29.8	0.0	29.8	0.0	29.8	0.0	29.8	0.0	29.8	0.0	29.8	0.0	30.0	0.7	29.9	-0.3	30.0	0.3	30.0	0.0	30.0	0.0	30.0	0.0
1962	30.0	0.0	30.1	0.3	30.1	0.0	30.2	0.3	30.2	0.0	30.2	0.0	30.3	0.3	30.3	0.0	30.4	0.3	30.4	0.0	30.4	0.0	30.4	0.0
1963	30.4	0.0	30.4	0.0	30.5	0.3	30.5	0.0	30.5	0.0	30.6	0.3	30.7	0.3	30.7	0.0	30.7	0.0	30.8	0.3	30.8	0.0	30.9	0.3
1964	30.9	0.0	30.9	0.0	30.9	0.0	30.9	0.0	30.9	0.0	31.0	0.3	31.1	0.3	31.0	-0.3	31.1	0.3	31.1	0.0	31.2	0.3	31.2	0.0
1965	31.2	0.0	31.2	0.0	31.3	0.3	31.4	0.3	31.4	0.0	31.6	0.6	31.6	0.0	31.6	0.0	31.6	0.0	31.7	0.3	31.7	0.0	31.8	0.3
1966	31.8	0.0	32.0	0.6	32.1	0.3	32.3	0.6	32.3	0.0	32.4	0.3	32.5	0.3	32.7	0.6	32.7	0.0	32.9	0.6	32.9	0.0	32.9	0.0
1967	32.9	0.0	32.9	0.0	33.0	0.3	33.1	0.3	33.2	0.3	33.3	0.3	33.4	0.3	33.5	0.3	33.6	0.3	33.7	0.3	33.8	0.3	33.9	0.3
1968	34.1	0.6	34.2	0.3	34.3	0.3	34.4	0.3	34.5	0.3	34.7	0.6	34.9	0.6	35.0	0.3	35.1	0.3	35.3	0.6	35.4	0.3	35.5	0.3
1969	35.6	0.3	35.8	0.6	36.1	0.8	36.3	0.6	36.4	0.3	36.6	0.5	36.8	0.5	37.0	0.5	37.1	0.3	37.3	0.5	37.5	0.5	37.7	0.5
1970	37.8	0.3	38.0	0.5	38.2	0.5	38.5	0.8	38.6	0.3	38.8	0.5	39.0	0.5	39.0	0.0	39.2	0.5	39.4	0.5	39.6	0.5	39.8	0.5
1971	39.8	0.0	39.9	0.3	40.0	0.3	40.1	0.2	40.3	0.5	40.6	0.7	40.7	0.2	40.8	0.2	40.8	0.0	40.9	0.2	40.9	0.0	41.1	0.5
1972	41.1	0.0	41.3	0.5	41.4	0.2	41.5	0.2	41.6	0.2	41.7	0.2	41.9	0.5	42.0	0.2	42.1	0.2	42.3	0.5	42.4	0.2	42.5	0.2
1973	42.6	0.2	42.9	0.7	43.3	0.9	43.6	0.7	43.9	0.7	44.2	0.7	44.3	0.2	45.1	1.8	45.2	0.2	45.6	0.9	45.9	0.7	46.2	0.7
1974	46.6	0.9	47.2	1.3	47.8	1.3	48.0	0.4	48.6	1.2	49.0	0.8	49.4	0.8	50.0	1.2	50.6	1.2	51.1	1.0	51.5	0.8	51.9	0.8
1975	52.1	0.4	52.5	0.8	52.7	0.4	52.9	0.4	53.2	0.6	53.6	0.8	54.2	1.1	54.3	0.2	54.6	0.6	54.9	0.5	55.3	0.7	55.5	0.4
1976	55.6	0.2	55.8	0.4	55.9	0.2	56.1	0.4	56.5	0.7	56.8	0.5	57.1	0.5	57.4	0.5	57.6	0.3	57.9	0.5	58.0	0.2	58.2	0.3
1977	58.5	0.5	59.1	1.0	59.5	0.7	60.0	0.8	60.3	0.5	60.7	0.7	61.0	0.5	61.2	0.3	61.4	0.3	61.6	0.3	61.9	0.5	62.1	0.3
1978	62.5	0.6	62.9	0.6	63.4	0.8	63.9	0.8	64.5	0.9	65.2	1.1	65.7	0.8	66.0	0.5	66.5	0.8	67.1	0.9	67.4	0.4	67.7	0.4
1979	68.3	0.9	69.1	1.2	69.8	1.0	70.6	1.1	71.5	1.3	72.3	1.1	73.1	1.1	73.8	1.0	74.6	1.1	75.2	0.8	75.9	0.9	76.7	1.1
1980	77.8	1.4	78.9	1.4	80.1	1.5	81.0	1.1	81.8	1.0	82.7	1.1	82.7	0.0	83.3	0.7	84.0	0.8	84.8	1.0	85.5	0.8	86.3	0.9
1981	87.0	0.8	87.9	1.0	88.5	0.7	89.1	0.7	89.8	0.8	90.6	0.9	91.6	1.1	92.3	0.8	93.2	1.0	93.4	0.2	93.7	0.3	94.0	0.3
1982	94.3	0.3	94.6	0.3	94.5	-0.1	94.9	0.4	95.8	0.9	97.0	1.3	97.5	0.5	97.7	0.2	97.9	0.2	98.2	0.3	98.0	-0.2	97.6	-0.4
1983	97.8	0.2	97.9	0.1	97.9	0.0	98.6	0.7	99.2	0.6	99.5	0.3	99.9	0.4	100.2	0.3	100.7	0.5	101.0	0.3	101.2	0.2	101.3	0.1
1984	101.9	0.6	102.4	0.5	102.6	0.2	103.1	0.5	103.4	0.3	103.7	0.3	104.1	0.4	104.5	0.4	105.0	0.5	105.3	0.3	105.3	0.0	105.3	0.0
1985	105.5	0.2	106.0	0.5	106.4	0.4	106.9	0.5	107.3	0.4	107.6	0.3	107.8	0.2	108.0	0.2	108.3	0.3	108.7	0.4	109.0	0.3	109.3	0.3
1986	109.6	0.3	109.3	-0.3	108.8	-0.5	108.6	-0.2	108.9	0.3	109.5	0.6	109.5	0.0	109.7	0.2	110.2	0.5	110.3	0.1	110.4	0.1	110.5	0.1
1987	111.2	0.6	111.6	0.4	112.1	0.4	112.7	0.5	113.1	0.4	113.5	0.4	113.8	0.3	114.4	0.5	115.0	0.5	115.3	0.3	115.4	0.1	115.4	0.0
1988	115.7	0.3	116.0	0.3	116.5	0.4	117.1	0.5	117.5	0.3	118.0	0.4	118.5	0.4	119.0	0.4	119.8	0.7	120.2	0.3	120.3	0.1	120.5	0.2
1989	121.1	0.5	121.6	0.4	122.3	0.6	123.1	0.7	123.8	0.6	124.1	0.2	124.4	0.2	124.6	0.2	125.0	0.3	125.6	0.5	125.9	0.2	126.1	0.2
1990	127.4	1.0	128.0	0.5	128.7	0.5	128.9	0.2	129.2	0.2	129.9	0.5	130.4	0.4	131.6	0.9	132.7	0.8	133.5	0.6	133.8	0.2	133.8	0.0
1991	134.6	0.6	134.8	0.1	135.0	0.1	135.2	0.1	135.6	0.3	136.0	0.3	136.2	0.1	136.6	0.3	137.2	0.4	137.4	0.1	137.8	0.3	137.9	0.1
1992	138.1	0.1	138.6	0.4	139.3	0.5	139.5	0.1	139.7	0.1	140.2	0.4	140.5	0.2	140.9	0.3	141.3	0.3	141.8	0.4	142.0	0.1	141.9	-0.1
1993	142.6	0.5	143.1	0.4	143.6	0.3	144.0	0.3	144.2	0.1	144.4	0.1	144.4	0.0	144.8	0.3	145.1	0.2	145.7	0.4	145.8	0.1	145.8	0.0
1994	146.2	0.3	146.7	0.3	147.2	0.3	147.4	0.1	147.5	0.1	148.0	0.3	148.4	0.3	149.0	0.4	149.4	0.3	149.5	0.1	149.7	0.1	149.7	0.0
1995	150.3	0.4	150.9	0.4	151.4	0.3	151.9	0.3	152.2	0.2	152.5	0.2	152.5	0.0	152.9	0.3	153.2	0.2	153.7	0.3	153.6	-0.1	153.5	-0.1
1996	154.4	0.6	154.9	0.3	155.7	0.5	156.3	0.4	156.6	0.2	156.7	0.1	157.0	0.2	157.3	0.2	157.8	0.3	158.3	0.3	158.6	0.2	158.6	0.0
1997	159.1	0.3	159.6	0.3	160.0	0.3	160.2	0.1	160.1	-0.1	160.3	0.1	160.5	0.1	160.8	0.2	161.2	0.2	161.6	0.2	161.5	-0.1	161.3	-0.1
1998	161.6	0.2	161.9	0.2	162.2	0.2	162.5	0.2	162.8	0.2	163.0	0.1	163.2	0.1	163.4	0.1	163.6	0.1	164.0	0.2	164.0	0.0	163.9	-0.1
1999	164.3	0.2	164.5	0.1	165.0	0.3	166.2	0.7	166.2	0.0	166.2	0.0	166.7	0.3	167.1	0.2	167.9	0.5	168.2	0.2	168.3	0.1	168.3	0.0
2000	168.8	0.3	169.8	0.6	171.2	0.8	171.3	0.1	171.5	0.1	172.4	0.5	172.8	0.2	172.8	0.0	173.7	0.5	174.0	0.2	174.1	0.1	174.0	-0.1
2001	175.1	0.6	175.8	0.4	176.2	0.2	176.9	0.4	177.7	0.5	178.0	0.2	177.5	-0.3	177.5	0.0	178.3	0.5	177.7	-0.3	177.4	-0.2	176.7	-0.4

Source: U.S. Department of Labor, Bureau of Labor Statistics, Division of Consumer Prices and Price Indexes.

U.S. CITY AVERAGE
Consumer Price Index - Urban Wage Earners
Base 1982-1984 = 100
All Items

For 1913-2001. Columns headed % show percentile change in the index from the previous period for which an index is available.

Year	Jan Index	%	Feb Index	%	Mar Index	%	Apr Index	%	May Index	%	Jun Index	%	Jul Index	%	Aug Index	%	Sep Index	%	Oct Index	%	Nov Index	%	Dec Index	%
1913	9.9	-	9.8	-1.0	9.8	0.0	9.9	1.0	9.8	-1.0	9.8	0.0	9.9	1.0	10.0	1.0	10.0	0.0	10.1	1.0	10.1	0.0	10.1	0.0
1914	10.1	0.0	10.0	-1.0	10.0	0.0	9.9	-1.0	9.9	0.0	10.0	1.0	10.1	1.0	10.2	1.0	10.3	1.0	10.2	-1.0	10.2	0.0	10.2	0.0
1915	10.2	0.0	10.1	-1.0	10.0	-1.0	10.1	1.0	10.1	0.0	10.2	1.0	10.2	0.0	10.2	0.0	10.2	0.0	10.3	1.0	10.4	1.0	10.4	0.0
1916	10.5	1.0	10.5	0.0	10.6	1.0	10.7	0.9	10.7	0.0	10.9	1.9	10.9	0.0	11.0	0.9	11.2	1.8	11.3	0.9	11.5	1.8	11.6	0.9
1917	11.8	1.7	12.0	1.7	12.1	0.8	12.6	4.1	12.9	2.4	13.0	0.8	12.9	-0.8	13.1	1.6	13.3	1.5	13.6	2.3	13.6	0.0	13.8	1.5
1918	14.0	1.4	14.2	1.4	14.1	-0.7	14.3	1.4	14.5	1.4	14.8	2.1	15.2	2.7	15.4	1.3	15.8	2.6	16.1	1.9	16.3	1.2	16.6	1.8
1919	16.6	0.0	16.2	-2.4	16.5	1.9	16.8	1.8	17.0	1.2	17.0	0.0	17.5	2.9	17.8	1.7	17.9	0.6	18.2	1.7	18.6	2.2	19.0	2.2
1920	19.4	2.1	19.6	1.0	19.8	1.0	20.4	3.0	20.7	1.5	21.0	1.4	20.9	-0.5	20.4	-2.4	20.1	-1.5	20.0	-0.5	19.9	-0.5	19.5	-2.0
1921	19.1	-2.1	18.5	-3.1	18.4	-0.5	18.2	-1.1	17.8	-2.2	17.7	-0.6	17.8	0.6	17.8	0.0	17.6	-1.1	17.6	0.0	17.5	-0.6	17.4	-0.6
1922	17.0	-2.3	17.0	0.0	16.8	-1.2	16.8	0.0	16.8	0.0	16.8	0.0	16.9	0.6	16.7	-1.2	16.7	0.0	16.8	0.6	16.9	0.6	17.0	0.6
1923	16.9	-0.6	16.9	0.0	16.9	0.0	17.0	0.6	17.0	0.0	17.1	0.6	17.3	1.2	17.2	-0.6	17.3	0.6	17.4	0.6	17.4	0.0	17.4	0.0
1924	17.4	0.0	17.3	-0.6	17.2	-0.6	17.1	-0.6	17.1	0.0	17.1	0.0	17.2	0.6	17.1	-0.6	17.2	0.6	17.3	0.6	17.3	0.0	17.4	0.6
1925	17.4	0.0	17.3	-0.6	17.4	0.6	17.3	-0.6	17.4	0.6	17.6	1.1	17.8	1.1	17.8	0.0	17.8	0.0	17.8	0.0	18.1	1.7	18.0	-0.6
1926	18.0	0.0	18.0	0.0	17.9	-0.6	18.0	0.6	17.9	-0.6	17.8	-0.6	17.6	-1.1	17.5	-0.6	17.6	0.6	17.7	0.6	17.8	0.6	17.8	0.0
1927	17.6	-1.1	17.5	-0.6	17.4	-0.6	17.4	0.0	17.5	0.6	17.7	1.1	17.4	-1.7	17.3	-0.6	17.4	0.6	17.5	0.6	17.4	-0.6	17.4	0.0
1928	17.4	0.0	17.2	-1.1	17.2	0.0	17.2	0.0	17.3	0.6	17.2	-0.6	17.2	0.0	17.2	0.0	17.4	1.2	17.3	-0.6	17.3	0.0	17.3	-0.6
1929	17.2	0.0	17.2	0.0	17.1	-0.6	17.0	-0.6	17.1	0.6	17.2	0.6	17.4	1.2	17.4	0.0	17.4	0.0	17.4	0.0	17.4	0.0	17.3	-0.6
1930	17.2	-0.6	17.1	-0.6	17.0	-0.6	17.1	0.6	17.0	-0.6	16.9	-0.6	16.7	-1.2	16.6	-0.6	16.7	0.6	16.6	-0.6	16.5	-0.6	16.2	-1.8
1931	16.0	-1.2	15.7	-1.9	15.6	-0.6	15.5	-0.6	15.4	-0.6	15.2	-1.3	15.2	0.0	15.1	-0.7	15.1	0.0	15.0	-0.7	14.8	-1.3	14.7	-0.7
1932	14.4	-2.0	14.2	-1.4	14.1	-0.7	14.0	-0.7	13.8	-1.4	13.7	-0.7	13.7	0.0	13.5	-1.5	13.5	0.0	13.4	-0.7	13.3	-0.7	13.2	-0.8
1933	13.0	-1.5	12.8	-1.5	12.7	-0.8	12.6	-0.8	12.7	0.8	12.8	0.8	13.2	3.1	13.3	0.8	13.3	0.0	13.3	0.0	13.3	0.0	13.2	-0.8
1934	13.3	0.8	13.4	0.8	13.4	0.0	13.4	0.0	13.4	0.0	13.4	0.0	13.4	0.0	13.5	0.7	13.7	1.5	13.6	-0.7	13.5	-0.7	13.5	0.0
1935	13.7	1.5	13.8	0.7	13.8	0.0	13.9	0.7	13.8	-0.7	13.8	0.0	13.7	-0.7	13.7	0.0	13.8	0.7	13.8	0.0	13.9	0.7	13.9	0.0
1936	13.9	0.0	13.8	-0.7	13.8	0.0	13.8	0.0	13.8	0.0	13.9	0.7	14.0	0.7	14.1	0.7	14.1	0.0	14.1	0.0	14.1	0.0	14.1	0.0
1937	14.2	0.7	14.2	0.0	14.3	0.7	14.4	0.7	14.4	0.0	14.5	0.7	14.5	0.0	14.6	0.7	14.7	0.7	14.6	-0.7	14.5	-0.7	14.5	0.0
1938	14.3	-1.4	14.2	-0.7	14.2	0.0	14.2	0.0	14.2	0.0	14.2	0.0	14.2	0.0	14.2	0.0	14.2	0.0	14.1	-0.7	14.1	0.0	14.1	0.0
1939	14.0	-0.7	14.0	0.0	13.9	-0.7	13.9	0.0	13.9	0.0	13.9	0.0	13.9	0.0	13.9	0.0	14.2	2.2	14.1	-0.7	14.1	0.0	14.0	-0.7
1940	14.0	0.0	14.1	0.7	14.1	0.0	14.1	0.0	14.1	0.0	14.1	0.0	14.1	0.0	14.1	0.0	14.1	0.0	14.1	0.0	14.1	0.0	14.2	0.7
1941	14.2	0.0	14.2	0.0	14.2	0.0	14.4	1.4	14.5	0.7	14.7	1.4	14.8	0.7	14.9	0.7	15.2	2.0	15.4	1.3	15.5	0.6	15.5	0.0
1942	15.7	1.3	15.9	1.3	16.1	1.3	16.2	0.6	16.3	0.6	16.4	0.6	16.5	0.6	16.6	0.6	16.6	0.0	16.8	1.2	16.9	0.6	17.0	0.6
1943	17.0	0.0	17.0	0.0	17.3	1.8	17.5	1.2	17.6	0.6	17.6	0.0	17.5	-0.6	17.4	-0.6	17.5	0.6	17.5	0.0	17.5	0.0	17.5	0.0
1944	17.5	0.0	17.5	0.0	17.5	0.0	17.6	0.6	17.6	0.0	17.7	0.6	17.8	0.6	17.8	0.0	17.8	0.0	17.8	0.0	17.8	0.0	17.9	0.6
1945	17.9	0.0	17.9	0.0	17.9	0.0	17.9	0.0	18.0	0.6	18.2	1.1	18.2	0.0	18.2	0.0	18.2	0.0	18.2	0.0	18.2	0.0	18.3	0.5
1946	18.3	0.0	18.2	-0.5	18.4	1.1	18.5	0.5	18.6	0.5	18.8	1.1	19.9	5.9	20.3	2.0	20.5	1.0	20.9	2.0	21.5	2.9	21.6	0.5
1947	21.6	0.0	21.6	0.0	22.1	2.3	22.1	0.0	22.0	-0.5	22.2	0.9	22.4	0.9	22.6	0.9	23.1	2.2	23.1	0.0	23.3	0.9	23.6	1.3
1948	23.8	0.8	23.6	-0.8	23.6	0.0	23.9	1.3	24.1	0.8	24.2	0.4	24.5	1.2	24.6	0.4	24.6	0.0	24.5	-0.4	24.4	-0.4	24.2	-0.8
1949	24.2	0.0	23.9	-1.2	24.0	0.4	24.0	0.0	24.0	0.0	24.0	0.0	23.8	-0.8	23.9	0.4	24.0	0.4	23.9	-0.4	23.9	0.0	23.8	-0.4
1950	23.7	-0.4	23.6	-0.4	23.7	0.4	23.7	0.0	23.8	0.4	24.0	0.8	24.2	0.8	24.4	0.8	24.6	0.8	24.7	0.4	24.8	0.4	25.1	1.2
1951	25.5	1.6	25.9	1.6	26.0	0.4	26.0	0.0	26.1	0.4	26.1	0.0	26.1	0.0	26.1	0.0	26.3	0.8	26.4	0.4	26.5	0.4	26.6	0.4
1952	26.6	0.0	26.5	-0.4	26.5	0.0	26.6	0.4	26.6	0.0	26.7	0.4	26.9	0.7	26.9	0.0	26.9	0.0	26.9	0.0	26.9	0.0	26.9	0.0
1953	26.8	-0.4	26.7	-0.4	26.7	0.0	26.8	0.4	26.8	0.0	26.9	0.4	27.0	0.4	27.1	0.4	27.1	0.0	27.2	0.4	27.1	-0.4	27.0	-0.4
1954	27.1	0.4	27.1	0.0	27.0	-0.4	27.0	0.0	27.1	0.4	27.1	0.0	27.1	0.0	27.1	0.0	27.0	-0.4	26.9	-0.4	27.0	0.4	26.9	-0.4
1955	26.9	0.0	26.9	0.0	26.9	0.0	26.9	0.0	26.9	0.0	26.9	0.0	27.0	0.4	26.9	-0.4	27.0	0.4	27.0	0.0	27.1	0.4	27.0	-0.4
1956	27.0	0.0	27.0	0.0	27.0	0.0	27.0	0.0	27.2	0.7	27.3	0.4	27.5	0.7	27.5	0.0	27.5	0.0	27.7	0.7	27.7	0.0	27.8	0.4
1957	27.8	0.0	27.9	0.4	28.0	0.4	28.1	0.4	28.1	0.0	28.3	0.7	28.4	0.4	28.5	0.4	28.5	0.0	28.5	0.0	28.6	0.4	28.6	0.0
1958	28.8	0.7	28.8	0.0	29.0	0.7	29.1	0.3	29.1	0.0	29.1	0.0	29.1	0.0	29.1	0.0	29.1	0.0	29.1	0.0	29.1	0.0	29.1	0.0

[Continued]

U.S. City Average
Consumer Price Index - Urban Wage Earners
Base 1982-1984 = 100
All Items
[Continued]

For 1913-2001. Columns headed % show percentile change in the index from the previous period for which an index is available.

Year	Jan Index	%	Feb Index	%	Mar Index	%	Apr Index	%	May Index	%	Jun Index	%	Jul Index	%	Aug Index	%	Sep Index	%	Oct Index	%	Nov Index	%	Dec Index	%
1959	29.1	0.0	29.1	0.0	29.1	0.0	29.1	0.0	29.2	0.3	29.3	0.3	29.4	0.3	29.3	-0.3	29.4	0.3	29.5	0.3	29.5	0.0	29.5	0.0
1960	29.5	0.0	29.5	0.0	29.5	0.0	29.7	0.7	29.7	0.0	29.8	0.3	29.8	0.0	29.8	0.0	29.8	0.0	29.9	0.3	30.0	0.3	30.0	0.0
1961	30.0	0.0	30.0	0.0	30.0	0.0	30.0	0.0	30.0	0.0	30.0	0.0	30.1	0.3	30.1	0.0	30.2	0.3	30.2	0.0	30.2	0.0	30.2	0.0
1962	30.2	0.0	30.2	0.0	30.3	0.3	30.4	0.3	30.4	0.0	30.4	0.0	30.4	0.3	30.4	0.0	30.6	0.7	30.6	0.0	30.6	0.0	30.6	0.0
1963	30.6	0.0	30.6	0.0	30.7	0.3	30.7	0.0	30.7	0.0	30.8	0.3	30.9	0.3	30.9	0.0	30.9	0.0	31.0	0.3	31.0	0.0	31.1	0.3
1964	31.1	0.0	31.1	0.0	31.1	0.0	31.1	0.0	31.1	0.0	31.2	0.3	31.3	0.3	31.2	-0.3	31.3	0.3	31.3	0.0	31.4	0.3	31.4	0.0
1965	31.4	0.0	31.4	0.0	31.5	0.3	31.6	0.3	31.6	0.0	31.8	0.6	31.8	0.0	31.8	0.0	31.8	0.0	31.9	0.3	31.9	0.0	32.0	0.3
1966	32.0	0.0	32.2	0.6	32.3	0.3	32.5	0.6	32.5	0.0	32.6	0.3	32.7	0.3	32.9	0.6	32.9	0.0	33.1	0.6	33.1	0.0	33.1	0.0
1967	33.1	0.0	33.1	0.0	33.2	0.3	33.3	0.3	33.4	0.3	33.5	0.3	33.6	0.3	33.7	0.3	33.8	0.3	33.9	0.3	34.0	0.3	34.1	0.3
1968	34.2	0.3	34.3	0.3	34.5	0.6	34.6	0.3	34.7	0.3	34.9	0.6	35.1	0.6	35.2	0.3	35.3	0.3	35.5	0.6	35.6	0.3	35.7	0.3
1969	35.8	0.3	36.0	0.6	36.3	0.8	36.5	0.6	36.6	0.3	36.8	0.5	37.0	0.5	37.2	0.5	37.3	0.3	37.5	0.5	37.7	0.5	37.9	0.5
1970	38.0	0.3	38.2	0.5	38.4	0.5	38.7	0.8	38.8	0.3	39.0	0.5	39.2	0.5	39.2	0.0	39.4	0.5	39.6	0.5	39.8	0.5	40.0	0.5
1971	40.0	0.0	40.1	0.2	40.2	0.2	40.4	0.5	40.6	0.5	40.8	0.5	40.9	0.2	41.0	0.2	41.0	0.0	41.1	0.2	41.2	0.2	41.3	0.2
1972	41.4	0.2	41.6	0.5	41.6	0.0	41.7	0.2	41.9	0.5	42.0	0.2	42.1	0.2	42.2	0.2	42.4	0.5	42.5	0.2	42.6	0.2	42.7	0.2
1973	42.9	0.5	43.2	0.7	43.6	0.9	43.9	0.7	44.1	0.5	44.4	0.7	44.5	0.2	45.4	2.0	45.5	0.2	45.9	0.9	46.2	0.7	46.5	0.6
1974	46.9	0.9	47.5	1.3	48.0	1.1	48.3	0.6	48.8	1.0	49.3	1.0	49.7	0.8	50.3	1.2	50.9	1.2	51.4	1.0	51.8	0.8	52.2	0.8
1975	52.4	0.4	52.8	0.8	53.0	0.4	53.2	0.4	53.5	0.6	53.9	0.7	54.5	1.1	54.7	0.4	54.9	0.4	55.3	0.7	55.6	0.5	55.8	0.4
1976	56.0	0.4	56.1	0.2	56.2	0.2	56.5	0.5	56.8	0.5	57.1	0.5	57.4	0.5	57.7	0.5	57.9	0.3	58.2	0.5	58.3	0.2	58.5	0.3
1977	58.9	0.7	59.5	1.0	59.8	0.5	60.3	0.8	60.6	0.5	61.0	0.7	61.3	0.5	61.5	0.3	61.8	0.5	61.9	0.2	62.2	0.5	62.5	0.5
1978	62.8	0.5	63.2	0.6	63.7	0.8	64.3	0.9	64.9	0.9	65.6	1.1	66.0	0.6	66.4	0.6	66.8	0.6	67.4	0.9	67.7	0.4	68.1	0.6
1979	68.7	0.9	69.5	1.2	70.3	1.2	71.1	1.1	71.9	1.1	72.8	1.3	73.7	1.2	74.4	0.9	75.1	0.9	75.7	0.8	76.4	0.9	77.2	1.0
1980	78.3	1.4	79.4	1.4	80.5	1.4	81.4	1.1	82.3	1.1	83.2	1.1	83.3	0.1	83.8	0.6	84.6	1.0	85.3	0.8	86.1	0.9	86.9	0.9
1981	87.5	0.7	88.5	1.1	89.0	0.6	89.6	0.7	90.3	0.8	91.1	0.9	92.2	1.2	92.8	0.7	93.7	1.0	93.9	0.2	94.1	0.2	94.4	0.3
1982	94.7	0.3	95.0	0.3	94.8	-0.2	95.2	0.4	96.2	1.1	97.4	1.2	98.0	0.6	98.2	0.2	98.3	0.1	98.6	0.3	98.4	-0.2	98.0	-0.4
1983	98.1	0.1	98.1	0.0	98.4	0.3	99.0	0.6	99.5	0.5	99.8	0.3	100.1	0.3	100.5	0.4	101.0	0.5	101.2	0.2	101.2	0.0	101.2	0.0
1984	101.6	0.4	101.8	0.2	101.8	0.0	102.1	0.3	102.5	0.4	102.8	0.3	103.2	0.4	104.2	1.0	104.8	0.6	104.8	0.0	104.7	-0.1	104.8	0.1
1985	104.9	0.1	105.4	0.5	105.9	0.5	106.3	0.4	106.7	0.4	107.0	0.3	107.1	0.1	107.3	0.2	107.6	0.3	107.9	0.3	108.3	0.4	108.6	0.3
1986	108.9	0.3	108.5	-0.4	107.9	-0.6	107.6	-0.3	107.9	0.3	108.4	0.5	108.4	0.0	108.6	0.2	109.1	0.5	109.1	0.0	109.2	0.1	109.3	0.1
1987	110.0	0.6	110.5	0.5	111.0	0.5	111.6	0.5	111.9	0.3	112.4	0.4	112.7	0.3	113.3	0.5	113.8	0.4	114.1	0.3	114.3	0.2	114.2	-0.1
1988	114.5	0.3	114.7	0.2	115.1	0.3	115.7	0.5	116.2	0.4	116.7	0.4	117.2	0.4	117.7	0.4	118.5	0.7	118.9	0.3	119.0	0.1	119.2	0.2
1989	119.7	0.4	120.2	0.4	120.8	0.5	121.8	0.8	122.5	0.6	122.8	0.2	123.2	0.3	123.2	0.0	123.6	0.3	124.2	0.5	124.4	0.2	124.6	0.2
1990	125.9	1.0	126.4	0.4	127.1	0.6	127.3	0.2	127.5	0.2	128.3	0.6	128.7	0.3	129.9	0.9	131.1	0.9	131.9	0.6	132.2	0.2	132.2	0.0
1991	132.8	0.5	132.8	0.0	133.0	0.2	133.3	0.2	133.8	0.4	134.1	0.2	134.3	0.1	134.6	0.2	135.2	0.4	135.4	0.1	135.8	0.3	135.9	0.1
1992	136.0	0.1	136.4	0.3	137.0	0.4	137.3	0.2	137.6	0.2	138.1	0.4	138.4	0.2	138.8	0.3	139.1	0.2	139.6	0.4	139.8	0.1	139.8	0.0
1993	140.3	0.4	140.7	0.3	141.1	0.3	141.6	0.4	141.9	0.2	142.0	0.1	142.1	0.1	142.4	0.2	142.6	0.1	143.3	0.5	143.4	0.1	143.3	-0.1
1994	143.6	0.2	144.0	0.3	144.4	0.3	144.7	0.2	144.9	0.1	145.4	0.3	145.8	0.3	146.5	0.5	146.9	0.3	147.0	0.1	147.3	0.2	147.2	-0.1
1995	147.8	0.4	148.3	0.3	148.7	0.3	149.3	0.4	149.6	0.2	149.9	0.2	149.9	0.0	150.2	0.2	150.6	0.3	151.0	0.3	150.9	-0.1	150.9	0.0
1996	151.7	0.5	152.2	0.3	152.9	0.5	153.6	0.5	154.0	0.3	154.1	0.1	154.3	0.1	154.5	0.1	155.1	0.4	155.5	0.3	155.9	0.3	155.9	0.0
1997	156.3	0.3	156.8	0.3	157.0	0.1	157.2	0.1	157.2	0.0	157.4	0.1	157.5	0.1	157.8	0.2	158.3	0.3	158.5	0.1	158.5	0.0	158.2	-0.2
1998	158.4	0.1	158.5	0.1	158.7	0.1	159.1	0.3	159.5	0.3	159.7	0.1	159.8	0.1	160.0	0.1	160.2	0.1	160.6	0.2	160.7	0.1	160.7	0.0
1999	161.0	0.2	161.1	0.1	161.4	0.2	162.7	0.8	162.8	0.1	162.8	0.0	163.3	0.3	163.8	0.3	164.7	0.5	165.0	0.2	165.1	0.1	165.1	0.0
2000	165.6	0.3	166.5	0.5	167.9	0.8	168.0	0.1	168.2	0.1	169.2	0.6	169.4	0.1	169.3	-0.1	170.4	0.6	170.6	0.1	170.9	0.2	170.7	-0.1
2001	171.7	0.6	172.4	0.4	172.6	0.1	173.5	0.5	174.4	0.5	174.6	0.1	173.8	-0.5	173.8	0.0	174.8	0.6	174.0	-0.5	173.7	-0.2	172.9	-0.5

Source: U.S. Department of Labor, Bureau of Labor Statistics, Division of Consumer Prices and Price Indexes.

U.S. City Average

Consumer Price Index - All Urban Consumers
Base 1982-1984 = 100

Food and Beverages

For 1967-2001. Columns headed % show percentile change in the index from the previous period for which an index is available.

Year	Jan Index	%	Feb Index	%	Mar Index	%	Apr Index	%	May Index	%	Jun Index	%	Jul Index	%	Aug Index	%	Sep Index	%	Oct Index	%	Nov Index	%	Dec Index	%
1967	34.8	-	34.7	-0.3	34.7	0.0	34.6	-0.3	34.6	0.0	34.9	0.9	35.2	0.9	35.4	0.6	35.2	-0.6	35.2	0.0	35.2	0.0	35.3	0.3
1968	35.6	0.8	35.7	0.3	35.8	0.3	36.0	0.6	36.1	0.3	36.2	0.3	36.4	0.6	36.6	0.5	36.6	0.0	36.7	0.3	36.6	-0.3	36.8	0.5
1969	37.0	0.5	37.0	0.0	37.2	0.5	37.4	0.5	37.5	0.3	38.0	1.3	38.4	1.1	38.6	0.5	38.7	0.3	38.6	-0.3	38.9	0.8	39.4	1.3
1970	39.6	0.5	39.8	0.5	39.8	0.0	40.0	0.5	40.1	0.2	40.2	0.2	40.4	0.5	40.4	0.0	40.4	0.0	40.4	0.0	40.2	-0.5	40.3	0.2
1971	40.4	0.2	40.5	0.2	40.9	1.0	41.2	0.7	41.3	0.2	41.6	0.7	41.8	0.5	41.9	0.2	41.6	-0.7	41.6	0.0	41.6	0.0	42.0	1.0
1972	42.0	0.0	42.6	1.4	42.7	0.2	42.7	0.0	42.7	0.0	42.9	0.5	43.3	0.9	43.4	0.2	43.5	0.2	43.5	0.0	43.7	0.5	43.9	0.5
1973	44.7	1.8	45.5	1.8	46.6	2.4	47.2	1.3	47.7	1.1	48.3	1.3	48.7	0.8	51.3	5.3	51.0	-0.6	51.0	0.0	51.6	1.2	52.0	0.8
1974	52.8	1.5	54.0	2.3	54.5	0.9	54.4	-0.2	54.8	0.7	55.0	0.4	55.1	0.2	55.9	1.5	56.7	1.4	57.1	0.7	57.6	0.9	58.3	1.2
1975	58.7	0.7	58.9	0.3	58.9	0.0	58.8	-0.2	59.0	0.3	59.9	1.5	61.2	2.2	61.1	-0.2	61.0	-0.2	61.4	0.7	61.6	0.3	61.9	0.5
1976	61.9	0.0	61.7	-0.3	61.3	-0.6	61.5	0.3	61.8	0.5	62.1	0.5	62.5	0.6	62.6	0.2	62.3	-0.5	62.4	0.2	62.2	-0.3	62.4	0.3
1977	62.9	0.8	64.3	2.2	64.6	0.5	65.3	1.1	65.6	0.5	66.2	0.9	66.5	0.5	66.7	0.3	66.5	-0.3	66.5	0.0	66.9	0.6	67.1	0.3
1978	68.1	1.5	69.0	1.3	69.8	1.2	70.9	1.6	71.8	1.3	72.9	1.5	73.4	0.7	73.5	0.1	73.6	0.1	74.0	0.5	74.3	0.4	74.9	0.8
1979	76.4	2.0	77.8	1.8	78.5	0.9	79.2	0.9	79.8	0.8	80.2	0.5	80.7	0.6	80.5	-0.2	80.8	0.4	81.2	0.5	81.5	0.4	82.4	1.1
1980	83.1	0.8	83.5	0.5	84.3	1.0	84.9	0.7	85.4	0.6	85.9	0.6	86.9	1.2	88.1	1.4	88.9	0.9	89.4	0.6	90.0	0.7	90.7	0.8
1981	91.4	0.8	92.2	0.9	92.7	0.5	92.9	0.2	92.8	-0.1	93.2	0.4	94.1	1.0	94.5	0.4	94.7	0.2	94.5	-0.2	94.4	-0.1	94.6	0.2
1982	95.7	1.2	96.5	0.8	96.4	-0.1	96.7	0.3	97.3	0.6	98.0	0.7	98.2	0.2	97.9	-0.3	98.0	0.1	97.8	-0.2	97.6	-0.2	97.6	0.0
1983	98.2	0.6	98.5	0.3	99.1	0.6	99.6	0.5	99.7	0.1	99.6	-0.1	99.6	0.0	99.7	0.1	99.8	0.1	99.9	0.1	99.8	-0.1	100.2	0.4
1984	102.0	1.8	102.9	0.9	102.9	0.0	103.0	0.1	102.7	-0.3	102.9	0.2	103.3	0.4	103.9	0.6	103.7	-0.2	103.7	0.0	103.6	-0.1	104.0	0.4
1985	104.7	0.7	105.4	0.7	105.5	0.1	105.5	0.0	105.3	-0.2	105.4	0.1	105.5	0.1	105.6	0.1	105.7	0.1	105.8	0.1	106.2	0.4	106.9	0.7
1986	107.7	0.7	107.6	-0.1	107.7	0.1	107.9	0.2	108.2	0.3	108.3	0.1	109.2	0.8	110.0	0.7	110.2	0.2	110.4	0.2	110.7	0.3	110.9	0.2
1987	112.1	1.1	112.5	0.4	112.5	0.0	112.8	0.3	113.3	0.4	113.8	0.4	113.7	-0.1	113.8	0.1	114.2	0.4	114.3	0.1	114.3	0.0	114.8	0.4
1988	115.7	0.8	115.8	0.1	116.0	0.2	116.7	0.6	117.1	0.3	117.6	0.4	118.8	1.0	119.4	0.5	120.1	0.6	120.3	0.2	120.2	-0.1	120.6	0.3
1989	122.0	1.2	122.7	0.6	123.3	0.5	124.0	0.6	124.7	0.6	124.9	0.2	125.4	0.4	125.6	0.2	125.9	0.2	126.3	0.3	126.7	0.3	127.2	0.4
1990	130.0	2.2	130.9	0.7	131.2	0.2	131.0	-0.2	131.1	0.1	131.7	0.5	132.4	0.5	132.7	0.2	133.0	0.2	133.4	0.3	133.7	0.2	133.9	0.1
1991	135.9	1.5	136.0	0.1	136.3	0.2	137.2	0.7	137.3	0.1	137.7	0.3	137.1	-0.4	136.6	-0.4	136.7	0.1	136.5	-0.1	136.9	0.3	137.3	0.3
1992	137.9	0.4	138.1	0.1	138.8	0.5	138.8	0.0	138.3	-0.4	138.3	0.0	138.1	-0.1	138.8	0.5	139.3	0.4	139.2	-0.1	139.1	-0.1	139.5	0.3
1993	140.5	0.7	140.7	0.1	140.9	0.1	141.4	0.4	141.8	0.3	141.1	-0.5	141.1	0.0	141.5	0.3	141.8	0.2	142.3	0.4	142.6	0.2	143.3	0.5
1994	144.3	0.7	143.6	-0.5	143.9	0.2	144.0	0.1	144.1	0.1	144.2	0.1	144.8	0.4	145.3	0.3	145.6	0.2	145.6	0.0	145.9	0.2	147.2	0.9
1995	147.9	0.5	147.8	-0.1	147.9	0.1	148.9	0.7	148.7	-0.1	148.4	-0.2	148.6	0.1	148.9	0.2	149.4	0.3	149.8	0.3	149.8	0.0	150.3	0.3
1996	151.4	0.7	151.3	-0.1	152.1	0.5	152.7	0.4	152.5	-0.1	153.1	0.4	153.6	0.3	154.2	0.4	155.0	0.5	155.8	0.5	156.2	0.3	156.6	0.3
1997	156.9	0.2	156.9	0.0	157.1	0.1	157.1	0.0	157.1	0.0	157.1	0.0	157.5	0.3	158.1	0.4	158.4	0.2	158.7	0.2	158.9	0.1	159.1	0.1
1998	160.3	0.8	159.8	-0.3	160.1	0.2	160.2	0.1	160.7	0.3	160.6	-0.1	160.9	0.2	161.4	0.3	161.5	0.1	162.4	0.6	162.5	0.1	162.7	0.1
1999	163.9	0.7	163.8	-0.1	163.7	-0.1	163.9	0.1	164.2	0.2	164.1	-0.1	164.2	0.1	164.7	0.3	165.1	0.2	165.5	0.2	165.7	0.1	165.9	0.1
2000	166.6	0.4	166.8	0.1	167.1	0.2	167.2	0.1	167.8	0.4	167.9	0.1	168.7	0.5	169.2	0.3	169.4	0.1	169.6	0.1	169.5	-0.1	170.5	0.6
2001	171.4	0.5	171.8	0.2	172.2	0.2	172.4	0.1	172.9	0.3	173.4	0.3	174.0	0.3	174.4	0.2	174.6	0.1	175.3	0.4	175.2	-0.1	175.2	0.0

Source: U.S. Department of Labor, Bureau of Labor Statistics, Division of Consumer Prices and Price Indexes.

U.S. City Average
Consumer Price Index - Urban Wage Earners
Base 1982-1984 = 100
Food and Beverages

For 1967-2001. Columns headed % show percentile change in the index from the previous period for which an index is available.

Year	Jan Index	%	Feb Index	%	Mar Index	%	Apr Index	%	May Index	%	Jun Index	%	Jul Index	%	Aug Index	%	Sep Index	%	Oct Index	%	Nov Index	%	Dec Index	%
1967	34.8	-	34.6	-0.6	34.6	0.0	34.5	-0.3	34.6	0.3	34.9	0.9	35.2	0.9	35.4	0.6	35.2	-0.6	35.1	-0.3	35.1	0.0	35.3	0.6
1968	35.5	0.6	35.7	0.6	35.8	0.3	35.9	0.3	36.0	0.3	36.1	0.3	36.4	0.8	36.6	0.5	36.5	-0.3	36.7	0.5	36.6	-0.3	36.8	0.5
1969	37.0	0.5	37.0	0.0	37.2	0.5	37.4	0.5	37.5	0.3	38.0	1.3	38.3	0.8	38.6	0.8	38.6	0.0	38.6	0.0	38.8	0.5	39.3	1.3
1970	39.6	0.8	39.8	0.5	39.8	0.0	39.9	0.3	40.1	0.5	40.2	0.2	40.4	0.5	40.4	0.0	40.4	0.0	40.3	-0.2	40.2	-0.2	40.3	0.2
1971	40.4	0.2	40.5	0.2	40.9	1.0	41.1	0.5	41.3	0.5	41.6	0.7	41.8	0.5	41.9	0.2	41.6	-0.7	41.5	-0.2	41.6	0.2	42.0	1.0
1972	42.0	0.0	42.6	1.4	42.7	0.2	42.7	0.0	42.7	0.0	42.9	0.5	43.3	0.9	43.4	0.2	43.5	0.2	43.5	0.0	43.7	0.5	43.9	0.5
1973	44.7	1.8	45.5	1.8	46.6	2.4	47.2	1.3	47.6	0.8	48.3	1.5	48.6	0.6	51.3	5.6	51.0	-0.6	51.0	0.0	51.5	1.0	52.0	1.0
1974	52.7	1.3	54.0	2.5	54.5	0.9	54.4	-0.2	54.7	0.6	55.0	0.5	55.1	0.2	55.9	1.5	56.7	1.4	57.0	0.5	57.6	1.1	58.2	1.0
1975	58.6	0.7	58.9	0.5	58.8	-0.2	58.8	0.0	59.0	0.3	59.8	1.4	61.1	2.2	61.0	-0.2	60.9	-0.2	61.3	0.7	61.5	0.3	61.9	0.7
1976	61.9	0.0	61.7	-0.3	61.3	-0.6	61.5	0.3	61.7	0.3	62.0	0.5	62.4	0.6	62.5	0.2	62.3	-0.3	62.3	0.0	62.1	-0.3	62.4	0.5
1977	62.9	0.8	64.2	2.1	64.5	0.5	65.3	1.2	65.5	0.3	66.2	1.1	66.5	0.5	66.7	0.3	66.5	-0.3	66.4	-0.2	66.8	0.6	67.1	0.4
1978	68.0	1.3	68.9	1.3	69.6	1.0	70.7	1.6	71.7	1.4	72.8	1.5	73.2	0.5	73.4	0.3	73.4	0.0	73.9	0.7	74.2	0.4	74.8	0.8
1979	76.3	2.0	77.8	2.0	78.7	1.2	79.2	0.6	79.8	0.8	80.1	0.4	80.7	0.7	80.5	-0.2	80.8	0.4	81.2	0.5	81.5	0.4	82.4	1.1
1980	83.1	0.8	83.5	0.5	84.3	1.0	85.0	0.8	85.5	0.6	86.1	0.7	87.1	1.2	88.3	1.4	89.2	1.0	89.7	0.6	90.4	0.8	91.0	0.7
1981	91.6	0.7	92.4	0.9	92.8	0.4	93.0	0.2	92.9	-0.1	93.3	0.4	94.2	1.0	94.6	0.4	94.7	0.1	94.6	-0.1	94.5	-0.1	94.6	0.1
1982	95.7	1.2	96.5	0.8	96.4	-0.1	96.7	0.3	97.3	0.6	98.0	0.7	98.3	0.3	97.9	-0.4	98.0	0.1	97.8	-0.2	97.7	-0.1	97.7	0.0
1983	98.2	0.5	98.6	0.4	99.1	0.5	99.6	0.5	99.8	0.2	99.6	-0.2	99.6	0.0	99.6	0.0	99.8	0.2	99.9	0.1	99.8	-0.1	100.2	0.4
1984	102.0	1.8	102.9	0.9	102.9	0.0	103.0	0.1	102.7	-0.3	102.9	0.2	103.2	0.3	103.8	0.6	103.6	-0.2	103.6	0.0	103.5	-0.1	103.8	0.3
1985	104.5	0.7	105.3	0.8	105.4	0.1	105.3	-0.1	105.1	-0.2	105.3	0.2	105.3	0.0	105.4	0.1	105.5	0.1	105.6	0.1	106.0	0.4	106.7	0.7
1986	107.5	0.7	107.5	0.0	107.5	0.0	107.8	0.3	108.0	0.2	108.1	0.1	109.0	0.8	109.9	0.8	110.1	0.2	110.2	0.1	110.5	0.3	110.7	0.2
1987	111.9	1.1	112.3	0.4	112.3	0.0	112.6	0.3	113.1	0.4	113.6	0.4	113.5	-0.1	113.6	0.1	114.0	0.4	114.1	0.1	114.1	0.0	114.5	0.4
1988	115.4	0.8	115.5	0.1	115.7	0.2	116.3	0.5	116.8	0.4	117.4	0.5	118.5	0.9	119.1	0.5	119.8	0.6	120.0	0.2	119.9	-0.1	120.3	0.3
1989	121.7	1.2	122.4	0.6	123.1	0.6	123.7	0.5	124.4	0.6	124.6	0.2	125.1	0.4	125.3	0.2	125.6	0.2	126.0	0.3	126.4	0.3	126.9	0.4
1990	129.7	2.2	130.6	0.7	130.9	0.2	130.7	-0.2	130.7	0.0	131.5	0.6	132.1	0.5	132.4	0.2	132.7	0.2	133.1	0.3	133.5	0.3	133.6	0.1
1991	135.6	1.5	135.7	0.1	136.1	0.3	136.9	0.6	137.0	0.1	137.4	0.3	136.8	-0.4	136.4	-0.3	136.5	0.1	136.2	-0.2	136.5	0.2	136.9	0.3
1992	137.4	0.4	137.8	0.3	138.4	0.4	138.5	0.1	137.9	-0.4	137.9	0.0	137.8	-0.1	138.5	0.5	138.9	0.3	138.8	-0.1	138.8	0.0	139.1	0.2
1993	140.1	0.7	140.2	0.1	140.5	0.2	140.9	0.3	141.4	0.4	140.8	-0.4	140.8	0.0	141.2	0.3	141.5	0.2	142.0	0.4	142.2	0.1	142.9	0.5
1994	143.8	0.6	143.2	-0.4	143.4	0.1	143.6	0.1	143.7	0.1	143.8	0.1	144.4	0.4	144.9	0.3	145.1	0.1	145.1	0.0	145.3	0.1	146.6	0.9
1995	147.2	0.4	147.3	0.1	147.3	0.0	148.3	0.7	148.1	-0.1	147.8	-0.2	148.0	0.1	148.3	0.2	148.9	0.4	149.3	0.3	149.3	0.0	149.8	0.3
1996	150.8	0.7	150.7	-0.1	151.5	0.5	152.2	0.5	151.9	-0.2	152.6	0.5	153.1	0.3	153.7	0.4	154.5	0.5	155.2	0.5	155.7	0.3	156.1	0.3
1997	156.4	0.2	156.4	0.0	156.5	0.1	156.5	0.0	156.6	0.1	156.6	0.0	157.0	0.3	157.6	0.4	157.8	0.1	158.1	0.2	158.3	0.1	158.5	0.1
1998	159.6	0.7	159.2	-0.3	159.4	0.1	159.5	0.1	159.9	0.3	159.9	0.0	160.2	0.2	160.7	0.3	160.8	0.1	161.6	0.5	161.7	0.1	161.9	0.1
1999	163.1	0.7	163.0	-0.1	162.9	-0.1	163.0	0.1	163.3	0.2	163.3	0.0	163.4	0.1	163.9	0.3	164.3	0.2	164.7	0.2	164.9	0.1	165.2	0.2
2000	165.9	0.4	166.1	0.1	166.4	0.2	166.5	0.1	167.2	0.4	167.3	0.1	168.0	0.4	168.6	0.4	168.8	0.1	169.0	0.1	168.8	-0.1	169.8	0.6
2001	170.8	0.6	171.2	0.2	171.6	0.2	171.9	0.2	172.3	0.2	172.8	0.3	173.4	0.3	173.8	0.2	174.0	0.1	174.8	0.5	174.5	-0.2	174.6	0.1

Source: U.S. Department of Labor, Bureau of Labor Statistics, Division of Consumer Prices and Price Indexes.

U.S. City Average
Consumer Price Index - All Urban Consumers
Base 1982-1984 = 100
Housing

For 1967-2001. Columns headed % show percentile change in the index from the previous period for which an index is available.

Year	Jan Index	%	Feb Index	%	Mar Index	%	Apr Index	%	May Index	%	Jun Index	%	Jul Index	%	Aug Index	%	Sep Index	%	Oct Index	%	Nov Index	%	Dec Index	%
1967	30.5	-	30.5	0.0	30.5	0.0	30.6	0.3	30.7	0.3	30.7	0.0	30.8	0.3	30.9	0.3	30.9	0.0	31.0	0.3	31.1	0.3	31.2	0.3
1968	31.3	0.3	31.5	0.6	31.5	0.0	31.6	0.3	31.7	0.3	31.9	0.6	32.1	0.6	32.3	0.6	32.4	0.3	32.5	0.3	32.7	0.6	32.9	0.6
1969	32.9	0.0	33.1	0.6	33.4	0.9	33.6	0.6	33.8	0.6	33.9	0.3	34.1	0.6	34.3	0.6	34.5	0.6	34.6	0.3	34.8	0.6	35.0	0.6
1970	35.1	0.3	35.4	0.9	35.8	1.1	36.0	0.6	36.2	0.6	36.3	0.3	36.5	0.6	36.7	0.5	36.9	0.5	37.1	0.5	37.3	0.5	37.5	0.5
1971	37.5	0.0	37.5	0.0	37.4	-0.3	37.4	0.0	37.7	0.8	37.9	0.5	38.1	0.5	38.2	0.3	38.3	0.3	38.5	0.5	38.6	0.3	38.7	0.3
1972	38.9	0.5	39.0	0.3	39.1	0.3	39.2	0.3	39.3	0.3	39.4	0.3	39.5	0.3	39.7	0.5	39.8	0.3	39.8	0.0	39.9	0.3	40.1	0.5
1973	40.1	0.0	40.3	0.5	40.4	0.2	40.5	0.2	40.7	0.5	40.8	0.2	40.9	0.2	41.2	0.7	41.6	1.0	42.1	1.2	42.5	1.0	42.8	0.7
1974	43.3	1.2	43.7	0.9	44.1	0.9	44.5	0.9	44.9	0.9	45.4	1.1	45.9	1.1	46.5	1.3	47.1	1.3	47.6	1.1	48.1	1.1	48.6	1.0
1975	49.0	0.8	49.5	1.0	49.7	0.4	50.0	0.6	50.2	0.4	50.5	0.6	50.7	0.4	50.9	0.4	51.3	0.8	51.5	0.4	52.0	1.0	52.3	0.6
1976	52.6	0.6	52.7	0.2	53.0	0.6	53.1	0.2	53.3	0.4	53.5	0.4	53.9	0.7	54.1	0.4	54.4	0.6	54.6	0.4	54.8	0.4	55.1	0.5
1977	55.5	0.7	55.9	0.7	56.2	0.5	56.6	0.7	56.8	0.4	57.3	0.9	57.7	0.7	58.0	0.5	58.4	0.7	58.6	0.3	58.9	0.5	59.2	0.5
1978	59.7	0.8	60.0	0.5	60.6	1.0	61.1	0.8	61.6	0.8	62.2	1.0	62.8	1.0	63.2	0.6	63.9	1.1	64.5	0.9	64.9	0.6	65.1	0.3
1979	65.6	0.8	66.4	1.2	67.0	0.9	67.7	1.0	68.5	1.2	69.4	1.3	70.3	1.3	71.3	1.4	72.2	1.3	73.2	1.4	74.1	1.2	75.0	1.2
1980	76.2	1.6	77.1	1.2	78.4	1.7	79.4	1.3	80.6	1.5	82.1	1.9	81.6	-0.6	81.8	0.2	82.4	0.7	83.5	1.3	84.3	1.0	85.3	1.2
1981	85.9	0.7	86.5	0.7	87.0	0.6	87.7	0.8	88.8	1.3	90.0	1.4	91.5	1.7	92.3	0.9	93.5	1.3	93.5	0.0	93.7	0.2	94.0	0.3
1982	94.3	0.3	94.6	0.3	94.4	-0.2	95.3	1.0	96.6	1.4	97.8	1.2	98.3	0.5	98.6	0.3	98.4	-0.2	98.8	0.4	98.2	-0.6	97.4	-0.8
1983	97.9	0.5	98.1	0.2	98.1	0.0	98.6	0.5	99.1	0.5	99.5	0.4	99.9	0.4	100.0	0.1	100.5	0.5	100.6	0.1	100.7	0.1	100.8	0.1
1984	101.4	0.6	101.9	0.5	102.1	0.2	102.6	0.5	103.0	0.4	103.5	0.5	104.1	0.6	104.5	0.4	105.1	0.6	105.1	0.0	105.0	-0.1	105.1	0.1
1985	105.3	0.2	105.8	0.5	106.1	0.3	106.5	0.4	107.3	0.8	107.9	0.6	108.3	0.4	108.7	0.4	108.9	0.2	109.1	0.2	109.3	0.2	109.6	0.3
1986	109.9	0.3	109.8	-0.1	109.9	0.1	110.2	0.3	110.4	0.2	111.2	0.7	111.3	0.1	111.6	0.3	112.0	0.4	111.8	-0.2	111.4	-0.4	111.5	0.1
1987	112.0	0.4	112.4	0.4	112.8	0.4	113.2	0.4	113.6	0.4	114.3	0.6	114.7	0.3	115.4	0.6	115.6	0.2	115.5	-0.1	115.5	0.0	115.6	0.1
1988	116.2	0.5	116.6	0.3	117.0	0.3	117.3	0.3	117.7	0.3	118.6	0.8	119.1	0.4	119.5	0.3	119.9	0.3	119.9	0.0	119.9	0.0	120.2	0.3
1989	120.7	0.4	121.1	0.3	121.5	0.3	121.6	0.1	122.1	0.4	122.9	0.7	123.9	0.8	124.2	0.2	124.3	0.1	124.4	0.1	124.5	0.1	124.9	0.3
1990	125.9	0.8	126.1	0.2	126.8	0.6	126.8	0.0	127.1	0.2	128.3	0.9	129.2	0.7	130.2	0.8	130.5	0.2	130.6	0.1	130.4	-0.2	130.5	0.1
1991	131.8	1.0	132.4	0.5	132.6	0.2	132.5	-0.1	132.8	0.2	133.4	0.5	134.2	0.6	134.5	0.2	134.7	0.1	134.7	0.0	134.7	0.0	135.0	0.2
1992	135.7	0.5	136.1	0.3	136.6	0.4	136.5	-0.1	136.7	0.1	137.7	0.7	138.3	0.4	138.6	0.2	138.4	-0.1	138.5	0.1	138.5	0.0	138.5	0.0
1993	139.3	0.6	139.7	0.3	140.2	0.4	140.4	0.1	140.5	0.1	141.5	0.7	141.9	0.3	142.3	0.3	142.3	0.0	142.2	-0.1	142.0	-0.1	142.3	0.2
1994	142.9	0.4	143.7	0.6	144.1	0.3	143.9	-0.1	144.1	0.1	144.9	0.6	145.4	0.3	145.9	0.3	145.8	-0.1	145.7	-0.1	145.5	-0.1	145.4	-0.1
1995	146.4	0.7	147.0	0.4	147.4	0.3	147.4	0.0	147.6	0.1	148.5	0.6	149.2	0.5	149.6	0.3	149.5	-0.1	149.7	0.1	149.4	-0.2	149.7	0.2
1996	150.6	0.6	151.2	0.4	151.7	0.3	151.8	0.1	152.0	0.1	152.7	0.5	153.6	0.6	154.0	0.3	153.9	-0.1	154.0	0.1	153.9	-0.1	154.0	0.1
1997	155.1	0.7	155.8	0.5	155.9	0.1	155.8	-0.1	155.9	0.1	156.9	0.6	157.5	0.4	157.6	0.1	157.7	0.1	157.7	0.0	157.7	0.0	157.7	0.0
1998	158.3	0.4	158.8	0.3	159.2	0.3	159.5	0.2	159.7	0.1	160.6	0.6	161.2	0.4	161.5	0.2	161.5	0.0	161.4	-0.1	161.3	-0.1	161.3	0.0
1999	161.8	0.3	162.3	0.3	162.8	0.3	163.0	0.1	163.0	0.0	164.1	0.7	164.7	0.4	165.0	0.2	165.2	0.1	165.0	-0.1	164.9	-0.1	164.8	-0.1
2000	166.0	0.7	167.1	0.7	167.8	0.4	167.9	0.1	168.1	0.1	169.6	0.9	170.6	0.6	170.9	0.2	171.4	0.3	171.7	0.2	171.6	-0.1	171.9	0.2
2001	174.1	1.3	174.7	0.3	175.4	0.4	175.4	0.0	175.9	0.3	177.3	0.8	177.6	0.2	178.0	0.2	177.4	-0.3	176.7	-0.4	176.9	0.1	176.9	0.0

Source: U.S. Department of Labor, Bureau of Labor Statistics, Division of Consumer Prices and Price Indexes.

U.S. City Average
Consumer Price Index - Urban Wage Earners
Base 1982-1984 = 100
Housing

For 1967-2001. Columns headed % show percentile change in the index from the previous period for which an index is available.

Year	Jan Index	%	Feb Index	%	Mar Index	%	Apr Index	%	May Index	%	Jun Index	%	Jul Index	%	Aug Index	%	Sep Index	%	Oct Index	%	Nov Index	%	Dec Index	%
1967	30.7	-	30.8	0.3	30.8	0.0	30.9	0.3	31.0	0.3	31.0	0.0	31.1	0.3	31.1	0.0	31.2	0.3	31.3	0.3	31.3	0.0	31.5	0.6
1968	31.6	0.3	31.7	0.3	31.8	0.3	31.9	0.3	32.0	0.3	32.2	0.6	32.4	0.6	32.6	0.6	32.6	0.0	32.8	0.6	33.0	0.6	33.1	0.3
1969	33.2	0.3	33.4	0.6	33.7	0.9	33.9	0.6	34.1	0.6	34.2	0.3	34.4	0.6	34.6	0.6	34.8	0.6	34.9	0.3	35.1	0.6	35.3	0.6
1970	35.4	0.3	35.7	0.8	36.1	1.1	36.3	0.6	36.5	0.6	36.6	0.3	36.8	0.5	37.0	0.5	37.2	0.5	37.4	0.5	37.6	0.5	37.8	0.5
1971	37.8	0.0	37.8	0.0	37.7	-0.3	37.8	0.3	38.0	0.5	38.2	0.5	38.4	0.5	38.5	0.3	38.7	0.5	38.8	0.3	38.9	0.3	39.1	0.5
1972	39.2	0.3	39.3	0.3	39.4	0.3	39.5	0.3	39.6	0.3	39.7	0.3	39.9	0.5	40.0	0.3	40.1	0.2	40.2	0.2	40.3	0.2	40.4	0.2
1973	40.5	0.2	40.6	0.2	40.7	0.2	40.9	0.5	41.0	0.2	41.2	0.5	41.3	0.2	41.6	0.7	42.0	1.0	42.5	1.2	42.8	0.7	43.2	0.9
1974	43.7	1.2	44.1	0.9	44.5	0.9	44.8	0.7	45.3	1.1	45.8	1.1	46.3	1.1	46.9	1.3	47.5	1.3	48.0	1.1	48.5	1.0	49.0	1.0
1975	49.4	0.8	49.9	1.0	50.1	0.4	50.5	0.8	50.7	0.4	51.0	0.6	51.2	0.4	51.4	0.4	51.7	0.6	52.0	0.6	52.5	1.0	52.7	0.4
1976	53.0	0.6	53.2	0.4	53.4	0.4	53.5	0.2	53.7	0.4	54.0	0.6	54.3	0.6	54.6	0.6	54.9	0.5	55.1	0.4	55.3	0.4	55.5	0.4
1977	56.0	0.9	56.3	0.5	56.7	0.7	57.1	0.7	57.3	0.4	57.8	0.9	58.2	0.7	58.5	0.5	58.9	0.7	59.1	0.3	59.4	0.5	59.8	0.7
1978	60.2	0.7	60.6	0.7	61.1	0.8	61.5	0.7	62.1	1.0	62.7	1.0	63.2	0.8	63.6	0.6	64.3	1.1	64.9	0.9	65.3	0.6	65.6	0.5
1979	66.1	0.8	66.9	1.2	67.6	1.0	68.2	0.9	69.0	1.2	70.0	1.4	70.9	1.3	71.9	1.4	72.8	1.3	73.8	1.4	74.8	1.4	75.7	1.2
1980	76.8	1.5	77.8	1.3	79.0	1.5	80.1	1.4	81.3	1.5	82.9	2.0	82.3	-0.7	82.6	0.4	83.1	0.6	84.2	1.3	85.0	1.0	86.1	1.3
1981	86.7	0.7	87.2	0.6	87.6	0.5	88.3	0.8	89.5	1.4	90.7	1.3	92.2	1.7	93.1	1.0	94.3	1.3	94.2	-0.1	94.4	0.2	94.6	0.2
1982	94.9	0.3	95.3	0.4	95.1	-0.2	96.0	0.9	97.4	1.5	98.6	1.2	99.2	0.6	99.5	0.3	99.4	-0.1	99.8	0.4	99.3	-0.5	98.4	-0.9
1983	98.5	0.1	98.6	0.1	99.1	0.5	99.5	0.4	99.8	0.3	100.1	0.3	100.3	0.2	100.7	0.4	101.0	0.3	101.0	0.0	100.8	-0.2	100.7	-0.1
1984	100.8	0.1	100.7	-0.1	100.3	-0.4	100.2	-0.1	101.0	0.8	101.3	0.3	102.1	0.8	103.8	1.7	104.6	0.8	104.2	-0.4	103.9	-0.3	104.0	0.1
1985	104.3	0.3	104.7	0.4	105.0	0.3	105.4	0.4	106.3	0.9	106.8	0.5	107.2	0.4	107.5	0.3	107.8	0.3	107.9	0.1	108.2	0.3	108.4	0.2
1986	108.7	0.3	108.6	-0.1	108.7	0.1	109.0	0.3	109.2	0.2	110.0	0.7	110.1	0.1	110.4	0.3	110.8	0.4	110.4	-0.4	110.0	-0.4	110.2	0.2
1987	110.7	0.5	111.0	0.3	111.4	0.4	111.8	0.4	112.2	0.4	112.9	0.6	113.2	0.3	114.0	0.7	114.1	0.1	114.0	-0.1	113.9	-0.1	114.1	0.2
1988	114.6	0.4	115.0	0.3	115.4	0.3	115.6	0.2	116.0	0.3	116.9	0.8	117.4	0.4	117.8	0.3	118.2	0.3	118.2	0.0	118.3	0.1	118.5	0.2
1989	119.0	0.4	119.3	0.3	119.6	0.3	119.8	0.2	120.3	0.4	121.1	0.7	122.1	0.8	122.4	0.2	122.5	0.1	122.5	0.0	122.7	0.2	123.1	0.3
1990	123.9	0.6	124.1	0.2	124.7	0.5	124.7	0.0	125.1	0.3	126.2	0.9	127.0	0.6	127.9	0.7	128.3	0.3	128.3	0.0	128.2	-0.1	128.3	0.1
1991	129.4	0.9	130.0	0.5	130.2	0.2	130.1	-0.1	130.5	0.3	131.1	0.5	131.8	0.5	132.0	0.2	132.4	0.3	132.3	-0.1	132.4	0.1	132.7	0.2
1992	133.3	0.5	133.6	0.2	134.0	0.3	133.9	-0.1	134.1	0.1	135.1	0.7	135.7	0.4	135.9	0.1	135.8	-0.1	135.9	0.1	136.0	0.1	136.1	0.1
1993	136.7	0.4	137.0	0.2	137.4	0.3	137.7	0.2	137.9	0.1	138.8	0.7	139.1	0.2	139.5	0.3	139.7	0.1	139.6	-0.1	139.4	-0.1	139.7	0.2
1994	140.2	0.4	140.9	0.5	141.3	0.3	141.1	-0.1	141.3	0.1	142.1	0.6	142.5	0.3	143.0	0.4	143.0	0.0	142.8	-0.1	142.7	-0.1	142.7	0.0
1995	143.5	0.6	144.0	0.3	144.3	0.2	144.4	0.1	144.6	0.1	145.5	0.6	146.1	0.4	146.5	0.3	146.5	0.0	146.6	0.1	146.4	-0.1	146.7	0.2
1996	147.5	0.5	148.0	0.3	148.5	0.3	148.6	0.1	148.9	0.2	149.6	0.5	150.4	0.5	150.7	0.2	150.8	0.1	150.7	-0.1	150.7	0.0	151.0	0.2
1997	151.8	0.5	152.4	0.4	152.5	0.1	152.4	-0.1	152.6	0.1	153.6	0.7	154.1	0.3	154.2	0.1	154.4	0.1	154.4	0.0	154.5	0.1	154.4	-0.1
1998	154.8	0.3	155.1	0.2	155.5	0.3	155.8	0.2	156.1	0.2	157.0	0.6	157.6	0.4	157.7	0.1	157.8	0.1	157.6	-0.1	157.7	0.1	157.8	0.1
1999	158.1	0.2	158.4	0.2	158.8	0.3	159.1	0.2	159.2	0.1	160.2	0.6	160.7	0.3	161.0	0.2	161.3	0.2	161.0	-0.2	161.1	0.1	161.1	0.0
2000	162.0	0.6	162.9	0.6	163.4	0.3	163.6	0.1	163.9	0.2	165.5	1.0	166.4	0.5	166.6	0.1	167.3	0.4	167.5	0.1	167.6	0.1	168.1	0.3
2001	170.2	1.2	170.5	0.2	171.0	0.3	171.0	0.0	171.7	0.4	173.0	0.8	173.3	0.2	173.5	0.1	173.2	-0.2	172.5	-0.4	172.8	0.2	172.9	0.1

Source: U.S. Department of Labor, Bureau of Labor Statistics, Division of Consumer Prices and Price Indexes.

U.S. City Average
Consumer Price Index - All Urban Consumers
Base 1982-1984 = 100
Apparel

For 1913-2001. Columns headed % show percentile change in the index from the previous period for which an index is available.

Year	Jan Index	%	Feb Index	%	Mar Index	%	Apr Index	%	May Index	%	Jun Index	%	Jul Index	%	Aug Index	%	Sep Index	%	Oct Index	%	Nov Index	%	Dec Index	%
1913	-	-	-	-	-	-	-	-	-	-	-	-	-	-	-	-	-	-	-	-	-	-	15.0	-
1914	-	-	-	-	-	-	-	-	-	-	-	-	-	-	-	-	-	-	-	-	-	-	15.6	4.0
1915	-	-	-	-	-	-	-	-	-	-	-	-	-	-	-	-	-	-	-	-	-	-	17.9	14.7
1916	-	-	-	-	-	-	-	-	-	-	-	-	-	-	-	-	-	-	-	-	-	-	22.2	24.0
1917	-	-	-	-	-	-	-	-	-	-	-	-	-	-	-	-	-	-	-	-	-	-	31.8	43.2
1918	-	-	-	-	-	-	-	-	-	-	-	-	-	-	-	-	-	-	-	-	-	-	42.6	23.8
1919	-	-	-	-	-	-	-	-	-	-	34.4	8.2	-	-	-	-	-	-	-	-	-	-	40.3	-10.4
1920	-	-	-	-	-	-	-	-	-	-	45.0	5.6	-	-	-	-	-	-	-	-	-	-	-	-
1921	-	-	-	-	-	-	-	-	34.7	-13.9	-	-	-	-	-	-	30.0	-13.5	-	-	-	-	28.6	-4.7
1922	-	-	-	-	27.3	-4.5	-	-	-	-	26.8	-1.8	-	-	-	-	26.6	-0.7	-	-	-	-	26.6	0.0
1923	-	-	-	-	27.0	1.5	-	-	-	-	27.0	0.0	-	-	-	-	27.2	0.7	-	-	-	-	27.2	0.0
1924	-	-	-	-	27.1	-0.4	-	-	-	-	26.9	-0.7	-	-	-	-	26.6	-1.1	-	-	-	-	26.4	-0.8
1925	-	-	-	-	-	-	-	-	-	-	26.4	0.0	-	-	-	-	-	-	-	-	-	-	26.2	-0.8
1926	-	-	-	-	-	-	-	-	-	-	25.9	-1.1	-	-	-	-	-	-	-	-	-	-	25.7	-0.8
1927	-	-	-	-	-	-	-	-	-	-	25.4	-1.2	-	-	-	-	-	-	-	-	-	-	25.1	-1.2
1928	-	-	-	-	-	-	-	-	-	-	25.0	-0.4	-	-	-	-	-	-	-	-	-	-	24.9	-0.4
1929	-	-	-	-	-	-	-	-	-	-	24.7	-0.8	-	-	-	-	-	-	-	-	-	-	24.6	-0.4
1930	-	-	-	-	-	-	-	-	-	-	24.5	-0.4	-	-	-	-	-	-	-	-	-	-	23.5	-4.1
1931	-	-	-	-	-	-	-	-	-	-	22.2	-5.5	-	-	-	-	-	-	-	-	-	-	20.6	-7.2
1932	-	-	-	-	-	-	-	-	-	-	19.5	-5.3	-	-	-	-	-	-	-	-	-	-	18.6	-4.6
1933	-	-	-	-	-	-	-	-	-	-	18.2	-2.2	-	-	-	-	-	-	-	-	-	-	20.2	11.0
1934	-	-	-	-	-	-	-	-	-	-	20.7	2.5	-	-	-	-	-	-	-	-	20.7	0.0	-	-
1935	-	-	-	-	20.8	0.5	-	-	-	-	-	-	20.7	-0.5	-	-	-	-	20.9	1.0	-	-	-	-
1936	21.0	0.5	-	-	-	-	21.0	0.0	-	-	-	-	20.9	-0.5	-	-	21.0	0.5	-	-	-	-	21.3	1.4
1937	-	-	-	-	21.7	1.9	-	-	-	-	22.0	1.4	-	-	-	-	22.5	2.3	-	-	-	-	22.5	0.0
1938	-	-	-	-	22.1	-1.8	-	-	-	-	21.9	-0.9	-	-	-	-	21.7	-0.9	-	-	-	-	21.7	0.0
1939	-	-	-	-	21.6	-0.5	-	-	-	-	21.6	0.0	-	-	-	-	21.6	0.0	-	-	-	-	21.7	0.5
1940	-	-	-	-	21.9	0.9	-	-	-	-	21.8	-0.5	-	-	-	-	21.8	0.0	21.8	0.0	21.8	0.0	21.8	0.0
1941	21.6	-0.9	21.6	0.0	21.9	1.4	22.0	0.5	22.0	0.0	22.2	0.9	22.5	1.4	22.9	1.8	23.8	3.9	24.2	1.7	24.5	1.2	24.6	0.4
1942	24.9	1.2	25.5	2.4	26.6	4.3	27.2	2.3	27.1	-0.4	26.9	-0.7	26.9	0.0	26.9	0.0	27.1	0.7	27.1	0.0	27.1	0.0	27.1	0.0
1943	27.1	0.0	27.1	0.0	27.4	1.1	27.5	0.4	27.5	0.0	27.5	0.0	27.7	0.7	27.8	0.4	28.4	2.2	28.6	0.7	28.7	0.3	29.0	1.0
1944	29.0	0.0	29.1	0.3	29.4	1.0	29.5	0.3	29.5	0.0	29.7	0.7	29.7	0.0	30.0	1.0	30.3	1.0	30.4	0.3	30.5	0.3	30.6	0.3
1945	30.7	0.3	30.8	0.3	30.8	0.0	30.9	0.3	31.0	0.3	31.2	0.6	31.4	0.6	31.5	0.3	31.9	1.3	31.9	0.0	31.9	0.0	32.1	0.6
1946	32.2	0.3	32.3	0.3	32.9	1.9	33.2	0.9	33.4	0.6	33.7	0.9	34.1	1.2	34.6	1.5	35.6	2.9	36.1	1.4	36.7	1.7	37.9	3.3
1947	38.4	1.3	38.9	1.3	39.5	1.5	39.7	0.5	39.7	0.0	39.9	0.5	39.6	-0.8	39.9	0.8	40.3	1.0	40.6	0.7	40.8	0.5	41.0	0.5
1948	41.3	0.7	41.9	1.5	42.1	0.5	42.2	0.2	42.4	0.5	42.3	-0.2	42.3	0.0	42.9	1.4	43.1	0.5	43.3	0.5	43.2	-0.2	43.1	-0.2
1949	42.2	-2.1	41.9	-0.7	41.7	-0.5	41.3	-1.0	41.1	-0.5	40.9	-0.5	40.5	-1.0	40.2	-0.7	40.2	0.0	40.1	-0.2	40.0	-0.2	39.9	-0.2
1950	39.7	-0.5	39.7	0.0	39.8	0.3	39.7	-0.3	39.6	-0.3	39.6	0.0	39.6	0.0	39.9	0.8	40.7	2.0	41.4	1.7	41.7	0.7	42.0	0.7
1951	42.6	1.4	43.4	1.9	43.6	0.5	43.7	0.2	43.8	0.2	43.8	0.0	43.7	-0.2	43.7	0.0	44.9	2.7	44.9	0.0	44.6	-0.7	44.4	-0.4
1952	43.9	-1.1	43.9	0.0	43.7	-0.5	43.5	-0.5	43.5	0.0	43.4	-0.2	43.2	-0.5	43.1	-0.2	43.5	0.9	43.4	-0.2	43.2	-0.5	43.1	-0.2
1953	43.0	-0.2	43.0	0.0	43.0	0.0	43.0	0.0	43.1	0.2	43.1	0.0	43.1	0.0	43.0	-0.2	43.4	0.9	43.5	0.2	43.5	0.0	43.4	-0.2
1954	43.2	-0.5	43.1	-0.2	43.0	-0.2	42.9	-0.2	43.0	0.2	43.0	0.0	42.9	-0.2	42.8	-0.2	43.0	0.5	43.1	0.2	43.1	0.0	43.1	0.0
1955	42.7	-0.9	42.7	0.0	42.7	0.0	42.6	-0.2	42.7	0.2	42.7	0.0	42.7	0.0	42.8	0.2	43.2	0.9	43.2	0.0	43.3	0.2	43.3	0.0
1956	43.2	-0.2	43.4	0.5	43.4	0.0	43.5	0.2	43.5	0.0	43.5	0.0	43.6	0.2	43.7	0.2	44.1	0.9	44.3	0.5	44.4	0.2	44.4	0.0
1957	44.2	-0.5	44.1	-0.2	44.4	0.7	44.3	-0.2	44.4	0.2	44.4	0.0	44.4	0.0	44.4	0.0	44.7	0.7	44.9	0.4	44.8	0.2	45.0	0.4
1958	44.6	-0.4	44.6	0.0	44.6	0.0	44.6	0.0	44.6	0.0	44.6	0.0	44.6	0.0	44.5	-0.2	44.7	0.4	44.8	0.2	45.0	0.4	44.9	-0.2

[Continued]

U.S. City Average
Consumer Price Index - All Urban Consumers
Base 1982-1984 = 100
Apparel

[Continued]

For 1913-2001. Columns headed % show percentile change in the index from the previous period for which an index is available.

Year	Jan Index	%	Feb Index	%	Mar Index	%	Apr Index	%	May Index	%	Jun Index	%	Jul Index	%	Aug Index	%	Sep Index	%	Oct Index	%	Nov Index	%	Dec Index	%
1959	44.6	-0.7	44.6	0.0	44.6	0.0	44.7	0.2	44.8	0.2	44.8	0.0	44.9	0.2	45.1	0.4	45.5	0.9	45.6	0.2	45.6	0.0	45.5	-0.2
1960	45.1	-0.9	45.3	0.4	45.4	0.2	45.5	0.2	45.5	0.0	45.5	0.0	45.6	0.2	45.7	0.2	46.1	0.9	46.3	0.4	46.2	-0.2	46.2	0.0
1961	45.8	-0.9	45.8	0.0	45.9	0.2	45.8	-0.2	45.9	0.2	45.8	-0.2	46.0	0.4	46.0	0.0	46.4	0.9	46.5	0.2	46.4	-0.2	46.4	0.0
1962	45.7	-1.5	45.9	0.4	46.1	0.4	46.1	0.0	46.1	0.0	46.2	0.2	46.2	0.0	46.1	-0.2	46.9	1.7	47.0	0.2	46.8	-0.4	46.7	-0.2
1963	46.4	-0.6	46.5	0.2	46.6	0.2	46.7	0.2	46.6	-0.2	46.7	0.2	46.7	0.0	46.8	0.2	47.2	0.9	47.4	0.4	47.5	0.2	47.5	0.0
1964	47.0	-1.1	47.0	0.0	47.1	0.2	47.2	0.2	47.3	0.2	47.3	0.0	47.2	-0.2	47.1	-0.2	47.4	0.6	47.5	0.2	47.6	0.2	47.7	0.2
1965	47.2	-1.0	47.3	0.2	47.4	0.2	47.5	0.2	47.8	0.6	47.8	0.0	47.5	-0.6	47.6	0.2	47.9	0.6	48.2	0.6	48.3	0.2	48.3	0.0
1966	48.0	-0.6	48.1	0.2	48.4	0.6	48.6	0.4	48.9	0.6	48.9	0.0	48.8	-0.2	48.8	0.0	49.5	1.4	49.9	0.8	50.1	0.4	50.2	0.2
1967	49.8	-0.8	50.1	0.6	50.4	0.6	50.5	0.2	50.9	0.8	50.9	0.0	50.8	-0.2	50.9	0.2	51.5	1.2	51.9	0.8	52.2	0.6	52.3	0.2
1968	51.8	-1.0	52.2	0.8	52.6	0.8	53.0	0.8	53.4	0.8	53.6	0.4	53.5	-0.2	53.8	0.6	54.7	1.7	55.2	0.9	55.5	0.5	55.6	0.2
1969	55.2	-0.7	55.4	0.4	55.9	0.9	56.2	0.5	56.6	0.7	56.8	0.4	56.7	-0.2	56.6	-0.2	57.6	1.8	58.1	0.9	58.4	0.5	58.5	0.2
1970	57.8	-1.2	58.1	0.5	58.4	0.5	58.6	0.3	59.0	0.7	59.1	0.2	58.8	-0.5	58.8	0.0	59.7	1.5	60.3	1.0	60.7	0.7	60.8	0.2
1971	60.0	-1.3	60.2	0.3	60.5	0.5	60.7	0.3	61.3	1.0	61.2	-0.2	60.8	-0.7	60.7	-0.2	61.5	1.3	62.0	0.8	62.1	0.2	62.1	0.0
1972	61.3	-1.3	61.5	0.3	61.8	0.5	62.1	0.5	62.5	0.6	62.2	-0.5	61.7	-0.8	61.6	-0.2	62.8	1.9	63.4	1.0	63.7	0.5	63.7	0.0
1973	62.7	-1.6	63.0	0.5	63.6	1.0	64.1	0.8	64.6	0.8	64.6	0.0	64.1	-0.8	64.5	0.6	65.4	1.4	66.1	1.1	66.5	0.6	66.5	0.0
1974	65.7	-1.2	66.5	1.2	67.4	1.4	68.1	1.0	68.8	1.0	69.2	0.6	69.0	-0.3	70.4	2.0	71.3	1.3	71.9	0.6	72.6	1.0	72.3	-0.4
1975	71.1	-1.7	71.5	0.6	71.8	0.4	72.0	0.3	72.3	0.4	72.1	-0.3	71.9	-0.3	72.5	0.8	73.2	1.0	73.7	0.7	74.2	0.7	74.0	-0.3
1976	73.1	-1.2	73.4	0.4	73.9	0.7	74.3	0.5	74.8	0.7	74.9	0.1	74.7	-0.3	75.5	1.1	76.6	1.5	76.9	0.4	77.4	0.7	77.4	0.0
1977	76.5	-1.2	76.9	0.5	77.3	0.5	77.6	0.4	78.2	0.8	78.5	0.4	78.2	-0.4	78.9	0.9	79.6	0.9	80.1	0.6	80.8	0.9	80.7	-0.1
1978	79.4	-1.6	78.8	-0.8	79.8	1.3	80.8	1.3	81.5	0.9	81.5	0.0	80.5	-1.2	81.4	1.1	82.5	1.4	83.3	1.0	83.7	0.5	83.2	-0.6
1979	81.9	-1.6	82.3	0.5	83.8	1.8	84.3	0.6	84.7	0.5	84.5	-0.2	83.8	-0.8	84.8	1.2	86.6	2.1	87.2	0.7	87.5	0.3	87.8	0.3
1980	87.2	-0.7	87.6	0.5	89.7	2.4	90.4	0.8	90.5	0.1	90.3	-0.2	89.8	-0.6	91.1	1.4	92.9	2.0	93.8	1.0	94.2	0.4	93.8	-0.4
1981	92.3	-1.6	92.8	0.5	94.4	1.7	95.0	0.6	95.0	0.0	94.7	-0.3	94.2	-0.5	95.5	1.4	97.2	1.8	97.6	0.4	97.5	-0.1	97.1	-0.4
1982	95.5	-1.6	95.8	0.3	97.4	1.7	97.8	0.4	97.6	-0.2	97.3	-0.3	96.7	-0.6	97.8	1.1	99.4	1.6	99.7	0.3	99.6	-0.1	98.7	-0.9
1983	97.4	-1.3	97.9	0.5	99.2	1.3	99.7	0.5	100.0	0.3	99.7	-0.3	99.4	-0.3	100.6	1.2	102.2	1.6	102.3	0.1	102.3	0.0	101.6	-0.7
1984	100.1	-1.5	100.0	-0.1	101.3	1.3	101.6	0.3	101.4	-0.2	100.6	-0.8	100.2	-0.4	102.0	1.8	104.1	2.1	104.9	0.8	104.6	-0.3	103.6	-1.0
1985	101.9	-1.6	102.9	1.0	104.7	1.7	105.0	0.3	104.7	-0.3	104.3	-0.4	103.4	-0.9	104.7	1.3	106.9	2.1	107.6	0.7	107.7	0.1	106.5	-1.1
1986	104.5	-1.9	104.1	-0.4	105.2	1.1	105.7	0.5	105.2	-0.5	104.3	-0.9	103.6	-0.7	105.5	1.8	108.1	2.5	108.7	0.6	108.6	-0.1	107.5	-1.0
1987	105.6	-1.8	106.2	0.6	109.7	3.3	111.5	1.6	111.1	-0.4	109.3	-1.6	107.3	-1.8	109.4	2.0	113.3	3.6	115.4	1.9	115.4	0.0	112.7	-2.3
1988	110.4	-2.0	110.2	-0.2	114.3	3.7	117.0	2.4	116.3	-0.6	114.6	-1.5	112.7	-1.7	112.6	-0.1	117.8	4.6	120.7	2.5	119.9	-0.7	118.0	-1.6
1989	115.3	-2.3	115.3	0.0	119.3	3.5	120.9	1.3	120.4	-0.4	117.8	-2.2	115.0	-2.4	115.0	0.0	120.0	4.3	122.7	2.2	122.1	-0.5	119.2	-2.4
1990	116.7	-2.1	120.4	3.2	125.4	4.2	126.7	1.0	125.5	-0.9	123.3	-1.8	120.8	-2.0	122.2	1.2	126.8	3.8	128.4	1.3	127.5	-0.7	125.3	-1.7
1991	123.8	-1.2	126.2	1.9	128.8	2.1	130.1	1.0	129.4	-0.5	126.9	-1.9	125.2	-1.3	127.6	1.9	131.3	2.9	132.7	1.1	132.9	0.2	129.6	-2.5
1992	127.9	-1.3	130.2	1.8	133.4	2.5	133.3	-0.1	133.1	-0.2	131.0	-1.6	129.2	-1.4	130.2	0.8	133.3	2.4	135.0	1.3	134.5	-0.4	131.4	-2.3
1993	129.7	-1.3	133.4	2.9	136.2	2.1	136.9	0.5	135.0	-1.4	131.9	-2.3	129.4	-1.9	131.9	1.9	134.6	2.0	136.1	1.1	136.2	0.1	132.6	-2.6
1994	130.4	-1.7	132.4	1.5	136.1	2.8	136.4	0.2	135.6	-0.6	133.8	-1.3	130.9	-2.2	131.1	0.2	134.2	2.4	135.2	0.7	134.2	-0.7	130.5	-2.8
1995	129.4	-0.8	131.1	1.3	134.4	2.5	134.8	0.3	133.4	-1.0	130.5	-2.2	128.3	-1.7	130.1	1.4	132.7	2.0	134.5	1.4	133.7	-0.6	130.6	-2.3
1996	130.0	-0.5	131.2	0.9	134.8	2.7	134.9	0.1	133.7	-0.9	130.8	-2.2	128.3	-1.9	128.1	-0.2	131.5	2.7	133.4	1.4	133.4	0.0	130.3	-2.3
1997	129.6	-0.5	131.9	1.8	134.5	2.0	136.1	1.2	135.3	-0.6	132.4	-2.1	130.2	-1.7	130.0	-0.2	133.0	2.3	134.9	1.4	134.7	-0.1	131.6	-2.3
1998	129.8	-1.4	131.9	1.6	134.9	2.3	135.8	0.7	135.3	-0.4	132.5	-2.1	129.6	-2.2	131.6	1.5	133.6	1.5	135.6	1.5	135.0	-0.4	130.7	-3.2
1999	127.9	-2.1	129.7	1.4	132.7	2.3	135.2	1.9	134.2	-0.7	130.9	-2.5	127.3	-2.8	127.5	0.2	131.8	3.4	134.6	2.1	133.6	-0.7	130.1	-2.6
2000	126.8	-2.5	129.2	1.9	132.5	2.6	133.3	0.6	132.2	-0.8	128.3	-3.0	124.5	-3.0	125.3	0.6	130.4	4.1	132.8	1.8	131.8	-0.8	127.8	-3.0
2001	125.4	-1.9	128.4	2.4	132.2	3.0	131.9	-0.2	129.8	-1.6	126.3	-2.7	122.6	-2.9	122.6	0.0	126.8	3.4	129.5	2.1	128.0	-1.2	123.7	-3.4

Source: U.S. Department of Labor, Bureau of Labor Statistics, Division of Consumer Prices and Price Indexes.

U.S. City Average
Consumer Price Index - Urban Wage Earners
Base 1982-1984 = 100
Apparel

For 1913-2001. Columns headed % show percentile change in the index from the previous period for which an index is available.

Year	Jan Index	%	Feb Index	%	Mar Index	%	Apr Index	%	May Index	%	Jun Index	%	Jul Index	%	Aug Index	%	Sep Index	%	Oct Index	%	Nov Index	%	Dec Index	%
1913	-	-	-	-	-	-	-	-	-	-	-	-	-	-	-	-	-	-	-	-	-	-	-	-
1914	-	-	-	-	-	-	-	-	-	-	-	-	-	-	-	-	-	-	-	-	-	-	15.1	-
1915	-	-	-	-	-	-	-	-	-	-	-	-	-	-	-	-	-	-	-	-	-	-	15.7	4.0
1916	-	-	-	-	-	-	-	-	-	-	-	-	-	-	-	-	-	-	-	-	-	-	18.0	14.6
1917	-	-	-	-	-	-	-	-	-	-	-	-	-	-	-	-	-	-	-	-	-	-	22.3	23.9
1918	-	-	-	-	-	-	-	-	-	-	-	-	-	-	-	-	-	-	-	-	-	-	31.9	43.0
1919	-	-	-	-	-	-	-	-	-	-	34.6	8.5	-	-	-	-	-	-	-	-	-	-	42.8	23.7
1920	-	-	-	-	-	-	-	-	-	-	45.2	5.6	-	-	-	-	-	-	-	-	-	-	40.5	-10.4
1921	-	-	-	-	-	-	-	-	34.8	-14.1	-	-	-	-	-	-	30.1	-13.5	-	-	-	-	28.7	-4.7
1922	-	-	-	-	27.5	-4.2	-	-	-	-	26.9	-2.2	-	-	-	-	26.7	-0.7	-	-	-	-	26.7	0.0
1923	-	-	-	-	27.1	1.5	-	-	-	-	27.2	0.4	-	-	-	-	27.4	0.7	-	-	-	-	27.4	0.0
1924	-	-	-	-	27.3	-0.4	-	-	-	-	27.0	-1.1	-	-	-	-	26.7	-1.1	-	-	-	-	26.5	-0.7
1925	-	-	-	-	-	-	-	-	-	-	26.5	0.0	-	-	-	-	-	-	-	-	-	-	26.3	-0.8
1926	-	-	-	-	-	-	-	-	-	-	26.1	-0.8	-	-	-	-	-	-	-	-	-	-	25.8	-1.1
1927	-	-	-	-	-	-	-	-	-	-	25.5	-1.2	-	-	-	-	-	-	-	-	-	-	25.2	-1.2
1928	-	-	-	-	-	-	-	-	-	-	25.2	0.0	-	-	-	-	-	-	-	-	-	-	25.0	-0.8
1929	-	-	-	-	-	-	-	-	-	-	24.8	-0.8	-	-	-	-	-	-	-	-	-	-	24.7	-0.4
1930	-	-	-	-	-	-	-	-	-	-	24.6	-0.4	-	-	-	-	-	-	-	-	-	-	23.6	-4.1
1931	-	-	-	-	-	-	-	-	-	-	22.3	-5.5	-	-	-	-	-	-	-	-	-	-	20.7	-7.2
1932	-	-	-	-	-	-	-	-	-	-	19.6	-5.3	-	-	-	-	-	-	-	-	-	-	18.6	-5.1
1933	-	-	-	-	-	-	-	-	-	-	18.3	-1.6	-	-	-	-	-	-	-	-	-	-	20.3	10.9
1934	-	-	-	-	-	-	-	-	-	-	20.8	2.5	-	-	-	-	-	-	-	-	20.8	0.0	-	-
1935	-	-	-	-	20.9	0.5	-	-	-	-	-	-	20.8	-0.5	-	-	-	-	21.0	1.0	-	-	-	-
1936	21.1	0.5	-	-	-	-	21.1	0.0	-	-	-	-	21.0	-0.5	-	-	21.1	0.5	-	-	-	-	21.4	1.4
1937	-	-	-	-	21.8	1.9	-	-	-	-	22.1	1.4	-	-	-	-	22.6	2.3	-	-	-	-	22.6	0.0
1938	-	-	-	-	22.2	-1.8	-	-	-	-	22.0	-0.9	-	-	-	-	21.8	-0.9	-	-	-	-	21.8	0.0
1939	-	-	-	-	21.7	-0.5	-	-	-	-	21.7	0.0	-	-	-	-	21.7	0.0	-	-	-	-	21.8	0.5
1940	-	-	-	-	22.0	0.9	-	-	-	-	21.9	-0.5	-	-	-	-	21.9	0.0	21.9	0.0	21.9	0.0	21.9	0.0
1941	21.7	-0.9	21.7	0.0	22.0	1.4	22.1	0.5	22.1	0.0	22.3	0.9	22.6	1.3	23.1	2.2	23.9	3.5	24.3	1.7	24.6	1.2	24.7	0.4
1942	25.1	1.6	25.7	2.4	26.7	3.9	27.3	2.2	27.3	0.0	27.0	-1.1	27.0	0.0	27.0	0.0	27.2	0.7	27.2	0.0	27.2	0.0	27.2	0.0
1943	27.3	0.4	27.3	0.0	27.5	0.7	27.6	0.4	27.6	0.0	27.6	0.0	27.9	1.1	28.0	0.4	28.6	2.1	28.7	0.3	28.8	0.3	29.1	1.0
1944	29.1	0.0	29.2	0.3	29.5	1.0	29.6	0.3	29.7	0.3	29.8	0.3	29.8	0.0	30.1	1.0	30.5	1.3	30.6	0.3	30.6	0.0	30.8	0.7
1945	30.9	0.3	30.9	0.0	31.0	0.3	31.0	0.0	31.2	0.6	31.4	0.6	31.5	0.3	31.6	0.3	32.0	1.3	32.0	0.0	32.1	0.3	32.3	0.6
1946	32.3	0.0	32.5	0.6	33.0	1.5	33.3	0.9	33.6	0.9	33.9	0.9	34.2	0.9	34.8	1.8	35.8	2.9	36.3	1.4	36.9	1.7	38.1	3.3
1947	38.6	1.3	39.1	1.3	39.7	1.5	39.9	0.5	39.9	0.0	40.1	0.5	39.8	-0.7	40.1	0.8	40.5	1.0	40.8	0.7	41.0	0.5	41.2	0.5
1948	41.5	0.7	42.1	1.4	42.3	0.5	42.4	0.2	42.6	0.5	42.5	-0.2	42.5	0.0	43.1	1.4	43.3	0.5	43.5	0.5	43.4	-0.2	43.3	-0.2
1949	42.4	-2.1	42.1	-0.7	41.9	-0.5	41.5	-1.0	41.3	-0.5	41.1	-0.5	40.7	-1.0	40.4	-0.7	40.4	0.0	40.3	-0.2	40.2	-0.2	40.1	-0.2
1950	39.9	-0.5	39.9	0.0	40.0	0.3	39.9	-0.2	39.8	-0.3	39.8	0.0	39.8	0.0	40.1	0.8	40.9	2.0	41.6	1.7	41.9	0.7	42.2	0.7
1951	42.8	1.4	43.6	1.9	43.9	0.7	44.0	0.2	44.0	0.0	44.0	0.0	43.9	-0.2	44.0	0.2	45.1	2.5	45.1	0.0	44.8	-0.7	44.6	-0.4
1952	44.2	-0.9	44.1	-0.2	44.0	-0.2	43.7	-0.7	43.7	0.0	43.6	-0.2	43.4	-0.5	43.3	-0.2	43.7	0.9	43.6	-0.2	43.4	-0.5	43.3	-0.2
1953	43.2	-0.2	43.2	0.0	43.2	0.0	43.2	0.0	43.3	0.2	43.3	0.0	43.3	0.0	43.2	-0.2	43.6	0.9	43.7	0.2	43.7	0.0	43.6	-0.2
1954	43.4	-0.5	43.3	-0.2	43.2	-0.2	43.1	-0.2	43.2	0.2	43.2	0.0	43.1	-0.2	43.0	-0.2	43.2	0.5	43.3	0.2	43.3	0.0	43.3	0.0
1955	42.9	-0.9	42.9	0.0	42.9	0.0	42.8	-0.2	42.9	0.2	42.9	0.0	42.9	0.0	43.0	0.2	43.4	0.9	43.4	0.0	43.5	0.2	43.5	0.0
1956	43.4	-0.2	43.6	0.5	43.6	0.0	43.7	0.2	43.7	0.0	43.7	0.0	43.9	0.5	44.0	0.2	44.4	0.9	44.5	0.2	44.6	0.2	44.6	0.0
1957	44.4	-0.4	44.4	0.0	44.6	0.5	44.5	-0.2	44.6	0.2	44.6	0.0	44.6	0.0	44.6	0.0	44.9	0.7	45.1	0.4	45.2	0.2	45.0	-0.4
1958	44.8	-0.4	44.8	0.0	44.8	0.0	44.8	0.0	44.8	0.0	44.8	0.0	44.8	0.0	44.7	-0.2	44.9	0.4	45.0	0.2	45.2	0.4	45.1	-0.2

[Continued]

218

U.S. City Average
Consumer Price Index - Urban Wage Earners
Base 1982-1984 = 100
Apparel
[Continued]

For 1913-2001. Columns headed % show percentile change in the index from the previous period for which an index is available.

Year	Jan Index	%	Feb Index	%	Mar Index	%	Apr Index	%	May Index	%	Jun Index	%	Jul Index	%	Aug Index	%	Sep Index	%	Oct Index	%	Nov Index	%	Dec Index	%
1959	44.8	-0.7	44.8	0.0	44.8	0.0	44.9	0.2	45.0	0.2	45.0	0.0	45.1	0.2	45.3	0.4	45.7	0.9	45.8	0.2	45.8	0.0	45.7	-0.2
1960	45.3	-0.9	45.5	0.4	45.6	0.2	45.7	0.2	45.7	0.0	45.7	0.0	45.8	0.2	45.9	0.2	46.4	1.1	46.6	0.4	46.5	-0.2	46.4	-0.2
1961	46.0	-0.9	46.1	0.2	46.1	0.0	46.1	0.0	46.1	0.0	46.1	0.0	46.2	0.2	46.2	0.0	46.7	1.1	46.7	0.0	46.7	0.0	46.6	-0.2
1962	46.0	-1.3	46.1	0.2	46.4	0.7	46.4	0.0	46.4	0.0	46.5	0.2	46.5	0.0	46.3	-0.4	47.1	1.7	47.2	0.2	47.0	-0.4	46.9	-0.2
1963	46.6	-0.6	46.7	0.2	46.8	0.2	46.9	0.2	46.9	0.0	47.0	0.2	47.0	0.0	47.0	0.0	47.4	0.9	47.6	0.4	47.7	0.2	47.7	0.0
1964	47.2	-1.0	47.2	0.0	47.3	0.2	47.4	0.2	47.5	0.2	47.5	0.0	47.4	-0.2	47.3	-0.2	47.6	0.6	47.7	0.2	47.8	0.2	47.9	0.2
1965	47.4	-1.0	47.5	0.2	47.6	0.2	47.7	0.2	48.0	0.6	48.1	0.2	47.7	-0.8	47.8	0.2	48.2	0.8	48.5	0.6	48.6	0.2	48.6	0.0
1966	48.2	-0.8	48.4	0.4	48.6	0.4	48.9	0.6	49.1	0.4	49.2	0.2	49.1	-0.2	49.1	0.0	49.7	1.2	50.1	0.8	50.3	0.4	50.5	0.4
1967	50.0	-1.0	50.3	0.6	50.6	0.6	50.8	0.4	51.1	0.6	51.2	0.2	51.1	-0.2	51.1	0.0	51.7	1.2	52.2	1.0	52.4	0.4	52.5	0.2
1968	52.1	-0.8	52.4	0.6	52.9	1.0	53.2	0.6	53.7	0.9	53.9	0.4	53.8	-0.2	54.0	0.4	54.9	1.7	55.4	0.9	55.7	0.5	55.8	0.2
1969	55.4	-0.7	55.7	0.5	56.1	0.7	56.5	0.7	56.9	0.7	57.1	0.4	57.0	-0.2	56.9	-0.2	57.8	1.6	58.3	0.9	58.7	0.7	58.8	0.2
1970	58.1	-1.2	58.4	0.5	58.7	0.5	58.9	0.3	59.3	0.7	59.4	0.2	59.1	-0.5	59.1	0.0	60.0	1.5	60.6	1.0	61.0	0.7	61.1	0.2
1971	60.2	-1.5	60.5	0.5	60.8	0.5	61.0	0.3	61.6	1.0	61.5	-0.2	61.1	-0.7	61.0	-0.2	61.8	1.3	62.3	0.8	62.4	0.2	62.4	0.0
1972	61.6	-1.3	61.8	0.3	62.1	0.5	62.4	0.5	62.8	0.6	62.5	-0.5	62.0	-0.8	61.9	-0.2	63.1	1.9	63.7	1.0	64.0	0.5	64.0	0.0
1973	63.0	-1.6	63.3	0.5	63.9	0.9	64.4	0.8	64.9	0.8	65.0	0.2	64.4	-0.9	64.8	0.6	65.7	1.4	66.4	1.1	66.9	0.8	66.9	0.0
1974	66.0	-1.3	66.8	1.2	67.7	1.3	68.4	1.0	69.2	1.2	69.5	0.4	69.3	-0.3	70.7	2.0	71.7	1.4	72.3	0.8	72.9	0.8	72.7	-0.3
1975	71.4	-1.8	71.8	0.6	72.2	0.6	72.4	0.3	72.6	0.3	72.4	-0.3	72.3	-0.1	72.9	0.8	73.5	0.8	74.1	0.8	74.5	0.5	74.4	-0.1
1976	73.4	-1.3	73.8	0.5	74.3	0.7	74.6	0.4	75.2	0.8	75.3	0.1	75.0	-0.4	75.9	1.2	76.9	1.3	77.3	0.5	77.8	0.6	77.8	0.0
1977	76.8	-1.3	77.3	0.7	77.7	0.5	78.0	0.4	78.6	0.8	78.8	0.3	78.6	-0.3	79.3	0.9	80.0	0.9	80.5	0.6	81.2	0.9	81.0	-0.2
1978	79.6	-1.7	79.1	-0.6	79.9	1.0	81.0	1.4	81.8	1.0	81.9	0.1	81.0	-1.1	81.8	1.0	82.9	1.3	83.8	1.1	84.0	0.2	83.7	-0.4
1979	82.5	-1.4	82.8	0.4	84.1	1.6	84.7	0.7	84.9	0.2	84.7	-0.2	84.3	-0.5	85.1	0.9	86.7	1.9	87.5	0.9	87.8	0.3	87.8	0.0
1980	87.0	-0.9	87.9	1.0	89.7	2.0	90.2	0.6	90.6	0.4	90.2	-0.4	89.9	-0.3	91.1	1.3	92.9	2.0	93.6	0.8	93.9	0.3	93.7	-0.2
1981	92.6	-1.2	93.1	0.5	94.4	1.4	95.3	1.0	95.4	0.1	95.2	-0.2	95.0	-0.2	96.3	1.4	97.6	1.3	97.6	0.0	97.6	0.0	97.0	-0.6
1982	95.5	-1.5	96.0	0.5	97.6	1.7	97.9	0.3	97.6	-0.3	97.1	-0.5	96.7	-0.4	97.7	1.0	99.4	1.7	99.7	0.3	99.6	-0.1	98.8	-0.8
1983	97.3	-1.5	97.8	0.5	99.4	1.6	99.8	0.4	100.0	0.2	99.7	-0.3	99.4	-0.3	100.6	1.2	102.1	1.5	102.4	0.3	102.3	-0.1	101.5	-0.8
1984	100.0	-1.5	100.1	0.1	101.4	1.3	101.5	0.1	101.3	-0.2	100.5	-0.8	100.0	-0.5	101.9	1.9	104.1	2.2	104.9	0.8	104.6	-0.3	103.5	-1.1
1985	101.7	-1.7	102.8	1.1	104.6	1.8	105.0	0.4	104.6	-0.4	104.4	-0.2	103.4	-1.0	104.7	1.3	106.9	2.1	107.7	0.7	107.7	0.0	106.6	-1.0
1986	104.6	-1.9	104.0	-0.6	105.1	1.1	105.6	0.5	105.1	-0.5	104.0	-1.0	103.4	-0.6	105.5	2.0	108.1	2.5	108.6	0.5	108.3	-0.3	107.4	-0.8
1987	105.4	-1.9	106.0	0.6	109.5	3.3	111.4	1.7	110.9	-0.4	109.1	-1.6	107.1	-1.8	109.1	1.9	112.9	3.5	115.2	2.0	115.2	0.0	112.6	-2.3
1988	110.3	-2.0	110.0	-0.3	113.9	3.5	116.3	2.1	115.7	-0.5	114.1	-1.4	112.4	-1.5	112.2	-0.2	117.2	4.5	120.1	2.5	119.5	-0.5	117.6	-1.6
1989	114.8	-2.4	114.7	-0.1	118.4	3.2	120.0	1.4	119.4	-0.5	116.9	-2.1	114.4	-2.1	114.5	0.1	119.3	4.2	122.0	2.3	121.4	-0.5	118.5	-2.4
1990	116.1	-2.0	119.3	2.8	124.4	4.3	125.8	1.1	124.7	-0.9	122.4	-1.8	119.8	-2.1	121.3	1.3	125.7	3.6	127.1	1.1	126.5	-0.5	124.5	-1.6
1991	122.9	-1.3	124.8	1.5	127.5	2.2	128.8	1.0	127.9	-0.7	125.7	-1.7	124.1	-1.3	126.4	1.9	129.7	2.6	131.1	1.1	131.4	0.2	128.4	-2.3
1992	126.8	-1.2	128.8	1.6	132.1	2.6	132.1	0.0	131.8	-0.2	129.8	-1.5	128.1	-1.3	129.5	1.1	132.1	2.0	133.8	1.3	133.4	-0.3	130.4	-2.2
1993	128.4	-1.5	132.0	2.8	134.8	2.1	135.2	0.3	133.6	-1.2	130.7	-2.2	128.4	-1.8	130.5	1.6	133.3	2.1	135.1	1.4	135.0	-0.1	131.3	-2.7
1994	129.4	-1.4	131.4	1.5	134.7	2.5	135.0	0.2	134.3	-0.5	132.4	-1.4	129.8	-2.0	130.2	0.3	133.1	2.2	133.9	0.6	133.0	-0.7	129.3	-2.8
1995	128.3	-0.8	130.0	1.3	133.2	2.5	133.6	0.3	132.1	-1.1	129.6	-1.9	127.4	-1.7	129.1	1.3	131.6	1.9	133.4	1.4	132.5	-0.7	129.5	-2.3
1996	129.1	-0.3	130.2	0.9	133.9	2.8	134.2	0.2	133.2	-0.7	130.2	-2.3	127.9	-1.8	127.5	-0.3	130.6	2.4	132.4	1.4	132.4	0.0	129.3	-2.3
1997	128.7	-0.5	131.1	1.9	133.8	2.1	135.5	1.3	134.7	-0.6	131.8	-2.2	129.8	-1.5	129.4	-0.3	132.1	2.1	133.9	1.4	133.6	-0.2	130.3	-2.5
1998	128.7	-1.2	130.4	1.3	133.0	2.0	134.0	0.8	133.7	-0.2	131.0	-2.0	128.2	-2.1	129.9	1.3	132.0	1.6	134.3	1.7	134.0	-0.2	129.8	-3.1
1999	127.1	-2.1	128.5	1.1	131.1	2.0	133.7	2.0	133.0	-0.5	129.6	-2.6	126.4	-2.5	126.4	0.0	130.5	3.2	133.1	2.0	132.3	-0.6	129.0	-2.5
2000	125.9	-2.4	127.9	1.6	131.0	2.4	131.8	0.6	130.9	-0.7	127.3	-2.8	123.6	-2.9	124.0	0.3	128.7	3.8	131.3	2.0	130.5	-0.6	126.6	-3.0
2001	124.1	-2.0	127.0	2.3	130.6	2.8	130.5	-0.1	128.5	-1.5	125.2	-2.6	121.9	-2.6	121.6	-0.2	125.6	3.3	128.3	2.1	127.2	-0.9	123.0	-3.3

Source: U.S. Department of Labor, Bureau of Labor Statistics, Division of Consumer Prices and Price Indexes.

U.S. City Average
Consumer Price Index - All Urban Consumers
Base 1982-1984 = 100
Transportation

For 1935-2001. Columns headed % show percentile change in the index from the previous period for which an index is available.

Year	Jan Index	%	Feb Index	%	Mar Index	%	Apr Index	%	May Index	%	Jun Index	%	Jul Index	%	Aug Index	%	Sep Index	%	Oct Index	%	Nov Index	%	Dec Index	%
1935	-	-	-	-	14.2	-	-	-	-	-	-	-	14.3	0.7	-	-	-	-	14.1	-1.4	-	-	-	-
1936	14.1	0.0	-	-	-	-	14.3	1.4	-	-	-	-	14.3	0.0	-	-	14.3	0.0	-	-	-	-	14.3	0.0
1937	-	-	-	-	14.5	1.4	-	-	-	-	14.5	0.0	-	-	-	-	14.6	0.7	-	-	-	-	14.7	0.7
1938	-	-	-	-	14.7	0.0	-	-	-	-	14.7	0.0	-	-	-	-	14.7	0.0	-	-	-	-	14.4	-2.0
1939	-	-	-	-	14.3	-0.7	-	-	-	-	14.3	0.0	-	-	-	-	14.3	0.0	-	-	-	-	14.3	0.0
1940	-	-	-	-	14.3	0.0	-	-	-	-	14.1	-1.4	-	-	-	-	14.2	0.7	-	-	-	-	14.3	0.7
1941	-	-	-	-	14.3	0.0	-	-	-	-	14.6	2.1	-	-	-	-	14.8	1.4	-	-	-	-	15.4	4.1
1942	-	-	-	-	16.0	3.9	-	-	-	-	16.1	0.6	-	-	-	-	16.0	-0.6	-	-	-	-	16.0	0.0
1943	-	-	-	-	16.0	0.0	-	-	-	-	15.9	-0.6	-	-	-	-	15.9	0.0	-	-	-	-	15.9	0.0
1944	-	-	-	-	15.9	0.0	-	-	-	-	15.9	0.0	-	-	-	-	15.9	0.0	-	-	-	-	15.9	0.0
1945	-	-	-	-	15.9	0.0	-	-	-	-	15.9	0.0	-	-	-	-	15.9	0.0	-	-	-	-	15.9	0.0
1946	-	-	-	-	16.0	0.6	-	-	-	-	16.2	1.3	-	-	-	-	17.5	8.0	-	-	-	-	17.9	2.3
1947	17.9	0.0	17.9	0.0	18.1	1.1	18.2	0.6	18.3	0.5	18.3	0.0	18.4	0.5	18.5	0.5	18.7	1.1	18.9	1.1	19.0	0.5	19.2	1.1
1948	19.5	1.6	19.6	0.5	19.6	0.0	19.8	1.0	19.8	0.0	19.9	0.5	21.0	5.5	21.4	1.9	21.5	0.5	21.6	0.5	21.6	0.0	21.6	0.0
1949	21.6	0.0	21.8	0.9	21.9	0.5	22.0	0.5	22.1	0.5	22.0	-0.5	22.1	0.5	22.3	0.9	22.3	0.0	22.4	0.4	22.4	0.0	22.5	0.4
1950	22.5	0.0	22.4	-0.4	22.4	0.0	22.3	-0.4	22.4	0.4	22.4	0.0	22.7	1.3	22.9	0.9	23.0	0.4	22.9	-0.4	23.0	0.4	23.3	1.3
1951	23.4	0.4	23.6	0.9	23.8	0.8	23.9	0.4	24.0	0.4	24.0	0.0	24.0	0.0	24.2	0.8	24.4	0.8	24.6	0.8	24.9	1.2	24.9	0.0
1952	25.0	0.4	25.2	0.8	25.4	0.8	25.4	0.0	25.5	0.4	25.7	0.8	25.9	0.8	25.9	0.0	26.0	0.4	26.2	0.8	26.3	0.4	26.3	0.0
1953	26.4	0.4	26.3	-0.4	26.4	0.4	26.4	0.0	26.4	0.0	26.4	0.0	26.5	0.4	26.6	0.4	26.7	0.4	26.7	0.0	26.5	-0.7	26.3	-0.8
1954	26.6	1.1	26.4	-0.8	26.3	-0.4	26.3	0.0	26.3	0.0	26.3	0.0	25.8	-1.9	25.8	0.0	25.8	0.0	25.5	-1.2	26.0	2.0	25.9	-0.4
1955	26.0	0.4	26.0	0.0	25.9	-0.4	25.5	-1.5	25.6	0.4	25.6	0.0	25.6	0.0	25.6	0.0	25.5	-0.4	25.8	1.2	26.2	1.6	25.9	-1.1
1956	25.9	0.0	25.9	0.0	25.8	-0.4	25.8	0.0	25.9	0.4	25.9	0.0	26.0	0.4	26.2	0.8	26.2	0.0	27.0	3.1	27.1	0.4	27.1	0.0
1957	27.2	0.4	27.4	0.7	27.5	0.4	27.6	0.4	27.5	-0.4	27.5	0.0	27.7	0.7	27.7	0.0	27.7	0.0	27.7	0.0	28.5	2.9	28.3	-0.7
1958	28.2	-0.4	28.2	0.0	28.2	0.0	28.2	0.0	28.2	0.0	28.3	0.4	28.6	1.1	28.7	0.3	28.8	0.3	29.1	1.0	29.4	1.0	29.4	0.0
1959	29.4	0.0	29.4	0.0	29.5	0.3	29.6	0.3	29.6	0.0	29.7	0.3	29.8	0.3	29.9	0.3	29.8	-0.3	30.2	1.3	30.3	0.3	30.3	0.0
1960	30.1	-0.7	30.0	-0.3	29.8	-0.7	29.8	0.0	29.6	-0.7	29.7	0.3	29.7	0.0	29.8	0.3	29.5	-1.0	29.8	1.0	29.8	0.0	29.8	0.0
1961	29.8	0.0	29.8	0.0	29.7	-0.3	29.7	0.0	29.8	0.3	30.1	1.0	30.2	0.3	30.4	0.7	30.4	0.0	30.6	0.7	30.6	0.0	30.4	-0.7
1962	30.4	0.0	30.4	0.0	30.4	0.0	30.8	1.3	30.8	0.0	30.8	0.0	30.6	-0.6	30.8	0.7	30.9	0.3	31.0	0.3	31.1	0.3	31.0	-0.3
1963	30.6	-1.3	30.6	0.0	30.7	0.3	30.7	0.0	30.8	0.3	30.8	0.0	30.9	0.3	31.1	0.6	31.0	-0.3	31.3	1.0	31.3	0.0	31.3	0.0
1964	31.4	0.3	31.2	-0.6	31.3	0.3	31.3	0.0	31.3	0.0	31.3	0.0	31.4	0.3	31.4	0.0	31.3	-0.3	31.4	0.3	31.6	0.6	31.7	0.3
1965	31.9	0.6	31.7	-0.6	31.7	0.0	31.9	0.6	32.0	0.3	31.9	-0.3	32.0	0.3	31.9	-0.3	31.9	0.0	31.9	0.0	32.0	0.3	32.0	0.0
1966	31.9	-0.3	31.9	0.0	32.0	0.3	32.1	0.3	32.1	0.0	32.2	0.3	32.6	1.2	32.6	0.0	32.5	-0.3	32.8	0.9	32.9	0.3	32.7	-0.6
1967	32.5	-0.6	32.7	0.6	32.8	0.3	33.0	0.6	33.2	0.6	33.2	0.0	33.4	0.6	33.4	0.0	33.5	0.3	33.8	0.9	34.0	0.6	33.8	-0.6
1968	34.1	0.9	34.0	-0.3	34.2	0.6	34.2	0.0	34.2	0.0	34.4	0.6	34.4	0.0	34.4	0.0	34.3	-0.3	34.6	0.9	34.8	0.6	34.5	-0.9
1969	34.6	0.3	35.0	1.2	35.7	2.0	35.8	0.3	35.6	-0.6	35.8	0.6	35.7	-0.3	35.7	0.0	35.5	-0.6	36.1	1.7	36.1	0.0	36.3	0.6
1970	36.5	0.6	36.5	0.0	36.5	0.0	37.0	1.4	37.3	0.8	37.5	0.5	37.7	0.5	37.5	-0.5	37.6	0.3	38.3	1.9	38.6	0.8	38.9	0.8
1971	39.1	0.5	39.1	0.0	39.2	0.3	39.3	0.3	39.5	0.5	39.8	0.8	39.7	-0.3	39.7	0.0	39.5	-0.5	39.7	0.5	39.5	-0.5	39.4	-0.3
1972	39.6	0.5	39.4	-0.5	39.4	0.0	39.5	0.3	39.8	0.8	39.9	0.3	40.0	0.3	40.1	0.2	40.3	0.5	40.3	0.0	40.4	0.2	40.4	0.0
1973	40.3	-0.2	40.3	0.0	40.4	0.2	40.8	1.0	41.1	0.7	41.5	1.0	41.5	0.0	41.4	-0.2	41.2	-0.5	41.6	1.0	41.9	0.7	42.2	0.7
1974	42.6	0.9	43.0	0.9	43.9	2.1	44.5	1.4	45.4	2.0	46.2	1.8	46.8	1.3	47.0	0.4	47.3	0.6	47.5	0.4	47.7	0.4	47.7	0.0
1975	47.6	-0.2	47.7	0.2	48.2	1.0	48.6	0.8	49.0	0.8	49.8	1.6	50.8	2.0	51.1	0.6	51.7	1.2	51.9	0.4	52.4	1.0	52.4	0.0
1976	52.6	0.4	52.7	0.2	53.2	0.9	53.7	0.9	54.4	1.3	55.2	1.5	55.8	1.1	56.1	0.5	56.4	0.5	56.9	0.9	57.0	0.2	57.0	0.0
1977	57.3	0.5	57.6	0.5	58.1	0.9	58.8	1.2	59.3	0.9	59.6	0.5	59.6	0.0	59.5	-0.2	59.4	-0.2	59.4	0.0	59.5	0.2	59.5	0.0
1978	59.6	0.2	59.7	0.2	59.9	0.3	60.3	0.7	61.0	1.2	61.7	1.1	62.3	1.0	62.6	0.5	62.8	0.3	63.1	0.5	63.7	1.0	64.1	0.6
1979	64.5	0.6	65.1	0.9	65.9	1.2	67.5	2.4	69.1	2.4	70.7	2.3	72.1	2.0	73.1	1.4	73.7	0.8	74.1	0.5	74.8	0.9	75.8	1.3
1980	77.7	2.5	79.7	2.6	81.1	1.8	82.1	1.2	82.8	0.9	83.1	0.4	83.5	0.5	84.1	0.7	84.7	0.7	85.2	0.6	86.2	1.2	86.9	0.8

[Continued]

U.S. City Average
Consumer Price Index - All Urban Consumers
Base 1982-1984 = 100
Transportation
[Continued]

For 1935-2001. Columns headed % show percentile change in the index from the previous period for which an index is available.

Year	Jan Index	%	Feb Index	%	Mar Index	%	Apr Index	%	May Index	%	Jun Index	%	Jul Index	%	Aug Index	%	Sep Index	%	Oct Index	%	Nov Index	%	Dec Index	%
1981	88.1	1.4	90.1	2.3	91.0	1.0	91.6	0.7	92.4	0.9	93.1	0.8	94.0	1.0	94.4	0.4	94.9	0.5	95.6	0.7	96.2	0.6	96.4	0.2
1982	96.5	0.1	95.8	-0.7	94.9	-0.9	94.1	-0.8	95.0	1.0	97.4	2.5	98.5	1.1	98.6	0.1	98.3	-0.3	98.3	0.0	98.4	0.1	98.1	-0.3
1983	97.5	-0.6	96.5	-1.0	95.6	-0.9	97.3	1.8	98.6	1.3	99.3	0.7	100.0	0.7	100.6	0.6	101.0	0.4	101.5	0.5	101.9	0.4	101.9	0.0
1984	101.8	-0.1	101.7	-0.1	102.1	0.4	103.0	0.9	103.9	0.9	104.2	0.3	104.1	-0.1	104.1	0.0	104.4	0.3	105.0	0.6	105.2	0.2	105.1	-0.1
1985	104.7	-0.4	104.6	-0.1	105.4	0.8	106.5	1.0	106.9	0.4	107.1	0.2	107.1	0.0	106.7	-0.4	106.4	-0.3	106.8	0.4	107.5	0.7	107.8	0.3
1986	107.8	0.0	106.2	-1.5	103.0	-3.0	100.9	-2.0	101.7	0.8	102.7	1.0	101.4	-1.3	100.3	-1.1	100.5	0.2	100.7	0.2	101.2	0.5	101.4	0.2
1987	102.6	1.2	103.1	0.5	103.3	0.2	104.2	0.9	104.7	0.5	105.4	0.7	106.0	0.6	106.5	0.5	106.6	0.1	107.1	0.5	107.8	0.7	107.6	-0.2
1988	107.1	-0.5	106.8	-0.3	106.5	-0.3	107.2	0.7	108.1	0.8	108.5	0.4	108.9	0.4	109.6	0.6	109.7	0.1	110.0	0.3	110.7	0.6	110.8	0.1
1989	111.1	0.3	111.6	0.5	111.9	0.3	114.6	2.4	116.0	1.2	115.9	-0.1	115.4	-0.4	114.3	-1.0	113.7	-0.5	114.5	0.7	115.0	0.4	115.2	0.2
1990	117.2	1.7	117.1	-0.1	116.8	-0.3	117.3	0.4	117.7	0.3	118.2	0.4	118.4	0.2	120.6	1.9	123.0	2.0	125.8	2.3	126.9	0.9	127.2	0.2
1991	125.5	-1.3	123.7	-1.4	122.3	-1.1	122.2	-0.1	123.3	0.9	123.7	0.3	123.4	-0.2	123.8	0.3	123.8	0.0	124.0	0.2	125.0	0.8	125.3	0.2
1992	124.5	-0.6	124.1	-0.3	124.4	0.2	125.2	0.6	126.3	0.9	126.9	0.5	127.2	0.2	126.9	-0.2	126.8	-0.1	128.0	0.9	129.2	0.9	129.0	-0.2
1993	129.1	0.1	129.2	0.1	129.0	-0.2	129.4	0.3	130.2	0.6	130.3	0.1	130.3	0.0	130.2	-0.1	130.1	-0.1	131.8	1.3	132.6	0.6	132.1	-0.4
1994	131.6	-0.4	131.9	0.2	132.2	0.2	132.6	0.3	132.8	0.2	133.8	0.8	134.6	0.6	135.9	1.0	135.9	0.0	136.1	0.1	137.1	0.7	137.1	0.0
1995	137.3	0.1	137.5	0.1	138.0	0.4	139.1	0.8	140.3	0.9	141.1	0.6	140.1	-0.7	139.2	-0.6	138.8	-0.3	139.4	0.4	139.4	0.0	139.1	-0.2
1996	139.9	0.6	140.4	0.4	141.2	0.6	143.1	1.3	144.4	0.9	144.0	-0.3	143.5	-0.3	142.8	-0.5	143.2	0.3	143.9	0.5	144.8	0.6	145.2	0.3
1997	145.0	-0.1	144.8	-0.1	144.9	0.1	144.8	-0.1	144.4	-0.3	144.0	-0.3	143.7	-0.2	143.8	0.1	144.3	0.3	144.5	0.1	143.9	-0.4	143.2	-0.5
1998	142.7	-0.3	142.1	-0.4	141.4	-0.5	141.5	0.1	142.0	0.4	141.7	-0.2	141.8	0.1	141.2	-0.4	140.7	-0.4	141.3	0.4	141.5	0.1	140.7	-0.6
1999	140.4	-0.2	139.8	-0.4	140.6	0.6	144.3	2.6	144.2	-0.1	143.4	-0.6	144.7	0.9	145.7	0.7	146.5	0.5	147.3	0.5	147.6	0.2	148.3	0.5
2000	148.3	0.0	149.7	0.9	153.4	2.5	152.9	-0.3	153.1	0.1	155.7	1.7	155.0	-0.4	153.2	-1.2	154.7	1.0	154.4	-0.2	155.2	0.5	154.4	-0.5
2001	154.4	0.0	154.9	0.3	153.9	-0.6	156.1	1.4	159.2	2.0	158.3	-0.6	154.4	-2.5	153.3	-0.7	155.5	1.4	152.3	-2.1	150.2	-1.4	148.5	-1.1

Source: U.S. Department of Labor, Bureau of Labor Statistics, Division of Consumer Prices and Price Indexes.

U.S. City Average
Consumer Price Index - Urban Wage Earners
Base 1982-1984 = 100
Transportation

For 1935-2001. Columns headed % show percentile change in the index from the previous period for which an index is available.

Year	Jan Index	%	Feb Index	%	Mar Index	%	Apr Index	%	May Index	%	Jun Index	%	Jul Index	%	Aug Index	%	Sep Index	%	Oct Index	%	Nov Index	%	Dec Index	%
1935	-	-	-	-	14.1	-	-	-	-	-	-	-	14.2	0.7	-	-	-	-	14.0	-1.4	-	-	-	-
1936	14.1	0.7	-	-	-	-	14.2	0.7	-	-	-	-	14.3	0.7	-	-	14.3	0.0	-	-	-	-	14.3	0.0
1937	-	-	-	-	14.4	0.7	-	-	-	-	14.4	0.0	-	-	-	-	14.5	0.7	-	-	-	-	14.6	0.7
1938	-	-	-	-	14.6	0.0	-	-	-	-	14.6	0.0	-	-	-	-	14.6	0.0	-	-	-	-	14.3	-2.1
1939	-	-	-	-	14.2	-0.7	-	-	-	-	14.2	0.0	-	-	-	-	14.3	0.7	-	-	-	-	14.2	-0.7
1940	-	-	-	-	14.2	0.0	-	-	-	-	14.1	-0.7	-	-	-	-	14.1	0.0	-	-	-	-	14.2	0.7
1941	-	-	-	-	14.3	0.7	-	-	-	-	14.6	2.1	-	-	-	-	14.7	0.7	-	-	-	-	15.3	4.1
1942	-	-	-	-	15.9	3.9	-	-	-	-	16.0	0.6	-	-	-	-	15.9	-0.6	-	-	-	-	15.9	0.0
1943	-	-	-	-	15.9	0.0	-	-	-	-	15.8	-0.6	-	-	-	-	15.8	0.0	-	-	-	-	15.8	0.0
1944	-	-	-	-	15.8	0.0	-	-	-	-	15.8	0.0	-	-	-	-	15.8	0.0	-	-	-	-	15.8	0.0
1945	-	-	-	-	15.8	0.0	-	-	-	-	15.8	0.0	-	-	-	-	15.8	0.0	-	-	-	-	15.8	0.0
1946	-	-	-	-	15.9	0.6	-	-	-	-	16.1	1.3	-	-	-	-	17.4	8.1	-	-	-	-	17.8	2.3
1947	17.8	0.0	17.8	0.0	18.0	1.1	18.1	0.6	18.2	0.6	18.2	0.0	18.3	0.5	18.4	0.5	18.6	1.1	18.8	1.1	18.9	0.5	19.1	1.1
1948	19.4	1.6	19.4	0.0	19.4	0.0	19.7	1.5	19.7	0.0	19.8	0.5	20.8	5.1	21.2	1.9	21.3	0.5	21.5	0.9	21.5	0.0	21.5	0.0
1949	21.5	0.0	21.7	0.9	21.8	0.5	21.9	0.5	22.0	0.5	21.9	-0.5	22.0	0.5	22.2	0.9	22.2	0.0	22.3	0.5	22.2	-0.4	22.4	0.9
1950	22.3	-0.4	22.3	0.0	22.2	-0.4	22.2	0.0	22.3	0.5	22.3	0.0	22.5	0.9	22.8	1.3	22.8	0.0	22.8	0.0	22.9	0.4	23.1	0.9
1951	23.2	0.4	23.5	1.3	23.7	0.9	23.7	0.0	23.8	0.4	23.8	0.0	23.8	0.0	24.0	0.8	24.2	0.8	24.4	0.8	24.7	1.2	24.7	0.0
1952	24.9	0.8	25.1	0.8	25.2	0.4	25.3	0.4	25.3	0.0	25.6	1.2	25.7	0.4	25.7	0.0	25.9	0.8	26.0	0.4	26.1	0.4	26.1	0.0
1953	26.2	0.4	26.1	-0.4	26.2	0.4	26.2	0.0	26.2	0.0	26.2	0.0	26.3	0.4	26.5	0.8	26.5	0.0	26.5	0.0	26.3	-0.8	26.1	-0.8
1954	26.4	1.1	26.2	-0.8	26.1	-0.4	26.1	0.0	26.1	0.0	26.1	0.0	25.7	-1.5	25.7	0.0	25.6	-0.4	25.3	-1.2	25.9	2.4	25.8	-0.4
1955	25.9	0.4	25.8	-0.4	25.8	0.0	25.4	-1.6	25.4	0.0	25.5	0.4	25.4	-0.4	25.4	0.0	25.4	0.0	25.7	1.2	26.0	1.2	25.8	-0.8
1956	25.7	-0.4	25.7	0.0	25.7	0.0	25.6	-0.4	25.7	0.4	25.7	0.0	25.9	0.8	26.0	0.4	26.1	0.4	26.9	3.1	27.0	0.4	27.0	0.0
1957	27.1	0.4	27.2	0.4	27.4	0.7	27.5	0.4	27.4	-0.4	27.4	0.0	27.5	0.4	27.6	0.4	27.6	0.0	27.5	-0.4	28.4	3.3	28.1	-1.1
1958	28.1	0.0	28.1	0.0	28.1	0.0	28.0	-0.4	28.1	0.4	28.1	0.0	28.4	1.1	28.6	0.7	28.6	0.0	28.9	1.0	29.3	1.4	29.2	-0.3
1959	29.2	0.0	29.2	0.0	29.3	0.3	29.4	0.3	29.4	0.0	29.5	0.3	29.6	0.3	29.7	0.3	29.6	-0.3	30.1	1.7	30.2	0.3	30.1	-0.3
1960	29.9	-0.7	29.9	0.0	29.7	-0.7	29.6	-0.3	29.5	-0.3	29.5	0.0	29.5	0.0	29.6	0.3	29.3	-1.0	29.6	1.0	29.7	0.3	29.7	0.0
1961	29.6	-0.3	29.6	0.0	29.5	-0.3	29.5	0.0	29.7	0.7	29.9	0.7	30.1	0.7	30.3	0.7	30.3	0.0	30.5	0.7	30.5	0.0	30.3	-0.7
1962	30.3	0.0	30.3	0.0	30.2	-0.3	30.6	1.3	30.6	0.0	30.6	0.0	30.5	-0.3	30.7	0.7	30.8	0.3	30.9	0.3	30.9	0.0	30.8	-0.3
1963	30.4	-1.3	30.5	0.3	30.5	0.0	30.5	0.0	30.7	0.7	30.7	0.0	30.8	0.3	30.9	0.3	30.8	-0.3	31.1	1.0	31.1	0.0	31.1	0.0
1964	31.2	0.3	31.0	-0.6	31.1	0.3	31.1	0.0	31.1	0.0	31.2	0.3	31.2	0.0	31.2	0.0	31.1	-0.3	31.2	0.3	31.4	0.6	31.5	0.3
1965	31.7	0.6	31.6	-0.3	31.6	0.0	31.7	0.3	31.8	0.3	31.7	-0.3	31.8	0.3	31.7	-0.3	31.7	0.0	31.7	0.0	31.8	0.3	31.9	0.3
1966	31.7	-0.6	31.7	0.0	31.8	0.3	32.0	0.6	32.0	0.0	32.0	0.0	32.4	1.3	32.4	0.0	32.4	0.0	32.6	0.6	32.7	0.3	32.5	-0.6
1967	32.4	-0.3	32.5	0.3	32.6	0.3	32.8	0.6	33.0	0.6	33.0	0.0	33.2	0.6	33.2	0.0	33.3	0.3	33.6	0.9	33.8	0.6	33.6	-0.6
1968	33.9	0.9	33.8	-0.3	34.0	0.6	34.0	0.0	34.0	0.0	34.2	0.6	34.2	0.0	34.2	0.0	34.1	-0.3	34.4	0.9	34.6	0.6	34.3	-0.9
1969	34.4	0.3	34.8	1.2	35.5	2.0	35.6	0.3	35.4	-0.6	35.6	0.6	35.5	-0.3	35.5	0.0	35.3	-0.6	35.9	1.7	35.9	0.0	36.1	0.6
1970	36.3	0.6	36.3	0.0	36.3	0.0	36.8	1.4	37.1	0.8	37.3	0.5	37.5	0.5	37.3	-0.5	37.4	0.3	38.1	1.9	38.4	0.8	38.7	0.8
1971	38.9	0.5	38.9	0.0	39.0	0.3	39.1	0.3	39.3	0.5	39.6	0.8	39.5	-0.3	39.5	0.0	39.2	-0.8	39.5	0.8	39.3	-0.5	39.2	-0.3
1972	39.3	0.3	39.1	-0.5	39.2	0.3	39.2	0.0	39.5	0.8	39.6	0.3	39.8	0.5	39.9	0.3	40.0	0.3	40.1	0.2	40.2	0.2	40.1	-0.2
1973	40.0	-0.2	40.1	0.2	40.2	0.2	40.6	1.0	40.9	0.7	41.2	0.7	41.3	0.2	41.2	-0.2	41.0	-0.5	41.3	0.7	41.6	0.7	41.9	0.7
1974	42.4	1.2	42.8	0.9	43.7	2.1	44.2	1.1	45.1	2.0	45.9	1.8	46.5	1.3	46.7	0.4	47.0	0.6	47.3	0.6	47.4	0.2	47.5	0.2
1975	47.4	-0.2	47.5	0.2	47.9	0.8	48.4	1.0	48.8	0.8	49.6	1.6	50.5	1.8	50.8	0.6	51.4	1.2	51.6	0.4	52.1	1.0	52.1	0.0
1976	52.3	0.4	52.4	0.2	52.9	1.0	53.4	0.9	54.1	1.3	54.9	1.5	55.4	0.9	55.7	0.5	56.1	0.7	56.5	0.7	56.7	0.4	56.7	0.0
1977	57.0	0.5	57.3	0.5	57.8	0.9	58.4	1.0	58.9	0.9	59.2	0.5	59.3	0.2	59.1	-0.3	59.0	-0.2	59.1	0.2	59.1	0.0	59.1	0.0
1978	59.2	0.2	59.4	0.3	59.5	0.2	60.0	0.8	60.7	1.2	61.5	1.3	62.1	1.0	62.4	0.5	62.6	0.3	62.9	0.5	63.5	1.0	63.9	0.6
1979	64.3	0.6	64.9	0.9	65.7	1.2	67.4	2.6	69.0	2.4	70.7	2.5	72.0	1.8	73.0	1.4	73.6	0.8	73.9	0.4	74.7	1.1	75.5	1.1
1980	77.4	2.5	79.5	2.7	80.8	1.6	81.9	1.4	82.7	1.0	82.9	0.2	83.3	0.5	83.9	0.7	84.4	0.6	84.9	0.6	85.9	1.2	86.6	0.8

[Continued]

U.S. City Average
Consumer Price Index - Urban Wage Earners
Base 1982-1984 = 100
Transportation

[Continued]

For 1935-2001. Columns headed % show percentile change in the index from the previous period for which an index is available.

Year	Jan Index	%	Feb Index	%	Mar Index	%	Apr Index	%	May Index	%	Jun Index	%	Jul Index	%	Aug Index	%	Sep Index	%	Oct Index	%	Nov Index	%	Dec Index	%
1981	87.9	1.5	90.0	2.4	90.8	0.9	91.4	0.7	92.3	1.0	92.9	0.7	93.9	1.1	94.3	0.4	94.8	0.5	95.6	0.8	96.2	0.6	96.4	0.2
1982	96.5	0.1	95.8	-0.7	94.8	-1.0	94.0	-0.8	95.0	1.1	97.4	2.5	98.5	1.1	98.6	0.1	98.2	-0.4	98.2	0.0	98.3	0.1	98.0	-0.3
1983	97.3	-0.7	96.3	-1.0	95.5	-0.8	97.1	1.7	98.4	1.3	99.1	0.7	99.9	0.8	100.6	0.7	101.1	0.5	101.5	0.4	101.9	0.4	101.9	0.0
1984	101.8	-0.1	101.8	0.0	102.2	0.4	103.2	1.0	104.1	0.9	104.4	0.3	104.3	-0.1	104.3	0.0	104.5	0.2	105.1	0.6	105.3	0.2	105.2	-0.1
1985	104.8	-0.4	104.6	-0.2	105.4	0.8	106.5	1.0	106.9	0.4	107.0	0.1	107.0	0.0	106.6	-0.4	106.2	-0.4	106.6	0.4	107.4	0.8	107.6	0.2
1986	107.5	-0.1	105.9	-1.5	102.6	-3.1	100.4	-2.1	101.2	0.8	102.1	0.9	100.8	-1.3	99.5	-1.3	99.8	0.3	100.0	0.2	100.6	0.6	100.6	0.0
1987	101.9	1.3	102.5	0.6	102.8	0.3	103.8	1.0	104.4	0.6	105.1	0.7	105.8	0.7	106.3	0.5	106.4	0.1	106.9	0.5	107.6	0.7	107.3	-0.3
1988	106.8	-0.5	106.4	-0.4	106.2	-0.2	106.8	0.6	107.8	0.9	108.2	0.4	108.6	0.4	109.4	0.7	109.4	0.0	109.8	0.4	110.3	0.5	110.4	0.1
1989	110.7	0.3	111.2	0.5	111.6	0.4	114.5	2.6	116.0	1.3	116.0	0.0	115.4	-0.5	114.2	-1.0	113.5	-0.6	114.3	0.7	114.6	0.3	114.8	0.2
1990	116.8	1.7	116.6	-0.2	116.2	-0.3	116.6	0.3	117.1	0.4	117.7	0.5	117.8	0.1	120.3	2.1	122.9	2.2	125.7	2.3	126.6	0.7	126.7	0.1
1991	124.7	-1.6	122.6	-1.7	121.2	-1.1	121.3	0.1	122.7	1.2	123.1	0.3	122.9	-0.2	123.2	0.2	123.3	0.1	123.4	0.1	124.5	0.9	124.5	0.0
1992	123.5	-0.8	122.9	-0.5	123.2	0.2	124.1	0.7	125.5	1.1	126.5	0.8	126.7	0.2	126.5	-0.2	126.5	0.0	127.5	0.8	128.5	0.8	128.2	-0.2
1993	128.0	-0.2	128.0	0.0	127.8	-0.2	128.4	0.5	129.2	0.6	129.5	0.2	129.4	-0.1	129.4	0.0	129.2	-0.2	131.0	1.4	131.6	0.5	130.8	-0.6
1994	130.2	-0.5	130.4	0.2	130.5	0.1	131.2	0.5	131.8	0.5	132.9	0.8	133.9	0.8	135.2	1.0	135.3	0.1	135.6	0.2	136.7	0.8	136.7	0.0
1995	136.9	0.1	137.1	0.1	137.6	0.4	138.7	0.8	140.1	1.0	140.8	0.5	139.8	-0.7	138.9	-0.6	138.5	-0.3	139.0	0.4	139.0	0.0	138.9	-0.1
1996	139.7	0.6	140.0	0.2	140.9	0.6	143.0	1.5	144.4	1.0	143.8	-0.4	143.3	-0.3	142.6	-0.5	142.9	0.2	143.5	0.4	144.5	0.7	144.8	0.2
1997	144.6	-0.1	144.4	-0.1	144.2	-0.1	144.2	0.0	143.8	-0.3	143.4	-0.3	142.9	-0.3	143.3	0.3	143.6	0.2	143.6	0.0	143.1	-0.3	142.4	-0.5
1998	141.7	-0.5	140.9	-0.6	140.1	-0.6	140.3	0.1	141.1	0.6	140.9	-0.1	140.8	-0.1	140.2	-0.4	139.6	-0.4	140.4	0.6	140.6	0.1	139.6	-0.7
1999	139.1	-0.4	138.3	-0.6	139.1	0.6	142.9	2.7	143.1	0.1	142.4	-0.5	143.7	0.9	145.0	0.9	146.0	0.7	146.6	0.4	146.9	0.2	147.6	0.5
2000	147.7	0.1	149.1	0.9	152.9	2.5	152.2	-0.5	152.5	0.2	155.5	2.0	154.4	-0.7	152.3	-1.4	154.2	1.2	154.0	-0.1	154.9	0.6	153.9	-0.6
2001	154.0	0.1	154.5	0.3	153.3	-0.8	155.8	1.6	159.2	2.2	157.9	-0.8	153.4	-2.8	152.5	-0.6	155.1	1.7	151.4	-2.4	149.2	-1.5	147.4	-1.2

Source: U.S. Department of Labor, Bureau of Labor Statistics, Division of Consumer Prices and Price Indexes.

U.S. City Average
Consumer Price Index - All Urban Consumers
Base 1982-1984 = 100
Medical Care

For 1935-2001. Columns headed % show percentile change in the index from the previous period for which an index is available.

Year	Jan Index	%	Feb Index	%	Mar Index	%	Apr Index	%	May Index	%	Jun Index	%	Jul Index	%	Aug Index	%	Sep Index	%	Oct Index	%	Nov Index	%	Dec Index	%
1935	-	-	-	-	10.2	-	-	-	-	-	-	-	10.2	0.0	-	-	-	-	10.2	0.0	-	-	-	-
1936	10.2	0.0	-	-	-	-	10.2	0.0	-	-	-	-	10.2	0.0	-	-	10.2	0.0	-	-	-	-	10.2	0.0
1937	-	-	-	-	10.3	1.0	-	-	-	-	10.3	0.0	-	-	-	-	10.3	0.0	-	-	-	-	10.3	0.0
1938	-	-	-	-	10.3	0.0	-	-	-	-	10.3	0.0	-	-	-	-	10.3	0.0	-	-	-	-	10.3	0.0
1939	-	-	-	-	10.3	0.0	-	-	-	-	10.4	1.0	-	-	-	-	10.4	0.0	-	-	-	-	10.4	0.0
1940	-	-	-	-	10.4	0.0	-	-	-	-	10.3	-1.0	-	-	-	-	10.3	0.0	-	-	-	-	10.4	1.0
1941	-	-	-	-	10.4	0.0	-	-	-	-	10.4	0.0	-	-	-	-	10.4	0.0	-	-	-	-	10.5	1.0
1942	-	-	-	-	10.6	1.0	-	-	-	-	10.7	0.9	-	-	-	-	10.8	0.9	-	-	-	-	10.9	0.9
1943	-	-	-	-	11.1	1.8	-	-	-	-	11.2	0.9	-	-	-	-	11.4	1.8	-	-	-	-	11.4	0.0
1944	-	-	-	-	11.5	0.9	-	-	-	-	11.5	0.0	-	-	-	-	11.6	0.9	-	-	-	-	11.7	0.9
1945	-	-	-	-	11.8	0.9	-	-	-	-	11.9	0.8	-	-	-	-	11.9	0.0	-	-	-	-	12.0	0.8
1946	-	-	-	-	12.2	1.7	-	-	-	-	12.4	1.6	-	-	-	-	12.7	2.4	-	-	-	-	13.0	2.4
1947	13.2	1.5	13.3	0.8	13.3	0.0	13.4	0.8	13.5	0.7	13.5	0.0	13.5	0.0	13.6	0.7	13.7	0.7	13.8	0.7	13.8	0.0	13.9	0.7
1948	14.0	0.7	14.0	0.0	14.1	0.7	14.3	1.4	14.3	0.0	14.3	0.0	14.5	1.4	14.5	0.0	14.5	0.0	14.6	0.7	14.7	0.7	14.7	0.0
1949	14.8	0.7	14.8	0.0	14.8	0.0	14.8	0.0	14.8	0.0	14.8	0.0	14.8	0.0	14.8	0.0	14.9	0.7	14.9	0.0	14.9	0.0	14.9	0.0
1950	15.0	0.7	15.0	0.0	15.0	0.0	15.0	0.0	15.0	0.0	15.0	0.0	15.1	0.7	15.1	0.0	15.2	0.7	15.3	0.7	15.3	0.0	15.4	0.7
1951	15.5	0.6	15.5	0.0	15.7	1.3	15.7	0.0	15.8	0.6	15.8	0.0	15.8	0.0	15.9	0.6	15.9	0.0	16.0	0.6	16.1	0.6	16.3	1.2
1952	16.4	0.6	16.4	0.0	16.5	0.6	16.5	0.0	16.5	0.0	16.8	1.8	16.8	0.0	16.8	0.0	16.9	0.6	16.9	0.0	16.9	0.0	17.0	0.6
1953	17.0	0.0	17.0	0.0	17.0	0.0	17.1	0.6	17.2	0.6	17.3	0.6	17.3	0.0	17.4	0.6	17.5	0.6	17.5	0.0	17.6	0.6	17.6	0.0
1954	17.6	0.0	17.7	0.6	17.7	0.0	17.8	0.6	17.8	0.0	17.8	0.0	17.8	0.0	17.9	0.6	17.9	0.0	17.9	0.0	18.0	0.6	18.0	0.0
1955	18.0	0.0	18.1	0.6	18.1	0.0	18.1	0.0	18.2	0.6	18.2	0.0	18.2	0.0	18.2	0.0	18.3	0.5	18.4	0.5	18.5	0.5	18.6	0.5
1956	18.6	0.0	18.7	0.5	18.7	0.0	18.8	0.5	18.8	0.0	18.8	0.0	18.9	0.5	19.0	0.5	19.1	0.5	19.1	0.0	19.2	0.5	19.2	0.0
1957	19.3	0.5	19.3	0.0	19.5	1.0	19.5	0.0	19.6	0.5	19.7	0.5	19.7	0.0	19.8	0.5	19.8	0.0	19.9	0.5	20.0	0.5	20.1	0.5
1958	20.2	0.5	20.2	0.0	20.3	0.5	20.4	0.5	20.5	0.5	20.6	0.5	20.7	0.5	20.7	0.0	20.9	1.0	21.0	0.5	21.0	0.0	21.0	0.0
1959	21.1	0.5	21.2	0.5	21.3	0.5	21.3	0.0	21.4	0.5	21.5	0.5	21.5	0.0	21.6	0.5	21.7	0.5	21.7	0.0	21.8	0.5	21.8	0.0
1960	21.9	0.5	22.0	0.5	22.1	0.5	22.2	0.5	22.2	0.0	22.2	0.0	22.3	0.5	22.3	0.0	22.4	0.4	22.4	0.0	22.5	0.4	22.5	0.0
1961	22.6	0.4	22.7	0.4	22.7	0.0	22.8	0.4	22.9	0.4	22.9	0.0	23.0	0.4	23.0	0.0	23.1	0.4	23.1	0.0	23.1	0.0	23.2	0.4
1962	23.2	0.0	23.3	0.4	23.4	0.4	23.5	0.4	23.5	0.0	23.6	0.4	23.6	0.0	23.6	0.0	23.6	0.0	23.7	0.4	23.7	0.0	23.7	0.0
1963	23.8	0.4	23.9	0.4	23.9	0.0	24.0	0.4	24.0	0.0	24.1	0.4	24.2	0.4	24.2	0.0	24.2	0.0	24.2	0.0	24.3	0.4	24.3	0.0
1964	24.4	0.4	24.4	0.0	24.4	0.0	24.5	0.4	24.5	0.0	24.6	0.4	24.6	0.0	24.7	0.4	24.7	0.0	24.7	0.0	24.7	0.0	24.8	0.4
1965	24.8	0.0	24.9	0.4	25.0	0.4	25.1	0.4	25.1	0.0	25.2	0.4	25.3	0.4	25.3	0.0	25.3	0.0	25.3	0.0	25.4	0.4	25.5	0.4
1966	25.6	0.4	25.6	0.0	25.8	0.8	25.9	0.4	26.0	0.4	26.2	0.8	26.3	0.4	26.4	0.4	26.7	1.1	26.9	0.7	27.0	0.4	27.2	0.7
1967	27.4	0.7	27.5	0.4	27.7	0.7	27.8	0.4	28.0	0.7	28.1	0.4	28.2	0.4	28.3	0.4	28.5	0.7	28.6	0.4	28.8	0.7	28.9	0.3
1968	29.1	0.7	29.2	0.3	29.4	0.7	29.6	0.7	29.6	0.0	29.7	0.3	29.9	0.7	30.0	0.3	30.2	0.7	30.4	0.7	30.5	0.3	30.7	-0.7
1969	30.9	0.7	31.2	1.0	31.4	0.6	31.6	0.6	31.8	0.6	32.0	0.6	32.1	0.3	32.3	0.6	32.5	0.6	32.3	-0.6	32.4	0.3	32.6	0.6
1970	32.7	0.3	33.0	0.9	33.3	0.9	33.5	0.6	33.7	0.6	33.9	0.6	34.2	0.9	34.3	0.3	34.5	0.6	34.6	0.3	34.7	0.3	35.0	0.9
1971	35.2	0.6	35.4	0.6	35.7	0.8	35.9	0.6	36.1	0.6	36.2	0.3	36.4	0.6	36.6	0.5	36.7	0.3	36.5	-0.5	36.5	0.0	36.6	0.3
1972	36.7	0.3	36.9	0.5	37.0	0.3	37.1	0.3	37.2	0.3	37.3	0.3	37.4	0.3	37.4	0.0	37.5	0.3	37.7	0.5	37.8	0.3	37.8	0.0
1973	38.0	0.5	38.1	0.3	38.2	0.3	38.3	0.3	38.5	0.5	38.6	0.3	38.7	0.3	38.7	0.0	38.9	0.5	39.6	1.8	39.7	0.3	39.8	0.3
1974	40.0	0.5	40.4	1.0	40.8	1.0	41.0	0.5	41.4	1.0	42.1	1.7	42.6	1.2	43.3	1.6	43.7	0.9	44.0	0.7	44.3	0.7	44.8	1.1
1975	45.3	1.1	45.9	1.3	46.3	0.9	46.7	0.9	47.0	0.6	47.3	0.6	47.8	1.1	48.1	0.6	48.5	0.8	48.8	0.6	48.8	0.0	49.2	0.8
1976	49.7	1.0	50.3	1.2	50.8	1.0	51.1	0.6	51.4	0.6	51.7	0.6	52.2	1.0	52.6	0.8	52.9	0.6	53.2	0.6	53.9	1.3	54.1	0.4
1977	54.6	0.9	55.1	0.9	55.6	0.9	56.1	0.9	56.4	0.5	56.8	0.7	57.3	0.9	57.7	0.7	58.1	0.7	58.3	0.3	58.6	0.5	58.9	0.5
1978	59.5	1.0	60.1	1.0	60.4	0.5	60.7	0.5	61.1	0.7	61.3	0.3	61.8	0.8	62.3	0.8	62.7	0.6	63.3	1.0	63.9	0.9	64.1	0.3
1979	65.0	1.4	65.5	0.8	65.9	0.6	66.2	0.5	66.5	0.5	66.9	0.6	67.5	0.9	68.1	0.9	68.6	0.7	69.2	0.9	69.8	0.9	70.6	1.1
1980	71.5	1.3	72.6	1.5	73.3	1.0	73.8	0.7	74.2	0.5	74.5	0.4	75.1	0.8	75.6	0.7	76.2	0.8	76.8	0.8	77.3	0.7	77.6	0.4

[Continued]

U.S. City Average
Consumer Price Index - All Urban Consumers
Base 1982-1984 = 100
Medical Care
[Continued]

For 1935-2001. Columns headed % show percentile change in the index from the previous period for which an index is available.

Year	Jan Index	%	Feb Index	%	Mar Index	%	Apr Index	%	May Index	%	Jun Index	%	Jul Index	%	Aug Index	%	Sep Index	%	Oct Index	%	Nov Index	%	Dec Index	%
1981	78.7	1.4	79.6	1.1	80.2	0.8	80.8	0.7	81.4	0.7	82.1	0.9	83.2	1.3	84.3	1.3	84.9	0.7	85.8	1.1	86.8	1.2	87.3	0.6
1982	88.2	1.0	89.0	0.9	89.8	0.9	90.6	0.9	91.2	0.7	91.9	0.8	92.9	1.1	93.8	1.0	94.6	0.9	95.4	0.8	96.3	0.9	96.9	0.6
1983	97.9	1.0	98.9	1.0	99.2	0.3	99.5	0.3	99.7	0.2	100.1	0.4	100.7	0.6	101.4	0.7	101.7	0.3	102.2	0.5	102.7	0.5	103.1	0.4
1984	104.0	0.9	105.1	1.1	105.4	0.3	105.8	0.4	106.1	0.3	106.4	0.3	107.1	0.7	107.5	0.4	107.9	0.4	108.5	0.6	109.1	0.6	109.4	0.3
1985	110.1	0.6	110.9	0.7	111.6	0.6	112.1	0.4	112.5	0.4	113.1	0.5	113.7	0.5	114.5	0.7	115.0	0.4	115.6	0.5	116.3	0.6	116.8	0.4
1986	117.7	0.8	118.9	1.0	119.9	0.8	120.5	0.5	121.0	0.4	121.6	0.5	122.4	0.7	123.2	0.7	123.8	0.5	124.5	0.6	125.2	0.6	125.8	0.5
1987	126.6	0.6	127.4	0.6	128.1	0.5	128.7	0.5	129.2	0.4	129.9	0.5	130.7	0.6	131.2	0.4	131.7	0.4	132.3	0.5	132.8	0.4	133.1	0.2
1988	134.4	1.0	135.5	0.8	136.3	0.6	136.9	0.4	137.5	0.4	138.2	0.5	139.3	0.8	139.9	0.4	140.4	0.4	141.2	0.6	141.8	0.4	142.3	0.4
1989	143.8	1.1	145.2	1.0	146.1	0.6	146.8	0.5	147.5	0.5	148.5	0.7	149.7	0.8	150.7	0.7	151.7	0.7	152.7	0.7	153.9	0.8	154.4	0.3
1990	155.9	1.0	157.5	1.0	158.7	0.8	159.8	0.7	160.8	0.6	161.9	0.7	163.5	1.0	165.0	0.9	165.8	0.5	167.1	0.8	168.4	0.8	169.2	0.5
1991	171.0	1.1	172.5	0.9	173.7	0.7	174.4	0.4	175.2	0.5	176.2	0.6	177.5	0.7	178.9	0.8	179.7	0.4	180.7	0.6	181.8	0.6	182.6	0.4
1992	184.3	0.9	186.2	1.0	187.3	0.6	188.1	0.4	188.7	0.3	189.4	0.4	190.7	0.7	191.5	0.4	192.3	0.4	193.3	0.5	194.3	0.5	194.7	0.2
1993	196.4	0.9	198.0	0.8	198.6	0.3	199.4	0.4	200.5	0.6	201.1	0.3	202.2	0.5	202.9	0.3	203.3	0.2	204.4	0.5	204.9	0.2	205.2	0.1
1994	206.4	0.6	207.7	0.6	208.3	0.3	209.2	0.4	209.7	0.2	210.4	0.3	211.5	0.5	212.2	0.3	212.8	0.3	214.0	0.6	214.7	0.3	215.3	0.3
1995	216.6	0.6	217.9	0.6	218.4	0.2	218.9	0.2	219.3	0.2	219.8	0.2	220.8	0.5	221.6	0.4	222.1	0.2	222.9	0.4	223.5	0.3	223.8	0.1
1996	225.2	0.6	226.2	0.4	226.6	0.2	227.0	0.2	227.4	0.2	227.8	0.2	228.7	0.4	229.2	0.2	229.4	0.1	230.1	0.3	230.5	0.2	230.6	0.0
1997	231.8	0.5	232.7	0.4	233.4	0.3	233.8	0.2	234.2	0.2	234.4	0.1	234.8	0.2	235.2	0.2	235.4	0.1	235.8	0.2	236.4	0.3	237.1	0.3
1998	238.1	0.4	239.3	0.5	239.8	0.2	240.7	0.4	241.4	0.3	242.0	0.2	242.7	0.3	243.5	0.3	243.9	0.2	244.3	0.2	244.7	0.2	245.2	0.2
1999	246.6	0.6	247.7	0.4	248.3	0.2	249.1	0.3	249.5	0.2	250.2	0.3	251.1	0.4	251.9	0.3	252.3	0.2	252.8	0.2	253.3	0.2	254.2	0.4
2000	255.5	0.5	257.0	0.6	258.1	0.4	258.8	0.3	259.4	0.2	260.5	0.4	261.4	0.3	262.6	0.5	263.1	0.2	263.7	0.2	264.1	0.2	264.8	0.3
2001	267.1	0.9	268.9	0.7	270.0	0.4	270.8	0.3	271.4	0.2	272.5	0.4	273.1	0.2	274.4	0.5	275.0	0.2	275.9	0.3	276.7	0.3	277.3	0.2

Source: U.S. Department of Labor, Bureau of Labor Statistics, Division of Consumer Prices and Price Indexes.

U.S. City Average
Consumer Price Index - Urban Wage Earners
Base 1982-1984 = 100
Medical Care

For 1935-2001. Columns headed % show percentile change in the index from the previous period for which an index is available.

Year	Jan Index	%	Feb Index	%	Mar Index	%	Apr Index	%	May Index	%	Jun Index	%	Jul Index	%	Aug Index	%	Sep Index	%	Oct Index	%	Nov Index	%	Dec Index	%
1935	-	-	-	-	10.2	-	-	-	-	-	-	-	10.2	0.0	-	-	-	-	10.2	0.0	-	-	-	-
1936	10.2	0.0	-	-	-	-	10.2	0.0	-	-	-	-	10.2	0.0	-	-	10.3	1.0	-	-	-	-	10.3	0.0
1937	-	-	-	-	10.4	1.0	-	-	-	-	10.4	0.0	-	-	-	-	10.4	0.0	-	-	-	-	10.4	0.0
1938	-	-	-	-	10.4	0.0	-	-	-	-	10.4	0.0	-	-	-	-	10.4	0.0	-	-	-	-	10.4	0.0
1939	-	-	-	-	10.4	0.0	-	-	-	-	10.4	0.0	-	-	-	-	10.4	0.0	-	-	-	-	10.4	0.0
1940	-	-	-	-	10.4	0.0	-	-	-	-	10.4	0.0	-	-	-	-	10.4	0.0	-	-	-	-	10.4	0.0
1941	-	-	-	-	10.4	0.0	-	-	-	-	10.4	0.0	-	-	-	-	10.5	1.0	-	-	-	-	10.6	1.0
1942	-	-	-	-	10.6	0.0	-	-	-	-	10.8	1.9	-	-	-	-	10.9	0.9	-	-	-	-	11.0	0.9
1943	-	-	-	-	11.2	1.8	-	-	-	-	11.3	0.9	-	-	-	-	11.4	0.9	-	-	-	-	11.5	0.9
1944	-	-	-	-	11.5	0.0	-	-	-	-	11.6	0.9	-	-	-	-	11.7	0.9	-	-	-	-	11.8	0.9
1945	-	-	-	-	11.8	0.0	-	-	-	-	11.9	0.8	-	-	-	-	11.9	0.0	-	-	-	-	12.1	1.7
1946	-	-	-	-	12.3	1.7	-	-	-	-	12.5	1.6	-	-	-	-	12.8	2.4	-	-	-	-	13.1	2.3
1947	13.3	1.5	13.3	0.0	13.4	0.8	13.5	0.7	13.5	0.0	13.6	0.7	13.6	0.0	13.6	0.0	13.8	1.5	13.8	0.0	13.9	0.7	13.9	0.0
1948	14.1	1.4	14.1	0.0	14.2	0.7	14.4	1.4	14.4	0.0	14.4	0.0	14.6	1.4	14.6	0.0	14.6	0.0	14.7	0.7	14.7	0.0	14.7	0.0
1949	14.8	0.7	14.8	0.0	14.9	0.7	14.9	0.0	14.9	0.0	14.9	0.0	14.9	0.0	14.9	0.0	15.0	0.7	14.9	-0.7	14.9	0.0	15.0	0.7
1950	15.1	0.7	15.1	0.0	15.1	0.0	15.1	0.0	15.1	0.0	15.1	0.0	15.1	0.0	15.2	0.7	15.3	0.7	15.3	0.0	15.4	0.7	15.5	0.6
1951	15.5	0.0	15.6	0.6	15.8	1.3	15.8	0.0	15.9	0.6	15.9	0.0	15.9	0.0	15.9	0.0	16.0	0.6	16.1	0.6	16.2	0.6	16.4	1.2
1952	16.4	0.0	16.4	0.0	16.6	1.2	16.6	0.0	16.6	0.0	16.9	1.8	16.9	0.0	16.9	0.0	17.0	0.6	17.0	0.0	17.0	0.0	17.1	0.6
1953	17.1	0.0	17.1	0.0	17.1	0.0	17.2	0.6	17.3	0.6	17.4	0.6	17.4	0.0	17.5	0.6	17.6	0.6	17.6	0.0	17.7	0.6	17.7	0.0
1954	17.7	0.0	17.8	0.6	17.8	0.0	17.9	0.6	17.9	0.0	17.9	0.0	17.9	0.0	18.0	0.6	18.0	0.0	18.0	0.0	18.1	0.6	18.1	0.0
1955	18.1	0.0	18.2	0.6	18.2	0.0	18.2	0.0	18.3	0.5	18.3	0.0	18.3	0.0	18.3	0.0	18.4	0.5	18.5	0.5	18.6	0.5	18.7	0.5
1956	18.7	0.0	18.8	0.5	18.8	0.0	18.9	0.5	18.9	0.0	18.9	0.0	19.0	0.5	19.1	0.5	19.2	0.5	19.2	0.0	19.3	0.5	19.3	0.0
1957	19.4	0.5	19.4	0.0	19.6	1.0	19.6	0.0	19.7	0.5	19.8	0.5	19.8	0.0	19.9	0.5	19.9	0.0	20.0	0.5	20.1	0.5	20.2	0.5
1958	20.3	0.5	20.3	0.0	20.4	0.5	20.5	0.5	20.6	0.5	20.7	0.5	20.8	0.5	20.8	0.0	21.0	1.0	21.1	0.5	21.1	0.0	21.1	0.0
1959	21.2	0.5	21.3	0.5	21.4	0.5	21.4	0.0	21.5	0.5	21.6	0.5	21.6	0.0	21.7	0.5	21.8	0.5	21.9	0.5	21.9	0.0	21.9	0.0
1960	22.0	0.5	22.2	0.9	22.2	0.0	22.3	0.5	22.3	0.0	22.4	0.4	22.4	0.0	22.4	0.0	22.5	0.4	22.6	0.4	22.6	0.0	22.6	0.0
1961	22.7	0.4	22.8	0.4	22.9	0.4	22.9	0.0	23.0	0.4	23.0	0.0	23.1	0.4	23.1	0.0	23.2	0.4	23.3	0.4	23.3	0.0	23.3	0.0
1962	23.3	0.0	23.4	0.4	23.5	0.4	23.6	0.4	23.6	0.0	23.7	0.4	23.7	0.0	23.7	0.0	23.8	0.4	23.8	0.0	23.8	0.0	23.9	0.4
1963	24.0	0.4	24.0	0.0	24.0	0.0	24.1	0.4	24.2	0.4	24.3	0.4	24.3	0.0	24.3	0.0	24.3	0.0	24.4	0.4	24.4	0.0	24.4	0.0
1964	24.5	0.4	24.5	0.0	24.6	0.4	24.7	0.4	24.7	0.0	24.7	0.0	24.7	0.0	24.8	0.4	24.8	0.0	24.8	0.0	24.9	0.4	24.9	0.0
1965	25.0	0.4	25.1	0.4	25.1	0.0	25.2	0.4	25.2	0.0	25.3	0.4	25.4	0.4	25.4	0.0	25.4	0.0	25.5	0.4	25.6	0.4	25.6	0.0
1966	25.7	0.4	25.8	0.4	26.0	0.8	26.0	0.0	26.2	0.8	26.3	0.4	26.4	0.4	26.6	0.8	26.8	0.8	27.0	0.7	27.2	0.7	27.3	0.4
1967	27.5	0.7	27.7	0.7	27.9	0.7	28.0	0.4	28.1	0.4	28.2	0.4	28.3	0.4	28.5	0.7	28.7	0.7	28.8	0.3	28.9	0.3	29.1	0.7
1968	29.2	0.3	29.4	0.7	29.6	0.7	29.7	0.3	29.8	0.3	29.9	0.3	30.0	0.3	30.1	0.3	30.3	0.7	30.5	0.7	30.7	0.7	30.9	0.7
1969	31.1	0.6	31.3	0.6	31.6	1.0	31.8	0.6	32.0	0.6	32.1	0.3	32.3	0.6	32.5	0.6	32.6	0.3	32.5	-0.3	32.6	0.3	32.8	0.6
1970	32.9	0.3	33.1	0.6	33.5	1.2	33.7	0.6	33.9	0.6	34.1	0.6	34.3	0.6	34.5	0.6	34.7	0.6	34.8	0.3	34.9	0.3	35.2	0.9
1971	35.4	0.6	35.6	0.6	35.9	0.8	36.1	0.6	36.3	0.6	36.4	0.3	36.6	0.5	36.8	0.5	36.9	0.3	36.7	-0.5	36.7	0.0	36.8	0.3
1972	36.9	0.3	37.1	0.5	37.2	0.3	37.3	0.3	37.4	0.3	37.5	0.3	37.6	0.3	37.6	0.0	37.7	0.3	37.9	0.5	38.0	0.3	38.0	0.0
1973	38.2	0.5	38.3	0.3	38.4	0.3	38.6	0.5	38.7	0.3	38.8	0.3	38.9	0.3	39.0	0.3	39.2	0.5	39.8	1.5	39.9	0.3	40.0	0.3
1974	40.3	0.7	40.6	0.7	41.0	1.0	41.2	0.5	41.7	1.2	42.3	1.4	42.9	1.4	43.5	1.4	43.9	0.9	44.2	0.7	44.6	0.9	45.0	0.9
1975	45.6	1.3	46.1	1.1	46.6	1.1	46.9	0.6	47.2	0.6	47.6	0.8	48.1	1.1	48.4	0.6	48.7	0.6	49.1	0.8	49.1	0.0	49.5	0.8
1976	50.0	1.0	50.6	1.2	51.1	1.0	51.4	0.6	51.7	0.6	52.0	0.6	52.5	1.0	52.9	0.8	53.2	0.6	53.5	0.6	54.2	1.3	54.4	0.4
1977	54.9	0.9	55.4	0.9	55.9	0.9	56.4	0.9	56.8	0.7	57.1	0.5	57.6	0.9	58.0	0.7	58.4	0.7	58.7	0.5	58.9	0.3	59.2	0.5
1978	59.8	1.0	60.4	1.0	60.7	0.5	61.0	0.5	61.4	0.7	61.7	0.5	62.1	0.6	62.6	0.8	63.1	0.8	63.7	1.0	64.2	0.8	64.5	0.5
1979	65.2	1.1	65.7	0.8	66.2	0.8	66.6	0.6	66.9	0.5	67.4	0.7	68.1	1.0	68.7	0.9	69.3	0.9	70.0	1.0	70.5	0.7	71.3	1.1
1980	72.2	1.3	73.2	1.4	73.9	1.0	74.5	0.8	75.0	0.7	75.3	0.4	75.8	0.7	76.4	0.8	77.1	0.9	77.7	0.8	78.2	0.6	78.6	0.5

[Continued]

U.S. City Average
Consumer Price Index - Urban Wage Earners
Base 1982-1984 = 100
Medical Care
[Continued]

For 1935-2001. Columns headed % show percentile change in the index from the previous period for which an index is available.

Year	Jan Index	%	Feb Index	%	Mar Index	%	Apr Index	%	May Index	%	Jun Index	%	Jul Index	%	Aug Index	%	Sep Index	%	Oct Index	%	Nov Index	%	Dec Index	%
1981	79.7	1.4	80.5	1.0	81.2	0.9	81.8	0.7	82.3	0.6	82.9	0.7	83.6	0.8	84.5	1.1	85.2	0.8	86.1	1.1	86.9	0.9	87.5	0.7
1982	88.3	0.9	89.1	0.9	89.9	0.9	90.6	0.8	91.2	0.7	91.9	0.8	92.9	1.1	93.8	1.0	94.5	0.7	95.3	0.8	96.2	0.9	96.8	0.6
1983	97.7	0.9	98.8	1.1	99.1	0.3	99.4	0.3	99.7	0.3	100.0	0.3	100.7	0.7	101.3	0.6	101.7	0.4	102.2	0.5	102.7	0.5	103.1	0.4
1984	104.0	0.9	105.1	1.1	105.5	0.4	105.8	0.3	106.2	0.4	106.5	0.3	107.1	0.6	107.6	0.5	107.9	0.3	108.6	0.6	109.2	0.6	109.5	0.3
1985	110.2	0.6	111.0	0.7	111.7	0.6	112.1	0.4	112.6	0.4	113.2	0.5	113.8	0.5	114.5	0.6	115.0	0.4	115.6	0.5	116.3	0.6	116.8	0.4
1986	117.8	0.9	118.9	0.9	119.9	0.8	120.5	0.5	121.0	0.4	121.6	0.5	122.4	0.7	123.1	0.6	123.7	0.5	124.5	0.6	125.0	0.4	125.7	0.6
1987	126.5	0.6	127.3	0.6	128.1	0.6	128.8	0.5	129.3	0.4	130.0	0.5	130.8	0.6	131.4	0.5	132.0	0.5	132.6	0.5	133.0	0.3	133.4	0.3
1988	134.6	0.9	135.8	0.9	136.5	0.5	137.1	0.4	137.8	0.5	138.5	0.5	139.6	0.8	140.3	0.5	140.8	0.4	141.7	0.6	142.2	0.4	142.8	0.4
1989	144.2	1.0	145.6	1.0	146.5	0.6	147.2	0.5	147.9	0.5	148.8	0.6	150.1	0.9	151.1	0.7	152.1	0.7	153.0	0.6	154.2	0.8	154.7	0.3
1990	156.1	0.9	157.6	1.0	158.8	0.8	159.8	0.6	160.8	0.6	161.8	0.6	163.3	0.9	164.7	0.9	165.5	0.5	166.8	0.8	168.1	0.8	168.8	0.4
1991	170.5	1.0	172.1	0.9	173.2	0.6	173.9	0.4	174.6	0.4	175.6	0.6	176.9	0.7	178.3	0.8	179.2	0.5	180.2	0.6	181.2	0.6	182.0	0.4
1992	183.7	0.9	185.7	1.1	186.8	0.6	187.6	0.4	188.2	0.3	188.9	0.4	190.2	0.7	191.2	0.5	191.9	0.4	193.0	0.6	193.8	0.4	194.3	0.3
1993	196.0	0.9	197.6	0.8	198.2	0.3	199.0	0.4	200.1	0.6	200.7	0.3	201.7	0.5	202.4	0.3	202.8	0.2	203.8	0.5	204.2	0.2	204.5	0.1
1994	205.8	0.6	207.0	0.6	207.7	0.3	208.6	0.4	209.1	0.2	209.7	0.3	210.8	0.5	211.5	0.3	212.0	0.2	213.4	0.7	214.0	0.3	214.6	0.3
1995	215.9	0.6	217.3	0.6	217.7	0.2	218.2	0.2	218.7	0.2	219.2	0.2	220.2	0.5	221.1	0.4	221.5	0.2	222.3	0.4	222.8	0.2	223.1	0.1
1996	224.5	0.6	225.6	0.5	226.0	0.2	226.4	0.2	226.8	0.2	227.3	0.2	228.2	0.4	228.5	0.1	228.8	0.1	229.4	0.3	229.9	0.2	230.1	0.1
1997	231.1	0.4	232.1	0.4	232.8	0.3	233.2	0.2	233.6	0.2	233.8	0.1	234.2	0.2	234.6	0.2	234.7	0.0	235.2	0.2	235.8	0.3	236.5	0.3
1998	237.4	0.4	238.7	0.5	239.1	0.2	239.9	0.3	240.6	0.3	241.4	0.3	242.1	0.3	242.8	0.3	243.2	0.2	243.7	0.2	244.0	0.1	244.4	0.2
1999	245.8	0.6	246.9	0.4	247.5	0.2	248.2	0.3	248.7	0.2	249.4	0.3	250.3	0.4	251.0	0.3	251.4	0.2	251.9	0.2	252.5	0.2	253.2	0.3
2000	254.5	0.5	256.2	0.7	257.3	0.4	258.0	0.3	258.5	0.2	259.7	0.5	260.6	0.3	261.7	0.4	262.2	0.2	262.8	0.2	263.1	0.1	263.8	0.3
2001	266.3	0.9	268.1	0.7	269.1	0.4	269.9	0.3	270.4	0.2	271.5	0.4	272.0	0.2	273.4	0.5	273.9	0.2	274.9	0.4	275.6	0.3	276.2	0.2

Source: U.S. Department of Labor, Bureau of Labor Statistics, Division of Consumer Prices and Price Indexes.

U.S. City Average
Consumer Price Index - All Urban Consumers
Base December 1997 = 100
Recreation

For 1993-2001. Columns headed % show percentile change in the index from the previous period for which an index is available.

Year	Jan Index	%	Feb Index	%	Mar Index	%	Apr Index	%	May Index	%	Jun Index	%	Jul Index	%	Aug Index	%	Sep Index	%	Oct Index	%	Nov Index	%	Dec Index	%
1993	89.5	-	89.9	0.4	90.3	0.4	90.6	0.3	90.2	-0.4	90.6	0.4	90.5	-0.1	90.8	0.3	91.2	0.4	91.6	0.4	91.7	0.1	91.7	0.0
1994	92.1	0.4	92.4	0.3	92.6	0.2	92.7	0.1	92.7	0.0	92.6	-0.1	92.7	0.1	92.6	-0.1	92.8	0.2	92.9	0.1	93.2	0.3	93.0	-0.2
1995	93.5	0.5	93.8	0.3	93.9	0.1	94.4	0.5	94.5	0.1	94.2	-0.3	94.3	0.1	94.6	0.3	95.0	0.4	95.1	0.1	95.5	0.4	95.6	0.1
1996	96.0	0.4	96.8	0.8	96.9	0.1	97.1	0.2	97.1	0.0	97.3	0.2	97.5	0.2	97.6	0.1	97.8	0.2	98.1	0.3	98.4	0.3	98.5	0.1
1997	98.8	0.3	99.2	0.4	99.4	0.2	99.3	-0.1	99.4	0.1	99.8	0.4	99.8	0.0	100.0	0.2	99.9	-0.1	100.0	0.1	100.0	0.0	100.0	0.0
1998	100.3	0.3	100.7	0.4	101.0	0.3	101.1	0.1	101.0	-0.1	101.2	0.2	101.1	-0.1	101.3	0.2	101.3	0.0	101.1	-0.2	101.3	0.2	101.2	-0.1
1999	101.7	0.5	101.8	0.1	101.8	0.0	102.0	0.2	102.2	0.2	102.2	0.0	102.2	0.0	102.2	0.0	101.7	-0.5	101.8	0.1	101.9	0.1	102.0	0.1
2000	102.3	0.3	102.5	0.2	102.9	0.4	102.9	0.0	103.1	0.2	103.4	0.3	103.7	0.3	103.9	0.2	103.8	-0.1	103.8	0.0	103.7	-0.1	103.7	0.0
2001	104.1	0.4	104.3	0.2	104.3	0.0	105.0	0.7	105.0	0.0	104.8	-0.2	105.0	0.2	105.1	0.1	105.2	0.1	105.3	0.1	105.5	0.2	105.3	-0.2

Source: U.S. Department of Labor, Bureau of Labor Statistics, Division of Consumer Prices and Price Indexes.

U.S. City Average
Consumer Price Index - Urban Wage Earners
Base December 1997 = 100
Recreation

For 1993-2001. Columns headed % show percentile change in the index from the previous period for which an index is available.

Year	Jan Index	%	Feb Index	%	Mar Index	%	Apr Index	%	May Index	%	Jun Index	%	Jul Index	%	Aug Index	%	Sep Index	%	Oct Index	%	Nov Index	%	Dec Index	%
1993	90.0	-	90.4	0.4	90.9	0.6	91.1	0.2	90.7	-0.4	91.1	0.4	91.1	0.0	91.4	0.3	91.6	0.2	92.0	0.4	92.2	0.2	92.2	0.0
1994	92.5	0.3	92.7	0.2	93.0	0.3	93.0	0.0	93.1	0.1	93.0	-0.1	93.0	0.0	92.9	-0.1	93.0	0.1	93.1	0.1	93.4	0.3	93.2	-0.2
1995	93.7	0.5	94.0	0.3	94.1	0.1	94.5	0.4	94.7	0.2	94.4	-0.3	94.5	0.1	94.7	0.2	95.1	0.4	95.1	0.0	95.5	0.4	95.6	0.1
1996	96.0	0.4	96.8	0.8	97.0	0.2	97.1	0.1	97.2	0.1	97.4	0.2	97.6	0.2	97.7	0.1	97.9	0.2	98.1	0.2	98.4	0.3	98.5	0.1
1997	98.7	0.2	99.2	0.5	99.4	0.2	99.3	-0.1	99.4	0.1	99.8	0.4	99.8	0.0	100.1	0.3	100.0	-0.1	100.1	0.1	100.0	-0.1	100.0	0.0
1998	100.3	0.3	100.7	0.4	101.0	0.3	101.0	0.0	100.9	-0.1	101.0	0.1	100.9	-0.1	101.1	0.2	101.0	-0.1	100.8	-0.2	100.8	0.0	100.8	0.0
1999	101.2	0.4	101.3	0.1	101.3	0.0	101.4	0.1	101.5	0.1	101.6	0.1	101.6	0.0	101.5	-0.1	101.0	-0.5	101.1	0.1	101.0	-0.1	101.2	0.2
2000	101.4	0.2	101.6	0.2	102.0	0.4	102.0	0.0	102.3	0.3	102.5	0.2	102.7	0.2	102.9	0.2	102.8	-0.1	102.8	0.0	102.7	-0.1	102.6	-0.1
2001	103.0	0.4	103.1	0.1	103.0	-0.1	103.7	0.7	103.7	0.0	103.5	-0.2	103.7	0.2	103.9	0.2	103.8	-0.1	103.8	0.0	104.0	0.2	103.8	-0.2

Source: U.S. Department of Labor, Bureau of Labor Statistics, Division of Consumer Prices and Price Indexes.

U.S. City Average
Consumer Price Index - All Urban Consumers
Base December 1997 = 100
Education & Communication

For 1993-2001. Columns headed % show percentile change in the index from the previous period for which an index is available.

Year	Jan Index	%	Feb Index	%	Mar Index	%	Apr Index	%	May Index	%	Jun Index	%	Jul Index	%	Aug Index	%	Sep Index	%	Oct Index	%	Nov Index	%	Dec Index	%
1993	84.3	-	84.3	0.0	84.4	0.1	84.3	-0.1	84.5	0.2	84.5	0.0	84.8	0.4	85.6	0.9	87.0	1.6	87.2	0.2	87.3	0.1	87.4	0.1
1994	87.5	0.1	87.9	0.5	87.8	-0.1	87.8	0.0	87.9	0.1	88.1	0.2	88.2	0.1	89.0	0.9	90.2	1.3	90.3	0.1	90.3	0.0	90.3	0.0
1995	91.3	1.1	91.3	0.0	91.2	-0.1	91.2	0.0	91.1	-0.1	91.3	0.2	91.5	0.2	92.4	1.0	93.7	1.4	93.7	0.0	93.7	0.0	93.9	0.2
1996	94.1	0.2	94.2	0.1	94.4	0.2	93.9	-0.5	94.4	0.5	94.6	0.2	94.7	0.1	95.7	1.1	96.8	1.1	97.0	0.2	97.0	0.0	97.1	0.1
1997	97.4	0.3	97.5	0.1	97.5	0.0	97.5	0.0	97.6	0.1	97.7	0.1	97.9	0.2	98.6	0.7	99.7	1.1	99.9	0.2	100.0	0.1	100.0	0.0
1998	99.9	-0.1	99.8	-0.1	99.9	0.1	99.9	0.0	100.1	0.2	100.1	0.0	100.0	-0.1	100.1	0.1	100.9	0.8	101.0	0.1	101.0	0.0	100.7	-0.3
1999	100.9	0.2	100.9	0.0	100.8	-0.1	100.7	-0.1	100.4	-0.3	100.3	-0.1	100.4	0.1	101.2	0.8	101.9	0.7	102.1	0.2	102.2	0.1	102.3	0.1
2000	102.7	0.4	102.2	-0.5	102.0	-0.2	101.8	-0.2	101.8	0.0	101.5	-0.3	102.0	0.5	102.8	0.8	102.9	0.1	103.6	0.7	103.2	-0.4	103.6	0.4
2001	103.9	0.3	104.0	0.1	104.3	0.3	104.1	-0.2	104.0	-0.1	104.4	0.4	104.8	0.4	105.8	1.0	106.6	0.8	107.1	0.5	107.0	-0.1	106.9	-0.1

Source: U.S. Department of Labor, Bureau of Labor Statistics, Division of Consumer Prices and Price Indexes.

U.S. City Average
Consumer Price Index - Urban Wage Earners
Base December 1997 = 100
Education & Communication

For 1993-2001. Columns headed % show percentile change in the index from the previous period for which an index is available.

Year	Jan Index	%	Feb Index	%	Mar Index	%	Apr Index	%	May Index	%	Jun Index	%	Jul Index	%	Aug Index	%	Sep Index	%	Oct Index	%	Nov Index	%	Dec Index	%
1993	84.9	-	84.9	0.0	85.0	0.1	84.9	-0.1	85.1	0.2	85.2	0.1	85.4	0.2	86.2	0.9	87.4	1.4	87.5	0.1	87.6	0.1	87.8	0.2
1994	87.9	0.1	88.2	0.3	88.2	0.0	88.2	0.0	88.3	0.1	88.5	0.2	88.6	0.1	89.3	0.8	90.3	1.1	90.4	0.1	90.4	0.0	90.4	0.0
1995	91.5	1.2	91.4	-0.1	91.3	-0.1	91.3	0.0	91.3	0.0	91.5	0.2	91.7	0.2	92.5	0.9	93.7	1.3	93.8	0.1	93.8	0.0	94.0	0.2
1996	94.1	0.1	94.2	0.1	94.4	0.2	94.0	-0.4	94.5	0.5	94.7	0.2	94.8	0.1	95.8	1.1	96.8	1.0	97.0	0.2	97.0	0.0	97.1	0.1
1997	97.5	0.4	97.5	0.0	97.6	0.1	97.6	0.0	97.8	0.2	97.9	0.1	98.1	0.2	98.5	0.4	99.7	1.2	99.9	0.2	100.0	0.1	100.0	0.0
1998	100.0	0.0	99.8	-0.2	100.0	0.2	100.1	0.1	100.3	0.2	100.3	0.0	100.2	-0.1	100.3	0.1	101.1	0.8	101.1	0.0	101.2	0.1	100.9	-0.3
1999	101.2	0.3	101.2	0.0	101.0	-0.2	100.9	-0.1	100.7	-0.2	100.7	0.0	100.8	0.1	101.5	0.7	102.1	0.6	102.3	0.2	102.5	0.2	102.5	0.0
2000	103.0	0.5	102.5	-0.5	102.2	-0.3	102.1	-0.1	102.1	0.0	101.7	-0.4	102.2	0.5	103.0	0.8	102.9	-0.1	103.7	0.8	103.2	-0.5	103.7	0.5
2001	104.0	0.3	104.1	0.1	104.4	0.3	104.2	-0.2	104.1	-0.1	104.5	0.4	104.9	0.4	105.8	0.9	106.5	0.7	107.1	0.6	106.9	-0.2	106.9	0.0

Source: U.S. Department of Labor, Bureau of Labor Statistics, Division of Consumer Prices and Price Indexes.

U.S. City Average
Consumer Price Index - All Urban Consumers
Base 1982-1984 = 100
Other Goods and Services

For 1967-2001. Columns headed % show percentile change in the index from the previous period for which an index is available.

Year	Jan Index	%	Feb Index	%	Mar Index	%	Apr Index	%	May Index	%	Jun Index	%	Jul Index	%	Aug Index	%	Sep Index	%	Oct Index	%	Nov Index	%	Dec Index	%
1967	34.4	-	34.5	0.3	34.5	0.0	34.6	0.3	34.7	0.3	34.8	0.3	35.0	0.6	35.3	0.9	35.5	0.6	35.6	0.3	35.8	0.6	35.9	0.3
1968	36.1	0.6	36.1	0.0	36.5	1.1	36.5	0.0	36.6	0.3	36.9	0.8	36.9	0.0	37.1	0.5	37.2	0.3	37.4	0.5	37.6	0.5	37.7	0.3
1969	37.8	0.3	37.8	0.0	38.0	0.5	38.1	0.3	38.2	0.3	38.5	0.8	38.8	0.8	39.0	0.5	39.3	0.8	39.4	0.3	39.7	0.8	39.8	0.3
1970	39.9	0.3	40.0	0.3	40.2	0.5	40.5	0.7	40.6	0.2	40.9	0.7	41.2	0.7	41.3	0.2	41.5	0.5	41.6	0.2	41.8	0.5	41.9	0.2
1971	42.2	0.7	42.2	0.0	42.3	0.2	42.4	0.2	42.5	0.2	42.6	0.2	42.9	0.7	43.1	0.5	43.5	0.9	43.6	0.2	43.6	0.0	43.7	0.2
1972	43.9	0.5	44.2	0.7	44.3	0.2	44.4	0.2	44.6	0.5	44.8	0.4	44.8	0.0	44.8	0.0	45.0	0.4	45.2	0.4	45.2	0.0	45.3	0.2
1973	45.4	0.2	45.5	0.2	45.8	0.7	46.0	0.4	46.2	0.4	46.4	0.4	46.5	0.2	46.6	0.2	46.9	0.6	47.1	0.4	47.4	0.6	47.5	0.2
1974	47.7	0.4	47.9	0.4	48.2	0.6	48.4	0.4	48.9	1.0	49.4	1.0	50.0	1.2	50.3	0.6	50.9	1.2	51.4	1.0	51.9	1.0	52.4	1.0
1975	52.7	0.6	53.1	0.8	53.3	0.4	53.5	0.4	53.6	0.2	53.7	0.2	53.9	0.4	54.0	0.2	54.4	0.7	54.7	0.6	54.9	0.4	55.3	0.7
1976	55.7	0.7	56.1	0.7	56.2	0.2	56.4	0.4	56.6	0.4	56.8	0.4	56.9	0.2	57.1	0.4	57.6	0.9	58.0	0.7	58.4	0.7	58.6	0.3
1977	59.0	0.7	59.2	0.3	59.3	0.2	59.5	0.3	59.7	0.3	60.0	0.5	60.2	0.3	60.4	0.3	61.1	1.2	61.7	1.0	62.1	0.6	62.3	0.3
1978	62.6	0.5	62.7	0.2	62.9	0.3	63.0	0.2	63.2	0.3	63.4	0.3	64.2	1.3	64.5	0.5	65.8	2.0	66.0	0.3	66.2	0.3	66.3	0.2
1979	66.8	0.8	67.3	0.7	67.6	0.4	67.7	0.1	68.0	0.4	68.2	0.3	68.4	0.3	69.1	1.0	70.7	2.3	70.9	0.3	71.1	0.3	71.5	0.6
1980	72.3	1.1	72.9	0.8	73.2	0.4	73.5	0.4	74.0	0.7	74.5	0.7	74.8	0.4	75.2	0.5	77.3	2.8	77.6	0.4	78.1	0.6	78.7	0.8
1981	79.3	0.8	79.7	0.5	80.2	0.6	80.6	0.5	81.4	1.0	81.8	0.5	82.2	0.5	82.6	0.5	85.2	3.1	86.0	0.9	86.2	0.2	86.5	0.3
1982	87.1	0.7	87.7	0.7	88.4	0.8	89.0	0.7	89.4	0.4	89.7	0.3	90.2	0.6	90.5	0.3	93.5	3.3	95.1	1.7	96.0	0.9	97.0	1.0
1983	98.1	1.1	98.7	0.6	98.8	0.1	99.3	0.5	99.4	0.1	99.7	0.3	100.8	1.1	101.3	0.5	103.2	1.9	104.0	0.8	104.5	0.5	104.7	0.2
1984	105.3	0.6	105.7	0.4	105.9	0.2	106.1	0.2	106.3	0.2	106.7	0.4	107.4	0.7	107.7	0.3	110.3	2.4	110.7	0.4	110.9	0.2	111.0	0.1
1985	111.9	0.8	112.3	0.4	112.6	0.3	112.8	0.2	113.0	0.2	113.2	0.2	113.9	0.6	114.3	0.4	116.8	2.2	117.4	0.5	117.5	0.1	118.0	0.4
1986	118.9	0.8	119.3	0.3	119.6	0.3	119.8	0.2	119.9	0.1	120.1	0.2	120.9	0.7	121.4	0.4	123.8	2.0	124.3	0.4	124.4	0.1	124.5	0.1
1987	125.5	0.8	126.1	0.5	126.3	0.2	126.6	0.2	126.9	0.2	127.2	0.2	128.0	0.6	128.5	0.4	131.1	2.0	131.6	0.4	131.8	0.2	132.1	0.2
1988	133.4	1.0	134.2	0.6	134.6	0.3	134.8	0.1	135.1	0.2	135.5	0.3	136.5	0.7	137.5	0.7	140.0	1.8	140.6	0.4	141.0	0.3	141.3	0.2
1989	143.4	1.5	144.1	0.5	144.4	0.2	144.7	0.2	145.4	0.5	146.3	0.6	147.3	0.7	148.7	1.0	151.2	1.7	151.8	0.4	151.9	0.1	152.9	0.7
1990	154.0	0.7	154.7	0.5	155.2	0.3	155.8	0.4	156.6	0.5	157.8	0.8	159.2	0.9	160.4	0.8	162.6	1.4	163.2	0.4	163.6	0.2	164.5	0.6
1991	166.5	1.2	167.4	0.5	167.9	0.3	168.8	0.5	169.1	0.2	170.0	0.5	170.8	0.5	172.2	0.8	175.8	2.1	176.2	0.2	176.9	0.4	177.6	0.4
1992	178.6	0.6	179.4	0.4	179.8	0.2	180.3	0.3	181.3	0.6	181.5	0.1	182.3	0.4	183.9	0.9	187.0	1.7	187.9	0.5	188.0	0.1	189.1	0.6
1993	191.0	1.0	191.5	0.3	192.0	0.3	192.4	0.2	193.2	0.4	193.1	-0.1	193.7	0.3	193.4	-0.2	193.1	-0.2	193.4	0.2	193.8	0.2	194.2	0.2
1994	195.1	0.5	195.2	0.1	195.5	0.2	196.4	0.5	197.1	0.4	197.6	0.3	198.0	0.2	199.4	0.7	201.4	1.0	201.9	0.2	202.3	0.2	202.4	0.0
1995	203.0	0.3	204.1	0.5	204.0	-0.0	204.3	0.1	204.9	0.3	205.3	0.2	205.7	0.2	207.7	1.0	210.2	1.2	210.7	0.2	211.2	0.2	211.1	-0.0
1996	212.0	0.4	212.6	0.3	213.0	0.2	213.3	0.1	214.1	0.4	214.0	-0.0	214.6	0.3	216.3	0.8	218.3	0.9	218.8	0.2	219.2	0.2	218.7	-0.2
1997	220.0	0.6	220.7	0.3	221.4	0.3	222.7	0.6	223.1	0.2	223.1	0.0	223.5	0.2	225.7	1.0	228.1	1.1	229.4	0.6	229.9	0.2	230.1	0.1
1998	231.3	0.5	233.1	0.8	232.4	-0.3	234.7	1.0	236.7	0.9	236.4	-0.1	237.8	0.6	238.0	0.1	240.4	1.0	241.3	0.4	240.5	-0.3	250.3	4.1
1999	255.4	2.0	255.0	-0.2	253.3	-0.7	256.1	1.1	255.8	-0.1	255.9	0.0	258.3	0.9	257.6	-0.3	262.6	1.9	263.2	0.2	263.0	-0.1	263.0	0.0
2000	264.7	0.6	266.7	0.8	268.0	0.5	271.9	1.5	270.2	-0.6	269.6	-0.2	272.2	1.0	271.6	-0.2	274.7	1.1	273.0	-0.6	276.2	1.2	274.0	-0.8
2001	275.9	0.7	277.2	0.5	277.7	0.2	281.3	1.3	280.2	-0.4	281.2	0.4	285.8	1.6	283.3	-0.9	287.8	1.6	285.6	-0.8	289.2	1.3	286.4	-1.0

Source: U.S. Department of Labor, Bureau of Labor Statistics, Division of Consumer Prices and Price Indexes.

U.S. City Average
Consumer Price Index - Urban Wage Earners
Base 1982-1984 = 100
Other Goods and Services

For 1967-2001. Columns headed % show percentile change in the index from the previous period for which an index is available.

Year	Jan Index	%	Feb Index	%	Mar Index	%	Apr Index	%	May Index	%	Jun Index	%	Jul Index	%	Aug Index	%	Sep Index	%	Oct Index	%	Nov Index	%	Dec Index	%
1967	34.7	-	34.8	0.3	34.8	0.0	34.9	0.3	35.0	0.3	35.1	0.3	35.3	0.6	35.6	0.8	35.8	0.6	36.0	0.6	36.1	0.3	36.3	0.6
1968	36.4	0.3	36.4	0.0	36.8	1.1	36.8	0.0	36.9	0.3	37.2	0.8	37.3	0.3	37.4	0.3	37.6	0.5	37.8	0.5	37.9	0.3	38.1	0.5
1969	38.1	0.0	38.2	0.3	38.3	0.3	38.5	0.5	38.6	0.3	38.8	0.5	39.1	0.8	39.4	0.8	39.6	0.5	39.8	0.5	40.0	0.5	40.1	0.2
1970	40.3	0.5	40.4	0.2	40.5	0.2	40.8	0.7	41.0	0.5	41.3	0.7	41.5	0.5	41.7	0.5	41.8	0.2	42.0	0.5	42.2	0.5	42.3	0.2
1971	42.6	0.7	42.6	0.0	42.7	0.2	42.8	0.2	42.9	0.2	43.0	0.2	43.3	0.7	43.5	0.5	43.9	0.9	44.0	0.2	44.0	0.0	44.1	0.2
1972	44.3	0.5	44.6	0.7	44.7	0.2	44.8	0.2	45.0	0.4	45.2	0.4	45.2	0.0	45.2	0.0	45.5	0.7	45.6	0.2	45.6	0.0	45.7	0.2
1973	45.8	0.2	46.0	0.4	46.2	0.4	46.4	0.4	46.6	0.4	46.8	0.4	46.9	0.2	47.0	0.2	47.3	0.6	47.6	0.6	47.8	0.4	48.0	0.4
1974	48.1	0.2	48.4	0.6	48.6	0.4	48.9	0.6	49.3	0.8	49.9	1.2	50.4	1.0	50.8	0.8	51.4	1.2	51.9	1.0	52.4	1.0	52.8	0.8
1975	53.2	0.8	53.6	0.8	53.8	0.4	53.9	0.2	54.1	0.4	54.2	0.2	54.4	0.4	54.5	0.2	54.9	0.7	55.2	0.5	55.4	0.4	55.9	0.9
1976	56.2	0.5	56.6	0.7	56.7	0.2	57.0	0.5	57.1	0.2	57.3	0.4	57.4	0.2	57.7	0.5	58.2	0.9	58.5	0.5	58.9	0.7	59.1	0.3
1977	59.5	0.7	59.7	0.3	59.9	0.3	60.1	0.3	60.3	0.3	60.5	0.3	60.7	0.3	60.9	0.3	61.7	1.3	62.3	1.0	62.7	0.6	62.9	0.3
1978	63.1	0.3	63.4	0.5	63.5	0.2	63.7	0.3	63.9	0.3	64.2	0.5	65.0	1.2	65.2	0.3	66.2	1.5	66.4	0.3	66.6	0.3	66.6	0.0
1979	67.3	1.1	67.9	0.9	68.1	0.3	68.3	0.3	68.6	0.4	68.7	0.1	69.0	0.4	69.8	1.2	71.0	1.7	71.2	0.3	71.5	0.4	71.8	0.4
1980	72.9	1.5	73.5	0.8	73.7	0.3	74.0	0.4	74.5	0.7	75.0	0.7	75.3	0.4	75.7	0.5	77.5	2.4	77.8	0.4	78.2	0.5	78.9	0.9
1981	79.4	0.6	79.8	0.5	80.2	0.5	80.6	0.5	81.5	1.1	81.9	0.5	82.2	0.4	82.6	0.5	84.6	2.4	85.4	0.9	85.8	0.5	86.1	0.3
1982	86.7	0.7	87.4	0.8	88.2	0.9	88.8	0.7	89.3	0.6	89.5	0.2	90.0	0.6	90.5	0.6	93.0	2.8	94.7	1.8	95.8	1.2	96.9	1.1
1983	98.3	1.4	98.9	0.6	99.0	0.1	99.5	0.5	99.7	0.2	100.0	0.3	101.3	1.3	101.9	0.6	103.3	1.4	104.0	0.7	104.5	0.5	104.7	0.2
1984	105.4	0.7	105.8	0.4	106.0	0.2	106.3	0.3	106.4	0.1	106.9	0.5	107.7	0.7	108.0	0.3	110.0	1.9	110.3	0.3	110.6	0.3	110.6	0.0
1985	111.6	0.9	112.2	0.5	112.3	0.1	112.6	0.3	112.8	0.2	113.0	0.2	113.8	0.7	114.2	0.4	116.3	1.8	116.8	0.4	116.9	0.1	117.4	0.4
1986	118.5	0.9	118.9	0.3	119.2	0.3	119.4	0.2	119.6	0.2	119.7	0.1	120.7	0.8	121.2	0.4	122.9	1.4	123.4	0.4	123.5	0.1	123.6	0.1
1987	124.8	1.0	125.4	0.5	125.6	0.2	125.9	0.2	126.2	0.2	126.6	0.3	127.5	0.7	128.0	0.4	130.3	1.8	130.8	0.4	131.0	0.2	131.3	0.2
1988	132.7	1.1	133.6	0.7	134.0	0.3	134.2	0.1	134.5	0.2	135.0	0.4	136.3	1.0	137.2	0.7	139.3	1.5	139.9	0.4	140.3	0.3	140.6	0.2
1989	143.0	1.7	143.7	0.5	144.0	0.2	144.4	0.3	145.2	0.6	146.3	0.8	147.5	0.8	148.8	0.9	150.8	1.3	151.4	0.4	151.5	0.1	152.7	0.8
1990	153.9	0.8	154.6	0.5	155.1	0.3	155.7	0.4	156.3	0.4	157.8	1.0	159.4	1.0	160.5	0.7	162.4	1.2	162.8	0.2	163.4	0.4	164.4	0.6
1991	166.6	1.3	167.5	0.5	168.1	0.4	169.1	0.6	169.4	0.2	170.5	0.6	171.2	0.4	172.6	0.8	175.5	1.7	175.9	0.2	176.8	0.5	177.7	0.5
1992	178.6	0.5	179.4	0.4	179.7	0.2	180.3	0.3	181.6	0.7	181.8	0.1	182.7	0.5	184.2	0.8	186.7	1.4	187.7	0.5	187.7	0.0	189.0	0.7
1993	191.2	1.2	191.6	0.2	192.2	0.3	192.8	0.3	193.6	0.4	193.3	-0.2	193.8	0.3	192.7	-0.6	190.9	-0.9	191.1	0.1	191.6	0.3	192.0	0.2
1994	193.1	0.6	193.2	0.1	193.4	0.1	194.4	0.5	195.3	0.5	195.8	0.3	196.3	0.3	197.5	0.6	198.9	0.7	199.4	0.3	199.8	0.2	200.0	0.1
1995	200.5	0.3	201.5	0.5	201.4	-0.0	201.7	0.1	202.5	0.4	203.0	0.2	203.3	0.1	205.0	0.8	207.2	1.1	207.8	0.3	208.3	0.2	208.1	-0.1
1996	209.0	0.4	209.6	0.3	209.9	0.1	210.1	0.1	211.2	0.5	211.0	-0.1	211.6	0.3	213.0	0.7	214.7	0.8	215.3	0.3	215.8	0.2	215.2	-0.3
1997	216.7	0.7	217.4	0.3	218.0	0.3	219.8	0.8	220.2	0.2	219.9	-0.1	220.3	0.2	222.1	0.8	224.6	1.1	226.1	0.7	226.7	0.3	226.9	0.1
1998	228.2	0.6	230.6	1.1	229.3	-0.6	232.3	1.3	234.8	1.1	234.0	-0.3	236.0	0.9	236.2	0.1	239.4	1.4	240.4	0.4	239.2	-0.5	252.6	5.6
1999	259.2	2.6	258.3	-0.3	255.6	-1.0	259.5	1.5	258.8	-0.3	258.7	-0.0	262.0	1.3	260.7	-0.5	267.3	2.5	267.9	0.2	267.4	-0.2	267.3	-0.0
2000	269.3	0.7	271.7	0.9	273.3	0.6	278.0	1.7	275.4	-0.9	274.5	-0.3	277.9	1.2	276.8	-0.4	280.9	1.5	278.2	-1.0	282.3	1.5	279.2	-1.1
2001	281.5	0.8	283.2	0.6	283.5	0.1	288.2	1.7	286.8	-0.5	287.9	0.4	293.8	2.0	290.0	-1.3	295.5	1.9	292.4	-1.0	297.3	1.7	293.3	-1.3

Source: U.S. Department of Labor, Bureau of Labor Statistics, Division of Consumer Prices and Price Indexes.

Anchorage, AK
Consumer Price Index - All Urban Consumers
Base 1982-1984 = 100
Annual Averages

For 1960-2001. Columns headed % show percentile change in the index from the previous period for which an index is available.

Year	All Items Index	%	Food & Beverage Index	%	Housing Index	%	Apparel Index	%	Transportation Index	%	Medical Care Index	%	Recreation* Index	%	Education & Communic.* Index	%	Other Goods & Services Index	%
1960	-	-	-	-	-	-	-	-	-	-	-	-	-	-	-	-	-	-
1961	34.5	-	-	-	-	-	-	-	-	-	-	-	-	-	-	-	-	-
1962	34.7	0.6	-	-	-	-	-	-	-	-	-	-	-	-	-	-	-	-
1963	34.8	0.3	-	-	-	-	-	-	-	-	-	-	-	-	-	-	-	-
1964	35.0	0.6	-	-	-	-	-	-	-	-	-	-	-	-	-	-	-	-
1965	35.3	0.9	-	-	-	-	-	-	-	-	-	-	-	-	-	-	-	-
1966	36.3	2.8	-	-	-	-	-	-	-	-	-	-	-	-	-	-	-	-
1967	37.2	2.5	-	-	-	-	-	-	-	-	-	-	-	-	-	-	-	-
1968	38.1	2.4	-	-	-	-	-	-	-	-	-	-	-	-	-	-	-	-
1969	39.6	3.9	-	-	-	-	-	-	-	-	-	-	-	-	-	-	-	-
1970	41.1	3.8	-	-	-	-	-	-	-	-	-	-	-	-	-	-	-	-
1971	42.3	2.9	-	-	-	-	56.5	-	40.8	-	35.2	-	-	-	-	-	-	-
1972	43.4	2.6	-	-	-	-	58.3	3.2	40.9	0.2	35.8	1.7	-	-	-	-	-	-
1973	45.3	4.4	-	-	-	-	60.7	4.1	41.4	1.2	37.3	4.2	-	-	-	-	-	-
1974	50.2	10.8	-	-	-	-	64.7	6.6	44.9	8.5	41.5	11.3	-	-	-	-	-	-
1975	57.1	13.7	-	-	-	-	69.8	7.9	49.3	9.8	46.9	13.0	-	-	-	-	63.8	-
1976	61.5	7.7	64.2	-	62.6	-	74.1	6.2	54.9	11.4	52.6	12.2	-	-	-	-	68.1	6.7
1977	65.6	6.7	68.9	7.3	65.5	4.6	79.2	6.9	60.2	9.7	57.9	10.1	-	-	-	-	71.7	5.3
1978	70.2	7.0	75.9	10.2	69.7	6.4	79.7	0.6	64.5	7.1	63.4	9.5	-	-	-	-	76.9	7.3
1979	77.6	10.5	84.0	10.7	78.0	11.9	81.7	2.5	71.3	10.5	69.1	9.0	-	-	-	-	83.1	8.1
1980	85.5	10.2	89.7	6.8	85.9	10.1	89.7	9.8	82.2	15.3	78.8	14.0	-	-	-	-	88.1	6.0
1981	92.4	8.1	94.3	5.1	92.5	7.7	94.1	4.9	92.7	12.8	86.9	10.3	-	-	-	-	93.2	5.8
1982	97.4	5.4	97.2	3.1	98.2	6.2	96.6	2.7	96.8	4.4	94.8	9.1	-	-	-	-	101.5	8.9
1983	99.2	1.8	99.7	2.6	99.0	0.8	101.6	5.2	98.5	1.8	99.7	5.2	-	-	-	-	105.3	3.7
1984	103.3	4.1	103.2	3.5	102.7	3.7	101.7	0.1	104.6	6.2	105.5	5.8	-	-	-	-	114.2	8.5
1985	105.8	2.4	106.2	2.9	103.0	0.3	105.8	4.0	108.2	3.4	110.9	5.1	-	-	-	-	123.2	7.9
1986	107.8	1.9	110.8	4.3	102.6	-0.4	109.0	3.0	107.8	-0.4	127.8	15.2	-	-	-	-	-	-
1987	108.2	0.4	113.1	2.1	97.5	-5.0	116.6	7.0	111.3	3.2	137.0	7.2	-	-	-	-	138.1	12.1
1988	108.6	0.4	113.8	0.6	95.4	-2.2	119.1	2.1	113.0	1.5	145.8	6.4	-	-	-	-	143.7	4.1
1989	111.7	2.9	117.2	3.0	96.3	0.9	125.0	5.0	116.7	3.3	154.4	5.9	-	-	-	-	155.7	8.4
1990	118.6	6.2	123.7	5.5	103.9	7.9	127.7	2.2	120.7	3.4	161.2	4.4	-	-	-	-	166.9	7.2
1991	124.0	4.6	127.7	3.2	111.2	7.0	126.6	-0.9	121.7	0.8	173.5	7.6	-	-	-	-	175.2	5.0
1992	128.2	3.4	130.3	2.0	116.6	4.9	130.2	2.8	123.3	1.3	183.0	5.5	-	-	-	-	177.8	1.5
1993	132.2	3.1	131.2	0.7	121.1	3.9	131.2	0.8	128.7	4.4	189.6	3.6	-	-	-	-	171.6	-3.5
1994	135.0	2.1	131.9	0.5	122.9	1.5	128.9	-1.8	136.9	6.4	197.8	4.3	-	-	-	-	163.3	-4.8
1995	138.9	2.9	138.5	5.0	124.9	1.6	130.0	0.9	143.8	5.0	211.6	7.0	-	-	-	-	164.6	0.8
1996	142.7	2.7	143.4	3.5	127.9	2.4	128.7	-1.0	147.2	2.4	231.1	9.2	-	-	-	-	171.3	4.1
1997	144.8	1.5	145.8	1.7	129.4	1.2	127.0	-1.3	147.0	-0.1	248.9	7.7	-	-	-	-	188.2	9.9
1998	146.9	1.5	147.3	1.0	131.0	1.2	125.6	-1.1	144.9	-1.4	255.7	2.7	104.7	-	97.9	-	204.2	8.5
1999	148.4	1.0	148.4	0.7	132.7	1.3	125.8	0.2	143.7	-0.8	260.8	2.0	107.1	2.3	97.0	-0.9	212.7	4.2
2000	150.9	1.7	151.7	2.2	134.2	1.1	124.5	-1.0	150.5	4.7	272.1	4.3	105.5	-1.5	94.8	-2.3	217.2	2.1
2001	155.2	2.8	156.4	3.1	139.0	3.6	131.1	5.3	153.0	1.7	282.9	4.0	106.4	0.9	94.3	-0.5		

Source: U.S. Department of Labor, Bureau of Labor Statistics, Division of Consumer Prices and Price Indexes. *Base is December 1997 = 100. - indicates no data collected for period.

Anchorage, AK
Consumer Price Index - Urban Wage Earners
Base 1982-1984 = 100
Annual Averages

For 1960-2001. Columns headed % show percentile change in the index from the previous period for which an index is available.

Year	All Items		Food & Beverage		Housing		Apparel		Trans-portation		Medical Care		Recrea-tion*		Education & Communic.*		Other Goods & Services	
	Index	%	Index	%	Index	%	Index	%	Index	%	Index	%	Index	%	Index	%	Index	%
1960	-		-		-		-		-		-						-	
1961	35.4		-		-		-		-		-		-		-		-	
1962	35.5	0.3	-		-		-		-		-		-		-		-	-
1963	35.7	0.6	-		-		-		-		-		-		-		-	
1964	35.9	0.6	-		-		-		-		-		-		-		-	
1965	36.2	0.8	-		-		-		-		-		-		-		-	
1966	37.2	2.8	-		-		-		-		-		-		-		-	
1967	38.2	2.7	-		-		-		-		-		-		-		-	
1968	39.1	2.4	-		-		-		-		-		-		-		-	
1969	40.7	4.1	-		-		-		-		-		-		-		-	
1970	42.1	3.4	-		-		-		-		-		-		-		-	
1971	43.4	3.1	-		-	-	57.1		40.4		36.2		-		-		-	
1972	44.5	2.5	-		-	-	58.9	3.2	40.5	0.2	36.9	1.9	-		-		-	
1973	46.4	4.3	-		-	-	61.4	4.2	41.0	1.2	38.4	4.1	-		-		-	
1974	51.4	10.8	-		-	-	65.4	6.5	44.4	8.3	42.7	11.2	-		-		-	
1975	58.5	13.8	-		-	-	70.5	7.8	48.8	9.9	48.3	13.1	-		-		-	
1976	63.1	7.9	64.5	-	65.7	-	74.9	6.2	54.3	11.3	54.1	12.0	-		-		62.6	-
1977	67.2	6.5	69.3	7.4	68.8	4.7	80.0	6.8	59.6	9.8	59.7	10.4	-		-		66.9	6.9
1978	72.0	7.1	76.9	11.0	73.0	6.1	80.3	0.4	64.1	7.6	67.1	12.4	-		-		70.1	4.8
1979	79.0	9.7	86.1	12.0	80.5	10.3	81.6	1.6	71.2	11.1	72.8	8.5	-		-		75.0	7.0
1980	86.3	9.2	90.3	4.9	87.6	8.8	86.5	6.0	82.9	16.4	79.3	8.9	-		-		81.9	9.2
1981	92.9	7.6	94.2	4.3	93.9	7.2	92.6	7.1	93.4	12.7	86.8	9.5					86.4	5.5
1982	98.2	5.7	97.2	3.2	100.1	6.6	96.3	4.0	97.3	4.2	94.9	9.3					92.4	6.9
1983	98.9	0.7	99.7	2.6	98.2	-1.9	101.6	5.5	98.4	1.1	99.8	5.2					101.9	10.3
1984	102.9	4.0	103.2	3.5	101.6	3.5	102.1	0.5	104.3	6.0	105.3	5.5					105.7	3.7
1985	105.8	2.8	106.2	2.9	103.4	1.8	105.5	3.3	107.6	3.2	110.5	4.9					114.1	7.9
1986	107.7	1.8	110.9	4.4	103.1	-0.3	108.1	2.5	106.5	-1.0	125.3	13.4					123.2	8.0
1987	107.9	0.2	113.2	2.1	97.8	-5.1	115.9	7.2	109.5	2.8	133.6	6.6					-	
1988	108.3	0.4	113.9	0.6	95.8	-2.0	116.3	0.3	111.0	1.4	142.1	6.4					137.3	11.4
1989	111.3	2.8	117.4	3.1	96.6	0.8	120.3	3.4	114.6	3.2	150.9	6.2	-		-		143.9	4.8
1990	118.4	6.4	124.1	5.7	104.1	7.8	125.7	4.5	118.5	3.4	157.9	4.6	-		-		158.4	10.1
1991	123.8	4.6	128.1	3.2	111.4	7.0	125.5	-0.2	119.4	0.8	169.7	7.5	-		-		170.8	7.8
1992	128.0	3.4	130.7	2.0	116.6	4.7	129.8	3.4	121.6	1.8	178.5	5.2	-		-		179.7	5.2
1993	132.0	3.1	131.7	0.8	121.1	3.9	131.4	1.2	126.8	4.3	185.6	4.0	-		-		182.0	1.3
1994	134.8	2.1	132.5	0.6	123.0	1.6	129.5	-1.4	134.5	6.1	193.6	4.3	-		-		173.0	-4.9
1995	138.5	2.7	139.1	5.0	125.0	1.6	130.7	0.9	140.7	4.6	206.5	6.7	-		-		160.9	-7.0
1996	142.4	2.8	144.0	3.5	127.8	2.2	130.5	-0.2	144.8	2.9	223.9	8.4	-		-		161.6	0.4
1997	144.5	1.5	146.2	1.5	129.3	1.2	128.0	-1.9	145.1	0.2	241.0	7.6	-		-		169.3	4.8
1998	146.3	1.2	147.6	1.0	130.8	1.2	125.6	-1.9	142.0	-2.1	249.7	3.6	104.2	-	98.8	-	187.6	10.8
1999	147.8	1.0	148.7	0.7	132.3	1.1	126.0	0.3	140.6	-1.0	259.2	3.8	104.9	0.7	98.5	-0.3	203.6	8.5
2000	151.1	2.2	152.1	2.3	133.9	1.2	125.0	-0.8	148.2	5.4	275.2	6.2	104.8	-0.1	97.1	-1.4	213.8	5.0
2001	155.8	3.1	156.7	3.0	138.9	3.7	131.7	5.4	151.6	2.3	290.3	5.5	105.5	0.7	97.3	0.2	218.7	2.3

Source: U.S. Department of Labor, Bureau of Labor Statistics, Division of Consumer Prices and Price Indexes. *Base is December 1997 = 100. - indicates no data collected for period.

Anchorage, AK
Consumer Price Index - All Urban Consumers
Base 1982-1984 = 100
All Items

For 1960-2001. Columns headed % show percentile change in the index from the previous period for which an index is available.

Year	Jan Index	%	Feb Index	%	Mar Index	%	Apr Index	%	May Index	%	Jun Index	%	Jul Index	%	Aug Index	%	Sep Index	%	Oct Index	%	Nov Index	%	Dec Index	%
1960	-	-	-	-	-	-	-	-	34.2	-	-	-	-	-	-	-	-	-	34.4	0.6	-	-	-	-
1961	-	-	-	-	-	-	-	-	34.4	0.0	-	-	-	-	-	-	-	-	34.8	1.2	-	-	-	-
1962	-	-	-	-	-	-	-	-	34.6	-0.6	-	-	-	-	-	-	-	-	34.7	0.3	-	-	-	-
1963	-	-	-	-	-	-	34.8	0.3	-	-	-	-	-	-	-	-	-	-	34.9	0.3	-	-	-	-
1964	-	-	-	-	-	-	34.8	-0.3	-	-	-	-	-	-	-	-	-	-	35.2	1.1	-	-	-	-
1965	-	-	-	-	-	-	35.3	0.3	-	-	-	-	-	-	-	-	-	-	35.3	0.0	-	-	-	-
1966	-	-	-	-	-	-	-	-	-	-	-	-	-	-	-	-	-	-	36.7	4.0	-	-	-	-
1967	-	-	-	-	-	-	-	-	-	-	-	-	-	-	-	-	-	-	37.5	2.2	-	-	-	-
1968	-	-	-	-	-	-	-	-	-	-	-	-	-	-	-	-	-	-	38.4	2.4	-	-	-	-
1969	38.9	1.3	-	-	-	-	39.5	1.5	-	-	-	-	39.6	0.3	-	-	-	-	40.2	1.5	-	-	-	-
1970	40.4	0.5	-	-	-	-	40.5	0.2	-	-	-	-	41.1	1.5	-	-	-	-	41.8	1.7	-	-	-	-
1971	41.8	0.0	-	-	-	-	41.8	0.0	-	-	-	-	42.3	1.2	-	-	-	-	42.8	1.2	-	-	-	-
1972	42.8	0.0	-	-	-	-	43.4	1.4	-	-	-	-	43.4	0.0	-	-	-	-	43.8	0.9	-	-	-	-
1973	43.6	-0.5	-	-	-	-	44.7	2.5	-	-	-	-	45.1	0.9	-	-	-	-	46.4	2.9	-	-	-	-
1974	47.1	1.5	-	-	-	-	48.7	3.4	-	-	-	-	50.3	3.3	-	-	-	-	52.5	4.4	-	-	-	-
1975	53.5	1.9	-	-	-	-	56.2	5.0	-	-	-	-	57.6	2.5	-	-	-	-	59.0	2.4	-	-	-	-
1976	59.5	0.8	-	-	-	-	60.6	1.8	-	-	-	-	61.8	2.0	-	-	-	-	62.8	1.6	-	-	-	-
1977	63.5	1.1	-	-	-	-	64.7	1.9	-	-	-	-	66.5	2.8	-	-	-	-	66.4	-0.2	-	-	-	-
1978	67.1	1.1	-	-	67.7	0.9	-	-	69.0	1.9	-	-	70.6	2.3	-	-	72.4	2.5	-	-	72.9	0.7	-	-
1979	74.2	1.8	-	-	75.3	1.5	-	-	76.2	1.2	-	-	77.7	2.0	-	-	79.9	2.8	-	-	80.1	0.3	-	-
1980	81.7	2.0	-	-	83.7	2.4	-	-	84.9	1.4	-	-	85.6	0.8	-	-	86.5	1.1	-	-	88.6	2.4	-	-
1981	90.0	1.6	-	-	90.3	0.3	-	-	91.6	1.4	-	-	92.2	0.7	-	-	93.9	1.8	-	-	95.0	1.2	-	-
1982	94.8	-0.2	-	-	97.4	2.7	-	-	98.8	1.4	-	-	98.8	0.0	-	-	98.7	-0.1	-	-	96.4	-2.3	-	-
1983	96.5	0.1	-	-	97.8	1.3	-	-	98.3	0.5	-	-	99.6	1.3	-	-	100.4	0.8	-	-	101.3	0.9	-	-
1984	101.7	0.4	-	-	102.8	1.1	-	-	103.1	0.3	-	-	103.2	0.1	-	-	104.1	0.9	-	-	104.0	-0.1	-	-
1985	104.3	0.3	-	-	104.9	0.6	-	-	104.5	-0.4	-	-	106.1	1.5	-	-	106.6	0.5	-	-	107.5	0.8	-	-
1986	107.6	0.1	-	-	109.1	1.4	-	-	108.2	-0.8	-	-	107.3	-0.8	-	-	107.2	-0.1	-	-	107.8	0.6	107.4	-0.4
1987	-	-	-	-	-	-	-	-	-	-	108.3	0.8	-	-	-	-	-	-	-	-	-	-	108.1	-0.2
1988	-	-	-	-	-	-	-	-	-	-	108.4	0.3	-	-	-	-	-	-	-	-	-	-	108.9	0.5
1989	-	-	-	-	-	-	-	-	-	-	110.9	1.8	-	-	-	-	-	-	-	-	-	-	112.5	1.4
1990	-	-	-	-	-	-	-	-	-	-	116.9	3.9	-	-	-	-	-	-	-	-	-	-	120.4	3.0
1991	-	-	-	-	-	-	-	-	-	-	123.3	2.4	-	-	-	-	-	-	-	-	-	-	124.7	1.1
1992	-	-	-	-	-	-	-	-	-	-	127.3	2.1	-	-	-	-	-	-	-	-	-	-	129.1	1.4
1993	-	-	-	-	-	-	-	-	-	-	131.5	1.9	-	-	-	-	-	-	-	-	-	-	132.8	1.0
1994	-	-	-	-	-	-	-	-	-	-	134.3	1.1	-	-	-	-	-	-	-	-	-	-	135.8	1.1
1995	-	-	-	-	-	-	-	-	-	-	138.2	1.8	-	-	-	-	-	-	-	-	-	-	139.5	0.9
1996	-	-	-	-	-	-	-	-	-	-	141.8	1.6	-	-	-	-	-	-	-	-	-	-	143.7	1.3
1997	-	-	-	-	-	-	-	-	-	-	144.1	0.3	-	-	-	-	-	-	-	-	-	-	145.4	0.9
1998	-	-	-	-	-	-	-	-	-	-	146.7	0.9	-	-	-	-	-	-	-	-	-	-	147.0	0.2
1999	-	-	-	-	-	-	-	-	-	-	148.6	1.1	-	-	-	-	-	-	-	-	-	-	148.3	-0.2
2000	-	-	-	-	-	-	-	-	-	-	150.0	1.1	-	-	-	-	-	-	-	-	-	-	151.9	1.3
2001	-	-	-	-	-	-	-	-	-	-	154.4	1.6	-	-	-	-	-	-	-	-	-	-	-	-

Source: U.S. Department of Labor, Bureau of Labor Statistics, Division of Consumer Prices and Price Indexes. - indicates no data collected for period.

Anchorage, AK
Consumer Price Index - Urban Wage Earners
Base 1982-1984 = 100
All Items

For 1960-2001. Columns headed % show percentile change in the index from the previous period for which an index is available.

Year	Jan Index	Jan %	Feb Index	Feb %	Mar Index	Mar %	Apr Index	Apr %	May Index	May %	Jun Index	Jun %	Jul Index	Jul %	Aug Index	Aug %	Sep Index	Sep %	Oct Index	Oct %	Nov Index	Nov %	Dec Index	Dec %
1960	-	-	-	-	-	-	-	-	35.1	-	-	-	-	-	-	-	-	-	35.3	0.6	-	-	-	-
1961	-	-	-	-	-	-	-	-	35.2	-0.3	-	-	-	-	-	-	-	-	35.7	1.4	-	-	-	-
1962	-	-	-	-	-	-	-	-	35.5	-0.6	-	-	-	-	-	-	-	-	35.5	0.0	-	-	-	-
1963	-	-	-	-	-	-	35.7	0.6	-	-	-	-	-	-	-	-	-	-	35.8	0.3	-	-	-	-
1964	-	-	-	-	-	-	35.7	-0.3	-	-	-	-	-	-	-	-	-	-	36.1	1.1	-	-	-	-
1965	-	-	-	-	-	-	36.2	0.3	-	-	-	-	-	-	-	-	-	-	36.2	0.0	-	-	-	-
1966	-	-	-	-	-	-	-	-	-	-	-	-	-	-	-	-	-	-	37.6	3.9	-	-	-	-
1967	-	-	-	-	-	-	-	-	-	-	-	-	-	-	-	-	-	-	38.4	2.1	-	-	-	-
1968	-	-	-	-	-	-	-	-	-	-	-	-	-	-	-	-	-	-	39.4	2.6	-	-	-	-
1969	39.8	1.0	-	-	-	-	40.5	1.8	-	-	-	-	40.6	0.2	-	-	-	-	41.2	1.5	-	-	-	-
1970	41.4	0.5	-	-	-	-	41.6	0.5	-	-	-	-	42.1	1.2	-	-	-	-	42.8	1.7	-	-	-	-
1971	42.8	0.0	-	-	-	-	42.9	0.2	-	-	-	-	43.4	1.2	-	-	-	-	43.9	1.2	-	-	-	-
1972	43.9	0.0	-	-	-	-	44.5	1.4	-	-	-	-	44.5	0.0	-	-	-	-	44.9	0.9	-	-	-	-
1973	44.7	-0.4	-	-	-	-	45.9	2.7	-	-	-	-	46.3	0.9	-	-	-	-	47.6	2.8	-	-	-	-
1974	48.3	1.5	-	-	-	-	49.9	3.3	-	-	-	-	51.6	3.4	-	-	-	-	53.9	4.5	-	-	-	-
1975	54.9	1.9	-	-	-	-	57.6	4.9	-	-	-	-	59.1	2.6	-	-	-	-	60.5	2.4	-	-	-	-
1976	61.0	0.8	-	-	-	-	62.1	1.8	-	-	-	-	63.4	2.1	-	-	-	-	64.4	1.6	-	-	-	-
1977	65.1	1.1	-	-	-	-	66.3	1.8	-	-	-	-	68.2	2.9	-	-	-	-	68.1	-0.1	-	-	-	-
1978	68.9	1.2	-	-	69.5	0.9	-	-	70.7	1.7	-	-	72.5	2.5	-	-	74.1	2.2	-	-	74.8	0.9	-	-
1979	75.8	1.3	-	-	77.0	1.6	-	-	77.8	1.0	-	-	79.3	1.9	-	-	81.0	2.1	-	-	81.4	0.5	-	-
1980	83.0	2.0	-	-	84.6	1.9	-	-	85.7	1.3	-	-	86.4	0.8	-	-	87.1	0.8	-	-	89.1	2.3	-	-
1981	90.3	1.3	-	-	90.8	0.6	-	-	92.3	1.7	-	-	92.9	0.7	-	-	94.5	1.7	-	-	95.8	1.4	-	-
1982	95.5	-0.3	-	-	97.8	2.4	-	-	99.1	1.3	-	-	99.6	0.5	-	-	99.5	-0.1	-	-	97.7	-1.8	-	-
1983	96.3	-1.4	-	-	97.6	1.3	-	-	97.9	0.3	-	-	98.9	1.0	-	-	100.2	1.3	-	-	101.4	1.2	-	-
1984	101.4	0.0	-	-	102.2	0.8	-	-	102.1	-0.1	-	-	102.5	0.4	-	-	104.1	1.6	-	-	104.1	0.0	-	-
1985	104.4	0.3	-	-	104.9	0.5	-	-	104.5	-0.4	-	-	106.0	1.4	-	-	106.5	0.5	-	-	107.6	1.0	-	-
1986	107.7	0.1	-	-	109.3	1.5	-	-	108.3	-0.9	-	-	107.0	-1.2	-	-	106.8	-0.2	-	-	107.5	0.7	107.2	-0.3
1987	-	-	-	-	-	-	-	-	-	-	108.0	0.7	-	-	-	-	-	-	-	-	-	-	107.9	-0.1
1988	-	-	-	-	-	-	-	-	-	-	108.1	0.2	-	-	-	-	-	-	-	-	-	-	108.5	0.4
1989	-	-	-	-	-	-	-	-	-	-	110.5	1.8	-	-	-	-	-	-	-	-	-	-	112.1	1.4
1990	-	-	-	-	-	-	-	-	-	-	116.6	4.0	-	-	-	-	-	-	-	-	-	-	120.2	3.1
1991	-	-	-	-	-	-	-	-	-	-	123.0	2.3	-	-	-	-	-	-	-	-	-	-	124.5	1.2
1992	-	-	-	-	-	-	-	-	-	-	127.0	2.0	-	-	-	-	-	-	-	-	-	-	129.1	1.7
1993	-	-	-	-	-	-	-	-	-	-	131.4	1.8	-	-	-	-	-	-	-	-	-	-	132.6	0.9
1994	-	-	-	-	-	-	-	-	-	-	134.1	1.1	-	-	-	-	-	-	-	-	-	-	135.5	1.0
1995	-	-	-	-	-	-	-	-	-	-	137.8	1.7	-	-	-	-	-	-	-	-	-	-	139.1	0.9
1996	-	-	-	-	-	-	-	-	-	-	141.4	1.7	-	-	-	-	-	-	-	-	-	-	143.5	1.5
1997	-	-	-	-	-	-	-	-	-	-	144.0	0.3	-	-	-	-	-	-	-	-	-	-	145.0	0.7
1998	-	-	-	-	-	-	-	-	-	-	146.1	0.8	-	-	-	-	-	-	-	-	-	-	146.6	0.3
1999	-	-	-	-	-	-	-	-	-	-	147.7	0.8	-	-	-	-	-	-	-	-	-	-	148.0	0.2
2000	-	-	-	-	-	-	-	-	-	-	150.0	1.4	-	-	-	-	-	-	-	-	-	-	152.2	1.5
2001	-	-	-	-	-	-	-	-	-	-	154.9	1.8	-	-	-	-	-	-	-	-	-	-	-	-

Source: U.S. Department of Labor, Bureau of Labor Statistics, Division of Consumer Prices and Price Indexes. - indicates no data collected for period.

Anchorage, AK
Consumer Price Index - All Urban Consumers
Base 1982-1984 = 100
Food and Beverages

For 1976-2001. Columns headed % show percentile change in the index from the previous period for which an index is available.

Year	Jan Index	%	Feb Index	%	Mar Index	%	Apr Index	%	May Index	%	Jun Index	%	Jul Index	%	Aug Index	%	Sep Index	%	Oct Index	%	Nov Index	%	Dec Index	%
1976	63.2	-	-	-	-	-	63.4	0.3	-	-	-	-	64.4	1.6	-	-	-	-	64.8	0.6	-	-	-	-
1977	65.4	0.9	-	-	-	-	67.3	2.9	-	-	-	-	70.9	5.3	-	-	-	-	69.8	-1.6	-	-	-	-
1978	71.6	2.6	-	-	73.2	2.2	-	-	76.2	4.1	-	-	76.2	0.0	-	-	77.7	2.0	-	-	78.2	0.6	-	-
1979	80.6	3.1	-	-	82.7	2.6	-	-	82.7	0.0	-	-	84.5	2.2	-	-	85.7	1.4	-	-	86.2	0.6	-	-
1980	86.8	0.7	-	-	87.3	0.6	-	-	88.6	1.5	-	-	89.9	1.5	-	-	91.0	1.2	-	-	93.0	2.2	-	-
1981	92.9	-0.1	-	-	92.6	-0.3	-	-	93.1	0.5	-	-	94.6	1.6	-	-	95.7	1.2	-	-	96.0	0.3	-	-
1982	96.5	0.5	-	-	95.6	-0.9	-	-	96.7	1.2	-	-	98.2	1.6	-	-	97.8	-0.4	-	-	97.9	0.1	-	-
1983	97.8	-0.1	-	-	98.4	0.6	-	-	99.2	0.8	-	-	100.2	1.0	-	-	100.3	0.1	-	-	101.0	0.7	-	-
1984	102.2	1.2	-	-	102.9	0.7	-	-	103.3	0.4	-	-	103.2	-0.1	-	-	103.2	0.0	-	-	103.7	0.5	-	-
1985	103.8	0.1	-	-	104.5	0.7	-	-	105.1	0.6	-	-	106.5	1.3	-	-	107.1	0.6	-	-	108.6	1.4	-	-
1986	109.7	1.0	-	-	109.8	0.1	-	-	110.5	0.6	-	-	111.1	0.5	-	-	111.5	0.4	-	-	111.6	0.1	111.9	0.3
1987	-	-	-	-	-	-	-	-	-	-	113.6	1.5	-	-	-	-	-	-	-	-	-	-	112.7	-0.8
1988	-	-	-	-	-	-	-	-	-	-	113.5	0.7	-	-	-	-	-	-	-	-	-	-	114.2	0.6
1989	-	-	-	-	-	-	-	-	-	-	116.4	1.9	-	-	-	-	-	-	-	-	-	-	118.0	1.4
1990	-	-	-	-	-	-	-	-	-	-	122.5	3.8	-	-	-	-	-	-	-	-	-	-	125.0	2.0
1991	-	-	-	-	-	-	-	-	-	-	128.2	2.6	-	-	-	-	-	-	-	-	-	-	127.2	-0.8
1992	-	-	-	-	-	-	-	-	-	-	129.9	2.1	-	-	-	-	-	-	-	-	-	-	130.7	0.6
1993	-	-	-	-	-	-	-	-	-	-	131.6	0.7	-	-	-	-	-	-	-	-	-	-	130.8	-0.6
1994	-	-	-	-	-	-	-	-	-	-	131.3	0.4	-	-	-	-	-	-	-	-	-	-	132.5	0.9
1995	-	-	-	-	-	-	-	-	-	-	138.6	4.6	-	-	-	-	-	-	-	-	-	-	138.4	-0.1
1996	-	-	-	-	-	-	-	-	-	-	142.0	2.6	-	-	-	-	-	-	-	-	-	-	144.7	1.9
1997	-	-	-	-	-	-	-	-	-	-	145.6	0.6	-	-	-	-	-	-	-	-	-	-	146.1	0.3
1998	-	-	-	-	-	-	-	-	-	-	147.8	1.2	-	-	-	-	-	-	-	-	-	-	146.9	-0.6
1999	-	-	-	-	-	-	-	-	-	-	147.9	0.7	-	-	-	-	-	-	-	-	-	-	149.0	0.7
2000	-	-	-	-	-	-	-	-	-	-	150.4	0.9	-	-	-	-	-	-	-	-	-	-	153.1	1.8
2001	-	-	-	-	-	-	-	-	-	-	156.0	1.9	-	-	-	-	-	-	-	-	-	-	-	-

Source: U.S. Department of Labor, Bureau of Labor Statistics, Division of Consumer Prices and Price Indexes. - indicates no data collected for period.

Anchorage, AK
Consumer Price Index - Urban Wage Earners
Base 1982-1984 = 100
Food and Beverages

For 1976-2001. Columns headed % show percentile change in the index from the previous period for which an index is available.

Year	Jan Index	%	Feb Index	%	Mar Index	%	Apr Index	%	May Index	%	Jun Index	%	Jul Index	%	Aug Index	%	Sep Index	%	Oct Index	%	Nov Index	%	Dec Index	%
1976	63.6	-	-	-	-	-	63.7	0.2	-	-	-	-	64.8	1.7	-	-	-	-	65.2	0.6	-	-	-	-
1977	65.8	0.9	-	-	-	-	67.7	2.9	-	-	-	-	71.3	5.3	-	-	-	-	70.2	-1.5	-	-	-	-
1978	72.0	2.6	-	-	73.3	1.8	-	-	76.0	3.7	-	-	78.0	2.6	-	-	79.5	1.9	-	-	80.4	1.1	-	-
1979	81.6	1.5	-	-	84.9	4.0	-	-	85.5	0.7	-	-	86.8	1.5	-	-	88.0	1.4	-	-	88.3	0.3	-	-
1980	88.8	0.6	-	-	88.1	-0.8	-	-	89.2	1.2	-	-	90.6	1.6	-	-	91.3	0.8	-	-	93.0	1.9	-	-
1981	92.4	-0.6	-	-	92.2	-0.2	-	-	93.2	1.1	-	-	94.2	1.1	-	-	95.9	1.8	-	-	96.0	0.1	-	-
1982	96.4	0.4	-	-	95.6	-0.8	-	-	96.6	1.0	-	-	98.1	1.6	-	-	97.8	-0.3	-	-	97.9	0.1	-	-
1983	98.1	0.2	-	-	98.5	0.4	-	-	99.1	0.6	-	-	100.2	1.1	-	-	100.4	0.2	-	-	100.9	0.5	-	-
1984	102.1	1.2	-	-	102.9	0.8	-	-	103.3	0.4	-	-	103.3	0.0	-	-	103.3	0.0	-	-	103.8	0.5	-	-
1985	103.8	0.0	-	-	104.6	0.8	-	-	105.2	0.6	-	-	106.6	1.3	-	-	107.0	0.4	-	-	108.5	1.4	-	-
1986	109.6	1.0	-	-	110.0	0.4	-	-	110.5	0.5	-	-	111.1	0.5	-	-	111.6	0.5	-	-	111.8	0.2	111.9	0.1
1987	-	-	-	-	-	-	-	-	-	-	113.6	1.5	-	-	-	-	-	-	-	-	-	-	112.8	-0.7
1988	-	-	-	-	-	-	-	-	-	-	113.5	0.6	-	-	-	-	-	-	-	-	-	-	114.3	0.7
1989	-	-	-	-	-	-	-	-	-	-	116.5	1.9	-	-	-	-	-	-	-	-	-	-	118.2	1.5
1990	-	-	-	-	-	-	-	-	-	-	122.9	4.0	-	-	-	-	-	-	-	-	-	-	125.3	2.0
1991	-	-	-	-	-	-	-	-	-	-	128.7	2.7	-	-	-	-	-	-	-	-	-	-	127.4	-1.0
1992	-	-	-	-	-	-	-	-	-	-	130.3	2.3	-	-	-	-	-	-	-	-	-	-	131.1	0.6
1993	-	-	-	-	-	-	-	-	-	-	132.2	0.8	-	-	-	-	-	-	-	-	-	-	131.2	-0.8
1994	-	-	-	-	-	-	-	-	-	-	132.0	0.6	-	-	-	-	-	-	-	-	-	-	133.0	0.8
1995	-	-	-	-	-	-	-	-	-	-	139.2	4.7	-	-	-	-	-	-	-	-	-	-	139.0	-0.1
1996	-	-	-	-	-	-	-	-	-	-	142.6	2.6	-	-	-	-	-	-	-	-	-	-	145.5	2.0
1997	-	-	-	-	-	-	-	-	-	-	146.1	0.4	-	-	-	-	-	-	-	-	-	-	146.2	0.1
1998	-	-	-	-	-	-	-	-	-	-	148.0	1.2	-	-	-	-	-	-	-	-	-	-	147.3	-0.5
1999	-	-	-	-	-	-	-	-	-	-	148.2	0.6	-	-	-	-	-	-	-	-	-	-	149.3	0.7
2000	-	-	-	-	-	-	-	-	-	-	150.7	0.9	-	-	-	-	-	-	-	-	-	-	153.4	1.8
2001	-	-	-	-	-	-	-	-	-	-	156.3	1.9	-	-	-	-	-	-	-	-	-	-	-	-

Source: U.S. Department of Labor, Bureau of Labor Statistics, Division of Consumer Prices and Price Indexes. - indicates no data collected for period.

Anchorage, AK
Consumer Price Index - All Urban Consumers
Base 1982-1984 = 100
Housing

For 1976-2001. Columns headed % show percentile change in the index from the previous period for which an index is available.

Year	Jan Index	Jan %	Feb Index	Feb %	Mar Index	Mar %	Apr Index	Apr %	May Index	May %	Jun Index	Jun %	Jul Index	Jul %	Aug Index	Aug %	Sep Index	Sep %	Oct Index	Oct %	Nov Index	Nov %	Dec Index	Dec %
1976	61.0	-	-	-	-	-	61.7	1.1	-	-	-	-	62.8	1.8	-	-	-	-	63.7	1.4	-	-	-	-
1977	64.3	0.9	-	-	-	-	64.6	0.5	-	-	-	-	66.0	2.2	-	-	-	-	66.4	0.6	-	-	-	-
1978	66.6	0.3	-	-	66.9	0.5	-	-	67.5	0.9	-	-	70.1	3.9	-	-	72.5	3.4	-	-	73.0	0.7	-	-
1979	74.4	1.9	-	-	75.7	1.7	-	-	76.7	1.3	-	-	78.3	2.1	-	-	80.5	2.8	-	-	80.4	-0.1	-	-
1980	82.4	2.5	-	-	84.6	2.7	-	-	85.4	0.9	-	-	85.9	0.6	-	-	86.4	0.6	-	-	88.8	2.8	-	-
1981	90.8	2.3	-	-	90.7	-0.1	-	-	91.6	1.0	-	-	91.9	0.3	-	-	93.7	2.0	-	-	95.2	1.6	-	-
1982	94.4	-0.8	-	-	99.4	5.3	-	-	101.4	2.0	-	-	100.1	-1.3	-	-	99.6	-0.5	-	-	94.8	-4.8	-	-
1983	95.2	0.4	-	-	97.8	2.7	-	-	98.1	0.3	-	-	99.7	1.6	-	-	100.7	1.0	-	-	100.9	0.2	-	-
1984	101.7	0.8	-	-	102.9	1.2	-	-	103.0	0.1	-	-	102.2	-0.8	-	-	103.2	1.0	-	-	102.7	-0.5	-	-
1985	103.0	0.3	-	-	102.7	-0.3	-	-	101.4	-1.3	-	-	104.2	2.8	-	-	103.8	-0.4	-	-	103.2	-0.6	-	-
1986	103.3	0.1	-	-	105.8	2.4	-	-	105.5	-0.3	-	-	101.1	-4.2	-	-	100.2	-0.9	-	-	100.1	-0.1	100.1	0.0
1987	-	-	-	-	-	-	-	-	-	-	99.0	-1.1	-	-	-	-	-	-	-	-	-	-	96.1	-2.9
1988	-	-	-	-	-	-	-	-	-	-	95.8	-0.3	-	-	-	-	-	-	-	-	-	-	94.9	-0.9
1989	-	-	-	-	-	-	-	-	-	-	95.8	0.9	-	-	-	-	-	-	-	-	-	-	96.8	1.0
1990	-	-	-	-	-	-	-	-	-	-	102.2	5.6	-	-	-	-	-	-	-	-	-	-	105.7	3.4
1991	-	-	-	-	-	-	-	-	-	-	109.5	3.6	-	-	-	-	-	-	-	-	-	-	113.0	3.2
1992	-	-	-	-	-	-	-	-	-	-	115.5	2.2	-	-	-	-	-	-	-	-	-	-	117.8	2.0
1993	-	-	-	-	-	-	-	-	-	-	120.6	2.4	-	-	-	-	-	-	-	-	-	-	121.6	0.8
1994	-	-	-	-	-	-	-	-	-	-	122.8	1.0	-	-	-	-	-	-	-	-	-	-	123.1	0.2
1995	-	-	-	-	-	-	-	-	-	-	124.3	1.0	-	-	-	-	-	-	-	-	-	-	125.5	1.0
1996	-	-	-	-	-	-	-	-	-	-	127.1	1.3	-	-	-	-	-	-	-	-	-	-	128.7	1.3
1997	-	-	-	-	-	-	-	-	-	-	129.4	0.5	-	-	-	-	-	-	-	-	-	-	129.5	0.1
1998	-	-	-	-	-	-	-	-	-	-	130.7	0.9	-	-	-	-	-	-	-	-	-	-	131.4	0.5
1999	-	-	-	-	-	-	-	-	-	-	132.6	0.9	-	-	-	-	-	-	-	-	-	-	132.8	0.2
2000	-	-	-	-	-	-	-	-	-	-	133.9	0.8	-	-	-	-	-	-	-	-	-	-	134.4	0.4
2001	-	-	-	-	-	-	-	-	-	-	137.8	2.5	-	-	-	-	-	-	-	-	-	-	-	-

Source: U.S. Department of Labor, Bureau of Labor Statistics, Division of Consumer Prices and Price Indexes. - indicates no data collected for period.

Anchorage, AK
Consumer Price Index - Urban Wage Earners
Base 1982-1984 = 100
Housing

For 1976-2001. Columns headed % show percentile change in the index from the previous period for which an index is available.

Year	Jan Index	%	Feb Index	%	Mar Index	%	Apr Index	%	May Index	%	Jun Index	%	Jul Index	%	Aug Index	%	Sep Index	%	Oct Index	%	Nov Index	%	Dec Index	%
1976	64.1	-	-	-	-	-	64.8	1.1	-	-	-	-	66.0	1.9	-	-	-	-	66.9	1.4	-	-	-	-
1977	67.5	0.9	-	-	-	-	67.8	0.4	-	-	-	-	69.3	2.2	-	-	-	-	69.7	0.6	-	-	-	-
1978	69.9	0.3	-	-	70.3	0.6	-	-	70.9	0.9	-	-	73.3	3.4	-	-	75.6	3.1	-	-	76.2	0.8	-	-
1979	77.4	1.6	-	-	78.7	1.7	-	-	79.2	0.6	-	-	80.7	1.9	-	-	82.6	2.4	-	-	82.6	0.0	-	-
1980	84.3	2.1	-	-	86.3	2.4	-	-	87.3	1.2	-	-	87.6	0.3	-	-	87.9	0.3	-	-	90.3	2.7	-	-
1981	92.1	2.0	-	-	92.0	-0.1	-	-	93.1	1.2	-	-	93.3	0.2	-	-	95.0	1.8	-	-	96.8	1.9	-	-
1982	96.0	-0.8	-	-	100.8	5.0	-	-	103.0	2.2	-	-	102.3	-0.7	-	-	101.7	-0.6	-	-	97.6	-4.0	-	-
1983	94.5	-3.2	-	-	97.1	2.8	-	-	97.0	-0.1	-	-	98.1	1.1	-	-	99.9	1.8	-	-	101.1	1.2	-	-
1984	100.8	-0.3	-	-	101.4	0.6	-	-	100.4	-1.0	-	-	100.6	0.2	-	-	103.0	2.4	-	-	102.9	-0.1	-	-
1985	103.3	0.4	-	-	102.9	-0.4	-	-	101.5	-1.4	-	-	104.4	2.9	-	-	104.2	-0.2	-	-	103.8	-0.4	-	-
1986	103.6	-0.2	-	-	106.6	2.9	-	-	106.3	-0.3	-	-	101.7	-4.3	-	-	100.9	-0.8	-	-	100.4	-0.5	100.6	0.2
1987	-	-	-	-	-	-	-	-	-	-	99.1	-1.5	-	-	-	-	-	-	-	-	-	-	96.4	-2.7
1988	-	-	-	-	-	-	-	-	-	-	96.3	-0.1	-	-	-	-	-	-	-	-	-	-	95.3	-1.0
1989	-	-	-	-	-	-	-	-	-	-	96.1	0.8	-	-	-	-	-	-	-	-	-	-	97.2	1.1
1990	-	-	-	-	-	-	-	-	-	-	102.4	5.3	-	-	-	-	-	-	-	-	-	-	105.8	3.3
1991	-	-	-	-	-	-	-	-	-	-	109.7	3.7	-	-	-	-	-	-	-	-	-	-	113.1	3.1
1992	-	-	-	-	-	-	-	-	-	-	115.4	2.0	-	-	-	-	-	-	-	-	-	-	117.9	2.2
1993	-	-	-	-	-	-	-	-	-	-	120.7	2.4	-	-	-	-	-	-	-	-	-	-	121.6	0.7
1994	-	-	-	-	-	-	-	-	-	-	122.7	0.9	-	-	-	-	-	-	-	-	-	-	123.3	0.5
1995	-	-	-	-	-	-	-	-	-	-	124.4	0.9	-	-	-	-	-	-	-	-	-	-	125.5	0.9
1996	-	-	-	-	-	-	-	-	-	-	127.0	1.2	-	-	-	-	-	-	-	-	-	-	128.5	1.2
1997	-	-	-	-	-	-	-	-	-	-	129.3	0.6	-	-	-	-	-	-	-	-	-	-	129.4	0.1
1998	-	-	-	-	-	-	-	-	-	-	130.4	0.8	-	-	-	-	-	-	-	-	-	-	131.1	0.5
1999	-	-	-	-	-	-	-	-	-	-	132.1	0.8	-	-	-	-	-	-	-	-	-	-	132.5	0.3
2000	-	-	-	-	-	-	-	-	-	-	133.7	0.9	-	-	-	-	-	-	-	-	-	-	134.2	0.4
2001	-	-	-	-	-	-	-	-	-	-	137.8	2.7	-	-	-	-	-	-	-	-	-	-	-	-

Source: U.S. Department of Labor, Bureau of Labor Statistics, Division of Consumer Prices and Price Indexes. - indicates no data collected for period.

Anchorage, AK
Consumer Price Index - All Urban Consumers
Base 1982-1984 = 100
Apparel

For 1971-2001. Columns headed % show percentile change in the index from the previous period for which an index is available.

Year	Jan Index	%	Feb Index	%	Mar Index	%	Apr Index	%	May Index	%	Jun Index	%	Jul Index	%	Aug Index	%	Sep Index	%	Oct Index	%	Nov Index	%	Dec Index	%
1971	55.3	-	-	-	-	-	56.1	1.4	-	-	-	-	56.8	1.2	-	-	-	-	57.0	0.4	-	-	-	-
1972	56.7	-0.5	-	-	-	-	58.5	3.2	-	-	-	-	58.3	-0.3	-	-	-	-	59.0	1.2	-	-	-	-
1973	58.9	-0.2	-	-	-	-	59.9	1.7	-	-	-	-	61.1	2.0	-	-	-	-	62.1	1.6	-	-	-	-
1974	61.7	-0.6	-	-	-	-	62.8	1.8	-	-	-	-	64.9	3.3	-	-	-	-	67.4	3.9	-	-	-	-
1975	67.6	0.3	-	-	-	-	70.1	3.7	-	-	-	-	69.6	-0.7	-	-	-	-	71.2	2.3	-	-	-	-
1976	70.3	-1.3	-	-	-	-	72.3	2.8	-	-	-	-	73.5	1.7	-	-	-	-	77.4	5.3	-	-	-	-
1977	78.7	1.7	-	-	-	-	79.1	0.5	-	-	-	-	79.0	-0.1	-	-	-	-	80.3	1.6	-	-	-	-
1978	77.5	-3.5	-	-	78.2	0.9	-	-	80.1	2.4	-	-	79.1	-1.2	-	-	81.4	2.9	-	-	81.5	0.1	-	-
1979	79.6	-2.3	-	-	79.3	-0.4	-	-	79.7	0.5	-	-	78.9	-1.0	-	-	86.5	9.6	-	-	85.0	-1.7	-	-
1980	83.8	-1.4	-	-	86.4	3.1	-	-	88.4	2.3	-	-	91.7	3.7	-	-	92.1	0.4	-	-	93.5	1.5	-	-
1981	92.7	-0.9	-	-	94.3	1.7	-	-	95.0	0.7	-	-	91.5	-3.7	-	-	95.7	4.6	-	-	95.0	-0.7	-	-
1982	93.9	-1.2	-	-	93.9	0.0	-	-	96.3	2.6	-	-	96.7	0.4	-	-	99.0	2.4	-	-	99.4	0.4	-	-
1983	95.7	-3.7	-	-	101.5	6.1	-	-	101.9	0.4	-	-	102.4	0.5	-	-	102.3	-0.1	-	-	104.8	2.4	-	-
1984	100.8	-3.8	-	-	102.3	1.5	-	-	99.9	-2.3	-	-	101.5	1.6	-	-	104.7	3.2	-	-	101.6	-3.0	-	-
1985	100.4	-1.2	-	-	107.3	6.9	-	-	106.1	-1.1	-	-	103.2	-2.7	-	-	108.7	5.3	-	-	107.6	-1.0	-	-
1986	105.5	-2.0	-	-	110.2	4.5	-	-	107.7	-2.3	-	-	109.0	1.2	-	-	110.3	1.2	-	-	110.7	0.4	108.9	-1.6
1987	-	-	-	-	-	-	-	-	-	-	115.4	6.0	-	-	-	-	-	-	-	-	-	-	117.8	2.1
1988	-	-	-	-	-	-	-	-	-	-	118.6	0.7	-	-	-	-	-	-	-	-	-	-	119.6	0.8
1989	-	-	-	-	-	-	-	-	-	-	124.4	4.0	-	-	-	-	-	-	-	-	-	-	125.6	1.0
1990	-	-	-	-	-	-	-	-	-	-	127.8	1.8	-	-	-	-	-	-	-	-	-	-	127.6	-0.2
1991	-	-	-	-	-	-	-	-	-	-	124.4	-2.5	-	-	-	-	-	-	-	-	-	-	128.9	3.6
1992	-	-	-	-	-	-	-	-	-	-	131.1	1.7	-	-	-	-	-	-	-	-	-	-	129.4	-1.3
1993	-	-	-	-	-	-	-	-	-	-	128.5	-0.7	-	-	-	-	-	-	-	-	-	-	133.8	4.1
1994	-	-	-	-	-	-	-	-	-	-	125.8	-6.0	-	-	-	-	-	-	-	-	-	-	131.9	4.8
1995	-	-	-	-	-	-	-	-	-	-	128.5	-2.6	-	-	-	-	-	-	-	-	-	-	131.6	2.4
1996	-	-	-	-	-	-	-	-	-	-	124.3	-5.5	-	-	-	-	-	-	-	-	-	-	133.1	7.1
1997	-	-	-	-	-	-	-	-	-	-	124.3	-6.6	-	-	-	-	-	-	-	-	-	-	129.6	4.3
1998	-	-	-	-	-	-	-	-	-	-	126.8	-2.2	-	-	-	-	-	-	-	-	-	-	124.4	-1.9
1999	-	-	-	-	-	-	-	-	-	-	126.9	2.0	-	-	-	-	-	-	-	-	-	-	124.7	-1.7
2000	-	-	-	-	-	-	-	-	-	-	119.5	-4.2	-	-	-	-	-	-	-	-	-	-	129.4	8.3
2001	-	-	-	-	-	-	-	-	-	-	131.3	1.5	-	-	-	-	-	-	-	-	-	-	-	-

Source: U.S. Department of Labor, Bureau of Labor Statistics, Division of Consumer Prices and Price Indexes. - indicates no data collected for period.

Anchorage, AK
Consumer Price Index - Urban Wage Earners
Base 1982-1984 = 100
Apparel

For 1971-2001. Columns headed % show percentile change in the index from the previous period for which an index is available.

Year	Jan Index	%	Feb Index	%	Mar Index	%	Apr Index	%	May Index	%	Jun Index	%	Jul Index	%	Aug Index	%	Sep Index	%	Oct Index	%	Nov Index	%	Dec Index	%
1971	55.9	-	-	-	-	-	56.7	1.4	-	-	-	-	57.4	1.2	-	-	-	-	57.6	0.3	-	-	-	-
1972	57.3	-0.5	-	-	-	-	59.1	3.1	-	-	-	-	58.9	-0.3	-	-	-	-	59.7	1.4	-	-	-	-
1973	59.6	-0.2	-	-	-	-	60.5	1.5	-	-	-	-	61.8	2.1	-	-	-	-	62.8	1.6	-	-	-	-
1974	62.4	-0.6	-	-	-	-	63.5	1.8	-	-	-	-	65.6	3.3	-	-	-	-	68.2	4.0	-	-	-	-
1975	68.4	0.3	-	-	-	-	70.8	3.5	-	-	-	-	70.3	-0.7	-	-	-	-	71.9	2.3	-	-	-	-
1976	71.1	-1.1	-	-	-	-	73.0	2.7	-	-	-	-	74.3	1.8	-	-	-	-	78.2	5.2	-	-	-	-
1977	79.6	1.8	-	-	-	-	80.0	0.5	-	-	-	-	79.8	-0.2	-	-	-	-	81.2	1.8	-	-	-	-
1978	78.3	-3.6	-	-	78.9	0.8	-	-	80.5	2.0	-	-	80.0	-0.6	-	-	81.6	2.0	-	-	82.0	0.5	-	-
1979	81.1	-1.1	-	-	80.0	-1.4	-	-	80.0	0.0	-	-	80.7	0.9	-	-	84.0	4.1	-	-	83.5	-0.6	-	-
1980	83.1	-0.5	-	-	84.1	1.2	-	-	84.6	0.6	-	-	87.2	3.1	-	-	88.4	1.4	-	-	89.6	1.4	-	-
1981	91.6	2.2	-	-	92.3	0.8	-	-	92.3	0.0	-	-	90.9	-1.5	-	-	93.9	3.3	-	-	94.3	0.4	-	-
1982	92.7	-1.7	-	-	93.5	0.9	-	-	95.0	1.6	-	-	96.9	2.0	-	-	99.3	2.5	-	-	99.8	0.5	-	-
1983	95.7	-4.1	-	-	101.7	6.3	-	-	102.2	0.5	-	-	102.1	-0.1	-	-	102.6	0.5	-	-	104.2	1.6	-	-
1984	100.6	-3.5	-	-	101.8	1.2	-	-	100.2	-1.6	-	-	102.1	1.9	-	-	105.4	3.2	-	-	102.4	-2.8	-	-
1985	101.2	-1.2	-	-	106.5	5.2	-	-	105.8	-0.7	-	-	103.3	-2.4	-	-	108.4	4.9	-	-	106.9	-1.4	-	-
1986	105.0	-1.8	-	-	109.6	4.4	-	-	107.0	-2.4	-	-	108.2	1.1	-	-	108.9	0.6	-	-	109.4	0.5	108.2	-1.1
1987	-	-	-	-	-	-	-	-	-	-	114.6	5.9	-	-	-	-	-	-	-	-	-	-	117.3	2.4
1988	-	-	-	-	-	-	-	-	-	-	116.3	-0.9	-	-	-	-	-	-	-	-	-	-	116.3	0.0
1989	-	-	-	-	-	-	-	-	-	-	119.6	2.8	-	-	-	-	-	-	-	-	-	-	121.0	1.2
1990	-	-	-	-	-	-	-	-	-	-	125.5	3.7	-	-	-	-	-	-	-	-	-	-	126.0	0.4
1991	-	-	-	-	-	-	-	-	-	-	122.3	-2.9	-	-	-	-	-	-	-	-	-	-	128.7	5.2
1992	-	-	-	-	-	-	-	-	-	-	131.1	1.9	-	-	-	-	-	-	-	-	-	-	128.6	-1.9
1993	-	-	-	-	-	-	-	-	-	-	127.9	-0.5	-	-	-	-	-	-	-	-	-	-	134.8	5.4
1994	-	-	-	-	-	-	-	-	-	-	126.6	-6.1	-	-	-	-	-	-	-	-	-	-	132.4	4.6
1995	-	-	-	-	-	-	-	-	-	-	128.8	-2.7	-	-	-	-	-	-	-	-	-	-	132.5	2.9
1996	-	-	-	-	-	-	-	-	-	-	126.2	-4.8	-	-	-	-	-	-	-	-	-	-	134.7	6.7
1997	-	-	-	-	-	-	-	-	-	-	125.8	-6.6	-	-	-	-	-	-	-	-	-	-	130.2	3.5
1998	-	-	-	-	-	-	-	-	-	-	126.8	-2.6	-	-	-	-	-	-	-	-	-	-	124.5	-1.8
1999	-	-	-	-	-	-	-	-	-	-	126.5	1.6	-	-	-	-	-	-	-	-	-	-	125.5	-0.8
2000	-	-	-	-	-	-	-	-	-	-	120.2	-4.2	-	-	-	-	-	-	-	-	-	-	129.8	8.0
2001	-	-	-	-	-	-	-	-	-	-	132.1	1.8	-	-	-	-	-	-	-	-	-	-	-	-

Source: U.S. Department of Labor, Bureau of Labor Statistics, Division of Consumer Prices and Price Indexes. - indicates no data collected for period.

Anchorage, AK
Consumer Price Index - All Urban Consumers
Base 1982-1984 = 100
Transportation

For 1971-2001. Columns headed % show percentile change in the index from the previous period for which an index is available.

Year	Jan Index	%	Feb Index	%	Mar Index	%	Apr Index	%	May Index	%	Jun Index	%	Jul Index	%	Aug Index	%	Sep Index	%	Oct Index	%	Nov Index	%	Dec Index	%
1971	40.3	-	-	-	-	-	40.6	0.7	-	-	-	-	41.2	1.5	-	-	-	-	40.8	-1.0	-	-	-	-
1972	40.7	-0.2	-	-	-	-	40.6	-0.2	-	-	-	-	41.0	1.0	-	-	-	-	41.2	0.5	-	-	-	-
1973	41.0	-0.5	-	-	-	-	41.1	0.2	-	-	-	-	41.6	1.2	-	-	-	-	41.5	-0.2	-	-	-	-
1974	42.0	1.2	-	-	-	-	43.3	3.1	-	-	-	-	45.6	5.3	-	-	-	-	46.9	2.9	-	-	-	-
1975	46.8	-0.2	-	-	-	-	48.0	2.6	-	-	-	-	50.1	4.4	-	-	-	-	50.7	1.2	-	-	-	-
1976	51.5	1.6	-	-	-	-	53.8	4.5	-	-	-	-	55.4	3.0	-	-	-	-	57.0	2.9	-	-	-	-
1977	57.1	0.2	-	-	-	-	59.8	4.7	-	-	-	-	61.6	3.0	-	-	-	-	60.9	-1.1	-	-	-	-
1978	61.6	1.1	-	-	61.9	0.5	-	-	64.2	3.7	-	-	65.5	2.0	-	-	65.7	0.3	-	-	66.8	1.7	-	-
1979	67.3	0.7	-	-	67.7	0.6	-	-	69.7	3.0	-	-	72.1	3.4	-	-	73.9	2.5	-	-	74.9	1.4	-	-
1980	77.1	2.9	-	-	79.6	3.2	-	-	80.8	1.5	-	-	82.3	1.9	-	-	84.0	2.1	-	-	86.7	3.2	-	-
1981	87.7	1.2	-	-	89.7	2.3	-	-	92.1	2.7	-	-	93.6	1.6	-	-	95.0	1.5	-	-	96.0	1.1	-	-
1982	95.7	-0.3	-	-	95.8	0.1	-	-	95.8	0.0	-	-	97.3	1.6	-	-	97.8	0.5	-	-	98.1	0.3	-	-
1983	97.6	-0.5	-	-	95.8	-1.8	-	-	97.1	1.4	-	-	98.3	1.2	-	-	99.4	1.1	-	-	101.9	2.5	-	-
1984	101.6	-0.3	-	-	102.6	1.0	-	-	104.3	1.7	-	-	105.0	0.7	-	-	106.0	1.0	-	-	107.0	0.9	-	-
1985	107.2	0.2	-	-	107.4	0.2	-	-	107.6	0.2	-	-	107.5	-0.1	-	-	107.9	0.4	-	-	110.6	2.5	-	-
1986	111.1	0.5	-	-	110.8	-0.3	-	-	107.1	-3.3	-	-	105.5	-1.5	-	-	105.0	-0.5	-	-	108.1	3.0	107.9	-0.2
1987	-	-	-	-	-	-	-	-	-	-	109.8	1.8	-	-	-	-	-	-	-	-	-	-	112.8	2.7
1988	-	-	-	-	-	-	-	-	-	-	112.2	-0.5	-	-	-	-	-	-	-	-	-	-	113.8	1.4
1989	-	-	-	-	-	-	-	-	-	-	116.3	2.2	-	-	-	-	-	-	-	-	-	-	117.1	0.7
1990	-	-	-	-	-	-	-	-	-	-	118.4	1.1	-	-	-	-	-	-	-	-	-	-	123.1	4.0
1991	-	-	-	-	-	-	-	-	-	-	123.4	0.2	-	-	-	-	-	-	-	-	-	-	120.0	-2.8
1992	-	-	-	-	-	-	-	-	-	-	122.7	2.2	-	-	-	-	-	-	-	-	-	-	123.8	0.9
1993	-	-	-	-	-	-	-	-	-	-	126.7	2.3	-	-	-	-	-	-	-	-	-	-	130.8	3.2
1994	-	-	-	-	-	-	-	-	-	-	134.6	2.9	-	-	-	-	-	-	-	-	-	-	139.3	3.5
1995	-	-	-	-	-	-	-	-	-	-	143.7	3.2	-	-	-	-	-	-	-	-	-	-	143.8	0.1
1996	-	-	-	-	-	-	-	-	-	-	147.4	2.5	-	-	-	-	-	-	-	-	-	-	147.0	-0.3
1997	-	-	-	-	-	-	-	-	-	-	146.6	-0.3	-	-	-	-	-	-	-	-	-	-	147.5	0.6
1998	-	-	-	-	-	-	-	-	-	-	145.6	-1.3	-	-	-	-	-	-	-	-	-	-	144.2	-1.0
1999	-	-	-	-	-	-	-	-	-	-	144.1	-0.1	-	-	-	-	-	-	-	-	-	-	143.4	-0.5
2000	-	-	-	-	-	-	-	-	-	-	148.7	3.7	-	-	-	-	-	-	-	-	-	-	152.3	2.4
2001	-	-	-	-	-	-	-	-	-	-	152.9	0.4	-	-	-	-	-	-	-	-	-	-	-	-

Source: U.S. Department of Labor, Bureau of Labor Statistics, Division of Consumer Prices and Price Indexes. - indicates no data collected for period.

Anchorage, AK
Consumer Price Index - Urban Wage Earners
Base 1982-1984 = 100
Transportation

For 1971-2001. Columns headed % show percentile change in the index from the previous period for which an index is available.

Year	Jan Index	%	Feb Index	%	Mar Index	%	Apr Index	%	May Index	%	Jun Index	%	Jul Index	%	Aug Index	%	Sep Index	%	Oct Index	%	Nov Index	%	Dec Index	%
1971	39.9	-	-	-	-	-	40.2	0.8	-	-	-	-	40.8	1.5	-	-	-	-	40.4	-1.0	-	-	-	-
1972	40.3	-0.2	-	-	-	-	40.2	-0.2	-	-	-	-	40.6	1.0	-	-	-	-	40.8	0.5	-	-	-	-
1973	40.6	-0.5	-	-	-	-	40.7	0.2	-	-	-	-	41.2	1.2	-	-	-	-	41.1	-0.2	-	-	-	-
1974	41.6	1.2	-	-	-	-	42.9	3.1	-	-	-	-	45.1	5.1	-	-	-	-	46.4	2.9	-	-	-	-
1975	46.3	-0.2	-	-	-	-	47.5	2.6	-	-	-	-	49.6	4.4	-	-	-	-	50.1	1.0	-	-	-	-
1976	51.0	1.8	-	-	-	-	53.2	4.3	-	-	-	-	54.8	3.0	-	-	-	-	56.4	2.9	-	-	-	-
1977	56.5	0.2	-	-	-	-	59.2	4.8	-	-	-	-	60.9	2.9	-	-	-	-	60.2	-1.1	-	-	-	-
1978	61.0	1.3	-	-	61.3	0.5	-	-	63.8	4.1	-	-	65.2	2.2	-	-	65.3	0.2	-	-	66.5	1.8	-	-
1979	66.9	0.6	-	-	67.4	0.7	-	-	69.5	3.1	-	-	72.0	3.6	-	-	73.8	2.5	-	-	74.7	1.2	-	-
1980	77.4	3.6	-	-	80.2	3.6	-	-	81.7	1.9	-	-	83.2	1.8	-	-	84.8	1.9	-	-	87.4	3.1	-	-
1981	88.3	1.0	-	-	90.3	2.3	-	-	92.9	2.9	-	-	94.5	1.7	-	-	95.8	1.4	-	-	96.8	1.0	-	-
1982	96.5	-0.3	-	-	96.5	0.0	-	-	96.2	-0.3	-	-	97.9	1.8	-	-	98.1	0.2	-	-	98.5	0.4	-	-
1983	97.7	-0.8	-	-	95.7	-2.0	-	-	96.8	1.1	-	-	98.2	1.4	-	-	99.3	1.1	-	-	101.7	2.4	-	-
1984	101.6	-0.1	-	-	102.3	0.7	-	-	104.0	1.7	-	-	104.7	0.7	-	-	105.5	0.8	-	-	106.5	0.9	-	-
1985	106.6	0.1	-	-	106.7	0.1	-	-	107.0	0.3	-	-	106.8	-0.2	-	-	107.2	0.4	-	-	110.1	2.7	-	-
1986	110.5	0.4	-	-	109.8	-0.6	-	-	105.7	-3.7	-	-	104.0	-1.6	-	-	103.5	-0.5	-	-	106.8	3.2	106.6	-0.2
1987	-	-	-	-	-	-	-	-	-	-	108.0	1.3	-	-	-	-	-	-	-	-	-	-	111.1	2.9
1988	-	-	-	-	-	-	-	-	-	-	110.4	-0.6	-	-	-	-	-	-	-	-	-	-	111.7	1.2
1989	-	-	-	-	-	-	-	-	-	-	114.1	2.1	-	-	-	-	-	-	-	-	-	-	115.0	0.8
1990	-	-	-	-	-	-	-	-	-	-	116.1	1.0	-	-	-	-	-	-	-	-	-	-	120.9	4.1
1991	-	-	-	-	-	-	-	-	-	-	120.8	-0.1	-	-	-	-	-	-	-	-	-	-	118.0	-2.3
1992	-	-	-	-	-	-	-	-	-	-	120.4	2.0	-	-	-	-	-	-	-	-	-	-	122.8	2.0
1993	-	-	-	-	-	-	-	-	-	-	125.2	2.0	-	-	-	-	-	-	-	-	-	-	128.5	2.6
1994	-	-	-	-	-	-	-	-	-	-	132.2	2.9	-	-	-	-	-	-	-	-	-	-	136.8	3.5
1995	-	-	-	-	-	-	-	-	-	-	140.4	2.6	-	-	-	-	-	-	-	-	-	-	140.9	0.4
1996	-	-	-	-	-	-	-	-	-	-	144.3	2.4	-	-	-	-	-	-	-	-	-	-	145.3	0.7
1997	-	-	-	-	-	-	-	-	-	-	145.1	-0.1	-	-	-	-	-	-	-	-	-	-	145.1	0.0
1998	-	-	-	-	-	-	-	-	-	-	142.8	-1.6	-	-	-	-	-	-	-	-	-	-	141.2	-1.1
1999	-	-	-	-	-	-	-	-	-	-	140.7	-0.4	-	-	-	-	-	-	-	-	-	-	140.6	-0.1
2000	-	-	-	-	-	-	-	-	-	-	146.1	3.9	-	-	-	-	-	-	-	-	-	-	150.4	2.9
2001	-	-	-	-	-	-	-	-	-	-	151.1	0.5	-	-	-	-	-	-	-	-	-	-	-	-

Source: U.S. Department of Labor, Bureau of Labor Statistics, Division of Consumer Prices and Price Indexes. - indicates no data collected for period.

Anchorage, AK
Consumer Price Index - All Urban Consumers
Base 1982-1984 = 100
Medical Care

For 1971-2001. Columns headed % show percentile change in the index from the previous period for which an index is available.

Year	Jan Index	%	Feb Index	%	Mar Index	%	Apr Index	%	May Index	%	Jun Index	%	Jul Index	%	Aug Index	%	Sep Index	%	Oct Index	%	Nov Index	%	Dec Index	%
1971	34.4	-	-	-	-	-	35.0	1.7	-	-	-	-	35.1	0.3	-	-	-	-	35.5	1.1	-	-	-	-
1972	35.7	0.6	-	-	-	-	35.7	0.0	-	-	-	-	35.7	0.0	-	-	-	-	36.1	1.1	-	-	-	-
1973	36.2	0.3	-	-	-	-	36.5	0.8	-	-	-	-	37.3	2.2	-	-	-	-	38.3	2.7	-	-	-	-
1974	38.7	1.0	-	-	-	-	39.7	2.6	-	-	-	-	41.9	5.5	-	-	-	-	43.6	4.1	-	-	-	-
1975	44.7	2.5	-	-	-	-	45.6	2.0	-	-	-	-	47.0	3.1	-	-	-	-	48.3	2.8	-	-	-	-
1976	49.9	3.3	-	-	-	-	51.1	2.4	-	-	-	-	53.3	4.3	-	-	-	-	54.1	1.5	-	-	-	-
1977	55.4	2.4	-	-	-	-	57.0	2.9	-	-	-	-	58.1	1.9	-	-	-	-	59.0	1.5	-	-	-	-
1978	62.0	5.1	-	-	62.1	0.2	-	-	62.2	0.2	-	-	63.5	2.1	-	-	64.7	1.9	-	-	64.8	0.2	-	-
1979	67.9	4.8	-	-	67.6	-0.4	-	-	69.4	2.7	-	-	69.2	-0.3	-	-	69.4	0.3	-	-	69.8	0.6	-	-
1980	73.4	5.2	-	-	77.4	5.4	-	-	79.0	2.1	-	-	79.8	1.0	-	-	80.2	0.5	-	-	80.9	0.9	-	-
1981	82.7	2.2	-	-	84.7	2.4	-	-	87.2	3.0	-	-	87.7	0.6	-	-	87.5	-0.2	-	-	89.0	1.7	-	-
1982	92.9	4.4	-	-	92.9	0.0	-	-	93.6	0.8	-	-	95.2	1.7	-	-	96.1	0.9	-	-	96.7	0.6	-	-
1983	99.0	2.4	-	-	99.2	0.2	-	-	99.0	-0.2	-	-	99.6	0.6	-	-	100.0	0.4	-	-	100.0	0.0	-	-
1984	103.7	3.7	-	-	104.7	1.0	-	-	104.8	0.1	-	-	105.6	0.8	-	-	106.7	1.0	-	-	106.7	0.0	-	-
1985	107.2	0.5	-	-	108.5	1.2	-	-	108.8	0.3	-	-	112.8	3.7	-	-	112.9	0.1	-	-	113.5	0.5	-	-
1986	115.0	1.3	-	-	118.2	2.8	-	-	119.1	0.8	-	-	137.2	15.2	-	-	137.3	0.1	-	-	137.7	0.3	131.5	-4.5
1987	-	-	-	-	-	-	-	-	-	-	135.0	2.7	-	-	-	-	-	-	-	-	-	-	139.1	3.0
1988	-	-	-	-	-	-	-	-	-	-	143.0	2.8	-	-	-	-	-	-	-	-	-	-	148.6	3.9
1989	-	-	-	-	-	-	-	-	-	-	153.1	3.0	-	-	-	-	-	-	-	-	-	-	155.7	1.7
1990	-	-	-	-	-	-	-	-	-	-	160.1	2.8	-	-	-	-	-	-	-	-	-	-	162.3	1.4
1991	-	-	-	-	-	-	-	-	-	-	170.1	4.8	-	-	-	-	-	-	-	-	-	-	176.9	4.0
1992	-	-	-	-	-	-	-	-	-	-	181.5	2.6	-	-	-	-	-	-	-	-	-	-	184.6	1.7
1993	-	-	-	-	-	-	-	-	-	-	188.5	2.1	-	-	-	-	-	-	-	-	-	-	190.7	1.2
1994	-	-	-	-	-	-	-	-	-	-	195.8	2.7	-	-	-	-	-	-	-	-	-	-	199.7	2.0
1995	-	-	-	-	-	-	-	-	-	-	207.5	3.9	-	-	-	-	-	-	-	-	-	-	215.7	4.0
1996	-	-	-	-	-	-	-	-	-	-	228.1	5.7	-	-	-	-	-	-	-	-	-	-	234.0	2.6
1997	-	-	-	-	-	-	-	-	-	-	247.4	5.7	-	-	-	-	-	-	-	-	-	-	250.4	1.2
1998	-	-	-	-	-	-	-	-	-	-	256.5	2.4	-	-	-	-	-	-	-	-	-	-	254.9	-0.6
1999	-	-	-	-	-	-	-	-	-	-	257.9	1.2	-	-	-	-	-	-	-	-	-	-	263.7	2.2
2000	-	-	-	-	-	-	-	-	-	-	269.5	2.2	-	-	-	-	-	-	-	-	-	-	274.7	1.9
2001	-	-	-	-	-	-	-	-	-	-	280.5	2.1	-	-	-	-	-	-	-	-	-	-	-	-

Source: U.S. Department of Labor, Bureau of Labor Statistics, Division of Consumer Prices and Price Indexes. - indicates no data collected for period.

Anchorage, AK
Consumer Price Index - Urban Wage Earners
Base 1982-1984 = 100
Medical Care

For 1971-2001. Columns headed % show percentile change in the index from the previous period for which an index is available.

Year	Jan Index	%	Feb Index	%	Mar Index	%	Apr Index	%	May Index	%	Jun Index	%	Jul Index	%	Aug Index	%	Sep Index	%	Oct Index	%	Nov Index	%	Dec Index	%
1971	35.4	-	-	-	-	-	36.1	2.0	-	-	-	-	36.1	0.0	-	-	-	-	36.6	1.4	-	-	-	-
1972	36.8	0.5	-	-	-	-	36.8	0.0	-	-	-	-	36.8	0.0	-	-	-	-	37.2	1.1	-	-	-	-
1973	37.3	0.3	-	-	-	-	37.6	0.8	-	-	-	-	38.4	2.1	-	-	-	-	39.5	2.9	-	-	-	-
1974	39.8	0.8	-	-	-	-	40.9	2.8	-	-	-	-	43.2	5.6	-	-	-	-	44.9	3.9	-	-	-	-
1975	46.1	2.7	-	-	-	-	47.0	2.0	-	-	-	-	48.4	3.0	-	-	-	-	49.8	2.9	-	-	-	-
1976	51.4	3.2	-	-	-	-	52.6	2.3	-	-	-	-	54.9	4.4	-	-	-	-	55.7	1.5	-	-	-	-
1977	57.0	2.3	-	-	-	-	58.8	3.2	-	-	-	-	59.9	1.9	-	-	-	-	60.7	1.3	-	-	-	-
1978	63.9	5.3	-	-	66.0	3.3	-	-	66.1	0.2	-	-	66.4	0.5	-	-	67.6	1.8	-	-	70.5	4.3	-	-
1979	72.7	3.1	-	-	72.3	-0.6	-	-	72.4	0.1	-	-	72.8	0.6	-	-	72.9	0.1	-	-	73.3	0.5	-	-
1980	75.0	2.3	-	-	77.5	3.3	-	-	79.0	1.9	-	-	80.4	1.8	-	-	80.9	0.6	-	-	80.9	0.0	-	-
1981	82.9	2.5	-	-	84.6	2.1	-	-	86.6	2.4	-	-	87.4	0.9	-	-	87.6	0.2	-	-	89.3	1.9	-	-
1982	92.7	3.8	-	-	92.8	0.1	-	-	93.7	1.0	-	-	95.3	1.7	-	-	96.4	1.2	-	-	97.0	0.6	-	-
1983	99.1	2.2	-	-	99.3	0.2	-	-	99.0	-0.3	-	-	99.8	0.8	-	-	100.3	0.5	-	-	100.3	0.0	-	-
1984	103.3	3.0	-	-	104.5	1.2	-	-	104.6	0.1	-	-	105.4	0.8	-	-	106.6	1.1	-	-	106.4	-0.2	-	-
1985	106.8	0.4	-	-	108.2	1.3	-	-	108.5	0.3	-	-	112.3	3.5	-	-	112.4	0.1	-	-	113.1	0.6	-	-
1986	114.4	1.1	-	-	117.8	3.0	-	-	118.7	0.8	-	-	132.8	11.9	-	-	132.8	0.0	-	-	133.3	0.4	128.4	-3.7
1987	-	-	-	-	-	-	-	-	-	-	131.8	2.6	-	-	-	-	-	-	-	-	-	-	135.6	2.9
1988	-	-	-	-	-	-	-	-	-	-	139.7	3.0	-	-	-	-	-	-	-	-	-	-	144.6	3.5
1989	-	-	-	-	-	-	-	-	-	-	149.4	3.3	-	-	-	-	-	-	-	-	-	-	152.4	2.0
1990	-	-	-	-	-	-	-	-	-	-	156.9	3.0	-	-	-	-	-	-	-	-	-	-	158.9	1.3
1991	-	-	-	-	-	-	-	-	-	-	166.6	4.8	-	-	-	-	-	-	-	-	-	-	172.8	3.7
1992	-	-	-	-	-	-	-	-	-	-	177.1	2.5	-	-	-	-	-	-	-	-	-	-	179.9	1.6
1993	-	-	-	-	-	-	-	-	-	-	184.5	2.6	-	-	-	-	-	-	-	-	-	-	186.8	1.2
1994	-	-	-	-	-	-	-	-	-	-	191.9	2.7	-	-	-	-	-	-	-	-	-	-	195.4	1.8
1995	-	-	-	-	-	-	-	-	-	-	202.6	3.7	-	-	-	-	-	-	-	-	-	-	210.4	3.8
1996	-	-	-	-	-	-	-	-	-	-	221.1	5.1	-	-	-	-	-	-	-	-	-	-	226.8	2.6
1997	-	-	-	-	-	-	-	-	-	-	239.3	5.5	-	-	-	-	-	-	-	-	-	-	242.6	1.4
1998	-	-	-	-	-	-	-	-	-	-	248.1	2.3	-	-	-	-	-	-	-	-	-	-	251.3	1.3
1999	-	-	-	-	-	-	-	-	-	-	254.1	1.1	-	-	-	-	-	-	-	-	-	-	264.3	4.0
2000	-	-	-	-	-	-	-	-	-	-	270.5	2.3	-	-	-	-	-	-	-	-	-	-	279.9	3.5
2001	-	-	-	-	-	-	-	-	-	-	285.5	2.0	-	-	-	-	-	-	-	-	-	-	-	-

Source: U.S. Department of Labor, Bureau of Labor Statistics, Division of Consumer Prices and Price Indexes. - indicates no data collected for period.

Anchorage, AK
Consumer Price Index - All Urban Consumers
Base December 1997 = 100
Recreation

For 1997-2001. Columns headed % show percentile change in the index from the previous period for which an index is available.

Year	Jan		Feb		Mar		Apr		May		Jun		Jul		Aug		Sep		Oct		Nov		Dec	
	Index	%	Index	%	Index	%	Index	%	Index	%	Index	%	Index	%	Index	%	Index	%	Index	%	Index	%	Index	%
1997	-	-	-	-	-	-	-	-	-	-	-	-	-	-	-	-	-	-	-	-	-	-	100.0	-
1998	-	-	-	-	-	-	-	-	-	-	103.3	3.3	-	-	-	-	-	-	-	-	-	-	106.1	2.7
1999	-	-	-	-	-	-	-	-	-	-	109.5	3.2	-	-	-	-	-	-	-	-	-	-	104.7	-4.4
2000	-	-	-	-	-	-	-	-	-	-	105.6	0.9	-	-	-	-	-	-	-	-	-	-	105.5	-0.1
2001	-	-	-	-	-	-	-	-	-	-	105.7	0.2	-	-	-	-	-	-	-	-	-	-	-	-

Source: U.S. Department of Labor, Bureau of Labor Statistics, Division of Consumer Prices and Price Indexes. - indicates no data collected for period.

Anchorage, AK
Consumer Price Index - Urban Wage Earners
Base December 1997 = 100
Recreation

For 1997-2001. Columns headed % show percentile change in the index from the previous period for which an index is available.

Year	Jan Index	%	Feb Index	%	Mar Index	%	Apr Index	%	May Index	%	Jun Index	%	Jul Index	%	Aug Index	%	Sep Index	%	Oct Index	%	Nov Index	%	Dec Index	%
1997	-	-	-	-	-	-	-	-	-	-	-	-	-	-	-	-	-	-	-	-	-	-	100.0	-
1998	-	-	-	-	-	-	-	-	-	-	102.4	2.4	-	-	-	-	-	-	-	-	-	-	106.0	3.5
1999	-	-	-	-	-	-	-	-	-	-	107.5	1.4	-	-	-	-	-	-	-	-	-	-	102.3	-4.8
2000	-	-	-	-	-	-	-	-	-	-	105.0	2.6	-	-	-	-	-	-	-	-	-	-	104.6	-0.4
2001	-	-	-	-	-	-	-	-	-	-	105.1	0.5	-	-	-	-	-	-	-	-	-	-	-	-

Source: U.S. Department of Labor, Bureau of Labor Statistics, Division of Consumer Prices and Price Indexes. - indicates no data collected for period.

Anchorage, AK
Consumer Price Index - All Urban Consumers
Base December 1997 = 100
Education & Communication

For 1997-2001. Columns headed % show percentile change in the index from the previous period for which an index is available.

Year	Jan Index	%	Feb Index	%	Mar Index	%	Apr Index	%	May Index	%	Jun Index	%	Jul Index	%	Aug Index	%	Sep Index	%	Oct Index	%	Nov Index	%	Dec Index	%
1997	-	-	-	-	-	-	-	-	-	-	-	-	-	-	-	-	-	-	-	-	-	-	100.0	-
1998	-	-	-	-	-	-	-	-	-	-	98.6	-1.4	-	-	-	-	-	-	-	-	-	-	97.3	-1.3
1999	-	-	-	-	-	-	-	-	-	-	97.2	-0.1	-	-	-	-	-	-	-	-	-	-	96.8	-0.4
2000	-	-	-	-	-	-	-	-	-	-	95.2	-1.7	-	-	-	-	-	-	-	-	-	-	94.4	-0.8
2001	-	-	-	-	-	-	-	-	-	-	94.1	-0.3	-	-	-	-	-	-	-	-	-	-	-	-

Source: U.S. Department of Labor, Bureau of Labor Statistics, Division of Consumer Prices and Price Indexes. - indicates no data collected for period.

Anchorage, AK
Consumer Price Index - Urban Wage Earners
Base December 1997 = 100
Education & Communication

For 1997-2001. Columns headed % show percentile change in the index from the previous period for which an index is available.

Year	Jan		Feb		Mar		Apr		May		Jun		Jul		Aug		Sep		Oct		Nov		Dec	
	Index	%	Index	%	Index	%	Index	%	Index	%	Index	%	Index	%	Index	%	Index	%	Index	%	Index	%	Index	%
1997	-	-	-	-	-	-	-	-	-	-	-	-	-	-	-	-	-	-	-	-	-	-	-	-
1998	-	-	-	-	-	-	-	-	-	-	-	-	-	-	-	-	-	-	-	-	-	-	100.0	-
1999	-	-	-	-	-	-	-	-	-	-	99.2	-0.8	-	-	-	-	-	-	-	-	-	-	98.4	-0.8
2000	-	-	-	-	-	-	-	-	-	-	98.6	0.2	-	-	-	-	-	-	-	-	-	-	98.4	-0.2
2001	-	-	-	-	-	-	-	-	-	-	97.3	-1.1	-	-	-	-	-	-	-	-	-	-	96.9	-0.4
	-	-	-	-	-	-	-	-	-	-	97.0	0.1	-	-	-	-	-	-	-	-	-	-	-	-

Source: U.S. Department of Labor, Bureau of Labor Statistics, Division of Consumer Prices and Price Indexes. - indicates no data collected for period.

Atlanta, GA
Consumer Price Index - All Urban Consumers
Base 1982-1984 = 100
Annual Averages

For 1917-2001. Columns headed % show percentile change in the index from the previous period for which an index is available.

Year	All Items		Food & Beverage		Housing		Apparel		Trans-portation		Medical Care		Recrea-tion*		Education & Communic.*		Other Goods & Services	
	Index	%	Index	%	Index	%	Index	%	Index	%	Index	%	Index	%	Index	%	Index	%
1917	-	-	-	-	-	-	-	-	-	-	-	-	-	-	-	-	-	-
1918	16.6	-	-	-	-	-	-	-	-	-	-	-	-	-	-	-	-	-
1919	19.3	16.3	-	-	-	-	-	-	-	-	-	-	-	-	-	-	-	-
1920	21.9	13.5	-	-	-	-	-	-	-	-	-	-	-	-	-	-	-	-
1921	19.0	-13.2	-	-	-	-	-	-	-	-	-	-	-	-	-	-	-	-
1922	17.5	-7.9	-	-	-	-	-	-	-	-	-	-	-	-	-	-	-	-
1923	17.6	0.6	-	-	-	-	-	-	-	-	-	-	-	-	-	-	-	-
1924	17.3	-1.7	-	-	-	-	-	-	-	-	-	-	-	-	-	-	-	-
1925	17.9	3.5	-	-	-	-	-	-	-	-	-	-	-	-	-	-	-	-
1926	18.1	1.1	-	-	-	-	-	-	-	-	-	-	-	-	-	-	-	-
1927	17.5	-3.3	-	-	-	-	-	-	-	-	-	-	-	-	-	-	-	-
1928	17.3	-1.1	-	-	-	-	-	-	-	-	-	-	-	-	-	-	-	-
1929	17.2	-0.6	-	-	-	-	-	-	-	-	-	-	-	-	-	-	-	-
1930	16.5	-4.1	-	-	-	-	-	-	-	-	-	-	-	-	-	-	-	-
1931	14.9	-9.7	-	-	-	-	-	-	-	-	-	-	-	-	-	-	-	-
1932	13.3	-10.7	-	-	-	-	-	-	-	-	-	-	-	-	-	-	-	-
1933	12.6	-5.3	-	-	-	-	-	-	-	-	-	-	-	-	-	-	-	-
1934	13.2	4.8	-	-	-	-	-	-	-	-	-	-	-	-	-	-	-	-
1935	13.5	2.3	-	-	-	-	-	-	-	-	-	-	-	-	-	-	-	-
1936	13.7	1.5	-	-	-	-	-	-	-	-	-	-	-	-	-	-	-	-
1937	14.1	2.9	-	-	-	-	-	-	-	-	-	-	-	-	-	-	-	-
1938	13.7	-2.8	-	-	-	-	-	-	-	-	-	-	-	-	-	-	-	-
1939	13.6	-0.7	-	-	-	-	-	-	-	-	-	-	-	-	-	-	-	-
1940	13.6	0.0	-	-	-	-	-	-	-	-	-	-	-	-	-	-	-	-
1941	14.4	5.9	-	-	-	-	-	-	-	-	-	-	-	-	-	-	-	-
1942	15.9	10.4	-	-	-	-	-	-	-	-	-	-	-	-	-	-	-	-
1943	17.0	6.9	-	-	-	-	-	-	-	-	-	-	-	-	-	-	-	-
1944	17.3	1.8	-	-	-	-	-	-	-	-	-	-	-	-	-	-	-	-
1945	17.9	3.5	-	-	-	-	-	-	-	-	-	-	-	-	-	-	-	-
1946	19.3	7.8	-	-	-	-	-	-	-	-	-	-	-	-	-	-	-	-
1947	22.3	15.5	-	-	-	-	-	-	20.4	-	15.2	-	-	-	-	-	-	-
1948	23.8	6.7	-	-	-	-	-	-	22.4	9.8	15.7	3.3	-	-	-	-	-	-
1949	23.8	0.0	-	-	-	-	-	-	24.1	7.6	16.1	2.5	-	-	-	-	-	-
1950	24.1	1.3	-	-	-	-	-	-	24.6	2.1	16.1	0.0	-	-	-	-	-	-
1951	26.4	9.5	-	-	-	-	-	-	26.4	7.3	16.9	5.0	-	-	-	-	-	-
1952	27.0	2.3	-	-	-	-	-	-	28.1	6.4	18.1	7.1	-	-	-	-	-	-
1953	27.3	1.1	-	-	-	-	42.2	-	28.9	2.8	18.5	2.2	-	-	-	-	-	-
1954	27.2	-0.4	-	-	-	-	42.4	0.5	28.0	-3.1	18.9	2.2	-	-	-	-	-	-
1955	27.1	-0.4	-	-	-	-	42.1	-0.7	27.5	-1.8	19.6	3.7	-	-	-	-	-	-
1956	27.5	1.5	-	-	-	-	42.9	1.9	28.2	2.5	20.2	3.1	-	-	-	-	-	-
1957	28.3	2.9	-	-	-	-	43.7	1.9	30.0	6.4	20.7	2.5	-	-	-	-	-	-
1958	29.0	2.5	-	-	-	-	44.3	1.4	31.3	4.3	21.4	3.4	-	-	-	-	-	-
1959	29.2	0.7	-	-	-	-	44.3	0.0	32.4	3.5	22.3	4.2	-	-	-	-	-	-
1960	29.6	1.4	-	-	-	-	45.0	1.6	32.0	-1.2	23.0	3.1	-	-	-	-	-	-
1961	29.7	0.3	-	-	-	-	45.1	0.2	32.4	1.3	23.2	0.9	-	-	-	-	-	-

[Continued]

Atlanta, GA
Consumer Price Index - All Urban Consumers
Base 1982-1984 = 100
Annual Averages

[Continued]

For 1917-2001. Columns headed % show percentile change in the index from the previous period for which an index is available.

Year	All Items		Food & Beverage		Housing		Apparel		Trans-portation		Medical Care		Recrea-tion*		Education & Communic.*		Other Goods & Services	
	Index	%	Index	%	Index	%	Index	%	Index	%	Index	%	Index	%	Index	%	Index	%
1962	30.0	1.0	-	-	-	-	45.1	0.0	33.1	2.2	23.9	3.0	-	-	-	-	-	-
1963	30.3	1.0	-	-	-	-	46.1	2.2	33.8	2.1	24.2	1.3	-	-	-	-	-	-
1964	30.8	1.7	-	-	-	-	46.2	0.2	34.7	2.7	24.8	2.5	-	-	-	-	-	-
1965	31.2	1.3	-	-	-	-	46.7	1.1	34.6	-0.3	25.4	2.4	-	-	-	-	-	-
1966	32.2	3.2	-	-	-	-	48.9	4.7	34.6	0.0	26.7	5.1	-	-	-	-	-	-
1967	33.2	3.1	-	-	-	-	51.6	5.5	35.2	1.7	28.4	6.4	-	-	-	-	-	-
1968	34.5	3.9	-	-	-	-	53.8	4.3	36.1	2.6	30.3	6.7	-	-	-	-	-	-
1969	36.5	5.8	-	-	-	-	56.0	4.1	37.3	3.3	33.3	9.9	-	-	-	-	-	-
1970	38.6	5.8	-	-	-	-	58.4	4.3	38.2	2.4	35.8	7.5	-	-	-	-	-	-
1971	40.4	4.7	-	-	-	-	59.9	2.6	40.6	6.3	38.6	7.8	-	-	-	-	-	-
1972	41.6	3.0	-	-	-	-	61.3	2.3	39.8	-2.0	39.6	2.6	-	-	-	-	-	-
1973	44.3	6.5	-	-	-	-	63.8	4.1	41.1	3.3	41.5	4.8	-	-	-	-	-	-
1974	49.2	11.1	-	-	-	-	69.1	8.3	46.5	13.1	46.1	11.1	-	-	-	-	-	-
1975	53.6	8.9	-	-	-	-	71.6	3.6	50.4	8.4	52.1	13.0	-	-	-	-	-	-
1976	56.1	4.7	62.5	-	51.9	-	74.3	3.8	54.2	7.5	56.0	7.5	-	-	-	-	55.4	-
1977	59.6	6.2	65.9	5.4	55.2	6.4	79.5	7.0	57.3	5.7	60.7	8.4	-	-	-	-	58.5	5.6
1978	63.9	7.2	72.2	9.6	59.8	8.3	84.0	5.7	59.6	4.0	63.8	5.1	-	-	-	-	62.7	7.2
1979	70.5	10.3	79.5	10.1	65.9	10.2	87.6	4.3	69.5	16.6	68.1	6.7	-	-	-	-	68.9	9.9
1980	80.3	13.9	85.8	7.9	76.1	15.5	93.1	6.3	84.8	22.0	74.7	9.7	-	-	-	-	75.6	9.7
1981	90.2	12.3	93.1	8.5	87.7	15.2	96.2	3.3	94.9	11.9	82.3	10.2	-	-	-	-	84.1	11.2
1982	96.0	6.4	97.1	4.3	95.4	8.8	96.8	0.6	97.5	2.7	92.6	12.5	-	-	-	-	91.7	9.0
1983	99.9	4.1	99.8	2.8	100.0	4.8	100.5	3.8	99.4	1.9	101.2	9.3	-	-	-	-	100.5	9.6
1984	104.1	4.2	103.1	3.3	104.6	4.6	102.7	2.2	103.0	3.6	106.2	4.9	-	-	-	-	107.9	7.4
1985	108.9	4.6	106.1	2.9	109.9	5.1	111.7	8.8	106.7	3.6	112.9	6.3	-	-	-	-	113.0	4.7
1986	112.2	3.0	111.2	4.8	115.2	4.8	110.4	-1.2	102.9	-3.6	123.7	9.6	-	-	-	-	119.8	6.0
1987	116.5	3.8	112.3	1.0	119.5	3.7	125.8	13.9	103.7	0.8	136.5	10.3	-	-	-	-	125.4	4.7
1988	120.4	3.3	117.4	4.5	122.6	2.6	129.2	2.7	105.6	1.8	150.1	10.0	-	-	-	-	129.3	3.1
1989	126.1	4.7	123.7	5.4	125.8	2.6	137.1	6.1	110.9	5.0	165.7	10.4	-	-	-	-	138.9	7.4
1990	131.7	4.4	131.9	6.6	128.8	2.4	133.8	-2.4	117.7	6.1	177.6	7.2	-	-	-	-	155.1	11.7
1991	135.9	3.2	135.3	2.6	130.6	1.4	148.4	10.9	118.7	0.8	191.6	7.9	-	-	-	-	166.5	7.4
1992	138.5	1.9	135.7	0.3	132.7	1.6	152.6	2.8	119.5	0.7	202.7	5.8	-	-	-	-	173.1	4.0
1993	143.4	3.5	139.6	2.9	136.6	2.9	158.0	3.5	124.2	3.9	213.0	5.1	-	-	-	-	181.3	4.7
1994	146.7	2.3	141.1	1.1	140.1	2.6	167.3	5.9	123.8	-0.3	227.0	6.6	-	-	-	-	183.4	1.2
1995	150.9	2.9	146.5	3.8	146.2	4.4	153.4	-8.3	128.1	3.5	236.0	4.0	-	-	-	-	194.8	6.2
1996	156.0	3.4	153.4	4.7	151.8	3.8	145.4	-5.2	134.7	5.2	240.7	2.0	-	-	-	-	200.7	3.0
1997	158.9	1.9	159.5	4.0	156.4	3.0	137.0	-5.8	132.5	-1.6	243.5	1.2	-	-	-	-	212.4	5.8
1998	161.2	1.4	164.7	3.3	161.1	3.0	137.6	0.4	127.8	-3.5	245.0	0.6	100.3	-	100.4	-	221.2	4.1
1999	164.8	2.2	167.6	1.8	165.1	2.5	132.4	-3.8	130.3	2.0	254.0	3.7	101.5	1.2	101.5	1.1	243.2	9.9
2000	170.6	3.5	171.8	2.5	171.0	3.6	132.3	-0.1	137.6	5.6	264.2	4.0	103.6	2.1	103.8	2.3	249.8	2.7
2001	176.2	3.3	180.1	4.8	178.4	4.3	127.0	-4.0	-	-	276.7	4.7	106.6	2.9	107.2	3.3	264.0	5.7

Source: U.S. Department of Labor, Bureau of Labor Statistics, Division of Consumer Prices and Price Indexes. *Base is December 1997 = 100. - indicates no data collected for period.

Atlanta, GA
Consumer Price Index - Urban Wage Earners
Base 1982-1984 = 100
Annual Averages

For 1917-2001. Columns headed % show percentile change in the index from the previous period for which an index is available.

Year	All Items		Food & Beverage		Housing		Apparel		Trans-portation		Medical Care		Recrea-tion*		Education & Communic.*		Other Goods & Services	
	Index	%	Index	%	Index	%	Index	%	Index	%	Index	%	Index	%	Index	%	Index	%
1917	-	-	-	-	-	-	-	-	-	-	-	-	-	-	-	-	-	-
1918	16.6	-	-	-	-	-	-	-	-	-	-	-	-	-	-	-	-	-
1919	19.3	16.3	-	-	-	-	-	-	-	-	-	-	-	-	-	-	-	-
1920	21.8	13.0	-	-	-	-	-	-	-	-	-	-	-	-	-	-	-	-
1921	18.9	-13.3	-	-	-	-	-	-	-	-	-	-	-	-	-	-	-	-
1922	17.5	-7.4	-	-	-	-	-	-	-	-	-	-	-	-	-	-	-	-
1923	17.5	0.0	-	-	-	-	-	-	-	-	-	-	-	-	-	-	-	-
1924	17.3	-1.1	-	-	-	-	-	-	-	-	-	-	-	-	-	-	-	-
1925	17.8	2.9	-	-	-	-	-	-	-	-	-	-	-	-	-	-	-	-
1926	18.0	1.1	-	-	-	-	-	-	-	-	-	-	-	-	-	-	-	-
1927	17.5	-2.8	-	-	-	-	-	-	-	-	-	-	-	-	-	-	-	-
1928	17.3	-1.1	-	-	-	-	-	-	-	-	-	-	-	-	-	-	-	-
1929	17.2	-0.6	-	-	-	-	-	-	-	-	-	-	-	-	-	-	-	-
1930	16.5	-4.1	-	-	-	-	-	-	-	-	-	-	-	-	-	-	-	-
1931	14.8	-10.3	-	-	-	-	-	-	-	-	-	-	-	-	-	-	-	-
1932	13.2	-10.8	-	-	-	-	-	-	-	-	-	-	-	-	-	-	-	-
1933	12.6	-4.5	-	-	-	-	-	-	-	-	-	-	-	-	-	-	-	-
1934	13.2	4.8	-	-	-	-	-	-	-	-	-	-	-	-	-	-	-	-
1935	13.5	2.3	-	-	-	-	-	-	-	-	-	-	-	-	-	-	-	-
1936	13.7	1.5	-	-	-	-	-	-	-	-	-	-	-	-	-	-	-	-
1937	14.1	2.9	-	-	-	-	-	-	-	-	-	-	-	-	-	-	-	-
1938	13.7	-2.8	-	-	-	-	-	-	-	-	-	-	-	-	-	-	-	-
1939	13.6	-0.7	-	-	-	-	-	-	-	-	-	-	-	-	-	-	-	-
1940	13.6	0.0	-	-	-	-	-	-	-	-	-	-	-	-	-	-	-	-
1941	14.3	5.1	-	-	-	-	-	-	-	-	-	-	-	-	-	-	-	-
1942	15.9	11.2	-	-	-	-	-	-	-	-	-	-	-	-	-	-	-	-
1943	17.0	6.9	-	-	-	-	-	-	-	-	-	-	-	-	-	-	-	-
1944	17.3	1.8	-	-	-	-	-	-	-	-	-	-	-	-	-	-	-	-
1945	17.9	3.5	-	-	-	-	-	-	-	-	-	-	-	-	-	-	-	-
1946	19.2	7.3	-	-	-	-	-	-	-	-	-	-	-	-	-	-	-	-
1947	22.3	16.1	-	-	-	-	-	-	19.8	-	14.6		-	-	-	-	-	-
1948	23.7	6.3	-	-	-	-	-	-	21.8	10.1	15.1	3.4	-	-	-	-	-	-
1949	23.7	0.0	-	-	-	-	-	-	23.5	7.8	15.5	2.6	-	-	-	-	-	-
1950	24.0	1.3	-	-	-	-	-	-	24.0	2.1	15.5	0.0	-	-	-	-	-	-
1951	26.3	9.6	-	-	-	-	-	-	25.7	7.1	16.3	5.2	-	-	-	-	-	-
1952	27.0	2.7	-	-	-	-	-	-	27.4	6.6	17.4	6.7	-	-	-	-	-	-
1953	27.2	0.7	-	-	-	-	40.0	-	28.1	2.6	17.8	2.3	-	-	-	-	-	-
1954	27.1	-0.4	-	-	-	-	40.1	0.2	27.2	-3.2	18.2	2.2	-	-	-	-	-	-
1955	27.0	-0.4	-	-	-	-	39.9	-0.5	26.8	-1.5	18.8	3.3	-	-	-	-	-	-
1956	27.5	1.9	-	-	-	-	40.7	2.0	27.5	2.6	19.5	3.7	-	-	-	-	-	-
1957	28.2	2.5	-	-	-	-	41.5	2.0	29.2	6.2	19.9	2.1	-	-	-	-	-	-
1958	28.9	2.5	-	-	-	-	42.0	1.2	30.5	4.5	20.6	3.5	-	-	-	-	-	-
1959	29.1	0.7	-	-	-	-	42.0	0.0	31.5	3.3	21.5	4.4	-	-	-	-	-	-
1960	29.5	1.4	-	-	-	-	42.7	1.7	31.2	-1.0	22.1	2.8	-	-	-	-	-	-
1961	29.7	0.7	-	-	-	-	42.7	0.0	31.6	1.3	22.3	0.9	-	-	-	-	-	-

[Continued]

Atlanta, GA
Consumer Price Index - Urban Wage Earners
Base 1982-1984 = 100
Annual Averages
[Continued]

For 1917-2001. Columns headed % show percentile change in the index from the previous period for which an index is available.

Year	All Items		Food & Beverage		Housing		Apparel		Trans-portation		Medical Care		Recrea-tion*		Education & Communic.*		Other Goods & Services	
	Index	%	Index	%	Index	%	Index	%	Index	%	Index	%	Index	%	Index	%	Index	%
1962	29.9	0.7	-	-	-	-	42.7	0.0	32.2	1.9	23.0	3.1	-	-	-	-	-	-
1963	30.2	1.0	-	-	-	-	43.7	2.3	32.9	2.2	23.3	1.3	-	-	-	-	-	-
1964	30.7	1.7	-	-	-	-	43.8	0.2	33.8	2.7	23.9	2.6	-	-	-	-	-	-
1965	31.1	1.3	-	-	-	-	44.3	1.1	33.7	-0.3	24.4	2.1	-	-	-	-	-	-
1966	32.1	3.2	-	-	-	-	46.4	4.7	33.7	0.0	25.7	5.3	-	-	-	-	-	-
1967	33.1	3.1	-	-	-	-	49.0	5.6	34.3	1.8	27.3	6.2	-	-	-	-	-	-
1968	34.4	3.9	-	-	-	-	51.0	4.1	35.1	2.3	29.1	6.6	-	-	-	-	-	-
1969	36.4	5.8	-	-	-	-	53.1	4.1	36.3	3.4	32.1	10.3	-	-	-	-	-	-
1970	38.5	5.8	-	-	-	-	55.3	4.1	37.2	2.5	34.5	7.5	-	-	-	-	-	-
1971	40.2	4.4	-	-	-	-	56.8	2.7	39.5	6.2	37.2	7.8	-	-	-	-	-	-
1972	41.5	3.2	-	-	-	-	58.1	2.3	38.8	-1.8	38.1	2.4	-	-	-	-	-	-
1973	44.2	6.5	-	-	-	-	60.5	4.1	40.0	3.1	40.0	5.0	-	-	-	-	-	-
1974	49.1	11.1	-	-	-	-	65.5	8.3	45.3	13.2	44.3	10.8	-	-	-	-	-	-
1975	53.5	9.0	-	-	-	-	67.9	3.7	49.0	8.2	50.2	13.3	-	-	-	-	-	-
1976	56.0	4.7	61.8	-	52.6	-	70.4	3.7	52.8	7.8	53.9	7.4	-	-	-	-	58.1	-
1977	59.4	6.1	65.2	5.5	56.0	6.5	75.3	7.0	55.8	5.7	58.4	8.3	-	-	-	-	61.3	5.5
1978	63.8	7.4	71.9	10.3	60.6	8.2	78.2	3.9	58.3	4.5	62.4	6.8	-	-	-	-	65.2	6.4
1979	71.0	11.3	79.4	10.4	67.0	10.6	84.4	7.9	69.0	18.4	68.1	9.1	-	-	-	-	70.2	7.7
1980	81.1	14.2	85.7	7.9	76.7	14.5	89.9	6.5	86.1	24.8	73.0	7.2	-	-	-	-	75.7	7.8
1981	90.8	12.0	93.2	8.8	87.9	14.6	95.9	6.7	96.0	11.5	81.8	12.1	-	-	-	-	83.6	10.4
1982	96.4	6.2	97.1	4.2	95.8	9.0	97.9	2.1	98.2	2.3	92.5	13.1	-	-	-	-	91.4	9.3
1983	100.1	3.8	99.9	2.9	100.7	5.1	100.0	2.1	99.5	1.3	101.3	9.5	-	-	-	-	100.7	10.2
1984	103.5	3.4	103.0	3.1	103.6	2.9	102.1	2.1	102.3	2.8	106.3	4.9	-	-	-	-	107.9	7.1
1985	107.9	4.3	105.9	2.8	108.4	4.6	109.4	7.1	106.0	3.6	113.0	6.3	-	-	-	-	112.8	4.5
1986	110.8	2.7	111.0	4.8	113.1	4.3	108.2	-1.1	101.9	-3.9	124.0	9.7	-	-	-	-	119.7	6.1
1987	114.8	3.6	111.9	0.8	117.5	3.9	122.3	13.0	102.7	0.8	136.7	10.2	-	-	-	-	126.4	5.6
1988	118.6	3.3	117.0	4.6	120.6	2.6	126.0	3.0	104.5	1.8	150.4	10.0	-	-	-	-	130.5	3.2
1989	124.4	4.9	123.3	5.4	123.9	2.7	134.2	6.5	109.7	5.0	165.6	10.1	-	-	-	-	141.2	8.2
1990	130.0	4.5	131.4	6.6	126.6	2.2	131.5	-2.0	115.8	5.6	177.1	6.9	-	-	-	-	158.0	11.9
1991	133.9	3.0	135.1	2.8	128.4	1.4	143.8	9.4	116.7	0.8	191.4	8.1	-	-	-	-	169.4	7.2
1992	136.6	2.0	135.4	0.2	130.5	1.6	148.4	3.2	117.5	0.7	202.3	5.7	-	-	-	-	178.1	5.1
1993	141.4	3.5	139.1	2.7	134.5	3.1	153.0	3.1	122.0	3.8	212.2	4.9	-	-	-	-	185.5	4.2
1994	144.3	2.1	140.7	1.2	138.0	2.6	162.3	6.1	121.6	-0.3	225.8	6.4	-	-	-	-	187.1	0.9
1995	148.7	3.0	145.0	3.1	144.2	4.5	149.3	-8.0	125.9	3.5	234.3	3.8	-	-	-	-	200.2	7.0
1996	153.6	3.3	151.9	4.8	149.3	3.5	141.0	-5.6	132.4	5.2	238.5	1.8	-	-	-	-	205.9	2.8
1997	156.5	1.9	158.2	4.1	153.7	2.9	132.4	-6.1	130.3	-1.6	241.1	1.1	-	-	-	-	218.1	5.9
1998	158.4	1.2	163.5	3.4	158.2	2.9	133.0	0.5	125.8	-3.5	241.9	0.3	98.9	-	100.7	-	225.1	3.2
1999	162.0	2.3	166.1	1.6	162.0	2.4	128.5	-3.4	128.6	2.2	250.3	3.5	97.9	-1.0	101.9	1.2	256.9	14.1
2000	168.1	3.8	170.5	2.6	167.8	3.6	129.0	0.4	136.5	6.1	259.9	3.8	99.5	1.6	103.6	1.7	269.2	4.8
2001	173.6	3.3	179.1	5.0	175.6	4.6	123.4	-4.3	-	-	270.1	3.9	101.8	2.3	106.8	3.1	286.1	6.3

Source: U.S. Department of Labor, Bureau of Labor Statistics, Division of Consumer Prices and Price Indexes. *Base is December 1997 = 100. - indicates no data collected for period.

Atlanta, GA
Consumer Price Index - All Urban Consumers
Base 1982-1984 = 100
All Items

For 1917-2001. Columns headed % show percentile change in the index from the previous period for which an index is available.

Year	Jan Index	%	Feb Index	%	Mar Index	%	Apr Index	%	May Index	%	Jun Index	%	Jul Index	%	Aug Index	%	Sep Index	%	Oct Index	%	Nov Index	%	Dec Index	%
1917	-	-	-	-	-	-	-	-	-	-	-	-	-	-	-	-	-	-	-	-	-	-	15.2	-
1918	-	-	-	-	-	-	-	-	-	-	-	-	-	-	-	-	-	-	-	-	-	-	18.2	19.7
1919	-	-	-	-	-	-	-	-	-	-	18.9	3.8	-	-	-	-	-	-	-	-	-	-	20.8	10.1
1920	-	-	-	-	-	-	-	-	-	-	23.0	10.6	-	-	-	-	-	-	-	-	-	-	20.8	-9.6
1921	-	-	-	-	-	-	-	-	19.0	-8.7	-	-	-	-	-	-	18.5	-2.6	-	-	-	-	18.0	-2.7
1922	-	-	-	-	17.4	-3.3	-	-	-	-	17.5	0.6	-	-	-	-	17.4	-0.6	-	-	-	-	17.3	-0.6
1923	-	-	-	-	17.4	0.6	-	-	-	-	17.6	1.1	-	-	-	-	17.8	1.1	-	-	-	-	17.5	-1.7
1924	-	-	-	-	17.3	-1.1	-	-	-	-	17.3	0.0	-	-	-	-	17.3	0.0	-	-	-	-	17.3	-0.6
1925	-	-	-	-	-	-	-	-	-	-	17.9	3.5	-	-	-	-	-	-	-	-	-	-	18.3	2.2
1926	-	-	-	-	-	-	-	-	-	-	18.0	-1.6	-	-	-	-	-	-	-	-	-	-	17.8	-1.1
1927	-	-	-	-	-	-	-	-	-	-	18.1	1.7	-	-	-	-	-	-	-	-	-	-	17.2	-5.0
1928	-	-	-	-	-	-	-	-	-	-	17.4	1.2	-	-	-	-	-	-	-	-	-	-	17.3	-0.6
1929	-	-	-	-	-	-	-	-	-	-	17.1	-1.2	-	-	-	-	-	-	-	-	-	-	17.1	0.0
1930	-	-	-	-	-	-	-	-	-	-	16.5	-3.5	-	-	-	-	-	-	-	-	-	-	15.8	-4.2
1931	-	-	-	-	-	-	-	-	-	-	14.8	-6.3	-	-	-	-	-	-	-	-	-	-	14.0	-5.4
1932	-	-	-	-	-	-	-	-	-	-	13.4	-4.3	-	-	-	-	-	-	-	-	-	-	12.6	-6.0
1933	-	-	-	-	-	-	-	-	-	-	12.5	-0.8	-	-	-	-	-	-	-	-	-	-	12.9	3.2
1934	-	-	-	-	-	-	-	-	-	-	13.1	1.6	-	-	-	-	-	-	-	-	13.4	2.3	-	-
1935	-	-	-	-	13.4	0.0	-	-	-	-	-	-	13.4	0.0	-	-	-	-	13.7	2.2	-	-	-	-
1936	13.8	0.7	-	-	-	-	13.5	-2.2	-	-	-	-	13.7	1.5	-	-	13.9	1.5	-	-	-	-	13.9	0.0
1937	-	-	-	-	14.0	0.7	-	-	-	-	14.1	0.7	-	-	-	-	14.3	1.4	-	-	-	-	14.1	-1.4
1938	-	-	-	-	13.8	-2.1	-	-	-	-	13.6	-1.4	-	-	-	-	13.8	1.5	-	-	-	-	13.8	0.0
1939	-	-	-	-	13.6	-1.4	-	-	-	-	13.5	-0.7	-	-	-	-	13.8	2.2	-	-	-	-	13.6	-1.4
1940	-	-	-	-	13.7	0.7	-	-	-	-	13.5	-1.5	-	-	-	-	13.6	0.7	-	-	-	-	13.8	1.5
1941	-	-	-	-	13.8	0.0	-	-	-	-	14.2	2.9	-	-	-	-	14.8	4.2	-	-	-	-	15.2	2.7
1942	-	-	-	-	15.7	3.3	-	-	-	-	15.9	1.3	-	-	-	-	16.1	1.3	-	-	-	-	16.4	1.9
1943	-	-	-	-	16.9	3.0	-	-	-	-	17.2	1.8	-	-	-	-	17.1	-0.6	-	-	-	-	17.1	0.0
1944	-	-	-	-	17.0	-0.6	-	-	-	-	17.3	1.8	-	-	-	-	17.5	1.2	-	-	-	-	17.7	1.1
1945	-	-	-	-	17.7	0.0	-	-	-	-	17.9	1.1	-	-	-	-	18.1	1.1	-	-	-	-	18.1	0.0
1946	-	-	-	-	18.1	0.0	-	-	-	-	18.4	1.7	-	-	-	-	20.2	9.8	-	-	-	-	21.4	5.9
1947	-	-	-	-	22.2	3.7	-	-	-	-	21.9	-1.4	-	-	22.3	1.8	-	-	-	-	23.1	3.6	-	-
1948	-	-	23.3	0.9	-	-	-	-	23.6	1.3	-	-	-	-	24.4	3.4	-	-	-	-	24.0	-1.6	-	-
1949	-	-	23.6	-1.7	-	-	-	-	23.7	0.4	-	-	-	-	24.0	1.3	-	-	-	-	23.8	-0.8	-	-
1950	-	-	23.4	-1.7	-	-	-	-	23.6	0.9	-	-	-	-	24.4	3.4	-	-	-	-	24.8	1.6	-	-
1951	-	-	25.8	4.0	-	-	-	-	26.5	2.7	-	-	-	-	26.5	0.0	-	-	-	-	26.9	1.5	-	-
1952	-	-	26.8	-0.4	-	-	-	-	26.7	-0.4	-	-	-	-	27.3	2.2	-	-	-	-	27.3	0.0	27.2	-0.4
1953	-	-	-	-	27.2	0.0	-	-	-	-	27.3	0.4	-	-	-	-	27.4	0.4	-	-	-	-	27.3	-0.4
1954	-	-	-	-	27.3	0.0	-	-	-	-	27.4	0.4	-	-	-	-	27.1	-1.1	-	-	-	-	27.0	-0.4
1955	-	-	-	-	26.9	-0.4	-	-	-	-	27.0	0.4	-	-	-	-	27.3	1.1	-	-	-	-	27.3	0.0
1956	-	-	-	-	27.2	-0.4	-	-	-	-	27.5	1.1	-	-	-	-	27.7	0.7	-	-	-	-	27.8	0.4
1957	-	-	-	-	28.1	1.1	-	-	-	-	28.2	0.4	-	-	-	-	28.5	1.1	-	-	-	-	28.5	0.0
1958	-	-	-	-	29.1	2.1	-	-	-	-	29.1	0.0	-	-	-	-	29.0	-0.3	-	-	-	-	29.0	0.0
1959	-	-	-	-	28.9	-0.3	-	-	-	-	29.2	1.0	-	-	-	-	29.3	0.3	-	-	-	-	29.4	0.3
1960	-	-	-	-	29.5	0.3	-	-	-	-	29.6	0.3	-	-	-	-	29.8	0.7	-	-	-	-	29.7	-0.3
1961	-	-	-	-	29.7	0.0	-	-	-	-	29.7	0.0	-	-	-	-	29.9	0.7	-	-	-	-	29.8	-0.3
1962	-	-	-	-	29.9	0.3	-	-	-	-	30.0	0.3	-	-	-	-	30.2	0.7	-	-	-	-	30.1	-0.3

[Continued]

Atlanta, GA
Consumer Price Index - All Urban Consumers
Base 1982-1984 = 100
All Items
[Continued]

For 1917-2001. Columns headed % show percentile change in the index from the previous period for which an index is available.

Year	Jan Index	%	Feb Index	%	Mar Index	%	Apr Index	%	May Index	%	Jun Index	%	Jul Index	%	Aug Index	%	Sep Index	%	Oct Index	%	Nov Index	%	Dec Index	%
1963	-		-		30.2	0.3	-		-		30.2	0.0	-		-		30.3	0.3	-		-		30.5	0.7
1964	-		-		30.7	0.7	-		-		30.6	-0.3	-		-		30.9	1.0	-		-		31.0	0.3
1965	-		-		31.0	0.0	-		-		31.1	0.3	-		-		31.2	0.3	-		-		31.5	1.0
1966	-		-		31.8	1.0	-		-		32.0	0.6	-		-		32.5	1.6	-		-		32.7	0.6
1967	-		-		32.9	0.6	-		-		33.1	0.6	-		-		33.3	0.6	-		-		33.7	1.2
1968	-		-		34.0	0.9	-		-		34.3	0.9	-		-		35.0	2.0	-		-		35.2	0.6
1969	-		-		36.0	2.3	-		-		36.4	1.1	-		-		37.1	1.9	-		-		37.5	1.1
1970	-		-		38.0	1.3	-		-		38.6	1.6	-		-		39.0	1.0	-		-		39.6	1.5
1971	-		-		39.9	0.8	-		-		40.6	1.8	-		-		40.5	-0.2	-		-		41.0	1.2
1972	-		-		41.1	0.2	-		-		41.4	0.7	-		-		42.1	1.7	-		-		42.3	0.5
1973	-		-		43.1	1.9	-		-		44.0	2.1	-		-		45.4	3.2	-		-		46.1	1.5
1974	-		-		47.8	3.7	-		-		48.8	2.1	-		-		50.6	3.7	-		-		51.7	2.2
1975	-		-		52.6	1.7	-		-		53.4	1.5	-		-		54.6	2.2	-		-		55.1	0.9
1976	-		-		55.2	0.2	-		-		55.9	1.3	-		-		56.9	1.8	-		-		57.0	0.2
1977	-		-		58.4	2.5	-		-		59.4	1.7	-		-		60.7	2.2	-		-		61.2	0.8
1978	-		61.7	0.8	-		62.5	1.3	-		63.6	1.8	-		64.7	1.7	-		65.9	1.9	-		65.9	0.0
1979	-		66.9	1.5	-		68.5	2.4	-		70.5	2.9	-		71.9	2.0	-		73.2	1.8	-		74.0	1.1
1980	-		76.4	3.2	-		78.0	2.1	-		80.3	2.9	-		81.7	1.7	-		83.0	1.6	-		85.7	3.3
1981	-		87.2	1.8	-		88.2	1.1	-		89.3	1.2	-		91.6	2.6	-		93.3	1.9	-		93.6	0.3
1982	-		92.8	-0.9	-		92.9	0.1	-		96.5	3.9	-		98.0	1.6	-		98.8	0.8	-		98.2	-0.6
1983	-		97.9	-0.3	-		98.7	0.8	-		100.2	1.5	-		100.8	0.6	-		100.9	0.1	-		101.9	1.0
1984	-		102.6	0.7	-		103.2	0.6	-		104.1	0.9	-		104.8	0.7	-		105.4	0.6	-		105.5	0.1
1985	-		107.0	1.4	-		107.6	0.6	-		108.8	1.1	-		109.9	1.0	-		110.4	0.5	-		111.2	0.7
1986	-		111.7	0.4	-		111.1	-0.5	-		112.2	1.0	-		112.4	0.2	-		112.7	0.3	-		113.5	0.7
1987	-		-		-		-		-		115.5	1.8	-		-		-		-		-		117.5	1.7
1988	-		-		-		-		-		119.1	1.4	-		-		-		-		-		121.7	2.2
1989	-		-		-		-		-		124.9	2.6	-		-		-		-		-		127.3	1.9
1990	-		-		-		-		-		130.8	2.7	-		-		-		-		-		132.6	1.4
1991	-		-		-		-		-		135.5	2.2	-		-		-		-		-		136.2	0.5
1992	-		-		-		-		-		138.6	1.8	-		-		-		-		-		138.5	-0.1
1993	-		-		-		-		-		142.2	2.7	-		-		-		-		-		144.7	1.8
1994	-		-		-		-		-		146.7	1.4	-		-		-		-		-		146.7	0.0
1995	-		-		-		-		-		150.3	2.5	-		-		-		-		-		151.5	0.8
1996	-		-		-		-		-		154.7	2.1	-		-		-		-		-		157.2	1.6
1997	-		-		-		-		-		-		-		-		-		-		-		159.4	1.4
1998	-		159.5	0.1	-		160.8	0.8	-		162.0	0.7	-		161.9	-0.1	-		162.0	0.1	-		161.6	-0.2
1999	-		161.9	0.2	-		164.0	1.3	-		164.8	0.5	-		165.9	0.7	-		166.5	0.4	-		167.0	0.3
2000	-		167.5	0.3	-		170.0	1.5	-		171.3	0.8	-		172.1	0.5	-		171.9	-0.1	-		171.9	0.0
2001	-		175.3	2.0	-		176.6	0.7	-		177.8	0.7	-		176.9	-0.5	-		176.7	-0.1	-		174.8	-1.1

Source: U.S. Department of Labor, Bureau of Labor Statistics, Division of Consumer Prices and Price Indexes. - indicates no data collected for period.

Atlanta, GA
Consumer Price Index - Urban Wage Earners
Base 1982-1984 = 100
All Items

For 1917-2001. Columns headed % show percentile change in the index from the previous period for which an index is available.

Year	Jan Index	%	Feb Index	%	Mar Index	%	Apr Index	%	May Index	%	Jun Index	%	Jul Index	%	Aug Index	%	Sep Index	%	Oct Index	%	Nov Index	%	Dec Index	%
1917	-	-	-	-	-	-	-	-	-	-	-	-	-	-	-	-	-	-	-	-	-	-	15.1	-
1918	-	-	-	-	-	-	-	-	-	-	-	-	-	-	-	-	-	-	-	-	-	-	18.1	19.9
1919	-	-	-	-	-	-	-	-	-	-	18.9	4.4	-	-	-	-	-	-	-	-	-	-	20.7	9.5
1920	-	-	-	-	-	-	-	-	-	-	23.0	11.1	-	-	-	-	-	-	-	-	-	-	20.8	-9.6
1921	-	-	-	-	-	-	-	-	18.9	-9.1	-	-	-	-	-	-	18.4	-2.6	-	-	-	-	17.9	-2.7
1922	-	-	-	-	17.4	-2.8	-	-	-	-	17.5	0.6	-	-	-	-	17.3	-1.1	-	-	-	-	17.3	0.0
1923	-	-	-	-	17.3	0.0	-	-	-	-	17.5	1.2	-	-	-	-	17.8	1.7	-	-	-	-	17.5	-1.7
1924	-	-	-	-	17.2	-1.7	-	-	-	-	17.3	0.6	-	-	-	-	17.3	0.0	-	-	-	-	17.3	0.0
1925	-	-	-	-	-	-	-	-	-	-	17.8	2.9	-	-	-	-	-	-	-	-	-	-	18.2	2.2
1926	-	-	-	-	-	-	-	-	-	-	18.0	-1.1	-	-	-	-	-	-	-	-	-	-	17.7	-1.7
1927	-	-	-	-	-	-	-	-	-	-	18.1	2.3	-	-	-	-	-	-	-	-	-	-	17.2	-5.0
1928	-	-	-	-	-	-	-	-	-	-	17.3	0.6	-	-	-	-	-	-	-	-	-	-	17.3	0.0
1929	-	-	-	-	-	-	-	-	-	-	17.1	-1.2	-	-	-	-	-	-	-	-	-	-	17.1	0.0
1930	-	-	-	-	-	-	-	-	-	-	16.4	-4.1	-	-	-	-	-	-	-	-	-	-	15.7	-4.3
1931	-	-	-	-	-	-	-	-	-	-	14.8	-5.7	-	-	-	-	-	-	-	-	-	-	14.0	-5.4
1932	-	-	-	-	-	-	-	-	-	-	13.3	-5.0	-	-	-	-	-	-	-	-	-	-	12.6	-5.3
1933	-	-	-	-	-	-	-	-	-	-	12.5	-0.8	-	-	-	-	-	-	-	-	-	-	12.9	3.2
1934	-	-	-	-	-	-	-	-	-	-	13.1	1.6	-	-	-	-	-	-	-	-	13.3	1.5	-	-
1935	-	-	-	-	13.3	0.0	-	-	-	-	-	-	13.3	0.0	-	-	-	-	13.7	3.0	-	-	-	-
1936	13.7	0.0	-	-	-	-	13.5	-1.5	-	-	-	-	13.7	1.5	-	-	13.8	0.7	-	-	-	-	13.8	0.0
1937	-	-	-	-	14.0	1.4	-	-	-	-	14.1	0.7	-	-	-	-	14.3	1.4	-	-	-	-	14.1	-1.4
1938	-	-	-	-	13.7	-2.8	-	-	-	-	13.6	-0.7	-	-	-	-	13.7	0.7	-	-	-	-	13.7	0.0
1939	-	-	-	-	13.6	-0.7	-	-	-	-	13.4	-1.5	-	-	-	-	13.7	2.2	-	-	-	-	13.5	-1.5
1940	-	-	-	-	13.6	0.7	-	-	-	-	13.5	-0.7	-	-	-	-	13.6	0.7	-	-	-	-	13.7	0.7
1941	-	-	-	-	13.8	0.7	-	-	-	-	14.2	2.9	-	-	-	-	14.7	3.5	-	-	-	-	15.1	2.7
1942	-	-	-	-	15.6	3.3	-	-	-	-	15.8	1.3	-	-	-	-	16.1	1.9	-	-	-	-	16.3	1.2
1943	-	-	-	-	16.9	3.7	-	-	-	-	17.2	1.8	-	-	-	-	17.1	-0.6	-	-	-	-	17.0	-0.6
1944	-	-	-	-	16.9	-0.6	-	-	-	-	17.2	1.8	-	-	-	-	17.5	1.7	-	-	-	-	17.7	1.1
1945	-	-	-	-	17.7	0.0	-	-	-	-	17.8	0.6	-	-	-	-	18.1	1.7	-	-	-	-	18.0	-0.6
1946	-	-	-	-	18.1	0.6	-	-	-	-	18.4	1.7	-	-	-	-	20.1	9.2	-	-	-	-	21.4	6.5
1947	-	-	-	-	22.1	3.3	-	-	-	-	21.8	-1.4	-	-	22.3	2.3	-	-	-	-	23.0	3.1	-	-
1948	-	-	23.3	1.3	-	-	-	-	23.5	0.9	-	-	-	-	24.3	3.4	-	-	-	-	24.0	-1.2	-	-
1949	-	-	23.5	-2.1	-	-	-	-	23.6	0.4	-	-	-	-	23.9	1.3	-	-	-	-	23.7	-0.8	-	-
1950	-	-	23.4	-1.3	-	-	-	-	23.5	0.4	-	-	-	-	24.4	3.8	-	-	-	-	24.7	1.2	-	-
1951	-	-	25.7	4.0	-	-	-	-	26.4	2.7	-	-	-	-	26.5	0.4	-	-	-	-	26.9	1.5	-	-
1952	-	-	26.8	-0.4	-	-	-	-	26.6	-0.7	-	-	-	-	27.2	2.3	-	-	-	-	27.2	0.0	27.1	-0.4
1953	-	-	-	-	27.1	0.0	-	-	-	-	27.2	0.4	-	-	-	-	27.3	0.4	-	-	-	-	27.2	-0.4
1954	-	-	-	-	27.2	0.0	-	-	-	-	27.3	0.4	-	-	-	-	27.0	-1.1	-	-	-	-	26.9	-0.4
1955	-	-	-	-	26.8	-0.4	-	-	-	-	27.0	0.7	-	-	-	-	27.2	0.7	-	-	-	-	27.2	0.0
1956	-	-	-	-	27.1	-0.4	-	-	-	-	27.4	1.1	-	-	-	-	27.6	0.7	-	-	-	-	27.7	0.4
1957	-	-	-	-	28.0	1.1	-	-	-	-	28.1	0.4	-	-	-	-	28.4	1.1	-	-	-	-	28.4	0.0
1958	-	-	-	-	29.0	2.1	-	-	-	-	29.0	0.0	-	-	-	-	28.9	-0.3	-	-	-	-	28.9	0.0
1959	-	-	-	-	28.9	0.0	-	-	-	-	29.2	1.0	-	-	-	-	29.3	0.3	-	-	-	-	29.4	0.3
1960	-	-	-	-	29.4	0.0	-	-	-	-	29.5	0.3	-	-	-	-	29.7	0.7	-	-	-	-	29.7	0.0
1961	-	-	-	-	29.7	0.0	-	-	-	-	29.6	-0.3	-	-	-	-	29.8	0.7	-	-	-	-	29.7	-0.3
1962	-	-	-	-	29.8	0.3	-	-	-	-	29.9	0.3	-	-	-	-	30.1	0.7	-	-	-	-	30.1	0.0

[Continued]

Atlanta, GA
Consumer Price Index - Urban Wage Earners
Base 1982-1984 = 100
All Items
[Continued]

For 1917-2001. Columns headed % show percentile change in the index from the previous period for which an index is available.

Year	Jan Index	Jan %	Feb Index	Feb %	Mar Index	Mar %	Apr Index	Apr %	May Index	May %	Jun Index	Jun %	Jul Index	Jul %	Aug Index	Aug %	Sep Index	Sep %	Oct Index	Oct %	Nov Index	Nov %	Dec Index	Dec %
1963	-	-	-	-	30.2	0.3	-	-	-	-	30.2	0.0	-	-	-	-	30.3	0.3	-	-	-	-	30.4	0.3
1964	-	-	-	-	30.7	1.0	-	-	-	-	30.6	-0.3	-	-	-	-	30.8	0.7	-	-	-	-	30.9	0.3
1965	-	-	-	-	31.0	0.3	-	-	-	-	31.0	0.0	-	-	-	-	31.1	0.3	-	-	-	-	31.4	1.0
1966	-	-	-	-	31.7	1.0	-	-	-	-	31.9	0.6	-	-	-	-	32.4	1.6	-	-	-	-	32.6	0.6
1967	-	-	-	-	32.8	0.6	-	-	-	-	33.0	0.6	-	-	-	-	33.2	0.6	-	-	-	-	33.6	1.2
1968	-	-	-	-	33.9	0.9	-	-	-	-	34.2	0.9	-	-	-	-	34.9	2.0	-	-	-	-	35.1	0.6
1969	-	-	-	-	35.9	2.3	-	-	-	-	36.3	1.1	-	-	-	-	37.0	1.9	-	-	-	-	37.4	1.1
1970	-	-	-	-	37.9	1.3	-	-	-	-	38.5	1.6	-	-	-	-	38.9	1.0	-	-	-	-	39.5	1.5
1971	-	-	-	-	39.8	0.8	-	-	-	-	40.4	1.5	-	-	-	-	40.3	-0.2	-	-	-	-	40.8	1.2
1972	-	-	-	-	40.9	0.2	-	-	-	-	41.3	1.0	-	-	-	-	42.0	1.7	-	-	-	-	42.2	0.5
1973	-	-	-	-	43.0	1.9	-	-	-	-	43.9	2.1	-	-	-	-	45.3	3.2	-	-	-	-	45.9	1.3
1974	-	-	-	-	47.7	3.9	-	-	-	-	48.7	2.1	-	-	-	-	50.5	3.7	-	-	-	-	51.6	2.2
1975	-	-	-	-	52.4	1.6	-	-	-	-	53.2	1.5	-	-	-	-	54.5	2.4	-	-	-	-	55.0	0.9
1976	-	-	-	-	55.1	0.2	-	-	-	-	55.7	1.1	-	-	-	-	56.8	2.0	-	-	-	-	56.9	0.2
1977	-	-	-	-	58.2	2.3	-	-	-	-	59.2	1.7	-	-	-	-	60.5	2.2	-	-	-	-	61.0	0.8
1978	-	-	61.7	1.1	-	-	62.5	1.3	-	-	63.7	1.9	-	-	64.6	1.4	-	-	65.6	1.5	-	-	65.9	0.5
1979	-	-	67.0	1.7	-	-	68.9	2.8	-	-	70.9	2.9	-	-	72.4	2.1	-	-	73.9	2.1	-	-	75.1	1.6
1980	-	-	77.2	2.8	-	-	79.1	2.5	-	-	80.9	2.3	-	-	82.6	2.1	-	-	83.5	1.1	-	-	86.1	3.1
1981	-	-	88.1	2.3	-	-	88.9	0.9	-	-	90.2	1.5	-	-	92.0	2.0	-	-	93.6	1.7	-	-	94.0	0.4
1982	-	-	93.5	-0.5	-	-	93.6	0.1	-	-	96.9	3.5	-	-	98.3	1.4	-	-	98.8	0.5	-	-	98.5	-0.3
1983	-	-	98.2	-0.3	-	-	99.3	1.1	-	-	99.9	0.6	-	-	100.6	0.7	-	-	101.3	0.7	-	-	102.4	1.1
1984	-	-	102.4	0.0	-	-	102.3	-0.1	-	-	102.8	0.5	-	-	100.6	0.7	-	-	105.2	1.0	-	-	104.5	-0.7
1985	-	-	105.9	1.3	-	-	106.6	0.7	-	-	107.8	1.1	-	-	104.2	1.4	-	-	109.1	0.2	-	-	110.0	0.8
1986	-	-	110.6	0.5	-	-	109.7	-0.8	-	-	111.0	1.2	-	-	108.9	1.0	-	-	111.1	0.2	-	-	111.7	0.5
1987	-	-	-	-	-	-	-	-	-	-	113.7	1.8	-	-	110.9	-0.1	-	-	-	-	-	-	115.8	1.8
1988	-	-	-	-	-	-	-	-	-	-	117.2	1.2	-	-	-	-	-	-	-	-	-	-	120.1	2.5
1989	-	-	-	-	-	-	-	-	-	-	123.2	2.6	-	-	-	-	-	-	-	-	-	-	125.5	1.9
1990	-	-	-	-	-	-	-	-	-	-	128.9	2.7	-	-	-	-	-	-	-	-	-	-	131.1	1.7
1991	-	-	-	-	-	-	-	-	-	-	133.5	1.8	-	-	-	-	-	-	-	-	-	-	134.4	0.7
1992	-	-	-	-	-	-	-	-	-	-	136.3	1.4	-	-	-	-	-	-	-	-	-	-	136.9	0.4
1993	-	-	-	-	-	-	-	-	-	-	140.2	2.4	-	-	-	-	-	-	-	-	-	-	142.6	1.7
1994	-	-	-	-	-	-	-	-	-	-	144.1	1.1	-	-	-	-	-	-	-	-	-	-	144.5	0.3
1995	-	-	-	-	-	-	-	-	-	-	147.9	2.4	-	-	-	-	-	-	-	-	-	-	149.4	1.0
1996	-	-	-	-	-	-	-	-	-	-	152.3	1.9	-	-	-	-	-	-	-	-	-	-	155.0	1.8
1997	-	-	-	-	-	-	-	-	-	-	-	-	-	-	-	-	-	-	-	-	-	-	156.8	1.2
1998	-	-	156.6	-0.1	-	-	157.7	0.7	-	-	159.3	1.0	-	-	159.1	-0.1	-	-	159.2	0.1	-	-	158.8	-0.3
1999	-	-	159.1	0.2	-	-	160.9	1.1	-	-	161.9	0.6	-	-	163.2	0.8	-	-	164.0	0.5	-	-	164.6	0.4
2000	-	-	165.0	0.2	-	-	167.3	1.4	-	-	168.9	1.0	-	-	169.6	0.4	-	-	169.6	0.0	-	-	169.7	0.1
2001	-	-	172.7	1.8	-	-	173.8	0.6	-	-	175.4	0.9	-	-	174.2	-0.7	-	-	174.1	-0.1	-	-	172.0	-1.2

Source: U.S. Department of Labor, Bureau of Labor Statistics, Division of Consumer Prices and Price Indexes. - indicates no data collected for period.

Atlanta, GA
Consumer Price Index - All Urban Consumers
Base 1982-1984 = 100
Food and Beverages

For 1975-2001. Columns headed % show percentile change in the index from the previous period for which an index is available.

Year	Jan Index	%	Feb Index	%	Mar Index	%	Apr Index	%	May Index	%	Jun Index	%	Jul Index	%	Aug Index	%	Sep Index	%	Oct Index	%	Nov Index	%	Dec Index	%
1975	-	-	-	-	-	-	-	-	-	-	-	-	-	-	-	-	-	-	-	-	-	-	63.2	-
1976	-	-	-	-	62.1	-1.7	-	-	-	-	62.2	0.2	-	-	-	-	63.0	1.3	-	-	-	-	62.4	-1.0
1977	-	-	-	-	64.9	4.0	-	-	-	-	65.9	1.5	-	-	-	-	67.2	2.0	-	-	-	-	67.6	0.6
1978	-	-	69.0	2.1	-	-	70.2	1.7	-	-	73.1	4.1	-	-	73.8	1.0	-	-	74.0	0.3	-	-	74.9	1.2
1979	-	-	77.7	3.7	-	-	78.8	1.4	-	-	79.1	0.4	-	-	80.8	2.1	-	-	80.7	-0.1	-	-	81.6	1.1
1980	-	-	82.4	1.0	-	-	82.9	0.6	-	-	84.4	1.8	-	-	87.6	3.8	-	-	88.6	1.1	-	-	91.4	3.2
1981	-	-	92.2	0.9	-	-	92.2	0.0	-	-	92.5	0.3	-	-	93.5	1.1	-	-	94.1	0.6	-	-	95.0	1.0
1982	-	-	96.1	1.2	-	-	96.3	0.2	-	-	97.5	1.2	-	-	97.4	-0.1	-	-	97.7	0.3	-	-	98.2	0.5
1983	-	-	98.8	0.6	-	-	100.2	1.4	-	-	100.0	-0.2	-	-	99.9	-0.1	-	-	100.1	0.2	-	-	100.4	0.3
1984	-	-	103.4	3.0	-	-	102.7	-0.7	-	-	102.2	-0.5	-	-	103.8	1.6	-	-	103.5	-0.3	-	-	104.3	0.8
1985	-	-	106.2	1.8	-	-	105.5	-0.7	-	-	105.5	0.0	-	-	105.3	-0.2	-	-	106.3	0.9	-	-	108.6	2.2
1986	-	-	109.4	0.7	-	-	110.5	1.0	-	-	110.6	0.1	-	-	113.0	2.2	-	-	112.5	-0.4	-	-	112.1	-0.4
1987	-	-	-	-	-	-	-	-	-	-	112.2	0.1	-	-	-	-	-	-	-	-	-	-	112.3	0.1
1988	-	-	-	-	-	-	-	-	-	-	115.6	2.9	-	-	-	-	-	-	-	-	-	-	119.2	3.1
1989	-	-	-	-	-	-	-	-	-	-	121.4	1.8	-	-	-	-	-	-	-	-	-	-	125.9	3.7
1990	-	-	-	-	-	-	-	-	-	-	130.5	3.7	-	-	-	-	-	-	-	-	-	-	133.3	2.1
1991	-	-	-	-	-	-	-	-	-	-	135.3	1.5	-	-	-	-	-	-	-	-	-	-	135.3	0.0
1992	-	-	-	-	-	-	-	-	-	-	135.8	0.4	-	-	-	-	-	-	-	-	-	-	135.7	-0.1
1993	-	-	-	-	-	-	-	-	-	-	138.4	2.0	-	-	-	-	-	-	-	-	-	-	140.7	1.7
1994	-	-	-	-	-	-	-	-	-	-	140.8	0.1	-	-	-	-	-	-	-	-	-	-	141.4	0.4
1995	-	-	-	-	-	-	-	-	-	-	145.4	2.8	-	-	-	-	-	-	-	-	-	-	147.6	1.5
1996	-	-	-	-	-	-	-	-	-	-	150.5	2.0	-	-	-	-	-	-	-	-	-	-	156.4	3.9
1997	-	-	-	-	-	-	-	-	-	-	-	-	-	-	-	-	-	-	-	-	-	-	161.0	2.9
1998	-	-	161.7	0.4	-	-	163.7	1.2	-	-	164.8	0.7	-	-	166.1	0.8	-	-	166.8	0.4	-	-	166.6	-0.1
1999	-	-	166.8	0.1	-	-	167.1	0.2	-	-	166.2	-0.5	-	-	167.0	0.5	-	-	169.1	1.3	-	-	170.2	0.7
2000	-	-	170.2	0.0	-	-	172.8	1.5	-	-	171.7	-0.6	-	-	172.1	0.2	-	-	172.2	0.1	-	-	172.6	0.2
2001	-	-	176.5	2.3	-	-	180.9	2.5	-	-	180.3	-0.3	-	-	180.1	-0.1	-	-	182.6	1.4	-	-	182.9	0.2

Source: U.S. Department of Labor, Bureau of Labor Statistics, Division of Consumer Prices and Price Indexes. - indicates no data collected for period.

Atlanta, GA
Consumer Price Index - Urban Wage Earners
Base 1982-1984 = 100
Food and Beverages

For 1975-2001. Columns headed % show percentile change in the index from the previous period for which an index is available.

Year	Jan Index	%	Feb Index	%	Mar Index	%	Apr Index	%	May Index	%	Jun Index	%	Jul Index	%	Aug Index	%	Sep Index	%	Oct Index	%	Nov Index	%	Dec Index	%
1975	-		-		-		-		-		-				-		-		-		-		-	
1976	-		-		61.4	-1.8	-		-		61.5	0.2	-		-		62.3	1.3	-		-		62.5	-
1977	-		-		64.1	3.9	-		-		65.1	1.6	-		-		66.5	2.2	-		-		61.7	-1.0
1978	-		68.3	2.2	-		70.1	2.6	-		72.8	3.9	-		73.8	1.4	-		73.7	-0.1	-		66.8	0.5
1979	-		77.4	4.0	-		78.7	1.7	-		79.1	0.5	-		80.5	1.8	-		80.7	0.2	-		74.4	0.9
1980	-		82.4	1.0	-		83.6	1.5	-		84.3	0.8	-		87.1	3.3	-		88.4	1.5	-		81.6	1.1
1981	-		91.9	1.2	-		92.6	0.8	-		93.1	0.5	-		93.7	0.6	-		94.2	0.5	-		94.8	0.6
1982	-		95.9	1.2	-		96.3	0.4	-		97.5	1.2	-		97.5	0.0	-		97.9	0.4	-		98.4	0.5
1983	-		98.9	0.5	-		100.3	1.4	-		100.1	-0.2	-		99.9	-0.2	-		97.9	0.4	-		98.4	0.5
1984	-		103.1	2.7	-		102.5	-0.6	-		102.3	-0.2	-		99.9	-0.2	-		100.1	0.2	-		100.4	0.3
1985	-		106.0	1.7	-		105.3	-0.7	-		105.4	0.1	-		103.6	1.3	-		103.4	-0.2	-		104.2	0.8
1986	-		109.2	0.7	-		110.3	1.0	-		110.3	0.0	-		112.9	2.4	-		112.5	-0.4	-		108.4	2.2
1987	-		-		-		-		-		111.9	0.1	-		-		-		-		-		111.8	-0.6
1988	-		-		-		-		-		115.0	2.8	-		-		-		-		-		111.9	0.0
1989	-		-		-		-		-		121.1	1.8	-		-		-		-		-		119.0	3.5
1990	-		-		-		-		-		129.9	3.6	-		-		-		-		-		125.4	3.6
1991	-		-		-		-		-		135.1	1.7	-		-		-		-		-		132.9	2.3
1992	-		-		-		-		-		135.4	0.2	-		-		-		-		-		135.1	0.0
1993	-		-		-		-		-		137.8	1.8	-		-		-		-		-		135.4	0.0
1994	-		-		-		-		-		140.6	0.1	-		-		-		-		-		140.4	1.9
1995	-		-		-		-		-		143.9	2.2	-		-		-		-		-		140.8	0.1
1996	-		-		-		-		-		149.4	2.2	-		-		-		-		-		146.2	1.6
1997	-		-		-		-		-		-		-		-		-		-		-		154.5	3.4
1998	-		160.5	0.4	-		162.5	1.2	-		163.7	0.7	-		164.9	0.7	-		165.3	0.2	-		159.9	3.5
1999	-		165.4	0.1	-		165.7	0.2	-		164.6	-0.7	-		165.6	0.6	-		167.4	1.1	-		165.3	0.0
2000	-		168.6	-0.1	-		171.4	1.7	-		170.5	-0.5	-		165.6	0.6	-		167.4	1.1	-		168.7	0.8
2001	-		175.6	2.5	-		180.1	2.6	-		179.2	-0.5	-		179.3	0.1	-		181.7	1.3	-		171.3	0.2

Source: U.S. Department of Labor, Bureau of Labor Statistics, Division of Consumer Prices and Price Indexes. - indicates no data collected for period.

Atlanta, GA
Consumer Price Index - All Urban Consumers
Base 1982-1984 = 100
Housing

For 1975-2001. Columns headed % show percentile change in the index from the previous period for which an index is available.

Year	Jan Index	%	Feb Index	%	Mar Index	%	Apr Index	%	May Index	%	Jun Index	%	Jul Index	%	Aug Index	%	Sep Index	%	Oct Index	%	Nov Index	%	Dec Index	%
1975	-	-	-	-	-	-	-	-	-	-	-	-	-	-	-	-	-	-	-	-	-	-	50.7	-
1976	-	-	-	-	51.2	1.0	-	-	-	-	51.8	1.2	-	-	-	-	52.5	1.4	-	-	-	-	52.8	0.6
1977	-	-	-	-	53.7	1.7	-	-	-	-	55.1	2.6	-	-	-	-	56.4	2.4	-	-	-	-	57.2	1.4
1978	-	-	57.6	0.7	-	-	58.5	1.6	-	-	59.2	1.2	-	-	60.4	2.0	-	-	62.2	3.0	-	-	62.0	-0.3
1979	-	-	62.3	0.5	-	-	63.5	1.9	-	-	66.0	3.9	-	-	66.9	1.4	-	-	68.9	3.0	-	-	69.6	1.0
1980	-	-	71.5	2.7	-	-	73.6	2.9	-	-	77.0	4.6	-	-	76.8	-0.3	-	-	78.4	2.1	-	-	82.4	5.1
1981	-	-	83.6	1.5	-	-	84.3	0.8	-	-	86.4	2.5	-	-	90.0	4.2	-	-	92.3	2.6	-	-	92.4	0.1
1982	-	-	90.7	-1.8	-	-	91.7	1.1	-	-	96.4	5.1	-	-	98.5	2.2	-	-	98.7	0.2	-	-	97.7	-1.0
1983	-	-	98.0	0.3	-	-	98.9	0.9	-	-	101.1	2.2	-	-	100.5	-0.6	-	-	100.2	-0.3	-	-	102.5	2.3
1984	-	-	102.7	0.2	-	-	103.4	0.7	-	-	105.3	1.8	-	-	106.0	0.7	-	-	105.4	-0.6	-	-	105.7	0.3
1985	-	-	107.4	1.6	-	-	108.4	0.9	-	-	110.2	1.7	-	-	111.6	1.3	-	-	111.2	-0.4	-	-	112.3	1.0
1986	-	-	112.7	0.4	-	-	114.1	1.2	-	-	116.1	1.8	-	-	116.3	0.2	-	-	115.9	-0.3	-	-	117.4	1.3
1987	-	-	-	-	-	-	-	-	-	-	118.2	0.7	-	-	-	-	-	-	-	-	-	-	120.8	2.2
1988	-	-	-	-	-	-	-	-	-	-	122.0	1.0	-	-	-	-	-	-	-	-	-	-	123.2	1.0
1989	-	-	-	-	-	-	-	-	-	-	124.7	1.2	-	-	-	-	-	-	-	-	-	-	126.9	1.8
1990	-	-	-	-	-	-	-	-	-	-	129.0	1.7	-	-	-	-	-	-	-	-	-	-	128.7	-0.2
1991	-	-	-	-	-	-	-	-	-	-	129.3	0.5	-	-	-	-	-	-	-	-	-	-	131.8	1.9
1992	-	-	-	-	-	-	-	-	-	-	132.4	0.5	-	-	-	-	-	-	-	-	-	-	133.0	0.5
1993	-	-	-	-	-	-	-	-	-	-	135.7	2.0	-	-	-	-	-	-	-	-	-	-	137.4	1.3
1994	-	-	-	-	-	-	-	-	-	-	139.9	1.8	-	-	-	-	-	-	-	-	-	-	140.4	0.4
1995	-	-	-	-	-	-	-	-	-	-	145.0	3.3	-	-	-	-	-	-	-	-	-	-	147.3	1.6
1996	-	-	-	-	-	-	-	-	-	-	150.5	2.2	-	-	-	-	-	-	-	-	-	-	153.0	1.7
1997	-	-	-	-	-	-	-	-	-	-	-	-	-	-	-	-	-	-	-	-	-	-	155.7	1.8
1998	-	-	157.9	1.4	-	-	159.2	0.8	-	-	163.9	3.0	-	-	164.1	0.1	-	-	160.9	-2.0	-	-	161.9	0.6
1999	-	-	162.1	0.1	-	-	163.9	1.1	-	-	167.3	2.1	-	-	167.3	0.0	-	-	165.4	-1.1	-	-	165.3	-0.1
2000	-	-	167.1	1.1	-	-	169.4	1.4	-	-	172.7	1.9	-	-	174.0	0.8	-	-	172.2	-1.0	-	-	172.6	0.2
2001	-	-	177.2	2.7	-	-	177.8	0.3	-	-	181.2	1.9	-	-	181.1	-0.1	-	-	177.3	-2.1	-	-	177.1	-0.1

Source: U.S. Department of Labor, Bureau of Labor Statistics, Division of Consumer Prices and Price Indexes. - indicates no data collected for period.

Atlanta, GA
Consumer Price Index - Urban Wage Earners
Base 1982-1984 = 100
Housing

For 1975-2001. Columns headed % show percentile change in the index from the previous period for which an index is available.

Year	Jan Index	%	Feb Index	%	Mar Index	%	Apr Index	%	May Index	%	Jun Index	%	Jul Index	%	Aug Index	%	Sep Index	%	Oct Index	%	Nov Index	%	Dec Index	%
1975	-		-		-		-		-		-		-		-		-		-		-		51.3	-
1976	-		-		51.9	1.2	-		-		52.5	1.2	-		-		53.2	1.3	-		-		53.5	0.6
1977	-		-		54.5	1.9	-		-		55.8	2.4	-		-		57.2	2.5	-		-		58.0	1.4
1978	-		58.6	1.0	-		59.3	1.2	-		60.1	1.3	-		61.1	1.7	-		62.6	2.5	-		62.9	0.5
1979	-		63.3	0.6	-		64.6	2.1	-		67.3	4.2	-		68.0	1.0	-		69.8	2.6	-		70.7	1.3
1980	-		72.4	2.4	-		74.6	3.0	-		77.8	4.3	-		77.6	-0.3	-		78.4	1.0	-		82.4	5.1
1981	-		83.6	1.5	-		84.4	1.0	-		86.8	2.8	-		90.2	3.9	-		92.3	2.3	-		92.6	0.3
1982	-		91.2	-1.5	-		92.4	1.3	-		96.8	4.8	-		98.8	2.1	-		98.7	-0.1	-		98.0	-0.7
1983	-		99.0	1.0	-		100.2	1.2	-		100.3	0.1	-		100.7	0.4	-		101.7	1.0	-		103.8	2.1
1984	-		102.5	-1.3	-		101.7	-0.8	-		102.4	0.7	-		104.8	2.3	-		105.7	0.9	-		104.4	-1.2
1985	-		106.1	1.6	-		107.0	0.8	-		108.8	1.7	-		110.2	1.3	-		109.4	-0.7	-		110.4	0.9
1986	-		110.7	0.3	-		111.9	1.1	-		114.2	2.1	-		114.2	0.0	-		113.7	-0.4	-		115.3	1.4
1987	-		-		-		-		-		116.2	0.8	-		-		-		-		-		118.8	2.2
1988	-		-		-		-		-		120.0	1.0	-		-		-		-		-		121.3	1.1
1989	-		-		-		-		-		122.9	1.3	-		-		-		-		-		124.8	1.5
1990	-		-		-		-		-		126.7	1.5	-		-		-		-		-		126.4	-0.2
1991	-		-		-		-		-		127.1	0.6	-		-		-		-		-		129.7	2.0
1992	-		-		-		-		-		130.2	0.4	-		-		-		-		-		130.9	0.5
1993	-		-		-		-		-		133.6	2.1	-		-		-		-		-		135.5	1.4
1994	-		-		-		-		-		137.6	1.5	-		-		-		-		-		138.4	0.6
1995	-		-		-		-		-		142.9	3.3	-		-		-		-		-		145.5	1.8
1996	-		-		-		-		-		148.0	1.7	-		-		-		-		-		150.6	1.8
1997	-		-		-		-		-		-		-		-		-		-		-		153.2	1.7
1998	-		154.8	1.0	-		156.1	0.8	-		161.3	3.3	-		161.5	0.1	-		158.1	-2.1	-		159.1	0.6
1999	-		159.1	0.0	-		160.4	0.8	-		164.1	2.3	-		164.3	0.1	-		162.3	-1.2	-		162.4	0.1
2000	-		163.8	0.9	-		165.5	1.0	-		169.5	2.4	-		170.8	0.8	-		169.0	-1.1	-		169.9	0.5
2001	-		174.0	2.4	-		174.4	0.2	-		178.5	2.4	-		178.4	-0.1	-		174.7	-2.1	-		174.8	0.1

Source: U.S. Department of Labor, Bureau of Labor Statistics, Division of Consumer Prices and Price Indexes. - indicates no data collected for period.

Atlanta, GA
Consumer Price Index - All Urban Consumers
Base 1982-1984 = 100
Apparel

For 1952-2001. Columns headed % show percentile change in the index from the previous period for which an index is available.

Year	Jan Index	Jan %	Feb Index	Feb %	Mar Index	Mar %	Apr Index	Apr %	May Index	May %	Jun Index	Jun %	Jul Index	Jul %	Aug Index	Aug %	Sep Index	Sep %	Oct Index	Oct %	Nov Index	Nov %	Dec Index	Dec %
1952	-		-		-		-		-		-		-		-		-		-		42.1		42.2	-0.7
1953	-		-		42.2	0.2	-		-		42.1	-0.2	-		-		42.5	1.0	-		-		42.1	-0.2
1954	-		-		42.5	0.7	-		-		42.6	0.2	-		-		42.2	-0.9	-		-		42.5	0.0
1955	-		-		41.5	-1.4	-		-		42.1	1.4	-		-		42.5	1.0	-		-		43.2	-0.5
1956	-		-		42.6	0.2	-		-		42.8	0.5	-		-		43.4	1.4	-		-		44.1	0.0
1957	-		-		43.7	1.2	-		-		43.6	-0.2	-		-		44.1	1.1	-		-		44.3	0.0
1958	-		-		44.3	0.5	-		-		44.1	-0.5	-		-		44.3	0.5	-		-		44.7	0.7
1959	-		-		44.0	-0.7	-		-		44.0	0.0	-		-		44.4	0.9	-		-		45.3	-0.4
1960	-		-		44.7	0.0	-		-		44.7	0.0	-		-		45.5	1.8	-		-		44.9	-0.2
1961	-		-		45.1	-0.4	-		-		45.1	0.0	-		-		45.0	-0.2	-		-		45.5	0.7
1962	-		-		45.0	0.2	-		-		44.9	-0.2	-		-		45.2	0.7	-		-		46.2	-0.6
1963	-		-		45.9	0.9	-		-		46.0	0.2	-		-		46.5	1.1	-		-		46.3	0.2
1964	-		-		46.2	0.0	-		-		46.0	-0.4	-		-		46.2	0.4	-		-		47.1	0.2
1965	-		-		46.4	0.2	-		-		46.4	0.0	-		-		47.0	1.3	-		-		50.8	1.6
1966	-		-		47.8	1.5	-		-		48.4	1.3	-		-		50.0	3.3	-		-		52.3	0.6
1967	-		-		51.3	1.0	-		-		51.4	0.2	-		-		52.0	1.2	-		-		55.0	1.3
1968	-		-		53.3	1.9	-		-		53.4	0.2	-		-		54.3	1.7	-		-		57.1	0.7
1969	-		-		55.0	0.0	-		-		55.8	1.5	-		-		56.7	1.6	-		-		59.4	0.7
1970	-		-		57.8	1.2	-		-		57.9	0.2	-		-		59.0	1.9	-		-		60.2	0.0
1971	-		-		60.1	1.2	-		-		59.3	-1.3	-		-		60.2	1.5	-		-		60.2	0.0
1972	-		-		60.4	0.3	-		-		60.3	-0.2	-		-		62.6	3.8	-		-		62.6	0.0
1973	-		-		63.0	0.6	-		-		62.7	-0.5	-		-		65.0	3.7	-		-		65.4	0.6
1974	-		-		67.3	2.9	-		-		69.1	2.7	-		-		71.1	2.9	-		-		70.3	-1.1
1975	-		-		71.6	1.8	-		-		70.5	-1.5	-		-		72.7	3.1	-		-		72.4	-0.4
1976	-		-		73.1	1.0	-		-		72.8	-0.4	-		-		76.3	4.8	-		-		76.4	0.1
1977	-		-		78.7	3.0	-		-		77.0	-2.2	-		-		82.2	6.8	-		-		82.0	-0.2
1978	-		81.7	-0.4	-		83.8	2.6	-		83.6	-0.2	-		85.9	2.8	-		85.1	-0.9	-		84.4	-0.8
1979	-		85.0	0.7	-		86.8	2.1	-		88.0	1.4	-		88.8	0.9	-		89.0	0.2	-		89.4	0.4
1980	-		92.1	3.0	-		90.8	-1.4	-		92.1	1.4	-		94.1	2.2	-		96.0	2.0	-		95.0	-1.0
1981	-		94.1	-0.9	-		96.9	3.0	-		94.1	-2.9	-		99.6	5.8	-		96.5	-3.1	-		96.4	-0.1
1982	-		94.9	-1.6	-		93.9	-1.1	-		93.9	0.0	-		96.9	3.2	-		102.5	5.8	-		99.3	-3.1
1983	-		97.7	-1.6	-		93.8	-4.0	-		99.1	5.7	-		107.0	8.0	-		105.1	-1.8	-		101.0	-3.9
1984	-		98.4	-2.6	-		101.0	2.6	-		101.0	0.0	-		101.1	0.1	-		109.4	8.2	-		106.7	-2.5
1985	-		113.3	6.2	-		107.9	-4.8	-		109.1	1.1	-		114.0	4.5	-		116.9	2.5	-		109.5	-6.3
1986	-		108.0	-1.4	-		110.4	2.2	-		107.0	-3.1	-		107.9	0.8	-		115.8	7.3	-		114.4	-1.2
1987	-		-		-		-		-		124.9	9.2	-		-		-		-		-		126.6	1.4
1988	-		-		-		-		-		129.0	1.9	-		-		-		-		-		129.4	0.3
1989	-		-		-		-		-		138.4	7.0	-		-		-		-		-		135.9	-1.8
1990	-		-		-		-		-		137.3	1.0	-		-		-		-		-		130.3	-5.1
1991	-		-		-		-		-		154.3	18.4	-		-		-		-		-		142.5	-7.6
1992	-		-		-		-		-		161.4	13.3	-		-		-		-		-		143.7	-11.0
1993	-		-		-		-		-		153.8	7.0	-		-		-		-		-		162.3	5.5
1994	-		-		-		-		-		173.2	6.7	-		-		-		-		-		161.4	-6.8
1995	-		-		-		-		-		160.5	-0.6	-		-		-		-		-		146.4	-8.8
1996	-		-		-		-		-		146.8	0.3	-		-		-		-		-		143.9	-2.0
1997	-		-		-		-		-		-		-		-		-		-		-		142.6	-0.9

[Continued]

Atlanta, GA
Consumer Price Index - All Urban Consumers
Base 1982-1984 = 100
Apparel

[Continued]

For 1952-2001. Columns headed % show percentile change in the index from the previous period for which an index is available.

Year	Jan Index	%	Feb Index	%	Mar Index	%	Apr Index	%	May Index	%	Jun Index	%	Jul Index	%	Aug Index	%	Sep Index	%	Oct Index	%	Nov Index	%	Dec Index	%
1998	-	-	138.3	-3.0	-	-	141.3	2.2	-	-	139.0	-1.6	-	-	135.6	-2.4	-	-	140.2	3.4	-	-	127.9	-8.8
1999	-	-	128.2	0.2	-	-	132.9	3.7	-	-	126.9	-4.5	-	-	135.1	6.5	-	-	138.3	2.4	-	-	134.6	-2.7
2000	-	-	129.1	-4.1	-	-	139.3	7.9	-	-	132.5	-4.9	-	-	130.3	-1.7	-	-	132.5	1.7	-	-	128.7	-2.9
2001	-	-	132.8	3.2	-	-	133.9	0.8	-	-	123.6	-7.7	-	-	119.1	-3.6	-	-	128.5	7.9	-	-	122.7	-4.5

Source: U.S. Department of Labor, Bureau of Labor Statistics, Division of Consumer Prices and Price Indexes. - indicates no data collected for period.

Atlanta, GA
Consumer Price Index - Urban Wage Earners
Base 1982-1984 = 100
Apparel

For 1952-2001. Columns headed % show percentile change in the index from the previous period for which an index is available.

Year	Jan Index	%	Feb Index	%	Mar Index	%	Apr Index	%	May Index	%	Jun Index	%	Jul Index	%	Aug Index	%	Sep Index	%	Oct Index	%	Nov Index	%	Dec Index	%
1952	-	-	-	-	-	-	-	-	-	-	-	-	-	-	-	-	-	-	-	-	39.9	-	40.0	-0.5
1953	-	-	-	-	40.0	0.3	-	-	-	-	39.9	-0.2	-	-	-	-	40.2	0.8	-	-	-	-	39.9	-0.2
1954	-	-	-	-	40.3	0.7	-	-	-	-	40.3	0.0	-	-	-	-	40.0	-0.7	-	-	-	-	40.2	-0.2
1955	-	-	-	-	39.3	-1.5	-	-	-	-	39.9	1.5	-	-	-	-	40.3	1.0	-	-	-	-	41.0	-0.2
1956	-	-	-	-	40.4	0.5	-	-	-	-	40.5	0.2	-	-	-	-	41.1	1.5	-	-	-	-	41.8	0.0
1957	-	-	-	-	41.4	1.0	-	-	-	-	41.3	-0.2	-	-	-	-	41.8	1.2	-	-	-	-	42.0	0.0
1958	-	-	-	-	42.0	0.5	-	-	-	-	41.8	-0.5	-	-	-	-	42.0	0.5	-	-	-	-	42.4	0.7
1959	-	-	-	-	41.7	-0.7	-	-	-	-	41.7	0.0	-	-	-	-	42.1	1.0	-	-	-	-	43.0	-0.2
1960	-	-	-	-	42.3	-0.2	-	-	-	-	42.4	0.2	-	-	-	-	43.1	1.7	-	-	-	-	42.5	-0.2
1961	-	-	-	-	42.8	-0.5	-	-	-	-	42.8	0.0	-	-	-	-	42.6	-0.5	-	-	-	-	43.1	0.7
1962	-	-	-	-	42.6	0.2	-	-	-	-	42.5	-0.2	-	-	-	-	42.8	0.7	-	-	-	-	43.8	-0.7
1963	-	-	-	-	43.5	0.9	-	-	-	-	43.6	0.2	-	-	-	-	44.1	1.1	-	-	-	-	43.9	0.2
1964	-	-	-	-	43.8	0.0	-	-	-	-	43.6	-0.5	-	-	-	-	43.8	0.5	-	-	-	-	44.6	0.2
1965	-	-	-	-	44.0	0.2	-	-	-	-	44.0	0.0	-	-	-	-	44.5	1.1	-	-	-	-	48.1	1.5
1966	-	-	-	-	45.3	1.6	-	-	-	-	45.9	1.3	-	-	-	-	47.4	3.3	-	-	-	-	49.6	0.6
1967	-	-	-	-	48.7	1.2	-	-	-	-	48.8	0.2	-	-	-	-	49.3	1.0	-	-	-	-	52.1	1.2
1968	-	-	-	-	50.5	1.8	-	-	-	-	50.6	0.2	-	-	-	-	51.5	1.8	-	-	-	-	54.1	0.6
1969	-	-	-	-	52.1	0.0	-	-	-	-	52.9	1.5	-	-	-	-	53.8	1.7	-	-	-	-	56.3	0.5
1970	-	-	-	-	54.8	1.3	-	-	-	-	54.9	0.2	-	-	-	-	56.0	2.0	-	-	-	-	57.1	0.2
1971	-	-	-	-	57.0	1.2	-	-	-	-	56.2	-1.4	-	-	-	-	57.0	1.4	-	-	-	-	59.3	0.2
1972	-	-	-	-	57.3	0.4	-	-	-	-	57.2	-0.2	-	-	-	-	59.3	3.7	-	-	-	-	59.3	0.0
1973	-	-	-	-	59.7	0.7	-	-	-	-	59.4	-0.5	-	-	-	-	61.6	3.7	-	-	-	-	62.0	0.6
1974	-	-	-	-	63.8	2.9	-	-	-	-	65.5	2.7	-	-	-	-	67.4	2.9	-	-	-	-	66.7	-1.0
1975	-	-	-	-	67.9	1.8	-	-	-	-	66.8	-1.6	-	-	-	-	68.9	3.1	-	-	-	-	68.6	-0.4
1976	-	-	-	-	69.3	1.0	-	-	-	-	69.0	-0.4	-	-	-	-	72.4	4.9	-	-	-	-	72.5	0.1
1977	-	-	-	-	74.6	2.9	-	-	-	-	72.9	-2.3	-	-	-	-	77.9	6.9	-	-	-	-	77.7	-0.3
1978	-	-	77.3	-0.5	-	-	77.5	0.3	-	-	77.5	0.0	-	-	78.1	0.8	-	-	79.7	2.0	-	-	79.7	0.0
1979	-	-	79.3	-0.5	-	-	82.5	4.0	-	-	84.1	1.9	-	-	86.7	3.1	-	-	87.1	0.5	-	-	88.6	1.7
1980	-	-	86.5	-2.4	-	-	86.5	0.0	-	-	87.9	1.6	-	-	92.3	5.0	-	-	92.9	0.7	-	-	95.1	2.4
1981	-	-	93.4	-1.8	-	-	94.6	1.3	-	-	94.7	0.1	-	-	95.9	1.3	-	-	99.5	3.8	-	-	97.7	-1.8
1982	-	-	96.8	-0.9	-	-	95.5	-1.3	-	-	95.2	-0.3	-	-	98.4	3.4	-	-	102.6	4.3	-	-	99.8	-2.7
1983	-	-	97.5	-2.3	-	-	94.4	-3.2	-	-	98.5	4.3	-	-	105.3	6.9	-	-	104.4	-0.9	-	-	100.1	-4.1
1984	-	-	97.6	-2.5	-	-	100.6	3.1	-	-	101.2	0.6	-	-	101.4	0.2	-	-	108.6	7.1	-	-	104.1	-4.1
1985	-	-	110.8	6.4	-	-	106.0	-4.3	-	-	108.2	2.1	-	-	111.9	3.4	-	-	113.1	1.1	-	-	107.5	-5.0
1986	-	-	106.1	-1.3	-	-	108.9	2.6	-	-	105.6	-3.0	-	-	105.5	-0.1	-	-	112.7	6.8	-	-	111.2	-1.3
1987	-	-	-	-	-	-	-	-	-	-	121.3	9.1	-	-	-	-	-	-	-	-	-	-	123.4	1.7
1988	-	-	-	-	-	-	-	-	-	-	125.5	1.7	-	-	-	-	-	-	-	-	-	-	126.5	0.8
1989	-	-	-	-	-	-	-	-	-	-	135.4	7.0	-	-	-	-	-	-	-	-	-	-	133.0	-1.8
1990	-	-	-	-	-	-	-	-	-	-	134.6	1.2	-	-	-	-	-	-	-	-	-	-	128.3	-4.7
1991	-	-	-	-	-	-	-	-	-	-	148.4	15.7	-	-	-	-	-	-	-	-	-	-	139.2	-6.2
1992	-	-	-	-	-	-	-	-	-	-	155.7	11.9	-	-	-	-	-	-	-	-	-	-	141.2	-9.3
1993	-	-	-	-	-	-	-	-	-	-	148.9	5.5	-	-	-	-	-	-	-	-	-	-	157.2	5.6
1994	-	-	-	-	-	-	-	-	-	-	167.6	6.6	-	-	-	-	-	-	-	-	-	-	157.1	-6.3
1995	-	-	-	-	-	-	-	-	-	-	156.0	-0.7	-	-	-	-	-	-	-	-	-	-	142.7	-8.5
1996	-	-	-	-	-	-	-	-	-	-	142.3	-0.3	-	-	-	-	-	-	-	-	-	-	139.8	-1.8
1997	-	-	-	-	-	-	-	-	-	-	-	-	-	-	-	-	-	-	-	-	-	-	137.6	-1.6

[Continued]

Atlanta, GA
Consumer Price Index - Urban Wage Earners
Base 1982-1984 = 100
Apparel
[Continued]

For 1952-2001. Columns headed % show percentile change in the index from the previous period for which an index is available.

Year	Jan		Feb		Mar		Apr		May		Jun		Jul		Aug		Sep		Oct		Nov		Dec	
	Index	%	Index	%	Index	%	Index	%	Index	%	Index	%	Index	%	Index	%	Index	%	Index	%	Index	%	Index	%
1998	-	-	134.0	-2.6	-	-	136.2	1.6	-	-	133.4	-2.1	-	-	131.3	-1.6	-	-	135.8	3.4	-	-	123.9	-8.8
1999	-	-	124.8	0.7	-	-	128.9	3.3	-	-	123.6	-4.1	-	-	131.2	6.1	-	-	134.3	2.4	-	-	129.9	-3.3
2000	-	-	125.9	-3.1	-	-	135.0	7.2	-	-	129.2	-4.3	-	-	131.2	-1.0	-	-	129.2	1.0	-	-	129.9	-3.3
2001	-	-	129.1	2.8	-	-	130.3	0.9	-	-	119.9	-8.0	-	-	115.3	-3.8	-	-	125.2	8.6	-	-	118.8	-5.1

Source: U.S. Department of Labor, Bureau of Labor Statistics, Division of Consumer Prices and Price Indexes. - indicates no data collected for period.

Atlanta, GA
Consumer Price Index - All Urban Consumers
Base 1982-1984 = 100
Transportation

For 1947-2000. Columns headed % show percentile change in the index from the previous period for which an index is available.

Year	Jan Index	%	Feb Index	%	Mar Index	%	Apr Index	%	May Index	%	Jun Index	%	Jul Index	%	Aug Index	%	Sep Index	%	Oct Index	%	Nov Index	%	Dec Index	%
1947	-		-		20.0	-	-	-	-	-	20.2	1.0	-	-	20.4	1.0	-	-	-	-	21.0	2.9	-	-
1948	-		21.5	2.4	-	-	-	-	22.0	2.3	-	-	-	-	23.1	5.0	-	-	-	-	23.1	0.0	-	-
1949	-		23.5	1.7	-	-	-	-	24.1	2.6	-	-	-	-	24.4	1.2	-	-	-	-	24.4	0.0	-	-
1950	-		24.4	0.0	-	-	-	-	24.4	0.0	-	-	-	-	24.8	1.6	-	-	-	-	25.0	0.8	-	-
1951	-		24.9	-0.4	-	-	-	-	26.6	6.8	-	-	-	-	26.6	0.0	-	-	-	-	27.2	2.3	-	-
1952	-		27.7	1.8	-	-	-	-	27.7	0.0	-	-	-	-	28.0	1.1	-	-	-	-	29.2	4.3	-	-
1953	-		-		29.1	-0.3	-	-	-	-	28.8	-1.0	-	-	-	-	28.8	0.0	-	-	-	-	28.8	0.0
1954	-		-		28.4	-1.4	-	-	-	-	28.4	0.0	-	-	-	-	26.8	-5.6	-	-	-	-	28.0	4.5
1955	-		-		27.5	-1.8	-	-	-	-	27.7	0.7	-	-	-	-	27.2	-1.8	-	-	-	-	27.7	1.8
1956	-		-		27.7	0.0	-	-	-	-	27.7	0.0	-	-	-	-	28.7	3.6	-	-	-	-	29.1	1.4
1957	-		-		30.2	3.8	-	-	-	-	29.8	-1.3	-	-	-	-	29.5	-1.0	-	-	-	-	31.0	5.1
1958	-		-		31.2	0.6	-	-	-	-	31.1	-0.3	-	-	-	-	31.2	0.3	-	-	-	-	32.2	3.2
1959	-		-		32.3	0.3	-	-	-	-	31.9	-1.2	-	-	-	-	32.5	1.9	-	-	-	-	33.1	1.8
1960	-		-		32.2	-2.7	-	-	-	-	32.0	-0.6	-	-	-	-	31.8	-0.6	-	-	-	-	31.4	-1.3
1961	-		-		32.1	2.2	-	-	-	-	32.6	1.6	-	-	-	-	32.5	-0.3	-	-	-	-	32.9	1.2
1962	-		-		32.4	-1.5	-	-	-	-	33.0	1.9	-	-	-	-	33.4	1.2	-	-	-	-	33.8	1.2
1963	-		-		33.5	-0.9	-	-	-	-	33.8	0.9	-	-	-	-	33.4	-1.2	-	-	-	-	34.8	4.2
1964	-		-		34.6	-0.6	-	-	-	-	34.5	-0.3	-	-	-	-	34.7	0.6	-	-	-	-	35.0	0.9
1965	-		-		35.0	0.0	-	-	-	-	34.0	-2.9	-	-	-	-	34.5	1.5	-	-	-	-	34.8	0.9
1966	-		-		34.4	-1.1	-	-	-	-	34.5	0.3	-	-	-	-	34.6	0.3	-	-	-	-	34.7	0.3
1967	-		-		34.7	0.0	-	-	-	-	35.2	1.4	-	-	-	-	35.5	0.9	-	-	-	-	35.9	1.1
1968	-		-		35.9	0.0	-	-	-	-	36.1	0.6	-	-	-	-	36.0	-0.3	-	-	-	-	36.5	1.4
1969	-		-		37.3	2.2	-	-	-	-	37.3	0.0	-	-	-	-	37.1	-0.5	-	-	-	-	37.6	1.3
1970	-		-		37.2	-1.1	-	-	-	-	38.1	2.4	-	-	-	-	38.4	0.8	-	-	-	-	40.1	4.4
1971	-		-		40.3	0.5	-	-	-	-	41.2	2.2	-	-	-	-	40.4	-1.9	-	-	-	-	40.7	0.7
1972	-		-		39.2	-3.7	-	-	-	-	39.5	0.8	-	-	-	-	40.1	1.5	-	-	-	-	40.4	0.7
1973	-		-		40.4	0.0	-	-	-	-	41.3	2.2	-	-	-	-	41.1	-0.5	-	-	-	-	42.2	2.7
1974	-		-		44.2	4.7	-	-	-	-	47.0	6.3	-	-	-	-	48.5	3.2	-	-	-	-	48.5	0.0
1975	-		-		48.6	0.2	-	-	-	-	50.4	3.7	-	-	-	-	51.5	2.2	-	-	-	-	52.2	1.4
1976	-		-		52.4	0.4	-	-	-	-	54.4	3.8	-	-	-	-	55.5	2.0	-	-	-	-	56.0	0.9
1977	-		-		56.5	0.9	-	-	-	-	57.9	2.5	-	-	-	-	57.5	-0.7	-	-	-	-	58.0	0.9
1978	-		57.9	-0.2	-	-	58.1	0.3	-	-	59.5	2.4	-	-	60.3	1.3	-	-	61.3	1.7	-	-	61.8	0.8
1979	-		63.0	1.9	-	-	66.3	5.2	-	-	69.4	4.7	-	-	72.3	4.2	-	-	73.8	2.1	-	-	75.6	2.4
1980	-		80.4	6.3	-	-	83.4	3.7	-	-	84.0	0.7	-	-	87.3	3.9	-	-	88.2	1.0	-	-	89.3	1.2
1981	-		92.5	3.6	-	-	94.4	2.1	-	-	95.2	0.8	-	-	95.1	-0.1	-	-	97.0	2.0	-	-	97.5	0.5
1982	-		96.4	-1.1	-	-	94.4	-2.1	-	-	98.3	4.1	-	-	99.2	0.9	-	-	98.7	-0.5	-	-	98.6	-0.1
1983	-		96.4	-2.2	-	-	97.9	1.6	-	-	99.5	1.6	-	-	100.6	1.1	-	-	101.3	0.7	-	-	101.8	0.5
1984	-		101.6	-0.2	-	-	102.7	1.1	-	-	103.3	0.6	-	-	103.1	-0.2	-	-	103.9	0.8	-	-	104.0	0.1
1985	-		103.3	-0.7	-	-	106.1	2.7	-	-	106.6	0.5	-	-	107.5	0.8	-	-	108.2	0.7	-	-	109.7	1.4
1986	-		108.4	-1.2	-	-	101.5	-6.4	-	-	103.3	1.8	-	-	100.6	-2.6	-	-	100.1	-0.5	-	-	101.0	0.9
1987	-		-		-	-	-	-	-	-	102.8	1.8	-	-	-	-	-	-	-	-	-	-	104.7	
1988	-		-		-	-	-	-	-	-	104.5	-0.2	-	-	-	-	-	-	-	-	-	-	106.7	2.1
1989	-		-		-	-	-	-	-	-	110.7	3.7	-	-	-	-	-	-	-	-	-	-	111.2	0.5
1990	-		-		-	-	-	-	-	-	114.4	2.9	-	-	-	-	-	-	-	-	-	-	120.9	5.7
1991	-		-		-	-	-	-	-	-	119.0	-1.6	-	-	-	-	-	-	-	-	-	-	118.4	-0.5
1992	-		-		-	-	-	-	-	-	117.8	-0.5	-	-	-	-	-	-	-	-	-	-	121.2	2.9

[Continued]

Atlanta, GA
Consumer Price Index - All Urban Consumers
Base 1982-1984 = 100
Transportation

[Continued]

For 1947-2000. Columns headed % show percentile change in the index from the previous period for which an index is available.

Year	Jan Index	%	Feb Index	%	Mar Index	%	Apr Index	%	May Index	%	Jun Index	%	Jul Index	%	Aug Index	%	Sep Index	%	Oct Index	%	Nov Index	%	Dec Index	%
1993	-	-	-	-	-	-	-	-	-	-	123.1	1.6	-	-	-	-	-	-	-	-	-	-	-	-
1994	-	-	-	-	-	-	-	-	-	-	123.6	-1.4	-	-	-	-	-	-	-	-	-	-	125.3	1.8
1995	-	-	-	-	-	-	-	-	-	-	126.9	2.3	-	-	-	-	-	-	-	-	-	-	124.0	0.3
1996	-	-	-	-	-	-	-	-	-	-	133.6	3.3	-	-	-	-	-	-	-	-	-	-	129.3	1.9
1997	-	-	-	-	-	-	-	-	-	-	-	-	-	-	-	-	-	-	-	-	-	-	135.7	1.6
1998	-	-	127.9	-2.0	-	-	128.1	0.2	-	-	127.1	-0.8	-	-	126.5	-0.5	-	-	128.4	1.5	-	-	130.5	-3.8
1999	-	-	126.6	-1.1	-	-	129.3	2.1	-	-	129.5	0.2	-	-	130.2	0.5	-	-	133.1	2.2	-	-	128.0	-0.3
2000	-	-	134.4	-0.1	-	-	137.0	1.9	-	-	139.0	1.5	-	-	138.2	-0.6	-	-	139.4	0.9	-	-	134.5	1.1

Source: U.S. Department of Labor, Bureau of Labor Statistics, Division of Consumer Prices and Price Indexes. - indicates no data collected for period.

Atlanta, GA
Consumer Price Index - Urban Wage Earners
Base 1982-1984 = 100
Transportation

For 1947-2000. Columns headed % show percentile change in the index from the previous period for which an index is available.

Year	Jan Index	Jan %	Feb Index	Feb %	Mar Index	Mar %	Apr Index	Apr %	May Index	May %	Jun Index	Jun %	Jul Index	Jul %	Aug Index	Aug %	Sep Index	Sep %	Oct Index	Oct %	Nov Index	Nov %	Dec Index	Dec %
1947	-	-	-	-	19.5	-	-	-	-	-	19.6	0.5	-	-	19.9	1.5	-	-	-	-	20.4	2.5	-	-
1948	-	-	20.9	2.5	-	-	-	-	21.4	2.4	-	-	-	-	22.5	5.1	-	-	-	-	22.5	0.0	-	-
1949	-	-	22.9	1.8	-	-	-	-	23.5	2.6	-	-	-	-	23.8	1.3	-	-	-	-	23.8	0.0	-	-
1950	-	-	23.8	0.0	-	-	-	-	23.8	0.0	-	-	-	-	24.1	1.3	-	-	-	-	24.3	0.8	-	-
1951	-	-	24.3	0.0	-	-	-	-	25.9	6.6	-	-	-	-	25.9	0.0	-	-	-	-	26.5	2.3	-	-
1952	-	-	27.0	1.9	-	-	-	-	27.0	0.0	-	-	-	-	27.3	1.1	-	-	-	-	28.4	4.0	-	-
1953	-	-	-	-	28.3	-0.4	-	-	-	-	28.0	-1.1	-	-	-	-	28.0	0.0	-	-	-	-	28.0	0.0
1954	-	-	-	-	27.6	-1.4	-	-	-	-	27.6	0.0	-	-	-	-	26.0	-5.8	-	-	-	-	27.3	5.0
1955	-	-	-	-	26.8	-1.8	-	-	-	-	26.9	0.4	-	-	-	-	26.5	-1.5	-	-	-	-	27.0	1.9
1956	-	-	-	-	27.0	0.0	-	-	-	-	27.0	0.0	-	-	-	-	28.0	3.7	-	-	-	-	28.3	1.1
1957	-	-	-	-	29.4	3.9	-	-	-	-	29.0	-1.4	-	-	-	-	28.7	-1.0	-	-	-	-	30.2	5.2
1958	-	-	-	-	30.3	0.3	-	-	-	-	30.2	-0.3	-	-	-	-	30.4	0.7	-	-	-	-	31.3	3.0
1959	-	-	-	-	31.4	0.3	-	-	-	-	31.1	-1.0	-	-	-	-	31.6	1.6	-	-	-	-	32.2	1.9
1960	-	-	-	-	31.4	-2.5	-	-	-	-	31.2	-0.6	-	-	-	-	31.0	-0.6	-	-	-	-	30.6	-1.3
1961	-	-	-	-	31.3	2.3	-	-	-	-	31.7	1.3	-	-	-	-	31.7	0.0	-	-	-	-	32.0	0.9
1962	-	-	-	-	31.6	-1.2	-	-	-	-	32.1	1.6	-	-	-	-	32.5	1.2	-	-	-	-	32.9	1.2
1963	-	-	-	-	32.6	-0.9	-	-	-	-	32.9	0.9	-	-	-	-	32.5	-1.2	-	-	-	-	33.9	4.3
1964	-	-	-	-	33.7	-0.6	-	-	-	-	33.6	-0.3	-	-	-	-	33.8	0.6	-	-	-	-	34.1	0.9
1965	-	-	-	-	34.1	0.0	-	-	-	-	33.1	-2.9	-	-	-	-	33.6	1.5	-	-	-	-	33.9	0.9
1966	-	-	-	-	33.5	-1.2	-	-	-	-	33.6	0.3	-	-	-	-	33.7	0.3	-	-	-	-	33.8	0.3
1967	-	-	-	-	33.8	0.0	-	-	-	-	34.3	1.5	-	-	-	-	34.6	0.9	-	-	-	-	35.0	1.2
1968	-	-	-	-	34.9	-0.3	-	-	-	-	35.2	0.9	-	-	-	-	35.1	-0.3	-	-	-	-	35.5	1.1
1969	-	-	-	-	36.3	2.3	-	-	-	-	36.3	0.0	-	-	-	-	36.1	-0.6	-	-	-	-	36.6	1.4
1970	-	-	-	-	36.2	-1.1	-	-	-	-	37.1	2.5	-	-	-	-	37.4	0.8	-	-	-	-	39.0	4.3
1971	-	-	-	-	39.2	0.5	-	-	-	-	40.1	2.3	-	-	-	-	39.4	-1.7	-	-	-	-	39.7	0.8
1972	-	-	-	-	38.2	-3.8	-	-	-	-	38.5	0.8	-	-	-	-	39.0	1.3	-	-	-	-	39.3	0.8
1973	-	-	-	-	39.3	0.0	-	-	-	-	40.2	2.3	-	-	-	-	40.0	-0.5	-	-	-	-	41.1	2.8
1974	-	-	-	-	43.1	4.9	-	-	-	-	45.7	6.0	-	-	-	-	47.2	3.3	-	-	-	-	47.2	0.0
1975	-	-	-	-	47.3	0.2	-	-	-	-	49.1	3.8	-	-	-	-	50.1	2.0	-	-	-	-	50.8	1.4
1976	-	-	-	-	51.0	0.4	-	-	-	-	53.0	3.9	-	-	-	-	54.0	1.9	-	-	-	-	54.5	0.9
1977	-	-	-	-	55.0	0.9	-	-	-	-	56.3	2.4	-	-	-	-	56.0	-0.5	-	-	-	-	56.5	0.9
1978	-	-	56.6	0.2	-	-	56.8	0.4	-	-	58.0	2.1	-	-	58.9	1.6	-	-	59.9	1.7	-	-	60.5	1.0
1979	-	-	61.8	2.1	-	-	65.5	6.0	-	-	68.5	4.6	-	-	71.6	4.5	-	-	74.3	3.8	-	-	76.5	3.0
1980	-	-	81.0	5.9	-	-	84.5	4.3	-	-	84.7	0.2	-	-	89.3	5.4	-	-	89.9	0.7	-	-	90.8	1.0
1981	-	-	94.5	4.1	-	-	95.7	1.3	-	-	96.0	0.3	-	-	95.9	-0.1	-	-	97.5	1.7	-	-	98.5	1.0
1982	-	-	97.5	-1.0	-	-	95.1	-2.5	-	-	99.0	4.1	-	-	99.8	0.8	-	-	99.1	-0.7	-	-	98.9	-0.2
1983	-	-	96.5	-2.4	-	-	98.1	1.7	-	-	99.7	1.6	-	-	100.6	0.9	-	-	101.1	0.5	-	-	101.4	0.3
1984	-	-	101.2	-0.2	-	-	102.2	1.0	-	-	102.6	0.4	-	-	102.3	-0.3	-	-	103.0	0.7	-	-	103.1	0.1
1985	-	-	102.3	-0.8	-	-	105.2	2.8	-	-	105.9	0.7	-	-	107.1	1.1	-	-	107.7	0.6	-	-	109.4	1.6
1986	-	-	108.1	-1.2	-	-	100.6	-6.9	-	-	102.5	1.9	-	-	99.6	-2.8	-	-	98.7	-0.9	-	-	99.6	0.9
1987	-	-	-	-	-	-	-	-	-	-	101.5	1.9	-	-	-	-	-	-	-	-	-	-	103.8	2.3
1988	-	-	-	-	-	-	-	-	-	-	103.5	-0.3	-	-	-	-	-	-	-	-	-	-	105.6	2.0
1989	-	-	-	-	-	-	-	-	-	-	109.6	3.8	-	-	-	-	-	-	-	-	-	-	109.7	0.1
1990	-	-	-	-	-	-	-	-	-	-	112.6	2.6	-	-	-	-	-	-	-	-	-	-	118.9	5.6
1991	-	-	-	-	-	-	-	-	-	-	116.9	-1.7	-	-	-	-	-	-	-	-	-	-	116.5	-0.3
1992	-	-	-	-	-	-	-	-	-	-	115.8	-0.6	-	-	-	-	-	-	-	-	-	-	119.1	2.8

[Continued]

Atlanta, GA
Consumer Price Index - Urban Wage Earners
Base 1982-1984 = 100
Transportation

[Continued]

For 1947-2000. Columns headed % show percentile change in the index from the previous period for which an index is available.

Year	Jan Index	%	Feb Index	%	Mar Index	%	Apr Index	%	May Index	%	Jun Index	%	Jul Index	%	Aug Index	%	Sep Index	%	Oct Index	%	Nov Index	%	Dec Index	%
1993	-		-		-		-		-		120.9	1.5	-		-		-		-		-		123.2	1.9
1994	-		-		-		-		-		121.0	-1.8	-		-		-		-		-		122.2	1.0
1995	-		-		-		-		-		124.8	2.1	-		-		-		-		-		127.0	1.8
1996	-		-		-		-		-		131.3	3.4					-		-		-		133.4	1.6
1997	-		-		-		-										-		-		-		128.2	-3.9
1998	-		125.7	-2.0	-		125.9	0.2	-		125.4	-0.4	-		124.6	-0.6	-		126.5	1.5	-		126.1	-0.3
1999	-		124.2	-1.5	-		127.2	2.4	-		127.7	0.4	-		129.2	1.2	-		131.9	2.1	-		133.2	1.0
2000	-		133.1	-0.1	-		136.0	2.2	-		138.2	1.6	-		137.1	-0.8	-		138.6	1.1	-		137.3	-0.9

Source: U.S. Department of Labor, Bureau of Labor Statistics, Division of Consumer Prices and Price Indexes. - indicates no data collected for period.

Atlanta, GA
Consumer Price Index - All Urban Consumers
Base 1982-1984 = 100
Medical Care

For 1947-2001. Columns headed % show percentile change in the index from the previous period for which an index is available.

Year	Jan Index	%	Feb Index	%	Mar Index	%	Apr Index	%	May Index	%	Jun Index	%	Jul Index	%	Aug Index	%	Sep Index	%	Oct Index	%	Nov Index	%	Dec Index	%
1947	-	-	-	-	15.1	-	-	-	-	-	15.1	0.0	-	-	15.3	1.3	-	-	-	-	15.3	0.0	-	-
1948	-	-	15.5	1.3	-	-	-	-	15.6	0.6	-	-	-	-	15.8	1.3	-	-	-	-	16.0	1.3	-	-
1949	-	-	16.1	0.6	-	-	-	-	16.1	0.0	-	-	-	-	16.1	0.0	-	-	-	-	16.1	0.0	-	-
1950	-	-	16.1	0.0	-	-	-	-	16.1	0.0	-	-	-	-	16.1	0.0	-	-	-	-	16.3	1.2	-	-
1951	-	-	16.6	1.8	-	-	-	-	17.0	2.4	-	-	-	-	17.0	0.0	-	-	-	-	17.1	0.6	-	-
1952	-	-	17.5	2.3	-	-	-	-	18.2	4.0	-	-	-	-	18.2	0.0	-	-	-	-	18.5	1.6	-	-
1953	-	-	-	-	18.5	0.0	-	-	-	-	18.6	0.5	-	-	-	-	18.4	-1.1	-	-	-	-	18.7	1.6
1954	-	-	-	-	18.9	1.1	-	-	-	-	18.9	0.0	-	-	-	-	19.0	0.5	-	-	-	-	19.0	0.0
1955	-	-	-	-	19.2	1.1	-	-	-	-	19.2	0.0	-	-	-	-	20.0	4.2	-	-	-	-	20.1	0.5
1956	-	-	-	-	20.1	0.0	-	-	-	-	20.3	1.0	-	-	-	-	20.2	-0.5	-	-	-	-	20.3	0.5
1957	-	-	-	-	20.7	2.0	-	-	-	-	20.7	0.0	-	-	-	-	20.8	0.5	-	-	-	-	20.9	0.5
1958	-	-	-	-	21.3	1.9	-	-	-	-	21.4	0.5	-	-	-	-	21.4	0.0	-	-	-	-	21.6	0.9
1959	-	-	-	-	21.6	0.0	-	-	-	-	22.6	4.6	-	-	-	-	22.6	0.0	-	-	-	-	22.8	0.9
1960	-	-	-	-	23.0	0.9	-	-	-	-	23.0	0.0	-	-	-	-	23.0	0.0	-	-	-	-	22.8	-0.9
1961	-	-	-	-	22.8	0.0	-	-	-	-	23.0	0.9	-	-	-	-	23.4	1.7	-	-	-	-	23.6	0.9
1962	-	-	-	-	23.8	0.8	-	-	-	-	23.9	0.4	-	-	-	-	23.9	0.0	-	-	-	-	23.9	0.0
1963	-	-	-	-	23.9	0.0	-	-	-	-	24.4	2.1	-	-	-	-	24.4	0.0	-	-	-	-	24.4	0.0
1964	-	-	-	-	24.6	0.8	-	-	-	-	24.7	0.4	-	-	-	-	25.0	1.2	-	-	-	-	25.1	0.4
1965	-	-	-	-	25.3	0.8	-	-	-	-	25.3	0.0	-	-	-	-	25.5	0.8	-	-	-	-	25.6	0.4
1966	-	-	-	-	26.1	2.0	-	-	-	-	26.6	1.9	-	-	-	-	27.3	2.6	-	-	-	-	27.4	0.4
1967	-	-	-	-	28.1	2.6	-	-	-	-	28.3	0.7	-	-	-	-	28.8	1.8	-	-	-	-	28.9	0.3
1968	-	-	-	-	29.7	2.8	-	-	-	-	30.0	1.0	-	-	-	-	30.8	2.7	-	-	-	-	31.4	1.9
1969	-	-	-	-	32.7	4.1	-	-	-	-	33.3	1.8	-	-	-	-	34.0	2.1	-	-	-	-	34.2	0.6
1970	-	-	-	-	35.1	2.6	-	-	-	-	35.9	2.3	-	-	-	-	36.2	0.8	-	-	-	-	36.9	1.9
1971	-	-	-	-	38.3	3.8	-	-	-	-	38.8	1.3	-	-	-	-	39.1	0.8	-	-	-	-	38.9	-0.5
1972	-	-	-	-	39.2	0.8	-	-	-	-	39.8	1.5	-	-	-	-	39.8	0.0	-	-	-	-	40.1	0.8
1973	-	-	-	-	40.4	0.7	-	-	-	-	41.5	2.7	-	-	-	-	42.3	1.9	-	-	-	-	42.9	1.4
1974	-	-	-	-	43.9	2.3	-	-	-	-	46.4	5.7	-	-	-	-	47.6	2.6	-	-	-	-	48.3	1.5
1975	-	-	-	-	51.3	6.2	-	-	-	-	51.8	1.0	-	-	-	-	53.5	3.3	-	-	-	-	53.7	0.4
1976	-	-	-	-	55.0	2.4	-	-	-	-	55.3	0.5	-	-	-	-	57.0	3.1	-	-	-	-	58.0	1.8
1977	-	-	-	-	59.9	3.3	-	-	-	-	60.9	1.7	-	-	-	-	61.7	1.3	-	-	-	-	61.7	0.0
1978	-	-	62.9	1.9	-	-	63.3	0.6	-	-	63.8	0.8	-	-	64.3	0.8	-	-	64.7	0.6	-	-	64.6	-0.2
1979	-	-	65.9	2.0	-	-	67.2	2.0	-	-	68.0	1.2	-	-	68.8	1.2	-	-	69.4	0.9	-	-	70.5	1.6
1980	-	-	71.5	1.4	-	-	72.1	0.8	-	-	75.0	4.0	-	-	76.4	1.9	-	-	77.0	0.8	-	-	78.3	1.7
1981	-	-	80.6	2.9	-	-	80.9	0.4	-	-	81.6	0.9	-	-	82.9	1.6	-	-	84.9	2.4	-	-	84.5	-0.5
1982	-	-	85.2	0.8	-	-	87.0	2.1	-	-	92.7	6.6	-	-	95.7	3.2	-	-	99.2	3.7	-	-	100.0	0.8
1983	-	-	100.9	0.9	-	-	101.1	0.2	-	-	101.2	0.1	-	-	101.1	-0.1	-	-	101.5	0.4	-	-	101.8	0.3
1984	-	-	103.5	1.7	-	-	104.6	1.1	-	-	106.0	1.3	-	-	107.3	1.2	-	-	108.8	1.4	-	-	109.0	0.2
1985	-	-	110.9	1.7	-	-	111.6	0.6	-	-	113.1	1.3	-	-	113.5	0.4	-	-	115.0	1.3	-	-	114.7	-0.3
1986	-	-	120.4	5.0	-	-	120.9	0.4	-	-	123.2	1.9	-	-	125.3	1.7	-	-	127.2	1.5	-	-	128.6	1.1
1987	-	-	-	-	-	-	-	-	-	-	133.4	3.7	-	-	-	-	-	-	-	-	-	-	139.5	4.6
1988	-	-	-	-	-	-	-	-	-	-	143.8	3.1	-	-	-	-	-	-	-	-	-	-	156.5	8.8
1989	-	-	-	-	-	-	-	-	-	-	162.4	3.8	-	-	-	-	-	-	-	-	-	-	169.1	4.1
1990	-	-	-	-	-	-	-	-	-	-	174.7	3.3	-	-	-	-	-	-	-	-	-	-	180.4	3.3
1991	-	-	-	-	-	-	-	-	-	-	187.8	4.1	-	-	-	-	-	-	-	-	-	-	195.5	4.1
1992	-	-	-	-	-	-	-	-	-	-	202.1	3.4	-	-	-	-	-	-	-	-	-	-	203.3	0.6

[Continued]

Atlanta, GA
Consumer Price Index - All Urban Consumers
Base 1982-1984 = 100
Medical Care
[Continued]

For 1947-2001. Columns headed % show percentile change in the index from the previous period for which an index is available.

Year	Jan Index	%	Feb Index	%	Mar Index	%	Apr Index	%	May Index	%	Jun Index	%	Jul Index	%	Aug Index	%	Sep Index	%	Oct Index	%	Nov Index	%	Dec Index	%
1993	-	-	-	-	-	-	-	-	-	-	210.9	3.7	-	-	-	-	-	-	-	-	-	-	-	-
1994	-	-	-	-	-	-	-	-	-	-	223.3	3.8	-	-	-	-	-	-	-	-	-	-	215.1	2.0
1995	-	-	-	-	-	-	-	-	-	-	234.1	1.5	-	-	-	-	-	-	-	-	-	-	230.7	3.3
1996	-	-	-	-	-	-	-	-	-	-	239.7	0.8	-	-	-	-	-	-	-	-	-	-	237.9	1.6
1997	-	-	-	-	-	-	-	-	-	-	-	-	-	-	-	-	-	-	-	-	-	-	241.7	0.8
1998	-	-	244.3	0.1	-	-	244.0	-0.1	-	-	243.8	-0.1	-	-	245.3	0.6	-	-	246.1	0.3	-	-	244.1	1.0
1999	-	-	248.7	0.7	-	-	251.4	1.1	-	-	251.7	0.1	-	-	257.6	2.3	-	-	258.2	0.2	-	-	247.0	0.4
2000	-	-	260.9	0.5	-	-	261.2	0.1	-	-	262.0	0.3	-	-	266.8	1.8	-	-	266.8	0.0	-	-	259.6	0.5
2001	-	-	275.3	2.0	-	-	277.2	0.7	-	-	278.0	0.3	-	-	276.9	-0.4	-	-	279.2	0.8	-	-	275.1	-1.5

Source: U.S. Department of Labor, Bureau of Labor Statistics, Division of Consumer Prices and Price Indexes. - indicates no data collected for period.

Atlanta, GA
Consumer Price Index - Urban Wage Earners
Base 1982-1984 = 100
Medical Care

For 1947-2001. Columns headed % show percentile change in the index from the previous period for which an index is available.

Year	Jan Index	%	Feb Index	%	Mar Index	%	Apr Index	%	May Index	%	Jun Index	%	Jul Index	%	Aug Index	%	Sep Index	%	Oct Index	%	Nov Index	%	Dec Index	%
1947	-		-		14.6	-	-		-		14.6	0.0	-		14.7	0.7	-		-		14.7	0.0	-	
1948	-		14.9	1.4	-		-		15.0	0.7	-		-		15.2	1.3	-		-		15.4	1.3	-	
1949	-		15.5	0.6	-		-		15.5	0.0	-		-		15.5	0.0	-		-		15.5	0.0	-	
1950	-		15.5	0.0	-		-		15.5	0.0	-		-		15.5	0.0	-		-		15.6	0.6	-	
1951	-		16.0	2.6	-		-		16.4	2.5	-		-		16.3	-0.6	-		-		16.4	0.6	-	
1952	-		16.8	2.4	-		-		17.6	4.8	-		-		17.5	-0.6	-		-		17.8	1.7	-	
1953	-		-		17.8	0.0	-		-		17.9	0.6	-		-		17.7	-1.1	-		-		18.0	1.7
1954	-		-		18.2	1.1	-		-		18.2	0.0	-		-		18.2	0.0	-		-		18.3	0.5
1955	-		-		18.5	1.1	-		-		18.5	0.0	-		-		19.2	3.8	-		-		19.4	1.0
1956	-		-		19.4	0.0	-		-		19.6	1.0	-		-		19.5	-0.5	-		-		19.6	0.5
1957	-		-		19.9	1.5	-		-		19.9	0.0	-		-		20.0	0.5	-		-		20.1	0.5
1958	-		-		20.5	2.0	-		-		20.6	0.5	-		-		20.6	0.0	-		-		20.8	1.0
1959	-		-		20.8	0.0	-		-		21.8	4.8	-		-		21.8	0.0	-		-		22.0	0.9
1960	-		-		22.1	0.5	-		-		22.1	0.0	-		-		22.2	0.5	-		-		21.9	-1.4
1961	-		-		21.9	0.0	-		-		22.2	1.4	-		-		22.6	1.8	-		-		22.7	0.4
1962	-		-		22.9	0.9	-		-		23.0	0.4	-		-		23.0	0.0	-		-		23.0	0.0
1963	-		-		23.0	0.0	-		-		23.5	2.2	-		-		23.5	0.0	-		-		23.5	0.0
1964	-		-		23.7	0.9	-		-		23.7	0.0	-		-		24.1	1.7	-		-		24.1	0.0
1965	-		-		24.3	0.8	-		-		24.4	0.4	-		-		24.5	0.4	-		-		24.6	0.4
1966	-		-		25.2	2.4	-		-		25.6	1.6	-		-		26.2	2.3	-		-		26.3	0.4
1967	-		-		27.0	2.7	-		-		27.2	0.7	-		-		27.7	1.8	-		-		27.9	0.7
1968	-		-		28.6	2.5	-		-		28.8	0.7	-		-		29.6	2.8	-		-		30.2	2.0
1969	-		-		31.5	4.3	-		-		32.0	1.6	-		-		32.7	2.2	-		-		32.9	0.6
1970	-		-		33.8	2.7	-		-		34.5	2.1	-		-		34.8	0.9	-		-		35.6	2.3
1971	-		-		36.9	3.7	-		-		37.3	1.1	-		-		37.6	0.8	-		-		37.5	-0.3
1972	-		-		37.7	0.5	-		-		38.3	1.6	-		-		38.3	0.0	-		-		38.6	0.8
1973	-		-		38.8	0.5	-		-		40.0	3.1	-		-		40.7	1.7	-		-		41.3	1.5
1974	-		-		42.2	2.2	-		-		44.6	5.7	-		-		45.8	2.7	-		-		46.5	1.5
1975	-		-		49.4	6.2	-		-		49.8	0.8	-		-		51.5	3.4	-		-		51.7	0.4
1976	-		-		52.9	2.3	-		-		53.2	0.6	-		-		54.8	3.0	-		-		55.8	1.8
1977	-		-		57.7	3.4	-		-		58.6	1.6	-		-		59.3	1.2	-		-		59.3	0.0
1978	-		60.4	1.9	-		61.8	2.3	-		62.3	0.8	-		63.1	1.3	-		63.6	0.8	-		64.4	1.3
1979	-		66.0	2.5	-		67.1	1.7	-		68.2	1.6	-		69.3	1.6	-		69.6	0.4	-		70.0	0.6
1980	-		70.7	1.0	-		70.8	0.1	-		72.3	2.1	-		74.1	2.5	-		75.0	1.2	-		76.5	2.0
1981	-		80.6	5.4	-		80.8	0.2	-		81.0	0.2	-		82.2	1.5	-		83.9	2.1	-		84.1	0.2
1982	-		84.8	0.8	-		86.6	2.1	-		92.7	7.0	-		95.5	3.0	-		99.2	3.9	-		100.0	0.8
1983	-		101.0	1.0	-		101.2	0.2	-		101.2	0.0	-		101.3	0.1	-		101.7	0.4	-		102.0	0.3
1984	-		103.6	1.6	-		104.7	1.1	-		106.0	1.2	-		107.3	1.2	-		108.7	1.3	-		109.0	0.3
1985	-		111.0	1.8	-		111.6	0.5	-		113.2	1.4	-		113.7	0.4	-		115.1	1.2	-		114.6	-0.4
1986	-		120.6	5.2	-		121.1	0.4	-		123.6	2.1	-		125.8	1.8	-		127.6	1.4	-		128.8	0.9
1987	-		-		-		-		-		133.5	3.6	-		-		-		-		-		139.8	4.7
1988	-		-		-		-		-		144.1	3.1	-		-		-		-		-		156.7	8.7
1989	-		-		-		-		-		162.3	3.6	-		-		-		-		-		168.8	4.0
1990	-		-		-		-		-		174.0	3.1	-		-		-		-		-		180.2	3.6
1991	-		-		-		-		-		187.6	4.1	-		-		-		-		-		195.2	4.1
1992	-		-		-		-		-		202.0	3.5	-		-		-		-		-		202.7	0.3

[Continued]

Atlanta, GA
Consumer Price Index - Urban Wage Earners
Base 1982-1984 = 100
Medical Care
[Continued]

For 1947-2001. Columns headed % show percentile change in the index from the previous period for which an index is available.

Year	Jan Index	%	Feb Index	%	Mar Index	%	Apr Index	%	May Index	%	Jun Index	%	Jul Index	%	Aug Index	%	Sep Index	%	Oct Index	%	Nov Index	%	Dec Index	%
1993	-		-		-		-		-		210.2	3.7	-		-		-		-		-		214.3	2.0
1994	-		-		-		-		-		222.1	3.6	-		-		-		-		-		229.5	3.3
1995	-		-		-		-		-		232.5	1.3	-		-		-		-		-		236.0	1.5
1996	-		-		-		-		-		237.4	0.6	-		-		-		-		-		239.6	0.9
1997	-		-		-		-		-		-		-		-		-		-		-		241.9	1.0
1998	-		241.9	0.0	-		241.0	-0.4	-		240.9	-0.0	-		241.9	0.4	-		242.6	0.3	-		243.5	0.4
1999	-		244.7	0.5	-		248.0	1.3	-		248.2	0.1	-		253.9	2.3	-		254.6	0.3	-		255.3	0.3
2000	-		256.7	0.5	-		257.0	0.1	-		257.8	0.3	-		262.5	1.8	-		262.6	0.0	-		265.4	1.1
2001	-		269.4	1.5	-		270.8	0.5	-		271.6	0.3	-		270.7	-0.3	-		271.2	0.2	-		267.3	-1.4

Source: U.S. Department of Labor, Bureau of Labor Statistics, Division of Consumer Prices and Price Indexes. - indicates no data collected for period.

Atlanta, GA
Consumer Price Index - All Urban Consumers
Base December 1997 = 100
Recreation

For 1997-2001. Columns headed % show percentile change in the index from the previous period for which an index is available.

Year	Jan Index	%	Feb Index	%	Mar Index	%	Apr Index	%	May Index	%	Jun Index	%	Jul Index	%	Aug Index	%	Sep Index	%	Oct Index	%	Nov Index	%	Dec Index	%
1997	-	-	-	-	-	-	-	-	-	-	-	-	-	-	-	-	-	-	-	-	-	-	100.0	-
1998	-	-	100.5	0.5	-	-	103.4	2.9	-	-	98.5	-4.7	-	-	99.2	0.7	-	-	99.4	0.2	-	-	100.9	1.5
1999	-	-	99.5	-1.4	-	-	101.7	2.2	-	-	101.1	-0.6	-	-	102.1	1.0	-	-	102.2	0.1	-	-	103.1	0.9
2000	-	-	103.2	0.1	-	-	103.5	0.3	-	-	104.3	0.8	-	-	104.0	-0.3	-	-	103.4	-0.6	-	-	103.2	-0.2
2001	-	-	105.5	2.2	-	-	107.9	2.3	-	-	105.4	-2.3	-	-	107.6	2.1	-	-	107.6	0.0	-	-	106.1	-1.4

Source: U.S. Department of Labor, Bureau of Labor Statistics, Division of Consumer Prices and Price Indexes. - indicates no data collected for period.

Atlanta, GA
Consumer Price Index - Urban Wage Earners
Base December 1997 = 100
Recreation

For 1997-2001. Columns headed % show percentile change in the index from the previous period for which an index is available.

Year	Jan Index	%	Feb Index	%	Mar Index	%	Apr Index	%	May Index	%	Jun Index	%	Jul Index	%	Aug Index	%	Sep Index	%	Oct Index	%	Nov Index	%	Dec Index	%
1997	-	-	-	-	-	-	-	-	-	-	-	-	-	-	-	-	-	-	-	-	-	-	100.0	-
1998	-	-	100.6	0.6	-	-	102.3	1.7	-	-	97.2	-5.0	-	-	97.7	0.5	-	-	97.4	-0.3	-	-	97.9	0.5
1999	-	-	96.9	-1.0	-	-	97.9	1.0	-	-	97.2	-0.7	-	-	98.5	1.3	-	-	98.3	-0.2	-	-	99.2	0.9
2000	-	-	99.3	0.1	-	-	99.6	0.3	-	-	100.0	0.4	-	-	99.5	-0.5	-	-	99.5	0.0	-	-	98.9	-0.6
2001	-	-	101.6	2.7	-	-	103.0	1.4	-	-	100.7	-2.2	-	-	102.1	1.4	-	-	102.1	0.0	-	-	101.8	-0.3

Source: U.S. Department of Labor, Bureau of Labor Statistics, Division of Consumer Prices and Price Indexes. - indicates no data collected for period.

Atlanta, GA
Consumer Price Index - All Urban Consumers
Base December 1997 = 100
Education & Communication

For 1997-2001. Columns headed % show percentile change in the index from the previous period for which an index is available.

Year	Jan Index	%	Feb Index	%	Mar Index	%	Apr Index	%	May Index	%	Jun Index	%	Jul Index	%	Aug Index	%	Sep Index	%	Oct Index	%	Nov Index	%	Dec Index	%
1997	-	-	-	-	-	-	-	-	-	-	-	-	-	-	-	-	-	-	-	-	-	-	100.0	-
1998	-	-	100.4	0.4	-	-	100.2	-0.2	-	-	99.7	-0.5	-	-	99.9	0.2	-	-	101.7	1.8	-	-	100.6	-1.1
1999	-	-	101.3	0.7	-	-	101.2	-0.1	-	-	100.5	-0.7	-	-	100.4	-0.1	-	-	102.9	2.5	-	-	103.7	0.8
2000	-	-	103.9	0.2	-	-	102.7	-1.2	-	-	102.3	-0.4	-	-	103.9	1.6	-	-	105.5	1.5	-	-	105.1	-0.4
2001	-	-	106.1	1.0	-	-	105.9	-0.2	-	-	105.6	-0.3	-	-	108.8	3.0	-	-	108.8	0.0	-	-	108.9	0.1

Source: U.S. Department of Labor, Bureau of Labor Statistics, Division of Consumer Prices and Price Indexes. - indicates no data collected for period.

Atlanta, GA
Consumer Price Index - Urban Wage Earners
Base December 1997 = 100
Education & Communication

For 1997-2001. Columns headed % show percentile change in the index from the previous period for which an index is available.

Year	Jan		Feb		Mar		Apr		May		Jun		Jul		Aug		Sep		Oct		Nov		Dec	
	Index	%	Index	%	Index	%	Index	%	Index	%	Index	%	Index	%	Index	%	Index	%	Index	%	Index	%	Index	%
1997	-	-	-	-	-	-	-	-	-	-	-	-	-	-	-	-	-	-	-	-	-	-	-	-
1998	-	-	100.7	0.7	-	-	100.5	-0.2	-	-	100.0	-0.5	-	-	100.2	0.2	-	-	102.0	1.8	-	-	100.0	-
1999	-	-	101.8	0.8	-	-	101.8	0.0	-	-	101.2	-0.6	-	-	100.7	-0.5	-	-	103.0	2.3	-	-	101.0	-1.0
2000	-	-	104.1	0.3	-	-	102.5	-1.5	-	-	102.1	-0.4	-	-	103.2	1.1	-	-	105.0	1.7	-	-	103.8	0.8
2001	-	-	105.8	1.1	-	-	105.6	-0.2	-	-	105.3	-0.3	-	-	108.3	2.8	-	-	108.3	0.0	-	-	104.7	-0.3

Source: U.S. Department of Labor, Bureau of Labor Statistics, Division of Consumer Prices and Price Indexes. - indicates no data collected for period.

279

Boston-Brockton-Nashua, MA-NH-ME-CT
Consumer Price Index - All Urban Consumers
Base 1982-1984 = 100
Annual Averages

For 1914-2001. Columns headed % show percentile change in the index from the previous period for which an index is available.

Year	All Items		Food & Beverage		Housing		Apparel		Trans-portation		Medical Care		Recrea-tion*		Education & Communic.*		Other Goods & Services	
	Index	%	Index	%	Index	%	Index	%	Index	%	Index	%	Index	%	Index	%	Index	%
1914	-	-	-	-	-	-	-	-	-	-	-	-	-	-	-	-	-	-
1915	10.5	-	-	-	-	-	-	-	-	-	-	-	-	-	-	-	-	-
1916	11.3	7.6	-	-	-	-	-	-	-	-	-	-	-	-	-	-	-	-
1917	13.3	17.7	-	-	-	-	-	-	-	-	-	-	-	-	-	-	-	-
1918	15.7	18.0	-	-	-	-	-	-	-	-	-	-	-	-	-	-	-	-
1919	18.0	14.6	-	-	-	-	-	-	-	-	-	-	-	-	-	-	-	-
1920	20.6	14.4	-	-	-	-	-	-	-	-	-	-	-	-	-	-	-	-
1921	18.3	-11.2	-	-	-	-	-	-	-	-	-	-	-	-	-	-	-	-
1922	17.0	-7.1	-	-	-	-	-	-	-	-	-	-	-	-	-	-	-	-
1923	17.4	2.4	-	-	-	-	-	-	-	-	-	-	-	-	-	-	-	-
1924	17.4	0.0	-	-	-	-	-	-	-	-	-	-	-	-	-	-	-	-
1925	17.9	2.9	-	-	-	-	-	-	-	-	-	-	-	-	-	-	-	-
1926	18.2	1.7	-	-	-	-	-	-	-	-	-	-	-	-	-	-	-	-
1927	17.9	-1.6	-	-	-	-	-	-	-	-	-	-	-	-	-	-	-	-
1928	17.7	-1.1	-	-	-	-	-	-	-	-	-	-	-	-	-	-	-	-
1929	17.8	0.6	-	-	-	-	-	-	-	-	-	-	-	-	-	-	-	-
1930	17.3	-2.8	-	-	-	-	-	-	-	-	-	-	-	-	-	-	-	-
1931	15.8	-8.7	-	-	-	-	-	-	-	-	-	-	-	-	-	-	-	-
1932	14.2	-10.1	-	-	-	-	-	-	-	-	-	-	-	-	-	-	-	-
1933	13.6	-4.2	-	-	-	-	-	-	-	-	-	-	-	-	-	-	-	-
1934	14.1	3.7	-	-	-	-	-	-	-	-	-	-	-	-	-	-	-	-
1935	14.3	1.4	-	-	-	-	-	-	-	-	-	-	-	-	-	-	-	-
1936	14.3	0.0	-	-	-	-	-	-	-	-	-	-	-	-	-	-	-	-
1937	14.8	3.5	-	-	-	-	-	-	-	-	-	-	-	-	-	-	-	-
1938	14.3	-3.4	-	-	-	-	-	-	-	-	-	-	-	-	-	-	-	-
1939	14.1	-1.4	-	-	-	-	-	-	-	-	-	-	-	-	-	-	-	-
1940	14.3	1.4	-	-	-	-	-	-	-	-	-	-	-	-	-	-	-	-
1941	14.9	4.2	-	-	-	-	-	-	-	-	-	-	-	-	-	-	-	-
1942	16.5	10.7	-	-	-	-	-	-	-	-	-	-	-	-	-	-	-	-
1943	17.4	5.5	-	-	-	-	-	-	-	-	-	-	-	-	-	-	-	-
1944	17.6	1.1	-	-	-	-	-	-	-	-	-	-	-	-	-	-	-	-
1945	17.9	1.7	-	-	-	-	-	-	-	-	-	-	-	-	-	-	-	-
1946	19.4	8.4	-	-	-	-	-	-	-	-	-	-	-	-	-	-	-	-
1947	22.1	13.9	-	-	-	-	-	-	16.4	-	13.4	-	-	-	-	-	-	-
1948	23.9	8.1	-	-	-	-	-	-	16.9	3.0	14.3	6.7	-	-	-	-	-	-
1949	23.6	-1.3	-	-	-	-	-	-	18.6	10.1	15.1	5.6	-	-	-	-	-	-
1950	23.9	1.3	-	-	-	-	-	-	20.6	10.8	15.7	4.0	-	-	-	-	-	-
1951	25.5	6.7	-	-	-	-	-	-	21.2	2.9	16.3	3.8	-	-	-	-	-	-
1952	26.0	2.0	-	-	-	-	-	-	22.6	6.6	17.2	5.5	-	-	-	-	-	-
1953	26.1	0.4	-	-	-	-	39.4	-	23.5	4.0	17.6	2.3	-	-	-	-	-	-
1954	26.3	0.8	-	-	-	-	39.1	-0.8	23.6	0.4	17.7	0.6	-	-	-	-	-	-
1955	26.4	0.4	-	-	-	-	39.2	0.3	23.2	-1.7	17.9	1.1	-	-	-	-	-	-
1956	27.1	2.7	-	-	-	-	39.8	1.5	24.0	3.4	19.0	6.1	-	-	-	-	-	-
1957	28.1	3.7	-	-	-	-	40.5	1.8	25.0	4.2	20.8	9.5	-	-	-	-	-	-
1958	28.9	2.8	-	-	-	-	41.1	1.5	25.8	3.2	22.2	6.7	-	-	-	-	-	-

[Continued]

Boston-Brockton-Nashua, MA-NH-ME-CT
Consumer Price Index - All Urban Consumers
Base 1982-1984 = 100
Annual Averages
[Continued]

For 1914-2001. Columns headed % show percentile change in the index from the previous period for which an index is available.

Year	All Items		Food & Beverage		Housing		Apparel		Trans- portation		Medical Care		Recrea- tion*		Education & Communic.*		Other Goods & Services	
	Index	%	Index	%	Index	%	Index	%	Index	%	Index	%	Index	%	Index	%	Index	%
1959	29.1	0.7	-	-	-	-	40.8	-0.7	26.4	2.3	22.8	2.7	-	-	-	-	-	-
1960	29.8	2.4	-	-	-	-	42.0	2.9	25.8	-2.3	23.2	1.8	-	-	-	-	-	-
1961	30.2	1.3	-	-	-	-	42.4	1.0	26.2	1.6	23.9	3.0	-	-	-	-	-	-
1962	30.8	2.0	-	-	-	-	43.0	1.4	28.2	7.6	24.8	3.8	-	-	-	-	-	-
1963	31.4	1.9	-	-	-	-	43.3	0.7	28.3	0.4	25.3	2.0	-	-	-	-	-	-
1964	31.9	1.6	-	-	-	-	43.6	0.7	28.5	0.7	26.1	3.2	-	-	-	-	-	-
1965	32.5	1.9	-	-	-	-	43.9	0.7	29.2	2.5	27.1	3.8	-	-	-	-	-	-
1966	33.6	3.4	-	-	-	-	45.0	2.5	29.9	2.4	28.2	4.1	-	-	-	-	-	-
1967	34.4	2.4	-	-	-	-	46.5	3.3	30.6	2.3	30.1	6.7	-	-	-	-	-	-
1968	35.8	4.1	-	-	-	-	49.3	6.0	31.6	3.3	32.5	8.0	-	-	-	-	-	-
1969	37.8	5.6	-	-	-	-	52.1	5.7	33.5	6.0	35.1	8.0	-	-	-	-	-	-
1970	40.2	6.3	-	-	-	-	54.6	4.8	34.9	4.2	37.4	6.6	-	-	-	-	-	-
1971	42.2	5.0	-	-	-	-	56.6	3.7	36.6	4.9	39.2	4.8	-	-	-	-	-	-
1972	43.7	3.6	-	-	-	-	57.8	2.1	36.6	0.0	40.5	3.3	-	-	-	-	-	-
1973	46.3	5.9	-	-	-	-	59.8	3.5	37.6	2.7	41.8	3.2	-	-	-	-	-	-
1974	51.2	10.6	-	-	-	-	64.1	7.2	41.0	9.0	44.8	7.2	-	-	-	-	-	-
1975	55.8	9.0	-	-	-	-	68.3	6.6	47.0	14.6	50.1	11.8	-	-	-	-	-	-
1976	60.0	7.5	67.0	-	56.3	-	71.5	4.7	59.3	26.2	53.4	6.6	-	-	-	-	56.4	-
1977	63.1	5.2	69.7	4.0	59.5	5.7	73.2	2.4	63.4	6.9	57.8	8.2	-	-	-	-	59.4	5.3
1978	66.4	5.2	75.3	8.0	63.1	6.1	78.7	7.5	63.0	-0.6	62.0	7.3	-	-	-	-	62.5	5.2
1979	73.2	10.2	83.2	10.5	69.9	10.8	84.9	7.9	69.4	10.2	69.5	12.1	-	-	-	-	67.4	7.8
1980	82.6	12.8	89.1	7.1	80.5	15.2	89.5	5.4	82.7	19.2	76.9	10.6	-	-	-	-	73.6	9.2
1981	91.8	11.1	94.3	5.8	92.0	14.3	93.8	4.8	94.1	13.8	83.7	8.8	-	-	-	-	81.0	10.1
1982	95.5	4.0	96.6	2.4	94.6	2.8	97.4	3.8	98.3	4.5	92.6	10.6	-	-	-	-	90.5	11.7
1983	99.8	4.5	99.1	2.6	100.3	6.0	99.8	2.5	99.2	0.9	98.8	6.7	-	-	-	-	100.1	10.6
1984	104.7	4.9	104.2	5.1	105.0	4.7	102.7	2.9	102.5	3.3	108.6	9.9	-	-	-	-	109.4	9.3
1985	109.4	4.5	108.6	4.2	109.1	3.9	106.1	3.3	105.3	2.7	120.5	11.0	-	-	-	-	118.9	8.7
1986	112.2	2.6	113.7	4.7	111.6	2.3	108.3	2.1	101.6	-3.5	131.8	9.4	-	-	-	-	128.8	8.3
1987	117.1	4.4	119.4	5.0	116.8	4.7	115.8	6.9	103.3	1.7	139.2	5.6	-	-	-	-	136.0	5.6
1988	124.2	6.1	124.4	4.2	123.7	5.9	125.8	8.6	108.3	4.8	152.1	9.3	-	-	-	-	147.1	8.2
1989	131.3	5.7	132.2	6.3	131.3	6.1	125.1	-0.6	113.7	5.0	165.3	8.7	-	-	-	-	157.9	7.3
1990	138.9	5.8	138.6	4.8	137.0	4.3	138.2	10.5	119.7	5.3	181.6	9.9	-	-	-	-	173.4	9.8
1991	145.0	4.4	142.5	2.8	140.9	2.8	144.6	4.6	125.5	4.8	202.7	11.6	-	-	-	-	188.4	8.7
1992	148.6	2.5	143.3	0.6	143.5	1.8	145.1	0.3	129.1	2.9	224.2	10.6	-	-	-	-	197.9	5.0
1993	152.9	2.9	146.3	2.1	146.4	2.0	157.6	8.6	132.5	2.6	239.0	6.6	-	-	-	-	202.6	2.4
1994	154.9	1.3	150.0	2.5	147.9	1.0	146.8	-6.9	135.0	1.9	251.1	5.1	-	-	-	-	206.6	2.0
1995	158.6	2.4	153.6	2.4	151.6	2.5	143.7	-2.1	137.1	1.6	266.1	6.0	-	-	-	-	213.3	3.2
1996	163.3	3.0	157.7	2.7	157.2	3.7	142.9	-0.6	139.5	1.8	280.8	5.5	-	-	-	-	220.2	3.2
1997	167.9	2.8	160.4	1.7	162.5	3.4	143.8	0.6	141.6	1.5	293.1	4.4	-	-	-	-	229.1	4.0
1998	171.7	2.3	165.8	3.4	165.8	2.0	147.0	2.2	139.5	-1.5	313.9	7.1	103.9	-	100.3	-	239.7	4.6
1999	176.0	2.5	170.6	2.9	170.3	2.7	143.6	-2.3	142.3	2.0	330.2	5.2	105.1	1.2	101.5	1.2	255.7	6.7
2000	183.6	4.3	174.8	2.5	179.6	5.5	139.6	-2.8	152.2	7.0	348.6	5.6	104.0	-1.0	102.9	1.4	275.6	7.8
2001	-		-		-		-		-		-		-		-		-	

Source: U.S. Department of Labor, Bureau of Labor Statistics, Division of Consumer Prices and Price Indexes. *Base is December 1997 = 100. - indicates no data collected for period.

Boston-Brockton-Nashua, MA-NH-ME-CT
Consumer Price Index - Urban Wage Earners
Base 1982-1984 = 100
Annual Averages

For 1914-2001. Columns headed % show percentile change in the index from the previous period for which an index is available.

Year	All Items		Food & Beverage		Housing		Apparel		Trans- portation		Medical Care		Recrea- tion*		Education & Communic.*		Other Goods & Services	
	Index	%	Index	%	Index	%	Index	%	Index	%	Index	%	Index	%	Index	%	Index	%
1914	-	-	-	-	-	-	-	-	-	-	-	-	-	-	-	-	-	-
1915	10.5	-	-	-	-	-	-	-	-	-	-	-	-	-	-	-	-	-
1916	11.3	7.6	-	-	-	-	-	-	-	-	-	-	-	-	-	-	-	-
1917	13.4	18.6	-	-	-	-	-	-	-	-	-	-	-	-	-	-	-	-
1918	15.8	17.9	-	-	-	-	-	-	-	-	-	-	-	-	-	-	-	-
1919	18.1	14.6	-	-	-	-	-	-	-	-	-	-	-	-	-	-	-	-
1920	20.8	14.9	-	-	-	-	-	-	-	-	-	-	-	-	-	-	-	-
1921	18.4	-11.5	-	-	-	-	-	-	-	-	-	-	-	-	-	-	-	-
1922	17.1	-7.1	-	-	-	-	-	-	-	-	-	-	-	-	-	-	-	-
1923	17.5	2.3	-	-	-	-	-	-	-	-	-	-	-	-	-	-	-	-
1924	17.5	0.0	-	-	-	-	-	-	-	-	-	-	-	-	-	-	-	-
1925	18.0	2.9	-	-	-	-	-	-	-	-	-	-	-	-	-	-	-	-
1926	18.3	1.7	-	-	-	-	-	-	-	-	-	-	-	-	-	-	-	-
1927	18.0	-1.6	-	-	-	-	-	-	-	-	-	-	-	-	-	-	-	-
1928	17.8	-1.1	-	-	-	-	-	-	-	-	-	-	-	-	-	-	-	-
1929	17.9	0.6	-	-	-	-	-	-	-	-	-	-	-	-	-	-	-	-
1930	17.4	-2.8	-	-	-	-	-	-	-	-	-	-	-	-	-	-	-	-
1931	15.9	-8.6	-	-	-	-	-	-	-	-	-	-	-	-	-	-	-	-
1932	14.3	-10.1	-	-	-	-	-	-	-	-	-	-	-	-	-	-	-	-
1933	13.7	-4.2	-	-	-	-	-	-	-	-	-	-	-	-	-	-	-	-
1934	14.2	3.6	-	-	-	-	-	-	-	-	-	-	-	-	-	-	-	-
1935	14.4	1.4	-	-	-	-	-	-	-	-	-	-	-	-	-	-	-	-
1936	14.4	0.0	-	-	-	-	-	-	-	-	-	-	-	-	-	-	-	-
1937	14.8	2.8	-	-	-	-	-	-	-	-	-	-	-	-	-	-	-	-
1938	14.4	-2.7	-	-	-	-	-	-	-	-	-	-	-	-	-	-	-	-
1939	14.2	-1.4	-	-	-	-	-	-	-	-	-	-	-	-	-	-	-	-
1940	14.4	1.4	-	-	-	-	-	-	-	-	-	-	-	-	-	-	-	-
1941	15.0	4.2	-	-	-	-	-	-	-	-	-	-	-	-	-	-	-	-
1942	16.6	10.7	-	-	-	-	-	-	-	-	-	-	-	-	-	-	-	-
1943	17.5	5.4	-	-	-	-	-	-	-	-	-	-	-	-	-	-	-	-
1944	17.7	1.1	-	-	-	-	-	-	-	-	-	-	-	-	-	-	-	-
1945	18.0	1.7	-	-	-	-	-	-	-	-	-	-	-	-	-	-	-	-
1946	19.5	8.3	-	-	-	-	-	-	-	-	-	-	-	-	-	-	-	-
1947	22.2	13.8	-	-	-	-	-	-	16.4	-	13.6	-	-	-	-	-	-	-
1948	24.0	8.1	-	-	-	-	-	-	16.9	3.0	14.5	6.6	-	-	-	-	-	-
1949	23.7	-1.2	-	-	-	-	-	-	18.5	9.5	15.3	5.5	-	-	-	-	-	-
1950	24.0	1.3	-	-	-	-	-	-	20.5	10.8	16.0	4.6	-	-	-	-	-	-
1951	25.6	6.7	-	-	-	-	-	-	21.2	3.4	16.5	3.1	-	-	-	-	-	-
1952	26.2	2.3	-	-	-	-	-	-	22.6	6.6	17.4	5.5	-	-	-	-	-	-
1953	26.3	0.4	-	-	-	-	39.7	-	23.4	3.5	17.9	2.9	-	-	-	-	-	-
1954	26.4	0.4	-	-	-	-	39.4	-0.8	23.6	0.9	18.0	0.6	-	-	-	-	-	-
1955	26.5	0.4	-	-	-	-	39.5	0.3	23.1	-2.1	18.1	0.6	-	-	-	-	-	-
1956	27.3	3.0	-	-	-	-	40.1	1.5	24.0	3.9	19.3	6.6	-	-	-	-	-	-
1957	28.2	3.3	-	-	-	-	40.8	1.7	24.9	3.8	21.1	9.3	-	-	-	-	-	-
1958	29.1	3.2	-	-	-	-	41.4	1.5	25.7	3.2	22.6	7.1	-	-	-	-	-	-

[Continued]

282

Boston-Brockton-Nashua, MA-NH-ME-CT
Consumer Price Index - Urban Wage Earners
Base 1982-1984 = 100
Annual Averages
[Continued]

For 1914-2001. Columns headed % show percentile change in the index from the previous period for which an index is available.

Year	All Items Index	%	Food & Beverage Index	%	Housing Index	%	Apparel Index	%	Transportation Index	%	Medical Care Index	%	Recreation* Index	%	Education & Communic.* Index	%	Other Goods & Services Index	%
1959	29.3	0.7	-	-	-	-	41.1	-0.7	26.3	2.3	23.1	2.2	-	-	-	-	-	-
1960	29.9	2.0	-	-	-	-	42.4	3.2	25.7	-2.3	23.5	1.7	-	-	-	-	-	-
1961	30.3	1.3	-	-	-	-	42.7	0.7	26.2	1.9	24.3	3.4	-	-	-	-	-	-
1962	31.0	2.3	-	-	-	-	43.3	1.4	28.1	7.3	25.1	3.3	-	-	-	-	-	-
1963	31.6	1.9	-	-	-	-	43.7	0.9	28.2	0.4	25.7	2.4	-	-	-	-	-	-
1964	32.1	1.6	-	-	-	-	43.9	0.5	28.4	0.7	26.5	3.1	-	-	-	-	-	-
1965	32.7	1.9	-	-	-	-	44.3	0.9	29.1	2.5	27.5	3.8	-	-	-	-	-	-
1966	33.8	3.4	-	-	-	-	45.3	2.3	29.8	2.4	28.6	4.0	-	-	-	-	-	-
1967	34.6	2.4	-	-	-	-	46.8	3.3	30.6	2.7	30.5	6.6	-	-	-	-	-	-
1968	36.0	4.0	-	-	-	-	49.7	6.2	31.5	2.9	33.0	8.2	-	-	-	-	-	-
1969	38.1	5.8	-	-	-	-	52.5	5.6	33.4	6.0	35.6	7.9	-	-	-	-	-	-
1970	40.4	6.0	-	-	-	-	55.0	4.8	34.8	4.2	38.0	6.7	-	-	-	-	-	-
1971	42.5	5.2	-	-	-	-	57.1	3.8	36.5	4.9	39.8	4.7	-	-	-	-	-	-
1972	44.0	3.5	-	-	-	-	58.2	1.9	36.5	0.0	41.1	3.3	-	-	-	-	-	-
1973	46.6	5.9	-	-	-	-	60.2	3.4	37.5	2.7	42.4	3.2	-	-	-	-	-	-
1974	51.4	10.3	-	-	-	-	64.6	7.3	40.9	9.1	45.4	7.1	-	-	-	-	-	-
1975	56.1	9.1	-	-	-	-	68.8	6.5	46.9	14.7	50.8	11.9	-	-	-	-	-	-
1976	60.4	7.7	67.6	-	56.2	-	72.0	4.7	59.2	26.2	54.2	6.7	-	-	-	-	57.1	-
1977	63.5	5.1	70.3	4.0	59.4	5.7	73.7	2.4	63.2	6.8	58.7	8.3	-	-	-	-	60.2	5.4
1978	66.7	5.0	75.8	7.8	63.0	6.1	78.2	6.1	62.9	-0.5	62.8	7.0	-	-	-	-	63.3	5.1
1979	73.5	10.2	83.3	9.9	70.1	11.3	82.6	5.6	70.0	11.3	69.4	10.5	-	-	-	-	68.1	7.6
1980	83.0	12.9	89.6	7.6	81.3	16.0	86.8	5.1	83.4	19.1	76.4	10.1	-	-	-	-	73.7	8.2
1981	92.2	11.1	94.6	5.6	93.2	14.6	92.9	7.0	94.0	12.7	83.8	9.7	-	-	-	-	81.1	10.0
1982	95.9	4.0	96.5	2.0	95.4	2.4	98.0	5.5	98.4	4.7	92.3	10.1	-	-	-	-	90.3	11.3
1983	99.7	4.0	99.1	2.7	100.2	5.0	100.2	2.2	99.1	0.7	98.8	7.0	-	-	-	-	100.1	10.9
1984	104.3	4.6	104.4	5.3	104.2	4.0	101.8	1.6	102.5	3.4	108.9	10.2	-	-	-	-	109.6	9.5
1985	109.3	4.8	108.4	3.8	109.6	5.2	104.8	2.9	105.1	2.5	119.3	9.6	-	-	-	-	119.1	8.7
1986	111.8	2.3	113.1	4.3	111.9	2.1	107.0	2.1	101.1	-3.8	130.6	9.5	-	-	-	-	128.8	8.1
1987	117.1	4.7	118.9	5.1	116.8	4.4	121.3	13.4	103.7	2.6	138.8	6.3	-	-	-	-	136.0	5.6
1988	124.1	6.0	123.8	4.1	123.5	5.7	132.6	9.3	109.2	5.3	151.4	9.1	-	-	-	-	147.0	8.1
1989	131.5	6.0	131.5	6.2	131.0	6.1	134.0	1.1	115.6	5.9	163.9	8.3	-	-	-	-	158.6	7.9
1990	138.8	5.6	137.9	4.9	136.0	3.8	146.9	9.6	122.0	5.5	179.7	9.6	-	-	-	-	174.3	9.9
1991	144.6	4.2	141.6	2.7	139.6	2.6	153.1	4.2	128.3	5.2	199.7	11.1	-	-	-	-	189.6	8.8
1992	148.0	2.4	142.4	0.6	142.0	1.7	153.2	0.1	131.9	2.8	219.9	10.1	-	-	-	-	200.0	5.5
1993	152.1	2.8	145.4	2.1	144.9	2.0	165.9	8.3	134.9	2.3	234.6	6.7	-	-	-	-	203.8	1.9
1994	153.8	1.1	148.7	2.3	146.4	1.0	152.2	-8.3	137.7	2.1	245.7	4.7	-	-	-	-	204.9	0.5
1995	157.4	2.3	152.1	2.3	150.0	2.5	150.7	-1.0	140.1	1.7	259.9	5.8	-	-	-	-	211.1	3.0
1996	162.2	3.0	156.2	2.7	155.5	3.7	150.5	-0.1	143.0	2.1	273.9	5.4	-	-	-	-	218.4	3.5
1997	166.6	2.7	158.7	1.6	160.6	3.3	150.9	0.3	144.8	1.3	285.2	4.1	-	-	-	-	229.9	5.3
1998	169.7	1.9	164.0	3.3	163.6	1.9	149.2	-1.1	141.6	-2.2	304.2	6.7	103.9	-	100.2	-	244.4	6.3
1999	174.2	2.7	168.6	2.8	168.1	2.8	145.7	-2.3	144.4	2.0	320.8	5.5	105.2	1.3	101.1	0.9	268.0	9.7
2000	182.4	4.7	173.0	2.6	177.6	5.7	142.9	-1.9	156.2	8.2	338.9	5.6	104.8	-0.4	102.3	1.2	290.9	8.5
2001	-	-	-	-	-	-	-	-	-	-	-	-	-	-	-	-	-	-

Source: U.S. Department of Labor, Bureau of Labor Statistics, Division of Consumer Prices and Price Indexes. *Base is December 1997 = 100. - indicates no data collected for period.

Boston-Brockton-Nashua, MA-NH-ME-CT
Consumer Price Index - All Urban Consumers
Base 1982-1984 = 100
All Items

For 1914-2001. Columns headed % show percentile change in the index from the previous period for which an index is available.

Year	Jan Index	%	Feb Index	%	Mar Index	%	Apr Index	%	May Index	%	Jun Index	%	Jul Index	%	Aug Index	%	Sep Index	%	Oct Index	%	Nov Index	%	Dec Index	%
1914	-	-	-	-	-	-	-	-	-	-	-	-	-	-	-	-	-	-	-	-	-	-	10.5	-
1915	-	-	-	-	-	-	-	-	-	-	-	-	-	-	-	-	-	-	-	-	-	-	10.7	1.9
1916	-	-	-	-	-	-	-	-	-	-	-	-	-	-	-	-	-	-	-	-	-	-	12.1	13.1
1917	-	-	-	-	-	-	-	-	-	-	-	-	-	-	-	-	-	-	-	-	-	-	14.2	17.4
1918	-	-	-	-	-	-	-	-	-	-	-	-	-	-	-	-	-	-	-	-	-	-	17.3	21.8
1919	-	-	-	-	-	-	-	-	-	-	17.4	0.6	-	-	-	-	-	-	-	-	-	-	19.5	12.1
1920	-	-	-	-	-	-	-	-	-	-	21.5	10.3	-	-	-	-	-	-	-	-	-	-	20.2	-6.0
1921	-	-	-	-	-	-	-	-	18.0	-10.9	-	-	-	-	-	-	18.0	0.0	-	-	-	-	17.8	-1.1
1922	-	-	-	-	16.9	-5.1	-	-	-	-	16.8	-0.6	-	-	-	-	16.9	0.6	-	-	-	-	17.3	2.4
1923	-	-	-	-	17.1	-1.2	-	-	-	-	17.1	0.0	-	-	-	-	17.6	2.9	-	-	-	-	17.8	1.1
1924	-	-	-	-	17.3	-2.8	-	-	-	-	17.2	-0.6	-	-	-	-	17.5	1.7	-	-	-	-	17.6	0.6
1925	-	-	-	-	-	-	-	-	-	-	17.5	-0.6	-	-	-	-	-	-	-	-	-	-	18.5	5.7
1926	-	-	-	-	-	-	-	-	-	-	18.1	-2.2	-	-	-	-	-	-	-	-	-	-	18.2	0.6
1927	-	-	-	-	-	-	-	-	-	-	18.0	-1.1	-	-	-	-	-	-	-	-	-	-	18.0	0.0
1928	-	-	-	-	-	-	-	-	-	-	17.5	-2.8	-	-	-	-	-	-	-	-	-	-	17.8	1.7
1929	-	-	-	-	-	-	-	-	-	-	17.5	-1.7	-	-	-	-	-	-	-	-	-	-	17.8	1.7
1930	-	-	-	-	-	-	-	-	-	-	17.4	-2.2	-	-	-	-	-	-	-	-	-	-	16.9	-2.9
1931	-	-	-	-	-	-	-	-	-	-	15.7	-7.1	-	-	-	-	-	-	-	-	-	-	15.3	-2.5
1932	-	-	-	-	-	-	-	-	-	-	14.1	-7.8	-	-	-	-	-	-	-	-	-	-	13.8	-2.1
1933	-	-	-	-	-	-	-	-	-	-	13.4	-2.9	-	-	-	-	-	-	-	-	-	-	13.9	3.7
1934	-	-	-	-	-	-	-	-	-	-	14.1	1.4	-	-	-	-	-	-	-	-	14.2	0.7	-	-
1935	-	-	-	-	14.5	2.1	-	-	-	-	-	-	14.2	-2.1	-	-	-	-	14.3	0.7	-	-	-	-
1936	14.4	0.7	-	-	-	-	14.3	-0.7	-	-	-	-	14.5	1.4	-	-	14.5	0.0	-	-	-	-	14.3	-1.4
1937	-	-	-	-	14.6	2.1	-	-	-	-	14.8	1.4	-	-	-	-	15.1	2.0	-	-	-	-	14.7	-2.6
1938	-	-	-	-	14.3	-2.7	-	-	-	-	14.3	0.0	-	-	-	-	14.3	0.0	-	-	-	-	14.2	-0.7
1939	-	-	-	-	14.1	-0.7	-	-	-	-	14.0	-0.7	-	-	-	-	14.3	2.1	-	-	-	-	14.1	-1.4
1940	-	-	-	-	14.3	1.4	-	-	-	-	14.4	0.7	-	-	-	-	14.3	-0.7	14.2	-0.7	14.2	0.0	14.3	0.7
1941	14.3	0.0	14.3	0.0	14.3	0.0	14.5	1.4	14.6	0.7	14.8	1.4	15.0	1.4	15.1	0.7	15.3	1.3	15.4	0.7	15.7	1.9	15.6	-0.6
1942	15.8	1.3	16.0	1.3	16.1	0.6	16.1	0.0	16.3	1.2	16.4	0.6	16.7	1.8	16.6	-0.6	16.8	1.2	17.0	1.2	17.1	0.6	17.1	0.0
1943	17.1	0.0	17.1	0.0	17.4	1.8	17.5	0.6	17.6	0.6	17.5	-0.6	17.3	-1.1	17.3	0.0	17.3	0.0	17.5	1.2	17.4	-0.6	17.4	0.0
1944	17.4	0.0	17.3	-0.6	17.3	0.0	17.5	1.2	17.5	0.0	17.5	0.0	17.6	0.6	17.7	0.6	17.8	0.6	17.6	-1.1	17.7	0.6	17.8	0.6
1945	17.8	0.0	17.8	0.0	17.7	-0.6	17.7	0.0	17.8	0.6	18.1	1.7	18.1	0.0	18.1	0.0	18.0	-0.6	17.9	-0.6	18.0	0.6	18.0	0.0
1946	18.1	0.6	18.0	-0.6	18.1	0.6	18.2	0.6	18.2	0.0	18.4	1.1	19.8	7.6	20.2	2.0	20.4	1.0	20.8	2.0	21.1	1.4	21.3	0.9
1947	21.4	0.5	21.3	-0.5	21.7	1.9	21.5	-0.9	21.4	-0.5	21.7	1.4	21.9	0.9	22.3	1.8	22.9	2.7	22.7	-0.9	22.8	0.4	23.2	1.8
1948	23.5	1.3	23.3	-0.9	23.2	-0.4	23.6	1.7	23.7	0.4	24.0	1.3	24.3	1.2	24.4	0.4	24.4	0.0	24.3	-0.4	24.1	-0.8	23.8	-1.2
1949	23.7	-0.4	23.3	-1.7	23.5	0.9	23.5	0.0	23.5	0.0	23.6	0.4	23.5	-0.4	23.7	0.9	23.9	0.8	23.7	-0.8	23.7	0.0	23.5	-0.8
1950	23.4	-0.4	23.3	-0.4	23.5	0.9	23.5	0.0	23.5	0.0	23.8	1.3	24.0	0.8	24.2	0.8	24.2	0.0	24.4	0.8	24.4	0.0	24.6	0.8
1951	25.0	1.6	25.3	1.2	25.3	0.0	25.3	0.0	25.4	0.4	25.4	0.0	25.5	0.4	25.5	0.0	25.6	0.4	25.8	0.8	25.9	0.4	26.0	0.4
1952	25.9	-0.4	25.8	-0.4	25.8	0.0	25.8	0.0	25.9	0.4	26.0	0.4	26.4	1.5	26.4	0.0	26.3	-0.4	26.3	0.0	26.1	-0.8	26.0	-0.4
1953	26.0	0.0	-	-	-	-	-	-	-	-	-	-	26.2	1.2	-	-	-	-	26.4	0.8	-	-	-	-
1954	26.1	-1.1	-	-	-	-	26.1	0.0	-	-	-	-	26.4	1.1	-	-	-	-	26.3	-0.4	-	-	-	-
1955	26.2	-0.4	-	-	-	-	26.3	0.4	-	-	-	-	26.4	0.4	-	-	-	-	26.5	0.4	-	-	-	-
1956	26.6	0.4	-	-	-	-	26.7	0.4	-	-	-	-	27.3	2.2	-	-	-	-	27.7	1.5	-	-	-	-
1957	27.6	-0.4	-	-	-	-	27.9	1.1	-	-	-	-	28.3	1.4	-	-	-	-	28.3	0.0	-	-	-	-
1958	28.6	1.1	-	-	-	-	28.9	1.0	-	-	-	-	29.1	0.7	-	-	-	-	29.1	0.0	-	-	-	-
1959	29.1	0.0	-	-	-	-	29.0	-0.3	-	-	-	-	29.1	0.3	-	-	-	-	29.4	1.0	-	-	-	-

[Continued]

Boston-Brockton-Nashua, MA-NH-ME-CT
Consumer Price Index - All Urban Consumers
Base 1982-1984 = 100
All Items
[Continued]

For 1914-2001. Columns headed % show percentile change in the index from the previous period for which an index is available.

Year	Jan Index	%	Feb Index	%	Mar Index	%	Apr Index	%	May Index	%	Jun Index	%	Jul Index	%	Aug Index	%	Sep Index	%	Oct Index	%	Nov Index	%	Dec Index	%
1960	29.3	-0.3	-	-	-	-	29.8	1.7	-	-	-	-	29.8	0.0	-	-	-	-	29.9	0.3	-	-	-	-
1961	30.0	0.3	-	-	-	-	30.1	0.3	-	-	-	-	30.2	0.3	-	-	-	-	30.3	0.3	-	-	-	-
1962	30.5	0.7	-	-	-	-	30.8	1.0	-	-	-	-	30.8	0.0	-	-	-	-	31.1	1.0	-	-	-	-
1963	31.2	0.3	-	-	-	-	31.4	0.6	-	-	-	-	31.5	0.3	-	-	-	-	31.6	0.3	-	-	-	-
1964	31.6	0.0	-	-	-	-	31.8	0.6	-	-	-	-	31.9	0.3	-	-	-	-	32.1	0.6	-	-	-	-
1965	32.2	0.3	-	-	-	-	32.4	0.6	-	-	-	-	32.6	0.6	-	-	-	-	32.6	0.0	-	-	-	-
1966	32.7	0.3	-	-	-	-	33.5	2.4	-	-	-	-	33.6	0.3	-	-	-	-	34.0	1.2	-	-	-	-
1967	34.1	0.3	-	-	-	-	34.1	0.0	-	-	-	-	34.4	0.9	-	-	-	-	34.7	0.9	-	-	-	-
1968	35.0	0.9	-	-	-	-	35.5	1.4	-	-	-	-	35.8	0.8	-	-	-	-	36.4	1.7	-	-	-	-
1969	36.7	0.8	-	-	-	-	37.3	1.6	-	-	-	-	37.9	1.6	-	-	-	-	38.7	2.1	-	-	-	-
1970	39.1	1.0	-	-	-	-	39.6	1.3	-	-	-	-	40.0	1.0	-	-	-	-	41.1	2.8	-	-	-	-
1971	41.5	1.0	-	-	-	-	41.8	0.7	-	-	-	-	42.2	1.0	-	-	-	-	42.8	1.4	-	-	-	-
1972	42.9	0.2	-	-	-	-	43.4	1.2	-	-	-	-	43.7	0.7	-	-	-	-	44.3	1.4	-	-	-	-
1973	44.6	0.7	-	-	-	-	45.6	2.2	-	-	-	-	46.1	1.1	-	-	-	-	47.7	3.5	-	-	-	-
1974	48.9	2.5	-	-	-	-	50.0	2.2	-	-	-	-	51.5	3.0	-	-	-	-	52.6	2.1	-	-	-	-
1975	53.8	2.3	-	-	-	-	54.7	1.7	-	-	-	-	56.1	2.6	-	-	-	-	56.7	1.1	-	-	-	-
1976	59.1	4.2	-	-	-	-	59.3	0.3	-	-	-	-	60.3	1.7	-	-	-	-	60.6	0.5	-	-	-	-
1977	61.6	1.7	-	-	-	-	62.5	1.5	-	-	-	-	63.5	1.6	-	-	-	-	63.9	0.6	-	-	-	-
1978	64.5	0.9	-	-	64.8	0.5	-	-	65.6	1.2	-	-	66.4	1.2	-	-	67.4	1.5	-	-	68.7	1.9	-	-
1979	69.4	1.0	-	-	70.6	1.7	-	-	72.1	2.1	-	-	73.7	2.2	-	-	75.0	1.8	-	-	76.6	2.1	-	-
1980	78.2	2.1	-	-	80.6	3.1	-	-	81.5	1.1	-	-	82.9	1.7	-	-	84.1	1.4	-	-	85.6	1.8	-	-
1981	88.2	3.0	-	-	90.2	2.3	-	-	90.7	0.6	-	-	91.6	1.0	-	-	93.9	2.5	-	-	94.3	0.4	-	-
1982	94.3	0.0	-	-	92.8	-1.6	-	-	93.8	1.1	-	-	96.1	2.5	-	-	97.3	1.2	-	-	98.1	0.8	-	-
1983	98.7	0.6	-	-	98.6	-0.1	-	-	99.1	0.5	-	-	99.7	0.6	-	-	100.2	0.5	-	-	101.4	1.2	-	-
1984	102.3	0.9	-	-	103.9	1.6	-	-	104.3	0.4	-	-	104.9	0.6	-	-	105.8	0.9	-	-	105.9	0.1	-	-
1985	106.5	0.6	-	-	108.2	1.6	-	-	108.4	0.2	-	-	109.3	0.8	-	-	110.5	1.1	-	-	112.0	1.4	-	-
1986	112.5	0.4	-	-	111.8	-0.6	-	-	111.0	-0.7	-	-	111.3	0.3	-	-	112.9	1.4	-	-	113.3	0.4	-	-
1987	114.6	1.1	-	-	115.9	1.1	-	-	115.3	-0.5	-	-	116.3	0.9	-	-	119.5	2.8	-	-	119.9	0.3	-	-
1988	120.1	0.2	-	-	122.1	1.7	-	-	123.1	0.8	-	-	123.8	0.6	-	-	126.2	1.9	-	-	127.4	1.0	-	-
1989	129.0	1.3	-	-	129.7	0.5	-	-	130.5	0.6	-	-	130.3	-0.2	-	-	132.2	1.5	-	-	134.3	1.6	-	-
1990	136.0	1.3	-	-	136.3	0.2	-	-	136.6	0.2	-	-	137.6	0.7	-	-	141.3	2.7	-	-	143.7	1.7	-	-
1991	143.8	0.1	-	-	143.9	0.1	-	-	143.5	-0.3	-	-	145.1	1.1	-	-	146.3	0.8	-	-	146.6	0.2	-	-
1992	146.3	-0.2	-	-	147.9	1.1	-	-	147.5	-0.3	-	-	148.9	0.9	-	-	149.4	0.3	-	-	150.4	0.7	-	-
1993	151.9	1.0	-	-	154.1	1.4	-	-	151.9	-1.4	-	-	152.5	0.4	-	-	152.0	-0.3	-	-	154.5	1.6	-	-
1994	153.6	-0.6	-	-	155.0	0.9	-	-	153.6	-0.9	-	-	153.9	0.2	-	-	155.7	1.2	-	-	156.7	0.6	-	-
1995	158.0	0.8	-	-	158.4	0.3	-	-	157.7	-0.4	-	-	157.8	0.1	-	-	158.6	0.5	-	-	160.3	1.1	-	-
1996	162.2	1.2	-	-	162.8	0.4	-	-	161.8	-0.6	-	-	162.0	0.1	-	-	163.5	0.9	-	-	166.3	1.7	-	-
1997	167.7	0.8	-	-	168.1	0.2	-	-	166.7	-0.8	-	-	167.1	0.2	-	-	167.8	0.4	-	-	169.4	1.0	-	-
1998	171.2	1.1	-	-	171.3	0.1	-	-	170.9	-0.2	-	-	170.7	-0.1	-	-	172.1	0.8	-	-	173.3	0.7	-	-
1999	174.1	0.5	-	-	174.8	0.4	-	-	174.2	-0.3	-	-	175.3	0.6	-	-	176.8	0.9	-	-	179.2	1.4	-	-
2000	180.2	0.6	-	-	182.8	1.4	-	-	181.7	-0.6	-	-	183.2	0.8	-	-	184.3	0.6	-	-	187.4	1.7	-	-
2001	189.0	0.9	-	-	190.9	1.0	-	-	190.9	0.0	-	-	192.1	0.6	-	-	192.7	0.3	-	-	192.7	0.0	-	-

Source: U.S. Department of Labor, Bureau of Labor Statistics, Division of Consumer Prices and Price Indexes. - indicates no data collected for period.

Boston-Brockton-Nashua, MA-NH-ME-CT
Consumer Price Index - Urban Wage Earners
Base 1982-1984 = 100
All Items

For 1914-2001. Columns headed % show percentile change in the index from the previous period for which an index is available.

Year	Jan Index	Jan %	Feb Index	Feb %	Mar Index	Mar %	Apr Index	Apr %	May Index	May %	Jun Index	Jun %	Jul Index	Jul %	Aug Index	Aug %	Sep Index	Sep %	Oct Index	Oct %	Nov Index	Nov %	Dec Index	Dec %
1914	-	-	-	-	-	-	-	-	-	-	-	-	-	-	-	-	-	-	-	-	-	-	10.6	-
1915	-	-	-	-	-	-	-	-	-	-	-	-	-	-	-	-	-	-	-	-	-	-	10.7	0.9
1916	-	-	-	-	-	-	-	-	-	-	-	-	-	-	-	-	-	-	-	-	-	-	12.1	13.1
1917	-	-	-	-	-	-	-	-	-	-	-	-	-	-	-	-	-	-	-	-	-	-	14.3	18.2
1918	-	-	-	-	-	-	-	-	-	-	-	-	-	-	-	-	-	-	-	-	-	-	17.4	21.7
1919	-	-	-	-	-	-	-	-	-	-	17.5	0.6	-	-	-	-	-	-	-	-	-	-	19.6	12.0
1920	-	-	-	-	-	-	-	-	-	-	21.6	10.2	-	-	-	-	-	-	-	-	-	-	20.3	-6.0
1921	-	-	-	-	-	-	-	-	18.1	-10.8	-	-	-	-	-	-	18.1	0.0	-	-	-	-	17.9	-1.1
1922	-	-	-	-	17.0	-5.0	-	-	-	-	16.8	-1.2	-	-	-	-	17.0	1.2	-	-	-	-	17.4	2.4
1923	-	-	-	-	17.2	-1.1	-	-	-	-	17.2	0.0	-	-	-	-	17.7	2.9	-	-	-	-	17.9	1.1
1924	-	-	-	-	17.4	-2.8	-	-	-	-	17.3	-0.6	-	-	-	-	17.6	1.7	-	-	-	-	17.7	0.6
1925	-	-	-	-	-	-	-	-	-	-	17.6	-0.6	-	-	-	-	-	-	-	-	-	-	18.6	5.7
1926	-	-	-	-	-	-	-	-	-	-	18.2	-2.2	-	-	-	-	-	-	-	-	-	-	18.3	0.5
1927	-	-	-	-	-	-	-	-	-	-	18.1	-1.1	-	-	-	-	-	-	-	-	-	-	18.1	
1928	-	-	-	-	-	-	-	-	-	-	17.6	-2.8	-	-	-	-	-	-	-	-	-	-	17.9	1.7
1929	-	-	-	-	-	-	-	-	-	-	17.6	-1.7	-	-	-	-	-	-	-	-	-	-	17.9	1.7
1930	-	-	-	-	-	-	-	-	-	-	17.5	-2.2	-	-	-	-	-	-	-	-	-	-	17.0	-2.9
1931	-	-	-	-	-	-	-	-	-	-	15.8	-7.1	-	-	-	-	-	-	-	-	-	-	15.4	-2.5
1932	-	-	-	-	-	-	-	-	-	-	14.2	-7.8	-	-	-	-	-	-	-	-	-	-	13.9	-2.1
1933	-	-	-	-	-	-	-	-	-	-	13.5	-2.9	-	-	-	-	-	-	-	-	-	-	13.9	3.0
1934	-	-	-	-	-	-	-	-	-	-	14.2	2.2	-	-	-	-	-	-	-	-	14.3	0.7	-	-
1935	-	-	-	-	14.5	1.4	-	-	-	-	-	-	14.3	-1.4	-	-	-	-	14.4	0.7	-	-	-	-
1936	14.5	0.7	-	-	-	-	14.4	-0.7	-	-	-	-	14.6	1.4	-	-	14.5	-0.7	-	-	-	-	14.4	-0.7
1937	-	-	-	-	14.7	2.1	-	-	-	-	14.8	0.7	-	-	-	-	15.2	2.7	-	-	-	-	14.8	-2.6
1938	-	-	-	-	14.4	-2.7	-	-	-	-	14.4	0.0	-	-	-	-	14.4	0.0	-	-	-	-	14.3	-0.7
1939	-	-	-	-	14.2	-0.7	-	-	-	-	14.1	-0.7	-	-	-	-	14.4	2.1	-	-	-	-	14.2	-1.4
1940	-	-	-	-	14.4	1.4	-	-	-	-	14.5	0.7	-	-	-	-	14.4	-0.7	14.3	-0.7	14.3	0.0	14.4	0.7
1941	14.4	0.0	14.4	0.0	14.4	0.0	14.6	1.4	14.7	0.7	14.8	0.7	15.1	2.0	15.2	0.7	15.4	1.3	15.5	0.6	15.7	1.3	15.6	-0.6
1942	15.8	1.3	16.1	1.9	16.2	0.6	16.2	0.0	16.4	1.2	16.5	0.6	16.7	1.2	16.7	0.0	16.8	0.6	17.1	1.8	17.2	0.6	17.2	0.0
1943	17.2	0.0	17.2	0.0	17.5	1.7	17.6	0.6	17.7	0.6	17.6	-0.6	17.4	-1.1	17.4	0.0	17.4	0.0	17.6	1.1	17.5	-0.6	17.5	0.0
1944	17.5	0.0	17.4	-0.6	17.4	0.0	17.6	1.1	17.6	0.0	17.6	0.0	17.7	0.6	17.8	0.6	17.9	0.6	17.7	-1.1	17.8	0.6	17.9	0.6
1945	17.9	0.0	17.9	0.0	17.8	-0.6	17.8	0.0	17.9	0.6	18.2	1.7	18.2	0.0	18.2	0.0	18.1	-0.5	18.0	-0.6	18.1	0.6	18.1	0.0
1946	18.2	0.6	18.1	-0.5	18.2	0.6	18.3	0.5	18.3	0.0	18.5	1.1	19.9	7.6	20.3	2.0	20.5	1.0	21.0	2.4	21.2	1.0	21.5	1.4
1947	21.6	0.5	21.4	-0.9	21.8	1.9	21.7	-0.5	21.6	-0.5	21.8	0.9	22.0	0.9	22.4	1.8	23.0	2.7	22.8	-0.9	23.0	0.9	23.3	1.3
1948	23.7	1.7	23.4	-1.3	23.4	0.0	23.7	1.3	23.8	0.4	24.1	1.3	24.5	1.7	24.5	0.0	24.6	0.4	24.4	-0.8	24.2	-0.8	23.9	-1.2
1949	23.8	-0.4	23.5	-1.3	23.6	0.4	23.6	0.0	23.6	0.0	23.7	0.4	23.7	0.0	23.8	0.4	24.0	0.8	23.8	-0.8	23.8	0.0	23.7	-0.4
1950	23.5	-0.8	23.5	0.0	23.6	0.4	23.6	0.0	23.7	0.4	24.0	1.3	24.2	0.8	24.4	0.8	24.4	0.0	24.6	0.8	24.6	0.0	24.8	0.8
1951	25.1	1.2	25.4	1.2	25.4	0.0	25.4	0.0	25.5	0.4	25.6	0.4	25.6	0.0	25.7	0.4	25.7	0.0	25.9	0.8	26.1	0.8	26.2	0.4
1952	26.1	-0.4	25.9	-0.8	25.9	0.0	25.9	0.0	26.1	0.8	26.1	0.0	26.5	1.5	26.5	0.0	26.4	-0.4	26.4	0.0	26.3	-0.4	26.2	-0.4
1953	26.1	-0.4	-	-	-	-	26.1	0.0	-	-	-	-	26.4	1.1	-	-	-	-	26.5	0.4	-	-	-	-
1954	26.3	-0.8	-	-	-	-	26.3	0.0	-	-	-	-	26.5	0.8	-	-	-	-	26.5	0.0	-	-	-	-
1955	26.3	-0.8	-	-	-	-	26.4	0.4	-	-	-	-	26.5	0.4	-	-	-	-	26.7	0.8	-	-	-	-
1956	26.7	0.0	-	-	-	-	26.8	0.4	-	-	-	-	27.5	2.6	-	-	-	-	27.8	1.1	-	-	-	-
1957	27.7	-0.4	-	-	-	-	28.0	1.1	-	-	-	-	28.4	1.4	-	-	-	-	28.4	0.0	-	-	-	-
1958	28.8	1.4	-	-	-	-	29.0	0.7	-	-	-	-	29.2	0.7	-	-	-	-	29.2	0.0	-	-	-	-
1959	29.2	0.0	-	-	-	-	29.2	0.0	-	-	-	-	29.3	0.3	-	-	-	-	29.5	0.7	-	-	-	-

[Continued]

Boston-Brockton-Nashua, MA-NH-ME-CT
Consumer Price Index - Urban Wage Earners
Base 1982-1984 = 100
All Items
[Continued]

For 1914-2001. Columns headed % show percentile change in the index from the previous period for which an index is available.

Year	Jan Index	%	Feb Index	%	Mar Index	%	Apr Index	%	May Index	%	Jun Index	%	Jul Index	%	Aug Index	%	Sep Index	%	Oct Index	%	Nov Index	%	Dec Index	%
1960	29.4	-0.3	-	-	-	-	29.9	1.7	-	-	-	-	30.0	0.3	-	-	-	-	30.1	0.3	-	-	-	-
1961	30.1	0.0	-	-	-	-	30.3	0.7	-	-	-	-	30.4	0.3	-	-	-	-	30.4	0.0	-	-	-	-
1962	30.7	1.0	-	-	-	-	30.9	0.7	-	-	-	-	31.0	0.3	-	-	-	-	31.2	0.6	-	-	-	-
1963	31.4	0.6	-	-	-	-	31.6	0.6	-	-	-	-	31.7	0.3	-	-	-	-	31.8	0.3	-	-	-	-
1964	31.8	0.0	-	-	-	-	31.9	0.3	-	-	-	-	32.1	0.6	-	-	-	-	32.2	0.3	-	-	-	-
1965	32.4	0.6	-	-	-	-	32.6	0.6	-	-	-	-	32.8	0.6	-	-	-	-	32.8	0.0	-	-	-	-
1966	32.9	0.3	-	-	-	-	33.7	2.4	-	-	-	-	33.8	0.3	-	-	-	-	34.2	1.2	-	-	-	-
1967	34.3	0.3	-	-	-	-	34.3	0.0	-	-	-	-	34.6	0.9	-	-	-	-	34.9	0.9	-	-	-	-
1968	35.2	0.9	-	-	-	-	35.7	1.4	-	-	-	-	36.0	0.8	-	-	-	-	36.6	1.7	-	-	-	-
1969	37.0	1.1	-	-	-	-	37.5	1.4	-	-	-	-	38.2	1.9	-	-	-	-	38.9	1.8	-	-	-	-
1970	39.3	1.0	-	-	-	-	39.8	1.3	-	-	-	-	40.3	1.3	-	-	-	-	41.3	2.5	-	-	-	-
1971	41.8	1.2	-	-	-	-	42.1	0.7	-	-	-	-	42.5	1.0	-	-	-	-	43.0	1.2	-	-	-	-
1972	43.2	0.5	-	-	-	-	43.7	1.2	-	-	-	-	43.9	0.5	-	-	-	-	44.6	1.6	-	-	-	-
1973	44.9	0.7	-	-	-	-	45.8	2.0	-	-	-	-	46.4	1.3	-	-	-	-	48.0	3.4	-	-	-	-
1974	49.1	2.3	-	-	-	-	50.2	2.2	-	-	-	-	51.8	3.2	-	-	-	-	52.9	2.1	-	-	-	-
1975	54.1	2.3	-	-	-	-	55.0	1.7	-	-	-	-	56.4	2.5	-	-	-	-	57.0	1.1	-	-	-	-
1976	59.5	4.4	-	-	-	-	59.7	0.3	-	-	-	-	60.6	1.5	-	-	-	-	60.9	0.5	-	-	-	-
1977	61.9	1.6	-	-	-	-	62.8	1.5	-	-	-	-	63.8	1.6	-	-	-	-	64.2	0.6	-	-	-	-
1978	64.9	1.1	-	-	65.0	0.2	-	-	65.8	1.2	-	-	66.7	1.4	-	-	67.6	1.3	-	-	68.9	1.9	-	-
1979	69.4	0.7	-	-	70.7	1.9	-	-	72.2	2.1	-	-	73.9	2.4	-	-	75.4	2.0	-	-	77.0	2.1	-	-
1980	78.5	1.9	-	-	81.0	3.2	-	-	81.9	1.1	-	-	83.3	1.7	-	-	84.6	1.6	-	-	86.2	1.9	-	-
1981	88.5	2.7	-	-	90.6	2.4	-	-	91.2	0.7	-	-	92.2	1.1	-	-	94.7	2.7	-	-	94.9	0.2	-	-
1982	94.6	-0.3	-	-	93.3	-1.4	-	-	94.1	0.9	-	-	96.4	2.4	-	-	97.8	1.5	-	-	98.4	0.6	-	-
1983	98.4	0.0	-	-	98.6	0.2	-	-	98.9	0.3	-	-	99.9	1.0	-	-	100.1	0.2	-	-	101.4	1.3	-	-
1984	102.1	0.7	-	-	103.2	1.1	-	-	104.1	0.9	-	-	104.1	0.0	-	-	105.6	1.4	-	-	106.0	0.4	-	-
1985	106.5	0.5	-	-	108.0	1.4	-	-	108.4	0.4	-	-	109.2	0.7	-	-	110.5	1.2	-	-	111.8	1.2	-	-
1986	112.3	0.4	-	-	111.5	-0.7	-	-	110.5	-0.9	-	-	111.0	0.5	-	-	112.5	1.4	-	-	112.8	0.3	-	-
1987	114.5	1.5	-	-	115.8	1.1	-	-	115.2	-0.5	-	-	116.4	1.0	-	-	119.5	2.7	-	-	119.9	0.3	-	-
1988	120.2	0.3	-	-	121.8	1.3	-	-	123.1	1.1	-	-	123.7	0.5	-	-	126.1	1.9	-	-	127.4	1.0	-	-
1989	128.9	1.2	-	-	129.7	0.6	-	-	130.6	0.7	-	-	130.8	0.2	-	-	132.6	1.4	-	-	134.7	1.6	-	-
1990	136.0	1.0	-	-	136.5	0.4	-	-	136.8	0.2	-	-	137.4	0.4	-	-	140.9	2.5	-	-	143.5	1.8	-	-
1991	143.3	-0.1	-	-	143.3	0.0	-	-	143.4	0.1	-	-	144.7	0.9	-	-	145.8	0.8	-	-	146.2	0.3	-	-
1992	146.1	-0.1	-	-	147.2	0.8	-	-	146.8	-0.3	-	-	148.2	1.0	-	-	148.7	0.3	-	-	150.0	0.9	-	-
1993	151.1	0.7	-	-	154.0	1.9	-	-	151.4	-1.7	-	-	151.6	0.1	-	-	151.0	-0.4	-	-	153.4	1.6	-	-
1994	152.5	-0.6	-	-	153.5	0.7	-	-	152.2	-0.8	-	-	152.9	0.5	-	-	154.7	1.2	-	-	155.8	0.7	-	-
1995	157.0	0.8	-	-	156.9	-0.1	-	-	156.5	-0.3	-	-	156.6	0.1	-	-	157.4	0.5	-	-	159.3	1.2	-	-
1996	161.1	1.1	-	-	161.7	0.4	-	-	160.8	-0.6	-	-	160.9	0.1	-	-	162.1	0.7	-	-	165.4	2.0	-	-
1997	166.6	0.7	-	-	166.8	0.1	-	-	165.6	-0.7	-	-	165.8	0.1	-	-	166.2	0.2	-	-	167.8	1.0	-	-
1998	169.3	0.9	-	-	169.3	0.0	-	-	168.9	-0.2	-	-	168.8	-0.1	-	-	169.9	0.7	-	-	171.5	0.9	-	-
1999	172.2	0.4	-	-	172.3	0.1	-	-	172.6	0.2	-	-	173.3	0.4	-	-	175.2	1.1	-	-	177.8	1.5	-	-
2000	178.6	0.4	-	-	181.1	1.4	-	-	180.6	-0.3	-	-	182.3	0.9	-	-	183.2	0.5	-	-	186.2	1.6	-	-
2001	187.4	0.6	-	-	189.3	1.0	-	-	190.1	0.4	-	-	191.3	0.6	-	-	192.0	0.4	-	-	191.9	-0.1	-	-

Source: U.S. Department of Labor, Bureau of Labor Statistics, Division of Consumer Prices and Price Indexes. - indicates no data collected for period.

Boston-Brockton-Nashua, MA-NH-ME-CT
Consumer Price Index - All Urban Consumers
Base 1982-1984 = 100
Food and Beverages

For 1976-2001. Columns headed % show percentile change in the index from the previous period for which an index is available.

Year	Jan Index	%	Feb Index	%	Mar Index	%	Apr Index	%	May Index	%	Jun Index	%	Jul Index	%	Aug Index	%	Sep Index	%	Oct Index	%	Nov Index	%	Dec Index	%
1976	66.9	-	-	-	-	-	66.6	-0.4	-	-	-	-	67.6	1.5	-	-	-	-	67.0	-0.9	-	-	-	-
1977	66.8	-0.3	-	-	-	-	69.0	3.3	-	-	-	-	70.8	2.6	-	-	-	-	70.6	-0.3	-	-	-	-
1978	71.5	1.3	-	-	72.7	1.7	-	-	74.6	2.6	-	-	76.5	2.5	-	-	77.1	0.8	-	-	77.4	0.4	-	-
1979	78.7	1.7	-	-	81.0	2.9	-	-	83.7	3.3	-	-	85.7	2.4	-	-	84.1	-1.9	-	-	84.1	0.0	-	-
1980	86.2	2.5	-	-	87.4	1.4	-	-	87.6	0.2	-	-	89.6	2.3	-	-	90.2	0.7	-	-	91.6	1.6	-	-
1981	94.4	3.1	-	-	94.6	0.2	-	-	94.2	-0.4	-	-	94.4	0.2	-	-	93.8	-0.6	-	-	94.1	0.3	-	-
1982	95.9	1.9	-	-	95.9	0.0	-	-	96.5	0.6	-	-	97.2	0.7	-	-	97.1	-0.1	-	-	96.8	-0.3	-	-
1983	97.4	0.6	-	-	99.1	1.7	-	-	98.6	-0.5	-	-	99.5	0.9	-	-	99.2	-0.3	-	-	100.0	0.8	-	-
1984	102.2	2.2	-	-	103.8	1.6	-	-	104.0	0.2	-	-	104.4	0.4	-	-	105.0	0.6	-	-	104.9	-0.1	-	-
1985	106.6	1.6	-	-	107.7	1.0	-	-	107.8	0.1	-	-	109.2	1.3	-	-	109.0	-0.2	-	-	110.1	1.0	-	-
1986	111.9	1.6	-	-	110.8	-1.0	-	-	112.2	1.3	-	-	114.1	1.7	-	-	116.2	1.8	-	-	115.4	-0.7	-	-
1987	119.3	3.4	-	-	118.4	-0.8	-	-	119.0	0.5	-	-	119.4	0.3	-	-	120.2	0.7	-	-	119.7	-0.4	-	-
1988	122.0	1.9	-	-	120.8	-1.0	-	-	123.5	2.2	-	-	124.8	1.1	-	-	127.3	2.0	-	-	126.4	-0.7	-	-
1989	128.1	1.3	-	-	130.2	1.6	-	-	131.5	1.0	-	-	133.5	1.5	-	-	133.8	0.2	-	-	133.9	0.1	-	-
1990	137.1	2.4	-	-	138.3	0.9	-	-	138.0	-0.2	-	-	138.3	0.2	-	-	139.4	0.8	-	-	139.5	0.1	-	-
1991	142.2	1.9	-	-	141.3	-0.6	-	-	143.2	1.3	-	-	143.0	-0.1	-	-	141.9	-0.8	-	-	142.9	0.7	-	-
1992	143.5	0.4	-	-	143.7	0.1	-	-	142.4	-0.9	-	-	143.1	0.5	-	-	143.3	0.1	-	-	143.5	0.1	-	-
1993	145.4	1.3	-	-	145.2	-0.1	-	-	146.3	0.8	-	-	146.7	0.3	-	-	146.6	-0.1	-	-	146.9	0.2	-	-
1994	148.0	0.7	-	-	149.4	0.9	-	-	148.6	-0.5	-	-	149.8	0.8	-	-	151.4	1.1	-	-	150.8	-0.4	-	-
1995	155.0	2.8	-	-	153.1	-1.2	-	-	154.0	0.6	-	-	152.5	-1.0	-	-	153.4	0.6	-	-	153.7	0.2	-	-
1996	156.0	1.5	-	-	157.6	1.0	-	-	156.9	-0.4	-	-	157.4	0.3	-	-	158.4	0.6	-	-	159.1	0.4	-	-
1997	159.2	0.1	-	-	160.1	0.6	-	-	159.6	-0.3	-	-	160.3	0.4	-	-	160.8	0.3	-	-	161.2	0.2	-	-
1998	164.5	2.0	-	-	163.6	-0.5	-	-	164.8	0.7	-	-	165.4	0.4	-	-	166.5	0.7	-	-	168.9	1.4	-	-
1999	169.4	0.3	-	-	168.7	-0.4	-	-	170.2	0.9	-	-	171.2	0.6	-	-	170.6	-0.4	-	-	172.5	1.1	-	-
2000	173.0	0.3	-	-	172.4	-0.3	-	-	173.6	0.7	-	-	175.3	1.0	-	-	176.2	0.5	-	-	177.3	0.6	-	-
2001	178.4	0.6	-	-	179.4	0.6	-	-	179.5	0.1	-	-	183.1	2.0	-	-	182.8	-0.2	-	-	184.4	0.9	-	-

Source: U.S. Department of Labor, Bureau of Labor Statistics, Division of Consumer Prices and Price Indexes. - indicates no data collected for period.

Boston-Brockton-Nashua, MA-NH-ME-CT
Consumer Price Index - Urban Wage Earners
Base 1982-1984 = 100
Food and Beverages

For 1976-2001. Columns headed % show percentile change in the index from the previous period for which an index is available.

Year	Jan Index	%	Feb Index	%	Mar Index	%	Apr Index	%	May Index	%	Jun Index	%	Jul Index	%	Aug Index	%	Sep Index	%	Oct Index	%	Nov Index	%	Dec Index	%
1976	67.5	-	-	-	-	-	67.2	-0.4	-	-	-	-	68.1	1.3	-	-	-	-	67.5	-0.9	-	-	-	-
1977	67.4	-0.1	-	-	-	-	69.7	3.4	-	-	-	-	71.4	2.4	-	-	-	-	71.2	-0.3	-	-	-	-
1978	72.1	1.3	-	-	73.3	1.7	-	-	74.9	2.2	-	-	77.6	3.6	-	-	77.5	-0.1	-	-	78.0	0.6	-	-
1979	78.6	0.8	-	-	81.3	3.4	-	-	83.5	2.7	-	-	85.8	2.8	-	-	84.0	-2.1	-	-	84.6	0.7	-	-
1980	86.1	1.8	-	-	87.7	1.9	-	-	88.6	1.0	-	-	90.1	1.7	-	-	90.9	0.9	-	-	92.2	1.4	-	-
1981	94.3	2.3	-	-	95.2	1.0	-	-	94.7	-0.5	-	-	94.7	0.0	-	-	94.4	-0.3	-	-	94.2	-0.2	-	-
1982	95.6	1.5	-	-	95.7	0.1	-	-	96.3	0.6	-	-	97.3	1.0	-	-	97.2	-0.1	-	-	96.7	-0.5	-	-
1983	97.2	0.5	-	-	99.0	1.9	-	-	98.6	-0.4	-	-	99.6	1.0	-	-	99.2	-0.4	-	-	99.9	0.7	-	-
1984	102.3	2.4	-	-	104.1	1.8	-	-	104.2	0.1	-	-	104.8	0.6	-	-	104.9	0.1	-	-	104.7	-0.2	-	-
1985	106.5	1.7	-	-	107.7	1.1	-	-	107.6	-0.1	-	-	109.1	1.4	-	-	108.7	-0.4	-	-	109.4	0.6	-	-
1986	111.3	1.7	-	-	110.3	-0.9	-	-	111.4	1.0	-	-	113.8	2.2	-	-	115.9	1.8	-	-	114.7	-1.0	-	-
1987	119.1	3.8	-	-	117.9	-1.0	-	-	118.2	0.3	-	-	118.8	0.5	-	-	119.6	0.7	-	-	119.0	-0.5	-	-
1988	121.3	1.9	-	-	120.1	-1.0	-	-	123.0	2.4	-	-	124.4	1.1	-	-	126.9	2.0	-	-	125.7	-0.9	-	-
1989	127.5	1.4	-	-	129.5	1.6	-	-	130.8	1.0	-	-	133.0	1.7	-	-	133.1	0.1	-	-	132.9	-0.2	-	-
1990	136.2	2.5	-	-	137.4	0.9	-	-	137.2	-0.1	-	-	137.7	0.4	-	-	138.9	0.9	-	-	138.8	-0.1	-	-
1991	141.3	1.8	-	-	140.4	-0.6	-	-	142.5	1.5	-	-	142.1	-0.3	-	-	141.2	-0.6	-	-	142.1	0.6	-	-
1992	142.6	0.4	-	-	142.8	0.1	-	-	141.6	-0.8	-	-	142.0	0.3	-	-	142.4	0.3	-	-	142.5	0.1	-	-
1993	144.6	1.5	-	-	144.4	-0.1	-	-	145.3	0.6	-	-	145.9	0.4	-	-	145.7	-0.1	-	-	145.9	0.1	-	-
1994	147.0	0.8	-	-	148.3	0.9	-	-	147.4	-0.6	-	-	148.6	0.8	-	-	150.1	1.0	-	-	149.2	-0.6	-	-
1995	153.6	2.9	-	-	151.6	-1.3	-	-	152.4	0.5	-	-	150.8	-1.0	-	-	152.0	0.8	-	-	152.1	0.1	-	-
1996	154.4	1.5	-	-	155.9	1.0	-	-	155.5	-0.3	-	-	156.1	0.4	-	-	157.0	0.6	-	-	157.6	0.4	-	-
1997	157.8	0.1	-	-	158.4	0.4	-	-	157.9	-0.3	-	-	158.8	0.6	-	-	159.0	0.1	-	-	159.4	0.3	-	-
1998	162.7	2.1	-	-	161.9	-0.5	-	-	163.0	0.7	-	-	163.6	0.4	-	-	164.7	0.7	-	-	167.2	1.5	-	-
1999	167.4	0.1	-	-	166.6	-0.5	-	-	168.2	1.0	-	-	169.2	0.6	-	-	168.6	-0.4	-	-	170.8	1.3	-	-
2000	171.1	0.2	-	-	170.4	-0.4	-	-	171.7	0.8	-	-	173.7	1.2	-	-	174.3	0.3	-	-	175.5	0.7	-	-
2001	176.5	0.6	-	-	177.5	0.6	-	-	177.7	0.1	-	-	181.3	2.0	-	-	181.1	-0.1	-	-	182.8	0.9	-	-

Source: U.S. Department of Labor, Bureau of Labor Statistics, Division of Consumer Prices and Price Indexes. - indicates no data collected for period.

Boston-Brockton-Nashua, MA-NH-ME-CT
Consumer Price Index - All Urban Consumers
Base 1982-1984 = 100
Housing

For 1976-2001. Columns headed % show percentile change in the index from the previous period for which an index is available.

Year	Jan Index	%	Feb Index	%	Mar Index	%	Apr Index	%	May Index	%	Jun Index	%	Jul Index	%	Aug Index	%	Sep Index	%	Oct Index	%	Nov Index	%	Dec Index	%
1976	55.2	-	-	-	-	-	55.6	0.7	-	-	-	-	56.4	1.4	-	-	-	-	56.7	0.5	-	-	-	-
1977	58.7	3.5	-	-	-	-	58.9	0.3	-	-	-	-	59.8	1.5	-	-	-	-	60.0	0.3	-	-	-	-
1978	61.2	2.0	-	-	61.9	1.1	-	-	62.1	0.3	-	-	62.9	1.3	-	-	63.6	1.1	-	-	65.4	2.8	-	-
1979	67.1	2.6	-	-	67.4	0.4	-	-	67.9	0.7	-	-	69.2	1.9	-	-	71.7	3.6	-	-	74.1	3.3	-	-
1980	75.6	2.0	-	-	78.4	3.7	-	-	79.3	1.1	-	-	81.0	2.1	-	-	82.0	1.2	-	-	83.4	1.7	-	-
1981	87.8	5.3	-	-	90.0	2.5	-	-	90.1	0.1	-	-	91.7	1.8	-	-	95.5	4.1	-	-	95.2	-0.3	-	-
1982	94.1	-1.2	-	-	89.6	-4.8	-	-	91.7	2.3	-	-	95.2	3.8	-	-	97.1	2.0	-	-	98.6	1.5	-	-
1983	100.1	1.5	-	-	98.8	-1.3	-	-	99.3	0.5	-	-	99.7	0.4	-	-	100.8	1.1	-	-	102.5	1.7	-	-
1984	103.1	0.6	-	-	104.0	0.9	-	-	104.3	0.3	-	-	105.5	1.2	-	-	106.1	0.6	-	-	106.4	0.3	-	-
1985	106.9	0.5	-	-	107.6	0.7	-	-	107.6	0.0	-	-	109.4	1.7	-	-	110.1	0.6	-	-	112.2	1.9	-	-
1986	111.8	-0.4	-	-	111.4	-0.4	-	-	110.1	-1.2	-	-	110.2	0.1	-	-	112.4	2.0	-	-	113.5	1.0	-	-
1987	114.2	0.6	-	-	115.3	1.0	-	-	114.7	-0.5	-	-	116.1	1.2	-	-	119.1	2.6	-	-	119.9	0.7	-	-
1988	119.8	-0.1	-	-	121.0	1.0	-	-	122.9	1.6	-	-	123.9	0.8	-	-	125.5	1.3	-	-	126.6	0.9	-	-
1989	130.0	2.7	-	-	130.5	0.4	-	-	129.2	-1.0	-	-	129.7	0.4	-	-	132.8	2.4	-	-	134.1	1.0	-	-
1990	136.0	1.4	-	-	135.4	-0.4	-	-	134.4	-0.7	-	-	136.4	1.5	-	-	137.4	0.7	-	-	140.9	2.5	-	-
1991	142.3	1.0	-	-	142.3	0.0	-	-	139.4	-2.0	-	-	140.6	0.9	-	-	140.7	0.1	-	-	140.7	0.0	-	-
1992	140.9	0.1	-	-	143.9	2.1	-	-	142.0	-1.3	-	-	144.1	1.5	-	-	143.7	-0.3	-	-	145.5	1.3	-	-
1993	146.7	0.8	-	-	147.1	0.3	-	-	144.8	-1.6	-	-	146.0	0.8	-	-	145.4	-0.4	-	-	148.1	1.9	-	-
1994	147.0	-0.7	-	-	148.1	0.7	-	-	145.8	-1.6	-	-	147.1	0.9	-	-	148.1	0.7	-	-	150.2	1.4	-	-
1995	151.7	1.0	-	-	153.1	0.9	-	-	149.4	-2.4	-	-	149.9	0.3	-	-	151.0	0.7	-	-	153.4	1.6	-	-
1996	157.1	2.4	-	-	157.3	0.1	-	-	154.7	-1.7	-	-	155.5	0.5	-	-	156.3	0.5	-	-	160.6	2.8	-	-
1997	163.1	1.6	-	-	164.4	0.8	-	-	160.4	-2.4	-	-	161.9	0.9	-	-	161.4	-0.3	-	-	163.4	1.2	-	-
1998	165.7	1.4	-	-	165.9	0.1	-	-	164.2	-1.0	-	-	164.4	0.1	-	-	166.0	1.0	-	-	167.6	1.0	-	-
1999	169.1	0.9	-	-	170.0	0.5	-	-	167.0	-1.8	-	-	169.2	1.3	-	-	170.6	0.8	-	-	174.2	2.1	-	-
2000	176.0	1.0	-	-	179.3	1.9	-	-	176.5	-1.6	-	-	178.2	1.0	-	-	179.6	0.8	-	-	184.8	2.9	-	-
2001	188.3	1.9	-	-	190.4	1.1	-	-	188.9	-0.8	-	-	191.6	1.4	-	-	192.9	0.7	-	-	194.0	0.6	-	-

Source: U.S. Department of Labor, Bureau of Labor Statistics, Division of Consumer Prices and Price Indexes. - indicates no data collected for period.

Boston-Brockton-Nashua, MA-NH-ME-CT
Consumer Price Index - Urban Wage Earners
Base 1982-1984 = 100
Housing

For 1976-2001. Columns headed % show percentile change in the index from the previous period for which an index is available.

Year	Jan Index	%	Feb Index	%	Mar Index	%	Apr Index	%	May Index	%	Jun Index	%	Jul Index	%	Aug Index	%	Sep Index	%	Oct Index	%	Nov Index	%	Dec Index	%
1976	55.1	-	-	-	-	-	55.5	0.7	-	-	-	-	56.3	1.4	-	-	-	-	56.6	0.5	-	-	-	-
1977	58.6	3.5	-	-	-	-	58.8	0.3	-	-	-	-	59.7	1.5	-	-	-	-	59.9	0.3	-	-	-	-
1978	61.1	2.0	-	-	61.8	1.1	-	-	61.9	0.2	-	-	62.8	1.5	-	-	63.7	1.4	-	-	65.5	2.8	-	-
1979	67.1	2.4	-	-	67.4	0.4	-	-	68.1	1.0	-	-	69.5	2.1	-	-	71.9	3.5	-	-	74.4	3.5	-	-
1980	76.2	2.4	-	-	79.2	3.9	-	-	80.1	1.1	-	-	81.7	2.0	-	-	82.7	1.2	-	-	84.6	2.3	-	-
1981	88.9	5.1	-	-	91.0	2.4	-	-	91.3	0.3	-	-	93.5	2.4	-	-	97.1	3.9	-	-	96.2	-0.9	-	-
1982	95.1	-1.1	-	-	90.2	-5.2	-	-	92.5	2.5	-	-	96.1	3.9	-	-	98.0	2.0	-	-	99.6	1.6	-	-
1983	99.8	0.2	-	-	98.7	-1.1	-	-	98.8	0.1	-	-	100.3	1.5	-	-	100.5	0.2	-	-	102.6	2.1	-	-
1984	102.6	0.0	-	-	102.3	-0.3	-	-	103.8	1.5	-	-	103.3	-0.5	-	-	105.9	2.5	-	-	106.9	0.9	-	-
1985	107.4	0.5	-	-	108.0	0.6	-	-	108.1	0.1	-	-	109.9	1.7	-	-	110.5	0.5	-	-	112.6	1.9	-	-
1986	112.4	-0.2	-	-	111.8	-0.5	-	-	110.3	-1.3	-	-	110.4	0.1	-	-	112.5	1.9	-	-	113.6	1.0	-	-
1987	114.0	0.4	-	-	115.4	1.2	-	-	114.8	-0.5	-	-	116.1	1.1	-	-	119.1	2.6	-	-	120.1	0.8	-	-
1988	119.7	-0.3	-	-	120.8	0.9	-	-	122.8	1.7	-	-	123.6	0.7	-	-	125.2	1.3	-	-	126.6	1.1	-	-
1989	129.6	2.4	-	-	130.1	0.4	-	-	128.7	-1.1	-	-	129.5	0.6	-	-	132.5	2.3	-	-	134.1	1.2	-	-
1990	135.3	0.9	-	-	134.8	-0.4	-	-	133.6	-0.9	-	-	135.2	1.2	-	-	136.1	0.7	-	-	140.0	2.9	-	-
1991	140.6	0.4	-	-	140.5	-0.1	-	-	138.1	-1.7	-	-	139.1	0.7	-	-	139.5	0.3	-	-	139.9	0.3	-	-
1992	139.6	-0.2	-	-	142.2	1.9	-	-	140.4	-1.3	-	-	142.5	1.5	-	-	142.1	-0.3	-	-	144.5	1.7	-	-
1993	145.4	0.6	-	-	145.5	0.1	-	-	143.5	-1.4	-	-	144.2	0.5	-	-	143.9	-0.2	-	-	147.2	2.3	-	-
1994	145.7	-1.0	-	-	146.4	0.5	-	-	144.5	-1.3	-	-	145.4	0.6	-	-	146.5	0.8	-	-	149.0	1.7	-	-
1995	150.2	0.8	-	-	151.1	0.6	-	-	147.8	-2.2	-	-	148.1	0.2	-	-	149.3	0.8	-	-	152.1	1.9	-	-
1996	155.5	2.2	-	-	155.7	0.1	-	-	153.0	-1.7	-	-	153.7	0.5	-	-	154.5	0.5	-	-	159.1	3.0	-	-
1997	161.5	1.5	-	-	162.4	0.6	-	-	158.5	-2.4	-	-	159.7	0.8	-	-	159.1	-0.4	-	-	161.7	1.6	-	-
1998	163.3	1.0	-	-	163.3	0.0	-	-	161.9	-0.9	-	-	162.5	0.4	-	-	163.7	0.7	-	-	166.0	1.4	-	-
1999	167.2	0.7	-	-	167.3	0.1	-	-	165.3	-1.2	-	-	166.6	0.8	-	-	168.2	1.0	-	-	172.2	2.4	-	-
2000	173.8	0.9	-	-	176.9	1.8	-	-	174.7	-1.2	-	-	176.3	0.9	-	-	177.6	0.7	-	-	183.0	3.0	-	-
2001	186.4	1.9	-	-	188.7	1.2	-	-	188.2	-0.3	-	-	191.2	1.6	-	-	192.6	0.7	-	-	193.9	0.7	-	-

Source: U.S. Department of Labor, Bureau of Labor Statistics, Division of Consumer Prices and Price Indexes. - indicates no data collected for period.

Boston-Brockton-Nashua, MA-NH-ME-CT
Consumer Price Index - All Urban Consumers
Base 1982-1984 = 100
Apparel

For 1952-2001. Columns headed % show percentile change in the index from the previous period for which an index is available.

Year	Jan Index	%	Feb Index	%	Mar Index	%	Apr Index	%	May Index	%	Jun Index	%	Jul Index	%	Aug Index	%	Sep Index	%	Oct Index	%	Nov Index	%	Dec Index	%
1952	-	-	-	-	-	-	-	-	-	-	-	-	-	-	-	-	-	-	39.6	-	-	-	-	-
1953	39.2	-1.0	-	-	-	-	39.5	0.8	-	-	-	-	39.5	0.0	-	-	-	-	39.6	0.3	-	-	-	-
1954	38.6	-2.5	-	-	-	-	38.8	0.5	-	-	-	-	39.1	0.8	-	-	-	-	39.9	2.0	-	-	-	-
1955	39.0	-2.3	-	-	-	-	39.3	0.8	-	-	-	-	39.1	-0.5	-	-	-	-	39.5	1.0	-	-	-	-
1956	39.0	-1.3	-	-	-	-	39.6	1.5	-	-	-	-	39.7	0.3	-	-	-	-	40.6	2.3	-	-	-	-
1957	39.7	-2.2	-	-	-	-	40.5	2.0	-	-	-	-	40.3	-0.5	-	-	-	-	41.1	2.0	-	-	-	-
1958	40.8	-0.7	-	-	-	-	40.9	0.2	-	-	-	-	41.2	0.7	-	-	-	-	41.8	1.5	-	-	-	-
1959	40.3	-3.6	-	-	-	-	40.3	0.0	-	-	-	-	40.7	1.0	-	-	-	-	41.7	2.5	-	-	-	-
1960	41.3	-1.0	-	-	-	-	41.9	1.5	-	-	-	-	42.3	1.0	-	-	-	-	42.6	0.7	-	-	-	-
1961	42.1	-1.2	-	-	-	-	42.0	-0.2	-	-	-	-	42.3	0.7	-	-	-	-	43.0	1.7	-	-	-	-
1962	41.9	-2.6	-	-	-	-	43.0	2.6	-	-	-	-	43.1	0.2	-	-	-	-	43.7	1.4	-	-	-	-
1963	43.0	-1.6	-	-	-	-	43.3	0.7	-	-	-	-	43.0	-0.7	-	-	-	-	44.1	2.6	-	-	-	-
1964	43.0	-2.5	-	-	-	-	43.8	1.9	-	-	-	-	43.5	-0.7	-	-	-	-	44.1	1.4	-	-	-	-
1965	43.2	-2.0	-	-	-	-	43.7	1.2	-	-	-	-	44.0	0.7	-	-	-	-	44.5	1.1	-	-	-	-
1966	44.4	-0.2	-	-	-	-	44.9	1.1	-	-	-	-	44.6	-0.7	-	-	-	-	45.9	2.9	-	-	-	-
1967	45.3	-1.3	-	-	-	-	46.3	2.2	-	-	-	-	46.3	0.0	-	-	-	-	47.5	2.6	-	-	-	-
1968	46.9	-1.3	-	-	-	-	49.3	5.1	-	-	-	-	48.8	-1.0	-	-	-	-	51.0	4.5	-	-	-	-
1969	50.4	-1.2	-	-	-	-	51.4	2.0	-	-	-	-	51.4	0.0	-	-	-	-	54.4	5.8	-	-	-	-
1970	52.6	-3.3	-	-	-	-	54.9	4.4	-	-	-	-	53.7	-2.2	-	-	-	-	56.5	5.2	-	-	-	-
1971	55.4	-1.9	-	-	-	-	56.6	2.2	-	-	-	-	56.2	-0.7	-	-	-	-	57.9	3.0	-	-	-	-
1972	56.7	-2.1	-	-	-	-	57.2	0.9	-	-	-	-	57.3	0.2	-	-	-	-	59.5	3.8	-	-	-	-
1973	58.1	-2.4	-	-	-	-	59.6	2.6	-	-	-	-	59.2	-0.7	-	-	-	-	61.3	3.5	-	-	-	-
1974	60.7	-1.0	-	-	-	-	63.4	4.4	-	-	-	-	63.8	0.6	-	-	-	-	66.6	4.4	-	-	-	-
1975	66.0	-0.9	-	-	-	-	67.5	2.3	-	-	-	-	67.6	0.1	-	-	-	-	70.4	4.1	-	-	-	-
1976	70.6	0.3	-	-	-	-	71.2	0.8	-	-	-	-	71.1	-0.1	-	-	-	-	72.7	2.3	-	-	-	-
1977	71.4	-1.8	-	-	-	-	72.5	1.5	-	-	-	-	72.0	-0.7	-	-	-	-	75.6	5.0	-	-	-	-
1978	74.8	-1.1	-	-	76.9	2.8	-	-	79.4	3.3	-	-	76.2	-4.0	-	-	81.2	6.6	-	-	83.0	2.2	-	-
1979	78.7	-5.2	-	-	84.6	7.5	-	-	84.6	0.0	-	-	83.7	-1.1	-	-	88.0	5.1	-	-	88.1	0.1	-	-
1980	85.7	-2.7	-	-	88.4	3.2	-	-	88.8	0.5	-	-	87.2	-1.8	-	-	92.5	6.1	-	-	93.2	0.8	-	-
1981	90.6	-2.8	-	-	95.3	5.2	-	-	93.4	-2.0	-	-	92.3	-1.2	-	-	95.6	3.6	-	-	95.6	0.0	-	-
1982	92.5	-3.2	-	-	97.0	4.9	-	-	95.8	-1.2	-	-	95.9	0.1	-	-	101.0	5.3	-	-	100.6	-0.4	-	-
1983	99.3	-1.3	-	-	101.3	2.0	-	-	100.8	-0.5	-	-	99.8	-1.0	-	-	98.4	-1.4	-	-	99.8	1.4	-	-
1984	98.7	-1.1	-	-	103.3	4.7	-	-	102.9	-0.4	-	-	101.0	-1.8	-	-	106.2	5.1	-	-	103.8	-2.3	-	-
1985	100.7	-3.0	-	-	106.8	6.1	-	-	107.1	0.3	-	-	101.7	-5.0	-	-	110.4	8.6	-	-	108.8	-1.4	-	-
1986	106.2	-2.4	-	-	108.4	2.1	-	-	107.8	-0.6	-	-	106.6	-1.1	-	-	111.2	4.3	-	-	108.5	-2.4	-	-
1987	107.4	-1.0	-	-	122.6	14.2	-	-	112.4	-8.3	-	-	110.3	-1.9	-	-	123.4	11.9	-	-	117.8	-4.5	-	-
1988	112.6	-4.4	-	-	134.7	19.6	-	-	128.4	-4.7	-	-	118.9	-7.4	-	-	126.7	6.6	-	-	130.8	3.2	-	-
1989	124.6	-4.7	-	-	121.4	-2.6	-	-	126.3	4.0	-	-	117.6	-6.9	-	-	121.5	3.3	-	-	137.5	13.2	-	-
1990	132.0	-4.0	-	-	129.7	-1.7	-	-	135.2	4.2	-	-	124.7	-7.8	-	-	154.6	24.0	-	-	152.5	-1.4	-	-
1991	135.6	-11.1	-	-	139.3	2.7	-	-	140.8	1.1	-	-	138.1	-1.9	-	-	157.9	14.3	-	-	154.1	-2.4	-	-
1992	144.5	-6.2	-	-	142.5	-1.4	-	-	142.7	0.1	-	-	141.4	-0.9	-	-	152.7	8.0	-	-	145.8	-4.5	-	-
1993	148.6	1.9	-	-	182.1	22.5	-	-	155.8	-14.4	-	-	150.1	-3.7	-	-	151.4	0.9	-	-	158.0	4.4	-	-
1994	149.9	-5.1	-	-	156.2	4.2	-	-	153.3	-1.9	-	-	140.1	-8.6	-	-	144.7	3.3	-	-	139.6	-3.5	-	-
1995	139.0	-0.4	-	-	142.3	2.4	-	-	145.5	2.2	-	-	145.5	0.0	-	-	145.8	0.2	-	-	144.3	-1.0	-	-
1996	138.5	-4.0	-	-	145.2	4.8	-	-	142.0	-2.2	-	-	138.1	-2.7	-	-	145.2	5.1	-	-	146.9	1.2	-	-
1997	144.3	-1.8	-	-	141.1	-2.2	-	-	146.8	4.0	-	-	140.1	-4.6	-	-	143.7	2.6	-	-	147.6	2.7	-	-

[Continued]

Boston-Brockton-Nashua, MA-NH-ME-CT
Consumer Price Index - All Urban Consumers
Base 1982-1984 = 100
Apparel
[Continued]

For 1952-2001. Columns headed % show percentile change in the index from the previous period for which an index is available.

Year	Jan		Feb		Mar		Apr		May		Jun		Jul		Aug		Sep		Oct		Nov		Dec	
	Index	%	Index	%	Index	%	Index	%	Index	%	Index	%	Index	%	Index	%	Index	%	Index	%	Index	%	Index	%
1998	144.0	-2.4	-	-	149.8	4.0	-	-	151.8	1.3	-	-	143.2	-5.7	-	-	146.2	2.1	-	-	147.6	1.0	-	-
1999	140.7	-4.7	-	-	146.9	4.4	-	-	145.6	-0.9	-	-	137.4	-5.6	-	-	145.1	5.6	-	-	146.5	1.0	-	-
2000	139.0	-5.1	-	-	147.0	5.8	-	-	141.7	-3.6	-	-	135.9	-4.1	-	-	137.7	1.3	-	-	138.2	0.4	-	-
2001	132.2	-4.3	-	-	143.1	8.2	-	-	144.6	1.0	-	-	137.6	-4.8	-	-	143.1	4.0	-	-	138.8	-3.0	-	-

Source: U.S. Department of Labor, Bureau of Labor Statistics, Division of Consumer Prices and Price Indexes. - indicates no data collected for period.

Boston-Brockton-Nashua, MA-NH-ME-CT
Consumer Price Index - Urban Wage Earners
Base 1982-1984 = 100
Apparel

For 1952-2001. Columns headed % show percentile change in the index from the previous period for which an index is available.

Year	Jan Index	%	Feb Index	%	Mar Index	%	Apr Index	%	May Index	%	Jun Index	%	Jul Index	%	Aug Index	%	Sep Index	%	Oct Index	%	Nov Index	%	Dec Index	%
1952	-	-	-	-	-	-	-	-	-	-	-	-	-	-	-	-	-	-	39.9	-	-	-	-	-
1953	39.4	-1.3	-	-	-	-	39.8	1.0	-	-	-	-	39.8	0.0	-	-	-	-	39.9	0.3	-	-	-	-
1954	38.9	-2.5	-	-	-	-	39.1	0.5	-	-	-	-	39.4	0.8	-	-	-	-	40.1	1.8	-	-	-	-
1955	39.3	-2.0	-	-	-	-	39.6	0.8	-	-	-	-	39.4	-0.5	-	-	-	-	39.8	1.0	-	-	-	-
1956	39.3	-1.3	-	-	-	-	39.9	1.5	-	-	-	-	40.0	0.3	-	-	-	-	40.9	2.3	-	-	-	-
1957	40.0	-2.2	-	-	-	-	40.8	2.0	-	-	-	-	40.6	-0.5	-	-	-	-	41.4	2.0	-	-	-	-
1958	41.1	-0.7	-	-	-	-	41.2	0.2	-	-	-	-	41.5	0.7	-	-	-	-	42.1	1.4	-	-	-	-
1959	40.6	-3.6	-	-	-	-	40.6	0.0	-	-	-	-	41.0	1.0	-	-	-	-	42.0	2.4	-	-	-	-
1960	41.6	-1.0	-	-	-	-	42.2	1.4	-	-	-	-	42.6	0.9	-	-	-	-	42.9	0.7	-	-	-	-
1961	42.4	-1.2	-	-	-	-	42.4	0.0	-	-	-	-	42.6	0.5	-	-	-	-	43.3	1.6	-	-	-	-
1962	42.3	-2.3	-	-	-	-	43.3	2.4	-	-	-	-	43.4	0.2	-	-	-	-	44.0	1.4	-	-	-	-
1963	43.3	-1.6	-	-	-	-	43.6	0.7	-	-	-	-	43.3	-0.7	-	-	-	-	44.4	2.5	-	-	-	-
1964	43.3	-2.5	-	-	-	-	44.1	1.8	-	-	-	-	43.8	-0.7	-	-	-	-	44.4	1.4	-	-	-	-
1965	43.6	-1.8	-	-	-	-	44.0	0.9	-	-	-	-	44.3	0.7	-	-	-	-	44.8	1.1	-	-	-	-
1966	44.7	-0.2	-	-	-	-	45.3	1.3	-	-	-	-	44.9	-0.9	-	-	-	-	46.2	2.9	-	-	-	-
1967	45.7	-1.1	-	-	-	-	46.7	2.2	-	-	-	-	46.7	0.0	-	-	-	-	47.9	2.6	-	-	-	-
1968	47.2	-1.5	-	-	-	-	49.7	5.3	-	-	-	-	49.1	-1.2	-	-	-	-	51.3	4.5	-	-	-	-
1969	50.7	-1.2	-	-	-	-	51.8	2.2	-	-	-	-	51.8	0.0	-	-	-	-	54.8	5.8	-	-	-	-
1970	53.0	-3.3	-	-	-	-	55.3	4.3	-	-	-	-	54.1	-2.2	-	-	-	-	57.0	5.4	-	-	-	-
1971	55.8	-2.1	-	-	-	-	57.0	2.2	-	-	-	-	56.6	-0.7	-	-	-	-	58.4	3.2	-	-	-	-
1972	57.2	-2.1	-	-	-	-	57.7	0.9	-	-	-	-	57.7	0.0	-	-	-	-	59.9	3.8	-	-	-	-
1973	58.5	-2.3	-	-	-	-	60.0	2.6	-	-	-	-	59.6	-0.7	-	-	-	-	61.8	3.7	-	-	-	-
1974	61.1	-1.1	-	-	-	-	63.9	4.6	-	-	-	-	64.3	0.6	-	-	-	-	67.1	4.4	-	-	-	-
1975	66.5	-0.9	-	-	-	-	68.0	2.3	-	-	-	-	68.1	0.1	-	-	-	-	70.9	4.1	-	-	-	-
1976	71.2	0.4	-	-	-	-	71.7	0.7	-	-	-	-	71.6	-0.1	-	-	-	-	73.3	2.4	-	-	-	-
1977	72.0	-1.8	-	-	-	-	73.0	1.4	-	-	-	-	72.5	-0.7	-	-	-	-	76.1	5.0	-	-	-	-
1978	75.4	-0.9	-	-	76.3	1.2	-	-	79.2	3.8	-	-	75.9	-4.2	-	-	81.4	7.2	-	-	80.9	-0.6	-	-
1979	77.2	-4.6	-	-	80.8	4.7	-	-	82.0	1.5	-	-	79.7	-2.8	-	-	87.7	10.0	-	-	86.8	-1.0	-	-
1980	83.0	-4.4	-	-	85.5	3.0	-	-	85.2	-0.4	-	-	84.4	-0.9	-	-	90.3	7.0	-	-	91.4	1.2	-	-
1981	87.6	-4.2	-	-	93.9	7.2	-	-	93.1	-0.9	-	-	89.6	-3.8	-	-	95.9	7.0	-	-	96.3	0.4	-	-
1982	92.2	-4.3	-	-	99.4	7.8	-	-	95.8	-3.6	-	-	95.9	0.1	-	-	102.3	6.7	-	-	101.0	-1.3	-	-
1983	98.5	-2.5	-	-	103.9	5.5	-	-	102.2	-1.6	-	-	99.2	-2.9	-	-	98.4	-0.8	-	-	99.0	0.6	-	-
1984	97.7	-1.3	-	-	101.9	4.3	-	-	101.6	-0.3	-	-	100.3	-1.3	-	-	105.8	5.5	-	-	103.4	-2.3	-	-
1985	99.6	-3.7	-	-	105.4	5.8	-	-	104.8	-0.6	-	-	100.0	-4.6	-	-	110.0	10.0	-	-	107.9	-1.9	-	-
1986	104.4	-3.2	-	-	107.8	3.3	-	-	106.2	-1.5	-	-	105.2	-0.9	-	-	110.1	4.7	-	-	107.2	-2.6	-	-
1987	112.2	4.7	-	-	127.6	13.7	-	-	115.9	-9.2	-	-	115.7	-0.2	-	-	130.1	12.4	-	-	124.3	-4.5	-	-
1988	120.9	-2.7	-	-	139.3	15.2	-	-	134.6	-3.4	-	-	125.9	-6.5	-	-	134.1	6.5	-	-	138.4	3.2	-	-
1989	130.5	-5.7	-	-	128.6	-1.5	-	-	134.9	4.9	-	-	126.8	-6.0	-	-	132.6	4.6	-	-	148.3	11.8	-	-
1990	141.4	-4.7	-	-	139.5	-1.3	-	-	147.3	5.6	-	-	134.5	-8.7	-	-	158.8	18.1	-	-	159.7	0.6	-	-
1991	143.7	-10.0	-	-	151.4	5.4	-	-	151.5	0.1	-	-	149.4	-1.4	-	-	162.6	8.8	-	-	157.7	-3.0	-	-
1992	154.2	-2.2	-	-	149.8	-2.9	-	-	150.1	0.2	-	-	149.1	-0.7	-	-	161.3	8.2	-	-	155.1	-3.8	-	-
1993	153.9	-0.8	-	-	202.4	31.5	-	-	164.3	-18.8	-	-	155.2	-5.5	-	-	157.8	1.7	-	-	163.1	3.4	-	-
1994	154.4	-5.3	-	-	157.5	2.0	-	-	156.5	-0.6	-	-	148.3	-5.2	-	-	152.1	2.6	-	-	146.7	-3.6	-	-
1995	146.5	-0.1	-	-	148.5	1.4	-	-	151.8	2.2	-	-	152.8	0.7	-	-	152.5	-0.2	-	-	151.9	-0.4	-	-
1996	147.4	-3.0	-	-	152.2	3.3	-	-	149.9	-1.5	-	-	146.0	-2.6	-	-	151.8	4.0	-	-	154.5	1.8	-	-
1997	152.7	-1.2	-	-	146.9	-3.8	-	-	157.0	6.9	-	-	148.7	-5.3	-	-	150.4	1.1	-	-	150.9	0.3	-	-

[Continued]

Boston-Brockton-Nashua, MA-NH-ME-CT
Consumer Price Index - Urban Wage Earners
Base 1982-1984 = 100
Apparel
[Continued]

For 1952-2001. Columns headed % show percentile change in the index from the previous period for which an index is available.

Year	Jan		Feb		Mar		Apr		May		Jun		Jul		Aug		Sep		Oct		Nov		Dec	
	Index	%	Index	%	Index	%	Index	%	Index	%	Index	%	Index	%	Index	%	Index	%	Index	%	Index	%	Index	%
1998	145.7	-3.4	-	-	153.3	5.2	-	-	154.7	0.9	-	-	144.6	-6.5	-	-	148.0	2.4	-	-	149.6	1.1	-	-
1999	142.0	-5.1	-	-	147.3	3.7	-	-	148.0	0.5	-	-	139.5	-5.7	-	-	148.5	6.5	-	-	149.2	0.5	-	-
2000	140.9	-5.6	-	-	148.1	5.1	-	-	145.3	-1.9	-	-	139.2	-4.2	-	-	143.9	3.4	-	-	142.2	-1.2	-	-
2001	133.4	-6.2	-	-	144.8	8.5	-	-	146.0	0.8	-	-	136.6	-6.4	-	-	146.4	7.2	-	-	143.1	-2.3	-	-

Source: U.S. Department of Labor, Bureau of Labor Statistics, Division of Consumer Prices and Price Indexes. - indicates no data collected for period.

Boston-Brockton-Nashua, MA-NH-ME-CT
Consumer Price Index - All Urban Consumers
Base 1982-1984 = 100
Transportation

For 1947-2000. Columns headed % show percentile change in the index from the previous period for which an index is available.

Year	Jan Index	%	Feb Index	%	Mar Index	%	Apr Index	%	May Index	%	Jun Index	%	Jul Index	%	Aug Index	%	Sep Index	%	Oct Index	%	Nov Index	%	Dec Index	%
1947	16.2	-	16.2	0.0	16.3	0.6	16.3	0.0	16.3	0.0	16.4	0.6	16.4	0.0	16.5	0.6	16.6	0.6	16.6	0.0	16.6	0.0	16.6	0.0
1948	16.7	0.6	16.8	0.6	16.8	0.0	16.8	0.0	16.8	0.0	16.8	0.0	16.9	0.6	17.1	1.2	17.1	0.0	17.1	0.0	17.1	0.0	17.1	0.0
1949	17.1	0.0	17.2	0.6	17.2	0.0	17.3	0.6	17.3	0.0	17.3	0.0	17.3	0.0	20.4	17.9	20.4	0.0	20.4	0.0	20.4	0.0	20.5	0.5
1950	20.5	0.0	20.4	-0.5	20.4	0.0	20.4	0.0	20.5	0.5	20.5	0.0	20.6	0.5	20.6	0.0	20.7	0.5	20.7	0.0	20.7	0.0	20.8	0.5
1951	20.8	0.0	20.8	0.0	20.8	0.0	20.8	0.0	20.8	0.0	20.8	0.0	20.8	0.0	21.6	3.8	21.6	0.0	21.8	0.9	21.9	0.5	21.9	0.0
1952	22.0	0.5	22.3	1.4	22.3	0.0	22.3	0.0	22.3	0.0	22.3	0.0	23.0	3.1	23.0	0.0	23.1	0.4	23.1	0.0	23.1	0.0	23.1	0.0
1953	23.2	0.4	-	-	-	-	23.5	1.3	-	-	-	-	23.7	0.9	-	-	-	-	23.7	0.0	-	-	-	-
1954	23.4	-1.3	-	-	-	-	24.4	4.3	-	-	-	-	23.7	-2.9	-	-	-	-	23.0	-3.0	-	-	-	-
1955	23.2	0.9	-	-	-	-	23.2	0.0	-	-	-	-	22.9	-1.3	-	-	-	-	23.5	2.6	-	-	-	-
1956	23.5	0.0	-	-	-	-	23.6	0.4	-	-	-	-	23.5	-0.4	-	-	-	-	25.1	6.8	-	-	-	-
1957	24.7	-1.6	-	-	-	-	24.9	0.8	-	-	-	-	25.0	0.4	-	-	-	-	25.2	0.8	-	-	-	-
1958	25.4	0.8	-	-	-	-	25.9	2.0	-	-	-	-	25.8	-0.4	-	-	-	-	25.7	-0.4	-	-	-	-
1959	26.5	3.1	-	-	-	-	26.4	-0.4	-	-	-	-	26.4	0.0	-	-	-	-	26.4	0.0	-	-	-	-
1960	25.7	-2.7	-	-	-	-	25.7	0.0	-	-	-	-	25.9	0.8	-	-	-	-	25.9	0.0	-	-	-	-
1961	25.6	-1.2	-	-	-	-	26.0	1.6	-	-	-	-	26.4	1.5	-	-	-	-	26.2	-0.8	-	-	-	-
1962	28.1	7.3	-	-	-	-	28.3	0.7	-	-	-	-	28.0	-1.1	-	-	-	-	28.3	1.1	-	-	-	-
1963	28.0	-1.1	-	-	-	-	28.3	1.1	-	-	-	-	28.5	0.7	-	-	-	-	28.3	-0.7	-	-	-	-
1964	28.4	0.4	-	-	-	-	28.3	-0.4	-	-	-	-	28.6	1.1	-	-	-	-	28.3	-1.0	-	-	-	-
1965	28.9	2.1	-	-	-	-	29.0	0.3	-	-	-	-	29.2	0.7	-	-	-	-	29.5	1.0	-	-	-	-
1966	29.3	-0.7	-	-	-	-	29.9	2.0	-	-	-	-	30.1	0.7	-	-	-	-	30.1	0.0	-	-	-	-
1967	30.1	0.0	-	-	-	-	30.4	1.0	-	-	-	-	30.7	1.0	-	-	-	-	30.9	0.7	-	-	-	-
1968	31.2	1.0	-	-	-	-	31.5	1.0	-	-	-	-	31.5	0.0	-	-	-	-	31.7	0.6	-	-	-	-
1969	32.9	3.8	-	-	-	-	33.6	2.1	-	-	-	-	33.6	0.0	-	-	-	-	33.6	0.0	-	-	-	-
1970	33.7	0.3	-	-	-	-	34.0	0.9	-	-	-	-	34.5	1.5	-	-	-	-	36.3	5.2	-	-	-	-
1971	36.6	0.8	-	-	-	-	36.2	-1.1	-	-	-	-	36.9	1.9	-	-	-	-	36.7	-0.5	-	-	-	-
1972	36.5	-0.5	-	-	-	-	36.3	-0.5	-	-	-	-	36.5	0.6	-	-	-	-	37.0	1.4	-	-	-	-
1973	37.0	0.0	-	-	-	-	37.1	0.3	-	-	-	-	37.8	1.9	-	-	-	-	37.8	0.0	-	-	-	-
1974	38.6	2.1	-	-	-	-	39.8	3.1	-	-	-	-	42.0	5.5	-	-	-	-	42.3	0.7	-	-	-	-
1975	42.8	1.2	-	-	-	-	45.1	5.4	-	-	-	-	47.0	4.2	-	-	-	-	47.6	1.3	-	-	-	-
1976	57.8	21.4	-	-	-	-	58.1	0.5	-	-	-	-	59.8	2.9	-	-	-	-	60.2	0.7	-	-	-	-
1977	62.2	3.3	-	-	-	-	63.3	1.8	-	-	-	-	63.9	0.9	-	-	-	-	63.6	-0.5	-	-	-	-
1978	63.7	0.2	-	-	61.2	-3.9	-	-	62.2	1.6	-	-	63.3	1.8	-	-	63.6	0.5	-	-	64.2	0.9	-	-
1979	63.6	-0.9	-	-	64.8	1.9	-	-	68.0	4.9	-	-	70.9	4.3	-	-	72.1	1.7	-	-	74.0	2.6	-	-
1980	76.6	3.5	-	-	80.5	5.1	-	-	81.8	1.6	-	-	83.5	2.1	-	-	84.7	1.4	-	-	86.3	1.9	-	-
1981	87.6	1.5	-	-	91.3	4.2	-	-	94.0	3.0	-	-	94.5	0.5	-	-	96.6	2.2	-	-	98.0	1.4	-	-
1982	97.6	-0.4	-	-	97.0	-0.6	-	-	96.1	-0.9	-	-	99.3	3.3	-	-	99.8	0.5	-	-	99.7	-0.1	-	-
1983	98.7	-1.0	-	-	97.2	-1.5	-	-	98.5	1.3	-	-	99.6	1.1	-	-	100.1	0.5	-	-	100.5	0.4	-	-
1984	100.7	0.2	-	-	101.8	1.1	-	-	102.9	1.1	-	-	103.0	0.1	-	-	103.0	0.0	-	-	103.1	0.1	-	-
1985	102.9	-0.2	-	-	104.3	1.4	-	-	105.4	1.1	-	-	105.7	0.3	-	-	105.7	0.0	-	-	106.8	1.0	-	-
1986	106.9	0.1	-	-	103.8	-2.9	-	-	100.5	-3.2	-	-	100.5	0.0	-	-	99.4	-1.1	-	-	100.1	0.7	-	-
1987	101.4	1.3	-	-	100.6	-0.8	-	-	101.8	1.2	-	-	103.4	1.6	-	-	104.9	1.5	-	-	106.8	1.8	-	-
1988	106.1	-0.7	-	-	105.5	-0.6	-	-	106.2	0.7	-	-	107.9	1.6	-	-	109.6	1.6	-	-	112.8	2.9	-	-
1989	112.5	-0.3	-	-	113.5	0.9	-	-	115.8	2.0	-	-	112.6	-2.8	-	-	112.6	0.0	-	-	114.6	1.8	-	-
1990	115.7	1.0	-	-	116.1	0.3	-	-	117.1	0.9	-	-	117.3	0.2	-	-	122.3	4.3	-	-	127.4	4.2	-	-
1991	125.3	-1.6	-	-	123.0	-1.8	-	-	124.3	1.1	-	-	125.7	1.1	-	-	126.2	0.4	-	-	127.8	1.3	-	-
1992	127.2	-0.5	-	-	128.6	1.1	-	-	129.1	0.4	-	-	129.9	0.6	-	-	128.9	-0.8	-	-	129.8	0.7	-	-

[Continued]

Boston-Brockton-Nashua, MA-NH-ME-CT
Consumer Price Index - All Urban Consumers
Base 1982-1984 = 100
Transportation
[Continued]

For 1947-2000. Columns headed % show percentile change in the index from the previous period for which an index is available.

Year	Jan		Feb		Mar		Apr		May		Jun		Jul		Aug		Sep		Oct		Nov		Dec	
	Index	%	Index	%	Index	%	Index	%	Index	%	Index	%	Index	%	Index	%	Index	%	Index	%	Index	%	Index	%
1993	131.9	1.6	-	-	132.4	0.4	-	-	132.1	-0.2	-	-	132.2	0.1	-	-	131.4	-0.6	-	-	134.4	2.3	-	-
1994	133.4	-0.7	-	-	134.1	0.5	-	-	132.5	-1.2	-	-	134.6	1.6	-	-	136.8	1.6	-	-	137.9	0.8	-	-
1995	137.1	-0.6	-	-	135.9	-0.9	-	-	137.5	1.2	-	-	137.4	-0.1	-	-	136.4	-0.7	-	-	137.7	1.0	-	-
1996	138.7	0.7	-	-	137.1	-1.2	-	-	139.6	1.8	-	-	139.1	-0.4	-	-	140.2	0.8	-	-	141.4	0.9	-	-
1997	142.3	0.6	-	-	141.6	-0.5	-	-	140.2	-1.0	-	-	140.5	0.2	-	-	142.1	1.1	-	-	142.8	0.5	-	-
1998	142.4	-0.3	-	-	139.7	-1.9	-	-	138.9	-0.6	-	-	139.0	0.1	-	-	138.7	-0.2	-	-	139.5	0.6	-	-
1999	138.6	-0.6	-	-	138.9	0.2	-	-	141.7	2.0	-	-	142.2	0.4	-	-	144.1	1.3	-	-	146.0	1.3	-	-
2000	147.2	0.8	-	-	150.4	2.2	-	-	151.2	0.5	-	-	154.5	2.2	-	-	153.7	-0.5	-	-	154.7	0.7	-	-

Source: U.S. Department of Labor, Bureau of Labor Statistics, Division of Consumer Prices and Price Indexes. - indicates no data collected for period.

Boston-Brockton-Nashua, MA-NH-ME-CT
Consumer Price Index - Urban Wage Earners
Base 1982-1984 = 100
Transportation

For 1947-2000. Columns headed % show percentile change in the index from the previous period for which an index is available.

Year	Jan Index	%	Feb Index	%	Mar Index	%	Apr Index	%	May Index	%	Jun Index	%	Jul Index	%	Aug Index	%	Sep Index	%	Oct Index	%	Nov Index	%	Dec Index	%
1947	16.2	-	16.2	0.0	16.2	0.0	16.3	0.6	16.3	0.0	16.3	0.0	16.4	0.6	16.4	0.0	16.5	0.6	16.5	0.0	16.5	0.0	16.6	0.6
1948	16.7	0.6	16.7	0.0	16.8	0.6	16.7	-0.6	16.8	0.6	16.8	0.0	16.9	0.6	17.0	0.6	17.1	0.6	17.1	0.0	17.1	0.0	17.1	0.0
1949	17.1	0.0	17.2	0.6	17.2	0.0	17.2	0.0	17.2	0.0	17.2	0.0	17.2	0.0	20.4	18.6	20.4	0.0	20.4	0.0	20.4	0.0	20.4	0.0
1950	20.4	0.0	20.4	0.0	20.4	0.0	20.4	0.0	20.4	0.0	20.5	0.5	20.5	0.0	20.6	0.5	20.6	0.0	20.6	0.0	20.6	0.0	20.7	0.5
1951	20.7	0.0	20.7	0.0	20.8	0.5	20.8	0.0	20.8	0.0	20.8	0.0	20.7	-0.5	21.5	3.9	21.5	0.0	21.8	1.4	21.9	0.5	21.9	0.0
1952	21.9	0.0	22.2	1.4	22.3	0.5	22.3	0.0	22.3	0.0	22.2	-0.4	23.0	3.6	23.0	0.0	23.0	0.0	23.0	0.0	23.0	0.0	23.0	0.0
1953	23.1	0.4	-		-		23.4	1.3	-		-		23.6	0.9	-		-		23.6	0.0	-		-	
1954	23.4	-0.8	-		-		24.3	3.8	-		-		23.7	-2.5	-		-		22.9	-3.4	-		-	
1955	23.1	0.9	-		-		23.1	0.0	-		-		22.9	-0.9	-		-		23.4	2.2	-		-	
1956	23.4	0.0	-		-		23.5	0.4	-		-		23.4	-0.4	-		-		25.1	7.3	-		-	
1957	24.7	-1.6	-		-		24.8	0.4	-		-		24.9	0.4	-		-		25.2	1.2	-		-	
1958	25.4	0.8	-		-		25.8	1.6	-		-		25.7	-0.4	-		-		25.6	-0.4	-		-	
1959	26.4	3.1	-		-		26.4	0.0	-		-		26.4	0.0	-		-		26.3	-0.4	-		-	
1960	25.6	-2.7	-		-		25.7	0.4	-		-		25.8	0.4	-		-		25.8	0.0	-		-	
1961	25.5	-1.2	-		-		25.9	1.6	-		-		26.3	1.5	-		-		26.1	-0.8	-		-	
1962	28.0	7.3	-		-		28.3	1.1	-		-		27.9	-1.4	-		-		28.2	1.1	-		-	
1963	27.9	-1.1	-		-		28.2	1.1	-		-		28.4	0.7	-		-		28.2	-0.7	-		-	
1964	28.3	0.4	-		-		28.2	-0.4	-		-		28.6	1.4	-		-		28.2	-1.4	-		-	
1965	28.9	2.5	-		-		28.9	0.0	-		-		29.1	0.7	-		-		29.4	1.0	-		-	
1966	29.2	-0.7	-		-		29.9	2.4	-		-		30.0	0.3	-		-		30.0	0.0	-		-	
1967	30.1	0.3	-		-		30.3	0.7	-		-		30.7	1.3	-		-		30.9	0.7	-		-	
1968	31.2	1.0	-		-		31.4	0.6	-		-		31.4	0.0	-		-		31.6	0.6	-		-	
1969	32.8	3.8	-		-		33.6	2.4	-		-		33.5	-0.3	-		-		33.5	0.0	-		-	
1970	33.6	0.3	-		-		33.9	0.9	-		-		34.5	1.8	-		-		36.2	4.9	-		-	
1971	36.6	1.1	-		-		36.1	-1.4	-		-		36.8	1.9	-		-		36.6	-0.5	-		-	
1972	36.4	-0.5	-		-		36.2	-0.5	-		-		36.4	0.6	-		-		36.9	1.4	-		-	
1973	36.9	0.0	-		-		37.1	0.5	-		-		37.7	1.6	-		-		37.8	0.3	-		-	
1974	38.5	1.9	-		-		39.7	3.1	-		-		41.9	5.5	-		-		42.2	0.7	-		-	
1975	42.7	1.2	-		-		45.0	5.4	-		-		46.9	4.2	-		-		47.5	1.3	-		-	
1976	57.6	21.3	-		-		57.9	0.5	-		-		59.7	3.1	-		-		60.1	0.7	-		-	
1977	62.1	3.3	-		-		63.2	1.8	-		-		63.7	0.8	-		-		63.4	-0.5	-		-	
1978	63.6	0.3	-		60.9	-4.2	-		62.1	2.0	-		63.0	1.4	-		63.4	0.6	-		64.3	1.4	-	
1979	63.8	-0.8	-		65.2	2.2	-		68.4	4.9	-		71.6	4.7	-		72.9	1.8	-		74.6	2.3	-	
1980	77.3	3.6	-		81.1	4.9	-		82.3	1.5	-		84.6	2.8	-		85.4	0.9	-		86.7	1.5	-	
1981	88.0	1.5	-		90.8	3.2	-		93.0	2.4	-		94.3	1.4	-		96.9	2.8	-		98.4	1.5	-	
1982	97.9	-0.5	-		97.3	-0.6	-		96.2	-1.1	-		99.3	3.2	-		99.8	0.5	-		99.6	-0.2	-	
1983	98.6	-1.0	-		97.1	-1.5	-		98.4	1.3	-		99.5	1.1	-		100.1	0.6	-		100.6	0.5	-	
1984	100.6	0.0	-		101.8	1.2	-		103.0	1.2	-		102.9	-0.1	-		102.9	0.0	-		103.2	0.3	-	
1985	103.0	-0.2	-		104.2	1.2	-		105.3	1.1	-		105.5	0.2	-		105.3	-0.2	-		106.4	1.0	-	
1986	106.6	0.2	-		103.3	-3.1	-		100.0	-3.2	-		100.0	0.0	-		98.9	-1.1	-		99.5	0.6	-	
1987	100.8	1.3	-		100.4	-0.4	-		101.9	1.5	-		103.8	1.9	-		105.9	2.0	-		107.7	1.7	-	
1988	107.3	-0.4	-		106.4	-0.8	-		107.0	0.6	-		108.7	1.6	-		110.6	1.7	-		113.9	3.0	-	
1989	113.6	-0.3	-		115.3	1.5	-		117.9	2.3	-		114.8	-2.6	-		114.6	-0.2	-		116.5	1.7	-	
1990	117.4	0.8	-		117.8	0.3	-		118.7	0.8	-		119.1	0.3	-		125.6	5.5	-		131.0	4.3	-	
1991	127.9	-2.4	-		124.9	-2.3	-		127.4	2.0	-		128.7	1.0	-		129.6	0.7	-		130.7	0.8	-	
1992	130.5	-0.2	-		130.8	0.2	-		131.5	0.5	-		133.0	1.1	-		132.2	-0.6	-		132.7	0.4	-	

[Continued]

Boston-Brockton-Nashua, MA-NH-ME-CT
Consumer Price Index - Urban Wage Earners
Base 1982-1984 = 100
Transportation
[Continued]

For 1947-2000. Columns headed % show percentile change in the index from the previous period for which an index is available.

Year	Jan		Feb		Mar		Apr		May		Jun		Jul		Aug		Sep		Oct		Nov		Dec	
	Index	%	Index	%	Index	%	Index	%	Index	%	Index	%	Index	%	Index	%	Index	%	Index	%	Index	%	Index	%
1993	134.6	1.4	-	-	134.9	0.2	-	-	134.6	-0.2	-	-	134.7	0.1	-	-	133.7	-0.7	-	-	136.5	2.1	-	-
1994	135.6	-0.7	-	-	136.2	0.4	-	-	134.9	-1.0	-	-	137.2	1.7	-	-	140.0	2.0	-	-	141.2	0.9	-	-
1995	140.0	-0.8	-	-	138.4	-1.1	-	-	140.2	1.3	-	-	140.8	0.4	-	-	139.8	-0.7	-	-	141.1	0.9	-	-
1996	141.9	0.6	-	-	140.3	-1.1	-	-	143.4	2.2	-	-	142.9	-0.3	-	-	143.5	0.4	-	-	145.2	1.2	-	-
1997	146.2	0.7	-	-	145.4	-0.5	-	-	143.6	-1.2	-	-	143.5	-0.1	-	-	145.4	1.3	-	-	145.5	0.1	-	-
1998	144.8	-0.5	-	-	141.8	-2.1	-	-	141.0	-0.6	-	-	141.1	0.1	-	-	140.5	-0.4	-	-	141.4	0.6	-	-
1999	140.2	-0.8	-	-	140.2	0.0	-	-	143.8	2.6	-	-	144.3	0.3	-	-	146.8	1.7	-	-	148.9	1.4	-	-
2000	150.2	0.9	-	-	154.2	2.7	-	-	155.0	0.5	-	-	158.9	2.5	-	-	158.1	-0.5	-	-	159.0	0.6	-	-

Source: U.S. Department of Labor, Bureau of Labor Statistics, Division of Consumer Prices and Price Indexes. - indicates no data collected for period.

Boston-Brockton-Nashua, MA-NH-ME-CT
Consumer Price Index - All Urban Consumers
Base 1982-1984 = 100
Medical Care

For 1947-2001. Columns headed % show percentile change in the index from the previous period for which an index is available.

Year	Jan Index	%	Feb Index	%	Mar Index	%	Apr Index	%	May Index	%	Jun Index	%	Jul Index	%	Aug Index	%	Sep Index	%	Oct Index	%	Nov Index	%	Dec Index	%
1947	13.3	-	13.3	0.0	13.4	0.8	13.4	0.0	13.4	0.0	13.4	0.0	13.3	-0.7	13.3	0.0	13.4	0.8	13.4	0.0	13.4	0.0	13.4	0.0
1948	13.8	3.0	13.8	0.0	14.3	3.6	14.4	0.7	14.5	0.7	14.3	-1.4	14.3	0.0	14.4	0.7	14.4	0.0	14.4	0.0	14.4	0.0	14.4	0.0
1949	14.8	2.8	14.8	0.0	14.9	0.7	14.9	0.0	14.9	0.0	15.0	0.7	15.3	2.0	15.3	0.0	15.4	0.7	15.4	0.0	15.4	0.0		
1950	15.6	1.3	15.6	0.0	15.7	0.6	15.7	0.0	15.7	0.0	15.7	0.0	15.7	0.0	15.7	0.0	15.7	0.0	15.7	0.0	15.8	0.6	16.0	1.3
1951	16.1	0.6	16.1	0.0	16.2	0.6	16.2	0.0	16.2	0.0	16.3	0.6	16.3	0.0	16.3	0.0	16.2	-0.6	16.3	0.6	16.3	0.0	16.7	2.5
1952	16.8	0.6	16.8	0.0	16.8	0.0	16.9	0.6	16.9	0.0	17.1	1.2	17.2	0.6	17.2	0.0	17.5	1.7	17.5	0.0	17.5	0.0	17.5	0.0
1953	17.6	0.6	-		-		17.6	0.0	-		-		17.6	0.0	-		-		17.7	0.6	-		-	
1954	17.7	0.0	-		-		17.7	0.0	-		-		17.7	0.0	-		-		17.7	0.0	-		-	
1955	17.7	0.0	-		-		17.7	0.0	-		-		17.8	0.6	-		-		18.0	1.1	-		-	
1956	18.3	1.7	-		-		18.3	0.0	-		-		19.5	6.6	-		-		19.6	0.5	-		-	
1957	19.7	0.5	-		-		20.1	2.0	-		-		21.2	5.5	-		-		21.2	0.0	-		-	
1958	22.0	3.8	-		-		22.1	0.5	-		-		22.3	0.9	-		-		22.4	0.4	-		-	
1959	22.6	0.9	-		-		22.7	0.4	-		-		22.7	0.0	-		-		22.9	0.9	-		-	
1960	23.0	0.4	-		-		23.1	0.4	-		-		23.2	0.4	-		-		23.3	0.4	-		-	
1961	23.7	1.7	-		-		23.8	0.4	-		-		23.9	0.4	-		-		24.1	0.8	-		-	
1962	24.5	1.7	-		-		24.8	1.2	-		-		24.8	0.0	-		-		24.9	0.4	-		-	
1963	24.9	0.0	-		-		25.3	1.6	-		-		25.3	0.0	-		-		25.5	0.8	-		-	
1964	25.6	0.4	-		-		25.9	1.2	-		-		25.9	0.0	-		-		26.5	2.3	-		-	
1965	26.8	1.1	-		-		26.8	0.0	-		-		27.1	1.1	-		-		27.3	0.7	-		-	
1966	27.4	0.4	-		-		27.9	1.8	-		-		28.0	0.4	-		-		28.8	2.9	-		-	
1967	29.3	1.7	-		-		29.3	0.0	-		-		29.9	2.0	-		-		31.0	3.7	-		-	
1968	31.7	2.3	-		-		31.8	0.3	-		-		32.2	1.3	-		-		33.6	4.3	-		-	
1969	34.2	1.8	-		-		34.5	0.9	-		-		34.9	1.2	-		-		36.0	3.2	-		-	
1970	36.5	1.4	-		-		36.8	0.8	-		-		37.2	1.1	-		-		38.5	3.5	-		-	
1971	38.8	0.8	-		-		39.2	1.0	-		-		39.4	0.5	-		-		39.2	-0.5	-		-	
1972	40.0	2.0	-		-		40.4	1.0	-		-		40.5	0.2	-		-		40.9	1.0	-		-	
1973	41.2	0.7	-		-		41.4	0.5	-		-		41.6	0.5	-		-		42.5	2.2	-		-	
1974	42.8	0.7	-		-		43.3	1.2	-		-		44.7	3.2	-		-		46.6	4.3	-		-	
1975	47.9	2.8	-		-		49.2	2.7	-		-		50.2	2.0	-		-		51.9	3.4	-		-	
1976	51.6	-0.6	-		-		51.8	0.4	-		-		53.9	4.1	-		-		54.9	1.9	-		-	
1977	56.2	2.4	-		-		56.9	1.2	-		-		57.9	1.8	-		-		59.2	2.2	-		-	
1978	59.4	0.3	-		59.8	0.7	-		60.6	1.3	-		61.5	1.5	-		62.8	2.1	-		66.1	5.3	-	
1979	66.9	1.2	-		67.7	1.2	-		68.2	0.7	-		69.8	2.3	-		70.2	0.6	-		72.1	2.7	-	
1980	74.3	3.1	-		74.9	0.8	-		76.6	2.3	-		76.4	-0.3	-		76.5	0.1	-		80.9	5.8	-	
1981	81.6	0.9	-		82.0	0.5	-		82.3	0.4	-		82.7	0.5	-		83.4	0.8	-		88.0	5.5	-	
1982	90.3	2.6	-		90.6	0.3	-		91.4	0.9	-		93.2	2.0	-		93.4	0.2	-		95.1	1.8	-	
1983	96.9	1.9	-		96.6	-0.3	-		96.9	0.3	-		98.3	1.4	-		100.3	2.0	-		102.1	1.8	-	
1984	104.2	2.1	-		106.7	2.4	-		107.8	1.0	-		109.4	1.5	-		109.1	-0.3	-		112.2	2.8	-	
1985	112.2	0.0	-		119.7	6.7	-		121.5	1.5	-		121.6	0.1	-		120.9	-0.6	-		123.5	2.2	-	
1986	126.5	2.4	-		130.2	2.9	-		131.9	1.3	-		132.9	0.8	-		133.8	0.7	-		133.5	-0.2	-	
1987	135.0	1.1	-		137.7	2.0	-		138.5	0.6	-		138.7	0.1	-		139.4	0.5	-		143.3	2.8	-	
1988	146.2	2.0	-		149.3	2.1	-		150.7	0.9	-		153.4	1.8	-		155.0	1.0	-		154.9	-0.1	-	
1989	157.7	1.8	-		160.3	1.6	-		164.3	2.5	-		166.4	1.3	-		169.3	1.7	-		170.1	0.5	-	
1990	173.2	1.8	-		177.9	2.7	-		181.7	2.1	-		182.3	0.3	-		182.7	0.2	-		187.5	2.6	-	
1991	189.7	1.2	-		198.4	4.6	-		201.8	1.7	-		205.4	1.8	-		204.6	-0.4	-		210.4	2.8	-	
1992	213.8	1.6	-		218.6	2.2	-		223.9	2.4	-		223.9	0.0	-		227.4	1.6	-		232.5	2.2	-	

[Continued]

Boston-Brockton-Nashua, MA-NH-ME-CT
Consumer Price Index - All Urban Consumers
Base 1982-1984 = 100
Medical Care
[Continued]

For 1947-2001. Columns headed % show percentile change in the index from the previous period for which an index is available.

Year	Jan Index	%	Feb Index	%	Mar Index	%	Apr Index	%	May Index	%	Jun Index	%	Jul Index	%	Aug Index	%	Sep Index	%	Oct Index	%	Nov Index	%	Dec Index	%
1993	233.9	0.6	-	-	232.7	-0.5	-	-	237.7	2.1	-	-	240.1	1.0	-	-	240.2	0.0	-	-	246.1	2.5	-	-
1994	247.3	0.5	-	-	249.3	0.8	-	-	250.4	0.4	-	-	250.2	-0.1	-	-	251.8	0.6	-	-	255.0	1.3	-	-
1995	257.9	1.1	-	-	262.7	1.9	-	-	265.1	0.9	-	-	266.7	0.6	-	-	265.9	-0.3	-	-	273.9	3.0	-	-
1996	275.2	0.5	-	-	278.5	1.2	-	-	278.5	0.0	-	-	279.8	0.5	-	-	282.3	0.9	-	-	286.5	1.5	-	-
1997	291.4	1.7	-	-	289.8	-0.5	-	-	292.0	0.8	-	-	292.8	0.3	-	-	291.8	-0.3	-	-	298.2	2.2	-	-
1998	303.5	1.8	-	-	308.9	1.8	-	-	313.6	1.5	-	-	316.3	0.9	-	-	316.5	0.1	-	-	320.0	1.1	-	-
1999	322.7	0.8	-	-	327.2	1.4	-	-	326.7	-0.2	-	-	330.1	1.0	-	-	331.9	0.5	-	-	337.2	1.6	-	-
2000	343.5	1.9	-	-	344.3	0.2	-	-	344.8	0.1	-	-	346.3	0.4	-	-	353.1	2.0	-	-	355.6	0.7	-	-
2001	359.9	1.2	-	-	364.3	1.2	-	-	369.4	1.4	-	-	368.6	-0.2	-	-	369.0	0.1	-	-	373.9	1.3	-	-

Source: U.S. Department of Labor, Bureau of Labor Statistics, Division of Consumer Prices and Price Indexes. - indicates no data collected for period.

Boston-Brockton-Nashua, MA-NH-ME-CT
Consumer Price Index - Urban Wage Earners
Base 1982-1984 = 100
Medical Care

For 1947-2001. Columns headed % show percentile change in the index from the previous period for which an index is available.

Year	Jan Index	%	Feb Index	%	Mar Index	%	Apr Index	%	May Index	%	Jun Index	%	Jul Index	%	Aug Index	%	Sep Index	%	Oct Index	%	Nov Index	%	Dec Index	%
1947	13.5	-	13.5	0.0	13.6	0.7	13.6	0.0	13.6	0.0	13.6	0.0	13.5	-0.7	13.5	0.0	13.6	0.7	13.6	0.0	13.6	0.0	13.6	0.0
1948	14.0	2.9	14.0	0.0	14.5	3.6	14.7	1.4	14.7	0.0	14.5	-1.4	14.5	0.0	14.6	0.7	14.6	0.0	14.6	0.0	14.6	0.0	14.6	0.0
1949	15.0	2.7	15.0	0.0	15.1	0.7	15.1	0.0	15.1	0.0	15.2	0.7	15.5	2.0	15.6	0.6	15.6	0.0	15.6	0.0	15.6	0.0	15.6	0.0
1950	15.8	1.3	15.8	0.0	15.9	0.6	15.9	0.0	15.9	0.0	16.0	0.6	16.0	0.0	16.0	0.0	16.0	0.0	16.0	0.0	16.0	0.0	16.2	1.3
1951	16.3	0.6	16.3	0.0	16.5	1.2	16.5	0.0	16.5	0.0	16.5	0.0	16.5	0.0	16.5	0.0	16.5	0.0	16.5	0.0	16.6	0.6	17.0	2.4
1952	17.1	0.6	17.1	0.0	17.1	0.0	17.1	0.0	17.1	0.0	17.3	1.2	17.4	0.6	17.4	0.0	17.7	1.7	17.7	0.0	17.7	0.0	17.8	0.6
1953	17.8	0.0	-	-	-	-	17.8	0.0	-	-	-	-	17.9	0.6	-	-	-	-	18.0	0.6	-	-	-	-
1954	18.0	0.0	-	-	-	-	18.0	0.0	-	-	-	-	18.0	0.0	-	-	-	-	18.0	0.0	-	-	-	-
1955	18.0	0.0	-	-	-	-	18.0	0.0	-	-	-	-	18.1	0.6	-	-	-	-	18.3	1.1	-	-	-	-
1956	18.6	1.6	-	-	-	-	18.6	0.0	-	-	-	-	19.8	6.5	-	-	-	-	19.9	0.5	-	-	-	-
1957	20.0	0.5	-	-	-	-	20.4	2.0	-	-	-	-	21.5	5.4	-	-	-	-	21.6	0.5	-	-	-	-
1958	22.3	3.2	-	-	-	-	22.4	0.4	-	-	-	-	22.6	0.9	-	-	-	-	22.7	0.4	-	-	-	-
1959	23.0	1.3	-	-	-	-	23.0	0.0	-	-	-	-	23.1	0.4	-	-	-	-	23.2	0.4	-	-	-	-
1960	23.3	0.4	-	-	-	-	23.4	0.4	-	-	-	-	23.5	0.4	-	-	-	-	23.6	0.4	-	-	-	-
1961	24.1	2.1	-	-	-	-	24.1	0.0	-	-	-	-	24.3	0.8	-	-	-	-	24.4	0.4	-	-	-	-
1962	24.9	2.0	-	-	-	-	25.1	0.8	-	-	-	-	25.1	0.0	-	-	-	-	25.2	0.4	-	-	-	-
1963	25.3	0.4	-	-	-	-	25.7	1.6	-	-	-	-	25.7	0.0	-	-	-	-	25.9	0.8	-	-	-	-
1964	26.0	0.4	-	-	-	-	26.3	1.2	-	-	-	-	26.3	0.0	-	-	-	-	26.9	2.3	-	-	-	-
1965	27.2	1.1	-	-	-	-	27.2	0.0	-	-	-	-	27.5	1.1	-	-	-	-	27.7	0.7	-	-	-	-
1966	27.8	0.4	-	-	-	-	28.3	1.8	-	-	-	-	28.4	0.4	-	-	-	-	29.2	2.8	-	-	-	-
1967	29.8	2.1	-	-	-	-	29.8	0.0	-	-	-	-	30.4	2.0	-	-	-	-	31.4	3.3	-	-	-	-
1968	32.1	2.2	-	-	-	-	32.3	0.6	-	-	-	-	32.7	1.2	-	-	-	-	34.1	4.3	-	-	-	-
1969	34.7	1.8	-	-	-	-	35.0	0.9	-	-	-	-	35.4	1.1	-	-	-	-	36.5	3.1	-	-	-	-
1970	37.0	1.4	-	-	-	-	37.4	1.1	-	-	-	-	37.8	1.1	-	-	-	-	39.0	3.2	-	-	-	-
1971	39.4	1.0	-	-	-	-	39.7	0.8	-	-	-	-	40.0	0.8	-	-	-	-	39.8	-0.5	-	-	-	-
1972	40.6	2.0	-	-	-	-	41.0	1.0	-	-	-	-	41.1	0.2	-	-	-	-	41.5	1.0	-	-	-	-
1973	41.8	0.7	-	-	-	-	42.0	0.5	-	-	-	-	42.2	0.5	-	-	-	-	43.2	2.4	-	-	-	-
1974	43.4	0.5	-	-	-	-	44.0	1.4	-	-	-	-	45.3	3.0	-	-	-	-	47.3	4.4	-	-	-	-
1975	48.6	2.7	-	-	-	-	49.9	2.7	-	-	-	-	50.9	2.0	-	-	-	-	52.7	3.5	-	-	-	-
1976	52.4	-0.6	-	-	-	-	52.6	0.4	-	-	-	-	54.7	4.0	-	-	-	-	55.7	1.8	-	-	-	-
1977	57.0	2.3	-	-	-	-	57.8	1.4	-	-	-	-	58.7	1.6	-	-	-	-	60.1	2.4	-	-	-	-
1978	60.3	0.3	-	-	61.2	1.5	-	-	61.9	1.1	-	-	62.0	0.2	-	-	63.9	3.1	-	-	65.8	3.0	-	-
1979	66.7	1.4	-	-	67.3	0.9	-	-	68.2	1.3	-	-	69.8	2.3	-	-	69.9	0.1	-	-	72.5	3.7	-	-
1980	73.6	1.5	-	-	74.4	1.1	-	-	77.0	3.5	-	-	75.6	-1.8	-	-	76.1	0.7	-	-	79.7	4.7	-	-
1981	80.5	1.0	-	-	81.9	1.7	-	-	83.9	2.4	-	-	82.8	-1.3	-	-	83.5	0.8	-	-	87.7	5.0	-	-
1982	89.8	2.4	-	-	90.3	0.6	-	-	91.2	1.0	-	-	93.0	2.0	-	-	93.1	0.1	-	-	94.6	1.6	-	-
1983	96.6	2.1	-	-	96.4	-0.2	-	-	96.7	0.3	-	-	98.4	1.8	-	-	100.5	2.1	-	-	102.3	1.8	-	-
1984	104.9	2.5	-	-	107.2	2.2	-	-	108.3	1.0	-	-	109.8	1.4	-	-	109.5	-0.3	-	-	112.0	2.3	-	-
1985	111.8	-0.2	-	-	118.1	5.6	-	-	119.9	1.5	-	-	120.5	0.5	-	-	120.0	-0.4	-	-	122.4	2.0	-	-
1986	125.1	2.2	-	-	128.8	3.0	-	-	130.6	1.4	-	-	131.7	0.8	-	-	132.8	0.8	-	-	132.7	-0.1	-	-
1987	134.6	1.4	-	-	137.1	1.9	-	-	138.2	0.8	-	-	138.2	0.0	-	-	139.3	0.8	-	-	142.8	2.5	-	-
1988	145.7	2.0	-	-	148.5	1.9	-	-	150.2	1.1	-	-	152.6	1.6	-	-	154.0	0.9	-	-	154.5	0.3	-	-
1989	157.1	1.7	-	-	159.5	1.5	-	-	162.7	2.0	-	-	164.5	1.1	-	-	167.7	1.9	-	-	168.4	0.4	-	-
1990	171.3	1.7	-	-	175.8	2.6	-	-	180.0	2.4	-	-	180.7	0.4	-	-	181.1	0.2	-	-	185.3	2.3	-	-
1991	187.4	1.1	-	-	194.9	4.0	-	-	198.9	2.1	-	-	202.5	1.8	-	-	201.9	-0.3	-	-	207.1	2.6	-	-
1992	210.2	1.5	-	-	214.4	2.0	-	-	219.1	2.2	-	-	219.1	0.0	-	-	223.7	2.1	-	-	228.4	2.1	-	-

[Continued]

Boston-Brockton-Nashua, MA-NH-ME-CT
Consumer Price Index - Urban Wage Earners
Base 1982-1984 = 100
Medical Care

[Continued]

For 1947-2001. Columns headed % show percentile change in the index from the previous period for which an index is available.

Year	Jan Index	%	Feb Index	%	Mar Index	%	Apr Index	%	May Index	%	Jun Index	%	Jul Index	%	Aug Index	%	Sep Index	%	Oct Index	%	Nov Index	%	Dec Index	%
1993	229.5	0.5	-	-	228.7	-0.3	-	-	233.8	2.2	-	-	236.1	1.0	-	-	236.1	0.0	-	-	240.4	1.8	-	-
1994	241.7	0.5	-	-	243.8	0.9	-	-	245.1	0.5	-	-	245.1	0.0	-	-	246.5	0.6	-	-	249.3	1.1	-	-
1995	252.1	1.1	-	-	256.7	1.8	-	-	258.9	0.9	-	-	260.8	0.7	-	-	260.1	-0.3	-	-	267.0	2.7	-	-
1996	268.3	0.5	-	-	271.8	1.3	-	-	272.1	0.1	-	-	273.3	0.4	-	-	275.2	0.7	-	-	279.2	1.5	-	-
1997	283.6	1.6	-	-	281.8	-0.6	-	-	284.3	0.9	-	-	285.1	0.3	-	-	284.3	-0.3	-	-	290.0	2.0	-	-
1998	294.0	1.4	-	-	299.2	1.8	-	-	303.9	1.6	-	-	306.5	0.9	-	-	306.7	0.1	-	-	309.9	1.0	-	-
1999	314.0	1.3	-	-	318.0	1.3	-	-	317.7	-0.1	-	-	320.7	0.9	-	-	322.1	0.4	-	-	327.5	1.7	-	-
2000	333.6	1.9	-	-	334.6	0.3	-	-	335.4	0.2	-	-	337.1	0.5	-	-	343.6	1.9	-	-	345.2	0.5	-	-
2001	350.3	1.5	-	-	354.5	1.2	-	-	358.1	1.0	-	-	358.3	0.1	-	-	358.8	0.1	-	-	363.4	1.3	-	-

Source: U.S. Department of Labor, Bureau of Labor Statistics, Division of Consumer Prices and Price Indexes. - indicates no data collected for period.

Boston-Brockton-Nashua, MA-NH-ME-CT
Consumer Price Index - All Urban Consumers
Base December 1997 = 100
Recreation

For 1997-2001. Columns headed % show percentile change in the index from the previous period for which an index is available.

Year	Jan		Feb		Mar		Apr		May		Jun		Jul		Aug		Sep		Oct		Nov		Dec	
	Index	%	Index	%	Index	%	Index	%	Index	%	Index	%	Index	%	Index	%	Index	%	Index	%	Index	%	Index	%
1997	-	-	-	-	-	-	-	-	-	-	-	-	-	-	-	-	-	-	-	-	-	-	100.0	-
1998	102.4	2.4	-	-	104.5	2.1	-	-	104.1	-0.4	-	-	103.2	-0.9	-	-	104.6	1.4	-	-	104.2	-0.4	-	-
1999	104.9	0.7	-	-	105.6	0.7	-	-	105.8	0.2	-	-	105.7	-0.1	-	-	104.8	-0.9	-	-	103.9	-0.9	-	-
2000	103.8	-0.1	-	-	103.9	0.1	-	-	103.3	-0.6	-	-	104.8	1.5	-	-	104.3	-0.5	-	-	103.8	-0.5	-	-
2001	104.4	0.6	-	-	105.1	0.7	-	-	105.8	0.7	-	-	105.9	0.1	-	-	105.1	-0.8	-	-	105.7	0.6	-	-

Source: U.S. Department of Labor, Bureau of Labor Statistics, Division of Consumer Prices and Price Indexes. - indicates no data collected for period.

Boston-Brockton-Nashua, MA-NH-ME-CT
Consumer Price Index - Urban Wage Earners
Base December 1997 = 100
Recreation

For 1997-2001. Columns headed % show percentile change in the index from the previous period for which an index is available.

Year	Jan Index	%	Feb Index	%	Mar Index	%	Apr Index	%	May Index	%	Jun Index	%	Jul Index	%	Aug Index	%	Sep Index	%	Oct Index	%	Nov Index	%	Dec Index	%
1997	-	-	-	-	-	-	-	-	-	-	-	-	-	-	-	-	-	-	-	-	-	-	100.0	-
1998	103.4	3.4	-	-	105.5	2.0	-	-	103.5	-1.9	-	-	102.9	-0.6	-	-	104.0	1.1	-	-	103.9	-0.1	-	-
1999	104.4	0.5	-	-	105.0	0.6	-	-	105.5	0.5	-	-	105.7	0.2	-	-	105.6	-0.1	-	-	104.9	-0.7	-	-
2000	104.7	-0.2	-	-	104.8	0.1	-	-	104.0	-0.8	-	-	105.6	1.5	-	-	104.7	-0.9	-	-	105.0	0.3	-	-
2001	105.6	0.6	-	-	106.4	0.8	-	-	107.0	0.6	-	-	107.1	0.1	-	-	106.4	-0.7	-	-	107.0	0.6	-	-

Source: U.S. Department of Labor, Bureau of Labor Statistics, Division of Consumer Prices and Price Indexes. - indicates no data collected for period.

Boston-Brockton-Nashua, MA-NH-ME-CT
Consumer Price Index - All Urban Consumers
Base December 1997 = 100
Education & Communication

For 1997-2001. Columns headed % show percentile change in the index from the previous period for which an index is available.

Year	Jan Index	%	Feb Index	%	Mar Index	%	Apr Index	%	May Index	%	Jun Index	%	Jul Index	%	Aug Index	%	Sep Index	%	Oct Index	%	Nov Index	%	Dec Index	%
1997	-	-	-	-	-	-	-	-	-	-	-	-	-	-	-	-	-	-	-	-	-	-	100.0	-
1998	100.1	0.1	-	-	99.0	-1.1	-	-	100.3	1.3	-	-	100.4	0.1	-	-	100.9	0.5	-	-	100.9	0.0	-	-
1999	100.9	0.0	-	-	101.0	0.1	-	-	100.2	-0.8	-	-	101.6	1.4	-	-	102.3	0.7	-	-	102.5	0.2	-	-
2000	102.2	-0.3	-	-	101.1	-1.1	-	-	101.3	0.2	-	-	102.0	0.7	-	-	103.8	1.8	-	-	105.6	1.7	-	-
2001	106.9	1.2	-	-	107.4	0.5	-	-	105.9	-1.4	-	-	105.8	-0.1	-	-	107.9	2.0	-	-	107.8	-0.1	-	-

Source: U.S. Department of Labor, Bureau of Labor Statistics, Division of Consumer Prices and Price Indexes. - indicates no data collected for period.

Boston-Brockton-Nashua, MA-NH-ME-CT
Consumer Price Index - Urban Wage Earners
Base December 1997 = 100
Education & Communication

For 1997-2001. Columns headed % show percentile change in the index from the previous period for which an index is available.

Year	Jan Index	%	Feb Index	%	Mar Index	%	Apr Index	%	May Index	%	Jun Index	%	Jul Index	%	Aug Index	%	Sep Index	%	Oct Index	%	Nov Index	%	Dec Index	%
1997	-	-	-	-	-	-	-	-	-	-	-	-	-	-	-	-	-	-	-	-	-	-	100.0	-
1998	100.1	0.1	-	-	98.9	-1.2	-	-	100.3	1.4	-	-	100.3	0.0	-	-	100.6	0.3	-	-	100.6	0.0	-	-
1999	100.6	0.0	-	-	100.7	0.1	-	-	99.9	-0.8	-	-	101.1	1.2	-	-	101.9	0.8	-	-	102.3	0.4	-	-
2000	101.9	-0.4	-	-	100.6	-1.3	-	-	100.8	0.2	-	-	101.5	0.7	-	-	103.2	1.7	-	-	104.9	1.6	-	-
2001	106.4	1.4	-	-	106.9	0.5	-	-	105.2	-1.6	-	-	105.1	-0.1	-	-	107.0	1.8	-	-	106.9	-0.1	-	-

Source: U.S. Department of Labor, Bureau of Labor Statistics, Division of Consumer Prices and Price Indexes. - indicates no data collected for period.

Chicago-Gary-Kenosha, IL-IN-WI
Consumer Price Index - All Urban Consumers
Base 1982-1984 = 100
Annual Averages

For 1914-2001, Columns headed % show percentile change in the index from the previous period for which an index is available.

Year	All Items		Food & Beverages		Housing		Apparel		Trans- portation		Medical Care		Recrea- tion*		Education & Communic.*		Other Goods & Services	
	Index	%	Index	%	Index	%	Index	%	Index	%	Index	%	Index	%	Index	%	Index	%
1914	-	-	-	-	-	-	-	-	-	-	-	-	-	-	-	-	-	-
1915	10.1	-	-	-	-	-	-	-	-	-	-	-	-	-	-	-	-	-
1916	10.9	7.9	-	-	-	-	-	-	-	-	-	-	-	-	-	-	-	-
1917	12.9	18.3	-	-	-	-	-	-	-	-	-	-	-	-	-	-	-	-
1918	14.9	15.5	-	-	-	-	-	-	-	-	-	-	-	-	-	-	-	-
1919	17.3	16.1	-	-	-	-	-	-	-	-	-	-	-	-	-	-	-	-
1920	19.8	14.5	-	-	-	-	-	-	-	-	-	-	-	-	-	-	-	-
1921	18.0	-9.1	-	-	-	-	-	-	-	-	-	-	-	-	-	-	-	-
1922	17.0	-5.6	-	-	-	-	-	-	-	-	-	-	-	-	-	-	-	-
1923	17.4	2.4	-	-	-	-	-	-	-	-	-	-	-	-	-	-	-	-
1924	17.7	1.7	-	-	-	-	-	-	-	-	-	-	-	-	-	-	-	-
1925	18.2	2.8	-	-	-	-	-	-	-	-	-	-	-	-	-	-	-	-
1926	18.3	0.5	-	-	-	-	-	-	-	-	-	-	-	-	-	-	-	-
1927	17.9	-2.2	-	-	-	-	-	-	-	-	-	-	-	-	-	-	-	-
1928	17.7	-1.1	-	-	-	-	-	-	-	-	-	-	-	-	-	-	-	-
1929	17.6	-0.6	-	-	-	-	-	-	-	-	-	-	-	-	-	-	-	-
1930	17.2	-2.3	-	-	-	-	-	-	-	-	-	-	-	-	-	-	-	-
1931	15.6	-9.3	-	-	-	-	-	-	-	-	-	-	-	-	-	-	-	-
1932	13.7	-12.2	-	-	-	-	-	-	-	-	-	-	-	-	-	-	-	-
1933	12.6	-8.0	-	-	-	-	-	-	-	-	-	-	-	-	-	-	-	-
1934	12.8	1.6	-	-	-	-	-	-	-	-	-	-	-	-	-	-	-	-
1935	13.4	4.7	-	-	-	-	-	-	-	-	-	-	-	-	-	-	-	-
1936	13.5	0.7	-	-	-	-	-	-	-	-	-	-	-	-	-	-	-	-
1937	14.2	5.2	-	-	-	-	-	-	-	-	-	-	-	-	-	-	-	-
1938	13.9	-2.1	-	-	-	-	-	-	-	-	-	-	-	-	-	-	-	-
1939	13.7	-1.4	-	-	-	-	-	-	-	-	-	-	-	-	-	-	-	-
1940	13.8	0.7	-	-	-	-	-	-	-	-	-	-	-	-	-	-	-	-
1941	14.5	5.1	-	-	-	-	-	-	-	-	-	-	-	-	-	-	-	-
1942	16.0	10.3	-	-	-	-	-	-	-	-	-	-	-	-	-	-	-	-
1943	16.9	5.6	-	-	-	-	-	-	-	-	-	-	-	-	-	-	-	-
1944	17.1	1.2	-	-	-	-	-	-	-	-	-	-	-	-	-	-	-	-
1945	17.5	2.3	-	-	-	-	-	-	-	-	-	-	-	-	-	-	-	-
1946	19.0	8.6	-	-	-	-	-	-	-	-	-	-	-	-	-	-	-	-
1947	22.1	16.3	-	-	-	-	-	-	17.5	-	12.1	-	-	-	-	-	-	-
1948	24.0	8.6	-	-	-	-	-	-	20.2	15.4	12.9	6.6	-	-	-	-	-	-
1949	24.0	0.0	-	-	-	-	-	-	22.0	8.9	13.5	4.7	-	-	-	-	-	-
1950	24.2	0.8	-	-	-	-	-	-	22.6	2.7	13.7	1.5	-	-	-	-	-	-
1951	26.1	7.9	-	-	-	-	-	-	23.9	5.8	14.5	5.8	-	-	-	-	-	-
1952	26.7	2.3	-	-	-	-	-	-	26.0	8.8	14.9	2.8	-	-	-	-	-	-
1953	26.9	0.7	-	-	-	-	52.4	-	26.6	2.3	15.5	4.0	-	-	-	-	-	-
1954	27.4	1.9	-	-	-	-	52.7	0.6	26.4	-0.8	15.9	2.6	-	-	-	-	-	-
1955	27.5	0.4	-	-	-	-	52.3	-0.8	26.2	-0.8	16.6	4.4	-	-	-	-	-	-
1956	27.9	1.5	-	-	-	-	54.0	3.3	26.7	1.9	17.6	6.0	-	-	-	-	-	-
1957	28.8	3.2	-	-	-	-	54.8	1.5	28.4	6.4	18.3	4.0	-	-	-	-	-	-
1958	29.7	3.1	-	-	-	-	55.0	0.4	30.0	5.6	19.4	6.0	-	-	-	-	-	-

[Continued]

Chicago-Gary-Kenosha, IL-IN-WI
Consumer Price Index - All Urban Consumers
Base 1982-1984 = 100
Annual Averages
[Continued]

For 1914-2001. Columns headed % show percentile change in the index from the previous period for which an index is available.

Year	All Items		Food & Beverage		Housing		Apparel		Trans-portation		Medical Care		Recrea-tion*		Education & Communic.*		Other Goods & Services	
	Index	%	Index	%	Index	%	Index	%	Index	%	Index	%	Index	%	Index	%	Index	%
1959	29.9	0.7	-	-	-	-	55.5	0.9	31.0	3.3	20.3	4.6	-	-	-	-	-	-
1960	30.4	1.7	-	-	-	-	56.4	1.6	31.1	0.3	21.5	5.9	-	-	-	-	-	-
1961	30.5	0.3	-	-	-	-	56.0	-0.7	30.9	-0.6	22.0	2.3	-	-	-	-	-	-
1962	30.8	1.0	-	-	-	-	55.8	-0.4	31.5	1.9	22.7	3.2	-	-	-	-	-	-
1963	31.1	1.0	-	-	-	-	56.0	0.4	31.7	0.6	24.3	7.0	-	-	-	-	-	-
1964	31.3	0.6	-	-	-	-	56.2	0.4	31.8	0.3	24.7	1.6	-	-	-	-	-	-
1965	31.7	1.3	-	-	-	-	56.8	1.1	32.6	2.5	25.1	1.6	-	-	-	-	-	-
1966	32.6	2.8	-	-	-	-	58.3	2.6	32.6	0.0	25.9	3.2	-	-	-	-	-	-
1967	33.5	2.8	-	-	-	-	60.6	3.9	33.5	2.8	28.0	8.1	-	-	-	-	-	-
1968	34.9	4.2	-	-	-	-	63.8	5.3	35.0	4.5	29.6	5.7	-	-	-	-	-	-
1969	36.8	5.4	-	-	-	-	66.9	4.9	37.2	6.3	31.4	6.1	-	-	-	-	-	-
1970	38.9	5.7	-	-	-	-	68.6	2.5	39.7	6.7	33.5	6.7	-	-	-	-	-	-
1971	40.4	3.9	-	-	-	-	71.1	3.6	42.1	6.0	35.9	7.2	-	-	-	-	-	-
1972	41.6	3.0	-	-	-	-	72.5	2.0	41.7	-1.0	36.8	2.5	-	-	-	-	-	-
1973	44.2	6.3	-	-	-	-	76.0	4.8	42.9	2.9	38.3	4.1	-	-	-	-	-	-
1974	48.9	10.6	-	-	-	-	80.4	5.8	47.2	10.0	42.0	9.7	-	-	-	-	-	-
1975	52.8	8.0	-	-	-	-	82.7	2.9	50.9	7.8	47.3	12.6	-	-	-	-	-	-
1976	55.3	4.7	64.2	-	48.5	-	83.7	1.2	56.1	10.2	52.8	11.6	-	-	-	-	58.0	-
1977	58.8	6.3	67.9	5.8	51.5	6.2	86.2	3.0	60.8	8.4	58.0	9.8	-	-	-	-	62.2	7.2
1978	63.8	8.5	75.8	11.6	57.3	11.3	88.0	2.1	63.1	3.8	62.1	7.1	-	-	-	-	65.8	5.8
1979	71.8	12.5	83.8	10.6	66.1	15.4	90.5	2.8	71.7	13.6	67.6	8.9	-	-	-	-	69.7	5.9
1980	82.2	14.5	91.2	8.8	77.4	17.1	95.6	5.6	85.0	18.5	76.3	12.9	-	-	-	-	76.1	9.2
1981	90.0	9.5	96.4	5.7	85.6	10.6	96.4	0.8	95.6	12.5	84.3	10.5	-	-	-	-	84.5	11.0
1982	96.2	6.9	98.7	2.4	94.7	10.6	97.7	1.3	98.3	2.8	92.1	9.3	-	-	-	-	91.9	8.8
1983	100.0	4.0	99.4	0.7	100.6	6.2	100.2	2.6	99.0	0.7	101.1	9.8	-	-	-	-	100.5	9.4
1984	103.8	3.8	102.0	2.6	104.7	4.1	102.1	1.9	102.7	3.7	106.8	5.6	-	-	-	-	107.6	7.1
1985	107.7	3.8	104.2	2.2	109.6	4.7	106.0	3.8	105.3	2.5	112.8	5.6	-	-	-	-	115.1	7.0
1986	110.0	2.1	108.9	4.5	112.9	3.0	103.9	-2.0	101.2	-3.9	120.1	6.5	-	-	-	-	124.2	7.9
1987	114.5	4.1	113.2	3.9	116.3	3.0	109.2	5.1	106.1	4.8	129.2	7.6	-	-	-	-	129.6	4.3
1988	119.0	3.9	117.1	3.4	120.7	3.8	116.6	6.8	107.6	1.4	138.0	6.8	-	-	-	-	138.0	6.5
1989	125.0	5.0	122.5	4.6	126.4	4.7	118.1	1.3	112.1	4.2	149.2	8.1	-	-	-	-	153.1	10.9
1990	131.7	5.4	130.3	6.4	131.4	4.0	124.3	5.2	118.7	5.9	163.0	9.2	-	-	-	-	164.3	7.3
1991	137.0	4.0	135.5	4.0	136.4	3.8	125.3	0.8	121.2	2.1	177.9	9.1	-	-	-	-	179.0	8.9
1992	141.1	3.0	139.2	2.7	139.9	2.6	126.2	0.7	123.2	1.7	190.7	7.2	-	-	-	-	192.0	7.3
1993	145.4	3.0	143.1	2.8	143.3	2.4	131.1	3.9	126.2	2.4	203.1	6.5	-	-	-	-	202.5	5.5
1994	148.6	2.2	147.0	2.7	144.8	1.0	131.0	-0.1	130.3	3.2	213.2	5.0	-	-	-	-	208.8	3.1
1995	153.3	3.2	151.3	2.9	150.6	4.0	126.3	-3.6	135.1	3.7	223.3	4.7	-	-	-	-	216.8	3.8
1996	157.4	2.7	156.1	3.2	155.1	3.0	120.6	-4.5	139.9	3.6	229.4	2.7	-	-	-	-	222.4	2.6
1997	161.7	2.7	160.5	2.8	160.2	3.3	122.3	1.4	140.2	0.2	235.5	2.7	-	-	-	-	233.3	4.9
1998	165.0	2.0	164.8	2.7	164.2	2.5	121.6	-0.6	138.0	-1.6	244.3	3.7	101.3	-	104.4	-	245.7	5.3
1999	168.4	2.1	168.4	2.2	168.0	2.3	117.2	-3.6	140.5	1.8	253.6	3.8	103.0	1.7	106.7	2.2	259.3	5.5
2000	173.8	3.2	171.4	1.8	175.3	4.3	112.5	-4.0	148.4	5.6	259.5	2.3	102.2	-0.8	109.9	3.0	267.7	3.2
2001	178.3	2.6	176.3	2.9	181.5	3.5	106.3	-5.5	-	-	272.2	4.9	107.0	4.7	112.5	2.4	277.7	3.7

Source: U.S. Department of Labor, Bureau of Labor Statistics, Division of Consumer Prices and Price Indexes. *Base is December 1997 = 100. - indicates no data collected for period.

Chicago-Gary-Kenosha, IL-IN-WI
Consumer Price Index - Urban Wage Earners
Base 1982-1984 = 100
Annual Averages

For 1914-2001. Columns headed % show percentile change in the index from the previous period for which an index is available.

Year	All Items		Food & Beverage		Housing		Apparel		Trans-portation		Medical Care		Recrea-tion*		Education & Communic.*		Other Goods & Services	
	Index	%	Index	%	Index	%	Index	%	Index	%	Index	%	Index	%	Index	%	Index	%
1914	-	-	-	-	-	-	-	-	-	-	-	-	-	-	-	-	-	-
1915	10.2	-	-	-	-	-	-	-	-	-	-	-	-	-	-	-	-	-
1916	11.1	8.8	-	-	-	-	-	-	-	-	-	-	-	-	-	-	-	-
1917	13.1	18.0	-	-	-	-	-	-	-	-	-	-	-	-	-	-	-	-
1918	15.2	16.0	-	-	-	-	-	-	-	-	-	-	-	-	-	-	-	-
1919	17.6	15.8	-	-	-	-	-	-	-	-	-	-	-	-	-	-	-	-
1920	20.2	14.8	-	-	-	-	-	-	-	-	-	-	-	-	-	-	-	-
1921	18.3	-9.4	-	-	-	-	-	-	-	-	-	-	-	-	-	-	-	-
1922	17.3	-5.5	-	-	-	-	-	-	-	-	-	-	-	-	-	-	-	-
1923	17.7	2.3	-	-	-	-	-	-	-	-	-	-	-	-	-	-	-	-
1924	18.0	1.7	-	-	-	-	-	-	-	-	-	-	-	-	-	-	-	-
1925	18.5	2.8	-	-	-	-	-	-	-	-	-	-	-	-	-	-	-	-
1926	18.6	0.5	-	-	-	-	-	-	-	-	-	-	-	-	-	-	-	-
1927	18.2	-2.2	-	-	-	-	-	-	-	-	-	-	-	-	-	-	-	-
1928	18.0	-1.1	-	-	-	-	-	-	-	-	-	-	-	-	-	-	-	-
1929	17.9	-0.6	-	-	-	-	-	-	-	-	-	-	-	-	-	-	-	-
1930	17.5	-2.2	-	-	-	-	-	-	-	-	-	-	-	-	-	-	-	-
1931	15.9	-9.1	-	-	-	-	-	-	-	-	-	-	-	-	-	-	-	-
1932	13.9	-12.6	-	-	-	-	-	-	-	-	-	-	-	-	-	-	-	-
1933	12.8	-7.9	-	-	-	-	-	-	-	-	-	-	-	-	-	-	-	-
1934	13.0	1.6	-	-	-	-	-	-	-	-	-	-	-	-	-	-	-	-
1935	13.6	4.6	-	-	-	-	-	-	-	-	-	-	-	-	-	-	-	-
1936	13.7	0.7	-	-	-	-	-	-	-	-	-	-	-	-	-	-	-	-
1937	14.4	5.1	-	-	-	-	-	-	-	-	-	-	-	-	-	-	-	-
1938	14.2	-1.4	-	-	-	-	-	-	-	-	-	-	-	-	-	-	-	-
1939	13.9	-2.1	-	-	-	-	-	-	-	-	-	-	-	-	-	-	-	-
1940	14.1	1.4	-	-	-	-	-	-	-	-	-	-	-	-	-	-	-	-
1941	14.7	4.3	-	-	-	-	-	-	-	-	-	-	-	-	-	-	-	-
1942	16.2	10.2	-	-	-	-	-	-	-	-	-	-	-	-	-	-	-	-
1943	17.2	6.2	-	-	-	-	-	-	-	-	-	-	-	-	-	-	-	-
1944	17.4	1.2	-	-	-	-	-	-	-	-	-	-	-	-	-	-	-	-
1945	17.8	2.3	-	-	-	-	-	-	-	-	-	-	-	-	-	-	-	-
1946	19.4	9.0	-	-	-	-	-	-	-	-	-	-	-	-	-	-	-	-
1947	22.4	15.5	-	-	-	-	-	-	17.2	-	11.9	-	-	-	-	-	-	-
1948	24.4	8.9	-	-	-	-	-	-	19.9	15.7	12.7	6.7	-	-	-	-	-	-
1949	24.4	0.0	-	-	-	-	-	-	21.6	8.5	13.3	4.7	-	-	-	-	-	-
1950	24.7	1.2	-	-	-	-	-	-	22.3	3.2	13.5	1.5	-	-	-	-	-	-
1951	26.6	7.7	-	-	-	-	-	-	23.5	5.4	14.3	5.9	-	-	-	-	-	-
1952	27.2	2.3	-	-	-	-	-	-	25.6	8.9	14.7	2.8	-	-	-	-	-	-
1953	27.4	0.7	-	-	-	-	50.8	-	26.2	2.3	15.2	3.4	-	-	-	-	-	-
1954	27.9	1.8	-	-	-	-	51.1	0.6	26.0	-0.8	15.6	2.6	-	-	-	-	-	-
1955	28.0	0.4	-	-	-	-	50.7	-0.8	25.7	-1.2	16.3	4.5	-	-	-	-	-	-
1956	28.4	1.4	-	-	-	-	52.3	3.2	26.2	1.9	17.3	6.1	-	-	-	-	-	-
1957	29.3	3.2	-	-	-	-	53.1	1.5	27.9	6.5	18.0	4.0	-	-	-	-	-	-
1958	30.2	3.1	-	-	-	-	53.3	0.4	29.5	5.7	19.1	6.1	-	-	-	-	-	-

[Continued]

Chicago-Gary-Kenosha, IL-IN-WI
Consumer Price Index - Urban Wage Earners
Base 1982-1984 = 100
Annual Averages
[Continued]

For 1914-2001. Columns headed % show percentile change in the index from the previous period for which an index is available.

Year	All Items		Food & Beverage		Housing		Apparel		Trans-portation		Medical Care		Recrea-tion*		Education & Communic.*		Other Goods & Services	
	Index	%	Index	%	Index	%	Index	%	Index	%	Index	%	Index	%	Index	%	Index	%
1959	30.4	0.7	-	-	-	-	53.8	0.9	30.5	3.4	20.0	4.7	-	-	-	-	-	-
1960	30.9	1.6	-	-	-	-	54.7	1.7	30.6	0.3	21.1	5.5	-	-	-	-	-	-
1961	31.1	0.6	-	-	-	-	54.3	-0.7	30.4	-0.7	21.6	2.4	-	-	-	-	-	-
1962	31.4	1.0	-	-	-	-	54.1	-0.4	31.0	2.0	22.4	3.7	-	-	-	-	-	-
1963	31.7	1.0	-	-	-	-	54.3	0.4	31.2	0.6	23.9	6.7	-	-	-	-	-	-
1964	31.8	0.3	-	-	-	-	54.5	0.4	31.3	0.3	24.3	1.7	-	-	-	-	-	-
1965	32.2	1.3	-	-	-	-	55.1	1.1	32.0	2.2	24.7	1.6	-	-	-	-	-	-
1966	33.2	3.1	-	-	-	-	56.5	2.5	32.1	0.3	25.5	3.2	-	-	-	-	-	-
1967	34.0	2.4	-	-	-	-	58.7	3.9	33.0	2.8	27.5	7.8	-	-	-	-	-	-
1968	35.5	4.4	-	-	-	-	61.8	5.3	34.5	4.5	29.1	5.8	-	-	-	-	-	-
1969	37.4	5.4	-	-	-	-	64.8	4.9	36.6	6.1	30.9	6.2	-	-	-	-	-	-
1970	39.6	5.9	-	-	-	-	66.5	2.6	39.1	6.8	33.0	6.8	-	-	-	-	-	-
1971	41.1	3.8	-	-	-	-	68.9	3.6	41.4	5.9	35.3	7.0	-	-	-	-	-	-
1972	42.3	2.9	-	-	-	-	70.3	2.0	41.0	-1.0	36.2	2.5	-	-	-	-	-	-
1973	44.9	6.1	-	-	-	-	73.7	4.8	42.2	2.9	37.7	4.1	-	-	-	-	-	-
1974	49.7	10.7	-	-	-	-	77.9	5.7	46.4	10.0	41.3	9.5	-	-	-	-	-	-
1975	53.7	8.0	-	-	-	-	80.2	3.0	50.1	8.0	46.5	12.6	-	-	-	-	-	-
1976	56.2	4.7	65.2	-	50.7	-	81.1	1.1	55.2	10.2	51.9	11.6	-	-	-	-	59.6	-
1977	59.8	6.4	69.0	5.8	53.8	6.1	83.5	3.0	59.8	8.3	57.1	10.0	-	-	-	-	63.9	7.2
1978	64.8	8.4	76.3	10.6	59.6	10.8	86.8	4.0	62.1	3.8	61.3	7.4	-	-	-	-	68.1	6.6
1979	72.9	12.5	84.5	10.7	68.4	14.8	89.7	3.3	71.1	14.5	67.5	10.1	-	-	-	-	71.8	5.4
1980	83.5	14.5	92.3	9.2	79.8	16.7	94.9	5.8	84.5	18.8	76.9	13.9	-	-	-	-	78.1	8.8
1981	91.4	9.5	96.3	4.3	88.3	10.7	95.9	1.1	95.5	13.0	84.4	9.8	-	-	-	-	84.9	8.7
1982	97.7	6.9	98.7	2.5	97.9	10.9	97.9	2.1	98.7	3.4	92.1	9.1	-	-	-	-	91.9	8.2
1983	100.4	2.8	99.4	0.7	101.6	3.8	100.0	2.1	98.8	0.1	101.0	9.7	-	-	-	-	100.6	9.5
1984	101.9	1.5	102.0	2.6	100.6	-1.0	102.2	2.2	102.4	3.6	106.8	5.7	-	-	-	-	107.5	6.9
1985	105.1	3.1	104.2	2.2	103.9	3.3	105.6	3.3	104.8	2.3	112.7	5.5	-	-	-	-	115.2	7.2
1986	106.8	1.6	109.0	4.6	106.9	2.9	104.1	-1.4	99.8	-4.8	119.9	6.4	-	-	-	-	124.8	8.3
1987	111.1	4.0	113.3	3.9	109.7	2.6	109.4	5.1	104.3	4.5	128.9	7.5	-	-	-	-	130.3	4.4
1988	115.3	3.8	117.2	3.4	113.6	3.6	116.1	6.1	106.3	1.9	138.4	7.4	-	-	-	-	138.5	6.3
1989	121.2	5.1	122.6	4.6	118.9	4.7	117.6	1.3	111.0	4.4	150.4	8.7	-	-	-	-	153.6	10.9
1990	127.8	5.4	130.4	6.4	123.8	4.1	124.5	5.9	117.2	5.6	164.3	9.2	-	-	-	-	166.2	8.2
1991	132.9	4.0	135.7	4.1	128.4	3.7	125.6	0.9	119.3	1.8	179.4	9.2	-	-	-	-	182.4	9.7
1992	136.7	2.9	139.2	2.6	131.7	2.6	125.9	0.2	121.2	1.6	192.4	7.2	-	-	-	-	195.9	7.4
1993	140.9	3.1	143.3	2.9	135.0	2.5	130.5	3.7	124.0	2.3	205.6	6.9	-	-	-	-	207.0	5.7
1994	144.0	2.2	147.2	2.7	136.3	1.0	130.0	-0.4	128.4	3.5	215.9	5.0	-	-	-	-	211.3	2.1
1995	148.4	3.1	151.6	3.0	141.4	3.7	125.1	-3.8	133.5	4.0	227.0	5.1	-	-	-	-	217.3	2.8
1996	152.4	2.7	156.3	3.1	145.7	3.0	119.6	-4.4	138.1	3.4	234.0	3.1	-	-	-	-	221.2	1.8
1997	156.2	2.5	160.7	2.8	150.4	3.2	119.6	0.0	137.6	-0.4	240.2	2.6	-	-	-	-	232.4	5.1
1998	159.3	2.0	165.0	2.7	154.2	2.5	118.9	-0.6	135.3	-1.7	249.3	3.8	-	-	-	-	246.9	6.2
1999	162.6	2.1	168.5	2.1	157.8	2.3	114.7	-3.5	137.5	1.6	258.8	3.8	101.0	-	105.1	-	264.1	7.0
2000	168.2	3.4	171.5	1.8	164.8	4.4	109.7	-4.4	145.2	5.6	265.0	2.4	102.1	1.1	107.8	2.6	273.8	3.7
2001	172.4	2.5	176.4	2.9	170.7	3.6	103.3	-5.8	-	-	278.4	5.1	105.1	3.3	114.4	2.6	284.6	3.9

Source: U.S. Department of Labor, Bureau of Labor Statistics, Division of Consumer Prices and Price Indexes. *Base is December 1997 = 100. - indicates no data collected for period.

Chicago-Gary-Kenosha, IL-IN-WI
Consumer Price Index - All Urban Consumers
Base 1982-1984 = 100
All Items

For 1914-2001. Columns headed % show percentile change in the index from the previous period for which an index is available.

Year	Jan Index	%	Feb Index	%	Mar Index	%	Apr Index	%	May Index	%	Jun Index	%	Jul Index	%	Aug Index	%	Sep Index	%	Oct Index	%	Nov Index	%	Dec Index	%
1914	-	-	-	-	-	-	-	-	-	-	-	-	-	-	-	-	-	-	-	-	-	-	10.0	-
1915	-	-	-	-	-	-	-	-	-	-	-	-	-	-	-	-	-	-	-	-	-	-	10.2	2.0
1916	-	-	-	-	-	-	-	-	-	-	-	-	-	-	-	-	-	-	-	-	-	-	11.6	13.7
1917	-	-	-	-	-	-	-	-	-	-	-	-	-	-	-	-	-	-	-	-	-	-	13.5	16.4
1918	-	-	-	-	-	-	-	-	-	-	-	-	-	-	-	-	-	-	-	-	-	-	16.3	20.7
1919	-	-	-	-	-	-	-	-	-	-	16.6	1.8	-	-	-	-	-	-	-	-	-	-	18.9	13.9
1920	-	-	-	-	-	-	-	-	-	-	20.8	10.1	-	-	-	-	-	-	-	-	-	-	18.9	-9.1
1921	-	-	-	-	-	-	-	-	17.9	-5.3	-	-	-	-	-	-	17.8	-0.6	-	-	-	-	17.5	-1.7
1922	-	-	-	-	-	-	-	-	16.9	-3.4	17.0	0.6	-	-	-	-	17.0	0.0	-	-	-	-	17.1	0.6
1923	-	-	-	-	17.2	0.6	-	-	-	-	17.3	0.6	-	-	-	-	17.7	2.3	-	-	-	-	17.7	0.0
1924	-	-	-	-	17.6	-0.6	-	-	-	-	17.7	0.6	-	-	-	-	17.8	0.6	-	-	-	-	17.9	0.6
1925	-	-	-	-	-	-	-	-	-	-	18.2	1.7	-	-	-	-	-	-	-	-	-	-	18.6	2.2
1926	-	-	-	-	-	-	-	-	-	-	18.3	-1.6	-	-	-	-	-	-	-	-	-	-	18.3	0.0
1927	-	-	-	-	-	-	-	-	-	-	18.3	0.0	-	-	-	-	-	-	-	-	-	-	17.8	-2.7
1928	-	-	-	-	-	-	-	-	-	-	17.6	-1.1	-	-	-	-	-	-	-	-	-	-	17.7	0.6
1929	-	-	-	-	-	-	-	-	-	-	17.6	-0.6	-	-	-	-	-	-	-	-	-	-	17.7	0.6
1930	-	-	-	-	-	-	-	-	-	-	17.4	-1.7	-	-	-	-	-	-	-	-	-	-	16.6	-4.6
1931	-	-	-	-	-	-	-	-	-	-	15.6	-6.0	-	-	-	-	-	-	-	-	-	-	14.9	-4.5
1932	-	-	-	-	-	-	-	-	-	-	13.6	-8.7	-	-	-	-	-	-	-	-	-	-	12.9	-5.1
1933	-	-	-	-	-	-	-	-	-	-	12.4	-3.9	-	-	-	-	-	-	-	-	-	-	12.7	2.4
1934	-	-	-	-	-	-	-	-	-	-	12.7	0.0	-	-	-	-	-	-	-	-	12.8	0.8	-	-
1935	-	-	-	-	13.3	3.9	-	-	-	-	-	-	13.4	0.8	-	-	-	-	13.4	0.0	-	-	-	-
1936	13.4	0.0	-	-	-	-	13.3	-0.7	-	-	-	-	13.6	2.3	-	-	13.8	1.5	13.4	-	-	-	13.7	-0.7
1937	-	-	-	-	13.9	1.5	-	-	-	-	-	-	14.2	2.2	-	-	14.4	1.4	-	-	-	-	14.2	-1.4
1938	-	-	-	-	13.9	-2.1	-	-	-	-	-	-	14.0	0.7	-	-	14.0	0.0	-	-	-	-	13.8	-1.4
1939	-	-	-	-	13.7	-0.7	-	-	-	-	-	-	13.6	-0.7	-	-	13.8	1.5	-	-	-	-	13.7	-0.7
1940	-	-	-	-	13.7	0.0	-	-	-	-	-	-	13.9	1.5	-	-	13.8	-0.7	13.8	0.0	13.8	0.0	13.9	0.7
1941	13.9	0.0	13.9	0.0	13.9	0.0	14.1	1.4	14.2	0.7	14.4	1.4	14.6	1.4	14.7	0.7	15.0	2.0	15.1	0.7	15.2	0.7	15.2	0.0
1942	15.4	1.3	15.4	0.0	15.6	1.3	15.8	1.3	16.0	1.3	16.0	0.0	16.0	0.0	16.1	0.6	16.1	0.0	16.3	1.2	16.4	0.6	16.4	0.0
1943	16.4	0.0	16.5	0.6	16.8	1.8	16.9	0.6	17.1	1.2	17.0	-0.6	16.8	-1.2	16.9	0.6	17.0	0.6	17.0	0.0	16.9	-0.6	16.9	0.0
1944	16.8	-0.6	16.8	0.0	16.8	0.0	17.0	1.2	17.0	0.0	17.1	0.6	17.3	1.2	17.3	0.0	17.3	0.0	17.3	0.0	17.3	0.0	17.3	0.0
1945	17.3	0.0	17.3	0.0	17.3	0.0	17.3	0.0	17.6	1.7	17.6	0.0	17.6	0.0	17.6	0.0	17.5	-0.6	17.5	0.0	17.5	0.0	17.6	0.6
1946	17.6	0.0	17.6	0.0	17.6	0.0	17.8	1.1	17.9	0.6	18.0	0.6	19.4	7.8	19.8	2.1	20.0	1.0	20.6	3.0	21.0	1.9	21.1	0.5
1947	21.1	0.0	21.0	-0.5	21.5	2.4	21.4	-0.5	21.5	0.5	21.8	1.4	22.0	0.9	22.4	1.8	23.1	3.1	23.0	-0.4	23.1	0.4	23.4	1.3
1948	23.5	0.4	23.2	-1.3	23.2	0.0	23.7	2.2	24.0	1.3	24.2	0.8	24.5	1.2	24.6	0.4	24.7	0.4	24.5	-0.8	24.2	-1.2	24.1	-0.4
1949	24.0	-0.4	23.8	-0.8	24.0	0.8	24.1	0.4	24.0	-0.4	24.2	0.8	23.9	-1.2	24.0	0.4	24.2	0.8	24.0	-0.8	24.1	0.4	23.8	-1.2
1950	23.7	-0.4	23.7	0.0	23.8	0.4	23.7	-0.4	24.0	1.3	24.0	0.0	24.3	1.2	24.5	0.8	24.6	0.4	24.7	0.4	24.8	0.4	25.2	1.6
1951	25.5	1.2	25.9	1.6	25.9	0.0	26.0	0.4	26.0	0.0	26.1	0.4	26.2	0.4	26.2	0.0	26.3	0.4	26.5	0.8	26.7	0.8	26.6	-0.4
1952	26.6	0.0	26.3	-1.1	26.4	0.4	26.5	0.4	26.7	0.8	26.8	0.4	26.9	0.4	27.0	0.4	26.9	-0.4	26.9	0.0	26.9	0.0	26.8	-0.4
1953	26.7	-0.4	26.6	-0.4	26.6	0.0	26.7	0.4	26.8	0.4	26.9	0.4	27.0	0.4	27.2	0.7	27.2	0.0	27.4	0.7	27.2	-0.7	27.2	0.0
1954	27.2	0.0	27.2	0.0	27.2	0.0	27.2	0.0	27.4	0.7	27.4	0.0	27.6	0.7	27.5	-0.4	27.4	-0.4	27.4	0.0	27.5	0.4	27.3	-0.7
1955	27.3	0.0	27.4	0.4	27.3	-0.4	27.3	0.0	27.4	0.4	27.4	0.0	27.6	0.7	27.7	0.4	27.8	0.4	27.8	0.0	27.8	0.0	27.7	-0.4
1956	27.6	-0.4	27.6	0.0	27.5	-0.4	27.6	0.4	27.7	0.4	27.9	0.7	28.2	1.1	28.0	-0.7	28.1	0.4	28.3	0.7	28.3	0.0	28.3	0.0
1957	28.3	0.0	28.4	0.4	28.4	0.0	28.5	0.4	28.6	0.4	28.7	0.3	29.0	1.0	29.0	0.0	29.1	0.3	29.2	0.3	29.4	0.7	29.4	0.0
1958	29.5	0.3	29.5	0.0	29.7	0.7	29.7	0.0	29.7	0.0	29.8	0.3	29.8	0.0	29.7	-0.3	29.8	0.3	29.8	0.0	29.8	0.0	29.7	-0.3
1959	29.7	0.0	29.7	0.0	29.7	0.0	29.8	0.3	29.8	0.0	29.9	0.3	30.0	0.3	30.0	0.0	30.2	0.7	30.2	0.0	30.2	0.0	30.2	0.0

[Continued]

Chicago-Gary-Kenosha, IL-IN-WI
Consumer Price Index - All Urban Consumers
Base 1982-1984 = 100
All Items
[Continued]

For 1914-2001. Columns headed % show percentile change in the index from the previous period for which an index is available.

Year	Jan Index	%	Feb Index	%	Mar Index	%	Apr Index	%	May Index	%	Jun Index	%	Jul Index	%	Aug Index	%	Sep Index	%	Oct Index	%	Nov Index	%	Dec Index	%
1960	30.1	-0.3	30.2	0.3	30.2	0.0	30.3	0.3	30.3	0.0	30.4	0.3	30.5	0.3	30.4	-0.3	30.5	0.3	30.5	0.0	30.5	0.0	30.5	0.0
1961	30.5	0.0	30.5	0.0	30.4	-0.3	30.4	0.0	30.4	0.0	30.3	-0.3	30.6	1.0	30.6	0.0	30.6	0.0	30.7	0.3	30.6	-0.3	30.6	0.0
1962	30.6	0.0	30.8	0.7	30.8	0.0	30.9	0.3	30.8	-0.3	30.8	0.0	30.8	0.0	30.8	0.0	31.0	0.6	30.9	-0.3	30.9	0.0	30.9	0.0
1963	31.0	0.3	31.0	0.0	31.1	0.3	31.1	0.0	31.0	-0.3	31.1	0.3	31.3	0.6	31.2	-0.3	31.2	0.0	31.2	0.0	31.2	0.0	31.3	0.3
1964	31.2	-0.3	31.1	-0.3	31.1	0.0	31.1	0.0	31.2	0.3	31.3	0.3	31.4	0.3	31.3	-0.3	31.3	0.0	31.4	0.3	31.4	0.0	31.4	0.0
1965	31.4	0.0	31.4	0.0	31.4	0.0	31.5	0.3	31.6	0.3	31.8	0.6	31.7	-0.3	31.7	0.0	31.8	0.3	31.9	0.3	31.9	0.0	32.1	0.6
1966	32.0	-0.3	32.2	0.6	32.4	0.6	32.4	0.0	32.5	0.3	32.6	0.3	32.6	0.0	32.8	0.6	33.0	0.6	33.0	0.0	33.0	0.0	33.1	0.3
1967	32.9	-0.6	33.1	0.6	33.1	0.0	33.1	0.0	33.2	0.3	33.3	0.3	33.5	0.6	33.7	0.6	33.9	0.6	33.9	0.0	34.0	0.3	34.1	0.3
1968	34.1	0.0	34.3	0.6	34.5	0.6	34.6	0.3	34.7	0.3	34.8	0.3	35.0	0.6	35.1	0.3	35.3	0.6	35.4	0.3	35.4	0.0	35.6	0.6
1969	35.8	0.6	35.9	0.3	36.2	0.8	36.3	0.3	36.4	0.3	36.7	0.8	36.9	0.5	37.2	0.8	37.5	0.8	37.4	-0.3	37.6	0.5	37.8	0.5
1970	38.0	0.5	38.1	0.3	38.3	0.5	38.4	0.3	38.6	0.5	38.8	0.5	39.0	0.5	39.2	0.5	39.4	0.5	39.6	0.5	39.7	0.3	39.9	0.5
1971	39.9	0.0	40.0	0.3	40.1	0.2	40.2	0.2	40.4	0.5	40.5	0.2	40.5	0.0	40.7	0.5	40.7	0.0	40.7	0.0	40.8	0.2	40.9	0.2
1972	40.9	0.0	41.2	0.7	41.2	0.0	41.3	0.2	41.4	0.2	41.6	0.5	41.6	0.0	41.8	0.5	41.9	0.2	42.0	0.2	42.1	0.2	42.2	0.2
1973	42.3	0.2	42.7	0.9	43.2	1.2	43.5	0.7	43.8	0.7	44.1	0.7	44.0	-0.2	45.0	2.3	45.1	0.2	45.4	0.7	45.6	0.4	45.8	0.4
1974	46.4	1.3	47.1	1.5	47.6	1.1	47.8	0.4	48.2	0.8	48.7	1.0	48.9	0.4	49.5	1.2	49.9	0.8	50.4	1.0	50.8	0.8	51.3	1.0
1975	51.3	0.0	51.7	0.8	52.1	0.8	52.2	0.2	52.0	-0.4	52.4	0.8	53.0	1.1	53.3	0.6	53.4	0.2	53.7	0.6	53.8	0.2	54.0	0.4
1976	53.7	-0.6	54.1	0.7	54.2	0.2	54.5	0.6	54.8	0.6	55.2	0.7	55.5	0.5	55.8	0.5	56.1	0.5	56.3	0.4	56.4	0.2	56.6	0.4
1977	56.7	0.2	57.3	1.1	57.7	0.7	58.2	0.9	58.4	0.3	58.6	0.3	59.0	0.7	59.3	0.5	59.7	0.7	59.8	0.2	60.0	0.3	60.2	0.3
1978	61.1	1.5	61.7	1.0	62.4	1.1	62.7	0.5	63.3	1.0	63.7	0.6	64.1	0.6	64.1	0.0	64.9	1.2	65.4	0.8	66.3	1.4	66.5	0.3
1979	66.8	0.5	67.8	1.5	69.2	2.1	69.9	1.0	70.3	0.6	71.5	1.7	72.8	1.8	73.2	0.5	74.1	1.2	74.2	0.1	75.6	1.9	76.4	1.1
1980	77.1	0.9	77.9	1.0	78.8	1.2	80.4	2.0	81.4	1.2	83.1	2.1	82.6	-0.6	82.1	-0.6	83.7	1.9	84.9	1.4	87.0	2.5	87.1	0.1
1981	86.7	-0.5	86.9	0.2	86.9	0.0	88.3	1.6	88.5	0.2	90.1	1.8	91.3	1.3	92.3	1.1	92.7	0.4	92.4	-0.3	92.7	0.3	91.7	-1.1
1982	92.2	0.5	92.0	-0.2	92.5	0.5	93.8	1.4	96.3	2.7	97.7	1.5	98.1	0.4	98.1	0.0	98.4	0.3	98.5	0.1	98.5	0.0	98.1	-0.4
1983	98.4	0.3	98.3	-0.1	98.3	0.0	98.8	0.5	99.2	0.4	99.9	0.7	100.3	0.4	101.0	0.7	101.4	0.4	101.2	-0.2	101.7	0.5	101.7	0.0
1984	102.2	0.5	102.1	-0.1	102.3	0.2	102.7	0.4	102.8	0.1	103.7	0.9	104.0	0.3	104.9	0.9	105.5	0.6	105.1	-0.4	105.1	0.0	105.1	0.0
1985	105.5	0.4	106.0	0.5	106.2	0.2	106.8	0.6	107.0	0.2	108.5	1.4	108.6	0.1	109.1	0.5	109.2	0.1	108.0	-1.1	108.5	0.5	109.1	0.6
1986	109.2	0.1	109.3	0.1	108.4	-0.8	108.3	-0.1	108.5	0.2	110.6	1.9	110.8	0.2	110.9	0.1	111.8	0.8	110.0	-1.6	110.9	0.8	110.8	-0.1
1987	111.9	1.0	111.9	0.0	112.3	0.4	112.8	0.4	113.3	0.4	115.5	1.9	115.9	0.3	116.7	0.7	117.1	0.3	115.1	-1.7	115.7	0.5	115.7	0.0
1988	115.3	-0.3	116.6	1.1	116.9	0.3	117.1	0.2	117.0	-0.1	118.9	1.6	119.8	0.8	120.1	0.3	122.0	1.6	121.6	-0.3	121.0	-0.5	121.3	0.2
1989	121.5	0.2	122.2	0.6	123.0	0.7	123.6	0.5	123.9	0.2	125.7	1.5	126.4	0.6	126.4	0.0	127.1	0.6	126.8	-0.2	126.7	-0.1	126.5	-0.2
1990	128.1	1.3	129.2	0.9	129.5	0.2	130.4	0.7	130.4	0.0	131.7	1.0	132.0	0.2	133.2	0.9	133.8	0.5	133.3	-0.4	134.2	0.7	134.6	0.3
1991	135.1	0.4	135.5	0.3	136.2	0.5	136.1	-0.1	136.8	0.5	137.3	0.4	137.3	0.0	137.6	0.2	138.3	0.5	138.0	-0.2	138.0	0.0	138.3	0.2
1992	138.9	0.4	139.2	0.2	139.7	0.4	139.8	0.1	140.5	0.5	141.2	0.5	141.4	0.1	141.9	0.4	142.7	0.6	142.1	-0.4	142.4	0.2	142.9	0.4
1993	143.2	0.2	143.6	0.3	144.1	0.3	144.7	0.4	145.7	0.7	145.6	-0.1	145.5	-0.1	146.1	0.4	146.7	0.4	147.2	0.3	146.4	-0.5	146.1	-0.2
1994	146.5	0.3	146.8	0.2	147.6	0.5	147.9	0.2	147.6	-0.2	148.1	0.3	148.3	0.1	149.8	1.0	150.2	0.3	149.4	-0.5	150.4	0.7	150.5	0.1
1995	151.8	0.9	152.3	0.3	152.6	0.2	153.1	0.3	153.0	-0.1	153.5	0.3	153.6	0.1	153.8	0.1	154.0	0.1	154.3	0.2	154.0	-0.2	153.8	-0.1
1996	154.6	0.5	155.2	0.4	156.3	0.7	156.4	0.1	156.9	0.3	157.6	0.4	157.7	0.1	158.1	0.3	158.3	0.1	158.8	0.3	159.4	0.4	159.7	0.2
1997	160.4	0.4	161.1	0.4	161.0	-0.1	160.9	-0.1	161.1	0.1	161.7	0.4	161.7	0.0	162.5	0.5	162.1	-0.2	162.5	0.2	162.9	0.2	162.8	-0.1
1998	162.8	0.0	163.1	0.2	164.1	0.6	164.8	0.4	165.6	0.5	166.0	0.2	166.5	0.3	165.4	-0.7	165.3	-0.1	165.7	0.2	165.4	-0.2	165.1	-0.2
1999	166.1	0.6	166.4	0.2	167.0	0.4	167.6	0.4	168.2	0.4	168.9	0.4	169.4	0.3	169.3	-0.1	169.7	0.2	169.7	0.0	169.3	-0.2	169.2	-0.1
2000	170.2	0.6	171.4	0.7	172.2	0.5	171.9	-0.2	173.7	1.0	176.0	1.3	174.6	-0.8	173.7	-0.5	174.8	0.6	175.4	0.3	176.0	0.3	175.8	-0.1
2001	178.1	1.3	178.5	0.2	177.1	-0.8	178.4	0.7	179.8	0.8	179.2	-0.3	177.7	-0.8	178.1	0.2	179.7	0.9	178.1	-0.9	177.4	-0.4	177.9	0.3

Source: U.S. Department of Labor, Bureau of Labor Statistics, Division of Consumer Prices and Price Indexes. - indicates no data collected for period.

Chicago-Gary-Kenosha, IL-IN-WI
Consumer Price Index - Urban Wage Earners
Base 1982-1984 = 100
All Items

For 1914-2001. Columns headed % show percentile change in the index from the previous period for which an index is available.

Year	Jan Index	%	Feb Index	%	Mar Index	%	Apr Index	%	May Index	%	Jun Index	%	Jul Index	%	Aug Index	%	Sep Index	%	Oct Index	%	Nov Index	%	Dec Index	%
1914	-		-		-		-		-		-		-		-		-		-		-		10.1	-
1915	-		-		-		-		-		-		-		-		-		-		-		10.4	3.0
1916	-		-		-		-		-		-		-		-		-		-		-		11.8	13.5
1917	-		-		-		-		-		-		-		-		-		-		-		13.7	16.1
1918	-		-		-		-		-		-		-		-		-		-		-		16.6	21.2
1919	-		-		-		-		-		16.9	1.8	-		-		-		-		-		19.2	13.6
1920	-		-		-		-		-		21.2	10.4	-		-		-		-		-		19.2	-9.4
1921	-		-		-		-		18.2	-5.2	-		-		-		18.1	-0.5	-		-		17.8	-1.7
1922	-		-		-		-		17.2	-3.4	17.3	0.6	-		-		17.3	0.0	-		-		17.4	0.6
1923	-		-		17.5	0.6	-		-		17.6	0.6	-		-		18.0	2.3	-		-		18.0	0.0
1924	-		-		17.9	-0.6	-		-		18.0	0.6	-		-		18.1	0.6	-		-		18.2	0.6
1925	-		-		-		-		-		18.5	1.6	-		-		-		-		-		18.9	2.2
1926	-		-		-		-		-		18.7	-1.1	-		-		-		-		-		18.6	-0.5
1927	-		-		-		-		-		18.6	0.0	-		-		-		-		-		18.1	-2.7
1928	-		-		-		-		-		17.9	-1.1	-		-		-		-		-		18.0	0.6
1929	-		-		-		-		-		17.9	-0.6	-		-		-		-		-		18.0	0.6
1930	-		-		-		-		-		17.7	-1.7	-		-		-		-		-		16.9	-4.5
1931	-		-		-		-		-		15.8	-6.5	-		-		-		-		-		15.2	-3.8
1932	-		-		-		-		-		13.8	-9.2	-		-		-		-		-		13.1	-5.1
1933	-		-		-		-		-		12.6	-3.8	-		-		-		-		-		12.9	2.4
1934	-		-		-		-		-		12.9	0.0	-		-		-		-		13.0	0.8	-	
1935	-		-		13.6	4.6	-		-		-		13.6	0.0	-		-		13.6	0.0	-		-	
1936	13.7	0.7	-		-		13.5	-1.5	-		-		13.8	2.2	-		14.0	1.4	-		-		13.9	-0.7
1937	-		-		14.1	1.4	-		-		14.4	2.1	-		-		14.6	1.4	-		-		14.4	-1.4
1938	-		-		14.1	-2.1	-		-		14.3	1.4	-		-		14.3	0.0	-		-		14.1	-1.4
1939	-		-		13.9	-1.4	-		-		13.8	-0.7	-		-		14.1	2.2	-		-		13.9	-1.4
1940	-		-		13.9	0.0	-		-		14.1	1.4	-		-		14.1	0.0	14.1	0.0	14.0	-0.7	14.1	0.7
1941	14.1	0.0	14.1	0.0	14.2	0.7	14.3	0.7	14.4	0.7	14.6	1.4	14.8	1.4	14.9	0.7	15.3	2.7	15.4	0.7	15.5	0.6	15.4	-0.6
1942	15.7	1.9	15.7	0.0	15.9	1.3	16.1	1.3	16.2	0.6	16.2	0.0	16.2	0.0	16.4	1.2	16.4	0.0	16.6	1.2	16.7	0.6	16.7	0.0
1943	16.7	0.0	16.8	0.6	17.1	1.8	17.2	0.6	17.4	1.2	17.3	-0.6	17.1	-1.2	17.2	0.6	17.3	0.6	17.3	0.0	17.2	-0.6	17.2	0.0
1944	17.1	-0.6	17.1	0.0	17.1	0.0	17.3	1.2	17.3	0.0	17.4	0.6	17.6	1.1	17.6	0.0	17.6	0.0	17.6	0.0	17.6	0.0	17.6	0.0
1945	17.6	0.0	17.6	0.0	17.6	0.0	17.6	0.0	17.9	1.7	17.9	0.0	17.9	0.0	17.9	0.0	17.8	-0.6	17.8	0.0	17.8	0.0	17.9	0.6
1946	17.9	0.0	17.9	0.0	17.9	0.0	18.1	1.1	18.2	0.6	18.3	0.5	19.7	7.7	20.2	2.5	20.4	1.0	20.9	2.5	21.3	1.9	21.4	0.5
1947	21.4	0.0	21.3	-0.5	21.8	2.3	21.8	0.0	21.9	0.5	22.1	0.9	22.4	1.4	22.7	1.3	23.5	3.5	23.4	-0.4	23.5	0.4	23.8	1.3
1948	23.9	0.4	23.6	-1.3	23.6	0.0	24.1	2.1	24.4	1.2	24.7	1.2	25.0	1.2	25.0	0.0	25.1	0.4	24.9	-0.8	24.6	-1.2	24.5	-0.4
1949	24.4	-0.4	24.2	-0.8	24.4	0.8	24.5	0.4	24.4	-0.4	24.6	0.8	24.3	-1.2	24.4	0.4	24.6	0.8	24.4	-0.8	24.5	0.4	24.2	-1.2
1950	24.1	-0.4	24.1	0.0	24.2	0.4	24.1	-0.4	24.4	1.2	24.4	0.0	24.8	1.6	25.0	0.8	25.1	0.4	25.2	0.4	25.2	0.0	25.6	1.6
1951	25.9	1.2	26.3	1.5	26.4	0.4	26.4	0.0	26.5	0.4	26.5	0.0	26.7	0.8	26.7	0.0	26.8	0.4	27.0	0.7	27.1	0.4	27.1	0.0
1952	27.1	0.0	26.8	-1.1	26.9	0.4	26.9	0.0	27.2	1.1	27.3	0.4	27.3	0.0	27.4	0.4	27.3	-0.4	27.3	0.0	27.4	0.4	27.2	-0.7
1953	27.2	0.0	27.1	-0.4	27.0	-0.4	27.2	0.7	27.2	0.0	27.4	0.7	27.5	0.4	27.6	0.4	27.7	0.4	27.9	0.7	27.7	-0.7	27.7	0.0
1954	27.7	0.0	27.7	0.0	27.7	0.0	27.7	0.0	27.9	0.7	27.9	0.0	28.1	0.7	28.0	-0.4	27.9	-0.4	27.9	0.0	28.0	0.4	27.8	-0.7
1955	27.8	0.0	27.9	0.4	27.8	-0.4	27.8	0.0	27.9	0.4	27.9	0.0	28.1	0.7	28.2	0.4	28.3	0.4	28.3	0.0	28.3	0.0	28.2	-0.4
1956	28.1	-0.4	28.1	0.0	28.0	-0.4	28.1	0.4	28.2	0.4	28.4	0.7	28.7	1.1	28.5	-0.7	28.6	0.4	28.8	0.7	28.8	0.0	28.8	0.0
1957	28.8	0.0	28.9	0.3	28.9	0.0	29.0	0.3	29.0	0.0	29.2	0.7	29.5	1.0	29.5	0.0	29.6	0.3	29.7	0.3	29.9	0.7	29.9	0.0
1958	30.0	0.3	30.0	0.0	30.2	0.7	30.2	0.0	30.2	0.0	30.3	0.3	30.3	0.0	30.2	-0.3	30.3	0.3	30.3	0.0	30.3	0.0	30.2	-0.3
1959	30.2	0.0	30.2	0.0	30.2	0.0	30.3	0.3	30.3	0.0	30.4	0.3	30.5	0.3	30.5	0.0	30.7	0.7	30.7	0.0	30.7	0.0	30.7	0.0

[Continued]

Chicago-Gary-Kenosha, IL-IN-WI
Consumer Price Index - Urban Wage Earners
Base 1982-1984 = 100
All Items
[Continued]

For 1914-2001. Columns headed % show percentile change in the index from the previous period for which an index is available.

Year	Jan		Feb		Mar		Apr		May		Jun		Jul		Aug		Sep		Oct		Nov		Dec	
	Index	%	Index	%	Index	%	Index	%	Index	%	Index	%	Index	%	Index	%	Index	%	Index	%	Index	%	Index	%
1960	30.6	-0.3	30.7	0.3	30.7	0.0	30.8	0.3	30.8	0.0	30.9	0.3	31.0	0.3	31.0	0.0	31.0	0.0	31.1	0.3	31.0	-0.3	31.1	0.3
1961	31.0	-0.3	31.0	0.0	31.0	0.0	30.9	-0.3	30.9	0.0	30.8	-0.3	31.1	1.0	31.1	0.0	31.2	0.3	31.2	0.0	31.1	-0.3	31.1	0.0
1962	31.2	0.3	31.3	0.3	31.3	0.0	31.4	0.3	31.4	0.0	31.3	-0.3	31.3	0.0	31.3	0.0	31.5	0.6	31.5	0.0	31.5	0.0	31.4	-0.3
1963	31.5	0.3	31.5	0.0	31.6	0.3	31.6	0.0	31.6	0.0	31.6	0.0	31.9	0.9	31.8	-0.3	31.8	0.0	31.8	0.0	31.7	-0.3	31.8	0.3
1964	31.7	-0.3	31.7	0.0	31.7	0.0	31.7	0.0	31.7	0.0	31.8	0.3	31.9	0.3	31.9	0.0	31.9	0.0	31.9	0.0	31.9	0.0	31.9	0.0
1965	31.9	0.0	31.9	0.0	32.0	0.3	32.0	0.0	32.1	0.3	32.3	0.6	32.3	0.0	32.3	0.0	32.4	0.3	32.4	0.0	32.5	0.3	32.6	0.3
1966	32.6	0.0	32.8	0.6	32.9	0.3	32.9	0.0	33.0	0.3	33.2	0.6	33.1	-0.3	33.4	0.9	33.5	0.3	33.6	0.3	33.5	-0.3	33.6	0.3
1967	33.5	-0.3	33.6	0.3	33.7	0.3	33.6	-0.3	33.7	0.3	33.8	0.3	34.1	0.9	34.3	0.6	34.5	0.6	34.5	0.0	34.6	0.3	34.7	0.3
1968	34.7	0.0	34.9	0.6	35.1	0.6	35.2	0.3	35.3	0.3	35.4	0.3	35.7	0.8	35.8	0.3	35.9	0.3	36.0	0.3	36.1	0.3	36.3	0.6
1969	36.4	0.3	36.5	0.3	36.8	0.8	36.9	0.3	37.0	0.3	37.4	1.1	37.6	0.5	37.8	0.5	38.1	0.8	38.0	-0.3	38.3	0.8	38.4	0.3
1970	38.7	0.8	38.7	0.0	38.9	0.5	39.0	0.3	39.3	0.8	39.4	0.3	39.7	0.8	39.9	0.5	40.1	0.5	40.3	0.5	40.4	0.2	40.6	0.5
1971	40.6	0.0	40.7	0.2	40.8	0.2	40.9	0.2	41.1	0.5	41.2	0.2	41.2	0.0	41.4	0.5	41.4	0.0	41.4	0.0	41.5	0.2	41.6	0.2
1972	41.6	0.0	41.9	0.7	41.9	0.0	42.0	0.2	42.1	0.2	42.3	0.5	42.4	0.2	42.6	0.5	42.7	0.2	42.7	0.0	42.8	0.2	42.9	0.2
1973	43.0	0.2	43.4	0.9	43.9	1.2	44.2	0.7	44.5	0.7	44.8	0.7	44.7	-0.2	45.8	2.5	45.8	0.0	46.2	0.9	46.3	0.2	46.6	0.6
1974	47.2	1.3	47.9	1.5	48.4	1.0	48.7	0.6	49.0	0.6	49.6	1.2	49.8	0.4	50.4	1.2	50.7	0.6	51.3	1.2	51.7	0.8	52.2	1.0
1975	52.2	0.0	52.6	0.8	53.0	0.8	53.1	0.2	52.9	-0.4	53.3	0.8	53.9	1.1	54.2	0.6	54.3	0.2	54.7	0.7	54.7	0.0	54.9	0.4
1976	54.7	-0.4	55.0	0.5	55.2	0.4	55.5	0.5	55.7	0.4	56.1	0.7	56.4	0.5	56.8	0.7	57.0	0.4	57.3	0.5	57.4	0.2	57.6	0.3
1977	57.7	0.2	58.3	1.0	58.7	0.7	59.2	0.9	59.4	0.3	59.6	0.3	60.1	0.8	60.4	0.5	60.8	0.7	60.9	0.2	61.1	0.3	61.3	0.3
1978	62.1	1.3	62.6	0.8	63.2	1.0	63.5	0.5	64.1	0.9	64.7	0.9	65.2	0.8	65.0	-0.3	65.7	1.1	66.5	1.2	67.3	1.2	67.6	0.4
1979	68.0	0.6	68.9	1.3	70.2	1.9	70.9	1.0	71.4	0.7	72.6	1.7	73.8	1.7	74.3	0.7	75.1	1.1	75.5	0.5	76.8	1.7	77.6	1.0
1980	78.3	0.9	79.2	1.1	80.1	1.1	81.7	2.0	82.7	1.2	84.4	2.1	84.1	-0.4	83.6	-0.6	85.0	1.7	86.1	1.3	88.2	2.4	88.2	0.0
1981	87.9	-0.3	88.1	0.2	88.2	0.1	89.6	1.6	89.9	0.3	91.2	1.4	92.5	1.4	93.5	1.1	93.9	0.4	94.1	0.2	94.4	0.3	93.4	-1.1
1982	93.9	0.5	93.8	-0.1	94.1	0.3	95.3	1.3	97.7	2.5	99.3	1.6	99.7	0.4	99.6	-0.1	99.7	0.1	99.8	0.1	99.8	0.0	99.4	-0.4
1983	99.7	0.3	99.2	-0.5	99.2	0.0	100.0	0.8	100.4	0.4	100.7	0.3	100.9	0.2	101.3	0.4	101.8	0.5	100.3	-1.5	100.7	0.4	100.2	-0.5
1984	101.6	1.4	101.1	-0.5	100.9	-0.2	100.9	0.0	101.0	0.1	101.5	0.5	101.8	0.3	102.6	0.8	103.6	1.0	102.8	-0.8	103.0	0.2	102.7	-0.3
1985	103.0	0.1	103.5	0.5	103.8	0.3	104.3	0.5	104.5	0.2	105.9	1.3	105.9	0.0	106.3	0.4	106.3	0.0	105.2	-1.0	105.9	0.7	106.4	0.5
1986	106.5	0.1	106.5	0.0	105.5	-0.9	105.2	-0.3	105.4	0.2	107.5	2.0	107.6	0.1	107.7	0.1	108.4	0.6	106.7	-1.6	107.6	0.8	107.5	-0.1
1987	108.7	1.1	108.6	-0.1	109.0	0.4	109.5	0.5	109.9	0.4	112.0	1.9	112.4	0.4	113.0	0.5	113.6	0.4	111.7	-1.7	112.2	0.4	112.2	0.0
1988	111.9	-0.3	112.9	0.9	113.2	0.3	113.3	0.1	113.3	0.0	115.2	1.7	116.2	0.9	116.4	0.2	118.2	1.5	117.8	-0.3	117.4	-0.3	117.7	0.3
1989	117.9	0.2	118.4	0.4	119.1	0.6	119.8	0.6	120.1	0.3	121.8	1.4	122.6	0.7	122.5	-0.1	123.1	0.5	122.9	-0.2	122.9	0.0	122.8	-0.1
1990	124.4	1.3	125.4	0.8	125.6	0.2	126.5	0.7	126.5	0.0	127.9	1.1	128.0	0.1	129.3	1.0	129.9	0.5	129.4	-0.4	130.3	0.7	130.7	0.3
1991	131.1	0.3	131.5	0.3	132.0	0.4	132.1	0.1	132.7	0.5	133.1	0.3	133.2	0.1	133.4	0.2	133.9	0.4	133.6	-0.2	133.8	0.1	134.1	0.2
1992	134.4	0.2	134.7	0.2	135.2	0.4	135.4	0.1	136.2	0.6	136.9	0.5	137.0	0.1	137.5	0.4	138.3	0.6	137.7	-0.4	138.2	0.4	138.5	0.2
1993	138.9	0.3	139.1	0.1	139.5	0.3	140.3	0.6	141.4	0.8	141.2	-0.1	141.1	-0.1	141.6	0.4	142.1	0.4	142.6	0.4	141.8	-0.6	141.7	-0.1
1994	142.0	0.2	142.3	0.2	143.0	0.5	143.3	0.2	143.1	-0.1	143.6	0.3	143.7	0.1	145.1	1.0	145.4	0.2	144.6	-0.6	145.7	0.8	145.8	0.1
1995	147.1	0.9	147.5	0.3	147.8	0.2	148.3	0.3	148.2	-0.1	148.5	0.2	148.7	0.1	148.8	0.1	149.0	0.1	149.2	0.1	149.0	-0.1	149.0	0.0
1996	149.7	0.5	150.2	0.3	151.3	0.7	151.5	0.1	151.9	0.3	152.6	0.5	152.7	0.1	152.9	0.1	153.2	0.2	153.7	0.3	154.4	0.5	154.6	0.1
1997	155.3	0.5	155.9	0.4	155.6	-0.2	155.3	-0.2	155.5	0.1	156.0	0.3	156.0	0.0	156.7	0.4	156.4	-0.2	156.9	0.3	157.2	0.2	157.3	0.1
1998	157.3	0.0	157.4	0.1	158.3	0.6	159.0	0.4	159.9	0.6	160.2	0.2	160.6	0.2	159.6	-0.6	159.6	0.0	160.0	0.3	159.9	-0.1	159.6	-0.2
1999	160.5	0.6	160.6	0.1	161.1	0.3	161.7	0.4	162.3	0.4	163.0	0.4	163.4	0.2	163.5	0.1	164.1	0.4	164.0	-0.1	163.7	-0.2	163.7	0.0
2000	164.6	0.5	165.8	0.7	166.5	0.4	166.3	-0.1	168.1	1.1	170.4	1.4	168.9	-0.9	168.0	-0.5	169.2	0.7	169.8	0.4	170.4	0.4	170.3	-0.1
2001	172.6	1.4	172.9	0.2	171.4	-0.9	172.6	0.7	174.0	0.8	173.4	-0.3	171.7	-1.0	172.0	0.2	173.7	1.0	171.9	-1.0	171.2	-0.4	171.7	0.3

Source: U.S. Department of Labor, Bureau of Labor Statistics, Division of Consumer Prices and Price Indexes. - indicates no data collected for period.

Chicago-Gary-Kenosha, IL-IN-WI
Consumer Price Index - All Urban Consumers
Base 1982-1984 = 100
Food and Beverages

For 1976-2001. Columns headed % show percentile change in the index from the previous period for which an index is available.

Year	Jan Index	%	Feb Index	%	Mar Index	%	Apr Index	%	May Index	%	Jun Index	%	Jul Index	%	Aug Index	%	Sep Index	%	Oct Index	%	Nov Index	%	Dec Index	%
1976	63.6	-	63.7	0.2	63.3	-0.6	64.0	1.1	63.7	-0.5	64.4	1.1	64.9	0.8	65.0	0.2	64.7	-0.5	64.9	0.3	64.5	-0.6	64.4	-0.2
1977	64.7	0.5	65.9	1.9	66.5	0.9	67.3	1.2	67.3	0.0	67.9	0.9	68.6	1.0	69.0	0.6	69.4	0.6	69.5	0.1	69.4	-0.1	70.0	0.9
1978	71.8	2.6	72.8	1.4	73.5	1.0	74.4	1.2	75.1	0.9	76.0	1.2	76.4	0.5	77.0	0.8	77.4	0.5	77.5	0.1	78.4	1.2	78.6	0.3
1979	80.0	1.8	81.2	1.5	82.3	1.4	82.9	0.7	83.7	1.0	83.9	0.2	84.7	1.0	84.1	-0.7	84.3	0.2	85.0	0.8	86.1	1.3	87.0	1.0
1980	86.8	-0.2	87.6	0.9	88.8	1.4	89.5	0.8	90.1	0.7	90.2	0.1	91.4	1.3	92.7	1.4	93.5	0.9	94.1	0.6	94.5	0.4	95.0	0.5
1981	95.6	0.6	96.2	0.6	96.3	0.1	95.9	-0.4	95.4	-0.5	96.2	0.8	96.5	0.3	97.1	0.6	96.9	-0.2	97.1	0.2	96.7	-0.4	96.7	0.0
1982	97.5	0.8	97.6	0.1	97.4	-0.2	98.5	1.1	99.4	0.9	99.9	0.5	99.5	-0.4	99.1	-0.4	98.9	-0.2	98.9	0.0	98.7	-0.2	98.8	0.1
1983	99.7	0.9	99.7	0.0	99.6	-0.1	99.8	0.2	99.4	-0.4	99.3	-0.1	98.5	-0.8	98.4	-0.1	99.3	0.9	99.3	0.0	99.8	0.5	99.5	-0.3
1984	101.8	2.3	102.7	0.9	102.2	-0.5	102.0	-0.2	101.7	-0.3	101.4	-0.3	102.0	0.6	102.5	0.5	102.1	-0.4	102.0	-0.1	101.2	-0.8	101.9	0.7
1985	102.6	0.7	104.0	1.4	104.1	0.1	103.5	-0.6	103.2	-0.3	104.1	0.9	103.8	-0.3	104.0	0.2	104.3	0.3	104.4	0.1	105.6	1.1	107.0	1.3
1986	106.9	-0.1	107.9	0.9	107.7	-0.2	107.8	0.1	107.4	-0.4	108.5	1.0	109.3	0.7	110.4	1.0	110.1	-0.3	109.1	-0.9	111.1	1.8	110.9	-0.2
1987	113.1	2.0	112.7	-0.4	112.0	-0.6	112.9	0.8	112.7	-0.2	113.6	0.8	113.2	-0.4	113.5	0.3	113.7	0.2	113.5	-0.2	113.7	0.2	113.7	0.0
1988	114.4	0.6	114.9	0.4	115.0	0.1	115.2	0.2	115.8	0.5	116.1	0.3	117.9	1.6	118.8	0.8	119.3	0.4	119.2	-0.1	118.9	-0.3	119.3	0.3
1989	120.7	1.2	121.5	0.7	121.5	0.0	122.7	1.0	122.3	-0.3	122.3	0.0	122.7	0.3	122.4	-0.2	122.9	0.4	123.2	0.2	123.6	0.3	124.2	0.5
1990	128.0	3.1	128.7	0.5	129.0	0.2	128.9	-0.1	129.1	0.2	129.8	0.5	131.3	1.2	131.0	-0.2	131.3	0.2	131.1	-0.2	132.2	0.8	132.9	0.5
1991	134.7	1.4	134.8	0.1	135.3	0.4	136.0	0.5	136.5	0.4	136.2	-0.2	136.0	-0.1	134.8	-0.9	135.5	0.5	134.6	-0.7	135.6	0.7	135.9	0.2
1992	136.6	0.5	137.7	0.8	138.8	0.8	139.1	0.2	139.8	0.5	138.9	-0.6	138.8	-0.1	139.2	0.3	140.4	0.9	139.6	-0.6	140.2	0.4	140.8	0.4
1993	142.5	1.2	140.8	-1.2	142.2	1.0	141.9	-0.2	143.3	1.0	142.7	-0.4	142.9	0.1	143.1	0.1	143.3	0.1	144.3	0.7	144.4	0.1	145.6	0.8
1994	147.2	1.1	146.4	-0.5	147.0	0.4	147.4	0.3	146.8	-0.4	145.9	-0.6	146.2	0.2	147.2	0.7	147.2	0.0	147.5	0.2	147.3	-0.1	147.6	0.2
1995	150.2	1.8	151.4	0.8	151.3	-0.1	151.7	0.3	150.9	-0.5	150.8	-0.1	151.2	0.3	150.9	-0.2	150.6	-0.2	151.4	0.5	152.3	0.6	152.9	0.4
1996	153.3	0.3	153.1	-0.1	154.2	0.7	154.8	0.4	154.0	-0.5	155.6	1.0	156.1	0.3	156.5	0.3	157.5	0.6	158.4	0.6	159.3	0.6	160.2	0.6
1997	160.2	0.0	159.5	-0.4	159.7	0.1	159.0	-0.4	159.6	0.4	159.6	0.0	160.3	0.4	160.5	0.1	160.3	-0.1	161.8	0.9	161.8	0.0	163.1	0.8
1998	163.1	0.0	163.0	-0.1	163.9	0.6	164.1	0.1	165.0	0.5	163.5	-0.9	165.8	1.4	165.5	-0.2	165.0	-0.3	167.0	1.2	166.1	-0.5	166.0	-0.1
1999	168.1	1.3	168.6	0.3	168.5	-0.1	168.2	-0.2	168.3	0.1	167.6	-0.4	168.6	0.6	168.6	0.0	169.1	0.3	168.4	-0.4	168.1	-0.2	168.9	0.5
2000	169.5	0.4	171.1	0.9	169.7	-0.8	168.8	-0.5	171.6	1.7	172.1	0.3	172.1	0.0	172.7	0.3	172.6	-0.1	172.6	0.0	171.5	-0.6	172.1	0.3
2001	175.2	1.8	175.8	0.3	175.0	-0.5	174.7	-0.2	176.3	0.9	176.7	0.2	176.8	0.1	176.5	-0.2	176.9	0.2	178.2	0.7	176.2	-1.1	177.0	0.5

Source: U.S. Department of Labor, Bureau of Labor Statistics, Division of Consumer Prices and Price Indexes. - indicates no data collected for period.

Chicago-Gary-Kenosha, IL-IN-WI
Consumer Price Index - Urban Wage Earners
Base 1982-1984 = 100
Food and Beverages

For 1976-2001. Columns headed % show percentile change in the index from the previous period for which an index is available.

Year	Jan Index	%	Feb Index	%	Mar Index	%	Apr Index	%	May Index	%	Jun Index	%	Jul Index	%	Aug Index	%	Sep Index	%	Oct Index	%	Nov Index	%	Dec Index	%
1976	64.6	-	64.6	0.0	64.2	-0.6	64.9	1.1	64.7	-0.3	65.3	0.9	65.9	0.9	66.0	0.2	65.6	-0.6	65.9	0.5	65.5	-0.6	65.4	-0.2
1977	65.7	0.5	66.9	1.8	67.5	0.9	68.3	1.2	68.3	0.0	68.9	0.9	69.6	1.0	70.1	0.7	70.4	0.4	70.6	0.3	70.5	-0.1	71.1	0.9
1978	72.6	2.1	73.1	0.7	73.6	0.7	74.7	1.5	75.5	1.1	76.5	1.3	77.1	0.8	77.5	0.5	78.0	0.6	78.4	0.5	79.1	0.9	79.3	0.3
1979	81.1	2.3	81.9	1.0	83.3	1.7	83.7	0.5	84.4	0.8	84.6	0.2	85.2	0.7	84.4	-0.9	84.7	0.4	85.9	1.4	86.8	1.0	87.6	0.9
1980	87.9	0.3	88.4	0.6	89.7	1.5	90.5	0.9	91.5	1.1	91.7	0.2	93.0	1.4	93.6	0.6	94.8	1.3	95.0	0.2	95.8	0.8	95.4	-0.4
1981	95.5	0.1	95.9	0.4	95.9	0.0	96.0	0.1	95.4	-0.6	96.2	0.8	96.5	0.3	96.9	0.4	96.8	-0.1	97.1	0.3	96.6	-0.5	96.7	0.1
1982	97.5	0.8	97.6	0.1	97.3	-0.3	98.5	1.2	99.4	0.9	99.8	0.4	99.5	-0.3	99.1	-0.4	98.8	-0.3	98.7	-0.1	98.7	0.0	98.8	0.1
1983	99.6	0.8	99.7	0.1	99.6	-0.1	99.7	0.1	99.4	-0.3	99.3	-0.1	98.5	-0.8	98.4	-0.1	99.3	0.9	99.5	0.2	99.8	0.3	99.7	-0.1
1984	101.9	2.2	102.7	0.8	102.2	-0.5	102.1	-0.1	101.8	-0.3	101.5	-0.3	101.9	0.4	102.5	0.6	102.0	-0.5	101.9	-0.1	101.3	-0.6	102.0	0.7
1985	102.6	0.6	104.0	1.4	104.1	0.1	103.6	-0.5	103.2	-0.4	104.1	0.9	103.7	-0.4	103.9	0.2	104.3	0.4	104.5	0.2	105.7	1.1	106.9	1.1
1986	107.0	0.1	107.9	0.8	107.8	-0.1	107.9	0.1	107.5	-0.4	108.6	1.0	109.4	0.7	110.5	1.0	110.2	-0.3	109.2	-0.9	111.3	1.9	110.9	-0.4
1987	113.2	2.1	112.8	-0.4	112.1	-0.6	113.0	0.8	112.8	-0.2	113.7	0.8	113.3	-0.4	113.6	0.3	113.8	0.2	113.6	-0.2	113.8	0.2	113.8	0.0
1988	114.5	0.6	114.9	0.3	115.1	0.2	115.3	0.2	115.9	0.5	116.1	0.2	118.0	1.6	118.9	0.8	119.4	0.4	119.3	-0.1	119.0	-0.3	119.4	0.3
1989	120.8	1.2	121.5	0.6	121.5	0.0	122.7	1.0	122.3	-0.3	122.4	0.1	122.8	0.3	122.5	-0.2	123.1	0.5	123.3	0.2	123.7	0.3	124.3	0.5
1990	128.3	3.2	128.8	0.4	129.1	0.2	129.1	0.0	129.2	0.1	130.0	0.6	131.4	1.1	131.2	-0.2	131.5	0.2	131.2	-0.2	132.4	0.9	133.0	0.5
1991	134.8	1.4	134.9	0.1	135.5	0.4	136.2	0.5	136.7	0.4	136.4	-0.2	136.2	-0.1	135.0	-0.9	135.7	0.5	134.7	-0.7	135.8	0.8	135.9	0.1
1992	136.6	0.5	137.7	0.8	138.9	0.9	139.2	0.2	139.8	0.4	139.0	-0.6	138.8	-0.1	139.2	0.3	140.4	0.9	139.7	-0.5	140.3	0.4	140.9	0.4
1993	142.6	1.2	140.9	-1.2	142.3	1.0	142.1	-0.1	143.4	0.9	142.8	-0.4	143.1	0.2	143.3	0.1	143.5	0.1	144.5	0.7	144.7	0.1	145.9	0.8
1994	147.4	1.0	146.5	-0.6	147.3	0.5	147.6	0.2	147.0	-0.4	146.1	-0.6	146.4	0.2	147.4	0.7	147.4	0.0	147.7	0.2	147.4	-0.2	147.8	0.3
1995	150.5	1.8	151.7	0.8	151.6	-0.1	151.9	0.2	151.1	-0.5	151.0	-0.1	151.4	0.3	151.1	-0.2	150.9	-0.1	151.7	0.5	152.6	0.6	153.2	0.4
1996	153.5	0.2	153.3	-0.1	154.4	0.7	155.0	0.4	154.0	-0.6	155.8	1.2	156.3	0.3	156.7	0.3	157.7	0.6	158.7	0.6	159.6	0.6	160.6	0.6
1997	160.5	-0.1	159.7	-0.5	160.0	0.2	159.3	-0.4	159.8	0.3	159.9	0.1	160.5	0.4	160.7	0.1	160.5	-0.1	162.0	0.9	162.0	0.0	163.4	0.9
1998	163.2	-0.1	163.2	0.0	164.1	0.6	164.2	0.1	165.1	0.5	163.7	-0.8	166.1	1.5	165.6	-0.3	165.2	-0.2	167.1	1.2	166.3	-0.5	166.2	-0.1
1999	168.3	1.3	168.9	0.4	168.8	-0.1	168.2	-0.4	168.4	0.1	167.6	-0.5	168.6	0.6	168.6	0.0	169.1	0.3	168.5	-0.4	168.3	-0.1	169.1	0.5
2000	169.5	0.2	171.3	1.1	169.7	-0.9	168.6	-0.6	171.7	1.8	172.2	0.3	172.2	0.0	173.0	0.5	172.7	-0.2	172.6	-0.1	171.7	-0.5	172.2	0.3
2001	175.3	1.8	176.0	0.4	175.1	-0.5	174.9	-0.1	176.1	0.7	176.8	0.4	176.8	0.0	176.6	-0.1	177.0	0.2	178.3	0.7	176.3	-1.1	177.2	0.5

Source: U.S. Department of Labor, Bureau of Labor Statistics, Division of Consumer Prices and Price Indexes. - indicates no data collected for period.

Chicago-Gary-Kenosha, IL-IN-WI
Consumer Price Index - All Urban Consumers
Base 1982-1984 = 100
Housing

For 1976-2001. Columns headed % show percentile change in the index from the previous period for which an index is available.

Year	Jan Index	%	Feb Index	%	Mar Index	%	Apr Index	%	May Index	%	Jun Index	%	Jul Index	%	Aug Index	%	Sep Index	%	Oct Index	%	Nov Index	%	Dec Index	%
1976	47.5	-	47.6	0.2	47.8	0.4	47.9	0.2	48.1	0.4	48.3	0.4	48.6	0.6	48.8	0.4	49.1	0.6	49.3	0.4	49.3	0.0	49.9	1.2
1977	50.0	0.2	50.4	0.8	50.5	0.2	50.9	0.8	51.0	0.2	51.0	0.0	51.6	1.2	51.9	0.6	52.4	1.0	52.6	0.4	52.9	0.6	53.0	0.2
1978	54.2	2.3	55.0	1.5	56.1	2.0	56.2	0.2	56.6	0.7	57.0	0.7	57.5	0.9	57.0	-0.9	58.2	2.1	58.9	1.2	60.1	2.0	60.3	0.3
1979	60.3	0.0	61.5	2.0	63.3	2.9	64.1	1.3	63.8	-0.5	65.6	2.8	67.2	2.4	68.0	1.2	68.9	1.3	68.6	-0.4	70.6	2.9	71.1	0.7
1980	71.5	0.6	72.0	0.7	72.3	0.4	74.6	3.2	76.2	2.1	79.6	4.5	78.1	-1.9	76.2	-2.4	78.7	3.3	80.7	2.5	84.3	4.5	84.1	-0.2
1981	81.8	-2.7	81.4	-0.5	81.0	-0.5	83.3	2.8	83.6	0.4	86.3	3.2	88.0	2.0	89.3	1.5	89.4	0.1	88.5	-1.0	88.8	0.3	86.3	-2.8
1982	87.5	1.4	87.2	-0.3	88.8	1.8	91.0	2.5	95.6	5.1	97.1	1.6	98.0	0.9	97.9	-0.1	98.5	0.6	98.5	0.0	98.5	0.0	97.8	-0.7
1983	98.2	0.4	98.6	0.4	98.8	0.2	99.1	0.3	99.4	0.3	101.5	2.1	102.1	0.6	102.4	0.3	102.2	-0.2	100.8	-1.4	101.8	1.0	102.3	0.5
1984	102.5	0.2	102.1	-0.4	102.5	0.4	103.0	0.5	103.0	0.0	105.1	2.0	105.0	-0.1	106.7	1.6	107.8	1.0	106.1	-1.6	106.2	0.1	106.3	0.1
1985	107.1	0.8	107.2	0.1	106.8	-0.4	107.6	0.7	108.1	0.5	111.6	3.2	111.7	0.1	113.2	1.3	113.3	0.1	109.4	-3.4	109.2	-0.2	109.6	0.4
1986	110.3	0.6	110.5	0.2	110.4	-0.1	111.3	0.8	111.0	-0.3	115.5	4.1	116.0	0.4	116.1	0.1	117.1	0.9	112.1	-4.3	112.7	0.5	112.1	-0.5
1987	113.1	0.9	113.3	0.2	113.3	0.0	113.9	0.5	114.1	0.2	118.7	4.0	119.6	0.8	120.3	0.6	120.6	0.2	115.4	-4.3	116.6	1.0	117.0	0.3
1988	115.7	-1.1	118.0	2.0	118.0	0.0	118.1	0.1	118.1	0.0	121.9	3.2	122.7	0.7	122.1	-0.5	124.6	2.0	123.7	-0.7	122.3	-1.1	123.1	0.7
1989	123.1	0.0	123.8	0.6	124.2	0.3	124.2	0.0	124.5	0.2	128.2	3.0	128.9	0.5	128.8	-0.1	129.9	0.9	126.9	-2.3	126.9	0.0	127.2	0.2
1990	128.0	0.6	129.2	0.9	129.3	0.1	130.2	0.7	129.6	-0.5	133.2	2.8	133.4	0.2	134.3	0.7	134.2	-0.1	130.8	-2.5	131.7	0.7	132.5	0.6
1991	134.2	1.3	134.3	0.1	135.8	1.1	134.9	-0.7	136.1	0.9	137.6	1.1	138.3	0.5	137.9	-0.3	137.7	-0.1	137.0	-0.5	135.6	-1.0	137.4	1.3
1992	138.9	1.1	138.3	-0.4	138.2	-0.1	138.2	0.0	139.1	0.7	141.4	1.7	140.7	-0.5	140.6	-0.1	141.6	0.7	139.5	-1.5	140.5	0.7	141.8	0.9
1993	141.8	0.0	141.3	-0.4	141.0	-0.2	142.5	1.1	142.9	0.3	144.3	1.0	143.3	-0.7	144.3	0.7	145.2	0.6	145.6	0.3	143.4	-1.5	143.4	0.0
1994	143.2	-0.1	143.2	0.0	143.6	0.3	144.2	0.4	144.1	-0.1	145.3	0.8	144.7	-0.4	145.4	0.5	145.9	0.3	144.2	-1.2	146.4	1.5	147.9	1.0
1995	149.2	0.9	149.1	-0.1	149.1	0.0	149.7	0.4	149.9	0.1	150.7	0.5	151.7	0.7	151.9	0.1	151.3	-0.4	151.3	0.0	151.4	0.1	152.1	0.5
1996	152.4	0.2	153.0	0.4	153.8	0.5	154.1	0.2	154.5	0.3	155.8	0.8	155.9	0.1	156.8	0.6	156.2	-0.4	156.3	0.1	156.0	-0.2	156.9	0.6
1997	158.6	1.1	159.2	0.4	158.7	-0.3	157.7	-0.6	158.1	0.3	159.7	1.0	160.1	0.3	161.0	0.6	161.4	0.2	161.8	0.2	163.2	0.9	162.3	-0.6
1998	162.3	0.0	162.5	0.1	163.5	0.6	164.4	0.6	164.3	-0.1	166.0	1.0	166.3	0.2	164.5	-1.1	164.0	-0.3	164.3	0.2	163.9	-0.2	164.5	0.4
1999	165.3	0.5	165.1	-0.1	165.3	0.1	166.7	0.8	167.0	0.2	169.2	1.3	169.6	0.2	169.7	0.1	170.4	0.4	169.8	-0.4	168.9	-0.5	169.3	0.2
2000	169.8	0.3	170.6	0.5	171.4	0.5	171.3	-0.1	173.4	1.2	175.9	1.4	177.5	0.9	176.8	-0.4	178.2	0.8	178.7	0.3	179.7	0.6	179.9	0.1
2001	183.6	2.1	183.8	0.1	182.2	-0.9	180.7	-0.8	181.1	0.2	181.2	0.1	181.0	-0.1	181.1	0.1	180.8	-0.2	179.5	-0.7	180.6	0.6	182.1	0.8

Source: U.S. Department of Labor, Bureau of Labor Statistics, Division of Consumer Prices and Price Indexes. - indicates no data collected for period.

Chicago-Gary-Kenosha, IL-IN-WI
Consumer Price Index - Urban Wage Earners
Base 1982-1984 = 100
Housing

For 1976-2001. Columns headed % show percentile change in the index from the previous period for which an index is available.

Year	Jan Index	%	Feb Index	%	Mar Index	%	Apr Index	%	May Index	%	Jun Index	%	Jul Index	%	Aug Index	%	Sep Index	%	Oct Index	%	Nov Index	%	Dec Index	%
1976	49.6	-	49.7	0.2	50.0	0.6	50.1	0.2	50.3	0.4	50.5	0.4	50.7	0.4	51.0	0.6	51.3	0.6	51.5	0.4	51.5	0.0	52.1	1.2
1977	52.3	0.4	52.7	0.8	52.8	0.2	53.2	0.8	53.3	0.2	53.3	0.0	53.9	1.1	54.2	0.6	54.7	0.9	54.9	0.4	55.3	0.7	55.4	0.2
1978	56.6	2.2	57.4	1.4	58.5	1.9	58.5	0.0	59.0	0.9	59.4	0.7	60.0	1.0	59.1	-1.5	60.3	2.0	61.3	1.7	62.4	1.8	62.9	0.8
1979	62.8	-0.2	63.9	1.8	65.7	2.8	66.3	0.9	66.1	-0.3	67.9	2.7	69.5	2.4	70.3	1.2	71.2	1.3	71.0	-0.3	73.0	2.8	73.4	0.5
1980	73.8	0.5	74.3	0.7	74.9	0.8	77.0	2.8	78.6	2.1	82.1	4.5	80.6	-1.8	78.7	-2.4	81.1	3.0	82.9	2.2	86.4	4.2	86.5	0.1
1981	84.3	-2.5	83.8	-0.6	83.4	-0.5	85.8	2.9	86.2	0.5	88.9	3.1	90.7	2.0	92.1	1.5	92.3	0.2	91.4	-1.0	91.8	0.4	89.2	-2.8
1982	90.4	1.3	90.2	-0.2	91.8	1.8	94.0	2.4	98.8	5.1	100.5	1.7	101.4	0.9	101.2	-0.2	101.8	0.6	101.8	0.0	101.7	-0.1	101.0	-0.7
1983	101.6	0.6	101.1	-0.5	101.3	0.2	102.1	0.8	102.5	0.4	103.2	0.7	103.4	0.2	103.0	-0.4	103.3	0.3	99.1	-4.1	99.6	0.5	98.8	-0.8
1984	101.4	2.6	100.1	-1.3	99.4	-0.7	99.0	-0.4	98.9	-0.1	99.9	1.0	100.0	0.1	101.3	1.3	103.3	2.0	100.7	-2.5	101.6	0.9	100.9	-0.7
1985	101.5	0.6	101.7	0.2	101.3	-0.4	102.0	0.7	102.4	0.4	106.0	3.5	106.1	0.1	107.4	1.2	107.5	0.1	103.6	-3.6	103.5	-0.1	103.9	0.4
1986	104.5	0.6	104.7	0.2	104.4	-0.3	105.3	0.9	105.0	-0.3	109.4	4.2	110.1	0.6	110.3	0.2	111.0	0.6	105.9	-4.6	106.5	0.6	105.9	-0.6
1987	106.8	0.8	107.0	0.2	106.9	-0.1	107.3	0.4	107.5	0.2	112.0	4.2	112.8	0.7	113.6	0.7	113.8	0.2	108.7	-4.5	109.8	1.0	110.3	0.5
1988	109.1	-1.1	111.2	1.9	110.9	-0.3	111.0	0.1	111.0	0.0	114.7	3.3	115.6	0.8	114.8	-0.7	117.2	2.1	116.4	-0.7	115.3	-0.9	116.1	0.7
1989	116.0	-0.1	116.6	0.5	116.7	0.1	116.7	0.0	117.0	0.3	120.7	3.2	121.3	0.5	121.3	0.0	122.3	0.8	119.3	-2.5	119.6	0.3	119.8	0.2
1990	120.6	0.7	121.7	0.9	121.7	0.0	122.7	0.8	122.1	-0.5	125.5	2.8	125.7	0.2	126.6	0.7	126.7	0.1	123.2	-2.8	124.1	0.7	125.0	0.7
1991	126.4	1.1	126.5	0.1	127.8	1.0	127.0	-0.6	128.0	0.8	129.4	1.1	130.2	0.6	129.7	-0.4	129.6	-0.1	128.8	-0.6	127.6	-0.9	129.5	1.5
1992	130.7	0.9	130.1	-0.5	129.9	-0.2	130.0	0.1	130.9	0.7	133.0	1.6	132.4	-0.5	132.2	-0.2	133.3	0.8	131.4	-1.4	132.5	0.8	133.7	0.9
1993	133.8	0.1	133.3	-0.4	132.8	-0.4	134.3	1.1	134.7	0.3	135.9	0.9	135.0	-0.7	135.9	0.7	136.7	0.6	137.2	0.4	135.1	-1.5	135.3	0.1
1994	135.1	-0.1	134.9	-0.1	135.3	0.3	135.8	0.4	135.5	-0.2	136.8	1.0	136.0	-0.6	136.7	0.5	137.2	0.4	135.6	-1.2	137.7	1.5	139.3	1.2
1995	140.4	0.8	140.3	-0.1	140.2	-0.1	140.7	0.4	140.8	0.1	141.4	0.4	142.2	0.6	142.4	0.1	142.0	-0.3	142.0	0.0	142.2	0.1	142.7	0.4
1996	143.2	0.4	143.7	0.3	144.5	0.6	144.8	0.2	145.1	0.2	146.2	0.8	146.3	0.1	147.1	0.5	146.8	-0.2	146.8	0.0	146.7	-0.1	147.6	0.6
1997	149.2	1.1	149.7	0.3	149.2	-0.3	148.1	-0.7	148.3	0.1	149.8	1.0	150.2	0.3	151.0	0.5	151.5	0.3	151.9	0.3	153.3	0.9	152.6	-0.5
1998	152.6	0.0	152.6	0.0	153.6	0.7	154.4	0.5	154.4	0.0	156.0	1.0	156.3	0.2	154.5	-1.2	154.0	-0.3	154.1	0.1	153.8	-0.2	154.4	0.4
1999	155.1	0.5	155.0	-0.1	155.2	0.1	156.5	0.8	156.8	0.2	158.9	1.3	159.3	0.3	159.4	0.1	160.1	0.4	159.5	-0.4	158.7	-0.5	159.1	0.3
2000	159.4	0.2	160.3	0.6	160.9	0.4	160.9	0.0	162.8	1.2	165.4	1.6	166.9	0.9	166.4	-0.3	167.7	0.8	168.2	0.3	169.2	0.6	169.4	0.1
2001	173.2	2.2	173.4	0.1	171.7	-1.0	170.1	-0.9	170.5	0.2	170.6	0.1	170.2	-0.2	170.3	0.1	169.9	-0.2	168.4	-0.9	169.5	0.7	171.0	0.9

Source: U.S. Department of Labor, Bureau of Labor Statistics, Division of Consumer Prices and Price Indexes. - indicates no data collected for period.

Chicago-Gary-Kenosha, IL-IN-WI
Consumer Price Index - All Urban Consumers
Base 1982-1984 = 100
Apparel

For 1952-2001. Columns headed % show percentile change in the index from the previous period for which an index is available.

Year	Jan Index	%	Feb Index	%	Mar Index	%	Apr Index	%	May Index	%	Jun Index	%	Jul Index	%	Aug Index	%	Sep Index	%	Oct Index	%	Nov Index	%	Dec Index	%
1952	-	-	-	-	-	-	-	-	-	-	-	-	-	-	-	-	-	-	-	-	-	-	52.2	-
1953	51.8	-0.8	51.9	0.2	52.0	0.2	52.1	0.2	52.3	0.4	52.4	0.2	52.4	0.0	52.6	0.4	53.1	1.0	53.1	0.0	53.1	0.0	52.9	-0.4
1954	52.9	0.0	52.9	0.0	53.0	0.2	52.9	-0.2	52.9	0.0	52.9	0.0	52.9	0.0	52.4	-0.9	52.5	0.2	52.4	-0.2	52.3	-0.2	52.2	-0.2
1955	51.4	-1.5	51.6	0.4	51.7	0.2	51.3	-0.8	51.4	0.2	51.5	0.2	52.1	1.2	52.3	0.4	53.3	1.9	53.4	0.2	53.7	0.6	53.4	-0.6
1956	53.4	0.0	53.4	0.0	53.5	0.2	53.6	0.2	53.5	-0.2	53.5	0.0	53.8	0.6	54.1	0.6	54.5	0.7	54.8	0.6	54.6	-0.4	54.8	0.4
1957	53.9	-1.6	54.1	0.4	54.7	1.1	54.6	-0.2	54.6	0.0	54.8	0.4	54.7	-0.2	54.8	0.2	55.7	1.6	55.6	-0.2	55.4	-0.4	55.4	0.0
1958	54.9	-0.9	54.8	-0.2	54.8	0.0	54.7	-0.2	54.7	0.0	54.9	0.4	55.2	0.5	54.8	-0.7	55.4	1.1	55.3	-0.2	55.4	0.2	55.1	-0.5
1959	54.8	-0.5	54.6	-0.4	54.5	-0.2	54.9	0.7	55.1	0.4	54.9	-0.4	55.4	0.9	55.6	0.4	56.6	1.8	56.6	0.0	56.6	0.0	56.6	0.0
1960	56.0	-1.1	56.1	0.2	56.2	0.2	55.7	-0.9	56.0	0.5	56.0	0.0	56.4	0.7	56.6	0.4	56.7	0.2	56.8	0.2	56.7	-0.2	56.9	0.4
1961	56.0	-1.6	56.0	0.0	56.0	0.0	56.0	0.0	55.8	-0.4	55.5	-0.5	55.8	0.5	55.5	-0.5	56.7	2.2	56.6	-0.2	56.4	-0.4	56.4	0.0
1962	55.4	-1.8	55.3	-0.2	55.6	0.5	55.5	-0.2	55.6	0.2	55.5	-0.2	55.7	0.4	55.4	-0.5	56.3	1.6	56.3	0.0	56.3	0.0	56.4	0.2
1963	55.6	-1.4	55.7	0.2	55.8	0.2	55.9	0.2	55.8	-0.2	55.4	-0.7	55.7	0.5	55.5	-0.4	56.9	2.5	57.0	0.2	56.6	-0.7	56.8	0.4
1964	55.4	-2.5	55.8	0.7	56.4	1.1	56.4	0.0	56.4	0.0	56.3	-0.2	56.1	-0.4	55.7	-0.7	56.7	1.8	56.6	-0.2	56.4	-0.4	56.5	0.2
1965	56.0	-0.9	55.8	-0.4	56.3	0.9	56.4	0.2	56.9	0.9	57.0	0.2	56.1	-1.6	56.4	0.5	57.5	2.0	57.7	0.3	57.7	0.0	57.9	0.3
1966	56.8	-1.9	56.7	-0.2	58.0	2.3	57.8	-0.3	58.1	0.5	58.3	0.3	57.4	-1.5	57.9	0.9	59.7	3.1	59.7	0.0	59.4	-0.5	59.7	0.5
1967	59.1	-1.0	59.2	0.2	59.7	0.8	59.8	0.2	60.3	0.8	60.4	0.2	59.8	-1.0	60.3	0.8	61.7	2.3	61.9	0.3	62.1	0.3	62.3	0.3
1968	60.5	-2.9	61.2	1.2	62.8	2.6	63.2	0.6	63.9	1.1	64.0	0.2	63.2	-1.2	63.4	0.3	65.2	2.8	65.7	0.8	65.8	0.2	65.9	0.2
1969	64.1	-2.7	65.7	2.5	66.3	0.9	66.0	-0.5	66.6	0.9	67.0	0.6	66.6	-0.6	65.2	-2.1	68.6	5.2	68.5	-0.1	68.9	0.6	68.8	-0.1
1970	66.2	-3.8	66.8	0.9	68.2	2.1	67.6	-0.9	68.7	1.6	68.3	-0.6	67.1	-1.8	67.9	1.2	71.0	4.6	70.7	-0.4	70.7	0.0	70.4	-0.4
1971	68.1	-3.3	69.8	2.5	70.7	1.3	70.5	-0.3	71.1	0.9	71.3	0.3	69.7	-2.2	70.3	0.9	72.9	3.7	72.8	-0.1	73.0	0.3	73.0	0.0
1972	70.4	-3.6	72.0	2.3	72.4	0.6	72.1	-0.4	72.2	0.1	72.1	-0.1	70.2	-2.6	70.4	0.3	74.3	5.5	74.3	0.0	74.7	0.5	74.7	0.0
1973	73.0	-2.3	74.1	1.5	76.1	2.7	76.1	0.0	76.5	0.5	76.2	-0.4	74.7	-2.0	75.5	1.1	77.5	2.6	77.3	-0.3	77.8	0.6	77.5	-0.4
1974	75.5	-2.6	77.2	2.3	78.4	1.6	79.3	1.1	79.6	0.4	80.1	0.6	79.0	-1.4	82.3	4.2	82.6	0.4	82.9	0.4	83.7	1.0	83.7	0.0
1975	81.0	-3.2	81.5	0.6	82.7	1.5	82.9	0.2	82.6	-0.4	82.1	-0.6	81.6	-0.6	82.7	1.3	84.3	1.9	84.1	-0.2	84.1	0.0	83.5	-0.7
1976	80.9	-3.1	82.0	1.4	82.6	0.7	82.2	-0.5	83.0	1.0	83.6	0.7	82.7	-1.1	84.2	1.8	86.0	2.1	85.6	-0.5	85.9	0.4	85.7	-0.2
1977	83.0	-3.2	84.1	1.3	85.4	1.5	85.3	-0.1	85.3	0.0	86.4	1.3	85.9	-0.6	87.0	1.3	88.7	2.0	87.3	-1.6	88.0	0.8	87.8	-0.2
1978	85.2	-3.0	85.0	-0.2	86.4	1.6	87.9	1.7	88.6	0.8	88.4	-0.2	87.7	-0.8	88.8	1.3	89.5	0.8	89.5	0.0	90.2	0.8	88.8	-1.6
1979	87.5	-1.5	88.2	0.8	90.4	2.5	89.6	-0.9	90.2	0.7	89.4	-0.9	89.9	0.6	89.3	-0.7	91.9	2.9	91.9	0.0	93.5	1.7	93.8	0.3
1980	93.7	-0.1	93.0	-0.7	95.1	2.3	94.8	-0.3	94.2	-0.6	95.2	1.1	95.5	0.3	96.2	0.7	97.4		97.9	0.5	98.3	0.4	95.8	-2.5
1981	93.1	-2.8	93.0	-0.1	94.4	1.5	94.9	0.5	95.1	0.2	94.0	-1.2	94.1	0.1	99.0	5.2	100.8	1.8	99.9	-0.9	100.8	0.9	98.1	-2.7
1982	95.6	-2.5	96.9	1.4	95.7	-1.2	97.2	1.6	98.7	1.5	97.8	-0.9	94.3	-3.6	99.3	5.3	100.5	1.2	99.8	-0.7	99.2	-0.6	97.4	-1.8
1983	96.4	-1.0	95.6	-0.8	98.6	3.1	97.9	-0.7	99.0	1.1	96.8	-2.2	97.4	0.6	102.2	4.9	104.7	2.4	104.7	0.0	106.0	1.2	103.5	-2.4
1984	99.0	-4.3	96.5	-2.5	98.7	2.3	99.7	1.0	100.4	0.7	98.8	-1.6	102.4	3.6	104.9	2.4	106.1	1.1	106.1	0.0	107.8	1.6	104.7	-2.9
1985	100.7	-3.8	103.8	3.1	105.7	1.8	106.7	0.9	105.7	-0.9	104.9	-0.8	105.6	0.7	106.4	0.8	108.4	1.9	108.3	-0.1	108.6	0.3	106.9	-1.6
1986	102.5	-4.1	102.4	-0.1	101.1	-1.3	100.2	-0.9	100.3	0.1	99.3	-1.0	101.1	1.8	105.0	3.9	109.4	4.2	109.4	0.0	108.6	-0.7	107.0	-1.5
1987	104.4	-2.4	102.7	-1.6	108.0	5.2	107.6	-0.4	108.6	0.9	106.7	-1.7	105.1	-1.5	112.7	7.2	114.3	1.4	114.2	-0.1	114.5	0.3	112.0	-2.2
1988	111.1	-0.8	112.2	1.0	115.8	3.2	115.3	-0.4	113.6	-1.5	115.6	1.8	114.7	-0.8	116.8	1.8	122.8	5.1	121.1	-1.4	120.4	-0.6	119.8	-0.5
1989	114.1	-4.8	112.3	-1.6	119.3	6.2	117.8	-1.3	116.0	-1.5	113.5	-2.2	118.1	4.1	119.6	1.3	120.5	0.8	124.8	3.6	123.2	-1.3	117.5	-4.6
1990	114.5	-2.6	121.4	6.0	126.1	3.9	129.4	2.6	129.4	0.0	123.0	-4.9	119.8	-2.6	123.5	3.1	126.7	2.6	126.6	-0.1	127.9	1.0	122.8	-4.0
1991	116.5	-5.1	124.1	6.5	127.1	2.4	128.9	1.4	125.2	-2.9	122.3	-2.3	119.6	-2.2	127.1	6.3	128.8	1.3	129.5	0.5	130.0	0.4	124.0	-4.6
1992	120.8	-2.6	126.5	4.7	129.3	2.2	124.7	-3.6	124.5	-0.2	123.5	-0.8	124.7	1.0	132.3	6.1	130.8	-1.1	129.4	-1.1	125.2	-3.2	123.1	-1.7
1993	121.2	-1.5	133.3	10.0	137.0	2.8	133.4	-2.6	133.9	0.4	126.6	-5.5	128.2	1.3	134.0	4.5	134.3	0.2	133.9	-0.3	131.9	-1.5	125.8	-4.6
1994	126.6	0.6	132.4	4.6	136.5	3.1	133.1	-2.5	129.0	-3.1	128.6	-0.3	126.5	-1.6	135.1	6.8	134.2	-0.7	131.8	-1.8	132.0	0.2	126.0	-4.5
1995	125.3	-0.6	128.2	2.3	130.1	1.5	130.0	-0.1	126.6	-2.6	123.8	-2.2	121.6	-1.8	124.2	2.1	131.0	5.5	131.4	0.3	125.4	-4.6	118.5	-5.5
1996	120.8	1.9	124.5	3.1	127.7	2.6	122.1	-4.4	122.1	0.0	118.0	-3.4	118.4	0.3	118.8	0.3	119.2	0.3	119.8	0.5	120.6	0.7	115.4	-4.3
1997	116.9	1.3	124.0	6.1	124.8	0.6	131.5	5.4	127.5	-3.0	124.6	-2.3	120.4	-3.4	122.2	1.5	120.0	-1.8	118.4	-1.3	119.7	1.1	117.9	-1.5

[Continued]

Chicago-Gary-Kenosha, IL-IN-WI
Consumer Price Index - All Urban Consumers
Base 1982-1984 = 100
Apparel

[Continued]

For 1952-2001. Columns headed % show percentile change in the index from the previous period for which an index is available.

Year	Jan Index	%	Feb Index	%	Mar Index	%	Apr Index	%	May Index	%	Jun Index	%	Jul Index	%	Aug Index	%	Sep Index	%	Oct Index	%	Nov Index	%	Dec Index	%
1998	117.7	-0.2	119.2	1.3	122.2	2.5	123.6	1.1	126.7	2.5	121.4	-4.2	121.0	-0.3	120.8	-0.2	125.2	3.6	122.4	-2.2	122.7	0.2	115.9	-5.5
1999	113.3	-2.2	121.1	6.9	122.8	1.4	127.2	3.6	122.6	-3.6	114.4	-6.7	115.5	1.0	115.0	-0.4	115.4	0.3	114.7	-0.6	115.0	0.3	109.7	-4.6
2000	109.4	-0.3	113.8	4.0	116.4	2.3	115.8	-0.5	115.2	-0.5	112.1	-2.7	108.0	-3.7	105.7	-2.1	111.3	5.3	115.4	3.7	115.5	0.1	111.6	-3.4
2001	107.1	-4.0	109.3	2.1	109.9	0.5	109.3	-0.5	109.7	0.4	106.5	-2.9	101.9	-4.3	103.5	1.6	108.0	4.3	107.5	-0.5	103.4	-3.8	99.3	-4.0

Source: U.S. Department of Labor, Bureau of Labor Statistics, Division of Consumer Prices and Price Indexes. - indicates no data collected for period.

Chicago-Gary-Kenosha, IL-IN-WI
Consumer Price Index - Urban Wage Earners
Base 1982-1984 = 100
Apparel

For 1952-2001. Columns headed % show percentile change in the index from the previous period for which an index is available.

Year	Jan Index	%	Feb Index	%	Mar Index	%	Apr Index	%	May Index	%	Jun Index	%	Jul Index	%	Aug Index	%	Sep Index	%	Oct Index	%	Nov Index	%	Dec Index	%
1952	-	-	-	-	-	-	-	-	-	-	-	-	-	-	-	-	-	-	-	-	-	-	50.6	-
1953	50.2	-0.8	50.3	0.2	50.4	0.2	50.5	0.2	50.7	0.4	50.8	0.2	50.8	0.0	51.0	0.4	51.4	0.8	51.4	0.0	51.5	0.2	51.3	-0.4
1954	51.2	-0.2	51.3	0.2	51.4	0.2	51.3	-0.2	51.3	0.0	51.3	0.0	51.3	0.0	50.8	-1.0	50.9	0.2	50.8	-0.2	50.7	-0.2	50.6	-0.2
1955	49.8	-1.6	50.0	0.4	50.1	0.2	49.7	-0.8	49.8	0.2	50.0	0.4	50.5	1.0	50.7	0.4	51.7	2.0	51.7	0.0	52.0	0.6	51.8	-0.4
1956	51.8	0.0	51.7	-0.2	51.9	0.4	52.0	0.2	51.8	-0.4	51.8	0.0	52.2	0.8	52.4	0.4	52.8	0.8	53.1	0.6	52.9	-0.4	53.1	0.4
1957	52.2	-1.7	52.4	0.4	53.0	1.1	52.9	-0.2	52.9	0.0	53.1	0.4	53.0	-0.2	53.1	0.2	54.0	1.7	53.9	-0.2	53.7	-0.4	53.7	0.0
1958	53.2	-0.9	53.1	-0.2	53.1	0.0	53.0	-0.2	53.0	0.0	53.2	0.4	53.5	0.6	53.1	-0.7	53.7	1.1	53.6	-0.2	53.7	0.2	53.4	-0.6
1959	53.1	-0.6	52.9	-0.4	52.8	-0.2	53.2	0.8	53.4	0.4	53.2	-0.4	53.7	0.9	53.9	0.4	54.8	1.7	54.8	0.0	54.8	0.0	54.8	0.0
1960	54.2	-1.1	54.4	0.4	54.5	0.2	54.0	-0.9	54.3	0.6	54.2	-0.2	54.7	0.9	54.8	0.2	55.0	0.4	55.1	0.2	55.0	-0.2	55.1	0.2
1961	54.3	-1.5	54.2	-0.2	54.2	0.0	54.2	0.0	54.1	-0.2	53.8	-0.6	54.1	0.6	53.8	-0.6	54.9	2.0	54.8	-0.2	54.7	-0.2	54.7	0.0
1962	53.7	-1.8	53.6	-0.2	53.9	0.6	53.8	-0.2	53.9	0.2	53.8	-0.2	53.9	0.2	53.7	-0.4	54.6	1.7	54.6	0.0	54.5	-0.2	54.7	0.4
1963	53.9	-1.5	53.9	0.0	54.1	0.4	54.2	0.2	54.1	-0.2	53.7	-0.7	54.0	0.6	53.8	-0.4	55.1	2.4	55.2	0.2	54.9	-0.5	55.1	0.4
1964	53.7	-2.5	54.1	0.7	54.7	1.1	54.7	0.0	54.7	0.0	54.5	-0.4	54.4	-0.2	54.0	-0.7	54.9	1.7	54.9	0.0	54.7	-0.4	54.8	0.2
1965	54.2	-1.1	54.1	-0.2	54.5	0.7	54.7	0.4	55.1	0.7	55.2	0.2	54.4	-1.4	54.7	0.6	55.7	1.8	55.9	0.4	55.9	0.0	56.1	0.4
1966	55.1	-1.8	55.0	-0.2	56.2	2.2	56.1	-0.2	56.3	0.4	56.5	0.4	55.6	-1.6	56.1	0.9	57.8	3.0	57.8	0.0	57.6	-0.3	57.9	0.5
1967	57.2	-1.2	57.4	0.3	57.8	0.7	57.9	0.2	58.4	0.9	58.6	0.3	58.0	-1.0	58.5	0.9	59.8	2.2	60.0	0.3	60.2	0.3	60.3	0.2
1968	58.6	-2.8	59.3	1.2	60.9	2.7	61.3	0.7	61.9	1.0	62.0	0.2	61.2	-1.3	61.5	0.5	63.2	2.8	63.7	0.8	63.8	0.2	63.9	0.2
1969	62.2	-2.7	63.6	2.3	64.2	0.9	64.0	-0.3	64.5	0.8	65.0	0.8	64.6	-0.6	63.2	-2.2	66.5	5.2	66.4	-0.2	66.7	0.5	66.7	0.0
1970	64.2	-3.7	64.7	0.8	66.1	2.2	65.5	-0.9	66.6	1.7	66.2	-0.6	65.0	-1.8	65.8	1.2	68.8	4.6	68.6	-0.3	68.5	-0.1	68.3	-0.3
1971	66.0	-3.4	67.6	2.4	68.5	1.3	68.3	-0.3	68.9	0.9	69.1	0.3	67.5	-2.3	68.1	0.9	70.7	3.8	70.6	-0.1	70.8	0.3	70.7	-0.1
1972	68.3	-3.4	69.7	2.0	70.2	0.7	69.9	-0.4	70.0	0.1	69.9	-0.1	68.0	-2.7	68.2	0.3	72.0	5.6	72.0	0.0	72.4	0.6	72.4	0.0
1973	70.8	-2.2	71.9	1.6	73.7	2.5	73.8	0.1	74.1	0.4	73.8	-0.4	72.4	-1.9	73.2	1.1	75.1	2.6	74.9	-0.3	75.4	0.7	75.1	-0.4
1974	73.1	-2.7	74.8	2.3	76.0	1.6	76.9	1.2	77.1	0.3	77.7	0.8	76.5	-1.5	79.8	4.3	80.1	0.4	80.3	0.2	81.1	1.0	81.1	0.0
1975	78.5	-3.2	79.0	0.6	80.2	1.5	80.4	0.2	80.1	-0.4	79.6	-0.6	79.1	-0.6	80.2	1.4	81.7	1.9	81.5	-0.2	81.5	0.0	80.9	-0.7
1976	78.4	-3.1	79.5	1.4	80.1	0.8	79.7	-0.5	80.4	0.9	81.0	0.7	80.1	-1.1	81.6	1.9	83.4	2.2	82.9	-0.6	83.2	0.4	83.1	-0.1
1977	80.5	-3.1	81.5	1.2	82.8	1.6	82.7	-0.1	82.7	0.0	83.8	1.3	83.3	-0.6	84.3	1.2	85.9	1.9	84.6	-1.5	85.3	0.8	85.1	-0.2
1978	84.4	-0.8	84.6	0.2	84.5	-0.1	86.4	2.2	86.2	-0.2	86.9	0.8	86.9	0.0	86.6	-0.3	87.9	1.5	89.3	1.6	89.6	0.3	88.2	-1.6
1979	85.7	-2.8	87.9	2.6	89.4	1.7	88.8	-0.7	88.9	0.1	88.2	-0.8	88.5	0.3	88.6	0.1	91.8	3.6	91.9	0.1	93.6	1.8	93.3	-0.3
1980	91.5	-1.9	93.0	1.6	93.6	0.6	93.3	-0.3	94.4	1.2	95.7	1.4	95.5	-0.2	96.1	0.6	95.9	-0.2	97.6	1.8	97.0	-0.6	95.1	-2.0
1981	92.2	-3.0	90.8	-1.5	91.8	1.1	93.2	1.5	94.0	0.9	93.2	-0.9	94.9	1.8	99.0	4.3	101.4	2.4	100.7	-0.7	100.7	0.0	98.5	-2.2
1982	96.0	-2.5	97.2	1.2	95.4	-1.9	97.2	1.9	99.1	2.0	98.1	-1.0	95.0	-3.2	98.7	3.9	100.4	1.7	100.0	-0.4	99.3	-0.7	97.6	-1.7
1983	96.2	-1.4	94.9	-1.4	98.1	3.4	97.5	-0.6	98.7	1.2	96.6	-2.1	97.2	0.6	101.8	4.7	104.6	2.8	104.6	0.0	106.0	1.3	103.6	-2.3
1984	98.6	-4.8	96.4	-2.2	99.0	2.7	99.5	0.5	100.4	0.9	99.4	-1.0	101.9	2.5	105.0	3.0	106.5	1.4	106.3	-0.2	108.2	1.8	105.0	-3.0
1985	100.5	-4.3	103.3	2.8	105.4	2.0	106.2	0.8	105.6	-0.6	104.5	-1.0	104.5	0.0	105.3	0.8	108.5	3.0	108.1	-0.4	108.2	0.1	107.0	-1.1
1986	102.9	-3.8	103.1	0.2	101.4	-1.6	100.6	-0.8	100.8	0.2	99.9	-0.9	101.2	1.3	104.7	3.5	109.4	4.5	109.4	0.0	108.7	-0.6	107.3	-1.3
1987	104.5	-2.6	102.9	-1.5	108.4	5.3	108.8	0.4	109.1	0.3	107.2	-1.7	105.5	-1.6	112.3	6.4	113.9	1.4	114.8	0.8	114.0	-0.7	111.9	-1.8
1988	110.5	-1.3	110.8	0.3	115.0	3.8	114.7	-0.3	112.1	-2.3	115.2	2.8	114.6	-0.5	115.8	1.0	122.9	6.1	121.2	-1.4	120.3	-0.7	119.8	-0.4
1989	114.0	-4.8	112.0	-1.8	118.8	6.1	117.9	-0.8	115.1	-2.4	113.2	-1.7	117.4	3.7	118.2	0.7	119.3	0.9	124.5	4.4	122.8	-1.4	117.7	-4.2
1990	114.3	-2.9	121.4	6.2	126.4	4.1	130.4	3.2	130.0	-0.3	123.8	-4.8	120.1	-3.0	123.6	2.9	126.9	2.7	126.6	-0.2	127.8	0.9	123.1	-3.7
1991	117.1	-4.9	125.6	7.3	128.0	1.9	130.2	1.7	126.0	-3.2	122.7	-2.6	120.3	-2.0	126.8	5.4	128.1	1.0	129.1	0.8	130.2	0.9	123.6	-5.1
1992	120.0	-2.9	125.6	4.7	129.2	2.9	125.8	-2.6	125.2	-0.5	123.9	-1.0	124.4	0.4	132.3	6.4	130.2	-1.6	128.7	-1.2	124.1	-3.6	121.3	-2.3
1993	119.3	-1.6	131.1	9.9	135.4	3.3	133.0	-1.8	134.1	0.8	126.9	-5.4	128.5	1.3	133.2	3.7	134.2	0.8	133.7	-0.4	131.6	-1.6	125.5	-4.6
1994	125.9	0.3	132.9	5.6	136.4	2.6	132.6	-2.8	128.8	-2.9	128.4	-0.3	126.5	-1.5	133.0	5.1	132.2	-0.6	129.5	-2.0	129.9	0.3	124.3	-4.3
1995	124.3	0.0	126.6	1.9	128.9	1.8	128.6	-0.2	125.3	-2.6	122.0	-2.6	120.7	-1.1	124.0	2.7	129.6	4.5	129.7	0.1	123.8	-4.5	117.5	-5.1
1996	120.6	2.6	122.8	1.8	125.8	2.4	120.8	-4.0	120.7	-0.1	117.1	-3.0	118.6	1.3	117.8	-0.7	118.4	0.5	118.5	0.1	119.8	1.1	114.0	-4.8
1997	115.8	1.6	121.8	5.2	122.7	0.7	127.7	4.1	123.7	-3.1	121.6	-1.7	118.2	-2.8	118.7	0.4	117.3	-1.2	116.4	-0.8	116.6	0.2	115.2	-1.2

[Continued]

Chicago-Gary-Kenosha, IL-IN-WI
Consumer Price Index - Urban Wage Earners
Base 1982-1984 = 100
Apparel
[Continued]

For 1952-2001. Columns headed % show percentile change in the index from the previous period for which an index is available.

Year	Jan		Feb		Mar		Apr		May		Jun		Jul		Aug		Sep		Oct		Nov		Dec	
	Index	%	Index	%	Index	%	Index	%	Index	%	Index	%	Index	%	Index	%	Index	%	Index	%	Index	%	Index	%
1998	115.8	0.5	116.5	0.6	119.3	2.4	120.1	0.7	123.8	3.1	118.8	-4.0	118.5	-0.3	118.5	0.0	122.0	3.0	119.8	-1.8	120.0	0.2	114.0	-5.0
1999	111.7	-2.0	119.5	7.0	120.2	0.6	124.1	3.2	119.9	-3.4	112.2	-6.4	113.4	1.1	112.2	-1.1	112.3	0.1	111.7	-0.5	112.1	0.4	107.2	-4.4
2000	107.5	0.3	111.2	3.4	113.5	2.1	112.7	-0.7	112.2	-0.4	109.2	-2.7	106.0	-2.9	103.1	-2.7	108.4	5.1	112.1	3.4	111.9	-0.2	108.5	-3.0
2001	104.4	-3.8	106.4	1.9	106.2	-0.2	105.9	-0.3	106.5	0.6	103.5	-2.8	99.2	-4.2	100.8	1.6	104.4	3.6	104.3	-0.1	100.9	-3.3	97.4	-3.5

Source: U.S. Department of Labor, Bureau of Labor Statistics, Division of Consumer Prices and Price Indexes. - indicates no data collected for period.

Chicago-Gary-Kenosha, IL-IN-WI
Consumer Price Index - All Urban Consumers
Base 1982-1984 = 100
Transportation

For 1947-2000. Columns headed % show percentile change in the index from the previous period for which an index is available.

Year	Jan Index	%	Feb Index	%	Mar Index	%	Apr Index	%	May Index	%	Jun Index	%	Jul Index	%	Aug Index	%	Sep Index	%	Oct Index	%	Nov Index	%	Dec Index	%
1947	16.8	-	16.8	0.0	16.8	0.0	17.1	1.8	17.4	1.8	17.4	0.0	17.4	0.0	17.5	0.6	17.7	1.1	18.1	2.3	18.2	0.6	18.3	0.5
1948	18.6	1.6	18.6	0.0	18.6	0.0	18.6	0.0	19.3	3.8	19.3	0.0	21.2	9.8	21.5	1.4	21.6	0.5	21.6	0.0	21.6	0.0	21.6	0.0
1949	21.6	0.0	21.7	0.5	21.7	0.0	21.7	0.0	21.7	0.0	21.7	0.0	21.7	0.0	21.7	0.0	21.7	0.0	22.9	5.5	22.9	0.0	22.8	-0.4
1950	22.8	0.0	22.7	-0.4	22.6	-0.4	22.4	-0.9	22.4	0.0	22.4	0.0	22.5	0.4	22.8	1.3	22.6	-0.9	22.6	0.0	22.7	0.4	22.9	0.9
1951	22.9	0.0	23.0	0.4	23.3	1.3	23.3	0.0	23.3	0.0	23.3	0.0	23.8	2.1	24.6	3.4	24.8	0.8	24.9	0.4	25.1	0.8	24.4	-2.8
1952	25.2	3.3	25.3	0.4	25.3	0.0	25.3	0.0	25.4	0.4	26.5	4.3	26.5	0.0	26.6	0.4	26.6	0.0	26.6	0.0	26.6	0.0	26.6	0.0
1953	26.8	0.8	26.7	-0.4	26.7	0.0	26.6	-0.4	26.5	-0.4	26.6	0.4	26.7	0.4	26.7	0.0	26.6	-0.4	26.5	-0.4	26.4	-0.4	26.4	0.0
1954	26.6	0.8	26.4	-0.8	26.4	0.0	26.3	-0.4	26.6	1.1	26.7	0.4	26.6	-0.4	26.5	-0.4	26.5	0.0	25.4	-4.2	26.7	5.1	26.5	-0.7
1955	26.6	0.4	26.4	-0.8	26.5	0.4	25.8	-2.6	25.9	0.4	25.9	0.0	25.9	0.0	26.0	0.4	26.0	0.0	26.3	1.2	26.5	0.8	26.1	-1.5
1956	26.0	-0.4	26.1	0.4	26.0	-0.4	26.1	0.4	26.2	0.4	26.2	0.0	26.6	1.5	26.6	0.0	26.6	0.0	27.8	4.5	27.8	0.0	27.7	-0.4
1957	28.0	1.1	27.7	-1.1	27.8	0.4	27.8	0.0	27.7	-0.4	27.7	0.0	28.7	3.6	28.9	0.7	28.6	-1.0	28.5	-0.3	29.6	3.9	30.0	1.4
1958	30.1	0.3	29.7	-1.3	29.5	-0.7	29.4	-0.3	29.5	0.3	29.7	0.7	29.6	-0.3	29.8	0.7	29.8	0.0	30.4	2.0	30.6	0.7	30.9	1.0
1959	30.8	-0.3	30.7	-0.3	30.8	0.3	30.8	0.0	30.7	-0.3	30.6	-0.3	30.9	1.0	30.9	0.0	30.9	0.0	31.5	1.9	31.7	0.6	31.9	0.6
1960	31.5	-1.3	31.4	-0.3	31.2	-0.6	31.0	-0.6	30.8	-0.6	30.9	0.3	31.0	0.3	31.1	0.3	31.0	-0.3	31.4	1.3	31.2	-0.6	31.0	-0.6
1961	30.8	-0.6	30.7	-0.3	30.3	-1.3	30.5	0.7	30.5	0.0	30.2	-1.0	31.2	3.3	31.4	0.6	31.3	-0.3	31.8	1.6	31.3	-1.6	31.1	-0.6
1962	31.2	0.3	31.4	0.6	31.4	0.0	31.8	1.3	31.8	0.0	31.3	-1.6	31.0	-1.0	30.8	-0.6	31.8	3.2	31.8	0.0	31.8	0.0	31.7	-0.3
1963	31.4	-0.9	31.5	0.3	31.8	1.0	31.7	-0.3	32.0	0.9	31.9	-0.3	31.9	0.0	31.8	-0.3	31.5	-0.9	31.9	1.3	31.6	-0.9	31.9	0.9
1964	31.5	-1.3	31.4	-0.3	31.3	-0.3	31.3	0.0	31.8	1.6	31.9	0.3	32.1	0.6	32.0	-0.3	31.7	-0.9	31.9	0.6	32.2	0.9	32.2	0.0
1965	32.4	0.6	32.3	-0.3	32.4	0.3	32.7	0.9	32.8	0.3	32.7	-0.3	32.7	0.0	32.5	-0.6	32.3	-0.6	32.6	0.9	32.6	0.0	32.7	0.3
1966	32.4	-0.9	32.4	0.0	32.4	0.0	32.5	0.3	32.5	0.0	32.6	0.3	32.6	0.0	32.8	0.6	32.8	0.0	32.9	0.3	32.9	0.0	32.7	-0.6
1967	32.6	-0.3	33.0	1.2	33.0	0.0	33.1	0.3	33.3	0.6	33.3	0.0	33.5	0.6	33.5	0.0	33.8	0.9	33.9	0.3	34.8	2.7	34.6	-0.6
1968	34.7	0.3	34.7	0.0	34.9	0.6	35.0	0.3	34.9	-0.3	35.0	0.3	35.0	0.0	35.0	0.0	34.9	-0.3	35.2	0.9	35.3	0.3	36.0	2.0
1969	36.2	0.6	36.5	0.8	37.2	1.9	37.4	0.5	37.1	-0.8	37.3	0.5	37.3	0.0	37.3	0.0	37.2	-0.3	37.7	1.3	37.8	0.3	38.0	0.5
1970	38.4	1.1	38.1	-0.8	38.1	0.0	38.7	1.6	38.9	0.5	39.1	0.5	40.3	3.1	40.3	0.0	40.0	-0.7	41.2	3.0	41.7	1.2	42.0	0.7
1971	41.9	-0.2	42.2	0.7	42.0	-0.5	42.0	0.0	42.5	1.2	42.0	-1.2	42.3	0.7	42.5	0.5	42.2	-0.7	41.9	-0.7	41.8	-0.2	42.0	0.5
1972	41.5	-1.2	40.9	-1.4	40.9	0.0	41.2	0.7	41.6	1.0	41.5	-0.2	41.9	1.0	42.1	0.5	42.1	0.0	42.0	-0.2	42.1	0.2	42.1	0.0
1973	41.8	-0.7	41.8	0.0	42.0	0.5	42.4	1.0	42.9	1.2	43.2	0.7	43.2	0.0	43.0	-0.5	42.9	-0.2	43.5	1.4	43.6	0.2	44.0	0.9
1974	44.5	1.1	44.6	0.2	45.3	1.6	45.7	0.9	46.7	2.2	47.4	1.5	48.1	1.5	48.4	0.6	48.6	0.4	48.8	0.4	49.0	0.4	49.0	0.0
1975	48.5	-1.0	48.5	0.0	49.0	1.0	49.4	0.8	49.8	0.8	50.5	1.4	51.6	2.2	52.4	1.6	52.6	0.4	52.7	0.2	52.9	0.4	52.8	-0.2
1976	52.6	-0.4	53.4	1.5	53.8	0.7	54.3	0.9	55.4	2.0	56.2	1.4	56.7	0.9	57.2	0.9	57.8	1.0	58.3	0.9	58.9	1.0	58.8	-0.2
1977	59.0	0.3	59.6	1.0	60.0	0.7	60.9	1.5	61.4	0.8	61.6	0.3	61.5	-0.2	61.4	-0.2	61.0	-0.7	61.1	0.2	61.0	-0.2	61.2	0.3
1978	61.3	0.2	61.3	0.0	61.3	0.0	61.5	0.3	62.4	1.5	63.2	1.3	63.5	0.5	63.9	0.6	63.9	0.0	64.6	1.1	65.0	0.6	65.4	0.6
1979	66.0	0.9	66.5	0.8	67.2	1.1	68.6	2.1	69.9	1.9	71.5	2.3	72.7	1.7	73.8	1.5	74.7	1.2	75.7	1.3	76.3	0.8	77.4	1.4
1980	79.8	3.1	81.2	1.8	83.1	2.3	84.7	1.9	85.5	0.9	85.4	-0.1	85.2	-0.2	85.7	0.6	86.2	0.6	86.6	0.5	88.1	1.7	88.8	0.8
1981	91.1	2.6	92.5	1.5	93.4	1.0	93.6	0.2	94.4	0.9	95.0	0.6	96.6	1.7	96.7	0.1	97.3	0.6	98.3	1.0	98.9	0.6	99.2	0.3
1982	98.7	-0.5	97.7	-1.0	96.7	-1.0	96.3	-0.4	96.9	0.6	99.6	2.8	100.1	0.5	99.8	-0.3	98.6	-1.2	98.9	0.3	98.8	-0.1	98.0	-0.8
1983	97.4	-0.6	96.4	-1.0	95.4	-1.0	97.0	1.7	98.2	1.2	98.4	0.2	99.3	0.9	100.7	1.4	100.6	-0.1	101.6	1.0	101.8	0.2	101.3	-0.5
1984	101.3	0.0	100.9	-0.4	101.5	0.6	102.2	0.7	102.6	0.4	103.0	0.4	103.2	0.2	103.0	-0.2	103.0	0.0	103.8	0.8	103.8	0.0	103.6	-0.2
1985	103.6	0.0	103.3	-0.3	104.2	0.9	105.3	1.1	106.1	0.8	106.0	-0.1	106.3	0.3	105.7	-0.6	104.7	-0.9	105.3	0.6	106.6	1.2	106.6	0.0
1986	106.1	-0.5	104.8	-1.2	101.3	-3.3	99.2	-2.1	100.8	1.6	101.9	1.1	99.9	-2.0	98.9	-1.0	99.0	0.1	99.7	0.7	100.7	1.0	101.9	1.2
1987	103.4	1.5	103.3	-0.1	104.0	0.7	104.6	0.6	105.9	1.2	106.5	0.6	107.2	0.7	107.2	0.0	107.1	-0.1	108.1	0.9	108.1	0.0	107.7	-0.4
1988	107.0	-0.6	107.1	0.1	107.0	-0.1	107.5	0.5	106.6	-0.8	107.1	0.5	107.1	0.0	108.1	0.9	108.3	0.2	108.1	-0.2	109.0	0.8	108.6	-0.4
1989	109.3	0.6	109.5	0.2	109.9	0.4	112.1	2.0	113.7	1.4	114.0	0.3	112.8	-1.1	111.9	-0.8	111.6	-0.3	113.9	2.1	113.1	-0.7	113.1	0.0
1990	116.6	3.1	115.4	-1.0	114.3	-1.0	115.5	1.0	115.9	0.3	116.6	0.6	116.1	-0.4	118.9	2.4	119.8	0.8	124.5	3.9	125.3	0.6	125.5	0.2
1991	123.5	-1.6	121.7	-1.5	120.0	-1.4	119.3	-0.6	121.1	1.5	121.1	0.0	120.4	-0.6	120.4	0.0	120.6	0.2	121.1	0.4	122.5	1.2	122.1	-0.3
1992	121.9	-0.2	120.7	-1.0	120.6	-0.1	121.9	1.1	123.1	1.0	123.2	0.1	123.6	0.3	122.6	-0.8	122.8	0.2	125.6	2.3	126.3	0.6	125.6	-0.6

[Continued]

Chicago-Gary-Kenosha, IL-IN-WI
Consumer Price Index - All Urban Consumers
Base 1982-1984 = 100
Transportation

[Continued]

For 1947-2000. Columns headed % show percentile change in the index from the previous period for which an index is available.

Year	Jan Index	%	Feb Index	%	Mar Index	%	Apr Index	%	May Index	%	Jun Index	%	Jul Index	%	Aug Index	%	Sep Index	%	Oct Index	%	Nov Index	%	Dec Index	%
1993	124.9	-0.6	125.0	0.1	124.8	-0.2	126.2	1.1	127.4	1.0	126.8	-0.5	126.6	-0.2	125.4	-0.9	125.6	0.2	127.0	1.1	127.7	0.6	126.6	-0.9
1994	125.7	-0.7	126.7	0.8	126.9	0.2	128.1	0.9	128.5	0.3	129.9	1.1	131.9	1.5	133.3	1.1	133.4	0.1	132.7	-0.5	133.7	0.8	133.0	-0.5
1995	133.2	0.2	133.0	-0.2	134.6	1.2	135.2	0.4	136.1	0.7	138.0	1.4	136.3	-1.2	135.2	-0.8	134.8	-0.3	135.9	0.8	134.8	-0.8	134.3	-0.4
1996	136.0	1.3	136.4	0.3	138.3	1.4	139.6	0.9	142.3	1.9	141.4	-0.6	140.2	-0.8	139.6	-0.4	139.6	0.0	140.3	0.5	142.5	1.6	142.9	0.3
1997	141.9	-0.7	142.0	0.1	141.5	-0.4	140.6	-0.6	141.2	0.4	140.0	-0.8	139.6	-0.3	139.8	0.1	139.6	-0.1	139.5	-0.1	138.6	-0.6	138.6	0.0
1998	137.7	-0.6	137.5	-0.1	137.4	-0.1	137.3	-0.1	138.6	0.9	138.4	-0.1	138.5	0.1	137.9	-0.4	137.5	-0.3	138.7	0.9	138.7	0.0	138.1	-0.4
1999	137.8	-0.2	136.9	-0.7	138.0	0.8	139.5	1.1	140.1	0.4	139.9	-0.1	140.6	0.5	140.6	0.0	142.3	1.2	143.1	0.6	143.5	0.3	143.8	0.2
2000	144.5	0.5	146.7	1.5	148.8	1.4	147.7	-0.7	151.3	2.4	156.6	3.5	148.2	-5.4	145.0	-2.2	147.6	1.8	147.6	0.0	149.2	1.1	148.1	-0.7

Source: U.S. Department of Labor, Bureau of Labor Statistics, Division of Consumer Prices and Price Indexes. - indicates no data collected for period.

Chicago-Gary-Kenosha, IL-IN-WI
Consumer Price Index - Urban Wage Earners
Base 1982-1984 = 100
Transportation

For 1947-2000. Columns headed % show percentile change in the index from the previous period for which an index is available.

Year	Jan Index	%	Feb Index	%	Mar Index	%	Apr Index	%	May Index	%	Jun Index	%	Jul Index	%	Aug Index	%	Sep Index	%	Oct Index	%	Nov Index	%	Dec Index	%
1947	16.5	-	16.5	0.0	16.6	0.6	16.8	1.2	17.2	2.4	17.2	0.0	17.2	0.0	17.3	0.6	17.5	1.2	17.8	1.7	17.9	0.6	18.0	0.6
1948	18.3	1.7	18.3	0.0	18.3	0.0	18.3	0.0	19.0	3.8	19.0	0.0	20.9	10.0	21.1	1.0	21.2	0.5	21.2	0.0	21.2	0.0	21.2	0.0
1949	21.2	0.0	21.3	0.5	21.3	0.0	21.4	0.5	21.4	0.0	21.3	-0.5	21.3	0.0	21.3	0.0	21.3	0.0	22.5	5.6	22.5	0.0	22.4	-0.4
1950	22.4	0.0	22.4	0.0	22.3	-0.4	22.0	-1.3	22.0	0.0	22.1	0.5	22.1	0.0	22.4	1.4	22.3	-0.4	22.3	0.0	22.3	0.0	22.5	0.9
1951	22.5	0.0	22.6	0.4	23.0	1.8	23.0	0.0	23.0	0.0	23.0	0.0	23.4	1.7	24.2	3.4	24.4	0.8	24.5	0.4	24.7	0.8	24.0	-2.8
1952	24.7	2.9	24.9	0.8	24.9	0.0	24.9	0.0	24.9	0.0	26.1	4.8	26.1	0.0	26.1	0.0	26.1	0.0	26.1	0.0	26.1	0.0	26.1	0.0
1953	26.3	0.8	26.3	0.0	26.2	-0.4	26.2	0.0	26.1	-0.4	26.2	0.4	26.3	0.4	26.3	0.0	26.2	-0.4	26.1	-0.4	26.0	-0.4	26.0	0.0
1954	26.2	0.8	26.0	-0.8	26.0	0.0	25.9	-0.4	26.2	1.2	26.3	0.4	26.2	-0.4	26.1	-0.4	26.1	0.0	25.0	-4.2	26.2	4.8	26.1	-0.4
1955	26.2	0.4	26.0	-0.8	26.0	0.0	25.3	-2.7	25.5	0.8	25.5	0.0	25.4	-0.4	25.5	0.4	25.5	0.0	25.9	1.6	26.1	0.8	25.7	-1.5
1956	25.6	-0.4	25.6	0.0	25.5	-0.4	25.6	0.4	25.8	0.8	25.8	0.0	26.1	1.2	26.2	0.4	26.2	0.0	27.3	4.2	27.3	0.0	27.3	0.0
1957	27.5	0.7	27.3	-0.7	27.4	0.4	27.3	-0.4	27.2	-0.4	27.2	0.0	28.3	4.0	28.4	0.4	28.1	-1.1	28.0	-0.4	29.2	4.3	29.5	1.0
1958	29.6	0.3	29.2	-1.4	29.0	-0.7	29.0	0.0	29.0	0.0	29.2	0.7	29.1	-0.3	29.3	0.7	29.4	0.3	29.9	1.7	30.1	0.7	30.4	1.0
1959	30.3	-0.3	30.2	-0.3	30.3	0.3	30.3	0.0	30.2	-0.3	30.1	-0.3	30.4	1.0	30.4	0.0	30.4	0.0	31.0	2.0	31.2	0.6	31.3	0.3
1960	30.9	-1.3	30.9	0.0	30.7	-0.6	30.5	-0.7	30.3	-0.7	30.4	0.3	30.5	0.3	30.6	0.3	30.5	-0.3	30.8	1.0	30.7	-0.3	30.5	-0.7
1961	30.3	-0.7	30.2	-0.3	29.8	-1.3	30.0	0.7	30.0	0.0	29.7	-1.0	30.7	3.4	30.8	0.3	30.8	0.0	31.3	1.6	30.8	-1.6	30.5	-1.0
1962	30.7	0.7	30.8	0.3	30.9	0.3	31.3	1.3	31.3	0.0	30.8	-1.6	30.5	-1.0	30.3	-0.7	31.2	3.0	31.3	0.3	31.2	-0.3	31.2	0.0
1963	30.8	-1.3	30.9	0.3	31.3	1.3	31.2	-0.3	31.5	1.0	31.4	-0.3	31.4	0.0	31.3	-0.3	31.0	-1.0	31.4	1.3	31.0	-1.3	31.3	1.0
1964	31.0	-1.0	30.8	-0.6	30.8	0.0	30.7	-0.3	31.3	2.0	31.4	0.3	31.6	0.6	31.4	-0.6	31.2	-0.6	31.4	0.6	31.6	0.6	31.6	0.0
1965	31.9	0.9	31.8	-0.3	31.8	0.0	32.2	1.3	32.2	0.0	32.2	0.0	32.2	0.0	32.0	-0.6	31.8	-0.6	32.1	0.9	32.1	0.0	32.2	0.3
1966	31.9	-0.9	31.9	0.0	31.8	-0.3	31.9	0.3	32.0	0.3	32.1	0.3	32.1	0.0	32.3	0.6	32.2	-0.3	32.3	0.3	32.3	0.0	32.2	-0.3
1967	32.1	-0.3	32.4	0.9	32.5	0.3	32.6	0.3	32.7	0.3	32.8	0.3	32.9	0.3	33.0	0.3	33.3	0.9	33.3	0.0	34.2	2.7	34.1	-0.3
1968	34.2	0.3	34.2	0.0	34.3	0.3	34.4	0.3	34.3	-0.3	34.4	0.3	34.5	0.3	34.4	-0.3	34.4	0.0	34.6	0.6	34.7	0.3	35.4	2.0
1969	35.6	0.6	35.9	0.8	36.6	1.9	36.8	0.5	36.5	-0.8	36.7	0.5	36.7	0.0	36.7	0.0	36.6	-0.3	37.1	1.4	37.1	0.0	37.4	0.8
1970	37.8	1.1	37.5	-0.8	37.4	-0.3	38.0	1.6	38.2	0.5	38.4	0.5	39.6	3.1	39.6	0.0	39.4	-0.5	40.5	2.8	41.0	1.2	41.3	0.7
1971	41.2	-0.2	41.5	0.7	41.3	-0.5	41.3	0.0	41.8	1.2	41.3	-1.2	41.6	0.7	41.8	0.5	41.5	-0.7	41.2	-0.7	41.1	-0.2	41.3	0.5
1972	40.8	-1.2	40.2	-1.5	40.2	0.0	40.5	0.7	40.9	1.0	40.8	-0.2	41.2	1.0	41.4	0.5	41.4	0.0	41.3	-0.2	41.4	0.2	41.4	0.0
1973	41.1	-0.7	41.1	0.0	41.3	0.5	41.7	1.0	42.2	1.2	42.5	0.7	42.5	0.0	42.3	-0.5	42.2	-0.2	42.8	1.4	42.9	0.2	43.3	0.9
1974	43.8	1.2	43.8	0.0	44.6	1.8	45.0	0.9	45.9	2.0	46.6	1.5	47.3	1.5	47.6	0.6	47.8	0.4	48.0	0.4	48.2	0.4	48.2	0.0
1975	47.7	-1.0	47.7	0.0	48.2	1.0	48.6	0.8	49.0	0.8	49.7	1.4	50.8	2.2	51.6	1.6	51.8	0.4	51.8	0.0	52.1	0.6	52.0	-0.2
1976	51.7	-0.6	52.6	1.7	52.9	0.6	53.4	0.9	54.5	2.1	55.3	1.5	55.8	0.9	56.2	0.7	56.9	1.2	57.3	0.7	57.9	1.0	57.8	-0.2
1977	58.1	0.5	58.6	0.9	59.0	0.7	59.9	1.5	60.4	0.8	60.6	0.3	60.5	-0.2	60.4	-0.2	60.0	-0.7	60.1	0.2	60.0	-0.2	60.2	0.3
1978	60.3	0.2	60.3	0.0	60.4	0.2	60.5	0.2	61.2	1.2	62.0	1.3	62.4	0.6	62.7	0.5	62.8	0.2	63.6	1.3	63.9	0.5	64.4	0.8
1979	65.0	0.9	65.6	0.9	66.4	1.2	67.8	2.1	69.3	2.2	71.0	2.5	72.4	2.0	73.6	1.7	74.4	1.1	75.1	0.9	76.0	1.2	77.0	1.3
1980	79.1	2.7	80.6	1.9	82.3	2.1	84.2	2.3	84.8	0.7	84.9	0.1	85.0	0.1	85.3	0.4	85.5	0.2	85.8	0.4	87.6	2.1	88.0	0.5
1981	90.7	3.1	92.2	1.7	93.0	0.9	93.9	1.0	94.5	0.6	94.9	0.4	96.4	1.6	96.6	0.2	97.2	0.6	98.4	1.2	98.9	0.5	99.7	0.8
1982	99.3	-0.4	98.1	-1.2	97.2	-0.9	96.5	-0.7	97.3	0.8	100.1	2.9	100.6	0.5	100.3	-0.3	98.9	-1.4	99.2	0.3	99.0	-0.2	98.0	-1.0
1983	97.3	-0.7	96.1	-1.2	95.2	-0.9	96.8	1.7	98.0	1.2	98.2	0.2	99.1	0.9	100.7	1.6	100.5	-0.2	101.5	1.0	101.7	0.2	101.2	-0.5
1984	101.1	-0.1	100.8	-0.3	101.2	0.4	102.1	0.9	102.4	0.3	102.8	0.4	103.0	0.2	102.7	-0.3	102.8	0.1	103.6	0.8	103.6	0.0	103.3	-0.3
1985	103.2	-0.1	102.9	-0.3	103.9	1.0	104.8	0.9	105.6	0.8	105.5	-0.1	105.7	0.2	105.1	-0.6	103.9	-1.1	104.6	0.7	106.0	1.3	106.0	0.0
1986	105.3	-0.7	103.9	-1.3	100.0	-3.8	97.8	-2.2	99.4	1.6	100.5	1.1	98.3	-2.2	97.3	-1.0	97.3	0.0	98.1	0.8	99.2	1.1	100.1	0.9
1987	101.9	1.8	101.7	-0.2	102.4	0.7	102.9	0.5	104.0	1.1	104.7	0.7	105.3	0.6	105.3	0.0	105.3	0.0	106.3	0.9	106.0	-0.3	105.7	-0.3
1988	105.2	-0.5	105.3	0.1	105.1	-0.2	105.3	0.2	105.4	0.1	105.9	0.5	106.1	0.2	107.2	1.0	107.4	0.2	107.2	-0.2	107.9	0.7	107.6	-0.3
1989	108.1	0.5	108.3	0.2	108.6	0.3	111.0	2.2	112.7	1.5	113.1	0.4	111.9	-1.1	110.9	-0.9	110.4	-0.5	112.8	2.2	112.0	-0.7	112.0	0.0
1990	115.4	3.0	114.4	-0.9	112.9	-1.3	114.0	1.0	114.4	0.4	115.1	0.6	114.5	-0.5	117.5	2.6	118.3	0.7	122.8	3.8	123.4	0.5	123.5	0.1
1991	121.4	-1.7	119.6	-1.5	117.8	-1.5	117.5	-0.3	119.3	1.5	119.4	0.1	118.6	-0.7	118.8	0.2	118.8	0.0	119.4	0.5	120.6	1.0	120.1	-0.4
1992	119.6	-0.4	118.5	-0.9	118.3	-0.2	119.5	1.0	121.2	1.4	121.8	0.5	121.8	0.0	121.0	-0.7	121.4	0.3	123.6	1.8	124.3	0.6	123.6	-0.6

[Continued]

Chicago-Gary-Kenosha, IL-IN-WI
Consumer Price Index - Urban Wage Earners
Base 1982-1984 = 100
Transportation
[Continued]

For 1947-2000. Columns headed % show percentile change in the index from the previous period for which an index is available.

Year	Jan		Feb		Mar		Apr		May		Jun		Jul		Aug		Sep		Oct		Nov		Dec	
	Index	%	Index	%	Index	%	Index	%	Index	%	Index	%	Index	%	Index	%	Index	%	Index	%	Index	%	Index	%
1993	122.8	-0.6	122.9	0.1	122.6	-0.2	123.9	1.1	125.3	1.1	124.9	-0.3	124.4	-0.4	123.4	-0.8	123.4	0.0	124.9	1.2	125.4	0.4	124.4	-0.8
1994	123.5	-0.7	124.4	0.7	124.5	0.1	125.7	1.0	126.7	0.8	128.2	1.2	129.9	1.3	131.4	1.2	131.5	0.1	131.0	-0.4	132.0	0.8	131.5	-0.4
1995	131.5	0.0	131.5	0.0	132.6	0.8	133.5	0.7	134.7	0.9	136.1	1.0	134.6	-1.1	133.6	-0.7	133.2	-0.3	134.0	0.6	133.1	-0.7	133.3	0.2
1996	134.6	1.0	134.7	0.1	136.5	1.3	138.0	1.1	140.2	1.6	139.6	-0.4	138.4	-0.9	137.6	-0.6	137.7	0.1	138.4	0.5	140.4	1.4	140.5	0.1
1997	139.8	-0.5	139.5	-0.2	138.7	-0.6	137.9	-0.6	138.4	0.4	137.6	-0.6	136.8	-0.6	137.3	0.4	136.9	-0.3	136.6	-0.2	135.8	-0.6	135.7	-0.1
1998	134.8	-0.7	134.6	-0.1	134.4	-0.1	134.5	0.1	135.9	1.0	135.7	-0.1	135.7	0.0	135.2	-0.4	134.9	-0.2	136.0	0.8	136.4	0.3	135.6	-0.6
1999	135.1	-0.4	133.9	-0.9	134.8	0.7	136.3	1.1	137.1	0.6	137.0	-0.1	137.6	0.4	137.9	0.2	139.6	1.2	140.1	0.4	140.4	0.2	140.6	0.1
2000	141.4	0.6	143.4	1.4	145.3	1.3	144.3	-0.7	147.7	2.4	152.9	3.5	144.9	-5.2	141.9	-2.1	144.4	1.8	144.5	0.1	146.0	1.0	145.1	-0.6

Source: U.S. Department of Labor, Bureau of Labor Statistics, Division of Consumer Prices and Price Indexes. - indicates no data collected for period.

Chicago-Gary-Kenosha, IL-IN-WI
Consumer Price Index - All Urban Consumers
Base 1982-1984 = 100
Medical Care

For 1947-2001. Columns headed % show percentile change in the index from the previous period for which an index is available.

Year	Jan Index	%	Feb Index	%	Mar Index	%	Apr Index	%	May Index	%	Jun Index	%	Jul Index	%	Aug Index	%	Sep Index	%	Oct Index	%	Nov Index	%	Dec Index	%
1947	11.7	-	11.7	0.0	11.9	1.7	12.0	0.8	12.1	0.8	12.2	0.8	12.2	0.0	12.4	1.6	12.4	0.0	12.4	0.0	12.4	0.0	12.5	0.8
1948	12.7	1.6	12.7	0.0	12.7	0.0	12.8	0.8	12.9	0.8	12.9	0.0	12.9	0.0	13.0	0.8	13.0	0.0	13.0	0.0	13.3	2.3	13.3	0.0
1949	13.4	0.8	13.4	0.0	13.6	1.5	13.6	0.0	13.6	0.0	13.6	0.0	13.6	0.0	13.6	0.0	13.6	0.0	13.6	0.0	13.6	0.0	13.6	0.0
1950	13.5	0.0	13.5	0.0	13.5	0.0	13.5	0.0	13.5	0.0	13.5	0.0	13.5	0.0	13.6	0.7	14.2	4.4	14.2	0.0	14.2	0.0	14.3	0.7
1951	14.3	0.0	14.3	0.0	14.4	0.7	14.5	0.7	14.5	0.0	14.5	0.0	14.5	0.0	14.5	0.0	14.7	1.4	14.7	0.0	14.8	0.7	14.8	0.0
1952	14.8	0.0	14.8	0.0	14.9	0.7	14.9	0.0	14.9	0.0	14.9	0.0	14.9	0.0	14.9	0.0	14.9	0.0	14.9	0.0	14.9	0.0	15.0	0.7
1953	15.0	0.0	15.0	0.0	15.0	0.0	15.4	2.7	15.4	0.0	15.4	0.0	15.6	1.3	15.6	0.0	15.6	0.0	15.7	0.6	15.8	0.6	15.8	0.0
1954	15.8	0.0	15.8	0.0	15.8	0.0	15.8	0.0	15.8	0.0	15.8	0.0	15.8	0.0	15.8	0.0	15.8	0.0	16.2	2.5	16.2	0.0	16.2	0.0
1955	16.4	1.2	16.4	0.0	16.4	0.0	16.5	0.6	16.5	0.0	16.5	0.0	16.5	0.0	16.5	0.0	16.5	0.0	16.6	0.6	17.2	3.6	17.2	0.0
1956	17.4	1.2	17.4	0.0	17.4	0.0	17.6	1.1	17.6	0.0	17.5	-0.6	17.6	0.6	17.6	0.0	17.6	0.0	17.7	0.6	17.8	0.6	17.8	0.0
1957	17.9	0.6	17.9	0.0	18.0	0.6	18.2	1.1	18.2	0.0	18.2	0.0	18.2	0.0	18.2	0.0	18.2	0.0	18.8	3.3	18.9	0.5	18.9	0.0
1958	19.3	2.1	19.3	0.0	19.3	0.0	19.4	0.5	19.4	0.0	19.4	0.0	19.4	0.0	19.4	0.0	19.4	0.0	19.5	0.5	19.5	0.0	19.5	0.0
1959	19.5	0.0	20.1	3.1	20.1	0.0	20.4	1.5	20.4	0.0	20.4	0.0	20.4	0.0	20.4	0.0	20.4	0.0	20.5	0.5	20.5	0.0	20.6	0.5
1960	20.7	0.5	21.5	3.9	21.5	0.0	21.6	0.5	21.6	0.0	21.6	0.0	21.4	-0.9	21.4	0.0	21.4	0.0	21.7	1.4	21.7	0.0	21.7	0.0
1961	21.9	0.9	21.9	0.0	21.9	0.0	21.9	0.0	21.9	0.0	21.9	0.0	21.9	0.0	21.9	0.0	21.9	0.0	22.3	1.8	22.3	0.0	22.3	0.0
1962	22.6	1.3	22.6	0.0	22.6	0.0	22.7	0.4	22.7	0.0	22.7	0.0	22.7	0.0	22.7	0.0	22.7	0.0	22.9	0.9	22.9	0.0	22.9	0.0
1963	24.1	5.2	24.1	0.0	24.1	0.0	24.2	0.4	24.3	0.4	24.3	0.0	24.4	0.4	24.4	0.0	24.4	0.0	24.5	0.4	24.5	0.0	24.5	0.0
1964	24.6	0.4	24.6	0.0	24.6	0.0	24.6	0.0	24.6	0.0	24.6	0.0	24.8	0.8	24.8	0.0	24.7	-0.4	24.8	0.4	24.9	0.4	24.9	0.0
1965	24.9	0.0	25.0	0.4	25.0	0.0	25.0	0.0	25.0	0.0	25.1	0.4	25.2	0.4	25.2	0.0	25.2	0.0	25.3	0.4	25.3	0.0	25.4	0.4
1966	25.5	0.4	25.6	0.4	25.6	0.0	25.6	0.0	25.7	0.4	25.8	0.4	25.9	0.4	26.0	0.4	26.3	1.2	26.4	0.4	26.5	0.4	26.7	0.8
1967	26.9	0.7	27.0	0.4	27.5	1.9	27.5	0.0	27.7	0.7	27.8	0.4	28.1	1.1	28.3	0.7	28.6	1.1	28.6	0.0	28.7	0.3	28.8	0.3
1968	29.0	0.7	29.3	1.0	29.4	0.3	29.6	0.7	29.5	-0.3	29.5	0.0	29.5	0.0	29.6	0.3	29.7	0.3	29.8	0.3	30.1	1.0	30.3	0.7
1969	30.4	0.3	30.6	0.7	30.7	0.3	31.3	2.0	31.4	0.3	31.5	0.3	31.5	0.0	31.6	0.3	32.0	1.3	31.9	-0.3	32.1	0.6	32.1	0.0
1970	32.3	0.6	32.5	0.6	33.0	1.5	33.1	0.3	33.2	0.3	33.2	0.0	33.3	0.3	33.8	1.5	34.2	1.2	34.5	0.9	34.6	0.3	34.8	0.6
1971	35.2	1.1	35.6	1.1	35.7	0.3	35.7	0.0	35.9	0.6	36.0	0.3	36.1	0.3	36.3	0.6	36.3	0.0	36.0	-0.8	36.0	0.0	36.1	0.3
1972	36.2	0.3	36.4	0.6	36.4	0.0	36.5	0.3	36.7	0.5	36.7	0.0	36.8	0.3	36.9	0.3	36.9	0.0	37.2	0.8	37.4	0.5	37.4	0.0
1973	37.6	0.5	37.6	0.0	37.8	0.5	37.8	0.0	38.0	0.5	38.0	0.0	38.2	0.5	38.2	0.0	38.6	1.0	39.2	1.6	39.3	0.3	39.3	0.0
1974	39.7	1.0	40.1	1.0	40.4	0.7	40.4	0.0	41.0	1.5	42.1	2.7	42.3	0.5	42.7	0.9	43.2	1.2	43.5	0.7	43.9	0.9	44.4	1.1
1975	45.0	1.4	45.3	0.7	45.8	1.1	45.9	0.2	46.2	0.7	47.0	1.7	47.7	1.5	48.3	1.3	48.7	0.8	49.2	1.0	48.8	-0.8	49.3	1.0
1976	49.7	0.8	50.6	1.8	51.5	1.8	51.8	0.6	52.2	0.8	52.5	0.6	53.2	1.3	53.5	0.6	54.0	0.9	54.3	0.6	54.8	0.9	55.1	0.5
1977	55.7	1.1	56.5	1.4	56.7	0.4	57.1	0.7	57.4	0.5	57.9	0.9	58.3	0.7	58.6	0.5	59.1	0.9	59.5	0.7	59.6	0.2	59.7	0.2
1978	60.4	1.2	60.7	0.5	60.9	0.3	61.3	0.7	61.5	0.3	61.6	0.2	62.2	1.0	62.1	-0.2	62.3	0.3	63.6	2.1	64.4	1.3	64.5	0.2
1979	65.4	1.4	65.4	0.0	65.5	0.2	65.9	0.6	67.1	1.8	67.1	0.0	68.4	1.9	68.5	0.1	68.6	0.1	68.7	0.1	69.0	0.4	71.5	3.6
1980	72.8	1.8	73.8	1.4	74.3	0.7	75.8	2.0	76.3	0.7	76.5	0.3	77.2	0.9	77.5	0.4	77.6	0.1	77.8	0.3	77.8	0.0	78.6	1.0
1981	80.1	1.9	80.7	0.7	81.2	0.6	82.8	2.0	83.1	0.4	84.6	1.8	84.9	0.4	86.1	1.4	86.2	0.1	86.6	0.5	87.0	0.5	88.0	1.1
1982	87.9	-0.1	88.8	1.0	89.3	0.6	90.2	1.0	90.6	0.4	91.8	1.3	93.0	1.3	93.3	0.3	93.5	0.2	94.3	0.9	95.7	1.5	97.2	1.6
1983	98.7	1.5	99.4	0.7	99.8	0.4	100.2	0.4	100.3	0.1	100.8	0.5	101.4	0.6	101.4	0.0	102.4	1.0	102.6	0.2	102.7	0.1	103.1	0.4
1984	104.6	1.5	105.1	0.5	105.1	0.0	105.1	0.0	105.0	-0.1	106.8	1.7	107.8	0.9	107.6	-0.2	107.7	0.1	108.8	1.0	108.9	0.1	109.3	0.4
1985	109.9	0.5	110.0	0.1	111.4	1.3	111.7	0.3	112.3	0.5	112.6	0.3	112.7	0.1	113.3	0.5	114.6	1.1	114.7	0.1	115.1	0.3	115.2	0.1
1986	116.3	1.0	117.1	0.7	118.0	0.8	118.7	0.6	119.2	0.4	119.5	0.3	121.0	1.3	121.1	0.1	122.0	0.7	122.6	0.5	122.7	0.1	123.1	0.3
1987	124.4	1.1	125.7	1.0	125.9	0.2	126.3	0.3	127.6	1.0	129.4	1.4	130.6	0.9	130.9	0.2	132.0	0.8	132.3	0.2	132.7	0.3	132.9	0.2
1988	134.2	1.0	134.8	0.4	135.6	0.6	135.9	0.2	136.4	0.4	137.4	0.7	139.9	1.8	139.5	-0.3	140.4	0.6	140.9	0.4	140.5	-0.3	140.8	0.2
1989	142.1	0.9	143.7	1.1	144.7	0.7	144.9	0.1	146.0	0.8	147.2	0.8	150.2	2.0	152.1	1.3	153.9	1.2	155.2	0.8	155.3	0.1	155.6	0.2
1990	156.2	0.4	157.6	0.9	158.9	0.8	160.2	0.8	161.5	0.8	162.0	0.3	164.3	1.4	165.3	0.6	166.8	0.9	167.4	0.4	168.0	0.4	168.2	0.1
1991	170.2	1.2	172.9	1.6	175.0	1.2	175.7	0.4	176.4	0.4	176.9	0.3	179.2	1.3	179.7	0.3	181.3	0.9	181.3	0.0	183.0	0.9	183.7	0.4
1992	185.1	0.8	186.9	1.0	189.4	1.3	189.5	0.1	189.9	0.2	190.2	0.2	191.3	0.6	191.7	0.2	193.1	0.7	192.9	-0.1	194.0	0.6	194.7	0.4

[Continued]

Chicago-Gary-Kenosha, IL-IN-WI
Consumer Price Index - All Urban Consumers
Base 1982-1984 = 100
Medical Care
[Continued]

For 1947-2001. Columns headed % show percentile change in the index from the previous period for which an index is available.

Year	Jan Index	%	Feb Index	%	Mar Index	%	Apr Index	%	May Index	%	Jun Index	%	Jul Index	%	Aug Index	%	Sep Index	%	Oct Index	%	Nov Index	%	Dec Index	%
1993	198.4	1.9	199.3	0.5	200.5	0.6	201.0	0.2	202.1	0.5	203.1	0.5	204.8	0.8	205.3	0.2	205.3	0.0	205.4	0.0	205.7	0.1	206.2	0.2
1994	209.6	1.6	210.8	0.6	211.1	0.1	211.1	0.0	211.6	0.2	212.9	0.6	214.5	0.8	214.2	-0.1	215.0	0.4	215.2	0.1	215.5	0.1	217.0	0.7
1995	220.8	1.8	221.7	0.4	221.9	0.1	222.3	0.2	223.2	0.4	222.6	-0.3	223.7	0.5	224.5	0.4	224.5	0.0	225.2	0.3	225.4	0.1	224.2	-0.5
1996	227.3	1.4	227.9	0.3	228.1	0.1	228.1	0.0	228.3	0.1	229.3	0.4	230.7	0.6	229.5	-0.5	230.0	0.2	231.3	0.6	231.0	-0.1	231.7	0.3
1997	233.4	0.7	234.2	0.3	234.4	0.1	234.7	0.1	235.3	0.3	235.6	0.1	236.6	0.4	235.6	-0.4	235.2	-0.2	236.8	0.7	236.7	-0.0	237.0	0.1
1998	238.7	0.7	239.3	0.3	241.3	0.8	244.4	1.3	244.8	0.2	244.2	-0.2	246.5	0.9	246.2	-0.1	246.5	0.1	246.6	0.0	246.7	0.0	246.6	-0.0
1999	250.0	1.4	251.4	0.6	250.4	-0.4	251.6	0.5	252.7	0.4	253.9	0.5	255.1	0.5	255.1	0.0	254.3	-0.3	256.5	0.9	255.5	-0.4	256.2	0.3
2000	256.9	0.3	257.7	0.3	258.2	0.2	259.2	0.4	257.4	-0.7	258.2	0.3	258.6	0.2	260.3	0.7	260.9	0.2	261.7	0.3	261.8	0.0	262.6	0.3
2001	266.7	1.6	270.1	1.3	271.1	0.4	270.8	-0.1	270.4	-0.1	272.4	0.7	272.4	0.0	272.8	0.1	273.6	0.3	274.4	0.3	275.7	0.5	275.8	0.0

Source: U.S. Department of Labor, Bureau of Labor Statistics, Division of Consumer Prices and Price Indexes. - indicates no data collected for period.

Chicago-Gary-Kenosha, IL-IN-WI
Consumer Price Index - Urban Wage Earners
Base 1982-1984 = 100
Medical Care

For 1947-2001. Columns headed % show percentile change in the index from the previous period for which an index is available.

Year	Jan Index	%	Feb Index	%	Mar Index	%	Apr Index	%	May Index	%	Jun Index	%	Jul Index	%	Aug Index	%	Sep Index	%	Oct Index	%	Nov Index	%	Dec Index	%
1947	11.5	-	11.5	0.0	11.7	1.7	11.8	0.9	11.9	0.8	12.0	0.8	12.0	0.0	12.2	1.7	12.2	0.0	12.2	0.0	12.2	0.0	12.3	0.8
1948	12.5	1.6	12.5	0.0	12.5	0.0	12.6	0.8	12.7	0.8	12.7	0.0	12.7	0.0	12.8	0.8	12.8	0.0	12.8	0.0	13.1	2.3	13.1	0.0
1949	13.2	0.8	13.2	0.0	13.4	1.5	13.4	0.0	13.4	0.0	13.3	-0.7	13.3	0.0	13.3	0.0	13.3	0.0	13.3	0.0	13.2	-0.8	13.2	0.0
1950	13.2	0.0	13.2	0.0	13.3	0.8	13.3	0.0	13.3	0.0	13.3	0.0	13.3	0.0	13.3	0.0	14.0	5.3	14.0	0.0	14.0	0.0	14.1	0.7
1951	14.1	0.0	14.1	0.0	14.2	0.7	14.3	0.7	14.3	0.0	14.3	0.0	14.3	0.0	14.3	0.0	14.4	0.7	14.4	0.0	14.6	1.4	14.6	0.0
1952	14.6	0.0	14.6	0.0	14.6	0.0	14.7	0.7	14.7	0.0	14.7	0.0	14.7	0.0	14.7	0.0	14.7	0.0	14.7	0.0	14.7	0.0	14.8	0.7
1953	14.8	0.0	14.8	0.0	14.8	0.0	15.1	2.0	15.2	0.7	15.2	0.0	15.3	0.7	15.3	0.0	15.3	0.0	15.5	1.3	15.5	0.0	15.5	0.0
1954	15.5	0.0	15.5	0.0	15.5	0.0	15.5	0.0	15.5	0.0	15.5	0.0	15.5	0.0	15.5	0.0	15.5	0.0	16.0	3.2	16.0	0.0	16.0	0.0
1955	16.1	0.6	16.1	0.0	16.1	0.0	16.2	0.6	16.2	0.0	16.3	0.6	16.3	0.0	16.3	0.0	16.3	0.0	16.3	0.0	16.9	3.7	16.9	0.0
1956	17.1	1.2	17.1	0.0	17.1	0.0	17.3	1.2	17.3	0.0	17.3	0.0	17.3	0.0	17.3	0.0	17.3	0.0	17.4	0.6	17.5	0.6	17.5	0.0
1957	17.6	0.6	17.6	0.0	17.7	0.6	17.9	1.1	17.9	0.0	17.9	0.0	17.9	0.0	17.9	0.0	17.9	0.0	18.5	3.4	18.6	0.5	18.6	0.0
1958	19.0	2.2	19.0	0.0	19.0	0.0	19.0	0.0	19.0	0.0	19.0	0.0	19.0	0.0	19.0	0.0	19.1	0.5	19.2	0.5	19.2	0.0	19.2	0.0
1959	19.2	0.0	19.7	2.6	19.7	0.0	20.1	2.0	20.1	0.0	20.1	0.0	20.1	0.0	20.1	0.0	20.1	0.0	20.1	0.0	20.1	0.0	20.2	0.5
1960	20.3	0.5	21.2	4.4	21.2	0.0	21.3	0.5	21.3	0.0	21.3	0.0	21.1	-0.9	21.1	0.0	21.1	0.0	21.3	0.9	21.3	0.0	21.3	0.0
1961	21.5	0.9	21.5	0.0	21.5	0.0	21.5	0.0	21.6	0.5	21.6	0.0	21.5	-0.5	21.5	0.0	21.5	0.0	21.9	1.9	21.9	0.0	21.9	0.0
1962	22.2	1.4	22.2	0.0	22.2	0.0	22.3	0.5	22.3	0.0	22.3	0.0	22.4	0.4	22.4	0.0	22.4	0.0	22.6	0.9	22.6	0.0	22.6	0.0
1963	23.7	4.9	23.7	0.0	23.7	0.0	23.9	0.8	23.9	0.0	23.9	0.0	24.0	0.4	24.0	0.0	24.0	0.0	24.1	0.4	24.1	0.0	24.1	0.0
1964	24.2	0.4	24.2	0.0	24.2	0.0	24.2	0.0	24.2	0.0	24.2	0.0	24.4	0.8	24.4	0.0	24.3	-0.4	24.4	0.4	24.5	0.4	24.5	0.0
1965	24.5	0.0	24.6	0.4	24.6	0.0	24.6	0.0	24.6	0.0	24.7	0.4	24.8	0.4	24.8	0.0	24.8	0.0	24.9	0.4	24.9	0.0	25.0	0.4
1966	25.1	0.4	25.1	0.0	25.1	0.0	25.2	0.4	25.3	0.4	25.3	0.0	25.5	0.8	25.5	0.0	25.8	1.2	25.9	0.4	26.1	0.8	26.3	0.8
1967	26.4	0.4	26.6	0.8	27.0	1.5	27.1	0.4	27.2	0.4	27.4	0.7	27.6	0.7	27.8	0.7	28.1	1.1	28.1	0.0	28.2	0.4	28.4	0.7
1968	28.5	0.4	28.8	1.1	29.0	0.7	29.1	0.3	29.0	-0.3	29.0	0.0	29.1	0.3	29.1	0.0	29.2	0.3	29.3	0.3	29.6	1.0	29.9	1.0
1969	29.9	0.0	30.1	0.7	30.2	0.3	30.8	2.0	30.9	0.3	31.0	0.3	31.0	0.0	31.1	0.3	31.5	1.3	31.4	-0.3	31.6	0.6	31.6	0.0
1970	31.8	0.6	32.0	0.6	32.5	1.6	32.6	0.3	32.7	0.3	32.7	0.0	32.8	0.3	33.2	1.2	33.7	1.5	33.9	0.6	34.0	0.3	34.3	0.9
1971	34.6	0.9	35.0	1.2	35.2	0.6	35.2	0.0	35.4	0.6	35.4	0.0	35.6	0.6	35.7	0.3	35.7	0.0	35.4	-0.8	35.4	0.0	35.5	0.3
1972	35.7	0.6	35.8	0.3	35.9	0.3	35.9	0.0	36.1	0.6	36.1	0.0	36.2	0.3	36.3	0.3	36.3	0.0	36.6	0.8	36.8	0.5	36.8	0.0
1973	37.0	0.5	37.0	0.0	37.2	0.5	37.2	0.0	37.4	0.5	37.4	0.0	37.6	0.5	37.6	0.0	37.9	0.8	38.6	1.8	38.7	0.3	38.7	0.0
1974	39.0	0.8	39.4	1.0	39.8	1.0	39.8	0.0	40.3	1.3	41.5	3.0	41.6	0.2	42.0	1.0	42.5	1.2	42.8	0.7	43.2	0.9	43.7	1.2
1975	44.3	1.4	44.6	0.7	45.1	1.1	45.2	0.2	45.5	0.7	46.3	1.8	46.9	1.3	47.5	1.3	47.9	0.8	48.4	1.0	48.0	-0.8	48.5	1.0
1976	48.9	0.8	49.8	1.8	50.7	1.8	51.0	0.6	51.4	0.8	51.7	0.6	52.4	1.4	52.6	0.4	53.2	1.1	53.4	0.4	53.9	0.9	54.2	0.6
1977	54.8	1.1	55.6	1.5	55.7	0.2	56.2	0.9	56.5	0.5	57.0	0.9	57.4	0.7	57.7	0.5	58.1	0.7	58.5	0.7	58.6	0.2	58.8	0.3
1978	59.2	0.7	59.5	0.5	59.8	0.5	60.3	0.8	60.6	0.5	60.8	0.3	61.5	1.2	61.5	0.0	61.6	0.2	62.9	2.1	63.9	1.6	64.2	0.5
1979	65.3	1.7	65.4	0.2	65.7	0.5	66.0	0.5	66.7	1.1	66.7	0.0	67.7	1.5	67.9	0.3	68.4	0.7	69.2	1.2	69.4	0.3	72.1	3.9
1980	73.9	2.5	74.6	0.9	74.7	0.1	76.1	1.9	76.7	0.8	76.5	-0.3	77.7	1.6	77.9	0.3	78.3	0.5	78.6	0.4	78.8	0.3	79.2	0.5
1981	80.6	1.8	81.5	1.1	81.9	0.5	82.9	1.2	83.6	0.8	84.4	1.0	84.8	0.5	84.8	0.0	85.8	1.2	86.3	0.6	87.6	1.5	88.1	0.6
1982	87.9	-0.2	88.8	1.0	89.3	0.6	90.1	0.9	90.6	0.6	91.8	1.3	93.0	1.3	93.3	0.3	93.4	0.1	94.3	1.0	95.6	1.4	97.1	1.6
1983	98.6	1.5	99.3	0.7	99.8	0.5	100.1	0.3	100.3	0.2	100.8	0.5	101.4	0.6	101.4	0.0	102.4	1.0	102.6	0.2	102.7	0.1	103.2	0.5
1984	104.7	1.5	105.2	0.5	105.2	0.0	105.2	0.0	105.1	-0.1	106.8	1.6	107.8	0.9	107.5	-0.3	107.7	0.2	108.7	0.9	108.9	0.2	109.2	0.3
1985	109.8	0.5	109.9	0.1	111.3	1.3	111.5	0.2	112.2	0.6	112.5	0.3	112.6	0.1	113.2	0.5	114.5	1.1	114.6	0.1	115.0	0.3	115.2	0.2
1986	116.2	0.9	117.0	0.7	117.8	0.7	118.5	0.6	119.1	0.5	119.3	0.2	120.8	1.3	120.8	0.0	121.8	0.8	122.3	0.4	122.4	0.1	122.8	0.3
1987	124.0	1.0	125.3	1.0	125.5	0.2	125.9	0.3	127.2	1.0	128.8	1.3	130.3	1.2	130.6	0.2	131.8	0.9	132.1	0.2	132.4	0.2	132.7	0.2
1988	134.1	1.1	134.9	0.6	135.5	0.4	136.1	0.4	136.6	0.4	137.4	0.6	140.4	2.2	140.1	-0.2	141.0	0.6	141.5	0.4	141.2	-0.2	141.5	0.2
1989	142.9	1.0	144.8	1.3	145.7	0.6	145.8	0.1	147.1	0.9	148.2	0.7	151.6	2.3	153.2	1.1	155.5	1.5	156.7	0.8	156.7	0.0	157.0	0.2
1990	157.5	0.3	158.8	0.8	159.8	0.6	161.4	1.0	162.7	0.8	163.1	0.2	165.8	1.7	166.6	0.5	168.2	1.0	168.6	0.2	169.2	0.4	169.3	0.1
1991	171.6	1.4	174.6	1.7	176.5	1.1	176.8	0.2	177.7	0.5	178.1	0.2	180.6	1.4	181.2	0.3	182.9	0.9	182.8	-0.1	184.8	1.1	185.5	0.4
1992	186.9	0.8	188.6	0.9	190.7	1.1	190.8	0.1	191.2	0.2	191.7	0.3	193.0	0.7	193.5	0.3	195.2	0.9	194.9	-0.2	195.8	0.5	196.7	0.5

[Continued]

Chicago-Gary-Kenosha, IL-IN-WI
Consumer Price Index - Urban Wage Earners
Base 1982-1984 = 100
Medical Care
[Continued]

For 1947-2001. Columns headed % show percentile change in the index from the previous period for which an index is available.

Year	Jan Index	%	Feb Index	%	Mar Index	%	Apr Index	%	May Index	%	Jun Index	%	Jul Index	%	Aug Index	%	Sep Index	%	Oct Index	%	Nov Index	%	Dec Index	%
1993	200.7	2.0	201.7	0.5	202.9	0.6	203.4	0.2	204.4	0.5	205.3	0.4	207.4	1.0	207.9	0.2	207.9	0.0	208.0	0.0	208.3	0.1	208.7	0.2
1994	212.4	1.8	213.4	0.5	213.6	0.1	213.6	0.0	214.1	0.2	215.5	0.7	217.3	0.8	217.1	-0.1	217.8	0.3	217.9	0.0	218.3	0.2	219.9	0.7
1995	223.9	1.8	225.1	0.5	225.2	0.0	225.7	0.2	226.6	0.4	226.1	-0.2	227.4	0.6	228.4	0.4	228.4	0.0	229.1	0.3	229.3	0.1	228.3	-0.4
1996	231.5	1.4	232.3	0.3	232.5	0.1	232.7	0.1	232.7	0.0	233.8	0.5	235.3	0.6	234.2	-0.5	234.8	0.3	236.1	0.6	235.8	-0.1	236.7	0.4
1997	238.3	0.7	239.0	0.3	239.3	0.1	239.5	0.1	240.1	0.3	240.4	0.1	241.5	0.5	240.3	-0.5	239.9	-0.2	241.4	0.6	241.4	0.0	241.8	0.2
1998	243.4	0.7	244.0	0.2	246.4	1.0	249.5	1.3	249.7	0.1	249.2	-0.2	251.4	0.9	251.2	-0.1	251.5	0.1	251.7	0.1	251.8	0.0	251.7	-0.0
1999	255.3	1.4	256.4	0.4	255.7	-0.3	256.7	0.4	257.6	0.4	259.3	0.7	260.3	0.4	260.5	0.1	259.8	-0.3	261.9	0.8	261.0	-0.3	261.6	0.2
2000	262.4	0.3	263.3	0.3	263.7	0.2	264.7	0.4	263.1	-0.6	263.8	0.3	264.3	0.2	265.8	0.6	266.4	0.2	267.2	0.3	267.3	0.0	268.0	0.3
2001	272.9	1.8	276.3	1.2	277.3	0.4	277.0	-0.1	276.7	-0.1	278.6	0.7	278.6	0.0	279.1	0.2	280.0	0.3	280.6	0.2	281.8	0.4	282.0	0.1

Source: U.S. Department of Labor, Bureau of Labor Statistics, Division of Consumer Prices and Price Indexes. - indicates no data collected for period.

Chicago-Gary-Kenosha, IL-IN-WI

Consumer Price Index - All Urban Consumers
Base December 1997 = 100
Recreation

For 1997-2001. Columns headed % show percentile change in the index from the previous period for which an index is available.

Year	Jan Index	%	Feb Index	%	Mar Index	%	Apr Index	%	May Index	%	Jun Index	%	Jul Index	%	Aug Index	%	Sep Index	%	Oct Index	%	Nov Index	%	Dec Index	%
1997	-	-	-	-	-	-	-	-	-	-	-	-	-	-	-	-	-	-	-	-	-	-	100.0	-
1998	100.2	0.2	100.7	0.5	100.7	0.0	100.7	0.0	99.7	-1.0	104.0	4.3	104.8	0.8	104.1	-0.7	100.8	-3.2	100.7	-0.1	100.1	-0.6	99.4	-0.7
1999	101.2	1.8	100.7	-0.5	101.9	1.2	101.1	-0.8	102.6	1.5	107.7	5.0	107.4	-0.3	106.3	-1.0	101.4	-4.6	102.1	0.7	102.1	0.0	101.1	-1.0
2000	103.0	1.9	101.6	-1.4	101.9	0.3	101.8	-0.1	100.7	-1.1	105.3	4.6	105.2	-0.1	105.3	0.1	100.2	-4.8	100.8	0.6	100.2	-0.6	100.1	-0.1
2001	100.6	0.5	101.6	1.0	101.4	-0.2	108.2	6.7	108.3	0.1	108.4	0.1	108.7	0.3	108.9	0.2	108.8	-0.1	109.4	0.6	109.2	-0.2	110.0	0.7

Source: U.S. Department of Labor, Bureau of Labor Statistics, Division of Consumer Prices and Price Indexes. - indicates no data collected for period.

Chicago-Gary-Kenosha, IL-IN-WI
Consumer Price Index - Urban Wage Earners
Base December 1997 = 100
Recreation

For 1997-2001. Columns headed % show percentile change in the index from the previous period for which an index is available.

Year	Jan Index	%	Feb Index	%	Mar Index	%	Apr Index	%	May Index	%	Jun Index	%	Jul Index	%	Aug Index	%	Sep Index	%	Oct Index	%	Nov Index	%	Dec Index	%
1997	-	-	-	-	-	-	-	-	-	-	-	-	-	-	-	-	-	-	-	-	-	-	100.0	-
1998	100.1	0.1	100.7	0.6	100.7	0.0	100.8	0.1	99.8	-1.0	102.8	3.0	103.4	0.6	103.0	-0.4	100.8	-2.1	100.5	-0.3	100.1	-0.4	99.3	-0.8
1999	100.9	1.6	100.1	-0.8	101.5	1.4	100.7	-0.8	101.8	1.1	105.7	3.8	105.2	-0.5	104.4	-0.8	100.8	-3.4	101.7	0.9	101.5	-0.2	100.7	-0.8
2000	102.5	1.8	101.4	-1.1	101.7	0.3	101.7	0.0	100.7	-1.0	103.7	3.0	103.8	0.1	104.0	0.2	100.0	-3.8	100.7	0.7	100.1	-0.6	99.9	-0.2
2001	100.2	0.3	101.1	0.9	100.9	-0.2	105.8	4.9	106.0	0.2	105.9	-0.1	106.2	0.3	106.3	0.1	106.6	0.3	107.0	0.4	106.9	-0.1	107.7	0.7

Source: U.S. Department of Labor, Bureau of Labor Statistics, Division of Consumer Prices and Price Indexes. - indicates no data collected for period.

Chicago-Gary-Kenosha, IL-IN-WI
Consumer Price Index - All Urban Consumers
Base December 1997 = 100
Education & Communication

For 1997-2001. Columns headed % show percentile change in the index from the previous period for which an index is available.

Year	Jan Index	%	Feb Index	%	Mar Index	%	Apr Index	%	May Index	%	Jun Index	%	Jul Index	%	Aug Index	%	Sep Index	%	Oct Index	%	Nov Index	%	Dec Index	%
1997	-	-	-	-	-	-	-	-	-	-	-	-	-	-	-	-	-	-	-	-	-	-	100.0	-
1998	101.1	1.1	101.3	0.2	103.7	2.4	104.7	1.0	105.8	1.1	106.2	0.4	104.7	-1.4	103.8	-0.9	105.2	1.3	105.9	0.7	105.9	0.0	105.0	-0.8
1999	107.1	2.0	107.4	0.3	107.3	-0.1	101.6	-5.3	106.9	5.2	106.7	-0.2	106.2	-0.5	106.5	0.3	107.2	0.7	107.7	0.5	107.9	0.2	108.2	0.3
2000	110.3	1.9	109.6	-0.6	109.6	0.0	109.2	-0.4	109.4	0.2	108.3	-1.0	108.9	0.6	110.0	1.0	109.9	-0.1	110.4	0.5	111.0	0.5	112.1	1.0
2001	112.7	0.5	111.9	-0.7	109.4	-2.2	112.0	2.4	112.7	0.6	112.6	-0.1	112.5	-0.1	112.5	0.0	113.3	0.7	113.6	0.3	113.2	-0.4	113.6	0.4

Source: U.S. Department of Labor, Bureau of Labor Statistics, Division of Consumer Prices and Price Indexes. - indicates no data collected for period.

Chicago-Gary-Kenosha, IL-IN-WI
Consumer Price Index - Urban Wage Earners
Base December 1997 = 100
Education & Communication

For 1997-2001. Columns headed % show percentile change in the index from the previous period for which an index is available.

Year	Jan Index	%	Feb Index	%	Mar Index	%	Apr Index	%	May Index	%	Jun Index	%	Jul Index	%	Aug Index	%	Sep Index	%	Oct Index	%	Nov Index	%	Dec Index	%
1997	-	-	-	-	-	-	-	-	-	-	-	-	-	-	-	-	-	-	-	-	-	-	100.0	-
1998	101.3	1.3	101.5	0.2	104.1	2.6	105.1	1.0	106.4	1.2	107.0	0.6	105.4	-1.5	104.5	-0.9	106.1	1.5	106.8	0.7	106.9	0.1	106.0	-0.8
1999	108.1	2.0	108.5	0.4	108.4	-0.1	102.1	-5.8	107.9	5.7	107.9	0.0	107.4	-0.5	107.7	0.3	108.4	0.6	108.9	0.5	109.1	0.2	109.5	0.4
2000	111.8	2.1	111.1	-0.6	111.1	0.0	110.7	-0.4	110.9	0.2	109.7	-1.1	110.4	0.6	111.7	1.2	111.4	-0.3	112.1	0.6	112.7	0.5	114.0	1.2
2001	114.5	0.4	113.7	-0.7	111.0	-2.4	113.9	2.6	114.7	0.7	114.7	0.0	114.5	-0.2	114.4	-0.1	115.1	0.6	115.5	0.3	115.0	-0.4	115.4	0.3

Source: U.S. Department of Labor, Bureau of Labor Statistics, Division of Consumer Prices and Price Indexes. - indicates no data collected for period.

Cincinnati-Hamilton, OH-KY-IN
Consumer Price Index - All Urban Consumers
Base 1982-1984 = 100
Annual Averages

For 1917-2001. Columns headed % show percentile change in the index from the previous period for which an index is available.

Year	All Items		Food & Beverage		Housing		Apparel		Trans-portation		Medical Care		Recrea-tion*		Education & Communic.*		Other Goods & Services	
	Index	%	Index	%	Index	%	Index	%	Index	%	Index	%	Index	%	Index	%	Index	%
1917	-	-	-	-	-	-	-	-	-	-	-	-	-	-	-	-	-	-
1918	14.5	-	-	-	-	-	-	-	-	-	-	-	-	-	-	-	-	-
1919	16.9	16.6	-	-	-	-	-	-	-	-	-	-	-	-	-	-	-	-
1920	19.3	14.2	-	-	-	-	-	-	-	-	-	-	-	-	-	-	-	-
1921	16.5	-14.5	-	-	-	-	-	-	-	-	-	-	-	-	-	-	-	-
1922	15.5	-6.1	-	-	-	-	-	-	-	-	-	-	-	-	-	-	-	-
1923	15.9	2.6	-	-	-	-	-	-	-	-	-	-	-	-	-	-	-	-
1924	16.0	0.6	-	-	-	-	-	-	-	-	-	-	-	-	-	-	-	-
1925	16.8	5.0	-	-	-	-	-	-	-	-	-	-	-	-	-	-	-	-
1926	17.1	1.8	-	-	-	-	-	-	-	-	-	-	-	-	-	-	-	-
1927	16.8	-1.8	-	-	-	-	-	-	-	-	-	-	-	-	-	-	-	-
1928	16.7	-0.6	-	-	-	-	-	-	-	-	-	-	-	-	-	-	-	-
1929	16.9	1.2	-	-	-	-	-	-	-	-	-	-	-	-	-	-	-	-
1930	16.7	-1.2	-	-	-	-	-	-	-	-	-	-	-	-	-	-	-	-
1931	15.1	-9.6	-	-	-	-	-	-	-	-	-	-	-	-	-	-	-	-
1932	13.3	-11.9	-	-	-	-	-	-	-	-	-	-	-	-	-	-	-	-
1933	12.8	-3.8	-	-	-	-	-	-	-	-	-	-	-	-	-	-	-	-
1934	13.3	3.9	-	-	-	-	-	-	-	-	-	-	-	-	-	-	-	-
1935	13.7	3.0	-	-	-	-	-	-	-	-	-	-	-	-	-	-	-	-
1936	13.9	1.5	-	-	-	-	-	-	-	-	-	-	-	-	-	-	-	-
1937	14.3	2.9	-	-	-	-	-	-	-	-	-	-	-	-	-	-	-	-
1938	14.0	-2.1	-	-	-	-	-	-	-	-	-	-	-	-	-	-	-	-
1939	13.7	-2.1	-	-	-	-	-	-	-	-	-	-	-	-	-	-	-	-
1940	13.8	0.7	-	-	-	-	-	-	-	-	-	-	-	-	-	-	-	-
1941	14.5	5.1	-	-	-	-	-	-	-	-	-	-	-	-	-	-	-	-
1942	16.2	11.7	-	-	-	-	-	-	-	-	-	-	-	-	-	-	-	-
1943	17.1	5.6	-	-	-	-	-	-	-	-	-	-	-	-	-	-	-	-
1944	17.5	2.3	-	-	-	-	-	-	-	-	-	-	-	-	-	-	-	-
1945	17.8	1.7	-	-	-	-	-	-	-	-	-	-	-	-	-	-	-	-
1946	19.3	8.4	-	-	-	-	-	-	-	-	-	-	-	-	-	-	-	-
1947	22.4	16.1	-	-	-	-	-	-	20.6	-	11.8	-	-	-	-	-	-	-
1948	24.1	7.6	-	-	-	-	-	-	23.3	13.1	13.1	11.0	-	-	-	-	-	-
1949	23.7	-1.7	-	-	-	-	-	-	25.1	7.7	13.4	2.3	-	-	-	-	-	-
1950	23.9	0.8	-	-	-	-	-	-	25.6	2.0	13.5	0.7	-	-	-	-	-	-
1951	25.8	7.9	-	-	-	-	-	-	27.5	7.4	13.8	2.2	-	-	-	-	-	-
1952	26.3	1.9	-	-	-	-	-	-	29.2	6.2	14.9	8.0	-	-	-	-	-	-
1953	26.7	1.5	-	-	-	-	37.5	-	30.0	2.7	15.6	4.7	-	-	-	-	-	-
1954	26.7	0.0	-	-	-	-	37.2	-0.8	29.2	-2.7	16.0	2.6	-	-	-	-	-	-
1955	26.6	-0.4	-	-	-	-	37.6	1.1	28.2	-3.4	16.5	3.1	-	-	-	-	-	-
1956	27.1	1.9	-	-	-	-	38.5	2.4	28.4	0.7	17.5	6.1	-	-	-	-	-	-
1957	28.0	3.3	-	-	-	-	38.8	0.8	30.1	6.0	18.0	2.9	-	-	-	-	-	-
1958	28.6	2.1	-	-	-	-	39.1	0.8	30.8	2.3	19.1	6.1	-	-	-	-	-	-
1959	28.8	0.7	-	-	-	-	39.5	1.0	32.8	6.5	19.6	2.6	-	-	-	-	-	-
1960	29.1	1.0	-	-	-	-	40.1	1.5	33.1	0.9	20.0	2.0	-	-	-	-	-	-
1961	29.2	0.3	-	-	-	-	40.3	0.5	33.1	0.0	20.6	3.0	-	-	-	-	-	-

[Continued]

Cincinnati-Hamilton, OH-KY-IN
Consumer Price Index - All Urban Consumers
Base 1982-1984 = 100
Annual Averages
[Continued]

For 1917-2001. Columns headed % show percentile change in the index from the previous period for which an index is available.

Year	All Items		Food & Beverage		Housing		Apparel		Trans-portation		Medical Care		Recrea-tion*		Education & Communic.*		Other Goods & Services	
	Index	%	Index	%	Index	%	Index	%	Index	%	Index	%	Index	%	Index	%	Index	%
1962	29.5	1.0	-	-	-	-	40.6	0.7	33.8	2.1	21.1	2.4	-	-	-	-	-	-
1963	29.8	1.0	-	-	-	-	41.0	1.0	34.0	0.6	21.8	3.3	-	-	-	-	-	-
1964	30.3	1.7	-	-	-	-	41.5	1.2	34.5	1.5	22.4	2.8	-	-	-	-	-	-
1965	30.5	0.7	-	-	-	-	41.8	0.7	34.5	0.0	23.9	6.7	-	-	-	-	-	-
1966	31.4	3.0	-	-	-	-	43.3	3.6	35.1	1.7	24.9	4.2	-	-	-	-	-	-
1967	32.3	2.9	-	-	-	-	45.0	3.9	35.9	2.3	26.7	7.2	-	-	-	-	-	-
1968	33.9	5.0	-	-	-	-	48.1	6.9	37.7	5.0	28.7	7.5	-	-	-	-	-	-
1969	35.5	4.7	-	-	-	-	51.2	6.4	38.8	2.9	31.1	8.4	-	-	-	-	-	-
1970	37.4	5.4	-	-	-	-	53.5	4.5	40.7	4.9	32.7	5.1	-	-	-	-	-	-
1971	39.0	4.3	-	-	-	-	55.0	2.8	43.0	5.7	35.2	7.6	-	-	-	-	-	-
1972	40.3	3.3	-	-	-	-	55.3	0.5	44.4	3.3	36.4	3.4	-	-	-	-	-	-
1973	42.7	6.0	-	-	-	-	57.6	4.2	44.3	-0.2	38.4	5.5	-	-	-	-	-	-
1974	47.3	10.8	-	-	-	-	61.6	6.9	47.7	7.7	42.4	10.4	-	-	-	-	-	-
1975	51.8	9.5	-	-	-	-	64.6	4.9	51.7	8.4	47.2	11.3	-	-	-	-	-	-
1976	55.0	6.2	60.1	-	50.8	-	68.8	6.5	56.0	8.3	52.6	11.4	-	-	-	-	-	-
1977	58.9	7.1	64.3	7.0	54.5	7.3	72.3	5.1	60.0	7.1	58.9	12.0	-	-	-	-	55.8	-
1978	64.3	9.2	71.1	10.6	60.4	10.8	77.7	7.5	62.5	4.2	65.5	11.2	-	-	-	-	59.2	6.1
1979	72.3	12.4	79.1	11.3	69.1	14.4	82.1	5.7	71.5	14.4	72.6	10.8	-	-	-	-	62.7	5.9
1980	82.1	13.6	85.9	8.6	80.1	15.9	89.1	8.5	84.1	17.6	79.2	9.1	-	-	-	-	67.6	7.8
1981	87.9	7.1	93.2	8.5	84.2	5.1	93.4	4.8	93.8	11.5	85.9	8.5	-	-	-	-	74.2	9.8
1982	94.9	8.0	97.0	4.1	93.6	11.2	97.6	4.5	97.3	3.7	93.6	9.0	-	-	-	-	81.6	10.0
1983	100.8	6.2	99.2	2.3	102.1	9.1	100.6	3.1	99.7	2.5	100.2	7.1	-	-	-	-	90.1	10.4
1984	104.3	3.5	103.8	4.6	104.2	2.1	101.7	1.1	103.0	3.3	106.3	6.1	-	-	-	-	101.5	12.7
1985	106.6	2.2	104.6	0.8	106.8	2.5	103.4	1.7	106.0	2.9	112.0	5.4	-	-	-	-	108.4	6.8
1986	107.6	0.9	107.2	2.5	108.6	1.7	105.5	2.0	99.7	-5.9	117.7	5.1	-	-	-	-	115.5	6.5
1987	111.9	4.0	110.7	3.3	112.0	3.1	115.8	9.8	102.8	3.1	125.7	6.8	-	-	-	-	120.9	4.7
1988	116.1	3.8	114.6	3.5	114.8	2.5	125.1	8.0	104.8	1.9	136.8	8.8	-	-	-	-	-	-
1989	120.9	4.1	119.6	4.4	119.2	3.8	119.7	-4.3	111.2	6.1	144.3	5.5	-	-	-	-	141.3	16.9
1990	126.5	4.6	128.3	7.3	121.1	1.6	121.2	1.3	117.7	5.8	157.4	9.1	-	-	-	-	149.9	6.1
1991	131.4	3.9	131.7	2.7	126.5	4.5	121.6	0.3	120.1	2.0	175.5	11.5	-	-	-	-	165.8	10.6
1992	134.1	2.1	129.6	-1.6	129.6	2.5	131.9	8.5	118.8	-1.1	188.0	7.1	-	-	-	-	174.4	5.2
1993	137.8	2.8	132.1	1.9	132.0	1.9	138.6	5.1	121.2	2.0	200.7	6.8	-	-	-	-	185.3	6.3
1994	142.4	3.3	135.6	2.6	135.2	2.4	140.5	1.4	129.4	6.8	213.8	6.5	-	-	-	-	197.4	6.5
1995	146.2	2.7	138.9	2.4	137.9	2.0	138.5	-1.4	135.0	4.3	222.4	4.0	-	-	-	-	197.5	0.1
1996	149.6	2.3	141.5	1.9	142.1	3.0	131.8	-4.8	138.5	2.6	225.8	1.5	-	-	-	-	209.3	6.0
1997	152.1	1.7	145.0	2.5	145.1	2.1	132.7	0.7	137.6	-0.6	221.1	-2.1	-	-	-	-	220.4	5.3
1998	155.1	2.0	148.4	2.3	149.9	3.3	129.0	-2.8	136.6	-0.7	224.5	1.5	105.6	-	99.4	-	234.2	6.3
1999	159.2	2.6	152.0	2.4	153.1	2.1	130.1	0.9	140.9	3.1	233.0	3.8	105.5	-0.1	99.6	0.2	246.4	5.2
2000	164.8	3.5	156.4	2.9	158.2	3.3	127.2	-2.2	148.8	5.6	253.9	9.0	106.0	0.5	98.8	-0.8	278.0	12.8
2001	-	-	-	-	-	-	-	-	-	-	-	-	-	-	-	-	295.2	6.2

Source: U.S. Department of Labor, Bureau of Labor Statistics, Division of Consumer Prices and Price Indexes. *Base is December 1997 = 100. - indicates no data collected for period.

Cincinnati-Hamilton, OH-KY-IN
Consumer Price Index - Urban Wage Earners
Base 1982-1984 = 100
Annual Averages

For 1917-2001. Columns headed % show percentile change in the index from the previous period for which an index is available.

Year	All Items		Food & Beverage		Housing		Apparel		Trans-portation		Medical Care		Recrea-tion*		Education & Communic.*		Other Goods & Services	
	Index	%	Index	%	Index	%	Index	%	Index	%	Index	%	Index	%	Index	%	Index	%
1917	-	-	-	-	-	-	-	-	-	-	-	-	-	-	-	-	-	-
1918	14.6	-	-	-	-	-	-	-	-	-	-	-	-	-	-	-	-	-
1919	17.0	16.4	-	-	-	-	-	-	-	-	-	-	-	-	-	-	-	-
1920	19.5	14.7	-	-	-	-	-	-	-	-	-	-	-	-	-	-	-	-
1921	16.7	-14.4	-	-	-	-	-	-	-	-	-	-	-	-	-	-	-	-
1922	15.7	-6.0	-	-	-	-	-	-	-	-	-	-	-	-	-	-	-	-
1923	16.0	1.9	-	-	-	-	-	-	-	-	-	-	-	-	-	-	-	-
1924	16.1	0.6	-	-	-	-	-	-	-	-	-	-	-	-	-	-	-	-
1925	17.0	5.6	-	-	-	-	-	-	-	-	-	-	-	-	-	-	-	-
1926	17.2	1.2	-	-	-	-	-	-	-	-	-	-	-	-	-	-	-	-
1927	16.9	-1.7	-	-	-	-	-	-	-	-	-	-	-	-	-	-	-	-
1928	16.8	-0.6	-	-	-	-	-	-	-	-	-	-	-	-	-	-	-	-
1929	17.0	1.2	-	-	-	-	-	-	-	-	-	-	-	-	-	-	-	-
1930	16.8	-1.2	-	-	-	-	-	-	-	-	-	-	-	-	-	-	-	-
1931	15.2	-9.5	-	-	-	-	-	-	-	-	-	-	-	-	-	-	-	-
1932	13.4	-11.8	-	-	-	-	-	-	-	-	-	-	-	-	-	-	-	-
1933	12.9	-3.7	-	-	-	-	-	-	-	-	-	-	-	-	-	-	-	-
1934	13.4	3.9	-	-	-	-	-	-	-	-	-	-	-	-	-	-	-	-
1935	13.8	3.0	-	-	-	-	-	-	-	-	-	-	-	-	-	-	-	-
1936	14.0	1.4	-	-	-	-	-	-	-	-	-	-	-	-	-	-	-	-
1937	14.4	2.9	-	-	-	-	-	-	-	-	-	-	-	-	-	-	-	-
1938	14.1	-2.1	-	-	-	-	-	-	-	-	-	-	-	-	-	-	-	-
1939	13.8	-2.1	-	-	-	-	-	-	-	-	-	-	-	-	-	-	-	-
1940	13.9	0.7	-	-	-	-	-	-	-	-	-	-	-	-	-	-	-	-
1941	14.6	5.0	-	-	-	-	-	-	-	-	-	-	-	-	-	-	-	-
1942	16.3	11.6	-	-	-	-	-	-	-	-	-	-	-	-	-	-	-	-
1943	17.2	5.5	-	-	-	-	-	-	-	-	-	-	-	-	-	-	-	-
1944	17.6	2.3	-	-	-	-	-	-	-	-	-	-	-	-	-	-	-	-
1945	18.0	2.3	-	-	-	-	-	-	-	-	-	-	-	-	-	-	-	-
1946	19.4	7.8	-	-	-	-	-	-	-	-	-	-	-	-	-	-	-	-
1947	22.6	16.5	-	-	-	-	-	-	20.8	-	11.3	-	-	-	-	-	-	-
1948	24.3	7.5	-	-	-	-	-	-	23.5	13.0	12.4	9.7	-	-	-	-	-	-
1949	23.9	-1.6	-	-	-	-	-	-	25.4	8.1	12.8	3.2	-	-	-	-	-	-
1950	24.1	0.8	-	-	-	-	-	-	25.9	2.0	12.8	0.0	-	-	-	-	-	-
1951	25.9	7.5	-	-	-	-	-	-	27.7	6.9	13.2	3.1	-	-	-	-	-	-
1952	26.5	2.3	-	-	-	-	-	-	29.5	6.5	14.2	7.6	-	-	-	-	-	-
1953	26.9	1.5	-	-	-	-	36.4	-	30.3	2.7	14.9	4.9	-	-	-	-	-	-
1954	26.9	0.0	-	-	-	-	36.2	-0.5	29.5	-2.6	15.2	2.0	-	-	-	-	-	-
1955	26.8	-0.4	-	-	-	-	36.5	0.8	28.5	-3.4	15.7	3.3	-	-	-	-	-	-
1956	27.3	1.9	-	-	-	-	37.4	2.5	28.7	0.7	16.7	6.4	-	-	-	-	-	-
1957	28.2	3.3	-	-	-	-	37.7	0.8	30.4	5.9	17.2	3.0	-	-	-	-	-	-
1958	28.8	2.1	-	-	-	-	37.9	0.5	31.1	2.3	18.2	5.8	-	-	-	-	-	-
1959	29.0	0.7	-	-	-	-	38.3	1.1	33.2	6.8	18.7	2.7	-	-	-	-	-	-
1960	29.3	1.0	-	-	-	-	38.9	1.6	33.4	0.6	19.0	1.6	-	-	-	-	-	-
1961	29.4	0.3	-	-	-	-	39.1	0.5	33.5	0.3	19.6	3.2	-	-	-	-	-	-

[Continued]

338

Cincinnati-Hamilton, OH-KY-IN
Consumer Price Index - Urban Wage Earners
Base 1982-1984 = 100
Annual Averages
[Continued]

For 1917-2001. Columns headed % show percentile change in the index from the previous period for which an index is available.

Year	All Items		Food & Beverage		Housing		Apparel		Transportation		Medical Care		Recreation*		Education & Communic.*		Other Goods & Services	
	Index	%	Index	%	Index	%	Index	%	Index	%	Index	%	Index	%	Index	%	Index	%
1962	29.7	1.0	-	-	-	-	39.4	0.8	34.1	1.8	20.1	2.6	-	-	-	-	-	-
1963	30.0	1.0	-	-	-	-	39.8	1.0	34.3	0.6	20.8	3.5	-	-	-	-	-	-
1964	30.5	1.7	-	-	-	-	40.3	1.3	34.8	1.5	21.4	2.9	-	-	-	-	-	-
1965	30.7	0.7	-	-	-	-	40.6	0.7	34.9	0.3	22.7	6.1	-	-	-	-	-	-
1966	31.6	2.9	-	-	-	-	42.0	3.4	35.5	1.7	23.8	4.8	-	-	-	-	-	-
1967	32.5	2.8	-	-	-	-	43.7	4.0	36.2	2.0	25.4	6.7	-	-	-	-	-	-
1968	34.1	4.9	-	-	-	-	46.7	6.9	38.1	5.2	27.4	7.9	-	-	-	-	-	-
1969	35.7	4.7	-	-	-	-	49.7	6.4	39.2	2.9	29.7	8.4	-	-	-	-	-	-
1970	37.6	5.3	-	-	-	-	52.0	4.6	41.1	4.8	31.2	5.1	-	-	-	-	-	-
1971	39.3	4.5	-	-	-	-	53.4	2.7	43.5	5.8	33.5	7.4	-	-	-	-	-	-
1972	40.6	3.3	-	-	-	-	53.7	0.6	44.8	3.0	34.7	3.6	-	-	-	-	-	-
1973	43.0	5.9	-	-	-	-	55.9	4.1	44.7	-0.2	36.6	5.5	-	-	-	-	-	-
1974	47.6	10.7	-	-	-	-	59.8	7.0	48.2	7.8	40.4	10.4	-	-	-	-	-	-
1975	52.2	9.7	-	-	-	-	62.7	4.8	52.2	8.3	45.0	11.4	-	-	-	-	-	-
1976	55.4	6.1	59.8	-	51.7	-	66.8	6.5	56.5	8.2	50.1	11.3	-	-	-	-	-	-
1977	59.3	7.0	64.1	7.2	55.5	7.4	70.2	5.1	60.6	7.3	56.1	12.0	-	-	-	-	55.6	-
1978	64.9	9.4	71.1	10.9	61.7	11.2	75.8	8.0	63.0	4.0	62.0	10.5	-	-	-	-	59.0	6.1
1979	73.3	12.9	79.7	12.1	70.8	14.7	81.0	6.9	72.0	14.3	70.2	13.2	-	-	-	-	63.1	6.9
1980	83.2	13.5	86.3	8.3	82.4	16.4	86.6	6.9	84.5	17.4	78.2	11.4	-	-	-	-	68.3	8.2
1981	89.2	7.2	92.9	7.6	86.3	4.7	93.1	7.5	94.0	11.2	85.6	9.5	-	-	-	-	74.6	9.2
1982	96.4	8.1	97.2	4.6	96.5	11.8	97.5	4.7	97.4	3.6	93.5	9.2	-	-	-	-	82.3	10.3
1983	100.8	4.6	99.2	2.1	102.0	5.7	100.9	3.5	99.7	2.4	100.2	7.2	-	-	-	-	90.2	9.6
1984	102.8	2.0	103.6	4.4	101.5	-0.5	101.6	0.7	102.9	3.2	106.3	6.1	-	-	-	-	101.7	12.7
1985	105.2	2.3	104.3	0.7	104.6	3.1	102.5	0.9	105.7	2.7	112.0	5.4	-	-	-	-	108.2	6.4
1986	105.8	0.6	106.8	2.4	106.3	1.6	104.5	2.0	99.7	-5.7	117.4	4.8	-	-	-	-	114.7	6.0
1987	109.8	3.8	110.2	3.2	109.6	3.1	111.5	6.7	103.1	3.4	125.5	6.9	-	-	-	-	119.9	4.5
1988	114.0	3.8	114.1	3.5	112.2	2.4	121.4	8.9	105.6	2.4	137.5	9.6	-	-	-	-	-	-
1989	118.6	4.0	119.1	4.4	116.4	3.7	115.7	-4.7	112.2	6.3	145.1	5.5	-	-	-	-	139.6	16.4
1990	124.3	4.8	128.0	7.5	118.5	1.8	118.3	2.2	118.9	6.0	157.8	8.8	-	-	-	-	147.5	5.7
1991	128.8	3.6	131.3	2.6	123.7	4.4	118.1	-0.2	121.2	1.9	175.2	11.0	-	-	-	-	161.7	9.6
1992	131.4	2.0	129.3	-1.5	126.8	2.5	128.3	8.6	120.2	-0.8	187.8	7.2	-	-	-	-	170.3	5.3
1993	135.1	2.8	132.0	2.1	129.2	1.9	133.2	3.8	122.9	2.2	199.7	6.3	-	-	-	-	181.7	6.7
1994	139.5	3.3	135.6	2.7	132.3	2.4	136.9	2.8	131.0	6.6	212.6	6.5	-	-	-	-	194.5	7.0
1995	143.4	2.8	138.8	2.4	134.8	1.9	135.7	-0.9	137.3	4.8	220.5	3.7	-	-	-	-	192.8	-0.9
1996	146.9	2.4	141.3	1.8	138.9	3.0	129.1	-4.9	141.9	3.4	223.5	1.4	-	-	-	-	203.8	5.7
1997	149.4	1.7	144.9	2.5	141.8	2.1	130.5	1.1	141.2	-0.5	218.7	-2.1	-	-	-	-	212.9	4.5
1998	151.9	1.7	148.5	2.5	146.4	3.2	126.5	-3.1	140.0	-0.8	220.9	1.0	104.4	-	97.9	-	225.3	5.8
1999	155.9	2.6	152.0	2.4	149.3	2.0	127.9	1.1	144.7	3.4	229.0	3.7	104.1	-0.3	96.6	-1.3	236.6	5.0
2000	161.8	3.8	156.3	2.8	154.2	3.3	125.4	-2.0	153.7	6.2	249.5	9.0	106.5	2.3	94.4	-2.3	270.2	14.2
2001	-		-		-		-		-		-		-		-		288.4	6.7

Source: U.S. Department of Labor, Bureau of Labor Statistics, Division of Consumer Prices and Price Indexes. *Base is December 1997 = 100. - indicates no data collected for period.

Cincinnati-Hamilton, OH-KY-IN

Consumer Price Index - All Urban Consumers
Base 1982-1984 = 100
All Items

For 1917-2001. Columns headed % show percentile change in the index from the previous period for which an index is available.

Year	Jan Index	%	Feb Index	%	Mar Index	%	Apr Index	%	May Index	%	Jun Index	%	Jul Index	%	Aug Index	%	Sep Index	%	Oct Index	%	Nov Index	%	Dec Index	%
1917	-		-		-		-		-		-		-		-		-		-		-		13.5	-
1918	-		-		-		-		-		-		-		-		-		-		-		15.7	16.3
1919	-		-		-		-		-		16.5	5.1	-		-		-		-		-		18.2	10.3
1920	-		-		-		-		-		20.4	12.1	-		-		-		-		-		18.3	-10.3
1921	-		-		-		-		16.6	-9.3	-		-		-		16.4	-1.2	-		-		15.8	-3.7
1922	-		-		15.4	-2.5	-		-		15.7	1.9	-		-		15.4	-1.9	-		-		15.5	0.6
1923	-		-		15.7	1.3	-		-		16.0	1.9	-		-		16.1	0.6	-		-		16.0	-0.6
1924	-		-		16.1	0.6	-		-		16.1	0.6	-		-		16.1	0.0	-		-		16.1	0.0
1925	-		-		-		-		-		17.0	5.6	-		-		-		-		-		17.1	0.6
1926	-		-		-		-		-		17.1		-		-		-		-		-		17.0	-0.6
1927	-		-		-		-		-		17.4	2.4	-		-		-		-		-		16.6	-4.6
1928	-		-		-		-		-		16.7	0.6	-		-		-		-		-		16.6	-0.6
1929	-		-		-		-		-		16.8	1.2	-		-		-		-		-		17.0	1.2
1930	-		-		-		-		-		16.7	-1.8	-		-		-		-		-		16.0	-4.2
1931	-		-		-		-		-		15.0	-6.3	-		-		-		-		-		14.4	-4.0
1932	-		-		-		-		-		13.3	-7.6	-		-		-		-		-		12.8	-3.8
1933	-		-		-		-		-		12.6	-1.6	-		-		-		-		-		12.9	2.4
1934	-		-		-		-		-		13.2	2.3	-		-		-		-		13.3	0.8	-	
1935	-		-		13.7	3.0	-		-		-		13.7	0.0	-		-		13.8	0.7	-		13.9	-1.4
1936	13.8	0.0	-		-		13.6	-1.4	-		-		14.0	2.9	-		14.1	0.7	-		-		14.3	-1.4
1937	-		-		14.3	2.9	-		-		14.3	0.0	-		-		14.5	1.4	-		-		13.8	-1.4
1938	-		-		14.0	-2.1	-		-		14.0	0.0	-		-		14.0	0.0	-		-		13.6	-1.4
1939	-		-		13.6	-1.4	-		-		13.5	-0.7	-		-		13.8	2.2	-		-		13.8	0.0
1940	-		-		13.7	0.7	-		-		13.7	0.0	-		-		13.9	1.5	13.8	-0.7	13.8	0.0	13.8	0.0
1941	13.8	0.0	13.8	0.0	14.0	1.4	14.1	0.7	14.2	0.7	14.4	1.4	14.5	0.7	14.8	2.1	15.0	1.4	15.3	2.0	15.4	0.7	15.3	-0.6
1942	15.5	1.3	15.7	1.3	15.9	1.3	16.0	0.6	16.1	0.6	16.2	0.6	16.2	0.0	16.3	0.6	16.4	0.6	16.6	1.2	16.6	0.0	16.7	0.6
1943	16.6	-0.6	16.7	0.6	16.9	1.2	17.1	1.2	17.2	0.6	17.3	0.6	17.3	0.0	17.3	0.0	17.2	-0.6	17.3	0.6	17.2	-0.6	17.3	0.6
1944	17.2	-0.6	17.1	-0.6	17.1	0.0	17.4	1.8	17.3	-0.6	17.6	1.7	17.6	0.0	17.6	0.0	17.6	0.0	17.5	-0.6	17.6	0.6	17.6	0.0
1945	17.6	0.0	17.6	0.0	17.6	0.0	17.6	0.0	17.8	1.1	18.0	1.1	18.0	0.0	18.0	0.0	17.9	-0.6	18.0	0.6	-		18.0	0.0
1946	18.0	0.0	17.9	-0.6	18.0	0.6	18.1	0.6	18.2	0.6	18.4	1.1	19.5	6.0	20.0	2.6	20.2	1.0	20.4	1.0	21.3	4.4	21.2	-0.5
1947	21.2	0.0	21.3	0.5	21.8	2.3	21.9	0.5	21.8	-0.5	22.1	1.4	22.4	1.4	22.6	0.9	23.1	2.2	23.3	0.9	23.3	0.0	23.7	1.7
1948	23.9	0.8	23.7	-0.8	23.6	-0.4	23.8	0.8	24.0	0.8	24.2	0.8	24.5	1.2	24.5	0.0	24.6	0.4	24.5	-0.4	24.2	-1.2	24.0	-0.8
1949	24.0	0.0	23.7	-1.2	23.8	0.4	23.8	0.0	23.6	-0.8	23.8	0.8	23.6	-0.8	23.6	0.0	23.8	0.8	23.6	-0.8	23.5	-0.4	23.4	-0.4
1950	23.4	0.0	23.3	-0.4	23.4	0.4	23.3	-0.4	23.6	1.3	23.7	0.4	23.9	0.8	24.2	1.3	24.4	0.8	24.5	0.4	24.5	0.0	24.8	1.2
1951	25.3	2.0	25.5	0.8	25.6	0.4	25.7	0.4	25.7	0.0	25.7	0.0	25.8	0.4	25.7	-0.4	26.0	1.2	26.0	0.0	26.1	0.4	26.1	0.0
1952	26.2	0.4	26.0	-0.8	26.0	0.0	26.2	0.8	26.3	0.4	26.4	0.4	26.5	0.4	26.5	0.0	26.5	0.0	26.5	0.0	26.3	-0.8	26.3	0.0
1953	-		-		26.3	0.0	-		-		26.8	1.9	-		-		27.0	0.7	-		-		26.8	-0.7
1954	-		-		26.7	-0.4	-		-		26.7	0.0	-		-		26.7	0.0	-		-		26.5	-0.7
1955	-		-		26.5	0.0	-		-		26.6	0.4	-		-		26.6	0.0	-		-		26.7	0.4
1956	-		-		26.7	0.0	-		-		27.2	1.9	-		-		27.4	0.7	-		-		27.5	0.4
1957	-		-		27.6	0.4	-		-		28.0	1.4	-		-		28.3	1.1	-		-		28.3	0.0
1958	-		-		28.6	1.1	-		-		28.7	0.3	-		-		28.7	0.0	-		-		28.6	-0.3
1959	-		-		28.6	0.0	-		-		28.8	0.7	-		-		28.9	0.3	-		-		29.0	0.3
1960	-		-		28.9	-0.3	-		-		29.2	1.0	-		-		29.2	0.0	-		-		29.2	0.0
1961	-		-		29.2	0.0	-		-		29.2	0.0	-		-		29.3	0.3	-		-		29.2	-0.3
1962	-		-		29.4	0.7	-		-		29.4	0.0	-		-		29.7	1.0	-		-		29.6	-0.3

[Continued]

340

Cincinnati-Hamilton, OH-KY-IN
Consumer Price Index - All Urban Consumers
Base 1982-1984 = 100
All Items
[Continued]

For 1917-2001. Columns headed % show percentile change in the index from the previous period for which an index is available.

Year	Jan Index	%	Feb Index	%	Mar Index	%	Apr Index	%	May Index	%	Jun Index	%	Jul Index	%	Aug Index	%	Sep Index	%	Oct Index	%	Nov Index	%	Dec Index	%
1963	-	-	-	-	29.8	0.7	-	-	-	-	29.8	0.0	-	-	-	-	29.9	0.3	-	-	-	-	29.9	0.0
1964	-	-	-	-	30.1	0.7	-	-	-	-	30.2	0.3	-	-	-	-	30.5	1.0	-	-	-	-	30.4	-0.3
1965	-	-	-	-	30.4	0.0	-	-	-	-	30.6	0.7	-	-	-	-	30.5	-0.3	-	-	-	-	30.7	0.7
1966	-	-	-	-	31.1	1.3	-	-	-	-	31.4	1.0	-	-	-	-	31.8	1.3	-	-	-	-	31.7	-0.3
1967	-	-	-	-	31.8	0.3	-	-	-	-	32.2	1.3	-	-	-	-	32.7	1.6	-	-	-	-	33.0	0.9
1968	-	-	-	-	33.4	1.2	-	-	-	-	33.8	1.2	-	-	-	-	34.3	1.5	-	-	-	-	34.5	0.6
1969	-	-	-	-	34.9	1.2	-	-	-	-	35.5	1.7	-	-	-	-	35.7	0.6	-	-	-	-	36.4	2.0
1970	-	-	-	-	36.8	1.1	-	-	-	-	37.4	1.6	-	-	-	-	37.7	0.8	-	-	-	-	38.3	1.6
1971	-	-	-	-	38.7	1.0	-	-	-	-	39.0	0.8	-	-	-	-	39.2	0.5	-	-	-	-	39.4	0.5
1972	-	-	-	-	39.8	1.0	-	-	-	-	40.3	1.3	-	-	-	-	40.8	1.2	-	-	-	-	40.9	0.2
1973	-	-	-	-	41.9	2.4	-	-	-	-	42.3	1.0	-	-	-	-	43.4	2.6	-	-	-	-	44.1	1.6
1974	-	-	-	-	45.7	3.6	-	-	-	-	47.1	3.1	-	-	-	-	48.6	3.2	-	-	-	-	49.7	2.3
1975	-	-	-	-	50.4	1.4	-	-	-	-	51.9	3.0	-	-	-	-	53.0	2.1	-	-	-	-	53.2	0.4
1976	-	-	-	-	54.0	1.5	-	-	-	-	54.9	1.7	-	-	-	-	55.6	1.3	-	-	-	-	56.4	1.4
1977	-	-	-	-	57.8	2.5	-	-	-	-	58.8	1.7	-	-	-	-	59.9	1.9	-	-	-	-	60.3	0.7
1978	-	-	-	-	62.1	3.0	-	-	63.8	2.7	-	-	64.7	1.4	-	-	65.8	1.7	-	-	66.9	1.7	-	-
1979	68.3	2.1	-	-	69.7	2.0	-	-	71.6	2.7	-	-	72.7	1.5	-	-	74.0	1.8	-	-	75.4	1.9	-	-
1980	77.4	2.7	-	-	80.1	3.5	-	-	81.3	1.5	-	-	83.0	2.1	-	-	84.0	1.2	-	-	84.7	0.8	-	-
1981	85.5	0.9	-	-	86.0	0.6	-	-	87.8	2.1	-	-	88.3	0.6	-	-	88.9	0.7	-	-	89.4	0.6	-	-
1982	92.3	3.2	-	-	92.1	-0.2	-	-	93.3	1.3	-	-	94.8	1.6	-	-	97.0	2.3	-	-	98.3	1.3	-	-
1983	98.9	0.6	-	-	99.4	0.5	-	-	100.6	1.2	-	-	101.0	0.4	-	-	101.7	0.7	-	-	102.4	0.7	-	-
1984	102.9	0.5	-	-	103.4	0.5	-	-	104.0	0.6	-	-	104.5	0.5	-	-	105.1	0.6	-	-	105.2	0.1	-	-
1985	105.1	-0.1	-	-	106.1	1.0	-	-	106.8	0.7	-	-	106.7	-0.1	-	-	106.6	-0.1	-	-	107.7	1.0	-	-
1986	107.7	0.0	-	-	106.5	-1.1	-	-	107.3	0.8	-	-	107.4	0.1	-	-	107.6	0.2	-	-	108.4	0.7	-	-
1987	-	-	-	-	-	-	-	-	-	-	110.6	2.0	-	-	-	-	-	-	-	-	-	-	113.2	2.4
1988	-	-	-	-	-	-	-	-	-	-	114.3	1.0	-	-	-	-	-	-	-	-	-	-	118.0	3.2
1989	-	-	-	-	-	-	-	-	-	-	119.9	1.6	-	-	-	-	-	-	-	-	-	-	121.8	1.6
1990	-	-	-	-	-	-	-	-	-	-	125.0	2.6	-	-	-	-	-	-	-	-	-	-	128.1	2.5
1991	-	-	-	-	-	-	-	-	-	-	130.5	1.9	-	-	-	-	-	-	-	-	-	-	132.3	1.4
1992	-	-	-	-	-	-	-	-	-	-	133.2	0.7	-	-	-	-	-	-	-	-	-	-	134.9	1.3
1993	-	-	-	-	-	-	-	-	-	-	137.0	1.6	-	-	-	-	-	-	-	-	-	-	138.7	1.2
1994	-	-	-	-	-	-	-	-	-	-	140.9	1.6	-	-	-	-	-	-	-	-	-	-	143.9	2.1
1995	-	-	-	-	-	-	-	-	-	-	145.0	0.8	-	-	-	-	-	-	-	-	-	-	147.3	1.6
1996	-	-	-	-	-	-	-	-	-	-	148.6	0.9	-	-	-	-	-	-	-	-	-	-	150.7	1.4
1997	-	-	-	-	-	-	-	-	-	-	151.4	0.5	-	-	-	-	-	-	-	-	-	-	152.8	0.9
1998	-	-	-	-	-	-	-	-	-	-	154.4	1.0	-	-	-	-	-	-	-	-	-	-	155.9	1.0
1999	-	-	-	-	-	-	-	-	-	-	157.7	1.2	-	-	-	-	-	-	-	-	-	-	160.8	2.0
2000	-	-	-	-	-	-	-	-	-	-	163.0	1.4	-	-	-	-	-	-	-	-	-	-	166.6	2.2
2001	-	-	-	-	-	-	-	-	-	-	167.2	0.4	-	-	-	-	-	-	-	-	-	-	-	-

Source: U.S. Department of Labor, Bureau of Labor Statistics, Division of Consumer Prices and Price Indexes. - indicates no data collected for period.

Cincinnati-Hamilton, OH-KY-IN

Consumer Price Index - Urban Wage Earners
Base 1982-1984 = 100

All Items

For 1917-2001. Columns headed % show percentile change in the index from the previous period for which an index is available.

Year	Jan Index	%	Feb Index	%	Mar Index	%	Apr Index	%	May Index	%	Jun Index	%	Jul Index	%	Aug Index	%	Sep Index	%	Oct Index	%	Nov Index	%	Dec Index	%
1917	-	-	-	-	-	-	-	-	-	-			-	-	-	-	-	-	-	-	-	-	13.6	-
1918	-	-	-	-	-	-	-	-	-	-			-	-	-	-	-	-	-	-	-	-	15.8	16.2
1919	-	-	-	-	-	-	-	-	-	-	16.6	5.1	-	-	-	-	-	-	-	-	-	-	18.4	10.8
1920	-	-	-	-	-	-	-	-	-	-	20.6	12.0	-	-	-	-	-	-	-	-	-	-	18.4	-10.7
1921	-	-	-	-	-	-	-	-	16.8	-8.7	-	-	-	-	-	-	16.5	-1.8	-	-	-	-	15.9	-3.6
1922	-	-	-	-	15.6	-1.9	-	-	-	-	15.8	1.3	-	-	-	-	15.6	-1.3	-	-	-	-	15.6	0.0
1923	-	-	-	-	15.8	1.3	-	-	-	-	16.1	1.9	-	-	-	-	16.2	0.6	-	-	-	-	16.1	-0.6
1924	-	-	-	-	16.2	0.6	-	-	-	-	16.2	0.0	-	-	-	-	16.2	0.0	-	-	-	-	16.2	0.0
1925	-	-	-	-	-	-	-	-	-	-	17.1	5.6	-	-	-	-	-	-	-	-	-	-	17.2	0.6
1926	-	-	-	-	-	-	-	-	-	-	17.2	0.0	-	-	-	-	-	-	-	-	-	-	17.1	-0.6
1927	-	-	-	-	-	-	-	-	-	-	17.5	2.3	-	-	-	-	-	-	-	-	-	-	16.7	-4.6
1928	-	-	-	-	-	-	-	-	-	-	16.8	0.6	-	-	-	-	-	-	-	-	-	-	16.7	-0.6
1929	-	-	-	-	-	-	-	-	-	-	17.0	1.8	-	-	-	-	-	-	-	-	-	-	17.1	0.6
1930	-	-	-	-	-	-	-	-	-	-	16.9	-1.2	-	-	-	-	-	-	-	-	-	-	16.1	-4.7
1931	-	-	-	-	-	-	-	-	-	-	15.1	-6.2	-	-	-	-	-	-	-	-	-	-	14.5	-4.0
1932	-	-	-	-	-	-	-	-	-	-	13.4	-7.6	-	-	-	-	-	-	-	-	-	-	12.9	-3.7
1933	-	-	-	-	-	-	-	-	-	-	12.7	-1.6	-	-	-	-	-	-	-	-	-	-	13.0	2.4
1934	-	-	-	-	-	-	-	-	-	-	13.3	2.3	-	-	-	-	-	-	-	-	13.4	0.8	-	-
1935	-	-	-	-	13.8	3.0	-	-	-	-	-	-	13.8	0.0	-	-	-	-	13.9	0.7	-	-	-	-
1936	13.9	0.0	-	-	-	-	13.7	-1.4	-	-	-	-	14.1	2.9	-	-	14.2	0.7	-	-	-	-	14.0	-1.4
1937	-	-	-	-	14.4	2.9	-	-	-	-	14.4	0.0	-	-	-	-	14.6	1.4	-	-	-	-	14.4	-1.4
1938	-	-	-	-	14.1	-2.1	-	-	-	-	14.1	0.0	-	-	-	-	14.1	0.0	-	-	-	-	13.9	-1.4
1939	-	-	-	-	13.7	-1.4	-	-	-	-	13.6	-0.7	-	-	-	-	13.9	2.2	-	-	-	-	13.7	-1.4
1940	-	-	-	-	13.8	0.7	-	-	-	-	13.8	0.0	-	-	-	-	14.0	1.4	13.9	-0.7	13.9	0.0	13.9	0.0
1941	13.9	0.0	13.9	0.0	14.1	1.4	14.2	0.7	14.3	0.7	14.5	1.4	14.6	0.7	14.9	2.1	15.1	1.3	15.4	2.0	15.5	0.6	15.4	-0.6
1942	15.7	1.9	15.8	0.6	16.0	1.3	16.1	0.6	16.2	0.6	16.3	0.6	16.3	0.0	16.4	0.6	16.5	0.6	16.7	1.2	16.7	0.0	16.8	0.6
1943	16.8	0.0	16.8	0.0	17.1	1.8	17.2	0.6	17.3	0.6	17.4	0.6	17.4	0.0	17.4	0.0	17.3	-0.6	17.4	0.6	17.3	-0.6	17.4	0.6
1944	17.3	-0.6	17.2	-0.6	17.2	0.0	17.5	1.7	17.4	-0.6	17.7	1.7	17.8	0.6	17.7	-0.6	17.7	0.0	17.6	-0.6	17.7	0.6	17.7	0.0
1945	17.8	0.6	17.7	-0.6	17.7	0.0	17.8	0.6	17.9	0.6	18.1	1.1	18.2	0.6	18.1	-0.5	18.0	-0.6	18.1	0.6	-	-	18.2	0.6
1946	18.2	0.0	18.1	-0.5	18.1	0.0	18.2	0.6	18.4	1.1	18.5	0.5	19.7	6.5	20.1	2.0	20.4	1.5	20.5	0.5	21.4	4.4	21.4	0.0
1947	21.3	-0.5	21.5	0.9	22.0	2.3	22.0	0.0	22.0	0.0	22.2	0.9	22.5	1.4	22.8	1.3	23.3	2.2	23.5	0.9	23.5	0.0	23.9	1.7
1948	24.0	0.4	23.9	-0.4	23.8	-0.4	24.0	0.8	24.2	0.8	24.4	0.8	24.7	1.2	24.7	0.0	24.8	0.4	24.6	-0.8	24.4	-0.8	24.2	-0.8
1949	24.2	0.0	23.9	-1.2	24.0	0.4	24.0	0.0	23.8	-0.8	24.0	0.8	23.7	-1.2	23.7	0.0	24.0	1.3	23.7	-1.2	23.7	0.0	23.6	-0.4
1950	23.6	0.0	23.5	-0.4	23.6	0.4	23.5	-0.4	23.8	1.3	23.9	0.4	24.0	0.4	24.3	1.2	24.5	0.8	24.6	0.4	24.6	0.0	25.0	1.6
1951	25.5	2.0	25.7	0.8	25.8	0.4	25.8	0.0	25.8	0.0	25.9	0.4	26.0	0.4	25.9	-0.4	26.1	0.8	26.2	0.4	26.3	0.4	26.3	0.0
1952	26.4	0.4	26.2	-0.8	26.2	0.0	26.4	0.8	26.5	0.4	26.6	0.4	26.7	0.4	26.7	0.0	26.7	0.0	26.7	0.0	26.5	-0.7	26.5	0.0
1953	-	-	-	-	26.5	0.0	-	-	-	-	27.0	1.9	-	-	-	-	27.1	0.4	-	-	-	-	27.0	-0.4
1954	-	-	-	-	26.9	-0.4	-	-	-	-	26.9	0.0	-	-	-	-	26.9	0.0	-	-	-	-	26.7	-0.7
1955	-	-	-	-	26.7	0.0	-	-	-	-	26.8	0.4	-	-	-	-	26.8	0.0	-	-	-	-	26.9	0.4
1956	-	-	-	-	26.9	0.0	-	-	-	-	27.4	1.9	-	-	-	-	27.6	0.7	-	-	-	-	27.7	0.4
1957	-	-	-	-	27.8	0.4	-	-	-	-	28.2	1.4	-	-	-	-	28.5	1.1	-	-	-	-	28.5	0.0
1958	-	-	-	-	28.8	1.1	-	-	-	-	28.9	0.3	-	-	-	-	28.9	0.0	-	-	-	-	28.8	-0.3
1959	-	-	-	-	28.8	0.0	-	-	-	-	29.0	0.7	-	-	-	-	29.1	0.3	-	-	-	-	29.2	0.3
1960	-	-	-	-	29.1	-0.3	-	-	-	-	29.4	1.0	-	-	-	-	29.4	0.0	-	-	-	-	29.4	0.0
1961	-	-	-	-	29.4	0.0	-	-	-	-	29.4	0.0	-	-	-	-	29.5	0.3	-	-	-	-	29.4	-0.3
1962	-	-	-	-	29.6	0.7	-	-	-	-	29.6	0.0	-	-	-	-	29.9	1.0	-	-	-	-	29.8	-0.3

[Continued]

Cincinnati-Hamilton, OH-KY-IN
Consumer Price Index - Urban Wage Earners
Base 1982-1984 = 100
All Items
[Continued]

For 1917-2001. Columns headed % show percentile change in the index from the previous period for which an index is available.

Year	Jan Index	%	Feb Index	%	Mar Index	%	Apr Index	%	May Index	%	Jun Index	%	Jul Index	%	Aug Index	%	Sep Index	%	Oct Index	%	Nov Index	%	Dec Index	%
1963	-	-	-	-	30.0	0.7	-	-	-	-	30.0	0.0	-	-	-	-	30.1	0.3	-	-	-	-	30.1	0.0
1964	-	-	-	-	30.3	0.7	-	-	-	-	30.4	0.3	-	-	-	-	30.7	1.0	-	-	-	-	30.7	0.0
1965	-	-	-	-	30.6	-0.3	-	-	-	-	30.8	0.7	-	-	-	-	30.7	-0.3	-	-	-	-	30.9	0.7
1966	-	-	-	-	31.3	1.3	-	-	-	-	31.6	1.0	-	-	-	-	32.0	1.3	-	-	-	-	31.9	-0.3
1967	-	-	-	-	32.0	0.3	-	-	-	-	32.4	1.3	-	-	-	-	32.9	1.5	-	-	-	-	33.3	1.2
1968	-	-	-	-	33.6	0.9	-	-	-	-	34.0	1.2	-	-	-	-	34.5	1.5	-	-	-	-	34.7	0.6
1969	-	-	-	-	35.2	1.4	-	-	-	-	35.7	1.4	-	-	-	-	36.0	0.8	-	-	-	-	36.6	1.7
1970	-	-	-	-	37.0	1.1	-	-	-	-	37.6	1.6	-	-	-	-	38.0	1.1	-	-	-	-	38.6	1.6
1971	-	-	-	-	39.0	1.0	-	-	-	-	39.3	0.8	-	-	-	-	39.5	0.5	-	-	-	-	39.7	0.5
1972	-	-	-	-	40.0	0.8	-	-	-	-	40.5	1.3	-	-	-	-	41.1	1.5	-	-	-	-	41.2	0.2
1973	-	-	-	-	42.2	2.4	-	-	-	-	42.6	0.9	-	-	-	-	43.7	2.6	-	-	-	-	44.5	1.8
1974	-	-	-	-	46.0	3.4	-	-	-	-	47.4	3.0	-	-	-	-	48.9	3.2	-	-	-	-	50.0	2.2
1975	-	-	-	-	50.7	1.4	-	-	-	-	52.3	3.2	-	-	-	-	53.3	1.9	-	-	-	-	53.6	0.6
1976	-	-	-	-	54.4	1.5	-	-	-	-	55.3	1.7	-	-	-	-	56.0	1.3	-	-	-	-	56.8	1.4
1977	-	-	-	-	58.2	2.5	-	-	-	-	59.2	1.7	-	-	-	-	60.3	1.9	-	-	-	-	60.8	0.8
1978	-	-	-	-	62.6	3.0	-	-	64.3	2.7	-	-	65.4	1.7	-	-	66.3	1.4	-	-	67.5	1.8	-	-
1979	69.1	2.4	-	-	70.5	2.0	-	-	72.6	3.0	-	-	73.7	1.5	-	-	75.1	1.9	-	-	76.7	2.1	-	-
1980	78.4	2.2	-	-	81.3	3.7	-	-	82.3	1.2	-	-	84.3	2.4	-	-	85.2	1.1	-	-	85.7	0.6	-	-
1981	86.7	1.2	-	-	87.1	0.5	-	-	88.9	2.1	-	-	89.9	1.1	-	-	90.2	0.3	-	-	90.8	0.7	-	-
1982	93.8	3.3	-	-	93.5	-0.3	-	-	94.8	1.4	-	-	96.3	1.6	-	-	98.5	2.3	-	-	99.9	1.4	-	-
1983	99.3	-0.6	-	-	100.1	0.8	-	-	100.7	0.6	-	-	100.2	-0.5	-	-	101.3	1.1	-	-	102.8	1.5	-	-
1984	102.0	-0.8	-	-	102.1	0.1	-	-	101.6	-0.5	-	-	102.3	0.7	-	-	104.4	2.1	-	-	103.9	-0.5	-	-
1985	103.8	-0.1	-	-	104.8	1.0	-	-	105.4	0.6	-	-	105.2	-0.2	-	-	105.0	-0.2	-	-	106.1	1.0	-	-
1986	106.1	0.0	-	-	104.7	-1.3	-	-	105.7	1.0	-	-	105.7	0.0	-	-	105.7	0.0	-	-	106.6	0.9	-	-
1987	-	-	-	-	-	-	-	-	-	-	108.6	1.9	-	-	-	-	-	-	-	-	-	-	111.1	2.3
1988	-	-	-	-	-	-	-	-	-	-	112.1	0.9	-	-	-	-	-	-	-	-	-	-	115.9	3.4
1989	-	-	-	-	-	-	-	-	-	-	117.7	1.6	-	-	-	-	-	-	-	-	-	-	119.6	1.6
1990	-	-	-	-	-	-	-	-	-	-	122.7	2.6	-	-	-	-	-	-	-	-	-	-	125.9	2.6
1991	-	-	-	-	-	-	-	-	-	-	127.9	1.6	-	-	-	-	-	-	-	-	-	-	129.7	1.4
1992	-	-	-	-	-	-	-	-	-	-	130.4	0.5	-	-	-	-	-	-	-	-	-	-	132.4	1.5
1993	-	-	-	-	-	-	-	-	-	-	134.1	1.3	-	-	-	-	-	-	-	-	-	-	136.0	1.4
1994	-	-	-	-	-	-	-	-	-	-	138.1	1.5	-	-	-	-	-	-	-	-	-	-	140.9	2.0
1995	-	-	-	-	-	-	-	-	-	-	142.3	1.0	-	-	-	-	-	-	-	-	-	-	144.4	1.5
1996	-	-	-	-	-	-	-	-	-	-	145.9	1.0	-	-	-	-	-	-	-	-	-	-	147.9	1.4
1997	-	-	-	-	-	-	-	-	-	-	148.7	0.5	-	-	-	-	-	-	-	-	-	-	150.0	0.9
1998	-	-	-	-	-	-	-	-	-	-	151.2	0.8	-	-	-	-	-	-	-	-	-	-	152.5	0.9
1999	-	-	-	-	-	-	-	-	-	-	154.2	1.1	-	-	-	-	-	-	-	-	-	-	157.6	2.2
2000	-	-	-	-	-	-	-	-	-	-	160.0	1.5	-	-	-	-	-	-	-	-	-	-	163.5	2.2
2001	-	-	-	-	-	-	-	-	-	-	164.0	0.3	-	-	-	-	-	-	-	-	-	-	-	-

Source: U.S. Department of Labor, Bureau of Labor Statistics, Division of Consumer Prices and Price Indexes. - indicates no data collected for period.

Cincinnati-Hamilton, OH-KY-IN
Consumer Price Index - All Urban Consumers
Base 1982-1984 = 100
Food and Beverages

For 1975-2001. Columns headed % show percentile change in the index from the previous period for which an index is available.

Year	Jan Index	%	Feb Index	%	Mar Index	%	Apr Index	%	May Index	%	Jun Index	%	Jul Index	%	Aug Index	%	Sep Index	%	Oct Index	%	Nov Index	%	Dec Index	%
1975	-	-	-	-	-	-	-	-	-	-	-	-	-	-	-	-	-	-	-	-	-	-	59.1	-
1976	-	-	-	-	59.2	0.2	-	-	-	-	60.2	1.7	-	-	-	-	60.7	0.8	-	-	-	-	60.7	0.0
1977	-	-	-	-	63.0	3.8	-	-	-	-	64.5	2.4	-	-	-	-	65.5	1.6	-	-	-	-	66.0	0.8
1978	-	-	-	-	68.5	3.8	-	-	70.4	2.8	-	-	72.7	3.3	-	-	72.4	-0.4	-	-	73.5	1.5	-	-
1979	75.6	2.9	-	-	77.5	2.5	-	-	79.5	2.6	-	-	79.7	0.3	-	-	79.9	0.3	-	-	80.8	1.1	-	-
1980	82.2	1.7	-	-	83.5	1.6	-	-	84.7	1.4	-	-	85.8	1.3	-	-	87.9	2.4	-	-	89.1	1.4	-	-
1981	91.4	2.6	-	-	92.5	1.2	-	-	93.1	0.6	-	-	93.2	0.1	-	-	94.0	0.9	-	-	93.8	-0.2	-	-
1982	95.2	1.5	-	-	95.3	0.1	-	-	96.6	1.4	-	-	98.4	1.9	-	-	98.1	-0.3	-	-	97.7	-0.4	-	-
1983	97.7	0.0	-	-	99.0	1.3	-	-	99.5	0.5	-	-	99.2	-0.3	-	-	98.8	-0.4	-	-	99.7	0.9	-	-
1984	102.4	2.7	-	-	103.5	1.1	-	-	103.9	0.4	-	-	103.7	-0.2	-	-	104.7	1.0	-	-	104.5	-0.2	-	-
1985	104.1	-0.4	-	-	105.4	1.2	-	-	105.1	-0.3	-	-	104.4	-0.7	-	-	104.1	-0.3	-	-	104.4	0.3	-	-
1986	105.0	0.6	-	-	105.2	0.2	-	-	106.0	0.8	-	-	107.8	1.7	-	-	109.0	1.1	-	-	109.2	0.2	-	-
1987	-	-	-	-	-	-	-	-	-	-	110.1	0.8	-	-	-	-	-	-	-	-	-	-	111.4	1.2
1988	-	-	-	-	-	-	-	-	-	-	112.8	1.3	-	-	-	-	-	-	-	-	-	-	116.3	3.1
1989	-	-	-	-	-	-	-	-	-	-	118.0	1.5	-	-	-	-	-	-	-	-	-	-	121.3	2.8
1990	-	-	-	-	-	-	-	-	-	-	127.2	4.9	-	-	-	-	-	-	-	-	-	-	129.4	1.7
1991	-	-	-	-	-	-	-	-	-	-	132.0	2.0	-	-	-	-	-	-	-	-	-	-	131.4	-0.5
1992	-	-	-	-	-	-	-	-	-	-	130.8	-0.5	-	-	-	-	-	-	-	-	-	-	128.5	-1.8
1993	-	-	-	-	-	-	-	-	-	-	131.5	2.3	-	-	-	-	-	-	-	-	-	-	132.7	0.9
1994	-	-	-	-	-	-	-	-	-	-	135.2	1.9	-	-	-	-	-	-	-	-	-	-	136.1	0.7
1995	-	-	-	-	-	-	-	-	-	-	137.6	1.1	-	-	-	-	-	-	-	-	-	-	140.2	1.9
1996	-	-	-	-	-	-	-	-	-	-	140.4	0.1	-	-	-	-	-	-	-	-	-	-	142.5	1.5
1997	-	-	-	-	-	-	-	-	-	-	144.4	1.3	-	-	-	-	-	-	-	-	-	-	145.7	0.9
1998	-	-	-	-	-	-	-	-	-	-	147.5	1.2	-	-	-	-	-	-	-	-	-	-	149.3	1.2
1999	-	-	-	-	-	-	-	-	-	-	151.3	1.3	-	-	-	-	-	-	-	-	-	-	152.7	0.9
2000	-	-	-	-	-	-	-	-	-	-	154.7	1.3	-	-	-	-	-	-	-	-	-	-	158.2	2.3
2001	-	-	-	-	-	-	-	-	-	-	160.5	1.5	-	-	-	-	-	-	-	-	-	-	-	-

Source: U.S. Department of Labor, Bureau of Labor Statistics, Division of Consumer Prices and Price Indexes. - indicates no data collected for period.

Cincinnati-Hamilton, OH-KY-IN
Consumer Price Index - Urban Wage Earners
Base 1982-1984 = 100
Food and Beverages

For 1975-2001. Columns headed % show percentile change in the index from the previous period for which an index is available.

Year	Jan		Feb		Mar		Apr		May		Jun		Jul		Aug		Sep		Oct		Nov		Dec	
	Index	%	Index	%	Index	%	Index	%	Index	%	Index	%	Index	%	Index	%	Index	%	Index	%	Index	%	Index	%
1975	-	-	-	-	-	-	-	-	-	-	-	-	-	-	-	-	-	-	-	-	-	-	58.9	-
1976	-	-	-	-	59.0	0.2	-	-	-	-	60.0	1.7	-	-	-	-	60.4	0.7	-	-	-	-	60.4	0.0
1977	-	-	-	-	62.7	3.8	-	-	-	-	64.3	2.6	-	-	-	-	65.3	1.6	-	-	-	-	65.8	0.8
1978	-	-	-	-	68.3	3.8	-	-	70.6	3.4	-	-	72.6	2.8	-	-	72.3	-0.4	-	-	73.7	1.9	-	-
1979	76.1	3.3	-	-	77.8	2.2	-	-	80.3	3.2	-	-	80.5	0.2	-	-	80.8	0.4	-	-	81.5	0.9	-	-
1980	82.2	0.9	-	-	83.8	1.9	-	-	85.0	1.4	-	-	86.4	1.6	-	-	88.6	2.5	-	-	89.3	0.8	-	-
1981	91.5	2.5	-	-	92.2	0.8	-	-	92.6	0.4	-	-	92.9	0.3	-	-	93.7	0.9	-	-	93.8	0.1	-	-
1982	95.6	1.9	-	-	95.7	0.1	-	-	96.9	1.3	-	-	98.4	1.5	-	-	98.2	-0.2	-	-	97.8	-0.4	-	-
1983	97.8	0.0	-	-	99.2	1.4	-	-	99.7	0.5	-	-	99.2	-0.5	-	-	98.8	-0.4	-	-	99.7	0.9	-	-
1984	102.3	2.6	-	-	103.3	1.0	-	-	103.7	0.4	-	-	103.3	-0.4	-	-	104.4	1.1	-	-	104.1	-0.3	-	-
1985	104.0	-0.1	-	-	105.3	1.3	-	-	104.8	-0.5	-	-	104.0	-0.8	-	-	103.8	-0.2	-	-	104.1	0.3	-	-
1986	104.7	0.6	-	-	105.0	0.3	-	-	105.7	0.7	-	-	107.4	1.6	-	-	108.4	0.9	-	-	108.8	0.4	-	-
1987	-	-	-	-	-	-	-	-	-	-	109.6	0.7	-	-	-	-	-	-	-	-	-	-	110.9	1.2
1988	-	-	-	-	-	-	-	-	-	-	112.4	1.4	-	-	-	-	-	-	-	-	-	-	115.8	3.0
1989	-	-	-	-	-	-	-	-	-	-	117.4	1.4	-	-	-	-	-	-	-	-	-	-	120.8	2.9
1990	-	-	-	-	-	-	-	-	-	-	126.9	5.0	-	-	-	-	-	-	-	-	-	-	129.1	1.7
1991	-	-	-	-	-	-	-	-	-	-	131.6	1.9	-	-	-	-	-	-	-	-	-	-	131.1	-0.4
1992	-	-	-	-	-	-	-	-	-	-	130.4	-0.5	-	-	-	-	-	-	-	-	-	-	128.3	-1.6
1993	-	-	-	-	-	-	-	-	-	-	131.2	2.3	-	-	-	-	-	-	-	-	-	-	132.8	1.2
1994	-	-	-	-	-	-	-	-	-	-	135.1	1.7	-	-	-	-	-	-	-	-	-	-	136.0	0.7
1995	-	-	-	-	-	-	-	-	-	-	137.5	1.1	-	-	-	-	-	-	-	-	-	-	140.2	2.0
1996	-	-	-	-	-	-	-	-	-	-	140.3	0.1	-	-	-	-	-	-	-	-	-	-	142.3	1.4
1997	-	-	-	-	-	-	-	-	-	-	144.2	1.3	-	-	-	-	-	-	-	-	-	-	145.5	0.9
1998	-	-	-	-	-	-	-	-	-	-	147.5	1.4	-	-	-	-	-	-	-	-	-	-	149.5	1.4
1999	-	-	-	-	-	-	-	-	-	-	151.3	1.2	-	-	-	-	-	-	-	-	-	-	152.7	0.9
2000	-	-	-	-	-	-	-	-	-	-	154.7	1.3	-	-	-	-	-	-	-	-	-	-	157.9	2.1
2001	-	-	-	-	-	-	-	-	-	-	160.3	1.5	-	-	-	-	-	-	-	-	-	-	-	-

Source: U.S. Department of Labor, Bureau of Labor Statistics, Division of Consumer Prices and Price Indexes. - indicates no data collected for period.

Cincinnati-Hamilton, OH-KY-IN
Consumer Price Index - All Urban Consumers
Base 1982-1984 = 100
Housing

For 1975-2001. Columns headed % show percentile change in the index from the previous period for which an index is available.

Year	Jan Index	%	Feb Index	%	Mar Index	%	Apr Index	%	May Index	%	Jun Index	%	Jul Index	%	Aug Index	%	Sep Index	%	Oct Index	%	Nov Index	%	Dec Index	%
1975	-	-	-	-	-	-	-	-	-	-	-	-	-	-	-	-	-	-	-	-	-	-	49.3	-
1976	-	-	-	-	50.2	1.8	-	-	-	-	50.6	0.8	-	-	-	-	51.0	0.8	-	-	-	-	52.5	2.9
1977	-	-	-	-	53.3	1.5	-	-	-	-	54.2	1.7	-	-	-	-	55.4	2.2	-	-	-	-	56.2	1.4
1978	-	-	-	-	58.0	3.2	-	-	59.9	3.3	-	-	60.4	0.8	-	-	62.2	3.0	-	-	63.5	2.1	-	-
1979	64.7	1.9	-	-	66.6	2.9	-	-	68.1	2.3	-	-	69.2	1.6	-	-	70.5	1.9	-	-	72.7	3.1	-	-
1980	74.7	2.8	-	-	78.1	4.6	-	-	79.3	1.5	-	-	82.2	3.7	-	-	82.1	-0.1	-	-	82.5	0.5	-	-
1981	82.2	-0.4	-	-	81.2	-1.2	-	-	84.7	4.3	-	-	85.4	0.8	-	-	84.6	-0.9	-	-	85.2	0.7	-	-
1982	90.0	5.6	-	-	89.4	-0.7	-	-	91.6	2.5	-	-	92.7	1.2	-	-	96.6	4.2	-	-	99.3	2.8	-	-
1983	99.6	0.3	-	-	101.1	1.5	-	-	102.4	1.3	-	-	102.6	0.2	-	-	103.1	0.5	-	-	103.0	-0.1	-	-
1984	103.3	0.3	-	-	103.6	0.3	-	-	104.0	0.4	-	-	104.6	0.6	-	-	104.6	0.0	-	-	104.7	0.1	-	-
1985	105.7	1.0	-	-	106.2	0.5	-	-	106.7	0.5	-	-	107.4	0.7	-	-	106.7	-0.7	-	-	107.4	0.7	-	-
1986	107.8	0.4	-	-	108.5	0.6	-	-	109.1	0.6	-	-	109.3	0.2	-	-	107.3	-1.8	-	-	109.1	1.7	-	-
1987	-	-	-	-	-	-	-	-	-	-	110.8	1.6	-	-	-	-	-	-	-	-	-	-	113.3	2.3
1988	-	-	-	-	-	-	-	-	-	-	113.3	0.0	-	-	-	-	-	-	-	-	-	-	116.3	2.6
1989	-	-	-	-	-	-	-	-	-	-	118.5	1.9	-	-	-	-	-	-	-	-	-	-	119.8	1.1
1990	-	-	-	-	-	-	-	-	-	-	120.2	0.3	-	-	-	-	-	-	-	-	-	-	122.0	1.5
1991	-	-	-	-	-	-	-	-	-	-	125.5	2.9	-	-	-	-	-	-	-	-	-	-	127.4	1.5
1992	-	-	-	-	-	-	-	-	-	-	128.7	1.0	-	-	-	-	-	-	-	-	-	-	130.5	1.4
1993	-	-	-	-	-	-	-	-	-	-	130.1	-0.3	-	-	-	-	-	-	-	-	-	-	133.9	2.9
1994	-	-	-	-	-	-	-	-	-	-	134.3	0.3	-	-	-	-	-	-	-	-	-	-	136.1	1.3
1995	-	-	-	-	-	-	-	-	-	-	136.5	0.3	-	-	-	-	-	-	-	-	-	-	139.3	2.1
1996	-	-	-	-	-	-	-	-	-	-	140.9	1.1	-	-	-	-	-	-	-	-	-	-	143.2	1.6
1997	-	-	-	-	-	-	-	-	-	-	144.0	0.6	-	-	-	-	-	-	-	-	-	-	146.3	1.6
1998	-	-	-	-	-	-	-	-	-	-	148.7	1.6	-	-	-	-	-	-	-	-	-	-	151.2	1.7
1999	-	-	-	-	-	-	-	-	-	-	151.9	0.5	-	-	-	-	-	-	-	-	-	-	154.4	1.6
2000	-	-	-	-	-	-	-	-	-	-	155.8	0.9	-	-	-	-	-	-	-	-	-	-	160.6	3.1
2001	-	-	-	-	-	-	-	-	-	-	160.0	-0.4	-	-	-	-	-	-	-	-	-	-	-	-

Source: U.S. Department of Labor, Bureau of Labor Statistics, Division of Consumer Prices and Price Indexes. - indicates no data collected for period.

Cincinnati-Hamilton, OH-KY-IN
Consumer Price Index - Urban Wage Earners
Base 1982-1984 = 100
Housing

For 1975-2001. Columns headed % show percentile change in the index from the previous period for which an index is available.

Year	Jan Index	%	Feb Index	%	Mar Index	%	Apr Index	%	May Index	%	Jun Index	%	Jul Index	%	Aug Index	%	Sep Index	%	Oct Index	%	Nov Index	%	Dec Index	%
1975	-	-	-	-	-	-	-	-	-	-	-	-	-	-	-	-	-	-	-	-	-	-	50.2	-
1976	-	-	-	-	51.1	1.8	-	-	-	-	51.5	0.8	-	-	-	-	51.9	0.8	-	-	-	-	53.5	3.1
1977	-	-	-	-	54.3	1.5	-	-	-	-	55.2	1.7	-	-	-	-	56.5	2.4	-	-	-	-	57.2	1.2
1978	-	-	-	-	59.1	3.3	-	-	61.0	3.2	-	-	61.7	1.1	-	-	63.3	2.6	-	-	65.0	2.7	-	-
1979	66.2	1.8	-	-	68.3	3.2	-	-	69.9	2.3	-	-	71.0	1.6	-	-	72.3	1.8	-	-	74.8	3.5	-	-
1980	76.9	2.8	-	-	80.5	4.7	-	-	81.5	1.2	-	-	84.5	3.7	-	-	84.3	-0.2	-	-	84.7	0.5	-	-
1981	84.4	-0.4	-	-	83.2	-1.4	-	-	86.6	4.1	-	-	87.7	1.3	-	-	86.7	-1.1	-	-	87.5	0.9	-	-
1982	92.7	5.9	-	-	91.9	-0.9	-	-	94.3	2.6	-	-	95.5	1.3	-	-	99.7	4.4	-	-	102.7	3.0	-	-
1983	100.5	-2.1	-	-	102.3	1.8	-	-	102.3	0.0	-	-	100.7	-1.6	-	-	102.0	1.3	-	-	104.1	2.1	-	-
1984	101.4	-2.6	-	-	101.0	-0.4	-	-	99.1	-1.9	-	-	100.4	1.3	-	-	103.9	3.5	-	-	102.7	-1.2	-	-
1985	103.7	1.0	-	-	104.2	0.5	-	-	104.5	0.3	-	-	105.2	0.7	-	-	104.4	-0.8	-	-	105.2	0.8	-	-
1986	105.6	0.4	-	-	106.3	0.7	-	-	107.0	0.7	-	-	107.0	0.0	-	-	104.8	-2.1	-	-	106.8	1.9	-	-
1987	-	-	-	-	-	-	-	-	-	-	108.4	1.5	-	-	-	-	-	-	-	-	-	-	110.9	2.3
1988	-	-	-	-	-	-	-	-	-	-	110.8	-0.1	-	-	-	-	-	-	-	-	-	-	113.7	2.6
1989	-	-	-	-	-	-	-	-	-	-	115.7	1.8	-	-	-	-	-	-	-	-	-	-	117.1	1.2
1990	-	-	-	-	-	-	-	-	-	-	117.5	0.3	-	-	-	-	-	-	-	-	-	-	119.4	1.6
1991	-	-	-	-	-	-	-	-	-	-	122.7	2.8	-	-	-	-	-	-	-	-	-	-	124.7	1.6
1992	-	-	-	-	-	-	-	-	-	-	125.9	1.0	-	-	-	-	-	-	-	-	-	-	127.7	1.4
1993	-	-	-	-	-	-	-	-	-	-	127.3	-0.3	-	-	-	-	-	-	-	-	-	-	131.1	3.0
1994	-	-	-	-	-	-	-	-	-	-	131.4	0.2	-	-	-	-	-	-	-	-	-	-	133.3	1.4
1995	-	-	-	-	-	-	-	-	-	-	133.5	0.2	-	-	-	-	-	-	-	-	-	-	136.2	2.0
1996	-	-	-	-	-	-	-	-	-	-	137.7	1.1	-	-	-	-	-	-	-	-	-	-	140.0	1.7
1997	-	-	-	-	-	-	-	-	-	-	140.7	0.5	-	-	-	-	-	-	-	-	-	-	143.0	1.6
1998	-	-	-	-	-	-	-	-	-	-	145.3	1.6	-	-	-	-	-	-	-	-	-	-	147.5	1.5
1999	-	-	-	-	-	-	-	-	-	-	148.1	0.4	-	-	-	-	-	-	-	-	-	-	150.5	1.6
2000	-	-	-	-	-	-	-	-	-	-	151.9	0.9	-	-	-	-	-	-	-	-	-	-	156.5	3.0
2001	-	-	-	-	-	-	-	-	-	-	156.0	-0.3	-	-	-	-	-	-	-	-	-	-	-	-

Source: U.S. Department of Labor, Bureau of Labor Statistics, Division of Consumer Prices and Price Indexes. - indicates no data collected for period.

Cincinnati-Hamilton, OH-KY-IN
Consumer Price Index - All Urban Consumers
Base 1982-1984 = 100
Apparel

For 1952-2001. Columns headed % show percentile change in the index from the previous period for which an index is available.

Year	Jan Index	%	Feb Index	%	Mar Index	%	Apr Index	%	May Index	%	Jun Index	%	Jul Index	%	Aug Index	%	Sep Index	%	Oct Index	%	Nov Index	%	Dec Index	%
1952	-	-	-	-	-	-	-	-	-	-	-	-	-	-	-	-	-	-	-	-	-	-	36.9	-
1953	-	-	-	-	37.1	0.5	-	-	-	-	37.7	1.6	-	-	-	-	37.8	0.3	-	-	-	-	37.4	-1.1
1954	-	-	-	-	37.1	-0.8	-	-	-	-	37.0	-0.3	-	-	-	-	37.5	1.4	-	-	-	-	37.2	-0.8
1955	-	-	-	-	37.3	0.3	-	-	-	-	37.2	-0.3	-	-	-	-	38.0	2.2	-	-	-	-	38.1	0.3
1956	-	-	-	-	38.6	1.3	-	-	-	-	38.4	-0.5	-	-	-	-	38.8	1.0	-	-	-	-	38.7	-0.3
1957	-	-	-	-	38.6	-0.3	-	-	-	-	38.6	0.0	-	-	-	-	39.4	2.1	-	-	-	-	38.9	-1.3
1958	-	-	-	-	39.0	0.3	-	-	-	-	38.7	-0.8	-	-	-	-	39.3	1.6	-	-	-	-	39.3	0.0
1959	-	-	-	-	39.3	0.0	-	-	-	-	39.3	0.0	-	-	-	-	39.7	1.0	-	-	-	-	39.7	0.0
1960	-	-	-	-	39.8	0.3	-	-	-	-	40.1	0.8	-	-	-	-	40.6	1.2	-	-	-	-	40.2	-1.0
1961	-	-	-	-	40.2	0.0	-	-	-	-	39.9	-0.7	-	-	-	-	40.6	1.8	-	-	-	-	40.5	-0.2
1962	-	-	-	-	40.5	0.0	-	-	-	-	40.5	0.0	-	-	-	-	40.9	1.0	-	-	-	-	40.8	-0.2
1963	-	-	-	-	40.9	0.2	-	-	-	-	40.7	-0.5	-	-	-	-	41.3	1.5	-	-	-	-	41.2	-0.2
1964	-	-	-	-	41.3	0.2	-	-	-	-	41.4	0.2	-	-	-	-	41.9	1.2	-	-	-	-	41.4	-1.2
1965	-	-	-	-	41.5	0.2	-	-	-	-	41.5	0.0	-	-	-	-	42.1	1.4	-	-	-	-	42.1	0.0
1966	-	-	-	-	42.7	1.4	-	-	-	-	43.3	1.4	-	-	-	-	44.0	1.6	-	-	-	-	44.0	0.0
1967	-	-	-	-	44.4	0.9	-	-	-	-	44.3	-0.2	-	-	-	-	45.7	3.2	-	-	-	-	46.0	0.7
1968	-	-	-	-	46.9	2.0	-	-	-	-	47.3	0.9	-	-	-	-	49.8	5.3	-	-	-	-	49.9	0.2
1969	-	-	-	-	50.3	0.8	-	-	-	-	50.9	1.2	-	-	-	-	52.3	2.8	-	-	-	-	52.3	0.0
1970	-	-	-	-	52.8	1.0	-	-	-	-	53.1	0.6	-	-	-	-	54.1	1.9	-	-	-	-	54.9	1.5
1971	-	-	-	-	55.2	0.5	-	-	-	-	54.7	-0.9	-	-	-	-	55.2	0.9	-	-	-	-	54.9	-0.5
1972	-	-	-	-	54.6	-0.5	-	-	-	-	54.7	0.2	-	-	-	-	55.9	2.2	-	-	-	-	56.2	0.5
1973	-	-	-	-	56.7	0.9	-	-	-	-	56.8	0.2	-	-	-	-	58.5	3.0	-	-	-	-	59.1	1.0
1974	-	-	-	-	59.8	1.2	-	-	-	-	60.8	1.7	-	-	-	-	63.5	4.4	-	-	-	-	63.7	0.3
1975	-	-	-	-	64.0	0.5	-	-	-	-	63.3	-1.1	-	-	-	-	65.6	3.6	-	-	-	-	66.1	0.8
1976	-	-	-	-	68.0	2.9	-	-	-	-	67.9	-0.1	-	-	-	-	70.6	4.0	-	-	-	-	70.0	-0.8
1977	-	-	-	-	71.1	1.6	-	-	-	-	71.1	0.0	-	-	-	-	73.9	3.9	-	-	-	-	74.7	1.1
1978	-	-	-	-	75.8	1.5	-	-	78.7	3.8	-	-	76.7	-2.5	-	-	78.9	2.9	-	-	80.0	1.4	-	-
1979	80.3	0.4	-	-	78.0	-2.9	-	-	83.1	6.5	-	-	81.5	-1.9	-	-	84.4	3.6	-	-	83.5	-1.1	-	-
1980	86.2	3.2	-	-	88.8	3.0	-	-	88.5	-0.3	-	-	85.2	-3.7	-	-	92.9	9.0	-	-	92.4	-0.5	-	-
1981	89.5	-3.1	-	-	94.7	5.8	-	-	91.5	-3.4	-	-	88.8	-3.0	-	-	97.7	10.0	-	-	96.9	-0.8	-	-
1982	94.3	-2.7	-	-	98.4	4.3	-	-	96.7	-1.7	-	-	95.5	-1.2	-	-	100.4	5.1	-	-	98.9	-1.5	-	-
1983	101.1	2.2	-	-	100.9	-0.2	-	-	98.6	-2.3	-	-	99.5	0.9	-	-	102.6	3.1	-	-	102.1	-0.5	-	-
1984	97.3	-4.7	-	-	101.5	4.3	-	-	102.7	1.2	-	-	101.8	-0.9	-	-	104.4	2.6	-	-	101.6	-2.7	-	-
1985	101.7	0.1	-	-	103.6	1.9	-	-	102.7	-0.9	-	-	98.0	-4.6	-	-	105.4	7.6	-	-	108.6	3.0	-	-
1986	103.3	-4.9	-	-	103.8	0.5	-	-	102.7	-1.1	-	-	101.7	-1.0	-	-	111.3	9.4	-	-	109.3	-1.8	-	-
1987	-	-	-	-	-	-	-	-	-	-	112.9	3.3	-	-	-	-	-	-	-	-	-	-	118.7	5.1
1988	-	-	-	-	-	-	-	-	-	-	120.9	1.9	-	-	-	-	-	-	-	-	-	-	129.4	7.0
1989	-	-	-	-	-	-	-	-	-	-	124.4	-3.9	-	-	-	-	-	-	-	-	-	-	114.9	-7.6
1990	-	-	-	-	-	-	-	-	-	-	121.5	5.7	-	-	-	-	-	-	-	-	-	-	121.0	-0.4
1991	-	-	-	-	-	-	-	-	-	-	120.1	-0.7	-	-	-	-	-	-	-	-	-	-	123.1	2.5
1992	-	-	-	-	-	-	-	-	-	-	127.1	3.2	-	-	-	-	-	-	-	-	-	-	136.6	7.5
1993	-	-	-	-	-	-	-	-	-	-	143.6	5.1	-	-	-	-	-	-	-	-	-	-	133.6	-7.0
1994	-	-	-	-	-	-	-	-	-	-	136.8	2.4	-	-	-	-	-	-	-	-	-	-	144.3	5.5
1995	-	-	-	-	-	-	-	-	-	-	139.2	-3.5	-	-	-	-	-	-	-	-	-	-	137.9	-0.9
1996	-	-	-	-	-	-	-	-	-	-	133.0	-3.6	-	-	-	-	-	-	-	-	-	-	130.6	-1.8
1997	-	-	-	-	-	-	-	-	-	-	130.8	0.2	-	-	-	-	-	-	-	-	-	-	134.6	2.9

[Continued]

Cincinnati-Hamilton, OH-KY-IN
Consumer Price Index - All Urban Consumers
Base 1982-1984 = 100
Apparel
[Continued]

For 1952-2001. Columns headed % show percentile change in the index from the previous period for which an index is available.

Year	Jan		Feb		Mar		Apr		May		Jun		Jul		Aug		Sep		Oct		Nov		Dec	
	Index	%	Index	%	Index	%	Index	%	Index	%	Index	%	Index	%	Index	%	Index	%	Index	%	Index	%	Index	%
1998	-	-	-	-	-	-	-	-	-	-	130.8	-2.8	-	-	-	-	-	-	-	-	-	-	127.1	-2.8
1999	-	-	-	-	-	-	-	-	-	-	129.1	1.6	-	-	-	-	-	-	-	-	-	-	131.2	1.6
2000	-	-	-	-	-	-	-	-	-	-	124.2	-5.3	-	-	-	-	-	-	-	-	-	-	130.2	4.8
2001	-	-	-	-	-	-	-	-	-	-	126.4	-2.9	-	-	-	-	-	-	-	-	-	-	-	-

Source: U.S. Department of Labor, Bureau of Labor Statistics, Division of Consumer Prices and Price Indexes. - indicates no data collected for period.

Cincinnati-Hamilton, OH-KY-IN
Consumer Price Index - Urban Wage Earners
Base 1982-1984 = 100
Apparel

For 1952-2001. Columns headed % show percentile change in the index from the previous period for which an index is available.

Year	Jan Index	%	Feb Index	%	Mar Index	%	Apr Index	%	May Index	%	Jun Index	%	Jul Index	%	Aug Index	%	Sep Index	%	Oct Index	%	Nov Index	%	Dec Index	%
1952	-	-	-	-	-	-	-	-	-	-	-	-	-	-	-	-	-	-	-	-	-	-	35.8	-
1953	-	-	-	-	36.1	0.8	-	-	-	-	36.6	1.4	-	-	-	-	36.7	0.3	-	-	-	-	36.3	-1.1
1954	-	-	-	-	36.1	-0.6	-	-	-	-	35.9	-0.6	-	-	-	-	36.4	1.4	-	-	-	-	36.1	-0.8
1955	-	-	-	-	36.2	0.3	-	-	-	-	36.1	-0.3	-	-	-	-	36.9	2.2	-	-	-	-	37.0	0.3
1956	-	-	-	-	37.5	1.4	-	-	-	-	37.2	-0.8	-	-	-	-	37.6	1.1	-	-	-	-	37.6	0.0
1957	-	-	-	-	37.5	-0.3	-	-	-	-	37.5	0.0	-	-	-	-	38.2	1.9	-	-	-	-	37.8	-1.0
1958	-	-	-	-	37.9	0.3	-	-	-	-	37.5	-1.1	-	-	-	-	38.2	1.9	-	-	-	-	38.2	0.0
1959	-	-	-	-	38.2	0.0	-	-	-	-	38.2		-	-	-	-	38.6	1.0	-	-	-	-	38.5	-0.3
1960	-	-	-	-	38.7	0.5	-	-	-	-	38.9	0.5	-	-	-	-	39.4	1.3	-	-	-	-	39.0	-1.0
1961	-	-	-	-	39.0	0.0	-	-	-	-	38.8	-0.5	-	-	-	-	39.4	1.5	-	-	-	-	39.3	-0.3
1962	-	-	-	-	39.3	0.0	-	-	-	-	39.3	0.0	-	-	-	-	39.7	1.0	-	-	-	-	39.6	-0.3
1963	-	-	-	-	39.7	0.3	-	-	-	-	39.6	-0.3	-	-	-	-	40.1	1.3	-	-	-	-	40.0	-0.2
1964	-	-	-	-	40.1	0.2	-	-	-	-	40.2	0.2	-	-	-	-	40.6	1.0	-	-	-	-	40.2	-1.0
1965	-	-	-	-	40.3	0.2	-	-	-	-	40.3	0.0	-	-	-	-	40.9	1.5	-	-	-	-	40.9	0.0
1966	-	-	-	-	41.4	1.2	-	-	-	-	42.0	1.4	-	-	-	-	42.7	1.7	-	-	-	-	42.7	0.0
1967	-	-	-	-	43.1	0.9	-	-	-	-	43.1	0.0	-	-	-	-	44.4	3.0	-	-	-	-	44.7	0.7
1968	-	-	-	-	45.5	1.8	-	-	-	-	46.0	1.1	-	-	-	-	48.4	5.2	-	-	-	-	48.4	0.0
1969	-	-	-	-	48.9	1.0	-	-	-	-	49.4	1.0	-	-	-	-	50.8	2.8	-	-	-	-	50.8	0.0
1970	-	-	-	-	51.3	1.0	-	-	-	-	51.5	0.4	-	-	-	-	52.6	2.1	-	-	-	-	53.3	1.3
1971	-	-	-	-	53.6	0.6	-	-	-	-	53.1	-0.9	-	-	-	-	53.6	0.9	-	-	-	-	53.3	-0.6
1972	-	-	-	-	53.0	-0.6	-	-	-	-	53.1	0.2	-	-	-	-	54.3	2.3	-	-	-	-	54.6	0.6
1973	-	-	-	-	55.1	0.9	-	-	-	-	55.1	0.0	-	-	-	-	56.8	3.1	-	-	-	-	57.4	1.1
1974	-	-	-	-	58.0	1.0	-	-	-	-	59.1	1.9	-	-	-	-	61.7	4.4	-	-	-	-	61.9	0.3
1975	-	-	-	-	62.1	0.3	-	-	-	-	61.5	-1.0	-	-	-	-	63.7	3.6	-	-	-	-	64.2	0.8
1976	-	-	-	-	66.0	2.8	-	-	-	-	66.0	0.0	-	-	-	-	68.5	3.8	-	-	-	-	67.9	-0.9
1977	-	-	-	-	69.1	1.8	-	-	-	-	69.1	0.0	-	-	-	-	71.7	3.8	-	-	-	-	72.5	1.1
1978	-	-	-	-	73.6	1.5	-	-	76.3	3.7	-	-	74.8	-2.0	-	-	77.7	3.9	-	-	77.6	-0.1	-	-
1979	79.5	2.4	-	-	76.6	-3.6	-	-	82.2	7.3	-	-	80.2	-2.4	-	-	83.6	4.2	-	-	83.4	-0.2	-	-
1980	81.9	-1.8	-	-	84.7	3.4	-	-	83.9	-0.9	-	-	85.5	1.9	-	-	90.9	6.3	-	-	91.1	0.2	-	-
1981	88.1	-3.3	-	-	92.7	5.2	-	-	91.2	-1.6	-	-	92.0	0.9	-	-	97.2	5.7	-	-	96.2	-1.0	-	-
1982	93.6	-2.7	-	-	97.7	4.4	-	-	96.8	-0.9	-	-	95.8	-1.0	-	-	100.9	5.3	-	-	99.1	-1.8	-	-
1983	100.2	1.1	-	-	101.7	1.5	-	-	98.6	-3.0	-	-	99.2	0.6	-	-	103.5	4.3	-	-	102.5	-1.0	-	-
1984	98.6	-3.8	-	-	101.7	3.1	-	-	102.3	0.6	-	-	100.8	-1.5	-	-	104.2	3.4	-	-	101.2	-2.9	-	-
1985	101.3	0.1	-	-	103.2	1.9	-	-	101.7	-1.5	-	-	97.2	-4.4	-	-	104.9	7.9	-	-	106.6	1.6	-	-
1986	101.9	-4.4	-	-	102.6	0.7	-	-	101.7	-0.9	-	-	102.6	0.9	-	-	109.5	6.7	-	-	108.2	-1.2	-	-
1987	-	-	-	-	-	-	-	-	-	-	109.2	0.9	-	-	-	-	-	-	-	-	-	-	113.8	4.2
1988	-	-	-	-	-	-	-	-	-	-	116.7	2.5	-	-	-	-	-	-	-	-	-	-	126.2	8.1
1989	-	-	-	-	-	-	-	-	-	-	119.8	-5.1	-	-	-	-	-	-	-	-	-	-	111.7	-6.8
1990	-	-	-	-	-	-	-	-	-	-	118.3	5.9	-	-	-	-	-	-	-	-	-	-	118.4	0.1
1991	-	-	-	-	-	-	-	-	-	-	116.9	-1.3	-	-	-	-	-	-	-	-	-	-	119.3	2.1
1992	-	-	-	-	-	-	-	-	-	-	123.5	3.5	-	-	-	-	-	-	-	-	-	-	133.1	7.8
1993	-	-	-	-	-	-	-	-	-	-	136.9	2.9	-	-	-	-	-	-	-	-	-	-	129.4	-5.5
1994	-	-	-	-	-	-	-	-	-	-	134.4	3.9	-	-	-	-	-	-	-	-	-	-	139.3	3.6
1995	-	-	-	-	-	-	-	-	-	-	137.6	-1.2	-	-	-	-	-	-	-	-	-	-	133.8	-2.8
1996	-	-	-	-	-	-	-	-	-	-	130.4	-2.5	-	-	-	-	-	-	-	-	-	-	127.8	-2.0
1997	-	-	-	-	-	-	-	-	-	-	129.1	1.0	-	-	-	-	-	-	-	-	-	-	131.9	2.2

[Continued]

Cincinnati-Hamilton, OH-KY-IN
Consumer Price Index - Urban Wage Earners
Base 1982-1984 = 100
Apparel
[Continued]

For 1952-2001. Columns headed % show percentile change in the index from the previous period for which an index is available.

Year	Jan Index	%	Feb Index	%	Mar Index	%	Apr Index	%	May Index	%	Jun Index	%	Jul Index	%	Aug Index	%	Sep Index	%	Oct Index	%	Nov Index	%	Dec Index	%
1998	-	-	-	-	-	-	-	-	-	-	128.3	-2.7	-	-	-	-	-	-	-	-	-	-	124.8	-2.7
1999	-	-	-	-	-	-	-	-	-	-	127.0	1.8	-	-	-	-	-	-	-	-	-	-	128.9	1.5
2000	-	-	-	-	-	-	-	-	-	-	122.2	-5.2	-	-	-	-	-	-	-	-	-	-	128.6	5.2
2001	-	-	-	-	-	-	-	-	-	-	124.8	-3.0	-	-	-	-	-	-	-	-	-	-	-	-

Source: U.S. Department of Labor, Bureau of Labor Statistics, Division of Consumer Prices and Price Indexes. - indicates no data collected for period.

Cincinnati-Hamilton, OH-KY-IN
Consumer Price Index - All Urban Consumers
Base 1982-1984 = 100
Transportation

For 1947-2001. Columns headed % show percentile change in the index from the previous period for which an index is available.

Year	Jan Index	%	Feb Index	%	Mar Index	%	Apr Index	%	May Index	%	Jun Index	%	Jul Index	%	Aug Index	%	Sep Index	%	Oct Index	%	Nov Index	%	Dec Index	%
1947	19.8	-	19.8	0.0	20.2	2.0	20.2	0.0	20.2	0.0	20.2	0.0	20.5	1.5	20.5	0.0	21.0	2.4	21.0	0.0	21.9	4.3	22.1	0.9
1948	22.2	0.5	22.2	0.0	22.2	0.0	22.2	0.0	22.2	0.0	22.7	2.3	23.8	4.8	24.2	1.7	24.3	0.4	24.3	0.0	24.3	0.0	24.3	0.0
1949	24.3	0.0	24.6	1.2	25.2	2.4	25.3	0.4	25.3	0.0	25.2	-0.4	25.2	0.0	25.2	0.0	25.2	0.0	25.2	0.0	25.2	0.0	25.1	-0.4
1950	25.1	0.0	25.1	0.0	25.1	0.0	24.9	-0.8	25.6	2.8	25.6	0.0	25.7	0.4	26.0	1.2	26.0	0.0	26.0	0.0	26.0	0.0	26.1	0.4
1951	26.7	2.3	26.7	0.0	27.0	1.1	27.0	0.0	27.0	0.0	27.0	0.0	27.0	0.0	27.4	1.5	28.1	2.6	28.3	0.7	28.6	1.1	28.6	0.0
1952	28.6	0.0	28.9	1.0	28.9	0.0	28.8	-0.3	29.4	2.1	29.4	0.0	29.4	0.0	29.4	0.0	29.4	0.0	29.4	0.0	29.4	0.0	29.4	0.0
1953	-		-		30.0	2.0	-		-		29.9	-0.3	-		-		30.2	1.0	-		-		30.0	-0.7
1954	-		-		29.4	-2.0	-		-		29.1	-1.0	-		-		29.2	0.3	-		-		28.4	-2.7
1955	-		-		28.5	0.4	-		-		28.3	-0.7	-		-		27.7	-2.1	-		-		28.1	1.4
1956	-		-		27.8	-1.1	-		-		28.1	1.1	-		-		28.5	1.4	-		-		29.5	3.5
1957	-		-		29.7	0.7	-		-		29.9	0.7	-		-		30.4	1.7	-		-		30.7	1.0
1958	-		-		30.4	-1.0	-		-		30.4	0.0	-		-		30.6	0.7	-		-		32.1	4.9
1959	-		-		32.5	1.2	-		-		32.8	0.9	-		-		32.7	-0.3	-		-		34.1	4.3
1960	-		-		33.5	-1.8	-		-		32.9	-1.8	-		-		32.8	-0.3	-		-		32.8	0.0
1961	-		-		32.8	0.0	-		-		33.3	1.5	-		-		33.6	0.9	-		-		32.9	-2.1
1962	-		-		33.8	2.7	-		-		33.8	0.0	-		-		33.9	0.3	-		-		33.8	-0.3
1963	-		-		33.9	0.3	-		-		33.8	-0.3	-		-		34.0	0.6	-		-		34.2	0.6
1964	-		-		34.4	0.6	-		-		34.4	0.0	-		-		34.5	0.3	-		-		34.5	0.0
1965	-		-		34.3	-0.6	--		-		34.5	0.6	-		-		34.6	0.3	-		-		34.8	0.6
1966	-		-		34.7	-0.3	-		-		35.1	1.2	-		-		35.5	1.1	-		-		35.3	-0.6
1967	-		-		35.1	-0.6	-		-		35.6	1.4	-		-		36.2	1.7	-		-		37.2	2.8
1968	-		-		37.4	0.5	-		-		37.9	1.3	-		-		37.9	0.0	-		-		37.6	-0.8
1969	-		-		38.9	3.5	-		-		38.9	0.0	-		-		38.5	-1.0	-		-		39.4	2.3
1970	-		-		39.0	-1.0	-		-		40.8	4.6	-		-		41.1	0.7	-		-		42.9	4.4
1971	-		-		42.3	-1.4	-		-		43.3	2.4	-		-		43.1	-0.5	-		-		43.6	1.2
1972	-		-		42.7	-2.1	-		-		44.5	4.2	-		-		45.6	2.5	-		-		45.2	-0.9
1973	-		-		45.5	0.7	-		-		43.8	-3.7	-		-		43.6	-0.5	-		-		43.8	0.5
1974	-		-		45.1	3.0	-		-		48.4	7.3	-		-		49.6	2.5	-		-		49.6	0.0
1975	-		-		49.7	0.2	-		-		51.7	4.0	-		-		53.3	3.1	-		-		53.2	-0.2
1976	-		-		53.2	0.0	-		-		56.5	6.2	-		-		57.5	1.8	-		-		58.2	1.2
1977	-		-		59.4	2.1	-		-		60.9	2.5	-		-		60.2	-1.1	-		-		60.1	-0.2
1978	-		-		60.7	1.0	-		61.7	1.6	-		62.9	1.9	-		63.5	1.0	-		64.5	1.6	-	
1979	65.2	1.1	-		66.4	1.8	-		69.6	4.8	-		72.6	4.3	-		75.1	3.4	-		76.5	1.9	-	
1980	79.0	3.3	-		81.3	2.9	-		83.6	2.8	-		85.0	1.7	-		86.1	1.3	-		87.2	1.3	-	
1981	89.8	3.0	-		92.2	2.7	-		93.5	1.4	-		94.0	0.5	-		95.0	1.1	-		96.3	1.4	-	
1982	97.2	0.9	-		95.4	-1.9	-		95.2	-0.2	-		98.8	3.8	-		98.5	-0.3	-		98.4	-0.1	-	
1983	98.0	-0.4	-		95.8	-2.2	-		99.1	3.4	-		100.0	0.9	-		101.4	1.4	-		102.6	1.2	-	
1984	101.8	-0.8	-		101.7	-0.1	-		102.9	1.2	-		103.2	0.3	-		103.7	0.5	-		104.8	1.1	-	
1985	103.3	-1.4	-		104.8	1.5	-		107.2	2.3	-		107.1	-0.1	-		105.4	-1.6	-		107.6	2.1	-	
1986	106.8	-0.7	-		98.4	-7.9	-		100.4	2.0	-		97.8	-2.6	-		98.0	0.2	-		98.7	0.7	-	
1987	-		-		-		-		-		101.7	3.0	-		-		-		-		-		104.0	2.3
1988	-		-		-		-		-		103.3	-0.7	-		-		-		-		-		106.3	2.9
1989	-		-		-		-		-		109.9	3.4	-		-		-		-		-		112.5	2.4
1990	-		-		-		-		-		115.0	2.2	-		-		-		-		-		120.4	4.7
1991	-		-		-		-		-		119.6	-0.7	-		-		-		-		-		120.7	0.9
1992	-		-		-		-		-		118.5	-1.8	-		-		-		-		-		119.1	0.5

[Continued]

Cincinnati-Hamilton, OH-KY-IN
Consumer Price Index - All Urban Consumers
Base 1982-1984 = 100
Transportation
[Continued]

For 1947-2001. Columns headed % show percentile change in the index from the previous period for which an index is available.

Year	Jan Index	%	Feb Index	%	Mar Index	%	Apr Index	%	May Index	%	Jun Index	%	Jul Index	%	Aug Index	%	Sep Index	%	Oct Index	%	Nov Index	%	Dec Index	%
1993	-		-		-		-		-		120.6	1.3	-		-		-		-		-		121.8	1.0
1994	-		-		-		-		-		127.0	4.3	-		-		-		-		-		131.9	3.9
1995	-		-		-		-		-		135.4	2.7	-		-		-		-		-		134.7	-0.5
1996	-		-		-		-		-		137.8	2.3	-		-		-		-		-		139.3	1.1
1997	-		-		-		-		-		138.5	-0.6	-		-		-		-		-		136.8	-1.2
1998	-		-		-		-		-		135.9	-0.7	-		-		-		-		-		137.3	1.0
1999	-		-		-		-		-		138.6	0.9	-		-		-		-		-		143.3	3.4
2000	-		-		-		-		-		148.2	3.4	-		-		-		-		-		149.5	0.9
2001	-		-		-		-		-		150.8	0.9	-		-		-		-		-		-	-

Source: U.S. Department of Labor, Bureau of Labor Statistics, Division of Consumer Prices and Price Indexes. - indicates no data collected for period.

Cincinnati-Hamilton, OH-KY-IN
Consumer Price Index - Urban Wage Earners
Base 1982-1984 = 100
Transportation

For 1947-2001. Columns headed % show percentile change in the index from the previous period for which an index is available.

Year	Jan Index	%	Feb Index	%	Mar Index	%	Apr Index	%	May Index	%	Jun Index	%	Jul Index	%	Aug Index	%	Sep Index	%	Oct Index	%	Nov Index	%	Dec Index	%
1947	20.0	-	20.0	0.0	20.4	2.0	20.4	0.0	20.4	0.0	20.4	0.0	20.7	1.5	20.8	0.5	21.2	1.9	21.2	0.0	22.1	4.2	22.3	0.9
1948	22.5	0.9	22.5	0.0	22.5	0.0	22.5	0.0	22.5	0.0	22.9	1.8	24.0	4.8	24.4	1.7	24.6	0.8	24.6	0.0	24.6	0.0	24.6	0.0
1949	24.6	0.0	24.8	0.8	25.4	2.4	25.5	0.4	25.5	0.0	25.5	0.0	25.4	-0.4	25.5	0.4	25.5	0.0	25.5	0.0	25.5	0.0	25.4	-0.4
1950	25.3	-0.4	25.3	0.0	25.3	0.0	25.2	-0.4	25.8	2.4	25.9	0.4	26.0	0.4	26.3	1.2	26.3	0.0	26.3	0.0	26.3	0.0	26.3	0.0
1951	26.9	2.3	27.0	0.4	27.3	1.1	27.3	0.0	27.3	0.0	27.3	0.0	27.3	0.0	27.6	1.1	28.4	2.9	28.6	0.7	28.9	1.0	28.9	0.0
1952	28.9	0.0	29.2	1.0	29.2	0.0	29.1	-0.3	29.7	2.1	29.7	0.0	29.7	0.0	29.7	0.0	29.7	0.0	29.7	0.0	29.7	0.0	30.3	-0.7
1953	-		-		30.3	2.0	-		-		30.2	-0.3	-		-		30.5	1.0	-		-		30.3	-0.7
1954	-		-		29.7	-2.0	-		-		29.4	-1.0	-		-		29.5	0.3	-		-		28.7	-2.7
1955	-		-		28.8	0.3	-		-		28.6	-0.7	-		-		28.0	-2.1	-		-		28.4	1.4
1956	-		-		28.1	-1.1	-		-		28.4	1.1	-		-		28.8	1.4	-		-		29.8	3.5
1957	-		-		30.0	0.7	-		-		30.2	0.7	-		-		30.7	1.7	-		-		31.0	1.0
1958	-		-		30.7	-1.0	-		-		30.7	0.0	-		-		30.9	0.7	-		-		32.4	4.9
1959	-		-		32.8	1.2	-		-		33.2	1.2	-		-		33.0	-0.6	-		-		34.4	4.2
1960	-		-		33.8	-1.7	-		-		33.3	-1.5	-		-		33.1	-0.6	-		-		33.2	0.3
1961	-		-		33.2	0.0	-		-		33.6	1.2	-		-		33.9	0.9	-		-		33.2	-2.1
1962	-		-		34.1	2.7	-		-		34.2	0.3	-		-		34.2	0.0	-		-		34.2	0.0
1963	-		-		34.2	0.0	-		-		34.2	0.0	-		-		34.3	0.3	-		-		34.5	0.6
1964	-		-		34.7	0.6	-		-		34.8	0.3	-		-		34.9	0.3	-		-		34.8	-0.3
1965	-		-		34.6	-0.6	-		-		34.8	0.6	-		-		35.0	0.6	-		-		35.1	0.3
1966	-		-		35.1	0.0	-		-		35.5	1.1	-		-		35.8	0.8	-		-		35.6	-0.6
1967	-		-		35.4	-0.6	-		-		36.0	1.7	-		-		36.6	1.7	-		-		37.6	2.7
1968	-		-		37.8	0.5	-		-		38.3	1.3	-		-		38.3	0.0	-		-		38.0	-0.8
1969	-		-		39.3	3.4	-		-		39.3	0.0	-		-		38.9	-1.0	-		-		39.8	2.3
1970	-		-		39.4	-1.0	-		-		41.2	4.6	-		-		41.5	0.7	-		-		43.3	4.3
1971	-		-		42.8	-1.2	-		-		43.7	2.1	-		-		43.5	-0.5	-		-		44.1	1.4
1972	-		-		43.2	-2.0	-		-		45.0	4.2	-		-		46.1	2.4	-		-		45.6	-1.1
1973	-		-		46.0	0.9	-		-		44.3	-3.7	-		-		44.0	-0.7	-		-		44.2	0.5
1974	-		-		45.6	3.2	-		-		48.9	7.2	-		-		50.1	2.5	-		-		50.1	0.0
1975	-		-		50.2	0.2	-		-		52.2	4.0	-		-		53.8	3.1	-		-		53.8	0.0
1976	-		-		53.7	-0.2	-		-		57.1	6.3	-		-		58.1	1.8	-		-		58.8	1.2
1977	-		-		60.0	2.0	-		-		61.5	2.5	-		-		60.8	-1.1	-		-		60.7	-0.2
1978	-		-		61.3	1.0	-		62.3	1.6	-		63.7	2.2	-		63.9	0.3	-		65.1	1.9	-	
1979	65.8	1.1	-		67.0	1.8	-		70.2	4.8	-		73.1	4.1	-		75.5	3.3	-		77.0	2.0	-	
1980	79.6	3.4	-		82.2	3.3	-		83.9	2.1	-		85.6	2.0	-		86.0	0.5	-		87.0	1.2	-	
1981	89.7	3.1	-		92.6	3.2	-		93.6	1.1	-		94.6	1.1	-		95.3	0.7	-		96.4	1.2	-	
1982	97.3	0.9	-		95.6	-1.7	-		95.4	-0.2	-		98.9	3.7	-		98.5	-0.4	-		98.5	0.0	-	
1983	98.2	-0.3	-		96.1	-2.1	-		99.1	3.1	-		99.9	0.8	-		101.3	1.4	-		102.6	1.3	-	
1984	101.7	-0.9	-		101.6	-0.1	-		102.8	1.2	-		103.0	0.2	-		103.5	0.5	-		104.6	1.1	-	
1985	103.1	-1.4	-		104.6	1.5	-		106.9	2.2	-		106.7	-0.2	-		105.0	-1.6	-		107.3	2.2	-	
1986	106.5	-0.7	-		98.4	-7.6	-		100.4	2.0	-		97.7	-2.7	-		97.9	0.2	-		98.7	0.8	-	
1987	-		-		-		-		-		101.9	3.2	-		-		-		-		-		104.4	2.5
1988	-		-		-		-		-		104.0	-0.4	-		-		-		-		-		107.1	3.0
1989	-		-		-		-		-		110.8	3.5	-		-		-		-		-		113.6	2.5
1990	-		-		-		-		-		116.1	2.2	-		-		-		-		-		121.7	4.8
1991	-		-		-		-		-		120.5	-1.0	-		-		-		-		-		121.8	1.1
1992	-		-		-		-		-		119.5	-1.9	-		-		-		-		-		120.9	1.2

[Continued]

Cincinnati-Hamilton, OH-KY-IN
Consumer Price Index - Urban Wage Earners
Base 1982-1984 = 100
Transportation
[Continued]

For 1947-2001. Columns headed % show percentile change in the index from the previous period for which an index is available.

Year	Jan Index	%	Feb Index	%	Mar Index	%	Apr Index	%	May Index	%	Jun Index	%	Jul Index	%	Aug Index	%	Sep Index	%	Oct Index	%	Nov Index	%	Dec Index	%
1993	-		-		-		-		-		122.1	1.0	-		-		-		-		-		123.6	1.2
1994	-		-		-		-		-		128.3	3.8	-		-		-		-		-		133.7	4.2
1995	-		-		-		-		-		137.5	2.8	-		-		-		-		-		137.2	-0.2
1996	-		-		-		-		-		141.1	2.8	-		-		-		-		-		142.7	1.1
1997	-		-		-		-		-		142.2	-0.4	-		-		-		-		-		140.2	-1.4
1998	-		-		-		-		-		139.0	-0.9	-		-		-		-		-		141.0	1.4
1999	-		-		-		-		-		141.7	0.5	-		-		-		-		-		147.7	4.2
2000	-		-		-		-		-		152.7	3.4	-		-		-		-		-		154.7	1.3
2001	-		-		-		-		-		155.9	0.8	-		-		-		-		-		-	

Source: U.S. Department of Labor, Bureau of Labor Statistics, Division of Consumer Prices and Price Indexes. - indicates no data collected for period.

Cincinnati-Hamilton, OH-KY-IN
Consumer Price Index - All Urban Consumers
Base 1982-1984 = 100
Medical Care

For 1947-2001. Columns headed % show percentile change in the index from the previous period for which an index is available.

Year	Jan Index	%	Feb Index	%	Mar Index	%	Apr Index	%	May Index	%	Jun Index	%	Jul Index	%	Aug Index	%	Sep Index	%	Oct Index	%	Nov Index	%	Dec Index	%
1947	11.3	-	11.3	0.0	11.3	0.0	11.4	0.9	11.6	1.8	11.7	0.9	12.1	3.4	12.2	0.8	12.2	0.0	12.3	0.8	12.3	0.0	12.4	0.8
1948	12.8	3.2	12.7	-0.8	12.7	0.0	13.1	3.1	13.1	0.0	13.1	0.0	13.2	0.8	13.2	0.0	13.2	0.0	13.2	0.0	13.2	0.0	13.2	0.0
1949	13.2	0.0	13.2	0.0	13.4	1.5	13.4	0.0	13.4	0.0	13.5	0.7	13.5	0.0	13.5	0.0	13.5	0.0	13.5	0.0	13.5	0.0	13.5	0.0
1950	13.5	0.0	13.5	0.0	13.5	0.0	13.5	0.0	13.5	0.0	13.5	0.0	13.5	0.0	13.5	0.0	13.5	0.0	13.5	0.0	13.5	0.0	13.6	0.7
1951	13.6	0.0	13.6	0.0	13.7	0.7	13.7	0.0	13.7	0.0	13.8	0.7	13.8	0.0	13.8	0.0	13.9	0.7	13.9	0.0	13.9	0.0	14.6	5.0
1952	14.6	0.0	14.7	0.7	14.9	1.4	14.9	0.0	14.9	0.0	14.9	0.0	15.0	0.7	15.0	0.0	15.0	0.0	15.0	0.0	15.0	0.0	15.0	0.0
1953	-		-		15.5	3.3	-		-		15.5	0.0	-		-		15.7	1.3	-		-		15.9	1.3
1954	-		-		15.9	0.0	-		-		15.9	0.0	-		-		15.9	0.0	-		-		16.1	1.3
1955	-		-		16.3	1.2	-		-		16.3	0.0	-		-		16.3	0.0	-		-		17.5	7.4
1956	-		-		17.5	0.0	-		-		17.5	0.0	-		-		17.5	0.0	-		-		17.6	0.6
1957	-		-		17.8	1.1	-		-		17.9	0.6	-		-		17.9	0.0	-		-		19.0	6.1
1958	-		-		19.0	0.0	-		-		19.0	0.0	-		-		19.0	0.0	-		-		19.4	2.1
1959	-		-		19.3	-0.5	-		-		19.7	2.1	-		-		19.7	0.0	-		-		19.7	0.0
1960	-		-		19.8	0.5	-		-		19.8	0.0	-		-		20.0	1.0	-		-		20.4	2.0
1961	-		-		20.5	0.5	-		-		20.6	0.5	-		-		20.7	0.5	-		-		20.7	0.0
1962	-		-		20.7	0.0	-		-		20.8	0.5	-		-		21.5	3.4	-		-		21.5	0.0
1963	-		-		21.7	0.9	-		-		21.9	0.9	-		-		21.9	0.0	-		-		21.9	0.0
1964	-		-		22.2	1.4	-		-		22.3	0.5	-		-		22.3	0.0	-		-		23.5	5.4
1965	-		-		23.6	0.4	-		-		23.9	1.3	-		-		23.9	0.0	-		-		24.2	1.3
1966	-		-		24.6	1.7	-		-		24.9	1.2	-		-		25.1	0.8	-		-		25.6	2.0
1967	-		-		26.5	3.5	-		-		26.6	0.4	-		-		27.0	1.5	-		-		27.4	1.5
1968	-		-		28.5	4.0	-		-		28.7	0.7	-		-		29.0	1.0	-		-		29.4	1.4
1969	-		-		30.8	4.8	-		-		31.2	1.3	-		-		31.7	1.6	-		-		31.7	0.0
1970	-		-		32.3	1.9	-		-		32.6	0.9	-		-		32.9	0.9	-		-		33.6	2.1
1971	-		-		35.0	4.2	-		-		35.4	1.1	-		-		35.6	0.6	-		-		35.4	-0.6
1972	-		-		36.4	2.8	-		-		36.5	0.3	-		-		36.5	0.0	-		-		36.9	1.1
1973	-		-		38.0	3.0	-		-		38.3	0.8	-		-		38.5	0.5	-		-		39.7	3.1
1974	-		-		41.4	4.3	-		-		42.0	1.4	-		-		43.3	3.1	-		-		44.4	2.5
1975	-		-		46.5	4.7	-		-		47.1	1.3	-		-		48.0	1.9	-		-		48.4	0.8
1976	-		-		51.6	6.6	-		-		52.3	1.4	-		-		53.6	2.5	-		-		55.1	2.8
1977	-		-		58.2	5.6	-		-		58.8	1.0	-		-		60.0	2.0	-		-		60.2	0.3
1978	-		-		63.3	5.1	-		64.5	1.9	-		65.4	1.4	-		68.1	4.1	-		68.2	0.1	-	
1979	71.6	5.0	-		72.1	0.7	-		71.8	-0.4	-		72.1	0.4	-		73.0	1.2	-		73.9	1.2	-	
1980	76.6	3.7	-		78.5	2.5	-		78.6	0.1	-		79.6	1.3	-		80.1	0.6	-		80.6	0.6	-	
1981	82.0	1.7	-		83.2	1.5	-		83.9	0.8	-		87.3	4.1	-		88.1	0.9	-		88.7	0.7	-	
1982	91.4	3.0	-		91.8	0.4	-		92.7	1.0	-		93.8	1.2	-		95.0	1.3	-		94.9	-0.1	-	
1983	98.5	3.8	-		98.9	0.4	-		99.4	0.5	-		100.6	1.2	-		100.5	-0.1	-		101.7	1.2	-	
1984	104.2	2.5	-		104.5	0.3	-		105.1	0.6	-		107.1	1.9	-		107.8	0.7	-		107.7	-0.1	-	
1985	109.2	1.4	-		110.4	1.1	-		111.5	1.0	-		112.2	0.6	-		113.2	0.9	-		114.3	1.0	-	
1986	115.1	0.7	-		115.8	0.6	-		116.3	0.4	-		119.0	2.3	-		118.8	-0.2	-		119.1	0.3	-	
1987	-		-		-		-		-		124.4	4.5	-		-		-		-		-		126.9	2.0
1988	-		-		-		-		-		135.3	6.6	-		-		-		-		-		138.2	2.1
1989	-		-		-		-		-		142.5	3.1	-		-		-		-		-		146.2	2.6
1990	-		-		-		-		-		153.9	5.3	-		-		-		-		-		161.0	4.6
1991	-		-		-		-		-		172.0	6.8	-		-		-		-		-		178.9	4.0
1992	-		-		-		-		-		185.4	3.6	-		-		-		-		-		190.6	2.8

[Continued]

Cincinnati-Hamilton, OH-KY-IN
Consumer Price Index - All Urban Consumers
Base 1982-1984 = 100
Medical Care
[Continued]

For 1947-2001. Columns headed % show percentile change in the index from the previous period for which an index is available.

Year	Jan Index	%	Feb Index	%	Mar Index	%	Apr Index	%	May Index	%	Jun Index	%	Jul Index	%	Aug Index	%	Sep Index	%	Oct Index	%	Nov Index	%	Dec Index	%
1993	-	-	-	-	-	-	-	-	-	-	197.9	3.8	-	-	-	-	-	-	-	-	-	-	203.4	2.8
1994	-	-	-	-	-	-	-	-	-	-	209.2	2.9	-	-	-	-	-	-	-	-	-	-	218.5	4.4
1995	-	-	-	-	-	-	-	-	-	-	221.4	1.3	-	-	-	-	-	-	-	-	-	-	223.5	0.9
1996	-	-	-	-	-	-	-	-	-	-	225.8	1.0	-	-	-	-	-	-	-	-	-	-	225.8	0.0
1997	-	-	-	-	-	-	-	-	-	-	220.2	-2.5	-	-	-	-	-	-	-	-	-	-	222.1	0.9
1998	-	-	-	-	-	-	-	-	-	-	223.4	0.6	-	-	-	-	-	-	-	-	-	-	225.7	1.0
1999	-	-	-	-	-	-	-	-	-	-	230.4	2.1	-	-	-	-	-	-	-	-	-	-	235.5	2.2
2000	-	-	-	-	-	-	-	-	-	-	249.9	6.1	-	-	-	-	-	-	-	-	-	-	257.9	3.2
2001	-	-	-	-	-	-	-	-	-	-	263.7	2.2	-	-	-	-	-	-	-	-	-	-	-	-

Source: U.S. Department of Labor, Bureau of Labor Statistics, Division of Consumer Prices and Price Indexes. - indicates no data collected for period.

357

Cincinnati-Hamilton, OH-KY-IN

Consumer Price Index - Urban Wage Earners
Base 1982-1984 = 100
Medical Care

For 1947-2001. Columns headed % show percentile change in the index from the previous period for which an index is available.

Year	Jan Index	%	Feb Index	%	Mar Index	%	Apr Index	%	May Index	%	Jun Index	%	Jul Index	%	Aug Index	%	Sep Index	%	Oct Index	%	Nov Index	%	Dec Index	%
1947	10.8	-	10.8	0.0	10.8	0.0	10.9	0.9	11.0	0.9	11.2	1.8	11.5	2.7	11.6	0.9	11.7	0.9	11.7	0.0	11.7	0.0	11.8	0.9
1948	12.2	3.4	12.1	-0.8	12.1	0.0	12.4	2.5	12.4	0.0	12.5	0.8	12.5	0.0	12.5	0.0	12.6	0.8	12.6	0.0	12.6	0.0	12.6	0.0
1949	12.6	0.0	12.6	0.0	12.7	0.8	12.8	0.8	12.8	0.0	12.8	0.0	12.8	0.0	12.8	0.0	12.8	0.0	12.8	0.0	12.8	0.0	13.0	1.6
1950	12.8	0.0	12.8	0.0	12.8	0.0	12.8	0.0	12.8	0.0	12.8	0.0	12.8	0.0	12.8	0.0	12.8	0.0	12.8	0.0	12.8	0.0	13.9	4.5
1951	13.0	0.0	13.0	0.0	13.0	0.0	13.1	0.8	13.1	0.0	13.1	0.0	13.1	0.0	13.1	0.0	13.3	1.5	13.3	0.0	13.3	0.0	14.3	0.0
1952	13.9	0.0	14.0	0.7	14.2	1.4	14.2	0.0	14.2	0.0	14.2	0.0	14.3	0.7	14.3	0.0	14.3	-	-	-	-	-	15.2	1.3
1953	-	-	-	-	14.7	2.8	-	-	-	-	14.8	0.7	-	-	-	-	15.0	1.4	-	-	-	-	15.4	1.3
1954	-	-	-	-	15.2	0.0	-	-	-	-	15.2	0.0	-	-	-	-	15.2	0.0	-	-	-	-	16.7	7.7
1955	-	-	-	-	15.5	0.6	-	-	-	-	15.5	0.0	-	-	-	-	15.5	0.0	-	-	-	-	16.7	0.0
1956	-	-	-	-	16.7	0.0	-	-	-	-	16.7	0.0	-	-	-	-	16.7	0.0	-	-	-	-	18.1	5.8
1957	-	-	-	-	17.0	1.8	-	-	-	-	17.0	0.0	-	-	-	-	17.1	0.6	-	-	-	-	18.5	2.2
1958	-	-	-	-	18.1	0.0	-	-	-	-	18.1	0.0	-	-	-	-	18.1	0.0	-	-	-	-	18.8	0.0
1959	-	-	-	-	18.4	-0.5	-	-	-	-	18.7	1.6	-	-	-	-	18.8	0.5	-	-	-	-	19.5	2.1
1960	-	-	-	-	18.9	0.5	-	-	-	-	18.9	0.0	-	-	-	-	19.1	1.1	-	-	-	-	19.7	0.0
1961	-	-	-	-	19.6	0.5	-	-	-	-	19.7	0.5	-	-	-	-	19.7	0.0	-	-	-	-	19.7	0.0
1962	-	-	-	-	19.7	0.0	-	-	-	-	19.8	0.5	-	-	-	-	20.5	3.5	-	-	-	-	20.5	0.0
1963	-	-	-	-	20.7	1.0	-	-	-	-	20.9	1.0	-	-	-	-	20.9	0.0	-	-	-	-	20.9	0.0
1964	-	-	-	-	21.2	1.4	-	-	-	-	21.2	0.0	-	-	-	-	21.2	0.0	-	-	-	-	22.4	5.7
1965	-	-	-	-	22.5	0.4	-	-	-	-	22.7	0.9	-	-	-	-	22.8	0.4	-	-	-	-	23.1	1.3
1966	-	-	-	-	23.5	1.7	-	-	-	-	23.7	0.9	-	-	-	-	23.9	0.8	-	-	-	-	24.4	2.1
1967	-	-	-	-	25.2	3.3	-	-	-	-	25.3	0.4	-	-	-	-	25.7	1.6	-	-	-	-	26.1	1.6
1968	-	-	-	-	27.2	4.2	-	-	-	-	27.3	0.4	-	-	-	-	27.6	1.1	-	-	-	-	28.0	1.4
1969	-	-	-	-	29.4	5.0	-	-	-	-	29.8	1.4	-	-	-	-	30.2	1.3	-	-	-	-	30.2	0.0
1970	-	-	-	-	30.8	2.0	-	-	-	-	31.0	0.6	-	-	-	-	31.3	1.0	-	-	-	-	32.1	2.6
1971	-	-	-	-	33.4	4.0	-	-	-	-	33.7	0.9	-	-	-	-	33.9	0.6	-	-	-	-	33.7	-0.6
1972	-	-	-	-	34.7	3.0	-	-	-	-	34.8	0.3	-	-	-	-	34.8	0.0	-	-	-	-	35.1	0.9
1973	-	-	-	-	36.2	3.1	-	-	-	-	36.5	0.8	-	-	-	-	36.7	0.5	-	-	-	-	37.8	3.0
1974	-	-	-	-	39.5	4.5	-	-	-	-	40.0	1.3	-	-	-	-	41.3	3.2	-	-	-	-	42.3	2.4
1975	-	-	-	-	44.3	4.7	-	-	-	-	44.8	1.1	-	-	-	-	45.8	2.2	-	-	-	-	46.1	0.7
1976	-	-	-	-	49.2	6.7	-	-	-	-	49.9	1.4	-	-	-	-	51.1	2.4	-	-	-	-	52.5	2.7
1977	-	-	-	-	55.4	5.5	-	-	-	-	56.1	1.3	-	-	-	-	57.2	2.0	-	-	-	-	57.4	0.3
1978	-	-	-	-	60.3	5.1	-	-	60.6	0.5	-	-	63.3	4.5	-	-	63.4	0.2	-	-	63.9	0.8	-	-
1979	68.2	6.7	-	-	68.5	0.4	-	-	69.8	1.9	-	-	70.5	1.0	-	-	71.2	1.0	-	-	71.5	0.4	-	-
1980	75.0	4.9	-	-	77.1	2.8	-	-	77.6	0.6	-	-	78.8	1.5	-	-	79.2	0.5	-	-	79.7	0.6	-	-
1981	82.0	2.9	-	-	82.6	0.7	-	-	83.4	1.0	-	-	86.6	3.8	-	-	87.8	1.4	-	-	88.8	1.1	-	-
1982	91.4	2.9	-	-	91.7	0.3	-	-	92.7	1.1	-	-	93.8	1.2	-	-	95.0	1.3	-	-	94.9	-0.1	-	-
1983	98.3	3.6	-	-	98.8	0.5	-	-	99.4	0.6	-	-	100.7	1.3	-	-	100.5	-0.2	-	-	101.8	1.3	-	-
1984	104.3	2.5	-	-	104.6	0.3	-	-	105.2	0.6	-	-	107.1	1.8	-	-	107.8	0.7	-	-	107.6	-0.2	-	-
1985	109.2	1.5	-	-	110.4	1.1	-	-	111.5	1.0	-	-	112.2	0.6	-	-	113.1	0.8	-	-	114.2	1.0	-	-
1986	114.9	0.6	-	-	115.6	0.6	-	-	116.0	0.3	-	-	118.7	2.3	-	-	118.5	-0.2	-	-	118.8	0.3	-	-
1987	-	-	-	-	-	-	-	-	-	-	124.1	4.5	-	-	-	-	-	-	-	-	-	-	127.0	2.3
1988	-	-	-	-	-	-	-	-	-	-	135.7	6.9	-	-	-	-	-	-	-	-	-	-	139.2	2.6
1989	-	-	-	-	-	-	-	-	-	-	143.3	2.9	-	-	-	-	-	-	-	-	-	-	146.9	2.5
1990	-	-	-	-	-	-	-	-	-	-	154.6	5.2	-	-	-	-	-	-	-	-	-	-	161.0	4.1
1991	-	-	-	-	-	-	-	-	-	-	171.7	6.6	-	-	-	-	-	-	-	-	-	-	178.7	4.1
1992	-	-	-	-	-	-	-	-	-	-	185.2	3.6	-	-	-	-	-	-	-	-	-	-	190.4	2.8

[Continued]

Cincinnati-Hamilton, OH-KY-IN
Consumer Price Index - Urban Wage Earners
Base 1982-1984 = 100
Medical Care
[Continued]

For 1947-2001. Columns headed % show percentile change in the index from the previous period for which an index is available.

Year	Jan		Feb		Mar		Apr		May		Jun		Jul		Aug		Sep		Oct		Nov		Dec	
	Index	%	Index	%	Index	%	Index	%	Index	%	Index	%	Index	%	Index	%	Index	%	Index	%	Index	%	Index	%
1993	-		-		-		-		-		197.0	3.5	-		-		-		-		-		-	
1994	-		-		-		-		-		207.9	2.7	-		-		-		-		-		202.4	2.7
1995	-		-		-		-		-		219.6	1.1	-		-		-		-		-		217.2	4.5
1996	-		-		-		-		-		223.6	0.9	-		-		-		-		-		221.5	0.9
1997	-		-		-		-		-		217.9	-2.5	-		-		-		-		-		223.5	-0.0
1998	-		-		-		-		-		220.0	0.2	-		-		-		-		-		219.5	0.7
1999	-		-		-		-		-		226.5	2.1	-		-		-		-		-		221.8	0.8
2000	-		-		-		-		-		245.6	6.1	-		-		-		-		-		231.5	2.2
2001	-		-		-		-		-		258.4	2.0	-		-		-		-		-		253.4	3.2

Source: U.S. Department of Labor, Bureau of Labor Statistics, Division of Consumer Prices and Price Indexes. - indicates no data collected for period.

Cincinnati-Hamilton, OH-KY-IN
Consumer Price Index - All Urban Consumers
Base December 1997 = 100
Recreation

For 1997-2001. Columns headed % show percentile change in the index from the previous period for which an index is available.

Year	Jan Index	%	Feb Index	%	Mar Index	%	Apr Index	%	May Index	%	Jun Index	%	Jul Index	%	Aug Index	%	Sep Index	%	Oct Index	%	Nov Index	%	Dec Index	%
1997	-	-	-	-	-	-	-	-	-	-	-	-	-	-	-	-	-	-	-	-	-	-	100.0	-
1998	-	-	-	-	-	-	-	-	-	-	105.7	5.7	-	-	-	-	-	-	-	-	-	-	105.4	-0.3
1999	-	-	-	-	-	-	-	-	-	-	105.4	0.0	-	-	-	-	-	-	-	-	-	-	105.6	0.2
2000	-	-	-	-	-	-	-	-	-	-	105.7	0.1	-	-	-	-	-	-	-	-	-	-	106.3	0.6
2001	-	-	-	-	-	-	-	-	-	-	107.5	1.1	-	-	-	-	-	-	-	-	-	-	-	-

Source: U.S. Department of Labor, Bureau of Labor Statistics, Division of Consumer Prices and Price Indexes. - indicates no data collected for period.

Cincinnati-Hamilton, OH-KY-IN
Consumer Price Index - Urban Wage Earners
Base December 1997 = 100
Recreation

For 1997-2001. Columns headed % show percentile change in the index from the previous period for which an index is available.

Year	Jan		Feb		Mar		Apr		May		Jun		Jul		Aug		Sep		Oct		Nov		Dec	
	Index	%	Index	%	Index	%	Index	%	Index	%	Index	%	Index	%	Index	%	Index	%	Index	%	Index	%	Index	%
1997	-	-	-	-	-	-	-	-	-	-	-	-	-	-	-	-	-	-	-	-	-	-	-	-
1998	-	-	-	-	-	-	-	-	-	-	104.7	4.7	-	-	-	-	-	-	-	-	-	-	100.0	-
1999	-	-	-	-	-	-	-	-	-	-	103.6	-0.5	-	-	-	-	-	-	-	-	-	-	104.1	-0.6
2000	-	-	-	-	-	-	-	-	-	-	106.3	1.6	-	-	-	-	-	-	-	-	-	-	104.6	1.0
2001	-	-	-	-	-	-	-	-	-	-	106.7	0.0	-	-	-	-	-	-	-	-	-	-	106.7	0.4

Source: U.S. Department of Labor, Bureau of Labor Statistics, Division of Consumer Prices and Price Indexes. - indicates no data collected for period.

Cincinnati-Hamilton, OH-KY-IN
Consumer Price Index - All Urban Consumers
Base December 1997 = 100
Education & Communication

For 1997-2001. Columns headed % show percentile change in the index from the previous period for which an index is available.

Year	Jan		Feb		Mar		Apr		May		Jun		Jul		Aug		Sep		Oct		Nov		Dec	
	Index	%	Index	%	Index	%	Index	%	Index	%	Index	%	Index	%	Index	%	Index	%	Index	%	Index	%	Index	%
1997	-	-	-	-	-	-	-	-	-	-	-	-	-	-	-	-	-	-	-	-	-	-	100.0	-
1998	-	-	-	-	-	-	-	-	-	-	99.4	-0.6	-	-	-	-	-	-	-	-	-	-	99.4	0.0
1999	-	-	-	-	-	-	-	-	-	-	99.1	-0.3	-	-	-	-	-	-	-	-	-	-	100.1	1.0
2000	-	-	-	-	-	-	-	-	-	-	98.7	-1.4	-	-	-	-	-	-	-	-	-	-	98.9	0.2
2001	-	-	-	-	-	-	-	-	-	-	100.4	1.5	-	-	-	-	-	-	-	-	-	-	-	-

Source: U.S. Department of Labor, Bureau of Labor Statistics, Division of Consumer Prices and Price Indexes. - indicates no data collected for period.

Cincinnati-Hamilton, OH-KY-IN
Consumer Price Index - Urban Wage Earners
Base December 1997 = 100
Education & Communication

For 1997-2001. Columns headed % show percentile change in the index from the previous period for which an index is available.

Year	Jan		Feb		Mar		Apr		May		Jun		Jul		Aug		Sep		Oct		Nov		Dec	
	Index	%	Index	%	Index	%	Index	%	Index	%	Index	%	Index	%	Index	%	Index	%	Index	%	Index	%	Index	%
1997	-	-	-	-	-	-	-	-	-	-	-	-	-	-	-	-	-	-	-	-	-	-	-	-
1998	-	-	-	-	-	-	-	-	-	-	98.7	-1.3	-	-	-	-	-	-	-	-	-	-	100.0	-
1999	-	-	-	-	-	-	-	-	-	-	96.3	-0.9	-	-	-	-	-	-	-	-	-	-	97.2	-1.5
2000	-	-	-	-	-	-	-	-	-	-	94.5	-2.4	-	-	-	-	-	-	-	-	-	-	96.8	0.5
2001	-	-	-	-	-	-	-	-	-	-	95.6	1.4	-	-	-	-	-	-	-	-	-	-	94.3	-0.2

Source: U.S. Department of Labor, Bureau of Labor Statistics, Division of Consumer Prices and Price Indexes. - indicates no data collected for period.

Cleveland-Akron, OH

Consumer Price Index - All Urban Consumers
Base 1982-1984 = 100
Annual Averages

For 1914-2001. Columns headed % show percentile change in the index from the previous period for which an index is available.

Year	All Items		Food & Beverage		Housing		Apparel		Trans-portation		Medical Care		Recrea-tion*		Education & Communic.*		Other Goods & Services	
	Index	%	Index	%	Index	%	Index	%	Index	%	Index	%	Index	%	Index	%	Index	%
1914	-	-	-	-	-	-	-	-	-	-	-	-	-	-	-	-	-	-
1915	8.7	-	-	-	-	-	-	-	-	-	-	-	-	-	-	-	-	-
1916	9.4	8.0	-	-	-	-	-	-	-	-	-	-	-	-	-	-	-	-
1917	11.4	21.3	-	-	-	-	-	-	-	-	-	-	-	-	-	-	-	-
1918	13.2	15.8	-	-	-	-	-	-	-	-	-	-	-	-	-	-	-	-
1919	15.5	17.4	-	-	-	-	-	-	-	-	-	-	-	-	-	-	-	-
1920	18.3	18.1	-	-	-	-	-	-	-	-	-	-	-	-	-	-	-	-
1921	16.6	-9.3	-	-	-	-	-	-	-	-	-	-	-	-	-	-	-	-
1922	15.1	-9.0	-	-	-	-	-	-	-	-	-	-	-	-	-	-	-	-
1923	15.7	4.0	-	-	-	-	-	-	-	-	-	-	-	-	-	-	-	-
1924	15.7	0.0	-	-	-	-	-	-	-	-	-	-	-	-	-	-	-	-
1925	16.0	1.9	-	-	-	-	-	-	-	-	-	-	-	-	-	-	-	-
1926	16.1	0.6	-	-	-	-	-	-	-	-	-	-	-	-	-	-	-	-
1927	15.8	-1.9	-	-	-	-	-	-	-	-	-	-	-	-	-	-	-	-
1928	15.6	-1.3	-	-	-	-	-	-	-	-	-	-	-	-	-	-	-	-
1929	15.5	-0.6	-	-	-	-	-	-	-	-	-	-	-	-	-	-	-	-
1930	15.2	-1.9	-	-	-	-	-	-	-	-	-	-	-	-	-	-	-	-
1931	13.7	-9.9	-	-	-	-	-	-	-	-	-	-	-	-	-	-	-	-
1932	12.4	-9.5	-	-	-	-	-	-	-	-	-	-	-	-	-	-	-	-
1933	11.8	-4.8	-	-	-	-	-	-	-	-	-	-	-	-	-	-	-	-
1934	12.2	3.4	-	-	-	-	-	-	-	-	-	-	-	-	-	-	-	-
1935	12.7	4.1	-	-	-	-	-	-	-	-	-	-	-	-	-	-	-	-
1936	12.8	0.8	-	-	-	-	-	-	-	-	-	-	-	-	-	-	-	-
1937	13.4	4.7	-	-	-	-	-	-	-	-	-	-	-	-	-	-	-	-
1938	13.3	-0.7	-	-	-	-	-	-	-	-	-	-	-	-	-	-	-	-
1939	13.2	-0.8	-	-	-	-	-	-	-	-	-	-	-	-	-	-	-	-
1940	13.2	0.0	-	-	-	-	-	-	-	-	-	-	-	-	-	-	-	-
1941	14.0	6.1	-	-	-	-	-	-	-	-	-	-	-	-	-	-	-	-
1942	15.5	10.7	-	-	-	-	-	-	-	-	-	-	-	-	-	-	-	-
1943	16.6	7.1	-	-	-	-	-	-	-	-	-	-	-	-	-	-	-	-
1944	16.9	1.8	-	-	-	-	-	-	-	-	-	-	-	-	-	-	-	-
1945	17.2	1.8	-	-	-	-	-	-	-	-	-	-	-	-	-	-	-	-
1946	18.5	7.6	-	-	-	-	-	-	-	-	-	-	-	-	-	-	-	-
1947	21.2	14.6	-	-	-	-	-	-	18.9	-	10.6	-	-	-	-	-	-	-
1948	23.0	8.5	-	-	-	-	-	-	21.8	15.3	11.2	5.7	-	-	-	-	-	-
1949	22.6	-1.7	-	-	-	-	-	-	23.1	6.0	11.7	4.5	-	-	-	-	-	-
1950	22.8	0.9	-	-	-	-	-	-	23.1	0.0	11.8	0.9	-	-	-	-	-	-
1951	24.6	7.9	-	-	-	-	-	-	24.6	6.5	12.6	6.8	-	-	-	-	-	-
1952	25.2	2.4	-	-	-	-	-	-	26.0	5.7	13.3	5.6	-	-	-	-	-	-
1953	25.4	0.8	-	-	-	-	44.1	-	26.3	1.2	13.8	3.8	-	-	-	-	-	-
1954	25.7	1.2	-	-	-	-	44.1	0.0	25.8	-1.9	14.5	5.1	-	-	-	-	-	-
1955	25.7	0.0	-	-	-	-	43.8	-0.7	25.6	-0.8	15.1	4.1	-	-	-	-	-	-
1956	26.2	1.9	-	-	-	-	44.8	2.3	26.7	4.3	16.1	6.6	-	-	-	-	-	-
1957	27.2	3.8	-	-	-	-	45.5	1.6	28.5	6.7	16.7	3.7	-	-	-	-	-	-
1958	27.8	2.2	-	-	-	-	45.9	0.9	29.0	1.8	17.1	2.4	-	-	-	-	-	-

[Continued]

Cleveland-Akron, OH
Consumer Price Index - All Urban Consumers
Base 1982-1984 = 100
Annual Averages
[Continued]

For 1914-2001. Columns headed % show percentile change in the index from the previous period for which an index is available.

Year	All Items Index	%	Food & Beverage Index	%	Housing Index	%	Apparel Index	%	Transportation Index	%	Medical Care Index	%	Recreation* Index	%	Education & Communic.* Index	%	Other Goods & Services Index	%
1959	27.9	0.4	-	-	-	-	46.2	0.7	30.1	3.8	18.7	9.4	-	-	-	-	-	-
1960	28.3	1.4	-	-	-	-	46.4	0.4	30.3	0.7	19.3	3.2	-	-	-	-	-	-
1961	28.5	0.7	-	-	-	-	46.8	0.9	31.0	2.3	20.7	7.3	-	-	-	-	-	-
1962	28.6	0.4	-	-	-	-	47.0	0.4	31.4	1.3	20.8	0.5	-	-	-	-	-	-
1963	28.9	1.0	-	-	-	-	47.7	1.5	31.5	0.3	21.9	5.3	-	-	-	-	-	-
1964	29.1	0.7	-	-	-	-	47.9	0.4	32.1	1.9	22.5	2.7	-	-	-	-	-	-
1965	29.6	1.7	-	-	-	-	48.3	0.8	32.6	1.6	23.2	3.1	-	-	-	-	-	-
1966	30.3	2.4	-	-	-	-	49.8	3.1	32.9	0.9	23.7	2.2	-	-	-	-	-	-
1967	31.2	3.0	-	-	-	-	51.3	3.0	33.9	3.0	25.2	6.3	-	-	-	-	-	-
1968	33.0	5.8	-	-	-	-	54.4	6.0	35.5	4.7	27.3	8.3	-	-	-	-	-	-
1969	34.9	5.8	-	-	-	-	57.6	5.9	37.0	4.2	30.5	11.7	-	-	-	-	-	-
1970	37.2	6.6	-	-	-	-	60.4	4.9	39.5	6.8	32.9	7.9	-	-	-	-	-	-
1971	38.3	3.0					62.4	3.3	42.2	6.8	35.2	7.0	-	-	-	-	-	-
1972	39.5	3.1					63.5	1.8	42.7	1.2	36.2	2.8	-	-	-	-	-	-
1973	41.8	5.8					66.5	4.7	44.1	3.3	38.0	5.0	-	-	-	-	-	-
1974	46.1	10.3	-	-	-	-	72.6	9.2	49.4	12.0	41.3	8.7	-	-	-	-	-	-
1975	50.2	8.9	-	-	-	-	74.4	2.5	52.1	5.5	46.0	11.4	-	-	-	-	-	-
1976	52.7	5.0	63.1	-	46.2	-	76.2	2.4	54.4	4.4	50.6	10.0	-	-	-	-	58.3	-
1977	56.3	6.8	66.4	5.2	49.7	7.6	80.5	5.6	57.8	6.3	56.7	12.1	-	-	-	-	61.8	6.0
1978	60.5	7.5	72.1	8.6	53.6	7.8	82.1	2.0	60.8	5.2	61.9	9.2	-	-	-	-	65.9	6.6
1979	68.5	13.2	79.6	10.4	63.0	17.5	84.5	2.9	69.2	13.8	66.0	6.6	-	-	-	-	71.1	7.9
1980	78.9	15.2	85.6	7.5	75.9	20.5	89.4	5.8	80.9	16.9	72.7	10.2	-	-	-	-	76.7	7.9
1981	87.2	10.5	93.2	8.9	83.8	10.4	95.0	6.3	92.0	13.7	81.2	11.7	-	-	-	-	84.9	10.7
1982	94.0	7.8	96.3	3.3	92.3	10.1	99.5	4.7	96.9	5.3	91.5	12.7	-	-	-	-	92.8	9.3
1983	101.2	7.7	99.8	3.6	102.6	11.2	99.3	-0.2	99.5	2.7	101.2	10.6	-	-	-	-	100.6	8.4
1984	104.8	3.6	103.9	4.1	105.1	2.4	101.3	2.0	103.6	4.1	107.4	6.1	-	-	-	-	106.7	6.1
1985	107.8	2.9	106.2	2.2	108.5	3.2	104.1	2.8	105.6	1.9	111.9	4.2	-	-	-	-	111.5	4.5
1986	109.4	1.5	107.6	1.3	111.8	3.0	102.4	-1.6	101.2	-4.2	122.3	9.3	-	-	-	-	117.0	4.9
1987	112.7	3.0	111.3	3.4	114.0	2.0	108.5	6.0	103.9	2.7	128.5	5.1	-	-	-	-	123.8	5.8
1988	116.7	3.5	116.4	4.6	117.8	3.3	105.8	-2.5	107.3	3.3	134.9	5.0	-	-	-	-	133.1	7.5
1989	122.7	5.1	124.0	6.5	122.7	4.2	111.4	5.3	113.0	5.3	143.5	6.4	-	-	-	-	141.0	5.9
1990	129.0	5.1	130.6	5.3	127.7	4.1	117.8	5.7	119.4	5.7	156.6	9.1	-	-	-	-	149.6	6.1
1991	134.2	4.0	135.4	3.7	132.5	3.8	121.9	3.5	123.1	3.1	171.7	9.6	-	-	-	-	160.1	7.0
1992	136.8	1.9	136.1	0.5	135.8	2.5	122.2	0.2	124.1	0.8	178.6	4.0	-	-	-	-	170.2	6.3
1993	140.3	2.6	139.7	2.6	139.0	2.4	125.1	2.4	125.0	0.7	187.2	4.8	-	-	-	-	180.3	5.9
1994	144.4	2.9	144.4	3.4	142.4	2.4	128.8	3.0	128.6	2.9	195.8	4.6	-	-	-	-	184.3	2.2
1995	147.9	2.4	148.9	3.1	145.1	1.9	127.1	-1.3	133.1	3.5	202.6	3.5	-	-	-	-	190.0	3.1
1996	152.0	2.8	154.2	3.6	148.6	2.4	128.8	1.3	138.5	4.1	209.4	3.4	-	-	-	-	193.0	1.6
1997	156.1	2.7	158.1	2.5	153.2	3.1	127.8	-0.8	141.8	2.4	211.5	1.0	-	-	-	-	204.6	6.0
1998	159.8	2.4	163.3	3.3	158.4	3.4	129.9	1.6	141.8	0.0	214.7	1.5	100.1	-	99.4	-	217.4	6.3
1999	162.5	1.7	169.5	3.8	160.2	1.1	124.1	-4.5	143.6	1.3	224.9	4.8	100.3	0.2	99.5	0.1	230.6	6.1
2000	168.0	3.4	172.9	2.0	166.1	3.7	123.1	-0.8	152.0	5.8	233.9	4.0	100.4	0.1	99.0	-0.5	245.0	6.2
2001	-	-	-	-	-	-	-	-	-	-	-	-	-	-	-	-	-	-

Source: U.S. Department of Labor, Bureau of Labor Statistics, Division of Consumer Prices and Price Indexes. *Base is December 1997 = 100. - indicates no data collected for period.

Cleveland-Akron, OH
Consumer Price Index - Urban Wage Earners
Base 1982-1984 = 100
Annual Averages

For 1914-2001. Columns headed % show percentile change in the index from the previous period for which an index is available.

Year	All Items		Food & Beverage		Housing		Apparel		Trans-portation		Medical Care		Recrea-tion*		Education & Communic.*		Other Goods & Services	
	Index	%	Index	%	Index	%	Index	%	Index	%	Index	%	Index	%	Index	%	Index	%
1914	-	-	-	-	-	-	-	-	-	-	-	-	-	-	-	-	-	-
1915	8.9	-	-	-	-	-	-	-	-	-	-	-	-	-	-	-	-	-
1916	9.7	9.0	-	-	-	-	-	-	-	-	-	-	-	-	-	-	-	-
1917	11.6	19.6	-	-	-	-	-	-	-	-	-	-	-	-	-	-	-	-
1918	13.6	17.2	-	-	-	-	-	-	-	-	-	-	-	-	-	-	-	-
1919	15.9	16.9	-	-	-	-	-	-	-	-	-	-	-	-	-	-	-	-
1920	18.8	18.2	-	-	-	-	-	-	-	-	-	-	-	-	-	-	-	-
1921	17.0	-9.6	-	-	-	-	-	-	-	-	-	-	-	-	-	-	-	-
1922	15.5	-8.8	-	-	-	-	-	-	-	-	-	-	-	-	-	-	-	-
1923	16.1	3.9	-	-	-	-	-	-	-	-	-	-	-	-	-	-	-	-
1924	16.1	0.0	-	-	-	-	-	-	-	-	-	-	-	-	-	-	-	-
1925	16.4	1.9	-	-	-	-	-	-	-	-	-	-	-	-	-	-	-	-
1926	16.5	0.6	-	-	-	-	-	-	-	-	-	-	-	-	-	-	-	-
1927	16.2	-1.8	-	-	-	-	-	-	-	-	-	-	-	-	-	-	-	-
1928	16.0	-1.2	-	-	-	-	-	-	-	-	-	-	-	-	-	-	-	-
1929	15.9	-0.6	-	-	-	-	-	-	-	-	-	-	-	-	-	-	-	-
1930	15.6	-1.9	-	-	-	-	-	-	-	-	-	-	-	-	-	-	-	-
1931	14.0	-10.3	-	-	-	-	-	-	-	-	-	-	-	-	-	-	-	-
1932	12.7	-9.3	-	-	-	-	-	-	-	-	-	-	-	-	-	-	-	-
1933	12.1	-4.7	-	-	-	-	-	-	-	-	-	-	-	-	-	-	-	-
1934	12.5	3.3	-	-	-	-	-	-	-	-	-	-	-	-	-	-	-	-
1935	13.0	4.0	-	-	-	-	-	-	-	-	-	-	-	-	-	-	-	-
1936	13.2	1.5	-	-	-	-	-	-	-	-	-	-	-	-	-	-	-	-
1937	13.7	3.8	-	-	-	-	-	-	-	-	-	-	-	-	-	-	-	-
1938	13.6	-0.7	-	-	-	-	-	-	-	-	-	-	-	-	-	-	-	-
1939	13.5	-0.7	-	-	-	-	-	-	-	-	-	-	-	-	-	-	-	-
1940	13.5	0.0	-	-	-	-	-	-	-	-	-	-	-	-	-	-	-	-
1941	14.3	5.9	-	-	-	-	-	-	-	-	-	-	-	-	-	-	-	-
1942	15.9	11.2	-	-	-	-	-	-	-	-	-	-	-	-	-	-	-	-
1943	17.0	6.9	-	-	-	-	-	-	-	-	-	-	-	-	-	-	-	-
1944	17.3	1.8	-	-	-	-	-	-	-	-	-	-	-	-	-	-	-	-
1945	17.6	1.7	-	-	-	-	-	-	-	-	-	-	-	-	-	-	-	-
1946	19.0	8.0	-	-	-	-	-	-	-	-	-	-	-	-	-	-	-	-
1947	21.7	14.2	-	-	-	-	-	-	19.1	-	10.4	-	-	-	-	-	-	-
1948	23.6	8.8	-	-	-	-	-	-	22.0	15.2	11.0	5.8	-	-	-	-	-	-
1949	23.2	-1.7	-	-	-	-	-	-	23.4	6.4	11.5	4.5	-	-	-	-	-	-
1950	23.4	0.9	-	-	-	-	-	-	23.4	0.0	11.6	0.9	-	-	-	-	-	-
1951	25.3	8.1	-	-	-	-	-	-	24.9	6.4	12.4	6.9	-	-	-	-	-	-
1952	25.9	2.4	-	-	-	-	-	-	26.3	5.6	13.1	5.6	-	-	-	-	-	-
1953	26.1	0.8	-	-	-	-	42.7	-	26.6	1.1	13.6	3.8	-	-	-	-	-	-
1954	26.3	0.8	-	-	-	-	42.7	0.0	26.1	-1.9	14.3	5.1	-	-	-	-	-	-
1955	26.4	0.4	-	-	-	-	42.5	-0.5	25.9	-0.8	14.9	4.2	-	-	-	-	-	-
1956	26.9	1.9	-	-	-	-	43.4	2.1	27.0	4.2	15.8	6.0	-	-	-	-	-	-
1957	27.9	3.7	-	-	-	-	44.1	1.6	28.9	7.0	16.4	3.8	-	-	-	-	-	-
1958	28.5	2.2	-	-	-	-	44.5	0.9	29.4	1.7	16.8	2.4	-	-	-	-	-	-

[Continued]

Cleveland-Akron, OH
Consumer Price Index - Urban Wage Earners
Base 1982-1984 = 100
Annual Averages
[Continued]

For 1914-2001. Columns headed % show percentile change in the index from the previous period for which an index is available.

Year	All Items		Food & Beverage		Housing		Apparel		Trans-portation		Medical Care		Recrea-tion*		Education & Communic.*		Other Goods & Services	
	Index	%	Index	%	Index	%	Index	%	Index	%	Index	%	Index	%	Index	%	Index	%
1959	28.6	0.4	-	-	-	-	44.8	0.7	30.4	3.4	18.4	9.5	-	-	-	-	-	-
1960	29.0	1.4	-	-	-	-	45.0	0.4	30.7	1.0	19.0	3.3	-	-	-	-	-	-
1961	29.3	1.0	-	-	-	-	45.4	0.9	31.3	2.0	20.3	6.8	-	-	-	-	-	-
1962	29.3	0.0	-	-	-	-	45.6	0.4	31.8	1.6	20.4	0.5	-	-	-	-	-	-
1963	29.7	1.4	-	-	-	-	46.3	1.5	31.9	0.3	21.5	5.4	-	-	-	-	-	-
1964	29.8	0.3	-	-	-	-	46.4	0.2	32.5	1.9	22.2	3.3	-	-	-	-	-	-
1965	30.3	1.7	-	-	-	-	46.8	0.9	33.0	1.5	22.8	2.7	-	-	-	-	-	-
1966	31.1	2.6	-	-	-	-	48.3	3.2	33.3	0.9	23.3	2.2	-	-	-	-	-	-
1967	32.0	2.9	-	-	-	-	49.8	3.1	34.3	3.0	24.7	6.0	-	-	-	-	-	-
1968	33.9	5.9	-	-	-	-	52.8	6.0	36.0	5.0	26.8	8.5	-	-	-	-	-	-
1969	35.8	5.6	-	-	-	-	55.9	5.9	37.5	4.2	30.0	11.9	-	-	-	-	-	-
1970	38.2	6.7	-	-	-	-	58.6	4.8	40.0	6.7	32.4	8.0	-	-	-	-	-	-
1971	39.3	2.9					60.5	3.2	42.7	6.8	34.6	6.8	-	-	-	-	-	-
1972	40.5	3.1	-	-	-	-	61.6	1.8	43.3	1.4	35.6	2.9	-	-	-	-	-	-
1973	42.9	5.9	-	-	-	-	64.5	4.7	44.6	3.0	37.3	4.8	-	-	-	-	-	-
1974	47.3	10.3	-	-	-	-	70.4	9.1	50.0	12.1	40.7	9.1	-	-	-	-	-	-
1975	51.5	8.9	-	-	-	-	72.2	2.6	52.7	5.4	45.3	11.3	-	-	-	-	-	-
1976	54.1	5.0	62.3	-	48.1	-	73.9	2.4	55.1	4.6	49.8	9.9	-	-	-	-	57.2	-
1977	57.8	6.8	65.6	5.3	51.8	7.7	78.1	5.7	58.5	6.2	55.8	12.0	-	-	-	-	60.6	5.9
1978	62.2	7.6	72.1	9.9	55.9	7.9	80.7	3.3	61.7	5.5	61.2	9.7	-	-	-	-	64.6	6.6
1979	70.6	13.5	80.4	11.5	65.3	16.8	83.6	3.6	70.6	14.4	66.5	8.7	-	-	-	-	69.8	8.0
1980	81.1	14.9	86.9	8.1	78.7	20.5	87.0	4.1	82.2	16.4	73.7	10.8	-	-	-	-	76.1	9.0
1981	89.2	10.0	94.0	8.2	86.8	10.3	93.2	7.1	92.4	12.4	81.4	10.4	-	-	-	-	84.3	10.8
1982	95.9	7.5	96.5	2.7	95.9	10.5	99.2	6.4	96.7	4.7	91.7	12.7	-	-	-	-	92.5	9.7
1983	101.1	5.4	99.9	3.5	102.4	6.8	99.3	0.1	99.6	3.0	101.1	10.3	-	-	-	-	100.7	8.9
1984	103.0	1.9	103.6	3.7	101.7	-0.7	101.5	2.2	103.7	4.1	107.1	5.9	-	-	-	-	106.8	6.1
1985	103.8	0.8	105.9	2.2	100.7	-1.0	105.0	3.4	105.6	1.8	111.5	4.1	-	-	-	-	111.2	4.1
1986	105.0	1.2	107.3	1.3	103.8	3.1	103.5	-1.4	100.1	-5.2	121.6	9.1	-	-	-	-	116.9	5.1
1987	108.0	2.9	110.9	3.4	105.7	1.8	109.2	5.5	102.1	2.0	127.9	5.2	-	-	-	-	124.7	6.7
1988	111.8	3.5	115.9	4.5	109.3	3.4	106.2	-2.7	105.4	3.2	134.1	4.8	-	-	-	-	134.8	8.1
1989	117.3	4.9	123.5	6.6	113.5	3.8	110.7	4.2	110.7	5.0	142.1	6.0	-	-	-	-	143.4	6.4
1990	123.0	4.9	130.2	5.4	117.9	3.9	117.0	5.7	116.6	5.3	154.6	8.8	-	-	-	-	150.7	5.1
1991	127.8	3.9	134.9	3.6	122.2	3.6	121.3	3.7	120.0	2.9	168.7	9.1	-	-	-	-	162.2	7.6
1992	130.3	2.0	135.7	0.6	125.4	2.6	122.4	0.9	120.8	0.7	175.6	4.1	-	-	-	-	173.3	6.8
1993	133.3	2.3	139.3	2.7	128.2	2.2	124.2	1.5	121.7	0.7	184.0	4.8	-	-	-	-	183.9	6.1
1994	137.0	2.8	143.9	3.3	131.1	2.3	127.5	2.7	125.3	3.0	192.3	4.5	-	-	-	-	186.3	1.3
1995	140.2	2.3	148.4	3.1	133.3	1.7	125.2	-1.8	129.8	3.6	199.2	3.6	-	-	-	-	191.3	2.7
1996	144.3	2.9	153.7	3.6	137.1	2.9	126.2	0.8	134.5	3.6	206.6	3.7	-	-	-	-	193.2	1.0
1997	148.1	2.6	157.5	2.5	141.5	3.2	124.9	-1.0	137.3	2.1	209.0	1.2	-	-	-	-	206.0	6.6
1998	151.7	2.4	162.5	3.2	146.3	3.4	127.7	2.2	138.1	0.6	211.1	1.0	-	-	-	-	219.7	6.7
1999	154.6	1.9	168.9	3.9	147.9	1.1	123.0	-3.7	140.0	1.4	220.8	4.6	100.2	-	99.0	-	241.1	9.7
2000	160.3	3.7	172.3	2.0	153.4	3.7	122.9	-0.1	148.6	6.1	229.9	4.1	100.1	-0.1	98.9	-0.1	263.0	9.1
2001	-	-	-	-	-	-	-	-					100.0	-0.1	97.3	-1.6		

Source: U.S. Department of Labor, Bureau of Labor Statistics, Division of Consumer Prices and Price Indexes. *Base is December 1997 = 100. - indicates no data collected for period.

Cleveland-Akron, OH
Consumer Price Index - All Urban Consumers
Base 1982-1984 = 100
All Items

For 1914-2001. Columns headed % show percentile change in the index from the previous period for which an index is available.

Year	Jan Index	Jan %	Feb Index	Feb %	Mar Index	Mar %	Apr Index	Apr %	May Index	May %	Jun Index	Jun %	Jul Index	Jul %	Aug Index	Aug %	Sep Index	Sep %	Oct Index	Oct %	Nov Index	Nov %	Dec Index	Dec %
1914	-	-	-	-	-	-	-	-	-	-	-	-	-	-	-	-	-	-	-	-	-	-	8.7	-
1915	-	-	-	-	-	-	-	-	-	-	-	-	-	-	-	-	-	-	-	-	-	-	8.8	1.1
1916	-	-	-	-	-	-	-	-	-	-	-	-	-	-	-	-	-	-	-	-	-	-	10.1	14.8
1917	-	-	-	-	-	-	-	-	-	-	-	-	-	-	-	-	-	-	-	-	-	-	12.0	18.8
1918	-	-	-	-	-	-	-	-	-	-	-	-	-	-	-	-	-	-	-	-	-	-	14.4	20.0
1919	-	-	-	-	-	-	-	-	-	-	15.1	4.9	-	-	-	-	-	-	-	-	-	-	16.9	11.9
1920	-	-	-	-	-	-	-	-	-	-	19.0	12.4	-	-	-	-	-	-	-	-	-	-	18.0	-5.3
1921	-	-	-	-	-	-	-	-	16.6	-7.8	-	-	-	-	-	-	16.2	-2.4	-	-	-	-	15.9	-1.9
1922	-	-	-	-	15.0	-5.7	-	-	-	-	15.1	0.7	-	-	-	-	14.9	-1.3	-	-	-	-	15.3	2.7
1923	-	-	-	-	15.4	0.7	-	-	-	-	15.8	2.6	-	-	-	-	16.0	1.3	-	-	-	-	15.9	-0.6
1924	-	-	-	-	15.7	-1.3	-	-	-	-	15.6	-0.6	-	-	-	-	15.7	0.6	-	-	-	-	15.7	0.0
1925	-	-	-	-	-	-	-	-	-	-	16.1	2.5	-	-	-	-	-	-	-	-	-	-	16.2	0.6
1926	-	-	-	-	-	-	-	-	-	-	16.2	0.0	-	-	-	-	-	-	-	-	-	-	16.1	-0.6
1927	-	-	-	-	-	-	-	-	-	-	16.1	0.0	-	-	-	-	-	-	-	-	-	-	15.7	-2.5
1928	-	-	-	-	-	-	-	-	-	-	15.7	0.0	-	-	-	-	-	-	-	-	-	-	15.5	-1.3
1929	-	-	-	-	-	-	-	-	-	-	15.6	0.6	-	-	-	-	-	-	-	-	-	-	15.4	-1.3
1930	-	-	-	-	-	-	-	-	-	-	15.4	0.0	-	-	-	-	-	-	-	-	-	-	14.6	-5.2
1931	-	-	-	-	-	-	-	-	-	-	13.6	-6.8	-	-	-	-	-	-	-	-	-	-	13.1	-3.7
1932	-	-	-	-	-	-	-	-	-	-	12.5	-4.6	-	-	-	-	-	-	-	-	-	-	11.8	-5.6
1933	-	-	-	-	-	-	-	-	-	-	11.6	-1.7	-	-	-	-	-	-	-	-	-	-	12.0	3.4
1934	-	-	-	-	-	-	-	-	-	-	12.2	1.7	-	-	-	-	-	-	-	-	12.2	0.0	-	-
1935	-	-	-	-	12.7	4.1	-	-	-	-	-	-	12.7	0.0	-	-	-	-	12.7	0.0	-	-	12.9	-1.5
1936	12.7	0.0	-	-	-	-	12.6	-0.8	-	-	-	-	12.9	2.4	-	-	13.1	1.6	-	-	-	-	13.4	-1.5
1937	-	-	-	-	13.1	1.6	-	-	-	-	13.4	2.3	-	-	-	-	13.6	1.5	-	-	-	-	13.2	-0.8
1938	-	-	-	-	13.2	-1.5	-	-	-	-	13.3	0.8	-	-	-	-	13.3	0.0	-	-	-	-	13.2	-0.8
1939	-	-	-	-	13.2	0.0	-	-	-	-	13.2	0.0	-	-	-	-	13.3	0.8	-	-	-	-	13.2	-0.8
1940	-	-	-	-	13.2	0.0	-	-	-	-	13.3	0.8	-	-	-	-	13.4	0.8	13.3	-0.7	13.2	-0.8	13.3	0.8
1941	13.3	0.0	13.4	0.8	13.4	0.0	13.5	0.7	13.6	0.7	13.9	2.2	14.0	0.7	14.2	1.4	14.5	2.1	14.6	0.7	14.8	1.4	14.8	0.0
1942	15.0	1.4	15.0	0.0	15.3	2.0	15.4	0.7	15.5	0.6	15.6	0.6	15.6	0.0	15.5	-0.6	15.6	0.6	15.9	1.9	15.9	0.0	16.1	1.3
1943	16.1	0.0	16.2	0.6	16.4	1.2	16.5	0.6	16.7	1.2	16.9	1.2	16.7	-1.2	16.7	0.0	16.8	0.6	16.8	0.0	16.8	0.0	16.8	0.0
1944	16.7	-0.6	16.7	0.0	16.7	0.0	16.9	1.2	16.9	0.0	16.9	0.0	17.1	1.2	17.1	0.0	17.1	0.0	17.0	-0.6	17.1	0.6	16.9	-1.2
1945	17.0	0.6	17.0	0.0	17.0	0.0	17.0	0.0	17.3	1.8	17.3	0.0	17.3	0.0	17.3	0.0	17.2	-0.6	17.3	0.6	17.3	0.0	17.3	0.0
1946	17.3	0.0	17.3	0.0	17.3	0.0	17.4	0.6	17.5	0.6	17.8	1.7	18.8	5.6	19.3	2.7	19.3	0.0	19.6	1.6	20.2	3.1	20.5	1.5
1947	20.4	-0.5	20.4	0.0	20.9	2.5	20.9	0.0	20.8	-0.5	21.0	1.0	-	-	21.4	1.9	-	-	-	-	21.9	2.3	-	-
1948	-	-	22.5	2.7	-	-	-	-	22.8	1.3	-	-	-	-	23.6	3.5	-	-	-	-	23.1	-2.1	-	-
1949	-	-	22.7	-1.7	-	-	-	-	22.6	-0.4	-	-	-	-	22.6	0.0	-	-	-	-	22.4	-0.9	-	-
1950	-	-	22.2	-0.9	-	-	-	-	22.3	0.5	-	-	-	-	23.1	3.6	-	-	-	-	23.5	1.7	-	-
1951	-	-	24.3	3.4	-	-	-	-	24.6	1.2	-	-	-	-	24.7	0.4	-	-	-	-	25.1	1.6	-	-
1952	-	-	25.1	0.0	-	-	-	-	25.2	0.4	-	-	-	-	25.4	0.8	-	-	-	-	25.3	-0.4	-	-
1953	-	-	25.0	-1.2	-	-	-	-	25.3	1.2	-	-	-	-	25.6	1.2	-	-	-	-	25.7	0.4	-	-
1954	-	-	25.7	0.0	-	-	-	-	25.7	0.0	-	-	-	-	25.7	0.0	-	-	-	-	25.7	0.0	-	-
1955	-	-	25.6	-0.4	-	-	-	-	25.7	0.4	-	-	-	-	25.8	0.4	-	-	-	-	25.9	0.4	-	-
1956	-	-	25.8	-0.4	-	-	-	-	26.1	1.2	-	-	-	-	26.5	1.5	-	-	-	-	26.7	0.8	-	-
1957	-	-	26.8	0.4	-	-	-	-	27.1	1.1	-	-	-	-	27.3	0.7	-	-	-	-	27.5	0.7	-	-
1958	-	-	27.7	0.7	-	-	-	-	27.8	0.4	-	-	-	-	27.8	0.0	-	-	-	-	27.7	-0.4	-	-
1959	-	-	27.8	0.4	-	-	-	-	27.9	0.4	-	-	-	-	28.0	0.4	-	-	-	-	28.1	0.4	-	-

[Continued]

Cleveland-Akron, OH
Consumer Price Index - All Urban Consumers
Base 1982-1984 = 100
All Items
[Continued]

For 1914-2001. Columns headed % show percentile change in the index from the previous period for which an index is available.

Year	Jan Index	Jan %	Feb Index	Feb %	Mar Index	Mar %	Apr Index	Apr %	May Index	May %	Jun Index	Jun %	Jul Index	Jul %	Aug Index	Aug %	Sep Index	Sep %	Oct Index	Oct %	Nov Index	Nov %	Dec Index	Dec %
1960	-		28.1	0.0	-		-		28.3	0.7	-		-		28.4	0.4	-		-		28.5	0.4	-	
1961	-		28.6	0.4	-		-		28.5	-0.3	-		-		28.6	0.4	-		-		28.5	-0.3	-	
1962	-		28.5	0.0	-		-		28.6	0.4	-		-		28.7	0.3	-		-		28.7	0.0	-	
1963	-		28.8	0.3	-		-		28.8	0.0	-		-		29.1	1.0	-		-		29.0	-0.3	-	
1964	-		29.1	0.3	-		-		28.9	-0.7	-		-		29.1	0.7	-		-		29.3	0.7	-	
1965	-		29.3	0.0	-		-		29.5	0.7	-		-		29.6	0.3	-		-		29.8	0.7	-	
1966	-		29.9	0.3	-		-		30.3	1.3	-		-		30.5	0.7	-		-		30.6	0.3	-	
1967	-		30.8	0.7	-		-		30.9	0.3	-		-		31.3	1.3	-		-		31.7	1.3	-	
1968	-		32.5	2.5	-		-		32.9	1.2	-		-		33.2	0.9	-		-		33.7	1.5	-	
1969	-		34.0	0.9	-		-		34.6	1.8	-		-		35.2	1.7	-		-		35.8	1.7	-	
1970	-		36.6	2.2	-		-		37.1	1.4	-		-		37.5	1.1	-		-		37.9	1.1	-	
1971	-		37.9	0.0	-		-		38.1	0.5	-		-		38.4	0.8	-		-		38.8	1.0	-	
1972	-		39.3	1.3	-		-		39.4	0.3	-		-		39.4	0.0	-		-		39.9	1.3	-	
1973	-		40.5	1.5	-		-		41.4	2.2	-		-		42.4	2.4	-		-		42.9	1.2	-	
1974	-		44.3	3.3	-		-		45.6	2.9	-		-		46.8	2.6	-		-		47.7	1.9	-	
1975	-		49.2	3.1	-		-		49.8	1.2	-		-		50.7	1.8	-		-		51.3	1.2	-	
1976	-		51.5	0.4	-		-		52.1	1.2	-		-		53.2	2.1	-		-		54.0	1.5	-	
1977	-		55.1	2.0	-		-		56.1	1.8	-		-		56.5	0.7	-		-		57.5	1.8	-	
1978	-		58.2	1.2	-		59.4	2.1	-		59.6	0.3	-		60.8	2.0	-		62.4	2.6	-		64.2	2.9
1979	-		65.6	2.2	-		67.1	2.3	-		68.6	2.2	-		69.1	0.7	-		70.1	1.4	-		72.6	3.6
1980	-		76.0	4.7	-		77.2	1.6	-		78.0	1.0	-		79.2	1.5	-		82.6	4.3	-		83.2	0.7
1981	-		85.3	2.5	-		84.9	-0.5	-		89.0	4.8	-		88.8	-0.2	-		88.3	-0.6	-		87.9	-0.5
1982	-		89.2	1.5	-		89.4	0.2	-		92.9	3.9	-		97.4	4.8	-		98.8	1.4	-		99.1	0.3
1983	-		99.5	0.4	-		99.7	0.2	-		101.2	1.5	-		101.8	0.6	-		103.2	1.4	-		102.6	-0.6
1984	-		103.3	0.7	-		103.9	0.6	-		105.1	1.2	-		105.3	0.2	-		106.1	0.8	-		106.0	-0.1
1985	-		106.2	0.2	-		106.9	0.7	-		108.1	1.1	-		108.6	0.5	-		108.8	0.2	-		108.8	0.0
1986	-		109.3	0.5	-		108.3	-0.9	-		109.4	1.0	-		110.1	0.6	-		109.9	-0.2	110.1	0.2	109.8	-0.3
1987	110.1	0.3	-		111.4	1.2	-		111.6	0.2	-		112.8	1.1	-		114.7	1.7	-		114.5	-0.2	-	
1988	113.9	-0.5	-		115.1	1.1	-		116.6	1.3	-		117.6	0.9	-		117.6	0.0	-		118.0	0.3	-	
1989	118.9	0.8	-		121.5	2.2	-		122.8	1.3	-		124.4	0.9	-		117.6	0.0	-		118.0	0.3	-	
1990	125.0	1.3	-		127.4	1.9	-		128.1	0.5	-		128.8	0.5	-		131.1	1.8	-		131.7	0.5	-	
1991	131.9	0.2	-		133.2	1.0	-		134.3	0.8	-		133.9	-0.3	-		135.4	1.1	-		135.7	0.2	-	
1992	136.2	0.4	-		136.3	0.1	-		136.1	-0.1	-		137.1	0.7	-		137.9	0.6	-		137.1	-0.6	-	
1993	137.5	0.3	-		138.8	0.9	-		139.6	0.6	-		140.9	0.9	-		141.7	0.6	-		142.1	0.3	-	
1994	142.4	0.2	-		143.3	0.6	-		143.7	0.3	-		143.7	0.0	-		146.3	1.8	-		146.0	-0.2	-	
1995	146.6	0.4	-		147.3	0.5	-		147.4	0.1	-		148.1	0.5	-		149.0	0.6	-		148.2	-0.5	-	
1996	149.0	0.5	-		150.9	1.3	-		151.8	0.6	-		152.1	0.2	-		153.5	0.9	-		153.8	0.2	-	
1997	153.8	0.0	-		155.4	1.0	-		155.6	0.1	-		156.3	0.4	-		157.3	0.6	-		157.1	-0.1	-	
1998	158.2	0.7	-		158.6	0.3	-		159.2	0.4	-		159.9	0.4	-		161.5	1.0	-		160.8	-0.4	-	
1999	160.6	-0.1	-		161.2	0.4	-		161.5	0.2	-		162.8	0.8	-		164.2	0.9	-		163.8	-0.2	-	
2000	164.5	0.4	-		166.9	1.5	-		166.6	-0.2	-		168.3	1.0	-		170.5	1.3	-		169.4	-0.6	-	
2001	171.3	1.1	-		172.3	0.6	-		173.7	0.8	-		173.4	-0.2	-		174.6	0.7	-		172.3	-1.3	-	

Source: U.S. Department of Labor, Bureau of Labor Statistics, Division of Consumer Prices and Price Indexes. - indicates no data collected for period.

Cleveland-Akron, OH
Consumer Price Index - Urban Wage Earners
Base 1982-1984 = 100
All Items

For 1914-2001. Columns headed % show percentile change in the index from the previous period for which an index is available.

Year	Jan Index	%	Feb Index	%	Mar Index	%	Apr Index	%	May Index	%	Jun Index	%	Jul Index	%	Aug Index	%	Sep Index	%	Oct Index	%	Nov Index	%	Dec Index	%
1914	-	-	-	-	-	-	-	-	-	-	-	-	-	-	-	-	-	-	-	-	-	-	8.9	-
1915	-	-	-	-	-	-	-	-	-	-	-	-	-	-	-	-	-	-	-	-	-	-	9.1	2.2
1916	-	-	-	-	-	-	-	-	-	-	-	-	-	-	-	-	-	-	-	-	-	-	10.4	14.3
1917	-	-	-	-	-	-	-	-	-	-	-	-	-	-	-	-	-	-	-	-	-	-	12.4	19.2
1918	-	-	-	-	-	-	-	-	-	-	-	-	-	-	-	-	-	-	-	-	-	-	14.8	19.4
1919	-	-	-	-	-	-	-	-	-	-	15.5	4.7	-	-	-	-	-	-	-	-	-	-	17.3	11.6
1920	-	-	-	-	-	-	-	-	-	-	19.5	12.7	-	-	-	-	-	-	-	-	-	-	18.5	-5.1
1921	-	-	-	-	-	-	-	-	17.0	-8.1	-	-	-	-	-	-	16.6	-2.4	-	-	-	-	16.3	-1.8
1922	-	-	-	-	15.4	-5.5	-	-	-	-	15.5	0.6	-	-	-	-	15.3	-1.3	-	-	-	-	15.7	2.6
1923	-	-	-	-	15.7	0.0	-	-	-	-	16.2	3.2	-	-	-	-	16.4	1.2	-	-	-	-	16.3	-0.6
1924	-	-	-	-	16.1	-1.2	-	-	-	-	16.0	-0.6	-	-	-	-	16.1	0.6	-	-	-	-	16.1	0.0
1925	-	-	-	-	-	-	-	-	-	-	16.5	2.5	-	-	-	-	-	-	-	-	-	-	16.6	0.6
1926	-	-	-	-	-	-	-	-	-	-	16.6	0.0	-	-	-	-	-	-	-	-	-	-	16.5	-0.6
1927	-	-	-	-	-	-	-	-	-	-	16.5	0.0	-	-	-	-	-	-	-	-	-	-	16.1	-2.4
1928	-	-	-	-	-	-	-	-	-	-	16.1	0.0	-	-	-	-	-	-	-	-	-	-	15.9	-1.2
1929	-	-	-	-	-	-	-	-	-	-	16.0	0.6	-	-	-	-	-	-	-	-	-	-	15.8	-1.2
1930	-	-	-	-	-	-	-	-	-	-	15.8	0.0	-	-	-	-	-	-	-	-	-	-	15.0	-5.1
1931	-	-	-	-	-	-	-	-	-	-	14.0	-6.7	-	-	-	-	-	-	-	-	-	-	13.4	-4.3
1932	-	-	-	-	-	-	-	-	-	-	12.8	-4.5	-	-	-	-	-	-	-	-	-	-	12.1	-5.5
1933	-	-	-	-	-	-	-	-	-	-	11.9	-1.7	-	-	-	-	-	-	-	-	-	-	12.3	3.4
1934	-	-	-	-	-	-	-	-	-	-	12.5	1.6	-	-	-	-	-	-	-	-	12.5	0.0	-	-
1935	-	-	-	-	13.0	4.0	-	-	-	-	-	-	13.0	0.0	-	-	-	-	13.1	0.8	-	-	-	-
1936	13.0	-0.8	-	-	-	-	13.0	0.0	-	-	-	-	13.2	1.5	-	-	13.4	1.5	-	-	-	-	13.2	-1.5
1937	-	-	-	-	13.5	2.3	-	-	-	-	13.8	2.2	-	-	-	-	14.0	1.4	-	-	-	-	13.8	-1.4
1938	-	-	-	-	13.5	-2.2	-	-	-	-	13.6	0.7	-	-	-	-	13.6	0.0	-	-	-	-	13.6	0.0
1939	-	-	-	-	13.5	-0.7	-	-	-	-	13.5	0.0	-	-	-	-	13.6	0.7	-	-	-	-	13.5	-0.7
1940	-	-	-	-	13.5	0.0	-	-	-	-	13.6	0.7	-	-	-	-	13.7	0.7	13.6	-0.7	13.5	-0.7	13.7	1.5
1941	13.7	0.0	13.7	0.0	13.8	0.7	13.9	0.7	14.0	0.7	14.2	1.4	14.3	0.7	14.6	2.1	14.8	1.4	15.0	1.4	15.1	0.7	15.2	0.7
1942	15.4	1.3	15.4	0.0	15.7	1.9	15.8	0.6	15.9	0.6	16.0	0.6	16.0	0.0	15.9	-0.6	16.0	0.6	16.3	1.9	16.4	0.6	16.5	0.6
1943	16.5	0.0	16.6	0.6	16.8	1.2	16.9	0.6	17.2	1.8	17.3	0.6	17.2	-0.6	17.2	0.0	17.2	0.0	17.2	0.0	17.2	0.0	17.2	0.0
1944	17.2	0.0	17.2	0.0	17.2	0.0	17.3	0.6	17.3	0.0	17.3	0.0	17.5	1.2	17.5	0.0	17.5	0.0	17.5	0.0	17.5	0.0	17.3	-1.1
1945	17.4	0.6	17.4	0.0	17.4	0.0	17.5	0.6	17.7	1.1	17.7	0.0	17.7	0.0	17.7	0.0	17.6	-0.6	17.7	0.6	17.7	0.0	17.8	0.6
1946	17.7	-0.6	17.7	0.0	17.7	0.0	17.8	0.6	18.0	1.1	18.2	1.1	19.3	6.0	19.7	2.1	19.8	0.5	20.1	1.5	20.7	3.0	21.0	1.4
1947	21.0	0.0	21.0	0.0	21.4	1.9	21.4	0.0	21.4	0.0	21.6	0.9	-	-	22.0	1.9	-	-	-	-	22.5	2.3	-	-
1948	-	-	23.1	2.7	-	-	-	-	23.4	1.3	-	-	-	-	24.2	3.4	-	-	-	-	23.7	-2.1	-	-
1949	-	-	23.2	-2.1	-	-	-	-	23.1	-0.4	-	-	-	-	23.2	0.4	-	-	-	-	23.0	-0.9	-	-
1950	-	-	22.8	-0.9	-	-	-	-	22.9	0.4	-	-	-	-	23.7	3.5	-	-	-	-	24.1	1.7	-	-
1951	-	-	24.9	3.3	-	-	-	-	25.2	1.2	-	-	-	-	25.3	0.4	-	-	-	-	25.7	1.6	-	-
1952	-	-	25.7	0.0	-	-	-	-	25.8	0.4	-	-	-	-	26.0	0.8	-	-	-	-	25.9	-0.4	-	-
1953	-	-	25.7	-0.8	-	-	-	-	25.9	0.8	-	-	-	-	26.3	1.5	-	-	-	-	26.4	0.4	-	-
1954	-	-	26.3	-0.4	-	-	-	-	26.3	0.0	-	-	-	-	26.3	0.0	-	-	-	-	26.3	0.0	-	-
1955	-	-	26.2	-0.4	-	-	-	-	26.3	0.4	-	-	-	-	26.5	0.8	-	-	-	-	26.5	0.0	-	-
1956	-	-	26.4	-0.4	-	-	-	-	26.8	1.5	-	-	-	-	27.2	1.5	-	-	-	-	27.4	0.7	-	-
1957	-	-	27.5	0.4	-	-	-	-	27.8	1.1	-	-	-	-	28.0	0.7	-	-	-	-	28.2	0.7	-	-
1958	-	-	28.4	0.7	-	-	-	-	28.5	0.4	-	-	-	-	28.5	0.0	-	-	-	-	28.4	-0.4	-	-
1959	-	-	28.5	0.4	-	-	-	-	28.6	0.4	-	-	-	-	28.7	0.3	-	-	-	-	28.9	0.7	-	-

[Continued]

Cleveland-Akron, OH
Consumer Price Index - Urban Wage Earners
Base 1982-1984 = 100
All Items
[Continued]

For 1914-2001. Columns headed % show percentile change in the index from the previous period for which an index is available.

Year	Jan Index	%	Feb Index	%	Mar Index	%	Apr Index	%	May Index	%	Jun Index	%	Jul Index	%	Aug Index	%	Sep Index	%	Oct Index	%	Nov Index	%	Dec Index	%
1960	-		28.8	-0.3	-		-		29.0	0.7	-		-		29.1	0.3	-		-		29.2	0.3	-	
1961	-		29.3	0.3	-		-		29.2	-0.3	-		-		29.4	0.7	-		-		29.2	-0.7	-	
1962	-		29.2	0.0	-		-		29.3	0.3	-		-		29.4	0.3	-		-		29.4	0.0	-	
1963	-		29.6	0.7	-		-		29.6	0.0	-		-		29.8	0.7	-		-		29.8	0.0	-	
1964	-		29.8	0.0	-		-		29.6	-0.7	-		-		29.8	0.7	-		-		30.0	0.7	-	
1965	-		30.1	0.3	-		-		30.3	0.7	-		-		30.4	0.3	-		-		30.6	0.7	-	
1966	-		30.6	0.0	-		-		31.1	1.6	-		-		31.2	0.3	-		-		31.4	0.6	-	
1967	-		31.6	0.6	-		-		31.7	0.3	-		-		32.1	1.3	-		-		32.5	1.2	-	
1968	-		33.4	2.8	-		-		33.8	1.2	-		-		34.0	0.6	-		-		34.5	1.5	-	
1969	-		34.9	1.2	-		-		35.5	1.7	-		-		36.1	1.7	-		-		36.7	1.7	-	
1970	-		37.5	2.2	-		-		38.1	1.6	-		-		38.4	0.8	-		-		38.8	1.0	-	
1971	-		38.9	0.3	-		-		39.0	0.3	-		-		39.4	1.0	-		-		39.8	1.0	-	
1972	-		40.3	1.3	-		-		40.4	0.2	-		-		40.4	0.0	-		-		40.9	1.2	-	
1973	-		41.6	1.7	-		-		42.5	2.2	-		-		43.5	2.4	-		-		44.0	1.1	-	
1974	-		45.5	3.4	-		-		46.8	2.9	-		-		48.0	2.6	-		-		49.0	2.1	-	
1975	-		50.5	3.1	-		-		51.0	1.0	-		-		52.0	2.0	-		-		52.6	1.2	-	
1976	-		52.8	0.4	-		-		53.4	1.1	-		-		54.6	2.2	-		-		55.4	1.5	-	
1977	-		56.5	2.0	-		-		57.6	1.9	-		-		58.0	0.7	-		-		59.0	1.7	-	
1978	-		59.7	1.2	-		61.0	2.2	-		61.5	0.8	-		62.7	2.0	-		64.2	2.4	-		65.9	2.6
1979	-		67.5	2.4	-		69.2	2.5	-		70.8	2.3	-		71.2	0.6	-		72.2	1.4	-		74.6	3.3
1980	-		78.1	4.7	-		79.5	1.8	-		80.2	0.9	-		81.4	1.5	-		84.6	3.9	-		74.6	3.3
1981	-		87.7	2.7	-		87.1	-0.7	-		90.8	4.2	-		90.6	-0.2	-		90.3	-0.3	-		85.4	0.9
1982	-		91.2	1.3	-		91.4	0.2	-		95.0	3.9	-		99.4	4.6	-		100.5	1.1	-		90.0	-0.3
1983	-		100.3	-0.5	-		100.9	0.6	-		101.3	0.4	-		101.6	0.3	-		101.5	-0.1	-		100.8	0.3
1984	-		101.8	1.1	-		102.6	0.8	-		103.0	0.4	-		105.0	1.9	-		103.8	-1.1	-		100.7	-0.8
1985	-		102.3	0.3	-		103.0	0.7	-		104.1	1.1	-		105.0	0.9	-		104.7	-0.3	-		102.0	-1.7
1986	-		105.1	0.3	-		103.8	-1.2	-		105.0	1.2	-		105.6	0.6	-		105.4	-0.2	105.5	0.1	105.3	-0.2
1987	105.6	0.3	-		106.7	1.0	-		107.0	0.3	-		108.1	1.0	-		109.9	1.7	-		109.9	0.0	-	
1988	109.3	-0.5	-		110.2	0.8	-		111.7	1.4	-		112.6	0.8	-		112.7	0.1	-		113.0	0.3	-	
1989	113.8	0.7	-		116.2	2.1	-		117.7	1.3	-		118.8	0.9	-		118.2	-0.5	-		118.0	-0.2	-	
1990	119.5	1.3	-		121.5	1.7	-		122.1	0.5	-		122.7	0.5	-		125.0	1.9	-		125.8	0.6	-	
1991	125.8	0.0	-		126.8	0.8	-		127.8	0.8	-		127.4	-0.3	-		129.0	1.3	-		129.3	0.2	-	
1992	129.6	0.2	-		129.7	0.1	-		129.6	-0.1	-		130.5	0.7	-		131.3	0.6	-		130.8	-0.4	-	
1993	130.8	0.0	-		131.8	0.8	-		132.7	0.7	-		133.9	0.9	-		134.6	0.5	-		135.1	0.4	-	
1994	135.1	0.0	-		135.7	0.4	-		136.1	0.3	-		136.3	0.1	-		138.9	1.9	-		138.8	-0.1	-	
1995	139.0	0.1	-		139.7	0.5	-		139.9	0.1	-		140.3	0.3	-		141.3	0.7	-		140.6	-0.5	-	
1996	141.5	0.6	-		143.1	1.1	-		144.0	0.6	-		144.3	0.2	-		145.8	1.0	-		146.2	0.3	-	
1997	146.2	0.0	-		147.5	0.9	-		147.8	0.2	-		148.2	0.3	-		149.2	0.7	-		149.1	-0.1	-	
1998	150.0	0.6	-		150.1	0.1	-		151.2	0.7	-		152.1	0.6	-		153.3	0.8	-		152.8	-0.3	-	
1999	152.7	-0.1	-		152.9	0.1	-		153.7	0.5	-		154.9	0.8	-		156.4	1.0	-		156.1	-0.2	-	
2000	156.9	0.5	-		159.3	1.5	-		159.0	-0.2	-		160.5	0.9	-		162.8	1.4	-		161.6	-0.7	-	
2001	163.3	1.1	-		163.9	0.4	-		165.6	1.0	-		164.9	-0.4	-		166.5	1.0	-		164.0	-1.5	-	

Source: U.S. Department of Labor, Bureau of Labor Statistics, Division of Consumer Prices and Price Indexes. - indicates no data collected for period.

Cleveland-Akron, OH
Consumer Price Index - All Urban Consumers
Base 1982-1984 = 100
Food and Beverages

For 1975-2001. Columns headed % show percentile change in the index from the previous period for which an index is available.

Year	Jan Index	%	Feb Index	%	Mar Index	%	Apr Index	%	May Index	%	Jun Index	%	Jul Index	%	Aug Index	%	Sep Index	%	Oct Index	%	Nov Index	%	Dec Index	%
1975	-	-	-	-	-	-	-	-	-	-	-	-	-	-	-	-	-	-	-	-	62.1	-	-	-
1976	-	-	62.1	0.0	-	-	-	-	63.0	1.4	-	-	-	-	63.2	0.3	-	-	-	-	63.7	0.8	-	-
1977	-	-	65.4	2.7	-	-	-	-	67.6	3.4	-	-	-	-	65.2	-3.6	-	-	-	-	67.4	3.4	-	-
1978	-	-	69.4	3.0	-	-	70.5	1.6	-	-	72.9	3.4	-	-	73.1	0.3	-	-	73.6	0.7	-	-	74.9	1.8
1979	-	-	77.9	4.0	-	-	79.4	1.9	-	-	79.8	0.5	-	-	80.2	0.5	-	-	80.6	0.5	-	-	81.4	1.0
1980	-	-	83.2	2.2	-	-	83.7	0.6	-	-	83.5	-0.2	-	-	86.6	3.7	-	-	89.0	2.8	-	-	89.5	0.6
1981	-	-	91.8	2.6	-	-	91.9	0.1	-	-	94.2	2.5	-	-	94.0	-0.2	-	-	94.4	0.4	-	-	94.2	-0.2
1982	-	-	95.4	1.3	-	-	95.5	0.1	-	-	96.7	1.3	-	-	96.7	0.0	-	-	97.1	0.4	-	-	97.2	0.1
1983	-	-	98.7	1.5	-	-	99.3	0.6	-	-	99.4	0.1	-	-	100.3	0.9	-	-	100.9	0.6	-	-	101.2	0.3
1984	-	-	103.6	2.4	-	-	103.2	-0.4	-	-	103.3	0.1	-	-	104.2	0.9	-	-	104.7	0.5	-	-	105.3	0.6
1985	-	-	107.0	1.6	-	-	106.2	-0.7	-	-	105.4	-0.8	-	-	106.0	0.6	-	-	106.1	0.1	-	-	106.5	0.4
1986	-	-	107.0	0.5	-	-	106.9	-0.1	-	-	106.3	-0.6	-	-	108.2	1.8	-	-	108.7	0.5	108.9	0.2	109.4	0.5
1987	110.6	1.1	-	-	110.7	0.1	-	-	110.9	0.2	-	-	110.6	-0.3	-	-	111.7	1.0	-	-	112.7	0.9	-	-
1988	113.3	0.5	-	-	114.8	1.3	-	-	114.2	-0.5	-	-	116.4	1.9	-	-	118.8	2.1	-	-	118.9	0.1	-	-
1989	121.0	1.8	-	-	121.8	0.7	-	-	123.3	1.2	-	-	124.9	1.3	-	-	125.4	0.4	-	-	125.6	0.2	-	-
1990	128.9	2.6	-	-	129.9	0.8	-	-	128.8	-0.8	-	-	131.2	1.9	-	-	131.5	0.2	-	-	131.6	0.1	-	-
1991	134.8	2.4	-	-	135.3	0.4	-	-	136.6	1.0	-	-	135.5	-0.8	-	-	134.8	-0.5	-	-	134.8	0.0	-	-
1992	136.4	1.2	-	-	136.4	0.0	-	-	136.4	0.0	-	-	134.9	-1.1	-	-	136.8	1.4	-	-	135.8	-0.7	-	-
1993	137.1	1.0	-	-	138.2	0.8	-	-	139.2	0.7	-	-	139.1	-0.1	-	-	141.5	1.7	-	-	141.9	0.3	-	-
1994	142.9	0.7	-	-	141.9	-0.7	-	-	143.7	1.3	-	-	143.6	-0.1	-	-	146.0	1.7	-	-	146.7	0.5	-	-
1995	149.1	1.6	-	-	146.9	-1.5	-	-	148.4	1.0	-	-	148.7	0.2	-	-	149.5	0.5	-	-	150.7	0.8	-	-
1996	150.7	0.0	-	-	151.6	0.6	-	-	153.4	1.2	-	-	153.9	0.3	-	-	156.3	1.6	-	-	157.5	0.8	-	-
1997	157.7	0.1	-	-	156.8	-0.6	-	-	157.5	0.4	-	-	157.7	0.1	-	-	158.4	0.4	-	-	159.4	0.6	-	-
1998	161.7	1.4	-	-	160.9	-0.5	-	-	163.1	1.4	-	-	163.0	-0.1	-	-	164.2	0.7	-	-	165.4	0.7	-	-
1999	167.2	1.1	-	-	168.2	0.6	-	-	169.6	0.8	-	-	168.5	-0.6	-	-	171.3	1.7	-	-	171.1	-0.1	-	-
2000	171.7	0.4	-	-	172.3	0.3	-	-	171.1	-0.7	-	-	172.6	0.9	-	-	174.6	1.2	-	-	174.0	-0.3	-	-
2001	175.1	0.6	-	-	175.4	0.2	-	-	175.6	0.1	-	-	176.4	0.5	-	-	177.1	0.4	-	-	178.3	0.7	-	-

Source: U.S. Department of Labor, Bureau of Labor Statistics, Division of Consumer Prices and Price Indexes. - indicates no data collected for period.

Cleveland-Akron, OH
Consumer Price Index - Urban Wage Earners
Base 1982-1984 = 100
Food and Beverages

For 1975-2001. Columns headed % show percentile change in the index from the previous period for which an index is available.

Year	Jan Index	%	Feb Index	%	Mar Index	%	Apr Index	%	May Index	%	Jun Index	%	Jul Index	%	Aug Index	%	Sep Index	%	Oct Index	%	Nov Index	%	Dec Index	%
1975	-	-	-	-	-	-	-	-	-	-	-	-	-	-	-	-	-	-	-	-	61.4	-	-	-
1976	-	-	61.4	0.0	-	-	-	-	62.2	1.3	-	-	-	-	62.5	0.5	-	-	-	-	62.9	0.6	-	-
1977	-	-	64.6	2.7	-	-	-	-	66.8	3.4	-	-	-	-	64.4	-3.6	-	-	-	-	66.6	3.4	-	-
1978	-	-	68.5	2.9	-	-	70.0	2.2	-	-	73.3	4.7	-	-	73.7	0.5	-	-	73.8	0.1	-	-	75.3	2.0
1979	-	-	78.4	4.1	-	-	80.3	2.4	-	-	80.8	0.6	-	-	80.9	0.1	-	-	81.2	0.4	-	-	83.0	2.2
1980	-	-	84.1	1.3	-	-	84.9	1.0	-	-	84.6	-0.4	-	-	88.1	4.1	-	-	90.1	2.3	-	-	91.5	1.6
1981	-	-	93.2	1.9	-	-	93.5	0.3	-	-	94.3	0.9	-	-	94.4	0.1	-	-	94.8	0.4	-	-	94.3	-0.5
1982	-	-	95.4	1.2	-	-	95.7	0.3	-	-	96.9	1.3	-	-	96.8	-0.1	-	-	97.4	0.6	-	-	97.6	0.2
1983	-	-	99.0	1.4	-	-	99.5	0.5	-	-	99.5	0.0	-	-	100.3	0.8	-	-	100.8	0.5	-	-	101.0	0.2
1984	-	-	103.3	2.3	-	-	102.9	-0.4	-	-	103.1	0.2	-	-	104.1	1.0	-	-	104.5	0.4	-	-	105.0	0.5
1985	-	-	106.7	1.6	-	-	106.0	-0.7	-	-	105.1	-0.8	-	-	105.8	0.7	-	-	105.9	0.1	-	-	106.2	0.3
1986	-	-	106.6	0.4	-	-	106.6	0.0	-	-	106.0	-0.6	-	-	107.9	1.8	-	-	108.3	0.4	108.6	0.3	109.0	0.4
1987	110.2	1.1	-	-	110.2	0.0	-	-	110.5	0.3	-	-	110.3	-0.2	-	-	111.4	1.0	-	-	112.3	0.8	-	-
1988	112.8	0.4	-	-	114.3	1.3	-	-	113.7	-0.5	-	-	115.9	1.9	-	-	118.3	2.1	-	-	118.4	0.1	-	-
1989	120.5	1.8	-	-	121.3	0.7	-	-	122.8	1.2	-	-	124.4	1.3	-	-	124.9	0.4	-	-	125.2	0.2	-	-
1990	128.5	2.6	-	-	129.5	0.8	-	-	128.4	-0.8	-	-	130.8	1.9	-	-	131.2	0.3	-	-	131.3	0.1	-	-
1991	134.4	2.4	-	-	134.9	0.4	-	-	136.2	1.0	-	-	135.1	-0.8	-	-	134.3	-0.6	-	-	134.3	0.0	-	-
1992	136.0	1.3	-	-	136.0	0.0	-	-	135.8	-0.1	-	-	134.3	-1.1	-	-	136.3	1.5	-	-	135.4	-0.7	-	-
1993	136.7	1.0	-	-	137.8	0.8	-	-	138.7	0.7	-	-	138.6	-0.1	-	-	141.0	1.7	-	-	141.4	0.3	-	-
1994	142.4	0.7	-	-	141.4	-0.7	-	-	143.3	1.3	-	-	143.1	-0.1	-	-	145.4	1.6	-	-	146.2	0.6	-	-
1995	148.5	1.6	-	-	146.3	-1.5	-	-	147.8	1.0	-	-	148.1	0.2	-	-	148.9	0.5	-	-	150.2	0.9	-	-
1996	150.2	0.0	-	-	151.2	0.7	-	-	152.9	1.1	-	-	153.4	0.3	-	-	155.8	1.6	-	-	157.0	0.8	-	-
1997	157.2	0.1	-	-	156.3	-0.6	-	-	156.9	0.4	-	-	157.1	0.1	-	-	157.9	0.5	-	-	158.9	0.6	-	-
1998	160.9	1.3	-	-	160.0	-0.6	-	-	162.2	1.4	-	-	162.2	0.0	-	-	163.5	0.8	-	-	164.7	0.7	-	-
1999	166.4	1.0	-	-	167.4	0.6	-	-	169.0	1.0	-	-	168.0	-0.6	-	-	170.6	1.5	-	-	170.6	0.0	-	-
2000	171.0	0.2	-	-	171.5	0.3	-	-	170.7	-0.5	-	-	172.1	0.8	-	-	174.1	1.2	-	-	173.3	-0.5	-	-
2001	174.6	0.8	-	-	175.2	0.3	-	-	175.2	0.0	-	-	176.1	0.5	-	-	176.9	0.5	-	-	177.8	0.5	-	-

Source: U.S. Department of Labor, Bureau of Labor Statistics, Division of Consumer Prices and Price Indexes. - indicates no data collected for period.

Cleveland-Akron, OH
Consumer Price Index - All Urban Consumers
Base 1982-1984 = 100
Housing

For 1975-2001. Columns headed % show percentile change in the index from the previous period for which an index is available.

Year	Jan Index	%	Feb Index	%	Mar Index	%	Apr Index	%	May Index	%	Jun Index	%	Jul Index	%	Aug Index	%	Sep Index	%	Oct Index	%	Nov Index	%	Dec Index	%
1975	-	-	-	-	-	-	-	-	-	-	-	-	-	-	-	-	-	-	-	-	45.1	-	-	-
1976	-	-	45.0	-0.2	-	-	-	-	45.2	0.4	-	-	-	-	46.8	3.5	-	-	-	-	47.4	1.3	-	-
1977	-	-	48.5	2.3	-	-	-	-	48.9	0.8	-	-	-	-	50.5	3.3	-	-	-	-	50.9	0.8	-	-
1978	-	-	51.1	0.4	-	-	52.7	3.1	-	-	51.8	-1.7	-	-	53.4	3.1	-	-	55.9	4.7	-	-	58.6	4.8
1979	-	-	59.7	1.9	-	-	61.5	3.0	-	-	63.7	3.6	-	-	63.3	-0.6	-	-	63.9	0.9	-	-	67.7	5.9
1980	-	-	72.5	7.1	-	-	73.8	1.8	-	-	75.2	1.9	-	-	75.6	0.5	-	-	80.7	6.7	-	-	80.6	-0.1
1981	-	-	82.4	2.2	-	-	80.4	-2.4	-	-	87.4	8.7	-	-	86.2	-1.4	-	-	84.1	-2.4	-	-	82.6	-1.8
1982	-	-	84.4	2.2	-	-	84.8	0.5	-	-	90.2	6.4	-	-	97.9	8.5	-	-	100.3	2.5	-	-	100.7	0.4
1983	-	-	101.1	0.4	-	-	101.0	-0.1	-	-	103.7	2.7	-	-	102.9	-0.8	-	-	104.7	1.7	-	-	102.8	-1.8
1984	-	-	102.7	-0.1	-	-	104.1	1.4	-	-	105.9	1.7	-	-	105.8	-0.1	-	-	106.9	1.0	-	-	106.0	-0.8
1985	-	-	106.3	0.3	-	-	106.3	0.0	-	-	110.4	3.9	-	-	110.6	0.2	-	-	109.4	-1.1	-	-	108.9	-0.5
1986	-	-	110.0	1.0	-	-	110.9	0.8	-	-	112.7	1.6	-	-	113.9	1.1	-	-	112.2	-1.5	112.5	0.3	111.7	-0.7
1987	111.3	-0.4	-	-	113.1	1.6	-	-	112.9	-0.2	-	-	115.1	1.9	-	-	115.8	0.6	-	-	114.8	-0.9	-	-
1988	114.5	-0.3	-	-	116.3	1.6	-	-	117.7	1.2	-	-	119.2	1.3	-	-	118.5	-0.6	-	-	119.3	0.7	-	-
1989	120.6	1.1	-	-	121.4	0.7	-	-	121.4	0.0	-	-	125.4	3.3	-	-	124.3	-0.9	-	-	122.5	-1.4	-	-
1990	123.7	1.0	-	-	125.6	1.5	-	-	126.9	1.0	-	-	128.5	1.3	-	-	130.7	1.7	-	-	129.2	-1.1	-	-
1991	129.7	0.4	-	-	131.2	1.2	-	-	132.3	0.8	-	-	132.8	0.4	-	-	133.9	0.8	-	-	133.4	-0.4	-	-
1992	136.0	1.9	-	-	134.1	-1.4	-	-	134.1	0.0	-	-	137.8	2.8	-	-	137.3	-0.4	-	-	135.1	-1.6	-	-
1993	136.7	1.2	-	-	138.5	1.3	-	-	137.3	-0.9	-	-	139.7	1.7	-	-	141.3	1.1	-	-	139.9	-1.0	-	-
1994	140.2	0.2	-	-	142.2	1.4	-	-	142.5	0.2	-	-	143.2	0.5	-	-	143.6	0.3	-	-	142.1	-1.0	-	-
1995	143.8	1.2	-	-	143.8	0.0	-	-	143.2	-0.4	-	-	146.6	2.4	-	-	147.0	0.3	-	-	145.7	-0.9	-	-
1996	145.7	0.0	-	-	148.0	1.6	-	-	147.8	-0.1	-	-	150.0	1.5	-	-	150.1	0.1	-	-	148.8	-0.9	-	-
1997	149.7	0.6	-	-	152.3	1.7	-	-	151.8	-0.3	-	-	154.7	1.9	-	-	154.5	-0.1	-	-	154.4	-0.1	-	-
1998	156.0	1.0	-	-	157.7	1.1	-	-	156.7	-0.6	-	-	159.0	1.5	-	-	161.5	1.6	-	-	159.2	-1.4	-	-
1999	158.7	-0.3	-	-	159.2	0.3	-	-	158.7	-0.3	-	-	161.7	1.9	-	-	162.0	0.2	-	-	160.5	-0.9	-	-
2000	161.4	0.6	-	-	163.7	1.4	-	-	164.2	0.3	-	-	167.7	2.1	-	-	169.8	1.3	-	-	167.7	-1.2	-	-
2001	169.5	1.1	-	-	174.1	2.7	-	-	173.8	-0.2	-	-	175.5	1.0	-	-	172.8	-1.5	-	-	170.0	-1.6	-	-

Source: U.S. Department of Labor, Bureau of Labor Statistics, Division of Consumer Prices and Price Indexes. - indicates no data collected for period.

Cleveland-Akron, OH
Consumer Price Index - Urban Wage Earners
Base 1982-1984 = 100
Housing

For 1975-2001. Columns headed % show percentile change in the index from the previous period for which an index is available.

Year	Jan Index	%	Feb Index	%	Mar Index	%	Apr Index	%	May Index	%	Jun Index	%	Jul Index	%	Aug Index	%	Sep Index	%	Oct Index	%	Nov Index	%	Dec Index	%
1975	-		-		-		-		-		-		-		-		-		-		-		-	
1976	-		46.9	-0.2	-		-		47.1	0.4	-		-		48.8	3.6	-		-		47.0		-	
1977	-		50.6	2.4	-		-		50.9	0.6	-		-		52.6	3.3	-		-		49.4	1.2	-	
1978	-		53.2	0.2	-		55.0	3.4	-		54.0	-1.8	=		55.7	3.1	-		-		53.1	1.0	-	
1979	-		62.1	2.0	-		63.8	2.7	-		66.2	3.8	-		65.8	-0.6	-		58.3	4.7	-		60.9	4.5
1980	-		75.3	7.3	-		77.0	2.3	-		77.9	1.2	-		78.4	0.6	-		66.3	0.8	-		70.2	5.9
1981	-		85.5	2.3	-		83.3	-2.6	-		90.7	8.9	-		89.2	-1.7	-		83.6	6.6	-		83.6	0.0
1982	-		87.7	2.2	-		88.2	0.6	-		94.0	6.6	-		89.2	-1.7	-		87.2	-2.2	-		85.8	-1.6
1983	-		102.9	-1.4	-		103.6	0.7	-		103.5	-0.1	-		102.0	8.5	-		104.0	2.0	-		104.4	0.4
1984	-		100.3	1.0	-		102.0	1.7	-		101.6	-0.4	-		102.6	-0.9	-		101.3	-1.3	-		99.3	-2.0
1985	-		98.6	0.5	-		98.6	0.0	-		102.6	4.1	-		105.6	3.9	-		102.3	-3.1	-		98.1	-4.1
1986	-		102.1	1.1	-		102.8	0.7	-		104.7	1.8	-		102.9	0.3	-		101.4	-1.5	-		101.0	-0.4
1987	103.3	-0.2	-		104.9	1.5	-		104.8	-0.1	-		106.7	1.8	-		105.8	1.1	107.5	0.7	104.2	-1.5	104.3	0.1	103.5	-0.8
1988	106.3	-0.2	-		108.0	1.6	-		109.2	1.1	-		110.5	1.2	-		-		109.9	-0.5	-		106.5	-0.9	-	
1989	111.6	1.1	-		112.2	0.5	-		112.4	0.2	-		115.7	2.9	-		-		115.1	-0.5	-		110.4	0.5	-	
1990	114.4	1.0	-		116.0	1.4	-		117.1	0.9	-		118.6	1.3	-		-		120.6	1.7	-		113.3	-1.6	-	
1991	119.7	0.3	-		120.9	1.0	-		121.8	0.7	-		122.3	0.4	-		-		123.8	1.2	-		119.3	-1.1	-	
1992	125.6	1.9	-		123.8	-1.4	-		123.9	0.1	-		127.1	2.6	-		-		126.6	-0.4	-		123.2	-0.5	-	
1993	126.2	1.0	-		127.7	1.2	-		126.7	-0.8	-		128.8	1.7	-		-		130.1	1.0	-		125.0	-1.3	-	
1994	129.1	-0.2	-		130.6	1.2	-		130.9	0.2	-		131.7	0.6	-		-		132.3	0.5	-		129.3	-0.6	-	
1995	132.3	1.0	-		132.2	-0.1	-		131.7	-0.4	-		134.6	2.2	-		-		135.1	0.4	-		131.0	-1.0	-	
1996	134.3	0.4	-		136.3	1.5	-		136.3	0.0	-		138.4	1.5	-		-		138.7	0.2	-		133.8	-1.0	-	
1997	138.4	0.6	-		140.6	1.6	-		140.3	-0.2	-		142.9	1.9	-		-		142.7	-0.1	-		137.6	-0.8	-	
1998	144.1	1.1	-		145.5	1.0	-		144.7	-0.5	-		146.9	1.5	-		-		149.3	1.6	-		142.6	-0.1	-	
1999	146.5	-0.3	-		146.9	0.3	-		146.5	-0.3	-		149.3	1.9	-		-		149.6	0.2	-		147.0	-1.5	-	
2000	149.0	0.6	-		151.1	1.4	-		151.6	0.3	-		154.9	2.2	-		-		156.9	1.3	-		148.1	-1.0	-	
2001	156.8	1.1	-		160.7	2.5	-		160.4	-0.2	-		162.5	1.3	-		-		159.8	-1.7	-		155.1	-1.1	-	

Source: U.S. Department of Labor, Bureau of Labor Statistics, Division of Consumer Prices and Price Indexes. - indicates no data collected for period.

Cleveland-Akron, OH
Consumer Price Index - All Urban Consumers
Base 1982-1984 = 100
Apparel

For 1952-2001. Columns headed % show percentile change in the index from the previous period for which an index is available.

Year	Jan Index	%	Feb Index	%	Mar Index	%	Apr Index	%	May Index	%	Jun Index	%	Jul Index	%	Aug Index	%	Sep Index	%	Oct Index	%	Nov Index	%	Dec Index	%
1952	-	-	-	-	-	-	-	-	-	-	-	-	-	-	-	-	-	-	-	-	43.7	-	-	-
1953	-	-	43.3	-0.9	-	-	-	-	44.4	2.5	-	-	-	-	44.2	-0.5	-	-	-	-	44.2	0.0	-	-
1954	-	-	44.1	-0.2	-	-	-	-	44.1	0.0	-	-	-	-	44.1	0.0	-	-	-	-	44.0	-0.2	-	-
1955	-	-	43.8	-0.5	-	-	-	-	43.8	0.0	-	-	-	-	43.7	-0.2	-	-	-	-	44.1	0.9	-	-
1956	-	-	44.2	0.2	-	-	-	-	44.6	0.9	-	-	-	-	45.0	0.9	-	-	-	-	45.3	0.7	-	-
1957	-	-	45.0	-0.7	-	-	-	-	45.4	0.9	-	-	-	-	45.5	0.2	-	-	-	-	45.8	0.7	-	-
1958	-	-	45.9	0.2	-	-	-	-	46.0	0.2	-	-	-	-	45.9	-0.2	-	-	-	-	45.9	0.0	-	-
1959	-	-	46.0	0.2	-	-	-	-	46.2	0.4	-	-	-	-	46.3	0.2	-	-	-	-	46.4	0.2	-	-
1960	-	-	46.4	0.0	-	-	-	-	46.3	-0.2	-	-	-	-	46.4	0.2	-	-	-	-	46.5	0.2	-	-
1961	-	-	46.5	0.0	-	-	-	-	46.7	0.4	-	-	-	-	46.9	0.4	-	-	-	-	47.0	0.2	-	-
1962	-	-	46.9	-0.2	-	-	-	-	47.1	0.4	-	-	-	-	46.9	-0.4	-	-	-	-	47.1	0.4	-	-
1963	-	-	47.3	0.4	-	-	-	-	47.8	1.1	-	-	-	-	48.1	0.6	-	-	-	-	47.7	-0.8	-	-
1964	-	-	47.8	0.2	-	-	-	-	48.0	0.4	-	-	-	-	47.7	-0.6	-	-	-	-	48.0	0.6	-	-
1965	-	-	47.9	-0.2	-	-	-	-	48.6	1.5	-	-	-	-	48.0	-1.2	-	-	-	-	48.5	1.0	-	-
1966	-	-	48.8	0.6	-	-	-	-	49.9	2.3	-	-	-	-	49.8	-0.2	-	-	-	-	50.4	1.2	-	-
1967	-	-	50.5	0.2	-	-	-	-	51.1	1.2	-	-	-	-	50.8	-0.6	-	-	-	-	52.7	3.7	-	-
1968	-	-	53.5	1.5	-	-	-	-	54.0	0.9	-	-	-	-	54.6	1.1	-	-	-	-	55.7	2.0	-	-
1969	-	-	56.1	0.7	-	-	-	-	57.3	2.1	-	-	-	-	57.7	0.7	-	-	-	-	59.3	2.8	-	-
1970	-	-	59.4	0.2	-	-	-	-	60.4	1.7	-	-	-	-	60.3	-0.2	-	-	-	-	61.4	1.8	-	-
1971	-	-	61.4	0.0	-	-	-	-	62.8	2.3	-	-	-	-	62.4	-0.6	-	-	-	-	63.0	1.0	-	-
1972	-	-	62.9	-0.2	-	-	-	-	63.5	1.0	-	-	-	-	63.4	-0.2	-	-	-	-	64.2	1.3	-	-
1973	-	-	64.2	0.0	-	-	-	-	65.7	2.3	-	-	-	-	66.6	1.4	-	-	-	-	69.3	4.1	-	-
1974	-	-	70.6	1.9	-	-	-	-	71.5	1.3	-	-	-	-	73.2	2.4	-	-	-	-	75.6	3.3	-	-
1975	-	-	74.0	-2.1	-	-	-	-	74.4	0.5	-	-	-	-	74.2	-0.3	-	-	-	-	74.9	0.9	-	-
1976	-	-	74.5	-0.5	-	-	-	-	75.3	1.1	-	-	-	-	76.3	1.3	-	-	-	-	78.6	3.0	-	-
1977	-	-	78.1	-0.6	-	-	-	-	79.7	2.0	-	-	-	-	81.4	2.1	-	-	-	-	82.8	1.7	-	-
1978	-	-	81.0	-2.2	-	-	80.2	-1.0	-	-	81.3	1.4	-	-	83.6	2.8	-	-	84.0	0.5	-	-	82.9	-1.3
1979	-	-	83.5	0.7	-	-	82.4	-1.3	-	-	81.4	-1.2	-	-	85.5	5.0	-	-	87.6	2.5	-	-	88.2	0.7
1980	-	-	87.7	-0.6	-	-	88.7	1.1	-	-	87.6	-1.2	-	-	90.4	3.2	-	-	91.6	1.3	-	-	91.4	-0.2
1981	-	-	93.2	2.0	-	-	96.1	3.1	-	-	94.6	-1.6	-	-	95.2	0.6	-	-	95.0	-0.2	-	-	97.3	2.4
1982	-	-	98.0	0.7	-	-	97.5	-0.5	-	-	98.4	0.9	-	-	102.1	3.8	-	-	101.6	-0.5	-	-	99.7	-1.9
1983	-	-	100.6	0.9	-	-	97.6	-3.0	-	-	98.7	1.1	-	-	99.1	0.4	-	-	99.9	0.8	-	-	99.5	-0.4
1984	-	-	101.2	1.7	-	-	98.4	-2.8	-	-	101.2	2.8	-	-	102.9	1.7	-	-	102.2	-0.7	-	-	102.8	0.6
1985	-	-	101.9	-0.9	-	-	103.2	1.3	-	-	101.5	-1.6	-	-	106.5	4.9	-	-	107.8	1.2	-	-	103.8	-3.7
1986	-	-	104.1	0.3	-	-	100.9	-3.1	-	-	99.3	-1.6	-	-	105.1	5.8	-	-	104.2	-0.9	103.1	-1.1	98.5	-4.5
1987	97.8	-0.7	-	-	105.5	7.9	-	-	104.0	-1.4	-	-	105.0	1.0	-	-	121.3	15.5	-	-	115.3	-4.9	-	-
1988	106.7	-7.5	-	-	111.0	4.0	-	-	111.8	0.7	-	-	108.0	-3.4	-	-	101.0	-6.5	-	-	100.1	-0.9	-	-
1989	91.9	-8.2	-	-	119.5	30.0	-	-	120.5	0.8	-	-	114.6	-4.9	-	-	111.2	-3.0	-	-	108.7	-2.2	-	-
1990	102.6	-5.6	-	-	128.8	25.5	-	-	127.6	-0.9	-	-	115.4	-9.6	-	-	115.5	0.1	-	-	115.0	-0.4	-	-
1991	112.8	-1.9	-	-	125.1	10.9	-	-	122.7	-1.9	-	-	115.2	-6.1	-	-	126.1	9.5	-	-	127.4	1.0	-	-
1992	121.0	-5.0	-	-	128.2	6.0	-	-	122.7	-4.3	-	-	116.8	-4.8	-	-	124.9	6.9	-	-	120.7	-3.4	-	-
1993	116.4	-3.6	-	-	119.7	2.8	-	-	126.7	5.8	-	-	127.2	0.4	-	-	129.3	1.7	-	-	128.6	-0.5	-	-
1994	126.9	-1.3	-	-	128.8	1.5	-	-	127.3	-1.2	-	-	116.3	-8.6	-	-	141.6	21.8	-	-	132.9	-6.1	-	-
1995	124.2	-6.5	-	-	136.5	9.9	-	-	129.9	-4.8	-	-	122.5	-5.7	-	-	126.3	3.1	-	-	123.9	-1.9	-	-
1996	120.9	-2.4	-	-	132.2	9.3	-	-	133.7	1.1	-	-	124.1	-7.2	-	-	133.2	7.3	-	-	128.7	-3.4	-	-
1997	121.6	-5.5	-	-	128.9	6.0	-	-	128.6	-0.2	-	-	124.7	-3.0	-	-	131.9	5.8	-	-	129.4	-1.9	-	-

[Continued]

Cleveland-Akron, OH
Consumer Price Index - All Urban Consumers
Base 1982-1984 = 100
Apparel
[Continued]

For 1952-2001. Columns headed % show percentile change in the index from the previous period for which an index is available.

Year	Jan		Feb		Mar		Apr		May		Jun		Jul		Aug		Sep		Oct		Nov		Dec	
	Index	%	Index	%	Index	%	Index	%	Index	%	Index	%	Index	%	Index	%	Index	%	Index	%	Index	%	Index	%
1998	130.0	0.5	-	-	127.2	-2.2	-	-	132.5	4.2	-	-	123.7	-6.6	-	-	134.0	8.3	-	-	134.3	0.2	-	-
1999	121.0	-9.9	-	-	126.5	4.5	-	-	123.0	-2.8	-	-	117.0	-4.9	-	-	130.6	11.6	-	-	126.6	-3.1	-	-
2000	120.2	-5.1	-	-	126.7	5.4	-	-	121.0	-4.5	-	-	114.1	-5.7	-	-	128.5	12.6	-	-	127.9	-0.5	-	-
2001	120.8	-5.6	-	-	121.7	0.7	-	-	122.2	0.4	-	-	117.8	-3.6	-	-	130.4	10.7	-	-	128.1	-1.8	-	-

Source: U.S. Department of Labor, Bureau of Labor Statistics, Division of Consumer Prices and Price Indexes. - indicates no data collected for period.

Cleveland-Akron, OH
Consumer Price Index - Urban Wage Earners
Base 1982-1984 = 100
Apparel

For 1952-2001. Columns headed % show percentile change in the index from the previous period for which an index is available.

Year	Jan Index	%	Feb Index	%	Mar Index	%	Apr Index	%	May Index	%	Jun Index	%	Jul Index	%	Aug Index	%	Sep Index	%	Oct Index	%	Nov Index	%	Dec Index	%
1952	-	-	-	-	-	-	-	-	-	-	-	-	-	-	-	-	-	-	-	-	42.4	-	-	-
1953	-	-	42.0	-0.9	-	-	-	-	43.0	2.4	-	-	-	-	42.9	-0.2	-	-	-	-	42.9	0.0	-	-
1954	-	-	42.8	-0.2	-	-	-	-	42.8	0.0	-	-	-	-	42.7	-0.2	-	-	-	-	42.6	-0.2	-	-
1955	-	-	42.4	-0.5	-	-	-	-	42.5	0.2	-	-	-	-	42.4	-0.2	-	-	-	-	42.7	0.7	-	-
1956	-	-	42.9	0.5	-	-	-	-	43.2	0.7	-	-	-	-	43.6	0.9	-	-	-	-	44.0	0.9	-	-
1957	-	-	43.6	-0.9	-	-	-	-	44.0	0.9	-	-	-	-	44.1	0.2	-	-	-	-	44.4	0.7	-	-
1958	-	-	44.5	0.2	-	-	-	-	44.6	0.2	-	-	-	-	44.5	-0.2	-	-	-	-	44.5	0.0	-	-
1959	-	-	44.6	0.2	-	-	-	-	44.8	0.4	-	-	-	-	44.9	0.2	-	-	-	-	45.0	0.2	-	-
1960	-	-	45.0	0.0	-	-	-	-	44.9	-0.2	-	-	-	-	45.0	0.2	-	-	-	-	45.1	0.2	-	-
1961	-	-	45.1	0.0	-	-	-	-	45.3	0.4	-	-	-	-	45.5	0.4	-	-	-	-	45.6	0.2	-	-
1962	-	-	45.5	-0.2	-	-	-	-	45.7	0.4	-	-	-	-	45.5	-0.4	-	-	-	-	45.7	0.4	-	-
1963	-	-	45.9	0.4	-	-	-	-	46.4	1.1	-	-	-	-	46.7	0.6	-	-	-	-	46.2	-1.1	-	-
1964	-	-	46.3	0.2	-	-	-	-	46.6	0.6	-	-	-	-	46.2	-0.9	-	-	-	-	46.5	0.6	-	-
1965	-	-	46.4	-0.2	-	-	-	-	47.2	1.7	-	-	-	-	46.6	-1.3	-	-	-	-	47.1	1.1	-	-
1966	-	-	47.3	0.4	-	-	-	-	48.4	2.3	-	-	-	-	48.3	-0.2	-	-	-	-	48.9	1.2	-	-
1967	-	-	49.0	0.2	-	-	-	-	49.6	1.2	-	-	-	-	49.3	-0.6	-	-	-	-	51.1	3.7	-	-
1968	-	-	51.8	1.4	-	-	-	-	52.3	1.0	-	-	-	-	53.0	1.3	-	-	-	-	54.0	1.9	-	-
1969	-	-	54.4	0.7	-	-	-	-	55.6	2.2	-	-	-	-	56.0	0.7	-	-	-	-	57.5	2.7	-	-
1970	-	-	57.6	0.2	-	-	-	-	58.6	1.7	-	-	-	-	58.5	-0.2	-	-	-	-	59.6	1.9	-	-
1971	-	-	59.6	0.0	-	-	-	-	60.9	2.2	-	-	-	-	60.5	-0.7	-	-	-	-	61.1	1.0	-	-
1972	-	-	61.1	0.0	-	-	-	-	61.6	0.8	-	-	-	-	61.5	-0.2	-	-	-	-	62.3	1.3	-	-
1973	-	-	62.2	-0.2	-	-	-	-	63.7	2.4	-	-	-	-	64.6	1.4	-	-	-	-	67.2	4.0	-	-
1974	-	-	68.5	1.9	-	-	-	-	69.3	1.2	-	-	-	-	71.0	2.5	-	-	-	-	73.3	3.2	-	-
1975	-	-	71.8	-2.0	-	-	-	-	72.2	0.6	-	-	-	-	72.0	-0.3	-	-	-	-	72.7	1.0	-	-
1976	-	-	72.3	-0.6	-	-	-	-	73.0	1.0	-	-	-	-	74.0	1.4	-	-	-	-	76.3	3.1	-	-
1977	-	-	75.8	-0.7	-	-	-	-	77.3	2.0	-	-	-	-	79.0	2.2	-	-	-	-	80.4	1.8	-	-
1978	-	-	78.5	-2.4	-	-	79.5	1.3	-	-	79.9	0.5	-	-	81.2	1.6	-	-	82.9	2.1	-	-	83.1	0.2
1979	-	-	83.6	0.6	-	-	83.2	-0.5	-	-	81.5	-2.0	-	-	83.3	2.2	-	-	85.3	2.4	-	-	85.7	0.5
1980	-	-	85.5	-0.2	-	-	86.9	1.6	-	-	85.3	-1.8	-	-	86.7	1.6	-	-	89.1	2.8	-	-	89.9	0.9
1981	-	-	91.1	1.3	-	-	92.8	1.9	-	-	92.3	-0.5	-	-	92.3	0.0	-	-	95.3	3.3	-	-	97.5	2.3
1982	-	-	97.6	0.1	-	-	97.3	-0.3	-	-	98.3	1.0	-	-	101.8	3.6	-	-	101.3	-0.5	-	-	99.7	-1.6
1983	-	-	101.0	1.3	-	-	97.7	-3.3	-	-	98.6	0.9	-	-	99.2	0.6	-	-	100.0	0.8	-	-	99.3	-0.7
1984	-	-	101.8	2.5	-	-	98.3	-3.4	-	-	101.4	3.2	-	-	103.4	2.0	-	-	102.7	-0.7	-	-	102.1	-0.6
1985	-	-	102.6	0.5	-	-	103.9	1.3	-	-	102.2	-1.6	-	-	107.8	5.5	-	-	109.1	1.2	-	-	105.3	-3.5
1986	-	-	104.9	-0.4	-	-	102.1	-2.7	-	-	100.5	-1.6	-	-	106.4	5.9	-	-	105.8	-0.6	103.8	-1.9	99.7	-3.9
1987	98.2	-1.5	-	-	105.9	7.8	-	-	104.6	-1.2	-	-	105.8	1.1	-	-	121.8	15.1	-	-	116.6	-4.3	-	-
1988	107.3	-8.0	-	-	111.5	3.9	-	-	112.4	0.8	-	-	108.4	-3.6	-	-	101.3	-6.5	-	-	100.0	-1.3	-	-
1989	92.0	-8.0	-	-	118.5	28.8	-	-	119.8	1.1	-	-	114.0	-4.8	-	-	109.9	-3.6	-	-	107.9	-1.8	-	-
1990	102.2	-5.3	-	-	127.3	24.6	-	-	126.3	-0.8	-	-	114.2	-9.6	-	-	115.2	0.9	-	-	114.7	-0.4	-	-
1991	112.2	-2.2	-	-	124.2	10.7	-	-	121.9	-1.9	-	-	114.9	-5.7	-	-	125.7	9.4	-	-	127.1	1.1	-	-
1992	120.9	-4.9	-	-	128.4	6.2	-	-	122.9	-4.3	-	-	116.7	-5.0	-	-	125.7	7.7	-	-	121.2	-3.6	-	-
1993	116.9	-3.5	-	-	119.5	2.2	-	-	125.3	4.9	-	-	126.3	0.8	-	-	128.0	1.3	-	-	127.2	-0.6	-	-
1994	125.9	-1.0	-	-	127.4	1.2	-	-	126.4	-0.8	-	-	115.5	-8.6	-	-	140.0	21.2	-	-	131.2	-6.3	-	-
1995	122.3	-6.8	-	-	134.3	9.8	-	-	127.7	-4.9	-	-	120.6	-5.6	-	-	124.8	3.5	-	-	125.7	-3.4	-	-
1996	118.5	-3.3	-	-	129.6	9.4	-	-	131.4	1.4	-	-	121.8	-7.3	-	-	130.1	6.8	-	-	125.7	-3.4	-	-
1997	119.7	-4.8	-	-	125.5	4.8	-	-	125.7	0.2	-	-	121.7	-3.2	-	-	129.0	6.0	-	-	126.1	-2.2	-	-

[Continued]

Cleveland-Akron, OH
Consumer Price Index - Urban Wage Earners
Base 1982-1984 = 100
Apparel
[Continued]

For 1952-2001. Columns headed % show percentile change in the index from the previous period for which an index is available.

Year	Jan		Feb		Mar		Apr		May		Jun		Jul		Aug		Sep		Oct		Nov		Dec	
	Index	%	Index	%	Index	%	Index	%	Index	%	Index	%	Index	%	Index	%	Index	%	Index	%	Index	%	Index	%
1998	125.7	-0.3	-	-	124.0	-1.4	-	-	128.9	4.0	-	-	125.2	-2.9	-	-	131.6	5.1	-	-	132.1	0.4	-	-
1999	120.7	-8.6	-	-	125.0	3.6	-	-	121.9	-2.5	-	-	116.2	-4.7	-	-	129.7	11.6	-	-	124.7	-3.9	-	-
2000	119.3	-4.3	-	-	126.4	6.0	-	-	120.5	-4.7	-	-	114.7	-4.8	-	-	128.4	11.9	-	-	128.4	0.0	-	-
2001	118.8	-7.5	-	-	122.4	3.0	-	-	121.0	-1.1	-	-	116.4	-3.8	-	-	129.5	11.3	-	-	128.0	-1.2	-	-

Source: U.S. Department of Labor, Bureau of Labor Statistics, Division of Consumer Prices and Price Indexes. - indicates no data collected for period.

Cleveland-Akron, OH
Consumer Price Index - All Urban Consumers
Base 1982-1984 = 100
Transportation

For 1947-2000. Columns headed % show percentile change in the index from the previous period for which an index is available.

Year	Jan Index	%	Feb Index	%	Mar Index	%	Apr Index	%	May Index	%	Jun Index	%	Jul Index	%	Aug Index	%	Sep Index	%	Oct Index	%	Nov Index	%	Dec Index	%
1947	18.3	-	18.3	0.0	18.6	1.6	18.7	0.5	18.6	-0.5	18.6	0.0	-	-	18.9	1.6	-	-	-	-	19.5	3.2	-	-
1948	-	-	20.7	6.2	-	-	-	-	20.8	0.5	-	-	-	-	22.8	9.6	-	-	-	-	22.9	0.4	-	-
1949	-	-	23.1	0.9	-	-	-	-	23.2	0.4	-	-	-	-	23.1	-0.4	-	-	-	-	23.1	0.0	-	-
1950	-	-	22.8	-1.3	-	-	-	-	22.7	-0.4	-	-	-	-	23.4	3.1	-	-	-	-	23.5	0.4	-	-
1951	-	-	23.7	0.9	-	-	-	-	23.9	0.8	-	-	-	-	24.9	4.2	-	-	-	-	25.6	2.8	-	-
1952	-	-	26.0	1.6	-	-	-	-	26.0	0.0	-	-	-	-	26.0	0.0	-	-	-	-	26.0		-	-
1953	-	-	26.1	0.4	-	-	-	-	26.2	0.4	-	-	-	-	26.6	1.5	-	-	-	-	26.4	-0.8	-	-
1954	-	-	26.1	-1.1	-	-	-	-	26.0	-0.4	-	-	-	-	25.0	-3.8	-	-	-	-	25.9	3.6	-	-
1955	-	-	25.4	-1.9	-	-	-	-	25.0	-1.6	-	-	-	-	25.4	1.6	-	-	-	-	26.5	4.3	-	-
1956	-	-	26.0	-1.9	-	-	-	-	26.1	0.4	-	-	-	-	26.7	2.3	-	-	-	-	27.8	4.1	-	-
1957	-	-	28.1	1.1	-	-	-	-	28.1	0.0	-	-	-	-	28.6	1.8	-	-	-	-	29.4	2.8	-	-
1958	-	-	28.7	-2.4	-	-	-	-	28.9	0.7	-	-	-	-	29.0	0.3	-	-	-	-	29.4	1.4	-	-
1959	-	-	29.6	0.7	-	-	-	-	29.7	0.3	-	-	-	-	30.3	2.0	-	-	-	-	30.7	1.3	-	-
1960	-	-	30.4	-1.0	-	-	-	-	30.2	-0.7	-	-	-	-	30.1	-0.3	-	-	-	-	30.5	1.3	-	-
1961	-	-	30.5	0.0	-	-	-	-	30.6	0.3	-	-	-	-	31.3	2.3	-	-	-	-	31.4	0.3	-	-
1962	-	-	31.1	-1.0	-	-	-	-	31.4	1.0	-	-	-	-	31.5	0.3	-	-	-	-	31.5	0.0	-	-
1963	-	-	31.3	-0.6	-	-	-	-	31.3	0.0	-	-	-	-	31.6	1.0	-	-	-	-	31.9	0.9	-	-
1964	-	-	31.9	0.0	-	-	-	-	32.0	0.3	-	-	-	-	32.0	0.0	-	-	-	-	32.4	1.3	-	-
1965	-	-	32.5	0.3	-	-	-	-	32.8	0.9	-	-	-	-	32.5	-0.9	-	-	-	-	32.7	0.6	-	-
1966	-	-	32.5	-0.6	-	-	-	-	33.0	1.5	-	-	-	-	32.9	-0.3	-	-	-	-	33.2	0.9	-	-
1967	-	-	33.2	0.0	-	-	-	-	33.4	0.6	-	-	-	-	34.0	1.8	-	-	-	-	34.9	2.6	-	-
1968	-	-	35.2	0.9	-	-	-	-	35.3	0.3	-	-	-	-	35.6	0.8	-	-	-	-	36.3	2.0	-	-
1969	-	-	35.9	-1.1	-	-	-	-	37.0	3.1	-	-	-	-	37.1	0.3	-	-	-	-	38.0	2.4	-	-
1970	-	-	38.4	1.1	-	-	-	-	38.8	1.0	-	-	-	-	39.2	1.0	-	-	-	-	41.9	6.9	-	-
1971	-	-	42.1	0.5	-	-	-	-	42.3	0.5	-	-	-	-	42.4	0.2	-	-	-	-	42.1	-0.7	-	-
1972	-	-	42.4	0.7	-	-	-	-	42.8	0.9	-	-	-	-	42.9	0.2	-	-	-	-	42.9	0.0	-	-
1973	-	-	43.1	0.5	-	-	-	-	44.0	2.1	-	-	-	-	44.2	0.5	-	-	-	-	44.8	1.4	-	-
1974	-	-	47.2	5.4	-	-	-	-	49.9	5.7	-	-	-	-	50.2	0.6	-	-	-	-	50.7	1.0	-	-
1975	-	-	50.7	0.0	-	-	-	-	51.9	2.4	-	-	-	-	53.5	3.1	-	-	-	-	52.1	-2.6	-	-
1976	-	-	52.2	0.2	-	-	-	-	53.7	2.9	-	-	-	-	55.5	3.4	-	-	-	-	56.2	1.3	-	-
1977	-	-	56.4	0.4	-	-	-	-	57.9	2.7	-	-	-	-	58.0	0.2	-	-	-	-	58.7	1.2	-	-
1978	-	-	58.8	0.2	-	-	59.6	1.4	-	-	60.9	2.2	-	-	61.8	1.5	-	-	62.1	0.5	-	-	62.8	1.1
1979	-	-	64.3	2.4	-	-	66.6	3.6	-	-	68.8	3.3	-	-	71.1	3.3	-	-	72.7	2.3	-	-	74.4	2.3
1980	-	-	77.4	4.0	-	-	79.5	2.7	-	-	80.7	1.5	-	-	82.4	2.1	-	-	82.9	0.6	-	-	85.4	3.0
1981	-	-	88.4	3.5	-	-	90.1	1.9	-	-	91.4	1.4	-	-	93.4	2.2	-	-	95.3	2.0	-	-	96.2	0.9
1982	-	-	95.1	-1.1	-	-	94.2	-0.9	-	-	97.2	3.2	-	-	99.1	2.0	-	-	98.0	-1.1	-	-	98.4	0.4
1983	-	-	96.0	-2.4	-	-	97.1	1.1	-	-	98.9	1.9	-	-	101.3	2.4	-	-	102.5	1.2	-	-	102.5	0.0
1984	-	-	101.8	-0.7	-	-	102.7	0.9	-	-	104.3	1.6	-	-	103.8	-0.5	-	-	104.8	1.0	-	-	104.7	-0.1
1985	-	-	103.5	-1.1	-	-	106.0	2.4	-	-	106.1	0.1	-	-	105.4	-0.7	-	-	106.2	0.8	-	-	107.2	0.9
1986	-	-	105.0	-2.1	-	-	99.5	-5.2	-	-	101.7	2.2	-	-	99.0	-2.7	-	-	99.6	0.6	100.3	0.7	100.9	0.6
1987	102.3	1.4	-	-	101.9	-0.4	-	-	103.0	1.1	-	-	104.5	1.5	-	-	104.7	0.2	-	-	106.4	1.6	-	-
1988	105.5	-0.8	-	-	103.7	-1.7	-	-	107.6	3.8	-	-	107.8	0.2	-	-	109.1	1.2	-	-	109.4	0.3	-	-
1989	109.3	-0.1	-	-	110.5	1.1	-	-	116.1	5.1	-	-	113.8	-2.0	-	-	111.9	-1.7	-	-	114.3	2.1	-	-
1990	117.0	2.4	-	-	114.7	-2.0	-	-	116.1	1.2	-	-	116.5	0.3	-	-	122.5	5.2	-	-	128.1	4.6	-	-
1991	123.9	-3.3	-	-	121.6	-1.9	-	-	122.7	0.9	-	-	123.1	0.3	-	-	123.1	0.0	-	-	124.7	1.3	-	-
1992	122.0	-2.2	-	-	123.1	0.9	-	-	124.4	1.1	-	-	124.9	0.4	-	-	123.7	-1.0	-	-	126.6	2.3	-	-

[Continued]

Cleveland-Akron, OH
Consumer Price Index - All Urban Consumers
Base 1982-1984 = 100
Transportation

[Continued]

For 1947-2000. Columns headed % show percentile change in the index from the previous period for which an index is available.

Year	Jan Index	%	Feb Index	%	Mar Index	%	Apr Index	%	May Index	%	Jun Index	%	Jul Index	%	Aug Index	%	Sep Index	%	Oct Index	%	Nov Index	%	Dec Index	%
1993	122.8	-3.0	-	-	123.3	0.4	-	-	125.9	2.1	-	-	126.1	0.2	-	-	124.7	-1.1	-	-	126.5	1.4	-	-
1994	125.5	-0.8	-	-	125.8	0.2	-	-	127.2	1.1	-	-	129.6	1.9	-	-	130.0	0.3	-	-	132.1	1.6	-	-
1995	131.0	-0.8	-	-	132.2	0.9	-	-	135.7	2.6	-	-	133.5	-1.6	-	-	133.7	0.1	-	-	131.5	-1.6	-	-
1996	134.0	1.9	-	-	136.0	1.5	-	-	138.8	2.1	-	-	138.1	-0.5	-	-	138.7	0.4	-	-	143.2	3.2	-	-
1997	142.1	-0.8	-	-	142.5	0.3	-	-	142.5	0.0	-	-	140.1	-1.7	-	-	142.5	1.7	-	-	141.1	-1.0	-	-
1998	141.6	0.4	-	-	141.7	0.1	-	-	141.8	0.1	-	-	142.6	0.6	-	-	141.2	-1.0	-	-	142.0	0.6	-	-
1999	140.5	-1.1	-	-	140.7	0.1	-	-	142.9	1.6	-	-	143.9	0.7	-	-	145.4	1.0	-	-	146.5	0.8	-	-
2000	148.3	1.2	-	-	151.7	2.3	-	-	150.6	-0.7	-	-	151.9	0.9	-	-	154.0	1.4	-	-	153.6	-0.3	-	-

Source: U.S. Department of Labor, Bureau of Labor Statistics, Division of Consumer Prices and Price Indexes. - indicates no data collected for period.

Cleveland-Akron, OH
Consumer Price Index - Urban Wage Earners
Base 1982-1984 = 100
Transportation

For 1947-2000. Columns headed % show percentile change in the index from the previous period for which an index is available.

Year	Jan Index	%	Feb Index	%	Mar Index	%	Apr Index	%	May Index	%	Jun Index	%	Jul Index	%	Aug Index	%	Sep Index	%	Oct Index	%	Nov Index	%	Dec Index	%
1947	18.6	-	18.6	0.0	18.8	1.1	18.9	0.5	18.8	-0.5	18.8	0.0	-	-	19.1	1.6	-	-	-	-	19.7	3.1	-	-
1948	-	-	20.9	6.1	-	-	-	-	21.0	0.5	-	-	-	-	23.1	10.0	-	-	-	-	23.1	0.0	-	-
1949	-	-	23.4	1.3	-	-	-	-	23.4	0.0	-	-	-	-	23.4	0.0	-	-	-	-	23.4	0.0	-	-
1950	-	-	23.1	-1.3	-	-	-	-	23.0	-0.4	-	-	-	-	23.7	3.0	-	-	-	-	23.8	0.4	-	-
1951	-	-	24.0	0.8	-	-	-	-	24.2	0.8	-	-	-	-	25.2	4.1	-	-	-	-	26.0	3.2	-	-
1952	-	-	26.3	1.2	-	-	-	-	26.3	0.0	-	-	-	-	26.3	0.0	-	-	-	-	26.4	0.4	-	-
1953	-	-	26.5	0.4	-	-	-	-	26.5	0.0	-	-	-	-	26.9	1.5	-	-	-	-	26.7	-0.7	-	-
1954	-	-	26.5	-0.7	-	-	-	-	26.4	-0.4	-	-	-	-	25.3	-4.2	-	-	-	-	26.2	3.6	-	-
1955	-	-	25.7	-1.9	-	-	-	-	25.3	-1.6	-	-	-	-	25.7	1.6	-	-	-	-	26.8	4.3	-	-
1956	-	-	26.3	-1.9	-	-	-	-	26.4	0.4	-	-	-	-	27.0	2.3	-	-	-	-	28.1	4.1	-	-
1957	-	-	28.4	1.1	-	-	-	-	28.4	0.0	-	-	-	-	28.9	1.8	-	-	-	-	29.7	2.8	-	-
1958	-	-	29.1	-2.0	-	-	-	-	29.2	0.3	-	-	-	-	29.3	0.3	-	-	-	-	29.8	1.7	-	-
1959	-	-	30.0	0.7	-	-	-	-	30.0	0.0	-	-	-	-	30.7	2.3	-	-	-	-	31.1	1.3	-	-
1960	-	-	30.7	-1.3	-	-	-	-	30.6	-0.3	-	-	-	-	30.5	-0.3	-	-	-	-	30.8	1.0	-	-
1961	-	-	30.9	0.3	-	-	-	-	31.0	0.3	-	-	-	-	31.7	2.3	-	-	-	-	31.8	0.3	-	-
1962	-	-	31.5	-0.9	-	-	-	-	31.8	1.0	-	-	-	-	31.9	0.3	-	-	-	-	31.9	0.0	-	-
1963	-	-	31.7	-0.6	-	-	-	-	31.7	0.0	-	-	-	-	32.0	0.9	-	-	-	-	32.3	0.9	-	-
1964	-	-	32.3	0.0	-	-	-	-	32.4	0.3	-	-	-	-	32.4	0.0	-	-	-	-	32.8	1.2	-	-
1965	-	-	32.9	0.3	-	-	-	-	33.2	0.9	-	-	-	-	32.9	-0.9	-	-	-	-	33.1	0.6	-	-
1966	-	-	32.9	-0.6	-	-	-	-	33.4	1.5	-	-	-	-	33.3	-0.3	-	-	-	-	33.6	0.9	-	-
1967	-	-	33.6	0.0	-	-	-	-	33.8	0.6	-	-	-	-	34.4	1.8	-	-	-	-	35.4	2.9	-	-
1968	-	-	35.6	0.6	-	-	-	-	35.7	0.3	-	-	-	-	36.0	0.8	-	-	-	-	36.7	1.9	-	-
1969	-	-	36.4	-0.8	-	-	-	-	37.5	3.0	-	-	-	-	37.6	0.3	-	-	-	-	38.5	2.4	-	-
1970	-	-	38.9	1.0	-	-	-	-	39.2	0.8	-	-	-	-	39.7	1.3	-	-	-	-	42.4	6.8	-	-
1971	-	-	42.6	0.5	-	-	-	-	42.8	0.5	-	-	-	-	42.9	0.2	-	-	-	-	42.6	-0.7	-	-
1972	-	-	42.9	0.7	-	-	-	-	43.3	0.9	-	-	-	-	43.5	0.5	-	-	-	-	43.4	-0.2	-	-
1973	-	-	43.6	0.5	-	-	-	-	44.5	2.1	-	-	-	-	44.7	0.4	-	-	-	-	45.3	1.3	-	-
1974	-	-	47.8	5.5	-	-	-	-	50.5	5.6	-	-	-	-	50.8	0.6	-	-	-	-	51.4	1.2	-	-
1975	-	-	51.3	-0.2	-	-	-	-	52.6	2.5	-	-	-	-	54.2	3.0	-	-	-	-	52.8	-2.6	-	-
1976	-	-	52.9	0.2	-	-	-	-	54.3	2.6	-	-	-	-	56.2	3.5	-	-	-	-	56.9	1.2	-	-
1977	-	-	57.1	0.4	-	-	-	-	58.6	2.6	-	-	-	-	58.7	0.2	-	-	-	-	59.5	1.4	-	-
1978	-	-	59.5	0.0	-	-	60.3	1.3	-	-	61.9	2.7	-	-	62.9	1.6	-	-	62.9	0.0	-	-	63.5	1.0
1979	-	-	65.5	3.1	-	-	68.1	4.0	-	-	70.5	3.5	-	-	72.7	3.1	-	-	74.4	2.3	-	-	75.5	1.5
1980	-	-	79.0	4.6	-	-	80.6	2.0	-	-	82.3	2.1	-	-	83.7	1.7	-	-	84.1	0.5	-	-	86.0	2.3
1981	-	-	89.6	4.2	-	-	90.9	1.5	-	-	91.6	0.8	-	-	93.7	2.3	-	-	95.3	1.7	-	-	95.9	0.6
1982	-	-	94.7	-1.3	-	-	93.6	-1.2	-	-	97.0	3.6	-	-	99.1	2.2	-	-	98.2	-0.9	-	-	98.5	0.3
1983	-	-	96.0	-2.5	-	-	97.1	1.1	-	-	99.2	2.2	-	-	101.4	2.2	-	-	102.5	1.1	-	-	102.5	0.0
1984	-	-	101.8	-0.7	-	-	102.8	1.0	-	-	104.5	1.7	-	-	104.0	-0.5	-	-	104.8	0.8	-	-	104.6	-0.2
1985	-	-	103.3	-1.2	-	-	106.1	2.7	-	-	106.2	0.1	-	-	105.4	-0.8	-	-	105.9	0.5	-	-	107.1	1.1
1986	-	-	104.4	-2.5	-	-	98.3	-5.8	-	-	100.7	2.4	-	-	97.6	-3.1	-	-	98.1	0.5	98.8	0.7	99.4	0.6
1987	100.6	1.2	-	-	100.2	-0.4	-	-	101.3	1.1	-	-	102.6	1.3	-	-	102.6	0.0	-	-	104.5	1.9	-	-
1988	103.8	-0.7	-	-	101.9	-1.8	-	-	105.5	3.5	-	-	105.6	0.1	-	-	107.0	1.3	-	-	107.5	0.5	-	-
1989	107.4	-0.1	-	-	108.5	1.0	-	-	113.7	4.8	-	-	111.4	-2.0	-	-	109.5	-1.7	-	-	112.1	2.4	-	-
1990	114.6	2.2	-	-	112.2	-2.1	-	-	113.6	1.2	-	-	114.0	0.4	-	-	119.3	4.6	-	-	124.4	4.3	-	-
1991	120.7	-3.0	-	-	118.6	-1.7	-	-	119.7	0.9	-	-	120.1	0.3	-	-	120.0	-0.1	-	-	121.4	1.2	-	-
1992	118.8	-2.1	-	-	119.6	0.7	-	-	121.0	1.2	-	-	121.6	0.5	-	-	120.6	-0.8	-	-	123.1	2.1	-	-

[Continued]

Cleveland-Akron, OH
Consumer Price Index - Urban Wage Earners
Base 1982-1984 = 100
Transportation
[Continued]

For 1947-2000. Columns headed % show percentile change in the index from the previous period for which an index is available.

Year	Jan Index	%	Feb Index	%	Mar Index	%	Apr Index	%	May Index	%	Jun Index	%	Jul Index	%	Aug Index	%	Sep Index	%	Oct Index	%	Nov Index	%	Dec Index	%
1993	119.6	-2.8	-	-	119.7	0.1	-	-	122.4	2.3	-	-	122.8	0.3	-	-	121.7	-0.9	-	-	123.4	1.4	-	-
1994	122.3	-0.9	-	-	122.4	0.1	-	-	123.9	1.2	-	-	126.3	1.9	-	-	126.7	0.3	-	-	129.0	1.8	-	-
1995	128.0	-0.8	-	-	129.0	0.8	-	-	132.2	2.5	-	-	130.2	-1.5	-	-	130.3	0.1	-	-	128.5	-1.4	-	-
1996	130.8	1.8	-	-	132.5	1.3	-	-	134.8	1.7	-	-	134.2	-0.4	-	-	134.7	0.4	-	-	138.6	2.9	-	-
1997	137.8	-0.6	-	-	137.9	0.1	-	-	138.1	0.1	-	-	135.6	-1.8	-	-	138.0	1.8	-	-	136.9	-0.8	-	-
1998	137.3	0.3	-	-	137.2	-0.1	-	-	138.6	1.0	-	-	139.0	0.3	-	-	137.7	-0.9	-	-	138.9	0.9	-	-
1999	136.9	-1.4	-	-	136.7	-0.1	-	-	139.4	2.0	-	-	140.0	0.4	-	-	141.9	1.4	-	-	142.9	0.7	-	-
2000	144.7	1.3	-	-	148.3	2.5	-	-	147.4	-0.6	-	-	148.8	0.9	-	-	150.6	1.2	-	-	149.7	-0.6	-	-

Source: U.S. Department of Labor, Bureau of Labor Statistics, Division of Consumer Prices and Price Indexes. - indicates no data collected for period.

Cleveland-Akron, OH
Consumer Price Index - All Urban Consumers
Base 1982-1984 = 100
Medical Care

For 1947-2001. Columns headed % show percentile change in the index from the previous period for which an index is available.

Year	Jan Index	%	Feb Index	%	Mar Index	%	Apr Index	%	May Index	%	Jun Index	%	Jul Index	%	Aug Index	%	Sep Index	%	Oct Index	%	Nov Index	%	Dec Index	%
1947	10.5	-	10.5	0.0	10.5	0.0	10.5	0.0	10.5	0.0	10.5	0.0	-		10.5	0.0	-		-		10.9	3.8	-	
1948	-		11.0	0.9	-		-		11.2	1.8	-		-		11.2	0.0	-		-		11.5	2.7	-	
1949	-		11.6	0.9	-		-		11.6	0.0	-		-		11.7	0.9	-		-		11.8	0.9	-	
1950	-		11.8	0.0	-		-		11.8	0.0	-		-		11.7	-0.8	-		-		11.9	1.7	-	
1951	-		12.2	2.5	-		-		12.6	3.3	-		-		12.6	0.0	-		-		13.2	4.8	-	
1952	-		13.2	0.0	-		-		13.3	0.8	-		-		13.4	0.8	-		-		13.3	-0.7	-	
1953	-		13.4	0.8	-		-		13.4	0.0	-		-		14.2	6.0	-		-		14.2	0.0	-	
1954	-		14.4	1.4	-		-		14.5	0.7	-		-		14.5	0.0	-		-		14.6	0.7	-	
1955	-		14.6	0.0	-		-		15.3	4.8	-		-		15.3	0.0	-		-		15.4	0.7	-	
1956	-		15.4	0.0	-		-		16.3	5.8	-		-		16.3	0.0	-		-		16.3	0.0	-	
1957	-		16.4	0.6	-		-		16.7	1.8	-		-		16.8	0.6	-		-		16.8	0.0	-	
1958	-		17.0	1.2	-		-		17.1	0.6	-		-		17.1	0.0	-		-		17.2	0.6	-	
1959	-		18.6	8.1	-		-		18.7	0.5	-		-		18.8	0.5	-		-		19.0	1.1	-	
1960	-		19.0	0.0	-		-		19.3	1.6	-		-		19.4	0.5	-		-		19.4	0.0	-	
1961	-		20.7	6.7	-		-		20.8	0.5	-		-		20.6	-1.0	-		-		20.7	0.5	-	
1962	-		20.7	0.0	-		-		20.8	0.5	-		-		20.8	0.0	-		-		20.8	0.0	-	
1963	-		20.8	0.0	-		-		22.1	6.3	-		-		22.2	0.5	-		-		22.3	0.5	-	
1964	-		22.4	0.4	-		-		22.5	0.4	-		-		22.5	0.0	-		-		22.7	0.9	-	
1965	-		23.1	1.8	-		-		23.2	0.4	-		-		23.2	0.0	-		-		23.3	0.4	-	
1966	-		23.5	0.9	-		-		23.6	0.4	-		-		23.7	0.4	-		-		24.2	2.1	-	
1967	-		24.4	0.8	-		-		25.1	2.9	-		-		25.4	1.2	-		-		25.7	1.2	-	
1968	-		26.4	2.7	-		-		26.9	1.9	-		-		27.2	1.1	-		-		28.5	4.8	-	
1969	-		29.4	3.2	-		-		30.3	3.1	-		-		31.2	3.0	-		-		31.4	0.6	-	
1970	-		32.3	2.9	-		-		32.8	1.5	-		-		33.4	1.8	-		-		33.3	-0.3	-	
1971	-		34.2	2.7	-		-		34.9	2.0	-		-		36.1	3.4	-		-		35.8	-0.8	-	
1972	-		35.7	-0.3	-		-		36.0	0.8	-		-		36.5	1.4	-		-		36.8	0.8	-	
1973	-		37.4	1.6	-		-		37.7	0.8	-		-		37.9	0.5	-		-		38.6	1.8	-	
1974	-		40.2	4.1	-		-		40.7	1.2	-		-		41.9	2.9	-		-		42.4	1.2	-	
1975	-		45.5	7.3	-		-		46.1	1.3	-		-		45.8	-0.7	-		-		46.9	2.4	-	
1976	-		49.5	5.5	-		-		50.2	1.4	-		-		50.9	1.4	-		-		51.9	2.0	-	
1977	-		55.0	6.0	-		-		56.4	2.5	-		-		57.4	1.8	-		-		58.3	1.6	-	
1978	-		61.0	4.6	-		61.2	0.3	-		61.9	1.1	-		62.4	0.8	-		62.7	0.5	-		63.2	0.8
1979	-		64.7	2.4	-		65.0	0.5	-		66.0	1.5	-		66.3	0.5	-		66.8	0.8	-		68.6	2.7
1980	-		71.9	4.8	-		71.6	-0.4	-		72.1	0.7	-		73.4	1.8	-		73.9	0.7	-		74.9	1.4
1981	-		79.7	6.4	-		80.6	1.1	-		81.3	0.9	-		82.1	1.0	-		82.1	0.0	-		83.4	1.6
1982	-		87.9	5.4	-		90.8	3.3	-		91.4	0.7	-		92.5	1.2	-		94.1	1.7	-		95.0	1.0
1983	-		99.8	5.1	-		101.3	1.5	-		101.5	0.2	-		101.9	0.4	-		101.7	-0.2	-		102.7	1.0
1984	-		106.6	3.8	-		107.3	0.7	-		108.1	0.7	-		107.8	-0.3	-		107.8	0.0	-		108.1	0.3
1985	-		110.4	2.1	-		111.1	0.6	-		111.5	0.4	-		112.0	0.4	-		112.5	0.4	-		116.0	3.1
1986	-		119.0	2.6	-		119.9	0.8	-		123.5	3.0	-		124.1	0.5	-		124.4	0.2	124.9	0.4	124.8	-0.1
1987	127.4	2.1	-		127.7	0.2	-		128.0	0.2	-		127.7	-0.2	-		129.4	1.3	-		129.8	0.3	-	
1988	132.4	2.0	-		132.9	0.4	-		133.1	0.2	-		133.8	0.5	-		137.7	2.9	-		137.5	-0.1	-	
1989	140.1	1.9	-		141.1	0.7	-		141.7	0.4	-		144.3	1.8	-		144.6	0.2	-		146.6	1.4	-	
1990	150.2	2.5	-		151.7	1.0	-		153.4	1.1	-		158.5	3.3	-		159.4	0.6	-		162.8	2.1	-	
1991	166.0	2.0	-		168.8	1.7	-		171.4	1.5	-		171.9	0.3	-		174.2	1.3	-		175.1	0.5	-	
1992	176.5	0.8	-		177.8	0.7	-		178.5	0.4	-		179.0	0.3	-		178.4	-0.3	-		179.0	0.3	-	

[Continued]

Cleveland-Akron, OH
Consumer Price Index - All Urban Consumers
Base 1982-1984 = 100
Medical Care
[Continued]

For 1947-2001. Columns headed % show percentile change in the index from the previous period for which an index is available.

Year	Jan Index	%	Feb Index	%	Mar Index	%	Apr Index	%	May Index	%	Jun Index	%	Jul Index	%	Aug Index	%	Sep Index	%	Oct Index	%	Nov Index	%	Dec Index	%
1993	185.5	3.6	-	-	185.1	-0.2	-	-	186.0	0.5	-	-	188.0	1.1	-	-	188.2	0.1	-	-	188.9	0.4	-	-
1994	192.6	2.0	-	-	195.3	1.4	-	-	194.5	-0.4	-	-	194.7	0.1	-	-	197.7	1.5	-	-	197.6	-0.1	-	-
1995	201.2	1.8	-	-	202.6	0.7	-	-	201.9	-0.3	-	-	202.4	0.2	-	-	202.4	0.0	-	-	203.3	0.4	-	-
1996	208.0	2.3	-	-	209.0	0.5	-	-	209.6	0.3	-	-	210.0	0.2	-	-	209.6	-0.2	-	-	209.8	0.1	-	-
1997	210.2	0.2	-	-	211.1	0.4	-	-	210.5	-0.3	-	-	212.3	0.9	-	-	212.2	-0.0	-	-	212.5	0.1	-	-
1998	211.6	-0.4	-	-	211.6	0.0	-	-	214.5	1.4	-	-	215.0	0.2	-	-	216.6	0.7	-	-	217.1	0.2	-	-
1999	219.8	1.2	-	-	223.7	1.8	-	-	223.2	-0.2	-	-	226.1	1.3	-	-	226.9	0.4	-	-	227.0	0.0	-	-
2000	229.8	1.2	-	-	233.5	1.6	-	-	234.1	0.3	-	-	234.5	0.2	-	-	234.8	0.1	-	-	234.3	-0.2	-	-
2001	238.6	1.8	-	-	238.2	-0.2	-	-	239.2	0.4	-	-	240.3	0.5	-	-	241.3	0.4	-	-	242.1	0.3	-	-

Source: U.S. Department of Labor, Bureau of Labor Statistics, Division of Consumer Prices and Price Indexes. - indicates no data collected for period.

385

Cleveland-Akron, OH
Consumer Price Index - Urban Wage Earners
Base 1982-1984 = 100
Medical Care

For 1947-2001. Columns headed % show percentile change in the index from the previous period for which an index is available.

Year	Jan Index	%	Feb Index	%	Mar Index	%	Apr Index	%	May Index	%	Jun Index	%	Jul Index	%	Aug Index	%	Sep Index	%	Oct Index	%	Nov Index	%	Dec Index	%
1947	10.3	-	10.3	0.0	10.3	0.0	10.3	0.0	10.3	0.0	10.3	0.0	-	-	10.4	1.0	-	-	-	-	10.8	3.8	-	-
1948	-	-	10.8	0.0	-	-	-	-	11.0	1.9	-	-	-	-	11.0	0.0	-	-	-	-	11.4	3.6	-	-
1949	-	-	11.4	0.0	-	-	-	-	11.4	0.0	-	-	-	-	11.5	0.9	-	-	-	-	11.6	0.9	-	-
1950	-	-	11.6	0.0	-	-	-	-	11.6	0.0	-	-	-	-	11.5	-0.9	-	-	-	-	11.7	1.7	-	-
1951	-	-	12.0	2.6	-	-	-	-	12.4	3.3	-	-	-	-	12.4	0.0	-	-	-	-	13.0	4.8	-	-
1952	-	-	13.0	0.0	-	-	-	-	13.0	0.0	-	-	-	-	13.1	0.8	-	-	-	-	13.1	0.0	-	-
1953	-	-	13.1	0.0	-	-	-	-	13.2	0.8	-	-	-	-	13.9	5.3	-	-	-	-	14.0	0.7	-	-
1954	-	-	14.2	1.4	-	-	-	-	14.2	0.0	-	-	-	-	14.2	0.0	-	-	-	-	14.4	1.4	-	-
1955	-	-	14.4	0.0	-	-	-	-	15.0	4.2	-	-	-	-	15.0	0.0	-	-	-	-	15.2	1.3	-	-
1956	-	-	15.2	0.0	-	-	-	-	16.0	5.3	-	-	-	-	16.1	0.6	-	-	-	-	16.1	0.0	-	-
1957	-	-	16.2	0.6	-	-	-	-	16.4	1.2	-	-	-	-	16.6	1.2	-	-	-	-	16.6	0.0	-	-
1958	-	-	16.8	1.2	-	-	-	-	16.8	0.0	-	-	-	-	16.8	0.0	-	-	-	-	16.9	0.6	-	-
1959	-	-	18.3	8.3	-	-	-	-	18.4	0.5	-	-	-	-	18.5	0.5	-	-	-	-	18.7	1.1	-	-
1960	-	-	18.7	0.0	-	-	-	-	19.0	1.6	-	-	-	-	19.1	0.5	-	-	-	-	19.1	0.0	-	-
1961	-	-	20.4	6.8	-	-	-	-	20.4	0.0	-	-	-	-	20.3	-0.5	-	-	-	-	20.3	0.0	-	-
1962	-	-	20.4	0.5	-	-	-	-	20.4	0.0	-	-	-	-	20.4	0.0	-	-	-	-	20.4	0.0	-	-
1963	-	-	20.5	0.5	-	-	-	-	21.8	6.3	-	-	-	-	21.9	0.5	-	-	-	-	21.9	0.0	-	-
1964	-	-	22.0	0.5	-	-	-	-	22.1	0.5	-	-	-	-	22.1	0.0	-	-	-	-	22.3	0.9	-	-
1965	-	-	22.7	1.8	-	-	-	-	22.8	0.4	-	-	-	-	22.8	0.0	-	-	-	-	22.9	0.4	-	-
1966	-	-	23.1	0.9	-	-	-	-	23.2	0.4	-	-	-	-	23.3	0.4	-	-	-	-	23.8	2.1	-	-
1967	-	-	24.0	0.8	-	-	-	-	24.7	2.9	-	-	-	-	25.0	1.2	-	-	-	-	25.2	0.8	-	-
1968	-	-	26.0	3.2	-	-	-	-	26.5	1.9	-	-	-	-	26.7	0.8	-	-	-	-	28.1	5.2	-	-
1969	-	-	28.9	2.8	-	-	-	-	29.8	3.1	-	-	-	-	30.7	3.0	-	-	-	-	30.8	0.3	-	-
1970	-	-	31.8	3.2	-	-	-	-	32.2	1.3	-	-	-	-	32.9	2.2	-	-	-	-	32.7	-0.6	-	-
1971	-	-	33.6	2.8	-	-	-	-	34.3	2.1	-	-	-	-	35.5	3.5	-	-	-	-	35.2	-0.8	-	-
1972	-	-	35.1	-0.3	-	-	-	-	35.4	0.9	-	-	-	-	35.9	1.4	-	-	-	-	36.2	0.8	-	-
1973	-	-	36.8	1.7	-	-	-	-	37.1	0.8	-	-	-	-	37.3	0.5	-	-	-	-	38.0	1.9	-	-
1974	-	-	39.5	3.9	-	-	-	-	40.0	1.3	-	-	-	-	41.2	3.0	-	-	-	-	41.7	1.2	-	-
1975	-	-	44.8	7.4	-	-	-	-	45.4	1.3	-	-	-	-	45.1	-0.7	-	-	-	-	46.1	2.2	-	-
1976	-	-	48.7	5.6	-	-	-	-	49.3	1.2	-	-	-	-	50.0	1.4	-	-	-	-	51.0	2.0	-	-
1977	-	-	54.1	6.1	-	-	-	-	55.4	2.4	-	-	-	-	56.4	1.8	-	-	-	-	57.3	1.6	-	-
1978	-	-	60.0	4.7	-	-	60.1	0.2	-	-	61.0	1.5	-	-	61.4	0.7	-	-	62.4	1.6	-	-	63.4	1.6
1979	-	-	65.0	2.5	-	-	65.2	0.3	-	-	65.9	1.1	-	-	67.1	1.8	-	-	67.8	1.0	-	-	69.5	2.5
1980	-	-	72.6	4.5	-	-	72.7	0.1	-	-	73.6	1.2	-	-	74.5	1.2	-	-	74.5	0.0	-	-	75.6	1.5
1981	-	-	80.6	6.6	-	-	80.8	0.2	-	-	80.9	0.1	-	-	81.8	1.1	-	-	82.7	1.1	-	-	83.9	1.5
1982	-	-	88.2	5.1	-	-	91.0	3.2	-	-	91.6	0.7	-	-	92.7	1.2	-	-	94.3	1.7	-	-	95.2	1.0
1983	-	-	100.0	5.0	-	-	101.3	1.3	-	-	101.5	0.2	-	-	101.7	0.2	-	-	101.6	-0.1	-	-	102.5	0.9
1984	-	-	106.4	3.8	-	-	107.1	0.7	-	-	107.9	0.7	-	-	107.5	-0.4	-	-	107.6	0.1	-	-	107.8	0.2
1985	-	-	110.0	2.0	-	-	110.6	0.5	-	-	111.0	0.4	-	-	111.6	0.5	-	-	112.0	0.4	-	-	115.3	2.9
1986	-	-	118.4	2.7	-	-	119.3	0.8	-	-	122.8	2.9	-	-	123.4	0.5	-	-	123.7	0.2	124.2	0.4	124.1	-0.1
1987	126.7	2.1	-	-	127.0	0.2	-	-	127.4	0.3	-	-	127.1	-0.2	-	-	128.8	1.3	-	-	129.0	0.2	-	-
1988	131.6	2.0	-	-	132.1	0.4	-	-	132.4	0.2	-	-	133.1	0.5	-	-	136.8	2.8	-	-	136.6	-0.1	-	-
1989	139.1	1.8	-	-	140.0	0.6	-	-	140.6	0.4	-	-	142.8	1.6	-	-	143.1	0.2	-	-	144.9	1.3	-	-
1990	148.3	2.3	-	-	149.6	0.9	-	-	151.0	0.9	-	-	156.8	3.8	-	-	157.5	0.4	-	-	160.8	2.1	-	-
1991	163.5	1.7	-	-	165.9	1.5	-	-	168.3	1.4	-	-	168.7	0.2	-	-	171.3	1.5	-	-	172.1	0.5	-	-
1992	173.5	0.8	-	-	174.6	0.6	-	-	175.6	0.6	-	-	176.2	0.3	-	-	175.6	-0.3	-	-	176.1	0.3	-	-

[Continued]

Cleveland-Akron, OH
Consumer Price Index - Urban Wage Earners
Base 1982-1984 = 100
Medical Care

[Continued]

For 1947-2001. Columns headed % show percentile change in the index from the previous period for which an index is available.

Year	Jan Index	%	Feb Index	%	Mar Index	%	Apr Index	%	May Index	%	Jun Index	%	Jul Index	%	Aug Index	%	Sep Index	%	Oct Index	%	Nov Index	%	Dec Index	%
1993	182.2	3.5	-	-	181.9	-0.2	-	-	182.7	0.4	-	-	185.0	1.3	-	-	185.0	0.0	-	-	185.7	0.4	-	-
1994	189.1	1.8	-	-	191.9	1.5	-	-	191.1	-0.4	-	-	191.3	0.1	-	-	194.4	1.6	-	-	194.1	-0.2	-	-
1995	197.5	1.8	-	-	198.8	0.7	-	-	198.5	-0.2	-	-	199.1	0.3	-	-	199.2	0.1	-	-	200.3	0.6	-	-
1996	205.0	2.3	-	-	206.0	0.5	-	-	206.6	0.3	-	-	207.1	0.2	-	-	206.9	-0.1	-	-	207.2	0.1	-	-
1997	207.4	0.1	-	-	208.7	0.6	-	-	208.2	-0.2	-	-	209.9	0.8	-	-	209.7	-0.1	-	-	209.9	0.1	-	-
1998	208.5	-0.7	-	-	208.5	0.0	-	-	210.7	1.1	-	-	211.3	0.3	-	-	212.7	0.7	-	-	213.3	0.3	-	-
1999	215.8	1.2	-	-	219.2	1.6	-	-	218.7	-0.2	-	-	221.8	1.4	-	-	223.3	0.7	-	-	223.4	0.0	-	-
2000	226.1	1.2	-	-	229.5	1.5	-	-	230.1	0.3	-	-	230.6	0.2	-	-	230.8	0.1	-	-	230.4	-0.2	-	-
2001	234.5	1.8	-	-	233.8	-0.3	-	-	234.7	0.4	-	-	235.9	0.5	-	-	236.9	0.4	-	-	237.5	0.3	-	-

Source: U.S. Department of Labor, Bureau of Labor Statistics, Division of Consumer Prices and Price Indexes. - indicates no data collected for period.

Cleveland-Akron, OH
Consumer Price Index - All Urban Consumers
Base December 1997 = 100
Recreation

For 1997-2001. Columns headed % show percentile change in the index from the previous period for which an index is available.

Year	Jan		Feb		Mar		Apr		May		Jun		Jul		Aug		Sep		Oct		Nov		Dec	
	Index	%	Index	%	Index	%	Index	%	Index	%	Index	%	Index	%	Index	%	Index	%	Index	%	Index	%	Index	%
1997	-	-	-	-	-	-	-	-	-	-	-	-	-	-	-	-	-	-	-	-	-	-	100.0	-
1998	100.9	0.9	-	-	99.3	-1.6	-	-	99.4	0.1	-	-	100.6	1.2	-	-	100.2	-0.4	-	-	100.2	0.0	-	-
1999	100.6	0.4	-	-	101.2	0.6	-	-	101.4	0.2	-	-	100.8	-0.6	-	-	99.2	-1.6	-	-	98.9	-0.3	-	-
2000	99.0	0.1	-	-	99.6	0.6	-	-	100.1	0.5	-	-	100.4	0.3	-	-	101.7	1.3	-	-	100.9	-0.8	-	-
2001	102.3	1.4	-	-	101.8	-0.5	-	-	101.5	-0.3	-	-	101.9	0.4	-	-	102.2	0.3	-	-	102.4	0.2	-	-

Source: U.S. Department of Labor, Bureau of Labor Statistics, Division of Consumer Prices and Price Indexes. - indicates no data collected for period.

Cleveland-Akron, OH
Consumer Price Index - Urban Wage Earners
Base December 1997 = 100
Recreation

For 1997-2001. Columns headed % show percentile change in the index from the previous period for which an index is available.

Year	Jan Index	%	Feb Index	%	Mar Index	%	Apr Index	%	May Index	%	Jun Index	%	Jul Index	%	Aug Index	%	Sep Index	%	Oct Index	%	Nov Index	%	Dec Index	%
1997	-	-	-	-	-	-	-	-	-	-	-	-	-	-	-	-	-	-	-	-	-	-	100.0	-
1998	101.0	1.0	-	-	99.5	-1.5	-	-	99.4	-0.1	-	-	100.7	1.3	-	-	100.4	-0.3	-	-	100.3	-0.1	-	-
1999	100.7	0.4	-	-	101.1	0.4	-	-	101.4	0.3	-	-	100.7	-0.7	-	-	98.7	-2.0	-	-	98.6	-0.1	-	-
2000	98.4	-0.2	-	-	99.2	0.8	-	-	99.8	0.6	-	-	100.1	0.3	-	-	101.3	1.2	-	-	100.4	-0.9	-	-
2001	101.8	1.4	-	-	101.2	-0.6	-	-	100.5	-0.7	-	-	101.2	0.7	-	-	101.4	0.2	-	-	101.6	0.2	-	-

Source: U.S. Department of Labor, Bureau of Labor Statistics, Division of Consumer Prices and Price Indexes. - indicates no data collected for period.

Cleveland-Akron, OH
Consumer Price Index - All Urban Consumers
Base December 1997 = 100
Education & Communication

For 1997-2001. Columns headed % show percentile change in the index from the previous period for which an index is available.

Year	Jan Index	%	Feb Index	%	Mar Index	%	Apr Index	%	May Index	%	Jun Index	%	Jul Index	%	Aug Index	%	Sep Index	%	Oct Index	%	Nov Index	%	Dec Index	%
1997	-	-	-	-	-	-	-	-	-	-	-	-	-	-	-	-	-	-	-	-	-	-	100.0	-
1998	99.9	-0.1	-	-	98.9	-1.0	-	-	99.3	0.4	-	-	98.9	-0.4	-	-	99.8	0.9	-	-	99.5	-0.3	-	-
1999	99.6	0.1	-	-	99.2	-0.4	-	-	98.9	-0.3	-	-	99.5	0.6	-	-	99.7	0.2	-	-	100.2	0.5	-	-
2000	100.1	-0.1	-	-	99.1	-1.0	-	-	99.1	0.0	-	-	100.6	1.5	-	-	97.5	-3.1	-	-	98.2	0.7	-	-
2001	99.0	0.8	-	-	99.1	0.1	-	-	99.9	0.8	-	-	100.5	0.6	-	-	102.1	1.6	-	-	102.5	0.4	-	-

Source: U.S. Department of Labor, Bureau of Labor Statistics, Division of Consumer Prices and Price Indexes. - indicates no data collected for period.

Cleveland-Akron, OH
Consumer Price Index - Urban Wage Earners
Base December 1997 = 100
Education & Communication

For 1997-2001. Columns headed % show percentile change in the index from the previous period for which an index is available.

Year	Jan		Feb		Mar		Apr		May		Jun		Jul		Aug		Sep		Oct		Nov		Dec	
	Index	%	Index	%	Index	%	Index	%	Index	%	Index	%	Index	%	Index	%	Index	%	Index	%	Index	%	Index	%
1997	-	-	-	-	-	-	-	-	-	-	-	-	-	-	-	-	-	-	-	-	-	-	100.0	-
1998	99.9	-0.1	-	-	98.8	-1.1	-	-	98.9	0.1	-	-	98.5	-0.4	-	-	99.3	0.8	-	-	99.0	-0.3	-	-
1999	99.3	0.3	-	-	98.8	-0.5	-	-	98.5	-0.3	-	-	98.6	0.1	-	-	98.8	0.2	-	-	99.3	0.5	-	-
2000	99.2	-0.1	-	-	98.1	-1.1	-	-	97.8	-0.3	-	-	98.2	0.4	-	-	95.1	-3.2	-	-	99.3	0.5	-	-
2001	96.7	0.8	-	-	96.8	0.1	-	-	97.8	1.0	-	-	98.6	0.8	-	-	99.2	0.6	-	-	99.4	0.2	-	-

Source: U.S. Department of Labor, Bureau of Labor Statistics, Division of Consumer Prices and Price Indexes. - indicates no data collected for period.

Dallas-Fort Worth, TX
Consumer Price Index - All Urban Consumers
Base 1982-1984 = 100
Annual Averages

For 1963-2001. Columns headed % show percentile change in the index from the previous period for which an index is available.

Year	All Items Index	%	Food & Beverage Index	%	Housing Index	%	Apparel Index	%	Transportation Index	%	Medical Care Index	%	Recreation* Index	%	Education & Communic.* Index	%	Other Goods & Services Index	%
1963	-	-	-	-	-	-	-	-	-	-	-	-	-	-	-	-	-	-
1964	29.5	-	-	-	-	-	45.4	-	31.3	-	24.5	-	-	-	-	-	-	-
1965	29.9	1.4	-	-	-	-	45.2	-0.4	31.6	1.0	25.0	2.0	-	-	-	-	-	-
1966	31.0	3.7	-	-	-	-	46.7	3.3	32.3	2.2	26.4	5.6	-	-	-	-	-	-
1967	31.9	2.9	-	-	-	-	48.7	4.3	33.3	3.1	28.3	7.2	-	-	-	-	-	-
1968	33.3	4.4	-	-	-	-	51.4	5.5	34.4	3.3	30.0	6.0	-	-	-	-	-	-
1969	35.5	6.6	-	-	-	-	54.8	6.6	35.6	3.5	32.4	8.0	-	-	-	-	-	-
1970	37.6	5.9	-	-	-	-	57.4	4.7	36.9	3.7	34.8	7.4	-	-	-	-	-	-
1971	38.7	2.9	-	-	-	-	57.6	0.3	39.1	6.0	36.4	4.6	-	-	-	-	-	-
1972	39.8	2.8	-	-	-	-	59.2	2.8	39.9	2.0	37.2	2.2	-	-	-	-	-	-
1973	42.1	5.8	-	-	-	-	62.6	5.7	41.1	3.0	38.7	4.0	-	-	-	-	-	-
1974	46.3	10.0	-	-	-	-	66.6	6.4	47.4	15.3	41.8	8.0	-	-	-	-	-	-
1975	50.4	8.9	-	-	-	-	68.8	3.3	52.1	9.9	46.0	10.0	-	-	-	-	-	-
1976	53.5	6.2	59.0	-	48.1	-	70.9	3.1	56.7	8.8	50.1	8.9	-	-	-	-	55.9	-
1977	57.4	7.3	63.7	8.0	51.7	7.5	74.8	5.5	61.0	7.6	55.2	10.2	-	-	-	-	59.5	6.4
1978	61.8	7.7	69.5	9.1	56.8	9.9	78.9	5.5	62.8	3.0	59.6	8.0	-	-	-	-	63.4	6.6
1979	69.7	12.8	78.1	12.4	65.3	15.0	83.6	6.0	71.9	14.5	62.9	5.5	-	-	-	-	68.8	8.5
1980	81.5	16.9	85.4	9.3	79.3	21.4	88.9	6.3	86.3	20.0	69.9	11.1	-	-	-	-	76.1	10.6
1981	90.8	11.4	92.4	8.2	90.1	13.6	95.0	6.9	95.5	10.7	80.3	14.9	-	-	-	-	84.0	10.4
1982	96.0	5.7	96.1	4.0	96.4	7.0	97.2	2.3	97.4	2.0	91.9	14.4	-	-	-	-	91.9	9.4
1983	99.7	3.9	99.6	3.6	99.6	3.3	99.7	2.6	99.2	1.8	101.2	10.1	-	-	-	-	100.9	9.8
1984	104.3	4.6	104.3	4.7	104.0	4.4	103.1	3.4	103.4	4.2	107.0	5.7	-	-	-	-	107.3	6.3
1985	108.2	3.7	107.1	2.7	107.3	3.2	107.7	4.5	107.2	3.7	113.9	6.4	-	-	-	-	112.5	4.8
1986	109.9	1.6	111.2	3.8	109.9	2.4	107.6	-0.1	101.1	-5.7	126.7	11.2	-	-	-	-	119.5	6.2
1987	112.9	2.7	115.9	4.2	109.5	-0.4	114.5	6.4	103.5	2.4	134.2	5.9	-	-	-	-	128.8	7.8
1988	116.1	2.8	120.1	3.6	109.8	0.3	123.1	7.5	108.0	4.3	141.9	5.7	-	-	-	-	135.2	5.0
1989	119.5	2.9	125.4	4.4	111.6	1.6	124.5	1.1	110.8	2.6	150.9	6.3	-	-	-	-	146.1	8.1
1990	125.1	4.7	131.1	4.5	114.3	2.4	137.5	10.4	117.2	5.8	161.9	7.3	-	-	-	-	156.3	7.0
1991	130.8	4.6	136.3	4.0	118.6	3.8	151.7	10.3	120.7	3.0	174.8	8.0	-	-	-	-	163.7	4.7
1992	133.9	2.4	138.3	1.5	121.8	2.7	151.3	-0.3	123.4	2.2	188.3	7.7	-	-	-	-	170.5	4.2
1993	137.3	2.5	139.0	0.5	125.3	2.9	147.8	-2.3	128.9	4.5	196.8	4.5	-	-	-	-	180.5	5.9
1994	141.2	2.8	142.2	2.3	129.0	3.0	148.2	0.3	134.5	4.3	205.6	4.5	-	-	-	-	181.0	0.3
1995	144.9	2.6	145.6	2.4	132.1	2.4	147.8	-0.3	139.4	3.6	216.9	5.5	-	-	-	-	185.7	2.6
1996	148.8	2.7	152.8	4.9	135.5	2.6	141.9	-4.0	142.1	1.9	224.6	3.6	-	-	-	-	195.6	5.3
1997	151.4	1.7	157.0	2.7	138.8	2.4	137.2	-3.3	142.9	0.6	225.3	0.3	-	-	-	-	205.6	5.1
1998	153.6	1.5	160.1	2.0	143.2	3.2	136.6	-0.4	138.5	-3.1	229.0	1.6	100.0	-	100.0	-	220.7	7.3
1999	158.0	2.9	165.1	3.1	146.8	2.5	140.7	3.0	141.0	1.8	233.2	1.8	102.3	2.3	104.0	4.0	241.7	9.5
2000	164.7	4.2	169.2	2.5	152.6	4.0	137.5	-2.3	152.3	8.0	243.2	4.3	106.6	4.2	107.3	3.2	256.1	6.0
2001	-	-	-	-	-	-	-	-	-	-	-	-	-	-	-	-	-	-

Source: U.S. Department of Labor, Bureau of Labor Statistics, Division of Consumer Prices and Price Indexes. *Base is December 1997 = 100. - indicates no data collected for period.

Dallas-Fort Worth, TX
Consumer Price Index - Urban Wage Earners
Base 1982-1984 = 100
Annual Averages

For 1963-2001. Columns headed % show percentile change in the index from the previous period for which an index is available.

Year	All Items Index	%	Food & Beverage Index	%	Housing Index	%	Apparel Index	%	Trans-portation Index	%	Medical Care Index	%	Recrea-tion* Index	%	Education & Communic.* Index	%	Other Goods & Services Index	%
1963	-	-	-	-	-	-	-	-	-	-	-	-	-	-	-	-	-	-
1964	30.0	-	-	-	-	-	47.9	-	31.3	-	24.9	-	-	-	-	-	-	-
1965	30.4	1.3	-	-	-	-	47.7	-0.4	31.6	1.0	25.4	2.0	-	-	-	-	-	-
1966	31.5	3.6	-	-	-	-	49.3	3.4	32.3	2.2	26.8	5.5	-	-	-	-	-	-
1967	32.4	2.9	-	-	-	-	51.4	4.3	33.3	3.1	28.7	7.1	-	-	-	-	-	-
1968	33.9	4.6	-	-	-	-	54.3	5.6	34.5	3.6	30.5	6.3	-	-	-	-	-	-
1969	36.1	6.5	-	-	-	-	57.9	6.6	35.6	3.2	32.9	7.9	-	-	-	-	-	-
1970	38.2	5.8	-	-	-	-	60.6	4.7	37.0	3.9	35.4	7.6	-	-	-	-	-	-
1971	39.3	2.9	-	-	-	-	60.9	0.5	39.1	5.7	37.0	4.5	-	-	-	-	-	-
1972	40.5	3.1	-	-	-	-	62.5	2.6	39.9	2.0	37.8	2.2	-	-	-	-	-	-
1973	42.8	5.7	-	-	-	-	66.1	5.8	41.1	3.0	39.3	4.0	-	-	-	-	-	-
1974	47.1	10.0	-	-	-	-	70.4	6.5	47.4	15.3	42.4	7.9	-	-	-	-	-	-
1975	51.3	8.9	-	-	-	-	72.7	3.3	52.1	9.9	46.8	10.4	-	-	-	-	-	-
1976	54.4	6.0	58.5	-	48.7	-	74.8	2.9	56.7	8.8	50.9	8.8	-	-	-	-	-	-
1977	58.4	7.4	63.2	8.0	52.4	7.6	78.9	5.5	61.0	7.6	56.1	10.2	-	-	-	-	58.6	-
1978	62.9	7.7	69.2	9.5	57.6	9.9	82.5	4.6	63.0	3.3	60.6	8.0	-	-	-	-	62.4	6.5
1979	70.9	12.7	77.9	12.6	66.1	14.8	87.3	5.8	72.3	14.8	65.2	7.6	-	-	-	-	66.5	6.6
1980	82.4	16.2	84.9	9.0	79.8	20.7	94.6	8.4	86.7	19.9	72.1	10.6	-	-	-	-	71.7	7.8
1981	91.5	11.0	92.2	8.6	90.5	13.4	98.9	4.5	96.4	11.2	81.2	12.6	-	-	-	-	79.4	10.7
1982	96.4	5.4	96.2	4.3	97.0	7.2	97.5	-1.4	97.6	1.2	91.7	12.9	-	-	-	-	84.4	6.3
1983	99.4	3.1	99.6	3.5	99.0	2.1	99.4	1.9	99.3	1.7	101.2	10.4	-	-	-	-	91.6	8.5
1984	104.2	4.8	104.2	4.6	104.0	5.1	103.0	3.6	103.2	3.9	107.1	5.8	-	-	-	-	101.3	10.6
1985	108.1	3.7	106.9	2.6	107.8	3.7	109.2	6.0	106.9	3.6	114.3	6.7	-	-	-	-	107.1	5.7
1986	109.4	1.2	110.8	3.6	110.3	2.3	109.3	0.1	100.5	-6.0	127.5	11.5	-	-	-	-	111.8	4.4
1987	112.6	2.9	115.6	4.3	109.8	-0.5	115.1	5.3	104.2	3.7	135.5	6.3	-	-	-	-	118.7	6.2
1988	115.8	2.8	119.7	3.5	110.1	0.3	123.1	7.0	108.5	4.1	143.5	5.9	-	-	-	-	126.3	6.4
1989	119.3	3.0	124.9	4.3	111.8	1.5	122.8	-0.2	111.8	3.0	153.2	6.8	-	-	-	-	132.6	5.0
1990	124.5	4.4	130.6	4.6	114.3	2.2	130.9	6.6	118.1	5.6	164.5	7.4	-	-	-	-	143.3	8.1
1991	129.6	4.1	135.7	3.9	118.7	3.8	138.7	6.0	121.6	3.0	177.7	8.0	-	-	-	-	153.7	7.3
1992	133.1	2.7	137.5	1.3	121.4	2.3	141.5	2.0	126.2	3.8	192.1	8.1	-	-	-	-	161.8	5.3
1993	137.0	2.9	138.2	0.5	124.6	2.6	143.0	1.1	132.8	5.2	200.8	4.5	-	-	-	-	168.7	4.3
1994	140.5	2.6	141.0	2.0	128.3	3.0	140.3	-1.9	138.1	4.0	209.2	4.2	-	-	-	-	178.2	5.6
1995	144.6	2.9	144.2	2.3	131.5	2.5	141.7	1.0	144.1	4.3	221.5	5.9	-	-	-	-	177.7	-0.3
1996	148.9	3.0	151.5	5.1	134.6	2.4	138.5	-2.3	147.1	2.1	228.7	3.3	-	-	-	-	182.1	2.5
1997	151.4	1.7	155.8	2.8	137.8	2.4	133.0	-4.0	147.7	0.4	229.7	0.4	-	-	-	-	191.9	5.4
1998	153.4	1.3	159.0	2.1	142.3	3.3	131.6	-1.1	143.2	-3.0	233.4	1.6	100.1	-	99.5	-	201.3	4.9
1999	157.7	2.8	163.7	3.0	146.0	2.6	134.1	1.9	145.3	1.5	237.7	1.8	102.5	2.4	103.2	3.7	217.2	7.9
2000	164.6	4.4	168.2	2.7	151.8	4.0	132.1	-1.5	156.5	7.7	247.7	4.2	107.0	4.4	105.9	2.6	239.5	10.3
2001	-	-	-	-	-	-	-	-	-	-	-	-	-	-	-	-	254.8	6.4

Source: U.S. Department of Labor, Bureau of Labor Statistics, Division of Consumer Prices and Price Indexes. *Base is December 1997 = 100. - indicates no data collected for period.

Dallas-Fort Worth, TX
Consumer Price Index - All Urban Consumers
Base 1982-1984 = 100
All Items

For 1963-2001. Columns headed % show percentile change in the index from the previous period for which an index is available.

Year	Jan Index	%	Feb Index	%	Mar Index	%	Apr Index	%	May Index	%	Jun Index	%	Jul Index	%	Aug Index	%	Sep Index	%	Oct Index	%	Nov Index	%	Dec Index	%
1963	-	-	-	-	-	-	-	-	-	-	-	-	-	-	-	-	-	-	-	-	29.5	-	-	-
1964	-	-	29.4	-0.3	-	-	-	-	29.6	0.7	-	-	-	-	29.5	-0.3	-	-	-	-	29.7	0.7	-	-
1965	-	-	29.5	-0.7	-	-	-	-	29.8	1.0	-	-	-	-	30.0	0.7	-	-	-	-	30.3	1.0	-	-
1966	-	-	30.5	0.7	-	-	-	-	30.9	1.3	-	-	-	-	31.1	0.6	-	-	-	-	31.4	1.0	-	-
1967	-	-	31.6	0.6	-	-	-	-	31.7	0.3	-	-	-	-	32.1	1.3	-	-	-	-	32.2	0.3	-	-
1968	-	-	32.5	0.9	-	-	-	-	33.2	2.2	-	-	-	-	33.5	0.9	-	-	-	-	34.0	1.5	-	-
1969	-	-	34.4	1.2	-	-	-	-	35.2	2.3	-	-	-	-	35.7	1.4	-	-	-	-	36.5	2.2	-	-
1970	-	-	37.0	1.4	-	-	-	-	37.5	1.4	-	-	-	-	37.8	0.8	-	-	-	-	37.9	0.3	-	-
1971	-	-	38.2	0.8	-	-	-	-	38.4	0.5	-	-	-	-	39.1	1.8	-	-	-	-	39.0	-0.3	-	-
1972	-	-	39.4	1.0	-	-	-	-	39.7	0.8	-	-	-	-	40.0	0.8	-	-	-	-	40.1	0.2	-	-
1973	-	-	40.7	1.5	-	-	-	-	41.6	2.2	-	-	-	-	42.6	2.4	-	-	-	-	43.2	1.4	-	-
1974	-	-	44.5	3.0	-	-	-	-	45.6	2.5	-	-	-	-	47.0	3.1	-	-	-	-	48.2	2.6	-	-
1975	-	-	49.1	1.9	-	-	-	-	49.7	1.2	-	-	-	-	51.2	3.0	-	-	-	-	51.8	1.2	-	-
1976	-	-	52.2	0.8	-	-	-	-	53.0	1.5	-	-	-	-	53.9	1.7	-	-	-	-	54.7	1.5	-	-
1977	-	-	55.9	2.2	-	-	-	-	57.2	2.3	-	-	-	-	58.1	1.6	-	-	-	-	58.6	0.9	-	-
1978	-	-	59.5	1.5	-	-	60.3	1.3	-	-	61.7	2.3	-	-	62.9	1.9	-	-	63.7	1.3	-	-	64.3	0.9
1979	-	-	65.6	2.0	-	-	67.3	2.6	-	-	69.3	3.0	-	-	71.1	2.6	-	-	72.7	2.3	-	-	74.6	2.6
1980	-	-	77.0	3.2	-	-	80.1	4.0	-	-	81.7	2.0	-	-	82.4	0.9	-	-	84.4	2.4	-	-	85.9	1.8
1981	-	-	87.5	1.9	-	-	89.1	1.8	-	-	91.2	2.4	-	-	91.9	0.8	-	-	93.2	1.4	-	-	94.1	1.0
1982	-	-	93.6	-0.5	-	-	94.7	1.2	-	-	97.2	2.6	-	-	97.0	-0.2	-	-	97.8	0.8	-	-	96.7	-1.1
1983	-	-	97.1	0.4	-	-	98.4	1.3	-	-	100.1	1.7	-	-	100.7	0.6	-	-	101.5	0.8	-	-	101.2	-0.3
1984	-	-	102.9	1.7	-	-	103.3	0.4	-	-	103.8	0.5	-	-	105.1	1.3	-	-	106.4	1.2	-	-	105.4	-0.9
1985	-	-	106.2	0.8	-	-	107.0	0.8	-	-	108.3	1.2	-	-	109.5	1.1	-	-	109.6	0.1	-	-	109.8	0.2
1986	-	-	110.6	0.7	-	-	108.8	-1.6	-	-	109.9	1.0	-	-	110.4	0.5	-	-	110.3	-0.1	-	-	109.3	-0.9
1987	-	-	110.9	1.5	-	-	112.2	1.2	-	-	112.9	0.6	-	-	113.5	0.5	-	-	114.9	1.2	-	-	113.9	-0.9
1988	-	-	114.0	0.1	-	-	115.4	1.2	-	-	115.6	0.2	-	-	117.2	1.4	-	-	117.9	0.6	-	-	117.2	-0.6
1989	-	-	117.5	0.3	-	-	118.7	1.0	-	-	120.0	1.1	-	-	120.0	0.0	-	-	121.4	1.2	-	-	120.5	-0.7
1990	-	-	122.2	1.4	-	-	122.9	0.6	-	-	123.8	0.7	-	-	126.0	1.8	-	-	129.5	2.8	-	-	128.4	-0.8
1991	-	-	129.4	0.8	-	-	129.5	0.1	-	-	130.1	0.5	-	-	131.1	0.8	-	-	133.6	1.9	-	-	132.0	-1.2
1992	-	-	132.4	0.3	-	-	132.5	0.1	-	-	134.2	1.3	-	-	134.4	0.1	-	-	136.1	1.3	-	-	134.6	-1.1
1993	-	-	135.4	0.6	-	-	137.0	1.2	-	-	136.2	-0.6	-	-	138.1	1.4	-	-	139.6	1.1	-	-	138.8	-0.6
1994	-	-	139.2	0.3	-	-	140.3	0.8	-	-	141.4	0.8	-	-	142.2	0.6	-	-	142.8	0.4	-	-	141.9	-0.6
1995	-	-	143.3	1.0	-	-	145.0	1.2	-	-	144.4	-0.4	-	-	145.1	0.5	-	-	146.8	1.2	-	-	145.5	-0.9
1996	-	-	146.2	0.5	-	-	148.5	1.6	-	-	149.4	0.6	-	-	149.5	0.1	-	-	150.7	0.8	-	-	150.0	-0.5
1997	-	-	150.7	0.5	-	-	150.6	-0.1	-	-	151.4	0.5	-	-	151.2	-0.1	-	-	152.8	1.1	-	-	152.5	-0.2
1998	152.1	-0.3	-	-	153.0	0.6	-	-	153.0	0.0	-	-	154.2	0.8	-	-	154.5	0.2	-	-	154.0	-0.3	-	-
1999	155.0	0.6	-	-	156.4	0.9	-	-	157.2	0.5	-	-	158.3	0.7	-	-	159.8	0.9	-	-	160.1	0.2	-	-
2000	160.4	0.2	-	-	163.1	1.7	-	-	163.2	0.1	-	-	166.2	1.8	-	-	166.9	0.4	-	-	166.8	-0.1	-	-
2001	167.3	0.3	-	-	168.9	1.0	-	-	169.4	0.3	-	-	171.5	1.2	-	-	172.8	0.8	-	-	171.5	-0.8	-	-

Source: U.S. Department of Labor, Bureau of Labor Statistics, Division of Consumer Prices and Price Indexes. - indicates no data collected for period.

Dallas-Fort Worth, TX
Consumer Price Index - Urban Wage Earners
Base 1982-1984 = 100
All Items

For 1963-2001. Columns headed % show percentile change in the index from the previous period for which an index is available.

Year	Jan Index	Jan %	Feb Index	Feb %	Mar Index	Mar %	Apr Index	Apr %	May Index	May %	Jun Index	Jun %	Jul Index	Jul %	Aug Index	Aug %	Sep Index	Sep %	Oct Index	Oct %	Nov Index	Nov %	Dec Index	Dec %
1963	-		-		-		-		-		-		-		-		-		-		-		-	
1964	-		29.9	-0.3	-		-		30.1	0.7	-		-		30.0	-0.3	-		-		30.0		-	
1965	-		30.0	-0.7	-		-		30.3	1.0	-		-		30.5	0.7	-		-		30.2	0.7	-	
1966	-		31.0	0.6	-		-		31.4	1.3	-		-		31.7	1.0	-		-		30.8	1.0	-	
1967	-		32.1	0.6	-		-		32.2	0.3	-		-		32.7	1.6	-		-		31.9	0.6	-	
1968	-		33.1	1.2	-		-		33.8	2.1	-		-		34.1	0.9	-		-		32.7	0.0	-	
1969	-		35.0	1.2	-		-		35.8	2.3	-		-		36.4	1.7	-		-		34.6	1.5	-	
1970	-		37.7	1.6	-		-		38.1	1.1	-		-		38.5	1.0	-		-		37.1	1.9	-	
1971	-		38.8	0.5	-		-		39.0	0.5	-		-		39.8	2.1	-		-		38.6	0.3	-	
1972	-		40.1	1.0	-		-		40.4	0.7	-		-		40.7	0.7	-		-		39.7	-0.3	-	
1973	-		41.4	1.5	-		-		42.4	2.4	-		-		43.4	2.4	-		-		40.8	0.2	-	
1974	-		45.3	3.0	-		-		46.4	2.4	-		-		47.8	3.0	-		-		44.0	1.4	-	
1975	-		49.9	1.6	-		-		50.5	1.2	-		-		52.1	3.2	-		-		49.1	2.7	-	
1976	-		53.1	0.8	-		-		53.9	1.5	-		-		54.8	1.7	-		-		52.7	1.2	-	
1977	-		56.8	2.0	-		-		58.2	2.5	-		-		59.2	1.7	-		-		55.7	1.6	-	
1978	-		60.5	1.5	-		61.5	1.7	-		62.7	2.0	-		64.0	2.1	-		64.9	1.4	59.6	0.7	65.2	0.5
1979	-		66.9	2.6	-		68.6	2.5	-		70.7	3.1	-		72.3	2.3	-		73.9	2.2	-		75.7	2.4
1980	-		78.1	3.2	-		80.9	3.6	-		82.5	2.0	-		83.5	1.2	-		85.3	2.2	-		87.0	2.0
1981	-		88.5	1.7	-		89.8	1.5	-		92.1	2.6	-		92.5	0.4	-		93.7	1.3	-		94.4	0.7
1982	-		94.0	-0.4	-		94.9	1.0	-		97.4	2.6	-		97.4	0.0	-		98.1	0.7	-		97.1	-1.0
1983	-		96.7	-0.4	-		97.8	1.1	-		99.3	1.5	-		100.2	0.9	-		102.1	1.9	-		101.7	-0.4
1984	-		103.0	1.3	-		102.6	-0.4	-		103.4	0.8	-		105.3	1.8	-		106.4	1.0	-		105.4	-0.9
1985	-		106.0	0.6	-		106.9	0.8	-		108.2	1.2	-		109.3	1.0	-		109.4	0.1	-		109.7	0.3
1986	-		110.4	0.6	-		108.3	-1.9	-		109.4	1.0	-		110.0	0.5	-		109.8	-0.2	-		108.6	-1.1
1987	-		110.6	1.8	-		111.7	1.0	-		112.6	0.8	-		113.3	0.6	-		114.7	1.2	-		113.8	-0.8
1988	-		113.8	0.0	-		114.8	0.9	-		115.4	0.5	-		117.0	1.4	-		117.7	0.6	-		117.0	-0.6
1989	-		117.2	0.2	-		118.6	1.2	-		120.0	1.2	-		119.8	-0.2	-		121.1	1.1	-		120.1	-0.8
1990	-		121.3	1.0	-		122.2	0.7	-		123.2	0.8	-		125.4	1.8	-		128.8	2.7	-		127.8	-0.8
1991	-		128.1	0.2	-		128.2	0.1	-		129.4	0.9	-		129.9	0.4	-		131.8	1.5	-		130.9	-0.7
1992	-		131.2	0.2	-		131.5	0.2	-		133.5	1.5	-		134.0	0.4	-		135.4	1.0	-		134.1	-1.0
1993	-		134.8	0.5	-		136.3	1.1	-		136.5	0.1	-		138.0	1.1	-		139.1	0.8	-		138.6	-0.4
1994	-		138.1	-0.4	-		139.3	0.9	-		140.6	0.9	-		141.6	0.7	-		142.4	0.6	-		141.7	-0.5
1995	-		142.7	0.7	-		144.5	1.3	-		144.4	-0.1	-		144.8	0.3	-		146.5	1.2	-		145.4	-0.8
1996	-		145.9	0.3	-		148.6	1.9	-		149.6	0.7	-		149.5	-0.1	-		150.7	0.8	-		150.2	-0.3
1997	-		150.8	0.4	-		150.4	-0.3	-		151.4	0.7	-		151.1	-0.2	-		152.8	1.1	-		152.7	-0.1
1998	152.2	-0.3	-		152.8	0.4	-		152.8	0.0	-		154.0	0.8	-		154.3	0.2	-		153.8	-0.3	-	
1999	154.6	0.5	-		155.8	0.8	-		157.0	0.8	-		158.0	0.6	-		159.6	1.0	-		159.8	0.1	-	
2000	160.3	0.3	-		162.9	1.6	-		163.1	0.1	-		166.2	1.9	-		166.8	0.4	-		166.6	-0.1	-	
2001	166.8	0.1	-		168.5	1.0	-		169.1	0.4	-		171.6	1.5	-		172.6	0.6	-		171.1	-0.9	-	

Source: U.S. Department of Labor, Bureau of Labor Statistics, Division of Consumer Prices and Price Indexes. - indicates no data collected for period.

Dallas-Fort Worth, TX
Consumer Price Index - All Urban Consumers
Base 1982-1984 = 100
Food and Beverages

For 1975-2001. Columns headed % show percentile change in the index from the previous period for which an index is available.

Year	Jan Index	%	Feb Index	%	Mar Index	%	Apr Index	%	May Index	%	Jun Index	%	Jul Index	%	Aug Index	%	Sep Index	%	Oct Index	%	Nov Index	%	Dec Index	%
1975	-	-	-	-	-	-	-	-	-	-	-	-	-	-	-	-	-	-	-	-	58.8	-	-	-
1976	-	-	58.7	-0.2	-	-	-	-	58.6	-0.2	-	-	-	-	59.3	1.2	-	-	-	-	59.2	-0.2	-	-
1977	-	-	62.3	5.2	-	-	-	-	63.4	1.8	-	-	-	-	64.5	1.7	-	-	-	-	64.9	0.6	-	-
1978	-	-	66.5	2.5	-	-	67.5	1.5	-	-	69.6	3.1	-	-	70.4	1.1	-	-	71.6	1.7	-	-	73.8	3.1
1979	-	-	75.8	2.7	-	-	77.2	1.8	-	-	78.3	1.4	-	-	78.2	-0.1	-	-	79.6	1.8	-	-	81.4	2.3
1980	-	-	81.9	0.6	-	-	82.9	1.2	-	-	84.5	1.9	-	-	86.3	2.1	-	-	88.8	2.9	-	-	90.0	1.4
1981	-	-	91.0	1.1	-	-	92.3	1.4	-	-	92.3	0.0	-	-	92.9	0.7	-	-	93.3	0.4	-	-	93.2	-0.1
1982	-	-	94.6	1.5	-	-	95.3	0.7	-	-	96.4	1.2	-	-	96.7	0.3	-	-	96.9	0.2	-	-	97.7	0.8
1983	-	-	98.3	0.6	-	-	99.3	1.0	-	-	99.4	0.1	-	-	99.7	0.3	-	-	100.9	1.2	-	-	100.9	0.0
1984	-	-	103.5	2.6	-	-	104.2	0.7	-	-	104.1	-0.1	-	-	105.0	0.9	-	-	104.7	-0.3	-	-	105.4	0.7
1985	-	-	106.3	0.9	-	-	107.0	0.7	-	-	107.5	0.5	-	-	106.9	-0.6	-	-	107.0	0.1	-	-	109.0	1.9
1986	-	-	110.0	0.9	-	-	110.1	0.1	-	-	110.6	0.5	-	-	111.9	1.2	-	-	112.6	0.6	-	-	112.8	0.2
1987	-	-	115.6	2.5	-	-	114.5	-1.0	-	-	116.2	1.5	-	-	116.1	-0.1	-	-	117.3	1.0	-	-	116.9	-0.3
1988	-	-	117.5	0.5	-	-	118.3	0.7	-	-	119.9	1.4	-	-	120.8	0.8	-	-	122.4	1.3	-	-	123.1	0.6
1989	-	-	124.4	1.1	-	-	124.8	0.3	-	-	124.9	0.1	-	-	125.3	0.3	-	-	126.6	1.0	-	-	127.9	1.0
1990	-	-	129.6	1.3	-	-	130.7	0.8	-	-	130.5	-0.2	-	-	131.5	0.8	-	-	132.0	0.4	-	-	134.1	1.6
1991	-	-	134.7	0.4	-	-	135.5	0.6	-	-	138.2	2.0	-	-	136.6	-1.2	-	-	135.6	-0.7	-	-	138.0	1.8
1992	-	-	139.6	1.2	-	-	138.6	-0.7	-	-	137.2	-1.0	-	-	138.1	0.7	-	-	138.6	0.4	-	-	137.9	-0.5
1993	-	-	138.1	0.1	-	-	139.3	0.9	-	-	139.1	-0.1	-	-	138.3	-0.6	-	-	137.6	-0.5	-	-	142.5	3.6
1994	-	-	140.2	-1.6	-	-	141.4	0.9	-	-	142.3	0.6	-	-	143.3	0.7	-	-	142.8	-0.3	-	-	143.9	0.8
1995	-	-	144.1	0.1	-	-	145.7	1.1	-	-	144.1	-1.1	-	-	145.5	1.0	-	-	146.8	0.9	-	-	148.2	1.0
1996	-	-	149.8	1.1	-	-	151.8	1.3	-	-	152.5	0.5	-	-	152.7	0.1	-	-	155.8	2.0	-	-	156.0	0.1
1997	-	-	155.7	-0.2	-	-	155.3	-0.3	-	-	157.1	1.2	-	-	157.4	0.2	-	-	158.1	0.4	-	-	159.6	0.9
1998	158.9	-0.4	-	-	159.0	0.1	-	-	159.4	0.3	-	-	160.5	0.7	-	-	160.9	0.2	-	-	161.2	0.2	-	-
1999	163.0	1.1	-	-	165.4	1.5	-	-	165.6	0.1	-	-	164.1	-0.9	-	-	165.0	0.5	-	-	166.3	0.8	-	-
2000	168.1	1.1	-	-	166.5	-1.0	-	-	168.8	1.4	-	-	168.9	0.1	-	-	171.6	1.6	-	-	170.3	-0.8	-	-
2001	171.4	0.6	-	-	170.4	-0.6	-	-	170.8	0.2	-	-	174.7	2.3	-	-	176.1	0.8	-	-	176.6	0.3	-	-

Source: U.S. Department of Labor, Bureau of Labor Statistics, Division of Consumer Prices and Price Indexes. - indicates no data collected for period.

Dallas-Fort Worth, TX

Consumer Price Index - Urban Wage Earners
Base 1982-1984 = 100

Food and Beverages

For 1975-2001. Columns headed % show percentile change in the index from the previous period for which an index is available.

Year	Jan Index	Jan %	Feb Index	Feb %	Mar Index	Mar %	Apr Index	Apr %	May Index	May %	Jun Index	Jun %	Jul Index	Jul %	Aug Index	Aug %	Sep Index	Sep %	Oct Index	Oct %	Nov Index	Nov %	Dec Index	Dec %
1975	-	-	-	-	-	-	-	-	-	-	-	-	-	-	-	-	-	-	-	-	-	-	-	-
1976	-	-	58.2	-0.2	-	-	-	-	58.1	-0.2	-	-	-	-	58.8	1.2	-	-	-	-	58.3	-	-	-
1977	-	-	61.8	5.3	-	-	-	-	62.9	1.8	-	-	-	-	64.0	1.7	-	-	-	-	58.7	-0.2	-	-
1978	-	-	65.9	2.3	-	-	67.8	2.9	-	-	69.0	1.8	-	-	70.0	1.4	-	-	71.9	2.7	64.4	0.6	72.5	0.8
1979	-	-	75.9	4.7	-	-	77.2	1.7	-	-	78.3	1.4	-	-	77.9	-0.5	-	-	79.4	1.9	-	-	80.7	1.6
1980	-	-	81.4	0.9	-	-	82.5	1.4	-	-	83.6	1.3	-	-	86.2	3.1	-	-	88.5	2.7	-	-	89.8	1.5
1981	-	-	90.3	0.6	-	-	91.1	0.9	-	-	92.1	1.1	-	-	93.7	1.7	-	-	93.6	-0.1	-	-	93.3	-0.3
1982	-	-	94.7	1.5	-	-	95.3	0.6	-	-	96.5	1.3	-	-	96.8	0.3	-	-	97.0	0.2	-	-	97.9	0.9
1983	-	-	98.3	0.4	-	-	99.2	0.9	-	-	99.5	0.3	-	-	99.7	0.2	-	-	100.9	1.2	-	-	100.8	-0.1
1984	-	-	103.5	2.7	-	-	104.2	0.7	-	-	104.0	-0.2	-	-	104.8	0.8	-	-	104.5	-0.3	-	-	105.3	0.8
1985	-	-	106.1	0.8	-	-	106.8	0.7	-	-	107.2	0.4	-	-	106.6	-0.6	-	-	106.5	-0.1	-	-	108.8	2.2
1986	-	-	109.6	0.7	-	-	109.6	0.0	-	-	110.2	0.5	-	-	111.7	1.4	-	-	112.3	0.5	-	-	112.4	0.1
1987	-	-	115.2	2.5	-	-	114.2	-0.9	-	-	115.8	1.4	-	-	115.8	0.0	-	-	116.9	0.9	-	-	116.6	-0.3
1988	-	-	117.1	0.4	-	-	117.9	0.7	-	-	119.5	1.4	-	-	120.4	0.8	-	-	122.0	1.3	-	-	122.7	0.6
1989	-	-	123.9	1.0	-	-	124.2	0.2	-	-	124.4	0.2	-	-	124.7	0.2	-	-	126.0	1.0	-	-	127.5	1.2
1990	-	-	129.1	1.3	-	-	130.0	0.7	-	-	129.8	-0.2	-	-	131.0	0.9	-	-	131.5	0.4	-	-	133.7	1.7
1991	-	-	134.2	0.4	-	-	135.1	0.7	-	-	137.7	1.9	-	-	136.0	-1.2	-	-	135.0	-0.7	-	-	137.1	1.6
1992	-	-	138.9	1.3	-	-	137.8	-0.8	-	-	136.3	-1.1	-	-	137.1	0.6	-	-	137.8	0.5	-	-	137.1	-0.5
1993	-	-	137.5	0.3	-	-	138.6	0.8	-	-	138.4	-0.1	-	-	137.6	-0.6	-	-	137.0	-0.4	-	-	141.4	3.2
1994	-	-	139.0	-1.7	-	-	140.4	1.0	-	-	141.0	0.4	-	-	141.8	0.6	-	-	141.4	-0.3	-	-	142.6	0.8
1995	-	-	142.6	0.0	-	-	144.5	1.3	-	-	142.7	-1.2	-	-	144.0	0.9	-	-	145.4	1.0	-	-	146.9	1.0
1996	-	-	148.8	1.3	-	-	150.5	1.1	-	-	151.1	0.4	-	-	151.3	0.1	-	-	154.6	2.2	-	-	155.0	0.3
1997	-	-	154.5	-0.3	-	-	154.3	-0.1	-	-	155.8	1.0	-	-	156.0	0.1	-	-	156.9	0.6	-	-	158.5	1.0
1998	157.9	-0.4	-	-	158.0	0.1	-	-	158.4	0.3	-	-	159.3	0.6	-	-	159.6	0.2	-	-	-	-	-	-
1999	161.9	1.2	-	-	164.0	1.3	-	-	164.2	0.1	-	-	162.8	-0.9	-	-	163.5	0.4	-	-	160.0	0.3	-	-
2000	166.7	1.1	-	-	165.3	-0.8	-	-	167.9	1.6	-	-	168.0	0.1	-	-	170.7	1.6	-	-	164.9	0.9	-	-
2001	170.9	0.9	-	-	169.8	-0.6	-	-	170.3	0.3	-	-	174.1	2.2	-	-	175.7	0.9	-	-	169.4	-0.8	-	-

Source: U.S. Department of Labor, Bureau of Labor Statistics, Division of Consumer Prices and Price Indexes. - indicates no data collected for period.

Dallas-Fort Worth, TX
Consumer Price Index - All Urban Consumers
Base 1982-1984 = 100
Housing

For 1975-2001. Columns headed % show percentile change in the index from the previous period for which an index is available.

Year	Jan Index	%	Feb Index	%	Mar Index	%	Apr Index	%	May Index	%	Jun Index	%	Jul Index	%	Aug Index	%	Sep Index	%	Oct Index	%	Nov Index	%	Dec Index	%
1975	-	-	-	-	-	-	-	-	-	-	-	-	-	-	-	-	-	-	-	-	46.0	-	-	-
1976	-	-	47.0	2.2	-	-	-	-	47.7	1.5	-	-	-	-	48.4	1.5	-	-	-	-	49.4	2.1	-	-
1977	-	-	50.0	1.2	-	-	-	-	51.4	2.8	-	-	-	-	52.4	1.9	-	-	-	-	53.0	1.1	-	-
1978	-	-	54.3	2.5	-	-	55.3	1.8	-	-	56.7	2.5	-	-	58.2	2.6	-	-	59.0	1.4	-	-	58.9	-0.2
1979	-	-	60.4	2.5	-	-	62.0	2.6	-	-	64.8	4.5	-	-	66.9	3.2	-	-	69.3	3.6	-	-	71.3	2.9
1980	-	-	73.6	3.2	-	-	77.7	5.6	-	-	80.2	3.2	-	-	80.1	-0.1	-	-	82.7	3.2	-	-	85.0	2.8
1981	-	-	86.1	1.3	-	-	87.6	1.7	-	-	90.8	3.7	-	-	91.0	0.2	-	-	92.9	2.1	-	-	94.5	1.7
1982	-	-	92.5	-2.1	-	-	95.9	3.7	-	-	98.5	2.7	-	-	97.4	-1.1	-	-	98.4	1.0	-	-	95.8	-2.6
1983	-	-	96.7	0.9	-	-	97.9	1.2	-	-	101.3	3.5	-	-	101.0	-0.3	-	-	101.3	0.3	-	-	100.7	-0.6
1984	-	-	103.0	2.3	-	-	102.8	-0.2	-	-	104.0	1.2	-	-	105.3	1.3	-	-	106.3	0.9	-	-	103.4	-2.7
1985	-	-	105.0	1.5	-	-	105.6	0.6	-	-	107.9	2.2	-	-	110.0	1.9	-	-	109.1	-0.8	-	-	107.7	-1.3
1986	-	-	109.7	1.9	-	-	109.8	0.1	-	-	111.3	1.4	-	-	111.6	0.3	-	-	110.0	-1.4	-	-	107.1	-2.6
1987	-	-	108.0	0.8	-	-	109.1	1.0	-	-	109.7	0.5	-	-	110.5	0.7	-	-	111.4	0.8	-	-	108.9	-2.2
1988	-	-	107.9	-0.9	-	-	109.2	1.2	-	-	109.4	0.2	-	-	111.9	2.3	-	-	111.2	-0.6	-	-	109.2	-1.8
1989	-	-	110.3	1.0	-	-	109.7	-0.5	-	-	112.4	2.5	-	-	112.9	0.4	-	-	113.7	0.7	-	-	111.2	-2.2
1990	-	-	111.6	0.4	-	-	112.2	0.5	-	-	114.0	1.6	-	-	116.1	1.8	-	-	118.3	1.9	-	-	114.8	-3.0
1991	-	-	116.8	1.7	-	-	117.1	0.3	-	-	117.8	0.6	-	-	119.1	1.1	-	-	121.9	2.4	-	-	120.3	-1.3
1992	-	-	118.4	-1.6	-	-	119.0	0.5	-	-	123.9	4.1	-	-	124.9	0.8	-	-	123.2	-1.4	-	-	121.7	-1.2
1993	-	-	123.9	1.8	-	-	123.7	-0.2	-	-	123.6	-0.1	-	-	127.6	3.2	-	-	128.1	0.4	-	-	126.1	-1.6
1994	-	-	126.6	0.4	-	-	128.5	1.5	-	-	129.5	0.8	-	-	130.1	0.5	-	-	131.0	0.7	-	-	128.9	-1.6
1995	-	-	131.6	2.1	-	-	131.5	-0.1	-	-	131.5	0.0	-	-	132.6	0.8	-	-	133.8	0.9	-	-	132.3	-1.1
1996	-	-	132.2	-0.1	-	-	134.1	1.4	-	-	136.2	1.6	-	-	137.5	1.0	-	-	138.1	0.4	-	-	136.1	-1.4
1997	-	-	137.9	1.3	-	-	136.7	-0.9	-	-	139.0	1.7	-	-	138.2	-0.6	-	-	141.5	2.4	-	-	140.5	-0.7
1998	140.6	0.1	-	-	141.2	0.4	-	-	141.9	0.5	-	-	145.2	2.3	-	-	145.9	0.5	-	-	143.6	-1.6	-	-
1999	144.6	0.7	-	-	145.1	0.3	-	-	145.4	0.2	-	-	148.7	2.3	-	-	148.7	0.0	-	-	147.5	-0.8	-	-
2000	148.3	0.5	-	-	149.7	0.9	-	-	150.4	0.5	-	-	155.1	3.1	-	-	155.8	0.5	-	-	154.5	-0.8	-	-
2001	155.4	0.6	-	-	158.2	1.8	-	-	157.4	-0.5	-	-	163.5	3.9	-	-	163.1	-0.2	-	-	162.7	-0.2	-	-

Source: U.S. Department of Labor, Bureau of Labor Statistics, Division of Consumer Prices and Price Indexes. - indicates no data collected for period.

Dallas-Fort Worth, TX
Consumer Price Index - Urban Wage Earners
Base 1982-1984 = 100
Housing

For 1975-2001. Columns headed % show percentile change in the index from the previous period for which an index is available.

Year	Jan Index	Jan %	Feb Index	Feb %	Mar Index	Mar %	Apr Index	Apr %	May Index	May %	Jun Index	Jun %	Jul Index	Jul %	Aug Index	Aug %	Sep Index	Sep %	Oct Index	Oct %	Nov Index	Nov %	Dec Index	Dec %
1975	-	-	-	-	-	-	-	-	-	-	-	-	-	-	-	-	-	-	-	-	-	-	-	-
1976	-	-	47.6	2.1	-	-	-	-	48.3	1.5	-	-	-	-	49.1	1.7	-	-	-	-	46.6	-	-	-
1977	-	-	50.6	1.2	-	-	-	-	52.1	3.0	-	-	-	-	53.0	1.7	-	-	-	-	50.0	1.8	-	-
1978	-	-	55.0	2.4	-	-	56.1	2.0	-	-	57.5	2.5	-	-	59.0	2.6	-	-	59.8	1.4	53.7	1.3	-	-
1979	-	-	61.2	2.7	-	-	62.8	2.6	-	-	65.6	4.5	-	-	67.7	3.2	-	-	70.1	3.5	-	-	59.6	-0.3
1980	-	-	74.1	2.9	-	-	78.3	5.7	-	-	80.8	3.2	-	-	80.6	-0.2	-	-	82.9	2.9	-	-	72.0	2.7
1981	-	-	86.6	1.3	-	-	87.9	1.5	-	-	91.2	3.8	-	-	91.3	0.1	-	-	93.2	2.1	-	-	85.5	3.1
1982	-	-	93.1	-2.1	-	-	96.4	3.5	-	-	99.2	2.9	-	-	98.1	-1.1	-	-	99.2	1.1	-	-	95.1	2.0
1983	-	-	95.8	-0.7	-	-	96.6	0.8	-	-	99.1	2.6	-	-	99.8	0.7	-	-	102.4	2.6	-	-	96.5	-2.7
1984	-	-	103.3	1.5	-	-	101.5	-1.7	-	-	102.9	1.4	-	-	105.8	2.8	-	-	106.9	1.0	-	-	101.8	-0.6
1985	-	-	105.4	1.3	-	-	105.9	0.5	-	-	108.4	2.4	-	-	110.5	1.9	-	-	109.7	-0.7	-	-	104.0	-2.7
1986	-	-	110.1	1.9	-	-	110.0	-0.1	-	-	111.8	1.6	-	-	112.1	0.3	-	-	110.3	-1.6	-	-	108.1	-1.5
1987	-	-	108.2	1.0	-	-	109.1	0.8	-	-	110.3	1.1	-	-	111.1	0.7	-	-	111.9	0.7	-	-	107.1	-2.9
1988	-	-	108.2	-0.7	-	-	109.4	1.1	-	-	110.0	0.5	-	-	112.2	2.0	-	-	111.6	-0.5	-	-	109.0	-2.6
1989	-	-	110.2	0.7	-	-	109.8	-0.4	-	-	112.7	2.6	-	-	113.2	0.4	-	-	114.0	0.7	-	-	109.4	-2.0
1990	-	-	111.3	0.0	-	-	112.2	0.8	-	-	113.9	1.5	-	-	116.1	1.9	-	-	118.7	2.2	-	-	111.3	-2.4
1991	-	-	117.1	2.4	-	-	117.1	0.0	-	-	118.0	0.8	-	-	119.4	1.2	-	-	122.1	2.3	-	-	120.0	-1.7
1992	-	-	118.6	-1.2	-	-	118.9	0.3	-	-	123.2	3.6	-	-	124.3	0.9	-	-	122.8	-1.2	-	-	121.1	-1.4
1993	-	-	123.1	1.7	-	-	122.6	-0.4	-	-	123.2	0.5	-	-	126.7	2.8	-	-	127.8	0.9	-	-	125.4	-1.9
1994	-	-	125.8	0.3	-	-	127.6	1.4	-	-	128.9	1.0	-	-	129.7	0.6	-	-	130.5	0.6	-	-	128.3	-1.7
1995	-	-	130.8	1.9	-	-	130.8	0.0	-	-	131.4	0.5	-	-	132.2	0.6	-	-	133.3	0.8	-	-	131.6	-1.3
1996	-	-	131.0	-0.5	-	-	133.1	1.6	-	-	135.5	1.8	-	-	136.5	0.7	-	-	137.0	0.4	-	-	135.3	-1.2
1997	-	-	137.1	1.3	-	-	135.3	-1.3	-	-	138.3	2.2	-	-	137.1	-0.9	-	-	140.6	2.6	-	-	139.6	-0.7
1998	139.7	0.1	-	-	140.2	0.4	-	-	140.8	0.4	-	-	144.4	2.6	-	-	145.2	0.6	-	-	142.7	-1.7	-	-
1999	143.6	0.6	-	-	144.2	0.4	-	-	144.6	0.3	-	-	148.1	2.4	-	-	148.0	-0.1	-	-	146.7	-0.9	-	-
2000	147.4	0.5	-	-	148.7	0.9	-	-	149.4	0.5	-	-	154.5	3.4	-	-	155.2	0.5	-	-	153.7	-1.0	-	-
2001	154.6	0.6	-	-	157.6	1.9	-	-	156.8	-0.5	-	-	163.6	4.3	-	-	162.9	-0.4	-	-	162.6	-0.2	-	-

Source: U.S. Department of Labor, Bureau of Labor Statistics, Division of Consumer Prices and Price Indexes. - indicates no data collected for period.

Dallas-Fort Worth, TX
Consumer Price Index - All Urban Consumers
Base 1982-1984 = 100
Apparel

For 1963-2001. Columns headed % show percentile change in the index from the previous period for which an index is available.

Year	Jan Index	%	Feb Index	%	Mar Index	%	Apr Index	%	May Index	%	Jun Index	%	Jul Index	%	Aug Index	%	Sep Index	%	Oct Index	%	Nov Index	%	Dec Index	%
1963	-		-		-		-		-		-		-		-		-		-		45.6	-	-	
1964	-		45.6	0.0	-		-		45.5	-0.2	-		-		45.1	-0.9	-		-		45.5	0.9	-	
1965	-		45.0	-1.1	-		-		45.2	0.4	-		-		44.8	-0.9	-		-		45.6	1.8	-	
1966	-		45.7	0.2	-		-		46.6	2.0	-		-		46.5	-0.2	-		-		47.9	3.0	-	
1967	-		48.2	0.6	-		-		48.6	0.8	-		-		48.8	0.4	-		-		49.0	0.4	-	
1968	-		49.6	1.2	-		-		51.4	3.6	-		-		51.8	0.8	-		-		52.9	2.1	-	
1969	-		53.3	0.8	-		-		54.6	2.4	-		-		54.8	0.4	-		-		56.7	3.5	-	
1970	-		57.6	1.6	-		-		57.3	-0.5	-		-		57.7	0.7	-		-		57.1	-1.0	-	
1971	-		56.9	-0.4	-		-		57.7	1.4	-		-		58.2	0.9	-		-		57.6	-1.0	-	
1972	-		58.4	1.4	-		-		59.1	1.2	-		-		59.2	0.2	-		-		60.3	1.9	-	
1973	-		61.1	1.3	-		-		62.4	2.1	-		-		63.1	1.1	-		-		63.9	1.3	-	
1974	-		65.2	2.0	-		-		66.1	1.4	-		-		67.0	1.4	-		-		68.3	1.9	-	
1975	-		68.2	-0.1	-		-		68.1	-0.1	-		-		69.3	1.8	-		-		69.6	0.4	-	
1976	-		69.4	-0.3	-		-		70.7	1.9	-		-		71.0	0.4	-		-		72.2	1.7	-	
1977	-		72.9	1.0	-		-		73.5	0.8	-		-		76.0	3.4	-		-		76.7	0.9	-	
1978	-		77.1	0.5	-		78.1	1.3	-		78.0	-0.1	-		79.8	2.3	-		80.3	0.6	-		81.6	1.6
1979	-		81.5	-0.1	-		83.4	2.3	-		82.2	-1.4	-		84.5	2.8	-		85.2	0.8	-		85.6	0.5
1980	-		86.8	1.4	-		88.2	1.6	-		87.3	-1.0	-		89.7	2.7	-		92.6	3.2	-		90.1	-2.7
1981	-		91.6	1.7	-		93.1	1.6	-		93.5	0.4	-		98.0	4.8	-		99.5	1.5	-		96.2	-3.3
1982	-		98.6	2.5	-		97.6	-1.0	-		97.6	0.0	-		96.2	-1.4	-		96.6	0.4	-		96.8	0.2
1983	-		98.4	1.7	-		101.1	2.7	-		98.6	-2.5	-		99.9	1.3	-		100.7	0.8	-		100.1	-0.6
1984	-		103.3	3.2	-		102.8	-0.5	-		99.6	-3.1	-		101.0	1.4	-		107.0	5.9	-		106.8	-0.2
1985	-		106.2	-0.6	-		105.8	-0.4	-		106.4	0.6	-		108.7	2.2	-		110.8	1.9	-		106.5	-2.9
1986	-		107.0	-1.4	-		106.2	-0.7	-		106.6	0.4	-		109.2	2.4	-		109.7	0.5	-		116.5	-1.7
1987	-		108.2	1.6	-		117.5	8.6	-		114.9	-2.2	-		113.9	-0.9	-		118.5	4.0	-		126.7	-1.6
1988	-		117.4	0.8	-		125.1	6.6	-		120.0	-4.1	-		123.0	2.5	-		128.8	4.7	-		124.9	-1.0
1989	-		118.4	-6.6	-		130.0	9.8	-		122.8	-5.5	-		124.6	1.5	-		126.1	1.2	-		142.7	-2.4
1990	-		133.6	7.0	-		136.1	1.9	-		133.0	-2.3	-		137.7	3.5	-		146.2	6.2	-		142.8	-14.1
1991	-		149.8	5.0	-		154.1	2.9	-		146.9	-4.7	-		150.6	2.5	-		166.3	10.4	-		149.9	-5.1
1992	-		157.5	10.3	-		152.4	-3.2	-		147.6	-3.1	-		144.5	-2.1	-		157.9	9.3	-		143.3	-6.9
1993	-		144.3	-3.7	-		161.5	11.9	-		142.8	-11.6	-		139.7	-2.2	-		153.9	10.2	-		146.2	-2.1
1994	-		148.0	3.3	-		147.6	-0.3	-		151.2	2.4	-		147.8	-2.2	-		149.3	1.0	-		143.7	-3.9
1995	-		145.6	-0.4	-		154.6	6.2	-		147.8	-4.4	-		145.0	-1.9	-		149.5	3.1	-		136.9	-2.0
1996	-		141.8	-1.3	-		149.4	5.4	-		141.4	-5.4	-		140.5	-0.6	-		139.7	-0.6	-		136.5	-1.4
1997	-		135.9	-0.7	-		139.8	2.9	-		137.3	-1.8	-		135.4	-1.4	-		138.4	2.2	-		-	
1998	130.2	-4.6	-		146.9	12.8	-		144.7	-1.5	-		135.2	-6.6	-		131.1	-3.0	-		130.6	-0.4	-	
1999	133.6	2.3	-		148.9	11.5	-		144.9	-2.7	-		134.5	-7.2	-		144.1	7.1	-		140.0	-2.8	-	
2000	128.6	-8.1	-		146.4	13.8	-		139.6	-4.6	-		133.2	-4.6	-		135.4	1.7	-		138.0	1.9	-	
2001	145.2	5.2	-		156.1	7.5	-		140.3	-10.1	-		134.7	-4.0	-		144.8	7.5	-		143.4	-1.0	-	

Source: U.S. Department of Labor, Bureau of Labor Statistics, Division of Consumer Prices and Price Indexes. - indicates no data collected for period.

Dallas-Fort Worth, TX
Consumer Price Index - Urban Wage Earners
Base 1982-1984 = 100
Apparel

For 1963-2001. Columns headed % show percentile change in the index from the previous period for which an index is available.

Year	Jan Index	Jan %	Feb Index	Feb %	Mar Index	Mar %	Apr Index	Apr %	May Index	May %	Jun Index	Jun %	Jul Index	Jul %	Aug Index	Aug %	Sep Index	Sep %	Oct Index	Oct %	Nov Index	Nov %	Dec Index	Dec %
1963	-	-	-	-	-	-	-	-	-	-	-	-	-	-	-	-	-	-	-	-	48.1	-	-	-
1964	-	-	48.1	0.0	-	-	-	-	48.0	-0.2	-	-	-	-	47.6	-0.8	-	-	-	-	48.0	0.8	-	-
1965	-	-	47.5	-1.0	-	-	-	-	47.7	0.4	-	-	-	-	47.3	-0.8	-	-	-	-	48.1	1.7	-	-
1966	-	-	48.3	0.4	-	-	-	-	49.2	1.9	-	-	-	-	49.1	-0.2	-	-	-	-	50.6	3.1	-	-
1967	-	-	50.9	0.6	-	-	-	-	51.3	0.8	-	-	-	-	51.5	0.4	-	-	-	-	51.7	0.4	-	-
1968	-	-	52.4	1.4	-	-	-	-	54.3	3.6	-	-	-	-	54.7	0.7	-	-	-	-	55.8	2.0	-	-
1969	-	-	56.3	0.9	-	-	-	-	57.7	2.5	-	-	-	-	57.9	0.3	-	-	-	-	59.9	3.5	-	-
1970	-	-	60.8	1.5	-	-	-	-	60.5	-0.5	-	-	-	-	60.9	0.7	-	-	-	-	60.3	-1.0	-	-
1971	-	-	60.1	-0.3	-	-	-	-	60.9	1.3	-	-	-	-	61.4	0.8	-	-	-	-	60.8	-1.0	-	-
1972	-	-	61.7	1.5	-	-	-	-	62.4	1.1	-	-	-	-	62.5	0.2	-	-	-	-	63.7	1.9	-	-
1973	-	-	64.6	1.4	-	-	-	-	65.9	2.0	-	-	-	-	66.6	1.1	-	-	-	-	67.5	1.4	-	-
1974	-	-	68.8	1.9	-	-	-	-	69.8	1.5	-	-	-	-	70.7	1.3	-	-	-	-	72.1	2.0	-	-
1975	-	-	72.1	0.0	-	-	-	-	72.0	-0.1	-	-	-	-	73.1	1.5	-	-	-	-	73.5	0.5	-	-
1976	-	-	73.2	-0.4	-	-	-	-	74.7	2.0	-	-	-	-	74.9	0.3	-	-	-	-	76.3	1.9	-	-
1977	-	-	76.9	0.8	-	-	-	-	77.6	0.9	-	-	-	-	80.2	3.4	-	-	-	-	81.0	1.0	-	-
1978	-	-	81.5	0.6	-	-	80.5	-1.2	-	-	80.7	0.2	-	-	84.3	4.5	-	-	84.3	0.0	-	-	85.0	0.8
1979	-	-	85.8	0.9	-	-	86.2	0.5	-	-	85.7	-0.6	-	-	88.6	3.4	-	-	89.2	0.7	-	-	89.2	0.0
1980	-	-	90.9	1.9	-	-	93.1	2.4	-	-	94.1	1.1	-	-	96.2	2.2	-	-	97.5	1.4	-	-	98.1	0.6
1981	-	-	98.6	0.5	-	-	99.9	1.3	-	-	100.9	1.0	-	-	99.5	-1.4	-	-	98.2	-1.3	-	-	95.7	-2.5
1982	-	-	98.4	2.8	-	-	97.4	-1.0	-	-	97.3	-0.1	-	-	97.2	-0.1	-	-	97.6	0.4	-	-	97.3	-0.3
1983	-	-	98.6	1.3	-	-	100.8	2.2	-	-	98.4	-2.4	-	-	98.9	0.5	-	-	101.2	2.3	-	-	99.3	-1.9
1984	-	-	103.9	4.6	-	-	102.3	-1.5	-	-	100.1	-2.2	-	-	100.7	0.6	-	-	106.3	5.6	-	-	106.9	0.6
1985	-	-	106.3	-0.6	-	-	107.8	1.4	-	-	108.7	0.8	-	-	110.1	1.3	-	-	112.9	2.5	-	-	110.1	-2.5
1986	-	-	107.7	-2.2	-	-	107.7	0.0	-	-	107.8	0.1	-	-	111.8	3.7	-	-	111.7	-0.1	-	-	108.5	-2.9
1987	-	-	110.6	1.9	-	-	118.2	6.9	-	-	113.8	-3.7	-	-	113.3	-0.4	-	-	119.1	5.1	-	-	117.9	-1.0
1988	-	-	118.8	0.8	-	-	124.1	4.5	-	-	119.6	-3.6	-	-	122.5	2.4	-	-	129.0	5.3	-	-	127.1	-1.5
1989	-	-	118.3	-6.9	-	-	129.7	9.6	-	-	121.0	-6.7	-	-	121.1	0.1	-	-	123.6	2.1	-	-	121.9	-1.4
1990	-	-	125.9	3.3	-	-	131.1	4.1	-	-	127.4	-2.8	-	-	131.2	3.0	-	-	137.2	4.6	-	-	135.8	-1.0
1991	-	-	138.1	1.7	-	-	142.9	3.5	-	-	138.4	-3.1	-	-	134.8	-2.6	-	-	146.4	8.6	-	-	130.5	-10.9
1992	-	-	143.7	10.1	-	-	142.3	-1.0	-	-	139.2	-2.2	-	-	135.8	-2.4	-	-	148.6	9.4	-	-	142.5	-4.1
1993	-	-	139.4	-2.2	-	-	155.9	11.8	-	-	142.5	-8.6	-	-	134.8	-5.4	-	-	145.3	7.8	-	-	139.6	-3.9
1994	-	-	138.7	-0.6	-	-	140.6	1.4	-	-	142.8	1.6	-	-	139.2	-2.5	-	-	142.2	2.2	-	-	138.2	-2.8
1995	-	-	137.2	-0.7	-	-	147.3	7.4	-	-	142.9	-3.0	-	-	137.8	-3.6	-	-	145.1	5.3	-	-	140.3	-3.3
1996	-	-	137.2	-2.2	-	-	146.0	6.4	-	-	138.8	-4.9	-	-	137.8	-0.7	-	-	136.1	-1.2	-	-	133.1	-2.2
1997	-	-	130.8	-1.7	-	-	135.4	3.5	-	-	132.3	-2.3	-	-	130.0	-1.7	-	-	135.6	4.3	-	-	134.0	-1.2
1998	127.8	-4.6	-	-	139.3	9.0	-	-	138.0	-0.9	-	-	129.4	-6.2	-	-	128.8	-0.5	-	-	126.9	-1.5	-	-
1999	126.6	-0.2	-	-	139.8	10.4	-	-	137.8	-1.4	-	-	128.3	-6.9	-	-	138.2	7.7	-	-	134.5	-2.7	-	-
2000	125.8	-6.5	-	-	139.7	11.0	-	-	133.9	-4.2	-	-	128.1	-4.3	-	-	129.0	0.7	-	-	133.6	3.6	-	-
2001	136.3	2.0	-	-	148.1	8.7	-	-	134.7	-9.0	-	-	131.2	-2.6	-	-	138.8	5.8	-	-	137.8	-0.7	-	-

Source: U.S. Department of Labor, Bureau of Labor Statistics, Division of Consumer Prices and Price Indexes. - indicates no data collected for period.

Dallas-Fort Worth, TX
Consumer Price Index - All Urban Consumers
Base 1982-1984 = 100
Transportation

For 1963-2000. Columns headed % show percentile change in the index from the previous period for which an index is available.

Year	Jan Index	%	Feb Index	%	Mar Index	%	Apr Index	%	May Index	%	Jun Index	%	Jul Index	%	Aug Index	%	Sep Index	%	Oct Index	%	Nov Index	%	Dec Index	%
1963	-	-	-	-	-	-	-	-	-	-	-	-	-	-	-	-	-	-	-	-	31.5	-	-	-
1964	-	-	30.7	-2.5	-	-	-	-	31.9	3.9	-	-	-	-	30.6	-4.1	-	-	-	-	31.9	4.2	-	-
1965	-	-	30.1	-5.6	-	-	-	-	31.9	6.0	-	-	-	-	32.0	0.3	-	-	-	-	32.2	0.6	-	-
1966	-	-	31.7	-1.6	-	-	-	-	32.3	1.9	-	-	-	-	32.4	0.3	-	-	-	-	32.7	0.9	-	-
1967	-	-	32.6	-0.3	-	-	-	-	33.1	1.5	-	-	-	-	33.8	2.1	-	-	-	-	33.6	-0.6	-	-
1968	-	-	33.6	0.0	-	-	-	-	34.5	2.7	-	-	-	-	34.8	0.9	-	-	-	-	34.9	0.3	-	-
1969	-	-	34.8	-0.3	-	-	-	-	35.5	2.0	-	-	-	-	35.6	0.3	-	-	-	-	36.4	2.2	-	-
1970	-	-	35.9	-1.4	-	-	-	-	36.8	2.5	-	-	-	-	37.3	1.4	-	-	-	-	37.4	0.3	-	-
1971	-	-	38.5	2.9	-	-	-	-	38.7	0.5	-	-	-	-	39.9	3.1	-	-	-	-	39.5	-1.0	-	-
1972	-	-	39.2	-0.8	-	-	-	-	40.2	2.6	-	-	-	-	40.4	0.5	-	-	-	-	39.8	-1.5	-	-
1973	-	-	39.6	-0.5	-	-	-	-	41.1	3.8	-	-	-	-	41.4	0.7	-	-	-	-	42.0	1.4	-	-
1974	-	-	43.9	4.5	-	-	-	-	47.0	7.1	-	-	-	-	49.2	4.7	-	-	-	-	49.6	0.8	-	-
1975	-	-	49.6	0.0	-	-	-	-	51.1	3.0	-	-	-	-	53.7	5.1	-	-	-	-	54.0	0.6	-	-
1976	-	-	53.6	-0.7	-	-	-	-	56.1	4.7	-	-	-	-	57.7	2.9	-	-	-	-	59.2	2.6	-	-
1977	-	-	59.4	0.3	-	-	-	-	61.5	3.5	-	-	-	-	61.7	0.3	-	-	-	-	61.3	-0.6	-	-
1978	-	-	61.0	-0.5	-	-	61.4	0.7	-	-	62.6	2.0	-	-	63.4	1.3	-	-	64.4	1.6	-	-	65.0	0.9
1979	-	-	66.1	1.7	-	-	68.9	4.2	-	-	72.3	4.9	-	-	74.4	2.9	-	-	75.4	1.3	-	-	77.8	3.2
1980	-	-	83.3	7.1	-	-	86.2	3.5	-	-	86.6	0.5	-	-	87.6	1.2	-	-	88.1	0.6	-	-	88.6	0.6
1981	-	-	92.3	4.2	-	-	95.1	3.0	-	-	96.5	1.5	-	-	96.5	0.0	-	-	97.2	0.7	-	-	97.6	0.4
1982	-	-	97.2	-0.4	-	-	93.8	-3.5	-	-	98.0	4.5	-	-	99.1	1.1	-	-	98.4	-0.7	-	-	97.9	-0.5
1983	-	-	95.6	-2.3	-	-	97.3	1.8	-	-	99.4	2.2	-	-	100.6	1.2	-	-	102.0	1.4	-	-	101.5	-0.5
1984	-	-	100.7	-0.8	-	-	101.7	1.0	-	-	102.4	0.7	-	-	104.8	2.3	-	-	105.9	1.0	-	-	105.6	-0.3
1985	-	-	104.9	-0.7	-	-	106.5	1.5	-	-	107.6	1.0	-	-	108.0	0.4	-	-	108.6	0.6	-	-	108.7	0.1
1986	-	-	107.9	-0.7	-	-	99.2	-8.1	-	-	100.2	1.0	-	-	98.7	-1.5	-	-	99.2	0.5	-	-	98.7	-0.5
1987	-	-	101.2	2.5	-	-	101.0	-0.2	-	-	103.2	2.2	-	-	104.7	1.5	-	-	105.8	1.1	-	-	107.2	1.3
1988	-	-	107.2	0.0	-	-	106.6	-0.6	-	-	108.2	1.5	-	-	108.4	0.2	-	-	108.8	0.4	-	-	109.0	0.2
1989	-	-	108.9	-0.1	-	-	109.5	0.6	-	-	112.6	2.8	-	-	110.4	-2.0	-	-	111.9	1.4	-	-	112.1	0.2
1990	-	-	113.9	1.6	-	-	113.1	-0.7	-	-	114.1	0.9	-	-	116.6	2.2	-	-	123.6	6.0	-	-	125.3	1.4
1991	-	-	121.0	-3.4	-	-	118.3	-2.2	-	-	119.5	1.0	-	-	120.8	1.1	-	-	121.1	0.2	-	-	123.1	1.7
1992	-	-	121.3	-1.5	-	-	122.4	0.9	-	-	123.0	0.5	-	-	122.9	-0.1	-	-	126.1	2.6	-	-	125.6	-0.4
1993	-	-	125.5	-0.1	-	-	126.1	0.5	-	-	127.9	1.4	-	-	130.4	2.0	-	-	132.1	1.3	-	-	133.1	0.8
1994	-	-	132.8	-0.2	-	-	133.1	0.2	-	-	133.3	0.2	-	-	135.7	1.8	-	-	136.4	0.5	-	-	136.5	0.1
1995	-	-	137.4	0.7	-	-	140.3	2.1	-	-	140.6	0.2	-	-	139.7	-0.6	-	-	140.9	0.9	-	-	138.3	-1.8
1996	-	-	139.6	0.9	-	-	141.9	1.6	-	-	143.5	1.1	-	-	141.2	-1.6	-	-	143.3	1.5	-	-	145.0	1.2
1997	-	-	144.1	-0.6	-	-	143.9	-0.1	-	-	143.3	-0.4	-	-	143.1	-0.1	-	-	141.6	-1.0	-	-	140.0	-1.1
1998	139.8	-0.1	-	-	139.2	-0.4	-	-	137.9	-0.9	-	-	138.5	0.4	-	-	137.4	-0.8	-	-	138.8	1.0	-	-
1999	136.9	-1.4	-	-	137.8	0.7	-	-	140.2	1.7	-	-	141.0	0.6	-	-	143.2	1.6	-	-	144.6	1.0	-	-
2000	146.3	1.2	-	-	151.9	3.8	-	-	150.9	-0.7	-	-	154.9	2.7	-	-	153.1	-1.2	-	-	154.8	1.1	-	-

Source: U.S. Department of Labor, Bureau of Labor Statistics, Division of Consumer Prices and Price Indexes. - indicates no data collected for period.

Dallas-Fort Worth, TX
Consumer Price Index - Urban Wage Earners
Base 1982-1984 = 100
Transportation

For 1963-2000. Columns headed % show percentile change in the index from the previous period for which an index is available.

Year	Jan Index	Jan %	Feb Index	Feb %	Mar Index	Mar %	Apr Index	Apr %	May Index	May %	Jun Index	Jun %	Jul Index	Jul %	Aug Index	Aug %	Sep Index	Sep %	Oct Index	Oct %	Nov Index	Nov %	Dec Index	Dec %
1963	-	-	-	-	-	-	-	-	-	-	-	-	-	-	-	-	-	-	-	-	31.5	-	-	-
1964	-	-	30.8	-2.2	-	-	-	-	31.9	3.6	-	-	-	-	30.7	-3.8	-	-	-	-	32.0	4.2	-	-
1965	-	-	30.2	-5.6	-	-	-	-	31.9	5.6	-	-	-	-	32.1	0.6	-	-	-	-	32.2	0.3	-	-
1966	-	-	31.7	-1.6	-	-	-	-	32.3	1.9	-	-	-	-	32.4	0.3	-	-	-	-	32.8	1.2	-	-
1967	-	-	32.6	-0.6	-	-	-	-	33.1	1.5	-	-	-	-	33.9	2.4	-	-	-	-	33.6	-0.9	-	-
1968	-	-	33.7	0.3	-	-	-	-	34.5	2.4	-	-	-	-	34.8	0.9	-	-	-	-	35.0	0.6	-	-
1969	-	-	34.8	-0.6	-	-	-	-	35.6	2.3	-	-	-	-	35.6	0.0	-	-	-	-	36.4	2.2	-	-
1970	-	-	36.0	-1.1	-	-	-	-	36.9	2.5	-	-	-	-	37.3	1.1	-	-	-	-	37.5	0.5	-	-
1971	-	-	38.5	2.7	-	-	-	-	38.8	0.8	-	-	-	-	39.9	2.8	-	-	-	-	39.5	-1.0	-	-
1972	-	-	39.2	-0.8	-	-	-	-	40.2	2.6	-	-	-	-	40.4	0.5	-	-	-	-	39.9	-1.2	-	-
1973	-	-	39.6	-0.8	-	-	-	-	41.2	4.0	-	-	-	-	41.4	0.5	-	-	-	-	42.0	1.4	-	-
1974	-	-	43.9	4.5	-	-	-	-	47.0	7.1	-	-	-	-	49.3	4.9	-	-	-	-	49.7	0.8	-	-
1975	-	-	49.6	-0.2	-	-	-	-	51.1	3.0	-	-	-	-	53.7	5.1	-	-	-	-	54.0	0.6	-	-
1976	-	-	53.7	-0.6	-	-	-	-	56.1	4.5	-	-	-	-	57.7	2.9	-	-	-	-	59.2	2.6	-	-
1977	-	-	59.5	0.5	-	-	-	-	61.6	3.5	-	-	-	-	61.7	0.2	-	-	-	-	61.3	-0.6	-	-
1978	-	-	61.0	-0.5	-	-	61.5	0.8	-	-	62.7	2.0	-	-	61.7	0.2	-	-	64.6	1.4	-	-	65.3	1.1
1979	-	-	66.4	1.7	-	-	69.3	4.4	-	-	62.7	2.0	-	-	63.7	1.6	-	-	64.6	1.4	-	-	65.3	1.1
1980	-	-	83.8	7.3	-	-	86.5	3.2	-	-	72.7	4.9	-	-	75.0	3.2	-	-	75.7	0.9	-	-	78.1	3.2
1981	-	-	93.3	4.4	-	-	95.6	2.5	-	-	86.7	0.2	-	-	87.8	1.3	-	-	88.7	1.0	-	-	89.4	0.8
1982	-	-	97.5	-0.5	-	-	94.0	-3.6	-	-	97.7	2.2	-	-	97.5	-0.2	-	-	98.6	1.1	-	-	98.0	-0.6
1983	-	-	95.6	-2.4	-	-	97.4	1.9	-	-	98.2	4.5	-	-	99.3	1.1	-	-	98.6	-0.7	-	-	98.0	-0.6
1984	-	-	100.6	-0.8	-	-	101.5	0.9	-	-	99.4	2.1	-	-	100.6	1.2	-	-	102.0	1.4	-	-	101.4	-0.6
1985	-	-	104.5	-0.8	-	-	106.2	1.6	-	-	102.3	0.8	-	-	104.6	2.2	-	-	105.7	1.1	-	-	105.3	-0.4
1986	-	-	107.6	-0.7	-	-	98.7	-8.3	-	-	107.3	1.0	-	-	107.6	0.3	-	-	108.3	0.7	-	-	108.4	0.1
1987	-	-	101.1	3.4	-	-	101.8	0.7	-	-	99.7	1.0	-	-	98.1	-1.6	-	-	98.4	0.3	-	-	97.8	-0.6
1988	-	-	107.7	-0.1	-	-	106.9	-0.7	-	-	104.3	2.5	-	-	106.0	1.6	-	-	106.8	0.8	-	-	107.8	0.9
1989	-	-	109.2	-0.3	-	-	110.8	1.5	-	-	108.4	1.4	-	-	109.2	0.7	-	-	109.5	0.3	-	-	109.5	0.0
1990	-	-	114.4	1.6	-	-	113.5	-0.8	-	-	114.3	3.2	-	-	111.9	-2.1	-	-	112.9	0.9	-	-	112.6	-0.3
1991	-	-	120.9	-4.2	-	-	118.5	-2.0	-	-	115.0	1.3	-	-	117.7	2.3	-	-	125.0	6.2	-	-	126.2	1.0
1992	-	-	121.8	-2.1	-	-	123.4	1.3	-	-	120.6	1.8	-	-	122.0	1.2	-	-	122.9	0.7	-	-	124.4	1.2
1993	-	-	128.3	-0.9	-	-	129.5	0.9	-	-	126.5	2.5	-	-	127.5	0.8	-	-	129.8	1.8	-	-	129.5	-0.2
1994	-	-	135.0	-1.2	-	-	135.5	0.4	-	-	132.1	2.0	-	-	135.1	2.3	-	-	136.9	1.3	-	-	136.6	-0.2
1995	-	-	142.3	0.4	-	-	144.5	1.5	-	-	136.8	1.0	-	-	139.8	2.2	-	-	141.3	1.1	-	-	141.8	0.4
1996	-	-	143.9	0.5	-	-	147.6	2.6	-	-	145.4	0.6	-	-	144.5	-0.6	-	-	145.0	0.3	-	-	143.2	-1.2
1997	-	-	149.0	-0.3	-	-	148.5	-0.3	-	-	148.7	0.7	-	-	146.5	-1.5	-	-	148.3	1.2	-	-	149.5	0.8
1998	144.5	-0.3	-	-	143.9	-0.4	-	-	142.8	-0.8	-	-	143.3	0.4	-	-	142.1	-0.8	-	-	143.6	1.1	-	-
1999	141.3	-1.6	-	-	142.0	0.5	-	-	144.7	1.9	-	-	145.0	0.2	-	-	147.6	1.8	-	-	148.8	0.8	-	-
2000	150.6	1.2	-	-	156.0	3.6	-	-	155.3	-0.4	-	-	159.0	2.4	-	-	157.2	-1.1	-	-	159.0	1.1	-	-

Source: U.S. Department of Labor, Bureau of Labor Statistics, Division of Consumer Prices and Price Indexes. - indicates no data collected for period.

Dallas-Fort Worth, TX
Consumer Price Index - All Urban Consumers
Base 1982-1984 = 100
Medical Care

For 1963-2001. Columns headed % show percentile change in the index from the previous period for which an index is available.

Year	Jan Index	%	Feb Index	%	Mar Index	%	Apr Index	%	May Index	%	Jun Index	%	Jul Index	%	Aug Index	%	Sep Index	%	Oct Index	%	Nov Index	%	Dec Index	%
1963	-		-		-		-		-		-		-		-		-		-		24.1	-	-	
1964	-		24.4	1.2	-		-		24.5	0.4	-		-		24.5	0.0	-		-		24.5	0.0	-	
1965	-		24.8	1.2	-		-		25.0	0.8	-		-		25.0	0.0	-		-		25.2	0.8	-	
1966	-		25.8	2.4	-		-		26.3	1.9	-		-		26.6	1.1	-		-		26.9	1.1	-	
1967	-		28.0	4.1	-		-		28.0	0.0	-		-		28.3	1.1	-		-		28.8	1.8	-	
1968	-		29.5	2.4	-		-		30.0	1.7	-		-		30.0	0.0	-		-		30.5	1.7	-	
1969	-		31.7	3.9	-		-		32.2	1.6	-		-		32.6	1.2	-		-		32.9	0.9	-	
1970	-		34.2	4.0	-		-		34.8	1.8	-		-		35.1	0.9	-		-		35.1	0.0	-	
1971	-		36.1	2.8	-		-		36.5	1.1	-		-		36.7	0.5	-		-		36.4	-0.8	-	
1972	-		36.9	1.4	-		-		37.1	0.5	-		-		37.2	0.3	-		-		37.5	0.8	-	
1973	-		38.2	1.9	-		-		38.6	1.0	-		-		38.5	-0.3	-		-		39.5	2.6	-	
1974	-		40.2	1.8	-		-		40.9	1.7	-		-		42.4	3.7	-		-		43.4	2.4	-	
1975	-		44.6	2.8	-		-		45.4	1.8	-		-		46.8	3.1	-		-		47.2	0.9	-	
1976	-		48.5	2.8	-		-		48.8	0.6	-		-		50.7	3.9	-		-		52.3	3.2	-	
1977	-		53.3	1.9	-		-		54.8	2.8	-		-		55.8	1.8	-		-		57.0	2.2	-	
1978	-		58.3	2.3	-		58.9	1.0	-		59.8	1.5	-		60.0	0.3	-		60.4	0.7	-		61.1	1.2
1979	-		61.3	0.3	-		62.2	1.5	-		62.4	0.3	-		63.5	1.8	-		63.6	0.2	-		65.2	2.5
1980	-		66.5	2.0	-		69.0	3.8	-		69.7	1.0	-		71.9	3.2	-		71.8	-0.1	-		72.4	0.8
1981	-		74.1	2.3	-		75.6	2.0	-		79.4	5.0	-		83.3	4.9	-		85.5	2.6	-		87.4	2.2
1982	-		89.2	2.1	-		90.3	1.2	-		91.6	1.4	-		92.2	0.7	-		94.2	2.2	-		96.0	1.9
1983	-		98.8	2.9	-		100.9	2.1	-		100.8	-0.1	-		102.3	1.5	-		102.3	0.0	-		104.1	1.8
1984	-		105.4	1.2	-		106.0	0.6	-		106.5	0.5	-		107.4	0.8	-		108.5	1.0	-		109.3	0.7
1985	-		110.5	1.1	-		111.3	0.7	-		112.1	0.7	-		114.7	2.3	-		116.1	1.2	-		122.1	5.2
1986	-		123.7	1.3	-		125.3	1.3	-		126.0	0.6	-		127.5	1.2	-		129.2	1.3	-		130.6	1.1
1987	-		130.3	-0.2	-		134.0	2.8	-		134.3	0.2	-		135.4	0.8	-		135.3	-0.1	-		137.9	1.9
1988	-		141.6	2.7	-		140.7	-0.6	-		140.9	0.1	-		141.6	0.5	-		142.9	0.9	-		145.7	2.0
1989	-		148.2	1.7	-		148.7	0.3	-		149.8	0.7	-		151.9	1.4	-		154.4	1.6	-		154.4	0.0
1990	-		156.4	1.3	-		156.9	0.3	-		162.1	3.3	-		163.7	1.0	-		167.3	2.2	-		168.2	0.5
1991	-		170.4	1.3	-		170.9	0.3	-		174.3	2.0	-		176.3	1.1	-		179.0	1.5	-		180.8	1.0
1992	-		182.7	1.1	-		185.7	1.6	-		187.7	1.1	-		188.9	0.6	-		193.8	2.6	-		194.1	0.2
1993	-		193.5	-0.3	-		194.0	0.3	-		196.7	1.4	-		197.9	0.6	-		199.7	0.9	-		200.6	0.5
1994	-		202.1	0.7	-		203.7	0.8	-		204.5	0.4	-		205.3	0.4	-		209.6	2.1	-		210.8	0.6
1995	-		212.8	0.9	-		216.2	1.6	-		215.6	-0.3	-		218.6	1.4	-		220.4	0.8	-		220.3	-0.0
1996	-		224.9	2.1	-		225.5	0.3	-		228.0	1.1	-		223.4	-2.0	-		224.1	0.3	-		222.6	-0.7
1997	-		222.6	0.0	-		224.1	0.7	-		224.2	0.0	-		226.7	1.1	-		227.3	0.3	-		228.1	0.4
1998	229.0	0.4	-		227.6	-0.6	-		228.2	0.3	-		229.5	0.6	-		231.1	0.7	-		228.8	-1.0	-	
1999	229.5	0.3	-		231.5	0.9	-		231.0	-0.2	-		233.4	1.0	-		234.0	0.3	-		237.8	1.6	-	
2000	237.9	0.0	-		240.8	1.2	-		239.8	-0.4	-		245.2	2.3	-		246.1	0.4	-		246.9	0.3	-	
2001	248.7	0.7	-		250.2	0.6	-		251.4	0.5	-		252.9	0.6	-		253.5	0.2	-		255.5	0.8	-	

Source: U.S. Department of Labor, Bureau of Labor Statistics, Division of Consumer Prices and Price Indexes. - indicates no data collected for period.

Dallas-Fort Worth, TX
Consumer Price Index - Urban Wage Earners
Base 1982-1984 = 100
Medical Care

For 1963-2001. Columns headed % show percentile change in the index from the previous period for which an index is available.

Year	Jan Index	%	Feb Index	%	Mar Index	%	Apr Index	%	May Index	%	Jun Index	%	Jul Index	%	Aug Index	%	Sep Index	%	Oct Index	%	Nov Index	%	Dec Index	%
1963	-		-												-		-		-		24.5		-	
1964	-		24.8	1.2	-		-		24.9	0.4			-		24.9	0.0	-		-		24.9	0.0	-	
1965	-		25.2	1.2	-		-		25.4	0.8			-		25.4	0.0	-		-		25.6	0.8	-	
1966	-		26.2	2.3	-		-		26.8	2.3			-		27.0	0.7	-		-		27.3	1.1	-	
1967	-		28.4	4.0	-		-		28.5	0.4			-		28.8	1.1	-		-		29.3	1.7	-	
1968	-		30.0	2.4	-		-		30.5	1.7			-		30.5	0.0	-		-		31.0	1.6	-	
1969	-		32.2	3.9	-		-		32.8	1.9			-		33.2	1.2	-		-		33.5	0.9	-	
1970	-		34.8	3.9	-		-		35.4	1.7			-		35.7	0.8	-		-		35.6	-0.3	-	
1971	-		36.7	3.1	-		-		37.1	1.1	-		-		37.3	0.5	-		-		37.0	-0.8		
1972	-		37.6	1.6	-		-		37.7	0.3	-		-		37.8	0.3	-		-		38.2	1.1		
1973	-		38.8	1.6	-		-		39.2	1.0	-		-		39.2	0.0	-		-		40.1	2.3		
1974	-		40.9	2.0	-		-		41.6	1.7	-		-		43.1	3.6	-		-		44.1	2.3		
1975	-		45.3	2.7	-		-		46.2	2.0	-		-		47.6	3.0	-		-		48.0	0.8		
1976	-		49.3	2.7	-		-		49.6	0.6	-		-		51.5	3.8	-		-		53.2	3.3		
1977	-		54.1	1.7	-		-		55.7	3.0	-		-		56.7	1.8	-		-		57.9	2.1		
1978	-		59.2	2.2	-		59.9	1.2	-		60.1	0.3	-		60.9	1.3	-		61.7	1.3	-		63.1	2.3
1979	-		63.1	0.0	-		64.5	2.2	-		65.1	0.9	-		66.1	1.5	-		66.0	-0.2	-		67.3	2.0
1980	-		68.2	1.3	-		70.2	2.9	-		71.1	1.3	-		74.6	4.9	-		74.5	-0.1	-		76.0	2.0
1981	-		76.8	1.1	-		77.6	1.0	-		80.4	3.6	-		83.3	3.6	-		84.8	1.8	-		87.0	2.6
1982	-		88.8	2.1	-		90.1	1.5	-		91.3	1.3	-		92.0	0.8	-		94.1	2.3	-		95.9	1.9
1983	-		98.8	3.0	-		101.0	2.2	-		100.7	-0.3	-		102.3	1.6	-		102.3	0.0	-		104.2	1.9
1984	-		105.7	1.4	-		106.1	0.4	-		106.6	0.5	-		107.6	0.9	-		108.7	1.0	-		109.6	0.8
1985	-		110.8	1.1	-		111.6	0.7	-		112.3	0.6	-		115.1	2.5	-		116.6	1.3	-		122.9	5.4
1986	-		124.5	1.3	-		126.0	1.2	-		126.8	0.6	-		128.4	1.3	-		130.1	1.3	-		131.5	1.1
1987	-		131.4	-0.1	-		135.1	2.8	-		135.5	0.3	-		136.8	1.0	-		136.8	0.0	-		139.8	2.2
1988	-		143.1	2.4	-		142.0	-0.8	-		142.4	0.3	-		143.4	0.7	-		144.4	0.7	-		148.1	2.6
1989	-		150.6	1.7	-		151.0	0.3	-		152.2	0.8	-		154.2	1.3	-		156.5	1.5	-		156.8	0.2
1990	-		158.8	1.3	-		159.3	0.3	-		164.7	3.4	-		166.6	1.2	-		170.1	2.1	-		170.8	0.4
1991	-		172.9	1.2	-		174.0	0.6	-		177.2	1.8	-		179.5	1.3	-		182.4	1.6	-		183.7	0.7
1992	-		185.7	1.1	-		189.5	2.0	-		191.9	1.3	-		193.1	0.6	-		198.1	2.6	-		198.0	-0.1
1993	-		197.2	-0.4	-		197.6	0.2	-		200.9	1.7	-		202.1	0.6	-		203.8	0.8	-		204.7	0.4
1994	-		205.9	0.6	-		207.4	0.7	-		207.9	0.2	-		208.8	0.4	-		213.3	2.2	-		214.6	0.4
1995	-		216.5	0.9	-		220.9	2.0	-		220.3	-0.3	-		223.3	1.4	-		225.3	0.9	-		225.1	-0.1
1996	-		229.0	1.7	-		229.4	0.2	-		232.0	1.1	-		226.5	-2.4	-		227.8	0.6	-		228.0	0.1
1997	-		227.7	-0.1	-		228.6	0.4	-		228.8	0.1	-		230.6	0.8	-		231.5	0.4	-		232.2	0.3
1998	232.9	0.3	-		232.1	-0.3	-		232.8	0.3	-		233.7	0.4	-		235.4	0.7	-		233.2	-0.9	-	
1999	233.9	0.3	-		235.8	0.8	-		235.5	-0.1	-		237.8	1.0	-		238.3	0.2	-		242.6	1.8	-	
2000	242.7	0.0	-		245.5	1.2	-		244.4	-0.4	-		249.7	2.2	-		250.5	0.3	-		251.2	0.3	-	
2001	252.9	0.7	-		254.5	0.6	-		255.5	0.4	-		257.1	0.6	-		257.3	0.1	-		259.3	0.8	-	

Source: U.S. Department of Labor, Bureau of Labor Statistics, Division of Consumer Prices and Price Indexes. - indicates no data collected for period.

Dallas-Fort Worth, TX
Consumer Price Index - All Urban Consumers
Base December 1997 = 100
Recreation

For 1997-2001. Columns headed % show percentile change in the index from the previous period for which an index is available.

Year	Jan Index	%	Feb Index	%	Mar Index	%	Apr Index	%	May Index	%	Jun Index	%	Jul Index	%	Aug Index	%	Sep Index	%	Oct Index	%	Nov Index	%	Dec Index	%
1997	-	-	-	-	-	-	-	-	-	-	-	-	-	-	-	-	-	-	-	-	-	-	100.0	-
1998	99.9	-0.1	-	-	99.7	-0.2	-	-	99.6	-0.1	-	-	99.9	0.3	-	-	100.1	0.2	-	-	100.7	0.6	-	-
1999	101.3	0.6	-	-	100.9	-0.4	-	-	101.6	0.7	-	-	102.7	1.1	-	-	103.2	0.5	-	-	103.9	0.7	-	-
2000	102.6	-1.3	-	-	105.5	2.8	-	-	106.2	0.7	-	-	108.5	2.2	-	-	108.0	-0.5	-	-	107.8	-0.2	-	-
2001	107.3	-0.5	-	-	107.4	0.1	-	-	109.5	2.0	-	-	109.1	-0.4	-	-	110.8	1.6	-	-	109.1	-1.5	-	-

Source: U.S. Department of Labor, Bureau of Labor Statistics, Division of Consumer Prices and Price Indexes. - indicates no data collected for period.

Dallas-Fort Worth, TX
Consumer Price Index - Urban Wage Earners
Base December 1997 = 100
Recreation

For 1997-2001. Columns headed % show percentile change in the index from the previous period for which an index is available.

Year	Jan		Feb		Mar		Apr		May		Jun		Jul		Aug		Sep		Oct		Nov		Dec	
	Index	%	Index	%	Index	%	Index	%	Index	%	Index	%	Index	%	Index	%	Index	%	Index	%	Index	%	Index	%
1997	-	-	-	-	-	-	-	-	-	-	-	-	-	-	-	-	-	-	-	-	-	-	100.0	-
1998	99.9	-0.1	-	-	99.7	-0.2	-	-	99.6	-0.1	-	-	100.0	0.4	-	-	100.1	0.1	-	-	100.8	0.7	-	-
1999	101.2	0.4	-	-	101.1	-0.1	-	-	101.6	0.5	-	-	102.8	1.2	-	-	103.5	0.7	-	-	104.2	0.7	-	-
2000	103.0	-1.2	-	-	105.7	2.6	-	-	106.7	0.9	-	-	108.9	2.1	-	-	108.4	-0.5	-	-	108.0	-0.4	-	-
2001	107.4	-0.6	-	-	107.5	0.1	-	-	109.5	1.9	-	-	109.6	0.1	-	-	110.8	1.1	-	-	109.5	-1.2	-	-

Source: U.S. Department of Labor, Bureau of Labor Statistics, Division of Consumer Prices and Price Indexes. - indicates no data collected for period.

Dallas-Fort Worth, TX
Consumer Price Index - All Urban Consumers
Base December 1997 = 100
Education & Communication

For 1997-2001. Columns headed % show percentile change in the index from the previous period for which an index is available.

Year	Jan Index	%	Feb Index	%	Mar Index	%	Apr Index	%	May Index	%	Jun Index	%	Jul Index	%	Aug Index	%	Sep Index	%	Oct Index	%	Nov Index	%	Dec Index	%
1997	-	-	-	-	-	-	-	-	-	-	-	-	-	-	-	-	-	-	-	-	-	-	100.0	-
1998	98.9	-1.1	-	-	99.1	0.2	-	-	99.0	-0.1	-	-	99.3	0.3	-	-	101.2	1.9	-	-	101.7	0.5	-	-
1999	101.8	0.1	-	-	102.1	0.3	-	-	103.0	0.9	-	-	104.0	1.0	-	-	106.0	1.9	-	-	105.9	-0.1	-	-
2000	107.1	1.1	-	-	106.2	-0.8	-	-	105.8	-0.4	-	-	107.4	1.5	-	-	108.0	0.6	-	-	108.9	0.8	-	-
2001	108.9	0.0	-	-	109.6	0.6	-	-	109.4	-0.2	-	-	109.5	0.1	-	-	113.3	3.5	-	-	113.6	0.3	-	-

Source: U.S. Department of Labor, Bureau of Labor Statistics, Division of Consumer Prices and Price Indexes. - indicates no data collected for period.

Dallas-Fort Worth, TX
Consumer Price Index - Urban Wage Earners
Base December 1997 = 100
Education & Communication

For 1997-2001. Columns headed % show percentile change in the index from the previous period for which an index is available.

Year	Jan Index	%	Feb Index	%	Mar Index	%	Apr Index	%	May Index	%	Jun Index	%	Jul Index	%	Aug Index	%	Sep Index	%	Oct Index	%	Nov Index	%	Dec Index	%
1997	-	-	-	-	-	-	-	-	-	-	-	-	-	-	-	-	-	-	-	-	-	-	100.0	-
1998	98.6	-1.4	-	-	98.8	0.2	-	-	98.8	0.0	-	-	99.3	0.5	-	-	100.0	0.7	-	-	100.8	0.8	-	-
1999	100.8	0.0	-	-	101.3	0.5	-	-	102.6	1.3	-	-	104.0	1.4	-	-	104.7	0.7	-	-	104.5	-0.2	-	-
2000	105.7	1.1	-	-	105.0	-0.7	-	-	104.5	-0.5	-	-	106.7	2.1	-	-	106.8	0.1	-	-	106.4	-0.4	-	-
2001	106.5	0.1	-	-	107.8	1.2	-	-	107.7	-0.1	-	-	107.8	0.1	-	-	111.7	3.6	-	-	111.2	-0.4	-	-

Source: U.S. Department of Labor, Bureau of Labor Statistics, Division of Consumer Prices and Price Indexes. - indicates no data collected for period.

Denver-Boulder-Greeley, CO
Consumer Price Index - All Urban Consumers
Base 1982-1984 = 100
Annual Averages

For 1964-2001. Columns headed % show percentile change in the index from the previous period for which an index is available.

Year	All Items		Food & Beverage		Housing		Apparel		Trans-portation		Medical Care		Recrea-tion*		Education & Communic.*		Other Goods & Services	
	Index	%	Index	%	Index	%	Index	%	Index	%	Index	%	Index	%	Index	%	Index	%
1964	28.3	-	-	-	-	-	-	-	-	-	-	-	-	-	-	-	-	-
1965	28.8	1.8	-	-	-	-	-	-	-	-	-	-	-	-	-	-	-	-
1966	29.7	3.1	-	-	-	-	-	-	-	-	-	-	-	-	-	-	-	-
1967	30.0	1.0	-	-	-	-	-	-	-	-	-	-	-	-	-	-	-	-
1968	30.7	2.3	-	-	-	-	-	-	-	-	-	-	-	-	-	-	-	-
1969	32.0	4.2	-	-	-	-	-	-	-	-	-	-	-	-	-	-	-	-
1970	34.5	7.8	-	-	-	-	-	-	-	-	-	-	-	-	-	-	-	-
1971	35.9	4.1	-	-	-	-	64.3	-	37.9	-	36.5	-	-	-	-	-	-	-
1972	37.0	3.1	-	-	-	-	66.1	2.8	37.8	-0.3	37.6	3.0	-	-	-	-	-	-
1973	39.6	7.0	-	-	-	-	68.8	4.1	39.6	4.8	39.0	3.7	-	-	-	-	-	-
1974	43.9	10.9	-	-	-	-	74.3	8.0	44.0	11.1	42.6	9.2	-	-	-	-	-	-
1975	48.4	10.3	-	-	-	-	78.6	5.8	48.3	9.8	47.4	11.3	-	-	-	-	52.2	-
1976	51.1	5.6	63.8	-	44.4	-	83.1	5.7	52.4	8.5	51.0	7.6	-	-	-	-	56.6	8.4
1977	55.4	8.4	68.9	8.0	48.6	9.5	88.0	5.9	56.3	7.4	55.8	9.4	-	-	-	-	60.8	7.4
1978	60.6	9.4	74.9	8.7	54.6	12.3	90.2	2.5	59.8	6.2	60.7	8.8	-	-	-	-	64.8	6.6
1979	70.0	15.5	82.8	10.5	65.6	20.1	92.1	2.1	70.3	17.6	66.2	9.1	-	-	-	-	72.2	11.4
1980	78.4	12.0	86.1	4.0	74.7	13.9	95.6	3.8	82.4	17.2	73.7	11.3	-	-	-	-	80.9	12.0
1981	87.2	11.2	93.2	8.2	84.7	13.4	96.4	0.8	91.7	11.3	81.0	9.9	-	-	-	-	89.4	10.5
1982	95.1	9.1	96.1	3.1	94.8	11.9	101.2	5.0	96.3	5.0	91.1	12.5	-	-	-	-	101.5	13.5
1983	100.5	5.7	99.6	3.6	100.9	6.4	98.8	-2.4	100.1	3.9	100.9	10.8	-	-	-	-	109.1	7.5
1984	104.3	3.8	104.3	4.7	104.1	3.2	100.0	1.2	103.6	3.5	108.0	7.0	-	-	-	-	115.5	5.9
1985	107.1	2.7	106.1	1.7	106.8	2.6	102.6	2.6	105.9	2.2	115.1	6.6	-	-	-	-	124.1	7.4
1986	107.9	0.7	107.2	1.0	108.2	1.3	102.8	0.2	100.9	-4.7	124.0	7.7	-	-	-	-	-	-
1987	110.8	2.7	108.3	1.0	109.6	1.3	102.0	-0.8	107.9	6.9	132.1	6.5	-	-	-	-	139.9	12.7
1988	113.7	2.6	110.4	1.9	110.0	0.4	106.8	4.7	114.1	5.7	142.6	7.9	-	-	-	-	148.6	6.2
1989	115.8	1.8	115.8	4.9	107.4	-2.4	93.8	-12.2	122.3	7.2	153.4	7.6	-	-	-	-	159.6	7.4
1990	120.9	4.4	124.1	7.2	109.8	2.2	91.2	-2.8	126.8	3.7	173.4	13.0	-	-	-	-	173.4	8.6
1991	125.6	3.9	128.3	3.4	114.1	3.9	94.8	3.9	127.8	0.8	191.8	10.6	-	-	-	-	186.4	7.5
1992	130.3	3.7	128.8	0.4	118.1	3.5	94.6	-0.2	134.2	5.0	206.5	7.7	-	-	-	-	191.5	2.7
1993	135.8	4.2	131.5	2.1	124.1	5.1	95.1	0.5	141.1	5.1	217.9	5.5	-	-	-	-	196.2	2.5
1994	141.8	4.4	134.4	2.2	131.1	5.6	96.8	1.8	148.4	5.2	230.3	5.7	-	-	-	-	202.5	3.2
1995	147.9	4.3	139.4	3.7	136.5	4.1	98.6	1.9	156.9	5.7	245.7	6.7	-	-	-	-	206.3	1.9
1996	153.1	3.5	142.2	2.0	142.6	4.5	103.6	5.1	162.7	3.7	250.8	2.1	-	-	-	-	212.8	3.2
1997	158.1	3.3	148.0	4.1	147.7	3.6	104.0	0.4	165.6	1.8	265.8	6.0	-	-	-	-	218.6	2.7
1998	161.9	2.4	151.6	2.4	154.4	4.5	100.6	-3.3	166.5	0.5	275.0	3.5	100.4	-	98.1	-	231.8	6.0
1999	166.6	2.9	157.0	3.6	161.9	4.9	94.0	-6.6	169.5	1.8	289.4	5.2	100.4	0.0	96.5	-1.6	240.2	3.6
2000	173.2	4.0	160.5	2.2	170.2	5.1	90.6	-3.6	179.3	5.8	303.7	4.9	102.1	1.7	96.9	0.4	-	-
2001	-	-	-	-	-	-	-	-	-	-	-	-	-	-	-	-	-	-

Source: U.S. Department of Labor, Bureau of Labor Statistics, Division of Consumer Prices and Price Indexes. *Base is December 1997 = 100. - indicates no data collected for period.

Denver-Boulder-Greeley, CO
Consumer Price Index - Urban Wage Earners
Base 1982-1984 = 100
Annual Averages

For 1964-2001. Columns headed % show percentile change in the index from the previous period for which an index is available.

Year	All Items Index	%	Food & Beverage Index	%	Housing Index	%	Apparel Index	%	Transportation Index	%	Medical Care Index	%	Recreation* Index	%	Education & Communic.* Index	%	Other Goods & Services Index	%
1964	28.4	-	-	-	-	-	-	-	-	-	-	-	-	-	-	-	-	-
1965	28.8	1.4	-	-	-	-	-	-	-	-	-	-	-	-	-	-	-	-
1966	29.7	3.1	-	-	-	-	-	-	-	-	-	-	-	-	-	-	-	-
1967	30.0	1.0	-	-	-	-	-	-	-	-	-	-	-	-	-	-	-	-
1968	30.8	2.7	-	-	-	-	-	-	-	-	-	-	-	-	-	-	-	-
1969	32.1	4.2	-	-	-	-	-	-	-	-	-	-	-	-	-	-	-	-
1970	34.5	7.5	-	-	-	-	-	-	-	-	-	-	-	-	-	-	-	-
1971	35.9	4.1	-	-	-	-	56.2	-	37.6	-	36.9	-	-	-	-	-	-	-
1972	37.1	3.3	-	-	-	-	57.9	3.0	37.5	-0.3	38.0	3.0	-	-	-	-	-	-
1973	39.6	6.7	-	-	-	-	60.2	4.0	39.3	4.8	39.4	3.7	-	-	-	-	-	-
1974	44.0	11.1	-	-	-	-	65.0	8.0	43.6	10.9	43.1	9.4	-	-	-	-	-	-
1975	48.5	10.2	-	-	-	-	68.8	5.8	48.0	10.1	47.8	10.9	-	-	-	-	-	-
1976	51.2	5.6	61.7	-	45.2	-	72.7	5.7	51.9	8.1	51.6	7.9	-	-	-	-	52.3	-
1977	55.5	8.4	66.6	7.9	49.5	9.5	77.0	5.9	55.9	7.7	56.4	9.3	-	-	-	-	56.8	8.6
1978	61.0	9.9	72.9	9.5	55.7	12.5	81.7	6.1	59.1	5.7	61.9	9.8	-	-	-	-	60.7	6.9
1979	70.9	16.2	80.3	10.2	67.5	21.2	88.3	8.1	69.8	18.1	66.4	7.3	-	-	-	-	65.6	8.1
1980	79.9	12.7	85.1	6.0	77.2	14.4	94.2	6.7	82.4	18.1	73.5	10.7	-	-	-	-	72.1	9.9
1981	88.9	11.3	92.9	9.2	87.5	13.3	95.4	1.3	91.8	11.4	81.6	11.0	-	-	-	-	80.3	11.4
1982	97.1	9.2	96.2	3.6	98.2	12.2	100.4	5.2	96.8	5.4	90.9	11.4	-	-	-	-	88.9	10.7
1983	99.8	2.8	99.6	3.5	99.5	1.3	99.0	-1.4	100.0	3.3	101.1	11.2	-	-	-	-	101.8	14.5
1984	103.2	3.4	104.2	4.6	102.3	2.8	100.6	1.6	103.3	3.3	108.0	6.8	-	-	-	-	109.3	7.4
1985	105.9	2.6	106.1	1.8	105.4	3.0	102.4	1.8	105.9	2.5	115.1	6.6	-	-	-	-	115.4	5.6
1986	106.3	0.4	106.9	0.8	106.6	1.1	101.3	-1.1	100.6	-5.0	124.1	7.8	-	-	-	-	124.1	7.5
1987	109.1	2.6	107.9	0.9	107.7	1.0	99.6	-1.7	108.4	7.8	132.8	7.0	-	-	-	-	-	-
1988	112.0	2.7	109.9	1.9	108.0	0.3	104.4	4.8	113.6	4.8	144.3	8.7	-	-	-	-	140.5	13.2
1989	114.2	2.0	115.3	4.9	106.0	-1.9	90.9	-12.9	121.4	6.9	154.6	7.1	-	-	-	-	149.5	6.4
1990	119.1	4.3	123.3	6.9	108.1	2.0	89.6	-1.4	125.5	3.4	174.8	13.1	-	-	-	-	159.5	6.7
1991	123.4	3.6	127.7	3.6	112.0	3.6	93.5	4.4	125.7	0.2	192.8	10.3	-	-	-	-	172.4	8.1
1992	127.9	3.6	128.2	0.4	115.8	3.4	92.9	-0.6	133.5	6.2	207.9	7.8	-	-	-	-	183.9	6.7
1993	133.2	4.1	131.1	2.3	121.6	5.0	94.4	1.6	140.5	5.2	218.9	5.3	-	-	-	-	188.9	2.7
1994	138.2	3.8	133.9	2.1	128.0	5.3	95.1	0.7	146.6	4.3	230.9	5.5	-	-	-	-	190.6	0.9
1995	144.0	4.2	138.8	3.7	133.1	4.0	96.9	1.9	155.2	5.9	245.5	6.3	-	-	-	-	195.1	2.4
1996	149.0	3.5	141.5	1.9	139.1	4.5	101.8	5.1	161.1	3.8	250.5	2.0	-	-	-	-	200.3	2.7
1997	153.6	3.1	147.0	3.9	143.9	3.5	102.3	0.5	163.9	1.7	264.6	5.6	-	-	-	-	206.8	3.2
1998	156.6	2.0	150.1	2.1	150.1	4.3	99.4	-2.8	162.7	-0.7	274.6	3.8	99.7	-	98.6	-	212.6	2.8
1999	161.1	2.9	155.6	3.7	157.5	4.9	92.0	-7.4	165.6	1.8	289.0	5.2	99.1	-0.6	97.3	-1.3	229.7	8.0
2000	167.7	4.1	159.1	2.2	166.2	5.5	87.5	-4.9	176.0	6.3	303.0	4.8	99.8	0.7	98.2	0.9	239.6	4.3
2001	-	-	-	-	-	-	-	-	-	-	-	-	-	-	-	-	-	-

Source: U.S. Department of Labor, Bureau of Labor Statistics, Division of Consumer Prices and Price Indexes. *Base is December 1997 = 100. - indicates no data collected for period.

Denver-Boulder-Greeley, CO
Consumer Price Index - All Urban Consumers
Base 1982-1984 = 100
All Items

For 1964-2001. Columns headed % show percentile change in the index from the previous period for which an index is available.

Year	Jan Index	%	Feb Index	%	Mar Index	%	Apr Index	%	May Index	%	Jun Index	%	Jul Index	%	Aug Index	%	Sep Index	%	Oct Index	%	Nov Index	%	Dec Index	%
1964	28.2	-	-		-		28.0	-0.7	-		-		28.5	1.8	-		-		28.5	0.0	-		-	
1965	28.5	0.0	-		-		28.6	0.4	-		-		28.9	1.0	-		-		28.9	0.0	-		-	
1966	29.2	1.0	-		-		29.6	1.4	-		-		29.7	0.3	-		-		29.9	0.7	-		-	
1967	29.7	-0.7	-		-		29.7	0.0	-		-		30.1	1.3	-		-		30.2	0.3	-		-	
1968	30.4	0.7	-		-		30.7	1.0	-		-		30.7	0.0	-		-		30.9	0.7	-		-	
1969	31.1	0.6	-		-		31.6	1.6	-		-		32.0	1.3	-		-		32.7	2.2	-		-	
1970	33.0	0.9	-		-		33.9	2.7	-		-		34.9	2.9	-		-		35.2	0.9	-		-	
1971	35.3	0.3	-		-		35.5	0.6	-		-		36.0	1.4	-		-		36.3	0.8	-		-	
1972	36.3	0.0	-		-		36.9	1.7	-		-		37.0	0.3	-		-		37.4	1.1	-		-	
1973	37.8	1.1	-		-		39.0	3.2	-		-		39.6	1.5	-		-		40.6	2.5	-		-	
1974	41.5	2.2	-		-		42.7	2.9	-		-		44.1	3.3	-		-		45.6	3.4	-		-	
1975	46.9	2.9	-		-		47.6	1.5	-		-		48.7	2.3	-		-		49.3	1.2	-		-	
1976	49.7	0.8	-		-		50.4	1.4	-		-		51.4	2.0	-		-		51.9	1.0	-		-	
1977	52.7	1.5	-		-		54.8	4.0	-		-		55.8	1.8	-		-		56.6	1.4	-		-	
1978	57.7	1.9	-		58.5	1.4	-		59.5	1.7	-		60.7	2.0	-		62.1	2.3	-		63.4	2.1	-	
1979	64.8	2.2	-		66.9	3.2	-		69.3	3.6	-		70.9	2.3	-		72.2	1.8	-		73.7	2.1	-	
1980	74.2	0.7	-		76.5	3.1	-		77.4	1.2	-		78.5	1.4	-		80.2	2.2	-		81.5	1.6	-	
1981	83.2	2.1	-		84.4	1.4	-		86.4	2.4	-		88.2	2.1	-		89.6	1.6	-		89.3	-0.3	-	
1982	91.6	2.6	-		92.7	1.2	-		94.0	1.4	-		95.9	2.0	-		97.3	1.5	-		97.8	0.5	-	
1983	98.2	0.4	-		98.8	0.6	-		100.4	1.6	-		100.7	0.3	-		101.8	1.1	-		101.9	0.1	-	
1984	103.0	1.1	-		103.5	0.5	-		103.9	0.4	-		104.9	1.0	-		105.4	0.5	-		104.8	-0.6	-	
1985	105.1	0.3	-		106.5	1.3	-		106.8	0.3	-		108.0	1.1	-		107.4	-0.6	-		107.8	0.4	-	
1986	109.3	1.4	-		106.7	-2.4	-		106.8	0.1	-		107.5	0.7	-		108.8	1.2	-		108.3	-0.5	108.4	0.1
1987	-		-		-		-		-		109.9	1.4	-		-		-		-		-		111.6	1.5
1988	-		-		-		-		-		112.8	1.1	-		-		-		-		-		114.7	1.7
1989	-		-		-		-		-		115.0	0.3	-		-		-		-		-		116.6	1.4
1990	-		-		-		-		-		119.4	2.4	-		-		-		-		-		122.5	2.6
1991	-		-		-		-		-		124.8	1.9	-		-		-		-		-		126.4	1.3
1992	-		-		-		-		-		129.0	2.1	-		-		-		-		-		131.6	2.0
1993	-		-		-		-		-		134.6	2.3	-		-		-		-		-		137.0	1.8
1994	-		-		-		-		-		140.0	2.2	-		-		-		-		-		143.6	2.6
1995	-		-		-		-		-		146.9	2.3	-		-		-		-		-		149.0	1.4
1996	-		-		-		-		-		152.0	2.0	-		-		-		-		-		154.2	1.4
1997	-		-		-		-		-		157.1	1.9	-		-		-		-		-		159.1	1.3
1998	-		-		-		-		-		160.5	0.9	-		-		-		-		-		163.3	1.7
1999	-		-		-		-		-		165.1	1.1	-		-		-		-		-		168.2	1.9
2000	-		-		-		-		-		171.4	1.9	-		-		-		-		-		175.1	2.2
2001	-		-		-		-		-		180.7	3.2	-		-		-		-		-		-	

Source: U.S. Department of Labor, Bureau of Labor Statistics, Division of Consumer Prices and Price Indexes. - indicates no data collected for period.

Denver-Boulder-Greeley, CO
Consumer Price Index - Urban Wage Earners
Base 1982-1984 = 100
All Items

For 1964-2001. Columns headed % show percentile change in the index from the previous period for which an index is available.

Year	Jan Index	Jan %	Feb Index	Feb %	Mar Index	Mar %	Apr Index	Apr %	May Index	May %	Jun Index	Jun %	Jul Index	Jul %	Aug Index	Aug %	Sep Index	Sep %	Oct Index	Oct %	Nov Index	Nov %	Dec Index	Dec %
1964	28.2	-	-	-	-	-	28.1	-0.4	-	-	-	-	28.5	1.4	-	-	-	-	28.5	0.0	-	-	-	-
1965	28.6	0.4	-	-	-	-	28.6	0.0	-	-	-	-	29.0	1.4	-	-	-	-	29.0	0.0	-	-	-	-
1966	29.2	0.7	-	-	-	-	29.7	1.7	-	-	-	-	29.8	0.3	-	-	-	-	30.0	0.7	-	-	-	-
1967	29.8	-0.7	-	-	-	-	29.8	0.0	-	-	-	-	30.1	1.0	-	-	-	-	30.3	0.7	-	-	-	-
1968	30.5	0.7	-	-	-	-	30.7	0.7	-	-	-	-	30.7	0.0	-	-	-	-	31.0	1.0	-	-	-	-
1969	31.1	0.3	-	-	-	-	31.7	1.9	-	-	-	-	32.1	1.3	-	-	-	-	32.8	2.2	-	-	-	-
1970	33.1	0.9	-	-	-	-	34.0	2.7	-	-	-	-	35.0	2.9	-	-	-	-	35.3	0.9	-	-	-	-
1971	35.4	0.3	-	-	-	-	35.6	0.6	-	-	-	-	36.1	1.4	-	-	-	-	36.4	0.8	-	-	-	-
1972	36.4	0.0	-	-	-	-	36.9	1.4	-	-	-	-	37.0	0.3	-	-	-	-	37.5	1.4	-	-	-	-
1973	37.8	0.8	-	-	-	-	39.1	3.4	-	-	-	-	39.7	1.5	-	-	-	-	40.7	2.5	-	-	-	-
1974	41.6	2.2	-	-	-	-	42.8	2.9	-	-	-	-	44.2	3.3	-	-	-	-	45.6	3.2	-	-	-	-
1975	47.0	3.1	-	-	-	-	47.7	1.5	-	-	-	-	48.8	2.3	-	-	-	-	49.4	1.2	-	-	-	-
1976	49.8	0.8	-	-	-	-	50.4	1.2	-	-	-	-	51.5	2.2	-	-	-	-	52.0	1.0	-	-	-	-
1977	52.8	1.5	-	-	-	-	54.9	4.0	-	-	-	-	55.9	1.8	-	-	-	-	56.7	1.4	-	-	-	-
1978	57.8	1.9	-	-	58.8	1.7	-	-	59.9	1.9	-	-	61.0	1.8	-	-	62.5	2.5	-	-	64.0	2.4	-	-
1979	65.5	2.3	-	-	67.6	3.2	-	-	70.1	3.7	-	-	71.9	2.6	-	-	73.2	1.8	-	-	74.7	2.0	-	-
1980	75.4	0.9	-	-	77.9	3.3	-	-	78.8	1.2	-	-	79.9	1.4	-	-	81.6	2.1	-	-	83.1	1.8	-	-
1981	84.8	2.0	-	-	85.9	1.3	-	-	88.1	2.6	-	-	90.1	2.3	-	-	91.4	1.4	-	-	91.0	-0.4	-	-
1982	93.3	2.5	-	-	94.6	1.4	-	-	96.0	1.5	-	-	98.0	2.1	-	-	99.5	1.5	-	-	99.9	0.4	-	-
1983	97.3	-2.6	-	-	98.2	0.9	-	-	99.7	1.5	-	-	99.7	0.0	-	-	101.3	1.6	-	-	101.7	0.4	-	-
1984	101.0	-0.7	-	-	102.7	1.7	-	-	102.4	-0.3	-	-	104.3	1.9	-	-	104.0	-0.3	-	-	103.7	-0.3	-	-
1985	104.0	0.3	-	-	105.4	1.3	-	-	105.7	0.3	-	-	106.9	1.1	-	-	106.1	-0.7	-	-	106.4	0.3	-	-
1986	107.9	1.4	-	-	105.2	-2.5	-	-	105.2	0.0	-	-	105.9	0.7	-	-	107.3	1.3	-	-	106.7	-0.6	106.7	0.0
1987	-	-	-	-	-	-	-	-	108.3	1.5	-	-	-	-	-	-	-	-	-	-	-	-	110.0	1.6
1988	-	-	-	-	-	-	-	-	111.0	0.9	-	-	-	-	-	-	-	-	-	-	-	-	112.9	1.7
1989	-	-	-	-	-	-	-	-	113.5	0.5	-	-	-	-	-	-	-	-	-	-	-	-	114.9	1.2
1990	-	-	-	-	-	-	-	-	117.5	2.3	-	-	-	-	-	-	-	-	-	-	-	-	120.8	2.8
1991	-	-	-	-	-	-	-	-	122.7	1.6	-	-	-	-	-	-	-	-	-	-	-	-	124.2	1.2
1992	-	-	-	-	-	-	-	-	126.5	1.9	-	-	-	-	-	-	-	-	-	-	-	-	129.4	2.3
1993	-	-	-	-	-	-	-	-	132.1	2.1	-	-	-	-	-	-	-	-	-	-	-	-	134.2	1.6
1994	-	-	-	-	-	-	-	-	136.4	1.6	-	-	-	-	-	-	-	-	-	-	-	-	140.1	2.7
1995	-	-	-	-	-	-	-	-	143.0	2.1	-	-	-	-	-	-	-	-	-	-	-	-	144.9	1.3
1996	-	-	-	-	-	-	-	-	147.9	2.1	-	-	-	-	-	-	-	-	-	-	-	-	150.1	1.5
1997	-	-	-	-	-	-	-	-	152.7	1.7	-	-	-	-	-	-	-	-	-	-	-	-	154.5	1.2
1998	-	-	-	-	-	-	-	-	155.2	0.5	-	-	-	-	-	-	-	-	-	-	-	-	157.9	1.7
1999	-	-	-	-	-	-	-	-	159.4	0.9	-	-	-	-	-	-	-	-	-	-	-	-	162.7	2.1
2000	-	-	-	-	-	-	-	-	165.5	1.7	-	-	-	-	-	-	-	-	-	-	-	-	169.8	2.6
2001	-	-	-	-	-	-	-	-	175.1	3.1	-	-	-	-	-	-	-	-	-	-	-	-	-	-

Source: U.S. Department of Labor, Bureau of Labor Statistics, Division of Consumer Prices and Price Indexes. - indicates no data collected for period.

Denver-Boulder-Greeley, CO
Consumer Price Index - All Urban Consumers
Base 1982-1984 = 100
Food and Beverages

For 1976-2001. Columns headed % show percentile change in the index from the previous period for which an index is available.

Year	Jan Index	%	Feb Index	%	Mar Index	%	Apr Index	%	May Index	%	Jun Index	%	Jul Index	%	Aug Index	%	Sep Index	%	Oct Index	%	Nov Index	%	Dec Index	%
1976	63.3	-	-	-	-	-	62.7	-0.9	-	-	-	-	64.1	2.2	-	-	-	-	64.3	0.3	-	-	-	-
1977	65.7	2.2	-	-	-	-	69.2	5.3	-	-	-	-	70.1	1.3	-	-	76.2	0.1	68.8	-1.9	-	-	-	-
1978	70.8	2.9	-	-	72.4	2.3	-	-	74.7	3.2	-	-	76.1	1.9	-	-	76.2	0.1	-	-	77.2	1.3	-	-
1979	80.2	3.9	-	-	82.4	2.7	-	-	83.4	1.2	-	-	84.1	0.8	-	-	83.0	-1.3	-	-	83.6	0.7	-	-
1980	81.9	-2.0	-	-	82.6	0.9	-	-	84.3	2.1	-	-	86.1	2.1	-	-	89.3	3.7	-	-	90.1	0.9	-	-
1981	90.8	0.8	-	-	92.0	1.3	-	-	92.9	1.0	-	-	94.2	1.4	-	-	94.6	0.4	-	-	93.9	-0.7	-	-
1982	94.9	1.1	-	-	95.6	0.7	-	-	95.9	0.3	-	-	96.5	0.6	-	-	96.5	0.0	-	-	96.7	0.2	-	-
1983	97.1	0.4	-	-	98.2	1.1	-	-	100.2	2.0	-	-	99.8	-0.4	-	-	100.2	0.4	-	-	100.7	0.5	-	-
1984	102.7	2.0	-	-	104.3	1.6	-	-	104.0	-0.3	-	-	104.8	0.8	-	-	104.9	0.1	-	-	104.5	-0.4	-	-
1985	104.9	0.4	-	-	107.4	2.4	-	-	105.9	-1.4	-	-	106.9	0.9	-	-	105.5	-1.3	-	-	108.1	-0.4	108.1	0.0
1986	107.8	2.2	-	-	107.3	-0.5	-	-	105.5	-1.7	-	-	106.0	0.5	-	-	108.5	2.4	-	-	-	-	107.9	-0.7
1987	-	-	-	-	-	-	-	-	-	-	108.7	0.6	-	-	-	-	-	-	-	-	-	-	111.2	1.5
1988	-	-	-	-	-	-	-	-	-	-	109.6	1.6	-	-	-	-	-	-	-	-	-	-	116.8	1.8
1989	-	-	-	-	-	-	-	-	-	-	114.7	3.1	-	-	-	-	-	-	-	-	-	-	126.2	3.4
1990	-	-	-	-	-	-	-	-	-	-	122.1	4.5	-	-	-	-	-	-	-	-	-	-	128.4	0.1
1991	-	-	-	-	-	-	-	-	-	-	128.3	1.7	-	-	-	-	-	-	-	-	-	-	129.2	0.5
1992	-	-	-	-	-	-	-	-	-	-	128.5	0.1	-	-	-	-	-	-	-	-	-	-	132.0	0.8
1993	-	-	-	-	-	-	-	-	-	-	131.0	1.4	-	-	-	-	-	-	-	-	-	-	135.0	1.0
1994	-	-	-	-	-	-	-	-	-	-	133.7	1.3	-	-	-	-	-	-	-	-	-	-	139.8	0.6
1995	-	-	-	-	-	-	-	-	-	-	139.0	3.0	-	-	-	-	-	-	-	-	-	-	143.1	1.2
1996	-	-	-	-	-	-	-	-	-	-	141.4	1.1	-	-	-	-	-	-	-	-	-	-	149.0	1.4
1997	-	-	-	-	-	-	-	-	-	-	147.0	2.7	-	-	-	-	-	-	-	-	-	-	153.3	2.3
1998	-	-	-	-	-	-	-	-	-	-	149.9	0.6	-	-	-	-	-	-	-	-	-	-	158.4	1.9
1999	-	-	-	-	-	-	-	-	-	-	155.5	1.4	-	-	-	-	-	-	-	-	-	-	161.3	1.1
2000	-	-	-	-	-	-	-	-	-	-	159.6	0.8	-	-	-	-	-	-	-	-	-	-	-	-
2001	-	-	-	-	-	-	-	-	-	-	166.6	3.3	-	-	-	-	-	-	-	-	-	-	-	-

Source: U.S. Department of Labor, Bureau of Labor Statistics, Division of Consumer Prices and Price Indexes. - indicates no data collected for period.

Denver-Boulder-Greeley, CO
Consumer Price Index - Urban Wage Earners
Base 1982-1984 = 100
Food and Beverages

For 1976-2001. Columns headed % show percentile change in the index from the previous period for which an index is available.

Year	Jan Index	%	Feb Index	%	Mar Index	%	Apr Index	%	May Index	%	Jun Index	%	Jul Index	%	Aug Index	%	Sep Index	%	Oct Index	%	Nov Index	%	Dec Index	%
1976	61.2	-	-	-	-	-	60.7	-0.8	-	-	-	-	62.0	2.1	-	-	-	-	62.2	0.3	-	-	-	-
1977	63.5	2.1	-	-	-	-	67.0	5.5	-	-	-	-	67.8	1.2	-	-	-	-	66.6	-1.8	-	-	-	-
1978	68.4	2.7	-	-	70.7	3.4	-	-	72.9	3.1	-	-	73.7	1.1	-	-	74.1	0.5	-	-	75.3	1.6	-	-
1979	78.0	3.6	-	-	79.5	1.9	-	-	80.3	1.0	-	-	81.4	1.4	-	-	80.3	-1.4	-	-	81.6	1.6	-	-
1980	80.8	-1.0	-	-	81.8	1.2	-	-	83.5	2.1	-	-	85.4	2.3	-	-	88.1	3.2	-	-	88.7	0.7	-	-
1981	90.1	1.6	-	-	91.5	1.6	-	-	92.1	0.7	-	-	93.9	2.0	-	-	94.1	0.2	-	-	94.2	0.1	-	-
1982	95.0	0.8	-	-	95.6	0.6	-	-	96.0	0.4	-	-	96.7	0.7	-	-	96.7	0.0	-	-	96.8	0.1	-	-
1983	97.2	0.4	-	-	98.3	1.1	-	-	100.1	1.8	-	-	99.8	-0.3	-	-	100.1	0.3	-	-	100.7	0.6	-	-
1984	102.6	1.9	-	-	104.1	1.5	-	-	103.8	-0.3	-	-	104.7	0.9	-	-	105.0	0.3	-	-	100.7	0.6	-	-
1984	102.6	1.9	-	-	104.1	1.5	-	-	103.8	-0.3	-	-	104.7	0.9	-	-	105.0	0.3	-	-	104.6	-0.4	-	-
1985	104.9	0.3	-	-	107.4	2.4	-	-	105.8	-1.5	-	-	106.8	0.9	-	-	105.5	-1.2	-	-	105.4	-0.1	-	-
1986	107.7	2.2	-	-	106.9	-0.7	-	-	105.1	-1.7	-	-	105.6	0.5	-	-	108.2	2.5	-	-	107.9	-0.3	107.8	-0.1
1987	-	-	-	-	-	-	-	-	-	-	108.3	0.5	-	-	-	-	-	-	-	-	-	-	107.5	-0.7
1988	-	-	-	-	-	-	-	-	-	-	109.1	1.5	-	-	-	-	-	-	-	-	-	-	110.8	1.6
1989	-	-	-	-	-	-	-	-	-	-	114.3	3.2	-	-	-	-	-	-	-	-	-	-	116.3	1.7
1990	-	-	-	-	-	-	-	-	-	-	121.4	4.4	-	-	-	-	-	-	-	-	-	-	125.3	3.2
1991	-	-	-	-	-	-	-	-	-	-	127.8	2.0	-	-	-	-	-	-	-	-	-	-	127.7	-0.1
1992	-	-	-	-	-	-	-	-	-	-	127.9	0.2	-	-	-	-	-	-	-	-	-	-	128.6	0.5
1993	-	-	-	-	-	-	-	-	-	-	130.6	1.6	-	-	-	-	-	-	-	-	-	-	131.7	0.8
1994	-	-	-	-	-	-	-	-	-	-	133.3	1.2	-	-	-	-	-	-	-	-	-	-	134.5	0.9
1995	-	-	-	-	-	-	-	-	-	-	138.5	3.0	-	-	-	-	-	-	-	-	-	-	139.2	0.5
1996	-	-	-	-	-	-	-	-	-	-	140.7	1.1	-	-	-	-	-	-	-	-	-	-	142.4	1.2
1997	-	-	-	-	-	-	-	-	-	-	146.2	2.7	-	-	-	-	-	-	-	-	-	-	147.9	1.2
1998	-	-	-	-	-	-	-	-	-	-	148.4	0.3	-	-	-	-	-	-	-	-	-	-	151.9	2.4
1999	-	-	-	-	-	-	-	-	-	-	154.1	1.4	-	-	-	-	-	-	-	-	-	-	157.1	1.9
2000	-	-	-	-	-	-	-	-	-	-	158.2	0.7	-	-	-	-	-	-	-	-	-	-	160.0	1.1
2001	-	-	-	-	-	-	-	-	-	-	165.6	3.5	-	-	-	-	-	-	-	-	-	-	-	-

Source: U.S. Department of Labor, Bureau of Labor Statistics, Division of Consumer Prices and Price Indexes. - indicates no data collected for period.

Denver-Boulder-Greeley, CO
Consumer Price Index - All Urban Consumers
Base 1982-1984 = 100
Housing

For 1976-2001. Columns headed % show percentile change in the index from the previous period for which an index is available.

Year	Jan Index	%	Feb Index	%	Mar Index	%	Apr Index	%	May Index	%	Jun Index	%	Jul Index	%	Aug Index	%	Sep Index	%	Oct Index	%	Nov Index	%	Dec Index	%
1976	43.1	-	-	-	-	-	43.8	1.6	-	-	-	-	44.8	2.3	-	-	-	-	44.9	0.2	-	-	-	-
1977	45.6	1.6	-	-	-	-	47.9	5.0	-	-	-	-	48.8	1.9	-	-	-	-	50.3	3.1	-	-	-	-
1978	51.4	2.2	-	-	52.5	2.1	-	-	53.1	1.1	-	-	54.3	2.3	-	-	56.2	3.5	-	-	58.1	3.4	-	-
1979	59.7	2.8	-	-	61.7	3.4	-	-	64.6	4.7	-	-	66.7	3.3	-	-	68.1	2.1	-	-	70.1	2.9	-	-
1980	70.4	0.4	-	-	73.0	3.7	-	-	73.6	0.8	-	-	74.8	1.6	-	-	76.3	2.0	-	-	77.9	2.1	-	-
1981	80.1	2.8	-	-	80.7	0.7	-	-	83.7	3.7	-	-	86.2	3.0	-	-	87.9	2.0	-	-	87.0	-1.0	-	-
1982	90.3	3.8	-	-	92.0	1.9	-	-	93.8	2.0	-	-	95.9	2.2	-	-	97.7	1.9	-	-	98.1	0.4	-	-
1983	99.4	1.3	-	-	100.6	1.2	-	-	101.0	0.4	-	-	100.5	-0.5	-	-	101.7	1.2	-	-	101.0	-0.7	-	-
1984	103.2	2.2	-	-	102.7	-0.5	-	-	102.9	0.2	-	-	105.5	2.5	-	-	105.5	0.0	-	-	104.3	-1.1	-	-
1985	105.9	1.5	-	-	106.1	0.2	-	-	106.1	0.0	-	-	107.9	1.7	-	-	106.6	-1.2	-	-	107.4	0.8	-	-
1986	110.6	3.0	-	-	107.3	-3.0	-	-	107.7	0.4	-	-	108.1	0.4	-	-	108.2	0.1	-	-	107.6	-0.6	108.2	0.6
1987	-	-	-	-	-	-	-	-	-	-	109.1	0.8	-	-	-	-	-	-	-	-	-	-	110.0	0.8
1988	-	-	-	-	-	-	-	-	-	-	110.5	0.5	-	-	-	-	-	-	-	-	-	-	109.5	-0.9
1989	-	-	-	-	-	-	-	-	-	-	107.6	-1.7	-	-	-	-	-	-	-	-	-	-	107.3	-0.3
1990	-	-	-	-	-	-	-	-	-	-	109.3	1.9	-	-	-	-	-	-	-	-	-	-	110.4	1.0
1991	-	-	-	-	-	-	-	-	-	-	113.7	3.0	-	-	-	-	-	-	-	-	-	-	114.5	0.7
1992	-	-	-	-	-	-	-	-	-	-	117.1	2.3	-	-	-	-	-	-	-	-	-	-	119.1	1.7
1993	-	-	-	-	-	-	-	-	-	-	123.0	3.3	-	-	-	-	-	-	-	-	-	-	125.3	1.9
1994	-	-	-	-	-	-	-	-	-	-	129.8	3.6	-	-	-	-	-	-	-	-	-	-	132.4	2.0
1995	-	-	-	-	-	-	-	-	-	-	134.8	1.8	-	-	-	-	-	-	-	-	-	-	138.2	2.5
1996	-	-	-	-	-	-	-	-	-	-	141.7	2.5	-	-	-	-	-	-	-	-	-	-	143.6	1.3
1997	-	-	-	-	-	-	-	-	-	-	146.5	2.0	-	-	-	-	-	-	-	-	-	-	148.9	1.6
1998	-	-	-	-	-	-	-	-	-	-	152.5	2.4	-	-	-	-	-	-	-	-	-	-	156.3	2.5
1999	-	-	-	-	-	-	-	-	-	-	160.4	2.6	-	-	-	-	-	-	-	-	-	-	163.4	1.9
2000	-	-	-	-	-	-	-	-	-	-	167.7	2.6	-	-	-	-	-	-	-	-	-	-	172.8	3.0
2001	-	-	-	-	-	-	-	-	-	-	180.6	4.5	-	-	-	-	-	-	-	-	-	-	-	-

Source: U.S. Department of Labor, Bureau of Labor Statistics, Division of Consumer Prices and Price Indexes. - indicates no data collected for period.

Denver-Boulder-Greeley, CO
Consumer Price Index - Urban Wage Earners
Base 1982-1984 = 100
Housing

For 1976-2001. Columns headed % show percentile change in the index from the previous period for which an index is available.

Year	Jan		Feb		Mar		Apr		May		Jun		Jul		Aug		Sep		Oct		Nov		Dec	
	Index	%	Index	%	Index	%	Index	%	Index	%	Index	%	Index	%	Index	%	Index	%	Index	%	Index	%	Index	%
1976	43.8	-	-	-	-	-	44.6	1.8	-	-	-	-	45.6	2.2	-	-	-	-	45.8	0.4	-	-	-	-
1977	46.4	1.3	-	-	-	-	48.8	5.2	-	-	-	-	49.7	1.8	-	-	-	-	51.2	3.0	-	-	-	-
1978	52.4	2.3	-	-	53.5	2.1	-	-	54.2	1.3	-	-	55.4	2.2	-	-	57.5	3.8	-	-	59.4	3.3	-	-
1979	61.2	3.0	-	-	63.4	3.6	-	-	66.5	4.9	-	-	68.7	3.3	-	-	70.1	2.0	-	-	72.2	3.0	-	-
1980	72.6	0.6	-	-	75.4	3.9	-	-	76.0	0.8	-	-	77.1	1.4	-	-	78.8	2.2	-	-	80.6	2.3	-	-
1981	82.8	2.7	-	-	83.2	0.5	-	-	86.6	4.1	-	-	89.1	2.9	-	-	90.8	1.9	-	-	89.8	-1.1	-	-
1982	93.3	3.9	-	-	95.3	2.1	-	-	97.2	2.0	-	-	99.5	2.4	-	-	101.4	1.9	-	-	101.6	0.2	-	-
1983	97.3	-4.2	-	-	98.6	1.3	-	-	99.6	1.0	-	-	98.8	-0.8	-	-	101.1	2.3	-	-	101.1	0.0	-	-
1984	99.7	-1.4	-	-	101.8	2.1	-	-	100.9	-0.9	-	-	104.3	3.4	-	-	103.1	-1.2	-	-	102.8	-0.3	-	-
1985	104.5	1.7	-	-	104.6	0.1	-	-	104.7	0.1	-	-	106.3	1.5	-	-	105.1	-1.1	-	-	105.9	0.8	-	-
1986	109.0	2.9	-	-	105.6	-3.1	-	-	106.1	0.5	-	-	106.6	0.5	-	-	106.7	0.1	-	-	106.1	-0.6	-	-
1987	-	-	-	-	-	-	-	-	-	-	107.4	0.7	-	-	-	-	-	-	-	-	-	-	106.7	0.6
1988	-	-	-	-	-	-	-	-	-	-	108.5	0.4	-	-	-	-	-	-	-	-	-	-	108.1	0.7
1989	-	-	-	-	-	-	-	-	-	-	106.0	-1.4	-	-	-	-	-	-	-	-	-	-	107.5	-0.9
1990	-	-	-	-	-	-	-	-	-	-	107.5	1.4	-	-	-	-	-	-	-	-	-	-	106.0	0.0
1991	-	-	-	-	-	-	-	-	-	-	111.7	2.9	-	-	-	-	-	-	-	-	-	-	108.6	1.0
1992	-	-	-	-	-	-	-	-	-	-	114.9	2.2	-	-	-	-	-	-	-	-	-	-	112.4	0.6
1993	-	-	-	-	-	-	-	-	-	-	120.6	3.3	-	-	-	-	-	-	-	-	-	-	116.7	1.6
1994	-	-	-	-	-	-	-	-	-	-	126.9	3.4	-	-	-	-	-	-	-	-	-	-	122.7	1.7
1995	-	-	-	-	-	-	-	-	-	-	131.4	1.7	-	-	-	-	-	-	-	-	-	-	129.2	1.8
1996	-	-	-	-	-	-	-	-	-	-	138.0	2.4	-	-	-	-	-	-	-	-	-	-	134.7	2.5
1997	-	-	-	-	-	-	-	-	-	-	142.8	1.9	-	-	-	-	-	-	-	-	-	-	140.2	1.6
1998	-	-	-	-	-	-	-	-	-	-	148.2	2.2	-	-	-	-	-	-	-	-	-	-	145.0	1.5
1999	-	-	-	-	-	-	-	-	-	-	155.7	2.4	-	-	-	-	-	-	-	-	-	-	152.1	2.6
2000	-	-	-	-	-	-	-	-	-	-	163.3	2.5	-	-	-	-	-	-	-	-	-	-	159.3	2.3
2001	-	-	-	-	-	-	-	-	-	-	176.8	4.6	-	-	-	-	-	-	-	-	-	-	169.0	3.5

Source: U.S. Department of Labor, Bureau of Labor Statistics, Division of Consumer Prices and Price Indexes. - indicates no data collected for period.

Denver-Boulder-Greeley, CO
Consumer Price Index - All Urban Consumers
Base 1982-1984 = 100
Apparel

For 1971-2001. Columns headed % show percentile change in the index from the previous period for which an index is available.

Year	Jan Index	%	Feb Index	%	Mar Index	%	Apr Index	%	May Index	%	Jun Index	%	Jul Index	%	Aug Index	%	Sep Index	%	Oct Index	%	Nov Index	%	Dec Index	%
1971	62.3	-	-	-	-	-	63.5	1.9	-	-	-	-	63.3	-0.3	-	-	-	-	66.9	5.7	-	-	-	-
1972	65.3	-2.4	-	-	-	-	66.2	1.4	-	-	-	-	65.4	-1.2	-	-	-	-	67.6	3.4	-	-	-	-
1973	65.6	-3.0	-	-	-	-	68.4	4.3	-	-	-	-	68.2	-0.3	-	-	-	-	71.2	4.4	-	-	-	-
1974	71.2	0.0	-	-	-	-	73.1	2.7	-	-	-	-	74.3	1.6	-	-	-	-	77.3	4.0	-	-	-	-
1975	75.8	-1.9	-	-	-	-	77.2	1.8	-	-	-	-	78.0	1.0	-	-	-	-	82.1	5.3	-	-	-	-
1976	79.9	-2.7	-	-	-	-	82.5	3.3	-	-	-	-	82.5	0.0	-	-	-	-	86.0	4.2	-	-	-	-
1977	83.8	-2.6	-	-	-	-	87.6	4.5	-	-	-	-	87.8	0.2	-	-	-	-	91.1	3.8	-	-	-	-
1978	89.0	-2.3	-	-	86.7	-2.6	-	-	90.3	4.2	-	-	90.9	0.7	-	-	93.4	2.8	-	-	91.4	-2.1	-	-
1979	86.7	-5.1	-	-	92.2	6.3	-	-	92.3	0.1	-	-	90.2	-2.3	-	-	94.7	5.0	-	-	95.7	1.1	-	-
1980	91.3	-4.6	-	-	96.3	5.5	-	-	95.1	-1.2	-	-	94.6	-0.5	-	-	97.7	3.3	-	-	98.0	0.3	-	-
1981	94.4	-3.7	-	-	97.2	3.0	-	-	96.0	-1.2	-	-	95.0	-1.0	-	-	98.1	3.3	-	-	96.9	-1.2	-	-
1982	97.2	0.3	-	-	102.4	5.3	-	-	102.5	0.1	-	-	99.1	-3.3	-	-	102.8	3.7	-	-	103.1	0.3	-	-
1983	97.8	-5.1	-	-	100.6	2.9	-	-	98.0	-2.6	-	-	96.6	-1.4	-	-	99.6	3.1	-	-	100.6	1.0	-	-
1984	97.4	-3.2	-	-	100.3	3.0	-	-	100.4	0.1	-	-	96.6	-3.8	-	-	102.2	5.8	-	-	102.5	0.3	-	-
1985	99.1	-3.3	-	-	103.8	4.7	-	-	104.5	0.7	-	-	102.1	-2.3	-	-	103.6	1.5	-	-	102.5	-1.1	-	-
1986	98.7	-3.7	-	-	101.6	2.9	-	-	102.5	0.9	-	-	100.8	-1.7	-	-	107.1	6.3	-	-	105.5	-1.5	103.1	-2.3
1987	-	-	-	-	-	-	-	-	-	-	100.1	-2.9	-	-	-	-	-	-	-	-	-	-	104.0	3.9
1988	-	-	-	-	-	-	-	-	-	-	106.2	2.1	-	-	-	-	-	-	-	-	-	-	107.4	1.1
1989	-	-	-	-	-	-	-	-	-	-	95.5	-11.1	-	-	-	-	-	-	-	-	-	-	92.0	-3.7
1990	-	-	-	-	-	-	-	-	-	-	91.5	-0.5	-	-	-	-	-	-	-	-	-	-	91.0	-0.5
1991	-	-	-	-	-	-	-	-	-	-	94.9	4.3	-	-	-	-	-	-	-	-	-	-	94.7	-0.2
1992	-	-	-	-	-	-	-	-	-	-	93.8	-1.0	-	-	-	-	-	-	-	-	-	-	95.5	1.8
1993	-	-	-	-	-	-	-	-	-	-	96.0	0.5	-	-	-	-	-	-	-	-	-	-	94.2	-1.9
1994	-	-	-	-	-	-	-	-	-	-	94.9	0.7	-	-	-	-	-	-	-	-	-	-	98.7	4.0
1995	-	-	-	-	-	-	-	-	-	-	97.5	-1.2	-	-	-	-	-	-	-	-	-	-	99.8	2.4
1996	-	-	-	-	-	-	-	-	-	-	106.9	7.1	-	-	-	-	-	-	-	-	-	-	100.3	-6.2
1997	-	-	-	-	-	-	-	-	-	-	103.9	3.6	-	-	-	-	-	-	-	-	-	-	104.1	0.2
1998	-	-	-	-	-	-	-	-	-	-	96.8	-7.0	-	-	-	-	-	-	-	-	-	-	104.4	7.9
1999	-	-	-	-	-	-	-	-	-	-	94.0	-10.0	-	-	-	-	-	-	-	-	-	-	93.9	-0.1
2000	-	-	-	-	-	-	-	-	-	-	91.4	-2.7	-	-	-	-	-	-	-	-	-	-	89.8	-1.8
2001	-	-	-	-	-	-	-	-	-	-	98.5	9.7	-	-	-	-	-	-	-	-	-	-	-	-

Source: U.S. Department of Labor, Bureau of Labor Statistics, Division of Consumer Prices and Price Indexes. - indicates no data collected for period.

Denver-Boulder-Greeley, CO
Consumer Price Index - Urban Wage Earners
Base 1982-1984 = 100
Apparel

For 1971-2001. Columns headed % show percentile change in the index from the previous period for which an index is available.

Year	Jan Index	Jan %	Feb Index	Feb %	Mar Index	Mar %	Apr Index	Apr %	May Index	May %	Jun Index	Jun %	Jul Index	Jul %	Aug Index	Aug %	Sep Index	Sep %	Oct Index	Oct %	Nov Index	Nov %	Dec Index	Dec %
1971	54.5	-	-	-	-	-	55.5	1.8	-	-	-	-	55.4	-0.2	-	-	-	-	58.6	5.8	-	-	-	-
1972	57.1	-2.6	-	-	-	-	57.9	1.4	-	-	-	-	57.2	-1.2	-	-	-	-	59.2	3.5	-	-	-	-
1973	57.3	-3.2	-	-	-	-	59.8	4.4	-	-	-	-	59.6	-0.3	-	-	-	-	62.3	4.5	-	-	-	-
1974	62.3	0.0	-	-	-	-	63.9	2.6	-	-	-	-	65.0	1.7	-	-	-	-	67.6	4.0	-	-	-	-
1975	66.3	-1.9	-	-	-	-	67.6	2.0	-	-	-	-	68.3	1.0	-	-	-	-	71.8	5.1	-	-	-	-
1976	69.9	-2.6	-	-	-	-	72.2	3.3	-	-	-	-	72.2	0.0	-	-	-	-	75.2	4.2	-	-	-	-
1977	73.3	-2.5	-	-	-	-	76.7	4.6	-	-	-	-	76.8	0.1	-	-	-	-	79.7	3.8	-	-	-	-
1978	77.9	-2.3	-	-	78.1	0.3	-	-	82.0	5.0	-	-	82.1	0.1	-	-	85.7	4.4	-	-	83.6	-2.5	-	-
1979	82.2	-1.7	-	-	86.5	5.2	-	-	87.5	1.2	-	-	87.4	-0.1	-	-	92.8	6.2	-	-	91.6	-1.3	-	-
1980	90.2	-1.5	-	-	96.4	6.9	-	-	93.6	-2.9	-	-	91.9	-1.8	-	-	96.4	4.9	-	-	96.2	-0.2	-	-
1981	92.3	-4.1	-	-	94.4	2.3	-	-	93.6	-0.8	-	-	95.4	1.9	-	-	98.7	3.5	-	-	97.0	-1.7	-	-
1982	96.6	-0.4	-	-	102.2	5.8	-	-	101.2	-1.0	-	-	97.8	-3.4	-	-	102.3	4.6	-	-	102.5	0.2	-	-
1983	97.7	-4.7	-	-	100.1	2.5	-	-	97.7	-2.4	-	-	96.7	-1.0	-	-	100.0	3.4	-	-	101.6	1.6	-	-
1984	97.9	-3.6	-	-	101.3	3.5	-	-	100.8	-0.5	-	-	97.0	-3.8	-	-	102.6	5.8	-	-	103.4	0.8	-	-
1985	100.2	-3.1	-	-	103.6	3.4	-	-	104.1	0.5	-	-	102.3	-1.7	-	-	103.1	0.8	-	-	101.6	-1.5	-	-
1986	98.2	-3.3	-	-	100.4	2.2	-	-	101.0	0.6	-	-	99.1	-1.9	-	-	105.9	6.9	-	-	103.5	-2.3	100.9	-2.5
1987	-	-	-	-	-	-	-	-	-	-	97.8	-3.1	-	-	-	-	-	-	-	-	-	-	101.5	3.8
1988	-	-	-	-	-	-	-	-	-	-	104.1	2.6	-	-	-	-	-	-	-	-	-	-	104.7	0.6
1989	-	-	-	-	-	-	-	-	-	-	92.5	-11.7	-	-	-	-	-	-	-	-	-	-	89.3	-3.5
1990	-	-	-	-	-	-	-	-	-	-	89.5	0.2	-	-	-	-	-	-	-	-	-	-	89.8	0.3
1991	-	-	-	-	-	-	-	-	-	-	93.7	4.3	-	-	-	-	-	-	-	-	-	-	93.2	-0.5
1992	-	-	-	-	-	-	-	-	-	-	91.8	-1.5	-	-	-	-	-	-	-	-	-	-	94.0	2.4
1993	-	-	-	-	-	-	-	-	-	-	95.2	1.3	-	-	-	-	-	-	-	-	-	-	93.7	-1.6
1994	-	-	-	-	-	-	-	-	-	-	93.4	-0.3	-	-	-	-	-	-	-	-	-	-	96.9	3.7
1995	-	-	-	-	-	-	-	-	-	-	95.5	-1.4	-	-	-	-	-	-	-	-	-	-	98.3	2.9
1996	-	-	-	-	-	-	-	-	-	-	104.8	6.6	-	-	-	-	-	-	-	-	-	-	98.7	-5.8
1997	-	-	-	-	-	-	-	-	-	-	101.6	2.9	-	-	-	-	-	-	-	-	-	-	103.0	1.4
1998	-	-	-	-	-	-	-	-	-	-	96.6	-6.2	-	-	-	-	-	-	-	-	-	-	102.3	5.9
1999	-	-	-	-	-	-	-	-	-	-	93.0	-9.1	-	-	-	-	-	-	-	-	-	-	91.1	-2.0
2000	-	-	-	-	-	-	-	-	-	-	88.0	-3.4	-	-	-	-	-	-	-	-	-	-	87.1	-1.0
2001	-	-	-	-	-	-	-	-	-	-	95.9	10.1	-	-	-	-	-	-	-	-	-	-	-	-

Source: U.S. Department of Labor, Bureau of Labor Statistics, Division of Consumer Prices and Price Indexes. - indicates no data collected for period.

Denver-Boulder-Greeley, CO
Consumer Price Index - All Urban Consumers
Base 1982-1984 = 100
Transportation

For 1971-2001. Columns headed % show percentile change in the index from the previous period for which an index is available.

Year	Jan Index	%	Feb Index	%	Mar Index	%	Apr Index	%	May Index	%	Jun Index	%	Jul Index	%	Aug Index	%	Sep Index	%	Oct Index	%	Nov Index	%	Dec Index	%
1971	38.0	-	-	-	-	-	38.0	0.0	-	-	-	-	37.8	-0.5	-	-	-	-	38.1	0.8	-	-	-	-
1972	37.1	-2.6	-	-	-	-	37.6	1.3	-	-	-	-	38.0	1.1	-	-	-	-	38.4	1.1	-	-	-	-
1973	38.0	-1.0	-	-	-	-	39.5	3.9	-	-	-	-	40.4	2.3	-	-	-	-	39.5	-2.2	-	-	-	-
1974	41.3	4.6	-	-	-	-	42.7	3.4	-	-	-	-	45.0	5.4	-	-	-	-	45.4	0.9	-	-	-	-
1975	45.9	1.1	-	-	-	-	47.0	2.4	-	-	-	-	49.3	4.9	-	-	-	-	49.8	1.0	-	-	-	-
1976	49.7	-0.2	-	-	-	-	50.8	2.2	-	-	-	-	53.2	4.7	-	-	-	-	53.9	1.3	-	-	-	-
1977	55.1	2.2	-	-	-	-	55.8	1.3	-	-	-	-	56.9	2.0	-	-	-	-	56.7	-0.4	-	-	-	-
1978	57.6	1.6	-	-	57.9	0.5	-	-	58.5	1.0	-	-	60.4	3.2	-	-	61.3	1.5	-	-	61.9	1.0	-	-
1979	63.3	2.3	-	-	65.2	3.0	-	-	68.9	5.7	-	-	71.6	3.9	-	-	73.7	2.9	-	-	75.1	1.9	-	-
1980	77.6	3.3	-	-	80.5	3.7	-	-	82.1	2.0	-	-	83.0	1.1	-	-	84.0	1.2	-	-	85.0	1.2	-	-
1981	87.0	2.4	-	-	89.7	3.1	-	-	91.1	1.6	-	-	92.7	1.8	-	-	93.5	0.9	-	-	94.7	1.3	-	-
1982	94.6	-0.1	-	-	94.0	-0.6	-	-	94.0	0.0	-	-	97.6	3.8	-	-	98.2	0.6	-	-	98.8	0.6	-	-
1983	97.0	-1.8	-	-	95.1	-2.0	-	-	99.6	4.7	-	-	101.5	1.9	-	-	102.7	1.2	-	-	103.3	0.6	-	-
1984	102.0	-1.3	-	-	102.6	0.6	-	-	104.1	1.5	-	-	103.8	-0.3	-	-	104.5	0.7	-	-	104.7	0.2	-	-
1985	102.5	-2.1	-	-	104.4	1.9	-	-	106.7	2.2	-	-	107.2	0.5	-	-	106.6	-0.6	-	-	107.2	0.6	-	-
1986	106.3	-0.8	-	-	98.8	-7.1	-	-	99.5	0.7	-	-	100.1	0.6	-	-	101.6	1.5	-	-	101.0	-0.6	100.3	-0.7
1987	-	-	-	-	-	-	-	-	-	-	105.6	5.3	-	-	-	-	-	-	-	-	-	-	110.2	4.4
1988	-	-	-	-	-	-	-	-	-	-	110.4	0.2	-	-	-	-	-	-	-	-	-	-	117.8	6.7
1989	-	-	-	-	-	-	-	-	-	-	121.6	3.2	-	-	-	-	-	-	-	-	-	-	123.0	1.2
1990	-	-	-	-	-	-	-	-	-	-	124.4	1.1	-	-	-	-	-	-	-	-	-	-	129.3	3.9
1991	-	-	-	-	-	-	-	-	-	-	126.6	-2.1	-	-	-	-	-	-	-	-	-	-	129.1	2.0
1992	-	-	-	-	-	-	-	-	-	-	131.9	2.2	-	-	-	-	-	-	-	-	-	-	136.6	3.6
1993	-	-	-	-	-	-	-	-	-	-	138.5	1.4	-	-	-	-	-	-	-	-	-	-	143.7	3.8
1994	-	-	-	-	-	-	-	-	-	-	145.3	1.1	-	-	-	-	-	-	-	-	-	-	151.5	4.3
1995	-	-	-	-	-	-	-	-	-	-	156.4	3.2	-	-	-	-	-	-	-	-	-	-	157.3	0.6
1996	-	-	-	-	-	-	-	-	-	-	159.6	1.5	-	-	-	-	-	-	-	-	-	-	165.8	3.9
1997	-	-	-	-	-	-	-	-	-	-	165.1	-0.4	-	-	-	-	-	-	-	-	-	-	166.2	0.7
1998	-	-	-	-	-	-	-	-	-	-	166.5	0.2	-	-	-	-	-	-	-	-	-	-	166.4	-0.1
1999	-	-	-	-	-	-	-	-	-	-	166.6	0.1	-	-	-	-	-	-	-	-	-	-	172.4	3.5
2000	-	-	-	-	-	-	-	-	-	-	177.8	3.1	-	-	-	-	-	-	-	-	-	-	180.8	1.7
2001	-	-	-	-	-	-	-	-	-	-	183.1	1.3	-	-	-	-	-	-	-	-	-	-	-	-

Source: U.S. Department of Labor, Bureau of Labor Statistics, Division of Consumer Prices and Price Indexes. - indicates no data collected for period.

Denver-Boulder-Greeley, CO
Consumer Price Index - Urban Wage Earners
Base 1982-1984 = 100
Transportation

For 1971-2001. Columns headed % show percentile change in the index from the previous period for which an index is available.

Year	Jan Index	Jan %	Feb Index	Feb %	Mar Index	Mar %	Apr Index	Apr %	May Index	May %	Jun Index	Jun %	Jul Index	Jul %	Aug Index	Aug %	Sep Index	Sep %	Oct Index	Oct %	Nov Index	Nov %	Dec Index	Dec %
1971	37.7	-	-	-	-	-	37.7	0.0	-	-	-	-	37.5	-0.5	-	-	-	-	37.8	0.8	-	-	-	-
1972	36.8	-2.6	-	-	-	-	37.3	1.4	-	-	-	-	37.7	1.1	-	-	-	-	38.1	1.1	-	-	-	-
1973	37.7	-1.0	-	-	-	-	39.2	4.0	-	-	-	-	40.1	2.3	-	-	-	-	39.2	-2.2	-	-	-	-
1974	40.9	4.3	-	-	-	-	42.3	3.4	-	-	-	-	44.6	5.4	-	-	-	-	45.0	0.9	-	-	-	-
1975	45.6	1.3	-	-	-	-	46.6	2.2	-	-	-	-	48.9	4.9	-	-	-	-	49.4	1.0	-	-	-	-
1976	49.3	-0.2	-	-	-	-	50.4	2.2	-	-	-	-	52.8	4.8	-	-	-	-	53.5	1.3	-	-	-	-
1977	54.6	2.1	-	-	-	-	55.4	1.5	-	-	-	-	56.5	2.0	-	-	-	-	56.2	-0.5	-	-	-	-
1978	57.1	1.6	-	-	57.2	0.2	-	-	58.1	1.6	-	-	59.4	2.2	-	-	60.2	1.3	-	-	61.3	1.8	-	-
1979	62.4	1.8	-	-	64.6	3.5	-	-	68.5	6.0	-	-	71.3	4.1	-	-	73.5	3.1	-	-	74.8	1.8	-	-
1980	77.4	3.5	-	-	80.3	3.7	-	-	82.2	2.4	-	-	83.1	1.1	-	-	83.8	0.8	-	-	85.1	1.6	-	-
1981	86.8	2.0	-	-	89.6	3.2	-	-	90.9	1.5	-	-	92.7	2.0	-	-	93.8	1.2	-	-	95.1	1.4	-	-
1982	95.0	-0.1	-	-	94.7	-0.3	-	-	94.3	-0.4	-	-	98.1	4.0	-	-	98.8	0.7	-	-	99.3	0.5	-	-
1983	97.1	-2.2	-	-	95.1	-2.1	-	-	99.6	4.7	-	-	101.4	1.8	-	-	102.6	1.2	-	-	103.0	0.4	-	-
1984	101.5	-1.5	-	-	102.3	0.8	-	-	103.7	1.4	-	-	103.5	-0.2	-	-	104.2	0.7	-	-	103.0	0.4	-	-
1985	102.0	-2.2	-	-	104.0	2.0	-	-	106.7	2.6	-	-	107.3	0.6	-	-	106.8	-0.5	-	-	107.3	0.5	-	-
1986	106.3	-0.9	-	-	98.6	-7.2	-	-	99.1	0.5	-	-	99.8	0.7	-	-	101.1	1.3	-	-	100.6	-0.5	99.9	-0.7
1987	-	-	-	-	-	-	-	-	-	-	105.8	5.9	-	-	-	-	-	-	-	-	-	-	110.9	4.8
1988	-	-	-	-	-	-	-	-	-	-	110.2	-0.6	-	-	-	-	-	-	-	-	-	-	117.0	6.2
1989	-	-	-	-	-	-	-	-	-	-	120.9	3.3	-	-	-	-	-	-	-	-	-	-	121.8	0.7
1990	-	-	-	-	-	-	-	-	-	-	122.5	0.6	-	-	-	-	-	-	-	-	-	-	128.4	4.8
1991	-	-	-	-	-	-	-	-	-	-	124.3	-3.2	-	-	-	-	-	-	-	-	-	-	127.2	2.3
1992	-	-	-	-	-	-	-	-	-	-	130.3	2.4	-	-	-	-	-	-	-	-	-	-	136.8	5.0
1993	-	-	-	-	-	-	-	-	-	-	138.1	1.0	-	-	-	-	-	-	-	-	-	-	142.9	3.5
1994	-	-	-	-	-	-	-	-	-	-	142.8	-0.1	-	-	-	-	-	-	-	-	-	-	150.4	5.3
1995	-	-	-	-	-	-	-	-	-	-	154.8	2.9	-	-	-	-	-	-	-	-	-	-	155.6	0.5
1996	-	-	-	-	-	-	-	-	-	-	157.9	1.5	-	-	-	-	-	-	-	-	-	-	164.2	4.0
1997	-	-	-	-	-	-	-	-	-	-	163.6	-0.4	-	-	-	-	-	-	-	-	-	-	164.1	0.3
1998	-	-	-	-	-	-	-	-	-	-	162.9	-0.7	-	-	-	-	-	-	-	-	-	-	162.6	-0.2
1999	-	-	-	-	-	-	-	-	-	-	162.4	-0.1	-	-	-	-	-	-	-	-	-	-	168.7	3.9
2000	-	-	-	-	-	-	-	-	-	-	173.7	3.0	-	-	-	-	-	-	-	-	-	-	178.4	2.7
2001	-	-	-	-	-	-	-	-	-	-	179.9	0.8	-	-	-	-	-	-	-	-	-	-	-	-

Source: U.S. Department of Labor, Bureau of Labor Statistics, Division of Consumer Prices and Price Indexes. - indicates no data collected for period.

Denver-Boulder-Greeley, CO
Consumer Price Index - All Urban Consumers
Base 1982-1984 = 100
Medical Care

For 1971-2001. Columns headed % show percentile change in the index from the previous period for which an index is available.

Year	Jan Index	%	Feb Index	%	Mar Index	%	Apr Index	%	May Index	%	Jun Index	%	Jul Index	%	Aug Index	%	Sep Index	%	Oct Index	%	Nov Index	%	Dec Index	%
1971	35.4	-	-	-	-	-	36.1	2.0	-	-	-	-	37.1	2.8	-	-	-	-	36.9	-0.5	-	-	-	-
1972	37.2	0.8	-	-	-	-	37.3	0.3	-	-	-	-	37.5	0.5	-	-	-	-	38.0	1.3	-	-	-	-
1973	38.1	0.3	-	-	-	-	38.5	1.0	-	-	-	-	38.8	0.8	-	-	-	-	39.7	2.3	-	-	-	-
1974	40.7	2.5	-	-	-	-	41.2	1.2	-	-	-	-	43.2	4.9	-	-	-	-	43.7	1.2	-	-	-	-
1975	45.7	4.6	-	-	-	-	46.7	2.2	-	-	-	-	47.6	1.9	-	-	-	-	48.3	1.5	-	-	-	-
1976	49.1	1.7	-	-	-	-	50.3	2.4	-	-	-	-	51.1	1.6	-	-	-	-	52.2	2.2	-	-	-	-
1977	53.3	2.1	-	-	-	-	54.6	2.4	-	-	-	-	56.2	2.9	-	-	-	-	57.3	2.0	-	-	-	-
1978	58.9	2.8	-	-	59.5	1.0	-	-	60.3	1.3	-	-	60.4	0.2	-	-	61.4	1.7	-	-	62.5	1.8	-	-
1979	63.3	1.3	-	-	64.1	1.3	-	-	65.7	2.5	-	-	66.1	0.6	-	-	67.2	1.7	-	-	68.5	1.9	-	-
1980	71.6	4.5	-	-	72.3	1.0	-	-	73.0	1.0	-	-	73.0	0.0	-	-	74.3	1.8	-	-	76.0	2.3	-	-
1981	78.4	3.2	-	-	78.8	0.5	-	-	79.4	0.8	-	-	80.1	0.9	-	-	82.4	2.9	-	-	84.3	2.3	-	-
1982	87.5	3.8	-	-	88.2	0.8	-	-	88.9	0.8	-	-	91.8	3.3	-	-	93.2	1.5	-	-	94.5	1.4	-	-
1983	97.4	3.1	-	-	99.0	1.6	-	-	99.4	0.4	-	-	102.4	3.0	-	-	102.5	0.1	-	-	102.8	0.3	-	-
1984	106.4	3.5	-	-	107.2	0.8	-	-	107.4	0.2	-	-	108.0	0.6	-	-	108.2	0.2	-	-	109.4	1.1	-	-
1985	110.8	1.3	-	-	112.5	1.5	-	-	113.2	0.6	-	-	115.9	2.4	-	-	117.6	1.5	-	-	118.5	0.8	126.1	0.3
1986	119.9	1.2	-	-	121.2	1.1	-	-	123.2	1.7	-	-	125.7	2.0	-	-	126.4	0.6	-	-	125.7	-0.6	133.3	1.9
1987	-	-	-	-	-	-	-	-	-	-	130.8	3.7	-	-	-	-	-	-	-	-	-	-	145.1	3.5
1988	-	-	-	-	-	-	-	-	-	-	140.2	5.2	-	-	-	-	-	-	-	-	-	-	156.8	4.5
1989	-	-	-	-	-	-	-	-	-	-	150.0	3.4	-	-	-	-	-	-	-	-	-	-	179.0	6.7
1990	-	-	-	-	-	-	-	-	-	-	167.8	7.0	-	-	-	-	-	-	-	-	-	-	195.3	3.7
1991	-	-	-	-	-	-	-	-	-	-	188.3	5.2	-	-	-	-	-	-	-	-	-	-	210.6	4.1
1992	-	-	-	-	-	-	-	-	-	-	202.3	3.6	-	-	-	-	-	-	-	-	-	-	219.5	1.5
1993	-	-	-	-	-	-	-	-	-	-	216.3	2.7	-	-	-	-	-	-	-	-	-	-	235.5	4.6
1994	-	-	-	-	-	-	-	-	-	-	225.1	2.6	-	-	-	-	-	-	-	-	-	-	246.6	0.7
1995	-	-	-	-	-	-	-	-	-	-	244.9	4.0	-	-	-	-	-	-	-	-	-	-	252.2	1.1
1996	-	-	-	-	-	-	-	-	-	-	249.4	1.1	-	-	-	-	-	-	-	-	-	-	268.1	1.8
1997	-	-	-	-	-	-	-	-	-	-	263.4	4.4	-	-	-	-	-	-	-	-	-	-	277.0	1.5
1998	-	-	-	-	-	-	-	-	-	-	273.0	1.8	-	-	-	-	-	-	-	-	-	-	293.7	3.0
1999	-	-	-	-	-	-	-	-	-	-	285.1	2.9	-	-	-	-	-	-	-	-	-	-	306.8	2.1
2000	-	-	-	-	-	-	-	-	-	-	300.6	2.3	-	-	-	-	-	-	-	-	-	-	-	-
2001	-	-	-	-	-	-	-	-	-	-	317.0	3.3	-	-	-	-	-	-	-	-	-	-	-	-

Source: U.S. Department of Labor, Bureau of Labor Statistics, Division of Consumer Prices and Price Indexes. - indicates no data collected for period.

Denver-Boulder-Greeley, CO
Consumer Price Index - Urban Wage Earners
Base 1982-1984 = 100
Medical Care

For 1971-2001. Columns headed % show percentile change in the index from the previous period for which an index is available.

Year	Jan		Feb		Mar		Apr		May		Jun		Jul		Aug		Sep		Oct		Nov		Dec	
	Index	%	Index	%	Index	%	Index	%	Index	%	Index	%	Index	%	Index	%	Index	%	Index	%	Index	%	Index	%
1971	35.8	-	-	-	-	-	36.5	2.0	-	-	-	-	37.5	2.7	-	-	-	-	37.3	-0.5	-	-	-	-
1972	37.6	0.8	-	-	-	-	37.7	0.3	-	-	-	-	37.9	0.5	-	-	-	-	38.4	1.3	-	-	-	-
1973	38.5	0.3	-	-	-	-	38.9	1.0	-	-	-	-	39.2	0.8	-	-	-	-	40.1	2.3	-	-	-	-
1974	41.1	2.5	-	-	-	-	41.7	1.5	-	-	-	-	43.7	4.8	-	-	-	-	44.1	0.9	-	-	-	-
1975	46.2	4.8	-	-	-	-	47.2	2.2	-	-	-	-	48.1	1.9	-	-	-	-	48.8	1.5	-	-	-	-
1976	49.6	1.6	-	-	-	-	50.8	2.4	-	-	-	-	51.7	1.8	-	-	-	-	52.7	1.9	-	-	-	-
1977	53.9	2.3	-	-	-	-	55.1	2.2	-	-	-	-	56.8	3.1	-	-	-	-	57.9	1.9	-	-	-	-
1978	59.5	2.8	-	-	60.3	1.3	-	-	61.4	1.8	-	-	62.1	1.1	-	-	62.9	1.3	-	-	64.0	1.7	-	-
1979	64.4	0.6	-	-	65.6	1.9	-	-	65.7	0.2	-	-	65.9	0.3	-	-	67.0	1.7	-	-	68.5	2.2	-	-
1980	70.0	2.2	-	-	71.5	2.1	-	-	72.3	1.1	-	-	73.0	1.0	-	-	75.6	3.6	-	-	76.2	0.8	-	-
1981	79.2	3.9	-	-	79.5	0.4	-	-	81.0	1.9	-	-	81.5	0.6	-	-	82.4	1.1	-	-	83.9	1.8	-	-
1982	86.9	3.6	-	-	87.8	1.0	-	-	88.6	0.9	-	-	91.6	3.4	-	-	93.1	1.6	-	-	94.5	1.5	-	-
1983	97.4	3.1	-	-	99.0	1.6	-	-	99.5	0.5	-	-	102.7	3.2	-	-	102.8	0.1	-	-	94.5	1.5	-	-
1984	106.5	3.2	-	-	107.3	0.8	-	-	107.5	0.2	-	-	108.0	0.5	-	-	102.8	0.1	-	-	103.2	0.4	-	-
1985	110.7	1.2	-	-	112.5	1.6	-	-	113.2	0.6	-	-	108.0	0.5	-	-	108.2	0.2	-	-	109.4	1.1	-	-
1986	120.0	1.1	-	-	121.2	1.0	-	-	123.3	1.7	-	-	115.9	2.4	-	-	117.6	1.5	-	-	118.7	0.9	-	-
1987	-	-	-	-	-	-	-	-	123.3	1.7	-	-	125.9	2.1	-	-	126.6	0.6	-	-	126.1	-0.4	126.5	0.3
1988	-	-	-	-	-	-	-	-	-	-	131.3	3.8	-	-	-	-	-	-	-	-	-	-	134.4	2.4
1989	-	-	-	-	-	-	-	-	-	-	141.8	5.5	-	-	-	-	-	-	-	-	-	-	146.9	3.6
1990	-	-	-	-	-	-	-	-	-	-	151.2	2.9	-	-	-	-	-	-	-	-	-	-	157.9	4.4
1991	-	-	-	-	-	-	-	-	-	-	169.4	7.3	-	-	-	-	-	-	-	-	-	-	180.2	6.4
1992	-	-	-	-	-	-	-	-	-	-	189.4	5.1	-	-	-	-	-	-	-	-	-	-	196.3	3.6
1993	-	-	-	-	-	-	-	-	-	-	203.4	3.6	-	-	-	-	-	-	-	-	-	-	212.5	4.5
1994	-	-	-	-	-	-	-	-	-	-	217.5	2.4	-	-	-	-	-	-	-	-	-	-	220.4	1.3
1995	-	-	-	-	-	-	-	-	-	-	226.1	2.6	-	-	-	-	-	-	-	-	-	-	235.6	4.2
1996	-	-	-	-	-	-	-	-	-	-	244.5	3.8	-	-	-	-	-	-	-	-	-	-	246.6	0.9
1997	-	-	-	-	-	-	-	-	-	-	249.4	1.1	-	-	-	-	-	-	-	-	-	-	251.5	0.8
1998	-	-	-	-	-	-	-	-	-	-	262.0	4.2	-	-	-	-	-	-	-	-	-	-	267.1	1.9
1999	-	-	-	-	-	-	-	-	-	-	272.7	2.1	-	-	-	-	-	-	-	-	-	-	276.4	1.4
2000	-	-	-	-	-	-	-	-	-	-	284.9	3.1	-	-	-	-	-	-	-	-	-	-	293.1	2.9
2001	-	-	-	-	-	-	-	-	-	-	300.1	2.4	-	-	-	-	-	-	-	-	-	-	305.8	1.9
	-	-	-	-	-	-	-	-	-	-	315.9	3.3	-	-	-	-	-	-	-	-	-	-	-	-

Source: U.S. Department of Labor, Bureau of Labor Statistics, Division of Consumer Prices and Price Indexes. - indicates no data collected for period.

Denver-Boulder-Greeley, CO
Consumer Price Index - All Urban Consumers
Base December 1997 = 100
Recreation

For 1997-2001. Columns headed % show percentile change in the index from the previous period for which an index is available.

Year	Jan Index	%	Feb Index	%	Mar Index	%	Apr Index	%	May Index	%	Jun Index	%	Jul Index	%	Aug Index	%	Sep Index	%	Oct Index	%	Nov Index	%	Dec Index	%
1997	-	-	-	-	-	-	-	-	-	-	-	-	-	-	-	-	-	-	-	-	-	-	100.0	-
1998	-	-	-	-	-	-	-	-	-	-	100.4	0.4	-	-	-	-	-	-	-	-	-	-	100.4	0.0
1999	-	-	-	-	-	-	-	-	-	-	100.8	0.4	-	-	-	-	-	-	-	-	-	-	100.1	-0.7
2000	-	-	-	-	-	-	-	-	-	-	100.6	0.5	-	-	-	-	-	-	-	-	-	-	103.7	3.1
2001	-	-	-	-	-	-	-	-	-	-	105.1	1.4	-	-	-	-	-	-	-	-	-	-	-	-

Source: U.S. Department of Labor, Bureau of Labor Statistics, Division of Consumer Prices and Price Indexes. - indicates no data collected for period.

Denver-Boulder-Greeley, CO
Consumer Price Index - Urban Wage Earners
Base December 1997 = 100
Recreation

For 1997-2001. Columns headed % show percentile change in the index from the previous period for which an index is available.

Year	Jan Index	%	Feb Index	%	Mar Index	%	Apr Index	%	May Index	%	Jun Index	%	Jul Index	%	Aug Index	%	Sep Index	%	Oct Index	%	Nov Index	%	Dec Index	%
1997	-	-	-	-	-	-	-	-	-	-	-	-	-	-	-	-	-	-	-	-	-	-	-	-
1998	-	-	-	-	-	-	-	-	-	-	-	-	-	-	-	-	-	-	-	-	-	-	100.0	-
1999	-	-	-	-	-	-	-	-	-	-	100.0	0.0	-	-	-	-	-	-	-	-	-	-	99.5	-0.5
2000	-	-	-	-	-	-	-	-	-	-	99.7	0.2	-	-	-	-	-	-	-	-	-	-	98.6	-1.1
2001	-	-	-	-	-	-	-	-	-	-	98.5	-0.1	-	-	-	-	-	-	-	-	-	-	101.2	2.7
	-	-	-	-	-	-	-	-	-	-	102.5	1.3	-	-	-	-	-	-	-	-	-	-	-	-

Source: U.S. Department of Labor, Bureau of Labor Statistics, Division of Consumer Prices and Price Indexes. - indicates no data collected for period.

Denver-Boulder-Greeley, CO
Consumer Price Index - All Urban Consumers
Base December 1997 = 100
Education & Communication

For 1997-2001. Columns headed % show percentile change in the index from the previous period for which an index is available.

Year	Jan Index	%	Feb Index	%	Mar Index	%	Apr Index	%	May Index	%	Jun Index	%	Jul Index	%	Aug Index	%	Sep Index	%	Oct Index	%	Nov Index	%	Dec Index	%
1997	-	-	-	-	-	-	-	-	-	-	-	-	-	-	-	-	-	-	-	-	-	-	100.0	-
1998	-	-	-	-	-	-	-	-	-	-	98.7	-1.3	-	-	-	-	-	-	-	-	-	-	97.6	-1.1
1999	-	-	-	-	-	-	-	-	-	-	96.5	-1.1	-	-	-	-	-	-	-	-	-	-	96.5	0.0
2000	-	-	-	-	-	-	-	-	-	-	96.1	-0.4	-	-	-	-	-	-	-	-	-	-	97.7	1.7
2001	-	-	-	-	-	-	-	-	-	-	97.9	0.2	-	-	-	-	-	-	-	-	-	-	-	-

Source: U.S. Department of Labor, Bureau of Labor Statistics, Division of Consumer Prices and Price Indexes. - indicates no data collected for period.

Denver-Boulder-Greeley, CO
Consumer Price Index - Urban Wage Earners
Base December 1997 = 100
Education & Communication

For 1997-2001. Columns headed % show percentile change in the index from the previous period for which an index is available.

Year	Jan		Feb		Mar		Apr		May		Jun		Jul		Aug		Sep		Oct		Nov		Dec	
	Index	%	Index	%	Index	%	Index	%	Index	%	Index	%	Index	%	Index	%	Index	%	Index	%	Index	%	Index	%
1997	-	-	-	-	-	-	-	-	-	-	-	-	-	-	-	-	-	-	-	-	-	-	-	-
1998	-	-	-	-	-	-	-	-	-	-	-	-	-	-	-	-	-	-	-	-	-	-	100.0	-
1999	-	-	-	-	-	-	-	-	-	-	99.1	-0.9	-	-	-	-	-	-	-	-	-	-	98.1	-1.0
2000	-	-	-	-	-	-	-	-	-	-	97.3	-0.8	-	-	-	-	-	-	-	-	-	-	97.4	0.1
2001	-	-	-	-	-	-	-	-	-	-	97.2	-0.2	-	-	-	-	-	-	-	-	-	-	99.1	2.0
	-	-	-	-	-	-	-	-	-	-	99.4	0.3	-	-	-	-	-	-	-	-	-	-	-	-

Source: U.S. Department of Labor, Bureau of Labor Statistics, Division of Consumer Prices and Price Indexes. - indicates no data collected for period.

Detroit-Ann Arbor-Flint, MI
Consumer Price Index - All Urban Consumers
Base 1982-1984 = 100
Annual Averages

For 1914-2001. Columns headed % show percentile change in the index from the previous period for which an index is available.

Year	All Items Index	%	Food & Beverage Index	%	Housing Index	%	Apparel Index	%	Trans-portation Index	%	Medical Care Index	%	Recrea-tion* Index	%	Education & Communic.* Index	%	Other Goods & Services Index	%
1914	-	-	-	-	-	-	-	-	-	-	-	-	-	-	-	-	-	-
1915	9.8	-	-	-	-	-	-	-	-	-	-	-	-	-	-	-	-	-
1916	10.8	10.2	-	-	-	-	-	-	-	-	-	-	-	-	-	-	-	-
1917	13.3	23.1	-	-	-	-	-	-	-	-	-	-	-	-	-	-	-	-
1918	15.7	18.0	-	-	-	-	-	-	-	-	-	-	-	-	-	-	-	-
1919	18.2	15.9	-	-	-	-	-	-	-	-	-	-	-	-	-	-	-	-
1920	21.8	19.8	-	-	-	-	-	-	-	-	-	-	-	-	-	-	-	-
1921	19.0	-12.8	-	-	-	-	-	-	-	-	-	-	-	-	-	-	-	-
1922	17.4	-8.4	-	-	-	-	-	-	-	-	-	-	-	-	-	-	-	-
1923	18.0	3.4	-	-	-	-	-	-	-	-	-	-	-	-	-	-	-	-
1924	18.0	0.0	-	-	-	-	-	-	-	-	-	-	-	-	-	-	-	-
1925	18.2	1.1	-	-	-	-	-	-	-	-	-	-	-	-	-	-	-	-
1926	18.3	0.5	-	-	-	-	-	-	-	-	-	-	-	-	-	-	-	-
1927	17.9	-2.2	-	-	-	-	-	-	-	-	-	-	-	-	-	-	-	-
1928	17.5	-2.2	-	-	-	-	-	-	-	-	-	-	-	-	-	-	-	-
1929	17.6	0.6	-	-	-	-	-	-	-	-	-	-	-	-	-	-	-	-
1930	16.9	-4.0	-	-	-	-	-	-	-	-	-	-	-	-	-	-	-	-
1931	14.8	-12.4	-	-	-	-	-	-	-	-	-	-	-	-	-	-	-	-
1932	12.8	-13.5	-	-	-	-	-	-	-	-	-	-	-	-	-	-	-	-
1933	12.1	-5.5	-	-	-	-	-	-	-	-	-	-	-	-	-	-	-	-
1934	12.8	5.8	-	-	-	-	-	-	-	-	-	-	-	-	-	-	-	-
1935	13.4	4.7	-	-	-	-	-	-	-	-	-	-	-	-	-	-	-	-
1936	13.8	3.0	-	-	-	-	-	-	-	-	-	-	-	-	-	-	-	-
1937	14.7	6.5	-	-	-	-	-	-	-	-	-	-	-	-	-	-	-	-
1938	14.4	-2.0	-	-	-	-	-	-	-	-	-	-	-	-	-	-	-	-
1939	14.0	-2.8	-	-	-	-	-	-	-	-	-	-	-	-	-	-	-	-
1940	14.1	0.7	-	-	-	-	-	-	-	-	-	-	-	-	-	-	-	-
1941	15.0	6.4	-	-	-	-	-	-	-	-	-	-	-	-	-	-	-	-
1942	16.7	11.3	-	-	-	-	-	-	-	-	-	-	-	-	-	-	-	-
1943	17.5	4.8	-	-	-	-	-	-	-	-	-	-	-	-	-	-	-	-
1944	17.8	1.7	-	-	-	-	-	-	-	-	-	-	-	-	-	-	-	-
1945	18.3	2.8	-	-	-	-	-	-	-	-	-	-	-	-	-	-	-	-
1946	19.9	8.7	-	-	-	-	-	-	-	-	-	-	-	-	-	-	-	-
1947	22.7	14.1	-	-	-	-	-	-	19.7	-	11.8	-	-	-	-	-	-	-
1948	24.5	7.9	-	-	-	-	-	-	22.2	12.7	12.3	4.2	-	-	-	-	-	-
1949	24.2	-1.2	-	-	-	-	-	-	23.4	5.4	12.6	2.4	-	-	-	-	-	-
1950	24.6	1.7	-	-	-	-	-	-	23.7	1.3	12.8	1.6	-	-	-	-	-	-
1951	26.5	7.7	-	-	-	-	-	-	24.7	4.2	13.4	4.7	-	-	-	-	-	-
1952	27.1	2.3	-	-	-	-	-	-	26.4	6.9	14.1	5.2	-	-	-	-	-	-
1953	27.6	1.8	-	-	-	-	52.1	-	27.5	4.2	14.7	4.3	-	-	-	-	-	-
1954	27.7	0.4	-	-	-	-	51.9	-0.4	26.3	-4.4	15.3	4.1	-	-	-	-	-	-
1955	27.7	0.0	-	-	-	-	51.8	-0.2	26.6	1.1	16.3	6.5	-	-	-	-	-	-
1956	28.2	1.8	-	-	-	-	52.6	1.5	27.5	3.4	17.4	6.7	-	-	-	-	-	-
1957	29.0	2.8	-	-	-	-	53.2	1.1	28.9	5.1	18.0	3.4	-	-	-	-	-	-
1958	29.4	1.4	-	-	-	-	53.0	-0.4	29.0	0.3	18.5	2.8	-	-	-	-	-	-

[Continued]

Detroit-Ann Arbor-Flint, MI
Consumer Price Index - All Urban Consumers
Base 1982-1984 = 100
Annual Averages
[Continued]

For 1914-2001. Columns headed % show percentile change in the index from the previous period for which an index is available.

Year	All Items		Food & Beverage		Housing		Apparel		Trans-portation		Medical Care		Recrea-tion*		Education & Communic.*		Other Goods & Services	
	Index	%	Index	%	Index	%	Index	%	Index	%	Index	%	Index	%	Index	%	Index	%
1959	29.4	0.0	-	-	-	-	53.9	1.7	30.1	3.8	19.3	4.3	-	-	-	-	-	-
1960	29.7	1.0	-	-	-	-	54.4	0.9	30.2	0.3	19.6	1.6	-	-	-	-	-	-
1961	29.8	0.3	-	-	-	-	55.2	1.5	29.7	-1.7	20.6	5.1	-	-	-	-	-	-
1962	29.9	0.3	-	-	-	-	55.5	0.5	30.3	2.0	21.2	2.9	-	-	-	-	-	-
1963	30.2	1.0	-	-	-	-	56.1	1.1	30.4	0.3	22.3	5.2	-	-	-	-	-	-
1964	30.4	0.7	-	-	-	-	56.8	1.2	30.7	1.0	23.2	4.0	-	-	-	-	-	-
1965	31.2	2.6	-	-	-	-	57.7	1.6	32.0	4.2	23.8	2.6	-	-	-	-	-	-
1966	32.5	4.2	-	-	-	-	59.0	2.3	32.8	2.5	25.1	5.5	-	-	-	-	-	-
1967	33.6	3.4	-	-	-	-	60.6	2.7	33.5	2.1	26.9	7.2	-	-	-	-	-	-
1968	35.1	4.5	-	-	-	-	63.2	4.3	34.9	4.2	28.7	6.7	-	-	-	-	-	-
1969	37.2	6.0	-	-	-	-	66.0	4.4	36.0	3.2	30.8	7.3	-	-	-	-	-	-
1970	39.5	6.2	-	-	-	-	67.9	2.9	36.9	2.5	33.5	8.8	-	-	-	-	-	-
1971	40.9	3.5	-	-	-	-	70.0	3.1	38.4	4.1	36.1	7.8	-	-	-	-	-	-
1972	42.5	3.9	-	-	-	-	71.7	2.4	39.1	1.8	38.0	5.3	-	-	-	-	-	-
1973	45.2	6.4	-	-	-	-	74.1	3.3	41.5	6.1	40.0	5.3	-	-	-	-	-	-
1974	50.1	10.8	-	-	-	-	80.2	8.2	46.5	12.0	43.8	9.5	-	-	-	-	-	-
1975	53.9	7.6	-	-	-	-	83.6	4.2	50.0	7.5	50.4	15.1	-	-	-	-	-	-
1976	56.8	5.4	63.8	-	52.3	-	86.0	2.9	53.7	7.4	56.3	11.7	-	-	-	-	57.5	-
1977	60.7	6.9	67.6	6.0	55.8	6.7	88.9	3.4	58.6	9.1	63.2	12.3	-	-	-	-	61.3	6.6
1978	65.3	7.6	74.5	10.2	60.3	8.1	89.7	0.9	62.0	5.8	67.7	7.1	-	-	-	-	65.8	7.3
1979	73.6	12.7	82.2	10.3	70.3	16.6	89.7	0.0	70.4	13.5	73.9	9.2	-	-	-	-	70.2	6.7
1980	85.3	15.9	88.9	8.2	85.5	21.6	94.3	5.1	82.8	17.6	80.1	8.4	-	-	-	-	75.1	7.0
1981	93.2	9.3	95.8	7.8	93.4	9.2	96.4	2.2	93.8	13.3	86.1	7.5	-	-	-	-	81.8	8.9
1982	97.0	4.1	99.3	3.7	96.3	3.1	98.3	2.0	97.9	4.4	93.2	8.2	-	-	-	-	91.8	12.2
1983	99.8	2.9	99.3	0.0	100.4	4.3	101.0	2.7	98.5	0.6	98.3	5.5	-	-	-	-	102.0	11.1
1984	103.2	3.4	101.4	2.1	103.3	2.9	100.8	-0.2	103.6	5.2	108.5	10.4	-	-	-	-	106.2	4.1
1985	106.8	3.5	103.2	1.8	107.5	4.1	102.6	1.8	106.6	2.9	116.4	7.3	-	-	-	-	111.6	5.1
1986	108.3	1.4	107.3	4.0	109.8	2.1	103.3	0.7	103.2	-3.2	125.0	7.4	-	-	-	-	114.6	2.7
1987	111.7	3.1	110.5	3.0	113.0	2.9	108.0	4.5	105.3	2.0	132.9	6.3	-	-	-	-	120.4	5.1
1988	116.1	3.9	114.7	3.8	116.1	2.7	115.2	6.7	109.5	4.0	140.2	5.5	-	-	-	-	130.0	8.0
1989	122.3	5.3	120.8	5.3	121.2	4.4	122.7	6.5	117.0	6.8	147.1	4.9	-	-	-	-	137.9	6.1
1990	128.6	5.2	126.5	4.7	126.4	4.3	127.9	4.2	124.0	6.0	159.8	8.6	-	-	-	-	147.5	7.0
1991	133.1	3.5	131.1	3.6	128.6	1.7	131.8	3.0	129.3	4.3	171.0	7.0	-	-	-	-	160.7	8.9
1992	135.9	2.1	133.4	1.8	131.8	2.5	129.9	-1.4	129.9	0.5	181.6	6.2	-	-	-	-	173.8	8.2
1993	139.6	2.7	135.2	1.3	134.4	2.0	137.9	6.2	132.5	2.0	190.9	5.1	-	-	-	-	183.5	5.6
1994	144.0	3.2	138.7	2.6	137.6	2.4	136.1	-1.3	138.6	4.6	199.7	4.6	-	-	-	-	197.1	7.4
1995	148.6	3.2	143.6	3.5	140.6	2.2	136.9	0.6	143.6	3.6	209.2	4.8	-	-	-	-	210.8	7.0
1996	152.5	2.6	147.9	3.0	145.5	3.5	131.7	-3.8	148.0	3.1	213.7	2.2	-	-	-	-	217.5	3.2
1997	156.3	2.5	151.4	2.4	149.9	3.0	135.2	2.7	149.0	0.7	214.1	0.2	-	-	-	-	228.4	5.0
1998	159.8	2.2	154.6	2.1	153.6	2.5	133.7	-1.1	148.9	-0.1	230.6	7.7	100.1	-	102.6	-	248.1	8.6
1999	163.9	2.6	158.3	2.4	156.3	1.8	133.4	-0.2	152.1	2.1	245.2	6.3	104.5	4.4	106.7	4.0	267.3	7.7
2000	169.8	3.6	163.9	3.5	161.7	3.5	127.9	-4.1	162.5	6.8	257.4	5.0	106.7	2.1	107.9	1.1	275.8	3.2
2001	174.4	2.7	168.5	2.8	166.3	2.8	125.1	-2.2	-		272.8	6.0	107.1	0.4	109.3	1.3	287.3	4.2

Source: U.S. Department of Labor, Bureau of Labor Statistics, Division of Consumer Prices and Price Indexes. *Base is December 1997 = 100. - indicates no data collected for period.

Detroit-Ann Arbor-Flint, MI
Consumer Price Index - Urban Wage Earners
Base 1982-1984 = 100
Annual Averages

For 1914-2001. Columns headed % show percentile change in the index from the previous period for which an index is available.

Year	All Items		Food & Beverage		Housing		Apparel		Trans-portation		Medical Care		Recrea-tion*		Education & Communic.*		Other Goods & Services	
	Index	%	Index	%	Index	%	Index	%	Index	%	Index	%	Index	%	Index	%	Index	%
1914	-	-	-	-	-	-	-	-	-	-	-	-	-	-	-	-	-	-
1915	9.8	-	-	-	-	-	-	-	-	-	-	-	-	-	-	-	-	-
1916	10.9	11.2	-	-	-	-	-	-	-	-	-	-	-	-	-	-	-	-
1917	13.4	22.9	-	-	-	-	-	-	-	-	-	-	-	-	-	-	-	-
1918	15.8	17.9	-	-	-	-	-	-	-	-	-	-	-	-	-	-	-	-
1919	18.4	16.5	-	-	-	-	-	-	-	-	-	-	-	-	-	-	-	-
1920	22.0	19.6	-	-	-	-	-	-	-	-	-	-	-	-	-	-	-	-
1921	19.2	-12.7	-	-	-	-	-	-	-	-	-	-	-	-	-	-	-	-
1922	17.6	-8.3	-	-	-	-	-	-	-	-	-	-	-	-	-	-	-	-
1923	18.2	3.4	-	-	-	-	-	-	-	-	-	-	-	-	-	-	-	-
1924	18.2	0.0	-	-	-	-	-	-	-	-	-	-	-	-	-	-	-	-
1925	18.4	1.1	-	-	-	-	-	-	-	-	-	-	-	-	-	-	-	-
1926	18.5	0.5	-	-	-	-	-	-	-	-	-	-	-	-	-	-	-	-
1927	18.0	-2.7	-	-	-	-	-	-	-	-	-	-	-	-	-	-	-	-
1928	17.7	-1.7	-	-	-	-	-	-	-	-	-	-	-	-	-	-	-	-
1929	17.7	0.0	-	-	-	-	-	-	-	-	-	-	-	-	-	-	-	-
1930	17.0	-4.0	-	-	-	-	-	-	-	-	-	-	-	-	-	-	-	-
1931	14.9	-12.4	-	-	-	-	-	-	-	-	-	-	-	-	-	-	-	-
1932	12.9	-13.4	-	-	-	-	-	-	-	-	-	-	-	-	-	-	-	-
1933	12.2	-5.4	-	-	-	-	-	-	-	-	-	-	-	-	-	-	-	-
1934	12.9	5.7	-	-	-	-	-	-	-	-	-	-	-	-	-	-	-	-
1935	13.5	4.7	-	-	-	-	-	-	-	-	-	-	-	-	-	-	-	-
1936	14.0	3.7	-	-	-	-	-	-	-	-	-	-	-	-	-	-	-	-
1937	14.8	5.7	-	-	-	-	-	-	-	-	-	-	-	-	-	-	-	-
1938	14.6	-1.4	-	-	-	-	-	-	-	-	-	-	-	-	-	-	-	-
1939	14.2	-2.7	-	-	-	-	-	-	-	-	-	-	-	-	-	-	-	-
1940	14.2	0.0	-	-	-	-	-	-	-	-	-	-	-	-	-	-	-	-
1941	15.1	6.3	-	-	-	-	-	-	-	-	-	-	-	-	-	-	-	-
1942	16.8	11.3	-	-	-	-	-	-	-	-	-	-	-	-	-	-	-	-
1943	17.7	5.4	-	-	-	-	-	-	-	-	-	-	-	-	-	-	-	-
1944	18.0	1.7	-	-	-	-	-	-	-	-	-	-	-	-	-	-	-	-
1945	18.4	2.2	-	-	-	-	-	-	-	-	-	-	-	-	-	-	-	-
1946	20.1	9.2	-	-	-	-	-	-	-	-	-	-	-	-	-	-	-	-
1947	22.9	13.9	-	-	-	-	-	-	20.5	-	12.0	-	-	-	-	-	-	-
1948	24.7	7.9	-	-	-	-	-	-	23.0	12.2	12.5	4.2	-	-	-	-	-	-
1949	24.4	-1.2	-	-	-	-	-	-	24.3	5.7	12.8	2.4	-	-	-	-	-	-
1950	24.8	1.6	-	-	-	-	-	-	24.6	1.2	13.1	2.3	-	-	-	-	-	-
1951	26.8	8.1	-	-	-	-	-	-	25.6	4.1	13.6	3.8	-	-	-	-	-	-
1952	27.4	2.2	-	-	-	-	-	-	27.4	7.0	14.3	5.1	-	-	-	-	-	-
1953	27.8	1.5	-	-	-	%	53.0	-	28.5	4.0	14.9	4.2	-	-	-	-	-	-
1954	27.9	0.4	-	-	-	-	52.9	-0.2	27.3	-4.2	15.5	4.0	-	-	-	-	-	-
1955	27.9	0.0	-	-	-	-	52.7	-0.4	27.6	1.1	16.6	7.1	-	-	-	-	-	-
1956	28.5	2.2	-	-	-	-	53.5	1.5	28.5	3.3	17.7	6.6	-	-	-	-	-	-
1957	29.3	2.8	-	-	-	-	54.2	1.3	30.0	5.3	18.3	3.4	-	-	-	-	-	-
1958	29.7	1.4	-	-	-	-	54.0	-0.4	30.1	0.3	18.9	3.3	-	-	-	-	-	-

[Continued]

Detroit-Ann Arbor-Flint, MI
Consumer Price Index - Urban Wage Earners
Base 1982-1984 = 100
Annual Averages
[Continued]

For 1914-2001. Columns headed % show percentile change in the index from the previous period for which an index is available.

Year	All Items Index	%	Food & Beverage Index	%	Housing Index	%	Apparel Index	%	Trans-portation Index	%	Medical Care Index	%	Recrea-tion* Index	%	Education & Communic.* Index	%	Other Goods & Services Index	%
1959	29.7	0.0	-	-	-	-	54.8	1.5	31.3	4.0	19.6	3.7	-	-	-	-	-	-
1960	29.9	0.7	-	-	-	-	55.4	1.1	31.3	0.0	20.0	2.0	-	-	-	-	-	-
1961	30.1	0.7	-	-	-	-	56.2	1.4	30.8	-1.6	21.0	5.0	-	-	-	-	-	-
1962	30.2	0.3	-	-	-	-	56.5	0.5	31.5	2.3	21.6	2.9	-	-	-	-	-	-
1963	30.5	1.0	-	-	-	-	57.1	1.1	31.6	0.3	22.7	5.1	-	-	-	-	-	-
1964	30.7	0.7	-	-	-	-	57.9	1.4	31.8	0.6	23.6	4.0	-	-	-	-	-	-
1965	31.4	2.3	-	-	-	-	58.8	1.6	33.2	4.4	24.2	2.5	-	-	-	-	-	-
1966	32.8	4.5	-	-	-	-	60.1	2.2	34.0	2.4	25.6	5.8	-	-	-	-	-	-
1967	34.0	3.7	-	-	-	-	61.7	2.7	34.8	2.4	27.4	7.0	-	-	-	-	-	-
1968	35.4	4.1	-	-	-	-	64.3	4.2	36.2	4.0	29.2	6.6	-	-	-	-	-	-
1969	37.6	6.2	-	-	-	-	67.2	4.5	37.4	3.3	31.4	7.5	-	-	-	-	-	-
1970	39.9	6.1	-	-	-	-	69.1	2.8	38.2	2.1	34.1	8.6	-	-	-	-	-	-
1971	41.3	3.5	-	-	-	-	71.3	3.2	39.9	4.5	36.8	7.9	-	-	-	-	-	-
1972	42.8	3.6	-	-	-	-	73.0	2.4	40.5	1.5	38.8	5.4	-	-	-	-	-	-
1973	45.7	6.8	-	-	-	-	75.4	3.3	43.0	6.2	40.7	4.9	-	-	-	-	-	-
1974	50.6	10.7	-	-	-	-	81.7	8.4	48.3	12.3	44.6	9.6	-	-	-	-	-	-
1975	54.4	7.5	-	-	-	-	85.1	4.2	51.9	7.5	51.4	15.2	-	-	-	-	-	-
1976	57.3	5.3	63.2	-	52.5	-	87.6	2.9	55.8	7.5	57.4	11.7	-	-	-	-	55.5	-
1977	61.3	7.0	66.9	5.9	56.0	6.7	90.5	3.3	60.8	9.0	64.4	12.2	-	-	-	-	59.1	6.5
1978	65.9	7.5	74.2	10.9	60.3	7.7	93.7	3.5	64.1	5.4	69.1	7.3	-	-	-	-	63.0	6.6
1979	74.3	12.7	82.2	10.8	70.3	16.6	93.6	-0.1	72.7	13.4	75.8	9.7	-	-	-	-	67.3	6.8
1980	85.6	15.2	88.7	7.9	85.2	21.2	97.7	4.4	84.5	16.2	81.3	7.3	-	-	-	-	73.5	9.2
1981	92.7	8.3	95.7	7.9	92.6	8.7	97.3	-0.4	93.1	10.2	86.8	6.8	-	-	-	-	80.5	9.5
1982	96.7	4.3	99.4	3.9	95.7	3.3	98.4	1.1	97.8	5.0	93.5	7.7	-	-	-	-	91.7	13.9
1983	101.1	4.6	99.2	-0.2	103.4	8.0	100.8	2.4	98.5	0.7	98.5	5.3	-	-	-	-	102.1	11.3
1984	102.2	1.1	101.4	2.2	100.9	-2.4	100.8	0.0	103.6	5.2	108.1	9.7	-	-	-	-	106.2	4.0
1985	104.5	2.3	102.9	1.5	102.7	1.8	103.5	2.7	106.7	3.0	115.6	6.9	-	-	-	-	111.5	5.0
1986	105.8	1.2	106.9	3.9	104.9	2.1	105.5	1.9	103.2	-3.3	123.6	6.9	-	-	-	-	114.1	2.3
1987	109.1	3.1	110.2	3.1	108.0	3.0	111.3	5.5	105.5	2.2	131.3	6.2	-	-	-	-	120.0	5.2
1988	113.3	3.8	114.2	3.6	110.9	2.7	119.1	7.0	109.5	3.8	139.6	6.3	-	-	-	-	130.1	8.4
1989	119.4	5.4	120.3	5.3	115.7	4.3	125.9	5.7	117.0	6.8	146.9	5.2	-	-	-	-	137.4	5.6
1990	125.6	5.2	126.1	4.8	120.7	4.3	131.8	4.7	124.1	6.1	159.1	8.3	-	-	-	-	147.3	7.2
1991	129.8	3.3	130.7	3.6	122.8	1.7	134.9	2.4	129.2	4.1	169.7	6.7	-	-	-	-	160.3	8.8
1992	132.1	1.8	133.1	1.8	125.7	2.4	133.3	-1.2	129.7	0.4	180.0	6.1	-	-	-	-	170.0	6.1
1993	135.4	2.5	134.8	1.3	128.1	1.9	140.6	5.5	132.4	2.1	189.3	5.2	-	-	-	-	175.8	3.4
1994	139.5	3.0	138.4	2.7	131.0	2.3	138.9	-1.2	138.6	4.7	197.4	4.3	-	-	-	-	186.7	6.2
1995	143.9	3.2	143.4	3.6	133.8	2.1	139.0	0.1	143.7	3.7	207.1	4.9	-	-	-	-	201.9	8.1
1996	147.7	2.6	147.6	2.9	138.2	3.3	134.6	-3.2	148.1	3.1	212.0	2.4	-	-	-	-	209.1	3.6
1997	151.0	2.2	151.1	2.4	142.2	2.9	137.9	2.5	149.0	0.6	212.3	0.1	-	-	-	-	218.9	4.7
1998	154.3	2.2	154.5	2.3	145.7	2.5	135.9	-1.5	148.8	-0.1	228.8	7.8	100.2	-	102.5	-	239.0	9.2
1999	158.5	2.7	158.3	2.5	148.3	1.8	135.5	-0.3	152.3	2.4	242.9	6.2	104.1	3.9	106.4	3.8	261.4	9.4
2000	164.4	3.7	163.9	3.5	153.5	3.5	130.3	-3.8	164.1	7.7	254.3	4.7	106.2	2.0	107.6	1.1	269.0	2.9
2001	168.9	2.7	168.6	2.9	157.7	2.7	128.0	-1.8	-	-	269.4	5.9	106.4	0.2	108.9	1.2	278.8	3.6

Source: U.S. Department of Labor, Bureau of Labor Statistics, Division of Consumer Prices and Price Indexes. *Base is December 1997 = 100. - indicates no data collected for period.

Detroit-Ann Arbor-Flint, MI
Consumer Price Index - All Urban Consumers
Base 1982-1984 = 100
All Items

For 1914-2001. Columns headed % show percentile change in the index from the previous period for which an index is available.

Year	Jan Index	%	Feb Index	%	Mar Index	%	Apr Index	%	May Index	%	Jun Index	%	Jul Index	%	Aug Index	%	Sep Index	%	Oct Index	%	Nov Index	%	Dec Index	%
1914	-	-	-	-	-	-	-	-	-	-	-	-	-	-	-	-	-	-	-	-	-	-	9.7	-
1915	-	-	-	-	-	-	-	-	-	-	-	-	-	-	-	-	-	-	-	-	-	-	10.1	4.1
1916	-	-	-	-	-	-	-	-	-	-	-	-	-	-	-	-	-	-	-	-	-	-	11.7	15.8
1917	-	-	-	-	-	-	-	-	-	-	-	-	-	-	-	-	-	-	-	-	-	-	14.3	22.2
1918	-	-	-	-	-	-	-	-	-	-	-	-	-	-	-	-	-	-	-	-	-	-	17.0	18.9
1919	-	-	-	-	-	-	-	-	-	-	17.8	4.7	-	-	-	-	-	-	-	-	-	-	19.9	11.8
1920	-	-	-	-	-	-	-	-	-	-	22.9	15.1	-	-	-	-	-	-	-	-	-	-	21.2	-7.4
1921	-	-	-	-	-	-	-	-	19.0	-10.4	-	-	-	-	-	-	18.5	-2.6	-	-	-	-	17.9	-3.2
1922	-	-	-	-	17.3	-3.4	-	-	-	-	17.4	0.6	-	-	-	-	17.3	-0.6	-	-	-	-	17.5	1.2
1923	-	-	-	-	17.7	1.1	-	-	-	-	18.0	1.7	-	-	-	-	18.4	2.2	-	-	-	-	18.2	-1.1
1924	-	-	-	-	18.1	-0.5	-	-	-	-	18.1	0.0	-	-	-	-	17.9	-1.1	-	-	-	-	17.9	0.0
1925	-	-	-	-	-	-	-	-	-	-	18.3	2.2	-	-	-	-	-	-	-	-	-	-	18.6	1.6
1926	-	-	-	-	-	-	-	-	-	-	18.4	-1.1	-	-	-	-	-	-	-	-	-	-	18.2	-1.1
1927	-	-	-	-	-	-	-	-	-	-	18.2	0.0	-	-	-	-	-	-	-	-	-	-	17.7	-2.7
1928	-	-	-	-	-	-	-	-	-	-	17.4	-1.7	-	-	-	-	-	-	-	-	-	-	17.4	0.0
1929	-	-	-	-	-	-	-	-	-	-	17.6	1.1	-	-	-	-	-	-	-	-	-	-	17.5	-0.6
1930	-	-	-	-	-	-	-	-	-	-	17.2	-1.7	-	-	-	-	-	-	-	-	-	-	15.9	-7.6
1931	-	-	-	-	-	-	-	-	-	-	14.8	-6.9	-	-	-	-	-	-	-	-	-	-	13.9	-6.1
1932	-	-	-	-	-	-	-	-	-	-	12.9	-7.2	-	-	-	-	-	-	-	-	-	-	12.1	-6.2
1933	-	-	-	-	-	-	-	-	-	-	11.7	-3.3	-	-	-	-	-	-	-	-	-	-	12.3	5.1
1934	-	-	-	-	-	-	-	-	-	-	12.8	4.1	-	-	-	-	-	-	-	-	12.8	0.0	-	-
1935	-	-	-	-	13.3	3.9	-	-	-	-	-	-	13.4	0.8	-	-	-	-	13.4	0.0	-	-	-	-
1936	13.6	1.5	-	-	-	-	13.6	0.0	-	-	-	-	14.0	2.9	-	-	14.1	0.7	-	-	-	-	14.0	-0.7
1937	-	-	-	-	14.4	2.9	-	-	-	-	14.8	2.8	-	-	-	-	14.9	0.7	-	-	-	-	15.0	0.7
1938	-	-	-	-	14.6	-2.7	-	-	-	-	14.5	-0.7	-	-	-	-	14.3	-1.4	-	-	-	-	14.2	-0.7
1939	-	-	-	-	14.0	-1.4	-	-	-	-	13.9	-0.7	-	-	-	-	14.1	1.4	-	-	-	-	14.0	-0.7
1940	-	-	-	-	14.1	0.7	-	-	-	-	14.2	0.7	-	-	-	-	14.1	-0.7	14.1	0.0	14.1	0.0	14.2	0.7
1941	14.2	0.0	14.3	0.7	14.4	0.7	14.6	1.4	14.6	0.0	15.0	2.7	15.0	0.0	15.1	0.7	15.4	2.0	15.7	1.9	15.8	0.6	15.9	0.6
1942	16.1	1.3	16.2	0.6	16.5	1.9	16.7	1.2	16.7	0.0	16.7	0.0	16.7	0.0	16.6	-0.6	16.7	0.6	16.9	1.2	17.0	0.6	17.1	0.6
1943	17.1	0.0	17.2	0.6	17.5	1.7	17.6	0.6	17.9	1.7	17.9	0.0	17.8	-0.6	17.5	-1.7	17.5	0.0	17.6	0.6	17.5	-0.6	17.7	1.1
1944	17.6	-0.6	17.5	-0.6	17.5	0.0	17.7	1.1	17.7	0.0	17.8	0.6	18.0	1.1	18.0	0.0	18.0	0.0	17.9	-0.6	17.9	0.0	18.0	0.6
1945	18.0	0.0	18.0	0.0	18.0	0.0	18.0	0.0	18.2	1.1	18.4	1.1	18.4	0.0	18.5	0.5	18.4	-0.5	18.4	0.0	18.5	0.5	18.5	0.0
1946	18.6	0.5	18.6	0.0	18.6	0.0	18.8	1.1	19.0	1.1	19.2	1.1	20.4	6.2	20.5	0.5	20.7	1.0	21.0	1.4	21.4	1.9	21.6	0.9
1947	21.6	0.0	21.6	0.0	22.1	2.3	22.1	0.0	22.1	0.0	22.4	1.4	22.6	0.9	23.0	1.8	23.2	0.9	23.6	1.7	23.5	-0.4	23.9	1.7
1948	24.1	0.8	23.9	-0.8	23.8	-0.4	24.3	2.1	24.5	0.8	24.7	0.8	24.9	0.8	24.9	0.0	24.8	-0.4	24.7	-0.4	24.5	-0.8	24.5	0.0
1949	24.3	-0.8	24.2	-0.4	24.2	0.0	24.2	0.0	24.3	0.4	24.3	0.0	24.1	-0.8	24.1	0.0	24.1	0.0	23.9	-0.8	24.1	0.8	24.0	-0.4
1950	23.9	-0.4	23.8	-0.4	24.0	0.8	24.0	0.0	24.2	0.8	24.4	0.8	24.6	0.8	24.7	0.4	25.0	1.2	25.2	0.8	25.3	0.4	25.5	0.8
1951	25.9	1.6	26.2	1.2	26.3	0.4	26.3	0.0	26.3	0.0	26.5	0.8	26.5	0.0	26.5	0.0	26.6	0.4	26.7	0.4	26.9	0.7	27.0	0.4
1952	27.0	0.0	26.8	-0.7	26.8	0.0	27.0	0.7	27.0	0.0	27.0	0.0	27.2	0.7	27.3	0.4	27.2	-0.4	27.4	0.7	27.4	0.0	27.6	0.7
1953	27.5	-0.4	27.3	-0.7	27.4	0.4	27.4	0.0	27.5	0.4	27.7	0.7	27.8	0.4	27.8	0.0	27.8	0.0	27.9	0.4	27.7	-0.7	27.7	0.0
1954	27.8	0.4	27.7	-0.4	27.7	0.0	27.7	0.0	27.8	0.4	27.8	0.0	27.9	0.4	27.7	-0.7	27.6	-0.4	27.6	0.0	27.8	0.7	27.6	-0.7
1955	27.6	0.0	27.6	0.0	27.6	0.0	27.6	0.0	27.7	0.4	27.7	0.0	27.7	0.0	27.7	0.0	27.8	0.4	27.7	-0.4	27.7	0.0	27.7	0.0
1956	27.6	-0.4	27.7	0.4	27.8	0.4	27.9	0.4	28.0	0.4	28.2	0.7	28.6	1.4	28.4	-0.7	28.4	0.0	28.5	0.4	28.6	0.4	28.6	0.0
1957	28.6	0.0	28.7	0.3	28.7	0.0	28.8	0.3	29.0	0.7	29.1	0.3	29.2	0.3	29.2	0.0	29.2	0.0	29.1	-0.3	29.3	0.7	29.3	0.0
1958	29.4	0.3	29.4	0.0	29.5	0.3	29.5	0.0	29.5	0.0	29.5	0.0	29.5	0.0	29.4	-0.3	29.4	0.0	29.3	-0.3	29.3	0.0	29.3	0.0
1959	29.3	0.0	29.3	0.0	29.2	-0.3	29.3	0.3	29.3	0.0	29.3	0.0	29.5	0.7	29.4	-0.3	29.6	0.7	29.7	0.3	29.5	-0.7	29.5	0.0

[Continued]

Detroit-Ann Arbor-Flint, MI
Consumer Price Index - All Urban Consumers
Base 1982-1984 = 100
All Items
[Continued]

For 1914-2001. Columns headed % show percentile change in the index from the previous period for which an index is available.

Year	Jan Index	%	Feb Index	%	Mar Index	%	Apr Index	%	May Index	%	Jun Index	%	Jul Index	%	Aug Index	%	Sep Index	%	Oct Index	%	Nov Index	%	Dec Index	%
1960	29.3	-0.7	29.4	0.3	29.4	0.0	29.5	0.3	29.5	0.0	29.7	0.7	29.9	0.7	29.8	-0.3	29.8	0.0	29.8	0.0	29.8	0.0	29.9	0.3
1961	30.0	0.3	30.0	0.0	29.9	-0.3	29.8	-0.3	29.8	0.0	29.9	0.3	29.8	-0.3	29.9	0.3	29.7	-0.7	29.8	0.3	29.7	-0.3	29.5	-0.7
1962	29.6	0.3	29.9	1.0	29.9	0.0	29.9	0.0	29.9	0.0	29.8	-0.3	29.8	0.0	29.9	0.3	30.1	0.7	30.1	0.0	30.0	-0.3	30.0	0.0
1963	30.0	0.0	30.0	0.0	30.0	0.0	29.9	-0.3	30.0	0.3	30.3	1.0	30.4	0.3	30.6	0.7	30.2	-1.3	30.3	0.3	30.4	0.3	30.3	-0.3
1964	30.4	0.3	30.2	-0.7	30.3	0.3	30.4	0.3	30.2	-0.7	30.3	0.3	30.5	0.7	30.5	0.0	30.6	0.3	30.7	0.3	30.6	-0.3	30.7	0.3
1965	30.7	0.0	30.6	-0.3	30.7	0.3	30.9	0.7	31.1	0.6	31.3	0.6	31.3	0.0	31.3	0.0	31.3	0.0	31.5	0.6	31.5	0.0	31.6	0.3
1966	31.7	0.3	31.9	0.6	32.1	0.6	32.3	0.6	32.4	0.3	32.6	0.6	32.6	0.0	32.8	0.6	32.8	0.0	33.0	0.6	33.0	0.0	33.2	0.6
1967	33.2	0.0	33.2	0.0	33.5	0.9	33.5	0.0	33.5	0.0	33.6	0.3	33.7	0.3	33.7	0.0	33.7	0.0	33.8	0.3	34.0	0.6	34.1	0.3
1968	34.1	0.0	34.3	0.6	34.6	0.9	34.7	0.3	34.8	0.3	35.1	0.9	35.2	0.3	35.3	0.3	35.5	0.6	35.6	0.3	35.8	0.6	35.9	0.3
1969	36.0	0.3	36.1	0.3	36.6	1.4	36.8	0.5	37.0	0.5	37.3	0.8	37.4	0.3	37.6	0.5	37.6	0.0	37.8	0.5	38.0	0.5	38.3	0.8
1970	38.4	0.3	38.7	0.8	39.0	0.8	39.2	0.5	39.5	0.8	39.6	0.3	39.7	0.3	39.6	-0.3	39.8	0.5	40.1	0.8	40.3	0.5	40.2	-0.2
1971	40.5	0.7	40.4	-0.2	40.4	0.0	40.4	0.0	40.7	0.7	41.0	0.7	41.0	0.0	41.3	0.7	41.3	0.0	41.3	0.0	41.5	0.5	41.6	0.2
1972	41.8	0.5	42.0	0.5	42.1	0.2	42.1	0.0	42.2	0.2	42.4	0.5	42.6	0.5	42.7	0.2	42.8	0.2	42.8	0.0	42.9	0.2	43.2	0.7
1973	43.2	0.0	43.6	0.9	44.1	1.1	44.5	0.9	44.9	0.9	45.0	0.2	45.0	0.0	46.0	2.2	46.2	0.4	46.4	0.4	46.8	0.9	47.1	0.6
1974	47.6	1.1	48.4	1.7	48.7	0.6	48.9	0.4	49.3	0.8	49.9	1.2	50.3	0.8	50.8	1.0	51.3	1.0	51.7	0.8	52.2	1.0	52.5	0.6
1975	52.3	-0.4	52.7	0.8	52.8	0.2	53.1	0.6	53.2	0.2	53.7	0.9	54.1	0.7	54.3	0.4	54.8	0.9	54.9	0.2	55.1	0.4	55.4	0.5
1976	55.7	0.5	55.8	0.2	55.7	-0.2	56.0	0.5	56.3	0.5	56.5	0.4	56.9	0.7	57.1	0.4	57.6	0.9	57.7	0.2	58.0	0.5	58.2	0.3
1977	58.5	0.5	58.9	0.7	59.5	1.0	60.2	1.2	60.3	0.2	60.9	1.0	61.4	0.8	61.4	0.0	61.5	0.2	61.6	0.2	62.1	0.8	62.0	-0.2
1978	62.2	0.3	62.4	0.3	63.4	1.6	64.0	0.9	64.7	1.1	65.4	1.1	65.5	0.2	65.9	0.6	66.5	0.9	67.6	1.7	68.0	0.6	68.0	0.0
1979	69.0	1.5	70.2	1.7	71.2	1.4	71.7	0.7	72.0	0.4	72.5	0.7	73.8	1.8	74.8	1.4	75.3	0.7	76.4	1.5	77.8	1.8	78.5	0.9
1980	79.8	1.7	80.9	1.4	81.7	1.0	83.5	2.2	83.6	0.1	86.4	3.3	85.4	-1.2	85.8	0.5	87.3	1.7	88.9	1.8	89.6	0.8	90.7	1.2
1981	90.3	-0.4	90.9	0.7	90.2	-0.8	91.6	1.6	92.6	1.1	94.4	1.9	95.2	0.8	95.4	0.2	95.6	0.2	94.7	-0.9	94.1	-0.6	93.6	-0.5
1982	94.5	1.0	93.5	-1.1	93.6	0.1	95.4	1.9	96.2	0.8	97.3	1.1	98.4	1.1	98.5	0.1	99.2	0.7	99.3	0.1	99.6	0.3	98.4	-1.2
1983	98.4	0.0	98.3	-0.1	98.4	0.1	99.2	0.8	99.2	0.0	99.8	0.6	100.4	0.6	100.5	0.1	100.7	0.2	100.3	-0.4	100.9	0.6	101.0	0.1
1984	101.4	0.4	102.0	0.6	102.3	0.3	102.8	0.5	102.8	0.0	103.0	0.2	103.5	0.5	103.6	0.1	104.8	1.2	104.9	0.1	103.9	-1.0	104.0	0.1
1985	104.6	0.6	105.5	0.9	106.1	0.6	106.2	0.1	106.3	0.1	106.6	0.3	107.0	0.4	107.0	0.0	107.8	0.7	107.6	-0.2	108.7	1.0	108.7	0.0
1986	108.7	0.0	108.6	-0.1	107.7	-0.8	107.3	-0.4	108.2	0.8	108.0	-0.2	107.1	-0.8	108.7	1.5	108.0	-0.6	109.1	1.0	109.4	0.3	109.2	-0.2
1987	-	-	110.2	0.9	-	-	111.2	0.9	-	-	111.1	-0.1	-	-	112.2	1.0	-	-	114.1	1.7	-	-	112.6	-1.3
1988	-	-	113.7	1.0	-	-	114.4	0.6	-	-	115.4	0.9	-	-	117.6	1.9	-	-	118.6	0.9	-	-	118.3	-0.3
1989	-	-	120.1	1.5	-	-	121.7	1.3	-	-	122.1	0.3	-	-	122.2	0.1	-	-	124.6	2.0	-	-	124.4	-0.2
1990	-	-	126.1	1.4	-	-	126.9	0.6	-	-	127.7	0.6	-	-	129.4	1.3	-	-	131.8	1.9	-	-	131.2	-0.5
1991	-	-	132.2	0.8	-	-	131.7	-0.4	-	-	133.5	1.4	-	-	133.2	-0.2	-	-	134.6	1.1	-	-	134.0	-0.4
1992	-	-	134.9	0.7	-	-	135.3	0.3	-	-	135.5	0.1	-	-	135.8	0.2	-	-	137.5	1.3	-	-	137.1	-0.3
1993	-	-	138.3	0.9	-	-	138.7	0.3	-	-	139.1	0.3	-	-	139.9	0.6	-	-	141.9	1.4	-	-	140.2	-1.2
1994	-	-	141.7	1.1	-	-	142.6	0.6	-	-	144.8	1.5	-	-	145.3	0.3	-	-	145.7	0.3	-	-	145.5	-0.1
1995	-	-	147.3	1.2	-	-	148.1	0.5	-	-	148.3	0.1	-	-	148.8	0.3	-	-	149.8	0.7	-	-	150.3	0.3
1996	-	-	151.3	0.7	-	-	152.3	0.7	-	-	151.9	-0.3	-	-	152.7	0.5	-	-	153.8	0.7	-	-	154.3	0.3
1997	-	-	155.4	0.7	-	-	156.0	0.4	-	-	155.0	-0.6	-	-	156.9	1.2	-	-	157.9	0.6	-	-	157.1	-0.5
1998	-	-	158.5	0.9	-	-	159.1	0.4	-	-	159.4	0.2	-	-	160.5	0.7	-	-	161.0	0.3	-	-	161.2	0.1
1999	-	-	161.2	0.0	-	-	164.1	1.8	-	-	163.8	-0.2	-	-	164.2	0.2	-	-	165.9	1.0	-	-	165.6	-0.2
2000	-	-	167.3	1.0	-	-	168.3	0.6	-	-	170.9	1.5	-	-	170.1	-0.5	-	-	171.9	1.1	-	-	171.7	-0.1
2001	-	-	173.2	0.9	-	-	174.5	0.8	-	-	175.8	0.7	-	-	175.1	-0.4	-	-	174.8	-0.2	-	-	173.5	-0.7

Source: U.S. Department of Labor, Bureau of Labor Statistics, Division of Consumer Prices and Price Indexes. - indicates no data collected for period.

Detroit-Ann Arbor-Flint, MI
Consumer Price Index - Urban Wage Earners
Base 1982-1984 = 100
All Items

For 1914-2001. Columns headed % show percentile change in the index from the previous period for which an index is available.

Year	Jan Index	%	Feb Index	%	Mar Index	%	Apr Index	%	May Index	%	Jun Index	%	Jul Index	%	Aug Index	%	Sep Index	%	Oct Index	%	Nov Index	%	Dec Index	%
1914	-	-	-	-	-	-	-	-	-	-	-	-	-	-	-	-	-	-	-	-	-	-	9.8	-
1915	-	-	-	-	-	-	-	-	-	-	-	-	-	-	-	-	-	-	-	-	-	-	10.2	4.1
1916	-	-	-	-	-	-	-	-	-	-	-	-	-	-	-	-	-	-	-	-	-	-	11.8	15.7
1917	-	-	-	-	-	-	-	-	-	-	-	-	-	-	-	-	-	-	-	-	-	-	14.4	22.0
1918	-	-	-	-	-	-	-	-	-	-	-	-	-	-	-	-	-	-	-	-	-	-	17.2	19.4
1919	-	-	-	-	-	-	-	-	-	-	17.9	4.1	-	-	-	-	-	-	-	-	-	-	20.1	12.3
1920	-	-	-	-	-	-	-	-	-	-	23.2	15.4	-	-	-	-	-	-	-	-	-	-	21.4	-7.8
1921	-	-	-	-	-	-	-	-	19.2	-10.3	-	-	-	-	-	-	18.6	-3.1	-	-	-	-	18.1	-2.7
1922	-	-	-	-	17.5	-3.3	-	-	-	-	17.6	0.6	-	-	-	-	17.5	-0.6	-	-	-	-	17.7	1.1
1923	-	-	-	-	17.9	1.1	-	-	-	-	18.2	1.7	-	-	-	-	18.5	1.6	-	-	-	-	18.4	-0.5
1924	-	-	-	-	18.3	-0.5	-	-	-	-	18.3	0.0	-	-	-	-	18.1	-1.1	-	-	-	-	18.1	0.0
1925	-	-	-	-	-	-	-	-	-	-	18.4	1.7	-	-	-	-	-	-	-	-	-	-	18.8	2.2
1926	-	-	-	-	-	-	-	-	-	-	18.6	-1.1	-	-	-	-	-	-	-	-	-	-	18.3	-1.6
1927	-	-	-	-	-	-	-	-	-	-	18.4	0.5	-	-	-	-	-	-	-	-	-	-	17.8	-3.3
1928	-	-	-	-	-	-	-	-	-	-	17.6	-1.1	-	-	-	-	-	-	-	-	-	-	17.6	0.0
1929	-	-	-	-	-	-	-	-	-	-	17.8	1.1	-	-	-	-	-	-	-	-	-	-	17.7	-0.6
1930	-	-	-	-	-	-	-	-	-	-	17.3	-2.3	-	-	-	-	-	-	-	-	-	-	16.1	-6.9
1931	-	-	-	-	-	-	-	-	-	-	14.9	-7.5	-	-	-	-	-	-	-	-	-	-	14.0	-6.0
1932	-	-	-	-	-	-	-	-	-	-	13.0	-7.1	-	-	-	-	-	-	-	-	-	-	12.2	-6.2
1933	-	-	-	-	-	-	-	-	-	-	11.8	-3.3	-	-	-	-	-	-	-	-	-	-	12.4	5.1
1934	-	-	-	-	-	-	-	-	-	-	12.9	4.0	-	-	-	-	-	-	-	-	12.9	0.0	-	-
1935	-	-	-	-	13.4	3.9	-	-	-	-	-	-	13.5	0.7	-	-	-	-	13.5	0.0	-	-	-	-
1936	13.7	1.5	-	-	-	-	13.7	0.0	-	-	-	-	14.1	2.9	-	-	14.2	0.7	-	-	-	-	14.1	-0.7
1937	-	-	-	-	14.6	3.5	-	-	-	-	14.9	2.1	-	-	-	-	15.1	1.3	-	-	-	-	15.1	0.0
1938	-	-	-	-	14.8	-2.0	-	-	-	-	14.6	-1.4	-	-	-	-	14.4	-1.4	-	-	-	-	14.3	-0.7
1939	-	-	-	-	14.2	-0.7	-	-	-	-	14.1	-0.7	-	-	-	-	14.2	0.7	-	-	-	-	14.2	0.0
1940	-	-	-	-	14.2	0.0	-	-	-	-	14.3	0.7	-	-	-	-	14.3	0.0	14.3	0.0	14.3	0.0	14.3	0.0
1941	14.4	0.7	14.4	0.0	14.5	0.7	14.7	1.4	14.7	0.0	15.1	2.7	15.2	0.7	15.3	0.7	15.6	2.0	15.9	1.9	16.0	0.6	16.0	0.0
1942	16.3	1.9	16.4	0.6	16.6	1.2	16.8	1.2	16.9	0.6	16.8	-0.6	16.8	0.0	16.8	0.0	16.8	0.0	17.0	1.2	17.1	0.6	17.2	0.6
1943	17.2	0.0	17.4	1.2	17.6	1.1	17.8	1.1	18.1	1.7	18.0	-0.6	17.9	-0.6	17.7	-1.1	17.7	0.0	17.8	0.6	17.7	-0.6	17.8	0.6
1944	17.8	0.0	17.7	-0.6	17.7	0.0	17.8	0.6	17.9	0.6	18.0	0.6	18.2	1.1	18.1	-0.5	18.1	0.0	18.1	0.0	18.1	0.0	18.1	0.0
1945	18.1	0.0	18.1	0.0	18.1	0.0	18.2	0.6	18.4	1.1	18.6	1.1	18.6	0.0	18.7	0.5	18.6	-0.5	18.6	0.0	18.6	0.0	18.7	0.5
1946	18.8	0.5	18.8	0.0	18.8	0.0	19.0	1.1	19.1	0.5	19.4	1.6	20.5	5.7	20.7	1.0	20.8	0.5	21.2	1.9	21.6	1.9	21.8	0.9
1947	21.8	0.0	21.8	0.0	22.3	2.3	22.3	0.0	22.3	0.0	22.6	1.3	22.9	1.3	23.2	1.3	23.4	0.9	23.8	1.7	23.8	0.0	24.1	1.3
1948	24.3	0.8	24.1	-0.8	24.0	-0.4	24.5	2.1	24.7	0.8	24.9	0.8	25.1	0.8	25.1	0.0	25.0	-0.4	24.9	-0.4	24.7	-0.8	24.7	0.0
1949	24.5	-0.8	24.4	-0.4	24.4	0.0	24.4	0.0	24.5	0.4	24.5	0.0	24.3	-0.8	24.3	0.0	24.3	0.0	24.1	-0.8	24.3	0.8	24.2	-0.4
1950	24.1	-0.4	24.0	-0.4	24.2	0.8	24.2	0.0	24.4	0.8	24.7	1.2	24.9	0.8	25.0	0.4	25.2	0.8	25.4	0.8	25.5	0.4	25.7	0.8
1951	26.1	1.6	26.4	1.1	26.6	0.8	26.5	-0.4	26.6	0.4	26.8	0.8	26.8	0.0	26.8	0.0	26.8	0.0	27.0	0.7	27.2	0.7	27.2	0.0
1952	27.2	0.0	27.1	-0.4	27.1	0.0	27.2	0.4	27.2	0.0	27.3	0.4	27.5	0.7	27.6	0.4	27.5	-0.4	27.7	0.7	27.6	-0.4	27.8	0.7
1953	27.7	-0.4	27.6	-0.4	27.6	0.0	27.6	0.0	27.7	0.4	27.9	0.7	28.0	0.4	28.0	0.0	28.0	0.0	28.1	0.4	27.9	-0.7	27.9	0.0
1954	28.0	0.4	27.9	-0.4	27.9	0.0	27.9	0.0	28.0	0.4	28.1	0.4	28.1	0.0	28.0	-0.4	27.8	-0.7	27.8	0.0	28.0	0.7	27.8	-0.7
1955	27.8	0.0	27.9	0.4	27.9	0.0	27.8	-0.4	27.9	0.4	27.9	0.0	28.0	0.4	27.9	-0.4	28.0	0.4	27.9	-0.4	28.0	0.4	27.9	-0.4
1956	27.9	0.0	27.9	0.0	28.0	0.4	28.1	0.4	28.3	0.7	28.5	0.7	28.8	1.1	28.7	-0.3	28.7	0.0	28.8	0.3	28.9	0.3	28.8	-0.3
1957	28.9	0.3	29.0	0.3	29.0	0.0	29.1	0.3	29.2	0.3	29.4	0.7	29.5	0.3	29.5	0.0	29.4	-0.3	29.4	0.0	29.6	0.7	29.5	-0.3
1958	29.6	0.3	29.6	0.0	29.7	0.3	29.8	0.3	29.8	0.0	29.7	-0.3	29.8	0.3	29.6	-0.7	29.7	0.3	29.5	-0.7	29.6	0.3	29.5	-0.3
1959	29.5	0.0	29.5	0.0	29.5	0.0	29.6	0.3	29.6	0.0	29.6	0.0	29.8	0.7	29.6	-0.7	29.9	1.0	29.9	0.0	29.7	-0.7	29.7	0.0

[Continued]

Detroit-Ann Arbor-Flint, MI
Consumer Price Index - Urban Wage Earners
Base 1982-1984 = 100
All Items
[Continued]

For 1914-2001. Columns headed % show percentile change in the index from the previous period for which an index is available.

Year	Jan Index	%	Feb Index	%	Mar Index	%	Apr Index	%	May Index	%	Jun Index	%	Jul Index	%	Aug Index	%	Sep Index	%	Oct Index	%	Nov Index	%	Dec Index	%
1960	29.6	-0.3	29.7	0.3	29.7	0.0	29.7	0.0	29.8	0.3	30.0	0.7	30.2	0.7	30.1	-0.3	30.0	-0.3	30.1	0.3	30.1	0.0	30.2	0.3
1961	30.3	0.3	30.3	0.0	30.2	-0.3	30.1	-0.3	30.1	0.0	30.2	0.3	30.1	-0.3	30.2	0.3	29.9	-1.0	30.0	0.3	30.0	0.0	29.8	-0.7
1962	29.9	0.3	30.2	1.0	30.2	0.0	30.2	0.0	30.2	0.0	30.1	-0.3	30.1	0.0	30.2	0.3	30.4	0.7	30.4	0.0	30.3	-0.3	30.3	0.0
1963	30.3	0.0	30.3	0.0	30.3	0.0	30.2	-0.3	30.3	0.3	30.6	1.0	30.7	0.3	30.9	0.7	30.5	-1.3	30.6	0.3	30.7	0.3	30.6	-0.3
1964	30.7	0.3	30.5	-0.7	30.6	0.3	30.7	0.3	30.5	-0.7	30.6	0.3	30.8	0.7	30.8	0.0	30.9	0.3	31.0	0.3	30.9	-0.3	31.0	0.3
1965	31.0	0.0	30.9	-0.3	31.0	0.3	31.2	0.6	31.3	0.3	31.6	1.0	31.6	0.0	31.6	0.0	31.6	0.0	31.7	0.3	31.8	0.3	31.9	0.3
1966	32.0	0.3	32.2	0.6	32.4	0.6	32.6	0.6	32.7	0.3	32.9	0.6	32.9	0.0	33.1	0.6	33.1	0.0	33.3	0.6	33.3	0.0	33.5	0.6
1967	33.5	0.0	33.5	0.0	33.8	0.9	33.9	0.3	33.9	0.0	33.9	0.0	34.0	0.3	34.1	0.3	34.1	0.0	34.1	0.0	34.3	0.6	34.4	0.3
1968	34.5	0.3	34.7	0.6	34.9	0.6	35.0	0.3	35.1	0.3	35.4	0.9	35.5	0.3	35.7	0.6	35.8	0.3	36.0	0.6	36.1	0.3	36.2	0.3
1969	36.3	0.3	36.5	0.6	37.0	1.4	37.1	0.3	37.3	0.5	37.6	0.8	37.7	0.3	38.0	0.8	38.0	0.0	38.2	0.5	38.4	0.5	38.6	0.5
1970	38.7	0.3	39.1	1.0	39.3	0.5	39.5	0.5	39.9	1.0	40.0	0.3	40.0	0.0	40.0	0.0	40.2	0.5	40.5	0.7	40.7	0.5	40.6	-0.2
1971	40.8	0.5	40.7	-0.2	40.8	0.2	40.8	0.0	41.0	0.5	41.4	1.0	41.4	0.0	41.7	0.7	41.7	0.0	41.7	0.0	41.9	0.5	42.0	0.2
1972	42.2	0.5	42.4	0.5	42.4	0.0	42.4	0.0	42.6	0.5	42.8	0.5	43.0	0.5	43.1	0.2	43.2	0.2	43.2	0.0	43.3	0.2	43.6	0.7
1973	43.6	0.0	44.0	0.9	44.5	1.1	45.0	1.1	45.3	0.7	45.4	0.2	45.4	0.0	46.4	2.2	46.6	0.4	46.8	0.4	47.2	0.9	47.5	0.6
1974	48.0	1.1	48.8	1.7	49.2	0.8	49.4	0.4	49.7	0.6	50.4	1.4	50.7	0.6	51.2	1.0	51.7	1.0	52.2	1.0	52.7	1.0	53.0	0.6
1975	52.8	-0.4	53.1	0.6	53.3	0.4	53.5	0.4	53.7	0.4	54.2	0.9	54.6	0.7	54.8	0.4	55.3	0.9	55.4	0.2	55.6	0.4	55.9	0.5
1976	56.3	0.7	56.3	0.0	56.2	-0.2	56.5	0.5	56.8	0.5	57.0	0.4	57.4	0.7	57.6	0.3	58.2	1.0	58.2	0.0	58.6	0.7	58.8	0.3
1977	59.0	0.3	59.5	0.8	60.0	0.8	60.8	1.3	60.9	0.2	61.5	1.0	62.0	0.8	62.0	0.0	62.1	0.2	62.2	0.2	62.6	0.6	62.6	0.0
1978	62.8	0.3	63.1	0.5	63.8	1.1	64.4	0.9	65.2	1.2	66.1	1.4	66.1	0.0	66.6	0.8	67.3	1.1	68.1	1.2	68.5	0.6	68.6	0.1
1979	69.6	1.5	70.9	1.9	71.8	1.3	72.4	0.8	72.7	0.4	73.2	0.7	74.6	1.9	75.6	1.3	75.9	0.4	77.0	1.4	78.4	1.8	78.8	0.5
1980	80.3	1.9	81.5	1.5	82.3	1.0	84.2	2.3	84.5	0.4	86.9	2.8	85.6	-1.5	86.2	0.7	87.5	1.5	88.8	1.5	89.5	0.8	90.1	0.7
1981	89.8	-0.3	90.1	0.3	89.5	-0.7	91.0	1.7	92.1	1.2	93.7	1.7	94.7	1.1	94.8	0.1	95.1	0.3	94.5	-0.6	93.8	-0.7	93.4	-0.4
1982	94.3	1.0	93.3	-1.1	93.4	0.1	95.2	1.9	96.0	0.8	97.1	1.1	98.2	1.1	98.2	0.0	98.9	0.7	98.9	0.0	99.2	0.3	98.0	-1.2
1983	97.8	-0.2	97.5	-0.3	98.4	0.9	100.2	1.8	101.5	1.3	102.1	0.6	103.2	1.1	103.1	-0.1	103.4	0.3	101.5	-1.8	102.5	1.0	102.3	-0.2
1984	104.5	2.2	103.5	-1.0	102.8	-0.7	101.4	-1.4	101.3	-0.1	100.8	-0.5	101.3	0.5	101.5	0.2	102.3	0.8	102.8	0.5	101.8	-1.0	101.9	0.1
1985	102.3	0.4	103.2	0.9	103.9	0.7	104.0	0.1	104.1	0.1	104.4	0.3	104.7	0.3	104.7	0.0	105.4	0.7	105.2	-0.2	106.3	1.0	106.3	0.0
1986	106.4	0.1	106.0	-0.4	105.0	-0.9	104.6	-0.4	105.6	1.0	105.3	-0.3	104.4	-0.9	106.2	1.7	105.4	-0.8	106.5	1.0	106.9	0.4	106.6	-0.3
1987	-		107.5	0.8	-		108.6	1.0	-		108.6	0.0	-		109.6	0.9	-		111.3	1.6	-		109.8	-1.3
1988	-		110.9	1.0	-		111.9	0.9	-		112.7	0.7	-		114.6	1.7	-		115.6	0.9	-		115.7	0.1
1989	-		117.3	1.4	-		119.0	1.4	-		119.3	0.3	-		119.2	-0.1	-		121.5	1.9	-		121.4	-0.1
1990	-		123.2	1.5	-		123.9	0.6	-		124.7	0.6	-		126.5	1.4	-		128.7	1.7	-		128.1	-0.5
1991	-		128.9	0.6	-		128.3	-0.5	-		130.1	1.4	-		130.2	0.1	-		131.1	0.7	-		130.6	-0.4
1992	-		131.3	0.5	-		131.7	0.3	-		131.8	0.1	-		132.0	0.2	-		133.5	1.1	-		133.1	-0.3
1993	-		134.4	1.0	-		134.6	0.1	-		135.1	0.4	-		135.7	0.4	-		137.5	1.3	-		135.7	-1.3
1994	-		137.0	1.0	-		137.9	0.7	-		140.2	1.7	-		141.0	0.6	-		141.1	0.1	-		141.0	-0.1
1995	-		142.7	1.2	-		143.6	0.6	-		143.7	0.1	-		144.0	0.2	-		145.0	0.7	-		145.5	0.3
1996	-		146.5	0.7	-		147.6	0.8	-		147.1	-0.3	-		148.0	0.6	-		148.8	0.5	-		149.4	0.4
1997	-		150.3	0.6	-		151.0	0.5	-		149.8	-0.8	-		151.6	1.2	-		152.4	0.5	-		151.7	-0.5
1998	-		152.9	0.8	-		153.5	0.4	-		154.0	0.3	-		155.1	0.7	-		155.7	0.4	-		155.9	0.1
1999	-		155.8	-0.1	-		158.7	1.9	-		158.3	-0.3	-		158.7	0.3	-		160.4	1.1	-		160.4	0.0
2000	-		162.1	1.1	-		163.0	0.6	-		165.8	1.7	-		164.6	-0.7	-		166.5	1.2	-		166.2	-0.2
2001	-		167.7	0.9	-		169.1	0.8	-		170.4	0.8	-		169.4	-0.6	-		169.1	-0.2	-		167.9	-0.7

Source: U.S. Department of Labor, Bureau of Labor Statistics, Division of Consumer Prices and Price Indexes. - indicates no data collected for period.

Detroit-Ann Arbor-Flint, MI
Consumer Price Index - All Urban Consumers
Base 1982-1984 = 100
Food and Beverages

For 1976-2001. Columns headed % show percentile change in the index from the previous period for which an index is available.

Year	Jan Index	%	Feb Index	%	Mar Index	%	Apr Index	%	May Index	%	Jun Index	%	Jul Index	%	Aug Index	%	Sep Index	%	Oct Index	%	Nov Index	%	Dec Index	%
1976	63.8	-	63.8	0.0	63.1	-1.1	63.5	0.6	63.9	0.6	63.9	0.0	64.3	0.6	64.0	-0.5	63.7	-0.5	63.6	-0.2	64.0	0.6	64.5	0.8
1977	64.8	0.5	65.9	1.7	65.8	-0.2	66.9	1.7	67.2	0.4	68.2	1.5	68.5	0.4	68.6	0.1	68.1	-0.7	68.4	0.4	69.2	1.2	69.2	0.0
1978	70.5	1.9	71.2	1.0	72.0	1.1	73.0	1.4	74.0	1.4	75.3	1.8	76.0	0.9	75.7	-0.4	75.9	0.3	76.2	0.4	76.8	0.8	77.6	1.0
1979	79.5	2.4	80.8	1.6	81.3	0.6	81.9	0.7	82.4	0.6	82.5	0.1	82.9	0.5	81.9	-1.2	82.4	0.6	82.9	0.6	83.3	0.5	84.2	1.1
1980	86.0	2.1	86.1	0.1	86.7	0.7	86.9	0.2	87.8	1.0	88.5	0.8	89.4	1.0	90.4	1.1	90.1	-0.3	90.6	0.6	92.1	1.7	92.8	0.8
1981	93.5	0.8	94.9	1.5	94.8	-0.1	95.1	0.3	95.3	0.2	95.4	0.1	96.1	0.7	96.1	0.0	96.6	0.5	96.7	0.1	97.3	0.6	97.4	0.1
1982	98.2	0.8	99.1	0.9	98.9	-0.2	99.1	0.2	99.3	0.2	100.1	0.8	100.2	0.1	99.5	-0.7	99.7	0.2	99.3	-0.4	99.6	0.3	99.2	-0.4
1983	99.7	0.5	100.1	0.4	100.8	0.7	100.7	-0.1	100.2	-0.5	99.9	-0.3	99.6	-0.3	99.3	-0.3	98.4	-0.9	97.1	-1.3	97.5	0.4	98.0	0.5
1984	100.2	2.2	101.1	0.9	101.1	0.0	102.1	1.0	101.6	-0.5	101.3	-0.3	102.1	0.8	101.9	-0.2	101.6	-0.3	101.0	-0.6	100.8	-0.2	101.8	1.0
1985	102.0	0.2	102.9	0.9	103.4	0.5	103.3	-0.1	103.1	-0.2	102.9	-0.2	103.1	0.2	102.5	-0.6	102.4	-0.1	103.3	0.9	104.3	1.0	104.8	0.5
1986	104.7	-0.1	105.3	0.6	105.8	0.5	105.7	-0.1	106.3	0.6	106.4	0.1	107.5	1.0	108.9	1.3	108.6	-0.3	109.3	0.6	109.5	0.2	109.2	-0.3
1987	-		109.7	0.5	-		109.4	-0.3	-		111.4	1.8	-		110.8	-0.5	-		111.5	0.6	-		110.9	-0.5
1988	-		112.3	1.3	-		113.0	0.6	-		114.4	1.2	-		115.5	1.0	-		116.9	1.2	-		117.8	0.8
1989	-		119.4	1.4	-		120.5	0.9	-		120.3	-0.2	-		121.2	0.7	-		121.5	0.2	-		123.0	1.2
1990	-		125.3	1.9	-		125.4	0.1	-		126.5	0.9	-		127.6	0.9	-		127.7	0.1	-		127.9	0.2
1991	-		129.0	0.9	-		130.3	1.0	-		131.6	1.0	-		131.6	0.0	-		132.6	0.8	-		133.0	0.3
1992	-		133.6	0.5	-		133.4	-0.1	-		132.9	-0.4	-		133.5	0.5	-		133.5	0.0	-		134.0	0.4
1993	-		134.1	0.1	-		134.2	0.1	-		135.1	0.7	-		135.8	0.5	-		136.8	0.7	-		136.1	-0.5
1994	-		136.4	0.2	-		136.9	0.4	-		138.9	1.5	-		140.1	0.9	-		139.7	-0.3	-		141.9	1.6
1995	-		142.8	0.6	-		143.1	0.2	-		143.5	0.3	-		143.9	0.3	-		144.2	0.2	-		144.9	0.5
1996	-		145.7	0.6	-		146.6	0.6	-		146.0	-0.4	-		149.2	2.2	-		150.4	0.8	-		151.2	0.5
1997	-		150.9	-0.2	-		151.0	0.1	-		151.2	0.1	-		151.9	0.5	-		151.8	-0.1	-		152.2	0.3
1998	-		153.3	0.7	-		153.9	0.4	-		153.8	-0.1	-		155.2	0.9	-		155.3	0.1	-		157.7	1.5
1999	-		156.7	-0.6	-		158.4	1.1	-		158.2	-0.1	-		157.4	-0.5	-		159.3	1.2	-		160.4	0.7
2000	-		161.4	0.6	-		162.6	0.7	-		163.9	0.8	-		164.4	0.3	-		165.6	0.7	-		167.2	1.0
2001	-		165.8	-0.8	-		167.0	0.7	-		169.7	1.6	-		168.9	-0.5	-		169.6	-0.4	-		170.6	0.6

Source: U.S. Department of Labor, Bureau of Labor Statistics, Division of Consumer Prices and Price Indexes. - indicates no data collected for period.

Detroit-Ann Arbor-Flint, MI
Consumer Price Index - Urban Wage Earners
Base 1982-1984 = 100
Food and Beverages

For 1976-2001. Columns headed % show percentile change in the index from the previous period for which an index is available.

Year	Jan Index	%	Feb Index	%	Mar Index	%	Apr Index	%	May Index	%	Jun Index	%	Jul Index	%	Aug Index	%	Sep Index	%	Oct Index	%	Nov Index	%	Dec Index	%
1976	63.2	-	63.1	-0.2	62.5	-1.0	62.9	0.6	63.2	0.5	63.2	0.0	63.6	0.6	63.4	-0.3	63.0	-0.6	62.9	-0.2	63.3	0.6	63.9	0.9
1977	64.2	0.5	65.2	1.6	65.2	0.0	66.2	1.5	66.6	0.6	67.5	1.4	67.8	0.4	67.9	0.1	67.4	-0.7	67.7	0.4	68.5	1.2	68.5	0.0
1978	70.0	2.2	70.8	1.1	71.4	0.8	72.5	1.5	73.5	1.4	75.2	2.3	76.0	1.1	75.9	-0.1	76.0	0.1	75.7	-0.4	76.5	1.1	77.3	1.0
1979	79.2	2.5	80.5	1.6	81.5	1.2	81.8	0.4	82.2	0.5	82.4	0.2	83.2	1.0	82.0	-1.4	82.4	0.5	83.0	0.7	83.3	0.4	84.3	1.2
1980	85.8	1.8	86.0	0.2	86.6	0.7	86.7	0.1	87.6	1.0	88.3	0.8	89.1	0.9	89.9	0.9	90.0	0.1	90.5	0.6	91.5	1.1	92.2	0.8
1981	92.9	0.8	94.2	1.4	94.3	0.1	95.1	0.8	95.3	0.2	95.6	0.3	96.4	0.8	96.3	-0.1	97.0	0.7	96.9	-0.1	97.4	0.5	97.3	-0.1
1982	98.3	1.0	99.0	0.7	98.9	-0.1	99.2	0.3	99.4	0.2	100.2	0.8	100.4	0.2	99.7	-0.7	99.9	0.2	99.4	-0.5	99.6	0.2	99.1	-0.5
1983	99.7	0.6	100.1	0.4	100.8	0.7	100.7	-0.1	100.2	-0.5	99.8	-0.4	99.5	-0.3	99.2	-0.3	98.3	-0.9	97.1	-1.2	97.4	0.3	97.9	0.5
1984	100.1	2.2	101.2	1.1	101.0	-0.2	102.1	1.1	101.5	-0.6	101.3	-0.2	102.0	0.7	102.1	0.1	101.7	-0.4	100.9	-0.8	100.6	-0.3	101.9	1.3
1985	101.8	-0.1	102.8	1.0	103.2	0.4	103.0	-0.2	102.9	-0.1	102.7	-0.2	102.9	0.2	102.2	-0.7	102.1	-0.1	102.9	0.8	104.0	1.1	104.5	0.5
1986	104.4	-0.1	104.7	0.3	105.5	0.8	105.3	-0.2	106.0	0.7	106.1	0.1	107.0	0.8	108.5	1.4	108.1	-0.4	109.0	0.8	109.1	0.1	109.0	-0.1
1987	-	-	109.5	0.5	-	-	109.1	-0.4	-	-	111.1	1.8	-	-	110.5	-0.5	-	-	111.2	0.6	-	-	110.4	-0.7
1988	-	-	112.0	1.4	-	-	112.5	0.4	-	-	113.9	1.2	-	-	115.0	1.0	-	-	116.4	1.2	-	-	117.3	0.8
1989	-	-	119.0	1.4	-	-	120.1	0.9	-	-	119.9	-0.2	-	-	120.8	0.8	-	-	121.0	0.2	-	-	122.7	1.4
1990	-	-	125.0	1.9	-	-	125.0	0.0	-	-	126.1	0.9	-	-	127.2	0.9	-	-	127.2	0.0	-	-	127.4	0.2
1991	-	-	128.6	0.9	-	-	129.9	1.0	-	-	131.2	1.0	-	-	131.1	-0.1	-	-	132.3	0.9	-	-	132.7	0.3
1992	-	-	133.3	0.5	-	-	133.0	-0.2	-	-	132.6	-0.3	-	-	133.1	0.4	-	-	133.0	-0.1	-	-	133.6	0.5
1993	-	-	133.7	0.1	-	-	133.8	0.1	-	-	134.7	0.7	-	-	135.3	0.4	-	-	136.4	0.8	-	-	135.7	-0.5
1994	-	-	136.0	0.2	-	-	136.5	0.4	-	-	138.6	1.5	-	-	139.9	0.9	-	-	139.5	-0.3	-	-	141.8	1.6
1995	-	-	142.5	0.5	-	-	142.8	0.2	-	-	143.2	0.3	-	-	143.6	0.3	-	-	144.0	0.3	-	-	144.8	0.6
1996	-	-	145.5	0.5	-	-	146.4	0.6	-	-	145.7	-0.5	-	-	149.0	2.3	-	-	149.9	0.6	-	-	151.0	0.7
1997	-	-	150.6	-0.3	-	-	150.6	0.0	-	-	150.9	0.2	-	-	151.6	0.5	-	-	151.5	-0.1	-	-	151.9	0.3
1998	-	-	153.3	0.9	-	-	153.8	0.3	-	-	153.7	-0.1	-	-	155.2	1.0	-	-	155.2	0.0	-	-	157.4	1.4
1999	-	-	156.5	-0.6	-	-	158.3	1.2	-	-	158.1	-0.1	-	-	157.6	-0.3	-	-	159.5	1.2	-	-	160.3	0.5
2000	-	-	161.4	0.7	-	-	162.6	0.7	-	-	163.9	0.8	-	-	164.4	0.3	-	-	165.8	0.9	-	-	167.1	0.8
2001	-	-	165.9	-0.7	-	-	167.1	0.7	-	-	169.8	1.6	-	-	169.2	-0.4	-	-	169.6	0.2	-	-	170.6	0.6

Source: U.S. Department of Labor, Bureau of Labor Statistics, Division of Consumer Prices and Price Indexes. - indicates no data collected for period.

Detroit-Ann Arbor-Flint, MI
Consumer Price Index - All Urban Consumers
Base 1982-1984 = 100
Housing

For 1976-2001. Columns headed % show percentile change in the index from the previous period for which an index is available.

Year	Jan Index	%	Feb Index	%	Mar Index	%	Apr Index	%	May Index	%	Jun Index	%	Jul Index	%	Aug Index	%	Sep Index	%	Oct Index	%	Nov Index	%	Dec Index	%
1976	51.2	-	51.2	0.0	51.2	0.0	51.2	0.0	51.5	0.6	51.8	0.6	52.2	0.8	52.6	0.8	53.7	2.1	53.4	-0.6	53.7	0.6	53.9	0.4
1977	54.1	0.4	54.4	0.6	55.1	1.3	55.6	0.9	55.2	-0.7	55.7	0.9	56.6	1.6	56.2	-0.7	56.4	0.4	56.4	0.0	56.9	0.9	56.9	0.0
1978	57.1	0.4	57.1	0.0	58.4	2.3	58.8	0.7	59.4	1.0	60.3	1.5	60.0	-0.5	60.6	1.0	61.8	2.0	63.2	2.3	63.6	0.6	63.4	-0.3
1979	64.4	1.6	66.3	3.0	67.7	2.1	67.7	0.0	67.6	-0.1	68.1	0.7	70.2	3.1	71.7	2.1	72.2	0.7	74.1	2.6	76.6	3.4	77.3	0.9
1980	78.5	1.6	79.8	1.7	80.5	0.9	83.2	3.4	82.6	-0.7	88.0	6.5	86.1	-2.2	85.9	-0.2	87.7	2.1	90.4	3.1	90.5	0.1	92.8	2.5
1981	91.2	-1.7	91.0	-0.2	88.9	-2.3	91.1	2.5	92.3	1.3	96.2	4.2	96.7	0.5	97.2	0.5	97.0	-0.2	94.3	-2.8	92.7	-1.7	91.8	-1.0
1982	93.2	1.5	90.8	-2.6	91.1	0.3	95.0	4.3	95.5	0.5	96.7	1.3	98.0	1.3	98.2	0.2	99.4	1.2	99.6	0.2	100.0	0.4	98.0	-2.0
1983	98.5	0.5	98.3	-0.2	98.3	0.0	100.3	2.0	99.6	-0.7	101.5	1.9	102.1	0.6	101.5	-0.6	101.3	-0.2	101.1	-0.2	101.5	0.4	101.5	0.0
1984	101.5	0.0	101.8	0.3	102.3	0.5	102.5	0.2	102.6	0.1	103.2	0.6	103.8	0.6	103.9	0.1	105.5	1.5	105.5	0.0	102.8	-2.6	103.5	0.7
1985	105.8	2.2	106.0	0.2	106.7	0.7	106.6	-0.1	106.8	0.2	107.8	0.9	107.8	0.0	107.3	-0.5	109.2	1.8	107.5	-1.6	109.3	1.7	109.1	-0.2
1986	109.6	0.5	110.6	0.9	109.6	-0.9	109.9	0.3	110.6	0.6	109.7	-0.8	107.5	-2.0	110.8	3.1	108.8	-1.8	110.5	1.6	110.2	-0.3	110.0	-0.2
1987	-	-	112.5	2.3	-	-	112.8	0.3	-	-	112.2	-0.5	-	-	114.1	1.7	-	-	114.7	0.5	-	-	112.4	-2.0
1988	-	-	115.0	2.3	-	-	114.2	-0.7	-	-	115.4	1.1	-	-	118.6	2.8	-	-	117.9	-0.6	-	-	116.7	-1.0
1989	-	-	119.6	2.5	-	-	119.5	-0.1	-	-	120.5	0.8	-	-	121.9	1.2	-	-	124.0	1.7	-	-	123.5	-0.4
1990	-	-	123.8	0.2	-	-	125.0	1.0	-	-	126.5	1.2	-	-	127.9	1.1	-	-	128.7	0.6	-	-	127.2	-1.2
1991	-	-	129.1	1.5	-	-	125.8	-2.6	-	-	129.9	3.3	-	-	128.9	-0.8	-	-	129.8	0.7	-	-	128.8	-0.8
1992	-	-	130.7	1.5	-	-	130.7	0.0	-	-	131.9	0.9	-	-	132.5	0.5	-	-	133.3	0.6	-	-	133.0	-0.2
1993	-	-	133.4	0.3	-	-	132.1	-1.0	-	-	133.9	1.4	-	-	135.0	0.8	-	-	137.0	1.5	-	-	135.6	-1.0
1994	-	-	136.4	0.6	-	-	136.7	0.2	-	-	137.6	0.7	-	-	138.3	0.5	-	-	138.8	0.4	-	-	138.5	-0.2
1995	-	-	139.1	0.4	-	-	139.3	0.1	-	-	140.2	0.6	-	-	141.2	0.7	-	-	142.1	0.6	-	-	143.1	0.7
1996	-	-	144.2	0.8	-	-	144.9	0.5	-	-	145.1	0.1	-	-	146.3	0.8	-	-	146.5	0.1	-	-	147.0	0.3
1997	-	-	148.8	1.2	-	-	149.4	0.4	-	-	148.9	-0.3	-	-	149.9	0.7	-	-	152.0	1.4	-	-	151.5	-0.3
1998	-	-	153.1	1.1	-	-	152.7	-0.3	-	-	152.8	0.1	-	-	154.0	0.8	-	-	155.1	0.7	-	-	154.8	-0.2
1999	-	-	154.7	-0.1	-	-	155.1	0.3	-	-	155.8	0.5	-	-	157.8	1.3	-	-	157.8	0.0	-	-	157.5	-0.2
2000	-	-	159.9	1.5	-	-	161.1	0.8	-	-	161.3	0.1	-	-	162.2	0.6	-	-	163.6	0.9	-	-	163.7	0.1
2001	-	-	165.3	1.0	-	-	164.9	-0.2	-	-	166.9	1.2	-	-	167.4	0.3	-	-	167.1	-0.2	-	-	166.9	-0.1

Source: U.S. Department of Labor, Bureau of Labor Statistics, Division of Consumer Prices and Price Indexes. - indicates no data collected for period.

Detroit-Ann Arbor-Flint, MI
Consumer Price Index - Urban Wage Earners
Base 1982-1984 = 100
Housing

For 1976-2001. Columns headed % show percentile change in the index from the previous period for which an index is available.

Year	Jan Index	%	Feb Index	%	Mar Index	%	Apr Index	%	May Index	%	Jun Index	%	Jul Index	%	Aug Index	%	Sep Index	%	Oct Index	%	Nov Index	%	Dec Index	%
1976	51.4	-	51.4	0.0	51.3	-0.2	51.4	0.2	51.7	0.6	52.0	0.6	52.3	0.6	52.7	0.8	53.9	2.3	53.6	-0.6	53.9	0.6	54.0	0.2
1977	54.3	0.6	54.5	0.4	55.2	1.3	55.7	0.9	55.4	-0.5	55.8	0.7	56.8	1.8	56.4	-0.7	56.6	0.4	56.6	0.0	57.0	0.7	57.0	0.0
1978	57.2	0.4	57.4	0.3	58.4	1.7	58.8	0.7	59.6	1.4	60.4	1.3	60.0	-0.7	60.6	1.0	61.8	2.0	63.2	2.3	63.4	0.3	63.1	-0.5
1979	64.2	1.7	66.3	3.3	67.7	2.1	67.9	0.3	67.7	-0.3	68.1	0.6	70.2	3.1	71.8	2.3	72.3	0.7	73.8	2.1	76.4	3.5	77.1	0.9
1980	78.3	1.6	79.6	1.7	80.2	0.8	82.8	3.2	82.3	-0.6	87.7	6.6	85.6	-2.4	85.5	-0.1	87.2	2.0	89.7	2.9	90.2	0.6	92.4	2.4
1981	90.7	-1.8	90.1	-0.7	87.9	-2.4	90.2	2.6	91.6	1.6	95.1	3.8	95.9	0.8	96.3	0.4	96.1	-0.2	93.8	-2.4	92.0	-1.9	91.1	-1.0
1982	92.5	1.5	90.0	-2.7	90.4	0.4	94.4	4.4	94.9	0.5	96.1	1.3	97.5	1.5	97.6	0.1	98.8	1.2	99.0	0.2	99.5	0.5	97.4	-2.1
1983	97.1	-0.3	96.5	-0.6	98.4	2.0	102.2	3.9	104.6	2.3	106.1	1.4	107.8	1.6	107.1	-0.6	107.5	0.4	103.6	-3.6	105.0	1.4	104.7	-0.3
1984	108.9	4.0	105.2	-3.4	103.6	-1.5	99.5	-4.0	99.2	-0.3	98.3	-0.9	99.1	0.8	99.2	0.1	99.8	0.6	100.8	1.0	98.7	-2.1	99.1	0.4
1985	101.2	2.1	101.3	0.1	102.0	0.7	101.9	-0.1	102.0	0.1	102.9	0.9	103.0	0.1	102.5	-0.5	104.3	1.8	102.6	-1.6	104.4	1.8	104.3	-0.1
1986	104.7	0.4	105.5	0.8	104.7	-0.8	105.1	0.4	105.6	0.5	104.7	-0.9	102.7	-1.9	105.9	3.1	103.9	-1.9	105.6	1.6	105.3	-0.3	105.1	-0.2
1987	-		107.4	2.2	-		107.7	0.3	-		107.4	-0.3	-		109.0	1.5	-		109.6	0.6	-		107.4	-2.0
1988	-		109.8	2.2	-		109.1	-0.6	-		110.3	1.1	-		112.9	2.4	-		112.5	-0.4	-		111.7	-0.7
1989	-		114.2	2.2	-		114.1	-0.1	-		114.9	0.7	-		116.3	1.2	-		118.2	1.6	-		118.1	-0.1
1990	-		118.3	0.2	-		119.4	0.9	-		120.9	1.3	-		122.1	1.0	-		123.0	0.7	-		121.5	-1.2
1991	-		123.3	1.5	-		119.7	-2.9	-		123.9	3.5	-		123.1	-0.6	-		123.9	0.6	-		123.0	-0.7
1992	-		124.7	1.4	-		124.6	-0.1	-		125.9	1.0	-		126.3	0.3	-		127.1	0.6	-		126.9	-0.2
1993	-		127.2	0.2	-		125.9	-1.0	-		127.7	1.4	-		128.6	0.7	-		130.6	1.6	-		129.4	-0.9
1994	-		129.9	0.4	-		130.2	0.2	-		131.0	0.6	-		131.6	0.5	-		132.2	0.5	-		131.9	-0.2
1995	-		132.4	0.4	-		132.6	0.2	-		133.5	0.7	-		134.3	0.6	-		135.1	0.6	-		136.1	0.7
1996	-		137.1	0.7	-		137.6	0.4	-		137.9	0.2	-		139.0	0.8	-		139.1	0.1	-		139.7	0.4
1997	-		141.2	1.1	-		141.7	0.4	-		141.3	-0.3	-		142.1	0.6	-		144.0	1.3	-		143.7	-0.2
1998	-		145.0	0.9	-		144.8	-0.1	-		145.0	0.1	-		146.1	0.8	-		147.3	0.8	-		147.0	-0.2
1999	-		146.9	-0.1	-		147.2	0.2	-		147.7	0.3	-		149.5	1.2	-		149.7	0.1	-		149.7	0.0
2000	-		152.0	1.5	-		152.9	0.6	-		152.9	0.0	-		153.7	0.5	-		155.3	1.0	-		155.5	0.1
2001	-		157.0	1.0	-		156.5	-0.3	-		158.2	1.1	-		158.5	0.2	-		158.4	-0.1	-		158.5	0.1

Source: U.S. Department of Labor, Bureau of Labor Statistics, Division of Consumer Prices and Price Indexes. - indicates no data collected for period.

Detroit-Ann Arbor-Flint, MI
Consumer Price Index - All Urban Consumers
Base 1982-1984 = 100
Apparel

For 1952-2001. Columns headed % show percentile change in the index from the previous period for which an index is available.

Year	Jan Index	%	Feb Index	%	Mar Index	%	Apr Index	%	May Index	%	Jun Index	%	Jul Index	%	Aug Index	%	Sep Index	%	Oct Index	%	Nov Index	%	Dec Index	%
1952	-	-	-	-	-	-	-	-	-	-	-	-	-	-	-	-	-	-	-	-	-	-	51.7	-
1953	51.7	0.0	51.8	0.2	51.9	0.2	52.0	0.2	52.2	0.4	52.2	0.0	52.2	0.0	52.1	-0.2	52.1	0.0	52.3	0.4	52.2	-0.2	52.1	-0.2
1954	52.0	-0.2	52.1	0.2	51.9	-0.4	51.9	0.0	51.9	0.0	52.1	0.4	52.1	0.0	51.9	-0.4	52.1	0.4	51.9	-0.4	51.9	0.0	51.9	0.0
1955	51.9	0.0	51.9	0.0	51.9	0.0	51.7	-0.4	51.7	0.0	51.8	0.2	51.9	0.2	51.7	-0.4	51.9	0.4	51.6	-0.6	51.7	0.2	51.8	0.2
1956	51.7	-0.2	52.0	0.6	52.1	0.2	52.4	0.6	52.3	-0.2	52.3	0.0	52.5	0.4	52.9	0.8	53.3	0.8	53.3	0.0	53.2	-0.2	52.9	-0.6
1957	53.1	0.4	53.2	0.2	53.2	0.0	53.3	0.2	53.4	0.2	53.2	-0.4	53.0	-0.4	53.1	0.2	53.3	0.4	53.2	-0.2	53.3	0.2	53.2	-0.2
1958	52.7	-0.9	52.7	0.0	52.8	0.2	52.9	0.2	52.8	-0.2	52.8	0.0	52.8	0.0	52.9	0.2	53.3	0.8	53.4	0.2	53.4	0.0	53.6	0.4
1959	53.5	-0.2	53.2	-0.6	53.5	0.6	53.6	0.2	53.6	0.0	53.6	0.0	53.3	-0.6	53.7	0.8	54.6	1.7	55.0	0.7	54.5	-0.9	54.5	0.0
1960	54.1	-0.7	54.0	-0.2	53.8	-0.4	53.8	0.0	54.1	0.6	54.2	0.2	54.3	0.2	54.2	-0.2	55.1	1.7	55.1	0.0	55.1	0.0	55.0	-0.2
1961	55.4	0.7	55.5	0.2	55.3	-0.4	55.3	0.0	55.1	-0.4	55.0	-0.2	54.8	-0.4	54.9	0.2	55.2	0.5	55.5	0.5	55.3	-0.4	55.5	0.4
1962	55.1	-0.7	55.4	0.5	55.4	0.0	55.4	0.0	55.5	0.2	55.6	0.2	55.4	-0.4	55.6	0.4	55.9	0.5	55.9	0.0	55.8	-0.2	55.3	-0.9
1963	55.3	0.0	55.6	0.5	55.4	-0.4	55.7	0.5	55.7	0.0	55.9	0.4	55.8	-0.2	56.2	0.7	56.7	0.9	56.6	-0.2	56.9	0.5	56.8	-0.2
1964	56.1	-1.2	56.4	0.5	56.9	0.9	56.9	0.0	56.8	-0.2	56.8	0.0	56.8	0.0	56.8	0.0	57.2	0.7	57.3	0.2	57.2	-0.2	57.4	0.3
1965	56.8	-1.0	57.2	0.7	57.6	0.7	58.1	0.9	57.9	-0.3	58.1	0.3	57.7	-0.7	57.6	-0.2	58.1	0.9	58.1	0.0	58.1	0.0	58.3	0.3
1966	57.6	-1.2	57.9	0.5	58.4	0.9	58.8	0.7	58.8	0.0	58.8	0.0	58.4	-0.7	58.9	0.9	59.9	1.7	60.0	0.2	60.1	0.2	60.2	0.2
1967	59.9	-0.5	60.1	0.3	60.6	0.8	60.6	0.0	60.7	0.2	60.7	0.0	59.8	-1.5	60.1	0.5	61.0	1.5	61.3	0.5	61.3	0.0	61.3	0.0
1968	60.3	-1.6	61.3	1.7	62.2	1.5	62.2	0.0	63.0	1.3	63.0	0.0	62.5	-0.8	63.4	1.4	64.6	1.9	65.1	0.8	65.6	0.8	65.7	0.2
1969	64.8	-1.4	65.6	1.2	65.8	0.3	65.6	-0.3	65.7	0.2	65.7	0.0	65.0	-1.1	65.2	0.3	67.1	2.9	67.1	0.0	67.1	0.0	67.2	0.1
1970	66.0	-1.8	67.1	1.7	68.9	2.7	67.6	-1.9	67.4	-0.3	67.7	0.4	67.1	-0.9	66.8	-0.4	68.8	3.0	68.9	0.1	69.1	0.3	68.6	-0.7
1971	66.8	-2.6	69.6	4.2	70.0	0.6	69.3	-1.0	70.1	1.2	70.0	-0.1	69.6	-0.6	69.9	0.4	70.5	0.9	71.4	1.3	71.6	0.3	71.0	-0.8
1972	69.4	-2.3	70.9	2.2	70.8	-0.1	71.0	0.3	71.6	0.8	71.1	-0.7	70.8	-0.4	71.3	0.7	72.8	2.1	73.4	0.8	73.6	0.3	73.2	-0.5
1973	71.1	-2.9	72.9	2.5	73.9	1.4	74.4	0.7	74.2	-0.3	73.9	-0.4	72.2	-2.3	73.8	2.2	75.3	2.0	76.0	0.9	75.8	-0.3	75.9	0.1
1974	74.2	-2.2	76.2	2.7	77.5	1.7	78.3	1.0	78.7	0.5	79.6	1.1	79.4	-0.3	83.9	5.7	84.5	0.7	83.4	-1.3	83.7	0.4	83.1	-0.7
1975	82.0	-1.3	81.5	-0.6	83.1	2.0	82.9	-0.2	82.8	-0.1	83.6	1.0	83.6	0.0	83.7	0.1	84.5	1.0	85.1	0.7	85.1	0.0	84.9	-0.2
1976	84.6	-0.4	85.2	0.7	85.4	0.2	86.2	0.9	85.3	-1.0	85.1	-0.2	85.0	-0.1	85.9	1.1	87.1	1.4	87.8	0.8	87.6	-0.2	87.5	-0.1
1977	87.0	-0.6	87.8	0.9	88.1	0.3	88.3	0.2	88.0	-0.3	89.2	1.4	89.0	-0.2	89.4	0.4	89.7	0.3	90.0	0.3	90.4	0.4	89.9	-0.6
1978	87.0	-3.2	86.5	-0.6	87.9	1.6	89.6	1.9	91.1	1.7	91.0	-0.1	88.1	-3.2	91.1	3.4	90.3	-0.9	91.9	1.8	91.6	-0.3	90.5	-1.2
1979	87.7	-3.1	87.3	-0.5	89.5	2.5	89.5	0.0	89.9	0.4	88.1	-2.0	88.2	0.1	91.6	3.9	92.1	0.5	91.9	-0.2	91.6	-0.3	89.7	-2.1
1980	89.1	-0.7	89.7	0.7	93.4	4.1	95.5	2.2	95.0	-0.5	93.3	-1.8	93.6	0.3	94.2	0.6	97.0	3.0	96.8	-0.2	98.1	1.3	96.2	-1.9
1981	95.1	-1.1	95.6	0.5	96.8	1.3	97.6	0.8	98.4	0.8	96.5	-1.9	97.0	0.5	95.4	-1.6	96.7	1.4	97.7	1.0	96.1	-1.6	94.3	-1.9
1982	92.7	-1.7	95.2	2.7	96.2	1.1	96.5	0.3	96.5	0.0	93.4	-3.2	98.3	5.2	100.0	1.7	104.8	4.8	103.7	-1.0	103.1	-0.6	99.2	-3.8
1983	96.2	-3.0	99.2	3.1	99.0	-0.2	99.7	0.7	101.1	1.4	99.4	-1.7	99.9	0.5	103.1	3.2	105.4	2.2	104.3	-1.0	104.3	0.0	100.0	-4.1
1984	96.7	-3.3	101.9	5.4	101.6	-0.3	98.8	-2.8	99.3	0.5	99.9	0.6	100.3	0.4	99.8	-0.5	105.7	5.9	103.4	-2.2	102.3	-1.1	99.1	-3.1
1985	93.1	-6.1	99.1	6.4	100.3	1.2	100.5	0.2	101.3	0.8	100.0	-1.3	101.3	1.3	105.3	3.9	108.6	3.1	107.1	-1.4	108.8	1.6	106.0	-2.6
1986	102.0	-3.8	103.1	1.1	102.9	-0.2	102.3	-0.6	101.9	-0.4	100.2	-1.7	98.4	-1.8	103.4	5.1	106.4	2.9	106.9	0.5	106.5	-0.4	105.2	-1.2
1987	-	-	103.0	-2.1	-	-	109.8	6.6	-	-	104.6	-4.7	-	-	104.0	-0.6	-	-	116.8	12.3	-	-	111.8	-4.3
1988	-	-	108.8	-2.7	-	-	118.5	8.9	-	-	111.3	-6.1	-	-	113.2	1.7	-	-	122.8	8.5	-	-	118.5	-3.5
1989	-	-	119.6	0.9	-	-	126.2	5.5	-	-	121.1	-4.0	-	-	118.8	-1.9	-	-	128.8	8.4	-	-	122.8	-4.7
1990	-	-	126.7	3.2	-	-	131.0	3.4	-	-	122.9	-6.2	-	-	127.8	4.0	-	-	131.4	2.8	-	-	129.0	-1.8
1991	-	-	129.6	0.5	-	-	134.1	3.5	-	-	130.0	-3.1	-	-	131.7	1.3	-	-	137.0	4.0	-	-	128.4	-6.3
1992	-	-	131.7	2.6	-	-	133.4	1.3	-	-	127.4	-4.5	-	-	127.8	0.3	-	-	130.1	1.8	-	-	129.6	-0.4
1993	-	-	134.8	4.0	-	-	144.1	6.9	-	-	134.2	-6.9	-	-	138.3	3.1	-	-	144.0	4.1	-	-	133.0	-7.6
1994	-	-	139.7	5.0	-	-	142.4	1.9	-	-	138.9	-2.5	-	-	130.9	-5.8	-	-	135.3	3.4	-	-	128.2	-5.2
1995	-	-	139.6	8.9	-	-	139.2	-0.3	-	-	132.8	-4.6	-	-	139.0	4.7	-	-	137.3	-1.2	-	-	135.7	-1.2
1996	-	-	136.1	0.3	-	-	137.0	0.7	-	-	131.3	-4.2	-	-	127.4	-3.0	-	-	130.5	2.4	-	-	125.6	-3.8
1997	-	-	137.8	9.7	-	-	142.1	3.1	-	-	128.2	-9.8	-	-	137.5	7.3	-	-	136.1	-1.0	-	-	130.8	-3.9

[Continued]

Detroit-Ann Arbor-Flint, MI
Consumer Price Index - All Urban Consumers
Base 1982-1984 = 100
Apparel
[Continued]

For 1952-2001. Columns headed % show percentile change in the index from the previous period for which an index is available.

Year	Jan Index	%	Feb Index	%	Mar Index	%	Apr Index	%	May Index	%	Jun Index	%	Jul Index	%	Aug Index	%	Sep Index	%	Oct Index	%	Nov Index	%	Dec Index	%
1998	-	-	131.8	0.8	-	-	138.5	5.1	-	-	130.8	-5.6	-	-	136.4	4.3	-	-	135.7	-0.5	-	-	128.2	-5.5
1999	-	-	130.9	2.1	-	-	142.9	9.2	-	-	136.0	-4.8	-	-	128.2	-5.7	-	-	135.2	5.5	-	-	127.0	-6.1
2000	-	-	134.2	5.7	-	-	129.9	-3.2	-	-	121.7	-6.3	-	-	129.8	6.7	-	-	131.4	1.2	-	-	118.5	-9.8
2001	-	-	129.9	9.6	-	-	129.4	-0.4	-	-	126.6	-2.2	-	-	125.0	-1.3	-	-	123.5	-1.2	-	-	115.3	-6.6

Source: U.S. Department of Labor, Bureau of Labor Statistics, Division of Consumer Prices and Price Indexes. - indicates no data collected for period.

Detroit-Ann Arbor-Flint, MI
Consumer Price Index - Urban Wage Earners
Base 1982-1984 = 100
Apparel

For 1952-2001. Columns headed % show percentile change in the index from the previous period for which an index is available.

Year	Jan		Feb		Mar		Apr		May		Jun		Jul		Aug		Sep		Oct		Nov		Dec	
	Index	%	Index	%	Index	%	Index	%	Index	%	Index	%	Index	%	Index	%	Index	%	Index	%	Index	%	Index	%
1952	-	-	-	-	-	-	-	-	-	-	-	-	-	-	-	-	-	-	-	-	-	-	52.6	-
1953	52.7	0.2	52.7	0.0	52.9	0.4	52.9	0.0	53.1	0.4	53.2	0.2	53.1	-0.2	53.1	0.0	53.1	0.0	53.2	0.2	53.1	-0.2	53.0	-0.2
1954	52.9	-0.2	53.0	0.2	52.8	-0.4	52.8	0.0	52.8	0.0	53.0	0.4	53.0	0.0	52.8	-0.4	53.0	0.4	52.9	-0.2	52.8	-0.2	52.8	0.0
1955	52.8	0.0	52.8	0.0	52.9	0.2	52.7	-0.4	52.7	0.0	52.7	0.0	52.8	0.2	52.6	-0.4	52.8	0.4	52.5	-0.6	52.6	0.2	52.7	0.2
1956	52.7	0.0	52.9	0.4	53.1	0.4	53.3	0.4	53.2	-0.2	53.2	0.0	53.4	0.4	53.9	0.9	54.3	0.7	54.2	-0.2	54.3	0.0	53.9	-0.6
1957	54.1	0.4	54.2	0.2	54.2	0.0	54.2	0.0	54.4	0.4	54.2	-0.4	53.9	-0.6	54.0	0.2	54.3	0.6	54.2	-0.2	54.3	0.2	54.2	-0.2
1958	53.7	-0.9	53.7	0.0	53.7	0.0	53.9	0.4	53.7	-0.4	53.7	0.0	53.7	0.0	53.9	0.4	54.2	0.6	54.4	0.4	54.4	0.0	54.5	0.2
1959	54.5	0.0	54.2	-0.6	54.5	0.6	54.5	0.0	54.6	0.2	54.5	-0.2	54.2	-0.6	54.7	0.9	55.6	1.6	56.0	0.7	55.5	-0.9	55.5	0.0
1960	55.0	-0.9	55.0	0.0	54.8	-0.4	54.8	0.0	55.0	0.4	55.2	0.4	55.3	0.2	55.2	-0.2	56.1	1.6	56.1	0.0	56.1	0.0	56.0	-0.2
1961	56.4	0.7	56.5	0.2	56.3	-0.4	56.3	0.0	56.1	-0.4	56.0	-0.2	55.8	-0.4	55.9	0.2	56.2	0.5	56.5	0.5	56.3	-0.4	56.5	0.4
1962	56.1	-0.7	56.4	0.5	56.4	0.0	56.4	0.0	56.5	0.2	56.6	0.2	56.4	-0.4	56.6	0.4	56.9	0.5	56.9	0.0	56.8	-0.2	56.3	-0.9
1963	56.3	0.0	56.6	0.5	56.4	-0.4	56.7	0.5	56.8	0.2	56.9	0.2	56.8	-0.2	57.2	0.7	57.7	0.9	57.6	-0.2	57.9	0.5	57.8	-0.2
1964	57.1	-1.2	57.4	0.5	57.9	0.9	57.9	0.0	57.9	0.0	57.8	-0.2	57.8	0.0	57.8	0.0	58.2	0.7	58.3	0.2	58.2	-0.2	58.4	0.3
1965	57.8	-1.0	58.2	0.7	58.7	0.9	59.1	0.7	58.9	-0.3	59.1	0.3	58.7	-0.7	58.7	0.0	59.2	0.9	59.2	0.0	59.2	0.0	59.3	0.2
1966	58.6	-1.2	58.9	0.5	59.5	1.0	59.8	0.5	59.8	0.0	59.8	0.0	59.5	-0.5	60.0	0.8	61.0	1.7	61.1	0.2	61.2	0.2	61.3	0.2
1967	61.0	-0.5	61.2	0.3	61.7	0.8	61.7	0.0	61.8	0.2	61.8	0.0	60.9	-1.5	61.1	0.3	62.1	1.6	62.4	0.5	62.4	0.0	62.4	0.0
1968	61.4	-1.6	62.4	1.6	63.3	1.4	63.3	0.0	64.1	1.3	64.2	0.2	63.7	-0.8	64.6	1.4	65.8	1.9	66.3	0.8	66.8	0.8	66.9	0.1
1969	65.9	-1.5	66.8	1.4	67.0	0.3	66.8	-0.3	66.9	0.1	66.9	0.0	66.1	-1.2	66.4	0.5	68.3	2.9	68.3	0.0	68.4	0.1	68.4	0.0
1970	67.2	-1.8	68.3	1.6	70.1	2.6	68.8	-1.9	68.7	-0.1	68.9	0.3	68.3	-0.9	68.0	-0.4	70.0	2.9	70.1	0.1	70.4	0.4	69.8	-0.9
1971	68.0	-2.6	70.8	4.1	71.3	0.7	70.6	-1.0	71.4	1.1	71.3	-0.1	70.9	-0.6	71.2	0.4	71.7	0.7	72.7	1.4	72.9	0.3	72.2	-1.0
1972	70.6	-2.2	72.2	2.3	72.1	-0.1	72.3	0.3	72.9	0.8	72.4	-0.7	72.1	-0.4	72.6	0.7	74.1	2.1	74.8	0.9	74.9	0.1	74.5	-0.5
1973	72.4	-2.8	74.2	2.5	75.2	1.3	75.7	0.7	75.6	-0.1	75.3	-0.4	73.5	-2.4	75.1	2.2	76.6	2.0	77.4	1.0	77.2	-0.3	77.2	0.0
1974	75.5	-2.2	77.5	2.6	78.9	1.8	79.7	1.0	80.1	0.5	81.0	1.1	80.9	-0.1	85.4	5.6	86.1	0.8	84.9	-1.4	85.3	0.5	84.6	-0.8
1975	83.5	-1.3	83.0	-0.6	84.6	1.9	84.4	-0.2	84.3	-0.1	85.1	0.9	85.1	0.0	85.2	0.1	86.0	0.9	86.6	0.7	86.6	0.0	86.4	-0.2
1976	86.1	-0.3	86.7	0.7	87.0	0.3	87.8	0.9	86.8	-1.1	86.7	-0.1	86.5	-0.2	87.4	1.0	88.7	1.5	89.4	0.8	89.1	-0.3	89.1	0.0
1977	88.6	-0.6	89.4	0.9	89.7	0.3	89.9	0.2	89.6	-0.3	90.8	1.3	90.6	-0.2	91.0	0.4	91.3	0.3	91.7	0.4	92.0	0.3	91.6	-0.4
1978	87.0	-5.0	87.5	0.6	87.9	0.5	90.5	3.0	93.5	3.3	95.2	1.8	92.5	-2.8	98.4	6.4	98.2	-0.2	98.0	-0.2	98.4	0.4	97.5	-0.9
1979	93.0	-4.6	92.5	-0.5	94.0	1.6	94.0	0.0	93.8	-0.2	90.8	-3.2	89.5	-1.4	95.9	7.2	96.1	0.2	95.9	-0.2	95.6	-0.3	92.0	-3.8
1980	92.4	0.4	96.6	4.5	99.4	2.9	100.4	1.0	102.6	2.2	94.1	-8.3	95.6	1.6	95.3	-0.3	96.7	1.5	100.1	3.5	100.9	0.8	97.9	-3.0
1981	97.2	-0.7	96.8	-0.4	98.6	1.9	99.4	0.8	99.4	0.0	97.7	-1.7	98.9	1.2	95.2	-3.7	97.1	2.0	97.5	0.4	95.7	-1.8	94.1	-1.7
1982	94.2	0.1	96.5	2.4	97.4	0.9	97.8	0.4	97.9	0.1	94.1	-3.9	99.1	5.3	99.5	0.4	104.3	4.8	101.4	-2.8	101.0	-0.4	97.6	-3.4
1983	95.3	-2.4	99.2	4.1	99.7	0.5	100.1	0.4	101.9	1.8	100.6	-1.3	100.4	-0.2	102.7	2.3	104.1	1.4	103.4	-0.7	103.7	0.3	98.4	-5.1
1984	95.1	-3.4	102.7	8.0	103.0	0.3	99.9	-3.0	100.3	0.4	100.5	0.2	98.8	-1.7	100.1	1.3	105.7	5.6	103.7	-1.9	101.3	-2.3	98.8	-2.5
1985	91.9	-7.0	98.6	7.3	101.2	2.6	101.4	0.2	102.2	0.8	102.0	-0.2	102.9	0.9	106.7	3.7	109.6	2.7	108.6	-0.9	110.6	1.8	106.7	-3.5
1986	105.2	-1.4	104.5	-0.7	104.0	-0.5	103.3	-0.7	102.8	-0.5	100.5	-2.2	98.3	-2.2	108.3	10.2	110.1	1.7	110.9	0.7	109.4	-1.4	108.2	-1.1
1987	-	-	105.9	-2.1	-	-	114.8	8.4	-	-	107.8	-6.1	-	-	107.6	-0.2	-	-	118.9	10.5	-	-	114.5	-3.7
1988	-	-	112.9	-1.4	-	-	123.0	8.9	-	-	115.4	-6.2	-	-	117.2	1.6	-	-	125.6	7.2	-	-	122.8	-2.2
1989	-	-	123.4	0.5	-	-	129.8	5.2	-	-	124.8	-3.9	-	-	121.1	-3.0	-	-	131.7	8.8	-	-	125.6	-4.6
1990	-	-	130.1	3.6	-	-	134.3	3.2	-	-	126.8	-5.6	-	-	133.4	5.2	-	-	135.7	1.7	-	-	132.3	-2.5
1991	-	-	132.5	0.2	-	-	135.4	2.2	-	-	131.5	-2.9	-	-	137.1	4.3	-	-	140.6	2.6	-	-	132.5	-5.8
1992	-	-	134.8	1.7	-	-	135.9	0.8	-	-	130.3	-4.1	-	-	131.3	0.8	-	-	134.0	2.1	-	-	134.0	0.0
1993	-	-	139.2	3.9	-	-	146.1	5.0	-	-	136.0	-6.9	-	-	140.4	3.2	-	-	146.9	4.6	-	-	135.7	-7.6
1994	-	-	141.7	4.4	-	-	144.2	1.8	-	-	140.9	-2.3	-	-	135.0	-4.2	-	-	139.2	3.1	-	-	131.8	-5.3
1995	-	-	142.0	7.7	-	-	142.1	0.1	-	-	134.3	-5.5	-	-	140.3	4.5	-	-	139.2	-0.8	-	-	137.9	-0.9
1996	-	-	138.8	0.7	-	-	140.8	1.4	-	-	133.9	-4.9	-	-	131.6	-1.7	-	-	132.3	0.5	-	-	127.7	-3.5
1997	-	-	140.3	9.9	-	-	146.2	4.2	-	-	130.0	-11.1	-	-	140.7	8.2	-	-	138.7	-1.4	-	-	133.4	-3.8

[Continued]

Detroit-Ann Arbor-Flint, MI
Consumer Price Index - Urban Wage Earners
Base 1982-1984 = 100
Apparel
[Continued]

For 1952-2001. Columns headed % show percentile change in the index from the previous period for which an index is available.

Year	Jan		Feb		Mar		Apr		May		Jun		Jul		Aug		Sep		Oct		Nov		Dec	
	Index	%	Index	%	Index	%	Index	%	Index	%	Index	%	Index	%	Index	%	Index	%	Index	%	Index	%	Index	%
1998	-	-	133.7	0.2	-	-	140.2	4.9	-	-	133.1	-5.1	-	-	139.0	4.4	-	-	138.1	-0.6	-	-	131.1	-5.1
1999	-	-	133.3	1.7	-	-	144.7	8.6	-	-	138.1	-4.6	-	-	130.0	-5.9	-	-	136.7	5.2	-	-	129.7	-5.1
2000	-	-	136.9	5.6	-	-	132.1	-3.5	-	-	124.0	-6.1	-	-	132.1	6.5	-	-	134.0	1.4	-	-	120.8	-9.9
2001	-	-	132.9	10.0	-	-	133.2	0.2	-	-	130.0	-2.4	-	-	127.3	-2.1	-	-	126.0	-1.0	-	-	117.9	-6.4

Source: U.S. Department of Labor, Bureau of Labor Statistics, Division of Consumer Prices and Price Indexes. - indicates no data collected for period.

Detroit-Ann Arbor-Flint, MI
Consumer Price Index - All Urban Consumers
Base 1982-1984 = 100
Transportation

For 1947-2000. Columns headed % show percentile change in the index from the previous period for which an index is available.

Year	Jan Index	%	Feb Index	%	Mar Index	%	Apr Index	%	May Index	%	Jun Index	%	Jul Index	%	Aug Index	%	Sep Index	%	Oct Index	%	Nov Index	%	Dec Index	%
1947	19.2	-	19.3	0.5	19.4	0.5	19.5	0.5	19.5	0.0	19.5	0.0	19.5	0.0	19.8	1.5	20.1	1.5	20.1	0.0	20.3	1.0	20.7	2.0
1948	20.7	0.0	20.7	0.0	20.7	0.0	21.8	5.3	21.8	0.0	22.0	0.9	22.6	2.7	23.0	1.8	23.1	0.4	23.1	0.0	23.1	0.0	23.1	0.0
1949	23.1	0.0	23.4	1.3	23.4	0.0	23.5	0.4	23.5	0.0	23.4	-0.4	23.4	0.0	23.4	0.0	23.4	0.0	23.4	0.0	23.4	0.0	23.4	0.0
1950	23.4	0.0	23.4	0.0	23.4	0.0	23.4	0.0	23.8	1.7	23.9	0.4	23.9	0.0	23.7	-0.8	23.8	0.4	23.7	-0.4	23.8	0.4	23.8	0.0
1951	23.8	0.0	23.8	0.0	24.1	1.3	24.1	0.0	24.1	0.0	24.6	2.1	24.8	0.8	24.8	0.0	25.1	1.2	25.5	1.6	25.9	1.6	25.9	0.0
1952	25.9	0.0	25.9	0.0	26.1	0.8	26.1	0.0	26.1	0.0	26.1	0.0	26.1	0.0	26.5	1.5	26.6	0.4	27.4	3.0	27.4	0.0	27.4	0.0
1953	27.4	0.0	27.4	0.0	27.3	-0.4	27.4	0.4	27.4	0.0	27.6	0.7	27.8	0.7	27.8	0.0	27.7	-0.4	27.6	-0.4	27.5	-0.4	26.7	-2.9
1954	27.3	2.2	26.5	-2.9	26.4	-0.4	26.3	-0.4	26.3	0.0	26.0	-1.1	26.1	0.4	25.7	-1.5	25.7	0.0	25.7	0.0	27.3	6.2	26.7	-2.2
1955	26.6	-0.4	26.4	-0.8	26.4	0.0	26.3	-0.4	26.3	0.0	26.7	1.5	26.6	-0.4	26.3	-1.1	26.4	0.4	26.7	1.1	27.2	1.9	27.2	0.0
1956	27.1	-0.4	27.1	0.0	27.0	-0.4	27.2	0.7	27.2	0.0	27.1	-0.4	27.5	1.5	27.6	0.4	27.5	-0.4	28.0	1.8	28.3	1.1	28.3	0.0
1957	28.6	1.1	28.5	-0.3	28.7	0.7	28.6	-0.3	28.8	0.7	28.8	0.0	28.8	0.0	28.9	0.3	28.7	-0.7	28.6	-0.3	30.0	4.9	29.7	-1.0
1958	29.3	-1.3	28.6	-2.4	28.6	0.0	28.5	-0.3	28.3	-0.7	28.7	1.4	28.7	0.0	29.2	1.7	29.3	0.3	29.2	-0.3	29.4	0.7	29.7	1.0
1959	29.8	0.3	29.5	-1.0	29.8	1.0	30.1	1.0	30.0	-0.3	29.1	-3.0	30.4	4.5	30.3	-0.3	30.7	1.3	30.7	0.0	30.5	-0.7	30.6	0.3
1960	29.9	-2.3	30.2	1.0	29.8	-1.3	29.3	-1.7	29.5	0.7	30.6	3.7	30.6	0.0	30.7	0.3	30.3	-1.3	30.4	0.3	30.4	0.0	30.0	-1.3
1961	30.2	0.7	30.1	-0.3	29.5	-2.0	29.1	-1.4	29.5	1.4	29.2	-1.0	28.9	-1.0	30.5	5.5	29.8	-2.3	30.1	1.0	30.2	0.3	28.7	-5.0
1962	29.0	1.0	30.6	5.5	30.6	0.0	31.0	1.3	29.8	-3.9	29.9	0.3	29.3	-2.0	30.3	3.4	30.8	1.7	31.0	0.6	30.4	-1.9	31.1	2.3
1963	30.6	-1.6	30.4	-0.7	30.6	0.7	29.5	-3.6	30.4	3.1	30.2	-0.7	30.3	0.3	31.4	3.6	29.7	-5.4	30.5	2.7	31.0	1.6	30.7	-1.0
1964	30.9	0.7	29.7	-3.9	30.3	2.0	30.3	0.0	29.8	-1.7	30.2	1.3	30.7	1.7	31.0	1.0	31.2	0.6	31.6	1.3	31.1	-1.6	31.3	0.6
1965	31.8	1.6	31.2	-1.9	31.1	-0.3	31.8	2.3	32.3	1.6	32.2	-0.3	32.2	0.0	32.0	-0.6	32.0	0.0	32.2	0.6	32.4	0.6	32.4	0.0
1966	32.5	0.3	32.3	-0.6	32.7	1.2	32.9	0.6	32.9	0.0	32.9	0.0	32.8	-0.3	32.9	0.3	32.6	-0.9	33.0	1.2	33.1	0.3	33.0	-0.3
1967	33.0	0.0	33.2	0.6	33.4	0.6	33.6	0.6	33.6	0.0	33.5	-0.3	33.5	0.0	33.4	-0.3	33.5	0.3	33.6	0.3	34.0	1.2	34.1	0.3
1968	34.4	0.9	34.4	0.0	34.9	1.5	34.9	0.0	35.0	0.3	35.1	0.3	35.0	-0.3	34.9	-0.3	34.8	-0.3	35.1	0.9	35.3	0.6	35.1	-0.6
1969	35.0	-0.3	35.4	1.1	36.6	3.4	36.5	-0.3	36.6	0.3	36.7	0.3	35.7	-2.7	36.7	2.8	35.6	-3.0	36.1	1.4	35.8	-0.8	36.0	0.6
1970	36.1	0.3	36.9	2.2	35.4	-4.1	36.5	3.1	37.2	1.9	36.4	-2.2	36.5	0.3	35.8	-1.9	36.0	0.6	38.7	7.5	38.9	0.5	37.8	-2.8
1971	39.5	4.5	38.1	-3.5	37.8	-0.8	38.1	0.8	38.7	1.6	38.8	0.3	37.8	-2.6	38.9	2.9	38.2	-1.8	38.2	0.0	38.6	1.0	38.4	-0.5
1972	39.1	1.8	39.2	0.3	38.8	-1.0	38.7	-0.3	38.7	0.0	39.2	1.3	39.1	-0.3	39.2	0.3	39.0	-0.5	39.2	0.5	39.2	0.0	39.6	1.0
1973	39.6	0.0	40.4	2.0	40.5	0.2	41.2	1.7	41.5	0.7	41.9	1.0	41.9	0.0	41.8	-0.2	41.5	-0.7	42.0	1.2	42.3	0.7	42.9	1.4
1974	43.4	1.2	43.9	1.2	45.2	3.0	45.9	1.5	46.3	0.9	47.1	1.7	47.5	0.8	47.6	0.2	47.8	0.4	47.9	0.2	47.9	0.0	47.9	0.0
1975	47.9	0.0	47.9	0.0	48.4	1.0	48.7	0.6	49.0	0.6	50.0	2.0	51.1	2.2	51.1	0.0	51.3	0.4	51.6	0.6	51.6	0.0	51.6	0.0
1976	51.8	0.4	51.8	0.0	51.9	0.2	52.3	0.8	53.1	1.5	53.8	1.3	54.2	0.7	54.4	0.4	54.8	0.7	55.1	0.5	55.8	1.3	55.9	0.2
1977	56.0	0.2	56.3	0.5	57.4	2.0	58.4	1.7	59.0	1.0	59.3	0.5	59.4	0.2	59.6	0.3	59.5	-0.2	59.5	0.0	59.5	0.0	59.5	0.0
1978	59.6	0.2	59.7	0.2	60.3	1.0	60.6	0.5	61.6	1.7	62.2	1.0	62.7	0.8	62.8	0.2	62.9	0.2	63.8	1.4	64.1	0.5	64.2	0.2
1979	65.3	1.7	65.8	0.8	66.3	0.8	68.0	2.6	68.9	1.3	70.3	2.0	71.5	1.7	72.5	1.4	73.1	0.8	74.0	1.2	74.4	0.5	75.3	1.2
1980	77.1	2.4	78.5	1.8	79.8	1.7	81.2	1.8	82.1	1.1	82.8	0.9	81.5	-1.6	83.2	2.1	85.2	2.4	86.4	1.4	87.9	1.7	87.7	-0.2
1981	88.9	1.4	90.0	1.2	91.1	1.2	92.0	1.0	93.1	1.2	93.3	0.2	95.4	2.3	95.4	0.0	95.4	0.0	96.8	1.5	97.1	0.3	97.0	-0.1
1982	97.4	0.4	96.2	-1.2	95.7	-0.5	95.4	-0.3	96.7	1.4	99.1	2.5	99.8	0.7	99.9	0.1	98.5	-1.4	98.6	0.1	98.6	0.0	98.4	-0.2
1983	97.3	-1.1	96.4	-0.9	96.1	-0.3	96.4	0.3	97.6	1.2	97.5	-0.1	98.7	1.2	99.6	0.9	100.2	0.6	100.3	0.1	101.2	0.9	101.0	-0.2
1984	101.1	0.1	101.4	0.3	102.0	0.6	103.1	1.1	103.6	0.5	103.5	-0.1	103.4	-0.1	103.4	0.0	104.5	1.1	106.0	1.4	106.1	0.1	105.3	-0.8
1985	104.6	-0.7	105.4	0.8	106.1	0.7	106.5	0.4	106.5	0.0	106.6	0.1	106.7	0.1	107.1	0.4	106.0	-1.0	107.2	1.1	107.9	0.7	108.3	0.4
1986	108.0	-0.3	106.0	-1.9	102.7	-3.1	101.2	-1.5	103.5	2.3	103.9	0.4	102.3	-1.5	101.7	-0.6	100.8	-0.9	102.2	1.4	103.6	1.4	103.1	-0.5
1987	-	-	102.9	-0.2	-	-	104.2	1.3	-	-	104.9	0.7	-	-	106.4	1.4	-	-	107.8	1.3	-	-	106.7	-1.0
1988	-	-	105.5	-1.1	-	-	106.8	1.2	-	-	110.3	3.3	-	-	111.3	0.9	-	-	111.7	0.4	-	-	112.8	1.0
1989	-	-	113.7	0.8	-	-	117.9	3.7	-	-	119.0	0.9	-	-	116.0	-2.5	-	-	118.4	2.1	-	-	118.3	-0.1
1990	-	-	120.5	1.9	-	-	120.2	-0.2	-	-	121.7	1.2	-	-	124.1	2.0	-	-	130.4	5.1	-	-	130.5	0.1
1991	-	-	128.3	-1.7	-	-	129.2	0.7	-	-	129.8	0.5	-	-	128.9	-0.7	-	-	129.1	0.2	-	-	130.9	1.4
1992	-	-	128.5	-1.8	-	-	130.0	1.2	-	-	130.1	0.1	-	-	128.6	-1.2	-	-	132.1	2.7	-	-	130.3	-1.4

[Continued]

Detroit-Ann Arbor-Flint, MI
Consumer Price Index - All Urban Consumers
Base 1982-1984 = 100
Transportation

[Continued]

For 1947-2000. Columns headed % show percentile change in the index from the previous period for which an index is available.

Year	Jan		Feb		Mar		Apr		May		Jun		Jul		Aug		Sep		Oct		Nov		Dec	
	Index	%	Index	%	Index	%	Index	%	Index	%	Index	%	Index	%	Index	%	Index	%	Index	%	Index	%	Index	%
1993	-	-	131.8	1.2	-	-	131.7	-0.1	-	-	132.7	0.8	-	-	132.7	0.0	-	-	134.4	1.3	-	-	132.6	-1.3
1994	-	-	134.9	1.7	-	-	136.3	1.0	-	-	139.9	2.6	-	-	142.2	1.6	-	-	140.4	-1.3	-	-	140.1	-0.2
1995	-	-	142.0	1.4	-	-	144.9	2.0	-	-	145.5	0.4	-	-	141.8	-2.5	-	-	144.4	1.8	-	-	143.8	-0.4
1996	-	-	145.1	0.9	-	-	147.6	1.7	-	-	148.5	0.6	-	-	147.0	-1.0	-	-	149.4	1.6	-	-	152.5	2.1
1997	-	-	148.4	-2.7	-	-	147.7	-0.5	-	-	148.7	0.7	-	-	149.5	0.5	-	-	150.4	0.6	-	-	148.2	-1.5
1998	-	-	149.3	0.7	-	-	148.8	-0.3	-	-	149.3	0.3	-	-	148.2	-0.7	-	-	149.3	0.7	-	-	148.7	-0.4
1999	-	-	148.0	-0.5	-	-	152.1	2.8	-	-	151.4	-0.5	-	-	152.2	0.5	-	-	154.5	1.5	-	-	156.7	1.4
2000	-	-	157.3	0.4	-	-	158.3	0.6	-	-	169.9	7.3	-	-	161.5	-4.9	-	-	164.8	2.0	-	-	165.3	0.3

Source: U.S. Department of Labor, Bureau of Labor Statistics, Division of Consumer Prices and Price Indexes. - indicates no data collected for period.

Detroit-Ann Arbor-Flint, MI
Consumer Price Index - Urban Wage Earners
Base 1982-1984 = 100
Transportation

For 1947-2000. Columns headed % show percentile change in the index from the previous period for which an index is available.

Year	Jan Index	%	Feb Index	%	Mar Index	%	Apr Index	%	May Index	%	Jun Index	%	Jul Index	%	Aug Index	%	Sep Index	%	Oct Index	%	Nov Index	%	Dec Index	%
1947	19.9	-	20.0	0.5	20.1	0.5	20.2	0.5	20.2	0.0	20.2	0.0	20.2	0.0	20.5	1.5	20.9	2.0	20.9	0.0	21.1	1.0	21.5	1.9
1948	21.5	0.0	21.5	0.0	21.5	0.0	22.6	5.1	22.6	0.0	22.8	0.9	23.4	2.6	23.9	2.1	24.0	0.4	24.0	0.0	24.0	0.0	24.0	0.0
1949	24.0	0.0	24.3	1.2	24.3	0.0	24.4	0.4	24.4	0.0	24.3	-0.4	24.3	0.0	24.3	0.0	24.3	0.0	24.3	0.0	24.3	0.0	24.3	0.0
1950	24.3	0.0	24.3	0.0	24.3	0.0	24.3	0.0	24.7	1.6	24.8	0.4	24.8	0.0	24.6	-0.8	24.7	0.4	24.6	-0.4	24.7	0.4	24.7	0.0
1951	24.7	0.0	24.7	0.0	25.0	1.2	25.1	0.4	25.1	0.0	25.5	1.6	25.8	1.2	25.8	0.0	26.1	1.2	26.5	1.5	26.8	1.1	26.8	0.0
1952	26.8	0.0	26.9	0.4	27.0	0.4	27.0	0.0	27.0	0.0	27.0	0.0	27.0	0.0	27.5	1.9	27.6	0.4	28.4	2.9	28.4	0.0	28.4	0.0
1953	28.5	0.4	28.4	-0.4	28.4	0.0	28.4	0.0	28.4	0.0	28.6	0.7	28.8	0.7	28.8	0.0	28.7	-0.3	28.6	-0.3	28.5	-0.3	27.7	-2.8
1954	28.4	2.5	27.5	-3.2	27.4	-0.4	27.3	-0.4	27.3	0.0	27.0	-1.1	27.0	0.0	26.7	-1.1	26.7	0.0	26.7	0.0	28.3	6.0	27.7	-2.1
1955	27.6	-0.4	27.4	-0.7	27.4	0.0	27.3	-0.4	27.3	0.0	27.7	1.5	27.6	-0.4	27.3	-1.1	27.4	0.4	27.7	1.1	28.2	1.8	28.3	0.4
1956	28.2	-0.4	28.1	-0.4	28.1	0.0	28.2	0.4	28.3	0.4	28.2	-0.4	28.5	1.1	28.6	0.4	28.6	0.0	29.0	1.4	29.4	1.4	29.4	0.0
1957	29.7	1.0	29.6	-0.3	29.8	0.7	29.7	-0.3	29.9	0.7	29.9	0.0	29.9	0.0	30.0	0.3	29.8	-0.7	29.7	-0.3	31.1	4.7	30.8	-1.0
1958	30.5	-1.0	29.7	-2.6	29.7	0.0	29.5	-0.7	29.4	-0.3	29.8	1.4	29.8	0.0	30.3	1.7	30.4	0.3	30.3	-0.3	30.5	0.7	30.8	1.0
1959	30.9	0.3	30.6	-1.0	30.9	1.0	31.3	1.3	31.1	-0.6	30.2	-2.9	31.6	4.6	31.4	-0.6	31.8	1.3	31.8	0.0	31.6	-0.6	31.8	0.6
1960	31.0	-2.5	31.4	1.3	30.9	-1.6	30.5	-1.3	30.6	0.3	31.8	3.9	31.8	0.0	31.8	0.0	31.4	-1.3	31.5	0.3	31.5	0.0	31.1	-1.3
1961	31.4	1.0	31.2	-0.6	30.6	-1.9	30.2	-1.3	30.7	1.7	30.3	-1.3	30.0	-1.0	31.6	5.3	30.9	-2.2	31.3	1.3	31.3	0.0	29.8	-4.8
1962	30.1	1.0	31.8	5.6	31.8	0.0	32.2	1.3	30.9	-4.0	31.0	0.3	30.4	-1.9	31.5	3.6	32.0	1.6	32.2	0.6	31.6	-1.9	32.3	2.2
1963	31.8	-1.5	31.5	-0.9	31.8	1.0	30.6	-3.8	31.5	2.9	31.3	-0.6	31.4	0.3	32.5	3.5	30.8	-5.2	31.7	2.9	32.2	1.6	31.9	-0.9
1964	32.0	0.3	30.8	-3.8	31.4	1.9	31.4	0.0	30.9	-1.6	31.3	1.3	31.8	1.6	32.2	1.3	32.3	0.3	32.7	1.2	32.3	-1.2	32.4	0.3
1965	33.0	1.9	32.3	-2.1	32.2	-0.3	33.0	2.5	33.5	1.5	33.4	-0.3	33.4	0.0	33.2	-0.6	33.2	0.0	33.4	0.6	33.6	0.6	33.6	0.0
1966	33.7	0.3	33.5	-0.6	34.0	1.5	34.2	0.6	34.1	-0.3	34.1	0.0	34.0	-0.3	34.1	0.3	33.8	-0.9	34.2	1.2	34.4	0.6	34.2	-0.6
1967	34.2	0.0	34.5	0.9	34.7	0.6	34.9	0.6	34.8	-0.3	34.8	0.0	34.7	-0.3	34.7	0.0	34.7	0.0	34.9	0.6	35.3	1.1	35.4	0.3
1968	35.7	0.8	35.7	0.0	36.2	1.4	36.2	0.0	36.3	0.3	36.4	0.3	36.3	-0.3	36.2	-0.3	36.1	-0.3	36.4	0.8	36.6	0.5	36.4	-0.5
1969	36.3	-0.3	36.8	1.4	38.0	3.3	37.9	-0.3	38.0	0.3	38.1	0.3	37.0	-2.9	38.0	2.7	37.0	-2.6	37.4	1.1	37.1	-0.8	37.3	0.5
1970	37.4	0.3	38.3	2.4	36.7	-4.2	37.9	3.3	38.6	1.8	37.8	-2.1	37.8	0.0	37.2	-1.6	37.3	0.3	40.1	7.5	40.4	0.7	39.2	-3.0
1971	41.0	4.6	39.5	-3.7	39.3	-0.5	39.6	0.8	40.1	1.3	40.3	0.5	39.2	-2.7	40.4	3.1	39.7	-1.7	39.7	0.0	40.1	1.0	39.9	-0.5
1972	40.6	1.8	40.7	0.2	40.2	-1.2	40.1	-0.2	40.2	0.2	40.6	1.0	40.5	-0.2	40.7	0.5	40.5	-0.5	40.6	0.2	40.7	0.2	41.1	1.0
1973	41.1	0.0	41.9	1.9	42.0	0.2	42.7	1.7	43.1	0.9	43.4	0.7	43.5	0.2	43.4	-0.2	43.1	-0.7	43.6	1.2	43.9	0.7	44.5	1.4
1974	45.0	1.1	45.6	1.3	46.9	2.9	47.6	1.5	48.0	0.8	48.8	1.7	49.2	0.8	49.4	0.4	49.6	0.4	49.7	0.2	49.7	0.0	49.7	0.0
1975	49.7	0.0	49.7	0.0	50.3	1.2	50.5	0.4	50.8	0.6	51.9	2.2	53.0	2.1	53.0	0.0	53.2	0.4	53.5	0.6	53.5	0.0	53.5	0.0
1976	53.7	0.4	53.7	0.0	53.8	0.2	54.3	0.9	55.1	1.5	55.9	1.5	56.2	0.5	56.4	0.4	56.8	0.7	57.2	0.7	57.9	1.2	58.0	0.2
1977	58.2	0.3	58.4	0.3	59.5	1.9	60.6	1.8	61.2	1.0	61.5	0.5	61.6	0.2	61.8	0.3	61.7	-0.2	61.7	0.0	61.8	0.2	61.8	0.0
1978	61.8	0.0	62.0	0.3	62.3	0.5	62.7	0.6	63.6	1.4	64.2	0.9	64.6	0.6	64.8	0.3	64.9	0.2	65.8	1.4	66.0	0.3	66.2	0.3
1979	67.5	2.0	68.0	0.7	68.6	0.9	70.1	2.2	71.1	1.4	72.6	2.1	74.2	2.2	75.0	1.1	74.9	-0.1	76.4	2.0	76.6	0.3	77.1	0.7
1980	79.1	2.6	80.4	1.6	81.7	1.6	84.3	3.2	85.3	1.2	85.5	0.2	83.4	-2.5	85.6	2.6	87.4	2.1	86.9	-0.6	88.1	1.4	86.9	-1.4
1981	88.0	1.3	89.3	1.5	90.0	0.8	90.9	1.0	92.4	1.7	92.6	0.2	94.3	1.8	94.5	0.2	95.2	0.7	96.4	1.3	96.9	0.5	97.0	0.1
1982	97.3	0.3	96.2	-1.1	95.7	-0.5	95.3	-0.4	96.6	1.4	99.1	2.6	99.8	0.7	99.8	0.0	98.5	-1.3	98.6	0.1	98.6	0.0	98.5	-0.1
1983	97.3	-1.2	96.4	-0.9	96.1	-0.3	96.4	0.3	97.7	1.3	97.6	-0.1	98.7	1.1	99.6	0.9	100.2	0.6	100.3	0.1	101.2	0.9	101.0	-0.2
1984	101.1	0.1	101.4	0.3	102.0	0.6	103.1	1.1	103.6	0.5	103.5	-0.1	103.4	-0.1	103.4	0.0	104.5	1.1	106.0	1.4	106.0	0.0	105.3	-0.7
1985	104.6	-0.7	105.5	0.9	106.1	0.6	106.6	0.5	106.6	0.0	106.7	0.1	106.9	0.2	107.3	0.4	106.1	-1.1	107.3	1.1	108.1	0.7	108.4	0.3
1986	108.1	-0.3	106.0	-1.9	102.6	-3.2	101.1	-1.5	103.5	2.4	103.9	0.4	102.3	-1.5	101.6	-0.7	100.8	-0.8	102.1	1.3	103.5	1.4	103.0	-0.5
1987	-		102.9	-0.1	-		104.3	1.4	-		105.0	0.7	-		106.6	1.5	-		108.1	1.4	-		106.9	-1.1
1988	-		105.6	-1.2	-		107.0	1.3	-		110.2	3.0	-		111.4	1.1	-		111.7	0.3	-		112.8	1.0
1989	-		113.6	0.7	-		118.0	3.9	-		119.2	1.0	-		116.0	-2.7	-		118.3	2.0	-		118.1	-0.2
1990	-		120.5	2.0	-		120.1	-0.3	-		121.7	1.3	-		124.2	2.1	-		130.7	5.2	-		130.6	-0.1
1991	-		128.1	-1.9	-		129.0	0.7	-		129.7	0.5	-		128.8	-0.7	-		129.0	0.2	-		130.7	1.3
1992	-		128.2	-1.9	-		129.8	1.2	-		129.9	0.1	-		128.4	-1.2	-		131.9	2.7	-		130.1	-1.4

[Continued]

Detroit-Ann Arbor-Flint, MI
Consumer Price Index - Urban Wage Earners
Base 1982-1984 = 100
Transportation
[Continued]

For 1947-2000. Columns headed % show percentile change in the index from the previous period for which an index is available.

Year	Jan Index	%	Feb Index	%	Mar Index	%	Apr Index	%	May Index	%	Jun Index	%	Jul Index	%	Aug Index	%	Sep Index	%	Oct Index	%	Nov Index	%	Dec Index	%
1993	-	-	131.6	1.2	-	-	131.6	0.0	-	-	132.7	0.8	-	-	132.6	-0.1	-	-	134.3	1.3	-	-	132.4	-1.4
1994	-	-	134.7	1.7	-	-	136.1	1.0	-	-	139.7	2.6	-	-	142.3	1.9	-	-	140.4	-1.3	-	-	140.1	-0.2
1995	-	-	142.0	1.4	-	-	145.1	2.2	-	-	145.8	0.5	-	-	141.9	-2.7	-	-	144.5	1.8	-	-	143.8	-0.5
1996	-	-	145.2	1.0	-	-	147.8	1.8	-	-	148.7	0.6	-	-	147.1	-1.1	-	-	149.6	1.7	-	-	152.7	2.1
1997	-	-	148.5	-2.8	-	-	147.7	-0.5	-	-	148.7	0.7	-	-	149.5	0.5	-	-	150.3	0.5	-	-	148.0	-1.5
1998	-	-	149.1	0.7	-	-	148.6	-0.3	-	-	149.4	0.5	-	-	148.2	-0.8	-	-	149.3	0.7	-	-	148.2	-0.7
1999	-	-	147.4	-0.5	-	-	151.9	3.1	-	-	151.8	-0.1	-	-	152.8	0.7	-	-	155.1	1.5	-	-	157.4	1.5
2000	-	-	158.7	0.8	-	-	159.7	0.6	-	-	172.8	8.2	-	-	162.4	-6.0	-	-	166.7	2.6	-	-	166.6	-0.1

Source: U.S. Department of Labor, Bureau of Labor Statistics, Division of Consumer Prices and Price Indexes. - indicates no data collected for period.

Detroit-Ann Arbor-Flint, MI
Consumer Price Index - All Urban Consumers
Base 1982-1984 = 100
Medical Care

For 1947-2001. Columns headed % show percentile change in the index from the previous period for which an index is available.

Year	Jan Index	%	Feb Index	%	Mar Index	%	Apr Index	%	May Index	%	Jun Index	%	Jul Index	%	Aug Index	%	Sep Index	%	Oct Index	%	Nov Index	%	Dec Index	%
1947	11.5	-	11.6	0.9	11.7	0.9	11.7	0.0	11.8	0.9	11.8	0.0	11.8	0.0	11.8	0.0	12.0	1.7	12.0	0.0	12.0	0.0	12.0	0.0
1948	12.1	0.8	12.1	0.0	12.2	0.8	12.2	0.0	12.2	0.0	12.2	0.0	12.2	0.0	12.3	0.8	12.4	0.8	12.4	0.0	12.4	0.0	12.4	0.0
1949	12.4	0.0	12.5	0.8	12.5	0.0	12.5	0.0	12.5	0.0	12.5	0.0	12.5	0.0	12.6	0.8	12.7	0.8	12.7	0.0	12.7	0.0	12.7	0.0
1950	12.7	0.0	12.8	0.8	12.8	0.0	12.8	0.0	12.8	0.0	12.8	0.0	12.8	0.0	12.8	0.0	12.8	0.0	12.9	0.8	12.9	0.0	12.9	0.0
1951	12.9	0.0	12.9	0.0	13.0	0.8	13.0	0.0	13.0	0.0	13.5	3.8	13.6	0.7	13.6	0.0	13.6	0.0	13.6	0.0	13.6	0.0	13.8	1.5
1952	13.7	-0.7	13.7	0.0	14.0	2.2	14.0	0.0	14.0	0.0	14.1	0.7	14.1	0.0	14.1	0.0	14.2	0.7	14.3	0.7	14.3	0.0	14.3	0.0
1953	14.3	0.0	14.3	0.0	14.3	0.0	14.3	0.0	14.8	3.5	14.8	0.0	14.8	0.0	14.9	0.7	14.8	-0.7	14.9	0.7	14.9	0.0	14.9	0.0
1954	14.9	0.0	15.0	0.7	15.0	0.0	15.0	0.0	15.2	1.3	15.2	0.0	15.2	0.0	15.5	2.0	15.5	0.0	15.5	0.0	15.6	0.6	15.6	0.0
1955	15.6	0.0	16.2	3.8	16.2	0.0	16.2	0.0	16.2	0.0	16.2	0.0	16.2	0.0	16.2	0.0	16.2	0.0	16.2	0.0	16.8	3.7	16.8	0.0
1956	16.8	0.0	16.8	0.0	17.4	3.6	17.4	0.0	17.4	0.0	17.4	0.0	17.4	0.0	17.5	0.6	17.5	0.0	17.5	0.0	17.6	0.6	17.6	0.0
1957	17.7	0.6	17.9	1.1	17.9	0.0	17.9	0.0	17.9	0.0	17.9	0.0	17.9	0.0	17.9	0.0	17.9	0.0	17.9	0.0	18.5	3.4	18.5	0.0
1958	18.5	0.0	18.4	-0.5	18.5	0.5	18.5	0.0	18.5	0.0	18.5	0.0	18.5	0.0	18.6	0.5	18.6	0.0	18.6	0.0	18.7	0.5	18.7	0.0
1959	18.7	0.0	19.3	3.2	19.3	0.0	19.3	0.0	19.3	0.0	19.3	0.0	19.3	0.0	19.3	0.0	19.3	0.0	19.3	0.0	19.3	0.0	19.3	0.0
1960	19.3	0.0	19.4	0.5	19.4	0.0	19.4	0.0	19.5	0.5	19.5	0.0	19.8	1.5	19.9	0.5	19.9	0.0	19.9	0.0	19.9	0.0	19.9	0.0
1961	20.0	0.5	20.0	0.0	20.0	0.0	20.0	0.0	20.0	0.0	20.9	4.5	21.0	0.5	21.0	0.0	21.0	0.0	21.0	0.0	21.0	0.0	21.0	0.0
1962	20.9	-0.5	21.0	0.5	21.1	0.5	21.1	0.0	21.3	0.9	21.3	0.0	21.3	0.0	21.3	0.0	21.3	0.0	21.3	0.0	21.3	0.0	21.3	0.0
1963	21.3	0.0	21.4	0.5	21.4	0.0	21.4	0.0	21.5	0.5	22.9	6.5	22.9	0.0	22.9	0.0	22.9	0.0	22.9	0.0	23.0	0.4	23.0	0.0
1964	23.0	0.0	23.0	0.0	23.2	0.9	23.2	0.0	23.2	0.0	23.2	0.0	23.2	0.0	23.2	0.0	23.2	0.0	23.1	-0.4	23.3	0.9	23.3	0.0
1965	23.4	0.4	23.4	0.0	23.7	1.3	23.7	0.0	23.8	0.4	23.8	0.0	23.8	0.0	24.0	0.8	23.9	-0.4	23.9	0.0	23.9	0.0	23.9	0.0
1966	24.3	1.7	24.4	0.4	24.8	1.6	24.8	0.0	24.9	0.4	25.1	0.8	25.2	0.4	25.3	0.4	25.5	0.8	25.6	0.4	25.9	1.2	26.1	0.8
1967	26.2	0.4	26.3	0.4	26.6	1.1	26.5	-0.4	26.6	0.4	26.7	0.4	26.8	0.4	26.8	0.0	27.3	1.9	27.3	0.0	27.7	1.5	27.8	0.4
1968	28.1	1.1	28.3	0.7	28.6	1.1	28.6	0.0	28.7	0.3	28.5	-0.7	28.5	0.0	28.6	0.4	28.8	0.7	29.0	0.7	29.0	0.0	29.4	1.4
1969	29.8	1.4	30.0	0.7	30.3	1.0	30.5	0.7	30.7	0.7	30.9	0.7	31.0	0.3	31.2	0.6	31.5	1.0	31.0	-1.6	31.2	0.6	31.4	0.6
1970	31.9	1.6	32.3	1.3	32.9	1.9	33.1	0.6	33.2	0.3	33.3	0.3	33.6	0.9	34.0	1.2	34.2	0.6	34.2	0.0	34.4	0.6	34.6	0.6
1971	35.1	1.4	35.4	0.9	35.5	0.3	35.6	0.3	35.7	0.3	36.0	0.8	36.2	0.6	36.4	0.6	36.7	0.8	36.6	-0.3	36.7	0.3	37.0	0.8
1972	37.5	1.4	37.6	0.3	37.7	0.3	37.8	0.3	37.8	0.0	38.0	0.5	38.0	0.0	38.2	0.5	38.2	0.0	38.6	1.0	38.6	0.0	38.6	0.0
1973	38.7	0.3	38.8	0.3	39.4	1.5	39.5	0.3	39.7	0.5	39.8	0.3	39.9	0.3	40.0	0.3	40.4	1.0	40.8	1.0	41.2	1.0	41.2	0.0
1974	41.5	0.7	42.0	1.2	42.2	0.5	42.4	0.5	42.9	1.2	43.3	0.9	43.8	1.2	44.5	1.6	45.3	1.8	45.6	0.7	46.0	0.9	46.1	0.2
1975	47.4	2.8	48.5	2.3	48.6	0.2	49.2	1.2	49.4	0.4	49.8	0.8	50.6	1.6	51.6	2.0	52.1	1.0	52.5	0.8	52.4	-0.2	52.7	0.6
1976	54.1	2.7	54.6	0.9	54.8	0.4	55.0	0.4	55.5	0.9	55.6	0.2	57.1	2.7	57.3	0.4	57.3	0.0	57.6	0.5	58.5	1.6	58.5	0.0
1977	59.0	0.9	59.1	0.2	60.5	2.4	61.6	1.8	62.7	1.8	63.4	1.1	63.8	0.6	65.1	2.0	65.4	0.5	65.5	0.2	65.9	0.6	65.8	-0.2
1978	65.8	0.0	66.3	0.8	66.8	0.8	67.2	0.6	67.4	0.3	67.4	0.0	67.5	0.1	67.6	0.1	67.7	0.1	69.5	2.7	69.5	0.0	70.3	1.2
1979	71.7	2.0	72.1	0.6	72.2	0.1	73.0	1.1	72.6	-0.5	73.4	1.1	74.0	0.8	74.2	0.3	74.4	0.3	74.9	0.7	75.8	1.2	78.0	2.9
1980	78.1	0.1	78.2	0.1	78.6	0.5	79.3	0.9	79.4	0.1	79.7	0.4	80.4	0.9	80.0	-0.5	80.9	1.1	81.7	1.0	82.3	0.7	82.4	0.1
1981	83.2	1.0	84.4	1.4	84.7	0.4	85.2	0.6	85.8	0.7	86.0	0.2	86.3	0.3	86.3	0.0	87.1	0.9	88.0	1.0	88.1	0.1	88.3	0.2
1982	89.2	1.0	90.1	1.0	91.0	1.0	91.6	0.7	92.7	1.2	92.7	0.0	93.8	1.2	94.6	0.9	95.5	1.0	95.8	0.3	95.8	0.0	95.8	0.0
1983	96.2	0.4	96.1	-0.1	96.8	0.7	96.7	-0.1	96.5	-0.2	96.3	-0.2	97.9	1.7	98.9	1.0	98.9	0.0	99.4	0.5	101.2	1.8	105.1	3.9
1984	105.8	0.7	106.5	0.7	106.9	0.4	107.7	0.7	107.7	0.0	107.7	0.0	108.9	1.1	109.4	0.5	109.9	0.5	110.0	0.1	110.5	0.5	110.6	0.1
1985	111.4	0.7	113.1	1.5	114.2	1.0	114.5	0.3	115.2	0.6	115.2	0.0	117.1	1.6	117.7	0.5	118.7	0.8	119.2	0.4	120.1	0.8	120.3	0.2
1986	121.7	1.2	122.0	0.2	122.7	0.6	123.0	0.2	123.6	0.5	124.1	0.4	126.5	1.9	126.6	0.1	126.8	0.2	127.2	0.3	127.4	0.2	128.2	0.6
1987	-	-	130.2	1.6	-	-	131.6	1.1	-	-	132.9	1.0	-	-	134.3	1.1	-	-	134.9	0.4	-	-	135.3	0.3
1988	-	-	138.6	2.4	-	-	138.5	-0.1	-	-	137.5	-0.7	-	-	142.7	3.8	-	-	142.1	-0.4	-	-	143.8	1.2
1989	-	-	142.9	-0.6	-	-	145.0	1.5	-	-	146.2	0.8	-	-	149.5	2.3	-	-	149.9	0.3	-	-	150.8	0.6
1990	-	-	154.7	2.6	-	-	156.5	1.2	-	-	158.9	1.5	-	-	163.7	3.0	-	-	163.9	0.1	-	-	164.6	0.4
1991	-	-	168.4	2.3	-	-	167.9	-0.3	-	-	169.5	1.0	-	-	173.0	2.1	-	-	174.4	0.8	-	-	175.6	0.7
1992	-	-	179.2	2.1	-	-	180.9	0.9	-	-	181.0	0.1	-	-	182.1	0.6	-	-	184.2	1.2	-	-	184.6	0.2

[Continued]

Detroit-Ann Arbor-Flint, MI
Consumer Price Index - All Urban Consumers
Base 1982-1984 = 100
Medical Care
[Continued]

For 1947-2001. Columns headed % show percentile change in the index from the previous period for which an index is available.

Year	Jan Index	%	Feb Index	%	Mar Index	%	Apr Index	%	May Index	%	Jun Index	%	Jul Index	%	Aug Index	%	Sep Index	%	Oct Index	%	Nov Index	%	Dec Index	%
1993	-		188.6	2.2	-		191.3	1.4	-		191.0	-0.2	-		191.6	0.3	-		192.3	0.4	-		192.5	0.1
1994	-		195.3	1.5	-		199.0	1.9	-		200.0	0.5	-		200.0	0.0	-		203.1	1.6	-		203.9	0.4
1995	-		206.2	1.1	-		208.8	1.3	-		209.8	0.5	-		209.9	0.0	-		210.0	0.0	-		212.8	1.3
1996	-		216.4	1.7	-		214.7	-0.8	-		213.8	-0.4	-		213.1	-0.3	-		212.2	-0.4	-		211.7	-0.2
1997	-		213.9	1.0	-		213.5	-0.2	-		213.7	0.1	-		213.7	0.0	-		214.8	0.5	-		216.1	0.6
1998	-		217.4	0.6	-		222.1	2.2	-		235.9	6.2	-		236.5	0.3	-		236.7	0.1	-		241.4	2.0
1999	-		243.3	0.8	-		244.9	0.7	-		246.1	0.5	-		246.2	0.0	-		246.6	0.2	-		245.3	-0.5
2000	-		248.9	1.5	-		251.1	0.9	-		259.6	3.4	-		261.5	0.7	-		262.5	0.4	-		265.8	1.3
2001	-		266.4	0.2	-		272.1	2.1	-		273.5	0.5	-		274.8	0.5	-		276.0	0.4	-		276.5	0.2

Source: U.S. Department of Labor, Bureau of Labor Statistics, Division of Consumer Prices and Price Indexes. - indicates no data collected for period.

Detroit-Ann Arbor-Flint, MI
Consumer Price Index - Urban Wage Earners
Base 1982-1984 = 100
Medical Care

For 1947-2001. Columns headed % show percentile change in the index from the previous period for which an index is available.

Year	Jan Index	%	Feb Index	%	Mar Index	%	Apr Index	%	May Index	%	Jun Index	%	Jul Index	%	Aug Index	%	Sep Index	%	Oct Index	%	Nov Index	%	Dec Index	%
1947	11.7	-	11.8	0.9	11.9	0.8	12.0	0.8	12.0	0.0	12.1	0.8	12.1	0.0	12.1	0.0	12.2	0.8	12.2	0.0	12.2	0.0	12.2	0.0
1948	12.4	1.6	12.4	0.0	12.4	0.0	12.5	0.8	12.5	0.0	12.5	0.0	12.5	0.0	12.6	0.8	12.6	0.0	12.6	0.0	12.6	0.0	12.6	0.0
1949	12.6	0.0	12.7	0.8	12.8	0.8	12.8	0.0	12.8	0.0	12.8	0.0	12.8	0.0	12.8	0.0	12.9	0.8	12.9	0.0	13.0	0.8	13.0	0.0
1950	13.0	0.0	13.0	0.0	13.0	0.0	13.0	0.0	13.0	0.0	13.1	0.8	13.1	0.0	13.1	0.0	13.1	0.0	13.1	0.0	13.2	0.8	13.2	0.0
1951	13.2	0.0	13.2	0.0	13.3	0.8	13.3	0.0	13.3	0.0	13.8	3.8	13.8	0.0	13.8	0.0	13.8	0.0	13.9	0.7	13.9	0.0	14.1	1.4
1952	14.0	-0.7	14.0	0.0	14.3	2.1	14.3	0.0	14.3	0.0	14.4	0.7	14.4	0.0	14.4	0.0	14.5	0.7	14.6	0.7	14.6	0.0	14.6	0.0
1953	14.5	-0.7	14.6	0.7	14.6	0.0	14.6	0.0	15.1	3.4	15.1	0.0	15.1	0.0	15.1	0.0	15.1	0.0	15.1	0.0	15.2	0.7	15.2	0.0
1954	15.2	0.0	15.2	0.0	15.2	0.0	15.2	0.0	15.5	2.0	15.5	0.0	15.5	0.0	15.8	1.9	15.8	0.0	15.8	0.0	15.9	0.6	15.9	0.0
1955	15.9	0.0	16.5	3.8	16.5	0.0	16.5	0.0	16.5	0.0	16.5	0.0	16.5	0.0	16.5	0.0	16.5	0.0	16.5	0.0	17.1	3.6	17.1	0.0
1956	17.1	0.0	17.1	0.0	17.7	3.5	17.7	0.0	17.7	0.0	17.8	0.6	17.8	0.0	17.9	0.6	17.9	0.0	17.8	-0.6	17.9	0.0	17.9	0.0
1957	18.0	0.6	18.3	1.7	18.3	0.0	18.3	0.0	18.2	-0.5	18.2	0.0	18.2	0.0	18.3	0.5	18.3	0.0	18.3	0.0	18.8	2.7	18.8	0.0
1958	18.8	0.0	18.8	0.0	18.8	0.0	18.8	0.0	18.8	0.0	18.9	0.5	18.9	0.0	19.0	0.5	19.0	0.0	19.0	0.0	19.1	0.5	19.1	0.0
1959	19.1	0.0	19.7	3.1	19.7	0.0	19.7	0.0	19.7	0.0	19.7	0.0	19.7	0.0	19.7	0.0	19.7	0.0	19.7	0.0	19.7	0.0	19.7	0.0
1960	19.7	0.0	19.8	0.5	19.8	0.0	19.8	0.0	19.9	0.5	19.9	0.0	20.2	1.5	20.2	0.0	20.2	0.0	20.3	0.5	20.3	0.0	20.3	0.0
1961	20.3	0.0	20.4	0.5	20.4	0.0	20.3	-0.5	20.4	0.5	21.3	4.4	21.4	0.5	21.4	0.0	21.4	0.0	21.4	0.0	21.4	0.0	21.4	0.0
1962	21.3	-0.5	21.4	0.5	21.5	0.5	21.5	0.0	21.7	0.9	21.7	0.0	21.7	0.0	21.7	0.0	21.7	0.0	21.7	0.0	21.7	0.0	21.7	0.0
1963	21.7	0.0	21.8	0.5	21.9	0.5	21.9	0.0	21.9	0.0	23.3	6.4	23.3	0.0	23.3	0.0	23.3	0.0	23.3	0.0	23.4	0.4	23.4	0.0
1964	23.4	0.0	23.5	0.4	23.6	0.4	23.6	0.0	23.6	0.0	23.6	0.0	23.6	0.0	23.7	0.4	23.6	-0.4	23.6	0.0	23.7	0.4	23.7	0.0
1965	23.9	0.8	23.9	0.0	24.1	0.8	24.2	0.4	24.2	0.0	24.3	0.4	24.3	0.0	24.5	0.8	24.4	-0.4	24.4	0.0	24.4	0.0	24.4	0.0
1966	24.8	1.6	24.9	0.4	25.3	1.6	25.3	0.0	25.4	0.4	25.6	0.8	25.6	0.0	25.7	0.4	26.0	1.2	26.1	0.4	26.4	1.1	26.6	0.8
1967	26.7	0.4	26.8	0.4	27.1	1.1	27.0	-0.4	27.1	0.4	27.3	0.7	27.3	0.0	27.3	0.0	27.8	1.8	27.9	0.4	28.2	1.1	28.4	0.7
1968	28.7	1.1	28.8	0.3	29.1	1.0	29.2	0.3	29.3	0.3	29.1	-0.7	29.1	0.0	29.1	0.0	29.3	0.7	29.6	1.0	29.6	0.0	30.0	1.4
1969	30.3	1.0	30.6	1.0	30.9	1.0	31.1	0.6	31.3	0.6	31.5	0.6	31.6	0.3	31.8	0.6	32.1	0.9	31.6	-1.6	31.8	0.6	32.0	0.6
1970	32.5	1.6	32.9	1.2	33.5	1.8	33.8	0.9	33.9	0.3	34.0	0.3	34.2	0.6	34.6	1.2	34.8	0.6	34.8	0.0	35.1	0.9	35.3	0.6
1971	35.8	1.4	36.1	0.8	36.1	0.0	36.3	0.6	36.4	0.3	36.7	0.8	36.9	0.5	37.1	0.5	37.4	0.8	37.3	-0.3	37.4	0.3	37.7	0.8
1972	38.2	1.3	38.4	0.5	38.5	0.3	38.5	0.0	38.5	0.0	38.7	0.5	38.7	0.0	38.9	0.5	38.9	0.0	39.3	1.0	39.3	0.0	39.3	0.0
1973	39.4	0.3	39.5	0.3	40.1	1.5	40.3	0.5	40.4	0.2	40.6	0.5	40.7	0.2	40.8	0.2	41.2	1.0	41.6	1.0	42.0	1.0	42.0	0.0
1974	42.3	0.7	42.8	1.2	43.0	0.5	43.2	0.5	43.7	1.2	44.1	0.9	44.6	1.1	45.4	1.8	46.1	1.5	46.5	0.9	46.9	0.9	47.0	0.2
1975	48.3	2.8	49.4	2.3	49.6	0.4	50.2	1.2	50.4	0.4	50.8	0.8	51.6	1.6	52.6	1.9	53.1	0.9	53.5	0.8	53.4	-0.2	53.7	0.6
1976	55.2	2.8	55.6	0.7	55.9	0.5	56.0	0.2	56.5	0.9	56.7	0.4	58.2	2.6	58.4	0.3	58.4	0.0	58.7	0.5	59.6	1.5	59.6	0.0
1977	60.1	0.8	60.3	0.3	61.6	2.2	62.8	1.9	63.9	1.8	64.6	1.1	65.1	0.8	66.3	1.8	66.7	0.6	66.7	0.0	67.2	0.7	67.1	-0.1
1978	67.2	0.1	67.4	0.3	67.7	0.4	68.4	1.0	68.4	0.0	68.4	0.0	68.4	0.0	68.5	0.1	69.7	1.8	71.5	2.6	71.7	0.3	71.8	0.1
1979	72.9	1.5	72.8	-0.1	73.3	0.7	75.0	2.3	75.3	0.4	75.8	0.7	76.3	0.7	76.6	0.4	76.8	0.3	77.4	0.8	78.1	0.9	79.1	1.3
1980	79.1	0.0	79.2	0.1	79.4	0.3	80.9	1.9	81.4	0.6	81.6	0.2	81.7	0.1	81.6	-0.1	82.1	0.6	82.6	0.6	82.8	0.2	83.4	0.7
1981	84.5	1.3	85.4	1.1	85.9	0.6	86.0	0.1	86.2	0.2	86.6	0.5	86.8	0.2	87.2	0.5	87.7	0.6	88.2	0.6	88.7	0.6	88.6	-0.1
1982	89.6	1.1	90.4	0.9	91.4	1.1	91.9	0.5	93.0	1.2	93.0	0.0	94.0	1.1	94.7	0.7	95.7	1.1	96.0	0.3	95.9	-0.1	95.9	0.0
1983	96.4	0.5	96.3	-0.1	96.9	0.6	96.9	0.0	96.7	-0.2	96.6	-0.1	98.2	1.7	99.0	0.8	99.0	0.0	99.6	0.6	101.2	1.6	104.8	3.6
1984	105.4	0.6	106.2	0.8	106.6	0.4	107.2	0.6	107.3	0.1	107.4	0.1	108.5	1.0	108.9	0.4	109.5	0.6	109.6	0.1	110.2	0.5	110.3	0.1
1985	111.0	0.6	112.6	1.4	113.6	0.9	113.8	0.2	114.6	0.7	114.5	-0.1	116.2	1.5	116.8	0.5	117.7	0.8	118.2	0.4	119.0	0.7	119.3	0.3
1986	120.4	0.9	120.8	0.3	121.4	0.5	121.8	0.3	122.4	0.5	122.9	0.4	125.0	1.7	125.0	0.0	125.2	0.2	125.8	0.5	125.9	0.1	126.7	0.6
1987	-		128.5	1.4	-		130.1	1.2	-		131.3	0.9	-		132.7	1.1	-		133.1	0.3	-		133.9	0.6
1988	-		137.7	2.8	-		137.7	0.0	-		136.5	-0.9	-		142.5	4.4	-		141.9	-0.4	-		143.4	1.1
1989	-		142.9	-0.3	-		144.7	1.3	-		145.9	0.8	-		149.4	2.4	-		149.7	0.2	-		150.5	0.5
1990	-		154.2	2.5	-		155.9	1.1	-		158.0	1.3	-		163.1	3.2	-		163.2	0.1	-		163.6	0.2
1991	-		167.7	2.5	-		166.8	-0.5	-		168.1	0.8	-		171.4	2.0	-		172.8	0.8	-		174.1	0.8
1992	-		177.6	2.0	-		179.3	1.0	-		179.5	0.1	-		180.4	0.5	-		182.7	1.3	-		182.9	0.1

[Continued]

Detroit-Ann Arbor-Flint, MI
Consumer Price Index - Urban Wage Earners
Base 1982-1984 = 100
Medical Care
[Continued]

For 1947-2001. Columns headed % show percentile change in the index from the previous period for which an index is available.

Year	Jan		Feb		Mar		Apr		May		Jun		Jul		Aug		Sep		Oct		Nov		Dec	
	Index	%	Index	%	Index	%	Index	%	Index	%	Index	%	Index	%	Index	%	Index	%	Index	%	Index	%	Index	%
1993	-	-	187.1	2.3	-	-	189.8	1.4	-	-	189.5	-0.2	-	-	190.0	0.3	-	-	190.7	0.4	-	-	190.7	0.0
1994	-	-	193.3	1.4	-	-	196.8	1.8	-	-	197.7	0.5	-	-	197.6	-0.1	-	-	200.7	1.6	-	-	201.3	0.3
1995	-	-	204.1	1.4	-	-	206.4	1.1	-	-	207.7	0.6	-	-	207.8	0.0	-	-	208.1	0.1	-	-	210.7	1.2
1996	-	-	214.7	1.9	-	-	213.0	-0.8	-	-	212.2	-0.4	-	-	211.6	-0.3	-	-	210.7	-0.4	-	-	209.8	-0.4
1997	-	-	211.9	1.0	-	-	211.7	-0.1	-	-	212.0	0.1	-	-	212.2	0.1	-	-	213.0	0.4	-	-	214.4	0.7
1998	-	-	215.6	0.6	-	-	220.4	2.2	-	-	234.4	6.4	-	-	234.7	0.1	-	-	234.7	0.0	-	-	239.5	2.0
1999	-	-	241.3	0.8	-	-	242.9	0.7	-	-	244.0	0.5	-	-	243.8	-0.1	-	-	244.1	0.1	-	-	242.0	-0.9
2000	-	-	245.3	1.4	-	-	248.0	1.1	-	-	257.0	3.6	-	-	258.6	0.6	-	-	259.6	0.4	-	-	262.6	1.2
2001	-	-	263.3	0.3	-	-	268.8	2.1	-	-	270.2	0.5	-	-	271.3	0.4	-	-	272.4	0.4	-	-	273.0	0.2

Source: U.S. Department of Labor, Bureau of Labor Statistics, Division of Consumer Prices and Price Indexes. - indicates no data collected for period.

Detroit-Ann Arbor-Flint, MI
Consumer Price Index - All Urban Consumers
Base December 1997 = 100
Recreation

For 1997-2001. Columns headed % show percentile change in the index from the previous period for which an index is available.

Year	Jan		Feb		Mar		Apr		May		Jun		Jul		Aug		Sep		Oct		Nov		Dec	
	Index	%	Index	%	Index	%	Index	%	Index	%	Index	%	Index	%	Index	%	Index	%	Index	%	Index	%	Index	%
1997	-	-	-	-	-	-	-	-	-	-	-	-	-	-	-	-	-	-	-	-	-	-	100.0	-
1998	-	-	100.9	0.9	-	-	100.8	-0.1	-	-	101.1	0.3	-	-	102.1	1.0	-	-	97.6	-4.4	-	-	97.6	0.0
1999	-	-	98.5	0.9	-	-	104.8	6.4	-	-	106.8	1.9	-	-	105.7	-1.0	-	-	107.5	1.7	-	-	106.1	-1.3
2000	-	-	103.2	-2.7	-	-	107.2	3.9	-	-	108.3	1.0	-	-	106.5	-1.7	-	-	107.7	1.1	-	-	107.4	-0.3
2001	-	-	105.7	-1.6	-	-	108.6	2.7	-	-	107.9	-0.6	-	-	108.9	0.9	-	-	106.7	-2.0	-	-	103.9	-2.6

Source: U.S. Department of Labor, Bureau of Labor Statistics, Division of Consumer Prices and Price Indexes. - indicates no data collected for period.

Detroit-Ann Arbor-Flint, MI
Consumer Price Index - Urban Wage Earners
Base December 1997 = 100
Recreation

For 1997-2001. Columns headed % show percentile change in the index from the previous period for which an index is available.

Year	Jan Index	%	Feb Index	%	Mar Index	%	Apr Index	%	May Index	%	Jun Index	%	Jul Index	%	Aug Index	%	Sep Index	%	Oct Index	%	Nov Index	%	Dec Index	%
1997	-	-	-	-	-	-	-	-	-	-	-	-	-	-	-	-	-	-	-	-	-	-	-	-
1998	-	-	100.6	0.6	-	-	100.8	0.2	-	-	101.1	0.3	-	-	102.1	1.0	-	-	-	-	-	-	100.0	-
1999	-	-	98.5	0.7	-	-	104.3	5.9	-	-	106.2	1.8	-	-	105.2	-0.9	-	-	98.1	-3.9	-	-	97.8	-0.3
2000	-	-	103.1	-2.3	-	-	106.7	3.5	-	-	107.6	0.8	-	-	105.2	-0.9	-	-	106.8	1.5	-	-	105.5	-1.2
2001	-	-	104.9	-1.6	-	-	107.9	2.9	-	-	107.5	-0.4	-	-	107.8	0.3	-	-	106.0	-1.7	-	-	103.3	-2.5

Source: U.S. Department of Labor, Bureau of Labor Statistics, Division of Consumer Prices and Price Indexes. - indicates no data collected for period.

Detroit-Ann Arbor-Flint, MI
Consumer Price Index - All Urban Consumers
Base December 1997 = 100
Education & Communication

For 1997-2001. Columns headed % show percentile change in the index from the previous period for which an index is available.

Year	Jan Index	%	Feb Index	%	Mar Index	%	Apr Index	%	May Index	%	Jun Index	%	Jul Index	%	Aug Index	%	Sep Index	%	Oct Index	%	Nov Index	%	Dec Index	%
1997	-	-	-	-	-	-	-	-	-	-	-	-	-	-	-	-	-	-	-	-	-	-	100.0	-
1998	-	-	99.8	-0.2	-	-	100.3	0.5	-	-	103.7	3.4	-	-	103.9	0.2	-	-	104.2	0.3	-	-	105.0	0.8
1999	-	-	105.0	0.0	-	-	106.8	1.7	-	-	105.8	-0.9	-	-	107.3	1.4	-	-	107.4	0.1	-	-	108.8	1.3
2000	-	-	109.1	0.3	-	-	106.8	-2.1	-	-	106.8	0.0	-	-	107.7	0.8	-	-	108.5	0.7	-	-	108.5	0.0
2001	-	-	108.8	0.3	-	-	108.5	-0.3	-	-	108.3	-0.2	-	-	108.9	0.6	-	-	109.5	0.6	-	-	112.9	3.1

Source: U.S. Department of Labor, Bureau of Labor Statistics, Division of Consumer Prices and Price Indexes. - indicates no data collected for period.

Detroit-Ann Arbor-Flint, MI
Consumer Price Index - Urban Wage Earners
Base December 1997 = 100
Education & Communication

For 1997-2001. Columns headed % show percentile change in the index from the previous period for which an index is available.

Year	Jan		Feb		Mar		Apr		May		Jun		Jul		Aug		Sep		Oct		Nov		Dec	
	Index	%	Index	%	Index	%	Index	%	Index	%	Index	%	Index	%	Index	%	Index	%	Index	%	Index	%	Index	%
1997	-	-	-	-	-	-	-	-	-	-	-	-	-	-	-	-	-	-	-	-	-	-	100.0	-
1998	-	-	99.7	-0.3	-	-	100.2	0.5	-	-	103.7	3.5	-	-	103.8	0.1	-	-	104.0	0.2	-	-	104.9	0.9
1999	-	-	104.8	-0.1	-	-	106.6	1.7	-	-	105.6	-0.9	-	-	107.0	1.3	-	-	107.1	0.1	-	-	108.5	1.3
2000	-	-	108.8	0.3	-	-	106.5	-2.1	-	-	106.5	0.0	-	-	107.4	0.8	-	-	108.2	0.7	-	-	108.1	-0.1
2001	-	-	108.5	0.4	-	-	108.2	-0.3	-	-	108.0	-0.2	-	-	108.4	0.4	-	-	109.0	0.6	-	-	112.5	3.2

Source: U.S. Department of Labor, Bureau of Labor Statistics, Division of Consumer Prices and Price Indexes. - indicates no data collected for period.

Honolulu, HI
Consumer Price Index - All Urban Consumers
Base 1982-1984 = 100
Annual Averages

For 1963-2001. Columns headed % show percentile change in the index from the previous period for which an index is available.

Year	All Items		Food & Beverage		Housing		Apparel		Trans-portation		Medical Care		Recrea-tion*		Education & Communic.*		Other Goods & Services	
	Index	%	Index	%	Index	%	Index	%	Index	%	Index	%	Index	%	Index	%	Index	%
1963	-	-	-	-	-	-	-	-	-	-	-	-	-	-	-	-	-	-
1964	33.7	-	-	-	-	-	46.7	-	37.7	-	25.1	-	-	-	-	-	-	-
1965	34.4	2.1	-	-	-	-	47.1	0.9	37.7	0.0	25.8	2.8	-	-	-	-	-	-
1966	35.3	2.6	-	-	-	-	47.9	1.7	37.8	0.3	26.6	3.1	-	-	-	-	-	-
1967	36.3	2.8	-	-	-	-	48.8	1.9	38.7	2.4	28.3	6.4	-	-	-	-	-	-
1968	37.7	3.9	-	-	-	-	50.7	3.9	40.1	3.6	29.9	5.7	-	-	-	-	-	-
1969	39.4	4.5	-	-	-	-	53.4	5.3	41.5	3.5	32.0	7.0	-	-	-	-	-	-
1970	41.5	5.3	-	-	-	-	56.2	5.2	43.4	4.6	33.5	4.7	-	-	-	-	-	-
1971	43.2	4.1					57.4	2.1	46.7	7.6	35.2	5.1	-	-	-	-	-	-
1972	44.6	3.2	-	-	-	-	58.9	2.6	47.6	1.9	36.0	2.3	-	-	-	-	-	-
1973	46.6	4.5	-	-	-	-	60.6	2.9	48.0	0.8	37.7	4.7	-	-	-	-	-	-
1974	51.5	10.5			-	-	65.1	7.4	52.3	9.0	41.5	10.1	-	-	-	-	-	-
1975	56.3	9.3	-	-	-	-	69.0	6.0	56.8	8.6	46.6	12.3	-	-	-	-	-	-
1976	59.1	5.0	59.7	-	59.2	-	71.6	3.8	59.5	4.8	51.5	10.5	-	-	-	-	53.8	-
1977	62.1	5.1	62.8	5.2	61.6	4.1	74.3	3.8	61.8	3.9	57.4	11.5	-	-	-	-	57.5	6.9
1978	66.9	7.7	69.0	9.9	66.0	7.1	78.8	6.1	66.0	6.8	62.5	8.9	-	-	-	-	61.4	6.8
1979	74.3	11.1	77.7	12.6	74.0	12.1	83.9	6.5	73.4	11.2	67.5	8.0	-	-	-	-	66.5	8.3
1980	83.0	11.7	84.2	8.4	83.2	12.4	89.8	7.0	86.6	18.0	73.1	8.3	-	-	-	-	73.3	10.2
1981	91.7	10.5	92.6	10.0	92.3	10.9	94.5	5.2	95.7	10.5	81.8	11.9	-	-	-	-	81.5	11.2
1982	97.2	6.0	96.9	4.6	98.0	6.2	98.4	4.1	99.0	3.4	91.6	12.0	-	-	-	-	92.0	12.9
1983	99.3	2.2	99.5	2.7	98.9	0.9	101.4	3.0	98.2	-0.8	101.1	10.4	-	-	-	-	101.4	10.2
1984	103.5	4.2	103.6	4.1	103.1	4.2	100.2	-1.2	102.9	4.8	107.3	6.1	-	-	-	-	106.6	5.1
1985	106.8	3.2	107.8	4.1	106.0	2.8	99.6	-0.6	104.9	1.9	113.2	5.5	-	-	-	-	112.5	5.5
1986	109.4	2.4	110.0	2.0	108.4	2.3	99.8	0.2	105.2	0.3	122.3	8.0	-	-	-	-	119.6	6.3
1987	114.9	5.0	114.1	3.7	115.0	6.1	102.5	2.7	109.7	4.3	127.9	4.6	-	-	-	-	-	-
1988	121.7	5.9	120.3	5.4	123.0	7.0	106.8	4.2	116.1	5.8	132.5	3.6	-	-	-	-	137.1	14.6
1989	128.7	5.8	128.1	6.5	131.1	6.6	104.3	-2.3	123.9	6.7	139.3	5.1	-	-	-	-	146.1	6.6
1990	138.1	7.3	137.8	7.6	141.5	7.9	107.0	2.6	131.1	5.8	154.2	10.7	-	-	-	-	160.4	9.8
1991	148.0	7.2	145.9	5.9	152.8	8.0	110.5	3.3	139.3	6.3	171.3	11.1	-	-	-	-	175.7	9.5
1992	155.1	4.8	148.5	1.8	161.7	5.8	114.2	3.3	147.4	5.8	182.6	6.6	-	-	-	-	189.0	7.6
1993	160.1	3.2	152.9	3.0	166.5	3.0	116.5	2.0	150.5	2.1	197.4	8.1	-	-	-	-	200.1	5.9
1994	164.5	2.7	153.4	0.3	171.6	3.1	118.7	1.9	156.4	3.9	206.0	4.4	-	-	-	-	209.6	4.7
1995	168.1	2.2	156.8	2.2	174.7	1.8	117.5	-1.0	162.4	3.8	209.8	1.8	-	-	-	-	216.8	3.4
1996	170.7	1.5	156.6	-0.1	176.8	1.2	118.5	0.9	167.0	2.8	215.0	2.5	-	-	-	-	226.5	4.5
1997	171.9	0.7	159.2	1.7	177.1	0.2	117.3	-1.0	166.2	-0.5	217.3	1.1	-	-	-	-	239.0	5.5
1998	171.5	-0.2	159.1	-0.1	176.0	-0.6	112.2	-4.3	162.5	-2.2	226.1	4.0	100.8	-	99.1	-	256.1	7.2
1999	173.3	1.0	162.9	2.4	175.8	-0.1	105.4	-6.1	162.2	-0.2	231.3	2.3	101.9	1.1	104.5	5.4	275.6	7.6
2000	176.3	1.7	164.8	1.2	177.9	1.2	103.5	-1.8	169.6	4.6	239.8	3.7	102.8	0.9	106.5	1.9	279.7	1.5
2001	-	-	-	-	-	-	-	-	-	-	-	-	-	-	-	-	-	-

Source: U.S. Department of Labor, Bureau of Labor Statistics, Division of Consumer Prices and Price Indexes. *Base is December 1997 = 100. - indicates no data collected for period.

Honolulu, HI
Consumer Price Index - Urban Wage Earners
Base 1982-1984 = 100
Annual Averages

For 1963-2001. Columns headed % show percentile change in the index from the previous period for which an index is available.

Year	All Items Index	%	Food & Beverage Index	%	Housing Index	%	Apparel Index	%	Transportation Index	%	Medical Care Index	%	Recreation* Index	%	Education & Communic.* Index	%	Other Goods & Services Index	%
1963	-	-	-	-	-	-	-	-	-	-	-	-	-	-	-	-	-	-
1964	33.3	-	-	-	-	-	45.2	-	37.8	-	24.6	-	-	-	-	-	-	-
1965	33.9	1.8	-	-	-	-	45.6	0.9	37.7	-0.3	25.3	2.8	-	-	-	-	-	-
1966	34.8	2.7	-	-	-	-	46.3	1.5	37.8	0.3	26.1	3.2	-	-	-	-	-	-
1967	35.8	2.9	-	-	-	-	47.2	1.9	38.7	2.4	27.7	6.1	-	-	-	-	-	-
1968	37.2	3.9	-	-	-	-	49.0	3.8	40.2	3.9	29.3	5.8	-	-	-	-	-	-
1969	38.8	4.3	-	-	-	-	51.7	5.5	41.5	3.2	31.3	6.8	-	-	-	-	-	-
1970	40.9	5.4	-	-	-	-	54.4	5.2	43.5	4.8	32.8	4.8	-	-	-	-	-	-
1971	42.6	4.2	-	-	-	-	55.6	2.2	46.7	7.4	34.5	5.2	-	-	-	-	-	-
1972	44.0	3.3	-	-	-	-	56.9	2.3	47.6	1.9	35.3	2.3	-	-	-	-	-	-
1973	45.9	4.3	-	-	-	-	58.6	3.0	48.0	0.8	36.9	4.5	-	-	-	-	-	-
1974	50.8	10.7	-	-	-	-	63.0	7.5	52.3	9.0	40.7	10.3	-	-	-	-	-	-
1975	55.5	9.3	-	-	-	-	66.7	5.9	56.9	8.8	45.6	12.0	-	-	-	-	-	-
1976	58.3	5.0	58.8	-	58.1	-	69.3	3.9	59.5	4.6	50.4	10.5	-	-	-	-	-	-
1977	61.2	5.0	61.9	5.3	60.4	4.0	71.9	3.8	61.9	4.0	56.2	11.5	-	-	-	-	54.8	-
1978	65.9	7.7	68.0	9.9	64.6	7.0	75.3	4.7	65.9	6.5	61.8	10.0	-	-	-	-	58.5	6.8
1979	73.2	11.1	76.4	12.4	72.2	11.8	79.9	6.1	73.5	11.5	66.3	7.3	-	-	-	-	61.9	5.8
1980	81.9	11.9	83.5	9.3	80.4	11.4	91.4	14.4	86.6	17.8	72.3	9.0	-	-	-	-	66.9	8.1
1981	90.5	10.5	92.3	10.5	89.0	10.7	95.3	4.3	96.2	11.1	81.9	13.3	-	-	-	-	72.8	8.8
1982	96.0	6.1	96.8	4.9	94.9	6.6	98.3	3.1	99.1	3.0	92.0	12.3	-	-	-	-	81.1	11.4
1983	99.8	4.0	99.5	2.8	100.1	5.5	101.4	3.2	98.1	-1.0	101.1	9.9	-	-	-	-	91.6	12.9
1984	104.3	4.5	103.7	4.2	104.9	4.8	100.3	-1.1	102.8	4.8	106.9	5.7	-	-	-	-	101.7	11.0
1985	107.9	3.5	108.3	4.4	108.6	3.5	99.4	-0.9	104.7	1.8	112.6	5.3	-	-	-	-	106.6	4.8
1986	110.3	2.2	110.8	2.3	111.0	2.2	100.1	0.7	104.7	0.0	121.1	7.5	-	-	-	-	112.5	5.5
1987	115.9	5.1	115.3	4.1	117.4	5.8	103.7	3.6	109.2	4.3	126.7	4.6	-	-	-	-	119.1	5.9
1988	122.8	6.0	121.7	5.6	125.5	6.9	108.2	4.3	115.7	6.0	131.4	3.7	-	-	-	-	-	-
1989	129.7	5.6	129.2	6.2	133.7	6.5	105.2	-2.8	123.7	6.9	138.3	5.3	-	-	-	-	136.4	14.5
1990	138.9	7.1	138.6	7.3	144.3	7.9	108.1	2.8	130.2	5.3	153.3	10.8	-	-	-	-	146.3	7.3
1991	148.9	7.2	146.5	5.7	155.7	7.9	111.9	3.5	138.6	6.5	170.3	11.1	-	-	-	-	161.9	10.7
1992	155.9	4.7	149.5	2.0	164.1	5.4	115.6	3.3	146.7	5.8	182.2	7.0	-	-	-	-	179.1	10.6
1993	160.7	3.1	153.8	2.9	169.1	3.0	118.5	2.5	148.9	1.5	197.5	8.4	-	-	-	-	193.7	8.2
1994	164.7	2.5	153.6	-0.1	173.9	2.8	120.0	1.3	154.3	3.6	206.9	4.8	-	-	-	-	204.5	5.6
1995	168.4	2.2	156.6	2.0	177.3	2.0	119.0	-0.8	160.2	3.8	213.1	3.0	-	-	-	-	212.4	3.9
1996	171.0	1.5	156.6	0.0	179.4	1.2	120.1	0.9	164.8	2.9	218.9	2.7	-	-	-	-	219.7	3.4
1997	172.2	0.7	159.2	1.7	179.7	0.2	119.0	-0.9	163.8	-0.6	221.6	1.2	-	-	-	-	227.6	3.6
1998	171.6	-0.3	159.0	-0.1	177.9	-1.0	115.6	-2.9	159.5	-2.6	230.7	4.1	-	-	-	-	239.8	5.4
1999	173.4	1.0	162.7	2.3	177.1	-0.4	109.6	-5.2	158.0	-0.9	235.4	2.0	100.9	-	99.6	-	258.5	7.8
2000	176.5	1.8	164.8	1.3	178.8	1.0	108.5	-1.0	165.7	4.9	242.8	3.1	101.7	0.8	105.0	5.4	287.3	11.1
2001	-	-	-	-	-	-	-	-	-	-	-	-	102.0	0.3	107.4	2.3	292.8	1.9

Source: U.S. Department of Labor, Bureau of Labor Statistics, Division of Consumer Prices and Price Indexes. *Base is December 1997 = 100. - indicates no data collected for period.

Honolulu, HI
Consumer Price Index - All Urban Consumers
Base 1982-1984 = 100
All Items

For 1963-2001. Columns headed % show percentile change in the index from the previous period for which an index is available.

Year	Jan Index	%	Feb Index	%	Mar Index	%	Apr Index	%	May Index	%	Jun Index	%	Jul Index	%	Aug Index	%	Sep Index	%	Oct Index	%	Nov Index	%	Dec Index	%
1963	-	-	-	-	-	-	-	-	-	-	-	-	-	-	-	-	-	-	-	-	-	-	33.7	-
1964	-	-	-	-	33.9	0.6	-	-	-	-	33.6	-0.9	-	-	-	-	33.7	0.3	-	-	-	-	34.0	0.9
1965	-	-	-	-	34.2	0.6	-	-	-	-	34.2	0.0	-	-	-	-	34.4	0.6	-	-	-	-	34.9	1.5
1966	-	-	-	-	35.1	0.6	-	-	-	-	35.2	0.3	-	-	-	-	35.6	1.1	-	-	-	-	35.9	0.8
1967	-	-	-	-	35.9	0.0	-	-	-	-	36.2	0.8	-	-	-	-	36.5	0.8	-	-	-	-	37.0	1.4
1968	-	-	-	-	37.3	0.8	-	-	-	-	37.6	0.8	-	-	-	-	38.0	1.1	-	-	-	-	38.4	1.1
1969	-	-	-	-	38.9	1.3	-	-	-	-	39.3	1.0	-	-	-	-	39.8	1.3	-	-	-	-	40.3	1.3
1970	-	-	-	-	41.1	2.0	-	-	-	-	41.6	1.2	-	-	-	-	41.7	0.2	-	-	-	-	42.0	0.7
1971	-	-	-	-	42.4	1.0	-	-	-	-	43.0	1.4	-	-	-	-	44.0	2.3	-	-	-	-	44.0	0.0
1972	-	-	-	-	44.5	1.1	-	-	-	-	44.4	-0.2	-	-	-	-	44.7	0.7	-	-	-	-	45.2	1.1
1973	-	-	-	-	45.8	1.3	-	-	-	-	46.3	1.1	-	-	-	-	47.1	1.7	-	-	-	-	48.2	2.3
1974	-	-	-	-	50.0	3.7	-	-	-	-	51.3	2.6	-	-	-	-	52.9	3.1	-	-	-	-	53.9	1.9
1975	-	-	-	-	55.2	2.4	-	-	-	-	56.0	1.4	-	-	-	-	57.2	2.1	-	-	-	-	58.0	1.4
1976	-	-	-	-	58.5	0.9	-	-	-	-	59.0	0.9	-	-	-	-	59.6	1.0	-	-	-	-	60.1	0.8
1977	-	-	-	-	61.1	1.7	-	-	-	-	61.9	1.3	-	-	-	-	63.0	1.8	-	-	-	-	63.5	0.8
1978	-	-	64.7	1.9	-	-	65.9	1.9	-	-	66.8	1.4	-	-	67.4	0.9	-	-	68.6	1.8	-	-	69.5	1.3
1979	-	-	71.3	2.6	-	-	72.9	2.2	-	-	74.2	1.8	-	-	75.3	1.5	-	-	76.5	1.6	-	-	78.0	2.0
1980	-	-	80.2	2.8	-	-	82.6	3.0	-	-	82.6	0.0	-	-	83.6	1.2	-	-	85.2	1.9	-	-	85.8	0.7
1981	-	-	88.4	3.0	-	-	90.8	2.7	-	-	91.8	1.1	-	-	93.2	1.5	-	-	94.2	1.1	-	-	93.8	-0.4
1982	-	-	95.2	1.5	-	-	95.6	0.4	-	-	97.7	2.2	-	-	97.9	0.2	-	-	100.0	2.1	-	-	98.0	-2.0
1983	-	-	98.2	0.2	-	-	99.1	0.9	-	-	98.6	-0.5	-	-	99.3	0.7	-	-	100.4	1.1	-	-	101.1	0.7
1984	-	-	102.0	0.9	-	-	102.9	0.9	-	-	103.4	0.5	-	-	103.9	0.5	-	-	104.4	0.5	-	-	105.3	0.9
1985	-	-	106.3	0.9	-	-	106.3	0.0	-	-	106.6	0.3	-	-	106.9	0.3	-	-	107.4	0.5	-	-	108.4	0.9
1986	-	-	109.4	0.9	-	-	108.6	-0.7	-	-	108.7	0.1	-	-	109.5	0.7	-	-	109.8	0.3	-	-	110.9	1.0
1987	-	-	-	-	-	-	-	-	-	-	113.3	2.2	-	-	-	-	-	-	-	-	-	-	116.5	2.8
1988	-	-	-	-	-	-	-	-	-	-	120.1	3.1	-	-	-	-	-	-	-	-	-	-	123.4	2.7
1989	-	-	-	-	-	-	-	-	-	-	126.4	2.4	-	-	-	-	-	-	-	-	-	-	131.1	3.7
1990	-	-	-	-	-	-	-	-	-	-	135.5	3.4	-	-	-	-	-	-	-	-	-	-	140.8	3.9
1991	-	-	-	-	-	-	-	-	-	-	146.8	4.3	-	-	-	-	-	-	-	-	-	-	149.1	1.6
1992	-	-	-	-	-	-	-	-	-	-	153.9	3.2	-	-	-	-	-	-	-	-	-	-	156.4	1.6
1993	-	-	-	-	-	-	-	-	-	-	158.6	1.4	-	-	-	-	-	-	-	-	-	-	161.6	1.9
1994	-	-	-	-	-	-	-	-	-	-	163.4	1.1	-	-	-	-	-	-	-	-	-	-	165.7	1.4
1995	-	-	-	-	-	-	-	-	-	-	166.9	0.7	-	-	-	-	-	-	-	-	-	-	169.4	1.5
1996	-	-	-	-	-	-	-	-	-	-	170.5	0.6	-	-	-	-	-	-	-	-	-	-	171.0	0.3
1997	-	-	-	-	-	-	-	-	-	-	172.1	0.6	-	-	-	-	-	-	-	-	-	-	171.8	-0.2
1998	-	-	-	-	-	-	-	-	-	-	172.0	0.1	-	-	-	-	-	-	-	-	-	-	171.0	-0.6
1999	-	-	-	-	-	-	-	-	-	-	172.7	1.0	-	-	-	-	-	-	-	-	-	-	173.8	0.6
2000	-	-	-	-	-	-	-	-	-	-	175.9	1.2	-	-	-	-	-	-	-	-	-	-	176.7	0.5
2001	-	-	-	-	-	-	-	-	-	-	178.1	0.8	-	-	-	-	-	-	-	-	-	-	-	-

Source: U.S. Department of Labor, Bureau of Labor Statistics, Division of Consumer Prices and Price Indexes. - indicates no data collected for period.

Honolulu, HI
Consumer Price Index - Urban Wage Earners
Base 1982-1984 = 100
All Items

For 1963-2001. Columns headed % show percentile change in the index from the previous period for which an index is available.

Year	Jan Index	%	Feb Index	%	Mar Index	%	Apr Index	%	May Index	%	Jun Index	%	Jul Index	%	Aug Index	%	Sep Index	%	Oct Index	%	Nov Index	%	Dec Index	%
1963	-	-	-	-	-	-	-	-	-	-	-	-	-	-	-	-	-	-	-	-	-	-	33.2	-
1964	-	-	-	-	33.4	0.6	-	-	-	-	33.1	-0.9	-	-	-	-	33.3	0.6	-	-	-	-	33.5	0.6
1965	-	-	-	-	33.7	0.6	-	-	-	-	33.7	0.0	-	-	-	-	33.9	0.6	-	-	-	-	34.4	1.5
1966	-	-	-	-	34.6	0.6	-	-	-	-	34.6	0.0	-	-	-	-	35.0	1.2	-	-	-	-	35.4	1.1
1967	-	-	-	-	35.4	0.0	-	-	-	-	35.7	0.8	-	-	-	-	36.0	0.8	-	-	-	-	36.4	1.1
1968	-	-	-	-	36.8	1.1	-	-	-	-	37.0	0.5	-	-	-	-	37.4	1.1	-	-	-	-	37.8	1.1
1969	-	-	-	-	38.4	1.6	-	-	-	-	38.7	0.8	-	-	-	-	39.2	1.3	-	-	-	-	39.7	1.3
1970	-	-	-	-	40.5	2.0	-	-	-	-	40.9	1.0	-	-	-	-	41.1	0.5	-	-	-	-	41.4	0.7
1971	-	-	-	-	41.8	1.0	-	-	-	-	42.4	1.4	-	-	-	-	43.4	2.4	-	-	-	-	43.3	-0.2
1972	-	-	-	-	43.8	1.2	-	-	-	-	43.7	-0.2	-	-	-	-	44.1	0.9	-	-	-	-	44.5	0.9
1973	-	-	-	-	45.1	1.3	-	-	-	-	45.6	1.1	-	-	-	-	46.4	1.8	-	-	-	-	47.5	2.4
1974	-	-	-	-	49.3	3.8	-	-	-	-	50.5	2.4	-	-	-	-	52.1	3.2	-	-	-	-	53.2	2.1
1975	-	-	-	-	54.4	2.3	-	-	-	-	55.2	1.5	-	-	-	-	56.4	2.2	-	-	-	-	57.2	1.4
1976	-	-	-	-	57.7	0.9	-	-	-	-	58.1	0.7	-	-	-	-	58.7	1.0	-	-	-	-	59.2	0.9
1977	-	-	-	-	60.2	1.7	-	-	-	-	61.0	1.3	-	-	-	-	62.1	1.8	-	-	-	-	62.6	0.8
1978	-	-	63.5	1.4	-	-	64.9	2.2	-	-	65.9	1.5	-	-	66.6	1.1	-	-	67.5	1.4	-	-	68.4	1.3
1979	-	-	70.2	2.6	-	-	71.6	2.0	-	-	72.9	1.8	-	-	74.2	1.8	-	-	75.6	1.9	-	-	77.1	2.0
1980	-	-	79.2	2.7	-	-	81.8	3.3	-	-	81.6	-0.2	-	-	82.1	0.6	-	-	83.6	1.8	-	-	84.8	1.4
1981	-	-	87.2	2.8	-	-	89.6	2.8	-	-	90.8	1.3	-	-	91.8	1.1	-	-	92.7	1.0	-	-	92.8	0.1
1982	-	-	94.1	1.4	-	-	94.6	0.5	-	-	96.3	1.8	-	-	96.5	0.2	-	-	98.3	1.9	-	-	97.0	-1.3
1983	-	-	98.4	1.4	-	-	99.1	0.7	-	-	97.9	-1.2	-	-	99.6	1.7	-	-	102.3	2.7	-	-	103.2	0.9
1984	-	-	101.8	-1.4	-	-	103.4	1.6	-	-	104.1	0.7	-	-	105.1	1.0	-	-	105.4	0.3	-	-	106.5	1.0
1985	-	-	107.5	0.9	-	-	107.4	-0.1	-	-	107.5	0.1	-	-	107.8	0.3	-	-	108.4	0.6	-	-	109.5	1.0
1986	-	-	110.4	0.8	-	-	109.5	-0.8	-	-	109.7	0.2	-	-	110.4	0.6	-	-	110.5	0.1	-	-	111.9	1.3
1987	-	-	-	-	-	-	-	-	-	-	114.3	2.1	-	-	-	-	-	-	-	-	-	-	117.6	2.9
1988	-	-	-	-	-	-	-	-	-	-	121.1	3.0	-	-	-	-	-	-	-	-	-	-	124.5	2.8
1989	-	-	-	-	-	-	-	-	-	-	127.4	2.3	-	-	-	-	-	-	-	-	-	-	132.0	3.6
1990	-	-	-	-	-	-	-	-	-	-	136.3	3.3	-	-	-	-	-	-	-	-	-	-	141.6	3.9
1991	-	-	-	-	-	-	-	-	-	-	147.7	4.3	-	-	-	-	-	-	-	-	-	-	150.1	1.6
1992	-	-	-	-	-	-	-	-	-	-	154.6	3.0	-	-	-	-	-	-	-	-	-	-	157.2	1.7
1993	-	-	-	-	-	-	-	-	-	-	159.4	1.4	-	-	-	-	-	-	-	-	-	-	162.0	1.6
1994	-	-	-	-	-	-	-	-	-	-	163.5	0.9	-	-	-	-	-	-	-	-	-	-	165.8	1.4
1995	-	-	-	-	-	-	-	-	-	-	167.2	0.8	-	-	-	-	-	-	-	-	-	-	169.7	1.5
1996	-	-	-	-	-	-	-	-	-	-	170.8	0.6	-	-	-	-	-	-	-	-	-	-	171.2	0.2
1997	-	-	-	-	-	-	-	-	-	-	172.4	0.7	-	-	-	-	-	-	-	-	-	-	172.0	-0.2
1998	-	-	-	-	-	-	-	-	-	-	172.3	0.2	-	-	-	-	-	-	-	-	-	-	171.0	-0.8
1999	-	-	-	-	-	-	-	-	-	-	173.0	1.2	-	-	-	-	-	-	-	-	-	-	173.9	0.5
2000	-	-	-	-	-	-	-	-	-	-	176.0	1.2	-	-	-	-	-	-	-	-	-	-	176.9	0.5
2001	-	-	-	-	-	-	-	-	-	-	178.6	1.0	-	-	-	-	-	-	-	-	-	-	-	-

Source: U.S. Department of Labor, Bureau of Labor Statistics, Division of Consumer Prices and Price Indexes. - indicates no data collected for period.

Honolulu, HI
Consumer Price Index - All Urban Consumers
Base 1982-1984 = 100
Food and Beverages

For 1975-2001. Columns headed % show percentile change in the index from the previous period for which an index is available.

Year	Jan Index	%	Feb Index	%	Mar Index	%	Apr Index	%	May Index	%	Jun Index	%	Jul Index	%	Aug Index	%	Sep Index	%	Oct Index	%	Nov Index	%	Dec Index	%
1975	-	-	-	-	-	-	-	-	-	-	-	-	-	-	-	-	-	-	-	-	-	-	59.4	-
1976	-	-	-	-	59.5	0.2	-	-	-	-	59.6	0.2	-	-	-	-	59.5	-0.2	-	-	-	-	60.5	1.7
1977	-	-	-	-	61.8	2.1	-	-	-	-	62.6	1.3	-	-	-	-	63.8	1.9	-	-	-	-	64.4	0.9
1978	-	-	65.9	2.3	-	-	67.6	2.6	-	-	69.2	2.4	-	-	70.0	1.2	-	-	71.2	1.7	-	-	72.3	1.5
1979	-	-	74.6	3.2	-	-	76.5	2.5	-	-	78.3	2.4	-	-	78.4	0.1	-	-	79.5	1.4	-	-	80.6	1.4
1980	-	-	81.6	1.2	-	-	83.0	1.7	-	-	83.3	0.4	-	-	85.1	2.2	-	-	86.5	1.6	-	-	87.8	1.5
1981	-	-	90.8	3.4	-	-	92.2	1.5	-	-	92.7	0.5	-	-	93.5	0.9	-	-	94.2	0.7	-	-	93.8	-0.4
1982	-	-	96.1	2.5	-	-	96.2	0.1	-	-	96.9	0.7	-	-	97.3	0.4	-	-	97.7	0.4	-	-	98.3	0.6
1983	-	-	98.8	0.5	-	-	99.6	0.8	-	-	99.4	-0.2	-	-	99.8	0.4	-	-	100.0	0.2	-	-	99.6	-0.4
1984	-	-	101.4	1.8	-	-	102.2	0.8	-	-	103.6	1.4	-	-	104.5	0.9	-	-	104.6	0.1	-	-	107.3	2.6
1985	-	-	108.1	0.7	-	-	108.2	0.1	-	-	107.6	-0.6	-	-	107.5	-0.1	-	-	106.9	-0.6	-	-	108.6	1.6
1986	-	-	108.7	0.1	-	-	107.9	-0.7	-	-	110.1	2.0	-	-	109.7	-0.4	-	-	111.7	1.8	-	-	113.0	1.2
1987	-	-	-	-	-	-	-	-	-	-	113.3	0.3	-	-	-	-	-	-	-	-	-	-	115.0	1.5
1988	-	-	-	-	-	-	-	-	-	-	118.9	3.4	-	-	-	-	-	-	-	-	-	-	121.7	2.4
1989	-	-	-	-	-	-	-	-	-	-	125.6	3.2	-	-	-	-	-	-	-	-	-	-	130.6	4.0
1990	-	-	-	-	-	-	-	-	-	-	136.6	4.6	-	-	-	-	-	-	-	-	-	-	139.0	1.8
1991	-	-	-	-	-	-	-	-	-	-	146.0	5.0	-	-	-	-	-	-	-	-	-	-	145.8	-0.1
1992	-	-	-	-	-	-	-	-	-	-	148.0	1.5	-	-	-	-	-	-	-	-	-	-	149.0	0.7
1993	-	-	-	-	-	-	-	-	-	-	153.0	2.7	-	-	-	-	-	-	-	-	-	-	152.8	-0.1
1994	-	-	-	-	-	-	-	-	-	-	151.6	-0.8	-	-	-	-	-	-	-	-	-	-	155.3	2.4
1995	-	-	-	-	-	-	-	-	-	-	156.5	0.8	-	-	-	-	-	-	-	-	-	-	157.1	0.4
1996	-	-	-	-	-	-	-	-	-	-	156.9	-0.1	-	-	-	-	-	-	-	-	-	-	156.3	-0.4
1997	-	-	-	-	-	-	-	-	-	-	159.4	2.0	-	-	-	-	-	-	-	-	-	-	159.0	-0.3
1998	-	-	-	-	-	-	-	-	-	-	160.0	0.6	-	-	-	-	-	-	-	-	-	-	158.2	-1.1
1999	-	-	-	-	-	-	-	-	-	-	162.4	2.7	-	-	-	-	-	-	-	-	-	-	163.5	0.7
2000	-	-	-	-	-	-	-	-	-	-	165.5	1.2	-	-	-	-	-	-	-	-	-	-	164.1	-0.8
2001	-	-	-	-	-	-	-	-	-	-	168.3	2.6	-	-	-	-	-	-	-	-	-	-	-	-

Source: U.S. Department of Labor, Bureau of Labor Statistics, Division of Consumer Prices and Price Indexes. - indicates no data collected for period.

Honolulu, HI
Consumer Price Index - Urban Wage Earners
Base 1982-1984 = 100
Food and Beverages

For 1975-2001. Columns headed % show percentile change in the index from the previous period for which an index is available.

Year	Jan Index	%	Feb Index	%	Mar Index	%	Apr Index	%	May Index	%	Jun Index	%	Jul Index	%	Aug Index	%	Sep Index	%	Oct Index	%	Nov Index	%	Dec Index	%
1975	-		-		-		-		-		-		-		-		-		-		-		-	
1976	-		-		58.7	0.3	-		-		58.7	0.0	-		-		-		-		-		58.5	-
1977	-		-		60.8	2.0	-		-		61.7	1.5	-		-		58.6	-0.2	-		-		59.6	1.7
1978	-		64.6	1.7	-		66.7	3.3	-		68.7	3.0	-		69.3	0.9	62.8	1.8	69.8	0.7	-		63.5	1.1
1979	-		74.0	4.7	-		75.5	2.0	-		76.2	0.9	-		76.9	0.9	-		78.3	1.8	-		70.7	1.3
1980	-		80.8	1.3	-		82.3	1.9	-		82.6	0.4	-		84.0	1.7	-		85.6	1.9	-		79.8	1.9
1981	-		90.5	3.3	-		91.9	1.5	-		92.2	0.3	-		93.0	0.9	-		93.6	0.6	-		87.6	2.3
1982	-		96.5	2.7	-		96.3	-0.2	-		96.7	0.4	-		96.9	0.2	-		97.4	0.5	-		94.0	0.4
1983	-		98.8	0.6	-		99.6	0.8	-		99.3	-0.3	-		99.8	0.5	-		99.8	0.0	-		98.2	0.8
1984	-		101.8	2.0	-		102.5	0.7	-		103.3	0.8	-		104.3	1.0	-		104.3	0.0	-		99.8	0.0
1985	-		109.1	0.6	-		108.6	-0.5	-		107.7	-0.8	-		107.9	0.2	-		107.3	-0.6	-		108.4	3.9
1986	-		109.6	0.4	-		108.9	-0.6	-		111.0	1.9	-		110.1	-0.8	-		112.5	2.2	-		109.2	1.8
1987	-		-		-		-		-		114.4	0.3	-		-		-		-		-		114.1	1.4
1988	-		-		-		-		-		120.2	3.4	-		-		-		-		-		116.2	1.6
1989	-		-		-		-		-		126.8	2.8	-		-		-		-		-		123.3	2.6
1990	-		-		-		-		-		137.1	4.3	-		-		-		-		-		131.5	3.7
1991	-		-		-		-		-		-		-		-		-		-		-		140.0	2.1
1992	-		-		-		-		-		146.6	4.7	-		-		-		-		-		146.5	-0.1
1993	-		-		-		-		-		149.0	1.7	-		-		-		-		-		150.0	0.7
1994	-		-		-		-		-		154.1	2.7	-		-		-		-		-		153.5	-0.4
1995	-		-		-		-		-		152.1	-0.9	-		-		-		-		-		155.2	2.0
1996	-		-		-		-		-		156.3	0.7	-		-		-		-		-		156.8	0.3
1997	-		-		-		-		-		156.9	0.1	-		-		-		-		-		156.4	-0.3
1998	-		-		-		-		-		159.4	1.9	-		-		-		-		-		159.1	-0.2
1999	-		-		-		-		-		159.9	0.5	-		-		-		-		-		158.1	-1.1
2000	-		-		-		-		-		162.2	2.6	-		-		-		-		-		163.2	0.6
2001	-		-		-		-		-		165.5	1.4	-		-		-		-		-		164.2	-0.8
	-		-		-		-		-		168.4	2.6	-		-		-		-		-		-	

Source: U.S. Department of Labor, Bureau of Labor Statistics, Division of Consumer Prices and Price Indexes. - indicates no data collected for period.

Honolulu, HI
Consumer Price Index - All Urban Consumers
Base 1982-1984 = 100
Housing

For 1975-2001. Columns headed % show percentile change in the index from the previous period for which an index is available.

Year	Jan Index	%	Feb Index	%	Mar Index	%	Apr Index	%	May Index	%	Jun Index	%	Jul Index	%	Aug Index	%	Sep Index	%	Oct Index	%	Nov Index	%	Dec Index	%
1975	-	-	-	-	-	-	-	-	-	-	-	-	-	-	-	-	-	-	-	-	-	-	58.6	-
1976	-	-	-	-	58.6	0.0	-	-	-	-	59.1	0.9	-	-	-	-	59.8	1.2	-	-	-	-	59.7	-0.2
1977	-	-	-	-	60.7	1.7	-	-	-	-	61.3	1.0	-	-	-	-	62.5	2.0	-	-	-	-	62.8	0.5
1978	-	-	63.7	1.4	-	-	65.0	2.0	-	-	65.9	1.4	-	-	66.2	0.5	-	-	67.9	2.6	-	-	68.7	1.2
1979	-	-	70.9	3.2	-	-	72.8	2.7	-	-	73.9	1.5	-	-	75.1	1.6	-	-	76.3	1.6	-	-	77.7	1.8
1980	-	-	80.3	3.3	-	-	83.7	4.2	-	-	83.2	-0.6	-	-	83.2	0.0	-	-	85.3	2.5	-	-	85.7	0.5
1981	-	-	88.3	3.0	-	-	91.8	4.0	-	-	93.0	1.3	-	-	94.4	1.5	-	-	94.8	0.4	-	-	93.8	-1.1
1982	-	-	95.3	1.6	-	-	95.7	0.4	-	-	99.3	3.8	-	-	98.7	-0.6	-	-	102.2	3.5	-	-	97.8	-4.3
1983	-	-	98.0	0.2	-	-	99.1	1.1	-	-	97.8	-1.3	-	-	98.2	0.4	-	-	100.0	1.8	-	-	101.7	1.7
1984	-	-	101.7	0.0	-	-	102.9	1.2	-	-	103.0	0.1	-	-	103.1	0.1	-	-	104.1	1.0	-	-	104.2	0.1
1985	-	-	105.6	1.3	-	-	105.4	-0.2	-	-	106.3	0.9	-	-	105.4	-0.8	-	-	106.1	0.7	-	-	108.1	1.9
1986	-	-	108.4	0.3	-	-	108.1	-0.3	-	-	107.2	-0.8	-	-	109.4	2.1	-	-	108.3	-1.0	-	-	109.6	1.2
1987	-	-	-	-	-	-	-	-	-	-	113.4	3.5	-	-	-	-	-	-	-	-	-	-	116.5	2.7
1988	-	-	-	-	-	-	-	-	-	-	121.1	3.9	-	-	-	-	-	-	-	-	-	-	124.9	3.1
1989	-	-	-	-	-	-	-	-	-	-	128.1	2.6	-	-	-	-	-	-	-	-	-	-	134.1	4.7
1990	-	-	-	-	-	-	-	-	-	-	139.0	3.7	-	-	-	-	-	-	-	-	-	-	144.1	3.7
1991	-	-	-	-	-	-	-	-	-	-	151.3	5.0	-	-	-	-	-	-	-	-	-	-	154.3	2.0
1992	-	-	-	-	-	-	-	-	-	-	160.3	3.9	-	-	-	-	-	-	-	-	-	-	163.0	1.7
1993	-	-	-	-	-	-	-	-	-	-	164.1	0.7	-	-	-	-	-	-	-	-	-	-	169.0	3.0
1994	-	-	-	-	-	-	-	-	-	-	170.4	0.8	-	-	-	-	-	-	-	-	-	-	172.8	1.4
1995	-	-	-	-	-	-	-	-	-	-	173.4	0.3	-	-	-	-	-	-	-	-	-	-	176.0	1.5
1996	-	-	-	-	-	-	-	-	-	-	176.8	0.5	-	-	-	-	-	-	-	-	-	-	177.0	-0.2
1997	-	-	-	-	-	-	-	-	-	-	177.3	0.3	-	-	-	-	-	-	-	-	-	-	175.7	-0.3
1998	-	-	-	-	-	-	-	-	-	-	176.3	-0.4	-	-	-	-	-	-	-	-	-	-	176.0	0.3
1999	-	-	-	-	-	-	-	-	-	-	175.5	-0.1	-	-	-	-	-	-	-	-	-	-	178.5	0.7
2000	-	-	-	-	-	-	-	-	-	-	177.3	0.7	-	-	-	-	-	-	-	-	-	-	-	-
2001	-	-	-	-	-	-	-	-	-	-	178.8	0.2	-	-	-	-	-	-	-	-	-	-	-	-

Source: U.S. Department of Labor, Bureau of Labor Statistics, Division of Consumer Prices and Price Indexes. - indicates no data collected for period.

Honolulu, HI
Consumer Price Index - Urban Wage Earners
Base 1982-1984 = 100
Housing

For 1975-2001. Columns headed % show percentile change in the index from the previous period for which an index is available.

Year	Jan Index	%	Feb Index	%	Mar Index	%	Apr Index	%	May Index	%	Jun Index	%	Jul Index	%	Aug Index	%	Sep Index	%	Oct Index	%	Nov Index	%	Dec Index	%
1975	-	-	-	-	-	-	-	-	-	-	-	-	-	-	-	-	-	-	-	-	-	-	-	-
1976	-	-	-	-	57.5	0.2	-	-	-	-	57.9	0.7	-	-	-	-	58.7	1.4	-	-	-	-	57.4	-
1977	-	-	-	-	59.5	1.7	-	-	-	-	60.1	1.0	-	-	-	-	61.3	2.0	-	-	-	-	58.5	-0.3
1978	-	-	62.2	1.0	-	-	63.5	2.1	-	-	64.4	1.4	-	-	65.0	0.9	-	-	66.4	2.2	-	-	61.6	0.5
1979	-	-	68.9	2.1	-	-	70.6	2.5	-	-	71.9	1.8	-	-	73.4	2.1	-	-	74.5	1.5	-	-	67.5	1.7
1980	-	-	77.7	2.1	-	-	81.5	4.9	-	-	80.8	-0.9	-	-	79.9	-1.1	-	-	81.4	1.9	-	-	76.1	2.1
1981	-	-	84.8	2.7	-	-	88.4	4.2	-	-	90.0	1.8	-	-	91.0	1.1	-	-	91.4	0.4	-	-	82.6	1.5
1982	-	-	92.3	1.7	-	-	92.8	0.5	-	-	96.0	3.4	-	-	95.5	-0.5	-	-	98.8	3.5	-	-	90.8	-0.7
1983	-	-	98.2	3.3	-	-	99.2	1.0	-	-	96.3	-2.9	-	-	98.9	2.7	-	-	104.8	6.0	-	-	95.1	-3.7
1984	-	-	101.1	-5.0	-	-	104.1	3.0	-	-	105.0	0.9	-	-	106.2	1.1	-	-	106.7	0.5	-	-	106.4	1.5
1985	-	-	108.2	1.4	-	-	108.2	0.0	-	-	108.9	0.6	-	-	107.9	-0.9	-	-	106.7	0.7	-	-	106.7	0.0
1986	-	-	111.0	0.3	-	-	110.7	-0.3	-	-	109.7	-0.9	-	-	112.2	2.3	-	-	108.7		-	-	110.7	1.8
1987	-	-	-	-	-	-	-	-	-	-	115.9	3.4	-	-	-	-	-	-	110.5	-1.5	-	-	112.1	1.4
1988	-	-	-	-	-	-	-	-	-	-	123.6	3.9	-	-	-	-	-	-	-	-	-	-	119.0	2.7
1989	-	-	-	-	-	-	-	-	-	-	130.7	2.6	-	-	-	-	-	-	-	-	-	-	127.4	3.1
1990	-	-	-	-	-	-	-	-	-	-	141.7	3.7	-	-	-	-	-	-	-	-	-	-	136.7	4.6
1991	-	-	-	-	-	-	-	-	-	-	154.3	5.0	-	-	-	-	-	-	-	-	-	-	146.9	3.7
1992	-	-	-	-	-	-	-	-	-	-	162.7	3.6	-	-	-	-	-	-	-	-	-	-	157.1	1.8
1993	-	-	-	-	-	-	-	-	-	-	166.7	0.7	-	-	-	-	-	-	-	-	-	-	165.5	1.7
1994	-	-	-	-	-	-	-	-	-	-	172.6	0.7	-	-	-	-	-	-	-	-	-	-	171.4	2.8
1995	-	-	-	-	-	-	-	-	-	-	176.0	0.5	-	-	-	-	-	-	-	-	-	-	175.2	1.5
1996	-	-	-	-	-	-	-	-	-	-	179.4	0.4	-	-	-	-	-	-	-	-	-	-	178.6	1.5
1997	-	-	-	-	-	-	-	-	-	-	179.9	0.3	-	-	-	-	-	-	-	-	-	-	179.4	0.0
1998	-	-	-	-	-	-	-	-	-	-	178.4	-0.6	-	-	-	-	-	-	-	-	-	-	179.5	-0.2
1999	-	-	-	-	-	-	-	-	-	-	176.9	-0.3	-	-	-	-	-	-	-	-	-	-	177.4	-0.6
2000	-	-	-	-	-	-	-	-	-	-	178.1	0.4	-	-	-	-	-	-	-	-	-	-	177.4	0.3
2001	-	-	-	-	-	-	-	-	-	-	179.9	0.2	-	-	-	-	-	-	-	-	-	-	179.6	0.8

Source: U.S. Department of Labor, Bureau of Labor Statistics, Division of Consumer Prices and Price Indexes. - indicates no data collected for period.

Honolulu, HI
Consumer Price Index - All Urban Consumers
Base 1982-1984 = 100
Apparel

For 1963-2001. Columns headed % show percentile change in the index from the previous period for which an index is available.

Year	Jan Index	%	Feb Index	%	Mar Index	%	Apr Index	%	May Index	%	Jun Index	%	Jul Index	%	Aug Index	%	Sep Index	%	Oct Index	%	Nov Index	%	Dec Index	%
1963	-	-	-	-	-	-	-	-	-	-	-	-	-	-	-	-	-	-	-	-	-	-	46.2	-
1964	-	-	-	-	46.4	0.4	-	-	-	-	46.4	0.0	-	-	-	-	47.1	1.5	-	-	-	-	47.0	-0.2
1965	-	-	-	-	46.8	-0.4	-	-	-	-	47.3	1.1	-	-	-	-	47.1	-0.4	-	-	-	-	47.4	0.6
1966	-	-	-	-	47.6	0.4	-	-	-	-	48.1	1.1	-	-	-	-	48.1	0.0	-	-	-	-	48.1	0.0
1967	-	-	-	-	48.2	0.2	-	-	-	-	48.8	1.2	-	-	-	-	49.3	1.0	-	-	-	-	49.5	0.4
1968	-	-	-	-	50.0	1.0	-	-	-	-	50.2	0.4	-	-	-	-	51.5	2.6	-	-	-	-	51.8	0.6
1969	-	-	-	-	52.5	1.4	-	-	-	-	53.5	1.9	-	-	-	-	54.0	0.9	-	-	-	-	54.4	0.7
1970	-	-	-	-	54.7	0.6	-	-	-	-	56.0	2.4	-	-	-	-	57.7	3.0	-	-	-	-	57.5	-0.3
1971	-	-	-	-	57.3	-0.3	-	-	-	-	56.9	-0.7	-	-	-	-	57.5	1.1	-	-	-	-	58.2	1.2
1972	-	-	-	-	58.8	1.0	-	-	-	-	58.8	0.0	-	-	-	-	59.1	0.5	-	-	-	-	58.9	-0.3
1973	-	-	-	-	59.9	1.7	-	-	-	-	59.8	-0.2	-	-	-	-	61.5	2.8	-	-	-	-	62.3	1.3
1974	-	-	-	-	63.6	2.1	-	-	-	-	64.7	1.7	-	-	-	-	66.6	2.9	-	-	-	-	67.2	0.9
1975	-	-	-	-	68.5	1.9	-	-	-	-	68.9	0.6	-	-	-	-	69.6	1.0	-	-	-	-	69.7	0.1
1976	-	-	-	-	70.9	1.7	-	-	-	-	71.7	1.1	-	-	-	-	72.6	1.3	-	-	-	-	72.3	-0.4
1977	-	-	-	-	73.9	2.2	-	-	-	-	73.9	0.0	-	-	-	-	74.7	1.1	-	-	-	-	75.9	1.6
1978	-	-	77.1	1.6	-	-	77.8	0.9	-	-	77.5	-0.4	-	-	80.5	3.9	-	-	80.2	-0.4	-	-	80.8	0.7
1979	-	-	83.1	2.8	-	-	82.5	-0.7	-	-	84.3	2.2	-	-	84.5	0.2	-	-	84.6	0.1	-	-	85.4	0.9
1980	-	-	88.2	3.3	-	-	88.5	0.3	-	-	88.6	0.1	-	-	91.6	3.4	-	-	92.0	0.4	-	-	91.6	-0.4
1981	-	-	93.2	1.7	-	-	93.0	-0.2	-	-	92.9	-0.1	-	-	94.6	1.8	-	-	97.5	3.1	-	-	96.8	-0.7
1982	-	-	97.4	0.6	-	-	98.2	0.8	-	-	99.0	0.8	-	-	98.1	-0.9	-	-	99.1	1.0	-	-	99.3	0.6
1983	-	-	100.4	1.1	-	-	101.9	1.5	-	-	100.4	-1.5	-	-	102.1	1.7	-	-	102.6	0.5	-	-	102.0	-0.6
1984	-	-	103.1	1.1	-	-	101.8	-1.3	-	-	101.0	-0.8	-	-	97.5	-3.5	-	-	97.7	0.2	-	-	99.2	1.5
1985	-	-	99.6	0.4	-	-	98.7	-0.9	-	-	98.4	-0.3	-	-	99.7	1.3	-	-	101.4	1.7	-	-	99.9	-1.5
1986	-	-	100.7	0.8	-	-	100.4	-0.3	-	-	96.4	-4.0	-	-	99.3	3.0	-	-	100.9	1.6	-	-	101.8	0.9
1987	-	-	-	-	-	-	-	-	-	-	101.0	-0.8	-	-	-	-	-	-	-	-	-	-	104.1	3.1
1988	-	-	-	-	-	-	-	-	-	-	105.7	1.5	-	-	-	-	-	-	-	-	-	-	108.0	2.2
1989	-	-	-	-	-	-	-	-	-	-	106.1	-1.8	-	-	-	-	-	-	-	-	-	-	102.5	-3.4
1990	-	-	-	-	-	-	-	-	-	-	106.2	3.6	-	-	-	-	-	-	-	-	-	-	107.8	1.5
1991	-	-	-	-	-	-	-	-	-	-	111.2	3.2	-	-	-	-	-	-	-	-	-	-	109.8	-1.3
1992	-	-	-	-	-	-	-	-	-	-	113.0	2.9	-	-	-	-	-	-	-	-	-	-	115.3	2.0
1993	-	-	-	-	-	-	-	-	-	-	117.3	1.7	-	-	-	-	-	-	-	-	-	-	115.6	-1.4
1994	-	-	-	-	-	-	-	-	-	-	119.1	3.0	-	-	-	-	-	-	-	-	-	-	118.2	-0.8
1995	-	-	-	-	-	-	-	-	-	-	118.1	-0.1	-	-	-	-	-	-	-	-	-	-	116.9	-1.0
1996	-	-	-	-	-	-	-	-	-	-	120.0	2.7	-	-	-	-	-	-	-	-	-	-	116.9	-2.6
1997	-	-	-	-	-	-	-	-	-	-	119.8	2.5	-	-	-	-	-	-	-	-	-	-	114.8	-4.2
1998	-	-	-	-	-	-	-	-	-	-	116.4	1.4	-	-	-	-	-	-	-	-	-	-	108.0	-7.2
1999	-	-	-	-	-	-	-	-	-	-	106.0	-1.9	-	-	-	-	-	-	-	-	-	-	104.9	-1.0
2000	-	-	-	-	-	-	-	-	-	-	104.5	-0.4	-	-	-	-	-	-	-	-	-	-	102.6	-1.8
2001	-	-	-	-	-	-	-	-	-	-	99.7	-2.8	-	-	-	-	-	-	-	-	-	-	-	-

Source: U.S. Department of Labor, Bureau of Labor Statistics, Division of Consumer Prices and Price Indexes. - indicates no data collected for period.

|

Honolulu, HI
Consumer Price Index - Urban Wage Earners
Base 1982-1984 = 100
Apparel

For 1963-2001. Columns headed % show percentile change in the index from the previous period for which an index is available.

Year	Jan Index	%	Feb Index	%	Mar Index	%	Apr Index	%	May Index	%	Jun Index	%	Jul Index	%	Aug Index	%	Sep Index	%	Oct Index	%	Nov Index	%	Dec Index	%
1963	-		-		-		-		-		-		-		-		-		-		-		-	
1964	-		-		44.9	0.7	-		-		44.9	0.0	-		-		-		-		-		44.6	-
1965	-		-		45.3	-0.4	-		-		45.8	1.1	-		-		45.6	1.6	-		-		45.5	-0.2
1966	-		-		46.0	0.2	-		-		46.5	1.1	-		-		45.5	-0.7	-		-		45.9	0.9
1967	-		-		46.6	0.2	-		-		47.2	1.3	-		-		46.5	0.0	-		-		46.5	0.0
1968	-		-		48.4	1.0	-		-		48.6	0.4	-		-		47.7	1.1	-		-		47.9	0.4
1969	-		-		50.7	1.2	-		-		51.8	2.2	-		-		49.8	2.5	-		-		50.1	0.6
1970	-		-		53.0	0.8	-		-		54.2	2.3	-		-		52.2	0.8	-		-		52.6	0.8
1971	-		-		55.5	-0.2	-		-		55.0	-0.9	-		-		55.8	3.0	-		-		55.6	-0.4
1972	-		-		56.9	1.1	-		-		56.8	-0.2	-		-		55.6	1.1	-		-		56.3	1.3
1973	-		-		58.0	1.8	-		-		57.9	-0.2	-		-		57.2	0.7	-		-		57.0	-0.3
1974	-		-		61.5	2.2	-		-		62.6	1.8	-		-		59.5	2.8	-		-		60.2	1.2
1975	-		-		66.2	1.8	-		-		66.7	0.8	-		-		64.4	2.9	-		-		65.0	0.9
1976	-		-		68.5	1.5	-		-		69.3	1.2	-		-		67.3	0.9	-		-		67.5	0.3
1977	-		-		71.5	2.3	-		-		71.5	0.0	-		-		70.2	1.3	-		-		69.9	-0.4
1978	-		73.4	-0.1	-		74.4	1.4	-		73.9	-0.7	-		75.9	2.7	72.2	1.0	77.6	2.2	-		73.5	1.8
1979	-		78.9	1.7	-		78.0	-1.1	-		79.1	1.4	-		79.8	0.9	-		82.4	3.3	-		77.6	0.0
1980	-		90.8	9.9	-		92.3	1.7	-		90.2	-2.3	-		92.0	2.0	-		92.6	0.7	-		82.6	0.2
1981	-		94.8	1.4	-		94.7	-0.1	-		95.0	0.3	-		95.3	0.3	-		96.2	0.9	-		93.5	1.0
1982	-		97.1	0.4	-		98.0	0.9	-		98.8	0.8	-		97.9	-0.9	-		99.1	1.2	-		96.7	0.5
1983	-		100.5	0.7	-		101.8	1.3	-		100.3	-1.5	-		101.8	1.5	-		102.4	0.6	-		99.8	0.7
1984	-		103.0	1.0	-		102.3	-0.7	-		100.3	-2.0	-		97.5	-2.8	-		98.5	1.0	-		102.0	-0.4
1985	-		100.1	0.5	-		98.0	-2.1	-		97.6	-0.4	-		99.3	1.7	-		101.9	2.6	-		99.6	1.1
1986	-		100.4	0.5	-		100.2	-0.2	-		97.1	-3.1	-		99.6	2.6	-		101.4	1.8	-		99.9	-2.0
1987	-		-		-		-		-		102.2	-0.6	-		-		-		-		-		102.8	1.4
1988	-		-		-		-		-		106.9	1.7	-		-		-		-		-		105.1	2.8
1989	-		-		-		-		-		107.5	-1.8	-		-		-		-		-		109.5	2.4
1990	-		-		-		-		-		107.4	4.3	-		-		-		-		-		103.0	-4.2
1991	-		-		-		-		-		112.8	3.7	-		-		-		-		-		108.8	1.3
1992	-		-		-		-		-		113.8	2.6	-		-		-		-		-		110.9	-1.7
1993	-		-		-		-		-		119.4	1.8	-		-		-		-		-		117.3	3.1
1994	-		-		-		-		-		120.3	2.3	-		-		-		-		-		117.6	-1.5
1995	-		-		-		-		-		119.4	-0.2	-		-		-		-		-		119.6	-0.6
1996	-		-		-		-		-		121.7	2.6	-		-		-		-		-		118.6	-0.7
1997	-		-		-		-		-		121.7	2.8	-		-		-		-		-		118.4	-2.7
1998	-		-		-		-		-		119.3	2.6	-		-		-		-		-		116.3	-4.4
1999	-		-		-		-		-		110.1	-1.6	-		-		-		-		-		111.9	-6.2
2000	-		-		-		-		-		110.0	0.8	-		-		-		-		-		109.1	-0.9
2001	-		-		-		-		-		104.1	-2.7	-		-		-		-		-		107.0	-2.7

Source: U.S. Department of Labor, Bureau of Labor Statistics, Division of Consumer Prices and Price Indexes. - indicates no data collected for period.

Honolulu, HI
Consumer Price Index - All Urban Consumers
Base 1982-1984 = 100
Transportation

For 1963-2001. Columns headed % show percentile change in the index from the previous period for which an index is available.

Year	Jan Index	%	Feb Index	%	Mar Index	%	Apr Index	%	May Index	%	Jun Index	%	Jul Index	%	Aug Index	%	Sep Index	%	Oct Index	%	Nov Index	%	Dec Index	%
1963	-	-	-	-	-	-	-	-	-	-	-	-	-	-	-	-	-	-	-	-	-	-	38.4	-
1964	-	-	-	-	38.0	-1.0	-	-	-	-	37.4	-1.6	-	-	-	-	37.4	0.0	-	-	-	-	38.0	1.6
1965	-	-	-	-	37.9	-0.3	-	-	-	-	37.5	-1.1	-	-	-	-	37.6	0.3	-	-	-	-	37.7	0.3
1966	-	-	-	-	37.5	-0.5	-	-	-	-	37.7	0.5	-	-	-	-	37.8	0.3	-	-	-	-	38.6	2.1
1967	-	-	-	-	38.4	-0.5	-	-	-	-	38.6	0.5	-	-	-	-	38.6	0.0	-	-	-	-	39.6	2.6
1968	-	-	-	-	40.1	1.3	-	-	-	-	40.0	-0.2	-	-	-	-	40.0	0.0	-	-	-	-	40.8	2.0
1969	-	-	-	-	41.7	2.2	-	-	-	-	41.5	-0.5	-	-	-	-	41.2	-0.7	-	-	-	-	42.2	2.4
1970	-	-	-	-	42.8	1.4	-	-	-	-	43.6	1.9	-	-	-	-	43.6	0.0	-	-	-	-	44.6	2.3
1971	-	-	-	-	45.7	2.5	-	-	-	-	47.7	4.4	-	-	-	-	47.2	-1.0	-	-	-	-	47.1	-0.2
1972	-	-	-	-	47.5	0.8	-	-	-	-	47.8	0.6	-	-	-	-	47.7	-0.2	-	-	-	-	47.7	0.0
1973	-	-	-	-	47.9	0.4	-	-	-	-	47.9	0.0	-	-	-	-	47.7	-0.4	-	-	-	-	48.7	2.1
1974	-	-	-	-	50.8	4.3	-	-	-	-	52.6	3.5	-	-	-	-	53.3	1.3	-	-	-	-	54.2	1.7
1975	-	-	-	-	55.2	1.8	-	-	-	-	57.1	3.4	-	-	-	-	58.1	1.8	-	-	-	-	58.0	-0.2
1976	-	-	-	-	58.7	1.2	-	-	-	-	59.3	1.0	-	-	-	-	60.0	1.2	-	-	-	-	60.9	1.5
1977	-	-	-	-	61.2	0.5	-	-	-	-	62.3	1.8	-	-	-	-	61.9	-0.6	-	-	-	-	62.6	1.1
1978	-	-	63.8	1.9	-	-	64.9	1.7	-	-	66.0	1.7	-	-	66.7	1.1	-	-	67.3	0.9	-	-	68.3	1.5
1979	-	-	68.6	0.4	-	-	70.5	2.8	-	-	72.8	3.3	-	-	74.7	2.6	-	-	76.5	2.4	-	-	79.9	4.4
1980	-	-	83.5	4.5	-	-	85.8	2.8	-	-	86.1	0.3	-	-	88.2	2.4	-	-	88.8	0.7	-	-	89.6	0.9
1981	-	-	92.5	3.2	-	-	94.7	2.4	-	-	95.9	1.3	-	-	97.1	1.3	-	-	97.6	0.5	-	-	98.3	0.7
1982	-	-	98.0	-0.3	-	-	97.6	-0.4	-	-	98.6	1.0	-	-	100.2	1.6	-	-	100.2	0.0	-	-	99.2	-1.0
1983	-	-	97.2	-2.0	-	-	96.6	-0.6	-	-	96.8	0.2	-	-	98.4	1.7	-	-	100.0	1.6	-	-	100.7	0.7
1984	-	-	101.2	0.5	-	-	101.8	0.6	-	-	103.2	1.4	-	-	104.0	0.8	-	-	103.9	-0.1	-	-	103.8	-0.1
1985	-	-	104.0	0.2	-	-	104.3	0.3	-	-	104.3	0.0	-	-	105.2	0.9	-	-	105.8	0.6	-	-	106.2	0.4
1986	-	-	108.1	1.8	-	-	104.6	-3.2	-	-	105.2	0.6	-	-	103.8	-1.3	-	-	103.5	-0.3	-	-	106.0	2.4
1987	-	-	-	-	-	-	-	-	-	-	107.3	1.2	-	-	-	-	-	-	-	-	-	-	112.1	4.5
1988	-	-	-	-	-	-	-	-	-	-	114.2	1.9	-	-	-	-	-	-	-	-	-	-	118.0	3.3
1989	-	-	-	-	-	-	-	-	-	-	121.8	3.2	-	-	-	-	-	-	-	-	-	-	126.0	3.4
1990	-	-	-	-	-	-	-	-	-	-	127.3	1.0	-	-	-	-	-	-	-	-	-	-	135.0	6.0
1991	-	-	-	-	-	-	-	-	-	-	138.1	2.3	-	-	-	-	-	-	-	-	-	-	140.4	1.7
1992	-	-	-	-	-	-	-	-	-	-	146.4	4.3	-	-	-	-	-	-	-	-	-	-	148.5	1.4
1993	-	-	-	-	-	-	-	-	-	-	149.5	0.7	-	-	-	-	-	-	-	-	-	-	151.4	1.3
1994	-	-	-	-	-	-	-	-	-	-	156.0	3.0	-	-	-	-	-	-	-	-	-	-	156.7	0.4
1995	-	-	-	-	-	-	-	-	-	-	160.0	2.1	-	-	-	-	-	-	-	-	-	-	164.9	3.1
1996	-	-	-	-	-	-	-	-	-	-	166.3	0.8	-	-	-	-	-	-	-	-	-	-	167.7	0.8
1997	-	-	-	-	-	-	-	-	-	-	167.8	0.1	-	-	-	-	-	-	-	-	-	-	164.6	-1.9
1998	-	-	-	-	-	-	-	-	-	-	163.2	-0.9	-	-	-	-	-	-	-	-	-	-	161.8	-0.9
1999	-	-	-	-	-	-	-	-	-	-	162.3	0.3	-	-	-	-	-	-	-	-	-	-	162.0	-0.2
2000	-	-	-	-	-	-	-	-	-	-	167.7	3.5	-	-	-	-	-	-	-	-	-	-	171.5	2.3
2001	-	-	-	-	-	-	-	-	-	-	176.0	2.6	-	-	-	-	-	-	-	-	-	-	-	-

Source: U.S. Department of Labor, Bureau of Labor Statistics, Division of Consumer Prices and Price Indexes. - indicates no data collected for period.

Honolulu, HI
Consumer Price Index - Urban Wage Earners
Base 1982-1984 = 100
Transportation

For 1963-2001. Columns headed % show percentile change in the index from the previous period for which an index is available.

Year	Jan Index	%	Feb Index	%	Mar Index	%	Apr Index	%	May Index	%	Jun Index	%	Jul Index	%	Aug Index	%	Sep Index	%	Oct Index	%	Nov Index	%	Dec Index	%
1963	-		-		-		-		-		-		-		-		-		-		-		-	
1964	-		-		38.0	-1.3	-		-		37.4	-1.6	-		-		-		-		-		38.5	-
1965	-		-		37.9	-0.3	-		-		37.5	-1.1	-		-		37.4	0.0	-		-		38.0	1.6
1966	-		-		37.5	-0.5	-		-		37.8	0.8	-		-		37.6	0.3	-		-		37.7	0.3
1967	-		-		38.5	-0.3	-		-		38.6	0.3	-		-		37.8	0.0	-		-		38.6	2.1
1968	-		-		40.1	1.0	-		-		40.1	0.0	-		-		38.7	0.3	-		-		39.7	2.6
1969	-		-		41.7	2.0	-		-		41.5	-0.5	-		-		40.0	-0.2	-		-		40.9	2.3
1970	-		-		42.8	1.4	-		-		43.6	1.9	-		-		41.2	-0.7	-		-		42.2	2.4
1971	-		-		45.7	2.5	-		-		47.7	4.4	-		-		43.6	0.0	-		-		44.6	2.3
1972	-		-		47.6	1.1	-		-		47.8	0.4	-		-		47.2	-1.0	-		-		47.1	-0.2
1973	-		-		48.0	0.6	-		-		47.9	-0.2	-		-		47.7	-0.2	-		-		47.7	0.0
1974	-		-		50.9	4.5	-		-		52.6	3.3	-		-		47.7	-0.4	-		-		48.7	2.1
1975	-		-		55.3	1.8	-		-		57.2	3.4	-		-		53.4	1.5	-		-		54.3	1.7
1976	-		-		58.7	1.2	-		-		59.3	1.0	-		-		58.2	1.7	-		-		58.0	-0.3
1977	-		-		61.2	0.5	-		-		62.3	1.8	-		-		60.1	1.3	-		-		60.9	1.3
1978	-		63.8	1.9	-		64.9	1.7	-		66.0	1.7	-		66.6	0.9	61.9	-0.6	67.2	0.9	-		62.6	1.1
1979	-		68.6	0.7	-		70.5	2.8	-		73.0	3.5	-		75.0	2.7	-		76.7	2.3	-		68.1	1.3
1980	-		83.4	4.5	-		86.0	3.1	-		86.2	0.2	-		88.0	2.1	-		76.7	2.3	-		79.8	4.0
1981	-		92.9	3.2	-		95.3	2.6	-		96.5	1.3	-		97.7	1.2	-		88.9	1.0	-		90.0	1.2
1982	-		98.4	-0.5	-		97.9	-0.5	-		98.8	0.9	-		100.3	1.5	-		98.4	0.7	-		98.9	0.5
1983	-		97.1	-2.0	-		96.4	-0.7	-		96.7	0.3	-		98.4	1.8	-		100.3	0.0	-		99.1	-1.2
1984	-		101.2	0.5	-		101.7	0.5	-		103.1	1.4	-		103.9	0.8	-		99.9	1.5	-		100.7	0.8
1985	-		103.9	0.2	-		104.1	0.2	-		104.1	0.0	-		105.0	0.9	-		103.9	0.0	-		103.7	-0.2
1986	-		107.9	1.8	-		104.1	-3.5	-		104.7	0.6	-		103.2	-1.4	-		105.6	0.6	-		106.0	0.4
1987	-		-		-		-		-		106.8	1.6	-		-		-		102.8	-0.4	-		105.1	2.2
1988	-		-		-		-		-		113.8	2.0	-		-		-		-		-		111.6	4.5
1989	-		-		-		-		-		121.4	3.3	-		-		-		-		-		117.5	3.3
1990	-		-		-		-		-		126.7	0.6	-		-		-		-		-		125.9	3.7
1991	-		-		-		-		-		137.1	2.5	-		-		-		-		-		133.8	5.6
1992	-		-		-		-		-		145.7	4.0	-		-		-		-		-		140.1	2.2
1993	-		-		-		-		-		148.0	0.2	-		-		-		-		-		147.7	1.4
1994	-		-		-		-		-		153.7	2.7	-		-		-		-		-		149.7	1.1
1995	-		-		-		-		-		157.9	2.0	-		-		-		-		-		154.8	0.7
1996	-		-		-		-		-		164.2	1.1	-		-		-		-		-		162.4	2.8
1997	-		-		-		-		-		165.5	0.0	-		-		-		-		-		165.5	0.8
1998	-		-		-		-		-		160.5	-1.0	-		-		-		-		-		162.1	-2.1
1999	-		-		-		-		-		158.4	-0.1	-		-		-		-		-		158.6	-1.2
2000	-		-		-		-		-		163.6	3.7	-		-		-		-		-		157.7	-0.4
2001	-		-		-		-		-		172.0	2.5	-		-		-		-		-		167.8	2.6

Source: U.S. Department of Labor, Bureau of Labor Statistics, Division of Consumer Prices and Price Indexes. - indicates no data collected for period.

Honolulu, HI
Consumer Price Index - All Urban Consumers
Base 1982-1984 = 100
Medical Care

For 1963-2001. Columns headed % show percentile change in the index from the previous period for which an index is available.

Year	Jan Index	%	Feb Index	%	Mar Index	%	Apr Index	%	May Index	%	Jun Index	%	Jul Index	%	Aug Index	%	Sep Index	%	Oct Index	%	Nov Index	%	Dec Index	%
1963	-	-	-	-	-	-	-	-	-	-	-	-	-	-	-	-	-	-	-	-	-	-	24.7	-
1964	-	-	-	-	25.0	1.2	-	-	-	-	25.1	0.4	-	-	-	-	25.2	0.4	-	-	-	-	25.3	0.4
1965	-	-	-	-	25.7	1.6	-	-	-	-	25.8	0.4	-	-	-	-	26.0	0.8	-	-	-	-	26.1	0.4
1966	-	-	-	-	26.3	0.8	-	-	-	-	26.5	0.8	-	-	-	-	26.8	1.1	-	-	-	-	27.4	2.2
1967	-	-	-	-	27.7	1.1	-	-	-	-	28.3	2.2	-	-	-	-	28.6	1.1	-	-	-	-	29.0	1.4
1968	-	-	-	-	29.3	1.0	-	-	-	-	29.8	1.7	-	-	-	-	30.3	1.7	-	-	-	-	30.7	1.3
1969	-	-	-	-	31.3	2.0	-	-	-	-	32.1	2.6	-	-	-	-	32.6	1.6	-	-	-	-	32.5	-0.3
1970	-	-	-	-	32.6	0.3	-	-	-	-	33.5	2.8	-	-	-	-	33.8	0.9	-	-	-	-	34.5	2.1
1971	-	-	-	-	35.0	1.4	-	-	-	-	35.2	0.6	-	-	-	-	35.6	1.1	-	-	-	-	35.6	0.0
1972	-	-	-	-	35.7	0.3	-	-	-	-	35.8	0.3	-	-	-	-	36.2	1.1	-	-	-	-	36.7	1.4
1973	-	-	-	-	37.1	1.1	-	-	-	-	37.5	1.1	-	-	-	-	38.0	1.3	-	-	-	-	38.7	1.8
1974	-	-	-	-	39.4	1.8	-	-	-	-	41.7	5.8	-	-	-	-	43.1	3.4	-	-	-	-	43.6	1.2
1975	-	-	-	-	45.5	4.4	-	-	-	-	46.5	2.2	-	-	-	-	47.6	2.4	-	-	-	-	48.1	1.1
1976	-	-	-	-	50.1	4.2	-	-	-	-	50.8	1.4	-	-	-	-	52.9	4.1	-	-	-	-	54.1	2.3
1977	-	-	-	-	55.6	2.8	-	-	-	-	56.7	2.0	-	-	-	-	59.3	4.6	-	-	-	-	59.7	0.7
1978	-	-	61.5	3.0	-	-	62.2	1.1	-	-	62.4	0.3	-	-	62.6	0.3	-	-	62.6	0.0	-	-	64.8	3.5
1979	-	-	66.1	2.0	-	-	66.9	1.2	-	-	67.1	0.3	-	-	68.2	1.6	-	-	68.4	0.3	-	-	69.2	1.2
1980	-	-	69.9	1.0	-	-	72.7	4.0	-	-	72.6	-0.1	-	-	74.1	2.1	-	-	75.5	1.9	-	-	75.3	-0.3
1981	-	-	76.9	2.1	-	-	79.3	3.1	-	-	81.1	2.3	-	-	84.1	3.7	-	-	85.8	2.0	-	-	86.4	0.7
1982	-	-	86.8	0.5	-	-	90.6	4.4	-	-	91.4	0.9	-	-	92.6	1.3	-	-	95.0	2.6	-	-	95.9	0.9
1983	-	-	98.6	2.8	-	-	100.4	1.8	-	-	100.6	0.2	-	-	103.3	2.7	-	-	102.5	-0.8	-	-	102.6	0.1
1984	-	-	105.2	2.5	-	-	106.9	1.6	-	-	107.0	0.1	-	-	108.5	1.4	-	-	108.6	0.1	-	-	109.3	0.6
1985	-	-	110.4	1.0	-	-	111.1	0.6	-	-	111.5	0.4	-	-	115.4	3.5	-	-	116.0	0.5	-	-	116.7	0.6
1986	-	-	120.0	2.8	-	-	120.4	0.3	-	-	121.2	0.7	-	-	124.6	2.8	-	-	125.2	0.5	-	-	124.5	-0.6
1987	-	-	-	-	-	-	-	-	-	-	126.5	1.6	-	-	-	-	-	-	-	-	-	-	129.2	2.1
1988	-	-	-	-	-	-	-	-	-	-	130.3	0.9	-	-	-	-	-	-	-	-	-	-	134.7	3.4
1989	-	-	-	-	-	-	-	-	-	-	136.0	1.0	-	-	-	-	-	-	-	-	-	-	142.7	4.9
1990	-	-	-	-	-	-	-	-	-	-	149.8	5.0	-	-	-	-	-	-	-	-	-	-	158.6	5.9
1991	-	-	-	-	-	-	-	-	-	-	168.0	5.9	-	-	-	-	-	-	-	-	-	-	174.6	3.9
1992	-	-	-	-	-	-	-	-	-	-	179.7	2.9	-	-	-	-	-	-	-	-	-	-	185.6	3.3
1993	-	-	-	-	-	-	-	-	-	-	192.8	3.9	-	-	-	-	-	-	-	-	-	-	202.0	4.8
1994	-	-	-	-	-	-	-	-	-	-	204.6	1.3	-	-	-	-	-	-	-	-	-	-	207.5	1.4
1995	-	-	-	-	-	-	-	-	-	-	207.8	0.1	-	-	-	-	-	-	-	-	-	-	211.8	1.9
1996	-	-	-	-	-	-	-	-	-	-	214.9	1.5	-	-	-	-	-	-	-	-	-	-	215.0	0.0
1997	-	-	-	-	-	-	-	-	-	-	215.6	0.3	-	-	-	-	-	-	-	-	-	-	219.1	1.6
1998	-	-	-	-	-	-	-	-	-	-	222.5	1.6	-	-	-	-	-	-	-	-	-	-	229.8	3.3
1999	-	-	-	-	-	-	-	-	-	-	231.0	0.5	-	-	-	-	-	-	-	-	-	-	231.5	0.2
2000	-	-	-	-	-	-	-	-	-	-	235.9	1.9	-	-	-	-	-	-	-	-	-	-	243.8	3.3
2001	-	-	-	-	-	-	-	-	-	-	246.1	0.9	-	-	-	-	-	-	-	-	-	-	-	-

Source: U.S. Department of Labor, Bureau of Labor Statistics, Division of Consumer Prices and Price Indexes. - indicates no data collected for period.

Honolulu, HI
Consumer Price Index - Urban Wage Earners
Base 1982-1984 = 100
Medical Care

For 1963-2001. Columns headed % show percentile change in the index from the previous period for which an index is available.

Year	Jan Index	Jan %	Feb Index	Feb %	Mar Index	Mar %	Apr Index	Apr %	May Index	May %	Jun Index	Jun %	Jul Index	Jul %	Aug Index	Aug %	Sep Index	Sep %	Oct Index	Oct %	Nov Index	Nov %	Dec Index	Dec %
1963	-	-	-	-	-	-	-	-	-	-	-	-	-	-	-	-	-	-	-	-	-	-	24.2	-
1964	-	-	-	-	24.5	1.2	-	-	-	-	24.5	0.0	-	-	-	-	24.7	0.8	-	-	-	-	24.8	0.4
1965	-	-	-	-	25.1	1.2	-	-	-	-	25.2	0.4	-	-	-	-	25.4	0.8	-	-	-	-	25.6	0.8
1966	-	-	-	-	25.7	0.4	-	-	-	-	26.0	1.2	-	-	-	-	26.2	0.8	-	-	-	-	26.8	2.3
1967	-	-	-	-	27.1	1.1	-	-	-	-	27.7	2.2	-	-	-	-	28.0	1.1	-	-	-	-	28.4	1.4
1968	-	-	-	-	28.7	1.1	-	-	-	-	29.2	1.7	-	-	-	-	29.7	1.7	-	-	-	-	30.1	1.3
1969	-	-	-	-	30.7	2.0	-	-	-	-	31.4	2.3	-	-	-	-	32.0	1.9	-	-	-	-	31.8	-0.6
1970	-	-	-	-	32.0	0.6	-	-	-	-	32.8	2.5	-	-	-	-	33.1	0.9	-	-	-	-	33.8	2.1
1971	-	-	-	-	34.2	1.2	-	-	-	-	34.5	0.9	-	-	-	-	34.8	0.9	-	-	-	-	34.9	0.3
1972	-	-	-	-	35.0	0.3	-	-	-	-	35.1	0.3	-	-	-	-	35.4	0.9	-	-	-	-	36.0	1.7
1973	-	-	-	-	36.3	0.8	-	-	-	-	36.7	1.1	-	-	-	-	37.3	1.6	-	-	-	-	37.9	1.6
1974	-	-	-	-	38.6	1.8	-	-	-	-	40.9	6.0	-	-	-	-	42.2	3.2	-	-	-	-	42.7	1.2
1975	-	-	-	-	44.6	4.4	-	-	-	-	45.6	2.2	-	-	-	-	46.6	2.2	-	-	-	-	47.1	1.1
1976	-	-	-	-	49.0	4.0	-	-	-	-	49.7	1.4	-	-	-	-	51.8	4.2	-	-	-	-	53.0	2.3
1977	-	-	-	-	54.4	2.6	-	-	-	-	55.5	2.0	-	-	-	-	58.1	4.7	-	-	-	-	58.5	0.7
1978	-	-	60.4	3.2	-	-	61.9	2.5	-	-	62.0	0.2	-	-	62.2	0.3	-	-	62.2	0.0	-	-	63.4	1.9
1979	-	-	64.8	2.2	-	-	65.3	0.8	-	-	66.4	1.7	-	-	66.3	-0.2	-	-	67.7	2.1	-	-	68.5	1.2
1980	-	-	68.9	0.6	-	-	71.0	3.0	-	-	71.3	0.4	-	-	73.7	3.4	-	-	75.5	2.4	-	-	75.2	-0.4
1981	-	-	76.8	2.1	-	-	78.8	2.6	-	-	81.8	3.8	-	-	84.5	3.3	-	-	85.8	1.5	-	-	86.7	1.0
1982	-	-	87.1	0.5	-	-	90.8	4.2	-	-	91.7	1.0	-	-	93.1	1.5	-	-	95.5	2.6	-	-	96.5	1.0
1983	-	-	99.0	2.6	-	-	100.5	1.5	-	-	100.6	0.1	-	-	103.1	2.5	-	-	102.3	-0.8	-	-	102.4	0.1
1984	-	-	105.0	2.5	-	-	106.6	1.5	-	-	106.7	0.1	-	-	108.0	1.2	-	-	108.0	0.0	-	-	108.7	0.6
1985	-	-	109.9	1.1	-	-	110.6	0.6	-	-	111.0	0.4	-	-	114.6	3.2	-	-	115.2	0.5	-	-	116.0	0.7
1986	-	-	119.0	2.6	-	-	119.4	0.3	-	-	120.2	0.7	-	-	123.1	2.4	-	-	123.7	0.5	-	-	123.2	-0.4
1987	-	-	-	-	-	-	-	-	-	-	125.1	1.5	-	-	-	-	-	-	-	-	-	-	128.3	2.6
1988	-	-	-	-	-	-	-	-	-	-	129.4	0.9	-	-	-	-	-	-	-	-	-	-	133.4	3.1
1989	-	-	-	-	-	-	-	-	-	-	134.8	1.0	-	-	-	-	-	-	-	-	-	-	141.9	5.3
1990	-	-	-	-	-	-	-	-	-	-	148.7	4.8	-	-	-	-	-	-	-	-	-	-	157.9	6.2
1991	-	-	-	-	-	-	-	-	-	-	166.9	5.7	-	-	-	-	-	-	-	-	-	-	173.8	4.1
1992	-	-	-	-	-	-	-	-	-	-	178.9	2.9	-	-	-	-	-	-	-	-	-	-	185.6	3.7
1993	-	-	-	-	-	-	-	-	-	-	192.6	3.8	-	-	-	-	-	-	-	-	-	-	202.3	5.0
1994	-	-	-	-	-	-	-	-	-	-	205.0	1.3	-	-	-	-	-	-	-	-	-	-	208.9	1.9
1995	-	-	-	-	-	-	-	-	-	-	210.6	0.8	-	-	-	-	-	-	-	-	-	-	215.5	2.3
1996	-	-	-	-	-	-	-	-	-	-	218.6	1.4	-	-	-	-	-	-	-	-	-	-	219.1	0.2
1997	-	-	-	-	-	-	-	-	-	-	219.8	0.3	-	-	-	-	-	-	-	-	-	-	223.5	1.7
1998	-	-	-	-	-	-	-	-	-	-	227.2	1.7	-	-	-	-	-	-	-	-	-	-	234.2	3.1
1999	-	-	-	-	-	-	-	-	-	-	235.4	0.5	-	-	-	-	-	-	-	-	-	-	235.4	0.0
2000	-	-	-	-	-	-	-	-	-	-	239.0	1.5	-	-	-	-	-	-	-	-	-	-	246.5	3.1
2001	-	-	-	-	-	-	-	-	-	-	249.3	1.1	-	-	-	-	-	-	-	-	-	-	-	-

Source: U.S. Department of Labor, Bureau of Labor Statistics, Division of Consumer Prices and Price Indexes. - indicates no data collected for period.

Honolulu, HI
Consumer Price Index - All Urban Consumers
Base December 1997 = 100
Recreation

For 1997-2001. Columns headed % show percentile change in the index from the previous period for which an index is available.

Year	Jan Index	%	Feb Index	%	Mar Index	%	Apr Index	%	May Index	%	Jun Index	%	Jul Index	%	Aug Index	%	Sep Index	%	Oct Index	%	Nov Index	%	Dec Index	%
1997	-	-	-	-	-	-	-	-	-	-	-	-	-	-	-	-	-	-	-	-	-	-	100.0	-
1998	-	-	-	-	-	-	-	-	-	-	101.4	1.4	-	-	-	-	-	-	-	-	-	-	100.3	-1.1
1999	-	-	-	-	-	-	-	-	-	-	101.3	1.0	-	-	-	-	-	-	-	-	-	-	102.5	1.2
2000	-	-	-	-	-	-	-	-	-	-	103.1	0.6	-	-	-	-	-	-	-	-	-	-	102.6	-0.5
2001	-	-	-	-	-	-	-	-	-	-	102.1	-0.5	-	-	-	-	-	-	-	-	-	-	-	-

Source: U.S. Department of Labor, Bureau of Labor Statistics, Division of Consumer Prices and Price Indexes. - indicates no data collected for period.

Honolulu, HI
Consumer Price Index - Urban Wage Earners
Base December 1997 = 100
Recreation

For 1997-2001. Columns headed % show percentile change in the index from the previous period for which an index is available.

Year	Jan		Feb		Mar		Apr		May		Jun		Jul		Aug		Sep		Oct		Nov		Dec	
	Index	%	Index	%	Index	%	Index	%	Index	%	Index	%	Index	%	Index	%	Index	%	Index	%	Index	%	Index	%
1997	-	-	-	-	-	-	-	-	-	-	-	-	-	-	-	-	-	-	-	-	-	-	-	-
1998	-	-	-	-	-	-	-	-	-	-	101.6	1.6	-	-	-	-	-	-	-	-	-	-	100.0	-
1999	-	-	-	-	-	-	-	-	-	-	101.2	0.9	-	-	-	-	-	-	-	-	-	-	100.3	-1.3
2000	-	-	-	-	-	-	-	-	-	-	102.3	0.1	-	-	-	-	-	-	-	-	-	-	102.2	1.0
2001	-	-	-	-	-	-	-	-	-	-	101.2	-0.5	-	-	-	-	-	-	-	-	-	-	101.7	-0.6

Source: U.S. Department of Labor, Bureau of Labor Statistics, Division of Consumer Prices and Price Indexes. - indicates no data collected for period.

Honolulu, HI
Consumer Price Index - All Urban Consumers
Base December 1997 = 100
Education & Communication

For 1997-2001. Columns headed % show percentile change in the index from the previous period for which an index is available.

Year	Jan		Feb		Mar		Apr		May		Jun		Jul		Aug		Sep		Oct		Nov		Dec	
	Index	%	Index	%	Index	%	Index	%	Index	%	Index	%	Index	%	Index	%	Index	%	Index	%	Index	%	Index	%
1997	-		-		-		-		-		-		-		-		-		-		-		100.0	-
1998	-		-		-		-		-		98.9	-1.1	-		-		-		-		-		99.3	0.4
1999	-		-		-		-		-		102.6	3.3	-		-		-		-		-		106.4	3.7
2000	-		-		-		-		-		107.3	0.8	-		-		-		-		-		105.6	-1.6
2001	-		-		-		-		-		103.5	-2.0	-		-		-		-		-		-	

Source: U.S. Department of Labor, Bureau of Labor Statistics, Division of Consumer Prices and Price Indexes. - indicates no data collected for period.

Honolulu, HI
Consumer Price Index - Urban Wage Earners
Base December 1997 = 100
Education & Communication

For 1997-2001. Columns headed % show percentile change in the index from the previous period for which an index is available.

Year	Jan		Feb		Mar		Apr		May		Jun		Jul		Aug		Sep		Oct		Nov		Dec	
	Index	%	Index	%	Index	%	Index	%	Index	%	Index	%	Index	%	Index	%	Index	%	Index	%	Index	%	Index	%
1997	-	-	-	-	-	-	-	-	-	-	-	-	-	-	-	-	-	-	-	-	-	-	100.0	-
1998	-	-	-	-	-	-	-	-	-	-	99.6	-0.4	-	-	-	-	-	-	-	-	-	-	99.6	0.0
1999	-	-	-	-	-	-	-	-	-	-	103.0	3.4	-	-	-	-	-	-	-	-	-	-	107.0	3.9
2000	-	-	-	-	-	-	-	-	-	-	108.2	1.1	-	-	-	-	-	-	-	-	-	-	106.6	-1.5
2001	-	-	-	-	-	-	-	-	-	-	104.4	-2.1	-	-	-	-	-	-	-	-	-	-	-	-

Source: U.S. Department of Labor, Bureau of Labor Statistics, Division of Consumer Prices and Price Indexes. - indicates no data collected for period.

Houston-Galveston-Brazoria, TX
Consumer Price Index - All Urban Consumers
Base 1982-1984 = 100
Annual Averages

For 1914-2001. Columns headed % show percentile change in the index from the previous period for which an index is available.

Year	All Items		Food & Beverage		Housing		Apparel		Trans-portation		Medical Care		Recrea-tion*		Education & Communic.*		Other Goods & Services	
	Index	%	Index	%	Index	%	Index	%	Index	%	Index	%	Index	%	Index	%	Index	%
1914	-	-	-	-	-	-	-	-	-	-	-	-	-	-	-	-	-	-
1915	9.4	-	-	-	-	-	-	-	-	-	-	-	-	-	-	-	-	-
1916	10.1	7.4	-	-	-	-	-	-	-	-	-	-	-	-	-	-	-	-
1917	12.4	22.8	-	-	-	-	-	-	-	-	-	-	-	-	-	-	-	-
1918	14.5	16.9	-	-	-	-	-	-	-	-	-	-	-	-	-	-	-	-
1919	16.9	16.6	-	-	-	-	-	-	-	-	-	-	-	-	-	-	-	-
1920	19.2	13.6	-	-	-	-	-	-	-	-	-	-	-	-	-	-	-	-
1921	17.0	-11.5	-	-	-	-	-	-	-	-	-	-	-	-	-	-	-	-
1922	15.9	-6.5	-	-	-	-	-	-	-	-	-	-	-	-	-	-	-	-
1923	15.9	0.0	-	-	-	-	-	-	-	-	-	-	-	-	-	-	-	-
1924	15.8	-0.6	-	-	-	-	-	-	-	-	-	-	-	-	-	-	-	-
1925	16.2	2.5	-	-	-	-	-	-	-	-	-	-	-	-	-	-	-	-
1926	16.0	-1.2	-	-	-	-	-	-	-	-	-	-	-	-	-	-	-	-
1927	15.7	-1.9	-	-	-	-	-	-	-	-	-	-	-	-	-	-	-	-
1928	15.6	-0.6	-	-	-	-	-	-	-	-	-	-	-	-	-	-	-	-
1929	15.7	0.6	-	-	-	-	-	-	-	-	-	-	-	-	-	-	-	-
1930	15.3	-2.5	-	-	-	-	-	-	-	-	-	-	-	-	-	-	-	-
1931	13.9	-9.2	-	-	-	-	-	-	-	-	-	-	-	-	-	-	-	-
1932	12.3	-11.5	-	-	-	-	-	-	-	-	-	-	-	-	-	-	-	-
1933	11.8	-4.1	-	-	-	-	-	-	-	-	-	-	-	-	-	-	-	-
1934	12.3	4.2	-	-	-	-	-	-	-	-	-	-	-	-	-	-	-	-
1935	12.7	3.3	-	-	-	-	-	-	-	-	-	-	-	-	-	-	-	-
1936	12.8	0.8	-	-	-	-	-	-	-	-	-	-	-	-	-	-	-	-
1937	13.3	3.9	-	-	-	-	-	-	-	-	-	-	-	-	-	-	-	-
1938	13.3	0.0	-	-	-	-	-	-	-	-	-	-	-	-	-	-	-	-
1939	13.2	-0.8	-	-	-	-	-	-	-	-	-	-	-	-	-	-	-	-
1940	13.2	0.0	-	-	-	-	-	-	-	-	-	-	-	-	-	-	-	-
1941	13.8	4.5	-	-	-	-	-	-	-	-	-	-	-	-	-	-	-	-
1942	15.2	10.1	-	-	-	-	-	-	-	-	-	-	-	-	-	-	-	-
1943	16.0	5.3	-	-	-	-	-	-	-	-	-	-	-	-	-	-	-	-
1944	16.2	1.3	-	-	-	-	-	-	-	-	-	-	-	-	-	-	-	-
1945	16.6	2.5	-	-	-	-	-	-	-	-	-	-	-	-	-	-	-	-
1946	17.9	7.8	-	-	-	-	-	-	-	-	-	-	-	-	-	-	-	-
1947	21.0	17.3	-	-	-	-	-	-	20.8	-	14.5	-	-	-	-	-	-	-
1948	22.7	8.1	-	-	-	-	-	-	23.2	11.5	14.9	2.8	-	-	-	-	-	-
1949	22.7	0.0	-	-	-	-	-	-	24.7	6.5	15.2	2.0	-	-	-	-	-	-
1950	23.4	3.1	-	-	-	-	-	-	25.7	4.0	15.6	2.6	-	-	-	-	-	-
1951	25.2	7.7	-	-	-	-	-	-	28.0	8.9	15.9	1.9	-	-	-	-	-	-
1952	25.5	1.2	-	-	-	-	-	-	28.5	1.8	16.8	5.7	-	-	-	-	-	-
1953	25.8	1.2	-	-	-	-	36.1	-	29.0	1.8	17.5	4.2	-	-	-	-	-	-
1954	25.8	0.0	-	-	-	-	36.0	-0.3	28.6	-1.4	17.7	1.1	-	-	-	-	-	-
1955	25.7	-0.4	-	-	-	-	36.0	0.0	28.3	-1.0	18.4	4.0	-	-	-	-	-	-
1956	26.1	1.6	-	-	-	-	36.7	1.9	28.9	2.1	18.9	2.7	-	-	-	-	-	-
1957	26.9	3.1	-	-	-	-	37.6	2.5	30.9	6.9	19.2	1.6	-	-	-	-	-	-
1958	27.3	1.5	-	-	-	-	38.3	1.9	31.5	1.9	19.7	2.6	-	-	-	-	-	-

[Continued]

Houston-Galveston-Brazoria, TX
Consumer Price Index - All Urban Consumers
Base 1982-1984 = 100
Annual Averages
[Continued]

For 1914-2001. Columns headed % show percentile change in the index from the previous period for which an index is available.

Year	All Items		Food & Beverage		Housing		Apparel		Trans-portation		Medical Care		Recrea-tion*		Education & Communic.*		Other Goods & Services	
	Index	%	Index	%	Index	%	Index	%	Index	%	Index	%	Index	%	Index	%	Index	%
1959	27.6	1.1	-	-	-	-	38.7	1.0	33.0	4.8	20.0	1.5	-	-	-	-	-	-
1960	27.8	0.7	-	-	-	-	38.7	0.0	32.9	-0.3	20.5	2.5	-	-	-	-	-	-
1961	28.0	0.7	-	-	-	-	38.9	0.5	33.1	0.6	20.8	1.5	-	-	-	-	-	-
1962	28.5	1.8	-	-	-	-	40.0	2.8	34.2	3.3	21.0	1.0	-	-	-	-	-	-
1963	28.8	1.1	-	-	-	-	40.5	1.3	33.5	-2.0	21.6	2.9	-	-	-	-	-	-
1964	29.2	1.4	-	-	-	-	40.8	0.7	34.3	2.4	22.2	2.8	-	-	-	-	-	-
1965	29.6	1.4	-	-	-	-	40.8	0.0	34.2	-0.3	22.8	2.7	-	-	-	-	-	-
1966	30.4	2.7	-	-	-	-	41.5	1.7	34.8	1.8	23.4	2.6	-	-	-	-	-	-
1967	31.2	2.6	-	-	-	-	42.2	1.7	36.0	3.4	24.9	6.4	-	-	-	-	-	-
1968	32.5	4.2	-	-	-	-	44.6	5.7	37.1	3.1	26.2	5.2	-	-	-	-	-	-
1969	34.6	6.5	-	-	-	-	48.1	7.8	38.4	3.5	28.5	8.8	-	-	-	-	-	-
1970	36.4	5.2	-	-	-	-	50.6	5.2	39.1	1.8	30.6	7.4	-	-	-	-	-	-
1971	37.7	3.6	-	-	-	-	51.5	1.8	40.8	4.3	32.4	5.9	-	-	-	-	-	-
1972	39.0	3.4	-	-	-	-	53.1	3.1	41.4	1.5	33.7	4.0	-	-	-	-	-	-
1973	41.2	5.6	-	-	-	-	55.1	3.8	42.2	1.9	35.0	3.9	-	-	-	-	-	-
1974	46.1	11.9	-	-	-	-	60.3	9.4	47.3	12.1	37.9	8.3	-	-	-	-	-	-
1975	51.4	11.5	-	-	-	-	64.2	6.5	51.9	9.7	43.2	14.0	-	-	-	-	-	-
1976	55.3	7.6	58.5	-	53.0	-	68.0	5.9	56.3	8.5	48.0	11.1	-	-	-	-	-	-
1977	59.3	7.2	61.6	5.3	57.4	8.3	72.0	5.9	60.5	7.5	54.2	12.9	-	-	-	-	56.3	-
1978	64.9	9.4	67.8	10.1	64.4	12.2	76.9	6.8	62.8	3.8	59.4	9.6	-	-	-	-	59.8	6.2
1979	73.5	13.3	76.8	13.3	73.6	14.3	83.1	8.1	72.3	15.1	65.1	9.6	-	-	-	-	65.5	9.5
1980	82.7	12.5	83.8	9.1	82.7	12.4	89.1	7.2	85.6	18.4	72.2	10.9	-	-	-	-	71.7	9.5
1981	91.0	10.0	91.8	9.5	91.2	10.3	95.6	7.3	94.8	10.7	80.0	10.8					79.3	10.6
1982	97.3	6.9	96.4	5.0	99.8	9.4	98.4	2.9	97.7	3.1	90.7	13.4					85.3	7.6
1983	100.0	2.8	99.3	3.0	100.3	0.5	99.8	1.4	99.1	1.4	101.1	11.5					91.8	7.6
1984	102.7	2.7	104.3	5.0	99.9	-0.4	101.9	2.1	103.3	4.2	108.1	6.9					101.0	10.0
1985	104.9	2.1	105.0	0.7	100.2	0.3	104.4	2.5	106.2	2.8	116.8	8.0					107.2	6.1
1986	103.9	-1.0	107.3	2.2	98.1	-2.1	106.1	1.6	99.2	-6.6	123.5	5.7					112.5	4.9
1987	106.5	2.5	111.8	4.2	97.0	-1.1	113.6	7.1	102.5	3.3	130.4	5.6					118.6	5.4
1988	109.5	2.8	116.2	3.9	98.0	1.0	121.1	6.6	104.5	2.0	136.7	4.8					124.8	5.2
1989	114.1	4.2	121.7	4.7	100.5	2.6	123.9	2.3	109.2	4.5	148.0	8.3					131.2	5.1
1990	120.6	5.7	128.7	5.8	104.8	4.3	132.5	6.9	116.0	6.2	161.2	8.9					138.5	5.6
1991	125.1	3.7	131.6	2.3	109.5	4.5	134.8	1.7	119.6	3.1	177.7	10.2	-	-	-	-	152.1	9.8
1992	129.1	3.2	130.8	-0.6	113.2	3.4	135.8	0.7	122.9	2.8	193.6	8.9					157.7	3.7
1993	133.4	3.3	132.4	1.2	116.8	3.2	142.1	4.6	128.2	4.3	200.8	3.7					172.1	9.1
1994	137.9	3.4	137.5	3.9	120.4	3.1	146.7	3.2	132.9	3.7	204.6	1.9					180.8	5.1
1995	139.8	1.4	140.2	2.0	121.1	0.6	138.3	-5.7	137.0	3.1	217.7	6.4					187.6	3.8
1996	142.7	2.1	142.9	1.9	123.9	2.3	137.7	-0.4	140.4	2.5	222.6	2.3					193.4	3.1
1997	145.4	1.9	147.7	3.4	126.1	1.8	142.1	3.2	141.4	0.7	228.4	2.6	-	-	-	-	197.6	2.2
1998	146.8	1.0	150.9	2.2	129.6	2.8	140.9	-0.8	135.7	-4.0	235.4	3.1	100.1	-	99.1	-	197.7	0.1
1999	148.7	1.3	152.8	1.3	132.1	1.9	139.9	-0.7	135.7	0.0	238.5	1.3	101.5	1.4	100.8	1.7	206.9	4.7
2000	154.2	3.7	157.7	3.2	137.2	3.9	146.5	4.7	142.4	4.9	242.9	1.8	105.7	4.1	100.3	-0.5	218.0	5.4
2001	158.8	3.0	163.5	3.7	144.1	5.0	142.4	-2.8	-	-	251.7	3.6	108.6	2.7	101.2	0.9	226.2	3.8
																	236.1	4.4

Source: U.S. Department of Labor, Bureau of Labor Statistics, Division of Consumer Prices and Price Indexes. *Base is December 1997 = 100. - indicates no data collected for period.

Houston-Galveston-Brazoria, TX
Consumer Price Index - Urban Wage Earners
Base 1982-1984 = 100
Annual Averages

For 1914-2001. Columns headed % show percentile change in the index from the previous period for which an index is available.

Year	All Items		Food & Beverage		Housing		Apparel		Trans-portation		Medical Care		Recrea-tion*		Education & Communic.*		Other Goods & Services	
	Index	%	Index	%	Index	%	Index	%	Index	%	Index	%	Index	%	Index	%	Index	%
1914	-	-	-	-	-	-	-	-	-	-	-	-	-	-	-	-	-	-
1915	9.5	-	-	-	-	-	-	-	-	-	-	-	-	-	-	-	-	-
1916	10.1	6.3	-	-	-	-	-	-	-	-	-	-	-	-	-	-	-	-
1917	12.5	23.8	-	-	-	-	-	-	-	-	-	-	-	-	-	-	-	-
1918	14.5	16.0	-	-	-	-	-	-	-	-	-	-	-	-	-	-	-	-
1919	17.0	17.2	-	-	-	-	-	-	-	-	-	-	-	-	-	-	-	-
1920	19.3	13.5	-	-	-	-	-	-	-	-	-	-	-	-	-	-	-	-
1921	17.1	-11.4	-	-	-	-	-	-	-	-	-	-	-	-	-	-	-	-
1922	16.0	-6.4	-	-	-	-	-	-	-	-	-	-	-	-	-	-	-	-
1923	16.0	0.0	-	-	-	-	-	-	-	-	-	-	-	-	-	-	-	-
1924	15.9	-0.6	-	-	-	-	-	-	-	-	-	-	-	-	-	-	-	-
1925	16.2	1.9	-	-	-	-	-	-	-	-	-	-	-	-	-	-	-	-
1926	16.1	-0.6	-	-	-	-	-	-	-	-	-	-	-	-	-	-	-	-
1927	15.8	-1.9	-	-	-	-	-	-	-	-	-	-	-	-	-	-	-	-
1928	15.6	-1.3	-	-	-	-	-	-	-	-	-	-	-	-	-	-	-	-
1929	15.7	0.6	-	-	-	-	-	-	-	-	-	-	-	-	-	-	-	-
1930	15.4	-1.9	-	-	-	-	-	-	-	-	-	-	-	-	-	-	-	-
1931	13.9	-9.7	-	-	-	-	-	-	-	-	-	-	-	-	-	-	-	-
1932	12.4	-10.8	-	-	-	-	-	-	-	-	-	-	-	-	-	-	-	-
1933	11.8	-4.8	-	-	-	-	-	-	-	-	-	-	-	-	-	-	-	-
1934	12.4	5.1	-	-	-	-	-	-	-	-	-	-	-	-	-	-	-	-
1935	12.8	3.2	-	-	-	-	-	-	-	-	-	-	-	-	-	-	-	-
1936	12.9	0.8	-	-	-	-	-	-	-	-	-	-	-	-	-	-	-	-
1937	13.4	3.9	-	-	-	-	-	-	-	-	-	-	-	-	-	-	-	-
1938	13.3	-0.7	-	-	-	-	-	-	-	-	-	-	-	-	-	-	-	-
1939	13.2	-0.8	-	-	-	-	-	-	-	-	-	-	-	-	-	-	-	-
1940	13.3	0.8	-	-	-	-	-	-	-	-	-	-	-	-	-	-	-	-
1941	13.8	3.8	-	-	-	-	-	-	-	-	-	-	-	-	-	-	-	-
1942	15.3	10.9	-	-	-	-	-	-	-	-	-	-	-	-	-	-	-	-
1943	16.1	5.2	-	-	-	-	-	-	-	-	-	-	-	-	-	-	-	-
1944	16.3	1.2	-	-	-	-	-	-	-	-	-	-	-	-	-	-	-	-
1945	16.6	1.8	-	-	-	-	-	-	-	-	-	-	-	-	-	-	-	-
1946	18.0	8.4	-	-	-	-	-	-	-	-	-	-	-	-	-	-	-	-
1947	21.1	17.2	-	-	-	-	-	-	20.7	-	13.9	-	-	-	-	-	-	-
1948	22.8	8.1	-	-	-	-	-	-	23.2	12.1	14.2	2.2	-	-	-	-	-	-
1949	22.8	0.0	-	-	-	-	-	-	24.6	6.0	14.6	2.8	-	-	-	-	-	-
1950	23.5	3.1	-	-	-	-	-	-	25.6	4.1	14.9	2.1	-	-	-	-	-	-
1951	25.3	7.7	-	-	-	-	-	-	27.9	9.0	15.3	2.7	-	-	-	-	-	-
1952	25.7	1.6	-	-	-	-	-	-	28.4	1.8	16.1	5.2	-	-	-	-	-	-
1953	26.0	1.2	-	-	-	-	36.8	-	28.9	1.8	16.8	4.3	-	-	-	-	-	-
1954	25.9	-0.4	-	-	-	-	36.7	-0.3	28.5	-1.4	17.0	1.2	-	-	-	-	-	-
1955	25.8	-0.4	-	-	-	-	36.7	0.0	28.1	-1.4	17.7	4.1	-	-	-	-	-	-
1956	26.2	1.6	-	-	-	-	37.4	1.9	28.8	2.5	18.2	2.8	-	-	-	-	-	-
1957	27.0	3.1	-	-	-	-	38.3	2.4	30.8	6.9	18.4	1.1	-	-	-	-	-	-
1958	27.5	1.9	-	-	-	-	39.1	2.1	31.3	1.6	18.8	2.2	-	-	-	-	-	-

[Continued]

Houston-Galveston-Brazoria, TX
Consumer Price Index - Urban Wage Earners
Base 1982-1984 = 100
Annual Averages
[Continued]

For 1914-2001. Columns headed % show percentile change in the index from the previous period for which an index is available.

Year	All Items		Food & Beverage		Housing		Apparel		Trans-portation		Medical Care		Recrea-tion*		Education & Communic.*		Other Goods & Services	
	Index	%	Index	%	Index	%	Index	%	Index	%	Index	%	Index	%	Index	%	Index	%
1959	27.7	0.7	-	-	-	-	39.5	1.0	32.8	4.8	19.2	2.1	-	-	-	-	-	-
1960	27.9	0.7	-	-	-	-	39.4	-0.3	32.8	0.0	19.6	2.1	-	-	-	-	-	-
1961	28.1	0.7	-	-	-	-	39.6	0.5	32.9	0.3	19.9	1.5	-	-	-	-	-	-
1962	28.6	1.8	-	-	-	-	40.8	3.0	34.0	3.3	20.2	1.5	-	-	-	-	-	-
1963	28.9	1.0	-	-	-	-	41.3	1.2	33.4	-1.8	20.7	2.5	-	-	-	-	-	-
1964	29.4	1.7	-	-	-	-	41.6	0.7	34.2	2.4	21.3	2.9	-	-	-	-	-	-
1965	29.7	1.0	-	-	-	-	41.6	0.0	34.1	-0.3	21.8	2.3	-	-	-	-	-	-
1966	30.5	2.7	-	-	-	-	42.3	1.7	34.7	1.8	22.5	3.2	-	-	-	-	-	-
1967	31.3	2.6	-	-	-	-	43.0	1.7	35.9	3.5	23.9	6.2	-	-	-	-	-	-
1968	32.7	4.5	-	-	-	-	45.4	5.6	36.9	2.8	25.1	5.0	-	-	-	-	-	-
1969	34.8	6.4	-	-	-	-	49.1	8.1	38.3	3.8	27.4	9.2	-	-	-	-	-	-
1970	36.6	5.2	-	-	-	-	51.6	5.1	39.0	1.8	29.3	6.9	-	-	-	-	-	-
1971	37.9	3.6	-	-	-	-	52.5	1.7	40.6	4.1	31.0	5.8	-	-	-	-	-	-
1972	39.2	3.4	-	-	-	-	54.1	3.0	41.2	1.5	32.3	4.2	-	-	-	-	-	-
1973	41.5	5.9	-	-	-	-	56.2	3.9	42.0	1.9	33.6	4.0	-	-	-	-	-	-
1974	46.3	11.6	-	-	-	-	61.4	9.3	47.1	12.1	36.4	8.3	-	-	-	-	-	-
1975	51.7	11.7	-	-	-	-	65.5	6.7	51.7	9.8	41.4	13.7	-	-	-	-	-	-
1976	55.6	7.5	59.5	-	53.0	-	69.3	5.8	56.0	8.3	46.0	11.1	-	-	-	-	-	-
1977	59.6	7.2	62.6	5.2	57.4	8.3	73.4	5.9	60.2	7.5	51.9	12.8	-	-	-	-	56.2	-
1978	65.1	9.2	68.6	9.6	64.3	12.0	78.5	6.9	62.7	4.2	57.0	9.8	-	-	-	-	59.6	6.0
1979	73.4	12.7	77.0	12.2	72.7	13.1	85.3	8.7	72.1	15.0	64.7	13.5	-	-	-	-	64.7	8.6
1980	82.1	11.9	83.8	8.8	81.4	12.0	90.3	5.9	84.3	16.9	71.7	10.8	-	-	-	-	70.6	9.1
1981	90.3	10.0	91.6	9.3	90.0	10.6	96.4	6.8	93.4	10.8	79.6	11.0	-	-	-	-	78.5	11.2
1982	96.9	7.3	96.4	5.2	98.7	9.7	98.5	2.2	97.1	4.0	90.5	13.7	-	-	-	-	84.6	7.8
1983	100.1	3.3	99.4	3.1	100.4	1.7	99.8	1.3	99.0	2.0	101.2	11.8	-	-	-	-	91.7	8.4
1984	103.1	3.0	104.2	4.8	100.8	0.4	101.8	2.0	103.9	4.9	108.3	7.0	-	-	-	-	101.0	10.1
1985	104.6	1.5	104.8	0.6	100.1	-0.7	104.2	2.4	106.7	2.7	117.0	8.0	-	-	-	-	107.3	6.2
1986	103.6	-1.0	107.3	2.4	98.0	-2.1	105.7	1.4	100.3	-6.0	123.7	5.7	-	-	-	-	112.4	4.8
1987	106.4	2.7	111.7	4.1	96.5	-1.5	112.7	6.6	104.7	4.4	130.9	5.8	-	-	-	-	117.4	4.4
1988	109.7	3.1	116.1	3.9	97.5	1.0	121.1	7.5	107.1	2.3	137.7	5.2	-	-	-	-	123.0	4.8
1989	114.4	4.3	121.7	4.8	100.2	2.8	124.0	2.4	111.9	4.5	149.3	8.4	-	-	-	-	130.4	6.0
1990	120.9	5.7	128.8	5.8	104.5	4.3	132.8	7.1	118.7	6.1	162.3	8.7	-	-	-	-	139.1	6.7
1991	125.3	3.6	131.7	2.3	109.4	4.7	133.9	0.8	122.1	2.9	178.9	10.2	-	-	-	-	152.8	9.8
1992	128.9	2.9	131.0	-0.5	113.3	3.6	134.4	0.4	125.2	2.5	195.3	9.2	-	-	-	-	157.7	3.2
1993	133.0	3.2	132.6	1.2	117.2	3.4	138.9	3.3	129.4	3.4	202.9	3.9	-	-	-	-	171.5	8.8
1994	137.4	3.3	137.7	3.8	120.7	3.0	145.4	4.7	134.0	3.6	206.6	1.8	-	-	-	-	179.6	4.7
1995	139.4	1.5	140.3	1.9	121.2	0.4	137.6	-5.4	138.6	3.4	219.5	6.2	-	-	-	-	185.1	3.1
1996	142.0	1.9	143.1	2.0	123.8	2.1	136.8	-0.6	142.2	2.6	224.6	2.3	-	-	-	-	190.0	2.6
1997	144.5	1.8	148.0	3.4	126.0	1.8	141.2	3.2	142.9	0.5	230.5	2.6	-	-	-	-	189.4	-0.3
1998	145.4	0.6	151.1	2.1	129.4	2.7	139.5	-1.2	136.9	-4.2	237.5	3.0	100.3	-	98.8	-	186.8	-1.4
1999	147.4	1.4	152.9	1.2	132.2	2.2	138.3	-0.9	136.9	0.0	240.1	1.1	102.7	2.4	100.4	1.6	195.9	4.9
2000	152.8	3.7	158.0	3.3	136.9	3.6	146.3	5.8	143.5	4.8	243.9	1.6	107.5	4.7	99.1	-1.3	208.9	6.6
2001	157.1	2.8	164.0	3.8	144.3	5.4	141.5	-3.3	-	-	252.9	3.7	109.7	2.0	99.2	0.1	218.0	4.4
																	228.3	4.7

Source: U.S. Department of Labor, Bureau of Labor Statistics, Division of Consumer Prices and Price Indexes. *Base is December 1997 = 100. - indicates no data collected for period.

Houston-Galveston-Brazoria, TX
Consumer Price Index - All Urban Consumers
Base 1982-1984 = 100
All Items

For 1914-2001. Columns headed % show percentile change in the index from the previous period for which an index is available.

Year	Jan Index	%	Feb Index	%	Mar Index	%	Apr Index	%	May Index	%	Jun Index	%	Jul Index	%	Aug Index	%	Sep Index	%	Oct Index	%	Nov Index	%	Dec Index	%
1914	-	-	-	-	-	-	-	-	-	-	-	-	-	-	-	-	-	-	-	-	-	-	9.5	-
1915	-	-	-	-	-	-	-	-	-	-	-	-	-	-	-	-	-	-	-	-	-	-	9.5	0.0
1916	-	-	-	-	-	-	-	-	-	-	-	-	-	-	-	-	-	-	-	-	-	-	10.9	14.7
1917	-	-	-	-	-	-	-	-	-	-	-	-	-	-	-	-	-	-	-	-	-	-	13.2	21.1
1918	-	-	-	-	-	-	-	-	-	-	-	-	-	-	-	-	-	-	-	-	-	-	15.9	20.5
1919	-	-	-	-	-	-	-	-	-	-	16.4	3.1	-	-	-	-	-	-	-	-	-	-	18.5	12.8
1920	-	-	-	-	-	-	-	-	-	-	19.7	6.5	-	-	-	-	-	-	-	-	-	-	18.9	-4.1
1921	-	-	-	-	-	-	-	-	16.9	-10.6	-	-	-	-	-	-	16.6	-1.8	-	-	-	-	16.4	-1.2
1922	-	-	-	-	15.9	-3.0	-	-	-	-	15.8	-0.6	-	-	-	-	15.7	-0.6	-	-	-	-	15.9	1.3
1923	-	-	-	-	15.7	-1.3	-	-	-	-	15.9	1.3	-	-	-	-	16.0	0.6	-	-	-	-	16.1	0.6
1924	-	-	-	-	15.9	-1.2	-	-	-	-	15.6	-1.9	-	-	-	-	15.8	1.3	-	-	-	-	16.0	1.3
1925	-	-	-	-	-	-	-	-	-	-	16.1	0.6	-	-	-	-	-	-	-	-	-	-	16.4	1.9
1926	-	-	-	-	-	-	-	-	-	-	16.0	-2.4	-	-	-	-	-	-	-	-	-	-	16.0	0.0
1927	-	-	-	-	-	-	-	-	-	-	15.7	-1.9	-	-	-	-	-	-	-	-	-	-	15.8	0.6
1928	-	-	-	-	-	-	-	-	-	-	15.5	-1.9	-	-	-	-	-	-	-	-	-	-	15.6	0.6
1929	-	-	-	-	-	-	-	-	-	-	15.6	0.0	-	-	-	-	-	-	-	-	-	-	15.8	1.3
1930	-	-	-	-	-	-	-	-	-	-	15.4	-2.5	-	-	-	-	-	-	-	-	-	-	14.7	-4.5
1931	-	-	-	-	-	-	-	-	-	-	13.8	-6.1	-	-	-	-	-	-	-	-	-	-	13.4	-2.9
1932	-	-	-	-	-	-	-	-	-	-	12.3	-8.2	-	-	-	-	-	-	-	-	-	-	11.7	-4.9
1933	-	-	-	-	-	-	-	-	-	-	11.6	-0.9	-	-	-	-	-	-	-	-	-	-	12.1	4.3
1934	-	-	-	-	-	-	-	-	-	-	12.2	0.8	-	-	-	-	-	-	-	-	12.6	3.3	-	-
1935	-	-	-	-	12.8	1.6	-	-	-	-	-	-	12.6	-1.6	-	-	-	-	12.7	0.8	-	-	-	-
1936	12.8	0.8	-	-	-	-	12.6	-1.6	-	-	-	-	12.9	2.4	-	-	13.0	0.8	-	-	-	-	13.0	0.0
1937	-	-	-	-	13.3	2.3	-	-	-	-	13.3	0.0	-	-	-	-	13.5	1.5	-	-	-	-	13.5	0.0
1938	-	-	-	-	13.3	-1.5	-	-	-	-	13.2	-0.8	-	-	-	-	13.3	0.8	-	-	-	-	13.3	0.0
1939	-	-	-	-	13.1	-1.5	-	-	-	-	13.1	0.0	-	-	-	-	13.3	1.5	-	-	-	-	13.2	-0.8
1940	-	-	-	-	13.2	0.0	-	-	-	-	13.2	0.0	-	-	-	-	13.2	0.0	13.3	0.8	13.3	0.0	13.3	0.0
1941	13.3	0.0	13.3	0.0	13.3	0.0	13.5	1.5	13.5	0.0	13.6	0.7	13.7	0.7	13.8	0.7	14.1	2.2	14.4	2.1	14.5	0.7	14.6	0.7
1942	14.7	0.7	14.9	1.4	15.1	1.3	15.1	0.0	15.2	0.7	15.1	-0.7	15.3	1.3	15.4	0.7	15.5	0.6	15.5	0.0	15.5	0.0	15.6	0.6
1943	15.7	0.6	15.8	0.6	16.2	2.5	16.2	0.0	16.3	0.6	16.1	-1.2	16.0	-0.6	15.9	-0.6	16.1	1.3	16.1	0.0	16.1	0.0	16.1	0.0
1944	16.1	0.0	16.1	0.0	16.0	-0.6	16.1	0.6	16.2	0.6	16.2	0.0	16.3	0.6	16.3	0.0	16.3	0.0	16.3	0.0	16.2	-0.6	16.3	0.6
1945	16.4	0.6	16.3	-0.6	16.3	0.0	16.4	0.6	16.5	0.6	16.6	0.6	16.7	0.6	16.7	0.0	16.7	0.0	16.6	-0.6	16.6	0.0	16.7	0.6
1946	16.6	-0.6	16.6	0.0	16.7	0.6	16.8	0.6	16.8	0.0	17.1	1.8	17.9	4.7	18.4	2.8	18.7	1.6	18.9	1.1	19.7	4.2	20.0	1.5
1947	20.2	1.0	20.2	0.0	20.6	2.0	20.8	1.0	20.7	-0.5	20.7	0.0	20.8	0.5	21.0	1.0	21.3	1.4	21.5	0.9	21.8	1.4	22.2	1.8
1948	22.4	0.9	22.4	0.0	22.4	0.0	22.5	0.4	22.5	0.0	22.7	0.9	22.9	0.9	23.1	0.9	23.1	0.0	23.0	-0.4	22.9	-0.4	22.9	0.0
1949	22.8	-0.4	22.5	-1.3	22.5	0.0	22.6	0.4	22.5	-0.4	22.5	0.0	22.5	0.0	22.6	0.4	22.7	0.4	22.8	0.4	23.0	0.9	23.0	0.0
1950	22.9	-0.4	22.9	0.0	23.0	0.4	22.9	-0.4	22.9	0.0	23.0	0.4	23.2	0.9	23.6	1.7	23.8	0.8	23.8	0.0	23.9	0.4	24.3	1.7
1951	24.8	2.1	25.0	0.8	25.1	0.4	25.2	0.4	25.2	0.0	25.1	-0.4	25.2	0.4	25.2	0.0	25.3	0.4	25.4	0.4	25.5	0.4	25.6	0.4
1952	25.5	-0.4	25.4	-0.4	25.4	0.0	25.4	0.0	25.4	0.0	25.4	0.0	25.5	0.4	25.6	0.4	25.5	-0.4	25.7	0.8	25.7	0.0	25.8	0.4
1953	-	-	25.7	-0.4	-	-	-	-	25.8	0.4	-	-	-	-	25.8	0.0	-	-	-	-	25.9	0.4	-	-
1954	-	-	25.9	0.0	-	-	-	-	25.8	-0.4	-	-	-	-	25.8	0.0	-	-	-	-	25.8	0.0	-	-
1955	-	-	25.6	-0.8	-	-	-	-	25.5	-0.4	-	-	-	-	25.5	0.0	-	-	-	-	25.8	1.2	-	-
1956	-	-	25.8	0.0	-	-	-	-	25.8	0.0	-	-	-	-	26.1	1.2	-	-	-	-	26.5	1.5	-	-
1957	-	-	26.7	0.8	-	-	-	-	26.8	0.4	-	-	-	-	27.0	0.7	-	-	-	-	27.1	0.4	-	-
1958	-	-	27.1	0.0	-	-	-	-	27.4	1.1	-	-	-	-	27.4	0.0	-	-	-	-	27.5	0.4	-	-
1959	-	-	27.4	-0.4	-	-	-	-	27.4	0.0	-	-	-	-	27.6	0.7	-	-	-	-	27.7	0.4	-	-

[Continued]

Houston-Galveston-Brazoria, TX
Consumer Price Index - All Urban Consumers
Base 1982-1984 = 100
All Items
[Continued]

For 1914-2001. Columns headed % show percentile change in the index from the previous period for which an index is available.

Year	Jan Index	%	Feb Index	%	Mar Index	%	Apr Index	%	May Index	%	Jun Index	%	Jul Index	%	Aug Index	%	Sep Index	%	Oct Index	%	Nov Index	%	Dec Index	%
1960	-	-	27.8	0.4	-	-	-	-	27.7	-0.4	-	-	-	-	27.9	0.7	-	-	-	-	28.0	0.4	-	-
1961	-	-	27.7	-1.1	-	-	-	-	27.9	0.7	-	-	-	-	27.9	0.0	-	-	-	-	28.3	1.4	-	-
1962	-	-	28.5	0.7	-	-	-	-	28.5	0.0	-	-	-	-	28.5	0.0	-	-	-	-	28.5	0.0	-	-
1963	-	-	28.6	0.4	-	-	-	-	28.5	-0.3	-	-	-	-	28.9	1.4	-	-	-	-	29.1	0.7	-	-
1964	-	-	29.2	0.3	-	-	-	-	29.1	-0.3	-	-	-	-	29.2	0.3	-	-	-	-	29.2	0.0	-	-
1965	-	-	29.3	0.3	-	-	29.4	0.3	-	-	-	-	29.6	0.7	-	-	-	-	29.8	0.7	-	-	-	-
1966	30.0	0.7	-	-	-	-	30.2	0.7	-	-	-	-	30.4	0.7	-	-	-	-	30.6	0.7	-	-	-	-
1967	30.8	0.7	-	-	-	-	31.0	0.6	-	-	-	-	31.1	0.3	-	-	-	-	31.5	1.3	-	-	-	-
1968	31.8	1.0	-	-	-	-	32.1	0.9	-	-	-	-	32.5	1.2	-	-	-	-	33.0	1.5	-	-	-	-
1969	33.6	1.8	-	-	-	-	34.2	1.8	-	-	-	-	34.6	1.2	-	-	-	-	33.0	1.5	-	-	-	-
1970	35.7	0.8	-	-	-	-	36.2	1.4	-	-	-	-	36.4	0.6	-	-	-	-	36.8	1.1	-	-	-	-
1971	37.2	1.1	-	-	-	-	37.3	0.3	-	-	-	-	37.8	1.3	-	-	-	-	38.2	1.1	-	-	-	-
1972	38.4	0.5	-	-	-	-	38.9	1.3	-	-	-	-	39.0	0.3	-	-	-	-	39.4	1.0	-	-	-	-
1973	39.7	0.8	-	-	-	-	40.7	2.5	-	-	-	-	41.0	0.7	-	-	-	-	42.5	3.7	-	-	-	-
1974	43.4	2.1	-	-	-	-	44.6	2.8	-	-	-	-	46.1	3.4	-	-	-	-	48.1	4.3	-	-	-	-
1975	49.7	3.3	-	-	-	-	50.3	1.2	-	-	-	-	51.8	3.0	-	-	-	-	52.6	1.5	-	-	-	-
1976	53.7	2.1	-	-	-	-	54.3	1.1	-	-	-	-	55.2	1.7	-	-	-	-	56.7	2.7	-	-	-	-
1977	57.2	0.9	-	-	-	-	58.8	2.8	-	-	-	-	59.7	1.5	-	-	-	-	60.1	0.7	-	-	-	-
1978	61.3	2.0	-	-	-	-	63.3	3.3	-	-	64.7	2.2	-	-	65.9	1.9	-	-	67.0	1.7	-	-	68.5	2.2
1979	-	-	69.9	2.0	-	-	71.1	1.7	-	-	73.4	3.2	-	-	75.0	2.2	-	-	76.1	1.5	-	-	77.5	1.8
1980	-	-	79.8	3.0	-	-	81.3	1.9	-	-	83.1	2.2	-	-	83.7	0.7	-	-	84.9	1.4	-	-	85.7	0.9
1981	-	-	87.8	2.5	-	-	89.3	1.7	-	-	91.3	2.2	-	-	91.9	0.7	-	-	93.5	1.7	-	-	94.4	1.0
1982	-	-	94.8	0.4	-	-	95.1	0.3	-	-	97.9	2.9	-	-	99.3	1.4	-	-	99.0	-0.3	-	-	99.2	0.2
1983	-	-	98.9	-0.3	-	-	98.7	-0.2	-	-	100.2	1.5	-	-	101.0	0.8	-	-	101.1	0.1	-	-	100.0	-1.1
1984	-	-	100.9	0.9	-	-	101.5	0.6	-	-	103.0	1.5	-	-	103.5	0.5	-	-	104.3	0.8	-	-	103.9	-0.4
1985	-	-	104.0	0.1	-	-	104.5	0.5	-	-	105.3	0.8	-	-	105.4	0.1	-	-	105.3	-0.1	-	-	105.0	-0.3
1986	-	-	105.1	0.1	-	-	102.9	-2.1	-	-	103.9	1.0	-	-	103.8	-0.1	-	-	104.1	0.3	-	-	103.2	-0.9
1987	-	-	104.4	1.2	-	-	106.4	1.9	-	-	106.5	0.1	-	-	107.3	0.8	-	-	108.0	0.7	-	-	107.3	-0.6
1988	-	-	108.0	0.7	-	-	108.2	0.2	-	-	109.4	1.1	-	-	110.3	0.8	-	-	111.1	0.7	-	-	111.3	0.2
1989	-	-	112.7	1.3	-	-	113.2	0.4	-	-	114.1	0.8	-	-	114.4	0.3	-	-	115.7	1.1	-	-	115.5	-0.2
1990	-	-	118.7	2.8	-	-	118.3	-0.3	-	-	119.7	1.2	-	-	121.5	1.5	-	-	124.0	2.1	-	-	123.0	-0.8
1991	-	-	124.3	1.1	-	-	123.5	-0.6	-	-	124.9	1.1	-	-	124.8	-0.1	-	-	127.3	2.0	-	-	127.0	-0.2
1992	-	-	127.0	0.0	-	-	128.7	1.3	-	-	129.4	0.5	-	-	129.9	0.4	-	-	130.8	0.7	-	-	129.3	-1.1
1993	-	-	131.7	1.9	-	-	131.8	0.1	-	-	132.9	0.8	-	-	133.0	0.1	-	-	136.6	2.7	-	-	136.5	-0.1
1994	-	-	137.0	0.4	-	-	136.8	-0.1	-	-	137.4	0.4	-	-	139.2	1.3	-	-	139.3	0.1	-	-	137.8	-1.1
1995	-	-	139.3	1.1	-	-	138.0	-0.9	-	-	139.9	1.4	-	-	140.1	0.1	-	-	141.6	1.1	-	-	140.9	-0.5
1996	-	-	141.5	0.4	-	-	143.1	1.1	-	-	142.8	-0.2	-	-	142.8	0.0	-	-	143.2	0.3	-	-	143.6	0.3
1997	-	-	144.5	0.6	-	-	145.2	0.5	-	-	144.8	-0.3	-	-	145.4	0.4	-	-	147.3	1.3	-	-	145.6	-1.2
1998	-	-	146.1	0.3	-	-	146.3	0.1	-	-	146.4	0.1	-	-	147.4	0.7	-	-	148.5	0.7	-	-	146.1	-1.6
1999	-	-	146.6	0.3	-	-	148.3	1.2	-	-	148.3	0.0	-	-	148.9	0.4	-	-	151.2	1.5	-	-	150.3	-0.6
2000	-	-	152.1	1.2	-	-	152.8	0.5	-	-	154.1	0.9	-	-	154.4	0.2	-	-	157.1	1.7	-	-	156.2	-0.6
2001	-	-	158.6	1.5	-	-	159.5	0.6	-	-	159.6	0.1	-	-	158.6	-0.6	-	-	159.4	0.5	-	-	157.1	-1.4

Source: U.S. Department of Labor, Bureau of Labor Statistics, Division of Consumer Prices and Price Indexes. - indicates no data collected for period.

Houston-Galveston-Brazoria, TX
Consumer Price Index - Urban Wage Earners
Base 1982-1984 = 100
All Items

For 1914-2001. Columns headed % show percentile change in the index from the previous period for which an index is available.

Year	Jan Index	%	Feb Index	%	Mar Index	%	Apr Index	%	May Index	%	Jun Index	%	Jul Index	%	Aug Index	%	Sep Index	%	Oct Index	%	Nov Index	%	Dec Index	%
1914	-	-	-	-	-	-	-	-	-	-	-	-	-	-	-	-	-	-	-	-	-	-	9.6	-
1915	-	-	-	-	-	-	-	-	-	-	-	-	-	-	-	-	-	-	-	-	-	-	9.5	-1.0
1916	-	-	-	-	-	-	-	-	-	-	-	-	-	-	-	-	-	-	-	-	-	-	10.9	14.7
1917	-	-	-	-	-	-	-	-	-	-	-	-	-	-	-	-	-	-	-	-	-	-	13.3	22.0
1918	-	-	-	-	-	-	-	-	-	-	-	-	-	-	-	-	-	-	-	-	-	-	16.0	20.3
1919	-	-	-	-	-	-	-	-	-	-	16.4	2.5	-	-	-	-	-	-	-	-	-	-	18.6	13.4
1920	-	-	-	-	-	-	-	-	-	-	19.8	6.5	-	-	-	-	-	-	-	-	-	-	19.0	-4.0
1921	-	-	-	-	-	-	-	-	17.0	-10.5	-	-	-	-	-	-	16.6	-2.4	-	-	-	-	16.4	-1.2
1922	-	-	-	-	16.0	-2.4	-	-	-	-	15.9	-0.6	-	-	-	-	15.8	-0.6	-	-	-	-	16.0	1.3
1923	-	-	-	-	15.8	-1.2	-	-	-	-	15.9	0.6	-	-	-	-	16.0	0.6	-	-	-	-	16.2	1.3
1924	-	-	-	-	16.0	-1.2	-	-	-	-	15.7	-1.9	-	-	-	-	15.9	1.3	-	-	-	-	16.0	0.6
1925	-	-	-	-	-	-	-	-	-	-	16.2	1.3	-	-	-	-	-	-	-	-	-	-	16.4	1.2
1926	-	-	-	-	-	-	-	-	-	-	16.0	-2.4	-	-	-	-	-	-	-	-	-	-	16.1	0.6
1927	-	-	-	-	-	-	-	-	-	-	15.8	-1.9	-	-	-	-	-	-	-	-	-	-	15.9	0.6
1928	-	-	-	-	-	-	-	-	-	-	15.5	-2.5	-	-	-	-	-	-	-	-	-	-	15.7	1.3
1929	-	-	-	-	-	-	-	-	-	-	15.6	-0.6	-	-	-	-	-	-	-	-	-	-	15.9	1.9
1930	-	-	-	-	-	-	-	-	-	-	15.4	-3.1	-	-	-	-	-	-	-	-	-	-	14.7	-4.5
1931	-	-	-	-	-	-	-	-	-	-	13.9	-5.4	-	-	-	-	-	-	-	-	-	-	13.5	-2.9
1932	-	-	-	-	-	-	-	-	-	-	12.3	-8.9	-	-	-	-	-	-	-	-	-	-	11.7	-4.9
1933	-	-	-	-	-	-	-	-	-	-	11.7	0.0	-	-	-	-	-	-	-	-	-	-	12.1	3.4
1934	-	-	-	-	-	-	-	-	-	-	12.2	0.8	-	-	-	-	-	-	-	-	12.6	3.3	-	-
1935	-	-	-	-	12.8	1.6	-	-	-	-	-	-	12.7	-0.8	-	-	-	-	12.7	0.0	-	-	-	-
1936	12.8	0.8	-	-	-	-	12.7	-0.8	-	-	-	-	12.9	1.6	-	-	13.1	1.6	-	-	-	-	13.1	0.0
1937	-	-	-	-	13.3	1.5	-	-	-	-	13.3	0.0	-	-	-	-	13.6	2.3	-	-	-	-	13.5	-0.7
1938	-	-	-	-	13.4	-0.7	-	-	-	-	13.3	-0.7	-	-	-	-	13.3	0.0	-	-	-	-	13.3	0.0
1939	-	-	-	-	13.2	-0.8	-	-	-	-	13.2	0.0	-	-	-	-	13.3	0.8	-	-	-	-	13.3	0.0
1940	-	-	-	-	13.2	-0.8	-	-	-	-	13.2	0.0	-	-	-	-	13.3	0.8	13.4	0.8	13.4	0.0	13.4	0.0
1941	13.4	0.0	13.4	0.0	13.4	0.0	13.6	1.5	13.6	0.0	13.6	0.0	13.8	1.5	13.9	0.7	14.2	2.2	14.5	2.1	14.6	0.7	14.7	0.7
1942	14.8	0.7	15.0	1.4	15.2	1.3	15.2	0.0	15.3	0.7	15.2	-0.7	15.4	1.3	15.4	0.0	15.5	0.6	15.6	0.6	15.6	0.0	15.7	0.6
1943	15.7	0.0	15.9	1.3	16.2	1.9	16.3	0.6	16.4	0.6	16.2	-1.2	16.1	-0.6	16.0	-0.6	16.2	1.3	16.2	0.0	16.2	0.0	16.2	0.0
1944	16.2	0.0	16.2	0.0	16.1	-0.6	16.2	0.6	16.3	0.6	16.2	-0.6	16.4	1.2	16.4	0.0	16.4	0.0	16.4	0.0	16.3	-0.6	16.4	0.6
1945	16.4	0.0	16.4	0.0	16.4	0.0	16.5	0.6	16.6	0.6	16.7	0.6	16.8	0.6	16.8	0.0	16.8	0.0	16.7	-0.6	16.7	0.0	16.8	0.6
1946	16.7	-0.6	16.7	0.0	16.8	0.6	16.9	0.6	16.9	0.0	17.2	1.8	18.0	4.7	18.5	2.8	18.8	1.6	19.0	1.1	19.8	4.2	20.1	1.5
1947	20.3	1.0	20.3	0.0	20.7	2.0	20.9	1.0	20.8	-0.5	20.8	0.0	20.9	0.5	21.1	1.0	21.4	1.4	21.6	0.9	21.9	1.4	22.3	1.8
1948	22.5	0.9	22.5	0.0	22.5	0.0	22.7	0.9	22.7	0.0	22.8	0.4	23.0	0.9	23.2	0.9	23.2	0.0	23.2	0.0	23.0	-0.9	23.0	0.0
1949	22.9	-0.4	22.6	-1.3	22.6	0.0	22.7	0.4	22.7	0.0	22.7	0.0	22.7	0.0	22.7	0.0	22.8	0.4	22.9	0.4	23.1	0.9	23.1	0.0
1950	23.1	0.0	23.0	-0.4	23.1	0.4	23.0	-0.4	23.0	0.0	23.1	0.4	23.3	0.9	23.7	1.7	23.9	0.8	23.9	0.0	24.0	0.4	24.4	1.7
1951	25.0	2.5	25.1	0.4	25.3	0.8	25.3	0.0	25.3	0.0	25.3	0.0	25.3	0.0	25.3	0.0	25.5	0.8	25.5	0.0	25.6	0.4	25.8	0.8
1952	25.7	-0.4	25.5	-0.8	25.5	0.0	25.6	0.4	25.5	-0.4	25.6	0.4	25.6	0.0	25.8	0.8	25.7	-0.4	25.8	0.4	25.8	0.0	25.9	0.4
1953	-	-	25.8	-0.4	-	-	-	-	26.0	0.8	-	-	-	-	26.0	0.0	-	-	-	-	26.1	0.4	-	-
1954	-	-	26.0	-0.4	-	-	-	-	25.9	-0.4	-	-	-	-	25.9	0.0	-	-	-	-	25.9	0.0	-	-
1955	-	-	25.7	-0.8	-	-	-	-	25.7	0.0	-	-	-	-	25.7	0.0	-	-	-	-	25.9	0.8	-	-
1956	-	-	25.9	0.0	-	-	-	-	26.0	0.4	-	-	-	-	26.3	1.2	-	-	-	-	26.6	1.1	-	-
1957	-	-	26.8	0.8	-	-	-	-	26.9	0.4	-	-	-	-	27.1	0.7	-	-	-	-	27.2	0.4	-	-
1958	-	-	27.2	0.0	-	-	-	-	27.5	1.1	-	-	-	-	27.5	0.0	-	-	-	-	27.6	0.4	-	-
1959	-	-	27.6	0.0	-	-	-	-	27.6	0.0	-	-	-	-	27.7	0.4	-	-	-	-	27.9	0.7	-	-

[Continued]

Houston-Galveston-Brazoria, TX
Consumer Price Index - Urban Wage Earners
Base 1982-1984 = 100
All Items

[Continued]

For 1914-2001. Columns headed % show percentile change in the index from the previous period for which an index is available.

Year	Jan Index	%	Feb Index	%	Mar Index	%	Apr Index	%	May Index	%	Jun Index	%	Jul Index	%	Aug Index	%	Sep Index	%	Oct Index	%	Nov Index	%	Dec Index	%
1960	-		27.9	0.0	-		-		27.8	-0.4	-		-		28.0	0.7	-		-		-		-	
1961	-		27.8	-1.1	-		-		28.0	0.7	-		-		28.1	0.4	-		-		28.1	0.4	-	
1962	-		28.6	0.4	-		-		28.7	0.3	-		-		28.6	-0.3	-		-		28.5	1.4	-	
1963	-		28.8	0.7	-		-		28.6	-0.7	-		-		29.1	1.7	-		-		28.6	0.0	-	
1964	-		29.4	0.7	-		-		29.3	-0.3	-		-		29.4	0.3	-		-		29.2	0.3	-	
1965	-		29.4	0.0	-		29.5	0.3	-		-		29.7	0.7	-		-		29.9	0.7	29.4	0.0	-	
1966	30.1	0.7	-		-		30.4	1.0	-		-		30.6	0.7	-		-		30.8	0.7	-		-	
1967	31.0	0.6	-		-		31.1	0.3	-		-		31.3	0.6	-		-		30.8	0.7	-		-	
1968	32.0	1.3	-		-		32.3	0.9	-		-		32.7	1.2	-		-		31.6	1.0	-		-	
1969	33.7	1.5	-		-		34.4	2.1	-		-		34.8	1.2	-		-		33.2	1.5	-		-	
1970	35.8	0.6	-		-		36.4	1.7	-		-		36.6	0.5	-		-		35.6	2.3	-		-	
1971	37.4	1.4	-		-		37.4	0.0	-		-		38.0	1.6	-		-		36.9	0.8	-		-	
1972	38.6	0.5	-		-		39.1	1.3	-		-		39.2	0.3	-		-		38.4	1.1	-		-	
1973	39.9	0.8	-		-		40.9	2.5	-		-		41.2	0.7	-		-		39.6	1.0	-		-	
1974	43.6	2.1	-		-		44.8	2.8	-		-		46.4	3.6	-		-		42.7	3.6	-		-	
1975	49.9	3.3	-		-		50.6	1.4	-		-		52.0	2.8	-		-		48.3	4.1	-		-	
1976	54.0	2.1	-		-		54.5	0.9	-		-		55.5	1.8	-		-		52.9	1.7	-		-	
1977	57.5	0.9	-		-		59.1	2.8	-		-		60.0	1.5	-		-		57.0	2.7	-		-	
1978	61.6	2.0	-		-		63.6	3.2	-		65.0	2.2	-		66.1	1.7	-		60.4	0.7	-		68.4	2.1
1979	-		69.9	2.2	-		71.3	2.0	-		73.5	3.1	-		66.1	1.7	-		67.0	1.4	-		68.4	2.1
1980	-		78.9	2.3	-		80.6	2.2	-		82.3	2.1	-		74.9	1.9	-		75.8	1.2	-		77.1	1.7
1981	-		87.0	2.0	-		88.7	2.0	-		90.7	2.3	-		83.2	1.1	-		84.4	1.4	-		85.3	1.1
1982	-		94.1	0.5	-		94.7	0.6	-		97.4	2.9	-		91.4	0.8	-		92.7	1.4	-		93.6	1.0
1983	-		99.4	0.4	-		99.5	0.1	-		100.2	0.7	-		98.8	1.4	-		98.7	-0.1	-		99.0	0.3
1984	-		101.4	1.8	-		101.8	0.4	-		103.2	1.4	-		100.8	0.6	-		101.0	0.2	-		99.6	-1.4
1985	-		103.7	0.0	-		104.3	0.6	-		105.0	0.7	-		104.5	1.3	-		104.8	0.3	-		103.7	-1.0
1986	-		104.7	0.0	-		102.7	-1.9	-		103.7	1.0	-		105.1	0.1	-		105.0	-0.1	-		104.7	-0.3
1987	-		104.3	1.4	-		106.1	1.7	-		106.4	0.3	-		103.6	-0.1	-		103.9	0.3	-		102.9	-1.0
1988	-		108.1	0.7	-		108.1	0.0	-		109.4	1.2	-		107.1	0.7	-		108.1	0.9	-		107.4	-0.6
1989	-		112.9	1.3	-		113.5	0.5	-		114.5	0.9	-		110.6	1.1	-		111.4	0.7	-		111.4	0.0
1990	-		118.9	2.7	-		118.6	-0.3	-		120.0	1.2	-		114.9	0.3	-		115.8	0.8	-		115.8	0.0
1991	-		124.4	0.8	-		123.6	-0.6	-		125.2	1.3	-		121.9	1.6	-		124.7	2.3	-		123.4	-1.0
1992	-		126.9	-0.2	-		128.4	1.2	-		129.2	0.6	-		124.9	-0.2	-		127.4	2.0	-		127.2	-0.2
1993	-		131.3	1.6	-		131.3	0.0	-		132.4	0.8	-		129.8	0.5	-		130.7	0.7	-		129.2	-1.1
1994	-		136.3	0.2	-		136.2	-0.1	-		137.0	0.6	-		132.7	0.2	-		136.1	2.6	-		136.0	-0.1
1995	-		138.9	0.8	-		137.6	-0.9	-		139.5	1.4	-		138.8	1.3	-		139.0	0.1	-		137.8	-0.9
1996	-		140.8	0.2	-		142.3	1.1	-		142.2	-0.1	-		139.8	0.2	-		140.9	0.8	-		140.5	-0.3
1997	-		143.6	0.4	-		144.1	0.3	-		144.1	0.0	-		142.2	0.0	-		142.5	0.2	-		143.0	0.4
1998	-		144.7	0.1	-		144.8	0.1	-		145.1	0.2	-		144.9	0.6	-		146.3	1.0	-		144.5	-1.2
1999	-		145.0	0.1	-		146.6	1.1	-		147.1	0.3	-		146.1	0.7	-		146.9	0.5	-		144.8	-1.4
2000	-		150.5	0.9	-		151.4	0.6	-		153.1	1.1	-		147.9	0.5	-		149.9	1.4	-		149.2	-0.5
2001	-		156.7	1.2	-		157.8	0.7	-		158.4	0.4	-		153.1	0.0	-		155.4	1.5	-		154.9	-0.3
													157.0	-0.9					157.8	0.5			155.2	-1.6

Source: U.S. Department of Labor, Bureau of Labor Statistics, Division of Consumer Prices and Price Indexes. - indicates no data collected for period.

Houston-Galveston-Brazoria, TX
Consumer Price Index - All Urban Consumers
Base 1982-1984 = 100
Food and Beverages

For 1976-2001. Columns headed % show percentile change in the index from the previous period for which an index is available.

Year	Jan Index	%	Feb Index	%	Mar Index	%	Apr Index	%	May Index	%	Jun Index	%	Jul Index	%	Aug Index	%	Sep Index	%	Oct Index	%	Nov Index	%	Dec Index	%
1976	58.0	-	-	-	-	-	57.7	-0.5	-	-	-	-	58.9	2.1	-	-	-	-	59.0	0.2	-	-	-	-
1977	59.3	0.5	-	-	-	-	61.3	3.4	-	-	-	-	62.3	1.6	-	-	-	-	62.0	-0.5	-	-	-	-
1978	63.5	2.4	-	-	-	-	66.0	3.9	-	-	68.1	3.2	-	-	68.7	0.9	-	-	70.0	1.9	-	-	71.7	2.4
1979	-	-	74.7	4.2	-	-	75.7	1.3	-	-	77.2	2.0	-	-	77.8	0.8	-	-	78.0	0.3	-	-	79.5	1.9
1980	-	-	80.8	1.6	-	-	81.8	1.2	-	-	82.2	0.5	-	-	84.7	3.0	-	-	87.3	3.1	-	-	88.1	0.9
1981	-	-	89.9	2.0	-	-	90.9	1.1	-	-	91.7	0.9	-	-	93.2	1.6	-	-	93.3	0.1	-	-	93.3	0.0
1982	-	-	94.6	1.4	-	-	95.2	0.6	-	-	96.7	1.6	-	-	97.6	0.9	-	-	97.5	-0.1	-	-	97.8	0.3
1983	-	-	98.3	0.5	-	-	99.0	0.7	-	-	99.7	0.7	-	-	100.0	0.3	-	-	99.8	-0.2	-	-	99.7	-0.1
1984	-	-	104.0	4.3	-	-	104.2	0.2	-	-	104.3	0.1	-	-	104.6	0.3	-	-	104.6	0.0	-	-	105.4	0.8
1985	-	-	105.4	0.0	-	-	104.6	-0.8	-	-	104.6	0.0	-	-	105.0	0.4	-	-	104.6	-0.4	-	-	105.8	1.1
1986	-	-	106.4	0.6	-	-	106.3	-0.1	-	-	106.7	0.4	-	-	107.8	1.0	-	-	108.4	0.6	-	-	109.3	0.8
1987	-	-	111.4	1.9	-	-	111.2	-0.2	-	-	111.8	0.5	-	-	111.6	-0.2	-	-	113.1	1.3	-	-	112.5	-0.5
1988	-	-	113.9	1.2	-	-	114.3	0.4	-	-	114.6	0.3	-	-	117.8	2.8	-	-	119.6	1.5	-	-	118.2	-1.2
1989	-	-	121.7	3.0	-	-	121.7	0.0	-	-	121.8	0.1	-	-	121.1	-0.6	-	-	121.8	0.6	-	-	123.5	1.4
1990	-	-	127.9	3.6	-	-	127.1	-0.6	-	-	128.6	1.2	-	-	129.5	0.7	-	-	131.3	1.4	-	-	129.2	-1.6
1991	-	-	132.2	2.3	-	-	132.3	0.1	-	-	130.9	-1.1	-	-	131.4	0.4	-	-	131.7	0.2	-	-	131.5	-0.2
1992	-	-	132.7	0.9	-	-	132.2	-0.4	-	-	129.9	-1.7	-	-	129.6	-0.2	-	-	129.7	0.1	-	-	130.4	0.5
1993	-	-	132.2	1.4	-	-	128.9	-2.5	-	-	130.2	1.0	-	-	133.4	2.5	-	-	134.9	1.1	-	-	136.5	1.2
1994	-	-	135.9	-0.4	-	-	137.3	1.0	-	-	137.1	-0.1	-	-	138.0	0.7	-	-	137.7	-0.2	-	-	139.7	1.5
1995	-	-	139.7	0.0	-	-	140.7	0.7	-	-	139.7	-0.7	-	-	140.1	0.3	-	-	140.5	0.3	-	-	141.0	0.4
1996	-	-	140.6	-0.3	-	-	140.9	0.2	-	-	141.8	0.6	-	-	144.5	1.9	-	-	144.9	0.3	-	-	145.9	0.7
1997	-	-	146.8	0.6	-	-	146.3	-0.3	-	-	147.3	0.7	-	-	148.3	0.7	-	-	149.4	0.7	-	-	149.0	-0.3
1998	-	-	150.0	0.7	-	-	150.3	0.2	-	-	151.1	0.5	-	-	151.6	0.3	-	-	151.9	0.2	-	-	151.1	-0.5
1999	-	-	150.8	-0.2	-	-	152.4	1.1	-	-	152.5	0.1	-	-	154.2	1.1	-	-	153.4	-0.5	-	-	154.7	0.8
2000	-	-	155.0	0.2	-	-	155.3	0.2	-	-	158.4	2.0	-	-	158.6	0.1	-	-	158.5	-0.1	-	-	162.3	2.4
2001	-	-	161.6	-0.4	-	-	162.1	0.3	-	-	163.1	0.6	-	-	164.1	0.6	-	-	165.1	0.6	-	-	165.6	0.3

Source: U.S. Department of Labor, Bureau of Labor Statistics, Division of Consumer Prices and Price Indexes. - indicates no data collected for period.

Houston-Galveston-Brazoria, TX
Consumer Price Index - Urban Wage Earners
Base 1982-1984 = 100
Food and Beverages

For 1976-2001. Columns headed % show percentile change in the index from the previous period for which an index is available.

Year	Jan Index	%	Feb Index	%	Mar Index	%	Apr Index	%	May Index	%	Jun Index	%	Jul Index	%	Aug Index	%	Sep Index	%	Oct Index	%	Nov Index	%	Dec Index	%
1976	59.0	-	-	-	-	-	58.7	-0.5	-	-	-	-	59.9	2.0	-	-	-	-	60.0	0.2	-	-	-	-
1977	60.3	0.5	-	-	-	-	62.3	3.3	-	-	-	-	63.3	1.6	-	-	-	-	63.1	-0.3	-	-	-	-
1978	64.6	2.4	-	-	-	-	67.1	3.9	-	-	69.3	3.3	-	-	69.4	0.1	-	-	70.4	1.4	-	-	72.0	2.3
1979	-	-	74.9	4.0	-	-	76.1	1.6	-	-	77.2	1.4	-	-	77.9	0.9	-	-	78.4	0.6	-	-	79.5	1.4
1980	-	-	80.1	0.8	-	-	81.8	2.1	-	-	82.6	1.0	-	-	84.8	2.7	-	-	87.3	2.9	-	-	88.5	1.4
1981	-	-	90.0	1.7	-	-	90.6	0.7	-	-	91.1	0.6	-	-	92.9	2.0	-	-	93.0	0.1	-	-	93.1	0.1
1982	-	-	94.6	1.6	-	-	95.3	0.7	-	-	96.7	1.5	-	-	97.6	0.9	-	-	97.6	0.0	-	-	97.9	0.3
1983	-	-	98.5	0.6	-	-	99.1	0.6	-	-	99.6	0.5	-	-	99.9	0.3	-	-	99.7	-0.2	-	-	99.7	0.0
1984	-	-	104.2	4.5	-	-	104.2	0.0	-	-	104.2	0.0	-	-	104.4	0.2	-	-	104.5	0.1	-	-	105.3	0.8
1985	-	-	105.1	-0.2	-	-	104.5	-0.6	-	-	104.5	0.0	-	-	104.8	0.3	-	-	104.5	-0.3	-	-	105.8	1.2
1986	-	-	106.3	0.5	-	-	106.4	0.1	-	-	106.7	0.3	-	-	107.7	0.9	-	-	108.5	0.7	-	-	109.3	0.7
1987	-	-	111.3	1.8	-	-	111.0	-0.3	-	-	111.6	0.5	-	-	111.4	-0.2	-	-	113.1	1.5	-	-	112.4	-0.6
1988	-	-	113.7	1.2	-	-	114.1	0.4	-	-	114.5	0.4	-	-	117.8	2.9	-	-	119.6	1.5	-	-	118.1	-1.3
1989	-	-	121.7	3.0	-	-	121.7	0.0	-	-	121.7	0.0	-	-	121.0	-0.6	-	-	121.8	0.7	-	-	123.6	1.5
1990	-	-	128.1	3.6	-	-	127.3	-0.6	-	-	128.7	1.1	-	-	129.6	0.7	-	-	131.4	1.4	-	-	129.4	-1.5
1991	-	-	132.2	2.2	-	-	132.4	0.2	-	-	130.9	-1.1	-	-	131.5	0.5	-	-	131.9	0.3	-	-	131.8	-0.1
1992	-	-	133.0	0.9	-	-	132.4	-0.5	-	-	130.0	-1.8	-	-	129.8	-0.2	-	-	129.8	0.0	-	-	130.4	0.5
1993	-	-	132.2	1.4	-	-	129.1	-2.3	-	-	130.3	0.9	-	-	133.6	2.5	-	-	135.2	1.2	-	-	136.9	1.3
1994	-	-	136.3	-0.4	-	-	137.6	1.0	-	-	137.4	-0.1	-	-	138.1	0.5	-	-	137.8	-0.2	-	-	139.8	1.5
1995	-	-	139.7	-0.1	-	-	140.7	0.7	-	-	139.7	-0.7	-	-	140.2	0.4	-	-	140.6	0.3	-	-	141.2	0.4
1996	-	-	140.8	-0.3	-	-	141.0	0.1	-	-	141.8	0.6	-	-	144.8	2.1	-	-	145.2	0.3	-	-	146.3	0.8
1997	-	-	147.1	0.5	-	-	146.7	-0.3	-	-	147.5	0.5	-	-	148.5	0.7	-	-	149.5	0.7	-	-	149.4	-0.1
1998	-	-	150.3	0.6	-	-	150.6	0.2	-	-	151.3	0.5	-	-	151.9	0.4	-	-	152.0	0.1	-	-	151.3	-0.5
1999	-	-	151.0	-0.2	-	-	152.5	1.0	-	-	152.5	0.0	-	-	154.4	1.2	-	-	153.5	-0.6	-	-	154.7	0.8
2000	-	-	155.2	0.3	-	-	155.5	0.2	-	-	158.8	2.1	-	-	158.9	0.1	-	-	159.1	0.1	-	-	162.6	2.2
2001	-	-	162.0	-0.4	-	-	162.3	0.2	-	-	163.8	0.9	-	-	164.7	0.5	-	-	166.0	0.8	-	-	166.2	0.1

Source: U.S. Department of Labor, Bureau of Labor Statistics, Division of Consumer Prices and Price Indexes. - indicates no data collected for period.

Houston-Galveston-Brazoria, TX
Consumer Price Index - All Urban Consumers
Base 1982-1984 = 100
Housing

For 1976-2001. Columns headed % show percentile change in the index from the previous period for which an index is available.

Year	Jan Index	%	Feb Index	%	Mar Index	%	Apr Index	%	May Index	%	Jun Index	%	Jul Index	%	Aug Index	%	Sep Index	%	Oct Index	%	Nov Index	%	Dec Index	%
1976	51.2	-	-	-	-	-	52.0	1.6	-	-	-	-	52.9	1.7	-	-	-	-	54.7	3.4	-	-	-	-
1977	55.3	1.1	-	-	-	-	56.7	2.5	-	-	-	-	57.8	1.9	-	-	-	-	58.2	0.7	-	-	-	-
1978	60.0	3.1	-	-	-	-	62.3	3.8	-	-	64.2	3.0	-	-	66.0	2.8	-	-	66.9	1.4	-	-	69.0	3.1
1979	-	-	70.0	1.4	-	-	70.5	0.7	-	-	73.5	4.3	-	-	75.3	2.4	-	-	76.7	1.9	-	-	78.1	1.8
1980	-	-	79.2	1.4	-	-	80.8	2.0	-	-	84.1	4.1	-	-	84.0	-0.1	-	-	84.8	1.0	-	-	85.4	0.7
1981	-	-	86.7	1.5	-	-	88.7	2.3	-	-	91.8	3.5	-	-	92.4	0.7	-	-	94.6	2.4	-	-	95.8	1.3
1982	-	-	96.4	0.6	-	-	97.6	1.2	-	-	100.8	3.3	-	-	102.8	2.0	-	-	101.5	-1.3	-	-	100.9	-0.6
1983	-	-	99.7	-1.2	-	-	98.3	-1.4	-	-	101.2	3.0	-	-	102.2	1.0	-	-	101.4	-0.8	-	-	98.8	-2.6
1984	-	-	98.4	-0.4	-	-	99.1	0.7	-	-	101.7	2.6	-	-	100.1	-1.6	-	-	101.0	0.9	-	-	99.2	-1.8
1985	-	-	100.0	0.8	-	-	100.0	0.0	-	-	101.1	1.1	-	-	101.0	-0.1	-	-	100.4	-0.6	-	-	98.4	-2.0
1986	-	-	99.2	0.8	-	-	97.6	-1.6	-	-	98.9	1.3	-	-	98.9	0.0	-	-	98.3	-0.6	-	-	95.2	-3.2
1987	-	-	94.8	-0.4	-	-	98.3	3.7	-	-	97.5	-0.8	-	-	97.9	0.4	-	-	97.5	-0.4	-	-	95.9	-1.6
1988	-	-	96.6	0.7	-	-	97.7	1.1	-	-	98.8	1.1	-	-	98.8	0.0	-	-	98.0	-0.8	-	-	99.3	1.3
1989	-	-	100.0	0.7	-	-	99.0	-1.0	-	-	100.6	1.6	-	-	101.7	1.1	-	-	101.8	0.1	-	-	100.4	-1.4
1990	-	-	103.1	2.7	-	-	102.8	-0.3	-	-	104.7	1.8	-	-	106.6	1.8	-	-	107.2	0.6	-	-	105.8	-1.3
1991	-	-	107.6	1.7	-	-	108.0	0.4	-	-	110.2	2.0	-	-	109.8	-0.4	-	-	111.4	1.5	-	-	111.0	-0.4
1992	-	-	109.9	-1.0	-	-	112.7	2.5	-	-	114.6	1.7	-	-	113.9	-0.6	-	-	115.4	1.3	-	-	113.3	-1.8
1993	-	-	114.7	1.2	-	-	114.7	0.0	-	-	117.5	2.4	-	-	117.2	-0.3	-	-	119.0	1.5	-	-	119.3	0.3
1994	-	-	119.9	0.5	-	-	119.0	-0.8	-	-	119.9	0.8	-	-	122.7	2.3	-	-	121.7	-0.8	-	-	119.5	-1.8
1995	-	-	122.3	2.3	-	-	116.5	-4.7	-	-	121.5	4.3	-	-	122.2	0.6	-	-	123.7	1.2	-	-	120.6	-2.5
1996	-	-	122.8	1.8	-	-	123.4	0.5	-	-	124.2	0.6	-	-	124.8	0.5	-	-	125.7	0.7	-	-	123.0	-2.1
1997	-	-	124.9	1.5	-	-	126.0	0.9	-	-	125.7	-0.2	-	-	126.4	0.6	-	-	128.5	1.7	-	-	126.0	-1.9
1998	-	-	127.4	1.1	-	-	127.8	0.3	-	-	130.0	1.7	-	-	131.2	0.9	-	-	132.9	1.3	-	-	129.2	-2.8
1999	-	-	130.6	1.1	-	-	131.3	0.5	-	-	132.8	1.1	-	-	132.5	-0.2	-	-	134.1	1.2	-	-	132.0	-1.6
2000	-	-	134.7	2.0	-	-	134.5	-0.1	-	-	136.7	1.6	-	-	137.5	0.6	-	-	141.8	3.1	-	-	140.0	-1.3
2001	-	-	144.1	2.9	-	-	144.2	0.1	-	-	145.1	0.6	-	-	144.3	-0.6	-	-	144.5	0.1	-	-	143.2	-0.9

Source: U.S. Department of Labor, Bureau of Labor Statistics, Division of Consumer Prices and Price Indexes. - indicates no data collected for period.

Houston-Galveston-Brazoria, TX
Consumer Price Index - Urban Wage Earners
Base 1982-1984 = 100
Housing

For 1976-2001. Columns headed % show percentile change in the index from the previous period for which an index is available.

Year	Jan Index	%	Feb Index	%	Mar Index	%	Apr Index	%	May Index	%	Jun Index	%	Jul Index	%	Aug Index	%	Sep Index	%	Oct Index	%	Nov Index	%	Dec Index	%
1976	51.2	-	-	-	-	-	52.0	1.6	-	-	-	-	52.9	1.7	-	-	-	-	54.8	3.6	-	-	-	-
1977	55.3	0.9	-	-	-	-	56.7	2.5	-	-	-	-	57.9	2.1	-	-	-	-	58.3	0.7	-	-	-	-
1978	60.1	3.1	-	-	-	-	62.3	3.7	-	-	64.1	2.9	-	-	65.8	2.7	-	-	66.4	0.9	-	-	68.4	3.0
1979	-	-	69.3	1.3	-	-	69.9	0.9	-	-	72.7	4.0	-	-	74.3	2.2	-	-	75.4	1.5	-	-	76.8	1.9
1980	-	-	77.7	1.2	-	-	79.4	2.2	-	-	82.5	3.9	-	-	82.7	0.2	-	-	83.5	1.0	-	-	84.2	0.8
1981	-	-	85.2	1.2	-	-	87.5	2.7	-	-	90.7	3.7	-	-	91.3	0.7	-	-	93.3	2.2	-	-	94.2	1.0
1982	-	-	94.9	0.7	-	-	96.6	1.8	-	-	99.8	3.3	-	-	101.6	1.8	-	-	100.6	-1.0	-	-	100.2	-0.4
1983	-	-	100.8	0.6	-	-	100.3	-0.5	-	-	101.0	0.7	-	-	101.3	0.3	-	-	101.0	-0.3	-	-	97.8	-3.2
1984	-	-	99.7	1.9	-	-	99.7	0.0	-	-	101.9	2.2	-	-	101.3	0.3	-	-	101.0	-0.3	-	-	97.8	-3.2
1985	-	-	100.0	1.0	-	-	99.9	-0.1	-	-	101.0	1.1	-	-	100.9	-0.1	-	-	100.3	-0.6	-	-	98.2	-2.1
1986	-	-	98.9	0.7	-	-	97.4	-1.5	-	-	98.8	1.4	-	-	98.7	-0.1	-	-	98.2	-0.5	-	-	94.9	-3.4
1987	-	-	94.5	-0.4	-	-	97.6	3.3	-	-	97.2	-0.4	-	-	97.1	-0.1	-	-	97.2	0.1	-	-	95.8	-1.4
1988	-	-	96.1	0.3	-	-	97.0	0.9	-	-	98.1	1.1	-	-	98.2	0.1	-	-	97.6	-0.6	-	-	98.7	1.1
1989	-	-	99.3	0.6	-	-	98.5	-0.8	-	-	100.3	1.8	-	-	101.6	1.3	-	-	101.4	-0.2	-	-	100.2	-1.2
1990	-	-	102.2	2.0	-	-	102.4	0.2	-	-	104.5	2.1	-	-	106.4	1.8	-	-	107.2	0.8	-	-	105.6	-1.5
1991	-	-	107.4	1.7	-	-	107.9	0.5	-	-	110.5	2.4	-	-	109.8	-0.6	-	-	111.1	1.2	-	-	111.3	0.2
1992	-	-	109.6	-1.5	-	-	112.6	2.7	-	-	114.7	1.9	-	-	114.2	-0.4	-	-	115.7	1.3	-	-	113.6	-1.8
1993	-	-	114.9	1.1	-	-	115.1	0.2	-	-	118.0	2.5	-	-	117.8	-0.2	-	-	119.4	1.4	-	-	119.7	0.3
1994	-	-	119.9	0.2	-	-	118.9	-0.8	-	-	120.1	1.0	-	-	123.0	2.4	-	-	122.2	-0.7	-	-	120.1	-1.7
1995	-	-	122.3	1.8	-	-	116.4	-4.8	-	-	121.6	4.5	-	-	122.5	0.7	-	-	123.6	0.9	-	-	121.0	-2.1
1996	-	-	122.7	1.4	-	-	122.8	0.1	-	-	124.3	1.2	-	-	125.0	0.6	-	-	125.7	0.6	-	-	123.2	-2.0
1997	-	-	124.3	0.9	-	-	125.5	1.0	-	-	126.0	0.4	-	-	126.9	0.7	-	-	128.2	1.0	-	-	125.7	-2.0
1998	-	-	126.8	0.9	-	-	127.2	0.3	-	-	130.1	2.3	-	-	131.4	1.0	-	-	132.8	1.1	-	-	129.2	-2.7
1999	-	-	130.5	1.0	-	-	130.9	0.3	-	-	133.3	1.8	-	-	133.1	-0.2	-	-	134.3	0.9	-	-	132.0	-1.7
2000	-	-	133.7	1.3	-	-	133.9	0.1	-	-	136.7	2.1	-	-	137.4	0.5	-	-	141.5	3.0	-	-	140.2	-0.9
2001	-	-	143.4	2.3	-	-	143.7	0.2	-	-	145.8	1.5	-	-	145.0	-0.5	-	-	145.1	0.1	-	-	143.6	-1.0

Source: U.S. Department of Labor, Bureau of Labor Statistics, Division of Consumer Prices and Price Indexes. - indicates no data collected for period.

Houston-Galveston-Brazoria, TX
Consumer Price Index - All Urban Consumers
Base 1982-1984 = 100
Apparel

For 1952-2001. Columns headed % show percentile change in the index from the previous period for which an index is available.

Year	Jan Index	%	Feb Index	%	Mar Index	%	Apr Index	%	May Index	%	Jun Index	%	Jul Index	%	Aug Index	%	Sep Index	%	Oct Index	%	Nov Index	%	Dec Index	%
1952	-	-	-	-	-	-	-	-	-	-	-	-	-	-	-	-	-	-	-	-	-	-	36.1	-
1953	-		36.0	-0.3	-	-	-	-	36.0	0.0	-	-	-	-	35.9	-0.3	-	-	-	-	36.4	1.4	-	-
1954	-		36.0	-1.1	-	-	-	-	36.0	0.0	-	-	-	-	36.1	0.3	-	-	-	-	36.1	0.0	-	-
1955	-		35.9	-0.6	-	-	-	-	36.1	0.6	-	-	-	-	35.8	-0.8	-	-	-	-	36.1	0.8	-	-
1956	-		36.4	0.8	-	-	-	-	36.2	-0.5	-	-	-	-	36.7	1.4	-	-	-	-	37.6	2.5	-	-
1957	-		37.2	-1.1	-	-	-	-	37.6	1.1	-	-	-	-	37.6	0.0	-	-	-	-	38.2	1.6	-	-
1958	-		38.3	0.3	-	-	-	-	38.4	0.3	-	-	-	-	38.3	-0.3	-	-	-	-	38.4	0.3	-	-
1959	-		38.7	0.8	-	-	-	-	38.6	-0.3	-	-	-	-	38.8	0.5	-	-	-	-	38.8	0.0	-	-
1960	-		38.2	-1.5	-	-	-	-	38.8	1.6	-	-	-	-	38.9	0.3	-	-	-	-	38.8	-0.3	-	-
1961	-		38.6	-0.5	-	-	-	-	38.8	0.5	-	-	-	-	38.7	-0.3	-	-	-	-	39.6	2.3	-	-
1962	-		39.7	0.3	-	-	-	-	40.0	0.8	-	-	-	-	40.2	0.5	-	-	-	-	40.3	0.2	-	-
1963	-		40.4	0.2	-	-	-	-	40.3	-0.2	-	-	-	-	40.8	1.2	-	-	-	-	40.6	-0.5	-	-
1964	-		41.0	1.0	-	-	-	-	40.7	-0.7	-	-	-	-	40.7	0.0	-	-	-	-	40.7	0.0	-	-
1965	-		40.2	-1.2	-	-	41.0	2.0	-	-	-	-	40.8	-0.5	-	-	-	-	41.3	1.2	-	-	-	-
1966	41.0	-0.7	-	-	-	-	41.4	1.0	-	-	-	-	41.6	0.5	-	-	-	-	42.0	1.0	-	-	-	-
1967	41.2	-1.9	-	-	-	-	41.9	1.7	-	-	-	-	42.0	0.2	-	-	-	-	43.2	2.9	-	-	-	-
1968	43.1	-0.2	-	-	-	-	43.9	1.9	-	-	-	-	44.3	0.9	-	-	-	-	46.0	3.8	-	-	-	-
1969	46.5	1.1	-	-	-	-	47.3	1.7	-	-	-	-	47.7	0.8	-	-	-	-	50.1	5.0	-	-	-	-
1970	49.7	-0.8	-	-	-	-	50.2	1.0	-	-	-	-	50.1	-0.2	-	-	-	-	52.2	4.2	-	-	-	-
1971	50.8	-2.7	-	-	-	-	51.4	1.2	-	-	-	-	50.8	-1.2	-	-	-	-	52.7	3.7	-	-	-	-
1972	52.3	-0.8	-	-	-	-	53.2	1.7	-	-	-	-	52.0	-2.3	-	-	-	-	54.4	4.6	-	-	-	-
1973	53.1	-2.4	-	-	-	-	55.1	3.8	-	-	-	-	53.5	-2.9	-	-	-	-	57.3	7.1	-	-	-	-
1974	57.6	0.5	-	-	-	-	59.3	3.0	-	-	-	-	60.5	2.0	-	-	-	-	62.2	2.8	-	-	-	-
1975	61.8	-0.6	-	-	-	-	63.3	2.4	-	-	-	-	64.3	1.6	-	-	-	-	66.3	3.1	-	-	-	-
1976	65.7	-0.9	-	-	-	-	67.4	2.6	-	-	-	-	66.9	-0.7	-	-	-	-	70.4	5.2	-	-	-	-
1977	70.0	-0.6	-	-	-	-	71.6	2.3	-	-	-	-	71.6	0.0	-	-	-	-	74.0	3.4	-	-	-	-
1978	72.8	-1.6	-	-	-	-	75.7	4.0	-	-	76.6	1.2	-	-	78.0	1.8	-	-	79.9	2.4	-	-	79.7	-0.3
1979	-		80.6	1.1	-	-	82.8	2.7	-	-	82.4	-0.5	-	-	83.2	1.0	-	-	85.1	2.3	-	-	86.0	1.1
1980	-		88.3	2.7	-	-	88.3	0.0	-	-	87.8	-0.6	-	-	89.4	1.8	-	-	91.6	2.5	-	-	90.7	-1.0
1981	-		93.4	3.0	-	-	94.8	1.5	-	-	95.0	0.2	-	-	95.5	0.5	-	-	97.8	2.4	-	-	99.5	1.7
1982	-		98.6	-0.9	-	-	98.6	0.0	-	-	97.5	-1.1	-	-	98.0	0.5	-	-	98.7	0.7	-	-	98.7	0.0
1983	-		101.5	2.8	-	-	100.0	-1.5	-	-	98.0	-2.0	-	-	98.8	0.8	-	-	100.3	1.5	-	-	100.6	0.3
1984	-		100.3	-0.3	-	-	100.8	0.5	-	-	102.1	1.3	-	-	102.1	0.0	-	-	102.6	0.5	-	-	104.0	1.4
1985	-		104.2	0.2	-	-	104.4	0.2	-	-	103.8	-0.6	-	-	104.2	0.4	-	-	104.9	0.7	-	-	105.5	0.6
1986	-		106.1	0.6	-	-	106.6	0.5	-	-	104.6	-1.9	-	-	107.6	2.9	-	-	105.7	-1.8	-	-	106.1	0.4
1987	-		107.9	1.7	-	-	112.8	4.5	-	-	111.6	-1.1	-	-	115.4	3.4	-	-	118.4	2.6	-	-	118.3	-0.1
1988	-		121.3	2.5	-	-	117.4	-3.2	-	-	122.0	3.9	-	-	121.1	-0.7	-	-	125.3	3.5	-	-	119.9	-4.3
1989	-		122.7	2.3	-	-	126.7	3.3	-	-	121.0	-4.5	-	-	122.0	0.8	-	-	127.5	4.5	-	-	124.9	-2.0
1990	-		136.9	9.6	-	-	130.0	-5.0	-	-	133.3	2.5	-	-	132.5	-0.6	-	-	134.9	1.8	-	-	128.6	-4.7
1991	-		138.2	7.5	-	-	133.3	-3.5	-	-	135.3	1.5	-	-	129.7	-4.1	-	-	138.8	7.0	-	-	135.0	-2.7
1992	-		137.1	1.6	-	-	135.8	-0.9	-	-	134.4	-1.0	-	-	141.4	5.2	-	-	137.8	-2.5	-	-	126.1	-8.5
1993	-		140.4	11.3	-	-	142.4	1.4	-	-	137.8	-3.2	-	-	132.2	-4.1	-	-	155.4	17.5	-	-	151.3	-2.6
1994	-		153.8	1.7	-	-	149.1	-3.1	-	-	145.3	-2.5	-	-	144.1	-0.8	-	-	147.3	2.2	-	-	136.8	-7.1
1995	-		139.1	1.7	-	-	140.9	1.3	-	-	131.5	-6.7	-	-	134.0	1.9	-	-	138.4	3.3	-	-	149.1	7.7
1996	-		138.0	-7.4	-	-	142.1	3.0	-	-	131.4	-7.5	-	-	135.3	3.0	-	-	133.9	-1.0	-	-	145.0	8.3
1997	-		140.4	-3.2	-	-	142.1	1.2	-	-	138.0	-2.9	-	-	139.9	1.4	-	-	147.8	5.6	-	-	144.4	-2.3

[Continued]

Houston-Galveston-Brazoria, TX
Consumer Price Index - All Urban Consumers
Base 1982-1984 = 100
Apparel
[Continued]

For 1952-2001. Columns headed % show percentile change in the index from the previous period for which an index is available.

Year	Jan Index	%	Feb Index	%	Mar Index	%	Apr Index	%	May Index	%	Jun Index	%	Jul Index	%	Aug Index	%	Sep Index	%	Oct Index	%	Nov Index	%	Dec Index	%
1998	-	-	141.7	-1.9	-	-	140.9	-0.6	-	-	134.9	-4.3	-	-	143.6	6.4	-	-	146.3	1.9	-	-	135.9	-7.1
1999	-	-	133.4	-1.8	-	-	139.0	4.2	-	-	136.0	-2.2	-	-	138.9	2.1	-	-	150.9	8.6	-	-	142.8	-5.4
2000	-	-	144.0	0.8	-	-	148.8	3.3	-	-	143.0	-3.9	-	-	138.9	-2.9	-	-	159.3	14.7	-	-	146.4	-8.1
2001	-	-	148.0	1.1	-	-	148.7	0.5	-	-	139.1	-6.5	-	-	135.9	-2.3	-	-	149.2	9.8	-	-	129.7	-13.1

Source: U.S. Department of Labor, Bureau of Labor Statistics, Division of Consumer Prices and Price Indexes. - indicates no data collected for period.

Houston-Galveston-Brazoria, TX
Consumer Price Index - Urban Wage Earners
Base 1982-1984 = 100
Apparel

For 1952-2001. Columns headed % show percentile change in the index from the previous period for which an index is available.

Year	Jan Index	%	Feb Index	%	Mar Index	%	Apr Index	%	May Index	%	Jun Index	%	Jul Index	%	Aug Index	%	Sep Index	%	Oct Index	%	Nov Index	%	Dec Index	%
1952	-	-	-	-	-	-	-	-	-	-	-	-	-	-	-	-	-	-	-	-	-	-	36.8	-
1953	-	-	36.7	-0.3	-	-	-	-	36.7	0.0	-	-	-	-	36.6	-0.3	-	-	-	-	37.1	1.4	-	-
1954	-	-	36.7	-1.1	-	-	-	-	36.7	0.0	-	-	-	-	36.8	0.3	-	-	-	-	36.8	0.0	-	-
1955	-	-	36.6	-0.5	-	-	-	-	36.8	0.5	-	-	-	-	36.4	-1.1	-	-	-	-	36.8	1.1	-	-
1956	-	-	37.1	0.8	-	-	-	-	36.9	-0.5	-	-	-	-	37.4	1.4	-	-	-	-	38.3	2.4	-	-
1957	-	-	37.9	-1.0	-	-	-	-	38.3	1.1	-	-	-	-	38.3	0.0	-	-	-	-	38.9	1.6	-	-
1958	-	-	39.1	0.5	-	-	-	-	39.1	0.0	-	-	-	-	39.0	-0.3	-	-	-	-	39.2	0.5	-	-
1959	-	-	39.4	0.5	-	-	-	-	39.3	-0.3	-	-	-	-	39.5	0.5	-	-	-	-	39.5	0.0	-	-
1960	-	-	38.9	-1.5	-	-	-	-	39.5	1.5	-	-	-	-	39.6	0.3	-	-	-	-	39.5	-0.3	-	-
1961	-	-	39.4	-0.3	-	-	-	-	39.5	0.3	-	-	-	-	39.4	-0.3	-	-	-	-	40.3	2.3	-	-
1962	-	-	40.4	0.2	-	-	-	-	40.8	1.0	-	-	-	-	40.9	0.2	-	-	-	-	41.1	0.5	-	-
1963	-	-	41.2	0.2	-	-	-	-	41.1	-0.2	-	-	-	-	41.6	1.2	-	-	-	-	41.4	-0.5	-	-
1964	-	-	41.8	1.0	-	-	-	-	41.4	-1.0	-	-	-	-	41.5	0.2	-	-	-	-	41.5	0.0	-	-
1965	-	-	41.0	-1.2	-	-	41.7	1.7	-	-	-	-	41.6	-0.2	-	-	-	-	42.0	1.0	-	-	-	-
1966	41.8	-0.5	-	-	-	-	42.2	1.0	-	-	-	-	42.3	0.2	-	-	-	-	42.8	1.2	-	-	-	-
1967	42.0	-1.9	-	-	-	-	42.7	1.7	-	-	-	-	42.8	0.2	-	-	-	-	44.0	2.8	-	-	-	-
1968	43.9	-0.2	-	-	-	-	44.8	2.1	-	-	-	-	45.1	0.7	-	-	-	-	46.9	4.0	-	-	-	-
1969	47.3	0.9	-	-	-	-	48.2	1.9	-	-	-	-	48.6	0.8	-	-	-	-	51.0	4.9	-	-	-	-
1970	50.6	-0.8	-	-	-	-	51.2	1.2	-	-	-	-	51.0	-0.4	-	-	-	-	53.2	4.3	-	-	-	-
1971	51.8	-2.6	-	-	-	-	52.4	1.2	-	-	-	-	51.7	-1.3	-	-	-	-	53.7	3.9	-	-	-	-
1972	53.3	-0.7	-	-	-	-	54.3	1.9	-	-	-	-	53.0	-2.4	-	-	-	-	55.5	4.7	-	-	-	-
1973	54.1	-2.5	-	-	-	-	56.1	3.7	-	-	-	-	54.5	-2.9	-	-	-	-	58.4	7.2	-	-	-	-
1974	58.7	0.5	-	-	-	-	60.5	3.1	-	-	-	-	61.7	2.0	-	-	-	-	63.4	2.8	-	-	-	-
1975	63.0	-0.6	-	-	-	-	64.5	2.4	-	-	-	-	65.5	1.6	-	-	-	-	67.6	3.2	-	-	-	-
1976	67.0	-0.9	-	-	-	-	68.6	2.4	-	-	-	-	68.2	-0.6	-	-	-	-	71.8	5.3	-	-	-	-
1977	71.4	-0.6	-	-	-	-	72.9	2.1	-	-	-	-	72.9	0.0	-	-	-	-	75.4	3.4	-	-	-	-
1978	74.1	-1.7	-	-	-	-	77.2	4.2	-	-	78.4	1.6	-	-	79.4	1.3	-	-	81.1	2.1	-	-	81.9	1.0
1979	-	-	83.1	1.5	-	-	85.3	2.6	-	-	84.4	-1.1	-	-	85.3	1.1	-	-	87.0	2.0	-	-	88.2	1.4
1980	-	-	89.2	1.1	-	-	89.7	0.6	-	-	89.4	-0.3	-	-	90.8	1.6	-	-	91.5	0.8	-	-	92.2	0.8
1981	-	-	94.6	2.6	-	-	95.8	1.3	-	-	95.2	-0.6	-	-	96.7	1.6	-	-	98.5	1.9	-	-	99.0	0.5
1982	-	-	98.3	-0.7	-	-	98.5	0.2	-	-	97.9	-0.6	-	-	98.2	0.3	-	-	98.8	0.6	-	-	99.2	0.4
1983	-	-	101.3	2.1	-	-	100.0	-1.3	-	-	98.0	-2.0	-	-	98.8	0.8	-	-	100.3	1.5	-	-	100.8	0.5
1984	-	-	100.4	-0.4	-	-	100.4	0.0	-	-	102.0	1.6	-	-	101.9	-0.1	-	-	102.7	0.8	-	-	103.8	1.1
1985	-	-	103.8	0.0	-	-	104.1	0.3	-	-	103.8	-0.3	-	-	104.1	0.3	-	-	104.7	0.6	-	-	105.3	0.6
1986	-	-	105.8	0.5	-	-	106.3	0.5	-	-	104.5	-1.7	-	-	106.9	2.3	-	-	105.5	-1.3	-	-	105.3	-0.2
1987	-	-	107.4	2.0	-	-	111.7	4.0	-	-	110.7	-0.9	-	-	114.7	3.6	-	-	117.2	2.2	-	-	117.6	0.3
1988	-	-	120.9	2.8	-	-	117.0	-3.2	-	-	122.1	4.4	-	-	121.2	-0.7	-	-	125.6	3.6	-	-	120.5	-4.1
1989	-	-	123.1	2.2	-	-	126.7	2.9	-	-	121.9	-3.8	-	-	122.0	0.1	-	-	126.8	3.9	-	-	124.8	-1.6
1990	-	-	137.4	10.1	-	-	130.7	-4.9	-	-	133.5	2.1	-	-	133.2	-0.2	-	-	134.8	1.2	-	-	127.8	-5.2
1991	-	-	137.1	7.3	-	-	132.7	-3.2	-	-	134.7	1.5	-	-	128.2	-4.8	-	-	137.9	7.6	-	-	134.2	-2.7
1992	-	-	136.4	1.6	-	-	134.7	-1.2	-	-	133.0	-1.3	-	-	139.2	4.7	-	-	136.5	-1.9	-	-	124.6	-8.7
1993	-	-	137.3	10.2	-	-	138.7	1.0	-	-	134.1	-3.3	-	-	130.2	-2.9	-	-	151.7	16.5	-	-	147.2	-3.0
1994	-	-	152.2	3.4	-	-	147.8	-2.9	-	-	144.3	-2.4	-	-	143.2	-0.8	-	-	146.1	2.0	-	-	136.1	-6.8
1995	-	-	139.0	2.1	-	-	139.8	0.6	-	-	132.2	-5.4	-	-	133.9	1.3	-	-	137.8	2.9	-	-	145.7	5.7
1996	-	-	138.4	-5.0	-	-	141.4	2.2	-	-	130.3	-7.9	-	-	134.5	3.2	-	-	132.4	-1.6	-	-	143.7	8.5
1997	-	-	139.3	-3.1	-	-	141.3	1.4	-	-	137.9	-2.4	-	-	140.0	1.5	-	-	146.4	4.6	-	-	142.1	-2.9

[Continued]

Houston-Galveston-Brazoria, TX
Consumer Price Index - Urban Wage Earners
Base 1982-1984 = 100
Apparel
[Continued]

For 1952-2001. Columns headed % show percentile change in the index from the previous period for which an index is available.

Year	Jan Index	%	Feb Index	%	Mar Index	%	Apr Index	%	May Index	%	Jun Index	%	Jul Index	%	Aug Index	%	Sep Index	%	Oct Index	%	Nov Index	%	Dec Index	%
1998	-	-	140.5	-1.1	-	-	139.5	-0.7	-	-	134.4	-3.7	-	-	142.6	6.1	-	-	144.1	1.1	-	-	133.7	-7.2
1999	-	-	132.5	-0.9	-	-	137.7	3.9	-	-	134.7	-2.2	-	-	136.8	1.6	-	-	147.8	8.0	-	-	142.4	-3.7
2000	-	-	144.0	1.1	-	-	148.0	2.8	-	-	144.2	-2.6	-	-	140.1	-2.8	-	-	157.5	12.4	-	-	142.4	-3.7
2001	-	-	146.8	1.1	-	-	147.7	0.6	-	-	139.3	-5.7	-	-	134.7	-3.3	-	-	147.4	9.4	-	-	129.4	-12.2

Source: U.S. Department of Labor, Bureau of Labor Statistics, Division of Consumer Prices and Price Indexes. - indicates no data collected for period.

Houston-Galveston-Brazoria, TX
Consumer Price Index - All Urban Consumers
Base 1982-1984 = 100
Transportation

For 1947-2000. Columns headed % show percentile change in the index from the previous period for which an index is available.

Year	Jan Index	Jan %	Feb Index	Feb %	Mar Index	Mar %	Apr Index	Apr %	May Index	May %	Jun Index	Jun %	Jul Index	Jul %	Aug Index	Aug %	Sep Index	Sep %	Oct Index	Oct %	Nov Index	Nov %	Dec Index	Dec %
1947	19.9	-	20.1	1.0	20.2	0.5	20.4	1.0	20.5	0.5	20.5	0.0	20.6	0.5	20.8	1.0	21.0	1.0	21.4	1.9	21.9	2.3	22.0	0.5
1948	22.6	2.7	22.7	0.4	22.7	0.0	22.7	0.0	22.7	0.0	22.8	0.4	23.2	1.8	23.7	2.2	23.8	0.4	23.9	0.4	24.0	0.4	24.0	0.0
1949	24.0	0.0	24.3	1.2	24.3	0.0	24.4	0.4	24.4	0.0	24.3	-0.4	25.0	2.9	25.0	0.0	25.0	0.0	25.1	0.4	25.2	0.4	25.2	0.0
1950	25.3	0.4	25.3	0.0	25.3	0.0	25.3	0.0	25.5	0.8	25.5	0.0	25.6	0.4	25.7	0.4	25.7	0.0	25.7	0.0	25.7	0.0	27.2	5.8
1951	27.3	0.4	27.5	0.7	27.8	1.1	27.7	-0.4	27.7	0.0	27.9	0.7	27.9	0.0	27.9	0.0	28.2	1.1	28.2	0.0	28.6	1.4	28.6	0.0
1952	28.0	-2.1	28.4	1.4	28.4	0.0	28.4	0.0	28.4	0.0	28.4	0.0	28.4	0.0	28.4	0.0	28.4	0.0	29.2	2.8	29.2	0.0	29.2	0.0
1953	-		29.0	-0.7	-		-		29.0	0.0	-		-		29.1	0.3	-		-		29.0	-0.3	-	
1954	-		28.7	-1.0	-		-		28.6	-0.3	-		-		28.2	-1.4	-		-		28.8	2.1	-	
1955	-		28.3	-1.7	-		-		27.9	-1.4	-		-		27.8	-0.4	-		-		28.9	4.0	-	
1956	-		28.7	-0.7	-		-		28.5	-0.7	-		-		28.9	1.4	-		-		29.7	2.8	-	
1957	-		30.3	2.0	-		-		30.8	1.7	-		-		31.1	1.0	-		-		31.8	2.3	-	
1958	-		29.0	-8.8	-		-		31.5	8.6	-		-		32.4	2.9	-		-		32.7	0.9	-	
1959	-		32.5	-0.6	-		-		32.9	1.2	-		-		33.2	0.9	-		-		33.4	0.6	-	
1960	-		33.7	0.9	-		-		31.4	-6.8	-		-		33.6	7.0	-		-		33.4	-0.6	-	
1961	-		31.5	-5.7	-		-		33.4	6.0	-		-		32.6	-2.4	-		-		34.7	6.4	-	
1962	-		34.6	-0.3	-		-		34.6	0.0	-		-		34.2	-1.2	-		-		33.2	-2.9	-	
1963	-		33.9	2.1	-		-		32.4	-4.4	-		-		33.8	4.3	-		-		34.3	1.5	-	
1964	-		34.0	-0.9	-		-		34.5	1.5	-		-		34.4	-0.3	-		-		34.6	0.6	-	
1965	-		33.8	-2.3	-		34.1	0.9	-		-		34.0	-0.3	-		-		34.6	1.8	-		-	
1966	34.6	0.0	-		-		34.6	0.0	-		-		35.0	1.2	-		-		35.0	0.0	-		-	
1967	35.4	1.1	-		-		35.7	0.8	-		-		35.9	0.6	-		-		36.7	2.2	-		-	
1968	36.7	0.0	-		-		37.0	0.8	-		-		37.0	0.0	-		-		37.3	0.8	-		-	
1969	37.7	1.1	-		-		38.4	1.9	-		-		38.3	-0.3	-		-		38.8	1.3	-		-	
1970	38.6	-0.5	-		-		39.0	1.0	-		-		38.9	-0.3	-		-		39.0	0.3	-		-	
1971	41.3	5.9	-		-		40.8	-1.2	-		-		40.3	-1.2	-		-		40.8	1.2	-		-	
1972	41.1	0.7	-		-		41.7	1.5	-		-		41.7	0.0	-		-		41.0	-1.7	-		-	
1973	41.1	0.2	-		-		41.9	1.9	-		-		42.3	1.0	-		-		42.4	0.2	-		-	
1974	43.9	3.5	-		-		45.9	4.6	-		-		48.0	4.6	-		-		49.6	3.3	-		-	
1975	49.1	-1.0	-		-		50.4	2.6	-		-		52.9	5.0	-		-		53.4	0.9	-		-	
1976	54.1	1.3	-		-		54.6	0.9	-		-		56.5	3.5	-		-		58.3	3.2	-		-	
1977	58.6	0.5	-		-		60.4	3.1	-		-		61.3	1.5	-		-		60.7	-1.0	-		-	
1978	61.1	0.7	-		-		61.6	0.8	-		62.5	1.5	-		63.3	1.3	-		64.1	1.3	-		65.1	1.6
1979	-		66.1	1.5	-		68.9	4.2	-		72.5	5.2	-		75.3	3.9	-		76.0	0.9	-		77.9	2.5
1980	-		82.8	6.3	-		85.4	3.1	-		86.1	0.8	-		86.6	0.6	-		87.0	0.5	-		88.2	1.4
1981	-		92.0	4.3	-		93.7	1.8	-		95.3	1.7	-		95.1	-0.2	-		97.0	2.0	-		97.9	0.9
1982	-		96.8	-1.1	-		93.9	-3.0	-		98.3	4.7	-		99.2	0.9	-		98.8	-0.4	-		99.2	0.4
1983	-		96.7	-2.5	-		97.3	0.6	-		98.8	1.5	-		99.9	1.1	-		101.1	1.2	-		100.9	-0.2
1984	-		100.2	-0.7	-		101.4	1.2	-		102.5	1.1	-		105.3	2.7	-		106.1	0.8	-		105.7	-0.4
1985	-		104.0	-1.6	-		105.7	1.6	-		106.9	1.1	-		106.8	-0.1	-		106.7	-0.1	-		107.1	0.4
1986	-		105.2	-1.8	-		97.2	-7.6	-		99.1	2.0	-		96.6	-2.5	-		97.7	1.1	-		97.3	-0.4
1987	-		100.3	3.1	-		101.3	1.0	-		102.8	1.5	-		103.9	1.1	-		104.3	0.4	-		104.2	-0.1
1988	-		102.9	-1.2	-		102.9	0.0	-		104.2	1.3	-		105.2	1.0	-		106.1	0.9	-		106.4	0.3
1989	-		106.9	0.5	-		108.5	1.5	-		110.3	1.7	-		109.1	-1.1	-		110.0	0.8	-		111.4	1.3
1990	-		112.8	1.3	-		112.5	-0.3	-		113.1	0.5	-		114.4	1.1	-		122.1	6.7	-		124.3	1.8
1991	-		120.1	-3.4	-		115.4	-3.9	-		118.4	2.6	-		118.3	-0.1	-		122.0	3.1	-		123.2	1.0
1992	-		121.0	-1.8	-		122.0	0.8	-		123.0	0.8	-		123.1	0.1	-		124.3	1.0	-		124.3	0.0

[Continued]

Houston-Galveston-Brazoria, TX
Consumer Price Index - All Urban Consumers
Base 1982-1984 = 100
Transportation
[Continued]

For 1947-2000. Columns headed % show percentile change in the index from the previous period for which an index is available.

Year	Jan Index	%	Feb Index	%	Mar Index	%	Apr Index	%	May Index	%	Jun Index	%	Jul Index	%	Aug Index	%	Sep Index	%	Oct Index	%	Nov Index	%	Dec Index	%
1993	-	-	124.8	0.4	-	-	127.2	1.9	-	-	127.8	0.5	-	-	128.8	0.8	-	-	131.2	1.9	-	-	130.9	-0.2
1994	-	-	130.6	-0.2	-	-	131.0	0.3	-	-	132.2	0.9	-	-	134.5	1.7	-	-	134.9	0.3	-	-	135.4	0.4
1995	-	-	135.9	0.4	-	-	136.7	0.6	-	-	139.0	1.7	-	-	136.6	-1.7	-	-	137.8	0.9	-	-	135.9	-1.4
1996	-	-	137.6	1.3	-	-	141.4	2.8	-	-	141.4	0.0	-	-	140.3	-0.8	-	-	140.5	0.1	-	-	143.0	1.8
1997	-	-	142.2	-0.6	-	-	143.2	0.7	-	-	141.4	-1.3	-	-	140.9	-0.4	-	-	141.0	0.1	-	-	139.0	-1.4
1998	-	-	137.1	-1.4	-	-	138.2	0.8	-	-	135.1	-2.2	-	-	133.9	-0.9	-	-	134.7	0.6	-	-	134.3	-0.3
1999	-	-	133.6	-0.5	-	-	135.7	1.6	-	-	133.5	-1.6	-	-	134.3	0.6	-	-	138.9	3.4	-	-	139.5	0.4
2000	-	-	140.9	1.0	-	-	143.0	1.5	-	-	144.4	1.0	-	-	143.3	-0.8	-	-	141.8	-1.0	-	-	141.7	-0.1

Source: U.S. Department of Labor, Bureau of Labor Statistics, Division of Consumer Prices and Price Indexes. - indicates no data collected for period.

Houston-Galveston-Brazoria, TX
Consumer Price Index - Urban Wage Earners
Base 1982-1984 = 100
Transportation

For 1947-2000. Columns headed % show percentile change in the index from the previous period for which an index is available.

Year	Jan Index	%	Feb Index	%	Mar Index	%	Apr Index	%	May Index	%	Jun Index	%	Jul Index	%	Aug Index	%	Sep Index	%	Oct Index	%	Nov Index	%	Dec Index	%
1947	19.8	-	20.1	1.5	20.1	0.0	20.3	1.0	20.4	0.5	20.4	0.0	20.5	0.5	20.7	1.0	21.0	1.4	21.3	1.4	21.8	2.3	21.9	0.5
1948	22.5	2.7	22.6	0.4	22.6	0.0	22.6	0.0	22.6	0.0	22.7	0.4	23.2	2.2	23.7	2.2	23.7	0.0	23.8	0.4	23.9	0.4	23.9	0.0
1949	23.9	0.0	24.2	1.3	24.2	0.0	24.3	0.4	24.3	0.0	24.2	-0.4	24.9	2.9	24.9	0.0	24.9	0.0	25.0	0.4	25.1	0.4	25.1	0.0
1950	25.2	0.4	25.2	0.0	25.2	0.0	25.2	0.0	25.4	0.8	25.4	0.0	25.5	0.4	25.6	0.4	25.6	0.0	25.6	0.0	25.6	0.0	27.1	5.9
1951	27.2	0.4	27.4	0.7	27.7	1.1	27.6	-0.4	27.6	0.0	27.8	0.7	27.8	0.0	27.8	0.0	28.1	1.1	28.1	0.0	28.5	1.4	28.5	0.0
1952	27.9	-2.1	28.2	1.1	28.2	0.0	28.2	0.0	28.2	0.0	28.2	0.0	28.2	0.0	28.2	0.0	28.3	0.4	29.0	2.5	29.0	0.0	29.0	0.0
1953	-		28.9	-0.3	-		-		28.9	0.0	-		-		29.0	0.3	-		-		28.9	-0.3	-	
1954	-		28.6	-1.0	-		-		28.5	-0.3	-		-		28.1	-1.4	-		-		28.7	2.1	-	
1955	-		28.2	-1.7	-		-		27.8	-1.4	-		-		27.7	-0.4	-		-		28.8	4.0	-	
1956	-		28.6	-0.7	-		-		28.4	-0.7	-		-		28.8	1.4	-		-		29.6	2.8	-	
1957	-		30.1	1.7	-		-		30.7	2.0	-		-		30.9	0.7	-		-		31.7	2.6	-	
1958	-		28.9	-8.8	-		-		31.4	8.7	-		-		32.2	2.5	-		-		32.6	1.2	-	
1959	-		32.4	-0.6	-		-		32.8	1.2	-		-		33.0	0.6	-		-		33.2	0.6	-	
1960	-		33.6	1.2	-		-		31.3	-6.8	-		-		33.5	7.0	-		-		33.2	-0.9	-	
1961	-		31.4	-5.4	-		-		33.2	5.7	-		-		32.5	-2.1	-		-		34.5	6.2	-	
1962	-		34.4	-0.3	-		-		34.5	0.3	-		-		34.1	-1.2	-		-		33.0	-3.2	-	
1963	-		33.8	2.4	-		-		32.3	-4.4	-		-		33.6	4.0	-		-		34.1	1.5	-	
1964	-		33.9	-0.6	-		-		34.3	1.2	-		-		34.2	-0.3	-		-		34.4	0.6	-	
1965	-		33.6	-2.3	-		34.0	1.2	-		-		33.9	-0.3	-		-		34.5	1.8	-		-	
1966	34.4	-0.3	-		-		34.5	0.3	-		-		34.9	1.2	-		-		34.9	0.0	-		-	
1967	35.2	0.9	-		-		35.6	1.1	-		-		35.7	0.3	-		-		36.6	2.5	-		-	
1968	36.6	0.0	-		-		36.8	0.5	-		-		36.9	0.3	-		-		37.1	0.5	-		-	
1969	37.5	1.1	-		-		38.3	2.1	-		-		38.2	-0.3	-		-		38.7	1.3	-		-	
1970	38.5	-0.5	-		-		38.8	0.8	-		-		38.8	0.0	-		-		38.9	0.3	-		-	
1971	41.1	5.7	-		-		40.6	-1.2	-		-		40.1	-1.2	-		-		40.6	1.2	-		-	
1972	41.0	1.0	-		-		41.5	1.2	-		-		41.5	0.0	-		-		40.8	-1.7	-		-	
1973	41.0	0.5	-		-		41.7	1.7	-		-		42.1	1.0	-		-		42.2	0.2	-		-	
1974	43.8	3.8	-		-		45.7	4.3	-		-		47.8	4.6	-		-		49.4	3.3	-		-	
1975	48.9	-1.0	-		-		50.2	2.7	-		-		52.7	5.0	-		-		53.2	0.9	-		-	
1976	53.9	1.3	-		-		54.4	0.9	-		-		56.2	3.3	-		-		58.1	3.4	-		-	
1977	58.4	0.5	-		-		60.2	3.1	-		-		61.1	1.5	-		-		60.4	-1.1	-		-	
1978	60.8	0.7	-		-		61.3	0.8	-		62.5	2.0	-		63.4	1.4	-		64.1	1.1	-		65.2	1.7
1979	-		66.2	1.5	-		69.2	4.5	-		72.7	5.1	-		75.0	3.2	-		75.4	0.5	-		77.1	2.3
1980	-		81.5	5.7	-		83.9	2.9	-		84.8	1.1	-		85.2	0.5	-		85.8	0.7	-		86.9	1.3
1981	-		90.4	4.0	-		92.2	2.0	-		93.9	1.8	-		94.2	0.3	-		95.4	1.3	-		97.0	1.7
1982	-		95.9	-1.1	-		93.5	-2.5	-		97.8	4.6	-		98.7	0.9	-		98.3	-0.4	-		98.7	0.4
1983	-		96.5	-2.2	-		97.1	0.6	-		98.6	1.5	-		99.8	1.2	-		101.2	1.4	-		101.2	0.0
1984	-		100.6	-0.6	-		102.1	1.5	-		103.3	1.2	-		106.0	2.6	-		106.8	0.8	-		106.4	-0.4
1985	-		104.8	-1.5	-		106.3	1.4	-		107.3	0.9	-		107.2	-0.1	-		107.2	0.0	-		107.5	0.3
1986	-		105.7	-1.7	-		98.5	-6.8	-		100.1	1.6	-		97.9	-2.2	-		98.9	1.0	-		98.5	-0.4
1987	-		102.2	3.8	-		103.4	1.2	-		105.0	1.5	-		106.2	1.1	-		107.0	0.8	-		106.7	-0.3
1988	-		105.5	-1.1	-		105.2	-0.3	-		106.6	1.3	-		108.0	1.3	-		108.7	0.6	-		109.0	0.3
1989	-		109.4	0.4	-		111.4	1.8	-		113.3	1.7	-		112.0	-1.1	-		112.6	0.5	-		113.9	1.2
1990	-		115.3	1.2	-		115.0	-0.3	-		115.6	0.5	-		117.1	1.3	-		125.4	7.1	-		127.5	1.7
1991	-		122.3	-4.1	-		117.6	-3.8	-		121.0	2.9	-		120.8	-0.2	-		124.6	3.1	-		125.6	0.8
1992	-		123.0	-2.1	-		123.9	0.7	-		125.6	1.4	-		125.8	0.2	-		126.5	0.6	-		126.5	0.0

[Continued]

492

Houston-Galveston-Brazoria, TX
Consumer Price Index - Urban Wage Earners
Base 1982-1984 = 100
Transportation

[Continued]

For 1947-2000. Columns headed % show percentile change in the index from the previous period for which an index is available.

Year	Jan Index	%	Feb Index	%	Mar Index	%	Apr Index	%	May Index	%	Jun Index	%	Jul Index	%	Aug Index	%	Sep Index	%	Oct Index	%	Nov Index	%	Dec Index	%
1993	-	-	126.1	-0.3	-	-	128.5	1.9	-	-	129.4	0.7	-	-	130.1	0.5	-	-	132.3	1.7	-	-	131.5	-0.6
1994	-	-	130.9	-0.5	-	-	131.6	0.5	-	-	133.4	1.4	-	-	135.9	1.9	-	-	136.6	0.5	-	-	137.4	0.6
1995	-	-	137.7	0.2	-	-	138.3	0.4	-	-	140.5	1.6	-	-	138.5	-1.4	-	-	138.9	0.3	-	-	137.7	-0.9
1996	-	-	139.1	1.0	-	-	143.2	2.9	-	-	143.5	0.2	-	-	142.0	-1.0	-	-	142.6	0.4	-	-	144.8	1.5
1997	-	-	144.0	-0.6	-	-	144.0	0.0	-	-	142.7	-0.9	-	-	142.8	0.1	-	-	142.4	-0.3	-	-	140.5	-1.3
1998	-	-	138.3	-1.6	-	-	138.7	0.3	-	-	136.3	-1.7	-	-	135.2	-0.8	-	-	136.0	0.6	-	-	135.5	-0.4
1999	-	-	134.2	-1.0	-	-	136.0	1.3	-	-	135.0	-0.7	-	-	136.4	1.0	-	-	140.4	2.9	-	-	140.7	0.2
2000	-	-	141.7	0.7	-	-	144.0	1.6	-	-	145.3	0.9	-	-	144.0	-0.9	-	-	143.2	-0.6	-	-	143.2	0.0

Source: U.S. Department of Labor, Bureau of Labor Statistics, Division of Consumer Prices and Price Indexes. - indicates no data collected for period.

Houston-Galveston-Brazoria, TX

Consumer Price Index - All Urban Consumers
Base 1982-1984 = 100

Medical Care

For 1947-2001. Columns headed % show percentile change in the index from the previous period for which an index is available.

Year	Jan Index	%	Feb Index	%	Mar Index	%	Apr Index	%	May Index	%	Jun Index	%	Jul Index	%	Aug Index	%	Sep Index	%	Oct Index	%	Nov Index	%	Dec Index	%
1947	14.1	-	14.2	0.7	14.2	0.0	14.3	0.7	14.5	1.4	14.6	0.7	14.5	-0.7	14.5	0.0	14.6	0.7	14.7	0.7	14.7	0.0	14.7	0.0
1948	14.7	0.0	14.7	0.0	14.9	1.4	14.8	-0.7	14.8	0.0	14.9	0.7	14.9	0.0	14.9	0.0	14.9	0.0	14.9	0.0	14.9	0.0	14.9	0.0
1949	15.1	1.3	15.1	0.0	15.1	0.0	15.1	0.0	15.2	0.7	15.3	0.7	15.3	0.0	15.3	0.0	15.3	0.0	15.3	0.0	15.2	-0.7	15.5	2.0
1950	15.5	0.0	15.5	0.0	15.5	0.0	15.5	0.0	15.5	0.0	15.5	0.0	15.5	0.0	15.6	0.6	15.6	0.0	15.6	0.0	15.6	0.0	15.6	0.0
1951	15.6	0.0	15.6	0.0	15.8	1.3	15.8	0.0	15.8	0.0	15.8	0.0	15.8	0.0	15.8	0.0	15.8	0.0	16.6	5.1	16.6	0.0	16.7	0.6
1952	16.6	-0.6	16.6	0.0	16.6	0.0	16.7	0.6	16.7	0.0	16.7	0.0	16.7	0.0	16.7	0.0	16.7	0.0	16.7	0.0	17.7	0.6	17.4	4.2
1953	-		17.4	0.0	-	-	-	-	17.6	1.1	-	-	-	-	17.6	0.0	-	-	-	-	17.7	0.6	-	-
1954	-		17.7	0.0	-	-	-	-	17.7	0.0	-	-	-	-	17.8	0.6	-	-	-	-	17.8	0.0	-	-
1955	-		17.8	0.0	-	-	-	-	18.5	3.9	-	-	-	-	18.5	0.0	-	-	-	-	18.9	2.2	-	-
1956	-		18.9	0.0	-	-	-	-	18.8	-0.5	-	-	-	-	19.0	1.1	-	-	-	-	19.1	0.5	-	-
1957	-		19.3	1.0	-	-	-	-	19.2	-0.5	-	-	-	-	19.1	-0.5	-	-	-	-	19.2	0.5	-	-
1958	-		19.6	2.1	-	-	-	-	19.6	0.0	-	-	-	-	19.6	0.0	-	-	-	-	19.8	1.0	-	-
1959	-		19.8	0.0	-	-	-	-	20.1	1.5	-	-	-	-	20.1	0.0	-	-	-	-	20.1	0.0	-	-
1960	-		20.3	1.0	-	-	-	-	20.6	1.5	-	-	-	-	20.6	0.0	-	-	-	-	20.6	0.0	-	-
1961	-		20.6	0.0	-	-	-	-	20.8	1.0	-	-	-	-	20.8	0.0	-	-	-	-	20.9	0.5	-	-
1962	-		20.9	0.0	-	-	-	-	21.0	0.5	-	-	-	-	21.0	0.0	-	-	-	-	21.2	1.0	-	-
1963	-		21.5	1.4	-	-	-	-	21.6	0.5	-	-	-	-	21.6	0.0	-	-	-	-	21.8	0.9	-	-
1964	-		22.0	0.9	-	-	-	-	22.2	0.9	-	-	-	-	22.2	0.0	-	-	-	-	22.2	0.0	-	-
1965	-		22.5	1.4	-	-	22.7	0.9	-	-	-	-	22.8	0.4	-	-	-	-	22.9	0.4	-	-	-	-
1966	23.0	0.4	-	-	-	-	23.1	0.4	-	-	-	-	23.3	0.9	-	-	-	-	23.9	2.6	-	-	-	-
1967	24.4	2.1	-	-	-	-	24.7	1.2	-	-	-	-	24.8	0.4	-	-	-	-	25.2	1.6	-	-	-	-
1968	25.7	2.0	-	-	-	-	25.8	0.4	-	-	-	-	26.1	1.2	-	-	-	-	26.7	2.3	-	-	-	-
1969	27.6	3.4	-	-	-	-	28.3	2.5	-	-	-	-	28.5	0.7	-	-	-	-	29.1	2.1	-	-	-	-
1970	29.8	2.4	-	-	-	-	30.5	2.3	-	-	-	-	30.6	0.3	-	-	-	-	30.8	0.7	-	-	-	-
1971	31.5	2.3	-	-	-	-	31.9	1.3	-	-	-	-	33.0	3.4	-	-	-	-	32.7	-0.9	-	-	-	-
1972	32.8	0.3	-	-	-	-	33.6	2.4	-	-	-	-	33.6	0.0	-	-	-	-	34.1	1.5	-	-	-	-
1973	34.4	0.9	-	-	-	-	34.7	0.9	-	-	-	-	34.8	0.3	-	-	-	-	35.6	2.3	-	-	-	-
1974	36.3	2.0	-	-	-	-	36.5	0.6	-	-	-	-	38.3	4.9	-	-	-	-	39.2	2.3	-	-	-	-
1975	40.6	3.6	-	-	-	-	42.0	3.4	-	-	-	-	43.6	3.8	-	-	-	-	45.0	3.2	-	-	-	-
1976	45.5	1.1	-	-	-	-	46.7	2.6	-	-	-	-	48.0	2.8	-	-	-	-	49.8	3.8	-	-	-	-
1977	51.3	3.0	-	-	-	-	53.5	4.3	-	-	-	-	54.4	1.7	-	-	-	-	55.5	2.0	-	-	-	-
1978	57.4	3.4	-	-	-	-	58.5	1.9	-	-	59.1	1.0	-	-	60.0	1.5	-	-	61.0	1.7	-	-	61.4	0.7
1979	-		63.0	2.6	-	-	63.9	1.4	-	-	64.5	0.9	-	-	65.3	1.2	-	-	67.6	3.5	-	-	67.9	0.4
1980	-		69.7	2.7	-	-	71.0	1.9	-	-	71.8	1.1	-	-	72.2	0.6	-	-	74.3	2.9	-	-	76.0	2.3
1981	-		76.7	0.9	-	-	77.6	1.2	-	-	80.2	3.4	-	-	80.9	0.9	-	-	82.8	2.3	-	-	84.1	1.6
1982	-		85.6	1.8	-	-	87.4	2.1	-	-	88.9	1.7	-	-	92.2	3.7	-	-	95.3	3.4	-	-	98.6	3.5
1983	-		100.2	1.6	-	-	101.7	1.5	-	-	101.4	-0.3	-	-	101.7	0.3	-	-	101.5	-0.2	-	-	100.9	-0.6
1984	-		104.2	3.3	-	-	105.0	0.8	-	-	108.8	3.6	-	-	109.7	0.8	-	-	111.4	1.5	-	-	112.5	1.0
1985	-		113.9	1.2	-	-	115.9	1.8	-	-	116.5	0.5	-	-	117.7	1.0	-	-	118.8	0.9	-	-	119.5	0.6
1986	-		120.8	1.1	-	-	121.8	0.8	-	-	123.5	1.4	-	-	124.5	0.8	-	-	125.6	0.9	-	-	126.4	0.6
1987	-		127.3	0.7	-	-	128.6	1.0	-	-	129.9	1.0	-	-	132.2	1.8	-	-	132.9	0.5	-	-	133.5	0.5
1988	-		134.7	0.9	-	-	135.6	0.7	-	-	136.5	0.7	-	-	136.0	-0.4	-	-	138.9	2.1	-	-	140.6	1.2
1989	-		144.0	2.4	-	-	145.7	1.2	-	-	148.3	1.8	-	-	149.9	1.1	-	-	151.1	0.8	-	-	152.2	0.7
1990	-		153.7	1.0	-	-	158.1	2.9	-	-	158.5	0.3	-	-	163.9	3.4	-	-	168.0	2.5	-	-	169.1	0.7
1991	-		170.4	0.8	-	-	173.8	2.0	-	-	174.9	0.6	-	-	180.3	3.1	-	-	185.1	2.7	-	-	186.0	0.5
1992	-		190.7	2.5	-	-	192.2	0.8	-	-	194.5	1.2	-	-	195.1	0.3	-	-	195.7	0.3	-	-	196.1	0.2

[Continued]

Houston-Galveston-Brazoria, TX
Consumer Price Index - All Urban Consumers
Base 1982-1984 = 100
Medical Care
[Continued]

For 1947-2001. Columns headed % show percentile change in the index from the previous period for which an index is available.

Year	Jan Index	%	Feb Index	%	Mar Index	%	Apr Index	%	May Index	%	Jun Index	%	Jul Index	%	Aug Index	%	Sep Index	%	Oct Index	%	Nov Index	%	Dec Index	%
1993	-		200.4	2.2	-		201.3	0.4	-		200.8	-0.2	-		200.8	0.0	-		201.9	0.5	-		201.2	-0.3
1994	-		200.9	-0.1	-		202.1	0.6	-		204.7	1.3	-		204.6	-0.0	-		208.5	1.9	-		208.7	0.1
1995	-		213.2	2.2	-		217.3	1.9	-		218.7	0.6	-		220.1	0.6	-		219.5	-0.3	-		220.6	0.5
1996	-		221.5	0.4	-		225.3	1.7	-		226.5	0.5	-		221.7	-2.1	-		220.4	-0.6	-		220.5	0.0
1997	-		226.0	2.5	-		228.2	1.0	-		228.0	-0.1	-		229.3	0.6	-		229.6	0.1	-		232.7	1.4
1998	-		234.6	0.8	-		235.4	0.3	-		235.2	-0.1	-		236.6	0.6	-		236.5	-0.0	-		234.7	-0.8
1999	-		237.8	1.3	-		238.2	0.2	-		238.4	0.1	-		239.2	0.3	-		238.5	-0.3	-		240.1	0.7
2000	-		241.5	0.6	-		241.3	-0.1	-		241.7	0.2	-		242.9	0.5	-		245.1	0.9	-		246.2	0.4
2001	-		248.6	1.0	-		248.8	0.1	-		250.4	0.6	-		253.1	1.1	-		253.9	0.3	-		258.2	1.7

Source: U.S. Department of Labor, Bureau of Labor Statistics, Division of Consumer Prices and Price Indexes. - indicates no data collected for period.

Houston-Galveston-Brazoria, TX
Consumer Price Index - Urban Wage Earners
Base 1982-1984 = 100
Medical Care

For 1947-2001. Columns headed % show percentile change in the index from the previous period for which an index is available.

Year	Jan Index	%	Feb Index	%	Mar Index	%	Apr Index	%	May Index	%	Jun Index	%	Jul Index	%	Aug Index	%	Sep Index	%	Oct Index	%	Nov Index	%	Dec Index	%
1947	13.5	-	13.6	0.7	13.6	0.0	13.7	0.7	13.9	1.5	14.0	0.7	13.9	-0.7	13.9	0.0	14.0	0.7	14.1	0.7	14.1	0.0	14.1	0.0
1948	14.1	0.0	14.1	0.0	14.3	1.4	14.2	-0.7	14.2	0.0	14.2	0.0	14.3	0.7	14.3	0.0	14.3	0.0	14.3	0.0	14.3	0.0	14.3	0.0
1949	14.4	0.7	14.4	0.0	14.4	0.0	14.5	0.7	14.6	0.7	14.7	0.7	14.6	-0.7	14.6	0.0	14.6	0.0	14.6	0.0	14.6	0.0	14.9	2.1
1950	14.9	0.0	14.9	0.0	14.9	0.0	14.9	0.0	14.9	0.0	14.9	0.0	14.9	0.0	14.9	0.0	15.0	0.7	15.0	0.0	15.0	0.0	15.0	0.0
1951	15.0	0.0	15.0	0.0	15.1	0.7	15.1	0.0	15.1	0.0	15.1	0.0	15.1	0.0	15.1	0.0	15.1	0.0	15.9	5.3	15.9	0.0	16.0	0.6
1952	15.9	-0.6	15.9	0.0	15.9	0.0	16.0	0.6	16.0	0.0	16.0	0.0	16.0	0.0	16.0	0.0	16.0	0.0	16.0	0.0	16.0	0.0	16.7	4.4
1953	-		16.7	0.0	-	-	-		16.8	0.6	-		-		16.8	0.0	-		-		17.0	1.2	-	
1954	-		17.0	0.0	-		-		17.0	0.0	-		-		17.1	0.6	-		-		17.1	0.0	-	
1955	-		17.1	0.0	-		-		17.7	3.5	-		-		17.8	0.6	-		-		18.1	1.7	-	
1956	-		18.2	0.6	-		-		18.0	-1.1	-		-		18.2	1.1	-		-		18.3	0.5	-	
1957	-		18.5	1.1	-		-		18.4	-0.5	-		-		18.3	-0.5	-		-		18.4	0.5	-	
1958	-		18.8	2.2	-		-		18.8	0.0	-		-		18.8	0.0	-		-		19.0	1.1	-	
1959	-		19.0	0.0	-		-		19.3	1.6	-		-		19.2	-0.5	-		-		19.2	0.0	-	
1960	-		19.4	1.0	-		-		19.7	1.5	-		-		19.7	0.0	-		-		19.8	0.5	-	
1961	-		19.7	-0.5	-		-		19.9	1.0	-		-		19.9	0.0	-		-		20.0	0.5	-	
1962	-		20.0	0.0	-		-		20.2	1.0	-		-		20.2	0.0	-		-		20.4	1.0	-	
1963	-		20.6	1.0	-		-		20.7	0.5	-		-		20.7	0.0	-		-		20.9	1.0	-	
1964	-		21.1	1.0	-		-		21.3	0.9	-		-		21.3	0.0	-		-		21.3	0.0	-	
1965	-		21.6	1.4	-		21.8	0.9	-		-		21.9	0.5	-		-		22.0	0.5	-		-	
1966	22.1	0.5	-		-		22.1	0.0	-		-		22.3	0.9	-		-		22.9	2.7	-		-	
1967	23.4	2.2	-		-		23.6	0.9	-		-		23.8	0.8	-		-		24.2	1.7	-		-	
1968	24.7	2.1	-		-		24.8	0.4	-		-		25.0	0.8	-		-		25.6	2.4	-		-	
1969	26.4	3.1	-		-		27.1	2.7	-		-		27.3	0.7	-		-		27.9	2.2	-		-	
1970	28.6	2.5	-		-		29.2	2.1	-		-		29.4	0.7	-		-		29.5	0.3	-		-	
1971	30.2	2.4	-		-		30.6	1.3	-		-		31.6	3.3	-		-		31.4	-0.6	-		-	
1972	31.5	0.3	-		-		32.2	2.2	-		-		32.2	0.0	-		-		32.7	1.6	-		-	
1973	33.0	0.9	-		-		33.3	0.9	-		-		33.4	0.3	-		-		34.1	2.1	-		-	
1974	34.8	2.1	-		-		35.0	0.6	-		-		36.7	4.9	-		-		37.6	2.5	-		-	
1975	38.9	3.5	-		-		40.3	3.6	-		-		41.8	3.7	-		-		43.2	3.3	-		-	
1976	43.6	0.9	-		-		44.8	2.8	-		-		46.1	2.9	-		-		47.8	3.7	-		-	
1977	49.2	2.9	-		-		51.3	4.3	-		-		52.2	1.8	-		-		53.2	1.9	-		-	
1978	55.0	3.4	-		-		56.1	2.0	-		56.3	0.4	-		57.8	2.7	-		58.4	1.0	-		59.0	1.0
1979	-		62.2	5.4	-		63.5	2.1	-		64.8	2.0	-		65.4	0.9	-		66.9	2.3	-		67.7	1.2
1980	-		68.6	1.3	-		70.5	2.8	-		70.6	0.1	-		72.9	3.3	-		74.0	1.5	-		75.4	1.9
1981	-		76.4	1.3	-		77.5	1.4	-		79.8	3.0	-		80.5	0.9	-		81.7	1.5	-		83.7	2.4
1982	-		85.3	1.9	-		87.1	2.1	-		88.6	1.7	-		92.1	4.0	-		95.3	3.5	-		98.8	3.7
1983	-		100.4	1.6	-		101.9	1.5	-		101.5	-0.4	-		101.7	0.2	-		101.3	-0.4	-		100.8	-0.5
1984	-		104.2	3.4	-		105.0	0.8	-		109.0	3.8	-		109.9	0.8	-		111.6	1.5	-		112.7	1.0
1985	-		114.2	1.3	-		116.2	1.8	-		116.8	0.5	-		117.9	0.9	-		119.0	0.9	-		119.6	0.5
1986	-		121.0	1.2	-		122.0	0.8	-		123.7	1.4	-		124.7	0.8	-		125.8	0.9	-		126.6	0.6
1987	-		127.6	0.8	-		129.0	1.1	-		130.4	1.1	-		132.7	1.8	-		133.4	0.5	-		134.3	0.7
1988	-		135.5	0.9	-		136.4	0.7	-		137.4	0.7	-		137.1	-0.2	-		140.1	2.2	-		141.8	1.2
1989	-		145.3	2.5	-		147.0	1.2	-		149.6	1.8	-		151.3	1.1	-		152.4	0.7	-		153.5	0.7
1990	-		154.7	0.8	-		159.3	3.0	-		159.5	0.1	-		165.0	3.4	-		169.2	2.5	-		170.3	0.7
1991	-		171.4	0.6	-		174.9	2.0	-		175.9	0.6	-		181.5	3.2	-		186.7	2.9	-		187.6	0.5
1992	-		192.4	2.6	-		193.8	0.7	-		196.1	1.2	-		196.7	0.3	-		197.5	0.4	-		197.9	0.2

[Continued]

496

Houston-Galveston-Brazoria, TX
Consumer Price Index - Urban Wage Earners
Base 1982-1984 = 100
Medical Care
[Continued]

For 1947-2001. Columns headed % show percentile change in the index from the previous period for which an index is available.

Year	Jan		Feb		Mar		Apr		May		Jun		Jul		Aug		Sep		Oct		Nov		Dec	
	Index	%	Index	%	Index	%	Index	%	Index	%	Index	%	Index	%	Index	%	Index	%	Index	%	Index	%	Index	%
1993	-	-	202.3	2.2	-	-	203.3	0.5	-	-	202.9	-0.2	-	-	202.9	0.0	-	-	203.9	0.5	-	-	203.2	-0.3
1994	-	-	202.9	-0.1	-	-	204.0	0.5	-	-	206.7	1.3	-	-	206.5	-0.1	-	-	210.5	1.9	-	-	210.8	0.1
1995	-	-	215.3	2.1	-	-	218.9	1.7	-	-	220.4	0.7	-	-	221.9	0.7	-	-	221.0	-0.4	-	-	222.4	0.6
1996	-	-	223.3	0.4	-	-	227.2	1.7	-	-	228.5	0.6	-	-	223.9	-2.0	-	-	222.5	-0.6	-	-	222.6	0.0
1997	-	-	227.9	2.4	-	-	230.0	0.9	-	-	229.9	-0.0	-	-	231.3	0.6	-	-	231.8	0.2	-	-	235.0	1.4
1998	-	-	236.6	0.7	-	-	237.5	0.4	-	-	237.3	-0.1	-	-	238.7	0.6	-	-	238.4	-0.1	-	-	236.7	-0.7
1999	-	-	239.7	1.3	-	-	240.1	0.2	-	-	240.2	0.0	-	-	241.0	0.3	-	-	239.7	-0.5	-	-	241.4	0.7
2000	-	-	242.9	0.6	-	-	242.5	-0.2	-	-	242.7	0.1	-	-	243.9	0.5	-	-	246.1	0.9	-	-	247.0	0.4
2001	-	-	249.7	1.1	-	-	249.7	0.0	-	-	251.8	0.8	-	-	254.5	1.1	-	-	255.3	0.3	-	-	259.5	1.6

Source: U.S. Department of Labor, Bureau of Labor Statistics, Division of Consumer Prices and Price Indexes. - indicates no data collected for period.

Houston-Galveston-Brazoria, TX
Consumer Price Index - All Urban Consumers
Base December 1997 = 100
Recreation

For 1997-2001. Columns headed % show percentile change in the index from the previous period for which an index is available.

Year	Jan Index	%	Feb Index	%	Mar Index	%	Apr Index	%	May Index	%	Jun Index	%	Jul Index	%	Aug Index	%	Sep Index	%	Oct Index	%	Nov Index	%	Dec Index	%
1997	-	-	-	-	-	-	-	-	-	-	-	-	-	-	-	-	-	-	-	-	-	-	100.0	-
1998	-	-	101.5	1.5	-	-	99.3	-2.2	-	-	99.8	0.5	-	-	100.5	0.7	-	-	99.9	-0.6	-	-	99.5	-0.4
1999	-	-	98.5	-1.0	-	-	101.9	3.5	-	-	102.3	0.4	-	-	102.9	0.6	-	-	101.5	-1.4	-	-	102.3	0.8
2000	-	-	104.7	2.3	-	-	105.7	1.0	-	-	105.3	-0.4	-	-	105.7	0.4	-	-	106.6	0.9	-	-	107.4	0.8
2001	-	-	107.8	0.4	-	-	108.6	0.7	-	-	110.5	1.7	-	-	110.4	-0.1	-	-	107.2	-2.9	-	-	107.4	0.2

Source: U.S. Department of Labor, Bureau of Labor Statistics, Division of Consumer Prices and Price Indexes. - indicates no data collected for period.

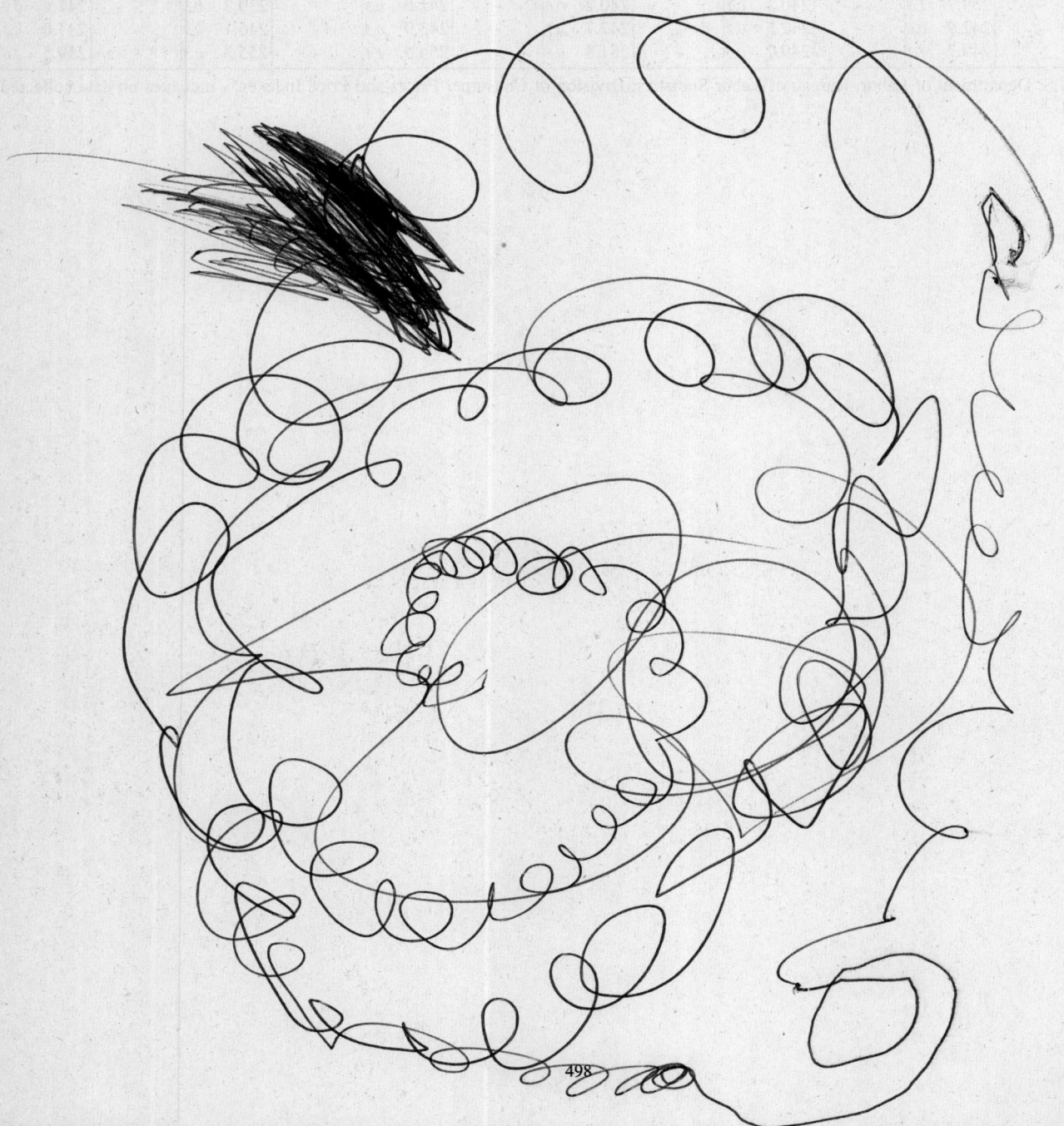

Houston-Galveston-Brazoria, TX
Consumer Price Index - Urban Wage Earners
Base December 1997 = 100
Recreation

For 1997-2001. Columns headed % show percentile change in the index from the previous period for which an index is available.

Year	Jan		Feb		Mar		Apr		May		Jun		Jul		Aug		Sep		Oct		Nov		Dec	
	Index	%	Index	%	Index	%	Index	%	Index	%	Index	%	Index	%	Index	%	Index	%	Index	%	Index	%	Index	%
1997	-	-	-	-	-	-	-	-	-	-	-	-	-	-	-	-	-	-	-	-	-		100.0	-
1998	-	-	101.3	1.3	-	-	99.6	-1.7	-	-	100.3	0.7	-	-	100.7	0.4	-	-	100.0	-0.7	-		100.1	0.1
1999	-	-	98.7	-1.4	-	-	103.1	4.5	-	-	103.9	0.8	-	-	104.2	0.3	-	-	103.1	-1.1	-		104.0	0.9
2000	-	-	106.7	2.6	-	-	107.6	0.8	-	-	107.5	-0.1	-	-	107.8	0.3	-	-	107.8	0.0	-		108.9	1.0
2001	-	-	108.7	-0.2	-	-	109.8	1.0	-	-	111.4	1.5	-	-	111.1	-0.3	-	-	108.5	-2.3	-		108.7	0.2

Source: U.S. Department of Labor, Bureau of Labor Statistics, Division of Consumer Prices and Price Indexes. - indicates no data collected for period.

Houston-Galveston-Brazoria, TX
Consumer Price Index - All Urban Consumers
Base December 1997 = 100
Education & Communication

For 1997-2001. Columns headed % show percentile change in the index from the previous period for which an index is available.

Year	Jan Index	%	Feb Index	%	Mar Index	%	Apr Index	%	May Index	%	Jun Index	%	Jul Index	%	Aug Index	%	Sep Index	%	Oct Index	%	Nov Index	%	Dec Index	%
1997	-	-	-	-	-	-	-	-	-	-	-	-	-	-	-	-	-	-	-	-	-	-	100.0	-
1998	-	-	99.8	-0.2	-	-	100.0	0.2	-	-	98.9	-1.1	-	-	98.7	-0.2	-	-	98.9	0.2	-	-	98.1	-0.8
1999	-	-	101.0	3.0	-	-	100.1	-0.9	-	-	101.1	1.0	-	-	101.3	0.2	-	-	101.2	-0.1	-	-	101.1	-0.1
2000	-	-	101.5	0.4	-	-	100.1	-1.4	-	-	99.0	-1.1	-	-	102.0	3.0	-	-	99.8	-2.2	-	-	99.2	-0.6
2001	-	-	99.7	0.5	-	-	101.1	1.4	-	-	100.1	-1.0	-	-	101.9	1.8	-	-	102.9	1.0	-	-	102.4	-0.5

Source: U.S. Department of Labor, Bureau of Labor Statistics, Division of Consumer Prices and Price Indexes. - indicates no data collected for period.

Houston-Galveston-Brazoria, TX
Consumer Price Index - Urban Wage Earners
Base December 1997 = 100
Education & Communication

For 1997-2001. Columns headed % show percentile change in the index from the previous period for which an index is available.

Year	Jan		Feb		Mar		Apr		May		Jun		Jul		Aug		Sep		Oct		Nov		Dec	
	Index	%	Index	%	Index	%	Index	%	Index	%	Index	%	Index	%	Index	%	Index	%	Index	%	Index	%	Index	%
1997	-	-	-	-	-	-	-	-	-	-	-	-	-	-	-	-	-	-	-	-	-	-	100.0	-
1998	-	-	99.8	-0.2	-	-	99.9	0.1	-	-	98.6	-1.3	-	-	98.3	-0.3	-	-	98.3	0.0	-	-	97.4	-0.9
1999	-	-	100.9	3.6	-	-	99.9	-1.0	-	-	101.1	1.2	-	-	101.0	-0.1	-	-	100.2	-0.8	-	-	100.2	0.0
2000	-	-	100.6	0.4	-	-	99.0	-1.6	-	-	98.1	-0.9	-	-	100.9	2.9	-	-	97.9	-3.0	-	-	97.3	-0.6
2001	-	-	97.8	0.5	-	-	99.4	1.6	-	-	98.7	-0.7	-	-	100.0	1.3	-	-	100.4	0.4	-	-	99.8	-0.6

Source: U.S. Department of Labor, Bureau of Labor Statistics, Division of Consumer Prices and Price Indexes. - indicates no data collected for period.

Kansas City, MO-KS
Consumer Price Index - All Urban Consumers
Base 1982-1984 = 100
Annual Averages

For 1917-2001. Columns headed % show percentile change in the index from the previous period for which an index is available.

Year	All Items		Food & Beverage		Housing		Apparel		Trans-portation		Medical Care		Recrea-tion*		Education & Communic.*		Other Goods & Services	
	Index	%	Index	%	Index	%	Index	%	Index	%	Index	%	Index	%	Index	%	Index	%
1917	-	-	-	-	-	-	-	-	-	-	-	-	-	-	-	-	-	-
1918	16.1	-	-	-	-	-	-	-	-	-	-	-	-	-	-	-	-	-
1919	18.5	14.9	-	-	-	-	-	-	-	-	-	-	-	-	-	-	-	-
1920	21.7	17.3	-	-	-	-	-	-	-	-	-	-	-	-	-	-	-	-
1921	19.2	-11.5	-	-	-	-	-	-	-	-	-	-	-	-	-	-	-	-
1922	17.5	-8.9	-	-	-	-	-	-	-	-	-	-	-	-	-	-	-	-
1923	17.4	-0.6	-	-	-	-	-	-	-	-	-	-	-	-	-	-	-	-
1924	17.3	-0.6	-	-	-	-	-	-	-	-	-	-	-	-	-	-	-	-
1925	17.5	1.2	-	-	-	-	-	-	-	-	-	-	-	-	-	-	-	-
1926	17.5	0.0	-	-	-	-	-	-	-	-	-	-	-	-	-	-	-	-
1927	17.0	-2.9	-	-	-	-	-	-	-	-	-	-	-	-	-	-	-	-
1928	16.7	-1.8	-	-	-	-	-	-	-	-	-	-	-	-	-	-	-	-
1929	16.8	0.6	-	-	-	-	-	-	-	-	-	-	-	-	-	-	-	-
1930	16.5	-1.8	-	-	-	-	-	-	-	-	-	-	-	-	-	-	-	-
1931	15.5	-6.1	-	-	-	-	-	-	-	-	-	-	-	-	-	-	-	-
1932	13.9	-10.3	-	-	-	-	-	-	-	-	-	-	-	-	-	-	-	-
1933	13.3	-4.3	-	-	-	-	-	-	-	-	-	-	-	-	-	-	-	-
1934	13.7	3.0	-	-	-	-	-	-	-	-	-	-	-	-	-	-	-	-
1935	14.0	2.2	-	-	-	-	-	-	-	-	-	-	-	-	-	-	-	-
1936	14.1	0.7	-	-	-	-	-	-	-	-	-	-	-	-	-	-	-	-
1937	14.6	3.5	-	-	-	-	-	-	-	-	-	-	-	-	-	-	-	-
1938	14.3	-2.1	-	-	-	-	-	-	-	-	-	-	-	-	-	-	-	-
1939	14.1	-1.4	-	-	-	-	-	-	-	-	-	-	-	-	-	-	-	-
1940	14.0	-0.7	-	-	-	-	-	-	-	-	-	-	-	-	-	-	-	-
1941	14.7	5.0	-	-	-	-	-	-	-	-	-	-	-	-	-	-	-	-
1942	16.3	10.9	-	-	-	-	-	-	-	-	-	-	-	-	-	-	-	-
1943	17.3	6.1	-	-	-	-	-	-	-	-	-	-	-	-	-	-	-	-
1944	17.6	1.7	-	-	-	-	-	-	-	-	-	-	-	-	-	-	-	-
1945	18.1	2.8	-	-	-	-	-	-	-	-	-	-	-	-	-	-	-	-
1946	19.3	6.6	-	-	-	-	-	-	-	-	-	-	-	-	-	-	-	-
1947	21.9	13.5	-	-	-	-	-	-	18.2	-	11.0	-	-	-	-	-	-	-
1948	23.6	7.8	-	-	-	-	-	-	20.2	11.0	11.9	8.2	-	-	-	-	-	-
1949	23.3	-1.3	-	-	-	-	-	-	21.5	6.4	12.2	2.5	-	-	-	-	-	-
1950	23.7	1.7	-	-	-	-	-	-	21.9	1.9	12.4	1.6	-	-	-	-	-	-
1951	25.5	7.6	-	-	-	-	-	-	23.2	5.9	13.0	4.8	-	-	-	-	-	-
1952	26.3	3.1	-	-	-	-	-	-	25.4	9.5	13.7	5.4	-	-	-	-	-	-
1953	26.4	0.4	-	-	-	-	39.2	-	26.0	2.4	14.0	2.2	-	-	-	-	-	-
1954	26.5	0.4	-	-	-	-	38.9	-0.8	25.2	-3.1	15.6	11.4	-	-	-	-	-	-
1955	26.5	0.0	-	-	-	-	38.9	0.0	25.0	-0.8	15.9	1.9	-	-	-	-	-	-
1956	26.9	1.5	-	-	-	-	39.4	1.3	25.4	1.6	16.6	4.4	-	-	-	-	-	-
1957	27.8	3.3	-	-	-	-	40.3	2.3	27.6	8.7	17.7	6.6	-	-	-	-	-	-
1958	28.5	2.5	-	-	-	-	40.4	0.2	29.1	5.4	19.0	7.3	-	-	-	-	-	-
1959	28.9	1.4	-	-	-	-	40.7	0.7	30.6	5.2	20.0	5.3	-	-	-	-	-	-
1960	29.3	1.4	-	-	-	-	41.7	2.5	30.6	0.0	20.3	1.5	-	-	-	-	-	-
1961	29.6	1.0	-	-	-	-	42.0	0.7	30.6	0.0	21.1	3.9	-	-	-	-	-	-

[Continued]

502

Kansas City, MO-KS

Consumer Price Index - All Urban Consumers

Base 1982-1984 = 100

Annual Averages

[Continued]

For 1917-2001. Columns headed % show percentile change in the index from the previous period for which an index is available.

Year	All Items		Food & Beverage		Housing		Apparel		Trans-portation		Medical Care		Recrea-tion*		Education & Communic.*		Other Goods & Services	
	Index	%	Index	%	Index	%	Index	%	Index	%	Index	%	Index	%	Index	%	Index	%
1962	30.1	1.7	-	-	-	-	42.0	0.0	31.3	2.3	21.5	1.9	-	-	-	-	-	-
1963	30.4	1.0	-	-	-	-	42.6	1.4	31.3	0.0	21.7	0.9	-	-	-	-	-	-
1964	31.2	2.6	-	-	-	-	43.6	2.3	31.6	1.0	22.8	5.1	-	-	-	-	-	-
1965	32.2	3.2	-	-	-	-	44.5	2.1	33.8	7.0	24.0	5.3	-	-	-	-	-	-
1966	33.0	2.5	-	-	-	-	45.7	2.7	34.5	2.1	25.3	5.4	-	-	-	-	-	-
1967	33.7	2.1	-	-	-	-	47.3	3.5	34.7	0.6	27.2	7.5	-	-	-	-	-	-
1968	35.0	3.9	-	-	-	-	50.8	7.4	35.5	2.3	28.9	6.3	-	-	-	-	-	-
1969	36.9	5.4	-	-	-	-	54.4	7.1	37.2	4.8	30.4	5.2	-	-	-	-	-	-
1970	39.0	5.7	-	-	-	-	57.4	5.5	38.2	2.7	31.8	4.6	-	-	-	-	-	-
1971	40.6	4.1	-	-	-	-	58.9	2.6	41.0	7.3	33.8	6.3	-	-	-	-	-	-
1972	41.8	3.0	-	-	-	-	60.3	2.4	41.0	0.0	35.1	3.8	-	-	-	-	-	-
1973	43.9	5.0	-	-	-	-	61.8	2.5	42.6	3.9	36.7	4.6	-	-	-	-	-	-
1974	48.6	10.7	-	-	-	-	65.7	6.3	47.3	11.0	40.1	9.3	-	-	-	-	-	-
1975	53.2	9.5	-	-	-	-	69.0	5.0	51.5	8.9	43.6	8.7	-	-	-	-	-	-
1976	56.1	5.5	62.9	-	52.7	-	70.7	2.5	55.5	7.8	47.3	8.5	-	-	-	-	57.7	-
1977	60.0	7.0	67.0	6.5	56.6	7.4	77.0	8.9	59.2	6.7	51.8	9.5	-	-	-	-	61.4	6.4
1978	64.6	7.7	74.6	11.3	61.5	8.7	79.0	2.6	62.1	4.9	56.7	9.5	-	-	-	-	64.7	5.4
1979	73.8	14.2	82.6	10.7	72.1	17.2	84.3	6.7	72.3	16.4	63.7	12.3	-	-	-	-	69.9	8.0
1980	83.6	13.3	89.6	8.5	82.7	14.7	87.6	3.9	85.0	17.6	70.9	11.3	-	-	-	-	76.7	9.7
1981	90.5	8.3	95.0	6.0	89.5	8.2	92.3	5.4	93.2	9.6	79.7	12.4	-	-	-	-	84.5	10.2
1982	95.0	5.0	97.5	2.6	93.8	4.8	95.7	3.7	97.5	4.6	91.0	14.2	-	-	-	-	91.3	8.0
1983	100.5	5.8	99.2	1.7	101.2	7.9	101.8	6.4	99.5	2.1	101.1	11.1	-	-	-	-	100.6	10.2
1984	104.5	4.0	103.3	4.1	105.0	3.8	102.5	0.7	103.0	3.5	107.8	6.6	-	-	-	-	108.1	7.5
1985	107.7	3.1	106.0	2.6	107.6	2.5	105.0	2.4	106.5	3.4	111.7	3.6	-	-	-	-	115.7	7.0
1986	108.7	0.9	109.5	3.3	109.4	1.7	107.0	1.9	100.0	-6.1	117.7	5.4	-	-	-	-	125.5	8.5
1987	113.1	4.0	112.8	3.0	113.6	3.8	109.7	2.5	102.9	2.9	123.4	4.8	-	-	-	-	-	-
1988	117.4	3.8	115.8	2.7	118.3	4.1	113.1	3.1	107.2	4.2	130.8	6.0	-	-	-	-	141.6	12.8
1989	121.6	3.6	119.9	3.5	119.6	1.1	119.7	5.8	112.2	4.7	142.0	8.6	-	-	-	-	152.3	7.6
1990	126.0	3.6	127.5	6.3	121.8	1.8	116.5	-2.7	116.2	3.6	156.8	10.4	-	-	-	-	159.6	4.8
1991	131.2	4.1	130.9	2.7	125.4	3.0	124.7	7.0	119.2	2.6	173.5	10.7	-	-	-	-	175.7	10.1
1992	134.3	2.4	132.9	1.5	127.2	1.4	124.8	0.1	121.8	2.2	183.8	5.9	-	-	-	-	189.4	7.8
1993	138.1	2.8	137.7	3.6	130.4	2.5	125.3	0.4	124.7	2.4	195.6	6.4	-	-	-	-	196.7	3.9
1994	141.3	2.3	140.2	1.8	133.1	2.1	123.3	-1.6	128.1	2.7	202.9	3.7	-	-	-	-	203.5	3.5
1995	145.3	2.8	144.6	3.1	136.7	2.7	125.8	2.0	133.4	4.1	208.5	2.8	-	-	-	-	208.4	2.4
1996	151.6	4.3	154.1	6.6	142.4	4.2	129.6	3.0	137.6	3.1	212.2	1.8	-	-	-	-	221.4	6.2
1997	155.8	2.8	160.0	3.8	146.1	2.6	133.4	2.9	140.7	2.3	210.0	-1.0	-	-	-	-	237.8	7.4
1998	157.8	1.3	159.7	-0.2	151.8	3.9	129.1	-3.2	137.2	-2.5	217.7	3.7	101.1	-	98.1	-	251.0	5.6
1999	160.1	1.5	161.0	0.8	154.6	1.8	121.6	-5.8	139.2	1.5	229.1	5.2	100.7	-0.4	98.3	0.2	277.6	10.6
2000	166.6	4.1	165.0	2.5	161.5	4.5	118.5	-2.5	147.5	6.0	245.1	7.0	102.8	2.1	101.1	2.8	295.1	6.3
2001	172.2	3.4	172.3	4.4	168.5	4.3	119.3	0.7	148.1	0.4	254.5	3.8	106.2	3.3	108.6	7.4	301.6	2.2

Source: U.S. Department of Labor, Bureau of Labor Statistics, Division of Consumer Prices and Price Indexes. *Base is December 1997 = 100. - indicates no data collected for period.

Kansas City, MO-KS
Consumer Price Index - Urban Wage Earners
Base 1982-1984 = 100
Annual Averages

For 1917-2001. Columns headed % show percentile change in the index from the previous period for which an index is available.

Year	All Items		Food & Beverage		Housing		Apparel		Trans-portation		Medical Care		Recrea-tion*		Education & Communic.*		Other Goods & Services	
	Index	%	Index	%	Index	%	Index	%	Index	%	Index	%	Index	%	Index	%	Index	%
1917	-	-	-	-	-	-	-	-	-	-	-	-	-	-	-	-	-	-
1918	16.3	-	-	-	-	-	-	-	-	-	-	-	-	-	-	-	-	-
1919	18.7	14.7	-	-	-	-	-	-	-	-	-	-	-	-	-	-	-	-
1920	22.0	17.6	-	-	-	-	-	-	-	-	-	-	-	-	-	-	-	-
1921	19.4	-11.8	-	-	-	-	-	-	-	-	-	-	-	-	-	-	-	-
1922	17.7	-8.8	-	-	-	-	-	-	-	-	-	-	-	-	-	-	-	-
1923	17.7	0.0	-	-	-	-	-	-	-	-	-	-	-	-	-	-	-	-
1924	17.5	-1.1	-	-	-	-	-	-	-	-	-	-	-	-	-	-	-	-
1925	17.8	1.7	-	-	-	-	-	-	-	-	-	-	-	-	-	-	-	-
1926	17.8	0.0	-	-	-	-	-	-	-	-	-	-	-	-	-	-	-	-
1927	17.2	-3.4	-	-	-	-	-	-	-	-	-	-	-	-	-	-	-	-
1928	16.9	-1.7	-	-	-	-	-	-	-	-	-	-	-	-	-	-	-	-
1929	17.0	0.6	-	-	-	-	-	-	-	-	-	-	-	-	-	-	-	-
1930	16.7	-1.8	-	-	-	-	-	-	-	-	-	-	-	-	-	-	-	-
1931	15.7	-6.0	-	-	-	-	-	-	-	-	-	-	-	-	-	-	-	-
1932	14.1	-10.2	-	-	-	-	-	-	-	-	-	-	-	-	-	-	-	-
1933	13.4	-5.0	-	-	-	-	-	-	-	-	-	-	-	-	-	-	-	-
1934	13.9	3.7	-	-	-	-	-	-	-	-	-	-	-	-	-	-	-	-
1935	14.2	2.2	-	-	-	-	-	-	-	-	-	-	-	-	-	-	-	-
1936	14.3	0.7	-	-	-	-	-	-	-	-	-	-	-	-	-	-	-	-
1937	14.8	3.5	-	-	-	-	-	-	-	-	-	-	-	-	-	-	-	-
1938	14.5	-2.0	-	-	-	-	-	-	-	-	-	-	-	-	-	-	-	-
1939	14.3	-1.4	-	-	-	-	-	-	-	-	-	-	-	-	-	-	-	-
1940	14.2	-0.7	-	-	-	-	-	-	-	-	-	-	-	-	-	-	-	-
1941	14.9	4.9	-	-	-	-	-	-	-	-	-	-	-	-	-	-	-	-
1942	16.5	10.7	-	-	-	-	-	-	-	-	-	-	-	-	-	-	-	-
1943	17.5	6.1	-	-	-	-	-	-	-	-	-	-	-	-	-	-	-	-
1944	17.8	1.7	-	-	-	-	-	-	-	-	-	-	-	-	-	-	-	-
1945	18.3	2.8	-	-	-	-	-	-	-	-	-	-	-	-	-	-	-	-
1946	19.6	7.1	-	-	-	-	-	-	-	-	-	-	-	-	-	-	-	-
1947	22.2	13.3	-	-	-	-	-	-	18.1	-	11.0	-	-	-	-	-	-	-
1948	23.9	7.7	-	-	-	-	-	-	20.1	11.0	11.9	8.2	-	-	-	-	-	-
1949	23.7	-0.8	-	-	-	-	-	-	21.3	6.0	12.2	2.5	-	-	-	-	-	-
1950	24.0	1.3	-	-	-	-	-	-	21.8	2.3	12.4	1.6	-	-	-	-	-	-
1951	25.8	7.5	-	-	-	-	-	-	23.0	5.5	13.0	4.8	-	-	-	-	-	-
1952	26.6	3.1	-	-	-	-	-	-	25.2	9.6	13.7	5.4	-	-	-	-	-	-
1953	26.7	0.4	-	-	-	-	40.5	-	25.8	2.4	14.0	2.2	-	-	-	-	-	-
1954	26.9	0.7	-	-	-	-	40.1	-1.0	25.1	-2.7	15.6	11.4	-	-	-	-	-	-
1955	26.9	0.0	-	-	-	-	40.1	0.0	24.9	-0.8	15.9	1.9	-	-	-	-	-	-
1956	27.3	1.5	-	-	-	-	40.6	1.2	25.3	1.6	16.6	4.4	-	-	-	-	-	-
1957	28.2	3.3	-	-	-	-	41.5	2.2	27.4	8.3	17.7	6.6	-	-	-	-	-	-
1958	28.8	2.1	-	-	-	-	41.6	0.2	28.9	5.5	19.0	7.3	-	-	-	-	-	-
1959	29.3	1.7	-	-	-	-	42.0	1.0	30.4	5.2	20.0	5.3	-	-	-	-	-	-
1960	29.7	1.4	-	-	-	-	43.0	2.4	30.4	0.0	20.3	1.5	-	-	-	-	-	-
1961	30.0	1.0	-	-	-	-	43.3	0.7	30.4	0.0	21.1	3.9	-	-	-	-	-	-

[Continued]

Kansas City, MO-KS
Consumer Price Index - Urban Wage Earners
Base 1982-1984 = 100
Annual Averages

[Continued]

For 1917-2001. Columns headed % show percentile change in the index from the previous period for which an index is available.

Year	All Items		Food & Beverage		Housing		Apparel		Trans-portation		Medical Care		Recrea-tion*		Education & Communic.*		Other Goods & Services	
	Index	%	Index	%	Index	%	Index	%	Index	%	Index	%	Index	%	Index	%	Index	%
1962	30.5	1.7	-	-	-	-	43.3	0.0	31.1	2.3	21.5	1.9	-	-	-	-	-	-
1963	30.8	1.0	-	-	-	-	43.9	1.4	31.1	0.0	21.7	0.9	-	-	-	-	-	-
1964	31.6	2.6	-	-	-	-	45.0	2.5	31.4	1.0	22.8	5.1	-	-	-	-	-	-
1965	32.6	3.2	-	-	-	-	45.9	2.0	33.6	7.0	24.0	5.3	-	-	-	-	-	-
1966	33.4	2.5	-	-	-	-	47.1	2.6	34.3	2.1	25.3	5.4	-	-	-	-	-	-
1967	34.1	2.1	-	-	-	-	48.8	3.6	34.5	0.6	27.2	7.5	-	-	-	-	-	-
1968	35.5	4.1	-	-	-	-	52.4	7.4	35.3	2.3	28.9	6.3	-	-	-	-	-	-
1969	37.4	5.4	-	-	-	-	56.1	7.1	36.9	4.5	30.4	5.2	-	-	-	-	-	-
1970	39.5	5.6	-	-	-	-	59.2	5.5	38.0	3.0	31.8	4.6	-	-	-	-	-	-
1971	41.1	4.1	-	-	-	-	60.7	2.5	40.8	7.4	33.8	6.3	-	-	-	-	-	-
1972	42.3	2.9			-	-	62.2	2.5	40.8	0.0	35.1	3.8	-	-	-	-	-	-
1973	44.5	5.2	-	-	-	-	63.7	2.4	42.4	3.9	36.7	4.6	-	-	-	-	-	-
1974	49.2	10.6	-	-	-	-	67.8	6.4	47.0	10.8	40.1	9.3	-	-	-	-	-	-
1975	53.9	9.6	-	-	-	-	71.1	4.9	51.2	8.9	43.6	8.7	-	-	-	-	-	-
1976	56.8	5.4	63.7	-	53.8	-	72.9	2.5	55.2	7.8	47.3	8.5	-	-	-	-	-	-
1977	60.9	7.2	67.8	6.4	57.8	7.4	79.4	8.9	58.8	6.5	51.8	9.5	-	-	-	-	57.9	-
1978	65.5	7.6	75.0	10.6	62.9	8.8	82.1	3.4	61.7	4.9	56.4	8.9	-	-	-	-	61.6	6.4
1979	74.4	13.6	82.0	9.3	73.2	16.4	84.4	2.8	72.2	17.0	63.9	13.3	-	-	-	-	65.1	5.7
1980	84.1	13.0	89.1	8.7	83.4	13.9	87.0	3.1	85.0	17.7	71.3	11.6	-	-	-	-	71.4	9.7
1981	91.2	8.4	94.7	6.3	90.3	8.3	92.3	6.1	93.7	10.2	79.2	11.1	-	-	-	-	78.6	10.1
1982	95.7	4.9	97.5	3.0	94.9	5.1	95.8	3.8	97.5	4.1	91.0	14.9	-	-	-	-	84.9	8.0
1983	101.3	5.9	99.3	1.8	103.2	8.7	102.2	6.7	99.5	2.1	101.1	11.1	-	-	-	-	91.2	7.4
1984	103.0	1.7	103.2	3.9	102.0	-1.2	102.1	-0.1	103.1	3.6	107.9	6.7	-	-	-	-	100.7	10.4
1985	105.7	2.6	105.8	2.5	103.5	1.5	105.7	3.5	106.5	3.3	111.8	3.6	-	-	-	-	108.0	7.2
1986	106.1	0.4	109.4	3.4	105.2	1.6	106.7	0.9	99.2	-6.9	117.6	5.2	-	-	-	-	115.5	6.9
1987	110.2	3.9	112.7	3.0	109.0	3.6	110.4	3.5	101.2	2.0	123.8	5.3	-	-	-	-	125.3	8.5
1988	114.4	3.8	115.8	2.8	113.4	4.0	114.2	3.4	105.5	4.2	131.6	6.3	-	-	-	-	-	-
1989	118.5	3.6	119.8	3.5	114.8	1.2	120.3	5.3	109.9	4.2	143.0	8.7	-	-	-	-	141.4	12.8
1990	122.4	3.3	127.4	6.3	117.0	1.9	116.8	-2.9	112.6	2.5	157.6	10.2	-	-	-	-	153.1	8.3
1991	127.4	4.1	131.0	2.8	120.2	2.7	125.6	7.5	115.9	2.9	173.7	10.2	-	-	-	-	160.1	4.6
1992	130.4	2.4	132.7	1.3	121.9	1.4	125.1	-0.4	119.1	2.8	184.2	6.0	-	-	-	-	176.8	10.4
1993	134.3	3.0	137.8	3.8	125.1	2.6	126.1	0.8	122.2	2.6	196.7	6.8	-	-	-	-	191.3	8.2
1994	137.5	2.4	140.2	1.7	127.7	2.1	124.2	-1.5	126.1	3.2	203.9	3.7	-	-	-	-	198.5	3.8
1995	141.7	3.1	144.6	3.1	131.0	2.6	126.8	2.1	131.8	4.5	209.0	2.5	-	-	-	-	205.5	3.5
1996	147.7	4.2	154.2	6.6	136.4	4.1	131.3	3.5	135.6	2.9	213.2	2.0	-	-	-	-	210.9	2.6
1997	151.5	2.6	160.1	3.8	139.9	2.6	133.2	1.4	137.8	1.6	211.5	-0.8	-	-	-	-	223.9	6.2
1998	152.9	0.9	159.7	-0.2	145.1	3.7	128.3	-3.7	134.3	-2.5	218.7	3.4	100.8	-	98.9	-	240.5	7.4
1999	154.8	1.2	161.1	0.9	146.9	1.2	119.5	-6.9	136.4	1.6	229.8	5.1	100.1	-0.7	99.6	0.7	254.5	5.8
2000	161.0	4.0	165.0	2.4	153.0	4.2	117.7	-1.5	144.7	6.1	244.7	6.5	101.9	1.8	102.5	2.9	284.3	11.7
2001	166.0	3.1	172.4	4.5	159.6	4.3	115.3	-2.0	145.1	0.3	251.6	2.8	105.3	3.3	110.5	7.8	304.1	7.0
																	310.1	2.0

Source: U.S. Department of Labor, Bureau of Labor Statistics, Division of Consumer Prices and Price Indexes. *Base is December 1997 = 100. - indicates no data collected for period.

Kansas City, MO-KS
Consumer Price Index - All Urban Consumers
Base 1982-1984 = 100
All Items

For 1917-2001. Columns headed % show percentile change in the index from the previous period for which an index is available.

Year	Jan Index	%	Feb Index	%	Mar Index	%	Apr Index	%	May Index	%	Jun Index	%	Jul Index	%	Aug Index	%	Sep Index	%	Oct Index	%	Nov Index	%	Dec Index	%
1917	-	-	-	-	-	-	-	-	-	-	-	-	-	-	-	-	-	-	-	-	-	-	14.8	-
1918	-	-	-	-	-	-	-	-	-	-	-	-	-	-	-	-	-	-	-	-	-	-	17.6	18.9
1919	-	-	-	-	-	-	-	-	-	-	17.7	0.6	-	-	-	-	-	-	-	-	-	-	20.4	15.3
1920	-	-	-	-	-	-	-	-	-	-	22.8	11.8	-	-	-	-	-	-	-	-	-	-	20.7	-9.2
1921	-	-	-	-	-	-	-	-	19.1	-7.7	-	-	-	-	-	-	18.7	-2.1	-	-	-	-	18.5	-1.1
1922	-	-	-	-	17.4	-5.9	-	-	-	-	17.4	0.0	-	-	-	-	17.3	-0.6	-	-	-	-	17.4	0.6
1923	-	-	-	-	17.4	0.0	-	-	-	-	17.4	0.0	-	-	-	-	17.5	0.6	-	-	-	-	17.5	0.0
1924	-	-	-	-	17.4	-0.6	-	-	-	-	17.2	-1.1	-	-	-	-	17.1	-0.6	-	-	-	-	17.3	1.2
1925	-	-	-	-	-	-	-	-	-	-	17.5	1.2	-	-	-	-	-	-	-	-	-	-	17.8	1.7
1926	-	-	-	-	-	-	-	-	-	-	17.7	-0.6	-	-	-	-	-	-	-	-	-	-	17.4	-1.7
1927	-	-	-	-	-	-	-	-	-	-	17.3	-0.6	-	-	-	-	-	-	-	-	-	-	16.7	-3.5
1928	-	-	-	-	-	-	-	-	-	-	16.7	0.0	-	-	-	-	-	-	-	-	-	-	16.7	0.0
1929	-	-	-	-	-	-	-	-	-	-	16.6	-0.6	-	-	-	-	-	-	-	-	-	-	16.8	1.2
1930	-	-	-	-	-	-	-	-	-	-	16.6	-1.2	-	-	-	-	-	-	-	-	-	-	16.1	-3.0
1931	-	-	-	-	-	-	-	-	-	-	15.5	-3.7	-	-	-	-	-	-	-	-	-	-	14.9	-3.9
1932	-	-	-	-	-	-	-	-	-	-	13.8	-7.4	-	-	-	-	-	-	-	-	-	-	13.5	-2.2
1933	-	-	-	-	-	-	-	-	-	-	13.2	-2.2	-	-	-	-	-	-	-	-	-	-	13.4	1.5
1934	-	-	-	-	-	-	-	-	-	-	13.6	1.5	-	-	-	-	-	-	-	-	13.8	1.5	-	-
1935	-	-	-	-	13.9	0.7	-	-	-	-	-	-	13.8	-0.7	-	-	-	-	13.9	0.7	-	-	-	-
1936	14.1	1.4	-	-	-	-	13.9	-1.4	-	-	-	-	14.1	1.4	-	-	14.3	1.4	-	-	-	-	14.2	-0.7
1937	-	-	-	-	14.5	2.1	-	-	-	-	14.7	1.4	-	-	-	-	14.8	0.7	-	-	-	-	14.6	-1.4
1938	-	-	-	-	14.4	-1.4	-	-	-	-	14.3	-0.7	-	-	-	-	14.3	0.0	-	-	-	-	14.2	-0.7
1939	-	-	-	-	14.1	-0.7	-	-	-	-	14.1	0.0	-	-	-	-	14.3	1.4	-	-	-	-	14.1	-1.4
1940	-	-	-	-	14.0	-0.7	-	-	-	-	14.0	0.0	-	-	-	-	13.9	-0.7	13.9	0.0	14.0	0.7	14.0	0.0
1941	14.0	0.0	14.0	0.0	14.1	0.7	14.3	1.4	14.3	0.0	14.5	1.4	14.5	0.0	14.7	1.4	15.1	2.7	15.3	1.3	15.4	0.7	15.5	0.6
1942	15.6	0.6	15.8	1.3	16.1	1.9	16.2	0.6	16.3	0.6	16.3	0.0	16.2	-0.6	16.4	1.2	16.3	-0.6	16.6	1.8	16.7	0.6	16.8	0.6
1943	16.8	0.0	16.9	0.6	17.2	1.8	17.4	1.2	17.4	0.0	17.4	0.0	17.2	-1.1	17.2	0.0	17.3	0.6	17.4	0.6	17.4	0.0	17.4	0.0
1944	17.4	0.0	17.4	0.0	17.4	0.0	17.5	0.6	17.6	0.6	17.6	0.0	17.7	0.6	17.6	-0.6	17.7	0.6	17.7	0.0	17.7	0.0	17.8	0.6
1945	17.8	0.0	17.8	0.0	17.8	0.0	17.9	0.6	18.0	0.6	18.1	0.6	18.2	0.6	18.2	0.0	18.1	-0.5	18.1	0.0	18.2	0.6	18.3	0.5
1946	18.3	0.0	18.2	-0.5	18.2	0.0	18.3	0.5	18.4	0.5	18.5	0.5	19.5	5.4	20.1	3.1	20.1	0.0	20.3	1.0	21.0	3.4	21.0	0.0
1947	21.1	0.5	21.2	0.5	21.5	1.4	21.6	0.5	21.5	-0.5	21.4	-0.5	21.5	0.5	-	-	-	-	22.6	5.1	-	-	-	-
1948	23.2	2.7	-	-	-	-	23.3	0.4	-	-	-	-	23.8	2.1	-	-	-	-	24.0	0.8	-	-	-	-
1949	23.6	-1.7	-	-	-	-	23.4	-0.8	-	-	-	-	23.3	-0.4	-	-	-	-	23.2	-0.4	-	-	-	-
1950	23.1	-0.4	-	-	-	-	23.3	0.9	-	-	-	-	23.8	2.1	-	-	-	-	24.1	1.3	-	-	-	-
1951	25.0	3.7	-	-	-	-	25.5	2.0	-	-	-	-	25.6	0.4	-	-	-	-	25.7	0.4	-	-	-	-
1952	26.0	1.2	-	-	-	-	26.1	0.4	-	-	-	-	26.4	1.1	-	-	-	-	26.4	0.0	-	-	-	-
1953	26.2	-0.8	-	-	-	-	26.2	0.0	-	-	-	-	26.4	0.8	-	-	-	-	26.5	0.4	-	-	-	-
1954	26.4	-0.4	-	-	-	-	26.5	0.4	-	-	-	-	26.5	0.0	-	-	-	-	26.5	0.0	-	-	-	-
1955	26.4	-0.4	-	-	-	-	26.4	0.0	-	-	-	-	26.6	0.8	-	-	-	-	26.6	0.0	-	-	-	-
1956	26.5	-0.4	-	-	-	-	26.7	0.8	-	-	-	-	27.0	1.1	-	-	-	-	27.3	1.1	-	-	-	-
1957	27.5	0.7	-	-	-	-	27.6	0.4	-	-	-	-	27.9	1.1	-	-	-	-	28.0	0.4	-	-	-	-
1958	28.1	0.4	-	-	-	-	28.4	1.1	-	-	-	-	28.6	0.7	-	-	-	-	28.7	0.3	-	-	-	-
1959	28.6	-0.3	-	-	-	-	28.8	0.7	-	-	-	-	28.9	0.3	-	-	-	-	29.1	0.7	-	-	-	-
1960	29.1	0.0	-	-	-	-	29.0	-0.3	-	-	-	-	29.3	1.0	-	-	-	-	29.4	0.3	-	-	-	-
1961	29.3	-0.3	-	-	-	-	29.7	1.4	-	-	-	-	29.8	0.3	-	-	-	-	29.7	-0.3	-	-	-	-
1962	29.8	0.3	-	-	-	-	30.0	0.7	-	-	-	-	30.1	0.3	-	-	-	-	30.4	1.0	-	-	-	-

[Continued]

Kansas City, MO-KS
Consumer Price Index - All Urban Consumers
Base 1982-1984 = 100
All Items
[Continued]

For 1917-2001. Columns headed % show percentile change in the index from the previous period for which an index is available.

Year	Jan Index	%	Feb Index	%	Mar Index	%	Apr Index	%	May Index	%	Jun Index	%	Jul Index	%	Aug Index	%	Sep Index	%	Oct Index	%	Nov Index	%	Dec Index	%
1963	30.0	-1.3	-	-	-	-	30.2	0.7	-	-	-	-	30.4	0.7	-	-	-	-	30.8	1.3	-	-	-	-
1964	30.8	0.0	-	-	-	-	30.9	0.3	-	-	-	-	31.3	1.3	-	-	-	-	31.4	0.3	-	-	-	-
1965	31.6	0.6	-	-	-	-	31.8	0.6	-	-	32.3	1.6	-	-	-	-	32.4	0.3	-	-	-	-	32.5	0.3
1966	-	-	-	-	32.7	0.6	-	-	-	-	33.0	0.9	-	-	-	-	33.2	0.6	-	-	-	-	33.3	0.3
1967	-	-	-	-	33.4	0.3	-	-	-	-	33.3	-0.3	-	-	-	-	34.1	2.4	-	-	-	-	34.1	0.0
1968	-	-	-	-	34.5	1.2	-	-	-	-	35.2	2.0	-	-	-	-	35.3	0.3	-	-	-	-	35.6	0.8
1969	-	-	-	-	36.3	2.0	-	-	-	-	37.0	1.9	-	-	-	-	37.3	0.8	-	-	-	-	37.8	1.3
1970	-	-	-	-	38.2	1.1	-	-	-	-	39.1	2.4	-	-	-	-	39.3	0.5	-	-	-	-	40.1	2.0
1971	-	-	-	-	40.1	0.0	-	-	-	-	40.6	1.2	-	-	-	-	40.9	0.7	-	-	-	-	40.9	0.0
1972	-	-	-	-	41.2	0.7	-	-	-	-	41.7	1.2	-	-	-	-	42.3	1.4	-	-	-	-	42.3	0.0
1973	-	-	-	-	42.9	1.4	-	-	-	-	43.7	1.9	-	-	-	-	44.6	2.1	-	-	-	-	45.3	1.6
1974	-	-	-	-	46.7	3.1	-	-	-	-	48.3	3.4	-	-	-	-	49.9	3.3	-	-	-	-	51.4	3.0
1975	-	-	-	-	52.1	1.4	-	-	-	-	52.9	1.5	-	-	-	-	54.0	2.1	-	-	-	-	54.9	1.7
1976	-	-	-	-	55.0	0.2	-	-	-	-	55.9	1.6	-	-	-	-	56.8	1.6	-	-	-	-	57.5	1.2
1977	-	-	-	-	58.9	2.4	-	-	-	-	60.3	2.4	-	-	-	-	60.8	0.8	-	-	-	-	61.5	1.2
1978	-	-	61.9	0.7	-	-	63.6	2.7	-	-	64.7	1.7	-	-	65.4	1.1	-	-	66.3	1.4	-	-	67.0	1.1
1979	-	-	68.9	2.8	-	-	71.2	3.3	-	-	73.9	3.8	-	-	75.6	2.3	-	-	77.4	2.4	-	-	78.7	1.7
1980	-	-	80.4	2.2	-	-	82.1	2.1	-	-	83.5	1.7	-	-	84.5	1.2	-	-	85.8	1.5	-	-	87.3	1.7
1981	-	-	88.2	1.0	-	-	89.4	1.4	-	-	91.1	1.9	-	-	91.4	0.3	-	-	91.8	0.4	-	-	92.1	0.3
1982	-	-	92.9	0.9	-	-	92.3	-0.6	-	-	94.8	2.7	-	-	96.0	1.3	-	-	97.4	1.5	-	-	97.9	0.5
1983	-	-	98.4	0.5	-	-	99.7	1.3	-	-	100.2	0.5	-	-	101.5	1.3	-	-	102.1	0.6	-	-	102.0	-0.1
1984	-	-	103.2	1.2	-	-	104.1	0.9	-	-	104.7	0.6	-	-	104.8	0.1	-	-	105.8	1.0	-	-	105.6	-0.2
1985	-	-	105.9	0.3	-	-	107.7	1.7	-	-	107.8	0.1	-	-	108.1	0.3	-	-	108.8	0.6	-	-	108.4	-0.4
1986	-	-	108.1	-0.3	-	-	108.0	-0.1	-	-	108.7	0.6	-	-	109.1	0.4	-	-	109.0	-0.1	-	-	109.3	0.3
1987	-	-	-	-	-	-	-	-	-	-	111.5	2.0	-	-	-	-	-	-	-	-	-	-	114.6	2.8
1988	-	-	-	-	-	-	-	-	-	-	116.3	1.5	-	-	-	-	-	-	-	-	-	-	118.4	1.8
1989	-	-	-	-	-	-	-	-	-	-	120.6	1.9	-	-	-	-	-	-	-	-	-	-	122.6	1.7
1990	-	-	-	-	-	-	-	-	-	-	124.3	1.4	-	-	-	-	-	-	-	-	-	-	127.7	2.7
1991	-	-	-	-	-	-	-	-	-	-	130.2	2.0	-	-	-	-	-	-	-	-	-	-	132.3	1.6
1992	-	-	-	-	-	-	-	-	-	-	133.4	0.8	-	-	-	-	-	-	-	-	-	-	135.2	1.3
1993	-	-	-	-	-	-	-	-	-	-	137.5	1.7	-	-	-	-	-	-	-	-	-	-	138.7	0.9
1994	-	-	-	-	-	-	-	-	-	-	140.6	1.4	-	-	-	-	-	-	-	-	-	-	141.9	0.9
1995	-	-	-	-	-	-	-	-	-	-	144.3	1.7	-	-	-	-	-	-	-	-	-	-	146.3	1.4
1996	-	-	-	-	-	-	-	-	-	-	150.6	2.9	-	-	-	-	-	-	-	-	-	-	152.6	1.3
1997	-	-	-	-	-	-	-	-	-	-	155.2	1.7	-	-	-	-	-	-	-	-	-	-	156.4	0.8
1998	-	-	-	-	-	-	-	-	-	-	157.5	0.7	-	-	-	-	-	-	-	-	-	-	158.1	0.4
1999	-	-	-	-	-	-	-	-	-	-	158.5	0.3	-	-	-	-	-	-	-	-	-	-	161.8	2.1
2000	-	-	-	-	-	-	-	-	-	-	165.0	2.0	-	-	-	-	-	-	-	-	-	-	168.2	1.9
2001	-	-	-	-	-	-	-	-	-	-	171.9	2.2	-	-	-	-	-	-	-	-	-	-	-	-

Source: U.S. Department of Labor, Bureau of Labor Statistics, Division of Consumer Prices and Price Indexes. - indicates no data collected for period.

Kansas City, MO-KS
Consumer Price Index - Urban Wage Earners
Base 1982-1984 = 100
All Items

For 1917-2001. Columns headed % show percentile change in the index from the previous period for which an index is available.

Year	Jan Index	%	Feb Index	%	Mar Index	%	Apr Index	%	May Index	%	Jun Index	%	Jul Index	%	Aug Index	%	Sep Index	%	Oct Index	%	Nov Index	%	Dec Index	%
1917	-	-	-	-	-	-	-	-	-	-	-	-	-	-	-	-	-	-	-	-	-	-	15.0	-
1918	-	-	-	-	-	-	-	-	-	-	-	-	-	-	-	-	-	-	-	-	-	-	17.8	18.7
1919	-	-	-	-	-	-	-	-	-	-	18.0	1.1	-	-	-	-	-	-	-	-	-	-	20.7	15.0
1920	-	-	-	-	-	-	-	-	-	-	23.1	11.6	-	-	-	-	-	-	-	-	-	-	21.0	-9.1
1921	-	-	-	-	-	-	-	-	19.4	-7.6	-	-	-	-	-	-	19.0	-2.1	-	-	-	-	18.7	-1.6
1922	-	-	-	-	17.7	-5.3	-	-	-	-	17.7	0.0	-	-	-	-	17.5	-1.1	-	-	-	-	17.6	0.6
1923	-	-	-	-	17.6	0.0	-	-	-	-	17.6	0.0	-	-	-	-	17.8	1.1	-	-	-	-	17.8	0.0
1924	-	-	-	-	17.6	-1.1	-	-	-	-	17.4	-1.1	-	-	-	-	17.4	0.0	-	-	-	-	17.5	0.6
1925	-	-	-	-	-	-	-	-	-	-	17.8	1.7	-	-	-	-	-	-	-	-	-	-	18.0	1.1
1926	-	-	-	-	-	-	-	-	-	-	17.9	-0.6	-	-	-	-	-	-	-	-	-	-	17.6	-1.7
1927	-	-	-	-	-	-	-	-	-	-	17.6	0.0	-	-	-	-	-	-	-	-	-	-	17.0	-3.4
1928	-	-	-	-	-	-	-	-	-	-	17.0	0.0	-	-	-	-	-	-	-	-	-	-	16.9	-0.6
1929	-	-	-	-	-	-	-	-	-	-	16.9	0.0	-	-	-	-	-	-	-	-	-	-	17.0	0.6
1930	-	-	-	-	-	-	-	-	-	-	16.8	-1.2	-	-	-	-	-	-	-	-	-	-	16.3	-3.0
1931	-	-	-	-	-	-	-	-	-	-	15.7	-3.7	-	-	-	-	-	-	-	-	-	-	15.1	-3.8
1932	-	-	-	-	-	-	-	-	-	-	14.0	-7.3	-	-	-	-	-	-	-	-	-	-	13.7	-2.1
1933	-	-	-	-	-	-	-	-	-	-	13.4	-2.2	-	-	-	-	-	-	-	-	-	-	13.5	0.7
1934	-	-	-	-	-	-	-	-	-	-	13.8	2.2	-	-	-	-	-	-	-	-	14.0	1.4	-	-
1935	-	-	-	-	14.1	0.7	-	-	-	-	-	-	14.0	-0.7	-	-	-	-	14.1	0.7	-	-	-	-
1936	14.3	1.4	-	-	-	-	14.1	-1.4	-	-	-	-	14.3	1.4	-	-	14.5	1.4	-	-	-	-	14.4	-0.7
1937	-	-	-	-	14.7	2.1	-	-	-	-	14.9	1.4	-	-	-	-	15.0	0.7	-	-	-	-	14.8	-1.3
1938	-	-	-	-	14.6	-1.4	-	-	-	-	14.5	-0.7	-	-	-	-	14.5	0.0	-	-	-	-	14.4	-0.7
1939	-	-	-	-	14.3	-0.7	-	-	-	-	14.3	0.0	-	-	-	-	14.5	1.4	-	-	-	-	14.3	-1.4
1940	-	-	-	-	14.2	-0.7	-	-	-	-	14.2	0.0	-	-	-	-	14.1	-0.7	14.1	0.0	14.2	0.7	14.2	0.0
1941	14.2	0.0	14.2	0.0	14.3	0.7	14.5	1.4	14.5	0.0	14.7	1.4	14.7	0.0	14.9	1.4	15.3	2.7	15.5	1.3	15.6	0.6	15.7	0.6
1942	15.8	0.6	16.0	1.3	16.3	1.9	16.4	0.6	16.5	0.6	16.5	0.0	16.5	0.0	16.6	0.6	16.6	0.0	16.8	1.2	16.9	0.6	17.0	0.6
1943	17.0	0.0	17.2	1.2	17.4	1.2	17.6	1.1	17.7	0.6	17.6	-0.6	17.4	-1.1	17.4	0.0	17.5	0.6	17.6	0.6	17.6	0.0	17.7	0.6
1944	17.6	-0.6	17.6	0.0	17.6	0.0	17.8	1.1	17.8	0.0	17.8	0.0	18.0	1.1	17.9	-0.6	18.0	0.6	17.9	-0.6	18.0	0.6	18.0	0.0
1945	18.1	0.6	18.1	0.0	18.1	0.0	18.2	0.6	18.3	0.5	18.4	0.5	18.4	0.0	18.5	0.5	18.4	-0.5	18.4	0.0	18.4	0.0	18.5	0.5
1946	18.5	0.0	18.4	-0.5	18.5	0.5	18.6	0.5	18.6	0.0	18.7	0.5	19.7	5.3	20.3	3.0	20.4	0.5	20.5	0.5	21.3	3.9	21.3	0.0
1947	21.4	0.5	21.5	0.5	21.8	1.4	21.8	0.0	21.8	0.0	21.6	-0.9	21.8	0.9	-	-	-	-	22.9	5.0	-	-	-	-
1948	23.5	2.6	-	-	-	-	23.7	0.9	-	-	-	-	24.1	1.7	-	-	-	-	24.3	0.8	-	-	-	-
1949	24.0	-1.2	-	-	-	-	23.8	-0.8	-	-	-	-	23.6	-0.8	-	-	-	-	23.5	-0.4	-	-	-	-
1950	23.4	-0.4	-	-	-	-	23.6	0.9	-	-	-	-	24.1	2.1	-	-	-	-	24.4	1.2	-	-	-	-
1951	25.4	4.1	-	-	-	-	25.8	1.6	-	-	-	-	25.9	0.4	-	-	-	-	26.0	0.4	-	-	-	-
1952	26.3	1.2	-	-	-	-	26.5	0.8	-	-	-	-	26.8	1.1	-	-	-	-	26.8	0.0	-	-	-	-
1953	26.6	-0.7	-	-	-	-	26.6	0.0	-	-	-	-	26.8	0.8	-	-	-	-	26.9	0.4	-	-	-	-
1954	26.7	-0.7	-	-	-	-	26.9	0.7	-	-	-	-	26.9	0.0	-	-	-	-	26.9	0.0	-	-	-	-
1955	26.8	-0.4	-	-	-	-	26.8	0.0	-	-	-	-	26.9	0.4	-	-	-	-	27.0	0.4	-	-	-	-
1956	26.9	-0.4	-	-	-	-	27.1	0.7	-	-	-	-	27.3	0.7	-	-	-	-	27.6	1.1	-	-	-	-
1957	27.8	0.7	-	-	-	-	28.0	0.7	-	-	-	-	28.3	1.1	-	-	-	-	28.3	0.0	-	-	-	-
1958	28.4	0.4	-	-	-	-	28.7	1.1	-	-	-	-	29.0	1.0	-	-	-	-	29.0	0.0	-	-	-	-
1959	28.9	-0.3	-	-	-	-	29.2	1.0	-	-	-	-	29.3	0.3	-	-	-	-	29.5	0.7	-	-	-	-
1960	29.5	0.0	-	-	-	-	29.4	-0.3	-	-	-	-	29.7	1.0	-	-	-	-	29.8	0.3	-	-	-	-
1961	29.7	-0.3	-	-	-	-	30.1	1.3	-	-	-	-	30.2	0.3	-	-	-	-	30.1	-0.3	-	-	-	-
1962	30.2	0.3	-	-	-	-	30.4	0.7	-	-	-	-	30.5	0.3	-	-	-	-	30.8	1.0	-	-	-	-

[Continued]

Kansas City, MO-KS
Consumer Price Index - Urban Wage Earners
Base 1982-1984 = 100
All Items
[Continued]

For 1917-2001. Columns headed % show percentile change in the index from the previous period for which an index is available.

Year	Jan Index	%	Feb Index	%	Mar Index	%	Apr Index	%	May Index	%	Jun Index	%	Jul Index	%	Aug Index	%	Sep Index	%	Oct Index	%	Nov Index	%	Dec Index	%
1963	30.4	-1.3	-	-	-	-	30.6	0.7	-	-	-	-	30.8	0.7	-	-	-	-	31.3	1.6	-	-	-	-
1964	31.2	-0.3	-	-	-	-	31.3	0.3	-	-	-	-	31.7	1.3	-	-	-	-	31.8	0.3	-	-	-	-
1965	32.0	0.6	-	-	-	-	32.2	0.6	-	-	32.8	1.9	-	-	-	-	32.9	0.3	-	-	-	-	32.9	0.0
1966	-	-	-	-	33.1	0.6	-	-	-	-	33.5	1.2	-	-	-	-	33.7	0.6	-	-	-	-	33.7	0.0
1967	-	-	-	-	33.9	0.6	-	-	-	-	33.8	-0.3	-	-	-	-	34.5	2.1	-	-	-	-	34.6	0.3
1968	-	-	-	-	35.0	1.2	-	-	-	-	35.7	2.0	-	-	-	-	35.8	0.3	-	-	-	-	36.1	0.8
1969	-	-	-	-	36.8	1.9	-	-	-	-	37.5	1.9	-	-	-	-	37.8	0.8	-	-	-	-	38.3	1.3
1970	-	-	-	-	38.7	1.0	-	-	-	-	39.7	2.6	-	-	-	-	39.8	0.3	-	-	-	-	40.6	2.0
1971	-	-	-	-	40.7	0.2	-	-	-	-	41.2	1.2	-	-	-	-	41.5	0.7	-	-	-	-	41.4	-0.2
1972	-	-	-	-	41.8	1.0	-	-	-	-	42.3	1.2	-	-	-	-	42.8	1.2	-	-	-	-	42.8	0.0
1973	-	-	-	-	43.5	1.6	-	-	-	-	44.3	1.8	-	-	-	-	45.2	2.0	-	-	-	-	45.9	1.5
1974	-	-	-	-	47.3	3.1	-	-	-	-	48.9	3.4	-	-	-	-	50.5	3.3	-	-	-	-	52.1	3.2
1975	-	-	-	-	52.8	1.3	-	-	-	-	53.7	1.7	-	-	-	-	54.7	1.9	-	-	-	-	55.6	1.6
1976	-	-	-	-	55.8	0.4	-	-	-	-	56.6	1.4	-	-	-	-	57.6	1.8	-	-	-	-	58.3	1.2
1977	-	-	-	-	59.7	2.4	-	-	-	-	61.1	2.3	-	-	-	-	61.6	0.8	-	-	-	-	62.4	1.3
1978	-	-	62.9	0.8	-	-	64.4	2.4	-	-	65.6	1.9	-	-	66.3	1.1	-	-	67.3	1.5	-	-	67.9	0.9
1979	-	-	69.7	2.7	-	-	72.0	3.3	-	-	74.5	3.5	-	-	76.1	2.1	-	-	77.8	2.2	-	-	79.3	1.9
1980	-	-	80.8	1.9	-	-	82.7	2.4	-	-	84.1	1.7	-	-	85.1	1.2	-	-	86.3	1.4	-	-	87.8	1.7
1981	-	-	88.8	1.1	-	-	90.2	1.6	-	-	91.8	1.8	-	-	92.2	0.4	-	-	92.6	0.4	-	-	92.8	0.2
1982	-	-	93.5	0.8	-	-	92.9	-0.6	-	-	95.6	2.9	-	-	96.8	1.3	-	-	98.1	1.3	-	-	98.5	0.4
1983	-	-	98.6	0.1	-	-	100.2	1.6	-	-	101.8	1.6	-	-	102.2	0.4	-	-	103.7	1.5	-	-	102.4	-1.3
1984	-	-	101.2	-1.2	-	-	102.3	1.1	-	-	102.4	0.1	-	-	103.9	1.5	-	-	105.0	1.1	-	-	103.8	-1.1
1985	-	-	103.9	0.1	-	-	105.7	1.7	-	-	106.0	0.3	-	-	106.2	0.2	-	-	106.8	0.6	-	-	106.4	-0.4
1986	-	-	105.8	-0.6	-	-	105.4	-0.4	-	-	106.3	0.9	-	-	106.5	0.2	-	-	106.2	-0.3	-	-	106.6	0.4
1987	-	-	-	-	-	-	-	-	-	-	108.6	1.9	-	-	-	-	-	-	-	-	-	-	111.7	2.9
1988	-	-	-	-	-	-	-	-	-	-	113.3	1.4	-	-	-	-	-	-	-	-	-	-	115.5	1.9
1989	-	-	-	-	-	-	-	-	-	-	117.6	1.8	-	-	-	-	-	-	-	-	-	-	119.4	1.5
1990	-	-	-	-	-	-	-	-	-	-	120.8	1.2	-	-	-	-	-	-	-	-	-	-	124.0	2.6
1991	-	-	-	-	-	-	-	-	-	-	126.2	1.8	-	-	-	-	-	-	-	-	-	-	128.5	1.8
1992	-	-	-	-	-	-	-	-	-	-	129.4	0.7	-	-	-	-	-	-	-	-	-	-	131.4	1.5
1993	-	-	-	-	-	-	-	-	-	-	133.5	1.6	-	-	-	-	-	-	-	-	-	-	135.0	1.1
1994	-	-	-	-	-	-	-	-	-	-	136.9	1.4	-	-	-	-	-	-	-	-	-	-	138.1	0.9
1995	-	-	-	-	-	-	-	-	-	-	140.9	2.0	-	-	-	-	-	-	-	-	-	-	142.6	1.2
1996	-	-	-	-	-	-	-	-	-	-	146.8	2.9	-	-	-	-	-	-	-	-	-	-	148.7	1.3
1997	-	-	-	-	-	-	-	-	-	-	151.0	1.5	-	-	-	-	-	-	-	-	-	-	151.9	0.6
1998	-	-	-	-	-	-	-	-	-	-	152.7	0.5	-	-	-	-	-	-	-	-	-	-	153.1	0.3
1999	-	-	-	-	-	-	-	-	-	-	153.2	0.1	-	-	-	-	-	-	-	-	-	-	156.5	2.2
2000	-	-	-	-	-	-	-	-	-	-	159.5	1.9	-	-	-	-	-	-	-	-	-	-	162.4	1.8
2001	-	-	-	-	-	-	-	-	-	-	165.9	2.2	-	-	-	-	-	-	-	-	-	-	-	-

Source: U.S. Department of Labor, Bureau of Labor Statistics, Division of Consumer Prices and Price Indexes. - indicates no data collected for period.

Kansas City, MO-KS
Consumer Price Index - All Urban Consumers
Base 1982-1984 = 100
Food and Beverages

For 1975-2001. Columns headed % show percentile change in the index from the previous period for which an index is available.

Year	Jan Index	%	Feb Index	%	Mar Index	%	Apr Index	%	May Index	%	Jun Index	%	Jul Index	%	Aug Index	%	Sep Index	%	Oct Index	%	Nov Index	%	Dec Index	%
1975	-	-	-	-	-	-	-	-	-	-	-	-	-	-	-	-	-	-	-	-	-	-	63.9	-
1976	-	-	-	-	62.7	-1.9	-	-	-	-	62.2	-0.8	-	-	-	-	63.4	1.9	-	-	-	-	63.2	-0.3
1977	-	-	-	-	65.6	3.8	-	-	-	-	67.7	3.2	-	-	-	-	68.0	0.4	-	-	-	-	68.5	0.7
1978	-	-	70.5	2.9	-	-	72.7	3.1	-	-	75.6	4.0	-	-	76.1	0.7	-	-	76.9	1.1	-	-	78.1	1.6
1979	-	-	81.3	4.1	-	-	82.3	1.2	-	-	82.6	0.4	-	-	83.1	0.6	-	-	83.3	0.2	-	-	84.9	1.9
1980	-	-	86.5	1.9	-	-	88.3	2.1	-	-	89.2	1.0	-	-	90.4	1.3	-	-	91.8	1.5	-	-	93.4	1.7
1981	-	-	95.0	1.7	-	-	95.5	0.5	-	-	93.5	-2.1	-	-	95.0	1.6	-	-	95.5	0.5	-	-	95.9	0.4
1982	-	-	96.9	1.0	-	-	96.2	-0.7	-	-	98.4	2.3	-	-	98.3	-0.1	-	-	98.1	-0.2	-	-	97.9	-0.2
1983	-	-	98.6	0.7	-	-	98.8	0.2	-	-	99.6	0.8	-	-	99.1	-0.5	-	-	99.8	0.7	-	-	99.6	-0.2
1984	-	-	102.6	3.0	-	-	103.2	0.6	-	-	102.6	-0.6	-	-	103.5	0.9	-	-	104.6	1.1	-	-	104.5	-0.1
1985	-	-	105.8	1.2	-	-	106.5	0.7	-	-	106.1	-0.4	-	-	105.7	-0.4	-	-	105.8	0.1	-	-	106.7	0.9
1986	-	-	107.9	1.1	-	-	108.6	0.6	-	-	109.0	0.4	-	-	110.8	1.7	-	-	110.7	-0.1	-	-	111.1	0.4
1987	-	-	-	-	-	-	-	-	-	-	112.7	1.4	-	-	-	-	-	-	-	-	-	-	112.9	0.2
1988	-	-	-	-	-	-	-	-	-	-	114.7	1.6	-	-	-	-	-	-	-	-	-	-	116.9	1.9
1989	-	-	-	-	-	-	-	-	-	-	118.8	1.6	-	-	-	-	-	-	-	-	-	-	120.9	1.8
1990	-	-	-	-	-	-	-	-	-	-	127.0	5.0	-	-	-	-	-	-	-	-	-	-	127.9	0.7
1991	-	-	-	-	-	-	-	-	-	-	131.1	2.5	-	-	-	-	-	-	-	-	-	-	130.8	-0.2
1992	-	-	-	-	-	-	-	-	-	-	130.7	-0.1	-	-	-	-	-	-	-	-	-	-	135.1	3.4
1993	-	-	-	-	-	-	-	-	-	-	137.4	1.7	-	-	-	-	-	-	-	-	-	-	138.1	0.5
1994	-	-	-	-	-	-	-	-	-	-	138.8	0.5	-	-	-	-	-	-	-	-	-	-	141.6	2.0
1995	-	-	-	-	-	-	-	-	-	-	142.8	0.8	-	-	-	-	-	-	-	-	-	-	146.5	2.6
1996	-	-	-	-	-	-	-	-	-	-	151.7	3.5	-	-	-	-	-	-	-	-	-	-	156.6	3.2
1997	-	-	-	-	-	-	-	-	-	-	158.8	1.4	-	-	-	-	-	-	-	-	-	-	161.2	1.5
1998	-	-	-	-	-	-	-	-	-	-	158.9	-1.4	-	-	-	-	-	-	-	-	-	-	160.5	1.0
1999	-	-	-	-	-	-	-	-	-	-	159.0	-0.9	-	-	-	-	-	-	-	-	-	-	163.0	2.5
2000	-	-	-	-	-	-	-	-	-	-	162.9	-0.1	-	-	-	-	-	-	-	-	-	-	167.0	2.5
2001	-	-	-	-	-	-	-	-	-	-	170.6	2.2	-	-	-	-	-	-	-	-	-	-	-	-

Source: U.S. Department of Labor, Bureau of Labor Statistics, Division of Consumer Prices and Price Indexes. - indicates no data collected for period.

Kansas City, MO-KS
Consumer Price Index - Urban Wage Earners
Base 1982-1984 = 100
Food and Beverages

For 1975-2001. Columns headed % show percentile change in the index from the previous period for which an index is available.

Year	Jan		Feb		Mar		Apr		May		Jun		Jul		Aug		Sep		Oct		Nov		Dec	
	Index	%	Index	%	Index	%	Index	%	Index	%	Index	%	Index	%	Index	%	Index	%	Index	%	Index	%	Index	%
1975	-	-	-	-	-	-	-	-	-	-	-	-	-	-	-	-	-	-	-	-	-	-	64.7	-
1976	-	-	-	-	63.4	-2.0	-	-	-	-	63.0	-0.6	-	-	-	-	64.2	1.9	-	-	-	-	63.9	-0.5
1977	-	-	-	-	66.4	3.9	-	-	-	-	68.6	3.3	-	-	-	-	68.8	0.3	-	-	-	-	69.3	0.7
1978	-	-	71.0	2.5	-	-	73.0	2.8	-	-	76.1	4.2	-	-	76.5	0.5	-	-	77.2	0.9	-	-	78.6	1.8
1979	-	-	81.0	3.1	-	-	81.8	1.0	-	-	81.9	0.1	-	-	82.2	0.4	-	-	82.4	0.2	-	-	83.9	1.8
1980	-	-	85.7	2.1	-	-	87.4	2.0	-	-	88.3	1.0	-	-	90.0	1.9	-	-	91.9	2.1	-	-	93.3	1.5
1981	-	-	94.2	1.0	-	-	94.8	0.6	-	-	93.6	-1.3	-	-	94.9	1.4	-	-	95.9	1.1	-	-	95.9	0.0
1982	-	-	96.8	0.9	-	-	96.1	-0.7	-	-	98.4	2.4	-	-	98.5	0.1	-	-	98.1	-0.4	-	-	97.9	-0.2
1983	-	-	98.8	0.9	-	-	99.0	0.2	-	-	99.6	0.6	-	-	99.3	-0.3	-	-	99.8	0.5	-	-	97.9	-0.2
1983	-	-	98.8	0.9	-	-	99.0	0.2	-	-	99.6	0.6	-	-	99.3	-0.3	-	-	99.8	0.5	-	-	99.6	-0.2
1984	-	-	102.5	2.9	-	-	103.1	0.6	-	-	102.5	-0.6	-	-	103.4	0.9	-	-	104.5	1.1	-	-	104.3	-0.2
1985	-	-	105.4	1.1	-	-	106.2	0.8	-	-	105.9	-0.3	-	-	105.6	-0.3	-	-	105.6	0.0	-	-	106.6	0.9
1986	-	-	107.9	1.2	-	-	108.5	0.6	-	-	108.7	0.2	-	-	110.7	1.8	-	-	110.7	0.0	-	-	111.1	0.4
1987	-	-	-	-	-	-	-	-	-	-	112.5	1.3	-	-	-	-	-	-	-	-	-	-	112.9	0.4
1988	-	-	-	-	-	-	-	-	-	-	114.7	1.6	-	-	-	-	-	-	-	-	-	-	116.9	1.9
1989	-	-	-	-	-	-	-	-	-	-	118.8	1.6	-	-	-	-	-	-	-	-	-	-	120.9	1.8
1990	-	-	-	-	-	-	-	-	-	-	126.9	5.0	-	-	-	-	-	-	-	-	-	-	127.9	0.8
1991	-	-	-	-	-	-	-	-	-	-	131.0	2.4	-	-	-	-	-	-	-	-	-	-	131.0	0.0
1992	-	-	-	-	-	-	-	-	-	-	130.4	-0.5	-	-	-	-	-	-	-	-	-	-	135.1	3.6
1993	-	-	-	-	-	-	-	-	-	-	137.3	1.6	-	-	-	-	-	-	-	-	-	-	138.2	0.7
1994	-	-	-	-	-	-	-	-	-	-	138.7	0.4	-	-	-	-	-	-	-	-	-	-	141.6	2.1
1995	-	-	-	-	-	-	-	-	-	-	142.7	0.8	-	-	-	-	-	-	-	-	-	-	146.5	2.7
1996	-	-	-	-	-	-	-	-	-	-	151.8	3.6	-	-	-	-	-	-	-	-	-	-	156.6	3.2
1997	-	-	-	-	-	-	-	-	-	-	158.9	1.5	-	-	-	-	-	-	-	-	-	-	161.3	1.5
1998	-	-	-	-	-	-	-	-	-	-	158.9	-1.5	-	-	-	-	-	-	-	-	-	-	160.6	1.1
1999	-	-	-	-	-	-	-	-	-	-	159.1	-0.9	-	-	-	-	-	-	-	-	-	-	163.0	2.5
2000	-	-	-	-	-	-	-	-	-	-	163.0	0.0	-	-	-	-	-	-	-	-	-	-	167.0	2.5
2001	-	-	-	-	-	-	-	-	-	-	170.7	2.2	-	-	-	-	-	-	-	-	-	-	-	-

Source: U.S. Department of Labor, Bureau of Labor Statistics, Division of Consumer Prices and Price Indexes. - indicates no data collected for period.

Kansas City, MO-KS
Consumer Price Index - All Urban Consumers
Base 1982-1984 = 100
Housing

For 1975-2001. Columns headed % show percentile change in the index from the previous period for which an index is available.

Year	Jan Index	%	Feb Index	%	Mar Index	%	Apr Index	%	May Index	%	Jun Index	%	Jul Index	%	Aug Index	%	Sep Index	%	Oct Index	%	Nov Index	%	Dec Index	%
1975	-	-	-	-	-	-	-	-	-	-	-	-	-	-	-	-	-	-	-	-	-	-	51.2	-
1976	-	-	-	-	51.6	0.8	-	-	-	-	52.5	1.7	-	-	-	-	53.4	1.7	-	-	-	-	54.4	1.9
1977	-	-	-	-	55.3	1.7	-	-	-	-	56.6	2.4	-	-	-	-	57.5	1.6	-	-	-	-	58.4	1.6
1978	-	-	58.8	0.7	-	-	60.9	3.6	-	-	61.7	1.3	-	-	62.2	0.8	-	-	63.0	1.3	-	-	63.2	0.3
1979	-	-	65.3	3.3	-	-	68.5	4.9	-	-	72.2	5.4	-	-	74.4	3.0	-	-	77.3	3.9	-	-	78.6	1.7
1980	-	-	79.3	0.9	-	-	80.6	1.6	-	-	83.0	3.0	-	-	83.8	1.0	-	-	85.2	1.7	-	-	86.6	1.6
1981	-	-	86.3	-0.3	-	-	88.0	2.0	-	-	91.5	4.0	-	-	91.0	-0.5	-	-	90.5	-0.5	-	-	90.5	0.0
1982	-	-	91.6	1.2	-	-	89.9	-1.9	-	-	93.1	3.6	-	-	94.5	1.5	-	-	97.1	2.8	-	-	98.4	1.3
1983	-	-	99.6	1.2	-	-	100.7	1.1	-	-	100.7	0.0	-	-	102.9	2.2	-	-	101.9	-1.0	-	-	102.2	0.3
1984	-	-	103.3	1.1	-	-	104.3	1.0	-	-	106.0	1.6	-	-	106.1	0.1	-	-	105.7	-0.4	-	-	105.8	0.1
1985	-	-	106.1	0.3	-	-	107.3	1.1	-	-	108.1	0.7	-	-	108.6	0.5	-	-	108.7	0.1	-	-	107.1	-1.5
1986	-	-	108.0	0.8	-	-	109.3	1.2	-	-	109.2	-0.1	-	-	111.3	1.9	-	-	109.5	-1.6	-	-	110.3	0.7
1987	-	-	-	-	-	-	-	-	-	-	112.2	1.7	-	-	-	-	-	-	-	-	-	-	114.9	2.4
1988	-	-	-	-	-	-	-	-	-	-	117.9	2.6	-	-	-	-	-	-	-	-	-	-	118.7	0.7
1989	-	-	-	-	-	-	-	-	-	-	119.6	0.8	-	-	-	-	-	-	-	-	-	-	119.7	0.1
1990	-	-	-	-	-	-	-	-	-	-	121.3	1.3	-	-	-	-	-	-	-	-	-	-	122.4	0.9
1991	-	-	-	-	-	-	-	-	-	-	124.5	1.7	-	-	-	-	-	-	-	-	-	-	126.3	1.4
1992	-	-	-	-	-	-	-	-	-	-	126.8	0.4	-	-	-	-	-	-	-	-	-	-	127.6	0.6
1993	-	-	-	-	-	-	-	-	-	-	129.3	1.3	-	-	-	-	-	-	-	-	-	-	131.6	1.8
1994	-	-	-	-	-	-	-	-	-	-	132.4	0.6	-	-	-	-	-	-	-	-	-	-	133.8	1.1
1995	-	-	-	-	-	-	-	-	-	-	135.0	0.9	-	-	-	-	-	-	-	-	-	-	138.3	2.4
1996	-	-	-	-	-	-	-	-	-	-	141.3	2.2	-	-	-	-	-	-	-	-	-	-	143.5	1.6
1997	-	-	-	-	-	-	-	-	-	-	145.1	1.1	-	-	-	-	-	-	-	-	-	-	147.2	1.4
1998	-	-	-	-	-	-	-	-	-	-	151.3	2.8	-	-	-	-	-	-	-	-	-	-	152.3	0.7
1999	-	-	-	-	-	-	-	-	-	-	153.6	0.9	-	-	-	-	-	-	-	-	-	-	155.7	1.4
2000	-	-	-	-	-	-	-	-	-	-	159.3	2.3	-	-	-	-	-	-	-	-	-	-	163.8	2.8
2001	-	-	-	-	-	-	-	-	-	-	168.4	2.8	-	-	-	-	-	-	-	-	-	-	-	-

Source: U.S. Department of Labor, Bureau of Labor Statistics, Division of Consumer Prices and Price Indexes. - indicates no data collected for period.

Kansas City, MO-KS
Consumer Price Index - Urban Wage Earners
Base 1982-1984 = 100
Housing

For 1975-2001. Columns headed % show percentile change in the index from the previous period for which an index is available.

Year	Jan Index	%	Feb Index	%	Mar Index	%	Apr Index	%	May Index	%	Jun Index	%	Jul Index	%	Aug Index	%	Sep Index	%	Oct Index	%	Nov Index	%	Dec Index	%
1975	-	-	-	-	-	-	-	-	-	-	-	-	-	-	-	-	-	-	-	-	-	-	52.2	-
1976	-	-	-	-	52.7	1.0	-	-	-	-	53.6	1.7	-	-	-	-	54.5	1.7	-	-	-	-	55.5	1.8
1977	-	-	-	-	56.4	1.6	-	-	-	-	57.8	2.5	-	-	-	-	58.7	1.6	-	-	-	-	59.6	1.5
1978	-	-	60.2	1.0	-	-	62.3	3.5	-	-	63.1	1.3	-	-	63.6	0.8	-	-	64.5	1.4	-	-	64.7	0.3
1979	-	-	66.8	3.2	-	-	69.8	4.5	-	-	73.4	5.2	-	-	75.4	2.7	-	-	78.1	3.6	-	-	64.7	0.3
1980	-	-	79.5	-0.1	-	-	81.1	2.0	-	-	83.8	3.3	-	-	84.6	1.0	-	-	85.8	1.4	-	-	87.3	1.7
1981	-	-	87.0	-0.3	-	-	88.8	2.1	-	-	92.2	3.8	-	-	91.9	-0.3	-	-	91.4	-0.5	-	-	91.4	0.0
1982	-	-	92.5	1.2	-	-	90.8	-1.8	-	-	94.2	3.7	-	-	95.7	1.6	-	-	98.2	2.6	-	-	99.8	1.6
1983	-	-	100.0	0.2	-	-	101.9	1.9	-	-	104.5	2.6	-	-	104.2	-0.3	-	-	106.0	1.7	-	-	103.4	-2.5
1984	-	-	99.3	-4.0	-	-	100.7	1.4	-	-	100.9	0.2	-	-	104.3	3.4	-	-	104.4	0.1	-	-	101.9	-2.4
1985	-	-	102.1	0.2	-	-	103.2	1.1	-	-	104.1	0.9	-	-	104.6	0.5	-	-	104.6	0.0	-	-	103.0	-1.5
1986	-	-	104.0	1.0	-	-	105.0	1.0	-	-	104.9	-0.1	-	-	107.1	2.1	-	-	105.1	-1.9	-	-	106.0	0.9
1987	-	-	-	-	-	-	-	-	-	-	107.8	1.7	-	-	-	-	-	-	-	-	-	-	110.3	2.3
1988	-	-	-	-	-	-	-	-	-	-	113.0	2.4	-	-	-	-	-	-	-	-	-	-	113.8	0.7
1989	-	-	-	-	-	-	-	-	-	-	114.8	0.9	-	-	-	-	-	-	-	-	-	-	114.8	0.0
1990	-	-	-	-	-	-	-	-	-	-	116.5	1.5	-	-	-	-	-	-	-	-	-	-	117.5	0.9
1991	-	-	-	-	-	-	-	-	-	-	119.4	1.6	-	-	-	-	-	-	-	-	-	-	121.0	1.3
1992	-	-	-	-	-	-	-	-	-	-	121.5	0.4	-	-	-	-	-	-	-	-	-	-	122.3	0.7
1993	-	-	-	-	-	-	-	-	-	-	123.9	1.3	-	-	-	-	-	-	-	-	-	-	126.3	1.9
1994	-	-	-	-	-	-	-	-	-	-	127.1	0.6	-	-	-	-	-	-	-	-	-	-	128.3	0.9
1995	-	-	-	-	-	-	-	-	-	-	129.5	0.9	-	-	-	-	-	-	-	-	-	-	132.6	2.4
1996	-	-	-	-	-	-	-	-	-	-	135.3	2.0	-	-	-	-	-	-	-	-	-	-	137.5	1.6
1997	-	-	-	-	-	-	-	-	-	-	138.9	1.0	-	-	-	-	-	-	-	-	-	-	140.9	1.4
1998	-	-	-	-	-	-	-	-	-	-	145.2	3.1	-	-	-	-	-	-	-	-	-	-	144.9	-0.2
1999	-	-	-	-	-	-	-	-	-	-	146.0	0.8	-	-	-	-	-	-	-	-	-	-	147.8	1.2
2000	-	-	-	-	-	-	-	-	-	-	151.0	2.2	-	-	-	-	-	-	-	-	-	-	155.0	2.6
2001	-	-	-	-	-	-	-	-	-	-	159.6	3.0	-	-	-	-	-	-	-	-	-	-	-	-

Source: U.S. Department of Labor, Bureau of Labor Statistics, Division of Consumer Prices and Price Indexes. - indicates no data collected for period.

Kansas City, MO-KS

Consumer Price Index - All Urban Consumers
Base 1982-1984 = 100
Apparel

For 1952-2001. Columns headed % show percentile change in the index from the previous period for which an index is available.

Year	Jan Index	%	Feb Index	%	Mar Index	%	Apr Index	%	May Index	%	Jun Index	%	Jul Index	%	Aug Index	%	Sep Index	%	Oct Index	%	Nov Index	%	Dec Index	%
1952	-		-		-		-		-		-		-		-		-		39.3		-		-	
1953	39.2	-0.3	-		-		39.2	0.0	-		-		39.4	0.5	-		-		39.3	-0.3	-		-	
1954	39.0	-0.8	-		-		38.8	-0.5	-		-		38.8	0.0	-		-		39.1	0.8	-		-	
1955	38.5	-1.5	-		-		38.6	0.3	-		-		38.6	0.0	-		-		39.4	2.1	-		-	
1956	39.1	-0.8	-		-		39.1	0.0	-		-		39.2	0.3	-		-		39.7	1.3	-		-	
1957	40.5	2.0	-		-		40.2	-0.7	-		-		39.9	-0.7	-		-		40.6	1.8	-		-	
1958	40.0	-1.5	-		-		40.4	1.0	-		-		40.2	-0.5	-		-		40.8	1.5	-		-	
1959	40.3	-1.2	-		-		40.5	0.5	-		-		40.5	0.0	-		-		41.4	2.2	-		-	
1960	40.8	-1.4	-		-		41.6	2.0	-		-		42.0	1.0	-		-		42.2	0.5	-		-	
1961	41.6	-1.4	-		-		41.9	0.7	-		-		42.1	0.5	-		-		42.5	1.0	-		-	
1962	41.9	-1.4	-		-		41.8	-0.2	-		-		41.4	-1.0	-		-		43.0	3.9	-		-	
1963	41.8	-2.8	-		-		42.2	1.0	-		-		42.1	-0.2	-		-		43.8	4.0	-		-	
1964	43.1	-1.6	-		-		43.3	0.5	-		-		43.3	0.0	-		-		44.4	2.5	-		-	
1965	43.6	-1.8	-		-		43.6	0.0	-		44.4	1.8	-		-		45.3	2.0	-		-		45.4	0.2
1966	-		-		45.0	-0.9	-		-		45.8	1.8	-		-		46.0	0.4	-		-		46.0	0.0
1967	-		-		46.3	0.7	-		-		46.7	0.9	-		-		48.6	4.1	-		-		48.6	0.0
1968	-		-		49.3	1.4	-		-		50.4	2.2	-		-		52.4	4.0	-		-		52.6	0.4
1969	-		-		53.1	1.0	-		-		54.2	2.1	-		-		55.6	2.6	-		-		55.8	0.4
1970	-		-		56.4	1.1	-		-		57.0	1.1	-		-		58.3	2.3	-		-		58.7	0.7
1971	-		-		58.6	-0.2	-		-		58.3	-0.5	-		-		59.8	2.6	-		-		58.9	-1.5
1972	-		-		59.7	1.4	-		-		59.9	0.3	-		-		61.5	2.7	-		-		61.1	-0.7
1973	-		-		61.2	0.2	-		-		61.6	0.7	-		-		62.6	1.6	-		-		62.3	-0.5
1974	-		-		63.6	2.1	-		-		64.9	2.0	-		-		68.2	5.1	-		-		68.3	0.1
1975	-		-		69.5	1.8	-		-		68.5	-1.4	-		-		69.5	1.5	-		-		68.3	-1.7
1976	-		-		69.5	1.8	-		-		71.0	2.2	-		-		73.2	3.1	-		-		73.0	-0.3
1977	-		-		75.9	4.0	-		-		76.3	0.5	-		-		78.8	3.3	-		-		79.0	0.3
1978	-		75.6	-4.3	-		79.2	4.8	-		78.1	-1.4	-		80.3	2.8	-		80.2	-0.1	-		81.0	1.0
1979	-		84.0	3.7	-		83.2	-1.0	-		83.1	-0.1	-		86.4	4.0	-		86.6	0.2	-		83.1	-4.0
1980	-		84.5	1.7	-		87.5	3.6	-		85.7	-2.1	-		87.9	2.6	-		91.1	3.6	-		91.1	0.0
1981	-		91.8	0.8	-		91.7	-0.1	-		91.1	-0.7	-		93.5	2.6	-		95.3	1.9	-		90.2	-5.4
1982	-		92.6	2.7	-		96.3	4.0	-		95.3	-1.0	-		97.8	2.6	-		96.1	-1.7	-		97.6	1.6
1983	-		98.6	1.0	-		102.6	4.1	-		101.3	-1.3	-		101.4	0.1	-		105.6	4.1	-		102.6	-2.8
1984	-		102.8	0.2	-		104.2	1.4	-		100.2	-3.8	-		101.9	1.7	-		104.0	2.1	-		102.0	-1.9
1985	-		104.8	2.7	-		108.1	3.1	-		102.8	-4.9	-		104.1	1.3	-		106.5	2.3	-		104.0	-2.3
1986	-		108.7	4.5	-		111.0	2.1	-		107.9	-2.8	-		106.2	-1.6	-		106.0	-0.2	-		101.4	-4.3
1987	-		-		-		-		-		104.8	3.4	-		-		-		-		-		114.6	9.4
1988	-		-		-		-		-		111.3	-2.9	-		-		-		-		-		115.0	3.3
1989	-		-		-		-		-		114.2	-0.7	-		-		-		-		-		125.1	9.5
1990	-		-		-		-		-		113.8	-9.0	-		-		-		-		-		119.3	4.8
1991	-		-		-		-		-		121.0	1.4	-		-		-		-		-		128.4	6.1
1992	-		-		-		-		-		125.3	-2.4	-		-		-		-		-		124.2	-0.9
1993	-		-		-		-		-		126.2	1.6	-		-		-		-		-		124.5	-1.3
1994	-		-		-		-		-		129.4	3.9	-		-		-		-		-		117.1	-9.5
1995	-		-		-		-		-		128.1	9.4	-		-		-		-		-		123.6	-3.5
1996	-		-		-		-		-		134.3	8.7	-		-		-		-		-		124.8	-7.1
1997	-		-		-		-		-		135.1	8.3	-		-		-		-		-		131.8	-2.4

[Continued]

Kansas City, MO-KS
Consumer Price Index - All Urban Consumers
Base 1982-1984 = 100
Apparel
[Continued]

For 1952-2001. Columns headed % show percentile change in the index from the previous period for which an index is available.

Year	Jan Index	%	Feb Index	%	Mar Index	%	Apr Index	%	May Index	%	Jun Index	%	Jul Index	%	Aug Index	%	Sep Index	%	Oct Index	%	Nov Index	%	Dec Index	%
1998	-	-	-	-	-	-	-	-	-	-	130.7	-0.8	-	-	-	-	-	-	-	-	-	-	127.5	-2.4
1999	-	-	-	-	-	-	-	-	-	-	119.1	-6.6	-	-	-	-	-	-	-	-	-	-	124.0	4.1
2000	-	-	-	-	-	-	-	-	-	-	118.1	-4.8	-	-	-	-	-	-	-	-	-	-	119.0	0.8
2001	-	-	-	-	-	-	-	-	-	-	120.4	1.2	-	-	-	-	-	-	-	-	-	-	-	-

Source: U.S. Department of Labor, Bureau of Labor Statistics, Division of Consumer Prices and Price Indexes. - indicates no data collected for period.

Kansas City, MO-KS
Consumer Price Index - Urban Wage Earners
Base 1982-1984 = 100
Apparel

For 1952-2001. Columns headed % show percentile change in the index from the previous period for which an index is available.

Year	Jan Index	%	Feb Index	%	Mar Index	%	Apr Index	%	May Index	%	Jun Index	%	Jul Index	%	Aug Index	%	Sep Index	%	Oct Index	%	Nov Index	%	Dec Index	%
1952	-		-		-		-		-		-		-		-		-		40.6		-		-	
1953	40.5	-0.2	-		-		40.4	-0.2	-		-		40.6	0.5	-		-		40.5	-0.2	-		-	
1954	40.3	-0.5	-		-		40.0	-0.7	-		-		40.0	0.0	-		-		40.3	0.7	-		-	
1955	39.7	-1.5	-		-		39.8	0.3	-		-		39.8	0.0	-		-		40.6	2.0	-		-	
1956	40.3	-0.7	-		-		40.3	0.0	-		-		40.5	0.5	-		-		41.0	1.2	-		-	
1957	41.8	2.0	-		-		41.5	-0.7	-		-		41.1	-1.0	-		-		41.9	1.9	-		-	
1958	41.3	-1.4	-		-		41.6	0.7	-		-		41.5	-0.2	-		-		42.1	1.4	-		-	
1959	41.5	-1.4	-		-		41.8	0.7	-		-		41.7	-0.2	-		-		42.7	2.4	-		-	
1960	42.1	-1.4	-		-		42.9	1.9	-		-		43.3	0.9	-		-		43.5	0.5	-		-	
1961	42.9	-1.4	-		-		43.2	0.7	-		-		43.4	0.5	-		-		43.8	0.9	-		-	
1962	43.2	-1.4	-		-		43.1	-0.2	-		-		42.7	-0.9	-		-		44.3	3.7	-		-	
1963	43.1	-2.7	-		-		43.5	0.9	-		-		43.4	-0.2	-		-		45.2	4.1	-		-	
1964	44.4	-1.8	-		-		44.7	0.7	-		-		44.7	0.0	-		-		45.8	2.5	-		-	
1965	45.0	-1.7	-		-		45.0	0.0	-		45.7	1.6	-		-		46.8	2.4	-		-		46.9	0.2
1966	-		-		46.4	-1.1	-		-		47.2	1.7	-		-		47.4	0.4	-		-		47.4	0.0
1967	-		-		47.7	0.6	-		-		48.1	0.8	-		-		50.1	4.2	-		-		50.1	0.0
1968	-		-		50.8	1.4	-		-		52.0	2.4	-		-		54.0	3.8	-		-		54.3	0.6
1969	-		-		54.7	0.7	-		-		55.9	2.2	-		-		57.3	2.5	-		-		57.5	0.3
1970	-		-		58.1	1.0	-		-		58.8	1.2	-		-		60.1	2.2	-		-		60.5	0.7
1971	-		-		60.4	-0.2	-		-		60.1	-0.5	-		-		61.6	2.5	-		-		60.7	-1.5
1972	-		-		61.6	1.5	-		-		61.7	0.2	-		-		63.4	2.8	-		-		63.0	-0.6
1973	-		-		63.1	0.2	-		-		63.6	0.8	-		-		64.5	1.4	-		-		64.2	-0.5
1974	-		-		65.6	2.2	-		-		66.9	2.0	-		-		70.3	5.1	-		-		70.5	0.3
1975	-		-		71.7	1.7	-		-		70.6	-1.5	-		-		71.7	1.6	-		-		70.5	-1.7
1976	-		-		71.7	1.7	-		-		73.2	2.1	-		-		75.5	3.1	-		-		75.3	-0.3
1977	-		-		78.3	4.0	-		-		78.7	0.5	-		-		81.3	3.3	-		-		81.5	0.2
1978	-		81.1	-0.5	-		82.2	1.4	-		79.9	-2.8	-		82.2	2.9	-		83.8	1.9	-		84.0	0.2
1979	-		84.3	0.4	-		84.9	0.7	-		82.7	-2.6	-		85.1	2.9	-		85.1	0.0	-		84.6	-0.6
1980	-		85.6	1.2	-		87.0	1.6	-		85.4	-1.8	-		86.5	1.3	-		89.7	3.7	-		88.8	-1.0
1981	-		91.6	3.2	-		92.8	1.3	-		91.7	-1.2	-		93.8	2.3	-		94.4	0.6	-		89.8	-4.9
1982	-		91.9	2.3	-		96.7	5.2	-		95.0	-1.8	-		98.4	3.6	-		96.6	-1.8	-		98.2	1.7
1983	-		98.8	0.6	-		102.8	4.0	-		101.6	-1.2	-		102.6	1.0	-		105.7	3.0	-		102.6	-2.9
1984	-		102.9	0.3	-		103.6	0.7	-		98.4	-5.0	-		101.2	2.8	-		104.2	3.0	-		102.1	-2.0
1985	-		104.5	2.4	-		108.5	3.8	-		104.1	-4.1	-		104.9	0.8	-		107.7	2.7	-		105.5	-2.0
1986	-		107.4	1.8	-		110.5	2.9	-		108.2	-2.1	-		106.4	-1.7	-		105.2	-1.1	-		101.8	-3.2
1987	-		-		-		-		-		105.6	3.7	-		-		-		-		-		115.3	9.2
1988	-		-		-		-		-		112.3	-2.6	-		-		-		-		-		116.2	3.5
1989	-		-		-		-		-		115.0	-1.0	-		-		-		-		-		125.6	9.2
1990	-		-		-		-		-		114.0	-9.2	-		-		-		-		-		119.6	4.9
1991	-		-		-		-		-		121.5	1.6	-		-		-		-		-		129.7	6.7
1992	-		-		-		-		-		125.1	-3.5	-		-		-		-		-		125.0	-0.1
1993	-		-		-		-		-		126.1	0.9	-		-		-		-		-		126.2	0.1
1994	-		-		-		-		-		131.4	4.1	-		-		-		-		-		117.1	-10.9
1995	-		-		-		-		-		129.3	10.4	-		-		-		-		-		124.3	-3.9
1996	-		-		-		-		-		136.5	9.8	-		-		-		-		-		126.0	-7.7
1997	-		-		-		-		-		135.5	7.5	-		-		-		-		-		130.9	-3.4

[Continued]

Kansas City, MO-KS
Consumer Price Index - Urban Wage Earners
Base 1982-1984 = 100
Apparel
[Continued]

For 1952-2001. Columns headed % show percentile change in the index from the previous period for which an index is available.

Year	Jan Index	%	Feb Index	%	Mar Index	%	Apr Index	%	May Index	%	Jun Index	%	Jul Index	%	Aug Index	%	Sep Index	%	Oct Index	%	Nov Index	%	Dec Index	%
1998	-	-	-	-	-	-	-	-	-	-	127.9	-2.3	-	-	-	-	-	-	-	-	-	-	128.8	0.7
1999	-	-	-	-	-	-	-	-	-	-	116.6	-9.5	-	-	-	-	-	-	-	-	-	-	122.5	5.1
2000	-	-	-	-	-	-	-	-	-	-	117.2	-4.3	-	-	-	-	-	-	-	-	-	-	118.2	0.9
2001	-	-	-	-	-	-	-	-	-	-	116.4	-1.5	-	-	-	-	-	-	-	-	-	-	-	-

Source: U.S. Department of Labor, Bureau of Labor Statistics, Division of Consumer Prices and Price Indexes. - indicates no data collected for period.

Kansas City, MO-KS
Consumer Price Index - All Urban Consumers
Base 1982-1984 = 100
Transportation

For 1947-2001. Columns headed % show percentile change in the index from the previous period for which an index is available.

Year	Jan Index	%	Feb Index	%	Mar Index	%	Apr Index	%	May Index	%	Jun Index	%	Jul Index	%	Aug Index	%	Sep Index	%	Oct Index	%	Nov Index	%	Dec Index	%
1947	17.7	-	17.7	0.0	17.7	0.0	18.0	1.7	18.0	0.0	18.0	0.0	18.1	0.6	-	-	-	-	18.7	3.3	-	-	-	-
1948	19.5	4.3	-	-	-	-	19.6	0.5	-	-	-	-	20.1	2.6	-	-	-	-	21.1	5.0	-	-	-	-
1949	21.1	0.0	-	-	-	-	21.5	1.9	-	-	-	-	21.3	-0.9	-	-	-	-	21.6	1.4	-	-	-	-
1950	21.7	0.5	-	-	-	-	21.7	0.0	-	-	-	-	22.3	2.8	-	-	-	-	21.9	-1.8	-	-	-	-
1951	22.5	2.7	-	-	-	-	22.9	1.8	-	-	-	-	23.1	0.9	-	-	-	-	23.6	2.2	-	-	-	-
1952	23.9	1.3	-	-	-	-	25.3	5.9	-	-	-	-	25.7	1.6	-	-	-	-	26.0	1.2	-	-	-	-
1953	26.1	0.4	-	-	-	-	26.0	-0.4	-	-	-	-	26.0	0.0	-	-	-	-	26.1	0.4	-	-	-	-
1954	25.1	-3.8	-	-	-	-	25.9	3.2	-	-	-	-	25.0	-3.5	-	-	-	-	24.8	-0.8	-	-	-	-
1955	25.1	1.2	-	-	-	-	24.6	-2.0	-	-	-	-	25.1	2.0	-	-	-	-	25.4	1.2	-	-	-	-
1956	25.0	-1.6	-	-	-	-	25.5	2.0	-	-	-	-	24.5	-3.9	-	-	-	-	26.1	6.5	-	-	-	-
1957	27.1	3.8	-	-	-	-	27.4	1.1	-	-	-	-	27.6	0.7	-	-	-	-	27.7	0.4	-	-	-	-
1958	28.1	1.4	-	-	-	-	28.4	1.1	-	-	-	-	29.7	4.6	-	-	-	-	30.1	1.3	-	-	-	-
1959	29.4	-2.3	-	-	-	-	30.6	4.1	-	-	-	-	30.7	0.3	-	-	-	-	31.2	1.6	-	-	-	-
1960	30.9	-1.0	-	-	-	-	29.8	-3.6	-	-	-	-	30.9	3.7	-	-	-	-	31.0	0.3	-	-	-	-
1961	30.0	-3.2	-	-	-	-	30.8	2.7	-	-	-	-	31.0	0.6	-	-	-	-	30.3	-2.3	-	-	-	-
1962	31.0	2.3	-	-	-	-	31.7	2.3	-	-	-	-	30.6	-3.5	-	-	-	-	31.9	4.2	-	-	-	-
1963	30.6	-4.1	-	-	-	-	31.3	2.3	-	-	-	-	30.9	-1.3	-	-	-	-	32.2	4.2	-	-	-	-
1964	31.5	-2.2	-	-	-	-	31.4	-0.3	-	-	-	-	31.7	1.0	-	-	-	-	31.4	-0.9	-	-	-	-
1965	32.8	4.5	-	-	-	-	33.0	0.6	-	-	34.5	4.5	-	-	-	-	34.3	-0.6	-	-	-	-	34.1	-0.6
1966	-	-	-	-	34.1	0.0	-	-	-	-	34.7	1.8	-	-	-	-	34.6	-0.3	-	-	-	-	34.8	0.6
1967	-	-	-	-	34.9	0.3	-	-	-	-	33.6	-3.7	-	-	-	-	35.5	5.7	-	-	-	-	34.8	-2.0
1968	-	-	-	-	35.0	0.6	-	-	-	-	36.7	4.9	-	-	-	-	35.0	-4.6	-	-	-	-	35.8	2.3
1969	-	-	-	-	37.6	5.0	-	-	-	-	37.5	-0.3	-	-	-	-	36.6	-2.4	-	-	-	-	37.7	3.0
1970	-	-	-	-	36.7	-2.7	-	-	-	-	38.5	4.9	-	-	-	-	37.9	-1.6	-	-	-	-	41.1	8.4
1971	-	-	-	-	41.0	-0.2	-	-	-	-	41.7	1.7	-	-	-	-	40.9	-1.9	-	-	-	-	40.2	-1.7
1972	-	-	-	-	40.0	-0.5	-	-	-	-	41.3	3.2	-	-	-	-	41.7	1.0	-	-	-	-	41.8	0.2
1973	-	-	-	-	42.1	0.7	-	-	-	-	42.9	1.9	-	-	-	-	42.6	-0.7	-	-	-	-	43.4	1.9
1974	-	-	-	-	45.4	4.6	-	-	-	-	47.7	5.1	-	-	-	-	48.8	2.3	-	-	-	-	49.3	1.0
1975	-	-	-	-	49.5	0.4	-	-	-	-	51.1	3.2	-	-	-	-	53.1	3.9	-	-	-	-	53.7	1.1
1976	-	-	-	-	53.7	0.0	-	-	-	-	55.8	3.9	-	-	-	-	56.4	1.1	-	-	-	-	57.5	2.0
1977	-	-	-	-	58.6	1.9	-	-	-	-	59.9	2.2	-	-	-	-	59.2	-1.2	-	-	-	-	59.9	1.2
1978	-	-	59.9	0.0	-	-	60.2	0.5	-	-	62.0	3.0	-	-	62.8	1.3	-	-	64.0	1.9	-	-	65.1	1.7
1979	-	-	65.9	1.2	-	-	69.3	5.2	-	-	73.0	5.3	-	-	75.1	2.9	-	-	75.8	0.9	-	-	78.1	3.0
1980	-	-	82.0	5.0	-	-	85.0	3.7	-	-	85.1	0.1	-	-	85.7	0.7	-	-	86.3	0.7	-	-	88.2	2.2
1981	-	-	90.9	3.1	-	-	92.2	1.4	-	-	93.4	1.3	-	-	93.6	0.2	-	-	94.6	1.1	-	-	96.5	2.0
1982	-	-	95.6	-0.9	-	-	95.0	-0.6	-	-	98.7	3.9	-	-	99.3	0.6	-	-	98.9	-0.4	-	-	97.8	-1.1
1983	-	-	96.1	-1.7	-	-	97.8	1.8	-	-	99.6	1.8	-	-	100.6	1.0	-	-	102.3	1.7	-	-	101.7	-0.6
1984	-	-	101.4	-0.3	-	-	102.4	1.0	-	-	103.6	1.2	-	-	102.5	-1.1	-	-	104.6	2.0	-	-	104.3	-0.3
1985	-	-	102.9	-1.3	-	-	106.9	3.9	-	-	107.6	0.7	-	-	106.9	-0.7	-	-	107.7	0.7	-	-	107.6	-0.1
1986	-	-	102.5	-4.7	-	-	98.5	-3.9	-	-	101.7	3.2	-	-	97.7	-3.9	-	-	98.7	1.0	-	-	98.9	0.2
1987	-	-	-	-	-	-	-	-	-	-	101.0	2.1	-	-	-	-	-	-	-	-	-	-	104.7	3.7
1988	-	-	-	-	-	-	-	-	-	-	105.5	0.8	-	-	-	-	-	-	-	-	-	-	108.8	3.1
1989	-	-	-	-	-	-	-	-	-	-	112.0	2.9	-	-	-	-	-	-	-	-	-	-	112.4	0.4
1990	-	-	-	-	-	-	-	-	-	-	112.8	0.4	-	-	-	-	-	-	-	-	-	-	119.5	5.9
1991	-	-	-	-	-	-	-	-	-	-	118.5	-0.8	-	-	-	-	-	-	-	-	-	-	119.9	1.2
1992	-	-	-	-	-	-	-	-	-	-	120.9	0.8	-	-	-	-	-	-	-	-	-	-	122.8	1.6

[Continued]

Kansas City, MO-KS
Consumer Price Index - All Urban Consumers
Base 1982-1984 = 100
Transportation

[Continued]

For 1947-2001. Columns headed % show percentile change in the index from the previous period for which an index is available.

Year	Jan Index	%	Feb Index	%	Mar Index	%	Apr Index	%	May Index	%	Jun Index	%	Jul Index	%	Aug Index	%	Sep Index	%	Oct Index	%	Nov Index	%	Dec Index	%
1993	-		-		-		-		-		124.6	1.5	-		-		-		-		-		124.7	0.1
1994	-		-		-		-		-		126.6	1.5	-		-		-		-		-		129.6	2.4
1995	-		-		-		-		-		133.3	2.9	-		-		-		-		-		133.5	0.2
1996	-		-		-		-		-		136.6	2.3	-		-		-		-		-		138.6	1.5
1997	-		-		-		-		-		141.1	1.8	-		-		-		-		-		140.4	-0.5
1998	-		-		-		-		-		137.4	-2.1	-		-		-		-		-		137.0	-0.3
1999	-		-		-		-		-		137.4	0.3	-		-		-		-		-		140.9	2.5
2000	-		-		-		-		-		146.8	4.2	-		-		-		-		-		148.1	0.9
2001	-		-		-		-		-		150.6	1.7	-		-		-		-		-		-	

Source: U.S. Department of Labor, Bureau of Labor Statistics, Division of Consumer Prices and Price Indexes. - indicates no data collected for period.

Kansas City, MO-KS
Consumer Price Index - Urban Wage Earners
Base 1982-1984 = 100
Transportation

For 1947-2001. Columns headed % show percentile change in the index from the previous period for which an index is available.

Year	Jan Index	%	Feb Index	%	Mar Index	%	Apr Index	%	May Index	%	Jun Index	%	Jul Index	%	Aug Index	%	Sep Index	%	Oct Index	%	Nov Index	%	Dec Index	%
1947	17.6	-	17.6	0.0	17.6	0.0	17.9	1.7	17.9	0.0	17.9	0.0	18.0	0.6	-	-	-	-	18.5	2.8	-	-	-	-
1948	19.4	4.9	-	-	-	-	19.5	0.5	-	-	-	-	20.0	2.6	-	-	-	-	21.0	5.0	-	-	-	-
1949	21.0	0.0	-	-	-	-	21.4	1.9	-	-	-	-	21.2	-0.9	-	-	-	-	21.5	1.4	-	-	-	-
1950	21.6	0.5	-	-	-	-	21.6	0.0	-	-	-	-	22.1	2.3	-	-	-	-	21.7	-1.8	-	-	-	-
1951	22.3	2.8	-	-	-	-	22.8	2.2	-	-	-	-	23.0	0.9	-	-	-	-	23.5	2.2	-	-	-	-
1952	23.7	0.9	-	-	-	-	25.2	6.3	-	-	-	-	25.5	1.2	-	-	-	-	25.8	1.2	-	-	-	-
1953	25.9	0.4	-	-	-	-	25.8	-0.4	-	-	-	-	25.9	0.4	-	-	-	-	25.9	0.0	-	-	-	-
1954	25.0	-3.5	-	-	-	-	25.7	2.8	-	-	-	-	24.9	-3.1	-	-	-	-	24.6	-1.2	-	-	-	-
1955	25.0	1.6	-	-	-	-	24.5	-2.0	-	-	-	-	24.9	1.6	-	-	-	-	25.2	1.2	-	-	-	-
1956	24.8	-1.6	-	-	-	-	25.3	2.0	-	-	-	-	24.3	-4.0	-	-	-	-	26.0	7.0	-	-	-	-
1957	27.0	3.8	-	-	-	-	27.3	1.1	-	-	-	-	27.4	0.4	-	-	-	-	27.5	0.4	-	-	-	-
1958	27.9	1.5	-	-	-	-	28.2	1.1	-	-	-	-	29.5	4.6	-	-	-	-	29.9	1.4	-	-	-	-
1959	29.2	-2.3	-	-	-	-	30.4	4.1	-	-	-	-	30.6	0.7	-	-	-	-	31.0	1.3	-	-	-	-
1960	30.7	-1.0	-	-	-	-	29.6	-3.6	-	-	-	-	30.7	3.7	-	-	-	-	30.8	0.3	-	-	-	-
1961	29.8	-3.2	-	-	-	-	30.6	2.7	-	-	-	-	30.8	0.7	-	-	-	-	30.2	-1.9	-	-	-	-
1962	30.8	2.0	-	-	-	-	31.5	2.3	-	-	-	-	30.5	-3.2	-	-	-	-	31.7	3.9	-	-	-	-
1963	30.4	-4.1	-	-	-	-	31.2	2.6	-	-	-	-	30.7	-1.6	-	-	-	-	32.0	4.2	-	-	-	-
1964	31.3	-2.2	-	-	-	-	31.3	0.0	-	-	-	-	31.5	0.6	-	-	-	-	31.2	-1.0	-	-	-	-
1965	32.6	4.5	-	-	-	-	32.8	0.6	-	-	34.3	4.6	-	-	-	-	34.1	-0.6	-	-	-	-	33.9	-0.6
1966	-	-	-	-	33.9	0.0	-	-	-	-	34.5	1.8	-	-	-	-	34.4	-0.3	-	-	-	-	34.6	0.6
1967	-	-	-	-	34.7	0.3	-	-	-	-	33.4	-3.7	-	-	-	-	35.3	5.7	-	-	-	-	34.6	-2.0
1968	-	-	-	-	34.8	0.6	-	-	-	-	36.5	4.9	-	-	-	-	34.8	-4.7	-	-	-	-	35.6	2.3
1969	-	-	-	-	37.4	5.1	-	-	-	-	37.3	-0.3	-	-	-	-	36.4	-2.4	-	-	-	-	37.5	3.0
1970	-	-	-	-	36.5	-2.7	-	-	-	-	38.3	4.9	-	-	-	-	37.6	-1.8	-	-	-	-	40.9	8.8
1971	-	-	-	-	40.8	-0.2	-	-	-	-	41.5	1.7	-	-	-	-	40.7	-1.9	-	-	-	-	39.9	-2.0
1972	-	-	-	-	39.8	-0.3	-	-	-	-	41.0	3.0	-	-	-	-	41.4	1.0	-	-	-	-	41.5	0.2
1973	-	-	-	-	41.8	0.7	-	-	-	-	42.7	2.2	-	-	-	-	42.4	-0.7	-	-	-	-	43.1	1.7
1974	-	-	-	-	45.1	4.6	-	-	-	-	47.5	5.3	-	-	-	-	48.6	2.3	-	-	-	-	49.0	0.8
1975	-	-	-	-	49.2	0.4	-	-	-	-	50.8	3.3	-	-	-	-	52.8	3.9	-	-	-	-	53.3	0.9
1976	-	-	-	-	53.4	0.2	-	-	-	-	55.5	3.9	-	-	-	-	56.1	1.1	-	-	-	-	57.2	2.0
1977	-	-	-	-	58.2	1.7	-	-	-	-	59.6	2.4	-	-	-	-	58.8	-1.3	-	-	-	-	59.5	1.2
1978	-	-	59.4	-0.2	-	-	59.6	0.3	-	-	61.5	3.2	-	-	62.4	1.5	-	-	63.7	2.1	-	-	64.8	1.7
1979	-	-	65.6	1.2	-	-	69.2	5.5	-	-	72.9	5.3	-	-	75.1	3.0	-	-	75.8	0.9	-	-	78.2	3.2
1980	-	-	82.1	5.0	-	-	85.2	3.8	-	-	85.3	0.1	-	-	85.6	0.4	-	-	86.2	0.7	-	-	88.1	2.2
1981	-	-	91.2	3.5	-	-	92.9	1.9	-	-	94.1	1.3	-	-	94.3	0.2	-	-	95.3	1.1	-	-	96.6	1.4
1982	-	-	95.6	-1.0	-	-	94.7	-0.9	-	-	98.7	4.2	-	-	99.4	0.7	-	-	98.9	-0.5	-	-	97.8	-1.1
1983	-	-	95.9	-1.9	-	-	97.7	1.9	-	-	99.6	1.9	-	-	100.7	1.1	-	-	102.3	1.6	-	-	101.6	-0.7
1984	-	-	101.3	-0.3	-	-	102.5	1.2	-	-	103.7	1.2	-	-	102.5	-1.2	-	-	104.7	2.1	-	-	104.4	-0.3
1985	-	-	102.8	-1.5	-	-	107.0	4.1	-	-	107.8	0.7	-	-	107.0	-0.7	-	-	107.6	0.6	-	-	107.5	-0.1
1986	-	-	102.1	-5.0	-	-	97.5	-4.5	-	-	101.0	3.6	-	-	96.6	-4.4	-	-	97.7	1.1	-	-	97.8	0.1
1987	-	-	-	-	-	-	-	-	-	-	99.4	1.6	-	-	-	-	-	-	-	-	-	-	103.0	3.6
1988	-	-	-	-	-	-	-	-	-	-	104.0	1.0	-	-	-	-	-	-	-	-	-	-	107.1	3.0
1989	-	-	-	-	-	-	-	-	-	-	109.8	2.5	-	-	-	-	-	-	-	-	-	-	110.1	0.3
1990	-	-	-	-	-	-	-	-	-	-	110.0	-0.1	-	-	-	-	-	-	-	-	-	-	115.2	4.7
1991	-	-	-	-	-	-	-	-	-	-	114.9	-0.3	-	-	-	-	-	-	-	-	-	-	116.8	1.7
1992	-	-	-	-	-	-	-	-	-	-	117.9	0.9	-	-	-	-	-	-	-	-	-	-	120.2	2.0

[Continued]

Kansas City, MO-KS
Consumer Price Index - Urban Wage Earners
Base 1982-1984 = 100
Transportation
[Continued]

For 1947-2001. Columns headed % show percentile change in the index from the previous period for which an index is available.

Year	Jan Index	%	Feb Index	%	Mar Index	%	Apr Index	%	May Index	%	Jun Index	%	Jul Index	%	Aug Index	%	Sep Index	%	Oct Index	%	Nov Index	%	Dec Index	%
1993	-	-	-	-	-	-	-	-	-	-	121.8	1.3	-	-	-	-	-	-	-	-	-	-	122.6	0.7
1994	-	-	-	-	-	-	-	-	-	-	124.5	1.5	-	-	-	-	-	-	-	-	-	-	127.7	2.6
1995	-	-	-	-	-	-	-	-	-	-	131.8	3.2	-	-	-	-	-	-	-	-	-	-	131.9	0.1
1996	-	-	-	-	-	-	-	-	-	-	134.8	2.2	-	-	-	-	-	-	-	-	-	-	136.5	1.3
1997	-	-	-	-	-	-	-	-	-	-	138.4	1.4	-	-	-	-	-	-	-	-	-	-	137.3	-0.8
1998	-	-	-	-	-	-	-	-	-	-	134.5	-2.0	-	-	-	-	-	-	-	-	-	-	134.1	-0.3
1999	-	-	-	-	-	-	-	-	-	-	134.5	0.3	-	-	-	-	-	-	-	-	-	-	138.4	2.9
2000	-	-	-	-	-	-	-	-	-	-	144.1	4.1	-	-	-	-	-	-	-	-	-	-	145.3	0.8
2001	-	-	-	-	-	-	-	-	-	-	147.8	1.7	-	-	-	-	-	-	-	-	-	-	-	-

Source: U.S. Department of Labor, Bureau of Labor Statistics, Division of Consumer Prices and Price Indexes. - indicates no data collected for period.

Kansas City, MO-KS
Consumer Price Index - All Urban Consumers
Base 1982-1984 = 100
Medical Care

For 1947-2001. Columns headed % show percentile change in the index from the previous period for which an index is available.

Year	Jan Index	%	Feb Index	%	Mar Index	%	Apr Index	%	May Index	%	Jun Index	%	Jul Index	%	Aug Index	%	Sep Index	%	Oct Index	%	Nov Index	%	Dec Index	%
1947	10.8	-	10.9	0.9	10.9	0.0	11.0	0.9	11.0	0.0	11.0	0.0	11.0	0.0	-	-	-	-	11.1	0.9	-	-	-	-
1948	11.5	3.6	-	-	-	-	11.9	3.5	-	-	-	-	11.9	0.0	-	-	-	-	12.1	1.7	-	-	-	-
1949	12.1	0.0	-	-	-	-	12.1	0.0	-	-	-	-	12.2	0.8	-	-	-	-	12.2	0.0	-	-	-	-
1950	12.2	0.0	-	-	-	-	12.3	0.8	-	-	-	-	12.3	0.0	-	-	-	-	12.7	3.3	-	-	-	-
1951	12.8	0.8	-	-	-	-	12.9	0.8	-	-	-	-	13.0	0.8	-	-	-	-	13.1	0.8	-	-	-	-
1952	13.3	1.5	-	-	-	-	13.4	0.8	-	-	-	-	13.9	3.7	-	-	-	-	13.9	0.0	-	-	-	-
1953	13.9	0.0	-	-	-	-	14.0	0.7	-	-	-	-	14.0	0.0	-	-	-	-	14.0	0.0	-	-	-	-
1954	14.0	0.0	-	-	-	-	15.8	12.9	-	-	-	-	15.9	0.6	-	-	-	-	15.9	0.0	-	-	-	-
1955	15.9	0.0	-	-	-	-	15.9	0.0	-	-	-	-	16.0	0.6	-	-	-	-	16.0	0.0	-	-	-	-
1956	16.0	0.0	-	-	-	-	16.2	1.3	-	-	-	-	16.2	0.0	-	-	-	-	17.5	8.0	-	-	-	-
1957	17.5	0.0	-	-	-	-	17.6	0.6	-	-	-	-	17.6	0.0	-	-	-	-	17.8	1.1	-	-	-	-
1958	17.9	0.6	-	-	-	-	17.9	0.0	-	-	-	-	19.9	11.2	-	-	-	-	19.9	0.0	-	-	-	-
1959	19.9	0.0	-	-	-	-	19.9	0.0	-	-	-	-	20.0	0.5	-	-	-	-	20.0	0.0	-	-	-	-
1960	20.1	0.5	-	-	-	-	20.2	0.5	-	-	-	-	20.5	1.5	-	-	-	-	20.4	-0.5	-	-	-	-
1961	20.4	0.0	-	-	-	-	21.2	3.9	-	-	-	-	21.1	-0.5	-	-	-	-	21.3	0.9	-	-	-	-
1962	21.4	0.5	-	-	-	-	21.4	0.0	-	-	-	-	21.5	0.5	-	-	-	-	21.6	0.5	-	-	-	-
1963	21.6	0.0	-	-	-	-	21.6	0.0	-	-	-	-	21.7	0.5	-	-	-	-	21.8	0.5	-	-	-	-
1964	21.8	0.0	-	-	-	-	22.0	0.9	-	-	-	-	23.5	6.8	-	-	-	-	23.5	0.0	-	-	-	-
1965	23.5	0.0	-	-	-	-	23.7	0.9	-	-	23.8	0.4	-	-	-	-	24.2	1.7	-	-	-	-	24.4	0.8
1966	-	-	-	-	25.2	3.3	-	-	-	-	25.4	0.8	-	-	-	-	25.5	0.4	-	-	-	-	25.7	0.8
1967	-	-	-	-	26.9	4.7	-	-	-	-	27.1	0.7	-	-	-	-	27.6	1.8	-	-	-	-	27.6	0.0
1968	-	-	-	-	28.7	4.0	-	-	-	-	29.0	1.0	-	-	-	-	29.1	0.3	-	-	-	-	29.6	1.7
1969	-	-	-	-	30.0	1.4	-	-	-	-	30.5	1.7	-	-	-	-	30.8	1.0	-	-	-	-	30.9	0.3
1970	-	-	-	-	31.2	1.0	-	-	-	-	31.7	1.6	-	-	-	-	32.1	1.3	-	-	-	-	32.7	1.9
1971	-	-	-	-	33.2	1.5	-	-	-	-	33.7	1.5	-	-	-	-	34.5	2.4	-	-	-	-	34.4	-0.3
1972	-	-	-	-	34.7	0.9	-	-	-	-	35.0	0.9	-	-	-	-	35.2	0.6	-	-	-	-	35.8	1.7
1973	-	-	-	-	36.4	1.7	-	-	-	-	36.5	0.3	-	-	-	-	36.7	0.5	-	-	-	-	37.7	2.7
1974	-	-	-	-	39.1	3.7	-	-	-	-	39.9	2.0	-	-	-	-	41.1	3.0	-	-	-	-	41.6	1.2
1975	-	-	-	-	43.3	4.1	-	-	-	-	43.3	0.0	-	-	-	-	44.0	1.6	-	-	-	-	44.9	2.0
1976	-	-	-	-	46.3	3.1	-	-	-	-	47.3	2.2	-	-	-	-	47.6	0.6	-	-	-	-	49.5	4.0
1977	-	-	-	-	51.1	3.2	-	-	-	-	51.7	1.2	-	-	-	-	52.5	1.5	-	-	-	-	53.3	1.5
1978	-	-	54.2	1.7	-	-	55.2	1.8	-	-	56.4	2.2	-	-	56.9	0.9	-	-	59.3	4.2	-	-	59.7	0.7
1979	-	-	61.8	3.5	-	-	62.8	1.6	-	-	63.4	1.0	-	-	63.9	0.8	-	-	65.3	2.2	-	-	66.6	2.0
1980	-	-	68.7	3.2	-	-	69.9	1.7	-	-	70.6	1.0	-	-	71.5	1.3	-	-	73.1	2.2	-	-	73.5	0.5
1981	-	-	77.7	5.7	-	-	78.2	0.6	-	-	79.0	1.0	-	-	80.2	1.5	-	-	82.5	2.9	-	-	83.2	0.8
1982	-	-	85.7	3.0	-	-	89.4	4.3	-	-	89.8	0.4	-	-	93.1	3.7	-	-	96.1	3.2	-	-	95.2	-0.9
1983	-	-	98.6	3.6	-	-	99.6	1.0	-	-	100.0	0.4	-	-	102.3	2.3	-	-	103.8	1.5	-	-	104.9	1.1
1984	-	-	107.0	2.0	-	-	108.0	0.9	-	-	107.5	-0.5	-	-	107.6	0.1	-	-	108.9	1.2	-	-	109.0	0.1
1985	-	-	109.4	0.4	-	-	109.9	0.5	-	-	111.0	1.0	-	-	113.2	2.0	-	-	113.5	0.3	-	-	114.5	0.9
1986	-	-	115.6	1.0	-	-	116.5	0.8	-	-	116.9	0.3	-	-	119.1	1.9	-	-	118.9	-0.2	-	-	120.9	1.7
1987	-	-	-	-	-	-	-	-	-	-	123.1	1.8	-	-	-	-	-	-	-	-	-	-	123.6	0.4
1988	-	-	-	-	-	-	-	-	-	-	128.8	4.2	-	-	-	-	-	-	-	-	-	-	132.9	3.2
1989	-	-	-	-	-	-	-	-	-	-	138.3	4.1	-	-	-	-	-	-	-	-	-	-	145.6	5.3
1990	-	-	-	-	-	-	-	-	-	-	152.8	4.9	-	-	-	-	-	-	-	-	-	-	160.8	5.2
1991	-	-	-	-	-	-	-	-	-	-	172.4	7.2	-	-	-	-	-	-	-	-	-	-	174.5	1.2
1992	-	-	-	-	-	-	-	-	-	-	181.7	4.1	-	-	-	-	-	-	-	-	-	-	185.9	2.3

[Continued]

Kansas City, MO-KS
Consumer Price Index - All Urban Consumers
Base 1982-1984 = 100
Medical Care
[Continued]

For 1947-2001. Columns headed % show percentile change in the index from the previous period for which an index is available.

Year	Jan		Feb		Mar		Apr		May		Jun		Jul		Aug		Sep		Oct		Nov		Dec	
	Index	%	Index	%	Index	%	Index	%	Index	%	Index	%	Index	%	Index	%	Index	%	Index	%	Index	%	Index	%
1993	-	-	-	-	-	-	-	-	-	-	195.5	5.2	-	-	-	-	-	-	-	-	-	-	195.8	0.2
1994	-	-	-	-	-	-	-	-	-	-	200.7	2.5	-	-	-	-	-	-	-	-	-	-	205.2	2.2
1995	-	-	-	-	-	-	-	-	-	-	207.8	1.3	-	-	-	-	-	-	-	-	-	-	209.1	0.6
1996	-	-	-	-	-	-	-	-	-	-	212.0	1.4	-	-	-	-	-	-	-	-	-	-	212.4	0.2
1997	-	-	-	-	-	-	-	-	-	-	210.9	-0.7	-	-	-	-	-	-	-	-	-	-	209.2	-0.8
1998	-	-	-	-	-	-	-	-	-	-	215.1	2.8	-	-	-	-	-	-	-	-	-	-	220.2	2.4
1999	-	-	-	-	-	-	-	-	-	-	226.2	2.7	-	-	-	-	-	-	-	-	-	-	232.0	2.6
2000	-	-	-	-	-	-	-	-	-	-	240.8	3.8	-	-	-	-	-	-	-	-	-	-	249.5	3.6
2001	-	-	-	-	-	-	-	-	-	-	252.4	1.2	-	-	-	-	-	-	-	-	-	-	-	-

Source: U.S. Department of Labor, Bureau of Labor Statistics, Division of Consumer Prices and Price Indexes. - indicates no data collected for period.

Kansas City, MO-KS
Consumer Price Index - Urban Wage Earners
Base 1982-1984 = 100
Medical Care

For 1947-2001. Columns headed % show percentile change in the index from the previous period for which an index is available.

Year	Jan Index	%	Feb Index	%	Mar Index	%	Apr Index	%	May Index	%	Jun Index	%	Jul Index	%	Aug Index	%	Sep Index	%	Oct Index	%	Nov Index	%	Dec Index	%
1947	10.8	-	10.9	0.9	10.9	0.0	11.0	0.9	11.0	0.0	11.0	0.0	11.0	0.0	-	-	-	-	11.1	0.9	-	-	-	-
1948	11.5	3.6	-	-	-	-	11.9	3.5	-	-	-	-	11.9	0.0	-	-	-	-	12.1	1.7	-	-	-	-
1949	12.1	0.0	-	-	-	-	12.1	0.0	-	-	-	-	12.2	0.8	-	-	-	-	12.2	0.0	-	-	-	-
1950	12.2	0.0	-	-	-	-	12.3	0.8	-	-	-	-	12.3	0.0	-	-	-	-	12.7	3.3	-	-	-	-
1951	12.8	0.8	-	-	-	-	12.9	0.8	-	-	-	-	13.0	0.8	-	-	-	-	13.1	0.8	-	-	-	-
1952	13.3	1.5	-	-	-	-	13.4	0.8	-	-	-	-	13.9	3.7	-	-	-	-	13.9	0.0	-	-	-	-
1953	13.9	0.0	-	-	-	-	14.0	0.7	-	-	-	-	14.0	0.0	-	-	-	-	14.0	0.0	-	-	-	-
1954	14.0	0.0	-	-	-	-	15.8	12.9	-	-	-	-	15.9	0.6	-	-	-	-	15.9	0.0	-	-	-	-
1955	15.9	0.0	-	-	-	-	15.9	0.0	-	-	-	-	16.0	0.6	-	-	-	-	16.0	0.0	-	-	-	-
1956	16.0	0.0	-	-	-	-	16.2	1.3	-	-	-	-	16.2	0.0	-	-	-	-	17.5	8.0	-	-	-	-
1957	17.5	0.0	-	-	-	-	17.6	0.6	-	-	-	-	17.6	0.0	-	-	-	-	17.8	1.1	-	-	-	-
1958	17.9	0.6	-	-	-	-	17.9	0.0	-	-	-	-	19.9	11.2	-	-	-	-	19.9	0.0	-	-	-	-
1959	19.9	0.0	-	-	-	-	19.9	0.0	-	-	-	-	20.0	0.5	-	-	-	-	20.0	0.0	-	-	-	-
1960	20.1	0.5	-	-	-	-	20.2	0.5	-	-	-	-	20.5	1.5	-	-	-	-	20.4	-0.5	-	-	-	-
1961	20.4	0.0	-	-	-	-	21.2	3.9	-	-	-	-	21.1	-0.5	-	-	-	-	21.3	0.9	-	-	-	-
1962	21.4	0.5	-	-	-	-	21.4	0.0	-	-	-	-	21.5	0.5	-	-	-	-	21.6	0.5	-	-	-	-
1963	21.6	0.0	-	-	-	-	21.6	0.0	-	-	-	-	21.7	0.5	-	-	-	-	21.8	0.5	-	-	-	-
1964	21.8	0.0	-	-	-	-	22.0	0.9	-	-	-	-	23.5	6.8	-	-	-	-	23.5	0.0	-	-	-	-
1965	23.5	0.0	-	-	-	-	23.7	0.9	-	-	23.8	0.4	-	-	-	-	24.2	1.7	-	-	-	-	24.4	0.8
1966	-	-	-	-	25.1	2.9	-	-	-	-	25.4	1.2	-	-	-	-	25.5	0.4	-	-	-	-	25.7	0.8
1967	-	-	-	-	26.9	4.7	-	-	-	-	27.1	0.7	-	-	-	-	27.6	1.8	-	-	-	-	27.6	0.0
1968	-	-	-	-	28.7	4.0	-	-	-	-	29.0	1.0	-	-	-	-	29.1	0.3	-	-	-	-	29.6	1.7
1969	-	-	-	-	30.0	1.4	-	-	-	-	30.5	1.7	-	-	-	-	30.8	1.0	-	-	-	-	30.9	0.3
1970	-	-	-	-	31.2	1.0	-	-	-	-	31.7	1.6	-	-	-	-	32.1	1.3	-	-	-	-	32.7	1.9
1971	-	-	-	-	33.2	1.5	-	-	-	-	33.6	1.2	-	-	-	-	34.5	2.7	-	-	-	-	34.4	-0.3
1972	-	-	-	-	34.7	0.9	-	-	-	-	35.0	0.9	-	-	-	-	35.2	0.6	-	-	-	-	35.8	1.7
1973	-	-	-	-	36.4	1.7	-	-	-	-	36.5	0.3	-	-	-	-	36.7	0.5	-	-	-	-	37.7	2.7
1974	-	-	-	-	39.1	3.7	-	-	-	-	39.9	2.0	-	-	-	-	41.1	3.0	-	-	-	-	41.6	1.2
1975	-	-	-	-	43.3	4.1	-	-	-	-	43.3	0.0	-	-	-	-	44.0	1.6	-	-	-	-	44.9	2.0
1976	-	-	-	-	46.3	3.1	-	-	-	-	47.3	2.2	-	-	-	-	47.6	0.6	-	-	-	-	49.5	4.0
1977	-	-	-	-	51.1	3.2	-	-	-	-	51.7	1.2	-	-	-	-	52.5	1.5	-	-	-	-	53.3	1.5
1978	-	-	54.2	1.7	-	-	55.0	1.5	-	-	56.3	2.4	-	-	56.8	0.9	-	-	58.4	2.8	-	-	59.3	1.5
1979	-	-	61.8	4.2	-	-	62.8	1.6	-	-	63.7	1.4	-	-	64.1	0.6	-	-	65.7	2.5	-	-	67.1	2.1
1980	-	-	67.8	1.0	-	-	69.9	3.1	-	-	70.2	0.4	-	-	72.8	3.7	-	-	74.2	1.9	-	-	74.7	0.7
1981	-	-	77.0	3.1	-	-	77.3	0.4	-	-	78.1	1.0	-	-	79.8	2.2	-	-	81.9	2.6	-	-	83.3	1.7
1982	-	-	85.9	3.1	-	-	89.5	4.2	-	-	89.9	0.4	-	-	93.0	3.4	-	-	95.9	3.1	-	-	95.0	-0.9
1983	-	-	98.4	3.6	-	-	99.5	1.1	-	-	100.1	0.6	-	-	102.3	2.2	-	-	103.7	1.4	-	-	104.9	1.2
1984	-	-	107.0	2.0	-	-	108.0	0.9	-	-	107.6	-0.4	-	-	107.7	0.1	-	-	109.1	1.3	-	-	109.2	0.1
1985	-	-	109.6	0.4	-	-	110.0	0.4	-	-	111.1	1.0	-	-	113.2	1.9	-	-	113.5	0.3	-	-	114.5	0.9
1986	-	-	115.6	1.0	-	-	116.4	0.7	-	-	116.8	0.3	-	-	119.0	1.9	-	-	118.8	-0.2	-	-	120.7	1.6
1987	-	-	-	-	-	-	-	-	-	-	123.4	2.2	-	-	-	-	-	-	-	-	-	-	124.2	0.6
1988	-	-	-	-	-	-	-	-	-	-	129.3	4.1	-	-	-	-	-	-	-	-	-	-	133.9	3.6
1989	-	-	-	-	-	-	-	-	-	-	139.4	4.1	-	-	-	-	-	-	-	-	-	-	146.5	5.1
1990	-	-	-	-	-	-	-	-	-	-	153.8	5.0	-	-	-	-	-	-	-	-	-	-	161.3	4.9
1991	-	-	-	-	-	-	-	-	-	-	172.7	7.1	-	-	-	-	-	-	-	-	-	-	174.7	1.2
1992	-	-	-	-	-	-	-	-	-	-	182.1	4.2	-	-	-	-	-	-	-	-	-	-	186.4	2.4

[Continued]

Kansas City, MO-KS
Consumer Price Index - Urban Wage Earners
Base 1982-1984 = 100
Medical Care

[Continued]

For 1947-2001. Columns headed % show percentile change in the index from the previous period for which an index is available.

Year	Jan Index	%	Feb Index	%	Mar Index	%	Apr Index	%	May Index	%	Jun Index	%	Jul Index	%	Aug Index	%	Sep Index	%	Oct Index	%	Nov Index	%	Dec Index	%
1993	-	-	-	-	-	-	-	-	-	-	196.7	5.5	-	-	-	-	-	-	-	-	-		196.7	0.0
1994	-	-	-	-	-	-	-	-	-	-	201.7	2.5	-	-	-	-	-	-	-	-	-		206.1	2.2
1995	-	-	-	-	-	-	-	-	-	-	208.4	1.1	-	-	-	-	-	-	-	-	-		209.6	0.6
1996	-	-	-	-	-	-	-	-	-	-	212.9	1.6	-	-	-	-	-	-	-	-	-		213.4	0.2
1997	-	-	-	-	-	-	-	-	-	-	212.3	-0.5	-	-	-	-	-	-	-	-	-		210.6	-0.8
1998	-	-	-	-	-	-	-	-	-	-	216.4	2.8	-	-	-	-	-	-	-	-	-		221.1	2.2
1999	-	-	-	-	-	-	-	-	-	-	227.0	2.7	-	-	-	-	-	-	-	-	-		232.6	2.5
2000	-	-	-	-	-	-	-	-	-	-	240.6	3.4	-	-	-	-	-	-	-	-	-		248.9	3.4
2001	-	-	-	-	-	-	-	-	-	-	249.7	0.3	-	-	-	-	-	-	-	-	-		-	-

Source: U.S. Department of Labor, Bureau of Labor Statistics, Division of Consumer Prices and Price Indexes. - indicates no data collected for period.

Kansas City, MO-KS
Consumer Price Index - All Urban Consumers
Base December 1997 = 100
Recreation

For 1997-2001. Columns headed % show percentile change in the index from the previous period for which an index is available.

Year	Jan Index	%	Feb Index	%	Mar Index	%	Apr Index	%	May Index	%	Jun Index	%	Jul Index	%	Aug Index	%	Sep Index	%	Oct Index	%	Nov Index	%	Dec Index	%
1997	-		-		-		-		-		-		-		-		-		-		-		100.0	-
1998	-		-		-		-		-		101.8	1.8	-		-		-		-		-		100.5	-1.3
1999	-		-		-		-		-		100.9	0.4	-		-		-		-		-		100.5	-0.4
2000	-		-		-		-		-		102.4	1.9	-		-		-		-		-		103.2	0.8
2001	-		-		-		-		-		106.0	2.7	-		-		-		-		-		-	

Source: U.S. Department of Labor, Bureau of Labor Statistics, Division of Consumer Prices and Price Indexes. - indicates no data collected for period.

Kansas City, MO-KS
Consumer Price Index - Urban Wage Earners
Base December 1997 = 100
Recreation

For 1997-2001. Columns headed % show percentile change in the index from the previous period for which an index is available.

Year	Jan		Feb		Mar		Apr		May		Jun		Jul		Aug		Sep		Oct		Nov		Dec	
	Index	%	Index	%	Index	%	Index	%	Index	%	Index	%	Index	%	Index	%	Index	%	Index	%	Index	%	Index	%
1997	-	-	-	-	-	-	-	-	-	-	-	-	-	-	-	-	-	-	-	-	-	-	100.0	-
1998	-	-	-	-	-	-	-	-	-	-	101.5	1.5	-	-	-	-	-	-	-	-	-	-	100.0	-1.5
1999	-	-	-	-	-	-	-	-	-	-	100.3	0.3	-	-	-	-	-	-	-	-	-	-	100.0	-0.3
2000	-	-	-	-	-	-	-	-	-	-	101.6	1.6	-	-	-	-	-	-	-	-	-	-	102.2	0.6
2001	-	-	-	-	-	-	-	-	-	-	105.3	3.0	-	-	-	-	-	-	-	-	-	-	-	-

Source: U.S. Department of Labor, Bureau of Labor Statistics, Division of Consumer Prices and Price Indexes. - indicates no data collected for period.

Kansas City, MO-KS
Consumer Price Index - All Urban Consumers
Base December 1997 = 100
Education & Communication

For 1997-2001. Columns headed % show percentile change in the index from the previous period for which an index is available.

Year	Jan		Feb		Mar		Apr		May		Jun		Jul		Aug		Sep		Oct		Nov		Dec	
	Index	%	Index	%	Index	%	Index	%	Index	%	Index	%	Index	%	Index	%	Index	%	Index	%	Index	%	Index	%
1997	-		-		-		-		-		-		-		-		-		-		-		100.0	-
1998	-		-		-		-		-		98.6	-1.4	-		-		-		-		-		97.7	-0.9
1999	-		-		-		-		-		97.5	-0.2	-		-		-		-		-		99.1	1.6
2000	-		-		-		-		-		100.3	1.2	-		-		-		-		-		102.0	1.7
2001	-		-		-		-		-		103.2	1.2	-		-		-		-					

Source: U.S. Department of Labor, Bureau of Labor Statistics, Division of Consumer Prices and Price Indexes. - indicates no data collected for period.

Kansas City, MO-KS
Consumer Price Index - Urban Wage Earners
Base December 1997 = 100
Education & Communication

For 1997-2001. Columns headed % show percentile change in the index from the previous period for which an index is available.

Year	Jan		Feb		Mar		Apr		May		Jun		Jul		Aug		Sep		Oct		Nov		Dec	
	Index	%	Index	%	Index	%	Index	%	Index	%	Index	%	Index	%	Index	%	Index	%	Index	%	Index	%	Index	%
1997	-	-	-	-	-	-	-	-	-	-	-	-	-	-	-	-	-	-	-	-	-	-	100.0	-
1998	-	-	-	-	-	-	-	-	-	-	99.0	-1.0	-	-	-	-	-	-	-	-	-	-	98.9	-0.1
1999	-	-	-	-	-	-	-	-	-	-	98.7	-0.2	-	-	-	-	-	-	-	-	-	-	100.4	1.7
2000	-	-	-	-	-	-	-	-	-	-	101.6	1.2	-	-	-	-	-	-	-	-	-	-	103.5	1.9
2001	-	-	-	-	-	-	-	-	-	-	105.0	1.4	-	-	-	-	-	-	-	-	-	-	-	-

Source: U.S. Department of Labor, Bureau of Labor Statistics, Division of Consumer Prices and Price Indexes. - indicates no data collected for period.

Los Angeles-Riverside-Orange County, CA
Consumer Price Index - All Urban Consumers
Base 1982-1984 = 100
Annual Averages

For 1914-2001. Columns headed % show percentile change in the index from the previous period for which an index is available.

Year	All Items		Food & Beverage		Housing		Apparel		Trans-portation		Medical Care		Recrea-tion*		Education & Communic.*		Other Goods & Services	
	Index	%	Index	%	Index	%	Index	%	Index	%	Index	%	Index	%	Index	%	Index	%
1914	-	-	-	-	-	-	-	-	-	-	-	-	-	-	-	-	-	-
1915	10.0	-	-	-	-	-	-	-	-	-	-	-	-	-	-	-	-	-
1916	10.5	5.0	-	-	-	-	-	-	-	-	-	-	-	-	-	-	-	-
1917	12.1	15.2	-	-	-	-	-	-	-	-	-	-	-	-	-	-	-	-
1918	14.4	19.0	-	-	-	-	-	-	-	-	-	-	-	-	-	-	-	-
1919	17.0	18.1	-	-	-	-	-	-	-	-	-	-	-	-	-	-	-	-
1920	19.9	17.1	-	-	-	-	-	-	-	-	-	-	-	-	-	-	-	-
1921	18.6	-6.5	-	-	-	-	-	-	-	-	-	-	-	-	-	-	-	-
1922	18.1	-2.7	-	-	-	-	-	-	-	-	-	-	-	-	-	-	-	-
1923	18.3	1.1	-	-	-	-	-	-	-	-	-	-	-	-	-	-	-	-
1924	18.4	0.5	-	-	-	-	-	-	-	-	-	-	-	-	-	-	-	-
1925	18.4	0.0	-	-	-	-	-	-	-	-	-	-	-	-	-	-	-	-
1926	17.9	-2.7	-	-	-	-	-	-	-	-	-	-	-	-	-	-	-	-
1927	17.6	-1.7	-	-	-	-	-	-	-	-	-	-	-	-	-	-	-	-
1928	17.3	-1.7	-	-	-	-	-	-	-	-	-	-	-	-	-	-	-	-
1929	17.3	0.0	-	-	-	-	-	-	-	-	-	-	-	-	-	-	-	-
1930	16.7	-3.5	-	-	-	-	-	-	-	-	-	-	-	-	-	-	-	-
1931	15.1	-9.6	-	-	-	-	-	-	-	-	-	-	-	-	-	-	-	-
1932	13.6	-9.9	-	-	-	-	-	-	-	-	-	-	-	-	-	-	-	-
1933	12.8	-5.9	-	-	-	-	-	-	-	-	-	-	-	-	-	-	-	-
1934	12.9	0.8	-	-	-	-	-	-	-	-	-	-	-	-	-	-	-	-
1935	13.3	3.1	-	-	-	-	-	-	-	-	-	-	-	-	-	-	-	-
1936	13.5	1.5	-	-	-	-	-	-	-	-	-	-	-	-	-	-	-	-
1937	14.2	5.2	-	-	-	-	-	-	-	-	-	-	-	-	-	-	-	-
1938	14.0	-1.4	-	-	-	-	-	-	-	-	-	-	-	-	-	-	-	-
1939	13.9	-0.7	-	-	-	-	-	-	-	-	-	-	-	-	-	-	-	-
1940	13.9	0.0	-	-	-	-	-	-	-	-	-	-	-	-	-	-	-	-
1941	14.7	5.8	-	-	-	-	-	-	-	-	-	-	-	-	-	-	-	-
1942	16.5	12.2	-	-	-	-	-	-	-	-	-	-	-	-	-	-	-	-
1943	17.3	4.8	-	-	-	-	-	-	-	-	-	-	-	-	-	-	-	-
1944	17.6	1.7	-	-	-	-	-	-	-	-	-	-	-	-	-	-	-	-
1945	18.1	2.8	-	-	-	-	-	-	-	-	-	-	-	-	-	-	-	-
1946	19.5	7.7	-	-	-	-	-	-	-	-	-	-	-	-	-	-	-	-
1947	22.0	12.8	-	-	-	-	-	-	17.9	-	13.4	-	-	-	-	-	-	-
1948	23.6	7.3	-	-	-	-	-	-	19.8	10.6	14.2	6.0	-	-	-	-	-	-
1949	23.6	0.0	-	-	-	-	-	-	21.0	6.1	14.7	3.5	-	-	-	-	-	-
1950	23.7	0.4	-	-	-	-	-	-	20.7	-1.4	15.0	2.0	-	-	-	-	-	-
1951	25.7	8.4	-	-	-	-	-	-	21.6	4.3	15.9	6.0	-	-	-	-	-	-
1952	26.5	3.1	-	-	-	-	-	-	23.8	10.2	16.5	3.8	-	-	-	-	-	-
1953	26.7	0.8	-	-	-	-	48.7	-	24.8	4.2	16.9	2.4	-	-	-	-	-	-
1954	26.7	0.0	-	-	-	-	48.9	0.4	24.6	-0.8	17.3	2.4	-	-	-	-	-	-
1955	26.7	0.0	-	-	-	-	48.9	0.0	24.4	-0.8	17.4	0.6	-	-	-	-	-	-
1956	27.1	1.5	-	-	-	-	49.8	1.8	24.8	1.6	17.9	2.9	-	-	-	-	-	-
1957	28.0	3.3	-	-	-	-	50.9	2.2	25.8	4.0	18.4	2.8	-	-	-	-	-	-
1958	28.9	3.2	-	-	-	-	51.0	0.2	26.5	2.7	19.9	8.2	-	-	-	-	-	-

[Continued]

Los Angeles-Riverside-Orange County, CA
Consumer Price Index - All Urban Consumers
Base 1982-1984 = 100
Annual Averages
[Continued]

For 1914-2001. Columns headed % show percentile change in the index from the previous period for which an index is available.

Year	All Items		Food & Beverage		Housing		Apparel		Trans- portation		Medical Care		Recrea- tion*		Education & Communic.*		Other Goods & Services	
	Index	%	Index	%	Index	%	Index	%	Index	%	Index	%	Index	%	Index	%	Index	%
1959	29.4	1.7	-	-	-	-	51.6	1.2	27.8	4.9	20.8	4.5	-	-	-	-	-	-
1960	30.0	2.0	-	-	-	-	52.8	2.3	28.0	0.7	21.4	2.9	-	-	-	-	-	-
1961	30.3	1.0	-	-	-	-	52.9	0.2	28.9	3.2	21.6	0.9	-	-	-	-	-	-
1962	30.7	1.3	-	-	-	-	53.0	0.2	29.9	3.5	22.3	3.2	-	-	-	-	-	-
1963	31.1	1.3	-	-	-	-	53.7	1.3	29.9	0.0	22.7	1.8	-	-	-	-	-	-
1964	31.7	1.9	-	-	-	-	54.5	1.5	31.1	4.0	23.2	2.2	-	-	-	-	-	-
1965	32.4	2.2	-	-	-	-	55.0	0.9	31.7	1.9	23.7	2.2	-	-	-	-	-	-
1966	33.0	1.9	-	-	-	-	55.9	1.6	31.9	0.6	24.6	3.8	-	-	-	-	-	-
1967	33.8	2.4	-	-	-	-	58.1	3.9	32.3	1.3	26.4	7.3	-	-	-	-	-	-
1968	35.2	4.1	-	-	-	-	61.2	5.3	33.3	3.1	27.8	5.3	-	-	-	-	-	-
1969	36.8	4.5	-	-	-	-	63.6	3.9	34.3	3.0	29.5	6.1	-	-	-	-	-	-
1970	38.7	5.2	-	-	-	-	66.5	4.6	35.4	3.2	31.6	7.1	-	-	-	-	-	-
1971	40.1	3.6	-	-	-	-	68.5	3.0	37.1	4.8	33.2	5.1	-	-	-	-	-	-
1972	41.4	3.2	-	-	-	-	69.7	1.8	38.0	2.4	33.9	2.1	-	-	-	-	-	-
1973	43.7	5.6	-	-	-	-	71.5	2.6	39.8	4.7	35.6	5.0	-	-	-	-	-	-
1974	48.2	10.3	-	-	-	-	76.7	7.3	44.5	11.8	39.0	9.6	-	-	-	-	-	-
1975	53.3	10.6	-	-	-	-	79.2	3.3	49.3	10.8	43.7	12.1	-	-	-	-	-	-
1976	56.9	6.8	60.5	-	54.4	-	80.9	2.1	54.2	9.9	49.3	12.8	-	-	-	-	57.3	-
1977	60.8	6.9	64.7	6.9	58.4	7.4	84.1	4.0	58.1	7.2	53.9	9.3	-	-	-	-	60.6	5.8
1978	65.3	7.4	71.6	10.7	63.2	8.2	85.8	2.0	60.6	4.3	58.6	8.7	-	-	-	-	65.1	7.4
1979	72.3	10.7	79.2	10.6	69.9	10.6	89.0	3.7	70.3	16.0	64.6	10.2	-	-	-	-	69.2	6.3
1980	83.7	15.8	85.7	8.2	83.7	19.7	98.3	10.4	82.5	17.4	72.7	12.5	-	-	-	-	76.4	10.4
1981	91.9	9.8	92.5	7.9	92.4	10.4	101.5	3.3	91.3	10.7	82.0	12.8	-	-	-	-	83.9	9.8
1982	97.3	5.9	96.8	4.6	97.8	5.8	98.9	-2.6	97.5	6.8	94.1	14.8	-	-	-	-	92.0	9.7
1983	99.1	1.8	100.1	3.4	98.3	0.5	99.7	0.8	98.8	1.3	100.7	7.0	-	-	-	-	101.2	10.0
1984	103.6	4.5	103.1	3.0	103.9	5.7	101.3	1.6	103.7	5.0	105.2	4.5	-	-	-	-	106.8	5.5
1985	108.4	4.6	105.5	2.3	109.7	5.6	105.1	3.8	107.5	3.7	112.9	7.3	-	-	-	-	115.3	8.0
1986	111.9	3.2	108.7	3.0	116.1	5.8	106.9	1.7	105.2	-2.1	120.9	7.1	-	-	-	-	122.3	6.1
1987	116.7	4.3	113.2	4.1	121.0	4.2	112.5	5.2	108.9	3.5	129.5	7.1	-	-	-	-	127.9	4.6
1988	122.1	4.6	117.2	3.5	126.6	4.6	114.3	1.6	113.8	4.5	139.6	7.8	-	-	-	-	139.9	9.4
1989	128.3	5.1	124.0	5.8	131.7	4.0	118.8	3.9	119.6	5.1	149.8	7.3	-	-	-	-	155.3	11.0
1990	135.9	5.9	130.9	5.6	139.3	5.8	126.4	6.4	126.5	5.8	163.3	9.0	-	-	-	-	166.3	7.1
1991	141.4	4.0	136.6	4.4	144.9	4.0	130.9	3.6	126.6	0.1	178.2	9.1	-	-	-	-	179.9	8.2
1992	146.5	3.6	140.9	3.1	148.6	2.6	133.2	1.8	133.0	5.1	192.4	8.0	-	-	-	-	197.1	9.6
1993	150.3	2.6	145.1	3.0	150.4	1.2	131.6	-1.2	137.5	3.4	206.6	7.4	-	-	-	-	211.9	7.5
1994	152.3	1.3	148.5	2.3	151.0	0.4	129.6	-1.5	140.5	2.2	215.2	4.2	-	-	-	-	218.0	2.9
1995	154.6	1.5	153.4	3.3	152.2	0.8	126.7	-2.2	142.3	1.3	221.8	3.1	-	-	-	-	225.6	3.5
1996	157.5	1.9	157.8	2.9	154.1	1.2	126.0	-0.6	144.3	1.4	228.9	3.2	-	-	-	-	232.8	3.2
1997	160.0	1.6	163.2	3.4	156.6	1.6	121.0	-4.0	145.2	0.6	232.0	1.4	-	-	-	-	240.7	3.4
1998	162.3	1.4	167.3	2.5	160.1	2.2	123.1	1.7	142.6	-1.8	236.7	2.0	101.0	-	99.5	-	248.5	3.2
1999	166.1	2.3	169.9	1.6	164.5	2.7	118.2	-4.0	146.8	2.9	244.5	3.3	101.9	0.9	99.2	-0.3	275.0	10.7
2000	171.6	3.3	173.6	2.2	170.8	3.8	117.0	-1.0	154.2	5.0	252.2	3.1	104.5	2.6	99.7	0.5	286.6	4.2
2001	177.3	3.3	181.1	4.3	179.5	5.1	112.1	-4.2	-	-	265.6	5.3	106.0	1.4	101.5	1.8	295.1	3.0

Source: U.S. Department of Labor, Bureau of Labor Statistics, Division of Consumer Prices and Price Indexes. *Base is December 1997 = 100. - indicates no data collected for period.

Los Angeles-Riverside-Orange County, CA
Consumer Price Index - Urban Wage Earners
Base 1982-1984 = 100
Annual Averages

For 1914-2001. Columns headed % show percentile change in the index from the previous period for which an index is available.

Year	All Items		Food & Beverage		Housing		Apparel		Trans-portation		Medical Care		Recrea-tion*		Education & Communic.*		Other Goods & Services	
	Index	%	Index	%	Index	%	Index	%	Index	%	Index	%	Index	%	Index	%	Index	%
1914	-	-	-	-	-	-	-	-	-	-	-	-	-	-	-	-	-	-
1915	9.9	-	-	-	-	-	-	-	-	-	-	-	-	-	-	-	-	-
1916	10.5	6.1	-	-	-	-	-	-	-	-	-	-	-	-	-	-	-	-
1917	12.1	15.2	-	-	-	-	-	-	-	-	-	-	-	-	-	-	-	-
1918	14.4	19.0	-	-	-	-	-	-	-	-	-	-	-	-	-	-	-	-
1919	17.0	18.1	-	-	-	-	-	-	-	-	-	-	-	-	-	-	-	-
1920	19.9	17.1	-	-	-	-	-	-	-	-	-	-	-	-	-	-	-	-
1921	18.6	-6.5	-	-	-	-	-	-	-	-	-	-	-	-	-	-	-	-
1922	18.1	-2.7	-	-	-	-	-	-	-	-	-	-	-	-	-	-	-	-
1923	18.3	1.1	-	-	-	-	-	-	-	-	-	-	-	-	-	-	-	-
1924	18.4	0.5	-	-	-	-	-	-	-	-	-	-	-	-	-	-	-	-
1925	18.4	0.0	-	-	-	-	-	-	-	-	-	-	-	-	-	-	-	-
1926	17.9	-2.7	-	-	-	-	-	-	-	-	-	-	-	-	-	-	-	-
1927	17.6	-1.7	-	-	-	-	-	-	-	-	-	-	-	-	-	-	-	-
1928	17.3	-1.7	-	-	-	-	-	-	-	-	-	-	-	-	-	-	-	-
1929	17.3	0.0	-	-	-	-	-	-	-	-	-	-	-	-	-	-	-	-
1930	16.7	-3.5	-	-	-	-	-	-	-	-	-	-	-	-	-	-	-	-
1931	15.1	-9.6	-	-	-	-	-	-	-	-	-	-	-	-	-	-	-	-
1932	13.6	-9.9	-	-	-	-	-	-	-	-	-	-	-	-	-	-	-	-
1933	12.8	-5.9	-	-	-	-	-	-	-	-	-	-	-	-	-	-	-	-
1934	12.9	0.8	-	-	-	-	-	-	-	-	-	-	-	-	-	-	-	-
1935	13.3	3.1	-	-	-	-	-	-	-	-	-	-	-	-	-	-	-	-
1936	13.5	1.5	-	-	-	-	-	-	-	-	-	-	-	-	-	-	-	-
1937	14.2	5.2	-	-	-	-	-	-	-	-	-	-	-	-	-	-	-	-
1938	14.0	-1.4	-	-	-	-	-	-	-	-	-	-	-	-	-	-	-	-
1939	13.9	-0.7	-	-	-	-	-	-	-	-	-	-	-	-	-	-	-	-
1940	13.9	0.0	-	-	-	-	-	-	-	-	-	-	-	-	-	-	-	-
1941	14.7	5.8	-	-	-	-	-	-	-	-	-	-	-	-	-	-	-	-
1942	16.5	12.2	-	-	-	-	-	-	-	-	-	-	-	-	-	-	-	-
1943	17.3	4.8	-	-	-	-	-	-	-	-	-	-	-	-	-	-	-	-
1944	17.6	1.7	-	-	-	-	-	-	-	-	-	-	-	-	-	-	-	-
1945	18.1	2.8	-	-	-	-	-	-	-	-	-	-	-	-	-	-	-	-
1946	19.5	7.7	-	-	-	-	-	-	-	-	-	-	-	-	-	-	-	-
1947	22.0	12.8	-	-	-	-	-	-	17.8	-	13.6	-	-	-	-	-	-	-
1948	23.6	7.3	-	-	-	-	-	-	19.7	10.7	14.4	5.9	-	-	-	-	-	-
1949	23.6	0.0	-	-	-	-	-	-	20.9	6.1	14.9	3.5	-	-	-	-	-	-
1950	23.7	0.4	-	-	-	-	-	-	20.6	-1.4	15.2	2.0	-	-	-	-	-	-
1951	25.7	8.4	-	-	-	-	-	-	21.5	4.4	16.1	5.9	-	-	-	-	-	-
1952	26.5	3.1	-	-	-	-	-	-	23.7	10.2	16.7	3.7	-	-	-	-	-	-
1953	26.7	0.8	-	-	-	-	48.9	-	24.6	3.8	17.2	3.0	-	-	-	-	-	-
1954	26.7	0.0	-	-	-	-	49.1	0.4	24.4	-0.8	17.5	1.7	-	-	-	-	-	-
1955	26.7	0.0	-	-	-	-	49.1	0.0	24.3	-0.4	17.6	0.6	-	-	-	-	-	-
1956	27.1	1.5	-	-	-	-	50.0	1.8	24.6	1.2	18.2	3.4	-	-	-	-	-	-
1957	28.0	3.3	-	-	-	-	51.1	2.2	25.6	4.1	18.7	2.7	-	-	-	-	-	-
1958	28.9	3.2	-	-	-	-	51.2	0.2	26.3	2.7	20.2	8.0	-	-	-	-	-	-

[Continued]

Los Angeles-Riverside-Orange County, CA
Consumer Price Index - Urban Wage Earners
Base 1982-1984 = 100
Annual Averages
[Continued]

For 1914-2001. Columns headed % show percentile change in the index from the previous period for which an index is available.

Year	All Items Index	%	Food & Beverage Index	%	Housing Index	%	Apparel Index	%	Trans-portation Index	%	Medical Care Index	%	Recrea-tion* Index	%	Education & Communic.* Index	%	Other Goods & Services Index	%
1959	29.4	1.7	-	-	-	-	51.8	1.2	27.7	5.3	21.1	4.5	-	-	-	-	-	-
1960	29.9	1.7			-	-	53.0	2.3	27.8	0.4	21.7	2.8	-	-	-	-	-	-
1961	30.3	1.3	-	-	-	-	53.1	0.2	28.7	3.2	22.0	1.4	-	-	-	-	-	-
1962	30.7	1.3			-	-	53.2	0.2	29.7	3.5	22.7	3.2	-	-	-	-	-	-
1963	31.1	1.3			-	-	53.9	1.3	29.8	0.3	23.0	1.3	-	-	-	-	-	-
1964	31.7	1.9			-	-	54.7	1.5	30.9	3.7	23.6	2.6	-	-	-	-	-	-
1965	32.4	2.2			-	-	55.2	0.9	31.6	2.3	24.0	1.7	-	-	-	-	-	-
1966	33.0	1.9			-	-	56.1	1.6	31.7	0.3	24.9	3.8	-	-	-	-	-	-
1967	33.8	2.4	-	-	-	-	58.3	3.9	32.1	1.3	26.8	7.6	-	-	-	-	-	-
1968	35.2	4.1	-	-	-	-	61.4	5.3	33.1	3.1	28.2	5.2	-	-	-	-	-	-
1969	36.8	4.5	-	-	-	-	63.9	4.1	34.1	3.0	29.9	6.0	-	-	-	-	-	-
1970	38.7	5.2	-	-	-	-	66.7	4.4	35.2	3.2	32.1	7.4	-	-	-	-	-	-
1971	40.1	3.6	-	-	-	-	68.8	3.1	36.9	4.8	33.7	5.0	-	-	-	-	-	-
1972	41.4	3.2	-	-	-	-	69.9	1.6	37.8	2.4	34.5	2.4	-	-	-	-	-	-
1973	43.7	5.6	-	-	-	-	71.8	2.7	39.6	4.8	36.1	4.6	-	-	-	-	-	-
1974	48.2	10.3	-	-	-	-	76.9	7.1	44.2	11.6	39.5	9.4	-	-	-	-	-	-
1975	53.3	10.6			-	-	79.5	3.4	49.1	11.1	44.4	12.4	-	-	-	-	-	-
1976	56.8	6.6	59.4		54.5		81.2	2.1	53.9	9.8	50.1	12.8	-	-	-	-	57.0	-
1977	60.8	7.0	63.5	6.9	58.5	7.3	84.4	3.9	57.8	7.2	54.7	9.2	-	-	-	-	60.2	5.6
1978	65.1	7.1	70.0	10.2	63.3	8.2	87.1	3.2	60.3	4.3	59.0	7.9	-	-	-	-	64.3	6.8
1979	72.8	11.8	78.0	11.4	70.6	11.5	91.5	5.1	70.5	16.9	65.3	10.7	-	-	-	-	68.6	6.7
1980	84.7	16.3	85.2	9.2	85.3	20.8	97.3	6.3	83.2	18.0	74.0	13.3	-	-	-	-	75.3	9.8
1981	93.1	9.9	92.2	8.2	94.8	11.1	100.7	3.5	92.0	10.6	83.5	12.8	-	-	-	-	82.9	10.1
1982	98.5	5.8	96.8	5.0	100.4	5.9	99.0	-1.7	97.8	6.3	94.1	12.7	-	-	-	-	91.7	10.6
1983	99.3	0.8	100.2	3.5	99.0	-1.4	99.6	0.6	98.6	0.8	100.7	7.0	-	-	-	-	101.7	10.9
1984	102.2	2.9	103.1	2.9	100.6	1.6	101.4	1.8	103.5	5.0	105.2	4.5	-	-	-	-	106.7	4.9
1985	106.5	4.2	105.4	2.2	106.2	5.6	105.0	3.6	107.0	3.4	112.9	7.3	-	-	-	-	113.7	6.6
1986	109.5	2.8	108.5	2.9	112.3	5.7	107.2	2.1	103.9	-2.9	120.7	6.9	-	-	-	-	120.7	6.2
1987	114.0	4.1	113.0	4.1	117.0	4.2	111.9	4.4	107.0	3.0	129.0	6.9	-	-	-	-	126.4	4.7
1988	119.0	4.4	117.1	3.6	122.3	4.5	114.0	1.9	111.4	4.1	139.1	7.8	-	-	-	-	137.6	8.9
1989	124.9	5.0	123.9	5.8	127.1	3.9	118.8	4.2	116.6	4.7	148.7	6.9	-	-	-	-	154.9	12.6
1990	131.9	5.6	131.0	5.7	134.1	5.5	126.1	6.1	122.2	4.8	161.5	8.6	-	-	-	-	166.1	7.2
1991	137.1	3.9	136.8	4.4	139.6	4.1	130.8	3.7	122.5	0.2	175.7	8.8	-	-	-	-	179.1	7.8
1992	142.0	3.6	141.4	3.4	143.0	2.4	133.6	2.1	128.6	5.0	190.0	8.1	-	-	-	-	194.2	8.4
1993	145.2	2.3	145.6	3.0	144.8	1.3	132.4	-0.9	132.5	3.0	203.9	7.3	-	-	-	-	204.6	5.4
1994	147.0	1.2	148.8	2.2	145.4	0.4	130.0	-1.8	135.7	2.4	211.7	3.8	-	-	-	-	207.4	1.4
1995	149.4	1.6	153.5	3.2	146.4	0.7	126.8	-2.5	138.4	2.0	218.8	3.4	-	-	-	-	213.9	3.1
1996	152.1	1.8	158.0	2.9	148.2	1.2	126.0	-0.6	140.6	1.6	226.4	3.5	-	-	-	-	220.4	3.0
1997	154.3	1.4	163.3	3.4	150.6	1.6	120.9	-4.0	141.0	0.3	229.4	1.3	-	-	-	-	227.3	3.1
1998	156.0	1.1	167.3	2.4	153.7	2.1	121.7	0.7	137.7	-2.3	234.1	2.0	100.4	-	99.5	-	234.5	3.2
1999	159.6	2.3	170.0	1.6	157.7	2.6	117.2	-3.7	141.8	3.0	241.3	3.1	100.2	-0.2	99.0	-0.5	264.2	12.7
2000	164.8	3.3	173.7	2.2	163.7	3.8	116.4	-0.7	149.1	5.1	248.6	3.0	101.2	1.0	99.7	0.7	276.1	4.5
2001	170.2	3.3	181.4	4.4	172.2	5.2	111.7	-4.0	-	-	261.9	5.3	102.8	1.6	101.4	1.7	285.3	3.3

Source: U.S. Department of Labor, Bureau of Labor Statistics, Division of Consumer Prices and Price Indexes. *Base is December 1997 = 100. - indicates no data collected for period.

Los Angeles-Riverside-Orange County, CA
Consumer Price Index - All Urban Consumers
Base 1982-1984 = 100
All Items

For 1914-2001. Columns headed % show percentile change in the index from the previous period for which an index is available.

Year	Jan Index	%	Feb Index	%	Mar Index	%	Apr Index	%	May Index	%	Jun Index	%	Jul Index	%	Aug Index	%	Sep Index	%	Oct Index	%	Nov Index	%	Dec Index	%
1914	-	-	-	-	-	-	-	-	-	-	-	-	-	-	-	-	-	-	-	-	-	-	10.2	-
1915	-	-	-	-	-	-	-	-	-	-	-	-	-	-	-	-	-	-	-	-	-	-	10.1	-1.0
1916	-	-	-	-	-	-	-	-	-	-	-	-	-	-	-	-	-	-	-	-	-	-	11.0	8.9
1917	-	-	-	-	-	-	-	-	-	-	-	-	-	-	-	-	-	-	-	-	-	-	13.0	18.2
1918	-	-	-	-	-	-	-	-	-	-	-	-	-	-	-	-	-	-	-	-	-	-	15.8	21.5
1919	-	-	-	-	-	-	-	-	-	-	16.4	3.8	-	-	-	-	-	-	-	-	-	-	18.6	13.4
1920	-	-	-	-	-	-	-	-	-	-	20.4	9.7	-	-	-	-	-	-	-	-	-	-	19.9	-2.5
1921	-	-	-	-	-	-	-	-	18.5	-7.0	-	-	-	-	-	-	18.3	-1.1	-	-	-	-	18.4	0.5
1922	-	-	-	-	18.2	-1.1	-	-	-	-	18.1	-0.5	-	-	-	-	18.0	-0.6	-	-	-	-	18.1	0.6
1923	-	-	-	-	18.0	-0.6	-	-	-	-	18.3	1.7	-	-	-	-	18.5	1.1	-	-	-	-	18.6	0.5
1924	-	-	-	-	18.5	-0.5	-	-	-	-	18.3	-1.1	-	-	-	-	18.4	0.5	-	-	-	-	18.2	-1.1
1925	-	-	-	-	-	-	-	-	-	-	18.5	1.6	-	-	-	-	-	-	-	-	-	-	18.5	0.0
1926	-	-	-	-	-	-	-	-	-	-	17.8	-3.8	-	-	-	-	-	-	-	-	-	-	17.8	0.0
1927	-	-	-	-	-	-	-	-	-	-	17.8	0.0	-	-	-	-	-	-	-	-	-	-	17.5	-1.7
1928	-	-	-	-	-	-	-	-	-	-	17.2	-1.7	-	-	-	-	-	-	-	-	-	-	17.4	1.2
1929	-	-	-	-	-	-	-	-	-	-	17.2	-1.1	-	-	-	-	-	-	-	-	-	-	17.2	0.0
1930	-	-	-	-	-	-	-	-	-	-	16.7	-2.9	-	-	-	-	-	-	-	-	-	-	16.0	-4.2
1931	-	-	-	-	-	-	-	-	-	-	14.9	-6.9	-	-	-	-	-	-	-	-	-	-	14.6	-2.0
1932	-	-	-	-	-	-	-	-	-	-	13.6	-6.8	-	-	-	-	-	-	-	-	-	-	13.1	-3.7
1933	-	-	-	-	-	-	-	-	-	-	12.5	-4.6	-	-	-	-	-	-	-	-	-	-	13.0	4.0
1934	-	-	-	-	-	-	-	-	-	-	12.9	-0.8	-	-	-	-	-	-	-	-	13.3	3.1	-	-
1935	-	-	-	-	13.6	2.3	-	-	-	-	-	-	13.2	-2.9	-	-	-	-	13.1	-0.8	-	-	-	-
1936	13.4	2.3	-	-	-	-	13.2	-1.5	-	-	-	-	13.4	1.5	-	-	13.7	2.2	-	-	-	-	13.7	0.0
1937	-	-	-	-	14.3	4.4	-	-	-	-	14.2	-0.7	-	-	-	-	14.4	1.4	-	-	-	-	14.3	-0.7
1938	-	-	-	-	14.0	-2.1	-	-	-	-	14.0	0.0	-	-	-	-	14.0	0.0	-	-	-	-	14.1	0.7
1939	-	-	-	-	14.0	-0.7	-	-	-	-	13.8	-1.4	-	-	-	-	14.1	2.2	-	-	-	-	13.9	-1.4
1940	-	-	-	-	13.9	0.0	-	-	-	-	13.9	0.0	-	-	-	-	14.0	0.7	14.0	0.0	14.1	0.7	14.1	0.0
1941	14.2	0.7	14.0	-1.4	14.1	0.7	14.3	1.4	14.4	0.7	14.6	1.4	14.6	0.0	14.7	0.7	15.0	2.0	15.2	1.3	15.3	0.7	15.5	1.3
1942	15.7	1.3	15.8	0.6	16.1	1.9	16.2	0.6	16.3	0.6	16.4	0.6	16.6	1.2	16.8	1.2	16.8	0.0	17.0	1.2	17.1	0.6	17.1	0.0
1943	17.1	0.0	17.0	-0.6	17.2	1.2	17.4	1.2	17.4	0.0	17.4	0.0	17.3	-0.6	17.2	-0.6	17.3	0.6	17.4	0.6	17.5	0.6	17.5	0.0
1944	17.4	-0.6	17.4	0.0	17.4	0.0	17.4	0.0	17.6	1.1	17.5	-0.6	17.5	0.0	17.6	0.6	17.7	0.6	17.8	0.6	17.8	0.0	17.9	0.6
1945	17.9	0.0	17.8	-0.6	17.9	0.6	18.0	0.6	18.0	0.0	18.0	0.0	18.1	0.6	18.1	0.0	18.3	1.1	18.3	0.0	18.4	0.5	18.5	0.5
1946	18.4	-0.5	18.4	0.0	18.4	0.0	18.5	0.5	18.6	0.5	18.8	1.1	19.7	4.8	20.0	1.5	20.1	0.5	20.5	2.0	21.4	4.4	21.4	0.0
1947	21.5	0.5	21.6	0.5	21.7	0.5	21.8	0.5	21.8	0.0	21.7	-0.5	21.8	0.5	21.9	0.5	22.4	2.3	22.4	0.0	22.8	1.8	23.0	0.9
1948	23.3	1.3	23.4	0.4	23.3	-0.4	23.5	0.9	23.5	0.0	23.5	0.0	23.7	0.9	23.8	0.4	23.8	0.0	23.9	0.4	24.0	0.4	24.1	0.4
1949	24.1	0.0	23.9	-0.8	23.9	0.0	23.9	0.0	23.7	-0.8	23.6	-0.4	23.4	-0.8	23.4	0.0	23.4	0.0	23.3	-0.4	23.4	0.4	23.2	-0.9
1950	23.4	0.9	23.3	-0.4	23.4	0.4	23.4	0.0	23.4	0.0	23.4	0.0	23.5	0.4	23.8	1.3	23.9	0.4	24.1	0.8	24.3	0.8	24.6	1.2
1951	25.0	1.6	25.5	2.0	25.7	0.8	25.7	0.0	25.7	0.0	25.7	0.0	25.8	0.4	25.8	0.0	25.9	0.4	25.9	0.0	26.2	1.2	26.3	0.4
1952	26.3	0.0	26.3	0.0	26.4	0.4	26.4	0.0	26.4	0.0	26.5	0.4	26.5	0.0	26.5	0.0	26.5	0.0	26.5	0.0	26.6	0.4	26.6	0.0
1953	26.6	0.0	26.5	-0.4	26.6	0.4	26.7	0.4	26.6	-0.4	26.6	0.0	26.7	0.4	26.7	0.0	26.8	0.4	26.8	0.0	26.8	0.0	26.7	-0.4
1954	27.0	1.1	26.9	-0.4	26.8	-0.4	26.7	-0.4	26.7	0.0	26.7	0.0	26.5	-0.7	26.6	0.4	26.6	0.0	26.5	-0.4	26.5	0.0	26.6	0.4
1955	26.6	0.0	26.5	-0.4	26.6	0.4	26.4	-0.8	26.6	0.8	26.6	0.0	26.7	0.4	26.6	-0.4	26.8	0.8	26.8	0.0	26.8	0.0	26.8	0.0
1956	26.8	0.0	26.7	-0.4	26.8	0.4	26.8	0.0	27.0	0.7	27.1	0.4	27.2	0.4	27.1	-0.4	27.2	0.4	27.3	0.4	27.5	0.7	27.6	0.4
1957	27.6	0.0	27.8	0.7	27.8	0.0	27.8	0.0	27.9	0.4	27.9	0.0	28.0	0.4	28.0	0.0	28.2	0.7	28.2	0.0	28.4	0.7	28.4	0.0
1958	28.6	0.7	28.6	0.0	28.8	0.7	29.0	0.7	28.9	-0.3	28.9	0.0	29.0	0.3	28.9	-0.3	29.1	0.7	29.1	0.0	29.2	0.3	29.2	0.0
1959	29.2	0.0	29.2	0.0	29.2	0.0	29.2	0.0	29.3	0.3	29.3	0.0	29.4	0.3	29.4	0.0	29.5	0.3	29.7	0.7	29.7	0.0	29.8	0.3

[Continued]

Los Angeles-Riverside-Orange County, CA
Consumer Price Index - All Urban Consumers
Base 1982-1984 = 100
All Items
[Continued]

For 1914-2001. Columns headed % show percentile change in the index from the previous period for which an index is available.

Year	Jan Index	%	Feb Index	%	Mar Index	%	Apr Index	%	May Index	%	Jun Index	%	Jul Index	%	Aug Index	%	Sep Index	%	Oct Index	%	Nov Index	%	Dec Index	%
1960	29.8	0.0	29.7	-0.3	29.9	0.7	30.0	0.3	30.0	0.0	29.9	-0.3	29.9	0.0	29.8	-0.3	30.0	0.7	30.1	0.3	30.1	0.0	30.3	0.7
1961	30.3	0.0	30.3	0.0	30.2	-0.3	30.3	0.3	30.3	0.0	30.3	0.0	30.3	0.0	30.3	0.0	30.3	0.0	30.4	0.3	30.5	0.3	30.5	0.0
1962	30.4	-0.3	30.4	0.0	30.5	0.3	30.6	0.3	30.8	0.7	30.8	0.0	30.7	-0.3	30.7	0.0	30.9	0.7	30.9	0.0	30.8	-0.3	30.9	0.3
1963	30.9	0.0	31.0	0.3	31.0	0.0	31.1	0.3	31.0	-0.3	30.9	-0.3	31.1	0.6	31.2	0.3	31.2	0.0	31.4	0.6	31.4	0.0	31.3	-0.3
1964	31.5	0.6	31.4	-0.3	31.6	0.6	31.6	0.0	31.6	0.0	31.6	0.0	31.6	0.0	31.7	0.3	31.6	-0.3	32.0	1.3	32.0	0.0	32.1	0.3
1965	32.1	0.0	32.2	0.3	32.3	0.3	32.4	0.3	32.4	0.0	32.5	0.3	32.4	-0.3	32.1	-0.9	32.5	1.2	32.4	-0.3	32.5	0.3	32.6	0.3
1966	32.5	-0.3	32.6	0.3	32.7	0.3	32.9	0.6	32.9	0.0	33.0	0.3	33.1	0.3	33.0	-0.3	33.3	0.9	33.4	0.3	33.5	0.3	33.5	0.0
1967	33.3	-0.6	33.3	0.0	33.2	-0.3	33.5	0.9	33.6	0.3	33.7	0.3	33.8	0.3	34.1	0.9	34.3	0.6	34.2	-0.3	34.5	0.9	34.5	0.0
1968	34.7	0.6	34.7	0.0	34.9	0.6	34.9	0.0	34.8	-0.3	35.1	0.9	35.2	0.3	35.3	0.3	35.3	0.0	35.6	0.8	35.7	0.3	35.7	0.0
1969	35.9	0.6	36.0	0.3	36.5	1.4	36.5	0.0	36.5	0.0	36.8	0.8	37.0	0.5	37.1	0.3	37.3	0.5	37.4	0.3	37.4	0.0	37.7	0.8
1970	37.8	0.3	37.9	0.3	38.0	0.3	38.4	1.1	38.5	0.3	38.6	0.3	38.9	0.8	38.7	-0.5	39.2	1.3	39.3	0.3	39.3	0.0	39.5	0.5
1971	39.5	0.0	39.3	-0.5	39.6	0.8	39.5	-0.3	40.0	1.3	40.2	0.5	40.3	0.2	40.4	0.2	40.6	0.5	40.7	0.2	40.6	-0.2	40.6	0.0
1972	40.6	0.0	40.7	0.2	41.0	0.7	41.0	0.0	41.1	0.2	41.2	0.2	41.5	0.7	41.6	0.2	41.9	0.7	41.9	0.0	42.1	0.5	42.1	0.0
1973	42.2	0.2	42.5	0.7	42.8	0.7	43.0	0.5	43.1	0.2	43.5	0.9	43.7	0.5	44.3	1.4	44.4	0.2	44.8	0.9	45.2	0.9	45.4	0.4
1974	45.8	0.9	46.1	0.7	46.6	1.1	47.0	0.9	47.5	1.1	47.9	0.8	48.4	1.0	49.0	1.2	49.8	1.6	49.8	0.0	50.3	1.0	50.8	1.0
1975	51.0	0.4	51.5	1.0	52.2	1.4	52.7	1.0	53.1	0.8	53.0	-0.2	53.5	0.9	53.7	0.4	54.3	1.1	54.7	0.7	55.0	0.5	55.4	0.7
1976	55.7	0.5	55.4	-0.5	55.5	0.2	55.5	0.0	56.3	1.4	56.5	0.4	57.1	1.1	57.4	0.5	57.8	0.7	58.0	0.3	58.3	0.5	58.5	0.3
1977	59.2	1.2	59.7	0.8	59.8	0.2	60.2	0.7	60.4	0.3	60.8	0.7	61.1	0.5	61.1	0.0	61.5	0.7	61.5	0.0	61.9	0.7	62.4	0.8
1978	62.8	0.6	63.1	0.5	63.4	0.5	64.2	1.3	64.8	0.9	65.5	1.1	65.8	0.5	66.0	0.3	66.8	1.2	66.9	0.1	67.1	0.3	66.7	-0.6
1979	67.6	1.3	68.3	1.0	69.0	1.0	70.3	1.9	71.4	1.6	72.1	1.0	72.7	0.8	73.6	1.2	74.7	1.5	75.1	0.5	75.9	1.1	77.2	1.7
1980	78.7	1.9	80.4	2.2	81.7	1.6	82.8	1.3	84.3	1.8	84.7	0.5	84.2	-0.6	83.7	-0.6	84.5	1.0	85.5	1.2	86.5	1.2	87.6	1.3
1981	87.8	0.2	88.5	0.8	89.1	0.7	89.9	0.9	90.5	0.7	90.7	0.2	92.1	1.5	93.0	1.0	94.5	1.6	95.2	0.7	95.3	0.1	95.5	0.2
1982	96.7	1.3	96.6	-0.1	96.9	0.3	97.0	0.1	97.2	0.2	98.2	1.0	97.9	-0.3	97.9	0.0	97.5	-0.4	98.0	0.5	97.6	-0.4	96.6	-1.0
1983	96.7	0.1	97.1	0.4	97.2	0.1	98.0	0.8	98.8	0.8	99.4	0.6	99.7	0.3	99.9	0.2	100.3	0.4	100.5	0.2	100.4	-0.1	100.8	0.4
1984	101.2	0.4	101.6	0.4	101.8	0.2	102.5	0.7	103.4	0.9	103.4	0.0	103.5	0.1	104.5	1.0	105.0	0.5	105.5	0.5	105.5	0.0	105.3	-0.2
1985	105.9	0.6	106.3	0.4	106.5	0.2	106.9	0.4	108.0	1.0	108.1	0.1	108.8	0.6	109.6	0.7	109.6	0.0	110.4	0.7	110.0	-0.4	110.4	0.4
1986	110.6	0.2	110.5	-0.1	111.1	0.5	110.6	-0.5	111.5	0.8	112.1	0.5	112.0	-0.1	112.0	0.0	113.3	1.2	113.8	0.4	113.0	-0.7	112.7	-0.3
1987	113.4	0.6	114.7	1.1	115.5	0.7	116.0	0.4	116.8	0.7	116.5	-0.3	116.5	0.0	117.3	0.7	118.0	0.6	118.6	0.5	118.2	-0.3	118.5	0.3
1988	118.9	0.3	119.7	0.7	120.6	0.8	121.1	0.4	122.0	0.7	122.0	0.0	122.1	0.1	122.6	0.4	123.4	0.7	124.0	0.5	124.1	0.1	124.2	0.1
1989	124.6	0.3	125.5	0.7	126.2	0.6	127.2	0.8	128.3	0.9	128.7	0.3	129.0	0.2	128.9	-0.1	130.1	0.9	130.0	-0.1	130.0	0.0	130.6	0.5
1990	132.1	1.1	133.6	1.1	134.5	0.7	134.2	-0.2	134.6	0.3	135.0	0.3	135.6	0.4	136.3	0.5	137.7	1.0	138.7	0.7	138.9	0.1	139.2	0.2
1991	140.0	0.6	139.9	-0.1	139.7	-0.1	140.7	0.7	140.8	0.1	140.8	0.0	141.5	0.5	141.7	0.1	142.6	0.6	142.9	0.2	143.5	0.4	143.1	-0.3
1992	144.3	0.8	144.9	0.4	145.5	0.4	145.8	0.2	146.0	0.1	146.2	0.1	146.7	0.3	146.9	0.1	147.4	0.3	148.4	0.7	148.2	-0.1	148.2	0.0
1993	149.2	0.7	150.0	0.5	149.8	-0.1	149.9	0.1	150.1	0.1	149.7	-0.3	149.8	0.1	149.9	0.1	150.2	0.2	150.9	0.5	151.6	0.5	151.9	0.2
1994	152.2	0.2	152.2	0.0	152.5	0.2	152.0	-0.3	151.4	-0.4	151.3	-0.1	151.7	0.3	152.0	0.2	152.7	0.5	153.4	0.5	152.9	-0.3	153.4	0.3
1995	154.3	0.6	154.5	0.1	154.6	0.1	154.7	0.1	155.1	0.3	154.8	-0.2	154.5	-0.2	154.4	-0.1	154.6	0.1	155.2	0.4	154.4	-0.5	154.6	0.1
1996	155.7	0.7	156.2	0.3	157.3	0.7	157.7	0.3	157.5	-0.1	156.7	-0.5	157.6	0.6	157.3	-0.2	158.2	0.6	158.8	0.4	158.4	-0.3	158.3	-0.1
1997	159.1	0.5	159.2	0.1	159.8	0.4	159.9	0.1	159.5	-0.3	159.4	-0.1	159.5	0.1	159.7	0.1	160.5	0.5	161.1	0.4	160.7	-0.2	161.2	0.3
1998	161.0	-0.1	161.1	0.1	161.4	0.2	161.8	0.2	162.3	0.3	162.2	-0.1	162.1	-0.1	162.6	0.3	162.6	0.0	163.2	0.4	163.4	0.1	163.5	0.1
1999	164.2	0.4	164.6	0.2	165.0	0.2	166.6	1.0	166.2	-0.2	165.4	-0.5	165.8	0.2	166.3	0.3	167.2	0.5	167.2	0.0	167.1	-0.1	167.3	0.1
2000	167.9	0.4	169.3	0.8	170.7	0.8	170.6	-0.1	171.1	0.3	171.0	-0.1	171.7	0.4	172.2	0.3	173.3	0.6	173.8	0.3	173.5	-0.2	173.5	0.0
2001	174.2	0.4	175.4	0.7	176.2	0.5	176.6	0.2	177.5	0.5	178.9	0.8	178.3	-0.3	178.4	0.1	178.8	0.2	178.3	-0.3	178.1	-0.1	177.1	-0.6

Source: U.S. Department of Labor, Bureau of Labor Statistics, Division of Consumer Prices and Price Indexes. - indicates no data collected for period.

Los Angeles-Riverside-Orange County, CA
Consumer Price Index - Urban Wage Earners
Base 1982-1984 = 100
All Items

For 1914-2001. Columns headed % show percentile change in the index from the previous period for which an index is available.

Year	Jan Index	%	Feb Index	%	Mar Index	%	Apr Index	%	May Index	%	Jun Index	%	Jul Index	%	Aug Index	%	Sep Index	%	Oct Index	%	Nov Index	%	Dec Index	%
1914	-	-	-	-	-	-	-	-	-	-	-	-	-	-	-	-	-	-	-	-	-	-	10.2	-
1915	-	-	-	-	-	-	-	-	-	-	-	-	-	-	-	-	-	-	-	-	-	-	10.0	-2.0
1916	-	-	-	-	-	-	-	-	-	-	-	-	-	-	-	-	-	-	-	-	-	-	11.0	10.0
1917	-	-	-	-	-	-	-	-	-	-	-	-	-	-	-	-	-	-	-	-	-	-	13.0	18.2
1918	-	-	-	-	-	-	-	-	-	-	-	-	-	-	-	-	-	-	-	-	-	-	15.8	21.5
1919	-	-	-	-	-	-	-	-	-	-	16.4	3.8	-	-	-	-	-	-	-	-	-	-	18.6	13.4
1920	-	-	-	-	-	-	-	-	-	-	20.4	9.7	-	-	-	-	-	-	-	-	-	-	19.9	-2.5
1921	-	-	-	-	-	-	-	-	18.5	-7.0	-	-	-	-	-	-	18.3	-1.1	-	-	-	-	18.4	0.5
1922	-	-	-	-	18.2	-1.1	-	-	-	-	18.1	-0.5	-	-	-	-	18.0	-0.6	-	-	-	-	18.1	0.6
1923	-	-	-	-	18.0	-0.6	-	-	-	-	18.3	1.7	-	-	-	-	18.5	1.1	-	-	-	-	18.6	0.5
1924	-	-	-	-	18.5	-0.5	-	-	-	-	18.3	-1.1	-	-	-	-	18.4	0.5	-	-	-	-	18.2	-1.1
1925	-	-	-	-	-	-	-	-	-	-	18.5	1.6	-	-	-	-	-	-	-	-	-	-	18.5	0.0
1926	-	-	-	-	-	-	-	-	-	-	17.8	-3.8	-	-	-	-	-	-	-	-	-	-	17.8	0.0
1927	-	-	-	-	-	-	-	-	-	-	17.8	0.0	-	-	-	-	-	-	-	-	-	-	17.5	-1.7
1928	-	-	-	-	-	-	-	-	-	-	17.2	-1.7	-	-	-	-	-	-	-	-	-	-	17.4	1.2
1929	-	-	-	-	-	-	-	-	-	-	17.2	-1.1	-	-	-	-	-	-	-	-	-	-	17.2	0.0
1930	-	-	-	-	-	-	-	-	-	-	16.7	-2.9	-	-	-	-	-	-	-	-	-	-	16.0	-4.2
1931	-	-	-	-	-	-	-	-	-	-	14.9	-6.9	-	-	-	-	-	-	-	-	-	-	14.6	-2.0
1932	-	-	-	-	-	-	-	-	-	-	13.6	-6.8	-	-	-	-	-	-	-	-	-	-	13.1	-3.7
1933	-	-	-	-	-	-	-	-	-	-	12.5	-4.6	-	-	-	-	-	-	-	-	-	-	13.0	4.0
1934	-	-	-	-	-	-	-	-	-	-	12.9	-0.8	-	-	-	-	-	-	-	-	13.3	3.1	-	-
1935	-	-	-	-	13.6	2.3	-	-	-	-	-	-	13.2	-2.9	-	-	-	-	13.1	-0.8	-	-	-	-
1936	13.4	2.3	-	-	-	-	13.2	-1.5	-	-	-	-	13.4	1.5	-	-	13.7	2.2	-	-	-	-	13.7	0.0
1937	-	-	-	-	14.3	4.4	-	-	-	-	14.2	-0.7	-	-	-	-	14.4	1.4	-	-	-	-	14.3	-0.7
1938	-	-	-	-	14.0	-2.1	-	-	-	-	14.0	0.0	-	-	-	-	14.0	0.0	-	-	-	-	14.1	0.7
1939	-	-	-	-	14.0	-0.7	-	-	-	-	13.8	-1.4	-	-	-	-	14.1	2.2	-	-	-	-	13.9	-1.4
1940	-	-	-	-	13.9	0.0	-	-	-	-	13.9	0.0	-	-	-	-	14.0	0.7	14.0	0.0	14.1	0.7	14.1	0.0
1941	14.2	0.7	14.0	-1.4	14.1	0.7	14.3	1.4	14.4	0.7	14.6	1.4	14.6	0.0	14.7	0.7	15.0	2.0	15.2	1.3	15.3	0.7	15.5	1.3
1942	15.7	1.3	15.8	0.6	16.1	1.9	16.2	0.6	16.3	0.6	16.4	0.6	16.6	1.2	16.7	0.6	16.8	0.6	17.0	1.2	17.1	0.6	17.1	0.0
1943	17.1	0.0	17.0	-0.6	17.2	1.2	17.4	1.2	17.4	0.0	17.4	0.0	17.3	-0.6	17.2	-0.6	17.3	0.6	17.4	0.6	17.5	0.6	17.5	0.0
1944	17.4	-0.6	17.4	0.0	17.4	0.0	17.4	0.0	17.6	1.1	17.5	-0.6	17.5	0.0	17.6	0.6	17.7	0.6	17.8	0.6	17.8	0.0	17.9	0.6
1945	17.9	0.0	17.8	-0.6	17.9	0.6	18.0	0.6	18.0	0.0	18.0	0.0	18.1	0.6	18.1	0.0	18.3	1.1	18.3	0.0	18.4	0.5	18.5	0.5
1946	18.4	-0.5	18.4	0.0	18.4	0.0	18.5	0.5	18.6	0.5	18.8	1.1	19.7	4.8	20.0	1.5	20.1	0.5	20.5	2.0	21.4	4.4	21.4	0.0
1947	21.5	0.5	21.6	0.5	21.7	0.5	21.8	0.5	21.8	0.0	21.7	-0.5	21.8	0.5	21.9	0.5	22.4	2.3	22.4	0.0	22.8	1.8	23.0	0.9
1948	23.2	0.9	23.3	0.4	23.2	-0.4	23.5	1.3	23.5	0.0	23.5	0.0	23.7	0.9	23.8	0.4	23.8	0.0	23.9	0.4	24.0	0.4	24.1	0.4
1949	24.1	0.0	23.9	-0.8	23.9	0.0	23.9	0.0	23.7	-0.8	23.6	-0.4	23.3	-1.3	23.3	0.0	23.3	0.0	23.3	0.0	23.3	0.0	23.2	-0.4
1950	23.4	0.9	23.3	-0.4	23.3	0.0	23.4	0.4	23.4	0.0	23.3	-0.4	23.5	0.9	23.8	1.3	23.9	0.4	24.1	0.8	24.3	0.8	24.6	1.2
1951	25.0	1.6	25.4	1.6	25.6	0.8	25.6	0.0	25.7	0.4	25.7	0.0	25.8	0.4	25.8	0.0	25.9	0.4	25.9	0.0	26.2	1.2	26.3	0.4
1952	26.3	0.0	26.3	0.0	26.4	0.4	26.4	0.0	26.4	0.0	26.5	0.4	26.5	0.0	26.5	0.0	26.5	0.0	26.5	0.0	26.6	0.4	26.6	0.0
1953	26.6	0.0	26.5	-0.4	26.6	0.4	26.7	0.4	26.6	-0.4	26.6	0.0	26.7	0.4	26.7	0.0	26.8	0.4	26.8	0.0	26.8	0.0	26.7	-0.4
1954	27.0	1.1	26.9	-0.4	26.8	-0.4	26.7	-0.4	26.7	0.0	26.7	0.0	26.5	-0.7	26.6	0.4	26.6	0.0	26.5	-0.4	26.5	0.0	26.6	0.4
1955	26.6	0.0	26.5	-0.4	26.6	0.4	26.4	-0.8	26.6	0.8	26.6	0.0	26.7	0.4	26.6	-0.4	26.8	0.8	26.8	0.0	26.8	0.0	26.8	0.0
1956	26.8	0.0	26.7	-0.4	26.8	0.4	26.8	0.0	27.0	0.7	27.1	0.4	27.2	0.4	27.1	-0.4	27.2	0.4	27.3	0.4	27.5	0.7	27.5	0.0
1957	27.6	0.4	27.8	0.7	27.8	0.0	27.8	0.0	27.9	0.4	27.9	0.0	27.9	0.0	28.0	0.4	28.2	0.7	28.2	0.0	28.4	0.7	28.4	0.0
1958	28.6	0.7	28.6	0.0	28.8	0.7	29.0	0.7	28.9	-0.3	28.9	0.0	29.0	0.3	28.9	-0.3	29.1	0.7	29.1	0.0	29.2	0.3	29.2	0.0
1959	29.2	0.0	29.2	0.0	29.2	0.0	29.2	0.0	29.3	0.3	29.3	0.0	29.4	0.3	29.4	0.0	29.5	0.3	29.6	0.3	29.7	0.3	29.7	0.0

[Continued]

Los Angeles-Riverside-Orange County, CA
Consumer Price Index - Urban Wage Earners
Base 1982-1984 = 100
All Items
[Continued]

For 1914-2001. Columns headed % show percentile change in the index from the previous period for which an index is available.

Year	Jan Index	%	Feb Index	%	Mar Index	%	Apr Index	%	May Index	%	Jun Index	%	Jul Index	%	Aug Index	%	Sep Index	%	Oct Index	%	Nov Index	%	Dec Index	%
1960	29.8	0.3	29.7	-0.3	29.8	0.3	30.0	0.7	29.9	-0.3	29.9	0.0	29.9	0.0	29.8	-0.3	29.9	0.3	30.1	0.7	30.1	0.0	30.3	0.7
1961	30.3	0.0	30.3	0.0	30.2	-0.3	30.3	0.3	30.3	0.0	30.3	0.0	30.3	0.0	30.3	0.0	30.3	0.0	30.4	0.3	30.5	0.3	30.5	0.0
1962	30.4	-0.3	30.4	0.0	30.5	0.3	30.6	0.3	30.8	0.7	30.8	0.0	30.7	-0.3	30.7	0.0	30.9	0.7	30.9	0.0	30.8	-0.3	30.9	0.3
1963	30.9	0.0	31.0	0.3	31.0	0.0	31.1	0.3	31.0	-0.3	30.9	-0.3	31.1	0.6	31.2	0.3	31.2	0.0	31.4	0.6	31.4	0.0	31.3	-0.3
1964	31.5	0.6	31.4	-0.3	31.6	0.6	31.6	0.0	31.6	0.0	31.6	0.0	31.6	0.0	31.7	0.3	31.6	-0.3	31.9	0.9	32.0	0.3	32.0	0.0
1965	32.1	0.3	32.2	0.3	32.3	0.3	32.4	0.3	32.4	0.0	32.5	0.3	32.4	-0.3	32.1	-0.9	32.5	1.2	32.4	-0.3	32.5	0.3	32.6	0.3
1966	32.5	-0.3	32.6	0.3	32.7	0.3	32.9	0.6	32.9	0.0	33.0	0.3	33.1	0.3	33.0	-0.3	33.3	0.9	33.4	0.3	33.5	0.3	33.5	0.0
1967	33.3	-0.6	33.3	0.0	33.2	-0.3	33.5	0.9	33.6	0.3	33.7	0.3	33.8	0.3	34.0	0.6	34.3	0.9	34.2	-0.3	34.5	0.9	34.5	0.0
1968	34.7	0.6	34.7	0.0	34.9	0.6	34.9	0.0	34.8	-0.3	35.1	0.9	35.2	0.3	35.3	0.3	35.3	0.0	35.6	0.8	35.7	0.3	35.7	0.0
1969	35.9	0.6	36.0	0.3	36.4	1.1	36.5	0.3	36.5	0.0	36.8	0.8	37.0	0.5	37.1	0.3	37.3	0.5	37.4	0.3	37.4	0.0	37.7	0.8
1970	37.8	0.3	37.9	0.3	38.0	0.3	38.4	1.1	38.5	0.3	38.5	0.0	38.9	1.0	38.6	-0.8	39.2	1.6	39.3	0.3	39.3	0.0	39.5	0.5
1971	39.5	0.0	39.3	-0.5	39.6	0.8	39.5	-0.3	40.0	1.3	40.2	0.5	40.3	0.2	40.4	0.2	40.6	0.5	40.7	0.2	40.6	-0.2	40.6	0.0
1972	40.6	0.0	40.7	0.2	41.0	0.7	41.0	0.0	41.0	0.0	41.1	0.2	41.5	1.0	41.6	0.2	41.9	0.7	41.9	0.0	42.1	0.5	42.1	0.0
1973	42.2	0.2	42.5	0.7	42.8	0.7	42.9	0.2	43.1	0.5	43.5	0.9	43.7	0.5	44.3	1.4	44.4	0.2	44.8	0.9	45.2	0.9	45.4	0.4
1974	45.7	0.7	46.1	0.9	46.6	1.1	47.0	0.9	47.5	1.1	47.8	0.6	48.4	1.3	49.0	1.2	49.7	1.4	49.8	0.2	50.3	1.0	50.8	1.0
1975	51.0	0.4	51.5	1.0	52.2	1.4	52.7	1.0	53.1	0.8	53.0	-0.2	53.5	0.9	53.7	0.4	54.3	1.1	54.6	0.6	55.0	0.7	55.4	0.7
1976	55.7	0.5	55.4	-0.5	55.5	0.2	55.5	0.0	56.3	1.4	56.5	0.4	57.1	1.1	57.4	0.5	57.8	0.7	58.0	0.3	58.2	0.3	58.5	0.5
1977	59.1	1.0	59.7	1.0	59.8	0.2	60.2	0.7	60.4	0.3	60.7	0.5	61.0	0.5	61.1	0.2	61.4	0.5	61.4	0.0	61.9	0.8	62.4	0.8
1978	62.8	0.6	63.2	0.6	63.3	0.2	63.9	0.9	64.7	1.3	65.3	0.9	65.7	0.6	65.9	0.3	66.6	1.1	66.7	0.2	66.8	0.1	66.7	-0.1
1979	67.6	1.3	68.5	1.3	69.2	1.0	70.7	2.2	71.9	1.7	72.6	1.0	73.4	1.1	74.3	1.2	75.5	1.6	75.8	0.4	76.4	0.8	77.8	1.8
1980	79.5	2.2	81.2	2.1	82.5	1.6	83.8	1.6	85.5	2.0	85.7	0.2	85.1	-0.7	84.6	-0.6	85.3	0.8	86.3	1.2	87.4	1.3	88.7	1.5
1981	88.9	0.2	89.7	0.9	90.2	0.6	91.1	1.0	91.6	0.5	91.9	0.3	93.5	1.7	94.3	0.9	95.7	1.5	96.4	0.7	96.5	0.1	96.7	0.2
1982	98.0	1.3	97.9	-0.1	98.2	0.3	98.2	0.0	98.3	0.1	99.4	1.1	99.1	-0.3	99.1	0.0	98.7	-0.4	99.1	0.4	98.7	-0.4	97.5	-1.2
1983	97.5	0.0	98.2	0.7	98.0	-0.2	98.2	0.2	98.8	0.6	98.8	0.0	99.2	0.4	99.4	0.2	100.4	1.0	101.2	0.8	100.8	-0.4	101.5	0.7
1984	100.8	-0.7	101.2	0.4	100.8	-0.4	101.1	0.3	102.6	1.5	102.7	0.1	101.6	-1.1	103.2	1.6	102.9	-0.3	102.4	-0.5	102.9	0.5	103.7	0.8
1985	104.3	0.6	104.6	0.3	104.8	0.2	105.3	0.5	106.3	0.9	106.3	0.0	106.9	0.6	107.6	0.7	107.5	-0.1	108.3	0.7	108.0	-0.3	108.3	0.3
1986	108.6	0.3	108.4	-0.2	108.8	0.4	108.3	-0.5	109.2	0.8	109.8	0.5	109.6	-0.2	109.5	-0.1	110.6	1.0	111.1	0.5	110.4	-0.6	110.1	-0.3
1987	110.8	0.6	112.1	1.2	112.8	0.6	113.3	0.4	114.1	0.7	113.8	-0.3	113.8	0.0	114.6	0.7	115.2	0.5	115.8	0.5	115.4	-0.3	115.7	0.3
1988	115.9	0.2	116.6	0.6	117.5	0.8	118.0	0.4	118.9	0.8	118.9	0.0	119.0	0.1	119.5	0.4	120.3	0.7	121.0	0.6	120.9	-0.1	121.1	0.2
1989	121.4	0.2	122.3	0.7	122.9	0.5	124.0	0.9	125.0	0.8	125.3	0.2	125.7	0.3	125.5	-0.2	126.5	0.8	126.5	0.0	126.4	-0.1	127.0	0.5
1990	128.5	1.2	129.8	1.0	130.5	0.5	130.2	-0.2	130.7	0.4	131.1	0.3	131.6	0.4	132.3	0.5	133.5	0.9	134.5	0.7	134.8	0.2	135.2	0.3
1991	135.8	0.4	135.5	-0.2	135.3	-0.1	136.3	0.7	136.5	0.1	136.4	-0.1	137.3	0.7	137.4	0.1	138.2	0.6	138.5	0.2	139.0	0.4	138.6	-0.3
1992	139.6	0.7	140.3	0.5	141.0	0.5	141.3	0.2	141.4	0.1	141.8	0.3	142.2	0.3	142.4	0.1	142.8	0.3	143.6	0.6	143.5	-0.1	143.5	0.0
1993	144.4	0.6	145.0	0.4	144.8	-0.1	144.9	0.1	145.1	0.1	144.8	-0.2	144.8	0.0	144.9	0.1	145.0	0.1	145.7	0.5	146.4	0.5	146.7	0.2
1994	146.8	0.1	146.9	0.1	147.0	0.1	146.6	-0.3	146.2	-0.3	146.1	-0.1	146.5	0.3	146.8	0.2	147.3	0.3	148.0	0.5	147.7	-0.2	148.1	0.3
1995	149.0	0.6	149.2	0.1	149.3	0.1	149.5	0.1	149.8	0.2	149.7	-0.1	149.3	-0.3	149.2	-0.1	149.3	0.1	149.9	0.4	149.2	-0.5	149.4	0.1
1996	150.4	0.7	150.9	0.3	151.9	0.7	152.4	0.3	152.3	-0.1	151.5	-0.5	152.3	0.5	151.9	-0.3	152.7	0.5	153.2	0.3	152.9	-0.2	152.7	-0.1
1997	153.6	0.6	153.6	0.0	154.2	0.4	154.3	0.1	154.0	-0.2	153.8	-0.1	153.8	0.0	154.0	0.1	154.7	0.5	155.4	0.5	154.9	-0.3	155.3	0.3
1998	155.1	-0.1	155.0	-0.1	155.1	0.1	155.6	0.3	156.2	0.4	156.1	-0.1	155.9	-0.1	156.1	0.1	156.1	0.0	156.8	0.4	157.0	0.1	157.2	0.1
1999	157.8	0.4	158.1	0.2	158.3	0.1	160.1	1.1	159.7	-0.2	158.9	-0.5	159.2	0.2	159.8	0.4	160.7	0.6	160.7	0.0	160.6	-0.1	160.9	0.2
2000	161.3	0.2	162.4	0.7	163.9	0.9	164.0	0.1	164.4	0.2	164.3	-0.1	165.0	0.4	165.3	0.2	166.3	0.6	166.9	0.4	166.6	-0.1	166.7	0.1
2001	167.3	0.4	168.3	0.6	169.1	0.5	169.6	0.3	170.5	0.5	171.9	0.8	171.3	-0.3	171.1	-0.1	171.5	0.2	171.0	-0.3	170.7	-0.2	169.7	-0.6

Source: U.S. Department of Labor, Bureau of Labor Statistics, Division of Consumer Prices and Price Indexes. - indicates no data collected for period.

Los Angeles-Riverside-Orange County, CA
Consumer Price Index - All Urban Consumers
Base 1982-1984 = 100
Food and Beverages

For 1976-2001. Columns headed % show percentile change in the index from the previous period for which an index is available.

Year	Jan Index	%	Feb Index	%	Mar Index	%	Apr Index	%	May Index	%	Jun Index	%	Jul Index	%	Aug Index	%	Sep Index	%	Oct Index	%	Nov Index	%	Dec Index	%
1976	60.6	-	59.8	-1.3	59.5	-0.5	59.5	0.0	60.2	1.2	60.4	0.3	61.0	1.0	61.0	0.0	60.6	-0.7	60.7	0.2	61.0	0.5	61.5	0.8
1977	62.3	1.3	62.9	1.0	63.3	0.6	63.9	0.9	64.3	0.6	64.9	0.9	65.2	0.5	65.4	0.3	65.5	0.2	65.7	0.3	66.1	0.6	66.6	0.8
1978	67.6	1.5	68.4	1.2	69.2	1.2	70.7	2.2	71.1	0.6	72.2	1.5	72.3	0.1	72.6	0.4	73.1	0.7	73.7	0.8	73.8	0.1	74.6	1.1
1979	75.9	1.7	77.2	1.7	77.9	0.9	79.0	1.4	79.9	1.1	79.6	-0.4	79.2	-0.5	79.1	-0.1	79.7	0.8	80.3	0.8	80.9	0.7	82.0	1.4
1980	82.5	0.6	82.4	-0.1	83.4	1.2	84.1	0.8	84.5	0.5	84.9	0.5	85.6	0.8	86.9	1.5	88.3	1.6	88.3	0.0	88.7	0.5	89.2	0.6
1981	89.7	0.6	91.3	1.8	91.9	0.7	92.2	0.3	92.3	0.1	92.4	0.1	92.7	0.3	93.4	0.8	93.4	0.0	93.5	0.1	93.1	-0.4	93.9	0.9
1982	95.0	1.2	95.4	0.4	95.7	0.3	95.8	0.1	96.5	0.7	96.7	0.2	97.6	0.9	97.5	-0.1	97.5	0.0	98.2	0.7	98.4	0.2	97.8	-0.6
1983	98.9	1.1	99.2	0.3	100.1	0.9	100.5	0.4	101.1	0.6	100.2	-0.9	100.0	-0.2	99.9	-0.1	99.9	0.0	100.4	0.5	100.1	-0.3	100.8	0.7
1984	102.3	1.5	102.6	0.3	102.9	0.3	102.6	-0.3	102.3	-0.3	102.0	-0.3	102.9	0.9	103.6	0.7	103.6	0.0	103.7	0.1	104.1	0.4	104.2	0.1
1985	105.0	0.8	105.2	0.2	104.8	-0.4	104.9	0.1	105.4	0.5	105.4	0.0	104.8	-0.6	105.2	0.4	105.5	0.3	105.9	0.4	106.8	0.8	107.9	1.0
1986	108.3	0.4	107.8	-0.5	107.8	0.0	107.7	-0.1	108.1	0.4	108.4	0.3	108.4	0.0	108.9	0.5	108.8	-0.1	109.3	0.5	110.3	0.9	110.5	0.2
1987	112.3	1.6	113.7	1.2	112.8	-0.8	112.9	0.1	113.6	0.6	113.0	-0.5	112.8	-0.2	113.2	0.4	113.4	0.2	113.6	0.2	113.3	-0.3	114.0	0.6
1988	114.6	0.5	114.8	0.2	115.4	0.5	116.0	0.5	116.2	0.2	116.2	0.0	117.8	1.4	118.8	0.8	118.8	0.0	119.1	0.3	119.1	0.0	120.0	0.8
1989	121.5	1.3	122.2	0.6	122.8	0.5	123.6	0.7	124.1	0.4	123.5	-0.5	123.6	0.1	124.1	0.4	124.6	0.4	125.2	0.5	126.1	0.7	126.8	0.6
1990	129.6	2.2	130.9	1.0	130.6	-0.2	130.1	-0.4	130.4	0.2	130.5	0.1	130.6	0.1	130.7	0.1	131.0	0.2	131.5	0.4	132.5	0.8	132.7	0.2
1991	135.9	2.4	135.6	-0.2	135.7	0.1	137.4	1.3	137.0	-0.3	137.3	0.2	136.9	-0.3	135.8	-0.8	135.6	-0.1	136.3	0.5	137.3	0.7	138.0	0.5
1992	139.4	1.0	139.5	0.1	141.1	1.1	140.9	-0.1	139.6	-0.9	140.3	0.5	140.1	-0.1	141.0	0.6	142.2	0.9	142.7	0.4	142.3	-0.3	142.2	-0.1
1993	144.2	1.4	143.4	-0.6	143.9	0.3	144.6	0.5	145.4	0.6	144.9	-0.3	144.3	-0.4	144.3	0.0	145.1	0.6	146.2	0.8	146.4	0.1	148.6	1.5
1994	149.0	0.3	147.7	-0.9	147.8	0.1	147.1	-0.5	146.7	-0.3	147.0	0.2	147.6	0.4	147.7	0.1	148.7	0.7	149.9	0.8	150.1	0.1	153.1	2.0
1995	153.4	0.2	152.7	-0.5	152.7	0.0	153.8	0.7	152.8	-0.7	152.8	0.0	152.2	-0.4	152.7	0.3	153.2	0.3	154.7	1.0	154.5	-0.1	154.8	0.2
1996	154.8	0.0	155.4	0.4	157.0	1.0	156.9	-0.1	156.3	-0.4	156.4	0.1	157.2	0.5	157.6	0.3	158.7	0.7	160.0	0.8	161.0	0.6	162.0	0.6
1997	163.8	1.1	162.4	-0.9	163.3	0.6	163.0	-0.2	161.6	-0.9	162.6	0.6	161.9	-0.4	163.3	0.9	163.4	0.1	164.2	0.5	164.4	0.1	164.8	0.2
1998	166.5	1.0	165.7	-0.5	166.2	0.3	166.4	0.1	167.4	0.6	166.6	-0.5	167.2	0.4	167.8	0.4	167.9	0.1	168.6	0.4	168.4	-0.1	168.5	0.1
1999	170.3	1.1	170.4	0.1	170.5	0.1	169.8	-0.4	169.4	-0.2	169.6	0.1	169.1	-0.3	169.4	0.2	169.8	0.2	170.7	0.5	169.9	-0.5	170.3	0.2
2000	171.1	0.5	171.4	0.2	171.9	0.3	171.8	-0.1	172.6	0.5	173.0	0.2	174.1	0.6	175.1	0.6	174.4	-0.4	175.9	0.9	174.9	-0.6	176.9	1.1
2001	178.0	0.6	179.9	1.1	180.1	0.1	180.0	-0.1	179.9	-0.1	180.9	0.6	181.5	0.3	182.6	0.6	182.2	-0.2	183.2	0.5	182.7	-0.3	182.2	-0.3

Source: U.S. Department of Labor, Bureau of Labor Statistics, Division of Consumer Prices and Price Indexes. - indicates no data collected for period.

Los Angeles-Riverside-Orange County, CA
Consumer Price Index - Urban Wage Earners
Base 1982-1984 = 100
Food and Beverages

For 1976-2001. Columns headed % show percentile change in the index from the previous period for which an index is available.

Year	Jan Index	%	Feb Index	%	Mar Index	%	Apr Index	%	May Index	%	Jun Index	%	Jul Index	%	Aug Index	%	Sep Index	%	Oct Index	%	Nov Index	%	Dec Index	%
1976	59.5	-	58.7	-1.3	58.4	-0.5	58.5	0.2	59.1	1.0	59.3	0.3	59.9	1.0	59.9	0.0	59.5	-0.7	59.7	0.3	59.9	0.3	60.4	0.8
1977	61.2	1.3	61.8	1.0	62.1	0.5	62.8	1.1	63.1	0.5	63.8	1.1	64.1	0.5	64.3	0.3	64.3	0.0	64.5	0.3	64.9	0.6	65.4	0.8
1978	66.5	1.7	67.4	1.4	67.7	0.4	68.9	1.8	69.6	1.0	70.4	1.1	70.7	0.4	70.9	0.3	71.4	0.7	71.8	0.6	71.7	-0.1	72.6	1.3
1979	73.9	1.8	75.3	1.9	76.6	1.7	77.5	1.2	78.1	0.8	78.4	0.4	78.3	-0.1	78.3	0.0	79.0	0.9	79.5	0.6	79.7	0.3	80.9	1.5
1980	81.3	0.5	81.4	0.1	82.3	1.1	83.5	1.5	83.9	0.5	84.3	0.5	85.1	0.9	86.4	1.5	88.0	1.9	87.9	-0.1	88.7	0.9	89.1	0.5
1981	89.6	0.6	90.8	1.3	91.5	0.8	91.8	0.3	91.5	-0.3	92.2	0.8	92.5	0.3	93.3	0.9	93.1	-0.2	92.9	-0.2	92.8	-0.1	93.7	1.0
1982	94.9	1.3	95.4	0.5	95.7	0.3	95.9	0.2	96.4	0.5	96.6	0.2	97.4	0.8	97.4	0.0	97.3	-0.1	98.1	0.8	98.3	0.2	97.8	-0.5
1983	98.9	1.1	99.3	0.4	100.2	0.9	100.6	0.4	101.2	0.6	100.3	-0.9	100.0	-0.3	100.0	0.0	99.9	-0.1	100.5	0.6	100.2	-0.3	100.9	0.7
1984	102.4	1.5	102.8	0.4	103.1	0.3	102.7	-0.4	102.3	-0.4	102.0	-0.3	102.9	0.9	103.5	0.6	103.5	0.0	103.6	0.1	103.9	0.3	104.1	0.2
1985	104.8	0.7	105.0	0.2	104.7	-0.3	104.8	0.1	105.2	0.4	105.2	0.0	104.6	-0.6	105.0	0.4	105.3	0.3	105.7	0.4	106.6	0.9	107.6	0.9
1986	108.1	0.5	107.6	-0.5	107.6	0.0	107.6	0.0	107.8	0.2	108.1	0.3	108.1	0.0	108.5	0.4	108.5	0.0	109.1	0.6	110.1	0.9	110.3	0.2
1987	112.0	1.5	113.4	1.3	112.5	-0.8	112.7	0.2	113.4	0.6	112.7	-0.6	112.6	-0.1	113.1	0.4	113.2	0.1	113.5	0.3	113.2	-0.3	113.9	0.6
1988	114.3	0.4	114.6	0.3	115.2	0.5	115.9	0.6	116.1	0.2	116.1	0.0	117.7	1.4	118.7	0.8	118.6	-0.1	119.0	0.3	119.0	0.0	119.9	0.8
1989	121.3	1.2	122.0	0.6	122.6	0.5	123.4	0.7	123.9	0.4	123.3	-0.5	123.5	0.2	124.1	0.5	124.6	0.4	125.1	0.4	126.1	0.8	126.9	0.6
1990	129.6	2.1	130.9	1.0	130.7	-0.2	130.2	-0.4	130.4	0.2	130.6	0.2	130.8	0.2	130.9	0.1	131.1	0.2	131.6	0.4	132.6	0.8	132.8	0.2
1991	136.0	2.4	135.7	-0.2	136.0	0.2	137.6	1.2	137.2	-0.3	137.5	0.2	137.2	-0.2	136.2	-0.7	135.9	-0.2	136.7	0.6	137.5	0.6	138.2	0.5
1992	139.6	1.0	139.8	0.1	141.6	1.3	141.4	-0.1	140.0	-1.0	140.7	0.5	140.6	-0.1	141.4	0.6	142.5	0.8	143.1	0.4	142.8	-0.2	142.7	-0.1
1993	144.6	1.3	143.8	-0.6	144.3	0.3	145.0	0.5	145.9	0.6	145.5	-0.3	144.8	-0.5	144.9	0.1	145.7	0.6	146.8	0.8	146.9	0.1	149.0	1.4
1994	149.4	0.3	148.2	-0.8	148.1	-0.1	147.4	-0.5	147.0	-0.3	147.4	0.3	147.9	0.3	148.0	0.1	148.9	0.6	149.9	0.7	150.0	0.1	153.1	2.1
1995	153.4	0.2	152.8	-0.4	152.9	0.1	153.8	0.6	152.9	-0.6	153.0	0.1	152.3	-0.5	152.9	0.4	153.3	0.3	154.8	1.0	154.7	-0.1	155.0	0.2
1996	155.0	0.0	155.7	0.5	157.3	1.0	157.1	-0.1	156.6	-0.3	156.7	0.1	157.4	0.4	158.0	0.4	159.0	0.6	160.2	0.8	161.1	0.6	162.1	0.6
1997	163.8	1.0	162.5	-0.8	163.3	0.5	163.0	-0.2	161.7	-0.8	162.6	0.6	162.0	-0.4	163.3	0.8	163.3	0.0	164.2	0.6	164.4	0.1	164.9	0.3
1998	166.5	1.0	165.6	-0.5	166.2	0.4	166.2	0.0	167.6	0.8	166.6	-0.6	167.2	0.4	167.8	0.4	167.9	0.1	168.7	0.5	168.6	-0.1	168.7	0.1
1999	170.3	0.9	170.6	0.2	170.6	0.0	169.7	-0.5	169.5	-0.1	169.7	0.1	169.1	-0.4	169.4	0.2	169.8	0.2	170.7	0.5	170.0	-0.4	170.3	0.2
2000	170.8	0.3	171.4	0.4	172.1	0.4	172.0	-0.1	172.7	0.4	173.2	0.3	174.3	0.6	175.4	0.6	174.6	-0.5	176.0	0.8	175.1	-0.5	177.0	1.1
2001	178.1	0.6	180.1	1.1	180.4	0.2	180.4	0.0	180.2	-0.1	181.1	0.5	181.9	0.4	183.0	0.6	182.5	-0.3	183.5	0.5	183.1	-0.2	182.4	-0.4

Source: U.S. Department of Labor, Bureau of Labor Statistics, Division of Consumer Prices and Price Indexes. - indicates no data collected for period.

Los Angeles-Riverside-Orange County, CA
Consumer Price Index - All Urban Consumers
Base 1982-1984 = 100
Housing

For 1976-2001. Columns headed % show percentile change in the index from the previous period for which an index is available.

Year	Jan Index	%	Feb Index	%	Mar Index	%	Apr Index	%	May Index	%	Jun Index	%	Jul Index	%	Aug Index	%	Sep Index	%	Oct Index	%	Nov Index	%	Dec Index	%
1976	53.9	-	53.2	-1.3	53.1	-0.2	52.9	-0.4	53.9	1.9	53.8	-0.2	54.4	1.1	54.7	0.6	55.4	1.3	55.7	0.5	55.7	0.0	56.0	0.5
1977	57.1	2.0	57.5	0.7	57.5	0.0	57.8	0.5	58.0	0.3	58.1	0.2	58.6	0.9	58.5	-0.2	59.1	1.0	58.8	-0.5	59.6	1.4	60.5	1.5
1978	60.9	0.7	61.2	0.5	61.4	0.3	62.2	1.3	62.9	1.1	63.5	1.0	63.8	0.5	64.0	0.3	65.1	1.7	65.0	-0.2	64.9	-0.2	63.7	-1.8
1979	64.7	1.6	65.6	1.4	66.1	0.8	67.4	2.0	68.6	1.8	69.4	1.2	70.1	1.0	71.3	1.7	72.6	1.8	73.0	0.6	74.1	1.5	75.9	2.4
1980	77.7	2.4	79.6	2.4	81.2	2.0	82.7	1.8	85.6	3.5	86.2	0.7	84.7	-1.7	83.0	-2.0	83.4	0.5	85.2	2.2	86.6	1.6	88.4	2.1
1981	88.4	0.0	88.6	0.2	88.8	0.2	89.6	0.9	90.4	0.9	90.3	-0.1	92.3	2.2	93.4	1.2	96.2	3.0	97.0	0.8	96.7	-0.3	96.7	0.0
1982	97.9	1.2	97.5	-0.4	98.3	0.8	98.4	0.1	98.3	-0.1	99.4	1.1	98.1	-1.3	98.0	-0.1	97.5	-0.5	97.8	0.3	97.0	-0.8	95.3	-1.8
1983	95.4	0.1	96.6	1.3	96.5	-0.1	97.0	0.5	97.8	0.8	98.4	0.6	98.7	0.3	99.1	0.4	100.2	1.1	100.4	0.2	100.0	-0.4	99.9	-0.1
1984	99.9	0.0	101.2	1.3	101.5	0.3	102.2	0.7	103.7	1.5	104.3	0.6	104.7	0.4	105.8	1.1	106.3	0.5	106.1	-0.2	105.6	-0.5	105.3	-0.3
1985	106.6	1.2	107.0	0.4	106.4	-0.6	106.6	0.2	109.1	2.3	108.4	-0.6	110.6	2.0	112.7	1.9	112.3	-0.4	113.5	1.1	111.7	-1.6	111.6	-0.1
1986	111.6	0.0	112.6	0.9	114.9	2.0	114.0	-0.8	115.4	1.2	115.9	0.4	116.9	0.9	117.2	0.3	120.0	2.4	120.4	0.3	117.5	-2.4	116.8	-0.6
1987	116.7	-0.1	118.3	1.4	119.5	1.0	120.4	0.8	121.6	1.0	120.7	-0.7	121.1	0.3	122.2	0.9	122.8	0.5	123.6	0.7	122.7	-0.7	122.9	0.2
1988	123.0	0.1	124.5	1.2	125.2	0.6	125.4	0.2	126.8	1.1	126.6	-0.2	126.4	-0.2	127.1	0.6	128.2	0.9	128.7	0.4	128.9	0.2	128.9	0.0
1989	128.7	-0.2	129.2	0.4	128.8	-0.3	128.6	-0.2	130.4	1.4	131.7	1.0	133.0	1.0	133.0	0.0	134.6	1.2	134.5	-0.1	134.0	-0.4	134.3	0.2
1990	135.8	1.1	136.7	0.7	138.1	1.0	137.1	-0.7	137.8	0.5	138.5	0.5	139.9	1.0	140.8	0.6	141.5	0.5	142.0	0.4	141.3	-0.5	141.5	0.1
1991	142.8	0.9	143.4	0.4	143.9	0.3	144.7	0.6	144.5	-0.1	144.4	-0.1	145.4	0.7	145.6	0.1	146.0	0.3	145.9	-0.1	146.3	0.3	146.1	-0.1
1992	147.0	0.6	147.7	0.5	147.9	0.1	147.9	0.0	148.1	0.1	148.8	0.5	149.0	0.1	149.3	0.2	149.2	-0.1	149.5	0.2	149.4	-0.1	148.9	-0.3
1993	149.9	0.7	150.8	0.6	150.0	-0.5	150.4	0.3	150.6	0.1	150.6	0.0	150.7	0.1	150.7	0.0	149.8	-0.6	150.2	0.3	150.4	0.1	151.0	0.4
1994	151.5	0.3	151.9	0.3	151.6	-0.2	150.8	-0.5	150.7	-0.1	150.6	-0.1	151.2	0.4	151.4	0.1	151.2	-0.1	151.2	0.0	149.9	-0.9	150.4	0.3
1995	151.3	0.6	152.0	0.5	152.0	0.0	151.6	-0.3	152.5	0.6	153.0	0.3	152.4	-0.4	152.5	0.1	152.7	0.1	152.7	0.0	150.9	-1.2	152.4	1.0
1996	153.1	0.5	153.4	0.2	153.4	0.0	153.6	0.1	153.4	-0.1	152.2	-0.8	154.4	1.4	154.6	0.1	155.4	0.5	155.6	0.1	155.1	-0.3	154.9	-0.1
1997	155.4	0.3	155.6	0.1	155.5	-0.1	155.2	-0.2	156.1	0.6	156.4	0.2	156.9	0.3	156.7	-0.1	157.1	0.3	157.9	0.5	157.7	-0.1	158.8	0.7
1998	158.4	-0.3	158.7	0.2	159.2	0.3	159.4	0.1	159.6	0.1	159.6	0.0	159.9	0.2	160.7	0.5	161.3	0.4	161.2	-0.1	161.4	0.1	161.8	0.2
1999	162.3	0.3	162.6	0.2	162.9	0.2	163.4	0.3	163.4	0.0	164.0	0.4	165.0	0.6	165.2	0.1	166.4	0.7	166.3	-0.1	166.2	-0.1	166.0	-0.1
2000	167.4	0.8	168.5	0.7	169.1	0.4	169.1	0.0	169.3	0.1	170.1	0.5	171.1	0.6	171.9	0.5	172.7	0.5	173.2	0.3	173.3	0.1	173.6	0.2
2001	175.1	0.9	175.4	0.2	176.3	0.5	176.7	0.2	177.9	0.7	181.1	1.8	180.7	-0.2	182.1	0.8	182.0	-0.1	181.6	-0.2	182.4	0.4	182.5	0.1

Source: U.S. Department of Labor, Bureau of Labor Statistics, Division of Consumer Prices and Price Indexes. - indicates no data collected for period.

Los Angeles-Riverside-Orange County, CA
Consumer Price Index - Urban Wage Earners
Base 1982-1984 = 100
Housing

For 1976-2001. Columns headed % show percentile change in the index from the previous period for which an index is available.

Year	Jan Index	%	Feb Index	%	Mar Index	%	Apr Index	%	May Index	%	Jun Index	%	Jul Index	%	Aug Index	%	Sep Index	%	Oct Index	%	Nov Index	%	Dec Index	%
1976	54.0	-	53.3	-1.3	53.1	-0.4	53.0	-0.2	54.0	1.9	53.9	-0.2	54.5	1.1	54.8	0.6	55.4	1.1	55.8	0.7	55.8	0.0	56.0	0.4
1977	57.2	2.1	57.6	0.7	57.5	-0.2	57.9	0.7	58.0	0.2	58.2	0.3	58.6	0.7	58.6	0.0	59.1	0.9	58.9	-0.3	59.7	1.4	60.6	1.5
1978	61.0	0.7	61.3	0.5	61.6	0.5	62.3	1.1	62.9	1.0	63.5	1.0	63.9	0.6	64.1	0.3	65.1	1.6	64.9	-0.3	64.8	-0.2	63.8	-1.5
1979	64.9	1.7	65.9	1.5	66.5	0.9	68.0	2.3	69.4	2.1	70.1	1.0	70.8	1.0	72.3	2.1	73.7	1.9	74.0	0.4	75.1	1.5	76.9	2.4
1980	79.2	3.0	81.2	2.5	82.9	2.1	84.4	1.8	87.6	3.8	88.1	0.6	86.4	-1.9	84.6	-2.1	84.7	0.1	86.6	2.2	88.2	1.8	90.3	2.4
1981	90.3	0.0	90.4	0.1	90.7	0.3	91.7	1.1	92.5	0.9	92.4	-0.1	95.1	2.9	96.2	1.2	99.1	3.0	99.9	0.8	99.5	-0.4	99.6	0.1
1982	100.9	1.3	100.3	-0.6	101.1	0.8	101.2	0.1	101.0	-0.2	102.2	1.2	100.7	-1.5	100.6	-0.1	100.0	-0.6	100.3	0.3	99.3	-1.0	97.4	-1.9
1983	97.3	-0.1	98.9	1.6	98.4	-0.5	97.6	-0.8	97.9	0.3	97.3	-0.6	97.7	0.4	98.0	0.3	100.3	2.3	101.7	1.4	100.9	-0.8	101.4	0.5
1984	99.1	-2.3	100.2	1.1	99.2	-1.0	99.1	-0.1	101.6	2.5	102.3	0.7	100.2	-2.1	102.8	2.6	101.6	-1.2	99.2	-2.4	100.2	1.0	102.0	1.8
1985	103.2	1.2	103.6	0.4	103.0	-0.6	103.2	0.2	105.8	2.5	104.9	-0.9	107.0	2.0	109.1	2.0	108.7	-0.4	109.8	1.0	108.1	-1.5	107.9	-0.2
1986	107.9	0.0	108.9	0.9	111.2	2.1	110.3	-0.8	111.7	1.3	112.2	0.4	113.1	0.8	113.4	0.3	116.1	2.4	116.5	0.3	113.6	-2.5	113.0	-0.5
1987	112.9	-0.1	114.4	1.3	115.4	0.9	116.3	0.8	117.6	1.1	116.7	-0.8	117.1	0.3	118.2	0.9	118.7	0.4	119.4	0.6	118.6	-0.7	118.9	0.3
1988	118.9	0.0	120.1	1.0	121.0	0.7	121.1	0.1	122.5	1.2	122.3	-0.2	122.1	-0.2	122.6	0.4	123.9	1.1	124.5	0.5	124.5	0.0	124.5	0.0
1989	124.2	-0.2	124.7	0.4	124.2	-0.4	124.1	-0.1	125.8	1.4	127.0	1.0	128.4	1.1	128.3	-0.1	129.7	1.1	129.7	0.0	129.1	-0.5	129.4	0.2
1990	130.9	1.2	131.7	0.6	133.0	1.0	132.0	-0.8	132.8	0.6	133.4	0.5	134.8	1.0	135.5	0.5	136.2	0.5	136.8	0.4	136.1	-0.5	136.3	0.1
1991	137.5	0.9	138.1	0.4	138.5	0.3	139.4	0.6	139.2	-0.1	139.1	-0.1	140.1	0.7	140.2	0.1	140.7	0.4	140.7	0.0	141.0	0.2	140.7	-0.2
1992	141.4	0.5	142.2	0.6	142.4	0.1	142.4	0.0	142.5	0.1	143.2	0.5	143.3	0.1	143.6	0.2	143.5	-0.1	143.9	0.3	143.8	-0.1	143.4	-0.3
1993	144.4	0.7	145.1	0.5	144.3	-0.6	144.7	0.3	144.9	0.1	144.9	0.0	144.9	0.0	145.0	0.1	144.1	-0.6	144.5	0.3	144.9	0.3	145.4	0.3
1994	145.8	0.3	146.3	0.3	145.9	-0.3	145.1	-0.5	145.1	0.0	144.9	-0.1	145.6	0.5	145.8	0.1	145.5	-0.2	145.4	-0.1	144.3	-0.8	144.7	0.3
1995	145.5	0.6	146.2	0.5	146.1	-0.1	145.9	-0.1	146.7	0.5	147.3	0.4	146.6	-0.5	146.7	0.1	147.0	0.2	146.9	-0.1	145.1	-1.2	146.8	1.2
1996	147.4	0.4	147.5	0.1	147.6	0.1	147.8	0.1	147.6	-0.1	146.5	-0.7	148.5	1.4	148.7	0.1	149.4	0.5	149.5	0.1	149.2	-0.2	149.0	-0.1
1997	149.3	0.2	149.5	0.1	149.5	0.0	149.2	-0.2	150.2	0.7	150.6	0.3	151.0	0.3	150.6	-0.3	151.1	0.3	151.8	0.5	151.7	-0.1	152.8	0.7
1998	152.3	-0.3	152.3	0.0	152.8	0.3	153.1	0.2	153.2	0.1	153.3	0.1	153.6	0.2	154.1	0.3	154.7	0.4	154.7	0.0	155.1	0.3	155.7	0.4
1999	155.9	0.1	156.0	0.1	156.3	0.2	156.6	0.2	156.8	0.1	157.1	0.2	157.9	0.5	158.2	0.2	159.5	0.8	159.4	-0.1	159.6	0.1	159.4	-0.1
2000	160.5	0.7	161.4	0.6	161.9	0.3	162.1	0.1	162.5	0.2	163.2	0.4	164.0	0.5	164.4	0.2	165.5	0.7	166.0	0.3	166.2	0.1	166.7	0.3
2001	168.0	0.8	168.3	0.2	169.1	0.5	169.5	0.2	170.6	0.6	173.6	1.8	173.1	-0.3	174.3	0.7	174.6	0.2	174.5	-0.1	175.3	0.5	175.7	0.2

Source: U.S. Department of Labor, Bureau of Labor Statistics, Division of Consumer Prices and Price Indexes. - indicates no data collected for period.

Los Angeles-Riverside-Orange County, CA
Consumer Price Index - All Urban Consumers
Base 1982-1984 = 100
Apparel

For 1952-2001. Columns headed % show percentile change in the index from the previous period for which an index is available.

Year	Jan Index	%	Feb Index	%	Mar Index	%	Apr Index	%	May Index	%	Jun Index	%	Jul Index	%	Aug Index	%	Sep Index	%	Oct Index	%	Nov Index	%	Dec Index	%
1952	-	-	-	-	-	-	-	-	-	-	-	-	-	-	-	-	-	-	-	-	-	-	49.2	-
1953	48.9	-0.6	48.9	0.0	48.7	-0.4	48.6	-0.2	48.6	0.0	48.5	-0.2	48.7	0.4	48.4	-0.6	48.9	1.0	48.8	-0.2	48.8	0.0	48.9	0.2
1954	48.7	-0.4	48.9	0.4	49.0	0.2	48.7	-0.6	48.5	-0.4	48.9	0.8	48.8	-0.2	48.7	-0.2	49.3	1.2	49.3	0.0	49.2	-0.2	49.2	0.0
1955	48.8	-0.8	48.9	0.2	48.7	-0.4	48.7	0.0	48.8	0.2	48.7	-0.2	48.8	0.2	48.8	0.0	49.2	0.8	49.2	0.0	49.0	-0.4	49.2	0.4
1956	49.1	-0.2	49.3	0.4	49.4	0.2	49.3	-0.2	49.8	1.0	49.8	0.0	49.9	0.2	49.8	-0.2	50.5	1.4	50.5	0.0	50.5	0.0	50.6	0.2
1957	50.4	-0.4	50.5	0.2	50.7	0.4	50.7	0.0	50.8	0.2	50.8	0.0	50.8	0.0	50.6	-0.4	51.3	1.4	51.2	-0.2	51.3	0.2	51.3	0.0
1958	51.0	-0.6	51.4	0.8	51.1	-0.6	50.9	-0.4	50.9	0.0	50.6	-0.6	50.8	0.4	50.6	-0.4	51.0	0.8	51.0	0.0	51.1	0.2	51.0	-0.2
1959	51.0	0.0	51.0	0.0	51.0	0.0	51.0	0.0	51.3	0.6	51.0	-0.6	51.6	1.2	51.4	-0.4	52.2	1.6	52.4	0.4	52.6	0.4	52.6	0.0
1960	52.5	-0.2	52.7	0.4	52.7	0.0	52.9	0.4	52.9	0.0	52.6	-0.6	52.7	0.2	52.6	-0.2	52.9	0.6	53.0	0.2	53.0	0.0	53.0	0.0
1961	52.7	-0.6	53.1	0.8	53.1	0.0	52.7	-0.8	53.0	0.6	52.7	-0.6	53.1	0.8	52.8	-0.6	53.0	0.4	52.9	-0.2	52.9	0.0	53.0	0.2
1962	52.7	-0.6	52.7	0.0	52.8	0.2	52.6	-0.4	52.7	0.2	52.7	0.0	52.8	0.2	52.5	-0.6	53.7	2.3	53.6	-0.2	53.6	0.0	53.7	0.2
1963	53.5	-0.4	53.5	0.0	53.6	0.2	53.4	-0.4	53.6	0.4	53.4	-0.4	53.5	0.2	53.6	0.2	54.1	0.9	54.1	0.0	54.1	0.0	54.5	0.7
1964	53.8	-1.3	54.3	0.9	54.4	0.2	54.5	0.2	54.5	0.0	54.6	0.2	54.6	0.0	54.4	-0.4	54.6	0.4	54.6	0.0	54.6	0.0	54.8	0.4
1965	54.6	-0.4	55.0	0.7	55.1	0.2	55.1	0.0	55.3	0.4	55.4	0.2	54.7	-1.3	54.5	-0.4	54.9	0.7	55.0	0.2	55.2	0.4	55.0	-0.4
1966	55.1	0.2	55.4	0.5	55.3	-0.2	55.5	0.4	55.9	0.7	55.9	0.0	55.7	-0.4	55.5	-0.4	56.6	2.0	56.4	-0.4	56.7	0.5	57.0	0.5
1967	56.4	-1.1	57.0	1.1	57.0	0.0	57.1	0.2	57.4	0.5	57.6	0.3	57.7	0.2	58.7	1.7	59.5	1.4	59.4	-0.2	59.6	0.3	59.6	0.0
1968	59.2	-0.7	59.8	1.0	60.4	1.0	60.4	0.0	60.6	0.3	60.8	0.3	61.2	0.7	61.2	0.0	62.2	1.6	62.5	0.5	62.5	0.0	63.0	0.8
1969	62.5	-0.8	62.9	0.6	63.1	0.3	62.7	-0.6	63.2	0.8	63.4	0.3	63.5	0.2	63.1	-0.6	64.6	2.4	64.6	0.0	64.9	0.5	65.1	0.3
1970	64.9	-0.3	65.4	0.8	65.7	0.5	66.0	0.5	66.7	1.1	66.8	0.1	66.3	-0.7	66.1	-0.3	67.2	1.7	67.2	0.0	67.7	0.7	67.9	0.3
1971	67.1	-1.2	67.5	0.6	67.7	0.3	67.7	0.0	68.8	1.6	68.9	0.1	68.9	0.0	68.5	-0.6	69.6	1.6	69.3	-0.4	69.3	0.0	69.1	-0.3
1972	68.6	-0.7	68.9	0.4	69.7	1.2	69.8	0.1	69.8	0.0	69.7	-0.1	69.2	-0.7	69.0	-0.3	70.3	1.9	70.3	0.0	70.3	0.0	70.6	0.4
1973	69.3	-1.8	69.7	0.6	71.2	2.2	71.0	-0.3	71.3	0.4	71.4	0.1	71.0	-0.6	71.6	0.8	73.0	2.0	72.6	-0.5	72.7	0.1	72.8	0.1
1974	71.8	-1.4	73.0	1.7	75.0	2.7	75.8	1.1	76.9	1.5	77.1	0.3	76.9	-0.3	78.3	1.8	79.0	0.9	78.6	-0.5	79.2	0.8	78.6	-0.8
1975	77.6	-1.3	78.0	0.5	78.0	0.0	78.5	0.6	79.1	0.8	79.4	0.4	78.6	-1.0	79.7	1.4	80.6	1.1	80.7	0.1	80.2	-0.6	80.1	-0.1
1976	79.0	-1.4	79.1	0.1	80.5	1.8	79.9	-0.7	80.7	1.0	80.5	-0.2	79.8	-0.9	81.4	2.0	82.3	1.1	82.2	-0.1	82.3	0.1	82.8	0.6
1977	82.8	0.0	83.7	1.1	84.0	0.4	83.7	-0.4	83.9	0.2	83.6	-0.4	82.7	-1.1	83.4	0.8	84.3	1.1	85.3	1.2	85.7	0.5	86.1	0.5
1978	86.2	0.1	85.0	-1.4	85.1	0.1	84.7	-0.5	85.5	0.9	85.5	0.0	85.4	-0.1	85.8	0.5	86.2	0.5	86.2	0.0	87.2	1.2	87.3	0.1
1979	85.9	-1.6	86.4	0.6	87.3	1.0	88.6	1.5	88.8	0.2	89.5	0.8	87.6	-2.1	88.0	0.5	90.7	3.1	90.5	-0.2	92.5	2.2	91.9	-0.6
1980	94.6	2.9	97.2	2.7	98.5	1.3	98.3	-0.2	97.8	-0.5	98.3	0.5	98.0	-0.3	98.4	0.4	99.0	0.6	99.7	0.7	100.1	0.4	99.7	-0.4
1981	97.7	-2.0	98.4	0.7	101.0	2.6	102.1	1.1	103.0	0.9	102.7	-0.3	101.6	-1.1	101.9	0.3	102.8	0.9	102.6	-0.2	102.8	0.2	101.5	-1.3
1982	99.9	-1.6	101.7	1.8	100.6	-1.1	99.5	-1.1	99.0	-0.5	98.6	-0.4	97.9	-0.7	97.7	-0.2	97.3	-0.4	97.9	0.6	98.8	0.9	98.1	-0.7
1983	95.3	-2.9	98.0	2.8	98.1	0.1	98.6	0.5	98.4	-0.2	99.9	1.5	99.9	0.0	101.7	1.8	102.0	0.3	101.8	-0.2	101.7	-0.1	101.2	-0.5
1984	101.3	0.1	101.2	-0.1	100.1	-1.1	100.5	0.4	100.3	-0.2	98.0	-2.3	97.7	-0.3	103.0	5.4	104.0	1.0	104.4	0.4	103.5	-0.9	102.3	-1.2
1985	99.8	-2.4	103.7	3.9	104.4	0.7	103.3	-1.1	103.5	0.2	104.3	0.8	103.0	-1.2	105.8	2.7	108.7	2.7	108.0	-0.6	108.0	0.0	108.4	0.4
1986	107.3	-1.0	106.4	-0.8	106.8	0.4	106.6	-0.2	105.9	-0.7	106.4	0.5	106.3	-0.1	105.9	-0.4	108.0	2.0	107.7	-0.3	108.4	0.6	107.3	-1.0
1987	109.6	2.1	108.8	-0.7	114.3	5.1	111.6	-2.4	112.2	0.5	113.5	1.2	110.1	-3.0	113.5	3.1	115.1	1.4	113.9	-1.0	113.1	-0.7	113.8	0.6
1988	113.2	-0.5	114.1	0.8	118.5	3.9	116.7	-1.5	117.6	0.8	115.9	-1.4	113.8	-1.8	109.7	-3.6	110.5	0.7	113.3	2.5	114.1	0.7	113.9	-0.2
1989	111.7	-1.9	114.1	2.1	122.0	6.9	122.1	0.1	122.7	0.5	120.3	-2.0	117.1	-2.7	116.8	-0.3	120.3	3.0	119.4	-0.7	119.3	-0.1	119.4	0.1
1990	119.3	-0.1	128.3	7.5	129.6	1.0	130.4	0.6	129.2	-0.9	126.3	-2.2	123.1	-2.5	122.3	-0.6	125.7	2.8	127.4	1.4	127.7	0.2	127.3	-0.3
1991	127.5	0.2	129.1	1.3	129.2	0.1	132.8	2.8	130.2	-2.0	125.2	-3.8	128.2	2.4	130.2	1.6	136.3	4.7	136.2	-0.1	136.1	-0.1	130.3	-4.3
1992	132.7	1.8	135.2	1.9	136.9	1.3	136.3	-0.4	136.0	-0.2	130.4	-4.1	130.8	0.3	132.0	0.9	131.8	-0.2	134.6	2.1	131.6	-2.2	129.5	-1.6
1993	128.9	-0.5	134.7	4.5	135.7	0.7	133.7	-1.5	129.8	-2.9	127.8	-1.5	127.4	-0.3	130.7	2.6	134.9	3.2	131.9	-2.2	133.9	1.5	130.2	-2.8
1994	129.1	-0.8	131.0	1.5	133.2	1.7	133.8	0.5	131.3	-1.9	125.0	-4.8	122.4	-2.1	123.7	1.1	132.2	6.9	133.3	0.8	132.3	-0.8	128.0	-3.3
1995	129.7	1.3	130.5	0.6	131.0	0.4	129.1	-1.5	128.8	-0.2	123.7	-4.0	128.0	3.5	123.8	-3.3	124.7	0.7	125.9	1.0	125.2	-0.6	120.1	-4.1
1996	126.8	5.6	127.4	0.5	134.0	5.2	130.0	-3.0	125.8	-3.2	124.4	-1.1	122.6	-1.4	122.0	-0.5	125.0	2.5	129.9	3.9	125.2	-3.6	118.6	-5.3
1997	122.3	3.1	122.2	-0.1	124.5	1.9	125.1	0.5	123.6	-1.2	121.4	-1.8	119.2	-1.8	117.0	-1.8	119.4	2.1	120.7	1.1	118.8	-1.6	117.4	-1.2

[Continued]

Los Angeles-Riverside-Orange County, CA
Consumer Price Index - All Urban Consumers
Base 1982-1984 = 100
Apparel

[Continued]

For 1952-2001. Columns headed % show percentile change in the index from the previous period for which an index is available.

Year	Jan Index	%	Feb Index	%	Mar Index	%	Apr Index	%	May Index	%	Jun Index	%	Jul Index	%	Aug Index	%	Sep Index	%	Oct Index	%	Nov Index	%	Dec Index	%
1998	118.5	0.9	125.0	5.5	129.3	3.4	130.3	0.8	126.2	-3.1	125.1	-0.9	119.7	-4.3	122.8	2.6	119.5	-2.7	123.5	3.3	120.6	-2.3	116.4	-3.5
1999	114.0	-2.1	121.1	6.2	122.2	0.9	123.7	1.2	122.7	-0.8	117.9	-3.9	111.2	-5.7	117.5	5.7	118.7	1.0	118.4	-0.3	117.0	-1.2	113.6	-2.9
2000	113.5	-0.1	118.4	4.3	118.0	-0.3	116.2	-1.5	121.7	4.7	116.2	-4.5	113.5	-2.3	115.2	1.5	119.3	3.6	119.5	0.2	118.2	-1.1	114.6	-3.0
2001	115.1	0.4	119.5	3.8	120.4	0.8	116.7	-3.1	113.4	-2.8	107.9	-4.9	106.2	-1.6	108.0	1.7	111.8	3.5	113.5	1.5	108.6	-4.3	104.4	-3.9

Source: U.S. Department of Labor, Bureau of Labor Statistics, Division of Consumer Prices and Price Indexes. - indicates no data collected for period.

Los Angeles-Riverside-Orange County, CA
Consumer Price Index - Urban Wage Earners
Base 1982-1984 = 100
Apparel

For 1952-2001. Columns headed % show percentile change in the index from the previous period for which an index is available.

Year	Jan Index	%	Feb Index	%	Mar Index	%	Apr Index	%	May Index	%	Jun Index	%	Jul Index	%	Aug Index	%	Sep Index	%	Oct Index	%	Nov Index	%	Dec Index	%
1952	-	-	-	-	-	-	-	-	-	-	-	-	-	-	-	-	-	-	-	-	-	-	49.4	-
1953	49.1	-0.6	49.1	0.0	48.9	-0.4	48.8	-0.2	48.8	0.0	48.7	-0.2	48.8	0.2	48.6	-0.4	49.1	1.0	49.0	-0.2	49.0	0.0	49.1	0.2
1954	48.9	-0.4	49.1	0.4	49.1	0.0	48.9	-0.4	48.7	-0.4	49.1	0.8	49.0	-0.2	48.8	-0.4	49.5	1.4	49.5	0.0	49.4	-0.2	49.4	0.0
1955	49.0	-0.8	49.1	0.2	48.9	-0.4	48.8	-0.2	49.0	0.4	48.8	-0.4	49.0	0.4	49.0	0.0	49.4	0.8	49.4	0.0	49.2	-0.4	49.4	0.4
1956	49.3	-0.2	49.5	0.4	49.5	0.0	49.5	0.0	50.0	1.0	50.0	0.0	50.1	0.2	50.0	-0.2	50.7	1.4	50.7	0.0	50.7	0.0	50.8	0.2
1957	50.6	-0.4	50.7	0.2	50.9	0.4	50.9	0.0	51.0	0.2	50.9	-0.2	51.0	0.2	50.8	-0.4	51.5	1.4	51.4	-0.2	51.5	0.2	51.5	0.0
1958	51.2	-0.6	51.6	0.8	51.3	-0.6	51.1	-0.4	51.1	0.0	50.8	-0.6	50.9	0.2	50.8	-0.2	51.2	0.8	51.2	0.0	51.3	0.2	51.2	-0.2
1959	51.2	0.0	51.2	0.0	51.2	0.0	51.2	0.0	51.5	0.6	51.2	-0.6	51.8	1.2	51.6	-0.4	52.4	1.6	52.6	0.4	52.8	0.4	52.8	0.0
1960	52.7	-0.2	52.9	0.4	52.9	0.0	53.1	0.4	53.1	0.0	52.8	-0.6	52.9	0.2	52.8	-0.2	53.1	0.6	53.2	0.2	53.2	0.0	53.2	0.0
1961	52.9	-0.6	53.3	0.8	53.3	0.0	52.9	-0.8	53.2	0.6	52.9	-0.6	53.3	0.8	53.0	-0.6	53.2	0.4	53.1	-0.2	53.1	0.0	53.2	0.2
1962	52.9	-0.6	52.9	0.0	53.0	0.2	52.8	-0.4	52.9	0.2	52.9	0.0	53.0	0.2	52.7	-0.6	53.9	2.3	53.8	-0.2	53.8	0.0	53.9	0.2
1963	53.7	-0.4	53.7	0.0	53.8	0.2	53.6	-0.4	53.8	0.4	53.6	-0.4	53.7	0.2	53.8	0.2	54.3	0.9	54.3	0.0	54.3	0.0	54.7	0.7
1964	54.0	-1.3	54.5	0.9	54.6	0.2	54.7	0.2	54.7	0.0	54.8	0.2	54.8	0.0	54.6	-0.4	54.8	0.4	54.8	0.0	54.8	0.0	55.0	0.4
1965	54.8	-0.4	55.2	0.7	55.3	0.2	55.3	0.0	55.5	0.4	55.6	0.2	54.9	-1.3	54.7	-0.4	55.1	0.7	55.2	0.2	55.4	0.4	55.2	-0.4
1966	55.3	0.2	55.6	0.5	55.5	-0.2	55.7	0.4	56.1	0.7	56.1	0.0	55.9	-0.4	55.7	-0.4	56.8	2.0	56.7	-0.2	56.9	0.4	57.2	0.5
1967	56.6	-1.0	57.2	1.1	57.2	0.0	57.4	0.3	57.6	0.3	57.8	0.3	57.9	0.2	58.9	1.7	59.7	1.4	59.6	-0.2	59.8	0.3	59.8	0.0
1968	59.4	-0.7	60.0	1.0	60.6	1.0	60.6	0.0	60.9	0.5	61.0	0.2	61.4	0.7	61.4	0.0	62.4	1.6	62.8	0.6	62.7	-0.2	63.2	0.8
1969	62.8	-0.6	63.1	0.5	63.3	0.3	63.0	-0.5	63.5	0.8	63.7	0.3	63.7	0.0	63.3	-0.6	64.9	2.5	64.9	0.0	65.2	0.5	65.3	0.2
1970	65.2	-0.2	65.6	0.6	65.9	0.5	66.2	0.5	67.0	1.2	67.1	0.1	66.6	-0.7	66.4	-0.3	67.5	1.7	67.5	0.0	67.9	0.6	68.1	0.3
1971	67.4	-1.0	67.8	0.6	68.0	0.3	68.0	0.0	69.0	1.5	69.2	0.3	69.1	-0.1	68.7	-0.6	69.8	1.6	69.6	-0.3	69.5	-0.1	69.4	-0.1
1972	68.9	-0.7	69.2	0.4	69.9	1.0	70.1	0.3	70.1	0.0	69.9	-0.3	69.4	-0.7	69.2	-0.3	70.6	2.0	70.6	0.0	70.6	0.0	70.8	0.3
1973	69.6	-1.7	69.9	0.4	71.5	2.3	71.2	-0.4	71.5	0.4	71.7	0.3	71.3	-0.6	71.9	0.8	73.3	1.9	72.9	-0.5	73.0	0.1	73.0	0.0
1974	72.0	-1.4	73.3	1.8	75.3	2.7	76.1	1.1	77.2	1.4	77.3	0.1	77.2	-0.1	78.6	1.8	79.3	0.9	78.9	-0.5	79.4	0.6	78.9	-0.6
1975	77.9	-1.3	78.3	0.5	78.3	0.0	78.7	0.5	79.4	0.9	79.7	0.4	78.9	-1.0	80.0	1.4	80.9	1.1	81.0	0.1	80.5	-0.6	80.4	-0.1
1976	79.3	-1.4	79.4	0.1	80.8	1.8	80.2	-0.7	81.0	1.0	80.8	-0.2	80.1	-0.9	81.7	2.0	82.6	1.1	82.5	-0.1	82.6	0.1	83.1	0.6
1977	83.1	0.0	84.1	1.2	84.3	0.2	84.1	-0.2	84.2	0.1	83.9	-0.4	83.0	-1.1	83.7	0.8	84.6	1.1	85.6	1.2	86.0	0.5	86.4	0.5
1978	85.5	-1.0	85.2	-0.4	85.6	0.5	85.7	0.1	86.6	1.1	87.7	1.3	86.1	-1.8	87.0	1.0	88.2	1.4	88.1	-0.1	89.7	1.8	89.5	-0.2
1979	89.1	-0.4	90.1	1.1	90.1	0.0	90.8	0.8	90.8	0.0	91.5	0.8	90.2	-1.4	91.2	1.1	93.2	2.2	93.8	0.6	93.8	0.0	93.7	-0.1
1980	95.5	1.9	96.8	1.4	98.2	1.4	97.8	-0.4	96.8	-1.0	96.9	0.1	96.7	-0.2	97.0	0.3	97.3	0.3	97.2	-0.1	98.7	1.5	99.3	0.6
1981	96.9	-2.4	98.7	1.9	99.3	0.6	100.6	1.3	101.1	0.5	100.7	-0.4	100.6	-0.1	101.8	1.2	102.4	0.6	101.9	-0.5	102.7	0.8	101.8	-0.9
1982	99.9	-1.9	101.8	1.9	100.7	-1.1	99.6	-1.1	99.1	-0.5	98.7	-0.4	98.2	-0.5	97.8	-0.4	97.6	-0.2	97.9	0.3	98.9	1.0	98.2	-0.7
1983	95.2	-3.1	97.9	2.8	97.9	0.0	98.5	0.6	98.2	-0.3	99.8	1.6	100.1	0.3	101.7	1.6	101.9	0.2	101.6	-0.3	101.5	-0.1	101.2	-0.3
1984	101.1	-0.1	101.0	-0.1	100.2	-0.8	100.8	0.6	100.3	-0.5	97.9	-2.4	97.7	-0.2	102.8	5.2	103.8	1.0	104.6	0.8	103.6	-1.0	102.2	-1.4
1985	100.0	-2.2	103.5	3.5	104.3	0.8	103.0	-1.2	103.3	0.3	104.0	0.7	102.8	-1.2	105.9	3.0	108.4	2.4	107.9	-0.5	108.0	0.1	108.6	0.6
1986	107.7	-0.8	106.8	-0.8	106.9	0.1	106.9	0.0	106.3	-0.6	106.9	0.6	106.5	-0.4	105.9	-0.6	108.2	2.2	108.1	-0.1	108.6	0.5	107.5	-1.0
1987	109.0	1.4	108.5	-0.5	113.7	4.8	111.0	-2.4	111.3	0.3	113.1	1.6	109.9	-2.8	113.1	2.9	114.4	1.1	113.3	-1.0	112.6	-0.6	113.4	0.7
1988	112.5	-0.8	113.8	1.2	116.6	2.5	115.5	-0.9	116.3	0.7	114.7	-1.4	113.1	-1.4	109.9	-2.8	111.1	1.1	114.2	2.8	115.2	0.9	115.1	-0.1
1989	112.1	-2.6	114.3	2.0	120.7	5.6	121.2	0.4	121.9	0.6	119.8	-1.7	117.2	-2.2	117.2	0.0	120.6	2.9	120.1	-0.4	120.0	-0.1	119.9	-0.1
1990	120.1	0.2	127.4	6.1	128.8	1.1	129.7	0.7	128.6	-0.8	125.7	-2.3	122.7	-2.4	122.2	-0.4	125.2	2.5	127.2	1.6	127.7	0.4	127.5	-0.2
1991	127.3	-0.2	128.6	1.0	128.8	0.2	132.8	3.1	129.9	-2.2	125.1	-3.7	128.5	2.7	130.4	1.5	135.8	4.1	135.9	0.1	136.2	0.2	130.4	-4.3
1992	132.4	1.5	135.7	2.5	137.3	1.2	136.2	-0.8	135.9	-0.2	131.2	-3.5	131.8	0.5	132.4	0.5	132.1	-0.2	135.2	2.3	132.4	-2.1	130.4	-1.5
1993	129.5	-0.7	134.9	4.2	136.2	1.0	134.1	-1.5	130.3	-2.8	128.6	-1.3	128.1	-0.4	131.7	2.8	136.0	3.3	132.8	-2.4	135.0	1.7	131.2	-2.8
1994	130.2	-0.8	132.1	1.5	133.6	1.1	134.1	0.4	131.3	-2.1	125.4	-4.5	123.2	-1.8	124.9	1.4	132.2	5.8	133.2	0.8	132.2	-0.8	127.7	-3.4
1995	129.7	1.6	130.3	0.5	131.3	0.8	129.6	-1.3	129.0	-0.5	124.0	-3.9	127.8	3.1	124.0	-3.0	124.5	0.4	126.3	1.4	125.1	-1.0	120.4	-3.8
1996	126.7	5.2	127.8	0.9	133.5	4.5	129.8	-2.8	125.7	-3.2	124.4	-1.0	123.3	-0.9	122.2	-0.9	125.1	2.4	129.9	3.8	125.3	-3.5	118.2	-5.7
1997	122.0	3.2	122.3	0.2	124.4	1.7	125.0	0.5	123.9	-0.9	121.3	-2.1	119.4	-1.6	117.1	-1.9	118.9	1.5	120.6	1.4	119.0	-1.3	117.0	-1.7

[Continued]

Los Angeles-Riverside-Orange County, CA
Consumer Price Index - Urban Wage Earners
Base 1982-1984 = 100
Apparel
[Continued]

For 1952-2001. Columns headed % show percentile change in the index from the previous period for which an index is available.

Year	Jan		Feb		Mar		Apr		May		Jun		Jul		Aug		Sep		Oct		Nov		Dec	
	Index	%	Index	%	Index	%	Index	%	Index	%	Index	%	Index	%	Index	%	Index	%	Index	%	Index	%	Index	%
1998	118.0	0.9	123.1	4.3	127.3	3.4	128.5	0.9	125.5	-2.3	124.2	-1.0	119.6	-3.7	120.5	0.8	117.3	-2.7	121.3	3.4	119.4	-1.6	115.3	-3.4
1999	114.2	-1.0	118.7	3.9	119.9	1.0	122.3	2.0	121.6	-0.6	116.9	-3.9	111.2	-4.9	116.7	4.9	117.6	0.8	117.0	-0.5	116.4	-0.5	113.8	-2.2
2000	113.8	0.0	117.6	3.3	117.1	-0.4	115.2	-1.6	120.6	4.7	115.9	-3.9	113.5	-2.1	115.4	1.7	116.8	1.2	118.0	1.0	117.7	-0.3	114.7	-2.5
2001	115.5	0.7	117.9	2.1	118.4	0.4	115.5	-2.4	112.2	-2.9	107.9	-3.8	107.7	-0.2	108.3	0.6	110.9	2.4	112.3	1.3	108.8	-3.1	104.7	-3.8

Source: U.S. Department of Labor, Bureau of Labor Statistics, Division of Consumer Prices and Price Indexes. - indicates no data collected for period.

Los Angeles-Riverside-Orange County, CA
Consumer Price Index - All Urban Consumers
Base 1982-1984 = 100
Transportation

For 1947-2000. Columns headed % show percentile change in the index from the previous period for which an index is available.

Year	Jan Index	%	Feb Index	%	Mar Index	%	Apr Index	%	May Index	%	Jun Index	%	Jul Index	%	Aug Index	%	Sep Index	%	Oct Index	%	Nov Index	%	Dec Index	%
1947	17.3	-	17.5	1.2	17.5	0.0	17.7	1.1	17.6	-0.6	17.6	0.0	18.0	2.3	18.1	0.6	18.3	1.1	18.4	0.5	18.4	0.0	18.4	0.0
1948	19.2	4.3	19.2	0.0	19.2	0.0	19.3	0.5	19.2	-0.5	19.2	0.0	20.1	4.7	20.4	1.5	20.5	0.5	20.5	0.0	20.5	0.0	20.6	0.5
1949	20.6	0.0	21.0	1.9	20.9	-0.5	21.0	0.5	21.0	0.0	21.0	0.0	21.0	0.0	21.0	0.0	21.0	0.0	21.0	0.0	21.0	0.0	21.0	0.0
1950	21.0	0.0	20.9	-0.5	20.7	-1.0	20.5	-1.0	20.5	0.0	20.5	0.0	20.6	0.5	20.7	0.5	20.7	0.0	20.8	0.5	20.9	0.5	21.0	0.5
1951	21.0	0.0	21.3	1.4	21.5	0.9	21.5	0.0	21.5	0.0	21.5	0.0	21.6	0.5	21.6	0.0	21.8	0.9	22.0	0.9	22.3	1.4	22.3	0.0
1952	22.2	-0.4	23.5	5.9	23.5	0.0	23.5	0.0	23.7	0.9	23.7	0.0	24.2	2.1	24.2	0.0	24.2	0.0	24.2	0.0	24.4	0.8	24.4	0.0
1953	24.6	0.8	24.6	0.0	24.9	1.2	24.9	0.0	24.8	-0.4	24.8	0.0	25.0	0.8	25.1	0.4	24.9	-0.8	25.0	0.4	24.9	-0.4	24.1	-3.2
1954	25.2	4.6	25.1	-0.4	25.0	-0.4	24.9	-0.4	24.9	0.0	24.6	-1.2	23.7	-3.7	23.9	0.8	24.1	0.8	23.6	-2.1	24.7	4.7	24.7	0.0
1955	24.7	0.0	24.7	0.0	24.9	0.8	23.9	-4.0	24.2	1.3	24.0	-0.8	24.0	0.0	24.0	0.0	24.1	0.4	24.3	0.8	24.9	2.5	24.7	-0.8
1956	24.5	-0.8	24.4	-0.4	24.5	0.4	24.2	-1.2	24.6	1.7	24.6	0.0	25.0	1.6	24.7	-1.2	24.7	0.0	25.3	2.4	25.5	0.8	25.6	0.4
1957	25.5	-0.4	25.9	1.6	25.9	0.0	25.9	0.0	26.1	0.8	25.9	-0.8	25.9	0.0	25.4	-1.9	25.7	1.2	25.7	0.0	26.0	1.2	25.7	-1.2
1958	25.6	-0.4	26.0	1.6	26.0	0.0	26.2	0.8	26.3	0.4	26.2	-0.4	26.7	1.9	26.8	0.4	26.9	0.4	26.8	-0.4	27.1	1.1	27.1	0.0
1959	27.2	0.4	27.5	1.1	27.5	0.0	27.7	0.7	27.8	0.4	27.7	-0.4	27.6	-0.4	27.9	1.1	27.7	-0.7	28.3	2.2	28.5	0.7	28.5	0.0
1960	28.1	-1.4	27.9	-0.7	28.3	1.4	28.2	-0.4	28.0	-0.7	28.0	0.0	27.9	-0.4	27.8	-0.4	27.6	-0.7	27.9	1.1	27.9	0.0	28.2	1.1
1961	28.6	1.4	28.6	0.0	27.9	-2.4	27.9	0.0	28.1	0.7	29.3	4.3	29.3	0.0	29.5	0.7	29.2	-1.0	29.2	0.0	29.6	1.4	29.6	0.0
1962	29.3	-1.0	29.2	-0.3	29.3	0.3	29.6	1.0	30.0	1.4	30.2	0.7	30.1	-0.3	30.2	0.3	30.1	-0.3	30.3	0.7	30.2	-0.3	30.2	0.0
1963	29.8	-1.3	29.9	0.3	29.7	-0.7	30.0	1.0	29.8	-0.7	29.1	-2.3	29.1	0.0	30.2	3.8	30.1	-0.3	30.7	2.0	30.8	0.3	29.6	-3.9
1964	31.3	5.7	29.8	-4.8	31.0	4.0	31.1	0.3	31.0	-0.3	31.3	1.0	30.5	-2.6	31.1	2.0	30.5	-1.9	31.4	3.0	31.8	1.3	31.8	0.0
1965	31.6	-0.6	31.6	0.0	31.6	0.0	31.9	0.9	31.9	0.0	31.8	-0.3	32.0	0.6	31.1	-2.8	31.8	2.3	31.3	-1.6	32.0	2.2	32.0	0.0
1966	31.0	-3.1	31.3	1.0	31.5	0.6	31.9	1.3	31.6	-0.9	31.8	0.6	32.4	1.9	31.3	-3.4	32.3	3.2	32.5	0.6	32.7	0.6	32.2	-1.5
1967	31.6	-1.9	31.5	-0.3	31.2	-1.0	32.3	3.5	32.4	0.3	32.4	0.0	32.4	0.0	32.5	0.3	33.2	2.2	32.4	-2.4	33.5	3.4	32.3	-3.6
1968	33.3	3.1	33.3	0.0	33.6	0.9	32.9	-2.1	32.8	-0.3	33.7	2.7	33.3	-1.2	33.6	0.9	32.9	-2.1	33.6	2.1	34.0	1.2	32.8	-3.5
1969	33.6	2.4	33.6	0.0	34.6	3.0	34.3	-0.9	33.6	-2.0	34.5	2.7	34.5	0.0	34.3	-0.6	34.2	-0.3	35.0	2.3	33.8	-3.4	34.9	3.3
1970	34.4	-1.4	33.9	-1.5	33.9	0.0	35.5	4.7	35.0	-1.4	34.7	-0.9	36.0	3.7	34.7	-3.6	36.4	4.9	36.8	1.1	36.5	-0.8	37.1	1.6
1971	36.8	-0.8	36.2	-1.6	37.5	3.6	36.5	-2.7	36.8	0.8	37.1	0.8	37.1	0.0	37.5	1.1	37.5	0.0	37.9	1.1	37.3	-1.6	37.1	-0.5
1972	37.0	-0.3	36.3	-1.9	37.5	3.3	37.4	-0.3	37.8	1.1	37.3	-1.3	38.1	2.1	38.2	0.3	38.9	1.8	39.1	0.5	39.2	0.3	39.2	0.0
1973	38.8	-1.0	38.9	0.3	39.0	0.3	39.4	1.0	39.7	0.8	40.0	0.8	40.4	1.0	40.2	-0.5	39.9	-0.7	40.1	0.5	40.5	1.0	40.5	0.0
1974	41.3	2.0	41.8	1.2	42.7	2.2	43.3	1.4	44.0	1.6	44.9	2.0	45.4	1.1	45.6	0.4	45.8	0.4	45.9	0.2	46.3	0.9	46.5	0.4
1975	46.6	0.2	46.8	0.4	47.1	0.6	47.9	1.7	48.5	1.3	49.4	1.9	50.4	2.0	50.8	0.8	50.8	0.0	51.4	1.2	51.4	0.0	51.2	-0.4
1976	51.3	0.2	51.4	0.2	51.7	0.6	52.3	1.2	53.0	1.3	53.8	1.5	55.3	2.8	55.7	0.7	56.2	0.9	56.6	0.7	56.7	0.2	56.6	-0.2
1977	56.7	0.2	57.0	0.5	57.3	0.5	57.9	1.0	58.3	0.7	58.8	0.9	59.2	0.7	58.9	-0.5	58.7	-0.3	58.5	-0.3	58.2	-0.5	58.1	-0.2
1978	58.2	0.2	58.6	0.7	58.7	0.2	58.9	0.3	59.8	1.5	60.5	1.2	61.1	1.0	61.3	0.3	61.7	0.7	62.1	0.6	62.8	1.1	63.0	0.3
1979	63.4	0.6	63.9	0.8	65.0	1.7	67.4	3.7	69.1	2.5	70.3	1.7	71.8	2.1	73.4	2.2	74.3	1.2	74.4	0.1	74.7	0.4	75.8	1.5
1980	77.8	2.6	80.3	3.2	81.3	1.2	82.2	1.1	82.3	0.1	82.0	-0.4	82.3	0.4	82.8	0.6	83.9	1.3	84.2	0.4	85.0	1.0	85.4	0.5
1981	86.1	0.8	87.9	2.1	88.6	0.8	89.7	1.2	90.5	0.9	91.3	0.9	92.3	1.1	92.3	0.0	92.8	0.5	94.2	1.5	94.8	0.6	94.9	0.1
1982	97.1	2.3	96.7	-0.4	95.8	-0.9	95.5	-0.3	96.1	0.6	98.2	2.2	99.1	0.9	99.0	-0.1	98.5	-0.5	98.8	0.3	98.2	-0.6	96.8	-1.4
1983	96.4	-0.4	94.7	-1.8	94.1	-0.6	96.7	2.8	98.5	1.9	100.1	1.6	100.9	0.8	100.9	0.0	100.6	-0.3	100.4	-0.2	100.3	-0.1	102.0	1.7
1984	102.2	0.2	101.0	-1.2	101.1	0.1	103.1	2.0	104.9	1.7	104.6	-0.3	103.1	-1.4	103.4	0.3	103.4	0.0	105.6	2.1	106.1	0.5	106.1	0.0
1985	105.6	-0.5	105.2	-0.4	106.5	1.2	108.4	1.8	108.3	-0.1	108.8	0.5	108.6	-0.2	107.4	-1.1	106.7	-0.7	107.5	0.7	108.0	0.5	108.6	0.6
1986	108.9	0.3	107.2	-1.6	105.3	-1.8	104.6	-0.7	105.6	1.0	106.8	1.1	104.6	-2.1	103.2	-1.3	103.4	0.2	104.3	0.9	104.3	0.0	104.0	-0.3
1987	105.3	1.3	106.9	1.5	107.8	0.8	108.4	0.6	108.9	0.5	109.1	0.2	108.9	-0.2	109.5	0.6	109.6	0.1	110.8	1.1	110.9	0.1	110.7	-0.2
1988	111.0	0.3	110.6	-0.4	110.8	0.2	112.9	1.9	114.1	1.1	114.7	0.5	114.6	-0.1	115.5	0.8	115.4	-0.1	115.5	0.1	115.0	-0.4	115.0	0.0
1989	114.6	-0.3	116.0	1.2	117.5	1.3	121.9	3.7	122.7	0.7	122.8	0.1	121.8	-0.8	120.3	-1.2	119.1	-1.0	119.0	-0.1	119.0	0.0	120.0	0.8
1990	121.4	1.2	122.3	0.7	123.2	0.7	123.5	0.2	123.9	0.3	125.1	1.0	125.3	0.2	127.1	1.4	129.0	1.5	131.5	1.9	132.5	0.8	133.6	0.8
1991	129.9	-2.8	127.1	-2.2	124.2	-2.3	123.8	-0.3	125.8	1.6	126.2	0.3	126.2	0.0	126.4	0.2	126.4	0.0	126.6	0.2	127.4	0.6	128.6	0.9
1992	129.3	0.5	129.6	0.2	130.1	0.4	130.6	0.4	132.3	1.3	132.7	0.3	134.6	1.4	133.8	-0.6	134.5	0.5	135.5	0.7	136.1	0.4	137.0	0.7

[Continued]

Los Angeles-Riverside-Orange County, CA
Consumer Price Index - All Urban Consumers
Base 1982-1984 = 100
Transportation
[Continued]

For 1947-2000. Columns headed % show percentile change in the index from the previous period for which an index is available.

Year	Jan Index	%	Feb Index	%	Mar Index	%	Apr Index	%	May Index	%	Jun Index	%	Jul Index	%	Aug Index	%	Sep Index	%	Oct Index	%	Nov Index	%	Dec Index	%
1993	137.5	0.4	137.9	0.3	137.7	-0.1	136.6	-0.8	137.0	0.3	136.4	-0.4	136.9	0.4	135.9	-0.7	136.7	0.6	138.2	1.1	139.6	1.0	139.4	-0.1
1994	139.0	-0.3	139.0	0.0	140.3	0.9	139.2	-0.8	137.9	-0.9	139.5	1.2	140.4	0.6	141.3	0.6	140.9	-0.3	142.5	1.1	142.9	0.3	142.6	-0.2
1995	143.3	0.5	142.3	-0.7	142.8	0.4	143.5	0.5	144.2	0.5	143.4	-0.6	142.2	-0.8	142.0	-0.1	140.9	-0.8	141.6	0.5	141.5	-0.1	140.1	-1.0
1996	141.2	0.8	142.2	0.7	143.7	1.1	146.5	1.9	148.6	1.4	146.9	-1.1	145.9	-0.7	144.5	-1.0	144.0	-0.3	143.0	-0.7	142.2	-0.6	143.4	0.8
1997	143.1	-0.2	143.8	0.5	146.0	1.5	146.7	0.5	145.0	-1.2	144.1	-0.6	144.5	0.3	145.1	0.4	147.1	1.4	146.3	-0.5	145.2	-0.8	144.9	-0.2
1998	143.4	-1.0	141.4	-1.4	140.1	-0.9	140.9	0.6	142.8	1.3	142.9	0.1	143.0	0.1	142.5	-0.3	142.8	0.2	143.4	0.4	143.9	0.3	143.8	-0.1
1999	142.8	-0.7	142.1	-0.5	143.2	0.8	149.4	4.3	148.4	-0.7	146.1	-1.5	147.6	1.0	148.1	0.3	148.7	0.4	148.0	-0.5	148.1	0.1	148.6	0.3
2000	147.6	-0.7	149.8	1.5	155.7	3.9	155.4	-0.2	154.9	-0.3	153.9	-0.6	155.4	1.0	154.3	-0.7	156.4	1.4	156.1	-0.2	156.1	0.0	155.0	-0.7

Source: U.S. Department of Labor, Bureau of Labor Statistics, Division of Consumer Prices and Price Indexes. - indicates no data collected for period.

Los Angeles-Riverside-Orange County, CA
Consumer Price Index - Urban Wage Earners
Base 1982-1984 = 100
Transportation

For 1947-2000. Columns headed % show percentile change in the index from the previous period for which an index is available.

Year	Jan Index	%	Feb Index	%	Mar Index	%	Apr Index	%	May Index	%	Jun Index	%	Jul Index	%	Aug Index	%	Sep Index	%	Oct Index	%	Nov Index	%	Dec Index	%
1947	17.2	-	17.4	1.2	17.4	0.0	17.6	1.1	17.5	-0.6	17.5	0.0	17.9	2.3	18.0	0.6	18.2	1.1	18.3	0.5	18.3	0.0	18.3	0.0
1948	19.1	4.4	19.1	0.0	19.1	0.0	19.2	0.5	19.1	-0.5	19.1	0.0	20.0	4.7	20.3	1.5	20.3	0.0	20.3	0.0	20.3	0.0	20.5	1.0
1949	20.5	0.0	20.9	2.0	20.8	-0.5	20.9	0.5	20.9	0.0	20.9	0.0	20.9	0.0	20.9	0.0	20.9	0.0	20.9	0.0	20.9	0.0	20.9	0.0
1950	20.9	0.0	20.8	-0.5	20.6	-1.0	20.4	-1.0	20.4	0.0	20.4	0.0	20.4	0.0	20.6	1.0	20.6	0.0	20.7	0.5	20.8	0.5	20.9	0.5
1951	20.9	0.0	21.2	1.4	21.4	0.9	21.4	0.0	21.4	0.0	21.4	0.0	21.4	0.0	21.4	0.0	21.7	1.4	21.9	0.9	22.1	0.9	22.1	0.0
1952	22.1	0.0	23.4	5.9	23.4	0.0	23.4	0.0	23.6	0.9	23.6	0.0	24.0	1.7	24.0	0.0	24.1	0.4	24.1	0.0	24.3	0.8	24.3	0.0
1953	24.5	0.8	24.4	-0.4	24.8	1.6	24.7	-0.4	24.6	-0.4	24.6	0.0	24.9	1.2	24.9	0.0	24.8	-0.4	24.8	0.0	24.8	0.0	24.0	-3.2
1954	25.1	4.6	25.0	-0.4	24.8	-0.8	24.7	-0.4	24.8	0.4	24.5	-1.2	23.5	-4.1	23.8	1.3	23.9	0.4	23.5	-1.7	24.6	4.7	24.6	0.0
1955	24.6	0.0	24.6	0.0	24.8	0.8	23.8	-4.0	24.1	1.3	23.8	-1.2	23.9	0.4	23.8	-0.4	23.9	0.4	24.2	1.3	24.7	2.1	24.6	-0.4
1956	24.4	-0.8	24.2	-0.8	24.4	0.8	24.1	-1.2	24.4	1.2	24.4	0.0	24.9	2.0	24.6	-1.2	24.6	0.0	25.2	2.4	25.4	0.8	25.4	0.0
1957	25.4	0.0	25.8	1.6	25.7	-0.4	25.8	0.4	25.9	0.4	25.8	-0.4	25.7	-0.4	25.3	-1.6	25.6	1.2	25.6	0.0	25.9	1.2	25.6	-1.2
1958	25.5	-0.4	25.8	1.2	25.9	0.4	26.0	0.4	26.1	0.4	26.1	0.0	26.5	1.5	26.6	0.4	26.7	0.4	26.7	0.0	26.9	0.7	27.0	0.4
1959	27.1	0.4	27.4	1.1	27.4	0.0	27.5	0.4	27.6	0.4	27.6	0.0	27.5	-0.4	27.8	1.1	27.5	-1.1	28.1	2.2	28.3	0.7	28.3	0.0
1960	27.9	-1.4	27.7	-0.7	28.2	1.8	28.1	-0.4	27.9	-0.7	27.8	-0.4	27.8	0.0	27.7	-0.4	27.5	-0.7	27.7	0.7	27.8	0.4	28.1	1.1
1961	28.4	1.1	28.5	0.4	27.7	-2.8	27.7	0.0	28.0	1.1	29.1	3.9	29.1	0.0	29.3	0.7	29.1	-0.7	29.1	0.0	29.5	1.4	29.4	-0.3
1962	29.2	-0.7	29.0	-0.7	29.1	0.3	29.5	1.4	29.8	1.0	30.0	0.7	30.0	0.0	30.0	0.0	29.9	-0.3	30.1	0.7	30.0	-0.3	30.0	0.0
1963	29.6	-1.3	29.7	0.3	29.5	-0.7	29.9	1.4	29.6	-1.0	29.0	-2.0	29.0	0.0	30.0	3.4	30.0	0.0	30.5	1.7	30.6	0.3	29.4	-3.9
1964	31.2	6.1	29.6	-5.1	30.9	4.4	30.9	0.0	30.9	0.0	31.1	0.6	30.4	-2.3	30.9	1.6	30.3	-1.9	31.2	3.0	31.6	1.3	31.6	0.0
1965	31.5	-0.3	31.5	0.0	31.4	-0.3	31.7	1.0	31.8	0.3	31.6	-0.6	31.8	0.6	30.9	-2.8	31.6	2.3	31.2	-1.3	31.8	1.9	31.8	0.0
1966	30.8	-3.1	31.1	1.0	31.3	0.6	31.8	1.6	31.4	-1.3	31.6	0.6	32.2	1.9	31.1	-3.4	32.1	3.2	32.3	0.6	32.5	0.6	32.0	-1.5
1967	31.4	-1.9	31.3	-0.3	31.0	-1.0	32.1	3.5	32.2	0.3	32.2	0.0	32.2	0.0	32.3	0.3	33.0	2.2	32.2	-2.4	33.4	3.7	32.1	-3.9
1968	33.2	3.4	33.1	-0.3	33.4	0.9	32.7	-2.1	32.6	-0.3	33.5	2.8	33.1	-1.2	33.5	1.2	32.7	-2.4	33.4	2.1	33.8	1.2	32.6	-3.6
1969	33.5	2.8	33.5	0.0	34.5	3.0	34.1	-1.2	33.4	-2.1	34.4	3.0	34.4	0.0	34.1	-0.9	34.0	-0.3	34.8	2.4	33.6	-3.4	34.7	3.3
1970	34.2	-1.4	33.7	-1.5	33.7	0.0	35.3	4.7	34.8	-1.4	34.5	-0.9	35.8	3.8	34.5	-3.6	36.2	4.9	36.6	1.1	36.3	-0.8	36.9	1.7
1971	36.6	-0.8	36.0	-1.6	37.3	3.6	36.3	-2.7	36.6	0.8	36.9	0.8	36.9	0.0	37.2	0.8	37.3	0.3	37.7	1.1	37.1	-1.6	36.9	-0.5
1972	36.8	-0.3	36.1	-1.9	37.2	3.0	37.2	0.0	37.6	1.1	37.1	-1.3	37.9	2.2	38.0	0.3	38.7	1.8	38.9	0.5	39.0	0.3	39.0	0.0
1973	38.6	-1.0	38.7	0.3	38.8	0.3	39.2	1.0	39.5	0.8	39.8	0.8	40.1	0.8	39.9	-0.5	39.7	-0.5	39.9	0.5	40.3	1.0	40.3	0.0
1974	41.1	2.0	41.5	1.0	42.5	2.4	43.1	1.4	43.8	1.6	44.6	1.8	45.1	1.1	45.4	0.7	45.6	0.4	45.7	0.2	46.1	0.9	46.2	0.2
1975	46.3	0.2	46.5	0.4	46.9	0.9	47.7	1.7	48.2	1.0	49.1	1.9	50.1	2.0	50.5	0.8	50.5	0.0	51.1	1.2	51.1	0.0	50.9	-0.4
1976	51.0	0.2	51.2	0.4	51.4	0.4	52.0	1.2	52.7	1.3	53.5	1.5	55.0	2.8	55.4	0.7	55.9	0.9	56.3	0.7	56.4	0.2	56.3	-0.2
1977	56.4	0.2	56.7	0.5	57.0	0.5	57.6	1.1	58.0	0.7	58.5	0.9	58.9	0.7	58.6	-0.5	58.4	-0.3	58.2	-0.3	57.9	-0.5	57.8	-0.2
1978	58.0	0.3	58.0	0.0	58.3	0.5	58.7	0.7	59.5	1.4	60.3	1.3	60.9	1.0	61.2	0.5	61.5	0.5	61.9	0.7	62.7	1.3	63.0	0.5
1979	63.4	0.6	63.9	0.8	65.0	1.7	67.6	4.0	69.4	2.7	70.6	1.7	72.3	2.4	73.8	2.1	74.5	0.9	74.4	-0.1	75.0	0.8	76.1	1.5
1980	77.9	2.4	80.8	3.7	82.0	1.5	83.5	1.8	83.5	0.0	83.3	-0.2	83.3	0.0	83.8	0.6	84.4	0.7	84.6	0.2	85.4	0.9	85.8	0.5
1981	86.6	0.9	88.4	2.1	89.1	0.8	90.6	1.7	91.5	1.0	92.4	1.0	93.3	1.0	93.0	-0.3	93.0	0.0	94.9	2.0	95.5	0.6	95.5	0.0
1982	97.6	2.2	97.0	-0.6	96.2	-0.8	95.7	-0.5	96.3	0.6	98.7	2.5	99.6	0.9	99.6	0.0	99.0	-0.6	99.1	0.1	98.2	-0.9	96.8	-1.4
1983	96.2	-0.6	94.6	-1.7	93.9	-0.7	96.4	2.7	98.3	2.0	100.0	1.7	100.8	0.8	100.8	0.0	100.4	-0.4	100.1	-0.3	100.1	0.0	101.8	1.7
1984	101.9	0.1	100.8	-1.1	101.0	0.2	103.0	2.0	104.9	1.8	104.5	-0.4	102.9	-1.5	103.1	0.2	103.4	0.3	105.5	2.0	105.9	0.4	105.8	-0.1
1985	105.3	-0.5	104.8	-0.5	106.2	1.3	108.1	1.8	107.9	-0.2	108.4	0.5	108.2	-0.2	106.9	-1.2	106.0	-0.8	106.8	0.8	107.4	0.6	107.8	0.4
1986	108.0	0.2	106.2	-1.7	104.3	-1.8	103.5	-0.8	104.4	0.9	105.6	1.1	103.3	-2.2	101.7	-1.5	101.8	0.1	102.5	0.7	102.7	0.2	102.4	-0.3
1987	103.4	1.0	105.1	1.6	105.9	0.8	106.6	0.7	107.1	0.5	107.3	0.2	107.1	-0.2	107.6	0.5	107.6	0.0	108.9	1.2	109.0	0.1	108.8	-0.2
1988	109.0	0.2	108.7	-0.3	108.8	0.1	110.6	1.7	111.8	1.1	112.2	0.4	111.9	-0.3	112.8	0.8	112.9	0.1	113.2	0.3	112.5	-0.6	112.6	0.1
1989	112.1	-0.4	113.5	1.2	114.8	1.1	119.0	3.7	119.7	0.6	119.7	0.0	118.7	-0.8	117.1	-1.3	116.0	-0.9	115.8	-0.2	115.6	-0.2	116.7	1.0
1990	117.9	1.0	118.5	0.5	119.0	0.4	119.3	0.3	119.6	0.3	120.7	0.9	121.1	0.3	122.8	1.4	124.5	1.4	126.6	1.7	127.6	0.8	128.5	0.7
1991	125.1	-2.6	122.4	-2.2	119.8	-2.1	119.6	-0.2	121.7	1.8	122.2	0.4	122.2	0.0	122.5	0.2	122.8	0.2	123.0	0.2	123.6	0.5	124.6	0.8
1992	125.1	0.4	125.4	0.2	125.7	0.2	126.3	0.5	128.0	1.3	128.8	0.6	129.9	0.9	129.6	-0.2	130.0	0.3	130.9	0.7	131.7	0.6	132.2	0.4

[Continued]

Los Angeles-Riverside-Orange County, CA
Consumer Price Index - Urban Wage Earners
Base 1982-1984 = 100
Transportation
[Continued]

For 1947-2000. Columns headed % show percentile change in the index from the previous period for which an index is available.

Year	Jan Index	%	Feb Index	%	Mar Index	%	Apr Index	%	May Index	%	Jun Index	%	Jul Index	%	Aug Index	%	Sep Index	%	Oct Index	%	Nov Index	%	Dec Index	%
1993	132.4	0.2	132.7	0.2	132.5	-0.2	131.7	-0.6	131.9	0.2	131.7	-0.2	132.0	0.2	131.4	-0.5	131.9	0.4	133.5	1.2	134.5	0.7	134.0	-0.4
1994	133.7	-0.2	133.4	-0.2	134.4	0.7	134.0	-0.3	133.7	-0.2	135.1	1.0	135.9	0.6	136.6	0.5	136.4	-0.1	137.9	1.1	138.6	0.5	138.4	-0.1
1995	138.7	0.2	138.1	-0.4	138.5	0.3	139.1	0.4	139.8	0.5	139.4	-0.3	138.4	-0.7	138.0	-0.3	137.3	-0.5	138.0	0.5	138.0	0.0	137.1	-0.7
1996	137.8	0.5	138.6	0.6	139.7	0.8	142.6	2.1	144.7	1.5	143.0	-1.2	142.2	-0.6	140.6	-1.1	140.1	-0.4	139.3	-0.6	138.6	-0.5	139.4	0.6
1997	139.5	0.1	140.1	0.4	141.8	1.2	142.6	0.6	141.0	-1.1	140.0	-0.7	140.0	0.0	141.0	0.7	142.6	1.1	142.1	-0.4	140.9	-0.8	140.5	-0.3
1998	138.9	-1.1	136.8	-1.5	135.3	-1.1	136.2	0.7	138.1	1.4	138.0	-0.1	138.0	0.0	137.5	-0.4	137.7	0.1	138.3	0.4	138.9	0.4	138.8	-0.1
1999	137.8	-0.7	137.0	-0.6	137.9	0.7	144.3	4.6	143.3	-0.7	140.9	-1.7	142.3	1.0	143.3	0.7	143.8	0.3	143.4	-0.3	143.4	0.0	143.9	0.3
2000	143.0	-0.6	144.7	1.2	150.7	4.1	150.5	-0.1	149.7	-0.5	148.8	-0.6	150.1	0.9	148.8	-0.9	151.1	1.5	151.2	0.1	151.1	-0.1	149.9	-0.8

Source: U.S. Department of Labor, Bureau of Labor Statistics, Division of Consumer Prices and Price Indexes. - indicates no data collected for period.

Los Angeles-Riverside-Orange County, CA
Consumer Price Index - All Urban Consumers
Base 1982-1984 = 100
Medical Care

For 1947-2001. Columns headed % show percentile change in the index from the previous period for which an index is available.

Year	Jan Index	%	Feb Index	%	Mar Index	%	Apr Index	%	May Index	%	Jun Index	%	Jul Index	%	Aug Index	%	Sep Index	%	Oct Index	%	Nov Index	%	Dec Index	%
1947	13.3	-	13.3	0.0	13.3	0.0	13.4	0.8	13.3	-0.7	13.3	0.0	13.3	0.0	13.3	0.0	13.4	0.8	13.6	1.5	13.6	0.0	13.6	0.0
1948	13.7	0.7	13.7	0.0	13.7	0.0	14.0	2.2	14.0	0.0	14.1	0.7	14.4	2.1	14.4	0.0	14.5	0.7	14.6	0.7	14.6	0.0	14.6	0.0
1949	14.7	0.7	14.7	0.0	14.7	0.0	14.7	0.0	14.7	0.0	14.7	0.0	14.7	0.0	14.7	0.0	14.7	0.0	14.7	0.0	14.7	0.0	14.7	0.0
1950	14.7	0.0	14.8	0.7	14.8	0.0	14.8	0.0	14.8	0.0	14.8	0.0	14.8	0.0	14.8	0.0	15.3	3.4	15.4	0.7	15.4	0.0	15.7	1.9
1951	15.7	0.0	15.7	0.0	15.9	1.3	15.9	0.0	15.9	0.0	15.9	0.0	16.0	0.6	16.0	0.0	16.0	0.0	16.0	0.0	16.0	0.0	16.0	0.0
1952	16.1	0.6	16.1	0.0	16.1	0.0	16.1	0.0	16.1	0.0	16.7	3.7	16.7	0.0	16.7	0.0	16.7	0.0	16.7	0.0	16.7	0.0	16.7	0.0
1953	16.7	0.0	16.7	0.0	16.7	0.0	16.9	1.2	16.9	0.0	16.9	0.0	16.9	0.0	17.0	0.6	17.0	0.0	17.1	0.6	17.1	0.0	17.1	0.0
1954	17.1	0.0	17.1	0.0	17.1	0.0	17.3	1.2	17.3	0.0	17.3	0.0	17.3	0.0	17.3	0.0	17.3	0.0	17.3	0.0	17.3	0.0	17.3	0.0
1955	17.3	0.0	17.3	0.0	17.3	0.0	17.1	-1.2	17.1	0.0	17.1	0.0	17.5	2.3	17.5	0.0	17.5	0.0	17.5	0.0	17.5	0.0	17.6	0.6
1956	17.8	1.1	17.8	0.0	17.8	0.0	17.9	0.6	17.9	0.0	17.9	0.0	17.9	0.0	18.0	0.6	18.0	0.0	18.1	0.6	18.1	0.0	18.0	-0.6
1957	18.3	1.7	18.3	0.0	18.3	0.0	18.3	0.0	18.3	0.0	18.4	0.5	18.4	0.0	18.5	0.5	18.5	0.0	18.5	0.0	18.5	0.0	18.6	0.5
1958	18.9	1.6	18.9	0.0	18.9	0.0	19.3	2.1	19.3	0.0	20.3	5.2	20.3	0.0	20.4	0.5	20.4	0.0	20.5	0.5	20.5	0.0	20.5	0.0
1959	20.6	0.5	20.6	0.0	20.6	0.0	20.6	0.0	20.7	0.5	20.7	0.0	20.7	0.0	20.7	0.0	20.7	0.0	21.1	1.9	21.1	0.0	21.1	0.0
1960	21.1	0.0	21.1	0.0	21.1	0.0	21.3	0.9	21.3	0.0	21.3	0.0	21.5	0.9	21.5	0.0	21.5	0.0	21.6	0.5	21.6	0.0	21.6	0.0
1961	21.6	0.0	21.6	0.0	21.6	0.0	21.6	0.0	21.6	0.0	21.6	0.0	21.6	0.0	21.7	0.5	21.7	0.0	21.7	0.0	21.7	0.0	21.7	0.0
1962	21.7	0.0	21.7	0.0	22.3	2.8	22.4	0.4	22.4	0.0	22.4	0.0	22.5	0.4	22.4	-0.4	22.4	0.0	22.4	0.0	22.4	0.0	22.4	0.0
1963	22.5	0.4	22.5	0.0	22.5	0.0	22.6	0.4	22.7	0.4	22.7	0.0	22.7	0.0	22.7	0.0	22.7	0.0	22.9	0.9	22.9	0.0	22.9	0.0
1964	23.0	0.4	23.1	0.4	23.1	0.0	23.2	0.4	23.2	0.0	23.2	0.0	23.3	0.4	23.3	0.0	23.3	0.0	23.5	0.9	23.5	0.0	23.4	-0.4
1965	23.4	0.0	23.5	0.4	23.5	0.0	23.6	0.4	23.7	0.4	23.7	0.0	23.7	0.0	23.7	0.0	23.7	0.0	23.7	0.0	23.8	0.4	23.8	0.0
1966	23.9	0.4	24.0	0.4	24.0	0.0	24.2	0.8	24.1	-0.4	24.2	0.4	24.3	0.4	24.3	0.0	25.2	3.7	25.4	0.8	25.5	0.4	25.7	0.8
1967	25.7	0.0	25.7	0.0	25.8	0.4	26.0	0.8	26.3	1.2	26.4	0.4	26.6	0.8	26.6	0.0	26.7	0.4	26.8	0.4	26.9	0.4	27.0	0.4
1968	27.2	0.7	27.3	0.4	27.3	0.0	27.5	0.7	27.8	1.1	27.8	0.0	28.0	0.7	28.1	0.4	28.1	0.0	28.2	0.4	28.3	0.4	28.5	0.7
1969	28.6	0.4	28.8	0.7	28.9	0.3	29.3	1.4	29.4	0.3	29.5	0.3	29.6	0.3	29.8	0.7	29.9	0.3	29.8	-0.3	30.0	0.7	30.4	1.3
1970	30.4	0.0	30.7	1.0	31.0	1.0	31.6	1.9	31.8	0.6	31.8	0.0	31.9	0.3	32.0	0.3	32.0	0.0	31.9	-0.3	31.9	0.0	32.1	0.6
1971	32.1	0.0	32.2	0.3	32.4	0.6	33.2	2.5	33.4	0.6	33.5	0.3	33.6	0.3	33.6	0.0	33.7	0.3	33.4	-0.9	33.4	0.0	33.4	0.0
1972	33.5	0.3	33.6	0.3	33.6	0.0	33.7	0.3	33.7	0.0	33.8	0.3	34.1	0.9	34.1	0.0	34.2	0.3	34.4	0.6	34.3	-0.3	34.5	0.6
1973	34.6	0.3	34.7	0.3	35.0	0.9	35.2	0.6	35.3	0.3	35.4	0.3	35.6	0.6	35.8	0.6	35.9	0.3	36.6	1.9	36.6	0.0	36.6	0.0
1974	36.9	0.8	37.2	0.8	37.5	0.8	37.6	0.3	38.4	2.1	38.8	1.0	39.3	1.3	39.8	1.3	40.0	0.5	40.3	0.7	40.9	1.5	41.1	0.5
1975	41.3	0.5	42.1	1.9	42.4	0.7	42.9	1.2	43.3	0.9	43.6	0.7	43.9	0.7	44.3	0.9	44.5	0.5	44.8	0.7	45.5	1.6	46.1	1.3
1976	46.4	0.7	47.7	2.8	47.9	0.4	48.3	0.8	48.9	1.2	49.3	0.8	49.7	0.8	50.1	0.8	50.3	0.4	50.6	0.6	51.3	1.4	51.3	0.0
1977	51.6	0.6	52.4	1.6	52.6	0.4	53.0	0.8	53.2	0.4	53.6	0.8	54.1	0.9	54.5	0.7	54.9	0.7	55.3	0.7	55.5	0.4	55.6	0.2
1978	56.0	0.7	56.3	0.5	56.4	0.2	56.6	0.4	58.2	2.8	58.4	0.3	58.7	0.5	60.0	2.2	60.2	0.3	60.6	0.7	61.1	0.8	61.1	0.0
1979	62.1	1.6	62.3	0.3	62.6	0.5	62.7	0.2	63.6	1.4	64.1	0.8	65.2	1.7	65.1	-0.2	66.2	1.7	66.6	0.6	66.8	0.3	67.7	1.3
1980	68.3	0.9	70.4	3.1	70.8	0.6	72.5	2.4	72.5	0.0	72.5	0.0	73.4	1.2	73.2	-0.3	73.6	0.5	74.7	1.5	75.2	0.7	75.3	0.1
1981	76.2	1.2	77.0	1.0	77.2	0.3	77.9	0.9	78.2	0.4	78.7	0.6	84.5	7.4	85.1	0.7	85.5	0.5	85.5	0.0	88.7	3.7	89.2	0.6
1982	90.0	0.9	90.1	0.1	90.6	0.6	91.6	1.1	92.6	1.1	94.4	1.9	94.8	0.4	95.9	1.2	97.1	1.3	96.9	-0.2	97.5	0.6	97.7	0.2
1983	99.3	1.6	99.6	0.3	99.7	0.1	100.2	0.5	100.2	0.0	101.0	0.8	101.6	0.6	101.2	-0.4	101.2	0.0	101.3	0.1	101.6	0.3	101.6	0.0
1984	103.2	1.6	103.3	0.1	103.6	0.3	104.0	0.4	104.5	0.5	104.5	0.0	105.6	1.1	106.1	0.5	106.0	-0.1	107.0	0.9	107.1	0.1	107.4	0.3
1985	110.1	2.5	110.5	0.4	111.1	0.5	111.2	0.1	111.3	0.1	112.2	0.8	112.8	0.5	113.7	0.8	114.6	0.8	115.1	0.4	115.7	0.5	116.4	0.6
1986	117.0	0.5	118.1	0.9	118.9	0.7	119.4	0.4	119.7	0.3	120.2	0.4	120.7	0.4	121.7	0.8	121.9	0.2	123.0	0.9	124.5	1.2	125.3	0.6
1987	126.6	1.0	127.2	0.5	127.6	0.3	128.1	0.4	128.1	0.0	129.3	0.9	129.6	0.2	130.2	0.5	130.6	0.3	131.7	0.8	132.3	0.5	132.6	0.2
1988	135.5	2.2	136.5	0.7	137.3	0.6	137.4	0.1	137.9	0.4	139.1	0.9	139.6	0.4	140.8	0.9	141.6	0.6	143.1	1.1	143.0	-0.1	143.1	0.1
1989	145.0	1.3	145.2	0.1	146.1	0.6	147.4	0.9	148.0	0.4	149.1	0.7	150.6	1.0	151.5	0.6	152.5	0.7	152.9	0.3	154.2	0.9	154.6	0.3
1990	157.0	1.6	158.2	0.8	159.0	0.5	160.0	0.6	160.8	0.5	161.7	0.6	163.6	1.2	164.0	0.2	165.9	1.2	168.5	1.6	170.1	0.9	170.4	0.2
1991	172.9	1.5	172.9	0.0	174.7	1.0	174.9	0.1	176.1	0.7	177.6	0.9	180.1	1.4	179.9	-0.1	180.4	0.3	181.0	0.3	183.4	1.3	184.2	0.4
1992	186.5	1.2	187.8	0.7	188.7	0.5	189.5	0.4	190.8	0.7	191.9	0.6	193.5	0.8	193.9	0.2	194.6	0.4	197.0	1.2	196.7	-0.2	197.9	0.6

[Continued]

Los Angeles-Riverside-Orange County, CA
Consumer Price Index - All Urban Consumers
Base 1982-1984 = 100
Medical Care

[Continued]

For 1947-2001. Columns headed % show percentile change in the index from the previous period for which an index is available.

Year	Jan Index	%	Feb Index	%	Mar Index	%	Apr Index	%	May Index	%	Jun Index	%	Jul Index	%	Aug Index	%	Sep Index	%	Oct Index	%	Nov Index	%	Dec Index	%
1993	199.0	0.6	202.3	1.7	201.9	-0.2	202.6	0.3	207.2	2.3	207.0	-0.1	207.3	0.1	207.8	0.2	208.8	0.5	211.3	1.2	211.4	0.0	212.0	0.3
1994	212.7	0.3	213.3	0.3	213.4	0.0	214.0	0.3	214.2	0.1	214.4	0.1	215.7	0.6	216.0	0.1	216.2	0.1	216.5	0.1	217.6	0.5	217.8	0.1
1995	219.1	0.6	219.6	0.2	220.7	0.5	220.4	-0.1	220.9	0.2	222.1	0.5	221.8	-0.1	222.3	0.2	222.3	0.0	223.5	0.5	224.1	0.3	224.2	0.0
1996	226.3	0.9	226.5	0.1	227.7	0.5	228.8	0.5	228.9	0.0	229.3	0.2	229.5	0.1	229.3	-0.1	229.4	0.0	229.9	0.2	230.1	0.1	230.5	0.2
1997	231.7	0.5	231.8	0.0	231.9	0.0	231.5	-0.2	231.2	-0.1	231.4	0.1	232.0	0.3	232.0	0.0	231.9	-0.0	232.4	0.2	232.9	0.2	232.7	-0.1
1998	233.1	0.2	234.9	0.8	234.4	-0.2	234.3	-0.0	234.8	0.2	236.9	0.9	237.6	0.3	238.3	0.3	237.5	-0.3	238.1	0.3	239.8	0.7	241.0	0.5
1999	241.2	0.1	242.4	0.5	241.9	-0.2	245.1	1.3	244.5	-0.2	244.4	-0.0	244.7	0.1	244.8	0.0	245.8	0.4	245.5	-0.1	245.9	0.2	248.1	0.9
2000	249.7	0.6	250.6	0.4	249.8	-0.3	249.8	0.0	252.2	1.0	252.4	0.1	252.7	0.1	252.4	-0.1	253.8	0.6	253.8	0.0	254.0	0.1	255.1	0.4
2001	257.7	1.0	260.2	1.0	260.7	0.2	261.9	0.5	263.1	0.5	264.1	0.4	263.8	-0.1	269.3	2.1	270.6	0.5	271.7	0.4	271.5	-0.1	272.7	0.4

Source: U.S. Department of Labor, Bureau of Labor Statistics, Division of Consumer Prices and Price Indexes. - indicates no data collected for period.

Los Angeles-Riverside-Orange County, CA
Consumer Price Index - Urban Wage Earners
Base 1982-1984 = 100
Medical Care

For 1947-2001. Columns headed % show percentile change in the index from the previous period for which an index is available.

Year	Jan Index	%	Feb Index	%	Mar Index	%	Apr Index	%	May Index	%	Jun Index	%	Jul Index	%	Aug Index	%	Sep Index	%	Oct Index	%	Nov Index	%	Dec Index	%
1947	13.5	-	13.5	0.0	13.5	0.0	13.6	0.7	13.5	-0.7	13.5	0.0	13.5	0.0	13.5	0.0	13.6	0.7	13.8	1.5	13.8	0.0	13.8	0.0
1948	13.9	0.7	13.9	0.0	13.9	0.0	14.2	2.2	14.2	0.0	14.3	0.7	14.6	2.1	14.6	0.0	14.7	0.7	14.8	0.7	14.8	0.0	14.8	0.0
1949	14.9	0.7	14.9	0.0	14.9	0.0	14.9	0.0	14.9	0.0	14.9	0.0	14.9	0.0	14.9	0.0	15.0	0.7	15.0	0.0	15.0	0.0	15.0	0.0
1950	15.0	0.0	15.0	0.0	15.0	0.0	15.0	0.0	15.0	0.0	15.0	0.0	15.0	0.0	15.0	0.0	15.5	3.3	15.6	0.6	15.7	0.6	16.0	1.9
1951	16.0	0.0	16.0	0.0	16.2	1.3	16.2	0.0	16.2	0.0	16.2	0.0	16.2	0.0	16.2	0.0	16.2	0.0	16.2	0.0	16.2	0.0	16.2	0.0
1952	16.3	0.6	16.3	0.0	16.4	0.6	16.4	0.0	16.4	0.0	16.9	3.0	16.9	0.0	16.9	0.0	16.9	0.0	16.9	0.0	16.9	0.0	16.9	0.0
1953	16.9	0.0	16.9	0.0	16.9	0.0	17.1	1.2	17.2	0.6	17.2	0.0	17.2	0.0	17.2	0.0	17.2	0.0	17.3	0.6	17.3	0.0	17.4	0.6
1954	17.3	-0.6	17.3	0.0	17.4	0.6	17.5	0.6	17.5	0.0	17.5	0.0	17.6	0.6	17.6	0.0	17.6	0.0	17.6	0.0	17.6	0.0	17.6	0.0
1955	17.6	0.0	17.6	0.0	17.6	0.0	17.4	-1.1	17.4	0.0	17.4	0.0	17.8	2.3	17.8	0.0	17.8	0.0	17.8	0.0	17.8	0.0	17.9	0.6
1956	18.1	1.1	18.1	0.0	18.1	0.0	18.1	0.0	18.2	0.6	18.2	0.0	18.2	0.0	18.2	0.0	18.3	0.5	18.3	0.0	18.3	0.0	18.3	0.0
1957	18.5	1.1	18.5	0.0	18.5	0.0	18.6	0.5	18.6	0.0	18.6	0.0	18.7	0.5	18.7	0.0	18.7	0.0	18.7	0.0	18.8	0.5	18.9	0.5
1958	19.2	1.6	19.2	0.0	19.2	0.0	19.6	2.1	19.6	0.0	20.6	5.1	20.6	0.0	20.7	0.5	20.7	0.0	20.9	1.0	20.9	0.0	20.9	0.0
1959	20.9	0.0	20.9	0.0	20.9	0.0	20.9	0.0	21.0	0.5	21.0	0.0	21.0	0.0	21.0	0.0	21.0	0.0	21.4	1.9	21.4	0.0	21.4	0.0
1960	21.4	0.0	21.4	0.0	21.4	0.0	21.6	0.9	21.6	0.0	21.6	0.0	21.8	0.9	21.8	0.0	21.8	0.0	21.9	0.5	21.9	0.0	21.9	0.0
1961	21.9	0.0	21.9	0.0	21.9	0.0	21.9	0.0	21.9	0.0	22.0	0.5	22.0	0.0	22.0	0.0	22.1	0.5	22.1	0.0	22.1	0.0	22.1	0.0
1962	22.0	-0.5	22.0	0.0	22.7	3.2	22.8	0.4	22.8	0.0	22.8	0.0	22.8	0.0	22.8	0.0	22.8	0.0	22.8	0.0	22.8	0.0	22.8	0.0
1963	22.9	0.4	22.9	0.0	22.9	0.0	23.0	0.4	23.0	0.0	23.0	0.0	23.1	0.4	23.1	0.0	23.0	-0.4	23.2	0.9	23.2	0.0	23.2	0.0
1964	23.3	0.4	23.4	0.4	23.4	0.0	23.6	0.9	23.6	0.0	23.6	0.0	23.7	0.4	23.7	0.0	23.6	-0.4	23.8	0.8	23.8	0.0	23.8	0.0
1965	23.8	0.0	23.8	0.0	23.9	0.4	24.0	0.4	24.0	0.0	24.0	0.0	24.1	0.4	24.1	0.0	24.0	-0.4	24.1	0.4	24.1	0.0	24.2	0.4
1966	24.2	0.0	24.3	0.4	24.4	0.4	24.5	0.4	24.5	0.0	24.6	0.4	24.6	0.0	24.7	0.4	25.6	3.6	25.8	0.8	25.9	0.4	26.1	0.8
1967	26.1	0.0	26.1	0.0	26.2	0.4	26.4	0.8	26.7	1.1	26.8	0.4	27.0	0.7	27.0	0.0	27.2	0.7	27.2	0.0	27.3	0.4	27.4	0.4
1968	27.6	0.7	27.7	0.4	27.7	0.0	28.0	1.1	28.2	0.7	28.2	0.0	28.4	0.7	28.5	0.4	28.5	0.0	28.6	0.4	28.7	0.3	28.9	0.7
1969	29.0	0.3	29.2	0.7	29.3	0.3	29.7	1.4	29.9	0.7	30.0	0.3	30.0	0.0	30.2	0.7	30.3	0.3	30.2	-0.3	30.4	0.7	30.8	1.3
1970	30.9	0.3	31.2	1.0	31.5	1.0	32.1	1.9	32.2	0.3	32.3	0.3	32.4	0.3	32.5	0.3	32.5	0.0	32.3	-0.6	32.4	0.3	32.5	0.3
1971	32.6	0.3	32.7	0.3	32.9	0.6	33.7	2.4	33.9	0.6	34.0	0.3	34.1	0.3	34.1	0.0	34.2	0.3	34.0	-0.6	34.0	0.0	34.0	0.0
1972	34.0	0.0	34.1	0.3	34.1	0.0	34.2	0.3	34.2	0.0	34.4	0.6	34.6	0.6	34.6	0.0	34.7	0.3	34.9	0.6	34.9	0.0	35.0	0.3
1973	35.1	0.3	35.3	0.6	35.5	0.6	35.7	0.6	35.8	0.3	35.9	0.3	36.1	0.6	36.3	0.6	36.4	0.3	37.1	1.9	37.1	0.0	37.1	0.0
1974	37.4	0.8	37.7	0.8	38.1	1.1	38.2	0.3	38.9	1.8	39.3	1.0	39.9	1.5	40.4	1.3	40.6	0.5	40.9	0.7	41.5	1.5	41.7	0.5
1975	41.9	0.5	42.7	1.9	43.0	0.7	43.5	1.2	43.9	0.9	44.2	0.7	44.5	0.7	45.0	1.1	45.2	0.4	45.5	0.7	46.2	1.5	46.8	1.3
1976	47.1	0.6	48.4	2.8	48.6	0.4	49.0	0.8	49.7	1.4	50.1	0.8	50.4	0.6	50.9	1.0	51.0	0.2	51.4	0.8	52.1	1.4	52.1	0.0
1977	52.4	0.6	53.2	1.5	53.4	0.4	53.8	0.7	54.0	0.4	54.4	0.7	54.9	0.9	55.3	0.7	55.7	0.7	56.1	0.7	56.4	0.5	56.4	0.0
1978	56.8	0.7	57.1	0.5	57.2	0.2	57.4	0.3	58.7	2.3	58.7	0.0	59.1	0.7	59.8	1.2	60.2	0.7	60.8	1.0	61.4	1.0	61.2	-0.3
1979	62.3	1.8	62.5	0.3	62.7	0.3	62.8	0.2	63.6	1.3	64.1	0.8	66.0	3.0	66.8	1.2	67.7	1.3	67.8	0.1	68.1	0.4	68.6	0.7
1980	69.3	1.0	70.4	1.6	70.6	0.3	72.6	2.8	73.9	1.8	73.7	-0.3	74.5	1.1	74.7	0.3	75.4	0.9	76.4	1.3	77.8	1.8	78.3	0.6
1981	79.0	0.9	80.7	2.2	81.0	0.4	81.5	0.6	81.9	0.5	82.8	1.1	83.7	1.1	84.3	0.7	85.3	1.2	85.2	-0.1	87.7	2.9	89.3	1.8
1982	90.0	0.8	90.2	0.2	90.8	0.7	91.8	1.1	92.8	1.1	94.5	1.8	94.9	0.4	95.9	1.1	97.0	1.1	96.7	-0.3	97.4	0.7	97.5	0.1
1983	99.2	1.7	99.4	0.2	99.7	0.3	100.2	0.5	100.3	0.1	101.1	0.8	101.6	0.5	101.2	-0.4	101.2	0.0	101.3	0.1	101.5	0.2	101.6	0.1
1984	103.1	1.5	103.2	0.1	103.6	0.4	104.1	0.5	104.6	0.5	104.6	0.0	105.5	0.9	106.1	0.6	105.8	-0.3	107.0	1.1	107.1	0.1	107.3	0.2
1985	110.0	2.5	110.5	0.5	111.1	0.5	111.2	0.1	111.4	0.2	112.2	0.7	112.8	0.5	113.7	0.8	114.5	0.7	115.0	0.4	115.7	0.6	116.4	0.6
1986	117.0	0.5	118.1	0.9	118.8	0.6	119.2	0.3	119.6	0.3	120.0	0.3	120.5	0.4	121.5	0.8	121.7	0.2	122.8	0.9	124.1	1.1	124.9	0.6
1987	126.1	1.0	126.7	0.5	127.1	0.3	127.7	0.5	127.6	-0.1	128.9	1.0	129.1	0.2	129.8	0.5	130.3	0.4	131.2	0.7	131.8	0.5	132.1	0.2
1988	135.1	2.3	136.2	0.8	137.0	0.6	136.9	-0.1	137.4	0.4	138.8	1.0	139.3	0.4	140.3	0.7	140.9	0.4	142.5	1.1	142.2	-0.2	142.3	0.1
1989	144.2	1.3	144.4	0.1	145.3	0.6	146.5	0.8	147.2	0.5	148.2	0.7	149.4	0.8	150.1	0.5	151.4	0.9	151.8	0.3	153.0	0.8	153.4	0.3
1990	155.8	1.6	156.9	0.7	157.5	0.4	158.6	0.7	159.3	0.4	160.2	0.6	161.4	0.7	161.7	0.2	163.6	1.2	166.3	1.7	168.5	1.3	168.7	0.1
1991	170.9	1.3	170.6	-0.2	172.2	0.9	172.3	0.1	173.5	0.7	175.3	1.0	177.7	1.4	177.5	-0.1	178.0	0.3	178.2	0.1	180.9	1.5	181.6	0.4
1992	183.7	1.2	185.2	0.8	186.2	0.5	186.9	0.4	188.3	0.7	189.4	0.6	191.2	1.0	191.8	0.3	192.6	0.4	194.6	1.0	194.2	-0.2	195.5	0.7

[Continued]

Los Angeles-Riverside-Orange County, CA
Consumer Price Index - Urban Wage Earners
Base 1982-1984 = 100
Medical Care
[Continued]

For 1947-2001. Columns headed % show percentile change in the index from the previous period for which an index is available.

Year	Jan Index	%	Feb Index	%	Mar Index	%	Apr Index	%	May Index	%	Jun Index	%	Jul Index	%	Aug Index	%	Sep Index	%	Oct Index	%	Nov Index	%	Dec Index	%
1993	196.6	0.6	199.6	1.5	199.4	-0.1	200.1	0.4	204.8	2.3	204.3	-0.2	204.7	0.2	205.1	0.2	206.0	0.4	208.5	1.2	208.3	-0.1	208.9	0.3
1994	209.6	0.3	210.0	0.2	210.0	0.0	210.8	0.4	210.8	0.0	211.1	0.1	212.1	0.5	212.4	0.1	212.6	0.1	213.0	0.2	214.1	0.5	214.2	0.0
1995	215.6	0.7	216.0	0.2	217.5	0.7	217.1	-0.2	217.6	0.2	219.0	0.6	219.3	0.1	219.7	0.2	219.6	-0.0	220.8	0.5	221.5	0.3	221.6	0.0
1996	223.7	0.9	223.9	0.1	225.1	0.5	226.2	0.5	226.3	0.0	226.9	0.3	227.1	0.1	226.9	-0.1	227.0	0.0	227.7	0.3	227.7	0.0	228.3	0.3
1997	229.2	0.4	229.4	0.1	229.5	0.0	229.1	-0.2	228.8	-0.1	228.8	0.0	229.5	0.3	229.3	-0.1	228.9	-0.2	229.9	0.4	230.5	0.3	230.3	-0.1
1998	230.8	0.2	232.4	0.7	231.6	-0.3	231.3	-0.1	232.0	0.3	234.4	1.0	235.1	0.3	235.9	0.3	234.9	-0.4	235.4	0.2	237.3	0.8	238.3	0.4
1999	238.0	-0.1	239.5	0.6	238.2	-0.5	242.0	1.6	241.7	-0.1	241.2	-0.2	241.3	0.0	241.5	0.1	242.5	0.4	242.1	-0.2	242.7	0.2	245.2	1.0
2000	246.5	0.5	247.3	0.3	246.7	-0.2	246.2	-0.2	248.8	1.1	248.9	0.0	249.2	0.1	248.5	-0.3	250.2	0.7	250.2	0.0	250.2	0.0	250.8	0.2
2001	254.1	1.3	256.5	0.9	257.2	0.3	257.9	0.3	259.3	0.5	260.5	0.5	259.6	-0.3	265.4	2.2	266.9	0.6	268.2	0.5	268.0	-0.1	269.4	0.5

Source: U.S. Department of Labor, Bureau of Labor Statistics, Division of Consumer Prices and Price Indexes. - indicates no data collected for period.

Los Angeles-Riverside-Orange County, CA
Consumer Price Index - All Urban Consumers
Base December 1997 = 100
Recreation

For 1997-2001. Columns headed % show percentile change in the index from the previous period for which an index is available.

Year	Jan Index	%	Feb Index	%	Mar Index	%	Apr Index	%	May Index	%	Jun Index	%	Jul Index	%	Aug Index	%	Sep Index	%	Oct Index	%	Nov Index	%	Dec Index	%
1997	-	-	-	-	-	-	-	-	-	-	-	-	-	-	-	-	-	-	-	-	-	-	100.0	-
1998	99.4	-0.6	100.3	0.9	100.3	0.0	100.7	0.4	101.5	0.8	101.4	-0.1	100.7	-0.7	101.1	0.4	100.4	-0.7	101.2	0.8	103.1	1.9	101.8	-1.3
1999	102.5	0.7	103.6	1.1	103.0	-0.6	104.3	1.3	103.1	-1.2	100.3	-2.7	101.1	0.8	99.5	-1.6	99.2	-0.3	100.2	1.0	101.4	1.2	104.1	2.7
2000	104.0	-0.1	104.3	0.3	104.7	0.4	104.8	0.1	104.5	-0.3	104.4	-0.1	103.9	-0.5	104.5	0.6	104.3	-0.2	105.0	0.7	104.6	-0.4	104.6	0.0
2001	105.6	1.0	105.4	-0.2	105.1	-0.3	106.8	1.6	105.9	-0.8	104.5	-1.3	104.7	0.2	105.2	0.5	105.9	0.7	105.4	-0.5	108.9	3.3	108.6	-0.3

Source: U.S. Department of Labor, Bureau of Labor Statistics, Division of Consumer Prices and Price Indexes. - indicates no data collected for period.

Los Angeles-Riverside-Orange County, CA
Consumer Price Index - Urban Wage Earners
Base December 1997 = 100
Recreation

For 1997-2001. Columns headed % show percentile change in the index from the previous period for which an index is available.

Year	Jan Index	%	Feb Index	%	Mar Index	%	Apr Index	%	May Index	%	Jun Index	%	Jul Index	%	Aug Index	%	Sep Index	%	Oct Index	%	Nov Index	%	Dec Index	%
1997	-	-	-	-	-	-	-	-	-	-	-	-	-	-	-	-	-	-	-	-	-	-	100.0	-
1998	99.2	-0.8	100.3	1.1	100.1	-0.2	100.6	0.5	101.0	0.4	100.9	-0.1	100.0	-0.9	100.4	0.4	99.7	-0.7	100.4	0.7	101.5	1.1	100.1	-1.4
1999	101.0	0.9	102.1	1.1	101.3	-0.8	102.2	0.9	100.7	-1.5	99.5	-1.2	100.2	0.7	98.2	-2.0	97.8	-0.4	98.8	1.0	98.5	-0.3	101.5	3.0
2000	101.1	-0.4	101.2	0.1	101.5	0.3	101.5	0.0	101.3	-0.2	101.2	-0.1	100.6	-0.6	101.3	0.7	100.8	-0.5	101.5	0.7	101.1	-0.4	101.2	0.1
2001	101.9	0.7	101.3	-0.6	101.1	-0.2	103.1	2.0	102.2	-0.9	102.5	0.3	102.6	0.1	103.2	0.6	103.6	0.4	102.8	-0.8	105.0	2.1	104.7	-0.3

Source: U.S. Department of Labor, Bureau of Labor Statistics, Division of Consumer Prices and Price Indexes. - indicates no data collected for period.

Economic Indicators Handbook, 6th Edition

Los Angeles-Riverside-Orange County, CA
Consumer Price Index - All Urban Consumers
Base December 1997 = 100
Education & Communication

For 1997-2001. Columns headed % show percentile change in the index from the previous period for which an index is available.

Year	Jan Index	%	Feb Index	%	Mar Index	%	Apr Index	%	May Index	%	Jun Index	%	Jul Index	%	Aug Index	%	Sep Index	%	Oct Index	%	Nov Index	%	Dec Index	%
1997	-	-	-	-	-	-	-	-	-	-	-	-	-	-	-	-	-	-	-	-	-	-	100.0	-
1998	99.6	-0.4	99.6	0.0	99.9	0.3	99.8	-0.1	99.7	-0.1	99.6	-0.1	99.9	0.3	99.6	-0.3	99.0	-0.6	99.3	0.3	99.2	-0.1	99.0	-0.2
1999	99.6	0.6	98.9	-0.7	98.5	-0.4	99.2	0.7	98.9	-0.3	98.7	-0.2	98.7	0.0	99.1	0.4	99.4	0.3	99.5	0.1	99.5	0.0	100.1	0.6
2000	100.2	0.1	99.9	-0.3	99.2	-0.7	99.4	0.2	99.4	0.0	99.2	-0.2	99.4	0.2	100.2	0.8	100.7	0.5	100.7	0.0	99.1	-1.6	99.4	0.3
2001	99.7	0.3	100.0	0.3	101.1	1.1	100.8	-0.3	101.3	0.5	101.6	0.3	101.9	0.3	102.0	0.1	102.1	0.1	102.6	0.5	102.4	-0.2	102.1	-0.3

Source: U.S. Department of Labor, Bureau of Labor Statistics, Division of Consumer Prices and Price Indexes. - indicates no data collected for period.

Los Angeles-Riverside-Orange County, CA
Consumer Price Index - Urban Wage Earners
Base December 1997 = 100
Education & Communication

For 1997-2001. Columns headed % show percentile change in the index from the previous period for which an index is available.

Year	Jan Index	%	Feb Index	%	Mar Index	%	Apr Index	%	May Index	%	Jun Index	%	Jul Index	%	Aug Index	%	Sep Index	%	Oct Index	%	Nov Index	%	Dec Index	%
1997	-	-	-	-	-	-	-	-	-	-	-	-	-	-	-	-	-	-	-	-	-	-	100.0	-
1998	99.6	-0.4	99.6	0.0	99.9	0.3	99.8	-0.1	99.8	0.0	99.7	-0.1	100.0	0.3	99.5	-0.5	98.8	-0.7	99.1	0.3	99.1	0.0	98.9	-0.2
1999	99.4	0.5	98.7	-0.7	98.2	-0.5	99.0	0.8	98.7	-0.3	98.5	-0.2	98.6	0.1	98.8	0.2	99.2	0.4	99.3	0.1	99.4	0.1	100.1	0.7
2000	100.2	0.1	99.9	-0.3	99.1	-0.8	99.4	0.3	99.3	-0.1	99.1	-0.2	99.4	0.3	100.4	1.0	100.6	0.2	100.7	0.1	98.8	-1.9	99.2	0.4
2001	99.5	0.3	99.8	0.3	101.1	1.3	100.7	-0.4	101.3	0.6	101.7	0.4	101.9	0.2	101.9	0.0	101.9	0.0	102.5	0.6	102.2	-0.3	101.9	-0.3

Source: U.S. Department of Labor, Bureau of Labor Statistics, Division of Consumer Prices and Price Indexes. - indicates no data collected for period.

Miami-Fort Lauderdale, FL
Consumer Price Index - All Urban Consumers
Base 1982-1984 = 100
Annual Averages

For 1977-2001. Columns headed % show percentile change in the index from the previous period for which an index is available.

Year	All Items		Food & Beverage		Housing		Apparel		Trans-portation		Medical Care		Recrea-tion*		Education & Communic.*		Other Goods & Services	
	Index	%	Index	%	Index	%	Index	%	Index	%	Index	%	Index	%	Index	%	Index	%
1977	-	-	-	-	-	-	-	-	-	-	-	-	-	-	-	-	-	-
1978	64.8	-	69.8	-	62.9	-	77.6	-	59.6	-	61.4	-	-	-	-	-	63.7	-
1979	71.2	9.9	78.6	12.6	68.5	8.9	81.2	4.6	67.1	12.6	68.9	12.2	-	-	-	-	69.1	8.5
1980	81.1	13.9	84.7	7.8	80.8	18.0	87.0	7.1	78.5	17.0	75.6	9.7	-	-	-	-	76.2	10.3
1981	90.5	11.6	91.3	7.8	92.0	13.9	91.9	5.6	88.8	13.1	81.9	8.3	-	-	-	-	84.7	11.2
1982	96.7	6.9	96.8	6.0	97.8	6.3	98.2	6.9	94.8	6.8	93.8	14.5	-	-	-	-	93.1	9.9
1983	99.9	3.3	99.5	2.8	99.7	1.9	100.1	1.9	100.2	5.7	101.0	7.7	-	-	-	-	100.0	7.4
1984	103.5	3.6	103.6	4.1	102.6	2.9	101.7	1.6	105.0	4.8	105.1	4.1	-	-	-	-	106.9	6.9
1985	106.5	2.9	104.4	0.8	105.7	3.0	105.7	3.9	108.3	3.1	109.2	3.9	-	-	-	-	113.3	6.0
1986	107.9	1.3	107.1	2.6	107.0	1.2	109.0	3.1	103.7	-4.2	117.4	7.5	-	-	-	-	121.8	7.5
1987	111.8	3.6	113.0	5.5	108.7	1.6	115.6	6.1	106.6	2.8	126.6	7.8	-	-	-	-	128.3	5.3
1988	116.8	4.5	118.7	5.0	113.1	4.0	123.5	6.8	110.7	3.8	134.6	6.3	-	-	-	-	133.6	4.1
1989	121.5	4.0	125.6	5.8	116.2	2.7	131.3	6.3	114.8	3.7	140.5	4.4	-	-	-	-	139.8	4.6
1990	128.0	5.3	134.3	6.9	120.4	3.6	135.6	3.3	121.6	5.9	151.8	8.0	-	-	-	-	153.2	9.6
1991	132.3	3.4	137.7	2.5	123.7	2.7	140.4	3.5	126.0	3.6	162.8	7.2	-	-	-	-	161.5	5.4
1992	134.5	1.7	140.6	2.1	126.2	2.0	138.8	-1.1	127.8	1.4	172.3	5.8	-	-	-	-	160.5	-0.6
1993	139.1	3.4	146.9	4.5	130.4	3.3	140.1	0.9	131.9	3.2	181.9	5.6	-	-	-	-	162.5	1.2
1994	143.6	3.2	152.7	3.9	135.2	3.7	143.5	2.4	135.3	2.6	188.1	3.4	-	-	-	-	162.8	0.2
1995	148.9	3.7	157.1	2.9	139.9	3.5	147.0	2.4	139.8	3.3	203.0	7.9	-	-	-	-	169.7	4.2
1996	153.7	3.2	161.4	2.7	145.1	3.7	146.0	-0.7	144.3	3.2	214.4	5.6	-	-	-	-	175.0	3.1
1997	158.4	3.1	165.7	2.7	150.2	3.5	153.5	5.1	147.2	2.0	219.2	2.2	-	-	-	-	181.3	3.6
1998	160.5	1.3	169.0	2.0	153.5	2.2	152.1	-0.9	144.2	-2.0	227.3	3.7	100.3	-	100.5	-	190.5	5.1
1999	162.4	1.2	171.0	1.2	155.2	1.1	138.2	-9.1	148.8	3.2	231.3	1.8	99.2	-1.1	102.0	1.5	203.3	6.7
2000	167.8	3.3	174.8	2.2	158.6	2.2	151.1	9.3	158.6	6.6	241.2	4.3	99.4	0.2	103.1	1.1	212.6	4.6
2001	173.0	3.1	180.7	3.4	164.2	3.5	150.7	-0.3	-	-	253.3	5.0	103.6	4.2	106.5	3.3	229.6	8.0

Source: U.S. Department of Labor, Bureau of Labor Statistics, Division of Consumer Prices and Price Indexes. *Base is December 1997 = 100. - indicates no data collected for period.

Miami-Fort Lauderdale, FL
Consumer Price Index - Urban Wage Earners
Base 1982-1984 = 100
Annual Averages

For 1977-2001. Columns headed % show percentile change in the index from the previous period for which an index is available.

Year	All Items Index	%	Food & Beverage Index	%	Housing Index	%	Apparel Index	%	Transportation Index	%	Medical Care Index	%	Recreation* Index	%	Education & Communic.* Index	%	Other Goods & Services Index	%
1977	-	-	-	-	-	-	-	-	-	-	-	-	-	-	-	-	-	-
1978	64.5	-	68.6	-	62.9	-	76.0	-	59.4	-	61.9	-	-	-	-	-	-	-
1979	71.3	10.5	78.3	14.1	68.3	8.6	80.2	5.5	67.5	13.6	67.8	9.5	-	-	-	-	66.0	-
1980	81.4	14.2	85.4	9.1	80.4	17.7	86.7	8.1	79.5	17.8	74.3	9.6	-	-	-	-	71.3	8.0
1981	90.5	11.2	91.6	7.3	92.1	14.6	91.7	5.8	89.6	12.7	79.8	7.4	-	-	-	-	77.3	8.4
1982	96.8	7.0	96.9	5.8	98.1	6.5	97.8	6.7	94.9	5.9	93.7	17.4	-	-	-	-	84.4	9.2
1983	99.9	3.2	99.5	2.7	99.6	1.5	100.0	2.2	100.3	5.7	101.3	8.1	-	-	-	-	93.1	10.3
1984	103.3	3.4	103.6	4.1	102.2	2.6	102.2	2.2	104.8	4.5	105.0	3.7	-	-	-	-	100.1	7.5
1985	106.4	3.0	104.3	0.7	106.0	3.7	106.0	3.7	107.9	3.0	108.7	3.5	-	-	-	-	106.9	6.8
1986	107.4	0.9	107.5	3.1	107.3	1.2	109.6	3.4	102.3	-5.2	116.6	7.3	-	-	-	-	112.4	5.1
1987	111.1	3.4	113.0	5.1	109.0	1.6	115.7	5.6	105.1	2.7	125.8	7.9	-	-	-	-	120.8	7.5
1988	115.9	4.3	118.5	4.9	113.4	4.0	122.8	6.1	109.0	3.7	133.1	5.8	-	-	-	-	126.8	5.0
1989	120.3	3.8	126.3	6.6	116.2	2.5	129.7	5.6	112.6	3.3	139.0	4.4	-	-	-	-	132.6	4.6
1990	126.2	4.9	134.8	6.7	120.2	3.4	133.3	2.8	118.3	5.1	150.7	8.4	-	-	-	-	138.9	4.8
1991	130.4	3.3	137.8	2.2	123.3	2.6	139.7	4.8	122.6	3.6	161.7	7.3	-	-	-	-	151.5	9.1
1992	132.6	1.7	139.7	1.4	125.7	1.9	138.3	-1.0	125.3	2.2	171.5	6.1	-	-	-	-	159.7	5.4
1993	137.3	3.5	145.8	4.4	129.8	3.3	140.8	1.8	130.1	3.8	181.0	5.5	-	-	-	-	157.7	-1.3
1994	141.5	3.1	151.3	3.8	134.4	3.5	145.5	3.3	133.5	2.6	185.5	2.5	-	-	-	-	159.0	0.8
1995	146.9	3.8	155.7	2.9	139.2	3.6	149.4	2.7	138.9	4.0	200.0	7.8	-	-	-	-	157.2	-1.1
1996	151.8	3.3	160.5	3.1	144.5	3.8	147.9	-1.0	143.2	3.1	211.7	5.8	-	-	-	-	163.4	3.9
1997	156.1	2.8	164.7	2.6	149.3	3.3	156.1	5.5	145.0	1.3	216.3	2.2	-	-	-	-	167.7	2.6
1998	157.8	1.1	167.9	1.9	152.4	2.1	155.3	-0.5	141.7	-2.3	225.4	4.2	100.2	-	100.9	-	173.9	3.7
1999	160.1	1.5	169.9	1.2	153.9	1.0	146.0	-6.0	146.4	3.3	229.3	1.7	98.9	-1.3	102.9	2.0	183.1	5.3
2000	165.4	3.3	173.6	2.2	157.0	2.0	160.9	10.2	156.2	6.7	239.0	4.2	98.1	-0.8	103.8	0.9	196.7	7.4
2001	170.5	3.1	179.4	3.3	162.6	3.6	161.4	0.3	-	-	251.4	5.2	102.3	4.3	107.3	3.4	223.0	8.0

Source: U.S. Department of Labor, Bureau of Labor Statistics, Division of Consumer Prices and Price Indexes. *Base is December 1997 = 100. - indicates no data collected for period.

Miami-Fort Lauderdale, FL
Consumer Price Index - All Urban Consumers
Base 1982-1984 = 100
All Items

For 1977-2001. Columns headed % show percentile change in the index from the previous period for which an index is available.

Year	Jan Index	%	Feb Index	%	Mar Index	%	Apr Index	%	May Index	%	Jun Index	%	Jul Index	%	Aug Index	%	Sep Index	%	Oct Index	%	Nov Index	%	Dec Index	%
1977	-	-	-	-	-	-	-	-	-	-	-	-	-	-	-	-	-	-	-	-	62.0	-	-	-
1978	62.5	0.8	-	-	63.4	1.4	-	-	63.8	0.6	-	-	65.1	2.0	-	-	66.1	1.5	-	-	66.6	0.8	-	-
1979	67.6	1.5	-	-	69.0	2.1	-	-	69.8	1.2	-	-	71.8	2.9	-	-	72.8	1.4	-	-	74.1	1.8	-	-
1980	76.5	3.2	-	-	79.2	3.5	-	-	80.5	1.6	-	-	82.9	3.0	-	-	82.6	-0.4	-	-	83.1	0.6	-	-
1981	85.2	2.5	-	-	86.9	2.0	-	-	88.8	2.2	-	-	90.6	2.0	-	-	93.2	2.9	-	-	95.3	2.3	-	-
1982	96.3	1.0	-	-	96.2	-0.1	-	-	96.6	0.4	-	-	96.2	-0.4	-	-	96.8	0.6	-	-	97.3	0.5	-	-
1983	98.0	0.7	-	-	98.6	0.6	-	-	98.9	0.3	-	-	99.8	0.9	-	-	101.1	1.3	-	-	101.7	0.6	-	-
1984	102.4	0.7	-	-	102.7	0.3	-	-	103.2	0.5	-	-	103.6	0.4	-	-	104.2	0.6	-	-	104.4	0.2	-	-
1985	104.6	0.2	-	-	105.5	0.9	-	-	106.1	0.6	-	-	106.3	0.2	-	-	107.6	1.2	-	-	107.9	0.3	-	-
1986	108.3	0.4	-	-	108.3	0.0	-	-	107.3	-0.9	-	-	106.2	-1.0	-	-	108.1	1.8	-	-	109.1	0.9	-	-
1987	109.9	0.7	-	-	110.7	0.7	-	-	111.1	0.4	-	-	112.0	0.8	-	-	112.5	0.4	-	-	113.8	1.2	-	-
1988	114.5	0.6	-	-	115.1	0.5	-	-	116.2	1.0	-	-	116.8	0.5	-	-	118.8	1.7	-	-	118.3	-0.4	-	-
1989	120.0	1.4	-	-	119.8	-0.2	-	-	120.9	0.9	-	-	121.6	0.6	-	-	122.9	1.1	-	-	123.0	0.1	-	-
1990	124.6	1.3	-	-	125.1	0.4	-	-	126.4	1.0	-	-	128.7	1.8	-	-	130.1	1.1	-	-	131.2	0.8	-	-
1991	131.5	0.2	-	-	132.0	0.4	-	-	132.0	0.0	-	-	132.0	0.0	-	-	132.1	0.1	-	-	133.5	1.1	-	-
1992	133.7	0.1	-	-	134.5	0.6	-	-	133.7	-0.6	-	-	133.8	0.1	-	-	134.6	0.6	-	-	135.9	1.0	-	-
1993	137.8	1.4	-	-	139.2	1.0	-	-	139.0	-0.1	-	-	139.0	0.0	-	-	139.2	0.1	-	-	139.8	0.4	-	-
1994	141.0	0.9	-	-	143.5	1.8	-	-	143.3	-0.1	-	-	143.4	0.1	-	-	144.5	0.8	-	-	144.5	0.0	-	-
1995	147.3	1.9	-	-	148.7	1.0	-	-	148.6	-0.1	-	-	148.3	-0.2	-	-	148.9	0.4	-	-	150.2	0.9	-	-
1996	152.0	1.2	-	-	152.4	0.3	-	-	152.6	0.1	-	-	152.4	-0.1	-	-	154.6	1.4	-	-	156.4	1.2	-	-
1997	158.1	1.1	-	-	158.5	0.3	-	-	157.9	-0.4	-	-	157.9	0.0	-	-	158.5	0.4	-	-	159.5	0.6	159.3	-0.1
1998	-	-	160.2	0.6	-	-	160.2	0.0	-	-	160.2	0.0	-	-	160.8	0.4	-	-	161.1	0.2	-	-	161.1	0.0
1999	-	-	161.4	0.2	-	-	161.7	0.2	-	-	161.3	-0.2	-	-	162.3	0.6	-	-	164.1	1.1	-	-	164.8	0.4
2000	-	-	165.9	0.7	-	-	166.9	0.6	-	-	168.0	0.7	-	-	168.4	0.2	-	-	169.6	0.7	-	-	169.5	-0.1
2001	-	-	171.9	1.4	-	-	172.8	0.5	-	-	173.5	0.4	-	-	173.5	0.0	-	-	174.2	0.4	-	-	173.1	-0.6

Source: U.S. Department of Labor, Bureau of Labor Statistics, Division of Consumer Prices and Price Indexes. - indicates no data collected for period.

Miami-Fort Lauderdale, FL

Consumer Price Index - Urban Wage Earners
Base 1982-1984 = 100

All Items

For 1977-2001. Columns headed % show percentile change in the index from the previous period for which an index is available.

Year	Jan Index	Jan %	Feb Index	Feb %	Mar Index	Mar %	Apr Index	Apr %	May Index	May %	Jun Index	Jun %	Jul Index	Jul %	Aug Index	Aug %	Sep Index	Sep %	Oct Index	Oct %	Nov Index	Nov %	Dec Index	Dec %
1977	-	-	-	-	-	-	-	-	-	-	-	-	-	-	-	-	-	-	-	-	61.6	-	-	-
1978	61.9	0.5	-	-	63.0	1.8	-	-	63.6	1.0	-	-	65.0	2.2	-	-	65.9	1.4	-	-	66.4	0.8	-	-
1979	67.2	1.2	-	-	69.2	3.0	-	-	70.0	1.2	-	-	72.0	2.9	-	-	73.1	1.5	-	-	74.2	1.5	-	-
1980	76.9	3.6	-	-	79.3	3.1	-	-	80.6	1.6	-	-	82.9	2.9	-	-	83.0	0.1	-	-	83.5	0.6	-	-
1981	85.4	2.3	-	-	87.2	2.1	-	-	89.1	2.2	-	-	90.7	1.8	-	-	92.9	2.4	-	-	95.2	2.5	-	-
1982	96.3	1.2	-	-	96.3	0.0	-	-	96.6	0.3	-	-	96.6	0.0	-	-	96.9	0.3	-	-	97.3	0.4	-	-
1983	98.0	0.7	-	-	98.3	0.3	-	-	99.3	1.0	-	-	100.2	0.9	-	-	101.1	0.9	-	-	101.5	0.4	-	-
1984	102.1	0.6	-	-	102.4	0.3	-	-	102.9	0.5	-	-	103.4	0.5	-	-	104.5	1.1	-	-	104.4	-0.1	-	-
1985	104.5	0.1	-	-	105.4	0.9	-	-	106.0	0.6	-	-	106.3	0.3	-	-	107.4	1.0	-	-	107.7	0.3	-	-
1986	108.1	0.4	-	-	107.8	-0.3	-	-	106.7	-1.0	-	-	105.6	-1.0	-	-	107.4	1.7	-	-	108.4	0.9	-	-
1987	109.3	0.8	-	-	109.9	0.5	-	-	110.3	0.4	-	-	111.3	0.9	-	-	111.8	0.4	-	-	113.1	1.2	-	-
1988	113.8	0.6	-	-	114.3	0.4	-	-	115.1	0.7	-	-	116.0	0.8	-	-	117.8	1.6	-	-	117.2	-0.5	-	-
1989	118.8	1.4	-	-	118.7	-0.1	-	-	120.0	1.1	-	-	120.6	0.5	-	-	121.4	0.7	-	-	121.5	0.1	-	-
1990	123.2	1.4	-	-	123.4	0.2	-	-	124.6	1.0	-	-	126.7	1.7	-	-	128.2	1.2	-	-	129.3	0.9	-	-
1991	129.8	0.4	-	-	130.1	0.2	-	-	130.2	0.1	-	-	130.2	0.0	-	-	130.2	0.0	-	-	131.4	0.9	-	-
1992	131.7	0.2	-	-	132.3	0.5	-	-	131.6	-0.5	-	-	132.0	0.3	-	-	132.8	0.6	-	-	134.2	1.1	-	-
1993	135.9	1.3	-	-	137.1	0.9	-	-	137.2	0.1	-	-	137.2	0.0	-	-	137.5	0.2	-	-	138.0	0.4	-	-
1994	138.7	0.5	-	-	141.1	1.7	-	-	141.2	0.1	-	-	141.4	0.1	-	-	142.5	0.8	-	-	142.7	0.1	-	-
1995	145.3	1.8	-	-	146.6	0.9	-	-	146.8	0.1	-	-	146.5	-0.2	-	-	146.9	0.3	-	-	148.2	0.9	-	-
1996	150.0	1.2	-	-	150.3	0.2	-	-	151.0	0.5	-	-	150.8	-0.1	-	-	152.6	1.2	-	-	154.6	1.3	-	-
1997	156.0	0.9	-	-	156.2	0.1	-	-	155.6	-0.4	-	-	155.5	-0.1	-	-	156.1	0.4	-	-	157.0	0.6	156.8	-0.1
1998	-	-	157.3	0.3	-	-	157.4	0.1	-	-	157.6	0.1	-	-	158.0	0.3	-	-	158.6	0.4	-	-	158.7	0.1
1999	-	-	158.8	0.1	-	-	159.1	0.2	-	-	158.9	-0.1	-	-	160.0	0.3	-	-	158.6	0.4	-	-	162.7	0.5
2000	-	-	163.5	0.5	-	-	164.6	0.7	-	-	165.7	0.7	-	-	160.0	0.7	-	-	161.9	1.2	-	-	167.2	0.1
2001	-	-	169.3	1.3	-	-	170.4	0.6	-	-	171.2	0.5	-	-	165.8	0.1	-	-	167.1	0.8	-	-	170.5	-0.7

Source: U.S. Department of Labor, Bureau of Labor Statistics, Division of Consumer Prices and Price Indexes. - indicates no data collected for period.

Miami-Fort Lauderdale, FL
Consumer Price Index - All Urban Consumers
Base 1982-1984 = 100
Food and Beverages

For 1977-2001. Columns headed % show percentile change in the index from the previous period for which an index is available.

Year	Jan Index	%	Feb Index	%	Mar Index	%	Apr Index	%	May Index	%	Jun Index	%	Jul Index	%	Aug Index	%	Sep Index	%	Oct Index	%	Nov Index	%	Dec Index	%
1977	-	-	-	-	-	-	-	-	-	-	-	-	-	-	-	-	-	-	-	-	65.1	-	-	-
1978	65.9	1.2	-	-	67.5	2.4	-	-	69.2	2.5	-	-	71.0	2.6	-	-	71.1	0.1	-	-	72.1	1.4	-	-
1979	74.9	3.9	-	-	76.9	2.7	-	-	78.3	1.8	-	-	79.9	2.0	-	-	80.2	0.4	-	-	80.1	-0.1	-	-
1980	81.4	1.6	-	-	82.0	0.7	-	-	82.7	0.9	-	-	84.8	2.5	-	-	87.2	2.8	-	-	88.3	1.3	-	-
1981	89.4	1.2	-	-	89.6	0.2	-	-	89.8	0.2	-	-	91.1	1.4	-	-	92.8	1.9	-	-	93.9	1.2	-	-
1982	94.9	1.1	-	-	95.8	0.9	-	-	96.9	1.1	-	-	97.8	0.9	-	-	97.8	0.0	-	-	97.0	-0.8	-	-
1983	97.9	0.9	-	-	98.9	1.0	-	-	99.1	0.2	-	-	99.0	-0.1	-	-	100.2	1.2	-	-	100.8	0.6	-	-
1984	104.0	3.2	-	-	104.2	0.2	-	-	102.6	-1.5	-	-	103.2	0.6	-	-	103.5	0.3	-	-	104.3	0.8	-	-
1985	104.1	-0.2	-	-	105.2	1.1	-	-	103.5	-1.6	-	-	104.4	0.9	-	-	104.1	-0.3	-	-	104.7	0.6	-	-
1986	106.3	1.5	-	-	106.9	0.6	-	-	106.9	0.0	-	-	103.1	-3.6	-	-	108.3	5.0	-	-	110.0	1.6	-	-
1987	110.7	0.6	-	-	112.2	1.4	-	-	113.9	1.5	-	-	113.6	-0.3	-	-	113.4	-0.2	-	-	113.5	0.1	-	-
1988	114.8	1.1	-	-	116.9	1.8	-	-	117.6	0.6	-	-	118.4	0.7	-	-	121.1	2.3	-	-	121.7	0.5	-	-
1989	122.3	0.5	-	-	123.0	0.6	-	-	124.0	0.8	-	-	126.7	2.2	-	-	126.4	-0.2	-	-	128.5	1.7	-	-
1990	134.1	4.4	-	-	134.1	0.0	-	-	132.4	-1.3	-	-	134.2	1.4	-	-	134.4	0.1	-	-	136.1	1.3	-	-
1991	136.0	-0.1	-	-	137.7	1.2	-	-	137.7	0.0	-	-	138.0	0.2	-	-	138.2	0.1	-	-	138.1	-0.1	-	-
1992	138.7	0.4	-	-	140.5	1.3	-	-	138.9	-1.1	-	-	139.9	0.7	-	-	142.0	1.5	-	-	142.2	0.1	-	-
1993	144.9	1.9	-	-	145.7	0.6	-	-	146.1	0.3	-	-	145.9	-0.1	-	-	147.6	1.2	-	-	149.3	1.2	-	-
1994	151.8	1.7	-	-	151.7	-0.1	-	-	152.1	0.3	-	-	152.3	0.1	-	-	152.8	0.3	-	-	154.6	1.2	-	-
1995	156.2	1.0	-	-	156.4	0.1	-	-	157.0	0.4	-	-	156.8	-0.1	-	-	157.6	0.5	-	-	157.9	0.2	-	-
1996	158.9	0.6	-	-	159.2	0.2	-	-	159.4	0.1	-	-	161.6	1.4	-	-	163.6	1.2	-	-	164.4	0.5	-	-
1997	163.9	-0.3	-	-	165.3	0.9	-	-	166.0	0.4	-	-	166.2	0.1	-	-	165.6	-0.4	-	-	166.5	0.5	166.9	0.2
1998	-	-	167.7	0.5	-	-	167.8	0.1	-	-	169.8	1.2	-	-	169.5	-0.2	-	-	170.9	0.8	-	-	169.2	-1.0
1999	-	-	169.9	0.4	-	-	170.5	0.4	-	-	170.0	-0.3	-	-	171.6	0.9	-	-	172.9	0.8	-	-	171.9	-0.6
2000	-	-	171.9	0.0	-	-	173.1	0.7	-	-	175.1	1.2	-	-	175.2	0.1	-	-	177.1	1.1	-	-	178.1	0.6
2001	-	-	179.3	0.7	-	-	180.9	0.9	-	-	180.6	-0.2	-	-	181.7	0.6	-	-	181.8	0.1	-	-	180.7	-0.6

Source: U.S. Department of Labor, Bureau of Labor Statistics, Division of Consumer Prices and Price Indexes. - indicates no data collected for period.

Miami-Fort Lauderdale, FL
Consumer Price Index - Urban Wage Earners
Base 1982-1984 = 100
Food and Beverages

For 1977-2001. Columns headed % show percentile change in the index from the previous period for which an index is available.

Year	Jan		Feb		Mar		Apr		May		Jun		Jul		Aug		Sep		Oct		Nov		Dec	
	Index	%	Index	%	Index	%	Index	%	Index	%	Index	%	Index	%	Index	%	Index	%	Index	%	Index	%	Index	%
1977	-	-	-	-	-	-	-	-	-	-	-	-	-	-	-	-	-	-	-	-	-	-	-	-
1978	63.5	0.8	-	-	66.1	4.1	-	-	68.2	3.2	-	-	69.8	2.3	-	-	70.5	1.0	-	-	63.0	-	-	-
1979	73.1	2.2	-	-	77.1	5.5	-	-	78.2	1.4	-	-	79.3	1.4	-	-	79.7	0.5	-	-	71.5	1.4	-	-
1980	81.8	2.0	-	-	82.7	1.1	-	-	83.7	1.2	-	-	85.5	2.2	-	-	88.1	3.0	-	-	80.2	0.6	-	-
1981	89.5	1.1	-	-	89.8	0.3	-	-	90.0	0.2	-	-	91.8	2.0	-	-	93.8	2.2	-	-	88.5	0.5	-	-
1982	94.7	1.2	-	-	95.6	1.0	-	-	97.0	1.5	-	-	98.2	1.2	-	-	98.2	0.0	-	-	93.6	-0.2	-	-
1983	97.8	0.8	-	-	99.0	1.2	-	-	99.2	0.2	-	-	99.2	0.0	-	-	100.2	1.0	-	-	97.0	-1.2	-	-
1984	103.8	3.3	-	-	104.0	0.2	-	-	102.6	-1.3	-	-	103.1	0.5	-	-	103.6	0.5	-	-	100.5	0.3	-	-
1985	103.9	-0.4	-	-	105.1	1.2	-	-	103.4	-1.6	-	-	104.3	0.9	-	-	104.0	-0.3	-	-	104.3	0.7	-	-
1986	106.3	1.6	-	-	107.0	0.7	-	-	107.2	0.2	-	-	104.2	-2.8	-	-	108.7	4.3	-	-	104.6	0.6	-	-
1987	111.4	0.9	-	-	112.4	0.9	-	-	113.8	1.2	-	-	113.6	-0.2	-	-	113.1	-0.4	-	-	110.4	1.6	-	-
1988	114.2	1.0	-	-	116.5	2.0	-	-	116.9	0.3	-	-	118.2	1.1	-	-	121.4	2.7	-	-	113.1	0.0	-	-
1989	122.7	0.7	-	-	123.5	0.7	-	-	124.9	1.1	-	-	127.5	2.1	-	-	126.9	-0.5	-	-	121.9	0.4	-	-
1990	135.5	5.1	-	-	135.7	0.1	-	-	132.8	-2.1	-	-	134.1	1.0	-	-	134.2	0.1	-	-	128.9	1.6	-	-
1991	136.3	-0.1	-	-	138.1	1.3	-	-	138.2	0.1	-	-	138.4	0.1	-	-	138.0	-0.3	-	-	137.3	-0.5	-	-
1992	138.0	0.5	-	-	139.9	1.4	-	-	137.9	-1.4	-	-	138.7	0.6	-	-	141.2	1.8	-	-	141.0	-0.1	-	-
1993	143.7	1.9	-	-	144.8	0.8	-	-	145.2	0.3	-	-	144.5	-0.5	-	-	146.4	1.3	-	-	148.5	1.4	-	-
1994	150.1	1.1	-	-	150.5	0.3	-	-	151.1	0.4	-	-	150.8	-0.2	-	-	151.3	0.3	-	-	152.5	0.8	-	-
1995	155.1	1.7	-	-	155.1	0.0	-	-	155.6	0.3	-	-	155.2	-0.3	-	-	156.0	0.5	-	-	156.4	0.3	-	-
1996	157.4	0.6	-	-	157.8	0.3	-	-	158.4	0.4	-	-	160.9	1.6	-	-	163.1	1.4	-	-	163.9	0.5	-	-
1997	163.0	-0.5	-	-	164.3	0.8	-	-	165.0	0.4	-	-	165.0	0.0	-	-	164.6	-0.2	-	-	165.7	0.7	165.7	0.0
1998	-	-	166.5	0.5	-	-	166.6	0.1	-	-	168.8	1.3	-	-	168.4	-0.2	169.9	0.9	-	-	-	-	167.9	-1.2
1999	-	-	168.8	0.5	-	-	169.2	0.2	-	-	168.9	-0.2	-	-	170.6	1.0	171.9	0.8	-	-	-	-	170.6	-0.8
2000	-	-	170.9	0.2	-	-	172.0	0.6	-	-	173.8	1.0	-	-	173.8	0.0	175.9	1.2	-	-	-	-	176.8	0.5
2001	-	-	178.0	0.7	-	-	179.8	1.0	-	-	179.2	-0.3	-	-	180.3	0.6	180.5	0.1	-	-	-	-	179.5	-0.6

Source: U.S. Department of Labor, Bureau of Labor Statistics, Division of Consumer Prices and Price Indexes. - indicates no data collected for period.

Miami-Fort Lauderdale, FL
Consumer Price Index - All Urban Consumers
Base 1982-1984 = 100
Housing

For 1977-2001. Columns headed % show percentile change in the index from the previous period for which an index is available.

Year	Jan Index	%	Feb Index	%	Mar Index	%	Apr Index	%	May Index	%	Jun Index	%	Jul Index	%	Aug Index	%	Sep Index	%	Oct Index	%	Nov Index	%	Dec Index	%
1977	-	-	-	-	-	-	-	-	-	-	-	-	-	-	-	-	-	-	-	-	60.6	-	-	-
1978	61.0	0.7	-	-	62.0	1.6	-	-	61.7	-0.5	-	-	63.2	2.4	-	-	64.4	1.9	-	-	64.5	0.2	-	-
1979	65.1	0.9	-	-	66.4	2.0	-	-	66.3	-0.2	-	-	68.8	3.8	-	-	69.8	1.5	-	-	71.8	2.9	-	-
1980	74.7	4.0	-	-	78.8	5.5	-	-	80.6	2.3	-	-	84.4	4.7	-	-	82.1	-2.7	-	-	81.9	-0.2	-	-
1981	84.8	3.5	-	-	86.7	2.2	-	-	89.8	3.6	-	-	92.3	2.8	-	-	95.7	3.7	-	-	99.2	3.7	-	-
1982	99.9	0.7	-	-	99.2	-0.7	-	-	98.7	-0.5	-	-	95.8	-2.9	-	-	96.7	0.9	-	-	96.7	0.0	-	-
1983	98.2	1.6	-	-	99.4	1.2	-	-	98.8	-0.6	-	-	99.7	0.9	-	-	100.6	0.9	-	-	100.8	0.2	-	-
1984	101.1	0.3	-	-	101.2	0.1	-	-	102.5	1.3	-	-	102.9	0.4	-	-	103.9	1.0	-	-	103.2	-0.7	-	-
1985	103.7	0.5	-	-	104.0	0.3	-	-	105.2	1.2	-	-	105.2	0.0	-	-	107.9	2.6	-	-	107.2	-0.6	-	-
1986	106.7	-0.5	-	-	107.6	0.8	-	-	106.8	-0.7	-	-	106.0	-0.7	-	-	107.3	1.2	-	-	107.6	0.3	-	-
1987	108.1	0.5	-	-	108.0	-0.1	-	-	106.9	-1.0	-	-	108.3	1.3	-	-	109.3	0.9	-	-	110.8	1.4	-	-
1988	111.8	0.9	-	-	111.1	-0.6	-	-	112.9	1.6	-	-	113.6	0.6	-	-	114.9	1.1	-	-	113.4	-1.3	-	-
1989	115.2	1.6	-	-	115.0	-0.2	-	-	115.2	0.2	-	-	116.5	1.1	-	-	117.9	1.2	-	-	117.2	-0.6	-	-
1990	116.7	-0.4	-	-	116.1	-0.5	-	-	119.6	3.0	-	-	123.3	3.1	-	-	123.1	-0.2	-	-	122.3	-0.6	-	-
1991	122.3	0.0	-	-	122.5	0.2	-	-	123.0	0.4	-	-	124.2	1.0	-	-	123.7	-0.4	-	-	125.4	1.4	-	-
1992	126.0	0.5	-	-	126.6	0.5	-	-	126.2	-0.3	-	-	125.7	-0.4	-	-	125.1	-0.5	-	-	127.0	1.5	-	-
1993	128.5	1.2	-	-	130.3	1.4	-	-	129.8	-0.4	-	-	130.5	0.5	-	-	131.2	0.5	-	-	131.1	-0.1	-	-
1994	133.0	1.4	-	-	134.3	1.0	-	-	134.9	0.4	-	-	135.3	0.3	-	-	136.1	0.6	-	-	136.0	-0.1	-	-
1995	138.5	1.8	-	-	139.1	0.4	-	-	138.4	-0.5	-	-	139.0	0.4	-	-	140.6	1.2	-	-	142.6	1.4	-	-
1996	143.8	0.8	-	-	144.5	0.5	-	-	143.5	-0.7	-	-	144.5	0.7	-	-	145.7	0.8	-	-	147.0	0.9	-	-
1997	149.7	1.8	-	-	150.3	0.4	-	-	149.6	-0.5	-	-	149.8	0.1	-	-	149.8	0.0	-	-	151.6	1.2	151.6	0.0
1998	-	-	153.2	1.1	-	-	153.4	0.1	-	-	153.3	-0.1	-	-	153.6	0.2	-	-	153.9	0.2	-	-	154.4	0.3
1999	-	-	155.5	0.7	-	-	155.0	-0.3	-	-	154.6	-0.3	-	-	154.9	0.2	-	-	155.5	0.4	-	-	156.1	0.4
2000	-	-	157.2	0.7	-	-	158.2	0.6	-	-	158.7	0.3	-	-	159.1	0.3	-	-	159.8	0.4	-	-	159.7	-0.1
2001	-	-	162.8	1.9	-	-	164.1	0.8	-	-	164.4	0.2	-	-	165.0	0.4	-	-	164.8	-0.1	-	-	165.6	0.5

Source: U.S. Department of Labor, Bureau of Labor Statistics, Division of Consumer Prices and Price Indexes. - indicates no data collected for period.

Miami-Fort Lauderdale, FL
Consumer Price Index - Urban Wage Earners
Base 1982-1984 = 100
Housing

For 1977-2001. Columns headed % show percentile change in the index from the previous period for which an index is available.

Year	Jan Index	Jan %	Feb Index	Feb %	Mar Index	Mar %	Apr Index	Apr %	May Index	May %	Jun Index	Jun %	Jul Index	Jul %	Aug Index	Aug %	Sep Index	Sep %	Oct Index	Oct %	Nov Index	Nov %	Dec Index	Dec %
1977	-	-	-	-	-	-	-	-	-	-	-	-	-	-	-	-	-	-	-	-	60.6	-	-	-
1978	60.9	0.5	-	-	62.0	1.8	-	-	61.6	-0.6	-	-	63.2	2.6	-	-	64.2	1.6	-	-	64.4	0.3	-	-
1979	65.1	1.1	-	-	66.3	1.8	-	-	66.3	0.0	-	-	68.7	3.6	-	-	69.7	1.5	-	-	71.5	2.6	-	-
1980	74.4	4.1	-	-	78.3	5.2	-	-	80.0	2.2	-	-	84.1	5.1	-	-	81.7	-2.9	-	-	81.7	0.0	-	-
1981	84.6	3.5	-	-	86.6	2.4	-	-	89.9	3.8	-	-	92.3	2.7	-	-	95.7	3.7	-	-	99.5	4.0	-	-
1982	100.4	0.9	-	-	99.7	-0.7	-	-	99.1	-0.6	-	-	96.0	-3.1	-	-	96.9	0.9	-	-	97.0	0.1	-	-
1983	97.9	0.9	-	-	98.4	0.5	-	-	99.6	1.2	-	-	100.4	0.8	-	-	100.4	0.0	-	-	100.4	0.0	-	-
1984	100.6	0.2	-	-	100.4	-0.2	-	-	101.8	1.4	-	-	102.4	0.6	-	-	104.5	2.1	-	-	103.3	-1.1	-	-
1985	103.9	0.6	-	-	104.4	0.5	-	-	105.6	1.1	-	-	105.6	0.0	-	-	108.2	2.5	-	-	107.5	-0.6	-	-
1986	107.0	-0.5	-	-	107.9	0.8	-	-	107.0	-0.8	-	-	106.1	-0.8	-	-	107.5	1.3	-	-	107.9	0.4	-	-
1987	108.4	0.5	-	-	108.3	-0.1	-	-	107.1	-1.1	-	-	108.6	1.4	-	-	109.5	0.8	-	-	111.1	1.5	-	-
1988	112.2	1.0	-	-	111.4	-0.7	-	-	113.0	1.4	-	-	113.8	0.7	-	-	115.3	1.3	-	-	113.7	-1.4	-	-
1989	115.3	1.4	-	-	114.9	-0.3	-	-	115.4	0.4	-	-	116.7	1.1	-	-	117.7	0.9	-	-	117.1	-0.5	-	-
1990	116.7	-0.3	-	-	116.0	-0.6	-	-	119.3	2.8	-	-	122.9	3.0	-	-	122.8	-0.1	-	-	122.0	-0.7	-	-
1991	122.0	0.0	-	-	122.2	0.2	-	-	122.6	0.3	-	-	123.8	1.0	-	-	123.4	-0.3	-	-	125.0	1.3	-	-
1992	125.6	0.5	-	-	126.2	0.5	-	-	125.6	-0.5	-	-	125.3	-0.2	-	-	124.6	-0.6	-	-	126.5	1.5	-	-
1993	127.9	1.1	-	-	129.6	1.3	-	-	129.3	-0.2	-	-	129.9	0.5	-	-	130.6	0.5	-	-	130.3	-0.2	-	-
1994	132.2	1.5	-	-	133.5	1.0	-	-	134.2	0.5	-	-	134.4	0.1	-	-	135.2	0.6	-	-	135.5	0.2	-	-
1995	137.5	1.5	-	-	138.1	0.4	-	-	137.7	-0.3	-	-	138.3	0.4	-	-	140.0	1.2	-	-	142.0	1.4	-	-
1996	143.1	0.8	-	-	143.5	0.3	-	-	143.1	-0.3	-	-	144.1	0.7	-	-	145.0	0.6	-	-	146.6	1.1	-	-
1997	148.8	1.5	-	-	149.1	0.2	-	-	148.7	-0.3	-	-	149.0	0.2	-	-	149.0	0.0	-	-	150.7	1.1	150.8	0.1
1998	-	-	152.0	0.8	-	-	152.2	0.1	-	-	152.2	0.0	-	-	152.5	0.2	-	-	152.8	0.2	-	-	153.4	0.4
1999	-	-	154.2	0.5	-	-	153.6	-0.4	-	-	153.4	-0.1	-	-	153.6	0.1	-	-	154.1	0.3	-	-	154.7	0.4
2000	-	-	155.4	0.5	-	-	156.2	0.5	-	-	157.2	0.6	-	-	157.5	0.2	-	-	158.2	0.4	-	-	158.2	0.0
2001	-	-	160.9	1.7	-	-	162.3	0.9	-	-	162.9	0.4	-	-	163.6	0.4	-	-	163.5	-0.1	-	-	164.1	0.4

Source: U.S. Department of Labor, Bureau of Labor Statistics, Division of Consumer Prices and Price Indexes. - indicates no data collected for period.

Miami-Fort Lauderdale, FL
Consumer Price Index - All Urban Consumers
Base 1982-1984 = 100
Apparel

For 1977-2001. Columns headed % show percentile change in the index from the previous period for which an index is available.

Year	Jan Index	%	Feb Index	%	Mar Index	%	Apr Index	%	May Index	%	Jun Index	%	Jul Index	%	Aug Index	%	Sep Index	%	Oct Index	%	Nov Index	%	Dec Index	%
1977	-	-	-	-	-	-	-	-	-	-	-	-	-	-	-	-	-	-	-	-	74.8	-	-	-
1978	75.6	1.1	-	-	77.2	2.1	-	-	77.1	-0.1	-	-	77.6	0.6	-	-	78.7	1.4	-	-	78.9	0.3	-	-
1979	78.7	-0.3	-	-	79.8	1.4	-	-	80.3	0.6	-	-	81.5	1.5	-	-	82.2	0.9	-	-	83.7	1.8	-	-
1980	82.3	-1.7	-	-	86.0	4.5	-	-	87.2	1.4	-	-	87.8	0.7	-	-	88.0	0.2	-	-	88.8	0.9	-	-
1981	90.9	2.4	-	-	89.8	-1.2	-	-	90.3	0.6	-	-	92.3	2.2	-	-	93.2	1.0	-	-	93.6	0.4	-	-
1982	95.7	2.2	-	-	97.6	2.0	-	-	98.3	0.7	-	-	99.4	1.1	-	-	97.0	-2.4	-	-	100.3	3.4	-	-
1983	99.0	-1.3	-	-	99.8	0.8	-	-	99.2	-0.6	-	-	100.6	1.4	-	-	99.9	-0.7	-	-	102.2	2.3	-	-
1984	99.8	-2.3	-	-	100.6	0.8	-	-	101.8	1.2	-	-	102.0	0.2	-	-	102.7	0.7	-	-	102.7	0.0	-	-
1985	101.5	-1.2	-	-	104.9	3.3	-	-	104.5	-0.4	-	-	104.7	0.2	-	-	107.5	2.7	-	-	108.8	1.2	-	-
1986	109.5	0.6	-	-	108.5	-0.9	-	-	108.6	0.1	-	-	108.5	-0.1	-	-	108.6	0.1	-	-	110.4	1.7	-	-
1987	110.5	0.1	-	-	114.8	3.9	-	-	117.1	2.0	-	-	116.3	-0.7	-	-	115.8	-0.4	-	-	117.3	1.3	-	-
1988	119.0	1.4	-	-	121.7	2.3	-	-	121.4	-0.2	-	-	122.4	0.8	-	-	126.2	3.1	-	-	127.1	0.7	-	-
1989	131.0	3.1	-	-	129.0	-1.5	-	-	129.3	0.2	-	-	125.2	-3.2	-	-	138.0	10.2	-	-	135.8	-1.6	-	-
1990	130.4	-4.0	-	-	136.6	4.8	-	-	132.1	-3.3	-	-	134.9	2.1	-	-	138.6	2.7	-	-	139.5	0.6	-	-
1991	135.6	-2.8	-	-	143.6	5.9	-	-	142.3	-0.9	-	-	137.1	-3.7	-	-	140.6	2.6	-	-	142.2	1.1	-	-
1992	140.4	-1.3	-	-	140.7	0.2	-	-	138.8	-1.4	-	-	134.2	-3.3	-	-	144.2	7.5	-	-	134.8	-6.5	-	-
1993	139.4	3.4	-	-	148.9	6.8	-	-	144.5	-3.0	-	-	139.0	-3.8	-	-	137.5	-1.1	-	-	134.1	-2.5	-	-
1994	127.5	-4.9	-	-	154.9	21.5	-	-	149.1	-3.7	-	-	143.7	-3.6	-	-	144.4	0.5	-	-	136.6	-5.4	-	-
1995	148.2	8.5	-	-	158.9	7.2	-	-	150.2	-5.5	-	-	139.8	-6.9	-	-	142.1	1.6	-	-	142.4	0.2	-	-
1996	149.8	5.2	-	-	149.7	-0.1	-	-	145.4	-2.9	-	-	131.7	-9.4	-	-	146.8	11.5	-	-	149.6	1.9	-	-
1997	163.0	9.0	-	-	152.6	-6.4	-	-	151.1	-1.0	-	-	148.7	-1.6	-	-	153.3	3.1	-	-	155.3	1.3	152.8	-1.6
1998	-	-	158.5	3.7	-	-	154.9	-2.3	-	-	150.8	-2.6	-	-	154.4	2.4	-	-	148.5	-3.8	-	-	143.5	-3.4
1999	-	-	140.3	-2.2	-	-	136.2	-2.9	-	-	132.2	-2.9	-	-	135.8	2.7	-	-	140.0	3.1	-	-	145.1	3.6
2000	-	-	152.9	5.4	-	-	150.4	-1.6	-	-	150.0	-0.3	-	-	153.2	2.1	-	-	156.1	1.9	-	-	143.5	-8.1
2001	-	-	152.6	6.3	-	-	151.3	-0.9	-	-	147.7	-2.4	-	-	149.8	1.4	-	-	156.9	4.7	-	-	146.9	-6.4

Source: U.S. Department of Labor, Bureau of Labor Statistics, Division of Consumer Prices and Price Indexes. - indicates no data collected for period.

Miami-Fort Lauderdale, FL
Consumer Price Index - Urban Wage Earners
Base 1982-1984 = 100
Apparel

For 1977-2001. Columns headed % show percentile change in the index from the previous period for which an index is available.

Year	Jan		Feb		Mar		Apr		May		Jun		Jul		Aug		Sep		Oct		Nov		Dec	
	Index	%	Index	%	Index	%	Index	%	Index	%	Index	%	Index	%	Index	%	Index	%	Index	%	Index	%	Index	%
1977	-	-	-	-	-	-	-	-	-	-	-	-	-	-	-	-	-	-	-	-	74.5	-	-	-
1978	74.8	0.4	-	-	74.9	0.1	-	-	75.3	0.5	-	-	76.3	1.3	-	-	76.7	0.5	-	-	77.3	0.8	-	-
1979	76.9	-0.5	-	-	79.5	3.4	-	-	79.4	-0.1	-	-	80.1	0.9	-	-	81.6	1.9	-	-	82.5	1.1	-	-
1980	82.8	0.4	-	-	84.0	1.4	-	-	85.7	2.0	-	-	86.6	1.1	-	-	89.2	3.0	-	-	90.1	1.0	-	-
1981	90.7	0.7	-	-	91.2	0.6	-	-	91.5	0.3	-	-	91.3	-0.2	-	-	91.5	0.2	-	-	93.0	1.6	-	-
1982	95.1	2.3	-	-	97.1	2.1	-	-	97.9	0.8	-	-	99.2	1.3	-	-	96.5	-2.7	-	-	100.0	3.6	-	-
1983	98.9	-1.1	-	-	99.2	0.3	-	-	99.2	0.0	-	-	100.6	1.4	-	-	99.9	-0.7	-	-	101.9	2.0	-	-
1984	100.0	-1.9	-	-	100.9	0.9	-	-	102.4	1.5	-	-	102.8	0.4	-	-	103.4	0.6	-	-	103.5	0.1	-	-
1985	102.0	-1.4	-	-	105.5	3.4	-	-	104.7	-0.8	-	-	104.7	0.0	-	-	108.0	3.2	-	-	109.1	1.0	-	-
1986	110.0	0.8	-	-	109.0	-0.9	-	-	109.5	0.5	-	-	109.2	-0.3	-	-	109.1	-0.1	-	-	110.6	1.4	-	-
1987	110.8	0.2	-	-	114.9	3.7	-	-	117.1	1.9	-	-	116.1	-0.9	-	-	115.9	-0.2	-	-	117.2	1.1	-	-
1988	118.8	1.4	-	-	121.8	2.5	-	-	121.0	-0.7	-	-	122.5	1.2	-	-	124.5	1.6	-	-	125.6	0.9	-	-
1989	129.2	2.9	-	-	127.5	-1.3	-	-	127.9	0.3	-	-	123.4	-3.5	-	-	136.7	10.8	-	-	133.9	-2.0	-	-
1990	128.6	-4.0	-	-	134.3	4.4	-	-	129.6	-3.5	-	-	132.3	2.1	-	-	137.3	3.8	-	-	136.4	-0.7	-	-
1991	134.5	-1.4	-	-	142.4	5.9	-	-	141.3	-0.8	-	-	137.2	-2.9	-	-	139.9	2.0	-	-	141.8	1.4	-	-
1992	140.5	-0.9	-	-	140.5	0.0	-	-	138.0	-1.8	-	-	132.7	-3.8	-	-	143.5	8.1	-	-	134.9	-6.0	-	-
1993	139.5	3.4	-	-	147.7	5.9	-	-	145.6	-1.4	-	-	140.1	-3.8	-	-	139.5	-0.4	-	-	134.9	-3.3	-	-
1994	129.0	-4.4	-	-	157.0	21.7	-	-	150.6	-4.1	-	-	145.8	-3.2	-	-	146.8	0.7	-	-	139.0	-5.3	-	-
1995	150.5	8.3	-	-	162.5	8.0	-	-	152.5	-6.2	-	-	142.7	-6.4	-	-	145.1	1.7	-	-	139.0	-5.3	-	-
1996	151.6	6.2	-	-	151.3	-0.2	-	-	147.9	-2.2	-	-	133.7	-9.6	-	-	145.1	1.7	-	-	142.8	-1.6	-	-
1997	165.4	9.5	-	-	155.0	-6.3	-	-	153.4	-1.0	-	-	151.4	-1.3	-	-	156.4	3.3	-	-	158.2	1.2	155.5	-1.7
1998	-	-	158.7	2.1	-	-	155.8	-1.8	-	-	154.0	-1.2	-	-	157.1	2.0	-	-	154.4	-1.7	-	-	150.3	-2.7
1999	-	-	146.0	-2.9	-	-	141.6	-3.0	-	-	138.6	-2.1	-	-	145.2	4.8	-	-	149.9	3.2	-	-	156.0	4.1
2000	-	-	163.7	4.9	-	-	161.0	-1.6	-	-	160.0	-0.6	-	-	159.9	-0.1	-	-	165.0	3.2	-	-	156.0	-5.5
2001	-	-	161.9	3.8	-	-	161.2	-0.4	-	-	157.5	-2.3	-	-	161.1	2.3	-	-	168.9	4.8	-	-	158.5	-6.2

Source: U.S. Department of Labor, Bureau of Labor Statistics, Division of Consumer Prices and Price Indexes. - indicates no data collected for period.

Miami-Fort Lauderdale, FL
Consumer Price Index - All Urban Consumers
Base 1982-1984 = 100
Transportation

For 1977-2000. Columns headed % show percentile change in the index from the previous period for which an index is available.

Year	Jan Index	%	Feb Index	%	Mar Index	%	Apr Index	%	May Index	%	Jun Index	%	Jul Index	%	Aug Index	%	Sep Index	%	Oct Index	%	Nov Index	%	Dec Index	%
1977	-	-	-	-	-	-	-	-	-	-	-	-	-	-	-	-	-	-	-	-	58.0	-	-	-
1978	58.0	0.0	-	-	58.2	0.3	-	-	58.5	0.5	-	-	60.0	2.6	-	-	60.6	1.0	-	-	61.6	1.7	-	-
1979	62.2	1.0	-	-	63.4	1.9	-	-	66.0	4.1	-	-	68.5	3.8	-	-	69.5	1.5	-	-	70.0	0.7	-	-
1980	74.0	5.7	-	-	76.8	3.8	-	-	77.9	1.4	-	-	79.2	1.7	-	-	79.7	0.6	-	-	81.3	2.0	-	-
1981	83.0	2.1	-	-	86.8	4.6	-	-	88.4	1.8	-	-	89.8	1.6	-	-	90.5	0.8	-	-	91.8	1.4	-	-
1982	93.0	1.3	-	-	92.6	-0.4	-	-	93.4	0.9	-	-	96.1	2.9	-	-	96.0	-0.1	-	-	96.7	0.7	-	-
1983	96.9	0.2	-	-	96.6	-0.3	-	-	98.8	2.3	-	-	100.4	1.6	-	-	103.2	2.8	-	-	103.8	0.6	-	-
1984	103.1	-0.7	-	-	103.7	0.6	-	-	105.1	1.4	-	-	105.4	0.3	-	-	105.6	0.2	-	-	106.5	0.9	-	-
1985	106.1	-0.4	-	-	106.9	0.8	-	-	108.8	1.8	-	-	109.1	0.3	-	-	108.6	-0.5	-	-	109.3	0.6	-	-
1986	109.5	0.2	-	-	105.5	-3.7	-	-	102.5	-2.8	-	-	102.2	-0.3	-	-	101.4	-0.8	-	-	102.2	0.8	-	-
1987	104.0	1.8	-	-	104.8	0.8	-	-	106.2	1.3	-	-	107.0	0.8	-	-	107.3	0.3	-	-	109.3	1.9	-	-
1988	108.8	-0.5	-	-	109.0	0.2	-	-	109.8	0.7	-	-	110.7	0.8	-	-	112.2	1.4	-	-	112.3	0.1	-	-
1989	113.9	1.4	-	-	113.5	-0.4	-	-	116.3	2.5	-	-	115.9	-0.3	-	-	113.7	-1.9	-	-	114.3	0.5	-	-
1990	118.8	3.9	-	-	118.4	-0.3	-	-	119.8	1.2	-	-	119.0	-0.7	-	-	123.0	3.4	-	-	128.2	4.2	-	-
1991	129.4	0.9	-	-	126.2	-2.5	-	-	126.4	0.2	-	-	124.3	-1.7	-	-	124.4	0.1	-	-	126.3	1.5	-	-
1992	125.6	-0.6	-	-	125.5	-0.1	-	-	126.7	1.0	-	-	128.7	1.6	-	-	127.8	-0.7	-	-	131.3	2.7	-	-
1993	131.7	0.3	-	-	130.9	-0.6	-	-	131.7	0.6	-	-	132.0	0.2	-	-	130.7	-1.0	-	-	134.1	2.6	-	-
1994	133.8	-0.2	-	-	134.6	0.6	-	-	134.3	-0.2	-	-	135.3	0.7	-	-	136.0	0.5	-	-	137.1	0.8	-	-
1995	138.0	0.7	-	-	138.9	0.7	-	-	141.7	2.0	-	-	141.6	-0.1	-	-	138.0	-2.5	-	-	140.1	1.5	-	-
1996	141.4	0.9	-	-	141.1	-0.2	-	-	145.3	3.0	-	-	144.3	-0.7	-	-	144.0	-0.2	-	-	148.3	3.0	-	-
1997	146.8	-1.0	-	-	148.9	1.4	-	-	146.7	-1.5	-	-	146.7	0.0	-	-	147.6	0.6	-	-	146.6	-0.7	146.3	-0.2
1998	-	-	143.9	-1.6	-	-	143.6	-0.2	-	-	143.2	-0.3	-	-	143.7	0.3	-	-	145.3	1.1	-	-	145.2	-0.1
1999	-	-	143.8	-1.0	-	-	147.2	2.4	-	-	147.4	0.1	-	-	149.7	1.6	-	-	152.9	2.1	-	-	154.3	0.9
2000	-	-	154.6	0.2	-	-	158.9	2.8	-	-	160.0	0.7	-	-	159.4	-0.4	-	-	159.8	0.3	-	-	160.9	0.7

Source: U.S. Department of Labor, Bureau of Labor Statistics, Division of Consumer Prices and Price Indexes. - indicates no data collected for period.

Miami-Fort Lauderdale, FL
Consumer Price Index - Urban Wage Earners
Base 1982-1984 = 100
Transportation

For 1977-2000. Columns headed % show percentile change in the index from the previous period for which an index is available.

Year	Jan Index	%	Feb Index	%	Mar Index	%	Apr Index	%	May Index	%	Jun Index	%	Jul Index	%	Aug Index	%	Sep Index	%	Oct Index	%	Nov Index	%	Dec Index	%
1977	-	-	-	-	-	-	-	-	-	-	-	-	-	-	-	-	-	-	-	-	57.6	-	-	-
1978	57.6	0.0	-	-	57.7	0.2	-	-	58.4	1.2	-	-	59.8	2.4	-	-	60.5	1.2	-	-	61.2	1.2	-	-
1979	62.0	1.3	-	-	63.5	2.4	-	-	66.4	4.6	-	-	69.0	3.9	-	-	70.0	1.4	-	-	70.5	0.7	-	-
1980	75.0	6.4	-	-	77.6	3.5	-	-	79.0	1.8	-	-	80.0	1.3	-	-	81.0	1.3	-	-	82.4	1.7	-	-
1981	84.4	2.4	-	-	88.0	4.3	-	-	89.4	1.6	-	-	90.1	0.8	-	-	91.0	1.0	-	-	92.6	1.8	-	-
1982	93.5	1.0	-	-	93.0	-0.5	-	-	93.1	0.1	-	-	96.2	3.3	-	-	96.1	-0.1	-	-	96.8	0.7	-	-
1983	97.4	0.6	-	-	96.6	-0.8	-	-	98.8	2.3	-	-	100.5	1.7	-	-	103.4	2.9	-	-	103.7	0.3	-	-
1984	102.9	-0.8	-	-	103.5	0.6	-	-	104.9	1.4	-	-	105.2	0.3	-	-	105.4	0.2	-	-	106.1	0.7	-	-
1985	105.7	-0.4	-	-	106.5	0.8	-	-	108.4	1.8	-	-	108.7	0.3	-	-	108.2	-0.5	-	-	108.8	0.6	-	-
1986	109.0	0.2	-	-	104.5	-4.1	-	-	101.0	-3.3	-	-	100.6	-0.4	-	-	99.9	-0.7	-	-	100.7	0.8	-	-
1987	102.0	1.3	-	-	103.0	1.0	-	-	104.7	1.7	-	-	105.8	1.1	-	-	105.9	0.1	-	-	107.8	1.8	-	-
1988	107.4	-0.4	-	-	107.5	0.1	-	-	108.1	0.6	-	-	109.0	0.8	-	-	110.3	1.2	-	-	110.4	0.1	-	-
1989	112.0	1.4	-	-	111.6	-0.4	-	-	114.0	2.2	-	-	113.7	-0.3	-	-	111.6	-1.8	-	-	112.0	0.4	-	-
1990	115.9	3.5	-	-	115.3	-0.5	-	-	116.6	1.1	-	-	116.0	-0.5	-	-	119.7	3.2	-	-	124.1	3.7	-	-
1991	125.1	0.8	-	-	122.3	-2.2	-	-	122.9	0.5	-	-	121.3	-1.3	-	-	121.5	0.2	-	-	123.1	1.3	-	-
1992	122.3	-0.6	-	-	121.9	-0.3	-	-	123.8	1.6	-	-	126.5	2.2	-	-	126.3	-0.2	-	-	129.2	2.3	-	-
1993	129.5	0.2	-	-	128.6	-0.7	-	-	129.6	0.8	-	-	130.3	0.5	-	-	129.6	-0.5	-	-	132.3	2.1	-	-
1994	131.5	-0.6	-	-	131.6	0.1	-	-	132.1	0.4	-	-	133.7	1.2	-	-	134.8	0.8	-	-	136.1	1.0	-	-
1995	137.0	0.7	-	-	137.5	0.4	-	-	140.7	2.3	-	-	140.6	-0.1	-	-	137.4	-2.3	-	-	139.4	1.5	-	-
1996	140.7	0.9	-	-	140.2	-0.4	-	-	144.5	3.1	-	-	143.3	-0.8	-	-	143.1	-0.1	-	-	146.6	2.4	-	-
1997	145.3	-0.9	-	-	146.7	1.0	-	-	144.8	-1.3	-	-	144.3	-0.3	-	-	144.9	0.4	-	-	144.2	-0.5	143.9	-0.2
1998	-	-	141.3	-1.8	-	-	141.0	-0.2	-	-	140.8	-0.1	-	-	141.1	0.2	-	-	142.9	1.3	-	-	142.9	0.0
1999	-	-	141.3	-1.1	-	-	144.6	2.3	-	-	145.1	0.3	-	-	147.3	1.5	-	-	150.5	2.2	-	-	151.9	0.9
2000	-	-	152.3	0.3	-	-	156.4	2.7	-	-	157.6	0.8	-	-	156.8	-0.5	-	-	157.2	0.3	-	-	158.2	0.6

Source: U.S. Department of Labor, Bureau of Labor Statistics, Division of Consumer Prices and Price Indexes. - indicates no data collected for period.

Miami-Fort Lauderdale, FL
Consumer Price Index - All Urban Consumers
Base 1982-1984 = 100
Medical Care

For 1977-2001. Columns headed % show percentile change in the index from the previous period for which an index is available.

Year	Jan Index	%	Feb Index	%	Mar Index	%	Apr Index	%	May Index	%	Jun Index	%	Jul Index	%	Aug Index	%	Sep Index	%	Oct Index	%	Nov Index	%	Dec Index	%
1977	-	-	-	-	-	-	-	-	-	-	-	-	-	-	-	-	-	-	-	-	57.9	-	-	-
1978	59.3	2.4	-	-	59.5	0.3	-	-	60.3	1.3	-	-	60.6	0.5	-	-	63.0	4.0	-	-	64.4	2.2	-	-
1979	65.2	1.2	-	-	67.4	3.4	-	-	67.5	0.1	-	-	68.4	1.3	-	-	70.5	3.1	-	-	72.3	2.6	-	-
1980	74.6	3.2	-	-	75.5	1.2	-	-	75.6	0.1	-	-	75.4	-0.3	-	-	75.8	0.5	-	-	75.7	-0.1	-	-
1981	77.8	2.8	-	-	79.1	1.7	-	-	80.2	1.4	-	-	81.6	1.7	-	-	84.6	3.7	-	-	85.6	1.2	-	-
1982	87.8	2.6	-	-	89.1	1.5	-	-	92.0	3.3	-	-	95.1	3.4	-	-	96.5	1.5	-	-	99.8	3.4	-	-
1983	99.7	-0.1	-	-	100.0	0.3	-	-	100.0	0.0	-	-	101.0	1.0	-	-	101.5	0.5	-	-	102.9	1.4	-	-
1984	103.9	1.0	-	-	105.0	1.1	-	-	105.0	0.0	-	-	105.0	0.0	-	-	104.8	-0.2	-	-	106.3	1.4	-	-
1985	107.0	0.7	-	-	108.6	1.5	-	-	108.4	-0.2	-	-	108.7	0.3	-	-	109.7	0.9	-	-	111.2	1.4	-	-
1986	113.4	2.0	-	-	115.4	1.8	-	-	115.6	0.2	-	-	116.0	0.3	-	-	120.1	3.5	-	-	121.1	0.8	-	-
1987	122.9	1.5	-	-	123.7	0.7	-	-	124.8	0.9	-	-	128.4	2.9	-	-	127.7	-0.5	-	-	130.2	2.0	-	-
1988	131.4	0.9	-	-	133.3	1.4	-	-	134.0	0.5	-	-	134.4	0.3	-	-	136.1	1.3	-	-	136.7	0.4	-	-
1989	137.9	0.9	-	-	137.9	0.0	-	-	140.5	1.9	-	-	140.9	0.3	-	-	141.7	0.6	-	-	142.6	0.6	-	-
1990	143.3	0.5	-	-	145.0	1.2	-	-	150.1	3.5	-	-	153.5	2.3	-	-	156.4	1.9	-	-	158.3	1.2	-	-
1991	159.7	0.9	-	-	160.4	0.4	-	-	161.8	0.9	-	-	163.1	0.8	-	-	162.9	-0.1	-	-	166.7	2.3	-	-
1992	169.6	1.7	-	-	171.0	0.8	-	-	171.7	0.4	-	-	171.2	-0.3	-	-	171.3	0.1	-	-	176.4	3.0	-	-
1993	179.2	1.6	-	-	180.1	0.5	-	-	182.0	1.1	-	-	183.1	0.6	-	-	183.1	0.0	-	-	182.7	-0.2	-	-
1994	184.7	1.1	-	-	185.2	0.3	-	-	187.0	1.0	-	-	186.4	-0.3	-	-	190.7	2.3	-	-	191.6	0.5	-	-
1995	196.6	2.6	-	-	200.1	1.8	-	-	201.7	0.8	-	-	204.3	1.3	-	-	204.9	0.3	-	-	206.2	0.6	-	-
1996	212.8	3.2	-	-	213.6	0.4	-	-	214.9	0.6	-	-	214.6	-0.1	-	-	216.3	0.8	-	-	214.0	-1.1	-	-
1997	215.1	0.5	-	-	219.1	1.9	-	-	219.6	0.2	-	-	220.1	0.2	-	-	219.6	-0.2	-	-	220.5	0.4	220.7	0.1
1998	-	-	225.1	2.0	-	-	225.4	0.1	-	-	226.0	0.3	-	-	228.9	1.3	-	-	230.3	0.6	-	-	230.7	0.2
1999	-	-	230.1	-0.3	-	-	230.8	0.3	-	-	231.0	0.1	-	-	232.0	0.4	-	-	232.3	0.1	-	-	232.3	0.0
2000	-	-	236.0	1.6	-	-	236.7	0.3	-	-	243.8	3.0	-	-	244.0	0.1	-	-	244.6	0.2	-	-	245.5	0.4
2001	-	-	249.0	1.4	-	-	249.2	0.1	-	-	251.3	0.8	-	-	252.4	0.4	-	-	261.6	3.6	-	-	260.1	-0.6

Source: U.S. Department of Labor, Bureau of Labor Statistics, Division of Consumer Prices and Price Indexes. - indicates no data collected for period.

Miami-Fort Lauderdale, FL
Consumer Price Index - Urban Wage Earners
Base 1982-1984 = 100
Medical Care

For 1977-2001. Columns headed % show percentile change in the index from the previous period for which an index is available.

Year	Jan Index	%	Feb Index	%	Mar Index	%	Apr Index	%	May Index	%	Jun Index	%	Jul Index	%	Aug Index	%	Sep Index	%	Oct Index	%	Nov Index	%	Dec Index	%
1977	-		-		-		-		-		-		-		-		-		-		58.2		-	
1978	59.3	1.9	-		59.5	0.3	-		61.9	4.0	-		62.2	0.5	-		63.4	1.9	-		64.0	0.9	-	
1979	64.7	1.1	-		65.5	1.2	-		65.8	0.5	-		66.8	1.5	-		70.4	5.4	-		71.4	1.4	-	
1980	73.5	2.9	-		74.3	1.1	-		74.2	-0.1	-		74.0	-0.3	-		74.4	0.5	-		74.8	0.5	-	
1981	76.0	1.6	-		77.1	1.4	-		77.5	0.5	-		79.5	2.6	-		80.7	1.5	-		85.4	5.8	-	
1982	87.6	2.6	-		89.1	1.7	-		91.9	3.1	-		94.7	3.0	-		96.1	1.5	-		99.9	4.0	-	
1983	100.0	0.1	-		100.4	0.4	-		100.4	0.0	-		101.3	0.9	-		101.8	0.5	-		103.0	1.2	-	
1984	103.9	0.9	-		104.9	1.0	-		104.9	0.0	-		104.9	0.0	-		104.6	-0.3	-		106.0	1.3	-	
1985	106.5	0.5	-		108.1	1.5	-		108.0	-0.1	-		108.2	0.2	-		109.2	0.9	-		110.6	1.3	-	
1986	112.5	1.7	-		114.6	1.9	-		114.8	0.2	-		115.3	0.4	-		119.4	3.6	-		120.4	0.8	-	
1987	122.2	1.5	-		123.0	0.7	-		124.2	1.0	-		127.6	2.7	-		126.9	-0.5	-		129.0	1.7	-	
1988	130.4	1.1	-		131.8	1.1	-		132.6	0.6	-		132.8	0.2	-		134.5	1.3	-		134.8	0.2	-	
1989	136.2	1.0	-		136.4	0.1	-		138.9	1.8	-		139.3	0.3	-		140.5	0.9	-		141.5	0.7	-	
1990	142.1	0.4	-		143.7	1.1	-		149.0	3.7	-		152.2	2.1	-		155.6	2.2	-		157.3	1.1	-	
1991	158.7	0.9	-		159.4	0.4	-		160.8	0.9	-		162.0	0.7	-		161.8	-0.1	-		165.4	2.2	-	
1992	168.3	1.8	-		169.9	1.0	-		170.9	0.6	-		171.0	0.1	-		170.8	-0.1	-		175.6	2.8	-	
1993	178.5	1.7	-		179.5	0.6	-		181.4	1.1	-		182.0	0.3	-		181.8	-0.1	-		181.6	-0.1	-	
1994	182.6	0.6	-		182.8	0.1	-		184.0	0.7	-		183.6	-0.2	-		188.1	2.5	-		189.2	0.6	-	
1995	193.6	2.3	-		196.9	1.7	-		198.6	0.9	-		201.3	1.4	-		202.1	0.4	-		203.4	0.6	-	
1996	210.0	3.2	-		210.9	0.4	-		211.9	0.5	-		211.8	-0.0	-		213.5	0.8	-		211.7	-0.8	-	
1997	212.0	0.1	-		216.1	1.9	-		216.5	0.2	-		217.0	0.2	-		216.5	-0.2	-		218.0	0.7	218.2	0.1
1998	-		223.1	2.2	-		223.5	0.2	-		224.1	0.3	-		227.0	1.3	-		228.4	0.6	-		228.7	0.1
1999	-		228.1	-0.3	-		228.7	0.3	-		229.2	0.2	-		230.1	0.4	-		230.2	0.0	-		230.1	-0.0
2000	-		233.5	1.5	-		234.1	0.3	-		241.8	3.3	-		242.0	0.1	-		242.4	0.2	-		243.3	0.4
2001	-		246.8	1.4	-		247.1	0.1	-		249.2	0.8	-		250.1	0.4	-		260.3	4.1	-		258.7	-0.6

Source: U.S. Department of Labor, Bureau of Labor Statistics, Division of Consumer Prices and Price Indexes. - indicates no data collected for period.

Miami-Fort Lauderdale, FL
Consumer Price Index - All Urban Consumers
Base December 1997 = 100
Recreation

For 1997-2001. Columns headed % show percentile change in the index from the previous period for which an index is available.

Year	Jan		Feb		Mar		Apr		May		Jun		Jul		Aug		Sep		Oct		Nov		Dec	
	Index	%	Index	%	Index	%	Index	%	Index	%	Index	%	Index	%	Index	%	Index	%	Index	%	Index	%	Index	%
1997	-	-	-	-	-	-	-	-	-	-	-	-	-	-	-	-	-	-	-	-	-	-	100.0	-
1998	-	-	100.5	0.5	-	-	100.6	0.1	-	-	100.8	0.2	-	-	101.0	0.2	-	-	98.9	-2.1	-	-	99.7	0.8
1999	-	-	99.7	0.0	-	-	99.0	-0.7	-	-	99.1	0.1	-	-	96.9	-2.2	-	-	99.6	2.8	-	-	101.7	2.1
2000	-	-	100.4	-1.3	-	-	98.5	-1.9	-	-	99.1	0.6	-	-	99.3	0.2	-	-	98.3	-1.0	-	-	100.4	2.1
2001	-	-	100.2	-0.2	-	-	102.7	2.5	-	-	104.4	1.7	-	-	104.7	0.3	-	-	105.2	0.5	-	-	105.6	0.4

Source: U.S. Department of Labor, Bureau of Labor Statistics, Division of Consumer Prices and Price Indexes. - indicates no data collected for period.

Miami-Fort Lauderdale, FL
Consumer Price Index - Urban Wage Earners
Base December 1997 = 100
Recreation

For 1997-2001. Columns headed % show percentile change in the index from the previous period for which an index is available.

Year	Jan		Feb		Mar		Apr		May		Jun		Jul		Aug		Sep		Oct		Nov		Dec	
	Index	%	Index	%	Index	%	Index	%	Index	%	Index	%	Index	%	Index	%	Index	%	Index	%	Index	%	Index	%
1997	-	-	-	-	-	-	-	-	-	-	-	-	-	-	-	-	-	-	-	-	-	-	100.0	-
1998	-	-	100.3	0.3	-	-	100.6	0.3	-	-	100.7	0.1	-	-	101.0	0.3	-	-	98.7	-2.3	-	-	99.8	1.1
1999	-	-	99.9	0.1	-	-	98.9	-1.0	-	-	99.0	0.1	-	-	96.0	-3.0	-	-	98.6	2.7	-	-	101.1	2.5
2000	-	-	99.5	-1.6	-	-	97.2	-2.3	-	-	97.8	0.6	-	-	98.2	0.4	-	-	96.6	-1.6	-	-	99.0	2.5
2001	-	-	98.6	-0.4	-	-	101.6	3.0	-	-	103.2	1.6	-	-	103.5	0.3	-	-	104.0	0.5	-	-	104.3	0.3

Source: U.S. Department of Labor, Bureau of Labor Statistics, Division of Consumer Prices and Price Indexes. - indicates no data collected for period.

Miami-Fort Lauderdale, FL
Consumer Price Index - All Urban Consumers
Base December 1997 = 100
Education & Communication

For 1997-2001. Columns headed % show percentile change in the index from the previous period for which an index is available.

Year	Jan Index	%	Feb Index	%	Mar Index	%	Apr Index	%	May Index	%	Jun Index	%	Jul Index	%	Aug Index	%	Sep Index	%	Oct Index	%	Nov Index	%	Dec Index	%
1997	-	-	-	-	-	-	-	-	-	-	-	-	-	-	-	-	-	-	-	-	-	-	100.0	-
1998	-	-	100.3	0.3	-	-	100.7	0.4	-	-	99.8	-0.9	-	-	100.3	0.5	-	-	101.2	0.9	-	-	101.3	0.1
1999	-	-	102.3	1.0	-	-	102.2	-0.1	-	-	100.9	-1.3	-	-	102.0	1.1	-	-	-	-	-	-	102.9	0.9
2000	-	-	102.3	-0.6	-	-	102.1	-0.2	-	-	101.5	-0.6	-	-	102.5	1.0	-	-	105.6	3.0	-	-	104.9	-0.7
2001	-	-	105.2	0.3	-	-	104.9	-0.3	-	-	104.9	0.0	-	-	107.4	2.4	-	-	108.8	1.3	-	-	109.1	0.3

Source: U.S. Department of Labor, Bureau of Labor Statistics, Division of Consumer Prices and Price Indexes. - indicates no data collected for period.

Miami-Fort Lauderdale, FL
Consumer Price Index - Urban Wage Earners
Base December 1997 = 100
Education & Communication

For 1997-2001. Columns headed % show percentile change in the index from the previous period for which an index is available.

Year	Jan Index	%	Feb Index	%	Mar Index	%	Apr Index	%	May Index	%	Jun Index	%	Jul Index	%	Aug Index	%	Sep Index	%	Oct Index	%	Nov Index	%	Dec Index	%
1997	-	-	-		-		-		-		-		-		-		-		-		-	-	100.0	-
1998	-	-	100.5	0.5	-		101.2	0.7	-		100.5	-0.7	-		100.4	-0.1	-		101.5	1.1	-	-	101.6	0.1
1999	-	-	103.0	1.4	-		103.1	0.1	-		101.8	-1.3	-		102.7	0.9	-		-		-	-	104.0	1.3
2000	-	-	103.2	-0.8	-		103.2	0.0	-		102.5	-0.7	-		102.5	0.0	-		106.4	3.8	-	-	105.6	-0.8
2001	-	-	106.0	0.4	-		105.7	-0.3	-		105.7	0.0	-		107.8	2.0	-		109.7	1.8	-	-	110.2	0.5

Source: U.S. Department of Labor, Bureau of Labor Statistics, Division of Consumer Prices and Price Indexes. - indicates no data collected for period.

Milwaukee-Racine, WI
Consumer Price Index - All Urban Consumers
Base 1982-1984 = 100
Annual Averages

For 1935-2001. Columns headed % show percentile change in the index from the previous period for which an index is available.

Year	All Items		Food & Beverage		Housing		Apparel		Trans- portation		Medical Care		Recrea- tion*		Education & Communic.*		Other Goods & Services	
	Index	%	Index	%	Index	%	Index	%	Index	%	Index	%	Index	%	Index	%	Index	%
1935	13.4	-	-	-	-	-	-	-	-	-	-	-	-	-	-	-	-	-
1936	13.6	1.5	-	-	-	-	-	-	-	-	-	-	-	-	-	-	-	-
1937	14.2	4.4	-	-	-	-	-	-	-	-	-	-	-	-	-	-	-	-
1938	13.8	-2.8	-	-	-	-	-	-	-	-	-	-	-	-	-	-	-	-
1939	13.5	-2.2	-	-	-	-	-	-	-	-	-	-	-	-	-	-	-	-
1940	13.5	0.0	-	-	-	-	-	-	-	-	-	-	-	-	-	-	-	-
1941	14.2	5.2	-	-	-	-	-	-	-	-	-	-	-	-	-	-	-	-
1942	15.7	10.6	-	-	-	-	-	-	-	-	-	-	-	-	-	-	-	-
1943	16.6	5.7	-	-	-	-	-	-	-	-	-	-	-	-	-	-	-	-
1944	16.9	1.8	-	-	-	-	-	-	-	-	-	-	-	-	-	-	-	-
1945	17.3	2.4	-	-	-	-	-	-	-	-	-	-	-	-	-	-	-	-
1946	18.6	7.5	-	-	-	-	-	-	-	-	-	-	-	-	-	-	-	-
1947	21.7	16.7	-	-	-	-	-	-	20.3	-	12.8	-	-	-	-	-	-	-
1948	23.4	7.8	-	-	-	-	-	-	21.9	7.9	13.6	6.3	-	-	-	-	-	-
1949	23.1	-1.3	-	-	-	-	-	-	22.8	4.1	14.2	4.4	-	-	-	-	-	-
1950	23.9	3.5	-	-	-	-	-	-	23.2	1.8	14.9	4.9	-	-	-	-	-	-
1951	26.2	9.6	-	-	-	-	-	-	24.8	6.9	16.5	10.7	-	-	-	-	-	-
1952	27.0	3.1	-	-	-	-	-	-	26.2	5.6	17.3	4.8	-	-	-	-	-	-
1953	27.1	0.4	-	-	-	-	39.6	-	27.1	3.4	17.9	3.5	-	-	-	-	-	-
1954	27.1	0.0	-	-	-	-	39.5	-0.3	26.8	-1.1	19.0	6.1	-	-	-	-	-	-
1955	27.1	0.0	-	-	-	-	39.3	-0.5	26.5	-1.1	19.5	2.6	-	-	-	-	-	-
1956	27.5	1.5	-	-	-	-	40.3	2.5	27.2	2.6	19.9	2.1	-	-	-	-	-	-
1957	28.4	3.3	-	-	-	-	40.9	1.5	28.4	4.4	21.4	7.5	-	-	-	-	-	-
1958	28.8	1.4	-	-	-	-	40.9	0.0	28.9	1.8	22.1	3.3	-	-	-	-	-	-
1959	28.8	0.0	-	-	-	-	41.3	1.0	29.8	3.1	22.5	1.8	-	-	-	-	-	-
1960	29.2	1.4	-	-	-	-	41.8	1.2	29.5	-1.0	23.1	2.7	-	-	-	-	-	-
1961	29.4	0.7	-	-	-	-	42.0	0.5	29.8	1.0	23.2	0.4	-	-	-	-	-	-
1962	29.8	1.4	-	-	-	-	42.2	0.5	30.8	3.4	23.4	0.9	-	-	-	-	-	-
1963	30.1	1.0	-	-	-	-	42.2	0.0	31.0	0.6	23.9	2.1	-	-	-	-	-	-
1964	30.4	1.0	-	-	-	-	42.8	1.4	31.1	0.3	24.4	2.1	-	-	-	-	-	-
1965	31.0	2.0	-	-	-	-	43.5	1.6	32.2	3.5	25.3	3.7	-	-	-	-	-	-
1966	31.7	2.3	-	-	-	-	44.2	1.6	32.4	0.6	26.7	5.5	-	-	-	-	-	-
1967	32.4	2.2	-	-	-	-	45.8	3.6	32.9	1.5	28.8	7.9	-	-	-	-	-	-
1968	33.5	3.4	-	-	-	-	47.7	4.1	33.2	0.9	30.4	5.6	-	-	-	-	-	-
1969	35.5	6.0	-	-	-	-	51.7	8.4	35.0	5.4	32.6	7.2	-	-	-	-	-	-
1970	37.5	5.6	-	-	-	-	55.9	8.1	36.4	4.0	34.3	5.2	-	-	-	-	-	-
1971	38.9	3.7	-	-	-	-	56.9	1.8	38.5	5.8	36.3	5.8	-	-	-	-	-	-
1972	40.1	3.1	-	-	-	-	58.1	2.1	39.2	1.8	36.9	1.7	-	-	-	-	-	-
1973	42.6	6.2	-	-	-	-	60.9	4.8	41.4	5.6	38.6	4.6	-	-	-	-	-	-
1974	46.7	9.6	-	-	-	-	64.9	6.6	46.0	11.1	42.4	9.8	-	-	-	-	-	-
1975	50.8	8.8	-	-	-	-	70.0	7.9	49.9	8.5	47.1	11.1	-	-	-	-	-	-
1976	54.1	6.5	63.4	-	47.4	-	74.2	6.0	53.5	7.2	52.6	11.7	-	-	-	-	59.9	-
1977	57.6	6.5	66.9	5.5	50.9	7.4	77.5	4.4	57.0	6.5	57.3	8.9	-	-	-	-	63.1	5.3
1978	62.3	8.2	73.4	9.7	55.9	9.8	78.3	1.0	60.5	6.1	61.9	8.0	-	-	-	-	66.5	5.4
1979	70.8	13.6	81.6	11.2	65.2	16.6	82.2	5.0	70.5	16.5	69.3	12.0	-	-	-	-	70.5	6.0

[Continued]

Milwaukee-Racine, WI
Consumer Price Index - All Urban Consumers
Base 1982-1984 = 100
Annual Averages

[Continued]

For 1935-2001. Columns headed % show percentile change in the index from the previous period for which an index is available.

Year	All Items		Food & Beverage		Housing		Apparel		Trans- portation		Medical Care		Recrea- tion*		Education & Communic.*		Other Goods & Services	
	Index	%	Index	%	Index	%	Index	%	Index	%	Index	%	Index	%	Index	%	Index	%
1980	81.4	15.0	87.2	6.9	78.2	19.9	87.5	6.4	83.2	18.0	77.9	12.4	-	-	-	-	75.7	7.4
1981	90.7	11.4	94.9	8.8	88.3	12.9	92.3	5.5	93.5	12.4	86.7	11.3	-	-	-	-	83.2	9.9
1982	95.9	5.7	98.5	3.8	94.0	6.5	96.9	5.0	98.5	5.3	93.7	8.1	-	-	-	-	92.4	11.1
1983	100.2	4.5	99.6	1.1	100.7	7.1	101.8	5.1	99.0	0.5	100.6	7.4	-	-	-	-	100.8	9.1
1984	103.8	3.6	101.9	2.3	105.1	4.4	101.3	-0.5	102.5	3.5	105.7	5.1	-	-	-	-	106.8	6.0
1985	107.0	3.1	105.7	3.7	108.5	3.2	103.4	2.1	103.9	1.4	109.3	3.4	-	-	-	-	113.1	5.9
1986	107.4	0.4	107.9	2.1	109.5	0.9	105.1	1.6	98.7	-5.0	114.6	4.8	-	-	-	-	121.6	7.5
1987	111.5	3.8	112.0	3.8	114.3	4.4	111.4	6.0	101.5	2.8	119.3	4.1	-	-	-	-	-	-
1988	115.9	3.9	115.8	3.4	118.4	3.6	121.0	8.6	103.1	1.6	128.4	7.6	-	-	-	-	139.0	14.3
1989	120.8	4.2	121.1	4.6	122.1	3.1	121.2	0.2	110.0	6.7	139.3	8.5	-	-	-	-	146.9	5.7
1990	126.2	4.5	128.1	5.8	126.0	3.2	126.0	4.0	115.2	4.7	150.8	8.3	-	-	-	-	156.6	6.6
1991	132.2	4.8	135.2	5.5	132.2	4.9	125.4	-0.5	119.1	3.4	159.5	5.8	-	-	-	-	169.8	8.4
1992	137.1	3.7	135.4	0.1	137.7	4.2	124.2	-1.0	123.1	3.4	174.3	9.3	-	-	-	-	182.0	7.2
1993	142.1	3.6	138.1	2.0	142.8	3.7	123.2	-0.8	128.5	4.4	185.5	6.4	-	-	-	-	194.9	7.1
1994	147.0	3.4	141.5	2.5	148.0	3.6	122.5	-0.6	134.2	4.4	201.7	8.7	-	-	-	-	201.1	3.2
1995	151.0	2.7	146.6	3.6	152.2	2.8	121.4	-0.9	137.5	2.5	213.2	5.7	-	-	-	-	207.1	3.0
1996	154.7	2.5	151.9	3.6	154.4	1.4	123.2	1.5	141.6	3.0	220.1	3.2	-	-	-	-	216.6	4.6
1997	157.7	1.9	154.5	1.7	156.1	1.1	122.9	-0.2	143.7	1.5	230.5	4.7	-	-	-	-	225.6	4.2
1998	160.3	1.6	157.5	1.9	159.9	2.4	118.7	-3.4	140.8	-2.0	239.8	4.0	100.0	-	100.0	-	242.1	7.3
1999	163.7	2.1	163.7	3.9	162.6	1.7	116.8	-1.6	142.5	1.2	251.5	4.9	101.1	1.1	101.0	1.0	259.2	7.1
2000	168.6	3.0	168.9	3.2	166.4	2.3	119.7	2.5	149.4	4.8	257.7	2.5	102.6	1.5	105.0	4.0	268.0	3.4
2001	-	-	-	-	-	-	-	-	-	-	-	-	-	-	-	-	-	-

Source: U.S. Department of Labor, Bureau of Labor Statistics, Division of Consumer Prices and Price Indexes. *Base is December 1997 = 100. - indicates no data collected for period.

Milwaukee-Racine, WI
Consumer Price Index - Urban Wage Earners
Base 1982-1984 = 100
Annual Averages

For 1935-2001. Columns headed % show percentile change in the index from the previous period for which an index is available.

Year	All Items		Food & Beverage		Housing		Apparel		Trans-portation		Medical Care		Recrea-tion*		Education & Communic.*		Other Goods & Services	
	Index	%	Index	%	Index	%	Index	%	Index	%	Index	%	Index	%	Index	%	Index	%
1935	12.9	-	-	-	-	-	-	-	-	-	-	-	-	-	-	-	-	-
1936	13.2	2.3	-	-	-	-	-	-	-	-	-	-	-	-	-	-	-	-
1937	13.7	3.8	-	-	-	-	-	-	-	-	-	-	-	-	-	-	-	-
1938	13.4	-2.2	-	-	-	-	-	-	-	-	-	-	-	-	-	-	-	-
1939	13.0	-3.0	-	-	-	-	-	-	-	-	-	-	-	-	-	-	-	-
1940	13.0	0.0	-	-	-	-	-	-	-	-	-	-	-	-	-	-	-	-
1941	13.7	5.4	-	-	-	-	-	-	-	-	-	-	-	-	-	-	-	-
1942	15.1	10.2	-	-	-	-	-	-	-	-	-	-	-	-	-	-	-	-
1943	16.0	6.0	-	-	-	-	-	-	-	-	-	-	-	-	-	-	-	-
1944	16.3	1.9	-	-	-	-	-	-	-	-	-	-	-	-	-	-	-	-
1945	16.7	2.5	-	-	-	-	-	-	-	-	-	-	-	-	-	-	-	-
1946	18.0	7.8	-	-	-	-	-	-	-	-	-	-	-	-	-	-	-	-
1947	20.9	16.1	-	-	-	-	-	-	20.5	-	13.0	-	-	-	-	-	-	-
1948	22.6	8.1	-	-	-	-	-	-	22.1	7.8	13.8	6.2	-	-	-	-	-	-
1949	22.4	-0.9	-	-	-	-	-	-	23.1	4.5	14.4	4.3	-	-	-	-	-	-
1950	23.1	3.1	-	-	-	-	-	-	23.5	1.7	15.0	4.2	-	-	-	-	-	-
1951	25.3	9.5	-	-	-	-	-	-	25.1	6.8	16.6	10.7	-	-	-	-	-	-
1952	26.1	3.2	-	-	-	-	-	-	26.5	5.6	17.5	5.4	-	-	-	-	-	-
1953	26.2	0.4	-	-	-	-	40.5	-	27.4	3.4	18.1	3.4	-	-	-	-	-	-
1954	26.2	0.0	-	-	-	-	40.4	-0.2	27.1	-1.1	19.2	6.1	-	-	-	-	-	-
1955	26.2	0.0	-	-	-	-	40.2	-0.5	26.8	-1.1	19.7	2.6	-	-	-	-	-	-
1956	26.6	1.5	-	-	-	-	41.2	2.5	27.5	2.6	20.1	2.0	-	-	-	-	-	-
1957	27.5	3.4	-	-	-	-	41.8	1.5	28.7	4.4	21.6	7.5	-	-	-	-	-	-
1958	27.8	1.1	-	-	-	-	41.8	0.0	29.2	1.7	22.3	3.2	-	-	-	-	-	-
1959	27.8	0.0	-	-	-	-	42.2	1.0	30.1	3.1	22.8	2.2	-	-	-	-	-	-
1960	28.2	1.4	-	-	-	-	42.7	1.2	29.9	-0.7	23.3	2.2	-	-	-	-	-	-
1961	28.4	0.7	-	-	-	-	43.0	0.7	30.1	0.7	23.5	0.9	-	-	-	-	-	-
1962	28.8	1.4	-	-	-	-	43.1	0.2	31.1	3.3	23.7	0.9	-	-	-	-	-	-
1963	29.1	1.0	-	-	-	-	43.1	0.0	31.3	0.6	24.2	2.1	-	-	-	-	-	-
1964	29.4	1.0	-	-	-	-	43.8	1.6	31.4	0.3	24.6	1.7	-	-	-	-	-	-
1965	30.0	2.0	-	-	-	-	44.5	1.6	32.6	3.8	25.6	4.1	-	-	-	-	-	-
1966	30.7	2.3	-	-	-	-	45.2	1.6	32.8	0.6	27.0	5.5	-	-	-	-	-	-
1967	31.3	2.0	-	-	-	-	46.8	3.5	33.2	1.2	29.1	7.8	-	-	-	-	-	-
1968	32.4	3.5	-	-	-	-	48.8	4.3	33.6	1.2	30.8	5.8	-	-	-	-	-	-
1969	34.3	5.9	-	-	-	-	52.9	8.4	35.4	5.4	32.9	6.8	-	-	-	-	-	-
1970	36.2	5.5	-	-	-	-	57.2	8.1	36.8	4.0	34.7	5.5	-	-	-	-	-	-
1971	37.6	3.9	-	-	-	-	58.2	1.7	38.9	5.7	36.7	5.8	-	-	-	-	-	-
1972	38.7	2.9	-	-	-	-	59.4	2.1	39.7	2.1	37.3	1.6	-	-	-	-	-	-
1973	41.1	6.2	-	-	-	-	62.3	4.9	41.9	5.5	39.0	4.6	-	-	-	-	-	-
1974	45.1	9.7	-	-	-	-	66.3	6.4	46.5	11.0	42.9	10.0	-	-	-	-	-	-
1975	49.1	8.9	-	-	-	-	71.5	7.8	50.4	8.4	47.6	11.0	-	-	-	-	-	-
1976	52.3	6.5	61.9	-	43.7	-	75.9	6.2	54.1	7.3	53.2	11.8	-	-	-	-	57.4	-
1977	55.6	6.3	65.3	5.5	46.9	7.3	79.2	4.3	57.6	6.5	58.0	9.0	-	-	-	-	60.4	5.2
1978	60.5	8.8	72.0	10.3	51.8	10.4	80.2	1.3	61.3	6.4	63.6	9.7	-	-	-	-	64.9	7.5
1979	69.2	14.4	81.1	12.6	61.3	18.3	84.6	5.5	70.9	15.7	69.9	9.9	-	-	-	-	68.9	6.2

[Continued]

Milwaukee-Racine, WI
Consumer Price Index - Urban Wage Earners
Base 1982-1984 = 100
Annual Averages
[Continued]

For 1935-2001. Columns headed % show percentile change in the index from the previous period for which an index is available.

Year	All Items		Food & Beverage		Housing		Apparel		Transportation		Medical Care		Recreation*		Education & Communic.*		Other Goods & Services	
	Index	%	Index	%	Index	%	Index	%	Index	%	Index	%	Index	%	Index	%	Index	%
1980	80.2	15.9	87.8	8.3	74.7	21.9	89.8	6.1	83.3	17.5	79.1	13.2	-	-	-	-	75.1	9.0
1981	89.2	11.2	95.1	8.3	84.7	13.4	95.1	5.9	93.5	12.2	87.6	10.7	-	-	-	-	82.3	9.6
1982	93.8	5.2	98.5	3.6	89.7	5.9	97.8	2.8	98.0	4.8	93.9	7.2	-	-	-	-	92.1	11.9
1983	100.0	6.6	99.7	1.2	100.3	11.8	101.6	3.9	99.1	1.1	100.2	6.7	-	-	-	-	101.0	9.7
1984	106.2	6.2	101.9	2.2	110.0	9.7	100.6	-1.0	102.9	3.8	105.9	5.7	-	-	-	-	106.9	5.8
1985	109.4	3.0	105.6	3.6	113.3	3.0	103.0	2.4	104.5	1.6	110.0	3.9	-	-	-	-	112.9	5.6
1986	109.6	0.2	107.9	2.2	114.1	0.7	105.6	2.5	99.0	-5.3	115.5	5.0	-	-	-	-	121.1	7.3
1987	114.1	4.1	111.9	3.7	119.0	4.3	113.0	7.0	102.5	3.5	120.6	4.4	-	-	-	-	-	-
1988	118.6	3.9	115.8	3.5	123.2	3.5	123.2	9.0	104.3	1.8	129.9	7.7	-	-	-	-	139.2	14.9
1989	123.5	4.1	120.9	4.4	126.9	3.0	123.5	0.2	110.9	6.3	141.4	8.9	-	-	-	-	147.6	6.0
1990	128.9	4.4	128.0	5.9	130.9	3.2	127.4	3.2	116.0	4.6	152.3	7.7	-	-	-	-	157.5	6.7
1991	135.0	4.7	135.1	5.5	137.2	4.8	128.1	0.5	119.3	2.8	160.7	5.5	-	-	-	-	171.6	9.0
1992	139.8	3.6	135.3	0.1	143.0	4.2	126.2	-1.5	123.9	3.9	175.3	9.1	-	-	-	-	184.3	7.4
1993	144.8	3.6	138.0	2.0	148.3	3.7	125.9	-0.2	129.5	4.5	186.2	6.2	-	-	-	-	196.6	6.7
1994	149.4	3.2	141.5	2.5	153.6	3.6	125.0	-0.7	134.6	3.9	202.1	8.5	-	-	-	-	201.2	2.3
1995	153.5	2.7	146.6	3.6	157.9	2.8	125.4	0.3	137.8	2.4	213.3	5.5	-	-	-	-	206.7	2.7
1996	157.0	2.3	151.9	3.6	160.0	1.3	127.8	1.9	141.2	2.5	219.5	2.9	-	-	-	-	216.2	4.6
1997	159.8	1.8	154.5	1.7	161.9	1.2	128.0	0.2	141.9	0.5	230.8	5.1	-	-	-	-	225.3	4.2
1998	162.1	1.4	157.1	1.7	165.6	2.3	125.8	-1.7	137.9	-2.8	239.9	3.9	99.5	-	100.1	-	242.9	7.8
1999	165.5	2.1	163.2	3.9	168.2	1.6	123.1	-2.1	139.6	1.2	252.2	5.1	99.5	0.0	101.0	0.9	263.3	8.4
2000	170.7	3.1	168.8	3.4	172.0	2.3	125.7	2.1	147.8	5.9	258.5	2.5	100.5	1.0	104.6	3.6	272.6	3.5
2001	-		-		-		-		-		-		-		-		-	

Source: U.S. Department of Labor, Bureau of Labor Statistics, Division of Consumer Prices and Price Indexes. *Base is December 1997 = 100. - indicates no data collected for period.

Milwaukee-Racine, WI
Consumer Price Index - All Urban Consumers
Base 1982-1984 = 100
All Items

For 1935-2001. Columns headed % show percentile change in the index from the previous period for which an index is available.

Year	Jan Index	%	Feb Index	%	Mar Index	%	Apr Index	%	May Index	%	Jun Index	%	Jul Index	%	Aug Index	%	Sep Index	%	Oct Index	%	Nov Index	%	Dec Index	%
1935	-	-	-	-	13.3	-	-	-	-	-	-	-	13.3	0.0	-	-	-	-	13.4	0.8	-	-	-	-
1936	13.5	0.7	-	-	-	-	13.4	-0.7	-	-	-	-	13.6	1.5	-	-	13.9	2.2	-	-	-	-	13.7	-1.4
1937	-	-	-	-	14.0	2.2	-	-	-	-	14.3	2.1	-	-	-	-	14.4	0.7	-	-	-	-	14.2	-1.4
1938	-	-	-	-	13.9	-2.1	-	-	-	-	13.9	0.0	-	-	-	-	13.7	-1.4	-	-	-	-	13.6	-0.7
1939	-	-	-	-	13.4	-1.5	-	-	-	-	13.4	0.0	-	-	-	-	13.6	1.5	-	-	-	-	13.4	-1.5
1940	-	-	-	-	13.4	0.0	-	-	-	-	13.6	1.5	-	-	-	-	13.5	-0.7	-	-	-	-	13.6	0.7
1941	-	-	-	-	13.6	0.0	-	-	-	-	14.2	4.4	-	-	-	-	14.6	2.8	-	-	-	-	15.0	2.7
1942	-	-	-	-	15.4	2.7	-	-	-	-	15.8	2.6	-	-	-	-	15.8	0.0	-	-	-	-	16.2	2.5
1943	-	-	-	-	16.5	1.9	-	-	-	-	16.8	1.8	-	-	-	-	16.6	-1.2	-	-	-	-	16.6	0.0
1944	-	-	-	-	16.6	0.0	-	-	-	-	16.9	1.8	-	-	-	-	17.0	0.6	-	-	-	-	17.0	0.0
1945	-	-	-	-	17.0	0.0	-	-	-	-	17.4	2.4	-	-	-	-	17.3	-0.6	-	-	-	-	17.4	0.6
1946	-	-	-	-	17.4	0.0	-	-	-	-	17.9	2.9	-	-	-	-	19.6	9.5	-	-	-	-	20.6	5.1
1947	-	-	-	-	21.2	2.9	-	-	-	-	21.5	1.4	-	-	21.8	1.4	-	-	-	-	22.5	3.2	-	-
1948	-	-	22.9	1.8	-	-	-	-	23.5	2.6	-	-	-	-	24.0	2.1	-	-	-	-	23.5	-2.1	-	-
1949	-	-	23.2	-1.3	-	-	-	-	23.2	0.0	-	-	-	-	23.0	-0.9	-	-	-	-	23.2	0.9	-	-
1950	-	-	23.1	-0.4	-	-	-	-	23.5	1.7	-	-	-	-	24.2	3.0	-	-	-	-	24.7	2.1	-	-
1951	-	-	25.7	4.0	-	-	-	-	26.1	1.6	-	-	-	-	26.3	0.8	-	-	-	-	26.7	1.5	-	-
1952	-	-	26.7	0.0	-	-	-	-	27.1	1.5	-	-	-	-	27.3	0.7	-	-	-	-	27.2	-0.4	27.1	-0.4
1953	-	-	26.9	-0.7	-	-	-	-	27.1	0.7	-	-	-	-	27.3	0.7	-	-	-	-	27.1	-0.7	-	-
1954	-	-	27.1	0.0	-	-	-	-	27.2	0.4	-	-	-	-	27.1	-0.4	-	-	-	-	27.1	0.0	-	-
1955	-	-	27.0	-0.4	-	-	-	-	27.0	0.0	-	-	-	-	27.1	0.4	-	-	-	-	27.2	0.4	-	-
1956	-	-	27.1	-0.4	-	-	-	-	27.3	0.7	-	-	-	-	27.7	1.5	-	-	-	-	27.8	0.4	-	-
1957	-	-	28.1	1.1	-	-	-	-	28.4	1.1	-	-	-	-	28.6	0.7	-	-	-	-	28.6	0.0	-	-
1958	-	-	28.8	0.7	-	-	-	-	28.9	0.3	-	-	-	-	28.9	0.0	-	-	-	-	28.8	-0.3	-	-
1959	-	-	28.7	-0.3	-	-	-	-	28.7	0.0	-	-	-	-	28.9	0.7	-	-	-	-	29.0	0.3	-	-
1960	-	-	28.9	-0.3	-	-	-	-	29.2	1.0	-	-	-	-	29.3	0.3	-	-	-	-	29.4	0.3	-	-
1961	-	-	29.4	0.0	-	-	-	-	29.3	-0.3	-	-	-	-	29.4	0.3	-	-	-	-	29.4	0.0	-	-
1962	-	-	29.8	1.4	-	-	-	-	29.8	0.0	-	-	-	-	29.8	0.0	-	-	-	-	29.9	0.3	-	-
1963	-	-	29.9	0.0	-	-	-	-	30.0	0.3	-	-	-	-	30.1	0.3	-	-	-	-	30.2	0.3	-	-
1964	-	-	30.2	0.0	-	-	-	-	30.3	0.3	-	-	-	-	30.5	0.7	-	-	-	-	30.6	0.3	-	-
1965	-	-	30.7	0.3	-	-	-	-	31.0	1.0	-	-	-	-	31.2	0.6	-	-	-	-	31.2	0.0	-	-
1966	-	-	31.4	0.6	-	-	-	-	31.6	0.6	-	-	-	-	32.0	1.3	-	-	-	-	32.0	0.0	-	-
1967	-	-	32.0	0.0	-	-	-	-	32.2	0.6	-	-	-	-	32.6	1.2	-	-	-	-	32.8	0.6	-	-
1968	-	-	33.0	0.6	-	-	-	-	33.3	0.9	-	-	-	-	33.7	1.2	-	-	-	-	34.0	0.9	-	-
1969	-	-	34.6	1.8	-	-	-	-	35.2	1.7	-	-	-	-	35.5	0.9	-	-	-	-	36.4	2.5	-	-
1970	-	-	36.8	1.1	-	-	-	-	37.3	1.4	-	-	-	-	37.6	0.8	-	-	-	-	38.1	1.3	-	-
1971	-	-	38.5	1.0	-	-	-	-	38.6	0.3	-	-	-	-	39.3	1.8	-	-	-	-	39.1	-0.5	-	-
1972	-	-	39.6	1.3	-	-	-	-	39.8	0.5	-	-	-	-	40.3	1.3	-	-	-	-	40.5	0.5	-	-
1973	-	-	41.1	1.5	-	-	-	-	42.1	2.4	-	-	-	-	43.1	2.4	-	-	-	-	43.9	1.9	-	-
1974	-	-	45.0	2.5	-	-	-	-	46.0	2.2	-	-	-	-	47.2	2.6	-	-	-	-	48.6	3.0	-	-
1975	-	-	49.3	1.4	-	-	-	-	50.3	2.0	-	-	-	-	51.5	2.4	-	-	-	-	52.3	1.6	-	-
1976	-	-	52.6	0.6	-	-	-	-	53.7	2.1	-	-	-	-	54.7	1.9	-	-	-	-	55.2	0.9	-	-
1977	-	-	56.2	1.8	-	-	-	-	57.6	2.5	-	-	-	-	57.9	0.5	-	-	-	-	58.8	1.6	-	-
1978	59.4	1.0	-	-	60.3	1.5	-	-	61.1	1.3	-	-	62.7	2.6	-	-	64.2	2.4	-	-	64.4	0.3	-	-
1979	64.9	0.8	-	-	67.2	3.5	-	-	70.3	4.6	-	-	72.1	2.6	-	-	73.2	1.5	-	-	74.4	1.6	-	-
1980	76.5	2.8	-	-	78.6	2.7	-	-	81.0	3.1	-	-	81.5	0.6	-	-	83.7	2.7	-	-	84.9	1.4	-	-

[Continued]

Milwaukee-Racine, WI
Consumer Price Index - All Urban Consumers
Base 1982-1984 = 100
All Items
[Continued]

For 1935-2001. Columns headed % show percentile change in the index from the previous period for which an index is available.

Year	Jan Index	%	Feb Index	%	Mar Index	%	Apr Index	%	May Index	%	Jun Index	%	Jul Index	%	Aug Index	%	Sep Index	%	Oct Index	%	Nov Index	%	Dec Index	%
1981	86.2	1.5	-	-	87.4	1.4	-	-	90.2	3.2	-	-	92.5	2.5	-	-	92.9	0.4	-	-	93.1	0.2	-	-
1982	94.3	1.3	-	-	93.7	-0.6	-	-	94.8	1.2	-	-	96.0	1.3	-	-	97.9	2.0	-	-	98.1	0.2	-	-
1983	98.7	0.6	-	-	98.7	0.0	-	-	100.0	1.3	-	-	100.3	0.3	-	-	101.6	1.3	-	-	101.2	-0.4	-	-
1984	101.7	0.5	-	-	102.6	0.9	-	-	103.8	1.2	-	-	104.0	0.2	-	-	104.9	0.9	-	-	105.0	0.1	-	-
1985	105.1	0.1	-	-	106.1	1.0	-	-	107.1	0.9	-	-	107.2	0.1	-	-	107.6	0.4	-	-	108.1	0.5	-	-
1986	108.1	0.0	-	-	106.6	-1.4	-	-	107.5	0.8	-	-	107.3	-0.2	-	-	107.8	0.5	-	-	107.1	-0.6	-	-
1987	-	-	-	-	-	-	-	-	-	-	110.1	2.1	-	-	-	-	-	-	-	-	-	-	107.8	0.7
1988	-	-	-	-	-	-	-	-	-	-	114.5	1.3	-	-	-	-	-	-	-	-	-	-	113.0	2.6
1989	-	-	-	-	-	-	-	-	-	-	120.3	2.6	-	-	-	-	-	-	-	-	-	-	117.2	2.4
1990	-	-	-	-	-	-	-	-	-	-	123.9	2.2	-	-	-	-	-	-	-	-	-	-	121.2	0.7
1991	-	-	-	-	-	-	-	-	-	-	131.0	1.9	-	-	-	-	-	-	-	-	-	-	128.6	3.8
1992	-	-	-	-	-	-	-	-	-	-	135.9	1.8	-	-	-	-	-	-	-	-	-	-	133.5	1.9
1993	-	-	-	-	-	-	-	-	-	-	140.5	1.7	-	-	-	-	-	-	-	-	-	-	138.2	1.7
1994	-	-	-	-	-	-	-	-	-	-	146.0	1.6	-	-	-	-	-	-	-	-	-	-	143.7	2.3
1995	-	-	-	-	-	-	-	-	-	-	150.6	1.8	-	-	-	-	-	-	-	-	-	-	147.9	1.3
1996	-	-	-	-	-	-	-	-	-	-	153.7	1.5	-	-	-	-	-	-	-	-	-	-	151.5	0.6
1997	-	-	-	-	-	-	-	-	-	-	157.6	1.3	-	-	-	-	-	-	-	-	-	-	155.6	1.2
1998	-	-	-	-	-	-	-	-	-	-	159.6	1.1	-	-	-	-	-	-	-	-	-	-	157.8	0.1
1999	-	-	-	-	-	-	-	-	-	-	162.7	1.1	-	-	-	-	-	-	-	-	-	-	161.0	0.9
2000	-	-	-	-	-	-	-	-	-	-	167.6	1.8	-	-	-	-	-	-	-	-	-	-	164.6	1.2
2001	-	-	-	-	-	-	-	-	-	-	171.8	1.3	-	-	-	-	-	-	-	-	-	-	169.6	1.2

Source: U.S. Department of Labor, Bureau of Labor Statistics, Division of Consumer Prices and Price Indexes. - indicates no data collected for period.

Milwaukee-Racine, WI
Consumer Price Index - Urban Wage Earners
Base 1982-1984 = 100
All Items

For 1935-2001. Columns headed % show percentile change in the index from the previous period for which an index is available.

Year	Jan Index	%	Feb Index	%	Mar Index	%	Apr Index	%	May Index	%	Jun Index	%	Jul Index	%	Aug Index	%	Sep Index	%	Oct Index	%	Nov Index	%	Dec Index	%
1935	-		-		12.9	-	-		-		-		12.9	0.0	-		-		13.0	0.8	-		-	
1936	13.0	0.0	-		-		13.0	0.0	-		-		13.2	1.5	-		13.4	1.5	-		-		13.3	-0.7
1937	-		-		13.5	1.5	-		-		13.8	2.2	-		-		13.9	0.7	-		-		13.7	-1.4
1938	-		-		13.5	-1.5	-		-		13.5	0.0	-		-		13.2	-2.2	-		-		13.2	0.0
1939	-		-		13.0	-1.5	-		-		12.9	-0.8	-		-		13.1	1.6	-		-		13.0	-0.8
1940	-		-		13.0	0.0	-		-		13.2	1.5	-		-		13.0	-1.5	-		-		13.1	0.8
1941	-		-		13.2	0.8	-		-		13.7	3.8	-		-		14.1	2.9	-		-		14.5	2.8
1942	-		-		14.9	2.8	-		-		15.3	2.7	-		-		15.2	-0.7	-		-		15.6	2.6
1943	-		-		16.0	2.6	-		-		16.2	1.3	-		-		16.1	-0.6	-		-		16.1	0.0
1944	-		-		16.1	0.0	-		-		16.4	1.9	-		-		16.4	0.0	-		-		16.4	0.0
1945	-		-		16.4	0.0	-		-		16.8	2.4	-		-		16.7	-0.6	-		-		16.8	0.6
1946	-		-		16.8	0.0	-		-		17.3	3.0	-		-		18.9	9.2	-		-		19.9	5.3
1947	-		-		20.5	3.0	-		-		20.7	1.0	-		21.1	1.9	-		-		21.7	2.8	-	
1948	-		22.1	1.8	-		-		22.7	2.7	-		-		23.1	1.8	-		-		22.7	-1.7	-	
1949	-		22.4	-1.3	-		-		22.5	0.4	-		-		22.2	-1.3	-		-		22.4	0.9	-	
1950	-		22.3	-0.4	-		-		22.7	1.8	-		-		23.4	3.1	-		-		23.8	1.7	-	
1951	-		24.8	4.2	-		-		25.2	1.6	-		-		25.4	0.8	-		-		25.8	1.6	-	
1952	-		25.8	0.0	-		-		26.2	1.6	-		-		26.3	0.4	-		-		26.2	-0.4	26.2	0.0
1953	-		26.0	-0.8	-		-		26.2	0.8	-		-		26.3	0.4	-		-		26.2	-0.4	-	
1954	-		26.2	0.0	-		-		26.3	0.4	-		-		26.2	-0.4	-		-		26.2	0.0	-	
1955	-		26.1	-0.4	-		-		26.1	0.0	-		-		26.2	0.4	-		-		26.3	0.4	-	
1956	-		26.2	-0.4	-		-		26.3	0.4	-		-		26.7	1.5	-		-		26.9	0.7	-	
1957	-		27.1	0.7	-		-		27.4	1.1	-		-		27.7	1.1	-		-		27.7	0.0	-	
1958	-		27.8	0.4	-		-		27.9	0.4	-		-		27.9	0.0	-		-		27.8	-0.4	-	
1959	-		27.7	-0.4	-		-		27.7	0.0	-		-		27.9	0.7	-		-		28.1	0.7	-	
1960	-		27.9	-0.7	-		-		28.2	1.1	-		-		28.3	0.4	-		-		28.4	0.4	-	
1961	-		28.4	0.0	-		-		28.3	-0.4	-		-		28.4	0.4	-		-		28.4	0.0	-	
1962	-		28.8	1.4	-		-		28.8	0.0	-		-		28.7	-0.3	-		-		28.9	0.7	-	
1963	-		28.9	0.0	-		-		29.0	0.3	-		-		29.1	0.3	-		-		29.2	0.3	-	
1964	-		29.2	0.0	-		-		29.2	0.0	-		-		29.5	1.0	-		-		29.6	0.3	-	
1965	-		29.7	0.3	-		-		30.0	1.0	-		-		30.2	0.7	-		-		30.1	-0.3	-	
1966	-		30.3	0.7	-		-		30.5	0.7	-		-		30.9	1.3	-		-		30.9	0.0	-	
1967	-		30.9	0.0	-		-		31.1	0.6	-		-		31.5	1.3	-		-		31.7	0.6	-	
1968	-		31.9	0.6	-		-		32.1	0.6	-		-		32.5	1.2	-		-		32.9	1.2	-	
1969	-		33.5	1.8	-		-		34.0	1.5	-		-		34.3	0.9	-		-		35.2	2.6	-	
1970	-		35.6	1.1	-		-		36.0	1.1	-		-		36.3	0.8	-		-		36.8	1.4	-	
1971	-		37.2	1.1	-		-		37.3	0.3	-		-		38.0	1.9	-		-		37.8	-0.5	-	
1972	-		38.2	1.1	-		-		38.4	0.5	-		-		39.0	1.6	-		-		39.1	0.3	-	
1973	-		39.7	1.5	-		-		40.7	2.5	-		-		41.7	2.5	-		-		42.4	1.7	-	
1974	-		43.5	2.6	-		-		44.4	2.1	-		-		45.6	2.7	-		-		46.9	2.9	-	
1975	-		47.6	1.5	-		-		48.6	2.1	-		-		49.8	2.5	-		-		50.5	1.4	-	
1976	-		50.8	0.6	-		-		51.9	2.2	-		-		52.9	1.9	-		-		53.3	0.8	-	
1977	-		54.3	1.9	-		-		55.7	2.6	-		-		55.9	0.4	-		-		56.8	1.6	-	
1978	57.6	1.4	-		58.3	1.2	-		59.3	1.7	-		60.9	2.7	-		62.6	2.8	-		62.8	0.3	-	
1979	63.1	0.5	-		65.5	3.8	-		68.7	4.9	-		70.4	2.5	-		71.5	1.6	-		72.7	1.7	-	
1980	75.3	3.6	-		77.5	2.9	-		79.8	3.0	-		80.0	0.3	-		82.3	2.9	-		83.7	1.7	-	

[Continued]

Milwaukee-Racine, WI
Consumer Price Index - Urban Wage Earners
Base 1982-1984 = 100
All Items
[Continued]

For 1935-2001. Columns headed % show percentile change in the index from the previous period for which an index is available.

Year	Jan		Feb		Mar		Apr		May		Jun		Jul		Aug		Sep		Oct		Nov		Dec	
	Index	%	Index	%	Index	%	Index	%	Index	%	Index	%	Index	%	Index	%	Index	%	Index	%	Index	%	Index	%
1981	85.1	1.7	-	-	85.9	0.9	-	-	88.7	3.3	-	-	91.1	2.7	-	-	91.4	0.3	-	-	91.2	-0.2	-	-
1982	92.4	1.3	-	-	91.5	-1.0	-	-	92.6	1.2	-	-	93.7	1.2	-	-	95.8	2.2	-	-	96.0	0.2	-	-
1983	94.9	-1.1	-	-	97.3	2.5	-	-	98.7	1.4	-	-	101.6	2.9	-	-	102.9	1.3	-	-	102.9	0.0	-	-
1984	102.4	-0.5	-	-	104.9	2.4	-	-	105.8	0.9	-	-	106.9	1.0	-	-	108.8	1.8	-	-	107.2	-1.5	-	-
1985	107.4	0.2	-	-	108.5	1.0	-	-	109.5	0.9	-	-	109.6	0.1	-	-	109.9	0.3	-	-	110.5	0.5	-	-
1986	110.4	-0.1	-	-	108.6	-1.6	-	-	109.7	1.0	-	-	109.5	-0.2	-	-	110.0	0.5	-	-	109.3	-0.6	110.0	0.6
1987	-	-	-	-	-	-	-	-	-	-	112.6	2.4	-	-	-	-	-	-	-	-	-	-	115.6	2.7
1988	-	-	-	-	-	-	-	-	-	-	117.2	1.4	-	-	-	-	-	-	-	-	-	-	120.1	2.5
1989	-	-	-	-	-	-	-	-	-	-	123.1	2.5	-	-	-	-	-	-	-	-	-	-	124.0	0.7
1990	-	-	-	-	-	-	-	-	-	-	126.3	1.9	-	-	-	-	-	-	-	-	-	-	131.6	4.2
1991	-	-	-	-	-	-	-	-	-	-	133.6	1.5	-	-	-	-	-	-	-	-	-	-	136.3	2.0
1992	-	-	-	-	-	-	-	-	-	-	138.4	1.5	-	-	-	-	-	-	-	-	-	-	141.2	2.0
1993	-	-	-	-	-	-	-	-	-	-	143.3	1.5	-	-	-	-	-	-	-	-	-	-	146.4	2.2
1994	-	-	-	-	-	-	-	-	-	-	148.4	1.4	-	-	-	-	-	-	-	-	-	-	150.5	1.4
1995	-	-	-	-	-	-	-	-	-	-	153.0	1.7	-	-	-	-	-	-	-	-	-	-	153.9	0.6
1996	-	-	-	-	-	-	-	-	-	-	156.2	1.5	-	-	-	-	-	-	-	-	-	-	157.9	1.1
1997	-	-	-	-	-	-	-	-	-	-	159.8	1.2	-	-	-	-	-	-	-	-	-	-	159.8	0.0
1998	-	-	-	-	-	-	-	-	-	-	161.4	1.0	-	-	-	-	-	-	-	-	-	-	162.8	0.9
1999	-	-	-	-	-	-	-	-	-	-	164.6	1.1	-	-	-	-	-	-	-	-	-	-	166.5	1.2
2000	-	-	-	-	-	-	-	-	-	-	169.6	1.9	-	-	-	-	-	-	-	-	-	-	171.7	1.2
2001	-	-	-	-	-	-	-	-	-	-	174.0	1.3	-	-	-	-	-	-	-	-	-	-	-	-

Source: U.S. Department of Labor, Bureau of Labor Statistics, Division of Consumer Prices and Price Indexes. - indicates no data collected for period.

Milwaukee-Racine, WI
Consumer Price Index - All Urban Consumers
Base 1982-1984 = 100
Food and Beverages

For 1975-2001. Columns headed % show percentile change in the index from the previous period for which an index is available.

Year	Jan Index	%	Feb Index	%	Mar Index	%	Apr Index	%	May Index	%	Jun Index	%	Jul Index	%	Aug Index	%	Sep Index	%	Oct Index	%	Nov Index	%	Dec Index	%
1975	-	-	-	-	-	-	-	-	-	-	-	-	-	-	-	-	-	-	-	-	62.1	-	-	-
1976	-	-	62.6	0.8	-	-	-	-	63.0	0.6	-	-	-	-	64.1	1.7	-	-	-	-	63.9	-0.3	-	-
1977	-	-	65.6	2.7	-	-	-	-	66.9	2.0	-	-	-	-	67.7	1.2	-	-	-	-	67.3	-0.6	-	-
1978	69.5	3.3	-	-	70.9	2.0	-	-	72.7	2.5	-	-	74.3	2.2	-	-	75.2	1.2	-	-	75.5	0.4	-	-
1979	78.0	3.3	-	-	80.3	2.9	-	-	81.7	1.7	-	-	82.1	0.5	-	-	82.3	0.2	-	-	83.7	1.7	-	-
1980	84.0	0.4	-	-	84.9	1.1	-	-	85.5	0.7	-	-	87.3	2.1	-	-	89.2	2.2	-	-	90.4	1.3	-	-
1981	91.9	1.7	-	-	94.3	2.6	-	-	94.7	0.4	-	-	95.7	1.1	-	-	95.9	0.2	-	-	95.8	-0.1	-	-
1982	96.4	0.6	-	-	97.0	0.6	-	-	98.9	2.0	-	-	99.9	1.0	-	-	99.2	-0.7	-	-	98.6	-0.6	-	-
1983	99.2	0.6	-	-	99.8	0.6	-	-	100.0	0.2	-	-	99.7	-0.3	-	-	99.6	-0.1	-	-	98.9	-0.7	-	-
1984	100.7	1.8	-	-	100.8	0.1	-	-	101.6	0.8	-	-	103.0	1.4	-	-	102.2	-0.8	-	-	102.4	0.2	-	-
1985	104.8	2.3	-	-	105.8	1.0	-	-	106.0	0.2	-	-	106.0	0.0	-	-	105.6	-0.4	-	-	105.8	0.2	-	-
1986	105.6	-0.2	-	-	106.1	0.5	-	-	107.0	0.8	-	-	108.0	0.9	-	-	109.4	1.3	-	-	110.5	1.0	110.1	-0.4
1987	-	-	-	-	-	-	-	-	-	-	112.0	1.7	-	-	-	-	-	-	-	-	-	-	111.9	-0.1
1988	-	-	-	-	-	-	-	-	-	-	114.3	2.1	-	-	-	-	-	-	-	-	-	-	117.3	2.6
1989	-	-	-	-	-	-	-	-	-	-	120.1	2.4	-	-	-	-	-	-	-	-	-	-	122.0	1.6
1990	-	-	-	-	-	-	-	-	-	-	126.2	3.4	-	-	-	-	-	-	-	-	-	-	130.0	3.0
1991	-	-	-	-	-	-	-	-	-	-	134.8	3.7	-	-	-	-	-	-	-	-	-	-	135.7	0.7
1992	-	-	-	-	-	-	-	-	-	-	135.6	-0.1	-	-	-	-	-	-	-	-	-	-	135.3	-0.2
1993	-	-	-	-	-	-	-	-	-	-	137.0	1.3	-	-	-	-	-	-	-	-	-	-	139.2	1.6
1994	-	-	-	-	-	-	-	-	-	-	140.0	0.6	-	-	-	-	-	-	-	-	-	-	143.1	2.2
1995	-	-	-	-	-	-	-	-	-	-	145.7	1.8	-	-	-	-	-	-	-	-	-	-	147.4	1.2
1996	-	-	-	-	-	-	-	-	-	-	150.5	2.1	-	-	-	-	-	-	-	-	-	-	153.2	1.8
1997	-	-	-	-	-	-	-	-	-	-	154.4	0.8	-	-	-	-	-	-	-	-	-	-	154.6	0.1
1998	-	-	-	-	-	-	-	-	-	-	156.6	1.3	-	-	-	-	-	-	-	-	-	-	158.5	1.2
1999	-	-	-	-	-	-	-	-	-	-	162.7	2.6	-	-	-	-	-	-	-	-	-	-	164.8	1.3
2000	-	-	-	-	-	-	-	-	-	-	169.0	2.5	-	-	-	-	-	-	-	-	-	-	168.9	-0.1
2001	-	-	-	-	-	-	-	-	-	-	173.6	2.8	-	-	-	-	-	-	-	-	-	-	-	-

Source: U.S. Department of Labor, Bureau of Labor Statistics, Division of Consumer Prices and Price Indexes. - indicates no data collected for period.

Milwaukee-Racine, WI
Consumer Price Index - Urban Wage Earners
Base 1982-1984 = 100
Food and Beverages

For 1975-2001. Columns headed % show percentile change in the index from the previous period for which an index is available.

Year	Jan Index	%	Feb Index	%	Mar Index	%	Apr Index	%	May Index	%	Jun Index	%	Jul Index	%	Aug Index	%	Sep Index	%	Oct Index	%	Nov Index	%	Dec Index	%
1975	-		-		-		-		-		-		-		-		-		-		60.7		-	
1976	-		61.1	0.7	-		-		61.5	0.7	-		-		62.6	1.8	-		-		62.4	-0.3	-	
1977	-		64.1	2.7	-		-		65.3	1.9	-		-		66.1	1.2	-		-		65.7	-0.6	-	
1978	67.9	3.3	-		69.3	2.1	-		71.5	3.2	-		72.6	1.5	-		73.9	1.8	-		74.6	0.9	-	
1979	77.1	3.4	-		79.9	3.6	-		81.6	2.1	-		81.9	0.4	-		81.8	-0.1	-		82.6	1.0	-	
1980	83.8	1.5	-		85.4	1.9	-		86.3	1.1	-		87.9	1.9	-		90.0	2.4	-		91.2	1.3	-	
1981	93.1	2.1	-		94.5	1.5	-		94.3	-0.2	-		95.8	1.6	-		96.1	0.3	-		95.9	-0.2	-	
1982	96.5	0.6	-		96.8	0.3	-		99.0	2.3	-		100.1	1.1	-		99.3	-0.8	-		98.7	-0.6	-	
1983	99.2	0.5	-		99.9	0.7	-		100.1	0.2	-		99.8	-0.3	-		99.7	-0.1	-		98.9	-0.8	-	
1984	100.6	1.7	-		100.6	0.0	-		101.5	0.9	-		102.9	1.4	-		102.2	-0.7	-		102.2	0.0	-	
1985	104.7	2.4	-		105.8	1.1	-		106.0	0.2	-		106.0	0.0	-		105.5	-0.5	-		105.6	0.1	-	
1986	105.6	0.0	-		105.9	0.3	-		106.9	0.9	-		107.9	0.9	-		109.4	1.4	-		110.4	0.9	110.1	-0.3
1987	-		-		-		-		-		111.9	1.6	-		-		-		-		-		111.8	-0.1
1988	-		-		-		-		-		114.4	2.3	-		-		-		-		-		117.1	2.4
1989	-		-		-		-		-		119.9	2.4	-		-		-		-		-		121.9	1.7
1990	-		-		-		-		-		126.0	3.4	-		-		-		-		-		130.0	3.2
1991	-		-		-		-		-		134.7	3.6	-		-		-		-		-		135.5	0.6
1992	-		-		-		-		-		135.4	-0.1	-		-		-		-		-		135.3	-0.1
1993	-		-		-		-		-		136.8	1.1	-		-		-		-		-		139.1	1.7
1994	-		-		-		-		-		139.9	0.6	-		-		-		-		-		143.1	2.3
1995	-		-		-		-		-		145.7	1.8	-		-		-		-		-		147.5	1.2
1996	-		-		-		-		-		150.6	2.1	-		-		-		-		-		153.2	1.7
1997	-		-		-		-		-		154.4	0.8	-		-		-		-		-		154.6	0.1
1998	-		-		-		-		-		156.3	1.1	-		-		-		-		-		157.9	1.0
1999	-		-		-		-		-		162.0	2.6	-		-		-		-		-		164.4	1.5
2000	-		-		-		-		-		168.7	2.6	-		-		-		-		-		168.8	0.1
2001	-		-		-		-		-		173.6	2.8	-		-		-		-		-		-	

Source: U.S. Department of Labor, Bureau of Labor Statistics, Division of Consumer Prices and Price Indexes. - indicates no data collected for period.

Milwaukee-Racine, WI
Consumer Price Index - All Urban Consumers
Base 1982-1984 = 100
Housing

For 1975-2001. Columns headed % show percentile change in the index from the previous period for which an index is available.

Year	Jan Index	%	Feb Index	%	Mar Index	%	Apr Index	%	May Index	%	Jun Index	%	Jul Index	%	Aug Index	%	Sep Index	%	Oct Index	%	Nov Index	%	Dec Index	%
1975	-	-	-	-	-	-	-	-	-	-	-	-	-	-	-	-	-	-	-	-	45.7	-	-	-
1976	-	-	46.0	0.7	-	-	-	-	47.2	2.6	-	-	-	-	47.9	1.5	-	-	-	-	48.5	1.3	-	-
1977	-	-	49.5	2.1	-	-	-	-	50.8	2.6	-	-	-	-	50.8	0.0	-	-	-	-	52.4	3.1	-	-
1978	53.1	1.3	-	-	54.0	1.7	-	-	54.3	0.6	-	-	56.6	4.2	-	-	58.5	3.4	-	-	58.0	-0.9	-	-
1979	57.6	-0.7	-	-	60.6	5.2	-	-	64.9	7.1	-	-	67.0	3.2	-	-	68.1	1.6	-	-	69.2	1.6	-	-
1980	72.5	4.8	-	-	74.5	2.8	-	-	77.9	4.6	-	-	78.3	0.5	-	-	81.0	3.4	-	-	82.3	1.6	-	-
1981	83.0	0.9	-	-	83.0	0.0	-	-	88.1	6.1	-	-	92.2	4.7	-	-	91.3	-1.0	-	-	90.2	-1.2	-	-
1982	92.8	2.9	-	-	91.0	-1.9	-	-	92.4	1.5	-	-	92.8	0.4	-	-	96.9	4.4	-	-	97.5	0.6	-	-
1983	99.2	1.7	-	-	99.4	0.2	-	-	100.6	1.2	-	-	101.7	1.1	-	-	102.1	0.4	-	-	100.8	-1.3	-	-
1984	102.3	1.5	-	-	103.9	1.6	-	-	105.5	1.5	-	-	105.1	-0.4	-	-	106.5	1.3	-	-	106.1	-0.4	-	-
1985	106.5	0.4	-	-	107.2	0.7	-	-	108.8	1.5	-	-	108.7	-0.1	-	-	109.7	0.9	-	-	109.4	-0.3	-	-
1986	110.4	0.9	-	-	109.1	-1.2	-	-	110.2	1.0	-	-	109.8	-0.4	-	-	110.2	0.4	-	-	106.7	-3.2	109.2	2.3
1987	-	-	-	-	-	-	-	-	-	-	112.4	2.9	-	-	-	-	-	-	-	-	-	-	116.2	3.4
1988	-	-	-	-	-	-	-	-	-	-	117.3	0.9	-	-	-	-	-	-	-	-	-	-	119.5	1.9
1989	-	-	-	-	-	-	-	-	-	-	121.8	1.9	-	-	-	-	-	-	-	-	-	-	122.5	0.6
1990	-	-	-	-	-	-	-	-	-	-	123.6	0.9	-	-	-	-	-	-	-	-	-	-	128.5	4.0
1991	-	-	-	-	-	-	-	-	-	-	131.0	1.9	-	-	-	-	-	-	-	-	-	-	133.3	1.8
1992	-	-	-	-	-	-	-	-	-	-	136.4	2.3	-	-	-	-	-	-	-	-	-	-	139.1	2.0
1993	-	-	-	-	-	-	-	-	-	-	140.9	1.3	-	-	-	-	-	-	-	-	-	-	144.7	2.7
1994	-	-	-	-	-	-	-	-	-	-	147.5	1.9	-	-	-	-	-	-	-	-	-	-	148.4	0.6
1995	-	-	-	-	-	-	-	-	-	-	152.1	2.5	-	-	-	-	-	-	-	-	-	-	152.4	0.2
1996	-	-	-	-	-	-	-	-	-	-	154.1	1.1	-	-	-	-	-	-	-	-	-	-	154.6	0.3
1997	-	-	-	-	-	-	-	-	-	-	156.1	1.0	-	-	-	-	-	-	-	-	-	-	156.0	-0.1
1998	-	-	-	-	-	-	-	-	-	-	159.2	2.1	-	-	-	-	-	-	-	-	-	-	160.7	0.9
1999	-	-	-	-	-	-	-	-	-	-	162.6	1.2	-	-	-	-	-	-	-	-	-	-	162.6	0.0
2000	-	-	-	-	-	-	-	-	-	-	165.0	1.5	-	-	-	-	-	-	-	-	-	-	167.8	1.7
2001	-	-	-	-	-	-	-	-	-	-	170.9	1.8	-	-	-	-	-	-	-	-	-	-	-	-

Source: U.S. Department of Labor, Bureau of Labor Statistics, Division of Consumer Prices and Price Indexes. - indicates no data collected for period.

Milwaukee-Racine, WI
Consumer Price Index - Urban Wage Earners
Base 1982-1984 = 100
Housing

For 1975-2001. Columns headed % show percentile change in the index from the previous period for which an index is available.

Year	Jan Index	%	Feb Index	%	Mar Index	%	Apr Index	%	May Index	%	Jun Index	%	Jul Index	%	Aug Index	%	Sep Index	%	Oct Index	%	Nov Index	%	Dec Index	%
1975	-	-	-	-	-	-	-	-	-	-	-	-	-	-	-	-	-	-	-	-	-	-	-	-
1976	-	-	42.5	1.0	-	-	-	-	43.5	2.4	-	-	-	-	44.2	1.6	-	-	-	-	42.1	-	-	-
1977	-	-	45.7	2.2	-	-	-	-	46.9	2.6	-	-	-	-	46.9	0.0	-	-	-	-	44.7	1.1	-	-
1978	49.2	1.7	-	-	49.9	1.4	-	-	50.1	0.4	-	-	52.4	4.6	-	-	54.5	4.0	-	-	48.4	3.2	-	-
1979	53.3	-1.3	-	-	56.5	6.0	-	-	61.1	8.1	-	-	63.1	3.3	-	-	64.1	1.6	-	-	54.0	-0.9	-	-
1980	69.2	5.6	-	-	71.2	2.9	-	-	74.2	4.2	-	-	74.5	0.4	-	-	77.4	3.9	-	-	65.5	2.2	-	-
1981	79.3	0.1	-	-	78.9	-0.5	-	-	84.4	7.0	-	-	88.8	5.2	-	-	88.1	-0.8	-	-	79.2	2.3	-	-
1982	88.9	2.9	-	-	86.6	-2.6	-	-	87.9	1.5	-	-	88.1	0.2	-	-	92.6	5.1	-	-	86.4	-1.9	-	-
1983	90.9	-2.5	-	-	96.2	5.8	-	-	97.7	1.6	-	-	104.1	6.6	-	-	105.0	0.9	-	-	93.2	0.6	-	-
1984	104.0	-0.8	-	-	108.6	4.4	-	-	109.4	0.7	-	-	111.0	1.5	-	-	114.6	3.2	-	-	104.8	-0.2	-	-
1985	111.2	0.4	-	-	112.0	0.7	-	-	113.6	1.4	-	-	113.6	0.0	-	-	114.5	0.8	-	-	110.8	-3.3	-	-
1986	115.2	1.0	-	-	113.7	-1.3	-	-	115.0	1.1	-	-	114.5	-0.4	-	-	114.8	0.3	-	-	114.1	-0.3	-	-
1987	-	-	-	-	-	-	-	-	-	-	117.1	2.9	-	-	-	-	-	-	-	-	111.0	-3.3	113.8	2.5
1988	-	-	-	-	-	-	-	-	-	-	122.1	1.0	-	-	-	-	-	-	-	-	-	-	120.9	3.2
1989	-	-	-	-	-	-	-	-	-	-	126.6	1.8	-	-	-	-	-	-	-	-	-	-	124.4	1.9
1990	-	-	-	-	-	-	-	-	-	-	128.4	0.9	-	-	-	-	-	-	-	-	-	-	127.3	0.6
1991	-	-	-	-	-	-	-	-	-	-	136.1	2.0	-	-	-	-	-	-	-	-	-	-	133.4	3.9
1992	-	-	-	-	-	-	-	-	-	-	141.5	2.2	-	-	-	-	-	-	-	-	-	-	138.4	1.7
1993	-	-	-	-	-	-	-	-	-	-	146.3	1.3	-	-	-	-	-	-	-	-	-	-	144.4	2.0
1994	-	-	-	-	-	-	-	-	-	-	153.1	1.9	-	-	-	-	-	-	-	-	-	-	150.2	2.7
1995	-	-	-	-	-	-	-	-	-	-	157.7	2.4	-	-	-	-	-	-	-	-	-	-	154.0	0.6
1996	-	-	-	-	-	-	-	-	-	-	159.8	1.1	-	-	-	-	-	-	-	-	-	-	158.1	0.3
1997	-	-	-	-	-	-	-	-	-	-	161.9	1.0	-	-	-	-	-	-	-	-	-	-	160.3	0.3
1998	-	-	-	-	-	-	-	-	-	-	164.8	1.8	-	-	-	-	-	-	-	-	-	-	161.9	0.0
1999	-	-	-	-	-	-	-	-	-	-	168.2	1.0	-	-	-	-	-	-	-	-	-	-	166.5	1.0
2000	-	-	-	-	-	-	-	-	-	-	170.4	1.2	-	-	-	-	-	-	-	-	-	-	168.3	0.1
2001	-	-	-	-	-	-	-	-	-	-	176.7	1.8	-	-	-	-	-	-	-	-	-	-	-	-

Source: U.S. Department of Labor, Bureau of Labor Statistics, Division of Consumer Prices and Price Indexes. - indicates no data collected for period.

Milwaukee-Racine, WI
Consumer Price Index - All Urban Consumers
Base 1982-1984 = 100
Apparel

For 1952-2001. Columns headed % show percentile change in the index from the previous period for which an index is available.

Year	Jan Index	%	Feb Index	%	Mar Index	%	Apr Index	%	May Index	%	Jun Index	%	Jul Index	%	Aug Index	%	Sep Index	%	Oct Index	%	Nov Index	%	Dec Index	%
1952	-	-	-	-	-	-	-	-	-	-	-	-	-	-	39.7	0.5	-	-	-	-	39.4	-	-	-
1953	-	-	39.3	-0.3	-	-	-	-	39.5	0.5	-	-	-	-	39.7	0.5	-	-	-	-	39.7	0.0	-	-
1954	-	-	39.9	0.5	-	-	-	-	39.7	-0.5	-	-	-	-	39.4	-0.8	-	-	-	-	39.2	-0.5	-	-
1955	-	-	39.1	-0.3	-	-	-	-	39.2	0.3	-	-	-	-	39.3	0.3	-	-	-	-	39.7	1.0	-	-
1956	-	-	39.9	0.5	-	-	-	-	40.1	0.5	-	-	-	-	40.5	1.0	-	-	-	-	40.6	0.2	-	-
1957	-	-	40.7	0.2	-	-	-	-	40.9	0.5	-	-	-	-	41.1	0.5	-	-	-	-	41.0	-0.2	-	-
1958	-	-	41.1	0.2	-	-	-	-	40.9	-0.5	-	-	-	-	41.0	0.2	-	-	-	-	40.9	-0.2	-	-
1959	-	-	40.7	-0.5	-	-	-	-	41.3	1.5	-	-	-	-	41.4	0.2	-	-	-	-	41.6	0.5	-	-
1960	-	-	41.7	0.2	-	-	-	-	41.9	0.5	-	-	-	-	41.8	-0.2	-	-	-	-	41.8	0.0	-	-
1961	-	-	42.1	0.7	-	-	-	-	42.1	0.0	-	-	-	-	41.7	-1.0	-	-	-	-	42.2	1.2	-	-
1962	-	-	42.1	-0.2	-	-	-	-	42.3	0.5	-	-	-	-	42.2	-0.2	-	-	-	-	42.1	-0.2	-	-
1963	-	-	41.9	-0.5	-	-	-	-	42.0	0.2	-	-	-	-	42.4	1.0	-	-	-	-	42.4	0.0	-	-
1964	-	-	42.3	-0.2	-	-	-	-	42.8	1.2	-	-	-	-	43.1	0.7	-	-	-	-	43.3	0.5	-	-
1965	-	-	43.2	-0.2	-	-	-	-	43.8	1.4	-	-	-	-	43.6	-0.5	-	-	-	-	43.3	-0.7	-	-
1966	-	-	43.6	0.7	-	-	-	-	43.9	0.7	-	-	-	-	44.3	0.9	-	-	-	-	44.8	1.1	-	-
1967	-	-	45.3	1.1	-	-	-	-	46.0	1.5	-	-	-	-	45.7	-0.7	-	-	-	-	46.4	1.5	-	-
1968	-	-	46.5	0.2	-	-	-	-	47.8	2.8	-	-	-	-	48.0	0.4	-	-	-	-	48.7	1.5	-	-
1969	-	-	49.6	1.8	-	-	-	-	51.5	3.8	-	-	-	-	51.5	0.0	-	-	-	-	54.4	5.6	-	-
1970	-	-	54.6	0.4	-	-	-	-	55.5	1.6	-	-	-	-	56.2	1.3	-	-	-	-	57.5	2.3	-	-
1971	-	-	56.7	-1.4	-	-	-	-	56.7	0.0	-	-	-	-	55.8	-1.6	-	-	-	-	58.3	4.5	-	-
1972	-	-	57.2	-1.9	-	-	-	-	58.3	1.9	-	-	-	-	57.2	-1.9	-	-	-	-	59.4	3.8	-	-
1973	-	-	59.8	0.7	-	-	-	-	60.6	1.3	-	-	-	-	60.7	0.2	-	-	-	-	62.7	3.3	-	-
1974	-	-	61.6	-1.8	-	-	-	-	64.2	4.2	-	-	-	-	65.4	1.9	-	-	-	-	68.2	4.3	-	-
1975	-	-	67.7	-0.7	-	-	-	-	69.8	3.1	-	-	-	-	69.6	-0.3	-	-	-	-	72.8	4.6	-	-
1976	-	-	71.7	-1.5	-	-	-	-	74.5	3.9	-	-	-	-	74.8	0.4	-	-	-	-	75.9	1.5	-	-
1977	-	-	75.2	-0.9	-	-	-	-	77.8	3.5	-	-	-	-	77.0	-1.0	-	-	-	-	80.1	4.0	-	-
1978	75.2	-6.1	-	-	77.6	3.2	-	-	80.0	3.1	-	-	76.7	-4.1	-	-	80.1	4.4	-	-	79.6	-0.6	-	-
1979	77.2	-3.0	-	-	81.5	5.6	-	-	80.5	-1.2	-	-	81.4	1.1	-	-	85.4	4.9	-	-	85.7	0.4	-	-
1980	83.5	-2.6	-	-	89.0	6.6	-	-	86.6	-2.7	-	-	83.7	-3.3	-	-	91.3	9.1	-	-	89.3	-2.2	-	-
1981	89.1	-0.2	-	-	91.8	3.0	-	-	89.4	-2.6	-	-	89.2	-0.2	-	-	97.0	8.7	-	-	97.2	0.2	-	-
1982	89.2	-8.2	-	-	94.8	6.3	-	-	96.4	1.7	-	-	96.9	0.5	-	-	102.2	5.5	-	-	100.1	-2.1	-	-
1983	95.6	-4.5	-	-	100.5	5.1	-	-	101.5	1.0	-	-	97.3	-4.1	-	-	108.2	11.2	-	-	107.4	-0.7	-	-
1984	98.8	-8.0	-	-	101.3	2.5	-	-	101.3	0.0	-	-	100.5	-0.8	-	-	102.4	1.9	-	-	103.5	1.1	-	-
1985	98.6	-4.7	-	-	103.6	5.1	-	-	102.5	-1.1	-	-	102.1	-0.4	-	-	106.0	3.8	-	-	106.5	0.5	-	-
1986	102.9	-3.4	-	-	107.3	4.3	-	-	106.3	-0.9	-	-	104.6	-1.6	-	-	105.3	0.7	-	-	105.0	-0.3	103.0	-1.9
1987	-	-	-	-	-	-	-	-	-	-	107.8	4.7	-	-	-	-	-	-	-	-	-	-	115.0	6.7
1988	-	-	-	-	-	-	-	-	-	-	118.1	2.7	-	-	-	-	-	-	-	-	-	-	123.9	4.9
1989	-	-	-	-	-	-	-	-	-	-	123.4	-0.4	-	-	-	-	-	-	-	-	-	-	119.1	-3.5
1990	-	-	-	-	-	-	-	-	-	-	120.7	1.3	-	-	-	-	-	-	-	-	-	-	131.4	8.9
1991	-	-	-	-	-	-	-	-	-	-	124.1	-5.6	-	-	-	-	-	-	-	-	-	-	126.7	2.1
1992	-	-	-	-	-	-	-	-	-	-	123.6	-2.4	-	-	-	-	-	-	-	-	-	-	124.7	0.9
1993	-	-	-	-	-	-	-	-	-	-	120.5	-3.4	-	-	-	-	-	-	-	-	-	-	125.8	4.4
1994	-	-	-	-	-	-	-	-	-	-	121.3	-3.6	-	-	-	-	-	-	-	-	-	-	123.7	2.0
1995	-	-	-	-	-	-	-	-	-	-	119.6	-3.3	-	-	-	-	-	-	-	-	-	-	123.2	3.0
1996	-	-	-	-	-	-	-	-	-	-	122.8	-0.3	-	-	-	-	-	-	-	-	-	-	123.6	0.7
1997	-	-	-	-	-	-	-	-	-	-	126.4	2.3	-	-	-	-	-	-	-	-	-	-	119.4	-5.5

[Continued]

Milwaukee-Racine, WI
Consumer Price Index - All Urban Consumers
Base 1982-1984 = 100
Apparel
[Continued]

For 1952-2001. Columns headed % show percentile change in the index from the previous period for which an index is available.

Year	Jan Index	%	Feb Index	%	Mar Index	%	Apr Index	%	May Index	%	Jun Index	%	Jul Index	%	Aug Index	%	Sep Index	%	Oct Index	%	Nov Index	%	Dec Index	%
1998	-	-	-	-	-	-	-	-	-	-	118.5	-0.8	-	-	-	-	-	-	-	-	-	-	118.9	0.3
1999	-	-	-	-	-	-	-	-	-	-	112.8	-5.1	-	-	-	-	-	-	-	-	-	-	120.7	7.0
2000	-	-	-	-	-	-	-	-	-	-	117.4	-2.7	-	-	-	-	-	-	-	-	-	-	122.0	3.9
2001	-	-	-	-	-	-	-	-	-	-	117.3	-3.9	-	-	-	-	-	-	-	-	-	-	-	-

Source: U.S. Department of Labor, Bureau of Labor Statistics, Division of Consumer Prices and Price Indexes. - indicates no data collected for period.

Milwaukee-Racine, WI
Consumer Price Index - Urban Wage Earners
Base 1982-1984 = 100
Apparel

For 1952-2001. Columns headed % show percentile change in the index from the previous period for which an index is available.

Year	Jan Index	%	Feb Index	%	Mar Index	%	Apr Index	%	May Index	%	Jun Index	%	Jul Index	%	Aug Index	%	Sep Index	%	Oct Index	%	Nov Index	%	Dec Index	%
1952	-	-	-	-	-	-	-	-	-	-	-	-	-	-	-	-	-	-	-	-	40.3	-	-	-
1953	-	-	40.2	-0.2	-	-	-	-	40.4	0.5	-	-	-	-	40.6	0.5	-	-	-	-	40.6	0.0	-	-
1954	-	-	40.8	0.5	-	-	-	-	40.6	-0.5	-	-	-	-	40.3	-0.7	-	-	-	-	40.1	-0.5	-	-
1955	-	-	40.0	-0.2	-	-	-	-	40.1	0.2	-	-	-	-	40.1	0.0	-	-	-	-	40.6	1.2	-	-
1956	-	-	40.8	0.5	-	-	-	-	41.0	0.5	-	-	-	-	41.4	1.0	-	-	-	-	41.5	0.2	-	-
1957	-	-	41.6	0.2	-	-	-	-	41.8	0.5	-	-	-	-	42.0	0.5	-	-	-	-	41.9	-0.2	-	-
1958	-	-	42.0	0.2	-	-	-	-	41.8	-0.5	-	-	-	-	41.9	0.2	-	-	-	-	41.8	-0.2	-	-
1959	-	-	41.6	-0.5	-	-	-	-	42.3	1.7	-	-	-	-	42.3	0.0	-	-	-	-	42.5	0.5	-	-
1960	-	-	42.6	0.2	-	-	-	-	42.8	0.5	-	-	-	-	42.7	-0.2	-	-	-	-	42.7	0.0	-	-
1961	-	-	43.0	0.7	-	-	-	-	43.0	0.0	-	-	-	-	42.7	-0.7	-	-	-	-	43.1	0.9	-	-
1962	-	-	43.1	0.0	-	-	-	-	43.2	0.2	-	-	-	-	43.1	-0.2	-	-	-	-	43.0	-0.2	-	-
1963	-	-	42.8	-0.5	-	-	-	-	42.9	0.2	-	-	-	-	43.4	1.2	-	-	-	-	43.4	0.0	-	-
1964	-	-	43.3	-0.2	-	-	-	-	43.8	1.2	-	-	-	-	44.0	0.5	-	-	-	-	44.2	0.5	-	-
1965	-	-	44.2	0.0	-	-	-	-	44.8	1.4	-	-	-	-	44.6	-0.4	-	-	-	-	44.3	-0.7	-	-
1966	-	-	44.6	0.7	-	-	-	-	44.9	0.7	-	-	-	-	45.3	0.9	-	-	-	-	45.8	1.1	-	-
1967	-	-	46.3	1.1	-	-	-	-	47.0	1.5	-	-	-	-	46.7	-0.6	-	-	-	-	47.4	1.5	-	-
1968	-	-	47.5	0.2	-	-	-	-	48.9	2.9	-	-	-	-	49.0	0.2	-	-	-	-	49.8	1.6	-	-
1969	-	-	50.7	1.8	-	-	-	-	52.6	3.7	-	-	-	-	52.7	0.2	-	-	-	-	55.6	5.5	-	-
1970	-	-	55.8	0.4	-	-	-	-	56.7	1.6	-	-	-	-	57.5	1.4	-	-	-	-	58.8	2.3	-	-
1971	-	-	58.0	-1.4	-	-	-	-	58.0	0.0	-	-	-	-	57.1	-1.6	-	-	-	-	59.6	4.4	-	-
1972	-	-	58.5	-1.8	-	-	-	-	59.6	1.9	-	-	-	-	58.5	-1.8	-	-	-	-	60.8	3.9	-	-
1973	-	-	61.1	0.5	-	-	-	-	62.0	1.5	-	-	-	-	62.1	0.2	-	-	-	-	64.1	3.2	-	-
1974	-	-	63.0	-1.7	-	-	-	-	65.6	4.1	-	-	-	-	66.8	1.8	-	-	-	-	69.7	4.3	-	-
1975	-	-	69.2	-0.7	-	-	-	-	71.3	3.0	-	-	-	-	71.2	-0.1	-	-	-	-	74.4	4.5	-	-
1976	-	-	73.4	-1.3	-	-	-	-	76.2	3.8	-	-	-	-	76.5	0.4	-	-	-	-	77.6	1.4	-	-
1977	-	-	76.9	-0.9	-	-	-	-	79.6	3.5	-	-	-	-	78.7	-1.1	-	-	-	-	81.9	4.1	-	-
1978	76.3	-6.8	-	-	78.0	2.2	-	-	80.1	2.7	-	-	78.3	-2.2	-	-	83.6	6.8	-	-	83.7	0.1	-	-
1979	80.2	-4.2	-	-	83.4	4.0	-	-	82.4	-1.2	-	-	82.8	0.5	-	-	88.0	6.3	-	-	89.0	1.1	-	-
1980	87.1	-2.1	-	-	90.2	3.6	-	-	89.6	-0.7	-	-	87.1	-2.8	-	-	93.1	6.9	-	-	90.3	-3.0	-	-
1981	93.4	3.4	-	-	94.9	1.6	-	-	93.4	-1.6	-	-	94.7	1.4	-	-	97.2	2.6	-	-	97.6	0.4	-	-
1982	90.3	-7.5	-	-	96.4	6.8	-	-	97.4	1.0	-	-	97.9	0.5	-	-	102.9	5.1	-	-	100.4	-2.4	-	-
1983	96.3	-4.1	-	-	101.3	5.2	-	-	101.1	-0.2	-	-	96.9	-4.2	-	-	107.2	10.6	-	-	106.4	-0.7	-	-
1984	98.8	-7.1	-	-	101.0	2.2	-	-	101.0	0.0	-	-	99.2	-1.8	-	-	101.4	2.2	-	-	102.2	0.8	-	-
1985	98.8	-3.3	-	-	103.1	4.4	-	-	102.0	-1.1	-	-	101.4	-0.6	-	-	104.8	3.4	-	-	106.7	1.8	-	-
1986	103.2	-3.3	-	-	106.7	3.4	-	-	107.0	0.3	-	-	105.6	-1.3	-	-	105.6	0.0	-	-	105.8	0.2	104.1	-1.6
1987	-	-	-	-	-	-	-	-	-	-	109.7	5.4	-	-	-	-	-	-	-	-	-	-	116.3	6.0
1988	-	-	-	-	-	-	-	-	-	-	120.5	3.6	-	-	-	-	-	-	-	-	-	-	125.9	4.5
1989	-	-	-	-	-	-	-	-	-	-	125.9	0.0	-	-	-	-	-	-	-	-	-	-	121.1	-3.8
1990	-	-	-	-	-	-	-	-	-	-	120.9	-0.2	-	-	-	-	-	-	-	-	-	-	133.8	10.7
1991	-	-	-	-	-	-	-	-	-	-	126.0	-5.8	-	-	-	-	-	-	-	-	-	-	130.3	3.4
1992	-	-	-	-	-	-	-	-	-	-	125.1	-4.0	-	-	-	-	-	-	-	-	-	-	127.4	1.8
1993	-	-	-	-	-	-	-	-	-	-	123.8	-2.8	-	-	-	-	-	-	-	-	-	-	128.0	3.4
1994	-	-	-	-	-	-	-	-	-	-	123.4	-3.6	-	-	-	-	-	-	-	-	-	-	126.6	2.6
1995	-	-	-	-	-	-	-	-	-	-	122.8	-3.0	-	-	-	-	-	-	-	-	-	-	127.9	4.2
1996	-	-	-	-	-	-	-	-	-	-	127.7	-0.2	-	-	-	-	-	-	-	-	-	-	127.9	0.2
1997	-	-	-	-	-	-	-	-	-	-	131.8	3.0	-	-	-	-	-	-	-	-	-	-	124.3	-5.7

[Continued]

Milwaukee-Racine, WI
Consumer Price Index - Urban Wage Earners
Base 1982-1984 = 100
Apparel
[Continued]

For 1952-2001. Columns headed % show percentile change in the index from the previous period for which an index is available.

Year	Jan Index	%	Feb Index	%	Mar Index	%	Apr Index	%	May Index	%	Jun Index	%	Jul Index	%	Aug Index	%	Sep Index	%	Oct Index	%	Nov Index	%	Dec Index	%
1998	-	-	-	-	-	-	-	-	-	-	125.9	1.3	-	-	-	-	-	-	-	-	-	-	125.8	-0.1
1999	-	-	-	-	-	-	-	-	-	-	119.4	-5.1	-	-	-	-	-	-	-	-	-	-	126.7	6.1
2000	-	-	-	-	-	-	-	-	-	-	123.4	-2.6	-	-	-	-	-	-	-	-	-	-	127.9	3.6
2001	-	-	-	-	-	-	-	-	-	-	122.8	-4.0	-	-	-	-	-	-	-	-	-	-	-	-

Source: U.S. Department of Labor, Bureau of Labor Statistics, Division of Consumer Prices and Price Indexes. - indicates no data collected for period.

Milwaukee-Racine, WI

Consumer Price Index - All Urban Consumers
Base 1982-1984 = 100

Transportation

For 1946-2001. Columns headed % show percentile change in the index from the previous period for which an index is available.

Year	Jan Index	%	Feb Index	%	Mar Index	%	Apr Index	%	May Index	%	Jun Index	%	Jul Index	%	Aug Index	%	Sep Index	%	Oct Index	%	Nov Index	%	Dec Index	%
1946	-	-	-	-	-	-	-	-	-	-	-	-	-	-	-	-	-	-	-	-	19.9	-	-	-
1947	-	-	-	-	20.0	0.5	-	-	-	-	20.0	0.0	-	-	20.2	1.0	-	-	-	-	20.8	3.0	-	-
1948	-	-	21.2	1.9	-	-	-	-	21.3	0.5	-	-	-	-	22.6	6.1	-	-	-	-	22.7	0.4	-	-
1949	-	-	23.0	1.3	-	-	-	-	23.1	0.4	-	-	-	-	22.9	-0.9	-	-	-	-	22.3	-2.6	-	-
1950	-	-	22.0	-1.3	-	-	-	-	23.2	5.5	-	-	-	-	23.8	2.6	-	-	-	-	23.8	0.0	-	-
1951	-	-	23.9	0.4	-	-	-	-	24.8	3.8	-	-	-	-	24.8	0.0	-	-	-	-	25.6	3.2	-	-
1952	-	-	26.1	2.0	-	-	-	-	26.2	0.4	-	-	-	-	26.2	0.0	-	-	-	-	27.0	3.1	-	-
1953	-	-	27.0	0.0	-	-	-	-	27.0	0.0	-	-	-	-	27.3	1.1	-	-	-	-	27.1	-0.7	-	-
1954	-	-	26.8	-1.1	-	-	-	-	26.8	0.0	-	-	-	-	26.4	-1.5	-	-	-	-	27.2	3.0	-	-
1955	-	-	26.5	-2.6	-	-	-	-	26.4	-0.4	-	-	-	-	26.3	-0.4	-	-	-	-	26.9	2.3	-	-
1956	-	-	26.7	-0.7	-	-	-	-	26.6	-0.4	-	-	-	-	27.3	2.6	-	-	-	-	28.1	2.9	-	-
1957	-	-	28.2	0.4	-	-	-	-	28.2	0.0	-	-	-	-	28.3	0.4	-	-	-	-	28.8	1.8	-	-
1958	-	-	28.5	-1.0	-	-	-	-	28.4	-0.4	-	-	-	-	29.2	2.8	-	-	-	-	29.3	0.3	-	-
1959	-	-	29.4	0.3	-	-	-	-	29.5	0.3	-	-	-	-	29.9	1.4	-	-	-	-	30.5	2.0	-	-
1960	-	-	29.2	-4.3	-	-	-	-	29.5	1.0	-	-	-	-	29.8	1.0	-	-	-	-	29.5	-1.0	-	-
1961	-	-	29.9	1.4	-	-	-	-	29.0	-3.0	-	-	-	-	30.1	3.8	-	-	-	-	29.9	-0.7	-	-
1962	-	-	30.5	2.0	-	-	-	-	31.0	1.6	-	-	-	-	30.3	-2.3	-	-	-	-	31.2	3.0	-	-
1963	-	-	30.5	-2.2	-	-	-	-	31.1	2.0	-	-	-	-	30.8	-1.0	-	-	-	-	31.5	2.3	-	-
1964	-	-	30.9	-1.9	-	-	-	-	30.5	-1.3	-	-	-	-	31.3	2.6	-	-	-	-	31.7	1.3	-	-
1965	-	-	32.1	1.3	-	-	-	-	32.6	1.6	-	-	-	-	32.1	-1.5	-	-	-	-	32.1	0.0	-	-
1966	-	-	32.3	0.6	-	-	-	-	32.0	-0.9	-	-	-	-	32.8	2.5	-	-	-	-	32.7	-0.3	-	-
1967	-	-	32.5	-0.6	-	-	-	-	32.7	0.6	-	-	-	-	32.8	0.3	-	-	-	-	33.7	2.7	-	-
1968	-	-	33.6	-0.3	-	-	-	-	32.8	-2.4	-	-	-	-	32.9	0.3	-	-	-	-	33.6	2.1	-	-
1969	-	-	35.0	4.2	-	-	-	-	34.8	-0.6	-	-	-	-	34.5	-0.9	-	-	-	-	35.8	3.8	-	-
1970	-	-	34.9	-2.5	-	-	-	-	36.6	4.9	-	-	-	-	36.1	-1.4	-	-	-	-	37.8	4.7	-	-
1971	-	-	38.9	2.9	-	-	-	-	37.8	-2.8	-	-	-	-	39.3	4.0	-	-	-	-	38.1	-3.1	-	-
1972	-	-	37.9	-0.5	-	-	-	-	38.6	1.8	-	-	-	-	40.3	4.4	-	-	-	-	40.0	-0.7	-	-
1973	-	-	40.2	0.5	-	-	-	-	41.6	3.5	-	-	-	-	41.5	-0.2	-	-	-	-	42.2	1.7	-	-
1974	-	-	43.4	2.8	-	-	-	-	45.7	5.3	-	-	-	-	47.4	3.7	-	-	-	-	47.8	0.8	-	-
1975	-	-	48.3	1.0	-	-	-	-	49.2	1.9	-	-	-	-	50.9	3.5	-	-	-	-	51.1	0.4	-	-
1976	-	-	51.1	0.0	-	-	-	-	52.4	2.5	-	-	-	-	55.0	5.0	-	-	-	-	55.4	0.7	-	-
1977	-	-	55.7	0.5	-	-	-	-	57.3	2.9	-	-	-	-	57.5	0.3	-	-	-	-	57.7	0.3	-	-
1978	57.9	0.3	-	-	58.2	0.5	-	-	59.1	1.5	-	-	61.1	3.4	-	-	61.7	1.0	-	-	63.5	2.9	-	-
1979	64.4	1.4	-	-	65.5	1.7	-	-	69.1	5.5	-	-	72.5	4.9	-	-	73.3	1.1	-	-	75.0	2.3	-	-
1980	77.4	3.2	-	-	80.7	4.3	-	-	84.5	4.7	-	-	84.0	-0.6	-	-	83.9	-0.1	-	-	86.1	2.6	-	-
1981	88.9	3.3	-	-	90.6	1.9	-	-	92.5	2.1	-	-	93.7	1.3	-	-	95.0	1.4	-	-	98.1	3.3	-	-
1982	98.2	0.1	-	-	97.2	-1.0	-	-	96.8	-0.4	-	-	100.6	3.9	-	-	99.1	-1.5	-	-	98.9	-0.2	-	-
1983	98.1	-0.8	-	-	95.9	-2.2	-	-	98.3	2.5	-	-	99.0	0.7	-	-	100.8	1.8	-	-	101.3	0.5	-	-
1984	100.8	-0.5	-	-	101.3	0.5	-	-	102.8	1.5	-	-	102.7	-0.1	-	-	103.3	0.6	-	-	103.9	0.6	-	-
1985	102.1	-1.7	-	-	103.0	0.9	-	-	104.7	1.7	-	-	104.6	-0.1	-	-	103.4	-1.1	-	-	105.1	1.6	-	-
1986	104.2	-0.9	-	-	97.5	-6.4	-	-	98.8	1.3	-	-	97.7	-1.1	-	-	97.1	-0.6	-	-	98.7	1.6	98.2	-0.5
1987	-	-	-	-	-	-	-	-	-	-	100.1	1.9	-	-	-	-	-	-	-	-	-	-	103.0	2.9
1988	-	-	-	-	-	-	-	-	-	-	101.7	-1.3	-	-	-	-	-	-	-	-	-	-	104.4	2.7
1989	-	-	-	-	-	-	-	-	-	-	110.0	5.4	-	-	-	-	-	-	-	-	-	-	110.1	0.1
1990	-	-	-	-	-	-	-	-	-	-	112.9	2.5	-	-	-	-	-	-	-	-	-	-	117.4	4.0
1991	-	-	-	-	-	-	-	-	-	-	117.7	0.3	-	-	-	-	-	-	-	-	-	-	120.6	2.5

[Continued]

Milwaukee-Racine, WI
Consumer Price Index - All Urban Consumers
Base 1982-1984 = 100
Transportation
[Continued]

For 1946-2001. Columns headed % show percentile change in the index from the previous period for which an index is available.

Year	Jan Index	%	Feb Index	%	Mar Index	%	Apr Index	%	May Index	%	Jun Index	%	Jul Index	%	Aug Index	%	Sep Index	%	Oct Index	%	Nov Index	%	Dec Index	%
1992	-		-		-		-		-	-	122.1	1.2	-		-		-		-		-		124.1	1.6
1993	-		-		-		-		-	-	127.3	2.6	-		-		-		-		-		129.7	1.9
1994	-		-		-		-		-	-	132.6	2.2	-		-		-		-		-		135.8	2.4
1995	-		-		-		-		-	-	137.8	1.5	-		-		-		-		-		137.2	-0.4
1996	-		-		-		-		-	-	139.9	2.0	-		-		-		-		-		143.2	2.4
1997	-		-		-		-		-	-	144.5	0.9	-		-		-		-		-		142.8	-1.2
1998	-		-		-		-		-	-	140.8	-1.4	-		-		-		-		-		140.7	-0.1
1999	-		-		-		-		-	-	141.1	0.3	-		-		-		-		-		143.9	2.0
2000	-		-		-		-		-	-	149.3	3.8	-		-		-		-		-		149.6	0.2
2001	-		-	-	-		-		-	-	150.7	0.7	-		-		-		-		-		-	-

Source: U.S. Department of Labor, Bureau of Labor Statistics, Division of Consumer Prices and Price Indexes. - indicates no data collected for period.

Milwaukee-Racine, WI
Consumer Price Index - Urban Wage Earners
Base 1982-1984 = 100
Transportation

For 1946-2001. Columns headed % show percentile change in the index from the previous period for which an index is available.

Year	Jan Index	%	Feb Index	%	Mar Index	%	Apr Index	%	May Index	%	Jun Index	%	Jul Index	%	Aug Index	%	Sep Index	%	Oct Index	%	Nov Index	%	Dec Index	%
1946	-	-	-	-	-	-	-	-	-	-	-	-	-	-	-	-	-	-	-	-	20.1	-	-	-
1947	-	-	-	-	20.2	0.5	-	-	-	-	20.2	0.0	-	-	20.4	1.0	-	-	-	-	21.1	3.4	-	-
1948	-	-	21.5	1.9	-	-	-	-	21.5	0.0	-	-	-	-	22.8	6.0	-	-	-	-	22.9	0.4	-	-
1949	-	-	23.2	1.3	-	-	-	-	23.3	0.4	-	-	-	-	23.2	-0.4	-	-	-	-	22.6	-2.6	-	-
1950	-	-	22.2	-1.8	-	-	-	-	23.4	5.4	-	-	-	-	24.1	3.0	-	-	-	-	24.1	0.0	-	-
1951	-	-	24.1	0.0	-	-	-	-	25.0	3.7	-	-	-	-	25.1	0.4	-	-	-	-	25.9	3.2	-	-
1952	-	-	26.4	1.9	-	-	-	-	26.5	0.4	-	-	-	-	26.5	0.0	-	-	-	-	27.3	3.0	-	-
1953	-	-	27.3	0.0	-	-	-	-	27.3	0.0	-	-	-	-	27.6	1.1	-	-	-	-	27.4	-0.7	-	-
1954	-	-	27.1	-1.1	-	-	-	-	27.1	0.0	-	-	-	-	26.7	-1.5	-	-	-	-	27.5	3.0	-	-
1955	-	-	26.8	-2.5	-	-	-	-	26.7	-0.4	-	-	-	-	26.6	-0.4	-	-	-	-	27.2	2.3	-	-
1956	-	-	27.0	-0.7	-	-	-	-	26.9	-0.4	-	-	-	-	27.6	2.6	-	-	-	-	28.4	2.9	-	-
1957	-	-	28.6	0.7	-	-	-	-	28.6	0.0	-	-	-	-	28.7	0.3	-	-	-	-	29.1	1.4	-	-
1958	-	-	28.9	-0.7	-	-	-	-	28.7	-0.7	-	-	-	-	29.5	2.8	-	-	-	-	29.6	0.3	-	-
1959	-	-	29.7	0.3	-	-	-	-	29.8	0.3	-	-	-	-	30.3	1.7	-	-	-	-	30.8	1.7	-	-
1960	-	-	29.6	-3.9	-	-	-	-	29.8	0.7	-	-	-	-	30.1	1.0	-	-	-	-	29.9	-0.7	-	-
1961	-	-	30.2	1.0	-	-	-	-	29.4	-2.6	-	-	-	-	30.4	3.4	-	-	-	-	30.2	-0.7	-	-
1962	-	-	30.9	2.3	-	-	-	-	31.4	1.6	-	-	-	-	30.7	-2.2	-	-	-	-	31.6	2.9	-	-
1963	-	-	30.8	-2.5	-	-	-	-	31.4	1.9	-	-	-	-	31.1	-1.0	-	-	-	-	31.8	2.3	-	-
1964	-	-	31.3	-1.6	-	-	-	-	30.8	-1.6	-	-	-	-	31.6	2.6	-	-	-	-	32.0	1.3	-	-
1965	-	-	32.4	1.3	-	-	-	-	32.9	1.5	-	-	-	-	32.5	-1.2	-	-	-	-	32.5	0.0	-	-
1966	-	-	32.6	0.3	-	-	-	-	32.3	-0.9	-	-	-	-	33.1	2.5	-	-	-	-	33.1	0.0	-	-
1967	-	-	32.8	-0.9	-	-	-	-	33.0	0.6	-	-	-	-	33.1	0.3	-	-	-	-	34.0	2.7	-	-
1968	-	-	34.0	0.0	-	-	-	-	33.2	-2.4	-	-	-	-	33.3	0.3	-	-	-	-	33.9	1.8	-	-
1969	-	-	35.4	4.4	-	-	-	-	35.2	-0.6	-	-	-	-	34.9	-0.9	-	-	-	-	36.2	3.7	-	-
1970	-	-	35.2	-2.8	-	-	-	-	37.0	5.1	-	-	-	-	36.5	-1.4	-	-	-	-	38.2	4.7	-	-
1971	-	-	39.3	2.9	-	-	-	-	38.3	-2.5	-	-	-	-	39.8	3.9	-	-	-	-	38.5	-3.3	-	-
1972	-	-	38.4	-0.3	-	-	-	-	39.0	1.6	-	-	-	-	40.7	4.4	-	-	-	-	40.4	-0.7	-	-
1973	-	-	40.7	0.7	-	-	-	-	42.1	3.4	-	-	-	-	42.0	-0.2	-	-	-	-	42.7	1.7	-	-
1974	-	-	43.9	2.8	-	-	-	-	46.2	5.2	-	-	-	-	47.9	3.7	-	-	-	-	48.3	0.8	-	-
1975	-	-	48.8	1.0	-	-	-	-	49.7	1.8	-	-	-	-	51.4	3.4	-	-	-	-	51.7	0.6	-	-
1976	-	-	51.6	-0.2	-	-	-	-	53.0	2.7	-	-	-	-	55.6	4.9	-	-	-	-	56.0	0.7	-	-
1977	-	-	56.3	0.5	-	-	-	-	57.9	2.8	-	-	-	-	58.1	0.3	-	-	-	-	58.3	0.3	-	-
1978	58.6	0.5	-	-	58.9	0.5	-	-	60.2	2.2	-	-	62.1	3.2	-	-	62.7	1.0	-	-	63.7	1.6	-	-
1979	64.6	1.4	-	-	66.2	2.5	-	-	69.1	4.4	-	-	72.4	4.8	-	-	74.1	2.3	-	-	75.6	2.0	-	-
1980	78.1	3.3	-	-	81.1	3.8	-	-	84.3	3.9	-	-	83.6	-0.8	-	-	84.0	0.5	-	-	86.3	2.7	-	-
1981	88.9	3.0	-	-	91.1	2.5	-	-	92.7	1.8	-	-	93.6	1.0	-	-	94.9	1.4	-	-	97.7	3.0	-	-
1982	97.6	-0.1	-	-	96.6	-1.0	-	-	96.2	-0.4	-	-	100.2	4.2	-	-	98.9	-1.3	-	-	98.8	-0.1	-	-
1983	97.9	-0.9	-	-	95.7	-2.2	-	-	98.4	2.8	-	-	99.2	0.8	-	-	101.0	1.8	-	-	101.6	0.6	-	-
1984	101.0	-0.6	-	-	101.6	0.6	-	-	103.2	1.6	-	-	103.0	-0.2	-	-	103.7	0.7	-	-	104.3	0.6	-	-
1985	102.5	-1.7	-	-	103.5	1.0	-	-	105.3	1.7	-	-	105.2	-0.1	-	-	104.0	-1.1	-	-	105.7	1.6	-	-
1986	104.8	-0.9	-	-	97.7	-6.8	-	-	99.2	1.5	-	-	97.9	-1.3	-	-	97.6	-0.3	-	-	98.8	1.2	98.4	-0.4
1987	-	-	-	-	-	-	-	-	-	-	100.9	2.5	-	-	-	-	-	-	-	-	-	-	104.1	3.2
1988	-	-	-	-	-	-	-	-	-	-	102.9	-1.2	-	-	-	-	-	-	-	-	-	-	105.7	2.7
1989	-	-	-	-	-	-	-	-	-	-	110.9	4.9	-	-	-	-	-	-	-	-	-	-	110.8	-0.1
1990	-	-	-	-	-	-	-	-	-	-	113.3	2.3	-	-	-	-	-	-	-	-	-	-	118.7	4.8
1991	-	-	-	-	-	-	-	-	-	-	117.7	-0.8	-	-	-	-	-	-	-	-	-	-	120.9	2.7

[Continued]

Milwaukee-Racine, WI
Consumer Price Index - Urban Wage Earners
Base 1982-1984 = 100
Transportation
[Continued]

For 1946-2001. Columns headed % show percentile change in the index from the previous period for which an index is available.

Year	Jan		Feb		Mar		Apr		May		Jun		Jul		Aug		Sep		Oct		Nov		Dec	
	Index	%	Index	%	Index	%	Index	%	Index	%	Index	%	Index	%	Index	%	Index	%	Index	%	Index	%	Index	%
1992	-	-	-	-	-	-	-	-	-	-	122.2	1.1	-	-	-	-	-	-	-	-	-	-	125.6	2.8
1993	-	-	-	-	-	-	-	-	-	-	128.3	2.1	-	-	-	-	-	-	-	-	-	-	130.6	1.8
1994	-	-	-	-	-	-	-	-	-	-	132.7	1.6	-	-	-	-	-	-	-	-	-	-	136.6	2.9
1995	-	-	-	-	-	-	-	-	-	-	138.3	1.2	-	-	-	-	-	-	-	-	-	-	137.4	-0.7
1996	-	-	-	-	-	-	-	-	-	-	140.1	2.0	-	-	-	-	-	-	-	-	-	-	142.3	1.6
1997	-	-	-	-	-	-	-	-	-	-	143.1	0.6	-	-	-	-	-	-	-	-	-	-	140.8	-1.6
1998	-	-	-	-	-	-	-	-	-	-	138.1	-1.9	-	-	-	-	-	-	-	-	-	-	137.6	-0.4
1999	-	-	-	-	-	-	-	-	-	-	138.0	0.3	-	-	-	-	-	-	-	-	-	-	141.2	2.3
2000	-	-	-	-	-	-	-	-	-	-	147.5	4.5	-	-	-	-	-	-	-	-	-	-	148.1	0.4
2001	-	-	-	-	-	-	-	-	-	-	149.1	0.7	-	-	-	-	-	-	-	-	-	-	-	-

Source: U.S. Department of Labor, Bureau of Labor Statistics, Division of Consumer Prices and Price Indexes. - indicates no data collected for period.

Milwaukee-Racine, WI
Consumer Price Index - All Urban Consumers
Base 1982-1984 = 100
Medical Care

For 1946-2001. Columns headed % show percentile change in the index from the previous period for which an index is available.

Year	Jan Index	%	Feb Index	%	Mar Index	%	Apr Index	%	May Index	%	Jun Index	%	Jul Index	%	Aug Index	%	Sep Index	%	Oct Index	%	Nov Index	%	Dec Index	%
1946	-	-	-	-	-	-	-	-	-	-	-	-	-	-	-	-	-	-	-	-	-	-	12.3	-
1947	-	-	-	-	12.7	3.3	-	-	-	-	12.8	0.8	-	-	12.9	0.8	-	-	-	-	13.0	0.8	-	-
1948	-	-	13.3	2.3	-	-	-	-	13.4	0.8	-	-	-	-	13.6	1.5	-	-	-	-	14.1	3.7	-	-
1949	-	-	14.2	0.7	-	-	-	-	14.2	0.0	-	-	-	-	14.3	0.7	-	-	-	-	14.3	0.0	-	-
1950	-	-	14.4	0.7	-	-	-	-	14.5	0.7	-	-	-	-	15.1	4.1	-	-	-	-	15.6	3.3	-	-
1951	-	-	15.7	0.6	-	-	-	-	16.4	4.5	-	-	-	-	16.8	2.4	-	-	-	-	17.0	1.2	-	-
1952	-	-	17.1	0.6	-	-	-	-	17.3	1.2	-	-	-	-	17.5	1.2	-	-	-	-	17.5	0.0	-	-
1953	-	-	17.7	1.1	-	-	-	-	17.8	0.6	-	-	-	-	18.1	1.7	-	-	-	-	18.2	0.6	-	-
1954	-	-	18.3	0.5	-	-	-	-	19.2	4.9	-	-	-	-	19.2	0.0	-	-	-	-	19.3	0.5	-	-
1955	-	-	19.3	0.0	-	-	-	-	19.4	0.5	-	-	-	-	19.8	2.1	-	-	-	-	19.6	-1.0	-	-
1956	-	-	19.7	0.5	-	-	-	-	19.9	1.0	-	-	-	-	19.9	0.0	-	-	-	-	20.0	0.5	-	-
1957	-	-	20.4	2.0	-	-	-	-	21.6	5.9	-	-	-	-	21.6	0.0	-	-	-	-	21.9	1.4	-	-
1958	-	-	22.0	0.5	-	-	-	-	22.1	0.5	-	-	-	-	22.1	0.0	-	-	-	-	22.1	0.0	-	-
1959	-	-	22.2	0.5	-	-	-	-	22.2	0.0	-	-	-	-	22.8	2.7	-	-	-	-	23.0	0.9	-	-
1960	-	-	23.0	0.0	-	-	-	-	23.0	0.0	-	-	-	-	23.1	0.4	-	-	-	-	23.1	0.0	-	-
1961	-	-	23.1	0.0	-	-	-	-	23.2	0.4	-	-	-	-	23.3	0.4	-	-	-	-	23.3	0.0	-	-
1962	-	-	23.4	0.4	-	-	-	-	23.4	0.0	-	-	-	-	23.4	0.0	-	-	-	-	23.4	0.0	-	-
1963	-	-	23.5	0.4	-	-	-	-	24.0	2.1	-	-	-	-	24.0	0.0	-	-	-	-	24.2	0.8	-	-
1964	-	-	24.2	0.0	-	-	-	-	24.3	0.4	-	-	-	-	24.4	0.4	-	-	-	-	24.5	0.4	-	-
1965	-	-	25.1	2.4	-	-	-	-	25.2	0.4	-	-	-	-	25.3	0.4	-	-	-	-	25.6	1.2	-	-
1966	-	-	25.9	1.2	-	-	-	-	26.3	1.5	-	-	-	-	26.9	2.3	-	-	-	-	27.7	3.0	-	-
1967	-	-	28.1	1.4	-	-	-	-	28.3	0.7	-	-	-	-	29.0	2.5	-	-	-	-	29.8	2.8	-	-
1968	-	-	29.9	0.3	-	-	-	-	29.9	0.0	-	-	-	-	30.5	2.0	-	-	-	-	31.4	3.0	-	-
1969	-	-	32.0	1.9	-	-	-	-	32.4	1.3	-	-	-	-	32.8	1.2	-	-	-	-	33.0	0.6	-	-
1970	-	-	33.9	2.7	-	-	-	-	34.2	0.9	-	-	-	-	34.6	1.2	-	-	-	-	34.6	0.0	-	-
1971	-	-	35.9	3.8	-	-	-	-	36.2	0.8	-	-	-	-	36.8	1.7	-	-	-	-	36.5	-0.8	-	-
1972	-	-	36.6	0.3	-	-	-	-	36.7	0.3	-	-	-	-	36.9	0.5	-	-	-	-	37.2	0.8	-	-
1973	-	-	37.6	1.1	-	-	-	-	38.2	1.6	-	-	-	-	38.8	1.6	-	-	-	-	39.6	2.1	-	-
1974	-	-	40.5	2.3	-	-	-	-	41.9	3.5	-	-	-	-	43.4	3.6	-	-	-	-	44.0	1.4	-	-
1975	-	-	45.3	3.0	-	-	-	-	46.4	2.4	-	-	-	-	48.0	3.4	-	-	-	-	48.7	1.5	-	-
1976	-	-	50.7	4.1	-	-	-	-	52.1	2.8	-	-	-	-	53.4	2.5	-	-	-	-	54.3	1.7	-	-
1977	-	-	55.1	1.5	-	-	-	-	57.2	3.8	-	-	-	-	58.0	1.4	-	-	-	-	58.9	1.6	-	-
1978	59.7	1.4	-	-	60.9	2.0	-	-	61.4	0.8	-	-	61.9	0.8	-	-	63.0	1.8	-	-	63.2	0.3	-	-
1979	66.3	4.9	-	-	67.2	1.4	-	-	67.8	0.9	-	-	69.8	2.9	-	-	71.0	1.7	-	-	71.7	1.0	-	-
1980	73.6	2.6	-	-	75.4	2.4	-	-	75.9	0.7	-	-	78.0	2.8	-	-	80.8	3.6	-	-	81.2	0.5	-	-
1981	83.2	2.5	-	-	86.1	3.5	-	-	86.3	0.2	-	-	87.0	0.8	-	-	87.9	1.0	-	-	88.1	0.2	-	-
1982	90.1	2.3	-	-	90.4	0.3	-	-	92.5	2.3	-	-	93.4	1.0	-	-	95.4	2.1	-	-	98.0	2.7	-	-
1983	99.2	1.2	-	-	99.2	0.0	-	-	99.3	0.1	-	-	101.0	1.7	-	-	101.8	0.8	-	-	102.0	0.2	-	-
1984	104.5	2.5	-	-	104.9	0.4	-	-	105.2	0.3	-	-	106.1	0.9	-	-	106.3	0.2	-	-	106.5	0.2	-	-
1985	107.1	0.6	-	-	108.3	1.1	-	-	109.0	0.6	-	-	109.5	0.5	-	-	110.1	0.5	-	-	110.5	0.4	-	-
1986	112.1	1.4	-	-	113.1	0.9	-	-	113.8	0.6	-	-	114.9	1.0	-	-	115.3	0.3	-	-	117.0	1.5	117.0	0.0
1987	-	-	-	-	-	-	-	-	-	-	117.8	0.7	-	-	-	-	-	-	-	-	-	-	120.9	2.6
1988	-	-	-	-	-	-	-	-	-	-	127.4	5.4	-	-	-	-	-	-	-	-	-	-	129.4	1.6
1989	-	-	-	-	-	-	-	-	-	-	137.2	6.0	-	-	-	-	-	-	-	-	-	-	141.5	3.1
1990	-	-	-	-	-	-	-	-	-	-	149.5	5.7	-	-	-	-	-	-	-	-	-	-	152.1	1.7
1991	-	-	-	-	-	-	-	-	-	-	157.3	3.4	-	-	-	-	-	-	-	-	-	-	161.8	2.9

[Continued]

Milwaukee-Racine, WI
Consumer Price Index - All Urban Consumers
Base 1982-1984 = 100
Medical Care
[Continued]

For 1946-2001. Columns headed % show percentile change in the index from the previous period for which an index is available.

Year	Jan		Feb		Mar		Apr		May		Jun		Jul		Aug		Sep		Oct		Nov		Dec	
	Index	%	Index	%	Index	%	Index	%	Index	%	Index	%	Index	%	Index	%	Index	%	Index	%	Index	%	Index	%
1992	-	-	-	-	-	-	-	-	-	-	172.5	6.6	-	-	-	-	-	-	-	-	-	-	176.1	2.1
1993	-	-	-	-	-	-	-	-	-	-	183.0	3.9	-	-	-	-	-	-	-	-	-	-	188.0	2.7
1994	-	-	-	-	-	-	-	-	-	-	196.6	4.6	-	-	-	-	-	-	-	-	-	-	206.8	5.2
1995	-	-	-	-	-	-	-	-	-	-	212.1	2.6	-	-	-	-	-	-	-	-	-	-	214.3	1.0
1996	-	-	-	-	-	-	-	-	-	-	218.3	1.9	-	-	-	-	-	-	-	-	-	-	222.0	1.7
1997	-	-	-	-	-	-	-	-	-	-	228.0	2.7	-	-	-	-	-	-	-	-	-.	-	232.9	2.1
1998	-	-	-	-	-	-	-	-	-	-	237.1	1.8	-	-	-	-	-	-	-	-	-	-	242.5	2.3
1999	-	-	-	-	-	-	-	-	-	-	249.9	3.1	-	-	-	-	-	-	-	-	-	-	253.2	1.3
2000	-	-	-	-	-	-	-	-	-	-	256.2	1.2	-	-	-	-	-	-	-	-	-	-	259.2	1.2
2001	-	-	-	-	-	-	-	-	-	-	264.3	2.0	-	-	-	-	-	-	-	-	-	-	-	-

Source: U.S. Department of Labor, Bureau of Labor Statistics, Division of Consumer Prices and Price Indexes. - indicates no data collected for period.

Milwaukee-Racine, WI
Consumer Price Index - Urban Wage Earners
Base 1982-1984 = 100
Medical Care

For 1946-2001. Columns headed % show percentile change in the index from the previous period for which an index is available.

Year	Jan Index	%	Feb Index	%	Mar Index	%	Apr Index	%	May Index	%	Jun Index	%	Jul Index	%	Aug Index	%	Sep Index	%	Oct Index	%	Nov Index	%	Dec Index	%
1946	-		-		-		-		-		-		-		-		-		-		-		12.4	
1947	-		-		12.9	4.0	-		-		12.9	0.0	-		13.0	0.8	-		-		13.1	0.8	-	
1948	-		13.4	2.3	-		-		13.5	0.7	-		-		13.8	2.2	-		-		14.3	3.6	-	
1949	-		14.3	0.0	-		-		14.3	0.0	-		-		14.5	1.4	-		-		14.5	0.0	-	
1950	-		14.5	0.0	-		-		14.7	1.4	-		-		15.3	4.1	-		-		15.7	2.6	-	
1951	-		15.9	1.3	-		-		16.6	4.4	-		-		17.0	2.4	-		-		17.1	0.6	-	
1952	-		17.3	1.2	-		-		17.5	1.2	-		-		17.7	1.1	-		-		17.7	0.0	-	
1953	-		17.9	1.1	-		-		18.0	0.6	-		-		18.3	1.7	-		-		18.4	0.5	-	
1954	-		18.5	0.5	-		-		19.4	4.9	-		-		19.4	0.0	-		-		19.5	0.5	-	
1955	-		19.5	0.0	-		-		19.6	0.5	-		-		20.0	2.0	-		-		19.8	-1.0	-	
1956	-		20.0	1.0	-		-		20.1	0.5	-		-		20.1	0.0	-		-		20.3	1.0	-	
1957	-		20.6	1.5	-		-		21.8	5.8	-		-		21.9	0.5	-		-		22.1	0.9	-	
1958	-		22.3	0.9	-		-		22.3	0.0	-		-		22.3	0.0	-		-		22.4	0.4	-	
1959	-		22.4	0.0	-		-		22.5	0.4	-		-		23.1	2.7	-		-		23.2	0.4	-	
1960	-		23.3	0.4	-		-		23.3	0.0	-		-		23.4	0.4	-		-		23.4	0.0	-	
1961	-		23.4	0.0	-		-		23.5	0.4	-		-		23.6	0.4	-		-		23.6	0.0	-	
1962	-		23.7	0.4	-		-		23.7	0.0	-		-		23.7	0.0	-		-		23.7	0.0	-	
1963	-		23.8	0.4	-		-		24.2	1.7	-		-		24.3	0.4	-		-		24.5	0.8	-	
1964	-		24.5	0.0	-		-		24.6	0.4	-		-		24.7	0.4	-		-		24.7	0.0	-	
1965	-		25.3	2.4	-		-		25.5	0.8	-		-		25.6	0.4	-		-		25.9	1.2	-	
1966	-		26.2	1.2	-		-		26.6	1.5	-		-		27.2	2.3	-		-		28.0	2.9	-	
1967	-		28.4	1.4	-		-		28.6	0.7	-		-		29.3	2.4	-		-		30.2	3.1	-	
1968	-		30.2	0.0	-		-		30.3	0.3	-		-		30.9	2.0	-		-		31.8	2.9	-	
1969	-		32.4	1.9	-		-		32.7	0.9	-		-		33.1	1.2	-		-		33.4	0.9	-	
1970	-		34.3	2.7	-		-		34.6	0.9	-		-		35.0	1.2	-		-		35.0	0.0	-	
1971	-		36.3	3.7	-		-		36.6	0.8	-		-		37.2	1.6	-		-		36.9	-0.8	-	
1972	-		37.0	0.3	-		-		37.1	0.3	-		-		37.3	0.5	-		-		37.6	0.8	-	
1973	-		38.0	1.1	-		-		38.7	1.8	-		-		39.2	1.3	-		-		40.1	2.3	-	
1974	-		40.9	2.0	-		-		42.3	3.4	-		-		43.9	3.8	-		-		44.4	1.1	-	
1975	-		45.8	3.2	-		-		46.9	2.4	-		-		48.5	3.4	-		-		49.2	1.4	-	
1976	-		51.3	4.3	-		-		52.7	2.7	-		-		54.0	2.5	-		-		54.9	1.7	-	
1977	-		55.7	1.5	-		-		57.8	3.8	-		-		58.7	1.6	-		-		59.5	1.4	-	
1978	61.4	3.2	-		62.0	1.0	-		63.3	2.1	-		63.9	0.9	-		64.8	1.4	-		64.9	0.2	-	
1979	67.3	3.7	-		68.0	1.0	-		68.1	0.1	-		70.5	3.5	-		71.8	1.8	-		72.1	0.4	-	
1980	74.5	3.3	-		77.2	3.6	-		78.1	1.2	-		79.4	1.7	-		81.3	2.4	-		81.9	0.7	-	
1981	84.0	2.6	-		86.9	3.5	-		87.1	0.2	-		88.1	1.1	-		88.7	0.7	-		88.9	0.2	-	
1982	91.0	2.4	-		91.2	0.2	-		92.9	1.9	-		93.6	0.8	-		95.3	1.8	-		97.3	2.1	-	
1983	98.5	1.2	-		98.7	0.2	-		98.9	0.2	-		100.7	1.8	-		101.4	0.7	-		101.6	0.2	-	
1984	104.4	2.8	-		104.9	0.5	-		105.3	0.4	-		106.6	1.2	-		106.7	0.1	-		107.0	0.3	-	
1985	107.8	0.7	-		108.9	1.0	-		109.7	0.7	-		110.2	0.5	-		110.8	0.5	-		111.3	0.5	-	
1986	113.0	1.5	-		114.0	0.9	-		114.7	0.6	-		115.6	0.8	-		116.3	0.6	-		117.9	1.4	118.0	0.1
1987	-		-		-		-		-		118.9	0.8	-		-		-		-		-		122.3	2.9
1988	-		-		-		-		-		128.8	5.3	-		-		-		-		-		131.0	1.7
1989	-		-		-		-		-		139.3	6.3	-		-		-		-		-		143.5	3.0
1990	-		-		-		-		-		151.1	5.3	-		-		-		-		-		153.5	1.6
1991	-		-		-		-		-		158.5	3.3	-		-		-		-		-		163.0	2.8

[Continued]

Milwaukee-Racine, WI
Consumer Price Index - Urban Wage Earners
Base 1982-1984 = 100
Medical Care
[Continued]

For 1946-2001. Columns headed % show percentile change in the index from the previous period for which an index is available.

Year	Jan Index	%	Feb Index	%	Mar Index	%	Apr Index	%	May Index	%	Jun Index	%	Jul Index	%	Aug Index	%	Sep Index	%	Oct Index	%	Nov Index	%	Dec Index	%
1992	-		-		-		-		-		173.6	6.5	-		-		-		-		-		177.0	2.0
1993	-		-		-		-		-		183.7	3.8	-		-		-		-		-		188.6	2.7
1994	-		-		-		-		-		196.9	4.4	-		-		-		-		-		207.4	5.3
1995	-		-		-		-		-		212.3	2.4	-		-		-		-		-		214.3	0.9
1996	-		-		-		-		-		217.8	1.6	-		-		-		-		-		221.2	1.6
1997	-		-		-		-		-		228.2	3.2	-		-		-		-		-		233.3	2.2
1998	-		-		-		-		-		237.1	1.6	-		-		-		-		-		242.7	2.4
1999	-		-		-		-		-		250.2	3.1	-		-		-		-		-		254.2	1.6
2000	-		-		-		-		-		257.1	1.1	-		-		-		-		-		259.9	1.1
2001	-		-		-		-		-		264.9	1.9	-		-		-		-		-		-	

Source: U.S. Department of Labor, Bureau of Labor Statistics, Division of Consumer Prices and Price Indexes. - indicates no data collected for period.

Milwaukee-Racine, WI
Consumer Price Index - All Urban Consumers
Base December 1997 = 100
Recreation

For 1997-2001. Columns headed % show percentile change in the index from the previous period for which an index is available.

Year	Jan		Feb		Mar		Apr		May		Jun		Jul		Aug		Sep		Oct		Nov		Dec	
	Index	%	Index	%	Index	%	Index	%	Index	%	Index	%	Index	%	Index	%	Index	%	Index	%	Index	%	Index	%
1997	-	-	-	-	-	-	-	-	-	-	-	-	-	-	-	-	-	-	-	-	-	-	100.0	-
1998	-	-	-	-	-	-	-	-	-	-	100.5	0.5	-	-	-	-	-	-	-	-	-	-	99.6	-0.9
1999	-	-	-	-	-	-	-	-	-	-	100.5	0.9	-	-	-	-	-	-	-	-	-	-	101.7	1.2
2000	-	-	-	-	-	-	-	-	-	-	103.0	1.3	-	-	-	-	-	-	-	-	-	-	102.3	-0.7
2001	-	-	-	-	-	-	-	-	-	-	102.7	0.4	-	-	-	-	-	-	-	-	-	-	-	-

Source: U.S. Department of Labor, Bureau of Labor Statistics, Division of Consumer Prices and Price Indexes. - indicates no data collected for period.

Milwaukee-Racine, WI
Consumer Price Index - Urban Wage Earners
Base December 1997 = 100
Recreation

For 1997-2001. Columns headed % show percentile change in the index from the previous period for which an index is available.

Year	Jan		Feb		Mar		Apr		May		Jun		Jul		Aug		Sep		Oct		Nov		Dec	
	Index	%	Index	%	Index	%	Index	%	Index	%	Index	%	Index	%	Index	%	Index	%	Index	%	Index	%	Index	%
1997	-	-	-	-	-	-	-	-	-	-	-	-	-	-	-	-	-	-	-	-	-	-	-	-
1998	-	-	-	-	-	-	-	-	-	-	100.0	0.0	-	-	-	-	-	-	-	-	-	-	100.0	-
1999	-	-	-	-	-	-	-	-	-	-	99.2	0.3	-	-	-	-	-	-	-	-	-	-	98.9	-1.1
2000	-	-	-	-	-	-	-	-	-	-	100.9	1.0	-	-	-	-	-	-	-	-	-	-	99.9	0.7
2001	-	-	-	-	-	-	-	-	-	-	100.4	0.3	-	-	-	-	-	-	-	-	-	-	100.1	-0.8

Source: U.S. Department of Labor, Bureau of Labor Statistics, Division of Consumer Prices and Price Indexes. - indicates no data collected for period.

Milwaukee-Racine, WI
Consumer Price Index - All Urban Consumers
Base December 1997 = 100
Education & Communication

For 1997-2001. Columns headed % show percentile change in the index from the previous period for which an index is available.

Year	Jan Index	%	Feb Index	%	Mar Index	%	Apr Index	%	May Index	%	Jun Index	%	Jul Index	%	Aug Index	%	Sep Index	%	Oct Index	%	Nov Index	%	Dec Index	%
1997	-	-	-	-	-	-	-	-	-	-	-	-	-	-	-	-	-	-	-	-	-	-	100.0	-
1998	-	-	-	-	-	-	-	-	-	-	99.7	-0.3	-	-	-	-	-	-	-	-	-	-	100.3	0.6
1999	-	-	-	-	-	-	-	-	-	-	99.9	-0.4	-	-	-	-	-	-	-	-	-	-	102.2	2.3
2000	-	-	-	-	-	-	-	-	-	-	103.4	1.2	-	-	-	-	-	-	-	-	-	-	106.6	3.1
2001	-	-	-	-	-	-	-	-	-	-	108.7	2.0	-	-	-	-	-	-	-	-	-	-	-	-

Source: U.S. Department of Labor, Bureau of Labor Statistics, Division of Consumer Prices and Price Indexes. - indicates no data collected for period.

Milwaukee-Racine, WI
Consumer Price Index - Urban Wage Earners
Base December 1997 = 100
Education & Communication

For 1997-2001. Columns headed % show percentile change in the index from the previous period for which an index is available.

Year	Jan		Feb		Mar		Apr		May		Jun		Jul		Aug		Sep		Oct		Nov		Dec	
	Index	%	Index	%	Index	%	Index	%	Index	%	Index	%	Index	%	Index	%	Index	%	Index	%	Index	%	Index	%
1997	-	-	-	-	-	-	-	-	-	-	-	-	-	-	-	-	-	-	-	-	-	-	-	-
1998	-	-	-	-	-	-	-	-	-	-	99.8	-0.2	-	-	-	-	-	-	-	-	-	-	100.0	-
1999	-	-	-	-	-	-	-	-	-	-	100.0	-0.3	-	-	-	-	-	-	-	-	-	-	100.3	0.5
2000	-	-	-	-	-	-	-	-	-	-	103.3	1.2	-	-	-	-	-	-	-	-	-	-	102.1	2.1
2001	-	-	-	-	-	-	-	-	-	-	108.3	2.2	-	-	-	-	-	-	-	-	-	-	-	-

Source: U.S. Department of Labor, Bureau of Labor Statistics, Division of Consumer Prices and Price Indexes. - indicates no data collected for period.

Minneapolis-St. Paul, MN-WI
Consumer Price Index - All Urban Consumers
Base 1982-1984 = 100
Annual Averages

For 1917-2001. Columns headed % show percentile change in the index from the previous period for which an index is available.

Year	All Items		Food & Beverage		Housing		Apparel		Trans-portation		Medical Care		Recrea-tion*		Education & Communic.*		Other Goods & Services	
	Index	%	Index	%	Index	%	Index	%	Index	%	Index	%	Index	%	Index	%	Index	%
1917	-	-	-	-	-	-	-	-	-	-	-	-	-	-	-	-	-	-
1918	14.1	-	-	-	-	-	-	-	-	-	-	-	-	-	-	-	-	-
1919	16.0	13.5	-	-	-	-	-	-	-	-	-	-	-	-	-	-	-	-
1920	18.6	16.3	-	-	-	-	-	-	-	-	-	-	-	-	-	-	-	-
1921	16.7	-10.2	-	-	-	-	-	-	-	-	-	-	-	-	-	-	-	-
1922	15.8	-5.4	-	-	-	-	-	-	-	-	-	-	-	-	-	-	-	-
1923	15.9	0.6	-	-	-	-	-	-	-	-	-	-	-	-	-	-	-	-
1924	15.8	-0.6	-	-	-	-	-	-	-	-	-	-	-	-	-	-	-	-
1925	15.9	0.6	-	-	-	-	-	-	-	-	-	-	-	-	-	-	-	-
1926	16.1	1.3	-	-	-	-	-	-	-	-	-	-	-	-	-	-	-	-
1927	15.7	-2.5	-	-	-	-	-	-	-	-	-	-	-	-	-	-	-	-
1928	15.5	-1.3	-	-	-	-	-	-	-	-	-	-	-	-	-	-	-	-
1929	15.6	0.6	-	-	-	-	-	-	-	-	-	-	-	-	-	-	-	-
1930	15.3	-1.9	-	-	-	-	-	-	-	-	-	-	-	-	-	-	-	-
1931	14.2	-7.2	-	-	-	-	-	-	-	-	-	-	-	-	-	-	-	-
1932	12.9	-9.2	-	-	-	-	-	-	-	-	-	-	-	-	-	-	-	-
1933	12.2	-5.4	-	-	-	-	-	-	-	-	-	-	-	-	-	-	-	-
1934	12.6	3.3	-	-	-	-	-	-	-	-	-	-	-	-	-	-	-	-
1935	13.0	3.2	-	-	-	-	-	-	-	-	-	-	-	-	-	-	-	-
1936	13.2	1.5	-	-	-	-	-	-	-	-	-	-	-	-	-	-	-	-
1937	13.8	4.5	-	-	-	-	-	-	-	-	-	-	-	-	-	-	-	-
1938	13.6	-1.4	-	-	-	-	-	-	-	-	-	-	-	-	-	-	-	-
1939	13.5	-0.7	-	-	-	-	-	-	-	-	-	-	-	-	-	-	-	-
1940	13.5	0.0	-	-	-	-	-	-	-	-	-	-	-	-	-	-	-	-
1941	14.2	5.2	-	-	-	-	-	-	-	-	-	-	-	-	-	-	-	-
1942	15.5	9.2	-	-	-	-	-	-	-	-	-	-	-	-	-	-	-	-
1943	16.2	4.5	-	-	-	-	-	-	-	-	-	-	-	-	-	-	-	-
1944	16.4	1.2	-	-	-	-	-	-	-	-	-	-	-	-	-	-	-	-
1945	16.7	1.8	-	-	-	-	-	-	-	-	-	-	-	-	-	-	-	-
1946	18.2	9.0	-	-	-	-	-	-	-	-	-	-	-	-	-	-	-	-
1947	21.0	15.4	-	-	-	-	-	-	21.6	-	10.7	-	-	-	-	-	-	-
1948	22.9	9.0	-	-	-	-	-	-	24.7	14.4	11.8	10.3	-	-	-	-	-	-
1949	22.7	-0.9	-	-	-	-	-	-	26.4	6.9	12.2	3.4	-	-	-	-	-	-
1950	22.9	0.9	-	-	-	-	-	-	26.5	0.4	12.6	3.3	-	-	-	-	-	-
1951	24.6	7.4	-	-	-	-	-	-	26.9	1.5	13.6	7.9	-	-	-	-	-	-
1952	25.4	3.3	-	-	-	-	-	-	28.7	6.7	14.5	6.6	-	-	-	-	-	-
1953	25.7	1.2	-	-	-	-	45.9	-	29.5	2.8	15.6	7.6	-	-	-	-	-	-
1954	25.9	0.8	-	-	-	-	45.9	0.0	29.2	-1.0	16.4	5.1	-	-	-	-	-	-
1955	25.9	0.0	-	-	-	-	45.2	-1.5	28.3	-3.1	17.0	3.7	-	-	-	-	-	-
1956	26.0	0.4	-	-	-	-	46.5	2.9	27.9	-1.4	17.3	1.8	-	-	-	-	-	-
1957	26.9	3.5	-	-	-	-	47.1	1.3	29.3	5.0	18.7	8.1	-	-	-	-	-	-
1958	27.6	2.6	-	-	-	-	47.3	0.4	30.3	3.4	21.2	13.4	-	-	-	-	-	-
1959	27.9	1.1	-	-	-	-	47.0	-0.6	31.6	4.3	22.7	7.1	-	-	-	-	-	-
1960	28.3	1.4	-	-	-	-	48.0	2.1	32.0	1.3	24.3	7.0	-	-	-	-	-	-
1961	28.6	1.1	-	-	-	-	46.9	-2.3	32.2	0.6	25.8	6.2	-	-	-	-	-	-

[Continued]

Minneapolis-St. Paul, MN-WI
Consumer Price Index - All Urban Consumers
Base 1982-1984 = 100
Annual Averages

[Continued]

For 1917-2001. Columns headed % show percentile change in the index from the previous period for which an index is available.

Year	All Items		Food & Beverage		Housing		Apparel		Trans-portation		Medical Care		Recrea-tion*		Education & Communic.*		Other Goods & Services	
	Index	%	Index	%	Index	%	Index	%	Index	%	Index	%	Index	%	Index	%	Index	%
1962	29.0	1.4	-	-	-	-	47.9	2.1	32.7	1.6	26.7	3.5	-	-	-	-	-	-
1963	29.4	1.4	-	-	-	-	48.8	1.9	33.2	1.5	27.0	1.1	-	-	-	-	-	-
1964	29.7	1.0	-	-	-	-	48.8	0.0	33.2	0.0	27.5	1.9	-	-	-	-	-	-
1965	30.1	1.3	-	-	-	-	49.9	2.3	33.8	1.8	27.6	0.4	-	-	-	-	-	-
1966	30.8	2.3	-	-	-	-	51.2	2.6	34.4	1.8	28.9	4.7	-	-	-	-	-	-
1967	31.8	3.2	-	-	-	-	53.0	3.5	35.6	3.5	30.4	5.2	-	-	-	-	-	-
1968	33.3	4.7	-	-	-	-	55.3	4.3	36.7	3.1	32.0	5.3	-	-	-	-	-	-
1969	35.0	5.1	-	-	-	-	58.3	5.4	37.4	1.9	33.6	5.0	-	-	-	-	-	-
1970	37.4	6.9	-	-	-	-	61.2	5.0	39.7	6.1	35.8	6.5	-	-	-	-	-	-
1971	38.7	3.5	-	-	-	-	62.6	2.3	41.1	3.5	37.7	5.3	-	-	-	-	-	-
1972	39.9	3.1	-	-	-	-	63.4	1.3	41.4	0.7	38.4	1.9	-	-	-	-	-	-
1973	42.3	6.0	-	-	-	-	66.3	4.6	43.1	4.1	40.3	4.9	-	-	-	-	-	-
1974	47.2	11.6	-	-	-	-	72.6	9.5	47.8	10.9	43.9	8.9	-	-	-	-	-	-
1975	51.2	8.5	-	-	-	-	74.0	1.9	50.9	6.5	48.6	10.7	-	-	-	-	-	-
1976	54.4	6.3	62.5	-	49.0	-	75.0	1.4	55.4	8.8	52.3	7.6	-	-	-	-	56.8	-
1977	58.2	7.0	65.8	5.3	53.2	8.6	78.1	4.1	59.6	7.6	56.6	8.2	-	-	-	-	60.0	5.6
1978	63.5	9.1	72.3	9.9	59.3	11.5	81.3	4.1	62.5	4.9	61.2	8.1	-	-	-	-	64.9	8.2
1979	70.8	11.5	80.9	11.9	66.3	11.8	85.5	5.2	71.8	14.9	66.2	8.2	-	-	-	-	69.3	6.8
1980	78.9	11.4	87.6	8.3	74.0	11.6	90.8	6.2	83.7	16.6	73.7	11.3	-	-	-	-	75.3	8.7
1981	88.6	12.3	92.7	5.8	85.9	16.1	94.7	4.3	93.6	11.8	80.3	9.0	-	-	-	-	83.2	10.5
1982	97.4	9.9	96.6	4.2	98.7	14.9	99.7	5.3	97.5	4.2	90.0	12.1	-	-	-	-	91.7	10.2
1983	99.5	2.2	99.5	3.0	99.3	0.6	101.5	1.8	99.3	1.8	100.3	11.4	-	-	-	-	100.7	9.8
1984	103.1	3.6	104.0	4.5	102.0	2.7	98.8	-2.7	103.2	3.9	109.7	9.4	-	-	-	-	107.6	6.9
1985	107.0	3.8	106.5	2.4	105.8	3.7	106.2	7.5	106.1	2.8	116.9	6.6	-	-	-	-	114.5	6.4
1986	108.4	1.3	109.4	2.7	107.8	1.9	107.0	0.8	100.5	-5.3	126.8	8.5	-	-	-	-	120.9	5.6
1987	111.6	3.0	113.9	4.1	109.5	1.6	109.7	2.5	102.9	2.4	133.7	5.4	-	-	-	-	-	-
1988	117.2	5.0	119.9	5.3	112.0	2.3	126.6	15.4	107.2	4.2	140.7	5.2	-	-	-	-	137.3	13.6
1989	122.0	4.1	126.6	5.6	115.8	3.4	121.5	-4.0	114.8	7.1	149.1	6.0	-	-	-	-	143.9	4.8
1990	127.0	4.1	134.6	6.3	118.5	2.3	130.5	7.4	118.5	3.2	161.5	8.3	-	-	-	-	153.0	6.3
1991	130.4	2.7	141.5	5.1	120.6	1.8	130.9	0.3	119.4	0.8	171.8	6.4	-	-	-	-	164.0	7.2
1992	135.0	3.5	144.8	2.3	124.9	3.6	141.7	8.3	121.7	1.9	182.4	6.2	-	-	-	-	171.7	4.7
1993	139.2	3.1	147.2	1.7	128.1	2.6	141.5	-0.1	126.9	4.3	193.8	6.3	-	-	-	-	184.0	7.2
1994	143.6	3.2	149.1	1.3	129.6	1.2	148.1	4.7	134.2	5.8	205.4	6.0	-	-	-	-	199.1	8.2
1995	147.0	2.4	152.4	2.2	132.7	2.4	143.6	-3.0	138.6	3.3	209.9	2.2	-	-	-	-	207.3	4.1
1996	151.9	3.3	158.8	4.2	138.0	4.0	143.1	-0.3	141.9	2.4	215.5	2.7	-	-	-	-	213.1	2.8
1997	155.4	2.3	163.5	3.0	140.8	2.0	145.6	1.7	144.0	1.5	218.8	1.5	-	-	-	-	222.3	4.3
1998	158.3	1.9	166.6	1.9	145.0	3.0	144.2	-1.0	141.9	-1.5	229.6	4.9	101.2	-	99.4	-	234.2	5.4
1999	163.3	3.2	172.1	3.3	149.2	2.9	139.3	-3.4	148.6	4.7	241.1	5.0	103.3	2.1	99.2	-0.2	257.7	10.0
2000	170.1	4.2	177.9	3.4	156.2	4.7	138.2	-0.8	157.6	6.1	249.7	3.6	104.2	0.9	102.2	3.0	276.0	7.1
2001	-	-	-	-	-	-	-	-	-	-	-	-	-	-	-	-	-	-

Source: U.S. Department of Labor, Bureau of Labor Statistics, Division of Consumer Prices and Price Indexes. *Base is December 1997 = 100. - indicates no data collected for period.

Minneapolis-St. Paul, MN-WI
Consumer Price Index - Urban Wage Earners
Base 1982-1984 = 100
Annual Averages

For 1917-2001. Columns headed % show percentile change in the index from the previous period for which an index is available.

Year	All Items		Food & Beverage		Housing		Apparel		Trans-portation		Medical Care		Recrea-tion*		Education & Communic.*		Other Goods & Services	
	Index	%	Index	%	Index	%	Index	%	Index	%	Index	%	Index	%	Index	%	Index	%
1917	-	-	-	-	-	-	-	-	-	-	-	-	-	-	-	-	-	-
1918	14.1	-	-	-	-	-	-	-	-	-	-	-	-	-	-	-	-	-
1919	16.1	14.2	-	-	-	-	-	-	-	-	-	-	-	-	-	-	-	-
1920	18.6	15.5	-	-	-	-	-	-	-	-	-	-	-	-	-	-	-	-
1921	16.8	-9.7	-	-	-	-	-	-	-	-	-	-	-	-	-	-	-	-
1922	15.8	-6.0	-	-	-	-	-	-	-	-	-	-	-	-	-	-	-	-
1923	15.9	0.6	-	-	-	-	-	-	-	-	-	-	-	-	-	-	-	-
1924	15.8	-0.6	-	-	-	-	-	-	-	-	-	-	-	-	-	-	-	-
1925	15.9	0.6	-	-	-	-	-	-	-	-	-	-	-	-	-	-	-	-
1926	16.1	1.3	-	-	-	-	-	-	-	-	-	-	-	-	-	-	-	-
1927	15.7	-2.5	-	-	-	-	-	-	-	-	-	-	-	-	-	-	-	-
1928	15.5	-1.3	-	-	-	-	-	-	-	-	-	-	-	-	-	-	-	-
1929	15.6	0.6	-	-	-	-	-	-	-	-	-	-	-	-	-	-	-	-
1930	15.3	-1.9	-	-	-	-	-	-	-	-	-	-	-	-	-	-	-	-
1931	14.2	-7.2	-	-	-	-	-	-	-	-	-	-	-	-	-	-	-	-
1932	12.9	-9.2	-	-	-	-	-	-	-	-	-	-	-	-	-	-	-	-
1933	12.2	-5.4	-	-	-	-	-	-	-	-	-	-	-	-	-	-	-	-
1934	12.6	3.3	-	-	-	-	-	-	-	-	-	-	-	-	-	-	-	-
1935	13.0	3.2	-	-	-	-	-	-	-	-	-	-	-	-	-	-	-	-
1936	13.2	1.5	-	-	-	-	-	-	-	-	-	-	-	-	-	-	-	-
1937	13.8	4.5	-	-	-	-	-	-	-	-	-	-	-	-	-	-	-	-
1938	13.6	-1.4	-	-	-	-	-	-	-	-	-	-	-	-	-	-	-	-
1939	13.5	-0.7	-	-	-	-	-	-	-	-	-	-	-	-	-	-	-	-
1940	13.5	0.0	-	-	-	-	-	-	-	-	-	-	-	-	-	-	-	-
1941	14.2	5.2	-	-	-	-	-	-	-	-	-	-	-	-	-	-	-	-
1942	15.5	9.2	-	-	-	-	-	-	-	-	-	-	-	-	-	-	-	-
1943	16.2	4.5	-	-	-	-	-	-	-	-	-	-	-	-	-	-	-	-
1944	16.4	1.2	-	-	-	-	-	-	-	-	-	-	-	-	-	-	-	-
1945	16.7	1.8	-	-	-	-	-	-	-	-	-	-	-	-	-	-	-	-
1946	18.2	9.0	-	-	-	-	-	-	-	-	-	-	-	-	-	-	-	-
1947	21.0	15.4	-	-	-	-	-	-	21.3	-	10.8	-	-	-	-	-	-	-
1948	22.9	9.0	-	-	-	-	-	-	24.3	14.1	11.9	10.2	-	-	-	-	-	-
1949	22.7	-0.9	-	-	-	-	-	-	26.0	7.0	12.4	4.2	-	-	-	-	-	-
1950	22.9	0.9	-	-	-	-	-	-	26.1	0.4	12.8	3.2	-	-	-	-	-	-
1951	24.6	7.4	-	-	-	-	-	-	26.5	1.5	13.8	7.8	-	-	-	-	-	-
1952	25.4	3.3	-	-	-	-	-	-	28.3	6.8	14.7	6.5	-	-	-	-	-	-
1953	25.7	1.2	-	-	-	-	46.9	-	29.0	2.5	15.9	8.2	-	-	-	-	-	-
1954	25.9	0.8	-	-	-	-	47.0	0.2	28.8	-0.7	16.6	4.4	-	-	-	-	-	-
1955	25.9	0.0	-	-	-	-	46.3	-1.5	27.9	-3.1	17.2	3.6	-	-	-	-	-	-
1956	26.0	0.4	-	-	-	-	47.6	2.8	27.5	-1.4	17.5	1.7	-	-	-	-	-	-
1957	26.9	3.5	-	-	-	-	48.2	1.3	28.8	4.7	19.0	8.6	-	-	-	-	-	-
1958	27.6	2.6	-	-	-	-	48.4	0.4	29.8	3.5	21.5	13.2	-	-	-	-	-	-
1959	27.9	1.1	-	-	-	-	48.1	-0.6	31.1	4.4	23.0	7.0	-	-	-	-	-	-
1960	28.4	1.8	-	-	-	-	49.1	2.1	31.5	1.3	24.6	7.0	-	-	-	-	-	-
1961	28.6	0.7	-	-	-	-	48.0	-2.2	31.7	0.6	26.2	6.5	-	-	-	-	-	-

[Continued]

Minneapolis-St. Paul, MN-WI
Consumer Price Index - Urban Wage Earners
Base 1982-1984 = 100
Annual Averages
[Continued]

For 1917-2001. Columns headed % show percentile change in the index from the previous period for which an index is available.

Year	All Items		Food & Beverage		Housing		Apparel		Transportation		Medical Care		Recreation*		Education & Communic.*		Other Goods & Services	
	Index	%	Index	%	Index	%	Index	%	Index	%	Index	%	Index	%	Index	%	Index	%
1962	29.0	1.4	-	-	-	-	49.0	2.1	32.2	1.6	27.1	3.4	-	-	-	-	-	-
1963	29.4	1.4	-	-	-	-	50.0	2.0	32.7	1.6	27.4	1.1	-	-	-	-	-	-
1964	29.7	1.0	-	-	-	-	50.0	0.0	32.7	0.0	27.9	1.8	-	-	-	-	-	-
1965	30.1	1.3	-	-	-	-	51.0	2.0	33.3	1.8	28.0	0.4	-	-	-	-	-	-
1966	30.8	2.3	-	-	-	-	52.3	2.5	33.9	1.8	29.3	4.6	-	-	-	-	-	-
1967	31.9	3.6	-	-	-	-	54.2	3.6	35.0	3.2	30.9	5.5	-	-	-	-	-	-
1968	33.3	4.4	-	-	-	-	56.5	4.2	36.2	3.4	32.5	5.2	-	-	-	-	-	-
1969	35.0	5.1	-	-	-	-	59.7	5.7	36.8	1.7	34.1	4.9	-	-	-	-	-	-
1970	37.4	6.9	-	-	-	-	62.5	4.7	39.1	6.3	36.3	6.5	-	-	-	-	-	-
1971	38.8	3.7	-	-	-	-	64.1	2.6	40.5	3.6	38.2	5.2	-	-	-	-	-	-
1972	40.0	3.1	-	-	-	-	64.8	1.1	40.8	0.7	38.9	1.8	-	-	-	-	-	-
1973	42.4	6.0	-	-	-	-	67.9	4.8	42.4	3.9	40.9	5.1	-	-	-	-	-	-
1974	47.3	11.6	-	-	-	-	74.3	9.4	47.1	11.1	44.5	8.8	-	-	-	-	-	-
1975	51.3	8.5	-	-	-	-	75.7	1.9	50.1	6.4	49.3	10.8	-	-	-	-	-	-
1976	54.5	6.2	63.6	-	48.2	-	76.7	1.3	54.6	9.0	53.1	7.7	-	-	-	-	-	-
1977	58.3	7.0	66.9	5.2	52.4	8.7	79.9	4.2	58.7	7.5	57.4	8.1	-	-	-	-	58.5	-
1978	63.7	9.3	73.3	9.6	58.6	11.8	82.9	3.8	61.6	4.9	62.0	8.0	-	-	-	-	61.8	5.6
1979	71.2	11.8	81.6	11.3	65.7	12.1	86.0	3.7	71.5	16.1	66.3	6.9	-	-	-	-	66.7	7.9
1980	79.4	11.5	88.5	8.5	73.2	11.4	91.7	6.6	83.9	17.3	72.9	10.0	-	-	-	-	71.1	6.6
1981	88.9	12.0	92.7	4.7	85.7	17.1	96.3	5.0	93.9	11.9	79.5	9.1	-	-	-	-	76.5	7.6
1982	97.5	9.7	96.5	4.1	98.9	15.4	99.5	3.3	97.7	4.0	89.5	12.6	-	-	-	-	83.8	9.5
1983	99.1	1.6	99.5	3.1	98.2	-0.7	101.4	1.9	99.4	1.7	100.2	12.0	-	-	-	-	91.8	9.5
1984	103.5	4.4	104.1	4.6	102.9	4.8	99.2	-2.2	103.0	3.6	110.4	10.2	-	-	-	-	101.0	10.0
1985	105.7	2.1	106.5	2.3	103.5	0.6	106.6	7.5	105.8	2.7	117.6	6.5	-	-	-	-	107.2	6.1
1986	106.6	0.9	109.5	2.8	105.5	1.9	106.6	0.0	99.5	-6.0	127.4	8.3	-	-	-	-	114.1	6.4
1987	109.8	3.0	113.9	4.0	106.9	1.3	108.3	1.6	102.1	2.6	134.4	5.5	-	-	-	-	120.6	5.7
1988	115.5	5.2	119.9	5.3	109.4	2.3	127.6	17.8	106.4	4.2	141.7	5.4	-	-	-	-	138.1	14.5
1989	120.1	4.0	126.6	5.6	112.9	3.2	118.8	-6.9	114.1	7.2	149.8	5.7	-	-	-	-	145.3	5.2
1990	124.8	3.9	134.7	6.4	115.5	2.3	127.2	7.1	117.5	3.0	160.9	7.4	-	-	-	-	154.2	6.1
1991	128.1	2.6	141.8	5.3	117.7	1.9	128.6	1.1	118.3	0.7	171.3	6.5	-	-	-	-	165.6	7.4
1992	132.5	3.4	144.8	2.1	121.7	3.4	139.1	8.2	121.0	2.3	182.1	6.3	-	-	-	-	173.0	4.5
1993	136.7	3.2	147.1	1.6	125.0	2.7	138.6	-0.4	126.5	4.5	192.4	5.7	-	-	-	-	186.4	7.7
1994	141.4	3.4	149.5	1.6	126.4	1.1	148.7	7.3	133.7	5.7	204.0	6.0	-	-	-	-	203.6	9.2
1995	144.8	2.4	152.8	2.2	129.5	2.5	142.2	-4.4	138.6	3.7	209.0	2.5	-	-	-	-	211.8	4.0
1996	149.5	3.2	159.4	4.3	134.7	4.0	141.8	-0.3	141.7	2.2	214.7	2.7	-	-	-	-	217.4	2.6
1997	152.9	2.3	164.2	3.0	137.5	2.1	143.6	1.3	143.1	1.0	218.6	1.8	-	-	-	-	227.1	4.5
1998	155.0	1.4	166.9	1.6	141.3	2.8	141.4	-1.5	140.7	-1.7	229.2	4.8	101.5	-	98.9	-	239.5	5.5
1999	159.9	3.2	172.6	3.4	145.6	3.0	138.6	-2.0	146.3	4.0	240.6	5.0	103.2	1.7	97.6	-1.3	267.4	11.6
2000	166.6	4.2	178.2	3.2	152.3	4.6	134.8	-2.7	156.2	6.8	249.1	3.5	103.9	0.7	99.8	2.3	288.3	7.8
2001	-	-	-	-	-	-	-	-	-	-	-	-	-	-	-	-	-	-

Source: U.S. Department of Labor, Bureau of Labor Statistics, Division of Consumer Prices and Price Indexes. *Base is December 1997 = 100. - indicates no data collected for period.

Minneapolis-St. Paul, MN-WI

Consumer Price Index - All Urban Consumers
Base 1982-1984 = 100

All Items

For 1917-2001. Columns headed % show percentile change in the index from the previous period for which an index is available.

Year	Jan Index	%	Feb Index	%	Mar Index	%	Apr Index	%	May Index	%	Jun Index	%	Jul Index	%	Aug Index	%	Sep Index	%	Oct Index	%	Nov Index	%	Dec Index	%
1917	-		-		-		-		-		-		-		-		-		-		-		13.1	-
1918	-		-		-		-		-		-		-		-		-		-		-		15.2	16.0
1919	-		-		-		-		-		15.6	2.6	-		-		-		-		-		17.5	12.2
1920	-		-		-		-		-		19.4	10.9	-		-		-		-		-		18.1	-6.7
1921	-		-		-		-		16.6	-8.3	-		-		-		16.5	-0.6	-		-		16.3	-1.2
1922	-		-		15.8	-3.1	-		-		15.9	0.6	-		-		15.5	-2.5	-		-		15.8	1.9
1923	-		-		15.8	0.0	-		-		15.8	0.0	-		-		15.9	0.6	-		-		16.0	0.6
1924	-		-		15.9	-0.6	-		-		15.7	-1.3	-		-		15.5	-1.3	-		-		15.7	1.3
1925	-		-		-		-		-		15.8	0.6	-		-		-		-		-		16.3	3.2
1926	-		-		-		-		-		16.3	0.0	-		-		-		-		-		16.0	-1.8
1927	-		-		-		-		-		16.0	0.0	-		-		-		-		-		15.6	-2.5
1928	-		-		-		-		-		15.6	0.0	-		-		-		-		-		15.5	-0.6
1929	-		-		-		-		-		15.5	0.0	-		-		-		-		-		15.7	1.3
1930	-		-		-		-		-		15.5	-1.3	-		-		-		-		-		14.9	-3.9
1931	-		-		-		-		-		14.2	-4.7	-		-		-		-		-		13.7	-3.5
1932	-		-		-		-		-		12.9	-5.8	-		-		-		-		-		12.4	-3.9
1933	-		-		-		-		-		11.9	-4.0	-		-		-		-		-		12.4	4.2
1934	-		-		-		-		-		12.6	1.6	-		-		-		-		12.6	0.0	-	
1935	-		-		12.9	2.4	-		-		-		12.9	0.0	-		-		13.0	0.8	-		-	
1936	13.1	0.8	-		-		13.0	-0.8	-		-		13.1	0.8	-		13.4	2.3	-		-		13.4	0.0
1937	-		-		13.6	1.5	-		-		13.7	0.7	-		-		13.9	1.5	-		-		13.8	-0.7
1938	-		-		13.6	-1.4	-		-		13.7	0.7	-		-		13.6	-0.7	-		-		13.5	-0.7
1939	-		-		13.4	-0.7	-		-		13.4	0.0	-		-		13.6	1.5	-		-		13.6	0.0
1940	-		-		13.5	-0.7	-		-		13.5	0.0	-		-		13.5	0.0	13.5	0.0	13.6	0.7	13.7	0.7
1941	13.6	-0.7	13.7	0.7	13.7	0.0	13.7	0.0	13.9	1.5	14.2	2.2	14.3	0.7	14.4	0.7	14.6	1.4	14.8	1.4	14.8	0.0	14.8	0.0
1942	15.0	1.4	15.1	0.7	15.3	1.3	15.4	0.7	15.5	0.6	15.5	0.0	15.6	0.6	15.6	0.0	15.7	0.6	15.8	0.6	15.9	0.6	16.0	0.6
1943	15.9	-0.6	16.0	0.6	16.2	1.3	16.2	0.0	16.3	0.6	16.3	0.0	16.2	-0.6	16.2	0.0	16.2	0.0	16.3	0.6	16.3	0.0	16.4	0.6
1944	16.2	-1.2	16.2	0.0	16.3	0.6	16.3	0.0	16.4	0.6	16.4	0.0	16.5	0.6	16.5	0.0	16.5	0.0	16.5	0.0	16.5	0.0	16.5	0.0
1945	16.5	0.0	16.5	0.0	16.5	0.0	16.5	0.0	16.6	0.6	16.7	0.6	16.7	0.0	16.7	0.0	16.8	0.6	16.8	0.0	16.9	0.6	16.9	0.0
1946	16.9	0.0	16.9	0.0	16.9	0.0	17.0	0.6	17.1	0.6	17.3	1.2	18.5	6.9	18.7	1.1	19.1	2.1	19.6	2.6	20.0	2.0	20.1	0.5
1947	19.9	-1.0	20.0	0.5	20.3	1.5	20.3	0.0	20.3	0.0	20.5	1.0	-		-		21.8	6.3	-		-		22.3	2.3
1948	-		-		22.5	0.9	-		-		23.0	2.2	-		-		23.3	1.3	-		-		22.9	-1.7
1949	-		-		22.8	-0.4	-		-		22.7	-0.4	-		-		22.7	0.0	-		-		22.5	-0.9
1950	-		-		22.4	-0.4	-		-		22.7	1.3	-		-		23.1	1.8	-		-		23.8	3.0
1951	-		-		24.5	2.9	-		-		24.6	0.4	-		-		24.5	-0.4	-		-		25.1	2.4
1952	-		-		25.2	0.4	-		-		25.5	1.2	-		-		25.5	0.0	-		-		25.4	-0.4
1953	25.4	0.0	-		-		25.5	0.4	-		-		25.7	0.8	-		-		25.9	0.8	-		-	
1954	25.9	0.0	-		-		25.8	-0.4	-		-		26.0	0.8	-		-		25.9	-0.4	-		-	
1955	25.9	0.0	-		-		26.0	0.4	-		-		26.1	0.4	-		-		25.8	-1.1	-		-	
1956	25.8	0.0	-		-		25.7	-0.4	-		-		26.1	1.6	-		-		26.1	0.0	-		-	
1957	26.5	1.5	-		-		26.6	0.4	-		-		27.0	1.5	-		-		27.1	0.4	-		-	
1958	27.3	0.7	-		-		27.5	0.7	-		-		27.7	0.7	-		-		27.6	-0.4	-		-	
1959	27.8	0.7	-		-		27.7	-0.4	-		-		27.8	0.4	-		-		28.1	1.1	-		-	
1960	28.0	-0.4	-		-		28.2	0.7	-		-		28.3	0.4	-		-		28.5	0.7	-		-	
1961	28.4	-0.4	-		-		28.6	0.7	-		-		28.7	0.3	-		-		28.7	0.0	-		-	
1962	28.6	-0.3	-		-		29.0	1.4	-		-		29.0	0.0	-		-		29.1	0.3	-		-	

[Continued]

Minneapolis-St. Paul, MN-WI
Consumer Price Index - All Urban Consumers
Base 1982-1984 = 100
All Items
[Continued]

For 1917-2001. Columns headed % show percentile change in the index from the previous period for which an index is available.

Year	Jan Index	%	Feb Index	%	Mar Index	%	Apr Index	%	May Index	%	Jun Index	%	Jul Index	%	Aug Index	%	Sep Index	%	Oct Index	%	Nov Index	%	Dec Index	%
1963	29.1	0.0	-	-	-	-	29.2	0.3	-	-	-	-	29.6	1.4	-	-	-	-	29.5	-0.3	-	-	-	-
1964	29.5	0.0	-	-	-	-	29.5	0.0	-	-	-	-	29.7	0.7	-	-	-	-	29.8	0.3	-	-	-	-
1965	29.8	0.0	-	-	-	-	29.9	0.3	-	-	-	-	30.1	0.7	-	-	-	-	30.2	0.3	-	-	-	-
1966	30.3	0.3	-	-	-	-	30.7	1.3	-	-	-	-	30.7	0.0	-	-	-	-	31.1	1.3	-	-	-	-
1967	31.1	0.0	-	-	-	-	31.3	0.6	-	-	-	-	31.7	1.3	-	-	-	-	32.5	2.5	-	-	-	-
1968	32.7	0.6	-	-	-	-	33.1	1.2	-	-	-	-	33.4	0.9	-	-	-	-	33.5	0.3	-	-	-	-
1969	33.7	0.6	-	-	-	-	34.3	1.8	-	-	-	-	35.1	2.3	-	-	-	-	35.8	2.0	-	-	-	-
1970	36.5	2.0	-	-	-	-	37.1	1.6	-	-	-	-	37.5	1.1	-	-	-	-	37.9	1.1	-	-	-	-
1971	38.2	0.8	-	-	-	-	38.3	0.3	-	-	-	-	38.8	1.3	-	-	-	-	39.3	1.3	-	-	-	-
1972	39.4	0.3	-	-	-	-	39.5	0.3	-	-	-	-	39.9	1.0	-	-	-	-	40.5	1.5	-	-	-	-
1973	40.7	0.5	-	-	-	-	41.6	2.2	-	-	-	-	42.4	1.9	-	-	-	-	43.4	2.4	-	-	-	-
1974	44.6	2.8	-	-	-	-	46.2	3.6	-	-	-	-	47.3	2.4	-	-	-	-	49.0	3.6	-	-	-	-
1975	49.7	1.4	-	-	-	-	49.9	0.4	-	-	-	-	51.5	3.2	-	-	-	-	52.5	1.9	-	-	-	-
1976	53.2	1.3	-	-	-	-	53.7	0.9	-	-	-	-	54.6	1.7	-	-	-	-	55.2	1.1	-	-	-	-
1977	56.0	1.4	-	-	-	-	57.2	2.1	-	-	-	-	58.7	2.6	-	-	-	-	59.5	1.4	-	-	-	-
1978	60.7	2.0	-	-	-	-	62.0	2.1	-	-	63.2	1.9	-	-	64.5	2.1	-	-	65.6	1.7	-	-	66.4	1.2
1979	-	-	67.4	1.5	-	-	68.7	1.9	-	-	70.7	2.9	-	-	72.2	2.1	-	-	73.6	1.9	-	-	74.5	1.2
1980	-	-	75.7	1.6	-	-	77.7	2.6	-	-	78.4	0.9	-	-	79.6	1.5	-	-	81.3	2.1	-	-	82.4	1.4
1981	-	-	82.9	0.6	-	-	84.8	2.3	-	-	87.9	3.7	-	-	91.2	3.8	-	-	92.8	1.8	-	-	95.1	2.5
1982	-	-	97.4	2.4	-	-	96.0	-1.4	-	-	96.8	0.8	-	-	99.9	3.2	-	-	97.9	-2.0	-	-	97.4	-0.5
1983	-	-	97.3	-0.1	-	-	98.5	1.2	-	-	99.5	1.0	-	-	100.6	1.1	-	-	100.8	0.2	-	-	101.0	0.2
1984	-	-	101.7	0.7	-	-	102.5	0.8	-	-	103.1	0.6	-	-	103.4	0.3	-	-	104.4	1.0	-	-	104.3	-0.1
1985	-	-	105.1	0.8	-	-	106.2	1.0	-	-	107.1	0.8	-	-	107.8	0.7	-	-	108.4	0.6	-	-	108.3	-0.1
1986	-	-	108.2	-0.1	-	-	107.7	-0.5	-	-	108.9	1.1	-	-	108.3	-0.6	-	-	108.5	0.2	108.4	-0.1	109.0	0.6
1987	-	-	-	-	-	-	-	-	-	-	109.9	0.8	-	-	-	-	-	-	-	-	-	-	113.2	3.0
1988	-	-	-	-	-	-	-	-	-	-	115.7	2.2	-	-	-	-	-	-	-	-	-	-	118.6	2.5
1989	-	-	-	-	-	-	-	-	-	-	120.3	1.4	-	-	-	-	-	-	-	-	-	-	123.8	2.9
1990	-	-	-	-	-	-	-	-	-	-	125.5	1.4	-	-	-	-	-	-	-	-	-	-	128.5	2.4
1991	-	-	-	-	-	-	-	-	-	-	129.4	0.7	-	-	-	-	-	-	-	-	-	-	131.4	1.5
1992	-	-	-	-	-	-	-	-	-	-	133.6	1.7	-	-	-	-	-	-	-	-	-	-	136.4	2.1
1993	-	-	-	-	-	-	-	-	-	-	138.5	1.5	-	-	-	-	-	-	-	-	-	-	139.9	1.0
1994	-	-	-	-	-	-	-	-	-	-	142.5	1.9	-	-	-	-	-	-	-	-	-	-	144.7	1.5
1995	-	-	-	-	-	-	-	-	-	-	146.0	0.9	-	-	-	-	-	-	-	-	-	-	148.0	1.4
1996	-	-	-	-	-	-	-	-	-	-	150.8	1.9	-	-	-	-	-	-	-	-	-	-	153.0	1.5
1997	-	-	-	-	-	-	-	-	-	-	154.9	1.2	-	-	-	-	-	-	-	-	-	-	155.9	0.6
1998	-	-	-	-	-	-	-	-	-	-	157.3	0.9	-	-	-	-	-	-	-	-	-	-	159.4	1.3
1999	-	-	-	-	-	-	-	-	-	-	161.4	1.3	-	-	-	-	-	-	-	-	-	-	165.1	2.3
2000	-	-	-	-	-	-	-	-	-	-	168.2	1.9	-	-	-	-	-	-	-	-	-	-	172.0	2.3
2001	-	-	-	-	-	-	-	-	-	-	175.3	1.9	-	-	-	-	-	-	-	-	-	-	-	-

Source: U.S. Department of Labor, Bureau of Labor Statistics, Division of Consumer Prices and Price Indexes. - indicates no data collected for period.

Minneapolis-St. Paul, MN-WI
Consumer Price Index - Urban Wage Earners
Base 1982-1984 = 100
All Items

For 1917-2001. Columns headed % show percentile change in the index from the previous period for which an index is available.

Year	Jan Index	%	Feb Index	%	Mar Index	%	Apr Index	%	May Index	%	Jun Index	%	Jul Index	%	Aug Index	%	Sep Index	%	Oct Index	%	Nov Index	%	Dec Index	%
1917	-		-		-		-		-		-		-		-		-		-		-		13.2	-
1918	-		-		-		-		-		-		-		-		-		-		-		15.2	15.2
1919	-		-		-		-		-		15.6	2.6	-		-		-		-		-		17.5	12.2
1920	-		-		-		-		-		19.4	10.9	-		-		-		-		-		18.2	-6.2
1921	-		-		-		-		16.6	-8.8	-		-		-		16.5	-0.6	-		-		16.3	-1.2
1922	-		-		15.8	-3.1	-		-		15.9	0.6	-		-		15.5	-2.5	-		-		15.8	1.9
1923	-		-		15.9	0.6	-		-		15.8	-0.6	-		-		15.9	0.6	-		-		16.0	0.6
1924	-		-		15.9	-0.6	-		-		15.7	-1.3	-		-		15.5	-1.3	-		-		15.7	1.3
1925	-		-		-		-		-		15.8	0.6	-		-		-		-		-		16.3	3.2
1926	-		-		-		-		-		16.3	0.0	-		-		-		-		-		16.0	-1.8
1927	-		-		-		-		-		16.1	0.6	-		-		-		-		-		15.6	-3.1
1928	-		-		-		-		-		15.6	0.0	-		-		-		-		-		15.5	-0.6
1929	-		-		-		-		-		15.5	0.0	-		-		-		-		-		15.7	1.3
1930	-		-		-		-		-		15.5	-1.3	-		-		-		-		-		14.9	-3.9
1931	-		-		-		-		-		14.2	-4.7	-		-		-		-		-		13.8	-2.8
1932	-		-		-		-		-		12.9	-6.5	-		-		-		-		-		12.5	-3.1
1933	-		-		-		-		-		11.9	-4.8	-		-		-		-		-		12.5	5.0
1934	-		-		-		-		-		12.6	0.8	-		-		-		-		12.6	0.0	-	
1935	-		-		12.9	2.4	-		-		-		12.9	0.0	-		-		13.0	0.8	-		-	
1936	13.2	1.5	-		-		13.0	-1.5	-		-		13.2	1.5	-		13.4	1.5	-		-		13.4	0.0
1937	-		-		13.6	1.5	-		-		13.8	1.5	-		-		14.0	1.4	-		-		13.9	-0.7
1938	-		-		13.6	-2.2	-		-		13.7	0.7	-		-		13.6	-0.7	-		-		13.5	-0.7
1939	-		-		13.4	-0.7	-		-		13.4	0.0	-		-		13.6	1.5	-		-		13.6	0.0
1940	-		-		13.5	-0.7	-		-		13.5	0.0	-		-		13.5	0.0	13.5	0.0	13.6	0.7	13.7	0.7
1941	13.6	-0.7	13.7	0.7	13.7	0.0	13.8	0.7	13.9	0.7	14.2	2.2	14.3	0.7	14.4	0.7	14.6	1.4	14.8	1.4	14.8	0.0	14.8	0.0
1942	15.0	1.4	15.1	0.7	15.3	1.3	15.4	0.7	15.5	0.6	15.5	0.0	15.6	0.6	15.6	0.0	15.7	0.6	15.8	0.6	15.9	0.6	16.0	0.6
1943	16.0	0.0	16.1	0.6	16.2	0.6	16.2	0.0	16.3	0.6	16.3	0.0	16.2	-0.6	16.2	0.0	16.2	0.0	16.3	0.6	16.3	0.0	16.4	0.6
1944	16.2	-1.2	16.2	0.0	16.3	0.6	16.3	0.0	16.4	0.6	16.4	0.0	16.5	0.6	16.5	0.0	16.5	0.0	16.5	0.0	16.5	0.0	16.5	0.0
1945	16.5	0.0	16.5	0.0	16.5	0.0	16.5	0.0	16.6	0.6	16.7	0.6	16.8	0.6	16.8	0.0	16.8	0.0	16.8	0.0	16.9	0.6	16.9	0.0
1946	17.0	0.6	16.9	-0.6	16.9	0.0	17.0	0.6	17.1	0.6	17.4	1.8	18.5	6.3	18.7	1.1	19.1	2.1	19.6	2.6	20.0	2.0	20.1	0.5
1947	19.9	-1.0	20.0	0.5	20.4	2.0	20.3	-0.5	20.4	0.5	20.6	1.0	-		-		21.8	5.8	-		-		22.3	2.3
1948	-		-		22.6	1.3	-		-		23.0	1.8	-		-		23.4	1.7	-		-		23.0	-1.7
1949	-		-		22.8	-0.9	-		-		22.7	-0.4	-		-		22.7	0.0	-		-		22.6	-0.4
1950	-		-		22.5	-0.4	-		-		22.7	0.9	-		-		23.2	2.2	-		-		23.8	2.6
1951	-		-		24.6	3.4	-		-		24.7	0.4	-		-		24.6	-0.4	-		-		25.2	2.4
1952	-		-		25.2	0.0	-		-		25.6	1.6	-		-		25.5	-0.4	-		-		25.5	0.0
1953	25.4	-0.4	-		-		25.6	0.8	-		-		25.7	0.4	-		-		25.9	0.8	-		-	
1954	25.9	0.0	-		-		25.8	-0.4	-		-		26.1	1.2	-		-		26.0	-0.4	-		-	
1955	25.9	-0.4	-		-		26.0	0.4	-		-		26.1	0.4	-		-		25.9	-0.8	-		-	
1956	25.8	-0.4	-		-		25.7	-0.4	-		-		26.2	1.9	-		-		26.1	-0.4	-		-	
1957	26.5	1.5	-		-		26.6	0.4	-		-		27.0	1.5	-		-		27.1	0.4	-		-	
1958	27.4	1.1	-		-		27.6	0.7	-		-		27.8	0.7	-		-		27.7	-0.4	-		-	
1959	27.8	0.4	-		-		27.8	0.0	-		-		27.9	0.4	-		-		28.1	0.7	-		-	
1960	28.0	-0.4	-		-		28.2	0.7	-		-		28.4	0.7	-		-		28.5	0.4	-		-	
1961	28.4	-0.4	-		-		28.7	1.1	-		-		28.7	0.0	-		-		28.7	0.0	-		-	
1962	28.7	0.0	-		-		29.0	1.0	-		-		29.1	0.3	-		-		29.1	0.0	-		-	

[Continued]

Minneapolis-St. Paul, MN-WI
Consumer Price Index - Urban Wage Earners
Base 1982-1984 = 100
All Items
[Continued]

For 1917-2001. Columns headed % show percentile change in the index from the previous period for which an index is available.

Year	Jan Index	%	Feb Index	%	Mar Index	%	Apr Index	%	May Index	%	Jun Index	%	Jul Index	%	Aug Index	%	Sep Index	%	Oct Index	%	Nov Index	%	Dec Index	%
1963	29.2	0.3	-	-	-	-	29.3	0.3	-	-	-	-	29.6	1.0	-	-	-	-	29.5	-0.3	-	-	-	-
1964	29.6	0.3	-	-	-	-	29.5	-0.3	-	-	-	-	29.7	0.7	-	-	-	-	29.9	0.7	-	-	-	-
1965	29.9	0.0	-	-	-	-	29.9	0.0	-	-	-	-	30.2	1.0	-	-	-	-	30.3	0.3	-	-	-	-
1966	30.4	0.3	-	-	-	-	30.7	1.0	-	-	-	-	30.8	0.3	-	-	-	-	31.2	1.3	-	-	-	-
1967	31.2	0.0	-	-	-	-	31.4	0.6	-	-	-	-	31.8	1.3	-	-	-	-	32.6	2.5	-	-	-	-
1968	32.8	0.6	-	-	-	-	33.1	0.9	-	-	-	-	33.5	1.2	-	-	-	-	33.5	0.0	-	-	-	-
1969	33.8	0.9	-	-	-	-	34.4	1.8	-	-	-	-	35.2	2.3	-	-	-	-	35.8	1.7	-	-	-	-
1970	36.5	2.0	-	-	-	-	37.2	1.9	-	-	-	-	37.6	1.1	-	-	-	-	38.0	1.1	-	-	-	-
1971	38.3	0.8	-	-	-	-	38.3	0.0	-	-	-	-	38.8	1.3	-	-	-	-	39.3	1.3	-	-	-	-
1972	39.4	0.3	-	-	-	-	39.6	0.5	-	-	-	-	40.0	1.0	-	-	-	-	40.5	1.3	-	-	-	-
1973	40.7	0.5	-	-	-	-	41.7	2.5	-	-	-	-	42.4	1.7	-	-	-	-	43.4	2.4	-	-	-	-
1974	44.7	3.0	-	-	-	-	46.2	3.4	-	-	-	-	47.4	2.6	-	-	-	-	49.0	3.4	-	-	-	-
1975	49.8	1.6	-	-	-	-	50.0	0.4	-	-	-	-	51.6	3.2	-	-	-	-	52.6	1.9	-	-	-	-
1976	53.2	1.1	-	-	-	-	53.7	0.9	-	-	-	-	54.7	1.9	-	-	-	-	55.2	0.9	-	-	-	-
1977	56.0	1.4	-	-	-	-	57.2	2.1	-	-	-	-	58.8	2.8	-	-	-	-	59.6	1.4	-	-	-	-
1978	60.8	2.0	-	-	-	-	62.1	2.1	-	-	63.3	1.9	-	-	64.8	2.4	-	-	65.7	1.4	-	-	66.7	1.5
1979	-	-	67.7	1.5	-	-	68.8	1.6	-	-	71.2	3.5	-	-	72.8	2.2	-	-	74.2	1.9	-	-	74.8	0.8
1980	-	-	76.3	2.0	-	-	78.3	2.6	-	-	79.1	1.0	-	-	79.8	0.9	-	-	81.8	2.5	-	-	83.0	1.5
1981	-	-	83.6	0.7	-	-	85.2	1.9	-	-	88.1	3.4	-	-	91.4	3.7	-	-	92.9	1.6	-	-	95.0	2.3
1982	-	-	97.3	2.4	-	-	96.0	-1.3	-	-	96.8	0.8	-	-	99.8	3.1	-	-	98.0	-1.8	-	-	97.5	-0.5
1983	-	-	98.5	1.0	-	-	99.5	1.0	-	-	99.3	-0.2	-	-	98.3	-1.0	-	-	99.6	1.3	-	-	99.6	0.0
1984	-	-	101.5	1.9	-	-	102.3	0.8	-	-	104.8	2.4	-	-	105.9	1.0	-	-	104.2	-1.6	-	-	103.2	-1.0
1985	-	-	103.9	0.7	-	-	104.9	1.0	-	-	105.9	1.0	-	-	106.5	0.6	-	-	107.1	0.6	-	-	107.1	0.0
1986	-	-	106.7	-0.4	-	-	105.9	-0.7	-	-	107.1	1.1	-	-	106.6	-0.5	-	-	106.6	0.0	106.6	0.0	107.0	0.4
1987	-	-	-	-	-	-	-	-	-	-	108.0	0.9	-	-	-	-	-	-	-	-	-	-	111.5	3.2
1988	-	-	-	-	-	-	-	-	-	-	114.1	2.3	-	-	-	-	-	-	-	-	-	-	116.9	2.5
1989	-	-	-	-	-	-	-	-	-	-	118.3	1.2	-	-	-	-	-	-	-	-	-	-	121.8	3.0
1990	-	-	-	-	-	-	-	-	-	-	123.1	1.1	-	-	-	-	-	-	-	-	-	-	126.4	2.7
1991	-	-	-	-	-	-	-	-	-	-	127.1	0.6	-	-	-	-	-	-	-	-	-	-	129.2	1.7
1992	-	-	-	-	-	-	-	-	-	-	131.0	1.4	-	-	-	-	-	-	-	-	-	-	133.9	2.2
1993	-	-	-	-	-	-	-	-	-	-	136.0	1.6	-	-	-	-	-	-	-	-	-	-	137.4	1.0
1994	-	-	-	-	-	-	-	-	-	-	140.2	2.0	-	-	-	-	-	-	-	-	-	-	142.6	1.7
1995	-	-	-	-	-	-	-	-	-	-	144.0	1.0	-	-	-	-	-	-	-	-	-	-	145.7	1.2
1996	-	-	-	-	-	-	-	-	-	-	148.5	1.9	-	-	-	-	-	-	-	-	-	-	150.6	1.4
1997	-	-	-	-	-	-	-	-	-	-	152.5	1.3	-	-	-	-	-	-	-	-	-	-	153.3	0.5
1998	-	-	-	-	-	-	-	-	-	-	154.0	0.5	-	-	-	-	-	-	-	-	-	-	156.1	1.4
1999	-	-	-	-	-	-	-	-	-	-	158.0	1.2	-	-	-	-	-	-	-	-	-	-	161.8	2.4
2000	-	-	-	-	-	-	-	-	-	-	164.6	1.7	-	-	-	-	-	-	-	-	-	-	168.6	2.4
2001	-	-	-	-	-	-	-	-	-	-	171.7	1.8	-	-	-	-	-	-	-	-	-	-	-	-

Source: U.S. Department of Labor, Bureau of Labor Statistics, Division of Consumer Prices and Price Indexes. - indicates no data collected for period.

Minneapolis-St. Paul, MN-WI
Consumer Price Index - All Urban Consumers
Base 1982-1984 = 100
Food and Beverages

For 1976-2001. Columns headed % show percentile change in the index from the previous period for which an index is available.

Year	Jan Index	%	Feb Index	%	Mar Index	%	Apr Index	%	May Index	%	Jun Index	%	Jul Index	%	Aug Index	%	Sep Index	%	Oct Index	%	Nov Index	%	Dec Index	%
1976	62.4	-	-	-	-	-	62.0	-0.6	-	-	-	-	62.8	1.3	-	-	-	-	62.7	-0.2	-	-	-	-
1977	63.1	0.6	-	-	-	-	65.0	3.0	-	-	-	-	66.7	2.6	-	-	-	-	66.8	0.1	-	-	-	-
1978	67.9	1.6	-	-	-	-	70.6	4.0	-	-	72.9	3.3	-	-	73.6	1.0	-	-	74.3	1.0	-	-	75.5	1.6
1979	-	-	78.2	3.6	-	-	79.4	1.5	-	-	81.7	2.9	-	-	82.3	0.7	-	-	82.6	0.4	-	-	83.6	1.2
1980	-	-	84.4	1.0	-	-	86.0	1.9	-	-	87.6	1.9	-	-	88.6	1.1	-	-	89.9	1.5	-	-	90.7	0.9
1981	-	-	91.3	0.7	-	-	91.7	0.4	-	-	92.2	0.5	-	-	93.8	1.7	-	-	94.1	0.3	-	-	94.1	0.0
1982	-	-	94.9	0.9	-	-	95.4	0.5	-	-	96.8	1.5	-	-	97.5	0.7	-	-	97.9	0.4	-	-	97.9	0.0
1983	-	-	97.9	0.0	-	-	99.4	1.5	-	-	99.2	-0.2	-	-	99.6	0.4	-	-	100.0	0.4	-	-	101.5	1.5
1984	-	-	103.4	1.9	-	-	103.6	0.2	-	-	103.8	0.2	-	-	104.1	0.3	-	-	104.8	0.7	-	-	105.3	0.5
1985	-	-	106.5	1.1	-	-	106.3	-0.2	-	-	106.2	-0.1	-	-	106.3	0.1	-	-	106.9	0.6	-	-	107.7	0.7
1986	-	-	108.4	0.6	-	-	108.7	0.3	-	-	108.6	-0.1	-	-	109.4	0.7	-	-	110.4	0.9	111.1	0.6	112.2	1.0
1987	-	-	-	-	-	-	-	-	-	-	113.5	1.2	-	-	-	-	-	-	-	-	-	-	114.4	0.8
1988	-	-	-	-	-	-	-	-	-	-	118.5	3.6	-	-	-	-	-	-	-	-	-	-	121.4	2.4
1989	-	-	-	-	-	-	-	-	-	-	124.9	2.9	-	-	-	-	-	-	-	-	-	-	128.3	2.7
1990	-	-	-	-	-	-	-	-	-	-	133.5	4.1	-	-	-	-	-	-	-	-	-	-	135.7	1.6
1991	-	-	-	-	-	-	-	-	-	-	140.8	3.8	-	-	-	-	-	-	-	-	-	-	142.3	1.1
1992	-	-	-	-	-	-	-	-	-	-	144.4	1.5	-	-	-	-	-	-	-	-	-	-	145.1	0.5
1993	-	-	-	-	-	-	-	-	-	-	147.0	1.3	-	-	-	-	-	-	-	-	-	-	147.4	0.3
1994	-	-	-	-	-	-	-	-	-	-	148.5	0.7	-	-	-	-	-	-	-	-	-	-	149.7	0.8
1995	-	-	-	-	-	-	-	-	-	-	152.0	1.5	-	-	-	-	-	-	-	-	-	-	152.8	0.5
1996	-	-	-	-	-	-	-	-	-	-	156.8	2.6	-	-	-	-	-	-	-	-	-	-	160.8	2.6
1997	-	-	-	-	-	-	-	-	-	-	162.0	0.7	-	-	-	-	-	-	-	-	-	-	165.0	1.9
1998	-	-	-	-	-	-	-	-	-	-	164.7	-0.2	-	-	-	-	-	-	-	-	-	-	168.5	2.3
1999	-	-	-	-	-	-	-	-	-	-	170.8	1.4	-	-	-	-	-	-	-	-	-	-	173.4	1.5
2000	-	-	-	-	-	-	-	-	-	-	176.1	1.6	-	-	-	-	-	-	-	-	-	-	179.7	2.0
2001	-	-	-	-	-	-	-	-	-	-	181.6	1.1	-	-	-	-	-	-	-	-	-	-	-	-

Source: U.S. Department of Labor, Bureau of Labor Statistics, Division of Consumer Prices and Price Indexes. - indicates no data collected for period.

Minneapolis-St. Paul, MN-WI
Consumer Price Index - Urban Wage Earners
Base 1982-1984 = 100
Food and Beverages

For 1976-2001. Columns headed % show percentile change in the index from the previous period for which an index is available.

Year	Jan Index	%	Feb Index	%	Mar Index	%	Apr Index	%	May Index	%	Jun Index	%	Jul Index	%	Aug Index	%	Sep Index	%	Oct Index	%	Nov Index	%	Dec Index	%
1976	63.5	-	-	-	-	-	63.1	-0.6	-	-	-	-	63.9	1.3	-	-	-	-	63.8	-0.2	-	-	-	-
1977	64.2	0.6	-	-	-	-	66.1	3.0	-	-	-	-	67.9	2.7	-	-	-	-	68.0	0.1	-	-	-	-
1978	69.0	1.5	-	-	-	-	71.9	4.2	-	-	73.4	2.1	-	-	75.0	2.2	-	-	75.3	0.4	-	-	76.1	1.1
1979	-	-	79.1	3.9	-	-	79.3	0.3	-	-	82.2	3.7	-	-	83.5	1.6	-	-	83.9	0.5	-	-	83.3	-0.7
1980	-	-	85.3	2.4	-	-	86.9	1.9	-	-	88.3	1.6	-	-	89.3	1.1	-	-	91.3	2.2	-	-	91.8	0.5
1981	-	-	91.3	-0.5	-	-	91.7	0.4	-	-	92.1	0.4	-	-	94.1	2.2	-	-	94.0	-0.1	-	-	93.7	-0.3
1982	-	-	94.5	0.9	-	-	95.2	0.7	-	-	96.6	1.5	-	-	97.4	0.8	-	-	98.0	0.6	-	-	98.0	0.0
1983	-	-	97.9	-0.1	-	-	99.4	1.5	-	-	99.1	-0.3	-	-	99.6	0.5	-	-	100.1	0.5	-	-	101.6	1.5
1984	-	-	103.4	1.8	-	-	103.8	0.4	-	-	103.8	0.0	-	-	104.2	0.4	-	-	105.0	0.8	-	-	105.4	0.4
1985	-	-	106.6	1.1	-	-	106.4	-0.2	-	-	106.1	-0.3	-	-	106.2	0.1	-	-	106.8	0.6	-	-	107.6	0.7
1986	-	-	108.5	0.8	-	-	108.6	0.1	-	-	108.6	0.0	-	-	109.6	0.9	-	-	110.4	0.7	111.1	0.6	112.1	0.9
1987	-	-	-	-	-	-	-	-	-	-	113.3	1.1	-	-	-	-	-	-	-	-	-	-	114.5	1.1
1988	-	-	-	-	-	-	-	-	-	-	118.5	3.5	-	-	-	-	-	-	-	-	-	-	121.4	2.4
1989	-	-	-	-	-	-	-	-	-	-	124.8	2.8	-	-	-	-	-	-	-	-	-	-	128.4	2.9
1990	-	-	-	-	-	-	-	-	-	-	133.4	3.9	-	-	-	-	-	-	-	-	-	-	135.9	1.9
1991	-	-	-	-	-	-	-	-	-	-	140.9	3.7	-	-	-	-	-	-	-	-	-	-	142.6	1.2
1992	-	-	-	-	-	-	-	-	-	-	144.4	1.3	-	-	-	-	-	-	-	-	-	-	145.1	0.5
1993	-	-	-	-	-	-	-	-	-	-	146.8	1.2	-	-	-	-	-	-	-	-	-	-	147.4	0.4
1994	-	-	-	-	-	-	-	-	-	-	148.8	0.9	-	-	-	-	-	-	-	-	-	-	150.2	0.9
1995	-	-	-	-	-	-	-	-	-	-	152.3	1.4	-	-	-	-	-	-	-	-	-	-	153.2	0.6
1996	-	-	-	-	-	-	-	-	-	-	157.2	2.6	-	-	-	-	-	-	-	-	-	-	161.6	2.8
1997	-	-	-	-	-	-	-	-	-	-	162.5	0.6	-	-	-	-	-	-	-	-	-	-	166.0	2.2
1998	-	-	-	-	-	-	-	-	-	-	165.0	-0.6	-	-	-	-	-	-	-	-	-	-	168.8	2.3
1999	-	-	-	-	-	-	-	-	-	-	171.2	1.4	-	-	-	-	-	-	-	-	-	-	174.0	1.6
2000	-	-	-	-	-	-	-	-	-	-	176.5	1.4	-	-	-	-	-	-	-	-	-	-	180.0	2.0
2001	-	-	-	-	-	-	-	-	-	-	182.0	1.1	-	-	-	-	-	-	-	-	-	-	-	-

Source: U.S. Department of Labor, Bureau of Labor Statistics, Division of Consumer Prices and Price Indexes. - indicates no data collected for period.

Minneapolis-St. Paul, MN-WI
Consumer Price Index - All Urban Consumers
Base 1982-1984 = 100
Housing

For 1976-2001. Columns headed % show percentile change in the index from the previous period for which an index is available.

Year	Jan Index	%	Feb Index	%	Mar Index	%	Apr Index	%	May Index	%	Jun Index	%	Jul Index	%	Aug Index	%	Sep Index	%	Oct Index	%	Nov Index	%	Dec Index	%
1976	47.7	-	-	-	-	-	48.1	0.8	-	-	-	-	49.1	2.1	-	-	-	-	49.8	1.4	-	-	-	-
1977	50.8	2.0	-	-	-	-	51.6	1.6	-	-	-	-	53.7	4.1	-	-	-	-	54.9	2.2	-	-	-	-
1978	56.5	2.9	-	-	-	-	57.5	1.8	-	-	58.7	2.1	-	-	60.3	2.7	-	-	61.6	2.2	-	-	62.2	1.0
1979	-	-	63.0	1.3	-	-	64.1	1.7	-	-	65.8	2.7	-	-	67.2	2.1	-	-	69.6	3.6	-	-	70.0	0.6
1980	-	-	70.7	1.0	-	-	73.0	3.3	-	-	73.4	0.5	-	-	74.4	1.4	-	-	76.7	3.1	-	-	77.8	1.4
1981	-	-	77.5	-0.4	-	-	79.7	2.8	-	-	84.7	6.3	-	-	89.9	6.1	-	-	91.9	2.2	-	-	96.1	4.6
1982	-	-	100.3	4.4	-	-	98.1	-2.2	-	-	97.1	-1.0	-	-	102.2	5.3	-	-	98.2	-3.9	-	-	96.8	-1.4
1983	-	-	97.7	0.9	-	-	98.7	1.0	-	-	99.9	1.2	-	-	100.3	0.4	-	-	100.3	0.0	-	-	99.6	-0.7
1984	-	-	100.0	0.4	-	-	101.5	1.5	-	-	102.3	0.8	-	-	102.5	0.2	-	-	103.3	0.8	-	-	103.0	-0.3
1985	-	-	103.7	0.7	-	-	104.7	1.0	-	-	106.0	1.2	-	-	107.1	1.0	-	-	107.6	0.5	-	-	106.7	-0.8
1986	-	-	106.8	0.1	-	-	107.6	0.7	-	-	109.4	1.7	-	-	109.2	-0.2	-	-	107.2	-1.8	106.4	-0.7	107.5	1.0
1987	-	-	-	-	-	-	-	-	-	-	108.1	0.6	-	-	-	-	-	-	-	-	-	-	111.0	2.7
1988	-	-	-	-	-	-	-	-	-	-	110.8	-0.2	-	-	-	-	-	-	-	-	-	-	113.3	2.3
1989	-	-	-	-	-	-	-	-	-	-	115.0	1.5	-	-	-	-	-	-	-	-	-	-	116.6	1.4
1990	-	-	-	-	-	-	-	-	-	-	117.4	0.7	-	-	-	-	-	-	-	-	-	-	119.5	1.8
1991	-	-	-	-	-	-	-	-	-	-	120.1	0.5	-	-	-	-	-	-	-	-	-	-	121.2	0.9
1992	-	-	-	-	-	-	-	-	-	-	123.7	2.1	-	-	-	-	-	-	-	-	-	-	126.0	1.9
1993	-	-	-	-	-	-	-	-	-	-	128.0	1.6	-	-	-	-	-	-	-	-	-	-	128.3	0.2
1994	-	-	-	-	-	-	-	-	-	-	128.9	0.5	-	-	-	-	-	-	-	-	-	-	130.4	1.2
1995	-	-	-	-	-	-	-	-	-	-	131.1	0.5	-	-	-	-	-	-	-	-	-	-	134.4	2.5
1996	-	-	-	-	-	-	-	-	-	-	137.3	2.2	-	-	-	-	-	-	-	-	-	-	138.7	1.0
1997	-	-	-	-	-	-	-	-	-	-	140.0	0.9	-	-	-	-	-	-	-	-	-	-	141.6	1.1
1998	-	-	-	-	-	-	-	-	-	-	144.1	1.8	-	-	-	-	-	-	-	-	-	-	145.9	1.2
1999	-	-	-	-	-	-	-	-	-	-	147.6	1.2	-	-	-	-	-	-	-	-	-	-	150.8	2.2
2000	-	-	-	-	-	-	-	-	-	-	153.7	1.9	-	-	-	-	-	-	-	-	-	-	158.6	3.2
2001	-	-	-	-	-	-	-	-	-	-	162.2	2.3	-	-	-	-	-	-	-	-	-	-	-	-

Source: U.S. Department of Labor, Bureau of Labor Statistics, Division of Consumer Prices and Price Indexes. - indicates no data collected for period.

Minneapolis-St. Paul, MN-WI
Consumer Price Index - Urban Wage Earners
Base 1982-1984 = 100
Housing

For 1976-2001. Columns headed % show percentile change in the index from the previous period for which an index is available.

Year	Jan Index	%	Feb Index	%	Mar Index	%	Apr Index	%	May Index	%	Jun Index	%	Jul Index	%	Aug Index	%	Sep Index	%	Oct Index	%	Nov Index	%	Dec Index	%
1976	47.0	-	-	-	-	-	47.4	0.9	-	-	-	-	48.4	2.1	-	-	-	-	49.1	1.4	-	-	-	-
1977	50.1	2.0	-	-	-	-	50.9	1.6	-	-	-	-	52.9	3.9	-	-	-	-	54.0	2.1	-	-	-	-
1978	55.7	3.1	-	-	-	-	56.6	1.6	-	-	58.1	2.7	-	-	59.9	3.1	-	-	61.0	1.8	-	-	61.7	1.1
1979	-	-	62.5	1.3	-	-	63.5	1.6	-	-	65.4	3.0	-	-	66.8	2.1	-	-	68.8	3.0	-	-	69.3	0.7
1980	-	-	70.1	1.2	-	-	72.0	2.7	-	-	72.5	0.7	-	-	73.5	1.4	-	-	76.0	3.4	-	-	77.4	1.8
1981	-	-	77.3	-0.1	-	-	79.5	2.8	-	-	84.5	6.3	-	-	89.8	6.3	-	-	91.7	2.1	-	-	96.2	4.9
1982	-	-	100.5	4.5	-	-	98.3	-2.2	-	-	97.1	-1.2	-	-	102.5	5.6	-	-	98.3	-4.1	-	-	96.8	-1.5
1983	-	-	99.8	3.1	-	-	100.7	0.9	-	-	99.2	-1.5	-	-	95.2	-4.0	-	-	97.6	2.5	-	-	96.6	-1.0
1984	-	-	99.9	3.4	-	-	101.2	1.3	-	-	105.9	4.6	-	-	107.9	1.9	-	-	103.1	-4.4	-	-	100.7	-2.3
1985	-	-	101.5	0.8	-	-	102.3	0.8	-	-	103.6	1.3	-	-	104.7	1.1	-	-	105.3	0.6	-	-	104.4	-0.9
1986	-	-	104.5	0.1	-	-	105.2	0.7	-	-	107.1	1.8	-	-	106.9	-0.2	-	-	104.7	-2.1	103.9	-0.8	104.9	1.0
1987	-	-	-	-	-	-	-	-	-	-	105.5	0.6	-	-	-	-	-	-	-	-	-	-	108.3	2.7
1988	-	-	-	-	-	-	-	-	-	-	108.2	-0.1	-	-	-	-	-	-	-	-	-	-	110.6	2.2
1989	-	-	-	-	-	-	-	-	-	-	112.1	1.4	-	-	-	-	-	-	-	-	-	-	113.6	1.3
1990	-	-	-	-	-	-	-	-	-	-	114.5	0.8	-	-	-	-	-	-	-	-	-	-	116.6	1.8
1991	-	-	-	-	-	-	-	-	-	-	117.2	0.5	-	-	-	-	-	-	-	-	-	-	118.2	0.9
1992	-	-	-	-	-	-	-	-	-	-	120.6	2.0	-	-	-	-	-	-	-	-	-	-	122.9	1.9
1993	-	-	-	-	-	-	-	-	-	-	124.9	1.6	-	-	-	-	-	-	-	-	-	-	125.1	0.2
1994	-	-	-	-	-	-	-	-	-	-	125.7	0.5	-	-	-	-	-	-	-	-	-	-	127.2	1.2
1995	-	-	-	-	-	-	-	-	-	-	127.9	0.6	-	-	-	-	-	-	-	-	-	-	131.1	2.5
1996	-	-	-	-	-	-	-	-	-	-	134.0	2.2	-	-	-	-	-	-	-	-	-	-	135.4	1.0
1997	-	-	-	-	-	-	-	-	-	-	136.6	0.9	-	-	-	-	-	-	-	-	-	-	138.4	1.3
1998	-	-	-	-	-	-	-	-	-	-	140.2	1.3	-	-	-	-	-	-	-	-	-	-	142.4	1.6
1999	-	-	-	-	-	-	-	-	-	-	143.8	1.0	-	-	-	-	-	-	-	-	-	-	147.4	2.5
2000	-	-	-	-	-	-	-	-	-	-	149.8	1.6	-	-	-	-	-	-	-	-	-	-	154.9	3.4
2001	-	-	-	-	-	-	-	-	-	-	158.6	2.4	-	-	-	-	-	-	-	-	-	-	-	-

Source: U.S. Department of Labor, Bureau of Labor Statistics, Division of Consumer Prices and Price Indexes. - indicates no data collected for period.

Minneapolis-St. Paul, MN-WI
Consumer Price Index - All Urban Consumers
Base 1982-1984 = 100
Apparel

For 1952-2001. Columns headed % show percentile change in the index from the previous period for which an index is available.

Year	Jan Index	%	Feb Index	%	Mar Index	%	Apr Index	%	May Index	%	Jun Index	%	Jul Index	%	Aug Index	%	Sep Index	%	Oct Index	%	Nov Index	%	Dec Index	%
1952	-		-		-		-		-		-		-		-		-		-		-		46.0	
1953	45.6	-0.9	-		-		45.9	0.7	-		-		45.6	-0.7	-		-		46.4	1.8	-		-	
1954	45.9	-1.1	-		-		45.9	0.0	-		-		46.0	0.2	-		-		46.1	0.2	-		-	
1955	45.2	-2.0	-		-		45.0	-0.4	-		-		44.8	-0.4	-		-		45.7	2.0	-		-	
1956	46.0	0.7	-		-		46.1	0.2	-		-		46.5	0.9	-		-		47.1	1.3	-		-	
1957	46.9	-0.4	-		-		47.2	0.6	-		-		46.9	-0.6	-		-		47.4	1.1	-		-	
1958	47.4	0.0	-		-		47.3	-0.2	-		-		47.3	0.0	-		-		47.5	0.4	-		-	
1959	47.0	-1.1	-		-		46.9	-0.2	-		-		46.9	0.0	-		-		47.1	0.4	-		-	
1960	47.3	0.4	-		-		47.8	1.1	-		-		47.9	0.2	-		-		49.0	2.3	-		-	
1961	46.8	-4.5	-		-		46.6	-0.4	-		-		46.6	0.0	-		-		47.6	2.1	-		-	
1962	47.4	-0.4	-		-		47.7	0.6	-		-		47.6	-0.2	-		-		48.8	2.5	-		-	
1963	48.6	-0.4	-		-		48.8	0.4	-		-		49.0	0.4	-		-		49.3	0.6	-		-	
1964	48.1	-2.4	-		-		48.6	1.0	-		-		48.6	0.0	-		-		49.8	2.5	-		-	
1965	49.2	-1.2	-		-		49.7	1.0	-		-		49.4	-0.6	-		-		50.7	2.6	-		-	
1966	50.3	-0.8	-		-		50.7	0.8	-		-		51.2	1.0	-		-		52.2	2.0	-		-	
1967	51.6	-1.1	-		-		52.9	2.5	-		-		52.6	-0.6	-		-		54.3	3.2	-		-	
1968	53.7	-1.1	-		-		55.2	2.8	-		-		55.1	-0.2	-		-		56.2	2.0	-		-	
1969	56.3	0.2	-		-		57.8	2.7	-		-		58.3	0.9	-		-		60.1	3.1	-		-	
1970	59.3	-1.3	-		-		60.9	2.7	-		-		60.1	-1.3	-		-		63.3	5.3	-		-	
1971	62.1	-1.9	-		-		62.8	1.1	-		-		62.2	-1.0	-		-		63.3	1.8	-		-	
1972	62.4	-1.4	-		-		63.0	1.0	-		-		62.2	-1.3	-		-		65.2	4.8	-		-	
1973	64.5	-1.1	-		-		65.4	1.4	-		-		66.1	1.1	-		-		68.1	3.0	-		-	
1974	68.4	0.4	-		-		71.0	3.8	-		-		71.1	0.1	-		-		77.5	9.0	-		-	
1975	75.8	-2.2	-		-		73.9	-2.5	-		-		73.1	-1.1	-		-		73.8	1.0	-		-	
1976	73.7	-0.1	-		-		74.5	1.1	-		-		74.0	-0.7	-		-		77.0	4.1	-		-	
1977	75.8	-1.6	-		-		77.2	1.8	-		-		78.9	2.2	-		-		79.4	0.6	-		-	
1978	78.8	-0.8	-		-		81.1	2.9	-		80.3	-1.0	-		81.8	1.9	-		82.4	0.7	-		84.2	2.2
1979	-		82.8	-1.7	-		85.5	3.3	-		84.4	-1.3	-		86.8	2.8	-		86.4	-0.5	-		88.1	2.0
1980	-		88.5	0.5	-		91.2	3.1	-		91.5	0.3	-		92.1	0.7	-		90.9	-1.3	-		91.5	0.7
1981	-		91.6	0.1	-		94.2	2.8	-		94.2	0.0	-		95.7	1.6	-		97.0	1.4	-		96.8	-0.2
1982	-		97.9	1.1	-		99.1	1.2	-		97.4	-1.7	-		101.2	3.9	-		100.9	-0.3	-		103.0	2.1
1983	-		99.7	-3.2	-		104.0	4.3	-		101.5	-2.4	-		101.6	0.1	-		100.8	-0.8	-		101.2	0.4
1984	-		98.6	-2.6	-		99.8	1.2	-		98.4	-1.4	-		96.7	-1.7	-		99.9	3.3	-		98.9	-1.0
1985	-		103.3	4.4	-		107.7	4.3	-		108.0	0.3	-		104.7	-3.1	-		107.2	2.4	-		108.7	1.4
1986	-		104.5	-3.9	-		108.9	4.2	-		106.7	-2.0	-		105.9	-0.7	-		108.7	2.6	107.3	-1.3	107.0	-0.3
1987	-		-		-		-		-		106.2	-0.7	-		-		-		-		-		113.2	6.6
1988	-		-		-		-		-		125.3	10.7	-		-		-		-		-		127.9	2.1
1989	-		-		-		-		-		114.5	-10.5	-		-		-		-		-		128.5	12.2
1990	-		-		-		-		-		125.5	-2.3	-		-		-		-		-		135.4	7.9
1991	-		-		-		-		-		126.4	-6.6	-		-		-		-		-		135.4	7.1
1992	-		-		-		-		-		137.6	1.6	-		-		-		-		-		145.9	6.0
1993	-		-		-		-		-		138.0	-5.4	-		-		-		-		-		145.0	5.1
1994	-		-		-		-		-		150.0	3.4	-		-		-		-		-		146.3	-2.5
1995	-		-		-		-		-		141.4	-3.3	-		-		-		-		-		145.7	3.0
1996	-		-		-		-		-		145.7	0.0	-		-		-		-		-		140.5	-3.6
1997	-		-		-		-		-		149.4	6.3	-		-		-		-		-		141.9	-5.0

[Continued]

Minneapolis-St. Paul, MN-WI
Consumer Price Index - All Urban Consumers
Base 1982-1984 = 100
Apparel
[Continued]

For 1952-2001. Columns headed % show percentile change in the index from the previous period for which an index is available.

Year	Jan Index	%	Feb Index	%	Mar Index	%	Apr Index	%	May Index	%	Jun Index	%	Jul Index	%	Aug Index	%	Sep Index	%	Oct Index	%	Nov Index	%	Dec Index	%
1998	-	-	-	-	-	-	-	-	-	-	143.5	1.1	-	-	-	-	-	-	-	-	-	-	144.9	1.0
1999	-	-	-	-	-	-	-	-	-	-	140.2	-3.2	-	-	-	-	-	-	-	-	-	-	138.4	-1.3
2000	-	-	-	-	-	-	-	-	-	-	138.8	0.3	-	-	-	-	-	-	-	-	-	-	137.5	-0.9
2001	-	-	-	-	-	-	-	-	-	-	136.8	-0.5	-	-	-	-	-	-	-	-	-	-	-	-

Source: U.S. Department of Labor, Bureau of Labor Statistics, Division of Consumer Prices and Price Indexes. - indicates no data collected for period.

Minneapolis-St. Paul, MN-WI
Consumer Price Index - Urban Wage Earners
Base 1982-1984 = 100
Apparel

For 1952-2001. Columns headed % show percentile change in the index from the previous period for which an index is available.

Year	Jan Index	%	Feb Index	%	Mar Index	%	Apr Index	%	May Index	%	Jun Index	%	Jul Index	%	Aug Index	%	Sep Index	%	Oct Index	%	Nov Index	%	Dec Index	%
1952	-	-	-	-	-	-	-	-	-	-	-	-	-	-	-	-	-	-	-	-	-	-	47.0	-
1953	46.6	-0.9	-	-	-	-	47.0	0.9	-	-	-	-	46.6	-0.9	-	-	-	-	47.5	1.9	-	-	-	-
1954	47.0	-1.1	-	-	-	-	46.9	-0.2	-	-	-	-	47.0	0.2	-	-	-	-	47.1	0.2	-	-	-	-
1955	46.3	-1.7	-	-	-	-	46.0	-0.6	-	-	-	-	45.8	-0.4	-	-	-	-	46.8	2.2	-	-	-	-
1956	47.1	0.6	-	-	-	-	47.2	0.2	-	-	-	-	47.5	0.6	-	-	-	-	48.2	1.5	-	-	-	-
1957	47.9	-0.6	-	-	-	-	48.3	0.8	-	-	-	-	47.9	-0.8	-	-	-	-	48.4	1.0	-	-	-	-
1958	48.5	0.2	-	-	-	-	48.4	-0.2	-	-	-	-	48.3	-0.2	-	-	-	-	48.5	0.4	-	-	-	-
1959	48.1	-0.8	-	-	-	-	47.9	-0.4	-	-	-	-	47.9	0.0	-	-	-	-	48.2	0.6	-	-	-	-
1960	48.4	0.4	-	-	-	-	48.9	1.0	-	-	-	-	49.0	0.2	-	-	-	-	50.1	2.2	-	-	-	-
1961	47.9	-4.4	-	-	-	-	47.7	-0.4	-	-	-	-	47.7	0.0	-	-	-	-	48.7	2.1	-	-	-	-
1962	48.5	-0.4	-	-	-	-	48.8	0.6	-	-	-	-	48.7	-0.2	-	-	-	-	49.9	2.5	-	-	-	-
1963	49.7	-0.4	-	-	-	-	49.9	0.4	-	-	-	-	50.1	0.4	-	-	-	-	50.4	0.6	-	-	-	-
1964	49.2	-2.4	-	-	-	-	49.7	1.0	-	-	-	-	49.7	0.0	-	-	-	-	50.9	2.4	-	-	-	-
1965	50.3	-1.2	-	-	-	-	50.9	1.2	-	-	-	-	50.6	-0.6	-	-	-	-	51.8	2.4	-	-	-	-
1966	51.4	-0.8	-	-	-	-	51.8	0.8	-	-	-	-	52.4	1.2	-	-	-	-	53.4	1.9	-	-	-	-
1967	52.7	-1.3	-	-	-	-	54.1	2.7	-	-	-	-	53.8	-0.6	-	-	-	-	55.5	3.2	-	-	-	-
1968	54.9	-1.1	-	-	-	-	56.5	2.9	-	-	-	-	56.3	-0.4	-	-	-	-	57.4	2.0	-	-	-	-
1969	57.5	0.2	-	-	-	-	59.1	2.8	-	-	-	-	59.7	1.0	-	-	-	-	61.5	3.0	-	-	-	-
1970	60.7	-1.3	-	-	-	-	62.3	2.6	-	-	-	-	61.5	-1.3	-	-	-	-	64.8	5.4	-	-	-	-
1971	63.5	-2.0	-	-	-	-	64.3	1.3	-	-	-	-	63.6	-1.1	-	-	-	-	64.7	1.7	-	-	-	-
1972	63.8	-1.4	-	-	-	-	64.4	0.9	-	-	-	-	63.6	-1.2	-	-	-	-	66.7	4.9	-	-	-	-
1973	66.0	-1.0	-	-	-	-	66.9	1.4	-	-	-	-	67.6	1.0	-	-	-	-	69.6	3.0	-	-	-	-
1974	69.9	0.4	-	-	-	-	72.6	3.9	-	-	-	-	72.7	0.1	-	-	-	-	79.2	8.9	-	-	-	-
1975	77.5	-2.1	-	-	-	-	75.6	-2.5	-	-	-	-	74.8	-1.1	-	-	-	-	75.5	0.9	-	-	-	-
1976	75.4	-0.1	-	-	-	-	76.2	1.1	-	-	-	-	75.7	-0.7	-	-	-	-	78.7	4.0	-	-	-	-
1977	77.6	-1.4	-	-	-	-	79.0	1.8	-	-	-	-	80.7	2.2	-	-	-	-	81.3	0.7	-	-	-	-
1978	80.5	-1.0	-	-	-	-	82.9	3.0	-	-	83.1	0.2	-	-	83.0	-0.1	-	-	83.1	0.1	-	-	85.6	3.0
1979	-	-	83.0	-3.0	-	-	85.8	3.4	-	-	84.3	-1.7	-	-	87.3	3.6	-	-	87.9	0.7	-	-	88.2	0.3
1980	-	-	88.7	0.6	-	-	91.5	3.2	-	-	92.4	1.0	-	-	93.5	1.2	-	-	92.7	-0.9	-	-	92.4	-0.3
1981	-	-	94.1	1.8	-	-	95.8	1.8	-	-	96.7	0.9	-	-	97.8	1.1	-	-	98.1	0.3	-	-	96.7	-1.4
1982	-	-	97.6	0.9	-	-	99.0	1.4	-	-	97.0	-2.0	-	-	101.2	4.3	-	-	100.7	-0.5	-	-	103.3	2.6
1983	-	-	99.8	-3.4	-	-	103.9	4.1	-	-	100.9	-2.9	-	-	101.2	0.3	-	-	100.4	-0.8	-	-	101.6	1.2
1984	-	-	98.9	-2.7	-	-	100.5	1.6	-	-	98.4	-2.1	-	-	97.7	-0.7	-	-	99.8	2.1	-	-	98.8	-1.0
1985	-	-	104.0	5.3	-	-	108.0	3.8	-	-	108.6	0.6	-	-	105.2	-3.1	-	-	107.4	2.1	-	-	109.0	1.5
1986	-	-	104.3	-4.3	-	-	109.4	4.9	-	-	105.4	-3.7	-	-	105.9	0.5	-	-	108.2	2.2	106.9	-1.2	106.0	-0.8
1987	-	-	-	-	-	-	-	-	-	-	104.1	-1.8	-	-	-	-	-	-	-	-	-	-	112.6	8.2
1988	-	-	-	-	-	-	-	-	-	-	126.9	12.7	-	-	-	-	-	-	-	-	-	-	128.3	1.1
1989	-	-	-	-	-	-	-	-	-	-	112.7	-12.2	-	-	-	-	-	-	-	-	-	-	124.8	10.7
1990	-	-	-	-	-	-	-	-	-	-	121.5	-2.6	-	-	-	-	-	-	-	-	-	-	132.8	9.3
1991	-	-	-	-	-	-	-	-	-	-	123.4	-7.1	-	-	-	-	-	-	-	-	-	-	133.9	8.5
1992	-	-	-	-	-	-	-	-	-	-	135.1	0.9	-	-	-	-	-	-	-	-	-	-	143.0	5.8
1993	-	-	-	-	-	-	-	-	-	-	135.2	-5.5	-	-	-	-	-	-	-	-	-	-	142.0	5.0
1994	-	-	-	-	-	-	-	-	-	-	151.5	6.7	-	-	-	-	-	-	-	-	-	-	146.0	-3.6
1995	-	-	-	-	-	-	-	-	-	-	140.8	-3.6	-	-	-	-	-	-	-	-	-	-	143.6	2.0
1996	-	-	-	-	-	-	-	-	-	-	144.5	0.6	-	-	-	-	-	-	-	-	-	-	139.0	-3.8
1997	-	-	-	-	-	-	-	-	-	-	148.1	6.5	-	-	-	-	-	-	-	-	-	-	139.0	-6.1

[Continued]

Minneapolis-St. Paul, MN-WI
Consumer Price Index - Urban Wage Earners
Base 1982-1984 = 100
Apparel
[Continued]

For 1952-2001. Columns headed % show percentile change in the index from the previous period for which an index is available.

Year	Jan		Feb		Mar		Apr		May		Jun		Jul		Aug		Sep		Oct		Nov		Dec	
	Index	%	Index	%	Index	%	Index	%	Index	%	Index	%	Index	%	Index	%	Index	%	Index	%	Index	%	Index	%
1998	-	-	-	-	-	-	-	-	-	-	140.3	0.9	-	-	-	-	-	-	-	-	-	-	142.6	1.6
1999	-	-	-	-	-	-	-	-	-	-	139.8	-2.0	-	-	-	-	-	-	-	-	-	-	137.5	-1.6
2000	-	-	-	-	-	-	-	-	-	-	134.8	-2.0	-	-	-	-	-	-	-	-	-	-	134.7	-0.1
2001	-	-	-	-	-	-	-	-	-	-	134.3	-0.3	-	-	-	-	-	-	-	-	-	-	-	-

Source: U.S. Department of Labor, Bureau of Labor Statistics, Division of Consumer Prices and Price Indexes. - indicates no data collected for period.

Minneapolis-St. Paul, MN-WI
Consumer Price Index - All Urban Consumers
Base 1982-1984 = 100
Transportation

For 1947-2001. Columns headed % show percentile change in the index from the previous period for which an index is available.

Year	Jan Index	%	Feb Index	%	Mar Index	%	Apr Index	%	May Index	%	Jun Index	%	Jul Index	%	Aug Index	%	Sep Index	%	Oct Index	%	Nov Index	%	Dec Index	%
1947	20.9	-	21.0	0.5	21.1	0.5	21.1	0.0	21.3	0.9	21.3	0.0	-	-	-	-	21.9	2.8	-	-	-	-	23.3	6.4
1948	-	-	-	-	23.7	1.7	-	-	-	-	23.7	0.0	-	-	-	-	26.1	10.1	-	-	-	-	25.9	-0.8
1949	-	-	-	-	26.2	1.2	-	-	-	-	26.3	0.4	-	-	-	-	26.6	1.1	-	-	-	-	26.8	0.8
1950	-	-	-	-	26.3	-1.9	-	-	-	-	26.1	-0.8	-	-	-	-	26.7	2.3	-	-	-	-	26.8	0.4
1951	-	-	-	-	27.1	1.1	-	-	-	-	27.1	0.0	-	-	-	-	25.8	-4.8	-	-	-	-	27.8	7.8
1952	-	-	-	-	28.3	1.8	-	-	-	-	28.8	1.8	-	-	-	-	29.2	1.4	-	-	-	-	29.2	0.0
1953	29.3	0.3	-	-	-	-	29.5	0.7	-	-	-	-	29.5	0.0	-	-	-	-	29.4	-0.3	-	-	-	-
1954	29.5	0.3	-	-	-	-	29.3	-0.7	-	-	-	-	29.4	0.3	-	-	-	-	28.7	-2.4	-	-	-	-
1955	29.5	2.8	-	-	-	-	28.5	-3.4	-	-	-	-	28.8	1.1	-	-	-	-	27.1	-5.9	-	-	-	-
1956	27.6	1.8	-	-	-	-	27.0	-2.2	-	-	-	-	28.0	3.7	-	-	-	-	28.6	2.1	-	-	-	-
1957	29.3	2.4	-	-	-	-	29.4	0.3	-	-	-	-	29.4	0.0	-	-	-	-	28.8	-2.0	-	-	-	-
1958	30.1	4.5	-	-	-	-	29.6	-1.7	-	-	-	-	30.3	2.4	-	-	-	-	30.5	0.7	-	-	-	-
1959	31.7	3.9	-	-	-	-	31.5	-0.6	-	-	-	-	30.6	-2.9	-	-	-	-	32.2	5.2	-	-	-	-
1960	32.0	-0.6	-	-	-	-	31.4	-1.9	-	-	-	-	32.1	2.2	-	-	-	-	32.2	0.3	-	-	-	-
1961	32.0	-0.6	-	-	-	-	32.5	1.6	-	-	-	-	32.1	-1.2	-	-	-	-	32.2	0.3	-	-	-	-
1962	32.1	-0.3	-	-	-	-	32.9	2.5	-	-	-	-	32.4	-1.5	-	-	-	-	33.4	3.1	-	-	-	-
1963	32.6	-2.4	-	-	-	-	33.1	1.5	-	-	-	-	33.7	1.8	-	-	-	-	33.2	-1.5	-	-	-	-
1964	33.6	1.2	-	-	-	-	32.5	-3.3	-	-	-	-	33.1	1.8	-	-	-	-	33.5	1.2	-	-	-	-
1965	33.5	0.0	-	-	-	-	33.6	0.3	-	-	-	-	33.8	0.6	-	-	-	-	34.0	0.6	-	-	-	-
1966	34.1	0.3	-	-	-	-	34.2	0.3	-	-	-	-	34.4	0.6	-	-	-	-	34.7	0.9	-	-	-	-
1967	34.7	0.0	-	-	-	-	35.1	1.2	-	-	-	-	35.4	0.9	-	-	-	-	36.5	3.1	-	-	-	-
1968	36.7	0.5	-	-	-	-	36.4	-0.8	-	-	-	-	36.7	0.8	-	-	-	-	37.2	1.4	-	-	-	-
1969	36.6	-1.6	-	-	-	-	37.8	3.3	-	-	-	-	37.0	-2.1	-	-	-	-	37.6	1.6	-	-	-	-
1970	38.2	1.6	-	-	-	-	39.2	2.6	-	-	-	-	39.8	1.5	-	-	-	-	40.5	1.8	-	-	-	-
1971	41.9	3.5	-	-	-	-	40.7	-2.9	-	-	-	-	41.0	0.7	-	-	-	-	40.9	-0.2	-	-	-	-
1972	41.7	2.0	-	-	-	-	40.6	-2.6	-	-	-	-	41.4	2.0	-	-	-	-	41.9	1.2	-	-	-	-
1973	42.2	0.7	-	-	-	-	42.8	1.4	-	-	-	-	43.3	1.2	-	-	-	-	43.2	-0.2	-	-	-	-
1974	44.9	3.9	-	-	-	-	47.0	4.7	-	-	-	-	49.2	4.7	-	-	-	-	48.8	-0.8	-	-	-	-
1975	48.6	-0.4	-	-	-	-	49.2	1.2	-	-	-	-	51.6	4.9	-	-	-	-	52.5	1.7	-	-	-	-
1976	53.0	1.0	-	-	-	-	54.2	2.3	-	-	-	-	56.3	3.9	-	-	-	-	56.7	0.7	-	-	-	-
1977	57.9	2.1	-	-	-	-	59.5	2.8	-	-	-	-	60.3	1.3	-	-	-	-	60.0	-0.5	-	-	-	-
1978	60.4	0.7	-	-	-	-	60.9	0.8	-	-	62.4	2.5	-	-	63.3	1.4	-	-	63.9	0.9	-	-	64.6	1.1
1979	-	-	65.6	1.5	-	-	68.2	4.0	-	-	72.3	6.0	-	-	74.7	3.3	-	-	75.6	1.2	-	-	77.4	2.4
1980	-	-	80.4	3.9	-	-	83.2	3.5	-	-	83.9	0.8	-	-	84.2	0.4	-	-	85.9	2.0	-	-	87.3	1.6
1981	-	-	89.8	2.9	-	-	91.7	2.1	-	-	94.1	2.6	-	-	94.7	0.6	-	-	96.8	2.2	-	-	97.2	0.4
1982	-	-	96.0	-1.2	-	-	93.7	-2.4	-	-	99.2	5.9	-	-	99.3	0.1	-	-	98.7	-0.6	-	-	98.6	-0.1
1983	-	-	96.1	-2.5	-	-	96.9	0.8	-	-	99.1	2.3	-	-	101.1	2.0	-	-	101.4	0.3	-	-	101.9	0.5
1984	-	-	101.9	0.0	-	-	102.3	0.4	-	-	103.5	1.2	-	-	103.6	0.1	-	-	104.2	0.6	-	-	104.4	0.2
1985	-	-	103.4	-1.0	-	-	105.4	1.9	-	-	107.1	1.6	-	-	107.5	0.4	-	-	106.8	-0.7	-	-	107.3	0.5
1986	-	-	104.5	-2.6	-	-	98.8	-5.5	-	-	101.2	2.4	-	-	98.3	-2.9	-	-	98.9	0.6	99.3	0.4	99.0	-0.3
1987	-	-	-	-	-	-	-	-	-	-	101.2	2.2	-	-	-	-	-	-	-	-	-	-	104.5	3.3
1988	-	-	-	-	-	-	-	-	-	-	105.7	1.1	-	-	-	-	-	-	-	-	-	-	108.8	2.9
1989	-	-	-	-	-	-	-	-	-	-	112.7	3.6	-	-	-	-	-	-	-	-	-	-	116.8	3.6
1990	-	-	-	-	-	-	-	-	-	-	116.9	0.1	-	-	-	-	-	-	-	-	-	-	120.1	2.7
1991	-	-	-	-	-	-	-	-	-	-	119.3	-0.7	-	-	-	-	-	-	-	-	-	-	119.5	0.2
1992	-	-	-	-	-	-	-	-	-	-	119.8	0.3	-	-	-	-	-	-	-	-	-	-	123.7	3.3

[Continued]

Minneapolis-St. Paul, MN-WI
Consumer Price Index - All Urban Consumers
Base 1982-1984 = 100
Transportation
[Continued]

For 1947-2001. Columns headed % show percentile change in the index from the previous period for which an index is available.

Year	Jan		Feb		Mar		Apr		May		Jun		Jul		Aug		Sep		Oct		Nov		Dec	
	Index	%	Index	%	Index	%	Index	%	Index	%	Index	%	Index	%	Index	%	Index	%	Index	%	Index	%	Index	%
1993	-	-	-	-	-	-	-	-	-	-	125.9	1.8	-	-	-	-	-	-	-	-	-	-	127.9	1.6
1994	-	-	-	-	-	-	-	-	-	-	132.2	3.4	-	-	-	-	-	-	-	-	-	-	136.2	3.0
1995	-	-	-	-	-	-	-	-	-	-	139.2	2.2	-	-	-	-	-	-	-	-	-	-	138.0	-0.9
1996	-	-	-	-	-	-	-	-	-	-	140.0	1.4	-	-	-	-	-	-	-	-	-	-	143.9	2.8
1997	-	-	-	-	-	-	-	-	-	-	145.0	0.8	-	-	-	-	-	-	-	-	-	-	142.9	-1.4
1998	-	-	-	-	-	-	-	-	-	-	141.6	-0.9	-	-	-	-	-	-	-	-	-	-	142.1	0.4
1999	-	-	-	-	-	-	-	-	-	-	144.9	2.0	-	-	-	-	-	-	-	-	-	-	152.2	5.0
2000	-	-	-	-	-	-	-	-	-	-	155.6	2.2	-	-	-	-	-	-	-	-	-	-	159.6	2.6
2001	-	-	-	-	-	-	-	-	-	-	162.6	1.9	-	-	-	-	-	-	-	-	-	-	-	-

Source: U.S. Department of Labor, Bureau of Labor Statistics, Division of Consumer Prices and Price Indexes. - indicates no data collected for period.

Minneapolis-St. Paul, MN-WI
Consumer Price Index - Urban Wage Earners
Base 1982-1984 = 100
Transportation

For 1947-2001. Columns headed % show percentile change in the index from the previous period for which an index is available.

Year	Jan Index	%	Feb Index	%	Mar Index	%	Apr Index	%	May Index	%	Jun Index	%	Jul Index	%	Aug Index	%	Sep Index	%	Oct Index	%	Nov Index	%	Dec Index	%
1947	20.6	-	20.6	0.0	20.7	0.5	20.8	0.5	21.0	1.0	21.0	0.0	-	-	-	-	21.5	2.4	-	-	-	-	22.9	6.5
1948	-	-	-	-	23.3	1.7	-	-	-	-	23.4	0.4	-	-	-	-	25.7	9.8	-	-	-	-	25.5	-0.8
1949	-	-	-	-	25.8	1.2	-	-	-	-	25.9	0.4	-	-	-	-	26.2	1.2	-	-	-	-	26.4	0.8
1950	-	-	-	-	25.9	-1.9	-	-	-	-	25.7	-0.8	-	-	-	-	26.3	2.3	-	-	-	-	26.4	0.4
1951	-	-	-	-	26.7	1.1	-	-	-	-	26.7	0.0	-	-	-	-	25.4	-4.9	-	-	-	-	27.4	7.9
1952	-	-	-	-	27.8	1.5	-	-	-	-	28.3	1.8	-	-	-	-	28.8	1.8	-	-	-	-	28.8	0.0
1953	28.8	0.0	-	-	-	-	29.1	1.0	-	-	-	-	29.1	0.0	-	-	-	-	28.9	-0.7	-	-	-	-
1954	29.1	0.7	-	-	-	-	28.8	-1.0	-	-	-	-	29.0	0.7	-	-	-	-	28.2	-2.8	-	-	-	-
1955	29.0	2.8	-	-	-	-	28.0	-3.4	-	-	-	-	28.3	1.1	-	-	-	-	26.7	-5.7	-	-	-	-
1956	27.2	1.9	-	-	-	-	26.6	-2.2	-	-	-	-	27.5	3.4	-	-	-	-	28.1	2.2	-	-	-	-
1957	28.8	2.5	-	-	-	-	28.9	0.3	-	-	-	-	29.0	0.3	-	-	-	-	28.3	-2.4	-	-	-	-
1958	29.6	4.6	-	-	-	-	29.2	-1.4	-	-	-	-	29.8	2.1	-	-	-	-	30.1	1.0	-	-	-	-
1959	31.3	4.0	-	-	-	-	31.1	-0.6	-	-	-	-	30.2	-2.9	-	-	-	-	31.7	5.0	-	-	-	-
1960	31.5	-0.6	-	-	-	-	30.9	-1.9	-	-	-	-	31.6	2.3	-	-	-	-	31.7	0.3	-	-	-	-
1961	31.5	-0.6	-	-	-	-	32.0	1.6	-	-	-	-	31.6	-1.2	-	-	-	-	31.7	0.3	-	-	-	-
1962	31.6	-0.3	-	-	-	-	32.4	2.5	-	-	-	-	31.9	-1.5	-	-	-	-	32.9	3.1	-	-	-	-
1963	32.1	-2.4	-	-	-	-	32.6	1.6	-	-	-	-	33.2	1.8	-	-	-	-	32.7	-1.5	-	-	-	-
1964	33.1	1.2	-	-	-	-	32.0	-3.3	-	-	-	-	32.6	1.9	-	-	-	-	32.9	0.9	-	-	-	-
1965	32.9	0.0	-	-	-	-	33.1	0.6	-	-	-	-	33.3	0.6	-	-	-	-	33.5	0.6	-	-	-	-
1966	33.5	0.0	-	-	-	-	33.7	0.6	-	-	-	-	33.9	0.6	-	-	-	-	34.2	0.9	-	-	-	-
1967	34.1	-0.3	-	-	-	-	34.5	1.2	-	-	-	-	34.9	1.2	-	-	-	-	36.0	3.2	-	-	-	-
1968	36.2	0.6	-	-	-	-	35.9	-0.8	-	-	-	-	36.1	0.6	-	-	-	-	36.6	1.4	-	-	-	-
1969	36.0	-1.6	-	-	-	-	37.2	3.3	-	-	-	-	36.5	-1.9	-	-	-	-	37.0	1.4	-	-	-	-
1970	37.6	1.6	-	-	-	-	38.6	2.7	-	-	-	-	39.2	1.6	-	-	-	-	39.8	1.5	-	-	-	-
1971	41.2	3.5	-	-	-	-	40.1	-2.7	-	-	-	-	40.3	0.5	-	-	-	-	40.3	0.0	-	-	-	-
1972	41.0	1.7	-	-	-	-	40.0	-2.4	-	-	-	-	40.7	1.7	-	-	-	-	41.2	1.2	-	-	-	-
1973	41.6	1.0	-	-	-	-	42.2	1.4	-	-	-	-	42.6	0.9	-	-	-	-	42.5	-0.2	-	-	-	-
1974	44.2	4.0	-	-	-	-	46.3	4.8	-	-	-	-	48.5	4.8	-	-	-	-	48.1	-0.8	-	-	-	-
1975	47.9	-0.4	-	-	-	-	48.5	1.3	-	-	-	-	50.8	4.7	-	-	-	-	51.7	1.8	-	-	-	-
1976	52.1	0.8	-	-	-	-	53.4	2.5	-	-	-	-	55.5	3.9	-	-	-	-	55.8	0.5	-	-	-	-
1977	57.0	2.2	-	-	-	-	58.6	2.8	-	-	-	-	59.4	1.4	-	-	-	-	59.1	-0.5	-	-	-	-
1978	59.5	0.7	-	-	-	-	60.0	0.8	-	-	61.6	2.7	-	-	62.5	1.5	-	-	63.3	1.3	-	-	64.1	1.3
1979	-	-	65.0	1.4	-	-	67.8	4.3	-	-	72.2	6.5	-	-	74.5	3.2	-	-	75.5	1.3	-	-	77.4	2.5
1980	-	-	80.5	4.0	-	-	83.3	3.5	-	-	84.2	1.1	-	-	84.2	0.0	-	-	85.9	2.0	-	-	87.6	2.0
1981	-	-	90.5	3.3	-	-	92.2	1.9	-	-	94.1	2.1	-	-	95.0	1.0	-	-	96.9	2.0	-	-	97.4	0.5
1982	-	-	96.3	-1.1	-	-	93.7	-2.7	-	-	99.4	6.1	-	-	99.4	0.0	-	-	98.8	-0.6	-	-	98.8	0.0
1983	-	-	96.1	-2.7	-	-	96.9	0.8	-	-	99.4	2.6	-	-	101.3	1.9	-	-	101.4	0.1	-	-	101.8	0.4
1984	-	-	101.7	-0.1	-	-	102.1	0.4	-	-	103.1	1.0	-	-	103.4	0.3	-	-	104.0	0.6	-	-	104.1	0.1
1985	-	-	102.8	-1.2	-	-	105.1	2.2	-	-	106.9	1.7	-	-	107.3	0.4	-	-	106.4	-0.8	-	-	107.1	0.7
1986	-	-	103.9	-3.0	-	-	97.6	-6.1	-	-	100.3	2.8	-	-	97.1	-3.2	-	-	97.7	0.6	98.1	0.4	97.8	-0.3
1987	-	-	-	-	-	-	-	-	-	-	100.4	2.7	-	-	-	-	-	-	-	-	-	-	103.9	3.5
1988	-	-	-	-	-	-	-	-	-	-	104.8	0.9	-	-	-	-	-	-	-	-	-	-	108.1	3.1
1989	-	-	-	-	-	-	-	-	-	-	112.1	3.7	-	-	-	-	-	-	-	-	-	-	116.1	3.6
1990	-	-	-	-	-	-	-	-	-	-	115.7	-0.3	-	-	-	-	-	-	-	-	-	-	119.3	3.1
1991	-	-	-	-	-	-	-	-	-	-	118.0	-1.1	-	-	-	-	-	-	-	-	-	-	118.7	0.6
1992	-	-	-	-	-	-	-	-	-	-	118.8	0.1	-	-	-	-	-	-	-	-	-	-	123.2	3.7

[Continued]

Minneapolis-St. Paul, MN-WI
Consumer Price Index - Urban Wage Earners
Base 1982-1984 = 100
Transportation
[Continued]

For 1947-2001. Columns headed % show percentile change in the index from the previous period for which an index is available.

Year	Jan Index	%	Feb Index	%	Mar Index	%	Apr Index	%	May Index	%	Jun Index	%	Jul Index	%	Aug Index	%	Sep Index	%	Oct Index	%	Nov Index	%	Dec Index	%
1993	-		-		-		-		-		125.3	1.7	-		-		-		-		-		127.6	1.8
1994	-		-		-		-		-		131.1	2.7	-		-		-		-		-		136.2	3.9
1995	-		-		-		-		-		139.4	2.3	-		-		-		-		-		137.9	-1.1
1996	-		-		-		-		-		140.0	1.5	-		-		-		-		-		143.4	2.4
1997	-		-		-		-		-		144.1	0.5	-		-		-		-		-		142.1	-1.4
1998	-		-		-		-		-		140.6	-1.1	-		-		-		-		-		140.9	0.2
1999	-		-		-		-		-		142.6	1.2	-		-		-		-		-		150.0	5.2
2000	-		-		-		-		-		153.7	2.5	-		-		-		-		-		158.7	3.3
2001	-		-		-		-		-		161.5	1.8	-		-		-		-		-		-	

Source: U.S. Department of Labor, Bureau of Labor Statistics, Division of Consumer Prices and Price Indexes. - indicates no data collected for period.

Minneapolis-St. Paul, MN-WI
Consumer Price Index - All Urban Consumers
Base 1982-1984 = 100
Medical Care

For 1947-2001. Columns headed % show percentile change in the index from the previous period for which an index is available.

Year	Jan Index	%	Feb Index	%	Mar Index	%	Apr Index	%	May Index	%	Jun Index	%	Jul Index	%	Aug Index	%	Sep Index	%	Oct Index	%	Nov Index	%	Dec Index	%
1947	10.2	-	10.2	0.0	10.2	0.0	10.4	2.0	10.5	1.0	10.6	1.0	-	-	-	-	11.0	3.8	-	-	-	-	11.2	1.8
1948	-	-	-	-	11.4	1.8	-	-	-	-	11.8	3.5	-	-	-	-	11.9	0.8	-	-	-	-	12.1	1.7
1949	-	-	-	-	12.1	0.0	-	-	-	-	12.2	0.8	-	-	-	-	12.3	0.8	-	-	-	-	12.4	0.8
1950	-	-	-	-	12.4	0.0	-	-	-	-	12.4	0.0	-	-	-	-	12.8	3.2	-	-	-	-	12.9	0.8
1951	-	-	-	-	13.6	5.4	-	-	-	-	13.6	0.0	-	-	-	-	13.8	1.5	-	-	-	-	13.9	0.7
1952	-	-	-	-	14.5	4.3	-	-	-	-	14.5	0.0	-	-	-	-	14.6	0.7	-	-	-	-	14.5	-0.7
1953	14.5	0.0	-	-	-	-	15.8	9.0	-	-	-	-	15.9	0.6	-	-	-	-	15.9	0.0	-	-	-	-
1954	16.0	0.6	-	-	-	-	16.4	2.5	-	-	-	-	16.5	0.6	-	-	-	-	16.4	-0.6	-	-	-	-
1955	16.6	1.2	-	-	-	-	17.0	2.4	-	-	-	-	17.1	0.6	-	-	-	-	17.1	0.0	-	-	-	-
1956	17.2	0.6	-	-	-	-	17.2	0.0	-	-	-	-	17.3	0.6	-	-	-	-	17.3	0.0	-	-	-	-
1957	17.4	0.6	-	-	-	-	17.6	1.1	-	-	-	-	19.5	10.8	-	-	-	-	19.6	0.5	-	-	-	-
1958	19.8	1.0	-	-	-	-	20.2	2.0	-	-	-	-	21.9	8.4	-	-	-	-	22.0	0.5	-	-	-	-
1959	22.2	0.9	-	-	-	-	22.2	0.0	-	-	-	-	22.4	0.9	-	-	-	-	23.5	4.9	-	-	-	-
1960	23.5	0.0	-	-	-	-	24.1	2.6	-	-	-	-	24.7	2.5	-	-	-	-	24.4	-1.2	-	-	-	-
1961	24.4	0.0	-	-	-	-	25.4	4.1	-	-	-	-	26.4	3.9	-	-	-	-	26.5	0.4	-	-	-	-
1962	26.5	0.0	-	-	-	-	26.5	0.0	-	-	-	-	26.8	1.1	-	-	-	-	26.9	0.4	-	-	-	-
1963	27.0	0.4	-	-	-	-	27.0	0.0	-	-	-	-	27.0	0.0	-	-	-	-	27.1	0.4	-	-	-	-
1964	27.2	0.4	-	-	-	-	27.6	1.5	-	-	-	-	27.5	-0.4	-	-	-	-	27.5	0.0	-	-	-	-
1965	27.5	0.0	-	-	-	-	27.6	0.4	-	-	-	-	27.6	0.0	-	-	-	-	27.7	0.4	-	-	-	-
1966	27.9	0.7	-	-	-	-	28.6	2.5	-	-	-	-	29.0	1.4	-	-	-	-	29.4	1.4	-	-	-	-
1967	30.0	2.0	-	-	-	-	30.1	0.3	-	-	-	-	30.4	1.0	-	-	-	-	30.8	1.3	-	-	-	-
1968	31.4	1.9	-	-	-	-	31.8	1.3	-	-	-	-	32.0	0.6	-	-	-	-	32.4	1.3	-	-	-	-
1969	32.8	1.2	-	-	-	-	33.3	1.5	-	-	-	-	34.0	2.1	-	-	-	-	33.9	-0.3	-	-	-	-
1970	34.2	0.9	-	-	-	-	35.6	4.1	-	-	-	-	36.3	2.0	-	-	-	-	36.3	0.0	-	-	-	-
1971	36.9	1.7	-	-	-	-	37.5	1.6	-	-	-	-	38.1	1.6	-	-	-	-	37.9	-0.5	-	-	-	-
1972	37.9	0.0	-	-	-	-	38.0	0.3	-	-	-	-	38.3	0.8	-	-	-	-	38.8	1.3	-	-	-	-
1973	39.4	1.5	-	-	-	-	39.8	1.0	-	-	-	-	40.0	0.5	-	-	-	-	41.0	2.5	-	-	-	-
1974	42.0	2.4	-	-	-	-	42.6	1.4	-	-	-	-	43.8	2.8	-	-	-	-	45.3	3.4	-	-	-	-
1975	47.4	4.6	-	-	-	-	47.6	0.4	-	-	-	-	48.9	2.7	-	-	-	-	49.4	1.0	-	-	-	-
1976	50.5	2.2	-	-	-	-	51.4	1.8	-	-	-	-	52.4	1.9	-	-	-	-	53.5	2.1	-	-	-	-
1977	54.9	2.6	-	-	-	-	55.7	1.5	-	-	-	-	56.9	2.2	-	-	-	-	57.5	1.1	-	-	-	-
1978	59.1	2.8	-	-	-	-	60.3	2.0	-	-	60.9	1.0	-	-	62.3	2.3	-	-	62.2	-0.2	-	-	63.2	1.6
1979	-	-	65.1	3.0	-	-	64.0	-1.7	-	-	65.2	1.9	-	-	66.7	2.3	-	-	68.1	2.1	-	-	70.2	3.1
1980	-	-	72.7	3.6	-	-	72.9	0.3	-	-	73.0	0.1	-	-	74.6	2.2	-	-	74.6	0.0	-	-	75.5	1.2
1981	-	-	77.2	2.3	-	-	78.4	1.6	-	-	79.3	1.1	-	-	82.2	3.7	-	-	82.8	0.7	-	-	84.2	1.7
1982	-	-	86.5	2.7	-	-	87.7	1.4	-	-	89.0	1.5	-	-	92.0	3.4	-	-	92.9	1.0	-	-	94.3	1.5
1983	-	-	96.4	2.2	-	-	96.4	0.0	-	-	99.7	3.4	-	-	102.3	2.6	-	-	104.7	2.3	-	-	104.8	0.1
1984	-	-	107.3	2.4	-	-	107.5	0.2	-	-	109.5	1.9	-	-	110.8	1.2	-	-	112.7	1.7	-	-	112.6	-0.1
1985	-	-	114.8	2.0	-	-	115.4	0.5	-	-	116.1	0.6	-	-	117.4	1.1	-	-	119.6	1.9	-	-	120.3	0.6
1986	-	-	123.0	2.2	-	-	124.9	1.5	-	-	125.9	0.8	-	-	127.2	1.0	-	-	130.7	2.8	131.4	0.5	131.6	0.2
1987	-	-	-	-	-	-	-	-	-	-	132.3	0.5	-	-	-	-	-	-	-	-	-	-	135.2	2.2
1988	-	-	-	-	-	-	-	-	-	-	139.3	3.0	-	-	-	-	-	-	-	-	-	-	142.2	2.1
1989	-	-	-	-	-	-	-	-	-	-	146.9	3.3	-	-	-	-	-	-	-	-	-	-	151.3	3.0
1990	-	-	-	-	-	-	-	-	-	-	160.1	5.8	-	-	-	-	-	-	-	-	-	-	162.9	1.7
1991	-	-	-	-	-	-	-	-	-	-	171.2	5.1	-	-	-	-	-	-	-	-	-	-	172.4	0.7
1992	-	-	-	-	-	-	-	-	-	-	181.2	5.1	-	-	-	-	-	-	-	-	-	-	183.7	1.4

[Continued]

Minneapolis-St. Paul, MN-WI
Consumer Price Index - All Urban Consumers
Base 1982-1984 = 100
Medical Care
[Continued]

For 1947-2001. Columns headed % show percentile change in the index from the previous period for which an index is available.

Year	Jan		Feb		Mar		Apr		May		Jun		Jul		Aug		Sep		Oct		Nov		Dec	
	Index	%	Index	%	Index	%	Index	%	Index	%	Index	%	Index	%	Index	%	Index	%	Index	%	Index	%	Index	%
1993	-	-	-	-	-	-	-	-	-	-	192.3	4.7	-	-	-	-	-	-	-	-	-	-	195.2	1.5
1994	-	-	-	-	-	-	-	-	-	-	203.5	4.3	-	-	-	-	-	-	-	-	-	-	207.3	1.9
1995	-	-	-	-	-	-	-	-	-	-	207.8	0.2	-	-	-	-	-	-	-	-	-	-	211.9	2.0
1996	-	-	-	-	-	-	-	-	-	-	214.7	1.3	-	-	-	-	-	-	-	-	-	-	216.3	0.7
1997	-	-	-	-	-	-	-	-	-	-	217.2	0.4	-	-	-	-	-	-	-	-	-	-	220.4	1.5
1998	-	-	-	-	-	-	-	-	-	-	226.1	2.6	-	-	-	-	-	-	-	-	-	-	233.2	3.1
1999	-	-	-	-	-	-	-	-	-	-	240.6	3.2	-	-	-	-	-	-	-	-	-	-	241.7	0.5
2000	-	-	-	-	-	-	-	-	-	-	247.6	2.4	-	-	-	-	-	-	-	-	-	-	251.8	1.7
2001	-	-	-	-	-	-	-	-	-	-	264.8	5.2	-	-	-	-	-	-	-	-	-	-	-	-

Source: U.S. Department of Labor, Bureau of Labor Statistics, Division of Consumer Prices and Price Indexes. - indicates no data collected for period.

Minneapolis-St. Paul, MN-WI
Consumer Price Index - Urban Wage Earners
Base 1982-1984 = 100
Medical Care

For 1947-2001. Columns headed % show percentile change in the index from the previous period for which an index is available.

Year	Jan Index	%	Feb Index	%	Mar Index	%	Apr Index	%	May Index	%	Jun Index	%	Jul Index	%	Aug Index	%	Sep Index	%	Oct Index	%	Nov Index	%	Dec Index	%
1947	10.4	-	10.4	0.0	10.4	0.0	10.5	1.0	10.7	1.9	10.8	0.9	-	-	-	-	11.1	2.8	-	-	-	-	11.4	2.7
1948	-	-	-	-	11.5	0.9	-	-	-	-	12.0	4.3	-	-	-	-	12.1	0.8	-	-	-	-	12.3	1.7
1949	-	-	-	-	12.3	0.0	-	-	-	-	12.4	0.8	-	-	-	-	12.5	0.8	-	-	-	-	12.5	0.0
1950	-	-	-	-	12.6	0.8	-	-	-	-	12.6	0.0	-	-	-	-	12.9	2.4	-	-	-	-	13.1	1.6
1951	-	-	-	-	13.8	5.3	-	-	-	-	13.8	0.0	-	-	-	-	14.0	1.4	-	-	-	-	14.1	0.7
1952	-	-	-	-	14.7	4.3	-	-	-	-	14.7	0.0	-	-	-	-	14.8	0.7	-	-	-	-	14.7	-0.7
1953	14.7	0.0	-	-	-	-	16.0	8.8	-	-	-	-	16.1	0.6	-	-	-	-	16.2	0.6	-	-	-	-
1954	16.3	0.6	-	-	-	-	16.6	1.8	-	-	-	-	16.7	0.6	-	-	-	-	16.6	-0.6	-	-	-	-
1955	16.8	1.2	-	-	-	-	17.2	2.4	-	-	-	-	17.4	1.2	-	-	-	-	17.4	0.0	-	-	-	-
1956	17.4	0.0	-	-	-	-	17.4	0.0	-	-	-	-	17.5	0.6	-	-	-	-	17.5	0.0	-	-	-	-
1957	17.6	0.6	-	-	-	-	17.8	1.1	-	-	-	-	19.8	11.2	-	-	-	-	19.9	0.5	-	-	-	-
1958	20.1	1.0	-	-	-	-	20.4	1.5	-	-	-	-	22.2	8.8	-	-	-	-	22.3	0.5	-	-	-	-
1959	22.5	0.9	-	-	-	-	22.5	0.0	-	-	-	-	22.7	0.9	-	-	-	-	23.8	4.8	-	-	-	-
1960	23.8	0.0	-	-	-	-	24.5	2.9	-	-	-	-	25.0	2.0	-	-	-	-	24.8	-0.8	-	-	-	-
1961	24.7	-0.4	-	-	-	-	25.8	4.5	-	-	-	-	26.8	3.9	-	-	-	-	26.9	0.4	-	-	-	-
1962	26.9	0.0	-	-	-	-	26.9	0.0	-	-	-	-	27.1	0.7	-	-	-	-	27.3	0.7	-	-	-	-
1963	27.4	0.4	-	-	-	-	27.4	0.0	-	-	-	-	27.4	0.0	-	-	-	-	27.5	0.4	-	-	-	-
1964	27.6	0.4	-	-	-	-	27.9	1.1	-	-	-	-	27.9	0.0	-	-	-	-	27.9	0.0	-	-	-	-
1965	27.9	0.0	-	-	-	-	28.0	0.4	-	-	-	-	27.9	-0.4	-	-	-	-	28.1	0.7	-	-	-	-
1966	28.3	0.7	-	-	-	-	29.0	2.5	-	-	-	-	29.4	1.4	-	-	-	-	29.9	1.7	-	-	-	-
1967	30.4	1.7	-	-	-	-	30.6	0.7	-	-	-	-	30.8	0.7	-	-	-	-	31.2	1.3	-	-	-	-
1968	31.8	1.9	-	-	-	-	32.3	1.6	-	-	-	-	32.5	0.6	-	-	-	-	32.9	1.2	-	-	-	-
1969	33.3	1.2	-	-	-	-	33.8	1.5	-	-	-	-	34.5	2.1	-	-	-	-	34.4	-0.3	-	-	-	-
1970	34.7	0.9	-	-	-	-	36.2	4.3	-	-	-	-	36.8	1.7	-	-	-	-	36.9	0.3	-	-	-	-
1971	37.4	1.4	-	-	-	-	38.0	1.6	-	-	-	-	38.7	1.8	-	-	-	-	38.5	-0.5	-	-	-	-
1972	38.4	-0.3	-	-	-	-	38.5	0.3	-	-	-	-	38.9	1.0	-	-	-	-	39.3	1.0	-	-	-	-
1973	39.9	1.5	-	-	-	-	40.4	1.3	-	-	-	-	40.6	0.5	-	-	-	-	41.6	2.5	-	-	-	-
1974	42.6	2.4	-	-	-	-	43.2	1.4	-	-	-	-	44.5	3.0	-	-	-	-	46.0	3.4	-	-	-	-
1975	48.1	4.6	-	-	-	-	48.3	0.4	-	-	-	-	49.6	2.7	-	-	-	-	50.1	1.0	-	-	-	-
1976	51.2	2.2	-	-	-	-	52.2	2.0	-	-	-	-	53.1	1.7	-	-	-	-	54.3	2.3	-	-	-	-
1977	55.7	2.6	-	-	-	-	56.5	1.4	-	-	-	-	57.7	2.1	-	-	-	-	58.3	1.0	-	-	-	-
1978	60.0	2.9	-	-	-	-	61.2	2.0	-	-	61.9	1.1	-	-	62.8	1.5	-	-	63.3	0.8	-	-	63.7	0.6
1979	-	-	64.8	1.7	-	-	64.0	-1.2	-	-	65.1	1.7	-	-	66.1	1.5	-	-	68.6	3.8	-	-	70.7	3.1
1980	-	-	72.4	2.4	-	-	72.1	-0.4	-	-	72.1	0.0	-	-	72.9	1.1	-	-	73.8	1.2	-	-	75.1	1.8
1981	-	-	75.9	1.1	-	-	76.8	1.2	-	-	78.0	1.6	-	-	81.8	4.9	-	-	82.9	1.3	-	-	83.7	1.0
1982	-	-	86.1	2.9	-	-	87.3	1.4	-	-	88.5	1.4	-	-	91.5	3.4	-	-	92.3	0.9	-	-	93.7	1.5
1983	-	-	95.7	2.1	-	-	95.7	0.0	-	-	99.6	4.1	-	-	102.3	2.7	-	-	105.2	2.8	-	-	105.3	0.1
1984	-	-	107.8	2.4	-	-	108.0	0.2	-	-	110.2	2.0	-	-	111.5	1.2	-	-	113.4	1.7	-	-	113.3	-0.1
1985	-	-	115.5	1.9	-	-	116.0	0.4	-	-	116.7	0.6	-	-	118.1	1.2	-	-	120.3	1.9	-	-	121.1	0.7
1986	-	-	123.6	2.1	-	-	125.5	1.5	-	-	126.5	0.8	-	-	127.9	1.1	-	-	131.4	2.7	132.1	0.5	132.4	0.2
1987	-	-	-	-	-	-	-	-	-	-	132.8	0.3	-	-	-	-	-	-	-	-	-	-	136.0	2.4
1988	-	-	-	-	-	-	-	-	-	-	140.0	2.9	-	-	-	-	-	-	-	-	-	-	143.4	2.4
1989	-	-	-	-	-	-	-	-	-	-	147.8	3.1	-	-	-	-	-	-	-	-	-	-	151.8	2.7
1990	-	-	-	-	-	-	-	-	-	-	159.8	5.3	-	-	-	-	-	-	-	-	-	-	162.1	1.4
1991	-	-	-	-	-	-	-	-	-	-	170.1	4.9	-	-	-	-	-	-	-	-	-	-	172.5	1.4
1992	-	-	-	-	-	-	-	-	-	-	181.1	5.0	-	-	-	-	-	-	-	-	-	-	183.1	1.1

[Continued]

Minneapolis-St. Paul, MN-WI
Consumer Price Index - Urban Wage Earners
Base 1982-1984 = 100
Medical Care
[Continued]

For 1947-2001. Columns headed % show percentile change in the index from the previous period for which an index is available.

Year	Jan		Feb		Mar		Apr		May		Jun		Jul		Aug		Sep		Oct		Nov		Dec	
	Index	%	Index	%	Index	%	Index	%	Index	%	Index	%	Index	%	Index	%	Index	%	Index	%	Index	%	Index	%
1993	-	-	-	-	-	-	-	-	-	-	191.2	4.4	-	-	-	-	-	-	-	-	-	-	193.5	1.2
1994	-	-	-	-	-	-	-	-	-	-	202.1	4.4	-	-	-	-	-	-	-	-	-	-	206.0	1.9
1995	-	-	-	-	-	-	-	-	-	-	206.8	0.4	-	-	-	-	-	-	-	-	-	-	211.1	2.1
1996	-	-	-	-	-	-	-	-	-	-	213.5	1.1	-	-	-	-	-	-	-	-	-	-	215.9	1.1
1997	-	-	-	-	-	-	-	-	-	-	217.2	0.6	-	-	-	-	-	-	-	-	-	-	220.1	1.3
1998	-	-	-	-	-	-	-	-	-	-	225.7	2.5	-	-	-	-	-	-	-	-	-	-	232.7	3.1
1999	-	-	-	-	-	-	-	-	-	-	240.0	3.1	-	-	-	-	-	-	-	-	-	-	241.1	0.5
2000	-	-	-	-	-	-	-	-	-	-	246.9	2.4	-	-	-	-	-	-	-	-	-	-	251.4	1.8
2001	-	-	-	-	-	-	-	-	-	-	264.1	5.1	-	-	-	-	-	-	-	-	-	-	-	-

Source: U.S. Department of Labor, Bureau of Labor Statistics, Division of Consumer Prices and Price Indexes. - indicates no data collected for period.

Minneapolis-St. Paul, MN-WI
Consumer Price Index - All Urban Consumers
Base December 1997 = 100
Recreation

For 1997-2001. Columns headed % show percentile change in the index from the previous period for which an index is available.

Year	Jan		Feb		Mar		Apr		May		Jun		Jul		Aug		Sep		Oct		Nov		Dec	
	Index	%	Index	%	Index	%	Index	%	Index	%	Index	%	Index	%	Index	%	Index	%	Index	%	Index	%	Index	%
1997	-	-	-	-	-	-	-	-	-	-	-	-	-	-	-	-	-	-	-	-	-	-	100.0	-
1998	-	-	-	-	-	-	-	-	-	-	100.6	0.6	-	-	-	-	-	-	-	-	-	-	101.8	1.2
1999	-	-	-	-	-	-	-	-	-	-	103.4	1.6	-	-	-	-	-	-	-	-	-	-	103.2	-0.2
2000	-	-	-	-	-	-	-	-	-	-	103.7	0.5	-	-	-	-	-	-	-	-	-	-	104.7	1.0
2001	-	-	-	-	-	-	-	-	-	-	107.8	3.0	-	-	-	-	-	-	-	-	-	-	-	-

Source: U.S. Department of Labor, Bureau of Labor Statistics, Division of Consumer Prices and Price Indexes. - indicates no data collected for period.

Minneapolis-St. Paul, MN-WI
Consumer Price Index - Urban Wage Earners
Base December 1997 = 100
Recreation

For 1997-2001. Columns headed % show percentile change in the index from the previous period for which an index is available.

Year	Jan		Feb		Mar		Apr		May		Jun		Jul		Aug		Sep		Oct		Nov		Dec	
	Index	%	Index	%	Index	%	Index	%	Index	%	Index	%	Index	%	Index	%	Index	%	Index	%	Index	%	Index	%
1997	-	-	-	-	-	-	-	-	-	-			-	-	-	-	-	-	-	-	-	-		
1998	-	-	-	-	-	-	-	-	-	-	100.9	0.9	-	-	-	-	-	-	-	-	-	-	100.0	-
1999	-	-	-	-	-	-	-	-	-	-	103.3	1.3	-	-	-	-	-	-	-	-	-	-	102.0	1.1
2000	-	-	-	-	-	-	-	-	-	-	103.6	0.5	-	-	-	-	-	-	-	-	-	-	103.1	-0.2
2001	-	-	-	-	-	-	-	-	-	-	106.8	2.4	-	-	-	-	-	-	-	-	-	-	-	-

Source: U.S. Department of Labor, Bureau of Labor Statistics, Division of Consumer Prices and Price Indexes. - indicates no data collected for period.

Minneapolis-St. Paul, MN-WI
Consumer Price Index - All Urban Consumers
Base December 1997 = 100
Education & Communication

For 1997-2001. Columns headed % show percentile change in the index from the previous period for which an index is available.

Year	Jan Index	%	Feb Index	%	Mar Index	%	Apr Index	%	May Index	%	Jun Index	%	Jul Index	%	Aug Index	%	Sep Index	%	Oct Index	%	Nov Index	%	Dec Index	%
1997	-	-	-	-	-	-	-	-	-	-	-	-	-	-	-	-	-	-	-	-	-	-	100.0	-
1998	-	-	-	-	-	-	-	-	-	-	99.6	-0.4	-	-	-	-	-	-	-	-	-	-	99.3	-0.3
1999	-	-	-	-	-	-	-	-	-	-	97.6	-1.7	-	-	-	-	-	-	-	-	-	-	100.9	3.4
2000	-	-	-	-	-	-	-	-	-	-	102.5	1.6	-	-	-	-	-	-	-	-	-	-	101.9	-0.6
2001	-	-	-	-	-	-	-	-	-	-	103.0	1.1	-	-	-	-	-	-	-	-	-	-	-	-

Source: U.S. Department of Labor, Bureau of Labor Statistics, Division of Consumer Prices and Price Indexes. - indicates no data collected for period.

Minneapolis-St. Paul, MN-WI
Consumer Price Index - Urban Wage Earners
Base December 1997 = 100
Education & Communication

For 1997-2001. Columns headed % show percentile change in the index from the previous period for which an index is available.

Year	Jan		Feb		Mar		Apr		May		Jun		Jul		Aug		Sep		Oct		Nov		Dec	
	Index	%	Index	%	Index	%	Index	%	Index	%	Index	%	Index	%	Index	%	Index	%	Index	%	Index	%	Index	%
1997	-	-	-	-	-	-	-	-	-	-	-	-	-	-	-	-	-	-	-	-	-	-	100.0	-
1998	-	-	-	-	-	-	-	-	-	-	99.4	-0.6	-	-	-	-	-	-	-	-	-	-	98.4	-1.0
1999	-	-	-	-	-	-	-	-	-	-	96.3	-2.1	-	-	-	-	-	-	-	-	-	-	98.8	2.6
2000	-	-	-	-	-	-	-	-	-	-	100.2	1.4	-	-	-	-	-	-	-	-	-	-	99.3	-0.9
2001	-	-	-	-	-	-	-	-	-	-	99.3	0.0	-	-	-	-	-	-	-	-	-	-	-	-

Source: U.S. Department of Labor, Bureau of Labor Statistics, Division of Consumer Prices and Price Indexes. - indicates no data collected for period.

New York-Northern New Jersey-Long Island, NY-NJ-CT-PA
Consumer Price Index - All Urban Consumers
Base 1982-1984 = 100
Annual Averages

For 1914-2001. Columns headed % show percentile change in the index from the previous period for which an index is available.

Year	All Items		Food & Beverage		Housing		Apparel		Trans-portation		Medical Care		Recrea-tion*		Education & Communic.*		Other Goods & Services	
	Index	%	Index	%	Index	%	Index	%	Index	%	Index	%	Index	%	Index	%	Index	%
1914	-	-	-	-	-	-	-	-	-	-	-	-	-	-	-	-	-	-
1915	9.9	-	-	-	-	-	-	-	-	-	-	-	-	-	-	-	-	-
1916	10.6	7.1	-	-	-	-	-	-	-	-	-	-	-	-	-	-	-	-
1917	12.8	20.8	-	-	-	-	-	-	-	-	-	-	-	-	-	-	-	-
1918	15.1	18.0	-	-	-	-	-	-	-	-	-	-	-	-	-	-	-	-
1919	17.7	17.2	-	-	-	-	-	-	-	-	-	-	-	-	-	-	-	-
1920	20.2	14.1	-	-	-	-	-	-	-	-	-	-	-	-	-	-	-	-
1921	18.1	-10.4	-	-	-	-	-	-	-	-	-	-	-	-	-	-	-	-
1922	17.2	-5.0	-	-	-	-	-	-	-	-	-	-	-	-	-	-	-	-
1923	17.5	1.7	-	-	-	-	-	-	-	-	-	-	-	-	-	-	-	-
1924	17.5	0.0	-	-	-	-	-	-	-	-	-	-	-	-	-	-	-	-
1925	17.9	2.3	-	-	-	-	-	-	-	-	-	-	-	-	-	-	-	-
1926	18.1	1.1	-	-	-	-	-	-	-	-	-	-	-	-	-	-	-	-
1927	17.9	-1.1	-	-	-	-	-	-	-	-	-	-	-	-	-	-	-	-
1928	17.8	-0.6	-	-	-	-	-	-	-	-	-	-	-	-	-	-	-	-
1929	17.9	0.6	-	-	-	-	-	-	-	-	-	-	-	-	-	-	-	-
1930	17.4	-2.8	-	-	-	-	-	-	-	-	-	-	-	-	-	-	-	-
1931	16.1	-7.5	-	-	-	-	-	-	-	-	-	-	-	-	-	-	-	-
1932	14.7	-8.7	-	-	-	-	-	-	-	-	-	-	-	-	-	-	-	-
1933	13.9	-5.4	-	-	-	-	-	-	-	-	-	-	-	-	-	-	-	-
1934	14.3	2.9	-	-	-	-	-	-	-	-	-	-	-	-	-	-	-	-
1935	14.5	1.4	-	-	-	-	-	-	-	-	-	-	-	-	-	-	-	-
1936	14.5	0.0	-	-	-	-	-	-	-	-	-	-	-	-	-	-	-	-
1937	14.8	2.1	-	-	-	-	-	-	-	-	-	-	-	-	-	-	-	-
1938	14.6	-1.4	-	-	-	-	-	-	-	-	-	-	-	-	-	-	-	-
1939	14.5	-0.7	-	-	-	-	-	-	-	-	-	-	-	-	-	-	-	-
1940	14.7	1.4	-	-	-	-	-	-	-	-	-	-	-	-	-	-	-	-
1941	15.3	4.1	-	-	-	-	-	-	-	-	-	-	-	-	-	-	-	-
1942	16.7	9.2	-	-	-	-	-	-	-	-	-	-	-	-	-	-	-	-
1943	17.9	7.2	-	-	-	-	-	-	-	-	-	-	-	-	-	-	-	-
1944	18.4	2.8	-	-	-	-	-	-	-	-	-	-	-	-	-	-	-	-
1945	18.9	2.7	-	-	-	-	-	-	-	-	-	-	-	-	-	-	-	-
1946	20.7	9.5	-	-	-	-	-	-	-	-	-	-	-	-	-	-	-	-
1947	23.2	12.1	-	-	-	-	-	-	16.1	-	14.3	-	-	-	-	-	-	-
1948	24.7	6.5	-	-	-	-	-	-	18.8	16.8	15.7	9.8	-	-	-	-	-	-
1949	24.5	-0.8	-	-	-	-	-	-	21.5	14.4	16.0	1.9	-	-	-	-	-	-
1950	24.6	0.4	-	-	-	-	-	-	22.4	4.2	16.3	1.9	-	-	-	-	-	-
1951	26.5	7.7	-	-	-	-	-	-	23.5	4.9	17.0	4.3	-	-	-	-	-	-
1952	26.9	1.5	-	-	-	-	-	-	23.9	1.7	18.1	6.5	-	-	-	-	-	-
1953	27.1	0.7	-	-	-	-	44.9	-	24.5	2.5	18.6	2.8	-	-	-	-	-	-
1954	27.2	0.4	-	-	-	-	44.5	-0.9	24.9	1.6	19.0	2.2	-	-	-	-	-	-
1955	27.1	-0.4	-	-	-	-	43.9	-1.3	24.2	-2.8	19.3	1.6	-	-	-	-	-	-
1956	27.5	1.5	-	-	-	-	44.9	2.3	25.0	3.3	19.5	1.0	-	-	-	-	-	-
1957	28.4	3.3	-	-	-	-	45.7	1.8	25.9	3.6	19.8	1.5	-	-	-	-	-	-
1958	29.2	2.8	-	-	-	-	46.0	0.7	26.3	1.5	20.2	2.0	-	-	-	-	-	-

[Continued]

New York-Northern New Jersey-Long Island, NY-NJ-CT-PA
Consumer Price Index - All Urban Consumers
Base 1982-1984 = 100
Annual Averages
[Continued]

For 1914-2001. Columns headed % show percentile change in the index from the previous period for which an index is available.

Year	All Items		Food & Beverage		Housing		Apparel		Transportation		Medical Care		Recreation*		Education & Communic.*		Other Goods & Services	
	Index	%	Index	%	Index	%	Index	%	Index	%	Index	%	Index	%	Index	%	Index	%
1959	29.6	1.4	-	-	-	-	46.4	0.9	27.6	4.9	21.5	6.4	-	-	-	-	-	-
1960	30.2	2.0	-	-	-	-	47.3	1.9	27.7	0.4	22.2	3.3	-	-	-	-	-	-
1961	30.5	1.0	-	-	-	-	47.8	1.1	27.8	0.4	23.0	3.6	-	-	-	-	-	-
1962	30.9	1.3	-	-	-	-	48.3	1.0	28.0	0.7	23.5	2.2	-	-	-	-	-	-
1963	31.6	2.3	-	-	-	-	49.2	1.9	28.2	0.7	23.9	1.7	-	-	-	-	-	-
1964	32.1	1.6	-	-	-	-	50.0	1.6	28.3	0.4	24.4	2.1	-	-	-	-	-	-
1965	32.6	1.6	-	-	-	-	50.7	1.4	28.7	1.4	25.3	3.7	-	-	-	-	-	-
1966	33.7	3.4	-	-	-	-	51.9	2.4	29.8	3.8	26.6	5.1	-	-	-	-	-	-
1967	34.6	2.7	-	-	-	-	54.5	5.0	31.2	4.7	28.4	6.8	-	-	-	-	-	-
1968	36.1	4.3	-	-	-	-	57.6	5.7	32.0	2.6	30.3	6.7	-	-	-	-	-	-
1969	38.3	6.1	-	-	-	-	61.4	6.6	33.9	5.9	33.1	9.2	-	-	-	-	-	-
1970	41.2	7.6	-	-	-	-	64.1	4.4	38.1	12.4	35.6	7.6	-	-	-	-	-	-
1971	43.6	5.8	-	-	-	-	65.6	2.3	40.2	5.5	38.6	8.4	-	-	-	-	-	-
1972	45.5	4.4	-	-	-	-	67.0	2.1	41.5	3.2	39.8	3.1	-	-	-	-	-	-
1973	48.3	6.2	-	-	-	-	68.8	2.7	42.3	1.9	41.2	3.5	-	-	-	-	-	-
1974	53.5	10.8	-	-	-	-	74.2	7.8	45.6	7.8	45.6	10.7	-	-	-	-	-	-
1975	57.6	7.7	-	-	-	-	76.9	3.6	50.3	10.3	51.4	12.7	-	-	-	-	-	-
1976	61.0	5.9	62.7	-	59.9	-	78.9	2.6	57.5	14.3	56.8	10.5	-	-	-	-	58.6	-
1977	64.2	5.2	65.8	4.9	63.0	5.2	81.3	3.0	60.5	5.2	61.6	8.5	-	-	-	-	62.3	6.3
1978	67.8	5.6	71.4	8.5	66.3	5.2	85.1	4.7	62.6	3.5	65.4	6.2	-	-	-	-	65.1	4.5
1979	73.7	8.7	78.0	9.2	72.1	8.7	86.8	2.0	70.6	12.8	70.5	7.8	-	-	-	-	68.7	5.5
1980	82.1	11.4	85.1	9.1	80.8	12.1	92.7	6.8	82.5	16.9	77.3	9.6	-	-	-	-	74.1	7.9
1981	90.1	9.7	92.7	8.9	89.4	10.6	96.3	3.9	92.4	12.0	84.3	9.1	-	-	-	-	80.9	9.2
1982	95.3	5.8	97.3	5.0	95.0	6.3	97.3	1.0	95.9	3.8	91.8	8.9	-	-	-	-	89.7	10.9
1983	99.8	4.7	99.0	1.7	100.2	5.5	100.6	3.4	99.1	3.3	100.1	9.0	-	-	-	-	101.2	12.8
1984	104.8	5.0	103.7	4.7	104.8	4.6	102.0	1.4	105.0	6.0	108.1	8.0	-	-	-	-	109.0	7.7
1985	108.7	3.7	107.3	3.5	108.7	3.7	104.5	2.5	107.1	2.0	115.9	7.2	-	-	-	-	116.1	6.5
1986	112.3	3.3	112.2	4.6	112.8	3.8	104.2	-0.3	104.8	-2.1	125.6	8.4	-	-	-	-	123.6	6.5
1987	118.0	5.1	118.6	5.7	118.0	4.6	109.9	5.5	108.7	3.7	136.1	8.4	-	-	-	-	130.8	5.8
1988	123.7	4.8	124.8	5.2	125.1	6.0	107.4	-2.3	112.8	3.8	144.8	6.4	-	-	-	-	139.5	6.7
1989	130.6	5.6	132.1	5.8	131.8	5.4	114.0	6.1	116.5	3.3	155.8	7.6	-	-	-	-	151.9	8.9
1990	138.5	6.0	139.6	5.7	139.3	5.7	121.8	6.8	123.1	5.7	172.4	10.7	-	-	-	-	164.0	8.0
1991	144.8	4.5	144.3	3.4	145.7	4.6	124.5	2.2	127.9	3.9	186.6	8.2	-	-	-	-	177.2	8.0
1992	150.0	3.6	146.0	1.2	151.4	3.9	128.5	3.2	131.5	2.8	200.0	7.2	-	-	-	-	191.0	7.8
1993	154.5	3.0	149.0	2.1	155.5	2.7	129.3	0.6	137.7	4.7	209.1	4.6	-	-	-	-	200.1	4.8
1994	158.2	2.4	151.9	1.9	159.9	2.8	126.2	-2.4	141.8	3.0	217.6	4.1	-	-	-	-	204.9	2.4
1995	162.2	2.5	155.9	2.6	163.4	2.2	126.0	-0.2	145.9	2.9	226.8	4.2	-	-	-	-	213.5	4.2
1996	166.9	2.9	159.7	2.4	167.7	2.6	127.7	1.3	152.4	4.5	235.4	3.8	-	-	-	-	221.7	3.8
1997	170.8	2.3	163.0	2.1	171.7	2.4	130.3	2.0	154.1	1.1	244.5	3.9	-	-	-	-	230.1	3.8
1998	173.6	1.6	166.1	1.9	175.9	2.4	127.9	-1.8	151.1	-1.9	255.0	4.3	102.3	-	99.7	-	242.6	5.4
1999	177.0	2.0	170.5	2.6	179.6	2.1	125.5	-1.9	152.3	0.8	265.3	4.0	103.6	1.3	100.6	0.9	256.5	5.7
2000	182.5	3.1	172.8	1.3	186.1	3.6	123.7	-1.4	160.0	5.1	275.1	3.7	105.6	1.9	102.2	1.6	273.6	6.7
2001	187.1	2.5	177.5	2.7	192.6	3.5	117.2	-5.3	-	-	287.1	4.4	107.4	1.7	105.8	3.5	285.3	4.3

Source: U.S. Department of Labor, Bureau of Labor Statistics, Division of Consumer Prices and Price Indexes. *Base is December 1997 = 100. - indicates no data collected for period.

New York-Northern New Jersey-Long Island, NY-NJ-CT-PA
Consumer Price Index - Urban Wage Earners
Base 1982-1984 = 100
Annual Averages

For 1914-2001. Columns headed % show percentile change in the index from the previous period for which an index is available.

Year	All Items		Food & Beverage		Housing		Apparel		Trans-portation		Medical Care		Recrea-tion*		Education & Communic.*		Other Goods & Services	
	Index	%	Index	%	Index	%	Index	%	Index	%	Index	%	Index	%	Index	%	Index	%
1914	-	-	-	-	-	-	-	-	-	-	-	-	-	-	-	-	-	-
1915	10.0	-	-	-	-	-	-	-	-	-	-	-	-	-	-	-	-	-
1916	10.8	8.0	-	-	-	-	-	-	-	-	-	-	-	-	-	-	-	-
1917	13.0	20.4	-	-	-	-	-	-	-	-	-	-	-	-	-	-	-	-
1918	15.3	17.7	-	-	-	-	-	-	-	-	-	-	-	-	-	-	-	-
1919	18.0	17.6	-	-	-	-	-	-	-	-	-	-	-	-	-	-	-	-
1920	20.5	13.9	-	-	-	-	-	-	-	-	-	-	-	-	-	-	-	-
1921	18.4	-10.2	-	-	-	-	-	-	-	-	-	-	-	-	-	-	-	-
1922	17.5	-4.9	-	-	-	-	-	-	-	-	-	-	-	-	-	-	-	-
1923	17.7	1.1	-	-	-	-	-	-	-	-	-	-	-	-	-	-	-	-
1924	17.7	0.0	-	-	-	-	-	-	-	-	-	-	-	-	-	-	-	-
1925	18.2	2.8	-	-	-	-	-	-	-	-	-	-	-	-	-	-	-	-
1926	18.4	1.1	-	-	-	-	-	-	-	-	-	-	-	-	-	-	-	-
1927	18.2	-1.1	-	-	-	-	-	-	-	-	-	-	-	-	-	-	-	-
1928	18.1	-0.5	-	-	-	-	-	-	-	-	-	-	-	-	-	-	-	-
1929	18.2	0.6	-	-	-	-	-	-	-	-	-	-	-	-	-	-	-	-
1930	17.7	-2.7	-	-	-	-	-	-	-	-	-	-	-	-	-	-	-	-
1931	16.4	-7.3	-	-	-	-	-	-	-	-	-	-	-	-	-	-	-	-
1932	14.9	-9.1	-	-	-	-	-	-	-	-	-	-	-	-	-	-	-	-
1933	14.1	-5.4	-	-	-	-	-	-	-	-	-	-	-	-	-	-	-	-
1934	14.5	2.8	-	-	-	-	-	-	-	-	-	-	-	-	-	-	-	-
1935	14.7	1.4	-	-	-	-	-	-	-	-	-	-	-	-	-	-	-	-
1936	14.7	0.0	-	-	-	-	-	-	-	-	-	-	-	-	-	-	-	-
1937	15.1	2.7	-	-	-	-	-	-	-	-	-	-	-	-	-	-	-	-
1938	14.8	-2.0	-	-	-	-	-	-	-	-	-	-	-	-	-	-	-	-
1939	14.7	-0.7	-	-	-	-	-	-	-	-	-	-	-	-	-	-	-	-
1940	14.9	1.4	-	-	-	-	-	-	-	-	-	-	-	-	-	-	-	-
1941	15.5	4.0	-	-	-	-	-	-	-	-	-	-	-	-	-	-	-	-
1942	17.0	9.7	-	-	-	-	-	-	-	-	-	-	-	-	-	-	-	-
1943	18.2	7.1	-	-	-	-	-	-	-	-	-	-	-	-	-	-	-	-
1944	18.7	2.7	-	-	-	-	-	-	-	-	-	-	-	-	-	-	-	-
1945	19.1	2.1	-	-	-	-	-	-	-	-	-	-	-	-	-	-	-	-
1946	21.0	9.9	-	-	-	-	-	-	-	-	-	-	-	-	-	-	-	-
1947	23.5	11.9	-	-	-	-	-	-	15.9	-	14.9	-	-	-	-	-	-	-
1948	25.1	6.8	-	-	-	-	-	-	18.6	17.0	16.3	9.4	-	-	-	-	-	-
1949	24.8	-1.2	-	-	-	-	-	-	21.3	14.5	16.7	2.5	-	-	-	-	-	-
1950	25.0	0.8	-	-	-	-	-	-	22.2	4.2	17.0	1.8	-	-	-	-	-	-
1951	26.9	7.6	-	-	-	-	-	-	23.3	5.0	17.7	4.1	-	-	-	-	-	-
1952	27.3	1.5	-	-	-	-	-	-	23.7	1.7	18.9	6.8	-	-	-	-	-	-
1953	27.5	0.7	-	-	-	-	44.8	-	24.2	2.1	19.4	2.6	-	-	-	-	-	-
1954	27.6	0.4	-	-	-	-	44.4	-0.9	24.6	1.7	19.8	2.1	-	-	-	-	-	-
1955	27.5	-0.4	-	-	-	-	43.8	-1.4	24.0	-2.4	20.1	1.5	-	-	-	-	-	-
1956	27.9	1.5	-	-	-	-	44.9	2.5	24.8	3.3	20.3	1.0	-	-	-	-	-	-
1957	28.8	3.2	-	-	-	-	45.6	1.6	25.7	3.6	20.6	1.5	-	-	-	-	-	-
1958	29.7	3.1	-	-	-	-	46.0	0.9	26.1	1.6	21.1	2.4	-	-	-	-	-	-

[Continued]

634

New York-Northern New Jersey-Long Island, NY-NJ-CT-PA
Consumer Price Index - Urban Wage Earners
Base 1982-1984 = 100
Annual Averages
[Continued]

For 1914-2001. Columns headed % show percentile change in the index from the previous period for which an index is available.

Year	All Items		Food & Beverage		Housing		Apparel		Transportation		Medical Care		Recreation*		Education & Communic.*		Other Goods & Services	
	Index	%	Index	%	Index	%	Index	%	Index	%	Index	%	Index	%	Index	%	Index	%
1959	30.1	1.3	-	-	-	-	46.3	0.7	27.3	4.6	22.4	6.2	-	-	-	-	-	-
1960	30.7	2.0	-	-	-	-	47.2	1.9	27.5	0.7	23.1	3.1	-	-	-	-	-	-
1961	30.9	0.7	-	-	-	-	47.7	1.1	27.5	0.0	24.0	3.9	-	-	-	-	-	-
1962	31.4	1.6	-	-	-	-	48.2	1.0	27.7	0.7	24.5	2.1	-	-	-	-	-	-
1963	32.1	2.2	-	-	-	-	49.2	2.1	27.9	0.7	25.0	2.0	-	-	-	-	-	-
1964	32.6	1.6	-	-	-	-	49.9	1.4	28.0	0.4	25.5	2.0	-	-	-	-	-	-
1965	33.1	1.5	-	-	-	-	50.6	1.4	28.4	1.4	26.4	3.5	-	-	-	-	-	-
1966	34.2	3.3	-	-	-	-	51.8	2.4	29.5	3.9	27.7	4.9	-	-	-	-	-	-
1967	35.1	2.6	-	-	-	-	54.4	5.0	30.9	4.7	29.6	6.9	-	-	-	-	-	-
1968	36.6	4.3	-	-	-	-	57.5	5.7	31.7	2.6	31.6	6.8	-	-	-	-	-	-
1969	38.9	6.3	-	-	-	-	61.3	6.6	33.6	6.0	34.5	9.2	-	-	-	-	-	-
1970	41.8	7.5	-	-	-	-	64.0	4.4	37.8	12.5	37.1	7.5	-	-	-	-	-	-
1971	44.2	5.7	-	-	-	-	65.5	2.3	39.8	5.3	40.2	8.4	-	-	-	-	-	-
1972	46.1	4.3	-	-	-	-	66.9	2.1	41.1	3.3	41.5	3.2	-	-	-	-	-	-
1973	49.1	6.5	-	-	-	-	68.7	2.7	41.9	1.9	43.0	3.6	-	-	-	-	-	-
1974	54.4	10.8	-	-	-	-	74.1	7.9	45.1	7.6	47.6	10.7	-	-	-	-	-	-
1975	58.5	7.5	-	-	-	-	76.7	3.5	49.8	10.4	53.6	12.6	-	-	-	-	-	-
1976	61.9	5.8	63.4	-	61.6	-	78.8	2.7	57.0	14.5	59.2	10.4	-	-	-	-	59.3	-
1977	65.2	5.3	66.5	4.9	64.8	5.2	81.2	3.0	59.9	5.1	64.3	8.6	-	-	-	-	63.0	6.2
1978	68.6	5.2	72.0	8.3	67.7	4.5	84.1	3.6	62.2	3.8	67.8	5.4	-	-	-	-	66.0	4.8
1979	74.7	8.9	78.7	9.3	73.6	8.7	87.3	3.8	70.3	13.0	72.5	6.9	-	-	-	-	69.6	5.5
1980	83.2	11.4	85.9	9.1	82.5	12.1	93.2	6.8	82.2	16.9	78.7	8.6	-	-	-	-	74.8	7.5
1981	91.3	9.7	92.9	8.1	91.4	10.8	96.0	3.0	92.3	12.3	86.2	9.5	-	-	-	-	80.9	8.2
1982	96.3	5.5	97.3	4.7	97.2	6.3	97.2	1.2	95.8	3.8	91.9	6.6	-	-	-	-	89.7	10.9
1983	100.1	3.9	99.1	1.8	100.9	3.8	100.6	3.5	98.9	3.2	99.9	8.7	-	-	-	-	101.6	13.3
1984	103.6	3.5	103.6	4.5	101.9	1.0	102.1	1.5	105.2	6.4	108.3	8.4	-	-	-	-	108.7	7.0
1985	107.9	4.2	107.0	3.3	107.3	5.3	104.4	2.3	107.2	1.9	116.2	7.3	-	-	-	-	115.4	6.2
1986	111.0	2.9	111.9	4.6	111.2	3.6	104.0	-0.4	104.2	-2.8	125.8	8.3	-	-	-	-	122.7	6.3
1987	116.6	5.0	118.2	5.6	116.0	4.3	110.2	6.0	108.4	4.0	136.8	8.7	-	-	-	-	129.5	5.5
1988	121.8	4.5	124.3	5.2	122.5	5.6	106.3	-3.5	112.4	3.7	145.8	6.6	-	-	-	-	137.9	6.5
1989	128.6	5.6	131.7	6.0	129.0	5.3	112.5	5.8	116.1	3.3	157.0	7.7	-	-	-	-	150.7	9.3
1990	136.3	6.0	139.4	5.8	135.9	5.3	120.1	6.8	123.1	6.0	172.0	9.6	-	-	-	-	163.6	8.6
1991	142.1	4.3	144.0	3.3	141.6	4.2	122.1	1.7	127.8	3.8	186.2	8.3	-	-	-	-	177.5	8.5
1992	146.9	3.4	145.6	1.1	146.7	3.6	125.8	3.0	131.6	3.0	200.3	7.6	-	-	-	-	191.0	7.6
1993	151.1	2.9	148.6	2.1	150.6	2.7	126.2	0.3	137.4	4.4	209.0	4.3	-	-	-	-	200.4	4.9
1994	154.5	2.3	151.5	2.0	154.6	2.7	122.7	-2.8	141.6	3.1	217.9	4.3	-	-	-	-	204.8	2.2
1995	158.3	2.5	155.3	2.5	158.0	2.2	121.8	-0.7	146.0	3.1	227.6	4.5	-	-	-	-	213.1	4.1
1996	163.1	3.0	159.0	2.4	162.2	2.7	123.6	1.5	153.3	5.0	236.0	3.7	-	-	-	-	221.2	3.8
1997	166.8	2.3	162.1	1.9	165.9	2.3	126.2	2.1	154.7	0.9	244.9	3.8	-	-	-	-	231.4	4.6
1998	169.2	1.4	164.9	1.7	169.7	2.3	122.5	-2.9	151.4	-2.1	255.3	4.2	102.1	-	99.9	-	247.5	7.0
1999	172.5	2.0	169.1	2.5	173.3	2.1	119.7	-2.3	152.4	0.7	265.1	3.8	102.7	0.6	101.2	1.3	266.8	7.8
2000	178.0	3.2	171.6	1.5	179.6	3.6	117.6	-1.8	160.7	5.4	274.8	3.7	104.2	1.5	102.6	1.4	287.7	7.8
2001	182.7	2.6	176.4	2.8	186.1	3.6	111.4	-5.3	-	-	286.8	4.4	106.0	1.7	106.2	3.5	302.6	5.2

Source: U.S. Department of Labor, Bureau of Labor Statistics, Division of Consumer Prices and Price Indexes. *Base is December 1997 = 100. - indicates no data collected for period.

New York-Northern New Jersey-Long Island, NY-NJ-CT-PA
Consumer Price Index - All Urban Consumers
Base 1982-1984 = 100
All Items

For 1914-2001. Columns headed % show percentile change in the index from the previous period for which an index is available.

Year	Jan Index	%	Feb Index	%	Mar Index	%	Apr Index	%	May Index	%	Jun Index	%	Jul Index	%	Aug Index	%	Sep Index	%	Oct Index	%	Nov Index	%	Dec Index	%
1914	-	-	-	-	-	-	-	-	-	-	-	-	-	-	-	-	-	-	-	-	-	-	9.9	-
1915	-	-	-	-	-	-	-	-	-	-	-	-	-	-	-	-	-	-	-	-	-	-	10.1	2.0
1916	-	-	-	-	-	-	-	-	-	-	-	-	-	-	-	-	-	-	-	-	-	-	11.3	11.9
1917	-	-	-	-	-	-	-	-	-	-	-	-	-	-	-	-	-	-	-	-	-	-	13.8	22.1
1918	-	-	-	-	-	-	-	-	-	-	-	-	-	-	-	-	-	-	-	-	-	-	16.8	21.7
1919	-	-	-	-	-	-	-	-	-	-	17.1	1.8	-	-	-	-	-	-	-	-	-	-	19.3	12.9
1920	-	-	-	-	-	-	-	-	-	-	20.9	8.3	-	-	-	-	-	-	-	-	-	-	19.5	-6.7
1921	-	-	-	-	-	-	-	-	17.9	-8.2	-	-	-	-	-	-	17.8	-0.6	-	-	-	-	17.9	0.6
1922	-	-	-	-	17.1	-4.5	-	-	-	-	17.2	0.6	-	-	-	-	17.1	-0.6	-	-	-	-	17.4	1.8
1923	-	-	-	-	17.3	-0.6	-	-	-	-	17.4	0.6	-	-	-	-	17.6	1.1	-	-	-	-	17.8	1.1
1924	-	-	-	-	17.4	-2.2	-	-	-	-	17.4	0.0	-	-	-	-	17.4	0.0	-	-	-	-	17.7	1.7
1925	-	-	-	-	-	-	-	-	-	-	17.7	0.0	-	-	-	-	-	-	-	-	-	-	18.5	4.5
1926	-	-	-	-	-	-	-	-	-	-	18.1	-2.2	-	-	-	-	-	-	-	-	-	-	18.1	0.0
1927	-	-	-	-	-	-	-	-	-	-	18.0	-0.6	-	-	-	-	-	-	-	-	-	-	18.1	0.6
1928	-	-	-	-	-	-	-	-	-	-	17.7	-2.2	-	-	-	-	-	-	-	-	-	-	17.8	0.6
1929	-	-	-	-	-	-	-	-	-	-	17.8	0.0	-	-	-	-	-	-	-	-	-	-	17.9	0.6
1930	-	-	-	-	-	-	-	-	-	-	17.4	-2.8	-	-	-	-	-	-	-	-	-	-	17.0	-2.3
1931	-	-	-	-	-	-	-	-	-	-	16.0	-5.9	-	-	-	-	-	-	-	-	-	-	15.4	-3.8
1932	-	-	-	-	-	-	-	-	-	-	14.7	-4.5	-	-	-	-	-	-	-	-	-	-	14.2	-3.4
1933	-	-	-	-	-	-	-	-	-	-	13.7	-3.5	-	-	-	-	-	-	-	-	-	-	14.0	2.2
1934	-	-	-	-	-	-	-	-	-	-	14.3	2.1	-	-	-	-	-	-	-	-	14.4	0.7	-	-
1935	-	-	-	-	14.4	0.0	-	-	-	-	-	-	14.3	-0.7	-	-	-	-	14.4	0.7	-	-	-	-
1936	14.6	1.4	-	-	-	-	14.4	-1.4	-	-	-	-	14.5	0.7	-	-	14.7	1.4	-	-	-	-	14.5	-1.4
1937	-	-	-	-	14.8	2.1	-	-	-	-	14.8	0.0	-	-	-	-	15.2	2.7	-	-	-	-	15.0	-1.3
1938	-	-	-	-	14.5	-3.3	-	-	-	-	14.5	0.0	-	-	-	-	14.6	0.7	-	-	-	-	14.6	0.0
1939	-	-	-	-	14.5	-0.7	-	-	-	-	14.3	-1.4	-	-	-	-	14.8	3.5	-	-	-	-	14.6	-1.4
1940	-	-	-	-	14.7	0.7	-	-	-	-	14.8	0.7	-	-	-	-	14.7	-0.7	14.6	-0.7	14.7	0.7	14.7	0.0
1941	14.7	0.0	14.8	0.7	14.8	0.0	14.9	0.7	15.0	0.7	15.2	1.3	15.3	0.7	15.4	0.7	15.6	1.3	15.7	0.6	15.8	0.6	15.8	0.0
1942	16.1	1.9	16.2	0.6	16.3	0.6	16.4	0.6	16.5	0.6	16.7	1.2	16.8	0.6	16.9	0.6	16.9	0.0	17.1	1.2	17.3	1.2	17.4	0.6
1943	17.5	0.6	17.5	0.0	17.8	1.7	17.9	0.6	18.1	1.1	18.1	0.0	18.1	0.0	17.9	-1.1	18.1	1.1	18.2	0.6	18.2	0.0	18.2	0.0
1944	18.2	0.0	18.1	-0.5	18.2	0.6	18.3	0.5	18.4	0.5	18.4	0.0	18.5	0.5	18.5	0.0	18.5	0.0	18.5	0.0	18.6	0.5	18.6	0.0
1945	18.6	0.0	18.6	0.0	18.5	-0.5	18.6	0.5	18.7	0.5	18.9	1.1	19.1	1.1	19.0	-0.5	18.9	-0.5	18.9	0.0	19.0	0.5	19.1	0.5
1946	19.2	0.5	19.2	0.0	19.3	0.5	19.5	1.0	19.6	0.5	19.8	1.0	21.0	6.1	21.3	1.4	21.8	2.3	22.3	2.3	22.5	0.9	22.7	0.9
1947	22.6	-0.4	22.5	-0.4	23.0	2.2	22.9	-0.4	22.7	-0.9	22.9	0.9	23.0	0.4	23.2	0.9	23.6	1.7	23.6	0.0	23.9	1.3	24.1	0.8
1948	24.4	1.2	24.3	-0.4	24.0	-1.2	24.4	1.7	24.5	0.4	24.7	0.8	25.2	2.0	25.3	0.4	25.3	0.0	25.1	-0.8	25.0	-0.4	24.7	-1.2
1949	24.7	0.0	24.4	-1.2	24.5	0.4	24.6	0.4	24.5	-0.4	24.5	0.0	24.5	0.0	24.5	0.0	24.6	0.4	24.3	-1.2	24.3	0.0	24.2	-0.4
1950	24.0	-0.8	24.1	0.4	24.1	0.0	24.2	0.4	24.2	0.0	24.3	0.4	24.7	1.6	24.7	0.0	25.0	1.2	25.1	0.4	25.3	0.8	25.6	1.2
1951	25.9	1.2	26.3	1.5	26.3	0.0	26.3	0.0	26.5	0.8	26.3	-0.8	26.4	0.4	26.4	0.0	26.6	0.8	26.7	0.4	26.8	0.4	26.8	0.0
1952	26.8	0.0	26.7	-0.4	26.6	-0.4	26.7	0.4	26.7	0.0	26.7	0.0	27.1	1.5	27.1	0.0	27.1	0.0	27.1	0.0	27.2	0.4	27.0	-0.7
1953	26.9	-0.4	26.8	-0.4	26.8	0.0	26.8	0.0	26.8	0.0	27.0	0.7	27.1	0.4	27.2	0.4	27.3	0.4	27.3	0.0	27.2	-0.4	27.3	0.4
1954	27.3	0.0	27.2	-0.4	27.1	-0.4	27.2	0.4	27.2	0.0	27.2	0.0	27.3	0.4	27.3	0.0	27.2	-0.4	27.2	0.0	27.2	0.0	27.1	-0.4
1955	27.1	0.0	27.2	0.4	27.1	-0.4	27.1	0.0	27.0	-0.4	27.0	0.0	27.0	0.0	27.0	0.0	27.2	0.7	27.1	-0.4	27.2	0.4	27.0	-0.7
1956	27.1	0.4	27.1	0.0	27.1	0.0	27.1	0.0	27.3	0.7	27.4	0.4	27.6	0.7	27.6	0.0	27.8	0.7	27.9	0.4	27.9	0.0	27.9	0.0
1957	27.9	0.0	28.0	0.4	28.0	0.0	28.2	0.7	28.3	0.4	28.4	0.4	28.6	0.7	28.6	0.0	28.5	-0.3	28.6	0.4	28.6	0.0	28.6	0.0
1958	29.0	1.4	29.0	0.0	29.2	0.7	29.2	0.0	29.2	0.0	29.2	0.0	29.2	0.0	29.2	0.0	29.3	0.3	29.3	0.0	29.4	0.3	29.3	-0.3
1959	29.4	0.3	29.4	0.0	29.4	0.0	29.4	0.0	29.4	0.0	29.6	0.7	29.8	0.7	29.7	-0.3	29.8	0.3	29.9	0.3	30.0	0.3	30.0	0.0

[Continued]

New York-Northern New Jersey-Long Island, NY-NJ-CT-PA
Consumer Price Index - All Urban Consumers
Base 1982-1984 = 100
All Items
[Continued]

For 1914-2001. Columns headed % show percentile change in the index from the previous period for which an index is available.

Year	Jan Index	%	Feb Index	%	Mar Index	%	Apr Index	%	May Index	%	Jun Index	%	Jul Index	%	Aug Index	%	Sep Index	%	Oct Index	%	Nov Index	%	Dec Index	%
1960	30.0	0.0	30.0	0.0	30.0	0.0	30.1	0.3	30.1	0.0	30.1	0.0	30.1	0.0	30.2	0.3	30.3	0.3	30.4	0.3	30.5	0.3	30.5	0.0
1961	30.4	-0.3	30.4	0.0	30.4	0.0	30.3	-0.3	30.3	0.0	30.3	0.0	30.5	0.7	30.5	0.0	30.6	0.3	30.6	0.0	30.6	0.0	30.6	0.0
1962	30.7	0.3	30.8	0.3	30.8	0.0	30.8	0.0	30.7	-0.3	30.8	0.3	30.9	0.3	31.0	0.3	31.2	0.6	31.2	0.0	31.1	-0.3	31.1	0.0
1963	31.2	0.3	31.3	0.3	31.3	0.0	31.4	0.3	31.3	-0.3	31.6	1.0	31.8	0.6	31.8	0.0	31.8	0.0	31.8	0.0	31.9	0.3	32.0	0.3
1964	31.9	-0.3	32.0	0.3	32.0	0.0	32.0	0.0	32.0	0.0	32.0	0.0	32.1	0.3	32.1	0.0	32.2	0.3	32.2	0.0	32.3	0.3	32.3	0.0
1965	32.2	-0.3	32.3	0.3	32.3	0.0	32.4	0.3	32.5	0.3	32.6	0.3	32.7	0.3	32.7	0.0	32.8	0.3	32.9	0.3	32.9	0.0	33.0	0.3
1966	33.0	0.0	33.2	0.6	33.4	0.6	33.5	0.3	33.5	0.0	33.5	0.0	33.8	0.9	33.9	0.3	34.1	0.6	34.2	0.3	34.2	0.0	34.2	0.0
1967	34.1	-0.3	34.3	0.6	34.3	0.0	34.3	0.0	34.4	0.3	34.5	0.3	34.6	0.3	34.7	0.3	34.8	0.3	34.9	0.3	35.0	0.3	35.1	0.3
1968	35.1	0.0	35.3	0.6	35.5	0.6	35.6	0.3	35.7	0.3	35.9	0.6	36.1	0.6	36.4	0.8	36.6	0.5	36.8	0.5	36.9	0.3	37.0	0.3
1969	37.2	0.5	37.3	0.3	37.7	1.1	37.9	0.5	38.0	0.3	38.3	0.8	38.4	0.3	38.5	0.3	38.8	0.8	39.0	0.5	39.1	0.3	39.5	1.0
1970	39.8	0.8	40.2	1.0	40.4	0.5	40.7	0.7	40.9	0.5	41.2	0.7	41.3	0.2	41.4	0.2	41.7	0.7	41.9	0.5	42.0	0.2	42.3	0.7
1971	42.4	0.2	42.7	0.7	43.0	0.7	43.1	0.2	43.3	0.5	43.6	0.7	43.9	0.7	43.9	0.0	44.0	0.2	44.1	0.2	44.1	0.0	44.3	0.5
1972	44.5	0.5	44.8	0.7	45.0	0.4	45.1	0.2	45.2	0.2	45.3	0.2	45.5	0.4	45.6	0.2	46.0	0.9	46.1	0.2	46.1	0.0	46.2	0.2
1973	46.3	0.2	46.7	0.9	47.2	1.1	47.6	0.8	47.8	0.4	48.1	0.6	48.2	0.2	49.0	1.7	49.2	0.4	49.5	0.6	50.0	1.0	50.5	1.0
1974	50.8	0.6	51.6	1.6	52.2	1.2	52.2	0.0	52.8	1.1	53.2	0.8	53.4	0.4	54.3	1.7	54.9	1.1	55.4	0.9	55.7	0.5	56.0	0.5
1975	56.0	0.0	56.5	0.9	56.5	0.0	56.6	0.2	56.8	0.4	57.1	0.5	57.6	0.9	57.9	0.5	58.6	1.2	58.8	0.3	59.3	0.9	59.6	0.5
1976	59.7	0.2	60.0	0.5	60.2	0.3	60.3	0.2	60.5	0.3	60.9	0.7	61.1	0.3	61.4	0.5	61.8	0.7	61.9	0.2	61.9	0.0	62.2	0.5
1977	62.4	0.3	63.0	1.0	63.3	0.5	63.5	0.3	63.9	0.6	64.4	0.8	64.5	0.2	64.8	0.5	64.8	0.0	64.9	0.2	65.2	0.5	65.3	0.2
1978	65.7	0.6	66.0	0.5	66.5	0.8	66.9	0.6	67.3	0.6	68.0	1.0	68.1	0.1	68.4	0.4	68.8	0.6	69.3	0.7	69.5	0.3	69.7	0.3
1979	70.2	0.7	71.0	1.1	71.4	0.6	72.1	1.0	72.8	1.0	73.5	1.0	74.0	0.7	74.5	0.7	75.4	1.2	76.1	0.9	76.6	0.7	77.1	0.7
1980	78.2	1.4	78.9	0.9	80.0	1.4	80.6	0.7	81.1	0.6	82.1	1.2	82.6	0.6	83.3	0.8	83.6	0.4	84.1	0.6	84.6	0.6	85.5	1.1
1981	86.3	0.9	87.4	1.3	87.8	0.5	88.3	0.6	88.8	0.6	89.5	0.8	90.8	1.5	91.6	0.9	93.0	1.5	92.7	-0.3	92.6	-0.1	92.7	0.1
1982	92.9	0.2	93.1	0.2	92.5	-0.6	92.8	0.3	93.7	1.0	95.7	2.1	95.9	0.2	96.3	0.4	97.1	0.8	98.4	1.3	98.1	-0.3	97.5	-0.6
1983	97.8	0.3	98.0	0.2	98.1	0.1	99.1	1.0	99.4	0.3	99.7	0.3	100.0	0.3	100.1	0.1	101.0	0.9	101.3	0.3	101.7	0.4	101.8	0.1
1984	102.8	1.0	103.4	0.6	103.7	0.3	104.1	0.4	104.1	0.0	104.3	0.2	104.8	0.5	105.5	0.7	106.2	0.7	106.1	-0.1	106.5	0.4	106.5	0.0
1985	106.7	0.2	107.3	0.6	107.5	0.2	107.9	0.4	108.1	0.2	108.3	0.2	108.4	0.1	109.2	0.7	109.6	0.4	109.8	0.2	110.7	0.8	111.0	0.3
1986	111.8	0.7	111.5	-0.3	111.5	0.0	111.2	-0.3	110.9	-0.3	111.7	0.7	112.5	0.7	112.7	0.2	113.0	0.3	113.4	0.4	113.3	-0.1	113.8	0.4
1987	114.7	0.8	115.3	0.5	115.8	0.4	116.6	0.7	117.3	0.6	117.8	0.4	117.9	0.1	118.9	0.8	119.8	0.8	120.2	0.3	120.5	0.2	120.6	0.1
1988	121.3	0.6	121.1	-0.2	121.5	0.3	122.6	0.9	122.7	0.1	123.1	0.3	123.6	0.4	124.2	0.5	126.0	1.4	126.2	0.2	125.9	-0.2	126.0	0.1
1989	127.0	0.8	127.6	0.5	128.9	1.0	129.5	0.5	130.2	0.5	130.5	0.2	130.6	0.1	130.9	0.2	132.2	1.0	132.8	0.5	133.2	0.3	133.3	0.1
1990	135.1	1.4	135.3	0.1	136.6	1.0	137.3	0.5	137.2	-0.1	137.1	-0.1	138.4	0.9	140.0	1.2	140.8	0.6	141.6	0.6	141.5	-0.1	141.6	0.1
1991	143.0	1.0	143.6	0.4	143.4	-0.1	143.7	0.2	144.0	0.2	144.6	0.4	145.2	0.4	145.4	0.1	145.8	0.3	145.7	-0.1	146.6	0.6	146.6	0.0
1992	147.3	0.5	148.0	0.5	149.1	0.7	149.2	0.1	148.9	-0.2	149.5	0.4	149.9	0.3	150.8	0.6	151.4	0.4	152.1	0.5	152.2	0.1	151.9	-0.2
1993	153.0	0.7	153.6	0.4	154.1	0.3	154.0	-0.1	153.8	-0.1	154.2	0.3	154.3	0.1	155.3	0.6	155.3	0.0	155.5	0.1	155.4	-0.1	155.6	0.1
1994	156.0	0.3	157.4	0.9	157.9	0.3	157.7	-0.1	157.3	-0.3	157.8	0.3	158.2	0.3	159.1	0.6	159.0	-0.1	159.5	0.3	159.4	-0.1	158.9	-0.3
1995	159.9	0.6	160.3	0.3	160.9	0.4	161.4	0.3	161.8	0.2	162.2	0.2	162.3	0.1	162.8	0.3	163.2	0.2	163.6	0.2	163.8	0.1	163.7	-0.1
1996	164.8	0.7	165.7	0.5	166.5	0.5	166.0	-0.3	166.4	0.2	166.5	0.1	166.7	0.1	167.2	0.3	168.2	0.6	168.2	0.0	168.4	0.1	168.5	0.1
1997	169.1	0.4	170.1	0.6	170.7	0.4	170.2	-0.3	169.9	-0.2	170.3	0.2	170.8	0.3	170.8	0.0	171.7	0.5	172.3	0.3	172.0	-0.2	171.9	-0.1
1998	172.1	0.1	172.7	0.3	173.0	0.2	173.0	0.0	173.0	0.0	173.1	0.1	173.6	0.3	174.2	0.3	174.4	0.1	174.8	0.2	174.7	-0.1	174.7	0.0
1999	175.0	0.2	175.1	0.1	175.5	0.2	176.0	0.3	176.1	0.1	176.8	0.4	177.2	0.2	177.6	0.2	178.2	0.3	178.9	0.4	178.8	-0.1	178.6	-0.1
2000	179.3	0.4	180.5	0.7	181.5	0.6	181.4	-0.1	181.4	0.0	182.0	0.3	182.8	0.4	183.1	0.2	184.4	0.7	184.6	0.1	184.6	0.0	184.2	-0.2
2001	184.9	0.4	185.3	0.2	186.4	0.6	186.6	0.1	187.3	0.4	188.3	0.5	187.8	-0.3	188.1	0.2	188.0	-0.1	187.8	-0.1	187.8	0.0	187.3	-0.3

Source: U.S. Department of Labor, Bureau of Labor Statistics, Division of Consumer Prices and Price Indexes. - indicates no data collected for period.

New York-Northern New Jersey-Long Island, NY-NJ-CT-PA
Consumer Price Index - Urban Wage Earners
Base 1982-1984 = 100
All Items

For 1914-2001. Columns headed % show percentile change in the index from the previous period for which an index is available.

Year	Jan Index	%	Feb Index	%	Mar Index	%	Apr Index	%	May Index	%	Jun Index	%	Jul Index	%	Aug Index	%	Sep Index	%	Oct Index	%	Nov Index	%	Dec Index	%
1914	-	-	-	-	-	-	-	-	-	-	-	-	-	-	-	-	-	-	-	-	-	-	10.1	-
1915	-	-	-	-	-	-	-	-	-	-	-	-	-	-	-	-	-	-	-	-	-	-	10.3	2.0
1916	-	-	-	-	-	-	-	-	-	-	-	-	-	-	-	-	-	-	-	-	-	-	11.5	11.7
1917	-	-	-	-	-	-	-	-	-	-	-	-	-	-	-	-	-	-	-	-	-	-	14.0	21.7
1918	-	-	-	-	-	-	-	-	-	-	-	-	-	-	-	-	-	-	-	-	-	-	17.1	22.1
1919	-	-	-	-	-	-	-	-	-	-	17.4	1.8	-	-	-	-	-	-	-	-	-	-	19.6	12.6
1920	-	-	-	-	-	-	-	-	-	-	21.2	8.2	-	-	-	-	-	-	-	-	-	-	19.8	-6.6
1921	-	-	-	-	-	-	-	-	18.2	-8.1	-	-	-	-	-	-	18.1	-0.5	-	-	-	-	18.2	0.6
1922	-	-	-	-	17.4	-4.4	-	-	-	-	17.4	0.0	-	-	-	-	17.4	0.0	-	-	-	-	17.7	1.7
1923	-	-	-	-	17.6	-0.6	-	-	-	-	17.7	0.6	-	-	-	-	17.9	1.1	-	-	-	-	18.1	1.1
1924	-	-	-	-	17.7	-2.2	-	-	-	-	17.7	0.0	-	-	-	-	17.7	0.0	-	-	-	-	18.0	1.7
1925	-	-	-	-	-	-	-	-	-	-	18.0	0.0	-	-	-	-	-	-	-	-	-	-	18.8	4.4
1926	-	-	-	-	-	-	-	-	-	-	18.4	-2.1	-	-	-	-	-	-	-	-	-	-	18.4	0.0
1927	-	-	-	-	-	-	-	-	-	-	18.3	-0.5	-	-	-	-	-	-	-	-	-	-	18.4	0.5
1928	-	-	-	-	-	-	-	-	-	-	18.0	-2.2	-	-	-	-	-	-	-	-	-	-	18.1	0.6
1929	-	-	-	-	-	-	-	-	-	-	18.1	0.0	-	-	-	-	-	-	-	-	-	-	18.2	0.6
1930	-	-	-	-	-	-	-	-	-	-	17.7	-2.7	-	-	-	-	-	-	-	-	-	-	17.2	-2.8
1931	-	-	-	-	-	-	-	-	-	-	16.2	-5.8	-	-	-	-	-	-	-	-	-	-	15.7	-3.1
1932	-	-	-	-	-	-	-	-	-	-	15.0	-4.5	-	-	-	-	-	-	-	-	-	-	14.4	-4.0
1933	-	-	-	-	-	-	-	-	-	-	13.9	-3.5	-	-	-	-	-	-	-	-	-	-	14.3	2.9
1934	-	-	-	-	-	-	-	-	-	-	14.5	1.4	-	-	-	-	-	-	-	-	14.6	0.7	-	-
1935	-	-	-	-	14.6	0.0	-	-	-	-	-	-	14.5	-0.7	-	-	-	-	14.6	0.7	-	-	-	-
1936	14.8	1.4	-	-	-	-	14.6	-1.4	-	-	-	-	14.7	0.7	-	-	14.9	1.4	-	-	-	-	14.7	-1.3
1937	-	-	-	-	15.0	2.0	-	-	-	-	15.0	0.0	-	-	-	-	15.4	2.7	-	-	-	-	15.2	-1.3
1938	-	-	-	-	14.8	-2.6	-	-	-	-	14.8	0.0	-	-	-	-	14.9	0.7	-	-	-	-	14.8	-0.7
1939	-	-	-	-	14.7	-0.7	-	-	-	-	14.5	-1.4	-	-	-	-	15.0	3.4	-	-	-	-	14.8	-1.3
1940	-	-	-	-	15.0	1.4	-	-	-	-	15.1	0.7	-	-	-	-	14.9	-1.3	14.8	-0.7	14.9	0.7	14.9	0.0
1941	15.0	0.7	15.0	0.0	15.0	0.0	15.1	0.7	15.2	0.7	15.5	2.0	15.5	0.0	15.6	0.6	15.8	1.3	16.0	1.3	16.1	0.6	16.1	0.0
1942	16.4	1.9	16.4	0.0	16.6	1.2	16.7	0.6	16.8	0.6	16.9	0.6	17.1	1.2	17.2	0.6	17.2	0.0	17.4	1.2	17.6	1.1	17.7	0.6
1943	17.7	0.0	17.8	0.6	18.1	1.7	18.2	0.6	18.4	1.1	18.4	0.0	18.3	-0.5	18.2	-0.5	18.4	1.1	18.4	0.0	18.5	0.5	18.5	0.0
1944	18.5	0.0	18.4	-0.5	18.5	0.5	18.6	0.5	18.6	0.0	18.6	0.0	18.8	1.1	18.8	0.0	18.8	0.0	18.8	0.0	18.9	0.5	18.9	0.0
1945	18.9	0.0	18.9	0.0	18.8	-0.5	18.9	0.5	19.0	0.5	19.2	1.1	19.4	1.0	19.2	-1.0	19.2	0.0	19.1	-0.5	19.3	1.0	19.4	0.5
1946	19.5	0.5	19.5	0.0	19.6	0.5	19.8	1.0	19.9	0.5	20.1	1.0	21.4	6.5	21.6	0.9	22.1	2.3	22.7	2.7	22.9	0.9	23.0	0.4
1947	22.9	-0.4	22.8	-0.4	23.3	2.2	23.3	0.0	23.0	-1.3	23.3	1.3	23.4	0.4	23.5	0.4	24.0	2.1	24.0	0.0	24.2	0.8	24.4	0.8
1948	24.8	1.6	24.7	-0.4	24.4	-1.2	24.8	1.6	24.9	0.4	25.1	0.8	25.6	2.0	25.7	0.4	25.7	0.0	25.5	-0.8	25.4	-0.4	25.1	-1.2
1949	25.1	0.0	24.8	-1.2	24.9	0.4	25.0	0.4	24.8	-0.8	24.8	0.0	24.9	0.4	24.8	-0.4	24.9	0.4	24.7	-0.8	24.7	0.0	24.6	-0.4
1950	24.4	-0.8	24.4	0.0	24.5	0.4	24.6	0.4	24.6	0.0	24.7	0.4	25.1	1.6	25.1	0.0	25.4	1.2	25.5	0.4	25.6	0.4	26.0	1.6
1951	26.3	1.2	26.7	1.5	26.7	0.0	26.7	0.0	26.9	0.7	26.7	-0.7	26.8	0.4	26.8	0.0	27.0	0.7	27.1	0.4	27.3	0.7	27.3	0.0
1952	27.3	0.0	27.1	-0.7	27.0	-0.4	27.1	0.4	27.1	0.0	27.1	0.0	27.5	1.5	27.5	0.0	27.5	0.0	27.5	0.0	27.6	0.4	27.4	-0.7
1953	27.4	0.0	27.2	-0.7	27.3	0.4	27.2	-0.4	27.3	0.4	27.4	0.4	27.5	0.4	27.6	0.4	27.7	0.4	27.7	0.0	27.6	-0.4	27.7	0.4
1954	27.7	0.0	27.6	-0.4	27.5	-0.4	27.6	0.4	27.6	0.0	27.6	0.0	27.7	0.4	27.7	0.0	27.6	-0.4	27.6	0.0	27.6	0.0	27.5	-0.4
1955	27.5	0.0	27.6	0.4	27.5	-0.4	27.5	0.0	27.4	-0.4	27.4	0.0	27.4	0.0	27.4	0.0	27.6	0.7	27.5	-0.4	27.6	0.4	27.4	-0.7
1956	27.5	0.4	27.5	0.0	27.5	0.0	27.5	0.0	27.7	0.7	27.9	0.7	28.1	0.7	28.0	-0.4	28.2	0.7	28.3	0.4	28.3	0.0	28.3	0.0
1957	28.3	0.0	28.4	0.4	28.4	0.0	28.6	0.7	28.7	0.3	28.9	0.7	29.0	0.3	29.1	0.3	29.0	-0.3	29.0	0.0	29.0	0.0	29.1	0.3
1958	29.4	1.0	29.5	0.3	29.7	0.7	29.7	0.0	29.7	0.0	29.6	-0.3	29.7	0.3	29.7	0.0	29.7	0.0	29.7	0.0	29.8	0.3	29.7	-0.3
1959	29.9	0.7	29.8	-0.3	29.8	0.0	29.9	0.3	29.9	0.0	30.0	0.3	30.2	0.7	30.1	-0.3	30.2	0.3	30.3	0.3	30.4	0.3	30.4	0.0

[Continued]

New York-Northern New Jersey-Long Island, NY-NJ-CT-PA
Consumer Price Index - Urban Wage Earners
Base 1982-1984 = 100
All Items
[Continued]

For 1914-2001. Columns headed % show percentile change in the index from the previous period for which an index is available.

Year	Jan Index	%	Feb Index	%	Mar Index	%	Apr Index	%	May Index	%	Jun Index	%	Jul Index	%	Aug Index	%	Sep Index	%	Oct Index	%	Nov Index	%	Dec Index	%
1960	30.4	0.0	30.5	0.3	30.5	0.0	30.6	0.3	30.6	0.0	30.6	0.0	30.6	0.0	30.7	0.3	30.7	0.0	30.9	0.7	31.0	0.3	30.9	-0.3
1961	30.9	0.0	30.9	0.0	30.9	0.0	30.8	-0.3	30.8	0.0	30.8	0.0	31.0	0.6	31.0	0.0	31.0	0.0	31.1	0.3	31.0	-0.3	31.1	0.3
1962	31.2	0.3	31.3	0.3	31.3	0.0	31.3	0.0	31.2	-0.3	31.2	0.0	31.4	0.6	31.5	0.3	31.7	0.6	31.6	-0.3	31.6	0.0	31.5	-0.3
1963	31.7	0.6	31.7	0.0	31.7	0.0	31.9	0.6	31.8	-0.3	32.1	0.9	32.2	0.3	32.2	0.0	32.2	0.0	32.3	0.3	32.4	0.3	32.5	0.3
1964	32.4	-0.3	32.5	0.3	32.5	0.0	32.5	0.0	32.5	0.0	32.5	0.0	32.6	0.3	32.6	0.0	32.7	0.3	32.7	0.0	32.8	0.3	32.8	0.0
1965	32.7	-0.3	32.8	0.3	32.8	0.0	32.9	0.3	33.0	0.3	33.1	0.3	33.2	0.3	33.2	0.0	33.3	0.3	33.4	0.3	33.4	0.0	33.5	0.3
1966	33.5	0.0	33.7	0.6	33.9	0.6	34.0	0.3	34.0	0.0	34.0	0.0	34.3	0.9	34.5	0.6	34.6	0.3	34.8	0.6	34.7	-0.3	34.7	0.0
1967	34.7	0.0	34.8	0.3	34.9	0.3	34.9	0.0	34.9	0.0	35.0	0.3	35.2	0.6	35.2	0.0	35.3	0.3	35.5	0.6	35.5	0.0	35.6	0.3
1968	35.7	0.3	35.9	0.6	36.0	0.3	36.1	0.3	36.3	0.6	36.5	0.6	36.7	0.5	36.9	0.5	37.2	0.8	37.3	0.3	37.4	0.3	37.5	0.3
1969	37.7	0.5	37.9	0.5	38.2	0.8	38.5	0.8	38.6	0.3	38.8	0.5	39.0	0.5	39.1	0.3	39.4	0.8	39.6	0.5	39.7	0.3	40.1	1.0
1970	40.4	0.7	40.8	1.0	41.1	0.7	41.3	0.5	41.5	0.5	41.8	0.7	41.9	0.2	42.1	0.5	42.3	0.5	42.6	0.7	42.7	0.2	43.0	0.7
1971	43.0	0.0	43.4	0.9	43.7	0.7	43.8	0.2	44.0	0.5	44.3	0.7	44.5	0.5	44.6	0.2	44.7	0.2	44.8	0.2	44.8	0.0	45.0	0.4
1972	45.2	0.4	45.5	0.7	45.7	0.4	45.8	0.2	45.9	0.2	46.0	0.2	46.1	0.2	46.3	0.4	46.7	0.9	46.8	0.2	46.8	0.0	47.0	0.4
1973	47.0	0.0	47.4	0.9	47.9	1.1	48.3	0.8	48.5	0.4	48.9	0.8	48.9	0.0	49.8	1.8	50.0	0.4	50.3	0.6	50.7	0.8	51.2	1.0
1974	51.6	0.8	52.4	1.6	53.0	1.1	53.0	0.0	53.6	1.1	54.0	0.7	54.3	0.6	55.1	1.5	55.8	1.3	56.3	0.9	56.5	0.4	56.8	0.5
1975	56.9	0.2	57.3	0.7	57.4	0.2	57.5	0.2	57.7	0.3	58.0	0.5	58.5	0.9	58.8	0.5	59.5	1.2	59.7	0.3	60.2	0.8	60.5	0.5
1976	60.7	0.3	60.9	0.3	61.1	0.3	61.2	0.2	61.4	0.3	61.8	0.7	62.1	0.5	62.4	0.5	62.7	0.5	62.9	0.3	62.9	0.0	63.1	0.3
1977	63.4	0.5	64.0	0.9	64.2	0.3	64.5	0.5	64.8	0.5	65.4	0.9	65.5	0.2	65.7	0.3	65.8	0.2	65.9	0.2	66.2	0.5	66.3	0.2
1978	66.7	0.6	67.0	0.4	67.4	0.6	67.7	0.4	68.0	0.4	68.7	1.0	68.8	0.1	69.1	0.4	69.4	0.4	70.0	0.9	70.2	0.3	70.6	0.6
1979	71.1	0.7	71.9	1.1	72.5	0.8	73.1	0.8	73.9	1.1	74.5	0.8	75.2	0.9	75.6	0.5	76.5	1.2	77.0	0.7	77.5	0.6	78.1	0.8
1980	79.2	1.4	80.0	1.0	81.1	1.4	81.6	0.6	82.2	0.7	83.1	1.1	83.7	0.7	84.5	1.0	84.8	0.4	85.2	0.5	85.8	0.7	86.8	1.2
1981	87.5	0.8	88.8	1.5	89.1	0.3	89.5	0.4	89.9	0.4	90.6	0.8	92.1	1.7	92.7	0.7	94.1	1.5	93.8	-0.3	93.7	-0.1	93.7	0.0
1982	94.0	0.3	94.1	0.1	93.4	-0.7	93.6	0.2	94.6	1.1	96.7	2.2	97.0	0.3	97.3	0.3	98.0	0.7	99.3	1.3	99.0	-0.3	98.4	-0.6
1983	98.6	0.2	98.2	-0.4	98.4	0.2	99.1	0.7	99.7	0.6	100.4	0.7	100.5	0.1	101.3	0.8	101.2	-0.1	101.4	0.2	100.9	-0.5	101.2	0.3
1984	101.9	0.7	102.0	0.1	101.8	-0.2	102.3	0.5	102.4	0.1	102.9	0.5	103.5	0.6	104.3	0.8	105.3	1.0	105.5	0.2	105.8	0.3	105.9	0.1
1985	106.1	0.2	106.6	0.5	106.8	0.2	107.2	0.4	107.4	0.2	107.6	0.2	107.6	0.0	108.4	0.7	108.6	0.2	108.8	0.2	109.8	0.9	110.1	0.3
1986	110.9	0.7	110.5	-0.4	110.5	0.0	110.0	-0.5	109.7	-0.3	110.4	0.6	111.2	0.7	111.4	0.2	111.5	0.1	111.9	0.4	111.9	0.0	112.4	0.4
1987	113.2	0.7	113.8	0.5	114.4	0.5	115.3	0.8	116.0	0.6	116.5	0.4	116.5	0.0	117.4	0.8	118.5	0.9	118.8	0.3	119.1	0.3	119.1	0.0
1988	119.6	0.4	119.3	-0.3	119.7	0.3	120.6	0.8	120.7	0.1	121.2	0.4	121.7	0.4	122.2	0.4	124.1	1.6	124.3	0.2	124.1	-0.2	124.1	0.0
1989	125.1	0.8	125.5	0.3	126.8	1.0	127.5	0.6	128.2	0.5	128.7	0.4	128.7	0.0	128.9	0.2	130.3	1.1	130.8	0.4	131.3	0.4	131.3	0.0
1990	133.0	1.3	133.1	0.1	134.5	1.1	135.0	0.4	134.9	-0.1	135.0	0.1	136.0	0.7	137.4	1.0	138.7	0.9	139.5	0.6	139.5	0.0	139.5	0.0
1991	140.3	0.6	140.6	0.2	140.5	-0.1	141.0	0.4	141.4	0.3	142.1	0.5	142.3	0.1	142.6	0.2	143.2	0.4	143.0	-0.1	144.0	0.7	143.9	-0.1
1992	144.4	0.3	144.8	0.3	145.8	0.7	145.9	0.1	145.8	-0.1	146.5	0.5	146.6	0.1	147.6	0.7	148.3	0.5	149.1	0.5	149.2	0.1	149.1	-0.1
1993	149.9	0.5	150.3	0.3	150.7	0.3	150.7	0.0	150.4	-0.2	150.7	0.2	150.7	0.0	151.7	0.7	151.8	0.1	152.1	0.2	152.0	-0.1	152.1	0.1
1994	152.4	0.2	153.5	0.7	154.0	0.3	153.9	-0.1	153.6	-0.2	154.2	0.4	154.4	0.1	155.3	0.6	155.5	0.1	156.0	0.3	155.9	-0.1	155.4	-0.3
1995	156.3	0.6	156.6	0.2	157.1	0.3	157.5	0.3	158.0	0.3	158.4	0.3	158.3	-0.1	158.9	0.4	159.5	0.4	159.7	0.1	159.9	0.1	159.9	0.0
1996	160.9	0.6	161.7	0.5	162.5	0.5	162.2	-0.2	162.8	0.4	162.8	0.0	162.8	0.0	163.3	0.3	164.4	0.7	164.4	0.0	164.7	0.2	164.7	0.0
1997	165.1	0.2	166.2	0.7	166.6	0.2	166.1	-0.3	166.0	-0.1	166.2	0.1	166.6	0.2	166.7	0.1	167.7	0.6	168.1	0.2	168.0	-0.1	167.7	-0.2
1998	167.7	0.0	168.2	0.3	168.2	0.0	168.5	0.2	168.6	0.1	168.8	0.1	169.1	0.2	169.7	0.4	169.9	0.1	170.5	0.4	170.5	0.0	170.5	0.0
1999	170.8	0.2	170.6	-0.1	170.8	0.1	171.3	0.3	171.5	0.1	172.1	0.3	172.5	0.2	173.2	0.4	173.9	0.4	174.5	0.3	174.6	0.1	174.3	-0.2
2000	174.7	0.2	176.0	0.7	176.7	0.4	176.8	0.1	177.0	0.1	177.6	0.3	178.4	0.5	178.5	0.1	179.9	0.8	180.2	0.2	180.1	-0.1	180.0	-0.1
2001	180.6	0.3	180.8	0.1	181.8	0.6	181.9	0.1	183.0	0.6	183.8	0.4	183.5	-0.2	183.5	0.0	183.6	0.1	183.3	-0.2	183.3	0.0	182.8	-0.3

Source: U.S. Department of Labor, Bureau of Labor Statistics, Division of Consumer Prices and Price Indexes. - indicates no data collected for period.

New York-Northern New Jersey-Long Island, NY-NJ-CT-PA
Consumer Price Index - All Urban Consumers
Base 1982-1984 = 100
Food and Beverages

For 1976-2001. Columns headed % show percentile change in the index from the previous period for which an index is available.

Year	Jan Index	%	Feb Index	%	Mar Index	%	Apr Index	%	May Index	%	Jun Index	%	Jul Index	%	Aug Index	%	Sep Index	%	Oct Index	%	Nov Index	%	Dec Index	%
1976	62.5	-	62.3	-0.3	62.0	-0.5	62.1	0.2	62.4	0.5	62.8	0.6	63.2	0.6	63.2	0.0	63.0	-0.3	63.1	0.2	62.8	-0.5	63.2	0.6
1977	63.4	0.3	64.7	2.1	64.8	0.2	65.4	0.9	65.8	0.6	66.3	0.8	66.6	0.5	66.7	0.2	66.1	-0.9	66.2	0.2	66.8	0.9	66.8	0.0
1978	68.0	1.8	68.8	1.2	69.3	0.7	70.4	1.6	71.1	1.0	72.4	1.8	72.5	0.1	72.4	-0.1	72.4	0.0	72.8	0.6	73.3	0.7	73.6	0.4
1979	74.8	1.6	76.1	1.7	76.6	0.7	77.1	0.7	77.7	0.8	78.0	0.4	79.0	1.3	78.3	-0.9	78.9	0.8	79.5	0.8	79.6	0.1	80.3	0.9
1980	81.7	1.7	81.6	-0.1	82.6	1.2	83.3	0.8	83.6	0.4	84.2	0.7	85.1	1.1	86.6	1.8	87.3	0.8	87.6	0.3	88.4	0.9	88.7	0.3
1981	89.5	0.9	90.4	1.0	91.1	0.8	91.9	0.9	92.1	0.2	92.6	0.5	93.7	1.2	94.1	0.4	94.7	0.6	94.1	-0.6	93.8	-0.3	94.0	0.2
1982	96.0	2.1	96.8	0.8	96.9	0.1	97.0	0.1	97.3	0.3	98.6	1.3	98.3	-0.3	97.6	-0.7	97.9	0.3	97.9	0.0	96.8	-1.1	97.1	0.3
1983	97.5	0.4	98.1	0.6	98.5	0.4	98.7	0.2	98.8	0.1	98.9	0.1	98.9	0.0	99.0	0.1	99.9	0.9	99.8	-0.1	99.5	-0.3	100.3	0.8
1984	102.3	2.0	103.0	0.7	103.5	0.5	103.3	-0.2	102.9	-0.4	103.4	0.5	103.7	0.3	104.4	0.7	104.3	-0.1	104.4	0.1	104.1	-0.3	104.8	0.7
1985	105.8	1.0	106.5	0.7	106.8	0.3	107.0	0.2	106.8	-0.2	106.9	0.1	107.0	0.1	107.4	0.4	108.0	0.6	108.1	0.1	108.2	0.1	108.9	0.6
1986	110.1	1.1	109.9	-0.2	110.1	0.2	110.9	0.7	111.2	0.3	110.9	-0.3	112.8	1.7	113.6	0.7	113.5	-0.1	114.2	0.6	114.2	0.0	114.7	0.4
1987	116.3	1.4	116.5	0.2	116.8	0.3	117.2	0.3	117.8	0.5	119.2	1.2	118.9	-0.3	119.2	0.3	119.7	0.4	119.9	0.2	120.1	0.2	121.3	1.0
1988	122.5	1.0	122.7	0.2	122.5	-0.2	124.0	1.2	123.5	-0.4	124.5	0.8	125.5	0.8	126.3	0.6	126.8	0.4	126.2	-0.5	126.8	0.5	126.8	0.0
1989	129.2	1.9	130.2	0.8	130.6	0.3	131.2	0.5	132.2	0.8	132.6	0.3	133.0	0.3	133.3	0.2	133.1	-0.2	132.9	-0.2	133.4	0.4	133.7	0.2
1990	136.9	2.4	138.4	1.1	138.5	0.1	138.7	0.1	138.7	0.0	139.2	0.4	140.4	0.9	140.8	0.3	140.4	-0.3	141.1	0.5	141.1	0.0	141.2	0.1
1991	143.3	1.5	143.8	0.3	144.2	0.3	145.6	1.0	145.2	-0.3	146.1	0.6	144.6	-1.0	143.7	-0.6	143.9	0.1	143.5	-0.3	143.4	-0.1	144.1	0.5
1992	145.2	0.8	145.6	0.3	146.2	0.4	146.2	0.0	145.3	-0.6	145.8	0.3	144.9	-0.6	145.9	0.7	146.0	0.1	146.7	0.5	146.4	-0.2	147.2	0.5
1993	148.7	1.0	148.5	-0.1	148.8	0.2	149.3	0.3	149.3	0.0	147.9	-0.9	147.9	0.0	149.0	0.7	148.9	-0.1	149.1	0.1	149.9	0.5	151.0	0.7
1994	151.8	0.5	150.9	-0.6	150.8	-0.1	150.9	0.1	151.3	0.3	151.2	-0.1	152.3	0.7	152.7	0.3	152.7	0.0	152.8	0.1	152.9	0.1	153.0	0.1
1995	154.6	1.0	154.3	-0.2	154.4	0.1	156.0	1.0	155.5	-0.3	155.7	0.1	155.9	0.1	156.4	0.3	156.8	0.3	157.0	0.1	157.2	0.1	157.0	-0.1
1996	158.1	0.7	158.5	0.3	158.7	0.1	158.5	-0.1	158.8	0.2	159.7	0.6	159.4	-0.2	159.2	-0.1	160.9	1.1	161.0	0.1	161.6	0.4	161.5	-0.1
1997	161.6	0.1	162.3	0.4	162.9	0.4	162.3	-0.4	162.8	0.3	162.9	0.1	162.8	-0.1	163.1	0.2	163.5	0.2	163.5	0.0	164.4	0.6	163.9	-0.3
1998	164.9	0.6	164.6	-0.2	164.8	0.1	165.3	0.3	165.7	0.2	165.0	-0.4	166.1	0.7	166.4	0.2	166.6	0.1	167.4	0.5	167.8	0.2	168.3	0.3
1999	169.9	1.0	169.1	-0.5	168.5	-0.4	169.6	0.7	170.6	0.6	170.5	-0.1	170.6	0.1	171.9	0.8	171.0	-0.5	170.8	-0.1	171.7	0.5	171.5	-0.1
2000	171.7	0.1	171.4	-0.2	171.4	0.0	171.4	0.0	173.3	1.1	172.4	-0.5	173.1	0.4	173.3	0.1	173.9	0.3	174.2	0.2	173.4	-0.5	174.6	0.7
2001	175.5	0.5	175.7	0.1	176.6	0.5	176.5	-0.1	177.8	0.7	177.9	0.1	178.3	0.2	178.5	0.1	178.3	-0.1	178.3	-0.1	177.8	-0.3	178.6	0.4

Source: U.S. Department of Labor, Bureau of Labor Statistics, Division of Consumer Prices and Price Indexes. - indicates no data collected for period.

New York-Northern New Jersey-Long Island, NY-NJ-CT-PA
Consumer Price Index - Urban Wage Earners
Base 1982-1984 = 100
Food and Beverages

For 1976-2001. Columns headed % show percentile change in the index from the previous period for which an index is available.

Year	Jan Index	%	Feb Index	%	Mar Index	%	Apr Index	%	May Index	%	Jun Index	%	Jul Index	%	Aug Index	%	Sep Index	%	Oct Index	%	Nov Index	%	Dec Index	%
1976	63.2	-	63.0	-0.3	62.7	-0.5	62.8	0.2	63.1	0.5	63.5	0.6	63.9	0.6	63.9	0.0	63.7	-0.3	63.8	0.2	63.5	-0.5	63.9	0.6
1977	64.1	0.3	65.4	2.0	65.5	0.2	66.2	1.1	66.5	0.5	67.1	0.9	67.4	0.4	67.4	0.0	66.9	-0.7	66.9	0.0	67.6	1.0	67.5	-0.1
1978	68.5	1.5	69.3	1.2	70.0	1.0	70.7	1.0	71.7	1.4	73.0	1.8	72.9	-0.1	72.9	0.0	73.0	0.1	73.6	0.8	73.9	0.4	74.4	0.7
1979	75.7	1.7	77.2	2.0	77.8	0.8	78.2	0.5	78.5	0.4	78.7	0.3	79.8	1.4	79.0	-1.0	79.4	0.5	79.7	0.4	80.0	0.4	81.0	1.3
1980	82.5	1.9	82.8	0.4	83.3	0.6	84.0	0.8	84.4	0.5	85.2	0.9	85.9	0.8	87.1	1.4	87.9	0.9	88.6	0.8	89.2	0.7	89.6	0.4
1981	90.1	0.6	91.0	1.0	91.5	0.5	92.1	0.7	92.1	0.0	92.7	0.7	93.9	1.3	94.1	0.2	94.6	0.5	94.2	-0.4	94.0	-0.2	94.1	0.1
1982	96.1	2.1	96.8	0.7	96.9	0.1	96.9	0.0	97.3	0.4	98.4	1.1	98.1	-0.3	97.4	-0.7	97.7	0.3	97.5	-0.2	96.8	-0.7	97.2	0.4
1983	97.6	0.4	98.2	0.6	98.6	0.4	98.9	0.3	99.0	0.1	99.0	0.0	98.9	-0.1	99.0	0.1	100.0	1.0	99.9	-0.1	99.6	-0.3	100.5	0.9
1984	102.5	2.0	103.2	0.7	103.6	0.4	103.4	-0.2	102.9	-0.5	103.3	0.4	103.5	0.2	104.2	0.7	104.0	-0.2	104.2	0.2	104.0	-0.2	104.8	0.8
1985	105.8	1.0	106.3	0.5	106.7	0.4	106.7	0.0	106.6	-0.1	106.7	0.1	106.7	0.0	107.0	0.3	107.5	0.5	107.6	0.1	107.9	0.3	108.8	0.8
1986	110.0	1.1	109.7	-0.3	109.9	0.2	110.7	0.7	110.9	0.2	110.7	-0.2	112.5	1.6	113.2	0.6	113.2	0.0	113.9	0.6	113.9	0.0	114.5	0.5
1987	115.9	1.2	116.1	0.2	116.4	0.3	116.8	0.3	117.4	0.5	118.8	1.2	118.5	-0.3	118.8	0.3	119.2	0.3	119.5	0.3	119.6	0.1	120.8	1.0
1988	121.9	0.9	122.1	0.2	121.9	-0.2	123.4	1.2	123.0	-0.3	124.0	0.8	125.1	0.9	125.9	0.6	126.4	0.4	125.7	-0.6	126.2	0.4	126.3	0.1
1989	128.8	2.0	129.8	0.8	130.2	0.3	130.8	0.5	131.7	0.7	132.2	0.4	132.6	0.3	133.0	0.3	132.6	-0.3	132.5	-0.1	133.0	0.4	133.1	0.1
1990	136.6	2.6	138.2	1.2	138.2	0.0	138.4	0.1	138.4	0.0	139.0	0.4	140.2	0.9	140.6	0.3	140.2	-0.3	140.9	0.5	140.9	0.0	141.0	0.1
1991	143.1	1.5	143.6	0.3	143.9	0.2	145.3	1.0	144.9	-0.3	146.0	0.8	144.4	-1.1	143.5	-0.6	143.6	0.1	143.2	-0.3	143.0	-0.1	143.7	0.5
1992	144.8	0.8	145.3	0.3	145.9	0.4	145.9	0.0	144.8	-0.8	145.4	0.4	144.5	-0.6	145.5	0.7	145.6	0.1	146.3	0.5	146.1	-0.1	146.7	0.4
1993	148.3	1.1	147.9	-0.3	148.4	0.3	148.9	0.3	148.9	0.0	147.4	-1.0	147.4	0.0	148.5	0.7	148.5	0.0	148.6	0.1	149.4	0.5	150.4	0.7
1994	151.4	0.7	150.5	-0.6	150.4	-0.1	150.5	0.1	150.9	0.3	151.0	0.1	151.9	0.6	152.4	0.3	152.2	-0.1	152.4	0.1	152.4	0.0	152.5	0.1
1995	154.1	1.0	153.7	-0.3	153.9	0.1	155.5	1.0	154.8	-0.5	155.1	0.2	155.3	0.1	155.7	0.3	156.3	0.4	156.4	0.1	156.5	0.1	156.3	-0.1
1996	157.5	0.8	157.9	0.3	158.0	0.1	157.8	-0.1	158.0	0.1	159.1	0.7	158.7	-0.3	158.4	-0.2	160.3	1.2	160.3	0.0	160.9	0.4	160.7	-0.1
1997	160.8	0.1	161.5	0.4	162.0	0.3	161.4	-0.4	161.9	0.3	162.0	0.1	161.9	-0.1	162.2	0.2	162.6	0.2	162.6	0.0	163.5	0.6	162.7	-0.5
1998	163.9	0.7	163.6	-0.2	163.6	0.0	164.2	0.4	164.5	0.2	163.9	-0.4	165.0	0.7	165.4	0.2	165.5	0.1	166.2	0.4	166.6	0.2	166.9	0.2
1999	168.7	1.1	167.8	-0.5	167.2	-0.4	168.2	0.6	169.0	0.5	169.2	0.1	169.2	0.0	170.5	0.8	169.8	-0.4	169.5	-0.2	170.5	0.6	170.0	-0.3
2000	170.3	0.2	170.0	-0.2	170.1	0.1	170.1	0.0	172.0	1.1	171.2	-0.5	171.9	0.4	172.2	0.2	172.9	0.4	173.2	0.2	172.0	-0.7	173.3	0.8
2001	174.3	0.6	174.6	0.2	175.4	0.5	175.3	-0.1	176.6	0.7	176.8	0.1	177.3	0.3	177.5	0.1	177.2	-0.2	176.7	-0.3	177.5	0.5	177.4	-0.1

Source: U.S. Department of Labor, Bureau of Labor Statistics, Division of Consumer Prices and Price Indexes. - indicates no data collected for period.

New York-Northern New Jersey-Long Island, NY-NJ-CT-PA
Consumer Price Index - All Urban Consumers
Base 1982-1984 = 100
Housing

For 1976-2001. Columns headed % show percentile change in the index from the previous period for which an index is available.

Year	Jan Index	%	Feb Index	%	Mar Index	%	Apr Index	%	May Index	%	Jun Index	%	Jul Index	%	Aug Index	%	Sep Index	%	Oct Index	%	Nov Index	%	Dec Index	%
1976	58.8	-	59.1	0.5	59.3	0.3	59.4	0.2	59.5	0.2	59.9	0.7	59.9	0.0	60.1	0.3	60.3	0.3	60.6	0.5	60.6	0.0	61.0	0.7
1977	61.6	1.0	61.8	0.3	62.2	0.6	62.4	0.3	62.6	0.3	63.2	1.0	63.2	0.0	63.4	0.3	63.7	0.5	63.8	0.2	63.9	0.2	64.1	0.3
1978	64.4	0.5	64.5	0.2	65.0	0.8	65.2	0.3	65.5	0.5	66.2	1.1	66.4	0.3	66.9	0.8	67.4	0.7	67.9	0.7	67.9	0.0	68.2	0.4
1979	68.7	0.7	69.2	0.7	69.4	0.3	70.1	1.0	70.9	1.1	71.8	1.3	72.2	0.6	73.0	1.1	74.1	1.5	74.7	0.8	75.4	0.9	75.9	0.7
1980	76.9	1.3	77.3	0.5	78.5	1.6	79.0	0.6	79.9	1.1	81.5	2.0	82.0	0.6	82.5	0.6	82.1	-0.5	82.5	0.5	83.1	0.7	84.7	1.9
1981	85.4	0.8	86.4	1.2	86.4	0.0	86.8	0.5	87.5	0.8	88.5	1.1	90.1	1.8	91.3	1.3	93.2	2.1	92.6	-0.6	92.3	-0.3	92.2	-0.1
1982	91.8	-0.4	91.4	-0.4	90.0	-1.5	90.8	0.9	92.7	2.1	95.9	3.5	96.0	0.1	96.7	0.7	97.3	0.6	100.0	2.8	99.7	-0.3	98.1	-1.6
1983	98.4	0.3	98.4	0.0	98.3	-0.1	99.7	1.4	100.0	0.3	100.4	0.4	100.8	0.4	100.4	-0.4	100.9	0.5	101.2	0.3	101.8	0.6	102.0	0.2
1984	102.7	0.7	103.5	0.8	103.3	-0.2	104.0	0.7	103.8	-0.2	104.1	0.3	104.9	0.8	105.5	0.6	106.4	0.9	105.8	-0.6	106.9	1.0	106.6	-0.3
1985	106.5	-0.1	107.1	0.6	106.9	-0.2	107.4	0.5	108.1	0.7	108.4	0.3	108.5	0.1	109.6	1.0	109.6	0.0	109.4	-0.2	111.2	1.6	111.5	0.3
1986	112.0	0.4	111.6	-0.4	112.2	0.5	112.0	-0.2	111.1	-0.8	112.7	1.4	113.7	0.9	113.9	0.2	113.7	-0.2	113.6	-0.1	113.1	-0.4	114.0	0.8
1987	115.2	1.1	115.6	0.3	115.4	-0.2	115.8	0.3	117.1	1.1	118.0	0.8	118.3	0.3	119.5	1.0	119.8	0.3	120.0	0.2	120.3	0.3	121.5	1.0
1988	123.2	1.4	122.8	-0.3	123.0	0.2	123.7	0.6	124.3	0.5	124.9	0.5	125.8	0.7	126.0	0.2	126.9	0.7	126.7	-0.2	126.9	0.2	127.1	0.2
1989	128.2	0.9	128.8	0.5	129.6	0.6	130.2	0.5	131.1	0.7	132.2	0.8	132.7	0.4	132.7	0.0	133.0	0.2	133.7	0.5	134.5	0.6	135.3	0.6
1990	136.3	0.7	135.8	-0.4	137.5	1.3	138.2	0.5	138.3	0.1	138.3	0.0	140.3	1.4	142.1	1.3	141.4	-0.5	141.2	-0.1	140.8	-0.3	141.1	0.2
1991	143.6	1.8	144.8	0.8	144.4	-0.3	144.2	-0.1	144.4	0.1	145.5	0.8	147.4	1.3	147.3	-0.1	146.6	-0.5	145.7	-0.6	147.2	1.0	147.4	0.1
1992	148.3	0.6	149.4	0.7	150.9	1.0	150.8	-0.1	150.2	-0.4	151.6	0.9	152.4	0.5	152.9	0.3	152.6	-0.2	152.6	0.0	152.6	0.0	152.2	-0.3
1993	153.5	0.9	153.8	0.2	154.7	0.6	154.6	-0.1	154.7	0.1	156.5	1.2	156.7	0.1	157.2	0.3	156.4	-0.5	156.2	-0.1	155.6	-0.4	156.3	0.4
1994	157.1	0.5	159.8	1.7	160.3	0.3	159.2	-0.7	158.8	-0.3	159.5	0.4	160.4	0.6	161.8	0.9	160.9	-0.6	160.7	-0.1	160.0	-0.4	159.7	-0.2
1995	160.9	0.8	161.5	0.4	162.0	0.3	162.4	0.2	162.8	0.2	163.9	0.7	165.0	0.7	165.0	0.0	164.1	-0.5	164.2	0.1	164.4	0.1	164.6	0.1
1996	166.6	1.2	166.9	0.2	167.4	0.3	166.4	-0.6	166.7	0.2	167.4	0.4	168.4	0.6	168.9	0.3	168.3	-0.4	168.2	-0.1	168.2	0.0	168.9	0.4
1997	169.8	0.5	170.9	0.6	171.2	0.2	170.5	-0.4	170.2	-0.2	171.3	0.6	172.5	0.7	172.7	0.1	172.5	-0.1	172.6	0.1	172.7	0.1	173.4	0.4
1998	174.0	0.3	174.5	0.3	174.9	0.2	174.7	-0.1	174.8	0.1	176.1	0.7	176.8	0.4	177.1	0.2	176.8	-0.2	177.1	0.2	177.2	0.1	177.3	0.1
1999	177.7	0.2	178.4	0.4	178.3	-0.1	178.5	0.1	178.4	-0.1	179.7	0.7	180.4	0.4	180.4	0.0	180.6	0.1	180.5	-0.1	181.2	0.4	181.0	-0.1
2000	182.9	1.0	184.8	1.0	184.9	0.1	184.2	-0.4	183.9	-0.2	185.8	1.0	187.5	0.9	186.8	-0.4	187.8	0.5	187.7	-0.1	188.5	0.4	188.4	-0.1
2001	189.7	0.7	189.8	0.1	191.3	0.8	191.6	0.2	191.5	-0.1	193.7	1.1	194.3	0.3	194.6	0.2	193.7	-0.5	193.1	-0.3	194.1	0.5	194.3	0.1

Source: U.S. Department of Labor, Bureau of Labor Statistics, Division of Consumer Prices and Price Indexes. - indicates no data collected for period.

New York-Northern New Jersey-Long Island, NY-NJ-CT-PA
Consumer Price Index - Urban Wage Earners
Base 1982-1984 = 100
Housing

For 1976-2001. Columns headed % show percentile change in the index from the previous period for which an index is available.

Year	Jan Index	%	Feb Index	%	Mar Index	%	Apr Index	%	May Index	%	Jun Index	%	Jul Index	%	Aug Index	%	Sep Index	%	Oct Index	%	Nov Index	%	Dec Index	%
1976	60.6	-	60.9	0.5	61.0	0.2	61.1	0.2	61.2	0.2	61.7	0.8	61.7	0.0	61.8	0.2	62.1	0.5	62.4	0.5	62.4	0.0	62.8	0.6
1977	63.3	0.8	63.6	0.5	64.0	0.6	64.2	0.3	64.4	0.3	65.1	1.1	65.0	-0.2	65.3	0.5	65.5	0.3	65.6	0.2	65.7	0.2	66.0	0.5
1978	66.3	0.5	66.4	0.2	66.7	0.5	66.8	0.1	66.8	0.0	67.5	1.0	67.8	0.4	68.1	0.4	68.5	0.6	69.0	0.7	69.1	0.1	69.5	0.6
1979	70.0	0.7	70.5	0.7	70.8	0.4	71.4	0.8	72.4	1.4	73.3	1.2	73.7	0.5	74.4	0.9	75.6	1.6	76.4	1.1	77.0	0.8	77.5	0.6
1980	78.5	1.3	79.0	0.6	79.9	1.1	80.6	0.9	81.4	1.0	83.2	2.2	83.7	0.6	84.3	0.7	83.6	-0.8	84.0	0.5	84.7	0.8	86.6	2.2
1981	87.2	0.7	88.5	1.5	88.4	-0.1	88.5	0.1	89.2	0.8	90.4	1.3	92.2	2.0	93.3	1.2	95.4	2.3	94.8	-0.6	94.5	-0.3	94.3	-0.2
1982	93.9	-0.4	93.4	-0.5	91.6	-1.9	92.5	1.0	94.6	2.3	98.1	3.7	98.3	0.2	99.0	0.7	99.6	0.6	102.5	2.9	102.3	-0.2	100.5	-1.8
1983	100.6	0.1	99.1	-1.5	99.5	0.4	99.9	0.4	100.7	0.8	102.3	1.6	102.0	-0.3	103.3	1.3	101.5	-1.7	101.6	0.1	100.0	-1.6	100.5	0.5
1984	100.2	-0.3	99.8	-0.4	98.4	-1.4	99.5	1.1	99.6	0.1	100.6	1.0	101.8	1.2	102.8	1.0	104.7	1.8	104.8	0.1	105.4	0.6	105.3	-0.1
1985	105.2	-0.1	105.9	0.7	105.6	-0.3	106.1	0.5	106.7	0.6	107.1	0.4	107.0	-0.1	108.1	1.0	108.0	-0.1	108.0	0.0	109.7	1.6	110.2	0.5
1986	110.6	0.4	110.1	-0.5	110.8	0.6	110.4	-0.4	109.4	-0.9	111.1	1.6	112.0	0.8	112.2	0.2	112.0	-0.2	111.8	-0.2	111.3	-0.4	112.1	0.7
1987	113.1	0.9	113.5	0.4	113.3	-0.2	113.9	0.5	115.2	1.1	116.1	0.8	116.3	0.2	117.4	0.9	117.7	0.3	117.9	0.2	118.2	0.3	119.3	0.9
1988	120.6	1.1	120.2	-0.3	120.4	0.2	120.8	0.3	121.4	0.5	122.5	0.9	123.3	0.7	123.4	0.1	124.2	0.6	123.9	-0.2	124.3	0.3	124.5	0.2
1989	125.5	0.8	125.9	0.3	126.4	0.4	127.4	0.8	128.1	0.5	129.4	1.0	129.9	0.4	129.9	0.0	130.4	0.4	130.9	0.4	131.9	0.8	132.7	0.6
1990	133.3	0.5	132.8	-0.4	134.5	1.3	135.0	0.4	135.1	0.1	135.2	0.1	136.6	1.0	138.0	1.0	137.9	-0.1	137.8	-0.1	137.4	-0.3	137.6	0.1
1991	139.4	1.3	140.2	0.6	139.9	-0.2	140.1	0.1	140.7	0.4	141.7	0.7	143.1	1.0	142.9	-0.1	142.6	-0.2	141.8	-0.6	143.4	1.1	143.5	0.1
1992	144.0	0.3	144.8	0.6	146.0	0.8	146.1	0.1	145.8	-0.2	147.0	0.8	147.5	0.3	147.9	0.3	147.7	-0.1	147.9	0.1	148.1	0.1	148.0	-0.1
1993	149.0	0.7	149.1	0.1	149.8	0.5	149.9	0.1	149.9	0.0	151.6	1.1	151.7	0.1	152.0	0.2	151.4	-0.4	151.1	-0.2	150.6	-0.3	151.4	0.5
1994	151.9	0.3	154.3	1.6	154.9	0.4	154.0	-0.6	153.5	-0.3	154.1	0.4	154.9	0.5	156.2	0.8	156.0	-0.1	155.6	-0.3	155.1	-0.3	154.9	-0.1
1995	155.9	0.6	156.3	0.3	156.7	0.3	157.1	0.3	157.5	0.3	158.4	0.6	159.2	0.5	159.2	0.0	158.8	-0.3	158.7	-0.1	159.1	0.3	159.4	0.2
1996	160.9	0.9	161.1	0.1	161.7	0.4	160.8	-0.6	161.4	0.4	162.0	0.4	162.8	0.5	163.3	0.3	163.1	-0.1	162.9	-0.1	163.0	0.1	163.8	0.5
1997	164.2	0.2	165.2	0.6	165.3	0.1	164.7	-0.4	164.8	0.1	165.7	0.5	166.5	0.5	166.7	0.1	166.8	0.1	166.6	-0.1	166.9	0.2	167.6	0.4
1998	167.6	0.0	168.2	0.4	168.4	0.1	168.5	0.1	168.8	0.2	169.9	0.7	170.4	0.3	170.7	0.2	170.7	0.0	170.9	0.1	171.2	0.2	171.4	0.1
1999	171.7	0.2	172.1	0.2	171.9	-0.1	172.0	0.1	172.1	0.1	173.3	0.7	173.8	0.3	173.9	0.1	174.3	0.2	174.3	0.0	175.1	0.5	175.3	0.1
2000	176.4	0.6	178.2	1.0	178.0	-0.1	177.5	-0.3	177.5	0.0	179.1	0.9	180.9	1.0	180.1	-0.4	181.7	0.9	181.5	-0.1	182.1	0.3	182.5	0.2
2001	183.6	0.6	183.3	-0.2	184.5	0.7	184.9	0.2	185.3	0.2	187.0	0.9	187.7	0.4	187.6	-0.1	187.2	-0.2	186.5	-0.4	187.5	0.5	187.9	0.2

Source: U.S. Department of Labor, Bureau of Labor Statistics, Division of Consumer Prices and Price Indexes. - indicates no data collected for period.

New York-Northern New Jersey-Long Island, NY-NJ-CT-PA
Consumer Price Index - All Urban Consumers
Base 1982-1984 = 100
Apparel

For 1952-2001. Columns headed % show percentile change in the index from the previous period for which an index is available.

Year	Jan Index	%	Feb Index	%	Mar Index	%	Apr Index	%	May Index	%	Jun Index	%	Jul Index	%	Aug Index	%	Sep Index	%	Oct Index	%	Nov Index	%	Dec Index	%
1952	-	-	-	-	-	-	-	-	-	-	-	-	-	-	-	-	-	-	-	-	-	-	45.1	-
1953	45.0	-0.2	44.9	-0.2	45.0	0.2	44.7	-0.7	44.8	0.2	44.7	-0.2	44.6	-0.2	44.5	-0.2	45.1	1.3	45.1	0.0	45.1	0.0	45.0	-0.2
1954	44.8	-0.4	44.7	-0.2	44.6	-0.2	44.4	-0.4	44.4	0.0	44.4	0.0	44.2	-0.5	44.2	0.0	44.6	0.9	44.5	-0.2	44.6	0.2	44.3	-0.7
1955	43.8	-1.1	43.7	-0.2	43.7	0.0	43.5	-0.5	43.6	0.2	43.5	-0.2	43.3	-0.5	43.5	0.5	44.5	2.3	44.5	0.0	44.6	0.2	44.6	0.0
1956	44.2	-0.9	44.5	0.7	44.5	0.0	44.6	0.2	44.5	-0.2	44.7	0.4	44.8	0.2	44.8	0.0	45.6	1.8	45.8	0.4	45.7	-0.2	45.7	0.0
1957	45.5	-0.4	45.2	-0.7	45.7	1.1	45.4	-0.7	45.6	0.4	45.7	0.2	45.6	-0.2	45.7	0.2	46.0	0.7	46.1	0.2	46.2	0.2	46.1	-0.2
1958	46.2	0.2	46.2	0.0	46.2	0.0	45.9	-0.6	45.8	-0.2	45.8	0.0	45.8	0.0	46.0	0.4	46.3	0.7	46.1	-0.4	46.3	0.4	46.2	-0.2
1959	46.0	-0.4	46.0	0.0	46.1	0.2	46.0	-0.2	46.0	0.0	46.1	0.2	46.3	0.4	46.5	0.4	46.6	0.2	46.7	0.2	46.9	0.4	46.9	0.0
1960	46.6	-0.6	46.8	0.4	47.1	0.6	47.2	0.2	47.1	-0.2	47.1	0.0	47.0	-0.2	47.1	0.2	47.7	1.3	48.0	0.6	47.9	-0.2	48.0	0.2
1961	47.6	-0.8	47.6	0.0	47.5	-0.2	47.4	-0.2	47.3	-0.2	47.3	0.0	47.4	0.2	47.7	0.6	48.2	1.0	48.4	0.4	48.4	0.0	48.3	-0.2
1962	47.8	-1.0	47.8	0.0	48.0	0.4	47.9	-0.2	47.7	-0.4	47.9	0.4	48.0	0.2	47.8	-0.4	48.9	2.3	49.1	0.4	49.0	-0.2	48.9	-0.2
1963	48.8	-0.2	48.7	-0.2	48.7	0.0	48.8	0.2	48.5	-0.6	49.0	1.0	49.2	0.4	49.2	0.0	50.0	1.6	50.1	0.2	50.1	0.0	50.2	0.2
1964	49.2	-2.0	49.6	0.8	49.9	0.6	49.8	-0.2	50.0	0.4	49.9	-0.2	49.8	-0.2	49.6	-0.4	50.6	2.0	50.4	-0.4	50.4	0.0	50.6	0.4
1965	49.4	-2.4	50.1	1.4	50.2	0.2	50.2	0.0	50.4	0.4	50.6	0.4	50.0	-1.2	50.6	1.2	51.7	2.2	51.8	0.2	51.6	-0.4	51.4	-0.4
1966	50.3	-2.1	50.8	1.0	51.3	1.0	51.4	0.2	51.7	0.6	51.5	-0.4	51.4	-0.2	51.0	-0.8	53.0	3.9	53.4	0.8	53.3	-0.2	53.4	0.2
1967	52.4	-1.9	53.3	1.7	54.1	1.5	53.9	-0.4	54.3	0.7	54.3	0.0	54.3	0.0	54.1	-0.4	55.5	2.6	55.8	0.5	55.8	0.0	55.8	0.0
1968	54.7	-2.0	55.6	1.6	56.3	1.3	56.5	0.4	57.0	0.9	57.3	0.5	56.9	-0.7	57.5	1.1	59.4	3.3	59.6	0.3	59.9	0.5	60.0	0.2
1969	58.9	-1.8	59.4	0.8	60.8	2.4	60.8	0.0	61.2	0.7	61.3	0.2	61.1	-0.3	60.8	-0.5	62.9	3.5	63.1	0.3	63.2	0.2	63.0	-0.3
1970	61.6	-2.2	63.0	2.3	63.3	0.5	63.1	-0.3	63.5	0.6	63.8	0.5	63.0	-1.3	63.6	1.0	65.9	3.6	65.9	0.0	65.9	0.0	66.0	0.2
1971	64.2	-2.7	65.0	1.2	65.5	0.8	65.0	-0.8	65.7	1.1	65.5	-0.3	64.8	-1.1	64.8	0.0	67.0	3.4	66.9	-0.1	66.7	-0.3	66.7	0.0
1972	65.0	-2.5	66.5	2.3	67.5	1.5	67.3	-0.3	67.3	0.0	66.2	-1.6	65.5	-1.1	65.4	-0.2	68.5	4.7	68.5	0.0	68.4	-0.1	68.3	-0.1
1973	65.1	-4.7	66.3	1.8	68.4	3.2	68.5	0.1	69.0	0.7	68.6	-0.6	67.5	-1.6	68.6	1.6	70.4	2.6	70.7	0.4	71.1	0.6	71.0	-0.1
1974	68.5	-3.5	70.8	3.4	72.9	3.0	72.2	-1.0	73.3	1.5	73.3	0.0	72.3	-1.4	76.1	5.3	77.6	2.0	77.9	0.4	78.2	0.4	76.9	-1.7
1975	75.1	-2.3	77.0	2.5	77.0	0.0	76.2	-1.0	76.6	0.5	75.3	-1.7	75.1	-0.3	77.4	3.1	78.3	1.2	78.3	0.0	78.4	0.1	77.6	-1.0
1976	76.2	-1.8	77.6	1.8	77.7	0.1	77.8	0.1	77.9	0.1	77.4	-0.6	77.4	0.0	80.1	3.5	81.7	2.0	80.9	-1.0	81.3	0.5	81.3	0.0
1977	79.3	-2.5	79.4	0.1	79.5	0.1	79.4	-0.1	79.9	0.6	81.0	1.4	80.8	-0.2	82.7	2.4	83.3	0.7	83.0	-0.4	83.9	1.1	83.6	-0.4
1978	81.8	-2.2	82.2	0.5	83.7	1.8	85.6	2.3	86.2	0.7	86.5	0.3	84.0	-2.9	84.8	1.0	86.2	1.7	87.0	0.9	86.9	-0.1	86.5	-0.5
1979	83.6	-3.4	85.0	1.7	86.7	2.0	86.6	-0.1	87.5	1.0	85.9	-1.8	84.2	-2.0	86.2	2.4	88.4	2.6	88.9	0.6	88.8	-0.1	89.8	1.1
1980	88.5	-1.4	90.3	2.0	92.1	2.0	92.6	0.5	92.4	-0.2	92.3	-0.1	91.2	-1.2	91.9	0.8	94.1	2.4	95.8	1.8	95.8	0.0	95.3	-0.5
1981	93.3	-2.1	95.7	2.6	96.2	0.5	96.6	0.4	96.4	-0.2	95.9	-0.5	95.5	-0.4	96.9	1.5	98.4	1.5	97.1	-1.3	97.1	0.0	96.3	-0.8
1982	94.0	-2.4	96.5	2.7	97.7	1.2	97.5	-0.2	97.0	-0.5	97.2	0.2	97.1	-0.1	97.9	0.8	99.1	1.2	99.0	-0.1	98.2	-0.8	97.3	-0.9
1983	96.7	-0.6	97.9	1.2	99.6	1.7	100.2	0.6	101.9	1.7	100.9	-1.0	100.0	-0.9	100.9	0.9	102.9	2.0	103.2	0.3	102.3	-0.9	100.6	-1.7
1984	99.4	-1.2	99.0	-0.4	101.2	2.2	101.0	-0.2	101.9	0.9	100.3	-1.6	99.4	-0.9	103.9	4.5	104.9	1.0	105.5	0.6	105.0	-0.5	102.9	-2.0
1985	101.2	-1.7	102.8	1.6	104.5	1.7	104.6	0.1	103.6	-1.0	101.9	-1.6	101.6	-0.3	106.7	5.0	107.0	0.3	107.1	0.1	107.4	0.3	105.3	-2.0
1986	103.4	-1.8	102.7	-0.7	103.8	1.1	104.5	0.7	103.9	-0.6	102.4	-1.4	100.9	-1.5	104.3	3.4	107.2	2.8	106.3	-0.8	105.6	-0.7	105.2	-0.4
1987	102.7	-2.4	105.7	2.9	110.4	4.4	112.9	2.3	112.0	-0.8	108.0	-3.6	105.0	-2.8	108.8	3.6	115.2	5.9	115.6	0.3	115.4	-0.2	106.9	-7.4
1988	102.0	-4.6	100.2	-1.8	105.0	4.8	108.9	3.7	106.9	-1.8	103.6	-3.1	100.3	-3.2	102.4	2.1	116.2	13.5	119.9	3.2	112.7	-6.0	111.0	-1.5
1989	107.3	-3.3	108.1	0.7	117.4	8.6	117.0	-0.3	114.5	-2.1	110.7	-3.3	106.7	-3.6	108.7	1.9	120.8	11.1	121.7	0.7	119.8	-1.6	114.7	-4.3
1990	116.9	1.9	116.2	-0.6	122.6	5.5	126.0	2.8	122.1	-3.1	117.7	-3.6	115.1	-2.2	121.2	5.3	126.9	4.7	128.0	0.9	126.1	-1.5	122.9	-2.5
1991	121.0	-1.5	121.9	0.7	123.4	1.2	123.5	0.1	124.0	0.4	122.8	-1.0	120.6	-1.8	123.7	2.6	127.3	2.9	129.5	1.7	130.6	0.8	125.8	-3.7
1992	123.7	-1.7	123.4	-0.2	127.0	2.9	127.1	0.1	127.3	0.2	124.6	-2.1	124.5	-0.1	128.8	3.5	136.1	5.7	135.6	-0.4	134.1	-1.1	129.7	-3.3
1993	126.8	-2.2	133.8	5.5	134.2	0.3	131.7	-1.9	126.8	-3.7	124.6	-1.7	123.4	-1.0	128.5	4.1	132.4	3.0	133.0	0.5	131.4	-1.2	125.3	-4.6
1994	122.2	-2.5	125.9	3.0	129.5	2.9	131.7	1.7	128.4	-2.5	127.7	-0.5	123.4	-3.4	123.4	0.0	126.4	2.4	127.2	0.6	127.2	0.0	121.7	-4.3
1995	122.9	1.0	123.9	0.8	127.9	3.2	127.5	-0.3	127.3	-0.2	123.5	-3.0	119.0	-3.6	123.1	3.4	129.1	4.9	130.5	1.1	130.2	-0.2	126.7	-2.7
1996	123.6	-2.4	128.0	3.6	131.7	2.9	130.4	-1.0	130.1	-0.2	124.9	-4.0	122.0	-2.3	124.7	2.2	132.4	6.2	130.7	-1.3	128.8	-1.5	125.2	-2.8
1997	125.5	0.2	131.1	4.5	134.4	2.5	132.4	-1.5	130.9	-1.1	126.4	-3.4	126.8	0.3	127.0	0.2	132.0	3.9	135.5	2.7	133.1	-1.8	128.9	-3.2

[Continued]

New York-Northern New Jersey-Long Island, NY-NJ-CT-PA
Consumer Price Index - All Urban Consumers
Base 1982-1984 = 100
Apparel

[Continued]

For 1952-2001. Columns headed % show percentile change in the index from the previous period for which an index is available.

Year	Jan Index	%	Feb Index	%	Mar Index	%	Apr Index	%	May Index	%	Jun Index	%	Jul Index	%	Aug Index	%	Sep Index	%	Oct Index	%	Nov Index	%	Dec Index	%
1998	124.5	-3.4	129.8	4.3	131.0	0.9	129.6	-1.1	128.2	-1.1	125.8	-1.9	123.1	-2.1	129.6	5.3	129.8	0.2	131.4	1.2	128.0	-2.6	123.4	-3.6
1999	121.1	-1.9	120.8	-0.2	125.6	4.0	127.1	1.2	124.6	-2.0	124.5	-0.1	123.2	-1.0	123.7	0.4	130.2	5.3	134.7	3.5	127.8	-5.1	122.3	-4.3
2000	118.5	-3.1	123.1	3.9	125.9	2.3	125.0	-0.7	125.3	0.2	118.3	-5.6	115.6	-2.3	123.1	6.5	132.7	7.8	132.3	-0.3	125.6	-5.1	118.7	-5.5
2001	116.6	-1.8	119.9	2.8	124.6	3.9	122.2	-1.9	120.7	-1.2	116.3	-3.6	110.9	-4.6	113.6	2.4	118.2	4.0	119.2	0.8	114.3	-4.1	109.9	-3.8

Source: U.S. Department of Labor, Bureau of Labor Statistics, Division of Consumer Prices and Price Indexes. - indicates no data collected for period.

New York-Northern New Jersey-Long Island, NY-NJ-CT-PA
Consumer Price Index - Urban Wage Earners
Base 1982-1984 = 100
Apparel

For 1952-2001. Columns headed % show percentile change in the index from the previous period for which an index is available.

Year	Jan Index	%	Feb Index	%	Mar Index	%	Apr Index	%	May Index	%	Jun Index	%	Jul Index	%	Aug Index	%	Sep Index	%	Oct Index	%	Nov Index	%	Dec Index	%
1952	-	-	-	-	-	-	-	-	-	-	-	-	-	-	-	-	-	-	-	-	-	-	45.0	-
1953	45.0	0.0	44.9	-0.2	44.9	0.0	44.7	-0.4	44.7	0.0	44.7	0.0	44.5	-0.4	44.4	-0.2	45.0	1.4	45.0	0.0	45.0	0.0	44.9	-0.2
1954	44.7	-0.4	44.7	0.0	44.5	-0.4	44.4	-0.2	44.4	0.0	44.3	-0.2	44.2	-0.2	44.1	-0.2	44.5	0.9	44.4	-0.2	44.5	0.2	44.3	-0.4
1955	43.7	-1.4	43.6	-0.2	43.7	0.2	43.5	-0.5	43.5	0.0	43.4	-0.2	43.2	-0.5	43.4	0.5	44.4	2.3	44.4	0.0	44.5	0.2	44.5	0.0
1956	44.1	-0.9	44.4	0.7	44.4	0.0	44.5	0.2	44.4	-0.2	44.6	0.5	44.7	0.2	44.7	0.0	45.5	1.8	45.7	0.4	45.6	-0.2	45.6	0.0
1957	45.5	-0.2	45.1	-0.9	45.6	1.1	45.4	-0.4	45.6	0.4	45.6	0.0	45.6	0.0	45.6	0.0	45.9	0.7	46.0	0.2	46.1	0.2	46.0	-0.2
1958	46.1	0.2	46.2	0.2	46.2	0.0	45.8	-0.9	45.7	-0.2	45.7	0.0	45.7	0.0	45.9	0.4	46.2	0.7	46.1	-0.2	46.2	0.2	46.2	0.0
1959	45.9	-0.6	45.9	0.0	46.0	0.2	46.0	0.0	46.0	0.0	46.1	0.2	46.2	0.2	46.4	0.4	46.5	0.2	46.6	0.2	46.8	0.4	46.8	0.0
1960	46.5	-0.6	46.7	0.4	47.0	0.6	47.1	0.2	47.0	-0.2	47.0	0.0	46.9	-0.2	47.0	0.2	47.6	1.3	47.9	0.6	47.9	0.0	47.9	0.0
1961	47.5	-0.8	47.5	0.0	47.4	-0.2	47.3	-0.2	47.2	-0.2	47.3	0.2	47.4	0.2	47.6	0.4	48.1	1.1	48.3	0.4	48.4	0.2	48.2	-0.4
1962	47.7	-1.0	47.8	0.2	47.9	0.2	47.8	-0.2	47.6	-0.4	47.8	0.4	48.0	0.4	47.8	-0.4	48.8	2.1	49.1	0.6	48.9	-0.4	48.8	-0.2
1963	48.7	-0.2	48.6	-0.2	48.6	0.0	48.7	0.2	48.5	-0.4	48.9	0.8	49.1	0.4	49.2	0.2	49.9	1.4	50.0	0.2	50.0	0.0	50.1	0.2
1964	49.2	-1.8	49.5	0.6	49.8	0.6	49.8	0.0	49.9	0.2	49.8	-0.2	49.8	0.0	49.5	-0.6	50.5	2.0	50.4	-0.2	50.3	-0.2	50.5	0.4
1965	49.3	-2.4	50.0	1.4	50.1	0.2	50.1	0.0	50.4	0.6	50.5	0.2	49.9	-1.2	50.5	1.2	51.6	2.2	51.7	0.2	51.6	-0.2	51.3	-0.6
1966	50.3	-1.9	50.7	0.8	51.2	1.0	51.3	0.2	51.7	0.8	51.4	-0.6	51.3	-0.2	51.0	-0.6	52.9	3.7	53.3	0.8	53.2	-0.2	53.3	0.2
1967	52.3	-1.9	53.2	1.7	54.1	1.7	53.8	-0.6	54.2	0.7	54.2	0.0	54.2	0.0	54.1	-0.2	55.4	2.4	55.7	0.5	55.7	0.0	55.7	0.0
1968	54.6	-2.0	55.5	1.6	56.2	1.3	56.5	0.5	56.9	0.7	57.2	0.5	56.8	-0.7	57.4	1.1	59.3	3.3	59.5	0.3	59.8	0.5	59.9	0.2
1969	58.8	-1.8	59.3	0.9	60.8	2.5	60.8	0.0	61.1	0.5	61.2	0.2	61.0	-0.3	60.8	-0.3	62.8	3.3	63.0	0.3	63.1	0.2	62.9	-0.3
1970	61.5	-2.2	62.9	2.3	63.2	0.5	63.0	-0.3	63.4	0.6	63.7	0.5	62.9	-1.3	63.5	1.0	65.8	3.6	65.8	0.0	65.8	0.0	65.9	0.2
1971	64.1	-2.7	64.9	1.2	65.4	0.8	64.9	-0.8	65.6	1.1	65.4	-0.3	64.7	-1.1	64.7	0.0	66.9	3.4	66.8	-0.1	66.6	-0.3	66.6	0.0
1972	64.9	-2.6	66.4	2.3	67.4	1.5	67.2	-0.3	67.2	0.0	66.1	-1.6	65.4	-1.1	65.3	-0.2	68.4	4.7	68.4	0.0	68.3	-0.1	68.1	-0.3
1973	65.0	-4.6	66.2	1.8	68.3	3.2	68.4	0.1	68.9	0.7	68.5	-0.6	67.4	-1.6	68.5	1.6	70.3	2.6	70.6	0.4	71.0	0.6	70.9	-0.1
1974	68.4	-3.5	70.7	3.4	72.8	3.0	72.1	-1.0	73.2	1.5	73.2	0.0	72.2	-1.4	76.0	5.3	77.5	2.0	77.8	0.4	78.1	0.4	76.7	-1.8
1975	75.0	-2.2	76.9	2.5	76.9	0.0	76.0	-1.2	76.5	0.7	75.2	-1.7	75.0	-0.3	77.2	2.9	78.2	1.3	78.2	0.0	78.3	0.1	77.5	-1.0
1976	76.1	-1.8	77.4	1.7	77.6	0.3	77.7	0.1	77.8	0.1	77.2	-0.8	77.2	0.0	80.0	3.6	81.5	1.9	80.8	-0.9	81.2	0.5	81.1	-0.1
1977	79.1	-2.5	79.3	0.3	79.4	0.1	79.2	-0.3	79.7	0.6	80.9	1.5	80.7	-0.2	82.6	2.4	83.2	0.7	82.8	-0.5	83.8	1.2	83.5	-0.4
1978	81.7	-2.2	82.2	0.6	83.2	1.2	84.7	1.8	84.7	0.0	84.6	-0.1	83.1	-1.8	84.1	1.2	84.6	0.6	85.7	1.3	85.4	-0.4	84.8	-0.7
1979	82.9	-2.2	85.0	2.5	86.9	2.2	87.4	0.6	88.1	0.8	86.2	-2.2	85.4	-0.9	87.2	2.1	89.1	2.2	89.7	0.7	89.7	0.0	90.4	0.8
1980	88.1	-2.5	89.2	1.2	92.7	3.9	92.8	0.1	94.1	1.4	92.5	-1.7	91.6	-1.0	93.9	2.5	95.8	2.0	96.1	0.3	95.8	-0.3	95.6	-0.2
1981	94.7	-0.9	95.3	0.6	95.4	0.1	95.4	0.0	96.1	0.7	95.5	-0.6	95.3	-0.2	97.0	1.8	98.0	1.0	96.8	-1.2	96.3	-0.5	95.9	-0.4
1982	94.0	-2.0	96.4	2.6	97.6	1.2	97.6	0.0	97.0	-0.6	97.1	0.1	96.8	-0.3	97.6	0.8	98.8	1.2	98.9	0.1	97.8	-1.1	97.3	-0.5
1983	96.8	-0.5	98.0	1.2	99.5	1.5	100.3	0.8	102.1	1.8	101.0	-1.1	99.9	-1.1	100.8	0.9	102.8	2.0	103.1	0.3	102.2	-0.9	100.7	-1.5
1984	99.5	-1.2	99.3	-0.2	101.3	2.0	101.1	-0.2	101.8	0.7	100.2	-1.6	99.3	-0.9	104.0	4.7	105.2	1.2	105.6	0.4	105.1	-0.5	103.2	-1.8
1985	101.5	-1.6	102.7	1.2	104.5	1.8	104.6	0.1	103.3	-1.2	101.6	-1.6	101.0	-0.6	106.6	5.5	107.2	0.6	107.1	-0.1	107.4	0.3	105.3	-2.0
1986	103.2	-2.0	102.5	-0.7	103.4	0.9	104.2	0.8	103.4	-0.8	101.7	-1.6	100.6	-1.1	104.3	3.7	107.3	2.9	106.1	-1.1	105.8	-0.3	105.5	-0.3
1987	103.2	-2.2	105.9	2.6	111.3	5.1	114.1	2.5	113.0	-1.0	108.5	-4.0	105.1	-3.1	108.0	2.8	115.3	6.8	115.8	0.4	115.8	0.0	106.7	-7.9
1988	101.3	-5.1	98.8	-2.5	104.3	5.6	108.0	3.5	106.0	-1.9	102.3	-3.5	98.8	-3.4	100.5	1.7	115.1	14.5	118.7	3.1	111.6	-6.0	109.9	-1.5
1989	106.2	-3.4	106.4	0.2	116.2	9.2	115.6	-0.5	112.8	-2.4	109.0	-3.4	104.9	-3.8	106.8	1.8	119.6	12.0	120.3	0.6	118.8	-1.2	113.3	-4.6
1990	115.2	1.7	113.9	-1.1	121.1	6.3	124.4	2.7	120.3	-3.3	116.0	-3.6	113.2	-2.4	119.0	5.1	125.8	5.7	126.4	0.5	124.6	-1.4	121.1	-2.8
1991	119.0	-1.7	119.2	0.2	121.1	1.6	121.1	0.0	121.4	0.2	120.4	-0.8	117.7	-2.2	121.8	3.5	124.8	2.5	126.8	1.6	127.9	0.9	123.5	-3.4
1992	120.9	-2.1	119.4	-1.2	123.6	3.5	123.3	-0.2	124.3	0.8	121.7	-2.1	121.8	0.1	126.8	4.1	133.8	5.5	134.0	0.1	132.1	-1.4	127.9	-3.2
1993	124.6	-2.6	131.2	5.3	131.5	0.2	128.3	-2.4	123.1	-4.1	121.0	-1.7	119.5	-1.2	124.7	4.4	129.1	3.5	130.1	0.8	128.6	-1.2	122.1	-5.1
1994	119.5	-2.1	123.4	3.3	126.4	2.4	128.1	1.3	124.6	-2.7	124.2	-0.3	119.6	-3.7	119.9	0.3	122.3	2.0	122.9	0.5	123.5	0.5	117.7	-4.7
1995	119.2	1.3	120.0	0.7	123.6	3.0	123.2	-0.3	123.2	0.0	119.6	-2.9	114.5	-4.3	119.3	4.2	125.5	5.2	126.1	0.5	125.5	-0.5	122.0	-2.8
1996	119.8	-1.8	124.2	3.7	127.6	2.7	126.8	-0.6	126.4	-0.3	121.0	-4.3	118.3	-2.2	120.0	1.4	127.9	6.6	126.4	-1.2	124.4	-1.6	120.6	-3.1
1997	120.8	0.2	127.4	5.5	130.4	2.4	128.0	-1.8	126.9	-0.9	122.5	-3.5	123.6	0.9	123.5	-0.1	127.7	3.4	130.3	2.0	129.3	-0.8	124.5	-3.7

[Continued]

New York-Northern New Jersey-Long Island, NY-NJ-CT-PA
Consumer Price Index - Urban Wage Earners
Base 1982-1984 = 100
Apparel
[Continued]

For 1952-2001. Columns headed % show percentile change in the index from the previous period for which an index is available.

Year	Jan Index	%	Feb Index	%	Mar Index	%	Apr Index	%	May Index	%	Jun Index	%	Jul Index	%	Aug Index	%	Sep Index	%	Oct Index	%	Nov Index	%	Dec Index	%
1998	120.1	-3.5	124.0	3.2	124.6	0.5	123.5	-0.9	122.3	-1.0	120.7	-1.3	118.3	-2.0	123.4	4.3	124.0	0.5	126.2	1.8	123.2	-2.4	119.1	-3.3
1999	116.3	-2.4	115.4	-0.8	118.9	3.0	120.3	1.2	118.3	-1.7	117.6	-0.6	117.8	0.2	119.1	1.1	125.0	5.0	128.0	2.4	122.6	-4.2	116.6	-4.9
2000	113.6	-2.6	117.5	3.4	118.6	0.9	118.8	0.2	119.2	0.3	114.0	-4.4	110.9	-2.7	117.1	5.6	124.9	6.7	124.9	0.0	119.3	-4.5	112.9	-5.4
2001	110.5	-2.1	113.8	3.0	118.1	3.8	114.8	-2.8	114.0	-0.7	110.3	-3.2	106.6	-3.4	108.8	2.1	113.4	4.2	113.0	-0.4	109.0	-3.5	104.9	-3.8

Source: U.S. Department of Labor, Bureau of Labor Statistics, Division of Consumer Prices and Price Indexes. - indicates no data collected for period.

New York-Northern New Jersey-Long Island, NY-NJ-CT-PA
Consumer Price Index - All Urban Consumers
Base 1982-1984 = 100
Transportation

For 1947-2000. Columns headed % show percentile change in the index from the previous period for which an index is available.

Year	Jan Index	%	Feb Index	%	Mar Index	%	Apr Index	%	May Index	%	Jun Index	%	Jul Index	%	Aug Index	%	Sep Index	%	Oct Index	%	Nov Index	%	Dec Index	%
1947	15.8	-	15.8	0.0	15.8	0.0	15.9	0.6	16.0	0.6	16.0	0.0	16.1	0.6	16.1	0.0	16.2	0.6	16.2	0.0	16.3	0.6	16.5	1.2
1948	16.5	0.0	16.5	0.0	16.5	0.0	16.5	0.0	16.5	0.0	16.5	0.0	20.9	26.7	21.1	1.0	21.2	0.5	21.3	0.5	21.3	0.0	21.3	0.0
1949	21.4	0.5	21.4	0.0	21.4	0.0	21.5	0.5	21.5	0.0	21.5	0.0	21.5	0.0	21.5	0.0	21.5	0.0	21.5	0.0	21.5	0.0	21.6	0.5
1950	21.6	0.0	21.6	0.0	21.6	0.0	21.6	0.0	21.6	0.0	21.6	0.0	23.1	6.9	23.2	0.4	23.2	0.0	23.2	0.0	23.3	0.4	23.3	0.0
1951	23.3	0.0	23.3	0.0	23.4	0.4	23.4	0.0	23.4	0.0	23.4	0.0	23.5	0.4	23.5	0.0	23.6	0.4	23.7	0.4	23.8	0.4	23.8	0.0
1952	23.8	0.0	23.9	0.4	23.9	0.0	23.9	0.0	23.9	0.0	23.9	0.0	23.9	0.0	23.9	0.0	24.0	0.4	24.0	0.0	24.0	0.0	24.0	0.0
1953	24.0	0.0	23.9	-0.4	23.9	0.0	23.9	0.0	23.9	0.0	24.0	0.4	24.2	0.8	25.2	4.1	25.2	0.0	25.2	0.0	25.1	-0.4	25.1	0.0
1954	25.5	1.6	25.4	-0.4	25.3	-0.4	25.2	-0.4	25.2	0.0	25.3	0.4	24.3	-4.0	24.2	-0.4	24.3	0.4	24.4	0.4	24.7	1.2	24.6	-0.4
1955	24.4	-0.8	24.4	0.0	24.4	0.0	24.3	-0.4	24.2	-0.4	24.2	0.0	23.9	-1.2	23.8	-0.4	23.8	0.0	24.0	0.8	24.6	2.5	24.3	-1.2
1956	24.5	0.8	24.7	0.8	24.6	-0.4	24.7	0.4	24.7	0.0	24.7	0.0	24.8	0.4	25.1	1.2	25.0	-0.4	25.9	3.6	25.7	-0.8	25.7	0.0
1957	25.7	0.0	25.9	0.8	25.9	0.0	26.0	0.4	26.0	0.0	26.0	0.0	25.8	-0.8	25.8	0.0	25.8	0.0	25.7	-0.4	26.3	2.3	26.2	-0.4
1958	26.2	0.0	26.1	-0.4	26.1	0.0	26.2	0.4	26.2	0.0	26.1	-0.4	26.2	0.4	26.3	0.4	26.3	0.0	26.5	0.8	27.0	1.9	27.2	0.7
1959	27.1	-0.4	27.1	0.0	27.2	0.4	27.4	0.7	27.4	0.0	27.4	0.0	27.6	0.7	27.6	0.0	27.6	0.0	28.0	1.4	28.1	0.4	28.1	0.0
1960	28.1	0.0	28.1	0.0	27.9	-0.7	27.8	-0.4	27.8	0.0	27.7	-0.4	27.6	-0.4	27.6	0.0	27.4	-0.7	27.6	0.7	27.7	0.4	27.7	0.0
1961	27.6	-0.4	27.5	-0.4	27.6	0.4	27.7	0.4	27.8	0.4	27.9	0.4	27.9	0.0	27.9	0.0	27.9	0.0	28.1	0.7	28.0	-0.4	27.8	-0.7
1962	27.9	0.4	27.8	-0.4	27.8	0.0	27.9	0.4	28.1	0.7	28.1	0.0	28.0	-0.4	28.1	0.4	28.0	-0.4	28.1	0.4	28.1	0.0	28.0	-0.4
1963	28.0	0.0	27.9	-0.4	28.0	0.4	28.1	0.4	28.0	-0.4	28.3	1.1	28.3	0.0	28.3	0.0	28.3	0.0	28.4	0.4	28.6	0.7	28.5	-0.3
1964	28.4	-0.4	28.4	0.0	28.3	-0.4	28.3	0.0	28.3	0.0	28.2	-0.4	28.2	0.0	28.2	0.0	28.1	-0.4	28.2	0.4	28.5	1.1	28.6	0.4
1965	28.7	0.3	28.5	-0.7	28.6	0.4	28.6	0.0	28.5	-0.3	28.4	-0.4	28.6	0.7	28.7	0.3	28.7	0.0	28.9	0.7	28.9	0.0	28.9	0.0
1966	29.0	0.3	29.0	0.0	29.1	0.3	29.2	0.3	29.1	-0.3	29.2	0.3	30.5	4.5	30.5	0.0	30.3	-0.7	30.6	1.0	30.7	0.3	30.6	-0.3
1967	30.5	-0.3	30.7	0.7	30.8	0.3	30.9	0.3	31.0	0.3	31.0	0.0	31.2	0.6	31.4	0.6	31.3	-0.3	31.7	1.3	31.6	-0.3	31.7	0.3
1968	31.7	0.0	31.7	0.0	31.7	0.0	31.7	0.0	31.7	0.0	31.9	0.6	32.1	0.6	32.2	0.3	32.1	-0.3	32.4	0.9	32.5	0.3	32.2	-0.9
1969	33.0	2.5	33.3	0.9	33.8	1.5	33.9	0.3	33.7	-0.6	33.9	0.6	33.9	0.0	33.9	0.0	33.6	-0.9	34.2	1.8	34.2	0.0	35.1	2.6
1970	37.4	6.6	37.5	0.3	37.5	0.0	37.8	0.8	38.0	0.5	38.1	0.3	38.2	0.3	38.1	-0.3	38.1	0.0	38.6	1.3	38.9	0.8	39.1	0.5
1971	39.3	0.5	40.0	1.8	40.1	0.2	40.1	0.0	40.2	0.2	40.6	1.0	40.6	0.0	40.5	-0.2	40.1	-1.0	40.3	0.5	40.3	0.0	40.2	-0.2
1972	41.2	2.5	41.2	0.0	41.1	-0.2	41.1	0.0	41.3	0.5	41.4	0.2	41.5	0.2	41.6	0.2	41.7	0.2	41.7	0.0	41.8	0.2	41.8	0.0
1973	41.7	-0.2	41.8	0.2	41.8	0.0	42.0	0.5	42.1	0.2	42.4	0.7	42.4	0.0	42.4	0.0	42.2	-0.5	42.5	0.7	42.7	0.5	43.1	0.9
1974	43.2	0.2	43.4	0.5	43.9	1.2	44.3	0.9	45.0	1.6	45.8	1.8	46.4	1.3	46.5	0.2	46.8	0.6	47.0	0.4	47.1	0.2	47.4	0.6
1975	47.3	-0.2	47.3	0.0	47.8	1.1	48.1	0.6	48.2	0.2	48.8	1.2	49.5	1.4	49.7	0.4	53.3	7.2	53.6	0.6	54.7	2.1	55.3	1.1
1976	55.3	0.0	55.4	0.2	56.4	1.8	56.5	0.2	56.9	0.7	57.5	1.1	57.9	0.7	58.1	0.3	58.7	1.0	59.1	0.7	59.1	0.0	59.0	-0.2
1977	59.4	0.7	59.7	0.5	60.1	0.7	60.4	0.5	60.6	0.3	60.8	0.3	60.8	0.0	60.8	0.0	60.7	-0.2	60.9	0.3	61.0	0.2	61.1	0.2
1978	61.1	0.0	61.3	0.3	61.3	0.0	61.6	0.5	61.8	0.3	62.2	0.6	62.6	0.6	62.8	0.3	63.3	0.8	64.1	1.3	64.4	0.5	64.8	0.6
1979	65.1	0.5	65.7	0.9	66.4	1.1	67.7	2.0	69.0	1.9	70.6	2.3	72.2	2.3	72.9	1.0	73.6	1.0	74.1	0.7	74.7	0.8	75.4	0.9
1980	77.2	2.4	79.1	2.5	80.5	1.8	81.5	1.2	81.8	0.4	82.1	0.4	83.6	1.8	83.9	0.4	84.4	0.6	84.6	0.2	85.3	0.8	86.0	0.8
1981	87.4	1.6	89.3	2.2	90.1	0.9	90.7	0.7	91.0	0.3	91.5	0.5	93.9	2.6	94.0	0.1	94.4	0.4	94.7	0.3	95.4	0.7	95.6	0.2
1982	95.4	-0.2	95.0	-0.4	94.0	-1.1	93.3	-0.7	93.6	0.3	95.6	2.1	96.6	1.0	96.9	0.3	97.4	0.5	97.9	0.5	97.8	-0.1	97.8	0.0
1983	97.5	-0.3	96.9	-0.6	96.1	-0.8	97.8	1.8	98.1	0.3	98.7	0.6	99.2	0.5	99.9	0.7	100.5	0.6	100.9	0.4	101.6	0.7	101.5	-0.1
1984	103.3	1.8	103.5	0.2	104.1	0.6	104.5	0.4	105.0	0.5	105.1	0.1	105.5	0.4	105.5	0.0	105.5	0.0	105.8	0.3	106.1	0.3	106.1	0.0
1985	106.1	0.0	106.1	0.0	106.6	0.5	106.8	0.2	107.1	0.3	107.4	0.3	107.4	0.0	107.1	-0.3	106.8	-0.3	107.6	0.7	108.1	0.5	108.4	0.3
1986	109.5	1.0	108.5	-0.9	106.1	-2.2	103.4	-2.5	103.4	0.0	104.5	1.1	103.9	-0.6	102.9	-1.0	102.4	-0.5	104.0	1.6	104.5	0.5	104.8	0.3
1987	105.4	0.6	105.7	0.3	106.1	0.4	107.4	1.2	108.0	0.6	108.8	0.7	109.4	0.6	110.2	0.7	110.3	0.1	110.7	0.4	111.5	0.7	111.2	-0.3
1988	111.3	0.1	111.3	0.0	110.7	-0.5	111.2	0.5	111.8	0.5	112.6	0.7	113.0	0.4	113.4	0.4	113.7	0.3	114.4	0.6	114.7	0.3	114.9	0.2
1989	115.2	0.3	115.1	-0.1	115.3	0.2	116.3	0.9	117.5	1.0	117.3	-0.2	116.9	-0.3	116.4	-0.4	115.8	-0.5	116.9	0.9	117.3	0.3	117.5	0.2
1990	119.5	1.7	119.8	0.3	119.5	-0.3	119.2	-0.3	119.3	0.1	120.4	0.9	120.8	0.3	122.1	1.1	125.3	2.6	129.0	3.0	130.6	1.2	131.4	0.6
1991	129.1	-1.8	127.8	-1.0	126.6	-0.9	126.2	-0.3	127.3	0.9	127.6	0.2	127.7	0.1	127.6	-0.1	128.1	0.4	128.6	0.4	129.1	0.4	129.1	0.0
1992	129.5	0.3	129.7	0.2	129.9	0.2	129.6	-0.2	129.8	0.2	130.1	0.2	130.9	0.6	130.6	-0.2	130.9	0.2	134.6	2.8	135.5	0.7	136.3	0.6

[Continued]

New York-Northern New Jersey-Long Island, NY-NJ-CT-PA
Consumer Price Index - All Urban Consumers
Base 1982-1984 = 100
Transportation
[Continued]

For 1947-2000. Columns headed % show percentile change in the index from the previous period for which an index is available.

Year	Jan Index	%	Feb Index	%	Mar Index	%	Apr Index	%	May Index	%	Jun Index	%	Jul Index	%	Aug Index	%	Sep Index	%	Oct Index	%	Nov Index	%	Dec Index	%
1993	137.3	0.7	136.9	-0.3	136.2	-0.5	136.4	0.1	137.1	0.5	136.7	-0.3	137.1	0.3	137.2	0.1	137.1	-0.1	139.1	1.5	140.1	0.7	141.0	0.6
1994	140.4	-0.4	140.6	0.1	139.9	-0.5	140.5	0.4	140.3	-0.1	141.2	0.6	141.5	0.2	142.2	0.5	142.3	0.1	143.9	1.1	144.5	0.4	144.6	0.1
1995	144.4	-0.1	144.5	0.1	144.5	0.0	144.1	-0.3	146.0	1.3	147.4	1.0	146.5	-0.6	145.7	-0.5	145.9	0.1	146.8	0.6	146.9	0.1	147.8	0.6
1996	148.6	0.5	149.0	0.3	150.7	1.1	152.5	1.2	153.0	0.3	153.1	0.1	152.8	-0.2	152.3	-0.3	153.3	0.7	153.5	0.1	154.5	0.7	155.8	0.8
1997	154.6	-0.8	154.6	0.0	155.1	0.3	154.1	-0.6	153.6	-0.3	153.9	0.2	153.7	-0.1	152.8	-0.6	154.6	1.2	155.5	0.6	153.4	-1.4	153.3	-0.1
1998	152.3	-0.7	152.4	0.1	151.6	-0.5	151.1	-0.3	151.1	0.0	150.7	-0.3	151.5	0.5	151.1	-0.3	150.0	-0.7	150.6	0.4	150.6	0.0	150.4	-0.1
1999	149.6	-0.5	149.4	-0.1	149.7	0.2	150.4	0.5	151.7	0.9	151.6	-0.1	152.4	0.5	152.8	0.3	153.4	0.4	155.6	1.4	155.0	-0.4	156.1	0.7
2000	155.7	-0.3	156.4	0.4	159.4	1.9	159.5	0.1	159.3	-0.1	162.0	1.7	161.8	-0.1	161.1	-0.4	160.6	-0.3	161.4	0.5	161.7	0.2	161.3	-0.2

Source: U.S. Department of Labor, Bureau of Labor Statistics, Division of Consumer Prices and Price Indexes. - indicates no data collected for period.

New York-Northern New Jersey-Long Island, NY-NJ-CT-PA
Consumer Price Index - Urban Wage Earners
Base 1982-1984 = 100
Transportation

For 1947-2000. Columns headed % show percentile change in the index from the previous period for which an index is available.

Year	Jan Index	%	Feb Index	%	Mar Index	%	Apr Index	%	May Index	%	Jun Index	%	Jul Index	%	Aug Index	%	Sep Index	%	Oct Index	%	Nov Index	%	Dec Index	%
1947	15.7	-	15.7	0.0	15.7	0.0	15.8	0.6	15.8	0.0	15.9	0.6	15.9	0.0	16.0	0.6	16.1	0.6	16.1	0.0	16.1	0.0	16.3	1.2
1948	16.3	0.0	16.3	0.0	16.3	0.0	16.3	0.0	16.3	0.0	16.3	0.0	20.7	27.0	20.9	1.0	21.0	0.5	21.1	0.5	21.1	0.0	21.1	0.0
1949	21.1	0.0	21.2	0.5	21.2	0.0	21.3	0.5	21.3	0.0	21.3	0.0	21.3	0.0	21.3	0.0	21.3	0.0	21.3	0.0	21.3	0.0	21.4	0.5
1950	21.4	0.0	21.4	0.0	21.4	0.0	21.4	0.0	21.4	0.0	21.4	0.0	22.9	7.0	23.0	0.4	22.9	-0.4	22.9	0.0	23.0	0.4	23.0	0.0
1951	23.0	0.0	23.1	0.4	23.2	0.4	23.2	0.0	23.2	0.0	23.2	0.0	23.3	0.4	23.3	0.0	23.4	0.4	23.5	0.4	23.6	0.4	23.6	0.0
1952	23.6	0.0	23.7	0.4	23.7	0.0	23.7	0.0	23.7	0.0	23.7	0.0	23.7	0.0	23.7	0.0	23.8	0.4	23.8	0.0	23.8	0.0	23.7	-0.4
1953	23.8	0.4	23.7	-0.4	23.7	0.0	23.7	0.0	23.7	0.0	23.7	0.0	23.9	0.8	25.0	4.6	24.9	-0.4	25.0	0.4	24.8	-0.8	24.9	0.4
1954	25.2	1.2	25.1	-0.4	25.0	-0.4	24.9	-0.4	25.0	0.4	25.0	0.0	24.0	-4.0	24.0	0.0	24.1	0.4	24.1	0.0	24.4	1.2	24.3	-0.4
1955	24.2	-0.4	24.2	0.0	24.2	0.0	24.1	-0.4	24.0	-0.4	23.9	-0.4	23.7	-0.8	23.6	-0.4	23.6	0.0	23.8	0.8	24.4	2.5	24.1	-1.2
1956	24.3	0.8	24.4	0.4	24.4	0.0	24.4	0.0	24.5	0.4	24.4	-0.4	24.6	0.8	24.8	0.8	24.8	0.0	25.6	3.2	25.4	-0.8	25.4	0.0
1957	25.5	0.4	25.6	0.4	25.6	0.0	25.7	0.4	25.7	0.0	25.7	0.0	25.6	-0.4	25.6	0.0	25.5	-0.4	25.5	0.0	26.1	2.4	26.0	-0.4
1958	26.0	0.0	25.9	-0.4	25.8	-0.4	25.9	0.4	25.9	0.0	25.9	0.0	25.9	0.0	26.1	0.8	26.1	0.0	26.2	0.4	26.7	1.9	26.9	0.7
1959	26.9	0.0	26.9	0.0	27.0	0.4	27.2	0.7	27.2	0.0	27.2	0.0	27.3	0.4	27.4	0.4	27.3	-0.4	27.7	1.5	27.8	0.4	27.8	0.0
1960	27.8	0.0	27.8	0.0	27.6	-0.7	27.5	-0.4	27.5	0.0	27.4	-0.4	27.3	-0.4	27.3	0.0	27.2	-0.4	27.3	0.4	27.4	0.4	27.5	0.4
1961	27.3	-0.7	27.2	-0.4	27.3	0.4	27.5	0.7	27.5	0.0	27.6	0.4	27.6	0.0	27.6	0.0	27.6	0.0	27.8	0.7	27.8	0.0	27.5	-1.1
1962	27.6	0.4	27.5	-0.4	27.5	0.0	27.7	0.7	27.8	0.4	27.8	0.0	27.8	0.0	27.8	0.0	27.7	-0.4	27.8	0.4	27.9	0.4	27.7	-0.7
1963	27.7	0.0	27.7	0.0	27.7	0.0	27.8	0.4	27.7	-0.4	28.1	1.4	28.1	0.0	28.1	0.0	28.0	-0.4	28.1	0.4	28.3	0.7	28.2	-0.4
1964	28.1	-0.4	28.1	0.0	28.0	-0.4	28.0	0.0	28.0	0.0	27.9	-0.4	28.0	0.4	27.9	-0.4	27.8	-0.4	27.9	0.4	28.2	1.1	28.3	0.4
1965	28.4	0.4	28.2	-0.7	28.3	0.4	28.3	0.0	28.2	-0.4	28.1	-0.4	28.3	0.7	28.4	0.4	28.4	0.0	28.6	0.7	28.6	0.0	28.6	0.0
1966	28.7	0.3	28.7	0.0	28.8	0.3	29.0	0.7	28.9	-0.3	29.0	0.3	30.3	4.5	30.3	0.0	30.0	-1.0	30.3	1.0	30.4	0.3	30.3	-0.3
1967	30.3	0.0	30.4	0.3	30.5	0.3	30.6	0.3	30.7	0.3	30.7	0.0	30.9	0.7	31.1	0.6	31.0	-0.3	31.4	1.3	31.3	-0.3	31.4	0.3
1968	31.4	0.0	31.4	0.0	31.4	0.0	31.4	0.0	31.4	0.0	31.6	0.6	31.8	0.6	31.9	0.3	31.8	-0.3	32.1	0.9	32.2	0.3	31.9	-0.9
1969	32.7	2.5	33.0	0.9	33.5	1.5	33.6	0.3	33.4	-0.6	33.5	0.3	33.6	0.3	33.6	0.0	33.3	-0.9	33.8	1.5	33.8	0.0	34.7	2.7
1970	37.0	6.6	37.1	0.3	37.2	0.3	37.4	0.5	37.6	0.5	37.7	0.3	37.8	0.3	37.7	-0.3	37.7	0.0	38.2	1.3	38.6	1.0	38.7	0.3
1971	38.9	0.5	39.6	1.8	39.8	0.5	39.7	-0.3	39.8	0.3	40.2	1.0	40.3	0.2	40.1	-0.5	39.7	-1.0	39.9	0.5	39.9	0.0	39.8	-0.3
1972	40.8	2.5	40.8	0.0	40.7	-0.2	40.7	0.0	40.9	0.5	41.0	0.2	41.1	0.2	41.1	0.0	41.3	0.5	41.3	0.0	41.4	0.2	41.4	0.0
1973	41.3	-0.2	41.4	0.2	41.4	0.0	41.6	0.5	41.7	0.2	42.0	0.7	42.0	0.0	42.0	0.0	41.8	-0.5	42.1	0.7	42.3	0.5	42.7	0.9
1974	42.8	0.2	43.0	0.5	43.5	1.2	43.9	0.9	44.6	1.6	45.4	1.8	46.0	1.3	46.1	0.2	46.3	0.4	46.5	0.4	46.7	0.4	47.0	0.6
1975	46.9	-0.2	46.9	0.0	47.4	1.1	47.7	0.6	47.8	0.2	48.3	1.0	49.0	1.4	49.3	0.6	52.8	7.1	53.1	0.6	54.2	2.1	54.8	1.1
1976	54.8	0.0	54.9	0.2	55.8	1.6	56.0	0.4	56.4	0.7	57.0	1.1	57.3	0.5	57.5	0.3	58.1	1.0	58.6	0.9	58.6	0.0	58.5	-0.2
1977	58.8	0.5	59.1	0.5	59.5	0.7	59.8	0.5	60.0	0.3	60.2	0.3	60.2	0.0	60.2	0.0	60.1	-0.2	60.3	0.3	60.4	0.2	60.5	0.2
1978	60.5	0.0	60.7	0.3	60.8	0.2	61.1	0.5	61.4	0.5	61.9	0.8	62.3	0.6	62.6	0.5	63.0	0.6	63.6	1.0	64.0	0.6	64.4	0.6
1979	64.7	0.5	65.3	0.9	66.0	1.1	67.4	2.1	68.7	1.9	70.5	2.6	72.0	2.1	72.8	1.1	73.5	1.0	73.7	0.3	74.4	0.9	75.1	0.9
1980	77.0	2.5	78.8	2.3	80.2	1.8	81.1	1.1	81.3	0.2	81.6	0.4	83.3	2.1	83.7	0.5	84.1	0.5	84.4	0.4	85.1	0.8	85.9	0.9
1981	87.2	1.5	89.2	2.3	90.0	0.9	90.7	0.8	90.7	0.0	91.3	0.7	93.9	2.8	94.1	0.2	94.6	0.5	94.9	0.3	95.5	0.6	95.7	0.2
1982	95.5	-0.2	95.0	-0.5	94.0	-1.1	93.0	-1.1	93.4	0.4	95.5	2.2	96.7	1.3	97.0	0.3	97.3	0.3	97.8	0.5	97.5	-0.3	97.6	0.1
1983	97.3	-0.3	96.6	-0.7	95.7	-0.9	97.3	1.7	97.8	0.5	98.5	0.7	99.1	0.6	99.9	0.8	100.6	0.7	101.0	0.4	101.7	0.7	101.7	0.0
1984	103.5	1.8	103.6	0.1	104.2	0.6	104.6	0.4	105.2	0.6	105.5	0.3	105.7	0.2	105.7	0.0	105.8	0.1	106.1	0.3	106.3	0.2	106.3	0.0
1985	106.2	-0.1	106.2	0.0	106.7	0.5	107.0	0.3	107.2	0.2	107.5	0.3	107.5	0.0	107.1	-0.4	106.7	-0.4	107.5	0.7	108.1	0.6	108.3	0.2
1986	109.5	1.1	108.4	-1.0	105.8	-2.4	102.9	-2.7	102.8	-0.1	103.8	1.0	103.1	-0.7	102.1	-1.0	101.5	-0.6	103.1	1.6	103.4	0.3	103.6	0.2
1987	104.4	0.8	105.0	0.6	105.5	0.5	107.0	1.4	107.7	0.7	108.7	0.9	109.3	0.6	110.2	0.8	110.4	0.2	110.7	0.3	111.3	0.5	111.1	-0.2
1988	111.2	0.1	111.1	-0.1	110.5	-0.5	110.8	0.3	111.3	0.5	112.0	0.6	112.5	0.4	113.1	0.5	113.3	0.2	113.9	0.5	114.1	0.2	114.4	0.3
1989	114.5	0.1	114.4	-0.1	114.6	0.2	115.8	1.0	117.4	1.4	117.4	0.0	117.1	-0.3	116.5	-0.5	115.7	-0.7	116.5	0.7	116.9	0.3	116.9	0.0
1990	119.3	2.1	119.4	0.1	119.0	-0.3	118.8	-0.2	118.8	0.0	120.2	1.2	120.9	0.6	122.3	1.2	126.1	3.1	129.7	2.9	131.3	1.2	131.8	0.4
1991	129.1	-2.0	127.3	-1.4	126.0	-1.0	125.9	-0.1	127.2	1.0	127.6	0.3	127.8	0.2	127.7	-0.1	128.4	0.5	128.6	0.2	129.1	0.4	129.0	-0.1
1992	129.5	0.4	129.4	-0.1	129.6	0.2	129.3	-0.2	129.9	0.5	130.8	0.7	131.4	0.5	131.0	-0.3	131.5	0.4	134.9	2.6	135.7	0.6	136.5	0.6

[Continued]

New York-Northern New Jersey-Long Island, NY-NJ-CT-PA
Consumer Price Index - Urban Wage Earners
Base 1982-1984 = 100
Transportation
[Continued]

For 1947-2000. Columns headed % show percentile change in the index from the previous period for which an index is available.

Year	Jan Index	%	Feb Index	%	Mar Index	%	Apr Index	%	May Index	%	Jun Index	%	Jul Index	%	Aug Index	%	Sep Index	%	Oct Index	%	Nov Index	%	Dec Index	%
1993	137.0	0.4	136.5	-0.4	135.9	-0.4	135.8	-0.1	136.7	0.7	136.7	0.0	136.9	0.1	137.0	0.1	136.9	-0.1	139.2	1.7	139.9	0.5	140.6	0.5
1994	139.8	-0.6	139.6	-0.1	139.1	-0.4	139.6	0.4	139.8	0.1	140.9	0.8	141.4	0.4	142.2	0.6	142.7	0.4	144.4	1.2	145.0	0.4	144.9	-0.1
1995	144.5	-0.3	144.5	0.0	144.5	0.0	144.3	-0.1	146.2	1.3	147.5	0.9	147.0	-0.3	146.2	-0.5	146.0	-0.1	146.8	0.5	146.8	0.0	148.1	0.9
1996	149.2	0.7	149.4	0.1	151.5	1.4	153.3	1.2	154.4	0.7	154.3	-0.1	153.7	-0.4	153.4	-0.2	154.1	0.5	154.2	0.1	155.5	0.8	156.6	0.7
1997	155.7	-0.6	155.6	-0.1	155.6	0.0	154.7	-0.6	154.2	-0.3	154.3	0.1	153.8	-0.3	153.6	-0.1	155.3	1.1	155.7	0.3	153.9	-1.2	153.7	-0.1
1998	152.5	-0.8	152.3	-0.1	151.4	-0.6	151.3	-0.1	151.7	0.3	151.6	-0.1	151.9	0.2	151.6	-0.2	150.2	-0.9	151.1	0.6	150.9	-0.1	150.5	-0.3
1999	149.6	-0.6	149.0	-0.4	149.2	0.1	150.0	0.5	151.3	0.9	151.4	0.1	152.3	0.6	153.3	0.7	154.3	0.7	156.1	1.2	155.7	-0.3	156.5	0.5
2000	156.2	-0.2	156.9	0.4	159.9	1.9	160.4	0.3	160.0	-0.2	162.7	1.7	162.6	-0.1	161.7	-0.6	161.2	-0.3	162.0	0.5	162.5	0.3	162.1	-0.2

Source: U.S. Department of Labor, Bureau of Labor Statistics, Division of Consumer Prices and Price Indexes. - indicates no data collected for period.

New York-Northern New Jersey-Long Island, NY-NJ-CT-PA
Consumer Price Index - All Urban Consumers
Base 1982-1984 = 100
Medical Care

For 1947-2001. Columns headed % show percentile change in the index from the previous period for which an index is available.

Year	Jan Index	%	Feb Index	%	Mar Index	%	Apr Index	%	May Index	%	Jun Index	%	Jul Index	%	Aug Index	%	Sep Index	%	Oct Index	%	Nov Index	%	Dec Index	%
1947	14.0	-	14.1	0.7	14.1	0.0	14.1	0.0	14.2	0.7	14.3	0.7	14.3	0.0	14.3	0.0	14.4	0.7	14.5	0.7	14.5	0.0	14.5	0.0
1948	14.8	2.1	14.9	0.7	15.0	0.7	15.6	4.0	15.6	0.0	15.6	0.0	16.0	2.6	16.0	0.0	16.1	0.6	16.1	0.0	16.1	0.0	16.1	0.0
1949	16.2	0.6	16.2	0.0	16.0	-1.2	16.0	0.0	16.0	0.0	16.0	0.0	16.0	0.0	16.0	0.0	16.0	0.0	16.0	0.0	16.0	0.0	16.2	1.3
1950	16.3	0.6	16.3	0.0	16.3	0.0	16.3	0.0	16.3	0.0	16.4	0.6	16.4	0.0	16.4	0.0	16.3	-0.6	16.4	0.6	16.4	0.0	16.4	0.0
1951	16.6	1.2	16.6	0.0	16.9	1.8	17.0	0.6	17.0	0.0	17.0	0.0	17.0	0.0	17.0	0.0	17.2	1.2	17.2	0.0	17.2	0.0	17.4	1.2
1952	17.6	1.1	17.6	0.0	17.6	0.0	17.6	0.0	17.6	0.0	18.3	4.0	18.3	0.0	18.4	0.5	18.6	1.1	18.6	0.0	18.7	0.5	18.6	-0.5
1953	18.6	0.0	18.5	-0.5	18.5	0.0	18.5	0.0	18.5	0.0	18.5	0.0	18.5	0.0	18.6	0.5	18.6	0.0	18.6	0.0	18.9	1.6	18.9	0.0
1954	18.9	0.0	18.9	0.0	18.9	0.0	19.0	0.5	19.0	0.0	19.0	0.0	19.0	0.0	19.0	0.0	19.0	0.0	19.0	0.0	19.1	0.5	19.1	0.0
1955	19.1	0.0	19.2	0.5	19.2	0.0	19.2	0.0	19.3	0.5	19.3	0.0	19.4	0.5	19.4	0.0	19.4	0.0	19.4	0.0	19.4	0.0	19.4	0.0
1956	19.4	0.0	19.4	0.0	19.4	0.0	19.4	0.0	19.4	0.0	19.4	0.0	19.4	0.0	19.6	1.0	19.6	0.0	19.6	0.0	19.6	0.0	19.6	0.0
1957	19.7	0.5	19.7	0.0	19.7	0.0	19.7	0.0	19.8	0.5	19.9	0.5	19.9	0.0	19.8	-0.5	19.8	0.0	19.8	0.0	19.9	0.5	19.9	0.0
1958	19.9	0.0	19.9	0.0	20.0	0.5	20.0	0.0	20.0	0.0	20.0	0.0	20.0	0.0	20.1	0.5	20.7	3.0	20.7	0.0	20.8	0.5	20.8	0.0
1959	20.8	0.0	21.1	1.4	21.1	0.0	21.1	0.0	21.4	1.4	21.5	0.5	21.5	0.0	21.4	-0.5	22.0	2.8	22.0	0.0	22.0	0.0	22.0	0.0
1960	22.0	0.0	22.0	0.0	22.1	0.5	22.1	0.0	22.1	0.0	22.1	0.0	22.1	0.0	22.1	0.0	22.1	0.0	22.1	0.0	22.7	2.7	22.7	0.0
1961	22.7	0.0	22.7	0.0	22.8	0.4	22.8	0.0	23.0	0.9	23.0	0.0	23.0	0.0	23.1	0.4	23.1	0.0	23.1	0.0	23.1	0.0	23.1	0.0
1962	23.1	0.0	23.3	0.9	23.4	0.4	23.4	0.0	23.5	0.4	23.5	0.0	23.5	0.0	23.6	0.4	23.6	0.0	23.5	-0.4	23.6	0.4	23.7	0.4
1963	23.7	0.0	23.9	0.8	23.9	0.0	23.9	0.0	24.0	0.4	23.9	-0.4	23.9	0.0	24.0	0.4	24.0	0.0	24.0	0.0	24.1	0.4	24.1	0.0
1964	24.2	0.4	24.3	0.4	24.3	0.0	24.4	0.4	24.4	0.0	24.4	0.0	24.4	0.0	24.6	0.8	24.4	-0.8	24.5	0.4	24.7	0.8	24.7	0.0
1965	24.9	0.8	25.1	0.8	25.2	0.4	25.2	0.0	25.2	0.0	25.4	0.8	25.4	0.0	25.3	-0.4	25.3	0.0	25.3	0.0	25.4	0.4	25.6	0.8
1966	25.7	0.4	25.8	0.4	26.0	0.8	26.1	0.4	26.3	0.8	26.7	1.5	26.8	0.4	27.0	0.7	27.0	0.0	27.2	0.7	27.3	0.4	27.3	0.0
1967	27.6	1.1	27.8	0.7	27.9	0.4	28.0	0.4	28.1	0.4	28.3	0.7	28.5	0.7	28.7	0.7	28.8	0.3	28.9	0.3	28.9	0.0	29.2	1.0
1968	29.3	0.3	29.4	0.3	29.6	0.7	29.8	0.7	29.8	0.0	30.1	1.0	30.5	1.3	30.5	0.0	30.8	1.0	31.0	0.6	31.1	0.3	31.2	0.3
1969	31.9	2.2	32.0	0.3	32.5	1.6	32.8	0.9	33.0	0.6	33.4	1.2	33.4	0.0	33.6	0.6	33.6	0.0	33.5	-0.3	33.6	0.3	33.8	0.6
1970	34.0	0.6	34.1	0.3	34.6	1.5	34.9	0.9	34.9	0.0	35.6	2.0	35.9	0.8	36.1	0.6	36.4	0.8	36.5	0.3	36.8	0.8	37.3	1.4
1971	37.6	0.8	37.8	0.5	38.2	1.1	38.2	0.0	38.4	0.5	38.5	0.3	38.8	0.8	39.0	0.5	39.0	0.0	38.9	-0.3	39.0	0.3	39.1	0.3
1972	39.4	0.8	39.4	0.0	39.4	0.0	39.5	0.3	39.6	0.3	39.8	0.5	39.8	0.0	39.9	0.3	39.9	0.0	40.1	0.5	40.3	0.5	40.6	0.7
1973	40.7	0.2	40.7	0.0	40.6	-0.2	40.6	0.0	40.9	0.7	41.0	0.2	41.0	0.0	41.1	0.2	41.3	0.5	42.0	1.7	42.1	0.2	42.3	0.5
1974	42.8	1.2	43.2	0.9	43.8	1.4	44.1	0.7	44.7	1.4	45.4	1.6	45.7	0.7	46.9	2.6	47.4	1.1	47.5	0.2	47.8	0.6	48.2	0.8
1975	48.9	1.5	49.6	1.4	50.3	1.4	50.6	0.6	51.0	0.8	51.3	0.6	51.7	0.8	51.9	0.4	52.6	1.3	52.8	0.4	52.6	-0.4	53.4	1.5
1976	54.5	2.1	55.0	0.9	55.5	0.9	55.7	0.4	55.9	0.4	56.5	1.1	57.1	1.1	57.5	0.7	57.9	0.7	57.9	0.0	58.8	1.6	58.9	0.2
1977	59.7	1.4	59.9	0.3	60.7	1.3	61.2	0.8	61.4	0.3	61.7	0.5	62.0	0.5	62.2	0.3	62.3	0.2	62.6	0.5	62.8	0.3	63.3	0.8
1978	64.1	1.3	64.5	0.6	64.6	0.2	64.8	0.3	65.5	1.1	65.5	0.0	65.5	0.0	65.5	0.0	65.7	0.3	65.7	0.0	66.7	1.5	66.3	-0.6
1979	68.1	2.7	69.0	1.3	69.2	0.3	69.7	0.7	69.8	0.1	70.1	0.4	70.2	0.1	70.5	0.4	71.1	0.9	72.2	1.5	73.0	1.1	73.5	0.7
1980	74.5	1.4	75.4	1.2	76.2	1.1	76.9	0.9	76.9	Base	77.0	0.1	77.2	0.3	77.8	0.8	78.3	0.6	78.7	0.5	79.0	0.4	79.3	0.4
1981	80.2	1.1	80.6	0.5	81.6	1.2	82.5	1.1	82.7	0.2	84.1	1.7	85.0	1.1	85.2	0.2	86.2	1.2	87.2	1.2	87.7	0.6	88.1	0.5
1982	89.1	1.1	89.9	0.9	90.7	0.9	90.9	0.2	91.2	0.3	91.6	0.4	91.5	-0.1	91.9	0.4	92.8	1.0	93.3	0.5	94.1	0.9	94.4	0.3
1983	95.4	1.1	97.3	2.0	98.1	0.8	98.7	0.6	99.4	0.7	99.4	0.0	100.0	0.6	101.2	1.2	101.7	0.5	102.3	0.6	103.2	0.9	103.9	0.7
1984	104.7	0.8	106.1	1.3	106.7	0.6	106.7	0.0	107.3	0.6	107.2	-0.1	107.7	0.5	109.0	1.2	109.8	0.7	110.1	0.3	110.8	0.6	111.4	0.5
1985	112.0	0.5	113.8	1.6	114.3	0.4	114.6	0.3	115.4	0.7	116.2	0.7	116.7	0.4	116.8	0.1	117.2	0.3	117.5	0.3	117.8	0.3	117.7	-0.1
1986	120.0	2.0	122.2	1.8	123.7	1.2	124.2	0.4	124.6	0.3	125.1	0.4	126.0	0.7	126.4	0.3	127.8	1.1	128.7	0.7	128.7	0.0	130.3	1.2
1987	131.1	0.6	132.9	1.4	135.0	1.6	136.1	0.8	136.1	0.0	136.3	0.1	136.8	0.4	137.2	0.3	137.2	0.0	137.5	0.2	137.9	0.3	138.5	0.4
1988	139.7	0.9	141.3	1.1	142.7	1.0	143.2	0.4	144.1	0.6	144.7	0.4	146.1	1.0	145.9	-0.1	146.9	0.7	147.1	0.1	147.6	0.3	147.9	0.2
1989	149.5	1.1	151.1	1.1	152.9	1.2	153.4	0.3	154.3		155.6	0.8	156.2	0.4	157.1	0.6	157.7	0.4	159.7	1.3	160.5	0.5	161.5	0.6
1990	163.9	1.5	166.7	1.7	169.2	1.5	170.1	0.5	170.5	0.2	171.4	0.5	171.8	0.2	175.1	1.9	175.9	0.5	177.5	0.9	178.0	0.3	178.7	0.4
1991	180.8	1.2	182.8	1.1	183.9	0.6	184.2	0.2	183.9	-0.2	185.3	0.8	187.2	1.0	188.7	0.8	189.3	0.3	189.6	0.2	191.0	0.7	192.0	0.5
1992	195.1	1.6	196.4	0.7	197.7	0.7	198.4	0.4	199.1	0.4	200.0	0.5	201.2	0.6	200.8	-0.2	201.9	0.5	202.8	0.4	203.1	0.1	203.3	0.1

[Continued]

New York-Northern New Jersey-Long Island, NY-NJ-CT-PA
Consumer Price Index - All Urban Consumers
Base 1982-1984 = 100
Medical Care
[Continued]

For 1947-2001. Columns headed % show percentile change in the index from the previous period for which an index is available.

Year	Jan Index	%	Feb Index	%	Mar Index	%	Apr Index	%	May Index	%	Jun Index	%	Jul Index	%	Aug Index	%	Sep Index	%	Oct Index	%	Nov Index	%	Dec Index	%
1993	205.1	0.9	205.5	0.2	206.6	0.5	207.9	0.6	208.9	0.5	208.9	0.0	209.5	0.3	210.7	0.6	211.0	0.1	211.3	0.1	211.4	0.0	212.0	0.3
1994	213.5	0.7	214.2	0.3	215.1	0.4	215.8	0.3	216.5	0.3	217.7	0.6	218.2	0.2	218.7	0.2	218.6	-0.0	220.6	0.9	220.6	0.0	221.7	0.5
1995	223.2	0.7	225.1	0.9	225.3	0.1	225.6	0.1	226.0	0.2	226.0	0.0	226.2	0.1	227.4	0.5	228.0	0.3	229.5	0.7	229.6	0.0	230.0	0.2
1996	231.1	0.5	231.6	0.2	232.6	0.4	232.8	0.1	234.1	0.6	234.0	-0.0	235.0	0.4	237.4	1.0	237.6	0.1	239.2	0.7	239.6	0.2	239.3	-0.1
1997	242.6	1.4	243.1	0.2	243.6	0.2	243.4	-0.1	243.5	0.0	244.1	0.2	244.4	0.1	244.7	0.1	245.4	0.3	246.1	0.3	246.5	0.2	246.9	0.2
1998	249.2	0.9	250.6	0.6	250.9	0.1	254.9	1.6	255.0	0.0	254.9	-0.0	254.9	0.0	256.9	0.8	257.7	0.3	258.1	0.2	257.5	-0.2	258.8	0.5
1999	262.8	1.5	262.6	-0.1	263.7	0.4	263.9	0.1	264.0	0.0	264.9	0.3	265.8	0.3	266.3	0.2	266.6	0.1	266.8	0.1	267.3	0.2	268.3	0.4
2000	269.5	0.4	271.3	0.7	272.4	0.4	272.7	0.1	274.2	0.6	275.4	0.4	275.7	0.1	276.0	0.1	276.9	0.3	278.2	0.5	279.1	0.3	279.6	0.2
2001	281.0	0.5	283.5	0.9	283.8	0.1	286.1	0.8	287.4	0.5	288.2	0.3	288.2	0.0	289.0	0.3	288.8	-0.1	289.6	0.3	289.6	0.0	290.0	0.1

Source: U.S. Department of Labor, Bureau of Labor Statistics, Division of Consumer Prices and Price Indexes. - indicates no data collected for period.

New York-Northern New Jersey-Long Island, NY-NJ-CT-PA
Consumer Price Index - Urban Wage Earners
Base 1982-1984 = 100
Medical Care

For 1947-2001. Columns headed % show percentile change in the index from the previous period for which an index is available.

Year	Jan Index	%	Feb Index	%	Mar Index	%	Apr Index	%	May Index	%	Jun Index	%	Jul Index	%	Aug Index	%	Sep Index	%	Oct Index	%	Nov Index	%	Dec Index	%
1947	14.6	-	14.7	0.7	14.7	0.0	14.7	0.0	14.8	0.7	14.9	0.7	14.9	0.0	15.0	0.7	15.0	0.0	15.2	1.3	15.2	0.0	15.2	0.0
1948	15.5	2.0	15.5	0.0	15.6	0.6	16.3	4.5	16.3	0.0	16.3	0.0	16.7	2.5	16.7	0.0	16.8	0.6	16.8	0.0	16.8	0.0	16.8	0.0
1949	16.9	0.6	16.8	-0.6	16.7	-0.6	16.7	0.0	16.7	0.0	16.7	0.0	16.7	0.0	16.6	-0.6	16.6	0.0	16.7	0.6	16.7	0.0	16.9	1.2
1950	17.0	0.6	17.0	0.0	17.0	0.0	17.0	0.0	17.0	0.0	17.1	0.6	17.1	0.0	17.1	0.0	17.0	-0.6	17.1	0.6	17.1	0.0	17.1	0.0
1951	17.3	1.2	17.4	0.6	17.6	1.1	17.7	0.6	17.7	0.0	17.7	0.0	17.7	0.0	17.7	0.0	17.9	1.1	17.9	0.0	17.9	0.0	18.1	1.1
1952	18.3	1.1	18.4	0.5	18.4	0.0	18.4	0.0	18.4	0.0	19.1	3.8	19.1	0.0	19.2	0.5	19.4	1.0	19.4	0.0	19.5	0.5	19.4	-0.5
1953	19.4	0.0	19.3	-0.5	19.3	0.0	19.3	0.0	19.3	0.0	19.3	0.0	19.3	0.0	19.4	0.5	19.4	0.0	19.4	0.0	19.7	1.5	19.7	0.0
1954	19.7	0.0	19.7	0.0	19.7	0.0	19.8	0.5	19.8	0.0	19.8	0.0	19.8	0.0	19.8	0.0	19.8	0.0	19.8	0.0	19.9	0.5	19.9	0.0
1955	20.0	0.5	20.0	0.0	20.0	0.0	20.0	0.0	20.2	1.0	20.2	0.0	20.2	0.0	20.2	0.0	20.2	0.0	20.2	0.0	20.2	0.0	20.2	0.0
1956	20.3	0.5	20.3	0.0	20.3	0.0	20.2	-0.5	20.3	0.5	20.3	0.0	20.3	0.0	20.5	1.0	20.5	0.0	20.5	0.0	20.5	0.0	20.5	0.0
1957	20.5	0.0	20.5	0.0	20.5	0.0	20.5	0.0	20.7	1.0	20.7	0.0	20.7	0.0	20.7	0.0	20.7	0.0	20.7	0.0	20.7	0.0	20.7	0.0
1958	20.8	0.5	20.8	0.0	20.8	0.0	20.8	0.0	20.9	0.5	20.9	0.0	20.9	0.0	21.0	0.5	21.6	2.9	21.6	0.0	21.6	0.0	21.6	0.0
1959	21.7	0.5	22.0	1.4	22.0	0.0	22.0	0.0	22.4	1.8	22.4	0.0	22.4	0.0	22.4	0.0	22.9	2.2	22.9	0.0	22.9	0.0	22.9	0.0
1960	22.9	0.0	23.0	0.4	23.0	0.0	23.0	0.0	23.0	0.0	23.0	0.0	23.0	0.0	23.0	0.0	23.0	0.0	23.0	0.0	23.7	3.0	23.7	0.0
1961	23.7	0.0	23.7	0.0	23.7	0.0	23.8	0.4	24.0	0.8	24.0	0.0	24.0	0.0	24.1	0.4	24.1	0.0	24.1	0.0	24.1	0.0	24.1	0.0
1962	24.1	0.0	24.2	0.4	24.4	0.8	24.4	0.0	24.5	0.4	24.5	0.0	24.5	0.0	24.6	0.4	24.6	0.0	24.5	-0.4	24.6	0.4	24.7	0.4
1963	24.8	0.4	24.9	0.4	25.0	0.4	25.0	0.0	25.0	0.0	24.9	-0.4	24.9	0.0	25.0	0.4	25.0	0.0	25.0	0.0	25.1	0.4	25.1	0.0
1964	25.2	0.4	25.3	0.4	25.4	0.4	25.4	0.0	25.5	0.4	25.4	-0.4	25.4	0.0	25.6	0.8	25.5	-0.4	25.6	0.4	25.7	0.4	25.8	0.4
1965	26.0	0.8	26.1	0.4	26.2	0.4	26.2	0.0	26.3	0.4	26.4	0.4	26.5	0.4	26.4	-0.4	26.4	0.0	26.4	0.0	26.5	0.4	26.7	0.8
1966	26.8	0.4	26.9	0.4	27.1	0.7	27.2	0.4	27.4	0.7	27.8	1.5	28.0	0.7	28.2	0.7	28.2	0.0	28.3	0.4	28.5	0.7	28.5	0.0
1967	28.8	1.1	29.0	0.7	29.1	0.3	29.2	0.3	29.3	0.3	29.5	0.7	29.7	0.7	29.9	0.7	30.0	0.3	30.1	0.3	30.1	0.0	30.4	1.0
1968	30.6	0.7	30.6	0.0	30.9	1.0	31.0	0.3	31.1	0.3	31.4	1.0	31.8	1.3	31.8	0.0	32.1	0.9	32.3	0.6	32.4	0.3	32.5	0.3
1969	33.3	2.5	33.4	0.3	33.9	1.5	34.2	0.9	34.4	0.6	34.8	1.2	34.8	0.0	35.1	0.9	35.1	0.0	35.0	-0.3	35.0	0.0	35.3	0.9
1970	35.4	0.3	35.6	0.6	36.1	1.4	36.4	0.8	36.4	0.0	37.1	1.9	37.4	0.8	37.7	0.8	37.9	0.5	38.1	0.5	38.4	0.8	38.8	1.0
1971	39.2	1.0	39.4	0.5	39.8	1.0	39.8	0.0	40.1	0.8	40.1	0.0	40.5	1.0	40.7	0.5	40.7	0.0	40.5	-0.5	40.7	0.5	40.8	0.2
1972	41.0	0.5	41.0	0.0	41.1	0.2	41.2	0.2	41.2	0.0	41.5	0.7	41.5	0.0	41.6	0.2	41.6	0.0	41.8	0.5	42.0	0.5	42.3	0.7
1973	42.5	0.5	42.4	-0.2	42.3	-0.2	42.4	0.2	42.6	0.5	42.7	0.2	42.8	0.2	42.8	0.0	43.1	0.7	43.8	1.6	43.9	0.2	44.1	0.5
1974	44.6	1.1	45.1	1.1	45.7	1.3	46.0	0.7	46.6	1.3	47.3	1.5	47.7	0.8	48.9	2.5	49.4	1.0	49.5	0.2	49.9	0.8	50.2	0.6
1975	51.0	1.6	51.8	1.6	52.5	1.4	52.8	0.6	53.2	0.8	53.5	0.6	53.9	0.7	54.1	0.4	54.8	1.3	55.0	0.4	54.8	-0.4	55.7	1.6
1976	56.8	2.0	57.4	1.1	57.9	0.9	58.1	0.3	58.3	0.3	59.0	1.2	59.5	0.8	59.9	0.7	60.4	0.8	60.4	0.0	61.3	1.5	61.4	0.2
1977	62.3	1.5	62.4	0.2	63.3	1.4	63.8	0.8	64.0	0.3	64.3	0.5	64.7	0.6	64.8	0.2	65.0	0.3	65.3	0.5	65.5	0.3	66.0	0.8
1978	66.5	0.8	66.9	0.6	67.1	0.3	67.2	0.1	67.8	0.9	67.9	0.1	67.8	-0.1	67.9	0.1	68.0	0.1	68.3	0.4	69.1	1.2	69.5	0.6
1979	70.4	1.3	70.9	0.7	71.3	0.6	71.9	0.8	72.0	0.1	72.3	0.4	72.6	0.4	72.8	0.3	73.2	0.5	73.5	0.4	73.8	0.4	74.4	0.8
1980	75.4	1.3	76.6	1.6	77.5	1.2	78.1	0.8	78.4	0.4	78.3	-0.1	78.6	0.4	79.1	0.6	80.4	1.6	80.4	0.0	80.7	0.4	80.9	0.2
1981	82.3	1.7	82.8	0.6	84.9	2.5	85.9	1.2	86.0	0.1	86.5	0.6	87.2	0.8	87.1	-0.1	87.5	0.5	87.8	0.3	88.1	0.3	88.4	0.3
1982	89.3	1.0	90.2	1.0	91.0	0.9	91.1	0.1	91.5	0.4	91.8	0.3	91.5	-0.3	91.9	0.4	92.8	1.0	93.3	0.5	94.0	0.8	94.2	0.2
1983	95.3	1.2	97.1	1.9	97.8	0.7	98.4	0.6	99.0	0.6	99.2	0.2	99.8	0.6	101.1	1.3	101.6	0.5	102.2	0.6	103.1	0.9	103.8	0.7
1984	104.7	0.9	106.1	1.3	106.7	0.6	106.8	0.1	107.4	0.6	107.4	0.0	107.9	0.5	109.2	1.2	109.9	0.6	110.4	0.5	111.1	0.6	111.6	0.5
1985	112.4	0.7	114.1	1.5	114.6	0.4	115.0	0.3	115.8	0.7	116.5	0.6	117.1	0.5	117.2	0.1	117.6	0.3	117.9	0.3	118.2	0.3	117.8	-0.3
1986	120.3	2.1	122.5	1.8	123.8	1.1	124.4	0.5	124.9	0.4	125.2	0.2	126.2	0.8	126.6	0.3	128.0	1.1	128.8	0.6	128.7	-0.1	130.4	1.3
1987	131.1	0.5	133.1	1.5	135.4	1.7	136.7	1.0	136.7	0.0	137.1	0.3	137.6	0.4	138.1	0.4	138.2	0.1	138.5	0.2	139.3	0.6	140.0	0.5
1988	141.1	0.8	142.5	1.0	143.6	0.8	144.1	0.3	145.0	0.6	145.6	0.4	147.0	1.0	146.9	-0.1	148.1	0.8	148.3	0.1	148.8	0.3	149.1	0.2
1989	150.4	0.9	152.1	1.1	154.1	1.3	154.8	0.5	155.6	0.5	157.0	0.9	157.7	0.4	158.6	0.6	159.2	0.4	160.6	0.9	161.5	0.6	162.5	0.6
1990	164.4	1.2	166.9	1.5	169.3	1.4	170.2	0.5	170.5	0.2	171.4	0.5	172.0	0.4	174.2	1.3	174.9	0.4	176.3	0.8	176.7	0.2	177.3	0.3
1991	180.0	1.5	182.1	1.2	183.3	0.7	183.5	0.1	183.2	-0.2	184.8	0.9	186.9	1.1	188.6	0.9	189.2	0.3	189.7	0.3	191.3	0.8	192.3	0.5
1992	195.2	1.5	196.5	0.7	197.7	0.6	198.6	0.5	199.0	0.2	200.0	0.5	201.2	0.6	201.2	0.0	202.5	0.6	203.5	0.5	203.7	0.1	204.0	0.1

[Continued]

New York-Northern New Jersey-Long Island, NY-NJ-CT-PA
Consumer Price Index - Urban Wage Earners
Base 1982-1984 = 100
Medical Care
[Continued]

For 1947-2001. Columns headed % show percentile change in the index from the previous period for which an index is available.

Year	Jan Index	%	Feb Index	%	Mar Index	%	Apr Index	%	May Index	%	Jun Index	%	Jul Index	%	Aug Index	%	Sep Index	%	Oct Index	%	Nov Index	%	Dec Index	%
1993	205.6	0.8	205.7	0.0	206.8	0.5	208.1	0.6	208.9	0.4	208.9	0.0	209.6	0.3	210.4	0.4	210.7	0.1	211.1	0.2	211.1	0.0	211.6	0.2
1994	213.7	1.0	214.3	0.3	215.3	0.5	216.0	0.3	216.5	0.2	217.9	0.6	218.3	0.2	219.0	0.3	219.0	0.0	221.2	1.0	221.2	0.0	222.3	0.5
1995	224.2	0.9	226.0	0.8	226.2	0.1	226.3	0.0	226.6	0.1	226.7	0.0	226.9	0.1	228.1	0.5	228.7	0.3	230.1	0.6	230.3	0.1	230.6	0.1
1996	231.5	0.4	232.2	0.3	233.1	0.4	233.6	0.2	234.9	0.6	235.0	0.0	235.6	0.3	238.0	1.0	238.2	0.1	239.9	0.7	240.3	0.2	240.1	-0.1
1997	242.7	1.1	243.5	0.3	244.0	0.2	243.7	-0.1	243.8	0.0	244.4	0.2	244.9	0.2	245.1	0.1	245.8	0.3	246.6	0.3	247.0	0.2	247.5	0.2
1998	249.6	0.8	251.1	0.6	251.5	0.2	255.0	1.4	255.2	0.1	255.1	-0.0	255.2	0.0	257.2	0.8	257.9	0.3	258.4	0.2	257.9	-0.2	259.0	0.4
1999	262.8	1.5	262.6	-0.1	263.5	0.3	263.7	0.1	263.9	0.1	264.8	0.3	265.6	0.3	266.0	0.2	266.3	0.1	266.6	0.1	267.1	0.2	268.0	0.3
2000	269.3	0.5	271.0	0.6	272.1	0.4	272.6	0.2	273.8	0.4	275.2	0.5	275.5	0.1	275.7	0.1	276.7	0.4	277.8	0.4	278.8	0.4	279.3	0.2
2001	280.5	0.4	283.1	0.9	283.3	0.1	286.0	1.0	287.0	0.3	287.7	0.2	287.9	0.1	288.6	0.2	288.6	0.0	289.4	0.3	289.3	-0.0	289.7	0.1

Source: U.S. Department of Labor, Bureau of Labor Statistics, Division of Consumer Prices and Price Indexes. - indicates no data collected for period.

New York-Northern New Jersey-Long Island, NY-NJ-CT-PA
Consumer Price Index - All Urban Consumers
Base December 1997 = 100
Recreation

For 1997-2001. Columns headed % show percentile change in the index from the previous period for which an index is available.

Year	Jan Index	%	Feb Index	%	Mar Index	%	Apr Index	%	May Index	%	Jun Index	%	Jul Index	%	Aug Index	%	Sep Index	%	Oct Index	%	Nov Index	%	Dec Index	%
1997	-	-	-	-	-	-	-	-	-	-	-	-	-	-	-	-	-	-	-	-	-	-	100.0	-
1998	100.8	0.8	101.8	1.0	102.6	0.8	103.0	0.4	102.2	-0.8	102.4	0.2	101.8	-0.6	102.0	0.2	102.7	0.7	102.3	-0.4	103.4	1.1	102.7	-0.7
1999	102.1	-0.6	102.9	0.8	103.6	0.7	104.0	0.4	103.7	-0.3	103.7	0.0	103.6	-0.1	104.4	0.8	103.5	-0.9	103.6	0.1	104.2	0.6	104.3	0.1
2000	105.1	0.8	104.7	-0.4	105.3	0.6	105.7	0.4	104.7	-0.9	104.6	-0.1	106.2	1.5	106.1	-0.1	106.0	-0.1	106.0	0.0	106.4	0.4	105.8	-0.6
2001	106.4	0.6	106.5	0.1	106.7	0.2	107.1	0.4	107.2	0.1	107.4	0.2	107.1	-0.3	107.4	0.3	107.4	0.0	108.5	1.0	108.5	0.0	108.2	-0.3

Source: U.S. Department of Labor, Bureau of Labor Statistics, Division of Consumer Prices and Price Indexes. - indicates no data collected for period.

New York-Northern New Jersey-Long Island, NY-NJ-CT-PA
Consumer Price Index - Urban Wage Earners
Base December 1997 = 100
Recreation

For 1997-2001. Columns headed % show percentile change in the index from the previous period for which an index is available.

Year	Jan Index	%	Feb Index	%	Mar Index	%	Apr Index	%	May Index	%	Jun Index	%	Jul Index	%	Aug Index	%	Sep Index	%	Oct Index	%	Nov Index	%	Dec Index	%
1997	-	-	-	-	-	-	-	-	-	-	-	-	-	-	-	-	-	-	-	-	-	-	100.0	-
1998	100.7	0.7	101.9	1.2	102.7	0.8	103.0	0.3	102.3	-0.7	102.6	0.3	101.7	-0.9	101.9	0.2	102.0	0.1	101.7	-0.3	102.7	1.0	101.9	-0.8
1999	101.7	-0.2	102.2	0.5	102.8	0.6	103.0	0.2	102.9	-0.1	102.8	-0.1	102.7	-0.1	103.2	0.5	102.5	-0.7	102.6	0.1	102.8	0.2	103.0	0.2
2000	103.8	0.8	103.5	-0.3	103.9	0.4	104.3	0.4	103.7	-0.6	103.6	-0.1	104.8	1.2	104.6	-0.2	104.5	-0.1	104.5	0.0	105.0	0.5	104.6	-0.4
2001	105.1	0.5	105.3	0.2	105.7	0.4	105.9	0.2	105.9	0.0	106.1	0.2	105.7	-0.4	106.0	0.3	106.1	0.1	106.7	0.6	106.7	0.0	106.3	-0.4

Source: U.S. Department of Labor, Bureau of Labor Statistics, Division of Consumer Prices and Price Indexes. - indicates no data collected for period.

New York-Northern New Jersey-Long Island, NY-NJ-CT-PA
Consumer Price Index - All Urban Consumers
Base December 1997 = 100
Education & Communication

For 1997-2001. Columns headed % show percentile change in the index from the previous period for which an index is available.

Year	Jan Index	%	Feb Index	%	Mar Index	%	Apr Index	%	May Index	%	Jun Index	%	Jul Index	%	Aug Index	%	Sep Index	%	Oct Index	%	Nov Index	%	Dec Index	%
1997	-	-	-	-	-	-	-	-	-	-	-	-	-	-	-	-	-	-	-	-	-	-	100.0	-
1998	100.1	0.1	99.1	-1.0	99.2	0.1	99.0	-0.2	99.4	0.4	99.0	-0.4	99.0	0.0	98.9	-0.1	100.7	1.8	100.8	0.1	100.7	-0.1	100.4	-0.3
1999	100.5	0.1	100.3	-0.2	100.3	0.0	100.6	0.3	100.2	-0.4	100.1	-0.1	100.0	-0.1	100.3	0.3	101.1	0.8	101.2	0.1	101.4	0.2	101.7	0.3
2000	101.8	0.1	101.3	-0.5	101.3	0.0	101.3	0.0	101.4	0.1	101.0	-0.4	101.8	0.8	102.6	0.8	102.5	-0.1	103.2	0.7	103.9	0.7	104.5	0.6
2001	104.8	0.3	104.7	-0.1	105.1	0.4	104.7	-0.4	104.5	-0.2	105.0	0.5	105.2	0.2	106.4	1.1	107.0	0.6	107.6	0.6	107.4	-0.2	107.5	0.1

Source: U.S. Department of Labor, Bureau of Labor Statistics, Division of Consumer Prices and Price Indexes. - indicates no data collected for period.

New York-Northern New Jersey-Long Island, NY-NJ-CT-PA
Consumer Price Index - Urban Wage Earners
Base December 1997 = 100
Education & Communication

For 1997-2001. Columns headed % show percentile change in the index from the previous period for which an index is available.

Year	Jan Index	%	Feb Index	%	Mar Index	%	Apr Index	%	May Index	%	Jun Index	%	Jul Index	%	Aug Index	%	Sep Index	%	Oct Index	%	Nov Index	%	Dec Index	%
1997	-	-	-	-	-	-	-	-	-	-	-	-	-	-	-	-	-	-	-	-	-	-	100.0	-
1998	100.0	0.0	99.1	-0.9	99.2	0.1	99.2	0.0	99.6	0.4	99.3	-0.3	99.3	0.0	99.2	-0.1	101.1	1.9	101.2	0.1	101.2	0.0	100.9	-0.3
1999	100.9	0.0	100.8	-0.1	100.8	0.0	101.1	0.3	100.8	-0.3	100.7	-0.1	100.6	-0.1	101.0	0.4	101.7	0.7	101.8	0.1	102.0	0.2	102.3	0.3
2000	102.3	0.0	101.8	-0.5	101.6	-0.2	101.6	0.0	101.8	0.2	101.4	-0.4	102.2	0.8	102.9	0.7	102.7	-0.2	103.5	0.8	104.2	0.7	104.9	0.7
2001	105.1	0.2	105.1	0.0	105.5	0.4	105.1	-0.4	104.9	-0.2	105.4	0.5	105.7	0.3	106.9	1.1	107.4	0.5	108.0	0.6	107.8	-0.2	108.0	0.2

Source: U.S. Department of Labor, Bureau of Labor Statistics, Division of Consumer Prices and Price Indexes. - indicates no data collected for period.

Philadelphia-Wilmington-Atlantic City, PA-NJ-DE-MD
Consumer Price Index - All Urban Consumers
Base 1982-1984 = 100
Annual Averages

For 1914-2001. Columns headed % show percentile change in the index from the previous period for which an index is available.

Year	All Items		Food & Beverage		Housing		Apparel		Trans-portation		Medical Care		Recrea-tion*		Education & Communic.*		Other Goods & Services	
	Index	%	Index	%	Index	%	Index	%	Index	%	Index	%	Index	%	Index	%	Index	%
1914	-	-	-	-	-	-	-	-	-	-	-	-	-	-	-	-	-	-
1915	10.1	-	-	-	-	-	-	-	-	-	-	-	-	-	-	-	-	-
1916	10.8	6.9	-	-	-	-	-	-	-	-	-	-	-	-	-	-	-	-
1917	13.1	21.3	-	-	-	-	-	-	-	-	-	-	-	-	-	-	-	-
1918	15.5	18.3	-	-	-	-	-	-	-	-	-	-	-	-	-	-	-	-
1919	17.9	15.5	-	-	-	-	-	-	-	-	-	-	-	-	-	-	-	-
1920	20.5	14.5	-	-	-	-	-	-	-	-	-	-	-	-	-	-	-	-
1921	18.2	-11.2	-	-	-	-	-	-	-	-	-	-	-	-	-	-	-	-
1922	17.2	-5.5	-	-	-	-	-	-	-	-	-	-	-	-	-	-	-	-
1923	17.6	2.3	-	-	-	-	-	-	-	-	-	-	-	-	-	-	-	-
1924	17.7	0.6	-	-	-	-	-	-	-	-	-	-	-	-	-	-	-	-
1925	18.4	4.0	-	-	-	-	-	-	-	-	-	-	-	-	-	-	-	-
1926	18.7	1.6	-	-	-	-	-	-	-	-	-	-	-	-	-	-	-	-
1927	18.3	-2.1	-	-	-	-	-	-	-	-	-	-	-	-	-	-	-	-
1928	18.0	-1.6	-	-	-	-	-	-	-	-	-	-	-	-	-	-	-	-
1929	17.8	-1.1	-	-	-	-	-	-	-	-	-	-	-	-	-	-	-	-
1930	17.4	-2.2	-	-	-	-	-	-	-	-	-	-	-	-	-	-	-	-
1931	15.9	-8.6	-	-	-	-	-	-	-	-	-	-	-	-	-	-	-	-
1932	14.2	-10.7	-	-	-	-	-	-	-	-	-	-	-	-	-	-	-	-
1933	13.5	-4.9	-	-	-	-	-	-	-	-	-	-	-	-	-	-	-	-
1934	14.2	5.2	-	-	-	-	-	-	-	-	-	-	-	-	-	-	-	-
1935	14.3	0.7	-	-	-	-	-	-	-	-	-	-	-	-	-	-	-	-
1936	14.5	1.4	-	-	-	-	-	-	-	-	-	-	-	-	-	-	-	-
1937	14.9	2.8	-	-	-	-	-	-	-	-	-	-	-	-	-	-	-	-
1938	14.5	-2.7	-	-	-	-	-	-	-	-	-	-	-	-	-	-	-	-
1939	14.3	-1.4	-	-	-	-	-	-	-	-	-	-	-	-	-	-	-	-
1940	14.3	0.0	-	-	-	-	-	-	-	-	-	-	-	-	-	-	-	-
1941	15.0	4.9	-	-	-	-	-	-	-	-	-	-	-	-	-	-	-	-
1942	16.7	11.3	-	-	-	-	-	-	-	-	-	-	-	-	-	-	-	-
1943	17.8	6.6	-	-	-	-	-	-	-	-	-	-	-	-	-	-	-	-
1944	18.0	1.1	-	-	-	-	-	-	-	-	-	-	-	-	-	-	-	-
1945	18.5	2.8	-	-	-	-	-	-	-	-	-	-	-	-	-	-	-	-
1946	20.1	8.6	-	-	-	-	-	-	-	-	-	-	-	-	-	-	-	-
1947	23.0	14.4	-	-	-	-	-	-	16.8	-	12.4	-	-	-	-	-	-	-
1948	24.8	7.8	-	-	-	-	-	-	18.4	9.5	13.0	4.8	-	-	-	-	-	-
1949	24.5	-1.2	-	-	-	-	-	-	19.5	6.0	13.4	3.1	-	-	-	-	-	-
1950	24.7	0.8	-	-	-	-	-	-	19.5	0.0	13.6	1.5	-	-	-	-	-	-
1951	27.0	9.3	-	-	-	-	-	-	23.2	19.0	14.2	4.4	-	-	-	-	-	-
1952	27.5	1.9	-	-	-	-	-	-	24.1	3.9	15.0	5.6	-	-	-	-	-	-
1953	27.6	0.4	-	%	-	-	44.3	-	24.5	1.7	15.6	4.0	-	%	-	%	-	%
1954	27.9	1.1	-	-	-	-	44.6	0.7	25.1	2.4	16.4	5.1	-	-	-	-	-	-
1955	27.9	0.0	-	-	-	-	44.4	-0.4	24.9	-0.8	17.5	6.7	-	-	-	-	-	-
1956	28.2	1.1	-	-	-	-	44.8	0.9	24.9	0.0	17.8	1.7	-	-	-	-	-	-
1957	29.1	3.2	-	-	-	-	46.0	2.7	25.8	3.6	18.2	2.2	-	-	-	-	-	-
1958	29.7	2.1	-	-	-	-	45.6	-0.9	26.6	3.1	18.9	3.8	-	-	-	-	-	-

[Continued]

Philadelphia-Wilmington-Atlantic City, PA-NJ-DE-MD
Consumer Price Index - All Urban Consumers
Base 1982-1984 = 100
Annual Averages

[Continued]

For 1914-2001. Columns headed % show percentile change in the index from the previous period for which an index is available.

Year	All Items		Food & Beverage		Housing		Apparel		Trans-portation		Medical Care		Recrea-tion*		Education & Communic.*		Other Goods & Services	
	Index	%	Index	%	Index	%	Index	%	Index	%	Index	%	Index	%	Index	%	Index	%
1959	30.0	1.0	-	-	-	-	46.3	1.5	28.0	5.3	20.0	5.8	-	-	-	-	-	-
1960	30.6	2.0	-	-	-	-	48.0	3.7	28.3	1.1	20.8	4.0	-	-	-	-	-	-
1961	30.9	1.0	-	-	-	-	49.1	2.3	29.0	2.5	21.7	4.3	-	-	-	-	-	-
1962	31.2	1.0	-	-	-	-	49.6	1.0	29.2	0.7	22.6	4.1	-	-	-	-	-	-
1963	31.8	1.9	-	-	-	-	50.2	1.2	29.9	2.4	23.1	2.2	-	-	-	-	-	-
1964	32.3	1.6	-	-	-	-	50.3	0.2	30.5	2.0	23.4	1.3	-	-	-	-	-	-
1965	32.8	1.5	-	-	-	-	51.0	1.4	31.3	2.6	24.0	2.6	-	-	-	-	-	-
1966	33.7	2.7	-	-	-	-	52.9	3.7	31.8	1.6	25.1	4.6	-	-	-	-	-	-
1967	34.6	2.7	-	-	-	-	55.3	4.5	32.6	2.5	26.7	6.4	-	-	-	-	-	-
1968	36.3	4.9	-	-	-	-	58.5	5.8	34.3	5.2	28.9	8.2	-	-	-	-	-	-
1969	38.2	5.2	-	-	-	-	61.5	5.1	35.9	4.7	31.4	8.7	-	-	-	-	-	-
1970	40.8	6.8	-	-	-	-	64.1	4.2	37.9	5.6	34.0	8.3	-	-	-	-	-	-
1971	42.7	4.7	-	-	-	-	65.9	2.8	40.2	6.1	36.7	7.9	-	-	-	-	-	-
1972	44.0	3.0	-	-	-	-	66.4	0.8	40.8	1.5	38.0	3.5	-	-	-	-	-	-
1973	46.9	6.6	-	-	-	-	69.0	3.9	41.6	2.0	39.8	4.7	-	-	-	-	-	-
1974	52.5	11.9	-	-	-	-	73.1	5.9	45.9	10.3	43.4	9.0	-	-	-	-	-	-
1975	56.8	8.2	-	-	-	-	75.2	2.9	49.8	8.5	49.3	13.6	-	-	-	-	-	-
1976	59.7	5.1	62.2	-	59.1	-	77.1	2.5	54.0	8.4	53.7	8.9	-	-	-	-	-	-
1977	63.5	6.4	66.0	6.1	62.7	6.1	79.1	2.6	59.3	9.8	59.0	9.9	-	-	-	-	56.0	-
1978	67.3	6.0	72.4	9.7	65.7	4.8	80.9	2.3	62.5	5.4	63.2	7.1	-	-	-	-	59.2	5.7
1979	73.9	9.8	79.5	9.8	71.9	9.4	86.2	6.6	70.9	13.4	68.4	8.2	-	-	-	-	62.4	5.4
1980	83.6	13.1	86.0	8.2	83.5	16.1	94.4	9.5	83.6	17.9	75.4	10.2	-	-	-	-	67.0	7.4
1981	92.1	10.2	92.5	7.6	93.7	12.2	95.9	1.6	93.2	11.5	83.9	11.3	-	-	-	-	73.2	9.3
1982	96.6	4.9	97.7	5.6	97.6	4.2	98.8	3.0	96.1	3.1	91.7	9.3	-	-	-	-	79.5	8.6
1983	99.4	2.9	100.0	2.4	98.4	0.8	100.3	1.5	99.4	3.4	100.6	9.7	-	-	-	-	89.5	12.6
1984	104.1	4.7	102.4	2.4	104.0	5.7	100.9	0.6	104.5	5.1	107.7	7.1	-	-	-	-	101.0	12.8
1985	108.8	4.5	105.0	2.5	109.1	4.9	101.4	0.5	109.4	4.7	119.1	10.6	-	-	-	-	109.5	8.4
1986	111.5	2.5	107.8	2.7	112.9	3.5	101.3	-0.1	107.1	-2.1	126.6	6.3	-	-	-	-	117.1	6.9
1987	116.8	4.8	112.1	4.0	118.4	4.9	107.7	6.3	111.5	4.1	133.0	5.1	-	-	-	-	126.5	8.0
1988	122.4	4.8	116.0	3.5	124.8	5.4	109.9	2.0	115.6	3.7	142.2	6.9	-	-	-	-	135.9	7.4
1989	128.3	4.8	124.2	7.1	130.8	4.8	99.4	-9.6	121.5	5.1	155.3	9.2	-	-	-	-	145.1	6.8
1990	135.8	5.8	131.2	5.6	138.7	6.0	101.4	2.0	127.7	5.1	167.4	7.8	-	-	-	-	155.4	7.1
1991	142.2	4.7	135.4	3.2	145.6	5.0	103.7	2.3	132.3	3.6	183.5	9.6	-	-	-	-	171.9	10.6
1992	146.6	3.1	137.6	1.6	149.6	2.7	106.5	2.7	136.1	2.9	196.6	7.1	-	-	-	-	185.5	7.9
1993	150.2	2.5	139.7	1.5	151.9	1.5	106.0	-0.5	139.5	2.5	211.6	7.6	-	-	-	-	195.8	5.6
1994	154.6	2.9	142.7	2.1	155.1	2.1	105.8	-0.2	144.0	3.2	223.9	5.8	-	-	-	-	210.7	7.6
1995	158.7	2.7	148.8	4.3	158.4	2.1	102.1	-3.5	148.7	3.3	232.5	3.8	-	-	-	-	222.2	5.5
1996	162.8	2.6	152.2	2.3	162.4	2.5	103.8	1.7	151.5	1.9	242.2	4.2	-	-	-	-	227.1	2.2
1997	166.5	2.3	154.3	1.4	167.3	3.0	104.0	0.2	152.8	0.9	247.8	2.3	-	-	-	-	232.9	2.6
1998	168.2	1.0	155.1	0.5	170.1	1.7	106.2	2.1	149.3	-2.3	254.8	2.8	101.3	-	99.5	-	241.4	3.6
1999	171.9	2.2	159.4	2.8	172.5	1.4	107.5	1.2	152.2	1.9	264.8	3.9	102.8	1.5	100.9	1.4	254.8	5.6
2000	176.5	2.7	161.4	1.3	176.9	2.6	102.6	-4.6	160.6	5.5	278.7	5.2	107.3	4.4	102.1	1.2	274.9	7.9
2001	181.3	2.7	167.0	3.5	183.3	3.6	99.8	-2.7	-	-	305.3	9.5	107.7	0.4	104.0	1.9	286.0	4.0

Source: U.S. Department of Labor, Bureau of Labor Statistics, Division of Consumer Prices and Price Indexes. *Base is December 1997 = 100. - indicates no data collected for period.

Philadelphia-Wilmington-Atlantic City, PA-NJ-DE-MD
Consumer Price Index - Urban Wage Earners
Base 1982-1984 = 100
Annual Averages

For 1914-2001. Columns headed % show percentile change in the index from the previous period for which an index is available.

Year	All Items Index	%	Food & Beverage Index	%	Housing Index	%	Apparel Index	%	Trans-portation Index	%	Medical Care Index	%	Recrea-tion* Index	%	Education & Communic.* Index	%	Other Goods & Services Index	%
1914	-	-	-	-	-	-	-	-	-	-	-	-	-	-	-	-	-	-
1915	10.0	-	-	-	-	-	-	-	-	-	-	-	-	-	-	-	-	-
1916	10.8	8.0	-	-	-	-	-	-	-	-	-	-	-	-	-	-	-	-
1917	13.0	20.4	-	-	-	-	-	-	-	-	-	-	-	-	-	-	-	-
1918	15.5	19.2	-	-	-	-	-	-	-	-	-	-	-	-	-	-	-	-
1919	17.8	14.8	-	-	-	-	-	-	-	-	-	-	-	-	-	-	-	-
1920	20.3	14.0	-	-	-	-	-	-	-	-	-	-	-	-	-	-	-	-
1921	18.1	-10.8	-	-	-	-	-	-	-	-	-	-	-	-	-	-	-	-
1922	17.1	-5.5	-	-	-	-	-	-	-	-	-	-	-	-	-	-	-	-
1923	17.5	2.3	-	-	-	-	-	-	-	-	-	-	-	-	-	-	-	-
1924	17.6	0.6	-	-	-	-	-	-	-	-	-	-	-	-	-	-	-	-
1925	18.3	4.0	-	-	-	-	-	-	-	-	-	-	-	-	-	-	-	-
1926	18.6	1.6	-	-	-	-	-	-	-	-	-	-	-	-	-	-	-	-
1927	18.2	-2.2	-	-	-	-	-	-	-	-	-	-	-	-	-	-	-	-
1928	17.9	-1.6	-	-	-	-	-	-	-	-	-	-	-	-	-	-	-	-
1929	17.7	-1.1	-	-	-	-	-	-	-	-	-	-	-	-	-	-	-	-
1930	17.3	-2.3	-	-	-	-	-	-	-	-	-	-	-	-	-	-	-	-
1931	15.8	-8.7	-	-	-	-	-	-	-	-	-	-	-	-	-	-	-	-
1932	14.1	-10.8	-	-	-	-	-	-	-	-	-	-	-	-	-	-	-	-
1933	13.4	-5.0	-	-	-	-	-	-	-	-	-	-	-	-	-	-	-	-
1934	14.1	5.2	-	-	-	-	-	-	-	-	-	-	-	-	-	-	-	-
1935	14.3	1.4	-	-	-	-	-	-	-	-	-	-	-	-	-	-	-	-
1936	14.5	1.4	-	-	-	-	-	-	-	-	-	-	-	-	-	-	-	-
1937	14.8	2.1	-	-	-	-	-	-	-	-	-	-	-	-	-	-	-	-
1938	14.5	-2.0	-	-	-	-	-	-	-	-	-	-	-	-	-	-	-	-
1939	14.2	-2.1	-	-	-	-	-	-	-	-	-	-	-	-	-	-	-	-
1940	14.3	0.7	-	-	-	-	-	-	-	-	-	-	-	-	-	-	-	-
1941	14.9	4.2	-	-	-	-	-	-	-	-	-	-	-	-	-	-	-	-
1942	16.6	11.4	-	-	-	-	-	-	-	-	-	-	-	-	-	-	-	-
1943	17.7	6.6	-	-	-	-	-	-	-	-	-	-	-	-	-	-	-	-
1944	17.9	1.1	-	-	-	-	-	-	-	-	-	-	-	-	-	-	-	-
1945	18.4	2.8	-	-	-	-	-	-	-	-	-	-	-	-	-	-	-	-
1946	20.0	8.7	-	-	-	-	-	-	-	-	-	-	-	-	-	-	-	-
1947	22.9	14.5	-	-	-	-	-	-	16.3	-	11.7	-	-	-	-	-	-	-
1948	24.7	7.9	-	-	-	-	-	-	17.9	9.8	12.3	5.1	-	-	-	-	-	-
1949	24.4	-1.2	-	-	-	-	-	-	19.0	6.1	12.6	2.4	-	-	-	-	-	-
1950	24.5	0.4	-	-	-	-	-	-	19.0	0.0	12.8	1.6	-	-	-	-	-	-
1951	26.8	9.4	-	-	-	-	-	-	22.5	18.4	13.4	4.7	-	-	-	-	-	-
1952	27.4	2.2	-	-	-	-	-	-	23.4	4.0	14.1	5.2	-	-	-	-	-	-
1953	27.5	0.4	-	-	-	-	51.1	-	23.8	1.7	14.7	4.3	-	-	-	-	-	-
1954	27.8	1.1	-	-	-	-	51.5	0.8	24.3	2.1	15.5	5.4	-	-	-	-	-	-
1955	27.7	-0.4	-	-	-	-	51.2	-0.6	24.1	-0.8	16.5	6.5	-	-	-	-	-	-
1956	28.1	1.4	-	-	-	-	51.7	1.0	24.2	0.4	16.8	1.8	-	-	-	-	-	-
1957	29.0	3.2	-	-	-	-	53.0	2.5	25.0	3.3	17.1	1.8	-	-	-	-	-	-
1958	29.5	1.7	-	-	-	-	52.7	-0.6	25.8	3.2	17.8	4.1	-	-	-	-	-	-

[Continued]

Philadelphia-Wilmington-Atlantic City, PA-NJ-DE-MD
Consumer Price Index - Urban Wage Earners
Base 1982-1984 = 100
Annual Averages
[Continued]

For 1914-2001. Columns headed % show percentile change in the index from the previous period for which an index is available.

Year	All Items		Food & Beverage		Housing		Apparel		Transportation		Medical Care		Recreation*		Education & Communic.*		Other Goods & Services	
	Index	%	Index	%	Index	%	Index	%	Index	%	Index	%	Index	%	Index	%	Index	%
1959	29.9	1.4	-	-	-	-	53.4	1.3	27.2	5.4	18.9	6.2	-	-	-	-	-	-
1960	30.4	1.7	-	-	-	-	55.4	3.7	27.4	0.7	19.6	3.7	-	-	-	-	-	-
1961	30.8	1.3	-	-	-	-	56.7	2.3	28.2	2.9	20.5	4.6	-	-	-	-	-	-
1962	31.0	0.6	-	-	-	-	57.2	0.9	28.4	0.7	21.3	3.9	-	-	-	-	-	-
1963	31.6	1.9	-	-	-	-	58.0	1.4	29.0	2.1	21.8	2.3	-	-	-	-	-	-
1964	32.1	1.6	-	-	-	-	58.1	0.2	29.6	2.1	22.1	1.4	-	-	-	-	-	-
1965	32.6	1.6	-	-	-	-	58.9	1.4	30.4	2.7	22.7	2.7	-	-	-	-	-	-
1966	33.5	2.8	-	-	-	-	61.0	3.6	30.9	1.6	23.7	4.4	-	-	-	-	-	-
1967	34.4	2.7	-	-	-	-	63.8	4.6	31.7	2.6	25.2	6.3	-	-	-	-	-	-
1968	36.1	4.9	-	-	-	-	67.5	5.8	33.3	5.0	27.3	8.3	-	-	-	-	-	-
1969	38.0	5.3	-	-	-	-	70.9	5.0	34.9	4.8	29.6	8.4	-	-	-	-	-	-
1970	40.6	6.8	-	-	-	-	73.9	4.2	36.8	5.4	32.1	8.4	-	-	-	-	-	-
1971	42.5	4.7	-	-	-	-	76.1	3.0	39.0	6.0	34.7	8.1	-	-	-	-	-	-
1972	43.7	2.8	-	-	-	-	76.6	0.7	39.6	1.5	35.9	3.5	-	-	-	-	-	-
1973	46.6	6.6	-	-	-	-	79.6	3.9	40.4	2.0	37.6	4.7	-	-	-	-	-	-
1974	52.2	12.0	-	-	-	-	84.3	5.9	44.6	10.4	41.0	9.0	-	-	-	-	-	-
1975	56.5	8.2	-	-	-	-	86.8	3.0	48.4	8.5	46.5	13.4	-	-	-	-	-	-
1976	59.4	5.1	60.5	-	58.9	-	89.0	2.5	52.4	8.3	50.7	9.0	-	-	-	-	58.2	-
1977	63.2	6.4	64.3	6.3	62.6	6.3	91.3	2.6	57.6	9.9	55.7	9.9	-	-	-	-	61.5	5.7
1978	67.1	6.2	70.8	10.1	65.5	4.6	90.5	-0.9	61.3	6.4	60.2	8.1	-	-	-	-	64.7	5.2
1979	73.9	10.1	79.2	11.9	71.5	9.2	89.4	-1.2	70.1	14.4	66.6	10.6	-	-	-	-	68.4	5.7
1980	83.5	13.0	86.8	9.6	82.4	15.2	94.4	5.6	83.2	18.7	76.0	14.1	-	-	-	-	73.9	8.0
1981	91.9	10.1	93.2	7.4	92.1	11.8	96.3	2.0	93.6	12.5	83.9	10.4	-	-	-	-	80.4	8.8
1982	95.8	4.2	97.7	4.8	95.6	3.8	98.8	2.6	96.2	2.8	91.6	9.2	-	-	-	-	89.4	11.2
1983	99.7	4.1	99.9	2.3	99.3	3.9	100.2	1.4	99.4	3.3	100.6	9.8	-	-	-	-	101.2	13.2
1984	104.5	4.8	102.4	2.5	105.2	5.9	100.9	0.7	104.4	5.0	107.9	7.3	-	-	-	-	109.4	8.1
1985	109.2	4.5	105.1	2.6	110.8	5.3	100.5	-0.4	109.2	4.6	119.0	10.3	-	-	-	-	116.8	6.8
1986	111.5	2.1	107.9	2.7	114.5	3.3	99.7	-0.8	106.0	-2.9	126.3	6.1	-	-	-	-	125.9	7.8
1987	116.7	4.7	112.4	4.2	120.0	4.8	104.4	4.7	110.8	4.5	132.7	5.1	-	-	-	-	134.7	7.0
1988	122.2	4.7	116.5	3.6	126.3	5.2	106.0	1.5	115.1	3.9	141.5	6.6	-	-	-	-	144.3	7.1
1989	128.3	5.0	125.1	7.4	133.0	5.3	94.5	-10.8	121.6	5.6	154.0	8.8	-	-	-	-	153.8	6.6
1990	136.1	6.1	132.3	5.8	140.7	5.8	97.6	3.3	128.4	5.6	165.9	7.7	-	-	-	-	170.7	11.0
1991	142.2	4.5	136.5	3.2	147.5	4.8	99.0	1.4	132.8	3.4	180.9	9.0	-	-	-	-	184.3	8.0
1992	146.4	3.0	138.7	1.6	151.3	2.6	103.3	4.3	136.1	2.5	193.9	7.2	-	-	-	-	194.3	5.4
1993	150.1	2.5	140.9	1.6	153.8	1.7	104.7	1.4	139.2	2.3	208.8	7.7	-	-	-	-	208.5	7.3
1994	154.2	2.7	143.9	2.1	156.9	2.0	101.9	-2.7	144.0	3.4	220.5	5.6	-	-	-	-	218.2	4.7
1995	158.3	2.7	150.0	4.2	160.3	2.2	98.1	-3.7	149.5	3.8	228.5	3.6	-	-	-	-	222.2	1.8
1996	162.2	2.5	153.3	2.2	164.1	2.4	100.1	2.0	152.2	1.8	237.9	4.1	-	-	-	-	227.4	2.3
1997	165.7	2.2	155.3	1.3	168.9	2.9	101.2	1.1	153.5	0.9	243.6	2.4	-	-	-	-	235.4	3.5
1998	167.5	1.1	155.7	0.3	172.1	1.9	104.5	3.3	149.4	-2.7	250.2	2.7	101.0	-	98.7	-	250.9	6.6
1999	171.5	2.4	160.1	2.8	174.4	1.3	106.6	2.0	152.2	1.9	259.7	3.8	102.6	1.6	100.5	1.8	274.4	9.4
2000	176.1	2.7	162.5	1.5	178.8	2.5	101.1	-5.2	162.1	6.5	272.5	4.9	107.6	4.9	102.5	2.0	284.4	3.6
2001	180.7	2.6	168.4	3.6	185.5	3.7	99.2	-1.9	-	-	298.1	9.4	107.5	-0.1	104.7	2.1	293.8	3.3

Source: U.S. Department of Labor, Bureau of Labor Statistics, Division of Consumer Prices and Price Indexes. *Base is December 1997 = 100. - indicates no data collected for period.

Philadelphia-Wilmington-Atlantic City, PA-NJ-DE-MD
Consumer Price Index - All Urban Consumers
Base 1982-1984 = 100
All Items

For 1914-2001. Columns headed % show percentile change in the index from the previous period for which an index is available.

Year	Jan Index	%	Feb Index	%	Mar Index	%	Apr Index	%	May Index	%	Jun Index	%	Jul Index	%	Aug Index	%	Sep Index	%	Oct Index	%	Nov Index	%	Dec Index	%
1914	-		-		-		-		-		-		-		-		-		-		-		10.2	-
1915	-		-		-		-		-		-		-		-		-		-		-		10.3	1.0
1916	-		-		-		-		-		-		-		-		-		-		-		11.6	12.6
1917	-		-		-		-		-		-		-		-		-		-		-		14.1	21.6
1918	-		-		-		-		-		-		-		-		-		-		-		17.0	20.6
1919	-		-		-		-		-		17.5	2.9	-		-		-		-		-		19.2	9.7
1920	-		-		-		-		-		21.3	10.9	-		-		-		-		-		19.9	-6.6
1921	-		-		-		-		18.1	-9.0	-		-		-		17.9	-1.1	-		-		17.7	-1.1
1922	-		-		17.3	-2.3	-		-		17.3	0.0	-		-		16.9	-2.3	-		-		17.3	2.4
1923	-		-		17.3	0.0	-		-		17.6	1.7	-		-		17.8	1.1	-		-		17.8	0.0
1924	-		-		17.6	-1.1	-		-		17.7	0.6	-		-		17.6	-0.6	-		-		18.0	2.3
1925	-		-		-		-		-		18.4	2.2	-		-		-		-		-		18.9	2.7
1926	-		-		-		-		-		18.8	-0.5	-		-		-		-		-		18.7	-0.5
1927	-		-		-		-		-		18.5	-1.1	-		-		-		-		-		18.3	-1.1
1928	-		-		-		-		-		18.1	-1.1	-		-		-		-		-		17.8	-1.7
1929	-		-		-		-		-		17.8	0.0	-		-		-		-		-		17.9	0.6
1930	-		-		-		-		-		17.5	-2.2	-		-		-		-		-		16.8	-4.0
1931	-		-		-		-		-		15.9	-5.4	-		-		-		-		-		15.3	-3.8
1932	-		-		-		-		-		14.2	-7.2	-		-		-		-		-		13.5	-4.9
1933	-		-		-		-		-		13.2	-2.2	-		-		-		-		-		13.8	4.5
1934	-		-		-		-		-		14.2	2.9	-		-		-		-		14.1	-0.7	-	-
1935	-		-		14.2	0.7	-		-		-		14.2	0.0	-		-		-		14.4	1.4	-	
1936	14.5	0.7	-		-		14.4	-0.7	-		-		14.5	0.7	-		14.6	0.7	-		-		14.6	0.0
1937	-		-		14.8	1.4	-		-		14.9	0.7	-		-		15.1	1.3	-		-		14.7	-2.6
1938	-		-		14.5	-1.4	-		-		14.6	0.7	-		-		14.5	-0.7	-		-		14.4	-0.7
1939	-		-		14.2	-1.4	-		-		14.2	0.0	-		-		14.5	2.1	-		-		14.3	-1.4
1940	-		-		14.3	0.0	-		-		14.4	0.7	-		-		14.3	-0.7	14.3	0.0	14.3	0.0	14.4	0.7
1941	14.4	0.0	14.4	0.0	14.5	0.7	14.6	0.7	14.7	0.7	15.0	2.0	15.0	0.0	15.2	1.3	15.5	2.0	15.7	1.3	15.7	0.0	15.8	0.6
1942	16.1	1.9	16.1	0.0	16.3	1.2	16.5	1.2	16.6	0.6	16.7	0.6	16.9	1.2	16.9	0.0	17.0	0.6	17.1	0.6	17.2	0.6	17.4	1.2
1943	17.4	0.0	17.4	0.0	17.6	1.1	18.0	2.3	18.1	0.6	18.0	-0.6	17.8	-1.1	17.8	0.0	17.8	0.0	17.9	0.6	17.9	0.0	17.9	0.0
1944	17.9	0.0	17.9	0.0	17.8	-0.6	17.9	0.6	18.0	0.6	18.1	0.6	18.1	0.0	18.2	0.6	18.2	0.0	18.1	-0.5	18.1	0.0	18.2	0.6
1945	18.3	0.5	18.4	0.5	18.3	-0.5	18.3	0.0	18.5	1.1	18.6	0.5	18.7	0.5	18.7	0.0	18.6	-0.5	18.6	0.0	18.6	0.0	18.7	0.5
1946	18.7	0.0	18.7	0.0	18.8	0.5	18.9	0.5	19.0	0.5	19.2	1.1	20.3	5.7	20.9	3.0	21.2	1.4	21.5	1.4	21.9	1.9	22.2	1.4
1947	22.1	-0.5	22.0	-0.5	22.7	3.2	22.5	-0.9	22.5	0.0	22.8	1.3	23.0	0.9	23.2	0.9	23.7	2.2	23.6	-0.4	23.8	0.8	24.2	1.7
1948	24.4	0.8	24.2	-0.8	24.0	-0.8	24.6	2.5	24.8	0.8	25.0	0.8	25.1	0.4	25.4	1.2	25.4	0.0	25.3	-0.4	25.0	-1.2	24.8	-0.8
1949	24.6	-0.8	24.5	-0.4	24.6	0.4	24.6	0.0	24.7	0.4	24.6	-0.4	24.4	-0.8	24.5	0.4	24.6	0.4	24.6	0.0	24.5	-0.4	24.3	-0.8
1950	24.1	-0.8	24.1	0.0	24.2	0.4	24.2	0.0	24.3	0.4	24.5	0.8	24.7	0.8	24.9	0.8	25.1	0.8	25.2	0.4	25.2	0.0	25.8	2.4
1951	26.3	1.9	26.9	2.3	26.9	0.0	27.0	0.4	27.0	0.0	26.9	-0.4	26.9	0.0	26.9	0.0	27.0	0.4	27.1	0.4	27.4	1.1	27.4	0.0
1952	27.4	0.0	27.1	-1.1	27.2	0.4	27.3	0.4	27.3	0.0	27.4	0.4	27.7	1.1	27.7	0.0	27.7	0.0	27.7	0.0	27.7	0.0	27.7	0.0
1953	27.6	-0.4	27.4	-0.7	27.5	0.4	27.4	-0.4	27.5	0.4	27.7	0.7	27.7	0.0	27.7	0.0	27.8	0.4	27.8	0.0	27.7	-0.4	27.7	0.0
1954	27.8	0.4	27.8	0.0	27.7	-0.4	27.8	0.4	27.8	0.0	28.0	0.7	28.1	0.4	28.0	-0.4	28.0	0.0	28.0	0.0	28.0	0.0	27.9	-0.4
1955	27.9	0.0	27.9	0.0	27.9	0.0	27.9	0.0	27.9	0.0	27.9	0.0	27.9	0.0	27.9	0.0	27.8	-0.4	27.8	0.0	27.7	-0.4	27.7	0.0
1956	27.7	0.0	27.7	0.0	27.9	0.7	28.0	0.4	28.0	0.0	28.2	0.7	28.5	1.1	28.5	0.0	28.6	0.4	28.6	0.0	28.5	-0.3	28.6	0.4
1957	28.7	0.3	28.9	0.7	28.9	0.0	28.9	0.0	28.9	0.0	29.0	0.3	29.2	0.7	29.4	0.7	29.4	0.0	29.4	0.0	29.5	0.3	29.5	0.0
1958	29.5	0.0	29.5	0.0	29.7	0.7	29.7	0.0	29.7	0.0	29.7	0.0	29.8	0.3	29.8	0.0	29.8	0.0	29.8	0.0	29.8	0.0	29.8	0.0
1959	29.8	0.0	29.8	0.0	29.8	0.0	29.8	0.0	29.7	-0.3	29.9	0.7	30.0	0.3	30.0	0.0	30.4	1.3	30.4	0.0	30.5	0.3	30.5	0.0

[Continued]

Philadelphia-Wilmington-Atlantic City, PA-NJ-DE-MD
Consumer Price Index - All Urban Consumers
Base 1982-1984 = 100
All Items
[Continued]

For 1914-2001. Columns headed % show percentile change in the index from the previous period for which an index is available.

Year	Jan Index	%	Feb Index	%	Mar Index	%	Apr Index	%	May Index	%	Jun Index	%	Jul Index	%	Aug Index	%	Sep Index	%	Oct Index	%	Nov Index	%	Dec Index	%
1960	30.3	-0.7	30.3	0.0	30.4	0.3	30.5	0.3	30.5	0.0	30.5	0.0	30.6	0.3	30.6	0.0	30.7	0.3	30.8	0.3	30.9	0.3	30.9	0.0
1961	30.8	-0.3	30.9	0.3	30.8	-0.3	30.9	0.3	30.9	0.0	30.8	-0.3	31.0	0.6	30.9	-0.3	31.0	0.3	31.0	0.0	31.1	0.3	31.0	-0.3
1962	31.0	0.0	31.1	0.3	31.1	0.0	31.2	0.3	31.0	-0.6	31.1	0.3	31.2	0.3	31.2	0.0	31.4	0.6	31.4	0.0	31.4	0.0	31.3	-0.3
1963	31.4	0.3	31.5	0.3	31.5	0.0	31.5	0.0	31.5	0.0	31.8	1.0	31.8	0.0	31.8	0.0	31.9	0.3	32.1	0.6	32.1	0.0	32.2	0.3
1964	32.2	0.0	32.2	0.0	32.1	-0.3	32.1	0.0	32.1	0.0	32.2	0.3	32.3	0.3	32.2	-0.3	32.3	0.3	32.4	0.3	32.5	0.3	32.5	0.0
1965	32.5	0.0	32.6	0.3	32.6	0.0	32.5	-0.3	32.6	0.3	32.8	0.6	32.9	0.3	32.8	-0.3	32.8	0.0	32.9	0.3	33.0	0.3	33.1	0.3
1966	33.1	0.0	33.3	0.6	33.4	0.3	33.5	0.3	33.5	0.0	33.6	0.3	33.7	0.3	33.9	0.6	34.0	0.3	34.1	0.3	34.1	0.0	34.2	0.3
1967	34.1	-0.3	34.2	0.3	34.2	0.0	34.3	0.3	34.4	0.3	34.5	0.3	34.6	0.3	34.8	0.6	34.9	0.3	35.1	0.6	35.1	0.0	35.2	0.3
1968	35.4	0.6	35.6	0.6	35.8	0.6	35.9	0.3	36.0	0.3	36.2	0.6	36.3	0.3	36.4	0.3	36.7	0.8	36.9	0.5	37.0	0.3	37.1	0.3
1969	37.1	0.0	37.3	0.5	37.6	0.8	37.8	0.5	37.8	0.0	38.0	0.5	38.3	0.8	38.6	0.8	38.8	0.5	38.9	0.3	39.0	0.3	39.2	0.5
1970	39.4	0.5	39.8	1.0	40.1	0.8	40.2	0.2	40.5	0.7	40.6	0.2	40.7	0.2	40.9	0.5	41.4	1.2	41.7	0.7	41.9	0.5	42.0	0.2
1971	42.0	0.0	42.2	0.5	42.3	0.2	42.4	0.2	42.7	0.7	43.0	0.7	42.8	-0.5	42.8	0.0	43.1	0.7	43.3	0.5	43.2	-0.2	43.3	0.2
1972	43.2	-0.2	43.3	0.2	43.5	0.5	43.6	0.2	43.6	0.0	43.8	0.5	44.0	0.5	44.1	0.2	44.4	0.7	44.5	0.2	44.7	0.4	44.6	-0.2
1973	44.7	0.2	45.2	1.1	45.9	1.5	46.2	0.7	46.4	0.4	46.6	0.4	46.7	0.2	47.5	1.7	47.8	0.6	48.3	1.0	48.6	0.6	48.9	0.6
1974	49.4	1.0	50.2	1.6	50.9	1.4	51.3	0.8	51.7	0.8	52.2	1.0	52.5	0.6	53.1	1.1	53.9	1.5	54.4	0.9	54.9	0.9	55.1	0.4
1975	55.2	0.2	55.5	0.5	55.8	0.5	55.8	0.0	56.1	0.5	56.6	0.9	57.1	0.9	57.3	0.4	57.8	0.9	58.2	0.7	58.3	0.2	58.3	0.0
1976	58.5	0.3	58.7	0.3	58.7	0.0	58.9	0.3	59.2	0.5	59.5	0.5	59.8	0.5	59.9	0.2	60.4	0.8	60.6	0.3	60.8	0.3	60.7	-0.2
1977	61.2	0.8	61.9	1.1	62.4	0.8	63.0	1.0	63.4	0.6	63.6	0.3	64.0	0.6	64.0	0.0	64.6	0.9	64.7	0.2	64.9	0.3	64.7	-0.3
1978	64.9	0.3	65.1	0.3	65.6	0.8	66.0	0.6	66.4	0.6	67.1	1.1	67.9	1.2	68.0	0.1	68.5	0.7	68.7	0.3	69.1	0.6	69.6	0.7
1979	70.0	0.6	70.6	0.9	70.9	0.4	71.9	1.4	72.9	1.4	74.0	1.5	74.8	1.1	75.4	0.8	76.0	0.8	76.2	0.3	77.0	1.0	77.4	0.5
1980	78.6	1.6	80.0	1.8	81.2	1.5	82.2	1.2	82.9	0.9	83.9	1.2	84.5	0.7	85.2	0.8	85.6	0.5	85.8	0.2	86.3	0.6	86.7	0.5
1981	87.6	1.0	88.6	1.1	89.4	0.9	90.3	1.0	90.7	0.4	91.9	1.3	92.7	0.9	93.6	1.0	95.0	1.5	95.1	0.1	94.9	-0.2	95.2	0.3
1982	95.4	0.2	95.4	0.0	95.1	-0.3	95.2	0.1	95.2	0.0	96.8	1.7	97.3	0.5	97.4	0.1	98.0	0.6	97.5	-0.5	97.9	0.4	97.5	-0.4
1983	97.6	0.1	97.6	0.0	98.0	0.4	98.1	0.1	98.4	0.3	99.0	0.6	99.8	0.8	100.3	0.5	100.9	0.6	100.8	-0.1	101.0	0.2	101.0	0.0
1984	101.9	0.9	102.6	0.7	102.7	0.1	103.2	0.5	103.4	0.2	103.8	0.4	104.3	0.5	104.8	0.5	105.2	0.4	105.1	-0.1	105.9	0.8	105.6	-0.3
1985	106.0	0.4	107.0	0.9	107.4	0.4	108.1	0.7	108.8	0.6	108.8	0.0	109.2	0.4	109.3	0.1	109.6	0.3	109.9	0.3	110.4	0.5	110.7	0.3
1986	110.9	0.2	110.8	-0.1	110.5	-0.3	110.0	-0.5	110.4	0.4	111.4	0.9	111.8	0.4	111.8	0.0	112.8	0.9	112.4	-0.4	112.2	-0.2	112.6	0.4
1987	113.4	0.7	113.9	0.4	114.0	0.1	115.5	1.3	116.4	0.8	117.4	0.9	117.4	0.0	118.4	0.9	118.7	0.3	119.1	0.3	118.6	-0.4	118.9	0.3
1988	119.3	0.3	119.3	0.0	119.6	0.3	120.0	0.3	120.9	0.7	121.9	0.8	123.2	1.1	123.9	0.6	125.2	1.0	124.6	-0.5	125.3	0.6	125.6	0.2
1989	125.7	0.1	125.4	-0.2	126.0	0.5	126.7	0.6	127.9	0.9	128.8	0.7	129.3	0.4	129.1	-0.2	130.2	0.9	130.5	0.2	130.1	-0.3	129.9	-0.2
1990	131.2	1.0	132.2	0.8	133.6	1.1	134.3	0.5	134.6	0.2	135.1	0.4	136.3	0.9	137.3	0.7	138.2	0.7	138.8	0.4	139.1	0.2	139.4	0.2
1991	140.4	0.7	140.6	0.1	141.0	0.3	140.8	-0.1	141.3	0.4	141.8	0.4	142.4	0.4	143.3	0.6	143.8	0.3	143.1	-0.5	143.3	0.1	144.4	0.8
1992	144.4	0.0	144.2	-0.1	145.4	0.8	145.4	0.0	145.7	0.2	147.5	1.2	147.3	-0.1	148.0	0.5	148.1	0.1	148.0	-0.1	147.5	-0.3	147.5	0.0
1993	147.5	0.0	148.5	0.7	149.3	0.5	149.6	0.2	149.4	-0.1	150.5	0.7	150.7	0.1	150.6	-0.1	151.1	0.3	152.2	0.7	152.1	-0.1	151.3	-0.5
1994	152.5	0.8	152.9	0.3	153.5	0.4	153.1	-0.3	153.2	0.1	154.6	0.9	155.3	0.5	155.7	0.3	156.2	0.3	156.6	0.3	156.7	0.1	155.4	-0.8
1995	156.6	0.8	157.8	0.8	158.0	0.1	157.8	-0.1	157.8	0.0	158.4	0.4	158.9	0.3	159.6	0.4	160.3	0.4	160.4	0.1	159.6	-0.5	159.1	-0.3
1996	160.3	0.8	161.2	0.6	162.0	0.5	162.1	0.1	161.8	-0.2	162.3	0.3	162.8	0.3	163.6	0.5	164.5	0.6	164.9	0.2	164.3	-0.4	164.3	0.0
1997	165.1	0.5	165.8	0.4	166.1	0.2	166.0	-0.1	166.0	0.0	166.1	0.1	166.4	0.2	166.8	0.2	168.6	1.1	167.7	-0.5	166.4	-0.8	166.4	0.0
1998	-	-	167.0	0.4	-	-	167.1	0.1	-	-	168.0	0.5	-	-	168.6	0.4	-	-	170.3	1.0	-	-	169.0	-0.8
1999	-	-	168.6	-0.2	-	-	171.1	1.5	-	-	172.1	0.6	-	-	173.1	0.6	-	-	174.4	0.8	-	-	172.9	-0.9
2000	-	-	174.8	1.1	-	-	175.8	0.6	-	-	176.6	0.5	-	-	177.5	0.5	-	-	177.9	0.2	-	-	177.5	-0.2
2001	-	-	179.0	0.8	-	-	181.2	1.2	-	-	182.5	0.7	-	-	182.8	0.2	-	-	182.9	0.1	-	-	179.9	-1.6

Source: U.S. Department of Labor, Bureau of Labor Statistics, Division of Consumer Prices and Price Indexes. - indicates no data collected for period.

Philadelphia-Wilmington-Atlantic City, PA-NJ-DE-MD
Consumer Price Index - Urban Wage Earners
Base 1982-1984 = 100
All Items

For 1914-2001. Columns headed % show percentile change in the index from the previous period for which an index is available.

Year	Jan Index	%	Feb Index	%	Mar Index	%	Apr Index	%	May Index	%	Jun Index	%	Jul Index	%	Aug Index	%	Sep Index	%	Oct Index	%	Nov Index	%	Dec Index	%
1914	-	-	-	-	-	-	-	-	-	-	-	-	-	-	-	-	-	-	-	-	-	-	10.1	-
1915	-	-	-	-	-	-	-	-	-	-	-	-	-	-	-	-	-	-	-	-	-	-	10.3	2.0
1916	-	-	-	-	-	-	-	-	-	-	-	-	-	-	-	-	-	-	-	-	-	-	11.5	11.7
1917	-	-	-	-	-	-	-	-	-	-	-	-	-	-	-	-	-	-	-	-	-	-	14.0	21.7
1918	-	-	-	-	-	-	-	-	-	-	-	-	-	-	-	-	-	-	-	-	-	-	16.9	20.7
1919	-	-	-	-	-	-	-	-	-	-	17.4	3.0	-	-	-	-	-	-	-	-	-	-	19.1	9.8
1920	-	-	-	-	-	-	-	-	-	-	21.2	11.0	-	-	-	-	-	-	-	-	-	-	19.8	-6.6
1921	-	-	-	-	-	-	-	-	18.0	-9.1	-	-	-	-	-	-	17.8	-1.1	-	-	-	-	17.6	-1.1
1922	-	-	-	-	17.2	-2.3	-	-	-	-	17.2	0.0	-	-	-	-	16.8	-2.3	-	-	-	-	17.2	2.4
1923	-	-	-	-	17.2	0.0	-	-	-	-	17.5	1.7	-	-	-	-	17.7	1.1	-	-	-	-	17.7	0.0
1924	-	-	-	-	17.5	-1.1	-	-	-	-	17.6	0.6	-	-	-	-	17.5	-0.6	-	-	-	-	17.9	2.3
1925	-	-	-	-	-	-	-	-	-	-	18.3	2.2	-	-	-	-	-	-	-	-	-	-	18.8	2.7
1926	-	-	-	-	-	-	-	-	-	-	18.7	-0.5	-	-	-	-	-	-	-	-	-	-	18.6	-0.5
1927	-	-	-	-	-	-	-	-	-	-	18.4	-1.1	-	-	-	-	-	-	-	-	-	-	18.2	-1.1
1928	-	-	-	-	-	-	-	-	-	-	18.0	-1.1	-	-	-	-	-	-	-	-	-	-	17.7	-1.7
1929	-	-	-	-	-	-	-	-	-	-	17.7	0.0	-	-	-	-	-	-	-	-	-	-	17.8	0.6
1930	-	-	-	-	-	-	-	-	-	-	17.4	-2.2	-	-	-	-	-	-	-	-	-	-	16.7	-4.0
1931	-	-	-	-	-	-	-	-	-	-	15.8	-5.4	-	-	-	-	-	-	-	-	-	-	15.3	-3.2
1932	-	-	-	-	-	-	-	-	-	-	14.1	-7.8	-	-	-	-	-	-	-	-	-	-	13.5	-4.3
1933	-	-	-	-	-	-	-	-	-	-	13.2	-2.2	-	-	-	-	-	-	-	-	-	-	13.8	4.5
1934	-	-	-	-	-	-	-	-	-	-	14.1	2.2	-	-	-	-	-	-	-	-	14.0	-0.7	-	-
1935	-	-	-	-	14.1	0.7	-	-	-	-	-	-	14.1	0.0	-	-	-	-	14.3	1.4	-	-	-	-
1936	14.5	1.4	-	-	-	-	14.3	-1.4	-	-	-	-	14.5	1.4	-	-	14.6	0.7	-	-	-	-	14.5	-0.7
1937	-	-	-	-	14.7	1.4	-	-	-	-	14.8	0.7	-	-	-	-	15.0	1.4	-	-	-	-	14.7	-2.0
1938	-	-	-	-	14.5	-1.4	-	-	-	-	14.5	0.0	-	-	-	-	14.5	0.0	-	-	-	-	14.3	-1.4
1939	-	-	-	-	14.1	-1.4	-	-	-	-	14.1	0.0	-	-	-	-	14.4	2.1	-	-	-	-	14.3	-0.7
1940	-	-	-	-	14.2	-0.7	-	-	-	-	14.3	0.7	-	-	-	-	14.3	0.0	14.3	0.0	14.3	0.0	14.3	0.0
1941	14.3	0.0	14.3	0.0	14.4	0.7	14.5	0.7	14.7	1.4	14.9	1.4	14.9	0.0	15.1	1.3	15.4	2.0	15.6	1.3	15.6	0.0	15.7	0.6
1942	16.0	1.9	16.0	0.0	16.2	1.3	16.4	1.2	16.5	0.6	16.6	0.6	16.8	1.2	16.8	0.0	16.9	0.6	17.0	0.6	17.1	0.6	17.3	1.2
1943	17.3	0.0	17.3	0.0	17.5	1.2	17.9	2.3	18.0	0.6	17.9	-0.6	17.7	-1.1	17.7	0.0	17.7	0.0	17.8	0.6	17.8	0.0	17.8	0.0
1944	17.8	0.0	17.8	0.0	17.7	-0.6	17.8	0.6	17.9	0.6	18.0	0.6	18.0	0.0	18.1	0.6	18.1	0.0	18.0	-0.6	18.0	0.0	18.1	0.6
1945	18.2	0.6	18.3	0.5	18.2	-0.5	18.2	0.0	18.4	1.1	18.5	0.5	18.6	0.5	18.6	0.0	18.5	-0.5	18.5	0.0	18.5	0.0	18.6	0.5
1946	18.6	0.0	18.6	0.0	18.7	0.5	18.8	0.5	18.9	0.5	19.1	1.1	20.2	5.8	20.8	3.0	21.1	1.4	21.3	0.9	21.8	2.3	22.0	0.9
1947	22.0	0.0	21.9	-0.5	22.5	2.7	22.4	-0.4	22.4	0.0	22.7	1.3	22.9	0.9	23.1	0.9	23.6	2.2	23.4	-0.8	23.7	1.3	24.0	1.3
1948	24.3	1.2	24.1	-0.8	23.9	-0.8	24.5	2.5	24.6	0.4	24.9	1.2	25.0	0.4	25.3	1.2	25.3	0.0	25.2	-0.4	24.8	-1.6	24.7	-0.4
1949	24.5	-0.8	24.4	-0.4	24.4	0.0	24.4	0.0	24.5	0.4	24.5	0.0	24.2	-1.2	24.4	0.8	24.5	0.4	24.4	-0.4	24.4	0.0	24.2	-0.8
1950	24.0	-0.8	23.9	-0.4	24.1	0.8	24.1	0.0	24.1	0.0	24.4	1.2	24.6	0.8	24.8	0.8	25.0	0.8	25.1	0.4	25.1	0.0	25.7	2.4
1951	26.1	1.6	26.8	2.7	26.8	0.0	26.8	0.0	26.9	0.4	26.8	-0.4	26.8	0.0	26.8	0.0	26.8	0.0	27.0	0.7	27.3	1.1	27.3	0.0
1952	27.2	-0.4	27.0	-0.7	27.1	0.4	27.2	0.4	27.2	0.0	27.3	0.4	27.6	1.1	27.6	0.0	27.5	-0.4	27.5	0.0	27.5	0.0	27.5	0.0
1953	27.4	-0.4	27.3	-0.4	27.4	0.4	27.3	-0.4	27.3	0.0	27.5	0.7	27.5	0.0	27.6	0.4	27.6	0.0	27.7	0.4	27.5	-0.7	27.6	0.4
1954	27.7	0.4	27.6	-0.4	27.6	0.0	27.6	0.0	27.7	0.4	27.8	0.4	27.9	0.4	27.9	0.0	27.9	0.0	27.9	0.0	27.8	-0.4	27.7	-0.4
1955	27.7	0.0	27.8	0.4	27.8	0.0	27.8	0.0	27.7	-0.4	27.7	0.0	27.8	0.4	27.8	0.0	27.6	-0.7	27.7	0.4	27.6	-0.4	27.6	0.0
1956	27.5	-0.4	27.5	0.0	27.8	1.1	27.9	0.4	27.9	0.0	28.0	0.4	28.3	1.1	28.3	0.0	28.4	0.4	28.5	0.4	28.4	-0.4	28.5	0.4
1957	28.5	0.0	28.7	0.7	28.8	0.3	28.7	-0.3	28.8	0.3	28.8	0.0	29.1	1.0	29.2	0.3	29.3	0.3	29.3	0.0	29.3	0.0	29.3	0.0
1958	29.3	0.0	29.4	0.3	29.5	0.3	29.5	0.0	29.5	0.0	29.5	0.0	29.6	0.3	29.6	0.0	29.6	0.0	29.6	0.0	29.6	0.0	29.6	0.0
1959	29.6	0.0	29.6	0.0	29.6	0.0	29.7	0.3	29.6	-0.3	29.8	0.7	29.8	0.0	29.8	0.0	30.2	1.3	30.2	0.0	30.3	0.3	30.4	0.3

[Continued]

Philadelphia-Wilmington-Atlantic City, PA-NJ-DE-MD
Consumer Price Index - Urban Wage Earners
Base 1982-1984 = 100
All Items
[Continued]

For 1914-2001. Columns headed % show percentile change in the index from the previous period for which an index is available.

Year	Jan Index	%	Feb Index	%	Mar Index	%	Apr Index	%	May Index	%	Jun Index	%	Jul Index	%	Aug Index	%	Sep Index	%	Oct Index	%	Nov Index	%	Dec Index	%
1960	30.1	-1.0	30.1	0.0	30.2	0.3	30.3	0.3	30.3	0.0	30.3	0.0	30.4	0.3	30.4	0.0	30.5	0.3	30.6	0.3	30.7	0.3	30.7	0.0
1961	30.7	0.0	30.7	0.0	30.6	-0.3	30.7	0.3	30.7	0.0	30.7	0.0	30.8	0.3	30.7	-0.3	30.8	0.3	30.9	0.3	30.9	0.0	30.9	0.0
1962	30.8	-0.3	31.0	0.6	31.0	0.0	31.0	0.0	30.8	-0.6	30.9	0.3	31.1	0.6	31.0	-0.3	31.3	1.0	31.2	-0.3	31.2	0.0	31.2	0.0
1963	31.2	0.0	31.3	0.3	31.4	0.3	31.4	0.0	31.3	-0.3	31.6	1.0	31.7	0.3	31.7	0.0	31.7	0.0	31.9	0.6	31.9	0.0	32.0	0.3
1964	32.0	0.0	32.1	0.3	31.9	-0.6	31.9	0.0	31.9	0.0	32.0	0.3	32.1	0.3	32.0	-0.3	32.1	0.3	32.2	0.3	32.3	0.3	32.3	0.0
1965	32.3	0.0	32.4	0.3	32.4	0.0	32.3	-0.3	32.5	0.6	32.6	0.3	32.7	0.3	32.6	-0.3	32.7	0.3	32.7	0.0	32.8	0.3	32.9	0.3
1966	32.9	0.0	33.1	0.6	33.2	0.3	33.4	0.6	33.3	-0.3	33.4	0.3	33.5	0.3	33.7	0.6	33.8	0.3	33.9	0.3	33.9	0.0	34.0	0.3
1967	33.9	-0.3	34.0	0.3	34.0	0.0	34.1	0.3	34.2	0.3	34.4	0.6	34.4	0.0	34.6	0.6	34.7	0.3	34.9	0.6	34.9	0.0	35.0	0.3
1968	35.3	0.9	35.4	0.3	35.6	0.6	35.7	0.3	35.8	0.3	36.0	0.6	36.1	0.3	36.3	0.6	36.5	0.6	36.7	0.5	36.8	0.3	36.9	0.3
1969	36.9	0.0	37.1	0.5	37.4	0.8	37.6	0.5	37.6	0.0	37.8	0.5	38.1	0.8	38.4	0.8	38.6	0.5	38.7	0.3	38.8	0.3	39.0	0.5
1970	39.2	0.5	39.6	1.0	39.9	0.8	40.0	0.3	40.2	0.5	40.4	0.5	40.5	0.2	40.7	0.5	41.2	1.2	41.5	0.7	41.7	0.5	41.8	0.2
1971	41.8	0.0	41.9	0.2	42.1	0.5	42.2	0.2	42.5	0.7	42.7	0.5	42.6	-0.2	42.6	0.0	42.9	0.7	43.0	0.2	42.9	-0.2	43.1	0.5
1972	42.9	-0.5	43.1	0.5	43.3	0.5	43.4	0.2	43.4	0.0	43.6	0.5	43.7	0.2	43.9	0.5	44.2	0.7	44.3	0.2	44.4	0.2	44.4	0.0
1973	44.4	0.0	45.0	1.4	45.6	1.3	45.9	0.7	46.2	0.7	46.4	0.4	46.4	0.0	47.2	1.7	47.5	0.6	48.0	1.1	48.4	0.8	48.7	0.6
1974	49.2	1.0	49.9	1.4	50.6	1.4	51.0	0.8	51.4	0.8	52.0	1.2	52.3	0.6	52.8	1.0	53.6	1.5	54.1	0.9	54.6	0.9	54.8	0.4
1975	54.9	0.2	55.2	0.5	55.5	0.5	55.5	0.0	55.8	0.5	56.3	0.9	56.8	0.9	57.0	0.4	57.5	0.9	57.9	0.7	58.0	0.2	58.0	0.0
1976	58.2	0.3	58.4	0.3	58.4	0.0	58.6	0.3	58.9	0.5	59.2	0.5	59.5	0.5	59.6	0.2	60.1	0.8	60.3	0.3	60.5	0.3	60.4	-0.2
1977	60.8	0.7	61.5	1.2	62.1	1.0	62.6	0.8	63.0	0.6	63.3	0.5	63.6	0.5	63.7	0.2	64.2	0.8	64.4	0.3	64.5	0.2	64.3	-0.3
1978	64.5	0.3	65.0	0.8	65.3	0.5	65.9	0.9	66.3	0.6	67.0	1.1	67.4	0.6	68.0	0.9	68.2	0.3	68.5	0.4	69.1	0.9	69.7	0.9
1979	70.2	0.7	70.9	1.0	71.2	0.4	72.0	1.1	72.8	1.1	73.8	1.4	74.7	1.2	75.1	0.5	75.8	0.9	76.2	0.5	77.0	1.0	77.3	0.4
1980	78.5	1.6	79.7	1.5	80.9	1.5	81.9	1.2	82.6	0.9	83.9	1.6	84.5	0.7	85.1	0.7	85.5	0.5	85.9	0.5	86.4	0.6	86.9	0.6
1981	88.0	1.3	88.9	1.0	89.3	0.4	90.0	0.8	90.5	0.6	91.4	1.0	92.4	1.1	93.5	1.2	94.5	1.1	94.7	0.2	94.5	-0.2	94.4	-0.1
1982	94.7	0.3	94.7	0.0	94.4	-0.3	94.5	0.1	94.6	0.1	96.1	1.6	96.7	0.6	96.6	-0.1	97.1	0.5	96.8	-0.3	97.1	0.3	96.7	-0.4
1983	97.3	0.6	97.5	0.2	98.3	0.8	98.7	0.4	98.6	-0.1	99.4	0.8	100.2	0.8	101.0	0.8	101.3	0.3	101.3	0.0	101.5	0.2	101.3	-0.2
1984	102.1	0.8	102.8	0.7	102.9	0.1	102.9	0.0	103.5	0.6	104.2	0.7	104.8	0.6	105.4	0.6	106.2	0.8	106.3	0.1	106.4	0.1	106.0	-0.4
1985	106.5	0.5	107.6	1.0	107.9	0.3	108.5	0.6	109.2	0.6	109.2	0.0	109.7	0.5	109.7	0.0	109.9	0.2	110.3	0.4	110.7	0.4	111.0	0.3
1986	111.2	0.2	111.1	-0.1	110.6	-0.5	110.1	-0.5	110.4	0.3	111.4	0.9	111.8	0.4	111.7	-0.1	112.5	0.7	112.3	-0.2	112.0	-0.3	112.5	0.4
1987	113.3	0.7	113.6	0.3	113.8	0.2	115.3	1.3	116.2	0.8	117.2	0.9	117.3	0.1	118.4	0.9	118.5	0.1	119.0	0.4	118.6	-0.3	119.0	0.3
1988	119.3	0.3	119.0	-0.3	119.5	0.4	119.8	0.3	120.8	0.8	121.8	0.8	123.1	1.1	123.6	0.4	124.9	1.1	124.4	-0.4	125.0	0.5	125.2	0.2
1989	125.5	0.2	125.4	-0.1	125.8	0.3	126.7	0.7	127.9	0.9	128.9	0.8	129.3	0.3	129.3	0.0	130.4	0.9	130.6	0.2	130.1	-0.4	130.0	-0.1
1990	131.0	0.8	132.2	0.9	133.8	1.2	134.4	0.4	134.9	0.4	135.5	0.4	136.6	0.8	137.5	0.7	138.6	0.8	139.1	0.4	139.4	0.2	139.8	0.3
1991	140.4	0.4	140.5	0.1	141.0	0.4	140.8	-0.1	141.2	0.3	141.8	0.4	142.5	0.5	143.2	0.5	143.7	0.3	142.9	-0.6	143.4	0.3	144.4	0.7
1992	144.2	-0.1	143.9	-0.2	145.0	0.8	145.1	0.1	145.5	0.3	147.4	1.3	147.3	-0.1	147.8	0.3	147.9	0.1	147.8	-0.1	147.6	-0.1	147.4	-0.1
1993	147.4	0.0	148.6	0.8	149.0	0.3	149.4	0.3	149.3	-0.1	150.4	0.7	150.6	0.1	150.4	-0.1	150.9	0.3	151.9	0.7	151.9	0.0	151.2	-0.5
1994	152.1	0.6	152.2	0.1	152.8	0.4	152.6	-0.1	152.7	0.1	154.2	1.0	154.9	0.5	155.3	0.3	155.9	0.4	156.1	0.1	156.1	0.0	155.1	-0.6
1995	156.4	0.8	157.5	0.7	157.5	0.0	157.4	-0.1	157.4	0.0	158.1	0.4	158.5	0.3	159.2	0.4	159.8	0.4	159.7	-0.1	159.2	-0.3	158.7	-0.3
1996	159.7	0.6	160.5	0.5	161.3	0.5	161.3	0.0	161.3	0.0	161.7	0.2	162.1	0.2	163.0	0.6	163.7	0.4	164.2	0.3	164.0	-0.1	163.6	-0.2
1997	164.4	0.5	164.9	0.3	165.3	0.2	165.1	-0.1	165.2	0.1	165.3	0.1	165.5	0.1	165.9	0.2	167.9	1.2	166.8	-0.7	165.9	-0.5	165.7	-0.1
1998	-		166.1	0.2	-		166.5	0.2	-		167.4	0.5	-		167.9	0.3	-		169.3	0.8	-		168.5	-0.5
1999	-		167.8	-0.4	-		170.6	1.7	-		171.9	0.8	-		172.6	0.4	-		174.3	1.0	-		172.8	-0.9
2000	-		174.6	1.0	-		175.8	0.7	-		176.1	0.2	-		177.1	0.6	-		177.2	0.1	-		177.0	-0.1
2001	-		178.2	0.7	-		180.7	1.4	-		182.0	0.7	-		182.2	0.1	-		182.3	0.1	-		179.2	-1.7

Source: U.S. Department of Labor, Bureau of Labor Statistics, Division of Consumer Prices and Price Indexes. - indicates no data collected for period.

Philadelphia-Wilmington-Atlantic City, PA-NJ-DE-MD
Consumer Price Index - All Urban Consumers
Base 1982-1984 = 100
Food and Beverages

For 1976-2001. Columns headed % show percentile change in the index from the previous period for which an index is available.

Year	Jan Index	%	Feb Index	%	Mar Index	%	Apr Index	%	May Index	%	Jun Index	%	Jul Index	%	Aug Index	%	Sep Index	%	Oct Index	%	Nov Index	%	Dec Index	%
1976	62.3	-	62.3	0.0	61.7	-1.0	61.8	0.2	62.0	0.3	62.3	0.5	62.4	0.2	62.5	0.2	62.5	0.0	62.4	-0.2	62.3	-0.2	62.2	-0.2
1977	63.1	1.4	64.7	2.5	65.3	0.9	65.8	0.8	65.9	0.2	66.3	0.6	66.7	0.6	66.3	-0.6	66.5	0.3	66.9	0.6	67.4	0.7	67.5	0.1
1978	68.3	1.2	69.3	1.5	70.1	1.2	70.6	0.7	71.6	1.4	73.5	2.7	74.1	0.8	74.0	-0.1	73.9	-0.1	73.8	-0.1	74.7	1.2	75.0	0.4
1979	76.3	1.7	77.4	1.4	78.2	1.0	78.7	0.6	79.2	0.6	79.3	0.1	80.3	1.3	80.1	-0.2	79.8	-0.4	80.9	1.4	81.3	0.5	82.0	0.9
1980	82.3	0.4	82.1	-0.2	83.0	1.1	83.9	1.1	84.8	1.1	86.2	1.7	86.7	0.6	87.5	0.9	87.9	0.5	88.6	0.8	89.3	0.8	89.6	0.3
1981	90.7	1.2	90.8	0.1	90.9	0.1	91.2	0.3	91.6	0.4	91.9	0.3	93.0	1.2	93.4	0.4	94.5	1.2	94.1	-0.4	93.9	-0.2	94.6	0.7
1982	95.5	1.0	96.7	1.3	96.7	0.0	97.7	1.0	97.4	-0.3	98.2	0.8	98.8	0.6	98.5	-0.3	98.7	0.2	98.1	-0.6	98.0	-0.1	97.8	-0.2
1983	98.3	0.5	98.8	0.5	99.1	0.3	99.7	0.6	99.9	0.2	100.7	0.8	100.4	-0.3	100.8	0.4	100.8	0.0	100.6	-0.2	100.1	-0.5	100.2	0.1
1984	101.6	1.4	102.6	1.0	102.7	0.1	102.3	-0.4	102.2	-0.1	102.4	0.2	103.2	0.8	103.6	0.4	102.2	-1.4	102.2	0.0	101.9	-0.3	101.8	-0.1
1985	103.2	1.4	104.5	1.3	104.9	0.4	104.9	0.0	104.9	0.0	104.6	-0.3	105.6	1.0	104.9	-0.7	105.6	0.7	105.8	0.2	105.3	-0.5	106.0	0.7
1986	106.1	0.1	106.0	-0.1	106.9	0.8	106.9	0.0	107.1	0.2	107.1	0.0	107.8	0.7	108.5	0.6	109.4	0.8	109.5	0.1	108.9	-0.5	109.3	0.4
1987	110.8	1.4	110.8	0.0	110.5	-0.3	111.4	0.8	111.9	0.4	112.0	0.1	112.4	0.4	112.7	0.3	112.7	0.0	113.4	0.6	113.1	-0.3	113.0	-0.1
1988	114.2	1.1	113.7	-0.4	112.7	-0.9	114.4	1.5	115.1	0.6	116.1	0.9	117.3	1.0	117.1	-0.2	117.4	0.3	118.5	0.9	117.3	-1.0	118.2	0.8
1989	119.4	1.0	120.1	0.6	121.7	1.3	122.3	0.5	123.1	0.7	125.0	1.5	125.7	0.6	125.4	-0.2	126.0	0.5	127.0	0.8	127.4	0.3	127.7	0.2
1990	128.4	0.5	130.2	1.4	130.6	0.3	130.1	-0.4	130.4	0.2	130.6	0.2	131.6	0.8	132.3	0.5	131.6	-0.5	132.5	0.7	132.5	0.0	133.6	0.8
1991	134.6	0.7	135.2	0.4	135.5	0.2	135.9	0.3	136.0	0.1	136.1	0.1	135.7	-0.3	135.2	-0.4	135.0	-0.1	135.0	0.0	135.1	0.1	135.1	0.0
1992	136.0	0.7	136.4	0.3	137.1	0.5	137.7	0.4	138.0	0.2	137.7	-0.2	138.1	0.3	137.7	-0.3	138.3	0.4	138.1	-0.1	137.6	-0.4	138.4	0.6
1993	138.6	0.1	139.0	0.3	139.4	0.3	140.4	0.7	140.9	0.4	139.5	-1.0	138.6	-0.6	138.6	0.0	140.2	1.2	139.7	-0.4	141.0	0.9	140.3	-0.5
1994	142.0	1.2	140.6	-1.0	141.0	0.3	141.8	0.6	141.1	-0.5	141.7	0.4	142.5	0.6	142.4	-0.1	144.0	1.1	144.9	0.6	144.7	-0.1	146.2	1.0
1995	147.9	1.2	148.4	0.3	147.8	-0.4	148.5	0.5	149.2	0.5	148.2	-0.7	148.7	0.3	149.1	0.3	149.9	0.5	149.7	-0.1	149.6	-0.1	149.0	-0.4
1996	151.1	1.4	150.7	-0.3	150.2	-0.3	151.2	0.7	151.6	0.3	152.2	0.4	152.7	0.3	152.9	0.1	153.1	0.1	152.8	-0.2	153.7	0.6	153.6	-0.1
1997	153.9	0.2	153.7	-0.1	154.0	0.2	153.8	-0.1	155.4	1.0	154.6	-0.5	154.9	0.2	154.9	0.0	155.3	0.3	153.6	-1.1	153.9	0.2	153.8	-0.1
1998	-	-	154.2	0.3	-	-	153.8	-0.3	-	-	155.9	1.4	-	-	154.6	-0.8	-	-	156.4	1.2	-	-	156.3	-0.1
1999	-	-	156.9	0.4	-	-	158.4	1.0	-	-	160.1	1.1	-	-	160.8	0.4	-	-	161.4	0.4	-	-	159.8	-1.0
2000	-	-	161.6	1.1	-	-	160.8	-0.5	-	-	160.9	0.1	-	-	162.3	0.9	-	-	160.8	-0.9	-	-	163.1	1.4
2001	-	-	164.8	1.0	-	-	166.2	0.8	-	-	166.2	0.0	-	-	166.8	0.4	-	-	169.8	1.8	-	-	169.7	-0.1

Source: U.S. Department of Labor, Bureau of Labor Statistics, Division of Consumer Prices and Price Indexes. - indicates no data collected for period.

Philadelphia-Wilmington-Atlantic City, PA-NJ-DE-MD
Consumer Price Index - Urban Wage Earners
Base 1982-1984 = 100
Food and Beverages

For 1976-2001. Columns headed % show percentile change in the index from the previous period for which an index is available.

Year	Jan Index	%	Feb Index	%	Mar Index	%	Apr Index	%	May Index	%	Jun Index	%	Jul Index	%	Aug Index	%	Sep Index	%	Oct Index	%	Nov Index	%	Dec Index	%
1976	60.6	-	60.6	0.0	60.0	-1.0	60.1	0.2	60.3	0.3	60.6	0.5	60.7	0.2	60.8	0.2	60.8	0.0	60.7	-0.2	60.6	-0.2	60.5	-0.2
1977	61.4	1.5	63.0	2.6	63.5	0.8	64.1	0.9	64.2	0.2	64.5	0.5	64.9	0.6	64.5	-0.6	64.7	0.3	65.1	0.6	65.6	0.8	65.7	0.2
1978	66.3	0.9	68.2	2.9	68.7	0.7	69.3	0.9	70.3	1.4	71.4	1.6	72.0	0.8	72.7	1.0	72.1	-0.8	72.1	0.0	73.1	1.4	73.3	0.3
1979	75.5	3.0	76.9	1.9	78.2	1.7	78.7	0.6	78.9	0.3	78.7	-0.3	79.6	1.1	79.5	-0.1	79.9	0.5	80.9	1.3	81.3	0.5	81.9	0.7
1980	82.1	0.2	82.1	0.0	83.5	1.7	84.7	1.4	85.6	1.1	87.6	2.3	88.1	0.6	88.9	0.9	88.8	-0.1	89.8	1.1	90.3	0.6	90.4	0.1
1981	91.4	1.1	91.6	0.2	92.1	0.5	91.9	-0.2	92.5	0.7	92.9	0.4	93.9	1.1	94.4	0.5	94.7	0.3	94.3	-0.4	93.8	-0.5	94.5	0.7
1982	95.4	1.0	96.7	1.4	96.8	0.1	97.7	0.9	97.4	-0.3	98.3	0.9	98.8	0.5	98.6	-0.2	98.8	0.2	98.0	-0.8	97.8	-0.2	97.7	-0.1
1983	98.3	0.6	98.7	0.4	99.0	0.3	99.6	0.6	99.9	0.3	100.7	0.8	100.5	-0.2	100.9	0.4	100.8	-0.1	100.6	-0.2	100.0	-0.6	100.2	0.2
1984	101.5	1.3	102.6	1.1	102.7	0.1	102.2	-0.5	102.1	-0.1	102.5	0.4	103.2	0.7	103.7	0.5	102.5	-1.2	102.4	-0.1	101.9	-0.5	101.8	-0.1
1985	103.2	1.4	104.5	1.3	105.0	0.5	104.9	-0.1	105.0	0.1	104.6	-0.4	105.7	1.1	105.0	-0.7	105.6	0.6	105.8	0.2	105.3	-0.5	106.1	0.8
1986	106.1	0.0	106.0	-0.1	106.9	0.8	107.0	0.1	107.2	0.2	107.0	-0.2	107.9	0.8	108.6	0.6	109.5	0.8	109.7	0.2	109.0	-0.6	109.4	0.4
1987	111.2	1.6	110.9	-0.3	110.5	-0.4	111.7	1.1	112.2	0.4	112.3	0.1	112.7	0.4	113.2	0.4	113.1	-0.1	113.6	0.4	113.6	0.0	113.3	-0.3
1988	114.7	1.2	114.0	-0.6	113.0	-0.9	114.6	1.4	115.5	0.8	116.6	1.0	117.8	1.0	117.6	-0.2	117.9	0.3	119.1	1.0	117.9	-1.0	118.7	0.7
1989	120.0	1.1	120.8	0.7	122.7	1.6	123.2	0.4	124.0	0.6	125.8	1.5	126.5	0.6	126.1	-0.3	126.9	0.6	128.0	0.9	128.4	0.3	128.6	0.2
1990	129.2	0.5	131.3	1.6	131.6	0.2	131.0	-0.5	131.5	0.4	131.8	0.2	133.0	0.9	133.5	0.4	132.9	-0.4	133.7	0.6	133.8	0.1	134.8	0.7
1991	135.7	0.7	136.4	0.5	136.7	0.2	136.8	0.1	137.1	0.2	137.2	0.1	137.1	-0.1	136.5	-0.4	136.1	-0.3	135.9	-0.1	136.3	0.3	136.2	-0.1
1992	137.0	0.6	137.4	0.3	138.3	0.7	138.8	0.4	139.0	0.1	138.9	-0.1	139.4	0.4	138.9	-0.4	139.5	0.4	139.4	-0.1	138.9	-0.4	139.4	0.4
1993	139.8	0.3	140.0	0.1	140.5	0.4	141.4	0.6	142.0	0.4	140.8	-0.8	140.0	-0.6	139.9	-0.1	141.7	1.3	140.8	-0.6	142.2	1.0	141.5	-0.5
1994	143.2	1.2	141.6	-1.1	142.4	0.6	143.0	0.4	142.3	-0.5	143.1	0.6	143.9	0.6	143.5	-0.3	145.3	1.3	146.2	0.6	145.7	-0.3	147.0	0.9
1995	149.1	1.4	149.3	0.1	148.8	-0.3	149.6	0.5	150.4	0.5	149.4	-0.7	149.7	0.2	150.3	0.4	150.8	0.3	150.9	0.1	150.9	0.0	150.4	-0.3
1996	152.3	1.3	152.1	-0.1	151.6	-0.3	152.2	0.4	152.7	0.3	153.2	0.3	153.7	0.3	154.1	0.3	154.3	0.1	154.0	-0.2	155.2	0.8	154.5	-0.5
1997	155.0	0.3	154.8	-0.1	155.3	0.3	154.8	-0.3	156.5	1.1	155.7	-0.5	156.1	0.3	155.6	-0.3	156.1	0.3	154.3	-1.2	154.9	0.4	154.7	-0.1
1998	-	-	154.9	0.1	-	-	154.5	-0.3	-	-	156.5	1.3	-	-	155.5	-0.6	-	-	156.8	0.8	-	-	156.6	-0.1
1999	-	-	157.6	0.6	-	-	158.9	0.8	-	-	160.9	1.3	-	-	161.6	0.4	-	-	162.4	0.5	-	-	160.5	-1.2
2000	-	-	162.3	1.1	-	-	162.1	-0.1	-	-	162.0	-0.1	-	-	163.2	0.7	-	-	161.8	-0.9	-	-	164.4	1.6
2001	-	-	166.0	1.0	-	-	167.7	1.0	-	-	167.6	-0.1	-	-	168.3	0.4	-	-	171.4	1.8	-	-	171.1	-0.2

Source: U.S. Department of Labor, Bureau of Labor Statistics, Division of Consumer Prices and Price Indexes. - indicates no data collected for period.

Philadelphia-Wilmington-Atlantic City, PA-NJ-DE-MD
Consumer Price Index - All Urban Consumers
Base 1982-1984 = 100
Housing

For 1976-2001. Columns headed % show percentile change in the index from the previous period for which an index is available.

Year	Jan Index	%	Feb Index	%	Mar Index	%	Apr Index	%	May Index	%	Jun Index	%	Jul Index	%	Aug Index	%	Sep Index	%	Oct Index	%	Nov Index	%	Dec Index	%
1976	57.8	-	58.1	0.5	58.3	0.3	58.4	0.2	58.7	0.5	58.7	0.0	59.0	0.5	59.0	0.0	59.9	1.5	60.2	0.5	60.5	0.5	60.5	0.0
1977	60.8	0.5	61.0	0.3	61.7	1.1	62.1	0.6	62.6	0.8	62.7	0.2	63.0	0.5	63.4	0.6	64.2	1.3	64.1	-0.2	64.0	-0.2	63.5	-0.8
1978	63.7	0.3	63.8	0.2	64.2	0.6	64.4	0.3	64.5	0.2	64.8	0.5	65.8	1.5	66.3	0.8	67.1	1.2	67.5	0.6	67.8	0.4	68.3	0.7
1979	68.1	-0.3	68.2	0.1	68.1	-0.1	69.3	1.8	70.7	2.0	72.5	2.5	72.8	0.4	73.4	0.8	74.4	1.4	74.5	0.1	75.4	1.2	75.9	0.7
1980	77.6	2.2	79.3	2.2	80.5	1.5	82.1	2.0	82.9	1.0	84.7	2.2	85.3	0.7	85.5	0.2	85.8	0.4	85.7	-0.1	85.9	0.2	86.8	1.0
1981	87.7	1.0	88.8	1.3	90.2	1.6	91.7	1.7	91.8	0.1	94.0	2.4	95.2	1.3	96.5	1.4	97.8	1.3	97.4	-0.4	97.1	-0.3	96.6	-0.5
1982	97.2	0.6	96.9	-0.3	96.4	-0.5	96.0	-0.4	96.2	0.2	98.6	2.5	98.7	0.1	98.5	-0.2	99.2	0.7	97.9	-1.3	98.6	0.7	97.5	-1.1
1983	97.3	-0.2	97.3	0.0	97.4	0.1	97.1	-0.3	97.6	0.5	98.2	0.6	99.4	1.2	99.1	-0.3	99.5	0.4	98.6	-0.9	99.1	0.5	99.7	0.6
1984	100.9	1.2	102.1	1.2	102.2	0.1	102.7	0.5	103.4	0.7	104.3	0.9	104.3	0.0	104.6	0.3	105.4	0.8	105.4	0.0	106.8	1.3	105.8	-0.9
1985	106.0	0.2	107.2	1.1	107.3	0.1	108.2	0.8	109.6	1.3	109.9	0.3	110.2	0.3	110.3	0.1	109.6	-0.6	109.5	-0.1	110.6	1.0	111.5	0.8
1986	111.5	0.0	111.7	0.2	111.2	-0.4	111.5	0.3	111.7	0.2	113.8	1.9	113.7	-0.1	114.1	0.4	114.9	0.7	113.5	-1.2	113.3	-0.2	113.5	0.2
1987	113.5	0.0	114.9	1.2	115.0	0.1	116.2	1.0	118.4	1.9	120.6	1.9	120.1	-0.4	121.4	1.1	120.8	-0.5	120.7	-0.1	119.2	-1.2	120.0	0.7
1988	120.4	0.3	120.5	0.1	120.7	0.2	121.5	0.7	122.3	0.7	125.2	2.4	126.5	1.0	128.0	1.2	129.1	0.9	126.2	-2.2	128.2	1.6	128.6	0.3
1989	127.6	-0.8	127.2	-0.3	128.9	1.3	128.4	-0.4	129.5	0.9	131.3	1.4	132.4	0.8	132.7	0.2	134.2	1.1	132.9	-1.0	131.9	-0.8	132.7	0.6
1990	134.5	1.4	134.6	0.1	136.2	1.2	136.8	0.4	136.9	0.1	138.4	1.1	139.9	1.1	141.4	1.1	141.7	0.2	141.1	-0.4	141.1	0.0	141.3	0.1
1991	143.2	1.3	143.4	0.1	144.5	0.8	143.4	-0.8	144.2	0.6	146.2	1.4	147.8	1.1	148.1	0.2	147.9	-0.1	145.7	-1.5	145.0	-0.5	147.2	1.5
1992	147.9	0.5	148.0	0.1	148.5	0.3	147.3	-0.8	147.4	0.1	151.8	3.0	151.0	-0.5	152.2	0.8	151.8	-0.3	151.0	-0.5	149.1	-1.3	148.9	-0.1
1993	148.9	0.0	151.5	1.7	152.6	0.7	151.7	-0.6	150.3	-0.9	152.8	1.7	152.6	-0.1	153.1	0.3	153.2	0.1	153.1	-0.1	151.6	-1.0	151.6	0.0
1994	152.7	0.7	153.5	0.5	154.2	0.5	152.6	-1.0	153.1	0.3	156.1	2.0	156.6	0.3	157.3	0.4	157.4	0.1	157.0	-0.3	156.4	-0.4	154.0	-1.5
1995	155.5	1.0	156.9	0.9	157.3	0.3	156.8	-0.3	157.0	0.1	158.3	0.8	160.2	1.2	160.1	-0.1	160.3	0.1	160.2	-0.1	158.6	-1.0	159.0	0.3
1996	160.6	1.0	161.3	0.4	162.1	0.5	162.1	0.0	160.3	-1.1	161.3	0.6	163.0	1.1	163.6	0.4	164.6	0.6	164.4	-0.1	162.3	-1.3	162.9	0.4
1997	164.2	0.8	166.7	1.5	166.6	-0.1	166.7	0.1	166.5	-0.1	167.9	0.8	168.8	0.5	169.1	0.2	170.2	0.7	168.6	-0.9	166.0	-1.5	166.6	0.4
1998	-	-	168.5	1.1	-	-	168.6	0.1	-	-	170.4	1.1	-	-	170.8	0.2	-	-	172.7	1.1	-	-	170.4	-1.3
1999	-	-	170.7	0.2	-	-	171.7	0.6	-	-	173.8	1.2	-	-	173.8	0.0	-	-	173.8	0.0	-	-	171.7	-1.2
2000	-	-	174.7	1.7	-	-	175.0	0.2	-	-	177.7	1.5	-	-	178.2	0.3	-	-	179.1	0.5	-	-	178.1	-0.6
2001	-	-	182.0	2.2	-	-	183.0	0.5	-	-	184.8	1.0	-	-	185.1	0.2	-	-	184.5	-0.3	-	-	181.5	-1.6

Source: U.S. Department of Labor, Bureau of Labor Statistics, Division of Consumer Prices and Price Indexes. - indicates no data collected for period.

Philadelphia-Wilmington-Atlantic City, PA-NJ-DE-MD
Consumer Price Index - Urban Wage Earners
Base 1982-1984 = 100
Housing

For 1976-2001. Columns headed % show percentile change in the index from the previous period for which an index is available.

Year	Jan Index	%	Feb Index	%	Mar Index	%	Apr Index	%	May Index	%	Jun Index	%	Jul Index	%	Aug Index	%	Sep Index	%	Oct Index	%	Nov Index	%	Dec Index	%
1976	57.6	-	58.0	0.7	58.1	0.2	58.3	0.3	58.5	0.3	58.5	0.0	58.8	0.5	58.9	0.2	59.8	1.5	60.0	0.3	60.3	0.5	60.4	0.2
1977	60.6	0.3	60.9	0.5	61.5	1.0	62.0	0.8	62.4	0.6	62.6	0.3	62.8	0.3	63.2	0.6	64.0	1.3	63.9	-0.2	63.8	-0.2	63.3	-0.8
1978	63.5	0.3	63.5	0.0	63.9	0.6	64.4	0.8	64.4	0.0	64.7	0.5	65.6	1.4	66.1	0.8	66.8	1.1	67.1	0.4	67.5	0.6	68.1	0.9
1979	67.9	-0.3	68.1	0.3	67.9	-0.3	69.0	1.6	70.1	1.6	71.7	2.3	72.3	0.8	72.9	0.8	73.8	1.2	73.9	0.1	75.0	1.5	75.3	0.4
1980	76.9	2.1	78.1	1.6	79.4	1.7	81.0	2.0	81.5	0.6	83.4	2.3	84.1	0.8	84.5	0.5	84.5	0.0	84.4	-0.1	84.9	0.6	85.7	0.9
1981	86.7	1.2	87.5	0.9	88.3	0.9	89.8	1.7	90.4	0.7	92.1	1.9	93.5	1.5	94.7	1.3	96.0	1.4	95.8	-0.2	95.3	-0.5	94.4	-0.9
1982	95.0	0.6	94.8	-0.2	94.2	-0.6	93.9	-0.3	94.1	0.2	96.6	2.7	96.6	0.0	96.4	-0.2	97.1	0.7	95.9	-1.2	96.7	0.8	95.6	-1.1
1983	96.4	0.8	97.3	0.9	98.4	1.1	98.6	0.2	97.8	-0.8	99.0	1.2	100.4	1.4	100.7	0.3	100.7	0.0	100.2	-0.5	100.9	0.7	100.9	0.0
1984	101.8	0.9	102.7	0.9	102.4	-0.3	102.1	-0.3	103.6	1.5	105.2	1.5	105.4	0.2	106.0	0.6	108.2	2.1	108.7	0.5	108.7	0.0	107.5	-1.1
1985	107.7	0.2	109.0	1.2	109.0	0.0	109.9	0.8	111.3	1.3	111.6	0.3	111.8	0.2	111.9	0.1	111.2	-0.6	111.2	0.0	112.3	1.0	113.2	0.8
1986	113.2	0.0	113.4	0.2	112.9	-0.4	113.3	0.4	113.4	0.1	115.5	1.9	115.3	-0.2	115.7	0.3	116.5	0.7	115.1	-1.2	115.0	-0.1	115.2	0.2
1987	115.2	0.0	116.4	1.0	116.5	0.1	117.5	0.9	119.8	2.0	122.2	2.0	121.7	-0.4	123.0	1.1	122.4	-0.5	122.3	-0.1	120.9	-1.1	121.9	0.8
1988	122.2	0.2	122.0	-0.2	122.2	0.2	122.9	0.6	123.8	0.7	126.8	2.4	128.2	1.1	129.5	1.0	130.7	0.9	127.8	-2.2	129.8	1.6	130.2	0.3
1989	129.6	-0.5	129.1	-0.4	130.8	1.3	130.5	-0.2	131.7	0.9	133.5	1.4	134.7	0.9	135.1	0.3	136.6	1.1	135.0	-1.2	134.1	-0.7	134.9	0.6
1990	136.5	1.2	136.7	0.1	138.3	1.2	138.8	0.4	139.0	0.1	140.7	1.2	141.9	0.9	143.2	0.9	143.8	0.4	143.0	-0.6	143.1	0.1	143.3	0.1
1991	144.7	1.0	145.0	0.2	146.1	0.8	145.2	-0.6	146.2	0.7	148.3	1.4	149.8	1.0	150.1	0.2	150.1	0.0	147.8	-1.5	147.0	-0.5	149.2	1.5
1992	149.6	0.3	149.6	0.0	150.1	0.3	149.1	-0.7	149.3	0.1	153.7	2.9	152.8	-0.6	154.0	0.8	153.6	-0.3	152.3	-0.8	150.9	-0.9	150.9	0.0
1993	150.7	-0.1	153.1	1.6	154.2	0.7	153.7	-0.3	152.3	-0.9	154.8	1.6	154.5	-0.2	155.1	0.4	155.3	0.1	154.8	-0.3	153.7	-0.7	153.7	0.0
1994	154.5	0.5	155.2	0.5	155.8	0.4	154.6	-0.8	155.1	0.3	158.0	1.9	158.4	0.3	159.0	0.4	159.3	0.2	158.6	-0.4	158.0	-0.4	156.3	-1.1
1995	157.4	0.7	158.7	0.8	159.1	0.3	158.6	-0.3	158.9	0.2	160.4	0.9	162.1	1.1	162.0	-0.1	162.2	0.1	161.8	-0.2	160.8	-0.6	161.1	0.2
1996	162.4	0.8	163.0	0.4	163.7	0.4	163.6	-0.1	162.2	-0.9	163.3	0.7	164.8	0.9	165.3	0.3	166.1	0.5	165.7	-0.2	164.3	-0.8	165.0	0.4
1997	165.9	0.5	168.1	1.3	168.0	-0.1	168.1	0.1	167.9	-0.1	169.5	1.0	170.3	0.5	170.6	0.2	171.6	0.6	169.9	-1.0	168.0	-1.1	168.6	0.4
1998	-	-	170.3	1.0	-	-	170.7	0.2	-	-	172.7	1.2	-	-	173.1	0.2	-	-	174.0	0.5	-	-	172.8	-0.7
1999	-	-	172.7	-0.1	-	-	173.6	0.5	-	-	175.9	1.3	-	-	175.7	-0.1	-	-	175.3	-0.2	-	-	173.8	-0.9
2000	-	-	176.7	1.7	-	-	177.1	0.2	-	-	179.5	1.4	-	-	180.1	0.3	-	-	180.9	0.4	-	-	180.4	-0.3
2001	-	-	183.9	1.9	-	-	185.0	0.6	-	-	187.0	1.1	-	-	187.5	0.3	-	-	186.6	-0.5	-	-	183.8	-1.5

Source: U.S. Department of Labor, Bureau of Labor Statistics, Division of Consumer Prices and Price Indexes. - indicates no data collected for period.

Philadelphia-Wilmington-Atlantic City, PA-NJ-DE-MD
Consumer Price Index - All Urban Consumers
Base 1982-1984 = 100
Apparel

For 1952-2001. Columns headed % show percentile change in the index from the previous period for which an index is available.

Year	Jan Index	%	Feb Index	%	Mar Index	%	Apr Index	%	May Index	%	Jun Index	%	Jul Index	%	Aug Index	%	Sep Index	%	Oct Index	%	Nov Index	%	Dec Index	%
1952	-	-	-	-	-	-	-	-	-	-	-	-	-	-	-	-	-	-	-	-	-	-	44.2	-
1953	43.8	-0.9	44.0	0.5	44.1	0.2	43.8	-0.7	44.0	0.5	44.0	0.0	44.0	0.0	44.0	0.0	44.9	2.0	44.9	0.0	45.0	0.2	45.0	0.0
1954	44.7	-0.7	44.6	-0.2	44.5	-0.2	44.5	0.0	44.3	-0.4	44.3	0.0	44.4	0.2	44.5	0.2	44.7	0.4	44.8	0.2	44.9	0.2	44.7	-0.4
1955	44.6	-0.2	44.6	0.0	44.2	-0.9	44.1	-0.2	44.0	-0.2	44.0	0.0	43.8	-0.5	44.0	0.5	44.6	1.4	44.6	0.0	45.0	0.9	44.9	-0.2
1956	43.9	-2.2	44.3	0.9	44.4	0.2	44.4	0.0	44.4	0.0	44.4	0.0	44.5	0.2	44.5	0.0	45.9	3.1	45.6	-0.7	45.8	0.4	45.9	0.2
1957	45.4	-1.1	45.9	1.1	46.1	0.4	45.7	-0.9	45.4	-0.7	45.4	0.0	45.9	1.1	45.9	0.0	46.5	1.3	46.7	0.4	46.6	-0.2	46.2	-0.9
1958	45.2	-2.2	45.2	0.0	45.4	0.4	45.2	-0.4	45.5	0.7	45.4	-0.2	44.9	-1.1	45.1	0.4	46.5	3.1	46.4	-0.2	46.4	0.0	46.4	0.0
1959	45.3	-2.4	45.4	0.2	45.6	0.4	45.6	0.0	45.6	0.0	45.7	0.2	45.9	0.4	46.0	0.2	47.6	3.5	47.7	0.2	47.6	-0.2	47.5	-0.2
1960	46.9	-1.3	47.2	0.6	47.6	0.8	47.6	0.0	47.6	0.0	47.4	-0.4	47.6	0.4	47.6	0.0	48.9	2.7	49.2	0.6	49.2	0.0	49.4	0.4
1961	48.9	-1.0	48.8	-0.2	49.0	0.4	48.8	-0.4	48.6	-0.4	48.6	0.0	48.6	0.0	48.6	0.0	49.7	2.3	50.0	0.6	49.9	-0.2	50.0	0.2
1962	48.8	-2.4	48.9	0.2	49.0	0.2	49.2	0.4	49.2	0.0	49.3	0.2	49.2	-0.2	49.4	0.4	50.4	2.0	50.4	0.0	50.5	0.2	50.3	-0.4
1963	49.9	-0.8	49.9	0.0	50.1	0.4	50.2	0.2	49.8	-0.8	50.0	0.4	50.1	0.2	49.8	-0.6	50.6	1.6	50.8	0.4	50.8	0.0	50.8	0.0
1964	50.1	-1.4	50.2	0.2	50.2	0.0	50.3	0.2	50.1	-0.4	50.0	-0.2	49.7	-0.6	49.8	0.2	50.7	1.8	51.1	0.8	51.2	0.2	51.1	-0.2
1965	50.4	-1.4	50.6	0.4	50.7	0.2	50.6	-0.2	51.1	1.0	51.0	-0.2	50.3	-1.4	50.6	0.6	51.4	1.6	51.7	0.6	51.8	0.2	51.8	0.0
1966	51.0	-1.5	51.6	1.2	52.2	1.2	52.4	0.4	52.5	0.2	52.5	0.0	52.8	0.6	52.4	-0.8	54.1	3.2	54.0	-0.2	54.4	0.7	54.6	0.4
1967	53.5	-2.0	53.9	0.7	54.4	0.9	55.0	1.1	55.3	0.5	55.4	0.2	54.9	-0.9	55.0	0.2	56.3	2.4	56.5	0.4	56.6	0.2	56.6	0.0
1968	56.0	-1.1	56.8	1.4	57.4	1.1	57.9	0.9	58.1	0.3	58.0	-0.2	57.9	-0.2	57.9	0.0	59.8	3.3	60.5	1.2	60.4	-0.2	60.6	0.3
1969	59.6	-1.7	60.3	1.2	61.2	1.5	61.2	0.0	60.9	-0.5	60.6	-0.5	60.1	-0.8	60.6	0.8	62.8	3.6	63.1	0.5	63.3	0.3	63.2	-0.2
1970	62.7	-0.8	63.3	1.0	64.0	1.1	63.1	-1.4	63.3	0.3	63.4	0.2	62.2	-1.9	62.8	1.0	65.5	4.3	66.3	1.2	66.2	-0.2	65.5	-1.1
1971	63.9	-2.4	64.7	1.3	65.4	1.1	66.8	2.1	67.0	0.3	66.9	-0.1	65.0	-2.8	64.6	-0.6	66.9	3.6	67.2	0.4	66.7	-0.7	66.4	-0.4
1972	64.7	-2.6	64.2	-0.8	66.3	3.3	66.7	0.6	66.4	-0.4	66.4	0.0	65.1	-2.0	64.9	-0.3	67.8	4.5	68.1	0.4	67.9	-0.3	67.8	-0.1
1973	66.0	-2.7	67.8	2.7	69.2	2.1	69.4	0.3	69.4	0.0	69.3	-0.1	67.6	-2.5	67.5	-0.1	69.6	3.1	70.6	1.4	70.7	0.1	70.7	0.0
1974	68.6	-3.0	70.7	3.1	72.0	1.8	72.0	0.0	72.1	0.1	73.0	1.2	71.7	-1.8	73.3	2.2	75.2	2.6	75.8	0.8	76.6	1.1	76.0	-0.8
1975	74.2	-2.4	74.5	0.4	74.9	0.5	75.0	0.1	74.7	-0.4	74.3	-0.5	73.4	-1.2	75.2	2.5	76.1	1.2	76.1	0.0	76.8	0.9	76.6	-0.3
1976	74.8	-2.3	75.8	1.3	76.3	0.7	76.4	0.1	76.9	0.7	77.1	0.3	76.2	-1.2	76.8	0.8	78.4	2.1	78.9	0.6	79.2	0.4	78.7	-0.6
1977	77.8	-1.1	77.9	0.1	78.7	1.0	78.8	0.1	78.4	-0.5	78.3	-0.1	78.7	0.5	79.6	1.1	79.9	0.4	80.6	0.9	80.6	0.0	80.2	-0.5
1978	77.9	-2.9	76.1	-2.3	78.0	2.5	79.1	1.4	79.9	1.0	81.4	1.9	83.2	2.2	82.1	-1.3	82.4	0.4	83.6	1.5	83.9	0.4	82.7	-1.4
1979	81.9	-1.0	86.1	5.1	85.3	-0.9	85.5	0.2	85.3	-0.2	85.0	-0.4	83.9	-1.3	87.1	3.8	88.6	1.7	86.6	-2.3	89.0	2.8	89.6	0.7
1980	88.2	-1.6	92.6	5.0	96.7	4.4	96.5	-0.2	95.5	-1.0	93.4	-2.2	93.9	0.5	96.0	2.2	95.2	-0.8	96.9	1.8	95.2	-1.8	93.1	-2.2
1981	92.6	-0.5	92.6	0.0	95.4	3.0	95.4	0.0	95.1	-0.3	95.1	0.0	90.2	-5.2	97.7	8.3	100.4	2.8	100.4	0.0	98.2	-2.2	98.0	-0.2
1982	96.4	-1.6	95.7	-0.7	96.6	0.9	98.6	2.1	97.0	-1.6	98.9	2.0	97.5	-1.4	98.8	1.3	102.8	4.0	102.8	0.0	101.2	-1.6	99.3	-1.9
1983	97.6	-1.7	98.2	0.6	100.6	2.4	100.4	-0.2	98.1	-2.3	99.5	1.4	99.3	-0.2	101.8	2.5	102.7	0.9	103.7	1.0	102.4	-1.3	99.5	-2.8
1984	100.0	0.5	99.2	-0.8	99.2	0.0	100.5	1.3	99.0	-1.5	97.6	-1.4	99.0	1.4	102.4	3.4	103.8	1.4	104.3	0.5	103.1	-1.2	102.4	-0.7
1985	99.6	-2.7	100.3	0.7	101.1	0.8	103.3	2.2	102.4	-0.9	100.2	-2.1	100.0	-0.2	102.7	2.7	101.9	-0.8	101.8	-0.1	103.3	1.5	100.6	-2.6
1986	100.2	-0.4	100.0	-0.2	100.4	0.4	99.7	-0.7	100.0	0.3	97.1	-2.9	100.6	3.6	102.1	1.5	104.8	2.6	104.4	-0.4	103.5	-0.9	102.8	-0.7
1987	104.7	1.8	103.5	-1.1	104.3	0.8	110.6	6.0	106.6	-3.6	103.7	-2.7	102.0	-1.6	110.3	8.1	111.3	0.9	112.4	1.0	113.0	0.5	110.3	-2.4
1988	109.1	-1.1	106.9	-2.0	112.7	5.4	107.9	-4.3	109.2	1.2	104.6	-4.2	108.7	3.9	108.9	0.2	112.7	3.5	113.7	0.9	113.8	0.1	110.3	-3.1
1989	111.3	0.9	108.9	-2.2	101.0	-7.3	102.7	1.7	102.8	0.1	98.4	-4.3	96.4	-2.0	91.8	-4.8	93.4	1.7	97.8	4.7	95.8	-2.0	92.0	-4.0
1990	87.8	-4.6	94.4	7.5	101.4	7.4	107.1	5.6	108.7	1.5	102.8	-5.4	100.4	-2.3	100.7	0.3	105.9	5.2	105.1	-0.8	101.9	-3.0	100.6	-1.3
1991	103.0	2.4	103.1	0.1	106.6	3.4	105.5	-1.0	106.0	0.5	98.9	-6.7	92.8	-6.2	100.3	8.1	107.6	7.3	104.1	-3.3	108.4	4.1	108.6	0.2
1992	104.9	-3.4	100.5	-4.2	107.1	6.6	110.4	3.1	110.9	0.5	105.8	-4.6	103.6	-2.1	107.4	3.7	107.0	-0.4	107.0	0.0	108.8	1.7	104.0	-4.4
1993	103.2	-0.8	107.5	4.2	105.7	-1.7	108.8	2.9	101.0	-7.2	105.6	4.6	106.9	1.2	108.4	1.4	105.3	-2.9	111.8	6.2	108.6	-2.9	99.5	-8.4
1994	103.5	4.0	106.1	2.5	107.1	0.9	107.0	-0.1	107.8	0.7	105.4	-2.2	107.8	2.3	105.3	-2.3	105.2	-0.1	108.0	2.7	106.3	-1.6	99.8	-6.1
1995	101.4	1.6	107.7	6.2	107.0	-0.6	103.3	-3.5	99.8	-3.4	98.1	-1.7	95.4	-2.8	102.9	7.9	104.2	1.3	104.4	0.2	104.1	-0.3	96.7	-7.1
1996	97.5	0.8	101.2	3.8	106.9	5.6	105.3	-1.5	104.6	-0.7	101.2	-3.3	98.1	-3.1	102.2	4.2	105.2	2.9	110.8	5.3	108.9	-1.7	103.7	-4.8
1997	101.2	-2.4	101.2	0.0	104.4	3.2	104.8	0.4	102.9	-1.8	100.6	-2.2	99.5	-1.1	102.5	3.0	115.1	12.3	108.1	-6.1	104.9	-3.0	102.7	-2.1

[Continued]

Philadelphia-Wilmington-Atlantic City, PA-NJ-DE-MD
Consumer Price Index - All Urban Consumers
Base 1982-1984 = 100
Apparel

[Continued]

For 1952-2001. Columns headed % show percentile change in the index from the previous period for which an index is available.

Year	Jan		Feb		Mar		Apr		May		Jun		Jul		Aug		Sep		Oct		Nov		Dec	
	Index	%	Index	%	Index	%	Index	%	Index	%	Index	%	Index	%	Index	%	Index	%	Index	%	Index	%	Index	%
1998	-	-	104.2	1.5	-	-	107.6	3.3	-	-	103.2	-4.1	-	-	106.7	3.4	-	-	111.7	4.7	-	-	103.9	-7.0
1999	-	-	101.7	-2.1	-	-	109.6	7.8	-	-	108.2	-1.3	-	-	109.4	1.1	-	-	112.5	2.8	-	-	103.8	-7.7
2000	-	-	102.0	-1.7	-	-	108.5	6.4	-	-	101.6	-6.4	-	-	100.1	-1.5	-	-	103.0	2.9	-	-	99.6	-3.3
2001	-	-	94.3	-5.3	-	-	104.3	10.6	-	-	96.1	-7.9	-	-	100.2	4.3	-	-	106.0	5.8	-	-	97.9	-7.6

Source: U.S. Department of Labor, Bureau of Labor Statistics, Division of Consumer Prices and Price Indexes. - indicates no data collected for period.

Philadelphia-Wilmington-Atlantic City, PA-NJ-DE-MD
Consumer Price Index - Urban Wage Earners
Base 1982-1984 = 100
Apparel

For 1952-2001. Columns headed % show percentile change in the index from the previous period for which an index is available.

Year	Jan Index	%	Feb Index	%	Mar Index	%	Apr Index	%	May Index	%	Jun Index	%	Jul Index	%	Aug Index	%	Sep Index	%	Oct Index	%	Nov Index	%	Dec Index	%
1952	-	-	-	-	-	-	-	-	-	-	-	-	-	-	-	-	-	-	-	-	-	-	51.0	-
1953	50.5	-1.0	50.8	0.6	50.9	0.2	50.5	-0.8	50.8	0.6	50.8	0.0	50.8	0.0	50.8	0.0	51.8	2.0	51.8	0.0	51.9	0.2	51.9	0.0
1954	51.6	-0.6	51.5	-0.2	51.4	-0.2	51.4	0.0	51.1	-0.6	51.1	0.0	51.3	0.4	51.4	0.2	51.6	0.4	51.7	0.2	51.8	0.2	51.6	-0.4
1955	51.5	-0.2	51.5	0.0	51.0	-1.0	50.9	-0.2	50.8	-0.2	50.8	0.0	50.5	-0.6	50.8	0.6	51.5	1.4	51.5	0.0	52.0	1.0	51.8	-0.4
1956	50.7	-2.1	51.1	0.8	51.2	0.2	51.3	0.2	51.2	-0.2	51.2	0.0	51.3	0.2	51.4	0.2	52.9	2.9	52.7	-0.4	52.9	0.4	52.9	0.0
1957	52.3	-1.1	52.9	1.1	53.2	0.6	52.8	-0.8	52.3	-0.9	52.3	0.0	53.0	1.3	52.0	-0.2	53.6	1.3	53.9	0.6	53.8	-0.2	53.4	-0.7
1958	52.2	-2.2	52.2	0.0	52.3	0.2	52.2	-0.2	52.5	0.6	52.3	-0.4	51.8	-1.0	52.0	0.4	53.7	3.3	53.5	-0.4	53.6	0.2	53.5	-0.2
1959	52.3	-2.2	52.4	0.2	52.7	0.6	52.7	0.0	52.7	0.0	52.8	0.2	53.0	0.4	53.0	0.0	55.0	3.8	55.0	0.0	55.0	0.0	54.8	-0.4
1960	54.1	-1.3	54.5	0.7	54.9	0.7	54.9	0.0	54.9	0.0	54.7	-0.4	54.9	0.4	55.0	0.2	56.4	2.5	56.8	0.7	56.8	0.0	57.1	0.5
1961	56.4	-1.2	56.3	-0.2	56.6	0.5	56.3	-0.5	56.1	-0.4	56.1	0.0	56.0	-0.2	56.1	0.2	57.3	2.1	57.7	0.7	57.6	-0.2	57.7	0.2
1962	56.3	-2.4	56.4	0.2	56.6	0.4	56.8	0.4	56.8	0.0	56.9	0.2	56.8	-0.2	57.1	0.5	58.2	1.9	58.2	0.0	58.3	0.2	58.0	-0.5
1963	57.6	-0.7	57.6	0.0	57.8	0.3	57.9	0.2	57.5	-0.7	57.7	0.3	57.8	0.2	57.5	-0.5	58.3	1.4	58.7	0.7	58.6	-0.2	58.6	0.0
1964	57.8	-1.4	58.0	0.3	57.9	-0.2	58.0	0.2	57.8	-0.3	57.7	-0.2	57.4	-0.5	57.5	0.2	58.5	1.7	58.9	0.7	59.0	0.2	59.0	0.0
1965	58.2	-1.4	58.3	0.2	58.5	0.3	58.3	-0.3	58.9	1.0	58.9	0.0	58.0	-1.5	58.3	0.5	59.3	1.7	59.6	0.5	59.8	0.3	59.8	0.0
1966	58.9	-1.5	59.6	1.2	60.2	1.0	60.5	0.5	60.6	0.2	60.6	0.0	61.0	0.7	60.5	-0.8	62.4	3.1	62.4	0.0	62.8	0.6	63.1	0.5
1967	61.8	-2.1	62.2	0.6	62.8	1.0	63.5	1.1	63.8	0.5	64.0	0.3	63.3	-1.1	63.5	0.3	64.9	2.2	65.2	0.5	65.3	0.0	65.3	0.0
1968	64.6	-1.1	65.6	1.5	66.2	0.9	66.8	0.9	67.1	0.4	67.0	-0.1	66.8	-0.3	66.8	0.0	69.1	3.4	69.8	1.0	69.7	-0.1	69.9	0.3
1969	68.8	-1.6	69.6	1.2	70.7	1.6	70.6	-0.1	70.3	-0.4	70.0	-0.4	69.3	-1.0	70.0	1.0	72.5	3.6	72.8	0.4	73.1	0.4	73.0	-0.1
1970	72.3	-1.0	73.1	1.1	73.9	1.1	72.8	-1.5	73.1	0.4	73.2	0.1	71.8	-1.9	72.5	1.0	75.6	4.3	76.5	1.2	76.4	-0.1	75.6	-1.0
1971	73.8	-2.4	74.7	1.2	75.5	1.1	77.1	2.1	77.4	0.4	77.2	-0.3	75.0	-2.8	74.5	-0.7	77.2	3.6	77.5	0.4	76.9	-0.8	76.6	-0.4
1972	74.6	-2.6	74.1	-0.7	76.5	3.2	76.9	0.5	76.7	-0.3	76.6	-0.1	75.1	-2.0	74.9	-0.3	78.2	4.4	78.6	0.5	78.4	-0.3	78.2	-0.3
1973	76.2	-2.6	78.2	2.6	79.9	2.2	80.1	0.3	80.1	0.0	79.9	-0.2	78.0	-2.4	77.9	-0.1	80.4	3.2	81.5	1.4	81.6	0.1	81.6	0.0
1974	79.2	-2.9	81.6	3.0	83.1	1.8	83.1	0.0	83.2	0.1	84.2	1.2	82.8	-1.7	84.6	2.2	86.8	2.6	87.5	0.8	88.4	1.0	87.7	-0.8
1975	85.6	-2.4	86.0	0.5	86.4	0.5	86.6	0.2	86.2	-0.5	85.7	-0.6	84.7	-1.2	86.8	2.5	87.8	1.2	87.8	0.0	88.6	0.9	88.4	-0.2
1976	86.3	-2.4	87.5	1.4	88.1	0.7	88.2	0.1	88.8	0.7	88.9	0.1	87.9	-1.1	88.7	0.9	90.5	2.0	91.1	0.7	91.4	0.3	90.8	-0.7
1977	89.8	-1.1	89.9	0.1	90.8	1.0	91.0	0.2	90.5	-0.5	90.3	-0.2	90.8	0.6	91.9	1.2	92.2	0.3	93.0	0.9	93.1	0.1	92.6	-0.5
1978	89.1	-3.8	87.2	-2.1	87.5	0.3	91.4	4.5	92.2	0.9	92.6	0.4	88.2	-4.8	90.2	2.3	90.7	0.6	91.7	1.1	92.8	1.2	91.7	-1.2
1979	90.7	-1.1	90.8	0.1	89.4	-1.5	88.6	-0.9	88.6	0.0	89.2	0.7	87.2	-2.2	87.9	0.8	89.1	1.4	89.1	0.0	90.3	1.3	91.4	1.2
1980	90.5	-1.0	93.8	3.6	94.4	0.6	94.9	0.5	94.2	-0.7	93.1	-1.2	93.0	-0.1	94.6	1.7	96.6	2.1	96.9	0.3	95.9	-1.0	94.5	-1.5
1981	93.6	-1.0	95.1	1.6	94.3	-0.8	94.7	0.4	94.6	-0.1	95.3	0.7	91.4	-4.1	99.3	8.6	100.7	1.4	99.6	-1.1	99.6	0.0	96.6	-3.0
1982	96.4	-0.2	95.8	-0.6	98.1	2.4	99.5	1.4	98.3	-1.2	99.3	1.0	98.2	-1.1	97.9	-0.3	101.8	4.0	102.1	0.3	100.5	-1.6	98.1	-2.4
1983	96.3	-1.8	97.0	0.7	102.5	5.7	101.3	-1.2	99.3	-2.0	100.2	0.9	99.9	-0.3	101.0	1.1	102.3	1.3	103.0	0.7	101.4	-1.6	98.5	-2.9
1984	99.2	0.7	98.3	-0.9	100.4	2.1	100.9	0.5	98.9	-2.0	97.5	-1.4	99.6	2.2	102.7	3.1	104.4	1.7	104.3	-0.1	103.0	-1.2	101.9	-1.1
1985	99.1	-2.7	100.3	1.2	100.3	0.0	102.3	2.0	101.6	-0.7	99.8	-1.8	99.3	-0.5	100.9	1.6	100.2	-0.7	100.5	0.3	101.8	1.3	99.5	-2.3
1986	98.9	-0.6	99.3	0.4	99.7	0.4	98.7	-1.0	98.4	-0.3	96.1	-2.3	98.4	2.4	100.3	1.9	101.2	0.9	102.6	1.4	101.9	-0.7	101.3	-0.6
1987	101.5	0.2	99.5	-2.0	100.6	1.1	106.9	6.3	103.3	-3.4	100.2	-3.0	99.4	-0.8	106.7	7.3	106.9	0.2	109.8	2.7	110.0	0.2	108.3	-1.5
1988	106.1	-2.0	103.1	-2.8	110.3	7.0	104.8	-5.0	106.8	1.9	101.0	-5.4	103.9	2.9	103.4	-0.5	108.3	4.7	109.2	0.8	109.5	0.3	105.0	-4.1
1989	106.3	1.2	104.2	-2.0	95.2	-8.6	98.0	2.9	97.7	-0.3	93.2	-4.6	90.2	-3.2	87.2	-3.3	88.6	1.6	94.0	6.1	91.7	-2.4	88.0	-4.0
1990	82.6	-6.1	88.7	7.4	98.4	10.9	104.1	5.8	106.3	2.1	99.8	-6.1	96.9	-2.9	95.7	-1.2	101.3	5.9	100.2	-1.1	98.0	-2.2	99.2	1.2
1991	99.8	0.6	99.2	-0.6	102.2	3.0	101.5	-0.7	98.9	-2.6	93.1	-5.9	88.5	-4.9	95.0	7.3	101.1	6.4	98.1	-3.0	105.2	7.2	105.7	0.5
1992	101.5	-4.0	97.5	-3.9	104.1	6.8	107.7	3.5	105.9	-1.7	103.1	-2.6	101.0	-2.0	103.2	2.2	102.6	-0.6	104.0	1.4	107.4	3.3	101.9	-5.1
1993	101.4	-0.5	106.9	5.4	103.4	-3.3	107.5	4.0	99.9	-7.1	103.5	3.6	105.5	1.9	105.9	0.4	103.3	-2.5	110.7	7.2	108.4	-2.1	99.6	-8.1
1994	101.4	1.8	103.1	1.7	103.0	-0.1	103.0	0.0	102.4	-0.6	101.7	-0.7	103.9	2.2	102.3	-1.5	101.7	-0.6	103.4	1.7	101.2	-2.1	95.2	-5.9
1995	97.4	2.3	104.4	7.2	103.2	-1.1	99.6	-3.5	95.4	-4.2	94.0	-1.5	91.5	-2.7	98.9	8.1	100.5	1.6	100.0	-0.5	100.1	0.1	92.5	-7.6
1996	93.2	0.8	96.7	3.8	102.8	6.3	100.6	-2.1	100.1	-0.5	96.8	-3.3	94.2	-2.7	99.8	5.9	101.6	1.8	108.9	7.2	106.6	-2.1	100.4	-5.8
1997	97.4	-3.0	98.1	0.7	101.1	3.1	101.2	0.1	99.9	-1.3	97.5	-2.4	96.4	-1.1	99.3	3.0	113.1	13.9	106.8	-5.6	103.2	-3.4	100.0	-3.1

[Continued]

Philadelphia-Wilmington-Atlantic City, PA-NJ-DE-MD
Consumer Price Index - Urban Wage Earners
Base 1982-1984 = 100
Apparel
[Continued]

For 1952-2001. Columns headed % show percentile change in the index from the previous period for which an index is available.

Year	Jan Index	%	Feb Index	%	Mar Index	%	Apr Index	%	May Index	%	Jun Index	%	Jul Index	%	Aug Index	%	Sep Index	%	Oct Index	%	Nov Index	%	Dec Index	%
1998	-	-	101.8	1.8	-	-	106.2	4.3	-	-	101.9	-4.0	-	-	104.9	2.9	-	-	110.5	5.3	-	-	102.4	-7.3
1999	-	-	99.6	-2.7	-	-	108.9	9.3	-	-	107.9	-0.9	-	-	107.8	-0.1	-	-	112.5	4.4	-	-	103.6	-7.9
2000	-	-	100.5	-3.0	-	-	107.0	6.5	-	-	99.9	-6.6	-	-	98.6	-1.3	-	-	101.6	3.0	-	-	97.2	-4.3
2001	-	-	93.0	-4.3	-	-	103.2	11.0	-	-	96.2	-6.8	-	-	100.5	4.5	-	-	105.4	4.9	-	-	96.9	-8.1

Source: U.S. Department of Labor, Bureau of Labor Statistics, Division of Consumer Prices and Price Indexes. - indicates no data collected for period.

Philadelphia-Wilmington-Atlantic City, PA-NJ-DE-MD
Consumer Price Index - All Urban Consumers
Base 1982-1984 = 100
Transportation

For 1947-2000. Columns headed % show percentile change in the index from the previous period for which an index is available.

Year	Jan Index	%	Feb Index	%	Mar Index	%	Apr Index	%	May Index	%	Jun Index	%	Jul Index	%	Aug Index	%	Sep Index	%	Oct Index	%	Nov Index	%	Dec Index	%
1947	15.6	-	15.6	0.0	16.8	7.7	16.9	0.6	16.9	0.0	16.9	0.0	16.9	0.0	17.1	1.2	17.2	0.6	17.2	0.0	17.2	0.0	17.3	0.6
1948	17.4	0.6	17.5	0.6	17.5	0.0	18.2	4.0	18.2	0.0	18.4	1.1	18.7	1.6	19.0	1.6	19.0	0.0	19.0	0.0	19.0	0.0	19.1	0.5
1949	19.2	0.5	19.3	0.5	19.3	0.0	19.3	0.0	21.1	9.3	19.4	-8.1	19.5	0.5	19.5	0.0	19.5	0.0	19.5	0.0	19.5	0.0	19.5	0.0
1950	19.5	0.0	19.5	0.0	19.5	0.0	19.4	-0.5	19.4	0.0	19.4	0.0	19.4	0.0	19.5	0.5	19.4	-0.5	19.2	-1.0	19.2	0.0	21.0	9.4
1951	21.2	1.0	23.4	10.4	23.5	0.4	23.5	0.0	23.5	0.0	23.1	-1.7	22.8	-1.3	23.0	0.9	23.0	0.0	22.8	-0.9	23.9	4.8	23.9	0.0
1952	23.9	0.0	23.2	-2.9	24.1	3.9	24.1	0.0	24.1	0.0	24.2	0.4	24.2	0.0	24.2	0.0	24.2	0.0	24.2	0.0	24.2	0.0	24.2	0.0
1953	24.3	0.4	24.2	-0.4	24.2	0.0	24.3	0.4	24.4	0.4	24.4	0.0	24.6	0.8	24.6	0.0	24.7	0.4	24.8	0.4	24.7	-0.4	24.7	0.0
1954	24.8	0.4	25.0	0.8	25.1	0.4	25.0	-0.4	25.1	0.4	25.0	-0.4	25.0	0.0	25.0	0.0	25.1	0.4	25.1	0.0	25.3	0.8	25.2	-0.4
1955	25.1	-0.4	25.2	0.4	25.1	-0.4	25.0	-0.4	25.3	1.2	25.4	0.4	25.3	-0.4	25.3	0.0	23.6	-6.7	24.1	2.1	24.7	2.5	24.5	-0.8
1956	24.8	1.2	24.7	-0.4	24.8	0.4	24.6	-0.8	24.5	-0.4	24.4	-0.4	24.7	1.2	25.0	1.2	25.0	0.0	25.1	0.4	25.6	2.0	25.7	0.4
1957	25.8	0.4	25.8	0.0	25.8	0.0	25.8	0.0	25.8	0.0	25.5	-1.2	25.4	-0.4	25.5	0.4	25.5	0.0	25.5	0.0	26.5	3.9	26.3	-0.8
1958	25.9	-1.5	25.8	-0.4	26.4	2.3	26.5	0.4	26.3	-0.8	26.3	0.0	26.5	0.8	26.7	0.8	26.8	0.4	26.7	-0.4	27.3	2.2	27.4	0.4
1959	27.6	0.7	27.4	-0.7	27.5	0.4	27.6	0.4	27.8	0.7	27.9	0.4	28.1	0.7	28.2	0.4	28.2	0.0	28.4	0.7	28.5	0.4	28.5	0.0
1960	28.5	0.0	28.5	0.0	28.4	-0.4	28.3	-0.4	28.2	-0.4	28.1	-0.4	28.0	-0.4	28.0	0.0	27.9	-0.4	28.4	1.8	28.5	0.4	28.5	0.0
1961	28.4	-0.4	28.5	0.4	28.6	0.4	29.0	1.4	29.1	0.3	29.2	0.3	29.2	0.0	29.2	0.0	29.1	-0.3	29.4	1.0	29.3	-0.3	29.0	-1.0
1962	29.0	0.0	29.0	0.0	29.0	0.0	29.3	1.0	29.1	-0.7	29.1	0.0	29.2	0.3	29.2	0.0	29.4	0.7	29.2	-0.7	29.5	1.0	29.4	-0.3
1963	28.9	-1.7	29.7	2.8	29.8	0.3	29.9	0.3	29.9	0.0	29.9	0.0	29.9	0.0	29.9	0.0	29.9	0.0	30.2	1.0	30.3	0.3	30.3	0.0
1964	30.4	0.3	30.4	0.0	30.4	0.0	30.5	0.3	30.5	0.0	30.2	-1.0	30.5	1.0	30.5	0.0	30.3	-0.7	30.5	0.7	30.8	1.0	31.0	0.6
1965	31.1	0.3	31.4	1.0	31.3	-0.3	31.4	0.3	31.6	0.6	31.4	-0.6	31.4	0.0	31.3	-0.3	31.0	-1.0	31.4	1.3	31.4	0.0	31.4	0.0
1966	31.4	0.0	31.4	0.0	31.5	0.3	31.6	0.3	31.7	0.3	31.8	0.3	31.9	0.3	32.1	0.6	31.8	-0.9	32.1	0.9	32.1	0.0	31.9	-0.6
1967	31.9	0.0	32.0	0.3	32.4	1.3	32.4	0.0	32.4	0.0	32.5	0.3	32.7	0.6	32.8	0.3	32.7	-0.3	33.0	0.9	33.3	0.9	33.3	0.0
1968	33.9	1.8	33.9	0.0	34.0	0.3	33.9	-0.3	34.1	0.6	34.2	0.3	34.4	0.6	34.5	0.3	34.4	-0.3	34.6	0.6	34.9	0.9	34.7	-0.6
1969	34.7	0.0	35.6	2.6	36.0	1.1	36.1	0.3	35.9	-0.6	36.1	0.6	36.1	0.0	35.9	-0.6	35.6	-0.8	36.2	1.7	36.3	0.3	36.3	0.0
1970	36.2	-0.3	37.1	2.5	37.1	0.0	37.6	1.3	37.9	0.8	38.1	0.5	38.1	0.0	38.0	-0.3	37.9	-0.3	38.4	1.3	38.6	0.5	39.1	1.3
1971	39.4	0.8	39.9	1.3	39.8	-0.3	40.1	0.8	40.2	0.2	40.5	0.7	40.6	0.2	40.3	-0.7	40.0	-0.7	40.2	0.5	40.3	0.2	40.4	0.2
1972	40.5	0.2	40.3	-0.5	40.4	0.2	40.4	0.0	40.9	1.2	41.0	0.2	40.9	-0.2	41.0	0.2	41.0	0.0	40.9	-0.2	41.1	0.5	41.2	0.2
1973	41.1	-0.2	41.1	0.0	41.1	0.0	41.4	0.7	41.6	0.5	41.9	0.7	41.9	0.0	41.7	-0.5	41.4	-0.7	41.9	1.2	42.0	0.2	42.5	1.2
1974	42.9	0.9	43.4	1.2	44.3	2.1	44.6	0.7	45.3	1.6	46.1	1.8	46.7	1.3	46.9	0.4	47.2	0.6	47.4	0.4	47.8	0.8	47.9	0.2
1975	47.7	-0.4	47.9	0.4	48.3	0.8	48.6	0.6	48.9	0.6	49.8	1.8	50.4	1.2	50.6	0.4	50.8	0.4	51.3	1.0	51.8	1.0	51.8	0.0
1976	51.7	-0.2	51.7	0.0	52.3	1.2	52.9	1.1	53.5	1.1	54.2	1.3	54.7	0.9	54.9	0.4	55.1	0.4	55.4	0.5	55.6	0.4	55.6	0.0
1977	56.2	1.1	56.8	1.1	57.2	0.7	58.5	2.3	60.0	2.6	60.3	0.5	60.3	0.0	60.1	-0.3	60.6	0.8	60.6	0.0	60.6	0.0	60.5	-0.2
1978	60.7	0.3	60.7	0.0	61.1	0.7	61.4	0.5	61.9	0.8	62.7	1.3	63.1	0.6	63.2	0.2	63.2	0.0	63.0	-0.3	64.2	1.9	64.4	0.3
1979	65.0	0.9	65.4	0.6	66.2	1.2	67.6	2.1	69.3	2.5	71.5	3.2	73.1	2.2	73.7	0.8	74.1	0.5	74.1	0.0	74.7	0.8	75.8	1.5
1980	77.8	2.6	79.9	2.7	81.5	2.0	82.2	0.9	83.4	1.5	83.7	0.4	83.9	0.2	85.2	1.5	85.4	0.2	85.6	0.2	86.9	1.5	87.4	0.6
1981	88.6	1.4	90.6	2.3	91.0	0.4	91.7	0.8	92.3	0.7	92.7	0.4	93.9	1.3	93.8	-0.1	94.4	0.6	95.8	1.5	96.5	0.7	97.2	0.7
1982	96.6	-0.6	95.5	-1.1	94.8	-0.7	93.9	-0.9	94.1	0.2	95.6	1.6	97.1	1.6	96.9	-0.2	96.4	-0.5	97.0	0.6	97.1	0.1	97.5	0.4
1983	98.0	0.5	96.9	-1.1	96.4	-0.5	97.6	1.2	98.4	0.8	98.5	0.1	99.1	0.6	100.7	1.6	101.3	0.6	102.0	0.7	102.4	0.4	102.1	-0.3
1984	102.8	0.7	102.7	-0.1	103.0	0.3	103.8	0.8	104.0	0.2	104.4	0.4	104.8	0.4	105.4	0.6	105.7	0.3	105.3	-0.4	106.0	0.7	106.3	0.3
1985	106.3	0.0	107.1	0.8	107.8	0.7	108.7	0.8	109.2	0.5	109.7	0.5	109.9	0.2	110.0	0.1	110.4	0.4	111.4	0.9	111.5	0.1	111.7	0.2
1986	112.1	0.4	110.9	-1.1	108.4	-2.3	104.7	-3.4	105.8	1.1	107.1	1.2	106.9	-0.2	104.8	-2.0	105.1	0.3	106.1	1.0	106.2	0.1	107.0	0.8
1987	108.5	1.4	108.4	-0.1	108.9	0.5	110.4	1.4	110.7	0.3	111.5	0.7	112.2	0.6	112.0	-0.2	112.6	0.5	113.5	0.8	114.3	0.7	114.6	0.3
1988	114.5	-0.1	114.2	-0.3	114.5	0.3	114.2	-0.3	115.1	0.8	114.8	-0.3	115.3	0.4	115.1	-0.2	115.9	0.7	117.4	1.3	117.7	0.3	117.9	0.2
1989	118.5	0.5	118.0	-0.4	118.0	0.0	120.2	1.9	122.9	2.2	123.3	0.3	123.1	-0.2	122.3	-0.6	122.5	0.2	123.4	0.7	123.0	-0.3	123.1	0.1
1990	124.9	1.5	125.6	0.6	125.2	-0.3	125.2	0.0	125.4	0.2	125.9	0.4	125.3	-0.5	125.9	0.5	128.3	1.9	132.1	3.0	133.8	1.3	134.6	0.6
1991	132.7	-1.4	131.4	-1.0	130.2	-0.9	130.0	-0.2	130.5	0.4	131.0	0.4	132.2	0.9	132.3	0.1	132.5	0.2	134.0	1.1	135.3	1.0	135.7	0.3
1992	135.1	-0.4	134.6	-0.4	134.4	-0.1	134.8	0.3	135.0	0.1	136.0	0.7	136.6	0.4	135.9	-0.5	136.1	0.1	137.0	0.7	138.3	0.9	139.4	0.8

[Continued]

Philadelphia-Wilmington-Atlantic City, PA-NJ-DE-MD
Consumer Price Index - All Urban Consumers
Base 1982-1984 = 100
Transportation
[Continued]

For 1947-2000. Columns headed % show percentile change in the index from the previous period for which an index is available.

Year	Jan Index	%	Feb Index	%	Mar Index	%	Apr Index	%	May Index	%	Jun Index	%	Jul Index	%	Aug Index	%	Sep Index	%	Oct Index	%	Nov Index	%	Dec Index	%
1993	139.2	-0.1	138.4	-0.6	138.5	0.1	137.5	-0.7	139.0	1.1	138.4	-0.4	139.4	0.7	137.4	-1.4	139.2	1.3	140.9	1.2	143.2	1.6	143.0	-0.1
1994	142.6	-0.3	142.3	-0.2	142.6	0.2	141.8	-0.6	141.6	-0.1	143.2	1.1	143.5	0.2	144.9	1.0	145.1	0.1	145.7	0.4	147.5	1.2	146.9	-0.4
1995	147.6	0.5	148.0	0.3	148.5	0.3	148.7	0.1	148.5	-0.1	149.5	0.7	148.6	-0.6	148.4	-0.1	148.9	0.3	150.1	0.8	149.1	-0.7	148.6	-0.3
1996	149.2	0.4	150.3	0.7	150.1	-0.1	150.0	-0.1	151.1	0.7	151.9	0.5	151.2	-0.5	151.2	0.0	151.9	0.5	153.2	0.9	154.1	0.6	154.3	0.1
1997	154.5	0.1	153.6	-0.6	153.6	0.0	153.0	-0.4	151.9	-0.7	152.0	0.1	151.8	-0.1	150.8	-0.7	152.2	0.9	153.8	1.1	154.0	0.1	152.9	-0.7
1998	-	-	150.3	-1.7	-	-	149.0	-0.9	-	-	148.7	-0.2	-	-	148.8	0.1	-	-	149.2	0.3	-	-	149.0	-0.1
1999	-	-	147.5	-1.0	-	-	150.5	2.0	-	-	151.1	0.4	-	-	152.9	1.2	-	-	156.5	2.4	-	-	156.5	0.0
2000	-	-	157.3	0.5	-	-	160.4	2.0	-	-	162.3	1.2	-	-	161.3	-0.6	-	-	162.3	0.6	-	-	161.6	-0.4

Source: U.S. Department of Labor, Bureau of Labor Statistics, Division of Consumer Prices and Price Indexes. - indicates no data collected for period.

Philadelphia-Wilmington-Atlantic City, PA-NJ-DE-MD
Consumer Price Index - Urban Wage Earners
Base 1982-1984 = 100
Transportation

For 1947-2000. Columns headed % show percentile change in the index from the previous period for which an index is available.

Year	Jan Index	%	Feb Index	%	Mar Index	%	Apr Index	%	May Index	%	Jun Index	%	Jul Index	%	Aug Index	%	Sep Index	%	Oct Index	%	Nov Index	%	Dec Index	%
1947	15.1	-	15.1	0.0	16.3	7.9	16.4	0.6	16.4	0.0	16.4	0.0	16.4	0.0	16.6	1.2	16.7	0.6	16.7	0.0	16.7	0.0	16.8	0.6
1948	16.9	0.6	17.0	0.6	17.0	0.0	17.7	4.1	17.7	0.0	17.9	1.1	18.1	1.1	18.4	1.7	18.5	0.5	18.5	0.0	18.4	-0.5	18.5	0.5
1949	18.6	0.5	18.7	0.5	18.7	0.0	18.8	0.5	20.5	9.0	18.9	-7.8	18.9	0.0	18.9	0.0	18.9	0.0	18.9	0.0	19.0	0.5	19.0	0.0
1950	19.0	0.0	19.0	0.0	19.0	0.0	18.8	-1.1	18.9	0.5	18.9	0.0	18.9	0.0	19.0	0.5	18.8	-1.1	18.6	-1.1	18.7	0.5	20.4	9.1
1951	20.6	1.0	22.8	10.7	22.9	0.4	22.9	0.0	22.9	0.0	22.4	-2.2	22.2	-0.9	22.3	0.5	22.4	0.4	22.2	-0.9	23.2	4.5	23.2	0.0
1952	23.2	0.0	22.5	-3.0	23.4	4.0	23.4	0.0	23.4	0.0	23.5	0.4	23.5	0.0	23.5	0.0	23.5	0.0	23.5	0.0	23.5	0.0	23.5	0.0
1953	23.6	0.4	23.5	-0.4	23.5	0.0	23.6	0.4	23.7	0.4	23.7	0.0	23.9	0.8	23.9	0.0	24.0	0.4	24.1	0.4	24.0	-0.4	24.0	0.0
1954	24.1	0.4	24.3	0.8	24.4	0.4	24.3	-0.4	24.3	0.0	24.3	0.0	24.2	-0.4	24.3	0.4	24.3	0.0	24.4	0.4	24.6	0.8	24.4	-0.8
1955	24.4	0.0	24.4	0.0	24.3	-0.4	24.3	0.0	24.6	1.2	24.7	0.4	24.6	-0.4	24.5	-0.4	22.9	-6.5	23.4	2.2	24.0	2.6	23.8	-0.8
1956	24.1	1.3	24.0	-0.4	24.1	0.4	23.9	-0.8	23.8	-0.4	23.7	-0.4	24.0	1.3	24.3	1.2	24.2	-0.4	24.4	0.8	24.9	2.0	25.0	0.4
1957	25.1	0.4	25.1	0.0	25.1	0.0	25.0	-0.4	25.1	0.4	24.8	-1.2	24.7	-0.4	24.7	0.0	24.8	0.4	24.7	-0.4	25.7	4.0	25.6	-0.4
1958	25.2	-1.6	25.1	-0.4	25.6	2.0	25.7	0.4	25.5	-0.8	25.6	0.4	25.8	0.8	26.0	0.8	26.0	0.0	25.9	-0.4	26.6	2.7	26.7	0.4
1959	26.8	0.4	26.6	-0.7	26.7	0.4	26.8	0.4	27.0	0.7	27.1	0.4	27.3	0.7	27.4	0.4	27.4	0.0	27.6	0.7	27.7	0.4	27.7	0.0
1960	27.7	0.0	27.7	0.0	27.6	-0.4	27.5	-0.4	27.4	-0.4	27.3	-0.4	27.2	-0.4	27.2	0.0	27.1	-0.4	27.5	1.5	27.6	0.4	27.7	0.4
1961	27.6	-0.4	27.7	0.4	27.7	0.0	28.2	1.8	28.3	0.4	28.4	0.4	28.4	0.0	28.3	-0.4	28.2	-0.4	28.5	1.1	28.5	0.0	28.1	-1.4
1962	28.2	0.4	28.2	0.0	28.1	-0.4	28.4	1.1	28.3	-0.4	28.3	0.0	28.3	0.0	28.3	0.0	28.5	0.7	28.4	-0.4	28.6	0.7	28.5	-0.3
1963	28.1	-1.4	28.9	2.8	28.9	0.0	29.0	0.3	29.0	0.0	29.0	0.0	29.1	0.3	29.0	-0.3	29.1	0.3	29.3	0.7	29.4	0.3	29.4	0.0
1964	29.5	0.3	29.5	0.0	29.5	0.0	29.6	0.3	29.6	0.0	29.3	-1.0	29.6	1.0	29.7	0.3	29.5	-0.7	29.7	0.7	29.9	0.7	30.1	0.7
1965	30.2	0.3	30.5	1.0	30.4	-0.3	30.5	0.3	30.7	0.7	30.5	-0.7	30.5	0.0	30.4	-0.3	30.1	-1.0	30.5	1.3	30.5	0.0	30.5	0.0
1966	30.5	0.0	30.5	0.0	30.6	0.3	30.7	0.3	30.7	0.0	30.9	0.7	31.0	0.3	31.2	0.6	30.9	-1.0	31.2	1.0	31.2	0.0	31.0	-0.6
1967	31.0	0.0	31.1	0.3	31.5	1.3	31.5	0.0	31.5	0.0	31.6	0.3	31.8	0.6	31.9	0.3	31.8	-0.3	32.1	0.9	32.3	0.6	32.4	0.3
1968	32.9	1.5	32.9	0.0	33.0	0.3	33.0	0.0	33.1	0.3	33.2	0.3	33.4	0.6	33.5	0.3	33.4	-0.3	33.6	0.6	33.9	0.9	33.7	-0.6
1969	33.7	0.0	34.5	2.4	35.0	1.4	35.1	0.3	34.9	-0.6	35.1	0.6	35.0	-0.3	34.9	-0.3	34.6	-0.9	35.1	1.4	35.2	0.3	35.2	0.0
1970	35.2	0.0	36.0	2.3	36.1	0.3	36.5	1.1	36.8	0.8	37.0	0.5	37.0	0.0	37.0	0.0	36.8	-0.5	37.3	1.4	37.5	0.5	38.0	1.3
1971	38.2	0.5	38.8	1.6	38.7	-0.3	38.9	0.5	39.1	0.5	39.4	0.8	39.5	0.3	39.2	-0.8	38.8	-1.0	39.1	0.8	39.2	0.3	39.3	0.3
1972	39.3	0.0	39.2	-0.3	39.3	0.3	39.3	0.0	39.7	1.0	39.8	0.3	39.7	-0.3	39.8	0.3	39.8	0.0	39.7	-0.3	40.0	0.8	40.1	0.2
1973	39.9	-0.5	39.9	0.0	39.9	0.0	40.2	0.8	40.4	0.5	40.7	0.7	40.7	0.0	40.5	-0.5	40.2	-0.7	40.7	1.2	40.8	0.2	41.3	1.2
1974	41.7	1.0	42.1	1.0	43.0	2.1	43.3	0.7	44.0	1.6	44.8	1.8	45.4	1.3	45.6	0.4	45.9	0.7	46.1	0.4	46.5	0.9	46.5	0.0
1975	46.4	-0.2	46.5	0.2	46.9	0.9	47.2	0.6	47.5	0.6	48.4	1.9	48.9	1.0	49.2	0.6	49.3	0.2	49.8	1.0	50.3	1.0	50.3	0.0
1976	50.2	-0.2	50.2	0.0	50.8	1.2	51.3	1.0	52.0	1.4	52.7	1.3	53.1	0.8	53.3	0.4	53.6	0.6	53.8	0.4	54.0	0.4	54.0	0.0
1977	54.5	0.9	55.1	1.1	55.6	0.9	56.8	2.2	58.3	2.6	58.6	0.5	58.6	0.0	58.3	-0.5	58.9	1.0	58.8	-0.2	58.8	0.0	58.8	0.0
1978	58.9	0.2	59.1	0.3	59.6	0.8	59.9	0.5	60.6	1.2	61.4	1.3	61.9	0.8	62.2	0.5	62.1	-0.2	62.4	0.5	63.4	1.6	63.6	0.3
1979	64.0	0.6	64.6	0.9	65.4	1.2	66.9	2.3	68.3	2.1	70.5	3.2	72.3	2.6	72.7	0.6	73.6	1.2	73.4	-0.3	74.3	1.2	75.2	1.2
1980	77.6	3.2	79.8	2.8	81.3	1.9	82.0	0.9	82.9	1.1	83.5	0.7	83.6	0.1	84.6	1.2	84.6	0.0	85.3	0.8	86.4	1.3	87.2	0.9
1981	88.7	1.7	91.0	2.6	91.4	0.4	91.9	0.5	92.7	0.9	93.0	0.3	94.2	1.3	94.3	0.1	94.8	0.5	96.8	2.1	97.0	0.2	97.6	0.6
1982	97.0	-0.6	95.8	-1.2	95.0	-0.8	94.1	-0.9	94.2	0.1	95.8	1.7	97.4	1.7	97.1	-0.3	96.6	-0.5	97.2	0.6	97.2	0.0	97.6	0.4
1983	98.0	0.4	96.8	-1.2	96.2	-0.6	97.5	1.4	98.3	0.8	98.5	0.2	99.2	0.7	100.7	1.5	101.3	0.6	102.0	0.7	102.3	0.3	102.0	-0.3
1984	102.6	0.6	102.6	0.0	102.9	0.3	103.7	0.8	104.0	0.3	104.3	0.3	104.6	0.3	105.2	0.6	105.6	0.4	105.1	-0.5	105.7	0.6	105.9	0.2
1985	106.1	0.2	106.8	0.7	107.5	0.7	108.4	0.8	109.0	0.6	109.5	0.5	109.7	0.2	109.8	0.1	110.1	0.3	111.1	0.9	111.2	0.1	111.3	0.1
1986	111.8	0.4	110.4	-1.3	107.6	-2.5	103.5	-3.8	104.7	1.2	106.0	1.2	105.8	-0.2	103.5	-2.2	103.8	0.3	104.6	0.8	104.7	0.1	105.6	0.9
1987	107.2	1.5	107.3	0.1	107.9	0.6	109.6	1.6	110.1	0.5	110.9	0.7	111.7	0.7	111.8	0.1	112.0	0.2	113.0	0.9	113.7	0.6	113.9	0.2
1988	113.8	-0.1	113.5	-0.3	114.0	0.4	113.8	-0.2	114.7	0.8	114.5	-0.2	115.1	0.5	115.0	-0.1	115.7	0.6	116.9	1.0	117.2	0.3	117.4	0.2
1989	118.0	0.5	117.6	-0.3	117.7	0.1	120.2	2.1	123.2	2.5	123.7	0.4	123.4	-0.2	122.9	-0.4	123.1	0.2	123.9	0.6	123.0	-0.7	123.0	0.0
1990	124.6	1.3	125.8	1.0	125.4	-0.3	125.3	-0.1	125.6	0.2	126.6	0.8	125.8	-0.6	126.8	0.8	129.7	2.3	133.9	3.2	135.2	1.0	135.6	0.3
1991	133.2	-1.8	131.4	-1.4	130.3	-0.8	130.4	0.1	130.9	0.4	131.3	0.3	133.0	1.3	133.0	0.0	133.6	0.5	134.8	0.9	135.6	0.6	135.8	0.1
1992	135.1	-0.5	134.3	-0.6	133.7	-0.4	133.9	0.1	135.0	0.8	136.3	1.0	136.7	0.3	136.4	-0.2	136.4	0.0	137.3	0.7	138.5	0.9	139.1	0.4

[Continued]

Philadelphia-Wilmington-Atlantic City, PA-NJ-DE-MD
Consumer Price Index - Urban Wage Earners
Base 1982-1984 = 100
Transportation
[Continued]

For 1947-2000. Columns headed % show percentile change in the index from the previous period for which an index is available.

Year	Jan Index	%	Feb Index	%	Mar Index	%	Apr Index	%	May Index	%	Jun Index	%	Jul Index	%	Aug Index	%	Sep Index	%	Oct Index	%	Nov Index	%	Dec Index	%
1993	138.9	-0.1	138.4	-0.4	138.0	-0.3	137.0	-0.7	138.3	0.9	138.3	0.0	138.9	0.4	137.6	-0.9	138.9	0.9	140.9	1.4	142.8	1.3	142.4	-0.3
1994	141.7	-0.5	141.4	-0.2	141.6	0.1	141.1	-0.4	141.6	0.4	143.2	1.1	143.8	0.4	145.5	1.2	145.6	0.1	146.5	0.6	148.3	1.2	147.9	-0.3
1995	148.4	0.3	149.1	0.5	149.0	-0.1	149.3	0.2	149.6	0.2	150.5	0.6	149.7	-0.5	149.3	-0.3	149.6	0.2	150.5	0.6	149.6	-0.6	149.3	-0.2
1996	149.7	0.3	150.4	0.5	150.6	0.1	150.8	0.1	152.2	0.9	152.7	0.3	151.9	-0.5	152.0	0.1	152.5	0.3	154.1	1.0	154.9	0.5	154.6	-0.2
1997	155.5	0.6	154.2	-0.8	154.1	-0.1	153.6	-0.3	152.5	-0.7	152.7	0.1	152.1	-0.4	151.8	-0.2	153.1	0.9	154.5	0.9	154.6	0.1	153.3	-0.8
1998	-	-	150.4	-1.9	-	-	148.9	-1.0	-	-	149.1	0.1	-	-	148.9	-0.1	-	-	149.3	0.3	-	-	148.9	-0.3
1999	-	-	146.8	-1.4	-	-	150.2	2.3	-	-	151.2	0.7	-	-	153.5	1.5	-	-	156.8	2.1	-	-	157.1	0.2
2000	-	-	158.4	0.8	-	-	162.0	2.3	-	-	163.9	1.2	-	-	163.3	-0.4	-	-	163.4	0.1	-	-	163.1	-0.2

Source: U.S. Department of Labor, Bureau of Labor Statistics, Division of Consumer Prices and Price Indexes. - indicates no data collected for period.

Philadelphia-Wilmington-Atlantic City, PA-NJ-DE-MD
Consumer Price Index - All Urban Consumers
Base 1982-1984 = 100
Medical Care

For 1947-2001. Columns headed % show percentile change in the index from the previous period for which an index is available.

Year	Jan Index	%	Feb Index	%	Mar Index	%	Apr Index	%	May Index	%	Jun Index	%	Jul Index	%	Aug Index	%	Sep Index	%	Oct Index	%	Nov Index	%	Dec Index	%
1947	12.1	-	12.1	0.0	12.2	0.8	12.4	1.6	12.5	0.8	12.5	0.0	12.5	0.0	12.5	0.0	12.5	0.0	12.6	0.8	12.6	0.0	12.7	0.8
1948	12.8	0.8	12.9	0.8	12.8	-0.8	12.9	0.8	12.9	0.0	12.9	0.0	13.0	0.8	13.0	0.0	13.0	0.0	13.0	0.0	13.2	1.5	13.2	0.0
1949	13.2	0.0	13.3	0.8	13.3	0.0	13.3	0.0	13.3	0.0	13.4	0.8	13.4	0.0	13.4	0.0	13.4	0.0	13.4	0.0	13.4	0.0	13.5	0.7
1950	13.5	0.0	13.5	0.0	13.5	0.0	13.5	0.0	13.6	0.7	13.6	0.0	13.6	0.0	13.6	0.0	13.7	0.7	13.7	0.0	13.7	0.0	13.7	0.0
1951	13.9	1.5	14.0	0.7	14.2	1.4	14.2	0.0	14.2	0.0	14.2	0.0	14.2	0.0	14.2	0.0	14.2	0.0	14.3	0.7	14.3	0.0	14.3	0.0
1952	14.3	0.0	14.3	0.0	14.5	1.4	14.5	0.0	14.5	0.0	15.2	4.8	15.2	0.0	15.2	0.0	15.5	2.0	15.5	0.0	15.5	0.0	15.5	0.0
1953	15.5	0.0	15.5	0.0	15.5	0.0	15.5	0.0	15.5	0.0	15.6	0.6	15.6	0.0	15.6	0.0	15.6	0.0	15.6	0.0	15.6	0.0	15.9	1.9
1954	15.9	0.0	16.0	0.6	16.0	0.0	16.0	0.0	16.0	0.0	16.2	1.3	16.2	0.0	16.2	0.0	17.1	5.6	17.1	0.0	17.1	0.0	17.3	1.2
1955	17.3	0.0	17.3	0.0	17.5	1.2	17.5	0.0	17.5	0.0	17.5	0.0	17.5	0.0	17.5	0.0	17.5	0.0	17.5	0.0	17.5	0.0	17.6	0.6
1956	17.6	0.0	17.6	0.0	17.8	1.1	17.8	0.0	17.8	0.0	17.8	0.0	17.8	0.0	17.8	0.0	17.9	0.6	17.9	0.0	17.9	0.0	17.9	0.0
1957	17.9	0.0	17.9	0.0	18.2	1.7	18.2	0.0	18.2	0.0	18.2	0.0	18.2	0.0	18.2	0.0	18.2	0.0	18.2	0.0	18.2	0.0	18.5	1.6
1958	18.5	0.0	18.5	0.0	18.5	0.0	18.6	0.5	18.6	0.0	18.6	0.0	19.2	3.2	19.2	0.0	19.2	0.0	19.2	0.0	19.2	0.0	19.3	0.5
1959	19.3	0.0	19.3	0.0	19.7	2.1	19.7	0.0	19.7	0.0	19.9	1.0	19.9	0.0	20.5	3.0	20.5	0.0	20.5	0.0	20.5	0.0	20.6	0.5
1960	20.6	0.0	20.6	0.0	20.8	1.0	20.8	0.0	20.8	0.0	20.9	0.5	20.9	0.0	20.9	0.0	20.9	0.0	20.9	0.0	20.9	0.0	21.0	0.5
1961	21.0	0.0	21.0	0.0	21.0	0.0	21.4	1.9	22.0	2.8	22.0	0.0	22.0	0.0	22.0	0.0	22.1	0.5	22.1	0.0	22.1	0.0	22.1	0.0
1962	22.1	0.0	22.1	0.0	22.1	0.0	22.1	0.0	22.1	0.0	22.9	3.6	22.9	0.0	22.9	0.0	22.9	0.0	22.9	0.0	22.9	0.0	22.9	0.0
1963	22.9	0.0	23.0	0.4	23.0	0.0	23.0	0.0	23.0	0.0	23.1	0.4	23.1	0.0	23.1	0.0	23.2	0.4	23.2	0.0	23.2	0.0	23.2	0.0
1964	23.3	0.4	23.3	0.0	23.3	0.0	23.3	0.0	23.3	0.0	23.3	0.0	23.5	0.9	23.4	-0.4	23.5	0.4	23.5	0.0	23.6	0.4	23.6	0.0
1965	23.6	0.0	23.6	0.0	23.8	0.8	23.8	0.0	23.9	0.4	24.1	0.8	24.2	0.4	24.2	0.0	24.3	0.4	24.3	0.0	24.3	0.0	24.4	0.4
1966	24.4	0.0	24.5	0.4	24.7	0.8	24.8	0.4	24.8	0.0	24.9	0.4	25.2	1.2	25.3	0.4	25.3	0.0	25.4	0.4	25.6	0.8	25.9	1.2
1967	26.0	0.4	26.1	0.4	26.1	0.0	26.2	0.4	26.3	0.4	26.6	1.1	26.8	0.8	26.8	0.0	27.3	1.9	27.5	0.7	27.5	0.0	27.7	0.7
1968	27.9	0.7	27.9	0.0	28.0	0.4	28.1	0.4	28.5	1.4	28.7	0.7	29.3	2.1	29.4	0.3	29.5	0.3	29.8	1.0	29.8	0.0	30.0	0.7
1969	30.1	0.3	30.2	0.3	30.6	1.3	30.7	0.3	30.9	0.7	31.1	0.6	32.1	3.2	32.2	0.3	32.4	0.6	32.1	-0.9	32.1	0.0	32.2	0.3
1970	32.5	0.9	32.7	0.6	32.9	0.6	33.1	0.6	33.3	0.6	33.4	0.3	34.6	3.6	34.9	0.9	34.9	0.0	34.8	-0.3	35.6	2.3	35.6	0.0
1971	35.8	0.6	36.0	0.6	36.0	0.0	36.1	0.3	36.2	0.3	36.7	1.4	37.4	1.9	37.4	0.0	37.5	0.3	37.2	-0.8	37.3	0.3	37.3	0.0
1972	37.3	0.0	37.5	0.5	37.5	0.0	37.6	0.3	37.6	0.0	37.7	0.3	38.0	0.8	38.3	0.8	38.3	0.0	38.6	0.8	38.6	0.0	38.7	0.3
1973	38.7	0.0	38.7	0.0	39.2	1.3	39.4	0.5	39.4	0.0	39.4	0.0	39.6	0.5	40.1	1.3	40.2	0.2	41.0	2.0	41.1	0.2	41.1	0.0
1974	41.1	0.0	41.5	1.0	41.7	0.5	41.8	0.2	42.5	1.7	43.6	2.6	44.2	1.4	44.2	0.0	44.4	0.5	45.2	1.8	45.3	0.2	45.7	0.9
1975	46.5	1.8	47.2	1.5	47.7	1.1	47.9	0.4	48.0	0.2	48.7	1.5	50.3	3.3	50.3	0.0	50.9	1.2	51.5	1.2	51.0	-1.0	51.3	0.6
1976	51.7	0.8	52.0	0.6	52.1	0.2	52.4	0.6	52.5	0.2	53.2	1.3	54.5	2.4	54.6	0.2	55.0	0.7	55.3	0.5	55.7	0.7	55.6	-0.2
1977	56.1	0.9	56.8	1.2	57.6	1.4	57.7	0.2	58.1	0.7	58.6	0.9	60.2	2.7	60.4	0.3	60.7	0.5	60.6	-0.2	60.6	0.0	60.5	-0.2
1978	61.7	2.0	62.0	0.5	62.2	0.3	63.0	1.3	61.9	-1.7	61.9	0.0	63.0	1.8	63.6	1.0	64.7	1.7	64.7	0.0	65.1	0.6	65.1	0.0
1979	65.7	0.9	66.4	1.1	66.4	0.0	66.6	0.3	66.9	0.5	67.9	1.5	69.4	2.2	69.9	0.7	69.9	0.0	70.1	0.3	70.3	0.3	71.1	1.1
1980	71.7	0.8	73.6	2.6	73.5	-0.1	73.9	0.5	73.7	-0.3	73.9	0.3	76.3	3.2	77.2	1.2	77.5	0.4	77.7	0.3	78.3	0.8	78.4	0.1
1981	80.1	2.2	81.0	1.1	81.2	0.2	81.7	0.6	81.7	0.0	82.4	0.9	85.2	3.4	86.1	1.1	86.6	0.6	86.5	-0.1	86.7	0.2	87.3	0.7
1982	89.1	2.1	89.2	0.1	89.1	-0.1	89.4	0.3	89.5	0.1	89.9	0.4	93.5	4.0	93.9	0.4	93.3	-0.6	93.6	0.3	95.0	1.5	95.3	0.3
1983	96.1	0.8	97.7	1.7	97.9	0.2	98.3	0.4	98.6	0.3	99.5	0.9	102.4	2.9	103.0	0.6	103.1	0.1	103.7	0.6	103.5	-0.2	103.6	0.1
1984	103.9	0.3	104.8	0.9	104.7	-0.1	105.6	0.9	105.6	0.0	105.9	0.3	107.5	1.5	108.4	0.8	109.0	0.6	109.3	0.3	113.4	3.8	114.0	0.5
1985	115.8	1.6	116.1	0.3	117.1	0.9	117.4	0.3	117.7	0.3	118.5	0.7	119.3	0.7	119.8	0.4	121.0	1.0	121.7	0.6	122.6	0.7	122.2	-0.3
1986	122.5	0.2	123.5	0.8	124.3	0.6	125.5	1.0	125.0	-0.4	125.5	0.4	127.6	1.7	128.3	0.5	129.0	0.5	129.2	0.2	129.2	0.0	130.0	0.6
1987	129.9	-0.1	130.3	0.3	130.7	0.3	130.6	-0.1	131.7	0.8	132.9	0.9	134.0	0.8	134.0	0.0	135.3	1.0	135.3	0.0	135.2	-0.1	136.6	1.0
1988	137.7	0.8	138.7	0.7	138.4	-0.2	139.8	1.0	140.7	0.6	140.7	0.0	143.8	2.2	143.5	-0.2	144.7	0.8	145.5	0.6	146.1	0.4	146.2	0.1
1989	146.9	0.5	147.8	0.6	148.8	0.7	151.1	1.5	152.0	0.6	155.1	2.0	156.0	0.6	155.9	-0.1	159.9	2.6	164.1	2.6	166.1	1.2	159.8	-3.8
1990	160.4	0.4	160.1	-0.2	162.1	1.2	164.2	1.3	165.2	0.6	166.2	0.6	169.2	1.8	170.4	0.7	171.0	0.4	171.5	0.3	174.3	1.6	174.6	0.2
1991	176.0	0.8	178.4	1.4	178.8	0.2	180.5	1.0	181.3	0.4	182.0	0.4	184.7	1.5	186.5	1.0	186.7	0.1	188.4	0.9	188.5	0.1	189.6	0.6
1992	188.0	-0.8	188.7	0.4	192.1	1.8	193.0	0.5	195.6	1.3	196.4	0.4	199.4	1.5	199.5	0.1	200.4	0.5	202.0	0.8	202.0	0.0	202.2	0.1

[Continued]

Philadelphia-Wilmington-Atlantic City, PA-NJ-DE-MD
Consumer Price Index - All Urban Consumers
Base 1982-1984 = 100
Medical Care
[Continued]

For 1947-2001. Columns headed % show percentile change in the index from the previous period for which an index is available.

Year	Jan		Feb		Mar		Apr		May		Jun		Jul		Aug		Sep		Oct		Nov		Dec	
	Index	%	Index	%	Index	%	Index	%	Index	%	Index	%	Index	%	Index	%	Index	%	Index	%	Index	%	Index	%
1993	202.0	-0.1	205.0	1.5	206.3	0.6	207.3	0.5	209.7	1.2	211.2	0.7	214.7	1.7	214.2	-0.2	214.1	-0.0	218.1	1.9	217.8	-0.1	218.3	0.2
1994	219.7	0.6	220.8	0.5	220.3	-0.2	223.2	1.3	223.1	-0.0	222.3	-0.4	224.8	1.1	225.5	0.3	225.5	0.0	226.2	0.3	226.9	0.3	228.1	0.5
1995	228.9	0.4	228.9	0.0	229.1	0.1	229.2	0.0	229.8	0.3	231.7	0.8	234.2	1.1	234.7	0.2	234.9	0.1	235.6	0.3	236.1	0.2	236.6	0.2
1996	236.8	0.1	237.3	0.2	236.8	-0.2	236.8	0.0	240.0	1.4	242.0	0.8	244.4	1.0	247.6	1.3	246.9	-0.3	246.9	0.0	246.3	-0.2	244.8	-0.6
1997	245.7	0.4	246.2	0.2	247.1	0.4	247.0	-0.0	246.8	-0.1	247.5	0.3	249.2	0.7	248.7	-0.2	249.0	0.1	248.7	-0.1	248.9	0.1	249.3	0.2
1998	-	-	252.3	1.2	-	-	251.8	-0.2	-	-	254.4	1.0	-	-	258.0	1.4	-	-	257.0	-0.4	-	-	257.5	0.2
1999	-	-	258.9	0.5	-	-	262.8	1.5	-	-	263.3	0.2	-	-	267.0	1.4	-	-	269.1	0.8	-	-	271.6	0.9
2000	-	-	273.9	0.8	-	-	276.5	0.9	-	-	276.5	0.0	-	-	281.7	1.9	-	-	282.5	0.3	-	-	284.5	0.7
2001	-	-	291.9	2.6	-	-	293.6	0.6	-	-	309.6	5.4	-	-	314.8	1.7	-	-	314.1	-0.2	-	-	315.5	0.4

Source: U.S. Department of Labor, Bureau of Labor Statistics, Division of Consumer Prices and Price Indexes. - indicates no data collected for period.

Philadelphia-Wilmington-Atlantic City, PA-NJ-DE-MD
Consumer Price Index - Urban Wage Earners
Base 1982-1984 = 100
Medical Care

For 1947-2001. Columns headed % show percentile change in the index from the previous period for which an index is available.

Year	Jan Index	%	Feb Index	%	Mar Index	%	Apr Index	%	May Index	%	Jun Index	%	Jul Index	%	Aug Index	%	Sep Index	%	Oct Index	%	Nov Index	%	Dec Index	%
1947	11.4	-	11.5	0.9	11.5	0.0	11.7	1.7	11.8	0.9	11.8	0.0	11.8	0.0	11.8	0.0	11.8	0.0	11.9	0.8	11.9	0.0	12.0	0.8
1948	12.1	0.8	12.2	0.8	12.1	-0.8	12.2	0.8	12.2	0.0	12.2	0.0	12.3	0.8	12.3	0.0	12.3	0.0	12.3	0.0	12.5	1.6	12.5	0.0
1949	12.5	0.0	12.5	0.0	12.6	0.8	12.6	0.0	12.6	0.0	12.6	0.0	12.6	0.0	12.6	0.0	12.7	0.8	12.7	0.0	12.7	0.0	12.7	0.0
1950	12.7	0.0	12.7	0.0	12.7	0.0	12.7	0.0	12.8	0.8	12.8	0.0	12.8	0.0	12.8	0.0	12.9	0.8	12.9	0.0	12.9	0.0	13.0	0.8
1951	13.2	1.5	13.2	0.0	13.4	1.5	13.4	0.0	13.4	0.0	13.4	0.0	13.4	0.0	13.4	0.0	13.4	0.0	13.5	0.7	13.5	0.0	13.5	0.0
1952	13.5	0.0	13.5	0.0	13.7	1.5	13.7	0.0	13.7	0.0	14.4	5.1	14.4	0.0	14.4	0.0	14.6	1.4	14.6	0.0	14.6	0.0	14.6	0.0
1953	14.6	0.0	14.6	0.0	14.6	0.0	14.6	0.0	14.6	0.0	14.7	0.7	14.7	0.0	14.7	0.0	14.7	0.0	14.7	0.0	14.7	0.0	15.0	2.0
1954	15.0	0.0	15.1	0.7	15.1	0.0	15.1	0.0	15.1	0.0	15.3	1.3	15.3	0.0	15.3	0.0	16.1	5.2	16.1	0.0	16.2	0.6	16.3	0.6
1955	16.3	0.0	16.3	0.0	16.5	1.2	16.5	0.0	16.5	0.0	16.5	0.0	16.5	0.0	16.5	0.0	16.5	0.0	16.5	0.0	16.5	0.0	16.6	0.6
1956	16.6	0.0	16.6	0.0	16.8	1.2	16.8	0.0	16.8	0.0	16.8	0.0	16.8	0.0	16.8	0.0	16.9	0.6	16.9	0.0	16.9	0.0	16.9	0.0
1957	16.9	0.0	16.9	0.0	17.1	1.2	17.1	0.0	17.1	0.0	17.2	0.6	17.2	0.0	17.2	0.0	17.2	0.0	17.2	0.0	17.2	0.0	17.4	1.2
1958	17.4	0.0	17.4	0.0	17.5	0.6	17.5	0.0	17.5	0.0	17.6	0.6	18.1	2.8	18.1	0.0	18.1	0.0	18.1	0.0	18.1	0.0	18.2	0.6
1959	18.3	0.5	18.3	0.0	18.6	1.6	18.6	0.0	18.6	0.0	18.8	1.1	18.8	0.0	19.3	2.7	19.4	0.5	19.4	0.0	19.4	0.0	19.4	0.0
1960	19.4	0.0	19.4	0.0	19.6	1.0	19.6	0.0	19.6	0.0	19.7	0.5	19.7	0.0	19.7	0.0	19.7	0.0	19.7	0.0	19.7	0.0	19.8	0.5
1961	19.8	0.0	19.8	0.0	19.9	0.5	20.2	1.5	20.8	3.0	20.8	0.0	20.8	0.0	20.8	0.0	20.9	0.5	20.8	-0.5	20.8	0.0	20.8	0.0
1962	20.9	0.5	20.9	0.0	20.9	0.0	20.9	0.0	20.9	0.0	21.6	3.3	21.6	0.0	21.6	0.0	21.7	0.5	21.6	-0.5	21.6	0.0	21.7	0.5
1963	21.7	0.0	21.7	0.0	21.7	0.0	21.7	0.0	21.7	0.0	21.8	0.5	21.8	0.0	21.8	0.0	21.9	0.5	21.9	0.0	21.9	0.0	21.9	0.0
1964	22.0	0.5	22.0	0.0	22.0	0.0	22.0	0.0	22.0	0.0	22.0	0.0	22.2	0.9	22.1	-0.5	22.2	0.5	22.2	0.0	22.3	0.5	22.3	0.0
1965	22.3	0.0	22.3	0.0	22.5	0.9	22.5	0.0	22.6	0.4	22.7	0.4	22.8	0.4	22.8	0.0	22.9	0.4	22.9	0.0	22.9	0.0	23.0	0.4
1966	23.1	0.4	23.1	0.0	23.3	0.9	23.4	0.4	23.4	0.0	23.5	0.4	23.8	1.3	23.9	0.4	23.9	0.0	24.0	0.4	24.2	0.8	24.5	1.2
1967	24.6	0.4	24.6	0.0	24.6	0.0	24.7	0.4	24.9	0.8	25.1	0.8	25.3	0.8	25.3	0.0	25.8	2.0	25.9	0.4	26.0	0.4	26.2	0.8
1968	26.3	0.4	26.4	0.4	26.5	0.4	26.6	0.4	26.9	1.1	27.1	0.7	27.6	1.8	27.7	0.4	27.9	0.7	28.1	0.7	28.2	0.4	28.3	0.4
1969	28.4	0.4	28.5	0.4	28.9	1.4	29.0	0.3	29.2	0.7	29.3	0.3	30.3	3.4	30.4	0.3	30.6	0.7	30.3	-1.0	30.3	0.0	30.4	0.3
1970	30.7	1.0	30.9	0.7	31.0	0.3	31.3	1.0	31.4	0.3	31.6	0.6	32.6	3.2	33.0	1.2	33.0	0.0	32.9	-0.3	33.6	2.1	33.7	0.3
1971	33.8	0.3	34.0	0.6	34.0	0.0	34.1	0.3	34.2	0.3	34.6	1.2	35.3	2.0	35.3	0.0	35.4	0.3	35.2	-0.6	35.2	0.0	35.2	0.0
1972	35.2	0.0	35.4	0.6	35.4	0.0	35.5	0.3	35.5	0.0	35.6	0.3	35.9	0.8	36.2	0.8	36.2	0.0	36.4	0.6	36.5	0.3	36.5	0.0
1973	36.6	0.3	36.6	0.0	37.0	1.1	37.2	0.5	37.2	0.0	37.2	0.0	37.4	0.5	37.8	1.1	38.0	0.5	38.7	1.8	38.8	0.3	38.8	0.0
1974	38.8	0.0	39.2	1.0	39.4	0.5	39.5	0.3	40.1	1.5	41.2	2.7	41.7	1.2	41.7	0.0	41.9	0.5	42.6	1.7	42.7	0.2	43.1	0.9
1975	43.9	1.9	44.6	1.6	45.0	0.9	45.3	0.7	45.4	0.2	46.0	1.3	47.5	3.3	47.5	0.0	48.0	1.1	48.7	1.5	48.2	-1.0	48.4	0.4
1976	48.9	1.0	49.1	0.4	49.2	0.2	49.5	0.6	49.6	0.2	50.3	1.4	51.5	2.4	51.6	0.2	51.9	0.6	52.2	0.6	52.6	0.8	52.5	-0.2
1977	53.0	1.0	53.6	1.1	54.4	1.5	54.5	0.2	54.9	0.7	55.3	0.7	56.9	2.9	57.0	0.2	57.3	0.5	57.2	-0.2	57.3	0.2	57.2	-0.2
1978	58.2	1.7	58.6	0.7	58.6	0.0	58.8	0.3	58.8	0.0	58.8	0.0	59.7	1.5	60.6	1.5	62.2	2.6	62.2	0.0	62.5	0.5	63.3	1.3
1979	63.3	0.0	63.9	0.9	64.0	0.2	64.1	0.2	64.4	0.5	66.8	3.7	67.6	1.2	67.9	0.4	68.3	0.6	69.1	1.2	69.3	0.3	69.8	0.7
1980	70.5	1.0	73.3	4.0	73.2	-0.1	73.8	0.8	74.3	0.7	74.8	0.7	77.3	3.3	78.6	1.7	78.9	0.4	79.2	0.4	79.2	0.0	79.2	0.0
1981	81.0	2.3	80.6	-0.5	80.7	0.1	81.2	0.6	81.2	0.0	81.4	0.2	84.7	4.1	86.2	1.8	87.3	1.3	87.4	0.1	87.7	0.3	87.6	-0.1
1982	89.3	1.9	89.2	-0.1	89.0	-0.2	89.4	0.4	89.6	0.2	89.8	0.2	93.1	3.7	93.7	0.6	93.1	-0.6	93.3	0.2	94.6	1.4	94.8	0.2
1983	95.8	1.1	97.7	2.0	97.8	0.1	98.2	0.4	98.5	0.3	99.7	1.2	102.4	2.7	103.0	0.6	103.1	0.1	103.6	0.5	103.5	-0.1	103.7	0.2
1984	104.0	0.3	105.1	1.1	105.0	-0.1	106.0	1.0	106.0	0.0	106.4	0.4	107.5	1.0	108.5	0.9	109.1	0.6	109.5	0.4	113.3	3.5	113.8	0.4
1985	115.9	1.8	116.2	0.3	117.2	0.9	117.3	0.1	117.7	0.3	118.5	0.7	119.1	0.5	119.6	0.4	120.8	1.0	121.7	0.7	122.6	0.7	122.1	-0.4
1986	122.3	0.2	123.3	0.8	124.1	0.6	125.4	1.0	124.8	-0.5	125.4	0.5	127.0	1.3	127.7	0.6	128.6	0.7	128.8	0.2	128.7	-0.1	129.5	0.6
1987	129.5	0.0	129.9	0.3	130.3	0.3	130.3	0.0	131.5	0.9	132.9	1.1	133.7	0.6	133.6	-0.1	134.5	0.7	134.9	0.3	134.7	-0.1	136.2	1.1
1988	137.3	0.8	138.1	0.6	137.7	-0.3	139.2	1.1	140.2	0.7	140.3	0.1	143.2	2.1	142.8	-0.3	144.1	0.9	144.7	0.4	145.3	0.4	145.3	0.0
1989	146.1	0.6	146.9	0.5	147.9	0.7	150.4	1.7	151.3	0.6	153.8	1.7	154.6	0.5	154.8	0.1	158.2	2.2	161.9	2.3	163.8	1.2	158.4	-3.3
1990	159.1	0.4	158.8	-0.2	160.8	1.3	163.0	1.4	163.9	0.6	164.9	0.6	167.6	1.6	168.7	0.7	169.3	0.4	169.7	0.2	172.3	1.5	172.5	0.1
1991	173.8	0.8	176.2	1.4	176.4	0.1	178.1	1.0	178.8	0.4	179.7	0.5	182.0	1.3	184.0	1.1	184.1	0.1	185.6	0.8	185.7	0.1	186.8	0.6
1992	185.5	-0.7	186.1	0.3	189.1	1.6	189.9	0.4	192.8	1.5	193.6	0.4	196.7	1.6	196.7	0.0	197.7	0.5	199.2	0.8	199.5	0.2	199.7	0.1

[Continued]

Philadelphia-Wilmington-Atlantic City, PA-NJ-DE-MD
Consumer Price Index - Urban Wage Earners
Base 1982-1984 = 100
Medical Care
[Continued]

For 1947-2001. Columns headed % show percentile change in the index from the previous period for which an index is available.

Year	Jan Index	%	Feb Index	%	Mar Index	%	Apr Index	%	May Index	%	Jun Index	%	Jul Index	%	Aug Index	%	Sep Index	%	Oct Index	%	Nov Index	%	Dec Index	%
1993	199.4	-0.2	202.7	1.7	203.8	0.5	204.8	0.5	206.8	1.0	208.4	0.8	211.9	1.7	211.4	-0.2	211.2	-0.1	215.2	1.9	214.7	-0.2	215.3	0.3
1994	216.4	0.5	217.6	0.6	217.1	-0.2	219.8	1.2	219.9	0.0	218.9	-0.5	221.4	1.1	221.9	0.2	222.0	0.0	222.8	0.4	223.4	0.3	224.6	0.5
1995	225.1	0.2	225.1	0.0	225.3	0.1	225.3	0.0	225.9	0.3	227.9	0.9	230.0	0.9	230.6	0.3	230.7	0.0	231.3	0.3	231.9	0.3	232.3	0.2
1996	232.4	0.0	232.9	0.2	232.2	-0.3	232.1	-0.0	236.0	1.7	238.3	1.0	240.4	0.9	243.2	1.2	242.6	-0.2	242.5	-0.0	241.9	-0.2	240.6	-0.5
1997	241.5	0.4	241.8	0.1	243.0	0.5	243.0	0.0	242.7	-0.1	243.2	0.2	244.8	0.7	244.4	-0.2	244.7	0.1	244.4	-0.1	244.6	0.1	244.9	0.1
1998	-	-	247.9	1.2	-	-	247.4	-0.2	-	-	250.1	1.1	-	-	253.2	1.2	-	-	252.0	-0.5	-	-	252.6	0.2
1999	-	-	253.9	0.5	-	-	257.9	1.6	-	-	258.4	0.2	-	-	262.0	1.4	-	-	263.5	0.6	-	-	266.1	1.0
2000	-	-	268.3	0.8	-	-	270.4	0.8	-	-	270.4	0.0	-	-	275.0	1.7	-	-	276.0	0.4	-	-	277.9	0.7
2001	-	-	285.0	2.6	-	-	286.6	0.6	-	-	302.8	5.7	-	-	307.1	1.4	-	-	306.4	-0.2	-	-	308.1	0.6

Source: U.S. Department of Labor, Bureau of Labor Statistics, Division of Consumer Prices and Price Indexes. - indicates no data collected for period.

Philadelphia-Wilmington-Atlantic City, PA-NJ-DE-MD
Consumer Price Index - All Urban Consumers
Base December 1997 = 100
Recreation

For 1997-2001. Columns headed % show percentile change in the index from the previous period for which an index is available.

Year	Jan Index	%	Feb Index	%	Mar Index	%	Apr Index	%	May Index	%	Jun Index	%	Jul Index	%	Aug Index	%	Sep Index	%	Oct Index	%	Nov Index	%	Dec Index	%
1997	-	-	-	-	-	-	-	-	-	-	-	-	-	-	-	-	-	-	-	-	-	-	100.0	-
1998	-	-	100.3	0.3	-	-	99.9	-0.4	-	-	101.2	1.3	-	-	102.2	1.0	-	-	102.7	0.5	-	-	102.0	-0.7
1999	-	-	100.6	-1.4	-	-	102.9	2.3	-	-	102.4	-0.5	-	-	103.6	1.2	-	-	103.6	0.0	-	-	104.2	0.6
2000	-	-	107.5	3.2	-	-	106.7	-0.7	-	-	107.3	0.6	-	-	109.0	1.6	-	-	107.9	-1.0	-	-	105.8	-1.9
2001	-	-	106.1	0.3	-	-	107.9	1.7	-	-	108.0	0.1	-	-	109.4	1.3	-	-	108.9	-0.5	-	-	106.1	-2.6

Source: U.S. Department of Labor, Bureau of Labor Statistics, Division of Consumer Prices and Price Indexes. - indicates no data collected for period.

Philadelphia-Wilmington-Atlantic City, PA-NJ-DE-MD
Consumer Price Index - Urban Wage Earners
Base December 1997 = 100
Recreation

For 1997-2001. Columns headed % show percentile change in the index from the previous period for which an index is available.

Year	Jan		Feb		Mar		Apr		May		Jun		Jul		Aug		Sep		Oct		Nov		Dec	
	Index	%	Index	%	Index	%	Index	%	Index	%	Index	%	Index	%	Index	%	Index	%	Index	%	Index	%	Index	%
1997	-	-	-	-	-	-	-	-	-	-	-	-	-	-	-	-	-	-	-	-	-	-	100.0	-
1998	-	-	100.2	0.2	-	-	100.2	0.0	-	-	101.0	0.8	-	-	101.5	0.5	-	-	102.0	0.5	-	-	101.8	-0.2
1999	-	-	100.3	-1.5	-	-	102.6	2.3	-	-	102.0	-0.6	-	-	103.3	1.3	-	-	103.6	0.3	-	-	104.3	0.7
2000	-	-	108.1	3.6	-	-	106.9	-1.1	-	-	107.5	0.6	-	-	109.5	1.9	-	-	108.2	-1.2	-	-	105.8	-2.2
2001	-	-	105.8	0.0	-	-	107.6	1.7	-	-	107.6	0.0	-	-	108.9	1.2	-	-	108.4	-0.5	-	-	106.9	-1.4

Source: U.S. Department of Labor, Bureau of Labor Statistics, Division of Consumer Prices and Price Indexes. - indicates no data collected for period.

Philadelphia-Wilmington-Atlantic City, PA-NJ-DE-MD
Consumer Price Index - All Urban Consumers
Base December 1997 = 100
Education & Communication

For 1997-2001. Columns headed % show percentile change in the index from the previous period for which an index is available.

Year	Jan Index	%	Feb Index	%	Mar Index	%	Apr Index	%	May Index	%	Jun Index	%	Jul Index	%	Aug Index	%	Sep Index	%	Oct Index	%	Nov Index	%	Dec Index	%
1997	-	-	-	-	-	-	-	-	-	-	-	-	-	-	-	-	-	-	-	-	-	-	100.0	-
1998	-	-	99.1	-0.9	-	-	99.3	0.2	-	-	99.3	0.0	-	-	99.5	0.2	-	-	100.0	0.5	-	-	99.9	-0.1
1999	-	-	99.9	0.0	-	-	100.2	0.3	-	-	99.9	-0.3	-	-	101.3	1.4	-	-	-	-	-	-	102.8	1.5
2000	-	-	102.1	-0.7	-	-	101.8	-0.3	-	-	100.7	-1.1	-	-	102.7	2.0	-	-	102.1	-0.6	-	-	103.3	1.2
2001	-	-	103.1	-0.2	-	-	103.4	0.3	-	-	103.2	-0.2	-	-	104.6	1.4	-	-	105.1	0.5	-	-	105.0	-0.1

Source: U.S. Department of Labor, Bureau of Labor Statistics, Division of Consumer Prices and Price Indexes. - indicates no data collected for period.

Philadelphia-Wilmington-Atlantic City, PA-NJ-DE-MD
Consumer Price Index - Urban Wage Earners
Base December 1997 = 100
Education & Communication

For 1997-2001. Columns headed % show percentile change in the index from the previous period for which an index is available.

Year	Jan Index	%	Feb Index	%	Mar Index	%	Apr Index	%	May Index	%	Jun Index	%	Jul Index	%	Aug Index	%	Sep Index	%	Oct Index	%	Nov Index	%	Dec Index	%
1997	-	-	-	-	-	-	-	-	-	-	-	-	-	-	-	-	-	-	-	-	-	-	100.0	-
1998	-	-	98.0	-2.0	-	-	98.1	0.1	-	-	98.1	0.0	-	-	99.6	1.5	-	-	99.0	-0.6	-	-	99.6	0.6
1999	-	-	99.8	0.2	-	-	99.9	0.1	-	-	99.7	-0.2	-	-	100.1	0.4	-	-	-	-	-	-	103.0	2.9
2000	-	-	102.6	-0.4	-	-	102.2	-0.4	-	-	101.1	-1.1	-	-	102.9	1.8	-	-	102.2	-0.7	-	-	104.0	1.8
2001	-	-	103.9	-0.1	-	-	104.2	0.3	-	-	104.0	-0.2	-	-	105.2	1.2	-	-	105.7	0.5	-	-	105.7	0.0

Source: U.S. Department of Labor, Bureau of Labor Statistics, Division of Consumer Prices and Price Indexes. - indicates no data collected for period.

Pittsburgh, PA
Consumer Price Index - All Urban Consumers
Base 1982-1984 = 100
Annual Averages

For 1917-2001. Columns headed % show percentile change in the index from the previous period for which an index is available.

Year	All Items		Food & Beverage		Housing		Apparel		Trans-portation		Medical Care		Recrea-tion*		Education & Communic.*		Other Goods & Services	
	Index	%	Index	%	Index	%	Index	%	Index	%	Index	%	Index	%	Index	%	Index	%
1917	-	-	-	-	-	-	-	-	-	-	-	-	-	-	-	-	-	-
1918	14.8	-	-	-	-	-	-	-	-	-	-	-	-	-	-	-	-	-
1919	17.0	14.9	-	-	-	-	-	-	-	-	-	-	-	-	-	-	-	-
1920	19.5	14.7	-	-	-	-	-	-	-	-	-	-	-	-	-	-	-	-
1921	17.5	-10.3	-	-	-	-	-	-	-	-	-	-	-	-	-	-	-	-
1922	16.3	-6.9	-	-	-	-	-	-	-	-	-	-	-	-	-	-	-	-
1923	16.6	1.8	-	-	-	-	-	-	-	-	-	-	-	-	-	-	-	-
1924	16.8	1.2	-	-	-	-	-	-	-	-	-	-	-	-	-	-	-	-
1925	17.4	3.6	-	-	-	-	-	-	-	-	-	-	-	-	-	-	-	-
1926	17.5	0.6	-	-	-	-	-	-	-	-	-	-	-	-	-	-	-	-
1927	17.2	-1.7	-	-	-	-	-	-	-	-	-	-	-	-	-	-	-	-
1928	17.1	-0.6	-	-	-	-	-	-	-	-	-	-	-	-	-	-	-	-
1929	17.1	0.0	-	-	-	-	-	-	-	-	-	-	-	-	-	-	-	-
1930	16.5	-3.5	-	-	-	-	-	-	-	-	-	-	-	-	-	-	-	-
1931	15.0	-9.1	-	-	-	-	-	-	-	-	-	-	-	-	-	-	-	-
1932	13.3	-11.3	-	-	-	-	-	-	-	-	-	-	-	-	-	-	-	-
1933	12.5	-6.0	-	-	-	-	-	-	-	-	-	-	-	-	-	-	-	-
1934	12.9	3.2	-	-	-	-	-	-	-	-	-	-	-	-	-	-	-	-
1935	13.3	3.1	-	-	-	-	-	-	-	-	-	-	-	-	-	-	-	-
1936	13.5	1.5	-	-	-	-	-	-	-	-	-	-	-	-	-	-	-	-
1937	14.0	3.7	-	-	-	-	-	-	-	-	-	-	-	-	-	-	-	-
1938	13.7	-2.1	-	-	-	-	-	-	-	-	-	-	-	-	-	-	-	-
1939	13.4	-2.2	-	-	-	-	-	-	-	-	-	-	-	-	-	-	-	-
1940	13.6	1.5	-	-	-	-	-	-	-	-	-	-	-	-	-	-	-	-
1941	14.4	5.9	-	-	-	-	-	-	-	-	-	-	-	-	-	-	-	-
1942	15.8	9.7	-	-	-	-	-	-	-	-	-	-	-	-	-	-	-	-
1943	16.8	6.3	-	-	-	-	-	-	-	-	-	-	-	-	-	-	-	-
1944	17.2	2.4	-	-	-	-	-	-	-	-	-	-	-	-	-	-	-	-
1945	17.6	2.3	-	-	-	-	-	-	-	-	-	-	-	-	-	-	-	-
1946	19.1	8.5	-	-	-	-	-	-	-	-	-	-	-	-	-	-	-	-
1947	22.2	16.2	-	-	-	-	-	-	16.2	-	11.7	-	-	-	-	-	-	-
1948	23.8	7.2	-	-	-	-	-	-	17.9	10.5	12.4	6.0	-	-	-	-	-	-
1949	23.5	-1.3	-	-	-	-	-	-	18.9	5.6	12.6	1.6	-	-	-	-	-	-
1950	23.7	0.9	-	-	-	-	-	-	21.0	11.1	12.9	2.4	-	-	-	-	-	-
1951	25.6	8.0	-	-	-	-	-	-	22.8	8.6	13.5	4.7	-	-	-	-	-	-
1952	26.1	2.0	-	-	-	-	-	-	24.4	7.0	14.0	3.7	-	-	-	-	-	-
1953	26.3	0.8	-	-	-	-	42.9	-	24.7	1.2	14.7	5.0	-	-	-	-	-	-
1954	26.5	0.8	-	-	-	-	42.9	0.0	24.3	-1.6	15.4	4.8	-	-	-	-	-	-
1955	26.3	-0.8	-	-	-	-	42.2	-1.6	24.2	-0.4	15.8	2.6	-	-	-	-	-	-
1956	27.0	2.7	-	-	-	-	43.2	2.4	24.5	1.2	16.8	6.3	-	-	-	-	-	-
1957	27.8	3.0	-	-	-	-	44.4	2.8	25.7	4.9	17.7	5.4	-	-	-	-	-	-
1958	28.7	3.2	-	-	-	-	44.5	0.2	26.9	4.7	18.5	4.5	-	-	-	-	-	-
1959	29.0	1.0	-	-	-	-	44.6	0.2	28.5	5.9	19.7	6.5	-	-	-	-	-	-
1960	29.7	2.4	-	-	-	-	45.3	1.6	29.1	2.1	20.7	5.1	-	-	-	-	-	-
1961	29.9	0.7	-	-	-	-	45.6	0.7	29.2	0.3	21.4	3.4	-	-	-	-	-	-

[Continued]

Pittsburgh, PA
Consumer Price Index - All Urban Consumers
Base 1982-1984 = 100
Annual Averages
[Continued]

For 1917-2001. Columns headed % show percentile change in the index from the previous period for which an index is available.

Year	All Items Index	%	Food & Beverage Index	%	Housing Index	%	Apparel Index	%	Trans-portation Index	%	Medical Care Index	%	Recrea-tion* Index	%	Education & Communic.* Index	%	Other Goods & Services Index	%
1962	30.2	1.0	-	-	-	-	45.9	0.7	29.9	2.4	22.4	4.7	-	-	-	-	-	-
1963	30.5	1.0	-	-	-	-	46.9	2.2	29.9	0.0	23.0	2.7	-	-	-	-	-	-
1964	30.9	1.3	-	-	-	-	47.7	1.7	30.3	1.3	23.7	3.0	-	-	-	-	-	-
1965	31.4	1.6	-	-	-	-	48.6	1.9	30.8	1.7	24.3	2.5	-	-	-	-	-	-
1966	32.2	2.5	-	-	-	-	49.9	2.7	31.1	1.0	25.1	3.3	-	-	-	-	-	-
1967	32.8	1.9	-	-	-	-	51.2	2.6	31.6	1.6	26.9	7.2	-	-	-	-	-	-
1968	34.3	4.6	-	-	-	-	54.2	5.9	32.7	3.5	28.4	5.6	-	-	-	-	-	-
1969	36.2	5.5	-	-	-	-	57.8	6.6	34.1	4.3	30.1	6.0	-	-	-	-	-	-
1970	38.1	5.2	-	-	-	-	59.1	2.2	36.0	5.6	31.6	5.0	-	-	-	-	-	-
1971	39.8	4.5	-	-	-	-	61.2	3.6	37.9	5.3	32.9	4.1	-	-	-	-	-	-
1972	41.1	3.3	-	-	-	-	63.3	3.4	38.3	1.1	34.6	5.2	-	-	-	-	-	-
1973	43.6	6.1	-	-	-	-	65.4	3.3	39.3	2.6	36.0	4.0	-	-	-	-	-	-
1974	48.3	10.8	-	-	-	-	70.5	7.8	43.4	10.4	39.5	9.7	-	-	-	-	-	-
1975	52.4	8.5	-	-	-	-	72.5	2.8	47.0	8.3	43.7	10.6	-	-	-	-	-	-
1976	55.2	5.3	62.3	-	50.7	-	73.8	1.8	51.6	9.8	48.2	10.3	-	-	-	-	57.9	-
1977	58.9	6.7	66.4	6.6	54.4	7.3	75.2	1.9	56.3	9.1	53.3	10.6	-	-	-	-	61.8	6.7
1978	64.1	8.8	72.8	9.6	60.5	11.2	77.6	3.2	59.7	6.0	58.0	8.8	-	-	-	-	65.5	6.0
1979	71.2	11.1	80.0	9.9	67.9	12.2	82.6	6.4	68.5	14.7	64.2	10.7	-	-	-	-	70.3	7.3
1980	81.0	13.8	87.2	9.0	78.9	16.2	87.1	5.4	82.1	19.9	71.2	10.9	-	-	-	-	75.2	7.0
1981	89.3	10.2	93.8	7.6	86.7	9.9	93.7	7.6	93.6	14.0	79.7	11.9	-	-	-	-	82.4	9.6
1982	94.4	5.7	98.0	4.5	92.2	6.3	97.7	4.3	96.6	3.2	89.6	12.4	-	-	-	-	90.8	10.2
1983	101.1	7.1	101.1	3.2	101.7	10.3	101.2	3.6	99.8	3.3	100.9	12.6	-	-	-	-	101.0	11.2
1984	104.5	3.4	100.9	-0.2	106.1	4.3	101.2	0.0	103.6	3.8	109.6	8.6	-	-	-	-	108.2	7.1
1985	106.9	2.3	102.3	1.4	108.5	2.3	102.8	1.6	105.4	1.7	113.4	3.5	-	-	-	-	113.0	4.4
1986	108.2	1.2	105.0	2.6	111.3	2.6	100.4	-2.3	99.5	-5.6	121.2	6.9	-	-	-	-	118.0	4.4
1987	111.4	3.0	109.4	4.2	113.4	1.9	107.0	6.6	100.5	1.0	130.2	7.4	-	-	-	-	122.7	4.0
1988	114.9	3.1	111.9	2.3	115.7	2.0	114.2	6.7	102.3	1.8	138.2	6.1	-	-	-	-	132.7	8.1
1989	120.1	4.5	118.0	5.5	119.2	3.0	121.2	6.1	107.2	4.8	146.8	6.2	-	-	-	-	140.7	6.0
1990	126.2	5.1	124.3	5.3	124.8	4.7	125.0	3.1	112.1	4.6	160.6	9.4	-	-	-	-	150.4	6.9
1991	131.3	4.0	129.2	3.9	131.4	5.3	129.5	3.6	112.9	0.7	175.7	9.4	-	-	-	-	155.0	3.1
1992	136.0	3.6	132.9	2.9	135.8	3.3	133.0	2.7	115.6	2.4	185.9	5.8	-	-	-	-	168.1	8.5
1993	139.9	2.9	137.2	3.2	139.1	2.4	134.5	1.1	118.1	2.2	196.8	5.9	-	-	-	-	177.2	5.4
1994	144.6	3.4	140.6	2.5	145.2	4.4	133.2	-1.0	122.3	3.6	207.0	5.2	-	-	-	-	182.9	3.2
1995	149.2	3.2	143.6	2.1	150.1	3.4	135.3	1.6	127.6	4.3	212.6	2.7	-	-	-	-	192.2	5.1
1996	153.2	2.7	148.9	3.7	153.1	2.0	134.6	-0.5	129.2	1.3	225.4	6.0	-	-	-	-	202.9	5.6
1997	157.0	2.5	151.8	1.9	156.2	2.0	140.9	4.7	132.7	2.7	228.8	1.5	228.8	-	140.9	-	214.3	5.6
1998	159.2	1.4	153.6	1.2	160.1	2.5	142.5	1.1	130.3	-1.8	235.0	2.7	100.8	-55.9	99.7	-29.2	-	-
1999	162.5	2.1	156.0	1.6	162.2	1.3	144.5	1.4	131.9	1.2	244.4	4.0	103.9	3.1	102.3	2.6	244.4	14.0
2000	168.0	3.4	159.3	2.1	165.5	2.0	157.7	9.1	139.6	5.8	248.7	1.8	106.2	2.2	105.5	3.1	258.0	5.6
2001	172.5	2.7	165.1	3.6	172.3	4.1	156.6	-0.7	141.2	1.1	254.6	2.4	104.2	-1.9	109.9	4.2	266.2	3.2

Source: U.S. Department of Labor, Bureau of Labor Statistics, Division of Consumer Prices and Price Indexes. *Base is December 1997 = 100. - indicates no data collected for period.

Pittsburgh, PA
Consumer Price Index - Urban Wage Earners
Base 1982-1984 = 100
Annual Averages

For 1917-2001. Columns headed % show percentile change in the index from the previous period for which an index is available.

Year	All Items		Food & Beverage		Housing		Apparel		Trans-portation		Medical Care		Recrea-tion*		Education & Communic.*		Other Goods & Services	
	Index	%	Index	%	Index	%	Index	%	Index	%	Index	%	Index	%	Index	%	Index	%
1917	-	-	-	-	-	-	-	-	-	-	-	-	-	-	-	-	-	-
1918	15.2	-	-	-	-	-	-	-	-	-	-	-	-	-	-	-	-	-
1919	17.5	15.1	-	-	-	-	-	-	-	-	-	-	-	-	-	-	-	-
1920	20.0	14.3	-	-	-	-	-	-	-	-	-	-	-	-	-	-	-	-
1921	17.9	-10.5	-	-	-	-	-	-	-	-	-	-	-	-	-	-	-	-
1922	16.7	-6.7	-	-	-	-	-	-	-	-	-	-	-	-	-	-	-	-
1923	17.1	2.4	-	-	-	-	-	-	-	-	-	-	-	-	-	-	-	-
1924	17.2	0.6	-	-	-	-	-	-	-	-	-	-	-	-	-	-	-	-
1925	17.8	3.5	-	-	-	-	-	-	-	-	-	-	-	-	-	-	-	-
1926	18.0	1.1	-	-	-	-	-	-	-	-	-	-	-	-	-	-	-	-
1927	17.7	-1.7	-	-	-	-	-	-	-	-	-	-	-	-	-	-	-	-
1928	17.5	-1.1	-	-	-	-	-	-	-	-	-	-	-	-	-	-	-	-
1929	17.5	0.0	-	-	-	-	-	-	-	-	-	-	-	-	-	-	-	-
1930	16.9	-3.4	-	-	-	-	-	-	-	-	-	-	-	-	-	-	-	-
1931	15.4	-8.9	-	-	-	-	-	-	-	-	-	-	-	-	-	-	-	-
1932	13.7	-11.0	-	-	-	-	-	-	-	-	-	-	-	-	-	-	-	-
1933	12.8	-6.6	-	-	-	-	-	-	-	-	-	-	-	-	-	-	-	-
1934	13.3	3.9	-	-	-	-	-	-	-	-	-	-	-	-	-	-	-	-
1935	13.7	3.0	-	-	-	-	-	-	-	-	-	-	-	-	-	-	-	-
1936	13.9	1.5	-	-	-	-	-	-	-	-	-	-	-	-	-	-	-	-
1937	14.4	3.6	-	-	-	-	-	-	-	-	-	-	-	-	-	-	-	-
1938	14.1	-2.1	-	-	-	-	-	-	-	-	-	-	-	-	-	-	-	-
1939	13.8	-2.1	-	-	-	-	-	-	-	-	-	-	-	-	-	-	-	-
1940	14.0	1.4	-	-	-	-	-	-	-	-	-	-	-	-	-	-	-	-
1941	14.7	5.0	-	-	-	-	-	-	-	-	-	-	-	-	-	-	-	-
1942	16.2	10.2	-	-	-	-	-	-	-	-	-	-	-	-	-	-	-	-
1943	17.3	6.8	-	-	-	-	-	-	-	-	-	-	-	-	-	-	-	-
1944	17.6	1.7	-	-	-	-	-	-	-	-	-	-	-	-	-	-	-	-
1945	18.1	2.8	-	-	-	-	-	-	-	-	-	-	-	-	-	-	-	-
1946	19.6	8.3	-	-	-	-	-	-	-	-	-	-	-	-	-	-	-	-
1947	22.8	16.3	-	-	-	-	-	-	16.0	-	11.8	-	-	-	-	-	-	-
1948	24.4	7.0	-	-	-	-	-	-	17.7	10.6	12.4	5.1	-	-	-	-	-	-
1949	24.1	-1.2	-	-	-	-	-	-	18.7	5.6	12.7	2.4	-	-	-	-	-	-
1950	24.3	0.8	-	-	-	-	-	-	20.7	10.7	13.0	2.4	-	-	-	-	-	-
1951	26.3	8.2	-	-	-	-	-	-	22.5	8.7	13.6	4.6	-	-	-	-	-	-
1952	26.8	1.9	-	-	-	-	-	-	24.1	7.1	14.1	3.7	-	-	-	-	-	-
1953	27.0	0.7	-	-	-	-	44.4	-	24.4	1.2	14.8	5.0	-	-	-	-	-	-
1954	27.2	0.7	-	-	-	-	44.4	0.0	24.0	-1.6	15.5	4.7	-	-	-	-	-	-
1955	27.0	-0.7	-	-	-	-	43.8	-1.4	23.9	-0.4	15.9	2.6	-	-	-	-	-	-
1956	27.7	2.6	-	-	-	-	44.8	2.3	24.1	0.8	16.9	6.3	-	-	-	-	-	-
1957	28.5	2.9	-	-	-	-	46.0	2.7	25.3	5.0	17.9	5.9	-	-	-	-	-	-
1958	29.4	3.2	-	-	-	-	46.1	0.2	26.6	5.1	18.6	3.9	-	-	-	-	-	-
1959	29.8	1.4	-	-	-	-	46.3	0.4	28.1	5.6	19.8	6.5	-	-	-	-	-	-
1960	30.4	2.0	-	-	-	-	47.0	1.5	28.8	2.5	20.9	5.6	-	-	-	-	-	-
1961	30.7	1.0	-	-	-	-	47.3	0.6	28.8	0.0	21.6	3.3	-	-	-	-	-	-

[Continued]

Pittsburgh, PA
Consumer Price Index - Urban Wage Earners
Base 1982-1984 = 100
Annual Averages
[Continued]

For 1917-2001. Columns headed % show percentile change in the index from the previous period for which an index is available.

Year	All Items		Food & Beverage		Housing		Apparel		Trans-portation		Medical Care		Recrea-tion*		Education & Communic.*		Other Goods & Services	
	Index	%	Index	%	Index	%	Index	%	Index	%	Index	%	Index	%	Index	%	Index	%
1962	31.0	1.0	-	-	-	-	47.6	0.6	29.5	2.4	22.5	4.2	-	-	-	-	-	-
1963	31.3	1.0	-	-	-	-	48.7	2.3	29.5	0.0	23.2	3.1	-	-	-	-	-	-
1964	31.7	1.3	-	-	-	-	49.4	1.4	29.9	1.4	23.9	3.0	-	-	-	-	-	-
1965	32.2	1.6	-	-	-	-	50.4	2.0	30.4	1.7	24.5	2.5	-	-	-	-	-	-
1966	33.1	2.8	-	-	-	-	51.8	2.8	30.7	1.0	25.3	3.3	-	-	-	-	-	-
1967	33.6	1.5	-	-	-	-	53.1	2.5	31.2	1.6	27.0	6.7	-	-	-	-	-	-
1968	35.2	4.8	-	-	-	-	56.2	5.8	32.3	3.5	28.5	5.6	-	-	-	-	-	-
1969	37.1	5.4	-	-	-	-	59.9	6.6	33.7	4.3	30.3	6.3	-	-	-	-	-	-
1970	39.1	5.4	-	-	-	-	61.3	2.3	35.5	5.3	31.8	5.0	-	-	-	-	-	-
1971	40.9	4.6	-	-	-	-	63.5	3.6	37.4	5.4	33.1	4.1	-	-	-	-	-	-
1972	42.1	2.9	-	-	-	-	65.6	3.3	37.8	1.1	34.8	5.1	-	-	-	-	-	-
1973	44.7	6.2	-	-	-	-	67.8	3.4	38.8	2.6	36.3	4.3	-	-	-	-	-	-
1974	49.5	10.7	-	-	-	-	73.1	7.8	42.8	10.3	39.7	9.4	-	-	-	-	-	-
1975	53.8	8.7	-	-	-	-	75.2	2.9	46.4	8.4	44.0	10.8	-	-	-	-	-	-
1976	56.6	5.2	62.2	-	53.8	-	76.5	1.7	50.9	9.7	48.5	10.2	-	-	-	-	57.1	-
1977	60.5	6.9	66.2	6.4	57.7	7.2	77.9	1.8	55.6	9.2	53.7	10.7	-	-	-	-	61.0	6.8
1978	65.6	8.4	72.8	10.0	64.1	11.1	78.5	0.8	59.1	6.3	57.9	7.8	-	-	-	-	64.7	6.1
1979	73.1	11.4	80.5	10.6	72.0	12.3	83.8	6.8	67.9	14.9	64.4	11.2	-	-	-	-	69.2	7.0
1980	83.4	14.1	87.4	8.6	83.9	16.5	89.4	6.7	81.4	19.9	73.3	13.8	-	-	-	-	75.2	8.7
1981	92.0	10.3	94.1	7.7	92.5	10.3	93.3	4.4	93.7	15.1	80.6	10.0	-	-	-	-	82.1	9.2
1982	97.0	5.4	98.0	4.1	98.5	6.5	97.7	4.7	96.9	3.4	89.9	11.5					89.9	9.5
1983	101.3	4.4	101.1	3.2	102.8	4.4	100.9	3.3	99.4	2.6	100.6	11.9	-	-	-	-	101.1	12.5
1984	101.6	0.3	100.9	-0.2	98.7	-4.0	101.4	0.5	103.7	4.3	109.5	8.8	-	-	-	-	108.9	7.7
1985	103.7	2.1	102.1	1.2	100.4	1.7	102.8	1.4	105.2	1.4	113.6	3.7	-	-	-	-	113.7	4.4
1986	104.2	0.5	104.7	2.5	102.9	2.5	100.0	-2.7	98.2	-6.7	121.7	7.1	-	-	-	-	118.7	4.4
1987	107.1	2.8	109.1	4.2	104.8	1.8	106.1	6.1	99.3	1.1	130.9	7.6	-	-	-	-	123.1	3.7
1988	110.4	3.1	111.9	2.6	106.9	2.0	112.6	6.1	101.7	2.4	139.4	6.5	-	-	-	-	134.3	9.1
1989	115.4	4.5	118.0	5.5	110.3	3.2	118.6	5.3	106.8	5.0	147.5	5.8	-	-	-	-	142.5	6.1
1990	121.3	5.1	124.5	5.5	115.6	4.8	122.1	3.0	111.5	4.4	161.3	9.4	-	-	-	-	153.4	7.6
1991	125.9	3.8	129.6	4.1	121.6	5.2	124.5	2.0	111.9	0.4	175.4	8.7	-	-	-	-	158.6	3.4
1992	130.1	3.3	133.1	2.7	125.5	3.2	128.0	2.8	114.7	2.5	184.1	5.0	-	-	-	-	172.6	8.8
1993	133.9	2.9	137.4	3.2	128.6	2.5	128.8	0.6	117.5	2.4	194.1	5.4	-	-	-	-	181.6	5.2
1994	138.3	3.3	140.5	2.3	134.1	4.3	128.5	-0.2	121.7	3.6	203.8	5.0	-	-	-	-	186.6	2.8
1995	142.9	3.3	143.4	2.1	138.5	3.3	128.9	0.3	128.5	5.6	208.6	2.4	-	-	-	-	195.2	4.6
1996	146.8	2.7	148.8	3.8	141.3	2.0	129.1	0.2	130.2	1.3	220.0	5.5	-	-	-	-	207.3	6.2
1997	150.5	2.5	151.8	2.0	144.0	1.9	136.8	6.0	133.1	2.2	223.2	1.5	223.2	-	136.8	-	219.3	5.8
1998	152.4	1.3	153.5	1.1	147.3	2.3	138.4	1.2	129.4	-2.8	228.4	2.3	100.8	-54.8	99.9	-27.0	-	-
1999	156.2	2.5	155.9	1.6	149.1	1.2	143.7	3.8	132.0	2.0	236.5	3.5	103.9	3.1	102.1	2.2	265.7	21.2
2000	162.0	3.7	159.2	2.1	151.9	1.9	159.8	11.2	142.6	8.0	240.0	1.5	106.0	2.0	104.9	2.7	273.2	2.8
2001	165.9	2.4	164.9	3.6	158.4	4.3	158.9	-0.6	143.4	0.6	244.9	2.0	102.9	-2.9	108.9	3.8	281.2	2.9

Source: U.S. Department of Labor, Bureau of Labor Statistics, Division of Consumer Prices and Price Indexes. *Base is December 1997 = 100. - indicates no data collected for period.

Pittsburgh, PA
Consumer Price Index - All Urban Consumers
Base 1982-1984 = 100
All Items

For 1917-2001. Columns headed % show percentile change in the index from the previous period for which an index is available.

Year	Jan Index	%	Feb Index	%	Mar Index	%	Apr Index	%	May Index	%	Jun Index	%	Jul Index	%	Aug Index	%	Sep Index	%	Oct Index	%	Nov Index	%	Dec Index	%
1917	-		-		-		-		-		-		-		-		-		-		-		13.5	-
1918	-		-		-		-		-		-		-		-		-		-		-		16.2	20.0
1919	-		-		-		-		-		16.5	1.9	-		-		-		-		-		18.4	11.5
1920	-		-		-		-		-		20.4	10.9	-		-		-		-		-		18.9	-7.4
1921	-		-		-		-		17.5	-7.4	-		-		-		17.1	-2.3	-		-		16.7	-2.3
1922	-		-		16.2	-3.0	-		-		16.3	0.6	-		-		16.2	-0.6	-		-		16.4	1.2
1923	-		-		16.4	0.0	-		-		16.7	1.8	-		-		16.8	0.6	-		-		16.7	-0.6
1924	-		-		16.5	-1.2	-		-		16.8	1.8	-		-		16.9	0.6	-		-		17.0	0.6
1925	-		-		-		-		-		17.4	2.4	-		-		-		-		-		17.7	1.7
1926	-		-		-		-		-		17.6	-0.6	-		-		-		-		-		17.5	-0.6
1927	-		-		-		-		-		17.5	0.0	-		-		-		-		-		17.1	-2.3
1928	-		-		-		-		-		16.9	-1.2	-		-		-		-		-		17.1	1.2
1929	-		-		-		-		-		17.1	0.0	-		-		-		-		-		17.0	-0.6
1930	-		-		-		-		-		16.7	-1.8	-		-		-		-		-		15.9	-4.8
1931	-		-		-		-		-		14.9	-6.3	-		-		-		-		-		14.3	-4.0
1932	-		-		-		-		-		13.2	-7.7	-		-		-		-		-		12.8	-3.0
1933	-		-		-		-		-		12.2	-4.7	-		-		-		-		-		12.7	4.1
1934	-		-		-		-		-		13.0	2.4	-		-		-		-		13.0	0.0	-	
1935	-		-		13.2	1.5	-		-		-		13.2	0.0	-		-		13.4	1.5	-		-	
1936	13.4	0.0	-		-		13.3	-0.7	-		-		13.6	2.3	-		13.8	1.5	-		-		13.6	-1.4
1937	-		-		13.9	2.2	-		-		14.1	1.4	-		-		14.3	1.4	-		-		13.9	-2.8
1938	-		-		13.7	-1.4	-		-		13.8	0.7	-		-		13.8	0.0	-		-		13.7	-0.7
1939	-		-		13.3	-2.9	-		-		13.4	0.8	-		-		13.6	1.5	-		-		13.4	-1.5
1940	-		-		13.5	0.7	-		-		13.7	1.5	-		-		13.7	0.0	13.7	0.0	13.7	0.0	13.8	0.7
1941	13.8	0.0	13.7	-0.7	13.8	0.7	13.9	0.7	14.1	1.4	14.3	1.4	14.5	1.4	14.5	0.0	14.8	2.1	14.9	0.7	15.0	0.7	15.1	0.7
1942	15.2	0.7	15.4	1.3	15.5	0.6	15.5	0.0	15.8	1.9	15.9	0.6	15.9	0.0	15.9	0.0	16.0	0.6	16.2	1.3	16.2	0.0	16.3	0.6
1943	16.4	0.6	16.5	0.6	16.7	1.2	16.8	0.6	17.0	1.2	17.0	0.0	16.9	-0.6	16.8	-0.6	16.9	0.6	17.0	0.6	17.0	0.0	16.9	-0.6
1944	16.9	0.0	16.9	0.0	16.9	0.0	17.1	1.2	17.1	0.0	17.2	0.6	17.3	0.6	17.4	0.6	17.4	0.0	17.4	0.0	17.3	-0.6	17.4	0.6
1945	17.4	0.0	17.4	0.0	17.4	0.0	17.4	0.0	17.5	0.6	17.8	1.7	17.8	0.0	17.7	-0.6	17.7	0.0	17.7	0.0	17.7	0.0	17.8	0.6
1946	17.9	0.6	17.8	-0.6	17.9	0.6	17.9	0.0	18.0	0.6	18.3	1.7	19.4	6.0	19.8	2.1	20.1	1.5	20.3	1.0	20.9	3.0	21.1	1.0
1947	21.2	0.5	21.3	0.5	21.7	1.9	21.6	-0.5	21.7	0.5	21.9	0.9	22.2	1.4	22.4	0.9	22.9	2.2	22.8	-0.4	22.9	0.4	23.2	1.3
1948	23.5	1.3	23.1	-1.7	23.1	0.0	23.4	1.3	23.6	0.9	23.9	1.3	24.2	1.3	24.3	0.4	24.3	0.0	24.1	-0.8	23.9	-0.8	23.8	-0.4
1949	23.8	0.0	23.4	-1.7	23.5	0.4	23.5	0.0	23.5	0.0	23.6	0.4	23.4	-0.8	23.5	0.4	23.5	0.0	23.3	-0.9	23.3	0.0	23.2	-0.4
1950	23.1	-0.4	23.0	-0.4	23.0	0.0	23.1	0.4	23.3	0.9	23.4	0.4	23.5	0.4	23.9	1.7	24.2	1.3	24.3	0.4	24.3	0.0	24.5	0.8
1951	25.0	2.0	25.2	0.8	25.3	0.4	25.4	0.4	25.6	0.8	25.6	0.0	25.8	0.8	25.7	-0.4	25.9	0.8	26.0	0.4	26.1	0.4	26.1	0.0
1952	26.2	0.4	26.0	-0.8	25.9	-0.4	26.0	0.4	26.0	0.0	26.0	0.0	26.1	0.4	26.2	0.4	26.2	0.0	26.2	0.0	26.2	0.0	26.2	0.0
1953	26.1	-0.4	-		-		26.1	0.0	-		-		26.3	0.8	-		-		26.5	0.8	-		-	
1954	26.5	0.0	-		-		26.5	0.0	-		-		26.7	0.8	-		-		26.4	-1.1	-		-	
1955	26.3	-0.4	-		-		26.3	0.0	-		-		26.3	0.0	-		-		26.3	0.0	-		-	
1956	26.3	0.0	-		-		26.6	1.1	-		-		27.1	1.9	-		-		27.3	0.7	-		-	
1957	27.5	0.7	-		-		27.5	0.0	-		-		27.9	1.5	-		-		28.0	0.4	-		-	
1958	28.3	1.1	-		-		28.6	1.1	-		-		28.8	0.7	-		-		28.8	0.0	-		-	
1959	28.8	0.0	-		-		28.8	0.0	-		-		29.1	1.0	-		-		29.3	0.7	-		-	
1960	29.3	0.0	-		-		29.6	1.0	-		-		29.8	0.7	-		-		29.8	0.0	-		-	
1961	29.9	0.3	-		-		29.9	0.0	-		-		30.0	0.3	-		-		29.9	-0.3	-		-	
1962	30.0	0.3	-		-		30.1	0.3	-		-		30.2	0.3	-		-		30.3	0.3	-		-	

[Continued]

Pittsburgh, PA
Consumer Price Index - All Urban Consumers
Base 1982-1984 = 100
All Items
[Continued]

For 1917-2001. Columns headed % show percentile change in the index from the previous period for which an index is available.

Year	Jan Index	%	Feb Index	%	Mar Index	%	Apr Index	%	May Index	%	Jun Index	%	Jul Index	%	Aug Index	%	Sep Index	%	Oct Index	%	Nov Index	%	Dec Index	%
1963	30.3	0.0	-	-	-	-	30.3	0.0	-	-	-	-	30.7	1.3	-	-	-	-	30.6	-0.3	-	-	-	-
1964	30.7	0.3	-	-	-	-	30.8	0.3	-	-	-	-	31.0	0.6	-	-	-	-	31.0	0.0	-	-	-	-
1965	31.1	0.3	-	-	-	-	31.3	0.6	-	-	-	-	31.6	1.0	-	-	-	-	31.6	0.0	-	-	-	-
1966	31.6	0.0	-	-	-	-	32.2	1.9	-	-	-	-	32.1	-0.3	-	-	-	-	32.5	1.2	-	-	-	-
1967	32.5	0.0	-	-	-	-	32.5	0.0	-	-	-	-	32.8	0.9	-	-	-	-	32.9	0.3	-	-	-	-
1968	33.5	1.8	-	-	-	-	34.0	1.5	-	-	-	-	34.2	0.6	-	-	-	-	34.9	2.0	-	-	-	-
1969	35.3	1.1	-	-	-	-	35.9	1.7	-	-	-	-	36.4	1.4	-	-	-	-	36.6	0.5	-	-	-	-
1970	36.9	0.8	-	-	-	-	37.7	2.2	-	-	-	-	38.3	1.6	-	-	-	-	39.0	1.8	-	-	-	-
1971	39.1	0.3	-	-	-	-	39.6	1.3	-	-	-	-	39.9	0.8	-	-	-	-	40.3	1.0	-	-	-	-
1972	40.4	0.2	-	-	-	-	40.9	1.2	-	-	-	-	41.1	0.5	-	-	-	-	41.5	1.0	-	-	-	-
1973	41.7	0.5	-	-	-	-	43.0	3.1	-	-	-	-	43.5	1.2	-	-	-	-	44.8	3.0	-	-	-	-
1974	45.7	2.0	-	-	-	-	47.2	3.3	-	-	-	-	48.6	3.0	-	-	-	-	49.9	2.7	-	-	-	-
1975	50.6	1.4	-	-	-	-	51.7	2.2	-	-	-	-	53.0	2.5	-	-	-	-	53.4	0.8	-	-	-	-
1976	53.8	0.7	-	-	-	-	54.6	1.5	-	-	-	-	55.2	1.1	-	-	-	-	56.0	1.4	-	-	-	-
1977	56.7	1.3	-	-	-	-	58.4	3.0	-	-	-	-	59.2	1.4	-	-	-	-	60.1	1.5	-	-	-	-
1978	60.6	0.8	-	-	-	-	62.3	2.8	-	-	63.5	1.9	-	-	65.5	3.1	-	-	66.4	1.4	-	-	67.2	1.2
1979	-	-	68.6	2.1	-	-	69.5	1.3	-	-	70.3	1.2	-	-	71.8	2.1	-	-	74.1	3.2	-	-	75.1	1.3
1980	-	-	77.2	2.8	-	-	78.9	2.2	-	-	80.6	2.2	-	-	82.2	2.0	-	-	84.0	2.2	-	-	85.9	2.3
1981	-	-	87.0	1.3	-	-	87.1	0.1	-	-	88.9	2.1	-	-	91.0	2.4	-	-	91.0	0.0	-	-	92.3	1.4
1982	-	-	91.3	-1.1	-	-	90.2	-1.2	-	-	93.4	3.5	-	-	95.5	2.2	-	-	98.5	3.1	-	-	99.0	0.5
1983	-	-	99.9	0.9	-	-	100.0	0.1	-	-	100.1	0.1	-	-	101.7	1.6	-	-	102.8	1.1	-	-	103.0	0.2
1984	-	-	103.4	0.4	-	-	104.4	1.0	-	-	104.8	0.4	-	-	104.6	-0.2	-	-	105.2	0.6	-	-	105.6	0.4
1985	-	-	106.1	0.5	-	-	106.3	0.2	-	-	106.8	0.5	-	-	106.8	0.0	-	-	107.6	0.7	-	-	108.6	0.9
1986	-	-	108.2	-0.4	-	-	107.5	-0.6	-	-	107.7	0.2	-	-	108.2	0.5	-	-	108.7	0.5	-	-	109.1	0.4
1987	-	-	109.8	0.6	-	-	110.8	0.9	-	-	111.1	0.3	-	-	112.0	0.8	-	-	112.8	0.7	-	-	113.0	0.2
1988	-	-	113.3	0.3	-	-	114.5	1.1	-	-	114.3	-0.2	-	-	115.3	0.9	-	-	116.3	0.9	-	-	116.7	0.3
1989	-	-	117.9	1.0	-	-	119.2	1.1	-	-	120.4	1.0	-	-	120.8	0.3	-	-	121.7	0.7	-	-	121.8	0.1
1990	-	-	123.4	1.3	-	-	124.9	1.2	-	-	125.0	0.1	-	-	127.1	1.7	-	-	129.6	2.0	-	-	129.1	-0.4
1991	-	-	129.3	0.2	-	-	130.3	0.8	-	-	130.7	0.3	-	-	131.5	0.6	-	-	133.2	1.3	-	-	134.4	0.9
1992	-	-	134.3	-0.1	-	-	135.1	0.6	-	-	135.2	0.1	-	-	136.9	1.3	-	-	137.7	0.6	-	-	137.3	-0.3
1993	-	-	139.2	1.4	-	-	139.6	0.3	-	-	139.5	-0.1	-	-	140.4	0.6	-	-	140.6	0.1	-	-	141.1	0.4
1994	-	-	142.6	1.1	-	-	143.9	0.9	-	-	144.0	0.1	-	-	145.7	1.2	-	-	146.4	0.5	-	-	146.5	0.1
1995	-	-	147.3	0.5	-	-	148.9	1.1	-	-	149.2	0.2	-	-	150.1	0.6	-	-	150.5	0.3	-	-	150.0	-0.3
1996	-	-	151.1	0.7	-	-	152.8	1.1	-	-	153.2	0.3	-	-	153.6	0.3	-	-	154.5	0.6	-	-	155.4	0.6
1997	-	-	156.2	0.5	-	-	156.6	0.3	-	-	157.4	0.5	-	-	157.5	0.1	-	-	157.9	0.3	-	-	157.1	-0.5
1998	-	-	-	-	-	-	-	-	-	-	158.1	0.6	-	-	-	-	-	-	-	-	-	-	160.3	1.4
1999	-	-	-	-	-	-	-	-	-	-	161.4	0.7	-	-	-	-	-	-	-	-	-	-	163.6	1.4
2000	-	-	-	-	-	-	-	-	-	-	166.9	2.0	-	-	-	-	-	-	-	-	-	-	169.0	1.3
2001	-	-	-	-	-	-	-	-	-	-	172.4	2.0	-	-	-	-	-	-	-	-	-	-	-	-

Source: U.S. Department of Labor, Bureau of Labor Statistics, Division of Consumer Prices and Price Indexes. - indicates no data collected for period.

Pittsburgh, PA
Consumer Price Index - Urban Wage Earners
Base 1982-1984 = 100
All Items

For 1917-2001. Columns headed % show percentile change in the index from the previous period for which an index is available.

Year	Jan Index	%	Feb Index	%	Mar Index	%	Apr Index	%	May Index	%	Jun Index	%	Jul Index	%	Aug Index	%	Sep Index	%	Oct Index	%	Nov Index	%	Dec Index	%
1917	-	-	-	-	-	-	-	-	-	-	-	-	-	-	-	-	-	-	-	-	-	-	13.9	-
1918	-	-	-	-	-	-	-	-	-	-	-	-	-	-	-	-	-	-	-	-	-	-	16.6	19.4
1919	-	-	-	-	-	-	-	-	-	-	16.9	1.8	-	-	-	-	-	-	-	-	-	-	18.8	11.2
1920	-	-	-	-	-	-	-	-	-	-	20.9	11.2	-	-	-	-	-	-	-	-	-	-	19.4	-7.2
1921	-	-	-	-	-	-	-	-	17.9	-7.7	-	-	-	-	-	-	17.5	-2.2	-	-	-	-	17.2	-1.7
1922	-	-	-	-	16.6	-3.5	-	-	-	-	16.7	0.6	-	-	-	-	16.6	-0.6	-	-	-	-	16.8	1.2
1923	-	-	-	-	16.8	0.0	-	-	-	-	17.2	2.4	-	-	-	-	17.3	0.6	-	-	-	-	17.2	-0.6
1924	-	-	-	-	17.0	-1.2	-	-	-	-	17.3	1.8	-	-	-	-	17.3	0.0	-	-	-	-	17.5	1.2
1925	-	-	-	-	-	-	-	-	-	-	17.8	1.7	-	-	-	-	-	-	-	-	-	-	18.2	2.2
1926	-	-	-	-	-	-	-	-	-	-	18.0	-1.1	-	-	-	-	-	-	-	-	-	-	18.0	0.0
1927	-	-	-	-	-	-	-	-	-	-	17.9	-0.6	-	-	-	-	-	-	-	-	-	-	17.6	-1.7
1928	-	-	-	-	-	-	-	-	-	-	17.4	-1.1	-	-	-	-	-	-	-	-	-	-	17.6	1.1
1929	-	-	-	-	-	-	-	-	-	-	17.5	-0.6	-	-	-	-	-	-	-	-	-	-	17.5	0.0
1930	-	-	-	-	-	-	-	-	-	-	17.1	-2.3	-	-	-	-	-	-	-	-	-	-	16.3	-4.7
1931	-	-	-	-	-	-	-	-	-	-	15.3	-6.1	-	-	-	-	-	-	-	-	-	-	14.7	-3.9
1932	-	-	-	-	-	-	-	-	-	-	13.6	-7.5	-	-	-	-	-	-	-	-	-	-	13.1	-3.7
1933	-	-	-	-	-	-	-	-	-	-	12.5	-4.6	-	-	-	-	-	-	-	-	-	-	13.0	4.0
1934	-	-	-	-	-	-	-	-	-	-	13.3	2.3	-	-	-	-	-	-	-	-	13.3	0.0	-	-
1935	-	-	-	-	13.6	2.3	-	-	-	-	-	-	13.6	0.0	-	-	-	-	13.7	0.7	-	-	-	-
1936	13.8	0.7	-	-	-	-	13.6	-1.4	-	-	-	-	14.0	2.9	-	-	14.1	0.7	-	-	-	-	14.0	-0.7
1937	-	-	-	-	14.2	1.4	-	-	-	-	14.5	2.1	-	-	-	-	14.7	1.4	-	-	-	-	14.3	-2.7
1938	-	-	-	-	14.1	-1.4	-	-	-	-	14.1	0.0	-	-	-	-	14.1	0.0	-	-	-	-	14.0	-0.7
1939	-	-	-	-	13.7	-2.1	-	-	-	-	13.8	0.7	-	-	-	-	14.0	1.4	-	-	-	-	13.8	-1.4
1940	-	-	-	-	13.8	0.0	-	-	-	-	14.1	2.2	-	-	-	-	14.1	0.0	14.0	-0.7	14.1	0.7	14.1	0.0
1941	14.1	0.0	14.1	0.0	14.2	0.7	14.3	0.7	14.5	1.4	14.7	1.4	14.8	0.7	14.9	0.7	15.2	2.0	15.3	0.7	15.4	0.7	15.5	0.6
1942	15.6	0.6	15.8	1.3	15.9	0.6	15.9	0.0	16.2	1.9	16.3	0.6	16.3	0.0	16.3	0.0	16.4	0.6	16.6	1.2	16.6	0.0	16.7	0.6
1943	16.8	0.6	16.9	0.6	17.1	1.2	17.3	1.2	17.5	1.2	17.5	0.0	17.3	-1.1	17.3	0.0	17.4	0.6	17.5	0.6	17.5	0.0	17.4	-0.6
1944	17.4	0.0	17.3	-0.6	17.3	0.0	17.5	1.2	17.5	0.0	17.7	1.1	17.7	0.0	17.8	0.6	17.8	0.0	17.8	0.0	17.7	-0.6	17.9	1.1
1945	17.9	0.0	17.9	0.0	17.8	-0.6	17.9	0.6	18.0	0.6	18.2	1.1	18.3	0.5	18.2	-0.5	18.1	-0.5	18.2	0.6	18.2	0.0	18.3	0.5
1946	18.3	0.0	18.3	0.0	18.3	0.0	18.4	0.5	18.5	0.5	18.8	1.6	19.9	5.9	20.3	2.0	20.6	1.5	20.8	1.0	21.5	3.4	21.7	0.9
1947	21.8	0.5	21.9	0.5	22.2	1.4	22.2	0.0	22.3	0.5	22.5	0.9	22.7	0.9	23.0	1.3	23.5	2.2	23.4	-0.4	23.5	0.4	23.8	1.3
1948	24.1	1.3	23.7	-1.7	23.7	0.0	24.0	1.3	24.2	0.8	24.5	1.2	24.8	1.2	24.9	0.4	24.9	0.0	24.7	-0.8	24.5	-0.8	24.4	-0.4
1949	24.4	0.0	24.0	-1.6	24.1	0.4	24.1	0.0	24.1	0.0	24.2	0.4	24.0	-0.8	24.1	0.4	24.1	0.0	23.9	-0.8	23.9	0.0	23.8	-0.4
1950	23.7	-0.4	23.6	-0.4	23.6	0.0	23.7	0.4	23.9	0.8	24.0	0.4	24.1	0.4	24.5	1.7	24.8	1.2	25.0	0.8	24.9	-0.4	25.1	0.8
1951	25.6	2.0	25.9	1.2	26.0	0.4	26.1	0.4	26.2	0.4	26.2	0.0	26.4	0.8	26.4	0.0	26.5	0.4	26.7	0.8	26.8	0.4	26.8	0.0
1952	26.8	0.0	26.7	-0.4	26.6	-0.4	26.7	0.4	26.7	0.0	26.6	-0.4	26.8	0.8	26.9	0.4	26.9	0.0	26.9	0.0	26.9	0.0	26.9	0.0
1953	26.7	-0.7	-	-	-	-	26.8	0.4	-	-	-	-	27.0	0.7	-	-	-	-	27.2	0.7	-	-	-	-
1954	27.2	0.0	-	-	-	-	27.2	0.0	-	-	-	-	27.4	0.7	-	-	-	-	27.1	-1.1	-	-	-	-
1955	27.0	-0.4	-	-	-	-	27.0	0.0	-	-	-	-	27.0	0.0	-	-	-	-	27.0	0.0	-	-	-	-
1956	27.0	0.0	-	-	-	-	27.3	1.1	-	-	-	-	27.8	1.8	-	-	-	-	28.0	0.7	-	-	-	-
1957	28.2	0.7	-	-	-	-	28.2	0.0	-	-	-	-	28.6	1.4	-	-	-	-	28.7	0.3	-	-	-	-
1958	29.1	1.4	-	-	-	-	29.4	1.0	-	-	-	-	29.6	0.7	-	-	-	-	29.6	0.0	-	-	-	-
1959	29.5	-0.3	-	-	-	-	29.6	0.3	-	-	-	-	29.8	0.7	-	-	-	-	30.1	1.0	-	-	-	-
1960	30.1	0.0	-	-	-	-	30.4	1.0	-	-	-	-	30.6	0.7	-	-	-	-	30.6	0.0	-	-	-	-
1961	30.7	0.3	-	-	-	-	30.7	0.0	-	-	-	-	30.8	0.3	-	-	-	-	30.7	-0.3	-	-	-	-
1962	30.8	0.3	-	-	-	-	30.9	0.3	-	-	-	-	31.0	0.3	-	-	-	-	31.1	0.3	-	-	-	-

[Continued]

Pittsburgh, PA
Consumer Price Index - Urban Wage Earners
Base 1982-1984 = 100
All Items
[Continued]

For 1917-2001. Columns headed % show percentile change in the index from the previous period for which an index is available.

Year	Jan Index	%	Feb Index	%	Mar Index	%	Apr Index	%	May Index	%	Jun Index	%	Jul Index	%	Aug Index	%	Sep Index	%	Oct Index	%	Nov Index	%	Dec Index	%
1963	31.1	0.0	-	-	-	-	31.1	0.0	-	-	-	-	31.5	1.3	-	-	-	-	31.4	-0.3	-	-	-	-
1964	31.5	0.3	-	-	-	-	31.6	0.3	-	-	-	-	31.8	0.6	-	-	-	-	31.8	0.0	-	-	-	-
1965	31.9	0.3	-	-	-	-	32.1	0.6	-	-	-	-	32.4	0.9	-	-	-	-	32.4	0.0	-	-	-	-
1966	32.4	0.0	-	-	-	-	33.1	2.2	-	-	-	-	33.0	-0.3	-	-	-	-	33.4	1.2	-	-	-	-
1967	33.3	-0.3	-	-	-	-	33.4	0.3	-	-	-	-	33.6	0.6	-	-	-	-	33.8	0.6	-	-	-	-
1968	34.4	1.8	-	-	-	-	34.9	1.5	-	-	-	-	35.1	0.6	-	-	-	-	35.8	2.0	-	-	-	-
1969	36.2	1.1	-	-	-	-	36.9	1.9	-	-	-	-	37.3	1.1	-	-	-	-	37.6	0.8	-	-	-	-
1970	37.8	0.5	-	-	-	-	38.7	2.4	-	-	-	-	39.3	1.6	-	-	-	-	40.0	1.8	-	-	-	-
1971	40.1	0.2	-	-	-	-	40.7	1.5	-	-	-	-	41.0	0.7	-	-	-	-	41.3	0.7	-	-	-	-
1972	41.4	0.2	-	-	-	-	41.9	1.2	-	-	-	-	42.2	0.7	-	-	-	-	42.5	0.7	-	-	-	-
1973	42.8	0.7	-	-	-	-	44.1	3.0	-	-	-	-	44.6	1.1	-	-	-	-	45.9	2.9	-	-	-	-
1974	46.8	2.0	-	-	-	-	48.5	3.6	-	-	-	-	49.9	2.9	-	-	-	-	51.2	2.6	-	-	-	-
1975	51.9	1.4	-	-	-	-	53.0	2.1	-	-	-	-	54.4	2.6	-	-	-	-	54.7	0.6	-	-	-	-
1976	55.2	0.9	-	-	-	-	56.0	1.4	-	-	-	-	56.7	1.3	-	-	-	-	57.5	1.4	-	-	-	-
1977	58.1	1.0	-	-	-	-	59.9	3.1	-	-	-	-	60.7	1.3	-	-	-	-	61.7	1.6	-	-	-	-
1978	62.2	0.8	-	-	-	-	63.9	2.7	-	-	65.1	1.9	-	-	66.9	2.8	-	-	67.8	1.3	-	-	68.7	1.3
1979	-	-	70.1	2.0	-	-	71.4	1.9	-	-	72.3	1.3	-	-	74.0	2.4	-	-	76.0	2.7	-	-	77.2	1.6
1980	-	-	79.3	2.7	-	-	81.4	2.6	-	-	83.0	2.0	-	-	84.5	1.8	-	-	86.6	2.5	-	-	88.4	2.1
1981	-	-	89.6	1.4	-	-	89.9	0.3	-	-	91.8	2.1	-	-	93.5	1.9	-	-	93.6	0.1	-	-	95.0	1.5
1982	-	-	94.1	-0.9	-	-	93.0	-1.2	-	-	96.1	3.3	-	-	98.1	2.1	-	-	101.0	3.0	-	-	101.4	0.4
1983	-	-	99.7	-1.7	-	-	101.1	1.4	-	-	100.7	-0.4	-	-	102.3	1.6	-	-	102.4	0.1	-	-	101.7	-0.7
1984	-	-	100.7	-1.0	-	-	101.4	0.7	-	-	101.3	-0.1	-	-	102.0	0.7	-	-	102.3	0.3	-	-	102.4	0.1
1985	-	-	102.9	0.5	-	-	103.2	0.3	-	-	103.7	0.5	-	-	103.6	-0.1	-	-	104.2	0.6	-	-	105.2	1.0
1986	-	-	104.7	-0.5	-	-	103.5	-1.1	-	-	103.7	0.2	-	-	104.0	0.3	-	-	104.4	0.4	-	-	104.8	0.4
1987	-	-	105.7	0.9	-	-	106.4	0.7	-	-	106.8	0.4	-	-	107.7	0.8	-	-	108.3	0.6	-	-	108.6	0.3
1988	-	-	108.9	0.3	-	-	110.1	1.1	-	-	110.0	-0.1	-	-	110.7	0.6	-	-	111.7	0.9	-	-	112.2	0.4
1989	-	-	113.4	1.1	-	-	114.7	1.1	-	-	115.9	1.0	-	-	116.0	0.1	-	-	116.8	0.7	-	-	117.1	0.3
1990	-	-	118.6	1.3	-	-	120.1	1.3	-	-	120.3	0.2	-	-	122.0	1.4	-	-	124.6	2.1	-	-	124.2	-0.3
1991	-	-	124.1	-0.1	-	-	124.9	0.6	-	-	125.3	0.3	-	-	125.9	0.5	-	-	127.5	1.3	-	-	128.7	0.9
1992	-	-	128.7	0.0	-	-	129.4	0.5	-	-	129.5	0.1	-	-	131.0	1.2	-	-	131.6	0.5	-	-	131.4	-0.2
1993	-	-	133.2	1.4	-	-	133.6	0.3	-	-	133.7	0.1	-	-	134.2	0.4	-	-	134.5	0.2	-	-	135.1	0.4
1994	-	-	136.3	0.9	-	-	137.4	0.8	-	-	137.8	0.3	-	-	139.4	1.2	-	-	140.1	0.5	-	-	140.3	0.1
1995	-	-	141.1	0.6	-	-	142.6	1.1	-	-	143.0	0.3	-	-	143.7	0.5	-	-	144.2	0.3	-	-	143.7	-0.3
1996	-	-	144.7	0.7	-	-	146.5	1.2	-	-	146.9	0.3	-	-	147.2	0.2	-	-	148.0	0.5	-	-	148.8	0.5
1997	-	-	149.6	0.5	-	-	150.1	0.3	-	-	150.8	0.5	-	-	151.0	0.1	-	-	151.3	0.2	-	-	150.6	-0.5
1998	-	-	-	-	-	-	-	-	-	-	151.4	0.5	-	-	-	-	-	-	-	-	-	-	153.4	1.3
1999	-	-	-	-	-	-	-	-	-	-	154.8	0.9	-	-	-	-	-	-	-	-	-	-	157.6	1.8
2000	-	-	-	-	-	-	-	-	-	-	161.2	2.3	-	-	-	-	-	-	-	-	-	-	162.8	1.0
2001	-	-	-	-	-	-	-	-	-	-	166.2	2.1	-	-	-	-	-	-	-	-	-	-		

Source: U.S. Department of Labor, Bureau of Labor Statistics, Division of Consumer Prices and Price Indexes. - indicates no data collected for period.

Pittsburgh, PA
Consumer Price Index - All Urban Consumers
Base 1982-1984 = 100
Food and Beverages

For 1976-2001. Columns headed % show percentile change in the index from the previous period for which an index is available.

Year	Jan Index	%	Feb Index	%	Mar Index	%	Apr Index	%	May Index	%	Jun Index	%	Jul Index	%	Aug Index	%	Sep Index	%	Oct Index	%	Nov Index	%	Dec Index	%
1976	62.0	-	-	-	-	-	62.0	0.0	-	-	-	-	62.3	0.5	-	-	-	-	62.7	0.6	-	-	-	-
1977	62.9	0.3	-	-	-	-	66.0	4.9	-	-	-	-	67.1	1.7	-	-	-	-	67.6	0.7	-	-	-	-
1978	68.5	1.3	-	-	-	-	71.4	4.2	-	-	73.6	3.1	-	-	74.4	1.1	-	-	75.1	0.9	-	-	75.3	0.3
1979	-		78.5	4.2	-	-	78.8	0.4	-	-	80.0	1.5	-	-	80.4	0.5	-	-	81.7	1.6	-	-	82.6	1.1
1980	-		83.5	1.1	-	-	84.5	1.2	-	-	86.7	2.6	-	-	89.0	2.7	-	-	90.1	1.2	-	-	91.5	1.6
1981	-		92.5	1.1	-	-	93.2	0.8	-	-	93.4	0.2	-	-	94.8	1.5	-	-	95.1	0.3	-	-	94.9	-0.2
1982	-		96.4	1.6	-	-	96.5	0.1	-	-	98.9	2.5	-	-	97.8	-1.1	-	-	99.4	1.6	-	-	99.9	0.5
1983	-		100.5	0.6	-	-	101.1	0.6	-	-	101.4	0.3	-	-	101.1	-0.3	-	-	101.2	0.1	-	-	101.7	0.5
1984	-		100.4	-1.3	-	-	101.1	0.7	-	-	101.1	0.0	-	-	101.4	0.3	-	-	100.7	-0.7	-	-	100.7	0.0
1985	-		102.7	2.0	-	-	102.3	-0.4	-	-	102.5	0.2	-	-	102.3	-0.2	-	-	101.9	-0.4	-	-	102.5	0.6
1986	-		104.0	1.5	-	-	103.8	-0.2	-	-	104.0	0.2	-	-	106.7	2.6	-	-	105.6	-1.0	-	-	107.2	1.5
1987	-		108.4	1.1	-	-	109.4	0.9	-	-	110.6	1.1	-	-	109.4	-1.1	-	-	109.7	0.3	-	-	109.7	0.0
1988	-		110.6	0.8	-	-	112.0	1.3	-	-	111.2	-0.7	-	-	113.1	1.7	-	-	112.3	-0.7	-	-	113.4	1.0
1989	-		116.5	2.7	-	-	117.5	0.9	-	-	118.2	0.6	-	-	119.0	0.7	-	-	118.9	-0.1	-	-	119.7	0.7
1990	-		122.9	2.7	-	-	123.8	0.7	-	-	124.6	0.6	-	-	125.1	0.4	-	-	125.9	0.6	-	-	124.8	-0.9
1991	-		128.7	3.1	-	-	129.3	0.5	-	-	129.5	0.2	-	-	128.9	-0.5	-	-	129.1	0.2	-	-	131.4	1.8
1992	-		132.3	0.7	-	-	131.7	-0.5	-	-	133.7	1.5	-	-	133.5	-0.1	-	-	133.3	-0.1	-	-	133.2	-0.1
1993	-		135.6	1.8	-	-	137.5	1.4	-	-	137.5	0.0	-	-	137.2	-0.2	-	-	137.9	0.5	-	-	139.1	0.9
1994	-		138.4	-0.5	-	-	139.8	1.0	-	-	140.8	0.7	-	-	141.5	0.5	-	-	140.2	-0.9	-	-	143.9	2.6
1995	-		140.9	-2.1	-	-	143.9	2.1	-	-	141.9	-1.4	-	-	144.5	1.8	-	-	144.9	0.3	-	-	146.1	0.8
1996	-		146.5	0.3	-	-	149.8	2.3	-	-	148.8	-0.7	-	-	149.6	0.5	-	-	149.1	-0.3	-	-	151.1	1.3
1997	-		150.8	-0.2	-	-	152.1	0.9	-	-	152.3	0.1	-	-	150.3	-1.3	-	-	153.0	1.8	-	-	152.4	-0.4
1998	-		-	-	-	-	-	-	-	-	152.4	0.0	-	-	-	-	-	-	-	-	-	-	154.7	1.5
1999	-		-	-	-	-	-	-	-	-	155.5	0.5	-	-	-	-	-	-	-	-	-	-	156.6	0.7
2000	-		-	-	-	-	-	-	-	-	158.1	1.0	-	-	-	-	-	-	-	-	-	-	160.4	1.5
2001	-		-	-	-	-	-	-	-	-	163.1	1.7	-	-	-	-	-	-	-	-	-	-	-	-

Source: U.S. Department of Labor, Bureau of Labor Statistics, Division of Consumer Prices and Price Indexes. - indicates no data collected for period.

Pittsburgh, PA
Consumer Price Index - Urban Wage Earners
Base 1982-1984 = 100
Food and Beverages

For 1976-2001. Columns headed % show percentile change in the index from the previous period for which an index is available.

Year	Jan Index	%	Feb Index	%	Mar Index	%	Apr Index	%	May Index	%	Jun Index	%	Jul Index	%	Aug Index	%	Sep Index	%	Oct Index	%	Nov Index	%	Dec Index	%
1976	61.8	-	-	-	-	-	61.9	0.2	-	-	-	-	62.1	0.3	-	-	-	-	62.6	0.8	-	-	-	-
1977	62.7	0.2	-	-	-	-	65.9	5.1	-	-	-	-	66.9	1.5	-	-	-	-	67.4	0.7	-	-	-	-
1978	68.3	1.3	-	-	-	-	71.2	4.2	-	-	73.3	2.9	-	-	74.9	2.2	-	-	74.8	-0.1	-	-	75.4	0.8
1979	-	-	78.7	4.4	-	-	79.5	1.0	-	-	80.3	1.0	-	-	81.2	1.1	-	-	82.2	1.2	-	-	83.0	1.0
1980	-	-	83.7	0.8	-	-	85.5	2.2	-	-	86.6	1.3	-	-	88.8	2.5	-	-	90.1	1.5	-	-	92.1	2.2
1981	-	-	93.0	1.0	-	-	93.6	0.6	-	-	93.8	0.2	-	-	94.8	1.1	-	-	94.9	0.1	-	-	95.0	0.1
1982	-	-	96.4	1.5	-	-	96.6	0.2	-	-	99.0	2.5	-	-	97.8	-1.2	-	-	99.5	1.7	-	-	99.9	0.4
1983	-	-	100.4	0.5	-	-	101.1	0.7	-	-	101.4	0.3	-	-	101.2	-0.2	-	-	101.3	0.1	-	-	101.7	0.4
1984	-	-	100.3	-1.4	-	-	101.0	0.7	-	-	101.1	0.1	-	-	101.6	0.5	-	-	100.6	-1.0	-	-	100.6	0.0
1985	-	-	102.5	1.9	-	-	102.1	-0.4	-	-	102.4	0.3	-	-	102.1	-0.3	-	-	101.5	-0.6	-	-	102.2	0.7
1986	-	-	103.5	1.3	-	-	103.3	-0.2	-	-	103.6	0.3	-	-	106.5	2.8	-	-	105.3	-1.1	-	-	106.9	1.5
1987	-	-	108.0	1.0	-	-	109.0	0.9	-	-	110.1	1.0	-	-	109.2	-0.8	-	-	109.6	0.4	-	-	109.6	0.0
1988	-	-	110.5	0.8	-	-	111.7	1.1	-	-	111.2	-0.4	-	-	113.0	1.6	-	-	112.5	-0.4	-	-	113.6	1.0
1989	-	-	116.4	2.5	-	-	117.4	0.9	-	-	118.1	0.6	-	-	119.0	0.8	-	-	119.0	0.0	-	-	119.7	0.6
1990	-	-	122.8	2.6	-	-	124.0	1.0	-	-	124.8	0.6	-	-	125.4	0.5	-	-	126.2	0.6	-	-	125.3	-0.7
1991	-	-	129.1	3.0	-	-	129.7	0.5	-	-	129.9	0.2	-	-	129.2	-0.5	-	-	129.6	0.3	-	-	131.8	1.7
1992	-	-	132.6	0.6	-	-	132.1	-0.4	-	-	133.9	1.4	-	-	133.7	-0.1	-	-	133.4	-0.2	-	-	133.4	0.0
1993	-	-	135.7	1.7	-	-	137.7	1.5	-	-	137.7	0.0	-	-	137.6	-0.1	-	-	138.2	0.4	-	-	139.3	0.8
1994	-	-	138.4	-0.6	-	-	139.8	1.0	-	-	140.6	0.6	-	-	141.4	0.6	-	-	140.5	-0.6	-	-	143.6	2.2
1995	-	-	141.0	-1.8	-	-	143.6	1.8	-	-	141.4	-1.5	-	-	144.6	2.3	-	-	144.7	0.1	-	-	145.8	0.8
1996	-	-	146.3	0.3	-	-	149.4	2.1	-	-	148.5	-0.6	-	-	149.5	0.7	-	-	149.2	-0.2	-	-	151.0	1.2
1997	-	-	150.8	-0.1	-	-	152.3	1.0	-	-	152.3	0.0	-	-	150.4	-1.2	-	-	153.0	1.7	-	-	152.5	-0.3
1998	-	-	-	-	-	-	-	-	-	-	152.4	-0.1	-	-	-	-	-	-	-	-	-	-	154.7	1.5
1999	-	-	-	-	-	-	-	-	-	-	155.4	0.5	-	-	-	-	-	-	-	-	-	-	156.4	0.6
2000	-	-	-	-	-	-	-	-	-	-	158.0	1.0	-	-	-	-	-	-	-	-	-	-	160.3	1.5
2001	-	-	-	-	-	-	-	-	-	-	162.9	1.6	-	-	-	-	-	-	-	-	-	-	-	-

Source: U.S. Department of Labor, Bureau of Labor Statistics, Division of Consumer Prices and Price Indexes. - indicates no data collected for period.

Pittsburgh, PA
Consumer Price Index - All Urban Consumers
Base 1982-1984 = 100
Housing

For 1976-2001. Columns headed % show percentile change in the index from the previous period for which an index is available.

Year	Jan Index	%	Feb Index	%	Mar Index	%	Apr Index	%	May Index	%	Jun Index	%	Jul Index	%	Aug Index	%	Sep Index	%	Oct Index	%	Nov Index	%	Dec Index	%
1976	49.2	-	-	-	-	-	50.6	2.8	-	-	-	-	50.6	0.0	-	-	-	-	51.3	1.4	-	-	-	-
1977	52.6	2.5	-	-	-	-	53.7	2.1	-	-	-	-	54.2	0.9	-	-	-	-	55.7	2.8	-	-	-	-
1978	56.8	2.0	-	-	-	-	58.2	2.5	-	-	59.3	1.9	-	-	61.9	4.4	-	-	63.4	2.4	-	-	64.9	2.4
1979	-	-	65.8	1.4	-	-	66.4	0.9	-	-	66.7	0.5	-	-	67.5	1.2	-	-	71.1	5.3	-	-	72.1	1.4
1980	-	-	74.3	3.1	-	-	76.9	3.5	-	-	78.6	2.2	-	-	79.9	1.7	-	-	82.0	2.6	-	-	84.7	3.3
1981	-	-	84.5	-0.2	-	-	83.3	-1.4	-	-	86.6	4.0	-	-	89.1	2.9	-	-	87.6	-1.7	-	-	90.8	3.7
1982	-	-	87.3	-3.9	-	-	85.4	-2.2	-	-	90.9	6.4	-	-	94.1	3.5	-	-	98.8	5.0	-	-	99.2	0.4
1983	-	-	100.5	1.3	-	-	101.4	0.9	-	-	100.7	-0.7	-	-	102.3	1.6	-	-	103.0	0.7	-	-	103.2	0.2
1984	-	-	104.9	1.6	-	-	106.4	1.4	-	-	106.9	0.5	-	-	105.7	-1.1	-	-	106.4	0.7	-	-	107.4	0.9
1985	-	-	107.8	0.4	-	-	108.1	0.3	-	-	108.7	0.6	-	-	108.6	-0.1	-	-	108.2	-0.4	-	-	110.4	2.0
1986	-	-	109.9	-0.5	-	-	111.8	1.7	-	-	111.0	-0.7	-	-	111.5	0.5	-	-	112.2	0.6	-	-	111.9	-0.3
1987	-	-	113.0	1.0	-	-	112.8	-0.2	-	-	112.8	0.0	-	-	114.1	1.2	-	-	114.0	-0.1	-	-	114.7	0.6
1988	-	-	114.4	-0.3	-	-	115.8	1.2	-	-	116.7	0.8	-	-	115.6	-0.9	-	-	115.6	0.0	-	-	116.6	0.9
1989	-	-	117.8	1.0	-	-	118.0	0.2	-	-	118.8	0.7	-	-	119.7	0.8	-	-	120.8	0.9	-	-	121.2	0.3
1990	-	-	121.3	0.1	-	-	123.6	1.9	-	-	124.0	0.3	-	-	126.7	2.2	-	-	127.6	0.7	-	-	127.0	-0.5
1991	-	-	128.8	1.4	-	-	130.3	1.2	-	-	131.3	0.8	-	-	131.7	0.3	-	-	133.2	1.1	-	-	134.8	1.2
1992	-	-	134.2	-0.4	-	-	135.5	1.0	-	-	134.9	-0.4	-	-	137.7	2.1	-	-	136.6	-0.8	-	-	136.6	0.0
1993	-	-	138.7	1.5	-	-	138.0	-0.5	-	-	138.7	0.5	-	-	139.6	0.6	-	-	139.8	0.1	-	-	141.0	0.9
1994	-	-	144.1	2.2	-	-	144.2	0.1	-	-	144.2	0.0	-	-	146.1	1.3	-	-	147.5	1.0	-	-	146.9	-0.4
1995	-	-	149.0	1.4	-	-	149.6	0.4	-	-	150.2	0.4	-	-	151.0	0.5	-	-	151.0	0.0	-	-	150.4	-0.4
1996	-	-	151.5	0.7	-	-	152.7	0.8	-	-	154.2	1.0	-	-	154.8	0.4	-	-	153.2	-1.0	-	-	153.2	0.0
1997	-	-	155.1	1.2	-	-	155.4	0.2	-	-	157.9	1.6	-	-	157.7	-0.1	-	-	155.9	-1.1	-	-	156.2	0.2
1998	-	-	-	-	-	-	-	-	-	-	158.7	1.6	-	-	-	-	-	-	-	-	-	-	161.4	1.7
1999	-	-	-	-	-	-	-	-	-	-	161.9	0.3	-	-	-	-	-	-	-	-	-	-	162.5	0.4
2000	-	-	-	-	-	-	-	-	-	-	164.1	1.0	-	-	-	-	-	-	-	-	-	-	167.0	1.8
2001	-	-	-	-	-	-	-	-	-	-	172.2	3.1	-	-	-	-	-	-	-	-	-	-	-	-

Source: U.S. Department of Labor, Bureau of Labor Statistics, Division of Consumer Prices and Price Indexes. - indicates no data collected for period.

Pittsburgh, PA
Consumer Price Index - Urban Wage Earners
Base 1982-1984 = 100
Housing

For 1976-2001. Columns headed % show percentile change in the index from the previous period for which an index is available.

Year	Jan Index	%	Feb Index	%	Mar Index	%	Apr Index	%	May Index	%	Jun Index	%	Jul Index	%	Aug Index	%	Sep Index	%	Oct Index	%	Nov Index	%	Dec Index	%
1976	52.2	-	-	-	-	-	53.7	2.9	-	-	-	-	53.7	0.0	-	-	-	-	54.4	1.3	-	-	-	-
1977	55.7	2.4	-	-	-	-	57.0	2.3	-	-	-	-	57.4	0.7	-	-	-	-	59.1	3.0	-	-	-	-
1978	60.2	1.9	-	-	-	-	61.7	2.5	-	-	63.1	2.3	-	-	65.3	3.5	-	-	67.1	2.8	-	-	68.5	2.1
1979	-	-	69.5	1.5	-	-	70.3	1.2	-	-	70.6	0.4	-	-	71.6	1.4	-	-	75.4	5.3	-	-	76.6	1.6
1980	-	-	79.0	3.1	-	-	81.9	3.7	-	-	83.7	2.2	-	-	85.0	1.6	-	-	87.2	2.6	-	-	90.1	3.3
1981	-	-	90.1	0.0	-	-	88.8	-1.4	-	-	92.6	4.3	-	-	94.9	2.5	-	-	93.3	-1.7	-	-	96.9	3.9
1982	-	-	93.3	-3.7	-	-	91.3	-2.1	-	-	97.2	6.5	-	-	100.6	3.5	-	-	105.3	4.7	-	-	105.7	0.4
1983	-	-	100.7	-4.7	-	-	104.9	4.2	-	-	103.0	-1.8	-	-	104.3	1.3	-	-	102.5	-1.7	-	-	100.2	-2.2
1984	-	-	98.1	-2.1	-	-	98.7	0.6	-	-	97.9	-0.8	-	-	98.7	0.8	-	-	99.0	0.3	-	-	99.4	0.4
1985	-	-	99.8	0.4	-	-	100.0	0.2	-	-	100.6	0.6	-	-	100.5	-0.1	-	-	100.2	-0.3	-	-	102.2	2.0
1986	-	-	101.9	-0.3	-	-	103.3	1.4	-	-	102.5	-0.8	-	-	103.0	0.5	-	-	103.7	0.7	-	-	103.4	-0.3
1987	-	-	104.4	1.0	-	-	104.1	-0.3	-	-	104.3	0.2	-	-	105.5	1.2	-	-	105.4	-0.1	-	-	106.0	0.6
1988	-	-	105.7	-0.3	-	-	107.0	1.2	-	-	107.8	0.7	-	-	106.8	-0.9	-	-	106.9	0.1	-	-	107.9	0.9
1989	-	-	108.9	0.9	-	-	109.1	0.2	-	-	110.2	1.0	-	-	110.8	0.5	-	-	111.7	0.8	-	-	112.3	0.5
1990	-	-	112.4	0.1	-	-	114.6	2.0	-	-	114.9	0.3	-	-	117.2	2.0	-	-	118.1	0.8	-	-	117.6	-0.4
1991	-	-	119.2	1.4	-	-	120.6	1.2	-	-	121.5	0.7	-	-	121.9	0.3	-	-	123.3	1.1	-	-	124.7	1.1
1992	-	-	124.1	-0.5	-	-	125.2	0.9	-	-	124.6	-0.5	-	-	127.2	2.1	-	-	126.3	-0.7	-	-	126.3	0.0
1993	-	-	128.2	1.5	-	-	127.6	-0.5	-	-	128.3	0.5	-	-	129.0	0.5	-	-	129.1	0.1	-	-	130.3	0.9
1994	-	-	133.0	2.1	-	-	133.1	0.1	-	-	133.2	0.1	-	-	134.9	1.3	-	-	136.1	0.9	-	-	135.5	-0.4
1995	-	-	137.5	1.5	-	-	138.1	0.4	-	-	138.6	0.4	-	-	139.3	0.5	-	-	139.3	0.0	-	-	138.8	-0.4
1996	-	-	139.7	0.6	-	-	141.0	0.9	-	-	142.3	0.9	-	-	142.9	0.4	-	-	141.4	-1.0	-	-	141.5	0.1
1997	-	-	143.0	1.1	-	-	143.3	0.2	-	-	145.5	1.5	-	-	145.2	-0.2	-	-	143.7	-1.0	-	-	144.1	0.3
1998	-	-	-	-	-	-	-	-	-	-	146.2	1.5	-	-	-	-	-	-	-	-	-	-	148.5	1.6
1999	-	-	-	-	-	-	-	-	-	-	148.9	0.3	-	-	-	-	-	-	-	-	-	-	149.4	0.3
2000	-	-	-	-	-	-	-	-	-	-	150.6	0.8	-	-	-	-	-	-	-	-	-	-	153.2	1.7
2001	-	-	-	-	-	-	-	-	-	-	158.3	3.3	-	-	-	-	-	-	-	-	-	-	-	-

Source: U.S. Department of Labor, Bureau of Labor Statistics, Division of Consumer Prices and Price Indexes. - indicates no data collected for period.

Pittsburgh, PA
Consumer Price Index - All Urban Consumers
Base 1982-1984 = 100
Apparel

For 1952-2001. Columns headed % show percentile change in the index from the previous period for which an index is available.

Year	Jan Index	%	Feb Index	%	Mar Index	%	Apr Index	%	May Index	%	Jun Index	%	Jul Index	%	Aug Index	%	Sep Index	%	Oct Index	%	Nov Index	%	Dec Index	%
1952	-	-	-	-	-	-	-	-	-	-	-	-	-	-	-	-	-	-	42.4	-	-	-	-	-
1953	42.5	0.2	-	-	-	-	42.9	0.9	-	-	-	-	42.5	-0.9	-	-	-	-	43.1	1.4	-	-	-	-
1954	43.1	0.0	-	-	-	-	42.8	-0.7	-	-	-	-	42.9	0.2	-	-	-	-	42.9	0.0	-	-	-	-
1955	42.3	-1.4	-	-	-	-	42.5	0.5	-	-	-	-	41.9	-1.4	-	-	-	-	42.2	0.7	-	-	-	-
1956	42.7	1.2	-	-	-	-	43.0	0.7	-	-	-	-	43.0	0.0	-	-	-	-	43.5	1.2	-	-	-	-
1957	43.9	0.9	-	-	-	-	44.1	0.5	-	-	-	-	43.9	-0.5	-	-	-	-	45.3	3.2	-	-	-	-
1958	44.9	-0.9	-	-	-	-	44.6	-0.7	-	-	-	-	44.2	-0.9	-	-	-	-	44.5	0.7	-	-	-	-
1959	44.0	-1.1	-	-	-	-	44.5	1.1	-	-	-	-	44.7	0.4	-	-	-	-	45.2	1.1	-	-	-	-
1960	44.6	-1.3	-	-	-	-	45.3	1.6	-	-	-	-	45.3	0.0	-	-	-	-	45.9	1.3	-	-	-	-
1961	45.0	-2.0	-	-	-	-	45.2	0.4	-	-	-	-	45.5	0.7	-	-	-	-	46.3	1.8	-	-	-	-
1962	45.5	-1.7	-	-	-	-	45.7	0.4	-	-	-	-	46.0	0.7	-	-	-	-	46.2	0.4	-	-	-	-
1963	46.5	0.6	-	-	-	-	46.8	0.6	-	-	-	-	46.9	0.2	-	-	-	-	47.3	0.9	-	-	-	-
1964	47.2	-0.2	-	-	-	-	47.6	0.8	-	-	-	-	47.7	0.2	-	-	-	-	48.2	1.0	-	-	-	-
1965	47.6	-1.2	-	-	-	-	49.0	2.9	-	-	-	-	48.4	-1.2	-	-	-	-	49.3	1.9	-	-	-	-
1966	48.2	-2.2	-	-	-	-	49.8	3.3	-	-	-	-	49.7	-0.2	-	-	-	-	51.0	2.6	-	-	-	-
1967	50.8	-0.4	-	-	-	-	51.2	0.8	-	-	-	-	50.8	-0.8	-	-	-	-	51.8	2.0	-	-	-	-
1968	51.4	-0.8	-	-	-	-	54.1	5.3	-	-	-	-	53.7	-0.7	-	-	-	-	56.1	4.5	-	-	-	-
1969	55.9	-0.4	-	-	-	-	57.8	3.4	-	-	-	-	57.4	-0.7	-	-	-	-	59.5	3.7	-	-	-	-
1970	57.2	-3.9	-	-	-	-	58.7	2.6	-	-	-	-	58.3	-0.7	-	-	-	-	61.4	5.3	-	-	-	-
1971	59.1	-3.7	-	-	-	-	60.7	2.7	-	-	-	-	60.0	-1.2	-	-	-	-	64.0	6.7	-	-	-	-
1972	62.4	-2.5	-	-	-	-	63.5	1.8	-	-	-	-	62.4	-1.7	-	-	-	-	64.7	3.7	-	-	-	-
1973	63.0	-2.6	-	-	-	-	64.8	2.9	-	-	-	-	64.3	-0.8	-	-	-	-	68.1	5.9	-	-	-	-
1974	67.3	-1.2	-	-	-	-	70.2	4.3	-	-	-	-	71.4	1.7	-	-	-	-	72.2	1.1	-	-	-	-
1975	69.9	-3.2	-	-	-	-	72.5	3.7	-	-	-	-	71.8	-1.0	-	-	-	-	74.5	3.8	-	-	-	-
1976	73.5	-1.3	-	-	-	-	73.2	-0.4	-	-	-	-	72.9	-0.4	-	-	-	-	75.2	3.2	-	-	-	-
1977	74.5	-0.9	-	-	-	-	74.3	-0.3	-	-	-	-	75.4	1.5	-	-	-	-	76.9	2.0	-	-	-	-
1978	73.3	-4.7	-	-	-	-	75.1	2.5	-	-	75.3	0.3	-	-	80.5	6.9	-	-	81.6	1.4	-	-	81.0	-0.7
1979	-	-	81.3	0.4	-	-	81.5	0.2	-	-	79.7	-2.2	-	-	83.2	4.4	-	-	85.5	2.8	-	-	85.9	0.5
1980	-	-	85.8	-0.1	-	-	86.0	0.2	-	-	84.0	-2.3	-	-	86.9	3.5	-	-	91.1	4.8	-	-	89.6	-1.6
1981	-	-	92.1	2.8	-	-	92.6	0.5	-	-	92.9	0.3	-	-	95.9	3.2	-	-	96.3	0.4	-	-	94.0	-2.4
1982	-	-	95.7	1.8	-	-	96.9	1.3	-	-	95.4	-1.5	-	-	99.0	3.8	-	-	101.3	2.3	-	-	99.0	-2.3
1983	-	-	103.4	4.4	-	-	100.9	-2.4	-	-	98.2	-2.7	-	-	101.1	3.0	-	-	102.8	1.7	-	-	101.4	-1.4
1984	-	-	100.4	-1.0	-	-	103.2	2.8	-	-	99.3	-3.8	-	-	100.3	1.0	-	-	102.7	2.4	-	-	100.9	-1.8
1985	-	-	104.4	3.5	-	-	101.2	-3.1	-	-	99.5	-1.7	-	-	100.0	0.5	-	-	108.8	8.8	-	-	104.0	-4.4
1986	-	-	97.7	-6.1	-	-	98.7	1.0	-	-	96.5	-2.2	-	-	101.9	5.6	-	-	104.8	2.8	-	-	102.4	-2.3
1987	-	-	101.1	-1.3	-	-	107.5	6.3	-	-	104.3	-3.0	-	-	108.3	3.8	-	-	112.4	3.8	-	-	110.5	-1.7
1988	-	-	109.7	-0.7	-	-	114.8	4.6	-	-	107.7	-6.2	-	-	114.7	6.5	-	-	122.7	7.0	-	-	117.3	-4.4
1989	-	-	116.5	-0.7	-	-	119.6	2.7	-	-	119.9	0.3	-	-	123.3	2.8	-	-	127.4	3.3	-	-	121.4	-4.7
1990	-	-	124.3	2.4	-	-	125.7	1.1	-	-	121.0	-3.7	-	-	125.5	3.7	-	-	129.1	2.9	-	-	125.4	-2.9
1991	-	-	125.9	0.4	-	-	131.4	4.4	-	-	125.0	-4.9	-	-	129.4	3.5	-	-	135.5	4.7	-	-	131.7	-2.8
1992	-	-	129.3	-1.8	-	-	133.2	3.0	-	-	127.9	-4.0	-	-	130.8	2.3	-	-	143.2	9.5	-	-	134.8	-5.9
1993	-	-	135.9	0.8	-	-	139.9	2.9	-	-	130.0	-7.1	-	-	140.2	7.8	-	-	131.4	-6.3	-	-	127.7	-2.8
1994	-	-	133.5	4.5	-	-	141.6	6.1	-	-	131.4	-7.2	-	-	133.1	1.3	-	-	133.8	0.5	-	-	125.1	-6.5
1995	-	-	133.3	6.6	-	-	140.4	5.3	-	-	134.1	-4.5	-	-	137.3	2.4	-	-	138.2	0.7	-	-	129.5	-6.3
1996	-	-	135.0	4.2	-	-	134.3	-0.5	-	-	129.3	-3.7	-	-	129.4	0.1	-	-	144.0	11.3	-	-	137.5	-4.5
1997	-	-	-	-	-	-	-	-	-	-	139.3	1.3	-	-	-	-	-	-	-	-	-	-	142.6	2.4

[Continued]

Pittsburgh, PA
Consumer Price Index - All Urban Consumers
Base 1982-1984 = 100
Apparel
[Continued]

For 1952-2001. Columns headed % show percentile change in the index from the previous period for which an index is available.

Year	Jan Index	%	Feb Index	%	Mar Index	%	Apr Index	%	May Index	%	Jun Index	%	Jul Index	%	Aug Index	%	Sep Index	%	Oct Index	%	Nov Index	%	Dec Index	%
1998	-	-	-	-	-	-	-	-	-	-	141.7	-0.6	-	-	-	-	-	-	-	-	-	-	143.3	1.1
1999	-	-	-	-	-	-	-	-	-	-	143.4	0.1	-	-	-	-	-	-	-	-	-	-	145.6	1.5
2000	-	-	-	-	-	-	-	-	-	-	159.9	9.8	-	-	-	-	-	-	-	-	-	-	155.6	-2.7
2001	-	-	-	-	-	-	-	-	-	-	158.9	2.1	-	-	-	-	-	-	-	-	-	-	-	-

Source: U.S. Department of Labor, Bureau of Labor Statistics, Division of Consumer Prices and Price Indexes. - indicates no data collected for period.

Pittsburgh, PA
Consumer Price Index - Urban Wage Earners
Base 1982-1984 = 100
Apparel

For 1952-2001. Columns headed % show percentile change in the index from the previous period for which an index is available.

Year	Jan Index	%	Feb Index	%	Mar Index	%	Apr Index	%	May Index	%	Jun Index	%	Jul Index	%	Aug Index	%	Sep Index	%	Oct Index	%	Nov Index	%	Dec Index	%
1952	-	-	-	-	-	-	-	-	-	-	-	-	-	-	-	-	-	-	44.0		-	-	-	-
1953	44.1	0.2	-	-	-	-	44.5	0.9	-	-	-	-	44.1	-0.9	-	-	-	-	44.6	1.1	-	-	-	-
1954	44.7	0.2	-	-	-	-	44.4	-0.7	-	-	-	-	44.4	0.0	-	-	-	-	44.4	0.0	-	-	-	-
1955	43.9	-1.1	-	-	-	-	44.1	0.5	-	-	-	-	43.4	-1.6	-	-	-	-	43.7	0.7	-	-	-	-
1956	44.3	1.4	-	-	-	-	44.5	0.5	-	-	-	-	44.5	0.0	-	-	-	-	45.1	1.3	-	-	-	-
1957	45.6	1.1	-	-	-	-	45.8	0.4	-	-	-	-	45.5	-0.7	-	-	-	-	46.9	3.1	-	-	-	-
1958	46.6	-0.6	-	-	-	-	46.2	-0.9	-	-	-	-	45.8	-0.9	-	-	-	-	46.2	0.9	-	-	-	-
1959	45.7	-1.1	-	-	-	-	46.1	0.9	-	-	-	-	46.3	0.4	-	-	-	-	46.9	1.3	-	-	-	-
1960	46.2	-1.5	-	-	-	-	46.9	1.5	-	-	-	-	46.9	0.0	-	-	-	-	47.6	1.5	-	-	-	-
1961	46.7	-1.9	-	-	-	-	46.9	0.4	-	-	-	-	47.2	0.6	-	-	-	-	48.0	1.7	-	-	-	-
1962	47.1	-1.9	-	-	-	-	47.4	0.6	-	-	-	-	47.7	0.6	-	-	-	-	47.9	0.4	-	-	-	-
1963	48.3	0.8	-	-	-	-	48.6	0.6	-	-	-	-	48.7	0.2	-	-	-	-	49.1	0.8	-	-	-	-
1964	48.9	-0.4	-	-	-	-	49.3	0.8	-	-	-	-	49.5	0.4	-	-	-	-	50.0	1.0	-	-	-	-
1965	49.3	-1.4	-	-	-	-	50.8	3.0	-	-	-	-	50.2	-1.2	-	-	-	-	51.1	1.8	-	-	-	-
1966	50.0	-2.2	-	-	-	-	51.7	3.4	-	-	-	-	51.6	-0.2	-	-	-	-	52.9	2.5	-	-	-	-
1967	52.7	-0.4	-	-	-	-	53.1	0.8	-	-	-	-	52.7	-0.8	-	-	-	-	53.7	1.9	-	-	-	-
1968	53.3	-0.7	-	-	-	-	56.1	5.3	-	-	-	-	55.7	-0.7	-	-	-	-	58.1	4.3	-	-	-	-
1969	58.0	-0.2	-	-	-	-	59.9	3.3	-	-	-	-	59.6	-0.5	-	-	-	-	61.7	3.5	-	-	-	-
1970	59.3	-3.9	-	-	-	-	60.8	2.5	-	-	-	-	60.5	-0.5	-	-	-	-	63.7	5.3	-	-	-	-
1971	61.3	-3.8	-	-	-	-	62.9	2.6	-	-	-	-	62.2	-1.1	-	-	-	-	66.4	6.8	-	-	-	-
1972	64.7	-2.6	-	-	-	-	65.8	1.7	-	-	-	-	64.7	-1.7	-	-	-	-	67.1	3.7	-	-	-	-
1973	65.4	-2.5	-	-	-	-	67.2	2.8	-	-	-	-	66.6	-0.9	-	-	-	-	70.7	6.2	-	-	-	-
1974	69.8	-1.3	-	-	-	-	72.8	4.3	-	-	-	-	74.0	1.6	-	-	-	-	74.9	1.2	-	-	-	-
1975	72.5	-3.2	-	-	-	-	75.2	3.7	-	-	-	-	74.4	-1.1	-	-	-	-	77.3	3.9	-	-	-	-
1976	76.2	-1.4	-	-	-	-	75.9	-0.4	-	-	-	-	75.6	-0.4	-	-	-	-	78.0	3.2	-	-	-	-
1977	77.3	-0.9	-	-	-	-	77.0	-0.4	-	-	-	-	78.2	1.6	-	-	-	-	79.7	1.9	-	-	-	-
1978	76.0	-4.6	-	-	-	-	77.8	2.4	-	-	76.5	-1.7	-	-	80.3	5.0	-	-	80.3	0.0	-	-	81.0	0.9
1979	-	-	81.4	0.5	-	-	82.9	1.8	-	-	81.5	-1.7	-	-	84.1	3.2	-	-	87.5	4.0	-	-	87.2	-0.3
1980	-	-	86.6	-0.7	-	-	86.8	0.2	-	-	85.4	-1.6	-	-	91.5	7.1	-	-	96.3	5.2	-	-	90.5	-6.0
1981	-	-	90.4	-0.1	-	-	93.1	3.0	-	-	93.1	0.0	-	-	95.5	2.6	-	-	94.9	-0.6	-	-	93.9	-1.1
1982	-	-	95.9	2.1	-	-	97.3	1.5	-	-	95.3	-2.1	-	-	98.7	3.6	-	-	101.2	2.5	-	-	99.2	-2.0
1983	-	-	102.9	3.7	-	-	100.3	-2.5	-	-	97.2	-3.1	-	-	101.1	4.0	-	-	102.9	1.8	-	-	101.5	-1.4
1984	-	-	101.5	0.0	-	-	103.2	1.7	-	-	99.1	-4.0	-	-	100.8	1.7	-	-	102.6	1.8	-	-	100.9	-1.7
1985	-	-	103.5	2.6	-	-	101.6	-1.8	-	-	100.0	-1.6	-	-	100.3	0.3	-	-	108.6	8.3	-	-	103.6	-4.6
1986	-	-	97.8	-5.6	-	-	98.6	0.8	-	-	96.4	-2.2	-	-	100.9	4.7	-	-	104.1	3.2	-	-	101.5	-2.5
1987	-	-	101.6	0.1	-	-	106.3	4.6	-	-	104.0	-2.2	-	-	107.9	3.8	-	-	110.0	1.9	-	-	108.5	-1.4
1988	-	-	108.5	0.0	-	-	113.1	4.2	-	-	108.2	-4.3	-	-	112.1	3.6	-	-	120.6	7.6	-	-	114.6	-5.0
1989	-	-	113.7	-0.8	-	-	117.8	3.6	-	-	117.7	-0.1	-	-	120.2	2.1	-	-	124.1	3.2	-	-	119.1	-4.0
1990	-	-	121.5	2.0	-	-	124.5	2.5	-	-	119.0	-4.4	-	-	120.1	0.9	-	-	125.7	4.7	-	-	122.6	-2.5
1991	-	-	122.0	-0.5	-	-	126.7	3.9	-	-	121.3	-4.3	-	-	123.2	1.6	-	-	129.3	5.0	-	-	124.9	-3.4
1992	-	-	126.8	1.5	-	-	130.1	2.6	-	-	124.0	-4.7	-	-	123.7	-0.2	-	-	135.7	9.7	-	-	128.5	-5.3
1993	-	-	130.9	1.9	-	-	135.6	3.6	-	-	125.7	-7.3	-	-	132.1	5.1	-	-	125.0	-5.4	-	-	122.3	-2.2
1994	-	-	129.0	5.5	-	-	137.0	6.2	-	-	127.7	-6.8	-	-	128.2	0.4	-	-	128.7	0.4	-	-	119.6	-7.1
1995	-	-	127.4	6.5	-	-	134.1	5.3	-	-	128.3	-4.3	-	-	127.9	-0.3	-	-	133.0	4.0	-	-	123.8	-6.9
1996	-	-	130.0	5.0	-	-	129.8	-0.2	-	-	123.6	-4.8	-	-	124.0	0.3	-	-	138.6	11.8	-	-	130.5	-5.8
1997	-	-	-	-	-	-	-	-	-	-	134.5	3.1	-	-	-	-	-	-	-	-	-	-	139.1	3.4

[Continued]

Pittsburgh, PA
Consumer Price Index - Urban Wage Earners
Base 1982-1984 = 100
Apparel
[Continued]

For 1952-2001. Columns headed % show percentile change in the index from the previous period for which an index is available.

Year	Jan		Feb		Mar		Apr		May		Jun		Jul		Aug		Sep		Oct		Nov		Dec	
	Index	%	Index	%	Index	%	Index	%	Index	%	Index	%	Index	%	Index	%	Index	%	Index	%	Index	%	Index	%
1998	-	-	-	-	-	-	-	-	-	-	138.0	-0.8	-	-	-	-	-	-	-	-	-		138.9	0.7
1999	-	-	-	-	-	-	-	-	-	-	141.2	1.7	-	-	-	-	-	-	-	-	-		146.1	3.5
2000	-	-	-	-	-	-	-	-	-	-	162.1	11.0	-	-	-	-	-	-	-	-	-		157.5	-2.8
2001	-	-	-	-	-	-	-	-	-	-	161.9	2.8	-	-	-	-	-	-	-	-	-		-	-

Source: U.S. Department of Labor, Bureau of Labor Statistics, Division of Consumer Prices and Price Indexes. - indicates no data collected for period.

Pittsburgh, PA
Consumer Price Index - All Urban Consumers
Base 1982-1984 = 100
Transportation

For 1947-2001. Columns headed % show percentile change in the index from the previous period for which an index is available.

Year	Jan Index	%	Feb Index	%	Mar Index	%	Apr Index	%	May Index	%	Jun Index	%	Jul Index	%	Aug Index	%	Sep Index	%	Oct Index	%	Nov Index	%	Dec Index	%
1947	15.9	-	15.8	-0.6	15.9	0.6	16.1	1.3	16.1	0.0	16.1	0.0	16.1	0.0	16.3	1.2	16.5	1.2	16.5	0.0	16.5	0.0	16.5	0.0
1948	17.4	5.5	17.6	1.1	17.6	0.0	17.6	0.0	17.6	0.0	17.6	0.0	18.0	2.3	18.3	1.7	18.3	0.0	18.4	0.5	18.4	0.0	18.4	0.0
1949	18.5	0.5	18.7	1.1	18.6	-0.5	18.7	0.5	18.8	0.5	18.9	0.5	18.9	0.0	18.9	0.0	18.9	0.0	18.9	0.0	18.9	0.0	20.2	6.9
1950	20.3	0.5	20.3	0.0	20.2	-0.5	20.1	-0.5	20.3	1.0	20.3	0.0	20.4	0.5	22.0	7.8	22.1	0.5	22.1	0.0	22.1	0.0	22.1	0.0
1951	22.1	0.0	22.1	0.0	22.3	0.9	22.3	0.0	22.3	0.0	22.3	0.0	22.3	0.0	22.3	0.0	23.3	4.5	23.6	1.3	24.0	1.7	24.0	0.0
1952	24.3	1.2	24.4	0.4	24.4	0.0	24.4	0.0	24.4	0.0	24.4	0.0	24.4	0.0	24.4	0.0	24.4	0.0	24.4	0.0	24.4	0.0	24.6	0.8
1953	24.6	0.0	-	-	-	-	24.6	0.0	-	-	-	-	24.9	1.2	-	-	-	-	24.9	0.0	-	-	-	-
1954	24.6	-1.2	-	-	-	-	24.5	-0.4	-	-	-	-	24.3	-0.8	-	-	-	-	23.7	-2.5	-	-	-	-
1955	24.4	3.0	-	-	-	-	24.3	-0.4	-	-	-	-	24.3	0.0	-	-	-	-	24.0	-1.2	-	-	-	-
1956	23.6	-1.7	-	-	-	-	24.0	1.7	-	-	-	-	24.1	0.4	-	-	-	-	25.4	5.4	-	-	-	-
1957	25.7	1.2	-	-	-	-	25.5	-0.8	-	-	-	-	25.4	-0.4	-	-	-	-	25.7	1.2	-	-	-	-
1958	26.4	2.7	-	-	-	-	26.3	-0.4	-	-	-	-	26.9	2.3	-	-	-	-	27.5	2.2	-	-	-	-
1959	27.8	1.1	-	-	-	-	28.0	0.7	-	-	-	-	28.6	2.1	-	-	-	-	29.1	1.7	-	-	-	-
1960	29.1	0.0	-	-	-	-	29.4	1.0	-	-	-	-	29.1	-1.0	-	-	-	-	29.0	-0.3	-	-	-	-
1961	29.0	0.0	-	-	-	-	29.3	1.0	-	-	-	-	28.9	-1.4	-	-	-	-	29.3	1.4	-	-	-	-
1962	29.7	1.4	-	-	-	-	30.0	1.0	-	-	-	-	29.9	-0.3	-	-	-	-	30.0	0.3	-	-	-	-
1963	29.7	-1.0	-	-	-	-	29.8	0.3	-	-	-	-	30.1	1.0	-	-	-	-	29.7	-1.3	-	-	-	-
1964	30.3	2.0	-	-	-	-	30.2	-0.3	-	-	-	-	30.0	-0.7	-	-	-	-	30.3	1.0	-	-	-	-
1965	30.8	1.7	-	-	-	-	30.8	0.0	-	-	-	-	30.8	0.0	-	-	-	-	30.8	0.0	-	-	-	-
1966	30.7	-0.3	-	-	-	-	30.9	0.7	-	-	-	-	31.2	1.0	-	-	-	-	31.3	0.3	-	-	-	-
1967	31.1	-0.6	-	-	-	-	31.5	1.3	-	-	-	-	31.6	0.3	-	-	-	-	31.9	0.9	-	-	-	-
1968	32.4	1.6	-	-	-	-	32.4	0.0	-	-	-	-	32.6	0.6	-	-	-	-	33.1	1.5	-	-	-	-
1969	33.1	0.0	-	-	-	-	34.3	3.6	-	-	-	-	34.2	-0.3	-	-	-	-	34.3	0.3	-	-	-	-
1970	34.3	0.0	-	-	-	-	35.7	4.1	-	-	-	-	36.3	1.7	-	-	-	-	36.5	0.6	-	-	-	-
1971	37.0	1.4	-	-	-	-	37.8	2.2	-	-	-	-	38.6	2.1	-	-	-	-	38.1	-1.3	-	-	-	-
1972	37.8	-0.8	-	-	-	-	38.1	0.8	-	-	-	-	38.5	1.0	-	-	-	-	38.6	0.3	-	-	-	-
1973	38.5	-0.3	-	-	-	-	39.0	1.3	-	-	-	-	39.5	1.3	-	-	-	-	39.6	0.3	-	-	-	-
1974	40.5	2.3	-	-	-	-	42.2	4.2	-	-	-	-	44.3	5.0	-	-	-	-	45.1	1.8	-	-	-	-
1975	44.9	-0.4	-	-	-	-	45.9	2.2	-	-	-	-	47.7	3.9	-	-	-	-	48.3	1.3	-	-	-	-
1976	48.4	0.2	-	-	-	-	50.3	3.9	-	-	-	-	52.5	4.4	-	-	-	-	53.2	1.3	-	-	-	-
1977	53.9	1.3	-	-	-	-	56.5	4.8	-	-	-	-	57.0	0.9	-	-	-	-	56.8	-0.4	-	-	-	-
1978	56.9	0.2	-	-	-	-	58.4	2.6	-	-	60.0	2.7	-	-	61.0	1.7	-	-	61.1	0.2	-	-	61.9	1.3
1979	-	-	63.0	1.8	-	-	65.3	3.7	-	-	68.0	4.1	-	-	71.3	4.9	-	-	72.4	1.5	-	-	74.0	2.2
1980	-	-	78.0	5.4	-	-	80.0	2.6	-	-	82.4	3.0	-	-	83.2	1.0	-	-	85.0	2.2	-	-	87.3	2.7
1981	-	-	90.7	3.9	-	-	92.1	1.5	-	-	93.4	1.4	-	-	94.9	1.6	-	-	96.1	1.3	-	-	96.5	0.4
1982	-	-	95.7	-0.8	-	-	93.6	-2.2	-	-	95.6	2.1	-	-	97.3	1.8	-	-	98.8	1.5	-	-	99.6	0.8
1983	-	-	97.9	-1.7	-	-	97.1	-0.8	-	-	98.4	1.3	-	-	100.7	2.3	-	-	102.4	1.7	-	-	102.8	0.4
1984	-	-	101.9	-0.9	-	-	102.7	0.8	-	-	104.3	1.6	-	-	104.0	-0.3	-	-	104.6	0.6	-	-	104.7	0.1
1985	-	-	104.0	-0.7	-	-	105.0	1.0	-	-	105.8	0.8	-	-	105.3	-0.5	-	-	106.1	0.8	-	-	107.1	0.9
1986	-	-	105.3	-1.7	-	-	98.1	-6.8	-	-	99.9	1.8	-	-	96.4	-3.5	-	-	97.2	0.8	-	-	97.7	0.5
1987	-	-	98.5	0.8	-	-	99.9	1.4	-	-	100.2	0.3	-	-	101.3	1.1	-	-	101.9	0.6	-	-	102.3	0.4
1988	-	-	100.5	-1.8	-	-	100.3	-0.2	-	-	102.2	1.9	-	-	102.3	0.1	-	-	104.4	2.1	-	-	104.7	0.3
1989	-	-	105.3	0.6	-	-	108.2	2.8	-	-	109.6	1.3	-	-	106.6	-2.7	-	-	107.1	0.5	-	-	107.3	0.2
1990	-	-	109.3	1.9	-	-	108.4	-0.8	-	-	109.2	0.7	-	-	111.4	2.0	-	-	118.8	6.6	-	-	118.7	-0.1
1991	-	-	113.0	-4.8	-	-	110.7	-2.0	-	-	111.9	1.1	-	-	112.1	0.2	-	-	113.7	1.4	-	-	114.8	1.0
1992	-	-	113.5	-1.1	-	-	114.0	0.4	-	-	115.6	1.4	-	-	116.2	0.5	-	-	117.5	1.1	-	-	117.7	0.2

[Continued]

Pittsburgh, PA
Consumer Price Index - All Urban Consumers
Base 1982-1984 = 100
Transportation

[Continued]

For 1947-2001. Columns headed % show percentile change in the index from the previous period for which an index is available.

Year	Jan Index	%	Feb Index	%	Mar Index	%	Apr Index	%	May Index	%	Jun Index	%	Jul Index	%	Aug Index	%	Sep Index	%	Oct Index	%	Nov Index	%	Dec Index	%
1993	-	-	117.6	-0.1	-	-	116.9	-0.6	-	-	117.5	0.5	-	-	116.5	-0.9	-	-	120.8	3.7	-	-	119.8	-0.8
1994	-	-	119.5	-0.3	-	-	119.7	0.2	-	-	122.1	2.0	-	-	124.4	1.9	-	-	124.0	-0.3	-	-	125.3	1.0
1995	-	-	126.0	0.6	-	-	126.5	0.4	-	-	130.5	3.2	-	-	127.9	-2.0	-	-	128.2	0.2	-	-	127.3	-0.7
1996	-	-	127.1	-0.2	-	-	128.7	1.3	-	-	129.8	0.9	-	-	127.9	-1.5	-	-	129.7	1.4	-	-	133.5	2.9
1997	-	-	133.1	-0.3	-	-	132.5	-0.5	-	-	132.2	-0.2	-	-	131.2	-0.8	-	-	134.5	2.5	-	-	132.2	-1.7
1998	-	-	-	-	-	-	-	-	-	-	130.8	-1.1	-	-	-	-	-	-	-	-	-	-	129.7	-0.8
1999	-	-	-	-	-	-	-	-	-	-	129.6	-0.1	-	-	-	-	-	-	-	-	-	-	134.2	3.5
2000	-	-	-	-	-	-	-	-	-	-	138.7	3.4	-	-	-	-	-	-	-	-	-	-	140.5	1.3
2001	-	-	-	-	-	-	-	-	-	-	143.0	1.8	-	-	-	-	-	-	-	-	-	-	-	-

Source: U.S. Department of Labor, Bureau of Labor Statistics, Division of Consumer Prices and Price Indexes. - indicates no data collected for period.

Pittsburgh, PA
Consumer Price Index - Urban Wage Earners
Base 1982-1984 = 100
Transportation

For 1947-2001. Columns headed % show percentile change in the index from the previous period for which an index is available.

Year	Jan Index	%	Feb Index	%	Mar Index	%	Apr Index	%	May Index	%	Jun Index	%	Jul Index	%	Aug Index	%	Sep Index	%	Oct Index	%	Nov Index	%	Dec Index	%
1947	15.7	-	15.6	-0.6	15.7	0.6	15.9	1.3	15.9	0.0	15.9	0.0	15.9	0.0	16.1	1.3	16.3	1.2	16.3	0.0	16.3	0.0	16.3	0.0
1948	17.2	5.5	17.3	0.6	17.3	0.0	17.3	0.0	17.3	0.0	17.4	0.6	17.8	2.3	18.1	1.7	18.1	0.0	18.2	0.6	18.1	-0.5	18.2	0.6
1949	18.3	0.5	18.4	0.5	18.4	0.0	18.5	0.5	18.6	0.5	18.7	0.5	18.7	0.0	18.7	0.0	18.7	0.0	18.7	0.0	18.7	0.0	20.0	7.0
1950	20.0	0.0	20.0	0.0	20.0	0.0	19.9	-0.5	20.0	0.5	20.1	0.5	20.1	0.0	21.7	8.0	21.8	0.5	21.8	0.0	21.8	0.0	21.8	0.0
1951	21.8	0.0	21.8	0.0	22.0	0.9	22.0	0.0	22.0	0.0	22.0	0.0	22.0	0.0	22.0	0.0	23.0	4.5	23.3	1.3	23.7	1.7	23.7	0.0
1952	24.0	1.3	24.1	0.4	24.1	0.0	24.1	0.0	24.1	0.0	24.1	0.0	24.1	0.0	24.1	0.0	24.1	0.0	24.1	0.0	24.1	0.0	24.3	0.8
1953	24.3	0.0	-		-		24.3	0.0	-		-		24.6	1.2	-		-		24.6	0.0	-		-	
1954	24.3	-1.2	-		-		24.2	-0.4	-		-		24.0	-0.8	-		-		23.4	-2.5	-		-	
1955	24.1	3.0	-		-		24.0	-0.4	-		-		24.0	0.0	-		-		23.7	-1.2	-		-	
1956	23.3	-1.7	-		-		23.7	1.7	-		-		23.8	0.4	-		-		25.1	5.5	-		-	
1957	25.4	1.2	-		-		25.2	-0.8	-		-		25.1	-0.4	-		-		25.4	1.2	-		-	
1958	26.1	2.8	-		-		26.0	-0.4	-		-		26.6	2.3	-		-		27.1	1.9	-		-	
1959	27.5	1.5	-		-		27.6	0.4	-		-		28.2	2.2	-		-		28.8	2.1	-		-	
1960	28.8	0.0	-		-		29.0	0.7	-		-		28.8	-0.7	-		-		28.7	-0.3	-		-	
1961	28.6	-0.3	-		-		28.9	1.0	-		-		28.5	-1.4	-		-		28.9	1.4	-		-	
1962	29.3	1.4	-		-		29.6	1.0	-		-		29.5	-0.3	-		-		29.6	0.3	-		-	
1963	29.3	-1.0	-		-		29.5	0.7	-		-		29.7	0.7	-		-		29.3	-1.3	-		-	
1964	29.9	2.0	-		-		29.9	0.0	-		-		29.7	-0.7	-		-		30.0	1.0	-		-	
1965	30.4	1.3	-		-		30.4	0.0	-		-		30.5	0.3	-		-		30.5	0.0	-		-	
1966	30.3	-0.7	-		-		30.5	0.7	-		-		30.8	1.0	-		-		30.9	0.3	-		-	
1967	30.7	-0.6	-		-		31.1	1.3	-		-		31.2	0.3	-		-		31.5	1.0	-		-	
1968	32.0	1.6	-		-		32.0	0.0	-		-		32.2	0.6	-		-		32.7	1.6	-		-	
1969	32.7	0.0	-		-		33.9	3.7	-		-		33.8	-0.3	-		-		33.9	0.3	-		-	
1970	33.9	0.0	-		-		35.3	4.1	-		-		35.9	1.7	-		-		36.1	0.6	-		-	
1971	36.5	1.1	-		-		37.3	2.2	-		-		38.1	2.1	-		-		37.6	-1.3	-		-	
1972	37.3	-0.8	-		-		37.6	0.8	-		-		38.0	1.1	-		-		38.1	0.3	-		-	
1973	38.0	-0.3	-		-		38.5	1.3	-		-		39.0	1.3	-		-		39.1	0.3	-		-	
1974	40.0	2.3	-		-		41.7	4.2	-		-		43.7	4.8	-		-		44.5	1.8	-		-	
1975	44.4	-0.2	-		-		45.3	2.0	-		-		47.1	4.0	-		-		47.7	1.3	-		-	
1976	47.8	0.2	-		-		49.7	4.0	-		-		51.8	4.2	-		-		52.6	1.5	-		-	
1977	53.3	1.3	-		-		55.8	4.7	-		-		56.3	0.9	-		-		56.1	-0.4	-		-	
1978	56.2	0.2	-		-		57.7	2.7	-		59.3	2.8	-		60.3	1.7	-		60.8	0.8	-		61.3	0.8
1979	-		62.5	2.0	-		64.6	3.4	-		67.5	4.5	-		70.9	5.0	-		71.8	1.3	-		73.2	1.9
1980	-		77.4	5.7	-		79.4	2.6	-		81.8	3.0	-		82.0	0.2	-		84.7	3.3	-		86.9	2.6
1981	-		90.5	4.1	-		92.1	1.8	-		93.5	1.5	-		95.0	1.6	-		96.5	1.6	-		96.9	0.4
1982	-		96.0	-0.9	-		93.7	-2.4	-		95.7	2.1	-		97.9	2.3	-		99.1	1.2	-		99.6	0.5
1983	-		97.6	-2.0	-		96.6	-1.0	-		97.9	1.3	-		100.5	2.7	-		102.2	1.7	-		102.6	0.4
1984	-		101.7	-0.9	-		102.7	1.0	-		104.4	1.7	-		104.2	-0.2	-		104.7	0.5	-		104.8	0.1
1985	-		104.1	-0.7	-		105.0	0.9	-		105.7	0.7	-		105.1	-0.6	-		105.6	0.5	-		106.6	0.9
1986	-		104.7	-1.8	-		97.0	-7.4	-		98.5	1.5	-		94.8	-3.8	-		95.4	0.6	-		95.9	0.5
1987	-		97.0	1.1	-		98.5	1.5	-		99.1	0.6	-		100.4	1.3	-		101.0	0.6	-		101.4	0.4
1988	-		99.7	-1.7	-		99.7	0.0	-		101.5	1.8	-		101.7	0.2	-		103.9	2.2	-		104.1	0.2
1989	-		104.8	0.7	-		107.9	3.0	-		109.3	1.3	-		106.3	-2.7	-		106.7	0.4	-		106.8	0.1
1990	-		108.7	1.8	-		107.9	-0.7	-		108.8	0.8	-		110.8	1.8	-		117.9	6.4	-		117.7	-0.2
1991	-		111.8	-5.0	-		109.6	-2.0	-		111.0	1.3	-		111.5	0.5	-		113.0	1.3	-		113.9	0.8
1992	-		112.3	-1.4	-		112.9	0.5	-		114.7	1.6	-		115.4	0.6	-		116.9	1.3	-		116.9	0.0

[Continued]

Pittsburgh, PA
Consumer Price Index - Urban Wage Earners
Base 1982-1984 = 100
Transportation
[Continued]

For 1947-2001. Columns headed % show percentile change in the index from the previous period for which an index is available.

Year	Jan Index	%	Feb Index	%	Mar Index	%	Apr Index	%	May Index	%	Jun Index	%	Jul Index	%	Aug Index	%	Sep Index	%	Oct Index	%	Nov Index	%	Dec Index	%
1993	-	-	116.8	-0.1	-	-	116.2	-0.5	-	-	117.1	0.8	-	-	116.2	-0.8	-	-	120.2	3.4	-	-	119.2	-0.8
1994	-	-	118.4	-0.7	-	-	118.8	0.3	-	-	121.6	2.4	-	-	123.9	1.9	-	-	123.9	0.0	-	-	125.4	1.2
1995	-	-	126.4	0.8	-	-	127.3	0.7	-	-	131.6	3.4	-	-	129.1	-1.9	-	-	129.1	0.0	-	-	128.3	-0.6
1996	-	-	128.2	-0.1	-	-	129.8	1.2	-	-	130.9	0.8	-	-	129.0	-1.5	-	-	130.8	1.4	-	-	134.1	2.5
1997	-	-	133.6	-0.4	-	-	133.1	-0.4	-	-	132.6	-0.4	-	-	131.8	-0.6	-	-	134.8	2.3	-	-	132.5	-1.7
1998	-	-	-	-	-	-	-	-	-	-	130.0	-1.9	-	-	-	-	-	-	-	-	-	-	128.7	-1.0
1999	-	-	-	-	-	-	-	-	-	-	128.3	-0.3	-	-	-	-	-	-	-	-	-	-	135.6	5.7
2000	-	-	-	-	-	-	-	-	-	-	141.2	4.1	-	-	-	-	-	-	-	-	-	-	144.0	2.0
2001	-	-	-	-	-	-	-	-	-	-	146.2	1.5	-	-	-	-	-	-	-	-	-	-	-	-

Source: U.S. Department of Labor, Bureau of Labor Statistics, Division of Consumer Prices and Price Indexes. - indicates no data collected for period.

Pittsburgh, PA
Consumer Price Index - All Urban Consumers
Base 1982-1984 = 100
Medical Care

For 1947-2001. Columns headed % show percentile change in the index from the previous period for which an index is available.

Year	Jan Index	Jan %	Feb Index	Feb %	Mar Index	Mar %	Apr Index	Apr %	May Index	May %	Jun Index	Jun %	Jul Index	Jul %	Aug Index	Aug %	Sep Index	Sep %	Oct Index	Oct %	Nov Index	Nov %	Dec Index	Dec %
1947	11.5	-	11.5	0.0	11.6	0.9	11.6	0.0	11.6	0.0	11.6	0.0	11.7	0.9	11.6	-0.9	11.7	0.9	11.7	0.0	11.9	1.7	11.9	0.0
1948	12.2	2.5	12.2	0.0	12.2	0.0	12.2	0.0	12.4	1.6	12.4	0.0	12.4	0.0	12.4	0.0	12.4	0.0	12.4	0.0	12.5	0.8	12.6	0.8
1949	12.6	0.0	12.6	0.0	12.6	0.0	12.6	0.0	12.6	0.0	12.6	0.0	12.6	0.0	12.6	0.0	12.6	0.0	12.6	0.0	12.6	0.0	12.7	0.8
1950	12.7	0.0	12.7	0.0	12.9	1.6	12.9	0.0	12.9	0.0	12.9	0.0	12.9	0.0	12.9	0.0	13.0	0.8	12.9	-0.8	13.0	0.8	13.0	0.0
1951	13.1	0.8	13.1	0.0	13.2	0.8	13.3	0.8	13.3	0.0	13.7	3.0	13.7	0.0	13.7	0.0	13.7	0.0	13.7	0.0	13.7	0.0	13.7	0.0
1952	13.8	0.7	13.8	0.0	13.9	0.7	13.9	0.0	13.9	0.0	13.9	0.0	13.9	0.0	13.9	0.0	14.1	1.4	14.1	0.0	14.1	0.0	14.3	1.4
1953	14.3	0.0	-	-	-	-	14.8	3.5	-	-	-	-	14.8	0.0	-	-	-	-	14.7	-0.7	-	-	-	-
1954	14.8	0.7	-	-	-	-	15.6	5.4	-	-	-	-	15.6	0.0	-	-	-	-	15.4	-1.3	-	-	-	-
1955	15.4	0.0	-	-	-	-	15.5	0.6	-	-	-	-	16.1	3.9	-	-	-	-	16.1	0.0	-	-	-	-
1956	16.1	0.0	-	-	-	-	16.5	2.5	-	-	-	-	16.5	0.0	-	-	-	-	17.5	6.1	-	-	-	-
1957	17.6	0.6	-	-	-	-	17.7	0.6	-	-	-	-	17.7	0.0	-	-	-	-	17.9	1.1	-	-	-	-
1958	18.0	0.6	-	-	-	-	18.0	0.0	-	-	-	-	18.8	4.4	-	-	-	-	18.9	0.5	-	-	-	-
1959	19.1	1.1	-	-	-	-	19.3	1.0	-	-	-	-	19.3	0.0	-	-	-	-	20.5	6.2	-	-	-	-
1960	20.6	0.5	-	-	-	-	20.7	0.5	-	-	-	-	20.7	0.0	-	-	-	-	20.8	0.5	-	-	-	-
1961	20.9	0.5	-	-	-	-	21.5	2.9	-	-	-	-	21.5	0.0	-	-	-	-	21.6	0.5	-	-	-	-
1962	21.7	0.5	-	-	-	-	21.7	0.0	-	-	-	-	22.8	5.1	-	-	-	-	23.0	0.9	-	-	-	-
1963	23.0	0.0	-	-	-	-	23.0	0.0	-	-	-	-	23.0	0.0	-	-	-	-	23.1	0.4	-	-	-	-
1964	23.2	0.4	-	-	-	-	23.6	1.7	-	-	-	-	23.9	1.3	-	-	-	-	23.9	0.0	-	-	-	-
1965	24.0	0.4	-	-	-	-	24.2	0.8	-	-	-	-	24.4	0.8	-	-	-	-	24.5	0.4	-	-	-	-
1966	24.6	0.4	-	-	-	-	24.8	0.8	-	-	-	-	25.1	1.2	-	-	-	-	25.3	0.8	-	-	-	-
1967	26.5	4.7	-	-	-	-	26.7	0.8	-	-	-	-	26.8	0.4	-	-	-	-	27.1	1.1	-	-	-	-
1968	27.5	1.5	-	-	-	-	27.7	0.7	-	-	-	-	28.5	2.9	-	-	-	-	29.1	2.1	-	-	-	-
1969	29.4	1.0	-	-	-	-	29.9	1.7	-	-	-	-	30.2	1.0	-	-	-	-	30.4	0.7	-	-	-	-
1970	30.6	0.7	-	-	-	-	31.3	2.3	-	-	-	-	31.8	1.6	-	-	-	-	32.1	0.9	-	-	-	-
1971	32.5	1.2	-	-	-	-	32.8	0.9	-	-	-	-	32.9	0.3	-	-	-	-	33.2	0.9	-	-	-	-
1972	33.6	1.2	-	-	-	-	34.2	1.8	-	-	-	-	34.9	2.0	-	-	-	-	35.0	0.3	-	-	-	-
1973	35.4	1.1	-	-	-	-	35.6	0.6	-	-	-	-	35.9	0.8	-	-	-	-	36.7	2.2	-	-	-	-
1974	37.3	1.6	-	-	-	-	38.0	1.9	-	-	-	-	40.1	5.5	-	-	-	-	40.9	2.0	-	-	-	-
1975	41.6	1.7	-	-	-	-	42.5	2.2	-	-	-	-	44.2	4.0	-	-	-	-	45.3	2.5	-	-	-	-
1976	45.8	1.1	-	-	-	-	46.4	1.3	-	-	-	-	49.1	5.8	-	-	-	-	49.9	1.6	-	-	-	-
1977	50.7	1.6	-	-	-	-	51.7	2.0	-	-	-	-	54.1	4.6	-	-	-	-	55.1	1.8	-	-	-	-
1978	55.5	0.7	-	-	-	-	56.7	2.2	-	-	57.0	0.5	-	-	59.5	4.4	-	-	59.7	0.3	-	-	60.3	1.0
1979	-	-	61.3	1.7	-	-	62.4	1.8	-	-	63.7	2.1	-	-	65.7	3.1	-	-	66.7	1.5	-	-	66.9	0.3
1980	-	-	67.9	1.5	-	-	69.1	1.8	-	-	70.8	2.5	-	-	73.4	3.7	-	-	73.4	0.0	-	-	74.2	1.1
1981	-	-	75.8	2.2	-	-	77.6	2.4	-	-	78.1	0.6	-	-	81.7	4.6	-	-	83.5	2.2	-	-	84.2	0.8
1982	-	-	85.7	1.8	-	-	86.8	1.3	-	-	87.8	1.2	-	-	92.3	5.1	-	-	93.0	0.8	-	-	94.3	1.4
1983	-	-	97.8	3.7	-	-	97.7	-0.1	-	-	99.4	1.7	-	-	102.1	2.7	-	-	105.6	3.4	-	-	105.6	0.0
1984	-	-	108.5	2.7	-	-	109.0	0.5	-	-	109.4	0.4	-	-	110.1	0.6	-	-	110.8	0.6	-	-	110.9	0.1
1985	-	-	111.4	0.5	-	-	112.1	0.6	-	-	112.3	0.2	-	-	114.0	1.5	-	-	115.0	0.9	-	-	117.0	1.7
1986	-	-	118.6	1.4	-	-	119.2	0.5	-	-	120.9	1.4	-	-	122.0	0.9	-	-	123.9	1.6	-	-	124.5	0.5
1987	-	-	125.5	0.8	-	-	127.8	1.8	-	-	130.7	2.3	-	-	132.4	1.3	-	-	133.2	0.6	-	-	134.1	0.7
1988	-	-	135.5	1.0	-	-	136.0	0.4	-	-	137.8	1.3	-	-	139.2	1.0	-	-	140.8	1.1	-	-	142.2	1.0
1989	-	-	142.3	0.1	-	-	144.0	1.2	-	-	146.3	1.6	-	-	149.2	2.0	-	-	149.9	0.5	-	-	151.3	0.9
1990	-	-	154.4	2.0	-	-	159.1	3.0	-	-	159.6	0.3	-	-	162.4	1.8	-	-	165.1	1.7	-	-	166.7	1.0
1991	-	-	168.9	1.3	-	-	171.2	1.4	-	-	175.3	2.4	-	-	179.6	2.5	-	-	181.3	0.9	-	-	182.1	0.4
1992	-	-	184.6	1.4	-	-	184.5	-0.1	-	-	182.8	-0.9	-	-	186.6	2.1	-	-	189.1	1.3	-	-	190.2	0.6

[Continued]

Pittsburgh, PA
Consumer Price Index - All Urban Consumers
Base 1982-1984 = 100
Medical Care

[Continued]

For 1947-2001. Columns headed % show percentile change in the index from the previous period for which an index is available.

Year	Jan Index	%	Feb Index	%	Mar Index	%	Apr Index	%	May Index	%	Jun Index	%	Jul Index	%	Aug Index	%	Sep Index	%	Oct Index	%	Nov Index	%	Dec Index	%
1993	-		194.1	2.1	-		194.7	0.3	-		197.7	1.5	-		198.4	0.4	-		199.1	0.4	-		199.3	0.1
1994	-		202.4	1.6	-		204.8	1.2	-		207.0	1.1	-		208.5	0.7	-		211.0	1.2	-		211.6	0.3
1995	-		208.2	-1.6	-		210.2	1.0	-		210.9	0.3	-		215.3	2.1	-		214.3	-0.5	-		218.5	2.0
1996	-		223.4	2.2	-		224.7	0.6	-		226.0	0.6	-		226.9	0.4	-		226.8	-0.0	-		226.7	-0.0
1997	-		-		-		-		-		228.6	0.8	-		-		-		-		-		229.1	0.2
1998	-		-		-		-		-		232.7	1.6	-		-		-		-		-		237.3	2.0
1999	-		-		-		-		-		243.4	2.6	-		-		-		-		-		245.5	0.9
2000	-		-		-		-		-		247.6	0.9	-		-		-		-		-		249.8	0.9
2001	-		-		-		-		-		251.9	0.8	-		-		-		-		-		-	

Source: U.S. Department of Labor, Bureau of Labor Statistics, Division of Consumer Prices and Price Indexes. - indicates no data collected for period.

Pittsburgh, PA
Consumer Price Index - Urban Wage Earners
Base 1982-1984 = 100
Medical Care

For 1947-2001. Columns headed % show percentile change in the index from the previous period for which an index is available.

Year	Jan Index	%	Feb Index	%	Mar Index	%	Apr Index	%	May Index	%	Jun Index	%	Jul Index	%	Aug Index	%	Sep Index	%	Oct Index	%	Nov Index	%	Dec Index	%
1947	11.6	-	11.6	0.0	11.6	0.0	11.7	0.9	11.7	0.0	11.7	0.0	11.8	0.9	11.7	-0.8	11.7	0.0	11.8	0.9	11.9	0.8	11.9	0.0
1948	12.2	2.5	12.3	0.8	12.3	0.0	12.3	0.0	12.5	1.6	12.5	0.0	12.5	0.0	12.4	-0.8	12.4	0.0	12.4	0.0	12.6	1.6	12.7	0.8
1949	12.7	0.0	12.7	0.0	12.7	0.0	12.7	0.0	12.7	0.0	12.7	0.0	12.7	0.0	12.7	0.0	12.7	0.0	12.7	0.0	12.7	0.0	12.8	0.8
1950	12.8	0.0	12.8	0.0	12.9	0.8	12.9	0.0	12.9	0.0	13.0	0.8	13.0	0.0	13.0	0.0	13.1	0.8	13.0	-0.8	13.1	0.8	13.1	0.0
1951	13.2	0.8	13.2	0.0	13.3	0.8	13.4	0.8	13.4	0.0	13.8	3.0	13.8	0.0	13.8	0.0	13.8	0.0	13.8	0.0	13.8	0.0	13.8	0.0
1952	13.9	0.7	13.9	0.0	14.0	0.7	14.0	0.0	14.0	0.0	14.0	0.0	14.0	0.0	14.0	0.0	14.2	1.4	14.2	0.0	14.2	0.0	14.4	1.4
1953	14.4	0.0	-	-	-	-	14.9	3.5	-	-	-	-	14.9	0.0	-	-	-	-	14.8	-0.7	-	-	-	-
1954	14.9	0.7	-	-	-	-	15.7	5.4	-	-	-	-	15.7	0.0	-	-	-	-	15.5	-1.3	-	-	-	-
1955	15.5	0.0	-	-	-	-	15.6	0.6	-	-	-	-	16.2	3.8	-	-	-	-	16.2	0.0	-	-	-	-
1956	16.2	0.0	-	-	-	-	16.6	2.5	-	-	-	-	16.6	0.0	-	-	-	-	17.6	6.0	-	-	-	-
1957	17.7	0.6	-	-	-	-	17.8	0.6	-	-	-	-	17.8	0.0	-	-	-	-	18.0	1.1	-	-	-	-
1958	18.1	0.6	-	-	-	-	18.1	0.0	-	-	-	-	18.9	4.4	-	-	-	-	19.0	0.5	-	-	-	-
1959	19.2	1.1	-	-	-	-	19.4	1.0	-	-	-	-	19.4	0.0	-	-	-	-	20.7	6.7	-	-	-	-
1960	20.7	0.0	-	-	-	-	20.8	0.5	-	-	-	-	20.9	0.5	-	-	-	-	20.9	0.0	-	-	-	-
1961	21.1	1.0	-	-	-	-	21.6	2.4	-	-	-	-	21.7	0.5	-	-	-	-	21.7	0.0	-	-	-	-
1962	21.8	0.5	-	-	-	-	21.8	0.0	-	-	-	-	22.9	5.0	-	-	-	-	23.1	0.9	-	-	-	-
1963	23.1	0.0	-	-	-	-	23.1	0.0	-	-	-	-	23.2	0.4	-	-	-	-	23.2	0.0	-	-	-	-
1964	23.4	0.9	-	-	-	-	23.8	1.7	-	-	-	-	24.1	1.3	-	-	-	-	24.1	0.0	-	-	-	-
1965	24.2	0.4	-	-	-	-	24.4	0.8	-	-	-	-	24.5	0.4	-	-	-	-	24.7	0.8	-	-	-	-
1966	24.7	0.0	-	-	-	-	24.9	0.8	-	-	-	-	25.2	1.2	-	-	-	-	25.5	1.2	-	-	-	-
1967	26.7	4.7	-	-	-	-	26.9	0.7	-	-	-	-	27.0	0.4	-	-	-	-	27.2	0.7	-	-	-	-
1968	27.7	1.8	-	-	-	-	27.9	0.7	-	-	-	-	28.7	2.9	-	-	-	-	29.3	2.1	-	-	-	-
1969	29.6	1.0	-	-	-	-	30.1	1.7	-	-	-	-	30.4	1.0	-	-	-	-	30.6	0.7	-	-	-	-
1970	30.8	0.7	-	-	-	-	31.5	2.3	-	-	-	-	32.0	1.6	-	-	-	-	32.4	1.3	-	-	-	-
1971	32.7	0.9	-	-	-	-	33.0	0.9	-	-	-	-	33.1	0.3	-	-	-	-	33.4	0.9	-	-	-	-
1972	33.8	1.2	-	-	-	-	34.4	1.8	-	-	-	-	35.1	2.0	-	-	-	-	35.2	0.3	-	-	-	-
1973	35.6	1.1	-	-	-	-	35.8	0.6	-	-	-	-	36.2	1.1	-	-	-	-	36.9	1.9	-	-	-	-
1974	37.5	1.6	-	-	-	-	38.3	2.1	-	-	-	-	40.4	5.5	-	-	-	-	41.2	2.0	-	-	-	-
1975	41.9	1.7	-	-	-	-	42.8	2.1	-	-	-	-	44.5	4.0	-	-	-	-	45.6	2.5	-	-	-	-
1976	46.1	1.1	-	-	-	-	46.7	1.3	-	-	-	-	49.4	5.8	-	-	-	-	50.3	1.8	-	-	-	-
1977	51.0	1.4	-	-	-	-	52.1	2.2	-	-	-	-	54.5	4.6	-	-	-	-	55.4	1.7	-	-	-	-
1978	55.9	0.9	-	-	-	-	57.1	2.1	-	-	56.8	-0.5	-	-	58.6	3.2	-	-	59.1	0.9	-	-	60.5	2.4
1979	-	-	62.0	2.5	-	-	62.7	1.1	-	-	63.4	1.1	-	-	65.5	3.3	-	-	66.6	1.7	-	-	68.4	2.7
1980	-	-	68.8	0.6	-	-	70.7	2.8	-	-	73.4	3.8	-	-	76.2	3.8	-	-	76.2	0.0	-	-	76.4	0.3
1981	-	-	77.3	1.2	-	-	78.2	1.2	-	-	78.4	0.3	-	-	82.9	5.7	-	-	84.3	1.7	-	-	84.8	0.6
1982	-	-	86.3	1.8	-	-	87.5	1.4	-	-	88.4	1.0	-	-	92.4	4.5	-	-	93.1	0.8	-	-	94.3	1.3
1983	-	-	97.6	3.5	-	-	97.5	-0.1	-	-	99.2	1.7	-	-	101.7	2.5	-	-	105.0	3.2	-	-	105.1	0.1
1984	-	-	108.4	3.1	-	-	108.9	0.5	-	-	109.4	0.5	-	-	110.0	0.5	-	-	110.8	0.7	-	-	110.9	0.1
1985	-	-	111.4	0.5	-	-	112.2	0.7	-	-	112.5	0.3	-	-	114.2	1.5	-	-	115.3	1.0	-	-	117.5	1.9
1986	-	-	119.1	1.4	-	-	119.8	0.6	-	-	121.4	1.3	-	-	122.5	0.9	-	-	124.4	1.6	-	-	125.2	0.6
1987	-	-	126.0	0.6	-	-	128.6	2.1	-	-	131.6	2.3	-	-	133.0	1.1	-	-	133.8	0.6	-	-	135.0	0.9
1988	-	-	136.6	1.2	-	-	137.3	0.5	-	-	139.1	1.3	-	-	140.3	0.9	-	-	141.7	1.0	-	-	143.3	1.1
1989	-	-	143.2	-0.1	-	-	145.0	1.3	-	-	147.2	1.5	-	-	149.7	1.7	-	-	150.1	0.3	-	-	152.0	1.3
1990	-	-	155.4	2.2	-	-	160.0	3.0	-	-	160.5	0.3	-	-	163.0	1.6	-	-	165.8	1.7	-	-	167.2	0.8
1991	-	-	169.4	1.3	-	-	171.9	1.5	-	-	174.9	1.7	-	-	178.4	2.0	-	-	180.2	1.0	-	-	181.0	0.4
1992	-	-	183.3	1.3	-	-	183.1	-0.1	-	-	181.1	-1.1	-	-	184.2	1.7	-	-	186.9	1.5	-	-	187.8	0.5

[Continued]

Pittsburgh, PA
Consumer Price Index - Urban Wage Earners
Base 1982-1984 = 100
Medical Care
[Continued]

For 1947-2001. Columns headed % show percentile change in the index from the previous period for which an index is available.

Year	Jan Index	%	Feb Index	%	Mar Index	%	Apr Index	%	May Index	%	Jun Index	%	Jul Index	%	Aug Index	%	Sep Index	%	Oct Index	%	Nov Index	%	Dec Index	%
1993	-	-	191.9	2.2	-	-	192.0	0.1	-	-	195.0	1.6	-	-	195.7	0.4	-	-	196.1	0.2	-	-	196.1	0.0
1994	-	-	199.3	1.6	-	-	201.6	1.2	-	-	204.0	1.2	-	-	204.9	0.4	-	-	207.7	1.4	-	-	208.3	0.3
1995	-	-	204.2	-2.0	-	-	206.5	1.1	-	-	207.2	0.3	-	-	211.2	1.9	-	-	209.9	-0.6	-	-	214.5	2.2
1996	-	-	218.3	1.8	-	-	219.4	0.5	-	-	220.9	0.7	-	-	221.4	0.2	-	-	221.0	-0.2	-	-	220.9	-0.0
1997	-	-	-	-	-	-	-	-	-	-	223.0	1.0	-	-	-	-	-	-	-	-	-	-	223.4	0.2
1998	-	-	-	-	-	-	-	-	-	-	226.3	1.3	-	-	-	-	-	-	-	-	-	-	230.5	1.9
1999	-	-	-	-	-	-	-	-	-	-	235.6	2.2	-	-	-	-	-	-	-	-	-	-	237.4	0.8
2000	-	-	-	-	-	-	-	-	-	-	239.4	0.8	-	-	-	-	-	-	-	-	-	-	240.7	0.5
2001	-	-	-	-	-	-	-	-	-	-	242.5	0.7	-	-	-	-	-	-	-	-	-	-	-	-

Source: U.S. Department of Labor, Bureau of Labor Statistics, Division of Consumer Prices and Price Indexes. - indicates no data collected for period.

Pittsburgh, PA
Consumer Price Index - All Urban Consumers
Base December 1997 = 100
Recreation

For 1997-2001. Columns headed % show percentile change in the index from the previous period for which an index is available.

Year	Jan		Feb		Mar		Apr		May		Jun		Jul		Aug		Sep		Oct		Nov		Dec	
	Index	%	Index	%	Index	%	Index	%	Index	%	Index	%	Index	%	Index	%	Index	%	Index	%	Index	%	Index	%
1997	-	-	226.8	-	-	-	229.0	1.0	-	-	231.0	0.9	-	-	229.4	-0.7	-	-	227.9	-0.7	-	-	100.0	-56.1
1998	-	-	-	-	-	-	-	-	-	-	100.0	0.0	-	-	-	-	-	-	-	-	-	-	101.6	1.6
1999	-	-	-	-	-	-	-	-	-	-	103.4	1.8	-	-	-	-	-	-	-	-	-	-	104.3	0.9
2000	-	-	-	-	-	-	-	-	-	-	106.7	2.3	-	-	-	-	-	-	-	-	-	-	105.7	-0.9
2001	-	-	-	-	-	-	-	-	-	-	105.5	-0.2	-	-	-	-	-	-	-	-	-	-	-	-

Source: U.S. Department of Labor, Bureau of Labor Statistics, Division of Consumer Prices and Price Indexes. - indicates no data collected for period.

Pittsburgh, PA
Consumer Price Index - Urban Wage Earners
Base December 1997 = 100
Recreation

For 1997-2001. Columns headed % show percentile change in the index from the previous period for which an index is available.

Year	Jan		Feb		Mar		Apr		May		Jun		Jul		Aug		Sep		Oct		Nov		Dec	
	Index	%	Index	%	Index	%	Index	%	Index	%	Index	%	Index	%	Index	%	Index	%	Index	%	Index	%	Index	%
1997	-	-	221.1	-	-	-	223.5	1.1	-	-	225.6	0.9	-	-	223.8	-0.8	-	-	222.1	-0.8	-	-	100.0	-55.0
1998	-	-	-	-	-	-	-	-	-	-	100.1	0.1	-	-	-	-	-	-	-	-	-	-	101.5	1.4
1999	-	-	-	-	-	-	-	-	-	-	103.2	1.7	-	-	-	-	-	-	-	-	-	-	104.6	1.4
2000	-	-	-	-	-	-	-	-	-	-	106.6	1.9	-	-	-	-	-	-	-	-	-	-	105.4	-1.1
2001	-	-	-	-	-	-	-	-	-	-	104.5	-0.9	-	-	-	-	-	-	-	-	-	-	-	-

Source: U.S. Department of Labor, Bureau of Labor Statistics, Division of Consumer Prices and Price Indexes. - indicates no data collected for period.

Pittsburgh, PA
Consumer Price Index - All Urban Consumers
Base December 1997 = 100
Education & Communication

For 1997-2001, Columns headed % show percentile change in the index from the previous period for which an index is available.

Year	Jan Index	%	Feb Index	%	Mar Index	%	Apr Index	%	May Index	%	Jun Index	%	Jul Index	%	Aug Index	%	Sep Index	%	Oct Index	%	Nov Index	%	Dec Index	%
1997	-	-	140.7	-	-	-	140.3	-0.3	-	-	136.5	-2.7	-	-	145.7	6.7	-	-	145.4	-0.2	-	-	100.0	-31.2
1998	-	-	-	-	-	-	-	-	-	-	98.1	-1.9	-	-	-	-	-	-	-	-	-	-	101.3	3.3
1999	-	-	-	-	-	-	-	-	-	-	101.3	0.0	-	-	-	-	-	-	-	-	-	-	103.4	2.1
2000	-	-	-	-	-	-	-	-	-	-	103.4	0.0	-	-	-	-	-	-	-	-	-	-	107.6	4.1
2001	-	-	-	-	-	-	-	-	-	-	108.6	0.9	-	-	-	-	-	-	-	-	-	-	-	-

Source: U.S. Department of Labor, Bureau of Labor Statistics, Division of Consumer Prices and Price Indexes. - indicates no data collected for period.

Pittsburgh, PA
Consumer Price Index - Urban Wage Earners
Base December 1997 = 100
Education & Communication

For 1997-2001. Columns headed % show percentile change in the index from the previous period for which an index is available.

Year	Jan		Feb		Mar		Apr		May		Jun		Jul		Aug		Sep		Oct		Nov		Dec	
	Index	%	Index	%	Index	%	Index	%	Index	%	Index	%	Index	%	Index	%	Index	%	Index	%	Index	%	Index	%
1997	-	-	135.4	-	-	-	136.0	0.4	-	-	132.7	-2.4	-	-	143.2	7.9	-	-	140.9	-1.6	-	-	100.0	-29.0
1998	-	-	-	-	-	-	-	-	-	-	98.6	-1.4	-	-	-	-	-	-	-	-	-	-	101.1	2.5
1999	-	-	-	-	-	-	-	-	-	-	101.1	0.0	-	-	-	-	-	-	-	-	-	-	103.1	2.0
2000	-	-	-	-	-	-	-	-	-	-	103.1	0.0	-	-	-	-	-	-	-	-	-	-	106.7	3.5
2001	-	-	-	-	-	-	-	-	-	-	107.9	1.1	-	-	-	-	-	-	-	-	-	-	-	-

Source: U.S. Department of Labor, Bureau of Labor Statistics, Division of Consumer Prices and Price Indexes. - indicates no data collected for period.

Portland-Salem, OR-WA
Consumer Price Index - All Urban Consumers
Base 1982-1984 = 100
Annual Averages

For 1914-2001. Columns headed % show percentile change in the index from the previous period for which an index is available.

Year	All Items		Food & Beverage		Housing		Apparel		Trans-portation		Medical Care		Recrea-tion*		Education & Communic.*		Other Goods & Services	
	Index	%	Index	%	Index	%	Index	%	Index	%	Index	%	Index	%	Index	%	Index	%
1914	10.5	-	-	-	-	-	16.5	-	-	-	-	-	-	-	-	-	-	-
1915	10.2	-2.9	-	-	-	-	16.8	1.8	-	-	-	-	-	-	-	-	-	-
1916	10.5	2.9	-	-	-	-	18.2	8.3	-	-	-	-	-	-	-	-	-	-
1917	12.3	17.1	-	-	-	-	21.7	19.2	-	-	-	-	-	-	-	-	-	-
1918	15.1	22.8	-	-	-	-	28.6	31.8	-	-	-	-	-	-	-	-	-	-
1919	17.7	17.2	-	-	-	-	36.3	26.9	-	-	-	-	-	-	-	-	-	-
1920	20.0	13.0	-	-	-	-	40.5	11.6	-	-	-	-	-	-	-	-	-	-
1921	17.3	-13.5	-	-	-	-	30.8	-24.0	-	-	-	-	-	-	-	-	-	-
1922	16.4	-5.2	-	-	-	-	25.7	-16.6	-	-	-	-	-	-	-	-	-	-
1923	16.6	1.2	-	-	-	-	26.6	3.5	-	-	-	-	-	-	-	-	-	-
1924	16.5	-0.6	-	-	-	-	26.6	0.0	-	-	-	-	-	-	-	-	-	-
1925	16.6	0.6	-	-	-	-	26.1	-1.9	-	-	-	-	-	-	-	-	-	-
1926	16.4	-1.2	-	-	-	-	25.9	-0.8	-	-	-	-	-	-	-	-	-	-
1927	16.2	-1.2	-	-	-	-	25.2	-2.7	-	-	-	-	-	-	-	-	-	-
1928	16.0	-1.2	-	-	-	-	24.9	-1.2	-	-	-	-	-	-	-	-	-	-
1929	15.8	-1.2	-	-	-	-	24.5	-1.6	-	-	-	-	-	-	-	-	-	-
1930	15.5	-1.9	-	-	-	-	23.8	-2.9	-	-	-	-	-	-	-	-	-	-
1931	14.0	-9.7	-	-	-	-	21.7	-8.8	-	-	-	-	-	-	-	-	-	-
1932	12.7	-9.3	-	-	-	-	19.2	-11.5	-	-	-	-	-	-	-	-	-	-
1933	12.1	-4.7	-	-	-	-	18.8	-2.1	-	-	-	-	-	-	-	-	-	-
1934	12.5	3.3	-	-	-	-	20.5	9.0	-	-	-	-	-	-	-	-	-	-
1935	12.9	3.2	-	-	-	-	20.5	0.0	-	-	-	-	-	-	-	-	-	-
1936	13.2	2.3	-	-	-	-	20.6	0.5	-	-	-	-	-	-	-	-	-	-
1937	13.9	5.3	-	-	-	-	21.5	4.4	-	-	-	-	-	-	-	-	-	-
1938	13.7	-1.4	-	-	-	-	21.4	-0.5	-	-	-	-	-	-	-	-	-	-
1939	13.6	-0.7	-	-	-	-	21.3	-0.5	-	-	-	-	-	-	-	-	-	-
1940	13.6	0.0	-	-	-	-	21.7	1.9	-	-	-	-	-	-	-	-	-	-
1941	14.4	5.9	-	-	-	-	22.5	3.7	-	-	-	-	-	-	-	-	-	-
1942	16.5	14.6	-	-	-	-	26.0	15.6	-	-	-	-	-	-	-	-	-	-
1943	17.5	6.1	-	-	-	-	27.6	6.2	-	-	-	-	-	-	-	-	-	-
1944	17.7	1.1	-	-	-	-	29.4	6.5	-	-	-	-	-	-	-	-	-	-
1945	18.2	2.8	-	-	-	-	30.0	2.0	-	-	-	-	-	-	-	-	-	-
1946	19.5	7.1	-	-	-	-	32.1	7.0	-	-	-	-	-	-	-	-	-	-
1947	22.1	13.3	-	-	-	-	37.9	18.1	19.8	-	14.2	-	-	-	-	-	-	-
1948	24.1	9.0	-	-	-	-	41.2	8.7	21.9	10.6	14.7	3.5	-	-	-	-	-	-
1949	23.8	-1.2	-	-	-	-	39.8	-3.4	23.6	7.8	15.0	2.0	-	-	-	-	-	-
1950	24.3	2.1	-	-	-	-	39.5	-0.8	24.0	1.7	15.4	2.7	-	-	-	-	-	-
1951	26.2	7.8	-	-	-	-	42.3	7.1	25.1	4.6	16.3	5.8	-	-	-	-	-	-
1952	26.8	2.3	-	-	-	-	41.9	-0.9	26.8	6.8	17.1	4.9	-	-	-	-	-	-
1953	26.9	0.4	-	-	-	-	41.6	-0.7	27.6	3.0	17.5	2.3	-	-	-	-	-	-
1954	26.9	0.0	-	-	-	-	41.9	0.7	26.8	-2.9	17.9	2.3	-	-	-	-	-	-
1955	26.8	-0.4	-	-	-	-	42.2	0.7	26.9	0.4	18.6	3.9	-	-	-	-	-	-
1956	27.5	2.6	-	-	-	-	43.2	2.4	26.9	0.0	19.2	3.2	-	-	-	-	-	-
1957	28.4	3.3	-	-	-	-	44.1	2.1	28.2	4.8	20.3	5.7	-	-	-	-	-	-
1958	29.0	2.1	-	-	-	-	44.2	0.2	29.8	5.7	20.6	1.5	-	-	-	-	-	-

[Continued]

Portland-Salem, OR-WA
Consumer Price Index - All Urban Consumers
Base 1982-1984 = 100
Annual Averages
[Continued]

For 1914-2001. Columns headed % show percentile change in the index from the previous period for which an index is available.

Year	All Items Index	%	Food & Beverage Index	%	Housing Index	%	Apparel Index	%	Trans-portation Index	%	Medical Care Index	%	Recrea-tion* Index	%	Education & Communic.* Index	%	Other Goods & Services Index	%
1959	29.3	1.0	-	-	-	-	44.5	0.7	31.1	4.4	20.8	1.0	-	-	-	-	-	-
1960	29.8	1.7	-	-	-	-	45.5	2.2	30.8	-1.0	21.8	4.8	-	-	-	-	-	-
1961	30.1	1.0	-	-	-	-	45.8	0.7	30.9	0.3	22.4	2.8	-	-	-	-	-	-
1962	30.2	0.3	-	-	-	-	45.5	-0.7	31.2	1.0	22.5	0.4	-	-	-	-	-	-
1963	30.8	2.0	-	-	-	-	46.3	1.8	31.5	1.0	23.0	2.2	-	-	-	-	-	-
1964	31.5	2.3	-	-	-	-	46.8	1.1	32.0	1.6	24.4	6.1	-	-	-	-	-	-
1965	32.3	2.5	-	-	-	-	48.2	3.0	32.4	1.3	25.2	3.3	-	-	-	-	-	-
1966	33.3	3.1	-	-	-	-	49.8	3.3	32.7	0.9	26.0	3.2	-	-	-	-	-	-
1967	34.2	2.7	-	-	-	-	51.0	2.4	34.1	4.3	27.7	6.5	-	-	-	-	-	-
1968	35.4	3.5	-	-	-	-	53.2	4.3	34.9	2.3	29.2	5.4	-	-	-	-	-	-
1969	37.1	4.8	-	-	-	-	56.2	5.6	36.1	3.4	30.9	5.8	-	-	-	-	-	-
1970	38.7	4.3	-	-	-	-	58.8	4.6	37.1	2.8	32.9	6.5	-	-	-	-	-	-
1971	39.7	2.6	-	-	-	-	59.5	1.2	37.3	0.5	34.2	4.0	-	-	-	-	-	-
1972	40.8	2.8	-	-	-	-	61.1	2.7	37.6	0.8	35.3	3.2	-	-	-	-	-	-
1973	43.5	6.6	-	-	-	-	65.0	6.4	38.6	2.7	37.6	6.5	-	-	-	-	-	-
1974	48.8	12.2	-	-	-	-	68.9	6.0	42.4	9.8	41.4	10.1	-	-	-	-	-	-
1975	53.5	9.6	-	-	-	-	72.9	5.8	46.8	10.4	46.0	11.1	-	-	-	-	-	-
1976	57.0	6.5	60.8	-	56.3	-	76.7	5.2	51.3	9.6	50.1	8.9	-	-	-	-	52.2	-
1977	61.6	8.1	64.6	6.3	61.2	8.7	82.1	7.0	56.2	9.6	55.2	10.2	-	-	-	-	56.3	7.9
1978	67.8	10.1	71.1	10.1	69.1	12.9	84.5	2.9	60.4	7.5	60.2	9.1	-	-	-	-	60.3	7.1
1979	77.0	13.6	79.8	12.2	79.7	15.3	85.7	1.4	70.6	16.9	65.9	9.5	-	-	-	-	65.5	8.6
1980	87.2	13.2	85.5	7.1	92.4	15.9	87.8	2.5	81.7	15.7	74.3	12.7	-	-	-	-	73.6	12.4
1981	95.0	8.9	92.3	8.0	100.0	8.2	92.6	5.5	91.8	12.4	83.3	12.1	-	-	-	-	82.1	11.5
1982	98.0	3.2	97.2	5.3	100.1	0.1	95.5	3.1	97.8	6.5	93.6	12.4	-	-	-	-	92.5	12.7
1983	99.1	1.1	99.7	2.6	98.6	-1.5	99.6	4.3	98.5	0.7	100.6	7.5	-	-	-	-	101.5	9.7
1984	102.8	3.7	103.2	3.5	101.2	2.6	104.9	5.3	103.6	5.2	105.8	5.2	-	-	-	-	106.0	4.4
1985	106.7	3.8	105.6	2.3	104.8	3.6	107.5	2.5	108.3	4.5	111.2	5.1	-	-	-	-	111.6	5.3
1986	108.2	1.4	108.2	2.5	106.2	1.3	100.5	-6.5	107.4	-0.8	119.1	7.1	-	-	-	-	121.0	8.4
1987	110.9	2.5	111.3	2.9	108.1	1.8	102.1	1.6	109.2	1.7	126.8	6.5	-	-	-	-	-	-
1988	114.7	3.4	112.0	0.6	111.8	3.4	111.9	9.6	110.6	1.3	138.8	9.5	-	-	-	-	136.0	12.4
1989	120.4	5.0	118.7	6.0	116.5	4.2	114.4	2.2	118.3	7.0	145.2	4.6	-	-	-	-	145.1	6.7
1990	127.4	5.8	126.1	6.2	122.6	5.2	120.7	5.5	125.5	6.1	154.4	6.3	-	-	-	-	157.9	8.8
1991	133.9	5.1	130.7	3.6	130.4	6.4	122.3	1.3	130.1	3.7	166.0	7.5	-	-	-	-	172.2	9.1
1992	139.8	4.4	131.7	0.8	138.2	6.0	124.8	2.0	134.0	3.0	176.3	6.2	-	-	-	-	183.6	6.6
1993	144.7	3.5	134.0	1.7	143.7	4.0	122.2	-2.1	136.2	1.6	186.6	5.8	-	-	-	-	201.2	9.6
1994	148.9	2.9	135.9	1.4	149.5	4.0	123.7	1.2	138.6	1.8	192.8	3.3	-	-	-	-	203.1	0.9
1995	153.2	2.9	137.1	0.9	154.6	3.4	123.4	-0.2	141.9	2.4	198.1	2.7	-	-	-	-	217.2	6.9
1996	158.6	3.5	143.1	4.4	158.3	2.4	124.5	0.9	147.0	3.6	211.8	6.9	-	-	-	-	235.6	8.5
1997	164.0	3.4	148.4	3.7	162.5	2.7	131.4	5.5	150.9	2.7	217.6	2.7	-	-	-	-	254.7	8.1
1998	167.1	1.9	153.7	3.6	168.4	3.6	132.4	0.8	146.9	-2.7	223.1	2.5	98.9	-	98.5	-	265.6	4.3
1999	172.6	3.3	157.3	2.3	174.5	3.6	134.8	1.8	152.1	3.5	229.8	3.0	100.8	1.9	100.3	1.8	287.4	8.2
2000	178.0	3.1	158.4	0.7	178.1	2.1	135.3	0.4	165.2	8.6	247.3	7.6	102.1	1.3	101.4	1.1	301.3	4.8
2001	-	-	-	-	-	-	-	-	-	-	-	-	-	-	-	-	-	-

Source: U.S. Department of Labor, Bureau of Labor Statistics, Division of Consumer Prices and Price Indexes. *Base is December 1997 = 100. - indicates no data collected for period.

Portland-Salem, OR-WA
Consumer Price Index - Urban Wage Earners
Base 1982-1984 = 100
Annual Averages

For 1914-2001. Columns headed % show percentile change in the index from the previous period for which an index is available.

Year	All Items		Food & Beverage		Housing		Apparel		Trans- portation		Medical Care		Recrea- tion*		Education & Communic.*		Other Goods & Services	
	Index	%	Index	%	Index	%	Index	%	Index	%	Index	%	Index	%	Index	%	Index	%
1914	10.6	-	-	-	-	-	16.6	-	-	-	-	-	-	-	-	-	-	-
1915	10.4	-1.9	-	-	-	-	16.9	1.8	-	-	-	-	-	-	-	-	-	-
1916	10.7	2.9	-	-	-	-	18.3	8.3	-	-	-	-	-	-	-	-	-	-
1917	12.5	16.8	-	-	-	-	21.9	19.7	-	-	-	-	-	-	-	-	-	-
1918	15.3	22.4	-	-	-	-	28.8	31.5	-	-	-	-	-	-	-	-	-	-
1919	17.9	17.0	-	-	-	-	36.5	26.7	-	-	-	-	-	-	-	-	-	-
1920	20.3	13.4	-	-	-	-	40.7	11.5	-	-	-	-	-	-	-	-	-	-
1921	17.6	-13.3	-	-	-	-	31.0	-23.8	-	-	-	-	-	-	-	-	-	-
1922	16.7	-5.1	-	-	-	-	25.9	-16.5	-	-	-	-	-	-	-	-	-	-
1923	16.8	0.6	-	-	-	-	26.8	3.5	-	-	-	-	-	-	-	-	-	-
1924	16.8	0.0	-	-	-	-	26.7	-0.4	-	-	-	-	-	-	-	-	-	-
1925	16.8	0.0	-	-	-	-	26.3	-1.5	-	-	-	-	-	-	-	-	-	-
1926	16.7	-0.6	-	-	-	-	26.0	-1.1	-	-	-	-	-	-	-	-	-	-
1927	16.5	-1.2	-	-	-	-	25.4	-2.3	-	-	-	-	-	-	-	-	-	-
1928	16.2	-1.8	-	-	-	-	25.0	-1.6	-	-	-	-	-	-	-	-	-	-
1929	16.1	-0.6	-	-	-	-	24.7	-1.2	-	-	-	-	-	-	-	-	-	-
1930	15.7	-2.5	-	-	-	-	23.9	-3.2	-	-	-	-	-	-	-	-	-	-
1931	14.2	-9.6	-	-	-	-	21.9	-8.4	-	-	-	-	-	-	-	-	-	-
1932	12.9	-9.2	-	-	-	-	19.3	-11.9	-	-	-	-	-	-	-	-	-	-
1933	12.3	-4.7	-	-	-	-	18.9	-2.1	-	-	-	-	-	-	-	-	-	-
1934	12.7	3.3	-	-	-	-	20.6	9.0	-	-	-	-	-	-	-	-	-	-
1935	13.2	3.9	-	-	-	-	20.6	0.0	-	-	-	-	-	-	-	-	-	-
1936	13.4	1.5	-	-	-	-	20.7	0.5	-	-	-	-	-	-	-	-	-	-
1937	14.1	5.2	-	-	-	-	21.6	4.3	-	-	-	-	-	-	-	-	-	-
1938	13.9	-1.4	-	-	-	-	21.6	0.0	-	-	-	-	-	-	-	-	-	-
1939	13.8	-0.7	-	-	-	-	21.4	-0.9	-	-	-	-	-	-	-	-	-	-
1940	13.8	0.0	-	-	-	-	21.8	1.9	-	-	-	-	-	-	-	-	-	-
1941	14.7	6.5	-	-	-	-	22.6	3.7	-	-	-	-	-	-	-	-	-	-
1942	16.7	13.6	-	-	-	-	26.2	15.9	-	-	-	-	-	-	-	-	-	-
1943	17.8	6.6	-	-	-	-	27.8	6.1	-	-	-	-	-	-	-	-	-	-
1944	18.0	1.1	-	-	-	-	29.6	6.5	-	-	-	-	-	-	-	-	-	-
1945	18.5	2.8	-	-	-	-	30.2	2.0	-	-	-	-	-	-	-	-	-	-
1946	19.8	7.0	-	-	-	-	32.3	7.0	-	-	-	-	-	-	-	-	-	-
1947	22.4	13.1	-	-	-	-	38.2	18.3	19.7	-	15.8	-	-	-	-	-	-	-
1948	24.5	9.4	-	-	-	-	41.5	8.6	21.9	11.2	16.4	3.8	-	-	-	-	-	-
1949	24.2	-1.2	-	-	-	-	40.1	-3.4	23.6	7.8	16.7	1.8	-	-	-	-	-	-
1950	24.6	1.7	-	-	-	-	39.8	-0.7	24.0	1.7	17.2	3.0	-	-	-	-	-	-
1951	26.6	8.1	-	-	-	-	42.6	7.0	25.1	4.6	18.2	5.8	-	-	-	-	-	-
1952	27.2	2.3	-	-	-	-	42.2	-0.9	26.8	6.8	19.0	4.4	-	-	-	-	-	-
1953	27.3	0.4	-	-	-	-	41.8	-0.9	27.6	3.0	19.5	2.6	-	-	-	-	-	-
1954	27.3	0.0	-	-	-	-	42.1	0.7	26.8	-2.9	19.9	2.1	-	-	-	-	-	-
1955	27.3	0.0	-	-	-	-	42.5	1.0	26.9	0.4	20.7	4.0	-	-	-	-	-	-
1956	27.9	2.2	-	-	-	-	43.5	2.4	26.9	0.0	21.4	3.4	-	-	-	-	-	-
1957	28.8	3.2	-	-	-	-	44.3	1.8	28.2	4.8	22.6	5.6	-	-	-	-	-	-
1958	29.5	2.4	-	-	-	-	44.4	0.2	29.8	5.7	22.9	1.3	-	-	-	-	-	-

[Continued]

Portland-Salem, OR-WA
Consumer Price Index - Urban Wage Earners
Base 1982-1984 = 100
Annual Averages
[Continued]

For 1914-2001. Columns headed % show percentile change in the index from the previous period for which an index is available.

Year	All Items		Food & Beverage		Housing		Apparel		Trans-portation		Medical Care		Recrea-tion*		Education & Communic.*		Other Goods & Services	
	Index	%	Index	%	Index	%	Index	%	Index	%	Index	%	Index	%	Index	%	Index	%
1959	29.8	1.0	-	-	-	-	44.7	0.7	31.0	4.0	23.2	1.3	-	-	-	-	-	-
1960	30.2	1.3	-	-	-	-	45.8	2.5	30.8	-0.6	24.3	4.7	-	-	-	-	-	-
1961	30.6	1.3	-	-	-	-	46.1	0.7	30.9	0.3	25.0	2.9	-	-	-	-	-	-
1962	30.7	0.3	-	-	-	-	45.8	-0.7	31.1	0.6	25.1	0.4	-	-	-	-	-	-
1963	31.3	2.0	-	-	-	-	46.6	1.7	31.5	1.3	25.7	2.4	-	-	-	-	-	-
1964	32.0	2.2	-	-	-	-	47.1	1.1	31.9	1.3	27.2	5.8	-	-	-	-	-	-
1965	32.8	2.5	-	-	-	-	48.5	3.0	32.4	1.6	28.1	3.3	-	-	-	-	-	-
1966	33.8	3.0	-	-	-	-	50.1	3.3	32.7	0.9	29.0	3.2	-	-	-	-	-	-
1967	34.7	2.7	-	-	-	-	51.3	2.4	34.1	4.3	30.9	6.6	-	-	-	-	-	-
1968	35.9	3.5	-	-	-	-	53.6	4.5	34.9	2.3	32.5	5.2	-	-	-	-	-	-
1969	37.7	5.0	-	-	-	-	56.6	5.6	36.0	3.2	34.4	5.8	-	-	-	-	-	-
1970	39.3	4.2	-	-	-	-	59.2	4.6	37.0	2.8	36.6	6.4	-	-	-	-	-	-
1971	40.3	2.5	-	-	-	-	59.9	1.2	37.3	0.8	38.1	4.1	-	-	-	-	-	-
1972	41.5	3.0	-	-	-	-	61.5	2.7	37.6	0.8	39.4	3.4	-	-	-	-	-	-
1973	44.2	6.5	-	-	-	-	65.4	6.3	38.5	2.4	41.9	6.3	-	-	-	-	-	-
1974	49.5	12.0	-	-	-	-	69.4	6.1	42.3	9.9	46.1	10.0	-	-	-	-	-	-
1975	54.3	9.7	-	-	-	-	73.4	5.8	46.8	10.6	51.2	11.1	-	-	-	-	-	-
1976	57.9	6.6	60.6	-	57.1	-	77.2	5.2	51.2	9.4	55.8	9.0	-	-	-	-	55.7	-
1977	62.5	7.9	64.4	6.3	62.1	8.8	82.6	7.0	56.2	9.8	61.5	10.2	-	-	-	-	60.0	7.7
1978	69.0	10.4	71.8	11.5	70.1	12.9	85.3	3.3	61.3	9.1	66.1	7.5	-	-	-	-	63.4	5.7
1979	78.3	13.5	81.0	12.8	81.1	15.7	86.9	1.9	70.7	15.3	71.8	8.6	-	-	-	-	67.6	6.6
1980	88.2	12.6	86.3	6.5	94.2	16.2	88.8	2.2	80.6	14.0	77.6	8.1	-	-	-	-	74.0	9.5
1981	95.8	8.6	92.5	7.2	102.2	8.5	93.2	5.0	91.3	13.3	83.8	8.0	-	-	-	-	81.3	9.9
1982	98.8	3.1	97.1	5.0	101.9	-0.3	95.3	2.3	97.0	6.2	93.8	11.9	-	-	-	-	92.2	13.4
1983	99.2	0.4	99.7	2.7	98.7	-3.1	98.9	3.8	98.5	1.5	100.8	7.5	-	-	-	-	102.1	10.7
1984	102.1	2.9	103.2	3.5	99.4	0.7	105.8	7.0	104.4	6.0	105.4	4.6	-	-	-	-	105.8	3.6
1985	105.1	2.9	105.6	2.3	101.3	1.9	108.8	2.8	109.0	4.4	111.1	5.4	-	-	-	-	111.2	5.1
1986	106.0	0.9	108.0	2.3	102.6	1.3	100.4	-7.7	107.5	-1.4	118.7	6.8	-	-	-	-	120.2	8.1
1987	108.5	2.4	111.1	2.9	104.4	1.8	101.8	1.4	109.3	1.7	126.4	6.5	-	-	-	-	-	-
1988	112.0	3.2	111.9	0.7	107.8	3.3	112.0	10.0	110.7	1.3	138.3	9.4	-	-	-	-	135.7	12.9
1989	117.6	5.0	118.6	6.0	112.3	4.2	114.4	2.1	117.9	6.5	144.7	4.6	-	-	-	-	145.6	7.3
1990	124.2	5.6	125.9	6.2	118.1	5.2	120.9	5.7	124.2	5.3	153.2	5.9	-	-	-	-	158.4	8.8
1991	130.8	5.3	130.5	3.7	125.9	6.6	123.6	2.2	129.1	3.9	164.3	7.2	-	-	-	-	171.9	8.5
1992	136.6	4.4	131.7	0.9	133.7	6.2	125.1	1.2	133.1	3.1	174.9	6.5	-	-	-	-	183.0	6.5
1993	141.5	3.6	133.9	1.7	139.1	4.0	123.0	-1.7	136.0	2.2	185.0	5.8	-	-	-	-	200.1	9.3
1994	145.6	2.9	135.5	1.2	144.8	4.1	123.8	0.7	138.8	2.1	191.1	3.3	-	-	-	-	203.1	1.5
1995	149.9	3.0	136.4	0.7	149.4	3.2	124.3	0.4	143.0	3.0	197.0	3.1	-	-	-	-	216.9	6.8
1996	155.2	3.5	142.2	4.3	152.9	2.3	125.4	0.9	148.2	3.6	210.6	6.9	-	-	-	-	235.0	8.3
1997	160.4	3.4	147.4	3.7	157.1	2.7	131.1	4.5	151.8	2.4	216.4	2.8	-	-	-	-	255.0	8.5
1998	162.9	1.6	152.4	3.4	162.4	3.4	131.1	0.0	147.0	-3.2	221.9	2.5	99.2	-	98.8	-	267.5	4.9
1999	167.9	3.1	156.1	2.4	167.2	3.0	134.4	2.5	151.4	3.0	228.2	2.8	101.0	1.8	100.5	1.7	297.1	11.1
2000	173.2	3.2	157.7	1.0	170.5	2.0	132.3	-1.6	163.0	7.7	246.3	7.9	102.0	1.0	101.6	1.1	314.7	5.9
2001	-	-	-	-	-	-	-	-	-	-	-	-	-	-	-	-	-	-

Source: U.S. Department of Labor, Bureau of Labor Statistics, Division of Consumer Prices and Price Indexes. *Base is December 1997 = 100. - indicates no data collected for period.

Portland-Salem, OR-WA
Consumer Price Index - All Urban Consumers
Base 1982-1984 = 100
All Items

For 1914-2001. Columns headed % show percentile change in the index from the previous period for which an index is available.

Year	Jan Index	%	Feb Index	%	Mar Index	%	Apr Index	%	May Index	%	Jun Index	%	Jul Index	%	Aug Index	%	Sep Index	%	Oct Index	%	Nov Index	%	Dec Index	%
1914	-		-		-		-		-		-		-		-		-		-		-		10.5	-
1915	-		-		-		-		-		-		-		-		-		-		-		10.1	-3.8
1916	-		-		-		-		-		-		-		-		-		-		-		10.9	7.9
1917	-		-		-		-		-		-		-		-		-		-		-		13.2	21.1
1918	-		-		-		-		-		-		-		-		-		-		-		16.6	25.8
1919	-		-		-		-		-		17.3	4.2	-		-		-		-		-		19.0	9.8
1920	-		-		-		-		-		21.1	11.1	-		-		-		-		-		18.8	-10.9
1921	-		-		17.1	-9.0	-		-		-		-		-		17.0	-0.6	-		-		16.8	-1.2
1922	-		-		16.3	-3.0	-		-		16.2	-0.6	-		-		16.4	1.2	-		-		16.5	0.6
1923	-		-		16.4	-0.6	-		-		16.5	0.6	-		-		16.6	0.6	-		-		16.7	0.6
1924	-		-		16.6	-0.6	-		-		16.4	-1.2	-		-		16.5	0.6	-		-		16.5	0.0
1925	-		-		-		-		-		16.6	0.6	-		-		-		-		-		16.7	0.6
1926	-		-		-		-		-		16.5	-1.2	-		-		-		-		-		16.4	-0.6
1927	-		-		-		-		-		16.4	0.0	-		-		-		-		-		16.1	-1.8
1928	-		-		-		-		-		15.8	-1.9	-		-		-		-		-		15.9	0.6
1929	-		-		-		-		-		15.7	-1.3	-		-		-		-		-		15.8	0.6
1930	-		-		-		-		-		15.7	-0.6	-		-		-		-		-		14.8	-5.7
1931	-		-		-		-		-		14.1	-4.7	-		-		-		-		-		13.6	-3.5
1932	-		-		-		-		-		12.7	-6.6	-		-		-		-		-		12.4	-2.4
1933	-		-		-		-		-		11.9	-4.0	-		-		-		-		-		12.2	2.5
1934	-		-		-		-		-		12.4	1.6	-		-		-		-		12.7	2.4	-	
1935	-		-		13.0	2.4	-		-		-		12.8	-1.5	-		-		12.9	0.8	-		-	
1936	13.0	0.8	-		-		12.9	-0.8	-		-		13.2	2.3	-		13.4	1.5	-		-		13.4	0.0
1937	-		-		13.7	2.2	-		-		13.9	1.5	-		-		14.1	1.4	-		-		13.9	-1.4
1938	-		-		13.8	-0.7	-		-		13.7	-0.7	-		-		13.7	0.0	-		-		13.7	0.0
1939	-		-		13.6	-0.7	-		-		13.5	-0.7	-		-		13.7	1.5	-		-		13.6	-0.7
1940	-		-		13.4	-1.5	-		-		13.6	1.5	-		-		13.7	0.7	-		-		13.7	0.0
1941	-		-		13.8	0.7	-		-		14.3	3.6	-		-		14.9	4.2	-		-		15.3	2.7
1942	-		-		16.1	5.2	-		-		16.5	2.5	-		-		16.8	1.8	-		-		17.1	1.8
1943	-		-		17.4	1.8	-		-		17.7	1.7	-		-		17.5	-1.1	-		-		17.5	0.0
1944	-		-		17.5	0.0	-		-		17.5	0.0	-		-		17.8	1.7	-		-		18.0	1.1
1945	-		-		18.0	0.0	-		-		18.3	1.7	-		-		18.3	0.0	-		-		18.5	1.1
1946	-		-		18.4	-0.5	-		-		19.0	3.3	-		-		20.4	7.4	-		-		21.3	4.4
1947	-		-		21.7	1.9	-		-		21.8	0.5	21.9	0.5	-		-		22.5	2.7	-		-	
1948	23.6	4.9	-		-		23.8	0.8	-		-		24.4	2.5	-		-		24.4	0.0	-		-	
1949	24.1	-1.2	-		-		24.0	-0.4	-		-		23.7	-1.2	-		-		23.5	-0.8	-		-	
1950	23.6	0.4	-		-		23.7	0.4	-		-		24.1	1.7	-		-		24.8	2.9	-		-	
1951	25.6	3.2	-		-		26.2	2.3	-		-		26.4	0.8	-		-		26.4	0.0	-		-	
1952	26.8	1.5	-		-		26.7	-0.4	-		-		26.7	0.0	-		-		26.8	0.4	-		26.7	-0.4
1953	26.7	0.0	-		-		26.9	0.7	-		-		26.9	0.0	-		-		27.1	0.7	-		-	
1954	26.9	-0.7	-		-		26.8	-0.4	-		-		26.9	0.4	-		-		26.9	0.0	-		-	
1955	26.7	-0.7	-		-		26.6	-0.4	-		-		26.7	0.4	-		-		27.1	1.5	-		-	
1956	27.1	0.0	-		-		27.1	0.0	-		-		27.7	2.2	-		-		27.9	0.7	-		-	
1957	28.0	0.4	-		-		28.4	1.4	-		-		28.5	0.4	-		-		28.4	-0.4	-		-	
1958	28.8	1.4	-		-		29.2	1.4	-		-		29.1	-0.3	-		-		29.0	-0.3	-		-	
1959	29.0	0.0	-		-		29.2	0.7	-		-		29.4	0.7	-		-		29.4	0.0	-		-	

[Continued]

Portland-Salem, OR-WA
Consumer Price Index - All Urban Consumers
Base 1982-1984 = 100
All Items
[Continued]

For 1914-2001. Columns headed % show percentile change in the index from the previous period for which an index is available.

Year	Jan Index	%	Feb Index	%	Mar Index	%	Apr Index	%	May Index	%	Jun Index	%	Jul Index	%	Aug Index	%	Sep Index	%	Oct Index	%	Nov Index	%	Dec Index	%
1960	29.7	1.0	-	-	-	-	29.8	0.3	-	-	-	-	29.8	0.0	-	-	-	-	29.7	-0.3	-	-	-	-
1961	30.1	1.3	-	-	-	-	29.9	-0.7	-	-	-	-	30.2	1.0	-	-	-	-	30.2	0.0	-	-	-	-
1962	30.0	-0.7	-	-	-	-	30.0	0.0	-	-	-	-	30.3	1.0	-	-	-	-	30.4	0.3	-	-	-	-
1963	30.5	0.3	-	-	-	-	30.7	0.7	-	-	-	-	30.9	0.7	-	-	-	-	30.9	0.0	-	-	-	-
1964	31.1	0.6	-	-	-	-	31.4	1.0	-	-	-	-	31.6	0.6	-	-	-	-	31.7	0.3	-	-	-	-
1965	31.8	0.3	-	-	-	-	32.1	0.9	-	-	-	-	32.5	1.2	-	-	-	-	32.6	0.3	-	-	-	-
1966	32.6	0.0	-	-	-	-	33.1	1.5	-	-	-	-	33.4	0.9	-	-	-	-	33.7	0.9	-	-	-	-
1967	33.9	0.6	-	-	-	-	33.9	0.0	-	-	-	-	34.2	0.9	-	-	-	-	34.5	0.9	-	-	-	-
1968	34.6	0.3	-	-	-	-	35.0	1.2	-	-	-	-	35.4	1.1	-	-	-	-	35.8	1.1	-	-	-	-
1969	36.2	1.1	-	-	-	-	37.0	2.2	-	-	-	-	37.1	0.3	-	-	-	-	37.6	1.3	-	-	-	-
1970	37.8	0.5	-	-	-	-	38.6	2.1	-	-	-	-	38.8	0.5	-	-	-	-	39.1	0.8	-	-	-	-
1971	39.2	0.3	-	-	-	-	39.2	0.0	-	-	-	-	39.7	1.3	-	-	-	-	40.1	1.0	-	-	-	-
1972	40.3	0.5	-	-	-	-	40.4	0.2	-	-	-	-	40.9	1.2	-	-	-	-	41.2	0.7	-	-	-	-
1973	41.6	1.0	-	-	-	-	42.8	2.9	-	-	-	-	43.4	1.4	-	-	-	-	44.7	3.0	-	-	-	-
1974	45.7	2.2	-	-	-	-	47.5	3.9	-	-	-	-	49.1	3.4	-	-	-	-	50.6	3.1	-	-	-	-
1975	52.1	3.0	-	-	-	-	52.7	1.2	-	-	-	-	53.7	1.9	-	-	-	-	54.4	1.3	-	-	-	-
1976	55.4	1.8	-	-	-	-	56.2	1.4	-	-	-	-	57.4	2.1	-	-	-	-	58.0	1.0	-	-	-	-
1977	58.9	1.6	-	-	-	-	60.7	3.1	-	-	-	-	62.0	2.1	-	-	-	-	62.8	1.3	-	-	-	-
1978	64.2	2.2	-	-	65.5	2.0	-	-	66.7	1.8	-	-	68.0	1.9	-	-	69.4	2.1	-	-	70.7	1.9	-	-
1979	72.3	2.3	-	-	73.6	1.8	-	-	75.4	2.4	-	-	77.7	3.1	-	-	79.3	2.1	-	-	80.8	1.9	-	-
1980	83.6	3.5	-	-	86.6	3.6	-	-	87.9	1.5	-	-	86.3	-1.8	-	-	87.8	1.7	-	-	89.5	1.9	-	-
1981	91.0	1.7	-	-	91.6	0.7	-	-	95.1	3.8	-	-	95.9	0.8	-	-	99.4	3.6	-	-	95.2	-4.2	-	-
1982	98.5	3.5	-	-	97.9	-0.6	-	-	96.4	-1.5	-	-	99.9	3.6	-	-	98.4	-1.5	-	-	97.6	-0.8	-	-
1983	97.9	0.3	-	-	97.2	-0.7	-	-	98.5	1.3	-	-	99.6	1.1	-	-	100.2	0.6	-	-	100.4	0.2	-	-
1984	100.8	0.4	-	-	101.8	1.0	-	-	103.1	1.3	-	-	102.8	-0.3	-	-	103.3	0.5	-	-	104.1	0.8	-	-
1985	104.8	0.7	-	-	105.5	0.7	-	-	106.0	0.5	-	-	106.9	0.8	-	-	107.6	0.7	-	-	108.3	0.7	-	-
1986	109.7	1.3	-	-	107.6	-1.9	-	-	107.5	-0.1	-	-	107.5	0.0	-	-	108.6	1.0	-	-	108.6	0.0	-	-
1987	-	-	-	-	-	-	-	-	-	-	109.9	1.2	-	-	-	-	-	-	-	-	-	-	111.9	1.8
1988	-	-	-	-	-	-	-	-	-	-	113.6	1.5	-	-	-	-	-	-	-	-	-	-	115.9	2.0
1989	-	-	-	-	-	-	-	-	-	-	119.3	2.9	-	-	-	-	-	-	-	-	-	-	121.6	1.9
1990	-	-	-	-	-	-	-	-	-	-	124.9	2.7	-	-	-	-	-	-	-	-	-	-	129.8	3.9
1991	-	-	-	-	-	-	-	-	-	-	132.8	2.3	-	-	-	-	-	-	-	-	-	-	135.1	1.7
1992	-	-	-	-	-	-	-	-	-	-	138.8	2.7	-	-	-	-	-	-	-	-	-	-	140.9	1.5
1993	-	-	-	-	-	-	-	-	-	-	143.6	1.9	-	-	-	-	-	-	-	-	-	-	145.8	1.5
1994	-	-	-	-	-	-	-	-	-	-	147.7	1.3	-	-	-	-	-	-	-	-	-	-	150.1	1.6
1995	-	-	-	-	-	-	-	-	-	-	152.5	1.6	-	-	-	-	-	-	-	-	-	-	153.9	0.9
1996	-	-	-	-	-	-	-	-	-	-	157.2	2.1	-	-	-	-	-	-	-	-	-	-	160.0	1.8
1997	-	-	-	-	-	-	-	-	-	-	162.6	1.6	-	-	-	-	-	-	-	-	-	-	165.5	1.8
1998	-	-	-	-	-	-	-	-	-	-	166.1	0.4	-	-	-	-	-	-	-	-	-	-	168.1	1.2
1999	-	-	-	-	-	-	-	-	-	-	170.8	1.6	-	-	-	-	-	-	-	-	-	-	174.4	2.1
2000	-	-	-	-	-	-	-	-	-	-	176.4	1.1	-	-	-	-	-	-	-	-	-	-	179.5	1.8
2001	-	-	-	-	-	-	-	-	-	-	181.2	0.9	-	-	-	-	-	-	-	-	-	-	-	-

Source: U.S. Department of Labor, Bureau of Labor Statistics, Division of Consumer Prices and Price Indexes. - indicates no data collected for period.

Portland-Salem, OR-WA
Consumer Price Index - Urban Wage Earners
Base 1982-1984 = 100
All Items

For 1914-2001. Columns headed % show percentile change in the index from the previous period for which an index is available.

Year	Jan Index	%	Feb Index	%	Mar Index	%	Apr Index	%	May Index	%	Jun Index	%	Jul Index	%	Aug Index	%	Sep Index	%	Oct Index	%	Nov Index	%	Dec Index	%
1914	-	-	-	-	-	-	-	-	-	-	-	-	-	-	-	-	-	-	-	-	-	-	10.6	-
1915	-	-	-	-	-	-	-	-	-	-	-	-	-	-	-	-	-	-	-	-	-	-	10.2	-3.8
1916	-	-	-	-	-	-	-	-	-	-	-	-	-	-	-	-	-	-	-	-	-	-	11.0	7.8
1917	-	-	-	-	-	-	-	-	-	-	-	-	-	-	-	-	-	-	-	-	-	-	13.4	21.8
1918	-	-	-	-	-	-	-	-	-	-	-	-	-	-	-	-	-	-	-	-	-	-	16.9	26.1
1919	-	-	-	-	-	-	-	-	-	-	17.6	4.1	-	-	-	-	-	-	-	-	-	-	19.3	9.7
1920	-	-	-	-	-	-	-	-	-	-	21.4	10.9	-	-	-	-	-	-	-	-	-	-	19.1	-10.7
1921	-	-	-	-	17.4	-8.9	-	-	-	-	-	-	-	-	-	-	17.3	-0.6	-	-	-	-	17.1	-1.2
1922	-	-	-	-	16.5	-3.5	-	-	-	-	16.5	0.0	-	-	-	-	16.7	1.2	-	-	-	-	16.8	0.6
1923	-	-	-	-	16.7	-0.6	-	-	-	-	16.7	0.0	-	-	-	-	16.9	1.2	-	-	-	-	17.0	0.6
1924	-	-	-	-	16.8	-1.2	-	-	-	-	16.6	-1.2	-	-	-	-	16.7	0.6	-	-	-	-	16.8	0.6
1925	-	-	-	-	-	-	-	-	-	-	16.9	0.6	-	-	-	-	-	-	-	-	-	-	16.9	0.0
1926	-	-	-	-	-	-	-	-	-	-	16.7	-1.2	-	-	-	-	-	-	-	-	-	-	16.7	0.0
1927	-	-	-	-	-	-	-	-	-	-	16.7	0.0	-	-	-	-	-	-	-	-	-	-	16.4	-1.8
1928	-	-	-	-	-	-	-	-	-	-	16.1	-1.8	-	-	-	-	-	-	-	-	-	-	16.2	0.6
1929	-	-	-	-	-	-	-	-	-	-	16.0	-1.2	-	-	-	-	-	-	-	-	-	-	16.1	0.6
1930	-	-	-	-	-	-	-	-	-	-	16.0	-0.6	-	-	-	-	-	-	-	-	-	-	15.0	-6.3
1931	-	-	-	-	-	-	-	-	-	-	14.3	-4.7	-	-	-	-	-	-	-	-	-	-	13.8	-3.5
1932	-	-	-	-	-	-	-	-	-	-	12.9	-6.5	-	-	-	-	-	-	-	-	-	-	12.6	-2.3
1933	-	-	-	-	-	-	-	-	-	-	12.1	-4.0	-	-	-	-	-	-	-	-	-	-	12.4	2.5
1934	-	-	-	-	-	-	-	-	-	-	12.6	1.6	-	-	-	-	-	-	-	-	12.9	2.4	-	-
1935	-	-	-	-	13.2	2.3	-	-	-	-	-	-	13.0	-1.5	-	-	-	-	13.1	0.8	-	-	-	-
1936	13.3	1.5	-	-	-	-	13.2	-0.8	-	-	-	-	13.4	1.5	-	-	13.6	1.5	-	-	-	-	13.6	0.0
1937	-	-	-	-	13.9	2.2	-	-	-	-	14.1	1.4	-	-	-	-	14.3	1.4	-	-	-	-	14.1	-1.4
1938	-	-	-	-	14.1	0.0	-	-	-	-	13.9	-1.4	-	-	-	-	13.9	0.0	-	-	-	-	13.9	0.0
1939	-	-	-	-	13.8	-0.7	-	-	-	-	13.7	-0.7	-	-	-	-	13.9	1.5	-	-	-	-	13.8	-0.7
1940	-	-	-	-	13.6	-1.4	-	-	-	-	13.8	1.5	-	-	-	-	13.9	0.7	-	-	-	-	13.9	0.0
1941	-	-	-	-	14.1	1.4	-	-	-	-	14.5	2.8	-	-	-	-	15.2	4.8	-	-	-	-	15.5	2.0
1942	-	-	-	-	16.3	5.2	-	-	-	-	16.7	2.5	-	-	-	-	17.1	2.4	-	-	-	-	17.4	1.8
1943	-	-	-	-	17.6	1.1	-	-	-	-	17.9	1.7	-	-	-	-	17.7	-1.1	-	-	-	-	17.8	0.6
1944	-	-	-	-	17.8	0.0	-	-	-	-	17.8	0.0	-	-	-	-	18.1	1.7	-	-	-	-	18.3	1.1
1945	-	-	-	-	18.3	0.0	-	-	-	-	18.6	1.6	-	-	-	-	18.6	0.0	-	-	-	-	18.8	1.1
1946	-	-	-	-	18.7	-0.5	-	-	-	-	19.3	3.2	-	-	-	-	20.7	7.3	-	-	-	-	21.7	4.8
1947	-	-	-	-	22.0	1.4	-	-	-	-	22.2	0.9	22.2	0.0	-	-	-	-	22.9	3.2	-	-	-	-
1948	24.0	4.8	-	-	-	-	24.1	0.4	-	-	-	-	24.8	2.9	-	-	-	-	24.7	-0.4	-	-	-	-
1949	24.5	-0.8	-	-	-	-	24.4	-0.4	-	-	-	-	24.1	-1.2	-	-	-	-	23.9	-0.8	-	-	-	-
1950	23.9	0.0	-	-	-	-	24.0	0.4	-	-	-	-	24.5	2.1	-	-	-	-	25.2	2.9	-	-	-	-
1951	26.0	3.2	-	-	-	-	26.6	2.3	-	-	-	-	26.8	0.8	-	-	-	-	26.8	0.0	-	-	-	-
1952	27.2	1.5	-	-	-	-	27.2	0.0	-	-	-	-	27.2	0.0	-	-	-	-	27.2	0.0	-	-	27.2	0.0
1953	27.2	0.0	-	-	-	-	27.3	0.4	-	-	-	-	27.3	0.0	-	-	-	-	27.5	0.7	-	-	-	-
1954	27.3	-0.7	-	-	-	-	27.2	-0.4	-	-	-	-	27.3	0.4	-	-	-	-	27.3	0.0	-	-	-	-
1955	27.2	-0.4	-	-	-	-	27.1	-0.4	-	-	-	-	27.2	0.4	-	-	-	-	27.6	1.5	-	-	-	-
1956	27.6	0.0	-	-	-	-	27.6	0.0	-	-	-	-	28.1	1.8	-	-	-	-	28.3	0.7	-	-	-	-
1957	28.5	0.7	-	-	-	-	28.8	1.1	-	-	-	-	28.9	0.3	-	-	-	-	28.9	0.0	-	-	-	-
1958	29.2	1.0	-	-	-	-	29.6	1.4	-	-	-	-	29.5	-0.3	-	-	-	-	29.5	0.0	-	-	-	-
1959	29.4	-0.3	-	-	-	-	29.7	1.0	-	-	-	-	29.9	0.7	-	-	-	-	29.9	0.0	-	-	-	-

[Continued]

Portland-Salem, OR-WA
Consumer Price Index - Urban Wage Earners
Base 1982-1984 = 100
All Items
[Continued]

For 1914-2001. Columns headed % show percentile change in the index from the previous period for which an index is available.

Year	Jan Index	%	Feb Index	%	Mar Index	%	Apr Index	%	May Index	%	Jun Index	%	Jul Index	%	Aug Index	%	Sep Index	%	Oct Index	%	Nov Index	%	Dec Index	%
1960	30.2	1.0	-	-	-	-	30.2	0.0	-	-	-	-	30.2	0.0	-	-	-	-	30.2	0.0	-	-	-	-
1961	30.5	1.0	-	-	-	-	30.4	-0.3	-	-	-	-	30.6	0.7	-	-	-	-	30.7	0.3	-	-	-	-
1962	30.5	-0.7	-	-	-	-	30.5	0.0	-	-	-	-	30.8	1.0	-	-	-	-	30.9	0.3	-	-	-	-
1963	31.0	0.3	-	-	-	-	31.2	0.6	-	-	-	-	31.4	0.6	-	-	-	-	31.4	0.0	-	-	-	-
1964	31.6	0.6	-	-	-	-	31.9	0.9	-	-	-	-	32.1	0.6	-	-	-	-	32.2	0.3	-	-	-	-
1965	32.3	0.3	-	-	-	-	32.6	0.9	-	-	-	-	33.0	1.2	-	-	-	-	33.1	0.3	-	-	-	-
1966	33.1	0.0	-	-	-	-	33.7	1.8	-	-	-	-	33.9	0.6	-	-	-	-	34.2	0.9	-	-	-	-
1967	34.4	0.6	-	-	-	-	34.5	0.3	-	-	-	-	34.7	0.6	-	-	-	-	35.0	0.9	-	-	-	-
1968	35.2	0.6	-	-	-	-	35.6	1.1	-	-	-	-	35.9	0.8	-	-	-	-	36.4	1.4	-	-	-	-
1969	36.8	1.1	-	-	-	-	37.5	1.9	-	-	-	-	37.7	0.5	-	-	-	-	38.2	1.3	-	-	-	-
1970	38.4	0.5	-	-	-	-	39.2	2.1	-	-	-	-	39.4	0.5	-	-	-	-	39.7	0.8	-	-	-	-
1971	39.9	0.5	-	-	-	-	39.8	-0.3	-	-	-	-	40.3	1.3	-	-	-	-	40.7	1.0	-	-	-	-
1972	41.0	0.7	-	-	-	-	41.1	0.2	-	-	-	-	41.5	1.0	-	-	-	-	41.8	0.7	-	-	-	-
1973	42.3	1.2	-	-	-	-	43.5	2.8	-	-	-	-	44.1	1.4	-	-	-	-	45.4	2.9	-	-	-	-
1974	46.5	2.4	-	-	-	-	48.3	3.9	-	-	-	-	49.9	3.3	-	-	-	-	51.4	3.0	-	-	-	-
1975	52.9	2.9	-	-	-	-	53.5	1.1	-	-	-	-	54.5	1.9	-	-	-	-	55.2	1.3	-	-	-	-
1976	56.2	1.8	-	-	-	-	57.0	1.4	-	-	-	-	58.3	2.3	-	-	-	-	58.9	1.0	-	-	-	-
1977	59.8	1.5	-	-	-	-	61.7	3.2	-	-	-	-	63.0	2.1	-	-	-	-	63.8	1.3	-	-	-	-
1978	65.2	2.2	-	-	66.6	2.1	-	-	68.0	2.1	-	-	69.4	2.1	-	-	70.9	2.2	-	-	72.1	1.7	-	-
1979	73.6	2.1	-	-	74.9	1.8	-	-	77.0	2.8	-	-	79.1	2.7	-	-	80.7	2.0	-	-	82.1	1.7	-	-
1980	84.5	2.9	-	-	87.3	3.3	-	-	88.8	1.7	-	-	87.5	-1.5	-	-	88.6	1.3	-	-	90.5	2.1	-	-
1981	91.9	1.5	-	-	92.6	0.8	-	-	95.8	3.5	-	-	96.9	1.1	-	-	100.2	3.4	95.9	-4.3	-	-	-	-
1982	99.1	3.3	-	-	98.5	-0.6	-	-	97.0	-1.5	-	-	100.8	3.9	-	-	99.2	-1.6	98.4	-0.8	-	-	-	-
1983	97.7	-0.7	-	-	98.2	0.5	-	-	98.5	0.3	-	-	99.4	0.9	-	-	100.0	0.6	100.5	0.5	-	-	-	-
1984	100.5	0.0	-	-	101.4	0.9	-	-	103.2	1.8	-	-	102.2	-1.0	-	-	101.9	-0.3	102.6	0.7	-	-	-	-
1985	103.2	0.6	-	-	104.0	0.8	-	-	104.5	0.5	-	-	105.2	0.7	-	-	106.0	0.8	106.6	0.6	-	-	-	-
1986	107.9	1.2	-	-	105.6	-2.1	-	-	105.2	-0.4	-	-	105.3	0.1	-	-	106.3	0.9	106.2	-0.1	-	-	-	-
1987	-	-	-	-	-	-	-	-	-	-	107.5	1.2	-	-	-	-	-	-	-	-	-	-	109.5	1.9
1988	-	-	-	-	-	-	-	-	-	-	110.9	1.3	-	-	-	-	-	-	-	-	-	-	113.0	1.9
1989	-	-	-	-	-	-	-	-	-	-	116.4	3.0	-	-	-	-	-	-	-	-	-	-	118.7	2.0
1990	-	-	-	-	-	-	-	-	-	-	121.8	2.6	-	-	-	-	-	-	-	-	-	-	126.6	3.9
1991	-	-	-	-	-	-	-	-	-	-	129.6	2.4	-	-	-	-	-	-	-	-	-	-	132.1	1.9
1992	-	-	-	-	-	-	-	-	-	-	135.5	2.6	-	-	-	-	-	-	-	-	-	-	137.7	1.6
1993	-	-	-	-	-	-	-	-	-	-	140.3	1.9	-	-	-	-	-	-	-	-	-	-	142.6	1.6
1994	-	-	-	-	-	-	-	-	-	-	144.3	1.2	-	-	-	-	-	-	-	-	-	-	146.8	1.7
1995	-	-	-	-	-	-	-	-	-	-	149.1	1.6	-	-	-	-	-	-	-	-	-	-	150.7	1.1
1996	-	-	-	-	-	-	-	-	-	-	153.9	2.1	-	-	-	-	-	-	-	-	-	-	156.5	1.7
1997	-	-	-	-	-	-	-	-	-	-	159.0	1.6	-	-	-	-	-	-	-	-	-	-	161.7	1.7
1998	-	-	-	-	-	-	-	-	-	-	162.2	0.3	-	-	-	-	-	-	-	-	-	-	163.5	0.8
1999	-	-	-	-	-	-	-	-	-	-	166.2	1.7	-	-	-	-	-	-	-	-	-	-	169.6	2.0
2000	-	-	-	-	-	-	-	-	-	-	171.8	1.3	-	-	-	-	-	-	-	-	-	-	174.6	1.6
2001	-	-	-	-	-	-	-	-	-	-	176.4	1.0	-	-	-	-	-	-	-	-	-	-	-	-

Source: U.S. Department of Labor, Bureau of Labor Statistics, Division of Consumer Prices and Price Indexes. - indicates no data collected for period.

Portland-Salem, OR-WA
Consumer Price Index - All Urban Consumers
Base 1982-1984 = 100
Food and Beverages

For 1976-2001. Columns headed % show percentile change in the index from the previous period for which an index is available.

Year	Jan Index	%	Feb Index	%	Mar Index	%	Apr Index	%	May Index	%	Jun Index	%	Jul Index	%	Aug Index	%	Sep Index	%	Oct Index	%	Nov Index	%	Dec Index	%
1976	60.1	-	-	-	-	-	60.2	0.2	-	-	-	-	61.3	1.8	-	-	-	-	61.0	-0.5	-	-	-	-
1977	61.6	1.0	-	-	-	-	64.1	4.1	-	-	-	-	65.4	2.0	-	-	73.0	0.7	65.4	0.0	-	-	-	-
1978	66.7	2.0	-	-	68.3	2.4	-	-	70.6	3.4	-	-	72.5	2.7	-	-	73.0	0.7	-	-	73.3	0.4	-	-
1979	76.1	3.8	-	-	78.2	2.8	-	-	79.6	1.8	-	-	80.4	1.0	-	-	80.7	0.4	-	-	81.8	1.4	-	-
1980	82.7	1.1	-	-	84.0	1.6	-	-	84.7	0.8	-	-	85.8	1.3	-	-	86.4	0.7	-	-	87.9	1.7	-	-
1981	89.4	1.7	-	-	91.0	1.8	-	-	91.9	1.0	-	-	93.1	1.3	-	-	93.6	0.5	-	-	93.4	-0.2	-	-
1982	94.7	1.4	-	-	95.1	0.4	-	-	95.5	0.4	-	-	99.6	4.3	-	-	98.7	-0.9	-	-	98.4	-0.3	-	-
1983	98.7	0.3	-	-	99.0	0.3	-	-	99.6	0.6	-	-	100.0	0.4	-	-	100.0	0.0	-	-	100.2	0.2	-	-
1984	101.2	1.0	-	-	102.6	1.4	-	-	103.3	0.7	-	-	103.6	0.3	-	-	103.4	-0.2	-	-	104.1	0.7	-	-
1985	104.1	0.0	-	-	105.1	1.0	-	-	105.1	0.0	-	-	105.7	0.6	-	-	106.4	0.7	-	-	106.3	-0.1	-	-
1986	108.1	1.7	-	-	107.7	-0.4	-	-	107.2	-0.5	-	-	106.8	-0.4	-	-	108.9	2.0	-	-	109.6	0.6	-	-
1987	-	-	-	-	-	-	-	-	-	-	111.7	1.9	-	-	-	-	-	-	-	-	-	-	110.9	-0.7
1988	-	-	-	-	-	-	-	-	-	-	111.0	0.1	-	-	-	-	-	-	-	-	-	-	113.0	1.8
1989	-	-	-	-	-	-	-	-	-	-	118.0	4.4	-	-	-	-	-	-	-	-	-	-	119.5	1.3
1990	-	-	-	-	-	-	-	-	-	-	124.9	4.5	-	-	-	-	-	-	-	-	-	-	127.4	2.0
1991	-	-	-	-	-	-	-	-	-	-	131.4	3.1	-	-	-	-	-	-	-	-	-	-	129.9	-1.1
1992	-	-	-	-	-	-	-	-	-	-	132.1	1.7	-	-	-	-	-	-	-	-	-	-	131.3	-0.6
1993	-	-	-	-	-	-	-	-	-	-	133.8	1.9	-	-	-	-	-	-	-	-	-	-	134.3	0.4
1994	-	-	-	-	-	-	-	-	-	-	135.5	0.9	-	-	-	-	-	-	-	-	-	-	136.2	0.5
1995	-	-	-	-	-	-	-	-	-	-	137.3	0.8	-	-	-	-	-	-	-	-	-	-	136.8	-0.4
1996	-	-	-	-	-	-	-	-	-	-	141.6	3.5	-	-	-	-	-	-	-	-	-	-	144.7	2.2
1997	-	-	-	-	-	-	-	-	-	-	147.0	1.6	-	-	-	-	-	-	-	-	-	-	149.8	1.9
1998	-	-	-	-	-	-	-	-	-	-	153.5	2.5	-	-	-	-	-	-	-	-	-	-	153.9	0.3
1999	-	-	-	-	-	-	-	-	-	-	157.5	2.3	-	-	-	-	-	-	-	-	-	-	157.1	-0.3
2000	-	-	-	-	-	-	-	-	-	-	158.2	0.7	-	-	-	-	-	-	-	-	-	-	158.6	0.3
2001	-	-	-	-	-	-	-	-	-	-	159.2	0.4	-	-	-	-	-	-	-	-	-	-	-	-

Source: U.S. Department of Labor, Bureau of Labor Statistics, Division of Consumer Prices and Price Indexes. - indicates no data collected for period.

Portland-Salem, OR-WA
Consumer Price Index - Urban Wage Earners
Base 1982-1984 = 100
Food and Beverages

For 1976-2001. Columns headed % show percentile change in the index from the previous period for which an index is available.

Year	Jan Index	%	Feb Index	%	Mar Index	%	Apr Index	%	May Index	%	Jun Index	%	Jul Index	%	Aug Index	%	Sep Index	%	Oct Index	%	Nov Index	%	Dec Index	%
1976	59.9	-	-	-	-	-	60.1	0.3	-	-	-	-	61.1	1.7	-	-	-	-	60.8	-0.5	-	-	-	-
1977	61.5	1.2	-	-	-	-	63.9	3.9	-	-	-	-	65.2	2.0	-	-	-	-	65.2	0.0	-	-	-	-
1978	66.5	2.0	-	-	69.4	4.4	-	-	71.4	2.9	-	-	73.3	2.7	-	-	73.5	0.3	-	-	74.4	1.2	-	-
1979	77.3	3.9	-	-	79.2	2.5	-	-	81.3	2.7	-	-	81.8	0.6	-	-	82.3	0.6	-	-	82.5	0.2	-	-
1980	83.8	1.6	-	-	84.7	1.1	-	-	85.7	1.2	-	-	86.8	1.3	-	-	86.6	-0.2	-	-	88.3	2.0	-	-
1981	90.4	2.4	-	-	91.2	0.9	-	-	92.2	1.1	-	-	93.2	1.1	-	-	93.3	0.1	-	-	93.6	0.3	-	-
1982	94.8	1.3	-	-	95.0	0.2	-	-	95.7	0.7	-	-	99.4	3.9	-	-	98.5	-0.9	-	-	98.3	-0.2	-	-
1983	98.8	0.5	-	-	99.0	0.2	-	-	99.6	0.6	-	-	100.1	0.5	-	-	99.9	-0.2	-	-	100.3	0.4	-	-
1984	101.2	0.9	-	-	102.5	1.3	-	-	103.3	0.8	-	-	103.7	0.4	-	-	103.4	-0.3	-	-	104.2	0.8	-	-
1985	104.2	0.0	-	-	105.1	0.9	-	-	105.2	0.1	-	-	105.6	0.4	-	-	106.5	0.9	-	-	106.3	-0.2	-	-
1986	108.2	1.8	-	-	107.6	-0.6	-	-	107.1	-0.5	-	-	106.4	-0.7	-	-	108.6	2.1	-	-	109.4	0.7	-	-
1987	-	-	-	-	-	-	-	-	-	-	111.4	1.8	-	-	-	-	-	-	-	-	-	-	110.8	-0.5
1988	-	-	-	-	-	-	-	-	-	-	110.8	0.0	-	-	-	-	-	-	-	-	-	-	112.9	1.9
1989	-	-	-	-	-	-	-	-	-	-	117.8	4.3	-	-	-	-	-	-	-	-	-	-	119.4	1.4
1990	-	-	-	-	-	-	-	-	-	-	124.6	4.4	-	-	-	-	-	-	-	-	-	-	127.2	2.1
1991	-	-	-	-	-	-	-	-	-	-	131.1	3.1	-	-	-	-	-	-	-	-	-	-	130.0	-0.8
1992	-	-	-	-	-	-	-	-	-	-	132.1	1.6	-	-	-	-	-	-	-	-	-	-	131.4	-0.5
1993	-	-	-	-	-	-	-	-	-	-	133.8	1.8	-	-	-	-	-	-	-	-	-	-	134.1	0.2
1994	-	-	-	-	-	-	-	-	-	-	135.1	0.7	-	-	-	-	-	-	-	-	-	-	135.8	0.5
1995	-	-	-	-	-	-	-	-	-	-	136.6	0.6	-	-	-	-	-	-	-	-	-	-	136.1	-0.4
1996	-	-	-	-	-	-	-	-	-	-	140.6	3.3	-	-	-	-	-	-	-	-	-	-	143.7	2.2
1997	-	-	-	-	-	-	-	-	-	-	146.1	1.7	-	-	-	-	-	-	-	-	-	-	148.7	1.8
1998	-	-	-	-	-	-	-	-	-	-	152.3	2.4	-	-	-	-	-	-	-	-	-	-	152.4	0.1
1999	-	-	-	-	-	-	-	-	-	-	156.3	2.6	-	-	-	-	-	-	-	-	-	-	155.9	-0.3
2000	-	-	-	-	-	-	-	-	-	-	157.4	1.0	-	-	-	-	-	-	-	-	-	-	158.1	0.4
2001	-	-	-	-	-	-	-	-	-	-	158.7	0.4	-	-	-	-	-	-	-	-	-	-	-	-

Source: U.S. Department of Labor, Bureau of Labor Statistics, Division of Consumer Prices and Price Indexes. - indicates no data collected for period.

Portland-Salem, OR-WA
Consumer Price Index - All Urban Consumers
Base 1982-1984 = 100
Housing

For 1976-2001. Columns headed % show percentile change in the index from the previous period for which an index is available.

Year	Jan Index	%	Feb Index	%	Mar Index	%	Apr Index	%	May Index	%	Jun Index	%	Jul Index	%	Aug Index	%	Sep Index	%	Oct Index	%	Nov Index	%	Dec Index	%
1976	54.3	-	-	-	-	-	55.5	2.2	-	-	-	-	56.6	2.0	-	-	-	-	57.4	1.4	-	-	-	-
1977	58.2	1.4	-	-	-	-	60.0	3.1	-	-	-	-	61.7	2.8	-	-	-	-	62.9	1.9	-	-	-	-
1978	64.7	2.9	-	-	66.6	2.9	-	-	67.5	1.4	-	-	69.1	2.4	-	-	70.8	2.5	-	-	73.0	3.1	-	-
1979	74.8	2.5	-	-	75.3	0.7	-	-	77.2	2.5	-	-	80.3	4.0	-	-	82.5	2.7	-	-	84.9	2.9	-	-
1980	88.4	4.1	-	-	92.5	4.6	-	-	94.3	1.9	-	-	90.6	-3.9	-	-	92.2	1.8	-	-	94.4	2.4	-	-
1981	96.0	1.7	-	-	95.1	-0.9	-	-	101.2	6.4	-	-	101.6	0.4	-	-	107.2	5.5	-	-	97.6	-9.0	-	-
1982	102.8	5.3	-	-	101.7	-1.1	-	-	97.9	-3.7	-	-	102.5	4.7	-	-	99.4	-3.0	-	-	97.8	-1.6	-	-
1983	98.2	0.4	-	-	97.3	-0.9	-	-	98.4	1.1	-	-	98.9	0.5	-	-	99.2	0.3	-	-	99.3	0.1	-	-
1984	99.9	0.6	-	-	100.5	0.6	-	-	101.3	0.8	-	-	101.0	-0.3	-	-	101.7	0.7	-	-	102.2	0.5	-	-
1985	103.5	1.3	-	-	103.7	0.2	-	-	103.8	0.1	-	-	105.6	1.7	-	-	105.2	-0.4	-	-	105.8	0.6	-	-
1986	108.1	2.2	-	-	106.0	-1.9	-	-	105.6	-0.4	-	-	104.7	-0.9	-	-	106.5	1.7	-	-	106.7	0.2	-	-
1987	-	-	-	-	-	-	-	-	-	-	107.1	0.4	-	-	-	-	-	-	-	-	-	-	109.2	2.0
1988	-	-	-	-	-	-	-	-	-	-	111.0	1.6	-	-	-	-	-	-	-	-	-	-	112.7	1.5
1989	-	-	-	-	-	-	-	-	-	-	115.1	2.1	-	-	-	-	-	-	-	-	-	-	118.0	2.5
1990	-	-	-	-	-	-	-	-	-	-	120.7	2.3	-	-	-	-	-	-	-	-	-	-	124.6	3.2
1991	-	-	-	-	-	-	-	-	-	-	128.0	2.7	-	-	-	-	-	-	-	-	-	-	132.7	3.7
1992	-	-	-	-	-	-	-	-	-	-	137.4	3.5	-	-	-	-	-	-	-	-	-	-	139.0	1.2
1993	-	-	-	-	-	-	-	-	-	-	141.6	1.9	-	-	-	-	-	-	-	-	-	-	145.8	3.0
1994	-	-	-	-	-	-	-	-	-	-	148.3	1.7	-	-	-	-	-	-	-	-	-	-	150.8	1.7
1995	-	-	-	-	-	-	-	-	-	-	153.8	2.0	-	-	-	-	-	-	-	-	-	-	155.4	1.0
1996	-	-	-	-	-	-	-	-	-	-	157.0	1.0	-	-	-	-	-	-	-	-	-	-	159.6	1.7
1997	-	-	-	-	-	-	-	-	-	-	161.2	1.0	-	-	-	-	-	-	-	-	-	-	163.9	1.7
1998	-	-	-	-	-	-	-	-	-	-	166.2	1.4	-	-	-	-	-	-	-	-	-	-	170.5	2.6
1999	-	-	-	-	-	-	-	-	-	-	172.6	1.2	-	-	-	-	-	-	-	-	-	-	176.5	2.3
2000	-	-	-	-	-	-	-	-	-	-	176.6	0.1	-	-	-	-	-	-	-	-	-	-	179.6	1.7
2001	-	-	-	-	-	-	-	-	-	-	182.3	1.5	-	-	-	-	-	-	-	-	-	-	-	-

Source: U.S. Department of Labor, Bureau of Labor Statistics, Division of Consumer Prices and Price Indexes. - indicates no data collected for period.

Portland-Salem, OR-WA
Consumer Price Index - Urban Wage Earners
Base 1982-1984 = 100
Housing

For 1976-2001. Columns headed % show percentile change in the index from the previous period for which an index is available.

Year	Jan Index	%	Feb Index	%	Mar Index	%	Apr Index	%	May Index	%	Jun Index	%	Jul Index	%	Aug Index	%	Sep Index	%	Oct Index	%	Nov Index	%	Dec Index	%
1976	55.1	-	-	-	-	-	56.3	2.2	-	-	-	-	57.4	2.0	-	-	-	-	58.2	1.4	-	-	-	-
1977	59.0	1.4	-	-	-	-	60.9	3.2	-	-	-	-	62.6	2.8	-	-	-	-	63.8	1.9	-	-	-	-
1978	65.7	3.0	-	-	67.5	2.7	-	-	68.5	1.5	-	-	70.0	2.2	-	-	72.0	2.9	-	-	74.1	2.9	-	-
1979	76.0	2.6	-	-	76.6	0.8	-	-	78.6	2.6	-	-	81.6	3.8	-	-	84.0	2.9	-	-	86.6	3.1	-	-
1980	90.4	4.4	-	-	94.4	4.4	-	-	96.4	2.1	-	-	92.2	-4.4	-	-	93.7	1.6	-	-	96.2	2.7	-	-
1981	97.8	1.7	-	-	97.3	-0.5	-	-	103.0	5.9	-	-	104.0	1.0	-	-	110.2	6.0	-	-	99.2	-10.0	-	-
1982	104.6	5.4	-	-	103.7	-0.9	-	-	99.5	-4.1	-	-	104.7	5.2	-	-	101.0	-3.5	-	-	99.4	-1.6	-	-
1983	97.8	-1.6	-	-	99.6	1.8	-	-	98.2	-1.4	-	-	98.3	0.1	-	-	98.8	0.5	-	-	99.4	0.6	-	-
1984	98.9	-0.5	-	-	99.4	0.5	-	-	101.2	1.8	-	-	99.5	-1.7	-	-	98.4	-1.1	-	-	98.8	0.4	-	-
1985	100.0	1.2	-	-	100.2	0.2	-	-	100.3	0.1	-	-	102.2	1.9	-	-	101.8	-0.4	-	-	102.2	0.4	-	-
1986	104.3	2.1	-	-	102.4	-1.8	-	-	102.0	-0.4	-	-	101.3	-0.7	-	-	103.0	1.7	-	-	103.1	0.1	-	-
1987	-	-	-	-	-	-	-	-	-	-	103.3	0.2	-	-	-	-	-	-	-	-	-	-	105.3	1.9
1988	-	-	-	-	-	-	-	-	-	-	107.0	1.6	-	-	-	-	-	-	-	-	-	-	108.6	1.5
1989	-	-	-	-	-	-	-	-	-	-	110.9	2.1	-	-	-	-	-	-	-	-	-	-	113.7	2.5
1990	-	-	-	-	-	-	-	-	-	-	116.2	2.2	-	-	-	-	-	-	-	-	-	-	120.0	3.3
1991	-	-	-	-	-	-	-	-	-	-	123.5	2.9	-	-	-	-	-	-	-	-	-	-	128.2	3.8
1992	-	-	-	-	-	-	-	-	-	-	132.9	3.7	-	-	-	-	-	-	-	-	-	-	134.6	1.3
1993	-	-	-	-	-	-	-	-	-	-	137.1	1.9	-	-	-	-	-	-	-	-	-	-	141.1	2.9
1994	-	-	-	-	-	-	-	-	-	-	143.6	1.8	-	-	-	-	-	-	-	-	-	-	146.1	1.7
1995	-	-	-	-	-	-	-	-	-	-	148.7	1.8	-	-	-	-	-	-	-	-	-	-	150.2	1.0
1996	-	-	-	-	-	-	-	-	-	-	151.7	1.0	-	-	-	-	-	-	-	-	-	-	154.2	1.6
1997	-	-	-	-	-	-	-	-	-	-	155.7	1.0	-	-	-	-	-	-	-	-	-	-	158.5	1.8
1998	-	-	-	-	-	-	-	-	-	-	160.7	1.4	-	-	-	-	-	-	-	-	-	-	164.2	2.2
1999	-	-	-	-	-	-	-	-	-	-	165.8	1.0	-	-	-	-	-	-	-	-	-	-	168.6	1.7
2000	-	-	-	-	-	-	-	-	-	-	169.3	0.4	-	-	-	-	-	-	-	-	-	-	171.8	1.5
2001	-	-	-	-	-	-	-	-	-	-	174.5	1.6	-	-	-	-	-	-	-	-	-	-	-	-

Source: U.S. Department of Labor, Bureau of Labor Statistics, Division of Consumer Prices and Price Indexes. - indicates no data collected for period.

727

Portland-Salem, OR-WA
Consumer Price Index - All Urban Consumers
Base 1982-1984 = 100
Apparel

For 1914-2001. Columns headed % show percentile change in the index from the previous period for which an index is available.

Year	Jan Index	%	Feb Index	%	Mar Index	%	Apr Index	%	May Index	%	Jun Index	%	Jul Index	%	Aug Index	%	Sep Index	%	Oct Index	%	Nov Index	%	Dec Index	%
1914	-	-	-	-	-	-	-	-	-	-	-	-	-	-	-	-	-	-	-	-	-	-	16.5	-
1915	-	-	-	-	-	-	-	-	-	-	-	-	-	-	-	-	-	-	-	-	-	-	17.1	3.6
1916	-	-	-	-	-	-	-	-	-	-	-	-	-	-	-	-	-	-	-	-	-	-	19.2	12.3
1917	-	-	-	-	-	-	-	-	-	-	-	-	-	-	-	-	-	-	-	-	-	-	23.9	24.5
1918	-	-	-	-	-	-	-	-	-	-	-	-	-	-	-	-	-	-	-	-	-	-	32.5	36.0
1919	-	-	-	-	-	-	-	-	-	-	35.6	9.5	-	-	-	-	-	-	-	-	-	-	40.1	12.6
1920	-	-	-	-	-	-	-	-	-	-	42.8	6.7	-	-	-	-	-	-	-	-	-	-	36.8	-14.0
1921	-	-	-	-	31.7	-13.9	-	-	-	-	-	-	-	-	-	-	28.2	-11.0	-	-	-	-	27.4	-2.8
1922	-	-	-	-	25.8	-5.8	-	-	-	-	25.4	-1.6	-	-	-	-	25.4	0.0	-	-	-	-	25.6	0.8
1923	-	-	-	-	26.5	3.5	-	-	-	-	26.7	0.8	-	-	-	-	26.8	0.4	-	-	-	-	26.8	0.0
1924	-	-	-	-	26.8	0.0	-	-	-	-	26.7	-0.4	-	-	-	-	26.3	-1.5	-	-	-	-	26.4	0.4
1925	-	-	-	-	-	-	-	-	-	-	26.1	-1.1	-	-	-	-	-	-	-	-	-	-	26.0	-0.4
1926	-	-	-	-	-	-	-	-	-	-	25.9	-0.4	-	-	-	-	-	-	-	-	-	-	25.5	-1.5
1927	-	-	-	-	-	-	-	-	-	-	25.4	-0.4	-	-	-	-	-	-	-	-	-	-	25.0	-1.6
1928	-	-	-	-	-	-	-	-	-	-	25.0	0.0	-	-	-	-	-	-	-	-	-	-	24.8	-0.8
1929	-	-	-	-	-	-	-	-	-	-	24.5	-1.2	-	-	-	-	-	-	-	-	-	-	24.5	0.0
1930	-	-	-	-	-	-	-	-	-	-	24.0	-2.0	-	-	-	-	-	-	-	-	-	-	22.8	-5.0
1931	-	-	-	-	-	-	-	-	-	-	22.0	-3.5	-	-	-	-	-	-	-	-	-	-	20.4	-7.3
1932	-	-	-	-	-	-	-	-	-	-	19.2	-5.9	-	-	-	-	-	-	-	-	-	-	18.2	-5.2
1933	-	-	-	-	-	-	-	-	-	-	18.3	0.5	-	-	-	-	-	-	-	-	-	-	20.1	9.8
1934	-	-	-	-	-	-	-	-	-	-	20.6	2.5	-	-	-	-	-	-	-	-	20.5	-0.5	-	-
1935	-	-	-	-	20.5	0.0	-	-	-	-	-	-	20.5	0.0	-	-	-	-	20.5	0.0	-	-	-	-
1936	20.6	0.5	-	-	-	-	20.7	0.5	-	-	-	-	20.6	-0.5	-	-	20.6	0.0	-	-	-	-	20.8	1.0
1937	-	-	-	-	21.3	2.4	-	-	-	-	21.5	0.9	-	-	-	-	21.8	1.4	-	-	-	-	21.7	-0.5
1938	-	-	-	-	21.5	-0.9	-	-	-	-	21.4	-0.5	-	-	-	-	21.4	0.0	-	-	-	-	21.3	-0.5
1939	-	-	-	-	21.2	-0.5	-	-	-	-	21.2	0.0	-	-	-	-	21.3	0.5	-	-	-	-	21.4	0.5
1940	-	-	-	-	21.7	1.4	-	-	-	-	21.7	0.0	-	-	-	-	21.7	0.0	-	-	-	-	21.7	0.0
1941	-	-	-	-	21.7	0.0	-	-	-	-	21.8	0.5	-	-	-	-	23.2	6.4	-	-	-	-	23.8	2.6
1942	-	-	-	-	25.8	8.4	-	-	-	-	26.2	1.6	-	-	-	-	26.5	1.1	-	-	-	-	26.5	0.0
1943	-	-	-	-	27.1	2.3	-	-	-	-	27.2	0.4	-	-	-	-	28.2	3.7	-	-	-	-	28.5	1.1
1944	-	-	-	-	29.1	2.1	-	-	-	-	29.5	1.4	-	-	-	-	29.8	1.0	-	-	-	-	29.8	0.0
1945	-	-	-	-	29.9	0.3	-	-	-	-	30.0	0.3	-	-	-	-	30.2	0.7	-	-	-	-	30.0	-0.7
1946	-	-	-	-	30.2	0.7	-	-	-	-	31.5	4.3	-	-	-	-	32.9	4.4	-	-	-	-	35.2	7.0
1947	-	-	-	-	37.5	6.5	-	-	-	-	37.9	1.1	37.5	-1.1	-	-	-	-	38.9	3.7	-	-	-	-
1948	40.0	2.8	-	-	-	-	41.3	3.2	-	-	-	-	41.0	-0.7	-	-	-	-	42.3	3.2	-	-	-	-
1949	41.1	-2.8	-	-	-	-	40.2	-2.2	-	-	-	-	39.7	-1.2	-	-	-	-	39.2	-1.3	-	-	-	-
1950	38.7	-1.3	-	-	-	-	39.0	0.8	-	-	-	-	38.8	-0.5	-	-	-	-	40.7	4.9	-	-	-	-
1951	41.4	1.7	-	-	-	-	42.0	1.4	-	-	-	-	42.5	1.2	-	-	-	-	42.9	0.9	-	-	-	-
1952	42.8	-0.2	-	-	-	-	41.8	-2.3	-	-	-	-	41.6	-0.5	-	-	-	-	42.1	1.2	-	-	-	-
1953	41.4	-1.7	-	-	-	-	41.3	-0.2	-	-	-	-	41.2	-0.2	-	-	-	-	42.4	2.9	-	-	-	-
1954	41.8	-1.4	-	-	-	-	41.5	-0.7	-	-	-	-	41.5	0.0	-	-	-	-	42.6	2.7	-	-	-	-
1955	42.1	-1.2	-	-	-	-	42.1	0.0	-	-	-	-	41.7	-1.0	-	-	-	-	42.8	2.6	-	-	-	-
1956	43.1	0.7	-	-	-	-	43.0	-0.2	-	-	-	-	42.9	-0.2	-	-	-	-	43.7	1.9	-	-	-	-
1957	43.5	-0.5	-	-	-	-	44.0	1.1	-	-	-	-	44.1	0.2	-	-	-	-	44.4	0.7	-	-	-	-
1958	44.2	-0.5	-	-	-	-	44.3	0.2	-	-	-	-	44.2	-0.2	-	-	-	-	44.1	-0.2	-	-	-	-
1959	44.0	-0.2	-	-	-	-	44.0	0.0	-	-	-	-	44.4	0.9	-	-	-	-	45.2	1.8	-	-	-	-

[Continued]

Portland-Salem, OR-WA
Consumer Price Index - All Urban Consumers
Base 1982-1984 = 100
Apparel
[Continued]

For 1914-2001. Columns headed % show percentile change in the index from the previous period for which an index is available.

Year	Jan Index	%	Feb Index	%	Mar Index	%	Apr Index	%	May Index	%	Jun Index	%	Jul Index	%	Aug Index	%	Sep Index	%	Oct Index	%	Nov Index	%	Dec Index	%
1960	45.2	0.0	-		-		45.5	0.7	-		-		45.5	0.0	-		-		45.7	0.4	-		-	
1961	45.8	0.2	-		-		45.8	0.0	-		-		45.8	0.0	-		-		45.9	0.2	-		-	
1962	45.3	-1.3	-		-		45.2	-0.2	-		-		45.1	-0.2	-		-		46.2	2.4	-		-	
1963	46.2	0.0	-		-		46.4	0.4	-		-		46.2	-0.4	-		-		46.6	0.9	-		-	
1964	45.9	-1.5	-		-		46.8	2.0	-		-		46.5	-0.6	-		-		47.6	2.4	-		-	
1965	46.7	-1.9	-		-		47.5	1.7	-		-		47.9	0.8	-		-		50.0	4.4	-		-	
1966	49.2	-1.6	-		-		49.7	1.0	-		-		49.8	0.2	-		-		50.3	1.0	-		-	
1967	50.3	0.0	-		-		50.8	1.0	-		-		50.8	0.0	-		-		51.8	2.0	-		-	
1968	51.1	-1.4	-		-		53.0	3.7	-		-		53.2	0.4	-		-		54.5	2.4	-		-	
1969	54.2	-0.6	-		-		55.7	2.8	-		-		55.7	0.0	-		-		58.4	4.8	-		-	
1970	57.2	-2.1	-		-		58.6	2.4	-		-		59.1	0.9	-		-		60.0	1.5	-		-	
1971	58.2	-3.0	-		-		58.5	0.5	-		-		58.9	0.7	-		-		61.7	4.8	-		-	
1972	60.3	-2.3	-		-		60.4	0.2	-		-		61.0	1.0	-		-		62.3	2.1	-		-	
1973	61.9	-0.6	-		-		64.3	3.9	-		-		65.0	1.1	-		-		67.4	3.7	-		-	
1974	66.3	-1.6	-		-		67.3	1.5	-		-		69.0	2.5	-		-		71.4	3.5	-		-	
1975	71.3	-0.1	-		-		72.7	2.0	-		-		72.5	-0.3	-		-		74.6	2.9	-		-	
1976	73.3	-1.7	-		-		75.5	3.0	-		-		76.9	1.9	-		-		79.2	3.0	-		-	
1977	79.2	0.0	-		-		80.7	1.9	-		-		81.9	1.5	-		-		84.8	3.5	-		-	
1978	84.0	-0.9	-		84.4	0.5	-		84.8	0.5	-		81.9	-3.4	-		86.0	5.0	-		85.6	-0.5	-	
1979	83.9	-2.0	-		86.5	3.1	-		85.8	-0.8	-		84.5	-1.5	-		87.6	3.7	-		86.0	-1.8	-	
1980	84.4	-1.9	-		88.3	4.6	-		87.3	-1.1	-		87.5	0.2	-		88.6	1.3	-		89.3	0.8	-	
1981	89.6	0.3	-		93.1	3.9	-		92.2	-1.0	-		90.8	-1.5	-		94.6	4.2	-		94.4	-0.2	-	
1982	92.8	-1.7	-		95.1	2.5	-		95.8	0.7	-		93.4	-2.5	-		96.6	3.4	-		98.2	1.7	-	
1983	96.6	-1.6	-		98.2	1.7	-		98.8	0.6	-		98.8	0.0	-		103.4	4.7	-		101.4	-1.9	-	
1984	100.0	-1.4	-		107.7	7.7	-		107.0	-0.6	-		101.4	-5.2	-		107.0	5.5	-		106.1	-0.8	-	
1985	100.5	-5.3	-		110.6	10.0	-		113.6	2.7	-		103.3	-9.1	-		108.7	5.2	-		108.2	-0.5	-	
1986	102.3	-5.5	-		100.7	-1.6	-		100.1	-0.6	-		96.1	-4.0	-		102.8	7.0	-		102.3	-0.5	-	
1987	-		-		-		-		-		98.5	-3.7	-		-		-		-		-		105.7	7.3
1988	-		-		-		-		-		109.4	3.5	-		-		-		-		-		114.5	4.7
1989	-		-		-		-		-		114.5	0.0	-		-		-		-		-		114.3	-0.2
1990	-		-		-		-		-		118.4	3.6	-		-		-		-		-		123.0	3.9
1991	-		-		-		-		-		123.2	0.2	-		-		-		-		-		121.4	-1.5
1992	-		-		-		-		-		124.3	2.4	-		-		-		-		-		125.3	0.8
1993	-		-		-		-		-		124.8	-0.4	-		-		-		-		-		119.6	-4.2
1994	-		-		-		-		-		124.7	4.3	-		-		-		-		-		122.8	-1.5
1995	-		-		-		-		-		127.8	4.1	-		-		-		-		-		119.1	-6.8
1996	-		-		-		-		-		122.4	2.8	-		-		-		-		-		126.6	3.4
1997	-		-		-		-		-		128.7	1.7	-		-		-		-		-		134.2	4.3
1998	-		-		-		-		-		132.1	-1.6	-		-		-		-		-		132.8	0.5
1999	-		-		-		-		-		133.2	0.3	-		-		-		-		-		136.5	2.5
2000	-		-		-		-		-		135.7	-0.6	-		-		-		-		-		134.9	-0.6
2001	-		-		-		-		-		134.6	-0.2	-		-		-		-		-		-	

Source: U.S. Department of Labor, Bureau of Labor Statistics, Division of Consumer Prices and Price Indexes. - indicates no data collected for period.

Portland-Salem, OR-WA
Consumer Price Index - Urban Wage Earners
Base 1982-1984 = 100
Apparel

For 1914-2001. Columns headed % show percentile change in the index from the previous period for which an index is available.

Year	Jan Index	%	Feb Index	%	Mar Index	%	Apr Index	%	May Index	%	Jun Index	%	Jul Index	%	Aug Index	%	Sep Index	%	Oct Index	%	Nov Index	%	Dec Index	%
1914	-		-		-		-		-		-		-		-		-		-		-		16.6	-
1915	-		-		-		-		-		-		-		-		-		-		-		17.2	3.6
1916	-		-		-		-		-		-		-		-		-		-		-		19.3	12.2
1917	-		-		-		-		-		-		-		-		-		-		-		24.0	24.4
1918	-		-		-		-		-		-		-		-		-		-		-		32.7	36.3
1919	-		-		-		-		-		35.9	9.8	-		-		-		-		-		40.4	12.5
1920	-		-		-		-		-		43.1	6.7	-		-		-		-		-		37.0	-14.2
1921	-		-		31.9	-13.8	-		-		-		-		-		28.4	-11.0	-		-		27.6	-2.8
1922	-		-		25.9	-6.2	-		-		25.6	-1.2	-		-		25.6	0.0	-		-		25.8	0.8
1923	-		-		26.7	3.5	-		-		26.9	0.7	-		-		26.9	0.0	-		-		26.9	0.0
1924	-		-		27.0	0.4	-		-		26.9	-0.4	-		-		26.4	-1.9	-		-		26.5	0.4
1925	-		-		-		-		-		26.3	-0.8	-		-		-		-		-		26.1	-0.8
1926	-		-		-		-		-		26.1	0.0	-		-		-		-		-		25.7	-1.5
1927	-		-		-		-		-		25.6	-0.4	-		-		-		-		-		25.2	-1.6
1928	-		-		-		-		-		25.1	-0.4	-		-		-		-		-		24.9	-0.8
1929	-		-		-		-		-		24.7	-0.8	-		-		-		-		-		24.6	-0.4
1930	-		-		-		-		-		24.2	-1.6	-		-		-		-		-		23.0	-5.0
1931	-		-		-		-		-		22.2	-3.5	-		-		-		-		-		20.5	-7.7
1932	-		-		-		-		-		19.3	-5.9	-		-		-		-		-		18.3	-5.2
1933	-		-		-		-		-		18.4	0.5	-		-		-		-		-		20.3	10.3
1934	-		-		-		-		-		20.7	2.0	-		-		-		-		20.6	-0.5	-	
1935	-		-		20.6	0.0	-		-		-		20.6	0.0	-		-		20.6	0.0	-		-	
1936	20.7	0.5	-		-		20.8	0.5	-		-		20.7	-0.5	-		20.7	0.0	-		-		20.9	1.0
1937	-		-		21.4	2.4	-		-		21.6	0.9	-		-		21.9	1.4	-		-		21.9	0.0
1938	-		-		21.6	-1.4	-		-		21.5	-0.5	-		-		21.5	0.0	-		-		21.5	0.0
1939	-		-		21.3	-0.9	-		-		21.3	0.0	-		-		21.4	0.5	-		-		21.5	0.5
1940	-		-		21.9	1.9	-		-		21.9	0.0	-		-		21.8	-0.5	-		-		21.8	0.0
1941	-		-		21.8	0.0	-		-		22.0	0.9	-		-		23.3	5.9	-		-		24.0	3.0
1942	-		-		26.0	8.3	-		-		26.4	1.5	-		-		26.7	1.1	-		-		26.7	0.0
1943	-		-		27.3	2.2	-		-		27.4	0.4	-		-		28.4	3.6	-		-		28.6	0.7
1944	-		-		29.3	2.4	-		-		29.7	1.4	-		-		30.0	1.0	-		-		30.0	0.0
1945	-		-		30.1	0.3	-		-		30.2	0.3	-		-		30.4	0.7	-		-		30.2	-0.7
1946	-		-		30.4	0.7	-		-		31.7	4.3	-		-		33.1	4.4	-		-		35.5	7.3
1947	-		-		37.8	6.5	-		-		38.1	0.8	37.8	-0.8	-		-		39.2	3.7	-		-	
1948	40.2	2.6	-		-		41.5	3.2	-		-		41.3	-0.5	-		-		42.5	2.9	-		-	
1949	41.3	-2.8	-		-		40.4	-2.2	-		-		39.9	-1.2	-		-		39.4	-1.3	-		-	
1950	38.9	-1.3	-		-		39.2	0.8	-		-		39.0	-0.5	-		-		41.0	5.1	-		-	
1951	41.6	1.5	-		-		42.3	1.7	-		-		42.8	1.2	-		-		43.2	0.9	-		-	
1952	43.1	-0.2	-		-		42.1	-2.3	-		-		41.8	-0.7	-		-		42.4	1.4	-		-	
1953	41.6	-1.9	-		-		41.5	-0.2	-		-		41.5	0.0	-		-		42.6	2.7	-		-	
1954	42.1	-1.2	-		-		41.8	-0.7	-		-		41.8	0.0	-		-		42.9	2.6	-		-	
1955	42.3	-1.4	-		-		42.3	0.0	-		-		42.0	-0.7	-		-		43.1	2.6	-		-	
1956	43.4	0.7	-		-		43.3	-0.2	-		-		43.2	-0.2	-		-		43.9	1.6	-		-	
1957	43.8	-0.2	-		-		44.2	0.9	-		-		44.3	0.2	-		-		44.7	0.9	-		-	
1958	44.4	-0.7	-		-		44.6	0.5	-		-		44.4	-0.4	-		-		44.4	0.0	-		-	
1959	44.2	-0.5	-		-		44.2	0.0	-		-		44.7	1.1	-		-		45.5	1.8	-		-	

[Continued]

Portland-Salem, OR-WA
Consumer Price Index - Urban Wage Earners
Base 1982-1984 = 100
Apparel
[Continued]

For 1914-2001. Columns headed % show percentile change in the index from the previous period for which an index is available.

Year	Jan Index	%	Feb Index	%	Mar Index	%	Apr Index	%	May Index	%	Jun Index	%	Jul Index	%	Aug Index	%	Sep Index	%	Oct Index	%	Nov Index	%	Dec Index	%
1960	45.5	0.0	-		-		45.8	0.7	-		-		45.8	0.0	-		-		46.0	0.4	-		-	
1961	46.1	0.2	-		-		46.1	0.0	-		-		46.1	0.0	-		-		46.2	0.2	-		-	
1962	45.6	-1.3	-		-		45.5	-0.2	-		-		45.4	-0.2	-		-		46.4	2.2	-		-	
1963	46.4	0.0	-		-		46.7	0.6	-		-		46.4	-0.6	-		-		46.9	1.1	-		-	
1964	46.2	-1.5	-		-		47.1	1.9	-		-		46.8	-0.6	-		-		47.9	2.4	-		-	
1965	47.0	-1.9	-		-		47.8	1.7	-		-		48.2	0.8	-		-		50.3	4.4	-		-	
1966	49.5	-1.6	-		-		50.0	1.0	-		-		50.1	0.2	-		-		50.6	1.0	-		-	
1967	50.6	0.0	-		-		51.2	1.2	-		-		51.1	-0.2	-		-		52.1	2.0	-		-	
1968	51.5	-1.2	-		-		53.4	3.7	-		-		53.5	0.2	-		-		54.9	2.6	-		-	
1969	54.5	-0.7	-		-		56.1	2.9	-		-		56.1	0.0	-		-		58.8	4.8	-		-	
1970	57.5	-2.2	-		-		59.0	2.6	-		-		59.5	0.8	-		-		60.3	1.3	-		-	
1971	58.6	-2.8	-		-		58.9	0.5	-		-		59.3	0.7	-		-		62.1	4.7	-		-	
1972	60.7	-2.3	-		-		60.8	0.2	-		-		61.4	1.0	-		-		62.7	2.1	-		-	
1973	62.2	-0.8	-		-		64.7	4.0	-		-		65.4	1.1	-		-		67.8	3.7	-		-	
1974	66.8	-1.5	-		-		67.7	1.3	-		-		69.5	2.7	-		-		71.9	3.5	-		-	
1975	71.7	-0.3	-		-		73.1	2.0	-		-		72.9	-0.3	-		-		75.0	2.9	-		-	
1976	73.7	-1.7	-		-		76.0	3.1	-		-		77.3	1.7	-		-		79.7	3.1	-		-	
1977	79.7	0.0	-		-		81.2	1.9	-		-		82.4	1.5	-		-		85.3	3.5	-		-	
1978	84.5	-0.9	-		84.4	-0.1	-		85.9	1.8	-		82.8	-3.6	-		87.7	5.9	-		86.7	-1.1	-	
1979	85.4	-1.5	-		84.8	-0.7	-		85.4	0.7	-		85.4	0.0	-		90.3	5.7	-		90.3	0.0	-	
1980	85.0	-5.9	-		87.6	3.1	-		86.5	-1.3	-		89.0	2.9	-		91.1	2.4	-		92.1	1.1	-	
1981	92.0	-0.1	-		93.5	1.6	-		93.8	0.3	-		91.0	-3.0	-		94.5	3.8	-		94.4	-0.1	-	
1982	92.5	-2.0	-		95.1	2.8	-		96.2	1.2	-		93.8	-2.5	-		96.1	2.5	-		97.2	1.1	-	
1983	95.4	-1.9	-		98.1	2.8	-		99.0	0.9	-		98.0	-1.0	-		102.3	4.4	-		99.8	-2.4	-	
1984	99.7	-0.1	-		110.1	10.4	-		108.8	-1.2	-		102.4	-5.9	-		107.5	5.0	-		106.3	-1.1	-	
1985	99.6	-6.3	-		112.8	13.3	-		116.3	3.1	-		102.8	-11.6	-		110.6	7.6	-		110.0	-0.5	-	
1986	103.6	-5.8	-		100.7	-2.8	-		99.9	-0.8	-		95.6	-4.3	-		102.5	7.2	-		102.0	-0.5	-	
1987	-		-		-		-		-		98.5	-3.4	-		-		-		-		-		105.2	6.8
1988	-		-		-		-		-		109.3	3.9	-		-		-		-		-		114.8	5.0
1989	-		-		-		-		-		114.7	-0.1	-		-		-		-		-		114.1	-0.5
1990	-		-		-		-		-		118.7	4.0	-		-		-		-		-		123.2	3.8
1991	-		-		-		-		-		124.6	1.1	-		-		-		-		-		122.6	-1.6
1992	-		-		-		-		-		124.6	1.6	-		-		-		-		-		125.6	0.8
1993	-		-		-		-		-		125.4	-0.2	-		-		-		-		-		120.6	-3.8
1994	-		-		-		-		-		124.6	3.3	-		-		-		-		-		123.1	-1.2
1995	-		-		-		-		-		128.0	4.0	-		-		-		-		-		120.5	-5.9
1996	-		-		-		-		-		123.6	2.6	-		-		-		-		-		127.2	2.9
1997	-		-		-		-		-		129.1	1.5	-		-		-		-		-		133.1	3.1
1998	-		-		-		-		-		131.7	-1.1	-		-		-		-		-		130.5	-0.9
1999	-		-		-		-		-		133.2	2.1	-		-		-		-		-		135.6	1.8
2000	-		-		-		-		-		133.6	-1.5	-		-		-		-		-		131.0	-1.9
2001	-		-		-		-		-		131.3	0.2	-		-		-		-		-		-	

Source: U.S. Department of Labor, Bureau of Labor Statistics, Division of Consumer Prices and Price Indexes. - indicates no data collected for period.

Portland-Salem, OR-WA
Consumer Price Index - All Urban Consumers
Base 1982-1984 = 100
Transportation

For 1947-2001. Columns headed % show percentile change in the index from the previous period for which an index is available.

Year	Jan Index	%	Feb Index	%	Mar Index	%	Apr Index	%	May Index	%	Jun Index	%	Jul Index	%	Aug Index	%	Sep Index	%	Oct Index	%	Nov Index	%	Dec Index	%
1947	-		-		19.5		-		-		19.6	0.5	19.6	0.0	-		-		20.0	2.0	-		-	
1948	20.9	4.5	-		-		21.0	0.5	-		-		22.2	5.7	-		-		22.6	1.8	-		-	
1949	22.9	1.3	-		-		23.2	1.3	-		-		24.0	3.4	-		-		24.0	0.0	-		-	
1950	24.2	0.8	-		-		23.7	-2.1	-		-		23.8	0.4	-		-		24.2	1.7	-		-	
1951	24.4	0.8	-		-		24.8	1.6	-		-		25.0	0.8	-		-		25.5	2.0	-		-	
1952	26.0	2.0	-		-		26.7	2.7	-		-		26.7	0.0	-		-		27.3	2.2	-		-	
1953	27.5	0.7	-		-		27.7	0.7	-		-		27.5	-0.7	-		-		27.5	0.0	-		-	
1954	27.4	-0.4	-		-		27.1	-1.1	-		-		26.6	-1.8	-		-		26.4	-0.8	-		-	
1955	26.9	1.9	-		-		26.7	-0.7	-		-		26.6	-0.4	-		-		27.4	3.0	-		-	
1956	27.1	-1.1	-		-		26.1	-3.7	-		-		26.7	2.3	-		-		27.6	3.4	-		-	
1957	27.6	0.0	-		-		28.1	1.8	-		-		28.6	1.8	-		-		28.1	-1.7	-		-	
1958	29.0	3.2	-		-		29.8	2.8	-		-		30.0	0.7	-		-		30.3	1.0	-		-	
1959	29.6	-2.3	-		-		31.4	6.1	-		-		30.6	-2.5	-		-		31.8	3.9	-		-	
1960	31.6	-0.6	-		-		31.1	-1.6	-		-		30.6	-1.6	-		-		30.1	-1.6	-		-	
1961	31.1	3.3	-		-		29.2	-6.1	-		-		31.5	7.9	-		-		31.8	1.0	-		-	
1962	31.4	-1.3	-		-		30.7	-2.2	-		-		31.5	2.6	-		-		31.1	-1.3	-		-	
1963	31.0	-0.3	-		-		31.6	1.9	-		-		31.5	-0.3	-		-		31.7	0.6	-		-	
1964	32.0	0.9	-		-		32.1	0.3	-		-		32.2	0.3	-		-		31.5	-2.2	-		-	
1965	32.4	2.9	-		-		32.5	0.3	-		-		32.7	0.6	-		-		32.2	-1.5	-		-	
1966	32.1	-0.3	-		-		32.6	1.6	-		-		32.7	0.3	-		-		33.3	1.8	-		-	
1967	33.1	-0.6	-		-		33.9	2.4	-		-		34.4	1.5	-		-		34.6	0.6	-		-	
1968	34.7	0.3	-		-		34.7	0.0	-		-		35.0	0.9	-		-		35.0	0.0	-		-	
1969	35.6	1.7	-		-		36.1	1.4	-		-		35.9	-0.6	-		-		36.3	1.1	-		-	
1970	36.7	1.1	-		-		36.9	0.5	-		-		37.2	0.8	-		-		37.1	-0.3	-		-	
1971	38.1	2.7	-		-		36.9	-3.1	-		-		37.3	1.1	-		-		37.3	0.0	-		-	
1972	37.5	0.5	-		-		37.1	-1.1	-		-		37.4	0.8	-		-		38.1	1.9	-		-	
1973	37.9	-0.5	-		-		38.2	0.8	-		-		38.7	1.3	-		-		38.8	0.3	-		-	
1974	39.8	2.6	-		-		41.1	3.3	-		-		43.2	5.1	-		-		43.6	0.9	-		-	
1975	45.0	3.2	-		-		45.3	0.7	-		-		47.7	5.3	-		-		48.0	0.6	-		-	
1976	49.0	2.1	-		-		49.4	0.8	-		-		52.3	5.9	-		-		53.0	1.3	-		-	
1977	53.6	1.1	-		-		56.4	5.2	-		-		56.6	0.4	-		-		56.7	0.2	-		-	
1978	58.3	2.8	-		57.9	-0.7	-		59.5	2.8	-		60.9	2.4	-		61.9	1.6	-		62.8	1.5	-	
1979	63.3	0.8	-		65.9	4.1	-		69.2	5.0	-		73.0	5.5	-		74.1	1.5	-		74.5	0.5	-	
1980	77.6	4.2	-		79.9	3.0	-		80.8	1.1	-		81.6	1.0	-		83.1	1.8	-		85.0	2.3	-	
1981	85.9	1.1	-		88.7	3.3	-		90.5	2.0	-		92.3	2.0	-		94.1	2.0	-		96.2	2.2	-	
1982	97.9	1.8	-		96.1	-1.8	-		96.1	0.0	-		99.3	3.3	-		99.3	0.0	-		98.6	-0.7	-	
1983	97.2	-1.4	-		94.4	-2.9	-		96.9	2.6	-		99.9	3.1	-		100.7	0.8	-		101.2	0.5	-	
1984	100.8	-0.4	-		100.8	0.0	-		104.6	3.8	-		104.4	-0.2	-		104.2	-0.2	-		105.7	1.4	-	
1985	106.6	0.9	-		106.2	-0.4	-		107.4	1.1	-		108.3	0.8	-		109.3	0.9	-		110.9	1.5	-	
1986	112.5	1.4	-		107.3	-4.6	-		106.0	-1.2	-		108.1	2.0	-		106.8	-1.2	-		105.1	-1.6	-	
1987	-		-		-		-		-		108.1	2.9	-		-		-		-		-		110.2	1.9
1988	-		-		-		-		-		109.7	-0.5	-		-		-		-		-		111.5	1.6
1989	-		-		-		-		-		117.8	5.7	-		-		-		-		-		118.8	0.8
1990	-		-		-		-		-		120.1	1.1	-		-		-		-		-		130.8	8.9
1991	-		-		-		-		-		130.0	-0.6	-		-		-		-		-		130.1	0.1
1992	-		-		-		-		-		131.7	1.2	-		-		-		-		-		136.4	3.6

[Continued]

Portland-Salem, OR-WA
Consumer Price Index - All Urban Consumers
Base 1982-1984 = 100
Transportation
[Continued]

For 1947-2001. Columns headed % show percentile change in the index from the previous period for which an index is available.

Year	Jan Index	%	Feb Index	%	Mar Index	%	Apr Index	%	May Index	%	Jun Index	%	Jul Index	%	Aug Index	%	Sep Index	%	Oct Index	%	Nov Index	%	Dec Index	%
1993	-		-		-		-		-		135.5	-0.7	-		-		-		-		-		136.9	1.0
1994	-		-		-		-		-		136.6	-0.2	-		-		-		-		-		140.6	2.9
1995	-		-		-		-		-		141.6	0.7	-		-		-		-		-		142.2	0.4
1996	-		-		-		-		-		145.1	2.0	-		-		-		-		-		148.9	2.6
1997	-		-		-		-		-		150.8	1.3	-		-		-		-		-		151.0	0.1
1998	-		-		-		-		-		147.8	-2.1	-		-		-		-		-		146.1	-1.2
1999	-		-		-		-		-		148.9	1.9	-		-		-		-		-		155.4	4.4
2000	-		-		-		-		-		162.1	4.3	-		-		-		-		-		168.3	3.8
2001	-		-		-		-		-		167.9	-0.2	-		-		-		-		-		-	

Source: U.S. Department of Labor, Bureau of Labor Statistics, Division of Consumer Prices and Price Indexes. - indicates no data collected for period.

Portland-Salem, OR-WA
Consumer Price Index - Urban Wage Earners
Base 1982-1984 = 100
Transportation

For 1947-2001. Columns headed % show percentile change in the index from the previous period for which an index is available.

Year	Jan Index	%	Feb Index	%	Mar Index	%	Apr Index	%	May Index	%	Jun Index	%	Jul Index	%	Aug Index	%	Sep Index	%	Oct Index	%	Nov Index	%	Dec Index	%
1947	-	-	-	-	19.5	-	-	-	-	-	19.6	0.5	19.6	0.0	-	-	-	-	20.0	2.0	-	-	-	-
1948	20.9	4.5	-	-	-	-	21.0	0.5	-	-	-	-	22.2	5.7	-	-	-	-	22.6	1.8	-	-	-	-
1949	22.9	1.3	-	-	-	-	23.2	1.3	-	-	-	-	23.9	3.0	-	-	-	-	24.0	0.4	-	-	-	-
1950	24.1	0.4	-	-	-	-	23.7	-1.7	-	-	-	-	23.8	0.4	-	-	-	-	24.2	1.7	-	-	-	-
1951	24.4	0.8	-	-	-	-	24.8	1.6	-	-	-	-	25.0	0.8	-	-	-	-	25.5	2.0	-	-	-	-
1952	26.0	2.0	-	-	-	-	26.6	2.3	-	-	-	-	26.7	0.4	-	-	-	-	27.3	2.2	-	-	-	-
1953	27.4	0.4	-	-	-	-	27.7	1.1	-	-	-	-	27.5	-0.7	-	-	-	-	27.5	0.0	-	-	-	-
1954	27.3	-0.7	-	-	-	-	27.1	-0.7	-	-	-	-	26.6	-1.8	-	-	-	-	26.4	-0.8	-	-	-	-
1955	26.9	1.9	-	-	-	-	26.7	-0.7	-	-	-	-	26.6	-0.4	-	-	-	-	27.3	2.6	-	-	-	-
1956	27.1	-0.7	-	-	-	-	26.0	-4.1	-	-	-	-	26.7	2.7	-	-	-	-	27.6	3.4	-	-	-	-
1957	27.6	0.0	-	-	-	-	28.1	1.8	-	-	-	-	28.5	1.4	-	-	-	-	28.1	-1.4	-	-	-	-
1958	29.0	3.2	-	-	-	-	29.7	2.4	-	-	-	-	30.0	1.0	-	-	-	-	30.3	1.0	-	-	-	-
1959	29.6	-2.3	-	-	-	-	31.3	5.7	-	-	-	-	30.6	-2.2	-	-	-	-	31.8	3.9	-	-	-	-
1960	31.5	-0.9	-	-	-	-	31.1	-1.3	-	-	-	-	30.6	-1.6	-	-	-	-	30.0	-2.0	-	-	-	-
1961	31.1	3.7	-	-	-	-	29.2	-6.1	-	-	-	-	31.4	7.5	-	-	-	-	31.7	1.0	-	-	-	-
1962	31.4	-0.9	-	-	-	-	30.7	-2.2	-	-	-	-	31.4	2.3	-	-	-	-	31.1	-1.0	-	-	-	-
1963	31.0	-0.3	-	-	-	-	31.6	1.9	-	-	-	-	31.4	-0.6	-	-	-	-	31.6	0.6	-	-	-	-
1964	32.0	1.3	-	-	-	-	32.1	0.3	-	-	-	-	32.2	0.3	-	-	-	-	31.5	-2.2	-	-	-	-
1965	32.4	2.9	-	-	-	-	32.4	0.0	-	-	-	-	32.7	0.9	-	-	-	-	32.2	-1.5	-	-	-	-
1966	32.1	-0.3	-	-	-	-	32.6	1.6	-	-	-	-	32.7	0.3	-	-	-	-	33.2	1.5	-	-	-	-
1967	33.1	-0.3	-	-	-	-	33.8	2.1	-	-	-	-	34.3	1.5	-	-	-	-	34.6	0.9	-	-	-	-
1968	34.7	0.3	-	-	-	-	34.7	0.0	-	-	-	-	35.0	0.9	-	-	-	-	35.0	0.0	-	-	-	-
1969	35.6	1.7	-	-	-	-	36.1	1.4	-	-	-	-	35.8	-0.8	-	-	-	-	36.3	1.4	-	-	-	-
1970	36.7	1.1	-	-	-	-	36.8	0.3	-	-	-	-	37.1	0.8	-	-	-	-	37.1	0.0	-	-	-	-
1971	38.1	2.7	-	-	-	-	36.9	-3.1	-	-	-	-	37.2	0.8	-	-	-	-	37.3	0.3	-	-	-	-
1972	37.5	0.5	-	-	-	-	37.1	-1.1	-	-	-	-	37.4	0.8	-	-	-	-	38.1	1.9	-	-	-	-
1973	37.9	-0.5	-	-	-	-	38.2	0.8	-	-	-	-	38.7	1.3	-	-	-	-	38.7	0.0	-	-	-	-
1974	39.8	2.8	-	-	-	-	41.1	3.3	-	-	-	-	43.2	5.1	-	-	-	-	43.6	0.9	-	-	-	-
1975	45.0	3.2	-	-	-	-	45.2	0.4	-	-	-	-	47.6	5.3	-	-	-	-	48.0	0.8	-	-	-	-
1976	49.0	2.1	-	-	-	-	49.4	0.8	-	-	-	-	52.2	5.7	-	-	-	-	52.9	1.3	-	-	-	-
1977	53.6	1.3	-	-	-	-	56.4	5.2	-	-	-	-	56.6	0.4	-	-	-	-	56.6	0.0	-	-	-	-
1978	58.2	2.8	-	-	58.0	-0.3	-	-	60.7	4.7	-	-	62.3	2.6	-	-	63.3	1.6	-	-	63.8	0.8	-	-
1979	64.2	0.6	-	-	66.8	4.0	-	-	69.8	4.5	-	-	72.8	4.3	-	-	73.5	1.0	-	-	74.2	1.0	-	-
1980	76.3	2.8	-	-	78.5	2.9	-	-	79.8	1.7	-	-	80.8	1.3	-	-	82.1	1.6	-	-	83.9	2.2	-	-
1981	85.8	2.3	-	-	88.5	3.1	-	-	90.3	2.0	-	-	92.1	2.0	-	-	93.6	1.6	-	-	95.2	1.7	-	-
1982	96.8	1.7	-	-	95.1	-1.8	-	-	95.2	0.1	-	-	98.5	3.5	-	-	98.5	0.0	-	-	98.1	-0.4	-	-
1983	96.7	-1.4	-	-	94.0	-2.8	-	-	96.7	2.9	-	-	99.9	3.3	-	-	100.9	1.0	-	-	101.7	0.8	-	-
1984	101.4	-0.3	-	-	101.5	0.1	-	-	105.5	3.9	-	-	105.3	-0.2	-	-	105.1	-0.2	-	-	106.5	1.3	-	-
1985	107.4	0.8	-	-	107.0	-0.4	-	-	108.2	1.1	-	-	108.9	0.6	-	-	109.9	0.9	-	-	111.3	1.3	-	-
1986	112.7	1.3	-	-	107.6	-4.5	-	-	106.1	-1.4	-	-	108.0	1.8	-	-	106.8	-1.1	-	-	105.2	-1.5	-	-
1987	-	-	-	-	-	-	-	-	-	-	108.3	2.9	-	-	-	-	-	-	-	-	-	-	110.2	1.8
1988	-	-	-	-	-	-	-	-	-	-	109.9	-0.3	-	-	-	-	-	-	-	-	-	-	111.5	1.5
1989	-	-	-	-	-	-	-	-	-	-	117.4	5.3	-	-	-	-	-	-	-	-	-	-	118.3	0.8
1990	-	-	-	-	-	-	-	-	-	-	119.3	0.8	-	-	-	-	-	-	-	-	-	-	129.1	8.2
1991	-	-	-	-	-	-	-	-	-	-	128.9	-0.2	-	-	-	-	-	-	-	-	-	-	129.3	0.3
1992	-	-	-	-	-	-	-	-	-	-	130.8	1.2	-	-	-	-	-	-	-	-	-	-	135.4	3.5

[Continued]

Portland-Salem, OR-WA
Consumer Price Index - Urban Wage Earners
Base 1982-1984 = 100
Transportation
[Continued]

For 1947-2001. Columns headed % show percentile change in the index from the previous period for which an index is available.

Year	Jan Index	%	Feb Index	%	Mar Index	%	Apr Index	%	May Index	%	Jun Index	%	Jul Index	%	Aug Index	%	Sep Index	%	Oct Index	%	Nov Index	%	Dec Index	%
1993	-		-		-		-		-		135.1	-0.2	-		-		-		-		-		137.0	1.4
1994	-		-		-		-		-		136.7	-0.2	-		-		-		-		-		141.0	3.1
1995	-		-		-		-		-		142.5	1.1	-		-		-		-		-		143.5	0.7
1996	-		-		-		-		-		146.5	2.1	-		-		-		-		-		149.9	2.3
1997	-		-		-		-		-		151.9	1.3	-		-		-		-		-		151.8	-0.1
1998	-		-		-		-		-		147.7	-2.7	-		-		-		-		-		146.2	-1.0
1999	-		-		-		-		-		148.1	1.3	-		-		-		-		-		154.7	4.5
2000	-		-		-		-		-		159.9	3.4	-		-		-		-		-		166.1	3.9
2001	-		-		-		-		-		166.0	-0.1	-		-		-		-		-		-	

Source: U.S. Department of Labor, Bureau of Labor Statistics, Division of Consumer Prices and Price Indexes. - indicates no data collected for period.

Portland-Salem, OR-WA
Consumer Price Index - All Urban Consumers
Base 1982-1984 = 100
Medical Care

For 1947-2001. Columns headed % show percentile change in the index from the previous period for which an index is available.

Year	Jan Index	%	Feb Index	%	Mar Index	%	Apr Index	%	May Index	%	Jun Index	%	Jul Index	%	Aug Index	%	Sep Index	%	Oct Index	%	Nov Index	%	Dec Index	%
1947	-	-	-	-	14.1	-	-	-	-	-	14.1	0.0	14.1	0.0	-	-	-	-	14.5	2.8	-	-	-	-
1948	14.6	0.7	-	-	-	-	14.6	0.0	-	-	-	-	14.8	1.4	-	-	-	-	14.8	0.0	-	-	-	-
1949	14.9	0.7	-	-	-	-	15.0	0.7	-	-	-	-	15.0	0.0	-	-	-	-	15.1	0.7	-	-	-	-
1950	15.1	0.0	-	-	-	-	15.1	0.0	-	-	-	-	15.6	3.3	-	-	-	-	15.8	1.3	-	-	-	-
1951	15.8	0.0	-	-	-	-	16.2	2.5	-	-	-	-	16.2	0.0	-	-	-	-	16.7	3.1	-	-	-	-
1952	16.8	0.6	-	-	-	-	17.0	1.2	-	-	-	-	17.2	1.2	-	-	-	-	17.2	0.0	-	-	-	-
1953	17.2	0.0	-	-	-	-	17.3	0.6	-	-	-	-	17.5	1.2	-	-	-	-	17.7	1.1	-	-	-	-
1954	17.7	0.0	-	-	-	-	17.8	0.6	-	-	-	-	17.9	0.6	-	-	-	-	18.0	0.6	-	-	-	-
1955	18.4	2.2	-	-	-	-	18.5	0.5	-	-	-	-	18.4	-0.5	-	-	-	-	18.9	2.7	-	-	-	-
1956	18.9	0.0	-	-	-	-	19.0	0.5	-	-	-	-	19.2	1.1	-	-	-	-	19.5	1.6	-	-	-	-
1957	20.0	2.6	-	-	-	-	20.2	1.0	-	-	-	-	20.3	0.5	-	-	-	-	20.4	0.5	-	-	-	-
1958	20.5	0.5	-	-	-	-	20.6	0.5	-	-	-	-	20.6	0.0	-	-	-	-	20.7	0.5	-	-	-	-
1959	20.7	0.0	-	-	-	-	20.7	0.0	-	-	-	-	20.8	0.5	-	-	-	-	20.8	0.0	-	-	-	-
1960	20.8	0.0	-	-	-	-	21.8	4.8	-	-	-	-	21.9	0.5	-	-	-	-	22.2	1.4	-	-	-	-
1961	22.2	0.0	-	-	-	-	22.4	0.9	-	-	-	-	22.6	0.9	-	-	-	-	22.5	-0.4	-	-	-	-
1962	22.3	-0.9	-	-	-	-	22.4	0.4	-	-	-	-	22.5	0.4	-	-	-	-	22.6	0.4	-	-	-	-
1963	22.8	0.9	-	-	-	-	22.8	0.0	-	-	-	-	23.0	0.9	-	-	-	-	23.4	1.7	-	-	-	-
1964	23.4	0.0	-	-	-	-	24.1	3.0	-	-	-	-	24.7	2.5	-	-	-	-	24.8	0.4	-	-	-	-
1965	24.9	0.4	-	-	-	-	25.0	0.4	-	-	-	-	25.3	1.2	-	-	-	-	25.3	0.0	-	-	-	-
1966	25.6	1.2	-	-	-	-	25.7	0.4	-	-	-	-	25.9	0.8	-	-	-	-	26.4	1.9	-	-	-	-
1967	27.1	2.7	-	-	-	-	27.2	0.4	-	-	-	-	27.7	1.8	-	-	-	-	28.2	1.8	-	-	-	-
1968	28.8	2.1	-	-	-	-	28.8	0.0	-	-	-	-	29.0	0.7	-	-	-	-	29.6	2.1	-	-	-	-
1969	30.0	1.4	-	-	-	-	30.5	1.7	-	-	-	-	31.0	1.6	-	-	-	-	31.2	0.6	-	-	-	-
1970	32.1	2.9	-	-	-	-	32.6	1.6	-	-	-	-	33.1	1.5	-	-	-	-	33.2	0.3	-	-	-	-
1971	34.1	2.7	-	-	-	-	34.2	0.3	-	-	-	-	34.2	0.0	-	-	-	-	34.1	-0.3	-	-	-	-
1972	34.6	1.5	-	-	-	-	34.9	0.9	-	-	-	-	35.3	1.1	-	-	-	-	36.0	2.0	-	-	-	-
1973	36.3	0.8	-	-	-	-	37.3	2.8	-	-	-	-	37.3	0.0	-	-	-	-	38.6	3.5	-	-	-	-
1974	39.3	1.8	-	-	-	-	40.1	2.0	-	-	-	-	42.1	5.0	-	-	-	-	42.6	1.2	-	-	-	-
1975	44.1	3.5	-	-	-	-	45.0	2.0	-	-	-	-	46.6	3.6	-	-	-	-	46.9	0.6	-	-	-	-
1976	48.7	3.8	-	-	-	-	49.0	0.6	-	-	-	-	50.3	2.7	-	-	-	-	50.9	1.2	-	-	-	-
1977	53.3	4.7	-	-	-	-	54.4	2.1	-	-	-	-	55.7	2.4	-	-	-	-	56.1	0.7	-	-	-	-
1978	57.6	2.7	-	-	59.2	2.8	-	-	59.7	0.8	-	-	60.6	1.5	-	-	61.0	0.7	-	-	61.8	1.3	-	-
1979	63.5	2.8	-	-	64.0	0.8	-	-	64.5	0.8	-	-	65.6	1.7	-	-	67.2	2.4	-	-	68.8	2.4	-	-
1980	70.6	2.6	-	-	73.0	3.4	-	-	73.7	1.0	-	-	74.0	0.4	-	-	76.1	2.8	-	-	76.6	0.7	-	-
1981	78.6	2.6	-	-	79.3	0.9	-	-	81.2	2.4	-	-	84.5	4.1	-	-	85.3	0.9	-	-	88.0	3.2	-	-
1982	89.4	1.6	-	-	91.0	1.8	-	-	92.3	1.4	-	-	94.3	2.2	-	-	95.4	1.2	-	-	96.7	1.4	-	-
1983	99.0	2.4	-	-	99.8	0.8	-	-	100.3	0.5	-	-	100.7	0.4	-	-	100.4	-0.3	-	-	102.1	1.7	-	-
1984	104.7	2.5	-	-	105.0	0.3	-	-	104.8	-0.2	-	-	105.9	1.0	-	-	106.4	0.5	-	-	107.1	0.7	-	-
1985	108.7	1.5	-	-	109.0	0.3	-	-	109.6	0.6	-	-	112.0	2.2	-	-	112.3	0.3	-	-	114.0	1.5	-	-
1986	116.0	1.8	-	-	116.9	0.8	-	-	119.4	2.1	-	-	120.1	0.6	-	-	119.7	-0.3	-	-	121.1	1.2	-	-
1987	-	-	-	-	-	-	-	-	-	-	123.7	2.1	-	-	-	-	-	-	-	-	-	-	129.8	4.9
1988	-	-	-	-	-	-	-	-	-	-	136.2	4.9	-	-	-	-	-	-	-	-	-	-	141.3	3.7
1989	-	-	-	-	-	-	-	-	-	-	143.9	1.8	-	-	-	-	-	-	-	-	-	-	146.5	1.8
1990	-	-	-	-	-	-	-	-	-	-	152.0	3.8	-	-	-	-	-	-	-	-	-	-	156.7	3.1
1991	-	-	-	-	-	-	-	-	-	-	163.5	4.3	-	-	-	-	-	-	-	-	-	-	168.4	3.0
1992	-	-	-	-	-	-	-	-	-	-	174.5	3.6	-	-	-	-	-	-	-	-	-	-	178.2	2.1

[Continued]

Portland-Salem, OR-WA
Consumer Price Index - All Urban Consumers
Base 1982-1984 = 100
Medical Care
[Continued]

For 1947-2001. Columns headed % show percentile change in the index from the previous period for which an index is available.

Year	Jan Index	%	Feb Index	%	Mar Index	%	Apr Index	%	May Index	%	Jun Index	%	Jul Index	%	Aug Index	%	Sep Index	%	Oct Index	%	Nov Index	%	Dec Index	%
1993	-	-	-	-	-	-	-	-	-	-	184.8	3.7	-	-	-	-	-	-	-	-	-	-	188.4	1.9
1994	-	-	-	-	-	-	-	-	-	-	190.8	1.3	-	-	-	-	-	-	-	-	-	-	194.7	2.0
1995	-	-	-	-	-	-	-	-	-	-	195.9	0.6	-	-	-	-	-	-	-	-	-	-	200.2	2.2
1996	-	-	-	-	-	-	-	-	-	-	210.2	5.0	-	-	-	-	-	-	-	-	-	-	213.5	1.6
1997	-	-	-	-	-	-	-	-	-	-	216.6	1.5	-	-	-	-	-	-	-	-	-	-	218.5	0.9
1998	-	-	-	-	-	-	-	-	-	-	222.0	1.6	-	-	-	-	-	-	-	-	-	-	224.2	1.0
1999	-	-	-	-	-	-	-	-	-	-	227.4	1.4	-	-	-	-	-	-	-	-	-	-	232.2	2.1
2000	-	-	-	-	-	-	-	-	-	-	241.0	3.8	-	-	-	-	-	-	-	-	-	-	253.6	5.2
2001	-	-	-	-	-	-	-	-	-	-	266.9	5.2	-	-	-	-	-	-	-	-	-	-	-	-

Source: U.S. Department of Labor, Bureau of Labor Statistics, Division of Consumer Prices and Price Indexes. - indicates no data collected for period.

Portland-Salem, OR-WA
Consumer Price Index - Urban Wage Earners
Base 1982-1984 = 100
Medical Care

For 1947-2001. Columns headed % show percentile change in the index from the previous period for which an index is available.

Year	Jan Index	%	Feb Index	%	Mar Index	%	Apr Index	%	May Index	%	Jun Index	%	Jul Index	%	Aug Index	%	Sep Index	%	Oct Index	%	Nov Index	%	Dec Index	%
1947	-	-	-	-	15.7	-	-	-	-	-	15.7	0.0	15.7	0.0	-	-	-	-	16.2	3.2	-	-	-	-
1948	16.2	0.0	-	-	-	-	16.3	0.6	-	-	-	-	16.5	1.2	-	-	-	-	16.5	0.0	-	-	-	-
1949	16.6	0.6	-	-	-	-	16.7	0.6	-	-	-	-	16.7	0.0	-	-	-	-	16.8	0.6	-	-	-	-
1950	16.8	0.0	-	-	-	-	16.8	0.0	-	-	-	-	17.3	3.0	-	-	-	-	17.6	1.7	-	-	-	-
1951	17.6	0.0	-	-	-	-	18.1	2.8	-	-	-	-	18.1	0.0	-	-	-	-	18.6	2.8	-	-	-	-
1952	18.7	0.5	-	-	-	-	18.9	1.1	-	-	-	-	19.1	1.1	-	-	-	-	19.1	0.0	-	-	-	-
1953	19.2	0.5	-	-	-	-	19.2	0.0	-	-	-	-	19.5	1.6	-	-	-	-	19.7	1.0	-	-	-	-
1954	19.7	0.0	-	-	-	-	19.8	0.5	-	-	-	-	19.9	0.5	-	-	-	-	20.0	0.5	-	-	-	-
1955	20.4	2.0	-	-	-	-	20.6	1.0	-	-	-	-	20.5	-0.5	-	-	-	-	21.0	2.4	-	-	-	-
1956	21.0	0.0	-	-	-	-	21.2	1.0	-	-	-	-	21.4	0.9	-	-	-	-	21.7	1.4	-	-	-	-
1957	22.3	2.8	-	-	-	-	22.5	0.9	-	-	-	-	22.7	0.9	-	-	-	-	22.7	0.0	-	-	-	-
1958	22.8	0.4	-	-	-	-	22.9	0.4	-	-	-	-	22.9	0.0	-	-	-	-	23.0	0.4	-	-	-	-
1959	23.0	0.0	-	-	-	-	23.0	0.0	-	-	-	-	23.2	0.9	-	-	-	-	23.2	0.0	-	-	-	-
1960	23.2	0.0	-	-	-	-	24.3	4.7	-	-	-	-	24.4	0.4	-	-	-	-	24.7	1.2	-	-	-	-
1961	24.7	0.0	-	-	-	-	25.0	1.2	-	-	-	-	25.2	0.8	-	-	-	-	25.1	-0.4	-	-	-	-
1962	24.8	-1.2	-	-	-	-	24.9	0.4	-	-	-	-	25.1	0.8	-	-	-	-	25.2	0.4	-	-	-	-
1963	25.4	0.8	-	-	-	-	25.4	0.0	-	-	-	-	25.6	0.8	-	-	-	-	26.0	1.6	-	-	-	-
1964	26.1	0.4	-	-	-	-	26.8	2.7	-	-	-	-	27.5	2.6	-	-	-	-	27.6	0.4	-	-	-	-
1965	27.7	0.4	-	-	-	-	27.8	0.4	-	-	-	-	28.2	1.4	-	-	-	-	28.2	0.0	-	-	-	-
1966	28.5	1.1	-	-	-	-	28.6	0.4	-	-	-	-	28.8	0.7	-	-	-	-	29.4	2.1	-	-	-	-
1967	30.2	2.7	-	-	-	-	30.3	0.3	-	-	-	-	30.9	2.0	-	-	-	-	31.4	1.6	-	-	-	-
1968	32.1	2.2	-	-	-	-	32.1	0.0	-	-	-	-	32.3	0.6	-	-	-	-	33.0	2.2	-	-	-	-
1969	33.4	1.2	-	-	-	-	34.0	1.8	-	-	-	-	34.5	1.5	-	-	-	-	34.8	0.9	-	-	-	-
1970	35.7	2.6	-	-	-	-	36.3	1.7	-	-	-	-	36.9	1.7	-	-	-	-	36.9	0.0	-	-	-	-
1971	37.9	2.7	-	-	-	-	38.1	0.5	-	-	-	-	38.1	0.0	-	-	-	-	37.9	-0.5	-	-	-	-
1972	38.6	1.8	-	-	-	-	38.8	0.5	-	-	-	-	39.4	1.5	-	-	-	-	40.0	1.5	-	-	-	-
1973	40.4	1.0	-	-	-	-	41.5	2.7	-	-	-	-	41.5	0.0	-	-	-	-	42.9	3.4	-	-	-	-
1974	43.8	2.1	-	-	-	-	44.6	1.8	-	-	-	-	46.8	4.9	-	-	-	-	47.4	1.3	-	-	-	-
1975	49.1	3.6	-	-	-	-	50.1	2.0	-	-	-	-	51.9	3.6	-	-	-	-	52.2	0.6	-	-	-	-
1976	54.2	3.8	-	-	-	-	54.5	0.6	-	-	-	-	56.0	2.8	-	-	-	-	56.6	1.1	-	-	-	-
1977	59.4	4.9	-	-	-	-	60.5	1.9	-	-	-	-	62.0	2.5	-	-	-	-	62.4	0.6	-	-	-	-
1978	64.1	2.7	-	-	65.1	1.6	-	-	65.3	0.3	-	-	66.2	1.4	-	-	66.9	1.1	-	-	68.0	1.6	-	-
1979	68.8	1.2	-	-	70.2	2.0	-	-	71.4	1.7	-	-	72.6	1.7	-	-	72.7	0.1	-	-	73.8	1.5	-	-
1980	74.8	1.4	-	-	76.0	1.6	-	-	77.7	2.2	-	-	78.2	0.6	-	-	78.7	0.6	-	-	79.2	0.6	-	-
1981	79.7	0.6	-	-	80.5	1.0	-	-	82.4	2.4	-	-	85.3	3.5	-	-	84.8	-0.6	-	-	87.9	3.7	-	-
1982	89.5	1.8	-	-	91.0	1.7	-	-	92.4	1.5	-	-	94.6	2.4	-	-	95.7	1.2	-	-	97.0	1.4	-	-
1983	99.5	2.6	-	-	100.2	0.7	-	-	100.7	0.5	-	-	100.9	0.2	-	-	100.6	-0.3	-	-	102.0	1.4	-	-
1984	104.4	2.4	-	-	104.6	0.2	-	-	104.3	-0.3	-	-	105.4	1.1	-	-	106.1	0.7	-	-	106.6	0.5	-	-
1985	108.3	1.6	-	-	108.7	0.4	-	-	109.2	0.5	-	-	111.9	2.5	-	-	112.4	0.4	-	-	114.1	1.5	-	-
1986	115.8	1.5	-	-	116.8	0.9	-	-	119.0	1.9	-	-	119.6	0.5	-	-	119.0	-0.5	-	-	120.6	1.3	-	-
1987	-	-	-	-	-	-	-	-	-	-	123.3	2.2	-	-	-	-	-	-	-	-	-	-	129.5	5.0
1988	-	-	-	-	-	-	-	-	-	-	135.7	4.8	-	-	-	-	-	-	-	-	-	-	140.9	3.8
1989	-	-	-	-	-	-	-	-	-	-	143.6	1.9	-	-	-	-	-	-	-	-	-	-	145.9	1.6
1990	-	-	-	-	-	-	-	-	-	-	151.0	3.5	-	-	-	-	-	-	-	-	-	-	155.3	2.8
1991	-	-	-	-	-	-	-	-	-	-	161.8	4.2	-	-	-	-	-	-	-	-	-	-	166.8	3.1
1992	-	-	-	-	-	-	-	-	-	-	173.0	3.7	-	-	-	-	-	-	-	-	-	-	176.8	2.2

[Continued]

Portland-Salem, OR-WA
Consumer Price Index - Urban Wage Earners
Base 1982-1984 = 100
Medical Care
[Continued]

For 1947-2001. Columns headed % show percentile change in the index from the previous period for which an index is available.

Year	Jan Index	%	Feb Index	%	Mar Index	%	Apr Index	%	May Index	%	Jun Index	%	Jul Index	%	Aug Index	%	Sep Index	%	Oct Index	%	Nov Index	%	Dec Index	%
1993	-	-	-	-	-	-	-	-	-	-	183.1	3.6	-	-	-	-	-	-	-	-	-	-	186.8	2.0
1994	-	-	-	-	-	-	-	-	-	-	189.0	1.2	-	-	-	-	-	-	-	-	-	-	193.3	2.3
1995	-	-	-	-	-	-	-	-	-	-	194.7	0.7	-	-	-	-	-	-	-	-	-	-	199.3	2.4
1996	-	-	-	-	-	-	-	-	-	-	208.9	4.8	-	-	-	-	-	-	-	-	-	-	212.3	1.6
1997	-	-	-	-	-	-	-	-	-	-	215.5	1.5	-	-	-	-	-	-	-	-	-	-	217.4	0.9
1998	-	-	-	-	-	-	-	-	-	-	221.0	1.7	-	-	-	-	-	-	-	-	-	-	222.8	0.8
1999	-	-	-	-	-	-	-	-	-	-	225.8	1.3	-	-	-	-	-	-	-	-	-	-	230.6	2.1
2000	-	-	-	-	-	-	-	-	-	-	239.9	4.0	-	-	-	-	-	-	-	-	-	-	252.6	5.3
2001	-	-	-	-	-	-	-	-	-	-	266.7	5.6	-	-	-	-	-	-	-	-	-	-	-	-

Source: U.S. Department of Labor, Bureau of Labor Statistics, Division of Consumer Prices and Price Indexes. - indicates no data collected for period.

Portland-Salem, OR-WA
Consumer Price Index - All Urban Consumers
Base December 1997 = 100
Recreation

For 1997-2001. Columns headed % show percentile change in the index from the previous period for which an index is available.

Year	Jan		Feb		Mar		Apr		May		Jun		Jul		Aug		Sep		Oct		Nov		Dec	
	Index	%	Index	%	Index	%	Index	%	Index	%	Index	%	Index	%	Index	%	Index	%	Index	%	Index	%	Index	%
1997	-	-	-	-	-	-	-	-	-	-	-	-	-	-	-	-	-	-	-	-	-	-	100.0	-
1998	-	-	-	-	-	-	-	-	-	-	98.7	-1.3	-	-	-	-	-	-	-	-	-	-	99.2	0.5
1999	-	-	-	-	-	-	-	-	-	-	101.3	2.1	-	-	-	-	-	-	-	-	-	-	100.4	-0.9
2000	-	-	-	-	-	-	-	-	-	-	101.6	1.2	-	-	-	-	-	-	-	-	-	-	102.6	1.0
2001	-	-	-	-	-	-	-	-	-	-	102.8	0.2	-	-	-	-	-	-	-	-	-	-	-	-

Source: U.S. Department of Labor, Bureau of Labor Statistics, Division of Consumer Prices and Price Indexes. - indicates no data collected for period.

Portland-Salem, OR-WA
Consumer Price Index - Urban Wage Earners
Base December 1997 = 100
Recreation

For 1997-2001. Columns headed % show percentile change in the index from the previous period for which an index is available.

Year	Jan		Feb		Mar		Apr		May		Jun		Jul		Aug		Sep		Oct		Nov		Dec	
	Index	%	Index	%	Index	%	Index	%	Index	%	Index	%	Index	%	Index	%	Index	%	Index	%	Index	%	Index	%
1997	-	-	-	-	-	-	-	-	-	-	-	-	-	-	-	-	-	-	-	-	-	-	100.0	-
1998	-	-	-	-	-	-	-	-	-	-	98.9	-1.1	-	-	-	-	-	-	-	-	-	-	99.4	0.5
1999	-	-	-	-	-	-	-	-	-	-	101.5	2.1	-	-	-	-	-	-	-	-	-	-	100.6	-0.9
2000	-	-	-	-	-	-	-	-	-	-	101.4	0.8	-	-	-	-	-	-	-	-	-	-	102.5	1.1
2001	-	-	-	-	-	-	-	-	-	-	102.4	-0.1	-	-	-	-	-	-	-	-	-	-	-	-

Source: U.S. Department of Labor, Bureau of Labor Statistics, Division of Consumer Prices and Price Indexes. - indicates no data collected for period.

Portland-Salem, OR-WA
Consumer Price Index - All Urban Consumers
Base December 1997 = 100
Education & Communication

For 1997-2001. Columns headed % show percentile change in the index from the previous period for which an index is available.

Year	Jan		Feb		Mar		Apr		May		Jun		Jul		Aug		Sep		Oct		Nov		Dec	
	Index	%	Index	%	Index	%	Index	%	Index	%	Index	%	Index	%	Index	%	Index	%	Index	%	Index	%	Index	%
1997	-	-	-	-	-	-	-	-	-	-	-	-	-	-	-	-	-	-	-	-	-	-	100.0	-
1998	-	-	-	-	-	-	-	-	-	-	98.1	-1.9	-	-	-	-	-	-	-	-	-	-	98.9	0.8
1999	-	-	-	-	-	-	-	-	-	-	99.4	0.5	-	-	-	-	-	-	-	-	-	-	101.1	1.7
2000	-	-	-	-	-	-	-	-	-	-	101.6	0.5	-	-	-	-	-	-	-	-	-	-	101.2	-0.4
2001	-	-	-	-	-	-	-	-	-	-	101.7	0.5	-	-	-	-	-	-	-	-	-	-	-	-

Source: U.S. Department of Labor, Bureau of Labor Statistics, Division of Consumer Prices and Price Indexes. - indicates no data collected for period.

Portland-Salem, OR-WA
Consumer Price Index - Urban Wage Earners
Base December 1997 = 100
Education & Communication

For 1997-2001. Columns headed % show percentile change in the index from the previous period for which an index is available.

Year	Jan		Feb		Mar		Apr		May		Jun		Jul		Aug		Sep		Oct		Nov		Dec	
	Index	%	Index	%	Index	%	Index	%	Index	%	Index	%	Index	%	Index	%	Index	%	Index	%	Index	%	Index	%
1997	-	-	-	-	-	-	-	-	-	-	-	-	-	-	-	-	-	-	-	-	-	-	100.0	-
1998	-	-	-	-	-	-	-	-	-	-	98.3	-1.7	-	-	-	-	-	-	-	-	-	-	99.2	0.9
1999	-	-	-	-	-	-	-	-	-	-	99.7	0.5	-	-	-	-	-	-	-	-	-	-	101.3	1.6
2000	-	-	-	-	-	-	-	-	-	-	101.8	0.5	-	-	-	-	-	-	-	-	-	-	101.5	-0.3
2001	-	-	-	-	-	-	-	-	-	-	102.3	0.8	-	-	-	-	-	-	-	-	-	-	-	-

Source: U.S. Department of Labor, Bureau of Labor Statistics, Division of Consumer Prices and Price Indexes. - indicates no data collected for period.

St. Louis, MO-IL
Consumer Price Index - All Urban Consumers
Base 1982-1984 = 100
Annual Averages

For 1917-2001. Columns headed % show percentile change in the index from the previous period for which an index is available.

Year	All Items Index	%	Food & Beverage Index	%	Housing Index	%	Apparel Index	%	Transportation Index	%	Medical Care Index	%	Recreation* Index	%	Education & Communic.* Index	%	Other Goods & Services Index	%
1917	-	-	-	-	-	-	-	-	-	-	-	-	-	-	-	-	-	-
1918	14.8	-	-	-	-	-	-	-	-	-	-	-	-	-	-	-	-	-
1919	16.8	13.5	-	-	-	-	-	-	-	-	-	-	-	-	-	-	-	-
1920	19.9	18.5	-	-	-	-	-	-	-	-	-	-	-	-	-	-	-	-
1921	17.4	-12.6	-	-	-	-	-	-	-	-	-	-	-	-	-	-	-	-
1922	16.3	-6.3	-	-	-	-	-	-	-	-	-	-	-	-	-	-	-	-
1923	16.7	2.5	-	-	-	-	-	-	-	-	-	-	-	-	-	-	-	-
1924	16.8	0.6	-	-	-	-	-	-	-	-	-	-	-	-	-	-	-	-
1925	17.3	3.0	-	-	-	-	-	-	-	-	-	-	-	-	-	-	-	-
1926	17.6	1.7	-	-	-	-	-	-	-	-	-	-	-	-	-	-	-	-
1927	17.3	-1.7	-	-	-	-	-	-	-	-	-	-	-	-	-	-	-	-
1928	16.9	-2.3	-	-	-	-	-	-	-	-	-	-	-	-	-	-	-	-
1929	17.1	1.2	-	-	-	-	-	-	-	-	-	-	-	-	-	-	-	-
1930	16.7	-2.3	-	-	-	-	-	-	-	-	-	-	-	-	-	-	-	-
1931	15.0	-10.2	-	-	-	-	-	-	-	-	-	-	-	-	-	-	-	-
1932	13.4	-10.7	-	-	-	-	-	-	-	-	-	-	-	-	-	-	-	-
1933	12.8	-4.5	-	-	-	-	-	-	-	-	-	-	-	-	-	-	-	-
1934	13.3	3.9	-	-	-	-	-	-	-	-	-	-	-	-	-	-	-	-
1935	13.7	3.0	-	-	-	-	-	-	-	-	-	-	-	-	-	-	-	-
1936	13.8	0.7	-	-	-	-	-	-	-	-	-	-	-	-	-	-	-	-
1937	14.3	3.6	-	-	-	-	-	-	-	-	-	-	-	-	-	-	-	-
1938	13.9	-2.8	-	-	-	-	-	-	-	-	-	-	-	-	-	-	-	-
1939	13.8	-0.7	-	-	-	-	-	-	-	-	-	-	-	-	-	-	-	-
1940	13.9	0.7	-	-	-	-	-	-	-	-	-	-	-	-	-	-	-	-
1941	14.6	5.0	-	-	-	-	-	-	-	-	-	-	-	-	-	-	-	-
1942	16.2	11.0	-	-	-	-	-	-	-	-	-	-	-	-	-	-	-	-
1943	17.0	4.9	-	-	-	-	-	-	-	-	-	-	-	-	-	-	-	-
1944	17.3	1.8	-	-	-	-	-	-	-	-	-	-	-	-	-	-	-	-
1945	17.6	1.7	-	-	-	-	-	-	-	-	-	-	-	-	-	-	-	-
1946	19.1	8.5	-	-	-	-	-	-	-	-	-	-	-	-	-	-	-	-
1947	22.2	16.2	-	-	-	-	-	-	18.2	-	13.2	-	-	-	-	-	-	-
1948	23.9	7.7	-	-	-	-	-	-	19.8	8.8	14.0	6.1	-	-	-	-	-	-
1949	23.6	-1.3	-	-	-	-	-	-	20.8	5.1	14.4	2.9	-	-	-	-	-	-
1950	23.9	1.3	-	-	-	-	-	-	21.3	2.4	14.5	0.7	-	-	-	-	-	-
1951	25.9	8.4	-	-	-	-	-	-	23.5	10.3	15.5	6.9	-	-	-	-	-	-
1952	26.7	3.1	-	-	-	-	-	-	25.8	9.8	18.0	16.1	-	-	-	-	-	-
1953	27.0	1.1	-	-	-	-	44.1	-	26.8	3.9	18.5	2.8	-	-	-	-	-	-
1954	27.1	0.4	-	-	-	-	44.0	-0.2	26.0	-3.0	18.9	2.2	-	-	-	-	-	-
1955	27.0	-0.4	-	-	-	-	44.0	0.0	26.1	0.4	19.5	3.2	-	-	-	-	-	-
1956	27.2	0.7	-	-	-	-	44.4	0.9	26.3	0.8	19.9	2.1	-	-	-	-	-	-
1957	28.1	3.3	-	-	-	-	45.0	1.4	28.0	6.5	21.5	8.0	-	-	-	-	-	-
1958	29.0	3.2	-	-	-	-	45.8	1.8	29.6	5.7	22.2	3.3	-	-	-	-	-	-
1959	29.4	1.4	-	-	-	-	46.2	0.9	31.6	6.8	23.3	5.0	-	-	-	-	-	-
1960	29.5	0.3	-	-	-	-	47.1	1.9	31.4	-0.6	23.7	1.7	-	-	-	-	-	-
1961	30.0	1.7	-	-	-	-	47.6	1.1	32.0	1.9	24.2	2.1	-	-	-	-	-	-

[Continued]

St. Louis, MO-IL
Consumer Price Index - All Urban Consumers
Base 1982-1984 = 100
Annual Averages
[Continued]

For 1917-2001. Columns headed % show percentile change in the index from the previous period for which an index is available.

Year	All Items		Food & Beverage		Housing		Apparel		Trans- portation		Medical Care		Recrea- tion*		Education & Communic.*		Other Goods & Services	
	Index	%	Index	%	Index	%	Index	%	Index	%	Index	%	Index	%	Index	%	Index	%
1962	30.3	1.0	-	-	-	-	47.6	0.0	32.4	1.3	25.5	5.4	-	-	-	-	-	-
1963	30.6	1.0	-	-	-	-	48.0	0.8	32.3	-0.3	25.7	0.8	-	-	-	-	-	-
1964	31.2	2.0	-	-	-	-	48.7	1.5	32.7	1.2	25.9	0.8	-	-	-	-	-	-
1965	31.7	1.6	-	-	-	-	49.2	1.0	33.0	0.9	26.8	3.5	-	-	-	-	-	-
1966	32.7	3.2	-	-	-	-	50.7	3.0	34.0	3.0	28.2	5.2	-	-	-	-	-	-
1967	33.7	3.1	-	-	-	-	52.4	3.4	35.3	3.8	29.7	5.3	-	-	-	-	-	-
1968	35.0	3.9	-	-	-	-	55.4	5.7	36.0	2.0	31.1	4.7	-	-	-	-	-	-
1969	36.8	5.1	-	-	-	-	58.2	5.1	37.2	3.3	33.0	6.1	-	-	-	-	-	-
1970	38.8	5.4	-	-	-	-	60.4	3.8	39.4	5.9	35.2	6.7	-	-	-	-	-	-
1971	40.3	3.9	-	-	-	-	62.4	3.3	42.1	6.9	36.7	4.3	-	-	-	-	-	-
1972	41.2	2.2	-	-	-	-	63.0	1.0	42.4	0.7	37.4	1.9	-	-	-	-	-	-
1973	43.5	5.6	-	-	-	-	64.5	2.4	43.8	3.3	38.6	3.2	-	-	-	-	-	-
1974	47.9	10.1	-	-	-	-	68.0	5.4	47.4	8.2	41.8	8.3	-	-	-	-	-	-
1975	52.6	9.8	-	-	-	-	70.8	4.1	51.5	8.6	46.3	10.8	-	-	-	-	-	-
1976	55.6	5.7	62.5	-	50.5	-	74.3	4.9	56.1	8.9	50.2	8.4	-	-	-	-	57.2	-
1977	59.5	7.0	66.8	6.9	54.0	6.9	79.2	6.6	59.5	6.1	55.4	10.4	-	-	-	-	60.5	5.8
1978	64.5	8.4	72.7	8.8	59.4	10.0	80.2	1.3	63.5	6.7	59.6	7.6	-	-	-	-	64.6	6.8
1979	72.7	12.7	81.0	11.4	67.9	14.3	85.2	6.2	73.8	16.2	64.8	8.7	-	-	-	-	68.7	6.3
1980	82.5	13.5	87.1	7.5	79.8	17.5	91.7	7.6	85.1	15.3	72.9	12.5	-	-	-	-	74.7	8.7
1981	90.1	9.2	93.5	7.3	87.6	9.8	95.3	3.9	94.4	10.9	81.8	12.2	-	-	-	-	82.0	9.8
1982	96.6	7.2	97.1	3.9	96.6	10.3	97.6	2.4	97.8	3.6	93.4	14.2	-	-	-	-	90.6	10.5
1983	100.1	3.6	99.7	2.7	100.4	3.9	100.8	3.3	99.2	1.4	100.9	8.0	-	-	-	-	101.0	11.5
1984	103.3	3.2	103.2	3.5	102.9	2.5	101.6	0.8	102.9	3.7	105.8	4.9	-	-	-	-	108.5	7.4
1985	107.1	3.7	105.7	2.4	107.8	4.8	104.4	2.8	105.3	2.3	111.0	4.9	-	-	-	-	115.4	6.4
1986	108.6	1.4	109.7	3.8	110.4	2.4	102.7	-1.6	100.3	-4.7	120.3	8.4	-	-	-	-	122.1	5.8
1987	112.2	3.3	114.0	3.9	112.1	1.5	107.6	4.8	103.9	3.6	127.9	6.3	-	-	-	-	128.1	4.9
1988	115.7	3.1	117.7	3.2	114.9	2.5	112.5	4.6	106.0	2.0	135.6	6.0	-	-	-	-	136.8	6.8
1989	121.8	5.3	125.8	6.9	120.3	4.7	118.4	5.2	110.5	4.2	145.6	7.4	-	-	-	-	145.4	6.3
1990	128.1	5.2	134.9	7.2	124.9	3.8	120.9	2.1	117.4	6.2	159.0	9.2	-	-	-	-	153.6	5.6
1991	132.1	3.1	139.6	3.5	127.7	2.2	122.5	1.3	118.5	0.9	171.7	8.0	-	-	-	-	163.4	6.4
1992	134.7	2.0	140.1	0.4	129.7	1.6	121.7	-0.7	121.9	2.9	181.0	5.4	-	-	-	-	172.3	5.4
1993	137.5	2.1	140.1	0.0	133.0	2.5	122.8	0.9	125.1	2.6	191.5	5.8	-	-	-	-	175.9	2.1
1994	141.3	2.8	144.0	2.8	136.7	2.8	125.1	1.9	129.2	3.3	201.7	5.3	-	-	-	-	174.0	-1.1
1995	145.2	2.8	146.9	2.0	139.5	2.0	119.2	-4.7	136.0	5.3	210.0	4.1	-	-	-	-	180.4	3.7
1996	149.6	3.0	151.2	2.9	142.6	2.2	122.2	2.5	141.8	4.3	218.4	4.0	-	-	-	-	186.3	3.3
1997	-	-	-	-	145.5	2.0	123.8	1.3	143.8	1.4	226.4	3.7	-	-	-	-	-	-
1998	154.5	3.3	158.4	4.8	147.0	1.0	126.2	1.9	138.4	-3.8	233.9	3.3	102.0	-	102.4	-	-	-
1999	157.6	2.0	161.9	2.2	149.0	1.4	123.5	-2.1	141.7	2.4	245.7	5.0	104.3	2.3	103.9	1.5	219.7	17.9
2000	163.1	3.5	166.8	3.0	155.0	4.0	120.9	-2.1	150.6	6.3	256.8	4.5	103.2	-1.1	103.7	-0.2	228.4	4.0
2001	167.3	2.6	169.3	1.5	161.2	4.0	120.3	-0.5	151.5	0.6	268.2	4.4	105.9	2.6	105.2	1.4	240.4	5.3

Source: U.S. Department of Labor, Bureau of Labor Statistics, Division of Consumer Prices and Price Indexes. *Base is December 1997 = 100. - indicates no data collected for period.

St. Louis, MO-IL
Consumer Price Index - Urban Wage Earners
Base 1982-1984 = 100
Annual Averages

For 1917-2001. Columns headed % show percentile change in the index from the previous period for which an index is available.

Year	All Items		Food & Beverage		Housing		Apparel		Transportation		Medical Care		Recreation*		Education & Communic.*		Other Goods & Services	
	Index	%	Index	%	Index	%	Index	%	Index	%	Index	%	Index	%	Index	%	Index	%
1917	-	-	-	-					-	-	-	-			-	-	-	-
1918	15.0	-	-	-					-	-	-	-			-	-	-	-
1919	17.0	13.3	-	-					-	-	-	-			-	-	-	-
1920	20.1	18.2	-	-					-	-	-	-			-	-	-	-
1921	17.6	-12.4	-	-					-	-	-	-			-	-	-	-
1922	16.5	-6.3	-	-					-	-	-	-			-	-	-	-
1923	16.8	1.8	-	-					-	-	-	-			-	-	-	-
1924	17.0	1.2	-	-					-	-	-	-			-	-	-	-
1925	17.5	2.9	-	-					-	-	-	-			-	-	-	-
1926	17.7	1.1	-	-					-	-	-	-			-	-	-	-
1927	17.5	-1.1	-	-					-	-	-	-			-	-	-	-
1928	17.1	-2.3	-	-					-	-	-	-			-	-	-	-
1929	17.2	0.6	-	-					-	-	-	-			-	-	-	-
1930	16.9	-1.7	-	-					-	-	-	-			-	-	-	-
1931	15.1	-10.7	-	-	-	-	-	-	-	-	-	-			-	-	-	-
1932	13.6	-9.9	-	-	-	-	-	-	-	-	-	-			-	-	-	-
1933	12.9	-5.1	-	-	-	-	-	-	-	-	-	-			-	-	-	-
1934	13.4	3.9	-	-	-	-	-	-	-	-	-	-			-	-	-	-
1935	13.8	3.0	-	-	-	-	-	-	-	-	-	-			-	-	-	-
1936	14.0	1.4	-	-	-	-	-	-	-	-	-	-			-	-	-	-
1937	14.4	2.9	-	-	-	-	-	-	-	-	-	-			-	-	-	-
1938	14.1	-2.1	-	-	-	-	-	-	-	-	-	-			-	-	-	-
1939	13.9	-1.4	-	-	-	-	-	-	-	-	-	-			-	-	-	-
1940	14.0	0.7	-	-	-	-	-	-	-	-	-	-			-	-	-	-
1941	14.7	5.0	-	-	-	-	-	-	-	-	-	-			-	-	-	-
1942	16.3	10.9	-	-	-	-	-	-	-	-	-	-			-	-	-	-
1943	17.2	5.5	-	-	-	-	-	-	-	-	-	-			-	-	-	-
1944	17.5	1.7	-	-	-	-	-	-	-	-	-	-			-	-	-	-
1945	17.8	1.7	-	-	-	-	-	-	-	-	-	-			-	-	-	-
1946	19.3	8.4	-	-	-	-	-	-	-	-	-	-			-	-	-	-
1947	22.4	16.1	-	-	-	-	-	-	18.5	-	13.1	-			-	-	-	-
1948	24.1	7.6	-	-	-	-	-	-	20.1	8.6	13.9	6.1	-	-	-	-	-	-
1949	23.8	-1.2	-	-	-	-	-	-	21.2	5.5	14.3	2.9	-	-	-	-	-	-
1950	24.1	1.3	-	-	-	-	-	-	21.7	2.4	14.4	0.7	-	-	-	-	-	-
1951	26.1	8.3	-	-	-	-	-	-	23.9	10.1	15.3	6.3	-	-	-	-	-	-
1952	27.0	3.4	-	-	-	-	-	-	26.2	9.6	17.9	17.0	-	-	-	-	-	-
1953	27.2	0.7	-	-	-	-	45.0	-	27.2	3.8	18.3	2.2	-	-	-	-	-	-
1954	27.3	0.4	-	-	-	-	44.9	-0.2	26.4	-2.9	18.7	2.2	-	-	-	-	-	-
1955	27.2	-0.4	-	-	-	-	44.8	-0.2	26.5	0.4	19.3	3.2	-	-	-	-	-	-
1956	27.5	1.1	-	-	-	-	45.3	1.1	26.7	0.8	19.7	2.1	-	-	-	-	-	-
1957	28.4	3.3	-	-	-	-	45.9	1.3	28.5	6.7	21.3	8.1	-	-	-	-	-	-
1958	29.2	2.8	-	-	-	-	46.7	1.7	30.1	5.6	22.0	3.3	-	-	-	-	-	-
1959	29.6	1.4	-	-	-	-	47.1	0.9	32.1	6.6	23.1	5.0	-	-	-	-	-	-
1960	29.8	0.7	-	-	-	-	48.0	1.9	31.9	-0.6	23.5	1.7	-	-	-	-	-	-
1961	30.3	1.7	-	-	-	-	48.5	1.0	32.5	1.9	24.0	2.1	-	-	-	-	-	-

[Continued]

St. Louis, MO-IL
Consumer Price Index - Urban Wage Earners
Base 1982-1984 = 100
Annual Averages
[Continued]

For 1917-2001. Columns headed % show percentile change in the index from the previous period for which an index is available.

Year	All Items		Food & Beverage		Housing		Apparel		Trans-portation		Medical Care		Recrea-tion*		Education & Communic.*		Other Goods & Services	
	Index	%	Index	%	Index	%	Index	%	Index	%	Index	%	Index	%	Index	%	Index	%
1962	30.6	1.0	-	-	-	-	48.5	0.0	32.9	1.2	25.3	5.4	-	-	-	-	-	-
1963	30.9	1.0		-		-	48.9	0.8	32.8	-0.3	25.5	0.8	-	-	-	-	-	-
1964	31.5	1.9	-	-	-	-	49.6	1.4	33.2	1.2	25.6	0.4	-	-	-	-	-	-
1965	32.0	1.6	-	-	-	-	50.1	1.0	33.6	1.2	26.5	3.5	-	-	-	-	-	-
1966	33.0	3.1		-		-	51.6	3.0	34.6	3.0	28.0	5.7	-	-	-	-	-	-
1967	34.0	3.0		-		-	53.4	3.5	35.8	3.5	29.4	5.0	-	-	-	-	-	-
1968	35.3	3.8		-		-	56.5	5.8	36.6	2.2	30.8	4.8	-	-	-	-	-	-
1969	37.1	5.1		-		-	59.3	5.0	37.8	3.3	32.7	6.2	-	-	-	-	-	-
1970	39.2	5.7		-	-	-	61.6	3.9	40.1	6.1	34.8	6.4	-	-	-	-	-	-
1971	40.7	3.8	-	-	-	-	63.6	3.2	42.8	6.7	36.3	4.3	-	-	-	-	-	-
1972	41.6	2.2	-	-	-	-	64.2	0.9	43.1	0.7	37.0	1.9	-	-	-	-	-	-
1973	43.9	5.5	-	-	-	-	65.7	2.3	44.5	3.2	38.2	3.2	-	-	-	-	-	-
1974	48.3	10.0		-	-	-	69.3	5.5	48.2	8.3	41.4	8.4	-	-	-	-	-	-
1975	53.1	9.9	-	-	-	-	72.2	4.2	52.3	8.5	45.9	10.9	-	-	-	-	-	-
1976	56.1	5.6	62.5	-	51.0	-	75.7	4.8	57.0	9.0	49.7	8.3	-	-	-	-	56.8	-
1977	60.0	7.0	66.8	6.9	54.5	6.9	80.8	6.7	60.5	6.1	55.0	10.7	-	-	-	-	60.0	5.6
1978	64.7	7.8	72.5	8.5	59.9	9.9	80.9	0.1	63.1	4.3	59.5	8.2	-	-	-	-	64.2	7.0
1979	73.2	13.1	81.5	12.4	68.9	15.0	84.4	4.3	73.3	16.2	65.1	9.4	-	-	-	-	68.7	7.0
1980	83.4	13.9	87.4	7.2	81.0	17.6	90.5	7.2	85.6	16.8	73.5	12.9	-	-	-	-	75.5	9.9
1981	90.9	9.0	93.6	7.1	88.7	9.5	95.3	5.3	94.5	10.4	82.2	11.8	-	-	-	-	82.6	9.4
1982	97.1	6.8	97.1	3.7	97.8	10.3	97.5	2.3	97.8	3.5	93.4	13.6	-	-	-	-	90.6	9.7
1983	100.3	3.3	99.8	2.8	100.8	3.1	101.0	3.6	99.1	1.3	100.7	7.8	-	-	-	-	101.4	11.9
1984	102.6	2.3	103.2	3.4	101.3	0.5	101.5	0.5	103.2	4.1	105.9	5.2	-	-	-	-	108.0	6.5
1985	107.1	4.4	105.6	2.3	109.1	7.7	104.1	2.6	105.3	2.0	111.0	4.8	-	-	-	-	114.6	6.1
1986	108.2	1.0	109.8	4.0	111.9	2.6	102.4	-1.6	99.2	-5.8	119.8	7.9	-	-	-	-	121.1	5.7
1987	111.8	3.3	114.0	3.8	113.9	1.8	107.7	5.2	103.2	4.0	127.5	6.4	-	-	-	-	126.8	4.7
1988	115.4	3.2	117.8	3.3	116.6	2.4	112.6	4.5	105.8	2.5	135.2	6.0	-	-	-	-	135.7	7.0
1989	121.5	5.3	125.8	6.8	122.0	4.6	118.5	5.2	110.1	4.1	145.6	7.7	-	-	-	-	144.7	6.6
1990	127.5	4.9	134.8	7.2	126.7	3.9	121.2	2.3	115.5	4.9	158.3	8.7	-	-	-	-	153.7	6.2
1991	131.5	3.1	139.6	3.6	129.5	2.2	122.8	1.3	117.2	1.5	170.6	7.8	-	-	-	-	165.4	7.6
1992	134.3	2.1	140.2	0.4	131.9	1.9	122.1	-0.6	121.0	3.2	180.0	5.5	-	-	-	-	175.4	6.0
1993	136.9	1.9	140.3	0.1	135.2	2.5	123.0	0.7	124.6	3.0	190.5	5.8	-	-	-	-	175.9	0.3
1994	140.7	2.8	144.3	2.9	138.9	2.7	125.9	2.4	129.2	3.7	200.1	5.0	-	-	-	-	170.4	-3.1
1995	144.7	2.8	147.0	1.9	141.6	1.9	119.7	-4.9	138.0	6.8	208.2	4.0	-	-	-	-	175.4	2.9
1996	148.7	2.8	151.1	2.8	144.8	2.3	122.5	2.3	143.0	3.6	216.6	4.0	-	-	-	-	180.2	2.7
1997	-	-	-	-	147.8	2.1	123.9	1.1	144.0	0.7	224.9	3.8	-	-	-	-	-	-
1998	153.0	2.9	158.5	4.9	149.0	0.8	125.9	1.6	137.5	-4.5	232.2	3.2	102.3	-	102.3	-	-	-
1999	156.3	2.2	162.0	2.2	150.7	1.1	124.6	-1.0	141.4	2.8	243.7	5.0	104.7	2.3	103.6	1.3	219.9	22.0
2000	162.1	3.7	166.8	3.0	156.4	3.8	121.8	-2.2	152.5	7.9	254.5	4.4	103.2	-1.4	102.9	-0.7	229.9	4.5
2001	166.3	2.6	169.4	1.6	162.8	4.1	121.2	-0.5	153.4	0.6	265.4	4.3	106.2	2.9	104.5	1.6	243.4	5.9

Source: U.S. Department of Labor, Bureau of Labor Statistics, Division of Consumer Prices and Price Indexes. *Base is December 1997 = 100. - indicates no data collected for period.

St. Louis, MO-IL
Consumer Price Index - All Urban Consumers
Base 1982-1984 = 100
All Items

For 1917-2001. Columns headed % show percentile change in the index from the previous period for which an index is available.

Year	Jan Index	%	Feb Index	%	Mar Index	%	Apr Index	%	May Index	%	Jun Index	%	Jul Index	%	Aug Index	%	Sep Index	%	Oct Index	%	Nov Index	%	Dec Index	%
1917	-	-	-	-	-	-	-	-	-	-	-	-	-	-	-	-	-	-	-	-	-	-	13.7	-
1918	-	-	-	-	-	-	-	-	-	-	-	-	-	-	-	-	-	-	-	-	-	-	16.0	16.8
1919	-	-	-	-	-	-	-	-	-	-	16.2	1.3	-	-	-	-	-	-	-	-	-	-	18.4	13.6
1920	-	-	-	-	-	-	-	-	-	-	21.1	14.7	-	-	-	-	-	-	-	-	-	-	18.8	-10.9
1921	-	-	-	-	-	-	-	-	17.2	-8.5	-	-	-	-	-	-	17.2	0.0	-	-	-	-	16.7	-2.9
1922	-	-	-	-	16.3	-2.4	-	-	-	-	16.5	1.2	-	-	-	-	16.2	-1.8	-	-	-	-	16.4	1.2
1923	-	-	-	-	16.5	0.6	-	-	-	-	16.6	0.6	-	-	-	-	16.9	1.8	-	-	-	-	16.8	-0.6
1924	-	-	-	-	16.7	-0.6	-	-	-	-	16.7	0.0	-	-	-	-	16.7	0.0	-	-	-	-	16.9	1.2
1925	-	-	-	-	-	-	-	-	-	-	17.3	2.4	-	-	-	-	-	-	-	-	-	-	17.7	2.3
1926	-	-	-	-	-	-	-	-	-	-	17.6	-0.6	-	-	-	-	-	-	-	-	-	-	17.6	0.0
1927	-	-	-	-	-	-	-	-	-	-	17.6	0.0	-	-	-	-	-	-	-	-	-	-	17.1	-2.8
1928	-	-	-	-	-	-	-	-	-	-	16.9	-1.2	-	-	-	-	-	-	-	-	-	-	16.9	0.0
1929	-	-	-	-	-	-	-	-	-	-	17.1	1.2	-	-	-	-	-	-	-	-	-	-	17.2	0.6
1930	-	-	-	-	-	-	-	-	-	-	16.8	-2.3	-	-	-	-	-	-	-	-	-	-	16.0	-4.8
1931	-	-	-	-	-	-	-	-	-	-	14.9	-6.9	-	-	-	-	-	-	-	-	-	-	14.2	-4.7
1932	-	-	-	-	-	-	-	-	-	-	13.4	-5.6	-	-	-	-	-	-	-	-	-	-	12.9	-3.7
1933	-	-	-	-	-	-	-	-	-	-	12.6	-2.3	-	-	-	-	-	-	-	-	-	-	12.9	2.4
1934	-	-	-	-	-	-	-	-	-	-	13.2	2.3	-	-	-	-	-	-	-	-	13.3	0.8	-	-
1935	-	-	-	-	13.6	2.3	-	-	-	-	-	-	13.7	0.7	-	-	-	-	13.7	0.0	-	-	-	-
1936	13.8	0.7	-	-	-	-	13.7	-0.7	-	-	-	-	13.9	1.5	-	-	14.1	1.4	-	-	-	-	13.9	-1.4
1937	-	-	-	-	14.2	2.2	-	-	-	-	14.3	0.7	-	-	-	-	14.5	1.4	-	-	-	-	14.3	-1.4
1938	-	-	-	-	14.0	-2.1	-	-	-	-	14.0	0.0	-	-	-	-	14.0	0.0	-	-	-	-	13.8	-1.4
1939	-	-	-	-	13.8	0.0	-	-	-	-	13.6	-1.4	-	-	-	-	14.0	2.9	-	-	-	-	13.8	-1.4
1940	-	-	-	-	13.8	0.0	-	-	-	-	13.8	0.0	-	-	-	-	13.9	0.7	13.9	0.0	13.9	0.0	14.1	1.4
1941	14.1	0.0	14.0	-0.7	14.1	0.7	14.2	0.7	14.2	0.0	14.5	2.1	14.5	0.0	14.6	0.7	15.0	2.7	15.1	0.7	15.3	1.3	15.4	0.7
1942	15.6	1.3	15.7	0.6	16.0	1.9	16.1	0.6	16.1	0.0	16.2	0.6	16.2	0.0	16.3	0.6	16.2	-0.6	16.4	1.2	16.5	0.6	16.7	1.2
1943	16.6	-0.6	16.7	0.6	16.9	1.2	17.1	1.2	17.3	1.2	17.2	-0.6	17.1	-0.6	17.1	0.0	17.1	0.0	17.1	0.0	17.1	0.0	17.1	0.0
1944	17.1	0.0	17.0	-0.6	17.1	0.6	17.2	0.6	17.3	0.6	17.3	0.0	17.5	1.2	17.4	-0.6	17.4	0.0	17.3	-0.6	17.4	0.6	17.4	0.0
1945	17.5	0.6	17.4	-0.6	17.4	0.0	17.4	0.0	17.6	1.1	17.7	0.6	17.7	0.0	17.7	0.0	17.6	-0.6	17.7	0.6	17.6	-0.6	17.9	1.7
1946	17.9	0.0	17.8	-0.6	17.9	0.6	18.0	0.6	18.0	0.0	18.3	1.7	19.5	6.6	19.9	2.1	19.9	0.0	20.4	2.5	21.0	2.9	21.1	0.5
1947	21.1	0.0	21.1	0.0	21.7	2.8	21.6	-0.5	21.5	-0.5	21.7	0.9	-	-	-	-	23.1	6.5	-	-	-	-	23.4	1.3
1948	-	-	-	-	23.4	0.0	-	-	-	-	24.0	2.6	-	-	-	-	24.4	1.7	-	-	-	-	23.9	-2.0
1949	-	-	-	-	23.6	-1.3	-	-	-	-	23.7	0.4	-	-	-	-	23.6	-0.4	-	-	-	-	23.4	-0.8
1950	-	-	-	-	23.4	0.0	-	-	-	-	23.5	0.4	-	-	-	-	24.2	3.0	-	-	-	-	24.9	2.9
1951	-	-	-	-	25.8	3.6	-	-	-	-	25.8	0.0	-	-	-	-	25.9	0.4	-	-	-	-	26.5	2.3
1952	-	-	-	-	26.5	0.0	-	-	-	-	26.8	1.1	-	-	-	-	26.8	0.0	-	-	-	-	26.7	-0.4
1953	-	-	-	-	26.6	-0.4	-	-	-	-	26.9	1.1	-	-	-	-	27.2	1.1	-	-	-	-	27.2	0.0
1954	-	-	-	-	27.2	0.0	-	-	-	-	27.3	0.4	-	-	-	-	26.9	-1.5	-	-	-	-	26.8	-0.4
1955	-	-	-	-	26.9	0.4	-	-	-	-	26.9	0.0	-	-	-	-	27.1	0.7	-	-	-	-	27.0	-0.4
1956	-	-	-	-	26.9	-0.4	-	-	-	-	27.2	1.1	-	-	-	-	27.4	0.7	-	-	-	-	27.7	1.1
1957	-	-	-	-	27.9	0.7	-	-	-	-	28.1	0.7	-	-	-	-	28.3	0.7	-	-	-	-	28.4	0.4
1958	-	-	-	-	28.9	1.8	-	-	-	-	28.9	0.0	-	-	-	-	29.1	0.7	-	-	-	-	29.2	0.3
1959	-	-	-	-	29.3	0.3	-	-	-	-	29.4	0.3	-	-	-	-	29.4	0.0	-	-	-	-	29.4	0.0
1960	-	-	-	-	29.4	0.0	-	-	-	-	29.6	0.7	-	-	-	-	29.6	0.0	-	-	-	-	29.7	0.3
1961	-	-	-	-	30.0	1.0	-	-	-	-	30.0	0.0	-	-	-	-	30.0	0.0	-	-	-	-	30.1	0.3
1962	-	-	-	-	30.2	0.3	-	-	-	-	30.1	-0.3	-	-	-	-	30.4	1.0	-	-	-	-	30.6	0.7

[Continued]

St. Louis, MO-IL
Consumer Price Index - All Urban Consumers
Base 1982-1984 = 100
All Items
[Continued]

For 1917-2001. Columns headed % show percentile change in the index from the previous period for which an index is available.

Year	Jan Index	%	Feb Index	%	Mar Index	%	Apr Index	%	May Index	%	Jun Index	%	Jul Index	%	Aug Index	%	Sep Index	%	Oct Index	%	Nov Index	%	Dec Index	%
1963	-	-	-	-	30.5	-0.3	-	-	-	-	30.4	-0.3	-	-	-	-	30.7	1.0	-	-	-	-	30.9	0.7
1964	-	-	-	-	31.0	0.3	-	-	-	-	31.0	0.0	-	-	-	-	31.3	1.0	-	-	-	-	31.4	0.3
1965	-	-	-	-	31.4	0.0	-	-	-	-	31.7	1.0	-	-	-	-	31.7	0.0	-	-	-	-	32.2	1.6
1966	-	-	-	-	32.3	0.3	-	-	-	-	32.8	1.5	-	-	-	-	33.1	0.9	-	-	-	-	33.1	0.0
1967	-	-	-	-	33.3	0.6	-	-	-	-	33.6	0.9	-	-	-	-	33.9	0.9	-	-	-	-	34.3	1.2
1968	-	-	-	-	34.6	0.9	-	-	-	-	35.0	1.2	-	-	-	-	35.4	1.1	-	-	-	-	35.6	0.6
1969	-	-	-	-	36.2	1.7	-	-	-	-	36.6	1.1	-	-	-	-	37.2	1.6	-	-	-	-	37.7	1.3
1970	-	-	-	-	38.2	1.3	-	-	-	-	38.7	1.3	-	-	-	-	39.3	1.6	-	-	-	-	39.6	0.8
1971	-	-	-	-	39.8	0.5	-	-	-	-	40.4	1.5	-	-	-	-	40.6	0.5	-	-	-	-	40.7	0.2
1972	-	-	-	-	40.7	0.0	-	-	-	-	41.0	0.7	-	-	-	-	41.6	1.5	-	-	-	-	41.6	0.0
1973	-	-	-	-	42.5	2.2	-	-	-	-	43.1	1.4	-	-	-	-	44.5	3.2	-	-	-	-	45.0	1.1
1974	-	-	-	-	46.5	3.3	-	-	-	-	47.5	2.2	-	-	-	-	49.1	3.4	-	-	-	-	50.0	1.8
1975	-	-	-	-	51.3	2.6	-	-	-	-	52.8	2.9	-	-	-	-	53.5	1.3	-	-	-	-	54.0	0.9
1976	-	-	-	-	54.8	1.5	-	-	-	-	55.6	1.5	-	-	-	-	56.3	1.3	-	-	-	-	56.6	0.5
1977	-	-	-	-	58.3	3.0	-	-	-	-	59.7	2.4	-	-	-	-	60.4	1.2	-	-	-	-	60.8	0.7
1978	-	-	-	-	61.9	1.8	-	-	63.8	3.1	-	-	65.0	1.9	-	-	66.0	1.5	-	-	67.1	1.7	-	-
1979	68.5	2.1	-	-	70.2	2.5	-	-	71.1	1.3	-	-	73.0	2.7	-	-	74.8	2.5	-	-	76.0	1.6	-	-
1980	78.3	3.0	-	-	80.2	2.4	-	-	81.4	1.5	-	-	82.5	1.4	-	-	85.0	3.0	-	-	85.4	0.5	-	-
1981	86.1	0.8	-	-	87.3	1.4	-	-	90.2	3.3	-	-	90.7	0.6	-	-	92.0	1.4	-	-	92.2	0.2	-	-
1982	93.7	1.6	-	-	94.5	0.9	-	-	96.2	1.8	-	-	97.7	1.6	-	-	99.0	1.3	-	-	97.6	-1.4	-	-
1983	98.0	0.4	-	-	98.7	0.7	-	-	99.5	0.8	-	-	100.8	1.3	-	-	101.7	0.9	-	-	100.9	-0.8	-	-
1984	101.3	0.4	-	-	101.9	0.6	-	-	102.8	0.9	-	-	103.9	1.1	-	-	104.8	0.9	-	-	104.1	-0.7	-	-
1985	105.5	1.3	-	-	105.8	0.3	-	-	106.4	0.6	-	-	107.7	1.2	-	-	108.3	0.6	-	-	108.3	0.0	-	-
1986	108.5	0.2	-	-	107.5	-0.9	-	-	107.3	-0.2	-	-	109.6	2.1	-	-	109.7	0.1	-	-	109.0	-0.6	-	-
1987	110.0	0.9	-	-	110.7	0.6	-	-	111.3	0.5	-	-	112.7	1.3	-	-	114.3	1.4	-	-	113.1	-1.0	-	-
1988	113.4	0.3	-	-	114.2	0.7	-	-	114.1	-0.1	-	-	116.0	1.7	-	-	117.3	1.1	-	-	118.3	0.9	-	-
1989	118.4	0.1	-	-	119.4	0.8	-	-	121.5	1.8	-	-	123.1	1.3	-	-	123.9	0.6	-	-	123.1	-0.6	-	-
1990	125.1	1.6	-	-	127.2	1.7	-	-	126.7	-0.4	-	-	128.0	1.0	-	-	129.9	1.5	-	-	130.4	0.4	-	-
1991	131.0	0.5	-	-	130.7	-0.2	-	-	131.3	0.5	-	-	132.7	1.1	-	-	133.5	0.6	-	-	133.2	-0.2	-	-
1992	132.5	-0.5	-	-	132.6	0.1	-	-	134.0	1.1	-	-	135.7	1.3	-	-	136.6	0.7	-	-	136.0	-0.4	-	-
1993	135.9	-0.1	-	-	136.1	0.1	-	-	136.8	0.5	-	-	138.8	1.5	-	-	138.4	-0.3	-	-	138.1	-0.2	-	-
1994	138.6	0.4	-	-	139.7	0.8	-	-	140.0	0.2	-	-	141.9	1.4	-	-	143.4	1.1	-	-	143.3	-0.1	-	-
1995	142.9	-0.3	-	-	144.5	1.1	-	-	144.6	0.1	-	-	145.6	0.7	-	-	147.1	1.0	-	-	145.7	-1.0	-	-
1996	147.2	1.0	-	-	148.9	1.2	-	-	148.1	-0.5	-	-	149.9	1.2	-	-	151.0	0.7	-	-	151.4	0.3	-	-
1997	151.5	0.1	-	-	152.2	0.5	-	-	152.1	-0.1	-	-	153.3	0.8	-	-	155.1	1.2	-	-	152.9	-1.4	-	-
1998	-	-	-	-	-	-	-	-	-	-	154.0	0.7	-	-	-	-	-	-	-	-	-	-	155.0	0.6
1999	-	-	-	-	-	-	-	-	-	-	156.4	0.9	-	-	-	-	-	-	-	-	-	-	158.8	1.5
2000	-	-	-	-	-	-	-	-	-	-	162.1	2.1	-	-	-	-	-	-	-	-	-	-	164.0	1.2
2001	-	-	-	-	-	-	-	-	-	-	167.5	2.1	-	-	-	-	-	-	-	-	-	-	-	-

Source: U.S. Department of Labor, Bureau of Labor Statistics, Division of Consumer Prices and Price Indexes. - indicates no data collected for period.

St. Louis, MO-IL
Consumer Price Index - Urban Wage Earners
Base 1982-1984 = 100
All Items

For 1917-2001. Columns headed % show percentile change in the index from the previous period for which an index is available.

Year	Jan Index	%	Feb Index	%	Mar Index	%	Apr Index	%	May Index	%	Jun Index	%	Jul Index	%	Aug Index	%	Sep Index	%	Oct Index	%	Nov Index	%	Dec Index	%
1917	-		-		-		-		-		-		-		-		-		-		-		13.9	
1918	-		-		-		-		-		-		-		-		-		-		-		16.2	16.5
1919	-		-		-		-		-		16.4	1.2	-		-		-		-		-		18.6	13.4
1920	-		-		-		-		-		21.3	14.5	-		-		-		-		-		18.9	-11.3
1921	-		-		-		-		17.4	-7.9	-		-		-		17.4	0.0	-		-		16.9	-2.9
1922	-		-		16.5	-2.4	-		-		16.6	0.6	-		-		16.3	-1.8	-		-		16.5	1.2
1923	-		-		16.6	0.6	-		-		16.7	0.6	-		-		17.1	2.4	-		-		17.0	-0.6
1924	-		-		16.9	-0.6	-		-		16.9	0.0	-		-		16.9	0.0	-		-		17.1	1.2
1925	-		-		-		-		-		17.5	2.3	-		-		-		-		-		17.9	2.3
1926	-		-		-		-		-		17.8	-0.6	-		-		-		-		-		17.7	-0.6
1927	-		-		-		-		-		17.8	0.6	-		-		-		-		-		17.2	-3.4
1928	-		-		-		-		-		17.1	-0.6	-		-		-		-		-		17.1	0.0
1929	-		-		-		-		-		17.2	0.6	-		-		-		-		-		17.4	1.2
1930	-		-		-		-		-		17.0	-2.3	-		-		-		-		-		16.1	-5.3
1931	-		-		-		-		-		15.1	-6.2	-		-		-		-		-		14.3	-5.3
1932	-		-		-		-		-		13.5	-5.6	-		-		-		-		-		13.0	-3.7
1933	-		-		-		-		-		12.7	-2.3	-		-		-		-		-		13.1	3.1
1934	-		-		-		-		-		13.4	2.3	-		-		-		-		13.5	0.7	-	
1935	-		-		13.8	2.2	-		-		-		13.8	0.0	-		-		13.8	0.0	-		-	
1936	14.0	1.4	-		-		13.8	-1.4	-		-		14.0	1.4	-		14.2	1.4	-		-		14.0	-1.4
1937	-		-		14.3	2.1	-		-		14.5	1.4	-		-		14.6	0.7	-		-		14.4	-1.4
1938	-		-		14.1	-2.1	-		-		14.1	0.0	-		-		14.1	0.0	-		-		14.0	-0.7
1939	-		-		13.9	-0.7	-		-		13.7	-1.4	-		-		14.1	2.9	-		-		13.9	-1.4
1940	-		-		13.9	0.0	-		-		14.0	0.7	-		-		14.0	0.0	14.1	0.7	14.0	-0.7	14.2	1.4
1941	14.2	0.0	14.2	0.0	14.2	0.0	14.3	0.7	14.3	0.0	14.6	2.1	14.7	0.7	14.8	0.7	15.2	2.7	15.3	0.7	15.4	0.7	15.5	0.6
1942	15.7	1.3	15.9	1.3	16.1	1.3	16.2	0.6	16.2	0.0	16.4	1.2	16.3	-0.6	16.5	1.2	16.4	-0.6	16.6	1.2	16.6	0.0	16.9	1.8
1943	16.8	-0.6	16.9	0.6	17.1	1.2	17.3	1.2	17.4	0.6	17.4	0.0	17.3	-0.6	17.3	0.0	17.2	-0.6	17.3	0.6	17.3	0.0	17.3	0.0
1944	17.3	0.0	17.2	-0.6	17.2	0.0	17.4	1.2	17.4	0.0	17.5	0.6	17.7	1.1	17.6	-0.6	17.6	0.0	17.5	-0.6	17.6	0.6	17.6	0.0
1945	17.7	0.6	17.6	-0.6	17.6	0.0	17.6	0.0	17.8	1.1	17.9	0.6	17.9	0.0	17.9	0.0	17.8	-0.6	17.8	0.0	17.8	0.0	18.0	1.1
1946	18.1	0.6	18.0	-0.6	18.0	0.0	18.2	1.1	18.2	0.0	18.5	1.6	19.6	5.9	20.1	2.6	20.1	0.0	20.6	2.5	21.2	2.9	21.3	0.5
1947	21.3	0.0	21.3	0.0	21.9	2.8	21.8	-0.5	21.8	0.0	21.9	0.5	-		-		23.3	6.4	-		-		23.6	1.3
1948	-		-		23.6	0.0	-		-		24.2	2.5	-		-		24.6	1.7	-		-		24.1	-2.0
1949	-		-		23.8	-1.2	-		-		23.9	0.4	-		-		23.8	-0.4	-		-		23.6	-0.8
1950	-		-		23.6	0.0	-		-		23.7	0.4	-		-		24.4	3.0	-		-		25.1	2.9
1951	-		-		26.0	3.6	-		-		26.0	0.0	-		-		26.2	0.8	-		-		26.8	2.3
1952	-		-		26.8	0.0	-		-		27.1	1.1	-		-		27.1	0.0	-		-		27.0	-0.4
1953	-		-		26.9	-0.4	-		-		27.2	1.1	-		-		27.5	1.1	-		-		27.4	-0.4
1954	-		-		27.4	0.0	-		-		27.5	0.4	-		-		27.1	-1.5	-		-		27.1	0.0
1955	-		-		27.1	0.0	-		-		27.2	0.4	-		-		27.3	0.4	-		-		27.2	-0.4
1956	-		-		27.1	-0.4	-		-		27.4	1.1	-		-		27.7	1.1	-		-		27.9	0.7
1957	-		-		28.2	1.1	-		-		28.4	0.7	-		-		28.6	0.7	-		-		28.7	0.3
1958	-		-		29.2	1.7	-		-		29.2	0.0	-		-		29.4	0.7	-		-		29.5	0.3
1959	-		-		29.5	0.0	-		-		29.6	0.3	-		-		29.6	0.0	-		-		29.7	0.3
1960	-		-		29.6	-0.3	-		-		29.8	0.7	-		-		29.9	0.3	-		-		30.0	0.3
1961	-		-		30.3	1.0	-		-		30.3	0.0	-		-		30.3	0.0	-		-		30.4	0.3
1962	-		-		30.5	0.3	-		-		30.4	-0.3	-		-		30.7	1.0	-		-		30.9	0.7

[Continued]

St. Louis, MO-IL
Consumer Price Index - Urban Wage Earners
Base 1982-1984 = 100
All Items
[Continued]

For 1917-2001. Columns headed % show percentile change in the index from the previous period for which an index is available.

Year	Jan Index	%	Feb Index	%	Mar Index	%	Apr Index	%	May Index	%	Jun Index	%	Jul Index	%	Aug Index	%	Sep Index	%	Oct Index	%	Nov Index	%	Dec Index	%
1963	-		-		30.8	-0.3	-		-		30.7	-0.3	-		-		31.0	1.0	-		-		31.2	0.6
1964	-		-		31.3	0.3	-		-		31.3	0.0	-		-		31.6	1.0	-		-		31.7	0.3
1965	-		-		31.7	0.0	-		-		32.1	1.3	-		-		32.0	-0.3	-		-		32.5	1.6
1966	-		-		32.6	0.3	-		-		33.1	1.5	-		-		33.4	0.9	-		-		33.4	0.0
1967	-		-		33.6	0.6	-		-		33.9	0.9	-		-		34.3	1.2	-		-		34.6	0.9
1968	-		-		35.0	1.2	-		-		35.3	0.9	-		-		35.7	1.1	-		-		35.9	0.6
1969	-		-		36.5	1.7	-		-		36.9	1.1	-		-		37.6	1.9	-		-		38.0	1.1
1970	-		-		38.5	1.3	-		-		39.0	1.3	-		-		39.6	1.5	-		-		40.0	1.0
1971	-		-		40.2	0.5	-		-		40.8	1.5	-		-		41.0	0.5	-		-		41.1	0.2
1972	-		-		41.1	0.0	-		-		41.4	0.7	-		-		42.0	1.4	-		-		42.0	0.0
1973	-		-		42.9	2.1	-		-		43.5	1.4	-		-		45.0	3.4	-		-		45.5	1.1
1974	-		-		47.0	3.3	-		-		48.0	2.1	-		-		49.6	3.3	-		-		50.5	1.8
1975	-		-		51.8	2.6	-		-		53.3	2.9	-		-		54.0	1.3	-		-		54.5	0.9
1976	-		-		55.3	1.5	-		-		56.2	1.6	-		-		56.8	1.1	-		-		57.2	0.7
1977	-		-		58.9	3.0	-		-		60.3	2.4	-		-		60.9	1.0	-		-		61.4	0.8
1978	-		-		62.5	1.8	-		63.9	2.2	-		64.9	1.6	-		66.2	2.0	-		67.2	1.5	-	
1979	68.5	1.9	-		70.4	2.8	-		71.5	1.6	-		73.9	3.4	-		75.6	2.3	-		76.9	1.7	-	
1980	79.4	3.3	-		81.1	2.1	-		82.5	1.7	-		83.6	1.3	-		85.9	2.8	-		86.4	0.6	-	
1981	87.0	0.7	-		88.2	1.4	-		91.2	3.4	-		91.5	0.3	-		92.8	1.4	-		92.8	0.0	-	
1982	94.2	1.5	-		94.9	0.7	-		96.7	1.9	-		98.3	1.7	-		99.6	1.3	-		98.2	-1.4	-	
1983	97.0	-1.2	-		99.7	2.8	-		99.9	0.2	-		100.8	0.9	-		101.7	0.9	-		101.7	0.0	-	
1984	100.9	-0.8	-		101.1	0.2	-		101.1	0.0	-		102.4	1.3	-		104.7	2.2	-		104.4	-0.3	-	
1985	105.5	1.1	-		105.7	0.2	-		106.4	0.7	-		107.6	1.1	-		108.3	0.7	-		108.3	0.0	-	
1986	108.5	0.2	-		107.1	-1.3	-		106.8	-0.3	-		109.0	2.1	-		109.0	0.0	-		108.4	-0.6	-	
1987	109.4	0.9	-		110.2	0.7	-		110.9	0.6	-		112.5	1.4	-		114.1	1.4	-		112.7	-1.2	-	
1988	113.0	0.3	-		113.8	0.7	-		113.7	-0.1	-		115.7	1.8	-		117.1	1.2	-		117.8	0.6	-	
1989	118.0	0.2	-		119.1	0.9	-		121.2	1.8	-		122.8	1.3	-		123.5	0.6	-		122.6	-0.7	-	
1990	124.6	1.6	-		126.5	1.5	-		126.0	-0.4	-		127.3	1.0	-		129.3	1.6	-		129.9	0.5	-	
1991	130.3	0.3	-		130.1	-0.2	-		130.6	0.4	-		132.0	1.1	-		133.0	0.8	-		132.7	-0.2	-	
1992	132.0	-0.5	-		132.0	0.0	-		133.6	1.2	-		135.4	1.3	-		136.5	0.8	-		135.6	-0.7	-	
1993	135.4	-0.1	-		135.5	0.1	-		136.4	0.7	-		138.3	1.4	-		137.6	-0.5	-		137.5	-0.1	-	
1994	137.7	0.1	-		138.7	0.7	-		139.2	0.4	-		141.4	1.6	-		143.0	1.1	-		142.9	-0.1	-	
1995	142.3	-0.4	-		143.9	1.1	-		144.2	0.2	-		145.2	0.7	-		146.5	0.9	-		145.0	-1.0	-	
1996	146.5	1.0	-		148.0	1.0	-		147.4	-0.4	-		149.0	1.1	-		150.1	0.7	-		150.5	0.3	-	
1997	150.6	0.1	-		151.1	0.3	-		151.2	0.1	-		152.5	0.9	-		154.0	1.0	-		151.9	-1.4	-	
1998	-		-		-		-		-		152.5	0.4	-		-		-		-		-		153.6	0.7
1999	-		-		-		-		-		155.0	0.9	-		-		-		-		-		157.7	1.7
2000	-		-		-		-		-		161.1	2.2	-		-		-		-		-		163.2	1.3
2001	-		-		-		-		-		166.6	2.1	-		-		-		-		-		-	

Source: U.S. Department of Labor, Bureau of Labor Statistics, Division of Consumer Prices and Price Indexes. - indicates no data collected for period.

St. Louis, MO-IL
Consumer Price Index - All Urban Consumers
Base 1982-1984 = 100
Food and Beverages

For 1975-2001. Columns headed % show percentile change in the index from the previous period for which an index is available.

Year	Jan Index	%	Feb Index	%	Mar Index	%	Apr Index	%	May Index	%	Jun Index	%	Jul Index	%	Aug Index	%	Sep Index	%	Oct Index	%	Nov Index	%	Dec Index	%
1975	-	-	-	-	-	-	-	-	-	-	-	-	-	-	-	-	-	-	-	-	-	-	62.0	-
1976	-	-	-	-	61.8	-0.3	-	-	-	-	62.6	1.3	-	-	-	-	62.9	0.5	-	-	-	-	62.8	-0.2
1977	-	-	-	-	65.4	4.1	-	-	-	-	67.9	3.8	-	-	-	-	67.9	0.0	-	-	-	-	67.8	-0.1
1978	-	-	-	-	70.1	3.4	-	-	72.6	3.6	-	-	74.2	2.2	-	-	74.2	0.0	-	-	74.6	0.5	-	-
1979	77.6	4.0	-	-	79.5	2.4	-	-	81.3	2.3	-	-	82.4	1.4	-	-	82.1	-0.4	-	-	81.7	-0.5	-	-
1980	83.7	2.4	-	-	84.1	0.5	-	-	85.3	1.4	-	-	86.9	1.9	-	-	89.9	3.5	-	-	90.8	1.0	-	-
1981	91.2	0.4	-	-	92.3	1.2	-	-	92.7	0.4	-	-	94.2	1.6	-	-	94.6	0.4	-	-	94.8	0.2	-	-
1982	95.5	0.7	-	-	95.7	0.2	-	-	96.7	1.0	-	-	98.0	1.3	-	-	98.1	0.1	-	-	98.1	0.0	-	-
1983	98.2	0.1	-	-	99.5	1.3	-	-	99.8	0.3	-	-	99.7	-0.1	-	-	100.2	0.5	-	-	100.0	-0.2	-	-
1984	101.3	1.3	-	-	102.3	1.0	-	-	102.2	-0.1	-	-	103.8	1.6	-	-	104.3	0.5	-	-	104.3	0.0	-	-
1985	105.0	0.7	-	-	106.1	1.0	-	-	105.0	-1.0	-	-	105.4	0.4	-	-	106.7	1.2	-	-	105.7	-0.9	-	-
1986	107.3	1.5	-	-	107.6	0.3	-	-	108.1	0.5	-	-	110.0	1.8	-	-	111.9	1.7	-	-	112.1	0.2	-	-
1987	113.4	1.2	-	-	113.7	0.3	-	-	114.1	0.4	-	-	114.2	0.1	-	-	115.0	0.7	-	-	113.3	-1.5	-	-
1988	113.9	0.5	-	-	114.3	0.4	-	-	115.8	1.3	-	-	118.3	2.2	-	-	120.5	1.9	-	-	121.8	1.1	-	-
1989	121.3	-0.4	-	-	124.4	2.6	-	-	125.4	0.8	-	-	125.3	-0.1	-	-	127.2	1.5	-	-	128.4	0.9	-	-
1990	132.8	3.4	-	-	133.6	0.6	-	-	134.0	0.3	-	-	134.2	0.1	-	-	135.3	0.8	-	-	137.6	1.7	-	-
1991	139.8	1.6	-	-	139.1	-0.5	-	-	139.4	0.2	-	-	139.5	0.1	-	-	139.6	0.1	-	-	140.4	0.6	-	-
1992	140.5	0.1	-	-	139.2	-0.9	-	-	140.6	1.0	-	-	139.7	-0.6	-	-	139.9	0.1	-	-	140.8	0.6	-	-
1993	139.8	-0.7	-	-	138.9	-0.6	-	-	138.8	-0.1	-	-	140.0	0.9	-	-	140.9	0.6	-	-	141.1	0.1	-	-
1994	143.9	2.0	-	-	143.6	-0.2	-	-	143.6	0.0	-	-	143.6	0.0	-	-	143.8	0.1	-	-	145.2	1.0	-	-
1995	145.7	0.3	-	-	145.7	0.0	-	-	147.5	1.2	-	-	146.3	-0.8	-	-	147.2	0.6	-	-	148.3	0.7	-	-
1996	149.8	1.0	-	-	150.2	0.3	-	-	150.3	0.1	-	-	151.4	0.7	-	-	151.3	-0.1	-	-	153.6	1.5	-	-
1997	153.6	0.0	-	-	153.9	0.2	-	-	154.3	0.3	-	-	155.8	1.0	-	-	156.7	0.6	-	-	154.7	-1.3	-	-
1998	-	-	-	-	-	-	-	-	-	-	158.4	2.4	-	-	-	-	-	-	-	-	-	-	158.4	0.0
1999	-	-	-	-	-	-	-	-	-	-	161.0	1.6	-	-	-	-	-	-	-	-	-	-	162.9	1.2
2000	-	-	-	-	-	-	-	-	-	-	166.5	2.2	-	-	-	-	-	-	-	-	-	-	167.1	0.4
2001	-	-	-	-	-	-	-	-	-	-	168.5	0.8	-	-	-	-	-	-	-	-	-	-	-	-

Source: U.S. Department of Labor, Bureau of Labor Statistics, Division of Consumer Prices and Price Indexes. - indicates no data collected for period.

St. Louis, MO-IL
Consumer Price Index - Urban Wage Earners
Base 1982-1984 = 100
Food and Beverages

For 1975-2001. Columns headed % show percentile change in the index from the previous period for which an index is available.

Year	Jan Index	%	Feb Index	%	Mar Index	%	Apr Index	%	May Index	%	Jun Index	%	Jul Index	%	Aug Index	%	Sep Index	%	Oct Index	%	Nov Index	%	Dec Index	%
1975	-	-	-	-	-	-	-	-	-	-	-	-	-	-	-	-	-	-	-	-	-	-	62.0	-
1976	-	-	-	-	61.8	-0.3	-	-	-	-	62.6	1.3	-	-	-	-	62.9	0.5	-	-	-	-	62.8	-0.2
1977	-	-	-	-	65.4	4.1	-	-	-	-	67.9	3.8	-	-	-	-	67.9	0.0	-	-	-	-	67.8	-0.1
1978	-	-	-	-	70.1	3.4	-	-	72.3	3.1	-	-	73.1	1.1	-	-	74.2	1.5	-	-	74.5	0.4	-	-
1979	77.3	3.8	-	-	79.7	3.1	-	-	80.8	1.4	-	-	83.0	2.7	-	-	83.3	0.4	-	-	83.1	-0.2	-	-
1980	84.7	1.9	-	-	84.5	-0.2	-	-	85.0	0.6	-	-	87.2	2.6	-	-	90.5	3.8	-	-	91.1	0.7	-	-
1981	91.6	0.5	-	-	92.3	0.8	-	-	93.0	0.8	-	-	94.2	1.3	-	-	95.0	0.8	-	-	94.9	-0.1	-	-
1982	95.3	0.4	-	-	95.7	0.4	-	-	96.6	0.9	-	-	97.9	1.3	-	-	98.1	0.2	-	-	98.1	0.0	-	-
1983	98.3	0.2	-	-	99.6	1.3	-	-	99.9	0.3	-	-	99.8	-0.1	-	-	100.4	0.6	-	-	100.1	-0.3	-	-
1984	101.2	1.1	-	-	102.3	1.1	-	-	102.2	-0.1	-	-	103.8	1.6	-	-	104.2	0.4	-	-	104.3	0.1	-	-
1985	104.9	0.6	-	-	105.9	1.0	-	-	104.9	-0.9	-	-	105.3	0.4	-	-	106.5	1.1	-	-	105.6	-0.8	-	-
1986	107.1	1.4	-	-	107.6	0.5	-	-	108.1	0.5	-	-	109.9	1.7	-	-	112.0	1.9	-	-	112.2	0.2	-	-
1987	113.6	1.2	-	-	113.8	0.2	-	-	114.0	0.2	-	-	114.2	0.2	-	-	115.1	0.8	-	-	113.5	-1.4	-	-
1988	114.0	0.4	-	-	114.5	0.4	-	-	115.7	1.0	-	-	118.3	2.2	-	-	120.5	1.9	-	-	121.9	1.2	-	-
1989	121.2	-0.6	-	-	124.3	2.6	-	-	125.3	0.8	-	-	125.3	0.0	-	-	127.3	1.6	-	-	128.6	1.0	-	-
1990	132.6	3.1	-	-	133.6	0.8	-	-	134.1	0.4	-	-	134.3	0.1	-	-	135.3	0.7	-	-	137.4	1.6	-	-
1991	139.6	1.6	-	-	139.1	-0.4	-	-	139.3	0.1	-	-	139.5	0.1	-	-	139.8	0.2	-	-	140.3	0.4	-	-
1992	140.5	0.1	-	-	139.3	-0.9	-	-	140.6	0.9	-	-	140.0	-0.4	-	-	140.1	0.1	-	-	140.8	0.5	-	-
1993	140.0	-0.6	-	-	139.1	-0.6	-	-	139.1	0.0	-	-	140.3	0.9	-	-	141.1	0.6	-	-	141.3	0.1	-	-
1994	143.9	1.8	-	-	143.9	0.0	-	-	144.1	0.1	-	-	144.1	0.0	-	-	144.2	0.1	-	-	145.4	0.8	-	-
1995	145.7	0.2	-	-	145.9	0.1	-	-	147.7	1.2	-	-	146.4	-0.9	-	-	147.2	0.5	-	-	148.1	0.6	-	-
1996	149.6	1.0	-	-	149.9	0.2	-	-	150.3	0.3	-	-	151.2	0.6	-	-	151.2	0.0	-	-	153.4	1.5	-	-
1997	153.7	0.2	-	-	154.1	0.3	-	-	154.5	0.3	-	-	156.1	1.0	-	-	156.7	0.4	-	-	155.0	-1.1	-	-
1998	-	-	-	-	-	-	-	-	-	-	158.3	2.1	-	-	-	-	-	-	-	-	-	-	158.6	0.2
1999	-	-	-	-	-	-	-	-	-	-	160.9	1.5	-	-	-	-	-	-	-	-	-	-	163.0	1.3
2000	-	-	-	-	-	-	-	-	-	-	166.4	2.1	-	-	-	-	-	-	-	-	-	-	167.2	0.5
2001	-	-	-	-	-	-	-	-	-	-	168.5	0.8	-	-	-	-	-	-	-	-	-	-	-	-

Source: U.S. Department of Labor, Bureau of Labor Statistics, Division of Consumer Prices and Price Indexes. - indicates no data collected for period.

St. Louis, MO-IL
Consumer Price Index - All Urban Consumers
Base 1982-1984 = 100
Housing

For 1975-2001. Columns headed % show percentile change in the index from the previous period for which an index is available.

Year	Jan Index	%	Feb Index	%	Mar Index	%	Apr Index	%	May Index	%	Jun Index	%	Jul Index	%	Aug Index	%	Sep Index	%	Oct Index	%	Nov Index	%	Dec Index	%
1975	-	-	-	-	-	-	-	-	-	-	-	-	-	-	-	-	-	-	-	-	-	-	48.7	-
1976	-	-	-	-	50.1	2.9	-	-	-	-	50.5	0.8	-	-	-	-	51.1	1.2	-	-	-	-	51.3	0.4
1977	-	-	-	-	52.8	2.9	-	-	-	-	53.9	2.1	-	-	-	-	55.1	2.2	-	-	-	-	55.7	1.1
1978	-	-	-	-	56.9	2.2	-	-	58.5	2.8	-	-	59.6	1.9	-	-	61.0	2.3	-	-	62.3	2.1	-	-
1979	63.7	2.2	-	-	65.4	2.7	-	-	65.3	-0.2	-	-	67.4	3.2	-	-	70.6	4.7	-	-	72.2	2.3	-	-
1980	75.4	4.4	-	-	77.2	2.4	-	-	78.4	1.6	-	-	79.7	1.7	-	-	83.1	4.3	-	-	82.9	-0.2	-	-
1981	82.6	-0.4	-	-	83.1	0.6	-	-	88.7	6.7	-	-	88.7	0.0	-	-	90.5	2.0	-	-	89.4	-1.2	-	-
1982	92.4	3.4	-	-	94.3	2.1	-	-	96.9	2.8	-	-	98.0	1.1	-	-	100.5	2.6	-	-	97.1	-3.4	-	-
1983	97.8	0.7	-	-	98.9	1.1	-	-	99.3	0.4	-	-	102.0	2.7	-	-	103.0	1.0	-	-	100.6	-2.3	-	-
1984	101.3	0.7	-	-	100.9	-0.4	-	-	102.7	1.8	-	-	104.4	1.7	-	-	104.8	0.4	-	-	101.9	-2.8	-	-
1985	106.2	4.2	-	-	105.2	-0.9	-	-	105.9	0.7	-	-	109.5	3.4	-	-	110.0	0.5	-	-	109.4	-0.5	-	-
1986	109.3	-0.1	-	-	108.5	-0.7	-	-	108.2	-0.3	-	-	114.2	5.5	-	-	112.9	-1.1	-	-	108.8	-3.6	-	-
1987	109.9	1.0	-	-	110.3	0.4	-	-	110.8	0.5	-	-	114.1	3.0	-	-	114.5	0.4	-	-	112.3	-1.9	-	-
1988	112.8	0.4	-	-	113.7	0.8	-	-	112.8	-0.8	-	-	115.8	2.7	-	-	116.1	0.3	-	-	117.1	0.9	-	-
1989	117.8	0.6	-	-	117.2	-0.5	-	-	118.4	1.0	-	-	122.5	3.5	-	-	124.3	1.5	-	-	120.6	-3.0	-	-
1990	121.6	0.8	-	-	124.5	2.4	-	-	123.9	-0.5	-	-	126.4	2.0	-	-	126.4	0.0	-	-	125.6	-0.6	-	-
1991	125.6	0.0	-	-	126.4	0.6	-	-	127.1	0.6	-	-	129.8	2.1	-	-	129.5	-0.2	-	-	127.4	-1.6	-	-
1992	126.5	-0.7	-	-	126.8	0.2	-	-	128.0	0.9	-	-	132.1	3.2	-	-	133.1	0.8	-	-	130.4	-2.0	-	-
1993	131.0	0.5	-	-	131.3	0.2	-	-	131.1	-0.2	-	-	135.4	3.3	-	-	135.6	0.1	-	-	132.7	-2.1	-	-
1994	133.8	0.8	-	-	135.7	1.4	-	-	135.2	-0.4	-	-	138.8	2.7	-	-	139.0	0.1	-	-	137.0	-1.4	-	-
1995	137.0	0.0	-	-	138.9	1.4	-	-	137.3	-1.2	-	-	141.1	2.8	-	-	142.1	0.7	-	-	139.7	-1.7	-	-
1996	140.2	0.4	-	-	141.8	1.1	-	-	140.1	-1.2	-	-	144.4	3.1	-	-	144.9	0.3	-	-	143.1	-1.2	-	-
1997	-	-	-	-	-	-	-	-	-	-	144.6	1.0	-	-	-	-	-	-	-	-	-	-	146.3	1.2
1998	-	-	-	-	-	-	-	-	-	-	145.8	-0.3	-	-	-	-	-	-	-	-	-	-	148.1	1.6
1999	-	-	-	-	-	-	-	-	-	-	148.5	0.3	-	-	-	-	-	-	-	-	-	-	149.4	0.6
2000	-	-	-	-	-	-	-	-	-	-	152.9	2.3	-	-	-	-	-	-	-	-	-	-	157.0	2.7
2001	-	-	-	-	-	-	-	-	-	-	161.8	3.1	-	-	-	-	-	-	-	-	-	-	-	-

Source: U.S. Department of Labor, Bureau of Labor Statistics, Division of Consumer Prices and Price Indexes. - indicates no data collected for period.

St. Louis, MO-IL
Consumer Price Index - Urban Wage Earners
Base 1982-1984 = 100
Housing

For 1975-2001. Columns headed % show percentile change in the index from the previous period for which an index is available.

Year	Jan Index	%	Feb Index	%	Mar Index	%	Apr Index	%	May Index	%	Jun Index	%	Jul Index	%	Aug Index	%	Sep Index	%	Oct Index	%	Nov Index	%	Dec Index	%
1975	-	-	-	-	-	-	-	-	-	-	-	-	-	-	-	-	-	-	-	-	-	-	49.1	-
1976	-	-	-	-	50.5	2.9	-	-	-	-	51.0	1.0	-	-	-	-	51.6	1.2	-	-	-	-	51.8	0.4
1977	-	-	-	-	53.3	2.9	-	-	-	-	54.3	1.9	-	-	-	-	55.6	2.4	-	-	-	-	56.2	1.1
1978	-	-	-	-	57.4	2.1	-	-	58.8	2.4	-	-	60.0	2.0	-	-	61.7	2.8	-	-	63.1	2.3	-	-
1979	64.2	1.7	-	-	66.2	3.1	-	-	66.4	0.3	-	-	68.6	3.3	-	-	71.5	4.2	-	-	73.3	2.5	-	-
1980	76.5	4.4	-	-	78.4	2.5	-	-	80.0	2.0	-	-	81.2	1.5	-	-	84.1	3.6	-	-	84.1	0.0	-	-
1981	83.5	-0.7	-	-	84.0	0.6	-	-	90.1	7.3	-	-	89.8	-0.3	-	-	91.8	2.2	-	-	90.4	-1.5	-	-
1982	93.5	3.4	-	-	95.4	2.0	-	-	98.1	2.8	-	-	99.2	1.1	-	-	101.9	2.7	-	-	98.3	-3.5	-	-
1983	95.6	-2.7	-	-	101.4	6.1	-	-	100.4	-1.0	-	-	101.6	1.2	-	-	102.3	0.7	-	-	102.6	0.3	-	-
1984	100.4	-2.1	-	-	99.4	-1.0	-	-	98.5	-0.9	-	-	100.6	2.1	-	-	104.4	3.8	-	-	103.2	-1.1	-	-
1985	107.4	4.1	-	-	106.3	-1.0	-	-	107.0	0.7	-	-	110.6	3.4	-	-	111.4	0.7	-	-	110.8	-0.5	-	-
1986	110.8	0.0	-	-	110.0	-0.7	-	-	109.7	-0.3	-	-	115.6	5.4	-	-	114.4	-1.0	-	-	110.4	-3.5	-	-
1987	111.7	1.2	-	-	112.1	0.4	-	-	112.5	0.4	-	-	116.2	3.3	-	-	116.4	0.2	-	-	113.8	-2.2	-	-
1988	114.4	0.5	-	-	115.3	0.8	-	-	114.3	-0.9	-	-	117.6	2.9	-	-	117.9	0.3	-	-	118.7	0.7	-	-
1989	119.4	0.6	-	-	118.9	-0.4	-	-	120.1	1.0	-	-	124.4	3.6	-	-	126.2	1.4	-	-	122.1	-3.2	-	-
1990	123.3	1.0	-	-	126.3	2.4	-	-	125.5	-0.6	-	-	128.4	2.3	-	-	128.5	0.1	-	-	127.5	-0.8	-	-
1991	127.4	-0.1	-	-	128.1	0.5	-	-	128.8	0.5	-	-	131.7	2.3	-	-	131.6	-0.1	-	-	129.3	-1.7	-	-
1992	128.5	-0.6	-	-	128.9	0.3	-	-	130.1	0.9	-	-	134.6	3.5	-	-	135.5	0.7	-	-	132.6	-2.1	-	-
1993	133.2	0.5	-	-	133.4	0.2	-	-	133.2	-0.1	-	-	137.9	3.5	-	-	137.9	0.0	-	-	134.8	-2.2	-	-
1994	136.0	0.9	-	-	137.8	1.3	-	-	137.4	-0.3	-	-	141.2	2.8	-	-	141.4	0.1	-	-	139.1	-1.6	-	-
1995	139.1	0.0	-	-	141.0	1.4	-	-	139.3	-1.2	-	-	143.4	2.9	-	-	144.2	0.6	-	-	141.6	-1.8	-	-
1996	142.4	0.6	-	-	143.7	0.9	-	-	142.1	-1.1	-	-	146.7	3.2	-	-	147.4	0.5	-	-	145.2	-1.5	-	-
1997	-	-	-	-	-	-	-	-	-	-	146.9	1.2	-	-	-	-	-	-	-	-	-	-	148.7	1.2
1998	-	-	-	-	-	-	-	-	-	-	147.7	-0.7	-	-	-	-	-	-	-	-	-	-	150.3	1.8
1999	-	-	-	-	-	-	-	-	-	-	150.3	0.0	-	-	-	-	-	-	-	-	-	-	151.1	0.5
2000	-	-	-	-	-	-	-	-	-	-	154.1	2.0	-	-	-	-	-	-	-	-	-	-	158.7	3.0
2001	-	-	-	-	-	-	-	-	-	-	163.4	3.0	-	-	-	-	-	-	-	-	-	-	-	-

Source: U.S. Department of Labor, Bureau of Labor Statistics, Division of Consumer Prices and Price Indexes. - indicates no data collected for period.

St. Louis, MO-IL
Consumer Price Index - All Urban Consumers
Base 1982-1984 = 100
Apparel

For 1952-2001. Columns headed % show percentile change in the index from the previous period for which an index is available.

Year	Jan Index	%	Feb Index	%	Mar Index	%	Apr Index	%	May Index	%	Jun Index	%	Jul Index	%	Aug Index	%	Sep Index	%	Oct Index	%	Nov Index	%	Dec Index	%
1952	-	-	-	-	-	-	-	-	-	-	-	-	-	-	-	-	-	-	-	-	-	-	43.8	-
1953	-	-	-	-	43.9	0.2	-	-	-	-	44.0	0.2	-	-	-	-	44.5	1.1	-	-	-	-	44.3	-0.4
1954	-	-	-	-	44.0	-0.7	-	-	-	-	44.1	0.2	-	-	-	-	43.9	-0.5	-	-	-	-	43.8	-0.2
1955	-	-	-	-	44.0	0.5	-	-	-	-	43.8	-0.5	-	-	-	-	43.9	0.2	-	-	-	-	44.1	0.5
1956	-	-	-	-	44.2	0.2	-	-	-	-	44.4	0.5	-	-	-	-	44.6	0.5	-	-	-	-	44.8	0.4
1957	-	-	-	-	45.0	0.4	-	-	-	-	44.8	-0.4	-	-	-	-	45.1	0.7	-	-	-	-	45.4	0.7
1958	-	-	-	-	45.9	1.1	-	-	-	-	45.7	-0.4	-	-	-	-	46.0	0.7	-	-	-	-	45.9	-0.2
1959	-	-	-	-	45.9	0.0	-	-	-	-	45.9	0.0	-	-	-	-	46.5	1.3	-	-	-	-	46.6	0.2
1960	-	-	-	-	46.8	0.4	-	-	-	-	46.9	0.2	-	-	-	-	47.5	1.3	-	-	-	-	47.5	0.0
1961	-	-	-	-	47.7	0.4	-	-	-	-	47.6	-0.2	-	-	-	-	47.6	0.0	-	-	-	-	47.4	-0.4
1962	-	-	-	-	47.5	0.2	-	-	-	-	47.6	0.2	-	-	-	-	47.8	0.4	-	-	-	-	47.5	-0.6
1963	-	-	-	-	47.6	0.2	-	-	-	-	48.0	0.8	-	-	-	-	48.3	0.6	-	-	-	-	48.7	0.8
1964	-	-	-	-	48.5	-0.4	-	-	-	-	48.5	0.0	-	-	-	-	48.8	0.6	-	-	-	-	48.9	0.2
1965	-	-	-	-	48.8	-0.2	-	-	-	-	48.9	0.2	-	-	-	-	49.6	1.4	-	-	-	-	49.7	0.2
1966	-	-	-	-	49.9	0.4	-	-	-	-	50.7	1.6	-	-	-	-	51.2	1.0	-	-	-	-	51.4	0.4
1967	-	-	-	-	52.1	1.4	-	-	-	-	52.2	0.2	-	-	-	-	52.6	0.8	-	-	-	-	53.4	1.5
1968	-	-	-	-	54.7	2.4	-	-	-	-	54.8	0.2	-	-	-	-	56.5	3.1	-	-	-	-	56.8	0.5
1969	-	-	-	-	57.5	1.2	-	-	-	-	57.9	0.7	-	-	-	-	58.8	1.6	-	-	-	-	59.1	0.5
1970	-	-	-	-	59.3	0.3	-	-	-	-	60.1	1.3	-	-	-	-	61.6	2.5	-	-	-	-	61.3	-0.5
1971	-	-	-	-	61.8	0.8	-	-	-	-	61.9	0.2	-	-	-	-	63.4	2.4	-	-	-	-	63.3	-0.2
1972	-	-	-	-	63.0	-0.5	-	-	-	-	62.6	-0.6	-	-	-	-	63.4	1.3	-	-	-	-	63.1	-0.5
1973	-	-	-	-	63.2	0.2	-	-	-	-	63.3	0.2	-	-	-	-	66.5	5.1	-	-	-	-	66.0	-0.8
1974	-	-	-	-	66.1	0.2	-	-	-	-	67.5	2.1	-	-	-	-	69.8	3.4	-	-	-	-	70.0	0.3
1975	-	-	-	-	70.2	0.3	-	-	-	-	70.6	0.6	-	-	-	-	71.3	1.0	-	-	-	-	72.0	1.0
1976	-	-	-	-	73.5	2.1	-	-	-	-	73.8	0.4	-	-	-	-	75.4	2.2	-	-	-	-	75.7	0.4
1977	-	-	-	-	78.8	4.1	-	-	-	-	79.0	0.3	-	-	-	-	80.0	1.3	-	-	-	-	80.9	1.1
1978	-	-	-	-	79.6	-1.6	-	-	78.0	-2.0	-	-	77.9	-0.1	-	-	80.6	3.5	-	-	84.1	4.3	-	-
1979	81.8	-2.7	-	-	87.3	6.7	-	-	85.4	-2.2	-	-	81.4	-4.7	-	-	86.9	6.8	-	-	87.5	0.7	-	-
1980	85.4	-2.4	-	-	92.0	7.7	-	-	92.9	1.0	-	-	91.0	-2.0	-	-	94.4	3.7	-	-	93.2	-1.3	-	-
1981	91.6	-1.7	-	-	96.2	5.0	-	-	94.1	-2.2	-	-	95.4	1.4	-	-	97.7	2.4	-	-	95.9	-1.8	-	-
1982	94.1	-1.9	-	-	99.2	5.4	-	-	97.5	-1.7	-	-	97.6	0.1	-	-	99.4	1.8	-	-	97.1	-2.3	-	-
1983	97.4	0.3	-	-	103.3	6.1	-	-	100.9	-2.3	-	-	100.5	-0.4	-	-	102.0	1.5	-	-	100.5	-1.5	-	-
1984	98.0	-2.5	-	-	102.5	4.6	-	-	100.0	-2.4	-	-	99.8	-0.2	-	-	105.3	5.5	-	-	103.8	-1.4	-	-
1985	99.6	-4.0	-	-	106.9	7.3	-	-	107.4	0.5	-	-	104.3	-2.9	-	-	105.2	0.9	-	-	103.9	-1.2	-	-
1986	98.0	-5.7	-	-	103.5	5.6	-	-	103.2	-0.3	-	-	99.2	-3.9	-	-	104.7	5.5	-	-	106.1	1.3	-	-
1987	102.0	-3.9	-	-	107.1	5.0	-	-	107.1	0.0	-	-	100.2	-6.4	-	-	114.6	14.4	-	-	113.1	-1.3	-	-
1988	109.1	-3.5	-	-	115.1	5.5	-	-	110.6	-3.9	-	-	107.4	-2.9	-	-	116.1	8.1	-	-	116.2	0.1	-	-
1989	111.5	-4.0	-	-	119.6	7.3	-	-	121.0	1.2	-	-	118.5	-2.1	-	-	119.3	0.7	-	-	119.0	-0.3	-	-
1990	118.7	-0.3	-	-	128.6	8.3	-	-	119.2	-7.3	-	-	116.7	-2.1	-	-	121.2	3.9	-	-	121.0	-0.2	-	-
1991	119.1	-1.6	-	-	124.6	4.6	-	-	121.4	-2.6	-	-	119.1	-1.9	-	-	125.8	5.6	-	-	124.6	-1.0	-	-
1992	121.4	-2.6	-	-	122.6	1.0	-	-	119.7	-2.4	-	-	118.0	-1.4	-	-	124.5	5.5	-	-	123.9	-0.5	-	-
1993	120.9	-2.4	-	-	122.8	1.6	-	-	126.0	2.6	-	-	122.6	-2.7	-	-	121.2	-1.1	-	-	123.5	1.9	-	-
1994	120.8	-2.2	-	-	123.1	1.9	-	-	123.7	0.5	-	-	121.4	-1.9	-	-	131.3	8.2	-	-	130.7	-0.5	-	-
1995	120.5	-7.8	-	-	120.7	0.2	-	-	117.9	-2.3	-	-	117.5	-0.3	-	-	123.0	4.7	-	-	116.4	-5.4	-	-
1996	117.8	1.2	-	-	124.1	5.3	-	-	120.7	-2.7	-	-	119.7	-0.8	-	-	127.6	6.6	-	-	123.6	-3.1	-	-
1997	-	-	-	-	-	-	-	-	-	-	123.9	0.2	-	-	-	-	-	-	-	-	-	-	123.7	-0.2

[Continued]

St. Louis, MO-IL
Consumer Price Index - All Urban Consumers
Base 1982-1984 = 100
Apparel
[Continued]

For 1952-2001. Columns headed % show percentile change in the index from the previous period for which an index is available.

Year	Jan		Feb		Mar		Apr		May		Jun		Jul		Aug		Sep		Oct		Nov		Dec	
	Index	%	Index	%	Index	%	Index	%	Index	%	Index	%	Index	%	Index	%	Index	%	Index	%	Index	%	Index	%
1998	-	-	-	-	-	-	-	-	-	-	126.0	1.9	-	-	-	-	-	-	-	-	-	-	126.4	0.3
1999	-	-	-	-	-	-	-	-	-	-	121.7	-3.7	-	-	-	-	-	-	-	-	-	-	125.3	3.0
2000	-	-	-	-	-	-	-	-	-	-	121.1	-3.4	-	-	-	-	-	-	-	-	-	-	120.7	-0.3
2001	-	-	-	-	-	-	-	-	-	-	123.1	2.0	-	-	-	-	-	-	-	-	-	-	-	-

Source: U.S. Department of Labor, Bureau of Labor Statistics, Division of Consumer Prices and Price Indexes. - indicates no data collected for period.

St. Louis, MO-IL
Consumer Price Index - Urban Wage Earners
Base 1982-1984 = 100
Apparel

For 1952-2001. Columns headed % show percentile change in the index from the previous period for which an index is available.

Year	Jan Index	%	Feb Index	%	Mar Index	%	Apr Index	%	May Index	%	Jun Index	%	Jul Index	%	Aug Index	%	Sep Index	%	Oct Index	%	Nov Index	%	Dec Index	%
1952	-		-		-		-		-		-		-		-		-		-		-		44.6	-
1953	-		-		44.8	0.4	-		-		44.9	0.2	-		-		45.4	1.1	-		-		45.2	-0.4
1954	-		-		44.9	-0.7	-		-		44.9	0.0	-		-		44.7	-0.4	-		-		44.6	-0.2
1955	-		-		44.9	0.7	-		-		44.6	-0.7	-		-		44.8	0.4	-		-		44.9	0.2
1956	-		-		45.1	0.4	-		-		45.2	0.2	-		-		45.5	0.7	-		-		45.6	0.2
1957	-		-		45.8	0.4	-		-		45.6	-0.4	-		-		46.0	0.9	-		-		46.3	0.7
1958	-		-		46.8	1.1	-		-		46.6	-0.4	-		-		46.8	0.4	-		-		46.7	-0.2
1959	-		-		46.8	0.2	-		-		46.7	-0.2	-		-		47.4	1.5	-		-		47.5	0.2
1960	-		-		47.7	0.4	-		-		47.8	0.2	-		-		48.4	1.3	-		-		48.4	0.0
1961	-		-		48.6	0.4	-		-		48.5	-0.2	-		-		48.5	0.0	-		-		48.3	-0.4
1962	-		-		48.4	0.2	-		-		48.5	0.2	-		-		48.7	0.4	-		-		48.4	-0.6
1963	-		-		48.5	0.2	-		-		48.9	0.8	-		-		49.2	0.6	-		-		49.6	0.8
1964	-		-		49.4	-0.4	-		-		49.5	0.2	-		-		49.8	0.6	-		-		49.8	0.0
1965	-		-		49.7	-0.2	-		-		49.8	0.2	-		-		50.6	1.6	-		-		50.7	0.2
1966	-		-		50.9	0.4	-		-		51.6	1.4	-		-		52.2	1.2	-		-		52.4	0.4
1967	-		-		53.1	1.3	-		-		53.2	0.2	-		-		53.6	0.8	-		-		54.5	1.7
1968	-		-		55.7	2.2	-		-		55.8	0.2	-		-		57.6	3.2	-		-		57.8	0.3
1969	-		-		58.6	1.4	-		-		59.0	0.7	-		-		59.9	1.5	-		-		60.2	0.5
1970	-		-		60.5	0.5	-		-		61.2	1.2	-		-		62.8	2.6	-		-		62.4	-0.6
1971	-		-		63.0	1.0	-		-		63.1	0.2	-		-		64.6	2.4	-		-		64.5	-0.2
1972	-		-		64.2	-0.5	-		-		63.8	-0.6	-		-		64.6	1.3	-		-		64.4	-0.3
1973	-		-		64.4	0.0	-		-		64.5	0.2	-		-		67.8	5.1	-		-		67.3	-0.7
1974	-		-		67.3	0.0	-		-		68.8	2.2	-		-		71.1	3.3	-		-		71.4	0.4
1975	-		-		71.5	0.1	-		-		71.9	0.6	-		-		72.7	1.1	-		-		73.4	1.0
1976	-		-		74.9	2.0	-		-		75.2	0.4	-		-		76.8	2.1	-		-		77.2	0.5
1977	-		-		80.3	4.0	-		-		80.5	0.2	-		-		81.5	1.2	-		-		82.4	1.1
1978	-		-		81.1	-1.6	-		79.3	-2.2	-		79.4	0.1	-		82.1	3.4	-		82.0	-0.1	-	
1979	80.3	-2.1	-		85.3	6.2	-		84.7	-0.7	-		81.2	-4.1	-		86.6	6.7	-		87.1	0.6	-	
1980	85.6	-1.7	-		90.3	5.5	-		90.7	0.4	-		89.3	-1.5	-		93.1	4.3	-		92.3	-0.9	-	
1981	92.1	-0.2	-		97.0	5.3	-		95.2	-1.9	-		95.2	0.0	-		96.7	1.6	-		95.3	-1.4	-	
1982	93.1	-2.3	-		98.9	6.2	-		96.9	-2.0	-		97.5	0.6	-		99.4	1.9	-		98.0	-1.4	-	
1983	97.5	-0.5	-		102.8	5.4	-		101.4	-1.4	-		101.3	-0.1	-		102.5	1.2	-		100.6	-1.9	-	
1984	97.4	-3.2	-		101.1	3.8	-		98.6	-2.5	-		100.5	1.9	-		106.0	5.5	-		104.9	-1.0	-	
1985	99.9	-4.8	-		106.0	6.1	-		106.9	0.8	-		103.3	-3.4	-		105.2	1.8	-		104.1	-1.0	-	
1986	99.0	-4.9	-		102.6	3.6	-		102.1	-0.5	-		99.0	-3.0	-		105.1	6.2	-		105.9	0.8	-	
1987	101.9	-3.8	-		107.2	5.2	-		107.4	0.2	-		100.7	-6.2	-		114.5	13.7	-		112.9	-1.4	-	
1988	109.6	-2.9	-		115.3	5.2	-		110.8	-3.9	-		107.1	-3.3	-		116.4	8.7	-		116.1	-0.3	-	
1989	111.8	-3.7	-		119.4	6.8	-		120.7	1.1	-		119.0	-1.4	-		119.2	0.2	-		119.4	0.2	-	
1990	119.1	-0.3	-		129.6	8.8	Apr		119.2	-8.0	-		116.8	-2.0	-		121.4	3.9	Oct		121.0	-0.3	-	
1991	119.6	-1.2	-		125.0	4.5	-		121.4	-2.9	-		119.0	-2.0	-		126.3	6.1	-		125.2	-0.9	-	
1992	121.8	-2.7	-		123.1	1.1	-		119.9	-2.6	-		118.2	-1.4	-		125.3	6.0	-		124.7	-0.5	-	
1993	121.0	-3.0	-		123.4	2.0	-		126.3	2.4	-		122.5	-3.0	-		120.9	-1.3	-		124.3	2.8	-	
1994	120.6	-3.0	-		123.1	2.1	-		123.7	0.5	-		122.4	-1.1	-		133.0	8.7	-		132.7	-0.2	-	
1995	120.7	-9.0	-		120.9	0.2	-		117.7	-2.6	-		118.3	0.5	-		124.0	4.8	-		117.1	-5.6	-	
1996	118.2	0.9	-		124.9	5.7	-		121.5	-2.7	-		119.9	-1.3	-		127.7	6.5	-		123.4	-3.4	-	
1997	-		-		-		-		-		123.9	0.4	-		-		-		-		-		123.9	0.0

[Continued]

St. Louis, MO-IL
Consumer Price Index - Urban Wage Earners
Base 1982-1984 = 100
Apparel

[Continued]

For 1952-2001. Columns headed % show percentile change in the index from the previous period for which an index is available.

Year	Jan		Feb		Mar		Apr		May		Jun		Jul		Aug		Sep		Oct		Nov		Dec	
	Index	%	Index	%	Index	%	Index	%	Index	%	Index	%	Index	%	Index	%	Index	%	Index	%	Index	%	Index	%
1998	-	-	-	-	-	-	-	-	-	-	125.4	1.2	-	-	-	-	-	-	-	-	-	-	126.4	0.8
1999	-	-	-	-	-	-	-	-	-	-	122.9	-2.8	-	-	-	-	-	-	-	-	-	-	126.4	2.8
2000	-	-	-	-	-	-	-	-	-	-	122.4	-3.2	-	-	-	-	-	-	-	-	-	-	121.1	-1.1
2001	-	-	-	-	-	-	-	-	-	-	123.7	2.1	-	-	-	-	-	-	-	-	-	-	-	-

Source: U.S. Department of Labor, Bureau of Labor Statistics, Division of Consumer Prices and Price Indexes. - indicates no data collected for period.

St. Louis, MO-IL
Consumer Price Index - All Urban Consumers
Base 1982-1984 = 100
Transportation

For 1947-2001. Columns headed % show percentile change in the index from the previous period for which an index is available.

Year	Jan Index	%	Feb Index	%	Mar Index	%	Apr Index	%	May Index	%	Jun Index	%	Jul Index	%	Aug Index	%	Sep Index	%	Oct Index	%	Nov Index	%	Dec Index	%
1947	17.7	-	17.7	0.0	17.9	1.1	18.0	0.6	18.0	0.0	18.0	0.0	-	-	-	-	18.4	2.2	-	-	-	-	18.9	2.7
1948	-	-	-	-	19.2	1.6	-	-	-	-	19.6	2.1	-	-	-	-	20.4	4.1	-	-	-	-	20.4	0.0
1949	-	-	-	-	20.7	1.5	-	-	-	-	20.7	0.0	-	-	-	-	20.7	0.0	-	-	-	-	21.5	3.9
1950	-	-	-	-	21.3	-0.9	-	-	-	-	21.1	-0.9	-	-	-	-	21.4	1.4	-	-	-	-	21.6	0.9
1951	-	-	-	-	23.5	8.8	-	-	-	-	23.4	-0.4	-	-	-	-	23.7	1.3	-	-	-	-	24.3	2.5
1952	-	-	-	-	25.6	5.3	-	-	-	-	25.6	0.0	-	-	-	-	26.3	2.7	-	-	-	-	26.1	-0.8
1953	-	-	-	-	26.9	3.1	-	-	-	-	26.8	-0.4	-	-	-	-	26.8	0.0	-	-	-	-	26.7	-0.4
1954	-	-	-	-	26.7	0.0	-	-	-	-	26.7	0.0	-	-	-	-	24.5	-8.2	-	-	-	-	25.6	4.5
1955	-	-	-	-	26.4	3.1	-	-	-	-	26.4	0.0	-	-	-	-	25.7	-2.7	-	-	-	-	26.2	1.9
1956	-	-	-	-	25.9	-1.1	-	-	-	-	26.2	1.2	-	-	-	-	26.3	0.4	-	-	-	-	27.3	3.8
1957	-	-	-	-	27.6	1.1	-	-	-	-	28.0	1.4	-	-	-	-	28.3	1.1	-	-	-	-	28.6	1.1
1958	-	-	-	-	28.9	1.0	-	-	-	-	29.1	0.7	-	-	-	-	30.1	3.4	-	-	-	-	31.3	4.0
1959	-	-	-	-	31.7	1.3	-	-	-	-	31.7	0.0	-	-	-	-	31.3	-1.3	-	-	-	-	32.0	2.2
1960	-	-	-	-	31.6	-1.2	-	-	-	-	31.6	0.0	-	-	-	-	31.2	-1.3	-	-	-	-	30.6	-1.9
1961	-	-	-	-	32.0	4.6	-	-	-	-	32.2	0.6	-	-	-	-	32.0	-0.6	-	-	-	-	32.5	1.6
1962	-	-	-	-	32.1	-1.2	-	-	-	-	31.8	-0.9	-	-	-	-	32.8	3.1	-	-	-	-	33.2	1.2
1963	-	-	-	-	32.7	-1.5	-	-	-	-	31.3	-4.3	-	-	-	-	32.2	2.9	-	-	-	-	32.8	1.9
1964	-	-	-	-	32.7	-0.3	-	-	-	-	32.1	-1.8	-	-	-	-	32.9	2.5	-	-	-	-	33.3	1.2
1965	-	-	-	-	33.0	-0.9	-	-	-	-	32.9	-0.3	-	-	-	-	32.7	-0.6	-	-	-	-	33.5	2.4
1966	-	-	-	-	33.5	0.0	-	-	-	-	34.4	2.7	-	-	-	-	34.4	0.0	-	-	-	-	34.4	0.0
1967	-	-	-	-	34.8	1.2	-	-	-	-	35.2	1.1	-	-	-	-	35.7	1.4	-	-	-	-	36.0	0.8
1968	-	-	-	-	36.0	0.0	-	-	-	-	36.1	0.3	-	-	-	-	36.1	0.0	-	-	-	-	35.9	-0.6
1969	-	-	-	-	36.9	2.8	-	-	-	-	37.3	1.1	-	-	-	-	37.4	0.3	-	-	-	-	37.7	0.8
1970	-	-	-	-	37.4	-0.8	-	-	-	-	39.4	5.3	-	-	-	-	40.3	2.3	-	-	-	-	42.2	4.7
1971	-	-	-	-	41.2	-2.4	-	-	-	-	42.7	3.6	-	-	-	-	42.0	-1.6	-	-	-	-	42.6	1.4
1972	-	-	-	-	41.2	-3.3	-	-	-	-	42.3	2.7	-	-	-	-	42.9	1.4	-	-	-	-	43.3	0.9
1973	-	-	-	-	43.5	0.5	-	-	-	-	44.3	1.8	-	-	-	-	43.9	-0.9	-	-	-	-	43.6	-0.7
1974	-	-	-	-	45.5	4.4	-	-	-	-	47.9	5.3	-	-	-	-	49.0	2.3	-	-	-	-	49.2	0.4
1975	-	-	-	-	49.5	0.6	-	-	-	-	51.3	3.6	-	-	-	-	53.1	3.5	-	-	-	-	53.5	0.8
1976	-	-	-	-	54.0	0.9	-	-	-	-	56.5	4.6	-	-	-	-	57.4	1.6	-	-	-	-	58.3	1.6
1977	-	-	-	-	58.7	0.7	-	-	-	-	60.3	2.7	-	-	-	-	59.8	-0.8	-	-	-	-	60.0	0.3
1978	-	-	-	-	59.9	-0.2	-	-	63.4	5.8	-	-	64.4	1.6	-	-	65.2	1.2	-	-	66.5	2.0	-	-
1979	67.4	1.4	-	-	68.9	2.2	-	-	72.0	4.5	-	-	76.3	6.0	-	-	76.7	0.5	-	-	78.4	2.2	-	-
1980	80.9	3.2	-	-	83.3	3.0	-	-	84.8	1.8	-	-	85.5	0.8	-	-	86.0	0.6	-	-	88.1	2.4	-	-
1981	90.3	2.5	-	-	92.5	2.4	-	-	94.1	1.7	-	-	94.8	0.7	-	-	95.4	0.6	-	-	97.6	2.3	-	-
1982	96.9	-0.7	-	-	94.6	-2.4	-	-	97.1	2.6	-	-	100.0	3.0	-	-	99.2	-0.8	-	-	99.0	-0.2	-	-
1983	97.6	-1.4	-	-	95.8	-1.8	-	-	99.0	3.3	-	-	100.3	1.3	-	-	100.9	0.6	-	-	101.2	0.3	-	-
1984	100.5	-0.7	-	-	101.3	0.8	-	-	103.0	1.7	-	-	103.4	0.4	-	-	103.9	0.5	-	-	104.6	0.7	-	-
1985	103.9	-0.7	-	-	103.8	-0.1	-	-	106.0	2.1	-	-	105.8	-0.2	-	-	105.4	-0.4	-	-	106.5	1.0	-	-
1986	106.1	-0.4	-	-	100.7	-5.1	-	-	99.7	-1.0	-	-	99.3	-0.4	-	-	97.7	-1.6	-	-	99.8	2.1	-	-
1987	101.4	1.6	-	-	102.1	0.7	-	-	103.2	1.1	-	-	104.7	1.5	-	-	105.7	1.0	-	-	105.7	0.0	-	-
1988	105.2	-0.5	-	-	104.0	-1.1	-	-	105.8	1.7	-	-	106.5	0.7	-	-	106.7	0.2	-	-	107.1	0.4	-	-
1989	107.2	0.1	-	-	107.4	0.2	-	-	113.3	5.5	-	-	112.0	-1.1	-	-	109.2	-2.5	-	-	111.6	2.2	-	-
1990	115.4	3.4	-	-	114.0	-1.2	-	-	115.1	1.0	-	-	114.8	-0.3	-	-	120.9	5.3	-	-	122.6	1.4	-	-
1991	121.6	-0.8	-	-	115.8	-4.8	-	-	118.2	2.1	-	-	117.2	-0.8	-	-	118.9	1.5	-	-	120.3	1.2	-	-
1992	118.8	-1.2	-	-	119.0	0.2	-	-	122.7	3.1	-	-	122.6	-0.1	-	-	122.7	0.1	-	-	124.8	1.7	-	-

[Continued]

St. Louis, MO-IL
Consumer Price Index - All Urban Consumers
Base 1982-1984 = 100
Transportation

[Continued]

For 1947-2001. Columns headed % show percentile change in the index from the previous period for which an index is available.

Year	Jan Index	%	Feb Index	%	Mar Index	%	Apr Index	%	May Index	%	Jun Index	%	Jul Index	%	Aug Index	%	Sep Index	%	Oct Index	%	Nov Index	%	Dec Index	%
1993	122.8	-1.6	-	-	123.5	0.6	-	-	126.0	2.0	-	-	125.8	-0.2	-	-	125.1	-0.6	-	-	127.1	1.6	-	-
1994	124.7	-1.9	-	-	125.8	0.9	-	-	127.0	1.0	-	-	130.8	3.0	-	-	132.3	1.1	-	-	132.9	0.5	-	-
1995	131.4	-1.1	-	-	135.3	3.0	-	-	137.8	1.8	-	-	136.6	-0.9	-	-	136.9	0.2	-	-	136.1	-0.6	-	-
1996	138.7	1.9	-	-	141.5	2.0	-	-	142.6	0.8	-	-	141.0	-1.1	-	-	141.0	0.0	-	-	144.9	2.8	-	-
1997	-	-	-	-	-	-	-	-	-	-	144.3	-0.4	-	-	-	-	-	-	-	-	-	-	143.2	-0.8
1998	-	-	-	-	-	-	-	-	-	-	139.5	-2.6	-	-	-	-	-	-	-	-	-	-	137.3	-1.6
1999	-	-	-	-	-	-	-	-	-	-	139.6	1.7	-	-	-	-	-	-	-	-	-	-	143.7	2.9
2000	-	-	-	-	-	-	-	-	-	-	150.5	4.7	-	-	-	-	-	-	-	-	-	-	150.8	0.2
2001	-	-	-	-	-	-	-	-	-	-	153.6	1.9	-	-	-	-	-	-	-	-	-	-	-	-

Source: U.S. Department of Labor, Bureau of Labor Statistics, Division of Consumer Prices and Price Indexes. - indicates no data collected for period.

St. Louis, MO-IL
Consumer Price Index - Urban Wage Earners
Base 1982-1984 = 100
Transportation

For 1947-2001. Columns headed % show percentile change in the index from the previous period for which an index is available.

Year	Jan Index	%	Feb Index	%	Mar Index	%	Apr Index	%	May Index	%	Jun Index	%	Jul Index	%	Aug Index	%	Sep Index	%	Oct Index	%	Nov Index	%	Dec Index	%
1947	18.0	-	18.0	0.0	18.2	1.1	18.3	0.5	18.3	0.0	18.2	-0.5	-	-	-	-	18.7	2.7	-	-	-	-	19.2	2.7
1948	-	-	-	-	19.5	1.6	-	-	-	-	19.9	2.1	-	-	-	-	20.7	4.0	-	-	-	-	20.7	0.0
1949	-	-	-	-	21.1	1.9	-	-	-	-	21.1	0.0	-	-	-	-	21.0	-0.5	-	-	-	-	21.9	4.3
1950	-	-	-	-	21.7	-0.9	-	-	-	-	21.4	-1.4	-	-	-	-	21.8	1.9	-	-	-	-	22.0	0.9
1951	-	-	-	-	23.8	8.2	-	-	-	-	23.8	0.0	-	-	-	-	24.1	1.3	-	-	-	-	24.7	2.5
1952	-	-	-	-	26.0	5.3	-	-	-	-	26.1	0.4	-	-	-	-	26.7	2.3	-	-	-	-	26.5	-0.7
1953	-	-	-	-	27.3	3.0	-	-	-	-	27.3	0.0	-	-	-	-	27.3	0.0	-	-	-	-	27.2	-0.4
1954	-	-	-	-	27.1	-0.4	-	-	-	-	27.1	0.0	-	-	-	-	24.9	-8.1	-	-	-	-	26.0	4.4
1955	-	-	-	-	26.9	3.5	-	-	-	-	26.9	0.0	-	-	-	-	26.1	-3.0	-	-	-	-	26.6	1.9
1956	-	-	-	-	26.3	-1.1	-	-	-	-	26.6	1.1	-	-	-	-	26.7	0.4	-	-	-	-	27.7	3.7
1957	-	-	-	-	28.0	1.1	-	-	-	-	28.5	1.8	-	-	-	-	28.8	1.1	-	-	-	-	29.1	1.0
1958	-	-	-	-	29.4	1.0	-	-	-	-	29.5	0.3	-	-	-	-	30.5	3.4	-	-	-	-	31.8	4.3
1959	-	-	-	-	32.3	1.6	-	-	-	-	32.2	-0.3	-	-	-	-	31.8	-1.2	-	-	-	-	32.5	2.2
1960	-	-	-	-	32.1	-1.2	-	-	-	-	32.1	0.0	-	-	-	-	31.7	-1.2	-	-	-	-	31.1	-1.9
1961	-	-	-	-	32.5	4.5	-	-	-	-	32.7	0.6	-	-	-	-	32.5	-0.6	-	-	-	-	33.0	1.5
1962	-	-	-	-	32.6	-1.2	-	-	-	-	32.3	-0.9	-	-	-	-	33.4	3.4	-	-	-	-	33.7	0.9
1963	-	-	-	-	33.2	-1.5	-	-	-	-	31.8	-4.2	-	-	-	-	32.7	2.8	-	-	-	-	33.3	1.8
1964	-	-	-	-	33.2	-0.3	-	-	-	-	32.6	-1.8	-	-	-	-	33.5	2.8	-	-	-	-	33.9	1.2
1965	-	-	-	-	33.5	-1.2	-	-	-	-	33.4	-0.3	-	-	-	-	33.2	-0.6	-	-	-	-	34.1	2.7
1966	-	-	-	-	34.0	-0.3	-	-	-	-	34.9	2.6	-	-	-	-	35.0	0.3	-	-	-	-	35.0	0.0
1967	-	-	-	-	35.3	0.9	-	-	-	-	35.8	1.4	-	-	-	-	36.2	1.1	-	-	-	-	36.6	1.1
1968	-	-	-	-	36.6	0.0	-	-	-	-	36.6	0.0	-	-	-	-	36.7	0.3	-	-	-	-	36.5	-0.5
1969	-	-	-	-	37.5	2.7	-	-	-	-	37.9	1.1	-	-	-	-	38.0	0.3	-	-	-	-	38.3	0.8
1970	-	-	-	-	38.0	-0.8	-	-	-	-	40.0	5.3	-	-	-	-	40.9	2.3	-	-	-	-	42.9	4.9
1971	-	-	-	-	41.8	-2.6	-	-	-	-	43.4	3.8	-	-	-	-	42.7	-1.6	-	-	-	-	43.3	1.4
1972	-	-	-	-	41.9	-3.2	-	-	-	-	43.0	2.6	-	-	-	-	43.6	1.4	-	-	-	-	44.0	0.9
1973	-	-	-	-	44.2	0.5	-	-	-	-	45.0	1.8	-	-	-	-	44.6	-0.9	-	-	-	-	44.3	-0.7
1974	-	-	-	-	46.3	4.5	-	-	-	-	48.7	5.2	-	-	-	-	49.8	2.3	-	-	-	-	50.0	0.4
1975	-	-	-	-	50.3	0.6	-	-	-	-	52.1	3.6	-	-	-	-	54.0	3.6	-	-	-	-	54.4	0.7
1976	-	-	-	-	54.9	0.9	-	-	-	-	57.4	4.6	-	-	-	-	58.3	1.6	-	-	-	-	59.3	1.7
1977	-	-	-	-	59.6	0.5	-	-	-	-	61.2	2.7	-	-	-	-	60.8	-0.7	-	-	-	-	61.0	0.3
1978	-	-	-	-	60.9	-0.2	-	-	62.2	2.1	-	-	63.4	1.9	-	-	64.3	1.4	-	-	65.3	1.6	-	-
1979	66.4	1.7	-	-	67.8	2.1	-	-	71.3	5.2	-	-	76.3	7.0	-	-	76.5	0.3	-	-	78.1	2.1	-	-
1980	81.2	4.0	-	-	83.5	2.8	-	-	85.4	2.3	-	-	86.3	1.1	-	-	86.6	0.3	-	-	88.4	2.1	-	-
1981	90.6	2.5	-	-	92.8	2.4	-	-	94.3	1.6	-	-	94.9	0.6	-	-	95.5	0.6	-	-	97.7	2.3	-	-
1982	96.9	-0.8	-	-	94.3	-2.7	-	-	96.9	2.8	-	-	100.1	3.3	-	-	99.2	-0.9	-	-	99.0	-0.2	-	-
1983	97.3	-1.7	-	-	95.3	-2.1	-	-	98.7	3.6	-	-	100.2	1.5	-	-	101.0	0.8	-	-	101.3	0.3	-	-
1984	100.5	-0.8	-	-	101.5	1.0	-	-	103.4	1.9	-	-	103.8	0.4	-	-	104.2	0.4	-	-	104.9	0.7	-	-
1985	103.8	-1.0	-	-	103.7	-0.1	-	-	106.1	2.3	-	-	105.9	-0.2	-	-	105.3	-0.6	-	-	106.3	0.9	-	-
1986	105.8	-0.5	-	-	99.9	-5.6	-	-	98.6	-1.3	-	-	98.2	-0.4	-	-	96.4	-1.8	-	-	98.3	2.0	-	-
1987	99.6	1.3	-	-	100.7	1.1	-	-	102.3	1.6	-	-	104.4	2.1	-	-	105.5	1.1	-	-	105.4	-0.1	-	-
1988	105.0	-0.4	-	-	103.9	-1.0	-	-	105.6	1.6	-	-	106.2	0.6	-	-	106.6	0.4	-	-	106.8	0.2	-	-
1989	106.9	0.1	-	-	107.4	0.5	-	-	112.9	5.1	-	-	111.7	-1.1	-	-	109.2	-2.2	-	-	111.0	1.6	-	-
1990	114.0	2.7	-	-	112.0	-1.8	-	-	113.1	1.0	-	-	113.1	0.0	-	-	118.9	5.1	-	-	120.7	1.5	-	-
1991	119.4	-1.1	-	-	114.4	-4.2	-	-	116.8	2.1	-	-	116.1	-0.6	-	-	117.9	1.6	-	-	119.2	1.1	-	-
1992	117.5	-1.4	-	-	117.2	-0.3	-	-	121.3	3.5	-	-	122.1	0.7	-	-	122.4	0.2	-	-	124.2	1.5	-	-

[Continued]

St. Louis, MO-IL
Consumer Price Index - Urban Wage Earners
Base 1982-1984 = 100
Transportation

[Continued]

For 1947-2001. Columns headed % show percentile change in the index from the previous period for which an index is available.

Year	Jan Index	%	Feb Index	%	Mar Index	%	Apr Index	%	May Index	%	Jun Index	%	Jul Index	%	Aug Index	%	Sep Index	%	Oct Index	%	Nov Index	%	Dec Index	%
1993	122.2	-1.6	-	-	122.3	0.1	-	-	125.2	2.4	-	-	125.5	0.2	-	-	125.0	-0.4	-	-	126.9	1.5	-	-
1994	124.3	-2.0	-	-	124.7	0.3	-	-	126.6	1.5	-	-	130.9	3.4	-	-	132.8	1.5	-	-	134.0	0.9	-	-
1995	133.1	-0.7	-	-	136.5	2.6	-	-	139.9	2.5	-	-	139.1	-0.6	-	-	138.9	-0.1	-	-	138.4	-0.4	-	-
1996	140.6	1.6	-	-	142.4	1.3	-	-	144.0	1.1	-	-	142.3	-1.2	-	-	142.1	-0.1	-	-	145.8	2.6	-	-
1997	-	-	-	-	-	-	-	-	-	-	144.5	-0.9	-	-	-	-	-	-	-	-	-	-	143.4	-0.8
1998	-	-	-	-	-	-	-	-	-	-	138.9	-3.1	-	-	-	-	-	-	-	-	-	-	136.1	-2.0
1999	-	-	-	-	-	-	-	-	-	-	138.7	1.9	-	-	-	-	-	-	-	-	-	-	144.1	3.9
2000	-	-	-	-	-	-	-	-	-	-	152.4	5.8	-	-	-	-	-	-	-	-	-	-	152.7	0.2
2001	-	-	-	-	-	-	-	-	-	-	156.2	2.3	-	-	-	-	-	-	-	-	-	-	-	-

Source: U.S. Department of Labor, Bureau of Labor Statistics, Division of Consumer Prices and Price Indexes. - indicates no data collected for period.

St. Louis, MO-IL
Consumer Price Index - All Urban Consumers
Base 1982-1984 = 100
Medical Care

For 1947-2001. Columns headed % show percentile change in the index from the previous period for which an index is available.

Year	Jan Index	%	Feb Index	%	Mar Index	%	Apr Index	%	May Index	%	Jun Index	%	Jul Index	%	Aug Index	%	Sep Index	%	Oct Index	%	Nov Index	%	Dec Index	%
1947	12.9	-	12.9	0.0	13.0	0.8	13.0	0.0	13.0	0.0	13.0	0.0	-	-	-	-	13.4	3.1	-	-	-	-	13.7	2.2
1948	-	-	-	-	13.8	0.7	-	-	-	-	13.8	0.0	-	-	-	-	14.3	3.6	-	-	-	-	14.4	0.7
1949	-	-	-	-	14.5	0.7	-	-	-	-	14.4	-0.7	-	-	-	-	14.4	0.0	-	-	-	-	14.5	0.7
1950	-	-	-	-	14.5	0.0	-	-	-	-	14.5	0.0	-	-	-	-	14.6	0.7	-	-	-	-	14.7	0.7
1951	-	-	-	-	15.0	2.0	-	-	-	-	15.0	0.0	-	-	-	-	15.1	0.7	-	-	-	-	17.7	17.2
1952	-	-	-	-	17.8	0.6	-	-	-	-	18.1	1.7	-	-	-	-	18.1	0.0	-	-	-	-	18.3	1.1
1953	-	-	-	-	18.4	0.5	-	-	-	-	18.5	0.5	-	-	-	-	18.5	0.0	-	-	-	-	18.6	0.5
1954	-	-	-	-	18.7	0.5	-	-	-	-	18.7	0.0	-	-	-	-	18.9	1.1	-	-	-	-	19.4	2.6
1955	-	-	-	-	19.5	0.5	-	-	-	-	19.5	0.0	-	-	-	-	19.5	0.0	-	-	-	-	19.5	0.0
1956	-	-	-	-	19.5	0.0	-	-	-	-	19.5	0.0	-	-	-	-	19.9	2.1	-	-	-	-	21.2	6.5
1957	-	-	-	-	21.4	0.9	-	-	-	-	21.4	0.0	-	-	-	-	21.5	0.5	-	-	-	-	21.7	0.9
1958	-	-	-	-	22.0	1.4	-	-	-	-	22.0	0.0	-	-	-	-	22.1	0.5	-	-	-	-	23.1	4.5
1959	-	-	-	-	23.2	0.4	-	-	-	-	23.3	0.4	-	-	-	-	23.5	0.9	-	-	-	-	23.7	0.9
1960	-	-	-	-	23.7	0.0	-	-	-	-	23.6	-0.4	-	-	-	-	23.6	0.0	-	-	-	-	23.8	0.8
1961	-	-	-	-	24.0	0.8	-	-	-	-	24.0	0.0	-	-	-	-	24.2	0.8	-	-	-	-	25.3	4.5
1962	-	-	-	-	25.4	0.4	-	-	-	-	25.5	0.4	-	-	-	-	25.6	0.4	-	-	-	-	25.6	0.0
1963	-	-	-	-	25.7	0.4	-	-	-	-	25.7	0.0	-	-	-	-	25.8	0.4	-	-	-	-	25.8	0.0
1964	-	-	-	-	25.8	0.0	-	-	-	-	25.7	-0.4	-	-	-	-	25.9	0.8	-	-	-	-	26.0	0.4
1965	-	-	-	-	26.5	1.9	-	-	-	-	26.9	1.5	-	-	-	-	27.0	0.4	-	-	-	-	27.1	0.4
1966	-	-	-	-	27.6	1.8	-	-	-	-	28.2	2.2	-	-	-	-	28.7	1.8	-	-	-	-	29.1	1.4
1967	-	-	-	-	29.5	1.4	-	-	-	-	29.5	0.0	-	-	-	-	30.0	1.7	-	-	-	-	30.3	1.0
1968	-	-	-	-	30.9	2.0	-	-	-	-	30.9	0.0	-	-	-	-	31.4	1.6	-	-	-	-	31.7	1.0
1969	-	-	-	-	32.6	2.8	-	-	-	-	33.1	1.5	-	-	-	-	33.4	0.9	-	-	-	-	33.5	0.3
1970	-	-	-	-	34.7	3.6	-	-	-	-	35.3	1.7	-	-	-	-	35.6	0.8	-	-	-	-	35.7	0.3
1971	-	-	-	-	36.4	2.0	-	-	-	-	36.8	1.1	-	-	-	-	37.1	0.8	-	-	-	-	36.8	-0.8
1972	-	-	-	-	37.2	1.1	-	-	-	-	37.4	0.5	-	-	-	-	37.5	0.3	-	-	-	-	37.6	0.3
1973	-	-	-	-	38.2	1.6	-	-	-	-	38.3	0.3	-	-	-	-	38.8	1.3	-	-	-	-	39.7	2.3
1974	-	-	-	-	40.7	2.5	-	-	-	-	41.2	1.2	-	-	-	-	42.7	3.6	-	-	-	-	44.1	3.3
1975	-	-	-	-	45.2	2.5	-	-	-	-	46.2	2.2	-	-	-	-	47.4	2.6	-	-	-	-	47.5	0.2
1976	-	-	-	-	49.1	3.4	-	-	-	-	50.1	2.0	-	-	-	-	50.7	1.2	-	-	-	-	52.4	3.4
1977	-	-	-	-	54.4	3.8	-	-	-	-	55.2	1.5	-	-	-	-	56.5	2.4	-	-	-	-	57.2	1.2
1978	-	-	-	-	58.9	3.0	-	-	59.1	0.3	-	-	60.1	1.7	-	-	60.3	0.3	-	-	60.5	0.3	-	-
1979	62.4	3.1	-	-	62.5	0.2	-	-	63.5	1.6	-	-	65.6	3.3	-	-	65.7	0.2	-	-	66.8	1.7	-	-
1980	70.7	5.8	-	-	71.2	0.7	-	-	72.1	1.3	-	-	73.4	1.8	-	-	73.4	0.0	-	-	75.1	2.3	-	-
1981	77.7	3.5	-	-	79.6	2.4	-	-	81.2	2.0	-	-	81.6	0.5	-	-	83.0	1.7	-	-	84.6	1.9	-	-
1982	90.2	6.6	-	-	91.5	1.4	-	-	92.1	0.7	-	-	93.7	1.7	-	-	94.5	0.9	-	-	95.9	1.5	-	-
1983	99.9	4.2	-	-	100.0	0.1	-	-	100.0	0.0	-	-	101.2	1.2	-	-	101.1	-0.1	-	-	101.7	0.6	-	-
1984	104.6	2.9	-	-	105.1	0.5	-	-	105.3	0.2	-	-	105.6	0.3	-	-	106.2	0.6	-	-	106.8	0.6	-	-
1985	108.6	1.7	-	-	109.5	0.8	-	-	110.3	0.7	-	-	111.3	0.9	-	-	111.5	0.2	-	-	112.6	1.0	-	-
1986	117.4	4.3	-	-	118.4	0.9	-	-	119.2	0.7	-	-	121.4	1.8	-	-	121.3	-0.1	-	-	122.1	0.7	-	-
1987	124.5	2.0	-	-	126.5	1.6	-	-	127.0	0.4	-	-	128.6	1.3	-	-	129.3	0.5	-	-	129.8	0.4	-	-
1988	132.4	2.0	-	-	133.4	0.8	-	-	134.0	0.4	-	-	136.5	1.9	-	-	136.6	0.1	-	-	138.8	1.6	-	-
1989	140.5	1.2	-	-	142.3	1.3	-	-	143.7	1.0	-	-	146.9	2.2	-	-	148.4	1.0	-	-	148.9	0.3	-	-
1990	152.4	2.4	-	-	156.5	2.7	-	-	158.7	1.4	-	-	159.6	0.6	-	-	160.5	0.6	-	-	162.3	1.1	-	-
1991	168.0	3.5	-	-	169.5	0.9	-	-	170.0	0.3	-	-	172.9	1.7	-	-	173.6	0.4	-	-	174.1	0.3	-	-
1992	177.1	1.7	-	-	178.8	1.0	-	-	179.4	0.3	-	-	182.4	1.7	-	-	183.1	0.4	-	-	182.9	-0.1	-	-

[Continued]

St. Louis, MO-IL
Consumer Price Index - All Urban Consumers
Base 1982-1984 = 100
Medical Care

[Continued]

For 1947-2001. Columns headed % show percentile change in the index from the previous period for which an index is available.

Year	Jan Index	%	Feb Index	%	Mar Index	%	Apr Index	%	May Index	%	Jun Index	%	Jul Index	%	Aug Index	%	Sep Index	%	Oct Index	%	Nov Index	%	Dec Index	%
1993	186.3	1.9	-	-	188.7	1.3	-	-	190.2	0.8	-	-	192.0	0.9	-	-	194.3	1.2	-	-	195.0	0.4	-	-
1994	197.5	1.3	-	-	199.2	0.9	-	-	199.9	0.4	-	-	202.5	1.3	-	-	204.2	0.8	-	-	204.6	0.2	-	-
1995	207.0	1.2	-	-	208.3	0.6	-	-	210.6	1.1	-	-	210.0	-0.3	-	-	210.6	0.3	-	-	211.1	0.2	-	-
1996	215.9	2.3	-	-	216.1	0.1	-	-	216.8	0.3	-	-	219.0	1.0	-	-	218.7	-0.1	-	-	222.6	1.8	-	-
1997	-	-	-	-	-	-	-	-	-	-	224.7	0.9	-	-	-	-	-	-	-	-	-	-	228.2	1.6
1998	-	-	-	-	-	-	-	-	-	-	232.2	1.8	-	-	-	-	-	-	-	-	-	-	235.7	1.5
1999	-	-	-	-	-	-	-	-	-	-	242.9	3.1	-	-	-	-	-	-	-	-	-	-	248.5	2.3
2000	-	-	-	-	-	-	-	-	-	-	255.5	2.8	-	-	-	-	-	-	-	-	-	-	258.2	1.1
2001	-	-	-	-	-	-	-	-	-	-	264.9	2.6	-	-	-	-	-	-	-	-	-	-	-	-

Source: U.S. Department of Labor, Bureau of Labor Statistics, Division of Consumer Prices and Price Indexes. - indicates no data collected for period.

St. Louis, MO-IL
Consumer Price Index - Urban Wage Earners
Base 1982-1984 = 100
Medical Care

For 1947-2001. Columns headed % show percentile change in the index from the previous period for which an index is available.

Year	Jan Index	%	Feb Index	%	Mar Index	%	Apr Index	%	May Index	%	Jun Index	%	Jul Index	%	Aug Index	%	Sep Index	%	Oct Index	%	Nov Index	%	Dec Index	%
1947	12.8	-	12.8	0.0	12.9	0.8	12.9	0.0	12.9	0.0	12.9	0.0	-	-	-	-	13.2	2.3	-	-	-	-	13.6	3.0
1948	-	-	-	-	13.7	0.7	-	-	-	-	13.7	0.0	-	-	-	-	14.2	3.6	-	-	-	-	14.2	0.0
1949	-	-	-	-	14.3	0.7	-	-	-	-	14.3	0.0	-	-	-	-	14.3	0.0	-	-	-	-	14.3	0.0
1950	-	-	-	-	14.4	0.7	-	-	-	-	14.4	0.0	-	-	-	-	14.4	0.0	-	-	-	-	14.5	0.7
1951	-	-	-	-	14.9	2.8	-	-	-	-	14.9	0.0	-	-	-	-	14.9	0.0	-	-	-	-	17.6	18.1
1952	-	-	-	-	17.7	0.6	-	-	-	-	17.9	1.1	-	-	-	-	17.9	0.0	-	-	-	-	18.2	1.7
1953	-	-	-	-	18.2	0.0	-	-	-	-	18.3	0.5	-	-	-	-	18.3	0.0	-	-	-	-	18.4	0.5
1954	-	-	-	-	18.5	0.5	-	-	-	-	18.6	0.5	-	-	-	-	18.7	0.5	-	-	-	-	19.2	2.7
1955	-	-	-	-	19.3	0.5	-	-	-	-	19.3	0.0	-	-	-	-	19.3	0.0	-	-	-	-	19.3	0.0
1956	-	-	-	-	19.3	0.0	-	-	-	-	19.4	0.5	-	-	-	-	19.7	1.5	-	-	-	-	21.0	6.6
1957	-	-	-	-	21.3	1.4	-	-	-	-	21.3	0.0	-	-	-	-	21.3	0.0	-	-	-	-	21.5	0.9
1958	-	-	-	-	21.8	1.4	-	-	-	-	21.8	0.0	-	-	-	-	21.9	0.5	-	-	-	-	22.9	4.6
1959	-	-	-	-	23.0	0.4	-	-	-	-	23.0	0.0	-	-	-	-	23.3	1.3	-	-	-	-	23.5	0.9
1960	-	-	-	-	23.5	0.0	-	-	-	-	23.4	-0.4	-	-	-	-	23.4	0.0	-	-	-	-	23.6	0.9
1961	-	-	-	-	23.8	0.8	-	-	-	-	23.8	0.0	-	-	-	-	24.0	0.8	-	-	-	-	25.1	4.6
1962	-	-	-	-	25.1	0.0	-	-	-	-	25.3	0.8	-	-	-	-	25.3	0.0	-	-	-	-	25.3	0.0
1963	-	-	-	-	25.5	0.8	-	-	-	-	25.5	0.0	-	-	-	-	25.5	0.0	-	-	-	-	25.6	0.4
1964	-	-	-	-	25.6	0.0	-	-	-	-	25.5	-0.4	-	-	-	-	25.7	0.8	-	-	-	-	25.8	0.4
1965	-	-	-	-	26.3	1.9	-	-	-	-	26.7	1.5	-	-	-	-	26.7	0.0	-	-	-	-	26.9	0.7
1966	-	-	-	-	27.3	1.5	-	-	-	-	28.0	2.6	-	-	-	-	28.4	1.4	-	-	-	-	28.8	1.4
1967	-	-	-	-	29.2	1.4	-	-	-	-	29.2	0.0	-	-	-	-	29.7	1.7	-	-	-	-	30.0	1.0
1968	-	-	-	-	30.6	2.0	-	-	-	-	30.7	0.3	-	-	-	-	31.1	1.3	-	-	-	-	31.5	1.3
1969	-	-	-	-	32.3	2.5	-	-	-	-	32.8	1.5	-	-	-	-	33.1	0.9	-	-	-	-	33.2	0.3
1970	-	-	-	-	34.4	3.6	-	-	-	-	34.9	1.5	-	-	-	-	35.3	1.1	-	-	-	-	35.4	0.3
1971	-	-	-	-	36.0	1.7	-	-	-	-	36.4	1.1	-	-	-	-	36.8	1.1	-	-	-	-	36.5	-0.8
1972	-	-	-	-	36.8	0.8	-	-	-	-	37.1	0.8	-	-	-	-	37.1	0.0	-	-	-	-	37.3	0.5
1973	-	-	-	-	37.9	1.6	-	-	-	-	38.0	0.3	-	-	-	-	38.4	1.1	-	-	-	-	39.3	2.3
1974	-	-	-	-	40.4	2.8	-	-	-	-	40.8	1.0	-	-	-	-	42.3	3.7	-	-	-	-	43.7	3.3
1975	-	-	-	-	44.8	2.5	-	-	-	-	45.8	2.2	-	-	-	-	47.0	2.6	-	-	-	-	47.1	0.2
1976	-	-	-	-	48.6	3.2	-	-	-	-	49.6	2.1	-	-	-	-	50.2	1.2	-	-	-	-	51.9	3.4
1977	-	-	-	-	53.9	3.9	-	-	-	-	54.7	1.5	-	-	-	-	56.0	2.4	-	-	-	-	56.7	1.3
1978	-	-	-	-	58.4	3.0	-	-	59.0	1.0	-	-	59.6	1.0	-	-	60.2	1.0	-	-	61.3	1.8	-	-
1979	62.8	2.4	-	-	63.2	0.6	-	-	63.7	0.8	-	-	65.2	2.4	-	-	65.9	1.1	-	-	67.8	2.9	-	-
1980	70.9	4.6	-	-	72.3	2.0	-	-	72.6	0.4	-	-	73.7	1.5	-	-	74.0	0.4	-	-	75.8	2.4	-	-
1981	78.1	3.0	-	-	80.7	3.3	-	-	81.4	0.9	-	-	81.8	0.5	-	-	83.3	1.8	-	-	85.0	2.0	-	-
1982	90.4	6.4	-	-	91.6	1.3	-	-	92.1	0.5	-	-	93.7	1.7	-	-	94.4	0.7	-	-	95.8	1.5	-	-
1983	99.5	3.9	-	-	99.7	0.2	-	-	99.8	0.1	-	-	101.2	1.4	-	-	101.2	0.0	-	-	101.8	0.6	-	-
1984	104.6	2.8	-	-	105.1	0.5	-	-	105.3	0.2	-	-	105.7	0.4	-	-	106.4	0.7	-	-	107.0	0.6	-	-
1985	108.8	1.7	-	-	109.6	0.7	-	-	110.3	0.6	-	-	111.3	0.9	-	-	111.5	0.2	-	-	112.5	0.9	-	-
1986	117.2	4.2	-	-	118.1	0.8	-	-	118.9	0.7	-	-	121.0	1.8	-	-	120.7	-0.2	-	-	121.5	0.7	-	-
1987	123.9	2.0	-	-	126.0	1.7	-	-	126.7	0.6	-	-	128.3	1.3	-	-	129.1	0.6	-	-	129.3	0.2	-	-
1988	131.9	2.0	-	-	132.9	0.8	-	-	133.6	0.5	-	-	136.1	1.9	-	-	136.3	0.1	-	-	138.5	1.6	-	-
1989	140.4	1.4	-	-	142.2	1.3	-	-	143.6	1.0	-	-	147.1	2.4	-	-	148.6	1.0	-	-	148.8	0.1	-	-
1990	152.4	2.4	-	-	156.0	2.4	-	-	158.1	1.3	-	-	158.9	0.5	-	-	159.7	0.5	-	-	161.3	1.0	-	-
1991	167.0	3.5	-	-	168.4	0.8	-	-	169.0	0.4	-	-	171.8	1.7	-	-	172.4	0.3	-	-	172.9	0.3	-	-
1992	175.9	1.7	-	-	177.8	1.1	-	-	178.4	0.3	-	-	181.6	1.8	-	-	182.2	0.3	-	-	182.0	-0.1	-	-

[Continued]

St. Louis, MO-IL
Consumer Price Index - Urban Wage Earners
Base 1982-1984 = 100
Medical Care

[Continued]

For 1947-2001. Columns headed % show percentile change in the index from the previous period for which an index is available.

Year	Jan Index	%	Feb Index	%	Mar Index	%	Apr Index	%	May Index	%	Jun Index	%	Jul Index	%	Aug Index	%	Sep Index	%	Oct Index	%	Nov Index	%	Dec Index	%
1993	185.3	1.8	-	-	187.9	1.4	-	-	189.2	0.7	-	-	190.8	0.8	-	-	193.2	1.3	-	-	193.8	0.3	-	-
1994	196.2	1.2	-	-	197.7	0.8	-	-	198.3	0.3	-	-	200.8	1.3	-	-	202.5	0.8	-	-	202.9	0.2	-	-
1995	205.2	1.1	-	-	206.5	0.6	-	-	208.9	1.2	-	-	208.3	-0.3	-	-	208.8	0.2	-	-	209.5	0.3	-	-
1996	214.2	2.2	-	-	214.4	0.1	-	-	214.9	0.2	-	-	217.2	1.1	-	-	216.9	-0.1	-	-	220.7	1.8	-	-
1997	-	-	-	-	-	-	-	-	-	-	223.2	1.1	-	-	-	-	-	-	-	-	-	-	226.6	1.5
1998	-	-	-	-	-	-	-	-	-	-	230.4	1.7	-	-	-	-	-	-	-	-	-	-	234.0	1.6
1999	-	-	-	-	-	-	-	-	-	-	240.9	2.9	-	-	-	-	-	-	-	-	-	-	246.6	2.4
2000	-	-	-	-	-	-	-	-	-	-	253.2	2.7	-	-	-	-	-	-	-	-	-	-	255.7	1.0
2001	-	-	-	-	-	-	-	-	-	-	262.3	2.6	-	-	-	-	-	-	-	-	-	-	-	-

Source: U.S. Department of Labor, Bureau of Labor Statistics, Division of Consumer Prices and Price Indexes. - indicates no data collected for period.

St. Louis, MO-IL
Consumer Price Index - All Urban Consumers
Base December 1997 = 100
Recreation

For 1997-2001. Columns headed % show percentile change in the index from the previous period for which an index is available.

Year	Jan Index	%	Feb Index	%	Mar Index	%	Apr Index	%	May Index	%	Jun Index	%	Jul Index	%	Aug Index	%	Sep Index	%	Oct Index	%	Nov Index	%	Dec Index	%
1997	222.1	-	-	-	224.6	1.1	-	-	226.3	0.8	-	-	226.9	0.3	-	-	227.8	0.4	-	-	229.0	0.5	100.0	-56.3
1998	-	-	-	-	-	-	-	-	-	-	101.3	1.3	-	-	-	-	-	-	-	-	-	-	102.7	1.4
1999	-	-	-	-	-	-	-	-	-	-	103.4	0.7	-	-	-	-	-	-	-	-	-	-	105.3	1.8
2000	-	-	-	-	-	-	-	-	-	-	103.1	-2.1	-	-	-	-	-	-	-	-	-	-	103.3	0.2
2001	-	-	-	-	-	-	-	-	-	-	104.8	1.5	-	-	-	-	-	-	-	-	-	-	-	-

Source: U.S. Department of Labor, Bureau of Labor Statistics, Division of Consumer Prices and Price Indexes. - indicates no data collected for period.

St. Louis, MO-IL
Consumer Price Index - Urban Wage Earners
Base December 1997 = 100
Recreation

For 1997-2001. Columns headed % show percentile change in the index from the previous period for which an index is available.

Year	Jan Index	%	Feb Index	%	Mar Index	%	Apr Index	%	May Index	%	Jun Index	%	Jul Index	%	Aug Index	%	Sep Index	%	Oct Index	%	Nov Index	%	Dec Index	%
1997	220.5	-	-	-	223.0	1.1	-	-	225.0	0.9	-	-	225.5	0.2	-	-	226.3	0.4	-	-	227.4	0.5	100.0	-56.0
1998	-	-	-	-	-	-	-	-	-	-	101.5	1.5	-	-	-	-	-	-	-	-	-	-	103.0	1.5
1999	-	-	-	-	-	-	-	-	-	-	103.6	0.6	-	-	-	-	-	-	-	-	-	-	105.7	2.0
2000	-	-	-	-	-	-	-	-	-	-	103.0	-2.6	-	-	-	-	-	-	-	-	-	-	103.4	0.4
2001	-	-	-	-	-	-	-	-	-	-	105.1	1.6	-	-	-	-	-	-	-	-	-	-	-	-

Source: U.S. Department of Labor, Bureau of Labor Statistics, Division of Consumer Prices and Price Indexes. - indicates no data collected for period.

St. Louis, MO-IL
Consumer Price Index - All Urban Consumers
Base December 1997 = 100
Education & Communication

For 1997-2001. Columns headed % show percentile change in the index from the previous period for which an index is available.

Year	Jan Index	%	Feb Index	%	Mar Index	%	Apr Index	%	May Index	%	Jun Index	%	Jul Index	%	Aug Index	%	Sep Index	%	Oct Index	%	Nov Index	%	Dec Index	%
1997	117.6	-	-	-	125.6	6.8	-	-	128.7	2.5	-	-	117.5	-8.7	-	-	127.1	8.2	-	-	126.2	-0.7	100.0	-20.8
1998	-	-	-	-	-	-	-	-	-	-	101.2	1.2	-	-	-	-	-	-	-	-	-	-	103.6	2.4
1999	-	-	-	-	-	-	-	-	-	-	103.3	-0.3	-	-	-	-	-	-	-	-	-	-	104.6	1.3
2000	-	-	-	-	-	-	-	-	-	-	103.6	-1.0	-	-	-	-	-	-	-	-	-	-	103.8	0.2
2001	-	-	-	-	-	-	-	-	-	-	104.2	0.4	-	-	-	-	-	-	-	-	-	-	-	-

Source: U.S. Department of Labor, Bureau of Labor Statistics, Division of Consumer Prices and Price Indexes. - indicates no data collected for period.

St. Louis, MO-IL
Consumer Price Index - Urban Wage Earners
Base December 1997 = 100
Education & Communication

For 1997-2001. Columns headed % show percentile change in the index from the previous period for which an index is available.

Year	Jan Index	%	Feb Index	%	Mar Index	%	Apr Index	%	May Index	%	Jun Index	%	Jul Index	%	Aug Index	%	Sep Index	%	Oct Index	%	Nov Index	%	Dec Index	%
1997	116.8	-	-	-	125.6	7.5	-	-	129.0	2.7	-	-	117.8	-8.7	-	-	127.3	8.1	-	-	126.2	-0.9	100.0	-20.8
1998	-	-	-	-	-	-	-	-	-	-	101.3	1.3	-	-	-	-	-	-	-	-	-	-	103.4	2.1
1999	-	-	-	-	-	-	-	-	-	-	103.0	-0.4	-	-	-	-	-	-	-	-	-	-	104.1	1.1
2000	-	-	-	-	-	-	-	-	-	-	102.9	-1.2	-	-	-	-	-	-	-	-	-	-	103.0	0.1
2001	-	-	-	-	-	-	-	-	-	-	103.6	0.6	-	-	-	-	-	-	-	-	-	-	-	-

Source: U.S. Department of Labor, Bureau of Labor Statistics, Division of Consumer Prices and Price Indexes. - indicates no data collected for period.

San Diego, CA
Consumer Price Index - All Urban Consumers
Base 1982-1984 = 100
Annual Averages

For 1965-2001. Columns headed % show percentile change in the index from the previous period for which an index is available.

Year	All Items		Food & Beverage		Housing		Apparel		Trans-portation		Medical Care		Recrea-tion*		Education & Communic.*		Other Goods & Services	
	Index	%	Index	%	Index	%	Index	%	Index	%	Index	%	Index	%	Index	%	Index	%
1965	28.2	-	-	-	-	-	48.1	-	32.1	-	26.6	-	-	-	-	-	-	-
1966	28.7	1.8	-	-	-	-	48.7	1.2	32.1	0.0	28.0	5.3	-	-	-	-	-	-
1967	29.6	3.1	-	-	-	-	49.5	1.6	33.3	3.7	30.0	7.1	-	-	-	-	-	-
1968	30.8	4.1	-	-	-	-	52.4	5.9	34.1	2.4	30.8	2.7	-	-	-	-	-	-
1969	32.4	5.2	-	-	-	-	54.7	4.4	34.9	2.3	32.4	5.2	-	-	-	-	-	-
1970	34.1	5.2	-	-	-	-	56.8	3.8	35.9	2.9	34.5	6.5	-	-	-	-	-	-
1971	35.4	3.8	-	-	-	-	58.3	2.6	37.9	5.6	36.3	5.2	-	-	-	-	-	-
1972	36.8	4.0	-	-	-	-	60.4	3.6	39.0	2.9	37.2	2.5	-	-	-	-	-	-
1973	39.2	6.5	-	-	-	-	62.7	3.8	40.7	4.4	39.0	4.8	-	-	-	-	-	-
1974	43.5	11.0	-	-	-	-	67.9	8.3	46.1	13.3	43.2	10.8	-	-	-	-	-	-
1975	47.6	9.4	-	-	-	-	69.5	2.4	51.0	10.6	48.5	12.3	-	-	-	-	-	-
1976	50.5	6.1	59.3	-	44.3	-	71.4	2.7	54.6	7.1	53.6	10.5	-	-	-	-	58.0	-
1977	53.8	6.5	62.9	6.1	47.9	8.1	72.8	2.0	58.1	6.4	58.6	9.3	-	-	-	-	61.1	5.3
1978	59.2	10.0	69.7	10.8	53.8	12.3	76.9	5.6	61.2	5.3	63.6	8.5	-	-	-	-	66.2	8.3
1979	68.9	16.4	77.3	10.9	65.2	21.2	81.5	6.0	69.9	14.2	69.5	9.3	-	-	-	-	71.3	7.7
1980	79.4	15.2	84.4	9.2	76.8	17.8	87.4	7.2	82.2	17.6	76.2	9.6	-	-	-	-	77.2	8.3
1981	90.1	13.5	90.5	7.2	89.6	16.7	92.2	5.5	91.4	11.2	83.0	8.9	-	-	-	-	85.1	10.2
1982	96.2	6.8	94.8	4.8	96.3	7.5	96.5	4.7	95.7	4.7	93.1	12.2	-	-	-	-	91.5	7.5
1983	99.0	2.9	100.4	5.9	98.6	2.4	99.7	3.3	98.8	3.2	100.7	8.2	-	-	-	-	100.2	9.5
1984	104.8	5.9	104.8	4.4	104.9	6.4	103.8	4.1	105.5	6.8	106.2	5.5	-	-	-	-	108.4	8.2
1985	110.4	5.3	107.2	2.3	113.7	8.4	105.9	2.0	109.4	3.7	110.1	3.7	-	-	-	-	115.7	6.7
1986	113.5	2.8	111.2	3.7	119.2	4.8	107.3	1.3	105.6	-3.5	118.2	7.4	-	-	-	-	120.0	3.7
1987	117.5	3.5	115.8	4.1	122.2	2.5	110.2	2.7	107.6	1.9	129.4	9.5	-	-	-	-	-	-
1988	123.4	5.0	119.7	3.4	126.9	3.8	119.0	8.0	114.2	.6.1	141.9	9.7	-	-	-	-	140.4	17.0
1989	130.6	5.8	127.3	6.3	131.3	3.5	120.8	1.5	124.5	9.0	158.7	11.8	-	-	-	-	158.2	12.7
1990	138.4	6.0	134.1	5.3	139.2	6.0	131.9	9.2	131.7	5.8	173.3	9.2	-	-	-	-	165.9	4.9
1991	143.4	3.6	140.3	4.6	144.1	3.5	129.6	-1.7	133.8	1.6	188.3	8.7	-	-	-	-	178.4	7.5
1992	147.4	2.8	142.5	1.6	148.2	2.8	131.2	1.2	135.9	1.6	201.6	7.1	-	-	-	-	189.1	6.0
1993	150.6	2.2	145.3	2.0	149.5	0.9	135.6	3.4	138.0	1.5	213.7	6.0	-	-	-	-	208.4	10.2
1994	154.5	2.6	147.6	1.6	153.4	2.6	141.7	4.5	141.8	2.8	217.8	1.9	-	-	-	-	214.8	3.1
1995	156.8	1.5	151.1	2.4	155.8	1.6	133.3	-5.9	147.5	4.0	219.9	1.0	-	-	-	-	217.0	1.0
1996	160.9	2.6	157.0	3.9	159.9	2.6	129.8	-2.6	150.8	2.2	231.6	5.3	-	-	-	-	219.0	0.9
1997	163.7	1.7	161.4	2.8	163.5	2.3	126.1	-2.9	152.2	0.9	236.8	2.2	-	-	-	-	225.2	2.8
1998	166.9	2.0	165.0	2.2	170.1	4.0	125.1	-0.8	149.4	-1.8	240.9	1.7	100.0	-	98.8	-	233.3	3.6
1999	172.8	3.5	166.5	0.9	178.2	4.8	131.6	5.2	152.1	1.8	247.2	2.6	105.0	5.0	97.5	-1.3	259.8	11.4
2000	182.8	5.8	169.2	1.6	190.5	6.9	131.3	-0.2	162.4	6.8	256.5	3.8	119.3	13.6	97.9	0.4	273.6	5.3
2001	-	-	-	-	-	-	-	-	-	-	-	-	-	-	-	-	-	-

Source: U.S. Department of Labor, Bureau of Labor Statistics, Division of Consumer Prices and Price Indexes. *Base is December 1997 = 100. - indicates no data collected for period.

San Diego, CA
Consumer Price Index - Urban Wage Earners
Base 1982-1984 = 100
Annual Averages

For 1965-2001. Columns headed % show percentile change in the index from the previous period for which an index is available.

Year	All Items		Food & Beverage		Housing		Apparel		Trans-portation		Medical Care		Recrea-tion*		Education & Communic.*		Other Goods & Services	
	Index	%	Index	%	Index	%	Index	%	Index	%	Index	%	Index	%	Index	%	Index	%
1965	29.5	-	-	-	-	-	50.2	-	31.9	-	26.0	-	-	-	-	-	-	-
1966	30.1	2.0	-	-	-	-	50.8	1.2	31.9	0.0	27.4	5.4	-	-	-	-	-	-
1967	31.0	3.0	-	-	-	-	51.6	1.6	33.1	3.8	29.4	7.3	-	-	-	-	-	-
1968	32.3	4.2	-	-	-	-	54.7	6.0	33.9	2.4	30.1	2.4	-	-	-	-	-	-
1969	34.0	5.3	-	-	-	-	57.1	4.4	34.7	2.4	31.7	5.3	-	-	-	-	-	-
1970	35.8	5.3	-	-	-	-	59.3	3.9	35.7	2.9	33.7	6.3	-	-	-	-	-	-
1971	37.1	3.6	-	-	-	-	60.8	2.5	37.7	5.6	35.5	5.3	-	-	-	-	-	-
1972	38.6	4.0	-	-	-	-	63.1	3.8	38.8	2.9	36.4	2.5	-	-	-	-	-	-
1973	41.1	6.5	-	-	-	-	65.5	3.8	40.5	4.4	38.2	4.9	-	-	-	-	-	-
1974	45.6	10.9	-	-	-	-	70.9	8.2	45.8	13.1	42.3	10.7	-	-	-	-	-	-
1975	49.9	9.4	-	-	-	-	72.6	2.4	50.6	10.5	47.4	12.1	-	-	-	-	-	-
1976	52.9	6.0	57.9	-	48.1	-	74.6	2.8	54.2	7.1	52.4	10.5	-	-	-	-	59.3	-
1977	56.4	6.6	61.4	6.0	52.0	8.1	76.0	1.9	57.7	6.5	57.3	9.4	-	-	-	-	62.5	5.4
1978	61.9	9.8	67.9	10.6	58.4	12.3	77.9	2.5	61.0	5.7	62.0	8.2	-	-	-	-	67.6	8.2
1979	71.4	15.3	75.9	11.8	69.9	19.7	81.0	4.0	69.6	14.1	69.4	11.9	-	-	-	-	72.5	7.2
1980	82.1	15.0	82.9	9.2	82.4	17.9	88.5	9.3	81.2	16.7	76.2	9.8	-	-	-	-	78.5	8.3
1981	92.8	13.0	89.9	8.4	96.2	16.7	92.5	4.5	90.2	11.1	83.5	9.6	-	-	-	-	85.0	8.3
1982	99.4	7.1	94.6	5.2	103.7	7.8	96.5	4.3	95.4	5.8	93.1	11.5	-	-	-	-	91.4	7.5
1983	99.0	-0.4	100.5	6.2	98.2	-5.3	99.8	3.4	98.8	3.6	100.6	8.1	-	-	-	-	100.3	9.7
1984	101.7	2.7	104.9	4.4	98.1	-0.1	103.8	4.0	105.9	7.2	106.3	5.7	-	-	-	-	108.3	8.0
1985	104.5	2.8	107.4	2.4	100.8	2.8	106.3	2.4	109.6	3.5	110.6	4.0	-	-	-	-	115.0	6.2
1986	107.2	2.6	111.2	3.5	105.6	4.8	107.5	1.1	106.2	-3.1	118.9	7.5	-	-	-	-	118.9	3.4
1987	111.1	3.6	116.1	4.4	108.1	2.4	110.2	2.5	108.5	2.2	130.4	9.7	-	-	-	-	-	-
1988	116.5	4.9	120.0	3.4	112.0	3.6	118.8	7.8	114.7	5.7	143.9	10.4	-	-	-	-	138.3	16.3
1989	123.5	6.0	127.8	6.5	115.8	3.4	120.7	1.6	124.3	8.4	161.4	12.2	-	-	-	-	159.7	15.5
1990	130.5	5.7	134.9	5.6	122.2	5.5	131.1	8.6	131.4	5.7	175.7	8.9	-	-	-	-	167.9	5.1
1991	134.7	3.2	141.2	4.7	126.0	3.1	128.2	-2.2	133.5	1.6	190.2	8.3	-	-	-	-	179.7	7.0
1992	138.2	2.6	143.3	1.5	129.1	2.5	130.0	1.4	136.4	2.2	203.9	7.2	-	-	-	-	191.0	6.3
1993	140.9	2.0	145.9	1.8	130.0	0.7	134.1	3.2	138.9	1.8	215.8	5.8	-	-	-	-	205.9	7.8
1994	144.4	2.5	148.4	1.7	133.8	2.9	140.3	4.6	142.3	2.4	219.3	1.6	-	-	-	-	209.3	1.7
1995	147.0	1.8	151.8	2.3	135.9	1.6	131.7	-6.1	149.1	4.8	221.2	0.9	-	-	-	-	212.5	1.5
1996	150.6	2.4	157.8	4.0	138.7	2.1	128.1	-2.7	153.2	2.7	233.1	5.4	-	-	-	-	213.5	0.5
1997	152.9	1.5	162.1	2.7	141.8	2.2	123.7	-3.4	153.8	0.4	240.4	3.1	-	-	-	-	218.5	2.3
1998	155.4	1.6	165.5	2.1	147.2	3.8	122.3	-1.1	150.1	-2.4	246.1	2.4	99.7	-	99.0	-	227.4	4.1
1999	161.3	3.8	167.1	1.0	155.1	5.4	128.8	5.3	152.2	1.4	252.8	2.7	106.5	6.8	97.6	-1.4	258.3	13.6
2000	170.7	5.8	169.7	1.6	165.2	6.5	130.6	1.4	161.5	6.1	262.7	3.9	127.3	19.5	98.2	0.6	273.3	5.8
2001	-	-	-	-	-	-	-	-	-	-	-	-	-	-	-	-	-	-

Source: U.S. Department of Labor, Bureau of Labor Statistics, Division of Consumer Prices and Price Indexes. *Base is December 1997 = 100. - indicates no data collected for period.

San Diego, CA
Consumer Price Index - All Urban Consumers
Base 1982-1984 = 100
All Items

For 1965-2001. Columns headed % show percentile change in the index from the previous period for which an index is available.

Year	Jan Index	%	Feb Index	%	Mar Index	%	Apr Index	%	May Index	%	Jun Index	%	Jul Index	%	Aug Index	%	Sep Index	%	Oct Index	%	Nov Index	%	Dec Index	%
1965	-	-	28.1	-	-	-	-	-	28.3	0.7	-	-	-	-	28.0	-1.1	-	-	-	-	28.2	0.7	-	-
1966	-	-	28.5	1.1	-	-	-	-	28.6	0.4	-	-	-	-	28.7	0.3	-	-	-	-	29.1	1.4	-	-
1967	-	-	29.2	0.3	-	-	-	-	29.3	0.3	-	-	-	-	29.8	1.7	-	-	-	-	30.0	0.7	-	-
1968	-	-	30.3	1.0	-	-	-	-	30.6	1.0	-	-	-	-	31.0	1.3	-	-	-	-	31.3	1.0	-	-
1969	-	-	31.7	1.3	-	-	-	-	32.2	1.6	-	-	-	-	32.7	1.6	-	-	-	-	32.9	0.6	-	-
1970	-	-	33.4	1.5	-	-	-	-	34.0	1.8	-	-	-	-	34.3	0.9	-	-	-	-	34.8	1.5	-	-
1971	-	-	35.0	0.6	-	-	-	-	35.3	0.9	-	-	-	-	35.6	0.8	-	-	-	-	35.7	0.3	-	-
1972	-	-	36.1	1.1	-	-	-	-	36.6	1.4	-	-	-	-	37.0	1.1	-	-	-	-	37.5	1.4	-	-
1973	-	-	37.9	1.1	-	-	-	-	38.7	2.1	-	-	-	-	39.7	2.6	-	-	-	-	40.4	1.8	-	-
1974	-	-	41.5	2.7	-	-	-	-	42.9	3.4	-	-	-	-	44.3	3.3	-	-	-	-	45.4	2.5	-	-
1975	-	-	46.5	2.4	-	-	-	-	47.0	1.1	-	-	-	-	48.1	2.3	-	-	-	-	48.8	1.5	-	-
1976	-	-	49.5	1.4	-	-	-	-	50.1	1.2	-	-	-	-	50.9	1.6	-	-	-	-	51.4	1.0	-	-
1977	-	-	52.2	1.6	-	-	-	-	53.4	2.3	-	-	-	-	54.4	1.9	-	-	-	-	55.2	1.5	-	-
1978	55.9	1.3	-	-	56.6	1.3	-	-	57.8	2.1	-	-	59.7	3.3	-	-	61.1	2.3	-	-	62.0	1.5	-	-
1979	63.5	2.4	-	-	65.5	3.1	-	-	67.5	3.1	-	-	69.8	3.4	-	-	71.1	1.9	-	-	73.3	3.1	-	-
1980	75.1	2.5	-	-	76.4	1.7	-	-	79.8	4.5	-	-	79.8	0.0	-	-	80.4	0.8	-	-	82.5	2.6	-	-
1981	85.1	3.2	-	-	86.7	1.9	-	-	88.0	1.5	-	-	90.3	2.6	-	-	92.8	2.8	-	-	95.0	2.4	-	-
1982	95.6	0.6	-	-	94.3	-1.4	-	-	97.4	3.3	-	-	99.0	1.6	-	-	96.3	-2.7	-	-	95.1	-1.2	-	-
1983	96.1	1.1	-	-	96.9	0.8	-	-	98.2	1.3	-	-	99.1	0.9	-	-	100.7	1.6	-	-	101.2	0.5	-	-
1984	102.4	1.2	-	-	103.3	0.9	-	-	104.4	1.1	-	-	103.9	-0.5	-	-	105.6	1.6	-	-	107.6	1.9	-	-
1985	107.7	0.1	-	-	109.2	1.4	-	-	110.0	0.7	-	-	110.3	0.3	-	-	111.6	1.2	-	-	112.1	0.4	-	-
1986	112.9	0.7	-	-	112.1	-0.7	-	-	113.2	1.0	-	-	113.3	0.1	-	-	114.1	0.7	-	-	114.6	0.4	-	-
1987	-	-	-	-	-	-	-	-	-	-	116.6	1.7	-	-	-	-	-	-	-	-	-	-	118.3	1.5
1988	-	-	-	-	-	-	-	-	-	-	121.9	3.0	-	-	-	-	-	-	-	-	-	-	125.0	2.5
1989	-	-	-	-	-	-	-	-	-	-	128.9	3.1	-	-	-	-	-	-	-	-	-	-	132.3	2.6
1990	-	-	-	-	-	-	-	-	-	-	136.5	3.2	-	-	-	-	-	-	-	-	-	-	140.3	2.8
1991	-	-	-	-	-	-	-	-	-	-	142.2	1.4	-	-	-	-	-	-	-	-	-	-	144.7	1.8
1992	-	-	-	-	-	-	-	-	-	-	147.0	1.6	-	-	-	-	-	-	-	-	-	-	147.7	0.5
1993	-	-	-	-	-	-	-	-	-	-	150.4	1.8	-	-	-	-	-	-	-	-	-	-	150.8	0.3
1994	-	-	-	-	-	-	-	-	-	-	154.3	2.3	-	-	-	-	-	-	-	-	-	-	154.6	0.2
1995	-	-	-	-	-	-	-	-	-	-	156.3	1.1	-	-	-	-	-	-	-	-	-	-	157.3	0.6
1996	-	-	-	-	-	-	-	-	-	-	159.8	1.6	-	-	-	-	-	-	-	-	-	-	161.9	1.3
1997	-	-	-	-	-	-	-	-	-	-	163.7	1.1	-	-	-	-	-	-	-	-	-	-	163.7	0.0
1998	-	-	-	-	-	-	-	-	-	-	166.0	1.4	-	-	-	-	-	-	-	-	-	-	167.8	1.1
1999	-	-	-	-	-	-	-	-	-	-	171.7	2.3	-	-	-	-	-	-	-	-	-	-	173.9	1.3
2000	-	-	-	-	-	-	-	-	-	-	179.8	3.4	-	-	-	-	-	-	-	-	-	-	185.8	3.3
2001	-	-	-	-	-	-	-	-	-	-	190.1	2.3	-	-	-	-	-	-	-	-	-	-	-	-

Source: U.S. Department of Labor, Bureau of Labor Statistics, Division of Consumer Prices and Price Indexes. - indicates no data collected for period.

San Diego, CA
Consumer Price Index - Urban Wage Earners
Base 1982-1984 = 100
All Items

For 1965-2001. Columns headed % show percentile change in the index from the previous period for which an index is available.

Year	Jan Index	%	Feb Index	%	Mar Index	%	Apr Index	%	May Index	%	Jun Index	%	Jul Index	%	Aug Index	%	Sep Index	%	Oct Index	%	Nov Index	%	Dec Index	%
1965	-	-	29.5	-	-	-	-	-	29.6	0.3	-	-	-	-	29.4	-0.7	-	-	-	-	29.6	0.7	-	-
1966	-	-	29.9	1.0	-	-	-	-	30.0	0.3	-	-	-	-	30.1	0.3	-	-	-	-	30.5	1.3	-	-
1967	-	-	30.6	0.3	-	-	-	-	30.7	0.3	-	-	-	-	31.3	2.0	-	-	-	-	31.4	0.3	-	-
1968	-	-	31.8	1.3	-	-	-	-	32.1	0.9	-	-	-	-	32.5	1.2	-	-	-	-	32.8	0.9	-	-
1969	-	-	33.3	1.5	-	-	-	-	33.7	1.2	-	-	-	-	34.2	1.5	-	-	-	-	34.5	0.9	-	-
1970	-	-	35.0	1.4	-	-	-	-	35.7	2.0	-	-	-	-	35.9	0.6	-	-	-	-	36.5	1.7	-	-
1971	-	-	36.7	0.5	-	-	-	-	37.1	1.1	-	-	-	-	37.4	0.8	-	-	-	-	37.5	0.3	-	-
1972	-	-	37.9	1.1	-	-	-	-	38.3	1.1	-	-	-	-	38.8	1.3	-	-	-	-	39.3	1.3	-	-
1973	-	-	39.8	1.3	-	-	-	-	40.5	1.8	-	-	-	-	41.7	3.0	-	-	-	-	42.3	1.4	-	-
1974	-	-	43.5	2.8	-	-	-	-	45.0	3.4	-	-	-	-	46.5	3.3	-	-	-	-	47.6	2.4	-	-
1975	-	-	48.7	2.3	-	-	-	-	49.2	1.0	-	-	-	-	50.4	2.4	-	-	-	-	51.1	1.4	-	-
1976	-	-	51.9	1.6	-	-	-	-	52.5	1.2	-	-	-	-	53.4	1.7	-	-	-	-	53.9	0.9	-	-
1977	-	-	54.8	1.7	-	-	-	-	56.0	2.2	-	-	-	-	57.1	2.0	-	-	-	-	57.9	1.4	-	-
1978	58.6	1.2	-	-	59.3	1.2	-	-	60.6	2.2	-	-	62.5	3.1	-	-	63.7	1.9	-	-	64.7	1.6	-	-
1979	65.9	1.9	-	-	67.8	2.9	-	-	70.1	3.4	-	-	72.3	3.1	-	-	73.7	1.9	-	-	75.9	3.0	-	-
1980	77.8	2.5	-	-	79.3	1.9	-	-	82.1	3.5	-	-	82.4	0.4	-	-	83.0	0.7	-	-	85.3	2.8	-	-
1981	87.7	2.8	-	-	89.3	1.8	-	-	90.7	1.6	-	-	93.2	2.8	-	-	95.5	2.5	-	-	97.7	2.3	-	-
1982	98.4	0.7	-	-	97.3	-1.1	-	-	100.3	3.1	-	-	102.1	1.8	-	-	99.6	-2.4	-	-	98.7	-0.9	-	-
1983	97.2	-1.5	-	-	97.8	0.6	-	-	97.6	-0.2	-	-	99.2	1.6	-	-	100.4	1.2	-	-	100.4	0.0	-	-
1984	102.1	1.7	-	-	101.2	-0.9	-	-	101.6	0.4	-	-	100.7	-0.9	-	-	102.5	1.8	-	-	102.0	-0.5	-	-
1985	102.1	0.1	-	-	103.5	1.4	-	-	104.3	0.8	-	-	104.5	0.2	-	-	105.5	1.0	-	-	106.0	0.5	-	-
1986	106.9	0.8	-	-	106.0	-0.8	-	-	107.0	0.9	-	-	107.0	0.0	-	-	107.7	0.7	-	-	108.2	0.5	-	-
1987	-	-	-	-	-	-	-	-	-	-	110.2	1.8	-	-	-	-	-	-	-	-	-	-	111.9	1.5
1988	-	-	-	-	-	-	-	-	-	-	115.1	2.9	-	-	-	-	-	-	-	-	-	-	118.0	2.5
1989	-	-	-	-	-	-	-	-	-	-	122.0	3.4	-	-	-	-	-	-	-	-	-	-	125.0	2.5
1990	-	-	-	-	-	-	-	-	-	-	128.9	3.1	-	-	-	-	-	-	-	-	-	-	132.2	2.6
1991	-	-	-	-	-	-	-	-	-	-	133.6	1.1	-	-	-	-	-	-	-	-	-	-	135.9	1.7
1992	-	-	-	-	-	-	-	-	-	-	137.9	1.5	-	-	-	-	-	-	-	-	-	-	138.6	0.5
1993	-	-	-	-	-	-	-	-	-	-	140.9	1.7	-	-	-	-	-	-	-	-	-	-	141.0	0.1
1994	-	-	-	-	-	-	-	-	-	-	144.0	2.1	-	-	-	-	-	-	-	-	-	-	144.8	0.6
1995	-	-	-	-	-	-	-	-	-	-	146.5	1.2	-	-	-	-	-	-	-	-	-	-	147.5	0.7
1996	-	-	-	-	-	-	-	-	-	-	149.9	1.6	-	-	-	-	-	-	-	-	-	-	151.3	0.9
1997	-	-	-	-	-	-	-	-	-	-	152.6	0.9	-	-	-	-	-	-	-	-	-	-	153.1	0.3
1998	-	-	-	-	-	-	-	-	-	-	154.5	0.9	-	-	-	-	-	-	-	-	-	-	156.2	1.1
1999	-	-	-	-	-	-	-	-	-	-	160.2	2.6	-	-	-	-	-	-	-	-	-	-	162.4	1.4
2000	-	-	-	-	-	-	-	-	-	-	167.5	3.1	-	-	-	-	-	-	-	-	-	-	173.9	3.8
2001	-	-	-	-	-	-	-	-	-	-	177.5	2.1	-	-	-	-	-	-	-	-	-	-	-	-

Source: U.S. Department of Labor, Bureau of Labor Statistics, Division of Consumer Prices and Price Indexes. - indicates no data collected for period.

San Diego, CA
Consumer Price Index - All Urban Consumers
Base 1982-1984 = 100
Food and Beverages

For 1975-2001. Columns headed % show percentile change in the index from the previous period for which an index is available.

Year	Jan Index	%	Feb Index	%	Mar Index	%	Apr Index	%	May Index	%	Jun Index	%	Jul Index	%	Aug Index	%	Sep Index	%	Oct Index	%	Nov Index	%	Dec Index	%
1975	-	-	-	-	-	-	-	-	-	-	-	-	-	-	-	-	-	-	-	-	58.9	-	-	-
1976	-	-	58.9	0.0	-	-	-	-	59.2	0.5	-	-	-	-	59.7	0.8	-	-	-	-	59.6	-0.2	-	-
1977	-	-	61.0	2.3	-	-	-	-	62.8	3.0	-	-	-	-	63.6	1.3	-	-	-	-	64.3	1.1	-	-
1978	65.8	2.3	-	-	67.3	2.3	-	-	69.8	3.7	-	-	71.0	1.7	-	-	71.3	0.4	-	-	71.0	-0.4	-	-
1979	73.6	3.7	-	-	75.6	2.7	-	-	77.4	2.4	-	-	77.5	0.1	-	-	78.4	1.2	-	-	79.4	1.3	-	-
1980	81.0	2.0	-	-	82.2	1.5	-	-	83.5	1.6	-	-	84.1	0.7	-	-	86.2	2.5	-	-	87.5	1.5	-	-
1981	88.7	1.4	-	-	89.6	1.0	-	-	89.7	0.1	-	-	90.9	1.3	-	-	91.8	1.0	-	-	91.2	-0.7	-	-
1982	93.2	2.2	-	-	93.7	0.5	-	-	94.2	0.5	-	-	95.5	1.4	-	-	95.0	-0.5	-	-	96.7	1.8	-	-
1983	96.1	-0.6	-	-	100.3	4.4	-	-	100.5	0.2	-	-	100.2	-0.3	-	-	101.0	0.8	-	-	102.1	1.1	-	-
1984	104.7	2.5	-	-	105.3	0.6	-	-	103.6	-1.6	-	-	103.9	0.3	-	-	105.1	1.2	-	-	105.6	0.5	-	-
1985	107.4	1.7	-	-	106.9	-0.5	-	-	106.9	0.0	-	-	105.9	-0.9	-	-	106.8	0.8	-	-	108.0	1.1	-	-
1986	111.2	3.0	-	-	108.9	-2.1	-	-	111.0	1.9	-	-	110.1	-0.8	-	-	111.0	0.8	-	-	113.7	2.4	-	-
1987	-	-	-	-	-	-	-	-	-	-	115.7	1.8	-	-	-	-	-	-	-	-	-	-	115.9	0.2
1988	-	-	-	-	-	-	-	-	-	-	118.5	2.2	-	-	-	-	-	-	-	-	-	-	120.9	2.0
1989	-	-	-	-	-	-	-	-	-	-	125.9	4.1	-	-	-	-	-	-	-	-	-	-	128.8	2.3
1990	-	-	-	-	-	-	-	-	-	-	134.1	4.1	-	-	-	-	-	-	-	-	-	-	134.2	0.1
1991	-	-	-	-	-	-	-	-	-	-	140.4	4.6	-	-	-	-	-	-	-	-	-	-	140.2	-0.1
1992	-	-	-	-	-	-	-	-	-	-	142.3	1.5	-	-	-	-	-	-	-	-	-	-	142.7	0.3
1993	-	-	-	-	-	-	-	-	-	-	144.5	1.3	-	-	-	-	-	-	-	-	-	-	146.2	1.2
1994	-	-	-	-	-	-	-	-	-	-	147.5	0.9	-	-	-	-	-	-	-	-	-	-	147.7	0.1
1995	-	-	-	-	-	-	-	-	-	-	151.2	2.4	-	-	-	-	-	-	-	-	-	-	151.1	-0.1
1996	-	-	-	-	-	-	-	-	-	-	155.7	3.0	-	-	-	-	-	-	-	-	-	-	158.3	1.7
1997	-	-	-	-	-	-	-	-	-	-	161.0	1.7	-	-	-	-	-	-	-	-	-	-	161.9	0.6
1998	-	-	-	-	-	-	-	-	-	-	164.8	1.8	-	-	-	-	-	-	-	-	-	-	165.2	0.2
1999	-	-	-	-	-	-	-	-	-	-	167.2	1.2	-	-	-	-	-	-	-	-	-	-	165.9	-0.8
2000	-	-	-	-	-	-	-	-	-	-	167.1	0.7	-	-	-	-	-	-	-	-	-	-	171.2	2.5
2001	-	-	-	-	-	-	-	-	-	-	176.1	2.9	-	-	-	-	-	-	-	-	-	-	-	-

Source: U.S. Department of Labor, Bureau of Labor Statistics, Division of Consumer Prices and Price Indexes. - indicates no data collected for period.

San Diego, CA
Consumer Price Index - Urban Wage Earners
Base 1982-1984 = 100
Food and Beverages

For 1975-2001. Columns headed % show percentile change in the index from the previous period for which an index is available.

Year	Jan Index	%	Feb Index	%	Mar Index	%	Apr Index	%	May Index	%	Jun Index	%	Jul Index	%	Aug Index	%	Sep Index	%	Oct Index	%	Nov Index	%	Dec Index	%
1975	-	-	-	-	-	-	-	-	-	-	-	-	-	-	-	-	-	-	-	-	57.4	-	-	-
1976	-	-	57.5	0.2	-	-	-	-	57.7	0.3	-	-	-	-	58.2	0.9	-	-	-	-	58.1	-0.2	-	-
1977	-	-	59.6	2.6	-	-	-	-	61.3	2.9	-	-	-	-	62.1	1.3	-	-	-	-	62.7	1.0	-	-
1978	63.9	1.9	-	-	65.4	2.3	-	-	67.9	3.8	-	-	69.3	2.1	-	-	69.7	0.6	-	-	69.4	-0.4	-	-
1979	72.0	3.7	-	-	74.2	3.1	-	-	76.0	2.4	-	-	76.5	0.7	-	-	77.1	0.8	-	-	77.9	1.0	-	-
1980	79.5	2.1	-	-	80.9	1.8	-	-	81.5	0.7	-	-	82.1	0.7	-	-	84.6	3.0	-	-	86.8	2.6	-	-
1981	87.6	0.9	-	-	88.8	1.4	-	-	89.1	0.3	-	-	90.2	1.2	-	-	91.3	1.2	-	-	90.8	-0.5	-	-
1982	92.6	2.0	-	-	93.3	0.8	-	-	93.9	0.6	-	-	95.4	1.6	-	-	94.9	-0.5	-	-	96.7	1.9	-	-
1983	96.0	-0.7	-	-	100.5	4.7	-	-	100.6	0.1	-	-	100.2	-0.4	-	-	101.0	0.8	-	-	102.3	1.3	-	-
1984	104.8	2.4	-	-	105.2	0.4	-	-	103.8	-1.3	-	-	104.0	0.2	-	-	105.4	1.3	-	-	105.8	0.4	-	-
1985	107.5	1.6	-	-	107.1	-0.4	-	-	107.2	0.1	-	-	106.2	-0.9	-	-	107.0	0.8	-	-	108.4	1.3	-	-
1986	111.4	2.8	-	-	108.9	-2.2	-	-	110.9	1.8	-	-	110.2	-0.6	-	-	111.0	0.7	-	-	114.0	2.7	-	-
1987	-	-	-	-	-	-	-	-	-	-	116.0	1.8	-	-	-	-	-	-	-	-	-	-	116.2	0.2
1988	-	-	-	-	-	-	-	-	-	-	118.8	2.2	-	-	-	-	-	-	-	-	-	-	121.3	2.1
1989	-	-	-	-	-	-	-	-	-	-	126.2	4.0	-	-	-	-	-	-	-	-	-	-	129.3	2.5
1990	-	-	-	-	-	-	-	-	-	-	134.7	4.2	-	-	-	-	-	-	-	-	-	-	135.2	0.4
1991	-	-	-	-	-	-	-	-	-	-	141.3	4.5	-	-	-	-	-	-	-	-	-	-	141.1	-0.1
1992	-	-	-	-	-	-	-	-	-	-	143.0	1.3	-	-	-	-	-	-	-	-	-	-	143.6	0.4
1993	-	-	-	-	-	-	-	-	-	-	145.1	1.0	-	-	-	-	-	-	-	-	-	-	146.7	1.1
1994	-	-	-	-	-	-	-	-	-	-	148.2	1.0	-	-	-	-	-	-	-	-	-	-	148.7	0.3
1995	-	-	-	-	-	-	-	-	-	-	151.8	2.1	-	-	-	-	-	-	-	-	-	-	151.8	0.0
1996	-	-	-	-	-	-	-	-	-	-	156.5	3.1	-	-	-	-	-	-	-	-	-	-	159.1	1.7
1997	-	-	-	-	-	-	-	-	-	-	161.6	1.6	-	-	-	-	-	-	-	-	-	-	162.6	0.6
1998	-	-	-	-	-	-	-	-	-	-	165.3	1.7	-	-	-	-	-	-	-	-	-	-	165.7	0.2
1999	-	-	-	-	-	-	-	-	-	-	167.7	1.2	-	-	-	-	-	-	-	-	-	-	166.6	-0.7
2000	-	-	-	-	-	-	-	-	-	-	167.5	0.5	-	-	-	-	-	-	-	-	-	-	171.9	2.6
2001	-	-	-	-	-	-	-	-	-	-	176.5	2.7	-	-	-	-	-	-	-	-	-	-	-	-

Source: U.S. Department of Labor, Bureau of Labor Statistics, Division of Consumer Prices and Price Indexes. - indicates no data collected for period.

San Diego, CA
Consumer Price Index - All Urban Consumers
Base 1982-1984 = 100
Housing

For 1975-2001. Columns headed % show percentile change in the index from the previous period for which an index is available.

Year	Jan Index	%	Feb Index	%	Mar Index	%	Apr Index	%	May Index	%	Jun Index	%	Jul Index	%	Aug Index	%	Sep Index	%	Oct Index	%	Nov Index	%	Dec Index	%
1975	-	-	-	-	-	-	-	-	-	-	-	-	-	-	-	-	-	-	-	-	42.4	-	-	-
1976	-	-	43.5	2.6	-	-	-	-	43.8	0.7	-	-	-	-	44.6	1.8	-	-	-	-	45.4	1.8	-	-
1977	-	-	46.2	1.8	-	-	-	-	47.0	1.7	-	-	-	-	48.7	3.6	-	-	-	-	49.6	1.8	-	-
1978	50.3	1.4	-	-	51.0	1.4	-	-	51.9	1.8	-	-	54.1	4.2	-	-	56.1	3.7	-	-	57.3	2.1	-	-
1979	58.9	2.8	-	-	61.3	4.1	-	-	63.2	3.1	-	-	66.4	5.1	-	-	67.5	1.7	-	-	70.5	4.4	-	-
1980	72.5	2.8	-	-	72.8	0.4	-	-	77.7	6.7	-	-	77.3	-0.5	-	-	77.3	0.0	-	-	80.2	3.8	-	-
1981	83.7	4.4	-	-	85.3	1.9	-	-	86.8	1.8	-	-	89.5	3.1	-	-	92.9	3.8	-	-	96.2	3.6	-	-
1982	96.7	0.5	-	-	94.6	-2.2	-	-	99.3	5.0	-	-	100.4	1.1	-	-	95.5	-4.9	-	-	93.2	-2.4	-	-
1983	95.5	2.5	-	-	96.5	1.0	-	-	97.1	0.6	-	-	98.3	1.2	-	-	101.1	2.8	-	-	101.2	0.1	-	-
1984	101.3	0.1	-	-	103.1	1.8	-	-	104.1	1.0	-	-	103.8	-0.3	-	-	106.1	2.2	-	-	109.1	2.8	-	-
1985	108.9	-0.2	-	-	111.8	2.7	-	-	112.1	0.3	-	-	113.6	1.3	-	-	116.7	2.7	-	-	116.9	0.2	-	-
1986	117.1	0.2	-	-	117.2	0.1	-	-	118.3	0.9	-	-	119.8	1.3	-	-	120.8	0.8	-	-	121.1	0.2	-	-
1987	-	-	-	-	-	-	-	-	-	-	121.3	0.2	-	-	-	-	-	-	-	-	-	-	123.2	1.6
1988	-	-	-	-	-	-	-	-	-	-	126.1	2.4	-	-	-	-	-	-	-	-	-	-	127.6	1.2
1989	-	-	-	-	-	-	-	-	-	-	128.8	0.9	-	-	-	-	-	-	-	-	-	-	133.8	3.9
1990	-	-	-	-	-	-	-	-	-	-	136.7	2.2	-	-	-	-	-	-	-	-	-	-	141.6	3.6
1991	-	-	-	-	-	-	-	-	-	-	142.8	0.8	-	-	-	-	-	-	-	-	-	-	145.4	1.8
1992	-	-	-	-	-	-	-	-	-	-	148.2	1.9	-	-	-	-	-	-	-	-	-	-	148.3	0.1
1993	-	-	-	-	-	-	-	-	-	-	149.2	0.6	-	-	-	-	-	-	-	-	-	-	149.8	0.4
1994	-	-	-	-	-	-	-	-	-	-	152.3	1.7	-	-	-	-	-	-	-	-	-	-	154.6	1.5
1995	-	-	-	-	-	-	-	-	-	-	155.1	0.3	-	-	-	-	-	-	-	-	-	-	156.4	0.8
1996	-	-	-	-	-	-	-	-	-	-	158.1	1.1	-	-	-	-	-	-	-	-	-	-	161.7	2.3
1997	-	-	-	-	-	-	-	-	-	-	163.9	1.4	-	-	-	-	-	-	-	-	-	-	163.1	-0.5
1998	-	-	-	-	-	-	-	-	-	-	167.8	2.9	-	-	-	-	-	-	-	-	-	-	172.4	2.7
1999	-	-	-	-	-	-	-	-	-	-	176.4	2.3	-	-	-	-	-	-	-	-	-	-	179.9	2.0
2000	-	-	-	-	-	-	-	-	-	-	187.3	4.1	-	-	-	-	-	-	-	-	-	-	193.7	3.4
2001	-	-	-	-	-	-	-	-	-	-	200.7	3.6	-	-	-	-	-	-	-	-	-	-	-	-

Source: U.S. Department of Labor, Bureau of Labor Statistics, Division of Consumer Prices and Price Indexes. - indicates no data collected for period.

San Diego, CA
Consumer Price Index - Urban Wage Earners
Base 1982-1984 = 100
Housing

For 1975-2001. Columns headed % show percentile change in the index from the previous period for which an index is available.

Year	Jan Index	%	Feb Index	%	Mar Index	%	Apr Index	%	May Index	%	Jun Index	%	Jul Index	%	Aug Index	%	Sep Index	%	Oct Index	%	Nov Index	%	Dec Index	%
1975	-	-	-	-	-	-	-	-	-	-	-	-	-	-	-	-	-	-	-	-	46.0	-	-	-
1976	-	-	47.2	2.6	-	-	-	-	47.6	0.8	-	-	-	-	48.4	1.7	-	-	-	-	49.3	-	-	-
1977	-	-	50.2	1.8	-	-	-	-	51.1	1.8	-	-	-	-	52.8	3.3	-	-	-	-	53.9	2.1	-	-
1978	54.7	1.5	-	-	55.3	1.1	-	-	56.4	2.0	-	-	58.8	4.3	-	-	60.8	3.4	-	-	62.1	2.1	-	-
1979	63.3	1.9	-	-	65.8	3.9	-	-	67.8	3.0	-	-	70.9	4.6	-	-	72.3	2.0	-	-	75.8	4.8	-	-
1980	77.9	2.8	-	-	78.2	0.4	-	-	83.1	6.3	-	-	82.9	-0.2	-	-	82.9	0.0	-	-	86.0	3.7	-	-
1981	90.0	4.7	-	-	91.5	1.7	-	-	93.0	1.6	-	-	96.2	3.4	-	-	99.6	3.5	-	-	103.3	3.7	-	-
1982	104.1	0.8	-	-	101.8	-2.2	-	-	107.0	5.1	-	-	108.1	1.0	-	-	102.7	-5.0	-	-	100.4	-2.2	-	-
1983	97.7	-2.7	-	-	97.9	0.2	-	-	95.8	-2.1	-	-	98.3	2.6	-	-	99.9	1.6	-	-	98.8	-1.1	-	-
1984	100.4	1.6	-	-	98.2	-2.2	-	-	98.1	-0.1	-	-	96.6	-1.5	-	-	99.2	2.7	-	-	96.9	-2.3	-	-
1985	96.5	-0.4	-	-	99.1	2.7	-	-	99.5	0.4	-	-	100.9	1.4	-	-	103.5	2.6	-	-	103.6	0.1	-	-
1986	103.7	0.1	-	-	103.8	0.1	-	-	104.8	1.0	-	-	106.1	1.2	-	-	107.1	0.9	-	-	107.3	0.2	-	-
1987	-	-	-	-	-	-	-	-	-	-	107.3	0.0	-	-	-	-	-	-	-	-	-	-	109.0	1.6
1988	-	-	-	-	-	-	-	-	-	-	111.3	2.1	-	-	-	-	-	-	-	-	-	-	112.6	1.2
1989	-	-	-	-	-	-	-	-	-	-	113.7	1.0	-	-	-	-	-	-	-	-	-	-	118.0	3.8
1990	-	-	-	-	-	-	-	-	-	-	120.2	1.9	-	-	-	-	-	-	-	-	-	-	124.1	3.2
1991	-	-	-	-	-	-	-	-	-	-	124.9	0.6	-	-	-	-	-	-	-	-	-	-	127.1	1.8
1992	-	-	-	-	-	-	-	-	-	-	129.2	1.7	-	-	-	-	-	-	-	-	-	-	129.1	-0.1
1993	-	-	-	-	-	-	-	-	-	-	129.8	0.5	-	-	-	-	-	-	-	-	-	-	130.2	0.3
1994	-	-	-	-	-	-	-	-	-	-	132.6	1.8	-	-	-	-	-	-	-	-	-	-	135.0	1.8
1995	-	-	-	-	-	-	-	-	-	-	135.4	0.3	-	-	-	-	-	-	-	-	-	-	136.4	0.7
1996	-	-	-	-	-	-	-	-	-	-	137.6	0.9	-	-	-	-	-	-	-	-	-	-	139.9	1.7
1997	-	-	-	-	-	-	-	-	-	-	141.8	1.4	-	-	-	-	-	-	-	-	-	-	141.8	0.0
1998	-	-	-	-	-	-	-	-	-	-	145.0	2.3	-	-	-	-	-	-	-	-	-	-	149.5	3.1
1999	-	-	-	-	-	-	-	-	-	-	153.3	2.5	-	-	-	-	-	-	-	-	-	-	156.9	2.3
2000	-	-	-	-	-	-	-	-	-	-	161.9	3.2	-	-	-	-	-	-	-	-	-	-	168.5	4.1
2001	-	-	-	-	-	-	-	-	-	-	174.2	3.4	-	-	-	-	-	-	-	-	-	-	-	-

Source: U.S. Department of Labor, Bureau of Labor Statistics, Division of Consumer Prices and Price Indexes. - indicates no data collected for period.

San Diego, CA
Consumer Price Index - All Urban Consumers
Base 1982-1984 = 100
Apparel

For 1965-2001. Columns headed % show percentile change in the index from the previous period for which an index is available.

Year	Jan Index	%	Feb Index	%	Mar Index	%	Apr Index	%	May Index	%	Jun Index	%	Jul Index	%	Aug Index	%	Sep Index	%	Oct Index	%	Nov Index	%	Dec Index	%
1965	-	-	48.5	-	-	-	-	-	48.4	-0.2	-	-	-	-	47.7	-1.4	-	-	-	-	47.8	0.2	-	-
1966	-	-	48.0	0.4	-	-	-	-	48.8	1.7	-	-	-	-	48.9	0.2	-	-	-	-	49.2	0.6	-	-
1967	-	-	48.8	-0.8	-	-	-	-	49.3	1.0	-	-	-	-	49.2	-0.2	-	-	-	-	50.5	2.6	-	-
1968	-	-	50.9	0.8	-	-	-	-	51.9	2.0	-	-	-	-	52.8	1.7	-	-	-	-	54.2	2.7	-	-
1969	-	-	53.9	-0.6	-	-	-	-	54.4	0.9	-	-	-	-	55.0	1.1	-	-	-	-	55.2	0.4	-	-
1970	-	-	55.8	1.1	-	-	-	-	57.2	2.5	-	-	-	-	56.8	-0.7	-	-	-	-	57.5	1.2	-	-
1971	-	-	57.5	0.0	-	-	-	-	58.4	1.6	-	-	-	-	58.5	0.2	-	-	-	-	58.7	0.3	-	-
1972	-	-	59.8	1.9	-	-	-	-	60.7	1.5	-	-	-	-	59.8	-1.5	-	-	-	-	61.4	2.7	-	-
1973	-	-	60.9	-0.8	-	-	-	-	61.7	1.3	-	-	-	-	63.3	2.6	-	-	-	-	64.7	2.2	-	-
1974	-	-	66.2	2.3	-	-	-	-	68.6	3.6	-	-	-	-	67.9	-1.0	-	-	-	-	69.1	1.8	-	-
1975	-	-	68.6	-0.7	-	-	-	-	70.3	2.5	-	-	-	-	69.2	-1.6	-	-	-	-	70.0	1.2	-	-
1976	-	-	71.0	1.4	-	-	-	-	71.5	0.7	-	-	-	-	71.9	0.6	-	-	-	-	71.5	-0.6	-	-
1977	-	-	71.1	-0.6	-	-	-	-	73.0	2.7	-	-	-	-	73.0	0.0	-	-	-	-	73.8	1.1	-	-
1978	74.0	0.3	-	-	73.8	-0.3	-	-	76.9	4.2	-	-	77.3	0.5	-	-	78.5	1.6	-	-	79.5	1.3	-	-
1979	79.2	-0.4	-	-	79.7	0.6	-	-	81.8	2.6	-	-	81.2	-0.7	-	-	82.9	2.1	-	-	82.9	0.0	-	-
1980	83.4	0.6	-	-	88.6	6.2	-	-	87.5	-1.2	-	-	86.7	-0.9	-	-	87.8	1.3	-	-	89.5	1.9	-	-
1981	87.9	-1.8	-	-	90.8	3.3	-	-	90.3	-0.6	-	-	93.5	3.5	-	-	95.0	1.6	-	-	95.0	0.0	-	-
1982	92.2	-2.9	-	-	95.1	3.1	-	-	96.4	1.4	-	-	95.9	-0.5	-	-	99.4	3.6	-	-	98.7	-0.7	-	-
1983	97.8	-0.9	-	-	97.3	-0.5	-	-	98.4	1.1	-	-	101.3	2.9	-	-	101.6	0.3	-	-	100.5	-1.1	-	-
1984	101.8	1.3	-	-	101.6	-0.2	-	-	103.8	2.2	-	-	100.6	-3.1	-	-	106.4	5.8	-	-	108.0	1.5	-	-
1985	105.1	-2.7	-	-	105.5	0.4	-	-	107.5	1.9	-	-	105.1	-2.2	-	-	106.1	1.0	-	-	106.3	0.2	-	-
1986	105.1	-1.1	-	-	108.3	3.0	-	-	108.1	-0.2	-	-	104.5	-3.3	-	-	109.0	4.3	-	-	108.2	-0.7	-	-
1987	-	-	-	-	-	-	-	-	-	-	110.1	1.8	-	-	-	-	-	-	-	-	-	-	110.3	0.2
1988	-	-	-	-	-	-	-	-	-	-	118.4	7.3	-	-	-	-	-	-	-	-	-	-	119.7	1.1
1989	-	-	-	-	-	-	-	-	-	-	123.5	3.2	-	-	-	-	-	-	-	-	-	-	118.2	-4.3
1990	-	-	-	-	-	-	-	-	-	-	133.5	12.9	-	-	-	-	-	-	-	-	-	-	130.4	-2.3
1991	-	-	-	-	-	-	-	-	-	-	127.7	-2.1	-	-	-	-	-	-	-	-	-	-	131.4	2.9
1992	-	-	-	-	-	-	-	-	-	-	131.8	0.3	-	-	-	-	-	-	-	-	-	-	130.6	-0.9
1993	-	-	-	-	-	-	-	-	-	-	142.1	8.8	-	-	-	-	-	-	-	-	-	-	129.1	-9.1
1994	-	-	-	-	-	-	-	-	-	-	153.6	19.0	-	-	-	-	-	-	-	-	-	-	129.7	-15.6
1995	-	-	-	-	-	-	-	-	-	-	134.3	3.5	-	-	-	-	-	-	-	-	-	-	132.3	-1.5
1996	-	-	-	-	-	-	-	-	-	-	131.5	-0.6	-	-	-	-	-	-	-	-	-	-	128.1	-2.6
1997	-	-	-	-	-	-	-	-	-	-	127.8	-0.2	-	-	-	-	-	-	-	-	-	-	124.5	-2.6
1998	-	-	-	-	-	-	-	-	-	-	126.1	1.3	-	-	-	-	-	-	-	-	-	-	124.2	-1.5
1999	-	-	-	-	-	-	-	-	-	-	132.1	6.4	-	-	-	-	-	-	-	-	-	-	131.1	-0.8
2000	-	-	-	-	-	-	-	-	-	-	132.9	1.4	-	-	-	-	-	-	-	-	-	-	129.8	-2.3
2001	-	-	-	-	-	-	-	-	-	-	128.4	-1.1	-	-	-	-	-	-	-	-	-	-	-	-

Source: U.S. Department of Labor, Bureau of Labor Statistics, Division of Consumer Prices and Price Indexes. - indicates no data collected for period.

San Diego, CA
Consumer Price Index - Urban Wage Earners
Base 1982-1984 = 100
Apparel

For 1965-2001. Columns headed % show percentile change in the index from the previous period for which an index is available.

Year	Jan Index	%	Feb Index	%	Mar Index	%	Apr Index	%	May Index	%	Jun Index	%	Jul Index	%	Aug Index	%	Sep Index	%	Oct Index	%	Nov Index	%	Dec Index	%
1965	-	-	50.6	-	-	-	-	-	50.6	0.0	-	-	-	-	49.8	-1.6	-	-	-	-	49.9	0.2	-	-
1966	-	-	50.1	0.4	-	-	-	-	50.9	1.6	-	-	-	-	51.0	0.2	-	-	-	-	51.3	0.6	-	-
1967	-	-	51.0	-0.6	-	-	-	-	51.5	1.0	-	-	-	-	51.4	-0.2	-	-	-	-	52.7	2.5	-	-
1968	-	-	53.2	0.9	-	-	-	-	54.2	1.9	-	-	-	-	55.1	1.7	-	-	-	-	56.5	2.5	-	-
1969	-	-	56.2	-0.5	-	-	-	-	56.8	1.1	-	-	-	-	57.5	1.2	-	-	-	-	57.7	0.3	-	-
1970	-	-	58.3	1.0	-	-	-	-	59.7	2.4	-	-	-	-	59.3	-0.7	-	-	-	-	60.0	1.2	-	-
1971	-	-	60.0	0.0	-	-	-	-	60.9	1.5	-	-	-	-	61.0	0.2	-	-	-	-	61.2	0.3	-	-
1972	-	-	62.4	2.0	-	-	-	-	63.4	1.6	-	-	-	-	62.5	-1.4	-	-	-	-	64.1	2.6	-	-
1973	-	-	63.6	-0.8	-	-	-	-	64.4	1.3	-	-	-	-	66.0	2.5	-	-	-	-	67.5	2.3	-	-
1974	-	-	69.1	2.4	-	-	-	-	71.6	3.6	-	-	-	-	70.8	-1.1	-	-	-	-	72.2	2.0	-	-
1975	-	-	71.6	-0.8	-	-	-	-	73.4	2.5	-	-	-	-	72.2	-1.6	-	-	-	-	73.1	1.2	-	-
1976	-	-	74.1	1.4	-	-	-	-	74.6	0.7	-	-	-	-	75.0	0.5	-	-	-	-	74.7	-0.4	-	-
1977	-	-	74.2	-0.7	-	-	-	-	76.3	2.8	-	-	-	-	76.2	-0.1	-	-	-	-	77.0	1.0	-	-
1978	75.9	-1.4	-	-	76.7	1.1	-	-	77.8	1.4	-	-	78.2	0.5	-	-	79.0	1.0	-	-	79.6	0.8	-	-
1979	77.5	-2.6	-	-	77.0	-0.6	-	-	80.3	4.3	-	-	81.4	1.4	-	-	83.4	2.5	-	-	84.6	1.4	-	-
1980	84.5	-0.1	-	-	90.0	6.5	-	-	90.1	0.1	-	-	87.6	-2.8	-	-	87.9	0.3	-	-	89.6	1.9	-	-
1981	88.8	-0.9	-	-	91.1	2.6	-	-	92.5	1.5	-	-	93.2	0.8	-	-	93.9	0.8	-	-	94.6	0.7	-	-
1982	92.3	-2.4	-	-	95.0	2.9	-	-	95.9	0.9	-	-	95.8	-0.1	-	-	99.2	3.5	-	-	98.9	-0.3	-	-
1983	98.5	-0.4	-	-	97.9	-0.6	-	-	98.6	0.7	-	-	101.0	2.4	-	-	101.7	0.7	-	-	100.4	-1.3	-	-
1984	101.5	1.1	-	-	101.7	0.2	-	-	103.7	2.0	-	-	100.8	-2.8	-	-	106.2	5.4	-	-	107.8	1.5	-	-
1985	105.0	-2.6	-	-	105.8	0.8	-	-	107.8	1.9	-	-	105.5	-2.1	-	-	106.4	0.9	-	-	106.8	0.4	-	-
1986	106.4	-0.4	-	-	108.8	2.3	-	-	109.0	0.2	-	-	104.3	-4.3	-	-	107.9	3.5	-	-	108.0	0.1	-	-
1987	-	-	-	-	-	-	-	-	-	-	110.5	2.3	-	-	-	-	-	-	-	-	-	-	110.0	-0.5
1988	-	-	-	-	-	-	-	-	-	-	118.0	7.3	-	-	-	-	-	-	-	-	-	-	119.6	1.4
1989	-	-	-	-	-	-	-	-	-	-	123.5	3.3	-	-	-	-	-	-	-	-	-	-	117.8	-4.6
1990	-	-	-	-	-	-	-	-	-	-	132.6	12.6	-	-	-	-	-	-	-	-	-	-	129.5	-2.3
1991	-	-	-	-	-	-	-	-	-	-	126.4	-2.4	-	-	-	-	-	-	-	-	-	-	130.0	2.8
1992	-	-	-	-	-	-	-	-	-	-	131.0	0.8	-	-	-	-	-	-	-	-	-	-	129.1	-1.5
1993	-	-	-	-	-	-	-	-	-	-	140.6	8.9	-	-	-	-	-	-	-	-	-	-	127.6	-9.2
1994	-	-	-	-	-	-	-	-	-	-	152.2	19.3	-	-	-	-	-	-	-	-	-	-	128.5	-15.6
1995	-	-	-	-	-	-	-	-	-	-	132.3	3.0	-	-	-	-	-	-	-	-	-	-	131.1	-0.9
1996	-	-	-	-	-	-	-	-	-	-	129.7	-1.1	-	-	-	-	-	-	-	-	-	-	126.6	-2.4
1997	-	-	-	-	-	-	-	-	-	-	125.0	-1.3	-	-	-	-	-	-	-	-	-	-	122.3	-2.2
1998	-	-	-	-	-	-	-	-	-	-	123.7	1.1	-	-	-	-	-	-	-	-	-	-	120.9	-2.3
1999	-	-	-	-	-	-	-	-	-	-	129.1	6.8	-	-	-	-	-	-	-	-	-	-	128.4	-0.5
2000	-	-	-	-	-	-	-	-	-	-	131.5	2.4	-	-	-	-	-	-	-	-	-	-	129.8	-1.3
2001	-	-	-	-	-	-	-	-	-	-	129.7	-0.1	-	-	-	-	-	-	-	-	-	-	-	-

Source: U.S. Department of Labor, Bureau of Labor Statistics, Division of Consumer Prices and Price Indexes. - indicates no data collected for period.

San Diego, CA
Consumer Price Index - All Urban Consumers
Base 1982-1984 = 100
Transportation

For 1965-2001. Columns headed % show percentile change in the index from the previous period for which an index is available.

Year	Jan Index	%	Feb Index	%	Mar Index	%	Apr Index	%	May Index	%	Jun Index	%	Jul Index	%	Aug Index	%	Sep Index	%	Oct Index	%	Nov Index	%	Dec Index	%
1965	-	-	32.0	-	-	-	-	-	32.7	2.2	-	-	-	-	32.4	-0.9	-	-	-	-	31.4	-3.1	-	-
1966	-	-	31.7	1.0	-	-	-	-	31.8	0.3	-	-	-	-	31.9	0.3	-	-	-	-	33.2	4.1	-	-
1967	-	-	33.0	-0.6	-	-	-	-	33.0	0.0	-	-	-	-	33.7	2.1	-	-	-	-	33.5	-0.6	-	-
1968	-	-	33.8	0.9	-	-	-	-	34.0	0.6	-	-	-	-	34.2	0.6	-	-	-	-	34.4	0.6	-	-
1969	-	-	34.5	0.3	-	-	-	-	35.0	1.4	-	-	-	-	35.1	0.3	-	-	-	-	35.0	-0.3	-	-
1970	-	-	34.8	-0.6	-	-	-	-	35.6	2.3	-	-	-	-	35.7	0.3	-	-	-	-	37.5	5.0	-	-
1971	-	-	36.9	-1.6	-	-	-	-	38.0	3.0	-	-	-	-	38.6	1.6	-	-	-	-	38.2	-1.0	-	-
1972	-	-	37.5	-1.8	-	-	-	-	38.8	3.5	-	-	-	-	39.7	2.3	-	-	-	-	40.2	1.3	-	-
1973	-	-	39.5	-1.7	-	-	-	-	40.6	2.8	-	-	-	-	41.2	1.5	-	-	-	-	41.3	0.2	-	-
1974	-	-	43.4	5.1	-	-	-	-	45.8	5.5	-	-	-	-	47.4	3.5	-	-	-	-	48.1	1.5	-	-
1975	-	-	48.8	1.5	-	-	-	-	50.1	2.7	-	-	-	-	52.5	4.8	-	-	-	-	52.6	0.2	-	-
1976	-	-	52.5	-0.2	-	-	-	-	53.8	2.5	-	-	-	-	55.5	3.2	-	-	-	-	56.4	1.6	-	-
1977	-	-	56.8	0.7	-	-	-	-	58.1	2.3	-	-	-	-	58.6	0.9	-	-	-	-	58.9	0.5	-	-
1978	58.8	-0.2	-	-	58.8	0.0	-	-	60.1	2.2	-	-	62.2	3.5	-	-	62.4	0.3	-	-	63.4	1.6	-	-
1979	64.1	1.1	-	-	65.2	1.7	-	-	68.9	5.7	-	-	71.2	3.3	-	-	72.9	2.4	-	-	74.2	1.8	-	-
1980	77.0	3.8	-	-	80.7	4.8	-	-	82.0	1.6	-	-	82.9	1.1	-	-	84.0	1.3	-	-	84.6	0.7	-	-
1981	86.0	1.7	-	-	88.6	3.0	-	-	90.7	2.4	-	-	92.8	2.3	-	-	93.7	1.0	-	-	94.7	1.1	-	-
1982	94.6	-0.1	-	-	93.2	-1.5	-	-	93.4	0.2	-	-	98.2	5.1	-	-	97.8	-0.4	-	-	96.6	-1.2	-	-
1983	96.2	-0.4	-	-	94.4	-1.9	-	-	98.5	4.3	-	-	100.3	1.8	-	-	100.6	0.3	-	-	101.3	0.7	-	-
1984	103.1	1.8	-	-	103.3	0.2	-	-	106.9	3.5	-	-	105.2	-1.6	-	-	105.9	0.7	-	-	107.6	1.6	-	-
1985	107.5	-0.1	-	-	108.6	1.0	-	-	111.1	2.3	-	-	110.1	-0.9	-	-	108.9	-1.1	-	-	109.3	0.4	-	-
1986	110.0	0.6	-	-	106.3	-3.4	-	-	106.6	0.3	-	-	105.3	-1.2	-	-	104.1	-1.1	-	-	102.9	-1.2	-	-
1987	-	-	-	-	-	-	-	-	-	-	106.9	3.9	-	-	-	-	-	-	-	-	-	-	108.4	1.4
1988	-	-	-	-	-	-	-	-	-	-	111.5	2.9	-	-	-	-	-	-	-	-	-	-	116.9	4.8
1989	-	-	-	-	-	-	-	-	-	-	123.4	5.6	-	-	-	-	-	-	-	-	-	-	125.6	1.8
1990	-	-	-	-	-	-	-	-	-	-	128.9	2.6	-	-	-	-	-	-	-	-	-	-	134.5	4.3
1991	-	-	-	-	-	-	-	-	-	-	132.7	-1.3	-	-	-	-	-	-	-	-	-	-	134.9	1.7
1992	-	-	-	-	-	-	-	-	-	-	135.7	0.6	-	-	-	-	-	-	-	-	-	-	136.1	0.3
1993	-	-	-	-	-	-	-	-	-	-	137.5	1.0	-	-	-	-	-	-	-	-	-	-	138.4	0.7
1994	-	-	-	-	-	-	-	-	-	-	140.1	1.2	-	-	-	-	-	-	-	-	-	-	143.5	2.4
1995	-	-	-	-	-	-	-	-	-	-	146.9	2.4	-	-	-	-	-	-	-	-	-	-	148.1	0.8
1996	-	-	-	-	-	-	-	-	-	-	151.6	2.4	-	-	-	-	-	-	-	-	-	-	150.1	-1.0
1997	-	-	-	-	-	-	-	-	-	-	151.0	0.6	-	-	-	-	-	-	-	-	-	-	153.3	1.5
1998	-	-	-	-	-	-	-	-	-	-	150.4	-1.9	-	-	-	-	-	-	-	-	-	-	148.4	-1.3
1999	-	-	-	-	-	-	-	-	-	-	150.8	1.6	-	-	-	-	-	-	-	-	-	-	153.3	1.7
2000	-	-	-	-	-	-	-	-	-	-	159.6	4.1	-	-	-	-	-	-	-	-	-	-	165.2	3.5
2001	-	-	-	-	-	-	-	-	-	-	166.5	0.8	-	-	-	-	-	-	-	-	-	-	-	-

Source: U.S. Department of Labor, Bureau of Labor Statistics, Division of Consumer Prices and Price Indexes. - indicates no data collected for period.

San Diego, CA
Consumer Price Index - Urban Wage Earners
Base 1982-1984 = 100
Transportation

For 1965-2001. Columns headed % show percentile change in the index from the previous period for which an index is available.

Year	Jan Index	%	Feb Index	%	Mar Index	%	Apr Index	%	May Index	%	Jun Index	%	Jul Index	%	Aug Index	%	Sep Index	%	Oct Index	%	Nov Index	%	Dec Index	%
1965	-	-	31.8	-	-	-	-	-	32.5	2.2	-	-	-	-	32.1	-1.2	-	-	-	-	31.2	-2.8	-	-
1966	-	-	31.5	1.0	-	-	-	-	31.5	0.0	-	-	-	-	31.6	0.3	-	-	-	-	33.0	4.4	-	-
1967	-	-	32.8	-0.6	-	-	-	-	32.8	0.0	-	-	-	-	33.5	2.1	-	-	-	-	33.3	-0.6	-	-
1968	-	-	33.6	0.9	-	-	-	-	33.8	0.6	-	-	-	-	33.9	0.3	-	-	-	-	34.2	0.9	-	-
1969	-	-	34.3	0.3	-	-	-	-	34.8	1.5	-	-	-	-	34.9	0.3	-	-	-	-	34.7	-0.6	-	-
1970	-	-	34.6	-0.3	-	-	-	-	35.4	2.3	-	-	-	-	35.5	0.3	-	-	-	-	37.2	4.8	-	-
1971	-	-	36.6	-1.6	-	-	-	-	37.8	3.3	-	-	-	-	38.3	1.3	-	-	-	-	38.0	-0.8	-	-
1972	-	-	37.2	-2.1	-	-	-	-	38.6	3.8	-	-	-	-	39.4	2.1	-	-	-	-	39.9	1.3	-	-
1973	-	-	39.2	-1.8	-	-	-	-	40.3	2.8	-	-	-	-	40.9	1.5	-	-	-	-	41.0	0.2	-	-
1974	-	-	43.1	5.1	-	-	-	-	45.5	5.6	-	-	-	-	47.1	3.5	-	-	-	-	47.8	1.5	-	-
1975	-	-	48.4	1.3	-	-	-	-	49.8	2.9	-	-	-	-	52.1	4.6	-	-	-	-	52.2	0.2	-	-
1976	-	-	52.2	0.0	-	-	-	-	53.4	2.3	-	-	-	-	55.1	3.2	-	-	-	-	56.0	1.6	-	-
1977	-	-	56.4	0.7	-	-	-	-	57.7	2.3	-	-	-	-	58.2	0.9	-	-	-	-	58.5	0.5	-	-
1978	58.7	0.3	-	-	58.8	0.2	-	-	60.0	2.0	-	-	61.9	3.2	-	-	62.0	0.2	-	-	63.3	2.1	-	-
1979	64.0	1.1	-	-	65.1	1.7	-	-	68.8	5.7	-	-	70.9	3.1	-	-	72.6	2.4	-	-	73.5	1.2	-	-
1980	76.3	3.8	-	-	79.9	4.7	-	-	80.9	1.3	-	-	81.8	1.1	-	-	82.5	0.9	-	-	83.5	1.2	-	-
1981	84.7	1.4	-	-	87.1	2.8	-	-	89.3	2.5	-	-	91.5	2.5	-	-	92.4	1.0	-	-	93.8	1.5	-	-
1982	93.9	0.1	-	-	92.7	-1.3	-	-	93.0	0.3	-	-	98.0	5.4	-	-	97.6	-0.4	-	-	96.4	-1.2	-	-
1983	95.9	-0.5	-	-	94.4	-1.6	-	-	98.4	4.2	-	-	100.2	1.8	-	-	100.6	0.4	-	-	101.4	0.8	-	-
1984	103.3	1.9	-	-	103.6	0.3	-	-	107.1	3.4	-	-	105.8	-1.2	-	-	106.2	0.4	-	-	107.9	1.6	-	-
1985	107.9	0.0	-	-	108.8	0.8	-	-	111.3	2.3	-	-	110.4	-0.8	-	-	109.1	-1.2	-	-	109.5	0.4	-	-
1986	110.1	0.5	-	-	106.9	-2.9	-	-	107.2	0.3	-	-	105.8	-1.3	-	-	104.7	-1.0	-	-	103.5	-1.1	-	-
1987	-	-	-	-	-	-	-	-	-	-	107.5	3.9	-	-	-	-	-	-	-	-	-	-	109.5	1.9
1988	-	-	-	-	-	-	-	-	-	-	112.2	2.5	-	-	-	-	-	-	-	-	-	-	117.2	4.5
1989	-	-	-	-	-	-	-	-	-	-	123.2	5.1	-	-	-	-	-	-	-	-	-	-	125.5	1.9
1990	-	-	-	-	-	-	-	-	-	-	128.8	2.6	-	-	-	-	-	-	-	-	-	-	134.0	4.0
1991	-	-	-	-	-	-	-	-	-	-	132.1	-1.4	-	-	-	-	-	-	-	-	-	-	135.0	2.2
1992	-	-	-	-	-	-	-	-	-	-	135.6	0.4	-	-	-	-	-	-	-	-	-	-	137.2	1.2
1993	-	-	-	-	-	-	-	-	-	-	138.2	0.7	-	-	-	-	-	-	-	-	-	-	139.5	0.9
1994	-	-	-	-	-	-	-	-	-	-	140.1	0.4	-	-	-	-	-	-	-	-	-	-	144.5	3.1
1995	-	-	-	-	-	-	-	-	-	-	148.3	2.6	-	-	-	-	-	-	-	-	-	-	149.9	1.1
1996	-	-	-	-	-	-	-	-	-	-	153.9	2.7	-	-	-	-	-	-	-	-	-	-	152.5	-0.9
1997	-	-	-	-	-	-	-	-	-	-	153.1	0.4	-	-	-	-	-	-	-	-	-	-	154.5	0.9
1998	-	-	-	-	-	-	-	-	-	-	151.2	-2.1	-	-	-	-	-	-	-	-	-	-	149.0	-1.5
1999	-	-	-	-	-	-	-	-	-	-	151.3	1.5	-	-	-	-	-	-	-	-	-	-	153.1	1.2
2000	-	-	-	-	-	-	-	-	-	-	158.7	3.7	-	-	-	-	-	-	-	-	-	-	164.3	3.5
2001	-	-	-	-	-	-	-	-	-	-	165.4	0.7	-	-	-	-	-	-	-	-	-	-	-	-

Source: U.S. Department of Labor, Bureau of Labor Statistics, Division of Consumer Prices and Price Indexes. - indicates no data collected for period.

San Diego, CA
Consumer Price Index - All Urban Consumers
Base 1982-1984 = 100
Medical Care

For 1965-2001. Columns headed % show percentile change in the index from the previous period for which an index is available.

Year	Jan Index	%	Feb Index	%	Mar Index	%	Apr Index	%	May Index	%	Jun Index	%	Jul Index	%	Aug Index	%	Sep Index	%	Oct Index	%	Nov Index	%	Dec Index	%
1965	-	-	26.4	-	-	-	-	-	26.5	0.4	-	-	-	-	26.6	0.4	-	-	-	-	26.8	0.8	-	-
1966	-	-	27.2	1.5	-	-	-	-	27.7	1.8	-	-	-	-	27.9	0.7	-	-	-	-	29.2	4.7	-	-
1967	-	-	29.4	0.7	-	-	-	-	29.9	1.7	-	-	-	-	30.2	1.0	-	-	-	-	30.5	1.0	-	-
1968	-	-	30.5	0.0	-	-	-	-	30.5	0.0	-	-	-	-	30.9	1.3	-	-	-	-	31.2	1.0	-	-
1969	-	-	31.9	2.2	-	-	-	-	32.3	1.3	-	-	-	-	32.7	1.2	-	-	-	-	32.7	0.0	-	-
1970	-	-	33.4	2.1	-	-	-	-	34.3	2.7	-	-	-	-	34.9	1.7	-	-	-	-	35.2	0.9	-	-
1971	-	-	35.6	1.1	-	-	-	-	36.3	2.0	-	-	-	-	36.8	1.4	-	-	-	-	36.6	-0.5	-	-
1972	-	-	36.7	0.3	-	-	-	-	36.8	0.3	-	-	-	-	37.2	1.1	-	-	-	-	38.0	2.2	-	-
1973	-	-	38.1	0.3	-	-	-	-	38.5	1.0	-	-	-	-	39.3	2.1	-	-	-	-	40.2	2.3	-	-
1974	-	-	41.1	2.2	-	-	-	-	42.2	2.7	-	-	-	-	44.4	5.2	-	-	-	-	45.0	1.4	-	-
1975	-	-	47.1	4.7	-	-	-	-	47.8	1.5	-	-	-	-	49.0	2.5	-	-	-	-	50.1	2.2	-	-
1976	-	-	52.0	3.8	-	-	-	-	52.8	1.5	-	-	-	-	54.3	2.8	-	-	-	-	55.3	1.8	-	-
1977	-	-	56.7	2.5	-	-	-	-	58.3	2.8	-	-	-	-	59.3	1.7	-	-	-	-	60.0	1.2	-	-
1978	61.2	2.0	-	-	62.5	2.1	-	-	62.7	0.3	-	-	63.8	1.8	-	-	64.0	0.3	-	-	65.7	2.7	-	-
1979	67.2	2.3	-	-	67.6	0.6	-	-	68.4	1.2	-	-	69.2	1.2	-	-	71.1	2.7	-	-	72.3	1.7	-	-
1980	72.7	0.6	-	-	73.8	1.5	-	-	76.2	3.3	-	-	76.5	0.4	-	-	77.1	0.8	-	-	79.1	2.6	-	-
1981	79.4	0.4	-	-	79.5	0.1	-	-	80.4	1.1	-	-	84.1	4.6	-	-	84.9	1.0	-	-	87.4	2.9	-	-
1982	88.7	1.5	-	-	89.2	0.6	-	-	90.1	1.0	-	-	93.7	4.0	-	-	95.4	1.8	-	-	98.8	3.6	-	-
1983	99.9	1.1	-	-	99.9	0.0	-	-	99.9	0.0	-	-	99.7	-0.2	-	-	101.1	1.4	-	-	102.8	1.7	-	-
1984	104.3	1.5	-	-	105.2	0.9	-	-	105.5	0.3	-	-	107.5	1.9	-	-	106.9	-0.6	-	-	107.2	0.3	-	-
1985	106.9	-0.3	-	-	108.8	1.8	-	-	109.9	1.0	-	-	110.6	0.6	-	-	110.9	0.3	-	-	112.1	1.1	-	-
1986	112.8	0.6	-	-	115.0	2.0	-	-	116.4	1.2	-	-	117.8	1.2	-	-	121.4	3.1	-	-	123.0	1.3	-	-
1987	-	-	-	-	-	-	-	-	-	-	126.9	3.2	-	-	-	-	-	-	-	-	-	-	132.0	4.0
1988	-	-	-	-	-	-	-	-	-	-	137.9	4.5	-	-	-	-	-	-	-	-	-	-	145.9	5.8
1989	-	-	-	-	-	-	-	-	-	-	153.3	5.1	-	-	-	-	-	-	-	-	-	-	164.1	7.0
1990	-	-	-	-	-	-	-	-	-	-	169.0	3.0	-	-	-	-	-	-	-	-	-	-	177.6	5.1
1991	-	-	-	-	-	-	-	-	-	-	185.7	4.6	-	-	-	-	-	-	-	-	-	-	190.9	2.8
1992	-	-	-	-	-	-	-	-	-	-	198.5	4.0	-	-	-	-	-	-	-	-	-	-	204.7	3.1
1993	-	-	-	-	-	-	-	-	-	-	211.9	3.5	-	-	-	-	-	-	-	-	-	-	215.5	1.7
1994	-	-	-	-	-	-	-	-	-	-	218.1	1.2	-	-	-	-	-	-	-	-	-	-	217.5	-0.3
1995	-	-	-	-	-	-	-	-	-	-	217.9	0.2	-	-	-	-	-	-	-	-	-	-	221.9	1.8
1996	-	-	-	-	-	-	-	-	-	-	227.1	2.3	-	-	-	-	-	-	-	-	-	-	236.1	4.0
1997	-	-	-	-	-	-	-	-	-	-	237.6	0.6	-	-	-	-	-	-	-	-	-	-	236.1	-0.6
1998	-	-	-	-	-	-	-	-	-	-	238.5	1.0	-	-	-	-	-	-	-	-	-	-	243.4	2.1
1999	-	-	-	-	-	-	-	-	-	-	245.6	0.9	-	-	-	-	-	-	-	-	-	-	248.8	1.3
2000	-	-	-	-	-	-	-	-	-	-	255.0	2.5	-	-	-	-	-	-	-	-	-	-	257.9	1.1
2001	-	-	-	-	-	-	-	-	-	-	263.9	2.3	-	-	-	-	-	-	-	-	-	-	-	-

Source: U.S. Department of Labor, Bureau of Labor Statistics, Division of Consumer Prices and Price Indexes. - indicates no data collected for period.

San Diego, CA
Consumer Price Index - Urban Wage Earners
Base 1982-1984 = 100
Medical Care

For 1965-2001. Columns headed % show percentile change in the index from the previous period for which an index is available.

Year	Jan Index	%	Feb Index	%	Mar Index	%	Apr Index	%	May Index	%	Jun Index	%	Jul Index	%	Aug Index	%	Sep Index	%	Oct Index	%	Nov Index	%	Dec Index	%
1965	-	-	25.8	-	-	-	-	-	26.0	0.8	-	-	-	-	26.1	0.4	-	-	-	-	26.2	0.4	-	-
1966	-	-	26.6	1.5	-	-	-	-	27.1	1.9	-	-	-	-	27.3	0.7	-	-	-	-	28.6	4.8	-	-
1967	-	-	28.8	0.7	-	-	-	-	29.2	1.4	-	-	-	-	29.6	1.4	-	-	-	-	29.9	1.0	-	-
1968	-	-	29.9	0.0	-	-	-	-	29.9	0.0	-	-	-	-	30.2	1.0	-	-	-	-	30.5	1.0	-	-
1969	-	-	31.2	2.3	-	-	-	-	31.6	1.3	-	-	-	-	32.0	1.3	-	-	-	-	32.0	0.0	-	-
1970	-	-	32.7	2.2	-	-	-	-	33.5	2.4	-	-	-	-	34.1	1.8	-	-	-	-	34.4	0.9	-	-
1971	-	-	34.9	1.5	-	-	-	-	35.5	1.7	-	-	-	-	36.0	1.4	-	-	-	-	35.8	-0.6	-	-
1972	-	-	35.9	0.3	-	-	-	-	36.0	0.3	-	-	-	-	36.4	1.1	-	-	-	-	37.1	1.9	-	-
1973	-	-	37.3	0.5	-	-	-	-	37.7	1.1	-	-	-	-	38.4	1.9	-	-	-	-	39.3	2.3	-	-
1974	-	-	40.2	2.3	-	-	-	-	41.3	2.7	-	-	-	-	43.4	5.1	-	-	-	-	44.0	1.4	-	-
1975	-	-	46.0	4.5	-	-	-	-	46.8	1.7	-	-	-	-	47.9	2.4	-	-	-	-	49.0	2.3	-	-
1976	-	-	50.9	3.9	-	-	-	-	51.6	1.4	-	-	-	-	53.1	2.9	-	-	-	-	54.1	1.9	-	-
1977	-	-	55.5	2.6	-	-	-	-	57.1	2.9	-	-	-	-	58.0	1.6	-	-	-	-	58.8	1.4	-	-
1978	60.3	2.6	-	-	60.8	0.8	-	-	61.1	0.5	-	-	62.5	2.3	-	-	62.8	0.5	-	-	63.7	1.4	-	-
1979	65.2	2.4	-	-	66.2	1.5	-	-	68.7	3.8	-	-	69.4	1.0	-	-	72.0	3.7	-	-	73.0	1.4	-	-
1980	73.8	1.1	-	-	74.4	0.8	-	-	75.1	0.9	-	-	77.0	2.5	-	-	77.6	0.8	-	-	77.9	0.4	-	-
1981	79.5	2.1	-	-	79.4	-0.1	-	-	80.1	0.9	-	-	85.4	6.6	-	-	86.5	1.3	-	-	87.9	1.6	-	-
1982	89.1	1.4	-	-	89.5	0.4	-	-	90.3	0.9	-	-	93.5	3.5	-	-	95.0	1.6	-	-	98.6	3.8	-	-
1983	99.5	0.9	-	-	99.6	0.1	-	-	99.6	0.0	-	-	99.4	-0.2	-	-	101.2	1.8	-	-	102.9	1.7	-	-
1984	104.4	1.5	-	-	105.3	0.9	-	-	105.6	0.3	-	-	107.5	1.8	-	-	107.1	-0.4	-	-	107.4	0.3	-	-
1985	107.3	-0.1	-	-	109.3	1.9	-	-	110.5	1.1	-	-	111.1	0.5	-	-	111.5	0.4	-	-	112.6	1.0	-	-
1986	113.3	0.6	-	-	115.6	2.0	-	-	117.1	1.3	-	-	118.5	1.2	-	-	122.4	3.3	-	-	123.8	1.1	-	-
1987	-	-	-	-	-	-	-	-	-	-	127.7	3.2	-	-	-	-	-	-	-	-	-	-	133.1	4.2
1988	-	-	-	-	-	-	-	-	-	-	139.5	4.8	-	-	-	-	-	-	-	-	-	-	148.4	6.4
1989	-	-	-	-	-	-	-	-	-	-	155.7	4.9	-	-	-	-	-	-	-	-	-	-	167.2	7.4
1990	-	-	-	-	-	-	-	-	-	-	171.5	2.6	-	-	-	-	-	-	-	-	-	-	179.9	4.9
1991	-	-	-	-	-	-	-	-	-	-	187.4	4.2	-	-	-	-	-	-	-	-	-	-	193.0	3.0
1992	-	-	-	-	-	-	-	-	-	-	200.8	4.0	-	-	-	-	-	-	-	-	-	-	207.0	3.1
1993	-	-	-	-	-	-	-	-	-	-	214.2	3.5	-	-	-	-	-	-	-	-	-	-	217.5	1.5
1994	-	-	-	-	-	-	-	-	-	-	219.9	1.1	-	-	-	-	-	-	-	-	-	-	218.7	-0.5
1995	-	-	-	-	-	-	-	-	-	-	219.3	0.3	-	-	-	-	-	-	-	-	-	-	223.2	1.8
1996	-	-	-	-	-	-	-	-	-	-	228.2	2.2	-	-	-	-	-	-	-	-	-	-	238.0	4.3
1997	-	-	-	-	-	-	-	-	-	-	239.9	0.8	-	-	-	-	-	-	-	-	-	-	241.0	0.5
1998	-	-	-	-	-	-	-	-	-	-	243.9	1.2	-	-	-	-	-	-	-	-	-	-	248.4	1.8
1999	-	-	-	-	-	-	-	-	-	-	250.9	1.0	-	-	-	-	-	-	-	-	-	-	254.6	1.5
2000	-	-	-	-	-	-	-	-	-	-	261.2	2.6	-	-	-	-	-	-	-	-	-	-	264.2	1.1
2001	-	-	-	-	-	-	-	-	-	-	269.9	2.2	-	-	-	-	-	-	-	-	-	-	-	-

Source: U.S. Department of Labor, Bureau of Labor Statistics, Division of Consumer Prices and Price Indexes. - indicates no data collected for period.

San Diego, CA
Consumer Price Index - All Urban Consumers
Base December 1997 = 100
Recreation

For 1997-2001. Columns headed % show percentile change in the index from the previous period for which an index is available.

Year	Jan		Feb		Mar		Apr		May		Jun		Jul		Aug		Sep		Oct		Nov		Dec	
	Index	%	Index	%	Index	%	Index	%	Index	%	Index	%	Index	%	Index	%	Index	%	Index	%	Index	%	Index	%
1997	-	-	-	-	-	-	-	-	-	-	-	-	-	-	-	-	-	-	-	-	-	-	100.0	-
1998	-	-	-	-	-	-	-	-	-	-	99.6	-0.4	-	-	-	-	-	-	-	-	-	-	100.3	0.7
1999	-	-	-	-	-	-	-	-	-	-	104.6	4.3	-	-	-	-	-	-	-	-	-	-	105.3	0.7
2000	-	-	-	-	-	-	-	-	-	-	113.5	7.8	-	-	-	-	-	-	-	-	-	-	125.0	10.1
2001	-	-	-	-	-	-	-	-	-	-	125.4	0.3	-	-	-	-	-	-	-	-	-	-	-	-

Source: U.S. Department of Labor, Bureau of Labor Statistics, Division of Consumer Prices and Price Indexes. - indicates no data collected for period.

San Diego, CA
Consumer Price Index - Urban Wage Earners
Base December 1997 = 100
Recreation

For 1997-2001. Columns headed % show percentile change in the index from the previous period for which an index is available.

Year	Jan		Feb		Mar		Apr		May		Jun		Jul		Aug		Sep		Oct		Nov		Dec	
	Index	%	Index	%	Index	%	Index	%	Index	%	Index	%	Index	%	Index	%	Index	%	Index	%	Index	%	Index	%
1997	-	-	-	-	-	-	-	-	-	-	-	-	-	-	-	-	-	-	-	-	-	-	100.0	-
1998	-	-	-	-	-	-	-	-	-	-	99.3	-0.7	-	-	-	-	-	-	-	-	-	-	100.2	0.9
1999	-	-	-	-	-	-	-	-	-	-	106.3	6.1	-	-	-	-	-	-	-	-	-	-	106.7	0.4
2000	-	-	-	-	-	-	-	-	-	-	119.1	11.6	-	-	-	-	-	-	-	-	-	-	135.6	13.9
2001	-	-	-	-	-	-	-	-	-	-	134.3	-1.0	-	-	-	-	-	-	-	-	-	-	-	-

Source: U.S. Department of Labor, Bureau of Labor Statistics, Division of Consumer Prices and Price Indexes. - indicates no data collected for period.

San Diego, CA
Consumer Price Index - All Urban Consumers
Base December 1997 = 100
Education & Communication

For 1997-2001. Columns headed % show percentile change in the index from the previous period for which an index is available.

Year	Jan		Feb		Mar		Apr		May		Jun		Jul		Aug		Sep		Oct		Nov		Dec	
	Index	%	Index	%	Index	%	Index	%	Index	%	Index	%	Index	%	Index	%	Index	%	Index	%	Index	%	Index	%
1997	-	-	-	-	-	-	-	-	-	-	-	-	-	-	-	-	-	-	-	-	-	-	100.0	-
1998	-	-	-	-	-	-	-	-	-	-	99.4	-0.6	-	-	-	-	-	-	-	-	-	-	98.3	-1.1
1999	-	-	-	-	-	-	-	-	-	-	97.2	-1.1	-	-	-	-	-	-	-	-	-	-	97.7	0.5
2000	-	-	-	-	-	-	-	-	-	-	98.0	0.3	-	-	-	-	-	-	-	-	-	-	97.8	-0.2
2001	-	-	-	-	-	-	-	-	-	-	99.3	1.5	-	-	-	-	-	-	-	-	-	-	-	-

Source: U.S. Department of Labor, Bureau of Labor Statistics, Division of Consumer Prices and Price Indexes. - indicates no data collected for period.

San Diego, CA
Consumer Price Index - Urban Wage Earners
Base December 1997 = 100
Education & Communication

For 1997-2001. Columns headed % show percentile change in the index from the previous period for which an index is available.

Year	Jan Index	%	Feb Index	%	Mar Index	%	Apr Index	%	May Index	%	Jun Index	%	Jul Index	%	Aug Index	%	Sep Index	%	Oct Index	%	Nov Index	%	Dec Index	%
1997	-	-	-	-	-	-	-	-	-	-	-	-	-	-	-	-	-	-	-	-	-	-	-	-
1998	-	-	-	-	-	-	-	-	-	-	99.4	-0.6	-	-	-	-	-	-	-	-	-	-	100.0	-
1999	-	-	-	-	-	-	-	-	-	-	97.3	-1.2	-	-	-	-	-	-	-	-	-	-	98.5	-0.9
2000	-	-	-	-	-	-	-	-	-	-	98.3	0.3	-	-	-	-	-	-	-	-	-	-	98.0	0.7
2001	-	-	-	-	-	-	-	-	-	-	99.8	1.6	-	-	-	-	-	-	-	-	-	-	-	-

Source: U.S. Department of Labor, Bureau of Labor Statistics, Division of Consumer Prices and Price Indexes. - indicates no data collected for period.

San Francisco-Oakland-San Jose, CA
Consumer Price Index - All Urban Consumers
Base 1982-1984 = 100
Annual Averages

For 1914-2001. Columns headed % show percentile change in the index from the previous period for which an index is available.

Year	All Items		Food & Beverage		Housing		Apparel		Trans-portation		Medical Care		Recrea-tion*		Education & Communic.*		Other Goods & Services	
	Index	%	Index	%	Index	%	Index	%	Index	%	Index	%	Index	%	Index	%	Index	%
1914	-	-	-	-	-	-	-	-	-	-	-	-	-	-	-	-	-	-
1915	9.2	-	-	-	-	-	-	-	-	-	-	-	-	-	-	-	-	-
1916	9.5	3.3	-	-	-	-	-	-	-	-	-	-	-	-	-	-	-	-
1917	10.9	14.7	-	-	-	-	-	-	-	-	-	-	-	-	-	-	-	-
1918	12.9	18.3	-	-	-	-	-	-	-	-	-	-	-	-	-	-	-	-
1919	15.0	16.3	-	-	-	-	-	-	-	-	-	-	-	-	-	-	-	-
1920	17.0	13.3	-	-	-	-	-	-	-	-	-	-	-	-	-	-	-	-
1921	15.3	-10.0	-	-	-	-	-	-	-	-	-	-	-	-	-	-	-	-
1922	14.6	-4.6	-	-	-	-	-	-	-	-	-	-	-	-	-	-	-	-
1923	14.7	0.7	-	-	-	-	-	-	-	-	-	-	-	-	-	-	-	-
1924	14.7	0.0	-	-	-	-	-	-	-	-	-	-	-	-	-	-	-	-
1925	15.1	2.7	-	-	-	-	-	-	-	-	-	-	-	-	-	-	-	-
1926	15.0	-0.7	-	-	-	-	-	-	-	-	-	-	-	-	-	-	-	-
1927	14.9	-0.7	-	-	-	-	-	-	-	-	-	-	-	-	-	-	-	-
1928	14.8	-0.7	-	-	-	-	-	-	-	-	-	-	-	-	-	-	-	-
1929	14.9	0.7	-	-	-	-	-	-	-	-	-	-	-	-	-	-	-	-
1930	14.5	-2.7	-	-	-	-	-	-	-	-	-	-	-	-	-	-	-	-
1931	13.3	-8.3	-	-	-	-	-	-	-	-	-	-	-	-	-	-	-	-
1932	12.3	-7.5	-	-	-	-	-	-	-	-	-	-	-	-	-	-	-	-
1933	11.8	-4.1	-	-	-	-	-	-	-	-	-	-	-	-	-	-	-	-
1934	12.1	2.5	-	-	-	-	-	-	-	-	-	-	-	-	-	-	-	-
1935	12.4	2.5	-	-	-	-	-	-	-	-	-	-	-	-	-	-	-	-
1936	12.4	0.0	-	-	-	-	-	-	-	-	-	-	-	-	-	-	-	-
1937	12.8	3.2	-	-	-	-	-	-	-	-	-	-	-	-	-	-	-	-
1938	12.8	0.0	-	-	-	-	-	-	-	-	-	-	-	-	-	-	-	-
1939	12.6	-1.6	-	-	-	-	-	-	-	-	-	-	-	-	-	-	-	-
1940	12.7	0.8	-	-	-	-	-	-	-	-	-	-	-	-	-	-	-	-
1941	13.4	5.5	-	-	-	-	-	-	-	-	-	-	-	-	-	-	-	-
1942	15.0	11.9	-	-	-	-	-	-	-	-	-	-	-	-	-	-	-	-
1943	16.0	6.7	-	-	-	-	-	-	-	-	-	-	-	-	-	-	-	-
1944	16.4	2.5	-	-	-	-	-	-	-	-	-	-	-	-	-	-	-	-
1945	16.8	2.4	-	-	-	-	-	-	-	-	-	-	-	-	-	-	-	-
1946	18.2	8.3	-	-	-	-	-	-	-	-	-	-	-	-	-	-	-	-
1947	20.6	13.2	-	-	-	-	-	-	16.4	-	13.6	-	-	-	-	-	-	-
1948	22.0	6.8	-	-	-	-	-	-	18.0	9.8	14.3	5.1	-	-	-	-	-	-
1949	22.0	0.0	-	-	-	-	-	-	19.4	7.8	14.7	2.8	-	-	-	-	-	-
1950	22.0	0.0	-	-	-	-	-	-	19.5	0.5	15.1	2.7	-	-	-	-	-	-
1951	23.8	8.2	-	-	-	-	-	-	20.8	6.7	15.8	4.6	-	-	-	-	-	-
1952	24.6	3.4	-	-	-	-	-	-	23.7	13.9	16.8	6.3	-	-	-	-	-	-
1953	25.0	1.6	-	-	-	-	39.3	-	25.7	8.4	17.2	2.4	-	-	-	-	-	-
1954	25.1	0.4	-	-	-	-	38.8	-1.3	25.5	-0.8	17.5	1.7	-	-	-	-	-	-
1955	24.9	-0.8	-	-	-	-	39.0	0.5	25.1	-1.6	17.6	0.6	-	-	-	-	-	-
1956	25.5	2.4	-	-	-	-	39.8	2.1	25.4	1.2	18.6	5.7	-	-	-	-	-	-
1957	26.5	3.9	-	-	-	-	40.7	2.3	27.1	6.7	19.6	5.4	-	-	-	-	-	-
1958	27.5	3.8	-	-	-	-	41.0	0.7	28.3	4.4	21.0	7.1	-	-	-	-	-	-

[Continued]

San Francisco-Oakland-San Jose, CA
Consumer Price Index - All Urban Consumers
Base 1982-1984 = 100
Annual Averages
[Continued]

For 1914-2001. Columns headed % show percentile change in the index from the previous period for which an index is available.

Year	All Items		Food & Beverage		Housing		Apparel		Trans-portation		Medical Care		Recrea-tion*		Education & Communic.*		Other Goods & Services	
	Index	%	Index	%	Index	%	Index	%	Index	%	Index	%	Index	%	Index	%	Index	%
1959	28.0	1.8	-	-	-	-	41.4	1.0	29.8	5.3	21.9	4.3	-	-	-	-	-	-
1960	28.6	2.1	-	-	-	-	42.5	2.7	29.6	-0.7	22.5	2.7	-	-	-	-	-	-
1961	28.9	1.0	-	-	-	-	43.2	1.6	29.8	0.7	23.0	2.2	-	-	-	-	-	-
1962	29.4	1.7	-	-	-	-	43.8	1.4	30.4	2.0	24.1	4.8	-	-	-	-	-	-
1963	29.8	1.4	-	-	-	-	44.2	0.9	30.7	1.0	24.7	2.5	-	-	-	-	-	-
1964	30.2	1.3	-	-	-	-	44.7	1.1	31.5	2.6	25.3	2.4	-	-	-	-	-	-
1965	30.8	2.0	-	-	-	-	45.4	1.6	31.7	0.6	25.9	2.4	-	-	-	-	-	-
1966	31.6	2.6	-	-	-	-	46.5	2.4	32.0	0.9	27.3	5.4	-	-	-	-	-	-
1967	32.5	2.8	-	-	-	-	48.5	4.3	32.9	2.8	28.9	5.9	-	-	-	-	-	-
1968	34.0	4.6	-	-	-	-	51.2	5.6	33.8	2.7	30.4	5.2	-	-	-	-	-	-
1969	35.8	5.3	-	-	-	-	53.7	4.9	35.3	4.4	31.9	4.9	-	-	-	-	-	-
1970	37.7	5.3	-	-	-	-	55.3	3.0	36.7	4.0	33.6	5.3	-	-	-	-	-	-
1971	39.1	3.7	-	-	-	-	57.7	4.3	38.8	5.7	35.6	6.0	-	-	-	-	-	-
1972	40.4	3.3	-	-	-	-	59.0	2.3	39.6	2.1	36.8	3.4	-	-	-	-	-	-
1973	42.8	5.9	-	-	-	-	61.4	4.1	40.5	2.3	38.2	3.8	-	-	-	-	-	-
1974	47.0	9.8	-	-	-	-	65.9	7.3	44.8	10.6	41.5	8.6	-	-	-	-	-	-
1975	51.8	10.2	-	-	-	-	68.7	4.2	49.9	11.4	47.7	14.9	-	-	-	-	-	-
1976	54.6	5.4	59.5	-	50.5	-	70.5	2.6	54.2	8.6	52.5	10.1	-	-	-	-	54.3	-
1977	58.8	7.7	64.0	7.6	55.0	8.9	73.1	3.7	58.0	7.0	57.8	10.1	-	-	-	-	58.2	7.2
1978	64.3	9.4	70.7	10.5	61.6	12.0	77.2	5.6	61.4	5.9	63.3	9.5	-	-	-	-	63.4	8.9
1979	69.8	8.6	79.3	12.2	65.1	5.7	82.0	6.2	70.4	14.7	69.1	9.2	-	-	-	-	67.6	6.6
1980	80.4	15.2	85.2	7.4	77.2	18.6	88.6	8.0	83.7	18.9	76.6	10.9	-	-	-	-	72.7	7.5
1981	90.8	12.9	91.2	7.0	90.5	17.2	92.6	4.5	92.0	9.9	84.6	10.4	-	-	-	-	79.8	9.8
1982	97.6	7.5	97.1	6.5	97.8	8.1	97.6	5.4	97.2	5.7	94.2	11.3	-	-	-	-	90.7	13.7
1983	98.4	0.8	99.3	2.3	97.7	-0.1	97.8	0.2	99.1	2.0	100.7	6.9	-	-	-	-	101.2	11.6
1984	104.0	5.7	103.7	4.4	104.5	7.0	104.6	7.0	103.7	4.6	105.1	4.4	-	-	-	-	108.2	6.9
1985	108.4	4.2	105.9	2.1	111.2	6.4	103.5	-1.1	105.5	1.7	111.1	5.7	-	-	-	-	116.3	7.5
1986	111.6	3.0	109.5	3.4	117.5	5.7	101.7	-1.7	101.2	-4.1	119.7	7.7	-	-	-	-	123.2	5.9
1987	115.4	3.4	113.7	3.8	121.5	3.4	104.6	2.9	102.4	1.2	128.7	7.5	-	-	-	-	130.9	6.3
1988	120.5	4.4	120.4	5.9	126.9	4.4	102.4	-2.1	105.3	2.8	136.9	6.4	-	-	-	-	140.1	7.0
1989	126.4	4.9	128.2	6.5	132.4	4.3	104.2	1.8	109.6	4.1	147.9	8.0	-	-	-	-	152.2	8.6
1990	132.1	4.5	134.7	5.1	137.3	3.7	107.5	3.2	114.7	4.7	160.5	8.5	-	-	-	-	161.0	5.8
1991	137.9	4.4	140.3	4.2	142.7	3.9	113.1	5.2	117.1	2.1	172.9	7.7	-	-	-	-	174.5	8.4
1992	142.5	3.3	143.3	2.1	146.2	2.5	117.8	4.2	119.8	2.3	187.0	8.2	-	-	-	-	195.9	12.3
1993	146.3	2.7	146.2	2.0	149.2	2.1	118.2	0.3	123.7	3.3	199.1	6.5	-	-	-	-	207.0	5.7
1994	148.7	1.6	148.9	1.8	151.5	1.5	115.5	-2.3	125.7	1.6	204.3	2.6	-	-	-	-	213.2	3.0
1995	151.6	2.0	151.6	1.8	154.5	2.0	114.0	-1.3	129.0	2.6	209.0	2.3	-	-	-	-	220.6	3.5
1996	155.1	2.3	155.3	2.4	157.4	1.9	116.9	2.5	133.5	3.5	214.5	2.6	-	-	-	-	227.8	3.3
1997	160.4	3.4	160.1	3.1	165.6	5.2	116.1	-0.7	133.6	0.1	221.8	3.4	-	-	-	-	239.9	5.3
1998	165.5	3.2	166.3	3.9	174.4	5.3	115.9	-0.2	132.0	-1.2	228.0	2.8	98.2	-	101.3	-	252.2	5.1
1999	172.5	4.2	170.8	2.7	185.6	6.4	114.2	-1.5	135.8	2.9	232.6	2.0	96.6	-1.6	104.2	2.9	277.7	10.1
2000	180.2	4.5	175.1	2.5	197.0	6.1	115.4	1.1	143.1	5.4	242.9	4.4	95.3	-1.3	106.4	2.1	289.4	4.2
2001	189.9	5.4	181.8	3.8	216.5	9.9	111.2	-3.6	-	-	255.2	5.1	93.4	-2.0	107.7	1.2	301.5	4.2

Source: U.S. Department of Labor, Bureau of Labor Statistics, Division of Consumer Prices and Price Indexes. *Base is December 1997 = 100. - indicates no data collected for period.

San Francisco-Oakland-San Jose, CA
Consumer Price Index - Urban Wage Earners
Base 1982-1984 = 100
Annual Averages

For 1914-2001. Columns headed % show percentile change in the index from the previous period for which an index is available.

Year	All Items		Food & Beverage		Housing		Apparel		Trans-portation		Medical Care		Recrea-tion*		Education & Communic.*		Other Goods & Services	
	Index	%	Index	%	Index	%	Index	%	Index	%	Index	%	Index	%	Index	%	Index	%
1914	-	-	-	-	-	-	-	-	-	-	-	-	-	-	-	-	-	-
1915	9.3	-	-	-	-	-	-	-	-	-	-	-	-	-	-	-	-	-
1916	9.6	3.2	-	-	-	-	-	-	-	-	-	-	-	-	-	-	-	-
1917	11.0	14.6	-	-	-	-	-	-	-	-	-	-	-	-	-	-	-	-
1918	13.0	18.2	-	-	-	-	-	-	-	-	-	-	-	-	-	-	-	-
1919	15.2	16.9	-	-	-	-	-	-	-	-	-	-	-	-	-	-	-	-
1920	17.1	12.5	-	-	-	-	-	-	-	-	-	-	-	-	-	-	-	-
1921	15.5	-9.4	-	-	-	-	-	-	-	-	-	-	-	-	-	-	-	-
1922	14.8	-4.5	-	-	-	-	-	-	-	-	-	-	-	-	-	-	-	-
1923	14.8	0.0	-	-	-	-	-	-	-	-	-	-	-	-	-	-	-	-
1924	14.8	0.0	-	-	-	-	-	-	-	-	-	-	-	-	-	-	-	-
1925	15.2	2.7	-	-	-	-	-	-	-	-	-	-	-	-	-	-	-	-
1926	15.2	0.0	-	-	-	-	-	-	-	-	-	-	-	-	-	-	-	-
1927	15.0	-1.3	-	-	-	-	-	-	-	-	-	-	-	-	-	-	-	-
1928	15.0	0.0	-	-	-	-	-	-	-	-	-	-	-	-	-	-	-	-
1929	15.0	0.0	-	-	-	-	-	-	-	-	-	-	-	-	-	-	-	-
1930	14.7	-2.0	-	-	-	-	-	-	-	-	-	-	-	-	-	-	-	-
1931	13.4	-8.8	-	-	-	-	-	-	-	-	-	-	-	-	-	-	-	-
1932	12.4	-7.5	-	-	-	-	-	-	-	-	-	-	-	-	-	-	-	-
1933	11.9	-4.0	-	-	-	-	-	-	-	-	-	-	-	-	-	-	-	-
1934	12.2	2.5	-	-	-	-	-	-	-	-	-	-	-	-	-	-	-	-
1935	12.5	2.5	-	-	-	-	-	-	-	-	-	-	-	-	-	-	-	-
1936	12.5	0.0	-	-	-	-	-	-	-	-	-	-	-	-	-	-	-	-
1937	13.0	4.0	-	-	-	-	-	-	-	-	-	-	-	-	-	-	-	-
1938	12.9	-0.8	-	-	-	-	-	-	-	-	-	-	-	-	-	-	-	-
1939	12.7	-1.6	-	-	-	-	-	-	-	-	-	-	-	-	-	-	-	-
1940	12.8	0.8	-	-	-	-	-	-	-	-	-	-	-	-	-	-	-	-
1941	13.5	5.5	-	-	-	-	-	-	-	-	-	-	-	-	-	-	-	-
1942	15.1	11.9	-	-	-	-	-	-	-	-	-	-	-	-	-	-	-	-
1943	16.1	6.6	-	-	-	-	-	-	-	-	-	-	-	-	-	-	-	-
1944	16.5	2.5	-	-	-	-	-	-	-	-	-	-	-	-	-	-	-	-
1945	17.0	3.0	-	-	-	-	-	-	-	-	-	-	-	-	-	-	-	-
1946	18.3	7.6	-	-	-	-	-	-	-	-	-	-	-	-	-	-	-	-
1947	20.8	13.7	-	-	-	-	-	-	16.0	-	13.7	-	-	-	-	-	-	-
1948	22.2	6.7	-	-	-	-	-	-	17.6	10.0	14.4	5.1	-	-	-	-	-	-
1949	22.2	0.0	-	-	-	-	-	-	19.0	8.0	14.8	2.8	-	-	-	-	-	-
1950	22.2	0.0	-	-	-	-	-	-	19.0	0.0	15.2	2.7	-	-	-	-	-	-
1951	24.0	8.1	-	-	-	-	-	-	20.3	6.8	15.9	4.6	-	-	-	-	-	-
1952	24.9	3.8	-	-	-	-	-	-	23.2	14.3	16.9	6.3	-	-	-	-	-	-
1953	25.3	1.6	-	-	-	-	40.8	-	25.1	8.2	17.4	3.0	-	-	-	-	-	-
1954	25.3	0.0	-	-	-	-	40.3	-1.2	24.9	-0.8	17.6	1.1	-	-	-	-	-	-
1955	25.2	-0.4	-	-	-	-	40.4	0.2	24.5	-1.6	17.8	1.1	-	-	-	-	-	-
1956	25.7	2.0	-	-	-	-	41.3	2.2	24.8	1.2	18.7	5.1	-	-	-	-	-	-
1957	26.8	4.3	-	-	-	-	42.2	2.2	26.4	6.5	19.7	5.3	-	-	-	-	-	-
1958	27.7	3.4	-	-	-	-	42.5	0.7	27.6	4.5	21.2	7.6	-	-	-	-	-	-

[Continued]

San Francisco-Oakland-San Jose, CA
Consumer Price Index - Urban Wage Earners
Base 1982-1984 = 100
Annual Averages
[Continued]

For 1914-2001. Columns headed % show percentile change in the index from the previous period for which an index is available.

Year	All Items		Food & Beverage		Housing		Apparel		Trans-portation		Medical Care		Recrea-tion*		Education & Communic.*		Other Goods & Services	
	Index	%	Index	%	Index	%	Index	%	Index	%	Index	%	Index	%	Index	%	Index	%
1959	28.3	2.2	-	-	-	-	43.0	1.2	29.1	5.4	22.0	3.8	-	-	-	-	-	-
1960	28.8	1.8	-	-	-	-	44.2	2.8	28.9	-0.7	22.7	3.2	-	-	-	-	-	-
1961	29.2	1.4	-	-	-	-	44.8	1.4	29.1	0.7	23.2	2.2	-	-	-	-	-	-
1962	29.7	1.7	-	-	-	-	45.4	1.3	29.7	2.1	24.2	4.3	-	-	-	-	-	-
1963	30.0	1.0	-	-	-	-	45.9	1.1	30.0	1.0	24.8	2.5	-	-	-	-	-	-
1964	30.5	1.7	-	-	-	-	46.4	1.1	30.8	2.7	25.4	2.4	-	-	-	-	-	-
1965	31.1	2.0	-	-	-	-	47.1	1.5	31.0	0.6	26.1	2.8	-	-	-	-	-	-
1966	31.9	2.6	-	-	-	-	48.3	2.5	31.2	0.6	27.5	5.4	-	-	-	-	-	-
1967	32.8	2.8	-	-	-	-	50.3	4.1	32.1	2.9	29.1	5.8	-	-	-	-	-	-
1968	34.3	4.6	-	-	-	-	53.2	5.8	33.0	2.8	30.6	5.2	-	-	-	-	-	-
1969	36.2	5.5	-	-	-	-	55.7	4.7	34.5	4.5	32.1	4.9	-	-	-	-	-	-
1970	38.0	5.0	-	-	-	-	57.4	3.1	35.9	4.1	33.8	5.3	-	-	-	-	-	-
1971	39.4	3.7	-	-	-	-	59.8	4.2	37.9	5.6	35.9	6.2	-	-	-	-	-	-
1972	40.8	3.6	-	-	-	-	61.2	2.3	38.6	1.8	37.0	3.1	-	-	-	-	-	-
1973	43.2	5.9	-	-	-	-	63.7	4.1	39.5	2.3	38.5	4.1	-	-	-	-	-	-
1974	47.4	9.7	-	-	-	-	68.4	7.4	43.8	10.9	41.8	8.6	-	-	-	-	-	-
1975	52.2	10.1	-	-	-	-	71.3	4.2	48.7	11.2	48.0	14.8	-	-	-	-	-	-
1976	55.2	5.7	59.1	-	51.8	-	73.1	2.5	52.9	8.6	52.9	10.2	-	-	-	-	54.0	-
1977	59.4	7.6	63.6	7.6	56.4	8.9	75.8	3.7	56.6	7.0	58.2	10.0	-	-	-	-	57.9	7.2
1978	64.8	9.1	70.3	10.5	63.0	11.7	78.4	3.4	60.3	6.5	63.5	9.1	-	-	-	-	61.7	6.6
1979	70.5	8.8	78.4	11.5	66.5	5.6	82.9	5.7	69.5	15.3	69.2	9.0	-	-	-	-	66.7	8.1
1980	81.2	15.2	84.9	8.3	78.9	18.6	88.8	7.1	82.3	18.4	76.9	11.1	-	-	-	-	73.1	9.6
1981	91.6	12.8	91.8	8.1	92.3	17.0	95.1	7.1	91.1	10.7	85.1	10.7	-	-	-	-	80.2	9.7
1982	98.2	7.2	97.0	5.7	100.0	8.3	98.1	3.2	96.8	6.3	94.1	10.6	-	-	-	-	91.0	13.5
1983	98.2	0.0	99.3	2.4	96.9	-3.1	97.7	-0.4	99.2	2.5	100.6	6.9	-	-	-	-	101.1	11.1
1984	103.7	5.6	103.7	4.4	103.2	6.5	104.2	6.7	104.0	4.8	105.4	4.8	-	-	-	-	107.9	6.7
1985	107.8	4.0	105.9	2.1	109.6	6.2	103.9	-0.3	105.7	1.6	111.8	6.1	-	-	-	-	115.9	7.4
1986	110.7	2.7	109.5	3.4	115.9	5.7	102.3	-1.5	101.5	-4.0	120.5	7.8	-	-	-	-	122.5	5.7
1987	114.3	3.3	113.8	3.9	119.4	3.0	105.4	3.0	103.7	2.2	130.0	7.9	-	-	-	-	130.4	6.4
1988	119.4	4.5	120.4	5.8	124.6	4.4	104.4	-0.9	107.1	3.3	138.1	6.2	-	-	-	-	140.1	7.4
1989	125.5	5.1	128.3	6.6	129.7	4.1	107.0	2.5	111.8	4.4	149.0	7.9	-	-	-	-	154.6	10.3
1990	131.1	4.5	134.7	5.0	134.6	3.8	110.6	3.4	116.7	4.4	160.8	7.9	-	-	-	-	164.5	6.4
1991	136.3	4.0	140.4	4.2	139.7	3.8	116.2	5.1	118.6	1.6	172.1	7.0	-	-	-	-	177.8	8.1
1992	140.6	3.2	143.3	2.1	143.1	2.4	121.5	4.6	121.9	2.8	186.4	8.3	-	-	-	-	195.8	10.1
1993	144.3	2.6	146.4	2.2	146.1	2.1	122.7	1.0	125.7	3.1	197.9	6.2	-	-	-	-	204.8	4.6
1994	146.3	1.4	149.2	1.9	148.3	1.5	120.6	-1.7	127.9	1.8	202.4	2.3	-	-	-	-	208.8	2.0
1995	149.3	2.1	151.8	1.7	151.1	1.9	120.0	-0.5	132.1	3.3	206.8	2.2	-	-	-	-	215.1	3.0
1996	152.6	2.2	155.6	2.5	153.8	1.8	122.7	2.2	136.4	3.3	212.2	2.6	-	-	-	-	220.5	2.5
1997	157.4	3.1	160.4	3.1	161.8	5.2	121.5	-1.0	135.8	-0.4	219.4	3.4	-	-	-	-	230.8	4.7
1998	161.8	2.8	166.3	3.7	170.2	5.2	119.9	-1.3	133.2	-1.9	225.1	2.6	97.6	-	102.1	-	243.0	5.3
1999	168.8	4.3	170.5	2.5	181.2	6.5	118.4	-1.3	137.7	3.4	229.7	2.0	95.3	-2.4	105.6	3.4	275.8	13.5
2000	176.3	4.4	175.1	2.7	192.1	6.0	119.9	1.3	145.3	5.5	239.6	4.3	94.2	-1.2	107.5	1.8	288.8	4.7
2001	185.7	5.3	181.9	3.9	211.9	10.3	115.9	-3.3	-	-	251.1	4.8	92.2	-2.1	108.4	0.8	301.3	4.3

Source: U.S. Department of Labor, Bureau of Labor Statistics, Division of Consumer Prices and Price Indexes. *Base is December 1997 = 100. - indicates no data collected for period.

San Francisco-Oakland-San Jose, CA
Consumer Price Index - All Urban Consumers
Base 1982-1984 = 100
All Items

For 1914-2001. Columns headed % show percentile change in the index from the previous period for which an index is available.

Year	Jan Index	%	Feb Index	%	Mar Index	%	Apr Index	%	May Index	%	Jun Index	%	Jul Index	%	Aug Index	%	Sep Index	%	Oct Index	%	Nov Index	%	Dec Index	%
1914	-	-	-	-	-	-	-	-	-	-	-	-	-	-	-	-	-	-	-	-	-	-	9.2	-
1915	-	-	-	-	-	-	-	-	-	-	-	-	-	-	-	-	-	-	-	-	-	-	9.2	0.0
1916	-	-	-	-	-	-	-	-	-	-	-	-	-	-	-	-	-	-	-	-	-	-	10.0	8.7
1917	-	-	-	-	-	-	-	-	-	-	-	-	-	-	-	-	-	-	-	-	-	-	11.6	16.0
1918	-	-	-	-	-	-	-	-	-	-	-	-	-	-	-	-	-	-	-	-	-	-	14.1	21.6
1919	-	-	-	-	-	-	-	-	-	-	14.7	4.3	-	-	-	-	-	-	-	-	-	-	16.3	10.9
1920	-	-	-	-	-	-	-	-	-	-	17.5	7.4	-	-	-	-	-	-	-	-	-	-	16.5	-5.7
1921	-	-	-	-	-	-	-	-	15.2	-7.9	-	-	-	-	-	-	15.0	-1.3	-	-	-	-	15.0	0.0
1922	-	-	-	-	14.7	-2.0	-	-	-	-	14.6	-0.7	-	-	-	-	14.5	-0.7	-	-	-	-	14.6	0.7
1923	-	-	-	-	14.4	-1.4	-	-	-	-	14.6	1.4	-	-	-	-	14.8	1.4	-	-	-	-	15.0	1.4
1924	-	-	-	-	14.6	-2.7	-	-	-	-	14.6	0.0	-	-	-	-	14.7	0.7	-	-	-	-	14.8	0.7
1925	-	-	-	-	-	-	-	-	-	-	15.1	2.0	-	-	-	-	-	-	-	-	-	-	15.3	1.3
1926	-	-	-	-	-	-	-	-	-	-	15.0	-2.0	-	-	-	-	-	-	-	-	-	-	15.0	0.0
1927	-	-	-	-	-	-	-	-	-	-	15.0	0.0	-	-	-	-	-	-	-	-	-	-	14.9	-0.7
1928	-	-	-	-	-	-	-	-	-	-	14.8	-0.7	-	-	-	-	-	-	-	-	-	-	15.0	1.4
1929	-	-	-	-	-	-	-	-	-	-	14.8	-1.3	-	-	-	-	-	-	-	-	-	-	14.9	0.7
1930	-	-	-	-	-	-	-	-	-	-	14.6	-2.0	-	-	-	-	-	-	-	-	-	-	14.1	-3.4
1931	-	-	-	-	-	-	-	-	-	-	13.3	-5.7	-	-	-	-	-	-	-	-	-	-	12.9	-3.0
1932	-	-	-	-	-	-	-	-	-	-	12.2	-5.4	-	-	-	-	-	-	-	-	-	-	12.0	-1.6
1933	-	-	-	-	-	-	-	-	-	-	11.7	-2.5	-	-	-	-	-	-	-	-	-	-	12.1	3.4
1934	-	-	-	-	-	-	-	-	-	-	12.2	0.8	-	-	-	-	-	-	-	-	12.5	2.5	-	-
1935	-	-	-	-	12.6	0.8	-	-	-	-	-	-	12.3	-2.4	-	-	-	-	12.3	0.0	-	-	-	-
1936	12.4	0.8	-	-	-	-	12.2	-1.6	-	-	-	-	12.4	1.6	-	-	12.4	0.0	-	-	-	-	12.4	0.0
1937	-	-	-	-	12.8	3.2	-	-	-	-	12.8	0.0	-	-	-	-	12.9	0.8	-	-	-	-	13.0	0.8
1938	-	-	-	-	12.8	-1.5	-	-	-	-	12.8	0.0	-	-	-	-	12.8	0.0	-	-	-	-	12.8	0.0
1939	-	-	-	-	12.7	-0.8	-	-	-	-	12.5	-1.6	-	-	-	-	12.8	2.4	-	-	-	-	12.6	-1.6
1940	-	-	-	-	12.6	0.0	-	-	-	-	12.6	0.0	-	-	-	-	12.7	0.8	12.8	0.8	12.8	0.0	12.8	0.0
1941	12.8	0.0	12.9	0.8	12.9	0.0	13.1	1.6	13.1	0.0	13.3	1.5	13.3	0.0	13.4	0.8	13.6	1.5	13.8	1.5	14.0	1.4	14.0	0.0
1942	14.3	2.1	14.4	0.7	14.6	1.4	14.8	1.4	14.8	0.0	14.9	0.7	14.9	0.0	15.1	1.3	15.2	0.7	15.3	0.7	15.6	2.0	15.6	0.0
1943	15.7	0.6	15.7	0.0	15.9	1.3	16.2	1.9	16.2	0.0	16.2	0.0	15.8	-2.5	15.7	-0.6	15.8	0.6	16.0	1.3	16.1	0.6	16.1	0.0
1944	16.1	0.0	16.0	-0.6	16.1	0.6	16.2	0.6	16.4	1.2	16.3	-0.6	16.4	0.6	16.4	0.0	16.4	0.0	16.6	1.2	16.6	0.0	16.8	1.2
1945	16.7	-0.6	16.6	-0.6	16.7	0.6	16.8	0.6	16.7	-0.6	16.8	0.6	16.9	0.6	16.8	-0.6	16.8	0.0	16.8	0.0	17.0	1.2	17.2	1.2
1946	17.0	-1.2	16.8	-1.2	16.9	0.6	16.9	0.0	17.0	0.6	17.4	2.4	18.2	4.6	18.7	2.7	19.1	2.1	19.4	1.6	20.1	3.6	20.3	1.0
1947	20.1	-1.0	20.0	-0.5	20.3	1.5	20.4	0.5	20.3	-0.5	20.1	-1.0	-	-	-	-	21.0	4.5	-	-	-	-	21.4	1.9
1948	-	-	-	-	21.7	1.4	-	-	-	-	22.0	1.4	-	-	-	-	22.4	1.8	-	-	-	-	22.4	0.0
1949	-	-	-	-	22.1	-1.3	-	-	-	-	22.0	-0.5	-	-	-	-	21.9	-0.5	-	-	-	-	21.7	-0.9
1950	-	-	-	-	21.8	0.5	-	-	-	-	21.7	-0.5	-	-	-	-	22.1	1.8	-	-	-	-	22.9	3.6
1951	-	-	-	-	23.8	3.9	-	-	-	-	23.7	-0.4	-	-	-	-	23.7	0.0	-	-	-	-	24.3	2.5
1952	-	-	-	-	24.3	0.0	-	-	-	-	24.8	2.1	-	-	-	-	24.7	-0.4	-	-	-	-	24.9	0.8
1953	-	-	-	-	24.9	0.0	-	-	-	-	25.0	0.4	-	-	-	-	25.2	0.8	-	-	-	-	25.2	0.0
1954	-	-	-	-	25.1	-0.4	-	-	-	-	25.1	0.0	-	-	-	-	25.0	-0.4	-	-	-	-	24.9	-0.4
1955	-	-	-	-	24.9	0.0	-	-	-	-	24.9	0.0	-	-	-	-	24.9	0.0	-	-	-	-	24.9	0.0
1956	-	-	-	-	25.1	0.8	-	-	-	-	25.4	1.2	-	-	-	-	25.6	0.8	-	-	-	-	26.2	2.3
1957	-	-	-	-	26.3	0.4	-	-	-	-	26.4	0.4	-	-	-	-	26.6	0.8	-	-	-	-	26.9	1.1
1958	-	-	-	-	27.3	1.5	-	-	-	-	27.6	1.1	-	-	-	-	27.6	0.0	-	-	-	-	27.6	0.0
1959	-	-	-	-	27.8	0.7	-	-	-	-	27.9	0.4	-	-	-	-	28.2	1.1	-	-	-	-	28.4	0.7

[Continued]

San Francisco-Oakland-San Jose, CA
Consumer Price Index - All Urban Consumers
Base 1982-1984 = 100
All Items
[Continued]

For 1914-2001. Columns headed % show percentile change in the index from the previous period for which an index is available.

Year	Jan Index	%	Feb Index	%	Mar Index	%	Apr Index	%	May Index	%	Jun Index	%	Jul Index	%	Aug Index	%	Sep Index	%	Oct Index	%	Nov Index	%	Dec Index	%
1960	-	-	-	-	28.3	-0.4	-	-	-	-	28.5	0.7	-	-	-	-	28.7	0.7	-	-	-	-	28.9	0.7
1961	-	-	-	-	28.8	-0.3	-	-	-	-	28.8	0.0	-	-	-	-	29.0	0.7	-	-	-	-	29.1	0.3
1962	-	-	-	-	29.3	0.7	-	-	-	-	29.4	0.3	-	-	-	-	29.4	0.0	-	-	-	-	29.5	0.3
1963	-	-	-	-	29.6	0.3	-	-	-	-	29.8	0.7	-	-	-	-	29.9	0.3	-	-	-	-	30.1	0.7
1964	-	-	-	-	30.1	0.0	-	-	-	-	30.2	0.3	-	-	-	-	30.3	0.3	-	-	-	-	30.5	0.7
1965	-	-	-	-	30.7	0.7	-	-	-	-	30.9	0.7	-	-	-	-	30.8	-0.3	-	-	-	-	31.1	1.0
1966	-	-	-	-	31.4	1.0	-	-	-	-	31.5	0.3	-	-	-	-	31.8	1.0	-	-	-	-	32.0	0.6
1967	-	-	-	-	32.0	0.0	-	-	-	-	32.4	1.3	-	-	-	-	32.9	1.5	-	-	-	-	33.1	0.6
1968	-	-	-	-	33.5	1.2	-	-	-	-	34.0	1.5	-	-	-	-	34.3	0.9	-	-	-	-	34.6	0.9
1969	-	-	-	-	35.2	1.7	-	-	-	-	35.7	1.4	-	-	-	-	36.3	1.7	-	-	-	-	36.8	1.4
1970	-	-	-	-	37.2	1.1	-	-	-	-	37.6	1.1	-	-	-	-	38.0	1.1	-	-	-	-	38.5	1.3
1971	-	-	-	-	38.7	0.5	-	-	-	-	39.0	0.8	-	-	-	-	39.3	0.8	-	-	-	-	39.6	0.8
1972	-	-	-	-	39.9	0.8	-	-	-	-	40.4	1.3	-	-	-	-	40.9	1.2	-	-	-	-	41.1	0.5
1973	-	-	-	-	41.9	1.9	-	-	-	-	42.5	1.4	-	-	-	-	43.8	3.1	-	-	-	-	44.0	0.5
1974	-	-	-	-	45.3	3.0	-	-	-	-	46.8	3.3	-	-	-	-	48.2	3.0	-	-	-	-	49.5	2.7
1975	-	-	-	-	50.7	2.4	-	-	-	-	51.6	1.8	-	-	-	-	52.5	1.7	-	-	-	-	53.4	1.7
1976	-	-	-	-	53.8	0.7	-	-	-	-	54.3	0.9	-	-	-	-	55.3	1.8	-	-	-	-	56.0	1.3
1977	-	-	-	-	57.2	2.1	-	-	-	-	58.8	2.8	-	-	-	-	59.9	1.9	-	-	-	-	60.9	1.7
1978	-	-	61.5	1.0	-	-	62.7	2.0	-	-	64.8	3.3	-	-	66.6	2.8	-	-	66.1	-0.8	-	-	65.3	-1.2
1979	-	-	66.3	1.5	-	-	67.9	2.4	-	-	69.1	1.8	-	-	71.0	2.7	-	-	72.0	1.4	-	-	74.9	4.0
1980	-	-	78.3	4.5	-	-	79.2	1.1	-	-	80.7	1.9	-	-	81.6	1.1	-	-	81.9	0.4	-	-	82.9	1.2
1981	-	-	84.7	2.2	-	-	87.9	3.8	-	-	89.1	1.4	-	-	93.6	5.1	-	-	96.6	3.2	-	-	95.6	-1.0
1982	-	-	96.2	0.6	-	-	97.2	1.0	-	-	99.1	2.0	-	-	99.0	-0.1	-	-	98.4	-0.6	-	-	95.6	-2.8
1983	-	-	96.7	1.2	-	-	97.4	0.7	-	-	98.6	1.2	-	-	99.5	0.9	-	-	99.4	-0.1	-	-	100.0	0.6
1984	-	-	101.4	1.4	-	-	102.9	1.5	-	-	103.7	0.8	-	-	105.2	1.4	-	-	106.5	1.2	-	-	106.0	-0.5
1985	-	-	106.9	0.8	-	-	107.5	0.6	-	-	108.4	0.8	-	-	109.2	0.7	-	-	109.5	0.3	-	-	109.4	-0.1
1986	-	-	111.0	1.5	-	-	110.4	-0.5	-	-	111.9	1.4	-	-	112.4	0.4	-	-	113.1	0.6	-	-	111.8	-1.1
1987	112.5	0.6	113.4	0.8	113.7	0.3	114.8	1.0	115.0	0.2	115.0	0.0	115.8	0.7	116.1	0.3	116.6	0.4	117.1	0.4	117.3	0.2	117.4	0.1
1988	118.4	0.9	117.9	-0.4	119.1	1.0	118.7	-0.3	119.7	0.8	120.1	0.3	120.9	0.7	122.0	0.9	122.1	0.1	122.3	0.2	122.2	-0.1	122.6	0.3
1989	124.0	1.1	124.0	0.0	125.9	1.5	125.4	-0.4	126.3	0.7	126.2	-0.1	127.4	1.0	128.1	0.5	126.8	-1.0	127.5	0.6	127.2	-0.2	127.4	0.2
1990	128.5	0.9	129.2	0.5	130.0	0.6	130.7	0.5	130.8	0.1	131.6	0.6	132.3	0.5	133.1	0.6	134.0	0.7	134.6	0.4	134.7	0.1	135.1	0.3
1991	136.7	1.2	136.1	-0.4	136.3	0.1	135.8	-0.4	136.2	0.3	137.6	1.0	138.2	0.4	139.1	0.7	139.7	0.4	139.6	-0.1	139.8	0.1	139.8	0.0
1992	140.3	0.4	141.0	0.5	141.9	0.6	141.6	-0.2	141.9	0.2	141.9	0.0	142.2	0.2	142.7	0.4	143.7	0.7	144.3	0.4	144.2	-0.1	144.3	0.1
1993	145.1	0.6	145.5	0.3	145.7	0.1	146.8	0.8	146.9	0.1	146.1	-0.5	146.1	0.0	146.2	0.1	146.5	0.2	147.0	0.3	147.2	0.1	147.0	-0.1
1994	147.5	0.3	147.4	-0.1	148.2	0.5	148.0	-0.1	148.3	0.2	148.1	-0.1	148.9	0.5	149.4	0.3	149.4	0.0	149.4	0.0	149.8	0.3	149.4	-0.3
1995	150.3	0.6	150.5	0.1	151.1	0.4	151.5	0.3	151.3	-0.1	151.7	0.3	151.5	-0.1	151.5	0.0	152.3	0.5	152.6	0.2	152.4	-0.1	152.1	-0.2
1996	152.9	0.5	153.2	0.2	152.9	-0.2	153.9	0.7	155.1	0.8	155.2	0.1	155.9	0.5	155.6	-0.2	156.3	0.4	156.9	0.4	156.9	0.0	156.0	-0.6
1997	157.0	0.6	157.9	0.6	159.2	0.8	159.6	0.3	159.8	0.1	160.0	0.1	160.6	0.4	161.2	0.4	161.6	0.2	162.5	0.6	162.6	0.1	162.6	0.0
1998	-	-	163.2	0.4	-	-	164.6	0.9	-	-	165.5	0.5	-	-	166.6	0.7	-	-	167.2	0.4	-	-	167.4	0.1
1999	-	-	169.4	1.2	-	-	172.2	1.7	-	-	171.8	-0.2	-	-	173.5	1.0	-	-	175.2	1.0	-	-	174.5	-0.4
2000	-	-	176.5	1.1	-	-	178.7	1.2	-	-	179.1	0.2	-	-	181.7	1.5	-	-	183.4	0.9	-	-	184.1	0.4
2001	-	-	187.9	2.1	-	-	189.1	0.6	-	-	190.9	1.0	-	-	191.0	0.1	-	-	191.7	0.4	-	-	190.6	-0.6

Source: U.S. Department of Labor, Bureau of Labor Statistics, Division of Consumer Prices and Price Indexes. - indicates no data collected for period.

San Francisco-Oakland-San Jose, CA
Consumer Price Index - Urban Wage Earners
Base 1982-1984 = 100
All Items

For 1914-2001. Columns headed % show percentile change in the index from the previous period for which an index is available.

Year	Jan Index	%	Feb Index	%	Mar Index	%	Apr Index	%	May Index	%	Jun Index	%	Jul Index	%	Aug Index	%	Sep Index	%	Oct Index	%	Nov Index	%	Dec Index	%
1914	-	-	-	-	-	-	-	-	-	-	-	-	-	-	-	-	-	-	-	-	-	-	9.3	-
1915	-	-	-	-	-	-	-	-	-	-	-	-	-	-	-	-	-	-	-	-	-	-	9.3	0.0
1916	-	-	-	-	-	-	-	-	-	-	-	-	-	-	-	-	-	-	-	-	-	-	10.0	7.5
1917	-	-	-	-	-	-	-	-	-	-	-	-	-	-	-	-	-	-	-	-	-	-	11.7	17.0
1918	-	-	-	-	-	-	-	-	-	-	-	-	-	-	-	-	-	-	-	-	-	-	14.3	22.2
1919	-	-	-	-	-	-	-	-	-	-	14.8	3.5	-	-	-	-	-	-	-	-	-	-	16.4	10.8
1920	-	-	-	-	-	-	-	-	-	-	17.7	7.9	-	-	-	-	-	-	-	-	-	-	16.7	-5.6
1921	-	-	-	-	-	-	-	-	15.3	-8.4	-	-	-	-	-	-	15.2	-0.7	-	-	-	-	15.1	-0.7
1922	-	-	-	-	14.8	-2.0	-	-	-	-	14.7	-0.7	-	-	-	-	14.6	-0.7	-	-	-	-	14.8	1.4
1923	-	-	-	-	14.6	-1.4	-	-	-	-	14.7	0.7	-	-	-	-	14.9	1.4	-	-	-	-	15.1	1.3
1924	-	-	-	-	14.7	-2.6	-	-	-	-	14.7	0.0	-	-	-	-	14.8	0.7	-	-	-	-	14.9	0.7
1925	-	-	-	-	-	-	-	-	-	-	15.3	2.7	-	-	-	-	-	-	-	-	-	-	15.4	0.7
1926	-	-	-	-	-	-	-	-	-	-	15.1	-1.9	-	-	-	-	-	-	-	-	-	-	15.1	0.0
1927	-	-	-	-	-	-	-	-	-	-	15.2	0.7	-	-	-	-	-	-	-	-	-	-	15.0	-1.3
1928	-	-	-	-	-	-	-	-	-	-	14.9	-0.7	-	-	-	-	-	-	-	-	-	-	15.1	1.3
1929	-	-	-	-	-	-	-	-	-	-	15.0	-0.7	-	-	-	-	-	-	-	-	-	-	15.0	0.0
1930	-	-	-	-	-	-	-	-	-	-	14.7	-2.0	-	-	-	-	-	-	-	-	-	-	14.2	-3.4
1931	-	-	-	-	-	-	-	-	-	-	13.4	-5.6	-	-	-	-	-	-	-	-	-	-	13.0	-3.0
1932	-	-	-	-	-	-	-	-	-	-	12.3	-5.4	-	-	-	-	-	-	-	-	-	-	12.1	-1.6
1933	-	-	-	-	-	-	-	-	-	-	11.8	-2.5	-	-	-	-	-	-	-	-	-	-	12.2	3.4
1934	-	-	-	-	-	-	-	-	-	-	12.3	0.8	-	-	-	-	-	-	-	-	12.6	2.4	-	-
1935	-	-	-	-	12.7	0.8	-	-	-	-	-	-	12.4	-2.4	-	-	-	-	12.4	0.0	-	-	-	-
1936	12.5	0.8	-	-	-	-	12.3	-1.6	-	-	-	-	12.5	1.6	-	-	12.5	0.0	-	-	-	-	12.5	0.0
1937	-	-	-	-	12.9	3.2	-	-	-	-	12.9	0.0	-	-	-	-	13.1	1.6	-	-	-	-	13.1	0.0
1938	-	-	-	-	12.9	-1.5	-	-	-	-	12.9	0.0	-	-	-	-	12.9	0.0	-	-	-	-	12.9	0.0
1939	-	-	-	-	12.8	-0.8	-	-	-	-	12.6	-1.6	-	-	-	-	12.9	2.4	-	-	-	-	12.7	-1.6
1940	-	-	-	-	12.7	0.0	-	-	-	-	12.7	0.0	-	-	-	-	12.8	0.8	12.9	0.8	12.9	0.0	12.9	0.0
1941	13.0	0.8	13.0	0.0	13.0	0.0	13.2	1.5	13.3	0.8	13.4	0.8	13.4	0.0	13.5	0.7	13.7	1.5	13.9	1.5	14.1	1.4	14.2	0.7
1942	14.5	2.1	14.5	0.0	14.7	1.4	14.9	1.4	14.9	0.0	15.0	0.7	15.0	0.0	15.2	1.3	15.4	1.3	15.5	0.6	15.7	1.3	15.8	0.6
1943	15.8	0.0	15.8	0.0	16.1	1.9	16.4	1.9	16.3	-0.6	16.4	0.6	16.0	-2.4	15.8	-1.2	16.0	1.3	16.2	1.3	16.3	0.6	16.3	0.0
1944	16.3	0.0	16.2	-0.6	16.3	0.6	16.4	0.6	16.5	0.6	16.5	0.0	16.5	0.0	16.5	0.0	16.6	0.6	16.7	0.6	16.8	0.6	16.9	0.6
1945	16.8	-0.6	16.7	-0.6	16.8	0.6	16.9	0.6	16.8	-0.6	16.9	0.6	17.0	0.6	16.9	-0.6	16.9	0.0	17.0	0.6	17.2	1.2	17.3	0.6
1946	17.1	-1.2	17.0	-0.6	17.0	0.0	17.1	0.6	17.2	0.6	17.6	2.3	18.4	4.5	18.9	2.7	19.3	2.1	19.6	1.6	20.3	3.6	20.5	1.0
1947	20.3	-1.0	20.2	-0.5	20.5	1.5	20.6	0.5	20.5	-0.5	20.3	-1.0	-	-	-	-	21.2	4.4	-	-	-	-	21.6	1.9
1948	-	-	-	-	21.9	1.4	-	-	-	-	22.2	1.4	-	-	-	-	22.6	1.8	-	-	-	-	22.6	0.0
1949	-	-	-	-	22.3	-1.3	-	-	-	-	22.2	-0.4	-	-	-	-	22.1	-0.5	-	-	-	-	21.9	-0.9
1950	-	-	-	-	22.0	0.5	-	-	-	-	21.9	-0.5	-	-	-	-	22.3	1.8	-	-	-	-	23.1	3.6
1951	-	-	-	-	24.0	3.9	-	-	-	-	23.9	-0.4	-	-	-	-	23.9	0.0	-	-	-	-	24.6	2.9
1952	-	-	-	-	24.6	0.0	-	-	-	-	25.0	1.6	-	-	-	-	24.9	-0.4	-	-	-	-	25.2	1.2
1953	-	-	-	-	25.1	-0.4	-	-	-	-	25.3	0.8	-	-	-	-	25.4	0.4	-	-	-	-	25.4	0.0
1954	-	-	-	-	25.3	-0.4	-	-	-	-	25.4	0.4	-	-	-	-	25.3	-0.4	-	-	-	-	25.2	-0.4
1955	-	-	-	-	25.2	0.0	-	-	-	-	25.1	-0.4	-	-	-	-	25.2	0.4	-	-	-	-	25.2	0.0
1956	-	-	-	-	25.4	0.8	-	-	-	-	25.6	0.8	-	-	-	-	25.9	1.2	-	-	-	-	26.4	1.9
1957	-	-	-	-	26.6	0.8	-	-	-	-	26.7	0.4	-	-	-	-	26.9	0.7	-	-	-	-	27.1	0.7
1958	-	-	-	-	27.6	1.8	-	-	-	-	27.8	0.7	-	-	-	-	27.9	0.4	-	-	-	-	27.8	-0.4
1959	-	-	-	-	28.1	1.1	-	-	-	-	28.2	0.4	-	-	-	-	28.4	0.7	-	-	-	-	28.7	1.1

[Continued]

San Francisco-Oakland-San Jose, CA
Consumer Price Index - Urban Wage Earners
Base 1982-1984 = 100
All Items
[Continued]

For 1914-2001. Columns headed % show percentile change in the index from the previous period for which an index is available.

Year	Jan Index	%	Feb Index	%	Mar Index	%	Apr Index	%	May Index	%	Jun Index	%	Jul Index	%	Aug Index	%	Sep Index	%	Oct Index	%	Nov Index	%	Dec Index	%
1960	-	-	-	-	28.6	-0.3	-	-	-	-	28.8	0.7	-	-	-	-	28.9	0.3	-	-	-	-	29.1	0.7
1961	-	-	-	-	29.1	0.0	-	-	-	-	29.1	0.0	-	-	-	-	29.3	0.7	-	-	-	-	29.4	0.3
1962	-	-	-	-	29.6	0.7	-	-	-	-	29.7	0.3	-	-	-	-	29.7	0.0	-	-	-	-	29.8	0.3
1963	-	-	-	-	29.9	0.3	-	-	-	-	30.0	0.3	-	-	-	-	30.1	0.3	-	-	-	-	30.3	0.7
1964	-	-	-	-	30.3	0.0	-	-	-	-	30.5	0.7	-	-	-	-	30.6	0.3	-	-	-	-	30.8	0.7
1965	-	-	-	-	31.0	0.6	-	-	-	-	31.2	0.6	-	-	-	-	31.1	-0.3	-	-	-	-	31.4	1.0
1966	-	-	-	-	31.7	1.0	-	-	-	-	31.8	0.3	-	-	-	-	32.1	0.9	-	-	-	-	32.3	0.6
1967	-	-	-	-	32.3	0.0	-	-	-	-	32.7	1.2	-	-	-	-	33.2	1.5	-	-	-	-	33.5	0.9
1968	-	-	-	-	33.9	1.2	-	-	-	-	34.3	1.2	-	-	-	-	34.6	0.9	-	-	-	-	35.0	1.2
1969	-	-	-	-	35.6	1.7	-	-	-	-	36.1	1.4	-	-	-	-	36.6	1.4	-	-	-	-	37.1	1.4
1970	-	-	-	-	37.6	1.3	-	-	-	-	37.9	0.8	-	-	-	-	38.3	1.1	-	-	-	-	38.9	1.6
1971	-	-	-	-	39.1	0.5	-	-	-	-	39.4	0.8	-	-	-	-	39.6	0.5	-	-	-	-	39.9	0.8
1972	-	-	-	-	40.3	1.0	-	-	-	-	40.8	1.2	-	-	-	-	41.2	1.0	-	-	-	-	41.5	0.7
1973	-	-	-	-	42.3	1.9	-	-	-	-	42.9	1.4	-	-	-	-	44.2	3.0	-	-	-	-	44.4	0.5
1974	-	-	-	-	45.7	2.9	-	-	-	-	47.2	3.3	-	-	-	-	48.6	3.0	-	-	-	-	49.9	2.7
1975	-	-	-	-	51.2	2.6	-	-	-	-	52.1	1.8	-	-	-	-	53.0	1.7	-	-	-	-	53.9	1.7
1976	-	-	-	-	54.3	0.7	-	-	-	-	54.8	0.9	-	-	-	-	55.8	1.8	-	-	-	-	56.6	1.4
1977	-	-	-	-	57.8	2.1	-	-	-	-	59.3	2.6	-	-	-	-	60.4	1.9	-	-	-	-	61.5	1.8
1978	-	-	62.2	1.1	-	-	63.2	1.6	-	-	65.3	3.3	-	-	67.0	2.6	-	-	66.5	-0.7	-	-	65.8	-1.1
1979	-	-	67.1	2.0	-	-	68.7	2.4	-	-	70.2	2.2	-	-	71.8	2.3	-	-	72.5	1.0	-	-	75.2	3.7
1980	-	-	78.8	4.8	-	-	79.7	1.1	-	-	81.3	2.0	-	-	82.6	1.6	-	-	83.0	0.5	-	-	84.0	1.2
1981	-	-	85.9	2.3	-	-	89.0	3.6	-	-	90.1	1.2	-	-	94.3	4.7	-	-	97.1	3.0	-	-	96.1	-1.0
1982	-	-	96.8	0.7	-	-	97.8	1.0	-	-	99.6	1.8	-	-	99.4	-0.2	-	-	98.9	-0.5	-	-	96.4	-2.5
1983	-	-	96.5	0.1	-	-	96.8	0.3	-	-	98.1	1.3	-	-	99.0	0.9	-	-	99.0	0.0	-	-	100.5	1.5
1984	-	-	101.4	0.9	-	-	102.2	0.8	-	-	103.5	1.3	-	-	106.0	2.4	-	-	104.9	-1.0	-	-	105.6	0.7
1985	-	-	106.5	0.9	-	-	107.1	0.6	-	-	107.9	0.7	-	-	108.6	0.6	-	-	108.7	0.1	-	-	108.8	0.1
1986	-	-	110.3	1.4	-	-	109.4	-0.8	-	-	111.0	1.5	-	-	111.3	0.3	-	-	112.0	0.6	-	-	110.7	-1.2
1987	111.3	0.5	112.4	1.0	112.8	0.4	113.9	1.0	113.9	0.0	114.0	0.1	114.7	0.6	114.9	0.2	115.4	0.4	116.0	0.5	116.2	0.2	116.4	0.2
1988	117.5	0.9	117.0	-0.4	117.9	0.8	117.8	-0.1	118.7	0.8	119.0	0.3	119.7	0.6	120.5	0.7	121.1	0.5	121.3	0.2	121.1	-0.2	121.5	0.3
1989	122.8	1.1	122.9	0.1	124.6	1.4	124.8	0.2	125.7	0.7	125.6	-0.1	126.4	0.6	127.0	0.5	126.1	-0.7	126.7	0.5	126.4	-0.2	126.6	0.2
1990	127.6	0.8	128.2	0.5	129.0	0.6	129.8	0.6	129.9	0.1	130.7	0.6	131.3	0.5	132.0	0.5	132.9	0.7	133.6	0.5	133.7	0.1	133.9	0.1
1991	135.3	1.0	134.5	-0.6	134.7	0.1	134.2	-0.4	134.8	0.4	136.0	0.9	136.4	0.3	137.2	0.6	137.9	0.5	137.8	-0.1	138.1	0.2	138.2	0.1
1992	138.5	0.2	139.1	0.4	139.9	0.6	139.6	-0.2	140.1	0.4	140.3	0.1	140.4	0.1	141.0	0.4	141.8	0.6	142.3	0.4	142.3	0.0	142.3	0.0
1993	143.0	0.5	143.5	0.3	143.8	0.2	144.8	0.7	144.8	0.0	144.0	-0.6	144.1	0.1	144.0	-0.1	144.4	0.3	145.0	0.4	145.0	0.0	144.7	-0.2
1994	145.3	0.4	145.0	-0.2	145.6	0.4	145.6	0.0	146.1	0.3	145.7	-0.3	146.6	0.6	147.1	0.3	147.1	0.0	147.0	-0.1	147.6	0.4	147.4	-0.1
1995	148.2	0.5	148.3	0.1	148.9	0.4	149.4	0.3	149.0	-0.3	149.6	0.4	149.3	-0.2	149.3	0.0	150.0	0.5	150.2	0.1	149.9	-0.2	149.6	-0.2
1996	150.5	0.6	150.5	0.0	150.7	0.1	151.9	0.8	153.0	0.7	152.9	-0.1	153.4	0.3	153.0	-0.3	153.8	0.5	154.3	0.3	154.2	-0.1	153.1	-0.7
1997	154.1	0.7	155.0	0.6	156.2	0.8	156.7	0.3	156.8	0.1	157.0	0.1	157.5	0.3	158.1	0.4	158.6	0.3	159.5	0.6	159.5	0.0	159.4	-0.1
1998	-	-	159.6	0.1	-	-	160.8	0.8	-	-	161.7	0.6	-	-	162.7	0.6	-	-	163.4	0.4	-	-	163.7	0.2
1999	-	-	165.7	1.2	-	-	168.8	1.9	-	-	168.3	-0.3	-	-	170.0	1.0	-	-	171.2	0.7	-	-	170.9	-0.2
2000	-	-	172.6	1.0	-	-	174.9	1.3	-	-	175.2	0.2	-	-	177.8	1.5	-	-	179.3	0.8	-	-	180.2	0.5
2001	-	-	183.5	1.8	-	-	184.9	0.8	-	-	186.9	1.1	-	-	186.7	-0.1	-	-	187.5	0.4	-	-	186.5	-0.5

Source: U.S. Department of Labor, Bureau of Labor Statistics, Division of Consumer Prices and Price Indexes. - indicates no data collected for period.

San Francisco-Oakland-San Jose, CA
Consumer Price Index - All Urban Consumers
Base 1982-1984 = 100
Food and Beverages

For 1975-2001. Columns headed % show percentile change in the index from the previous period for which an index is available.

Year	Jan Index	%	Feb Index	%	Mar Index	%	Apr Index	%	May Index	%	Jun Index	%	Jul Index	%	Aug Index	%	Sep Index	%	Oct Index	%	Nov Index	%	Dec Index	%
1975	-	-	-	-	-	-	-	-	-	-	-	-	-	-	-	-	-	-	-	-	-	-	60.2	-
1976	-	-	-	-	59.1	-1.8	-	-	-	-	59.3	0.3	-	-	-	-	59.7	0.7	-	-	-	-	60.0	0.5
1977	-	-	-	-	62.5	4.2	-	-	-	-	64.6	3.4	-	-	-	-	65.0	0.6	-	-	-	-	65.9	1.4
1978	-	-	67.3	2.1	-	-	69.1	2.7	-	-	71.4	3.3	-	-	72.3	1.3	-	-	72.9	0.8	-	-	73.0	0.1
1979	-	-	76.5	4.8	-	-	78.8	3.0	-	-	79.6	1.0	-	-	79.8	0.3	-	-	81.3	1.9	-	-	81.9	0.7
1980	-	-	82.5	0.7	-	-	83.7	1.5	-	-	84.2	0.6	-	-	85.9	2.0	-	-	87.7	2.1	-	-	89.3	1.8
1981	-	-	90.1	0.9	-	-	91.0	1.0	-	-	90.1	-1.0	-	-	92.7	2.9	-	-	91.9	-0.9	-	-	92.3	0.4
1982	-	-	95.8	3.8	-	-	96.2	0.4	-	-	97.5	1.4	-	-	97.8	0.3	-	-	99.0	1.2	-	-	97.7	-1.3
1983	-	-	98.3	0.6	-	-	100.1	1.8	-	-	98.9	-1.2	-	-	98.9	0.0	-	-	99.4	0.5	-	-	100.7	1.3
1984	-	-	102.7	2.0	-	-	103.2	0.5	-	-	103.4	0.2	-	-	103.9	0.5	-	-	104.6	0.7	-	-	105.3	0.7
1985	-	-	106.1	0.8	-	-	105.8	-0.3	-	-	105.3	-0.5	-	-	106.0	0.7	-	-	105.3	-0.7	-	-	107.2	1.8
1986	-	-	107.9	0.7	-	-	108.8	0.8	-	-	109.1	0.3	-	-	110.5	1.3	-	-	111.0	0.5	-	-	110.7	-0.3
1987	112.5	1.6	111.9	-0.5	112.5	0.5	113.5	0.9	113.5	0.0	114.0	0.4	114.1	0.1	114.2	0.1	114.0	-0.2	114.0	0.0	114.1	0.1	115.8	1.5
1988	117.3	1.3	116.6	-0.6	117.8	1.0	118.5	0.6	119.4	0.8	119.9	0.4	121.2	1.1	121.6	0.3	122.8	1.0	122.8	0.0	122.6	-0.2	124.3	1.4
1989	126.1	1.4	126.8	0.6	126.9	0.1	127.0	0.1	128.2	0.9	127.8	-0.3	127.4	-0.3	128.2	0.6	129.0	0.6	130.0	0.8	130.5	0.4	131.0	0.4
1990	132.8	1.4	133.2	0.3	133.0	-0.2	133.6	0.5	133.0	-0.4	133.7	0.5	135.1	1.0	134.9	-0.1	135.7	0.6	136.5	0.6	137.2	0.5	137.1	-0.1
1991	140.0	2.1	139.1	-0.6	140.0	0.6	140.1	0.1	139.8	-0.2	140.2	0.3	139.3	-0.6	139.1	-0.1	139.8	0.5	140.1	0.2	142.4	1.6	143.6	0.8
1992	142.2	-1.0	142.9	0.5	143.1	0.1	142.8	-0.2	142.8	0.0	142.9	0.1	142.3	-0.4	144.0	1.2	143.9	-0.1	143.9	0.0	144.0	0.1	145.1	0.8
1993	146.6	1.0	146.6	0.0	146.6	0.0	146.9	0.2	146.5	-0.3	145.5	-0.7	145.8	0.2	145.1	-0.5	145.1	0.0	146.6	1.0	146.3	-0.2	147.3	0.7
1994	148.9	1.1	148.2	-0.5	148.4	0.1	149.2	0.5	148.0	-0.8	147.6	-0.3	148.7	0.7	148.2	-0.3	148.2	0.0	148.9	0.5	150.4	1.0	152.2	1.2
1995	152.9	0.5	151.7	-0.8	152.2	0.3	153.1	0.6	151.5	-1.0	150.9	-0.4	151.3	0.3	149.9	-0.9	151.5	1.1	151.8	0.2	150.7	-0.7	151.6	0.6
1996	152.7	0.7	152.2	-0.3	154.8	1.7	155.4	0.4	154.0	-0.9	154.8	0.5	155.1	0.2	155.9	0.5	156.3	0.3	157.7	0.9	157.5	-0.1	157.2	-0.2
1997	157.9	0.4	159.5	1.0	159.9	0.3	159.8	-0.1	158.8	-0.6	158.4	-0.3	158.8	0.3	160.7	1.2	160.6	-0.1	162.0	0.9	162.0	0.0	163.1	0.7
1998	-	-	165.0	1.2	-	-	165.7	0.4	-	-	166.3	0.4	-	-	166.6	0.2	-	-	167.3	0.4	-	-	168.5	0.7
1999	-	-	169.4	0.5	-	-	170.7	0.8	-	-	171.2	0.3	-	-	170.4	-0.5	-	-	172.0	0.9	-	-	171.7	-0.2
2000	-	-	173.2	0.9	-	-	173.3	0.1	-	-	175.3	1.2	-	-	177.0	1.0	-	-	175.7	-0.7	-	-	178.0	1.3
2001	-	-	179.4	0.8	-	-	180.3	0.5	-	-	182.8	1.4	-	-	183.5	0.4	-	-	183.3	-0.1	-	-	182.9	-0.2

Source: U.S. Department of Labor, Bureau of Labor Statistics, Division of Consumer Prices and Price Indexes. - indicates no data collected for period.

San Francisco-Oakland-San Jose, CA
Consumer Price Index - Urban Wage Earners
Base 1982-1984 = 100
Food and Beverages

For 1975-2001. Columns headed % show percentile change in the index from the previous period for which an index is available.

Year	Jan Index	%	Feb Index	%	Mar Index	%	Apr Index	%	May Index	%	Jun Index	%	Jul Index	%	Aug Index	%	Sep Index	%	Oct Index	%	Nov Index	%	Dec Index	%
1975	-		-		-		-		-		-		-		-		-		-		-		59.8	
1976	-		-		58.7	-1.8	-		-		58.8	0.2	-		-		59.3	0.9	-		-		59.6	0.5
1977	-		-		62.1	4.2	-		-		64.1	3.2	-		-		64.6	0.8	-		-		65.4	1.2
1978	-		67.0	2.4	-		68.7	2.5	-		70.9	3.2	-		71.9	1.4	-		72.3	0.6	-		72.7	0.6
1979	-		76.2	4.8	-		78.1	2.5	-		79.0	1.2	-		78.9	-0.1	-		79.9	1.3	-		80.5	0.8
1980	-		82.5	2.5	-		83.1	0.7	-		83.9	1.0	-		85.5	1.9	-		87.3	2.1	-		89.1	2.1
1981	-		90.6	1.7	-		92.1	1.7	-		91.2	-1.0	-		93.0	2.0	-		92.4	-0.6	-		92.4	0.0
1982	-		95.8	3.7	-		96.3	0.5	-		97.5	1.2	-		97.6	0.1	-		98.7	1.1	-		97.6	-1.1
1983	-		98.3	0.7	-		100.0	1.7	-		98.9	-1.1	-		99.0	0.1	-		99.5	0.5	-		100.9	1.4
1984	-		102.8	1.9	-		103.4	0.6	-		103.4	0.0	-		103.9	0.5	-		104.5	0.6	-		105.2	0.7
1985	-		106.1	0.9	-		105.9	-0.2	-		105.2	-0.7	-		106.0	0.8	-		105.3	-0.7	-		107.2	1.8
1986	-		108.0	0.7	-		108.8	0.7	-		109.0	0.2	-		110.5	1.4	-		110.8	0.3	-		110.7	-0.1
1987	112.6	1.7	111.9	-0.6	112.6	0.6	113.7	1.0	113.7	0.0	114.2	0.4	114.3	0.1	114.4	0.1	114.1	-0.3	114.0	-0.1	114.1	0.1	115.7	1.4
1988	117.2	1.3	116.6	-0.5	117.7	0.9	118.6	0.8	119.5	0.8	120.0	0.4	121.3	1.1	121.7	0.3	122.9	1.0	122.8	-0.1	122.6	-0.2	124.3	1.4
1989	125.9	1.3	126.9	0.8	127.0	0.1	127.2	0.2	128.4	0.9	128.0	-0.3	127.5	-0.4	128.3	0.6	129.1	0.6	130.1	0.8	130.6	0.4	131.1	0.4
1990	132.8	1.3	133.4	0.5	133.1	-0.2	133.7	0.5	133.1	-0.4	133.8	0.5	135.2	1.0	135.0	-0.1	135.8	0.6	136.6	0.6	137.2	0.4	137.2	0.0
1991	140.1	2.1	139.3	-0.6	140.2	0.6	140.3	0.1	139.9	-0.3	140.4	0.4	139.4	-0.7	139.1	-0.2	139.8	0.5	140.0	0.1	142.3	1.6	143.5	0.8
1992	142.2	-0.9	143.0	0.6	143.2	0.1	142.8	-0.3	142.7	-0.1	142.9	0.1	142.4	-0.3	144.0	1.1	143.8	-0.1	143.9	0.1	144.0	0.1	145.2	0.8
1993	146.6	1.0	146.8	0.1	146.8	0.0	147.1	0.2	146.7	-0.3	145.7	-0.7	146.0	0.2	145.3	-0.5	145.4	0.1	146.8	1.0	146.5	-0.2	147.4	0.6
1994	149.1	1.2	148.4	-0.5	148.7	0.2	149.6	0.6	148.4	-0.8	148.0	-0.3	149.1	0.7	148.5	-0.4	148.5	0.0	149.1	0.4	150.5	0.9	152.3	1.2
1995	152.9	0.4	151.8	-0.7	152.3	0.3	153.1	0.5	151.6	-1.0	151.1	-0.3	151.6	0.3	150.2	-0.9	151.9	1.1	152.1	0.1	150.9	-0.8	151.9	0.7
1996	152.9	0.7	152.4	-0.3	155.1	1.8	155.8	0.5	154.3	-1.0	155.1	0.5	155.4	0.2	156.3	0.6	156.7	0.3	158.0	0.8	157.8	-0.1	157.5	-0.2
1997	158.3	0.5	159.8	0.9	160.2	0.3	160.2	0.0	159.1	-0.7	158.8	-0.2	159.1	0.2	161.1	1.3	160.8	-0.2	162.2	0.9	162.1	-0.1	163.2	0.7
1998	-		165.0	1.1	-		165.5	0.3	-		166.1	0.4	-		166.5	0.2	-		167.3	0.5	-		168.5	0.7
1999	-		169.1	0.4	-		170.5	0.8	-		170.8	0.2	-		170.0	-0.5	-		171.8	1.1	-		171.5	-0.2
2000	-		173.1	0.9	-		173.2	0.1	-		175.2	1.2	-		177.0	1.0	-		175.7	-0.7	-		177.8	1.2
2001	-		179.6	1.0	-		180.4	0.4	-		182.8	1.3	-		183.4	0.3	-		183.3	-0.1	-		182.9	-0.2

Source: U.S. Department of Labor, Bureau of Labor Statistics, Division of Consumer Prices and Price Indexes. - indicates no data collected for period.

San Francisco-Oakland-San Jose, CA
Consumer Price Index - All Urban Consumers
Base 1982-1984 = 100
Housing

For 1975-2001. Columns headed % show percentile change in the index from the previous period for which an index is available.

Year	Jan Index	%	Feb Index	%	Mar Index	%	Apr Index	%	May Index	%	Jun Index	%	Jul Index	%	Aug Index	%	Sep Index	%	Oct Index	%	Nov Index	%	Dec Index	%
1975	-	-	-	-	-	-	-	-	-	-	-	-	-	-	-	-	-	-	-	-	-	-	49.3	-
1976	-	-	-	-	50.0	1.4	-	-	-	-	50.4	0.8	-	-	-	-	51.4	2.0	-	-	-	-	50.9	-1.0
1977	-	-	-	-	53.1	4.3	-	-	-	-	54.8	3.2	-	-	-	-	56.5	3.1	-	-	-	-	58.2	3.0
1978	-	-	58.9	1.2	-	-	59.7	1.4	-	-	62.5	4.7	-	-	64.9	3.8	-	-	63.1	-2.8	-	-	61.0	-3.3
1979	-	-	61.7	1.1	-	-	63.0	2.1	-	-	63.9	1.4	-	-	66.4	3.9	-	-	67.0	0.9	-	-	71.4	6.6
1980	-	-	75.8	6.2	-	-	75.2	-0.8	-	-	78.1	3.9	-	-	78.6	0.6	-	-	78.2	-0.5	-	-	79.1	1.2
1981	-	-	81.1	2.5	-	-	86.2	6.3	-	-	87.7	1.7	-	-	95.2	8.6	-	-	100.1	5.1	-	-	97.3	-2.8
1982	-	-	97.4	0.1	-	-	98.5	1.1	-	-	100.2	1.7	-	-	99.5	-0.7	-	-	97.3	-2.2	-	-	92.9	-4.5
1983	-	-	95.7	3.0	-	-	96.2	0.5	-	-	97.4	1.2	-	-	99.3	2.0	-	-	99.6	0.3	-	-	99.4	-0.2
1984	-	-	100.9	1.5	-	-	102.7	1.8	-	-	103.7	1.0	-	-	106.9	3.1	-	-	108.0	1.0	-	-	106.7	-1.2
1985	-	-	108.2	1.4	-	-	109.3	1.0	-	-	111.0	1.6	-	-	113.4	2.2	-	-	114.2	0.7	-	-	112.8	-1.2
1986	-	-	115.7	2.6	-	-	115.5	-0.2	-	-	117.9	2.1	-	-	119.4	1.3	-	-	120.1	0.6	-	-	117.8	-1.9
1987	118.5	0.6	119.5	0.8	119.1	-0.3	120.4	1.1	121.2	0.7	121.2	0.0	122.7	1.2	122.9	0.2	123.3	0.3	123.7	0.3	122.6	-0.9	122.6	0.0
1988	123.7	0.9	123.8	0.1	125.6	1.5	124.2	-1.1	126.1	1.5	126.7	0.5	127.9	0.9	130.0	1.6	128.5	-1.2	128.9	0.3	128.5	-0.3	128.9	0.3
1989	130.4	1.2	130.0	-0.3	133.0	2.3	130.1	-2.2	131.3	0.9	131.6	0.2	134.4	2.1	135.0	0.4	133.0	-1.5	133.4	0.3	132.7	-0.5	133.3	0.5
1990	134.2	0.7	135.1	0.7	135.7	0.4	135.9	0.1	136.5	0.4	137.5	0.7	138.1	0.4	138.5	0.3	138.8	0.2	138.6	-0.1	139.1	0.4	139.2	0.1
1991	141.2	1.4	140.9	-0.2	141.2	0.2	140.2	-0.7	140.8	0.4	142.8	1.4	143.8	0.7	144.5	0.5	145.0	0.3	144.1	-0.6	144.1	0.0	143.7	-0.3
1992	144.7	0.7	145.3	0.4	146.6	0.9	145.5	-0.8	145.6	0.1	145.3	-0.2	146.0	0.5	145.9	-0.1	147.5	1.1	147.9	0.3	147.1	-0.5	147.3	0.1
1993	147.5	0.1	147.6	0.1	147.8	0.1	149.5	1.2	150.0	0.3	149.4	-0.4	149.1	-0.2	149.4	0.2	149.7	0.2	149.8	0.1	150.3	0.3	150.4	0.1
1994	150.4	0.0	150.4	0.0	150.8	0.3	150.2	-0.4	151.2	0.7	151.7	0.3	152.5	0.5	153.0	0.3	152.7	-0.2	152.2	-0.3	151.7	-0.3	151.6	-0.1
1995	152.6	0.7	153.2	0.4	153.5	0.2	153.9	0.3	154.4	0.3	154.8	0.3	154.8	0.0	155.0	0.1	155.7	0.5	155.6	-0.1	155.5	-0.1	155.2	-0.2
1996	155.6	0.3	155.9	0.2	153.1	-1.8	153.7	0.4	156.8	2.0	157.3	0.3	158.7	0.9	158.9	0.1	159.2	0.2	159.9	0.4	160.0	0.1	159.8	-0.1
1997	161.2	0.9	161.7	0.3	162.7	0.6	163.2	0.3	164.5	0.8	165.1	0.4	165.8	0.4	167.0	0.7	167.6	0.4	169.0	0.8	169.3	0.2	169.7	0.2
1998	-	-	169.5	-0.1	-	-	172.6	1.8	-	-	174.4	1.0	-	-	176.1	1.0	-	-	177.5	0.8	-	-	178.7	0.7
1999	-	-	181.7	1.7	-	-	183.0	0.7	-	-	185.0	1.1	-	-	186.9	1.0	-	-	189.9	1.6	-	-	189.6	-0.2
2000	-	-	192.1	1.3	-	-	194.4	1.2	-	-	195.4	0.5	-	-	197.9	1.3	-	-	202.0	2.1	-	-	203.8	0.9
2001	-	-	211.8	3.9	-	-	213.6	0.8	-	-	217.9	2.0	-	-	219.7	0.8	-	-	219.9	0.1	-	-	220.2	0.1

Source: U.S. Department of Labor, Bureau of Labor Statistics, Division of Consumer Prices and Price Indexes. - indicates no data collected for period.

San Francisco-Oakland-San Jose, CA
Consumer Price Index - Urban Wage Earners
Base 1982-1984 = 100
Housing

For 1975-2001. Columns headed % show percentile change in the index from the previous period for which an index is available.

Year	Jan Index	%	Feb Index	%	Mar Index	%	Apr Index	%	May Index	%	Jun Index	%	Jul Index	%	Aug Index	%	Sep Index	%	Oct Index	%	Nov Index	%	Dec Index	%
1975	-	-	-	-			-	-	-	-	-	-	-	-	-	-	-	-	-	-	-	-	50.6	-
1976	-	-	-	-	51.2	1.2	-	-	-	-	51.7	1.0	-	-	-	-	52.7	1.9	-	-	-	-	52.1	-1.1
1977	-	-	-	-	54.4	4.4	-	-	-	-	56.2	3.3	-	-	-	-	57.9	3.0	-	-	-	-	59.7	3.1
1978	-	-	60.3	1.0	-	-	61.1	1.3	-	-	63.8	4.4	-	-	66.3	3.9	-	-	64.5	-2.7	-	-	62.4	-3.3
1979	-	-	63.2	1.3	-	-	64.4	1.9	-	-	65.4	1.6	-	-	67.7	3.5	-	-	68.3	0.9	-	-	72.8	6.6
1980	-	-	77.4	6.3	-	-	76.9	-0.6	-	-	80.1	4.2	-	-	80.6	0.6	-	-	79.8	-1.0	-	-	81.0	1.5
1981	-	-	83.0	2.5	-	-	87.8	5.8	-	-	89.4	1.8	-	-	96.9	8.4	-	-	101.9	5.2	-	-	99.3	-2.6
1982	-	-	99.6	0.3	-	-	100.7	1.1	-	-	102.4	1.7	-	-	101.5	-0.9	-	-	99.4	-2.1	-	-	95.0	-4.4
1983	-	-	95.5	0.5	-	-	95.2	-0.3	-	-	96.2	1.1	-	-	97.8	1.7	-	-	98.0	0.2	-	-	100.0	2.0
1984	-	-	100.5	0.5	-	-	100.5	0.0	-	-	102.8	2.3	-	-	107.7	4.8	-	-	103.6	-3.8	-	-	105.2	1.5
1985	-	-	106.7	1.4	-	-	107.8	1.0	-	-	109.5	1.6	-	-	111.6	1.9	-	-	112.2	0.5	-	-	111.1	-1.0
1986	-	-	114.1	2.7	-	-	113.9	-0.2	-	-	116.3	2.1	-	-	117.7	1.2	-	-	118.5	0.7	-	-	116.0	-2.1
1987	116.7	0.6	117.7	0.9	117.2	-0.4	118.5	1.1	119.0	0.4	119.0	0.0	120.4	1.2	120.5	0.1	120.9	0.3	121.4	0.4	120.5	-0.7	120.5	0.0
1988	121.7	1.0	121.9	0.2	123.1	1.0	122.2	-0.7	123.9	1.4	124.5	0.5	125.4	0.7	127.0	-1.3	126.2	-0.6	126.6	0.3	126.0	-0.5	126.4	0.3
1989	127.6	0.9	127.3	-0.2	129.8	2.0	127.8	-1.5	128.9	0.9	129.1	0.2	131.2	1.6	131.9	0.5	130.4	-1.1	131.0	0.5	130.3	-0.5	130.8	0.4
1990	131.7	0.7	132.6	0.7	133.0	0.3	133.4	0.3	134.1	0.5	135.0	0.7	135.4	0.3	135.8	0.3	136.0	0.1	136.0	0.0	136.4	0.3	136.3	-0.1
1991	138.2	1.4	137.9	-0.2	138.1	0.1	137.1	-0.7	138.1	0.7	140.0	1.4	140.8	0.6	141.3	0.4	141.9	0.4	141.0	-0.6	141.2	0.1	140.7	-0.4
1992	141.6	0.6	142.1	0.4	143.2	0.8	142.2	-0.7	142.5	0.2	142.5	0.0	143.0	0.4	142.8	-0.1	144.3	1.1	144.8	0.3	144.1	-0.5	144.1	0.0
1993	144.3	0.1	144.5	0.1	144.8	0.2	146.6	1.2	146.9	0.2	146.2	-0.5	146.0	-0.1	146.3	0.2	146.5	0.1	146.8	0.2	147.3	0.3	147.2	-0.1
1994	147.2	0.0	147.2	0.0	147.6	0.3	147.1	-0.3	148.0	0.6	148.6	0.4	149.3	0.5	149.6	0.2	149.4	-0.1	148.9	-0.3	148.5	-0.3	148.4	-0.1
1995	149.4	0.7	149.9	0.3	150.1	0.1	150.5	0.3	151.0	0.3	151.4	0.3	151.4	0.0	151.5	0.1	152.2	0.5	152.2	0.0	152.1	-0.1	151.8	-0.2
1996	152.1	0.2	152.4	0.2	149.5	-1.9	150.2	0.5	153.3	2.1	153.7	0.3	154.9	0.8	155.1	0.1	155.4	0.2	156.1	0.5	156.2	0.1	156.1	-0.1
1997	157.3	0.8	157.9	0.4	158.8	0.6	159.3	0.3	160.7	0.9	161.3	0.4	162.0	0.4	163.1	0.7	163.9	0.5	165.2	0.8	165.5	0.2	166.1	0.4
1998	-	-	165.4	-0.4	-	-	168.4	1.8	-	-	170.2	1.1	-	-	171.9	1.0	-	-	173.1	0.7	-	-	174.6	0.9
1999	-	-	177.5	1.7	-	-	178.7	0.7	-	-	180.8	1.2	-	-	182.5	0.9	-	-	184.9	1.3	-	-	185.3	0.2
2000	-	-	187.1	1.0	-	-	189.1	1.1	-	-	190.4	0.7	-	-	192.9	1.3	-	-	196.8	2.0	-	-	199.7	1.5
2001	-	-	206.7	3.5	-	-	208.4	0.8	-	-	213.3	2.4	-	-	215.2	0.9	-	-	215.6	0.2	-	-	216.7	0.5

Source: U.S. Department of Labor, Bureau of Labor Statistics, Division of Consumer Prices and Price Indexes. - indicates no data collected for period.

San Francisco-Oakland-San Jose, CA
Consumer Price Index - All Urban Consumers
Base 1982-1984 = 100
Apparel

For 1952-2001. Columns headed % show percentile change in the index from the previous period for which an index is available.

Year	Jan Index	%	Feb Index	%	Mar Index	%	Apr Index	%	May Index	%	Jun Index	%	Jul Index	%	Aug Index	%	Sep Index	%	Oct Index	%	Nov Index	%	Dec Index	%
1952	-	-	-	-	-	-	-	-	-	-	-	-	-	-	-	-	-	-	-	-	-	-	39.3	-
1953	-	-	-	-	39.4	0.3	-	-	-	-	38.9	-1.3	-	-	-	-	39.4	1.3	-	-	-	-	39.4	0.0
1954	-	-	-	-	38.9	-1.3	-	-	-	-	38.8	-0.3	-	-	-	-	38.8	0.0	-	-	-	-	38.4	-1.0
1955	-	-	-	-	38.8	1.0	-	-	-	-	38.8	0.0	-	-	-	-	39.3	1.3	-	-	-	-	39.3	0.0
1956	-	-	-	-	39.6	0.8	-	-	-	-	39.7	0.3	-	-	-	-	39.8	0.3	-	-	-	-	40.5	1.8
1957	-	-	-	-	40.7	0.5	-	-	-	-	40.6	-0.2	-	-	-	-	40.8	0.5	-	-	-	-	41.0	0.5
1958	-	-	-	-	41.0	0.0	-	-	-	-	40.9	-0.2	-	-	-	-	40.9	0.0	-	-	-	-	41.0	0.2
1959	-	-	-	-	41.0	0.0	-	-	-	-	41.2	0.5	-	-	-	-	41.9	1.7	-	-	-	-	42.1	0.5
1960	-	-	-	-	42.1	0.0	-	-	-	-	42.4	0.7	-	-	-	-	42.9	1.2	-	-	-	-	43.0	0.2
1961	-	-	-	-	43.0	0.0	-	-	-	-	43.2	0.5	-	-	-	-	43.2	0.0	-	-	-	-	43.4	0.5
1962	-	-	-	-	43.7	0.7	-	-	-	-	43.9	0.5	-	-	-	-	43.8	-0.2	-	-	-	-	44.0	0.5
1963	-	-	-	-	44.0	0.0	-	-	-	-	44.1	0.2	-	-	-	-	44.3	0.5	-	-	-	-	44.5	0.5
1964	-	-	-	-	44.6	0.2	-	-	-	-	44.6	0.0	-	-	-	-	44.6	0.0	-	-	-	-	44.9	0.7
1965	-	-	-	-	45.2	0.7	-	-	-	-	45.5	0.7	-	-	-	-	45.2	-0.7	-	-	-	-	45.6	0.9
1966	-	-	-	-	46.3	1.5	-	-	-	-	46.5	0.4	-	-	-	-	46.8	0.6	-	-	-	-	47.1	0.6
1967	-	-	-	-	47.7	1.3	-	-	-	-	47.8	0.2	-	-	-	-	49.5	3.6	-	-	-	-	49.7	0.4
1968	-	-	-	-	50.5	1.6	-	-	-	-	51.0	1.0	-	-	-	-	51.9	1.8	-	-	-	-	52.3	0.8
1969	-	-	-	-	53.1	1.5	-	-	-	-	53.3	0.4	-	-	-	-	54.5	2.3	-	-	-	-	54.7	0.4
1970	-	-	-	-	54.6	-0.2	-	-	-	-	54.5	-0.2	-	-	-	-	56.1	2.9	-	-	-	-	56.5	0.7
1971	-	-	-	-	57.2	1.2	-	-	-	-	57.5	0.5	-	-	-	-	58.5	1.7	-	-	-	-	58.0	-0.9
1972	-	-	-	-	58.2	0.3	-	-	-	-	58.0	-0.3	-	-	-	-	60.1	3.6	-	-	-	-	60.1	0.0
1973	-	-	-	-	60.4	0.5	-	-	-	-	61.0	1.0	-	-	-	-	62.4	2.3	-	-	-	-	62.7	0.5
1974	-	-	-	-	64.1	2.2	-	-	-	-	65.9	2.8	-	-	-	-	67.4	2.3	-	-	-	-	68.4	1.5
1975	-	-	-	-	68.4	0.0	-	-	-	-	68.1	-0.4	-	-	-	-	68.8	1.0	-	-	-	-	69.8	1.5
1976	-	-	-	-	70.5	1.0	-	-	-	-	69.8	-1.0	-	-	-	-	70.6	1.1	-	-	-	-	71.4	1.1
1977	-	-	-	-	72.6	1.7	-	-	-	-	72.7	0.1	-	-	-	-	73.7	1.4	-	-	-	-	74.1	0.5
1978	-	-	73.6	-0.7	-	-	78.3	6.4	-	-	76.5	-2.3	-	-	77.2	0.9	-	-	79.6	3.1	-	-	79.3	-0.4
1979	-	-	80.1	1.0	-	-	80.1	0.0	-	-	81.3	1.5	-	-	81.4	0.1	-	-	84.3	3.6	-	-	86.7	2.8
1980	-	-	86.9	0.2	-	-	88.3	1.6	-	-	85.4	-3.3	-	-	90.7	6.2	-	-	91.0	0.3	-	-	90.5	-0.5
1981	-	-	89.6	-1.0	-	-	91.0	1.6	-	-	92.2	1.3	-	-	94.3	2.3	-	-	93.8	-0.5	-	-	96.4	2.8
1982	-	-	97.3	0.9	-	-	97.3	0.0	-	-	97.1	-0.2	-	-	98.9	1.9	-	-	98.6	-0.3	-	-	96.4	-2.2
1983	-	-	98.8	2.5	-	-	99.1	0.3	-	-	97.8	-1.3	-	-	98.2	0.4	-	-	95.5	-2.7	-	-	98.0	2.6
1984	-	-	102.1	4.2	-	-	104.4	2.3	-	-	100.6	-3.6	-	-	107.1	6.5	-	-	109.5	2.2	-	-	105.7	-3.5
1985	-	-	108.1	2.3	-	-	105.0	-2.9	-	-	104.7	-0.3	-	-	100.6	-3.9	-	-	102.2	1.6	-	-	99.1	-3.0
1986	-	-	98.1	-1.0	-	-	103.9	5.9	-	-	100.0	-3.8	-	-	102.6	2.6	-	-	105.9	3.2	-	-	99.6	-5.9
1987	96.8	-2.8	103.1	6.5	106.6	3.4	108.6	1.9	103.7	-4.5	102.2	-1.4	100.4	-1.8	100.2	-0.2	105.1	4.9	107.4	2.2	112.2	4.5	108.4	-3.4
1988	108.9	0.5	106.3	-2.4	106.2	-0.1	105.4	-0.8	103.6	-1.7	99.7	-3.8	97.3	-2.4	95.2	-2.2	101.9	7.0	101.7	-0.2	102.7	1.0	99.5	-3.1
1989	100.6	1.1	100.2	-0.4	104.7	4.5	107.5	2.7	105.6	-1.8	103.5	-2.0	101.3	-2.1	103.1	1.8	106.9	3.7	108.2	1.2	105.5	-2.5	103.0	-2.4
1990	99.6	-3.3	104.5	4.9	107.3	2.7	108.4	1.0	106.5	-1.8	106.5	0.0	105.7	-0.8	107.6	1.8	112.2	4.3	113.2	0.9	109.2	-3.5	109.1	-0.1
1991	112.1	2.7	110.9	-1.1	112.0	1.0	114.0	1.8	111.3	-2.4	109.1	-2.0	109.2	0.1	115.6	5.9	115.8	0.2	116.6	0.7	115.8	-0.7	114.8	-0.9
1992	114.2	-0.5	117.7	3.1	121.6	3.3	119.5	-1.7	121.3	1.5	118.4	-2.4	115.4	-2.5	118.0	2.3	117.6	-0.3	117.0	-0.5	117.9	0.8	114.4	-3.0
1993	114.7	0.3	117.2	2.2	121.9	4.0	124.3	2.0	121.6	-2.2	117.1	-3.7	116.2	-0.8	115.2	-0.9	120.0	4.2	119.0	-0.8	117.3	-1.4	113.5	-3.2
1994	115.1	1.4	114.7	-0.3	116.3	1.4	116.1	-0.2	119.0	2.5	111.9	-6.0	114.5	2.3	116.4	1.7	117.8	1.2	113.7	-3.5	118.3	4.0	112.5	-4.9
1995	113.4	0.8	115.0	1.4	117.8	2.4	118.3	0.4	111.9	-5.4	115.0	2.8	110.5	-3.9	114.7	3.8	113.4	-1.1	114.6	1.1	114.1	-0.4	108.7	-4.7
1996	114.8	5.6	113.3	-1.3	122.2	7.9	122.8	0.5	121.5	-1.1	118.5	-2.5	116.7	-1.5	112.7	-3.4	117.9	4.6	116.6	-1.1	117.3	0.6	108.8	-7.2
1997	112.2	3.1	113.4	1.1	117.3	3.4	117.9	0.5	115.7	-1.9	117.3	1.4	121.7	3.8	119.2	-2.1	117.6	-1.3	115.9	-1.4	116.3	0.3	109.0	-6.3

[Continued]

San Francisco-Oakland-San Jose, CA
Consumer Price Index - All Urban Consumers
Base 1982-1984 = 100
Apparel
[Continued]

For 1952-2001. Columns headed % show percentile change in the index from the previous period for which an index is available.

Year	Jan Index	%	Feb Index	%	Mar Index	%	Apr Index	%	May Index	%	Jun Index	%	Jul Index	%	Aug Index	%	Sep Index	%	Oct Index	%	Nov Index	%	Dec Index	%
1998	-	-	114.8	5.3	-	-	118.1	2.9	-	-	113.2	-4.1	-	-	118.9	5.0	-	-	119.6	0.6	-	-	111.2	-7.0
1999	-	-	114.6	3.1	-	-	115.1	0.4	-	-	109.7	-4.7	-	-	112.9	2.9	-	-	120.4	6.6	-	-	112.9	-6.2
2000	-	-	115.1	1.9	-	-	117.1	1.7	-	-	113.3	-3.2	-	-	115.3	1.8	-	-	118.5	2.8	-	-	112.9	-4.7
2001	-	-	117.0	3.6	-	-	116.5	-0.4	-	-	108.6	-6.8	-	-	108.9	0.3	-	-	110.4	1.4	-	-	103.5	-6.3

Source: U.S. Department of Labor, Bureau of Labor Statistics, Division of Consumer Prices and Price Indexes. - indicates no data collected for period.

San Francisco-Oakland-San Jose, CA
Consumer Price Index - Urban Wage Earners
Base 1982-1984 = 100
Apparel

For 1952-2001. Columns headed % show percentile change in the index from the previous period for which an index is available.

Year	Jan Index	%	Feb Index	%	Mar Index	%	Apr Index	%	May Index	%	Jun Index	%	Jul Index	%	Aug Index	%	Sep Index	%	Oct Index	%	Nov Index	%	Dec Index	%
1952	-	-	-	-	-	-	-	-	-	-	-	-	-	-	-	-	-	-	-	-	-	-	40.8	-
1953	-	-	-	-	40.9	0.2	-	-	-	-	40.4	-1.2	-	-	-	-	40.9	1.2	-	-	-	-	40.9	0.0
1954	-	-	-	-	40.4	-1.2	-	-	-	-	40.3	-0.2	-	-	-	-	40.2	-0.2	-	-	-	-	39.8	-1.0
1955	-	-	-	-	40.3	1.3	-	-	-	-	40.3	0.0	-	-	-	-	40.8	1.2	-	-	-	-	40.8	0.0
1956	-	-	-	-	41.1	0.7	-	-	-	-	41.2	0.2	-	-	-	-	41.3	0.2	-	-	-	-	42.0	1.7
1957	-	-	-	-	42.2	0.5	-	-	-	-	42.1	-0.2	-	-	-	-	42.3	0.5	-	-	-	-	42.5	0.5
1958	-	-	-	-	42.5	0.0	-	-	-	-	42.5	0.0	-	-	-	-	42.5	0.0	-	-	-	-	42.5	0.0
1959	-	-	-	-	42.6	0.2	-	-	-	-	42.7	0.2	-	-	-	-	43.5	1.9	-	-	-	-	43.7	0.5
1960	-	-	-	-	43.7	0.0	-	-	-	-	44.0	0.7	-	-	-	-	44.6	1.4	-	-	-	-	44.7	0.2
1961	-	-	-	-	44.6	-0.2	-	-	-	-	44.9	0.7	-	-	-	-	44.9	0.0	-	-	-	-	45.0	0.2
1962	-	-	-	-	45.3	0.7	-	-	-	-	45.5	0.4	-	-	-	-	45.5	0.0	-	-	-	-	45.7	0.4
1963	-	-	-	-	45.7	0.0	-	-	-	-	45.8	0.2	-	-	-	-	46.0	0.4	-	-	-	-	46.2	0.4
1964	-	-	-	-	46.3	0.2	-	-	-	-	46.3	0.0	-	-	-	-	46.3	0.0	-	-	-	-	46.6	0.6
1965	-	-	-	-	46.9	0.6	-	-	-	-	47.2	0.6	-	-	-	-	46.9	-0.6	-	-	-	-	47.4	1.1
1966	-	-	-	-	48.0	1.3	-	-	-	-	48.2	0.4	-	-	-	-	48.5	0.6	-	-	-	-	48.9	0.8
1967	-	-	-	-	49.5	1.2	-	-	-	-	49.6	0.2	-	-	-	-	51.4	3.6	-	-	-	-	51.5	0.2
1968	-	-	-	-	52.4	1.7	-	-	-	-	52.9	1.0	-	-	-	-	53.9	1.9	-	-	-	-	54.3	0.7
1969	-	-	-	-	55.1	1.5	-	-	-	-	55.3	0.4	-	-	-	-	56.6	2.4	-	-	-	-	56.7	0.2
1970	-	-	-	-	56.7	0.0	-	-	-	-	56.5	-0.4	-	-	-	-	58.2	3.0	-	-	-	-	58.7	0.9
1971	-	-	-	-	59.4	1.2	-	-	-	-	59.6	0.3	-	-	-	-	60.8	2.0	-	-	-	-	60.1	-1.2
1972	-	-	-	-	60.4	0.5	-	-	-	-	60.2	-0.3	-	-	-	-	62.4	3.7	-	-	-	-	62.4	0.0
1973	-	-	-	-	62.7	0.5	-	-	-	-	63.3	1.0	-	-	-	-	64.8	2.4	-	-	-	-	65.0	0.3
1974	-	-	-	-	66.5	2.3	-	-	-	-	68.4	2.9	-	-	-	-	69.9	2.2	-	-	-	-	71.0	1.6
1975	-	-	-	-	71.0	0.0	-	-	-	-	70.7	-0.4	-	-	-	-	71.4	1.0	-	-	-	-	72.4	1.4
1976	-	-	-	-	73.2	1.1	-	-	-	-	72.4	-1.1	-	-	-	-	73.3	1.2	-	-	-	-	74.1	1.1
1977	-	-	-	-	75.3	1.6	-	-	-	-	75.4	0.1	-	-	-	-	76.5	1.5	-	-	-	-	76.9	0.5
1978	-	-	75.1	-2.3	-	-	79.0	5.2	-	-	78.1	-1.1	-	-	78.8	0.9	-	-	80.4	2.0	-	-	79.9	-0.6
1979	-	-	81.3	1.8	-	-	81.8	0.6	-	-	83.9	2.6	-	-	82.6	-1.5	-	-	83.6	1.2	-	-	85.9	2.8
1980	-	-	86.2	0.3	-	-	87.2	1.2	-	-	85.9	-1.5	-	-	90.8	5.7	-	-	92.3	1.7	-	-	91.7	-0.7
1981	-	-	92.7	1.1	-	-	94.5	1.9	-	-	95.1	0.6	-	-	96.1	1.1	-	-	97.0	0.9	-	-	96.6	-0.4
1982	-	-	97.7	1.1	-	-	97.8	0.1	-	-	98.3	0.5	-	-	99.1	0.8	-	-	98.9	-0.2	-	-	97.1	-1.8
1983	-	-	98.5	1.4	-	-	98.5	0.0	-	-	97.6	-0.9	-	-	98.2	0.6	-	-	95.8	-2.4	-	-	98.0	2.3
1984	-	-	102.0	4.1	-	-	103.6	1.6	-	-	100.0	-3.5	-	-	106.6	6.6	-	-	109.0	2.3	-	-	105.9	-2.8
1985	-	-	107.7	1.7	-	-	105.3	-2.2	-	-	104.7	-0.6	-	-	101.7	-2.9	-	-	102.7	1.0	-	-	100.2	-2.4
1986	-	-	99.5	-0.7	-	-	104.5	5.0	-	-	100.5	-3.8	-	-	103.0	2.5	-	-	106.1	3.0	-	-	100.4	-5.4
1987	97.5	-2.9	103.1	5.7	106.7	3.5	109.2	2.3	104.0	-4.8	103.0	-1.0	101.2	-1.7	100.8	-0.4	105.6	4.8	109.3	3.5	113.8	4.1	110.0	-3.3
1988	110.8	0.7	108.0	-2.5	108.1	0.1	107.2	-0.8	105.2	-1.9	101.4	-3.6	99.4	-2.0	97.0	-2.4	104.4	7.6	104.1	-0.3	105.2	1.1	101.9	-3.1
1989	103.7	1.8	103.2	-0.5	107.0	3.7	110.1	2.9	108.0	-1.9	106.9	-1.0	104.8	-2.0	106.4	1.5	109.5	2.9	111.3	1.6	108.1	-2.9	105.5	-2.4
1990	103.7	-1.7	106.9	3.1	110.1	3.0	111.3	1.1	109.6	-1.5	109.7	0.1	108.9	-0.7	110.2	1.2	115.4	4.7	116.7	1.1	112.2	-3.9	112.8	0.5
1991	115.8	2.7	113.5	-2.0	114.8	1.1	117.0	1.9	114.2	-2.4	111.7	-2.2	112.1	0.4	118.6	5.8	118.9	0.3	120.2	1.1	119.3	-0.7	118.4	-0.8
1992	117.6	-0.7	120.7	2.6	124.9	3.5	122.7	-1.8	124.8	1.7	122.0	-2.2	119.2	-2.3	121.9	2.3	121.4	-0.4	120.8	-0.5	122.4	1.3	119.1	-2.7
1993	118.8	-0.3	121.4	2.2	125.2	3.1	128.7	2.8	126.0	-2.1	121.1	-3.9	120.7	-0.3	119.2	-1.2	125.6	5.4	124.9	-0.6	122.7	-1.8	118.5	-3.4
1994	120.8	1.9	119.5	-1.1	120.9	1.2	120.9	0.0	125.4	3.7	116.3	-7.3	119.4	2.7	122.0	2.2	122.8	0.7	117.8	-4.1	123.7	5.0	117.4	-5.1
1995	119.8	2.0	121.1	1.1	124.4	2.7	125.2	0.6	116.8	-6.7	123.2	5.5	115.9	-5.9	122.3	5.5	120.0	-1.9	119.4	-0.5	119.1	-0.3	112.7	-5.4
1996	120.8	7.2	117.2	-3.0	128.9	10.0	129.2	0.2	128.4	-0.6	125.2	-2.5	122.2	-2.4	116.6	-4.6	124.3	6.6	122.8	-1.2	124.4	1.3	112.8	-9.3
1997	117.9	4.5	118.3	0.3	122.9	3.9	123.3	0.3	120.4	-2.4	123.1	2.2	128.1	4.1	125.1	-2.3	122.6	-2.0	121.7	-0.7	122.0	0.2	112.2	-8.0

[Continued]

San Francisco-Oakland-San Jose, CA
Consumer Price Index - Urban Wage Earners
Base 1982-1984 = 100
Apparel
[Continued]

For 1952-2001. Columns headed % show percentile change in the index from the previous period for which an index is available.

Year	Jan		Feb		Mar		Apr		May		Jun		Jul		Aug		Sep		Oct		Nov		Dec	
	Index	%	Index	%	Index	%	Index	%	Index	%	Index	%	Index	%	Index	%	Index	%	Index	%	Index	%	Index	%
1998	-	-	118.1	5.3	-	-	121.6	3.0	-	-	116.7	-4.0	-	-	122.9	5.3	-	-	124.6	1.4	-	-	116.6	-6.4
1999	-	-	119.9	2.8	-	-	118.7	-1.0	-	-	113.0	-4.8	-	-	116.6	3.2	-	-	124.6	6.9	-	-	118.2	-5.1
2000	-	-	119.6	1.2	-	-	121.7	1.8	-	-	118.5	-2.6	-	-	120.3	1.5	-	-	122.8	2.1	-	-	116.2	-5.4
2001	-	-	121.5	4.6	-	-	121.1	-0.3	-	-	113.1	-6.6	-	-	113.3	0.2	-	-	115.9	2.3	-	-	108.7	-6.2

Source: U.S. Department of Labor, Bureau of Labor Statistics, Division of Consumer Prices and Price Indexes. - indicates no data collected for period.

San Francisco-Oakland-San Jose, CA
Consumer Price Index - All Urban Consumers
Base 1982-1984 = 100
Transportation

For 1947-2000. Columns headed % show percentile change in the index from the previous period for which an index is available.

Year	Jan Index	%	Feb Index	%	Mar Index	%	Apr Index	%	May Index	%	Jun Index	%	Jul Index	%	Aug Index	%	Sep Index	%	Oct Index	%	Nov Index	%	Dec Index	%
1947	16.0	-	16.1	0.6	16.1	0.0	16.3	1.2	16.2	-0.6	16.2	0.0	-	-	-	-	16.7	3.1	-	-	-	-	17.0	1.8
1948	-	-	-	-	17.4	2.4	-	-	-	-	18.0	3.4	-	-	-	-	18.6	3.3	-	-	-	-	18.7	0.5
1949	-	-	-	-	19.3	3.2	-	-	-	-	19.5	1.0	-	-	-	-	19.5	0.0	-	-	-	-	19.6	0.5
1950	-	-	-	-	19.6	0.0	-	-	-	-	19.2	-2.0	-	-	-	-	19.4	1.0	-	-	-	-	19.5	0.5
1951	-	-	-	-	20.6	5.6	-	-	-	-	20.8	1.0	-	-	-	-	21.3	2.4	-	-	-	-	21.4	0.5
1952	-	-	-	-	21.6	0.9	-	-	-	-	24.1	11.6	-	-	-	-	25.2	4.6	-	-	-	-	25.2	0.0
1953	-	-	-	-	25.7	2.0	-	-	-	-	25.5	-0.8	-	-	-	-	25.8	1.2	-	-	-	-	25.9	0.4
1954	-	-	-	-	25.8	-0.4	-	-	-	-	25.7	-0.4	-	-	-	-	25.2	-1.9	-	-	-	-	25.4	0.8
1955	-	-	-	-	25.3	-0.4	-	-	-	-	24.8	-2.0	-	-	-	-	24.8	0.0	-	-	-	-	25.3	2.0
1956	-	-	-	-	25.0	-1.2	-	-	-	-	25.1	0.4	-	-	-	-	25.3	0.8	-	-	-	-	26.7	5.5
1957	-	-	-	-	27.1	1.5	-	-	-	-	26.9	-0.7	-	-	-	-	27.1	0.7	-	-	-	-	27.4	1.1
1958	-	-	-	-	28.0	2.2	-	-	-	-	28.4	1.4	-	-	-	-	28.8	1.4	-	-	-	-	28.4	-1.4
1959	-	-	-	-	29.7	4.6	-	-	-	-	29.6	-0.3	-	-	-	-	30.0	1.4	-	-	-	-	30.5	1.7
1960	-	-	-	-	29.6	-3.0	-	-	-	-	29.5	-0.3	-	-	-	-	29.3	-0.7	-	-	-	-	29.9	2.0
1961	-	-	-	-	29.6	-1.0	-	-	-	-	29.3	-1.0	-	-	-	-	30.1	2.7	-	-	-	-	30.5	1.3
1962	-	-	-	-	30.2	-1.0	-	-	-	-	30.5	1.0	-	-	-	-	30.5	0.0	-	-	-	-	30.4	-0.3
1963	-	-	-	-	30.5	0.3	-	-	-	-	30.6	0.3	-	-	-	-	30.8	0.7	-	-	-	-	31.4	1.9
1964	-	-	-	-	31.4	0.0	-	-	-	-	31.6	0.6	-	-	-	-	31.4	-0.6	-	-	-	-	31.9	1.6
1965	-	-	-	-	31.7	-0.6	-	-	-	-	31.7	0.0	-	-	-	-	31.6	-0.3	-	-	-	-	31.9	0.9
1966	-	-	-	-	31.9	0.0	-	-	-	-	31.6	-0.9	-	-	-	-	32.2	1.9	-	-	-	-	32.4	0.6
1967	-	-	-	-	32.4	0.0	-	-	-	-	32.9	1.5	-	-	-	-	33.2	0.9	-	-	-	-	33.4	0.6
1968	-	-	-	-	33.6	0.6	-	-	-	-	33.8	0.6	-	-	-	-	33.8	0.0	-	-	-	-	34.1	0.9
1969	-	-	-	-	35.0	2.6	-	-	-	-	35.3	0.9	-	-	-	-	35.4	0.3	-	-	-	-	36.1	2.0
1970	-	-	-	-	35.6	-1.4	-	-	-	-	36.5	2.5	-	-	-	-	37.0	1.4	-	-	-	-	38.6	4.3
1971	-	-	-	-	38.8	0.5	-	-	-	-	38.9	0.3	-	-	-	-	38.7	-0.5	-	-	-	-	38.6	-0.3
1972	-	-	-	-	39.0	1.0	-	-	-	-	39.5	1.3	-	-	-	-	40.1	1.5	-	-	-	-	40.2	0.2
1973	-	-	-	-	39.8	-1.0	-	-	-	-	40.7	2.3	-	-	-	-	40.6	-0.2	-	-	-	-	41.1	1.2
1974	-	-	-	-	42.6	3.6	-	-	-	-	45.0	5.6	-	-	-	-	46.5	3.3	-	-	-	-	47.3	1.7
1975	-	-	-	-	48.3	2.1	-	-	-	-	50.0	3.5	-	-	-	-	51.0	2.0	-	-	-	-	51.6	1.2
1976	-	-	-	-	52.5	1.7	-	-	-	-	53.9	2.7	-	-	-	-	55.7	3.3	-	-	-	-	56.3	1.1
1977	-	-	-	-	56.9	1.1	-	-	-	-	58.5	2.8	-	-	-	-	58.4	-0.2	-	-	-	-	59.1	1.2
1978	-	-	59.5	0.7	-	-	59.7	0.3	-	-	61.5	3.0	-	-	62.2	1.1	-	-	62.9	1.1	-	-	64.0	1.7
1979	-	-	64.7	1.1	-	-	67.4	4.2	-	-	70.5	4.6	-	-	72.9	3.4	-	-	74.3	1.9	-	-	76.0	2.3
1980	-	-	80.7	6.2	-	-	83.7	3.7	-	-	83.7	0.0	-	-	84.9	1.4	-	-	85.6	0.8	-	-	86.5	1.1
1981	-	-	88.6	2.4	-	-	90.6	2.3	-	-	92.8	2.4	-	-	93.0	0.2	-	-	94.1	1.2	-	-	94.9	0.9
1982	-	-	94.0	-0.9	-	-	94.5	0.5	-	-	98.1	3.8	-	-	99.6	1.5	-	-	99.8	0.2	-	-	98.2	-1.6
1983	-	-	96.2	-2.0	-	-	96.5	0.3	-	-	100.4	4.0	-	-	101.2	0.8	-	-	100.0	-1.2	-	-	100.8	0.8
1984	-	-	100.6	-0.2	-	-	103.2	2.6	-	-	104.9	1.6	-	-	103.8	-1.0	-	-	105.9	2.0	-	-	105.1	-0.8
1985	-	-	104.6	-0.5	-	-	105.9	1.2	-	-	106.7	0.8	-	-	105.3	-1.3	-	-	105.0	-0.3	-	-	105.5	0.5
1986	-	-	105.3	-0.2	-	-	99.8	-5.2	-	-	102.8	3.0	-	-	99.4	-3.3	-	-	99.7	0.3	-	-	98.5	-1.2
1987	99.4	0.9	100.2	0.8	101.4	1.2	101.8	0.4	102.0	0.2	102.1	0.1	102.6	0.5	103.2	0.6	103.3	0.1	103.5	0.2	104.6	1.1	104.5	-0.1
1988	104.4	-0.1	103.5	-0.9	103.4	-0.1	103.7	0.3	104.4	0.7	105.3	0.9	105.7	0.4	106.5	0.8	106.7	0.2	107.0	0.3	106.1	-0.8	106.4	0.3
1989	106.8	0.4	107.2	0.4	107.6	0.4	110.9	3.1	112.1	1.1	111.6	-0.4	111.5	-0.1	110.7	-0.7	108.7	-1.8	109.0	0.3	109.5	0.5	109.1	-0.4
1990	110.4	1.2	110.4	0.0	111.5	1.0	112.0	0.4	112.7	0.6	113.4	0.6	113.8	0.4	115.4	1.4	116.8	1.2	119.1	2.0	119.6	0.4	121.2	1.3
1991	119.5	-1.4	117.0	-2.1	115.2	-1.5	113.7	-1.3	115.9	1.9	117.6	1.5	117.7	0.1	118.4	0.6	117.5	-0.8	117.9	0.3	117.4	-0.4	117.0	-0.3
1992	116.6	-0.3	116.2	-0.3	116.7	0.4	117.6	0.8	119.1	1.3	120.1	0.8	121.4	1.1	121.5	0.1	120.7	-0.7	122.1	1.2	122.7	0.5	123.3	0.5

[Continued]

San Francisco-Oakland-San Jose, CA
Consumer Price Index - All Urban Consumers
Base 1982-1984 = 100
Transportation
[Continued]

For 1947-2000. Columns headed % show percentile change in the index from the previous period for which an index is available.

Year	Jan		Feb		Mar		Apr		May		Jun		Jul		Aug		Sep		Oct		Nov		Dec	
	Index	%	Index	%	Index	%	Index	%	Index	%	Index	%	Index	%	Index	%	Index	%	Index	%	Index	%	Index	%
1993	125.1	1.5	124.3	-0.6	123.5	-0.6	123.1	-0.3	123.4	0.2	123.1	-0.2	123.0	-0.1	123.6	0.5	122.2	-1.1	124.4	1.8	124.7	0.2	123.5	-1.0
1994	123.9	0.3	123.4	-0.4	124.9	1.2	125.3	0.3	125.1	-0.2	125.6	0.4	126.1	0.4	127.2	0.9	126.3	-0.7	127.3	0.8	127.2	-0.1	126.2	-0.8
1995	126.7	0.4	126.6	-0.1	127.4	0.6	128.2	0.6	129.1	0.7	130.4	1.0	130.3	-0.1	129.5	-0.6	129.8	0.2	130.4	0.5	130.0	-0.3	129.9	-0.1
1996	129.9	0.0	131.7	1.4	131.9	0.2	134.9	2.3	135.8	0.7	135.9	0.1	135.2	-0.5	134.2	-0.7	134.1	-0.1	134.2	0.1	132.8	-1.0	131.3	-1.1
1997	131.2	-0.1	133.1	1.4	134.7	1.2	135.3	0.4	134.7	-0.4	134.1	-0.4	134.0	-0.1	133.0	-0.7	133.4	0.3	133.5	0.1	133.0	-0.4	132.6	-0.3
1998	-	-	133.3	0.5	-	-	131.7	-1.2	-	-	132.4	0.5	-	-	131.5	-0.7	-	-	131.5	0.0	-	-	131.1	-0.3
1999	-	-	129.6	-1.1	-	-	140.2	8.2	-	-	135.0	-3.7	-	-	138.3	2.4	-	-	136.4	-1.4	-	-	136.6	0.1
2000	-	-	138.3	1.2	-	-	143.6	3.8	-	-	142.6	-0.7	-	-	145.6	2.1	-	-	145.6	0.0	-	-	145.1	-0.3

Source: U.S. Department of Labor, Bureau of Labor Statistics, Division of Consumer Prices and Price Indexes. - indicates no data collected for period.

San Francisco-Oakland-San Jose, CA
Consumer Price Index - Urban Wage Earners
Base 1982-1984 = 100
Transportation

For 1947-2000. Columns headed % show percentile change in the index from the previous period for which an index is available.

Year	Jan Index	%	Feb Index	%	Mar Index	%	Apr Index	%	May Index	%	Jun Index	%	Jul Index	%	Aug Index	%	Sep Index	%	Oct Index	%	Nov Index	%	Dec Index	%
1947	15.7	-	15.7	0.0	15.8	0.6	15.9	0.6	15.8	-0.6	15.8	0.0	-	-	-	-	16.3	3.2	-	-	-	-	16.6	1.8
1948	-	-	-	-	17.0	2.4	-	-	-	-	17.5	2.9	-	-	-	-	18.2	4.0	-	-	-	-	18.3	0.5
1949	-	-	-	-	18.9	3.3	-	-	-	-	19.0	0.5	-	-	-	-	19.1	0.5	-	-	-	-	19.2	0.5
1950	-	-	-	-	19.2	0.0	-	-	-	-	18.8	-2.1	-	-	-	-	19.0	1.1	-	-	-	-	19.0	0.0
1951	-	-	-	-	20.1	5.8	-	-	-	-	20.3	1.0	-	-	-	-	20.8	2.5	-	-	-	-	20.9	0.5
1952	-	-	-	-	21.1	1.0	-	-	-	-	23.6	11.8	-	-	-	-	24.6	4.2	-	-	-	-	24.6	0.0
1953	-	-	-	-	25.1	2.0	-	-	-	-	24.9	-0.8	-	-	-	-	25.2	1.2	-	-	-	-	25.3	0.4
1954	-	-	-	-	25.2	-0.4	-	-	-	-	25.1	-0.4	-	-	-	-	24.6	-2.0	-	-	-	-	24.8	0.8
1955	-	-	-	-	24.7	-0.4	-	-	-	-	24.2	-2.0	-	-	-	-	24.3	0.4	-	-	-	-	24.7	1.6
1956	-	-	-	-	24.4	-1.2	-	-	-	-	24.5	0.4	-	-	-	-	24.7	0.8	-	-	-	-	26.1	5.7
1957	-	-	-	-	26.5	1.5	-	-	-	-	26.3	-0.8	-	-	-	-	26.4	0.4	-	-	-	-	26.7	1.1
1958	-	-	-	-	27.3	2.2	-	-	-	-	27.7	1.5	-	-	-	-	28.2	1.8	-	-	-	-	27.7	-1.8
1959	-	-	-	-	29.0	4.7	-	-	-	-	28.9	-0.3	-	-	-	-	29.3	1.4	-	-	-	-	29.7	1.4
1960	-	-	-	-	28.9	-2.7	-	-	-	-	28.8	-0.3	-	-	-	-	28.6	-0.7	-	-	-	-	29.2	2.1
1961	-	-	-	-	28.9	-1.0	-	-	-	-	28.6	-1.0	-	-	-	-	29.4	2.8	-	-	-	-	29.8	1.4
1962	-	-	-	-	29.4	-1.3	-	-	-	-	29.7	1.0	-	-	-	-	29.8	0.3	-	-	-	-	29.7	-0.3
1963	-	-	-	-	29.7	0.0	-	-	-	-	29.9	0.7	-	-	-	-	30.0	0.3	-	-	-	-	30.6	2.0
1964	-	-	-	-	30.6	0.0	-	-	-	-	30.9	1.0	-	-	-	-	30.7	-0.6	-	-	-	-	31.1	1.3
1965	-	-	-	-	31.0	-0.3	-	-	-	-	31.0	0.0	-	-	-	-	30.8	-0.6	-	-	-	-	31.2	1.3
1966	-	-	-	-	31.2	0.0	-	-	-	-	30.9	-1.0	-	-	-	-	31.5	1.9	-	-	-	-	31.6	0.3
1967	-	-	-	-	31.6	0.0	-	-	-	-	32.1	1.6	-	-	-	-	32.4	0.9	-	-	-	-	32.6	0.6
1968	-	-	-	-	32.8	0.6	-	-	-	-	33.0	0.6	-	-	-	-	33.0	0.0	-	-	-	-	33.3	0.9
1969	-	-	-	-	34.2	2.7	-	-	-	-	34.4	0.6	-	-	-	-	34.6	0.6	-	-	-	-	35.2	1.7
1970	-	-	-	-	34.8	-1.1	-	-	-	-	35.7	2.6	-	-	-	-	36.2	1.4	-	-	-	-	37.7	4.1
1971	-	-	-	-	37.9	0.5	-	-	-	-	38.0	0.3	-	-	-	-	37.8	-0.5	-	-	-	-	37.7	-0.3
1972	-	-	-	-	38.1	1.1	-	-	-	-	38.5	1.0	-	-	-	-	39.2	1.8	-	-	-	-	39.2	0.0
1973	-	-	-	-	38.8	-1.0	-	-	-	-	39.8	2.6	-	-	-	-	39.7	-0.3	-	-	-	-	40.1	1.0
1974	-	-	-	-	41.6	3.7	-	-	-	-	44.0	5.8	-	-	-	-	45.4	3.2	-	-	-	-	46.2	1.8
1975	-	-	-	-	47.2	2.2	-	-	-	-	48.8	3.4	-	-	-	-	49.8	2.0	-	-	-	-	50.4	1.2
1976	-	-	-	-	51.2	1.6	-	-	-	-	52.6	2.7	-	-	-	-	54.4	3.4	-	-	-	-	55.0	1.1
1977	-	-	-	-	55.6	1.1	-	-	-	-	57.1	2.7	-	-	-	-	57.0	-0.2	-	-	-	-	57.7	1.2
1978	-	-	58.1	0.7	-	-	58.4	0.5	-	-	60.3	3.3	-	-	61.2	1.5	-	-	61.9	1.1	-	-	63.0	1.8
1979	-	-	63.6	1.0	-	-	66.6	4.7	-	-	69.8	4.8	-	-	72.1	3.3	-	-	73.2	1.5	-	-	75.0	2.5
1980	-	-	79.4	5.9	-	-	81.9	3.1	-	-	81.9	0.0	-	-	83.5	2.0	-	-	84.4	1.1	-	-	85.2	0.9
1981	-	-	87.8	3.1	-	-	89.8	2.3	-	-	91.5	1.9	-	-	92.3	0.9	-	-	93.5	1.3	-	-	94.3	0.9
1982	-	-	93.4	-1.0	-	-	94.2	0.9	-	-	97.6	3.6	-	-	99.2	1.6	-	-	99.4	0.2	-	-	98.0	-1.4
1983	-	-	96.0	-2.0	-	-	96.4	0.4	-	-	100.5	4.3	-	-	101.3	0.8	-	-	100.4	-0.9	-	-	101.3	0.9
1984	-	-	101.1	-0.2	-	-	103.6	2.5	-	-	105.1	1.4	-	-	103.9	-1.1	-	-	106.0	2.0	-	-	105.3	-0.7
1985	-	-	104.8	-0.5	-	-	106.1	1.2	-	-	107.0	0.8	-	-	105.6	-1.3	-	-	105.2	-0.4	-	-	105.7	0.5
1986	-	-	105.6	-0.1	-	-	100.0	-5.3	-	-	102.9	2.9	-	-	99.7	-3.1	-	-	100.0	0.3	-	-	98.8	-1.2
1987	99.3	0.5	100.8	1.5	102.3	1.5	103.2	0.9	103.5	0.3	103.8	0.3	104.1	0.3	104.8	0.7	104.8	0.0	105.3	0.5	105.9	0.6	106.1	0.2
1988	106.1	0.0	105.5	-0.6	105.4	-0.1	105.5	0.1	106.2	0.7	107.1	0.8	107.6	0.5	108.1	0.5	108.3	0.2	108.8	0.5	108.0	-0.7	108.0	0.0
1989	108.5	0.5	108.9	0.4	109.6	0.6	113.4	3.5	114.9	1.3	114.4	-0.4	114.1	-0.3	113.3	-0.7	111.3	-1.8	111.1	-0.2	111.5	0.4	111.1	-0.4
1990	111.7	0.5	112.1	0.4	113.2	1.0	113.7	0.4	114.4	0.6	115.4	0.9	115.7	0.3	117.6	1.6	119.2	1.4	122.0	2.3	122.3	0.2	123.2	0.7
1991	121.0	-1.8	118.1	-2.4	116.2	-1.6	114.8	-1.2	117.2	2.1	118.9	1.5	119.2	0.3	119.8	0.5	119.5	-0.3	120.0	0.4	119.1	-0.8	118.9	-0.2
1992	118.3	-0.5	118.0	-0.3	118.3	0.3	119.2	0.8	121.1	1.6	122.5	1.2	123.5	0.8	123.8	0.2	123.4	-0.3	124.3	0.7	125.0	0.6	125.3	0.2

[Continued]

San Francisco-Oakland-San Jose, CA
Consumer Price Index - Urban Wage Earners
Base 1982-1984 = 100
Transportation
[Continued]

For 1947-2000. Columns headed % show percentile change in the index from the previous period for which an index is available.

Year	Jan		Feb		Mar		Apr		May		Jun		Jul		Aug		Sep		Oct		Nov		Dec	
	Index	%	Index	%	Index	%	Index	%	Index	%	Index	%	Index	%	Index	%	Index	%	Index	%	Index	%	Index	%
1993	126.4	0.9	125.8	-0.5	125.2	-0.5	125.0	-0.2	125.3	0.2	125.3	0.0	125.3	0.0	125.7	0.3	125.1	-0.5	127.0	1.5	126.9	-0.1	125.6	-1.0
1994	125.5	-0.1	124.7	-0.6	125.6	0.7	126.3	0.6	126.5	0.2	127.4	0.7	128.3	0.7	129.6	1.0	129.3	-0.2	130.5	0.9	130.5	0.0	130.1	-0.3
1995	129.8	-0.2	129.7	-0.1	130.6	0.7	131.6	0.8	132.4	0.6	133.4	0.8	133.2	-0.1	132.6	-0.5	132.4	-0.2	133.5	0.8	133.2	-0.2	133.1	-0.1
1996	133.3	0.2	134.3	0.8	134.7	0.3	138.5	2.8	139.7	0.9	139.0	-0.5	138.3	-0.5	137.1	-0.9	136.7	-0.3	136.5	-0.1	135.1	-1.0	133.2	-1.4
1997	133.7	0.4	135.7	1.5	136.7	0.7	138.1	1.0	137.2	-0.7	136.2	-0.7	135.4	-0.6	134.9	-0.4	135.9	0.7	135.8	-0.1	135.2	-0.4	135.0	-0.1
1998	-	-	134.8	-0.1	-	-	133.0	-1.3	-	-	133.8	0.6	-	-	132.5	-1.0	-	-	132.4	-0.1	-	-	131.8	-0.5
1999	-	-	130.4	-1.1	-	-	142.8	9.5	-	-	137.2	-3.9	-	-	141.3	3.0	-	-	137.9	-2.4	-	-	138.0	0.1
2000	-	-	139.8	1.3	-	-	146.5	4.8	-	-	144.6	-1.3	-	-	147.5	2.0	-	-	148.5	0.7	-	-	147.5	-0.7

Source: U.S. Department of Labor, Bureau of Labor Statistics, Division of Consumer Prices and Price Indexes. - indicates no data collected for period.

San Francisco-Oakland-San Jose, CA
Consumer Price Index - All Urban Consumers
Base 1982-1984 = 100
Medical Care

For 1947-2001. Columns headed % show percentile change in the index from the previous period for which an index is available.

Year	Jan Index	%	Feb Index	%	Mar Index	%	Apr Index	%	May Index	%	Jun Index	%	Jul Index	%	Aug Index	%	Sep Index	%	Oct Index	%	Nov Index	%	Dec Index	%
1947	13.3	-	13.4	0.8	13.4	0.0	13.4	0.0	13.4	0.0	13.4	0.0	-	-	-	-	13.8	3.0	-	-	-	-	13.9	0.7
1948	-	-	-	-	14.0	0.7	-	-	-	-	14.2	1.4	-	-	-	-	14.4	1.4	-	-	-	-	14.6	1.4
1949	-	-	-	-	14.7	0.7	-	-	-	-	14.7	0.0	-	-	-	-	14.8	0.7	-	-	-	-	14.8	0.0
1950	-	-	-	-	14.8	0.0	-	-	-	-	14.8	0.0	-	-	-	-	15.5	4.7	-	-	-	-	15.7	1.3
1951	-	-	-	-	15.7	0.0	-	-	-	-	15.8	0.6	-	-	-	-	15.8	0.0	-	-	-	-	16.0	1.3
1952	-	-	-	-	16.8	5.0	-	-	-	-	16.9	0.6	-	-	-	-	16.9	0.0	-	-	-	-	17.0	0.6
1953	-	-	-	-	17.0	0.0	-	-	-	-	17.2	1.2	-	-	-	-	17.4	1.2	-	-	-	-	17.4	0.0
1954	-	-	-	-	17.5	0.6	-	-	-	-	17.5	0.0	-	-	-	-	17.5	0.0	-	-	-	-	17.5	0.0
1955	-	-	-	-	17.5	0.0	-	-	-	-	17.6	0.6	-	-	-	-	17.8	1.1	-	-	-	-	17.9	0.6
1956	-	-	-	-	18.2	1.7	-	-	-	-	18.2	0.0	-	-	-	-	19.2	5.5	-	-	-	-	19.3	0.5
1957	-	-	-	-	19.3	0.0	-	-	-	-	19.5	1.0	-	-	-	-	19.6	0.5	-	-	-	-	20.0	2.0
1958	-	-	-	-	20.3	1.5	-	-	-	-	21.4	5.4	-	-	-	-	21.5	0.5	-	-	-	-	21.6	0.5
1959	-	-	-	-	21.7	0.5	-	-	-	-	22.0	1.4	-	-	-	-	22.0	0.0	-	-	-	-	22.0	0.0
1960	-	-	-	-	22.4	1.8	-	-	-	-	22.5	0.4	-	-	-	-	22.7	0.9	-	-	-	-	22.8	0.4
1961	-	-	-	-	22.9	0.4	-	-	-	-	23.0	0.4	-	-	-	-	23.1	0.4	-	-	-	-	23.2	0.4
1962	-	-	-	-	24.0	3.4	-	-	-	-	24.1	0.4	-	-	-	-	24.2	0.4	-	-	-	-	24.4	0.8
1963	-	-	-	-	24.5	0.4	-	-	-	-	24.6	0.4	-	-	-	-	24.7	0.4	-	-	-	-	24.8	0.4
1964	-	-	-	-	25.1	1.2	-	-	-	-	25.3	0.8	-	-	-	-	25.5	0.8	-	-	-	-	25.5	0.0
1965	-	-	-	-	25.8	1.2	-	-	-	-	25.9	0.4	-	-	-	-	25.9	0.0	-	-	-	-	26.3	1.5
1966	-	-	-	-	26.6	1.1	-	-	-	-	27.1	1.9	-	-	-	-	27.8	2.6	-	-	-	-	28.2	1.4
1967	-	-	-	-	28.7	1.8	-	-	-	-	28.9	0.7	-	-	-	-	29.1	0.7	-	-	-	-	29.4	1.0
1968	-	-	-	-	30.1	2.4	-	-	-	-	30.3	0.7	-	-	-	-	30.5	0.7	-	-	-	-	30.9	1.3
1969	-	-	-	-	31.4	1.6	-	-	-	-	31.7	1.0	-	-	-	-	32.2	1.6	-	-	-	-	32.5	0.9
1970	-	-	-	-	33.2	2.2	-	-	-	-	33.5	0.9	-	-	-	-	34.1	1.8	-	-	-	-	34.2	0.3
1971	-	-	-	-	35.3	3.2	-	-	-	-	35.7	1.1	-	-	-	-	36.2	1.4	-	-	-	-	35.9	-0.8
1972	-	-	-	-	36.4	1.4	-	-	-	-	36.7	0.8	-	-	-	-	37.1	1.1	-	-	-	-	37.4	0.8
1973	-	-	-	-	37.9	1.3	-	-	-	-	38.0	0.3	-	-	-	-	38.4	1.1	-	-	-	-	39.0	1.6
1974	-	-	-	-	40.1	2.8	-	-	-	-	41.2	2.7	-	-	-	-	42.7	3.6	-	-	-	-	43.5	1.9
1975	-	-	-	-	45.7	5.1	-	-	-	-	48.3	5.7	-	-	-	-	49.1	1.7	-	-	-	-	49.8	1.4
1976	-	-	-	-	51.7	3.8	-	-	-	-	52.3	1.2	-	-	-	-	53.2	1.7	-	-	-	-	54.6	2.6
1977	-	-	-	-	56.4	3.3	-	-	-	-	57.4	1.8	-	-	-	-	59.3	3.3	-	-	-	-	59.7	0.7
1978	-	-	61.0	2.2	-	-	62.6	2.6	-	-	62.6	0.0	-	-	63.7	1.8	-	-	65.5	2.8	-	-	65.9	0.6
1979	-	-	67.0	1.7	-	-	67.3	0.4	-	-	67.8	0.7	-	-	69.3	2.2	-	-	72.1	4.0	-	-	73.2	1.5
1980	-	-	74.4	1.6	-	-	76.0	2.2	-	-	76.4	0.5	-	-	76.8	0.5	-	-	78.4	2.1	-	-	78.6	0.3
1981	-	-	81.1	3.2	-	-	82.9	2.2	-	-	84.0	1.3	-	-	85.7	2.0	-	-	87.2	1.8	-	-	89.1	2.2
1982	-	-	90.8	1.9	-	-	93.1	2.5	-	-	94.3	1.3	-	-	95.2	1.0	-	-	96.3	1.2	-	-	97.6	1.3
1983	-	-	99.5	1.9	-	-	99.7	0.2	-	-	101.2	1.5	-	-	101.9	0.7	-	-	101.6	-0.3	-	-	101.7	0.1
1984	-	-	103.8	2.1	-	-	104.4	0.6	-	-	104.6	0.2	-	-	105.4	0.8	-	-	106.4	0.9	-	-	107.0	0.6
1985	-	-	107.8	0.7	-	-	108.5	0.6	-	-	110.3	1.7	-	-	113.2	2.6	-	-	113.9	0.6	-	-	115.1	1.1
1986	-	-	115.9	0.7	-	-	117.4	1.3	-	-	118.9	1.3	-	-	121.9	2.5	-	-	122.4	0.4	-	-	124.0	1.3
1987	125.1	0.9	125.2	0.1	125.8	0.5	126.6	0.6	126.4	-0.2	127.3	0.7	130.1	2.2	131.3	0.9	131.1	-0.2	131.4	0.2	132.0	0.5	132.2	0.2
1988	133.2	0.8	133.1	-0.1	133.7	0.5	134.3	0.4	134.7	0.3	136.1	1.0	137.9	1.3	138.1	0.1	139.1	0.7	140.1	0.7	140.5	0.3	141.4	0.6
1989	143.0	1.1	144.6	1.1	145.0	0.3	145.7	0.5	145.8	0.1	146.6	0.5	147.8	0.8	148.4	0.4	149.9	1.0	150.4	0.3	154.1	2.5	152.9	-0.8
1990	155.2	1.5	156.1	0.6	158.3	1.4	158.3	0.0	158.3	0.0	158.7	0.3	161.3	1.6	162.7	0.9	163.1	0.2	164.2	0.7	164.8	0.4	164.9	0.1
1991	166.6	1.0	167.8	0.7	168.7	0.5	168.7	0.0	169.0	0.2	169.7	0.4	173.2	2.1	176.6	2.0	177.9	0.7	178.2	0.2	178.9	0.4	179.4	0.3
1992	180.1	0.4	182.2	1.2	183.1	0.5	185.3	1.2	185.2	-0.1	186.7	0.8	188.5	1.0	188.7	0.1	190.3	0.8	190.9	0.3	191.2	0.2	191.4	0.1

[Continued]

San Francisco-Oakland-San Jose, CA
Consumer Price Index - All Urban Consumers
Base 1982-1984 = 100
Medical Care

[Continued]

For 1947-2001. Columns headed % show percentile change in the index from the previous period for which an index is available.

Year	Jan		Feb		Mar		Apr		May		Jun		Jul		Aug		Sep		Oct		Nov		Dec	
	Index	%	Index	%	Index	%	Index	%	Index	%	Index	%	Index	%	Index	%	Index	%	Index	%	Index	%	Index	%
1993	193.1	0.9	194.9	0.9	194.7	-0.1	197.8	1.6	197.8	0.0	199.5	0.9	201.4	1.0	201.6	0.1	201.2	-0.2	202.2	0.5	202.0	-0.1	202.4	0.2
1994	202.4	0.0	202.5	0.0	203.1	0.3	203.9	0.4	203.5	-0.2	203.9	0.2	203.3	-0.3	204.9	0.8	205.7	0.4	205.8	0.0	206.3	0.2	206.8	0.2
1995	209.0	1.1	208.6	-0.2	209.2	0.3	207.7	-0.7	207.7	0.0	207.1	-0.3	208.8	0.8	208.8	0.0	209.9	0.5	210.1	0.1	210.6	0.2	210.6	0.0
1996	212.4	0.9	212.2	-0.1	213.3	0.5	214.1	0.4	213.2	-0.4	213.3	0.0	214.2	0.4	214.6	0.2	214.3	-0.1	217.3	1.4	217.2	-0.0	217.9	0.3
1997	218.3	0.2	218.6	0.1	219.3	0.3	220.6	0.6	222.2	0.7	222.3	0.0	222.3	0.0	222.7	0.2	221.8	-0.4	223.3	0.7	224.6	0.6	225.9	0.6
1998	-	-	227.3	0.6	-	-	227.4	0.0	-	-	228.3	0.4	-	-	228.2	-0.0	-	-	228.7	0.2	-	-	229.0	0.1
1999	-	-	230.7	0.7	-	-	229.2	-0.7	-	-	232.5	1.4	-	-	233.7	0.5	-	-	234.1	0.2	-	-	237.3	1.4
2000	-	-	236.8	-0.2	-	-	237.6	0.3	-	-	238.5	0.4	-	-	249.5	4.6	-	-	249.1	-0.2	-	-	249.0	-0.0
2001	-	-	253.3	1.7	-	-	254.1	0.3	-	-	254.4	0.1	-	-	255.5	0.4	-	-	255.8	0.1	-	-	261.0	2.0

Source: U.S. Department of Labor, Bureau of Labor Statistics, Division of Consumer Prices and Price Indexes. - indicates no data collected for period.

San Francisco-Oakland-San Jose, CA
Consumer Price Index - Urban Wage Earners
Base 1982-1984 = 100
Medical Care

For 1947-2001. Columns headed % show percentile change in the index from the previous period for which an index is available.

Year	Jan Index	%	Feb Index	%	Mar Index	%	Apr Index	%	May Index	%	Jun Index	%	Jul Index	%	Aug Index	%	Sep Index	%	Oct Index	%	Nov Index	%	Dec Index	%
1947	13.4	-	13.5	0.7	13.5	0.0	13.5	0.0	13.5	0.0	13.5	0.0	-	-	-	-	13.9	3.0	-	-	-	-	14.0	0.7
1948	-	-	-	-	14.1	0.7	-	-	-	-	14.3	1.4	-	-	-	-	14.5	1.4	-	-	-	-	14.7	1.4
1949	-	-	-	-	14.8	0.7	-	-	-	-	14.8	0.0	-	-	-	-	14.9	0.7	-	-	-	-	14.9	0.0
1950	-	-	-	-	14.9	0.0	-	-	-	-	14.9	0.0	-	-	-	-	15.6	4.7	-	-	-	-	15.8	1.3
1951	-	-	-	-	15.8	0.0	-	-	-	-	15.9	0.6	-	-	-	-	15.9	0.0	-	-	-	-	16.1	1.3
1952	-	-	-	-	16.9	5.0	-	-	-	-	17.0	0.6	-	-	-	-	17.0	0.0	-	-	-	-	17.1	0.6
1953	-	-	-	-	17.1	0.0	-	-	-	-	17.3	1.2	-	-	-	-	17.5	1.2	-	-	-	-	17.6	0.6
1954	-	-	-	-	17.6	0.0	-	-	-	-	17.6	0.0	-	-	-	-	17.6	0.0	-	-	-	-	17.7	0.6
1955	-	-	-	-	17.7	0.0	-	-	-	-	17.7	0.0	-	-	-	-	17.9	1.1	-	-	-	-	18.0	0.6
1956	-	-	-	-	18.3	1.7	-	-	-	-	18.3	0.0	-	-	-	-	19.4	6.0	-	-	-	-	19.4	0.0
1957	-	-	-	-	19.5	0.5	-	-	-	-	19.6	0.5	-	-	-	-	19.7	0.5	-	-	-	-	20.1	2.0
1958	-	-	-	-	20.4	1.5	-	-	-	-	21.6	5.9	-	-	-	-	21.6	0.0	-	-	-	-	21.7	0.5
1959	-	-	-	-	21.8	0.5	-	-	-	-	22.1	1.4	-	-	-	-	22.1	0.0	-	-	-	-	22.2	0.5
1960	-	-	-	-	22.5	1.4	-	-	-	-	22.7	0.9	-	-	-	-	22.8	0.4	-	-	-	-	22.9	0.4
1961	-	-	-	-	23.0	0.4	-	-	-	-	23.1	0.4	-	-	-	-	23.3	0.9	-	-	-	-	23.4	0.4
1962	-	-	-	-	24.2	3.4	-	-	-	-	24.3	0.4	-	-	-	-	24.4	0.4	-	-	-	-	24.5	0.4
1963	-	-	-	-	24.7	0.8	-	-	-	-	24.8	0.4	-	-	-	-	24.9	0.4	-	-	-	-	25.0	0.4
1964	-	-	-	-	25.2	0.8	-	-	-	-	25.4	0.8	-	-	-	-	25.7	1.2	-	-	-	-	25.7	0.0
1965	-	-	-	-	26.0	1.2	-	-	-	-	26.0	0.0	-	-	-	-	26.1	0.4	-	-	-	-	26.5	1.5
1966	-	-	-	-	26.8	1.1	-	-	-	-	27.3	1.9	-	-	-	-	28.0	2.6	-	-	-	-	28.4	1.4
1967	-	-	-	-	28.9	1.8	-	-	-	-	29.1	0.7	-	-	-	-	29.3	0.7	-	-	-	-	29.6	1.0
1968	-	-	-	-	30.3	2.4	-	-	-	-	30.5	0.7	-	-	-	-	30.7	0.7	-	-	-	-	31.1	1.3
1969	-	-	-	-	31.6	1.6	-	-	-	-	32.0	1.3	-	-	-	-	32.4	1.3	-	-	-	-	32.7	0.9
1970	-	-	-	-	33.4	2.1	-	-	-	-	33.7	0.9	-	-	-	-	34.3	1.8	-	-	-	-	34.5	0.6
1971	-	-	-	-	35.5	2.9	-	-	-	-	35.9	1.1	-	-	-	-	36.4	1.4	-	-	-	-	36.2	-0.5
1972	-	-	-	-	36.6	1.1	-	-	-	-	36.9	0.8	-	-	-	-	37.3	1.1	-	-	-	-	37.7	1.1
1973	-	-	-	-	38.2	1.3	-	-	-	-	38.3	0.3	-	-	-	-	38.6	0.8	-	-	-	-	39.3	1.8
1974	-	-	-	-	40.4	2.8	-	-	-	-	41.5	2.7	-	-	-	-	43.0	3.6	-	-	-	-	43.8	1.9
1975	-	-	-	-	46.0	5.0	-	-	-	-	48.6	5.7	-	-	-	-	49.5	1.9	-	-	-	-	50.1	1.2
1976	-	-	-	-	52.1	4.0	-	-	-	-	52.6	1.0	-	-	-	-	53.6	1.9	-	-	-	-	54.9	2.4
1977	-	-	-	-	56.8	3.5	-	-	-	-	57.8	1.8	-	-	-	-	59.7	3.3	-	-	-	-	60.1	0.7
1978	-	-	62.3	3.7	-	-	62.7	0.6	-	-	62.3	-0.6	-	-	64.4	3.4	-	-	65.0	0.9	-	-	65.8	1.2
1979	-	-	66.4	0.9	-	-	66.9	0.8	-	-	68.2	1.9	-	-	69.9	2.5	-	-	72.2	3.3	-	-	73.4	1.7
1980	-	-	74.7	1.8	-	-	75.8	1.5	-	-	76.0	0.3	-	-	77.4	1.8	-	-	79.1	2.2	-	-	80.0	1.1
1981	-	-	82.2	2.8	-	-	83.2	1.2	-	-	83.8	0.7	-	-	87.0	3.8	-	-	87.5	0.6	-	-	89.2	1.9
1982	-	-	90.9	1.9	-	-	93.1	2.4	-	-	94.3	1.3	-	-	95.0	0.7	-	-	96.0	1.1	-	-	97.1	1.1
1983	-	-	99.1	2.1	-	-	99.5	0.4	-	-	101.0	1.5	-	-	101.7	0.7	-	-	101.5	-0.2	-	-	101.7	0.2
1984	-	-	103.8	2.1	-	-	104.6	0.8	-	-	104.9	0.3	-	-	105.8	0.9	-	-	106.9	1.0	-	-	107.6	0.7
1985	-	-	108.5	0.8	-	-	109.1	0.6	-	-	110.8	1.6	-	-	113.8	2.7	-	-	114.5	0.6	-	-	115.8	1.1
1986	-	-	116.6	0.7	-	-	118.0	1.2	-	-	119.8	1.5	-	-	122.7	2.4	-	-	123.1	0.3	-	-	124.7	1.3
1987	126.0	1.0	126.3	0.2	126.9	0.5	127.7	0.6	127.7	0.0	128.7	0.8	131.5	2.2	132.6	0.8	132.4	-0.2	132.8	0.3	133.4	0.5	133.6	0.1
1988	134.4	0.6	134.4	0.0	135.0	0.4	135.6	0.4	136.0	0.3	137.3	1.0	138.9	1.2	139.3	0.3	140.0	0.5	141.5	1.1	142.0	0.4	142.5	0.4
1989	144.3	1.3	146.0	1.2	145.9	-0.1	147.0	0.8	147.1	0.1	147.9	0.5	149.1	0.8	149.4	0.2	151.0	1.1	151.5	0.3	155.1	2.4	153.6	-1.0
1990	156.1	1.6	156.8	0.4	158.9	1.3	158.8	-0.1	158.5	-0.2	158.9	0.3	161.3	1.5	163.1	1.1	163.4	0.2	164.3	0.6	164.9	0.4	164.1	-0.5
1991	166.3	1.3	167.1	0.5	168.0	0.5	168.3	0.2	168.6	0.2	169.3	0.4	172.3	1.8	175.8	2.0	177.1	0.7	176.6	-0.3	177.6	0.6	178.3	0.4
1992	178.6	0.2	181.4	1.6	182.2	0.4	184.7	1.4	184.4	-0.2	186.8	1.3	188.5	0.9	188.7	0.1	190.0	0.7	190.2	0.1	190.3	0.1	190.6	0.2

[Continued]

San Francisco-Oakland-San Jose, CA
Consumer Price Index - Urban Wage Earners
Base 1982-1984 = 100
Medical Care
[Continued]

For 1947-2001. Columns headed % show percentile change in the index from the previous period for which an index is available.

Year	Jan Index	%	Feb Index	%	Mar Index	%	Apr Index	%	May Index	%	Jun Index	%	Jul Index	%	Aug Index	%	Sep Index	%	Oct Index	%	Nov Index	%	Dec Index	%
1993	192.2	0.8	194.2	1.0	194.0	-0.1	196.8	1.4	196.8	0.0	198.3	0.8	200.1	0.9	200.5	0.2	199.4	-0.5	201.0	0.8	200.6	-0.2	201.0	0.2
1994	200.9	-0.0	200.3	-0.3	201.4	0.5	202.2	0.4	201.5	-0.3	201.9	0.2	201.4	-0.2	203.0	0.8	203.6	0.3	203.6	0.0	204.1	0.2	204.7	0.3
1995	206.7	1.0	206.4	-0.1	207.1	0.3	205.6	-0.7	205.6	0.0	204.9	-0.3	206.6	0.8	206.6	0.0	207.6	0.5	207.8	0.1	208.3	0.2	208.4	0.0
1996	210.1	0.8	209.9	-0.1	211.2	0.6	211.9	0.3	211.3	-0.3	211.3	0.0	212.2	0.4	212.6	0.2	212.0	-0.3	214.6	1.2	214.1	-0.2	215.2	0.5
1997	215.8	0.3	216.1	0.1	216.9	0.4	218.0	0.5	219.7	0.8	220.0	0.1	220.0	0.0	220.5	0.2	219.6	-0.4	220.9	0.6	222.3	0.6	223.2	0.4
1998	-	-	224.5	0.6	-	-	224.5	0.0	-	-	225.4	0.4	-	-	225.3	-0.0	-	-	225.6	0.1	-	-	225.9	0.1
1999	-	-	227.6	0.8	-	-	226.5	-0.5	-	-	229.7	1.4	-	-	230.8	0.5	-	-	231.2	0.2	-	-	234.4	1.4
2000	-	-	234.3	-0.0	-	-	235.2	0.4	-	-	235.8	0.3	-	-	245.3	4.0	-	-	244.8	-0.2	-	-	244.8	0.0
2001	-	-	249.2	1.8	-	-	250.0	0.3	-	-	250.4	0.2	-	-	251.6	0.5	-	-	252.0	0.2	-	-	256.1	1.6

Source: U.S. Department of Labor, Bureau of Labor Statistics, Division of Consumer Prices and Price Indexes. - indicates no data collected for period.

San Francisco-Oakland-San Jose, CA
Consumer Price Index - All Urban Consumers
Base December 1997 = 100
Recreation

For 1997-2001. Columns headed % show percentile change in the index from the previous period for which an index is available.

Year	Jan Index	%	Feb Index	%	Mar Index	%	Apr Index	%	May Index	%	Jun Index	%	Jul Index	%	Aug Index	%	Sep Index	%	Oct Index	%	Nov Index	%	Dec Index	%
1997	-	-	-	-	-	-	-	-	-	-	-	-	-	-	-	-	-	-	-	-	-	-	100.0	-
1998	-	-	98.2	-1.8	-	-	98.7	0.5	-	-	99.2	0.5	-	-	99.2	0.0	-	-	96.9	-2.3	-	-	96.3	-0.6
1999	-	-	98.0	1.8	-	-	97.3	-0.7	-	-	97.5	0.2	-	-	96.8	-0.7	-	-	95.6	-1.2	-	-	93.8	-1.9
2000	-	-	94.9	1.2	-	-	94.6	-0.3	-	-	95.5	1.0	-	-	95.8	0.3	-	-	95.8	0.0	-	-	95.4	-0.4
2001	-	-	94.6	-0.8	-	-	93.5	-1.2	-	-	92.0	-1.6	-	-	93.2	1.3	-	-	93.4	0.2	-	-	93.3	-0.1

Source: U.S. Department of Labor, Bureau of Labor Statistics, Division of Consumer Prices and Price Indexes. - indicates no data collected for period.

San Francisco-Oakland-San Jose, CA
Consumer Price Index - Urban Wage Earners
Base December 1997 = 100
Recreation

For 1997-2001. Columns headed % show percentile change in the index from the previous period for which an index is available.

Year	Jan Index	%	Feb Index	%	Mar Index	%	Apr Index	%	May Index	%	Jun Index	%	Jul Index	%	Aug Index	%	Sep Index	%	Oct Index	%	Nov Index	%	Dec Index	%
1997	-	-	-	-	-	-	-	-	-	-	-	-	-	-	-	-	-	-	-	-	-	-	100.0	-
1998	-	-	98.0	-2.0	-	-	98.4	0.4	-	-	98.7	0.3	-	-	98.0	-0.7	-	-	96.1	-1.9	-	-	95.4	-0.7
1999	-	-	96.7	1.4	-	-	95.7	-1.0	-	-	96.1	0.4	-	-	95.4	-0.7	-	-	94.4	-1.0	-	-	92.9	-1.6
2000	-	-	93.7	0.9	-	-	93.5	-0.2	-	-	94.4	1.0	-	-	94.7	0.3	-	-	94.8	0.1	-	-	94.3	-0.5
2001	-	-	93.6	-0.7	-	-	92.4	-1.3	-	-	90.9	-1.6	-	-	92.0	1.2	-	-	92.0	0.0	-	-	91.8	-0.2

Source: U.S. Department of Labor, Bureau of Labor Statistics, Division of Consumer Prices and Price Indexes. - indicates no data collected for period.

San Francisco-Oakland-San Jose, CA
Consumer Price Index - All Urban Consumers
Base December 1997 = 100
Education & Communication

For 1997-2001. Columns headed % show percentile change in the index from the previous period for which an index is available.

Year	Jan Index	%	Feb Index	%	Mar Index	%	Apr Index	%	May Index	%	Jun Index	%	Jul Index	%	Aug Index	%	Sep Index	%	Oct Index	%	Nov Index	%	Dec Index	%
1997	-	-	-	-	-	-	-	-	-	-	-	-	-	-	-	-	-	-	-	-	-	-	100.0	-
1998	-	-	99.9	-0.1	-	-	100.0	0.1	-	-	100.2	0.2	-	-	102.4	2.2	-	-	103.3	0.9	-	-	103.1	-0.2
1999	-	-	103.1	0.0	-	-	103.2	0.1	-	-	102.3	-0.9	-	-	104.9	2.5	-	-	105.9	1.0	-	-	106.4	0.5
2000	-	-	106.1	-0.3	-	-	105.6	-0.5	-	-	105.5	-0.1	-	-	107.6	2.0	-	-	107.6	0.0	-	-	106.0	-1.5
2001	-	-	105.8	-0.2	-	-	106.2	0.4	-	-	106.6	0.4	-	-	108.4	1.7	-	-	110.3	1.8	-	-	110.1	-0.2

Source: U.S. Department of Labor, Bureau of Labor Statistics, Division of Consumer Prices and Price Indexes. - indicates no data collected for period.

San Francisco-Oakland-San Jose, CA
Consumer Price Index - Urban Wage Earners
Base December 1997 = 100
Education & Communication

For 1997-2001. Columns headed % show percentile change in the index from the previous period for which an index is available.

Year	Jan Index	%	Feb Index	%	Mar Index	%	Apr Index	%	May Index	%	Jun Index	%	Jul Index	%	Aug Index	%	Sep Index	%	Oct Index	%	Nov Index	%	Dec Index	%
1997	-	-	-	-	-	-	-	-	-	-	-	-	-	-	-	-	-	-	-	-	-	-	100.0	-
1998	-	-	100.2	0.2	-	-	100.4	0.2	-	-	100.7	0.3	-	-	103.6	2.9	-	-	104.5	0.9	-	-	104.4	-0.1
1999	-	-	104.4	0.0	-	-	104.5	0.1	-	-	103.6	-0.9	-	-	106.9	3.2	-	-	107.1	0.2	-	-	107.7	0.6
2000	-	-	107.4	-0.3	-	-	106.8	-0.6	-	-	106.7	-0.1	-	-	108.6	1.8	-	-	108.7	0.1	-	-	106.8	-1.7
2001	-	-	106.6	-0.2	-	-	107.3	0.7	-	-	107.5	0.2	-	-	108.7	1.1	-	-	110.8	1.9	-	-	110.5	-0.3

Source: U.S. Department of Labor, Bureau of Labor Statistics, Division of Consumer Prices and Price Indexes. - indicates no data collected for period.

Seattle-Tacoma-Bremerton, WA
Consumer Price Index - All Urban Consumers
Base 1982-1984 = 100
Annual Averages

For 1914-2001. Columns headed % show percentile change in the index from the previous period for which an index is available.

Year	All Items		Food & Beverage		Housing		Apparel		Trans-portation		Medical Care		Recrea-tion*		Education & Communic.*		Other Goods & Services	
	Index	%	Index	%	Index	%	Index	%	Index	%	Index	%	Index	%	Index	%	Index	%
1914	-	-	-	-	-	-	-	-	-	-	-	-	-	-	-	-	-	-
1915	9.0	-	-	-	-	-	-	-	-	-	-	-	-	-	-	-	-	-
1916	9.4	4.4	-	-	-	-	-	-	-	-	-	-	-	-	-	-	-	-
1917	11.0	17.0	-	-	-	-	-	-	-	-	-	-	-	-	-	-	-	-
1918	13.7	24.5	-	-	-	-	-	-	-	-	-	-	-	-	-	-	-	-
1919	16.5	20.4	-	-	-	-	-	-	-	-	-	-	-	-	-	-	-	-
1920	18.8	13.9	-	-	-	-	-	-	-	-	-	-	-	-	-	-	-	-
1921	16.7	-11.2	-	-	-	-	-	-	-	-	-	-	-	-	-	-	-	-
1922	15.6	-6.6	-	-	-	-	-	-	-	-	-	-	-	-	-	-	-	-
1923	15.5	-0.6	-	-	-	-	-	-	-	-	-	-	-	-	-	-	-	-
1924	15.5	0.0	-	-	-	-	-	-	-	-	-	-	-	-	-	-	-	-
1925	15.8	1.9	-	-	-	-	-	-	-	-	-	-	-	-	-	-	-	-
1926	15.8	0.0	-	-	-	-	-	-	-	-	-	-	-	-	-	-	-	-
1927	15.5	-1.9	-	-	-	-	-	-	-	-	-	-	-	-	-	-	-	-
1928	15.4	-0.6	-	-	-	-	-	-	-	-	-	-	-	-	-	-	-	-
1929	15.5	0.6	-	-	-	-	-	-	-	-	-	-	-	-	-	-	-	-
1930	15.2	-1.9	-	-	-	-	-	-	-	-	-	-	-	-	-	-	-	-
1931	13.8	-9.2	-	-	-	-	-	-	-	-	-	-	-	-	-	-	-	-
1932	12.6	-8.7	-	-	-	-	-	-	-	-	-	-	-	-	-	-	-	-
1933	12.0	-4.8	-	-	-	-	-	-	-	-	-	-	-	-	-	-	-	-
1934	12.3	2.5	-	-	-	-	-	-	-	-	-	-	-	-	-	-	-	-
1935	12.6	2.4	-	-	-	-	-	-	-	-	-	-	-	-	-	-	-	-
1936	12.7	0.8	-	-	-	-	-	-	-	-	-	-	-	-	-	-	-	-
1937	13.4	5.5	-	-	-	-	-	-	-	-	-	-	-	-	-	-	-	-
1938	13.2	-1.5	-	-	-	-	-	-	-	-	-	-	-	-	-	-	-	-
1939	13.2	0.0	-	-	-	-	-	-	-	-	-	-	-	-	-	-	-	-
1940	13.2	0.0	-	-	-	-	-	-	-	-	-	-	-	-	-	-	-	-
1941	14.0	6.1	-	-	-	-	-	-	-	-	-	-	-	-	-	-	-	-
1942	15.8	12.9	-	-	-	-	-	-	-	-	-	-	-	-	-	-	-	-
1943	16.7	5.7	-	-	-	-	-	-	-	-	-	-	-	-	-	-	-	-
1944	16.9	1.2	-	-	-	-	-	-	-	-	-	-	-	-	-	-	-	-
1945	17.3	2.4	-	-	-	-	-	-	-	-	-	-	-	-	-	-	-	-
1946	18.6	7.5	-	-	-	-	-	-	-	-	-	-	-	-	-	-	-	-
1947	21.1	13.4	-	-	-	-	-	-	19.1	-	14.4	-	-	-	-	-	-	-
1948	22.8	8.1	-	-	-	-	-	-	20.8	8.9	15.1	4.9	-	-	-	-	-	-
1949	22.7	-0.4	-	-	-	-	-	-	22.2	6.7	15.8	4.6	-	-	-	-	-	-
1950	23.1	1.8	-	-	-	-	-	-	22.9	3.2	16.1	1.9	-	-	-	-	-	-
1951	24.8	7.4	-	-	-	-	-	-	24.2	5.7	17.1	6.2	-	-	-	-	-	-
1952	25.5	2.8	-	-	-	-	-	-	25.6	5.8	18.4	7.6	-	-	-	-	-	-
1953	25.8	1.2	-	-	-	-	43.9	-	27.4	7.0	19.0	3.3	-	-	-	-	-	-
1954	25.8	0.0	-	-	-	-	43.6	-0.7	26.9	-1.8	19.7	3.7	-	-	-	-	-	-
1955	25.9	0.4	-	-	-	-	43.8	0.5	26.4	-1.9	20.1	2.0	-	-	-	-	-	-
1956	26.2	1.2	-	-	-	-	44.2	0.9	26.6	0.8	20.6	2.5	-	-	-	-	-	-
1957	27.3	4.2	-	-	-	-	45.1	2.0	28.6	7.5	21.3	3.4	-	-	-	-	-	-
1958	27.9	2.2	-	-	-	-	44.9	-0.4	29.7	3.8	22.3	4.7	-	-	-	-	-	-

[Continued]

Seattle-Tacoma-Bremerton, WA
Consumer Price Index - All Urban Consumers
Base 1982-1984 = 100
Annual Averages
[Continued]

For 1914-2001. Columns headed % show percentile change in the index from the previous period for which an index is available.

Year	All Items		Food & Beverage		Housing		Apparel		Trans-portation		Medical Care		Recrea-tion*		Education & Communic.*		Other Goods & Services	
	Index	%	Index	%	Index	%	Index	%	Index	%	Index	%	Index	%	Index	%	Index	%
1959	28.5	2.2	-	-	-	-	45.4	1.1	31.1	4.7	22.8	2.2	-	-	-	-	-	-
1960	28.8	1.1	-	-	-	-	46.0	1.3	30.8	-1.0	23.9	4.8	-	-	-	-	-	-
1961	29.3	1.7	-	-	-	-	46.7	1.5	31.7	2.9	24.0	0.4	-	-	-	-	-	-
1962	29.7	1.4	-	-	-	-	47.5	1.7	32.6	2.8	24.3	1.2	-	-	-	-	-	-
1963	30.2	1.7	-	-	-	-	48.2	1.5	32.5	-0.3	24.5	0.8	-	-	-	-	-	-
1964	30.6	1.3	-	-	-	-	48.7	1.0	32.6	0.3	25.0	2.0	-	-	-	-	-	-
1965	31.0	1.3	-	-	-	-	49.0	0.6	33.5	2.8	26.0	4.0	-	-	-	-	-	-
1966	31.9	2.9	-	-	-	-	50.4	2.9	34.0	1.5	27.6	6.2	-	-	-	-	-	-
1967	32.8	2.8	-	-	-	-	52.2	3.6	35.3	3.8	29.1	5.4	-	-	-	-	-	-
1968	34.1	4.0	-	-	-	-	53.7	2.9	35.9	1.7	30.8	5.8	-	-	-	-	-	-
1969	35.8	5.0	-	-	-	-	55.8	3.9	36.2	0.8	32.9	6.8	-	-	-	-	-	-
1970	37.4	4.5	-	-	-	-	58.3	4.5	37.1	2.5	34.5	4.9	-	-	-	-	-	-
1971	38.2	2.1	-	-	-	-	60.6	3.9	37.8	1.9	35.8	3.8	-	-	-	-	-	-
1972	39.3	2.9	-	-	-	-	61.4	1.3	38.6	2.1	36.5	2.0	-	-	-	-	-	-
1973	41.8	6.4	-	-	-	-	64.2	4.6	39.6	2.6	37.8	3.6	-	-	-	-	-	-
1974	46.4	11.0	-	-	-	-	68.2	6.2	44.0	11.1	41.2	9.0	-	-	-	-	-	-
1975	51.1	10.1	-	-	-	-	72.7	6.6	48.1	9.3	46.1	11.9	-	-	-	-	-	-
1976	54.0	5.7	61.3	-	50.3	-	76.9	5.8	51.8	7.7	50.9	10.4	-	-	-	-	50.8	-
1977	58.3	8.0	65.6	7.0	54.8	8.9	80.4	4.6	56.9	9.8	56.0	10.0	-	-	-	-	54.2	6.7
1978	63.9	9.6	71.0	8.2	61.7	12.6	82.6	2.7	61.2	7.6	62.2	11.1	-	-	-	-	57.8	6.6
1979	71.0	11.1	78.3	10.3	68.1	10.4	87.9	6.4	71.1	16.2	67.4	8.4	-	-	-	-	64.2	11.1
1980	82.7	16.5	84.5	7.9	82.7	21.4	95.0	8.1	83.1	16.9	75.8	12.5	-	-	-	-	71.5	11.4
1981	91.8	11.0	91.6	8.4	92.2	11.5	99.0	4.2	94.2	13.4	84.9	12.0	-	-	-	-	80.0	11.9
1982	97.7	6.4	98.3	7.3	98.4	6.7	99.6	0.6	98.0	4.0	93.5	10.1	-	-	-	-	91.7	14.6
1983	99.3	1.6	100.1	1.8	98.7	0.3	101.2	1.6	98.9	0.9	100.9	7.9	-	-	-	-	101.1	10.3
1984	103.0	3.7	101.6	1.5	102.8	4.2	99.2	-2.0	103.1	4.2	105.6	4.7	-	-	-	-	107.3	6.1
1985	105.6	2.5	103.2	1.6	105.5	2.6	102.5	3.3	105.0	1.8	112.2	6.3	-	-	-	-	111.9	4.3
1986	106.7	1.0	106.8	3.5	106.8	1.2	104.7	2.1	101.7	-3.1	117.6	4.8	-	-	-	-	117.1	4.6
1987	109.2	2.3	111.9	4.8	108.1	1.2	109.4	4.5	102.3	0.6	124.6	6.0	-	-	-	-	122.5	4.6
1988	112.8	3.3	114.9	2.7	111.9	3.5	115.6	5.7	103.5	1.2	132.9	6.7	-	-	-	-	127.4	4.0
1989	118.1	4.7	123.1	7.1	116.3	3.9	107.4	-7.1	109.2	5.5	141.6	6.5	-	-	-	-	135.4	6.3
1990	126.8	7.4	133.0	8.0	125.4	7.8	112.0	4.3	116.1	6.3	154.6	9.2	-	-	-	-	146.8	8.4
1991	134.1	5.8	140.6	5.7	134.0	6.9	113.4	1.3	119.9	3.3	169.4	9.6	-	-	-	-	156.5	6.6
1992	139.0	3.7	141.1	0.4	139.3	4.0	118.7	4.7	123.9	3.3	184.2	8.7	-	-	-	-	169.1	8.1
1993	142.9	2.8	142.4	0.9	143.5	3.0	115.5	-2.7	128.4	3.6	193.1	4.8	-	-	-	-	179.5	6.2
1994	147.8	3.4	146.9	3.2	147.9	3.1	120.9	4.7	135.0	5.1	199.8	3.5	-	-	-	-	184.9	3.0
1995	152.3	3.0	152.0	3.5	151.5	2.4	121.2	0.2	139.5	3.3	209.4	4.8	-	-	-	-	198.0	7.1
1996	157.5	3.4	155.5	2.3	156.9	3.6	125.7	3.7	144.0	3.2	217.4	3.8	-	-	-	-	210.7	6.4
1997	163.0	3.5	160.2	3.0	164.4	4.8	125.9	0.2	145.6	1.1	224.7	3.4	-	-	-	-	223.1	5.9
1998	167.7	2.9	165.2	3.1	170.9	4.0	126.5	0.5	145.4	-0.1	232.7	3.6	99.1	-	102.9	-	238.5	6.9
1999	172.8	3.0	169.6	2.7	177.3	3.7	125.5	-0.8	149.9	3.1	240.3	3.3	100.1	1.0	104.1	1.2	256.7	7.6
2000	179.2	3.7	173.7	2.4	184.8	4.2	126.6	0.9	159.6	6.5	246.6	2.6	101.1	1.0	104.5	0.4	267.5	4.2
2001	185.7	3.6	181.2	4.3	195.6	5.8	124.2	-1.9	-	-	257.4	4.4	100.2	-0.9	106.3	1.7	275.6	3.0

Source: U.S. Department of Labor, Bureau of Labor Statistics, Division of Consumer Prices and Price Indexes. *Base is December 1997 = 100. - indicates no data collected for period.

Seattle-Tacoma-Bremerton, WA
Consumer Price Index - Urban Wage Earners
Base 1982-1984 = 100
Annual Averages

For 1914-2001. Columns headed % show percentile change in the index from the previous period for which an index is available.

Year	All Items		Food & Beverage		Housing		Apparel		Trans-portation		Medical Care		Recrea-tion*		Education & Communic.*		Other Goods & Services	
	Index	%	Index	%	Index	%	Index	%	Index	%	Index	%	Index	%	Index	%	Index	%
1914	-	-	-	-	-	-	-	-	-	-	-	-	-	-	-	-	-	-
1915	9.3	-	-	-	-	-	-	-	-	-	-	-	-	-	-	-	-	-
1916	9.6	3.2	-	-	-	-	-	-	-	-	-	-	-	-	-	-	-	-
1917	11.3	17.7	-	-	-	-	-	-	-	-	-	-	-	-	-	-	-	-
1918	14.1	24.8	-	-	-	-	-	-	-	-	-	-	-	-	-	-	-	-
1919	17.0	20.6	-	-	-	-	-	-	-	-	-	-	-	-	-	-	-	-
1920	19.4	14.1	-	-	-	-	-	-	-	-	-	-	-	-	-	-	-	-
1921	17.1	-11.9	-	-	-	-	-	-	-	-	-	-	-	-	-	-	-	-
1922	16.0	-6.4	-	-	-	-	-	-	-	-	-	-	-	-	-	-	-	-
1923	15.9	-0.6	-	-	-	-	-	-	-	-	-	-	-	-	-	-	-	-
1924	15.9	0.0	-	-	-	-	-	-	-	-	-	-	-	-	-	-	-	-
1925	16.3	2.5	-	-	-	-	-	-	-	-	-	-	-	-	-	-	-	-
1926	16.3	0.0	-	-	-	-	-	-	-	-	-	-	-	-	-	-	-	-
1927	15.9	-2.5	-	-	-	-	-	-	-	-	-	-	-	-	-	-	-	-
1928	15.8	-0.6	-	-	-	-	-	-	-	-	-	-	-	-	-	-	-	-
1929	15.9	0.6	-	-	-	-	-	-	-	-	-	-	-	-	-	-	-	-
1930	15.6	-1.9	-	-	-	-	-	-	-	-	-	-	-	-	-	-	-	-
1931	14.2	-9.0	-	-	-	-	-	-	-	-	-	-	-	-	-	-	-	-
1932	12.9	-9.2	-	-	-	-	-	-	-	-	-	-	-	-	-	-	-	-
1933	12.3	-4.7	-	-	-	-	-	-	-	-	-	-	-	-	-	-	-	-
1934	12.6	2.4	-	-	-	-	-	-	-	-	-	-	-	-	-	-	-	-
1935	12.9	2.4	-	-	-	-	-	-	-	-	-	-	-	-	-	-	-	-
1936	13.1	1.6	-	-	-	-	-	-	-	-	-	-	-	-	-	-	-	-
1937	13.7	4.6	-	-	-	-	-	-	-	-	-	-	-	-	-	-	-	-
1938	13.6	-0.7	-	-	-	-	-	-	-	-	-	-	-	-	-	-	-	-
1939	13.5	-0.7	-	-	-	-	-	-	-	-	-	-	-	-	-	-	-	-
1940	13.6	0.7	-	-	-	-	-	-	-	-	-	-	-	-	-	-	-	-
1941	14.4	5.9	-	-	-	-	-	-	-	-	-	-	-	-	-	-	-	-
1942	16.2	12.5	-	-	-	-	-	-	-	-	-	-	-	-	-	-	-	-
1943	17.1	5.6	-	-	-	-	-	-	-	-	-	-	-	-	-	-	-	-
1944	17.4	1.8	-	-	-	-	-	-	-	-	-	-	-	-	-	-	-	-
1945	17.8	2.3	-	-	-	-	-	-	-	-	-	-	-	-	-	-	-	-
1946	19.2	7.9	-	-	-	-	-	-	-	-	-	-	-	-	-	-	-	-
1947	21.7	13.0	-	-	-	-	-	-	19.5	-	14.3	-	-	-	-	-	-	-
1948	23.5	8.3	-	-	-	-	-	-	21.2	8.7	15.0	4.9	-	-	-	-	-	-
1949	23.4	-0.4	-	-	-	-	-	-	22.7	7.1	15.7	4.7	-	-	-	-	-	-
1950	23.7	1.3	-	-	-	-	-	-	23.3	2.6	15.9	1.3	-	-	-	-	-	-
1951	25.5	7.6	-	-	-	-	-	-	24.7	6.0	16.9	6.3	-	-	-	-	-	-
1952	26.2	2.7	-	-	-	-	-	-	26.1	5.7	18.2	7.7	-	-	-	-	-	-
1953	26.5	1.1	-	-	-	-	44.4	-	27.9	6.9	18.9	3.8	-	-	-	-	-	-
1954	26.5	0.0	-	-	-	-	44.1	-0.7	27.4	-1.8	19.5	3.2	-	-	-	-	-	-
1955	26.6	0.4	-	-	-	-	44.3	0.5	27.0	-1.5	19.9	2.1	-	-	-	-	-	-
1956	27.0	1.5	-	-	-	-	44.7	0.9	27.1	0.4	20.4	2.5	-	-	-	-	-	-
1957	28.1	4.1	-	-	-	-	45.6	2.0	29.2	7.7	21.1	3.4	-	-	-	-	-	-
1958	28.7	2.1	-	-	-	-	45.4	-0.4	30.3	3.8	22.1	4.7	-	-	-	-	-	-

[Continued]

Seattle-Tacoma-Bremerton, WA
Consumer Price Index - Urban Wage Earners
Base 1982-1984 = 100
Annual Averages
[Continued]

For 1914-2001. Columns headed % show percentile change in the index from the previous period for which an index is available.

Year	All Items		Food & Beverage		Housing		Apparel		Transportation		Medical Care		Recreation*		Education & Communic.*		Other Goods & Services	
	Index	%	Index	%	Index	%	Index	%	Index	%	Index	%	Index	%	Index	%	Index	%
1959	29.3	2.1	-	-	-	-	45.9	1.1	31.7	4.6	22.6	2.3	-	-	-	-	-	-
1960	29.6	1.0	-	-	-	-	46.5	1.3	31.4	-0.9	23.7	4.9	-	-	-	-	-	-
1961	30.1	1.7	-	-	-	-	47.2	1.5	32.3	2.9	23.8	0.4	-	-	-	-	-	-
1962	30.5	1.3	-	-	-	-	48.0	1.7	33.3	3.1	24.1	1.3	-	-	-	-	-	-
1963	31.1	2.0	-	-	-	-	48.8	1.7	33.2	-0.3	24.3	0.8	-	-	-	-	-	-
1964	31.5	1.3	-	-	-	-	49.3	1.0	33.3	0.3	24.7	1.6	-	-	-	-	-	-
1965	31.9	1.3	-	-	-	-	49.6	0.6	34.2	2.7	25.7	4.0	-	-	-	-	-	-
1966	32.7	2.5	-	-	-	-	51.0	2.8	34.7	1.5	27.4	6.6	-	-	-	-	-	-
1967	33.7	3.1	-	-	-	-	52.8	3.5	36.0	3.7	28.8	5.1	-	-	-	-	-	-
1968	35.1	4.2	-	-	-	-	54.3	2.8	36.6	1.7	30.5	5.9	-	-	-	-	-	-
1969	36.8	4.8	-	-	-	-	56.5	4.1	36.9	0.8	32.6	6.9	-	-	-	-	-	-
1970	38.4	4.3	-	-	-	-	59.0	4.4	37.9	2.7	34.1	4.6	-	-	-	-	-	-
1971	39.2	2.1	-	-	-	-	61.3	3.9	38.6	1.8	35.4	3.8	-	-	-	-	-	-
1972	40.4	3.1	-	-	-	-	62.1	1.3	39.4	2.1	36.2	2.3	-	-	-	-	-	-
1973	43.0	6.4	-	-	-	-	65.0	4.7	40.4	2.5	37.4	3.3	-	-	-	-	-	-
1974	47.7	10.9	-	-	-	-	69.1	6.3	44.9	11.1	40.8	9.1	-	-	-	-	-	-
1975	52.5	10.1	-	-	-	-	73.5	6.4	49.1	9.4	45.7	12.0	-	-	-	-	-	-
1976	55.5	5.7	61.6	-	52.5	-	77.8	5.9	52.8	7.5	50.4	10.3	-	-	-	-	52.6	-
1977	59.9	7.9	65.9	7.0	57.2	9.0	81.3	4.5	58.1	10.0	55.4	9.9	-	-	-	-	56.1	6.7
1978	65.3	9.0	71.2	8.0	64.4	12.6	83.5	2.7	61.4	5.7	61.1	10.3	-	-	-	-	60.0	7.0
1979	72.4	10.9	78.3	10.0	70.9	10.1	87.9	5.3	70.8	15.3	67.4	10.3	-	-	-	-	65.2	8.7
1980	84.0	16.0	84.8	8.3	85.9	21.2	93.9	6.8	82.3	16.2	75.1	11.4	-	-	-	-	71.6	9.8
1981	93.1	10.8	92.1	8.6	95.5	11.2	97.9	4.3	93.4	13.5	84.1	12.0	-	-	-	-	79.9	11.6
1982	99.1	6.4	98.3	6.7	101.7	6.5	99.7	1.8	97.8	4.7	93.4	11.1	-	-	-	-	91.2	14.1
1983	98.9	-0.2	100.1	1.8	97.6	-4.0	100.9	1.2	98.9	1.1	100.8	7.9	-	-	-	-	101.5	11.3
1984	102.1	3.2	101.6	1.5	100.8	3.3	99.4	-1.5	103.3	4.4	105.8	5.0	-	-	-	-	107.3	5.7
1985	104.2	2.1	103.3	1.7	102.2	1.4	102.5	3.1	105.4	2.0	112.6	6.4	-	-	-	-	111.9	4.3
1986	105.0	0.8	106.6	3.2	103.3	1.1	103.7	1.2	101.8	-3.4	118.4	5.2	-	-	-	-	117.2	4.7
1987	107.4	2.3	111.6	4.7	104.5	1.2	108.3	4.4	102.7	0.9	126.2	6.6	-	-	-	-	123.0	4.9
1988	110.9	3.3	114.6	2.7	108.0	3.3	114.1	5.4	104.6	1.9	134.7	6.7	-	-	-	-	128.0	4.1
1989	116.1	4.7	122.7	7.1	111.9	3.6	105.7	-7.4	110.2	5.4	143.4	6.5	-	-	-	-	136.3	6.5
1990	124.4	7.1	132.7	8.1	120.5	7.7	111.0	5.0	116.7	5.9	156.0	8.8	-	-	-	-	147.7	8.4
1991	131.3	5.5	140.2	5.7	128.4	6.6	112.2	1.1	120.6	3.3	170.0	9.0	-	-	-	-	157.4	6.6
1992	136.0	3.6	140.8	0.4	133.0	3.6	117.7	4.9	125.0	3.6	184.9	8.8	-	-	-	-	170.4	8.3
1993	140.0	2.9	142.5	1.2	137.0	3.0	115.0	-2.3	130.1	4.1	193.9	4.9	-	-	-	-	181.6	6.6
1994	145.1	3.6	146.6	2.9	141.4	3.2	120.5	4.8	137.8	5.9	200.2	3.2	-	-	-	-	186.7	2.8
1995	149.3	2.9	151.0	3.0	144.5	2.2	120.4	-0.1	143.1	3.8	209.1	4.4	-	-	-	-	200.3	7.3
1996	154.3	3.3	154.5	2.3	149.3	3.3	124.1	3.1	147.5	3.1	217.8	4.2	-	-	-	-	214.8	7.2
1997	159.0	3.0	159.1	3.0	155.8	4.4	125.2	0.9	148.4	0.6	225.0	3.3	-	-	-	-	225.4	4.9
1998	163.2	2.6	163.6	2.8	161.9	3.9	127.0	1.4	147.8	-0.4	232.8	3.5	99.1	-	102.5	-	240.4	6.7
1999	168.3	3.1	167.7	2.5	168.0	3.8	127.3	0.2	152.6	3.2	239.1	2.7	99.9	0.8	103.6	1.1	261.9	8.9
2000	174.6	3.7	171.9	2.5	175.0	4.2	128.2	0.7	162.9	6.7	244.8	2.4	100.7	0.8	104.8	1.2	274.4	4.8
2001	180.8	3.6	179.5	4.4	185.5	6.0	125.8	-1.9	-	-	254.8	4.1	99.6	-1.1	106.7	1.8	282.2	2.8

Source: U.S. Department of Labor, Bureau of Labor Statistics, Division of Consumer Prices and Price Indexes. *Base is December 1997 = 100. - indicates no data collected for period.

Seattle-Tacoma-Bremerton, WA
Consumer Price Index - All Urban Consumers
Base 1982-1984 = 100
All Items

For 1914-2001. Columns headed % show percentile change in the index from the previous period for which an index is available.

Year	Jan Index	%	Feb Index	%	Mar Index	%	Apr Index	%	May Index	%	Jun Index	%	Jul Index	%	Aug Index	%	Sep Index	%	Oct Index	%	Nov Index	%	Dec Index	%
1914	-	-	-	-	-	-	-	-	-	-	-	-	-	-	-	-	-	-	-	-	-	-	9.2	-
1915	-	-	-	-	-	-	-	-	-	-	-	-	-	-	-	-	-	-	-	-	-	-	9.1	-1.1
1916	-	-	-	-	-	-	-	-	-	-	-	-	-	-	-	-	-	-	-	-	-	-	9.7	6.6
1917	-	-	-	-	-	-	-	-	-	-	-	-	-	-	-	-	-	-	-	-	-	-	11.8	21.6
1918	-	-	-	-	-	-	-	-	-	-	-	-	-	-	-	-	-	-	-	-	-	-	15.4	30.5
1919	-	-	-	-	-	-	-	-	-	-	16.0	3.9	-	-	-	-	-	-	-	-	-	-	18.2	13.8
1920	-	-	-	-	-	-	-	-	-	-	19.6	7.7	-	-	-	-	-	-	-	-	-	-	17.9	-8.7
1921	-	-	-	-	-	-	-	-	16.8	-6.1	-	-	-	-	-	-	16.3	-3.0	-	-	-	-	16.0	-1.8
1922	-	-	-	-	15.7	-1.9	-	-	-	-	15.6	-0.6	-	-	-	-	15.5	-0.6	-	-	-	-	15.5	0.0
1923	-	-	-	-	15.1	-2.6	-	-	-	-	15.5	2.6	-	-	-	-	15.6	0.6	-	-	-	-	15.6	0.0
1924	-	-	-	-	15.5	-0.6	-	-	-	-	15.6	0.6	-	-	-	-	15.5	-0.6	-	-	-	-	15.6	0.6
1925	-	-	-	-	-	-	-	-	-	-	16.0	2.6	-	-	-	-	-	-	-	-	-	-	16.0	0.0
1926	-	-	-	-	-	-	-	-	-	-	15.8	-1.2	-	-	-	-	-	-	-	-	-	-	15.7	-0.6
1927	-	-	-	-	-	-	-	-	-	-	15.8	0.6	-	-	-	-	-	-	-	-	-	-	15.4	-2.5
1928	-	-	-	-	-	-	-	-	-	-	15.3	-0.6	-	-	-	-	-	-	-	-	-	-	15.4	0.7
1929	-	-	-	-	-	-	-	-	-	-	15.5	0.6	-	-	-	-	-	-	-	-	-	-	15.5	0.0
1930	-	-	-	-	-	-	-	-	-	-	15.5	0.0	-	-	-	-	-	-	-	-	-	-	14.4	-7.1
1931	-	-	-	-	-	-	-	-	-	-	13.9	-3.5	-	-	-	-	-	-	-	-	-	-	13.4	-3.6
1932	-	-	-	-	-	-	-	-	-	-	12.6	-6.0	-	-	-	-	-	-	-	-	-	-	12.1	-4.0
1933	-	-	-	-	-	-	-	-	-	-	12.0	-0.8	-	-	-	-	-	-	-	-	-	-	12.1	0.8
1934	-	-	-	-	-	-	-	-	-	-	12.2	0.8	-	-	-	-	-	-	-	-	12.4	1.6	-	-
1935	-	-	-	-	12.7	2.4	-	-	-	-	-	-	12.5	-1.6	-	-	-	-	12.5	0.0	-	-	-	-
1936	12.7	1.6	-	-	-	-	12.5	-1.6	-	-	-	-	12.7	1.6	-	-	12.9	1.6	-	-	-	-	12.9	0.0
1937	-	-	-	-	13.3	3.1	-	-	-	-	13.3	0.0	-	-	-	-	13.5	1.5	-	-	-	-	13.4	-0.7
1938	-	-	-	-	13.3	-0.7	-	-	-	-	13.2	-0.8	-	-	-	-	13.2	0.0	-	-	-	-	13.2	0.0
1939	-	-	-	-	13.1	-0.8	-	-	-	-	13.1	0.0	-	-	-	-	13.3	1.5	-	-	-	-	13.1	-1.5
1940	-	-	-	-	13.2	0.8	-	-	-	-	13.2	0.0	-	-	-	-	13.2	0.0	13.2	0.0	13.2	0.0	13.3	0.8
1941	13.3	0.0	13.3	0.0	13.4	0.8	13.5	0.7	13.8	2.2	13.9	0.7	14.0	0.7	14.1	0.7	14.5	2.8	14.7	1.4	14.7	0.0	14.9	1.4
1942	15.2	2.0	15.3	0.7	15.5	1.3	15.6	0.6	15.8	1.3	15.5	-1.9	15.6	0.6	15.8	1.3	16.0	1.3	16.1	0.6	16.2	0.6	16.4	1.2
1943	16.4	0.0	16.4	0.0	16.6	1.2	16.7	0.6	16.9	1.2	16.8	-0.6	16.5	-1.8	16.4	-0.6	16.7	1.8	16.8	0.6	16.8	0.0	16.8	0.0
1944	16.8	0.0	16.7	-0.6	16.8	0.6	16.8	0.0	16.9	0.6	16.9	0.0	17.0	0.6	17.0	0.0	17.0	0.0	17.1	0.6	17.1	0.0	17.2	0.6
1945	17.2	0.0	17.1	-0.6	17.2	0.6	17.2	0.0	17.3	0.6	17.3	0.0	17.4	0.6	17.4	0.0	17.4	0.0	17.3	-0.6	17.4	0.6	17.6	1.1
1946	17.5	-0.6	17.5	0.0	17.6	0.6	17.6	0.0	17.7	0.6	17.9	1.1	18.7	4.5	19.0	1.6	19.4	2.1	19.9	2.6	20.3	2.0	20.6	1.5
1947	20.4	-1.0	20.3	-0.5	20.7	2.0	20.8	0.5	20.8	0.0	20.7	-0.5	-	-	21.2	2.4	-	-	-	-	21.8	2.8	-	-
1948	-	-	22.4	2.8	-	-	-	-	22.9	2.2	-	-	-	-	23.2	1.3	-	-	-	-	22.9	-1.3	-	-
1949	-	-	23.0	0.4	-	-	-	-	22.8	-0.9	-	-	-	-	22.5	-1.3	-	-	-	-	22.7	0.9	-	-
1950	-	-	22.6	-0.4	-	-	-	-	22.6	0.0	-	-	-	-	23.0	1.8	-	-	-	-	23.8	3.5	-	-
1951	-	-	24.5	2.9	-	-	-	-	24.9	1.6	-	-	-	-	24.8	-0.4	-	-	-	-	25.3	2.0	-	-
1952	-	-	25.4	0.4	-	-	-	-	25.5	0.4	-	-	-	-	25.5	0.0	-	-	-	-	25.7	0.8	-	-
1953	-	-	25.5	-0.8	-	-	-	-	25.8	1.2	-	-	-	-	25.9	0.4	-	-	-	-	25.8	-0.4	-	-
1954	-	-	25.8	0.0	-	-	-	-	25.8	0.0	-	-	-	-	25.8	0.0	-	-	-	-	25.7	-0.4	-	-
1955	-	-	25.8	0.4	-	-	-	-	25.9	0.4	-	-	-	-	25.9	0.0	-	-	-	-	26.1	0.8	-	-
1956	-	-	25.8	-1.1	-	-	-	-	26.0	0.8	-	-	-	-	26.4	1.5	-	-	-	-	26.7	1.1	-	-
1957	-	-	27.1	1.5	-	-	-	-	27.3	0.7	-	-	-	-	27.5	0.7	-	-	-	-	27.5	0.0	-	-
1958	-	-	27.8	1.1	-	-	-	-	28.0	0.7	-	-	-	-	28.0	0.0	-	-	-	-	28.0	0.0	-	-
1959	-	-	28.2	0.7	-	-	-	-	28.4	0.7	-	-	-	-	28.6	0.7	-	-	-	-	28.7	0.3	-	-

[Continued]

Seattle-Tacoma-Bremerton, WA
Consumer Price Index - All Urban Consumers
Base 1982-1984 = 100
All Items
[Continued]

For 1914-2001. Columns headed % show percentile change in the index from the previous period for which an index is available.

Year	Jan Index	%	Feb Index	%	Mar Index	%	Apr Index	%	May Index	%	Jun Index	%	Jul Index	%	Aug Index	%	Sep Index	%	Oct Index	%	Nov Index	%	Dec Index	%
1960	-	-	28.6	-0.3	-	-	-	-	28.8	0.7	-	-	-	-	28.8	0.0	-	-	-	-	29.0	0.7	-	-
1961	-	-	29.1	0.3	-	-	-	-	29.3	0.7	-	-	-	-	29.3	0.0	-	-	-	-	29.5	0.7	-	-
1962	-	-	29.6	0.3	-	-	-	-	29.7	0.3	-	-	-	-	29.8	0.3	-	-	-	-	29.9	0.3	-	-
1963	-	-	29.9	0.0	-	-	-	-	30.0	0.3	-	-	-	-	30.5	1.7	-	-	-	-	30.5	0.0	-	-
1964	-	-	30.5	0.0	-	-	-	-	30.5	0.0	-	-	-	-	30.8	1.0	-	-	-	-	30.7	-0.3	-	-
1965	-	-	30.6	-0.3	-	-	-	-	30.9	1.0	-	-	-	-	31.1	0.6	-	-	-	-	31.2	0.3	-	-
1966	-	-	31.4	0.6	-	-	-	-	31.8	1.3	-	-	-	-	32.0	0.6	-	-	-	-	32.3	0.9	-	-
1967	-	-	32.3	0.0	-	-	-	-	32.6	0.9	-	-	-	-	33.0	1.2	-	-	-	-	33.3	0.9	-	-
1968	-	-	33.6	0.9	-	-	-	-	33.8	0.6	-	-	-	-	34.4	1.8	-	-	-	-	34.8	1.2	-	-
1969	-	-	35.1	0.9	-	-	-	-	35.6	1.4	-	-	-	-	36.2	1.7	-	-	-	-	36.3	0.3	-	-
1970	-	-	36.9	1.7	-	-	-	-	37.4	1.4	-	-	-	-	37.6	0.5	-	-	-	-	37.7	0.3	-	-
1971	-	-	37.6	-0.3	-	-	-	-	37.9	0.8	-	-	-	-	38.6	1.8	-	-	-	-	38.6	0.0	-	-
1972	-	-	39.0	1.0	-	-	-	-	39.0	0.0	-	-	-	-	39.3	0.8	-	-	-	-	39.8	1.3	-	-
1973	-	-	40.4	1.5	-	-	-	-	41.4	2.5	-	-	-	-	42.3	2.2	-	-	-	-	43.1	1.9	-	-
1974	-	-	44.5	3.2	-	-	-	-	45.7	2.7	-	-	-	-	46.9	2.6	-	-	-	-	48.5	3.4	-	-
1975	-	-	49.8	2.7	-	-	-	-	50.7	1.8	-	-	-	-	51.6	1.8	-	-	-	-	52.4	1.6	-	-
1976	-	-	53.0	1.1	-	-	-	-	53.3	0.6	-	-	-	-	54.4	2.1	-	-	-	-	55.1	1.3	-	-
1977	-	-	56.2	2.0	-	-	-	-	57.8	2.8	-	-	-	-	59.1	2.2	-	-	-	-	59.9	1.4	-	-
1978	60.4	0.8	-	-	61.4	1.7	-	-	63.5	3.4	-	-	63.9	0.6	-	-	65.9	3.1	-	-	66.8	1.4	-	-
1979	66.3	-0.7	-	-	67.9	2.4	-	-	69.7	2.7	-	-	71.3	2.3	-	-	73.0	2.4	-	-	74.7	2.3	-	-
1980	77.4	3.6	-	-	80.0	3.4	-	-	81.9	2.4	-	-	83.7	2.2	-	-	84.7	1.2	-	-	86.1	1.7	-	-
1981	86.9	0.9	-	-	88.9	2.3	-	-	90.1	1.3	-	-	92.6	2.8	-	-	94.7	2.3	-	-	94.9	0.2	-	-
1982	97.1	2.3	-	-	96.2	-0.9	-	-	98.8	2.7	-	-	97.3	-1.5	-	-	99.1	1.8	-	-	97.6	-1.5	-	-
1983	97.6	0.0	-	-	97.7	0.1	-	-	98.7	1.0	-	-	99.7	1.0	-	-	100.5	0.8	-	-	100.7	0.2	-	-
1984	101.3	0.6	-	-	101.8	0.5	-	-	102.7	0.9	-	-	103.1	0.4	-	-	103.8	0.7	-	-	104.4	0.6	-	-
1985	104.8	0.4	-	-	105.4	0.6	-	-	105.3	-0.1	-	-	105.6	0.3	-	-	105.6	0.0	-	-	106.3	0.7	-	-
1986	107.3	0.9	-	-	106.6	-0.7	-	-	106.1	-0.5	-	-	106.2	0.1	-	-	107.0	0.8	-	-	106.9	-0.1	106.8	-0.1
1987	-	-	-	-	-	-	-	-	-	-	108.2	1.3	-	-	-	-	-	-	-	-	-	-	110.3	1.9
1988	-	-	-	-	-	-	-	-	-	-	111.9	1.5	-	-	-	-	-	-	-	-	-	-	113.8	1.7
1989	-	-	-	-	-	-	-	-	-	-	116.7	2.5	-	-	-	-	-	-	-	-	-	-	119.6	2.5
1990	-	-	-	-	-	-	-	-	-	-	124.2	3.8	-	-	-	-	-	-	-	-	-	-	129.4	4.2
1991	-	-	-	-	-	-	-	-	-	-	133.0	2.8	-	-	-	-	-	-	-	-	-	-	135.2	1.7
1992	-	-	-	-	-	-	-	-	-	-	137.8	1.9	-	-	-	-	-	-	-	-	-	-	140.2	1.7
1993	-	-	-	-	-	-	-	-	-	-	141.9	1.2	-	-	-	-	-	-	-	-	-	-	143.9	1.4
1994	-	-	-	-	-	-	-	-	-	-	146.4	1.7	-	-	-	-	-	-	-	-	-	-	149.2	1.9
1995	-	-	-	-	-	-	-	-	-	-	151.2	1.3	-	-	-	-	-	-	-	-	-	-	153.3	1.4
1996	-	-	-	-	-	-	-	-	-	-	155.6	1.5	-	-	-	-	-	-	-	-	-	-	159.4	2.4
1997	-	-	-	-	-	-	-	-	-	-	-	-	-	-	-	-	-	-	-	-	-	-	165.0	3.5
1998	-	-	166.5	0.9	-	-	166.4	-0.1	-	-	167.5	0.7	-	-	168.5	0.6	-	-	169.3	0.5	-	-	169.4	0.1
1999	-	-	170.6	0.7	-	-	172.2	0.9	-	-	172.7	0.3	-	-	173.4	0.4	-	-	174.7	0.7	-	-	174.4	-0.2
2000	-	-	176.1	1.0	-	-	177.8	1.0	-	-	179.2	0.8	-	-	180.3	0.6	-	-	182.1	1.0	-	-	181.5	-0.3
2001	-	-	184.0	1.4	-	-	184.2	0.1	-	-	186.3	1.1	-	-	186.8	0.3	-	-	187.9	0.6	-	-	186.1	-1.0

Source: U.S. Department of Labor, Bureau of Labor Statistics, Division of Consumer Prices and Price Indexes. - indicates no data collected for period.

Seattle-Tacoma-Bremerton, WA
Consumer Price Index - Urban Wage Earners
Base 1982-1984 = 100
All Items

For 1914-2001. Columns headed % show percentile change in the index from the previous period for which an index is available.

Year	Jan Index	%	Feb Index	%	Mar Index	%	Apr Index	%	May Index	%	Jun Index	%	Jul Index	%	Aug Index	%	Sep Index	%	Oct Index	%	Nov Index	%	Dec Index	%
1914	-		-		-		-		-		-		-		-		-		-		-		9.4	-
1915	-		-		-		-		-		-		-		-		-		-		-		9.3	-1.1
1916	-		-		-		-		-		-		-		-		-		-		-		10.0	7.5
1917	-		-		-		-		-		-		-		-		-		-		-		12.1	21.0
1918	-		-		-		-		-		-		-		-		-		-		-		15.8	30.6
1919	-		-		-		-		-		16.5	4.4	-		-		-		-		-		18.7	13.3
1920	-		-		-		-		-		20.2	8.0	-		-		-		-		-		18.4	-8.9
1921	-		-		-		-		17.2	-6.5	-		-		-		16.7	-2.9	-		-		16.4	-1.8
1922	-		-		16.1	-1.8	-		-		16.0	-0.6	-		-		15.9	-0.6	-		-		15.9	0.0
1923	-		-		15.5	-2.5	-		-		15.9	2.6	-		-		16.1	1.3	-		-		16.0	-0.6
1924	-		-		15.9	-0.6	-		-		16.0	0.6	-		-		15.9	-0.6	-		-		16.0	0.6
1925	-		-		-		-		-		16.4	2.5	-		-		-		-		-		16.5	0.6
1926	-		-		-		-		-		16.3	-1.2	-		-		-		-		-		16.1	-1.2
1927	-		-		-		-		-		16.3	1.2	-		-		-		-		-		15.8	-3.1
1928	-		-		-		-		-		15.7	-0.6	-		-		-		-		-		15.8	0.6
1929	-		-		-		-		-		15.9	0.6	-		-		-		-		-		16.0	0.6
1930	-		-		-		-		-		15.9	-0.6	-		-		-		-		-		14.8	-6.9
1931	-		-		-		-		-		14.3	-3.4	-		-		-		-		-		13.8	-3.5
1932	-		-		-		-		-		13.0	-5.8	-		-		-		-		-		12.4	-4.6
1933	-		-		-		-		-		12.3	-0.8	-		-		-		-		-		12.4	0.8
1934	-		-		-		-		-		12.5	0.8	-		-		-		-		12.8	2.4	-	
1935	-		-		13.0	1.6	-		-		-		12.8	-1.5	-		-		12.8	0.0	-		-	
1936	13.0	1.6	-		-		12.9	-0.8	-		-		13.0	0.8	-		13.2	1.5	-		-		13.3	0.8
1937	-		-		13.6	2.3	-		-		13.7	0.7	-		-		13.9	1.5	-		-		13.8	-0.7
1938	-		-		13.7	-0.7	-		-		13.5	-1.5	-		-		13.5	0.0	-		-		13.5	0.0
1939	-		-		13.5	0.0	-		-		13.5	0.0	-		-		13.7	1.5	-		-		13.5	-1.5
1940	-		-		13.6	0.7	-		-		13.6	0.0	-		-		13.6	0.0	13.6	0.0	13.6	0.0	13.6	0.0
1941	13.7	0.7	13.7	0.0	13.8	0.7	13.9	0.7	14.2	2.2	14.3	0.7	14.4	0.7	14.5	0.7	14.9	2.8	15.1	1.3	15.1	0.0	15.3	1.3
1942	15.6	2.0	15.7	0.6	16.0	1.9	16.1	0.6	16.2	0.6	15.9	-1.9	16.0	0.6	16.3	1.9	16.5	1.2	16.6	0.6	16.7	0.6	16.8	0.6
1943	16.9	0.6	16.9	0.0	17.0	0.6	17.2	1.2	17.4	1.2	17.2	-1.1	17.0	-1.2	16.9	-0.6	17.2	1.8	17.2	0.0	17.3	0.6	17.3	0.0
1944	17.3	0.0	17.2	-0.6	17.2	0.0	17.2	0.0	17.4	1.2	17.3	-0.6	17.4	0.6	17.4	0.0	17.5	0.6	17.6	0.6	17.5	-0.6	17.6	0.6
1945	17.6	0.0	17.6	0.0	17.7	0.6	17.7	0.0	17.8	0.6	17.8	0.0	17.8	0.0	17.9	0.6	17.8	-0.6	17.8	0.0	17.9	0.6	18.1	1.1
1946	18.0	-0.6	18.0	0.0	18.0	0.0	18.1	0.6	18.2	0.6	18.4	1.1	19.3	4.9	19.5	1.0	19.9	2.1	20.4	2.5	20.9	2.5	21.1	1.0
1947	20.9	-0.9	20.9	0.0	21.3	1.9	21.4	0.5	21.3	-0.5	21.3	0.0	-		21.8	2.3	-		-		22.4	2.8	-	
1948	-		23.0	2.7	-		-		23.5	2.2	-		-		23.8	1.3	-		-		23.6	-0.8	-	
1949	-		23.6	0.0	-		-		23.4	-0.8	-		-		23.2	-0.9	-		-		23.3	0.4	-	
1950	-		23.3	0.0	-		-		23.3	0.0	-		-		23.7	1.7	-		-		24.4	3.0	-	
1951	-		25.2	3.3	-		-		25.6	1.6	-		-		25.5	-0.4	-		-		26.0	2.0	-	
1952	-		26.1	0.4	-		-		26.2	0.4	-		-		26.2	0.0	-		-		26.4	0.8	-	
1953	-		26.2	-0.8	-		-		26.5	1.1	-		-		26.7	0.8	-		-		26.6	-0.4	-	
1954	-		26.5	-0.4	-		-		26.5	0.0	-		-		26.5	0.0	-		-		26.4	-0.4	-	
1955	-		26.5	0.4	-		-		26.7	0.8	-		-		26.6	-0.4	-		-		26.8	0.8	-	
1956	-		26.5	-1.1	-		-		26.7	0.8	-		-		27.1	1.5	-		-		27.4	1.1	-	
1957	-		27.9	1.8	-		-		28.0	0.4	-		-		28.2	0.7	-		-		28.3	0.4	-	
1958	-		28.5	0.7	-		-		28.8	1.1	-		-		28.8	0.0	-		-		28.8	0.0	-	
1959	-		29.0	0.7	-		-		29.2	0.7	-		-		29.4	0.7	-		-		29.5	0.3	-	

[Continued]

Seattle-Tacoma-Bremerton, WA
Consumer Price Index - Urban Wage Earners
Base 1982-1984 = 100
All Items
[Continued]

For 1914-2001. Columns headed % show percentile change in the index from the previous period for which an index is available.

Year	Jan Index	%	Feb Index	%	Mar Index	%	Apr Index	%	May Index	%	Jun Index	%	Jul Index	%	Aug Index	%	Sep Index	%	Oct Index	%	Nov Index	%	Dec Index	%
1960	-	-	29.4	-0.3	-	-	-	-	29.6	0.7	-	-	-	-	29.6	0.0	-	-	-	-	29.8	0.7	-	-
1961	-	-	29.9	0.3	-	-	-	-	30.1	0.7	-	-	-	-	30.1	0.0	-	-	-	-	30.3	0.7	-	-
1962	-	-	30.4	0.3	-	-	-	-	30.5	0.3	-	-	-	-	30.6	0.3	-	-	-	-	30.7	0.3	-	-
1963	-	-	30.7	0.0	-	-	-	-	30.8	0.3	-	-	-	-	31.3	1.6	-	-	-	-	31.4	0.3	-	-
1964	-	-	31.4	0.0	-	-	-	-	31.3	-0.3	-	-	-	-	31.7	1.3	-	-	-	-	31.6	-0.3	-	-
1965	-	-	31.5	-0.3	-	-	-	-	31.8	1.0	-	-	-	-	32.0	0.6	-	-	-	-	32.1	0.3	-	-
1966	-	-	32.3	0.6	-	-	-	-	32.6	0.9	-	-	-	-	32.8	0.6	-	-	-	-	33.2	1.2	-	-
1967	-	-	33.2	0.0	-	-	-	-	33.5	0.9	-	-	-	-	33.9	1.2	-	-	-	-	34.2	0.9	-	-
1968	-	-	34.5	0.9	-	-	-	-	34.8	0.9	-	-	-	-	35.4	1.7	-	-	-	-	35.7	0.8	-	-
1969	-	-	36.1	1.1	-	-	-	-	36.6	1.4	-	-	-	-	37.2	1.6	-	-	-	-	37.3	0.3	-	-
1970	-	-	37.9	1.6	-	-	-	-	38.4	1.3	-	-	-	-	38.6	0.5	-	-	-	-	38.7	0.3	-	-
1971	-	-	38.6	-0.3	-	-	-	-	38.9	0.8	-	-	-	-	39.6	1.8	-	-	-	-	39.6	0.0	-	-
1972	-	-	40.1	1.3	-	-	-	-	40.1	0.0	-	-	-	-	40.4	0.7	-	-	-	-	40.9	1.2	-	-
1973	-	-	41.5	1.5	-	-	-	-	42.6	2.7	-	-	-	-	43.4	1.9	-	-	-	-	44.3	2.1	-	-
1974	-	-	45.8	3.4	-	-	-	-	47.0	2.6	-	-	-	-	48.2	2.6	-	-	-	-	49.9	3.5	-	-
1975	-	-	51.2	2.6	-	-	-	-	52.1	1.8	-	-	-	-	53.0	1.7	-	-	-	-	53.8	1.5	-	-
1976	-	-	54.5	1.3	-	-	-	-	54.8	0.6	-	-	-	-	55.9	2.0	-	-	-	-	56.6	1.3	-	-
1977	-	-	57.8	2.1	-	-	-	-	59.4	2.8	-	-	-	-	60.8	2.4	-	-	-	-	61.5	1.2	-	-
1978	62.0	0.8	-	-	63.0	1.6	-	-	64.9	3.0	-	-	65.4	0.8	-	-	67.3	2.9	-	-	68.1	1.2	-	-
1979	67.6	-0.7	-	-	69.4	2.7	-	-	71.1	2.4	-	-	72.8	2.4	-	-	74.5	2.3	-	-	76.0	2.0	-	-
1980	78.8	3.7	-	-	81.4	3.3	-	-	83.2	2.2	-	-	84.8	1.9	-	-	85.8	1.2	-	-	87.5	2.0	-	-
1981	88.4	1.0	-	-	90.3	2.1	-	-	91.5	1.3	-	-	93.7	2.4	-	-	95.9	2.3	-	-	96.3	0.4	-	-
1982	98.4	2.2	-	-	97.6	-0.8	-	-	100.2	2.7	-	-	98.8	-1.4	-	-	100.6	1.8	-	-	99.2	-1.4	-	-
1983	98.2	-1.0	-	-	98.0	-0.2	-	-	97.9	-0.1	-	-	98.5	0.6	-	-	99.7	1.2	-	-	100.1	0.4	-	-
1984	100.2	0.1	-	-	101.1	0.9	-	-	102.1	1.0	-	-	102.2	0.1	-	-	102.9	0.7	-	-	103.0	0.1	-	-
1985	103.4	0.4	-	-	104.2	0.8	-	-	104.0	-0.2	-	-	104.2	0.2	-	-	104.1	-0.1	-	-	104.8	0.7	-	-
1986	105.7	0.9	-	-	105.0	-0.7	-	-	104.3	-0.7	-	-	104.6	0.3	-	-	105.3	0.7	-	-	105.1	-0.2	105.1	0.0
1987	-	-	-	-	-	-	-	-	-	-	106.4	1.2	-	-	-	-	-	-	-	-	-	-	108.4	1.9
1988	-	-	-	-	-	-	-	-	-	-	109.9	1.4	-	-	-	-	-	-	-	-	-	-	112.0	1.9
1989	-	-	-	-	-	-	-	-	-	-	114.7	2.4	-	-	-	-	-	-	-	-	-	-	117.6	2.5
1990	-	-	-	-	-	-	-	-	-	-	122.0	3.7	-	-	-	-	-	-	-	-	-	-	126.9	4.0
1991	-	-	-	-	-	-	-	-	-	-	130.2	2.6	-	-	-	-	-	-	-	-	-	-	132.4	1.7
1992	-	-	-	-	-	-	-	-	-	-	134.8	1.8	-	-	-	-	-	-	-	-	-	-	137.2	1.8
1993	-	-	-	-	-	-	-	-	-	-	138.9	1.2	-	-	-	-	-	-	-	-	-	-	141.1	1.6
1994	-	-	-	-	-	-	-	-	-	-	143.7	1.8	-	-	-	-	-	-	-	-	-	-	146.5	1.9
1995	-	-	-	-	-	-	-	-	-	-	148.3	1.2	-	-	-	-	-	-	-	-	-	-	150.4	1.4
1996	-	-	-	-	-	-	-	-	-	-	152.6	1.5	-	-	-	-	-	-	-	-	-	-	155.9	2.2
1997	-	-	-	-	-	-	-	-	-	-	-	-	-	-	-	-	-	-	-	-	-	-	160.6	3.0
1998	-	-	162.2	1.0	-	-	161.9	-0.2	-	-	162.8	0.6	-	-	163.8	0.6	-	-	164.9	0.7	-	-	164.9	0.0
1999	-	-	166.0	0.7	-	-	167.8	1.1	-	-	168.0	0.1	-	-	168.8	0.5	-	-	170.2	0.8	-	-	170.1	-0.1
2000	-	-	171.6	0.9	-	-	173.3	1.0	-	-	174.5	0.7	-	-	175.4	0.5	-	-	177.5	1.2	-	-	177.0	-0.3
2001	-	-	179.2	1.2	-	-	179.4	0.1	-	-	181.3	1.1	-	-	181.5	0.1	-	-	183.1	0.9	-	-	181.1	-1.1

Source: U.S. Department of Labor, Bureau of Labor Statistics, Division of Consumer Prices and Price Indexes. - indicates no data collected for period.

Seattle-Tacoma-Bremerton, WA
Consumer Price Index - All Urban Consumers
Base 1982-1984 = 100
Food and Beverages

For 1975-2001. Columns headed % show percentile change in the index from the previous period for which an index is available.

Year	Jan Index	%	Feb Index	%	Mar Index	%	Apr Index	%	May Index	%	Jun Index	%	Jul Index	%	Aug Index	%	Sep Index	%	Oct Index	%	Nov Index	%	Dec Index	%
1975	-	-	-	-	-	-	-	-	-	-	-	-	-	-	-	-	-	-	-	-	60.8	-	-	-
1976	-	-	60.6	-0.3	-	-	-	-	60.8	0.3	-	-	-	-	61.8	1.6	-	-	-	-	61.8	0.0	-	-
1977	-	-	63.5	2.8	-	-	-	-	65.2	2.7	-	-	-	-	66.8	2.5	-	-	-	-	66.8	0.0	-	-
1978	67.1	0.4	-	-	69.2	3.1	-	-	72.5	4.8	-	-	70.9	-2.2	-	-	71.9	1.4	-	-	72.5	0.8	-	-
1979	74.1	2.2	-	-	77.5	4.6	-	-	78.8	1.7	-	-	78.8	0.0	-	-	78.5	-0.4	-	-	80.1	2.0	-	-
1980	81.4	1.6	-	-	82.5	1.4	-	-	83.6	1.3	-	-	84.4	1.0	-	-	86.4	2.4	-	-	87.2	0.9	-	-
1981	88.7	1.7	-	-	90.4	1.9	-	-	90.7	0.3	-	-	92.0	1.4	-	-	93.1	1.2	-	-	93.1	0.0	-	-
1982	95.1	2.1	-	-	94.6	-0.5	-	-	99.6	5.3	-	-	100.0	0.4	-	-	99.8	-0.2	-	-	99.5	-0.3	-	-
1983	100.0	0.5	-	-	101.5	1.5	-	-	102.4	0.9	-	-	98.9	-3.4	-	-	98.7	-0.2	-	-	99.0	0.3	-	-
1984	100.8	1.8	-	-	101.3	0.5	-	-	101.4	0.1	-	-	101.7	0.3	-	-	102.1	0.4	-	-	102.1	0.0	-	-
1985	101.7	-0.4	-	-	103.3	1.6	-	-	103.3	0.0	-	-	103.6	0.3	-	-	103.5	-0.1	-	-	103.3	-0.2	-	-
1986	104.9	1.5	-	-	105.9	1.0	-	-	107.1	1.1	-	-	106.7	-0.4	-	-	107.5	0.7	-	-	107.9	0.4	108.1	0.2
1987	-	-	-	-	-	-	-	-	-	-	111.7	3.3	-	-	-	-	-	-	-	-	-	-	112.2	0.4
1988	-	-	-	-	-	-	-	-	-	-	114.0	1.6	-	-	-	-	-	-	-	-	-	-	115.8	1.6
1989	-	-	-	-	-	-	-	-	-	-	121.7	5.1	-	-	-	-	-	-	-	-	-	-	124.4	2.2
1990	-	-	-	-	-	-	-	-	-	-	131.8	5.9	-	-	-	-	-	-	-	-	-	-	134.2	1.8
1991	-	-	-	-	-	-	-	-	-	-	141.1	5.1	-	-	-	-	-	-	-	-	-	-	140.2	-0.6
1992	-	-	-	-	-	-	-	-	-	-	141.1	0.6	-	-	-	-	-	-	-	-	-	-	141.1	0.0
1993	-	-	-	-	-	-	-	-	-	-	142.8	1.2	-	-	-	-	-	-	-	-	-	-	142.1	-0.5
1994	-	-	-	-	-	-	-	-	-	-	145.3	2.3	-	-	-	-	-	-	-	-	-	-	148.5	2.2
1995	-	-	-	-	-	-	-	-	-	-	151.9	2.3	-	-	-	-	-	-	-	-	-	-	152.1	0.1
1996	-	-	-	-	-	-	-	-	-	-	153.5	0.9	-	-	-	-	-	-	-	-	-	-	157.5	2.6
1997	-	-	-	-	-	-	-	-	-	-	-	-	-	-	-	-	-	-	-	-	-	-	161.5	2.5
1998	-	-	165.6	2.5	-	-	162.9	-1.6	-	-	163.9	0.6	-	-	165.6	1.0	-	-	167.7	1.3	-	-	167.3	-0.2
1999	-	-	169.5	1.3	-	-	168.8	-0.4	-	-	168.6	-0.1	-	-	170.0	0.8	-	-	170.6	0.4	-	-	170.7	0.1
2000	-	-	171.5	0.5	-	-	172.9	0.8	-	-	173.1	0.1	-	-	173.8	0.4	-	-	176.8	1.7	-	-	175.6	-0.7
2001	-	-	180.1	2.6	-	-	179.9	-0.1	-	-	182.9	1.7	-	-	180.6	-1.3	-	-	183.4	1.6	-	-	181.6	-1.0

Source: U.S. Department of Labor, Bureau of Labor Statistics, Division of Consumer Prices and Price Indexes. - indicates no data collected for period.

Seattle-Tacoma-Bremerton, WA
Consumer Price Index - Urban Wage Earners
Base 1982-1984 = 100
Food and Beverages

For 1975-2001. Columns headed % show percentile change in the index from the previous period for which an index is available.

Year	Jan Index	%	Feb Index	%	Mar Index	%	Apr Index	%	May Index	%	Jun Index	%	Jul Index	%	Aug Index	%	Sep Index	%	Oct Index	%	Nov Index	%	Dec Index	%
1975	-	-	-	-	-	-	-	-	-	-	-	-	-	-	-	-	-	-	-	-	61.1	-	-	-
1976	-	-	60.9	-0.3	-	-	-	-	61.1	0.3	-	-	-	-	62.1	1.6	-	-	-	-	62.1	0.0	-	-
1977	-	-	63.8	2.7	-	-	-	-	65.5	2.7	-	-	-	-	67.1	2.4	-	-	-	-	67.1	0.0	-	-
1978	67.7	0.9	-	-	69.8	3.1	-	-	72.1	3.3	-	-	71.0	-1.5	-	-	72.3	1.8	-	-	72.7	0.6	-	-
1979	74.4	2.3	-	-	77.8	4.6	-	-	78.8	1.3	-	-	78.7	-0.1	-	-	79.0	0.4	-	-	79.3	0.4	-	-
1980	81.4	2.6	-	-	82.6	1.5	-	-	83.7	1.3	-	-	84.7	1.2	-	-	86.6	2.2	-	-	87.6	1.2	-	-
1981	89.6	2.3	-	-	91.2	1.8	-	-	91.5	0.3	-	-	92.5	1.1	-	-	93.5	1.1	-	-	93.1	-0.4	-	-
1982	95.1	2.1	-	-	94.7	-0.4	-	-	99.5	5.1	-	-	99.9	0.4	-	-	99.7	-0.2	-	-	99.5	-0.2	-	-
1983	100.0	0.5	-	-	101.6	1.6	-	-	102.5	0.9	-	-	98.9	-3.5	-	-	98.6	-0.3	-	-	99.0	0.4	-	-
1984	100.7	1.7	-	-	101.3	0.6	-	-	101.4	0.1	-	-	101.6	0.2	-	-	102.2	0.6	-	-	102.2	0.0	-	-
1985	101.7	-0.5	-	-	103.4	1.7	-	-	103.3	-0.1	-	-	103.6	0.3	-	-	103.7	0.1	-	-	103.3	-0.4	-	-
1986	104.9	1.5	-	-	105.8	0.9	-	-	106.9	1.0	-	-	106.6	-0.3	-	-	107.2	0.6	-	-	107.6	0.4	107.9	0.3
1987	-	-	-	-	-	-	-	-	-	-	111.3	3.2	-	-	-	-	-	-	-	-	-	-	111.8	0.4
1988	-	-	-	-	-	-	-	-	-	-	113.6	1.6	-	-	-	-	-	-	-	-	-	-	115.6	1.8
1989	-	-	-	-	-	-	-	-	-	-	121.3	4.9	-	-	-	-	-	-	-	-	-	-	124.1	2.3
1990	-	-	-	-	-	-	-	-	-	-	131.5	6.0	-	-	-	-	-	-	-	-	-	-	134.0	1.9
1991	-	-	-	-	-	-	-	-	-	-	140.5	4.9	-	-	-	-	-	-	-	-	-	-	140.0	-0.4
1992	-	-	-	-	-	-	-	-	-	-	140.5	0.4	-	-	-	-	-	-	-	-	-	-	141.0	0.4
1993	-	-	-	-	-	-	-	-	-	-	142.4	1.0	-	-	-	-	-	-	-	-	-	-	142.5	0.1
1994	-	-	-	-	-	-	-	-	-	-	145.2	1.9	-	-	-	-	-	-	-	-	-	-	147.9	1.9
1995	-	-	-	-	-	-	-	-	-	-	150.8	2.0	-	-	-	-	-	-	-	-	-	-	151.3	0.3
1996	-	-	-	-	-	-	-	-	-	-	152.7	0.9	-	-	-	-	-	-	-	-	-	-	156.4	2.4
1997	-	-	-	-	-	-	-	-	-	-	-	-	-	-	-	-	-	-	-	-	-	-	159.8	2.2
1998	-	-	164.3	2.8	-	-	161.5	-1.7	-	-	162.1	0.4	-	-	163.9	1.1	-	-	165.8	1.2	-	-	165.3	-0.3
1999	-	-	167.9	1.6	-	-	166.9	-0.6	-	-	166.6	-0.2	-	-	168.1	0.9	-	-	168.8	0.4	-	-	169.0	0.1
2000	-	-	169.8	0.5	-	-	171.2	0.8	-	-	171.2	0.0	-	-	171.9	0.4	-	-	174.9	1.7	-	-	173.8	-0.6
2001	-	-	178.6	2.8	-	-	178.3	-0.2	-	-	181.3	1.7	-	-	178.7	-1.4	-	-	181.6	1.6	-	-	179.8	-1.0

Source: U.S. Department of Labor, Bureau of Labor Statistics, Division of Consumer Prices and Price Indexes. - indicates no data collected for period.

Seattle-Tacoma-Bremerton, WA
Consumer Price Index - All Urban Consumers
Base 1982-1984 = 100
Housing

For 1975-2001. Columns headed % show percentile change in the index from the previous period for which an index is available.

Year	Jan Index	%	Feb Index	%	Mar Index	%	Apr Index	%	May Index	%	Jun Index	%	Jul Index	%	Aug Index	%	Sep Index	%	Oct Index	%	Nov Index	%	Dec Index	%
1975	-	-	-	-	-	-	-	-	-	-	-	-	-	-	-	-	-	-	-	-	48.9	-	-	-
1976	-	-	49.8	1.8	-	-	-	-	49.2	-1.2	-	-	-	-	50.7	3.0	-	-	-	-	51.5	1.6	-	-
1977	-	-	52.2	1.4	-	-	-	-	54.2	3.8	-	-	-	-	55.8	3.0	-	-	-	-	57.0	2.2	-	-
1978	57.5	0.9	-	-	58.7	2.1	-	-	60.9	3.7	-	-	61.6	1.1	-	-	64.5	4.7	-	-	65.5	1.6	-	-
1979	63.6	-2.9	-	-	64.8	1.9	-	-	66.3	2.3	-	-	68.4	3.2	-	-	70.3	2.8	-	-	72.1	2.6	-	-
1980	76.3	5.8	-	-	79.2	3.8	-	-	82.0	3.5	-	-	84.5	3.0	-	-	84.8	0.4	-	-	86.7	2.2	-	-
1981	87.2	0.6	-	-	88.8	1.8	-	-	89.8	1.1	-	-	93.1	3.7	-	-	95.9	3.0	-	-	95.7	-0.2	-	-
1982	99.0	3.4	-	-	97.7	-1.3	-	-	101.1	3.5	-	-	96.6	-4.5	-	-	99.8	3.3	-	-	97.1	-2.7	-	-
1983	97.2	0.1	-	-	97.0	-0.2	-	-	97.7	0.7	-	-	99.2	1.5	-	-	100.0	0.8	-	-	100.2	0.2	-	-
1984	100.9	0.7	-	-	101.9	1.0	-	-	102.1	0.2	-	-	102.6	0.5	-	-	103.8	1.2	-	-	104.6	0.8	-	-
1985	105.2	0.6	-	-	105.4	0.2	-	-	105.3	-0.1	-	-	105.0	-0.3	-	-	104.8	-0.2	-	-	106.5	1.6	-	-
1986	107.7	1.1	-	-	107.0	-0.6	-	-	106.2	-0.7	-	-	105.9	-0.3	-	-	107.3	1.3	-	-	107.1	-0.2	106.6	-0.5
1987	-	-	-	-	-	-	-	-	-	-	107.2	0.6	-	-	-	-	-	-	-	-	-	-	109.1	1.8
1988	-	-	-	-	-	-	-	-	-	-	111.0	1.7	-	-	-	-	-	-	-	-	-	-	112.9	1.7
1989	-	-	-	-	-	-	-	-	-	-	114.6	1.5	-	-	-	-	-	-	-	-	-	-	118.1	3.1
1990	-	-	-	-	-	-	-	-	-	-	122.0	3.3	-	-	-	-	-	-	-	-	-	-	128.9	5.7
1991	-	-	-	-	-	-	-	-	-	-	132.3	2.6	-	-	-	-	-	-	-	-	-	-	135.8	2.6
1992	-	-	-	-	-	-	-	-	-	-	138.3	1.8	-	-	-	-	-	-	-	-	-	-	140.2	1.4
1993	-	-	-	-	-	-	-	-	-	-	142.0	1.3	-	-	-	-	-	-	-	-	-	-	144.9	2.0
1994	-	-	-	-	-	-	-	-	-	-	147.0	1.4	-	-	-	-	-	-	-	-	-	-	148.9	1.3
1995	-	-	-	-	-	-	-	-	-	-	150.5	1.1	-	-	-	-	-	-	-	-	-	-	152.5	1.3
1996	-	-	-	-	-	-	-	-	-	-	154.6	1.4	-	-	-	-	-	-	-	-	-	-	159.2	3.0
1997	-	-	-	-	-	-	-	-	-	-	-	-	-	-	-	-	-	-	-	-	-	-	167.4	5.2
1998	-	-	168.0	0.4	-	-	169.5	0.9	-	-	171.4	1.1	-	-	171.5	0.1	-	-	172.8	0.8	-	-	174.2	0.8
1999	-	-	175.0	0.5	-	-	175.4	0.2	-	-	177.6	1.3	-	-	178.6	0.6	-	-	179.1	0.3	-	-	179.4	0.2
2000	-	-	181.6	1.2	-	-	182.5	0.5	-	-	185.1	1.4	-	-	186.1	0.5	-	-	187.8	0.9	-	-	187.8	0.0
2001	-	-	191.5	2.0	-	-	193.6	1.1	-	-	196.1	1.3	-	-	198.7	1.3	-	-	198.4	-0.2	-	-	198.2	-0.1

Source: U.S. Department of Labor, Bureau of Labor Statistics, Division of Consumer Prices and Price Indexes. - indicates no data collected for period.

Seattle-Tacoma-Bremerton, WA
Consumer Price Index - Urban Wage Earners
Base 1982-1984 = 100
Housing

For 1975-2001. Columns headed % show percentile change in the index from the previous period for which an index is available.

Year	Jan Index	%	Feb Index	%	Mar Index	%	Apr Index	%	May Index	%	Jun Index	%	Jul Index	%	Aug Index	%	Sep Index	%	Oct Index	%	Nov Index	%	Dec Index	%
1975	-	-	-	-	-	-	-	-	-	-	-	-	-	-	-	-	-	-	-	-	51.0	-	-	-
1976	-	-	51.9	1.8	-	-	-	-	51.4	-1.0	-	-	-	-	52.9	2.9	-	-	-	-	53.7	1.5	-	-
1977	-	-	54.5	1.5	-	-	-	-	56.6	3.9	-	-	-	-	58.3	3.0	-	-	-	-	59.5	2.1	-	-
1978	60.1	1.0	-	-	61.3	2.0	-	-	63.5	3.6	-	-	64.2	1.1	-	-	67.3	4.8	-	-	68.2	1.3	-	-
1979	66.1	-3.1	-	-	67.6	2.3	-	-	69.1	2.2	-	-	71.1	2.9	-	-	73.1	2.8	-	-	75.1	2.7	-	-
1980	79.5	5.9	-	-	82.3	3.5	-	-	85.4	3.8	-	-	87.8	2.8	-	-	88.0	0.2	-	-	90.0	2.3	-	-
1981	90.4	0.4	-	-	92.4	2.2	-	-	93.2	0.9	-	-	96.0	3.0	-	-	99.1	3.2	-	-	99.0	-0.1	-	-
1982	102.3	3.3	-	-	100.9	-1.4	-	-	104.5	3.6	-	-	99.7	-4.6	-	-	103.1	3.4	-	-	100.5	-2.5	-	-
1983	98.7	-1.8	-	-	97.9	-0.8	-	-	96.1	-1.8	-	-	96.4	0.3	-	-	97.9	1.6	-	-	98.7	0.8	-	-
1984	98.7	0.0	-	-	100.3	1.6	-	-	100.7	0.4	-	-	100.6	-0.1	-	-	101.8	1.2	-	-	101.4	-0.4	-	-
1985	102.1	0.7	-	-	102.4	0.3	-	-	102.0	-0.4	-	-	101.5	-0.5	-	-	101.4	-0.1	-	-	103.0	1.6	-	-
1986	104.1	1.1	-	-	103.5	-0.6	-	-	102.6	-0.9	-	-	102.5	-0.1	-	-	103.9	1.4	-	-	103.6	-0.3	103.2	-0.4
1987	-	-	-	-	-	-	-	-	-	-	103.7	0.5	-	-	-	-	-	-	-	-	-	-	105.2	1.4
1988	-	-	-	-	-	-	-	-	-	-	107.1	1.8	-	-	-	-	-	-	-	-	-	-	108.9	1.7
1989	-	-	-	-	-	-	-	-	-	-	110.3	1.3	-	-	-	-	-	-	-	-	-	-	113.5	2.9
1990	-	-	-	-	-	-	-	-	-	-	117.4	3.4	-	-	-	-	-	-	-	-	-	-	123.6	5.3
1991	-	-	-	-	-	-	-	-	-	-	126.7	2.5	-	-	-	-	-	-	-	-	-	-	130.1	2.7
1992	-	-	-	-	-	-	-	-	-	-	132.2	1.6	-	-	-	-	-	-	-	-	-	-	133.8	1.2
1993	-	-	-	-	-	-	-	-	-	-	135.7	1.4	-	-	-	-	-	-	-	-	-	-	138.4	2.0
1994	-	-	-	-	-	-	-	-	-	-	140.5	1.5	-	-	-	-	-	-	-	-	-	-	142.3	1.3
1995	-	-	-	-	-	-	-	-	-	-	143.6	0.9	-	-	-	-	-	-	-	-	-	-	145.5	1.3
1996	-	-	-	-	-	-	-	-	-	-	147.5	1.4	-	-	-	-	-	-	-	-	-	-	151.2	2.5
1997	-	-	-	-	-	-	-	-	-	-	-	-	-	-	-	-	-	-	-	-	-	-	158.6	4.9
1998	-	-	159.5	0.6	-	-	160.5	0.6	-	-	162.0	0.9	-	-	162.2	0.1	-	-	163.9	1.0	-	-	165.3	0.9
1999	-	-	166.2	0.5	-	-	166.3	0.1	-	-	168.1	1.1	-	-	168.7	0.4	-	-	169.7	0.6	-	-	170.4	0.4
2000	-	-	172.4	1.2	-	-	173.0	0.3	-	-	174.9	1.1	-	-	175.8	0.5	-	-	177.8	1.1	-	-	178.3	0.3
2001	-	-	181.9	2.0	-	-	183.4	0.8	-	-	185.5	1.1	-	-	187.8	1.2	-	-	188.5	0.4	-	-	188.6	0.1

Source: U.S. Department of Labor, Bureau of Labor Statistics, Division of Consumer Prices and Price Indexes. - indicates no data collected for period.

Seattle-Tacoma-Bremerton, WA
Consumer Price Index - All Urban Consumers
Base 1982-1984 = 100
Apparel

For 1952-2001. Columns headed % show percentile change in the index from the previous period for which an index is available.

Year	Jan Index	%	Feb Index	%	Mar Index	%	Apr Index	%	May Index	%	Jun Index	%	Jul Index	%	Aug Index	%	Sep Index	%	Oct Index	%	Nov Index	%	Dec Index	%
1952	-	-	-	-	-	-	-	-	-	-	-	-	-	-	-	-	-	-	-	-	43.9	-	-	-
1953	-	-	43.9	0.0	-	-	-	-	43.8	-0.2	-	-	-	-	44.1	0.7	-	-	-	-	44.0	-0.2	-	-
1954	-	-	43.5	-1.1	-	-	-	-	43.7	0.5	-	-	-	-	43.6	-0.2	-	-	-	-	43.5	-0.2	-	-
1955	-	-	43.7	0.5	-	-	-	-	43.4	-0.7	-	-	-	-	43.9	1.2	-	-	-	-	44.1	0.5	-	-
1956	-	-	43.8	-0.7	-	-	-	-	44.0	0.5	-	-	-	-	44.1	0.2	-	-	-	-	45.0	2.0	-	-
1957	-	-	44.8	-0.4	-	-	-	-	45.0	0.4	-	-	-	-	45.3	0.7	-	-	-	-	45.2	-0.2	-	-
1958	-	-	45.1	-0.2	-	-	-	-	45.1	0.0	-	-	-	-	44.8	-0.7	-	-	-	-	44.7	-0.2	-	-
1959	-	-	44.7	0.0	-	-	-	-	45.1	0.9	-	-	-	-	45.5	0.9	-	-	-	-	46.1	1.3	-	-
1960	-	-	46.0	-0.2	-	-	-	-	45.4	-1.3	-	-	-	-	45.8	0.9	-	-	-	-	46.6	1.7	-	-
1961	-	-	46.5	-0.2	-	-	-	-	46.7	0.4	-	-	-	-	46.2	-1.1	-	-	-	-	47.4	2.6	-	-
1962	-	-	47.2	-0.4	-	-	-	-	47.4	0.4	-	-	-	-	47.5	0.2	-	-	-	-	47.8	0.6	-	-
1963	-	-	48.2	0.8	-	-	-	-	47.7	-1.0	-	-	-	-	48.1	0.8	-	-	-	-	48.8	1.5	-	-
1964	-	-	48.9	0.2	-	-	-	-	49.1	0.4	-	-	-	-	48.1	-2.0	-	-	-	-	48.9	1.7	-	-
1965	-	-	48.8	-0.2	-	-	-	-	49.0	0.4	-	-	-	-	48.7	-0.6	-	-	-	-	49.7	2.1	-	-
1966	-	-	50.1	0.8	-	-	-	-	50.6	1.0	-	-	-	-	50.2	-0.8	-	-	-	-	51.0	1.6	-	-
1967	-	-	51.4	0.8	-	-	-	-	52.2	1.6	-	-	-	-	52.3	0.2	-	-	-	-	53.1	1.5	-	-
1968	-	-	52.9	-0.4	-	-	-	-	53.5	1.1	-	-	-	-	53.6	0.2	-	-	-	-	54.6	1.9	-	-
1969	-	-	54.7	0.2	-	-	-	-	55.7	1.8	-	-	-	-	55.7	0.0	-	-	-	-	57.2	2.7	-	-
1970	-	-	57.1	-0.2	-	-	-	-	58.1	1.8	-	-	-	-	58.0	-0.2	-	-	-	-	60.0	3.4	-	-
1971	-	-	59.5	-0.8	-	-	-	-	61.1	2.7	-	-	-	-	60.3	-1.3	-	-	-	-	61.4	1.8	-	-
1972	-	-	61.0	-0.7	-	-	-	-	61.0	0.0	-	-	-	-	60.8	-0.3	-	-	-	-	62.6	3.0	-	-
1973	-	-	62.9	0.5	-	-	-	-	64.3	2.2	-	-	-	-	64.1	-0.3	-	-	-	-	65.5	2.2	-	-
1974	-	-	65.8	0.5	-	-	-	-	67.5	2.6	-	-	-	-	68.6	1.6	-	-	-	-	71.1	3.6	-	-
1975	-	-	71.8	1.0	-	-	-	-	72.9	1.5	-	-	-	-	72.5	-0.5	-	-	-	-	73.4	1.2	-	-
1976	-	-	75.4	2.7	-	-	-	-	77.4	2.7	-	-	-	-	76.9	-0.6	-	-	-	-	77.9	1.3	-	-
1977	-	-	78.5	0.8	-	-	-	-	79.9	1.8	-	-	-	-	80.6	0.9	-	-	-	-	82.4	2.2	-	-
1978	81.6	-1.0	-	-	81.4	-0.2	-	-	82.8	1.7	-	-	81.5	-1.6	-	-	84.2	3.3	-	-	84.0	-0.2	-	-
1979	82.8	-1.4	-	-	86.1	4.0	-	-	87.6	1.7	-	-	86.9	-0.8	-	-	89.4	2.9	-	-	92.7	3.7	-	-
1980	90.6	-2.3	-	-	93.7	3.4	-	-	92.3	-1.5	-	-	94.5	2.4	-	-	98.8	4.6	-	-	98.5	-0.3	-	-
1981	96.8	-1.7	-	-	98.0	1.2	-	-	98.8	0.8	-	-	99.4	0.6	-	-	100.4	1.0	-	-	100.6	0.2	-	-
1982	97.7	-2.9	-	-	99.9	2.3	-	-	99.3	-0.6	-	-	97.5	-1.8	-	-	102.9	5.5	-	-	100.5	-2.3	-	-
1983	96.9	-3.6	-	-	101.6	4.9	-	-	103.1	1.5	-	-	101.6	-1.5	-	-	103.6	2.0	-	-	100.3	-3.2	-	-
1984	97.3	-3.0	-	-	100.2	3.0	-	-	98.2	-2.0	-	-	97.8	-0.4	-	-	101.6	3.9	-	-	100.4	-1.2	-	-
1985	96.9	-3.5	-	-	104.6	7.9	-	-	100.6	-3.8	-	-	100.8	0.2	-	-	107.8	6.9	-	-	103.7	-3.8	-	-
1986	99.2	-4.3	-	-	104.0	4.8	-	-	103.9	-0.1	-	-	103.9	0.0	-	-	108.3	4.2	-	-	108.6	0.3	105.1	-3.2
1987	-	-	-	-	-	-	-	-	-	-	107.0	1.8	-	-	-	-	-	-	-	-	-	-	111.9	4.6
1988	-	-	-	-	-	-	-	-	-	-	115.7	3.4	-	-	-	-	-	-	-	-	-	-	115.6	-0.1
1989	-	-	-	-	-	-	-	-	-	-	110.4	-4.5	-	-	-	-	-	-	-	-	-	-	104.4	-5.4
1990	-	-	-	-	-	-	-	-	-	-	110.4	5.7	-	-	-	-	-	-	-	-	-	-	113.6	2.9
1991	-	-	-	-	-	-	-	-	-	-	112.3	-1.1	-	-	-	-	-	-	-	-	-	-	114.4	1.9
1992	-	-	-	-	-	-	-	-	-	-	118.5	3.6	-	-	-	-	-	-	-	-	-	-	118.9	0.3
1993	-	-	-	-	-	-	-	-	-	-	115.5	-2.9	-	-	-	-	-	-	-	-	-	-	115.5	0.0
1994	-	-	-	-	-	-	-	-	-	-	122.5	6.1	-	-	-	-	-	-	-	-	-	-	119.3	-2.6
1995	-	-	-	-	-	-	-	-	-	-	120.3	0.8	-	-	-	-	-	-	-	-	-	-	122.2	1.6
1996	-	-	-	-	-	-	-	-	-	-	125.2	2.5	-	-	-	-	-	-	-	-	-	-	126.3	0.9
1997	-	-	-	-	-	-	-	-	-	-	-	-	-	-	-	-	-	-	-	-	-	-	123.5	-2.2

[Continued]

Seattle-Tacoma-Bremerton, WA
Consumer Price Index - All Urban Consumers
Base 1982-1984 = 100
Apparel
[Continued]

For 1952-2001. Columns headed % show percentile change in the index from the previous period for which an index is available.

Year	Jan Index	%	Feb Index	%	Mar Index	%	Apr Index	%	May Index	%	Jun Index	%	Jul Index	%	Aug Index	%	Sep Index	%	Oct Index	%	Nov Index	%	Dec Index	%
1998	-	-	126.9	2.8	-	-	126.2	-0.6	-	-	122.8	-2.7	-	-	129.2	5.2	-	-	129.8	0.5	-	-	124.5	-4.1
1999	-	-	126.1	1.3	-	-	129.0	2.3	-	-	124.3	-3.6	-	-	120.3	-3.2	-	-	128.7	7.0	-	-	124.5	-3.3
2000	-	-	127.4	2.3	-	-	131.1	2.9	-	-	125.6	-4.2	-	-	123.5	-1.7	-	-	130.6	5.7	-	-	120.8	-7.5
2001	-	-	128.3	6.2	-	-	121.5	-5.3	-	-	122.8	1.1	-	-	126.3	2.9	-	-	126.4	0.1	-	-	119.8	-5.2

Source: U.S. Department of Labor, Bureau of Labor Statistics, Division of Consumer Prices and Price Indexes. - indicates no data collected for period.

Seattle-Tacoma-Bremerton, WA
Consumer Price Index - Urban Wage Earners
Base 1982-1984 = 100
Apparel

For 1952-2001. Columns headed % show percentile change in the index from the previous period for which an index is available.

Year	Jan Index	%	Feb Index	%	Mar Index	%	Apr Index	%	May Index	%	Jun Index	%	Jul Index	%	Aug Index	%	Sep Index	%	Oct Index	%	Nov Index	%	Dec Index	%
1952	-	-	-	-	-	-	-	-	-	-	-	-	-	-	-	-	-	-	-	-	44.4	-	-	-
1953	-	-	44.4	0.0	-	-	-	-	44.3	-0.2	-	-	-	-	44.6	0.7	-	-	-	-	44.5	-0.2	-	-
1954	-	-	44.1	-0.9	-	-	-	-	44.2	0.2	-	-	-	-	44.1	-0.2	-	-	-	-	44.0	-0.2	-	-
1955	-	-	44.2	0.5	-	-	-	-	43.9	-0.7	-	-	-	-	44.4	1.1	-	-	-	-	44.6	0.5	-	-
1956	-	-	44.3	-0.7	-	-	-	-	44.5	0.5	-	-	-	-	44.6	0.2	-	-	-	-	45.5	2.0	-	-
1957	-	-	45.3	-0.4	-	-	-	-	45.5	0.4	-	-	-	-	45.8	0.7	-	-	-	-	45.7	-0.2	-	-
1958	-	-	45.6	-0.2	-	-	-	-	45.6	0.0	-	-	-	-	45.3	-0.7	-	-	-	-	45.2	-0.2	-	-
1959	-	-	45.3	0.2	-	-	-	-	45.6	0.7	-	-	-	-	46.1	1.1	-	-	-	-	46.6	1.1	-	-
1960	-	-	46.5	-0.2	-	-	-	-	46.0	-1.1	-	-	-	-	46.4	0.9	-	-	-	-	47.1	1.5	-	-
1961	-	-	47.0	-0.2	-	-	-	-	47.2	0.4	-	-	-	-	46.7	-1.1	-	-	-	-	47.9	2.6	-	-
1962	-	-	47.8	-0.2	-	-	-	-	48.0	0.4	-	-	-	-	48.0	0.0	-	-	-	-	48.4	0.8	-	-
1963	-	-	48.8	0.8	-	-	-	-	48.3	-1.0	-	-	-	-	48.7	0.8	-	-	-	-	49.4	1.4	-	-
1964	-	-	49.5	0.2	-	-	-	-	49.7	0.4	-	-	-	-	48.7	-2.0	-	-	-	-	49.5	1.6	-	-
1965	-	-	49.4	-0.2	-	-	-	-	49.6	0.4	-	-	-	-	49.2	-0.8	-	-	-	-	50.2	2.0	-	-
1966	-	-	50.7	1.0	-	-	-	-	51.2	1.0	-	-	-	-	50.8	-0.8	-	-	-	-	51.6	1.6	-	-
1967	-	-	52.0	0.8	-	-	-	-	52.8	1.5	-	-	-	-	52.9	0.2	-	-	-	-	53.7	1.5	-	-
1968	-	-	53.5	-0.4	-	-	-	-	54.2	1.3	-	-	-	-	54.3	0.2	-	-	-	-	55.3	1.8	-	-
1969	-	-	55.4	0.2	-	-	-	-	56.4	1.8	-	-	-	-	56.4	0.0	-	-	-	-	57.9	2.7	-	-
1970	-	-	57.8	-0.2	-	-	-	-	58.8	1.7	-	-	-	-	58.7	-0.2	-	-	-	-	60.8	3.6	-	-
1971	-	-	60.2	-1.0	-	-	-	-	61.9	2.8	-	-	-	-	61.0	-1.5	-	-	-	-	62.1	1.8	-	-
1972	-	-	61.8	-0.5	-	-	-	-	61.7	-0.2	-	-	-	-	61.5	-0.3	-	-	-	-	63.3	2.9	-	-
1973	-	-	63.7	0.6	-	-	-	-	65.1	2.2	-	-	-	-	64.9	-0.3	-	-	-	-	66.3	2.2	-	-
1974	-	-	66.6	0.5	-	-	-	-	68.3	2.6	-	-	-	-	69.4	1.6	-	-	-	-	72.0	3.7	-	-
1975	-	-	72.6	0.8	-	-	-	-	73.8	1.7	-	-	-	-	73.4	-0.5	-	-	-	-	74.3	1.2	-	-
1976	-	-	76.3	2.7	-	-	-	-	78.3	2.6	-	-	-	-	77.8	-0.6	-	-	-	-	78.8	1.3	-	-
1977	-	-	79.5	0.9	-	-	-	-	80.9	1.8	-	-	-	-	81.5	0.7	-	-	-	-	83.4	2.3	-	-
1978	82.2	-1.4	-	-	82.7	0.6	-	-	84.3	1.9	-	-	81.9	-2.8	-	-	85.5	4.4	-	-	84.7	-0.9	-	-
1979	82.1	-3.1	-	-	85.6	4.3	-	-	87.6	2.3	-	-	88.1	0.6	-	-	90.1	2.3	-	-	92.0	2.1	-	-
1980	89.8	-2.4	-	-	92.8	3.3	-	-	91.8	-1.1	-	-	94.6	3.1	-	-	96.1	1.6	-	-	97.3	1.2	-	-
1981	95.4	-2.0	-	-	98.4	3.1	-	-	97.3	-1.1	-	-	97.0	-0.3	-	-	99.3	2.4	-	-	99.7	0.4	-	-
1982	97.3	-2.4	-	-	100.1	2.9	-	-	100.1	0.0	-	-	98.1	-2.0	-	-	102.6	4.6	-	-	100.4	-2.1	-	-
1983	96.3	-4.1	-	-	101.0	4.9	-	-	102.5	1.5	-	-	101.9	-0.6	-	-	103.4	1.5	-	-	100.3	-3.0	-	-
1984	97.2	-3.1	-	-	100.5	3.4	-	-	98.2	-2.3	-	-	98.0	-0.2	-	-	101.6	3.7	-	-	100.8	-0.8	-	-
1985	96.6	-4.2	-	-	104.7	8.4	-	-	101.0	-3.5	-	-	101.5	0.5	-	-	107.9	6.3	-	-	103.1	-4.4	-	-
1986	99.0	-4.0	-	-	103.0	4.0	-	-	103.4	0.4	-	-	102.9	-0.5	-	-	106.7	3.7	-	-	107.0	0.3	103.9	-2.9
1987	-	-	-	-	-	-	-	-	-	-	105.3	1.3	-	-	-	-	-	-	-	-	-	-	111.3	5.7
1988	-	-	-	-	-	-	-	-	-	-	114.2	2.6	-	-	-	-	-	-	-	-	-	-	114.0	-0.2
1989	-	-	-	-	-	-	-	-	-	-	108.5	-4.8	-	-	-	-	-	-	-	-	-	-	103.0	-5.1
1990	-	-	-	-	-	-	-	-	-	-	109.1	5.9	-	-	-	-	-	-	-	-	-	-	112.8	3.4
1991	-	-	-	-	-	-	-	-	-	-	111.1	-1.5	-	-	-	-	-	-	-	-	-	-	113.2	1.9
1992	-	-	-	-	-	-	-	-	-	-	117.0	3.4	-	-	-	-	-	-	-	-	-	-	118.4	1.2
1993	-	-	-	-	-	-	-	-	-	-	114.3	-3.5	-	-	-	-	-	-	-	-	-	-	115.7	1.2
1994	-	-	-	-	-	-	-	-	-	-	122.2	5.6	-	-	-	-	-	-	-	-	-	-	118.8	-2.8
1995	-	-	-	-	-	-	-	-	-	-	119.6	0.7	-	-	-	-	-	-	-	-	-	-	121.2	1.3
1996	-	-	-	-	-	-	-	-	-	-	123.4	1.8	-	-	-	-	-	-	-	-	-	-	124.8	1.1
1997	-	-	-	-	-	-	-	-	-	-	-	-	-	-	-	-	-	-	-	-	-	-	122.7	-1.7

[Continued]

Seattle-Tacoma-Bremerton, WA
Consumer Price Index - Urban Wage Earners
Base 1982-1984 = 100
Apparel
[Continued]

For 1952-2001. Columns headed % show percentile change in the index from the previous period for which an index is available.

Year	Jan		Feb		Mar		Apr		May		Jun		Jul		Aug		Sep		Oct		Nov		Dec	
	Index	%	Index	%	Index	%	Index	%	Index	%	Index	%	Index	%	Index	%	Index	%	Index	%	Index	%	Index	%
1998	-	-	126.5	3.1	-	-	126.8	0.2	-	-	122.7	-3.2	-	-	129.9	5.9	-	-	131.0	0.8	-	-	126.2	-3.7
1999	-	-	126.9	0.6	-	-	130.1	2.5	-	-	126.0	-3.2	-	-	123.0	-2.4	-	-	130.7	6.3	-	-	127.2	-2.7
2000	-	-	129.3	1.7	-	-	132.2	2.2	-	-	127.4	-3.6	-	-	124.6	-2.2	-	-	132.0	5.9	-	-	122.5	-7.2
2001	-	-	128.3	4.7	-	-	122.4	-4.6	-	-	125.5	2.5	-	-	127.5	1.6	-	-	128.6	0.9	-	-	122.9	-4.4

Source: U.S. Department of Labor, Bureau of Labor Statistics, Division of Consumer Prices and Price Indexes. - indicates no data collected for period.

Seattle-Tacoma-Bremerton, WA
Consumer Price Index - All Urban Consumers
Base 1982-1984 = 100
Transportation

For 1947-2000. Columns headed % show percentile change in the index from the previous period for which an index is available.

Year	Jan Index	%	Feb Index	%	Mar Index	%	Apr Index	%	May Index	%	Jun Index	%	Jul Index	%	Aug Index	%	Sep Index	%	Oct Index	%	Nov Index	%	Dec Index	%
1947	18.7	-	18.7	0.0	18.8	0.5	18.9	0.5	18.9	0.0	18.9	0.0	-	-	19.1	1.1	-	-	-	-	19.5	2.1	-	-
1948	-	-	20.4	4.6	-	-	-	-	20.4	0.0	-	-	-	-	21.1	3.4	-	-	-	-	21.4	1.4	-	-
1949	-	-	21.6	0.9	-	-	-	-	22.0	1.9	-	-	-	-	22.6	2.7	-	-	-	-	22.6	0.0	-	-
1950	-	-	22.8	0.9	-	-	-	-	22.3	-2.2	-	-	-	-	22.6	1.3	-	-	-	-	23.7	4.9	-	-
1951	-	-	23.8	0.4	-	-	-	-	24.0	0.8	-	-	-	-	24.2	0.8	-	-	-	-	24.8	2.5	-	-
1952	-	-	25.0	0.8	-	-	-	-	25.2	0.8	-	-	-	-	25.2	0.0	-	-	-	-	26.8	6.3	-	-
1953	-	-	26.9	0.4	-	-	-	-	27.6	2.6	-	-	-	-	27.6	0.0	-	-	-	-	27.4	-0.7	-	-
1954	-	-	27.5	0.4	-	-	-	-	26.9	-2.2	-	-	-	-	26.6	-1.1	-	-	-	-	26.7	0.4	-	-
1955	-	-	26.6	-0.4	-	-	-	-	26.2	-1.5	-	-	-	-	26.1	-0.4	-	-	-	-	26.9	3.1	-	-
1956	-	-	25.8	-4.1	-	-	-	-	25.9	0.4	-	-	-	-	26.7	3.1	-	-	-	-	27.6	3.4	-	-
1957	-	-	28.4	2.9	-	-	-	-	28.6	0.7	-	-	-	-	28.1	-1.7	-	-	-	-	29.2	3.9	-	-
1958	-	-	29.1	-0.3	-	-	-	-	29.4	1.0	-	-	-	-	30.1	2.4	-	-	-	-	29.9	-0.7	-	-
1959	-	-	30.7	2.7	-	-	-	-	30.8	0.3	-	-	-	-	32.0	3.9	-	-	-	-	31.0	-3.1	-	-
1960	-	-	30.3	-2.3	-	-	-	-	31.0	2.3	-	-	-	-	30.7	-1.0	-	-	-	-	31.0	1.0	-	-
1961	-	-	30.9	-0.3	-	-	-	-	31.4	1.6	-	-	-	-	31.8	1.3	-	-	-	-	32.6	2.5	-	-
1962	-	-	32.3	-0.9	-	-	-	-	32.5	0.6	-	-	-	-	32.6	0.3	-	-	-	-	33.0	1.2	-	-
1963	-	-	32.3	-2.1	-	-	-	-	32.2	-0.3	-	-	-	-	32.9	2.2	-	-	-	-	32.4	-1.5	-	-
1964	-	-	32.4	0.0	-	-	-	-	31.8	-1.9	-	-	-	-	33.5	5.3	-	-	-	-	32.8	-2.1	-	-
1965	-	-	32.4	-1.2	-	-	-	-	33.9	4.6	-	-	-	-	33.8	-0.3	-	-	-	-	33.8	0.0	-	-
1966	-	-	33.7	-0.3	-	-	-	-	33.4	-0.9	-	-	-	-	34.1	2.1	-	-	-	-	34.8	2.1	-	-
1967	-	-	34.6	-0.6	-	-	-	-	35.3	2.0	-	-	-	-	35.6	0.8	-	-	-	-	35.7	0.3	-	-
1968	-	-	35.7	0.0	-	-	-	-	35.6	-0.3	-	-	-	-	36.2	1.7	-	-	-	-	36.2	0.0	-	-
1969	-	-	36.3	0.3	-	-	-	-	36.0	-0.8	-	-	-	-	36.5	1.4	-	-	-	-	35.9	-1.6	-	-
1970	-	-	36.9	2.8	-	-	-	-	37.1	0.5	-	-	-	-	37.5	1.1	-	-	-	-	37.1	-1.1	-	-
1971	-	-	37.4	0.8	-	-	-	-	37.6	0.5	-	-	-	-	38.5	2.4	-	-	-	-	37.7	-2.1	-	-
1972	-	-	38.2	1.3	-	-	-	-	38.3	0.3	-	-	-	-	38.7	1.0	-	-	-	-	39.4	1.8	-	-
1973	-	-	39.0	-1.0	-	-	-	-	39.4	1.0	-	-	-	-	39.7	0.8	-	-	-	-	40.0	0.8	-	-
1974	-	-	41.3	3.2	-	-	-	-	43.6	5.6	-	-	-	-	45.4	4.1	-	-	-	-	45.8	0.9	-	-
1975	-	-	46.1	0.7	-	-	-	-	47.5	3.0	-	-	-	-	49.0	3.2	-	-	-	-	49.7	1.4	-	-
1976	-	-	49.7	0.0	-	-	-	-	51.1	2.8	-	-	-	-	52.8	3.3	-	-	-	-	53.3	0.9	-	-
1977	-	-	55.2	3.6	-	-	-	-	56.5	2.4	-	-	-	-	58.3	3.2	-	-	-	-	57.8	-0.9	-	-
1978	58.3	0.9	-	-	58.5	0.3	-	-	60.2	2.9	-	-	61.8	2.7	-	-	63.1	2.1	-	-	63.8	1.1	-	-
1979	64.5	1.1	-	-	66.0	2.3	-	-	69.6	5.5	-	-	72.5	4.2	-	-	74.7	3.0	-	-	76.1	1.9	-	-
1980	78.0	2.5	-	-	81.3	4.2	-	-	82.5	1.5	-	-	83.7	1.5	-	-	84.7	1.2	-	-	85.9	1.4	-	-
1981	86.8	1.0	-	-	91.0	4.8	-	-	93.6	2.9	-	-	96.2	2.8	-	-	97.1	0.9	-	-	97.7	0.6	-	-
1982	98.2	0.5	-	-	97.0	-1.2	-	-	96.6	-0.4	-	-	99.7	3.2	-	-	99.1	-0.6	-	-	97.8	-1.3	-	-
1983	96.4	-1.4	-	-	94.0	-2.5	-	-	96.8	3.0	-	-	100.9	4.2	-	-	102.0	1.1	-	-	102.2	0.2	-	-
1984	101.0	-1.2	-	-	99.9	-1.1	-	-	103.8	3.9	-	-	104.5	0.7	-	-	104.0	-0.5	-	-	104.4	0.4	-	-
1985	105.1	0.7	-	-	104.4	-0.7	-	-	105.0	0.6	-	-	105.5	0.5	-	-	104.5	-0.9	-	-	105.1	0.6	-	-
1986	106.5	1.3	-	-	102.9	-3.4	-	-	100.9	-1.9	-	-	100.9	0.0	-	-	100.4	-0.5	-	-	99.7	-0.7	100.4	0.7
1987	-	-	-	-	-	-	-	-	-	-	100.9	0.5	-	-	-	-	-	-	-	-	-	-	103.8	2.9
1988	-	-	-	-	-	-	-	-	-	-	102.5	-1.3	-	-	-	-	-	-	-	-	-	-	104.6	2.0
1989	-	-	-	-	-	-	-	-	-	-	107.5	2.8	-	-	-	-	-	-	-	-	-	-	110.8	3.1
1990	-	-	-	-	-	-	-	-	-	-	113.4	2.3	-	-	-	-	-	-	-	-	-	-	118.9	4.9
1991	-	-	-	-	-	-	-	-	-	-	119.3	0.3	-	-	-	-	-	-	-	-	-	-	120.6	1.1
1992	-	-	-	-	-	-	-	-	-	-	121.8	1.0	-	-	-	-	-	-	-	-	-	-	126.0	3.4

[Continued]

Seattle-Tacoma-Bremerton, WA

Consumer Price Index - All Urban Consumers
Base 1982-1984 = 100

Transportation

[Continued]

For 1947-2000. Columns headed % show percentile change in the index from the previous period for which an index is available.

Year	Jan		Feb		Mar		Apr		May		Jun		Jul		Aug		Sep		Oct		Nov		Dec	
	Index	%	Index	%	Index	%	Index	%	Index	%	Index	%	Index	%	Index	%	Index	%	Index	%	Index	%	Index	%
1993	-	-	-	-	-	-	-	-	-	-	126.6	0.5	-	-	-	-	-	-	-	-	-	-	130.1	2.8
1994	-	-	-	-	-	-	-	-	-	-	133.0	2.2	-	-	-	-	-	-	-	-	-	-	137.0	3.0
1995	-	-	-	-	-	-	-	-	-	-	138.2	0.9	-	-	-	-	-	-	-	-	-	-	140.8	1.9
1996	-	-	-	-	-	-	-	-	-	-	142.5	1.2	-	-	-	-	-	-	-	-	-	-	145.5	2.1
1997	-	-	-	-	-	-	-	-	-	-	-	-	-	-	-	-	-	-	-	-	-	-	145.8	0.2
1998	-	-	145.0	-0.5	-	-	143.8	-0.8	-	-	146.2	1.7	-	-	146.6	0.3	-	-	145.9	-0.5	-	-	145.0	-0.6
1999	-	-	144.6	-0.3	-	-	150.5	4.1	-	-	150.2	-0.2	-	-	152.0	1.2	-	-	152.2	0.1	-	-	151.6	-0.4
2000	-	-	152.7	0.7	-	-	158.5	3.8	-	-	160.3	1.1	-	-	162.3	1.2	-	-	163.0	0.4	-	-	163.8	0.5

Source: U.S. Department of Labor, Bureau of Labor Statistics, Division of Consumer Prices and Price Indexes. - indicates no data collected for period.

Seattle-Tacoma-Bremerton, WA
Consumer Price Index - Urban Wage Earners
Base 1982-1984 = 100
Transportation

For 1947-2000. Columns headed % show percentile change in the index from the previous period for which an index is available.

Year	Jan Index	%	Feb Index	%	Mar Index	%	Apr Index	%	May Index	%	Jun Index	%	Jul Index	%	Aug Index	%	Sep Index	%	Oct Index	%	Nov Index	%	Dec Index	%
1947	19.1	-	19.1	0.0	19.2	0.5	19.2	0.0	19.3	0.5	19.3	0.0	-	-	19.5	1.0	-	-	-	-	19.9	2.1	-	-
1948	-	-	20.8	4.5	-	-	-	-	20.8	0.0	-	-	-	-	21.5	3.4	-	-	-	-	21.8	1.4	-	-
1949	-	-	22.0	0.9	-	-	-	-	22.5	2.3	-	-	-	-	23.0	2.2	-	-	-	-	23.1	0.4	-	-
1950	-	-	23.3	0.9	-	-	-	-	22.8	-2.1	-	-	-	-	23.1	1.3	-	-	-	-	24.1	4.3	-	-
1951	-	-	24.3	0.8	-	-	-	-	24.5	0.8	-	-	-	-	24.6	0.4	-	-	-	-	25.3	2.8	-	-
1952	-	-	25.5	0.8	-	-	-	-	25.8	1.2	-	-	-	-	25.8	0.0	-	-	-	-	27.4	6.2	-	-
1953	-	-	27.4	0.0	-	-	-	-	28.2	2.9	-	-	-	-	28.1	-0.4	-	-	-	-	28.0	-0.4	-	-
1954	-	-	28.1	0.4	-	-	-	-	27.4	-2.5	-	-	-	-	27.1	-1.1	-	-	-	-	27.2	0.4	-	-
1955	-	-	27.1	-0.4	-	-	-	-	26.8	-1.1	-	-	-	-	26.6	-0.7	-	-	-	-	27.4	3.0	-	-
1956	-	-	26.3	-4.0	-	-	-	-	26.4	0.4	-	-	-	-	27.2	3.0	-	-	-	-	28.2	3.7	-	-
1957	-	-	29.0	2.8	-	-	-	-	29.2	0.7	-	-	-	-	28.7	-1.7	-	-	-	-	29.8	3.8	-	-
1958	-	-	29.7	-0.3	-	-	-	-	30.0	1.0	-	-	-	-	30.7	2.3	-	-	-	-	30.5	-0.7	-	-
1959	-	-	31.3	2.6	-	-	-	-	31.4	0.3	-	-	-	-	32.7	4.1	-	-	-	-	31.6	-3.4	-	-
1960	-	-	30.9	-2.2	-	-	-	-	31.6	2.3	-	-	-	-	31.3	-0.9	-	-	-	-	31.6	1.0	-	-
1961	-	-	31.5	-0.3	-	-	-	-	32.1	1.9	-	-	-	-	32.4	0.9	-	-	-	-	33.3	2.8	-	-
1962	-	-	33.0	-0.9	-	-	-	-	33.2	0.6	-	-	-	-	33.3	0.3	-	-	-	-	33.7	1.2	-	-
1963	-	-	33.0	-2.1	-	-	-	-	32.8	-0.6	-	-	-	-	33.6	2.4	-	-	-	-	33.0	-1.8	-	-
1964	-	-	33.1	0.3	-	-	-	-	32.5	-1.8	-	-	-	-	34.2	5.2	-	-	-	-	33.5	-2.0	-	-
1965	-	-	33.1	-1.2	-	-	-	-	34.6	4.5	-	-	-	-	34.5	-0.3	-	-	-	-	34.5	0.0	-	-
1966	-	-	34.4	-0.3	-	-	-	-	34.1	-0.9	-	-	-	-	34.8	2.1	-	-	-	-	35.6	2.3	-	-
1967	-	-	35.3	-0.8	-	-	-	-	36.1	2.3	-	-	-	-	36.3	0.6	-	-	-	-	36.4	0.3	-	-
1968	-	-	36.5	0.3	-	-	-	-	36.3	-0.5	-	-	-	-	36.9	1.7	-	-	-	-	37.0	0.3	-	-
1969	-	-	37.0	0.0	-	-	-	-	36.8	-0.5	-	-	-	-	37.3	1.4	-	-	-	-	36.6	-1.9	-	-
1970	-	-	37.7	3.0	-	-	-	-	37.9	0.5	-	-	-	-	38.3	1.1	-	-	-	-	37.8	-1.3	-	-
1971	-	-	38.2	1.1	-	-	-	-	38.3	0.3	-	-	-	-	39.3	2.6	-	-	-	-	38.4	-2.3	-	-
1972	-	-	39.0	1.6	-	-	-	-	39.1	0.3	-	-	-	-	39.5	1.0	-	-	-	-	40.2	1.8	-	-
1973	-	-	39.9	-0.7	-	-	-	-	40.2	0.8	-	-	-	-	40.5	0.7	-	-	-	-	40.9	1.0	-	-
1974	-	-	42.2	3.2	-	-	-	-	44.5	5.5	-	-	-	-	46.3	4.0	-	-	-	-	46.7	0.9	-	-
1975	-	-	47.1	0.9	-	-	-	-	48.5	3.0	-	-	-	-	50.1	3.3	-	-	-	-	50.7	1.2	-	-
1976	-	-	50.7	0.0	-	-	-	-	52.1	2.8	-	-	-	-	53.9	3.5	-	-	-	-	54.4	0.9	-	-
1977	-	-	56.4	3.7	-	-	-	-	57.7	2.3	-	-	-	-	59.5	3.1	-	-	-	-	59.0	-0.8	-	-
1978	59.0	0.0	-	-	59.2	0.3	-	-	60.6	2.4	-	-	62.2	2.6	-	-	62.8	1.0	-	-	63.5	1.1	-	-
1979	64.2	1.1	-	-	65.9	2.6	-	-	69.4	5.3	-	-	72.2	4.0	-	-	74.3	2.9	-	-	75.7	1.9	-	-
1980	77.2	2.0	-	-	80.9	4.8	-	-	81.9	1.2	-	-	82.7	1.0	-	-	83.8	1.3	-	-	85.3	1.8	-	-
1981	86.4	1.3	-	-	89.8	3.9	-	-	92.6	3.1	-	-	95.2	2.8	-	-	95.8	0.6	-	-	97.6	1.9	-	-
1982	98.1	0.5	-	-	96.8	-1.3	-	-	96.4	-0.4	-	-	99.5	3.2	-	-	98.8	-0.7	-	-	97.7	-1.1	-	-
1983	96.2	-1.5	-	-	93.9	-2.4	-	-	96.8	3.1	-	-	101.0	4.3	-	-	102.2	1.2	-	-	102.3	0.1	-	-
1984	101.2	-1.1	-	-	100.2	-1.0	-	-	103.9	3.7	-	-	104.5	0.6	-	-	104.1	-0.4	-	-	104.7	0.6	-	-
1985	105.4	0.7	-	-	104.7	-0.7	-	-	105.5	0.8	-	-	105.9	0.4	-	-	105.0	-0.8	-	-	105.6	0.6	-	-
1986	106.7	1.0	-	-	103.1	-3.4	-	-	101.0	-2.0	-	-	101.0	0.0	-	-	100.5	-0.5	-	-	99.8	-0.7	100.2	0.4
1987	-	-	-	-	-	-	-	-	-	-	101.1	0.9	-	-	-	-	-	-	-	-	-	-	104.2	3.1
1988	-	-	-	-	-	-	-	-	-	-	103.6	-0.6	-	-	-	-	-	-	-	-	-	-	105.7	2.0
1989	-	-	-	-	-	-	-	-	-	-	108.6	2.7	-	-	-	-	-	-	-	-	-	-	111.9	3.0
1990	-	-	-	-	-	-	-	-	-	-	113.8	1.7	-	-	-	-	-	-	-	-	-	-	119.5	5.0
1991	-	-	-	-	-	-	-	-	-	-	119.7	0.2	-	-	-	-	-	-	-	-	-	-	121.5	1.5
1992	-	-	-	-	-	-	-	-	-	-	122.8	1.1	-	-	-	-	-	-	-	-	-	-	127.2	3.6

[Continued]

Seattle-Tacoma-Bremerton, WA
Consumer Price Index - Urban Wage Earners
Base 1982-1984 = 100
Transportation
[Continued]

For 1947-2000. Columns headed % show percentile change in the index from the previous period for which an index is available.

Year	Jan Index	%	Feb Index	%	Mar Index	%	Apr Index	%	May Index	%	Jun Index	%	Jul Index	%	Aug Index	%	Sep Index	%	Oct Index	%	Nov Index	%	Dec Index	%
1993	-	-	-	-	-	-	-	-	-	-	127.9	0.6	-	-	-	-	-	-	-	-	-	-	132.3	3.4
1994	-	-	-	-	-	-	-	-	-	-	135.4	2.3	-	-	-	-	-	-	-	-	-	-	140.2	3.5
1995	-	-	-	-	-	-	-	-	-	-	141.9	1.2	-	-	-	-	-	-	-	-	-	-	144.3	1.7
1996	-	-	-	-	-	-	-	-	-	-	146.2	1.3	-	-	-	-	-	-	-	-	-	-	148.8	1.8
1997	-	-	-	-	-	-	-	-	-	-	-	-	-	-	-	-	-	-	-	-	-	-	148.3	-0.3
1998	-	-	147.0	-0.9	-	-	145.9	-0.7	-	-	148.7	1.9	-	-	148.9	0.1	-	-	148.4	-0.3	-	-	147.5	-0.6
1999	-	-	146.5	-0.7	-	-	153.4	4.7	-	-	152.8	-0.4	-	-	155.1	1.5	-	-	155.2	0.1	-	-	154.6	-0.4
2000	-	-	155.5	0.6	-	-	161.5	3.9	-	-	163.6	1.3	-	-	165.5	1.2	-	-	167.0	0.9	-	-	167.4	0.2

Source: U.S. Department of Labor, Bureau of Labor Statistics, Division of Consumer Prices and Price Indexes. - indicates no data collected for period.

Seattle-Tacoma-Bremerton, WA
Consumer Price Index - All Urban Consumers
Base 1982-1984 = 100
Medical Care

For 1947-2001. Columns headed % show percentile change in the index from the previous period for which an index is available.

Year	Jan Index	%	Feb Index	%	Mar Index	%	Apr Index	%	May Index	%	Jun Index	%	Jul Index	%	Aug Index	%	Sep Index	%	Oct Index	%	Nov Index	%	Dec Index	%
1947	14.1	-	14.3	1.4	14.3	0.0	14.4	0.7	14.4	0.0	14.4	0.0	-		14.4	0.0	-		-		14.6	1.4	-	-
1948	-		14.7	0.7	-		-		15.0	2.0	-		-		15.3	2.0	-		-		15.6	2.0	-	
1949	-		15.6	0.0	-		-		15.9	1.9	-		-		15.9	0.0	-		-		16.0	0.6	-	
1950	-		16.0	0.0	-		-		16.0	0.0	-		-		16.0	0.0	-		-		16.1	0.6	-	
1951	-		16.6	3.1	-		-		17.1	3.0	-		-		17.2	0.6	-		-		17.4	1.2	-	
1952	-		17.8	2.3	-		-		18.3	2.8	-		-		18.7	2.2	-		-		18.7	0.0	-	
1953	-		18.7	0.0	-		-		18.9	1.1	-		-		19.0	0.5	-		-		19.6	3.2	-	
1954	-		19.6	0.0	-		-		19.8	1.0	-		-		19.6	-1.0	-		-		19.7	0.5	-	
1955	-		19.8	0.5	-		-		19.8	0.0	-		-		19.9	0.5	-		-		21.1	6.0	-	
1956	-		20.4	-3.3	-		-		20.5	0.5	-		-		20.8	1.5	-		-		20.7	-0.5	-	
1957	-		20.9	1.0	-		-		21.0	0.5	-		-		21.6	2.9	-		-		21.7	0.5	-	
1958	-		22.1	1.8	-		-		22.2	0.5	-		-		22.4	0.9	-		-		22.5	0.4	-	
1959	-		22.6	0.4	-		-		22.6	0.0	-		-		22.9	1.3	-		-		23.3	1.7	-	
1960	-		23.9	2.6	-		-		23.9	0.0	-		-		24.1	0.8	-		-		23.9	-0.8	-	
1961	-		23.9	0.0	-		-		24.0	0.4	-		-		24.0	0.0	-		-		24.1	0.4	-	
1962	-		24.2	0.4	-		-		24.3	0.4	-		-		24.4	0.4	-		-		24.4	0.0	-	
1963	-		24.4	0.0	-		-		24.5	0.4	-		-		24.6	0.4	-		-		24.6	0.0	-	
1964	-		24.6	0.0	-		-		24.9	1.2	-		-		25.1	0.8	-		-		25.2	0.4	-	
1965	-		25.4	0.8	-		-		25.9	2.0	-		-		26.1	0.8	-		-		26.6	1.9	-	
1966	-		26.8	0.8	-		-		27.3	1.9	-		-		27.8	1.8	-		-		28.5	2.5	-	
1967	-		28.5	0.0	-		-		28.8	1.1	-		-		29.3	1.7	-		-		29.8	1.7	-	
1968	-		30.1	1.0	-		-		30.6	1.7	-		-		31.1	1.6	-		-		31.5	1.3	-	
1969	-		32.1	1.9	-		-		32.7	1.9	-		-		33.3	1.8	-		-		33.5	0.6	-	
1970	-		34.0	1.5	-		-		34.3	0.9	-		-		34.7	1.2	-		-		34.8	0.3	-	
1971	-		35.4	1.7	-		-		35.6	0.6	-		-		36.1	1.4	-		-		36.0	-0.3	-	
1972	-		36.2	0.6	-		-		36.4	0.6	-		-		36.7	0.8	-		-		36.7	0.0	-	
1973	-		37.2	1.4	-		-		37.4	0.5	-		-		37.9	1.3	-		-		38.6	1.8	-	
1974	-		39.4	2.1	-		-		40.7	3.3	-		-		41.7	2.5	-		-		42.8	2.6	-	
1975	-		44.8	4.7	-		-		45.7	2.0	-		-		46.7	2.2	-		-		47.4	1.5	-	
1976	-		49.4	4.2	-		-		50.5	2.2	-		-		51.1	1.2	-		-		52.8	3.3	-	
1977	-		54.6	3.4	-		-		55.5	1.6	-		-		56.4	1.6	-		-		57.3	1.6	-	
1978	60.6	5.8	-		60.7	0.2	-		61.3	1.0	-		62.4	1.8	-		62.8	0.6	-		64.0	1.9	-	
1979	64.7	1.1	-		66.1	2.2	-		66.3	0.3	-		67.4	1.7	-		68.1	1.0	-		69.8	2.5	-	
1980	72.6	4.0	-		73.9	1.8	-		75.1	1.6	-		76.4	1.7	-		76.4	0.0	-		78.4	2.6	-	
1981	81.2	3.6	-		83.2	2.5	-		83.8	0.7	-		85.3	1.8	-		86.1	0.9	-		87.5	1.6	-	
1982	89.7	2.5	-		91.7	2.2	-		92.4	0.8	-		93.8	1.5	-		94.8	1.1	-		96.1	1.4	-	
1983	99.5	3.5	-		101.1	1.6	-		100.6	-0.5	-		101.3	0.7	-		101.3	0.0	-		100.7	-0.6	-	
1984	103.2	2.5	-		104.6	1.4	-		104.7	0.1	-		105.7	1.0	-		106.5	0.8	-		107.4	0.8	-	
1985	109.7	2.1	-		111.9	2.0	-		112.3	0.4	-		113.1	0.7	-		113.2	0.1	-		112.1	-1.0	-	
1986	113.2	1.0	-		116.0	2.5	-		116.0	0.0	-		118.9	2.5	-		119.9	0.8	-		119.6	-0.3	120.5	0.8
1987	-		-		-		-		-		122.6	1.7	-		-		-		-		-		126.6	3.3
1988	-		-		-		-		-		131.2	3.6	-		-		-		-		-		134.6	2.6
1989	-		-		-		-		-		140.6	4.5	-		-		-		-		-		142.6	1.4
1990	-		-		-		-		-		152.6	7.0	-		-		-		-		-		156.6	2.6
1991	-		-		-		-		-		166.2	6.1	-		-		-		-		-		172.6	3.9
1992	-		-		-		-		-		181.2	5.0	-		-		-		-		-		187.1	3.3

[Continued]

Seattle-Tacoma-Bremerton, WA
Consumer Price Index - All Urban Consumers
Base 1982-1984 = 100
Medical Care
[Continued]

For 1947-2001. Columns headed % show percentile change in the index from the previous period for which an index is available.

Year	Jan Index	%	Feb Index	%	Mar Index	%	Apr Index	%	May Index	%	Jun Index	%	Jul Index	%	Aug Index	%	Sep Index	%	Oct Index	%	Nov Index	%	Dec Index	%
1993	-		-		-		-		-		192.4	2.8	-		-		-		-		-		193.8	0.7
1994	-		-		-		-		-		197.3	1.8	-		-		-		-		-		202.4	2.6
1995	-		-		-		-		-		207.5	2.5	-		-		-		-		-		211.3	1.8
1996	-		-		-		-		-		216.9	2.7	-		-		-		-		-		217.9	0.5
1997	-		-		-		-		-		-		-		-		-		-		-		227.1	4.2
1998	-		230.4	1.5	-		231.8	0.6	-		231.3	-0.2	-		233.9	1.1	-		234.8	0.4	-		236.0	0.5
1999	-		238.7	1.1	-		238.6	-0.0	-		239.6	0.4	-		242.2	1.1	-		242.0	-0.1	-		242.1	0.0
2000	-		244.9	1.2	-		242.8	-0.9	-		247.4	1.9	-		248.7	0.5	-		248.5	-0.1	-		249.2	0.3
2001	-		253.3	1.6	-		255.4	0.8	-		255.9	0.2	-		259.8	1.5	-		260.2	0.2	-		263.1	1.1

Source: U.S. Department of Labor, Bureau of Labor Statistics, Division of Consumer Prices and Price Indexes. - indicates no data collected for period.

Seattle-Tacoma-Bremerton, WA
Consumer Price Index - Urban Wage Earners
Base 1982-1984 = 100
Medical Care

For 1947-2001. Columns headed % show percentile change in the index from the previous period for which an index is available.

Year	Jan Index	Jan %	Feb Index	Feb %	Mar Index	Mar %	Apr Index	Apr %	May Index	May %	Jun Index	Jun %	Jul Index	Jul %	Aug Index	Aug %	Sep Index	Sep %	Oct Index	Oct %	Nov Index	Nov %	Dec Index	Dec %
1947	14.0	-	14.2	1.4	14.2	0.0	14.2	0.0	14.2	0.0	14.3	0.7	-	-	14.3	0.0	-	-	-	-	14.5	1.4	-	-
1948	-	-	14.6	0.7	-	-	-	-	14.8	1.4	-	-	-	-	15.2	2.7	-	-	-	-	15.4	1.3	-	-
1949	-	-	15.4	0.0	-	-	-	-	15.7	1.9	-	-	-	-	15.7	0.0	-	-	-	-	15.9	1.3	-	-
1950	-	-	15.9	0.0	-	-	-	-	15.9	0.0	-	-	-	-	15.9	0.0	-	-	-	-	16.0	0.6	-	-
1951	-	-	16.4	2.5	-	-	-	-	17.0	3.7	-	-	-	-	17.0	0.0	-	-	-	-	17.2	1.2	-	-
1952	-	-	17.7	2.9	-	-	-	-	18.1	2.3	-	-	-	-	18.5	2.2	-	-	-	-	18.5	0.0	-	-
1953	-	-	18.5	0.0	-	-	-	-	18.7	1.1	-	-	-	-	18.8	0.5	-	-	-	-	19.4	3.2	-	-
1954	-	-	19.4	0.0	-	-	-	-	19.6	1.0	-	-	-	-	19.4	-1.0	-	-	-	-	19.5	0.5	-	-
1955	-	-	19.6	0.5	-	-	-	-	19.6	0.0	-	-	-	-	19.7	0.5	-	-	-	-	20.9	6.1	-	-
1956	-	-	20.2	-3.3	-	-	-	-	20.3	0.5	-	-	-	-	20.6	1.5	-	-	-	-	20.5	-0.5	-	-
1957	-	-	20.7	1.0	-	-	-	-	20.8	0.5	-	-	-	-	21.4	2.9	-	-	-	-	21.5	0.5	-	-
1958	-	-	21.9	1.9	-	-	-	-	22.0	0.5	-	-	-	-	22.2	0.9	-	-	-	-	22.3	0.5	-	-
1959	-	-	22.4	0.4	-	-	-	-	22.4	0.0	-	-	-	-	22.7	1.3	-	-	-	-	23.1	1.8	-	-
1960	-	-	23.7	2.6	-	-	-	-	23.7	0.0	-	-	-	-	23.9	0.8	-	-	-	-	23.7	-0.8	-	-
1961	-	-	23.7	0.0	-	-	-	-	23.8	0.4	-	-	-	-	23.8	0.0	-	-	-	-	23.9	0.4	-	-
1962	-	-	24.0	0.4	-	-	-	-	24.1	0.4	-	-	-	-	24.1	0.0	-	-	-	-	24.2	0.4	-	-
1963	-	-	24.2	0.0	-	-	-	-	24.3	0.4	-	-	-	-	24.4	0.4	-	-	-	-	24.4	0.0	-	-
1964	-	-	24.4	0.0	-	-	-	-	24.6	0.8	-	-	-	-	24.8	0.8	-	-	-	-	25.0	0.8	-	-
1965	-	-	25.2	0.8	-	-	-	-	25.6	1.6	-	-	-	-	25.8	0.8	-	-	-	-	26.4	2.3	-	-
1966	-	-	26.6	0.8	-	-	-	-	27.0	1.5	-	-	-	-	27.5	1.9	-	-	-	-	28.3	2.9	-	-
1967	-	-	28.2	-0.4	-	-	-	-	28.5	1.1	-	-	-	-	29.1	2.1	-	-	-	-	29.5	1.4	-	-
1968	-	-	29.9	1.4	-	-	-	-	30.3	1.3	-	-	-	-	30.8	1.7	-	-	-	-	31.2	1.3	-	-
1969	-	-	31.8	1.9	-	-	-	-	32.4	1.9	-	-	-	-	33.0	1.9	-	-	-	-	33.2	0.6	-	-
1970	-	-	33.6	1.2	-	-	-	-	34.0	1.2	-	-	-	-	34.4	1.2	-	-	-	-	34.5	0.3	-	-
1971	-	-	35.0	1.4	-	-	-	-	35.3	0.9	-	-	-	-	35.8	1.4	-	-	-	-	35.7	-0.3	-	-
1972	-	-	35.9	0.6	-	-	-	-	36.1	0.6	-	-	-	-	36.4	0.8	-	-	-	-	36.3	-0.3	-	-
1973	-	-	36.9	1.7	-	-	-	-	37.1	0.5	-	-	-	-	37.6	1.3	-	-	-	-	38.3	1.9	-	-
1974	-	-	39.1	2.1	-	-	-	-	40.3	3.1	-	-	-	-	41.3	2.5	-	-	-	-	42.4	2.7	-	-
1975	-	-	44.3	4.5	-	-	-	-	45.2	2.0	-	-	-	-	46.3	2.4	-	-	-	-	47.0	1.5	-	-
1976	-	-	48.9	4.0	-	-	-	-	50.0	2.2	-	-	-	-	50.6	1.2	-	-	-	-	52.3	3.4	-	-
1977	-	-	54.0	3.3	-	-	-	-	55.0	1.9	-	-	-	-	55.8	1.5	-	-	-	-	56.8	1.8	-	-
1978	59.0	3.9	-	-	59.2	0.3	-	-	60.1	1.5	-	-	61.2	1.8	-	-	61.5	0.5	-	-	63.9	3.9	-	-
1979	64.6	1.1	-	-	65.5	1.4	-	-	66.2	1.1	-	-	67.8	2.4	-	-	68.2	0.6	-	-	69.9	2.5	-	-
1980	72.4	3.6	-	-	73.2	1.1	-	-	74.6	1.9	-	-	74.4	-0.3	-	-	76.0	2.2	-	-	78.0	2.6	-	-
1981	79.9	2.4	-	-	81.4	1.9	-	-	82.9	1.8	-	-	84.1	1.4	-	-	86.2	2.5	-	-	87.9	2.0	-	-
1982	89.8	2.2	-	-	91.7	2.1	-	-	92.4	0.8	-	-	93.8	1.5	-	-	94.5	0.7	-	-	95.9	1.5	-	-
1983	99.2	3.4	-	-	100.7	1.5	-	-	100.5	-0.2	-	-	101.3	0.8	-	-	101.2	-0.1	-	-	100.9	-0.3	-	-
1984	103.2	2.3	-	-	104.7	1.5	-	-	104.9	0.2	-	-	106.0	1.0	-	-	106.9	0.8	-	-	107.5	0.6	-	-
1985	109.9	2.2	-	-	112.2	2.1	-	-	112.5	0.3	-	-	113.3	0.7	-	-	113.6	0.3	-	-	112.8	-0.7	-	-
1986	114.0	1.1	-	-	116.9	2.5	-	-	116.8	-0.1	-	-	119.8	2.6	-	-	120.7	0.8	-	-	120.4	-0.2	121.5	0.9
1987	-	-	-	-	-	-	-	-	-	-	124.3	2.3	-	-	-	-	-	-	-	-	-	-	128.2	3.1
1988	-	-	-	-	-	-	-	-	-	-	133.0	3.7	-	-	-	-	-	-	-	-	-	-	136.5	2.6
1989	-	-	-	-	-	-	-	-	-	-	142.5	4.4	-	-	-	-	-	-	-	-	-	-	144.3	1.3
1990	-	-	-	-	-	-	-	-	-	-	154.0	6.7	-	-	-	-	-	-	-	-	-	-	157.9	2.5
1991	-	-	-	-	-	-	-	-	-	-	166.9	5.7	-	-	-	-	-	-	-	-	-	-	173.1	3.7
1992	-	-	-	-	-	-	-	-	-	-	181.9	5.1	-	-	-	-	-	-	-	-	-	-	188.0	3.4

[Continued]

Seattle-Tacoma-Bremerton, WA
Consumer Price Index - Urban Wage Earners
Base 1982-1984 = 100
Medical Care
[Continued]

For 1947-2001. Columns headed % show percentile change in the index from the previous period for which an index is available.

Year	Jan Index	%	Feb Index	%	Mar Index	%	Apr Index	%	May Index	%	Jun Index	%	Jul Index	%	Aug Index	%	Sep Index	%	Oct Index	%	Nov Index	%	Dec Index	%
1993	-	-	-	-	-	-	-	-	-	-	193.2	2.8	-	-	-	-	-	-	-	-	-	-	194.5	0.7
1994	-	-	-	-	-	-	-	-	-	-	197.7	1.6	-	-	-	-	-	-	-	-	-	-	202.7	2.5
1995	-	-	-	-	-	-	-	-	-	-	207.4	2.3	-	-	-	-	-	-	-	-	-	-	210.8	1.6
1996	-	-	-	-	-	-	-	-	-	-	217.3	3.1	-	-	-	-	-	-	-	-	-	-	218.3	0.5
1997	-	-	-	-	-	-	-	-	-	-	-	-	-	-	-	-	-	-	-	-	-	-	227.2	4.1
1998	-	-	230.6	1.5	-	-	231.9	0.6	-	-	231.5	-0.2	-	-	233.9	1.0	-	-	234.8	0.4	-	-	236.6	0.8
1999	-	-	237.9	0.5	-	-	237.8	-0.0	-	-	238.2	0.2	-	-	240.7	1.0	-	-	240.5	-0.1	-	-	240.5	0.0
2000	-	-	243.3	1.2	-	-	241.2	-0.9	-	-	245.5	1.8	-	-	246.8	0.5	-	-	246.5	-0.1	-	-	247.4	0.4
2001	-	-	251.1	1.5	-	-	252.9	0.7	-	-	253.4	0.2	-	-	257.1	1.5	-	-	257.5	0.2	-	-	260.1	1.0

Source: U.S. Department of Labor, Bureau of Labor Statistics, Division of Consumer Prices and Price Indexes. - indicates no data collected for period.

Seattle-Tacoma-Bremerton, WA
Consumer Price Index - All Urban Consumers
Base December 1997 = 100
Recreation

For 1997-2001. Columns headed % show percentile change in the index from the previous period for which an index is available.

Year	Jan		Feb		Mar		Apr		May		Jun		Jul		Aug		Sep		Oct		Nov		Dec	
	Index	%	Index	%	Index	%	Index	%	Index	%	Index	%	Index	%	Index	%	Index	%	Index	%	Index	%	Index	%
1997	-	-	-	-	-	-	-	-	-	-	-	-	-	-	-	-	-	-	-	-	-	-	100.0	-
1998	-	-	99.7	-0.3	-	-	99.4	-0.3	-	-	98.7	-0.7	-	-	98.7	0.0	-	-	98.8	0.1	-	-	99.0	0.2
1999	-	-	99.9	0.9	-	-	99.8	-0.1	-	-	100.5	0.7	-	-	99.2	-1.3	-	-	100.8	1.6	-	-	100.9	0.1
2000	-	-	100.8	-0.1	-	-	100.7	-0.1	-	-	101.3	0.6	-	-	101.2	-0.1	-	-	101.6	0.4	-	-	101.4	-0.2
2001	-	-	100.9	-0.5	-	-	100.4	-0.5	-	-	99.8	-0.6	-	-	99.7	-0.1	-	-	100.8	1.1	-	-	99.5	-1.3

Source: U.S. Department of Labor, Bureau of Labor Statistics, Division of Consumer Prices and Price Indexes. - indicates no data collected for period.

Seattle-Tacoma-Bremerton, WA
Consumer Price Index - Urban Wage Earners
Base December 1997 = 100
Recreation

For 1997-2001. Columns headed % show percentile change in the index from the previous period for which an index is available.

Year	Jan Index	%	Feb Index	%	Mar Index	%	Apr Index	%	May Index	%	Jun Index	%	Jul Index	%	Aug Index	%	Sep Index	%	Oct Index	%	Nov Index	%	Dec Index	%
1997	-	-	-	-	-	-	-	-	-	-	-	-	-	-	-	-	-	-	-	-	-	-	100.0	-
1998	-	-	100.0	0.0	-	-	99.6	-0.4	-	-	98.7	-0.9	-	-	98.5	-0.2	-	-	98.7	0.2	-	-	98.8	0.1
1999	-	-	99.7	0.9	-	-	99.6	-0.1	-	-	100.2	0.6	-	-	98.9	-1.3	-	-	100.8	1.9	-	-	101.0	0.2
2000	-	-	100.5	-0.5	-	-	100.4	-0.1	-	-	101.1	0.7	-	-	100.8	-0.3	-	-	100.8	0.0	-	-	100.6	-0.2
2001	-	-	100.2	-0.4	-	-	99.9	-0.3	-	-	99.3	-0.6	-	-	99.1	-0.2	-	-	100.1	1.0	-	-	98.7	-1.4

Source: U.S. Department of Labor, Bureau of Labor Statistics, Division of Consumer Prices and Price Indexes. - indicates no data collected for period.

Seattle-Tacoma-Bremerton, WA
Consumer Price Index - All Urban Consumers
Base December 1997 = 100
Education & Communication

For 1997-2001. Columns headed % show percentile change in the index from the previous period for which an index is available.

Year	Jan		Feb		Mar		Apr		May		Jun		Jul		Aug		Sep		Oct		Nov		Dec	
	Index	%	Index	%	Index	%	Index	%	Index	%	Index	%	Index	%	Index	%	Index	%	Index	%	Index	%	Index	%
1997	-	-	-	-	-	-	-	-	-	-	-	-	-	-	-	-	-	-	-	-	-	-	100.0	-
1998	-	-	102.9	2.9	-	-	102.9	0.0	-	-	103.3	0.4	-	-	102.9	-0.4	-	-	103.5	0.6	-	-	102.8	-0.7
1999	-	-	102.7	-0.1	-	-	104.2	1.5	-	-	103.8	-0.4	-	-	104.4	0.6	-	-	105.1	0.7	-	-	105.1	0.0
2000	-	-	105.1	0.0	-	-	103.3	-1.7	-	-	103.6	0.3	-	-	105.0	1.4	-	-	105.1	0.1	-	-	105.1	0.0
2001	-	-	105.8	0.7	-	-	106.0	0.2	-	-	106.0	0.0	-	-	106.4	0.4	-	-	107.1	0.7	-	-	107.0	-0.1

Source: U.S. Department of Labor, Bureau of Labor Statistics, Division of Consumer Prices and Price Indexes. - indicates no data collected for period.

Seattle-Tacoma-Bremerton, WA
Consumer Price Index - Urban Wage Earners
Base December 1997 = 100
Education & Communication

For 1997-2001. Columns headed % show percentile change in the index from the previous period for which an index is available.

Year	Jan Index	%	Feb Index	%	Mar Index	%	Apr Index	%	May Index	%	Jun Index	%	Jul Index	%	Aug Index	%	Sep Index	%	Oct Index	%	Nov Index	%	Dec Index	%
1997	-	-	-	-	-	-	-	-	-	-	-	-	-	-	-	-	-	-	-	-	-	-	100.0	-
1998	-	-	102.5	2.5	-	-	102.5	0.0	-	-	102.9	0.4	-	-	102.7	-0.2	-	-	102.9	0.2	-	-	101.9	-1.0
1999	-	-	102.0	0.1	-	-	103.4	1.4	-	-	102.9	-0.5	-	-	104.3	1.4	-	-	104.8	0.5	-	-	104.8	0.0
2000	-	-	105.1	0.3	-	-	103.4	-1.6	-	-	104.4	1.0	-	-	105.5	1.1	-	-	105.5	0.0	-	-	105.4	-0.1
2001	-	-	106.0	0.6	-	-	106.4	0.4	-	-	106.9	0.5	-	-	106.9	0.0	-	-	107.3	0.4	-	-	107.2	-0.1

Source: U.S. Department of Labor, Bureau of Labor Statistics, Division of Consumer Prices and Price Indexes. - indicates no data collected for period.

Tampa-St. Petersburg-Clearwater, FL
Consumer Price Index - All Urban Consumers
Base 1987 = 100
Annual Averages

For 1988-2001. Columns headed % show percentile change in the index from the previous period for which an index is available.

Year	All Items		Food & Beverage		Housing		Apparel		Trans-portation		Medical Care		Recrea-tion*		Education & Communic.*		Other Goods & Services	
	Index	%	Index	%	Index	%	Index	%	Index	%	Index	%	Index	%	Index	%	Index	%
1988	103.7	-	103.5	-	102.9	-	107.4	-	102.7	-	109.7	-	-	-	-	-	104.2	-
1989	107.2	3.4	106.3	2.7	104.8	1.8	111.7	4.0	106.6	3.8	124.3	13.3	-	-	-	-	109.2	4.8
1990	111.7	4.2	112.4	5.7	108.3	3.3	114.7	2.7	110.8	3.9	133.2	7.2	-	-	-	-	117.0	7.1
1991	116.4	4.2	116.4	3.6	111.2	2.7	127.9	11.5	112.2	1.3	147.2	10.5	-	-	-	-	125.9	7.6
1992	119.2	2.4	116.4	0.0	113.4	2.0	132.8	3.8	114.8	2.3	156.6	6.4	-	-	-	-	132.8	5.5
1993	124.0	4.0	118.2	1.5	116.7	2.9	157.7	18.8	116.6	1.6	165.8	5.9	-	-	-	-	137.9	3.8
1994	126.5	2.0	121.9	3.1	121.4	4.0	143.6	-8.9	118.8	1.9	172.8	4.2	-	-	-	-	141.4	2.5
1995	129.7	2.5	125.5	3.0	123.8	2.0	134.1	-6.6	124.9	5.1	181.5	5.0	-	-	-	-	147.6	4.4
1996	131.6	1.5	129.1	2.9	126.6	2.3	115.1	-14.2	127.3	1.9	188.7	4.0	-	-	-	-	156.1	5.8
1997	134.0	1.8	131.7	2.0	129.0	1.9	120.0	4.3	127.0	-0.2	190.5	1.0	-	-	-	-	163.3	4.6
1998	137.5	2.6	133.7	1.5	132.2	2.5	144.1	20.1	124.2	-2.2	192.1	0.8	100.4	-	99.4	-	178.2	9.1
1999	140.6	2.3	137.7	3.0	135.3	2.3	148.2	2.8	126.3	1.7	191.9	-0.1	100.6	0.2	99.5	0.1	192.6	8.1
2000	145.7	3.6	142.3	3.3	139.4	3.0	158.9	7.2	134.0	6.1	199.0	3.7	99.8	-0.8	101.6	2.1	199.0	3.3
2001	-	-	-	-	-	-	-	-	-	-	-	-	-	-	-	-	-	-

Source: U.S. Department of Labor, Bureau of Labor Statistics, Division of Consumer Prices and Price Indexes. *Base is December 1997 = 100. - indicates no data collected for period.

Tampa-St. Petersburg-Clearwater, FL
Consumer Price Index - Urban Wage Earners
Base 1987 = 100
Annual Averages

For 1988-2001. Columns headed % show percentile change in the index from the previous period for which an index is available.

Year	All Items		Food & Beverage		Housing		Apparel		Trans-portation		Medical Care		Recrea-tion*		Education & Communic.*		Other Goods & Services	
	Index	%	Index	%	Index	%	Index	%	Index	%	Index	%	Index	%	Index	%	Index	%
1988	103.4	-	103.3	-	103.0	-	105.4	-	102.7	-	109.3	-	-	-	-	-	104.1	-
1989	106.8	3.3	107.2	3.8	105.0	1.9	105.5	0.1	106.5	3.7	124.1	13.5	-	-	-	-	108.8	4.5
1990	111.3	4.2	112.9	5.3	108.5	3.3	108.1	2.5	110.6	3.8	132.6	6.8	-	-	-	-	117.0	7.5
1991	115.6	3.9	117.0	3.6	111.4	2.7	118.9	10.0	111.8	1.1	147.1	10.9	-	-	-	-	126.4	8.0
1992	118.2	2.2	117.2	0.2	113.4	1.8	122.2	2.8	114.9	2.8	157.5	7.1	-	-	-	-	132.9	5.1
1993	122.2	3.4	118.4	1.0	116.8	3.0	140.5	15.0	116.6	1.5	167.2	6.2	-	-	-	-	137.5	3.5
1994	124.8	2.1	121.5	2.6	121.3	3.9	129.4	-7.9	118.8	1.9	174.4	4.3	-	-	-	-	140.2	2.0
1995	128.0	2.6	124.8	2.7	123.5	1.8	123.3	-4.7	124.6	4.9	182.6	4.7	-	-	-	-	146.0	4.1
1996	131.0	2.3	130.0	4.2	126.2	2.2	112.1	-9.1	127.6	2.4	190.4	4.3	-	-	-	-	154.3	5.7
1997	133.1	1.6	132.6	2.0	128.5	1.8	115.2	2.8	127.4	-0.2	193.3	1.5	-	-	-	-	159.1	3.1
1998	135.9	2.1	134.4	1.4	131.5	2.3	131.3	14.0	124.7	-2.1	194.3	0.5	100.9	-	101.0	-	173.4	9.0
1999	139.1	2.4	138.3	2.9	134.4	2.2	135.0	2.8	126.8	1.7	193.7	-0.3	100.7	-0.2	102.4	1.4	191.9	10.7
2000	144.3	3.7	143.3	3.6	138.5	3.1	144.6	7.1	135.0	6.5	200.7	3.6	99.2	-1.5	104.5	2.1	200.3	4.4
2001	-	-	-	-	-	-	-	-	-	-	-	-	-	-	-	-	-	-

Source: U.S. Department of Labor, Bureau of Labor Statistics, Division of Consumer Prices and Price Indexes. *Base is December 1997 = 100. - indicates no data collected for period.

Tampa-St. Petersburg-Clearwater, FL
Consumer Price Index - All Urban Consumers
Base 1987 = 100
All Items

For 1988-2001. Columns headed % show percentile change in the index from the previous period for which an index is available.

Year	Jan		Feb		Mar		Apr		May		Jun		Jul		Aug		Sep		Oct		Nov		Dec	
	Index	%	Index	%	Index	%	Index	%	Index	%	Index	%	Index	%	Index	%	Index	%	Index	%	Index	%	Index	%
1988	-		-		-		-				-		-		-		-		-		-		-	
1989	-		-		-		-				-		-		-		-		-		-		-	
1990	-		-		-		-				-		-		-		-		-		-		-	
1991	-		-		-		-				-		-		-		-		-		-		-	
1992	-		-		-		-				-		-		-		-		-		-		-	
1993	-		-		-		-				-		-		-		-		-		-		-	
1994	-		-		-		-				-		-		-		-		-		-		-	
1995	-		-		-		-				-		-		-		-		-		-		-	
1996	-		-		-		-				-		-		-		-		-		-		-	
1997	-		-		-		-				-		-		-		-		-		-		134.6	-
1998	-		-		-		-		-		137.1	1.9	-		-		-		-		-		137.9	0.6
1999	-		-		-		-		-		139.4	1.1	-		-		-		-		-		141.8	1.7
2000	-		-		-		-		-		145.1	2.3	-		-		-		-		-		146.2	0.8
2001	-		-		-		-		-		148.0	1.2	-		-		-		-		-		-	

Source: U.S. Department of Labor, Bureau of Labor Statistics, Division of Consumer Prices and Price Indexes. - indicates no data collected for period.

Tampa-St. Petersburg-Clearwater, FL
Consumer Price Index - Urban Wage Earners
Base 1987 = 100
All Items

For 1988-2001. Columns headed % show percentile change in the index from the previous period for which an index is available.

Year	Jan Index	%	Feb Index	%	Mar Index	%	Apr Index	%	May Index	%	Jun Index	%	Jul Index	%	Aug Index	%	Sep Index	%	Oct Index	%	Nov Index	%	Dec Index	%
1988	-	-	-	-	-	-	-	-	-	-	-	-	-	-	-	-	-	-	-	-	-	-	-	-
1989	-	-	-	-	-	-	-	-	-	-	-	-	-	-	-	-	-	-	-	-	-	-	-	-
1990	-	-	-	-	-	-	-	-	-	-	-	-	-	-	-	-	-	-	-	-	-	-	-	-
1991	-	-	-	-	-	-	-	-	-	-	-	-	-	-	-	-	-	-	-	-	-	-	-	-
1992	-	-	-	-	-	-	-	-	-	-	-	-	-	-	-	-	-	-	-	-	-	-	-	-
1993	-	-	-	-	-	-	-	-	-	-	-	-	-	-	-	-	-	-	-	-	-	-	-	-
1994	-	-	-	-	-	-	-	-	-	-	-	-	-	-	-	-	-	-	-	-	-	-	-	-
1995	-	-	-	-	-	-	-	-	-	-	-	-	-	-	-	-	-	-	-	-	-	-	-	-
1996	-	-	-	-	-	-	-	-	-	-	-	-	-	-	-	-	-	-	-	-	-	-	-	-
1997	-	-	-	-	-	-	-	-	-	-	-	-	-	-	-	-	-	-	-	-	-	-	133.4	-
1998	-	-	-	-	-	-	-	-	-	-	135.2	1.3	-	-	-	-	-	-	-	-	-	-	136.5	1.0
1999	-	-	-	-	-	-	-	-	-	-	137.8	1.0	-	-	-	-	-	-	-	-	-	-	140.4	1.9
2000	-	-	-	-	-	-	-	-	-	-	143.7	2.4	-	-	-	-	-	-	-	-	-	-	145.0	0.9
2001	-	-	-	-	-	-	-	-	-	-	146.8	1.2	-	-	-	-	-	-	-	-	-	-	-	-

Source: U.S. Department of Labor, Bureau of Labor Statistics, Division of Consumer Prices and Price Indexes. - indicates no data collected for period.

Tampa-St. Petersburg-Clearwater, FL
Consumer Price Index - All Urban Consumers
Base 1987 = 100
Food and Beverages

For 1987-2001. Columns headed % show percentile change in the index from the previous period for which an index is available.

Year	Jan Index	%	Feb Index	%	Mar Index	%	Apr Index	%	May Index	%	Jun Index	%	Jul Index	%	Aug Index	%	Sep Index	%	Oct Index	%	Nov Index	%	Dec Index	%
1987	-	-	-	-	-	-	-	-	-	-	-	-	-	-	-	-	-	-	-	-	-	-	-	-
1988	-	-	-	-	-	-	-	-	-	-	-	-	-	-	-	-	-	-	-	-	-	-	-	-
1989	-	-	-	-	-	-	-	-	-	-	-	-	-	-	-	-	-	-	-	-	-	-	-	-
1990	-	-	-	-	-	-	-	-	-	-	-	-	-	-	-	-	-	-	-	-	-	-	-	-
1991	-	-	-	-	-	-	-	-	-	-	-	-	-	-	-	-	-	-	-	-	-	-	-	-
1992	-	-	-	-	-	-	-	-	-	-	-	-	-	-	-	-	-	-	-	-	-	-	-	-
1993	-	-	-	-	-	-	-	-	-	-	-	-	-	-	-	-	-	-	-	-	-	-	-	-
1994	-	-	-	-	-	-	-	-	-	-	-	-	-	-	-	-	-	-	-	-	-	-	-	-
1995	-	-	-	-	-	-	-	-	-	-	-	-	-	-	-	-	-	-	-	-	-	-	-	-
1996	-	-	-	-	-	-	-	-	-	-	-	-	-	-	-	-	-	-	-	-	-	-	-	-
1997	-	-	-	-	-	-	-	-	-	-	-	-	-	-	-	-	-	-	-	-	-	-	132.8	-
1998	-	-	-	-	-	-	-	-	-	-	132.6	-0.2	-	-	-	-	-	-	-	-	-	-	134.9	1.7
1999	-	-	-	-	-	-	-	-	-	-	136.2	1.0	-	-	-	-	-	-	-	-	-	-	139.2	2.2
2000	-	-	-	-	-	-	-	-	-	-	141.9	1.9	-	-	-	-	-	-	-	-	-	-	142.7	0.6
2001	-	-	-	-	-	-	-	-	-	-	145.7	2.1	-	-	-	-	-	-	-	-	-	-	-	-

Source: U.S. Department of Labor, Bureau of Labor Statistics, Division of Consumer Prices and Price Indexes. - indicates no data collected for period.

Tampa-St. Petersburg-Clearwater, FL
Consumer Price Index - Urban Wage Earners
Base 1987 = 100
Food and Beverages

For 1987-2001. Columns headed % show percentile change in the index from the previous period for which an index is available.

Year	Jan Index	%	Feb Index	%	Mar Index	%	Apr Index	%	May Index	%	Jun Index	%	Jul Index	%	Aug Index	%	Sep Index	%	Oct Index	%	Nov Index	%	Dec Index	%
1987	-		-		-		-		-		-		-		-		-		-		-		-	
1988	-		-		-		-		-		-		-		-		-		-		-		-	
1989	-		-		-		-		-		-		-		-		-		-		-		-	
1990	-		-		-		-		-		-		-		-		-		-		-		-	
1991	-		-		-		-		-		-		-		-		-		-		-		-	
1992	-		-		-		-		-		-		-		-		-		-		-		-	
1993	-		-		-		-		-		-		-		-		-		-		-		-	
1994	-		-		-		-		-		-		-		-		-		-		-		-	
1995	-		-		-		-		-		-		-		-		-		-		-		-	
1996	-		-		-		-		-		-		-		-		-		-		-		-	
1997	-		-		-		-		-		-		-		-		-		-		-		133.8	-
1998	-		-		-		-		-		133.3	-0.4	-		-		-		-		-		135.5	1.7
1999	-		-		-		-		-		136.8	1.0	-		-		-		-		-		139.8	2.2
2000	-		-		-		-		-		142.8	2.1	-		-		-		-		-		143.7	0.6
2001	-		-		-		-		-		146.6	2.0	-		-		-		-		-		-	

Source: U.S. Department of Labor, Bureau of Labor Statistics, Division of Consumer Prices and Price Indexes. - indicates no data collected for period.

Tampa-St. Petersburg-Clearwater, FL
Consumer Price Index - All Urban Consumers
Base 1987 = 100
Housing

For 1987-2001. Columns headed % show percentile change in the index from the previous period for which an index is available.

Year	Jan Index	%	Feb Index	%	Mar Index	%	Apr Index	%	May Index	%	Jun Index	%	Jul Index	%	Aug Index	%	Sep Index	%	Oct Index	%	Nov Index	%	Dec Index	%
1987	-	-	-	-	-	-	-	-	-	-	-	-	-	-	-	-	-	-	-	-	-	-	-	-
1988	-	-	-	-	-	-	-	-	-	-	-	-	-	-	-	-	-	-	-	-	-	-	-	-
1989	-	-	-	-	-	-	-	-	-	-	-	-	-	-	-	-	-	-	-	-	-	-	-	-
1990	-	-	-	-	-	-	-	-	-	-	-	-	-	-	-	-	-	-	-	-	-	-	-	-
1991	-	-	-	-	-	-	-	-	-	-	-	-	-	-	-	-	-	-	-	-	-	-	-	-
1992	-	-	-	-	-	-	-	-	-	-	-	-	-	-	-	-	-	-	-	-	-	-	-	-
1993	-	-	-	-	-	-	-	-	-	-	-	-	-	-	-	-	-	-	-	-	-	-	-	-
1994	-	-	-	-	-	-	-	-	-	-	-	-	-	-	-	-	-	-	-	-	-	-	-	-
1995	-	-	-	-	-	-	-	-	-	-	-	-	-	-	-	-	-	-	-	-	-	-	-	-
1996	-	-	-	-	-	-	-	-	-	-	-	-	-	-	-	-	-	-	-	-	-	-	-	-
1997	-	-	-	-	-	-	-	-	-	-	-	-	-	-	-	-	-	-	-	-	-	-	129.5	-
1998	-	-	-	-	-	-	-	-	-	-	131.8	1.8	-	-	-	-	-	-	-	-	-	-	132.6	0.6
1999	-	-	-	-	-	-	-	-	-	-	134.8	1.7	-	-	-	-	-	-	-	-	-	-	135.9	0.8
2000	-	-	-	-	-	-	-	-	-	-	138.2	1.7	-	-	-	-	-	-	-	-	-	-	140.5	1.7
2001	-	-	-	-	-	-	-	-	-	-	143.0	1.8	-	-	-	-	-	-	-	-	-	-	-	-

Source: U.S. Department of Labor, Bureau of Labor Statistics, Division of Consumer Prices and Price Indexes. - indicates no data collected for period.

Tampa-St. Petersburg-Clearwater, FL
Consumer Price Index - Urban Wage Earners
Base 1987 = 100
Housing

For 1987-2001. Columns headed % show percentile change in the index from the previous period for which an index is available.

Year	Jan		Feb		Mar		Apr		May		Jun		Jul		Aug		Sep		Oct		Nov		Dec	
	Index	%	Index	%	Index	%	Index	%	Index	%	Index	%	Index	%	Index	%	Index	%	Index	%	Index	%	Index	%
1987	-	-	-	-	-	-	-	-	-	-	-	-	-	-	-	-	-	-	-	-	-	-	-	-
1988	-	-	-	-	-	-	-	-	-	-	-	-	-	-	-	-	-	-	-	-	-	-	-	-
1989	-	-	-	-	-	-	-	-	-	-	-	-	-	-	-	-	-	-	-	-	-	-	-	-
1990	-	-	-	-	-	-	-	-	-	-	-	-	-	-	-	-	-	-	-	-	-	-	-	-
1991	-	-	-	-	-	-	-	-	-	-	-	-	-	-	-	-	-	-	-	-	-	-	-	-
1992	-	-	-	-	-	-	-	-	-	-	-	-	-	-	-	-	-	-	-	-	-	-	-	-
1993	-	-	-	-	-	-	-	-	-	-	-	-	-	-	-	-	-	-	-	-	-	-	-	-
1994	-	-	-	-	-	-	-	-	-	-	-	-	-	-	-	-	-	-	-	-	-	-	-	-
1995	-	-	-	-	-	-	-	-	-	-	-	-	-	-	-	-	-	-	-	-	-	-	-	-
1996	-	-	-	-	-	-	-	-	-	-	-	-	-	-	-	-	-	-	-	-	-	-	-	-
1997	-	-	-	-	-	-	-	-	-	-	-	-	-	-	-	-	-	-	-	-	-	-	129.1	-
1998	-	-	-	-	-	-	-	-	-	-	130.9	1.4	-	-	-	-	-	-	-	-	-	-	132.2	1.0
1999	-	-	-	-	-	-	-	-	-	-	133.8	1.2	-	-	-	-	-	-	-	-	-	-	135.1	1.0
2000	-	-	-	-	-	-	-	-	-	-	137.0	1.4	-	-	-	-	-	-	-	-	-	-	139.9	2.1
2001	-	-	-	-	-	-	-	-	-	-	142.2	1.6	-	-	-	-	-	-	-	-	-	-	-	-

Source: U.S. Department of Labor, Bureau of Labor Statistics, Division of Consumer Prices and Price Indexes. - indicates no data collected for period.

Tampa-St. Petersburg-Clearwater, FL
Consumer Price Index - All Urban Consumers
Base 1987 = 100
Apparel

For 1987-2001. Columns headed % show percentile change in the index from the previous period for which an index is available.

Year	Jan Index	%	Feb Index	%	Mar Index	%	Apr Index	%	May Index	%	Jun Index	%	Jul Index	%	Aug Index	%	Sep Index	%	Oct Index	%	Nov Index	%	Dec Index	%
1987	-	-	-	-	-	-	-	-	-	-	-	-	-	-	-	-	-	-	-	-	-	-	-	-
1988	-	-	-	-	-	-	-	-	-	-	-	-	-	-	-	-	-	-	-	-	-	-	-	-
1989	-	-	-	-	-	-	-	-	-	-	-	-	-	-	-	-	-	-	-	-	-	-	-	-
1990	-	-	-	-	-	-	-	-	-	-	-	-	-	-	-	-	-	-	-	-	-	-	-	-
1991	-	-	-	-	-	-	-	-	-	-	-	-	-	-	-	-	-	-	-	-	-	-	-	-
1992	-	-	-	-	-	-	-	-	-	-	-	-	-	-	-	-	-	-	-	-	-	-	-	-
1993	-	-	-	-	-	-	-	-	-	-	-	-	-	-	-	-	-	-	-	-	-	-	-	-
1994	-	-	-	-	-	-	-	-	-	-	-	-	-	-	-	-	-	-	-	-	-	-	-	-
1995	-	-	-	-	-	-	-	-	-	-	-	-	-	-	-	-	-	-	-	-	-	-	-	-
1996	-	-	-	-	-	-	-	-	-	-	-	-	-	-	-	-	-	-	-	-	-	-	-	-
1997	-	-	-	-	-	-	-	-	-	-	-	-	-	-	-	-	-	-	-	-	-	-	122.8	-
1998	-	-	-	-	-	-	-	-	-	-	144.4	17.6	-	-	-	-	-	-	-	-	-	-	143.8	-0.4
1999	-	-	-	-	-	-	-	-	-	-	147.8	2.8	-	-	-	-	-	-	-	-	-	-	148.7	0.6
2000	-	-	-	-	-	-	-	-	-	-	165.6	11.4	-	-	-	-	-	-	-	-	-	-	152.1	-8.2
2001	-	-	-	-	-	-	-	-	-	-	148.3	-2.5	-	-	-	-	-	-	-	-	-	-	-	-

Source: U.S. Department of Labor, Bureau of Labor Statistics, Division of Consumer Prices and Price Indexes. - indicates no data collected for period.

Tampa-St. Petersburg-Clearwater, FL
Consumer Price Index - Urban Wage Earners
Base 1987 = 100
Apparel

For 1987-2001. Columns headed % show percentile change in the index from the previous period for which an index is available.

Year	Jan		Feb		Mar		Apr		May		Jun		Jul		Aug		Sep		Oct		Nov		Dec	
	Index	%	Index	%	Index	%	Index	%	Index	%	Index	%	Index	%	Index	%	Index	%	Index	%	Index	%	Index	%
1987	-	-	-	-	-	-	-	-	-	-	-	-	-	-	-	-	-	-	-	-	-	-	-	-
1988	-	-	-	-	-	-	-	-	-	-	-	-	-	-	-	-	-	-	-	-	-	-	-	-
1989	-	-	-	-	-	-	-	-	-	-	-	-	-	-	-	-	-	-	-	-	-	-	-	-
1990	-	-	-	-	-	-	-	-	-	-	-	-	-	-	-	-	-	-	-	-	-	-	-	-
1991	-	-	-	-	-	-	-	-	-	-	-	-	-	-	-	-	-	-	-	-	-	-	-	-
1992	-	-	-	-	-	-	-	-	-	-	-	-	-	-	-	-	-	-	-	-	-	-	-	-
1993	-	-	-	-	-	-	-	-	-	-	-	-	-	-	-	-	-	-	-	-	-	-	-	-
1994	-	-	-	-	-	-	-	-	-	-	-	-	-	-	-	-	-	-	-	-	-	-	-	-
1995	-	-	-	-	-	-	-	-	-	-	-	-	-	-	-	-	-	-	-	-	-	-	-	-
1996	-	-	-	-	-	-	-	-	-	-	-	-	-	-	-	-	-	-	-	-	-	-	-	-
1997	-	-	-	-	-	-	-	-	-	-	-	-	-	-	-	-	-	-	-	-	-	-	-	-
1998	-	-	-	-	-	-	-	-	-	-	131.8	13.9	-	-	-	-	-	-	-	-	-	-	115.7	-
1999	-	-	-	-	-	-	-	-	-	-	134.7	3.1	-	-	-	-	-	-	-	-	-	-	130.7	-0.8
2000	-	-	-	-	-	-	-	-	-	-	151.2	11.8	-	-	-	-	-	-	-	-	-	-	135.3	0.4
2001	-	-	-	-	-	-	-	-	-	-	135.1	-2.1	-	-	-	-	-	-	-	-	-	-	138.0	-8.7

Source: U.S. Department of Labor, Bureau of Labor Statistics, Division of Consumer Prices and Price Indexes. - indicates no data collected for period.

Tampa-St. Petersburg-Clearwater, FL
Consumer Price Index - All Urban Consumers
Base 1987 = 100
Transportation

For 1987-2001. Columns headed % show percentile change in the index from the previous period for which an index is available.

Year	Jan		Feb		Mar		Apr		May		Jun		Jul		Aug		Sep		Oct		Nov		Dec	
	Index	%	Index	%	Index	%	Index	%	Index	%	Index	%	Index	%	Index	%	Index	%	Index	%	Index	%	Index	%
1987	-	-	-	-	-	-	-	-	-	-	-	-	-	-	-	-	-	-	-	-	-	-	-	-
1988	-	-	-	-	-	-	-	-	-	-	-	-	-	-	-	-	-	-	-	-	-	-	-	-
1989	-	-	-	-	-	-	-	-	-	-	-	-	-	-	-	-	-	-	-	-	-	-	-	-
1990	-	-	-	-	-	-	-	-	-	-	-	-	-	-	-	-	-	-	-	-	-	-	-	-
1991	-	-	-	-	-	-	-	-	-	-	-	-	-	-	-	-	-	-	-	-	-	-	-	-
1992	-	-	-	-	-	-	-	-	-	-	-	-	-	-	-	-	-	-	-	-	-	-	-	-
1993	-	-	-	-	-	-	-	-	-	-	-	-	-	-	-	-	-	-	-	-	-	-	-	-
1994	-	-	-	-	-	-	-	-	-	-	-	-	-	-	-	-	-	-	-	-	-	-	-	-
1995	-	-	-	-	-	-	-	-	-	-	-	-	-	-	-	-	-	-	-	-	-	-	-	-
1996	-	-	-	-	-	-	-	-	-	-	-	-	-	-	-	-	-	-	-	-	-	-	-	-
1997	-	-	-	-	-	-	-	-	-	-	-	-	-	-	-	-	-	-	-	-	-	-	126.1	-
1998	-	-	-	-	-	-	-	-	-	-	124.4	-1.3	-	-	-	-	-	-	-	-	-	-	124.0	-0.3
1999	-	-	-	-	-	-	-	-	-	-	124.1	0.1	-	-	-	-	-	-	-	-	-	-	128.6	3.6
2000	-	-	-	-	-	-	-	-	-	-	133.5	3.8	-	-	-	-	-	-	-	-	-	-	134.5	0.7
2001	-	-	-	-	-	-	-	-	-	-	135.0	0.4	-	-	-	-	-	-	-	-	-	-	-	-

Source: U.S. Department of Labor, Bureau of Labor Statistics, Division of Consumer Prices and Price Indexes. - indicates no data collected for period.

Tampa-St. Petersburg-Clearwater, FL
Consumer Price Index - Urban Wage Earners
Base 1987 = 100
Transportation

For 1987-2001. Columns headed % show percentile change in the index from the previous period for which an index is available.

Year	Jan Index	%	Feb Index	%	Mar Index	%	Apr Index	%	May Index	%	Jun Index	%	Jul Index	%	Aug Index	%	Sep Index	%	Oct Index	%	Nov Index	%	Dec Index	%
1987	-	-	-	-	-	-	-	-	-	-	-	-	-	-	-	-	-	-	-	-	-	-	-	-
1988	-	-	-	-	-	-	-	-	-	-	-	-	-	-	-	-	-	-	-	-	-	-	-	-
1989	-	-	-	-	-	-	-	-	-	-	-	-	-	-	-	-	-	-	-	-	-	-	-	-
1990	-	-	-	-	-	-	-	-	-	-	-	-	-	-	-	-	-	-	-	-	-	-	-	-
1991	-	-	-	-	-	-	-	-	-	-	-	-	-	-	-	-	-	-	-	-	-	-	-	-
1992	-	-	-	-	-	-	-	-	-	-	-	-	-	-	-	-	-	-	-	-	-	-	-	-
1993	-	-	-	-	-	-	-	-	-	-	-	-	-	-	-	-	-	-	-	-	-	-	-	-
1994	-	-	-	-	-	-	-	-	-	-	-	-	-	-	-	-	-	-	-	-	-	-	-	-
1995	-	-	-	-	-	-	-	-	-	-	-	-	-	-	-	-	-	-	-	-	-	-	-	-
1996	-	-	-	-	-	-	-	-	-	-	-	-	-	-	-	-	-	-	-	-	-	-	-	-
1997	-	-	-	-	-	-	-	-	-	-	-	-	-	-	-	-	-	-	-	-	-	-	126.3	-
1998	-	-	-	-	-	-	-	-	-	-	124.6	-1.3	-	-	-	-	-	-	-	-	-	-	124.8	0.2
1999	-	-	-	-	-	-	-	-	-	-	124.3	-0.4	-	-	-	-	-	-	-	-	-	-	129.4	4.1
2000	-	-	-	-	-	-	-	-	-	-	134.4	3.9	-	-	-	-	-	-	-	-	-	-	135.7	1.0
2001	-	-	-	-	-	-	-	-	-	-	136.3	0.4	-	-	-	-	-	-	-	-	-	-	-	-

Source: U.S. Department of Labor, Bureau of Labor Statistics, Division of Consumer Prices and Price Indexes. - indicates no data collected for period.

Tampa-St. Petersburg-Clearwater, FL
Consumer Price Index - All Urban Consumers
Base 1987 = 100
Medical Care

For 1987-2001. Columns headed % show percentile change in the index from the previous period for which an index is available.

Year	Jan Index	%	Feb Index	%	Mar Index	%	Apr Index	%	May Index	%	Jun Index	%	Jul Index	%	Aug Index	%	Sep Index	%	Oct Index	%	Nov Index	%	Dec Index	%
1987	-	-	-	-	-	-	-	-	-	-	-	-	-	-	-	-	-	-	-	-	-	-	-	-
1988	-	-	-	-	-	-	-	-	-	-	-	-	-	-	-	-	-	-	-	-	-	-	-	-
1989	-	-	-	-	-	-	-	-	-	-	-	-	-	-	-	-	-	-	-	-	-	-	-	-
1990	-	-	-	-	-	-	-	-	-	-	-	-	-	-	-	-	-	-	-	-	-	-	-	-
1991	-	-	-	-	-	-	-	-	-	-	-	-	-	-	-	-	-	-	-	-	-	-	-	-
1992	-	-	-	-	-	-	-	-	-	-	-	-	-	-	-	-	-	-	-	-	-	-	-	-
1993	-	-	-	-	-	-	-	-	-	-	-	-	-	-	-	-	-	-	-	-	-	-	-	-
1994	-	-	-	-	-	-	-	-	-	-	-	-	-	-	-	-	-	-	-	-	-	-	-	-
1995	-	-	-	-	-	-	-	-	-	-	-	-	-	-	-	-	-	-	-	-	-	-	-	-
1996	-	-	-	-	-	-	-	-	-	-	-	-	-	-	-	-	-	-	-	-	-	-	-	-
1997	-	-	-	-	-	-	-	-	-	-	-	-	-	-	-	-	-	-	-	-	-	-	191.3	-
1998	-	-	-	-	-	-	-	-	-	-	194.3	1.6	-	-	-	-	-	-	-	-	-	-	189.8	-2.3
1999	-	-	-	-	-	-	-	-	-	-	190.1	0.2	-	-	-	-	-	-	-	-	-	-	193.7	1.9
2000	-	-	-	-	-	-	-	-	-	-	196.6	1.5	-	-	-	-	-	-	-	-	-	-	201.4	2.4
2001	-	-	-	-	-	-	-	-	-	-	204.8	1.7	-	-	-	-	-	-	-	-	-	-	-	-

Source: U.S. Department of Labor, Bureau of Labor Statistics, Division of Consumer Prices and Price Indexes. - indicates no data collected for period.

Tampa-St. Petersburg-Clearwater, FL
Consumer Price Index - Urban Wage Earners
Base 1987 = 100
Medical Care

For 1987-2001. Columns headed % show percentile change in the index from the previous period for which an index is available.

Year	Jan Index	%	Feb Index	%	Mar Index	%	Apr Index	%	May Index	%	Jun Index	%	Jul Index	%	Aug Index	%	Sep Index	%	Oct Index	%	Nov Index	%	Dec Index	%
1987	-		-		-		-		-		-		-		-		-		-		-		-	
1988	-		-		-		-		-		-		-		-		-		-		-		-	
1989	-		-		-		-		-		-		-		-		-		-		-		-	
1990	-		-		-		-		-		-		-		-		-		-		-		-	
1991	-		-		-		-		-		-		-		-		-		-		-		-	
1992	-		-		-		-		-		-		-		-		-		-		-		-	
1993	-		-		-		-		-		-		-		-		-		-		-		-	
1994	-		-		-		-		-		-		-		-		-		-		-		-	
1995	-		-		-		-		-		-		-		-		-		-		-		-	
1996	-		-		-		-		-		-		-		-		-		-		-		-	
1997	-		-		-		-		-		-		-		-		-		-		-		-	
1998	-		-		-		-		-		196.9	1.6	-		-		-		-		-		193.8	-
1999	-		-		-		-		-		191.9	0.1	-		-		-		-		-		191.7	-2.6
2000	-		-		-		-		-		198.5	1.5	-		-		-		-		-		195.6	1.9
2001	-		-		-		-		-		206.0	1.5	-		-		-		-		-		202.9	2.2

Source: U.S. Department of Labor, Bureau of Labor Statistics, Division of Consumer Prices and Price Indexes. - indicates no data collected for period.

Tampa-St. Petersburg-Clearwater, FL
Consumer Price Index - All Urban Consumers
Base December 1997 = 100
Recreation

For 1998-2001. Columns headed % show percentile change in the index from the previous period for which an index is available.

Year	Jan		Feb		Mar		Apr		May		Jun		Jul		Aug		Sep		Oct		Nov		Dec	
	Index	%	Index	%	Index	%	Index	%	Index	%	Index	%	Index	%	Index	%	Index	%	Index	%	Index	%	Index	%
1998	-	-	-	-	-	-	-	-	-	-	99.6	-	-	-	-	-	-	-	-	-	-	-	101.2	1.6
1999	-	-	-	-	-	-	-	-	-	-	100.7	-0.5	-	-	-	-	-	-	-	-	-	-	100.6	-0.1
2000	-	-	-	-	-	-	-	-	-	-	99.9	-0.7	-	-	-	-	-	-	-	-	-	-	99.7	-0.2
2001	-	-	-	-	-	-	-	-	-	-	100.9	1.2	-	-	-	-	-	-	-	-	-	-	-	-

Source: U.S. Department of Labor, Bureau of Labor Statistics, Division of Consumer Prices and Price Indexes. - indicates no data collected for period.

Tampa-St. Petersburg-Clearwater, FL
Consumer Price Index - Urban Wage Earners
Base December 1997 = 100
Recreation

For 1998-2001. Columns headed % show percentile change in the index from the previous period for which an index is available.

Year	Jan		Feb		Mar		Apr		May		Jun		Jul		Aug		Sep		Oct		Nov		Dec	
	Index	%	Index	%	Index	%	Index	%	Index	%	Index	%	Index	%	Index	%	Index	%	Index	%	Index	%	Index	%
1998	-	-	-	-	-	-	-	-	-	-	100.2	-	-	-	-	-	-	-	-	-	-	-	101.5	1.3
1999	-	-	-	-	-	-	-	-	-	-	100.9	-0.6	-	-	-	-	-	-	-	-	-	-	100.5	-0.4
2000	-	-	-	-	-	-	-	-	-	-	99.5	-1.0	-	-	-	-	-	-	-	-	-	-	99.0	-0.5
2001	-	-	-	-	-	-	-	-	-	-	100.3	1.3	-	-	-	-	-	-	-	-	-	-	-	-

Source: U.S. Department of Labor, Bureau of Labor Statistics, Division of Consumer Prices and Price Indexes. - indicates no data collected for period.

Tampa-St. Petersburg-Clearwater, FL
Consumer Price Index - All Urban Consumers
Base December 1997 = 100
Education & Communication

For 1998-2001. Columns headed % show percentile change in the index from the previous period for which an index is available.

Year	Jan		Feb		Mar		Apr		May		Jun		Jul		Aug		Sep		Oct		Nov		Dec	
	Index	%	Index	%	Index	%	Index	%	Index	%	Index	%	Index	%	Index	%	Index	%	Index	%	Index	%	Index	%
1998	-	-	-	-	-	-	-	-	-	-	99.6	-	-	-	-	-	-	-	-	-	-	-	99.2	-0.4
1999	-	-	-	-	-	-	-	-	-	-	98.7	-0.5	-	-	-	-	-	-	-	-	-	-	100.3	1.6
2000	-	-	-	-	-	-	-	-	-	-	101.9	1.6	-	-	-	-	-	-	-	-	-	-	101.4	-0.5
2001	-	-	-	-	-	-	-	-	-	-	102.6	1.2	-	-	-	-	-	-	-	-	-	-	-	-

Source: U.S. Department of Labor, Bureau of Labor Statistics, Division of Consumer Prices and Price Indexes. - indicates no data collected for period.

Tampa-St. Petersburg-Clearwater, FL
Consumer Price Index - Urban Wage Earners
Base December 1997 = 100
Education & Communication

For 1998-2001. Columns headed % show percentile change in the index from the previous period for which an index is available.

Year	Jan		Feb		Mar		Apr		May		Jun		Jul		Aug		Sep		Oct		Nov		Dec	
	Index	%	Index	%	Index	%	Index	%	Index	%	Index	%	Index	%	Index	%	Index	%	Index	%	Index	%	Index	%
1998	-	-	-	-	-	-	-	-	-	-	100.2	-	-	-	-	-	-	-	-	-	-	-	101.8	1.6
1999	-	-	-	-	-	-	-	-	-	-	101.5	-0.3	-	-	-	-	-	-	-	-	-	-	103.3	1.8
2000	-	-	-	-	-	-	-	-	-	-	105.1	1.7	-	-	-	-	-	-	-	-	-	-	103.9	-1.1
2001	-	-	-	-	-	-	-	-	-	-	105.4	1.4	-	-	-	-	-	-	-	-	-	-	-	-

Source: U.S. Department of Labor, Bureau of Labor Statistics, Division of Consumer Prices and Price Indexes. - indicates no data collected for period.

Washington-Baltimore, DC-MD-VA-WV
Consumer Price Index - All Urban Consumers
Base November 1996 = 100
Annual Averages

For 1996-2001. Columns headed % show percentile change in the index from the previous period for which an index is available.

Year	All Items		Food & Beverage		Housing		Apparel		Trans-portation		Medical Care		Recrea-tion*		Education & Communic.*		Other Goods & Services	
	Index	%	Index	%	Index	%	Index	%	Index	%	Index	%	Index	%	Index	%	Index	%
1996	-	-	-	-	-	-	-	-	-	-	-	-	-	-	-	-	-	-
1997	100.8	-	100.1	-	101.0	-	98.5	-	100.3	-	102.1	-	-	-	-	-	102.6	-
1998	102.1	1.3	101.6	1.5	103.1	2.1	99.3	0.8	98.4	-1.9	104.4	2.3	101.4	-	101.4	-	106.6	3.9
1999	104.2	2.1	103.1	1.5	105.5	2.3	98.3	-1.0	100.3	1.9	106.9	2.4	102.8	1.4	102.6	1.2	114.7	7.6
2000	107.6	3.3	105.5	2.3	108.9	3.2	98.2	-0.1	107.3	7.0	109.7	2.6	103.7	0.9	104.0	1.4	120.7	5.2
2001	-	-	-	-	-	-	-	-	-	-	-	-	-	-	-	-	-	-

Source: U.S. Department of Labor, Bureau of Labor Statistics, Division of Consumer Prices and Price Indexes. *Base is December 1997 = 100. - indicates no data collected for period.

Washington-Baltimore, DC-MD-VA-WV
Consumer Price Index - Urban Wage Earners
Base November 1996 = 100
Annual Averages

For 1996-2001. Columns headed % show percentile change in the index from the previous period for which an index is available.

Year	All Items		Food & Beverage		Housing		Apparel		Trans- portation		Medical Care		Recrea- tion*		Education & Communic.*		Other Goods & Services	
	Index	%	Index	%	Index	%	Index	%	Index	%	Index	%	Index	%	Index	%	Index	%
1996	-	-	-	-	-	-	-	-	-	-	-	-	-	-	-	-	-	-
1997	100.8	-	100.0	-	101.0	-	99.1	-	100.3	-	101.4	-	-	-	-	-	103.0	-
1998	101.9	1.1	101.4	1.4	103.2	2.2	99.3	0.2	98.3	-2.0	103.7	2.3	101.4	-	101.6	-	107.8	4.7
1999	104.0	2.1	102.8	1.4	105.7	2.4	97.9	-1.4	100.2	1.9	105.6	1.8	102.0	0.6	102.3	0.7	120.0	11.3
2000	107.5	3.4	105.0	2.1	108.9	3.0	97.4	-0.5	107.1	6.9	108.5	2.7	102.6	0.6	102.7	0.4	128.8	7.3
2001	-	-	-	-	-	-	-	-	-	-	-	-	-	-	-	-	-	-

Source: U.S. Department of Labor, Bureau of Labor Statistics, Division of Consumer Prices and Price Indexes. *Base is December 1997 = 100. - indicates no data collected for period.

Washington-Baltimore, DC-MD-VA-WV
Consumer Price Index - All Urban Consumers
Base November 1996 = 100
All Items

For 1996-2001. Columns headed % show percentile change in the index from the previous period for which an index is available.

Year	Jan		Feb		Mar		Apr		May		Jun		Jul		Aug		Sep		Oct		Nov		Dec	
	Index	%	Index	%	Index	%	Index	%	Index	%	Index	%	Index	%	Index	%	Index	%	Index	%	Index	%	Index	%
1996	-	-	-	-	-	-	-	-	-	-	-	-	-	-	-	-	-	-	-	-	100.0	-	-	-
1997	100.4	0.4	-	-	100.8	0.4	-	-	100.5	-0.3	-	-	101.1	0.6	-	-	101.4	0.3	-	-	100.5	-0.9	-	-
1998	101.0	0.5	-	-	101.6	0.6	-	-	101.5	-0.1	-	-	102.8	1.3	-	-	102.9	0.1	-	-	102.4	-0.5	-	-
1999	102.8	0.4	-	-	103.2	0.4	-	-	103.6	0.4	-	-	104.6	1.0	-	-	105.4	0.8	-	-	105.0	-0.4	-	-
2000	105.4	0.4	-	-	107.1	1.6	-	-	106.7	-0.4	-	-	108.4	1.6	-	-	108.7	0.3	-	-	108.5	-0.2	-	-
2001	108.9	0.4	-	-	109.7	0.7	-	-	110.1	0.4	-	-	110.8	0.6	-	-	111.7	0.8	-	-	110.9	-0.7	-	-

Source: U.S. Department of Labor, Bureau of Labor Statistics, Division of Consumer Prices and Price Indexes. - indicates no data collected for period.

Washington-Baltimore, DC-MD-VA-WV
Consumer Price Index - Urban Wage Earners
Base November 1996 = 100
All Items

For 1996-2001. Columns headed % show percentile change in the index from the previous period for which an index is available.

Year	Jan Index	%	Feb Index	%	Mar Index	%	Apr Index	%	May Index	%	Jun Index	%	Jul Index	%	Aug Index	%	Sep Index	%	Oct Index	%	Nov Index	%	Dec Index	%
1996	-	-	-	-	-	-	-	-	-	-	-	-	-	-	-	-	-	-	-	-	100.0	-	-	-
1997	100.4	0.4	-	-	100.8	0.4	-	-	100.5	-0.3	-	-	101.1	0.6	-	-	101.4	0.3	-	-	100.4	-1.0	-	-
1998	100.8	0.4	-	-	101.3	0.5	-	-	101.3	0.0	-	-	102.5	1.2	-	-	102.7	0.2	-	-	102.2	-0.5	-	-
1999	102.7	0.5	-	-	102.8	0.1	-	-	103.4	0.6	-	-	104.3	0.9	-	-	105.3	1.0	-	-	104.9	-0.4	-	-
2000	105.3	0.4	-	-	106.9	1.5	-	-	106.7	-0.2	-	-	108.2	1.4	-	-	108.7	0.5	-	-	108.4	-0.3	-	-
2001	108.6	0.2	-	-	109.4	0.7	-	-	109.9	0.5	-	-	110.6	0.6	-	-	111.6	0.9	-	-	110.7	-0.8	-	-

Source: U.S. Department of Labor, Bureau of Labor Statistics, Division of Consumer Prices and Price Indexes. - indicates no data collected for period.

Washington-Baltimore, DC-MD-VA-WV
Consumer Price Index - All Urban Consumers
Base November 1996 = 100
Food and Beverages

For 1996-2001. Columns headed % show percentile change in the index from the previous period for which an index is available.

Year	Jan Index	%	Feb Index	%	Mar Index	%	Apr Index	%	May Index	%	Jun Index	%	Jul Index	%	Aug Index	%	Sep Index	%	Oct Index	%	Nov Index	%	Dec Index	%
1996	-	-	-	-	-	-	-	-	-	-	-	-	-	-	-	-	-	-	-	-	100.0	-	-	-
1997	99.9	-0.1	-	-	100.0	0.1	-	-	99.7	-0.3	-	-	100.1	0.4	-	-	100.0	-0.1	-	-	100.8	0.8	-	-
1998	101.7	0.9	-	-	101.3	-0.4	-	-	101.8	0.5	-	-	101.1	-0.7	-	-	101.3	0.2	-	-	102.1	0.8	-	-
1999	103.1	1.0	-	-	102.9	-0.2	-	-	103.4	0.5	-	-	102.5	-0.9	-	-	103.0	0.5	-	-	103.6	0.6	-	-
2000	104.0	0.4	-	-	104.4	0.4	-	-	105.5	1.1	-	-	106.3	0.8	-	-	106.5	0.2	-	-	105.6	-0.8	-	-
2001	107.0	1.3	-	-	107.6	0.6	-	-	108.4	0.7	-	-	108.8	0.4	-	-	109.7	0.8	-	-	109.8	0.1	-	-

Source: U.S. Department of Labor, Bureau of Labor Statistics, Division of Consumer Prices and Price Indexes. - indicates no data collected for period.

Washington-Baltimore, DC-MD-VA-WV
Consumer Price Index - Urban Wage Earners
Base November 1996 = 100
Food and Beverages

For 1996-2001. Columns headed % show percentile change in the index from the previous period for which an index is available.

Year	Jan		Feb		Mar		Apr		May		Jun		Jul		Aug		Sep		Oct		Nov		Dec	
	Index	%	Index	%	Index	%	Index	%	Index	%	Index	%	Index	%	Index	%	Index	%	Index	%	Index	%	Index	%
1996	-	-	-	-	-	-	-	-	-	-	-	-	-	-	-	-	-	-	-	-	100.0	-	-	-
1997	99.9	-0.1	-	-	100.0	0.1	-	-	99.7	-0.3	-	-	99.9	0.2	-	-	99.8	-0.1	-	-	100.6	0.8	-	-
1998	101.7	1.1	-	-	101.1	-0.6	-	-	101.6	0.5	-	-	100.9	-0.7	-	-	101.1	0.2	-	-	102.0	0.9	-	-
1999	102.9	0.9	-	-	102.7	-0.2	-	-	103.1	0.4	-	-	102.1	-1.0	-	-	102.6	0.5	-	-	103.2	0.6	-	-
2000	103.6	0.4	-	-	103.7	0.1	-	-	104.9	1.2	-	-	105.8	0.9	-	-	106.1	0.3	-	-	105.0	-1.0	-	-
2001	106.6	1.5	-	-	107.3	0.7	-	-	108.3	0.9	-	-	108.6	0.3	-	-	109.5	0.8	-	-	109.4	-0.1	-	-

Source: U.S. Department of Labor, Bureau of Labor Statistics, Division of Consumer Prices and Price Indexes. - indicates no data collected for period.

Washington-Baltimore, DC-MD-VA-WV
Consumer Price Index - All Urban Consumers
Base November 1996 = 100
Housing

For 1996-2001. Columns headed % show percentile change in the index from the previous period for which an index is available.

Year	Jan Index	%	Feb Index	%	Mar Index	%	Apr Index	%	May Index	%	Jun Index	%	Jul Index	%	Aug Index	%	Sep Index	%	Oct Index	%	Nov Index	%	Dec Index	%
1996	-	-	-	-	-	-	-	-	-	-	-	-	-	-	-	-	-	-	-	-	100.0	-	-	-
1997	100.4	0.4	-	-	100.6	0.2	-	-	100.4	-0.2	-	-	102.4	2.0	-	-	101.9	-0.5	-	-	99.9	-2.0	-	-
1998	100.9	1.0	-	-	101.8	0.9	-	-	101.5	-0.3	-	-	105.2	3.6	-	-	105.5	0.3	-	-	103.1	-2.3	-	-
1999	103.8	0.7	-	-	104.5	0.7	-	-	104.0	-0.5	-	-	107.4	3.3	-	-	107.2	-0.2	-	-	105.5	-1.6	-	-
2000	106.1	0.6	-	-	107.5	1.3	-	-	106.8	-0.7	-	-	110.5	3.5	-	-	110.8	0.3	-	-	110.2	-0.5	-	-
2001	111.4	1.1	-	-	112.0	0.5	-	-	111.7	-0.3	-	-	114.3	2.3	-	-	114.7	0.3	-	-	113.4	-1.1	-	-

Source: U.S. Department of Labor, Bureau of Labor Statistics, Division of Consumer Prices and Price Indexes. - indicates no data collected for period.

Washington-Baltimore, DC-MD-VA-WV
Consumer Price Index - Urban Wage Earners
Base November 1996 = 100
Housing

For 1996-2001. Columns headed % show percentile change in the index from the previous period for which an index is available.

Year	Jan		Feb		Mar		Apr		May		Jun		Jul		Aug		Sep		Oct		Nov		Dec	
	Index	%	Index	%	Index	%	Index	%	Index	%	Index	%	Index	%	Index	%	Index	%	Index	%	Index	%	Index	%
1996	-	-	-	-	-	-	-	-	-	-	-	-	-	-	-	-	-	-	-	-	100.0	-	-	-
1997	100.4	0.4	-	-	100.5	0.1	-	-	100.4	-0.1	-	-	102.4	2.0	-	-	102.2	-0.2	-	-	100.0	-2.2	-	-
1998	100.9	0.9	-	-	101.6	0.7	-	-	101.6	0.0	-	-	105.5	3.8	-	-	105.7	0.2	-	-	103.2	-2.4	-	-
1999	103.9	0.7	-	-	104.6	0.7	-	-	104.2	-0.4	-	-	107.7	3.4	-	-	107.4	-0.3	-	-	105.6	-1.7	-	-
2000	106.3	0.7	-	-	107.4	1.0	-	-	106.6	-0.7	-	-	110.7	3.8	-	-	110.9	0.2	-	-	110.3	-0.5	-	-
2001	111.1	0.7	-	-	111.7	0.5	-	-	111.6	-0.1	-	-	114.4	2.5	-	-	114.9	0.4	-	-	113.7	-1.0	-	-

Source: U.S. Department of Labor, Bureau of Labor Statistics, Division of Consumer Prices and Price Indexes. - indicates no data collected for period.

Washington-Baltimore, DC-MD-VA-WV
Consumer Price Index - All Urban Consumers
Base November 1996 = 100
Apparel

For 1996-2001. Columns headed % show percentile change in the index from the previous period for which an index is available.

Year	Jan Index	%	Feb Index	%	Mar Index	%	Apr Index	%	May Index	%	Jun Index	%	Jul Index	%	Aug Index	%	Sep Index	%	Oct Index	%	Nov Index	%	Dec Index	%
1996	-	-	-	-	-	-	-	-	-	-	-	-	-	-	-	-	-	-	-	-	100.0	-	-	-
1997	99.0	-1.0	-	-	100.3	1.3	-	-	101.4	1.1	-	-	97.3	-4.0	-	-	99.2	2.0	-	-	95.3	-3.9	-	-
1998	94.1	-1.3	-	-	105.2	11.8	-	-	100.9	-4.1	-	-	97.6	-3.3	-	-	98.0	0.4	-	-	99.5	1.5	-	-
1999	95.9	-3.6	-	-	98.5	2.7	-	-	100.4	1.9	-	-	94.5	-5.9	-	-	101.8	7.7	-	-	98.5	-3.2	-	-
2000	97.9	-0.6	-	-	104.2	6.4	-	-	97.6	-6.3	-	-	91.6	-6.1	-	-	100.1	9.3	-	-	99.1	-1.0	-	-
2001	94.2	-4.9	-	-	101.8	8.1	-	-	98.4	-3.3	-	-	93.1	-5.4	-	-	104.1	11.8	-	-	100.5	-3.5	-	-

Source: U.S. Department of Labor, Bureau of Labor Statistics, Division of Consumer Prices and Price Indexes. - indicates no data collected for period.

Washington-Baltimore, DC-MD-VA-WV
Consumer Price Index - Urban Wage Earners
Base November 1996 = 100
Apparel

For 1996-2001. Columns headed % show percentile change in the index from the previous period for which an index is available.

Year	Jan		Feb		Mar		Apr		May		Jun		Jul		Aug		Sep		Oct		Nov		Dec	
	Index	%	Index	%	Index	%	Index	%	Index	%	Index	%	Index	%	Index	%	Index	%	Index	%	Index	%	Index	%
1996	-	-	-	-	-	-	-	-	-	-	-	-	-	-	-	-	-	-	-	-	100.0	-	-	-
1997	98.7	-1.3	-	-	101.1	2.4	-	-	102.4	1.3	-	-	98.0	-4.3	-	-	99.4	1.4	-	-	96.1	-3.3	-	-
1998	94.0	-2.2	-	-	106.1	12.9	-	-	100.8	-5.0	-	-	96.5	-4.3	-	-	98.4	2.0	-	-	99.9	1.5	-	-
1999	94.9	-5.0	-	-	98.3	3.6	-	-	100.4	2.1	-	-	93.2	-7.2	-	-	102.1	9.5	-	-	98.3	-3.7	-	-
2000	96.6	-1.7	-	-	103.7	7.3	-	-	97.0	-6.5	-	-	89.5	-7.7	-	-	100.1	11.8	-	-	98.6	-1.5	-	-
2001	92.3	-6.4	-	-	102.0	10.5	-	-	97.5	-4.4	-	-	91.8	-5.8	-	-	104.9	14.3	-	-	100.8	-3.9	-	-

Source: U.S. Department of Labor, Bureau of Labor Statistics, Division of Consumer Prices and Price Indexes. - indicates no data collected for period.

Washington-Baltimore, DC-MD-VA-WV

Consumer Price Index - All Urban Consumers
Base November 1996 = 100

Transportation

For 1996-2000. Columns headed % show percentile change in the index from the previous period for which an index is available.

Year	Jan		Feb		Mar		Apr		May		Jun		Jul		Aug		Sep		Oct		Nov		Dec	
	Index	%	Index	%	Index	%	Index	%	Index	%	Index	%	Index	%	Index	%	Index	%	Index	%	Index	%	Index	%
1996	-	-	-	-	-	-	-	-	-	-	-	-	-	-	-	-	-	-	-	-	100.0	-	-	-
1997	100.4	0.4	-	-	100.9	0.5	-	-	100.1	-0.8	-	-	99.7	-0.4	-	-	100.7	1.0	-	-	100.2	-0.5	-	-
1998	99.5	-0.7	-	-	98.3	-1.2	-	-	98.1	-0.2	-	-	98.8	0.7	-	-	97.8	-1.0	-	-	98.3	0.5	-	-
1999	97.9	-0.4	-	-	97.8	-0.1	-	-	99.7	1.9	-	-	100.7	1.0	-	-	101.8	1.1	-	-	103.0	1.2	-	-
2000	102.9	-0.1	-	-	107.0	4.0	-	-	107.4	0.4	-	-	109.0	1.5	-	-	107.9	-1.0	-	-	108.4	0.5	-	-

Source: U.S. Department of Labor, Bureau of Labor Statistics, Division of Consumer Prices and Price Indexes. - indicates no data collected for period.

Washington-Baltimore, DC-MD-VA-WV
Consumer Price Index - Urban Wage Earners
Base November 1996 = 100
Transportation

For 1996-2000. Columns headed % show percentile change in the index from the previous period for which an index is available.

Year	Jan Index	%	Feb Index	%	Mar Index	%	Apr Index	%	May Index	%	Jun Index	%	Jul Index	%	Aug Index	%	Sep Index	%	Oct Index	%	Nov Index	%	Dec Index	%
1996	-	-	-	-	-	-	-	-	-	-	-	-	-	-	-	-	-	-	-	-	100.0	-	-	-
1997	100.6	0.6	-	-	101.0	0.4	-	-	100.2	-0.8	-	-	99.6	-0.6	-	-	100.7	1.1	-	-	100.0	-0.7	-	-
1998	99.2	-0.8	-	-	98.1	-1.1	-	-	98.0	-0.1	-	-	98.7	0.7	-	-	97.8	-0.9	-	-	98.3	0.5	-	-
1999	97.9	-0.4	-	-	97.5	-0.4	-	-	99.5	2.1	-	-	100.4	0.9	-	-	101.7	1.3	-	-	103.0	1.3	-	-
2000	103.0	0.0	-	-	106.6	3.5	-	-	107.2	0.6	-	-	108.5	1.2	-	-	107.7	-0.7	-	-	108.2	0.5	-	-

Source: U.S. Department of Labor, Bureau of Labor Statistics, Division of Consumer Prices and Price Indexes. - indicates no data collected for period.

Washington-Baltimore, DC-MD-VA-WV
Consumer Price Index - All Urban Consumers
Base November 1996 = 100
Medical Care

For 1996-2001. Columns headed % show percentile change in the index from the previous period for which an index is available.

Year	Jan		Feb		Mar		Apr		May		Jun		Jul		Aug		Sep		Oct		Nov		Dec	
	Index	%	Index	%	Index	%	Index	%	Index	%	Index	%	Index	%	Index	%	Index	%	Index	%	Index	%	Index	%
1996	-	-	-	-	-	-	-	-	-	-	-	-	-	-	-	-	-	-	-	-	100.0	-	-	-
1997	102.3	2.3	-	-	102.5	0.2	-	-	101.7	-0.8	-	-	101.3	-0.4	-	-	101.8	0.5	-	-	102.8	1.0	-	-
1998	103.9	1.1	-	-	104.1	0.2	-	-	103.9	-0.2	-	-	104.2	0.3	-	-	104.7	0.5	-	-	105.5	0.8	-	-
1999	105.5	0.0	-	-	106.8	1.2	-	-	106.6	-0.2	-	-	106.9	0.3	-	-	107.0	0.1	-	-	107.6	0.6	-	-
2000	108.6	0.9	-	-	109.2	0.6	-	-	109.8	0.5	-	-	110.5	0.6	-	-	108.9	-1.4	-	-	110.4	1.4	-	-
2001	110.8	0.4	-	-	111.4	0.5	-	-	110.3	-1.0	-	-	110.6	0.3	-	-	110.7	0.1	-	-	112.0	1.2	-	-

Source: U.S. Department of Labor, Bureau of Labor Statistics, Division of Consumer Prices and Price Indexes. - indicates no data collected for period.

Washington-Baltimore, DC-MD-VA-WV
Consumer Price Index - Urban Wage Earners
Base November 1996 = 100
Medical Care

For 1996-2001. Columns headed % show percentile change in the index from the previous period for which an index is available.

Year	Jan		Feb		Mar		Apr		May		Jun		Jul		Aug		Sep		Oct		Nov		Dec	
	Index	%	Index	%	Index	%	Index	%	Index	%	Index	%	Index	%	Index	%	Index	%	Index	%	Index	%	Index	%
1996	-	-	-	-	-	-	-	-	-	-	-	-	-	-	-	-	-	-	-	-	100.0	-	-	-
1997	101.7	1.7	-	-	102.0	0.3	-	-	101.0	-1.0	-	-	100.6	-0.4	-	-	100.9	0.3	-	-	102.1	1.2	-	-
1998	103.3	1.2	-	-	103.5	0.2	-	-	103.2	-0.3	-	-	103.5	0.3	-	-	104.2	0.7	-	-	104.6	0.4	-	-
1999	104.0	-0.6	-	-	105.5	1.4	-	-	105.1	-0.4	-	-	105.8	0.7	-	-	105.9	0.1	-	-	106.4	0.5	-	-
2000	107.4	0.9	-	-	107.9	0.5	-	-	108.5	0.6	-	-	109.4	0.8	-	-	107.8	-1.5	-	-	109.2	1.3	-	-
2001	109.7	0.5	-	-	110.3	0.5	-	-	109.3	-0.9	-	-	109.6	0.3	-	-	109.6	0.0	-	-	110.7	1.0	-	-

Source: U.S. Department of Labor, Bureau of Labor Statistics, Division of Consumer Prices and Price Indexes. - indicates no data collected for period.

Washington-Baltimore, DC-MD-VA-WV
Consumer Price Index - All Urban Consumers
Base December 1997 = 100
Recreation

For 1997-2001. Columns headed % show percentile change in the index from the previous period for which an index is available.

Year	Jan Index	%	Feb Index	%	Mar Index	%	Apr Index	%	May Index	%	Jun Index	%	Jul Index	%	Aug Index	%	Sep Index	%	Oct Index	%	Nov Index	%	Dec Index	%
1997	-	-	-	-	-	-	-	-	-	-	-	-	-	-	-	-	-	-	-	-	-	-	100.0	-
1998	101.0	1.0	-	-	101.3	0.3	-	-	101.6	0.3	-	-	101.0	-0.6	-	-	101.9	0.9	-	-	101.2	-0.7	-	-
1999	102.7	1.5	-	-	101.9	-0.8	-	-	102.9	1.0	-	-	103.2	0.3	-	-	102.7	-0.5	-	-	103.2	0.5	-	-
2000	103.5	0.3	-	-	103.8	0.3	-	-	104.0	0.2	-	-	103.8	-0.2	-	-	103.6	-0.2	-	-	103.4	-0.2	-	-
2001	104.0	0.6	-	-	104.4	0.4	-	-	104.8	0.4	-	-	105.4	0.6	-	-	105.9	0.5	-	-	106.0	0.1	-	-

Source: U.S. Department of Labor, Bureau of Labor Statistics, Division of Consumer Prices and Price Indexes. - indicates no data collected for period.

Washington-Baltimore, DC-MD-VA-WV
Consumer Price Index - Urban Wage Earners
Base December 1997 = 100
Recreation

For 1997-2001. Columns headed % show percentile change in the index from the previous period for which an index is available.

Year	Jan		Feb		Mar		Apr		May		Jun		Jul		Aug		Sep		Oct		Nov		Dec	
	Index	%	Index	%	Index	%	Index	%	Index	%	Index	%	Index	%	Index	%	Index	%	Index	%	Index	%	Index	%
1997	-	-	-	-	-	-	-	-	-	-	-	-	-	-	-	-	-	-	-	-	-	-	100.0	-
1998	101.4	1.4	-	-	101.2	-0.2	-	-	101.6	0.4	-	-	101.1	-0.5	-	-	101.8	0.7	-	-	101.1	-0.7	-	-
1999	102.7	1.6	-	-	101.6	-1.1	-	-	102.0	0.4	-	-	102.3	0.3	-	-	101.5	-0.8	-	-	102.2	0.7	-	-
2000	102.5	0.3	-	-	102.8	0.3	-	-	103.0	0.2	-	-	102.5	-0.5	-	-	102.4	-0.1	-	-	102.2	-0.2	-	-
2001	102.8	0.6	-	-	103.6	0.8	-	-	103.8	0.2	-	-	104.4	0.6	-	-	104.4	0.0	-	-	104.6	0.2	-	-

Source: U.S. Department of Labor, Bureau of Labor Statistics, Division of Consumer Prices and Price Indexes. - indicates no data collected for period.

Washington-Baltimore, DC-MD-VA-WV
Consumer Price Index - All Urban Consumers
Base December 1997 = 100
Education & Communication

For 1997-2001. Columns headed % show percentile change in the index from the previous period for which an index is available.

Year	Jan Index	%	Feb Index	%	Mar Index	%	Apr Index	%	May Index	%	Jun Index	%	Jul Index	%	Aug Index	%	Sep Index	%	Oct Index	%	Nov Index	%	Dec Index	%
1997	-	-	-	-	-	-	-	-	-	-	-	-	-	-	-	-	-	-	-	-	-	-	100.0	-
1998	99.9	-0.1	-	-	99.8	-0.1	-	-	101.2	1.4	-	-	101.3	0.1	-	-	102.6	1.3	-	-	102.9	0.3	-	-
1999	102.3	-0.6	-	-	102.0	-0.3	-	-	101.8	-0.2	-	-	101.6	-0.2	-	-	103.4	1.8	-	-	103.9	0.5	-	-
2000	103.8	-0.1	-	-	103.2	-0.6	-	-	102.8	-0.4	-	-	104.0	1.2	-	-	104.5	0.5	-	-	105.1	0.6	-	-
2001	105.9	0.8	-	-	106.5	0.6	-	-	106.0	-0.5	-	-	107.9	1.8	-	-	109.6	1.6	-	-	110.6	0.9	-	-

Source: U.S. Department of Labor, Bureau of Labor Statistics, Division of Consumer Prices and Price Indexes. - indicates no data collected for period.

Washington-Baltimore, DC-MD-VA-WV
Consumer Price Index - Urban Wage Earners
Base December 1997 = 100
Education & Communication

For 1997-2001. Columns headed % show percentile change in the index from the previous period for which an index is available.

Year	Jan		Feb		Mar		Apr		May		Jun		Jul		Aug		Sep		Oct		Nov		Dec	
	Index	%	Index	%	Index	%	Index	%	Index	%	Index	%	Index	%	Index	%	Index	%	Index	%	Index	%	Index	%
1997	-	-	-	-	-	-	-	-	-	-	-	-	-	-	-	-	-	-	-	-	-	-	100.0	-
1998	100.0	0.0	-	-	99.9	-0.1	-	-	101.8	1.9	-	-	101.9	0.1	-	-	102.8	0.9	-	-	102.9	0.1	-	-
1999	102.2	-0.7	-	-	102.0	-0.2	-	-	101.8	-0.2	-	-	101.5	-0.3	-	-	102.9	1.4	-	-	103.4	0.5	-	-
2000	103.2	-0.2	-	-	102.5	-0.7	-	-	102.0	-0.5	-	-	102.3	0.3	-	-	102.6	0.3	-	-	103.5	0.9	-	-
2001	104.6	1.1	-	-	105.2	0.6	-	-	104.5	-0.7	-	-	106.2	1.6	-	-	107.7	1.4	-	-	108.8	1.0	-	-

Source: U.S. Department of Labor, Bureau of Labor Statistics, Division of Consumer Prices and Price Indexes. - indicates no data collected for period.

CHAPTER 7

PRODUCER PRICE INDEX

PRODUCER PRICE INDEX

The Producer Price Index (PPI) is a program of the Bureau of Labor Statistics (BLS), U.S. Department of Labor. In one of its publications, BLS describes the Producer Price Index (PPI) as follows:

> The Producer Price Index . . . measures average changes in selling prices received by domestic producers for their output. Most of the information used in calculating the Producer Price Index is obtained through the systematic sampling of virtually every industry in the mining and manufacturing sectors of the economy. The PPI program (also known as the industrial price program) includes some data from other sectors as well—agriculture, fishing, forestry, services, and gas and electricity. Thus the title "Producer Price Index" refers to an entire "family" or system of indexes. (Reference 1, p. 125.)

Description of the PPI

The PPI covers nearly 500 mining and manufacturing industries and about 8,000 specific products and product categories. More than 3,000 commodity prices are included, organized by type of product and end use. Data are reported by product groupings and sub-groups as well as in large aggregates.

Important aspects of the PPI include the definition of *price*, the selection of a *sample universe*, *data collection*, and the analytical management of the collected data, including the use of *weights*. Data are expressed as an index; the base year at present (2000) continues to be 1982, meaning that prices for 1982 are indexed at 100.

Price. Price is defined as "the net revenue accruing to a specified producing establishment from a specified kind of buyer for a specified product shipped under specified transaction terms on a specified day of the month." (Reference 1). Under this definition, companies voluntarily providing pricing information to the BLS thus report on *actual* shipments in a given month rather than average price levels. Prices exclude taxes paid but reflect discounts, low-interest financing, and other forms of incentives, rebates, and the like.

Sampling. Samples are chosen from each industry surveyed using Unemployment Insurance System data for identifying establishments—because virtually all employers are required to report to the system. Establishments are stratified, meaning that they are assigned to groups with like characteristics within an industry. Within strata, units are ordered by size. The number of units required for the sample is selected within each stratum based on employment. Selection of each establishment is then accomplished systematically with a probability of selection proportionate to its size.

Data Collection. Data are collected by companies in the sample on a voluntary basis. Within each establishment, a portion of the transactions is selected by the BLS field representative; these transactions are then priced every month. The selection of the transactions is also made systematically so that the probability of a product or commodity being selected is proportional to its relative importance to the reporting unit.

Weights. In order to create price indexes for aggregations of products, price indexes for individual products/commodities must be combined to form a composite index. This is accomplished by giving each component a weight appropriate to its importance in the aggregate as a whole. Industrial products are weighted by their proportion of total industry shipments as measured by the Standard Industrial Classification (SIC) system and reported by the *Census of Manufactures*. Commodities are weighted based on gross value of shipments data.

Base of Index. The index shows prices relative to 1982, which is defined as 100. Changes in the index are usually expressed as increases or decreases in percent, derived by the following formula:

((Current Index / Previous Index) - 1) x 100.

If the current index is 220.5 and the last index is 219.7, the formula produces a 0.36% change. This is the actual price increase from the last measured index to the current index.

This brief description hides much of the complexity of the PPI. For more details, the reader is referred to Reference 1. In summary, the methodology used is designed to present an accurate picture of price movements. The accuracy of the index is dependent on voluntary reporting; however, price definitions, sampling, and analytical factors are designed to take into account producers of all sizes operating in all kinds of markets and geographies; prices are actual, excluding taxes but including sales incentives; industrial establishments as well as products and commodities are selected to reflect, in the index, in proportion to their relative importance overall.

History of the PPI

The PPI (then called the Wholesale Price Index or WPI), was first published in 1902 and covered the 1890-1901 period. The WPI was initially an average of prices. Weighting of components was first incorporated in 1914. Major sample expansions and reclassifications took place in 1952 and 1967. In 1978, the index was renamed Producer Price Index in recognition of the fact that the meaning of the word "wholesale"—which had been understood earlier to mean goods sold in large quantities—had come to mean prices charged by wholesalers, jobbers, and distributors. The PPI is based on prices received by producers from the party that makes the first purchase, be that a distributor, a retailer, or the final consumer. The last comprehensive revision of the PPI, begun in 1978, culminated in January 1986 with the introduction of the current methods of price definition, sampling, data collection, and analysis.

Uses of the PPI

The PPI is widely used by government, industry, labor organization, and in the academic sector. It is an early measure of inflation—because producer sales predate retail sales; the latter form the backbone of the Consumer Price Index (CPI). The CPI, however, does not mirror the movements of the PPI at some lag in time. The PPI excludes imported goods, the CPI does not; the CPI includes services, the PPI largely does not. The CPI does not directly include the prices of capital equipment (industrial tooling and the like); the PPI does. Sharp swings in the prices of goods and other items may not reflect in consumer prices in the same way—because distributors and retailers absorb price rises/drops rather than cause wide price swings at the consumer level. The PPI is used in the construction of the implicit GNP deflator. In addition to the use of the index for analytical purposes in industry, it is used in contracts in price escalation clauses and in inventory valuation.

Presentation of Data

Six summary tables of the Producer Price Index are presented in Chapter 4, Other Cyclic Indicators, in the section on Prices and Productivity. In this chapter, 120 detailed PPI tables are shown. The first four tables show annual averages for 15 major product and commodity groupings and 100 subdivisions from 1926 to 1999. Thereafter, monthly data, from 1913 or a later date to 1999 are shown, first by the major group ("Farm Products") and then followed by the next level of detail provided by the PPI ("Fruits & Melons, Fresh/Dry Vegetables & Nuts," "Grains," "Livestock," etc.). All tables show a 1982 base (1982 = 100). Percent changes in the index from month to month are precalculated.

Bibliography

1. U.S. Department of Labor, Bureau of Labor Statistics. *BLS Handbook of Methods*, Bulletin 2285, 1987. Washington, D.C.

Producer Price Index
Annual Averages, 1926-1934
Base 1982 = 100

Columns headed % show percentile change in the index from the previous period for which an index is available.

	1926		1927		1928		1929		1930		1931		1932		1933		1934	
	Index	%	Index	%	Index	%	Index	%	Index	%	Index	%	Index	%	Index	%	Index	%
Farm Products	25.3	-	25.1	-0.8	26.7	6.4	26.4	-1.1	22.4	-15.2	16.4	-26.8	12.2	-25.6	13.0	6.6	16.5	26.9
Fruits & Melons, Fresh/Dry Vegetables & Nuts	27.0	-	25.8	-4.4	25.6	-0.8	25.7	0.4	25.8	0.4	18.5	-28.3	14.3	-22.7	15.5	8.4	16.9	9.0
Grains	33.7	-	34.0	0.9	36.0	5.9	32.8	-8.9	26.4	-19.5	17.9	-32.2	13.3	-25.7	17.9	34.6	25.1	40.2
Slaughter Livestock	18.8	-	18.8	0.0	20.0	6.4	20.0	0.0	16.8	-16.0	11.9	-29.2	8.9	-25.2	8.2	-7.9	9.8	19.5
Slaughter Poultry	102.5	-	91.9	-10.3	98.5	7.2	109.0	10.7	88.4	-18.9	75.4	-14.7	60.0	-20.4	47.4	-21.0	53.3	12.4
Plant and Animal Fibers	45.0	-	44.0	-2.2	48.0	9.1	45.6	-5.0	32.3	-29.2	21.2	-34.4	15.4	-27.4	19.8	28.6	26.3	32.8
Fluid Milk	19.5	-	19.9	2.1	20.3	2.0	21.2	4.4	20.6	-2.8	18.5	-10.2	13.6	-26.5	13.2	-2.9	16.2	22.7
Chicken Eggs	67.4	-	60.5	-10.2	63.7	5.3	70.3	10.4	54.1	-23.0	41.7	-22.9	37.5	-10.1	32.9	-12.3	39.1	18.8
Hay, Hayseeds and Oilseeds	29.5	-	26.2	-11.2	28.9	10.3	30.4	5.2	27.7	-8.9	21.1	-23.8	15.4	-27.0	16.0	3.9	23.3	45.6
Other Farm Products	13.2	-	13.1	-0.8	14.8	13.0	14.4	-2.7	9.7	-32.6	6.8	-29.9	6.0	-11.8	6.6	10.0	8.2	24.2
Processed Foods and Feeds	-	-	-	-	-	-	-	-	-	-	-	-	-	-	-	-	-	-
Cereal and Bakery Products	18.8	-	17.8	-5.3	17.6	-1.1	16.5	-6.3	15.3	-7.3	13.8	-9.8	12.5	-9.4	14.1	12.8	16.7	18.4
Meats, Poultry, and Fish	17.5	-	16.2	-7.4	18.7	15.4	19.1	2.1	17.2	-9.9	13.2	-23.3	10.2	-22.7	8.8	-13.7	11.0	25.0
Dairy Products	17.5	-	18.1	3.4	18.4	1.7	18.4	0.0	16.7	-9.2	14.3	-14.4	10.7	-25.2	10.6	-0.9	12.7	19.8
Processed Fruits and Vegetables	20.3	-	20.1	-1.0	21.5	7.0	22.4	4.2	21.0	-6.3	17.6	-16.2	15.7	-10.8	15.9	1.3	17.9	12.6
Sugar and Confectionery	19.3	-	20.7	7.3	19.5	-5.8	17.5	-10.3	16.1	-8.0	15.5	-3.7	13.8	-11.0	14.9	8.0	14.9	0.0
Beverages and Beverage Materials	-	-	-	-	-	-	-	-	-	-	-	-	-	-	-	-	-	-
Fats and Oils	-	-	-	-	-	-	-	-	-	-	-	-	-	-	-	-	-	-
Miscellaneous Processed Foods	-	-	-	-	-	-	-	-	-	-	-	-	-	-	-	-	-	-
Prepared Animal Feeds	-	-	-	-	-	-	-	-	-	-	-	-	-	-	-	-	-	-
Textile Products and Apparel	-	-	-	-	-	-	-	-	-	-	-	-	-	-	-	-	-	-
Synthetic Fibers	-	-	-	-	-	-	-	-	-	-	-	-	-	-	-	-	-	-
Processed Yarns and Threads	-	-	-	-	-	-	-	-	-	-	-	-	-	-	-	-	-	-
Gray Fabrics	-	-	-	-	-	-	-	-	-	-	-	-	-	-	-	-	-	-
Finished Fabrics	-	-	-	-	-	-	-	-	-	-	-	-	-	-	-	-	-	-
Apparel	-	-	-	-	-	-	-	-	-	-	-	-	-	-	-	-	-	-
Textile Housefurnishings	-	-	-	-	-	-	-	-	-	-	-	-	-	-	-	-	-	-
Miscellaneous Textile Products	-	-	-	-	-	-	-	-	-	-	-	-	-	-	-	-	-	-
Apparel & Other Fabricated Textile Products	-	-	-	-	-	-	-	-	-	-	-	-	-	-	-	-	-	-
Miscellaneous Textile Products/ Services	-	-	-	-	-	-	-	-	-	-	-	-	-	-	-	-	-	-
Hides, Skins, Leather, and Related Products	17.1	-	18.4	7.6	20.7	12.5	18.6	-10.1	17.1	-8.1	14.7	-14.0	12.5	-15.0	13.8	10.4	14.8	7.2
Hides and Skins	20.5	-	24.6	20.0	30.4	23.6	23.0	-24.3	18.7	-18.7	12.3	-34.2	8.6	-30.1	13.6	58.1	14.0	2.9

Source: U.S. Department of Labor, Bureau of Labor Statistics, Division of Industry Prices and Price Indexes. n.e.c. stands for not elsewhere classified. - indicates no data collected for period or unavailable.

Producer Price Index
Annual Averages, 1935-1943
Base 1982 = 100

Columns headed % show percentile change in the index from the previous period for which an index is available.

	1935 Index	%	1936 Index	%	1937 Index	%	1938 Index	%	1939 Index	%	1940 Index	%	1941 Index	%	1942 Index	%	1943 Index	%
Farm Products	19.8	20.0	20.4	3.0	21.8	6.9	17.3	-20.6	16.5	-4.6	17.1	3.6	20.8	21.6	26.7	28.4	30.9	15.7
Fruits & Melons, Fresh/Dry Vegetables & Nuts	15.6	-7.7	18.4	17.9	18.9	2.7	14.2	-24.9	15.7	10.6	16.0	1.9	16.8	5.0	24.8	47.6	33.5	35.1
Grains	27.8	10.8	29.7	6.8	33.2	11.8	20.5	-38.3	19.8	-3.4	22.9	15.7	25.7	12.2	31.2	21.4	39.1	25.3
Slaughter Livestock	16.8	71.4	16.8	0.0	19.2	14.3	15.5	-19.3	13.7	-11.6	13.3	-2.9	18.0	35.3	23.7	31.7	25.4	7.2
Slaughter Poultry	71.1	33.4	70.9	-0.3	72.4	2.1	70.2	-3.0	58.5	-16.7	58.2	-0.5	74.9	28.7	86.1	15.0	97.8	13.6
Plant and Animal Fibers	25.7	-2.3	27.1	5.4	26.6	-1.8	20.4	-23.3	23.5	15.2	23.3	-0.9	29.9	28.3	38.7	29.4	40.3	4.1
Fluid Milk	17.0	4.9	17.0	0.0	16.4	-3.5	15.0	-8.5	14.2	-5.3	15.8	11.3	17.1	8.2	19.3	12.9	21.8	13.0
Chicken Eggs	50.7	29.7	48.6	-4.1	44.9	-7.6	44.1	-1.8	35.8	-18.8	38.1	6.4	50.4	32.3	64.5	28.0	76.8	19.1
Hay, Hayseeds and Oilseeds	23.0	-1.3	22.5	-2.2	26.8	19.1	22.4	-16.4	20.8	-7.1	20.5	-1.4	21.7	5.9	30.0	38.2	36.6	22.0
Other Farm Products	9.3	13.4	8.9	-4.3	10.7	20.2	8.9	-16.8	8.5	-4.5	7.7	-9.4	10.1	31.2	14.7	45.5	16.7	13.6
Processed Foods and Feeds	-		-		-		-		-		-		-		-		-	
Cereal and Bakery Products	17.7	6.0	16.2	-8.5	16.5	1.9	14.8	-10.3	14.1	-4.7	14.7	4.3	15.2	3.4	16.8	10.5	17.6	4.8
Meats, Poultry, and Fish	16.5	50.0	15.3	-7.3	17.3	13.1	14.6	-15.6	13.5	-7.5	12.8	-5.2	15.8	23.4	19.6	24.1	19.3	-1.5
Dairy Products	13.9	9.4	14.6	5.0	14.5	-0.7	12.7	-12.4	12.0	-5.5	13.5	12.5	15.2	12.6	17.4	14.5	19.4	11.5
Processed Fruits and Vegetables	17.8	-0.6	17.5	-1.7	18.2	4.0	16.3	-10.4	15.7	-3.7	15.9	1.3	18.4	15.7	21.8	18.5	22.5	3.2
Sugar and Confectionery	16.3	9.4	16.8	3.1	16.4	-2.4	14.9	-9.1	15.2	2.0	14.4	-5.3	16.7	16.0	18.5	10.8	18.6	0.5
Beverages and Beverage Materials	-		-		-		-		-		-		-		-		-	
Fats and Oils	-		-		-		-		-		-		-		-		-	
Miscellaneous Processed Foods	-		-		-		-		-		-		-		-		-	
Prepared Animal Feeds	-		-		-		-		-		-		-		-		-	
Textile Products and Apparel	-		-		-		-		-		-		-		-		-	
Synthetic Fibers	-		-		-		-		-		-		-		-		-	
Processed Yarns and Threads	-		-		-		-		-		-		-		-		-	
Gray Fabrics	-		-		-		-		-		-		-		-		-	
Finished Fabrics	-		-		-		-		-		-		-		-		-	
Apparel	-		-		-		-		-		-		-		-		-	
Textile Housefurnishings	-		-		-		-		-		-		-		-		-	
Miscellaneous Textile Products	-		-		-		-		-		-		-		-		-	
Apparel & Other Fabricated Textile Products	-		-		-		-		-		-		-		-		-	
Miscellaneous Textile Products/ Services	-		-		-		-		-		-		-		-		-	
Hides, Skins, Leather, and Related Products	15.3	3.4	16.3	6.5	17.9	9.8	15.8	-11.7	16.3	3.2	17.2	5.5	18.4	7.0	20.1	9.2	20.1	0.0
Hides and Skins	16.4	17.1	19.3	17.7	23.2	20.2	15.1	-34.9	17.3	14.6	18.8	8.7	22.2	18.1	24.1	8.6	23.5	-2.5

Source: U.S. Department of Labor, Bureau of Labor Statistics, Division of Industry Prices and Price Indexes. n.e.c. stands for not elsewhere classified. - indicates no data collected for period or unavailable.

Producer Price Index
Annual Averages, 1944-1952
Base 1982 = 100

Columns headed % show percentile change in the index from the previous period for which an index is available.

	1944		1945		1946		1947		1948		1949		1950		1951		1952	
	Index	%	Index	%	Index	%	Index	%	Index	%	Index	%	Index	%	Index	%	Index	%
Farm Products	31.2	1.0	32.4	3.8	37.5	15.7	45.1	20.3	48.5	7.5	41.9	-13.6	44.0	5.0	51.2	16.4	48.4	-5.5
Fruits & Melons, Fresh/Dry Vegetables & Nuts	33.4	-0.3	33.7	0.9	35.7	5.9	36.0	0.8	37.4	3.9	36.3	-2.9	33.4	-8.0	35.6	6.6	44.0	23.6
Grains	42.7	9.2	43.7	2.3	52.3	19.7	71.0	35.8	67.2	-5.4	54.0	-19.6	57.5	6.5	63.6	10.6	62.9	-1.1
Slaughter Livestock	24.8	-2.4	25.8	4.0	30.4	17.8	41.4	36.2	46.7	12.8	39.1	-16.3	42.7	9.2	50.8	19.0	44.1	-13.2
Slaughter Poultry	95.3	-2.6	100.7	5.7	108.9	8.1	111.8	2.7	128.7	15.1	105.6	-17.9	96.8	-8.3	106.4	9.9	101.4	-4.7
Plant and Animal Fibers	41.0	1.7	42.9	4.6	56.9	32.6	65.7	15.5	69.7	6.1	67.1	-3.7	78.4	16.8	97.1	23.9	77.7	-20.0
Fluid Milk	22.5	3.2	22.5	0.0	27.2	20.9	30.0	10.3	34.1	13.7	27.6	-19.1	27.1	-1.8	32.1	18.5	33.5	4.4
Chicken Eggs	67.8	-11.7	73.1	7.8	70.5	-3.6	85.1	20.7	92.2	8.3	88.7	-3.8	75.3	-15.1	95.7	27.1	84.9	-11.3
Hay, Hayseeds and Oilseeds	40.5	10.7	40.3	-0.5	43.5	7.9	55.5	27.6	56.9	2.5	43.2	-24.1	46.6	7.9	53.2	14.2	51.0	-4.1
Other Farm Products	17.5	4.8	17.2	-1.7	19.7	14.5	25.3	28.4	26.3	4.0	27.3	3.8	33.6	23.1	36.4	8.3	35.9	-1.4
Processed Foods and Feeds	-	-	-	-	-	-	33.0	-	35.3	7.0	32.1	-9.1	33.2	3.4	36.9	11.1	36.4	-1.4
Cereal and Bakery Products	17.9	1.7	17.9	0.0	21.5	20.1	28.7	33.5	29.2	1.7	27.7	-5.1	28.2	1.8	30.5	8.2	30.5	0.0
Meats, Poultry, and Fish	18.5	-4.1	18.8	1.6	25.3	34.6	35.3	39.5	41.0	16.1	35.8	-12.7	37.9	5.9	43.6	15.0	40.5	-7.1
Dairy Products	19.3	-0.5	19.4	0.5	25.4	30.9	28.0	10.2	31.3	11.8	28.2	-9.9	27.7	-1.8	31.5	13.7	33.1	5.1
Processed Fruits and Vegetables	22.8	1.3	23.0	0.9	24.4	6.1	31.7	29.9	31.6	-0.3	31.4	-0.6	31.6	0.6	33.3	5.4	33.2	-0.3
Sugar and Confectionery	18.6	0.0	18.5	-0.5	22.0	18.9	28.9	31.4	29.6	2.4	27.4	-7.4	27.9	1.8	30.3	8.6	31.1	2.6
Beverages and Beverage Materials	-	-	-	-	-	-	26.6	-	27.8	4.5	28.3	1.8	30.5	7.8	32.5	6.6	33.2	2.2
Fats and Oils	-	-	-	-	-	-	-	-	-	-	-	-	-	-	-	-	-	-
Miscellaneous Processed Foods	-	-	-	-	-	-	34.8	-	36.5	4.9	40.0	9.6	43.9	9.7	45.6	3.9	44.2	-3.1
Prepared Animal Feeds	-	-	-	-	-	-	55.3	-	56.0	1.3	49.0	-12.5	48.8	-0.4	53.7	10.0	57.7	7.4
Textile Products and Apparel	-	-	-	-	-	-	50.6	-	52.8	4.3	48.3	-8.5	50.2	3.9	56.0	11.6	50.5	-9.8
Synthetic Fibers	-	-	-	-	-	-	-	-	-	-	-	-	-	-	-	-	-	-
Processed Yarns and Threads	-	-	-	-	-	-	-	-	-	-	-	-	-	-	-	-	-	-
Gray Fabrics	-	-	-	-	-	-	-	-	-	-	-	-	-	-	-	-	-	-
Finished Fabrics	-	-	-	-	-	-	-	-	-	-	-	-	-	-	-	-	-	-
Apparel	-	-	-	-	-	-	95.1	-	97.0	2.0	89.9	-7.3	90.5	0.7	97.6	7.8	94.0	-3.7
Textile Housefurnishings	-	-	-	-	-	-	97.2	-	103.1	6.1	95.7	-7.2	99.9	4.4	111.5	11.6	100.8	-9.6
Miscellaneous Textile Products	-	-	-	-	-	-	-	-	-	-	-	-	-	-	-	-	-	-
Apparel & Other Fabricated Textile Products	-	-	-	-	-	-	-	-	-	-	-	-	-	-	-	-	-	-
Miscellaneous Textile Products/ Services	-	-	-	-	-	-	-	-	-	-	-	-	-	-	-	-	-	-
Hides, Skins, Leather, and Related Products	19.9	-1.0	20.1	1.0	23.3	15.9	31.7	36.1	32.1	1.3	30.4	-5.3	32.9	8.2	37.7	14.6	30.5	-19.1
Hides and Skins	22.4	-4.7	23.9	6.7	30.3	26.8	47.6	57.1	44.5	-6.5	38.8	-12.8	45.0	16.0	51.9	15.3	27.5	-47.0

Source: U.S. Department of Labor, Bureau of Labor Statistics, Division of Industry Prices and Price Indexes. n.e.c. stands for not elsewhere classified. - indicates no data collected for period or unavailable.

Producer Price Index
Annual Averages, 1953-1961
Base 1982 = 100

Columns headed % show percentile change in the index from the previous period for which an index is available.

	1953		1954		1955		1956		1957		1958		1959		1960		1961	
	Index	%	Index	%	Index	%	Index	%	Index	%	Index	%	Index	%	Index	%	Index	%
Farm Products	43.8	-9.5	43.2	-1.4	40.5	-6.3	40.0	-1.2	41.1	2.8	42.9	4.4	40.2	-6.3	40.1	-0.2	39.7	-1.0
Fruits & Melons, Fresh/Dry Vegetables & Nuts	36.7	-16.6	36.3	-1.1	38.1	5.0	38.1	0.0	37.9	-0.5	41.0	8.2	37.6	-8.3	39.0	3.7	36.3	-6.9
Grains	57.8	-8.1	58.6	1.4	55.8	-4.8	55.8	0.0	53.9	-3.4	50.9	-5.6	49.5	-2.8	48.5	-2.0	49.2	1.4
Slaughter Livestock	37.5	-15.0	37.0	-1.3	31.8	-14.1	30.6	-3.8	35.3	15.4	41.6	17.8	38.2	-8.2	36.6	-4.2	36.0	-1.6
Slaughter Poultry	100.5	-0.9	81.8	-18.6	87.0	6.4	71.4	-17.9	66.4	-7.0	65.1	-2.0	59.4	-8.8	63.4	6.7	52.7	-16.9
Plant and Animal Fibers	69.8	-10.2	71.7	2.7	69.2	-3.5	69.4	0.3	70.2	1.2	68.6	-2.3	66.3	-3.4	63.6	-4.1	64.8	1.9
Fluid Milk	30.2	-9.9	27.9	-7.6	28.0	0.4	28.9	3.2	29.3	1.4	28.9	-1.4	28.9	0.0	30.0	3.8	30.2	0.7
Chicken Eggs	93.7	10.4	70.8	-24.4	76.0	7.3	72.6	-4.5	68.5	-5.6	72.5	5.8	58.1	-19.9	68.5	17.9	65.7	-4.1
Hay, Hayseeds and Oilseeds	46.8	-8.2	48.3	3.2	44.0	-8.9	42.9	-2.5	42.6	-0.7	39.9	-6.3	39.8	-0.3	38.8	-2.5	43.7	12.6
Other Farm Products	37.1	3.3	45.0	21.3	37.5	-16.7	38.6	2.9	38.0	-1.6	36.9	-2.9	34.9	-5.4	33.8	-3.2	34.1	0.9
Processed Foods and Feeds	34.8	-4.4	35.4	1.7	33.8	-4.5	33.8	0.0	34.8	3.0	36.5	4.9	35.6	-2.5	35.6	0.0	36.2	1.7
Cereal and Bakery Products	31.2	2.3	32.5	4.2	33.1	1.8	32.8	-0.9	33.3	1.5	33.6	0.9	34.0	1.2	34.7	2.1	35.4	2.0
Meats, Poultry, and Fish	34.7	-14.3	34.4	-0.9	31.7	-7.8	30.5	-3.8	34.4	12.8	39.9	16.0	36.7	-8.0	36.1	-1.6	35.3	-2.2
Dairy Products	32.3	-2.4	31.0	-4.0	31.0	0.0	31.7	2.3	32.6	2.8	32.9	0.9	33.4	1.5	34.6	3.6	35.4	2.3
Processed Fruits and Vegetables	33.1	-0.3	33.0	-0.3	33.3	0.9	34.1	2.4	32.8	-3.8	34.7	5.8	34.5	-0.6	33.8	-2.0	34.6	2.4
Sugar and Confectionery	31.3	0.6	32.2	2.9	31.6	-1.9	31.4	-0.6	32.4	3.2	33.1	2.2	32.9	-0.6	33.4	1.5	33.2	-0.6
Beverages and Beverage Materials	33.8	1.8	37.6	11.2	36.2	-3.7	37.1	2.5	37.1	0.0	36.3	-2.2	36.2	-0.3	36.1	-0.3	36.1	0.0
Fats and Oils	-	-	-	-	-	-	-	-	-	-	-	-	-	-	-	-	-	-
Miscellaneous Processed Foods	43.4	-1.8	38.3	-11.8	36.9	-3.7	35.9	-2.7	35.4	-1.4	35.8	1.1	35.9	0.3	37.9	5.6	37.8	-0.3
Prepared Animal Feeds	46.9	-18.7	51.3	9.4	40.5	-21.1	38.5	-4.9	36.0	-6.5	39.8	10.6	40.2	1.0	37.2	-7.5	40.4	8.6
Textile Products and Apparel	49.3	-2.4	48.2	-2.2	48.2	0.0	48.2	0.0	48.3	0.2	47.4	-1.9	48.1	1.5	48.6	1.0	47.8	-1.6
Synthetic Fibers	-	-	-	-	-	-	-	-	-	-	-	-	-	-	-	-	-	-
Processed Yarns and Threads	-	-	-	-	-	-	-	-	-	-	-	-	-	-	-	-	-	-
Gray Fabrics	-	-	-	-	-	-	-	-	-	-	-	-	-	-	-	-	-	-
Finished Fabrics	-	-	-	-	-	-	-	-	-	-	-	-	-	-	-	-	-	-
Apparel	93.4	-0.6	92.6	-0.9	92.6	0.0	93.6	1.1	93.6	0.0	93.4	-0.2	94.0	0.6	94.9	1.0	94.6	-0.3
Textile Housefurnishings	96.6	-4.2	94.3	-2.4	94.9	0.6	95.8	0.9	96.5	0.7	92.7	-3.9	93.8	1.2	96.1	2.5	96.6	0.5
Miscellaneous Textile Products	-	-	-	-	-	-	-	-	-	-	-	-	-	-	-	-	-	-
Apparel & Other Fabricated Textile Products	-	-	-	-	-	-	-	-	-	-	-	-	-	-	-	-	-	-
Miscellaneous Textile Products/ Services	-	-	-	-	-	-	-	-	-	-	-	-	-	-	-	-	-	-
Hides, Skins, Leather, and Related Products	31.0	1.6	29.5	-4.8	29.4	-0.3	31.2	6.1	31.2	0.0	31.6	1.3	35.9	13.6	34.6	-3.6	34.9	0.9
Hides and Skins	29.8	8.4	24.1	-19.1	24.7	2.5	25.8	4.5	24.1	-6.6	25.1	4.1	39.6	57.8	29.7	-25.0	31.9	7.4

Source: U.S. Department of Labor, Bureau of Labor Statistics, Division of Industry Prices and Price Indexes. n.e.c. stands for not elsewhere classified. - indicates no data collected for period or unavailable.

Producer Price Index
Annual Averages, 1962-1970
Base 1982 = 100

Columns headed % show percentile change in the index from the previous period for which an index is available.

	1962		1963		1964		1965		1966		1967		1968		1969		1970	
	Index	%	Index	%	Index	%	Index	%	Index	%	Index	%	Index	%	Index	%	Index	%
Farm Products	40.4	1.8	39.6	-2.0	39.0	-1.5	40.7	4.4	43.7	7.4	41.3	-5.5	42.3	2.4	45.0	6.4	45.8	1.8
Fruits & Melons, Fresh/Dry Vegetables & Nuts	37.9	4.4	37.3	-1.6	40.1	7.5	39.5	-1.5	39.8	0.8	39.4	-1.0	42.0	6.6	43.4	3.3	44.0	1.4
Grains	50.8	3.3	52.4	3.1	48.4	-7.6	46.1	-4.8	50.0	8.5	47.4	-5.2	42.1	-11.2	42.8	1.7	46.8	9.3
Slaughter Livestock	37.4	3.9	34.2	-8.6	32.6	-4.7	38.6	18.4	42.2	9.3	38.8	-8.1	40.2	3.6	45.4	12.9	45.3	-0.2
Slaughter Poultry	54.3	3.0	53.9	-0.7	52.2	-3.2	55.0	5.4	58.2	5.8	52.1	-10.5	54.0	3.6	58.8	8.9	51.9	-11.7
Plant and Animal Fibers	67.3	3.9	68.7	2.1	67.2	-2.2	62.3	-7.3	56.2	-9.8	49.3	-12.3	51.5	4.5	45.9	-10.9	44.5	-3.1
Fluid Milk	29.4	-2.6	29.2	-0.7	29.6	1.4	30.1	1.7	34.2	13.6	35.4	3.5	37.5	5.9	39.2	4.5	40.8	4.1
Chicken Eggs	63.2	-3.8	62.4	-1.3	60.3	-3.4	62.1	3.0	71.6	15.3	56.0	-21.8	62.3	11.2	74.9	20.2	71.0	-5.2
Hay, Hayseeds and Oilseeds	42.9	-1.8	46.0	7.2	44.8	-2.6	46.0	2.7	37.1	3.9	36.4	-1.9	37.7	3.6	39.9	5.8	42.7	7.0
Other Farm Products	33.6	-1.5	32.7	-2.7	36.1	10.4	35.7	-1.1	38.0	3.5	39.8	-1.0	40.6	2.0	42.7	5.2	44.6	4.4
Processed Foods and Feeds	36.5	0.8	36.8	0.8	36.7	-0.3	36.8	0.3	40.2	5.8	39.8	-1.0	39.8	1.0	40.5	1.8	42.4	4.7
Cereal and Bakery Products	36.2	2.3	36.1	-0.3	36.3	0.6	36.7	1.1	38.8	5.7	39.4	1.5	39.8	1.0	40.5	1.8	42.4	4.7
Meats, Poultry, and Fish	36.6	3.7	34.5	-5.7	33.6	-2.6	37.3	11.0	40.8	9.4	38.8	-4.9	40.0	3.1	44.2	10.5	45.0	1.8
Dairy Products	35.2	-0.6	35.4	0.6	35.5	0.3	35.8	0.8	39.1	9.2	40.2	2.8	42.1	4.7	43.5	3.3	44.7	2.8
Processed Fruits and Vegetables	33.3	-3.8	35.3	6.0	35.6	0.8	34.7	-2.5	35.6	2.6	36.4	2.2	38.8	6.6	39.4	1.5	40.3	2.3
Sugar and Confectionery	33.5	0.9	38.9	16.1	36.7	-5.7	35.8	-2.5	36.3	1.4	37.1	2.2	38.1	2.7	40.8	7.1	42.9	5.1
Beverages and Beverage Materials	36.2	0.3	36.9	1.9	38.8	5.1	38.6	-0.5	38.7	0.3	38.9	0.5	40.0	2.8	41.3	3.2	44.0	6.5
Fats and Oils											46.5	-	44.8	-3.7	46.9	4.7	55.1	17.5
Miscellaneous Processed Foods	36.4	-3.7	37.3	2.5	38.9	4.3	40.6	4.4	40.7	0.2	40.2	-1.2	41.3	2.7	43.4	5.1	45.5	4.8
Prepared Animal Feeds	42.7	5.7	45.0	5.4	44.0	-2.2	44.9	2.0	48.9	8.9	47.3	-3.3	45.8	-3.2	45.7	-0.2	49.1	7.4
Textile Products and Apparel	48.2	0.8	48.2	0.0	48.5	0.6	48.8	0.6	48.9	0.2	48.9	0.0	50.7	3.7	51.8	2.2	52.4	1.2
Synthetic Fibers	-	-	-	-	-	-	-	-	-	-	-	-	-	-	-	-	-	-
Processed Yarns and Threads	-	-	-	-	-	-	-	-	-	-	-	-	-	-	-	-	-	-
Gray Fabrics	-	-	-	-	-	-	-	-	-	-	-	-	-	-	-	-	-	-
Finished Fabrics	-	-	-	-	-	-	-	-	-	-	-	-	-	-	-	-	-	-
Apparel	95.0	0.4	95.4	0.4	96.3	0.9	97.1	0.8	98.3	1.2	100.0	1.7	103.6	3.6	107.4	3.7	110.8	3.2
Textile Housefurnishings	98.3	1.8	97.1	-1.2	97.6	0.5	97.3	-0.3	98.5	1.2	100.0	1.5	104.2	4.2	100.8	-3.3	103.5	2.7
Miscellaneous Textile Products	-	-																
Apparel & Other Fabricated Textile Products	-	-															-	-
Miscellaneous Textile Products/ Services	-	-									-						-	
Hides, Skins, Leather, and Related Products	35.3	1.1	34.3	-2.8	34.4	0.3	35.9	4.4	39.4	9.7	38.1	-3.3	39.3	3.1	41.5	5.6	42.0	1.2
Hides and Skins	31.4	-1.6	24.9	-20.7	25.9	4.0	32.9	27.0	41.7	26.7	27.9	-33.1	29.6	6.1	34.6	16.9	29.0	-16.2

Source: U.S. Department of Labor, Bureau of Labor Statistics, Division of Industry Prices and Price Indexes. n.e.c. stands for not elsewhere classified. - indicates no data collected for period or unavailable.

Producer Price Index
Annual Averages, 1971-1979
Base 1982 = 100

Columns headed % show percentile change in the index from the previous period for which an index is available.

	1971		1972		1973		1974		1975		1976		1977		1978		1979	
	Index	%	Index	%	Index	%	Index	%	Index	%	Index	%	Index	%	Index	%	Index	%
Farm Products	46.6	1.7	51.6	10.7	72.7	40.9	77.4	6.5	77.0	-0.5	78.8	2.3	79.4	0.8	87.7	10.5	99.6	13.6
Fruits & Melons, Fresh/Dry Vegetables & Nuts	47.3	7.5	50.3	6.3	66.3	31.8	75.8	14.3	72.4	-4.5	70.3	-2.9	75.8	7.8	85.3	12.5	90.3	5.9
Grains	47.8	2.1	48.8	2.1	87.1	78.5	122.3	40.4	106.2	-13.2	97.6	-8.1	78.2	-19.9	86.5	10.6	101.8	17.7
Slaughter Livestock	45.9	1.3	55.3	20.5	73.8	33.5	66.2	-10.3	72.9	10.1	67.2	-7.8	67.1	-0.1	85.4	27.3	100.9	18.1
Slaughter Poultry	52.2	0.6	54.2	3.8	93.5	72.5	82.0	-12.3	98.9	20.6	87.0	-12.0	91.4	5.1	104.1	13.9	101.2	-2.8
Plant and Animal Fibers	45.7	2.7	57.9	26.7	97.5	68.4	95.6	-1.9	75.5	-21.0	110.3	46.1	99.7	-9.6	95.3	-4.4	103.4	8.5
Fluid Milk	42.0	2.9	43.3	3.1	51.3	18.5	61.2	19.3	63.8	4.2	71.2	11.6	71.8	0.8	77.8	8.4	88.5	13.8
Chicken Eggs	56.4	-20.6	58.0	2.8	92.7	59.8	89.9	-3.0	89.4	-0.6	100.2	12.1	90.6	-9.6	88.7	-2.1	98.8	11.4
Hay, Hayseeds and Oilseeds	51.3	9.9	55.5	8.2	103.4	86.3	107.4	3.9	94.1	-12.4	98.9	5.1	110.1	11.3	101.4	-7.9	114.8	13.2
Other Farm Products	42.1	-1.4	45.5	8.1	53.7	18.0	59.9	11.5	61.8	3.2	81.4	31.7	118.7	45.8	100.2	-15.6	105.3	5.1
Processed Foods and Feeds	45.5	2.0	48.0	5.5	58.9	22.7	68.0	15.4	72.6	6.8	70.8	-2.5	74.0	4.5	80.6	8.9	88.5	9.8
Cereal and Bakery Products	44.0	3.8	45.2	2.7	53.0	17.3	67.5	27.4	70.1	3.9	67.8	-3.3	68.3	0.7	75.0	9.8	82.9	10.5
Meats, Poultry, and Fish	45.0	0.0	50.5	12.2	65.0	28.7	63.5	-2.3	74.2	16.9	70.5	-5.0	70.7	0.3	84.3	19.2	93.9	11.4
Dairy Products	46.5	4.0	47.7	2.6	52.7	10.5	58.8	11.6	62.6	6.5	67.7	8.1	69.7	3.0	75.7	8.6	84.9	12.2
Processed Fruits and Vegetables	41.7	3.5	43.6	4.6	47.2	8.3	56.3	19.3	61.9	9.9	62.0	0.2	68.3	10.2	73.8	8.1	80.9	9.6
Sugar and Confectionery	44.3	3.3	45.1	1.8	49.1	8.9	96.0	95.5	94.3	-1.8	70.8	-24.9	65.8	-7.1	73.3	11.4	79.6	8.6
Beverages and Beverage Materials	45.2	2.7	45.9	1.5	47.4	3.3	54.8	15.6	63.2	15.3	67.5	6.8	78.3	16.0	77.9	-0.5	82.0	5.3
Fats and Oils	58.6	6.4	54.6	-6.8	75.6	38.5	120.5	59.4	104.7	-13.1	82.8	-20.9	96.5	16.5	104.7	8.5	113.1	8.0
Miscellaneous Processed Foods	45.6	0.2	46.2	1.3	49.6	7.4	63.8	28.6	71.8	12.5	70.3	-2.1	76.5	8.8	80.1	4.7	87.1	8.7
Prepared Animal Feeds	49.4	0.6	54.9	11.1	94.0	71.2	87.1	-7.3	81.5	-6.4	92.0	12.9	96.8	5.2	93.4	-3.5	103.8	11.1
Textile Products and Apparel	53.3	1.7	55.5	4.1	60.5	9.0	68.0	12.4	67.4	-0.9	72.4	7.4	75.3	4.0	78.1	3.7	82.5	5.6
Synthetic Fibers	-	-	-	-	-	-	-	-	-	-	63.2	-	66.2	4.7	67.6	2.1	73.4	8.6
Processed Yarns and Threads	-	-	-	-	-	-	-	-	-	-	71.9	-	73.0	1.5	74.0	1.4	78.9	6.6
Gray Fabrics	-	-	-	-	-	-	-	-	-	-	73.0	-	72.1	-1.2	81.6	13.2	87.5	7.2
Finished Fabrics	-	-	-	-	-	-	-	-	-	-	81.2	-	83.3	2.6	83.3	0.0	86.2	3.5
Apparel	113.6	2.5	114.8	1.1	119.0	3.7	129.5	8.8	133.4	3.0	139.9	4.9	-	-	-	-	-	-
Textile Housefurnishings	104.9	1.4	109.2	4.1	113.3	3.8	143.1	26.3	151.9	6.1	159.3	4.9	-	-	-	-	-	-
Miscellaneous Textile Products	-	-	-	-	-	-	-	-	-	-	-	-	-	-	-	-	-	-
Apparel & Other Fabricated Textile Products	-	-	-	-	-	-	-	-	-	-	-	-	-	-	77.9	-	82.1	5.4
Miscellaneous Textile Products/ Services	-	-	-	-	-	-	-	-	-	-	-	-	-	-				
Hides, Skins, Leather, and Related Products	43.4	3.3	50.0	15.2	54.5	9.0	55.2	1.3	56.5	2.4	63.9	13.1	68.3	6.9	76.1	11.4	96.1	26.3
Hides and Skins	32.1	10.7	59.6	85.7	70.8	18.8	54.6	-22.9	48.6	-11.0	72.0	48.1	79.9	11.0	100.5	25.8	149.2	48.5

Source: U.S. Department of Labor, Bureau of Labor Statistics, Division of Industry Prices and Price Indexes. n.e.c. stands for not elsewhere classified. - indicates no data collected for period or unavailable.

Producer Price Index
Annual Averages, 1980-1988
Base 1982 = 100

Columns headed % show percentile change in the index from the previous period for which an index is available.

	1980		1981		1982		1983		1984		1985		1986		1987		1988	
	Index	%	Index	%	Index	%	Index	%	Index	%	Index	%	Index	%	Index	%	Index	%
Farm Products	102.9	3.3	105.2	2.2	100.0	-4.9	102.4	2.4	105.5	3.0	95.1	-9.9	92.9	-2.3	95.5	2.8	104.9	9.8
Fruits & Melons, Fresh/Dry Vegetables & Nuts	94.1	4.2	105.4	12.0	100.0	-5.1	103.3	3.3	109.6	6.1	102.7	-6.3	103.9	1.2	106.8	2.8	108.5	1.6
Grains	113.3	11.3	117.8	4.0	100.0	-15.1	114.0	14.0	113.7	-0.3	96.1	-15.5	79.3	-17.5	71.1	-10.3	97.9	37.7
Slaughter Livestock	98.0	-2.9	96.2	-1.8	100.0	4.0	94.3	-5.7	97.7	3.6	89.2	-8.7	91.8	2.9	102.0	11.1	103.3	1.3
Slaughter Poultry	105.3	4.1	104.8	-0.5	100.0	-4.6	107.6	7.6	125.4	16.5	117.9	-6.0	129.7	10.0	101.2	-22.0	121.5	20.1
Plant and Animal Fibers	133.6	29.2	119.2	-10.8	100.0	-16.1	111.9	11.9	112.6	0.6	97.5	-13.4	88.4	-9.3	106.5	20.5	98.4	-7.6
Fluid Milk	96.0	8.5	101.7	5.9	100.0	-1.7	99.8	-0.2	98.5	-1.3	93.7	-4.9	91.0	-2.9	91.9	1.0	89.4	-2.7
Chicken Eggs	95.7	-3.1	104.7	9.4	100.0	-4.5	-		117.9	17.9	95.7	-18.8	99.6	4.1	87.6	-12.0	88.6	1.1
Hay, Hayseeds and Oilseeds	116.1	1.1	128.8	10.9	100.0	-22.4	116.0	16.0	120.5	3.9	96.8	-19.7	92.9	-4.0	101.4	9.1	138.4	36.5
Other Farm Products	108.9	3.4	99.7	-8.4	100.0	0.3	102.8	2.8	104.1	1.3	103.1	-1.0	96.3	-6.6	94.4	-2.0	95.4	1.1
Processed Foods and Feeds	95.9	8.4	98.9	3.1	100.0	1.1	101.8	1.8	105.4	3.5	103.5	-1.8	105.4	1.8	107.9	2.4	112.7	4.4
Cereal and Bakery Products	93.0	12.2	100.7	8.3	100.0	-0.7	102.8	2.8	106.6	3.7	110.3	3.5	111.0	0.6	112.6	1.4	123.0	9.2
Meats, Poultry, and Fish	94.4	0.5	95.6	1.3	100.0	4.6	96.7	-3.3	98.8	2.2	95.9	-2.9	100.2	4.5	104.9	4.7	106.6	1.6
Dairy Products	92.7	9.2	98.7	6.5	100.0	1.3	100.7	0.7	101.1	0.4	100.2	-0.9	99.9	-0.3	101.6	1.7	102.2	0.6
Processed Fruits and Vegetables	83.3	3.0	95.2	14.3	100.0	5.0	101.1	1.1	107.3	6.1	108.0	0.7	104.9	-2.9	108.6	3.5	113.8	4.8
Sugar and Confectionery	119.6	50.3	102.3	-14.5	100.0	-2.2	108.6	8.6	111.7	2.9	107.9	-3.4	109.7	1.7	112.7	2.7	114.7	1.8
Beverages and Beverage Materials	90.7	10.6	96.5	6.4	100.0	3.6	102.6	2.6	106.3	3.6	107.7	1.3	114.6	6.4	112.5	-1.8	114.3	1.6
Fats and Oils	105.4	-6.8	105.7	0.3	100.0	-5.4	111.0	11.0	140.1	26.2	125.5	-10.4	96.5	-23.1	97.9	1.5	117.2	19.7
Miscellaneous Processed Foods	91.4	4.9	100.6	10.1	100.0	-0.6	102.5	2.5	111.8	9.1	114.1	2.1	116.2	1.8	119.8	3.1	122.5	2.3
Prepared Animal Feeds	107.3	3.4	109.0	1.6	100.0	-8.3	108.3	8.3	104.4	-3.6	90.1	-13.7	94.6	5.0	98.5	4.1	116.0	17.8
Textile Products and Apparel	89.7	8.7	97.6	8.8	100.0	2.5	100.3	0.3	102.7	2.4	102.9	0.2	103.2	0.3	105.1	1.8	109.2	3.9
Synthetic Fibers	83.1	13.2	96.5	16.1	100.0	3.6	96.7	-3.3	98.5	1.9	95.5	-3.0	92.5	-3.1	91.8	-0.8	97.3	6.0
Processed Yarns and Threads	88.6	12.3	99.8	12.6	100.0	0.2	100.1	0.1	103.2	3.1	102.1	-1.1	101.7	-0.4	103.8	2.1	108.0	4.0
Gray Fabrics	95.0	8.6	101.0	6.3	100.0	-1.0	101.2	1.2	105.8	4.5	104.4	-1.3	103.7	-0.7	107.2	3.4	114.0	6.3
Finished Fabrics	92.9	7.8	100.5	8.2	100.0	-0.5	98.9	-1.1	101.7	2.8	101.4	-0.3	101.4	0.0	104.2	2.8	109.4	5.0
Apparel	-		-		-		-		-		-		-		-		-	
Textile Housefurnishings	-		-		-		-		-		-		-		-		-	
Miscellaneous Textile Products	-		-		-		-		-		-		-		-		-	
Apparel & Other Fabricated Textile Products	88.7	8.0	95.8	8.0	100.0	4.4	101.0	1.0	102.8	1.8	104.2	1.4	105.5	1.2	107.3	1.7	110.4	2.9
Miscellaneous Textile Products/ Services	-		-		-		-		-		-		96.4	-	98.7	2.4	105.3	6.7
Hides, Skins, Leather, and Related Products	94.7	-1.5	99.3	4.9	100.0	0.7	103.2	3.2	109.0	5.6	108.9	-0.1	113.0	3.8	120.4	6.5	131.4	9.1
Hides and Skins	103.4	-30.7	104.7	1.3	100.0	-4.5	109.8	9.8	143.8	31.0	126.1	-12.3	147.7	17.1	179.9	21.8	-	-

Source: U.S. Department of Labor, Bureau of Labor Statistics, Division of Industry Prices and Price Indexes. n.e.c. stands for not elsewhere classified. - indicates no data collected for period or unavailable.

Producer Price Index
Annual Averages, 1989-1997
Base 1982 = 100

Columns headed % show percentile change in the index from the previous period for which an index is available.

	1989		1990		1991		1992		1993		1994		1995		1996		1997	
	Index	%	Index	%	Index	%	Index	%	Index	%	Index	%	Index	%	Index	%	Index	%
Farm Products	110.9	5.7	112.2	1.2	105.7	-5.8	103.6	-2.0	107.1	3.4	106.3	-0.7	107.4	1.0	122.4	14.0	112.8	-7.8
Fruits & Melons, Fresh/Dry																		
Vegetables & Nuts	114.6	5.6	117.5	2.5	114.7	-2.4	96.9	-15.5	106.9	10.3	104.6	-2.2	108.5	3.7	122.5	12.9	115.1	-6.0
Grains	106.4	8.7	97.4	-8.5	92.0	-5.5	97.3	5.8	94.5	-2.9	102.7	8.7	112.6	9.6	151.1	34.2	111.2	-26.4
Slaughter Livestock	106.1	2.7	115.6	9.0	107.9	-6.7	104.7	-3.0	107.0	2.2	96.4	-9.9	92.8	-3.7	95.2	2.6	96.3	1.2
Slaughter Poultry	128.8	6.0	118.8	-7.8	111.2	-6.4	112.6	1.3	122.0	8.3	124.4	2.0	125.6	1.0	140.5	11.9	131.0	-6.8
Plant and Animal Fibers	107.8	9.6	117.8	9.3	115.1	-2.3	89.8	-22.0	91.3	1.7	120.7	32.2	155.3	28.7	129.3	-16.7	117.0	-9.5
Fluid Milk	98.8	10.5	100.8	2.0	89.5	-11.2	96.1	7.4	94.1	-2.1	95.7	1.7	93.6	-2.2	107.9	15.3	96.9	-10.2
Chicken Eggs	119.6	35.0	117.6	-1.7	110.7	-5.9	94.1	-15.0	105.9	12.5	97.8	-7.6	104.1	6.4	130.7	25.6	119.0	-9.0
Hay, Hayseeds and Oilseeds	137.0	-1.0	122.1	-10.9	112.1	-8.2	111.2	-0.8	126.2	13.5	132.4	4.9	122.9	-7.2	146.3	19.0	153.2	4.7
Other Farm Products	103.3	8.3	125.3	21.3	151.6	21.0	150.6	-0.7	149.6	-0.7	149.5	-0.1	152.9	2.3	156.8	2.6	-	
Processed Foods and Feeds	117.8	4.5	121.9	3.5	121.9	0.0	122.1	0.2	124.0	1.6	125.5	1.2	127.0	1.2	133.3	5.0	134.0	0.5
Cereal and Bakery Products	131.1	6.6	134.2	2.4	137.9	2.8	144.2	4.6	147.6	2.4	151.1	2.4	154.7	2.4	159.9	3.4	158.1	-1.1
Meats, Poultry, and Fish	111.0	4.1	119.6	7.7	116.6	-2.5	112.2	-3.8	115.5	2.9	112.2	-2.9	111.8	-0.4	116.5	4.2	118.6	1.8
Dairy Products	110.6	8.2	117.2	6.0	114.6	-2.2	117.9	2.9	118.1	0.2	119.4	1.1	119.7	0.3	130.4	8.9	128.1	-1.8
Processed Fruits and Vegetables	119.9	5.4	124.7	4.0	119.6	-4.1	120.8	1.0	118.2	-2.2	121.1	2.5	122.4	1.1	127.6	4.2	126.4	-0.9
Sugar and Confectionery	120.1	4.7	123.1	2.5	128.4	4.3	127.7	-0.5	127.9	0.2	132.5	3.6	134.0	1.1	137.5	2.6	137.4	-0.1
Beverages and Beverage Materials	118.4	3.6	120.8	2.0	124.1	2.7	124.4	0.2	124.8	0.3	127.7	2.3	133.8	4.8	134.6	0.6	137.7	2.3
Fats and Oils	112.1	-4.4	119.4	6.5	112.0	-6.2	108.8	-2.9	116.9	7.4	135.8	16.2	138.5	2.0	130.7	-5.6	130.8	0.1
Miscellaneous Processed Foods	129.4	5.6	134.2	3.7	138.3	3.1	139.2	0.7	142.3	2.2	144.3	1.4	146.2	1.3	149.9	2.5	152.9	2.0
Prepared Animal Feeds	116.6	0.5	107.4	-7.9	106.8	-0.6	108.3	1.4	111.0	2.5	111.3	0.3	109.1	-2.0	135.3	24.0	132.9	-1.8
Textile Products and Apparel	112.3	2.8	115.0	2.4	116.3	1.1	117.8	1.3	118.0	0.2	118.3	0.3	120.8	2.1	122.4	1.3	122.6	0.2
Synthetic Fibers	104.8	7.7	106.7	1.8	105.3	-1.3	103.4	-1.8	103.6	0.2	104.1	0.5	109.4	5.1	111.3	1.7	111.1	-0.2
Processed Yarns and Threads	110.4	2.2	112.6	2.0	112.6	0.0	110.8	-1.6	107.8	-2.7	108.4	0.6	112.8	4.1	114.7	1.7	113.8	-0.8
Gray Fabrics	115.2	1.1	117.2	1.7	117.4	0.2	120.6	2.7	118.6	-1.7	116.8	-1.5	121.2	3.8	121.4	0.2	121.8	0.3
Finished Fabrics	113.6	3.8	116.0	2.1	117.5	1.3	118.8	1.1	119.5	0.6	119.2	-0.3	121.7	2.1	123.6	1.6	123.9	0.2
Apparel	-		-		-		-		-		-		-		-		-	
Textile Housefurnishings	-		-		-		-		-		-		-		-		-	
Miscellaneous Textile Products	-		-		-		-		-		-		-		-		-	
Apparel & Other Fabricated																		
Textile Products	113.0	2.4	116.0	2.7	118.1	1.8	120.4	1.9	121.6	1.0	122.1	0.4	123.2	0.9	125.0	1.5	125.6	0.5
Miscellaneous Textile Products/																		
Services	111.8	6.2	114.0	2.0	113.5	-0.4	114.9	1.2	115.9	0.9	118.1	1.9	123.6	4.7	123.5	-0.1	120.1	-2.8
Hides, Skins, Leather, and Related																		
Products	136.3	3.7	141.7	4.0	138.9	-2.0	140.4	1.1	143.7	2.4	148.5	3.3	153.7	3.5	150.5	-2.1	154.3	2.5
Hides and Skins	212.9	-	217.9	2.3	174.2	-20.1	174.0	-0.1	184.2	5.9	206.3	12.0	215.5	4.5	191.8	-11.0	202.0	5.3

Source: U.S. Department of Labor, Bureau of Labor Statistics, Division of Industry Prices and Price Indexes. n.e.c. stands for not elsewhere classified. - indicates no data collected for period or unavailable.

Producer Price Index
Annual Averages, 1998-2001
Base 1982 = 100

Columns headed % show percentile change in the index from the previous period for which an index is available.

	1998		1999		2000		2001										
	Index	%	Index	%	Index	%	Index	%	Index	%	Index	%	Index	%	Index	%	Index	%
Farm Products	104.6	-7.3	98.4	-5.9	99.5	1.1	103.7	4.2								
Fruits & Melons, Fresh/Dry Vegetables & Nuts	117.5	2.1	117.4	-0.1	111.1	-5.4	114.1	2.7								
Grains	93.4	-16.0	80.1	-14.2	78.3	-2.2	81.2	3.7								
Slaughter Livestock	82.3	-14.5	86.4	5.0	96.5	11.7	99.6	3.2								
Slaughter Poultry	141.4	7.9	129.9	-8.1	124.7	-4.0	130.7	4.8								
Plant and Animal Fibers	110.4	-5.6	86.5	-21.6	93.9	8.6	67.2	-28.4								
Fluid Milk	112.9	16.5	106.3	-5.8	92.0	-13.5	112.0	21.7								
Chicken Eggs	107.6	-9.6	89.4	-16.9	97.8	9.4	93.7	-4.2								
Hay, Hayseeds and Oilseeds	125.9	-17.8	101.5	-19.4	105.0	3.4	106.8	1.7								
Other Farm Products	156.8	-	151.5	-3.4	-	-	156.8	3.5								
Processed Foods and Feeds	131.6	-1.8	131.1	-0.4	133.1	1.5	137.3	3.2								
Cereal and Bakery Products	157.4	-0.4	157.5	0.1	158.4	0.6	162.0	2.3								
Meats, Poultry, and Fish	113.0	-4.7	114.2	1.1	121.1	6.0	125.5	3.6								
Dairy Products	138.2	7.9	139.2	0.7	133.7	-4.0	145.3	8.7								
Processed Fruits and Vegetables	125.7	-0.6	128.1	1.9	128.6	0.4	129.4	0.6								
Sugar and Confectionery	134.4	-2.2	135.2	0.6	132.6	-1.9	136.1	2.6								
Beverages and Beverage Materials	137.4	-0.2	138.5	0.8	143.0	3.2	145.9	2.0								
Fats and Oils	141.0	7.8	121.8	-13.6	109.9	-9.8	107.4	-2.3								
Miscellaneous Processed Foods	154.1	0.8	155.4	0.8	156.6	0.8	160.1	2.2								
Prepared Animal Feeds	108.0	-18.7	98.3	-9.0	102.9	4.7	105.1	2.1								
Textile Products and Apparel	122.9	0.2	121.1	-1.5	121.4	0.2	121.3	-0.1								
Synthetic Fibers	109.9	-1.1	103.8	-5.6	107.2	3.3	108.6	1.3								
Processed Yarns and Threads	112.7	-1.0	108.6	-3.6	107.9	-0.6	105.6	-2.1								
Gray Fabrics	121.6	-0.2	114.4	-5.9	113.2	-1.0	114.1	0.8								
Finished Fabrics	123.9	0.0	122.6	-1.0	122.5	-0.1	122.6	0.1								
Apparel	-	-	-	-	-	-	-	-								
Textile Housefurnishings	-	-	-	-	-	-	-	-								
Miscellaneous Textile Products	-	-	-	-	-	-	-	-								
Apparel & Other Fabricated Textile Products	126.9	1.0	127.0	0.1	127.4	0.3	127.1	-0.2								
Miscellaneous Textile Products/ Services	117.4	-2.2	116.0	-1.2	115.3	-0.6	116.3	0.9								
Hides, Skins, Leather, and Related Products	148.0	-4.1	146.0	-1.4	151.5	3.8	158.2	4.4								
Hides and Skins	158.2	-21.7	145.9	-7.8	174.0	19.3	189.7	9.0								

Source: U.S. Department of Labor, Bureau of Labor Statistics, Division of Industry Prices and Price Indexes. n.e.c. stands for not elsewhere classified. - indicates no data collected for period or unavailable.

Producer Price Index
Annual Averages, 1926-1934
Base 1982 = 100

Columns headed % show percentile change in the index from the previous period for which an index is available.

	1926		1927		1928		1929		1930		1931		1932		1933		1934	
	Index	%	Index	%	Index	%	Index	%	Index	%	Index	%	Index	%	Index	%	Index	%
Leather	16.2	-	17.7	9.3	20.4	15.3	18.3	-10.3	16.4	-10.4	13.9	-15.2	10.5	-24.5	11.5	9.5	12.1	5.2
Footwear	14.6	-	14.9	2.1	16.0	7.4	15.5	-3.1	14.9	-3.9	13.7	-8.1	12.6	-8.0	13.1	4.0	14.3	9.2
Other Leather and Related Products	-	-	-	-	-	-	-	-	-	-	-	-	-	-	-	-	-	-
Fuels and Related Products and Power	10.3	-	9.1	-11.7	8.7	-4.4	8.6	-1.1	8.1	-5.8	7.0	-13.6	7.3	4.3	6.9	-5.5	7.6	10.1
Coal	8.5	-	8.4	-1.2	7.9	-6.0	7.7	-2.5	7.6	-1.3	7.3	-3.9	7.1	-2.7	7.0	-1.4	7.7	10.0
Coke Oven Products	6.0	-	5.6	-6.7	5.0	-10.7	5.0	0.0	5.0	0.0	4.9	-2.0	4.6	-6.1	4.6	0.0	5.0	8.7
Gas Fuels	-	-	-	-	-	-	-	-	-	-	-	-	-	-	-	-	-	-
Electric Power	-	-	-	-	-	-	-	-	-	-	-	-	-	-	-	-	-	-
Utility Natural Gas	-	-	-	-	-	-	-	-	-	-	-	-	-	-	-	-	-	-
Crude Petroleum (domestic production)	-	-	-	-	-	-	-	-	-	-	-	-	-	-	-	-	-	-
Petroleum Products, Refined	-	-	-	-	-	-	-	-	-	-	-	-	-	-	-	-	-	-
Petroleum and Coal Products, n.e.c.	-	-	-	-	-	-	-	-	-	-	-	-	-	-	-	-	-	-
Chemicals and Allied Products	-	-	-	-	-	-	-	-	-	-	-	-	-	-	16.2	-	17.0	4.9
Industrial Chemicals	19.9	-	19.8	-0.5	19.6	-1.0	19.8	1.0	19.3	-2.5	17.9	-7.3	17.7	-1.1	17.3	-2.3	17.3	0.0
Paints and Allied Products	-	-	-	-	-	-	-	-	-	-	-	-	-	-	-	-	-	-
Drugs and Pharmaceuticals	-	-	-	-	-	-	-	-	-	-	-	-	-	-	-	-	-	-
Fats and Oils, Inedible	52.9	-	49.0	-7.4	50.5	3.1	47.1	-6.7	37.6	-20.2	25.9	-31.1	21.2	-18.1	20.9	-1.4	21.5	2.9
Agricultural Chemicals and Chemical Products	-	-	-	-	-	-	-	-	-	-	-	-	-	-	-	-	-	-
Plastic Resins and Materials	-	-	-	-	-	-	-	-	-	-	-	-	-	-	-	-	-	-
Other Chemicals and Allied Products	-	-	-	-	-	-	-	-	-	-	-	-	-	-	-	-	-	-
Rubber and Plastic Products	47.1	-	35.7	-24.2	28.3	-20.7	24.6	-13.1	21.5	-12.6	18.3	-14.9	15.9	-13.1	16.7	5.0	19.5	16.8
Rubber and Rubber Products	-	-	-	-	-	-	-	-	-	-	-	-	-	-	-	-	-	-
Plastic Products	-	-	-	-	-	-	-	-	-	-	-	-	-	-	-	-	-	-
Lumber and Wood Products	9.3	-	8.8	-5.4	8.5	-3.4	8.8	3.5	8.0	-9.1	6.5	-18.8	5.6	-13.8	6.7	19.6	7.8	16.4
Lumber	8.1	-	7.6	-6.2	7.3	-3.9	7.6	4.1	6.9	-9.2	5.6	-18.8	4.8	-14.3	5.7	18.7	6.8	19.3
Millwork	10.7	-	10.7	0.0	10.7	0.0	10.8	0.9	10.2	-5.6	8.5	-16.7	8.4	-1.2	8.8	4.8	9.2	4.5
Plywood	-	-	-	-	-	-	-	-	-	-	-	-	-	-	-	-	-	-
Other Wood Products	-	-	-	-	-	-	-	-	-	-	-	-	-	-	-	-	-	-
Logs, Bolts, Timber and Pulpwood	-	-	-	-	-	-	-	-	-	-	-	-	-	-	-	-	-	-
Prefabricated Wood Buildings & Components	-	-	-	-	-	-	-	-	-	-	-	-	-	-	-	-	-	-
Treated Wood and Contract Wood Preserving	-	-	-	-	-	-	-	-	-	-	-	-	-	-	-	-	-	-

Source: U.S. Department of Labor, Bureau of Labor Statistics, Division of Industry Prices and Price Indexes. n.e.c. stands for not elsewhere classified. - indicates no data collected for period or unavailable.

Producer Price Index
Annual Averages, 1935-1943
Base 1982 = 100

Columns headed % show percentile change in the index from the previous period for which an index is available.

	1935		1936		1937		1938		1939		1940		1941		1942		1943	
	Index	%	Index	%	Index	%	Index	%	Index	%	Index	%	Index	%	Index	%	Index	%
Leather	13.0	7.4	13.8	6.2	15.7	13.8	13.6	-13.4	14.2	4.4	15.0	5.6	15.8	5.3	16.4	3.8	16.4	0.0
Footwear	14.3	0.0	14.6	2.1	15.3	4.8	14.9	-2.6	15.0	0.7	15.7	4.7	16.5	5.1	18.3	10.9	18.4	0.5
Other Leather and Related Products	-	-	-	-	-	-	-	-	-	-	-	-	-	-	-	-	-	-
Fuels and Related Products and Power	7.6	0.0	7.9	3.9	8.0	1.3	7.9	-1.2	7.5	-5.1	7.4	-1.3	7.9	6.8	8.1	2.5	8.3	2.5
Coal	7.8	1.3	7.9	1.3	7.9	0.0	7.9	0.0	7.8	-1.3	7.8	0.0	8.3	6.4	8.7	4.8	9.2	5.7
Coke Oven Products	5.3	6.0	5.6	5.7	6.1	8.9	6.2	1.6	6.3	1.6	6.6	4.8	7.1	7.6	7.3	2.8	7.3	0.0
Gas Fuels	-	-	-	-	-	-	-	-	-	-	-	-	-	-	-	-	-	-
Electric Power	-	-	-	-	-	-	-	-	-	-	-	-	-	-	-	-	-	-
Utility Natural Gas	-	-	-	-	-	-	-	-	-	-	-	-	-	-	-	-	-	-
Crude Petroleum (domestic production)	-	-	-	-	-	-	-	-	-	-	-	-	-	-	-	-	-	-
Petroleum Products, Refined	-	-	-	-	-	-	-	-	-	-	-	-	-	-	-	-	-	-
Petroleum and Coal Products, n.e.c.	-	-	-	-	-	-	-	-	-	-	-	-	-	-	-	-	-	-
Chemicals and Allied Products	17.7	4.1	17.8	0.6	18.6	4.5	17.7	-4.8	17.6	-0.6	17.9	1.7	19.5	8.9	21.7	11.3	21.9	0.9
Industrial Chemicals	17.6	1.7	17.5	-0.6	17.5	0.0	17.2	-1.7	16.8	-2.3	16.9	0.6	17.4	3.0	19.2	10.3	19.2	0.0
Paints and Allied Products	-	-	-	-	-	-	-	-	-	-	-	-	-	-	-	-	-	-
Drugs and Pharmaceuticals	-	-	-	-	-	-	-	-	-	-	-	-	-	-	-	-	-	-
Fats and Oils, Inedible	32.7	52.1	33.5	2.4	40.7	21.5	26.2	-35.6	25.7	-1.9	23.6	-8.2	41.0	73.7	55.7	35.9	53.9	-3.2
Agricultural Chemicals and Chemical Products	-	-	-	-	-	-	-	-	-	-	-	-	-	-	-	-	-	-
Plastic Resins and Materials	-	-	-	-	-	-	-	-	-	-	-	-	-	-	-	-	-	-
Other Chemicals and Allied Products	-	-	-	-	-	-	-	-	-	-	-	-	-	-	-	-	-	-
Rubber and Plastic Products	19.6	0.5	21.1	7.7	24.9	18.0	24.4	-2.0	25.4	4.1	23.7	-6.7	25.5	7.6	29.7	16.5	30.5	2.7
Rubber and Rubber Products	-	-	-	-	-	-	-	-	-	-	-	-	-	-	-	-	-	-
Plastic Products	-	-	-	-	-	-	-	-	-	-	-	-	-	-	-	-	-	-
Lumber and Wood Products	7.5	-3.8	7.9	5.3	9.3	17.7	8.5	-8.6	8.7	2.4	9.6	10.3	11.5	19.8	12.5	8.7	13.2	5.6
Lumber	6.6	-2.9	7.0	6.1	8.1	15.7	7.1	-12.3	7.5	5.6	8.3	10.7	9.9	19.3	10.7	8.1	11.4	6.5
Millwork	9.1	-1.1	9.7	6.6	11.7	20.6	10.5	-10.3	10.3	-1.9	11.2	8.7	12.8	14.3	14.0	9.4	14.1	0.7
Plywood	-	-	-	-	-	-	-	-	-	-	-	-	-	-	-	-	-	-
Other Wood Products	-	-	-	-	-	-	-	-	-	-	-	-	-	-	-	-	-	-
Logs, Bolts, Timber and Pulpwood	-	-	-	-	-	-	-	-	-	-	-	-	-	-	-	-	-	-
Prefabricated Wood Buildings & Components	-	-	-	-	-	-	-	-	-	-	-	-	-	-	-	-	-	-
Treated Wood and Contract Wood Preserving	-	-	-	-	-	-	-	-	-	-	-	-	-	-	-	-	-	-

Source: U.S. Department of Labor, Bureau of Labor Statistics, Division of Industry Prices and Price Indexes. n.e.c. stands for not elsewhere classified. - indicates no data collected for period or unavailable.

Producer Price Index
Annual Averages, 1944-1952
Base 1982 = 100

Columns headed % show percentile change in the index from the previous period for which an index is available.

	1944 Index	%	1945 Index	%	1946 Index	%	1947 Index	%	1948 Index	%	1949 Index	%	1950 Index	%	1951 Index	%	1952 Index	%
Leather	16.4	0.0	16.5	0.6	20.7	25.5	31.4	51.7	29.9	-4.8	27.7	-7.4	31.8	14.8	37.0	16.4	26.6	-28.1
Footwear	18.4	0.0	18.4	0.0	20.4	10.9	25.8	26.5	27.6	7.0	27.2	-1.4	28.7	5.5	32.7	13.9	30.2	-7.6
Other Leather and Related Products	-	-	-	-	-	-	35.1	-	36.0	2.6	34.3	-4.7	34.5	0.6	39.5	14.5	35.4	-10.4
Fuels and Related Products and Power	8.6	3.6	8.7	1.2	9.3	6.9	11.1	19.4	13.1	18.0	12.4	-5.3	12.6	1.6	13.0	3.2	13.0	0.0
Coal	9.6	4.3	9.9	3.1	10.6	7.1	12.9	21.7	15.6	20.9	15.5	-0.6	15.6	0.6	15.9	1.9	16.0	0.6
Coke Oven Products	7.7	5.5	7.9	2.6	8.4	6.3	9.9	17.9	12.3	24.2	13.1	6.5	13.6	3.8	14.6	7.4	14.7	0.7
Gas Fuels	-	-	-	-	-	-	-	-	-	-	-	-	-	-	-	-	-	-
Electric Power	-	-	-	-	-	-	-	-	-	-	-	-	-	-	-	-	-	-
Utility Natural Gas	-	-	-	-	-	-	-	-	-	-	-	-	-	-	-	-	-	-
Crude Petroleum (domestic production)	-	-	-	-	-	-	-	-	-	-	-	-	-	-	-	-	-	-
Petroleum Products, Refined	-	-	-	-	-	-	9.7	-	12.2	25.8	10.7	-12.3	11.2	4.7	12.1	8.0	11.9	-1.7
Petroleum and Coal Products, n.e.c.	-	-	-	-	-	-	-	-	-	-	-	-	-	-	-	-	-	-
Chemicals and Allied Products	22.2	1.4	22.3	0.5	24.1	8.1	32.1	33.2	32.8	2.2	30.0	-8.5	30.4	1.3	34.8	14.5	33.0	-5.2
Industrial Chemicals	19.1	-0.5	19.1	0.0	19.8	3.7	23.3	17.7	24.7	6.0	22.7	-8.1	23.8	4.8	28.4	19.3	27.1	-4.6
Paints and Allied Products	-	-	-	-	-	-	-	-	-	-	-	-	-	-	-	-	-	-
Drugs and Pharmaceuticals	-	-	-	-	-	-	57.0	-	54.7	-4.0	50.7	-7.3	50.1	-1.2	51.8	3.4	50.1	-3.3
Fats and Oils, Inedible	54.0	0.2	54.0	0.0	63.4	17.4	97.6	53.9	88.7	-9.1	43.2	-51.3	52.5	21.5	67.9	29.3	38.3	-43.6
Agricultural Chemicals and Chemical Products	-	-	-	-	-	-	29.0	-	30.4	4.8	31.4	3.3	30.6	-2.5	32.5	6.2	33.1	1.8
Plastic Resins and Materials	-	-	-	-	-	-	37.4	-	37.2	-0.5	37.7	1.3	37.9	0.5	47.4	25.1	47.1	-0.6
Other Chemicals and Allied Products	-	-	-	-	-	-	31.7	-	32.5	2.5	28.6	-12.0	28.5	-0.3	31.8	11.6	29.7	-6.6
Rubber and Plastic Products	30.1	-1.3	29.2	-3.0	29.3	0.3	29.2	-0.3	30.2	3.4	29.2	-3.3	35.6	21.9	43.7	22.8	39.6	-9.4
Rubber and Rubber Products	-	-	-	-	-	-	-	-	-	-	-	-	-	-	-	-	-	-
Plastic Products	-	-	-	-	-	-	-	-	-	-	-	-	-	-	-	-	-	-
Lumber and Wood Products	14.3	8.3	14.5	1.4	16.6	14.5	25.8	55.4	29.5	14.3	27.3	-7.5	31.4	15.0	34.1	8.6	33.2	-2.6
Lumber	12.4	8.8	12.5	0.8	14.4	15.2	23.0	59.7	26.1	13.5	23.9	-8.4	27.9	16.7	30.2	8.2	29.4	-2.6
Millwork	14.6	3.5	14.7	0.7	16.6	12.9	21.3	28.3	25.7	20.7	26.3	2.3	28.0	6.5	31.7	13.2	31.0	-2.2
Plywood	-	-	-	-	-	-	47.1	-	53.5	13.6	46.8	-12.5	52.3	11.8	56.6	8.2	51.6	-8.8
Other Wood Products	-	-	-	-	-	-	-	-	-	-	-	-	-	-	-	-	-	-
Logs, Bolts, Timber and Pulpwood	-	-	-	-	-	-	-	-	-	-	-	-	-	-	-	-	-	-
Prefabricated Wood Buildings & Components	-	-	-	-	-	-	-	-	-	-	-	-	-	-	-	-	-	-
Treated Wood and Contract Wood Preserving	-	-	-	-	-	-	-	-	-	-	-	-	-	-	-	-	-	-

Source: U.S. Department of Labor, Bureau of Labor Statistics, Division of Industry Prices and Price Indexes. n.e.c. stands for not elsewhere classified. - indicates no data collected for period or unavailable.

Producer Price Index
Annual Averages, 1953-1961
Base 1982 = 100

Columns headed % show percentile change in the index from the previous period for which an index is available.

	1953 Index	%	1954 Index	%	1955 Index	%	1956 Index	%	1957 Index	%	1958 Index	%	1959 Index	%	1960 Index	%	1961 Index	%
Leather	27.7	4.1	25.3	-8.7	25.1	-0.8	27.1	8.0	26.8	-1.1	27.4	2.2	33.2	21.2	30.1	-9.3	30.9	2.7
Footwear	30.1	-0.3	30.1	0.0	30.2	0.3	32.1	6.3	32.6	1.6	32.9	0.9	34.9	6.1	35.8	2.6	35.9	0.3
Other Leather and Related Products	34.9	-1.4	34.1	-2.3	33.7	-1.2	34.6	2.7	34.4	-0.6	34.2	-0.6	38.3	12.0	37.2	-2.9	36.8	-1.1
Fuels and Related Products and Power	13.4	3.1	13.2	-1.5	13.2	0.0	13.6	3.0	14.3	5.1	13.7	-4.2	13.7	0.0	13.9	1.5	14.0	0.7
Coal	16.6	3.8	15.6	-6.0	15.4	-1.3	16.8	9.1	18.3	8.9	18.0	-1.6	18.0	0.0	17.9	-0.6	17.7	-1.1
Coke Oven Products	15.5	5.4	15.6	0.6	15.9	1.9	17.6	10.7	19.0	8.0	19.0	0.0	19.9	4.7	20.0	0.5	20.0	0.0
Gas Fuels	-	-	-	-	-	-	-	-	-	-	7.2	-	7.8	8.3	8.2	5.1	8.4	2.4
Electric Power	-	-	-	-	-	-	-	-	-	-	24.5	-	24.6	0.4	24.9	1.2	25.0	0.4
Utility Natural Gas	-	-	-	-	-	-	-	-	-	-	-	-	-	-	-	-	-	-
Crude Petroleum (domestic production)	-	-	-	-	-	-	-	-	-	-	-	-	-	-	-	-	-	-
Petroleum Products, Refined	12.2	2.5	11.8	-3.3	12.1	2.5	12.8	5.8	13.7	7.0	12.5	-8.8	12.4	-0.8	12.5	0.8	12.8	2.4
Petroleum and Coal Products, n.e.c.	-	-	-	-	-	-	-	-	-	-	-	-	-	-	-	-	-	-
Chemicals and Allied Products	33.4	1.2	33.8	1.2	33.7	-0.3	33.9	0.6	34.6	2.1	34.9	0.9	34.8	-0.3	34.8	0.0	34.5	-0.9
Industrial Chemicals	27.7	2.2	27.7	0.0	27.9	0.7	28.6	2.5	29.1	1.7	29.1	0.0	29.2	0.3	29.3	0.3	28.6	-2.4
Paints and Allied Products	-	-	-	-	-	-	-	-	-	-	-	-	-	-	-	-	-	-
Drugs and Pharmaceuticals	50.3	0.4	50.8	1.0	50.3	-1.0	49.9	-0.8	50.6	1.4	50.9	0.6	50.5	-0.8	50.7	0.4	49.8	-1.8
Fats and Oils, Inedible	40.3	5.2	44.2	9.7	43.3	-2.0	43.0	-0.7	46.9	9.1	47.9	2.1	43.3	-9.6	37.5	-13.4	40.3	7.5
Agricultural Chemicals and Chemical Products	33.0	-0.3	33.2	0.6	33.0	-0.6	32.5	-1.5	32.6	0.3	33.2	1.8	33.3	0.3	33.7	1.2	33.8	0.3
Plastic Resins and Materials	47.1	0.0	46.8	-0.6	44.6	-4.7	40.5	-9.2	40.6	0.2	40.0	-1.5	38.3	-4.3	38.2	-0.3	36.5	-4.5
Other Chemicals and Allied Products	29.7	0.0	31.2	5.1	31.5	1.0	32.4	2.9	33.6	3.7	34.3	2.1	34.6	0.9	34.7	0.3	35.0	0.9
Rubber and Plastic Products	36.9	-6.8	37.5	1.6	42.4	13.1	43.0	1.4	42.8	-0.5	42.8	0.0	42.6	-0.5	42.7	0.2	41.1	-3.7
Rubber and Rubber Products	-	-	-	-	-	-	-	-	-	-	-	-	-	-	-	-	-	-
Plastic Products	-	-	-	-	-	-	-	-	-	-	-	-	-	-	-	-	-	-
Lumber and Wood Products	33.1	-0.3	32.5	-1.8	34.1	4.9	34.6	1.5	32.8	-5.2	32.5	-0.9	34.7	6.8	33.5	-3.5	32.0	-4.5
Lumber	29.1	-1.0	28.6	-1.7	30.4	6.3	31.1	2.3	29.2	-6.1	28.8	-1.4	31.0	7.6	29.6	-4.5	28.1	-5.1
Millwork	32.1	3.5	31.8	-0.9	31.4	-1.3	31.5	0.3	31.3	-0.6	31.2	-0.3	33.1	6.1	33.3	0.6	32.5	-2.4
Plywood	53.8	4.3	50.7	-5.8	51.9	2.4	50.0	-3.7	47.4	-5.2	47.8	0.8	49.8	4.2	47.2	-5.2	46.2	-2.1
Other Wood Products	-	-	-	-	-	-	-	-	-	-	-	-	-	-	-	-	-	-
Logs, Bolts, Timber and Pulpwood	-	-	-	-	-	-	-	-	-	-	-	-	-	-	-	-	-	-
Prefabricated Wood Buildings & Components	-	-	-	-	-	-	-	-	-	-	-	-	-	-	-	-	-	-
Treated Wood and Contract Wood Preserving	-	-	-	-	-	-	-	-	-	-	-	-	-	-	-	-	-	-

Source: U.S. Department of Labor, Bureau of Labor Statistics, Division of Industry Prices and Price Indexes. n.e.c. stands for not elsewhere classified. - indicates no data collected for period or unavailable.

Producer Price Index
Annual Averages, 1962-1970
Base 1982 = 100

Columns headed % show percentile change in the index from the previous period for which an index is available.

	1962		1963		1964		1965		1966		1967		1968		1969		1970	
	Index	%	Index	%	Index	%	Index	%	Index	%	Index	%	Index	%	Index	%	Index	%
Leather	31.6	2.3	29.7	-6.0	30.0	1.0	31.5	5.0	35.3	12.1	32.1	-9.1	32.8	2.2	34.9	6.4	34.6	-0.9
Footwear	36.3	1.1	36.2	-0.3	36.3	0.3	37.0	1.9	39.5	6.8	40.8	3.3	42.8	4.9	44.7	4.4	46.2	3.4
Other Leather and Related Products	37.2	1.1	37.1	-0.3	36.8	-0.8	37.8	2.7	40.8	7.9	40.4	-1.0	40.2	-0.5	41.8	4.0	43.0	2.9
Fuels and Related Products and Power	14.0	0.0	13.9	-0.7	13.5	-2.9	13.8	2.2	14.1	2.2	14.4	2.1	14.3	-0.7	14.6	2.1	15.3	4.8
Coal	17.5	-1.1	17.5	0.0	17.5	0.0	17.5	0.0	17.9	2.3	18.7	4.5	19.4	3.7	21.1	8.8	28.1	33.2
Coke Oven Products	20.0	0.0	20.0	0.0	20.6	3.0	20.8	1.0	21.2	1.9	21.7	2.4	22.4	3.2	23.6	5.4	27.6	16.9
Gas Fuels	8.4	0.0	8.7	3.6	8.5	-2.3	8.7	2.4	9.1	4.6	9.4	3.3	8.7	-7.4	8.8	1.1	9.8	11.4
Electric Power	25.1	0.4	24.9	-0.8	24.7	-0.8	24.6	-0.4	24.5	-0.4	24.6	0.4	24.8	0.8	25.0	0.8	26.1	4.4
Utility Natural Gas	-	-	-	-	-	-	-	-	-	-	-	-	-	-	-	-	-	-
Crude Petroleum (domestic production)	-	-	-	-	-	-	-	-	-	-	-	-	-	-	-	-	-	-
Petroleum Products, Refined	12.6	-1.6	12.5	-0.8	11.9	-4.8	12.3	3.4	12.8	4.1	13.1	2.3	12.9	-1.5	13.1	1.6	13.3	1.5
Petroleum and Coal Products, n.e.c.	-	-	-	-	-	-	-	-	-	-	-	-	-	-	-	-	-	-
Chemicals and Allied Products	33.9	-1.7	33.5	-1.2	33.6	0.3	33.9	0.9	34.0	0.3	34.2	0.6	34.1	-0.3	34.2	0.3	35.0	2.3
Industrial Chemicals	28.1	-1.7	27.6	-1.8	27.4	-0.7	27.7	1.1	27.9	0.7	28.4	1.8	28.6	0.7	28.4	-0.7	28.6	0.7
Paints and Allied Products	-	-	-	-	-	-	-	-	-	-	-	-	-	-	-	-	-	-
Drugs and Pharmaceuticals	48.6	-2.4	48.2	-0.8	48.1	-0.2	47.8	-0.6	47.8	0.0	47.6	-0.4	47.3	-0.6	47.6	0.6	48.2	1.3
Fats and Oils, Inedible	35.1	-12.9	37.0	5.4	44.6	20.5	51.9	16.4	47.3	-8.9	37.4	-20.9	34.0	-9.1	40.9	20.3	49.7	21.5
Agricultural Chemicals and Chemical Products	33.6	-0.6	33.1	-1.5	32.9	-0.6	33.6	2.1	33.9	0.9	34.2	0.9	32.9	-3.8	29.6	-10.0	30.3	2.4
Plastic Resins and Materials	36.3	-0.5	35.6	-1.9	35.3	-0.8	35.0	-0.8	35.3	0.9	35.3	0.0	32.4	-8.2	31.9	-1.5	32.0	0.3
Other Chemicals and Allied Products	34.9	-0.3	35.3	1.1	35.6	0.8	36.0	1.1	36.4	1.1	37.0	1.6	37.6	1.6	38.6	2.7	40.2	4.1
Rubber and Plastic Products	39.9	-2.9	40.1	0.5	39.6	-1.2	39.7	0.3	40.5	2.0	41.4	2.2	42.8	3.4	43.6	1.9	44.9	3.0
Rubber and Rubber Products	-	-	-	-	-	-	-	-	-	-	37.3	-	38.6	3.5	39.3	1.8	41.1	4.6
Plastic Products	-	-	-	-	-	-	-	-	-	-	-	-	-	-	-	-	-	-
Lumber and Wood Products	32.2	0.6	32.8	1.9	33.5	2.1	33.7	0.6	35.2	4.5	35.1	-0.3	39.8	13.4	44.0	10.6	39.9	-9.3
Lumber	28.6	1.8	29.3	2.4	29.9	2.0	30.2	1.0	32.2	6.6	32.2	0.0	37.8	17.4	42.3	11.9	36.6	-13.5
Millwork	32.5	0.0	33.2	2.2	34.6	4.2	34.4	-0.6	35.1	2.0	35.8	2.0	37.9	5.9	42.2	11.3	41.5	-1.7
Plywood	44.6	-3.5	45.1	1.1	44.6	-1.1	44.6	0.0	44.8	0.4	43.1	-3.8	49.8	15.5	52.8	6.0	46.7	-11.6
Other Wood Products	-	-	-	-	-	-	-	-	41.6	-	42.3	1.7	44.4	5.0	47.7	7.4	49.7	4.2
Logs, Bolts, Timber and Pulpwood	-	-	-	-	-	-	-	-	-	-	-	-	-	-	-	-	-	-
Prefabricated Wood Buildings & Components	-	-	-	-	-	-	-	-	-	-	-	-	-	-	-	-	-	-
Treated Wood and Contract Wood Preserving	-	-	-	-	-	-	-	-	-	-	-	-	-	-	-	-	-	-

Source: U.S. Department of Labor, Bureau of Labor Statistics, Division of Industry Prices and Price Indexes. n.e.c. stands for not elsewhere classified. - indicates no data collected for period or unavailable.

Producer Price Index
Annual Averages, 1971-1979
Base 1982 = 100

Columns headed % show percentile change in the index from the previous period for which an index is available.

	1971		1972		1973		1974		1975		1976		1977		1978		1979	
	Index	%	Index	%	Index	%	Index	%	Index	%	Index	%	Index	%	Index	%	Index	%
Leather	36.2	4.6	45.1	24.6	51.4	14.0	49.6	-3.5	48.7	-1.8	60.4	24.0	64.6	7.0	76.6	18.6	114.6	49.6
Footwear	47.7	3.2	50.8	6.5	53.3	4.9	57.1	7.1	60.3	5.6	64.8	7.5	68.8	6.2	74.7	8.6	89.0	19.1
Other Leather and Related Products	43.8	1.9	47.6	8.7	52.5	10.3	55.2	5.1	57.0	3.3	61.8	8.4	66.0	6.8	71.5	8.3	82.9	15.9
Fuels and Related Products and Power	16.6	8.5	17.1	3.0	19.4	13.5	30.1	55.2	35.4	17.6	38.3	8.2	43.6	13.8	46.5	6.7	58.9	26.7
Coal	34.0	21.0	36.2	6.5	40.8	12.7	62.2	52.5	72.2	16.1	68.9	-4.6	72.8	5.7	80.4	10.4	84.3	4.9
Coke Oven Products	32.2	16.7	33.7	4.7	36.1	7.1	53.7	48.8	71.7	33.5	75.1	4.7	82.2	9.5	89.2	8.5	93.0	4.3
Gas Fuels	10.2	4.1	10.8	5.9	11.9	10.2	15.3	28.6	20.4	33.3	27.0	32.4	36.6	35.6	40.4	10.4	51.3	27.0
Electric Power	28.6	9.6	29.9	4.5	31.8	6.4	40.1	26.1	47.6	18.7	51.1	7.4	57.3	12.1	61.6	7.5	66.5	8.0
Utility Natural Gas	-	-	-	-	-	-	-	-	-	-	-	-	-	-	-	-	-	-
Crude Petroleum (domestic production)	-	-	-	-	-	-	-	-	-	-	-	-	-	-	-	-	-	-
Petroleum Products, Refined	14.1	6.0	14.3	1.4	16.9	18.2	29.3	73.4	33.8	15.4	36.3	7.4	40.5	11.6	42.2	4.2	58.4	38.4
Petroleum and Coal Products, n.e.c.	-	-	-	-	-	-	-	-	-	-	-	-	-	-	-	-	-	-
Chemicals and Allied Products	35.6	1.7	35.6	0.0	37.6	5.6	50.2	33.5	62.0	23.5	64.0	3.2	65.9	3.0	68.0	3.2	76.0	11.8
Industrial Chemicals	28.9	1.0	28.7	-0.7	29.3	2.1	43.0	46.8	58.7	36.5	62.2	6.0	63.5	2.1	64.0	0.8	74.9	17.0
Paints and Allied Products	39.5	-	-	-	-	-	-	-	60.5	53.2	64.3	6.3	68.5	6.5	71.4	4.2	78.5	9.9
Drugs and Pharmaceuticals	48.8	1.2	49.0	0.4	49.6	1.2	53.6	8.1	60.3	12.5	63.8	5.8	66.9	4.9	70.5	5.4	75.9	7.7
Fats and Oils, Inedible	50.0	0.6	43.4	-13.2	85.5	97.0	126.6	48.1	95.5	-24.6	93.6	-2.0	104.5	11.6	118.3	13.2	141.0	19.2
Agricultural Chemicals and Chemical Products	31.5	4.0	31.4	-0.3	33.0	5.1	47.1	42.7	69.6	47.8	64.4	-7.5	64.2	-0.3	67.8	5.6	73.3	8.1
Plastic Resins and Materials	31.3	-2.2	31.3	0.0	32.5	3.8	50.7	56.0	63.8	25.8	68.4	7.2	69.7	1.9	70.5	1.1	83.2	18.0
Other Chemicals and Allied Products	41.5	3.2	42.0	1.2	43.7	4.0	54.6	24.9	62.4	14.3	63.2	1.3	65.1	3.0	67.3	3.4	71.0	5.5
Rubber and Plastic Products	45.2	0.7	45.3	0.2	46.6	2.9	56.4	21.0	62.2	10.3	66.0	6.1	69.4	5.2	72.4	4.3	80.5	11.2
Rubber and Rubber Products	41.9	1.9	42.5	1.4	44.1	3.8	51.5	16.8	56.7	10.1	60.9	7.4	64.9	6.6	69.2	6.6	78.1	12.9
Plastic Products	48.5	-	-	-	-	-	-	-	68.7	41.6	71.5	4.1	74.5	4.2	-	-	83.1	11.5
Lumber and Wood Products	44.7	12.0	50.7	13.4	62.2	22.7	64.5	3.7	62.1	-3.7	72.2	16.3	83.0	15.0	96.9	16.7	105.5	8.9
Lumber	43.8	19.7	51.3	17.1	66.0	28.7	66.6	0.9	61.9	-7.1	75.0	21.2	89.0	18.7	103.7	16.5	114.0	9.9
Millwork	43.2	4.1	46.0	6.5	51.6	12.2	56.2	8.9	57.4	2.1	63.3	10.3	69.3	9.5	84.3	21.6	91.0	7.9
Plywood	49.4	5.8	56.3	14.0	66.9	18.8	69.4	3.7	69.4	0.0	80.6	16.1	91.4	13.4	101.5	11.1	107.9	6.3
Other Wood Products	50.3	1.2	52.8	5.0	63.4	20.1	70.5	11.2	68.5	-2.8	70.4	2.8	78.0	10.8	89.7	15.0	99.7	11.1
Logs, Bolts, Timber and Pulpwood	-	-	-	-	-	-	-	-	-	-	-	-	-	-	-	-	-	-
Prefabricated Wood Buildings & Components	-	-	-	-	-	-	-	-	-	-	-	-	-	-	-	-	-	-
Treated Wood and Contract Wood Preserving	-	-	-	-	-	-	-	-	-	-	-	-	-	-	-	-	-	-

Source: U.S. Department of Labor, Bureau of Labor Statistics, Division of Industry Prices and Price Indexes. n.e.c. stands for not elsewhere classified. - indicates no data collected for period or unavailable.

Producer Price Index
Annual Averages, 1980-1988
Base 1982 = 100

Columns headed % show percentile change in the index from the previous period for which an index is available.

	1980		1981		1982		1983		1984		1985		1986		1987		1988	
	Index	%	Index	%	Index	%	Index	%	Index	%	Index	%	Index	%	Index	%	Index	%
Leather	99.8	-12.9	102.7	2.9	100.0	-2.6	106.2	6.2	119.6	12.6	113.4	-5.2	122.9	8.4	140.9	14.6	167.5	18.9
Footwear	95.2	7.0	98.3	3.3	100.0	1.7	102.1	2.1	102.7	0.6	104.8	2.0	106.9	2.0	109.4	2.3	115.1	5.2
Other Leather and Related Products	88.3	6.5	97.7	10.6	100.0	2.4	102.2	2.2	106.6	4.3	110.3	3.5	110.3	0.0	113.0	2.4	119.1	5.4
Fuels and Related Products and Power	82.8	40.6	100.2	21.0	100.0	-0.2	95.9	-4.1	94.8	-1.1	91.4	-3.6	69.8	-23.6	70.2	0.6	66.7	-5.0
Coal	87.4	3.7	93.0	6.4	100.0	7.5	100.5	0.5	102.2	1.7	102.2	0.0	100.8	-1.4	97.1	-3.7	95.4	-1.8
Coke Oven Products	93.3	0.3	98.8	5.9	100.0	1.2	96.3	-3.7	94.5	-1.9	93.2	-1.4	88.0	-5.6	82.8	-5.9	84.9	2.5
Gas Fuels	71.7	39.8	88.6	23.6	100.0	12.9	108.1	8.1	104.5	-3.3	98.7	-5.6	83.2	-15.7	74.1	-10.9	71.4	-3.6
Electric Power	79.1	18.9	90.3	14.2	100.0	10.7	102.8	2.8	108.2	5.3	111.6	3.1	112.6	0.9	110.6	-1.8	111.2	0.5
Utility Natural Gas	-	-	-	-	-	-	-	-	-	-	-	-	-	-	-	-	-	-
Crude Petroleum (domestic production)	-	-	-	-	-	-	-	-	-	-	-	-	-	-	-	-	-	-
Petroleum Products, Refined	88.6	51.7	105.9	19.5	100.0	-5.6	89.9	-10.1	87.4	-2.8	83.2	-4.8	53.2	-36.1	56.8	6.8	53.9	-5.1
Petroleum and Coal Products, n.e.c.	-	-	-	-	-	-	-	-	-	-	100.5	-	77.1	-23.3	63.7	-17.4	66.4	4.2
Chemicals and Allied Products	89.0	17.1	98.4	10.6	100.0	1.6	100.3	0.3	102.9	2.6	103.7	0.8	102.6	-1.1	106.4	3.7	116.3	9.3
Industrial Chemicals	91.9	22.7	103.1	12.2	100.0	-3.0	97.3	-2.7	96.8	-0.5	96.0	-0.8	91.5	-4.7	95.5	4.4	106.8	11.8
Paints and Allied Products	89.7	14.3	-	-	100.0	11.5	100.5	0.5	105.1	4.6	106.7	1.5	105.7	-0.9	107.4	1.6	113.1	5.3
Drugs and Pharmaceuticals	83.0	9.4	92.1	11.0	100.0	8.6	107.6	7.6	114.2	6.1	122.0	6.8	130.1	6.6	139.1	6.9	148.4	6.7
Fats and Oils, Inedible	111.6	-20.9	110.7	-0.8	100.0	-9.7	106.9	6.9	139.1	30.1	110.6	-20.5	80.1	-27.6	92.7	15.7	110.9	19.6
Agricultural Chemicals and Chemical Products	87.9	19.9	97.4	10.8	100.0	2.7	95.9	-4.1	97.4	1.6	96.2	-1.2	94.2	-2.1	96.4	2.3	104.5	8.4
Plastic Resins and Materials	98.5	18.4	102.0	3.6	100.0	-2.0	102.8	2.8	108.9	5.9	107.5	-1.3	104.4	-2.9	110.3	5.7	132.4	20.0
Other Chemicals and Allied Products	83.1	17.0	94.1	13.2	100.0	6.3	101.3	1.3	102.7	1.4	105.2	2.4	105.8	0.6	107.0	1.1	111.9	4.6
Rubber and Plastic Products	90.1	11.9	96.4	7.0	100.0	3.7	100.8	0.8	102.3	1.5	101.9	-0.4	101.9	0.0	103.0	1.1	109.3	6.1
Rubber and Rubber Products	88.7	13.6	95.7	7.9	100.0	4.5	99.3	-0.7	99.4	0.1	98.7	-0.7	98.1	-0.6	99.4	1.3	103.6	4.2
Plastic Products	91.5	10.1	97.1	6.1	100.0	3.0	102.3	2.3	105.5	3.1	105.4	-0.1	106.1	0.7	107.3	1.1	115.0	7.2
Lumber and Wood Products	101.5	-3.8	102.8	1.3	100.0	-2.7	107.9	7.9	108.0	0.1	106.6	-1.3	107.2	0.6	112.8	5.2	118.9	5.4
Lumber	104.9	-8.0	104.6	-0.3	100.0	-4.4	113.5	13.5	112.5	-0.9	109.6	-2.6	110.5	0.8	118.2	7.0	122.1	3.3
Millwork	93.2	2.4	97.8	4.9	100.0	2.2	108.2	8.2	110.2	1.8	111.7	1.4	113.7	1.8	117.7	3.5	121.9	3.6
Plywood	106.2	-1.6	105.9	-0.3	100.0	-5.6	105.2	5.2	104.1	-1.0	99.6	-4.3	101.4	1.8	102.6	1.2	103.4	0.8
Other Wood Products	101.2	1.5	101.2	0.0	100.0	-1.2	97.6	-2.4	99.3	1.7	100.1	0.8	100.9	0.8	103.7	2.8	107.2	3.4
Logs, Bolts, Timber and Pulpwood	-	-	-	-	100.0	-	96.6	-3.4	97.0	0.4	96.0	-1.0	92.3	-3.9	101.8	10.3	117.7	15.6
Prefabricated Wood Buildings & Components	-	-	-	-	-	-	-	-	-	-	101.4	-	104.1	2.7	105.5	1.3	108.2	2.6
Treated Wood and Contract Wood Preserving	-	-	-	-	-	-	-	-	-	-	-	-	98.0	-	98.8	0.8	102.2	3.4

Source: U.S. Department of Labor, Bureau of Labor Statistics, Division of Industry Prices and Price Indexes. n.e.c. stands for not elsewhere classified. - indicates no data collected for period or unavailable.

Producer Price Index
Annual Averages, 1989-1997
Base 1982 = 100

Columns headed % show percentile change in the index from the previous period for which an index is available.

	1989		1990		1991		1992		1993		1994		1995		1996		1997	
	Index	%	Index	%	Index	%	Index	%	Index	%	Index	%	Index	%	Index	%	Index	%
Leather	170.4	1.7	177.5	4.2	168.4	-5.1	163.7	-2.8	168.6	3.0	179.6	6.5	191.4	6.6	177.9	-7.1	182.7	2.7
Footwear	120.8	5.0	125.6	4.0	128.6	2.4	132.0	2.6	134.4	1.8	135.5	0.8	139.2	2.7	141.6	1.7	143.8	1.6
Other Leather and Related Products	123.1	3.4	128.9	4.7	132.6	2.9	134.9	1.7	136.3	1.0	136.8	0.4	138.9	1.5	141.0	1.5	143.5	1.8
Fuels and Related Products and Power	72.9	9.3	82.3	12.9	81.2	-1.3	80.4	-1.0	80.0	-0.5	77.8	-2.7	78.0	0.3	85.8	10.0	85.9	0.1
Coal	95.5	0.1	97.5	2.1	97.2	-0.3	95.0	-2.3	96.1	1.2	96.7	0.6	95.0	-1.8	94.5	-0.5	96.0	1.6
Coke Oven Products	89.9	5.9	91.4	1.7	93.9	2.7	91.3	-2.8	89.2	-2.3	88.6	-0.7	92.0	3.8	95.8	4.1	95.1	-0.7
Gas Fuels	75.3	5.5	78.4	4.1	77.0	-1.8	75.9	-1.4	78.5	3.4	72.8	-7.3	65.2	-10.4	88.3	35.4	95.1	7.7
Electric Power	114.8	3.2	117.6	2.4	124.3	5.7	126.3	1.6	128.6	1.8	128.7	0.1	130.9	1.7	131.6	0.5	131.5	-0.1
Utility Natural Gas	-	-	-	-	97.2	-	98.6	1.4	104.1	5.6	104.4	0.3	98.8	-5.4	105.2	6.5	112.0	6.5
Crude Petroleum (domestic production)	-	-	-	-	-	-	58.0	-	51.4	-11.4	47.1	-8.4	51.1	8.5	62.6	22.5	57.5	-8.1
Petroleum Products, Refined	61.2	13.5	74.8	22.2	67.2	-10.2	64.7	-3.7	62.0	-4.2	59.1	-4.7	60.8	2.9	70.1	15.3	67.9	-3.1
Petroleum and Coal Products, n.e.c.	65.0	-2.1	67.3	3.5	63.6	-5.5	58.8	-7.5	66.4	12.9	65.8	-0.9	69.8	6.1	70.2	0.6	72.5	3.3
Chemicals and Allied Products	123.0	5.8	123.6	0.5	125.6	1.6	125.9	0.2	128.2	1.8	132.1	3.0	142.5	7.9	142.1	-0.3	143.7	1.1
Industrial Chemicals	114.8	7.5	113.2	-1.4	111.8	-1.2	109.3	-2.2	110.4	1.0	114.3	3.5	128.4	12.3	126.7	-1.3	126.7	0.0
Paints and Allied Products	122.6	8.4	128.5	4.8	131.6	2.4	131.0	-0.5	132.2	0.9	133.9	1.3	141.0	5.3	144.8	2.7	148.1	2.3
Drugs and Pharmaceuticals	160.0	7.8	170.8	6.8	182.6	6.9	192.2	5.3	200.9	4.5	206.0	2.5	210.9	2.4	214.7	1.8	219.0	2.0
Fats and Oils, Inedible	95.5	-13.9	88.1	-7.7	86.8	-1.5	93.0	7.1	95.6	2.8	110.6	15.7	126.9	14.7	133.3	5.0	132.3	-0.8
Agricultural Chemicals and Chemical Products	108.7	4.0	107.4	-1.2	111.7	4.0	110.3	-1.3	109.9	-0.4	119.9	9.1	130.1	8.5	133.7	2.8	132.9	-0.6
Plastic Resins and Materials	133.4	0.8	124.1	-7.0	120.0	-3.3	116.4	-3.0	117.1	0.6	122.4	4.5	143.5	17.2	133.1	-7.2	137.3	3.2
Other Chemicals and Allied Products	117.3	4.8	118.9	1.4	121.5	2.2	123.3	1.5	125.5	1.8	127.1	1.3	130.6	2.8	132.4	1.4	133.3	0.7
Rubber and Plastic Products	112.6	3.0	113.6	0.9	115.1	1.3	115.1	0.0	116.0	0.8	117.6	1.4	124.3	5.7	123.8	-0.4	123.2	-0.5
Rubber and Rubber Products	107.0	3.3	108.6	1.5	109.6	0.9	109.8	0.2	110.8	0.9	111.9	1.0	117.1	4.6	116.4	-0.6	115.8	-0.5
Plastic Products	118.3	2.9	119.0	0.6	120.8	1.5	120.7	-0.1	121.6	0.7	123.5	1.6	131.1	6.2	130.5	-0.5	129.9	-0.5
Lumber and Wood Products	126.7	6.6	129.7	2.4	132.1	1.9	146.6	11.0	174.0	18.7	180.0	3.4	178.1	-1.1	176.1	-1.1	183.8	4.4
Lumber	125.7	2.9	124.6	-0.9	124.9	0.2	144.7	15.9	183.4	26.7	188.4	2.7	173.4	-8.0	179.8	3.7	194.6	8.2
Millwork	127.3	4.4	130.4	2.4	135.5	3.9	143.3	5.8	156.6	9.3	162.4	3.7	163.8	0.9	166.6	1.7	170.9	2.6
Plywood	115.9	12.1	114.2	-1.5	114.3	0.1	133.3	16.6	152.8	14.6	158.6	3.8	165.3	4.2	156.4	-5.4	159.3	1.9
Other Wood Products	113.1	5.5	114.7	1.4	118.6	3.4	124.5	5.0	135.3	8.7	137.7	1.8	143.7	4.4	127.5	-11.3	128.3	0.6
Logs, Bolts, Timber and Pulpwood	131.9	12.1	142.8	8.3	144.1	0.9	164.8	14.4	212.3	28.8	219.1	3.2	220.4	0.6	206.8	-6.2	214.5	3.7
Prefabricated Wood Buildings & Components	110.7	2.3	113.1	2.2	118.2	4.5	122.8	3.9	132.5	7.9	141.6	6.9	147.8	4.4	150.7	2.0	156.4	3.8
Treated Wood and Contract Wood Preserving	109.7	7.3	112.6	2.6	115.6	2.7	123.5	6.8	138.1	11.8	149.0	7.9	149.2	0.1	154.9	3.8	164.1	5.9

Source: U.S. Department of Labor, Bureau of Labor Statistics, Division of Industry Prices and Price Indexes. n.e.c. stands for not elsewhere classified. - indicates no data collected for period or unavailable.

Producer Price Index
Annual Averages, 1998-2001
Base 1982 = 100

Columns headed % show percentile change in the index from the previous period for which an index is available.

	1998		1999		2000		2001										
	Index	%	Index	%	Index	%	Index	%	Index	%	Index	%	Index	%	Index	%
Leather	178.4	-2.4	176.3	-1.2	182.2	3.3	200.0	9.8								
Footwear	144.7	0.6	144.5	-0.1	144.9	0.3	145.8	0.6								
Other Leather and Related Products	144.8	0.9	145.5	0.5	146.1	0.4	147.6	1.0								
Fuels and Related Products and Power	75.3	-12.3	80.5	6.9	103.5	28.6	105.5	1.9								
Coal	93.6	-2.5	90.7	-3.1	87.9	-3.1	96.2	9.4								
Coke Oven Products	98.0	3.0	94.3	-3.8	86.9	-7.8	87.7	0.9								
Gas Fuels	76.6	-19.5	85.5	11.6	146.1	70.9	157.4	7.7								
Electric Power	129.9	-1.2	128.6	-1.0	130.7	1.6	138.6	6.0								
Utility Natural Gas	108.1	-3.5	108.7	0.6	134.0	23.3	161.1	20.2								
Crude Petroleum (domestic production)	35.7	-37.9	50.3	40.9	85.2	69.4	69.6	-18.3								
Petroleum Products, Refined	51.3	-24.4	60.9	18.7	91.3	49.9	85.3	-6.6								
Petroleum and Coal Products, n.e.c.	68.0	-6.2	64.8	-4.7	83.4	28.7	76.8	-7.9								
Chemicals and Allied Products	143.9	0.1	144.2	0.2	151.0	4.7	151.9	0.6								
Industrial Chemicals	121.4	-4.2	118.9	-2.1	129.1	8.6	128.4	-0.5								
Paints and Allied Products	150.7	1.8	152.5	1.2	156.3	2.5	159.9	2.3								
Drugs and Pharmaceuticals	242.6	10.8	251.5	3.7	257.4	2.3	261.4	1.6								
Fats and Oils, Inedible	116.7	-11.8	88.4	-24.3	70.1	-20.7	77.5	10.6								
Agricultural Chemicals and Chemical Products	128.5	-3.3	123.6	-3.8	124.5	0.7	130.8	5.1								
Plastic Resins and Materials	125.3	-8.7	125.8	0.4	141.6	12.6	134.9	-4.7								
Other Chemicals and Allied Products	134.7	1.1	135.3	0.4	137.2	1.4	139.6	1.7								
Rubber and Plastic Products	122.6	-0.5	122.5	-0.1	125.5	2.4	127.2	1.4								
Rubber and Rubber Products	115.3	-0.4	114.2	-1.0	115.3	1.0	116.8	1.3								
Plastic Products	129.3	-0.5	129.6	0.2	133.4	2.9	135.3	1.4								
Lumber and Wood Products	179.1	-2.6	183.6	2.5	178.2	-2.9	174.3	-2.2								
Lumber	179.5	-7.8	188.2	4.8	178.8	-5.0	171.4	-4.1								
Millwork	171.1	0.1	174.7	2.1	176.4	1.0	179.1	1.5								
Plywood	157.3	-1.3	176.4	12.1	157.6	-10.7	154.1	-2.2								
Other Wood Products	135.2	5.4	131.1	-3.0	130.5	-0.5	130.5	0.0								
Logs, Bolts, Timber and Pulpwood	208.1	-3.0	202.0	-2.9	196.4	-2.8	182.7	-7.0								
Prefabricated Wood Buildings & Components	160.0	2.3	165.9	3.7	171.3	3.3	175.3	2.3								
Treated Wood and Contract Wood Preserving	162.1	-1.2	167.1	3.1	156.6	-6.3	153.8	-1.8								

Source: U.S. Department of Labor, Bureau of Labor Statistics, Division of Industry Prices and Price Indexes. n.e.c. stands for not elsewhere classified. - indicates no data collected for period or unavailable.

Producer Price Index
Annual Averages, 1926-1934
Base 1982 = 100

Columns headed % show percentile change in the index from the previous period for which an index is available.

	1926		1927		1928		1929		1930		1931		1932		1933		1934	
	Index	%	Index	%	Index	%	Index	%	Index	%	Index	%	Index	%	Index	%	Index	%
Pulp, Paper, and Allied Products	-	-	-	-	-	-	-	-	-	-	-	-	-	-	-	-	-	-
Pulp, Paper, and Products, ex. Building Paper	-	-	-	-	-	-	-	-	-	-	-	-			-	-	-	-
Building Paper & Building Board Mill Products	-	-	-	-	-	-	-	-	-	-	-	-			-	-	-	-
Publications, Printed Matter & Printing Materials	-	-	-	-	-	-	-	-							-	-	-	-
Metals and Metal Products	13.7	-	12.9	-5.8	12.9	0.0	13.3	3.1	12.0	-9.8	10.8	-10.0	9.9	-8.3	10.2	3.0	11.2	9.8
Iron and Steel	11.3	-	10.6	-6.2	10.6	0.0	10.7	0.9	10.1	-5.6	9.4	-6.9	9.0	-4.3	8.9	-1.1	9.8	10.1
Nonferrous Metals	16.5	-	15.3	-7.3	15.5	1.3	17.5	12.9	13.6	-22.3	10.2	-25.0	8.2	-19.6	9.8	19.5	11.2	14.3
Metal Containers	15.2	-	15.2	0.0	14.7	-3.3	14.9	1.4	14.7	-1.3	14.1	-4.1	13.5	-4.3	12.6	-6.7	14.5	15.1
Hardware	-	-	-	-	-	-	-	-	-	-	-	-	-	-	-	-	-	-
Plumbing Fixtures and Brass Fittings	26.2	-	23.4	-10.7	23.8	1.7	22.5	-5.5	21.3	-5.3	20.1	-5.6	16.4	-18.4	16.1	-1.8	16.8	4.3
Heating Equipment	-	-	-	-	-	-	-	-	-	-	-	-	-	-	-	-	-	-
Fabricated Structural Metal Products	-	-	-	-	-	-	-	-	-	-	-	-	-	-	-	-	-	-
Miscellaneous Metal Products	-	-	-	-	-	-	-	-	-	-	-	-	-	-	-	-	-	-
Metal Treatment Services	-	-	-	-	-	-	-	-	-	-	-	-	-	-	-	-	-	-
Machinery and Equipment	-	-	-	-	-	-	-	-	-	-	-	-	-	-	-	-	-	-
Agricultural Machinery and Equipment	14.1	-	14.1	0.0	14.0	-0.7	13.9	-0.7	13.4	-3.6	13.0	-3.0	12.0	-7.7	11.8	-1.7	12.7	7.6
Construction Machinery and Equipment	-	-	-	-	-	-	-	-	-	-	-	-	-	-	-	-	-	-
Metalworking Machinery and Equipment	-	-	-	-	-	-	-	-	-	-	-	-	-	-	-	-	-	-
General Purpose Machinery and Equipment	-	-	-	-	-	-	-	-	-	-	-	-	-	-	-	-	-	-
Electronic Computers and Computer Equipment	-	-	-	-	-	-	-	-	-	-	-	-	-	-	-	-	-	-
Special Industry Machinery and Equipment	-	-	-	-	-	-	-	-	-	-	-	-	-	-	-	-	-	-
Electrical Machinery and Equipment	-	-	-	-	-	-	-	-	-	-	-	-	-	-	-	-	-	-
Miscellaneous Instruments	-	-	-	-	-	-	-	-	-	-	-	-	-	-	-	-	-	-
Miscellaneous Machinery	-	-	-	-	-	-	-	-	-	-	-	-	-	-	-	-	-	-
Furniture and Household Durables	28.6	-	27.9	-2.4	27.2	-2.5	27.0	-0.7	26.5	-1.9	24.4	-7.9	21.5	-11.9	21.6	0.5	23.4	8.3
Household Furniture	22.9	-	22.3	-2.6	22.1	-0.9	21.7	-1.8	21.5	-0.9	20.1	-6.5	17.1	-14.9	17.2	0.6	18.1	5.2
Commercial Furniture	-	-	-	-	-	-	-	-	-	-	-	-	-	-	-	-	-	-

Source: U.S. Department of Labor, Bureau of Labor Statistics, Division of Industry Prices and Price Indexes. n.e.c. stands for not elsewhere classified. - indicates no data collected for period or unavailable.

Producer Price Index
Annual Averages, 1935-1943
Base 1982 = 100

Columns headed % show percentile change in the index from the previous period for which an index is available.

	1935		1936		1937		1938		1939		1940		1941		1942		1943	
	Index	%	Index	%	Index	%	Index	%	Index	%	Index	%	Index	%	Index	%	Index	%
Pulp, Paper, and Allied Products	-	-	-	-	-	-	-	-	-	-	-	-	-	-	-	-	-	-
Pulp, Paper, and Products, ex. Building Paper	-	-	-	-	-	-	-	-	-	-	-	-	-	-	-	-	-	-
Building Paper & Building Board Mill Products	-	-	-	-	-	-	-	-	-	-	-	-	-	-	-	-	-	-
Publications, Printed Matter & Printing Materials	-	-	-	-	-	-	-	-	-	-	-	-	-	-	-	-	-	-
Metals and Metal Products	11.2	0.0	11.4	1.8	13.1	14.9	12.6	-3.8	12.5	-0.8	12.5	0.0	12.8	2.4	13.0	1.6	12.9	-0.8
Iron and Steel	9.8	0.0	9.9	1.0	11.1	12.1	11.1	0.0	10.8	-2.7	10.7	-0.9	10.9	1.9	11.0	0.9	11.0	0.0
Nonferrous Metals	11.3	0.9	11.8	4.4	14.8	25.4	12.0	-18.9	12.9	7.5	13.4	3.9	13.9	3.7	14.1	1.4	14.2	0.7
Metal Containers	14.4	-0.7	14.5	0.7	13.5	-6.9	14.4	6.7	13.8	-4.2	13.5	-2.2	13.6	0.7	13.8	1.5	13.8	0.0
Hardware	-	-	-	-	-	-	-	-	-	-	-	-	-	-	-	-	-	-
Plumbing Fixtures and Brass Fittings	14.7	-12.5	16.8	14.3	17.1	1.8	16.9	-1.2	16.9	0.0	17.9	5.9	18.3	2.2	20.3	10.9	19.7	-3.0
Heating Equipment	-	-	-	-	-	-	-	-	-	-	-	-	-	-	-	-	-	-
Fabricated Structural Metal Products	-	-	-	-	-	-	-	-	-	-	-	-	-	-	-	-	-	-
Miscellaneous Metal Products	-	-	-	-	-	-	-	-	-	-	-	-	-	-	-	-	-	-
Metal Treatment Services	-	-	-	-	-	-	-	-	-	-	-	-	-	-	-	-	-	-
Machinery and Equipment	-	-	-	-	-	-	-	-	14.8	-	14.9	0.7	15.1	1.3	15.4	2.0	15.2	-1.3
Agricultural Machinery and Equipment	13.2	3.9	13.3	0.8	13.3	0.0	13.5	1.5	13.2	-2.2	13.1	-0.8	13.2	0.8	13.7	3.8	13.7	0.0
Construction Machinery and Equipment	-	-	-	-	-	-	-	-	9.3	-	9.5	2.2	10.0	5.3	10.3	3.0	10.3	0.0
Metalworking Machinery and Equipment	-	-	-	-	-	-	-	-	-	-	-	-	-	-	-	-	-	-
General Purpose Machinery and Equipment	-	-	-	-	-	-	-	-	13.3	-	13.3	0.0	13.6	2.3	13.7	0.7	13.4	-2.2
Electronic Computers and Computer Equipment	-	-	-	-	-	-	-	-	-	-	-	-	-	-	-	-	-	-
Special Industry Machinery and Equipment	-	-	-	-	-	-	-	-	-	-	-	-	-	-	-	-	-	-
Electrical Machinery and Equipment	-	-	-	-	-	-	-	-	19.6	-	19.5	-0.5	19.6	0.5	19.6	0.0	19.5	-0.5
Miscellaneous Instruments	-	-	-	-	-	-	-	-	-	-	-	-	-	-	-	-	-	-
Miscellaneous Machinery	-	-	-	-	-	-	-	-	-	-	-	-	-	-	-	-	-	-
Furniture and Household Durables	23.2	-0.9	23.6	1.7	26.1	10.6	25.5	-2.3	25.4	-0.4	26.0	2.4	27.6	6.2	29.9	8.3	29.7	-0.7
Household Furniture	17.7	-2.2	17.8	0.6	19.7	10.7	19.0	-3.6	18.6	-2.1	18.7	0.5	20.2	8.0	22.3	10.4	22.4	0.4
Commercial Furniture	-	-	-	-	-	-	-	-	-	-	-	-	-	-	-	-	-	-

Source: U.S. Department of Labor, Bureau of Labor Statistics, Division of Industry Prices and Price Indexes. n.e.c. stands for not elsewhere classified. - indicates no data collected for period or unavailable.

Producer Price Index
Annual Averages, 1944-1952
Base 1982 = 100

Columns headed % show percentile change in the index from the previous period for which an index is available.

	1944		1945		1946		1947		1948		1949		1950		1951		1952	
	Index	%	Index	%	Index	%	Index	%	Index	%	Index	%	Index	%	Index	%	Index	%
Pulp, Paper, and Allied Products	-	-	-	-	-	-	25.1	-	26.2	4.4	25.1	-4.2	25.7	2.4	30.5	18.7	29.7	-2.6
Pulp, Paper, and Products, ex. Building Paper	-	-	-	-	-	-	26.6	-	27.7	4.1	26.5	-4.3	27.1	2.3	32.2	18.8	31.4	-2.5
Building Paper & Building Board Mill Products	-	-	-	-	-	-	29.4	-	32.5	10.5	32.9	1.2	34.0	3.3	35.9	5.6	36.5	1.7
Publications, Printed Matter & Printing Materials	-	-	-	-	-	-	-	-	-	-	-	-	-	-	-	-	-	-
Metals and Metal Products	12.9	0.0	13.1	1.6	14.7	12.2	18.2	23.8	20.7	13.7	20.9	1.0	22.0	5.3	24.5	11.4	24.5	0.0
Iron and Steel	11.0	0.0	11.2	1.8	12.4	10.7	15.1	21.8	17.6	16.6	17.8	1.1	19.1	7.3	20.8	8.9	21.0	1.0
Nonferrous Metals	14.1	-0.7	14.1	0.0	16.3	15.6	22.4	37.4	24.8	10.7	23.1	-6.9	24.4	5.6	29.1	19.3	28.9	-0.7
Metal Containers	13.8	0.0	13.8	0.0	14.2	2.9	16.0	12.7	17.8	11.2	19.3	8.4	19.4	0.5	21.5	10.8	21.6	0.5
Hardware	-	-	-	-	-	-	17.2	-	18.7	8.7	19.6	4.8	21.1	7.7	23.3	10.4	23.2	-0.4
Plumbing Fixtures and Brass Fittings	19.0	-3.6	18.8	-1.1	20.1	6.9	24.0	19.4	26.1	8.7	26.1	0.0	27.4	5.0	31.1	13.5	29.8	-4.2
Heating Equipment	-	-	-	-	-	-	35.8	-	38.0	6.1	38.9	2.4	39.4	1.3	43.0	9.1	42.7	-0.7
Fabricated Structural Metal Products	-	-	-	-	-	-	22.6	-	23.9	5.8	23.5	-1.7	24.3	3.4	27.4	12.8	26.8	-2.2
Miscellaneous Metal Products	-	-	-	-	-	-	18.0	-	22.2	23.3	23.9	7.7	24.7	3.3	26.8	8.5	26.7	-0.4
Metal Treatment Services	-	-	-	-	-	-	-	-	-	-	-	-	-	-	-	-	-	-
Machinery and Equipment	15.1	-0.7	15.1	0.0	16.6	9.9	19.3	16.3	20.9	8.3	21.9	4.8	22.6	3.2	25.3	11.9	25.3	0.0
Agricultural Machinery and Equipment	13.7	0.0	13.8	0.7	14.8	7.2	17.1	15.5	19.2	12.3	20.5	6.8	21.0	2.4	22.8	8.6	23.0	0.9
Construction Machinery and Equipment	10.3	0.0	10.4	1.0	11.3	8.7	12.8	13.3	14.5	13.3	15.4	6.2	15.8	2.6	17.6	11.4	17.9	1.7
Metalworking Machinery and Equipment	-	-	-	-	-	-	14.3	-	15.4	7.7	16.2	5.2	17.2	6.2	19.2	11.6	19.5	1.6
General Purpose Machinery and Equipment	13.4	0.0	13.4	0.0	14.4	7.5	16.7	16.0	18.2	9.0	19.2	5.5	19.9	3.6	22.2	11.6	22.0	-0.9
Electronic Computers and Computer Equipment	-	-	-	-	-	-	-	-	-	-	-	-	-	-	-	-	-	-
Special Industry Machinery and Equipment	-	-	-	-	-	-	-	-	-	-	-	-	-	-	-	-	-	-
Electrical Machinery and Equipment	19.2	-1.5	19.3	0.5	22.0	14.0	26.9	22.3	28.1	4.5	28.8	2.5	29.8	3.5	34.1	14.4	33.6	-1.5
Miscellaneous Instruments	-	-	-	-	-	-	-	-	-	-	-	-	-	-	-	-	-	-
Miscellaneous Machinery	-	-	-	-	-	-	21.7	-	23.4	7.8	24.3	3.8	24.8	2.1	27.6	11.3	27.6	0.0
Furniture and Household Durables	30.5	2.7	30.5	0.0	32.4	6.2	37.2	14.8	39.4	5.9	40.1	1.8	40.9	2.0	44.4	8.6	43.5	-2.0
Household Furniture	23.1	3.1	23.4	1.3	25.0	6.8	29.9	19.6	32.2	7.7	31.8	-1.2	32.9	3.5	36.4	10.6	35.3	-3.0
Commercial Furniture	-	-	-	-	-	-	20.1	-	21.5	7.0	22.2	3.3	23.4	5.4	26.5	13.2	26.2	-1.1

Source: U.S. Department of Labor, Bureau of Labor Statistics, Division of Industry Prices and Price Indexes. n.e.c. stands for not elsewhere classified. - indicates no data collected for period or unavailable.

Producer Price Index
Annual Averages, 1953-1961
Base 1982 = 100

Columns headed % show percentile change in the index from the previous period for which an index is available.

	1953		1954		1955		1956		1957		1958		1959		1960		1961	
	Index	%	Index	%	Index	%	Index	%	Index	%	Index	%	Index	%	Index	%	Index	%
Pulp, Paper, and Allied Products	29.6	-0.3	29.6	0.0	30.4	2.7	32.4	6.6	33.0	1.9	33.4	1.2	33.7	0.9	34.0	0.9	33.0	-2.9
Pulp, Paper, and Products, ex. Building Paper	31.2	-0.6	31.2	0.0	32.0	2.6	34.1	6.6	34.8	2.1	35.2	1.1	35.4	0.6	35.8	1.1	34.7	-3.1
Building Paper & Building Board Mill Products	38.4	5.2	40.4	5.2	41.4	2.5	43.3	4.6	44.8	3.5	45.3	1.1	46.3	2.2	46.1	-0.4	45.8	-0.7
Publications, Printed Matter & Printing Materials	-	-	-	-	-	-	-	-	-	-	-	-	-	-	-	-	-	-
Metals and Metal Products	25.3	3.3	25.5	0.8	27.2	6.7	29.6	8.8	30.2	2.0	30.0	-0.7	30.6	2.0	30.6	0.0	30.5	-0.3
Iron and Steel	22.1	5.2	22.4	1.4	23.7	5.8	26.1	10.1	28.0	7.3	28.4	1.4	29.0	2.1	28.6	-1.4	28.7	0.3
Nonferrous Metals	29.3	1.4	29.1	-0.7	33.5	15.1	36.6	9.3	32.2	-12.0	30.0	-6.8	31.9	6.3	32.6	2.2	31.5	-3.4
Metal Containers	22.6	4.6	23.2	2.7	23.6	1.7	25.1	6.4	26.8	6.8	27.6	3.0	27.2	-1.4	27.3	0.4	27.8	1.8
Hardware	24.5	5.6	25.7	4.9	27.1	5.4	28.8	6.3	30.5	5.9	31.6	3.6	32.0	1.3	32.2	0.6	32.5	0.9
Plumbing Fixtures and Brass Fittings	29.4	-1.3	30.0	2.0	31.8	6.0	34.0	6.9	33.0	-2.9	31.4	-4.8	33.0	5.1	33.5	1.5	33.5	0.0
Heating Equipment	43.1	0.9	42.9	-0.5	43.2	0.7	44.6	3.2	45.7	2.5	45.3	-0.9	45.5	0.4	44.6	-2.0	42.9	-3.8
Fabricated Structural Metal Products	27.0	0.7	27.3	1.1	28.5	4.4	30.9	8.4	31.2	1.0	31.2	0.0	31.1	-0.3	31.4	1.0	30.8	-1.9
Miscellaneous Metal Products	26.8	0.4	26.9	0.4	27.4	1.9	28.9	5.5	31.0	7.3	31.2	0.6	31.2	0.0	31.3	0.3	32.1	2.6
Metal Treatment Services	-	-	-	-	-	-	-	-	-	-	-	-	-	-	-	-	-	-
Machinery and Equipment	25.9	2.4	26.3	1.5	27.2	3.4	29.3	7.7	31.4	7.2	32.1	2.2	32.8	2.2	33.0	0.6	33.0	0.0
Agricultural Machinery and Equipment	23.2	0.9	23.1	-0.4	23.3	0.9	24.2	3.9	25.3	4.5	26.3	4.0	27.2	3.4	27.7	1.8	28.2	1.8
Construction Machinery and Equipment	18.4	2.8	18.7	1.6	19.5	4.3	21.1	8.2	22.7	7.6	23.6	4.0	24.5	3.8	25.0	2.0	25.4	1.6
Metalworking Machinery and Equipment	19.8	1.5	20.1	1.5	21.2	5.5	23.2	9.4	24.6	6.0	25.2	2.4	25.8	2.4	26.5	2.7	26.8	1.1
General Purpose Machinery and Equipment	22.6	2.7	23.1	2.2	24.1	4.3	26.5	10.0	28.4	7.2	28.8	1.4	29.7	3.1	30.0	1.0	29.8	-0.7
Electronic Computers and Computer Equipment	-		-	-	-		-		-		-		-		-		-	
Special Industry Machinery and Equipment	-		-		-		-		-		-		-		-	-	26.5	-
Electrical Machinery and Equipment	34.5	2.7	35.2	2.0	35.8	1.7	38.7	8.1	41.6	7.5	42.5	2.2	43.1	1.4	43.0	-0.2	42.4	-1.4
Miscellaneous Instruments	-	-	-		-		-		-		-		-		-		-	
Miscellaneous Machinery	28.3	2.5	29.0	2.5	29.8	2.8	31.6	6.0	33.5	6.0	34.2	2.1	34.5	0.9	34.7	0.6	35.1	1.2
Furniture and Household Durables	44.4	2.1	44.9	1.1	45.1	0.4	46.3	2.7	47.5	2.6	47.9	0.8	48.0	0.2	47.8	-0.4	47.5	-0.6
Household Furniture	35.6	0.8	35.5	-0.3	35.6	0.3	37.2	4.5	38.3	3.0	38.5	0.5	38.8	0.8	39.2	1.0	39.6	1.0
Commercial Furniture	26.6	1.5	27.0	1.5	28.1	4.1	30.2	7.5	32.1	6.3	32.9	2.5	33.1	0.6	33.4	0.9	33.2	-0.6

Source: U.S. Department of Labor, Bureau of Labor Statistics, Division of Industry Prices and Price Indexes. n.e.c. stands for not elsewhere classified. - indicates no data collected for period or unavailable.

Producer Price Index
Annual Averages, 1962-1970
Base 1982 = 100

Columns headed % show percentile change in the index from the previous period for which an index is available.

	1962 Index	%	1963 Index	%	1964 Index	%	1965 Index	%	1966 Index	%	1967 Index	%	1968 Index	%	1969 Index	%	1970 Index	%
Pulp, Paper, and Allied Products	33.4	1.2	33.1	-0.9	33.0	-0.3	33.3	0.9	34.2	2.7	34.6	1.2	35.0	1.2	36.0	2.9	37.5	4.2
Pulp, Paper, and Products, ex. Building Paper	35.2	1.4	34.9	-0.9	34.9	0.0	35.2	0.9	36.2	2.8	36.6	1.1	37.0	1.1	38.1	3.0	39.7	4.2
Building Paper & Building Board Mill Products	44.2	-3.5	43.6	-1.4	42.7	-2.1	42.1	-1.4	42.1	0.0	41.8	-0.7	42.1	0.7	44.1	4.8	42.2	-4.3
Publications, Printed Matter & Printing Materials	-	-	-	-	-	-	-	-	-	-	-	-	-	-	-	-	-	-
Metals and Metal Products	30.2	-1.0	30.3	0.3	31.1	2.6	32.0	2.9	32.8	2.5	33.2	1.2	34.0	2.4	36.0	5.9	38.7	7.5
Iron and Steel	28.3	-1.4	28.2	-0.4	28.6	1.4	28.9	1.0	29.1	0.7	29.5	1.4	30.1	2.0	31.6	5.0	34.0	7.6
Nonferrous Metals	31.1	-1.3	31.1	0.0	33.2	6.8	36.2	9.0	37.9	4.7	37.9	0.0	39.3	3.7	43.1	9.7	47.3	9.7
Metal Containers	28.2	1.4	28.5	1.1	28.7	0.7	29.3	2.1	29.9	2.0	30.4	1.7	31.6	3.9	32.5	2.8	34.3	5.5
Hardware	32.6	0.3	32.6	0.0	32.9	0.9	33.2	0.9	34.4	3.6	35.7	3.8	36.6	2.5	37.9	3.6	39.8	5.0
Plumbing Fixtures and Brass Fittings	32.5	-3.0	32.5	0.0	32.8	0.9	33.5	2.1	35.2	5.1	35.9	2.0	37.1	3.3	38.5	3.8	39.9	3.6
Heating Equipment	42.4	-1.2	42.2	-0.5	41.8	-0.9	41.7	-0.2	42.1	1.0	42.2	0.2	43.3	2.6	44.4	2.5	46.6	5.0
Fabricated Structural Metal Products	30.6	-0.6	30.6	0.0	30.9	1.0	31.5	1.9	32.4	2.9	32.8	1.2	33.5	2.1	34.7	3.6	36.7	5.8
Miscellaneous Metal Products	32.3	0.6	32.7	1.2	33.8	3.4	34.0	0.6	34.7	2.1	35.4	2.0	36.1	2.0	38.0	5.3	40.5	6.6
Metal Treatment Services	-	-	-	-	-	-	-	-	-	-	-	-	-	-	-	-	-	-
Machinery and Equipment	33.0	0.0	33.1	0.3	33.3	0.6	33.7	1.2	34.7	3.0	35.9	3.5	37.0	3.1	38.2	3.2	40.0	4.7
Agricultural Machinery and Equipment	28.8	2.1	29.2	1.4	29.6	1.4	30.2	2.0	31.1	3.0	32.1	3.2	33.4	4.0	34.9	4.5	36.4	4.3
Construction Machinery and Equipment	25.4	0.0	25.9	2.0	26.5	2.3	27.2	2.6	28.1	3.3	29.1	3.6	30.7	5.5	32.1	4.6	33.7	5.0
Metalworking Machinery and Equipment	27.2	1.5	27.3	0.4	27.8	1.8	28.6	2.9	29.9	4.5	31.2	4.3	32.4	3.8	33.7	4.0	35.6	5.6
General Purpose Machinery and Equipment	29.9	0.3	30.1	0.7	30.2	0.3	30.4	0.7	31.8	4.6	32.9	3.5	34.0	3.3	35.2	3.5	37.4	6.3
Electronic Computers and Computer Equipment	-	-	-	-	-	-	-	-	-	-	-	-	-	-	-	-	-	-
Special Industry Machinery and Equipment	26.9	1.5	27.4	1.9	27.9	1.8	28.4	1.8	29.5	3.9	30.8	4.4	32.4	5.2	33.8	4.3	35.6	5.3
Electrical Machinery and Equipment	41.8	-1.4	41.3	-1.2	41.1	-0.5	41.1	0.0	42.0	2.2	43.2	2.9	43.7	1.2	44.4	1.6	45.9	3.4
Miscellaneous Instruments	-	-	-	-	-	-	-	-	-	-	-	-	-	-	-	-	-	-
Miscellaneous Machinery	35.2	0.3	35.3	0.3	35.6	0.8	35.8	0.6	36.3	1.4	37.3	2.8	38.9	4.3	40.3	3.6	42.0	4.2
Furniture and Household Durables	47.2	-0.6	46.9	-0.6	47.1	0.4	46.8	-0.6	47.4	1.3	48.3	1.9	49.7	2.9	50.7	2.0	51.9	2.4
Household Furniture	40.0	1.0	40.3	0.7	40.6	0.7	40.9	0.7	42.0	2.7	43.5	3.6	45.2	3.9	47.2	4.4	48.6	3.0
Commercial Furniture	33.4	0.6	33.5	0.3	33.7	0.6	33.9	0.6	34.5	1.8	36.3	5.2	37.7	3.9	39.2	4.0	41.6	6.1

Source: U.S. Department of Labor, Bureau of Labor Statistics, Division of Industry Prices and Price Indexes. n.e.c. stands for not elsewhere classified. - indicates no data collected for period or unavailable.

Producer Price Index
Annual Averages, 1971-1979
Base 1982 = 100

Columns headed % show percentile change in the index from the previous period for which an index is available.

	1971		1972		1973		1974		1975		1976		1977		1978		1979	
	Index	%	Index	%	Index	%	Index	%	Index	%	Index	%	Index	%	Index	%	Index	%
Pulp, Paper, and Allied Products	38.1	1.6	39.3	3.1	42.3	7.6	52.5	24.1	59.0	12.4	62.1	5.3	64.6	4.0	67.7	4.8	75.9	12.1
Pulp, Paper, and Products, ex. Building Paper	40.4	1.8	41.6	3.0	44.8	7.7	55.9	24.8	62.9	12.5	66.2	5.2	68.6	3.6	71.6	4.4	80.6	12.6
Building Paper & Building Board Mill Products	42.9	1.7	44.4	3.5	47.1	6.1	51.6	9.6	53.1	2.9	57.9	9.0	65.6	13.3	78.2	19.2	76.2	-2.6
Publications, Printed Matter & Printing Materials	-	-	-	-	-	-	-	-	-	-	-	-	-	-	-	-	-	-
Metals and Metal Products	39.4	1.8	40.9	3.8	44.0	7.6	57.0	29.5	61.5	7.9	65.0	5.7	69.3	6.6	75.3	8.7	86.0	14.2
Iron and Steel	35.9	5.6	37.9	5.6	40.2	6.1	52.7	31.1	59.3	12.5	63.7	7.4	68.0	6.8	74.8	10.0	83.6	11.8
Nonferrous Metals	43.5	-8.0	44.3	1.8	51.2	15.6	71.0	38.7	65.1	-8.3	68.9	5.8	74.1	7.5	78.8	6.3	99.3	26.0
Metal Containers	37.1	8.2	39.2	5.7	41.0	4.6	50.1	22.2	58.5	16.8	61.5	5.1	66.4	8.0	74.1	11.6	81.9	10.5
Hardware	41.7	4.8	42.9	2.9	44.5	3.7	50.2	12.8	58.2	15.9	61.8	6.2	66.2	7.1	71.5	8.0	78.0	9.1
Plumbing Fixtures and Brass Fittings	41.8	4.8	43.0	2.9	45.1	4.9	53.5	18.6	58.2	8.8	62.5	7.4	67.0	7.2	71.4	6.6	77.9	9.1
Heating Equipment	48.6	4.3	49.8	2.5	50.8	2.0	56.9	12.0	63.5	11.6	66.6	4.9	69.8	4.8	73.5	5.3	78.9	7.3
Fabricated Structural Metal Products	38.8	5.7	40.2	3.6	41.8	4.0	52.9	26.6	62.0	17.2	63.6	2.6	67.8	6.6	74.3	9.6	81.6	9.8
Miscellaneous Metal Products	42.1	4.0	44.0	4.5	45.9	4.3	55.7	21.4	64.1	15.1	66.2	3.3	69.5	5.0	75.1	8.1	81.9	9.1
Metal Treatment Services	-	-	-	-	-	-	-	-	-	-	-	-	-	-	-	-	-	-
Machinery and Equipment	41.4	3.5	42.3	2.2	43.7	3.3	50.0	14.4	57.9	15.8	61.3	5.9	65.2	6.4	70.3	7.8	76.7	9.1
Agricultural Machinery and Equipment	37.8	3.8	39.3	4.0	40.5	3.1	46.2	14.1	54.2	17.3	58.8	8.5	63.6	8.2	68.5	7.7	74.6	8.9
Construction Machinery and Equipment	35.4	5.0	36.6	3.4	38.0	3.8	44.3	16.6	53.8	21.4	57.8	7.4	62.1	7.4	67.7	9.0	74.5	10.0
Metalworking Machinery and Equipment	36.7	3.1	37.5	2.2	39.1	4.3	45.8	17.1	53.5	16.8	56.9	6.4	61.9	8.8	67.6	9.2	75.2	11.2
General Purpose Machinery and Equipment	39.2	4.8	40.3	2.8	41.8	3.7	49.7	18.9	58.7	18.1	62.4	6.3	66.4	6.4	71.2	7.2	77.8	9.3
Electronic Computers and Computer Equipment	-	-	-	-	-	-	-	-	-	-	-	-	-	-	-	-	-	-
Special Industry Machinery and Equipment	37.2	4.5	38.0	2.2	40.0	5.3	46.4	16.0	53.8	15.9	58.0	7.8	62.3	7.4	68.6	10.1	76.0	10.8
Electrical Machinery and Equipment	47.1	2.6	47.7	1.3	48.5	1.7	54.0	11.3	60.7	12.4	63.4	4.4	66.6	5.0	71.2	6.9	77.2	8.4
Miscellaneous Instruments	-	-	-	-	-	-	-	-	-	-	-	-	-	-	-	-	-	-
Miscellaneous Machinery	43.7	4.0	44.8	2.5	46.2	3.1	52.0	12.6	60.5	16.3	64.1	6.0	67.3	5.0	72.5	7.7	77.8	7.3
Furniture and Household Durables	53.1	2.3	53.8	1.3	55.7	3.5	61.8	11.0	67.5	9.2	70.3	4.1	73.2	4.1	77.5	5.9	82.8	6.8
Household Furniture	50.0	2.9	51.0	2.0	53.5	4.9	59.4	11.0	63.6	7.1	66.8	5.0	70.6	5.7	75.5	6.9	81.0	7.3
Commercial Furniture	42.9	3.1	43.6	1.6	47.0	7.8	55.3	17.7	60.5	9.4	63.0	4.1	67.5	7.1	73.1	8.3	80.5	10.1

Source: U.S. Department of Labor, Bureau of Labor Statistics, Division of Industry Prices and Price Indexes. n.e.c. stands for not elsewhere classified. - indicates no data collected for period or unavailable.

Producer Price Index
Annual Averages, 1980-1988
Base 1982 = 100

Columns headed % show percentile change in the index from the previous period for which an index is available.

	1980		1981		1982		1983		1984		1985		1986		1987		1988	
	Index	%	Index	%	Index	%	Index	%	Index	%	Index	%	Index	%	Index	%	Index	%
Pulp, Paper, and Allied Products	86.3	13.7	94.8	9.8	100.0	5.5	103.3	3.3	110.3	6.8	113.3	2.7	116.1	2.5	121.8	4.9	130.4	7.1
Pulp, Paper, and Products, ex. Building Paper	91.7	13.8	99.1	8.1	100.0	0.9	99.3	-0.7	107.3	8.1	106.9	-0.4	107.6	0.7	114.3	6.2	124.9	9.3
Building Paper & Building Board Mill Products	86.1	13.0	96.7	12.3	100.0	3.4	104.4	4.4	108.2	3.6	107.4	-0.7	108.8	1.3	111.2	2.2	113.3	1.9
Publications, Printed Matter & Printing Materials	-	-	91.4	-	100.0	9.4	106.3	6.3	112.7	6.0	118.7	5.3	123.3	3.9	128.1	3.9	134.7	5.2
Metals and Metal Products	95.0	10.5	99.6	4.8	100.0	0.4	101.8	1.8	104.8	2.9	104.4	-0.4	103.2	-1.1	107.1	3.8	118.7	10.8
Iron and Steel	90.0	7.7	98.5	9.4	100.0	1.5	101.3	1.3	105.3	3.9	104.8	-0.5	101.1	-3.5	104.6	3.5	115.7	10.6
Nonferrous Metals	115.7	16.5	108.4	-6.3	100.0	-7.7	104.7	4.7	105.1	0.4	99.6	-5.2	98.5	-1.1	108.8	10.5	133.2	22.4
Metal Containers	90.9	11.0	96.1	5.7	100.0	4.1	102.1	2.1	106.5	4.3	109.0	2.3	110.2	1.1	109.5	-0.6	110.2	0.6
Hardware	85.8	10.0	93.9	9.4	100.0	6.5	103.7	3.7	105.9	2.1	109.1	3.0	109.5	0.4	109.6	0.1	113.7	3.7
Plumbing Fixtures and Brass Fittings	88.5	13.6	96.0	8.5	100.0	4.2	103.8	3.8	108.6	4.6	111.9	3.0	115.5	3.2	119.7	3.6	128.7	7.5
Heating Equipment	87.0	10.3	94.5	8.6	100.0	5.8	102.7	2.7	106.6	3.8	109.5	2.7	113.0	3.2	115.5	2.2	119.2	3.2
Fabricated Structural Metal Products	88.8	8.8	96.9	9.1	100.0	3.2	99.6	-0.4	101.9	2.3	103.2	1.3	103.6	0.4	105.4	1.7	114.3	8.4
Miscellaneous Metal Products	88.5	8.1	95.8	8.2	100.0	4.4	100.5	0.5	104.6	4.1	107.1	2.4	107.0	-0.1	107.8	0.7	112.1	4.0
Metal Treatment Services	-	-	-	-	-	-	-	-	-	-	102.4	-	104.7	2.2	106.2	1.4	109.8	3.4
Machinery and Equipment	86.0	12.1	94.4	9.8	100.0	5.9	102.7	2.7	105.1	2.3	107.2	2.0	108.8	1.5	110.4	1.5	113.2	2.5
Agricultural Machinery and Equipment	83.3	11.7	92.7	11.3	100.0	7.9	104.9	4.9	108.0	3.0	108.7	0.6	109.2	0.5	109.6	0.4	112.7	2.8
Construction Machinery and Equipment	84.2	13.0	93.3	10.8	100.0	7.2	102.3	2.3	103.8	1.5	105.4	1.5	106.7	1.2	108.9	2.1	111.8	2.7
Metalworking Machinery and Equipment	85.5	13.7	93.9	9.8	100.0	6.5	101.7	1.7	104.1	2.4	106.6	2.4	108.4	1.7	110.1	1.6	113.5	3.1
General Purpose Machinery and Equipment	87.0	11.8	95.0	9.2	100.0	5.3	101.4	1.4	103.3	1.9	105.7	2.3	107.2	1.4	108.3	1.0	112.8	4.2
Electronic Computers and Computer Equipment	-	-	-	-	-	-	-	-	-	-	-	-	-	-	-	-	-	-
Special Industry Machinery and Equipment	84.8	11.6	94.7	11.7	100.0	5.6	103.7	3.7	107.3	3.5	110.8	3.3	114.2	3.1	117.3	2.7	121.7	3.8
Electrical Machinery and Equipment	87.1	12.8	95.1	9.2	100.0	5.2	103.7	3.7	107.4	3.6	109.6	2.0	111.2	1.5	112.6	1.3	114.5	1.7
Miscellaneous Instruments	-	-	91.9	-	100.0	8.8	105.3	5.3	106.6	1.2	109.8	3.0	112.7	2.6	115.7	2.7	118.9	2.8
Miscellaneous Machinery	85.7	10.2	94.1	9.8	100.0	6.3	102.1	2.1	102.2	0.1	103.3	1.1	104.2	0.9	105.7	1.4	108.6	2.7
Furniture and Household Durables	90.7	9.5	95.9	5.7	100.0	4.3	103.4	3.4	105.7	2.2	107.1	1.3	108.2	1.0	109.9	1.6	113.1	2.9
Household Furniture	89.1	10.0	95.4	7.1	100.0	4.8	102.1	2.1	105.3	3.1	108.5	3.0	110.3	1.7	113.0	2.4	117.6	4.1
Commercial Furniture	85.7	6.5	93.5	9.1	100.0	7.0	103.9	3.9	107.8	3.8	111.9	3.8	115.3	3.0	118.6	2.9	124.2	4.7

Source: U.S. Department of Labor, Bureau of Labor Statistics, Division of Industry Prices and Price Indexes. n.e.c. stands for not elsewhere classified. - indicates no data collected for period or unavailable.

Producer Price Index
Annual Averages, 1989-1997
Base 1982 = 100

Columns headed % show percentile change in the index from the previous period for which an index is available.

	1989 Index	%	1990 Index	%	1991 Index	%	1992 Index	%	1993 Index	%	1994 Index	%	1995 Index	%	1996 Index	%	1997 Index	%
Pulp, Paper, and Allied Products	137.8	5.7	141.2	2.5	142.9	1.2	145.2	1.6	147.3	1.4	152.5	3.5	172.2	12.9	168.7	-2.0	167.9	-0.5
Pulp, Paper, and Products, ex. Building Paper	132.4	6.0	132.9	0.4	129.8	-2.3	129.2	-0.5	127.6	-1.2	133.1	4.3	163.4	22.8	149.7	-8.4	144.7	-3.3
Building Paper & Building Board Mill Products	115.6	2.0	112.2	-2.9	111.8	-0.4	119.6	7.0	132.7	11.0	144.1	8.6	144.9	0.6	137.2	-5.3	130.0	-5.2
Publications, Printed Matter & Printing Materials	142.1	5.5	148.4	4.4	154.8	4.3	159.6	3.1	164.9	3.3	169.6	2.9	179.9	6.1	186.9	3.9	190.5	1.9
Metals and Metal Products	124.1	4.5	122.9	-1.0	120.2	-2.2	119.2	-0.8	119.2	0.0	124.8	4.7	134.5	7.8	131.0	-2.6	131.8	0.6
Iron and Steel	119.1	2.9	117.2	-1.6	114.1	-2.6	111.5	-2.3	116.0	4.0	122.0	5.2	128.8	5.6	125.8	-2.3	126.5	0.6
Nonferrous Metals	141.5	6.2	133.8	-5.4	123.4	-7.8	120.9	-2.0	114.4	-5.4	126.6	10.7	149.6	18.2	136.5	-8.8	136.6	0.1
Metal Containers	111.5	1.2	114.0	2.2	115.5	1.3	113.9	-1.4	109.7	-3.7	108.1	-1.5	117.2	8.4	110.0	-6.1	107.9	-1.9
Hardware	120.4	5.9	125.9	4.6	130.2	3.4	132.7	1.9	135.2	1.9	137.5	1.7	141.1	2.6	143.8	1.9	145.6	1.3
Plumbing Fixtures and Brass Fittings	137.7	7.0	144.3	4.8	149.7	3.7	153.1	2.3	155.9	1.8	159.6	2.4	166.0	4.0	171.1	3.1	174.6	2.0
Heating Equipment	125.1	4.9	131.6	5.2	134.1	1.9	137.3	2.4	140.4	2.3	142.5	1.5	147.5	3.5	151.2	2.5	152.6	0.9
Fabricated Structural Metal Products	120.3	5.2	121.8	1.2	122.4	0.5	122.1	-0.2	123.2	0.9	127.3	3.3	135.1	6.1	137.8	2.0	140.3	1.8
Miscellaneous Metal Products	117.0	4.4	119.4	2.1	120.4	0.8	121.4	0.8	122.3	0.7	123.6	1.1	125.9	1.9	126.9	0.8	127.6	0.6
Metal Treatment Services	114.5	4.3	116.3	1.6	117.4	0.9	118.2	0.7	119.8	1.4	121.4	1.3	123.5	1.7	124.8	1.1	126.0	1.0
Machinery and Equipment	117.4	3.7	120.7	2.8	123.0	1.9	123.4	0.3	124.0	0.5	125.1	0.9	126.6	1.2	126.5	-0.1	125.9	-0.5
Agricultural Machinery and Equipment	117.7	4.4	121.7	3.4	125.7	3.3	129.5	3.0	133.6	3.2	137.0	2.5	142.9	4.3	146.8	2.7	148.6	1.2
Construction Machinery and Equipment	117.2	4.8	121.6	3.8	125.2	3.0	128.7	2.8	132.0	2.6	133.7	1.3	136.7	2.2	139.8	2.3	142.2	1.7
Metalworking Machinery and Equipment	118.2	4.1	123.0	4.1	127.6	3.7	130.9	2.6	133.5	2.0	136.5	2.2	139.8	2.4	143.1	2.4	145.4	1.6
General Purpose Machinery and Equipment	119.0	5.5	123.7	3.9	127.8	3.3	129.9	1.6	132.2	1.8	134.8	2.0	139.1	3.2	142.5	2.4	145.0	1.8
Electronic Computers and Computer Equipment	-	-	-	-	88.9	-	73.2	-17.7	62.2	-15.0	57.0	-8.4	52.2	-8.4	45.5	-12.8	39.2	-13.8
Special Industry Machinery and Equipment	127.0	4.4	131.5	3.5	135.9	3.3	139.5	2.6	143.7	3.0	146.2	1.7	149.8	2.5	153.3	2.3	156.7	2.2
Electrical Machinery and Equipment	117.5	2.6	119.3	1.5	120.8	1.3	121.3	0.4	122.5	1.0	123.4	0.7	124.2	0.6	123.4	-0.6	122.4	-0.8
Miscellaneous Instruments	122.5	3.0	126.7	3.4	130.3	2.8	133.7	2.6	137.8	3.1	139.6	1.3	141.0	1.0	143.3	1.6	146.0	1.9
Miscellaneous Machinery	112.7	3.8	116.7	3.5	120.3	3.1	121.7	1.2	122.7	0.8	124.7	1.6	127.0	1.8	129.2	1.7	130.9	1.3
Furniture and Household Durables	116.9	3.4	119.2	2.0	121.2	1.7	122.2	0.8	123.7	1.2	126.1	1.9	128.2	1.7	130.4	1.7	130.8	0.3
Household Furniture	121.8	3.6	125.1	2.7	128.0	2.3	130.0	1.6	133.4	2.6	138.0	3.4	141.8	2.8	144.5	1.9	146.2	1.2
Commercial Furniture	129.0	3.9	133.4	3.4	136.2	2.1	138.1	1.4	140.5	1.7	144.7	3.0	148.2	2.4	151.7	2.4	154.2	1.6

Source: U.S. Department of Labor, Bureau of Labor Statistics, Division of Industry Prices and Price Indexes. n.e.c. stands for not elsewhere classified. - indicates no data collected for period or unavailable.

Producer Price Index
Annual Averages, 1998-2001
Base 1982 = 100

Columns headed % show percentile change in the index from the previous period for which an index is available.

	1998		1999		2000		2001												
	Index	%	Index	%	Index	%	Index	%	Index	%	Index	%	Index	%	Index	%	Index	%
Pulp, Paper, and Allied Products	171.7	2.3	174.1	1.4	183.7	5.5	184.7	0.5										
Pulp, Paper, and Products, ex. Building Paper	147.0	1.6	147.9	0.6	161.4	9.1	157.6	-2.4										
Building Paper & Building Board Mill Products	132.9	2.2	141.6	6.5	138.8	-2.0	128.9	-7.1										
Publications, Printed Matter & Printing Materials	195.8	2.8	199.6	1.9	205.4	2.9	211.8	3.1										
Metals and Metal Products	127.8	-3.0	124.6	-2.5	128.1	2.8	125.4	-2.1										
Iron and Steel	122.5	-3.2	114.0	-6.9	116.6	2.3	109.7	-5.9										
Nonferrous Metals	123.0	-10.0	119.1	-3.2	128.1	7.6	123.5	-3.6										
Metal Containers	108.3	0.4	106.4	-1.8	106.8	0.4	106.2	-0.6										
Hardware	147.0	1.0	148.7	1.2	151.2	1.7	154.4	2.1										
Plumbing Fixtures and Brass Fittings	175.1	0.3	176.7	0.9	180.4	2.1	180.7	0.2										
Heating Equipment	153.3	0.5	154.0	0.5	155.6	1.0	157.1	1.0										
Fabricated Structural Metal Products	142.5	1.6	143.3	0.6	144.9	1.1	144.6	-0.2										
Miscellaneous Metal Products	128.0	0.3	127.7	-0.2	128.0	0.2	128.6	0.5										
Metal Treatment Services	127.0	0.8	129.5	2.0	129.8	0.2	133.2	2.6										
Machinery and Equipment	124.9	-0.8	124.3	-0.5	124.0	-0.2	123.6	-0.3										
Agricultural Machinery and Equipment	150.4	1.2	152.1	1.1	153.7	1.1	155.7	1.3										
Construction Machinery and Equipment	145.2	2.1	147.2	1.4	148.6	1.0	149.1	0.3										
Metalworking Machinery and Equipment	147.2	1.2	148.1	0.6	149.6	1.0	150.6	0.7										
General Purpose Machinery and Equipment	147.2	1.5	149.3	1.4	150.7	0.9	152.7	1.3										
Electronic Computers and Computer Equipment	108.2	176.0	93.5	-13.6	86.3	-7.7	78.1	-9.5										
Special Industry Machinery and Equipment	159.1	1.5	161.3	1.4	163.1	1.1	164.8	1.0										
Electrical Machinery and Equipment	121.0	-1.1	119.8	-1.0	118.7	-0.9	117.3	-1.2										
Miscellaneous Instruments	147.7	1.2	148.6	0.6	150.3	1.1	152.1	1.2										
Miscellaneous Machinery	131.9	0.8	133.1	0.9	134.2	0.8	135.8	1.2										
Furniture and Household Durables	131.3	0.4	131.7	0.3	132.6	0.7	133.1	0.4										
Household Furniture	148.4	1.5	150.5	1.4	152.7	1.5	154.9	1.4										
Commercial Furniture	155.2	0.6	156.6	0.9	158.4	1.1	160.3	1.2										

Source: U.S. Department of Labor, Bureau of Labor Statistics, Division of Industry Prices and Price Indexes. n.e.c. stands for not elsewhere classified. - indicates no data collected for period or unavailable.

Producer Price Index
Annual Averages, 1926-1934
Base 1982 = 100

Columns headed % show percentile change in the index from the previous period for which an index is available.

	1926		1927		1928		1929		1930		1931		1932		1933		1934	
	Index	%	Index	%	Index	%	Index	%	Index	%	Index	%	Index	%	Index	%	Index	%
Floor Coverings	31.7	-	30.3	-4.4	29.7	-2.0	29.7	0.0	30.0	1.0	25.4	-15.3	22.7	-10.6	23.6	4.0	25.8	9.3
Household Appliances	-	-	-	-	-	-	-	-	-	-	-	-	-	-	-	-	-	-
Home Electronic Equipment	-	-	-	-	-	-	-	-	-	-	-	-	-	-	-	-	-	-
Other Household Durable Goods	-	-	-	-	-	-	-	-	-	-	-	-	-	-	-	-	-	-
Nonmetallic Mineral Products	16.4	-	15.7	-4.3	16.2	3.2	16.0	-1.2	15.9	-0.6	14.9	-6.3	13.9	-6.7	14.7	5.8	15.7	6.8
Glass	-	-	-	-	-	-	-	-	-	-	-	-	-	-	-	-	-	-
Concrete Ingredients and Related Products	14.9	-	14.5	-2.7	16.4	13.1	16.5	0.6	16.6	0.6	15.1	-9.0	14.4	-4.6	15.6	8.3	16.6	6.4
Concrete Products	23.7	-	23.7	0.0	23.7	0.0	23.3	-1.7	23.6	1.3	22.3	-5.5	20.5	-8.1	20.9	2.0	20.9	0.0
Clay Construction Products ex. Refractories	-	-	-	-	-	-	-	-	-	-	-	-	-	-	-	-	-	-
Refractories	-	-	-	-	-	-	-	-	-	-	-	-	-	-	-	-	-	-
Asphalt Felts and Coatings	21.2	-	20.0	-5.7	17.9	-10.5	15.8	-11.7	16.1	1.9	16.7	3.7	15.3	-8.4	15.7	2.6	16.9	7.6
Gypsum Products	-	-	-	-	-	-	-	-	-	-	-	-	-	-	-	-	-	-
Glass Containers	-	-	-	-	-	-	-	-	-	-	-	-	-	-	-	-	-	-
Other Nonmetallic Minerals	-	-	-	-	-	-	-	-	-	-	-	-	-	-	-	-	-	-
Transportation Equipment	-	-	-	-	-	-	-	-	-	-	-	-	-	-	-	-	-	-
Motor Vehicles and Equipment	16.7	-	16.0	-4.2	16.2	1.3	16.7	3.1	15.7	-6.0	14.9	-5.1	14.5	-2.7	13.9	-4.1	14.6	5.0
Aircraft and Aircraft Equipment	-	-	-	-	-	-	-	-	-	-	-	-	-	-	-	-	-	-
Ships and Boats	-	-	-	-	-	-	-	-	-	-	-	-	-	-	-	-	-	-
Railroad Equipment	-	-	-	-	-	-	-	-	-	-	-	-	-	-	-	-	-	-
Transportation Equipment, n.e.c.	-	-	-	-	-	-	-	-	-	-	-	-	-	-	-	-	-	-
Miscellaneous Products	-	-	-	-	-	-	-	-	-	-	-	-	-	-	-	-	-	-
Toys, Sporting Goods, Small Arms, etc.	-	-	-	-	-	-	-	-	-	-	-	-	-	-	-	-	-	-
Tobacco Products, incl. Stemmed & Redried	-	-	-	-	-	-	-	-	-	-	-	-	-	-	-	-	-	-
Notions	-	-	-	-	-	-	-	-	-	-	-	-	-	-	-	-	-	-
Photographic Equipment and Supplies	-	-	-	-	-	-	-	-	-	-	-	-	-	-	-	-	-	-
Mobile Homes	-	-	-	-	-	-	-	-	-	-	-	-	-	-	-	-	-	-
Medical, Surgical & Personal Aid Devices	-	-	-	-	-	-	-	-	-	-	-	-	-	-	-	-	-	-
Industrial Safety Equipment	-	-	-	-	-	-	-	-	-	-	-	-	-	-	-	-	-	-
Mining Services	-	-	-	-	-	-	-	-	-	-	-	-	-	-	-	-	-	-
Other Miscellaneous Products	-	-	-	-	-	-	-	-	-	-	-	-	-	-	-	-	-	-

Source: U.S. Department of Labor, Bureau of Labor Statistics, Division of Industry Prices and Price Indexes. n.e.c. stands for not elsewhere classified. - indicates no data collected for period or unavailable.

Producer Price Index
Annual Averages, 1935-1943
Base 1982 = 100

Columns headed % show percentile change in the index from the previous period for which an index is available.

	1935		1936		1937		1938		1939		1940		1941		1942		1943	
	Index	%	Index	%	Index	%	Index	%	Index	%	Index	%	Index	%	Index	%	Index	%
Floor Coverings	26.2	1.6	26.3	0.4	29.5	12.2	28.2	-4.4	28.9	2.5	31.2	8.0	32.1	2.9	33.2	3.4	33.2	0.0
Household Appliances	-	-	-	-	-	-	-	-	-	-	-	-	-	-	-	-	-	-
Home Electronic Equipment	-	-	-	-	-	-	-	-	-	-	-	-	-	-	-	-	-	-
Other Household Durable Goods	-	-	-	-	-	-	-	-	-	-	-	-	-	-	-	-	-	-
Nonmetallic Mineral Products	15.7	0.0	15.8	0.6	16.1	1.9	15.6	-3.1	15.3	-1.9	15.3	0.0	15.7	2.6	16.3	3.8	16.4	0.6
Glass	-	-	-	-	-	-	-	-	-	-	-	-	-	-	-	-	-	-
Concrete Ingredients and Related Products	16.6	0.0	16.7	0.6	16.6	-0.6	16.7	0.6	16.7	0.0	16.6	-0.6	16.8	1.2	17.3	3.0	17.3	0.0
Concrete Products	19.0	-9.1	20.2	6.3	20.3	0.5	18.7	-7.9	18.6	-0.5	16.6	-10.8	19.2	15.7	19.9	3.6	19.9	0.0
Clay Construction Products ex. Refractories	-	-	-	-	-	-	-	-	-	-	-	-	-	-	-	-	-	-
Refractories	-	-	-	-	-	-	-	-	-	-	-	-	-	-	-	-	-	-
Asphalt Felts and Coatings	17.7	4.7	17.4	-1.7	19.1	9.8	15.4	-19.4	15.9	3.2	17.4	9.4	17.9	2.9	17.5	-2.2	17.5	0.0
Gypsum Products	-	-	-	-	-	-	-	-	-	-	-	-	-	-	-	-	-	-
Glass Containers	-	-	-	-	-	-	-	-	-	-	-	-	-	-	-	-	-	-
Other Nonmetallic Minerals	-	-	-	-	-	-	-	-	-	-	-	-	-	-	-	-	-	-
Transportation Equipment	-	-	-	-	-	-	-	-	-	-	-	-	-	-	-	-	-	-
Motor Vehicles and Equipment	14.0	-4.1	13.9	-0.7	14.9	7.2	15.9	6.7	15.6	-1.9	16.1	3.2	17.2	6.8	18.8	9.3	18.8	0.0
Aircraft and Aircraft Equipment	-	-	-	-	-	-	-	-	-	-	-	-	-	-	-	-	-	-
Ships and Boats	-	-	-	-	-	-	-	-	-	-	-	-	-	-	-	-	-	-
Railroad Equipment	-	-	-	-	-	-	-	-	-	-	-	-	-	-	-	-	-	-
Transportation Equipment, n.e.c.	-	-	-	-	-	-	-	-	-	-	-	-	-	-	-	-	-	-
Miscellaneous Products	-	-	-	-	-	-	-	-	-	-	-	-	-	-	-	-	-	-
Toys, Sporting Goods, Small Arms, etc.	-	-	-	-	-	-	-	-	-	-	-	-	-	-	-	-	-	-
Tobacco Products, incl. Stemmed & Redried	-	-	-	-	-	-	-	-	-	-	-	-	-	-	-	-	-	-
Notions	-	-	-	-	-	-	-	-	-	-	-	-	-	-	-	-	-	-
Photographic Equipment and Supplies	-	-	-	-	-	-	-	-	-	-	-	-	-	-	-	-	-	-
Mobile Homes	-	-	-	-	-	-	-	-	-	-	-	-	-	-	-	-	-	-
Medical, Surgical & Personal Aid Devices	-	-	-	-	-	-	-	-	-	-	-	-	-	-	-	-	-	-
Industrial Safety Equipment	-	-	-	-	-	-	-	-	-	-	-	-	-	-	-	-	-	-
Mining Services	-	-	-	-	-	-	-	-	-	-	-	-	-	-	-	-	-	-
Other Miscellaneous Products	-	-	-	-	-	-	-	-	-	-	-	-	-	-	-	-	-	-

Source: U.S. Department of Labor, Bureau of Labor Statistics, Division of Industry Prices and Price Indexes. n.e.c. stands for not elsewhere classified. - indicates no data collected for period or unavailable.

Producer Price Index
Annual Averages, 1944-1952
Base 1982 = 100

Columns headed % show percentile change in the index from the previous period for which an index is available.

	1944		1945		1946		1947		1948		1949		1950		1951		1952	
	Index	%	Index	%	Index	%	Index	%	Index	%	Index	%	Index	%	Index	%	Index	%
Floor Coverings	33.2	0.0	33.1	-0.3	36.8	11.2	43.6	18.5	46.4	6.4	46.6	0.4	52.3	12.2	62.7	19.9	55.9	-10.8
Household Appliances	-	-	-	-	-	-	51.5	-	54.0	4.9	53.7	-0.6	54.0	0.6	57.3	6.1	57.0	-0.5
Home Electronic Equipment	-	-	-	-	-	-	141.0	-	146.7	4.0	151.8	3.5	141.8	-6.6	136.2	-3.9	135.9	-0.2
Other Household Durable Goods	-	-	-	-	-	-	19.5	-	20.0	2.6	20.9	4.5	21.5	2.9	23.1	7.4	23.3	0.9
Nonmetallic Mineral Products	16.7	1.8	17.4	4.2	18.5	6.3	20.7	11.9	22.4	8.2	23.0	2.7	23.5	2.2	25.0	6.4	25.0	0.0
Glass	-	-	-	-	-	-	30.2	-	31.8	5.3	33.4	5.0	34.1	2.1	36.3	6.5	36.3	0.0
Concrete Ingredients and Related Products	17.5	1.2	18.0	2.9	18.7	3.9	20.5	9.6	22.4	9.3	23.2	3.6	23.5	1.3	24.9	6.0	24.9	0.0
Concrete Products	19.9	0.0	19.9	0.0	21.1	6.0	23.9	13.3	25.1	5.0	25.7	2.4	26.3	2.3	28.0	6.5	28.0	0.0
Clay Construction Products ex. Refractories	-	-	-	-	-	-	23.9	-	25.7	7.5	26.5	3.1	27.6	4.2	29.9	8.3	29.8	-0.3
Refractories	-	-	-	-	-	-	14.3	-	15.8	10.5	16.5	4.4	18.2	10.3	19.6	7.7	19.8	1.0
Asphalt Felts and Coatings	17.6	0.6	18.0	2.3	18.8	4.4	21.4	13.8	23.5	9.8	23.4	-0.4	23.1	-1.3	23.9	3.5	23.4	-2.1
Gypsum Products	-	-	-	-	-	-	27.5	-	30.0	9.1	29.7	-1.0	30.4	2.4	34.1	12.2	34.2	0.3
Glass Containers	-	-	-	-	-	-	14.7	-	16.9	15.0	19.0	12.4	19.1	0.5	20.6	7.9	21.1	2.4
Other Nonmetallic Minerals	-	-	-	-	-	-	14.9	-	16.3	9.4	16.5	1.2	17.0	3.0	17.7	4.1	17.9	1.1
Transportation Equipment	-	-	-	-	-	-	-	-	-	-	-	-	-	-	-	-	-	-
Motor Vehicles and Equipment	18.9	0.5	19.2	1.6	22.3	16.1	25.5	14.3	28.2	10.6	30.1	6.7	30.0	-0.3	31.6	5.3	33.4	5.7
Aircraft and Aircraft Equipment	-	-	-	-	-	-	-	-	-	-	-	-	-	-	-	-	-	-
Ships and Boats	-	-	-	-	-	-	-	-	-	-	-	-	-	-	-	-	-	-
Railroad Equipment	-	-	-	-	-	-	-	-	-	-	-	-	-	-	-	-	-	-
Transportation Equipment, n.e.c.	-	-	-	-	-	-	-	-	-	-	-	-	-	-	-	-	-	-
Miscellaneous Products	-	-	-	-	-	-	26.6	-	27.7	4.1	28.2	1.8	28.6	1.4	30.3	5.9	30.2	-0.3
Toys, Sporting Goods, Small Arms, etc.	-	-	-	-	-	-	35.1	-	36.7	4.6	36.7	0.0	38.7	5.4	42.0	8.5	41.0	-2.4
Tobacco Products, incl. Stemmed & Redried	-	-	-	-	-	-	20.5	-	21.3	3.9	22.3	4.7	22.8	2.2	23.5	3.1	23.6	0.4
Notions	-	-	-	-	-	-	37.8	-	37.9	0.3	34.2	-9.8	33.7	-1.5	37.0	9.8	34.4	-7.0
Photographic Equipment and Supplies	-	-	-	-	-	-	32.2	-	35.3	9.6	36.6	3.7	36.3	-0.8	37.5	3.3	38.0	1.3
Mobile Homes	-	-	-	-	-	-	-	-	-	-	-	-	-	-	-	-	-	-
Medical, Surgical & Personal Aid Devices	-	-	-	-	-	-	-	-	-	-	-	-	-	-	-	-	-	-
Industrial Safety Equipment	-	-	-	-	-	-	-	-	-	-	-	-	-	-	-	-	-	-
Mining Services	-	-	-	-	-	-	-	-	-	-	-	-	-	-	-	-	-	-
Other Miscellaneous Products	-	-	-	-	-	-	23.2	-	23.8	2.6	23.9	0.4	24.1	0.8	25.7	6.6	25.7	0.0

Source: U.S. Department of Labor, Bureau of Labor Statistics, Division of Industry Prices and Price Indexes. n.e.c. stands for not elsewhere classified. - indicates no data collected for period or unavailable.

Producer Price Index
Annual Averages, 1953-1961
Base 1982 = 100

Columns headed % show percentile change in the index from the previous period for which an index is available.

	1953		1954		1955		1956		1957		1958		1959		1960		1961	
	Index	%	Index	%	Index	%	Index	%	Index	%	Index	%	Index	%	Index	%	Index	%
Floor Coverings	56.8	1.6	56.0	-1.4	57.6	2.9	59.7	3.6	60.7	1.7	58.1	-4.3	58.3	0.3	59.3	1.7	58.6	-1.2
Household Appliances	57.5	0.9	58.1	1.0	56.7	-2.4	56.0	-1.2	56.0	0.0	55.6	-0.7	55.5	-0.2	54.0	-2.7	53.0	-1.9
Home Electronic Equipment	-	-	-	-	136.3	0.3	136.4	0.1	138.3	1.4	138.2	-0.1	135.9	-1.7	133.8	-1.5	131.0	-2.1
Other Household Durable Goods	24.2	3.9	25.0	3.3	25.9	3.6	27.3	5.4	28.7	5.1	29.8	3.8	30.2	1.3	30.8	2.0	30.8	0.0
Nonmetallic Mineral Products	26.0	4.0	26.6	2.3	27.3	2.6	28.5	4.4	29.6	3.9	29.9	1.0	30.3	1.3	30.4	0.3	30.5	0.3
Glass	38.4	5.8	39.6	3.1	40.7	2.8	42.4	4.2	43.1	1.7	43.0	-0.2	43.0	0.0	42.1	-2.1	41.7	-1.0
Concrete Ingredients and Related Products	25.8	3.6	26.6	3.1	27.5	3.4	28.7	4.4	29.9	4.2	30.6	2.3	30.9	1.0	31.3	1.3	31.3	0.0
Concrete Products	28.7	2.5	29.2	1.7	29.5	1.0	30.6	3.7	31.4	2.6	31.9	1.6	32.3	1.3	32.6	0.9	32.6	0.0
Clay Construction Products ex. Refractories	30.4	2.0	30.9	1.6	32.1	3.9	33.8	5.3	34.3	1.5	34.5	0.6	35.4	2.6	35.9	1.4	36.1	0.6
Refractories	21.6	9.1	22.9	6.0	24.4	6.6	25.8	5.7	27.6	7.0	28.2	2.2	29.0	2.8	29.0	0.0	28.8	-0.7
Asphalt Felts and Coatings	24.4	4.3	23.7	-2.9	24.2	2.1	25.5	5.4	27.9	9.4	25.7	-7.9	26.5	3.1	24.4	-7.9	26.3	7.8
Gypsum Products	35.2	2.9	35.5	0.9	35.5	0.0	36.9	3.9	36.9	0.0	38.4	4.1	38.7	0.8	38.7	0.0	39.4	1.8
Glass Containers	22.7	7.6	23.8	4.8	24.1	1.3	25.4	5.4	26.8	5.5	28.3	5.6	28.3	0.0	27.6	-2.5	27.4	-0.7
Other Nonmetallic Minerals	18.6	3.9	19.1	2.7	19.3	1.0	19.6	1.6	20.4	4.1	20.9	2.5	21.1	1.0	21.4	1.4	21.2	-0.9
Transportation Equipment	-	-	-	-	-	-	-	-	-	-	-	-	-	-	-	-	-	-
Motor Vehicles and Equipment	33.3	-0.3	33.4	0.3	34.3	2.7	36.3	5.8	37.9	4.4	39.0	2.9	39.9	2.3	39.3	-1.5	39.2	-0.3
Aircraft and Aircraft Equipment	-	-	-	-	-	-	-	-	-	-	-	-	-	-	-	-	-	-
Ships and Boats	-	-	-	-	-	-	-	-	-	-	-	-	-	-	-	-	-	-
Railroad Equipment	-	-	-	-	-	-	-	-	-	-	-	-	-	-	-	-	27.9	-
Transportation Equipment, n.e.c.	-	-	-	-	-	-	-	-	-	-	-	-	-	-	-	-	-	-
Miscellaneous Products	31.0	2.6	31.3	1.0	31.3	0.0	31.7	1.3	32.6	2.8	33.3	2.1	33.4	0.3	33.6	0.6	33.7	0.3
Toys, Sporting Goods, Small Arms, etc.	41.1	0.2	40.9	-0.5	41.0	0.2	42.0	2.4	42.5	1.2	43.0	1.2	42.4	-1.4	42.8	0.9	43.1	0.7
Tobacco Products, incl. Stemmed & Redried	25.3	7.2	25.6	1.2	25.6	0.0	25.6	0.0	26.7	4.3	27.7	3.7	27.9	0.7	27.9	0.0	27.9	0.0
Notions	34.2	-0.6	34.8	1.8	33.7	-3.2	34.9	3.6	35.6	2.0	35.7	0.3	35.6	-0.3	35.5	-0.3	35.2	-0.8
Photographic Equipment and Supplies	38.3	0.8	38.7	1.0	39.1	1.0	39.8	1.8	41.5	4.3	42.6	2.7	44.0	3.3	44.4	0.9	45.0	1.4
Mobile Homes	-	-	-	-	-	-	-	-	-	-	-	-	-	-	-	-	-	-
Medical, Surgical & Personal Aid Devices	-	-	-	-	-	-	-	-	-	-	-	-	-	-	-	-	-	-
Industrial Safety Equipment	-	-	-	-	-	-	-	-	-	-	-	-	-	-	-	-	-	-
Mining Services	-	-	-	-	-	-	-	-	-	-	-	-	-	-	-	-	-	-
Other Miscellaneous Products	25.7	0.0	26.0	1.2	26.1	0.4	26.5	1.5	27.2	2.6	27.4	0.7	27.5	0.4	27.9	1.5	28.0	0.4

Source: U.S. Department of Labor, Bureau of Labor Statistics, Division of Industry Prices and Price Indexes. n.e.c. stands for not elsewhere classified. - indicates no data collected for period or unavailable.

Producer Price Index
Annual Averages, 1962-1970
Base 1982 = 100

Columns headed % show percentile change in the index from the previous period for which an index is available.

	1962		1963		1964		1965		1966		1967		1968		1969		1970	
	Index	%	Index	%	Index	%	Index	%	Index	%	Index	%	Index	%	Index	%	Index	%
Floor Coverings	57.2	-2.4	57.0	-0.3	58.7	3.0	57.7	-1.7	57.2	-0.9	55.2	-3.5	55.9	1.3	55.4	-0.9	54.9	-0.9
Household Appliances	52.3	-1.3	51.1	-2.3	50.8	-0.6	49.7	-2.2	49.6	-0.2	50.2	1.2	51.1	1.8	51.7	1.2	52.9	2.3
Home Electronic Equipment	125.3	-4.4	121.8	-2.8	119.9	-1.6	117.1	-2.3	114.9	-1.9	113.6	-1.1	111.4	-1.9	107.4	-3.6	106.0	-1.3
Other Household Durable Goods	31.3	1.6	31.4	0.3	31.8	1.3	32.2	1.3	33.0	2.5	34.6	4.8	36.9	6.6	38.6	4.6	40.1	3.9
Nonmetallic Mineral Products	30.5	0.0	30.3	-0.7	30.4	0.3	30.4	0.0	30.7	1.0	31.2	1.6	32.4	3.8	33.6	3.7	35.3	5.1
Glass	41.8	0.2	42.3	1.2	44.1	4.3	43.4	-1.6	43.3	-0.2	-	-	-	-	-	-	-	-
Concrete Ingredients and Related Products	31.5	0.6	31.4	-0.3	31.3	-0.3	31.5	0.6	31.6	0.3	32.3	2.2	33.3	3.1	34.4	3.3	36.3	5.5
Concrete Products	32.7	0.3	32.4	-0.9	32.1	-0.9	32.3	0.6	32.8	1.5	33.6	2.4	34.5	2.7	35.8	3.8	37.7	5.3
Clay Construction Products ex. Refractories	36.4	0.8	36.6	0.5	36.7	0.3	37.0	0.8	37.7	1.9	38.3	1.6	39.3	2.6	40.7	3.6	42.1	3.4
Refractories	28.7	-0.3	28.6	-0.3	28.8	0.7	29.1	1.0	29.3	0.7	29.7	1.4	31.7	6.7	32.5	2.5	35.9	10.5
Asphalt Felts and Coatings	25.3	-3.8	24.0	-5.1	23.7	-1.2	24.8	4.6	25.6	3.2	25.1	-2.0	25.9	3.2	25.8	-0.4	25.8	0.0
Gypsum Products	39.9	1.3	40.0	0.3	41.1	2.8	39.5	-3.9	38.9	-1.5	39.1	0.5	40.5	3.6	40.5	0.0	38.9	-4.0
Glass Containers	26.9	-1.8	26.9	0.0	27.0	0.4	27.3	1.1	27.8	1.8	28.1	1.1	30.2	7.5	32.3	7.0	33.9	5.0
Other Nonmetallic Minerals	21.2	0.0	21.1	-0.5	21.1	0.0	21.0	-0.5	21.1	0.5	21.2	0.5	21.9	3.3	22.7	3.7	23.8	4.8
Transportation Equipment	-	-	-	-	-	-	-	-	-	-	-	-	-	-	40.4	-	41.9	3.7
Motor Vehicles and Equipment	39.2	0.0	38.9	-0.8	39.1	0.5	39.2	0.3	39.2	0.0	39.8	1.5	40.9	2.8	41.7	2.0	43.3	3.8
Aircraft and Aircraft Equipment	-	-	-	-	-	-	-	-	-	-	-	-	-	-	-	-	-	-
Ships and Boats	-	-	-	-	-	-	-	-	-	-	-	-	-	-	-	-	-	-
Railroad Equipment	28.0	0.4	28.0	0.0	28.0	0.0	28.1	0.4	28.2	0.4	28.9	2.5	29.8	3.1	31.4	5.4	33.2	5.7
Transportation Equipment, n.e.c.	-	-	-	-	-	-	-	-	-	-	-	-	-	-	-	-	-	-
Miscellaneous Products	33.9	0.6	34.2	0.9	34.4	0.6	34.7	0.9	35.3	1.7	36.2	2.5	37.0	2.2	38.1	3.0	39.8	4.5
Toys, Sporting Goods, Small Arms, etc.	43.0	-0.2	43.1	0.2	43.1	0.0	43.8	1.6	44.4	1.4	45.2	1.8	46.2	2.2	47.6	3.0	49.5	4.0
Tobacco Products, incl. Stemmed & Redried	28.0	0.4	28.7	2.5	29.1	1.4	29.1	0.0	30.1	3.4	31.0	3.0	31.6	1.9	33.1	4.7	35.2	6.3
Notions	35.2	0.0	35.2	0.0	35.3	0.3	35.3	0.0	35.8	1.4	36.1	0.8	36.1	0.0	37.2	3.0	39.1	5.1
Photographic Equipment and Supplies	46.1	2.4	46.0	-0.2	46.3	0.7	46.7	0.9	46.5	-0.4	47.5	2.2	48.6	2.3	48.7	0.2	49.9	2.5
Mobile Homes	-	-	-	-	-	-	-	-	-	-	-	-	-	-	-	-	-	-
Medical, Surgical & Personal Aid Devices	-	-	-	-	-	-	-	-	-	-	-	-	-	-	-	-	-	-
Industrial Safety Equipment	-	-	-	-	-	-	-	-	-	-	-	-	-	-	-	-	-	-
Mining Services	-	-	-	-	-	-	-	-	-	-	-	-	-	-	-	-	-	-
Other Miscellaneous Products	28.1	0.4	28.0	-0.4	28.1	0.4	28.4	1.1	28.8	1.4	29.6	2.8	30.3	2.4	30.9	2.0	32.1	3.9

Source: U.S. Department of Labor, Bureau of Labor Statistics, Division of Industry Prices and Price Indexes. n.e.c. stands for not elsewhere classified. - indicates no data collected for period or unavailable.

Producer Price Index
Annual Averages, 1971-1979
Base 1982 = 100

Columns headed % show percentile change in the index from the previous period for which an index is available.

	1971		1972		1973		1974		1975		1976		1977		1978		1979	
	Index	%	Index	%	Index	%	Index	%	Index	%	Index	%	Index	%	Index	%	Index	%
Floor Coverings	54.6	-0.5	54.4	-0.4	56.4	3.7	63.7	12.9	69.0	8.3	72.5	5.1	75.3	3.9	78.2	3.9	81.7	4.5
Household Appliances	54.0	2.1	54.0	0.0	54.5	0.9	59.2	8.6	66.5	12.3	69.9	5.1	72.9	4.3	76.8	5.3	80.8	5.2
Home Electronic Equipment	106.1	0.1	105.3	-0.8	104.4	-0.9	105.7	1.2	106.2	0.5	103.7	-2.4	99.6	-4.0	102.4	2.8	103.7	1.3
Other Household Durable Goods	41.8	4.2	43.4	3.8	45.1	3.9	51.4	14.0	58.3	13.4	61.9	6.2	65.7	6.1	70.2	6.8	78.9	12.4
Nonmetallic Mineral Products	38.2	8.2	39.4	3.1	40.7	3.3	47.8	17.4	54.4	13.8	58.2	7.0	62.6	7.6	69.6	11.2	77.6	11.5
Glass	55.6	-	-	-	-	-	-	-	62.8	12.9	67.7	7.8	72.6	7.2	78.0	7.4	83.0	6.4
Concrete Ingredients and Related Products	39.3	8.3	40.9	4.1	42.3	3.4	48.0	13.5	55.6	15.8	60.2	8.3	64.2	6.6	70.2	9.3	78.7	12.1
Concrete Products	40.5	7.4	42.2	4.2	44.2	4.7	50.9	15.2	57.3	12.6	60.5	5.6	64.4	6.4	71.9	11.6	82.0	14.0
Clay Construction Products ex. Refractories	43.9	4.3	45.0	2.5	47.3	5.1	51.8	9.5	58.0	12.0	62.7	8.1	69.0	10.0	75.6	9.6	83.6	10.6
Refractories	37.6	4.7	38.3	1.9	40.4	5.5	42.6	5.4	49.2	15.5	54.6	11.0	59.2	8.4	64.2	8.4	70.2	9.3
Asphalt Felts and Coatings	31.5	22.1	32.9	4.4	34.0	3.3	49.2	44.7	56.7	15.2	59.8	5.5	63.5	6.2	73.3	15.4	81.7	11.5
Gypsum Products	42.7	9.8	44.8	4.9	47.2	5.4	53.7	13.8	56.2	4.7	60.3	7.3	71.7	18.9	89.5	24.8	98.5	10.1
Glass Containers	37.0	9.1	38.0	2.7	39.1	2.9	43.7	11.8	50.5	15.6	55.0	8.9	60.2	9.5	68.7	14.1	73.4	6.8
Other Nonmetallic Minerals	26.3	10.5	26.9	2.3	27.2	1.1	40.0	47.1	46.7	16.7	49.3	5.6	53.1	7.7	58.4	10.0	66.5	13.9
Transportation Equipment	44.2	5.5	45.5	2.9	46.1	1.3	50.3	9.1	56.7	12.7	60.5	6.7	64.6	6.8	69.5	7.6	75.3	8.3
Motor Vehicles and Equipment	45.7	5.5	47.0	2.8	47.4	0.9	51.4	8.4	57.6	12.1	61.2	6.3	65.2	6.5	70.0	7.4	75.8	8.3
Aircraft and Aircraft Equipment	36.6	-	-	-	-	-	-	-	48.5	32.5	54.5	12.4	59.3	8.8	64.1	8.1	69.9	9.0
Ships and Boats	-	-	-	-	-	-	-	-	-	-	-	-	-	-	-	-	-	-
Railroad Equipment	34.9	5.1	37.1	6.3	38.9	4.9	47.3	21.6	58.1	22.8	62.5	7.6	67.4	7.8	73.0	8.3	80.0	9.6
Transportation Equipment, n.e.c.	-	-	-	-	-	-	-	-	-	-	-	-	-	-	-	-	-	-
Miscellaneous Products	40.8	2.5	41.5	1.7	43.3	4.3	48.1	11.1	53.4	11.0	55.6	4.1	59.4	6.8	66.7	12.3	75.5	13.2
Toys, Sporting Goods, Small Arms, etc.	50.9	2.8	51.7	1.6	53.2	2.9	59.7	12.2	65.9	10.4	67.7	2.7	70.1	3.5	73.7	5.1	79.6	8.0
Tobacco Products, incl. Stemmed & Redried	36.1	2.6	36.4	0.8	37.7	3.6	41.1	9.0	46.3	12.7	50.5	9.1	55.6	10.1	61.4	10.4	67.4	9.8
Notions	40.4	3.3	40.5	0.2	41.3	2.0	49.6	20.1	54.5	9.9	58.6	7.5	62.2	6.1	65.7	5.6	69.3	5.5
Photographic Equipment and Supplies	50.5	1.2	50.7	0.4	51.5	1.6	55.5	7.8	62.1	11.9	64.7	4.2	66.5	2.8	69.3	4.2	73.0	5.3
Mobile Homes	-	-	-	-	-	-	-	-	-	-	-	-	-	-	-	-	-	-
Medical, Surgical & Personal Aid Devices									-		-		-		-		89.5	-
Industrial Safety Equipment	-		-		-		-		-		-		-		-		83.3	-
Mining Services	-	-	-	-	-	-	-	-	-	-	-	-	-	-	-	-	-	-
Other Miscellaneous Products	33.3	3.7	34.3	3.0	37.1	8.2	42.0	13.2	46.0	9.5	45.2	-1.7	49.5	9.5	62.2	25.7	77.9	25.2

Source: U.S. Department of Labor, Bureau of Labor Statistics, Division of Industry Prices and Price Indexes. n.e.c. stands for not elsewhere classified. - indicates no data collected for period or unavailable.

Producer Price Index
Annual Averages, 1980-1988
Base 1982 = 100

Columns headed % show percentile change in the index from the previous period for which an index is available.

	1980		1981		1982		1983		1984		1985		1986		1987		1988	
	Index	%	Index	%	Index	%	Index	%	Index	%	Index	%	Index	%	Index	%	Index	%
Floor Coverings	90.0	10.2	98.7	9.7	100.0	1.3	102.4	2.4	105.6	3.1	105.6	0.0	108.3	2.6	110.7	2.2	114.7	3.6
Household Appliances	87.5	8.3	94.1	7.5	100.0	6.3	103.9	3.9	106.0	2.0	106.7	0.7	105.7	-0.9	105.6	-0.1	106.0	0.4
Home Electronic Equipment	103.8	0.1	101.3	-2.4	100.0	-1.3	97.8	-2.2	95.2	-2.7	90.8	-4.6	89.9	-1.0	88.8	-1.2	87.2	-1.8
Other Household Durable Goods	96.3	22.1	97.1	0.8	100.0	3.0	108.2	8.2	110.1	1.8	111.7	1.5	112.9	1.1	115.4	2.2	119.8	3.8
Nonmetallic Mineral Products	88.4	13.9	96.7	9.4	100.0	3.4	101.6	1.6	105.4	3.7	108.6	3.0	110.0	1.3	110.0	0.0	111.2	1.1
Glass	88.7	6.9	96.0	8.2	100.0	4.2	104.0	4.0	105.6	1.5	104.7	-0.9	107.4	2.6	109.4	1.9	112.3	2.7
Concrete Ingredients and Related Products	88.4	12.3	95.6	8.1	100.0	4.6	101.1	1.1	105.1	4.0	108.5	3.2	109.4	0.8	110.4	0.9	112.0	1.4
Concrete Products	92.0	12.2	97.8	6.3	100.0	2.2	101.4	1.4	103.9	2.5	107.5	3.5	109.2	1.6	109.4	0.2	110.0	0.5
Clay Construction Products ex. Refractories	88.8	6.2	95.8	7.9	100.0	4.4	106.5	6.5	110.0	3.3	113.5	3.2	118.0	4.0	121.4	2.9	124.9	2.9
Refractories	78.5	11.8	89.7	14.3	100.0	11.5	101.2	1.2	107.1	5.8	109.7	2.4	110.2	0.5	110.5	0.3	113.8	3.0
Asphalt Felts and Coatings	99.6	21.9	102.3	2.7	100.0	-2.2	96.4	-3.6	100.3	4.0	102.6	2.3	97.9	-4.6	92.4	-5.6	94.7	2.5
Gypsum Products	100.1	1.6	100.1	0.0	100.0	-0.1	111.7	11.7	135.4	21.2	132.3	-2.3	137.0	3.6	125.2	-8.6	112.9	-9.8
Glass Containers	82.3	12.1	92.5	12.4	100.0	8.1	99.1	-0.9	101.4	2.3	106.8	5.3	111.9	4.8	113.0	1.0	112.3	-0.6
Other Nonmetallic Minerals	83.6	25.7	98.3	17.6	100.0	1.7	101.8	1.8	106.0	4.1	110.5	4.2	110.2	-0.3	110.3	0.1	112.9	2.4
Transportation Equipment	82.9	10.1	94.3	13.8	100.0	6.0	102.8	2.8	105.2	2.3	107.9	2.6	110.5	2.4	112.5	1.8	114.3	1.6
Motor Vehicles and Equipment	83.1	9.6	94.6	13.8	100.0	5.7	102.2	2.2	104.1	1.9	106.4	2.2	109.1	2.5	111.7	2.4	113.1	1.3
Aircraft and Aircraft Equipment	78.8	12.7	91.3	15.9	100.0	9.5	108.3	8.3	115.0	6.2	-		123.8	7.7	123.3	-0.4	126.0	2.2
Ships and Boats	-		-		100.0	-	103.0	3.0	107.3	4.2	110.3	2.8	113.4	2.8	114.1	0.6	115.1	0.9
Railroad Equipment	90.4	13.0	97.0	7.3	100.0	3.1	101.1	1.1	102.6	1.5	104.9	2.2	105.4	0.5	104.7	-0.7	107.5	2.7
Transportation Equipment, n.e.c.	-		-		-		-		-		-		100.2	-	102.0	1.8	106.1	4.0
Miscellaneous Products	93.6	24.0	96.1	2.7	100.0	4.1	104.8	4.8	107.0	2.1	109.4	2.2	111.6	2.0	114.9	3.0	120.2	4.6
Toys, Sporting Goods, Small Arms, etc.	89.7	12.7	95.7	6.7	100.0	4.5	101.7	1.7	102.6	0.9	104.5	1.9	106.6	2.0	107.8	1.1	111.8	3.7
Tobacco Products, incl. Stemmed & Redried	76.0	12.8	83.1	9.3	100.0	20.3	113.1	13.1	123.3	9.0	132.5	7.5	142.5	7.5	154.7	8.6	171.9	11.1
Notions	78.4	13.1	93.8	19.6	100.0	6.6	101.1	1.1	102.3	1.2	102.9	0.6	103.7	0.8	105.2	1.4	107.9	2.6
Photographic Equipment and Supplies	96.4	32.1	99.8	3.5	100.0	0.2	102.5	2.5	102.0	-0.5	102.6	0.6	104.0	1.4	105.4	1.3	107.2	1.7
Mobile Homes	-		96.9	-	100.0	3.2	100.9	0.9	100.9	0.0	101.7	0.8	102.8	1.1	104.3	1.5	109.3	4.8
Medical, Surgical & Personal Aid Devices	93.3	4.2	97.2	4.2	-		103.8	6.8	108.3	4.3	109.0	0.6	111.8	2.6	117.0	4.7	118.9	1.6
Industrial Safety Equipment	89.6	7.6	95.3	6.4	100.0	4.9	103.0	3.0	106.9	3.8	111.3	4.1	121.0	8.7	129.1	6.7	136.7	5.9
Mining Services	-		-		-		-		-		-		91.3	-	87.3	-4.4	90.6	3.8
Other Miscellaneous Products	107.4	37.9	102.7	-4.4	100.0	-2.6	104.0	4.0	103.6	-0.4	103.4	-0.2	104.8	1.4	108.0	3.1	111.0	2.8

Source: U.S. Department of Labor, Bureau of Labor Statistics, Division of Industry Prices and Price Indexes. n.e.c. stands for not elsewhere classified. - indicates no data collected for period or unavailable.

Producer Price Index
Annual Averages, 1989-1997
Base 1982 = 100

Columns headed % show percentile change in the index from the previous period for which an index is available.

	1989		1990		1991		1992		1993		1994		1995		1996		1997	
	Index	%	Index	%	Index	%	Index	%	Index	%	Index	%	Index	%	Index	%	Index	%
Floor Coverings	117.6	2.5	119.0	1.2	120.4	1.2	120.3	-0.1	120.2	-0.1	121.5	1.1	123.7	1.8	126.6	2.3	127.7	0.9
Household Appliances	108.7	2.5	110.8	1.9	111.3	0.5	111.4	0.1	112.9	1.3	112.8	-0.1	112.4	-0.4	112.7	0.3	110.2	-2.2
Home Electronic Equipment	86.9	-0.3	82.7	-4.8	83.2	0.6	82.0	-1.4	80.2	-2.2	80.3	0.1	78.9	-1.7	79.0	0.1	77.5	-1.9
Other Household Durable Goods	127.2	6.2	130.7	2.8	134.2	2.7	136.6	1.8	138.0	1.0	140.8	2.0	144.8	2.8	148.1	2.3	149.7	1.1
Nonmetallic Mineral Products	112.6	1.3	114.7	1.9	117.2	2.2	117.3	0.1	120.0	2.3	124.2	3.5	129.0	3.9	131.0	1.6	133.2	1.7
Glass	113.2	0.8	113.8	0.5	114.4	0.5	115.7	1.1	116.9	1.0	120.1	2.7	122.9	2.3	120.9	-1.6	120.3	-0.5
Concrete Ingredients and Related Products	113.2	1.1	115.3	1.9	118.4	2.7	119.4	0.8	123.4	3.4	128.7	4.3	134.7	4.7	138.8	3.0	142.5	2.7
Concrete Products	111.2	1.1	113.5	2.1	116.6	2.7	117.2	0.5	120.2	2.6	124.6	3.7	129.4	3.9	133.2	2.9	136.0	2.1
Clay Construction Products ex. Refractories	127.0	1.7	129.9	2.3	130.2	0.2	132.0	1.4	135.1	2.3	138.3	2.4	141.3	2.2	142.3	0.7	143.4	0.8
Refractories	119.4	4.9	122.3	2.4	125.4	2.5	126.4	0.8	127.1	0.6	128.2	0.9	132.1	3.0	136.8	3.6	138.7	1.4
Asphalt Felts and Coatings	95.8	1.2	97.1	1.4	98.2	1.1	96.2	-2.0	96.8	0.6	95.3	-1.5	100.0	4.9	100.0	0.0	99.9	-0.1
Gypsum Products	110.0	-2.6	105.2	-4.4	99.3	-5.6	99.9	0.6	108.3	8.4	136.1	25.7	154.5	13.5	154.0	-0.3	170.7	10.8
Glass Containers	115.2	2.6	120.4	4.5	125.4	4.2	125.1	-0.2	125.8	0.6	127.5	1.4	130.5	2.4	129.1	-1.1	125.7	-2.6
Other Nonmetallic Minerals	114.2	1.2	116.0	1.6	118.4	2.1	116.4	-1.7	119.2	2.4	121.6	2.0	125.4	3.1	127.7	1.8	130.2	2.0
Transportation Equipment	117.7	3.0	121.5	3.2	126.4	4.0	130.4	3.2	133.7	2.5	137.2	2.6	139.7	1.8	141.7	1.4	141.6	-0.1
Motor Vehicles and Equipment	116.2	2.7	118.2	1.7	122.1	3.3	124.9	2.3	128.0	2.5	131.4	2.7	133.0	1.2	134.1	0.8	132.8	-1.0
Aircraft and Aircraft Equipment	129.9	3.1	136.8	5.3	144.3	5.5	151.3	4.9	154.9	2.4	159.2	2.8	163.7	2.8	167.8	2.5	169.8	1.2
Ships and Boats	120.1	4.3	125.4	4.4	130.3	3.9	137.4	5.4	143.3	4.3	145.4	1.5	147.8	1.7	154.1	4.3	159.4	3.4
Railroad Equipment	114.0	6.0	118.6	4.0	122.2	3.0	123.7	1.2	125.2	1.2	129.2	3.2	134.8	4.3	137.2	1.8	134.8	-1.7
Transportation Equipment, n.e.c.	109.8	3.5	111.6	1.6	113.6	1.8	114.7	1.0	115.7	0.9	117.5	1.6	121.5	3.4	124.9	2.8	127.0	1.7
Miscellaneous Products	126.5	5.2	134.2	6.1	140.8	4.9	145.3	3.2	145.4	0.1	141.9	-2.4	145.4	2.5	147.7	1.6	150.9	2.2
Toys, Sporting Goods, Small Arms, etc.	116.7	4.4	119.6	2.5	122.6	2.5	124.6	1.6	125.5	0.7	127.0	1.2	129.1	1.7	130.4	1.0	131.5	0.8
Tobacco Products, incl. Stemmed & Redried	194.8	13.3	221.4	13.7	249.7	12.8	275.3	10.3	260.3	-5.4	224.7	-13.7	231.3	2.9	237.4	2.6	248.8	4.8
Notions	112.4	4.2	115.8	3.0	117.9	1.8	119.3	1.2	120.5	1.0	121.8	1.1	123.9	1.7	125.7	1.5	125.8	0.1
Photographic Equipment and Supplies	114.3	6.6	118.4	3.6	118.1	-0.3	118.6	0.4	117.9	-0.6	116.9	-0.8	118.4	1.3	119.9	1.3	118.7	-1.0
Mobile Homes	114.0	4.3	117.5	3.1	120.4	2.5	121.7	1.1	127.8	5.0	137.0	7.2	145.6	6.3	149.8	2.9	152.2	1.6
Medical, Surgical & Personal Aid Devices	123.0	3.4	127.3	3.5	130.3	2.4	133.9	2.8	137.8	2.9	140.4	1.9	141.3	0.6	143.1	1.3	143.0	-0.1
Industrial Safety Equipment	144.2	5.5	149.7	3.8	157.7	5.3	163.6	3.7	166.5	1.8	172.6	3.7	178.5	3.4	182.7	2.4	186.1	1.9
Mining Services	90.9	0.3	95.5	5.1	98.6	3.2	95.1	-3.5	100.0	5.2	102.9	2.9	106.1	3.1	107.6	1.4	118.9	10.5
Other Miscellaneous Products	114.0	2.7	117.7	3.2	120.5	2.4	122.4	1.6	125.3	2.4	127.5	1.8	131.9	3.5	132.8	0.7	133.5	0.5

Source: U.S. Department of Labor, Bureau of Labor Statistics, Division of Industry Prices and Price Indexes. n.e.c. stands for not elsewhere classified. - indicates no data collected for period or unavailable.

Producer Price Index
Annual Averages, 1998-2001
Base 1982 = 100

Columns headed % show percentile change in the index from the previous period for which an index is available.

	1998		1999		2000		2001											
	Index	%	Index	%	Index	%	Index	%	Index	%	Index	%	Index	%	Index	%	Index	%
Floor Coverings	128.3	0.5	127.2	-0.9	129.6	1.9	130.1	0.4										
Household Appliances	108.9	-1.2	108.5	-0.4	107.3	-1.1	105.3	-1.9										
Home Electronic Equipment	75.9	-2.1	73.7	-2.9	71.8	-2.6	70.4	-1.9										
Other Household Durable Goods	151.2	1.0	152.7	1.0	155.5	1.8	157.3	1.2										
Nonmetallic Mineral Products	135.4	1.7	138.9	2.6	142.5	2.6	144.3	1.3										
Glass	118.5	-1.5	117.5	-0.8	120.1	2.2	121.5	1.2										
Concrete Ingredients and Related Products	147.6	3.6	152.1	3.0	155.6	2.3	159.1	2.2										
Concrete Products	140.0	2.9	143.7	2.6	147.8	2.9	151.7	2.6										
Clay Construction Products ex. Refractories	144.9	1.0	148.3	2.3	152.8	3.0	158.0	3.4										
Refractories	141.1	1.7	142.3	0.9	144.0	1.2	150.8	4.7										
Asphalt Felts and Coatings	99.5	-0.4	99.2	-0.3	104.1	4.9	107.5	3.3										
Gypsum Products	177.6	4.0	208.0	17.1	201.4	-3.2	156.1	-22.5										
Glass Containers	125.9	0.2	125.9	0.0	127.4	1.2	132.8	4.2										
Other Nonmetallic Minerals	131.3	0.8	134.9	2.7	140.3	4.0	143.0	1.9										
Transportation Equipment	141.2	-0.3	141.8	0.4	143.8	1.4	145.1	0.9										
Motor Vehicles and Equipment	131.4	-1.1	131.7	0.2	132.3	0.5	131.5	-0.6										
Aircraft and Aircraft Equipment	170.9	0.6	172.3	0.8	177.5	3.0	183.5	3.4										
Ships and Boats	161.9	1.6	163.1	0.7	165.9	1.7	169.3	2.0										
Railroad Equipment	135.0	0.1	135.2	0.1	135.7	0.4	135.4	-0.2										
Transportation Equipment, n.e.c.	129.9	2.3	130.6	0.5	133.7	2.4	136.5	2.1										
Miscellaneous Products	156.0	3.4	166.6	6.8	170.8	2.5	181.3	6.1										
Toys, Sporting Goods, Small Arms, etc.	132.4	0.7	132.4	0.0	132.5	0.1	133.0	0.4										
Tobacco Products, incl. Stemmed & Redried	283.6	14.0	374.0	31.9	397.2	6.2	441.9	11.3										
Notions	125.9	0.1	128.3	1.9	129.8	1.2	130.0	0.2										
Photographic Equipment and Supplies	114.5	-3.5	111.5	-2.6	109.1	-2.2	111.2	1.9										
Mobile Homes	154.3	1.4	158.4	2.7	161.3	1.8	164.2	1.8										
Medical, Surgical & Personal Aid Devices	143.4	0.3	144.6	0.8	146.0	1.0	148.3	1.6										
Industrial Safety Equipment	189.9	2.0	193.4	1.8	197.6	2.2	203.0	2.7										
Mining Services	123.5	3.9	114.9	-7.0	120.9	5.2	143.1	18.4										
Other Miscellaneous Products	134.6	0.8	135.1	0.4	136.6	1.1	138.8	1.6										

Source: U.S. Department of Labor, Bureau of Labor Statistics, Division of Industry Prices and Price Indexes. n.e.c. stands for not elsewhere classified. - indicates no data collected for period or unavailable.

FARM PRODUCTS
Producer Price Index
Base 1982 = 100

For 1913-2001. Columns headed % show percentile change in the index from the previous period for which an index is available.

Year	Jan Index	%	Feb Index	%	Mar Index	%	Apr Index	%	May Index	%	Jun Index	%	Jul Index	%	Aug Index	%	Sep Index	%	Oct Index	%	Nov Index	%	Dec Index	%
1913	17.6	-	17.5	-0.6	17.6	0.6	17.5	-0.6	17.4	-0.6	17.6	1.1	18.1	2.8	18.2	0.6	18.8	3.3	18.8	0.0	18.9	0.5	18.5	-2.1
1914	18.4	-0.5	18.3	-0.5	18.2	-0.5	18.0	-1.1	18.0	0.0	18.1	0.6	18.0	-0.6	18.3	1.7	17.9	-2.2	17.2	-3.9	17.6	2.3	17.4	-1.1
1915	18.1	4.0	18.4	1.7	17.9	-2.7	18.2	1.7	18.2	0.0	17.7	-2.7	18.1	2.3	17.9	-1.1	17.5	-2.2	18.1	3.4	18.0	-0.6	18.4	2.2
1916	19.4	5.4	19.4	0.0	19.4	0.0	19.6	1.0	19.8	1.0	19.7	-0.5	20.3	3.0	21.7	6.9	22.6	4.1	23.7	4.9	25.3	6.8	25.0	-1.2
1917	26.2	4.8	27.2	3.8	28.6	5.1	31.6	10.5	33.6	6.3	33.8	0.6	34.0	0.6	34.6	1.8	34.3	-0.9	35.2	2.6	36.0	2.3	35.6	-1.1
1918	37.0	3.9	37.1	0.3	37.3	0.5	36.6	-1.9	35.4	-3.3	35.4	0.0	37.0	4.5	38.6	4.3	39.6	2.6	38.2	-3.5	38.0	-0.5	38.1	0.3
1919	38.9	2.1	37.5	-3.6	38.5	2.7	40.0	3.9	40.9	2.3	39.6	-3.2	41.5	4.8	41.3	-0.5	38.7	-6.3	38.5	-0.5	40.3	4.7	41.8	3.7
1920	43.0	2.9	41.2	-4.2	41.5	0.7	42.5	2.4	42.8	0.7	42.3	-1.2	40.5	-4.3	37.8	-6.7	36.4	-3.7	32.2	-11.5	30.0	-6.8	26.4	-12.0
1921	25.6	-3.0	23.4	-8.6	22.7	-3.0	20.9	-7.9	21.0	0.5	20.3	-3.3	21.8	7.4	22.5	3.2	22.7	0.9	22.7	0.0	22.1	-2.6	22.2	0.5
1922	22.2	0.0	24.0	8.1	23.6	-1.7	23.4	-0.8	23.8	1.7	23.4	-1.7	24.1	3.0	23.0	-4.6	23.3	1.3	23.8	2.1	24.7	3.8	25.0	1.2
1923	25.1	0.4	25.3	0.8	25.3	0.0	24.8	-2.0	24.4	-1.6	24.2	-0.8	23.7	-2.1	24.2	2.1	25.3	4.5	25.4	0.4	25.7	1.2	25.5	-0.8
1924	25.6	0.4	25.0	-2.3	24.2	-3.2	24.6	1.7	24.0	-2.4	23.8	-0.8	24.9	4.6	25.7	3.2	25.3	-1.6	26.0	2.8	26.2	0.8	27.3	4.2
1925	28.7	5.1	28.4	-1.0	28.5	0.4	27.1	-4.9	27.1	0.0	27.6	1.8	28.3	2.5	28.1	-0.7	27.7	-1.4	27.0	-2.5	27.3	1.1	26.6	-2.6
1926	27.1	1.9	26.5	-2.2	25.7	-3.0	26.0	1.2	25.8	-0.8	25.5	-1.2	24.9	-2.4	24.6	-1.2	25.1	2.0	24.7	-1.6	23.9	-3.2	24.0	0.4
1927	24.3	1.2	24.1	-0.8	23.8	-1.2	23.8	0.0	24.3	2.1	24.3	0.0	24.6	1.2	25.8	4.9	26.7	3.5	26.5	-0.7	26.3	-0.8	26.3	0.0
1928	26.8	1.9	26.4	-1.5	26.1	-1.1	27.1	3.8	27.7	2.2	26.9	-2.9	27.4	1.9	27.0	-1.5	27.5	1.9	26.1	-5.1	25.7	-1.5	26.2	1.9
1929	26.7	1.9	26.6	-0.4	27.1	1.9	26.5	-2.2	25.8	-2.6	26.1	1.2	27.1	3.8	27.1	0.0	26.9	-0.7	26.2	-2.6	25.5	-2.7	25.7	0.8
1930	25.5	-0.8	24.7	-3.1	23.9	-3.2	24.2	1.3	23.5	-2.9	22.5	-4.3	21.0	-6.7	21.4	1.9	21.5	0.5	20.8	-3.3	20.0	-3.8	19.0	-5.0
1931	18.4	-3.2	17.7	-3.8	17.8	0.6	17.7	-0.6	16.9	-4.5	16.5	-2.4	16.4	-0.6	16.1	-1.8	15.3	-5.0	14.8	-3.3	14.8	0.0	14.1	-4.7
1932	13.3	-5.7	12.8	-3.8	12.7	-0.8	12.4	-2.4	11.8	-4.8	11.6	-1.7	12.1	4.3	12.4	2.5	12.4	0.0	11.8	-4.8	11.8	0.0	11.1	-5.9
1933	10.8	-2.7	10.3	-4.6	10.8	4.9	11.2	3.7	12.7	13.4	13.4	5.5	15.2	13.4	14.6	-3.9	14.4	-1.4	14.1	-2.1	14.3	1.4	14.0	-2.1
1934	14.8	5.7	15.5	4.7	15.5	0.0	15.1	-2.6	15.1	0.0	16.0	6.0	16.3	1.9	17.6	8.0	18.5	5.1	17.8	-3.8	17.8	0.0	18.2	2.2
1935	19.6	7.7	20.0	2.0	19.7	-1.5	20.3	3.0	20.3	0.0	19.8	-2.5	19.5	-1.5	20.0	2.6	20.1	0.5	19.7	-2.0	19.6	-0.5	19.8	1.0
1936	19.7	-0.5	20.1	2.0	19.3	-4.0	19.4	0.5	19.0	-2.1	19.7	3.7	20.5	4.1	21.2	3.4	21.2	0.0	21.2	0.0	21.5	1.4	22.4	4.2
1937	23.1	3.1	23.1	0.0	23.8	3.0	23.3	-2.1	22.7	-2.6	22.3	-1.8	22.6	1.3	21.8	-3.5	21.7	-0.5	20.3	-6.5	19.1	-5.9	18.4	-3.7
1938	18.1	-1.6	17.6	-2.8	17.7	0.6	17.2	-2.8	17.0	-1.2	17.3	1.8	17.5	1.2	17.0	-2.9	17.2	1.2	16.8	-2.3	17.1	1.8	17.0	-0.6
1939	17.0	0.0	16.9	-0.6	16.6	-1.8	16.1	-3.0	16.1	0.0	15.7	-2.5	15.8	0.6	15.4	-2.5	17.3	12.3	16.9	-2.3	17.0	0.6	17.1	0.6
1940	17.4	1.8	17.3	-0.6	17.1	-1.2	17.5	2.3	17.1	-2.3	16.7	-2.3	16.8	0.6	16.5	-1.8	16.7	1.2	16.8	0.6	17.2	2.4	17.6	2.3
1941	18.1	2.8	17.7	-2.2	18.1	2.3	18.8	3.9	19.3	2.7	20.7	7.3	21.7	4.8	22.1	1.8	23.0	4.1	22.7	-1.3	22.9	0.9	23.9	4.4
1942	25.5	6.7	25.6	0.4	26.0	1.6	26.4	1.5	26.3	-0.4	26.3	0.0	26.6	1.1	26.8	0.8	27.2	1.5	27.5	1.1	27.9	1.5	28.7	2.9
1943	29.5	2.8	30.0	1.7	31.0	3.3	31.2	0.6	31.7	1.6	31.9	0.6	31.5	-1.3	31.2	-1.0	31.0	-0.6	30.9	-0.3	30.6	-1.0	30.7	0.3
1944	30.7	0.0	30.9	0.7	31.2	1.0	31.1	-0.3	31.0	-0.3	31.5	1.6	31.3	-0.6	30.9	-1.3	31.0	0.3	31.2	0.6	31.4	0.6	31.6	0.6
1945	31.9	0.9	32.1	0.6	32.1	0.0	32.5	1.2	32.8	0.9	32.9	0.3	32.5	-1.2	32.0	-1.5	31.4	-1.9	32.1	2.2	33.1	3.1	33.2	0.3
1946	32.7	-1.5	33.0	0.9	33.6	1.8	34.1	1.5	34.7	1.8	35.4	2.0	39.6	11.9	40.6	2.5	39.0	-3.9	41.7	6.9	42.8	2.6	42.4	-0.9
1947	41.6	-1.9	42.6	2.4	45.5	6.8	44.0	-3.3	43.6	-0.9	43.8	0.5	44.3	1.1	44.8	1.1	46.6	4.0	47.4	1.7	47.7	0.6	50.1	5.0
1948	51.2	2.2	47.7	-6.8	47.6	-0.2	48.3	1.5	49.4	2.3	50.4	2.0	50.2	-0.4	49.6	-1.2	48.8	-1.6	46.9	-3.9	46.3	-1.3	45.2	-2.4
1949	43.8	-3.1	42.0	-4.1	42.7	1.7	42.7	0.0	42.7	0.0	41.8	-2.1	41.7	-0.2	41.7	0.0	41.8	0.2	41.0	-1.9	40.9	-0.2	40.3	-1.5
1950	40.1	-0.5	41.0	2.2	41.7	1.7	41.5	-0.5	42.6	2.7	42.7	0.2	45.3	6.1	45.8	1.1	46.5	1.5	45.6	-1.9	47.1	3.3	48.8	3.6
1951	50.8	4.1	52.9	4.1	53.1	0.4	53.1	0.0	52.3	-1.5	51.5	-1.5	50.2	-2.5	49.9	-0.6	49.7	-0.4	50.4	1.4	50.6	0.4	50.3	-0.6
1952	49.7	-1.2	48.7	-2.0	48.9	0.4	49.1	0.4	48.8	-0.6	48.4	-0.8	49.8	2.9	49.7	-0.2	48.2	-3.0	47.4	-1.7	46.8	-1.3	44.8	-4.3
1953	45.0	0.4	44.2	-1.8	45.1	2.0	43.9	-2.7	44.2	0.7	43.1	-2.5	44.2	2.6	43.5	-1.6	44.3	1.8	43.0	-2.9	42.3	-1.6	42.7	0.9
1954	44.2	3.5	44.1	-0.2	44.4	0.7	44.9	1.1	44.2	-1.6	42.8	-3.2	43.4	1.4	43.3	-0.2	42.3	-2.3	42.0	-0.7	42.1	0.2	40.6	-3.6
1955	41.8	3.0	42.0	0.5	41.6	-1.0	42.5	2.2	41.2	-3.1	41.5	0.7	40.4	-2.7	39.8	-1.5	40.4	1.5	39.2	-3.0	38.0	-3.1	37.5	-1.3
1956	38.0	1.3	38.9	2.4	39.1	0.5	39.8	1.8	41.1	3.3	41.2	0.2	40.7	-1.2	40.3	-1.0	40.7	1.0	39.9	-2.0	39.7	-0.5	40.1	1.0
1957	40.4	0.7	40.1	-0.7	40.1	0.0	40.9	2.0	40.4	-1.2	41.1	1.7	41.9	1.9	42.0	0.2	41.1	-2.1	41.3	0.5	41.5	0.5	41.8	0.7

[Continued]

FARM PRODUCTS
Producer Price Index
Base 1982 = 100
[Continued]

For 1913-2001. Columns headed % show percentile change in the index from the previous period for which an index is available.

Year	Jan Index	%	Feb Index	%	Mar Index	%	Apr Index	%	May Index	%	Jun Index	%	Jul Index	%	Aug Index	%	Sep Index	%	Oct Index	%	Nov Index	%	Dec Index	%
1958	42.3	1.2	43.4	2.6	45.4	4.6	44.1	-2.9	44.5	0.9	43.2	-2.9	42.9	-0.7	42.1	-1.9	42.0	-0.2	41.7	-0.7	41.6	-0.2	40.9	-1.7
1959	41.3	1.0	41.2	-0.2	41.0	-0.5	41.8	2.0	41.0	-1.9	40.6	-1.0	39.9	-1.7	39.4	-1.3	40.1	1.8	39.1	-2.5	38.6	-1.3	38.8	0.5
1960	39.1	0.8	39.3	0.5	40.8	3.8	41.2	1.0	40.8	-1.0	40.2	-1.5	40.1	-0.2	39.1	-2.5	39.6	1.3	40.4	2.0	40.6	0.5	40.1	-1.2
1961	40.5	1.0	40.7	0.5	40.6	-0.2	40.0	-1.5	39.2	-2.0	38.5	-1.8	39.4	2.3	40.0	1.5	39.4	-1.5	39.4	0.0	39.6	0.5	39.7	0.3
1962	40.5	2.0	40.6	0.2	40.7	0.2	40.1	-1.5	39.8	-0.7	39.4	-1.0	39.9	1.3	40.4	1.3	41.6	3.0	40.8	-1.9	41.1	0.7	40.3	-1.9
1963	40.8	1.2	39.9	-2.2	39.5	-1.0	39.5	0.0	39.1	-1.0	39.3	0.5	40.1	2.0	39.9	-0.5	39.5	-1.0	39.4	-0.3	39.8	1.0	38.6	-3.0
1964	39.9	3.4	39.1	-2.0	39.4	0.8	39.1	-0.8	38.8	-0.8	38.6	-0.5	39.0	1.0	38.7	-0.8	39.6	2.3	38.8	-2.0	38.9	0.3	38.4	-1.3
1965	38.5	0.3	39.1	1.6	39.5	1.0	40.4	2.3	40.7	0.7	41.5	2.0	41.4	-0.2	41.0	-1.0	41.2	0.5	41.1	-0.2	41.5	1.0	42.6	2.7
1966	43.2	1.4	44.4	2.8	44.2	-0.5	44.0	-0.5	43.2	-1.8	43.1	-0.2	44.6	3.5	44.7	0.2	45.0	0.7	43.2	-4.0	42.4	-1.9	42.1	-0.7
1967	42.5	1.0	41.8	-1.6	41.3	-1.2	40.4	-2.2	41.7	3.2	42.4	1.7	42.5	0.2	41.1	-3.3	40.7	-1.0	40.2	-1.2	39.9	-0.7	41.0	2.8
1968	41.0	0.0	41.9	2.2	42.3	1.0	42.3	0.0	42.9	1.4	42.4	-1.2	43.0	1.4	42.0	-2.3	42.5	1.2	41.9	-1.4	42.7	1.9	42.8	0.2
1969	43.4	1.4	43.5	0.2	44.1	1.4	43.9	-0.5	45.9	4.6	46.2	0.7	46.0	-0.4	45.1	-2.0	44.9	-0.4	44.6	-0.7	46.0	3.1	46.4	0.9
1970	46.6	0.4	47.0	0.9	47.3	0.6	46.0	-2.7	45.9	-0.2	46.0	0.2	46.8	1.7	44.8	-4.3	46.3	3.3	44.5	-3.9	44.1	-0.9	44.2	0.2
1971	44.9	1.6	47.0	4.7	46.6	-0.9	46.6	0.0	47.0	0.9	47.9	1.9	46.8	-2.3	46.7	-0.2	45.6	-2.4	45.9	0.7	46.3	0.9	47.8	3.2
1972	48.6	1.7	49.8	2.5	49.4	-0.8	49.1	-0.6	50.4	2.6	51.1	1.4	52.8	3.3	52.9	0.2	53.1	0.4	51.8	-2.4	53.1	2.5	56.7	6.8
1973	59.5	4.9	62.3	4.7	66.4	6.6	66.3	-0.2	70.3	6.0	75.2	7.0	71.5	-4.9	88.0	23.1	82.7	-6.0	77.7	-6.0	75.9	-2.3	77.3	1.8
1974	83.6	8.2	84.8	1.4	81.3	-4.1	76.8	-5.5	74.6	-2.9	69.6	-6.7	74.6	7.2	78.1	4.7	75.4	-3.5	77.4	2.7	77.5	0.1	75.8	-2.2
1975	74.1	-2.2	72.1	-2.7	70.6	-2.1	73.3	3.8	76.1	3.8	76.8	0.9	79.9	4.0	79.7	-0.3	81.3	2.0	81.4	0.1	79.1	-2.8	80.0	1.1
1976	79.5	-0.6	78.7	-1.0	77.0	-2.2	79.6	3.4	79.5	-0.1	81.1	2.0	81.2	0.1	78.3	-3.6	79.2	1.1	77.0	-2.8	75.7	-1.7	79.1	4.5
1977	79.8	0.9	82.1	2.9	83.5	1.7	85.9	2.9	84.3	-1.9	79.5	-5.7	78.5	-1.3	75.0	-4.5	75.1	0.1	75.1	0.0	76.6	2.0	77.7	1.4
1978	79.3	2.1	82.1	3.5	84.2	2.6	88.2	4.8	89.0	0.9	90.6	1.8	90.7	0.1	86.8	-4.3	88.8	2.3	90.5	1.9	90.0	-0.6	91.9	2.1
1979	95.0	3.4	99.4	4.6	100.2	0.8	101.5	1.3	101.2	-0.3	100.2	-1.0	101.8	1.6	98.4	-3.3	99.5	1.1	98.9	-0.6	99.1	0.2	100.1	1.0
1980	97.6	-2.5	100.0	2.5	98.7	-1.3	94.5	-4.3	96.3	1.9	96.3	0.0	104.9	8.9	108.9	3.8	110.2	1.2	108.8	-1.3	109.3	0.5	109.5	0.2
1981	109.1	-0.4	108.3	-0.7	107.6	-0.6	108.7	1.0	107.1	-1.5	107.6	0.5	108.7	1.0	106.4	-2.1	103.6	-2.6	100.3	-3.2	97.9	-2.4	96.8	-1.1
1982	99.9	3.2	102.0	2.1	101.0	-1.0	103.4	2.4	105.8	2.3	104.3	-1.4	101.8	-2.4	99.4	-2.4	96.8	-2.6	94.6	-2.3	95.2	0.6	96.0	0.8
1983	96.2	0.2	99.3	3.2	99.6	0.3	103.4	3.8	103.3	-0.1	102.1	-1.2	100.8	-1.3	104.6	3.8	105.8	1.1	105.3	-0.5	103.6	-1.6	104.8	1.2
1984	108.7	3.7	107.9	-0.7	110.3	2.2	109.5	-0.7	107.6	-1.7	106.1	-1.4	106.7	0.6	104.5	-2.1	103.1	-1.3	99.1	-3.9	101.4	2.3	101.4	0.0
1985	100.4	-1.0	101.2	0.8	98.5	-2.7	97.7	-0.8	95.1	-2.7	94.7	-0.4	94.6	-0.1	90.0	-4.9	87.8	-2.4	90.7	3.3	95.1	4.9	95.8	0.7
1986	93.8	-2.1	91.5	-2.5	90.9	-0.7	90.2	-0.8	93.7	3.9	91.8	-2.0	94.3	2.7	93.7	-0.6	92.5	-1.3	93.8	1.4	95.0	1.3	93.8	-1.3
1987	91.1	-2.9	92.0	1.0	92.2	0.2	95.7	3.8	99.9	4.4	98.8	-1.1	97.9	-0.9	95.7	-2.2	96.1	0.4	94.9	-1.2	96.3	1.5	95.7	-0.6
1988	97.3	1.7	97.9	0.6	98.2	0.3	99.2	1.0	102.2	3.0	106.8	4.5	109.1	2.2	109.3	0.2	111.6	2.1	110.9	-0.6	107.9	-2.7	108.9	0.9
1989	112.0	2.8	110.8	-1.1	113.8	2.7	111.0	-2.5	115.1	3.7	111.8	-2.9	110.5	-1.2	109.3	-1.1	108.0	-1.2	107.8	-0.2	109.0	1.1	111.5	2.3
1990	114.9	3.0	115.7	0.7	115.3	-0.3	113.3	-1.7	113.7	0.4	113.6	-0.1	113.8	0.2	111.4	-2.1	109.2	-2.0	109.5	0.3	108.5	-0.9	107.2	-1.2
1991	106.9	-0.3	106.9	0.0	109.7	2.6	109.6	-0.1	110.4	0.7	109.1	-1.2	105.6	-3.2	102.9	-2.6	103.1	0.2	101.5	-1.6	101.6	0.1	100.6	-1.0
1992	102.8	2.2	105.5	2.6	106.4	0.9	103.2	-3.0	105.8	2.5	104.7	-1.0	102.5	-2.1	102.2	-0.3	101.6	-0.6	102.7	1.1	101.8	-0.9	103.7	1.9
1993	104.3	0.6	104.4	0.1	106.4	1.9	109.7	3.1	111.0	1.2	104.3	-6.0	105.4	1.1	106.6	1.1	106.3	-0.3	104.2	-2.0	110.1	5.7	113.0	2.6
1994	112.0	-0.9	112.3	0.3	112.8	0.4	111.5	-1.2	108.7	-2.5	107.2	-1.4	102.8	-4.1	101.0	-1.8	101.3	0.3	98.8	-2.5	101.4	2.6	105.5	4.0
1995	103.6	-1.8	104.9	1.3	105.1	0.2	104.8	-0.3	102.6	-2.1	104.2	1.6	106.2	1.9	105.1	-1.0	110.7	5.3	110.2	-0.5	115.4	4.7	116.5	1.0
1996	116.4	-0.1	116.6	0.2	119.5	2.5	121.7	1.8	128.1	5.3	129.6	1.2	129.9	0.2	128.6	-1.0	125.1	-2.7	120.2	-3.9	117.9	-1.9	114.8	-2.6
1997	113.0	-1.6	113.0	0.0	116.2	2.8	116.7	0.4	117.4	0.6	111.6	-4.9	111.6	0.0	111.4	-0.2	111.2	-0.2	110.4	-0.7	110.6	0.2	110.1	-0.5
1998	106.3	-3.5	106.3	0.0	107.4	1.0	106.5	-0.8	105.8	-0.7	105.7	-0.1	105.0	-0.7	102.9	-2.0	102.0	-0.9	104.8	2.7	103.1	-1.6	99.0	-4.0
1999	102.2	3.2	98.3	-3.8	99.2	0.9	96.5	-2.7	99.6	3.2	99.2	-0.4	95.2	-4.0	99.0	4.0	99.3	0.3	97.5	-1.8	97.8	0.3	96.9	-0.9
2000	95.9	-1.0	97.5	1.7	100.6	3.2	101.6	1.0	103.7	2.1	100.1	-3.5	97.3	-2.8	94.6	-2.8	98.0	3.6	100.3	2.3	101.5	1.2	103.4	1.9
2001	104.5	1.1	103.6	-0.9	107.3	3.6	106.0	-1.2	106.8	0.8	105.9	-0.8	105.0	-0.8	105.5	0.5	105.0	-0.5	101.6	-3.2	97.0	-4.5	96.6	-0.4

Source: U.S. Department of Labor, Bureau of Labor Statistics, Division of Industry Prices and Price Indexes. n.e.c. stands for not elsewhere classified. - indicates no data collected for period or unavailable.

925

Fruits & Melons, Fresh/Dry Vegetables & Nuts
Producer Price Index
Base 1982 = 100

For 1926-2001. Columns headed % show percentile change in the index from the previous period for which an index is available.

Year	Jan Index	%	Feb Index	%	Mar Index	%	Apr Index	%	May Index	%	Jun Index	%	Jul Index	%	Aug Index	%	Sep Index	%	Oct Index	%	Nov Index	%	Dec Index	%
1926	29.4	-	28.9	-1.7	28.8	-0.3	32.4	12.5	29.7	-8.3	28.0	-5.7	24.1	-13.9	22.7	-5.8	24.4	7.5	26.1	7.0	25.1	-3.8	24.2	-3.6
1927	25.4	5.0	25.0	-1.6	23.6	-5.6	24.3	3.0	28.4	16.9	28.6	0.7	25.6	-10.5	26.3	2.7	24.7	-6.1	25.0	1.2	26.8	7.2	25.7	-4.1
1928	26.4	2.7	27.5	4.2	28.6	4.0	28.6	0.0	28.3	-1.0	26.7	-5.7	25.4	-4.9	25.0	-1.6	24.6	-1.6	22.6	-8.1	22.0	-2.7	21.8	-0.9
1929	22.5	3.2	21.5	-4.4	20.9	-2.8	21.3	1.9	22.6	6.1	25.3	11.9	28.1	11.1	29.6	5.3	29.6	0.0	29.3	-1.0	28.5	-2.7	28.9	1.4
1930	27.6	-4.5	27.4	-0.7	27.1	-1.1	29.8	10.0	30.3	1.7	30.2	-0.3	25.5	-15.6	23.1	-9.4	23.8	3.0	23.8	0.0	21.4	-10.1	19.0	-11.2
1931	19.6	3.2	18.6	-5.1	18.8	1.1	19.6	4.3	19.8	1.0	20.0	1.0	19.2	-4.0	19.0	-1.0	18.3	-3.7	17.3	-5.5	16.5	-4.6	15.9	-3.6
1932	15.5	-2.5	15.4	-0.6	15.5	0.6	15.5	0.0	15.2	-1.9	15.6	2.6	14.9	-4.5	13.6	-8.7	12.7	-6.6	12.5	-1.6	12.6	0.8	12.7	0.8
1933	12.9	1.6	12.7	-1.6	13.4	5.5	14.5	8.2	14.8	2.1	16.2	9.5	20.1	24.1	18.4	-8.5	16.8	-8.7	15.4	-8.3	15.1	-1.9	15.6	3.3
1934	17.2	10.3	18.4	7.0	18.3	-0.5	17.0	-7.1	17.1	0.6	17.7	3.5	17.0	-4.0	16.3	-4.1	16.2	-0.6	16.6	2.5	15.9	-4.2	14.9	-6.3
1935	15.0	0.7	15.3	2.0	15.1	-1.3	16.5	9.3	16.2	-1.8	17.1	5.6	16.0	-6.4	14.7	-8.1	14.6	-0.7	14.3	-2.1	15.7	9.8	15.9	1.3
1936	15.5	-2.5	15.5	0.0	16.3	5.2	17.2	5.5	18.6	8.1	22.0	18.3	21.1	-4.1	19.6	-7.1	18.1	-7.7	18.8	3.9	19.1	1.6	19.3	1.0
1937	21.5	11.4	23.4	8.8	23.0	-1.7	22.0	-4.3	22.2	0.9	22.2	0.0	17.9	-19.4	16.1	-10.1	15.7	-2.5	15.1	-3.8	14.8	-2.0	13.6	-8.1
1938	13.6	0.0	13.4	-1.5	13.2	-1.5	13.5	2.3	14.1	4.4	15.3	8.5	13.8	-9.8	13.6	-1.4	14.1	3.7	13.9	-1.4	16.0	15.1	15.5	-3.1
1939	15.5	0.0	15.9	2.6	16.2	1.9	16.5	1.9	16.3	-1.2	15.8	-3.1	15.7	-0.6	14.5	-7.6	15.8	9.0	14.9	-5.7	15.2	2.0	15.8	3.9
1940	15.0	-5.1	14.4	-4.0	14.5	0.7	16.9	16.6	18.1	7.1	19.6	8.3	17.9	-8.7	16.0	-10.6	15.3	-4.4	14.6	-4.6	15.1	3.4	15.4	2.0
1941	14.9	-3.2	14.7	-1.3	15.0	2.0	15.9	6.0	15.9	0.0	18.7	17.6	17.1	-8.6	17.1	0.0	17.3	1.2	18.8	8.7	18.2	-3.2	17.9	-1.6
1942	19.0	6.1	20.9	10.0	21.7	3.8	25.0	15.2	25.3	1.2	27.9	10.3	26.3	-5.7	26.0	-1.1	25.6	-1.5	25.7	0.4	26.9	4.7	27.7	3.0
1943	27.0	-2.5	29.0	7.4	31.4	8.3	33.9	8.0	38.7	14.2	40.6	4.9	38.7	-4.7	34.7	-10.3	31.7	-8.6	31.2	-1.6	32.3	3.5	32.6	0.9
1944	32.2	-1.2	33.0	2.5	33.9	2.7	34.9	2.9	35.0	0.3	38.6	10.3	36.0	-6.7	33.6	-6.7	31.3	-6.8	30.2	-3.5	30.6	1.3	31.4	2.6
1945	30.8	-1.9	32.0	3.9	31.3	-2.2	33.8	8.0	36.4	7.7	37.5	3.0	36.0	-4.0	34.1	-5.3	31.8	-6.7	31.4	-1.3	33.9	8.0	35.6	5.0
1946	34.5	-3.1	35.2	2.0	37.0	5.1	38.6	4.3	39.3	1.8	37.8	-3.8	35.8	-5.3	32.6	-8.9	30.9	-5.2	33.3	7.8	37.1	11.4	35.4	-4.6
1947	33.7	-4.8	35.4	5.0	38.2	7.9	38.2	0.0	39.3	2.9	37.1	-5.6	33.9	-8.6	34.5	1.8	34.0	-1.4	33.5	-1.5	37.1	10.7	37.2	0.3
1948	38.7	4.0	39.6	2.3	39.5	-0.3	42.1	6.6	43.5	3.3	38.2	-12.2	36.1	-5.5	35.4	-1.9	33.8	-4.5	33.9	0.3	34.7	2.4	33.9	-2.3
1949	37.6	10.9	38.2	1.6	37.8	-1.0	40.8	7.9	42.4	3.9	36.7	-13.4	36.0	-1.9	34.1	-5.3	33.0	-3.2	31.4	-4.8	33.8	7.6	33.4	-1.2
1950	33.0	-1.2	32.5	-1.5	33.3	2.5	35.4	6.3	35.2	-0.6	32.8	-6.8	34.9	6.4	32.9	-5.7	31.5	-4.3	30.6	-2.9	34.1	11.4	35.0	2.6
1951	33.2	-5.1	35.8	7.8	32.4	-9.5	36.0	11.1	38.0	5.6	34.5	-9.2	33.2	-3.8	32.7	-1.5	33.9	3.7	35.2	3.8	39.1	11.1	43.0	10.0
1952	44.4	3.3	41.2	-7.2	45.3	10.0	46.6	2.9	47.1	1.1	45.5	-3.4	46.9	3.1	45.5	-3.0	42.3	-7.0	40.8	-3.5	41.4	1.5	41.0	-1.0
1953	39.2	-4.4	37.4	-4.6	38.7	3.5	39.1	1.0	38.5	-1.5	40.2	4.4	34.7	-13.7	35.8	3.2	35.1	-2.0	34.5	-1.7	34.5	0.0	32.8	-4.9
1954	33.3	1.5	32.8	-1.5	32.8	0.0	35.6	8.5	38.2	7.3	35.4	-7.3	40.6	14.7	39.6	-2.5	36.5	-7.8	37.3	2.2	37.8	1.3	35.4	-6.3
1955	38.5	8.8	38.0	-1.3	38.2	0.5	44.2	15.7	43.4	-1.8	38.3	-11.8	36.1	-5.7	36.4	0.8	37.3	2.5	34.0	-8.8	37.5	10.3	35.0	-6.7
1956	38.4	9.7	35.9	-6.5	38.9	8.4	37.3	-4.1	40.9	9.7	44.0	7.6	40.9	-7.0	34.7	-15.2	34.8	0.3	35.7	2.6	38.2	7.0	37.5	-1.8
1957	36.8	-1.9	35.2	-4.3	34.4	-2.3	37.7	9.6	39.9	5.8	38.5	-3.5	39.5	2.6	38.9	-1.5	36.1	-7.2	39.4	9.1	38.9	-1.3	39.6	1.8
1958	44.2	11.6	46.4	5.0	52.1	12.3	47.3	-9.2	44.6	-5.7	37.3	-16.4	38.9	4.3	35.6	-8.5	35.8	0.6	37.1	3.6	35.9	-3.2	36.3	1.1
1959	37.5	3.3	38.7	3.2	34.2	-11.6	41.7	21.9	39.1	-6.2	36.9	-5.6	36.0	-2.4	33.9	-5.8	37.7	11.2	37.4	-0.8	37.8	1.1	39.5	4.5
1960	38.4	-2.8	36.7	-4.4	38.2	4.1	40.8	6.8	42.8	4.9	40.1	-6.3	41.3	3.0	36.1	-12.6	38.3	6.1	39.9	4.2	39.3	-1.5	36.4	-7.4
1961	37.9	4.1	36.5	-3.7	38.7	6.0	36.6	-5.4	37.1	1.4	37.8	1.9	38.2	1.1	35.6	-6.8	34.7	-2.5	34.6	-0.3	34.9	0.9	33.8	-3.2
1962	37.6	11.2	40.5	7.7	41.1	1.5	38.4	-6.6	41.5	8.1	38.3	-7.7	35.8	-6.5	35.3	-1.4	36.8	4.2	37.8	2.7	37.4	-1.1	34.3	-8.3
1963	40.4	17.8	37.4	-7.4	38.4	2.7	38.6	0.5	38.7	0.3	37.7	-2.6	37.6	-0.3	35.9	-4.5	34.1	-5.0	34.6	1.5	37.3	7.8	36.8	-1.3
1964	37.2	1.1	38.0	2.2	40.7	7.1	41.1	1.0	41.7	1.5	43.9	5.3	42.3	-3.6	38.0	-10.2	39.4	3.7	38.1	-3.3	41.9	10.0	38.4	-8.4
1965	38.2	-0.5	39.8	4.2	41.8	5.0	45.6	9.1	46.0	0.9	42.3	-8.0	40.3	-4.7	33.2	-17.6	37.3	12.3	37.1	-0.5	36.5	-1.6	35.8	-1.9
1966	37.8	5.6	38.0	0.5	39.5	3.9	43.1	9.1	40.1	-7.0	38.7	-3.5	41.5	7.2	37.9	-8.7	42.8	12.9	38.0	-11.2	40.4	6.3	39.3	-2.7
1967	39.5	0.5	40.6	2.8	38.3	-5.7	38.7	1.0	40.6	4.9	44.3	9.1	41.9	-5.4	37.5	-10.5	35.8	-4.5	35.6	-0.6	39.8	11.8	40.7	2.3
1968	41.9	2.9	43.5	3.8	44.3	1.8	43.4	-2.0	47.9	10.4	41.3	-13.8	42.0	1.7	37.8	-10.0	37.9	0.3	38.7	2.1	42.7	10.3	42.8	0.2
1969	43.8	2.3	42.8	-2.3	44.1	3.0	41.9	-5.0	49.7	18.6	44.2	-11.1	40.6	-8.1	41.5	2.2	40.2	-3.1	39.3	-2.2	48.6	23.7	43.6	-10.3
1970	45.3	3.9	45.6	0.7	45.9	0.7	43.7	-4.8	48.0	9.8	47.4	-1.2	43.6	-8.0	38.6	-11.5	44.0	14.0	39.7	-9.8	42.3	6.5	43.8	3.5

[Continued]

Fruits & Melons, Fresh/Dry Vegetables & Nuts
Producer Price Index
Base 1982 = 100
[Continued]

For 1926-2001. Columns headed % show percentile change in the index from the previous period for which an index is available.

Year	Jan Index	%	Feb Index	%	Mar Index	%	Apr Index	%	May Index	%	Jun Index	%	Jul Index	%	Aug Index	%	Sep Index	%	Oct Index	%	Nov Index	%	Dec Index	%
1971	45.6	4.1	46.6	2.2	49.3	5.8	47.6	-3.4	50.2	5.5	53.7	7.0	43.1	-19.7	45.7	6.0	40.9	-10.5	45.6	11.5	50.1	9.9	49.8	-0.6
1972	49.2	-1.2	50.3	2.2	44.5	-11.5	46.3	4.0	47.5	2.6	48.0	1.1	51.2	6.7	54.7	6.8	54.4	-0.5	48.4	-11.0	55.9	15.5	53.1	-5.0
1973	59.6	12.2	57.9	-2.9	62.5	7.9	69.4	11.0	73.3	5.6	77.9	6.3	74.0	-5.0	63.9	-13.6	58.7	-8.1	63.9	8.9	66.3	3.8	67.6	2.0
1974	72.7	7.5	84.6	16.4	83.0	-1.9	89.5	7.8	93.3	4.2	80.6	-13.6	73.7	-8.6	64.1	-13.0	64.3	0.3	65.5	1.9	73.7	12.5	64.5	-12.5
1975	69.0	7.0	66.6	-3.5	64.6	-3.0	72.3	11.9	72.2	-0.1	81.5	12.9	82.2	0.9	70.8	-13.9	72.0	1.7	72.2	0.3	70.5	-2.4	75.0	6.4
1976	76.8	2.4	74.6	-2.9	72.7	-2.5	76.9	5.8	70.6	-8.2	63.3	-10.3	64.9	2.5	62.8	-3.2	71.0	13.1	75.9	6.9	65.7	-13.4	68.8	4.7
1977	78.3	13.8	83.9	7.2	86.4	3.0	81.1	-6.1	79.6	-1.8	69.5	-12.7	71.8	3.3	69.6	-3.1	72.1	3.6	74.1	2.8	76.3	3.0	66.8	-12.5
1978	77.5	16.0	80.5	3.9	79.3	-1.5	89.6	13.0	86.8	-3.1	90.8	4.6	99.5	9.6	84.9	-14.7	82.0	-3.4	84.4	2.9	81.6	-3.3	87.3	7.0
1979	92.1	5.5	103.7	12.6	92.9	-10.4	94.2	1.4	90.0	-4.5	89.2	-0.9	89.4	0.2	95.3	6.6	82.1	-13.9	85.9	4.6	85.3	-0.7	83.1	-2.6
1980	86.3	3.9	87.0	0.8	86.1	-1.0	88.0	2.2	96.2	9.3	92.1	-4.3	99.4	7.9	100.1	0.7	104.9	4.8	95.0	-9.4	97.2	2.3	96.6	-0.6
1981	102.0	5.6	107.0	4.9	115.4	7.9	112.8	-2.3	108.5	-3.8	103.8	-4.3	104.7	0.9	101.7	-2.9	99.7	-2.0	98.1	-1.6	100.1	2.0	110.6	10.5
1982	114.0	3.1	114.4	0.4	101.4	-11.4	105.5	4.0	107.0	1.4	104.3	-2.5	94.3	-9.6	94.1	-0.2	87.1	-7.4	87.9	0.9	92.0	4.7	98.1	6.6
1983	89.7	-8.6	89.8	0.1	92.6	3.1	105.1	13.5	102.5	-2.5	104.2	1.7	101.8	-2.3	106.6	4.7	108.8	2.1	121.5	11.7	108.5	-10.7	108.9	0.4
1984	114.8	5.4	123.1	7.2	121.4	-1.4	104.0	-14.3	99.3	-4.5	107.9	8.7	111.1	3.0	115.8	4.2	114.4	-1.2	105.4	-7.9	99.0	-6.1	99.3	0.3
1985	102.1	2.8	114.1	11.8	109.6	-3.9	109.6	0.0	99.0	-9.7	100.2	1.2	108.7	8.5	103.0	-5.2	93.9	-8.8	92.2	-1.8	94.6	2.6	105.3	11.3
1986	101.1	-4.0	92.5	-8.5	93.5	1.1	103.8	11.0	108.1	4.1	102.8	-4.9	105.2	2.3	104.5	-0.7	105.7	1.1	113.4	7.3	109.7	-3.3	107.3	-2.2
1987	98.4	-8.3	101.9	3.6	108.3	6.3	105.1	-3.0	104.5	-0.6	110.3	5.6	112.2	1.7	99.5	-11.3	102.5	3.0	101.5	-1.0	124.1	22.3	113.8	-8.3
1988	118.2	3.9	100.5	-15.0	101.5	1.0	101.0	-0.5	101.2	0.2	100.8	-0.4	109.9	9.0	105.9	-3.6	117.4	10.9	111.3	-5.2	119.0	6.9	114.7	-3.6
1989	109.4	-4.6	123.8	13.2	118.7	-4.1	115.3	-2.9	128.9	11.8	122.3	-5.1	120.8	-1.2	109.7	-9.2	101.8	-7.2	114.3	12.3	102.9	-10.0	106.7	3.7
1990	139.1	30.4	156.9	12.8	133.3	-15.0	106.9	-19.8	103.6	-3.1	106.9	3.2	117.3	9.7	107.4	-8.4	104.0	-3.2	109.0	4.8	119.3	9.4	106.7	-10.6
1991	109.8	2.9	111.4	1.5	113.3	1.7	124.4	9.8	141.9	14.1	137.0	-3.5	124.8	-8.9	110.9	-11.1	108.1	-2.5	98.1	-9.3	108.5	10.6	88.7	-18.2
1992	99.6	12.3	106.9	7.3	104.6	-2.2	92.7	-11.4	91.3	-1.5	83.3	-8.8	85.2	2.3	95.9	12.6	89.3	-6.9	105.2	17.8	102.0	-3.0	106.3	4.2
1993	103.7	-2.4	105.2	1.4	101.6	-3.4	118.3	16.4	120.8	2.1	93.9	-22.3	97.5	3.8	99.7	2.3	102.3	2.6	94.6	-7.5	118.4	25.2	126.4	6.8
1994	113.3	-10.4	99.4	-12.3	100.0	0.6	96.6	-3.4	101.4	5.0	99.2	-2.2	100.3	1.1	95.3	-5.0	97.2	2.0	99.9	2.8	115.7	15.8	137.1	18.5
1995	110.9	-19.1	105.9	-4.5	107.7	1.7	118.9	10.4	117.0	-1.6	101.3	-13.4	101.5	0.2	96.9	-4.5	113.5	17.1	98.6	-13.1	113.6	15.2	115.5	1.7
1996	117.3	1.6	115.7	-1.4	138.3	19.5	125.0	-9.6	117.1	-6.3	129.5	10.6	118.8	-8.3	112.1	-5.6	122.4	9.2	130.3	6.5	123.8	-5.0	119.6	-3.4
1997	117.0	-2.2	122.8	5.0	127.2	3.6	112.5	-11.6	117.5	4.4	105.8	-10.0	101.8	-3.8	109.0	7.1	112.8	3.5	122.7	8.8	111.8	-8.9	121.4	8.6
1998	118.0	-2.8	122.2	3.6	121.7	-0.4	128.4	5.5	116.2	-9.5	110.2	-5.2	119.9	8.8	108.9	-9.2	114.9	5.5	122.3	6.4	110.8	-9.4	116.5	5.1
1999	121.6	4.4	111.5	-8.3	115.8	3.9	123.5	6.6	122.3	-1.0	122.4	0.1	116.7	-4.7	112.1	-3.9	120.5	7.5	116.2	-3.6	105.9	-8.9	119.9	13.2
2000	107.9	-10.0	108.4	0.5	111.9	3.2	111.4	-0.4	119.3	7.1	104.8	-12.2	104.1	-0.7	100.3	-3.7	115.9	15.6	121.5	4.8	121.6	0.1	106.7	-12.3
2001	116.4	9.1	118.8	2.1	122.7	3.3	115.3	-6.0	119.0	3.2	114.6	-3.7	99.9	-12.8	107.6	7.7	113.1	5.1	110.6	-2.2	109.3	-1.2	122.1	11.7

Source: U.S. Department of Labor, Bureau of Labor Statistics, Division of Industry Prices and Price Indexes. n.e.c. stands for not elsewhere classified. - indicates no data collected for period or unavailable.

Grains
Producer Price Index
Base 1982 = 100

For 1926-2001. Columns headed % show percentile change in the index from the previous period for which an index is available.

Year	Jan Index	%	Feb Index	%	Mar Index	%	Apr Index	%	May Index	%	Jun Index	%	Jul Index	%	Aug Index	%	Sep Index	%	Oct Index	%	Nov Index	%	Dec Index	%
1926	37.9	-	36.5	-3.7	34.2	-6.3	34.7	1.5	33.7	-2.9	32.9	-2.4	33.9	3.0	32.2	-5.0	32.1	-0.3	32.8	2.2	31.5	-4.0	32.6	3.5
1927	32.3	-0.9	32.1	-0.6	31.3	-2.5	31.4	0.3	35.1	11.8	36.9	5.1	36.0	-2.4	36.5	1.4	34.7	-4.9	33.4	-3.7	33.6	0.6	34.4	2.4
1928	35.2	2.3	36.5	3.7	38.3	4.9	40.9	6.8	42.8	4.6	40.4	-5.6	37.5	-7.2	32.1	-14.4	32.8	2.2	32.6	-0.6	31.8	-2.5	31.8	0.0
1929	33.1	4.1	34.4	3.9	33.2	-3.5	31.8	-4.2	29.7	-6.6	30.6	3.0	34.4	12.4	33.4	-2.9	34.2	2.4	33.4	-2.3	32.0	-4.2	32.9	2.8
1930	31.6	-4.0	30.0	-5.1	28.1	-6.3	28.4	1.1	27.7	-2.5	26.4	-4.7	24.9	-5.7	27.1	8.8	25.9	-4.4	24.3	-6.2	21.5	-11.5	21.5	0.0
1931	21.1	-1.9	20.4	-3.3	20.0	-2.0	20.1	0.5	20.1	0.0	18.9	-6.0	16.5	-12.7	15.1	-8.5	14.8	-2.0	14.9	0.7	17.3	16.1	15.8	-8.7
1932	15.7	-0.6	15.5	-1.3	14.7	-5.2	15.0	2.0	14.4	-4.0	12.7	-11.8	12.3	-3.1	12.9	4.9	12.6	-2.3	11.6	-7.9	11.1	-4.3	10.7	-3.6
1933	11.0	2.8	11.0	0.0	12.1	10.0	15.1	24.8	17.7	17.2	19.3	9.0	24.8	28.5	21.8	-12.1	21.5	-1.4	19.6	-8.8	20.6	5.1	20.4	-1.0
1934	21.4	4.9	21.3	-0.5	20.9	-1.9	19.8	-5.3	21.5	8.6	24.4	13.5	25.1	2.9	29.0	15.5	29.7	2.4	28.6	-3.7	29.3	2.4	30.8	5.1
1935	29.9	-2.9	29.4	-1.7	27.9	-5.1	29.6	6.1	28.1	-5.1	25.9	-7.8	26.4	1.9	26.7	1.1	28.1	5.2	29.1	3.6	26.2	-10.0	25.8	-1.5
1936	26.6	3.1	26.3	-1.1	25.4	-3.4	24.9	-2.0	23.8	-4.4	24.6	3.4	29.9	21.5	34.5	15.4	34.4	-0.3	34.4	0.0	34.7	0.9	36.7	5.8
1937	38.1	3.8	37.6	-1.3	38.1	1.3	40.1	5.2	38.3	-4.5	35.5	-7.3	35.4	-0.3	31.0	-12.4	31.0	0.0	25.9	-16.5	23.3	-10.0	24.1	3.4
1938	25.3	5.0	24.6	-2.8	23.2	-5.7	22.2	-4.3	21.1	-5.0	21.1	0.0	19.6	-7.1	18.0	-8.2	17.9	-0.6	17.1	-4.5	17.1	0.0	18.3	7.0
1939	19.0	3.8	18.4	-3.2	18.3	-0.5	18.6	1.6	20.1	8.1	19.6	-2.5	17.6	-10.2	17.4	-1.1	21.9	25.9	20.8	-5.0	21.6	3.8	24.2	12.0
1940	24.8	2.5	24.5	-1.2	24.8	1.2	26.0	4.8	23.9	-8.1	21.7	-9.2	20.5	-5.5	20.0	-2.4	20.8	4.0	22.0	5.8	22.8	3.6	22.5	-1.3
1941	22.8	1.3	21.7	-4.8	22.8	5.1	23.9	4.8	25.1	5.0	25.6	2.0	25.7	0.4	26.8	4.3	28.7	7.1	27.4	-4.5	28.4	3.6	30.6	7.7
1942	32.3	5.6	32.1	-0.6	31.6	-1.6	30.8	-2.5	31.1	1.0	29.9	-3.9	30.0	0.3	30.3	1.0	31.5	4.0	30.8	-2.2	31.2	1.3	33.9	8.7
1943	36.1	6.5	36.6	1.4	37.8	3.3	37.8	0.0	38.1	0.8	38.3	0.5	39.1	2.1	39.4	0.8	40.3	2.3	41.3	2.5	41.5	0.5	43.2	4.1
1944	43.6	0.9	43.6	0.0	43.6	0.0	43.6	0.0	43.7	0.2	42.8	-2.1	42.2	-1.4	41.3	-2.1	41.0	-0.7	42.2	2.9	42.0	-0.5	43.0	2.4
1945	43.6	1.4	43.7	0.2	43.7	0.0	43.9	0.5	43.5	-0.9	43.8	0.7	43.3	-1.1	42.5	-1.8	42.7	0.5	43.8	2.6	44.8	2.3	44.9	0.2
1946	45.0	0.2	45.1	0.2	46.0	2.0	46.1	0.2	49.9	8.2	51.1	2.4	61.0	19.4	56.9	-6.7	57.4	0.9	58.7	2.3	55.7	-5.1	54.9	-1.4
1947	54.8	-0.2	57.7	5.3	68.9	19.4	67.9	-1.5	69.1	1.8	69.1	0.0	67.5	-2.3	70.0	3.7	77.2	10.3	81.4	5.4	83.2	2.2	85.5	2.8
1948	86.9	1.6	74.3	-14.5	73.5	-1.1	73.5	0.0	72.1	-1.9	69.9	-3.1	63.6	-9.0	60.1	-5.5	59.3	-1.3	57.5	-3.0	57.9	0.7	57.9	0.0
1949	56.8	-1.9	53.6	-5.6	55.5	3.5	55.9	0.7	54.6	-2.3	52.4	-4.0	52.0	-0.8	51.3	-1.3	53.5	4.3	53.4	-0.2	53.7	0.6	55.0	2.4
1950	54.8	-0.4	55.2	0.7	56.7	2.7	57.9	2.1	58.9	1.7	57.4	-2.5	58.8	2.4	56.9	-3.2	56.6	-0.5	56.6	0.0	58.5	3.4	61.5	5.1
1951	63.7	3.6	65.5	2.8	64.2	-2.0	64.2	0.0	63.0	-1.9	60.7	-3.7	60.4	-0.5	61.4	1.7	61.9	0.8	64.8	4.7	66.5	2.6	67.3	1.2
1952	66.3	-1.5	65.2	-1.7	65.3	0.2	64.6	-1.1	63.3	-2.0	61.1	-3.5	60.8	-0.5	62.1	2.1	62.1	0.0	60.8	-2.1	61.8	1.6	61.5	-0.5
1953	60.6	-1.5	59.7	-1.5	60.7	1.7	60.1	-1.0	59.8	-0.5	54.0	-9.7	54.7	1.3	55.4	1.3	56.6	2.2	56.3	-0.5	57.2	1.6	58.0	1.4
1954	58.5	0.9	58.7	0.3	59.6	1.5	59.5	-0.2	58.4	-1.8	55.4	-5.1	56.4	1.8	58.4	3.5	60.0	2.7	59.5	-0.8	59.9	0.7	59.2	-1.2
1955	59.9	1.2	59.7	-0.3	59.0	-1.2	58.3	-1.2	59.2	1.5	57.9	-2.2	55.5	-4.1	50.4	-9.2	52.2	3.6	52.8	1.1	51.1	-3.2	53.0	3.7
1956	52.2	-1.5	53.1	1.7	54.1	1.9	57.3	5.9	57.9	1.0	55.7	-3.8	56.6	1.6	56.9	0.5	58.1	2.1	53.8	-7.4	56.3	4.6	56.9	1.1
1957	57.3	0.7	55.8	-2.6	56.0	0.4	55.9	-0.2	54.7	-2.1	53.7	-1.8	53.0	-1.3	52.8	-0.4	52.0	-1.5	51.6	-0.8	51.8	0.4	51.6	-0.4
1958	50.6	-1.9	51.2	1.2	52.7	2.9	54.9	4.2	54.0	-1.6	52.1	-3.5	51.1	-1.9	49.5	-3.1	48.7	-1.6	49.2	1.0	48.2	-2.0	48.7	1.0
1959	48.7	0.0	49.3	1.2	49.8	1.0	51.1	2.6	50.4	-1.4	50.1	-0.6	50.1	0.0	49.8	-0.6	48.8	-2.0	48.5	-0.6	49.0	1.0	48.7	-0.6
1960	49.5	1.6	49.1	-0.8	50.1	2.0	50.9	1.6	49.8	-2.2	49.6	-0.4	48.4	-2.4	47.6	-1.7	48.0	0.8	47.0	-2.1	45.0	-4.3	46.6	3.6
1961	48.2	3.4	48.7	1.0	49.0	0.6	47.3	-3.5	47.9	1.3	47.5	-0.8	49.8	4.8	50.0	0.4	50.0	0.0	49.9	-0.2	50.8	1.8	50.6	-0.4
1962	50.0	-1.2	49.7	-0.6	50.1	0.8	50.6	1.0	51.9	2.6	51.4	-1.0	51.0	-0.8	50.5	-1.0	50.7	0.4	50.6	-0.2	51.2	1.2	52.0	1.6
1963	52.4	0.8	53.0	1.1	53.3	0.6	54.1	1.5	52.9	-2.2	52.2	-1.3	51.2	-1.9	50.6	-1.2	52.9	4.5	52.3	-1.1	51.6	-1.3	52.3	1.4
1964	53.4	2.1	52.4	-1.9	51.0	-2.7	53.1	4.1	53.1	0.0	46.2	-13.0	44.1	-4.5	44.1	0.0	46.4	5.2	45.7	-1.5	45.2	-1.1	46.3	2.4
1965	46.5	0.4	46.6	0.2	46.6	0.0	46.9	0.6	46.8	-0.2	46.1	-1.5	45.5	-1.3	45.4	-0.2	45.9	1.1	45.6	-0.7	45.0	-1.3	46.3	2.9
1966	47.5	2.6	47.8	0.6	46.7	-2.3	46.9	0.4	48.1	2.6	48.8	1.5	53.0	8.6	54.3	2.5	53.8	-0.9	50.9	-5.4	50.4	-1.0	52.2	3.6
1967	51.8	-0.8	49.3	-4.8	51.4	4.3	50.5	-1.8	50.4	-0.2	49.4	-2.0	47.6	-3.6	44.3	-6.9	44.0	-0.7	44.5	1.1	41.8	-6.1	43.9	5.0
1968	43.7	-0.5	44.4	1.6	43.8	-1.4	43.6	-0.5	44.4	1.8	42.2	-5.0	41.2	-2.4	38.6	-6.3	39.4	2.1	40.5	2.8	42.2	4.2	41.3	-2.1
1969	42.4	2.7	42.2	-0.5	42.0	-0.5	42.7	1.7	44.6	4.4	44.0	-1.3	43.1	-2.0	42.1	-2.3	42.9	1.9	43.6	1.6	42.0	-3.7	42.6	1.4
1970	44.2	3.8	44.2	0.0	44.0	-0.5	45.1	2.5	45.5	0.9	45.9	0.9	45.9	0.0	45.9	0.0	51.7	12.6	49.4	-4.4	49.4	0.0	51.2	3.6

[Continued]

Grains
Producer Price Index
Base 1982 = 100
[Continued]

For 1926-2001. Columns headed % show percentile change in the index from the previous period for which an index is available.

Year	Jan Index	%	Feb Index	%	Mar Index	%	Apr Index	%	May Index	%	Jun Index	%	Jul Index	%	Aug Index	%	Sep Index	%	Oct Index	%	Nov Index	%	Dec Index	%
1971	52.6	2.7	53.0	0.8	51.4	-3.0	50.7	-1.4	50.8	0.2	51.9	2.2	48.6	-6.4	44.0	-9.5	42.2	-4.1	41.9	-0.7	41.6	-0.7	45.3	8.9
1972	44.6	-1.5	44.1	-1.1	44.5	0.9	45.5	2.2	46.2	1.5	44.8	-3.0	45.7	2.0	47.3	3.5	51.9	9.7	51.8	-0.2	53.9	4.1	65.3	21.2
1973	64.3	-1.5	60.8	-5.4	59.8	-1.6	62.1	3.8	71.1	14.5	84.7	19.1	74.6	-11.9	126.3	69.3	109.8	-13.1	108.6	-1.1	104.7	-3.6	117.9	12.6
1974	128.4	8.9	131.9	2.7	124.7	-5.5	101.0	-19.0	99.8	-1.2	106.3	6.5	117.2	10.3	131.7	12.4	123.0	-6.6	138.1	12.3	134.4	-2.7	130.9	-2.6
1975	121.1	-7.5	115.2	-4.9	106.0	-8.0	103.6	-2.3	101.0	-2.5	96.4	-4.6	104.0	7.9	112.7	8.4	110.4	-2.0	107.8	-2.4	98.6	-8.5	97.5	-1.1
1976	99.8	2.4	101.6	1.8	103.3	1.7	99.1	-4.1	101.2	2.1	106.7	5.4	106.4	-0.3	98.5	-7.4	97.5	-1.0	88.5	-9.2	83.2	-6.0	85.7	3.0
1977	87.7	2.3	88.1	0.5	87.0	-1.2	87.4	0.5	81.2	-7.1	74.8	-7.9	71.7	-4.1	66.6	-7.1	68.4	2.7	68.6	0.3	78.0	13.7	79.3	1.7
1978	80.2	1.1	81.0	1.0	84.8	4.7	94.2	11.1	89.7	-4.8	89.2	-0.6	87.1	-2.4	84.8	-2.6	83.9	-1.1	86.3	2.9	89.6	3.8	87.6	-2.2
1979	87.4	-0.2	89.7	2.6	91.0	1.4	94.0	3.3	99.7	6.1	103.7	4.0	117.3	13.1	108.6	-7.4	106.4	-2.0	108.6	2.1	107.5	-1.0	108.1	0.6
1980	101.8	-5.8	105.9	4.0	103.3	-2.5	99.9	-3.3	103.8	3.9	102.1	-1.6	116.1	13.7	121.6	4.7	123.6	1.6	127.7	3.3	128.5	0.6	125.7	-2.2
1981	131.7	4.8	126.8	-3.7	124.1	-2.1	125.5	1.1	122.2	-2.6	121.9	-0.2	122.0	0.1	115.1	-5.7	107.7	-6.4	107.9	0.2	107.4	-0.5	101.3	-5.7
1982	106.8	5.4	105.8	-0.9	104.7	-1.0	107.1	2.3	108.2	1.0	107.0	-1.1	100.9	-5.7	93.5	-7.3	88.8	-5.0	86.9	-2.1	94.2	8.4	95.9	1.8
1983	97.8	2.0	105.4	7.8	107.8	2.3	115.6	7.2	114.8	-0.7	114.5	-0.3	112.2	-2.0	119.4	6.4	122.3	2.4	120.3	-1.6	122.1	1.5	115.5	-5.4
1984	116.4	0.8	111.6	-4.1	119.0	6.6	124.3	4.5	121.5	-2.3	122.3	0.7	118.0	-3.5	112.3	-4.8	109.7	-2.3	103.9	-5.3	104.2	0.3	100.8	-3.3
1985	103.1	2.3	103.0	-0.1	102.5	-0.5	104.6	2.0	101.5	-3.0	100.9	-0.6	97.2	-3.7	87.8	-9.7	85.9	-2.2	83.6	-2.7	91.0	8.9	92.8	2.0
1986	91.7	-1.2	91.8	0.1	90.8	-1.1	90.7	-0.1	94.6	4.3	86.4	-8.7	72.2	-16.4	65.9	-8.7	62.9	-4.6	63.9	1.6	69.4	8.6	71.0	2.3
1987	66.8	-5.9	66.7	-0.1	67.5	1.2	71.0	5.2	79.0	11.3	74.0	-6.3	68.8	-7.0	63.4	-7.8	69.5	9.6	72.8	4.7	74.9	2.9	78.9	5.3
1988	77.5	-1.8	83.5	7.7	80.6	-3.5	82.3	2.1	82.9	0.7	103.4	24.7	111.5	7.8	109.9	-1.4	112.9	2.7	114.2	1.2	107.4	-6.0	108.9	1.4
1989	115.2	5.8	111.3	-3.4	115.1	3.4	109.8	-4.6	114.1	3.9	105.8	-7.3	105.1	-0.7	100.3	-4.6	100.1	-0.2	98.2	-1.9	101.1	3.0	101.0	-0.1
1990	100.8	-0.2	100.4	-0.4	100.2	-0.2	107.2	7.0	108.6	1.3	110.4	1.7	103.1	-6.6	92.1	-10.7	88.3	-4.1	85.8	-2.8	85.1	-0.8	87.0	2.2
1991	85.9	-1.3	88.0	2.4	94.0	6.8	94.1	0.1	92.7	-1.5	90.2	-2.7	84.3	-6.5	93.2	10.6	92.4	-0.9	94.8	2.6	96.4	1.7	97.7	1.3
1992	103.1	5.5	106.2	3.0	108.5	2.2	102.7	-5.3	103.5	0.8	105.7	2.1	95.0	-10.1	88.5	-6.8	90.6	2.4	87.8	-3.1	86.6	-1.4	89.2	3.0
1993	89.9	0.8	88.1	-2.0	89.3	1.4	93.7	4.9	91.1	-2.8	85.3	-6.4	91.2	6.9	93.9	3.0	92.2	-1.8	96.4	4.6	106.1	10.1	116.4	9.7
1994	118.0	1.4	116.8	-1.0	112.5	-3.7	109.3	-2.8	106.8	-2.3	110.1	3.1	96.4	-12.4	90.2	-6.4	94.2	4.4	91.1	-3.3	91.2	0.1	95.3	4.5
1995	95.5	0.2	96.9	1.5	98.2	1.3	101.1	3.0	104.2	3.1	110.5	6.0	116.2	5.2	114.0	-1.9	119.3	4.6	126.2	5.8	131.1	3.9	137.6	5.0
1996	141.4	2.8	146.5	3.6	151.5	3.4	166.9	10.2	190.5	14.1	181.9	-4.5	184.9	1.6	170.6	-7.7	138.7	-18.7	118.8	-14.3	112.2	-5.6	109.6	-2.3
1997	111.1	1.4	111.0	-0.1	119.3	7.5	121.2	1.6	116.6	-3.8	112.4	-3.6	105.9	-5.8	106.3	0.4	107.2	0.8	109.1	1.8	107.1	-1.8	107.4	0.3
1998	104.4	-2.8	105.2	0.8	107.2	1.9	99.8	-6.9	98.7	-1.1	94.0	-4.8	92.0	-2.1	82.5	-10.3	76.3	-7.5	84.6	10.9	88.5	4.6	87.1	-1.6
1999	87.0	-0.1	86.4	-0.7	84.9	-1.7	83.1	-2.1	84.6	1.8	82.2	-2.8	71.7	-12.8	80.9	12.8	75.9	-6.2	72.7	-4.2	77.2	6.2	74.0	-4.1
2000	77.8	5.1	82.4	5.9	85.9	4.2	82.6	-3.8	85.8	3.9	78.6	-8.4	71.0	-9.7	66.8	-5.9	70.1	4.9	76.3	8.8	81.2	6.4	81.2	0.0
2001	85.7	5.5	80.1	-6.5	84.0	4.9	80.4	-4.3	79.7	-0.9	77.6	-2.6	81.0	4.4	83.1	2.6	81.7	-1.7	78.5	-3.9	80.2	2.2	82.6	3.0

Source: U.S. Department of Labor, Bureau of Labor Statistics, Division of Industry Prices and Price Indexes. n.e.c. stands for not elsewhere classified. - indicates no data collected for period or unavailable.

Slaughter Livestock
Producer Price Index
Base 1982 = 100

For 1926-2001. Columns headed % show percentile change in the index from the previous period for which an index is available.

Year	Jan Index	%	Feb Index	%	Mar Index	%	Apr Index	%	May Index	%	Jun Index	%	Jul Index	%	Aug Index	%	Sep Index	%	Oct Index	%	Nov Index	%	Dec Index	%
1926	-		-		-		-		-		-		-		-		-		-		-		-	
1927	-		-		-		-		-		-		-		-		-		-		-		-	
1928	-		-		-		-		-		-		-		-		-		-		-		-	
1929	-		-		-		-		-		-		-		-		-		-		-		-	
1930	-		-		-		-		-		-		-		-		-		-		-		-	
1931	-		-		-		-		-		-		-		-		-		-		-		-	
1932	-		-		-		-		-		-		-		-		-		-		-		-	
1933	-		-		-		-		-		-		-		-		-		-		-		-	
1934	-		-		-		-		-		-		-		-		-		-		-		-	
1935	-		-		-		-		-		-		-		-		-		-		-		-	
1936	-		-		-		-		-		-		-		-		-		-		-		-	
1937	-		-		-		-		-		-		-		-		-		-		-		-	
1938	-		-		-		-		-		-		-		-		-		-		-		-	
1939	-		-		15.0	-	-		-		13.6	-9.3	-		12.8	-5.9	14.7	14.8	-		-		12.3	-16.3
1940	-		-		12.6	2.4	-		-		12.6	0.0	-		-		14.0	11.1	-		-		14.1	0.7
1941	-		-		15.7	11.3	-		-		17.9	14.0	-		-		19.4	8.4	-		-		19.0	-2.1
1942	-		-		22.2	16.8	-		-		23.7	6.8	-		-		24.3	2.5	-		-		24.4	0.4
1943	-		-		27.3	11.9	-		-		25.3	-7.3			-		25.3	0.0	-		-		23.4	-7.5
1944	-		-		24.8	6.0	-		-		24.6	-0.8			-		25.0	1.6	-		-		24.8	-0.8
1945	-		-		26.1	5.2	-		-		26.1	0.0	-		-		25.1	-3.8	-		-		25.8	2.8
1946	26.2	1.6	26.1	-0.4	26.5	1.5	26.6	0.4	26.6	0.0	27.0	1.5	31.8	17.8	34.2	7.5	28.8	-15.8	33.7	17.0	38.7	14.8	38.5	-0.5
1947	37.2	-3.4	39.6	6.5	41.6	5.1	38.6	-7.2	39.5	2.3	40.4	2.3	42.0	4.0	42.0	0.0	44.1	5.0	44.4	0.7	42.3	-4.7	45.1	6.6
1948	47.5	5.3	43.0	-9.5	42.9	-0.2	42.4	-1.2	45.7	7.8	49.7	8.8	51.9	4.4	51.8	-0.2	50.9	-1.7	47.0	-7.7	44.9	-4.5	42.7	-4.9
1949	40.4	-5.4	38.4	-5.0	40.1	4.4	39.1	-2.5	40.1	2.6	40.8	1.7	40.0	-2.0	39.3	-1.7	39.6	0.8	38.2	-3.5	36.8	-3.7	36.7	-0.3
1950	37.7	2.7	39.2	4.0	39.1	-0.3	38.8	-0.8	42.6	9.8	43.3	1.6	46.7	7.9	46.8	0.2	45.9	-1.9	43.4	-5.4	43.8	0.9	45.5	3.9
1951	49.1	7.9	52.4	6.7	53.1	1.3	53.2	0.2	51.9	-2.4	52.0	0.2	51.5	-1.0	51.4	-0.2	50.7	-1.4	50.3	-0.8	47.5	-5.6	46.8	-1.5
1952	46.0	-1.7	45.6	-0.9	45.4	-0.4	46.3	2.0	47.7	3.0	46.8	-1.9	46.9	0.2	45.9	-2.1	42.5	-7.4	40.6	-4.5	39.2	-3.4	36.9	-5.9
1953	39.4	6.8	38.7	-1.8	38.8	0.3	36.6	-5.7	38.9	6.3	37.0	-4.9	40.8	10.3	37.3	-8.6	38.6	3.5	34.9	-9.6	33.2	-4.9	36.2	9.0
1954	39.6	9.4	39.5	-0.3	39.8	0.8	41.1	3.3	40.5	-1.5	37.9	-6.4	35.8	-5.5	35.9	0.3	34.9	-2.8	33.5	-4.0	33.2	-0.9	32.2	-3.0
1955	34.0	5.6	34.2	0.6	33.0	-3.5	35.2	6.7	32.8	-6.8	35.0	6.7	33.4	-4.6	31.3	-6.3	31.5	0.6	30.3	-3.8	25.8	-14.9	24.6	-4.7
1956	26.3	6.9	28.4	8.0	28.0	-1.4	30.0	7.1	31.7	5.7	32.3	1.9	31.1	-3.7	33.0	6.1	33.2	0.6	32.0	-3.6	29.7	-7.2	31.2	5.1
1957	32.3	3.5	32.6	0.9	33.3	2.1	34.7	4.2	34.5	-0.6	36.7	6.4	38.0	3.5	38.2	0.5	36.1	-5.5	34.8	-3.6	35.1	0.9	36.9	5.1
1958	38.0	3.0	40.4	6.3	42.4	5.0	42.4	0.0	44.6	5.2	44.0	-1.3	43.4	-1.4	42.3	-2.5	41.4	-2.1	40.1	-3.1	40.7	1.5	39.7	-2.5
1959	40.5	2.0	39.5	-2.5	40.9	3.5	41.7	2.0	40.9	-1.9	40.4	-1.2	38.1	-5.7	37.5	-1.6	37.0	-1.3	35.3	-4.6	33.5	-5.1	33.0	-1.5
1960	34.5	4.5	35.5	2.9	38.1	7.3	37.9	-0.5	38.1	0.5	37.8	-0.8	37.4	-1.1	35.9	-4.0	35.1	-2.2	36.0	2.6	36.5	1.4	36.9	1.1
1961	37.6	1.9	37.6	0.0	36.8	-2.1	36.7	-0.3	34.9	-4.9	34.4	-1.4	34.4	0.0	36.8	7.0	35.9	-2.4	35.4	-1.4	35.3	-0.3	35.9	1.7
1962	37.0	3.1	36.5	-1.4	37.0	1.4	36.7	-0.8	35.6	-3.0	35.8	0.6	37.3	4.2	38.5	3.2	40.7	5.7	38.5	-5.4	38.4	-0.3	37.3	-2.9
1963	36.5	-2.1	34.2	-6.3	32.6	-4.7	33.7	3.4	33.4	-0.9	34.4	3.0	36.7	6.7	36.5	-0.5	34.3	-6.0	34.0	-0.9	33.7	-0.9	30.8	-8.6
1964	32.4	5.2	31.7	-2.2	32.2	1.6	31.6	-1.9	31.3	-0.9	31.6	1.0	33.8	7.0	34.2	1.2	35.3	3.2	33.2	-5.9	32.0	-3.6	32.0	0.0
1965	32.9	2.8	34.0	3.3	34.4	1.2	35.3	2.6	37.5	6.2	41.0	9.3	41.1	0.2	41.8	1.7	40.2	-3.8	40.5	0.7	40.8	0.7	42.9	5.1
1966	44.2	3.0	45.8	3.6	44.4	-3.1	44.0	-0.9	42.8	-2.7	42.2	-1.4	41.7	-1.2	43.0	3.1	41.9	-2.6	40.8	-2.6	37.7	-7.6	37.5	-0.5
1967	38.9	3.7	38.2	-1.8	37.3	-2.4	36.1	-3.2	39.4	9.1	40.3	2.3	41.2	2.2	40.8	-1.0	39.7	-2.7	39.1	-1.5	37.0	-5.4	37.5	1.4
1968	37.9	1.1	39.4	4.0	40.5	2.8	40.4	-0.2	40.5	0.2	40.7	0.5	42.0	3.2	40.7	-3.1	40.6	-0.2	39.9	-1.7	39.9	0.0	40.0	0.3
1969	40.7	1.7	41.9	2.9	43.2	3.1	43.7	1.2	47.2	8.0	50.0	5.9	48.6	-2.8	47.4	-2.5	45.7	-3.6	45.5	-0.4	44.7	-1.8	46.1	3.1
1970	45.0	-2.4	47.9	6.4	49.7	3.8	47.9	-3.6	46.9	-2.1	47.2	0.6	48.4	2.5	45.5	-6.0	44.1	-3.1	42.9	-2.7	39.2	-8.6	38.6	-1.5

[Continued]

Slaughter Livestock
Producer Price Index
Base 1982 = 100
[Continued]

For 1926-2001. Columns headed % show percentile change in the index from the previous period for which an index is available.

Year	Jan Index	%	Feb Index	%	Mar Index	%	Apr Index	%	May Index	%	Jun Index	%	Jul Index	%	Aug Index	%	Sep Index	%	Oct Index	%	Nov Index	%	Dec Index	%
1971	39.7	2.8	46.1	16.1	44.5	-3.5	45.3	1.8	46.1	1.8	46.1	0.0	47.0	2.0	47.0	0.0	46.2	-1.7	46.9	1.5	46.9	0.0	48.4	3.2
1972	51.3	6.0	54.1	5.5	53.0	-2.0	51.9	-2.1	54.2	4.4	56.8	4.8	59.1	4.0	57.4	-2.9	56.2	-2.1	55.9	-0.5	54.1	-3.2	59.2	9.4
1973	61.8	4.4	69.0	11.7	75.4	9.3	71.4	-5.3	73.2	2.5	75.2	2.7	77.3	2.8	94.4	22.1	80.4	-14.8	72.0	-10.4	69.8	-3.1	66.3	-5.0
1974	76.5	15.4	75.6	-1.2	70.2	-7.1	65.5	-6.7	61.7	-5.8	53.5	-13.3	67.3	25.8	71.6	6.4	65.4	-8.7	64.0	-2.1	60.7	-5.2	61.9	2.0
1975	60.5	-2.3	59.0	-2.5	60.3	2.2	67.3	11.6	76.8	14.1	78.5	2.2	81.9	4.3	78.7	-3.9	81.4	3.4	80.6	-1.0	75.0	-6.9	74.3	-0.9
1976	71.6	-3.6	69.6	-2.8	66.3	-4.7	74.6	12.5	72.5	-2.8	71.8	-1.0	68.2	-5.0	64.4	-5.6	62.7	-2.6	60.5	-3.5	59.9	-1.0	64.4	7.5
1977	64.4	0.0	64.5	0.2	63.4	-1.7	65.1	2.7	69.9	7.4	66.8	-4.4	70.0	4.8	68.0	-2.9	67.0	-1.5	68.8	2.7	66.5	-3.3	70.8	6.5
1978	73.0	3.1	78.4	7.4	80.8	3.1	84.6	4.7	89.3	5.6	91.6	2.6	87.9	-4.0	84.0	-4.4	88.0	4.8	91.2	3.6	86.3	-5.4	89.3	3.5
1979	95.9	7.4	103.4	7.8	107.0	3.5	110.2	3.0	108.8	-1.3	102.4	-5.9	99.3	-3.0	93.1	-6.2	99.4	6.8	97.6	-1.8	96.3	-1.3	97.9	1.7
1980	96.1	-1.8	99.7	3.7	97.7	-2.0	89.4	-8.5	90.5	1.2	93.1	2.9	101.0	8.5	106.9	5.8	103.5	-3.2	102.0	-1.4	98.8	-3.1	97.5	-1.3
1981	94.7	-2.9	94.9	0.2	92.8	-2.2	95.7	3.1	97.6	2.0	102.0	4.5	103.4	1.4	101.6	-1.7	99.8	-1.8	94.8	-5.0	89.6	-5.5	87.3	-2.6
1982	91.8	5.2	97.4	6.1	99.1	1.7	103.8	4.7	109.7	5.7	107.6	-1.9	104.8	-2.6	104.1	-0.7	100.4	-3.6	96.4	-4.0	92.7	-3.8	92.0	-0.8
1983	94.0	2.2	97.4	3.6	97.5	0.1	101.1	3.7	100.0	-1.1	97.6	-2.4	93.3	-4.4	93.9	0.6	89.8	-4.4	89.0	-0.9	85.5	-3.9	92.4	8.1
1984	97.2	5.2	97.7	0.5	101.2	3.6	101.1	-0.1	98.8	-2.3	97.0	-1.8	100.9	4.0	98.4	-2.5	95.0	-3.5	90.7	-4.5	96.1	6.0	97.8	1.8
1985	96.0	-1.8	96.8	0.8	91.8	-5.2	89.7	-2.3	88.3	-1.6	87.9	-0.5	86.9	-1.1	82.1	-5.5	77.0	-6.2	88.2	14.5	92.8	5.2	92.8	0.0
1986	90.2	-2.8	87.7	-2.8	85.4	-2.6	82.9	-2.9	88.9	7.2	87.3	-1.8	95.1	8.9	98.1	3.2	98.2	0.1	95.9	-2.3	96.6	0.7	95.6	-1.0
1987	93.1	-2.6	95.9	3.0	96.0	0.1	104.3	8.6	109.6	5.1	109.8	0.2	107.3	-2.3	106.5	-0.7	104.1	-2.3	102.6	-1.4	96.8	-5.7	98.1	1.3
1988	99.3	1.2	105.7	6.4	106.3	0.6	107.7	1.3	111.8	3.8	106.1	-5.1	99.7	-6.0	100.6	0.9	100.7	0.1	101.8	1.1	98.3	-3.4	101.0	2.7
1989	104.5	3.5	104.6	0.1	106.8	2.1	106.4	-0.4	107.4	0.9	106.0	-1.3	104.8	-1.1	108.8	3.8	103.7	-4.7	104.6	0.9	105.6	1.0	110.5	4.6
1990	110.7	0.2	113.2	2.3	117.0	3.4	117.9	0.8	120.5	2.2	117.8	-2.2	114.7	-2.6	117.8	2.7	113.3	-3.8	116.5	2.8	113.9	-2.2	114.3	0.4
1991	112.8	-1.3	113.9	1.0	117.1	2.8	115.8	-1.1	115.2	-0.5	112.8	-2.1	110.2	-2.3	100.7	-8.6	101.1	0.4	100.9	-0.2	96.6	-4.3	97.7	1.1
1992	100.0	2.4	106.0	6.0	107.0	0.9	106.7	-0.3	108.0	1.2	105.3	-2.5	103.7	-1.5	104.2	0.5	103.4	-0.8	104.2	0.8	101.8	-2.3	106.3	4.4
1993	108.3	1.9	110.0	1.6	112.6	2.4	113.0	0.4	112.8	-0.2	109.8	-2.7	105.0	-4.4	107.1	2.0	105.7	-1.3	100.0	-5.4	100.5	0.5	99.2	-1.3
1994	100.7	1.5	103.6	2.9	104.7	1.1	104.9	0.2	98.5	-6.1	92.4	-6.2	94.3	2.1	96.8	2.7	91.3	-5.7	88.1	-3.5	89.6	1.7	91.6	2.2
1995	96.4	5.2	100.5	4.3	96.9	-3.6	92.3	-4.7	87.4	-5.3	90.7	3.8	90.7	0.0	90.8	0.1	92.0	1.3	91.4	-0.7	91.9	0.5	92.3	0.4
1996	89.6	-2.9	90.5	1.0	89.9	-0.7	89.6	-0.3	93.5	4.4	95.0	1.6	97.4	2.5	99.6	2.3	100.5	0.9	100.5	0.0	100.7	0.2	95.8	-4.9
1997	95.4	-0.4	93.8	-1.7	96.3	2.7	101.6	5.5	102.6	1.0	96.2	-6.2	98.8	2.7	97.9	-0.9	95.8	-2.1	93.0	-2.9	93.1	0.1	91.4	-1.8
1998	85.6	-6.3	83.6	-2.3	85.4	2.2	87.9	2.9	90.7	3.2	90.7	0.0	81.8	-9.8	82.1	0.4	79.0	-3.8	78.7	-0.4	74.9	-4.8	67.3	-10.1
1999	79.3	17.8	81.0	2.1	83.6	3.2	83.8	0.2	87.9	4.9	88.6	0.8	85.0	-4.1	88.6	4.2	86.7	-2.1	90.9	4.8	89.6	-1.4	91.9	2.6
2000	91.6	-0.3	92.4	0.9	98.3	6.4	102.3	4.1	102.5	0.2	100.4	-2.0	97.9	-2.5	92.8	-5.2	91.1	-1.8	93.1	2.2	94.3	1.3	100.9	7.0
2001	100.9	0.0	102.3	1.4	107.9	5.5	108.4	0.5	107.2	-1.1	106.0	-1.1	102.9	-2.9	100.1	-2.7	97.6	-2.5	93.5	-4.2	84.3	-9.8	84.0	-0.4

Source: U.S. Department of Labor, Bureau of Labor Statistics, Division of Industry Prices and Price Indexes. n.e.c. stands for not elsewhere classified. - indicates no data collected for period or unavailable.

Slaughter Poultry
Producer Price Index
Base 1982 = 100

For 1926-2001. Columns headed % show percentile change in the index from the previous period for which an index is available.

Year	Jan Index	%	Feb Index	%	Mar Index	%	Apr Index	%	May Index	%	Jun Index	%	Jul Index	%	Aug Index	%	Sep Index	%	Oct Index	%	Nov Index	%	Dec Index	%
1926	-	-	-	-	-	-	-	-	-	-	-	-	-	-	-	-	-	-	-	-	-	-	-	-
1927	-	-	-	-	-	-	-	-	-	-	-	-	-	-	-	-	-	-	-	-	-	-	-	-
1928	-	-	-	-	-	-	-	-	-	-	-	-	-	-	-	-	-	-	-	-	-	-	-	-
1929	-	-	-	-	-	-	-	-	-	-	-	-	-	-	-	-	-	-	-	-	-	-	-	-
1930	-	-	-	-	-	-	-	-	-	-	-	-	-	-	-	-	-	-	-	-	-	-	-	-
1931	-	-	-	-	-	-	-	-	-	-	-	-	-	-	-	-	-	-	-	-	-	-	-	-
1932	-	-	-	-	-	-	-	-	-	-	-	-	-	-	-	-	-	-	-	-	-	-	-	-
1933	-	-	-	-	-	-	-	-	-	-	-	-	-	-	-	-	-	-	-	-	-	-	-	-
1934	-	-	-	-	-	-	-	-	-	-	-	-	-	-	-	-	-	-	-	-	-	-	-	-
1935	-	-	-	-	-	-	-	-	-	-	-	-	-	-	-	-	-	-	-	-	-	-	-	-
1936	-	-	-	-	-	-	-	-	-	-	-	-	-	-	-	-	-	-	-	-	-	-	-	-
1937	-	-	-	-	-	-	-	-	-	-	-	-	-	-	-	-	-	-	-	-	-	-	-	-
1938	-	-	-	-	-	-	-	-	-	-	-	-	-	-	-	-	-	-	-	-	-	-	-	-
1939	-	-	-	-	67.7	-	-	-	-	-	55.3	-18.3	-	-	56.3	1.8	60.8	8.0	-	-	-	-	52.5	-13.7
1940	-	-	-	-	60.0	14.3	-	-	-	-	54.9	-8.5	-	-	-	-	59.6	8.6	-	-	-	-	58.2	-2.3
1941	-	-	-	-	72.2	24.1	-	-	-	-	77.2	6.9	-	-	-	-	76.8	-0.5	-	-	-	-	73.8	-3.9
1942	-	-	-	-	89.3	21.0	-	-	-	-	77.6	-13.1	-	-	-	-	87.0	12.1	-	-	-	-	90.9	4.5
1943	-	-	-	-	98.8	8.7	-	-	-	-	99.8	1.0	-	-	-	-	96.5	-3.3	-	-	-	-	96.2	-0.3
1944	-	-	-	-	98.8	2.7	-	-	-	-	89.2	-9.7	-	-	-	-	94.8	6.3	-	-	-	-	98.2	3.6
1945	-	-	-	-	104.0	5.9	-	-	-	-	103.0	-1.0	-	-	-	-	97.3	-5.5	-	-	-	-	98.4	1.1
1946	102.6	4.3	104.3	1.7	103.2	-1.1	108.9	5.5	108.9	0.0	108.0	-0.8	110.6	2.4	103.9	-6.1	125.7	21.0	121.0	-3.7	101.9	-15.8	107.9	5.9
1947	103.7	-3.9	103.7	0.0	115.2	11.1	115.4	0.2	116.9	1.3	111.9	-4.3	110.6	-1.2	111.9	1.2	119.5	6.8	108.2	-9.5	107.4	-0.7	117.5	9.4
1948	128.5	9.4	119.1	-7.3	131.4	10.3	135.1	2.8	131.7	-2.5	133.2	1.1	129.2	-3.0	131.0	1.4	130.3	-0.5	119.4	-8.4	123.9	3.8	131.5	6.1
1949	123.9	-5.8	116.4	-6.1	122.8	5.5	120.5	-1.9	108.3	-10.1	97.8	-9.7	98.1	0.3	102.8	4.8	97.6	-5.1	95.5	-2.2	97.9	2.5	85.0	-13.2
1950	79.5	-6.5	97.3	22.4	105.9	8.8	102.6	-3.1	95.6	-6.8	92.5	-3.2	104.9	13.4	108.0	3.0	102.5	-5.1	92.4	-9.9	89.3	-3.4	90.5	1.3
1951	100.4	10.9	111.7	11.3	120.0	7.4	120.9	0.7	114.1	-5.6	111.9	-1.9	108.6	-2.9	106.3	-2.1	102.3	-3.8	94.1	-8.0	91.0	-3.3	95.1	4.5
1952	104.5	9.9	108.5	3.8	102.9	-5.2	97.9	-4.9	89.0	-9.1	92.7	4.2	101.0	9.0	105.1	4.1	105.2	0.1	98.2	-6.7	112.7	14.8	99.1	-12.1
1953	106.2	7.2	105.3	-0.8	107.4	2.0	110.8	3.2	106.0	-4.3	94.4	-10.9	106.7	13.0	102.6	-3.8	99.4	-3.1	93.1	-6.3	91.6	-1.6	82.7	-9.7
1954	91.2	10.3	87.9	-3.6	91.8	4.4	88.4	-3.7	84.3	-4.6	83.6	-0.8	83.0	-0.7	83.3	0.4	77.9	-6.5	72.2	-7.3	70.4	-2.5	66.8	-5.1
1955	79.8	19.5	86.5	8.4	100.5	16.2	96.9	-3.6	91.1	-6.0	92.4	1.4	89.8	-2.8	91.4	1.8	89.0	-2.6	78.6	-11.7	75.4	-4.1	72.1	-4.4
1956	74.1	2.8	78.1	5.4	80.9	3.6	76.1	-5.9	77.4	1.7	72.0	-7.0	75.2	4.4	69.2	-8.0	63.7	-7.9	63.0	-1.1	63.4	0.6	64.3	1.4
1957	63.9	-0.6	68.6	7.4	70.9	3.4	67.6	-4.7	67.7	0.1	69.3	2.4	71.3	2.9	70.8	-0.7	63.7	-10.0	60.2	-5.5	61.9	2.8	60.6	-2.1
1958	68.4	12.9	69.3	1.3	73.7	6.3	65.9	-10.6	71.4	8.3	73.5	2.9	67.7	-7.9	64.0	-5.5	58.2	-9.1	56.1	-3.6	58.4	4.1	55.5	-5.0
1959	62.4	12.4	63.6	1.9	63.0	-0.9	58.2	-7.6	59.0	1.4	58.7	-0.5	58.2	-0.9	54.7	-6.0	55.3	1.1	53.6	-3.1	56.3	5.0	69.1	22.7
1960	64.7	-6.4	66.1	2.2	68.4	3.5	67.8	-0.9	65.6	-3.2	64.7	-1.4	62.7	-3.1	60.1	-4.1	59.2	-1.5	60.1	1.5	60.0	-0.2	60.8	1.3
1961	64.3	5.8	67.4	4.8	63.6	-5.6	58.8	-7.5	56.9	-3.2	46.0	-19.2	46.6	1.3	46.8	0.4	41.3	-11.8	43.5	5.3	44.0	1.1	53.0	20.5
1962	56.2	6.0	57.6	2.5	56.7	-1.6	52.2	-7.9	50.6	-3.1	50.2	-0.8	53.3	6.2	54.0	1.3	57.8	7.0	54.4	-5.9	53.5	-1.7	54.7	2.2
1963	54.6	-0.2	57.7	5.7	57.0	-1.2	57.0	0.0	53.2	-6.7	53.8	1.1	53.8	0.0	51.9	-3.5	52.1	0.4	52.2	0.2	55.0	5.4	48.8	-11.3
1964	53.9	10.5	53.2	-1.3	52.7	-0.9	52.1	-1.1	49.8	-4.4	50.7	1.8	53.8	6.1	51.7	-3.9	52.7	1.9	51.6	-2.1	53.0	2.7	50.7	-4.3
1965	53.2	4.9	54.6	2.6	57.1	4.6	55.3	-3.2	53.7	-2.9	56.0	4.3	56.3	0.5	55.0	-2.3	54.3	-1.3	54.4	0.2	54.1	-0.6	55.5	2.6
1966	58.5	5.4	60.7	3.8	64.2	5.8	60.5	-5.8	64.5	6.6	60.8	-5.7	59.9	-1.5	57.1	-4.7	55.7	-2.5	52.9	-5.0	54.1	2.3	49.1	-9.2
1967	56.1	14.3	61.8	10.2	57.8	-6.5	56.6	-2.1	54.5	-3.7	54.5	0.0	56.6	3.9	49.2	-13.1	46.4	-5.7	47.0	1.3	41.7	-11.3	43.4	4.1
1968	49.8	14.7	55.3	11.0	51.8	-6.3	51.6	-0.4	54.4	5.4	57.0	4.8	59.7	4.7	55.9	-6.4	53.9	-3.6	50.4	-6.5	55.7	10.5	52.7	-5.4
1969	57.5	9.1	59.9	4.2	60.8	1.5	57.9	-4.8	62.7	8.3	61.9	-1.3	65.3	5.5	58.7	-10.1	56.5	-3.7	54.2	-4.1	54.9	1.3	55.2	0.5
1970	60.2	9.1	55.3	-8.1	57.7	4.3	52.7	-8.7	53.2	0.9	49.5	-7.0	52.1	5.3	49.2	-5.6	51.9	5.5	48.7	-6.2	49.6	1.8	41.8	-15.7

[Continued]

Slaughter Poultry
Producer Price Index
Base 1982 = 100
[Continued]

For 1926-2001. Columns headed % show percentile change in the index from the previous period for which an index is available.

Year	Jan Index	%	Feb Index	%	Mar Index	%	Apr Index	%	May Index	%	Jun Index	%	Jul Index	%	Aug Index	%	Sep Index	%	Oct Index	%	Nov Index	%	Dec Index	%
1971	50.1	19.9	52.0	3.8	52.1	0.2	51.8	-0.6	52.8	1.9	56.3	6.6	63.0	11.9	52.5	-16.7	53.5	1.9	48.6	-9.2	48.0	-1.2	45.4	-5.4
1972	49.1	8.1	54.9	11.8	56.1	2.2	49.1	-12.5	50.2	2.2	53.6	6.8	61.7	15.1	55.7	-9.7	58.5	5.0	54.1	-7.5	53.6	-0.9	54.0	0.7
1973	66.6	23.3	71.4	7.2	85.9	20.3	96.8	12.7	93.9	-3.0	96.1	2.3	98.7	2.7	140.5	42.4	118.0	-16.0	98.6	-16.4	80.5	-18.4	75.3	-6.5
1974	74.6	-0.9	93.7	25.6	86.6	-7.6	76.1	-12.1	76.5	0.5	69.2	-9.5	77.2	11.6	78.1	1.2	90.4	15.7	81.8	-9.5	93.2	13.9	87.2	-6.4
1975	90.5	3.8	92.1	1.8	88.6	-3.8	87.7	-1.0	92.5	5.5	99.3	7.4	114.2	15.0	105.5	-7.6	106.3	0.8	109.8	3.3	106.1	-3.4	94.5	-10.9
1976	88.1	-6.8	90.2	2.4	95.2	5.5	86.2	-9.5	90.8	5.3	91.1	0.3	95.9	5.3	93.3	-2.7	85.9	-7.9	78.4	-8.7	72.5	-7.5	75.9	4.7
1977	80.1	5.5	95.7	19.5	92.3	-3.6	95.0	2.9	95.4	0.4	95.2	-0.2	101.0	6.1	91.8	-9.1	94.7	3.2	88.8	-6.2	84.8	-4.5	82.2	-3.1
1978	88.7	7.9	98.4	10.9	97.9	-0.5	102.1	4.3	101.3	-0.8	115.5	14.0	128.5	11.3	106.7	-17.0	110.0	3.1	96.4	-12.4	100.2	3.9	103.5	3.3
1979	107.3	3.7	113.5	5.8	113.4	-0.1	109.1	-3.8	112.7	3.3	95.3	-15.4	95.8	0.5	89.6	-6.5	90.4	0.9	84.4	-6.6	101.9	20.7	101.4	-0.5
1980	101.7	0.3	96.2	-5.4	93.8	-2.5	89.6	-4.5	89.2	-0.4	86.8	-2.7	118.4	36.4	117.0	-1.2	125.6	7.4	116.2	-7.5	115.2	-0.9	114.0	-1.0
1981	111.1	-2.5	115.1	3.6	111.2	-3.4	101.8	-8.5	108.0	6.1	109.4	1.3	112.2	2.6	109.6	-2.3	102.5	-6.5	96.8	-5.6	91.2	-5.8	89.3	-2.1
1982	97.3	9.0	102.8	5.7	103.0	0.2	97.0	-5.8	100.4	3.5	108.0	7.6	110.7	2.5	98.7	-10.8	102.4	3.7	92.3	-9.9	94.6	2.5	92.7	-2.0
1983	92.3	-0.4	104.3	13.0	92.7	-11.1	89.0	-4.0	97.4	9.4	103.9	6.7	111.8	7.6	115.4	3.2	126.2	9.4	108.6	-13.9	124.3	14.5	125.7	1.1
1984	131.6	4.7	131.0	-0.5	134.6	2.7	125.5	-6.8	125.4	-0.1	118.7	-5.3	135.1	13.8	113.9	-15.7	124.9	9.7	114.3	-8.5	128.8	12.7	120.8	-6.2
1985	121.3	0.4	115.9	-4.5	112.3	-3.1	105.4	-6.1	111.8	6.1	116.5	4.2	118.6	1.8	112.6	-5.1	127.4	13.1	117.4	-7.8	132.8	13.1	122.5	-7.8
1986	110.9	-9.5	102.9	-7.2	108.9	5.8	110.1	1.1	113.7	3.3	123.3	8.4	154.6	25.4	177.2	14.6	145.7	-17.8	163.6	12.3	130.8	-20.0	114.5	-12.5
1987	110.6	-3.4	104.1	-5.9	104.0	-0.1	105.3	1.3	112.8	7.1	94.2	-16.5	102.3	8.6	111.2	8.7	100.3	-9.8	88.5	-11.8	93.9	6.1	87.7	-6.6
1988	99.1	13.0	86.9	-12.3	96.9	11.5	97.6	0.7	112.2	15.0	130.4	16.2	156.4	19.9	145.1	-7.2	142.7	-1.7	141.0	-1.2	128.0	-9.2	121.7	-4.9
1989	122.4	0.6	121.5	-0.7	138.5	14.0	138.4	-0.1	155.0	12.0	148.5	-4.2	135.5	-8.8	125.4	-7.5	134.9	7.6	109.0	-19.2	111.8	2.6	104.3	-6.7
1990	108.9	4.4	115.5	6.1	129.1	11.8	117.3	-9.1	128.2	9.3	118.5	-7.6	134.7	13.7	122.1	-9.4	128.9	5.6	110.2	-14.5	108.3	-1.7	104.2	-3.8
1991	110.4	6.0	103.1	-6.6	110.2	6.9	107.3	-2.6	113.9	6.2	112.7	-1.1	119.2	5.8	120.4	1.0	116.7	-3.1	109.1	-6.5	106.8	-2.1	105.1	-1.6
1992	106.9	1.7	102.8	-3.8	105.4	2.5	102.8	-2.5	116.1	12.9	110.7	-4.7	124.1	12.1	120.5	-2.9	111.8	-7.2	119.3	6.7	121.7	2.0	108.8	-10.6
1993	112.0	2.9	110.4	-1.4	116.1	5.2	116.5	0.3	132.3	13.6	118.9	-10.1	124.4	4.6	125.9	1.2	135.1	7.3	126.1	-6.7	127.2	0.9	118.4	-6.9
1994	110.9	-6.3	119.6	7.8	129.5	8.3	126.8	-2.1	138.2	9.0	135.2	-2.2	131.0	-3.1	119.9	-8.5	128.3	7.0	125.0	-2.6	114.4	-8.5	114.2	-0.2
1995	108.6	-4.9	109.3	0.6	113.1	3.5	109.1	-3.5	111.0	1.7	121.1	9.1	130.0	7.3	139.7	7.5	147.2	5.4	135.7	-7.8	150.3	10.8	132.5	-11.8
1996	133.6	0.8	124.0	-7.2	120.0	-3.2	120.9	0.7	140.6	16.3	155.3	10.5	151.3	-2.6	148.6	-1.8	147.4	-0.8	144.3	-2.1	151.3	4.9	149.0	-1.5
1997	138.1	-7.3	130.2	-5.7	117.5	-9.8	127.0	8.1	130.9	3.1	133.4	1.9	146.9	10.1	147.9	0.7	139.9	-5.4	121.7	-13.0	122.3	0.5	115.9	-5.2
1998	116.9	0.9	116.1	-0.7	125.3	7.9	128.5	2.6	131.1	2.0	140.5	7.2	156.7	11.5	167.8	7.1	164.1	-2.2	161.8	-1.4	151.4	-6.4	136.2	-10.0
1999	129.5	-4.9	126.4	-2.4	124.8	-1.3	118.7	-4.9	136.6	15.1	135.6	-0.7	137.6	1.5	126.3	-8.2	132.6	5.0	122.7	-7.5	137.7	12.2	130.7	-5.1
2000	122.2	-6.5	113.4	-7.2	117.8	3.9	121.0	2.7	123.0	1.7	124.2	1.0	126.5	1.9	119.6	-5.5	133.6	11.7	130.8	-2.1	134.7	3.0	129.1	-4.2
2001	124.3	-3.7	123.6	-0.6	129.3	4.6	128.0	-1.0	132.0	3.1	131.9	-0.1	133.8	1.4	132.6	-0.9	139.5	5.2	137.2	-1.6	134.5	-2.0	121.4	-9.7

Source: U.S. Department of Labor, Bureau of Labor Statistics, Division of Industry Prices and Price Indexes. n.e.c. stands for not elsewhere classified. - indicates no data collected for period or unavailable.

Plant and Animal Fibers
Producer Price Index
Base 1982 = 100

For 1926-2001. Columns headed % show percentile change in the index from the previous period for which an index is available.

Year	Jan Index	%	Feb Index	%	Mar Index	%	Apr Index	%	May Index	%	Jun Index	%	Jul Index	%	Aug Index	%	Sep Index	%	Oct Index	%	Nov Index	%	Dec Index	%
1926	52.6	-	52.1	-1.0	48.5	-6.9	47.0	-3.1	46.4	-1.3	45.9	-1.1	46.2	0.7	48.3	4.5	43.6	-9.7	37.6	-13.8	36.4	-3.2	35.9	-1.4
1927	37.1	3.3	38.3	3.2	39.0	1.8	39.5	1.3	41.8	5.8	42.7	2.2	44.8	4.9	48.4	8.0	51.3	6.0	49.9	-2.7	48.4	-3.0	47.0	-2.9
1928	46.3	-1.5	45.6	-1.5	47.8	4.8	49.1	2.7	51.2	4.3	50.6	-1.2	50.9	0.6	46.8	-8.1	45.4	-3.0	47.1	3.7	47.5	0.8	48.2	1.5
1929	47.6	-1.2	47.7	0.2	48.9	2.5	47.2	-3.5	45.6	-3.4	45.2	-0.9	45.0	-0.4	45.4	0.9	45.6	0.4	44.7	-2.0	42.4	-5.1	41.7	-1.7
1930	41.3	-1.0	38.4	-7.0	37.3	-2.9	38.2	2.4	37.5	-1.8	33.1	-11.7	30.5	-7.9	28.7	-5.9	26.5	-7.7	25.6	-3.4	25.8	0.8	24.2	-6.2
1931	24.7	2.1	25.7	4.0	25.6	-0.4	24.2	-5.5	22.4	-7.4	22.0	-1.8	22.6	2.7	18.9	-16.4	17.5	-7.4	16.9	-3.4	17.3	2.4	16.5	-4.6
1932	16.7	1.2	16.8	0.6	16.4	-2.4	15.0	-8.5	13.7	-8.7	12.7	-7.3	13.6	7.1	16.6	22.1	17.8	7.2	15.9	-10.7	15.0	-5.7	14.3	-4.7
1933	14.5	1.4	13.9	-4.1	15.0	7.9	15.7	4.7	19.2	22.3	21.9	14.1	24.9	13.7	22.4	-10.0	22.5	0.4	27.0	-1.5	26.2	-3.0	26.5	1.1	26.8	1.7
1934	24.7	7.9	26.7	8.1	26.7	0.0	26.0	-2.6	24.9	-4.2	26.2	5.2	26.7	1.9	27.4	2.6	27.0	-1.5	26.2	-3.0	26.5	1.1	26.8	1.7
1935	26.9	0.4	26.5	-1.5	24.4	-7.9	24.8	1.6	25.8	4.0	25.4	-1.6	25.7	1.2	25.1	-2.3	24.5	-2.4	27.4	0.0	27.3	-0.4	27.7	1.5	26.9	-1.1
1936	26.7	-0.7	26.0	-2.6	26.1	0.4	26.2	0.4	26.0	-0.8	26.7	2.7	28.4	6.4	27.4	-3.5	22.5	-9.6	20.8	-7.6	19.8	-4.8	20.0	1.0
1937	29.8	2.8	29.9	0.3	31.9	6.7	31.6	-0.9	30.0	-5.1	28.9	-3.7	28.6	-1.0	24.9	-12.9	22.5	-9.6	20.8	-7.6	19.8	-4.8	20.0	1.0
1938	20.6	3.0	20.8	1.0	20.7	-0.5	20.5	-1.0	20.0	-2.4	19.8	-1.0	21.0	6.1	20.2	-3.8	19.5	-3.5	20.5	5.1	20.9	2.0	20.4	-2.4
1939	20.8	2.0	21.2	1.9	21.7	2.4	21.5	-0.9	23.1	7.4	23.5	1.7	23.3	-0.9	22.6	-3.0	24.0	6.2	25.3	5.4	26.3	4.0	29.3	11.4
1940	25.8	-11.9	25.0	-3.1	24.5	-2.0	24.0	-2.0	22.8	-5.0	23.5	3.1	22.9	-2.6	21.7	-5.2	21.7	0.0	22.0	1.4	22.8	3.6	23.0	0.9
1941	23.3	1.3	23.4	0.4	24.3	3.8	25.0	2.9	27.7	10.8	29.7	7.2	32.9	10.8	33.6	2.1	35.3	5.1	34.4	-2.5	34.1	-0.9	35.7	4.7
1942	38.7	8.4	38.7	0.0	39.5	2.1	40.4	2.3	40.3	-0.2	38.4	-4.7	39.0	1.6	37.3	-4.4	37.4	0.3	37.6	0.5	38.3	1.9	38.9	1.6
1943	40.1	3.1	40.6	1.2	41.2	1.5	41.3	0.2	41.2	-0.2	41.1	-0.2	40.7	-1.0	40.1	-1.5	40.1	0.0	39.6	-1.2	38.4	-3.0	38.5	0.3
1944	39.2	1.8	40.3	2.8	40.8	1.2	40.6	-0.5	40.7	0.2	41.5	2.0	41.7	0.5	41.1	-1.4	41.2	0.2	41.4	0.5	41.1	-0.7	41.4	0.7
1945	41.5	0.2	41.5	0.0	41.8	0.7	42.4	1.4	43.2	1.9	43.1	-0.2	42.6	-1.2	42.2	-0.9	42.4	0.5	43.5	2.6	44.9	3.2	45.3	0.9
1946	45.5	0.4	47.2	3.7	48.7	3.2	50.1	2.9	49.8	-0.6	52.1	4.6	63.1	21.1	67.5	7.0	68.7	1.8	67.7	-1.5	59.8	-11.7	61.9	3.5
1947	61.0	-1.5	62.9	3.1	65.6	4.3	66.3	1.1	67.5	1.8	69.3	2.7	70.3	1.4	65.7	-6.5	62.0	-5.6	62.7	1.1	65.9	5.1	69.5	5.5
1948	68.7	-1.2	65.7	-4.4	67.7	3.0	72.9	7.7	74.7	2.5	75.6	1.2	71.8	-5.0	67.8	-5.6	67.5	-0.4	67.1	-0.6	67.5	0.6	69.6	3.1
1949	70.7	1.6	70.6	-0.1	70.4	-0.3	70.8	0.6	69.4	-2.0	69.0	-0.6	67.1	-2.8	64.9	-3.3	63.6	-2.0	63.0	-0.9	62.0	-1.6	63.2	1.9
1950	65.0	2.8	67.4	3.7	67.1	-0.4	68.3	1.8	70.0	2.5	72.4	3.4	77.0	6.4	80.5	4.5	90.8	12.8	89.7	-1.2	94.7	5.6	98.0	3.5
1951	108.3	10.5	112.5	3.9	116.4	3.5	112.2	-3.6	107.9	-3.8	105.1	-2.6	92.6	-11.9	80.9	-12.6	77.0	-4.8	80.2	4.2	86.7	8.1	85.6	-1.3
1952	85.8	0.2	81.3	-5.2	80.2	-1.4	80.7	0.6	77.1	-4.5	80.1	3.9	77.9	-2.7	77.7	-0.3	76.5	-1.5	74.0	-3.3	72.3	-2.3	68.7	-5.0
1953	68.2	-0.7	69.3	1.6	70.6	1.9	69.8	-1.1	70.4	0.9	70.2	-0.3	70.9	1.0	70.1	-1.1	69.9	-0.3	69.6	-0.4	69.8	0.3	69.6	-0.3
1954	70.3	1.0	71.9	2.3	71.5	-0.6	71.2	-0.4	72.2	1.4	72.2	0.0	72.4	0.3	72.0	-0.6	72.5	0.7	72.3	-0.3	70.5	-2.5	70.9	0.6
1955	70.5	-0.6	70.4	-0.1	69.4	-1.4	69.3	-0.1	69.8	0.7	69.8	0.0	70.1	0.4	69.4	-1.0	68.1	-1.9	66.9	-1.8	68.2	1.9	68.1	-0.1
1956	68.7	0.9	71.4	3.9	71.2	-0.3	71.4	0.3	71.5	0.1	71.7	0.3	70.4	-1.8	66.3	-5.8	66.4	0.2	67.5	1.7	68.1	0.9	68.4	0.4
1957	69.4	1.5	70.1	1.0	70.2	0.1	70.4	0.3	70.4	0.0	70.8	0.6	70.9	0.1	70.2	-1.0	69.4	-1.1	69.7	0.4	70.7	1.4	70.0	-1.0
1958	69.8	-0.3	69.4	-0.6	68.6	-1.2	68.4	-0.3	68.6	0.3	68.7	0.1	68.7	0.0	68.7	0.0	68.0	-1.0	68.0	0.0	68.0	0.0	67.3	-1.0
1959	67.1	-0.3	66.9	-0.3	67.2	0.4	68.2	1.5	68.7	0.7	68.6	-0.1	67.5	-1.6	64.6	-4.3	64.5	-0.2	63.9	-0.9	63.9	0.0	64.6	1.1
1960	64.7	0.2	64.9	0.3	64.8	-0.2	65.0	0.3	65.2	0.3	65.3	0.2	65.1	-0.3	62.3	-4.3	62.2	-0.2	61.3	-1.4	61.3	0.0	61.3	0.0
1961	61.3	0.0	61.6	0.5	62.7	1.8	63.0	0.5	64.3	2.1	65.0	1.1	65.3	0.5	66.4	1.7	66.6	0.3	67.1	0.8	67.1	0.0	67.1	0.0
1962	67.0	-0.1	67.1	0.1	67.3	0.3	67.6	0.4	67.6	0.0	68.1	0.7	67.9	-0.3	67.3	-0.9	66.6	-1.0	66.6	0.0	66.7	0.2	67.1	0.6
1963	67.9	1.2	68.9	1.5	69.6	1.0	69.7	0.1	69.5	-0.3	69.3	-0.3	68.5	-1.2	68.1	-0.6	68.0	-0.1	68.0	0.0	68.2	0.3	69.3	1.6
1964	69.4	0.1	69.5	0.1	69.8	0.4	69.8	0.0	69.2	-0.9	69.2	0.0	68.0	-1.7	65.6	-3.5	64.5	-1.7	64.1	-0.6	64.2	0.2	63.3	-1.4
1965	63.2	-0.2	62.7	-0.8	62.6	-0.2	62.6	0.0	62.7	0.2	62.9	0.3	62.7	-0.3	61.8	-1.4	61.5	-0.5	61.5	0.0	61.4	-0.2	61.3	-0.2
1966	61.3	0.0	61.2	-0.2	61.3	0.2	61.5	0.3	61.7	0.3	61.7	0.0	61.8	0.2	49.4	-20.1	49.0	-0.8	48.8	-0.4	48.4	-0.8	48.5	0.2
1967	48.4	-0.2	48.0	-0.8	48.0	0.0	47.8	-0.4	47.8	0.0	48.4	1.3	48.4	0.0	48.8	0.8	49.5	1.4	49.5	0.0	51.2	3.4	55.2	7.8
1968	54.3	-1.6	52.3	-3.7	52.3	0.0	52.0	-0.6	51.8	-0.4	51.9	0.2	51.9	0.0	52.5	1.2	52.7	0.4	50.7	-3.8	48.7	-3.9	47.2	-3.1
1969	47.0	-0.4	46.3	-1.5	46.0	-0.6	46.0	0.0	46.3	0.7	46.3	0.0	46.3	0.0	45.7	-1.3	45.4	-0.7	45.2	-0.4	45.1	-0.2	44.9	-0.4
1970	44.6	-0.7	44.7	0.2	44.4	-0.7	44.7	0.7	44.8	0.2	44.9	0.2	45.2	0.7	45.2	0.0	44.4	-1.8	43.8	-1.4	43.3	-1.1	42.7	-1.4

[Continued]

Plant and Animal Fibers
Producer Price Index
Base 1982 = 100
[Continued]

For 1926-2001. Columns headed % show percentile change in the index from the previous period for which an index is available.

Year	Jan Index	%	Feb Index	%	Mar Index	%	Apr Index	%	May Index	%	Jun Index	%	Jul Index	%	Aug Index	%	Sep Index	%	Oct Index	%	Nov Index	%	Dec Index	%
1971	42.9	0.5	43.4	1.2	43.8	0.9	44.1	0.7	44.5	0.9	45.5	2.2	45.6	0.2	46.0	0.9	46.9	2.0	47.4	1.1	47.9	1.1	50.5	5.4
1972	54.0	6.9	55.8	3.3	56.3	0.9	60.2	6.9	64.1	6.5	62.7	-2.2	61.8	-1.4	59.4	-3.9	53.4	-10.1	52.1	-2.4	55.3	6.1	59.6	7.8
1973	66.1	10.9	69.0	4.4	75.2	9.0	76.2	1.3	84.5	10.9	87.6	3.7	91.9	4.9	112.6	22.5	132.0	17.2	131.3	-0.5	115.3	-12.2	127.8	10.8
1974	135.4	5.9	118.3	-12.6	108.1	-8.6	103.1	-4.6	96.7	-6.2	96.3	-0.4	92.6	-3.8	89.4	-3.5	83.6	-6.5	78.5	-6.1	74.3	-5.4	70.5	-5.1
1975	68.4	-3.0	66.7	-2.5	68.2	2.2	67.8	-0.6	75.5	11.4	71.7	-5.0	75.3	5.0	79.4	5.4	80.8	1.8	81.1	0.4	82.3	1.5	88.5	7.5
1976	95.3	7.7	91.9	-3.6	92.5	0.7	92.4	-0.1	99.3	7.5	116.2	17.0	132.6	14.1	116.1	-12.4	119.4	2.8	123.1	3.1	127.1	3.2	118.0	-7.2
1977	106.7	-9.6	118.3	10.9	124.4	5.2	123.0	-1.1	117.6	-4.4	97.3	-17.3	96.3	-1.0	88.8	-7.8	81.7	-8.0	82.3	0.7	80.9	-1.7	79.3	-2.0
1978	84.3	6.3	86.0	2.0	92.1	7.1	89.2	-3.1	94.5	5.9	95.1	0.6	93.6	-1.6	97.3	4.0	99.2	2.0	103.6	4.4	104.2	0.6	104.9	0.7
1979	105.3	0.4	101.1	-4.0	97.5	-3.6	97.5	0.0	102.3	4.9	108.2	5.8	102.3	-5.5	102.5	0.2	104.1	1.6	104.9	0.8	106.2	1.2	109.4	3.0
1980	117.8	7.7	132.8	12.7	125.6	-5.4	131.6	4.8	134.4	2.1	121.7	-9.4	131.6	8.1	138.4	5.2	145.5	5.1	137.2	-5.7	141.5	3.1	144.9	2.4
1981	140.0	-3.4	132.2	-5.6	133.1	0.7	135.1	1.5	127.3	-5.8	128.0	0.5	123.8	-3.3	114.6	-7.4	101.8	-11.2	104.3	2.5	97.8	-6.2	92.8	-5.1
1982	97.7	5.3	95.4	-2.4	98.3	3.0	102.2	4.0	105.5	3.2	100.1	-5.1	108.8	8.7	102.3	-6.0	97.0	-5.2	97.6	0.6	96.3	-1.3	98.8	2.6
1983	99.4	0.6	101.7	2.3	107.0	5.2	105.3	-1.6	110.3	4.7	113.2	2.6	113.5	0.3	118.6	4.5	117.6	-0.8	115.6	-1.7	120.1	3.9	120.3	0.2
1984	113.0	-6.1	114.7	1.5	123.4	7.6	124.3	0.7	127.7	2.7	124.5	-2.5	116.2	-6.7	104.2	-10.3	103.6	-0.6	100.0	-3.5	99.2	-0.8	100.1	0.9
1985	100.8	0.7	98.9	-1.9	98.8	-0.1	104.1	5.4	99.9	-4.0	98.1	-1.8	99.4	1.3	95.9	-3.5	94.2	-1.8	94.3	0.1	93.5	-0.8	91.9	-1.7
1986	96.8	5.3	97.8	1.0	101.9	4.2	103.8	1.9	106.2	2.3	108.2	1.9	108.7	0.5	46.5	-57.2	53.2	14.4	74.3	39.7	75.9	2.2	87.1	14.8
1987	94.7	8.7	93.1	-1.7	89.9	-3.4	98.4	9.5	108.7	10.5	116.1	6.8	120.1	3.4	123.4	2.7	118.5	-4.0	108.9	-8.1	105.1	-3.5	100.5	-4.4
1988	100.7	0.2	97.8	-2.9	103.2	5.5	103.6	0.4	103.7	0.1	107.6	3.8	99.4	-7.6	98.7	-0.7	89.6	-9.2	89.7	0.1	93.1	3.8	93.9	0.9
1989	95.8	2.0	94.8	-1.0	98.4	3.8	105.0	6.7	108.1	3.0	110.5	2.2	111.5	0.9	116.8	4.8	113.9	-2.5	116.9	2.6	115.3	-1.4	106.3	-7.8
1990	104.8	-1.4	108.7	3.7	114.7	5.5	118.7	3.5	121.9	2.7	125.9	3.3	129.4	2.8	125.1	-3.3	116.6	-6.8	116.4	-0.2	115.0	-1.2	116.9	1.7
1991	115.2	-1.5	126.3	9.6	129.1	2.2	134.0	3.8	139.2	3.9	130.8	-6.0	120.2	-8.1	106.7	-11.2	103.5	-3.0	96.3	-7.0	90.3	-6.2	89.7	-0.7
1992	85.4	-4.8	83.5	-2.2	84.7	1.4	89.0	5.1	93.4	4.9	96.2	3.0	102.0	6.0	96.6	-5.3	93.8	-2.9	82.8	-11.7	83.2	0.5	87.3	4.9
1993	89.5	2.5	89.5	0.0	94.2	5.3	91.5	-2.9	93.3	2.0	90.5	-3.0	90.8	0.3	88.5	-2.5	89.4	1.0	92.0	2.9	88.8	-3.5	98.1	10.5
1994	107.1	9.2	119.0	11.1	120.8	1.5	123.4	2.2	129.2	4.7	129.4	0.2	114.5	-11.5	118.7	3.7	122.1	2.9	111.1	-9.0	120.4	8.4	132.6	10.1
1995	143.5	8.2	149.4	4.1	180.2	20.6	175.2	-2.8	165.7	-5.4	178.9	8.0	163.5	-8.6	139.2	-14.9	147.6	6.0	142.6	-3.4	139.9	-1.9	137.9	-1.4
1996	136.2	-1.2	135.2	-0.7	132.4	-2.1	142.6	7.7	137.4	-3.6	135.7	-1.2	128.2	-5.5	128.3	0.1	122.8	-4.3	119.9	-2.4	113.1	-5.7	120.4	6.5
1997	116.4	-3.3	116.5	0.1	122.5	5.2	115.1	-6.0	116.0	0.8	117.5	1.3	120.0	2.1	121.1	0.9	118.3	-2.3	116.8	-1.3	115.5	-1.1	108.4	-6.1
1998	104.1	-4.0	108.1	3.8	110.1	1.9	101.5	-7.8	107.9	6.3	117.9	9.3	120.9	2.5	115.8	-4.2	117.8	1.7	112.6	-4.4	110.9	-1.5	97.7	-11.9
1999	93.5	-4.3	90.8	-2.9	96.3	6.1	94.4	-2.0	93.8	-0.6	89.6	-4.5	79.4	-11.4	82.7	4.2	80.0	-3.3	80.8	1.0	79.4	-1.7	77.3	-2.6
2000	83.9	8.5	88.1	5.0	97.6	10.8	86.2	-11.7	94.5	9.6	90.9	-3.8	86.9	-4.4	96.7	11.3	99.3	2.7	101.4	2.1	101.2	-0.2	100.2	-1.0
2001	92.8	-7.4	92.1	-0.8	80.5	-12.6	71.9	-10.7	69.6	-3.2	63.5	-8.8	62.7	-1.3	59.4	-5.3	56.6	-4.7	48.3	-14.7	54.2	12.2	54.8	1.1

Source: U.S. Department of Labor, Bureau of Labor Statistics, Division of Industry Prices and Price Indexes. n.e.c. stands for not elsewhere classified. - indicates no data collected for period or unavailable.

935

Fluid Milk
Producer Price Index
Base 1982 = 100

For 1926-2001. Columns headed % show percentile change in the index from the previous period for which an index is available.

Year	Jan Index	%	Feb Index	%	Mar Index	%	Apr Index	%	May Index	%	Jun Index	%	Jul Index	%	Aug Index	%	Sep Index	%	Oct Index	%	Nov Index	%	Dec Index	%
1926	19.6	-	19.6	0.0	19.6	0.0	19.8	1.0	19.2	-3.0	18.9	-1.6	19.1	1.1	19.3	1.0	19.9	3.1	19.8	-0.5	19.7	-0.5	19.7	0.0
1927	19.6	-0.5	19.6	0.0	19.6	0.0	19.4	-1.0	19.2	-1.0	19.2	0.0	19.4	1.0	19.4	0.0	20.9	7.7	20.9	0.0	21.0	0.5	21.0	0.0
1928	20.8	-1.0	20.8	0.0	19.4	-6.7	19.3	-0.5	19.1	-1.0	19.1	0.0	20.0	4.7	20.9	4.5	21.1	1.0	21.0	-0.5	21.0	0.0	21.0	0.0
1929	21.2	1.0	21.1	-0.5	21.1	0.0	21.1	0.0	21.1	0.0	21.4	1.4	21.1	-1.4	21.1	0.0	21.2	0.5	21.4	0.9	21.4	0.0	21.4	0.0
1930	21.1	-1.4	21.1	0.0	21.1	0.0	21.1	0.0	19.8	-6.2	19.8	0.0	19.8	0.0	20.7	4.5	21.1	1.9	21.1	0.0	21.1	0.0	19.8	-6.2
1931	18.7	-5.6	18.5	-1.1	18.5	0.0	18.5	0.0	18.5	0.0	18.9	2.2	19.2	1.6	18.8	-2.1	18.8	0.0	18.8	0.0	17.5	-6.9	17.5	0.0
1932	14.7	-16.0	13.8	-6.1	13.8	0.0	13.8	0.0	13.8	0.0	13.5	-2.2	13.5	0.0	13.5	0.0	13.5	0.0	13.5	0.0	13.5	0.0	11.9	-11.9
1933	11.5	-3.4	11.0	-4.3	10.8	-1.8	10.8	0.0	12.0	11.1	13.5	12.5	13.9	3.0	14.7	5.8	14.7	0.0	14.8	0.7	15.2	2.7	15.5	2.0
1934	15.2	-1.9	14.6	-3.9	14.4	-1.4	14.3	-0.7	15.9	11.2	16.9	6.3	17.3	2.4	17.3	0.0	17.3	0.0	17.5	1.2	17.0	-2.9	17.0	0.0
1935	17.2	1.2	17.4	1.2	17.4	0.0	17.3	-0.6	17.1	-1.2	16.9	-1.2	16.9	0.0	17.1	1.2	16.8	-1.8	16.5	-1.8	16.5	0.0	16.6	0.6
1936	16.5	-0.6	16.6	0.6	15.9	-4.2	15.8	-0.6	15.8	0.0	15.8	0.0	16.4	3.8	17.1	4.3	18.2	6.4	18.3	0.5	18.4	0.5	18.4	0.0
1937	18.4	0.0	18.5	0.5	18.5	0.0	15.1	-18.4	13.3	-11.9	13.3	0.0	14.6	9.8	15.5	6.2	16.7	7.7	16.7	0.0	17.6	5.4	17.8	1.1
1938	16.4	-7.9	15.6	-4.9	15.4	-1.3	14.8	-3.9	14.2	-4.1	14.1	-0.7	14.3	1.4	14.2	-0.7	15.2	7.0	15.2	0.0	15.3	0.7	15.4	0.7
1939	15.2	-1.3	15.1	-0.7	13.0	-13.9	10.9	-16.2	10.9	0.0	11.1	1.8	13.2	18.9	14.6	10.6	15.9	8.9	16.9	6.3	16.9	0.0	16.7	-1.2
1940	16.7	0.0	16.6	-0.6	16.5	-0.6	16.5	0.0	14.8	-10.3	14.8	0.0	15.2	2.7	15.3	0.7	15.1	-1.3	15.4	2.0	16.4	6.5	16.2	-1.2
1941	16.1	-0.6	16.0	-0.6	16.1	0.6	15.5	-3.7	14.6	-5.8	15.4	5.5	16.8	9.1	17.7	5.4	18.2	2.8	19.3	6.0	19.4	0.5	19.4	0.0
1942	19.4	0.0	19.2	-1.0	19.0	-1.0	17.9	-5.8	17.6	-1.7	17.5	-0.6	18.7	6.9	19.0	1.6	20.0	5.3	20.2	1.0	21.1	4.5	21.3	0.9
1943	21.6	1.4	21.6	0.0	21.6	0.0	21.6	0.0	21.6	0.0	21.6	0.0	21.6	0.0	21.6	0.0	21.6	0.0	21.7	0.5	22.5	3.7	22.5	0.0
1944	22.6	0.4	22.6	0.0	22.5	-0.4	22.4	-0.4	22.3	-0.4	22.3	0.0	22.3	0.0	22.4	0.4	22.5	0.4	22.5	0.0	22.5	0.0	22.5	0.0
1945	22.5	0.0	22.5	0.0	22.5	0.0	22.5	0.0	22.4	-0.4	22.4	0.0	22.4	0.0	22.4	0.0	22.4	0.0	22.4	0.0	22.5	0.4	22.6	0.4
1946	22.6	0.0	22.7	0.4	22.7	0.0	22.8	0.4	22.9	0.4	24.8	8.3	28.9	16.5	29.8	3.1	30.5	2.3	32.9	7.9	33.2	0.9	32.8	-1.2
1947	32.3	-1.5	30.6	-5.3	29.8	-2.6	28.4	-4.7	25.8	-9.2	26.1	1.2	27.4	5.0	29.6	8.0	31.0	4.7	32.0	3.2	32.8	2.5	34.0	3.7
1948	35.3	3.8	34.8	-1.4	33.6	-3.4	33.9	0.9	34.0	0.3	35.0	2.9	36.3	3.7	36.2	-0.3	34.9	-3.6	32.6	-6.6	31.5	-3.4	31.4	-0.3
1949	29.7	-5.4	28.5	-4.0	27.6	-3.2	26.7	-3.3	26.3	-1.5	26.3	0.0	26.7	1.5	27.6	3.4	27.8	0.7	27.9	0.4	28.2	1.1	27.9	-1.1
1950	27.3	-2.2	27.2	-0.4	26.9	-1.1	25.9	-3.7	25.3	-2.3	25.0	-1.2	25.8	3.2	26.7	3.5	27.6	3.4	28.4	2.9	29.1	2.5	30.1	3.4
1951	32.5	8.0	32.7	0.6	32.5	-0.6	31.5	-3.1	30.8	-2.2	30.9	0.3	31.3	1.3	31.8	1.6	31.8	0.0	32.2	1.3	32.9	2.2	33.5	1.8
1952	33.7	0.6	33.9	0.6	33.7	-0.6	33.1	-1.8	31.9	-3.6	31.6	-0.9	32.7	3.5	33.7	3.1	34.8	3.3	35.1	0.9	34.5	-1.7	33.3	-3.5
1953	32.2	-3.3	31.5	-2.2	30.7	-2.5	29.6	-3.6	28.6	-3.4	28.5	-0.3	29.5	3.5	29.8	1.0	30.3	1.7	30.8	1.7	31.2	1.3	30.4	-2.6
1954	29.8	-2.0	29.0	-2.7	28.5	-1.7	27.0	-5.3	25.7	-4.8	25.6	-0.4	26.8	4.7	27.4	2.2	28.0	2.2	28.7	2.5	29.1	1.4	28.6	-1.7
1955	28.2	-1.4	28.1	-0.4	27.7	-1.4	27.6	-0.4	26.7	-3.3	26.6	-0.4	27.2	2.3	28.0	2.9	28.6	2.1	29.1	1.7	29.0	-0.3	28.9	-0.3
1956	28.7	-0.7	28.7	0.0	27.7	-3.5	27.5	-0.7	28.4	3.3	28.4	0.0	28.9	1.8	29.1	0.7	29.3	0.7	29.7	1.4	30.2	1.7	30.3	0.3
1957	30.0	-1.0	29.8	-0.7	29.2	-2.0	29.0	-0.7	28.2	-2.8	28.1	-0.4	28.5	1.4	29.0	1.8	29.6	2.1	30.2	2.0	30.4	0.7	30.3	-0.3
1958	30.1	-0.7	29.9	-0.7	29.2	-2.3	28.0	-4.1	27.7	-1.1	27.6	-0.4	28.1	1.8	28.6	1.8	29.3	2.4	29.4	0.3	29.5	0.3	29.4	-0.3
1959	29.2	-0.7	29.2	0.0	28.6	-2.1	28.1	-1.7	27.6	-1.8	27.5	-0.4	28.2	2.5	28.9	2.5	29.3	1.4	29.7	1.4	30.0	1.0	30.1	0.3
1960	30.3	0.7	30.3	0.0	29.9	-1.3	29.2	-2.3	28.4	-2.7	28.5	0.4	29.2	2.5	29.7	1.7	30.5	2.7	31.0	1.6	31.3	1.0	31.3	0.0
1961	30.9	-1.3	30.4	-1.6	30.2	-0.7	29.7	-1.7	29.2	-1.7	29.0	-0.7	30.0	3.4	30.1	0.3	30.4	1.0	30.7	1.0	30.8	0.3	30.6	-0.6
1962	30.6	0.0	30.4	-0.7	29.8	-2.0	28.7	-3.7	28.1	-2.1	28.2	0.4	29.0	2.8	29.3	1.0	29.5	0.7	29.8	1.0	29.7	-0.3	29.6	-0.3
1963	29.4	-0.7	29.3	-0.3	28.9	-1.4	28.5	-1.4	28.2	-1.1	28.4	0.7	29.0	2.1	29.2	0.7	29.6	1.4	29.8	0.7	30.0	0.7	30.0	0.0
1964	29.8	-0.7	29.7	-0.3	29.4	-1.0	28.9	-1.7	28.6	-1.0	28.7	0.3	29.2	1.7	29.6	1.4	30.1	1.7	30.3	0.7	30.6	1.0	30.5	-0.3
1965	30.2	-1.0	30.1	-0.3	29.1	-3.3	29.4	1.0	29.1	-1.0	29.2	0.3	29.7	1.7	30.2	1.7	30.4	0.7	30.8	1.3	31.2	1.3	31.4	0.6
1966	31.5	0.3	32.4	2.9	32.7	0.9	32.5	-0.6	32.2	-0.9	32.7	1.6	34.7	6.1	36.0	3.7	36.4	1.1	36.5	0.3	36.1	-1.1	36.0	-0.3
1967	35.8	-0.6	35.5	-0.8	34.5	-2.8	34.6	0.3	35.0	1.2	35.2	0.6	35.2	0.0	35.1	-0.3	35.9	2.3	35.9	0.0	35.9	0.0	36.1	0.6
1968	36.2	0.3	36.2	0.0	36.0	-0.6	36.7	1.9	37.5	2.2	37.6	0.3	37.9	0.8	37.9	0.0	38.1	0.5	38.4	0.8	38.4	0.0	38.4	0.0
1969	38.3	-0.3	38.5	0.5	38.5	0.0	38.8	0.8	38.9	0.3	39.1	0.5	39.2	0.3	39.2	0.0	39.5	0.8	39.7	0.5	40.0	0.8	40.8	2.0
1970	41.0	0.5	40.9	-0.2	40.6	-0.7	41.0	1.0	40.5	-1.2	40.5	0.0	40.6	0.2	40.5	-0.2	40.7	0.5	40.8	0.2	41.3	1.2	41.6	0.7

[Continued]

Fluid Milk
Producer Price Index
Base 1982 = 100
[Continued]

For 1926-2001. Columns headed % show percentile change in the index from the previous period for which an index is available.

Year	Jan Index	%	Feb Index	%	Mar Index	%	Apr Index	%	May Index	%	Jun Index	%	Jul Index	%	Aug Index	%	Sep Index	%	Oct Index	%	Nov Index	%	Dec Index	%
1971	41.6	0.0	41.7	0.2	41.9	0.5	42.1	0.5	42.0	-0.2	42.2	0.5	42.3	0.2	42.2	-0.2	42.2	0.0	42.2	0.0	42.1	-0.2	42.1	0.0
1972	42.7	1.4	42.6	-0.2	43.1	1.2	43.2	0.2	43.4	0.5	43.1	-0.7	43.2	0.2	43.2	0.0	43.5	0.7	43.8	0.7	43.7	-0.2	43.7	0.0
1973	44.8	2.5	45.5	1.6	46.1	1.3	46.2	0.2	47.0	1.7	47.2	0.4	47.2	0.0	50.8	7.6	56.2	10.6	59.6	6.0	62.7	5.2	62.7	0.0
1974	65.4	4.3	65.9	0.8	65.8	-0.2	65.3	-0.8	63.2	-3.2	58.3	-7.8	55.8	-4.3	56.0	0.4	56.4	0.7	58.8	4.3	61.8	5.1	61.2	-1.0
1975	60.9	-0.5	60.9	0.0	60.1	-1.3	59.3	-1.3	59.0	-0.5	58.6	-0.7	59.7	1.9	62.3	4.4	65.8	5.6	69.9	6.2	73.6	5.3	75.3	2.3
1976	75.2	-0.1	73.5	-2.3	71.4	-2.9	69.7	-2.4	68.7	-1.4	67.3	-2.0	68.4	1.6	71.0	3.8	72.1	1.5	73.2	1.5	72.3	-1.2	71.8	-0.7
1977	70.9	-1.3	70.2	-1.0	69.1	-1.6	70.0	1.3	70.2	0.3	70.6	0.6	71.7	1.6	72.6	1.3	73.2	0.8	74.2	1.4	74.3	0.1	74.4	0.1
1978	73.8	-0.8	74.2	0.5	74.7	0.7	75.1	0.5	75.1	0.0	75.1	0.0	76.6	2.0	78.1	2.0	80.0	2.4	82.1	2.6	83.5	1.7	85.4	2.3
1979	85.6	0.2	86.6	1.2	86.3	-0.3	85.8	-0.6	85.7	-0.1	86.3	0.7	87.7	1.6	88.5	0.9	91.5	3.4	92.3	0.9	92.9	0.7	93.5	0.6
1980	92.8	-0.7	93.4	0.6	93.1	-0.3	93.9	0.9	93.9	0.0	94.0	0.1	94.1	0.1	96.1	2.1	97.5	1.5	99.4	1.9	100.8	1.4	102.8	2.0
1981	102.1	-0.7	102.5	0.4	102.5	0.0	101.7	-0.8	100.4	-1.3	100.9	0.5	100.6	-0.3	100.9	0.3	101.7	0.8	104.2	2.5	102.0	-2.1	101.5	-0.5
1982	101.8	0.3	101.2	-0.6	100.0	-1.2	99.2	-0.8	98.7	-0.5	98.7	0.0	98.8	0.1	98.7	-0.1	99.8	1.1	100.9	1.1	101.2	0.3	101.1	-0.1
1983	100.7	-0.4	100.6	-0.1	100.1	-0.5	99.4	-0.7	99.0	-0.4	98.6	-0.4	98.7	0.1	99.7	1.0	100.7	1.0	100.6	-0.1	100.3	-0.3	99.6	-0.7
1984	98.8	-0.8	97.6	-1.2	97.1	-0.5	96.5	-0.6	96.2	-0.3	96.2	0.0	97.0	0.8	98.0	1.0	99.9	1.9	101.5	1.6	101.8	0.3	101.8	0.0
1985	100.7	-1.1	99.5	-1.2	98.5	-1.0	96.0	-2.5	93.8	-2.3	91.9	-2.0	90.7	-1.3	90.3	-0.4	90.6	0.3	90.6	0.0	91.1	0.6	90.3	-0.9
1986	90.3	0.0	90.2	-0.1	88.9	-1.4	87.9	-1.1	88.2	0.3	88.5	0.3	89.0	0.6	90.7	1.9	91.6	1.0	94.4	3.1	95.7	1.4	96.1	0.4
1987	96.1	0.0	94.6	-1.6	92.2	-2.5	90.7	-1.6	89.4	-1.4	88.1	-1.5	89.7	1.8	91.1	1.6	92.7	1.8	93.2	0.5	93.1	-0.1	91.5	-1.7
1988	90.5	-1.1	89.1	-1.5	86.7	-2.7	85.4	-1.5	85.3	-0.1	83.8	-1.8	84.9	1.3	88.1	3.8	91.2	3.5	94.3	3.4	96.5	2.3	97.0	0.5
1989	96.4	-0.6	94.7	-1.8	91.3	-3.6	90.2	-1.2	89.7	-0.6	91.0	1.4	93.7	3.0	98.1	4.7	103.1	5.1	107.6	4.4	113.1	5.1	116.2	2.7
1990	114.7	-1.3	105.1	-8.4	100.5	-4.4	98.0	-2.5	100.3	2.3	103.1	2.8	105.3	2.1	105.5	0.2	104.6	-0.9	95.4	-8.8	91.8	-3.8	85.8	-6.5
1991	84.4	-1.6	84.1	-0.4	83.1	-1.2	82.9	-0.2	83.4	0.6	85.1	2.0	88.1	3.5	91.8	4.2	94.3	2.7	98.1	4.0	99.3	1.2	99.6	0.3
1992	97.7	-1.9	93.8	-4.0	91.3	-2.7	91.7	0.4	95.3	3.9	98.0	2.8	99.6	1.6	100.1	0.5	99.5	-0.6	98.1	-1.4	95.4	-2.8	92.4	-3.1
1993	91.0	-1.5	89.1	-2.1	89.4	0.3	92.5	3.5	95.9	3.7	96.5	0.6	94.9	-1.7	92.6	-2.4	94.0	1.5	95.6	1.7	98.7	3.2	98.6	-0.1
1994	99.3	0.7	98.2	-1.1	99.3	1.1	99.7	0.4	95.3	-4.4	94.0	-1.4	90.9	-3.3	92.1	1.3	94.9	3.0	95.9	1.1	95.2	-0.7	93.5	-1.8
1995	92.1	-1.5	91.6	-0.5	92.8	1.3	90.7	-2.3	90.8	0.1	89.9	-1.0	89.3	-0.7	92.3	3.4	94.1	2.0	98.0	4.1	100.7	2.8	101.4	0.7
1996	101.4	0.0	101.1	-0.3	99.9	-1.2	101.7	1.8	104.9	3.1	108.0	3.0	113.3	4.9	116.0	2.4	119.6	3.1	116.9	-2.3	109.1	-6.7	102.5	-6.0
1997	97.0	-5.4	97.8	0.8	98.7	0.9	97.6	-1.1	95.6	-2.0	91.0	-4.8	90.6	-0.4	93.7	3.4	97.0	3.5	98.4	1.4	103.0	4.7	104.7	1.7
1998	105.9	1.1	106.7	0.8	103.0	-3.5	101.4	-1.6	98.1	-3.3	104.1	6.1	105.9	1.7	115.8	9.3	123.3	6.5	127.7	3.6	130.5	2.2	132.4	1.5
1999	127.8	-3.5	113.4	-11.3	110.1	-2.9	93.4	-15.2	94.8	1.5	97.3	2.6	103.4	6.3	112.6	8.9	117.4	4.3	109.8	-6.5	104.6	-4.7	91.0	-13.0
2000	89.5	-1.6	88.6	-1.0	89.3	0.8	89.3	0.0	90.0	0.8	91.5	1.7	94.5	3.3	93.8	-0.7	96.1	2.5	93.8	-2.4	90.1	-3.9	97.4	8.1
2001	98.1	0.7	97.5	-0.6	103.6	6.3	108.2	4.4	115.2	6.5	121.2	5.2	121.9	0.6	123.4	1.2	125.7	1.9	121.2	-3.6	106.6	-12.0	101.6	-4.7

Source: U.S. Department of Labor, Bureau of Labor Statistics, Division of Industry Prices and Price Indexes. n.e.c. stands for not elsewhere classified. - indicates no data collected for period or unavailable.

Chicken Eggs
Producer Price Index
Base 1982 = 100

For 1926-2001. Columns headed % show percentile change in the index from the previous period for which an index is available.

Year	Jan Index	%	Feb Index	%	Mar Index	%	Apr Index	%	May Index	%	Jun Index	%	Jul Index	%	Aug Index	%	Sep Index	%	Oct Index	%	Nov Index	%	Dec Index	%
1926	-	-	-	-	-	-	-	-	-	-	-	-	-	-	-	-	-	-	-	-	-	-	-	-
1927	-	-	-	-	-	-	-	-	-	-	-	-	-	-	-	-	-	-	-	-	-	-	-	-
1928	-	-	-	-	-	-	-	-	-	-	-	-	-	-	-	-	-	-	-	-	-	-	-	-
1929	-	-	-	-	-	-	-	-	-	-	-	-	-	-	-	-	-	-	-	-	-	-	-	-
1930	-	-	-	-	-	-	-	-	-	-	-	-	-	-	-	-	-	-	-	-	-	-	-	-
1931	-	-	-	-	-	-	-	-	-	-	-	-	-	-	-	-	-	-	-	-	-	-	-	-
1932	-	-	-	-	-	-	-	-	-	-	-	-	-	-	-	-	-	-	-	-	-	-	-	-
1933	-	-	-	-	-	-	-	-	-	-	-	-	-	-	-	-	-	-	-	-	-	-	-	-
1934	-	-	-	-	-	-	-	-	-	-	-	-	-	-	-	-	-	-	-	-	-	-	-	-
1935	-	-	-	-	-	-	-	-	-	-	-	-	-	-	-	-	-	-	-	-	-	-	-	-
1936	-	-	-	-	-	-	-	-	-	-	-	-	-	-	-	-	-	-	-	-	-	-	-	-
1937	48.1	-	43.1	-10.4	44.3	2.8	43.3	-2.3	39.9	-7.9	39.4	-1.3	41.4	5.1	42.1	1.7	46.7	10.9	47.3	1.3	52.7	11.4	50.0	-5.1
1938	43.3	-13.4	35.1	-18.9	34.9	-0.6	35.2	0.9	39.6	12.5	39.7	0.3	42.2	6.3	44.1	4.5	50.5	14.5	52.8	4.6	57.2	8.3	54.3	-5.1
1939	38.6	-28.9	33.9	-12.2	33.2	-2.1	32.8	-1.2	31.7	-3.4	31.1	-1.9	31.8	2.3	32.0	0.6	37.3	16.6	40.9	9.7	46.8	14.4	39.3	-16.0
1940	40.7	3.6	43.4	6.6	33.2	-23.5	32.7	-1.5	32.7	0.0	31.4	-4.0	31.8	1.3	33.3	4.7	39.9	19.8	42.4	6.3	46.0	8.5	49.7	8.0
1941	37.8	-23.9	33.5	-11.4	36.1	7.8	42.5	17.7	44.5	4.7	49.3	10.8	51.8	5.1	54.1	4.4	57.7	6.7	61.0	5.7	69.4	13.8	66.7	-3.9
1942	65.0	-2.5	56.8	-12.6	54.6	-3.9	56.6	3.7	57.5	1.6	59.4	3.3	63.1	6.2	67.3	6.7	70.4	4.6	73.9	5.0	74.5	0.8	74.7	0.3
1943	74.0	-0.9	70.2	-5.1	72.9	3.8	71.6	-1.8	72.9	1.8	75.1	3.0	75.3	0.3	78.9	4.8	82.3	4.3	84.4	2.6	83.7	-0.8	80.2	-4.2
1944	72.6	-9.5	62.8	-13.5	60.2	-4.1	58.5	-2.8	57.5	-1.7	60.7	5.6	66.3	9.2	64.5	-2.7	70.3	9.0	74.5	6.0	82.4	10.6	83.8	1.7
1945	75.8	-9.5	68.2	-10.0	66.8	-2.1	67.0	0.3	67.0	0.0	68.3	1.9	69.9	2.3	74.0	5.9	67.5	-8.8	79.7	18.1	87.1	9.3	85.9	-1.4
1946	70.8	-17.6	65.8	-7.1	65.7	-0.2	64.5	-1.8	65.9	2.2	65.5	-0.6	65.3	-0.3	67.8	3.8	78.6	15.9	83.2	5.9	77.9	-6.4	75.2	-3.5
1947	76.0	1.1	74.5	-2.0	80.8	8.5	82.7	2.4	80.5	-2.7	82.0	1.9	86.6	5.6	84.5	-2.4	91.7	8.5	91.9	0.2	89.0	-3.2	100.7	13.1
1948	86.2	-14.4	83.3	-3.4	82.9	-0.5	83.3	0.5	81.9	-1.7	84.3	2.9	87.2	3.4	95.9	10.0	101.6	5.9	112.4	10.6	110.5	-1.7	96.5	-12.7
1949	85.1	-11.8	77.1	-9.4	79.8	3.5	85.6	7.3	86.0	0.5	87.2	1.4	95.2	9.2	100.6	5.7	108.7	8.1	101.2	-6.9	90.9	-10.2	67.9	-25.3
1950	58.9	-13.3	59.9	1.7	65.0	8.5	62.3	-4.2	58.5	-6.1	62.6	7.0	71.2	13.7	75.5	6.0	88.5	17.2	97.0	9.6	101.8	4.9	102.5	0.7
1951	79.9	-22.0	80.3	0.5	85.6	6.6	85.8	0.2	89.1	3.8	94.1	5.6	94.2	0.1	106.2	12.7	111.4	4.9	115.1	3.3	116.6	1.3	90.3	-22.6
1952	71.6	-20.7	65.9	-8.0	67.9	3.0	72.4	6.6	65.9	-9.0	71.8	9.0	100.1	39.4	101.2	1.1	99.8	-1.4	110.6	10.8	104.3	-5.7	88.3	-15.3
1953	83.3	-5.7	79.0	-5.2	89.2	12.9	90.9	1.9	87.5	-3.7	94.5	8.0	94.2	-0.3	100.9	7.1	108.6	7.6	112.0	3.1	99.0	-11.6	86.2	-12.9
1954	82.2	-4.6	79.5	-3.3	71.0	-10.7	69.1	-2.7	61.2	-11.4	62.8	2.6	74.8	19.1	76.6	2.4	68.5	-10.6	73.1	6.7	74.0	1.2	56.7	-23.4
1955	57.7	1.8	79.9	38.5	72.9	-8.8	69.1	-5.2	63.4	-8.2	66.0	4.1	69.8	5.8	84.6	21.2	91.3	7.9	82.1	-10.1	87.7	6.8	88.0	0.3
1956	76.2	-13.4	72.1	-5.4	75.3	4.4	70.8	-6.0	71.1	0.4	69.8	-1.8	72.8	4.3	68.9	-5.4	80.9	17.4	77.4	-4.3	70.3	-9.2	65.9	-6.3
1957	58.3	-11.5	58.8	0.9	56.6	-3.7	60.7	7.2	51.0	-16.0	54.1	6.1	67.6	25.0	70.7	4.6	80.9	14.4	91.8	13.5	88.7	-3.4	82.8	-6.7
1958	65.5	-20.9	65.8	0.5	83.0	26.1	68.4	-17.6	67.1	-1.9	66.4	-1.0	67.5	1.7	72.3	7.1	87.4	20.9	80.8	-7.6	76.7	-5.1	68.9	-10.2
1959	64.2	-6.8	61.4	-4.4	62.5	1.8	48.3	-22.7	45.3	-6.2	50.1	10.6	58.0	15.8	59.2	2.1	75.7	27.9	61.2	-19.2	56.2	-8.2	55.7	-0.9
1960	50.5	-9.3	51.8	2.6	67.3	29.9	71.1	5.6	61.7	-13.2	57.0	-7.6	58.0	1.8	67.8	16.9	75.8	11.8	87.7	15.7	95.9	9.4	77.8	-18.9
1961	66.7	-14.3	72.0	7.9	67.1	-6.8	58.9	-12.2	56.2	-4.6	56.2	0.0	67.0	19.2	71.6	6.9	67.9	-5.2	70.5	3.8	71.0	0.7	63.7	-10.3
1962	65.0	2.0	64.7	-0.5	60.3	-6.8	60.9	1.0	50.0	-17.9	53.1	6.2	57.2	7.7	65.1	13.8	73.5	12.9	68.4	-6.9	74.6	9.1	65.9	-11.7
1963	66.4	0.8	65.8	-0.9	66.3	0.8	53.9	-18.7	51.2	-5.0	52.6	2.7	58.1	10.5	63.7	9.6	71.6	12.4	65.0	-9.2	68.0	4.6	66.3	-2.5
1964	70.6	6.5	59.5	-15.7	60.1	1.0	52.8	-12.1	51.0	-3.4	58.9	15.5	58.0	-1.5	65.5	12.9	64.3	-1.8	64.9	0.9	60.8	-6.3	56.6	-6.9
1965	52.4	-7.4	50.9	-2.9	57.7	13.4	60.5	4.9	52.4	-13.4	54.4	3.8	56.2	3.3	66.4	18.1	70.3	5.9	69.8	-0.7	75.7	8.5	78.5	3.7
1966	66.3	-15.5	77.2	16.4	78.7	1.9	67.6	-14.1	57.7	-14.6	60.3	4.5	65.4	8.5	72.1	10.2	84.9	17.8	76.2	-10.2	80.9	6.2	72.4	-10.5
1967	66.4	-8.3	55.7	-16.1	60.3	8.3	51.1	-15.3	49.5	-3.1	50.5	2.0	57.1	13.1	54.5	-4.6	61.8	13.4	51.0	-17.5	53.6	5.1	60.3	12.5
1968	49.0	-18.7	53.1	8.4	53.7	1.1	54.9	2.2	48.2	-12.2	58.6	21.6	60.7	3.6	65.3	7.6	84.1	28.8	70.7	-15.9	71.4	1.0	78.2	9.5
1969	81.2	3.8	71.7	-11.7	73.6	2.6	64.6	-12.2	53.5	-17.2	57.0	6.5	77.7	36.3	66.7	-14.2	81.3	21.9	75.5	-7.1	92.8	22.9	103.4	11.4
1970	101.0	-2.3	90.9	-10.0	79.7	-12.3	63.0	-21.0	52.9	-16.0	56.6	7.0	73.8	30.4	59.5	-19.4	78.1	31.3	58.5	-25.1	65.9	12.6	71.2	8.0

[Continued]

Chicken Eggs
Producer Price Index
Base 1982 = 100
[Continued]

For 1926-2001. Columns headed % show percentile change in the index from the previous period for which an index is available.

Year	Jan Index	%	Feb Index	%	Mar Index	%	Apr Index	%	May Index	%	Jun Index	%	Jul Index	%	Aug Index	%	Sep Index	%	Oct Index	%	Nov Index	%	Dec Index	%
1971	63.4	-11.0	54.6	-13.9	56.6	3.7	58.4	3.2	51.7	-11.5	54.8	6.0	50.0	-8.8	61.6	23.2	60.3	-2.1	51.7	-14.3	49.5	-4.3	64.0	29.3
1972	51.8	-19.1	51.4	-0.8	60.3	17.3	48.8	-19.1	50.7	3.9	51.4	1.4	57.2	11.3	55.6	-2.8	64.3	15.6	55.4	-13.8	68.9	24.4	80.5	16.8
1973	88.5	9.9	72.8	-17.7	85.4	17.3	81.1	-5.0	76.7	-5.4	89.2	16.3	86.9	-2.6	117.3	35.0	107.2	-8.6	99.4	-7.3	101.4	2.0	106.6	5.1
1974	110.7	3.8	104.5	-5.6	93.9	-10.1	88.8	-5.4	70.5	-20.6	69.8	-1.0	73.8	5.7	83.7	13.4	95.0	13.5	93.9	-1.2	92.3	-1.7	101.3	9.8
1975	94.4	-6.8	90.9	-3.7	93.0	2.3	78.3	-15.8	81.4	4.0	77.1	-5.3	78.2	1.4	87.7	12.1	97.6	11.3	88.6	-9.2	98.4	11.1	107.6	9.3
1976	101.9	-5.3	99.0	-2.8	89.1	-10.0	91.0	2.1	96.0	5.5	92.8	-3.3	93.9	1.2	104.5	11.3	105.7	1.1	101.1	-4.4	107.9	6.7	119.5	10.8
1977	105.9	-11.4	109.0	2.9	97.1	-10.9	92.4	-4.8	80.8	-12.6	79.1	-2.1	87.6	10.7	90.7	3.5	91.4	0.8	77.0	-15.8	83.6	8.6	93.1	11.4
1978	81.2	-12.8	95.3	17.4	93.6	-1.8	85.2	-9.0	79.0	-7.3	71.3	-9.7	84.1	18.0	88.4	5.1	93.9	6.2	87.5	-6.8	99.6	13.8	105.7	6.1
1979	99.9	-5.5	98.9	-1.0	111.9	13.1	103.8	-7.2	91.7	-11.7	95.5	4.1	93.8	-1.8	93.3	-0.5	98.1	5.1	87.2	-11.1	100.0	14.7	111.0	11.0
1980	92.6	-16.6	84.2	-9.1	103.1	22.4	85.8	-16.8	78.6	-8.4	82.1	4.5	89.2	8.6	99.0	11.0	105.4	6.5	98.0	-7.0	108.6	10.8	121.7	12.1
1981	103.9	-14.6	103.4	-0.5	100.9	-2.4	109.8	8.8	92.3	-15.9	97.7	5.9	103.5	5.9	101.1	-2.3	108.1	6.9	108.4	0.3	117.3	8.2	109.4	-6.7
1982	104.7	-4.3	112.2	7.2	114.2	1.8	107.5	-5.9	91.9	-14.5	89.1	-3.0	96.1	7.9	96.1	0.0	97.0	0.9	99.5	2.6	96.5	-3.0	95.1	-1.5
1983	95.1	0.0	95.1	0.0	95.1	0.0	95.1	0.0	103.6	8.9	94.7	-8.6	99.2	4.8	106.0	6.9	112.0	5.7	-		-		-	
1984	158.0	41.1	157.1	-0.6	132.0	-16.0	147.9	12.0	112.5	-23.9	99.5	-11.6	103.5	4.0	101.4	-2.0	99.4	-2.0	100.7	1.3	98.5	-2.2	104.9	6.5
1985	79.4	-24.3	90.4	13.9	93.8	3.8	98.0	4.5	84.0	-14.3	82.7	-1.5	91.8	11.0	94.5	2.9	105.4	11.5	106.9	1.4	109.2	2.2	111.9	2.5
1986	107.2	-4.2	98.5	-8.1	101.9	3.5	94.9	-6.9	90.7	-4.4	83.4	-8.0	93.6	12.2	107.1	14.4	101.3	-5.4	97.1	-4.1	110.4	13.7	108.5	-1.7
1987	99.0	-8.8	98.2	-0.8	89.7	-8.7	90.1	0.4	84.4	-6.3	80.1	-5.1	85.3	6.5	79.7	-6.6	100.6	26.2	81.1	-19.4	92.6	14.2	70.6	-23.8
1988	76.5	8.4	73.8	-3.5	79.7	8.0	73.1	-8.3	70.8	-3.1	77.1	8.9	95.7	24.1	107.0	11.8	102.1	-4.6	107.4	5.2	99.7	-7.2	100.3	0.6
1989	127.3	26.9	96.7	-24.0	135.8	40.4	110.8	-18.4	107.0	-3.4	104.8	-2.1	111.0	5.9	116.7	5.1	124.6	6.8	124.3	-0.2	134.5	8.2	141.3	5.1
1990	154.8	9.6	114.0	-26.4	128.9	13.1	127.9	-0.8	95.3	-25.5	100.4	5.4	91.6	-8.8	114.4	24.9	112.6	-1.6	121.6	8.0	125.0	2.8	124.5	-0.4
1991	140.0	12.4	110.5	-21.1	131.7	19.2	113.2	-14.0	94.6	-16.4	96.9	2.4	100.7	3.9	109.0	8.2	105.8	-2.9	105.0	-0.8	102.1	-2.8	118.7	16.3
1992	91.9	-22.6	94.1	2.4	92.8	-1.4	90.1	-2.9	86.4	-4.1	84.6	-2.1	83.9	-0.8	87.3	4.1	103.6	18.7	94.7	-8.6	112.4	18.7	107.7	-4.2
1993	102.9	-4.5	107.0	4.0	121.3	13.4	111.1	-8.4	101.6	-8.6	109.5	7.8	95.5	-12.8	110.5	15.7	93.2	-15.7	105.2	12.9	108.6	3.2	103.8	-4.4
1994	100.1	-3.6	109.1	9.0	112.3	2.9	99.0	-11.8	84.2	-14.9	91.1	8.2	89.3	-2.0	100.1	12.1	98.8	-1.3	89.2	-9.7	100.5	12.7	100.0	-0.5
1995	92.6	-7.4	95.8	3.5	97.1	1.4	97.1	0.0	85.4	-12.0	88.8	4.0	97.4	9.7	99.2	1.8	108.9	9.8	111.1	2.0	136.9	23.2	138.8	1.4
1996	123.4	-11.1	126.7	2.7	138.5	9.3	132.1	-4.6	112.4	-14.9	119.2	6.0	116.7	-2.1	130.6	11.9	134.0	2.6	128.8	-3.9	143.9	11.7	161.8	12.4
1997	125.8	-22.2	129.4	2.9	119.7	-7.5	108.2	-9.6	106.2	-1.8	97.4	-8.3	117.7	20.8	107.7	-8.5	120.0	11.4	111.6	-7.0	148.5	33.1	136.2	-8.3
1998	117.4	-13.8	103.2	-12.1	118.5	14.8	99.5	-16.0	83.8	-15.8	100.7	20.2	95.2	-5.5	107.7	13.1	107.4	-0.3	111.7	4.0	124.6	11.5	121.5	-2.5
1999	109.7	-9.7	98.2	-10.5	104.9	6.8	85.3	-18.7	77.1	-9.6	80.8	4.8	80.7	-0.1	95.7	18.6	87.7	-8.4	68.8	-21.6	101.7	47.8	82.1	-19.3
2000	89.5	9.0	112.3	25.5	79.6	-29.1	98.5	23.7	73.8	-25.1	94.5	28.0	80.9	-14.4	108.6	34.2	92.4	-14.9	109.1	18.1	112.1	2.7	122.3	9.1
2001	108.8	-11.0	104.3	-4.1	103.0	-1.2	117.4	14.0	81.0	-31.0	79.1	-2.3	82.0	3.7	87.0	6.1	81.8	-6.0	86.5	5.7	103.3	19.4	89.7	-13.2

Source: U.S. Department of Labor, Bureau of Labor Statistics, Division of Industry Prices and Price Indexes. n.e.c. stands for not elsewhere classified. - indicates no data collected for period or unavailable.

Hay, Hayseeds and Oilseeds
Producer Price Index
Base 1982 = 100

For 1926-2001. Columns headed % show percentile change in the index from the previous period for which an index is available.

Year	Jan Index	%	Feb Index	%	Mar Index	%	Apr Index	%	May Index	%	Jun Index	%	Jul Index	%	Aug Index	%	Sep Index	%	Oct Index	%	Nov Index	%	Dec Index	%
1926	30.9	-	30.1	-2.6	30.1	0.0	31.9	6.0	31.3	-1.9	27.5	-12.1	28.2	2.5	28.7	1.8	29.0	1.0	28.8	-0.7	28.7	-0.3	28.9	0.7
1927	28.9	0.0	28.6	-1.0	27.6	-3.5	27.4	-0.7	27.3	-0.4	25.1	-8.1	24.0	-4.4	24.9	3.8	24.8	-0.4	25.3	2.0	24.8	-2.0	26.0	4.8
1928	27.0	3.8	26.9	-0.4	28.3	5.2	29.6	4.6	30.5	3.0	27.4	-10.2	26.9	-1.8	27.3	1.5	28.4	4.0	30.2	6.3	31.3	3.6	32.0	2.2
1929	33.1	3.4	33.3	0.6	33.1	-0.6	32.8	-0.9	30.1	-8.2	27.0	-10.3	27.3	1.1	28.1	2.9	29.7	5.7	30.8	3.7	30.4	-1.3	29.8	-2.0
1930	29.7	-0.3	28.7	-3.4	28.2	-1.7	29.0	2.8	28.4	-2.1	25.8	-9.2	25.6	-0.8	27.9	9.0	27.5	-1.4	27.6	0.4	27.6	0.0	26.7	-3.3
1931	25.8	-3.4	24.9	-3.5	24.5	-1.6	24.6	0.4	23.1	-6.1	20.3	-12.1	19.9	-2.0	18.4	-7.5	17.9	-2.7	17.3	-3.4	17.7	2.3	18.4	4.0
1932	18.3	-0.5	17.4	-4.9	18.0	3.4	18.0	0.0	16.2	-10.0	13.9	-14.2	13.5	-2.9	13.7	1.5	13.7	0.0	14.1	2.9	14.1	0.0	13.8	-2.1
1933	13.7	-0.7	13.3	-2.9	13.7	3.0	14.2	3.6	15.6	9.9	15.3	-1.9	16.5	7.8	17.9	8.5	18.0	0.6	17.5	-2.8	17.7	1.1	18.2	2.8
1934	18.8	3.3	19.2	2.1	19.2	0.0	19.7	2.6	20.0	1.5	21.2	6.0	23.3	9.9	26.4	13.3	28.3	7.2	27.6	-2.5	27.0	-2.2	28.3	4.8
1935	28.9	2.1	28.6	-1.0	28.1	-1.7	27.3	-2.8	26.0	-4.8	23.1	-11.2	19.8	-14.3	18.0	-9.1	18.6	3.3	19.3	3.8	19.4	0.5	19.1	-1.5
1936	19.3	1.0	19.3	0.0	18.9	-2.1	20.0	5.8	19.4	-3.0	18.4	-5.2	22.0	19.6	25.0	13.6	25.8	3.2	26.2	1.6	27.3	4.2	27.9	2.2
1937	28.9	3.6	28.9	0.0	28.4	-1.7	28.7	1.1	27.1	-5.6	25.6	-5.5	24.7	-3.5	24.8	0.4	25.5	2.8	26.4	3.5	26.0	-1.5	26.5	1.9
1938	26.8	1.1	26.4	-1.5	25.6	-3.0	24.7	-3.5	23.9	-3.2	22.4	-6.3	22.1	-1.3	20.5	-7.2	18.3	-10.7	19.1	4.4	19.5	2.1	20.1	3.1
1939	21.2	5.5	20.7	-2.4	20.8	0.5	20.7	-0.5	19.9	-3.9	19.6	-1.5	19.0	-3.1	21.5	13.2	20.6	-4.2	21.6	4.9	21.7	0.5	21.9	0.9
1940	22.3	1.8	22.4	0.4	22.1	-1.3	22.0	-0.5	21.8	-0.9	19.9	-8.7	19.4	-2.5	19.7	1.5	18.8	-4.6	18.8	0.0	19.0	1.1	19.4	2.1
1941	19.9	2.6	19.9	0.0	19.7	-1.0	19.9	1.0	20.3	2.0	20.6	1.5	20.9	1.5	21.2	1.4	22.3	5.2	23.5	5.4	25.3	7.7	26.5	4.7
1942	28.1	6.0	29.2	3.9	30.5	4.5	30.9	1.3	30.5	-1.3	29.7	-2.6	29.8	0.3	29.6	-0.7	29.4	-0.7	29.7	1.0	30.4	2.4	31.6	3.9
1943	32.8	3.8	34.3	4.6	35.5	3.5	36.4	2.5	36.5	0.3	34.9	-4.4	34.8	-0.3	34.9	0.3	36.4	4.3	38.9	6.9	41.5	6.7	42.2	1.7
1944	42.1	-0.2	41.7	-1.0	41.0	-1.7	41.0	0.0	41.6	1.5	38.6	-7.2	37.9	-1.8	38.1	0.5	38.7	1.6	41.4	7.0	42.1	1.7	42.2	0.2
1945	43.2	2.4	43.8	1.4	43.5	-0.7	41.8	-3.9	39.2	-6.2	39.4	0.5	39.1	-0.8	37.6	-3.8	37.7	0.3	38.3	1.6	39.7	3.7	39.7	0.0
1946	39.8	0.3	39.6	-0.5	40.4	2.0	40.2	-0.5	40.2	0.0	40.4	0.5	41.1	1.7	41.4	0.7	42.0	1.4	46.7	11.2	54.3	16.3	55.3	1.8
1947	55.7	0.7	55.8	0.2	61.8	10.8	60.2	-2.6	51.8	-14.0	50.9	-1.7	50.9	0.0	50.3	-1.2	51.7	2.8	55.7	7.7	58.8	5.6	61.7	4.9
1948	64.3	4.2	58.6	-8.9	59.4	1.4	60.9	2.5	61.7	1.3	62.1	0.6	59.5	-4.2	53.7	-9.7	51.7	-3.7	49.2	-4.8	50.8	3.3	50.9	0.2
1949	49.3	-3.1	45.9	-6.9	45.3	-1.3	44.7	-1.3	42.2	-5.6	40.8	-3.3	41.0	0.5	45.3	10.5	41.0	-9.5	40.4	-1.5	40.8	1.0	41.7	2.2
1950	42.1	1.0	41.5	-1.4	48.3	16.4	45.0	-6.8	45.3	0.7	45.4	0.2	46.5	2.4	48.1	3.4	46.7	-2.9	45.6	-2.4	51.1	12.1	53.3	4.3
1951	55.6	4.3	57.3	3.1	57.7	0.7	57.3	-0.7	56.3	-1.7	53.2	-5.5	49.7	-6.6	48.4	-2.6	48.5	0.2	50.2	3.5	52.4	4.4	52.9	1.0
1952	52.7	-0.4	52.4	-0.6	50.3	-4.0	49.5	-1.6	49.8	0.6	51.1	2.6	52.1	2.0	51.8	-0.6	50.0	-3.5	50.1	0.2	51.1	2.0	51.0	-0.2
1953	50.4	-1.2	49.2	-2.4	50.6	2.8	49.4	-2.4	48.6	-1.6	46.5	-4.3	44.4	-4.5	44.1	-0.7	42.1	-4.5	43.7	3.8	45.6	4.3	46.5	2.0
1954	46.9	0.9	47.5	1.3	48.4	1.9	50.0	3.3	49.4	-1.2	49.8	0.8	49.2	-1.2	48.8	-0.8	45.3	-7.2	47.6	5.1	47.7	0.2	48.6	1.9
1955	48.9	0.6	48.4	-1.0	48.3	-0.2	46.6	-3.5	46.0	-1.3	45.7	-0.7	44.4	-2.8	42.3	-4.7	38.9	-8.0	39.3	1.0	39.3	0.0	40.2	2.3
1956	40.9	1.7	41.7	2.0	42.8	2.6	45.0	5.1	46.7	3.8	45.3	-3.0	41.8	-7.7	41.5	-0.7	39.7	-4.3	40.7	2.5	43.6	7.1	44.3	1.6
1957	44.9	1.4	43.9	-2.2	44.1	0.5	44.2	0.2	43.8	-0.9	43.2	-1.4	42.7	-1.2	42.2	-1.2	40.4	-4.3	40.1	-0.7	40.2	0.2	40.7	1.2
1958	41.0	0.7	41.0	0.0	41.2	0.5	41.4	0.5	41.4	0.0	41.1	-0.7	39.5	-3.9	39.3	-0.5	37.4	-4.8	38.0	1.6	38.3	0.8	38.9	1.6
1959	39.6	1.8	40.4	2.0	40.7	0.7	41.2	1.2	41.6	1.0	40.4	-2.9	38.9	-3.7	37.9	-2.6	37.9	0.0	39.1	3.2	39.6	1.3	39.6	0.0
1960	40.2	1.5	40.0	-0.5	39.8	-0.5	39.6	-0.5	39.7	0.3	38.6	-2.8	38.1	-1.3	38.2	0.3	37.5	-1.8	37.4	-0.3	37.6	0.5	38.4	2.1
1961	41.2	7.3	42.2	2.4	45.3	7.3	50.0	10.4	47.7	-4.6	43.4	-9.0	43.4	0.0	43.0	-0.9	41.5	-3.5	41.4	-0.2	42.2	1.9	42.3	0.2
1962	42.4	0.2	42.6	0.5	43.0	0.9	43.8	1.9	43.8	0.0	43.3	-1.1	42.9	-0.9	42.9	0.0	40.7	-5.1	42.0	3.2	43.5	3.6	44.1	1.4
1963	45.6	3.4	46.2	1.3	46.3	0.2	45.1	-2.6	45.8	1.6	46.3	1.1	45.3	-2.2	45.3	0.0	45.0	-0.7	46.5	3.3	47.8	2.8	46.7	-2.3
1964	47.0	0.6	46.4	-1.3	45.1	-2.8	43.8	-2.9	42.7	-2.5	42.8	0.2	43.0	0.5	43.1	0.2	44.3	2.8	45.2	2.0	47.1	4.2	47.5	0.8
1965	48.5	2.1	49.1	1.2	48.5	-1.2	48.6	0.2	47.0	-3.3	46.7	-0.6	46.3	-0.9	43.4	-6.3	42.9	-1.2	41.8	-2.6	43.7	4.5	45.1	3.2
1966	46.2	2.4	47.5	2.8	47.1	-0.8	47.6	1.1	49.0	2.9	49.9	1.8	55.1	10.4	56.7	2.9	51.4	-9.3	49.5	-3.7	50.0	1.0	50.7	1.4
1967	50.3	-0.8	49.0	-2.6	49.1	0.2	48.2	-1.8	48.0	-0.4	47.5	-1.0	47.2	-0.6	45.4	-3.8	44.4	-2.2	44.2	-0.5	44.7	1.1	45.9	2.7
1968	46.0	0.2	46.0	0.0	46.5	1.1	46.4	-0.2	46.5	0.2	46.0	-1.1	46.1	0.2	46.0	-0.2	44.6	-3.0	42.9	-3.8	43.7	1.9	44.3	1.4
1969	45.4	2.5	45.8	0.9	45.8	0.0	46.3	1.1	46.9	1.3	45.0	-4.1	45.3	0.7	43.7	-3.5	43.1	-1.4	41.2	-4.4	42.1	2.2	42.8	1.7
1970	43.8	2.3	43.3	-1.1	43.3	0.0	44.7	3.2	45.3	1.3	45.9	1.3	47.6	3.7	47.5	-0.2	48.2	1.5	50.1	3.9	50.8	1.4	50.2	-1.2

[Continued]

Hay, Hayseeds and Oilseeds
Producer Price Index
Base 1982 = 100
[Continued]

For 1926-2001. Columns headed % show percentile change in the index from the previous period for which an index is available.

Year	Jan Index	%	Feb Index	%	Mar Index	%	Apr Index	%	May Index	%	Jun Index	%	Jul Index	%	Aug Index	%	Sep Index	%	Oct Index	%	Nov Index	%	Dec Index	%
1971	51.1	1.8	51.0	-0.2	50.5	-1.0	49.2	-2.6	50.1	1.8	51.6	3.0	53.7	4.1	53.7	0.0	51.1	-4.8	50.7	-0.8	51.4	1.4	51.3	-0.2
1972	51.1	-0.4	51.8	1.4	53.7	3.7	55.7	3.7	54.9	-1.4	54.9	0.0	54.9	0.0	54.5	-0.7	55.4	1.7	54.0	-2.5	58.6	8.5	66.5	13.5
1973	67.6	1.7	83.7	23.8	88.4	5.6	87.8	-0.7	114.2	30.1	140.9	23.4	88.1	-37.5	138.0	56.6	143.1	3.7	99.2	-30.7	91.3	-8.0	98.9	8.3
1974	101.9	3.0	102.5	0.6	102.9	0.4	92.3	-10.3	91.4	-1.0	89.9	-1.6	101.5	12.9	124.4	22.6	117.1	-5.9	126.9	8.4	122.7	-3.3	115.5	-5.9
1975	109.2	-5.5	99.4	-9.0	91.6	-7.8	100.6	9.8	94.1	-6.5	89.4	-5.0	96.2	7.6	100.2	4.2	93.2	-7.0	88.6	-4.9	83.3	-6.0	83.4	0.1
1976	85.3	2.3	86.7	1.6	84.9	-2.1	84.6	-0.4	89.0	5.2	103.1	15.8	112.0	8.6	105.5	-5.8	108.9	3.2	103.4	-5.1	109.0	5.4	113.9	4.5
1977	115.1	1.1	119.6	3.9	130.6	9.2	151.5	16.0	136.2	-10.1	127.0	-6.8	97.6	-23.1	92.1	-5.6	83.8	-9.0	84.0	0.2	90.9	8.2	92.5	1.8
1978	93.3	0.9	90.0	-3.5	98.5	9.4	101.8	3.4	103.2	1.4	103.6	0.4	104.6	1.0	101.2	-3.3	99.9	-1.3	104.0	4.1	107.0	2.9	110.0	2.8
1979	112.8	2.5	115.7	2.6	117.2	1.3	116.7	-0.4	113.1	-3.1	121.4	7.3	122.2	0.7	118.4	-3.1	113.2	-4.4	110.7	-2.2	108.0	-2.4	108.2	0.2
1980	102.5	-5.3	105.6	3.0	101.5	-3.9	96.4	-5.0	97.2	0.8	97.5	0.3	118.1	21.1	122.9	4.1	131.9	7.3	133.7	1.4	140.2	4.9	145.8	4.0
1981	146.5	0.5	138.6	-5.4	136.1	-1.8	139.2	2.3	140.5	0.9	134.1	-4.6	136.3	1.6	133.6	-2.0	125.5	-6.1	108.3	-13.7	103.9	-4.1	102.8	-1.1
1982	102.6	-0.2	102.3	-0.3	100.4	-1.9	104.7	4.3	106.8	2.0	103.1	-3.5	103.4	0.3	96.1	-7.1	94.8	-1.4	91.3	-3.7	96.2	5.4	98.2	2.1
1983	99.8	1.6	102.4	2.6	102.4	0.0	106.4	3.9	106.8	0.4	100.2	-6.2	106.8	6.6	123.5	15.6	139.9	13.3	135.7	-3.0	135.2	-0.4	132.6	-1.9
1984	135.0	1.8	124.7	-7.6	132.2	6.0	132.6	0.3	139.6	5.3	128.0	-8.3	115.5	-9.8	114.0	-1.3	107.3	-5.9	103.0	-4.0	106.8	3.7	106.9	0.1
1985	106.3	-0.6	100.8	-5.2	99.6	-1.2	100.5	0.9	100.3	-0.2	99.0	-1.3	97.2	-1.8	92.5	-4.8	91.3	-1.3	86.8	-4.9	94.0	8.3	93.7	-0.3
1986	94.3	0.6	95.2	1.0	96.0	0.8	91.1	-5.1	91.4	0.3	95.2	4.2	93.7	-1.6	89.4	-4.6	89.2	-0.2	88.0	-1.3	98.4	11.8	93.5	-5.0
1987	94.0	0.5	95.6	1.7	95.4	-0.2	97.7	2.4	104.3	6.8	106.4	2.0	105.1	-1.2	101.9	-3.0	99.7	-2.2	101.0	1.3	104.9	3.9	110.7	5.5
1988	113.7	2.7	114.7	0.9	114.2	-0.4	121.8	6.7	127.8	4.9	150.3	17.6	154.3	2.7	159.2	3.2	163.5	2.7	151.0	-7.6	142.8	-5.4	147.9	3.6
1989	153.2	3.6	144.2	-5.9	149.2	3.5	142.1	-4.8	149.7	5.3	143.8	-3.9	140.3	-2.4	129.8	-7.5	128.3	-1.2	118.2	-7.9	121.0	2.4	124.2	2.6
1990	121.0	-2.6	122.4	1.2	122.0	-0.3	122.6	0.5	116.8	-4.7	118.3	1.3	124.0	4.8	118.7	-4.3	121.4	2.3	128.3	5.7	123.1	-4.1	126.2	2.5
1991	121.3	-3.9	121.9	0.5	117.9	-3.3	116.1	-1.5	110.7	-4.7	114.4	3.3	104.5	-8.7	107.8	3.2	110.3	2.3	106.1	-3.8	106.8	0.7	106.8	0.0
1992	109.2	2.2	107.8	-1.3	111.7	3.6	109.3	-2.1	117.8	7.8	121.3	3.0	111.0	-8.5	107.2	-3.4	109.3	2.0	106.8	-2.3	109.0	2.1	114.5	5.0
1993	116.6	1.8	114.9	-1.5	118.3	3.0	123.2	4.1	128.1	4.0	119.7	-6.6	134.7	12.5	129.4	-3.9	127.3	-1.6	126.1	-0.9	132.9	5.4	142.7	7.4
1994	141.7	-0.7	141.7	0.0	144.7	2.1	143.3	-1.0	138.4	-3.4	141.8	2.5	130.0	-8.3	121.3	-6.7	122.4	0.9	117.2	-4.2	122.5	4.5	123.3	0.7
1995	121.2	-1.7	120.2	-0.8	119.3	-0.7	121.6	1.9	117.3	-3.5	117.4	0.1	120.5	2.6	114.2	-5.2	123.9	8.5	128.8	4.0	132.0	2.5	138.0	4.5
1996	141.3	2.4	138.0	-2.3	139.4	1.0	149.2	7.0	155.2	4.0	149.0	-4.0	149.9	0.6	155.9	4.0	158.1	1.4	140.4	-11.2	140.1	-0.2	138.9	-0.9
1997	147.6	6.3	149.6	1.4	164.2	9.8	164.4	0.1	170.4	3.6	161.5	-5.2	156.2	-3.3	145.4	-6.9	142.2	-2.2	142.5	0.2	146.8	3.0	140.7	-4.2
1998	136.6	-2.9	139.5	2.1	135.9	-2.6	131.7	-3.1	135.0	2.5	127.3	-5.7	130.4	2.4	115.9	-11.1	112.4	-3.0	113.8	1.2	117.8	3.5	113.9	-3.3
1999	112.0	-1.7	103.5	-7.6	102.2	-1.3	105.0	2.7	107.9	2.8	103.2	-4.4	94.4	-8.5	99.8	5.7	99.5	-0.3	97.5	-2.0	97.1	-0.4	95.9	-1.2
2000	98.3	2.5	103.6	5.4	106.8	3.1	107.4	0.6	115.0	7.1	108.1	-6.0	102.4	-5.3	99.4	-2.9	104.7	5.3	103.2	-1.4	103.5	0.3	107.7	4.1
2001	106.8	-0.8	101.7	-4.8	101.9	0.2	101.5	-0.4	108.8	7.2	108.4	-0.4	114.1	5.3	115.2	1.0	108.7	-5.6	106.0	-2.5	105.2	-0.8	102.9	-2.2

Source: U.S. Department of Labor, Bureau of Labor Statistics, Division of Industry Prices and Price Indexes. n.e.c. stands for not elsewhere classified. - indicates no data collected for period or unavailable.

Other Farm Products

Producer Price Index
Base 1982 = 100

For 1926-2001. Columns headed % show percentile change in the index from the previous period for which an index is available.

Year	Jan Index	%	Feb Index	%	Mar Index	%	Apr Index	%	May Index	%	Jun Index	%	Jul Index	%	Aug Index	%	Sep Index	%	Oct Index	%	Nov Index	%	Dec Index	%
1926	15.7	-	14.6	-7.0	12.8	-12.3	11.8	-7.8	12.3	4.2	12.5	1.6	12.6	0.8	12.6	0.0	12.9	2.4	12.9	0.0	13.6	5.4	14.2	4.4
1927	14.0	-1.4	12.9	-7.9	12.9	0.0	11.4	-11.6	11.0	-3.5	11.4	3.6	11.8	3.5	14.2	20.3	14.2	0.0	13.5	-4.9	13.3	-1.5	16.9	27.1
1928	18.1	7.1	16.8	-7.2	14.5	-13.7	14.4	-0.7	14.3	-0.7	12.4	-13.3	13.3	7.3	14.3	7.5	12.8	-10.5	14.3	11.7	13.3	-7.0	19.1	43.6
1929	20.3	6.3	18.0	-11.3	18.4	2.2	14.5	-21.2	14.2	-2.1	13.0	-8.5	12.8	-1.5	13.0	1.6	13.0	0.0	12.7	-2.3	11.9	-6.3	10.8	-9.2
1930	10.4	-3.7	10.2	-1.9	10.2	0.0	10.2	0.0	10.0	-2.0	9.9	-1.0	9.8	-1.0	9.6	-2.0	9.4	-2.1	9.5	1.1	8.7	-8.4	8.1	-6.9
1931	7.5	-7.4	7.3	-2.7	6.9	-5.5	6.8	-1.4	7.0	2.9	7.1	1.4	7.1	0.0	6.8	-4.2	6.6	-2.9	6.5	-1.5	6.5	0.0	6.3	-3.1
1932	5.9	-6.3	5.8	-1.7	5.8	0.0	5.9	1.7	5.9	0.0	5.8	-1.7	5.8	0.0	6.2	6.9	7.0	12.9	6.5	-7.1	6.1	-6.2	6.2	1.6
1933	6.2	0.0	6.3	1.6	6.3	0.0	6.2	-1.6	6.4	3.2	6.4	0.0	6.5	1.6	6.5	0.0	6.5	0.0	6.7	3.1	7.1	6.0	7.3	2.8
1934	7.6	4.1	7.9	3.9	7.9	0.0	7.8	-1.3	7.8	0.0	7.8	0.0	7.6	-2.6	8.0	5.3	8.5	6.3	9.2	8.2	9.4	2.2	9.4	0.0
1935	9.8	4.3	9.9	1.0	9.8	-1.0	9.7	-1.0	9.6	-1.0	9.5	-1.0	9.5	0.0	9.3	-2.1	8.9	-4.3	9.2	1.1	9.5	3.3	8.3	-1.2
1936	8.5	2.4	8.6	1.2	8.5	-1.2	8.4	-1.2	8.4	0.0	8.6	2.4	8.8	2.3	8.8	0.0	9.1	3.4	9.2	1.1	9.5	3.3	10.3	8.4
1937	10.9	5.8	11.1	1.8	11.0	-0.9	10.9	-0.9	10.8	-0.9	10.7	-0.9	10.7	0.0	10.8	0.9	10.7	-0.9	10.8	0.9	10.2	-5.6	9.8	-3.9
1938	9.2	-6.1	9.0	-2.2	8.9	-1.1	8.7	-2.2	8.7	0.0	8.7	0.0	8.9	2.3	9.1	2.2	9.1	0.0	9.0	-1.1	8.9	-1.1	8.8	-1.1
1939	8.8	0.0	8.9	1.1	8.7	-2.2	8.6	-1.1	8.6	0.0	8.6	0.0	8.6	0.0	8.5	-1.2	8.3	-2.4	7.8	-6.0	8.1	3.8	7.9	-2.5
1940	7.9	0.0	7.8	-1.3	7.9	1.3	7.9	0.0	7.7	-2.5	7.6	-1.3	7.5	-1.3	7.4	-1.3	7.5	1.4	7.7	2.7	7.8	1.3	8.1	3.8
1941	8.0	-1.2	8.2	2.5	8.7	6.1	9.0	3.4	9.4	4.4	9.7	3.2	9.8	1.0	10.4	6.1	11.3	8.7	11.8	4.4	12.2	3.4	13.1	7.4
1942	14.1	7.6	14.2	0.7	14.1	-0.7	14.1	0.0	14.1	0.0	14.1	0.0	14.1	0.0	14.5	2.8	15.1	4.1	15.7	4.0	15.9	1.3	16.3	2.5
1943	16.6	1.8	16.2	-2.4	16.3	0.6	16.6	1.8	16.6	0.0	16.6	0.0	16.7	0.6	16.8	0.6	17.0	1.2	16.9	-0.6	17.0	0.6	17.2	1.2
1944	17.4	1.2	17.5	0.6	17.5	0.0	17.5	0.0	17.5	0.0	17.5	0.0	17.4	-0.6	17.5	0.6	17.7	1.1	17.6	-0.6	17.7	0.6	17.7	0.0
1945	17.2	-2.8	17.1	-0.6	17.1	0.0	17.1	0.0	17.2	0.6	17.2	0.0	17.2	0.0	17.3	0.6	17.3	0.0	17.4	0.6	17.4	0.0	17.5	0.6
1946	17.8	1.7	17.7	-0.6	17.7	0.0	17.7	0.0	17.7	0.0	17.7	0.0	19.3	9.0	19.9	3.1	20.3	2.0	22.2	9.4	23.8	7.2	24.8	4.2
1947	25.4	2.4	25.1	-1.2	25.5	1.6	25.0	-2.0	24.2	-3.2	24.8	2.5	25.1	1.2	25.4	1.2	24.9	-2.0	25.7	3.2	25.9	0.8	26.2	1.2
1948	26.1	-0.4	25.9	-0.8	25.5	-1.5	25.2	-1.2	25.2	0.0	25.6	1.6	25.8	0.8	26.4	2.3	26.9	1.9	27.7	3.0	27.8	0.4	27.2	-2.2
1949	26.5	-2.6	26.0	-1.9	25.8	-0.8	25.6	-0.8	25.9	1.2	26.0	0.4	26.3	1.2	26.5	0.8	26.6	0.4	27.9	4.9	31.8	14.0	32.9	3.5
1950	32.4	-1.5	32.1	-0.9	31.3	-2.5	31.5	0.6	31.1	-1.3	32.2	3.5	34.0	5.6	35.2	3.5	36.8	4.5	35.5	-3.5	35.1	-1.1	36.0	2.6
1951	36.9	2.5	37.1	0.5	36.8	-0.8	36.8	0.0	36.7	-0.3	36.5	-0.5	36.1	-1.1	35.8	-0.8	35.7	-0.3	36.5	2.2	35.6	-2.5	36.3	2.0
1952	36.2	-0.3	36.4	0.6	36.4	0.0	35.9	-1.4	36.0	0.3	35.9	-0.3	36.3	1.1	36.2	-0.3	35.9	-0.8	35.7	-0.6	34.8	-2.5	35.4	1.7
1953	35.0	-1.1	35.3	0.9	37.5	6.2	36.0	-4.0	35.6	-1.1	35.9	0.8	37.0	3.1	37.9	2.4	39.2	3.4	38.4	-2.0	38.3	-0.3	38.9	1.6
1954	42.3	8.7	44.2	4.5	47.6	7.7	47.9	0.6	47.6	-0.6	47.7	0.2	48.3	1.3	44.4	-8.1	43.3	-2.5	42.0	-3.0	43.3	3.1	41.5	-4.2
1955	41.1	-1.0	36.7	-10.7	37.6	2.5	37.4	-0.5	36.4	-2.7	37.6	3.3	36.2	-3.7	36.4	0.6	38.4	5.5	38.2	-0.5	36.8	-3.7	36.5	-0.8
1956	36.7	0.5	38.3	4.4	37.7	-1.6	37.7	0.0	38.0	0.8	38.7	1.8	39.2	1.3	39.7	1.3	40.2	1.3	39.4	-2.0	38.7	-1.8	38.9	0.5
1957	39.1	0.5	38.9	-0.5	38.4	-1.3	38.0	-1.0	37.9	-0.3	38.3	1.1	37.6	-1.8	37.6	0.0	37.6	0.0	37.2	-1.1	37.9	1.9	37.5	-1.1
1958	37.7	0.5	37.4	-0.8	37.7	0.8	37.4	-0.8	37.3	-0.3	37.2	-0.3	36.8	-1.1	36.7	-0.3	36.1	-1.6	36.5	1.1	36.2	-0.8	35.8	-1.1
1959	35.3	-1.4	35.4	0.3	35.2	-0.6	35.1	-0.3	35.1	0.0	34.9	-0.6	34.8	-0.3	34.7	-0.3	35.0	0.9	34.6	-1.1	34.6	0.0	33.5	-3.2
1960	33.5	0.0	33.9	1.2	33.6	-0.9	33.8	0.6	33.7	-0.3	33.7	0.0	33.6	-0.3	33.0	-1.8	34.0	3.0	34.3	0.9	34.0	-0.9	34.3	0.9
1961	33.7	-1.7	34.1	1.2	34.1	0.0	34.0	-0.3	34.0	0.0	33.9	-0.3	34.0	0.3	34.0	0.0	34.5	1.5	34.2	-0.9	34.0	-0.6	34.6	1.8
1962	34.2	-1.2	34.2	0.0	34.2	0.0	34.1	-0.3	34.2	0.3	33.8	-1.2	33.8	0.0	32.9	-2.7	33.2	0.9	32.8	-1.2	33.0	0.6	32.6	-1.2
1963	32.0	-1.8	32.6	1.9	32.6	0.0	32.7	0.3	32.8	0.3	32.7	-0.3	32.6	-0.3	32.4	-0.6	32.6	0.6	33.1	1.5	33.2	0.3	33.2	0.0
1964	36.2	9.0	35.3	-2.5	36.8	4.2	36.4	-1.1	36.4	0.0	36.1	-0.8	36.0	-0.3	36.0	0.0	35.4	-1.7	36.3	2.5	36.0	-0.8	36.0	0.0
1965	34.9	-3.1	35.6	2.0	34.8	-2.2	35.0	0.6	34.7	-0.9	35.0	0.9	34.9	-0.3	36.0	3.2	36.9	2.5	36.6	-0.8	36.5	-0.3	37.9	3.8
1966	37.5	-1.1	37.4	-0.3	37.3	-0.3	37.5	0.5	37.1	-1.1	37.0	-0.3	37.1	0.3	37.5	1.1	37.4	-0.3	36.9	-1.3	36.1	-2.2	36.8	1.9
1967	36.4	-1.1	36.8	1.1	36.4	-1.1	36.3	-0.3	36.5	0.6	36.7	0.5	36.5	-0.5	36.3	-0.5	35.7	-1.7	35.6	-0.3	36.9	3.7	37.1	0.5
1968	37.2	0.3	37.0	-0.5	37.1	0.3	37.3	0.5	37.2	-0.3	37.2	0.0	37.2	0.0	37.7	1.3	38.1	1.1	38.1	0.0	39.1	2.6	39.4	0.8
1969	38.7	-1.8	38.9	0.5	39.1	0.5	38.8	-0.8	38.6	-0.5	38.8	0.5	39.1	0.8	40.0	2.3	40.7	1.7	42.7	4.9	42.4	-0.7	41.4	-2.4
1970	42.6	2.9	42.2	-0.9	42.0	-0.5	42.0	0.0	42.1	0.2	42.0	-0.2	42.6	1.4	43.3	1.6	43.4	0.2	42.8	-1.4	44.2	3.3	43.7	-1.1

[Continued]

Other Farm Products
Producer Price Index
Base 1982 = 100
[Continued]

For 1926-2001. Columns headed % show percentile change in the index from the previous period for which an index is available.

Year	Jan Index	%	Feb Index	%	Mar Index	%	Apr Index	%	May Index	%	Jun Index	%	Jul Index	%	Aug Index	%	Sep Index	%	Oct Index	%	Nov Index	%	Dec Index	%
1971	43.7	0.0	43.6	-0.2	42.3	-3.0	41.7	-1.4	41.4	-0.7	41.4	0.0	41.3	-0.2	41.8	1.2	42.1	0.7	42.1	0.0	41.2	-2.1	42.7	3.6
1972	43.0	0.7	42.5	-1.2	42.8	0.7	43.0	0.5	43.5	1.2	43.7	0.5	44.4	1.6	49.0	10.4	48.3	-1.4	48.2	-0.2	48.8	1.2	49.3	1.0
1973	49.7	0.8	51.2	3.0	52.2	2.0	51.8	-0.8	53.2	2.7	54.0	1.5	55.4	2.6	54.8	-1.1	55.8	1.8	56.3	0.9	55.6	-1.2	54.3	-2.3
1974	55.9	2.9	56.7	1.4	58.0	2.3	59.8	3.1	60.8	1.7	59.5	-2.1	58.3	-2.0	59.2	1.5	60.5	2.2	62.0	2.5	64.0	3.2	63.9	-0.2
1975	62.8	-1.7	63.6	1.3	62.3	-2.0	61.2	-1.8	60.2	-1.6	60.3	0.2	58.3	-3.3	61.2	5.0	61.9	1.1	63.7	2.9	62.8	-1.4	63.5	1.1
1976	64.8	2.0	66.0	1.9	65.6	-0.6	70.6	7.6	75.1	6.4	81.8	8.9	79.7	-2.6	82.9	4.0	92.1	11.1	93.6	1.6	98.8	5.6	105.9	7.2
1977	107.8	1.8	114.4	6.1	134.2	17.3	140.7	4.8	130.6	-7.2	124.5	-4.7	122.1	-1.9	106.4	-12.9	115.5	8.6	107.9	-6.6	110.5	2.4	110.2	-0.3
1978	103.7	-5.9	101.0	-2.6	100.1	-0.9	98.7	-1.4	98.9	0.2	99.3	0.4	97.7	-1.6	95.7	-2.0	103.3	7.9	100.7	-2.5	104.2	3.5	98.7	-5.3
1979	98.3	-0.4	92.4	-6.0	92.7	0.3	92.9	0.2	96.2	3.6	102.4	6.4	113.6	10.9	113.2	-0.4	115.1	1.7	114.2	-0.8	116.0	1.6	116.3	0.3
1980	109.7	-5.7	111.0	1.2	113.5	2.3	111.0	-2.2	113.3	2.1	112.7	-0.5	106.5	-5.5	103.0	-3.3	106.4	3.3	104.1	-2.2	108.1	3.8	107.8	-0.3
1981	107.9	0.1	107.5	-0.4	107.8	0.3	107.8	0.0	94.6	-12.2	88.4	-6.6	91.1	3.1	96.1	5.5	98.0	2.0	95.9	-2.1	99.5	3.8	102.1	2.6
1982	102.0	-0.1	99.7	-2.3	99.5	-0.2	99.9	0.4	99.8	-0.1	99.0	-0.8	96.7	-2.3	100.0	3.4	100.8	0.8	99.8	-1.0	100.7	0.9	102.1	1.4
1983	102.0	-0.1	102.4	0.4	102.1	-0.3	101.7	-0.4	102.4	0.7	103.6	1.2	102.9	-0.7	104.1	1.2	104.7	0.6	103.4	-1.2	103.3	-0.1	100.9	-2.3
1984	102.1	1.2	101.6	-0.5	101.2	-0.4	101.9	0.7	105.0	3.0	101.7	-3.1	101.1	-0.6	103.6	2.5	108.0	4.2	107.1	-0.8	108.5	1.3	107.0	-1.4
1985	105.5	-1.4	104.0	-1.4	104.1	0.1	103.4	-0.7	103.3	-0.1	103.3	0.0	103.2	-0.1	100.0	-3.1	103.0	3.0	102.9	-0.1	103.4	0.5	100.9	-2.4
1986	100.9	0.0	100.3	-0.6	99.1	-1.2	98.5	-0.6	97.9	-0.6	97.9	0.0	97.9	0.0	89.9	-8.2	94.8	5.5	91.1	-3.9	94.0	3.2	94.0	0.0
1987	93.5	-0.5	94.0	0.5	94.0	0.0	93.5	-0.5	93.5	0.0	93.5	0.0	92.0	-1.6	92.0	0.0	96.5	4.9	97.0	0.5	96.5	-0.5	96.5	0.0
1988	95.5	-1.0	95.5	0.0	95.5	0.0	91.5	-4.2	91.5	0.0	91.5	0.0	91.5	0.0	93.0	1.6	98.5	5.9	100.1	1.6	101.1	1.0	99.7	-1.4
1989	99.7	0.0	98.7	-1.0	98.7	0.0	99.2	0.5	99.2	0.0	99.2	0.0	98.7	-0.5	98.1	-0.6	101.2	3.2	114.2	12.8	114.5	0.3	117.8	2.9
1990	117.8	0.0	117.8	0.0	117.8	0.0	119.3	1.3	119.3	0.0	119.3	0.0	117.8	-1.3	117.3	-0.4	121.8	3.8	141.9	16.5	142.4	0.4	150.7	5.8
1991	151.6	0.6	151.6	0.0	151.2	-0.3	151.2	0.0	151.2	0.0	151.2	0.0	151.2	0.0	149.0	-1.5	154.3	3.6	142.7	-7.5	157.2	10.2	156.3	-0.6
1992	152.4	-2.5	152.4	0.0	169.9	11.5	140.8	-17.1	140.8	0.0	140.8	0.0	134.9	-4.2	143.7	6.5	158.2	10.1	157.3	-0.6	158.2	0.6	158.2	0.0
1993	156.3	-1.2	164.1	5.0	162.1	-1.2	145.6	-10.2	136.9	-6.0	136.9	0.0	136.9	0.0	138.8	1.4	150.5	8.4	152.4	1.3	157.3	3.2	157.3	0.0
1994	157.3	0.0	163.1	3.7	136.9	-16.1	147.6	7.8	147.6	0.0	147.6	0.0	130.1	-11.9	135.9	4.5	153.4	12.9	156.3	1.9	158.2	1.2	160.2	1.3
1995	164.7	2.8	167.8	1.9	149.5	-10.9	134.2	-10.2	-	-	-	-	154.3	15.0	152.1	-1.4	160.4	5.5	159.1	-0.8	161.7	1.6	161.7	0.0
1996	166.1	2.7	177.1	6.6	153.0	-13.6	140.7	-8.0	-	-	-	-	140.3	-0.3	153.0	9.1	164.8	7.7	167.9	1.9	168.3	0.2	168.8	0.3
1997	176.2	4.4	180.2	2.3	166.6	-7.5	-		-		-	-	139.0	-16.6	140.3	0.9	153.9	9.7	157.4	2.3	154.3	-2.0	167.9	8.8
1998	168.3	0.2	168.3	0.0	159.1	-5.5	148.6	-6.6	-	-	-	-	142.9	-3.8	142.0	-0.6	156.9	10.5	163.5	4.2	167.0	2.1	167.4	0.2
1999	167.7	0.2	167.9	0.1	172.3	2.6	131.9	-23.4	-	-	-	-	131.5	-0.3	143.8	9.4	153.4	6.7	158.7	3.5	160.0	0.8	167.0	4.4
2000	167.4	0.2	167.0	-0.2	156.9	-6.0	137.6	-12.3	-	-	-	-	-		148.6	8.0	159.6	7.4	158.7	-0.6	155.6	-2.0	172.7	11.0
2001	178.8	3.5	181.0	1.2	159.6	-11.8	121.0	-24.2	-	-	-	-	163.5	35.1	159.1	-2.7	164.4	3.3	167.0	1.6	173.6	4.0	171.8	-1.0

Source: U.S. Department of Labor, Bureau of Labor Statistics, Division of Industry Prices and Price Indexes. n.e.c. stands for not elsewhere classified. - indicates no data collected for period or unavailable.

PROCESSED FOODS AND FEEDS

Producer Price Index
Base 1982 = 100

For 1947-2001. Columns headed % show percentile change in the index from the previous period for which an index is available.

Year	Jan Index	%	Feb Index	%	Mar Index	%	Apr Index	%	May Index	%	Jun Index	%	Jul Index	%	Aug Index	%	Sep Index	%	Oct Index	%	Nov Index	%	Dec Index	%
1947	31.5	-	31.6	0.3	32.9	4.1	32.1	-2.4	31.5	-1.9	31.7	0.6	32.3	1.9	32.8	1.5	34.2	4.3	34.5	0.9	34.9	1.2	35.6	2.0
1948	36.7	3.1	35.0	-4.6	34.9	-0.3	35.4	1.4	35.7	0.8	35.9	0.6	36.1	0.6	35.8	-0.8	35.6	-0.6	34.5	-3.1	34.1	-1.2	33.6	-1.5
1949	32.9	-2.1	32.0	-2.7	32.1	0.3	32.0	-0.3	31.9	-0.3	31.9	0.0	32.1	0.6	32.5	1.2	32.2	-0.9	31.8	-1.2	31.6	-0.6	31.5	-0.3
1950	31.3	-0.6	31.5	0.6	31.7	0.6	31.7	0.0	32.4	2.2	32.4	0.0	34.2	5.6	34.7	1.5	34.9	0.6	34.1	-2.3	34.2	0.3	35.3	3.2
1951	36.4	3.1	37.2	2.2	37.0	-0.5	37.0	0.0	37.0	0.0	36.7	-0.8	36.6	-0.3	36.7	0.3	36.7	0.0	37.0	0.8	37.0	0.0	36.9	-0.3
1952	36.9	0.0	36.8	-0.3	36.6	-0.5	36.3	-0.8	36.4	0.3	36.3	-0.3	36.6	0.8	36.9	0.8	36.9	0.0	36.4	-1.4	36.0	-1.1	35.0	-2.8
1953	35.2	0.6	35.1	-0.3	34.8	-0.9	34.4	-1.1	34.8	1.2	34.2	-1.7	34.8	1.8	34.7	-0.3	35.2	1.4	34.7	-1.4	34.4	-0.9	34.9	1.5
1954	35.5	1.7	35.2	-0.8	35.4	0.6	36.0	1.7	36.2	0.6	35.4	-2.2	35.8	1.1	35.7	-0.3	35.3	-1.1	34.6	-2.0	34.7	0.3	34.6	-0.3
1955	34.7	0.3	34.5	-0.6	34.0	-1.4	34.2	0.6	33.9	-0.9	34.2	0.9	34.2	0.0	33.8	-1.2	33.6	-0.6	33.4	-0.6	32.8	-1.8	32.6	-0.6
1956	32.7	0.3	32.8	0.3	32.8	0.0	33.4	1.8	34.2	2.4	34.0	-0.6	33.8	-0.6	34.0	0.6	34.3	0.9	34.2	-0.3	34.3	0.3	34.2	-0.3
1957	34.6	1.2	34.4	-0.6	34.4	0.0	34.5	0.3	34.5	0.0	34.8	0.9	35.2	1.1	35.1	-0.3	35.0	-0.3	34.6	-1.1	34.8	0.6	35.1	0.9
1958	35.8	2.0	35.9	0.3	36.4	1.4	36.9	1.4	37.1	0.5	37.2	0.3	37.2	0.0	36.6	-1.6	36.4	-0.5	36.1	-0.8	36.1	0.0	36.3	0.6
1959	36.3	0.0	35.9	-1.1	35.8	-0.3	35.9	0.3	35.9	0.0	35.7	-0.6	35.6	-0.3	35.1	-1.4	35.4	0.9	35.2	-0.6	35.0	-0.6	34.9	-0.3
1960	35.2	0.9	35.1	-0.3	35.6	1.4	35.6	0.0	35.4	-0.6	35.5	0.3	35.8	0.8	35.5	-0.8	35.6	0.3	35.9	0.8	35.9	0.0	36.0	0.3
1961	36.5	1.4	36.6	0.3	36.5	-0.3	36.3	-0.5	36.1	-0.6	35.6	-1.4	35.9	0.8	36.0	0.3	36.0	0.0	35.9	-0.3	36.1	0.6	36.4	0.8
1962	36.7	0.8	36.6	-0.3	36.5	-0.3	36.2	-0.8	36.0	-0.6	36.0	0.0	36.5	1.4	36.6	0.3	37.3	1.9	36.7	-1.6	36.7	0.0	36.6	-0.3
1963	36.7	0.3	36.6	-0.3	36.1	-1.4	36.1	0.0	36.7	1.7	36.9	0.5	37.1	0.5	36.8	-0.8	36.9	0.3	37.2	0.8	36.6	-0.8	36.7	-1.3
1964	37.3	1.6	36.8	-1.3	36.6	-0.5	36.5	-0.3	36.1	-1.1	36.3	0.6	36.6	0.8	36.5	-0.3	37.1	1.6	36.9	-0.5	36.6	-0.8	36.7	0.3
1965	37.1	1.1	37.0	-0.3	36.9	-0.3	37.1	0.5	37.3	0.5	38.3	2.7	38.5	0.5	38.5	0.0	38.5	0.0	38.5	0.0	38.9	1.0	39.3	1.0
1966	39.7	1.0	40.2	1.3	39.9	-0.7	39.7	-0.5	39.8	0.3	39.9	0.3	40.5	1.5	41.2	1.7	41.1	-0.2	40.6	-1.2	40.1	-1.2	40.2	0.2
1967	40.2	0.0	39.7	-1.2	39.4	-0.8	39.2	-0.5	39.4	0.5	40.1	1.8	40.3	0.5	39.9	-1.0	40.1	0.5	39.8	-0.7	39.5	-0.8	39.7	0.5
1968	40.0	0.8	40.3	0.7	40.2	-0.2	40.2	0.0	40.5	0.7	40.9	1.0	41.3	1.0	41.0	-0.7	41.0	0.0	40.7	-0.7	40.8	0.2	40.9	0.2
1969	41.3	1.0	41.4	0.2	41.5	0.2	41.8	0.7	42.5	1.7	43.3	1.9	43.5	0.5	43.3	-0.5	43.2	-0.2	43.3	0.2	43.3	0.0	43.7	0.9
1970	44.6	2.1	44.7	0.2	44.5	-0.4	44.5	0.0	44.2	-0.7	44.5	0.7	45.1	1.3	44.9	-0.4	45.0	0.2	44.5	-1.1	44.5	0.0	44.0	-1.1
1971	44.5	1.1	45.1	1.3	45.2	0.2	45.2	0.0	45.6	0.9	45.8	0.4	46.2	0.9	46.0	-0.4	45.7	-0.7	45.4	-0.7	45.5	0.2	46.1	1.3
1972	46.6	1.1	47.3	1.5	47.2	-0.2	46.8	-0.8	47.2	0.9	47.6	0.8	48.3	1.5	48.1	-0.4	48.5	0.8	48.5	0.0	48.9	0.8	51.5	5.3
1973	52.6	2.1	54.5	3.6	56.2	3.1	55.6	-1.1	57.7	3.8	60.3	4.5	58.3	-3.3	66.1	13.4	62.2	-5.9	60.9	-2.1	60.4	-0.8	61.9	2.5
1974	64.4	4.0	65.5	1.7	64.8	-1.1	63.3	-2.3	63.2	-0.2	62.6	-0.9	66.6	6.4	71.4	7.2	70.3	-1.5	73.0	3.8	75.4	3.3	74.8	-0.8
1975	74.1	-0.9	72.6	-2.0	70.5	-2.9	71.4	1.3	71.2	-0.3	71.5	0.4	73.4	2.7	74.1	1.0	74.0	-0.1	74.0	0.0	72.6	-1.9	72.0	-0.8
1976	71.3	-1.0	70.2	-1.5	69.9	-0.4	70.8	1.3	71.5	1.0	72.3	1.1	72.6	0.4	70.3	-3.2	70.5	0.3	69.6	-1.3	69.5	-0.1	71.2	2.4
1977	71.3	0.1	72.3	1.4	73.1	1.1	75.0	2.6	76.3	1.7	75.6	-0.9	74.4	-1.6	73.5	-1.2	73.3	-0.3	73.3	0.0	74.3	1.4	75.3	1.3
1978	76.2	1.2	77.5	1.7	78.3	1.0	79.6	1.7	80.5	1.1	81.4	1.1	81.2	-0.2	80.2	-1.2	81.7	1.9	83.1	1.7	82.8	-0.4	84.2	1.7
1979	85.6	1.7	87.1	1.8	87.7	0.7	88.4	0.8	88.3	-0.1	87.7	-0.7	88.8	1.3	87.7	-1.2	89.8	2.4	89.4	-0.4	90.3	1.0	91.2	1.0
1980	90.9	-0.3	92.7	2.0	92.1	-0.6	90.9	-1.3	92.7	2.0	93.0	0.3	96.1	3.3	99.2	3.2	99.3	0.1	101.8	2.5	102.3	0.5	100.0	-2.2
1981	100.7	0.7	99.5	-1.2	98.8	-0.7	98.4	-0.4	98.7	0.3	99.4	0.7	100.3	0.9	99.9	-0.4	99.0	-0.9	98.0	-1.0	97.2	-0.8	96.9	-0.3
1982	98.2	1.3	98.7	0.5	98.7	0.0	99.8	1.1	101.2	1.4	101.7	0.5	101.2	-0.5	100.8	-0.4	100.8	0.0	99.7	-1.1	99.5	-0.2	99.6	0.1
1983	100.1	0.5	101.3	1.2	101.2	-0.1	101.8	0.6	101.8	0.0	101.1	-0.7	101.2	0.1	101.6	0.4	103.2	1.6	102.5	-0.7	102.5	0.0	103.0	0.5
1984	104.9	1.8	104.7	-0.2	106.2	1.4	106.3	0.1	106.4	0.1	105.3	-1.0	106.3	0.9	105.3	-0.9	104.8	-0.5	104.4	-0.4	104.9	0.5	105.2	0.3
1985	105.1	-0.1	104.9	-0.2	104.3	-0.6	103.8	-0.5	103.4	-0.4	102.9	-0.5	103.3	0.4	102.3	-1.0	101.5	-0.8	102.5	1.0	103.9	1.4	104.5	0.6
1986	104.7	0.2	104.0	-0.7	103.7	-0.3	103.3	-0.4	104.3	1.0	104.7	0.4	106.1	1.3	107.2	1.0	107.0	-0.2	106.7	-0.3	106.5	-0.2	106.7	0.2
1987	106.1	-0.6	106.4	0.3	105.9	-0.5	107.2	1.2	109.1	1.8	109.0	-0.1	109.0	0.0	108.2	-0.7	108.9	0.6	108.7	-0.2	108.1	-0.6	108.2	0.1
1988	109.3	1.0	109.1	-0.2	109.6	0.5	110.1	0.5	111.2	1.0	113.5	2.1	115.0	1.3	114.5	-0.4	115.4	0.8	115.0	-0.3	114.8	-0.2	115.0	0.2
1989	116.6	1.4	116.6	0.0	117.5	0.8	117.2	-0.3	117.9	0.6	117.4	-0.4	118.1	0.6	117.9	-0.2	117.9	0.0	117.9	0.0	118.9	0.8	119.3	0.3
1990	120.2	0.8	120.0	-0.2	120.9	0.7	121.2	0.2	123.5	1.9	122.8	-0.6	123.2	0.3	123.0	-0.2	122.4	-0.5	122.2	-0.2	121.7	-0.4	121.7	0.0
1991	122.1	0.3	122.3	0.2	122.6	0.2	122.5	-0.1	122.3	-0.2	121.9	-0.3	121.6	-0.2	121.4	-0.2	121.1	-0.2	121.9	0.7	121.4	-0.4	121.4	0.0

[Continued]

PROCESSED FOODS AND FEEDS
Producer Price Index
Base 1982 = 100
[Continued]

For 1947-2001. Columns headed % show percentile change in the index from the previous period for which an index is available.

Year	Jan Index	%	Feb Index	%	Mar Index	%	Apr Index	%	May Index	%	Jun Index	%	Jul Index	%	Aug Index	%	Sep Index	%	Oct Index	%	Nov Index	%	Dec Index	%
1992	121.3	-0.1	121.7	0.3	121.8	0.1	122.0	0.2	122.5	0.4	123.0	0.4	122.4	-0.5	122.1	-0.2	122.1	0.0	121.8	-0.2	121.6	-0.2	122.4	0.7
1993	122.7	0.2	122.7	0.0	122.9	0.2	123.7	0.7	124.2	0.4	124.0	-0.2	124.3	0.2	124.3	0.0	124.3	0.0	124.5	0.2	124.8	0.2	125.4	0.5
1994	126.0	0.5	126.2	0.2	126.8	0.5	126.6	-0.2	126.1	-0.4	125.4	-0.6	124.9	-0.4	125.2	0.2	125.0	-0.2	124.5	-0.4	124.7	0.2	124.3	-0.3
1995	125.2	0.7	125.9	0.6	126.2	0.2	125.6	-0.5	125.0	-0.5	125.3	0.2	126.7	1.1	127.5	0.6	127.8	0.2	128.9	0.9	130.0	0.9	130.2	0.2
1996	130.0	-0.2	130.3	0.2	130.3	0.0	130.9	0.5	132.7	1.4	134.0	1.0	134.8	0.6	136.1	1.0	136.0	-0.1	136.0	0.0	134.7	-1.0	134.2	-0.4
1997	133.4	-0.6	132.9	-0.4	134.5	1.2	134.5	0.0	135.4	0.7	134.3	-0.8	133.9	-0.3	134.3	0.3	134.1	-0.1	133.5	-0.4	133.7	0.1	132.9	-0.6
1998	131.3	-1.2	131.7	0.3	130.9	-0.6	130.8	-0.1	131.5	0.5	131.5	0.0	131.9	0.3	132.6	0.5	132.1	-0.4	131.8	-0.2	132.0	0.2	131.1	-0.7
1999	131.9	0.6	131.0	-0.7	130.8	-0.2	129.1	-1.3	130.3	0.9	130.8	0.4	130.5	-0.2	131.8	1.0	132.5	0.5	132.4	-0.1	131.8	-0.5	130.9	-0.7
2000	131.0	0.1	131.7	0.5	132.1	0.3	133.2	0.8	134.3	0.8	134.2	-0.1	134.1	-0.1	133.2	-0.7	132.9	-0.2	133.1	0.2	133.1	0.0	134.1	0.8
2001	134.8	0.5	135.6	0.6	136.3	0.5	137.1	0.6	137.8	0.5	138.0	0.1	138.5	0.4	139.5	0.7	139.4	-0.1	138.2	-0.9	136.6	-1.2	135.9	-0.5

Source: U.S. Department of Labor, Bureau of Labor Statistics, Division of Industry Prices and Price Indexes. n.e.c. stands for not elsewhere classified. - indicates no data collected for period or unavailable.

Cereal and Bakery Products

Producer Price Index
Base 1982 = 100

For 1926-2001. Columns headed % show percentile change in the index from the previous period for which an index is available.

Year	Jan Index	%	Feb Index	%	Mar Index	%	Apr Index	%	May Index	%	Jun Index	%	Jul Index	%	Aug Index	%	Sep Index	%	Oct Index	%	Nov Index	%	Dec Index	%
1926	20.1	-	19.8	-1.5	19.5	-1.5	19.3	-1.0	18.9	-2.1	19.0	0.5	18.8	-1.1	18.3	-2.7	18.1	-1.1	18.3	1.1	18.0	-1.6	17.9	-0.6
1927	17.8	-0.6	17.8	0.0	17.6	-1.1	17.6	0.0	18.2	3.4	18.3	0.5	18.2	-0.5	18.0	-1.1	17.5	-2.8	17.5	0.0	17.4	-0.6	17.4	0.0
1928	17.6	1.1	17.6	0.0	17.9	1.7	18.6	3.9	18.9	1.6	18.4	-2.6	17.9	-2.7	17.1	-4.5	17.0	-0.6	16.9	-0.6	16.7	-1.2	16.7	0.0
1929	16.7	0.0	16.9	1.2	16.4	-3.0	16.2	-1.2	15.9	-1.9	16.0	0.6	17.2	7.5	17.0	-1.2	16.9	-0.6	16.6	-1.8	16.5	-0.6	16.5	0.0
1930	16.5	0.0	16.2	-1.8	16.0	-1.2	15.9	-0.6	15.8	-0.6	15.6	-1.3	15.2	-2.6	15.1	-0.7	14.8	-2.0	14.6	-1.4	14.3	-2.1	14.3	0.0
1931	14.3	0.0	14.2	-0.7	14.0	-1.4	13.9	-0.7	14.0	0.7	13.9	-0.7	13.5	-2.9	13.4	-0.7	13.2	-1.5	13.3	0.8	13.7	3.0	13.6	-0.7
1932	13.4	-1.5	13.1	-2.2	12.8	-2.3	12.8	0.0	12.8	0.0	12.6	-1.6	12.4	-1.6	12.4	0.0	12.4	0.0	12.1	-2.4	11.8	-2.5	11.6	-1.7
1933	11.5	-0.9	11.4	-0.9	11.8	3.5	12.4	5.1	13.0	4.8	13.3	2.3	15.7	18.0	16.0	1.9	16.0	0.0	16.0	0.0	16.2	1.3	16.0	-1.2
1934	16.2	1.3	16.2	0.0	16.0	-1.2	16.0	0.0	16.4	2.5	16.7	1.8	16.7	0.0	17.1	2.4	17.3	1.2	17.1	-1.2	17.1	0.0	17.3	1.2
1935	17.3	0.0	17.3	0.0	17.3	0.0	17.5	1.2	17.4	-0.6	17.1	-1.7	17.5	2.3	17.9	2.3	18.2	1.7	18.6	2.2	18.3	-1.6	18.3	0.0
1936	17.3	-5.5	16.7	-3.5	16.2	-3.0	15.8	-2.5	15.5	-1.9	15.4	-0.6	15.9	3.2	16.5	3.8	16.5	0.0	16.5	0.0	16.2	-1.8	16.4	1.2
1937	16.6	1.2	16.8	1.2	16.9	0.6	16.9	0.0	16.7	-1.2	17.0	1.8	17.4	2.4	16.5	-5.2	16.2	-1.8	15.9	-1.9	15.3	-3.8	15.4	0.7
1938	15.6	1.3	15.6	0.0	15.2	-2.6	15.1	-0.7	14.7	-2.6	15.1	2.7	14.9	-1.3	14.5	-2.7	14.3	-1.4	14.1	-1.4	13.9	-1.4	14.1	1.4
1939	13.8	-2.1	13.7	-0.7	13.6	-0.7	13.6	0.0	13.9	2.2	14.3	2.9	13.5	-5.6	13.5	0.0	14.9	10.4	14.7	-1.3	14.7	0.0	15.2	3.4
1940	15.1	-0.7	15.5	2.6	15.5	0.0	15.6	0.6	15.2	-2.6	14.6	-3.9	14.3	-2.1	14.1	-1.4	14.3	1.4	14.5	1.4	14.1	-2.8	13.9	-1.4
1941	14.1	1.4	13.9	-1.4	14.1	1.4	14.5	2.8	14.7	1.4	15.1	2.7	15.1	0.0	15.3	1.3	16.2	5.9	16.2	0.0	16.2	0.0	16.8	3.7
1942	17.1	1.8	17.2	0.6	17.1	-0.6	17.0	-0.6	16.7	-1.8	16.4	-1.8	16.4	0.0	16.5	0.6	16.7	1.2	16.8	0.6	16.9	0.6	16.8	-0.6
1943	17.1	1.8	17.4	1.8	17.6	1.1	17.6	0.0	17.6	0.0	17.6	0.0	17.6	0.0	17.6	0.0	17.8	1.1	17.9	0.6	17.9	0.0	17.9	0.0
1944	17.9	0.0	17.9	0.0	17.9	0.0	17.9	0.0	17.9	0.0	17.9	0.0	17.8	-0.6	17.7	-0.6	17.8	0.6	17.9	0.6	17.9	0.0	17.9	0.0
1945	17.9	0.0	17.9	0.0	17.9	0.0	17.9	0.0	18.0	0.6	18.0	0.0	17.9	-0.6	17.9	0.0	17.9	0.0	17.9	0.0	18.0	0.6	18.0	0.0
1946	18.0	0.0	18.1	0.6	18.1	0.0	18.7	3.3	18.9	1.1	19.2	1.6	23.5	22.4	23.4	-0.4	24.0	2.6	24.2	0.8	25.6	5.8	26.2	2.3
1947	26.6	1.5	26.8	0.8	27.9	4.1	28.4	1.8	28.2	-0.7	27.7	-1.8	28.4	2.5	28.4	0.0	29.1	2.5	30.3	4.1	31.2	3.0	31.1	-0.3
1948	31.1	0.0	29.8	-4.2	29.6	-0.7	29.5	-0.3	29.2	-1.0	29.1	-0.3	29.2	0.3	28.8	-1.4	28.6	-0.7	28.3	-1.0	28.4	0.4	28.4	0.0
1949	28.2	-0.7	28.0	-0.7	28.0	0.0	27.9	-0.4	27.8	-0.4	27.8	0.0	27.9	0.4	27.5	-1.4	27.3	-0.7	27.3	0.0	27.3	0.0	27.3	0.0
1950	27.3	0.0	27.5	0.7	27.6	0.4	27.6	0.0	27.6	0.0	27.5	-0.4	28.4	3.3	29.0	2.1	29.1	0.3	28.8	-1.0	28.8	0.0	29.4	2.1
1951	30.3	3.1	30.7	1.3	30.5	-0.7	30.5	0.0	30.5	0.0	30.3	-0.7	30.3	0.0	30.4	0.3	30.3	-0.3	30.5	0.7	30.7	0.7	30.8	0.3
1952	30.7	-0.3	30.6	-0.3	30.7	0.3	30.6	-0.3	30.5	-0.3	30.4	-0.3	30.3	-0.3	30.3	0.0	30.3	0.0	30.3	0.0	30.5	0.7	30.5	0.0
1953	30.5	0.0	30.7	0.7	31.1	1.3	31.1	0.0	31.1	0.0	30.8	-1.0	30.9	0.3	30.9	0.0	31.6	2.3	31.9	0.9	32.1	0.6	32.0	-0.3
1954	32.0	0.0	32.2	0.6	32.1	-0.3	32.3	0.6	32.3	0.0	32.4	0.3	32.5	0.3	32.3	-0.6	32.4	0.3	32.6	0.6	33.2	1.8	33.3	0.3
1955	33.3	0.0	33.1	-0.6	33.2	0.3	33.3	0.3	33.7	1.2	33.5	-0.6	33.5	0.0	32.8	-2.1	32.6	-0.6	32.7	0.3	32.8	0.3	32.8	0.0
1956	32.8	0.0	32.9	0.3	32.9	0.0	32.9	0.0	32.9	0.0	32.9	0.0	32.7	-0.6	32.6	-0.3	32.7	0.3	32.9	0.6	33.0	0.3	32.9	-0.3
1957	33.0	0.3	33.1	0.3	33.3	0.6	33.3	0.0	33.2	-0.3	33.3	0.3	33.5	0.6	33.3	-0.6	33.3	0.0	33.5	0.6	33.5	0.0	33.7	0.6
1958	33.7	0.0	33.7	0.0	33.6	-0.3	33.8	0.6	33.6	-0.6	33.8	0.6	33.5	-0.9	33.3	-0.6	33.6	0.9	33.7	0.3	33.7	0.0	33.5	-0.6
1959	33.5	0.0	33.5	0.0	33.9	1.2	33.9	0.0	34.0	0.3	34.0	0.0	34.0	0.0	34.0	0.0	34.0	0.0	34.0	0.0	34.3	0.9	34.3	0.0	34.3	0.0
1960	34.4	0.3	34.4	0.0	34.4	0.0	34.4	0.0	34.6	0.6	34.6	0.0	34.9	0.9	34.8	-0.3	34.9	0.3	35.1	0.6	35.1	0.0	35.2	0.3
1961	35.2	0.0	35.2	0.0	35.2	0.0	35.2	0.0	35.2	0.0	35.3	0.3	35.3	0.0	35.3	0.0	35.4	0.3	35.7	0.8	35.7	0.0	35.7	0.0
1962	36.0	0.8	36.1	0.3	36.1	0.0	36.3	0.6	36.1	-0.6	36.2	0.3	36.3	0.3	36.3	0.0	36.2	-0.3	36.2	0.0	36.3	0.3	36.2	-0.3
1963	36.1	-0.3	36.5	1.1	36.3	-0.5	36.4	0.3	36.2	-0.5	36.0	-0.6	35.8	-0.6	35.7	-0.3	36.0	0.8	36.3	0.8	36.1	-0.6	36.0	-0.3
1964	36.0	0.0	36.1	0.3	35.9	-0.6	36.3	1.1	36.2	-0.3	36.3	0.3	36.5	0.6	36.4	-0.3	36.4	0.0	36.4	0.0	36.4	0.0	36.4	0.0
1965	36.4	0.0	36.3	-0.3	36.4	0.3	36.4	0.0	36.4	0.0	36.5	0.3	36.8	0.8	36.6	-0.5	36.7	0.3	36.8	0.3	37.2	1.1	37.4	0.5
1966	37.6	0.5	37.7	0.3	37.7	0.0	37.9	0.5	38.0	0.3	38.4	1.1	38.9	1.3	40.0	2.8	40.0	0.0	40.0	0.0	40.0	0.0	39.7	-0.7
1967	39.5	-0.5	39.5	0.0	39.4	-0.3	39.4	0.0	39.5	0.3	39.5	0.0	39.3	-0.5	39.3	0.0	39.3	0.0	39.3	0.0	39.4	0.3	39.4	0.0
1968	39.4	0.0	39.5	0.3	39.5	0.0	39.5	0.0	39.4	-0.3	39.4	0.0	39.8	1.0	40.2	1.0	40.0	-0.5	40.2	0.5	40.2	0.0	40.2	0.0
1969	40.2	0.0	40.2	0.0	40.2	0.0	40.2	0.0	40.2	0.0	40.3	0.2	40.4	0.2	40.5	0.2	40.6	0.2	40.8	0.5	41.0	0.5	41.1	0.2
1970	41.1	0.0	41.5	1.0	41.7	0.5	41.9	0.5	41.9	0.0	42.0	0.2	42.4	1.0	42.5	0.2	43.1	1.4	43.3	0.5	43.7	0.9	43.8	0.2

[Continued]

Cereal and Bakery Products
Producer Price Index
Base 1982 = 100
[Continued]

For 1926-2001. Columns headed % show percentile change in the index from the previous period for which an index is available.

Year	Jan Index	%	Feb Index	%	Mar Index	%	Apr Index	%	May Index	%	Jun Index	%	Jul Index	%	Aug Index	%	Sep Index	%	Oct Index	%	Nov Index	%	Dec Index	%
1971	44.0	0.5	44.0	0.0	44.1	0.2	44.1	0.0	44.1	0.0	44.1	0.0	43.9	-0.5	43.9	0.0	43.8	-0.2	43.9	0.2	43.9	0.0	44.0	0.2
1972	44.2	0.5	44.3	0.2	44.4	0.2	44.5	0.2	44.6	0.2	44.6	0.0	44.8	0.4	45.4	1.3	45.7	0.7	46.1	0.9	46.6	1.1	47.3	1.5
1973	47.7	0.8	47.6	-0.2	47.8	0.4	48.7	1.9	49.0	0.6	49.6	1.2	49.5	-0.2	53.7	8.5	58.2	8.4	59.3	1.9	61.5	3.7	63.1	2.6
1974	65.5	3.8	66.8	2.0	67.9	1.6	65.8	-3.1	65.8	0.0	65.4	-0.6	66.6	1.8	66.7	0.2	66.9	0.3	69.4	3.7	70.8	2.0	71.7	1.3
1975	71.8	0.1	72.3	0.7	71.7	-0.8	70.6	-1.5	69.4	-1.7	68.7	-1.0	69.6	1.3	69.3	-0.4	69.7	0.6	70.0	0.4	69.7	-0.4	68.8	-1.3
1976	69.0	0.3	69.1	0.1	68.8	-0.4	68.0	-1.2	68.3	0.4	68.5	0.3	68.4	-0.1	67.1	-1.9	66.9	-0.3	67.0	0.1	66.5	-0.7	66.4	-0.2
1977	66.4	0.0	67.0	0.9	67.6	0.9	67.6	0.0	67.8	0.3	67.4	-0.6	67.7	0.4	67.8	0.1	68.8	1.5	69.2	0.6	70.9	2.5	71.8	1.3
1978	72.6	1.1	72.9	0.4	73.4	0.7	74.4	1.4	74.2	-0.3	74.9	0.9	75.3	0.5	75.8	0.7	75.3	-0.7	76.2	1.2	77.3	1.4	77.5	0.3
1979	77.7	0.3	78.5	1.0	78.8	0.4	80.0	1.5	80.8	1.0	81.3	0.6	83.7	3.0	85.1	1.7	86.2	1.3	86.6	0.5	87.7	1.3	88.1	0.5
1980	88.8	0.8	90.6	2.0	91.3	0.8	91.6	0.3	92.5	1.0	91.9	-0.6	92.5	0.7	92.9	0.4	93.9	1.1	95.1	1.3	96.7	1.7	98.0	1.3
1981	99.1	1.1	99.4	0.3	99.4	0.0	100.0	0.6	101.0	1.0	101.0	0.0	101.8	0.8	101.5	-0.3	101.8	0.3	101.2	-0.6	101.1	-0.1	100.5	-0.6
1982	101.1	0.6	99.8	-1.3	99.8	0.0	99.9	0.1	99.6	-0.3	99.6	0.0	99.7	0.1	99.6	-0.1	100.1	0.5	99.7	-0.4	100.2	0.5	101.0	0.8
1983	101.4	0.4	101.2	-0.2	101.2	0.0	102.0	0.8	102.1	0.1	102.6	0.5	103.0	0.4	103.6	0.6	103.9	0.3	104.3	0.4	104.5	0.2	104.5	0.0
1984	105.1	0.6	105.3	0.2	105.4	0.1	105.7	0.3	105.9	0.2	106.9	0.9	107.3	0.4	107.1	-0.2	107.1	0.0	107.4	0.3	107.8	0.4	107.8	0.0
1985	109.0	1.1	109.4	0.4	109.5	0.1	109.9	0.4	109.6	-0.3	110.3	0.6	110.2	-0.1	110.3	0.1	110.8	0.5	111.4	0.5	111.3	-0.1	111.6	0.3
1986	111.6	0.0	111.6	0.0	111.6	0.0	111.4	-0.2	111.6	0.2	111.1	-0.4	110.7	-0.4	110.9	0.2	110.5	-0.4	110.6	0.1	110.5	-0.1	110.1	-0.4
1987	110.2	0.1	110.8	0.5	111.2	0.4	111.4	0.2	112.0	0.5	111.9	-0.1	111.9	0.0	112.6	0.6	113.0	0.4	114.5	1.3	115.3	0.7	116.7	1.2
1988	118.2	1.3	119.6	1.2	119.8	0.2	120.2	0.3	120.4	0.2	123.2	2.3	124.1	0.7	124.6	0.4	126.4	1.4	126.4	0.0	126.1	-0.2	126.5	0.3
1989	128.2	1.3	129.0	0.6	129.2	0.2	129.1	-0.1	130.8	1.3	131.2	0.3	132.1	0.7	132.9	0.6	132.8	-0.1	132.4	-0.3	132.4	0.0	133.3	0.7
1990	133.2	-0.1	133.8	0.5	133.9	0.1	134.6	0.5	135.1	0.4	134.7	-0.3	134.3	-0.3	134.2	-0.1	133.7	-0.4	134.2	0.4	134.2	0.0	134.6	0.3
1991	135.3	0.5	136.0	0.5	136.6	0.4	137.0	0.3	137.4	0.3	137.8	0.3	137.3	-0.4	138.3	0.7	138.6	0.2	139.9	0.9	140.0	0.1	141.0	0.7
1992	142.1	0.8	143.5	1.0	143.4	-0.1	143.5	0.1	144.0	0.3	145.3	0.9	144.8	-0.3	144.3	-0.3	144.6	0.2	144.9	0.2	145.1	0.1	144.7	-0.3
1993	145.7	0.7	146.5	0.5	146.1	-0.3	146.6	0.3	146.3	-0.2	146.4	0.1	146.6	0.1	147.6	0.7	147.1	-0.3	149.0	1.3	150.6	1.1	152.3	1.1
1994	152.0	-0.2	152.1	0.1	152.0	-0.1	151.5	-0.3	151.7	0.1	150.9	-0.5	150.0	-0.6	149.4	-0.4	150.4	0.7	151.0	0.4	151.1	0.1	151.0	-0.1
1995	151.2	0.1	151.4	0.1	151.1	-0.2	151.3	0.1	152.2	0.6	153.5	0.9	155.1	1.0	156.0	0.6	157.3	0.8	158.9	1.0	158.9	0.0	159.2	0.2
1996	158.4	-0.5	160.2	1.1	159.9	-0.2	160.3	0.3	163.6	2.1	160.9	-1.7	160.2	-0.4	159.6	-0.4	159.0	-0.4	159.6	0.4	158.7	-0.6	158.5	-0.1
1997	158.3	-0.1	158.4	0.1	158.0	-0.3	158.7	0.4	158.8	0.1	158.3	-0.3	157.4	-0.6	157.6	0.1	158.0	0.3	157.9	-0.1	157.9	0.0	157.6	-0.2
1998	157.3	-0.2	157.3	0.0	157.8	0.3	157.8	0.0	157.8	0.0	157.4	-0.3	157.3	-0.1	156.6	-0.4	156.3	-0.2	157.4	0.7	157.8	0.3	157.6	-0.1
1999	157.9	0.2	157.7	-0.1	157.6	-0.1	157.3	-0.2	157.8	0.3	157.8	0.0	157.5	-0.2	157.8	0.2	157.7	-0.1	157.0	-0.4	157.1	0.1	157.1	0.0
2000	157.4	0.2	157.5	0.1	157.7	0.1	157.8	0.1	158.1	0.2	158.4	0.2	158.3	-0.1	158.5	0.1	158.7	0.1	159.6	0.6	159.5	-0.1	160.0	0.3
2001	160.2	0.1	160.5	0.2	161.1	0.4	161.6	0.3	161.8	0.1	162.1	0.2	162.5	0.2	162.5	0.0	162.8	0.2	163.2	0.2	163.1	-0.1	162.9	-0.1

Source: U.S. Department of Labor, Bureau of Labor Statistics, Division of Industry Prices and Price Indexes. n.e.c. stands for not elsewhere classified. - indicates no data collected for period or unavailable.

947

Meats, Poultry, and Fish
Producer Price Index
Base 1982 = 100

For 1926-2001. Columns headed % show percentile change in the index from the previous period for which an index is available.

Year	Jan Index	%	Feb Index	%	Mar Index	%	Apr Index	%	May Index	%	Jun Index	%	Jul Index	%	Aug Index	%	Sep Index	%	Oct Index	%	Nov Index	%	Dec Index	%
1926	17.5	-	17.1	-2.3	17.2	0.6	17.4	1.2	17.5	0.6	17.9	2.3	17.7	-1.1	17.5	-1.1	17.8	1.7	17.7	-0.6	17.3	-2.3	17.2	-0.6
1927	15.6	-9.3	15.7	0.6	15.8	0.6	15.9	0.6	15.7	-1.3	15.5	-1.3	15.8	1.9	15.8	0.0	16.2	2.5	17.5	8.0	17.6	0.6	17.4	-1.1
1928	17.4	0.0	17.1	-1.7	16.6	-2.9	17.4	4.8	18.1	4.0	18.2	0.6	19.7	8.2	20.8	5.6	22.1	6.3	20.4	-7.7	19.0	-6.9	17.9	-5.8
1929	18.4	2.8	17.9	-2.7	19.0	6.1	19.5	2.6	19.5	0.0	19.5	0.0	20.4	4.6	20.3	-0.5	19.8	-2.5	18.6	-6.1	17.9	-3.8	18.1	1.1
1930	18.6	2.8	18.4	-1.1	18.2	-1.1	18.1	-0.5	17.7	-2.2	17.5	-1.1	16.0	-8.6	16.3	1.9	17.4	6.7	16.9	-2.9	16.0	-5.3	15.6	-2.5
1931	15.5	-0.6	14.6	-5.8	14.4	-1.4	14.0	-2.8	13.0	-7.1	12.5	-3.8	12.8	2.4	13.3	3.9	12.9	-3.0	12.5	-3.1	11.8	-5.6	11.1	-5.9
1932	10.8	-2.7	10.4	-3.7	10.7	2.9	10.5	-1.9	9.9	-5.7	9.8	-1.0	10.8	10.2	10.8	0.0	10.6	-1.9	9.9	-6.6	9.4	-5.1	8.6	-8.5
1933	8.7	1.2	8.8	1.1	8.9	1.1	8.8	-1.1	9.2	4.5	9.2	0.0	8.9	-3.3	8.9	0.0	9.0	1.1	8.9	-1.1	8.4	-5.6	8.0	-4.8
1934	8.5	6.3	9.4	10.6	9.9	5.3	10.0	1.0	10.5	5.0	10.9	3.8	11.1	1.8	12.2	9.9	13.4	9.8	12.2	-9.0	12.0	-1.6	12.0	0.0
1935	14.3	19.2	15.3	7.0	16.0	4.6	16.5	3.1	17.0	3.0	16.5	-2.9	16.3	-1.2	17.9	9.8	18.0	0.6	17.0	-5.6	16.5	-2.9	17.0	3.0
1936	16.6	-2.4	16.1	-3.0	15.7	-2.5	15.9	1.3	14.9	-6.3	14.9	0.0	14.8	-0.7	15.1	2.0	15.3	1.3	14.8	-3.3	14.9	0.7	15.2	2.0
1937	15.9	4.6	15.8	-0.6	16.1	1.9	16.6	3.1	16.8	1.2	17.2	2.4	18.5	7.6	19.6	5.9	19.8	1.0	18.8	-5.1	17.2	-8.5	15.5	-9.9
1938	14.4	-7.1	13.7	-4.9	14.3	4.4	14.4	0.7	14.4	0.0	14.8	2.8	15.7	6.1	15.0	-4.5	15.2	1.3	14.6	-3.9	14.3	-2.1	14.0	-2.1
1939	14.3	2.1	14.5	1.4	14.4	-0.7	14.2	-1.4	13.7	-3.5	13.2	-3.6	13.2	0.0	12.9	-2.3	14.2	10.1	13.1	-7.7	12.5	-4.6	12.0	-4.0
1940	12.2	1.7	12.0	-1.6	12.1	0.8	12.5	3.3	12.9	3.2	12.4	-3.9	12.8	3.2	13.3	3.9	13.8	3.8	13.2	-4.3	13.4	1.5	13.5	0.7
1941	14.5	7.4	14.6	0.7	14.6	0.0	15.0	2.7	15.2	1.3	15.9	4.6	16.4	3.1	17.0	3.7	17.4	2.4	16.4	-5.7	15.9	-3.0	16.7	5.0
1942	17.8	6.6	18.2	2.2	19.1	4.9	19.8	3.7	20.1	1.5	19.9	-1.0	19.8	-0.5	20.1	1.5	20.3	1.0	20.2	-0.5	19.6	-3.0	19.9	1.5
1943	20.2	1.5	20.2	0.0	20.2	0.0	20.3	0.5	20.3	0.0	19.5	-3.9	18.5	-5.1	18.5	0.0	18.5	0.0	18.6	0.5	18.6	0.0	18.5	-0.5
1944	18.5	0.0	18.5	0.0	18.5	0.0	18.6	0.5	18.6	0.0	18.5	-0.5	18.5	0.0	18.5	0.0	18.5	0.0	18.5	0.0	18.6	0.5	18.6	0.0
1945	18.6	0.0	18.6	0.0	18.8	1.1	18.9	0.5	19.0	0.5	18.9	-0.5	18.9	0.0	18.9	0.0	18.9	0.0	18.9	0.0	18.9	0.0	18.9	0.0
1946	18.9	0.0	18.9	0.0	19.2	1.6	19.3	0.5	19.3	0.0	19.3	0.0	29.7	53.9	34.6	16.5	22.9	-33.8	33.5	46.3	35.4	5.7	33.0	-6.8
1947	32.1	-2.7	32.8	2.2	34.5	5.2	33.1	-4.1	33.6	1.5	34.6	3.0	35.3	2.0	36.7	4.0	39.2	6.8	37.8	-3.6	36.4	-3.7	37.4	2.7
1948	40.3	7.8	37.8	-6.2	39.0	3.2	40.4	3.6	42.0	4.0	42.3	0.7	44.1	4.3	44.6	1.1	44.4	-0.4	41.0	-7.7	38.8	-5.4	37.7	-2.8
1949	36.6	-2.9	34.9	-4.6	36.5	4.6	36.6	0.3	36.7	0.3	36.8	0.3	36.2	-1.6	35.8	-1.1	36.8	2.8	35.3	-4.1	34.2	-3.1	33.4	-2.3
1950	33.7	0.9	34.6	2.7	34.4	-0.6	34.4	0.0	37.2	8.1	38.3	3.0	41.3	7.8	41.4	0.2	41.8	1.0	38.9	-6.9	38.8	-0.3	40.5	4.4
1951	41.9	3.5	43.9	4.8	43.8	-0.2	43.8	0.0	44.1	0.7	43.8	-0.7	43.7	-0.2	43.9	0.5	44.2	0.7	44.6	0.9	43.3	-2.9	42.4	-2.1
1952	42.4	0.0	41.4	-2.4	41.5	0.2	40.9	-1.4	41.9	2.4	41.2	-1.7	41.3	0.2	42.0	1.7	40.9	-2.6	38.9	-4.9	38.1	-2.1	35.1	-7.9
1953	37.1	5.7	36.7	-1.1	34.1	-7.1	33.3	-2.3	35.1	5.4	34.2	-2.6	36.2	5.8	35.0	-3.3	36.4	4.0	33.2	-8.8	32.2	-3.0	33.5	4.0
1954	36.0	7.5	34.7	-3.6	34.7	0.0	35.3	1.7	36.8	4.2	34.5	-6.3	35.2	2.0	34.4	-2.3	34.4	0.0	32.1	-6.7	32.2	0.3	31.8	-1.2
1955	32.7	2.8	32.5	-0.6	31.1	-4.3	32.1	3.2	32.0	-0.3	34.2	6.9	33.1	-3.2	32.2	-2.7	32.7	1.6	30.5	-6.7	29.1	-4.6	28.1	-3.4
1956	28.3	0.7	28.4	0.4	27.9	-1.8	29.7	6.5	30.7	3.4	31.1	1.3	31.3	0.6	31.8	1.6	33.4	5.0	32.0	-4.2	30.9	-3.4	30.5	-1.3
1957	31.7	3.9	31.4	-0.9	31.6	0.6	33.0	4.4	34.2	3.6	36.1	5.6	37.1	2.8	36.5	-1.6	35.8	-1.9	34.2	-4.5	35.0	2.3	35.7	2.0
1958	38.0	6.4	38.4	1.1	39.6	3.1	40.6	2.5	42.2	3.9	42.6	0.9	41.9	-1.6	40.5	-3.3	40.0	-1.2	38.7	-3.2	38.3	-1.0	37.9	-1.0
1959	38.6	1.8	37.7	-2.3	37.2	-1.3	37.7	1.3	37.9	0.5	38.1	0.5	37.1	-2.6	35.4	-4.6	37.3	5.4	35.5	-4.8	33.9	-4.5	33.8	-0.3
1960	34.6	2.4	34.8	0.6	36.6	5.2	36.1	-1.4	36.8	1.9	36.7	-0.3	37.2	1.4	36.1	-3.0	35.9	-0.6	36.6	1.9	36.1	-1.4	36.4	0.8
1961	36.8	1.1	37.2	1.1	35.9	-3.5	35.3	-1.7	34.3	-2.8	33.6	-2.0	34.6	3.0	35.4	2.3	35.3	-0.3	35.0	-0.8	34.6	-1.1	35.4	2.3
1962	36.7	3.7	36.5	-0.5	36.4	-0.3	35.3	-3.0	35.3	0.0	35.4	0.3	36.6	3.4	37.3	1.9	39.5	5.9	37.0	-6.3	37.0	0.0	36.8	-0.5
1963	36.2	-1.6	35.3	-2.5	33.9	-4.0	33.4	-1.5	34.0	1.8	34.8	2.4	35.6	2.3	35.2	-1.1	34.8	-1.1	34.5	-0.9	33.9	-1.7	32.4	-4.4
1964	33.9	4.6	32.9	-2.9	32.8	-0.3	32.7	-0.3	32.1	-1.8	33.3	3.7	34.5	3.6	34.5	0.0	35.5	2.9	34.5	-2.8	33.2	-3.8	32.8	-1.2
1965	34.0	3.7	34.0	0.0	34.2	0.6	34.6	1.2	36.1	4.3	39.0	8.0	39.3	0.8	39.3	0.0	38.9	-1.0	38.8	-0.3	39.0	0.5	40.8	4.6
1966	41.7	2.2	42.5	1.9	41.9	-1.4	41.0	-2.1	41.0	0.0	40.6	-1.0	40.7	0.2	41.1	1.0	41.5	1.0	40.0	-3.6	38.5	-3.8	38.6	0.3
1967	39.0	1.0	38.7	-0.8	37.6	-2.8	37.2	-1.1	38.4	3.2	40.0	4.2	40.6	1.5	39.7	-2.2	40.1	1.0	38.7	-3.5	37.8	-2.3	38.2	1.1
1968	39.1	2.4	39.8	1.8	39.6	-0.5	39.1	-1.3	39.5	1.0	40.6	2.8	42.0	3.4	40.6	-3.3	41.1	1.2	39.5	-3.9	39.8	0.8	39.7	-0.3
1969	41.1	3.5	41.2	0.2	41.5	0.7	42.2	1.7	44.7	5.9	46.8	4.7	47.1	0.6	46.0	-2.3	45.4	-1.3	44.5	-2.0	44.6	0.2	45.1	1.1
1970	46.6	3.3	46.2	-0.9	47.1	1.9	46.2	-1.9	45.3	-1.9	45.7	0.9	46.7	2.2	45.2	-3.2	44.7	-1.1	43.1	-3.6	42.2	-2.1	40.5	-4.0

[Continued]

Meats, Poultry, and Fish
Producer Price Index
Base 1982 = 100
[Continued]

For 1926-2001. Columns headed % show percentile change in the index from the previous period for which an index is available.

Year	Jan Index	%	Feb Index	%	Mar Index	%	Apr Index	%	May Index	%	Jun Index	%	Jul Index	%	Aug Index	%	Sep Index	%	Oct Index	%	Nov Index	%	Dec Index	%
1971	42.2	4.2	44.7	5.9	43.8	-2.0	44.0	0.5	45.2	2.7	45.3	0.2	46.4	2.4	45.7	-1.5	45.6	-0.2	45.4	-0.4	45.5	0.2	46.8	2.9
1972	48.7	4.1	50.7	4.1	49.4	-2.6	48.0	-2.8	49.2	2.5	51.0	3.7	52.7	3.3	51.3	-2.7	51.1	-0.4	50.6	-1.0	49.7	-1.8	52.9	6.4
1973	56.4	6.6	59.5	5.5	64.1	7.7	63.3	-1.2	63.1	-0.3	64.0	1.4	65.9	3.0	77.0	16.8	72.7	-5.6	66.1	-9.1	64.1	-3.0	64.0	-0.2
1974	69.0	7.8	69.8	1.2	64.3	-7.9	61.2	-4.8	59.5	-2.8	55.0	-7.6	64.9	18.0	65.9	1.5	64.3	-2.4	63.3	-1.6	62.3	-1.6	62.4	0.2
1975	64.3	3.0	63.9	-0.6	63.6	-0.5	67.7	6.4	74.0	9.3	77.5	4.7	81.4	5.0	79.4	-2.5	81.4	2.5	81.7	0.4	78.0	-4.5	76.9	-1.4
1976	75.0	-2.5	72.2	-3.7	70.1	-2.9	73.4	4.7	73.9	0.7	73.8	-0.1	71.9	-2.6	67.8	-5.7	68.4	0.9	65.4	-4.4	65.4	0.0	68.7	5.0
1977	68.6	-0.1	68.9	0.4	67.6	-1.9	67.9	0.4	71.3	5.0	71.2	-0.1	73.6	3.4	70.9	-3.7	71.0	0.1	71.7	1.0	71.2	-0.7	74.1	4.1
1978	75.2	1.5	79.8	6.1	79.5	-0.4	82.2	3.4	85.6	4.1	87.8	2.6	87.1	-0.8	83.8	-3.8	87.1	3.9	88.6	1.7	85.8	-3.2	89.0	3.7
1979	93.3	4.8	96.5	3.4	97.3	0.8	98.2	0.9	97.2	-1.0	93.7	-3.6	92.3	-1.5	87.6	-5.1	93.1	6.3	90.9	-2.4	92.9	2.2	94.3	1.5
1980	93.0	-1.4	93.0	0.0	92.9	-0.1	87.8	-5.5	87.1	-0.8	88.0	1.0	96.5	9.7	100.9	4.6	100.1	-0.8	99.4	-0.7	97.4	-2.0	96.3	-1.1
1981	96.3	0.0	94.6	-1.8	93.9	-0.7	92.8	-1.2	95.2	2.6	96.5	1.4	99.8	3.4	98.8	-1.0	98.3	-0.5	95.7	-2.6	93.2	-2.6	91.7	-1.6
1982	94.6	3.2	96.3	1.8	97.1	0.8	100.2	3.2	103.9	3.7	105.3	1.3	103.3	-1.9	101.8	-1.5	103.2	1.4	99.7	-3.4	97.7	-2.0	97.0	-0.7
1983	97.9	0.9	101.3	3.5	101.2	-0.1	100.6	-0.6	100.1	-0.5	97.1	-3.0	96.0	-1.1	94.4	-1.7	94.3	-0.1	92.0	-2.4	91.1	-1.0	94.1	3.3
1984	99.3	5.5	98.8	-0.5	102.6	3.8	101.6	-1.0	99.8	-1.8	96.1	-3.7	100.5	4.6	97.9	-2.6	96.9	-1.0	95.3	-1.7	97.2	2.0	99.4	2.3
1985	99.6	0.2	99.2	-0.4	97.0	-2.2	95.0	-2.1	94.7	-0.3	92.6	-2.2	94.4	1.9	92.9	-1.6	91.1	-1.9	94.5	3.7	99.1	4.9	100.5	1.4
1986	98.1	-2.4	95.1	-3.1	93.9	-1.3	92.4	-1.6	95.8	3.7	97.2	1.5	103.0	6.0	107.7	4.6	106.4	-1.2	105.2	-1.1	103.7	-1.4	103.6	-0.1
1987	101.9	-1.6	102.5	0.6	100.3	-2.1	104.5	4.2	109.7	5.0	108.9	-0.7	109.5	0.6	106.2	-3.0	108.0	1.7	106.1	-1.8	101.4	-4.4	99.9	-1.5
1988	103.8	3.9	102.7	-1.1	104.0	1.3	104.4	0.4	107.7	3.2	110.0	2.1	109.6	-0.4	107.8	-1.6	109.3	1.4	106.8	-2.3	106.0	-0.7	106.8	0.8
1989	109.8	2.8	109.9	0.1	111.8	1.7	111.4	-0.4	112.7	1.2	111.4	-1.2	111.6	0.2	111.3	-0.3	110.4	-0.8	109.6	-0.7	111.0	1.3	111.5	0.5
1990	114.0	2.2	114.9	0.8	116.9	1.7	118.4	1.3	124.1	4.8	121.5	-2.1	121.6	0.1	121.0	-0.5	119.5	-1.2	121.0	1.3	121.1	0.1	120.9	-0.2
1991	120.0	-0.7	119.6	-0.3	120.6	0.8	120.0	-0.5	121.0	0.8	119.1	-1.6	118.6	-0.4	114.4	-3.5	112.3	-1.8	113.3	0.9	110.9	-2.1	110.0	-0.8
1992	109.0	-0.9	110.8	1.7	112.2	1.3	113.5	1.2	113.7	0.2	113.5	-0.2	112.6	-0.8	111.8	-0.7	111.9	0.1	112.1	0.2	111.0	-1.0	113.8	2.5
1993	114.3	0.4	115.2	0.8	116.7	1.3	118.0	1.1	118.7	0.6	117.6	-0.9	115.0	-2.2	114.3	-0.6	115.2	0.8	114.4	-0.7	113.5	-0.8	112.5	-0.9
1994	113.9	1.2	114.2	0.3	116.7	2.2	116.1	-0.5	114.0	-1.8	112.0	-1.8	110.1	-1.7	112.3	2.0	110.8	-1.3	109.3	-1.4	109.1	-0.2	108.1	-0.9
1995	111.0	2.7	112.8	1.6	112.8	0.0	110.4	-2.1	108.5	-1.7	109.2	0.6	111.9	2.5	112.8	0.8	112.3	-0.4	113.2	0.8	113.8	0.5	112.5	-1.1
1996	111.5	-0.9	112.0	0.4	111.4	-0.5	111.2	-0.2	113.1	1.7	116.6	3.1	118.0	1.2	121.1	2.6	118.9	-1.8	121.0	1.8	121.7	0.6	121.5	-0.2
1997	119.1	-2.0	116.7	-2.0	119.5	2.4	118.9	-0.5	121.6	2.3	119.3	-1.9	119.4	0.1	120.8	1.2	118.9	-1.6	117.9	-0.8	116.9	-0.8	114.7	-1.9
1998	112.3	-2.1	113.3	0.9	111.5	-1.6	112.3	0.7	115.1	2.5	115.6	0.4	114.9	-0.6	116.8	1.7	113.9	-2.5	111.7	-1.9	111.2	-0.4	107.9	-3.0
1999	110.5	2.4	109.8	-0.6	112.0	2.0	110.0	-1.8	114.1	3.7	115.6	1.3	114.0	-1.4	116.5	2.2	117.8	1.1	117.1	-0.6	116.2	-0.8	117.1	0.8
2000	116.6	-0.4	118.9	2.0	119.3	0.3	122.6	2.8	124.5	1.5	124.0	-0.4	123.5	-0.4	122.0	-1.2	119.6	-2.0	120.2	0.5	119.9	-0.2	121.6	1.4
2001	121.0	-0.5	125.0	3.3	126.4	1.1	128.7	1.8	128.6	-0.1	126.8	-1.4	127.0	0.2	128.0	0.8	127.3	-0.5	124.7	-2.0	121.4	-2.6	120.7	-0.6

Source: U.S. Department of Labor, Bureau of Labor Statistics, Division of Industry Prices and Price Indexes. n.e.c. stands for not elsewhere classified. - indicates no data collected for period or unavailable.

Dairy Products

Producer Price Index
Base 1982 = 100

For 1926-2001. Columns headed % show percentile change in the index from the previous period for which an index is available.

Year	Jan Index	%	Feb Index	%	Mar Index	%	Apr Index	%	May Index	%	Jun Index	%	Jul Index	%	Aug Index	%	Sep Index	%	Oct Index	%	Nov Index	%	Dec Index	%
1926	17.9	-	17.7	-1.1	17.4	-1.7	17.0	-2.3	16.8	-1.2	16.6	-1.2	16.7	0.6	17.0	1.8	17.6	3.5	18.0	2.3	18.2	1.1	18.7	2.7
1927	18.4	-1.6	18.6	1.1	18.5	-0.5	18.3	-1.1	17.2	-6.0	17.0	-1.2	17.1	0.6	17.2	0.6	18.4	7.0	18.7	1.6	18.8	0.5	19.2	2.1
1928	18.8	-2.1	18.5	-1.6	18.2	-1.6	17.6	-3.3	17.4	-1.1	17.4	0.0	18.0	3.4	18.7	3.9	19.0	1.6	18.8	-1.1	19.0	1.1	19.2	1.1
1929	19.0	-1.0	19.1	0.5	19.0	-0.5	18.5	-2.6	18.2	-1.6	18.4	1.1	18.0	-2.2	18.2	1.1	18.5	1.6	18.5	0.0	18.1	-2.2	17.7	-2.2
1930	17.0	-4.0	17.0	0.0	17.2	1.2	17.3	0.6	16.1	-6.9	15.7	-2.5	16.0	1.9	17.0	6.3	17.4	2.4	17.2	-1.1	16.7	-2.9	15.5	-7.2
1931	14.6	-5.8	14.5	-0.7	14.6	0.7	14.1	-3.4	13.7	-2.8	13.7	0.0	14.1	2.9	14.3	1.4	14.7	2.8	15.0	2.0	14.1	-6.0	13.9	-1.4
1932	11.9	-14.4	11.2	-5.9	11.2	0.0	10.7	-4.5	10.4	-2.8	10.0	-3.8	10.2	2.0	10.5	2.9	10.6	1.0	10.6	0.0	10.8	1.9	10.4	-3.7
1933	9.6	-7.7	9.1	-5.2	8.9	-2.2	9.3	4.5	10.2	9.7	11.0	7.8	11.5	4.5	11.5	0.0	11.5	0.0	11.5	0.0	11.7	1.7	11.4	-2.6
1934	11.4	0.0	12.1	6.1	12.0	-0.8	11.6	-3.3	11.7	0.9	12.7	8.5	13.1	3.1	13.5	3.1	13.3	-1.5	13.5	1.5	13.7	1.5	13.9	1.5
1935	14.6	5.0	15.2	4.1	14.4	-5.3	14.8	2.8	13.6	-8.1	13.0	-4.4	12.9	-0.8	13.2	2.3	13.3	0.8	13.4	0.8	14.2	6.0	14.6	2.8
1936	14.7	0.7	14.9	1.4	14.0	-6.0	13.7	-2.1	13.1	-4.4	13.5	3.1	14.6	8.1	15.3	4.8	15.6	2.0	15.2	-2.6	15.4	1.3	15.5	0.6
1937	15.5	0.0	15.5	0.0	15.7	1.3	13.7	-12.7	12.7	-7.3	12.6	-0.8	13.3	5.6	13.9	4.5	14.8	6.5	14.9	0.7	15.5	4.0	15.7	1.3
1938	14.5	-7.6	13.7	-5.5	13.4	-2.2	12.5	-6.7	12.1	-3.2	12.0	-0.8	12.1	0.8	12.0	-0.8	12.4	3.3	12.5	0.8	12.7	1.6	12.9	1.6
1939	12.5	-3.1	12.5	0.0	11.3	-9.6	10.1	-10.6	10.2	1.0	10.5	2.9	10.4	-1.0	11.9	14.4	13.0	9.2	13.7	5.4	14.0	2.2	14.2	1.4
1940	14.3	0.7	13.9	-2.8	13.7	-1.4	13.5	-1.5	12.7	-5.9	12.6	-0.8	12.9	2.4	12.9	0.0	13.1	1.6	13.5	3.1	14.4	6.7	14.7	2.1
1941	14.0	-4.8	13.9	-0.7	14.0	0.7	14.1	0.7	14.2	0.7	14.7	3.5	15.3	4.1	15.7	2.6	16.2	3.2	16.6	2.5	16.8	1.2	16.7	-0.6
1942	16.8	0.6	16.6	-1.2	16.5	-0.6	16.4	-0.6	16.3	-0.6	16.1	-1.2	16.8	4.3	17.5	4.2	18.4	5.1	19.0	3.3	19.4	2.1	19.5	0.5
1943	19.8	1.5	19.8	0.0	19.8	0.0	19.8	0.0	19.7	-0.5	19.1	-3.0	19.0	-0.5	19.0	0.0	19.0	0.0	19.0	0.0	19.4	2.1	19.3	-0.5
1944	19.3	0.0	19.3	0.0	19.3	0.0	19.2	-0.5	19.2	0.0	19.2	0.0	19.2	0.0	19.3	0.5	19.3	0.0	19.3	0.0	19.3	0.0	19.3	0.0
1945	19.3	0.0	19.3	0.0	19.3	0.0	19.3	0.0	19.3	0.0	19.3	0.0	19.3	0.0	19.3	0.0	19.2	-0.5	19.3	0.5	19.7	2.1	19.8	0.5
1946	20.0	1.0	20.2	1.0	20.3	0.5	20.3	0.0	20.4	0.5	22.2	8.8	27.4	23.4	28.2	2.9	29.5	4.6	32.3	9.5	31.9	-1.2	31.4	-1.6
1947	28.7	-8.6	28.0	-2.4	27.4	-2.1	26.7	-2.6	26.1	-2.2	26.0	-0.4	26.9	3.5	27.8	3.3	28.5	2.5	29.3	2.8	30.3	3.4	30.9	2.0
1948	31.5	1.9	31.5	0.0	30.6	-2.9	30.9	1.0	30.8	-0.3	31.3	1.6	32.2	2.9	32.5	0.9	31.8	-2.2	31.3	-1.6	30.9	-1.3	30.5	-1.3
1949	29.8	-2.3	29.2	-2.0	28.3	-3.1	27.7	-2.1	27.3	-1.4	27.6	1.1	27.7	0.4	28.4	2.5	28.2	-0.7	28.2	0.0	28.0	-0.7	28.1	0.4
1950	27.4	-2.5	27.5	0.4	27.2	-1.1	26.9	-1.1	26.2	-2.6	26.3	0.4	27.0	2.7	27.7	2.6	28.5	2.9	28.9	1.4	29.0	0.3	29.5	1.7
1951	30.9	4.7	31.5	1.9	31.2	-1.0	30.9	-1.0	31.1	0.6	31.1	0.0	31.1	0.0	31.5	1.3	31.0	-1.6	31.7	2.3	32.4	2.2	33.0	1.9
1952	33.1	0.3	33.6	1.5	33.1	-1.5	32.7	-1.2	32.3	-1.2	32.1	-0.6	33.2	3.4	33.3	0.3	34.0	2.1	33.8	-0.6	33.7	-0.3	33.0	-2.1
1953	32.7	-0.9	32.4	-0.9	32.0	-1.2	31.7	-0.9	31.5	-0.6	31.5	0.0	32.1	1.9	32.3	0.6	32.5	0.6	32.9	1.2	33.3	1.2	32.5	-2.4
1954	31.9	-1.8	31.3	-1.9	31.0	-1.0	30.1	-2.9	29.7	-1.3	29.9	0.7	30.7	2.7	30.9	0.7	31.1	0.6	31.7	1.9	31.8	0.3	31.6	-0.6
1955	31.3	-0.9	31.3	0.0	31.3	0.0	31.2	-0.3	30.4	-2.6	30.5	0.3	30.9	1.3	31.5	1.9	30.5	-3.2	30.7	0.7	30.9	0.7	31.3	1.3
1956	31.0	-1.0	31.0	0.0	31.0	0.0	30.9	-0.3	31.5	1.9	31.5	0.0	31.5	0.0	31.8	1.0	32.0	0.6	32.4	1.3	33.1	2.2	32.9	-0.6
1957	32.8	-0.3	32.8	0.0	32.5	-0.9	32.5	0.0	32.3	-0.6	31.5	-2.5	31.6	0.3	32.2	1.9	32.8	1.9	33.2	1.2	33.4	0.6	33.5	0.3
1958	33.3	-0.6	33.3	0.0	33.1	-0.6	32.5	-1.8	32.3	-0.6	32.4	0.3	32.5	0.3	32.7	0.6	33.2	1.5	33.1	-0.3	33.1	0.0	33.1	0.0
1959	33.0	-0.3	33.0	0.0	33.0	0.0	32.7	-0.9	32.6	-0.3	32.7	0.3	33.3	1.8	33.5	0.6	33.9	1.2	34.1	0.6	34.4	0.9	34.5	0.3
1960	34.7	0.6	34.6	-0.3	34.4	-0.6	33.7	-2.0	33.5	-0.6	33.8	0.9	34.2	1.2	34.4	0.6	35.2	2.3	35.4	0.6	35.5	0.3	35.6	0.3
1961	35.4	-0.6	35.0	-1.1	35.2	0.6	35.0	-0.6	34.9	-0.3	35.0	0.3	35.1	0.3	35.3	0.6	35.6	0.8	36.1	1.4	36.1	0.0	36.3	0.6
1962	36.0	-0.8	36.0	0.0	35.6	-1.1	35.0	-1.7	34.4	-1.7	34.6	0.6	34.8	0.6	35.0	0.6	35.0	0.0	35.5	1.4	35.6	0.3	35.6	0.0
1963	35.5	-0.3	35.6	0.3	35.3	-0.8	35.2	-0.3	35.2	0.0	35.1	-0.3	35.4	0.9	35.6	0.6	35.6	0.0	35.4	-0.6	35.6	0.6	35.6	0.0
1964	35.6	0.0	35.4	-0.6	35.4	0.0	35.3	-0.3	35.1	-0.6	35.3	0.6	35.3	0.0	35.4	0.3	35.8	1.1	35.9	0.3	36.1	0.6	35.9	-0.6
1965	35.7	-0.6	35.5	-0.6	35.4	-0.3	35.4	0.0	35.2	-0.6	35.3	0.3	35.5	0.6	35.8	0.8	36.0	0.6	36.0	0.0	36.4	1.1	36.7	0.8
1966	36.6	-0.3	37.2	1.6	37.9	1.9	37.8	-0.3	37.9	0.3	38.4	1.3	39.5	2.9	40.9	3.5	40.9	0.0	41.0	0.2	40.4	-1.5	40.3	-0.2
1967	40.1	-0.5	39.9	-0.5	39.7	-0.5	39.6	-0.3	39.8	0.5	40.2	1.0	40.2	0.0	40.3	0.2	40.5	0.5	40.5	0.0	40.5	0.0	40.9	1.0
1968	40.8	-0.2	40.9	0.2	40.6	-0.7	41.5	2.2	42.5	2.4	42.4	-0.2	42.5	0.2	42.5	0.0	42.5	0.0	42.9	0.9	42.8	-0.2	43.0	0.5
1969	42.9	-0.2	42.9	0.0	43.0	0.2	43.3	0.7	43.6	0.7	43.8	0.5	43.8	0.0	43.8	0.0	44.1	0.7	43.1	-2.3	43.3	0.5	44.2	2.1
1970	44.2	0.0	44.3	0.2	43.9	-0.9	44.5	1.4	44.7	0.4	44.7	0.0	44.8	0.2	44.8	0.0	44.8	0.0	45.1	0.7	45.1	0.0	45.4	0.7

[Continued]

Dairy Products

Producer Price Index
Base 1982 = 100
[Continued]

For 1926-2001. Columns headed % show percentile change in the index from the previous period for which an index is available.

Year	Jan Index	%	Feb Index	%	Mar Index	%	Apr Index	%	May Index	%	Jun Index	%	Jul Index	%	Aug Index	%	Sep Index	%	Oct Index	%	Nov Index	%	Dec Index	%
1971	45.4	0.0	45.2	-0.4	46.2	2.2	46.4	0.4	46.7	0.6	46.7	0.0	46.7	0.0	46.8	0.2	46.8	0.0	46.8	0.0	46.7	-0.2	47.2	1.1
1972	47.1	-0.2	47.2	0.2	47.4	0.4	47.2	-0.4	47.2	0.0	46.3	-1.9	47.3	2.2	47.7	0.8	47.8	0.2	48.2	0.8	48.9	1.5	49.4	1.0
1973	49.7	0.6	49.8	0.2	51.0	2.4	51.1	0.2	50.8	-0.6	51.2	0.8	51.1	-0.2	52.8	3.3	55.1	4.4	56.1	1.8	56.2	0.2	57.2	1.8
1974	58.3	1.9	59.3	1.7	60.8	2.5	61.9	1.8	59.0	-4.7	57.4	-2.7	56.9	-0.9	57.2	0.5	58.2	1.7	58.8	1.0	59.0	0.3	59.0	0.0
1975	59.6	1.0	59.6	0.0	59.7	0.2	59.8	0.2	60.1	0.5	60.5	0.7	61.5	1.7	62.8	2.1	64.6	2.9	66.6	3.1	67.5	1.4	68.8	1.9
1976	68.2	-0.9	65.7	-3.7	67.0	2.0	67.4	0.6	67.2	-0.3	67.2	0.0	68.4	1.8	69.9	2.2	68.5	-2.0	68.2	-0.4	67.6	-0.9	67.2	-0.6
1977	67.0	-0.3	67.0	0.0	67.5	0.7	69.7	3.3	70.0	0.4	70.0	0.0	70.4	0.6	70.5	0.1	70.6	0.1	70.7	0.1	71.1	0.6	71.6	0.7
1978	71.5	-0.1	71.8	0.4	72.4	0.8	74.1	2.3	74.1	0.0	74.5	0.5	74.8	0.4	76.7	2.5	77.5	1.0	79.2	2.2	80.2	1.3	81.5	1.6
1979	81.8	0.4	81.6	-0.2	82.3	0.9	83.2	1.1	83.5	0.4	83.7	0.2	84.0	0.4	86.5	3.0	87.7	1.4	87.6	-0.1	88.1	0.6	88.3	0.2
1980	88.8	0.6	88.7	-0.1	89.6	1.0	91.4	2.0	91.8	0.4	92.2	0.4	92.4	0.2	93.5	1.2	93.9	0.4	95.6	1.8	96.5	0.9	97.4	0.9
1981	98.3	0.9	98.5	0.2	98.5	0.0	98.6	0.1	98.3	-0.3	98.5	0.2	98.5	0.0	98.5	0.0	98.6	0.1	99.2	0.6	99.2	0.0	99.3	0.1
1982	99.5	0.2	99.6	0.1	99.6	0.0	99.8	0.2	99.8	0.0	99.9	0.1	99.9	0.0	100.0	0.1	100.1	0.1	100.4	0.3	100.5	0.1	100.8	0.3
1983	100.7	-0.1	100.8	0.1	100.7	-0.1	100.8	0.1	100.8	0.0	100.6	-0.2	100.6	0.0	100.6	0.0	100.7	0.1	101.0	0.3	101.0	0.0	100.0	-1.0
1984	99.8	-0.2	99.8	0.0	100.0	0.2	100.0	0.0	100.0	0.0	100.3	0.3	101.0	0.7	100.9	-0.1	102.5	1.6	103.0	0.5	103.4	0.4	102.8	-0.6
1985	102.6	-0.2	102.1	-0.5	101.8	-0.3	101.0	-0.8	100.4	-0.6	100.2	-0.2	99.7	-0.5	99.2	-0.5	98.9	-0.3	98.8	-0.1	98.9	0.1	98.9	0.0
1986	98.8	-0.1	98.9	0.1	98.8	-0.1	98.8	0.0	99.2	0.4	99.2	0.0	99.5	0.3	100.3	0.8	100.6	0.3	101.2	0.6	101.8	0.6	102.1	0.3
1987	101.9	-0.2	101.4	-0.5	101.4	0.0	101.2	-0.2	100.9	-0.3	101.1	0.2	101.4	0.3	101.9	0.5	102.7	0.8	102.1	-0.6	102.0	-0.1	101.7	-0.3
1988	101.0	-0.7	100.5	-0.5	100.1	-0.4	100.0	-0.1	100.1	0.1	100.6	0.5	101.2	0.6	102.2	1.0	103.8	1.6	104.9	1.1	105.5	0.6	106.2	0.7
1989	107.1	0.8	106.5	-0.6	106.0	-0.5	105.6	-0.4	105.6	0.0	106.4	0.8	107.9	1.4	110.7	2.6	113.3	2.3	116.4	2.7	120.1	3.2	121.4	1.1
1990	120.5	-0.7	116.9	-3.0	116.1	-0.7	115.1	-0.9	116.6	1.3	118.0	1.2	119.5	1.3	120.2	0.6	119.0	-1.0	117.4	-1.3	114.8	-2.2	112.8	-1.7
1991	112.3	-0.4	112.0	-0.3	111.9	-0.1	111.5	-0.4	111.5	0.0	112.1	0.5	113.6	1.3	115.1	1.3	115.9	0.7	119.3	2.9	119.8	0.4	120.0	0.2
1992	118.3	-1.4	116.0	-1.9	115.0	-0.9	115.4	0.3	116.9	1.3	118.7	1.5	119.4	0.6	120.0	0.5	120.0	0.0	119.4	-0.5	118.7	-0.6	117.4	-1.1
1993	116.4	-0.9	115.4	-0.9	115.0	-0.3	117.2	1.9	118.5	1.1	119.5	0.8	119.2	-0.3	117.9	-1.1	118.4	0.4	119.0	0.5	120.3	1.1	121.0	0.6
1994	120.3	-0.6	119.9	-0.3	120.6	0.6	121.4	0.7	121.2	-0.2	118.7	-2.1	117.1	-1.3	118.2	0.9	118.8	0.5	119.2	0.3	119.4	0.2	118.6	-0.7
1995	117.1	-1.3	117.6	0.4	118.3	0.6	118.1	-0.2	117.7	-0.3	117.2	-0.4	118.0	0.7	119.0	0.8	120.5	1.3	122.6	1.7	125.0	2.0	125.0	0.0
1996	124.1	-0.7	123.4	-0.6	123.1	-0.2	123.2	0.1	126.9	3.0	131.8	3.9	134.6	2.1	137.2	1.9	139.7	1.8	140.7	0.7	132.1	-6.1	128.0	-3.1
1997	126.3	-1.3	127.3	0.8	128.4	0.9	127.8	-0.5	125.9	-1.5	125.3	-0.5	124.5	-0.6	126.0	1.2	127.1	0.9	130.3	2.5	134.1	2.9	134.2	0.1
1998	130.1	-3.1	133.1	2.3	132.2	-0.7	131.4	-0.6	131.3	-0.1	133.4	1.6	135.6	1.6	140.1	3.3	145.7	4.0	148.3	1.8	148.5	0.1	148.4	-0.1
1999	148.9	0.3	144.0	-3.3	141.8	-1.5	132.1	-6.8	133.0	0.7	135.3	1.7	136.4	0.8	139.9	2.6	142.9	2.1	143.5	0.4	141.3	-1.5	132.0	-6.6
2000	131.4	-0.5	130.7	-0.5	131.0	0.2	132.3	1.0	132.6	0.2	134.0	1.1	135.8	1.3	135.3	-0.4	135.6	0.2	134.4	-0.9	135.2	0.6	136.2	0.7
2001	137.0	0.6	135.9	-0.8	138.7	2.1	141.7	2.2	146.9	3.7	150.4	2.4	151.2	0.5	152.1	0.6	153.5	0.9	150.6	-1.9	145.4	-3.5	140.3	-3.5

Source: U.S. Department of Labor, Bureau of Labor Statistics, Division of Industry Prices and Price Indexes. n.e.c. stands for not elsewhere classified. - indicates no data collected for period or unavailable.

Processed Fruits and Vegetables
Producer Price Index
Base 1982 = 100

For 1926-2001. Columns headed % show percentile change in the index from the previous period for which an index is available.

Year	Jan Index	%	Feb Index	%	Mar Index	%	Apr Index	%	May Index	%	Jun Index	%	Jul Index	%	Aug Index	%	Sep Index	%	Oct Index	%	Nov Index	%	Dec Index	%
1926	20.6	-	20.5	-0.5	20.3	-1.0	20.3	0.0	20.1	-1.0	20.2	0.5	20.3	0.5	20.1	-1.0	20.3	1.0	20.5	1.0	20.4	-0.5	20.2	-1.0
1927	20.1	-0.5	20.4	1.5	20.4	0.0	20.0	-2.0	20.0	0.0	20.0	0.0	20.0	0.0	20.0	0.0	19.7	-1.5	19.6	-0.5	20.3	3.6	20.5	1.0
1928	21.4	4.4	21.5	0.5	21.7	0.9	21.8	0.5	21.8	0.0	21.8	0.0	21.6	-0.9	21.0	-2.8	21.1	0.5	21.3	0.9	21.4	0.5	21.5	0.5
1929	21.4	-0.5	21.7	1.4	21.8	0.5	22.1	1.4	22.7	2.7	23.0	1.3	23.5	2.2	22.7	-3.4	22.5	-0.9	22.4	-0.4	22.3	-0.4	22.5	0.9
1930	22.7	0.9	22.6	-0.4	22.5	-0.4	22.2	-1.3	20.7	-6.8	20.5	-1.0	20.4	-0.5	20.4	0.0	20.6	1.0	20.3	-1.5	19.6	-3.4	19.2	-2.0
1931	19.0	-1.0	19.1	0.5	18.6	-2.6	18.3	-1.6	17.7	-3.3	17.5	-1.1	17.5	0.0	17.3	-1.1	17.1	-1.2	16.8	-1.8	16.3	-3.0	16.3	0.0
1932	16.2	-0.6	16.1	-0.6	16.4	1.9	16.4	0.0	16.3	-0.6	16.1	-1.2	15.5	-3.7	15.4	-0.6	15.0	-2.6	15.2	1.3	15.1	-0.7	15.0	-0.7
1933	14.9	-0.7	14.8	-0.7	14.8	0.0	14.9	0.7	15.4	3.4	15.6	1.3	15.9	1.9	16.4	3.1	17.1	4.3	17.2	0.6	17.1	-0.6	17.1	0.0
1934	17.2	0.6	17.5	1.7	17.6	0.6	17.7	0.6	17.6	-0.6	17.6	0.0	17.8	1.1	17.5	-1.7	18.0	2.9	18.7	3.9	18.5	-1.1	18.5	0.0
1935	18.5	0.0	18.7	1.1	18.7	0.0	18.5	-1.1	18.3	-1.1	18.2	-0.5	17.9	-1.6	17.1	-4.5	17.1	0.0	16.9	-1.2	16.8	-0.6	16.8	0.0
1936	16.6	-1.2	16.6	0.0	16.9	1.8	17.1	1.2	17.1	0.0	16.9	-1.2	17.1	1.2	18.1	5.8	18.3	1.1	18.2	-0.5	18.3	0.5	18.4	0.5
1937	18.5	0.5	18.5	0.0	18.5	0.0	18.5	0.0	18.5	0.0	18.7	1.1	18.3	-2.1	17.9	-2.2	17.8	-0.6	17.7	-0.6	17.9	1.1	17.8	-0.6
1938	17.7	-0.6	17.6	-0.6	17.5	-0.6	17.2	-1.7	16.9	-1.7	16.3	-3.6	15.9	-2.5	15.3	-3.8	15.2	-0.7	15.2	0.0	15.1	-0.7	15.1	0.0
1939	15.2	0.7	15.2	0.0	15.3	0.7	15.5	1.3	15.5	0.0	15.6	0.6	15.6	0.0	15.5	-0.6	16.1	3.9	16.4	1.9	16.3	-0.6	16.2	-0.6
1940	16.1	-0.6	16.1	0.0	15.9	-1.2	15.9	0.0	15.9	0.0	16.0	0.6	16.0	0.0	15.8	-1.2	15.7	-0.6	15.7	0.0	15.7	0.0	15.7	0.0
1941	15.9	1.3	16.3	2.5	16.4	0.6	16.8	2.4	17.1	1.8	17.6	2.9	18.9	7.4	19.9	5.3	19.8	-0.5	20.4	3.0	20.7	1.5	21.0	1.4
1942	21.1	0.5	21.2	0.5	21.4	0.9	21.5	0.5	21.5	0.0	22.0	2.3	21.8	-0.9	21.8	0.0	22.0	0.9	22.5	2.3	22.5	0.0	22.5	0.0
1943	22.5	0.0	22.5	0.0	22.5	0.0	22.5	0.0	22.5	0.0	22.5	0.0	22.5	0.0	22.4	-0.4	22.4	0.0	22.5	0.4	22.5	0.0	22.5	0.0
1944	22.6	0.4	22.6	0.0	22.6	0.0	22.6	0.0	22.6	0.0	22.6	0.0	22.6	0.0	22.8	0.9	23.1	1.3	23.0	-0.4	23.0	0.0	23.1	0.4
1945	23.0	-0.4	23.0	0.0	23.0	0.0	23.0	0.0	23.1	0.4	23.1	0.0	23.1	0.0	23.1	0.0	23.1	0.0	23.0	-0.4	23.1	0.4	23.0	-0.4
1946	23.0	0.0	23.0	0.0	23.0	0.0	23.2	0.9	23.4	0.9	23.7	1.3	23.7	0.0	23.4	-1.3	23.5	0.4	23.7	0.9	29.4	24.1	29.4	0.0
1947	31.9	8.5	31.8	-0.3	31.8	0.0	31.8	0.0	32.2	1.3	31.9	-0.9	31.7	-0.6	31.3	-1.3	31.6	1.0	31.6	0.0	31.6	0.0	31.5	-0.3
1948	31.6	0.3	31.6	0.0	31.4	-0.6	31.2	-0.6	31.2	0.0	31.3	0.3	31.5	0.6	32.1	1.9	32.2	0.3	31.8	-1.2	32.0	0.6	31.8	-0.6
1949	31.7	-0.3	31.8	0.3	31.8	0.0	31.8	0.0	32.0	0.6	31.7	-0.9	31.4	-0.9	31.3	-0.3	31.3	0.0	31.3	0.0	31.1	-0.6	30.0	-3.5
1950	30.6	2.0	31.0	1.3	31.0	0.0	30.8	-0.6	30.9	0.3	31.0	0.3	31.2	0.6	32.1	2.9	32.4	0.9	32.6	0.6	32.1	-1.5	32.6	1.6
1951	33.4	2.5	33.7	0.9	33.7	0.0	33.7	0.0	33.4	-0.9	33.0	-1.2	32.7	-0.9	32.6	-0.3	33.1	1.5	33.4	0.9	33.6	0.6	33.6	0.0
1952	33.4	-0.6	33.1	-0.9	33.2	0.3	33.1	-0.3	32.9	-0.6	32.7	-0.6	32.8	0.3	33.2	1.2	33.5	0.9	33.5	0.0	33.5	0.0	33.2	-0.9
1953	33.3	0.3	33.3	0.0	33.2	-0.3	33.0	-0.6	32.9	-0.3	32.8	-0.3	33.2	1.2	33.1	-0.3	33.1	0.0	33.2	0.3	33.1	-0.3	32.8	-0.9
1954	32.8	0.0	32.6	-0.6	32.6	0.0	32.6	0.0	33.0	1.2	33.1	0.3	33.1	0.0	33.1	0.0	33.2	0.3	33.3	0.3	33.3	0.0	33.5	0.6
1955	33.1	-1.2	33.0	-0.3	33.1	0.3	33.1	0.0	32.9	-0.6	33.0	0.3	33.1	0.3	33.2	0.3	33.7	1.5	34.0	0.9	34.0	0.0	34.1	0.3
1956	34.1	0.0	34.4	0.9	34.3	-0.3	34.4	0.3	34.5	0.3	34.7	0.6	34.5	-0.6	33.9	-1.7	33.7	-0.6	33.6	-0.3	33.6	0.0	33.4	-0.6
1957	33.4	0.0	33.5	0.3	33.5	0.0	33.2	-0.9	32.7	-1.5	32.2	-1.5	32.3	0.3	32.2	-0.3	32.4	0.6	32.7	0.9	32.8	0.3	33.1	0.9
1958	33.4	0.9	33.4	0.0	33.7	0.9	34.0	0.9	34.2	0.6	34.9	2.0	35.2	0.9	35.3	0.3	35.2	-0.3	35.4	0.6	35.7	0.8	35.7	0.0
1959	35.0	-2.0	34.9	-0.3	35.2	0.9	34.9	-0.9	34.9	0.0	35.1	0.6	34.9	-0.6	34.1	-2.3	33.8	-0.9	34.0	0.6	33.6	-1.2	33.1	-1.5
1960	33.0	-0.3	33.2	0.6	33.4	0.6	33.4	0.0	33.6	0.6	33.8	0.6	33.9	0.3	33.7	-0.6	34.0	0.9	34.4	1.2	34.6	0.6	34.8	0.6
1961	35.3	1.4	35.4	0.3	35.2	-0.6	35.1	-0.3	34.4	-2.0	34.4	0.0	34.5	0.3	34.0	-1.4	33.9	-0.3	34.1	0.6	34.1	0.0	34.1	0.0
1962	33.7	-1.2	33.9	0.6	33.7	-0.6	33.7	0.0	33.5	-0.6	33.7	0.6	33.6	-0.3	33.0	-1.8	32.8	-0.6	32.8	0.0	32.7	-0.3	32.5	-0.6
1963	34.0	4.6	33.9	-0.3	34.4	1.5	35.0	1.7	35.2	0.6	35.6	1.1	35.9	0.8	35.6	-0.8	35.8	0.6	36.0	0.6	36.2	0.6	36.3	0.3
1964	36.4	0.3	36.5	0.3	36.5	0.0	36.5	0.0	36.1	-1.1	36.1	0.0	35.7	-1.1	34.7	-2.8	34.7	0.0	34.9	0.6	34.8	-0.3	34.7	-0.3
1965	34.7	0.0	34.1	-1.7	34.2	0.3	34.3	0.3	34.1	-0.6	34.5	1.2	34.6	0.3	34.1	-1.4	34.6	1.5	35.6	2.9	35.8	0.6	35.7	-0.3
1966	35.6	-0.3	35.7	0.3	35.6	-0.3	35.6	0.0	35.8	0.6	35.7	-0.3	35.5	-0.6	34.8	-2.0	35.2	1.1	35.9	2.0	36.0	0.3	36.0	0.0
1967	36.0	0.0	35.4	-1.7	35.4	0.0	35.5	0.3	35.7	0.6	36.2	1.4	36.3	0.3	36.4	0.3	36.7	0.8	37.2	1.4	38.1	2.4	38.4	0.8
1968	38.6	0.5	38.7	0.3	38.9	0.5	39.0	0.3	39.1	0.3	39.1	0.0	39.1	0.0	38.6	-1.3	38.6	0.0	38.8	0.5	38.8	0.0	38.6	-0.5
1969	38.7	0.3	39.0	0.8	39.1	0.3	39.3	0.5	39.4	0.3	39.4	0.0	39.7	0.8	39.7	0.0	39.7	0.0	39.5	-0.5	39.6	0.3	39.6	0.0
1970	39.8	0.5	39.9	0.3	39.7	-0.5	39.9	0.5	40.2	0.8	40.3	0.2	40.5	0.5	40.7	0.5	40.8	0.2	40.5	-0.7	40.7	0.5	40.5	-0.5

[Continued]

Processed Fruits and Vegetables
Producer Price Index
Base 1982 = 100
[Continued]

For 1926-2001. Columns headed % show percentile change in the index from the previous period for which an index is available.

Year	Jan Index	%	Feb Index	%	Mar Index	%	Apr Index	%	May Index	%	Jun Index	%	Jul Index	%	Aug Index	%	Sep Index	%	Oct Index	%	Nov Index	%	Dec Index	%
1971	40.6	0.2	40.7	0.2	40.9	0.5	41.2	0.7	41.5	0.7	42.1	1.4	42.3	0.5	42.3	0.0	42.2	-0.2	42.0	-0.5	42.0	0.0	42.2	0.5
1972	42.3	0.2	42.3	0.0	42.5	0.5	43.1	1.4	43.4	0.7	43.5	0.2	43.6	0.2	43.8	0.5	43.7	-0.2	44.4	1.6	45.1	1.6	45.5	0.9
1973	45.7	0.4	45.9	0.4	46.0	0.2	46.1	0.2	46.4	0.7	46.6	0.4	46.5	-0.2	47.1	1.3	47.4	0.6	49.2	3.8	49.7	1.0	50.2	1.0
1974	50.7	1.0	51.3	1.2	51.5	0.4	52.0	1.0	52.9	1.7	54.0	2.1	57.5	6.5	59.3	3.1	60.3	1.7	61.9	2.7	62.3	0.6	62.0	-0.5
1975	62.4	0.6	62.3	-0.2	61.8	-0.8	62.2	0.6	62.3	0.2	62.3	0.0	61.7	-1.0	61.4	-0.5	61.4	0.0	61.7	0.5	61.6	-0.2	61.4	-0.3
1976	61.0	-0.7	60.6	-0.7	60.6	0.0	60.8	0.3	61.2	0.7	61.5	0.5	61.8	0.5	62.3	0.8	62.7	0.6	63.5	1.3	64.0	0.8	64.0	0.0
1977	63.8	-0.3	66.6	4.4	67.1	0.8	67.5	0.6	67.7	0.3	68.4	1.0	68.6	0.3	69.4	1.2	69.6	0.3	69.4	-0.3	70.4	1.4	70.8	0.6
1978	70.8	0.0	70.9	0.1	71.3	0.6	71.6	0.4	71.9	0.4	72.4	0.7	73.0	0.8	74.1	1.5	74.7	0.8	76.6	2.5	78.8	2.9	79.6	1.0
1979	79.6	0.0	80.0	0.5	80.0	0.0	80.3	0.4	80.7	0.5	80.7	0.0	81.5	1.0	81.8	0.4	82.0	0.2	81.4	-0.7	81.0	-0.5	81.1	0.1
1980	81.2	0.1	81.4	0.2	81.5	0.1	81.9	0.5	82.1	0.2	82.8	0.9	83.7	1.1	84.1	0.5	84.3	0.2	85.2	1.1	85.5	0.4	86.2	0.8
1981	86.9	0.8	88.8	2.2	93.0	4.7	94.0	1.1	94.5	0.5	95.6	1.2	96.9	1.4	97.4	0.5	98.4	1.0	99.0	0.6	98.6	-0.4	99.0	0.4
1982	99.5	0.5	100.7	1.2	100.5	-0.2	100.3	-0.2	99.8	-0.5	100.5	0.7	100.0	-0.5	99.9	-0.1	99.4	-0.5	99.6	0.2	99.4	-0.2	100.4	1.0
1983	100.1	-0.3	99.9	-0.2	100.2	0.3	99.7	-0.5	100.3	0.6	101.0	0.7	101.0	0.0	101.4	0.4	101.5	0.1	102.4	0.9	102.3	-0.1	103.1	0.8
1984	104.8	1.6	106.7	1.8	107.6	0.8	107.5	-0.1	108.5	0.9	108.6	0.1	107.9	-0.6	107.8	-0.1	106.3	-1.4	107.8	1.4	106.5	-1.2	106.9	0.4
1985	108.1	1.1	108.1	0.0	109.3	1.1	108.8	-0.5	108.6	-0.2	109.7	1.0	109.2	-0.5	109.3	0.1	107.5	-1.6	106.9	-0.6	105.2	-1.6	105.0	-0.2
1986	104.5	-0.5	104.6	0.1	104.7	0.1	104.1	-0.6	104.3	0.2	105.4	1.1	104.5	-0.9	105.1	0.6	105.1	0.0	104.6	-0.5	105.6	1.0	106.6	0.9
1987	107.3	0.7	107.5	0.2	108.4	0.8	108.3	-0.1	108.4	0.1	109.5	1.0	108.7	-0.7	109.3	0.6	108.5	-0.7	108.4	-0.1	108.8	0.4	110.1	1.2
1988	110.9	0.7	111.4	0.5	111.8	0.4	111.5	-0.3	111.7	0.2	111.6	-0.1	113.4	1.6	115.2	1.6	115.5	0.3	116.5	0.9	117.9	1.2	118.5	0.5
1989	119.0	-0.4	118.8	-0.2	119.2	0.3	119.0	-0.2	119.8	0.7	120.5	0.6	120.8	0.2	121.2	0.3	120.7	-0.4	120.0	-0.6	119.9	-0.1	120.4	0.4
1990	122.4	1.7	125.7	2.7	126.9	1.0	126.9	0.0	127.0	0.1	126.5	-0.4	126.1	-0.3	125.8	-0.2	124.9	-0.7	123.6	-1.0	120.9	-2.2	120.2	-0.6
1991	120.0	-0.2	120.2	0.2	119.8	-0.3	119.2	-0.5	119.3	0.1	119.0	-0.3	119.6	0.5	118.7	-0.8	118.6	-0.1	119.2	0.5	120.4	1.0	121.6	1.0
1992	122.1	0.4	122.4	0.2	122.3	-0.1	122.0	-0.2	122.0	0.0	121.0	-0.8	120.6	-0.3	120.5	-0.1	119.8	-0.6	119.1	-0.6	118.9	-0.2	118.4	-0.4
1993	117.5	-0.8	117.0	-0.4	116.4	-0.5	116.1	-0.3	116.7	0.5	117.6	0.8	119.0	1.2	118.7	-0.3	118.9	0.2	119.5	0.5	120.3	0.7	120.4	0.1
1994	120.8	0.3	121.6	0.7	121.4	-0.2	121.7	0.2	122.0	0.2	122.0	0.0	121.9	-0.1	121.6	-0.2	120.6	-0.8	120.6	0.0	120.0	-0.5	119.6	-0.3
1995	120.2	0.5	120.7	0.4	121.3	0.5	120.7	-0.5	122.3	1.3	122.1	-0.2	122.7	0.5	122.9	0.2	122.9	0.0	123.1	0.2	124.3	1.0	125.1	0.6
1996	126.0	0.7	126.0	0.0	126.5	0.4	127.3	0.6	127.6	0.2	127.9	0.2	128.1	0.2	128.2	0.1	128.6	0.3	128.3	-0.2	128.4	0.1	128.1	-0.2
1997	127.8	-0.2	127.8	0.0	127.3	-0.4	127.2	-0.1	126.9	-0.2	126.5	-0.3	126.2	-0.2	125.9	-0.2	125.3	-0.5	125.6	0.2	124.9	-0.6	124.7	-0.2
1998	124.8	0.1	125.4	0.5	125.2	-0.2	125.3	0.1	125.7	0.3	125.6	-0.1	126.1	0.4	126.2	0.1	125.2	-0.8	125.1	-0.1	126.3	1.0	127.2	0.7
1999	128.0	0.6	128.1	0.1	128.4	0.2	128.4	0.0	127.9	-0.4	127.8	-0.1	128.0	0.2	127.7	-0.2	127.8	0.1	128.1	0.2	128.3	0.2	129.0	0.5
2000	129.1	0.1	129.1	0.0	129.1	0.0	129.0	-0.1	129.2	0.2	128.9	-0.2	128.7	-0.2	128.4	-0.2	128.1	-0.2	128.2	0.1	127.9	-0.2	127.6	-0.2
2001	128.4	0.6	128.4	0.0	128.2	-0.2	128.6	0.3	129.1	0.4	128.8	-0.2	129.6	0.6	129.9	0.2	129.7	-0.2	130.1	0.3	130.8	0.5	131.4	0.5

Source: U.S. Department of Labor, Bureau of Labor Statistics, Division of Industry Prices and Price Indexes. n.e.c. stands for not elsewhere classified. - indicates no data collected for period or unavailable.

Sugar and Confectionery
Producer Price Index
Base 1982 = 100

For 1926-2001. Columns headed % show percentile change in the index from the previous period for which an index is available.

Year	Jan Index	%	Feb Index	%	Mar Index	%	Apr Index	%	May Index	%	Jun Index	%	Jul Index	%	Aug Index	%	Sep Index	%	Oct Index	%	Nov Index	%	Dec Index	%
1926	18.2	-	18.5	1.6	17.7	-4.3	18.3	3.4	19.0	3.8	18.8	-1.1	19.1	1.6	19.3	1.0	19.8	2.6	20.2	2.0	20.6	2.0	22.0	6.8
1927	22.0	0.0	21.4	-2.7	20.9	-2.3	20.9	0.0	21.2	1.4	21.0	-0.9	20.5	-2.4	19.8	-3.4	20.8	5.1	20.4	-1.9	20.1	-1.5	19.9	-1.0
1928	20.0	0.5	19.3	-3.5	20.1	4.1	20.4	1.5	20.5	0.5	20.4	-0.5	19.7	-3.4	19.2	-2.5	19.5	1.6	18.2	-6.7	17.8	-2.2	18.2	2.2
1929	17.7	-2.7	17.2	-2.8	17.0	-1.2	16.9	-0.6	16.9	0.0	16.8	-0.6	17.8	6.0	18.3	2.8	18.4	0.5	18.7	1.6	17.5	-6.4	17.5	0.0
1930	17.6	0.6	17.2	-2.3	16.8	-2.3	16.7	-0.6	16.0	-4.2	15.6	-2.5	15.8	1.3	15.2	-3.8	15.1	-0.7	15.5	2.6	16.1	3.9	15.7	-2.5
1931	15.8	0.6	15.5	-1.9	15.2	-1.9	15.3	0.7	14.9	-2.6	15.3	2.7	16.1	5.2	16.0	-0.6	15.6	-2.5	15.6	0.0	15.5	-0.6	14.6	-5.8
1932	14.3	-2.1	14.2	-0.7	13.5	-4.9	13.0	-3.7	12.5	-3.8	12.9	3.2	13.8	7.0	14.4	4.3	14.4	0.0	14.4	0.0	14.2	-1.4	13.8	-2.8
1933	13.1	-5.1	13.1	0.0	14.0	6.9	14.4	2.9	15.2	5.6	15.6	2.6	15.9	1.9	16.0	0.6	16.2	1.3	15.5	-4.3	15.1	-2.6	15.0	-0.7
1934	14.7	-2.0	15.3	4.1	14.9	-2.6	14.4	-3.4	13.8	-4.2	14.8	7.2	15.6	5.4	15.9	1.9	15.2	-4.4	15.1	-0.7	14.9	-1.3	14.6	-2.0
1935	14.2	-2.7	14.4	1.4	14.8	2.8	16.4	10.8	16.9	3.0	17.0	0.6	17.0	-1.8	16.7	0.0	17.0	1.8	17.5	2.9	17.2	-1.7	16.7	-2.9
1936	16.9	1.2	17.0	0.6	16.7	-1.8	17.1	2.4	17.1	0.0	17.1	0.0	16.7	-2.3	16.7	0.0	16.5	-1.2	16.0	-3.0	16.4	2.5	16.9	3.0
1937	17.4	3.0	16.9	-2.9	16.4	-3.0	16.4	0.0	16.3	-0.6	16.1	-1.2	16.3	1.2	16.3	0.0	16.8	3.1	16.0	-4.8	16.1	0.6	15.9	-1.2
1938	15.8	-0.6	15.5	-1.9	15.3	-1.3	14.8	-3.3	14.6	-1.4	14.3	-2.1	14.4	0.7	14.2	-1.4	15.0	5.6	15.3	2.0	15.0	-2.0	14.6	-2.7
1939	14.3	-2.1	14.2	-0.7	14.4	1.4	14.7	2.1	14.7	0.0	14.6	-0.7	14.5	-0.7	14.4	-0.7	18.5	28.5	17.2	-7.0	15.5	-9.9	15.2	-1.9
1940	14.6	-3.9	14.6	0.0	14.5	-0.7	14.6	0.7	14.5	-0.7	14.4	-0.7	14.3	-0.7	14.0	-2.1	14.1	0.7	14.2	0.7	14.4	1.4	14.5	0.7
1941	14.7	1.4	14.9	1.4	16.2	8.7	16.8	3.7	16.7	-0.6	16.8	0.6	16.9	0.6	17.8	5.3	17.7	-0.6	17.3	-2.3	17.3	0.0	17.4	0.6
1942	18.1	4.0	18.2	0.6	18.2	0.0	18.6	2.2	18.6	0.0	18.6	0.0	18.6	0.0	18.6	0.0	18.6	0.0	18.6	0.0	18.6	0.0	18.6	0.0
1943	18.6	0.0	18.6	0.0	18.6	0.0	18.6	0.0	18.6	0.0	18.6	0.0	18.6	0.0	18.6	0.0	18.6	0.0	18.6	0.0	18.6	0.0	18.6	0.0
1944	18.6	0.0	18.6	0.0	18.6	0.0	18.6	0.0	18.6	0.0	18.7	0.5	18.7	0.0	18.7	0.0	18.5	-1.1	18.5	0.0	18.5	0.0	18.5	0.0
1945	18.5	0.0	18.5	0.0	18.5	0.0	18.5	0.0	18.5	0.0	18.5	0.0	18.5	0.0	18.5	0.0	18.5	0.0	18.5	0.0	18.5	0.0	18.5	0.0
1946	18.5	0.0	19.5	5.4	20.2	3.6	20.2	0.0	20.2	0.0	20.2	0.0	20.7	2.5	20.8	0.5	23.5	13.0	26.1	11.1	26.6	1.9	27.2	2.3
1947	27.4	0.7	27.8	1.5	28.1	1.1	28.3	0.7	28.3	0.0	28.4	0.4	28.5	0.4	29.3	2.8	29.4	0.3	29.4	0.0	30.4	3.4	30.6	0.7
1948	30.3	-1.0	30.4	0.3	30.2	-0.7	30.1	-0.3	29.0	-3.7	28.7	-1.0	29.4	2.4	29.5	0.3	29.7	0.7	29.4	-1.0	29.6	0.7	29.2	-1.4
1949	29.4	0.7	28.7	-2.4	27.8	-3.1	27.3	-1.8	26.9	-1.5	26.9	0.0	26.7	-0.7	26.7	0.0	26.9	0.7	27.1	0.7	27.1	0.0	27.0	-0.4
1950	27.1	0.4	26.8	-1.1	26.5	-1.1	26.4	-0.4	26.7	1.1	26.9	0.7	27.7	3.0	28.6	3.2	29.7	3.8	29.6	-0.3	29.6	0.0	29.6	0.0
1951	29.6	0.0	29.6	0.0	29.6	0.0	29.5	-0.3	30.4	3.1	31.3	3.0	31.2	-0.3	30.7	-1.6	30.7	0.0	30.1	-2.0	30.2	0.3	30.1	-0.3
1952	30.1	0.0	30.2	0.3	30.5	1.0	31.2	2.3	31.1	-0.3	31.6	1.6	31.8	0.6	31.5	-0.9	31.5	0.0	31.6	0.3	31.3	-0.9	30.9	-1.3
1953	30.9	0.0	30.9	0.0	31.3	1.3	31.4	0.3	31.3	-0.3	31.4	0.3	31.4	0.0	31.5	0.3	31.4	-0.3	31.5	0.3	31.0	-1.6	31.1	0.3
1954	31.5	1.3	31.5	0.0	32.3	2.5	32.2	-0.3	32.4	0.6	32.4	0.0	32.6	0.6	32.7	0.3	32.3	-1.2	32.1	-0.6	32.1	0.0	31.9	-0.6
1955	31.9	0.0	32.2	0.9	31.7	-1.6	31.7	0.0	31.6	-0.3	31.6	0.0	31.7	0.3	31.5	-0.6	31.4	-0.3	31.5	0.3	31.4	-0.3	31.3	-0.3
1956	31.3	0.0	31.3	0.0	31.4	0.3	30.1	-4.1	31.4	4.3	31.3	-0.3	31.5	0.6	31.4	-0.3	31.5	0.3	31.7	0.6	32.0	0.9	32.1	0.3
1957	32.4	0.9	32.1	-0.9	32.1	0.0	32.1	0.0	32.3	0.6	32.5	0.6	32.7	0.6	32.6	-0.3	32.6	0.0	32.6	0.0	32.7	0.3	32.7	0.0
1958	32.8	0.3	32.7	-0.3	32.4	-0.9	32.7	0.9	33.0	0.9	33.3	0.9	33.3	0.0	33.2	-0.3	33.3	0.3	33.4	0.3	33.3	-0.3	33.5	0.6
1959	33.0	-1.5	32.6	-1.2	32.3	-0.9	32.1	-0.6	32.7	1.9	33.1	1.2	33.0	-0.3	33.0	0.0	33.3	0.9	33.6	0.9	33.4	-0.6	33.1	-0.9
1960	32.4	-2.1	32.6	0.6	32.9	0.9	33.0	0.3	33.1	0.3	33.1	0.0	33.9	2.4	33.9	0.0	34.1	0.6	33.9	-0.6	34.0	0.3	33.7	-0.9
1961	33.7	0.0	33.6	-0.3	33.4	-0.6	33.3	-0.3	33.6	0.9	33.7	0.3	33.3	-1.2	32.8	-1.5	32.7	-0.3	32.7	0.0	32.8	0.3	33.2	1.2
1962	33.2	0.0	33.4	0.6	33.4	0.0	33.6	0.6	33.5	-0.3	33.6	0.3	33.5	-0.3	33.7	0.6	33.5	-0.6	33.8	0.9	33.6	-0.6	33.7	0.3
1963	34.5	2.4	34.5	0.0	34.8	0.9	37.4	7.5	43.8	17.1	43.4	-0.9	39.5	-9.0	36.5	-7.6	36.9	1.1	41.2	11.7	43.1	4.6	41.0	-4.9
1964	42.8	4.4	40.3	-5.8	38.5	-4.5	37.9	-1.6	36.7	-3.2	35.5	-3.3	35.0	-1.4	34.9	-0.3	34.5	-1.1	34.7	0.6	34.4	-0.9	35.2	2.3
1965	36.1	2.6	36.1	0.0	35.5	-1.7	35.5	0.0	35.7	0.6	35.8	0.3	35.8	0.0	35.7	-0.3	35.7	0.0	35.9	0.6	35.8	-0.3	35.7	-0.3
1966	35.9	0.6	36.1	0.6	36.0	-0.3	35.9	-0.3	35.9	0.0	35.9	0.0	36.0	0.3	36.4	1.1	36.6	0.5	36.6	0.0	36.8	0.5	36.9	0.3
1967	37.1	0.5	37.0	-0.3	36.9	-0.3	36.7	-0.5	36.7	0.0	37.0	0.8	37.3	0.8	37.4	0.3	37.1	-0.8	37.2	0.3	37.4	0.5	37.0	-1.1
1968	37.2	0.5	37.3	0.3	37.3	0.0	37.4	0.3	37.8	1.1	38.5	1.9	38.6	0.3	38.5	-0.3	38.6	0.3	38.8	0.5	38.7	-0.3	38.9	0.5
1969	39.1	0.5	39.1	0.0	39.2	0.3	39.4	0.5	40.2	2.0	41.5	3.2	41.3	-0.5	41.7	1.0	41.8	0.2	41.9	0.2	42.0	0.2	41.7	-0.7
1970	42.3	1.4	41.9	-0.9	41.8	-0.2	42.2	1.0	42.5	0.7	42.8	0.7	43.5	1.6	43.5	0.0	43.8	0.7	44.0	0.5	43.8	-0.5	43.5	-0.7

[Continued]

Sugar and Confectionery
Producer Price Index
Base 1982 = 100

[Continued]

For 1926-2001. Columns headed % show percentile change in the index from the previous period for which an index is available.

Year	Jan Index	%	Feb Index	%	Mar Index	%	Apr Index	%	May Index	%	Jun Index	%	Jul Index	%	Aug Index	%	Sep Index	%	Oct Index	%	Nov Index	%	Dec Index	%
1971	43.7	0.5	44.2	1.1	44.5	0.7	44.2	-0.7	44.5	0.7	44.4	-0.2	44.5	0.2	44.5	0.0	44.5	0.0	43.7	-1.8	44.2	1.1	44.6	0.9
1972	44.5	-0.2	44.9	0.9	45.2	0.7	44.9	-0.7	44.8	-0.2	45.0	0.4	45.3	0.7	45.0	-0.7	45.1	0.2	45.8	1.6	45.1	-1.5	45.3	0.4
1973	45.0	-0.7	46.1	2.4	46.6	1.1	47.0	0.9	47.8	1.7	48.6	1.7	48.6	0.0	50.3	3.5	50.8	1.0	51.8	2.0	53.3	2.9	52.7	-1.1
1974	56.3	6.8	62.0	10.1	70.5	13.7	70.4	-0.1	80.0	13.6	89.3	11.6	91.5	2.5	100.3	9.6	110.5	10.2	116.9	5.8	155.7	33.2	148.8	-4.4
1975	132.8	-10.8	128.8	-3.0	112.4	-12.7	103.9	-7.6	88.8	-14.5	80.8	-9.0	84.7	4.8	90.2	6.5	81.4	-9.8	77.3	-5.0	77.0	-0.4	73.8	-4.2
1976	75.1	1.8	74.3	-1.1	76.8	3.4	75.1	-2.2	77.4	3.1	73.2	-5.4	74.6	1.9	68.6	-8.0	62.0	-9.6	65.4	5.5	63.6	-2.8	63.2	-0.6
1977	63.8	0.9	65.9	3.3	66.8	1.4	69.1	3.4	68.4	-1.0	65.4	-4.4	63.5	-2.9	66.3	4.4	64.6	-2.6	63.1	-2.3	66.2	4.9	66.4	0.3
1978	68.9	3.8	71.9	4.4	71.5	-0.6	72.7	1.7	72.8	0.1	73.1	0.4	72.6	-0.7	74.3	2.3	75.1	1.1	76.2	1.5	75.1	-1.4	75.8	0.9
1979	75.9	0.1	77.3	1.8	77.3	0.0	77.4	0.1	77.0	-0.5	78.3	1.7	80.0	2.2	80.9	1.1	80.6	-0.4	81.2	0.7	82.7	1.8	86.9	5.1
1980	87.1	0.2	106.6	22.4	98.0	-8.1	102.0	4.1	121.6	19.2	120.7	-0.7	116.3	-3.6	128.7	10.7	126.6	-1.6	150.1	18.6	151.7	1.1	126.0	-16.9
1981	127.8	1.4	119.9	-6.2	112.0	-6.6	105.5	-5.8	97.4	-7.7	101.9	4.6	98.6	-3.2	99.1	0.5	91.5	-7.7	91.5	0.0	90.5	-1.1	91.8	1.4
1982	95.2	3.7	95.4	0.2	94.6	-0.8	94.9	0.3	98.4	3.7	99.8	1.4	102.2	2.4	105.9	3.6	103.3	-2.5	102.5	-0.8	104.0	1.5	103.9	-0.1
1983	104.6	0.7	106.2	1.5	105.2	-0.9	106.6	1.3	107.5	0.8	109.8	2.1	109.9	0.1	110.8	0.8	111.3	0.5	110.5	-0.7	110.4	-0.1	110.3	-0.1
1984	111.2	0.8	111.4	0.2	111.7	0.3	111.9	0.2	112.6	0.6	112.8	0.2	113.1	0.3	112.6	-0.4	112.1	-0.4	111.2	-0.8	110.1	-1.0	109.7	-0.4
1985	108.8	-0.8	107.9	-0.8	108.5	0.6	108.8	0.3	109.2	0.4	109.2	0.0	108.9	-0.3	108.1	-0.7	107.6	-0.5	106.1	-1.4	105.8	-0.3	106.0	0.2
1986	108.0	1.9	108.4	0.4	109.2	0.7	108.8	-0.4	109.0	0.2	109.4	0.4	109.8	0.4	109.8	0.0	110.4	0.5	110.9	0.5	111.1	0.2	111.2	0.1
1987	110.8	-0.4	110.8	0.0	111.2	0.4	111.9	0.6	112.8	0.8	112.9	0.1	113.7	0.7	113.9	0.2	114.0	0.1	113.6	-0.4	113.5	-0.1	113.0	-0.4
1988	112.5	-0.4	112.8	0.3	113.0	0.2	113.3	0.3	113.1	-0.2	113.6	0.4	115.9	2.0	115.9	0.0	115.9	0.0	116.5	0.5	116.8	0.3	117.3	0.4
1989	117.8	0.4	118.3	0.4	118.6	0.3	119.2	0.5	119.6	0.3	120.7	0.9	122.0	1.1	121.3	-0.6	121.6	0.2	120.1	-1.2	120.5	0.3	121.0	0.4
1990	121.1	0.1	121.8	0.6	121.7	-0.1	122.6	0.7	122.8	0.2	123.0	0.2	123.9	0.7	123.7	-0.2	123.9	0.2	123.0	-0.7	124.8	1.5	124.7	-0.1
1991	126.3	1.3	128.4	1.7	127.8	-0.5	128.3	0.4	127.8	-0.4	127.6	-0.2	129.1	1.2	129.4	0.2	129.8	0.3	128.5	-1.0	128.6	0.1	128.8	0.2
1992	128.6	-0.2	127.7	-0.7	127.4	-0.2	127.6	0.2	127.8	0.2	127.7	-0.1	129.0	1.0	129.3	0.2	129.2	-0.1	126.0	-2.5	125.8	-0.2	125.9	0.1
1993	125.4	-0.4	124.5	-0.7	124.6	0.1	124.8	0.2	125.5	0.6	126.6	0.9	129.3	2.1	129.3	0.0	130.6	1.0	131.7	0.8	131.5	-0.2	130.7	-0.6
1994	130.6	-0.1	130.5	-0.1	131.3	0.6	133.2	1.4	133.6	0.3	134.6	0.7	134.7	0.1	134.3	-0.3	133.9	-0.3	130.9	-2.2	131.2	0.2	131.3	0.1
1995	132.0	0.5	133.0	0.8	133.2	0.2	133.5	0.2	133.8	0.2	133.8	0.0	134.6	0.6	134.3	-0.2	134.6	0.2	134.6	0.0	134.9	0.2	135.9	0.7
1996	135.9	0.0	135.9	0.0	136.2	0.2	136.8	0.4	137.3	0.4	138.1	0.6	137.8	-0.2	137.9	0.1	138.5	0.4	138.5	0.0	138.6	0.1	138.8	0.1
1997	138.8	0.0	138.4	-0.3	138.6	0.1	138.4	-0.1	138.4	0.0	138.1	-0.2	138.2	0.1	138.1	-0.1	138.3	0.1	135.0	-2.4	135.0	0.0	133.7	-1.0
1998	134.0	0.2	134.4	0.3	134.7	0.2	133.9	-0.6	134.2	0.2	134.4	0.1	134.4	0.0	134.6	0.1	134.7	0.1	134.4	-0.2	134.4	0.0	134.4	0.0
1999	134.8	0.3	135.0	0.1	135.2	0.1	135.4	0.1	135.9	0.4	136.2	0.2	136.3	0.1	135.7	-0.4	135.0	-0.5	135.0	0.0	134.2	-0.6	133.6	-0.4
2000	133.6	0.0	132.6	-0.7	132.9	0.2	132.8	-0.1	132.9	0.1	133.0	0.1	132.7	-0.2	132.0	-0.5	132.0	0.0	132.2	0.2	132.2	0.0	132.2	0.0
2001	134.0	1.4	135.7	1.3	135.5	-0.1	135.2	-0.2	135.5	0.2	135.2	-0.2	135.6	0.3	136.0	0.3	136.3	0.2	137.1	0.6	137.9	0.6	139.3	1.0

Source: U.S. Department of Labor, Bureau of Labor Statistics, Division of Industry Prices and Price Indexes. n.e.c. stands for not elsewhere classified. - indicates no data collected for period or unavailable.

Beverages and Beverage Materials
Producer Price Index
Base 1982 = 100

For 1947-2001. Columns headed % show percentile change in the index from the previous period for which an index is available.

Year	Jan Index	%	Feb Index	%	Mar Index	%	Apr Index	%	May Index	%	Jun Index	%	Jul Index	%	Aug Index	%	Sep Index	%	Oct Index	%	Nov Index	%	Dec Index	%
1947	26.3	-	26.5	0.8	26.6	0.4	26.6	0.0	26.4	-0.8	26.2	-0.8	26.2	0.0	26.4	0.8	26.7	1.1	26.8	0.4	27.0	0.7	27.3	1.1
1948	27.5	0.7	27.7	0.7	27.7	0.0	27.7	0.0	27.7	0.0	27.8	0.4	27.8	0.0	27.8	0.0	27.8	0.0	27.8	0.0	27.9	0.4	27.9	0.0
1949	27.9	0.0	27.9	0.0	27.9	0.0	27.8	-0.4	27.8	0.0	27.8	0.0	27.8	0.0	27.8	0.0	28.0	0.7	28.1	0.4	29.7	5.7	30.2	1.7
1950	30.2	0.0	30.1	-0.3	30.1	0.0	29.7	-1.3	29.6	-0.3	29.7	0.3	30.3	2.0	30.7	1.3	31.0	1.0	31.5	1.6	31.3	-0.6	32.0	2.2
1951	32.5	1.6	32.6	0.3	32.6	0.0	32.6	0.0	32.6	0.0	32.6	0.0	32.5	-0.3	32.5	0.0	32.5	0.0	32.5	0.0	32.5	0.0	32.5	0.0
1952	32.5	0.0	33.3	2.5	33.3	0.0	33.2	-0.3	33.2	0.0	33.2	0.0	33.2	0.0	33.2	0.0	33.2	0.0	33.2	0.0	33.2	0.0	33.2	0.0
1953	33.2	0.0	33.2	0.0	33.6	1.2	33.5	-0.3	33.3	-0.6	33.3	0.0	33.8	1.5	33.8	0.0	34.0	0.6	34.5	1.5	34.6	0.3	34.6	0.0
1954	35.2	1.7	35.6	1.1	36.6	2.8	38.7	5.7	38.7	0.0	38.7	0.0	39.0	0.8	38.7	-0.8	37.6	-2.8	37.6	0.0	37.2	-1.1	37.5	0.8
1955	37.5	0.0	36.6	-2.4	36.2	-1.1	36.2	0.0	36.2	0.0	36.2	0.0	35.8	-1.1	35.8	0.0	35.9	0.3	36.1	0.6	36.4	0.8	36.1	-0.8
1956	36.1	0.0	36.4	0.8	36.9	1.4	36.7	-0.5	36.6	-0.3	36.8	0.5	37.1	0.8	37.4	0.8	37.8	1.1	37.8	0.0	38.0	0.5	37.6	-1.1
1957	37.8	0.5	37.6	-0.5	37.5	-0.3	37.2	-0.8	37.2	0.0	37.2	0.0	37.2	0.0	37.2	0.0	36.9	-0.8	36.6	-0.8	36.6	0.0	36.7	0.3
1958	36.7	0.0	36.7	0.0	36.4	-0.8	36.4	0.0	36.4	0.0	36.4	0.0	36.2	-0.5	36.1	-0.3	36.1	0.0	36.2	0.3	36.2	0.0	36.1	-0.3
1959	35.9	-0.6	35.7	-0.6	36.4	2.0	36.3	-0.3	36.3	0.0	36.3	0.0	36.3	0.0	36.2	-0.3	36.2	0.0	36.2	0.0	36.2	0.0	36.2	0.0
1960	36.2	0.0	36.2	0.0	36.2	0.0	36.2	0.0	36.2	0.0	36.2	0.0	36.1	-0.3	36.1	0.0	36.1	0.0	36.1	0.0	36.1	0.0	36.1	0.0
1961	35.9	-0.6	36.0	0.3	36.0	0.0	35.9	-0.3	35.9	0.0	35.9	0.0	36.1	0.6	36.1	0.0	36.3	0.6	36.1	-0.6	36.2	0.3	36.2	0.0
1962	36.2	0.0	36.2	0.0	36.2	0.0	36.2	0.0	36.2	0.0	36.2	0.0	36.2	0.0	36.3	0.3	36.2	-0.3	36.1	-0.3	36.1	0.0	36.0	-0.3
1963	36.0	0.0	36.0	0.0	36.0	0.0	36.2	0.6	36.3	0.3	36.8	1.4	37.4	1.6	37.5	0.3	37.5	0.0	37.5	0.0	37.7	0.5	37.9	0.5
1964	38.3	1.1	38.5	0.5	38.8	0.8	38.8	0.0	38.9	0.3	38.9	0.0	38.9	0.0	38.9	0.0	38.9	0.0	38.9	0.0	38.9	0.0	38.9	0.0
1965	38.8	-0.3	38.8	0.0	38.5	-0.8	38.6	0.3	38.6	0.0	38.6	0.0	38.6	0.0	38.6	0.0	38.6	0.0	38.6	0.0	38.6	0.0	38.7	0.3
1966	38.7	0.0	38.6	-0.3	38.6	0.0	38.6	0.0	38.6	0.0	38.8	0.5	38.9	0.3	38.9	0.0	38.6	-0.8	38.6	0.0	38.6	0.0	38.7	0.3
1967	38.7	0.0	38.7	0.0	38.6	-0.3	38.7	0.3	38.8	0.3	38.9	0.3	38.9	0.0	39.0	0.3	39.0	0.0	39.2	0.5	39.2	0.0	39.4	0.5
1968	39.4	0.0	39.7	0.8	39.8	0.3	39.9	0.3	40.0	0.3	40.0	0.0	40.0	0.0	40.1	0.2	40.2	0.2	40.4	0.5	40.4	0.0	40.4	0.0
1969	40.5	0.2	40.6	0.2	40.7	0.2	40.7	0.0	40.9	0.5	41.1	0.5	41.2	0.2	41.2	0.0	41.3	0.2	42.1	1.9	42.4	0.7	42.5	0.2
1970	42.9	0.9	43.3	0.9	43.3	0.0	43.4	0.2	44.0	1.4	44.0	0.0	44.1	0.2	44.3	0.5	44.5	0.5	44.6	0.2	44.7	0.2	44.5	-0.4
1971	44.8	0.7	44.9	0.2	44.9	0.0	45.1	0.4	45.1	0.0	45.1	0.0	45.2	0.2	45.3	0.2	45.4	0.2	45.4	0.0	45.4	0.0	45.3	-0.2
1972	45.3	0.0	45.5	0.4	45.4	-0.2	45.6	0.4	45.6	0.0	45.8	0.4	45.9	0.2	46.3	0.9	46.4	0.2	46.2	-0.4	46.5	0.6	46.6	0.2
1973	46.6	0.0	46.7	0.2	47.0	0.6	47.3	0.6	47.5	0.4	47.3	-0.4	47.1	-0.4	47.2	0.2	47.3	0.2	47.9	1.3	48.2	0.6	48.4	0.4
1974	48.9	1.0	49.1	0.4	50.3	2.4	51.5	2.4	52.4	1.7	53.9	2.9	55.9	3.7	56.9	1.8	57.5	1.1	59.4	3.3	60.1	1.2	61.6	2.5
1975	63.3	2.8	63.2	-0.2	63.1	-0.2	63.0	-0.2	62.7	-0.5	62.4	-0.5	62.1	-0.5	62.9	1.3	63.3	0.6	64.3	1.6	64.3	0.0	64.4	0.2
1976	64.3	-0.2	65.1	1.2	65.1	0.0	65.9	1.2	67.1	1.8	67.3	0.3	68.5	1.8	68.4	-0.1	68.7	0.4	69.1	0.6	69.6	0.7	71.6	2.9
1977	71.7	0.1	73.7	2.8	77.7	5.4	78.7	1.3	80.2	1.9	80.9	0.9	79.7	-1.5	80.0	0.4	79.7	-0.4	79.8	0.1	78.5	-1.6	78.4	-0.1
1978	78.7	0.4	78.4	-0.4	77.9	-0.6	77.9	0.0	77.7	-0.3	77.9	0.3	77.3	-0.8	76.6	-0.9	77.0	0.5	78.3	1.7	78.4	0.1	78.3	-0.1
1979	78.2	-0.1	78.3	0.1	78.3	0.0	78.5	0.3	79.9	1.8	81.2	1.6	83.4	2.7	84.3	1.1	84.8	0.6	85.2	0.5	86.1	1.1	86.3	0.2
1980	87.2	1.0	87.5	0.3	88.0	0.6	88.7	0.8	90.0	1.5	91.2	1.3	91.3	0.1	92.3	1.1	91.9	-0.4	93.3	1.5	93.7	0.4	93.6	-0.1
1981	94.6	1.1	95.3	0.7	95.5	0.2	95.8	0.3	96.4	0.6	96.6	0.2	96.9	0.3	97.1	0.2	97.0	-0.1	97.3	0.3	97.9	0.6	98.1	0.2
1982	98.8	0.7	99.3	0.5	99.8	0.5	99.9	0.1	99.9	0.0	99.9	0.0	100.0	0.1	100.4	0.4	100.1	-0.3	100.4	0.3	100.6	0.2	100.8	0.2
1983	101.3	0.5	101.7	0.4	102.0	0.3	102.4	0.4	102.6	0.2	102.4	-0.2	102.7	0.3	102.7	0.0	102.9	0.2	103.3	0.4	103.7	0.4	103.7	0.0
1984	104.6	0.9	105.2	0.6	105.1	-0.1	105.7	0.6	106.5	0.8	106.2	-0.3	106.6	0.4	106.9	0.3	106.9	0.0	107.5	0.6	107.4	-0.1	107.3	-0.1
1985	107.4	0.1	108.0	0.6	107.9	-0.1	107.8	-0.1	107.8	0.0	107.3	-0.5	107.5	0.2	107.1	-0.4	107.1	0.0	107.6	0.5	107.9	0.3	109.0	1.0
1986	112.9	3.6	114.5	1.4	115.0	0.4	115.9	0.8	115.9	0.0	115.5	-0.3	115.5	0.0	114.0	-1.3	113.7	-0.3	114.2	0.4	113.9	-0.3	113.8	-0.1
1987	112.6	-1.1	112.8	0.2	112.9	0.1	113.3	0.4	113.2	-0.1	113.0	-0.2	112.1	-0.8	112.3	0.2	111.6	-0.6	112.3	0.6	112.0	-0.3	112.2	0.2
1988	112.5	0.3	113.0	0.4	113.9	0.8	114.1	0.2	114.1	0.0	114.1	0.0	113.8	-0.3	114.6	0.7	114.7	0.1	115.3	0.5	115.8	0.4	115.8	0.0
1989	116.5	0.6	117.7	1.0	118.7	0.8	119.2	0.4	119.7	0.4	119.6	-0.1	119.4	-0.2	118.3	-0.9	117.1	-1.0	118.1	0.9	118.4	0.3	118.4	0.0
1990	119.7	1.1	120.7	0.8	121.5	0.7	121.5	0.0	121.0	-0.4	120.8	-0.2	120.9	0.1	120.6	-0.2	120.8	0.2	120.3	-0.4	120.5	0.2	121.1	0.5
1991	125.5	3.6	125.5	0.0	125.3	-0.2	125.5	0.2	124.3	-1.0	124.2	-0.1	123.5	-0.6	123.2	-0.2	123.1	-0.1	123.0	-0.1	123.0	0.0	123.2	0.2

[Continued]

Beverages and Beverage Materials
Producer Price Index
Base 1982 = 100
[Continued]

For 1947-2001. Columns headed % show percentile change in the index from the previous period for which an index is available.

Year	Jan Index	%	Feb Index	%	Mar Index	%	Apr Index	%	May Index	%	Jun Index	%	Jul Index	%	Aug Index	%	Sep Index	%	Oct Index	%	Nov Index	%	Dec Index	%
1992	124.8	1.3	125.2	0.3	124.5	-0.6	124.6	0.1	125.1	0.4	125.7	0.5	124.4	-1.0	124.1	-0.2	123.8	-0.2	123.4	-0.3	123.5	0.1	124.0	0.4
1993	124.5	0.4	125.4	0.7	125.4	0.0	125.2	-0.2	125.0	-0.2	124.8	-0.2	124.4	-0.3	124.5	0.1	124.4	-0.1	124.5	0.1	124.3	-0.2	124.6	0.2
1994	125.5	0.7	126.0	0.4	125.2	-0.6	124.8	-0.3	124.8	0.0	125.3	0.4	129.9	3.7	129.7	-0.2	129.7	0.0	130.1	0.3	130.4	0.2	130.5	0.1
1995	131.8	1.0	133.4	1.2	133.8	0.3	134.3	0.4	134.1	-0.1	134.0	-0.1	134.2	0.1	134.4	0.1	133.9	-0.4	134.0	0.1	134.0	0.0	134.3	0.2
1996	134.3	0.0	134.5	0.1	134.3	-0.1	134.8	0.4	134.3	-0.4	134.3	0.0	134.3	0.0	134.6	0.2	134.2	-0.3	135.4	0.9	134.5	-0.7	135.2	0.5
1997	135.3	0.1	135.2	-0.1	137.1	1.4	138.0	0.7	138.9	0.7	139.3	0.3	139.4	0.1	139.4	0.0	138.0	-1.0	137.8	-0.1	136.8	-0.7	136.9	0.1
1998	137.8	0.7	137.8	0.0	138.0	0.1	138.1	0.1	137.5	-0.4	137.2	-0.2	137.1	-0.1	137.0	-0.1	136.6	-0.3	137.1	0.4	137.2	0.1	137.3	0.1
1999	137.6	0.2	138.3	0.5	137.9	-0.3	138.2	0.2	138.2	0.0	137.9	-0.2	138.9	0.7	138.7	-0.1	138.6	-0.1	138.9	0.2	139.0	0.1	139.5	0.4
2000	141.0	1.1	142.0	0.7	142.0	0.0	142.1	0.1	144.0	1.3	143.5	-0.3	143.5	0.0	143.6	0.1	143.5	-0.1	143.8	0.2	143.2	-0.4	143.6	0.3
2001	145.2	1.1	145.7	0.3	146.2	0.3	145.7	-0.3	145.7	0.0	145.7	0.0	145.7	0.0	145.9	0.1	146.4	0.3	146.3	-0.1	146.4	0.1	146.3	-0.1

Source: U.S. Department of Labor, Bureau of Labor Statistics, Division of Industry Prices and Price Indexes. n.e.c. stands for not elsewhere classified. - indicates no data collected for period or unavailable.

Fats and Oils
Producer Price Index
Base 1982 = 100

For 1967-2001. Columns headed % show percentile change in the index from the previous period for which an index is available.

Year	Jan Index	%	Feb Index	%	Mar Index	%	Apr Index	%	May Index	%	Jun Index	%	Jul Index	%	Aug Index	%	Sep Index	%	Oct Index	%	Nov Index	%	Dec Index	%
1967	48.8	-	48.3	-1.0	47.7	-1.2	47.7	0.0	47.6	-0.2	46.6	-2.1	45.3	-2.8	46.2	2.0	45.9	-0.6	44.8	-2.4	44.3	-1.1	44.3	0.0
1968	44.5	0.5	46.6	4.7	46.1	-1.1	45.4	-1.5	46.0	1.3	44.8	-2.6	44.3	-1.1	45.5	2.7	43.9	-3.5	42.3	-3.6	43.8	3.5	43.9	0.2
1969	45.1	2.7	46.6	3.3	46.6	0.0	45.8	-1.7	45.8	0.0	46.0	0.4	45.8	-0.4	45.9	0.2	45.9	0.0	48.6	5.9	50.8	4.5	49.8	-2.0
1970	49.5	-0.6	51.6	4.2	56.3	9.1	55.6	-1.2	54.4	-2.2	53.6	-1.5	53.4	-0.4	55.3	3.6	54.3	-1.8	57.5	5.9	60.7	5.6	58.2	-4.1
1971	57.7	-0.9	59.0	2.3	58.9	-0.2	56.8	-3.6	56.6	-0.4	57.3	1.2	60.2	5.1	62.9	4.5	60.3	-4.1	58.7	-2.7	58.8	0.2	56.4	-4.1
1972	55.6	-1.4	56.3	1.3	56.0	-0.5	56.3	0.5	55.4	-1.6	55.4	0.0	54.5	-1.6	53.5	-1.8	53.2	-0.6	53.2	0.0	52.7	-0.9	52.5	-0.4
1973	52.2	-0.6	57.4	10.0	63.3	10.3	64.0	1.1	68.0	6.3	73.9	8.7	74.2	0.4	103.3	39.2	84.2	-18.5	92.5	9.9	80.4	-13.1	93.7	16.5
1974	96.9	3.4	112.6	16.2	108.2	-3.9	101.3	-6.4	109.2	7.8	107.6	-1.5	119.3	10.9	145.4	21.9	128.0	-12.0	144.6	13.0	143.0	-1.1	129.9	-9.2
1975	127.9	-1.5	117.1	-8.4	110.3	-5.8	108.4	-1.7	98.7	-8.9	94.5	-4.3	108.3	14.6	113.3	4.6	103.5	-8.6	98.9	-4.4	92.0	-7.0	83.2	-9.6
1976	80.4	-3.4	79.8	-0.7	80.3	0.6	77.8	-3.1	76.8	-1.3	78.3	2.0	87.0	11.1	82.5	-5.2	89.8	8.8	85.2	-5.1	88.8	4.2	86.9	-2.1
1977	86.2	-0.8	91.4	6.0	98.3	7.5	109.8	11.7	111.1	1.2	107.1	-3.6	95.5	-10.8	92.5	-3.1	88.4	-4.4	90.2	2.0	90.9	0.8	96.6	6.3
1978	94.3	-2.4	94.5	0.2	104.9	11.0	107.0	2.0	107.9	0.8	105.7	-2.0	106.6	0.9	104.8	-1.7	111.3	6.2	108.2	-2.8	105.8	-2.2	105.8	0.0
1979	106.8	0.9	110.4	3.4	110.9	0.5	114.4	3.2	112.4	-1.7	113.2	0.7	117.7	4.0	117.0	-0.6	117.7	0.6	114.3	-2.9	112.4	-1.7	109.5	-2.6
1980	104.6	-4.5	105.2	0.6	103.5	-1.6	99.7	-3.7	98.5	-1.2	98.9	0.4	105.5	6.7	111.7	5.9	110.8	-0.8	107.4	-3.1	110.6	3.0	108.8	-1.6
1981	107.0	-1.7	106.1	-0.8	106.8	0.7	108.0	1.1	106.1	-1.8	105.7	-0.4	109.1	3.2	106.7	-2.2	104.3	-2.2	103.8	-0.5	102.9	-0.9	101.8	-1.1
1982	100.7	-1.1	100.7	0.0	99.4	-1.3	101.4	2.0	103.3	1.9	103.1	-0.2	102.9	-0.2	100.2	-2.6	98.2	-2.0	99.4	1.2	96.3	-3.1	94.3	-2.1
1983	93.8	-0.5	95.4	1.7	95.8	0.4	99.7	4.1	102.3	2.6	101.9	-0.4	103.3	1.4	114.2	10.6	141.1	23.6	130.9	-7.2	127.6	-2.5	126.3	-1.0
1984	129.4	2.5	127.0	-1.9	133.0	4.7	136.4	2.6	152.7	12.0	152.5	-0.1	145.4	-4.7	142.2	-2.2	138.8	-2.4	140.2	1.0	145.0	3.4	138.3	-4.6
1985	130.4	-5.7	132.6	1.7	135.0	1.8	140.8	4.3	137.6	-2.3	137.8	0.1	132.0	-4.2	118.4	-10.3	113.6	-4.1	110.6	-2.6	109.6	-0.9	106.8	-2.6
1986	107.3	0.5	103.8	-3.3	99.1	-4.5	97.8	-1.3	97.0	-0.8	95.5	-1.5	94.4	-1.2	92.8	-1.7	91.0	-1.9	93.4	2.6	92.9	-0.5	93.3	0.4
1987	95.3	2.1	95.8	0.5	95.6	-0.2	95.4	-0.2	99.2	4.0	97.9	-1.3	97.6	-0.3	96.4	-1.2	97.7	1.3	99.4	1.7	101.1	1.7	103.6	2.5
1988	110.6	6.8	111.1	0.5	109.3	-1.6	111.9	2.4	114.0	1.9	120.1	5.4	132.1	10.0	127.1	-3.8	122.7	-3.5	118.4	-3.5	114.3	-3.5	114.8	0.4
1989	114.1	-0.6	111.6	-2.2	114.7	2.8	113.7	-0.9	117.5	3.3	112.6	-4.2	112.5	-0.1	108.5	-3.6	108.9	0.4	108.3	-0.6	112.5	3.9	110.2	-2.0
1990	111.3	1.0	111.8	0.4	117.8	5.4	116.2	-1.4	124.6	7.2	126.0	1.1	124.6	-1.1	126.3	1.4	124.0	-1.8	118.5	-4.4	115.1	-2.9	116.9	1.6
1991	115.8	-0.9	115.8	0.0	118.2	2.1	116.9	-1.1	111.6	-4.5	110.5	-1.0	107.0	-3.2	110.8	3.6	111.2	0.4	109.8	-1.3	107.9	-1.7	108.9	0.9
1992	108.4	-0.5	108.8	0.4	111.1	2.1	108.6	-2.3	111.1	2.3	113.6	2.3	108.3	-4.7	104.2	-3.8	105.7	1.4	104.9	-0.8	108.5	3.4	111.9	3.1
1993	113.1	1.1	110.7	-2.1	111.5	0.7	112.9	1.3	113.7	0.7	111.4	-2.0	121.5	9.1	119.5	-1.6	118.7	-0.7	117.7	-0.8	120.2	2.1	132.1	9.9
1994	137.3	3.9	136.1	-0.9	137.1	0.7	136.2	-0.7	137.8	1.2	136.9	-0.7	128.5	-6.1	128.3	-0.2	133.6	4.1	132.2	-1.0	141.7	7.2	144.4	1.9
1995	144.3	-0.1	143.3	-0.7	143.2	-0.1	138.2	-3.5	134.3	-2.8	135.2	0.7	138.5	2.4	138.6	0.1	137.3	-0.9	138.4	0.8	136.8	-1.2	134.0	-2.0
1996	130.5	-2.6	129.4	-0.8	127.5	-1.5	131.5	3.1	137.1	4.3	134.8	-1.7	132.3	-1.9	133.3	0.8	133.6	0.2	126.6	-5.2	125.9	-0.6	125.8	-0.1
1997	128.8	2.4	127.8	-0.8	131.3	2.7	128.8	-1.9	130.6	1.4	129.2	-1.1	127.6	-1.2	126.7	-0.7	128.9	1.7	135.2	4.9	139.4	3.1	135.2	-3.0
1998	135.2	0.0	137.7	1.8	138.6	0.7	142.9	3.1	148.2	3.7	140.5	-5.2	139.9	-0.4	139.9	0.0	143.3	2.4	141.4	-1.3	144.2	2.0	140.1	-2.8
1999	137.7	-1.7	132.4	-3.8	124.7	-5.8	124.4	-0.2	124.1	-0.2	119.9	-3.4	116.5	-2.8	118.8	2.0	118.9	0.1	116.7	-1.9	114.1	-2.2	113.0	-1.0
2000	112.3	-0.6	111.0	-1.2	112.8	1.6	114.2	1.2	114.1	-0.1	111.1	-2.6	109.1	-1.8	107.0	-1.9	107.8	0.7	107.5	-0.3	107.0	-0.5	105.5	-1.4
2001	103.9	-1.5	102.1	-1.7	104.5	2.4	104.0	-0.5	103.7	-0.3	104.9	1.2	108.3	3.2	117.7	8.7	114.5	-2.7	108.4	-5.3	107.4	-0.9	108.9	1.4

Source: U.S. Department of Labor, Bureau of Labor Statistics, Division of Industry Prices and Price Indexes. n.e.c. stands for not elsewhere classified. - indicates no data collected for period or unavailable.

Miscellaneous Processed Foods
Producer Price Index
Base 1982 = 100

For 1947-2001. Columns headed % show percentile change in the index from the previous period for which an index is available.

Year	Jan Index	%	Feb Index	%	Mar Index	%	Apr Index	%	May Index	%	Jun Index	%	Jul Index	%	Aug Index	%	Sep Index	%	Oct Index	%	Nov Index	%	Dec Index	%
1947	35.5	-	35.7	0.6	35.6	-0.3	34.7	-2.5	33.9	-2.3	33.7	-0.6	33.8	0.3	33.9	0.3	34.3	1.2	35.5	3.5	35.7	0.6	35.2	-1.4
1948	35.2	0.0	35.0	-0.6	34.8	-0.6	35.1	0.9	35.3	0.6	35.9	1.7	36.2	0.8	37.3	3.0	38.1	2.1	39.0	2.4	38.1	-2.3	37.9	-0.5
1949	37.2	-1.8	36.8	-1.1	38.3	4.1	38.5	0.5	38.4	-0.3	39.6	3.1	40.3	1.8	42.3	5.0	42.0	-0.7	42.6	1.4	42.3	-0.7	42.1	-0.5
1950	41.1	-2.4	42.2	2.7	42.2	0.0	41.8	-0.9	41.4	-1.0	39.5	-4.6	44.2	11.9	52.2	18.1	48.2	-7.7	44.9	-6.8	43.6	-2.9	44.7	2.5
1951	46.1	3.1	47.4	2.8	45.2	-4.6	45.6	0.9	45.8	0.4	45.5	-0.7	45.3	-0.4	45.9	1.3	46.0	0.2	45.3	-1.5	45.1	-0.4	44.3	-1.8
1952	42.5	-4.1	42.8	0.7	43.0	0.5	40.0	-7.0	41.9	4.8	43.9	4.8	47.0	7.1	46.5	-1.1	47.4	1.9	46.1	-2.7	45.3	-1.7	43.4	-4.2
1953	41.9	-3.5	42.4	1.2	44.9	5.9	44.7	-0.4	45.1	0.9	44.6	-1.1	43.5	-2.5	43.3	-0.5	43.3	0.0	43.4	0.2	40.9	-5.8	42.3	3.4
1954	41.4	-2.1	40.4	-2.4	39.5	-2.2	38.2	-3.3	37.6	-1.6	35.9	-4.5	37.6	4.7	40.7	8.2	38.4	-5.7	37.0	-3.6	36.3	-1.9	36.5	0.6
1955	36.4	-0.3	37.4	2.7	37.4	0.0	37.5	0.3	37.5	0.0	37.6	0.3	37.3	-0.8	36.9	-1.1	36.4	-1.4	36.5	0.3	36.2	-0.8	36.3	0.3
1956	36.4	0.3	36.2	-0.5	36.2	0.0	36.3	0.3	36.2	-0.3	36.2	0.0	36.0	-0.6	35.6	-1.1	35.6	0.0	35.4	-0.6	35.5	0.3	35.5	0.0
1957	35.3	-0.6	35.5	0.6	35.3	-0.6	35.3	0.0	35.4	0.3	35.4	0.0	35.2	-0.6	35.3	0.3	35.6	0.8	35.6	0.0	35.8	0.6	35.7	-0.3
1958	35.4	-0.8	35.3	-0.3	35.8	1.4	36.0	0.6	35.9	-0.3	35.9	0.0	36.0	0.3	35.8	-0.6	35.9	0.3	36.0	0.3	36.2	0.6	35.9	-0.8
1959	35.7	-0.6	36.0	0.8	35.5	-1.4	35.4	-0.3	35.6	0.6	35.4	-0.6	35.6	0.6	35.8	0.6	35.9	0.3	35.9	0.0	36.5	1.7	37.1	1.6
1960	38.5	3.8	37.7	-2.1	37.7	0.0	38.1	1.1	37.9	-0.5	38.5	1.6	38.3	-0.5	37.7	-1.6	37.6	-0.3	37.3	-0.8	38.1	2.1	37.4	-1.8
1961	38.1	1.9	37.9	-0.5	38.3	1.1	38.0	-0.8	38.1	0.3	38.3	0.5	38.1	-0.5	37.9	-0.5	37.9	0.0	37.6	-0.8	36.9	-1.9	36.6	-0.8
1962	36.5	-0.3	36.4	-0.3	36.7	0.8	36.2	-1.4	36.0	-0.6	36.4	1.1	36.1	-0.8	36.1	0.0	36.7	1.7	37.4	1.9	36.2	-3.2	35.9	-0.8
1963	35.8	-0.3	36.2	1.1	36.2	0.0	36.2	0.0	36.4	0.6	37.1	1.9	37.3	0.5	38.1	2.1	38.1	0.0	38.8	1.8	38.5	-0.8	38.4	-0.3
1964	38.4	0.0	38.1	-0.8	38.5	1.0	39.3	2.1	38.9	-1.0	38.7	-0.5	38.9	0.5	38.9	0.0	39.1	0.5	39.0	-0.3	39.4	1.0	39.7	0.8
1965	40.9	3.0	40.9	0.0	40.2	-1.7	39.9	-0.7	40.1	0.5	40.3	0.5	40.5	0.5	41.0	1.2	40.8	-0.5	40.8	0.0	40.8	0.0	40.8	0.0
1966	40.7	-0.2	40.8	0.2	40.9	0.2	40.7	-0.5	40.4	-0.7	40.2	-0.5	40.7	1.2	40.8	0.2	40.8	0.0	41.1	0.7	41.0	-0.2	40.6	-1.0
1967	40.2	-1.0	39.8	-1.0	40.0	0.5	40.4	1.0	40.2	-0.5	40.2	0.0	40.4	0.5	40.1	-0.7	40.2	0.2	40.2	0.0	40.4	0.5	40.6	0.5
1968	40.8	0.5	40.8	0.0	40.8	0.0	40.8	0.0	40.7	-0.2	40.9	0.5	41.0	0.2	41.0	0.0	41.8	2.0	42.3	1.2	42.3	0.0	42.2	-0.2
1969	42.2	0.0	42.6	0.9	42.6	0.0	42.4	-0.5	42.4	0.0	42.4	0.0	42.7	0.7	42.8	0.2	43.3	1.2	47.0	8.5	45.5	-3.2	45.2	-0.7
1970	45.2	0.0	45.5	0.7	45.4	-0.2	44.9	-1.1	44.3	-1.3	45.3	2.3	45.8	1.1	45.9	0.2	46.3	0.9	45.9	-0.9	45.5	-0.9	45.3	-0.4
1971	45.0	-0.7	45.0	0.0	45.7	1.6	46.0	0.7	45.8	-0.4	45.8	0.0	45.8	0.0	45.8	0.0	45.5	-0.7	45.4	-0.2	45.5	0.2	45.5	0.0
1972	45.7	0.4	45.8	0.2	45.7	-0.2	45.8	0.2	46.3	1.1	46.0	-0.6	46.0	0.0	45.8	-0.4	46.8	2.2	47.0	0.4	46.7	-0.6	46.6	-0.2
1973	46.9	0.6	47.2	0.6	47.8	1.3	47.7	-0.2	47.8	0.2	48.3	1.0	49.7	2.9	51.7	4.0	51.5	-0.4	52.0	1.0	52.0	0.0	52.6	1.2
1974	54.0	2.7	56.3	4.3	59.1	5.0	60.1	1.7	61.5	2.3	63.0	2.4	64.5	2.4	66.4	2.9	68.5	3.2	69.0	0.7	71.1	3.0	72.1	1.4
1975	73.2	1.5	72.9	-0.4	72.3	-0.8	72.5	0.3	72.0	-0.7	71.4	-0.8	70.8	-0.8	71.6	1.1	71.8	0.3	71.3	-0.7	70.9	-0.6	70.4	-0.7
1976	69.5	-1.3	68.8	-1.0	68.8	0.0	69.8	1.5	69.9	0.1	69.5	-0.6	69.6	0.1	69.9	0.4	70.6	1.0	71.5	1.3	71.7	0.3	73.5	2.5
1977	73.3	-0.3	74.0	1.0	74.0	0.0	74.3	0.4	77.4	4.2	77.6	0.3	78.2	0.8	78.2	0.0	78.1	-0.1	78.0	-0.1	77.2	-1.0	77.2	0.0
1978	77.8	0.8	78.1	0.4	78.8	0.9	80.2	1.8	80.6	0.5	80.4	-0.2	81.5	1.4	79.2	-2.8	79.4	0.3	80.6	1.5	82.0	1.7	82.1	0.1
1979	83.1	1.2	83.7	0.7	87.5	4.5	88.2	0.8	88.6	0.5	84.9	-4.2	85.6	0.8	87.6	2.3	88.1	0.6	88.8	0.8	89.4	0.7	89.7	0.3
1980	90.7	1.1	89.9	-0.9	90.4	0.6	90.6	0.2	90.0	-0.7	89.9	-0.1	89.9	0.0	90.1	0.2	91.2	1.2	92.8	1.8	94.6	1.9	96.7	2.2
1981	98.2	1.6	99.8	1.6	100.2	0.4	100.6	0.4	101.0	0.4	101.2	0.2	101.5	0.3	101.4	-0.1	101.8	0.4	100.5	-1.3	100.6	0.1	100.6	0.0
1982	101.0	0.4	100.9	-0.1	100.4	-0.5	100.4	0.0	99.8	-0.6	100.0	0.2	99.8	-0.2	98.9	-0.9	99.4	0.5	99.7	0.3	99.7	0.0	100.0	0.3
1983	100.1	0.1	100.3	0.2	100.0	-0.3	100.5	0.5	100.5	0.0	101.2	0.7	102.6	1.4	101.7	-0.9	104.0	2.3	105.4	1.3	106.5	1.0	107.1	0.6
1984	107.3	0.2	110.8	3.3	110.7	-0.1	111.2	0.5	111.1	-0.1	112.6	1.4	113.2	0.5	112.8	-0.4	113.1	0.3	113.1	0.0	113.0	-0.1	113.0	0.0
1985	113.2	0.2	113.2	0.0	113.2	0.0	113.5	0.3	114.1	0.5	114.1	0.0	114.5	0.4	115.1	0.5	114.5	-0.5	114.5	0.0	114.6	0.1	114.6	0.0
1986	115.4	0.7	115.1	-0.3	115.2	0.1	115.1	-0.1	115.4	0.3	115.7	0.3	116.1	0.3	116.4	0.3	116.6	0.2	117.4	0.7	117.7	0.3	118.3	0.5
1987	118.9	0.5	119.5	0.5	119.8	0.3	120.0	0.2	120.0	0.0	119.5	-0.4	119.5	0.0	119.7	0.2	119.6	-0.1	119.9	0.3	120.3	0.3	120.5	0.2
1988	119.9	-0.5	120.5	0.5	120.7	0.2	121.4	0.6	121.5	0.1	121.3	-0.2	122.7	1.2	123.4	0.6	123.8	0.3	124.3	0.4	125.1	0.6	125.3	0.2
1989	126.2	0.7	127.5	1.0	128.1	0.5	128.6	0.4	129.3	0.5	129.3	0.0	129.4	0.1	130.0	0.5	130.3	0.2	130.6	0.2	131.1	0.4	131.8	0.5
1990	131.6	-0.2	132.2	0.5	132.9	0.5	133.1	0.2	133.8	0.5	133.7	-0.1	134.1	0.3	134.8	0.5	135.0	0.1	134.8	-0.1	136.7	1.4	137.4	0.5
1991	137.6	0.1	137.9	0.2	137.8	-0.1	138.2	0.3	137.3	-0.7	137.8	0.4	137.9	0.1	139.0	0.8	138.8	-0.1	139.2	0.3	138.9	-0.2	138.8	-0.1

[Continued]

Miscellaneous Processed Foods
Producer Price Index
Base 1982 = 100
[Continued]

For 1947-2001. Columns headed % show percentile change in the index from the previous period for which an index is available.

Year	Jan Index	%	Feb Index	%	Mar Index	%	Apr Index	%	May Index	%	Jun Index	%	Jul Index	%	Aug Index	%	Sep Index	%	Oct Index	%	Nov Index	%	Dec Index	%
1992	139.1	0.2	139.1	0.0	138.8	-0.2	138.7	-0.1	138.7	0.0	138.4	-0.2	138.9	0.4	139.4	0.4	139.5	0.1	139.4	-0.1	140.2	0.6	140.2	0.0
1993	140.7	0.4	141.2	0.4	141.8	0.4	141.9	0.1	142.1	0.1	142.2	0.1	142.5	0.2	143.1	0.4	142.8	-0.2	143.1	0.2	143.3	0.1	143.4	0.1
1994	143.5	0.1	144.2	0.5	144.1	-0.1	144.1	0.0	144.0	-0.1	144.1	0.1	144.2	0.1	144.3	0.1	144.3	0.0	144.7	0.3	145.0	0.2	145.3	0.2
1995	145.6	0.2	145.0	-0.4	145.2	0.1	145.4	0.1	145.3	-0.1	145.3	0.0	146.2	0.6	146.6	0.3	146.8	0.1	147.4	0.4	147.6	0.1	147.8	0.1
1996	148.1	0.2	148.6	0.3	148.7	0.1	148.8	0.1	149.3	0.3	149.6	0.2	150.2	0.4	150.6	0.3	151.1	0.3	151.0	-0.1	151.5	0.3	151.9	0.3
1997	152.3	0.3	152.3	0.0	152.4	0.1	152.7	0.2	152.6	-0.1	152.7	0.1	153.3	0.4	153.4	0.1	153.3	-0.1	153.4	0.1	153.4	0.0	153.6	0.1
1998	153.6	0.0	153.5	-0.1	153.6	0.1	154.0	0.3	154.1	0.1	154.1	0.0	154.4	0.2	154.5	0.1	154.5	0.0	154.5	0.0	154.6	0.1	154.5	-0.1
1999	154.8	0.2	155.2	0.3	155.1	-0.1	155.2	0.1	155.0	-0.1	155.3	0.2	155.6	0.2	155.8	0.1	155.6	-0.1	155.4	-0.1	155.7	0.2	155.9	0.1
2000	155.9	0.0	156.1	0.1	155.8	-0.2	155.8	0.0	156.0	0.1	156.1	0.1	156.3	0.1	156.6	0.2	157.4	0.5	157.6	0.1	157.8	0.1	158.4	0.4
2001	159.0	0.4	159.1	0.1	159.2	0.1	159.4	0.1	159.7	0.2	160.2	0.3	160.5	0.2	160.8	0.2	160.6	-0.1	160.8	0.1	161.1	0.2	160.8	-0.2

Source: U.S. Department of Labor, Bureau of Labor Statistics, Division of Industry Prices and Price Indexes. n.e.c. stands for not elsewhere classified. - indicates no data collected for period or unavailable.

Prepared Animal Feeds
Producer Price Index
Base 1982 = 100

For 1947-2001. Columns headed % show percentile change in the index from the previous period for which an index is available.

Year	Jan Index	%	Feb Index	%	Mar Index	%	Apr Index	%	May Index	%	Jun Index	%	Jul Index	%	Aug Index	%	Sep Index	%	Oct Index	%	Nov Index	%	Dec Index	%
1947	45.3	-	42.0	-7.3	50.8	21.0	47.5	-6.5	48.7	2.5	52.8	8.4	57.3	8.5	58.4	1.9	65.4	12.0	63.8	-2.4	63.3	-0.8	67.9	7.3
1948	74.2	9.3	61.1	-17.7	60.2	-1.5	60.9	1.2	58.7	-3.6	60.3	2.7	55.4	-8.1	47.7	-13.9	48.5	1.7	44.9	-7.4	50.0	11.4	50.5	1.0
1949	49.5	-2.0	45.2	-8.7	47.4	4.9	50.5	6.5	48.7	-3.6	48.8	0.2	52.6	7.8	56.0	6.5	49.8	-11.1	47.5	-4.6	45.7	-3.8	46.5	1.8
1950	44.7	-3.9	43.8	-2.0	47.2	7.8	49.4	4.7	53.7	8.7	50.1	-6.7	56.7	13.2	49.2	-13.2	47.7	-3.0	45.5	-4.6	47.9	5.3	50.2	4.8
1951	51.4	2.4	52.7	2.5	52.9	0.4	54.4	2.8	51.7	-5.0	51.4	-0.6	52.4	1.9	51.2	-2.3	53.8	5.1	55.8	3.7	57.9	3.8	58.8	1.6
1952	60.2	2.4	60.7	0.8	58.5	-3.6	58.9	0.7	57.9	-1.7	57.7	-0.3	54.9	-4.9	58.5	6.6	57.9	-1.0	57.9	0.0	55.2	-4.7	54.6	-1.1
1953	52.3	-4.2	50.5	-3.4	50.8	0.6	47.4	-6.7	48.7	2.7	44.7	-8.2	44.2	-1.1	45.4	2.7	43.6	-4.0	43.3	-0.7	42.1	-2.8	49.3	17.1
1954	50.2	1.8	52.0	3.6	54.0	3.8	59.4	10.0	58.3	-1.9	53.8	-7.7	52.5	-2.4	50.9	-3.0	47.6	-6.5	45.1	-5.3	45.4	0.7	46.4	2.2
1955	45.3	-2.4	45.9	1.3	44.3	-3.5	42.8	-3.4	40.1	-6.3	37.8	-5.7	39.5	4.5	38.3	-3.0	38.8	1.3	39.9	2.8	36.3	-9.0	36.8	1.4
1956	37.3	1.4	36.4	-2.4	35.9	-1.4	39.8	10.9	43.7	9.8	40.6	-7.1	38.9	-4.2	38.5	-1.0	37.2	-3.4	36.4	-2.2	38.4	5.5	38.8	1.0
1957	39.8	2.6	38.9	-2.3	38.5	-1.0	38.0	-1.3	35.9	-5.5	33.9	-5.6	35.3	4.1	36.4	3.1	35.5	-2.5	33.7	-5.1	32.8	-2.7	33.2	1.2
1958	34.2	3.0	35.1	2.6	39.9	13.7	43.2	8.3	41.7	-3.5	39.2	-6.0	42.6	8.7	41.0	-3.8	38.2	-6.8	36.9	-3.4	38.8	5.1	46.2	19.1
1959	46.1	-0.2	43.9	-4.8	42.5	-3.2	44.3	4.2	40.9	-7.7	36.9	-9.8	38.6	4.6	37.8	-2.1	34.5	-8.7	37.6	9.0	39.4	4.8	39.6	0.5
1960	40.4	2.0	38.6	-4.5	39.1	1.3	40.4	3.3	36.3	-10.1	36.1	-0.6	36.0	-0.3	35.1	-2.5	36.2	3.1	35.4	-2.2	35.7	0.8	37.4	4.8
1961	39.9	6.7	39.6	-0.8	40.7	2.8	41.4	1.7	42.9	3.6	40.1	-6.5	39.9	-0.5	39.7	-0.5	39.7	0.0	38.0	-4.3	41.0	7.9	42.0	2.4
1962	42.4	1.0	41.6	-1.9	41.6	0.0	41.8	0.5	41.8	0.0	41.4	-1.0	42.9	3.6	42.6	-0.7	43.9	3.1	43.6	-0.7	44.4	1.8	44.7	0.7
1963	45.7	2.2	45.7	0.0	45.2	-1.1	43.2	-4.4	43.0	-0.5	43.3	0.7	44.9	3.7	45.5	1.3	46.0	1.1	45.5	-1.1	45.3	-0.4	46.2	2.0
1964	46.5	0.6	45.3	-2.6	44.5	-1.8	44.3	-0.4	42.7	-3.6	42.4	-0.7	42.8	0.9	42.6	-0.5	43.9	3.1	44.5	1.4	43.4	-2.5	45.0	3.7
1965	44.5	-1.1	44.2	-0.7	44.1	-0.2	44.6	1.1	43.6	-2.2	45.1	3.4	45.9	1.8	45.2	-1.5	45.1	-0.2	44.9	-0.4	46.3	3.1	45.8	-1.1
1966	47.0	2.6	48.2	2.6	46.2	-4.1	46.1	-0.2	47.6	3.3	47.9	0.6	51.2	6.9	51.6	0.8	51.1	-1.0	49.5	-3.1	49.6	0.2	51.0	2.8
1967	51.0	0.0	48.7	-4.5	48.2	-1.0	47.5	-1.5	45.9	-3.4	47.3	3.1	47.6	0.6	46.2	-2.9	47.0	1.7	46.6	-0.9	45.9	-1.5	46.2	0.7
1968	46.5	0.6	46.2	-0.6	46.0	-0.4	45.3	-1.5	45.5	0.4	46.2	1.5	46.2	0.0	45.8	-0.9	45.4	-0.9	45.4	0.0	45.3	-0.2	45.7	0.9
1969	45.7	0.0	45.4	-0.7	44.7	-1.5	45.8	2.5	44.4	-3.1	45.2	1.8	45.9	1.5	45.7	-0.4	46.1	0.9	46.4	0.7	46.2	-0.4	47.1	1.9
1970	51.0	8.3	50.9	-0.2	46.1	-9.4	46.9	1.7	46.3	-1.3	46.9	1.3	49.3	5.1	49.5	0.4	50.7	2.4	49.4	-2.6	50.0	1.2	51.7	3.4
1971	51.1	-1.2	49.7	-2.7	50.8	2.2	49.4	-2.8	49.5	0.2	50.9	2.8	50.6	-0.6	49.6	-2.0	48.0	-3.2	46.7	-2.7	47.5	1.7	49.5	4.2
1972	49.1	-0.8	49.1	0.0	51.4	4.7	51.3	-0.2	51.3	0.0	51.0	-0.6	52.5	2.9	52.9	0.8	55.8	5.5	55.1	-1.3	61.7	12.0	77.4	25.4
1973	78.7	1.7	86.4	9.8	86.3	-0.1	78.9	-8.6	100.0	26.7	122.0	22.0	93.3	-23.5	123.9	32.8	90.0	-27.4	87.3	-3.0	86.8	-0.6	95.1	9.6
1974	96.2	1.2	90.3	-6.1	85.7	-5.1	78.7	-8.2	73.4	-6.7	72.2	-1.6	73.9	2.4	102.8	39.1	87.4	-15.0	100.0	14.4	92.6	-7.4	92.1	-0.5
1975	87.8	-4.7	79.3	-9.7	75.4	-4.9	81.1	7.6	78.0	-3.8	80.0	2.6	80.2	0.2	84.0	4.7	83.9	-0.1	84.0	0.1	81.3	-3.2	82.6	1.6
1976	83.6	1.2	82.9	-0.8	82.9	0.0	82.2	-0.8	85.8	4.4	100.8	17.5	102.3	1.5	93.2	-8.9	100.1	7.4	94.6	-5.5	94.7	0.1	100.9	6.5
1977	103.6	2.7	103.6	0.0	105.0	1.4	115.0	9.5	113.3	-1.5	106.7	-5.8	89.1	-16.5	83.2	-6.6	82.7	-0.6	79.7	-3.6	91.7	15.1	88.6	-3.4
1978	92.0	3.8	88.4	-3.9	94.9	7.4	93.5	-1.5	91.7	-1.9	93.6	2.1	92.9	-0.7	89.9	-3.2	91.7	2.0	95.2	3.8	97.2	2.1	100.3	3.2
1979	100.0	-0.3	102.8	2.8	102.1	-0.7	102.0	-0.1	99.8	-2.2	104.3	4.5	111.2	6.6	102.3	-8.0	103.8	1.5	106.0	2.1	105.3	-0.7	106.5	1.1
1980	104.0	-2.3	104.0	0.0	102.5	-1.4	97.0	-5.4	98.0	1.0	97.0	-1.0	106.0	9.3	110.0	3.8	115.2	4.7	116.8	1.4	120.5	3.2	116.9	-3.0
1981	117.8	0.8	111.6	-5.3	109.4	-2.0	112.5	2.8	114.1	1.4	110.9	-2.8	109.9	-0.9	108.4	-1.4	105.5	-2.7	103.2	-2.2	101.6	-1.6	102.8	1.2
1982	102.9	0.1	101.7	-1.2	100.0	-1.7	102.4	2.4	102.9	0.5	102.4	-0.5	101.3	-1.1	98.2	-3.1	96.7	-1.5	94.6	-2.2	97.5	3.1	99.4	1.9
1983	100.2	0.8	100.5	0.3	100.5	0.0	105.5	5.0	104.8	-0.7	102.8	-1.9	104.1	1.3	110.3	6.0	118.0	7.0	117.7	-0.3	119.3	1.4	116.2	-2.6
1984	116.1	-0.1	109.4	-5.8	111.4	1.8	111.8	0.4	109.9	-1.7	106.7	-2.9	102.5	-3.9	101.3	-1.2	99.0	-2.3	95.8	-3.2	94.5	-1.4	94.1	-0.4
1985	93.7	-0.4	91.6	-2.2	89.7	-2.1	88.1	-1.8	86.3	-2.0	87.0	0.8	88.0	1.1	88.4	0.5	89.1	0.8	91.0	2.1	93.2	2.4	94.5	1.4
1986	95.6	1.2	94.1	-1.6	95.0	1.0	95.5	0.5	95.2	-0.3	95.5	0.3	94.4	-1.2	93.5	-1.0	95.7	2.4	92.5	-3.3	93.9	1.5	94.5	0.6
1987	93.8	-0.7	94.1	0.3	92.4	-1.8	93.8	1.5	98.4	4.9	99.9	1.5	99.4	-0.5	98.4	-1.0	99.9	1.5	100.3	0.4	104.8	4.5	107.3	2.4
1988	105.8	-1.4	102.9	-2.7	104.0	1.1	106.0	1.9	107.1	1.0	120.2	12.2	127.3	5.9	123.6	-2.9	125.4	1.5	125.5	0.1	123.3	-1.8	120.9	-1.9
1989	124.3	2.8	121.1	-2.6	122.0	0.7	119.0	-2.5	117.8	-1.0	114.9	-2.5	117.6	2.3	114.2	-2.9	115.3	1.0	112.3	-2.6	110.9	-1.2	110.3	-0.5
1990	110.7	0.4	106.1	-4.2	105.9	-0.2	106.2	0.3	109.1	2.7	107.4	-1.6	109.3	1.8	107.4	-1.7	107.7	0.3	108.0	0.3	105.6	-2.2	105.9	0.3
1991	104.5	-1.3	105.1	0.6	106.3	1.1	105.9	-0.4	105.8	-0.1	106.0	0.2	104.1	-1.8	107.9	3.7	109.0	1.0	108.7	-0.3	109.4	0.6	109.0	-0.4

[Continued]

Prepared Animal Feeds
Producer Price Index
Base 1982 = 100
[Continued]

For 1947-2001. Columns headed % show percentile change in the index from the previous period for which an index is available.

Year	Jan Index	%	Feb Index	%	Mar Index	%	Apr Index	%	May Index	%	Jun Index	%	Jul Index	%	Aug Index	%	Sep Index	%	Oct Index	%	Nov Index	%	Dec Index	%
1992	108.7	-0.3	108.9	0.2	109.3	0.4	107.9	-1.3	108.7	0.7	109.3	0.6	107.7	-1.5	106.9	-0.7	107.9	0.9	107.3	-0.6	107.3	0.0	109.6	2.1
1993	110.0	0.4	107.9	-1.9	107.0	-0.8	108.2	1.1	108.5	0.3	107.9	-0.6	113.2	4.9	114.9	1.5	112.6	-2.0	111.7	-0.8	113.3	1.4	116.2	2.6
1994	115.9	-0.3	116.6	0.6	116.0	-0.5	113.8	-1.9	113.2	-0.5	114.3	1.0	112.1	-1.9	109.4	-2.4	109.0	-0.4	107.1	-1.7	104.7	-2.2	103.9	-0.8
1995	104.1	0.2	102.8	-1.2	103.9	1.1	105.2	1.3	103.7	-1.4	104.7	1.0	105.7	1.0	108.4	2.6	110.3	1.8	114.7	4.0	120.6	5.1	125.3	3.9
1996	129.1	3.0	129.4	0.2	131.4	1.5	134.8	2.6	138.6	2.8	138.1	-0.4	139.8	1.2	140.2	0.3	142.8	1.9	135.3	-5.3	131.7	-2.7	132.1	0.3
1997	131.2	-0.7	131.7	0.4	136.1	3.3	137.5	1.0	139.7	1.6	136.6	-2.2	132.6	-2.9	131.7	-0.7	135.0	2.5	126.8	-6.1	128.0	0.9	127.7	-0.2
1998	121.2	-5.1	117.3	-3.2	113.8	-3.0	109.1	-4.1	107.3	-1.6	106.8	-0.5	109.0	2.1	106.0	-2.8	101.8	-4.0	99.5	-2.3	101.6	2.1	101.9	0.3
1999	101.5	-0.4	99.8	-1.7	97.0	-2.8	97.7	0.7	97.0	-0.7	97.3	0.3	96.5	-0.8	97.0	0.5	97.9	0.9	99.3	1.4	99.6	0.3	99.1	-0.5
2000	99.2	0.1	101.3	2.1	102.9	1.6	102.7	-0.2	105.1	2.3	105.0	-0.1	103.3	-1.6	99.6	-3.6	102.0	2.4	102.9	0.9	103.6	0.7	107.3	3.6
2001	110.5	3.0	106.5	-3.6	104.2	-2.2	102.3	-1.8	102.2	-0.1	104.0	1.8	104.7	0.7	107.2	2.4	106.4	-0.7	105.3	-1.0	104.5	-0.8	103.6	-0.9

Source: U.S. Department of Labor, Bureau of Labor Statistics, Division of Industry Prices and Price Indexes. n.e.c. stands for not elsewhere classified. - indicates no data collected for period or unavailable.

TEXTILE PRODUCTS AND APPAREL
Producer Price Index
Base 1982 = 100

For 1947-2001. Columns headed % show percentile change in the index from the previous period for which an index is available.

Year	Jan Index	%	Feb Index	%	Mar Index	%	Apr Index	%	May Index	%	Jun Index	%	Jul Index	%	Aug Index	%	Sep Index	%	Oct Index	%	Nov Index	%	Dec Index	%
1947	49.8	-	50.1	0.6	50.3	0.4	50.3	0.0	50.2	-0.2	50.0	-0.4	50.2	0.4	50.4	0.4	51.0	1.2	51.2	0.4	51.7	1.0	52.6	1.7
1948	53.2	1.1	53.5	0.6	53.4	-0.2	52.9	-0.9	53.1	0.4	52.8	-0.6	52.9	0.2	52.9	0.0	52.8	-0.2	52.6	-0.4	52.2	-0.8	52.1	-0.2
1949	51.0	-2.1	50.5	-1.0	49.8	-1.4	48.9	-1.8	47.8	-2.2	47.5	-0.6	47.3	-0.4	47.3	0.0	47.4	0.2	47.6	0.4	47.7	0.2	47.7	0.0
1950	47.7	0.0	47.8	0.2	47.7	-0.2	47.1	-1.3	47.0	-0.2	47.3	0.6	48.7	3.0	50.8	4.3	52.8	3.9	54.4	3.0	55.2	1.5	56.4	2.2
1951	58.0	2.8	58.6	1.0	58.7	0.2	58.5	-0.3	58.1	-0.7	57.2	-1.5	56.5	-1.2	54.9	-2.8	53.6	-2.4	52.6	-1.9	52.6	0.0	52.6	0.0
1952	52.3	-0.6	51.7	-1.1	50.9	-1.5	50.6	-0.6	50.3	-0.6	50.1	-0.4	50.1	0.0	50.2	0.2	50.4	0.4	50.2	-0.4	50.0	-0.4	49.8	-0.4
1953	50.1	0.6	49.9	-0.4	49.4	-1.0	49.3	-0.2	49.4	0.2	49.3	-0.2	49.4	0.2	49.4	0.0	49.1	-0.6	48.9	-0.4	48.7	-0.4	48.5	-0.4
1954	48.6	0.2	48.2	-0.8	48.1	-0.2	48.0	-0.2	48.0	0.0	48.1	0.2	48.2	0.2	48.2	0.0	48.2	0.0	48.3	0.2	48.2	-0.2	48.2	0.0
1955	48.2	0.0	48.2	0.0	48.2	0.0	48.1	-0.2	48.1	0.0	48.2	0.2	48.2	0.0	48.2	0.0	48.3	0.2	48.3	0.0	48.4	0.2	48.4	0.0
1956	48.4	0.0	48.6	0.4	48.5	-0.2	48.2	-0.6	48.1	-0.2	48.1	0.0	48.1	0.0	48.0	-0.2	48.0	0.0	48.3	0.6	48.3	0.0	48.4	0.2
1957	48.5	0.2	48.4	-0.2	48.3	-0.2	48.2	-0.2	48.3	0.2	48.3	0.0	48.3	0.0	48.3	0.0	48.3	0.0	48.2	-0.2	48.1	-0.2	48.1	0.0
1958	47.9	-0.4	47.7	-0.4	47.6	-0.2	47.5	-0.2	47.4	-0.2	47.3	-0.2	47.3	0.0	47.3	0.0	47.3	0.0	47.2	-0.2	47.2	0.0	47.3	0.2
1959	47.3	0.0	47.5	0.4	47.6	0.2	47.7	0.2	47.8	0.2	48.1	0.6	48.2	0.2	48.4	0.4	48.5	0.2	48.5	0.0	48.7	0.4	49.0	0.6
1960	48.9	-0.2	48.9	0.0	48.7	-0.4	48.7	0.0	48.7	0.0	48.7	0.0	48.7	0.0	48.6	-0.2	48.5	-0.2	48.5	0.0	48.3	-0.4	48.2	-0.2
1961	48.0	-0.4	48.0	0.0	47.8	-0.4	47.7	-0.2	47.6	-0.2	47.5	-0.2	47.6	0.2	47.7	0.2	47.8	0.2	48.0	0.4	48.0	0.0	48.1	0.2
1962	48.1	0.0	48.1	0.0	48.2	0.2	48.2	0.0	48.2	0.0	48.3	0.2	48.3	0.0	48.3	0.0	48.2	-0.2	48.2	0.0	48.2	0.0	48.2	0.0
1963	48.1	-0.2	48.1	0.0	48.0	-0.2	48.0	0.0	48.0	0.0	48.1	0.2	48.1	0.0	48.1	0.0	48.2	0.2	48.2	0.0	48.4	0.4	48.5	0.2
1964	48.5	0.0	48.5	0.0	48.5	0.0	48.4	-0.2	48.5	0.2	48.4	-0.2	48.4	0.0	48.5	0.2	48.5	0.0	48.6	0.2	48.6	0.0	48.6	0.0
1965	48.6	0.0	48.6	0.0	48.6	0.0	48.6	0.0	48.7	0.2	48.8	0.2	48.8	0.0	48.8	0.0	48.9	0.2	48.9	0.0	48.8	-0.2	48.9	0.2
1966	48.8	-0.2	48.9	0.2	48.9	0.0	49.0	0.2	49.0	0.0	49.0	0.0	49.1	0.2	49.1	0.0	49.0	-0.2	49.0	0.0	48.9	-0.2	48.8	-0.2
1967	48.9	0.2	48.9	0.0	48.8	-0.2	48.7	-0.2	48.6	-0.2	48.6	0.0	48.6	0.0	48.6	0.0	48.8	0.4	48.9	0.2	49.3	0.8	49.7	0.8
1968	50.0	0.6	50.1	0.2	50.2	0.2	50.2	0.0	50.3	0.2	50.5	0.4	50.7	0.4	50.9	0.4	51.1	0.4	51.3	0.4	51.5	0.4	51.4	-0.2
1969	51.6	0.4	51.5	-0.2	51.4	-0.2	51.4	0.0	51.4	0.0	51.7	0.6	51.9	0.4	52.1	0.4	52.1	0.0	52.2	0.2	52.3	0.2	52.2	-0.2
1970	52.4	0.4	52.3	-0.2	52.4	0.2	52.4	0.0	52.3	-0.2	52.4	0.2	52.4	0.0	52.4	0.0	52.4	0.0	52.3	-0.2	52.2	-0.2	52.2	0.0
1971	52.2	0.0	52.3	0.2	52.4	0.2	52.7	0.6	52.8	0.2	53.4	1.1	53.6	0.4	53.9	0.6	53.8	-0.2	53.8	0.0	53.9	0.2	54.3	0.7
1972	54.4	0.2	54.7	0.6	54.8	0.2	55.0	0.4	55.4	0.7	55.5	0.2	55.7	0.4	55.8	0.2	55.9	0.2	56.1	0.4	56.3	0.4	56.5	0.4
1973	57.0	0.9	57.4	0.7	58.2	1.4	59.0	1.4	59.8	1.4	60.5	1.2	60.7	0.3	61.2	0.8	62.0	1.3	62.8	1.3	63.5	1.1	64.2	1.1
1974	65.4	1.9	66.1	1.1	66.5	0.6	67.2	1.1	68.0	1.2	69.3	1.9	69.5	0.3	69.6	0.1	69.5	-0.1	68.7	-1.2	68.3	-0.6	67.7	-0.9
1975	67.2	-0.7	66.7	-0.7	65.7	-1.5	65.7	0.0	66.1	0.6	66.4	0.5	66.9	0.8	67.3	0.6	67.6	0.4	69.1	2.2	70.0	1.3	70.4	0.6
1976	71.2	1.1	71.5	0.4	71.7	0.3	72.0	0.4	72.0	0.0	72.5	0.7	72.8	0.4	73.1	0.4	72.8	-0.4	73.0	0.3	73.4	0.5	73.3	-0.1
1977	73.7	0.5	74.2	0.7	74.5	0.4	75.1	0.8	75.3	0.3	75.6	0.4	75.5	-0.1	75.6	0.1	75.8	0.3	75.9	0.1	75.9	0.0	76.2	0.4
1978	76.5	0.4	76.8	0.4	76.9	0.1	77.2	0.4	77.5	0.4	77.8	0.4	78.2	0.5	78.5	0.4	78.9	0.5	79.3	0.5	79.8	0.6	80.0	0.3
1979	80.2	0.2	80.3	0.1	80.8	0.6	81.4	0.7	81.7	0.4	82.3	0.7	82.8	0.6	83.4	0.7	83.7	0.4	84.1	0.5	84.5	0.5	84.6	0.1
1980	85.7	1.3	86.3	0.7	87.6	1.5	88.6	1.1	89.0	0.5	89.4	0.4	90.3	1.0	90.7	0.4	91.2	0.6	92.0	0.9	92.7	0.8	93.1	0.4
1981	94.4	1.4	94.8	0.4	95.4	0.6	96.6	1.3	97.4	0.8	97.8	0.4	98.4	0.6	98.9	0.5	99.2	0.3	99.7	0.5	99.5	-0.2	99.4	-0.1
1982	100.2	0.8	100.5	0.3	100.2	-0.3	100.4	0.2	100.4	0.0	100.2	-0.2	99.8	-0.4	99.8	0.0	99.9	0.1	99.8	-0.1	99.7	-0.1	99.0	-0.7
1983	99.1	0.1	99.0	-0.1	99.4	0.4	99.5	0.1	99.9	0.4	100.1	0.2	100.4	0.3	100.7	0.3	100.8	0.1	101.2	0.4	101.5	0.3	101.6	0.1
1984	101.8	0.2	102.5	0.7	102.6	0.1	102.6	0.0	102.9	0.3	102.8	-0.1	102.9	0.1	102.7	-0.2	103.0	0.3	102.9	-0.1	102.7	-0.2	102.6	-0.1
1985	102.8	0.2	103.0	0.2	102.9	-0.1	103.0	0.1	102.9	-0.1	102.8	-0.1	102.7	-0.1	102.9	0.2	102.8	-0.1	102.7	-0.1	102.9	0.2	103.0	0.1
1986	103.0	0.0	103.1	0.1	103.3	0.2	103.2	-0.1	103.2	0.0	103.2	0.0	103.3	0.1	103.2	-0.1	103.2	0.0	103.2	0.0	103.3	0.1	103.4	0.1
1987	103.6	0.2	103.7	0.1	103.9	0.2	104.2	0.3	104.4	0.2	104.8	0.4	105.3	0.5	105.6	0.3	106.0	0.4	106.4	0.4	106.6	0.2	107.0	0.4
1988	107.6	0.6	108.1	0.5	108.4	0.3	108.7	0.3	108.9	0.2	109.3	0.4	109.5	0.2	109.6	0.1	109.8	0.2	110.0	0.2	110.2	0.2	110.5	0.3
1989	111.0	0.5	111.3	0.3	111.2	-0.1	111.6	0.4	111.8	0.2	112.2	0.4	112.6	0.4	112.9	0.3	113.0	0.1	113.3	0.3	113.5	0.2	113.6	0.1
1990	114.6	0.9	114.6	0.0	114.7	0.1	114.9	0.2	114.8	-0.1	115.0	0.2	115.1	0.1	115.1	0.0	115.1	0.0	115.1	0.0	115.3	0.2	115.2	-0.1
1991	115.7	0.4	115.8	0.1	115.9	0.1	116.0	0.1	116.0	0.0	116.2	0.2	116.3	0.1	116.5	0.2	116.6	0.1	116.7	0.1	116.8	0.1	116.9	0.1

[Continued]

TEXTILE PRODUCTS AND APPAREL
Producer Price Index
Base 1982 = 100

[Continued]

For 1947-2001. Columns headed % show percentile change in the index from the previous period for which an index is available.

Year	Jan Index	%	Feb Index	%	Mar Index	%	Apr Index	%	May Index	%	Jun Index	%	Jul Index	%	Aug Index	%	Sep Index	%	Oct Index	%	Nov Index	%	Dec Index	%
1992	117.4	0.4	117.6	0.2	117.7	0.1	117.8	0.1	117.7	-0.1	117.9	0.2	117.8	-0.1	117.8	0.0	118.0	0.2	118.1	0.1	118.0	-0.1	118.0	0.0
1993	118.0	0.0	117.9	-0.1	117.9	0.0	118.1	0.2	118.0	-0.1	118.0	0.0	118.2	0.2	118.3	0.1	118.1	-0.2	118.1	0.0	118.0	-0.1	117.9	-0.1
1994	117.9	0.0	117.9	0.0	117.9	0.0	117.9	0.0	118.0	0.1	118.1	0.1	118.4	0.3	118.5	0.1	118.7	0.2	118.6	-0.1	118.6	0.0	118.8	0.2
1995	119.4	0.5	119.9	0.4	120.1	0.2	120.4	0.2	120.8	0.3	120.8	0.0	121.0	0.2	121.1	0.1	121.5	0.3	121.6	0.1	121.3	-0.2	121.3	0.0
1996	121.8	0.4	121.9	0.1	122.0	0.1	122.0	0.0	122.3	0.2	122.3	0.0	122.6	0.2	122.5	-0.1	123.0	0.4	122.9	-0.1	122.7	-0.2	122.7	0.0
1997	122.6	-0.1	122.5	-0.1	122.6	0.1	122.5	-0.1	122.6	0.1	122.6	0.0	122.6	0.0	122.6	0.0	122.7	0.1	122.5	-0.2	122.5	0.0	122.5	0.0
1998	123.2	0.6	123.2	0.0	123.1	-0.1	123.2	0.1	123.2	0.0	123.2	0.0	123.0	-0.2	122.9	-0.1	122.8	-0.1	122.5	-0.2	122.2	-0.2	122.0	-0.2
1999	121.8	-0.2	121.5	-0.2	121.5	0.0	121.3	-0.2	121.2	-0.1	121.0	-0.2	120.8	-0.2	120.9	0.1	120.8	-0.1	120.8	0.0	120.6	-0.2	120.6	0.0
2000	120.8	0.2	121.0	0.2	121.2	0.2	121.3	0.1	121.4	0.1	121.4	0.0	121.6	0.2	121.7	0.1	121.6	-0.1	121.6	0.0	121.7	0.1	121.7	0.0
2001	121.7	0.0	121.9	0.2	122.0	0.1	122.0	0.0	121.6	-0.3	121.5	-0.1	121.2	-0.2	121.1	-0.1	121.1	0.0	120.8	-0.2	120.7	-0.1	120.4	-0.2

Source: U.S. Department of Labor, Bureau of Labor Statistics, Division of Industry Prices and Price Indexes. n.e.c. stands for not elsewhere classified. - indicates no data collected for period or unavailable.

Synthetic Fibers
Producer Price Index
Base 1982 = 100

For 1975-2001. Columns headed % show percentile change in the index from the previous period for which an index is available.

Year	Jan Index	%	Feb Index	%	Mar Index	%	Apr Index	%	May Index	%	Jun Index	%	Jul Index	%	Aug Index	%	Sep Index	%	Oct Index	%	Nov Index	%	Dec Index	%
1975	-	-	-	-	-	-	-	-	-	-	-	-	-	-	-	-	-	-	-	-	-	-	61.7	-
1976	62.8	1.8	63.1	0.5	63.0	-0.2	63.5	0.8	63.4	-0.2	63.2	-0.3	63.3	0.2	63.7	0.6	63.6	-0.2	62.8	-1.3	62.7	-0.2	62.7	0.0
1977	63.2	0.8	63.8	0.9	63.7	-0.2	65.7	3.1	66.1	0.6	67.4	2.0	67.2	-0.3	67.4	0.3	67.5	0.1	67.4	-0.1	67.4	0.0	67.4	0.0
1978	67.9	0.7	67.8	-0.1	67.8	0.0	67.4	-0.6	67.6	0.3	67.2	-0.6	67.2	0.0	67.3	0.1	67.3	0.0	67.5	0.3	68.2	1.0	68.2	0.0
1979	69.7	2.2	70.0	0.4	70.1	0.1	71.0	1.3	72.4	2.0	73.1	1.0	73.8	1.0	74.4	0.8	76.2	2.4	76.9	0.9	76.6	-0.4	76.9	0.4
1980	78.4	2.0	78.5	0.1	79.6	1.4	80.5	1.1	82.2	2.1	83.0	1.0	83.9	1.1	84.8	1.1	86.1	1.5	86.5	0.5	86.8	0.3	86.9	0.1
1981	90.4	4.0	90.7	0.3	91.9	1.3	93.5	1.7	96.5	3.2	97.4	0.9	98.5	1.1	99.5	1.0	99.3	-0.2	100.4	1.1	99.7	-0.7	99.6	-0.1
1982	100.5	0.9	100.7	0.2	99.5	-1.2	100.6	1.1	100.8	0.2	100.5	-0.3	99.6	-0.9	100.1	0.5	100.3	0.2	99.4	-0.9	99.5	0.1	98.5	-1.0
1983	96.7	-1.8	94.5	-2.3	95.0	0.5	94.9	-0.1	96.0	1.2	96.2	0.2	97.7	1.6	97.2	-0.5	97.5	0.3	99.1	1.6	98.3	-0.8	97.5	-0.8
1984	98.3	0.8	99.6	1.3	99.2	-0.4	99.1	-0.1	99.1	0.0	99.0	-0.1	98.8	-0.2	98.7	-0.1	98.2	-0.5	97.6	-0.6	97.2	-0.4	97.3	0.1
1985	97.2	-0.1	97.2	0.0	96.6	-0.6	97.1	0.5	96.9	-0.2	96.5	-0.4	95.4	-1.1	95.5	0.1	95.6	0.1	92.4	-3.3	92.8	0.4	93.0	0.2
1986	93.6	0.6	93.5	-0.1	93.5	0.0	92.4	-1.2	92.3	-0.1	92.1	-0.2	92.5	0.4	92.3	-0.2	92.2	-0.1	91.7	-0.5	91.7	0.0	91.6	-0.1
1987	92.1	0.5	91.4	-0.8	91.3	-0.1	90.8	-0.5	90.8	0.0	91.0	0.2	91.4	0.4	91.7	0.3	91.9	0.2	92.8	1.0	93.3	0.5	93.6	0.3
1988	94.4	0.9	94.7	0.3	95.1	0.4	96.3	1.3	97.0	0.7	96.6	-0.4	97.6	1.0	98.0	0.4	98.6	0.6	99.4	0.8	99.4	0.0	99.9	0.5
1989	100.6	0.7	101.1	0.5	101.6	0.5	104.1	2.5	105.0	0.9	106.2	1.1	106.5	0.3	106.2	-0.3	105.9	-0.3	107.1	1.1	106.7	-0.4	106.9	0.2
1990	106.9	0.0	107.3	0.4	107.4	0.1	106.6	-0.7	106.7	0.1	106.4	-0.3	107.5	1.0	107.1	-0.4	107.2	0.1	105.4	-1.7	105.8	0.4	106.0	0.2
1991	106.8	0.8	106.9	0.1	106.6	-0.3	105.5	-1.0	105.3	-0.2	105.3	0.0	105.1	-0.2	105.0	-0.1	105.0	0.0	104.2	-0.8	104.0	-0.2	103.5	-0.5
1992	103.1	-0.4	103.6	0.5	103.5	-0.1	104.2	0.7	103.4	-0.8	103.9	0.5	103.9	0.0	103.6	-0.3	103.2	-0.4	103.3	0.1	102.4	-0.9	102.5	0.1
1993	102.6	0.1	102.3	-0.3	102.4	0.1	102.8	0.4	102.9	0.1	103.5	0.6	103.8	0.3	105.1	1.3	104.5	-0.6	104.4	-0.1	104.2	-0.2	104.2	0.0
1994	103.8	-0.4	103.5	-0.3	103.1	-0.4	103.0	-0.1	103.2	0.2	103.4	0.2	104.6	1.2	105.6	1.0	105.9	0.3	104.8	-1.0	104.2	-0.6	104.3	0.1
1995	106.8	2.4	107.0	0.2	106.4	-0.6	108.4	1.9	108.6	0.2	108.4	-0.2	109.6	1.1	111.0	1.3	111.6	0.5	112.4	0.7	111.8	-0.5	110.9	-0.8
1996	111.0	0.1	111.2	0.2	111.2	0.0	111.2	0.0	111.0	-0.2	109.5	-1.4	111.7	2.0	111.8	0.1	112.1	0.3	112.0	-0.1	111.7	-0.3	111.6	-0.1
1997	112.7	1.0	111.4	-1.2	111.4	0.0	111.5	0.1	111.3	-0.2	111.0	-0.3	110.9	-0.1	111.0	0.1	110.5	-0.5	110.6	0.1	110.5	-0.1	110.2	-0.3
1998	111.2	0.9	111.2	0.0	110.9	-0.3	111.0	0.1	110.9	-0.1	110.7	-0.2	110.8	0.1	110.8	0.0	109.5	-1.2	107.9	-1.5	107.2	-0.6	106.9	-0.3
1999	105.5	-1.3	105.5	0.0	104.7	-0.8	104.0	-0.7	103.5	-0.5	103.7	0.2	103.2	-0.5	103.0	-0.2	102.9	-0.1	103.6	0.7	103.4	-0.2	103.4	0.0
2000	103.3	-0.1	104.7	1.4	105.0	0.3	105.7	0.7	107.9	2.1	108.1	0.2	107.3	-0.7	108.0	0.7	108.3	0.3	108.5	0.2	109.9	1.3	109.4	-0.5
2001	109.3	-0.1	111.4	1.9	111.0	-0.4	111.2	0.2	108.9	-2.1	107.7	-1.1	107.8	0.1	106.9	-0.8	107.8	0.8	107.7	-0.1	107.2	-0.5	106.7	-0.5

Source: U.S. Department of Labor, Bureau of Labor Statistics, Division of Industry Prices and Price Indexes. n.e.c. stands for not elsewhere classified. - indicates no data collected for period or unavailable.

Processed Yarns and Threads
Producer Price Index
Base 1982 = 100

For 1975-2001. Columns headed % show percentile change in the index from the previous period for which an index is available.

Year	Jan Index	%	Feb Index	%	Mar Index	%	Apr Index	%	May Index	%	Jun Index	%	Jul Index	%	Aug Index	%	Sep Index	%	Oct Index	%	Nov Index	%	Dec Index	%
1975	-	-	-	-	-	-	-	-	-	-	-	-	-	-	-	-	-	-	-	-	-	-	72.3	-
1976	73.4	1.5	73.3	-0.1	72.8	-0.7	71.8	-1.4	71.6	-0.3	72.1	0.7	73.1	1.4	72.1	-1.4	71.5	-0.8	70.9	-0.8	70.5	-0.6	70.3	-0.3
1977	70.0	-0.4	70.5	0.7	71.4	1.3	73.4	2.8	74.0	0.8	74.8	1.1	74.8	0.0	74.3	-0.7	73.8	-0.7	73.2	-0.8	72.6	-0.8	72.7	0.1
1978	72.8	0.1	73.1	0.4	73.2	0.1	73.1	-0.1	73.0	-0.1	73.5	0.7	73.7	0.3	74.0	0.4	74.7	0.9	75.2	0.7	76.2	1.3	75.7	-0.7
1979	76.2	0.7	76.2	0.0	77.4	1.6	77.2	-0.3	78.0	1.0	78.5	0.6	79.2	0.9	80.0	1.0	80.8	1.0	81.0	0.2	81.4	0.5	81.5	0.1
1980	82.8	1.6	85.3	3.0	86.3	1.2	88.3	2.3	89.8	1.7	88.8	-1.1	88.5	-0.3	89.1	0.7	89.9	0.9	90.5	0.7	91.0	0.6	92.7	1.9
1981	93.9	1.3	94.2	0.3	97.3	3.3	97.6	0.3	100.2	2.7	100.7	0.5	101.5	0.8	102.7	1.2	102.9	0.2	104.4	1.5	101.5	-2.8	101.0	-0.5
1982	100.7	-0.3	101.7	1.0	101.6	-0.1	101.6	0.0	101.9	0.3	100.8	-1.1	98.3	-2.5	98.3	0.0	98.8	0.5	98.7	-0.1	98.9	0.2	98.9	0.0
1983	97.4	-1.5	97.7	0.3	98.2	0.5	98.3	0.1	99.3	1.0	99.5	0.2	100.2	0.7	101.4	1.2	101.4	0.0	102.2	0.8	102.5	0.3	103.3	0.8
1984	102.9	-0.4	104.1	1.2	104.1	0.0	103.8	-0.3	104.3	0.5	104.0	-0.3	103.9	-0.1	102.8	-1.1	102.8	0.0	102.3	-0.5	101.8	-0.5	101.8	0.0
1985	102.2	0.4	102.6	0.4	102.3	-0.3	102.2	-0.1	102.2	0.0	102.1	-0.1	102.2	0.1	101.9	-0.3	101.8	-0.1	101.8	0.0	101.8	0.0	101.6	-0.2
1986	101.3	-0.3	101.2	-0.1	101.3	0.1	101.9	0.6	101.7	-0.2	101.5	-0.2	101.7	0.2	102.1	0.4	102.3	0.2	101.9	-0.4	101.6	-0.3	102.1	0.5
1987	101.5	-0.6	101.3	-0.2	101.1	-0.2	101.6	0.5	102.6	1.0	103.4	0.8	104.3	0.9	104.8	0.5	105.3	0.5	106.2	0.9	106.4	0.2	106.9	0.5
1988	107.6	0.7	107.8	0.2	107.8	0.0	107.9	0.1	107.8	-0.1	108.1	0.3	108.2	0.1	108.0	-0.2	108.1	0.1	108.3	0.2	108.2	-0.1	108.5	0.3
1989	108.5	0.0	108.9	0.4	109.6	0.6	110.0	0.4	110.2	0.2	110.5	0.3	110.8	0.3	111.2	0.4	111.1	-0.1	111.4	0.3	111.7	0.3	111.4	-0.3
1990	113.1	1.5	113.4	0.3	113.4	0.0	113.6	0.2	113.6	0.0	113.8	0.2	112.4	-1.2	111.3	-1.0	111.2	-0.1	111.2	0.0	112.2	0.9	112.4	0.2
1991	112.8	0.4	112.7	-0.1	112.8	0.1	112.9	0.1	112.6	-0.3	113.1	0.4	113.1	0.0	112.4	-0.6	112.1	-0.3	112.0	-0.1	112.2	0.2	112.0	-0.2
1992	111.8	-0.2	111.6	-0.2	111.7	0.1	111.7	0.0	111.6	-0.1	111.7	0.1	110.1	-1.4	110.2	0.1	109.8	-0.4	109.7	-0.1	109.8	0.1	109.6	-0.2
1993	108.5	-1.0	108.2	-0.3	108.0	-0.2	107.9	-0.1	107.7	-0.2	107.9	0.2	107.9	0.0	107.7	-0.2	107.8	0.1	107.7	-0.1	107.3	-0.4	107.1	-0.2
1994	107.1	0.0	107.0	-0.1	107.1	0.1	107.2	0.1	107.3	0.1	108.4	1.0	109.1	0.6	108.9	-0.2	109.0	0.1	109.4	0.4	109.8	0.4	109.9	0.1
1995	110.6	0.6	111.1	0.5	112.0	0.8	112.2	0.2	113.1	0.8	113.2	0.1	112.9	-0.3	113.5	0.5	113.4	-0.1	113.5	0.1	113.9	0.4	113.8	-0.1
1996	114.4	0.5	114.5	0.1	114.1	-0.3	114.7	0.5	114.5	-0.2	114.6	0.1	114.5	-0.1	114.3	-0.2	116.4	1.8	114.9	-1.3	114.8	-0.1	114.6	-0.2
1997	114.2	-0.3	114.4	0.2	114.4	0.0	114.0	-0.3	113.9	-0.1	113.7	-0.2	113.5	-0.2	113.6	0.1	113.7	0.1	113.9	0.2	113.6	-0.3	113.3	-0.3
1998	113.3	0.0	113.4	0.1	113.3	-0.1	113.3	0.0	113.2	-0.1	113.3	0.1	113.0	-0.3	112.8	-0.2	112.7	-0.1	111.9	-0.7	111.3	-0.5	111.3	0.0
1999	110.4	-0.8	109.5	-0.8	108.9	-0.5	108.7	-0.2	108.5	-0.2	108.4	-0.1	108.1	-0.3	108.9	0.7	108.7	-0.2	107.9	-0.7	107.8	-0.1	107.6	-0.2
2000	108.0	0.4	107.8	-0.2	107.7	-0.1	108.1	0.4	108.1	0.0	108.1	0.0	108.0	-0.1	108.0	0.0	107.7	-0.3	107.7	0.0	107.7	0.0	107.6	-0.1
2001	108.3	0.7	108.1	-0.2	107.6	-0.5	107.3	-0.3	106.8	-0.5	106.5	-0.3	105.0	-1.4	104.4	-0.6	104.2	-0.2	103.4	-0.8	102.5	-0.9	102.5	0.0

Source: U.S. Department of Labor, Bureau of Labor Statistics, Division of Industry Prices and Price Indexes. n.e.c. stands for not elsewhere classified. - indicates no data collected for period or unavailable.

Gray Fabrics
Producer Price Index
Base 1982 = 100

For 1975-2001. Columns headed % show percentile change in the index from the previous period for which an index is available.

Year	Jan Index	%	Feb Index	%	Mar Index	%	Apr Index	%	May Index	%	Jun Index	%	Jul Index	%	Aug Index	%	Sep Index	%	Oct Index	%	Nov Index	%	Dec Index	%
1975	-	-	-	-	-	-	-	-	-	-	-	-	-	-	-	-	-	-	-	-	-	-	68.8	-
1976	70.3	2.2	71.2	1.3	71.2	0.0	71.6	0.6	72.4	1.1	73.4	1.4	74.7	1.8	74.7	0.0	73.7	-1.3	73.9	0.3	75.1	1.6	74.1	-1.3
1977	73.0	-1.5	72.1	-1.2	71.9	-0.3	72.3	0.6	72.0	-0.4	71.9	-0.1	72.2	0.4	71.1	-1.5	70.9	-0.3	71.4	0.7	72.4	1.4	73.8	1.9
1978	75.0	1.6	75.7	0.9	77.2	2.0	78.4	1.6	80.7	2.9	81.1	0.5	82.0	1.1	83.2	1.5	85.5	2.8	87.1	1.9	87.2	0.1	86.7	-0.6
1979	86.4	-0.3	84.8	-1.9	84.7	-0.1	85.7	1.2	85.8	0.1	86.3	0.6	88.3	2.3	88.6	0.3	88.6	0.0	89.2	0.7	89.9	0.8	91.1	1.3
1980	91.3	0.2	91.1	-0.2	94.1	3.3	94.3	0.2	93.9	-0.4	92.7	-1.3	93.4	0.8	94.6	1.3	97.0	2.5	98.7	1.8	99.8	1.1	99.1	-0.7
1981	98.8	-0.3	99.1	0.3	99.6	0.5	100.9	1.3	100.4	-0.5	101.5	1.1	102.0	0.5	102.5	0.5	102.6	0.1	101.9	-0.7	101.4	-0.5	101.3	-0.1
1982	102.0	0.7	101.4	-0.6	100.9	-0.5	100.7	-0.2	100.4	-0.3	100.5	0.1	99.7	-0.8	99.5	-0.2	98.8	-0.7	98.9	0.1	98.5	-0.4	98.6	0.1
1983	99.4	0.8	99.3	-0.1	99.8	0.5	100.3	0.5	100.6	0.3	100.4	-0.2	100.6	0.2	101.0	0.4	101.4	0.4	102.9	1.5	104.2	1.3	104.6	0.4
1984	104.0	-0.6	105.2	1.2	105.4	0.2	105.3	-0.1	105.8	0.5	106.2	0.4	106.2	0.0	106.3	0.1	106.4	0.1	106.5	0.1	105.8	-0.7	106.0	0.2
1985	105.8	-0.2	105.0	-0.8	104.6	-0.4	104.4	-0.2	104.7	0.3	104.4	-0.3	104.0	-0.4	103.5	-0.5	103.5	0.0	104.0	0.5	104.2	0.2	104.3	0.1
1986	104.2	-0.1	104.1	-0.1	103.9	-0.2	104.1	0.2	103.9	-0.2	104.0	0.1	104.2	0.2	103.5	-0.7	102.9	-0.6	103.2	0.3	103.3	0.1	103.2	-0.1
1987	103.7	0.5	103.7	0.0	103.9	0.2	105.4	1.4	105.8	0.4	106.7	0.9	108.0	1.2	107.9	-0.1	109.3	1.3	110.3	0.9	110.8	0.5	111.1	0.3
1988	111.8	0.6	112.8	0.9	113.2	0.4	113.9	0.6	114.2	0.3	114.6	0.4	114.9	0.3	115.1	0.2	114.3	-0.7	114.2	-0.1	114.5	0.3	115.0	0.4
1989	115.5	0.4	113.9	-1.4	114.0	0.1	114.0	0.0	113.9	-0.1	114.5	0.5	115.5	0.9	115.7	0.2	115.8	0.1	116.5	0.6	116.5	0.0	116.7	0.2
1990	117.2	0.4	117.3	0.1	117.2	-0.1	117.3	0.1	117.2	-0.1	116.4	-0.7	117.6	1.0	117.2	-0.3	116.7	-0.4	116.8	0.1	117.5	0.6	117.8	0.3
1991	117.2	-0.5	116.7	-0.4	116.6	-0.1	116.6	0.0	116.8	0.2	116.6	-0.2	117.1	0.4	117.9	0.7	118.0	0.1	118.1	0.1	118.3	0.2	119.2	0.8
1992	119.8	0.5	120.2	0.3	120.3	0.1	120.7	0.3	121.2	0.4	121.5	0.2	121.5	0.0	121.2	-0.2	121.0	-0.2	120.5	-0.4	119.8	-0.6	120.1	0.3
1993	120.1	0.0	119.8	-0.2	119.5	-0.3	119.6	0.1	118.4	-1.0	119.0	0.5	118.8	-0.2	118.8	0.0	117.5	-1.1	118.1	0.5	117.0	-0.9	116.9	-0.1
1994	116.5	-0.3	116.3	-0.2	116.4	0.1	116.6	0.2	116.4	-0.2	116.4	0.0	116.3	-0.1	117.2	0.8	117.6	0.3	116.5	-0.9	117.2	0.6	117.7	0.4
1995	118.6	0.8	120.5	1.6	120.7	0.2	121.0	0.2	121.7	0.6	122.0	0.2	121.4	-0.5	121.4	0.0	122.5	0.9	121.8	-0.6	120.9	-0.7	121.6	0.6
1996	120.8	-0.7	120.8	0.0	121.9	0.9	122.4	0.4	121.6	-0.7	120.9	-0.6	121.1	0.2	121.4	0.2	121.3	-0.1	121.6	0.2	121.2	-0.3	121.5	0.2
1997	121.4	-0.1	121.7	0.2	121.6	-0.1	121.4	-0.2	121.8	0.3	121.9	0.1	121.9	0.0	121.7	-0.2	122.4	0.6	122.1	-0.2	121.4	-0.6	121.8	0.3
1998	123.4	1.3	123.4	0.0	123.0	-0.3	123.2	0.2	123.0	-0.2	122.8	-0.2	121.6	-1.0	121.4	-0.2	120.6	-0.7	118.7	-1.6	118.9	0.2	118.8	-0.1
1999	117.8	-0.8	116.6	-1.0	117.6	0.9	116.0	-1.4	115.5	-0.4	114.1	-1.2	113.4	-0.6	112.2	-1.1	112.0	-0.2	113.3	1.2	112.4	-0.8	111.8	-0.5
2000	112.9	1.0	113.3	0.4	112.9	-0.4	113.2	0.3	112.5	-0.6	111.6	-0.8	112.8	1.1	113.4	0.5	113.1	-0.3	113.2	0.1	114.4	1.1	114.6	0.2
2001	114.3	-0.3	115.0	0.6	115.6	0.5	115.4	-0.2	114.0	-1.2	114.5	0.4	113.3	-1.0	113.8	0.4	114.7	0.8	113.7	-0.9	112.3	-1.2	112.6	0.3

Source: U.S. Department of Labor, Bureau of Labor Statistics, Division of Industry Prices and Price Indexes. n.e.c. stands for not elsewhere classified. - indicates no data collected for period or unavailable.

Finished Fabrics
Producer Price Index
Base 1982 = 100

For 1975-2001. Columns headed % show percentile change in the index from the previous period for which an index is available.

Year	Jan Index	%	Feb Index	%	Mar Index	%	Apr Index	%	May Index	%	Jun Index	%	Jul Index	%	Aug Index	%	Sep Index	%	Oct Index	%	Nov Index	%	Dec Index	%
1975	-	-	-	-	-	-	-	-	-	-	-	-	-	-	-	-	-	-	-	-	-	-	80.3	-
1976	79.8	-0.6	80.9	1.4	81.7	1.0	82.4	0.9	81.8	-0.7	81.4	-0.5	81.1	-0.4	81.2	0.1	80.7	-0.6	80.5	-0.2	81.4	1.1	81.5	0.1
1977	80.9	-0.7	81.7	1.0	82.7	1.2	83.7	1.2	84.3	0.7	84.2	-0.1	83.9	-0.4	83.9	0.0	83.8	-0.1	83.7	-0.1	83.1	-0.7	83.2	0.1
1978	83.2	0.0	83.3	0.1	82.7	-0.7	82.8	0.1	82.9	0.1	82.8	-0.1	82.9	0.1	83.0	0.1	83.6	0.7	83.9	0.4	84.2	0.4	85.1	1.1
1979	83.1	-2.4	83.6	0.6	84.6	1.2	85.0	0.5	85.9	1.1	86.4	0.6	86.9	0.6	87.5	0.7	87.6	0.1	87.4	-0.2	88.1	0.8	88.2	0.1
1980	88.7	0.6	89.2	0.6	90.9	1.9	91.9	1.1	92.6	0.8	93.0	0.4	93.6	0.6	93.8	0.2	93.9	0.1	95.0	1.2	95.6	0.6	96.5	0.9
1981	98.1	1.7	98.7	0.6	98.9	0.2	100.3	1.4	100.9	0.6	100.8	-0.1	101.1	0.3	101.8	0.7	101.8	0.0	101.7	-0.1	101.6	-0.1	100.8	-0.8
1982	101.8	1.0	102.1	0.3	100.8	-1.3	100.6	-0.2	100.5	-0.1	99.5	-1.0	99.4	-0.1	99.8	0.4	99.3	-0.5	98.9	-0.4	98.7	-0.2	98.6	-0.1
1983	98.1	-0.5	98.2	0.1	98.3	0.1	98.9	0.6	98.6	-0.3	98.3	-0.3	98.3	0.0	99.2	0.9	99.0	-0.2	99.4	0.4	99.9	0.5	100.2	0.3
1984	100.2	0.0	101.4	1.2	101.9	0.5	101.9	0.0	102.2	0.3	102.0	-0.2	101.9	-0.1	102.1	0.2	102.2	0.1	101.8	-0.4	101.7	-0.1	101.6	-0.1
1985	101.6	0.0	102.0	0.4	102.0	0.0	102.1	0.1	101.0	-1.1	100.9	-0.1	100.8	-0.1	101.1	0.3	101.3	0.2	101.3	0.0	101.2	-0.1	101.1	-0.1
1986	101.3	0.2	101.1	-0.2	101.3	0.2	101.3	0.0	101.5	0.2	101.5	0.0	101.6	0.1	101.6	0.0	101.4	-0.2	101.3	-0.1	101.3	0.0	101.3	0.0
1987	102.7	1.4	103.0	0.3	103.1	0.1	103.4	0.3	103.7	0.3	104.0	0.3	104.0	0.0	104.6	0.6	104.7	0.1	105.5	0.8	105.9	0.4	106.2	0.3
1988	106.9	0.7	108.2	1.2	109.0	0.7	109.2	0.2	109.3	0.1	109.6	0.3	109.4	-0.2	109.4	0.0	109.9	0.5	110.1	0.2	111.0	0.8	110.8	-0.2
1989	111.7	0.8	112.1	0.4	112.6	0.4	112.9	0.3	113.5	0.5	113.8	0.3	113.9	0.1	114.1	0.2	114.2	0.1	114.6	0.4	114.9	0.3	115.0	0.1
1990	115.5	0.4	115.6	0.1	115.7	0.1	116.0	0.3	115.9	-0.1	116.0	0.1	115.8	-0.2	115.8	0.0	115.8	0.0	116.4	0.5	116.4	0.0	116.5	0.1
1991	116.7	0.2	117.1	0.3	117.3	0.2	117.4	0.1	117.5	0.1	117.4	-0.1	117.6	0.2	117.8	0.2	118.0	0.2	117.9	-0.1	118.0	0.1	117.8	-0.2
1992	118.1	0.3	118.4	0.3	118.4	0.0	118.6	0.2	118.7	0.1	119.1	0.3	118.9	-0.2	119.0	0.1	119.0	0.0	119.2	0.2	119.3	0.1	119.2	-0.1
1993	119.4	0.2	119.4	0.0	119.4	0.0	119.5	0.1	120.0	0.4	119.8	-0.2	119.6	-0.2	119.5	-0.1	119.4	-0.1	119.4	0.0	119.3	-0.1	119.1	-0.2
1994	119.2	0.1	118.9	-0.3	118.9	0.0	119.2	0.3	119.2	0.0	119.2	0.0	119.1	-0.1	119.1	0.0	119.1	0.0	119.5	0.3	119.6	0.1	119.5	-0.1
1995	120.0	0.4	120.6	0.5	121.0	0.3	121.3	0.2	121.7	0.3	121.8	0.1	122.0	0.2	122.3	0.2	122.3	0.0	122.4	0.1	122.3	-0.1	122.3	0.0
1996	123.1	0.7	123.2	0.1	123.1	-0.1	123.6	0.4	123.5	-0.1	123.7	0.2	123.7	0.0	123.9	0.2	123.8	-0.1	123.7	-0.1	123.9	0.2	123.6	-0.2
1997	123.7	0.1	123.8	0.1	123.6	-0.2	123.9	0.2	124.0	0.1	123.9	-0.1	123.9	0.0	123.8	-0.1	123.9	0.1	124.1	0.2	124.0	-0.1	123.7	-0.2
1998	123.6	-0.1	123.9	0.2	124.5	0.5	124.6	0.1	124.7	0.1	124.2	-0.4	124.0	-0.2	124.2	0.2	123.7	-0.4	123.5	-0.2	122.7	-0.6	122.5	-0.2
1999	122.3	-0.2	122.5	0.2	123.0	0.4	122.8	-0.2	122.6	-0.2	122.6	0.0	122.5	-0.1	122.8	0.2	123.1	0.2	123.0	-0.1	121.9	-0.9	121.9	0.0
2000	122.0	0.1	121.8	-0.2	122.7	0.7	122.9	0.2	123.0	0.1	122.6	-0.3	123.0	0.3	122.8	-0.2	123.0	0.2	122.8	-0.2	121.8	-0.8	121.8	0.0
2001	121.7	-0.1	121.7	0.0	122.9	1.0	123.1	0.2	123.1	0.0	123.4	0.2	123.2	-0.2	122.7	-0.4	122.5	-0.2	122.5	0.0	122.6	0.1	121.4	-1.0

Source: U.S. Department of Labor, Bureau of Labor Statistics, Division of Industry Prices and Price Indexes. n.e.c. stands for not elsewhere classified. - indicates no data collected for period or unavailable.

Apparel & Other Fabricated Textile Products
Producer Price Index
Base 1982 = 100

For 1977-2001. Columns headed % show percentile change in the index from the previous period for which an index is available.

Year	Jan Index	%	Feb Index	%	Mar Index	%	Apr Index	%	May Index	%	Jun Index	%	Jul Index	%	Aug Index	%	Sep Index	%	Oct Index	%	Nov Index	%	Dec Index	%
1977	-	-	-	-	-	-	-	-	-	-	-	-	-	-	-	-	-	-	-	-	-	-	76.2	-
1978	76.5	0.4	76.7	0.3	76.9	0.3	77.1	0.3	77.3	0.3	77.8	0.6	78.2	0.5	78.4	0.3	78.3	-0.1	78.6	0.4	79.1	0.6	79.4	0.4
1979	80.1	0.9	80.4	0.4	80.8	0.5	81.4	0.7	81.4	0.0	82.1	0.9	82.2	0.1	82.8	0.7	83.1	0.4	83.4	0.4	83.8	0.5	83.7	-0.1
1980	85.0	1.6	85.6	0.7	86.6	1.2	87.5	1.0	87.6	0.1	88.6	1.1	89.7	1.2	90.0	0.3	90.1	0.1	90.6	0.6	91.3	0.8	91.6	0.3
1981	92.9	1.4	93.3	0.4	93.6	0.3	94.8	1.3	95.3	0.5	95.7	0.4	96.3	0.6	96.6	0.3	97.0	0.4	97.8	0.8	98.2	0.4	98.3	0.1
1982	99.3	1.0	99.6	0.3	99.8	0.2	100.1	0.3	100.1	0.0	100.3	0.2	100.1	-0.2	100.2	0.1	100.4	0.2	100.5	0.1	100.3	-0.2	99.4	-0.9
1983	100.0	0.6	100.1	0.1	100.5	0.4	100.3	-0.2	100.8	0.5	101.2	0.4	101.4	0.2	101.5	0.1	101.6	0.1	101.5	-0.1	101.8	0.3	101.7	-0.1
1984	102.2	0.5	102.4	0.2	102.5	0.1	102.6	0.1	102.8	0.2	102.6	-0.2	102.9	0.3	102.8	-0.1	103.3	0.5	103.3	0.0	103.4	0.1	103.2	-0.2
1985	103.5	0.3	103.7	0.2	103.8	0.1	104.0	0.2	104.0	0.0	104.0	0.0	104.2	0.2	104.5	0.3	104.4	-0.1	104.5	0.1	104.8	0.3	105.0	0.2
1986	105.0	0.0	105.3	0.3	105.6	0.3	105.4	-0.2	105.5	0.1	105.5	0.0	105.6	0.1	105.5	-0.1	105.6	0.1	105.8	0.2	105.9	0.1	105.9	0.0
1987	106.0	0.1	106.2	0.2	106.5	0.3	106.7	0.2	106.7	0.0	107.0	0.3	107.4	0.4	107.7	0.3	108.0	0.3	108.1	0.1	108.1	0.0	108.6	0.5
1988	109.1	0.5	109.3	0.2	109.6	0.3	109.7	0.1	109.9	0.2	110.4	0.5	110.7	0.3	110.8	0.1	111.1	0.3	111.2	0.1	111.3	0.1	111.6	0.3
1989	112.1	0.4	112.5	0.4	112.2	-0.3	112.4	0.2	112.5	0.1	112.6	0.1	113.0	0.4	113.4	0.4	113.6	0.2	113.7	0.1	114.0	0.3	114.2	0.2
1990	115.3	1.0	115.3	0.0	115.4	0.1	115.7	0.3	115.7	0.0	116.0	0.3	116.1	0.1	116.4	0.3	116.5	0.1	116.6	0.1	116.6	0.0	116.3	-0.3
1991	116.9	0.5	117.3	0.3	117.5	0.2	117.8	0.3	117.8	0.0	118.1	0.3	118.2	0.1	118.4	0.2	118.5	0.1	118.7	0.2	118.9	0.2	119.0	0.1
1992	119.8	0.7	120.0	0.2	120.2	0.2	120.2	0.0	120.1	-0.1	120.2	0.1	120.3	0.1	120.5	0.2	120.8	0.2	121.0	0.2	121.1	0.1	121.1	0.0
1993	121.3	0.2	121.3	0.0	121.4	0.1	121.5	0.1	121.6	0.1	121.3	-0.2	121.7	0.3	121.7	0.0	121.7	0.0	121.7	0.0	121.7	0.0	121.6	-0.1
1994	121.8	0.2	121.9	0.1	122.0	0.1	121.8	-0.2	122.0	0.2	121.8	-0.2	122.2	0.3	122.1	-0.1	122.2	0.1	122.3	0.1	122.2	-0.1	122.4	0.2
1995	122.6	0.2	122.8	0.2	123.1	0.2	122.9	-0.2	123.1	0.2	123.1	0.0	123.4	0.2	123.2	-0.2	123.6	0.3	123.8	0.2	123.4	-0.3	123.5	0.1
1996	124.2	0.6	124.3	0.1	124.4	0.1	124.2	-0.2	124.9	0.6	125.1	0.2	125.4	0.2	125.1	-0.2	125.6	0.4	125.8	0.2	125.5	-0.2	125.7	0.2
1997	125.5	-0.2	125.3	-0.2	125.6	0.2	125.4	-0.2	125.6	0.2	125.7	0.1	125.7	0.0	125.8	0.1	125.9	0.1	125.5	-0.3	125.8	0.2	125.9	0.1
1998	126.8	0.7	126.7	-0.1	126.7	0.0	126.8	0.1	126.8	0.0	126.8	0.0	126.8	0.0	126.7	-0.1	127.0	0.2	127.2	0.2	127.1	-0.1	126.9	-0.2
1999	127.1	0.2	127.0	-0.1	127.0	0.0	127.0	0.0	127.1	0.1	127.0	-0.1	126.9	-0.1	126.9	0.0	127.0	0.1	126.8	-0.2	126.8	0.0	127.1	0.2
2000	127.1	0.0	127.2	0.1	127.5	0.2	127.4	-0.1	127.3	-0.1	127.4	0.0	127.6	0.2	127.6	0.0	127.5	-0.1	127.4	-0.1	127.4	0.0	127.4	0.0
2001	127.4	0.0	127.4	0.0	127.2	-0.2	127.2	0.0	127.2	0.0	127.1	-0.1	127.2	0.1	127.3	0.1	127.0	-0.2	126.9	-0.1	127.0	0.1	126.8	-0.2

Source: U.S. Department of Labor, Bureau of Labor Statistics, Division of Industry Prices and Price Indexes. n.e.c. stands for not elsewhere classified. - indicates no data collected for period or unavailable.

Miscellaneous Textile Products/Services
Producer Price Index
Base 1982 = 100

For 1985-2001. Columns headed % show percentile change in the index from the previous period for which an index is available.

Year	Jan Index	%	Feb Index	%	Mar Index	%	Apr Index	%	May Index	%	Jun Index	%	Jul Index	%	Aug Index	%	Sep Index	%	Oct Index	%	Nov Index	%	Dec Index	%
1985	-	-	-	-	-	-	-	-	-	-	100.0	-	99.7	-0.3	99.3	-0.4	99.2	-0.1	99.2	0.0	99.2	0.0	97.7	-1.5
1986	97.8	0.1	98.2	0.4	98.3	0.1	96.4	-1.9	96.6	0.2	96.5	-0.1	95.4	-1.1	94.1	-1.4	94.0	-0.1	95.2	1.3	96.2	1.1	97.5	1.4
1987	97.2	-0.3	97.8	0.6	97.8	0.0	97.8	0.0	97.7	-0.1	98.1	0.4	98.5	0.4	99.2	0.7	99.8	0.6	99.8	0.0	100.1	0.3	100.7	0.6
1988	102.7	2.0	103.4	0.7	104.3	0.9	104.9	0.6	105.0	0.1	105.2	0.2	105.3	0.1	105.3	0.0	105.2	-0.1	106.2	1.0	107.8	1.5	107.9	0.1
1989	109.3	1.3	109.8	0.5	109.6	-0.2	109.4	-0.2	109.5	0.1	110.9	1.3	113.6	2.4	113.8	0.2	113.9	0.1	113.7	-0.2	113.8	0.1	113.7	-0.1
1990	113.7	0.0	113.9	0.2	114.0	0.1	113.9	-0.1	113.6	-0.3	114.0	0.4	114.0	0.0	114.1	0.1	113.9	-0.2	113.9	0.0	114.3	0.4	114.3	0.0
1991	115.9	1.4	112.6	-2.8	112.0	-0.5	111.4	-0.5	111.7	0.3	111.9	0.2	111.7	-0.2	115.2	3.1	115.1	-0.1	114.6	-0.4	115.0	0.3	114.2	-0.7
1992	114.4	0.2	114.5	0.1	114.7	0.2	114.5	-0.2	114.7	0.2	114.8	0.1	114.8	0.0	114.8	0.0	115.3	0.4	115.3	0.0	115.3	0.0	115.3	0.0
1993	115.6	0.3	115.4	-0.2	115.5	0.1	115.9	0.3	115.7	-0.2	116.0	0.3	116.1	0.1	115.9	-0.2	116.2	0.3	116.4	0.2	116.2	-0.2	116.2	0.0
1994	116.4	0.2	116.6	0.2	117.1	0.4	117.0	-0.1	117.8	0.7	118.8	0.8	118.6	-0.2	118.3	-0.3	118.4	0.1	118.8	0.3	119.4	0.5	119.6	0.2
1995	120.2	0.5	120.8	0.5	122.2	1.2	123.0	0.7	124.1	0.9	124.1	0.0	124.3	0.2	124.6	0.2	124.2	-0.3	125.3	0.9	125.3	0.0	124.9	-0.3
1996	124.6	-0.2	124.8	0.2	124.5	-0.2	124.4	-0.1	124.0	-0.3	123.6	-0.3	123.6	0.0	123.4	-0.2	122.7	-0.6	122.2	-0.4	122.1	-0.1	122.0	-0.1
1997	121.7	-0.2	121.2	-0.4	121.0	-0.2	121.2	0.2	121.1	-0.1	121.1	0.0	120.3	-0.7	119.7	-0.5	119.1	-0.5	118.5	-0.5	118.3	-0.2	118.3	0.0
1998	118.3	0.0	118.0	-0.3	117.1	-0.8	117.7	0.5	117.8	0.1	117.7	-0.1	117.4	-0.3	117.6	0.2	116.8	-0.7	116.9	0.1	116.8	-0.1	116.4	-0.3
1999	116.4	0.0	116.1	-0.3	116.0	-0.1	116.2	0.2	116.1	-0.1	116.2	0.1	116.4	0.2	116.7	0.3	116.1	-0.5	115.4	-0.6	115.3	-0.1	115.1	-0.2
2000	115.1	0.0	114.8	-0.3	114.8	0.0	115.0	0.2	115.0	0.0	115.0	0.0	115.1	0.1	115.5	0.3	115.4	-0.1	115.7	0.3	116.1	0.3	116.0	-0.1
2001	116.1	0.1	116.2	0.1	116.1	-0.1	116.5	0.3	116.5	0.0	116.2	-0.3	116.3	0.1	116.5	0.2	116.2	-0.3	116.1	-0.1	116.1	0.0	116.8	0.6

Source: U.S. Department of Labor, Bureau of Labor Statistics, Division of Industry Prices and Price Indexes. n.e.c. stands for not elsewhere classified. - indicates no data collected for period or unavailable.

HIDES, SKINS, LEATHER, AND RELATED PRODUCTS
Producer Price Index
Base 1982 = 100

For 1926-2001. Columns headed % show percentile change in the index from the previous period for which an index is available.

Year	Jan		Feb		Mar		Apr		May		Jun		Jul		Aug		Sep		Oct		Nov		Dec	
	Index	%	Index	%	Index	%	Index	%	Index	%	Index	%	Index	%	Index	%	Index	%	Index	%	Index	%	Index	%
1926	17.6	-	17.3	-1.7	17.1	-1.2	16.9	-1.2	16.9	0.0	16.9	0.0	16.9	0.0	17.0	0.6	16.9	-0.6	17.2	1.8	17.1	-0.6	17.1	0.0
1927	17.2	0.6	17.1	-0.6	17.1	0.0	17.4	1.8	17.7	1.7	18.3	3.4	19.0	3.8	19.0	0.0	19.2	1.1	19.2	0.0	19.4	1.0	19.9	2.6
1928	20.6	3.5	21.1	2.4	21.1	0.0	21.6	2.4	21.5	-0.5	21.1	-1.9	21.1	0.0	20.6	-2.4	20.6	0.0	20.0	-2.9	19.7	-1.5	19.7	0.0
1929	19.3	-2.0	18.6	-3.6	18.4	-1.1	18.4	0.0	18.2	-1.1	18.4	1.1	18.6	1.1	18.7	0.5	18.9	1.1	18.8	-0.5	18.5	-1.6	18.4	-0.5
1930	17.9	-2.7	17.7	-1.1	17.6	-0.6	17.5	-0.6	17.5	0.0	17.5	0.0	17.2	-1.7	16.9	-1.7	17.0	0.6	16.5	-2.9	16.1	-2.4	15.6	-3.1
1931	15.1	-3.2	14.8	-2.0	14.9	0.7	14.9	0.0	14.9	0.0	15.0	0.7	15.3	2.0	15.1	-1.3	14.5	-4.0	14.1	-2.8	13.9	-1.4	13.6	-2.2
1932	13.5	-0.7	13.4	-0.7	13.2	-1.5	12.8	-3.0	12.4	-3.1	12.1	-2.4	11.7	-3.3	11.9	1.7	12.3	3.4	12.4	0.8	12.2	-1.6	11.9	-2.5
1933	11.8	-0.8	11.6	-1.7	11.6	0.0	11.8	1.7	13.1	11.0	14.1	7.6	14.7	4.3	15.6	6.1	15.8	1.3	15.2	-3.8	15.1	-0.7	15.2	0.7
1934	15.3	0.7	15.3	0.0	15.1	-1.3	15.2	0.7	15.0	-1.3	14.9	-0.7	14.7	-1.3	14.3	-2.7	14.4	0.7	14.3	-0.7	14.4	0.7	14.5	0.7
1935	14.7	1.4	14.7	0.0	14.6	-0.7	14.7	0.7	15.1	2.7	15.2	0.7	15.2	0.0	15.3	0.7	15.5	1.3	16.0	3.2	16.3	1.9	16.3	0.0
1936	16.6	1.8	16.4	-1.2	16.2	-1.2	16.1	-0.6	16.0	-0.6	16.0	0.0	16.0	0.0	16.0	0.0	16.1	0.6	16.3	1.2	16.5	1.2	17.0	3.0
1937	17.4	2.4	17.5	0.6	17.7	1.1	18.2	2.8	18.2	0.0	18.2	0.0	18.2	0.0	18.4	1.1	18.4	0.0	18.2	-1.1	17.3	-4.9	16.7	-3.5
1938	16.5	-1.2	16.2	-1.8	16.0	-1.2	15.7	-1.9	15.6	-0.6	15.4	-1.3	15.6	1.3	15.7	0.6	15.7	0.0	16.0	1.9	16.1	0.6	15.9	-1.2
1939	15.9	0.0	15.7	-1.3	15.6	-0.6	15.5	-0.6	15.6	0.6	15.8	1.3	15.8	0.0	15.8	0.0	16.8	6.3	17.9	6.5	17.7	-1.1	17.7	0.0
1940	17.7	0.0	17.5	-1.1	17.4	-0.6	17.4	0.0	17.3	-0.6	16.9	-2.3	16.9	0.0	16.5	-2.4	16.8	1.8	17.1	1.8	17.5	2.3	17.5	0.0
1941	17.5	0.0	17.4	-0.6	17.5	0.6	17.7	1.1	18.2	2.8	18.4	1.1	18.7	1.6	18.8	0.5	19.0	1.1	19.2	1.1	19.5	1.6	19.6	0.5
1942	19.6	0.0	19.7	0.5	19.9	1.0	20.4	2.5	20.3	-0.5	20.2	-0.5	20.2	0.0	20.2	0.0	20.1	-0.5	20.1	0.0	20.1	0.0	20.1	0.0
1943	20.1	0.0	20.1	0.0	20.1	0.0	20.1	0.0	20.1	0.0	20.1	0.0	20.1	0.0	20.1	0.0	20.1	0.0	20.1	0.0	19.9	-1.0	20.0	0.5
1944	20.0	0.0	20.0	0.0	20.0	0.0	20.0	0.0	20.0	0.0	19.9	-0.5	19.8	-0.5	19.8	0.0	19.8	0.0	19.8	0.0	19.8	0.0	20.0	1.0
1945	20.1	0.5	20.1	0.0	20.1	0.0	20.1	0.0	20.1	0.0	20.1	0.0	20.1	0.0	20.1	0.0	20.3	1.0	20.3	0.0	20.3	0.0	20.3	0.0
1946	20.4	0.5	20.4	0.0	20.4	0.0	20.4	0.0	20.6	1.0	20.9	1.5	24.1	15.3	23.7	-1.7	24.2	2.1	24.3	0.4	29.4	21.0	30.2	2.7
1947	30.1	-0.3	30.3	0.7	30.5	0.7	30.2	-1.0	30.0	-0.7	30.2	0.7	31.0	2.6	31.9	2.9	32.2	0.9	34.0	5.6	35.2	3.5	35.0	-0.6
1948	34.2	-2.3	32.6	-4.7	31.3	-4.0	31.7	1.3	32.2	1.6	32.1	-0.3	32.4	0.9	31.9	-1.5	31.6	-0.9	31.3	-0.9	31.9	1.9	31.6	-0.9
1949	31.5	-0.3	30.7	-2.5	30.2	-1.6	30.1	-0.3	30.0	-0.3	30.0	0.0	29.7	-1.0	30.0	1.0	30.4	1.3	30.7	1.0	30.8	0.3	30.7	-0.3
1950	30.2	-1.6	30.2	0.0	30.5	1.0	30.5	0.0	30.8	1.0	31.1	1.0	32.5	4.5	33.4	2.8	34.7	3.9	35.4	2.0	36.6	3.4	38.1	4.1
1951	39.9	4.7	40.1	0.5	39.8	-0.7	39.7	-0.3	39.6	-0.3	39.1	-1.3	38.4	-1.8	37.0	-3.6	37.0	0.0	35.7	-3.5	33.6	-5.9	33.0	-1.8
1952	32.1	-2.7	31.2	-2.8	30.8	-1.3	29.5	-4.2	29.7	0.7	30.1	1.3	30.2	0.3	30.3	0.3	30.3	0.0	30.3	0.0	30.7	1.3	31.1	1.3
1953	30.5	-1.9	30.8	1.0	30.8	0.0	30.7	-0.3	31.5	2.6	31.7	0.6	31.4	-0.9	31.4	0.0	31.3	-0.3	30.5	-2.6	30.5	0.0	30.0	-1.6
1954	29.9	-0.3	29.8	-0.3	29.7	-0.3	29.7	0.0	30.1	1.3	30.0	-0.3	29.8	-0.7	29.5	-1.0	29.2	-1.0	29.0	-0.7	29.1	0.3	28.8	-1.0
1955	28.8	0.0	29.0	0.7	28.9	-0.3	29.3	1.4	29.2	-0.3	29.2	0.0	29.4	0.7	29.4	0.0	29.5	0.3	29.9	1.4	30.2	1.0	30.3	0.3
1956	30.3	0.0	30.5	0.7	30.7	0.7	31.6	2.9	31.4	-0.6	31.4	0.0	31.4	0.0	31.4	0.0	31.4	0.0	31.3	-0.3	31.3	0.0	31.1	-0.6
1957	30.9	-0.6	30.8	-0.3	30.9	0.3	31.0	0.3	31.0	0.0	31.3	1.0	31.6	1.0	31.5	-0.3	31.4	-0.3	31.4	0.0	31.4	0.0	31.2	-0.6
1958	31.2	0.0	31.3	0.3	31.2	-0.3	31.3	0.3	31.4	0.3	31.5	0.3	31.5	0.0	31.5	0.0	31.4	-0.3	31.8	1.3	32.1	0.9	32.5	1.2
1959	32.7	0.6	33.1	1.2	34.1	3.0	37.0	8.5	37.2	0.5	37.3	0.3	37.5	0.5	37.6	0.3	37.4	-0.5	36.5	-2.4	35.1	-3.8	35.3	0.6
1960	35.4	0.3	35.1	-0.8	35.1	0.0	35.2	0.3	34.9	-0.9	34.6	-0.9	34.6	0.0	34.1	-1.4	33.9	-0.6	34.1	0.6	34.1	0.0	34.2	0.3
1961	34.0	-0.6	33.9	-0.3	34.3	1.2	34.5	0.6	34.8	0.9	34.6	-0.6	34.9	0.9	35.5	1.7	35.6	0.3	35.8	0.6	35.7	-0.3	35.6	-0.3
1962	35.6	0.0	35.4	-0.6	35.3	-0.3	35.1	-0.6	35.3	0.6	35.5	0.6	35.3	-0.6	35.2	-0.3	35.3	0.3	35.3	0.0	35.3	0.0	35.1	-0.6
1963	34.8	-0.9	34.6	-0.6	34.6	0.0	34.3	-0.9	34.5	0.6	34.3	-0.6	34.3	0.0	34.1	-0.6	33.9	-0.6	34.0	0.3	34.0	0.0	33.8	-0.6
1964	33.8	0.0	33.7	-0.3	33.7	0.0	34.3	1.8	34.4	0.3	34.5	0.3	34.6	0.3	34.7	0.3	34.6	-0.3	34.8	0.6	34.7	-0.3	34.6	-0.3
1965	34.5	-0.3	34.6	0.3	34.8	0.6	35.0	0.6	35.3	0.9	35.4	0.3	35.8	1.1	36.9	3.1	36.6	-0.8	37.2	1.6	37.4	0.5	37.7	0.8
1966	38.2	1.3	38.7	1.3	39.0	0.8	39.6	1.5	40.4	2.0	40.4	0.0	40.4	0.0	39.9	-1.2	39.4	-1.3	39.0	-1.0	38.6	-1.0	38.6	0.0
1967	38.8	0.5	38.8	0.6	38.5	-0.8	38.0	-1.3	37.9	-0.3	38.0	0.3	37.9	-0.3	37.5	-1.1	37.7	0.5	37.7	0.0	38.0	0.8	38.2	0.5
1968	38.3	0.3	38.4	0.3	38.8	1.0	38.9	0.3	39.1	0.5	39.0	-0.3	39.3	0.8	39.3	0.0	39.7	1.0	40.2	1.3	40.2	0.0	40.4	0.5
1969	40.6	0.5	40.6	0.0	40.6	0.0	41.5	2.2	41.5	0.0	41.3	-0.5	41.6	0.7	41.7	0.2	42.3	1.4	42.0	-0.7	42.0	0.0	41.8	-0.5
1970	42.0	0.5	42.0	0.0	42.0	0.0	42.3	0.7	42.1	-0.5	41.8	-0.7	41.8	0.0	41.8	0.0	41.8	0.0	42.0	0.5	42.2	0.5	42.0	-0.5

[Continued]

HIDES, SKINS, LEATHER, AND RELATED PRODUCTS
Producer Price Index
Base 1982 = 100
[Continued]

For 1926-2001. Columns headed % show percentile change in the index from the previous period for which an index is available.

Year	Jan Index	%	Feb Index	%	Mar Index	%	Apr Index	%	May Index	%	Jun Index	%	Jul Index	%	Aug Index	%	Sep Index	%	Oct Index	%	Nov Index	%	Dec Index	%
1971	42.6	1.4	42.8	0.5	42.8	0.0	43.4	1.4	43.6	0.5	43.5	-0.2	43.5	0.0	43.6	0.2	43.7	0.2	43.7	0.0	43.8	0.2	44.2	0.9
1972	44.9	1.6	45.4	1.1	46.8	3.1	48.4	3.4	49.3	1.9	49.8	1.0	50.1	0.6	51.3	2.4	51.7	0.8	53.2	2.9	54.8	3.0	54.1	-1.3
1973	54.8	1.3	55.2	0.7	54.6	-1.1	55.2	1.1	54.1	-2.0	53.6	-0.9	53.8	0.4	54.4	1.1	54.7	0.6	54.7	0.0	54.5	-0.4	54.0	-0.9
1974	54.3	0.6	54.6	0.6	54.6	0.0	55.4	1.5	55.7	0.5	55.6	-0.2	55.8	0.4	55.7	-0.2	56.4	1.3	55.3	-2.0	55.0	-0.5	54.5	-0.9
1975	54.1	-0.7	54.0	-0.2	54.5	0.9	56.2	3.1	56.2	0.0	56.6	0.7	56.8	0.4	56.9	0.2	57.6	1.2	58.0	0.7	58.8	1.4	58.9	0.2
1976	60.2	2.2	61.2	1.7	62.0	1.3	63.3	2.1	64.8	2.4	64.0	-1.2	64.9	1.4	65.3	0.6	66.1	1.2	65.1	-1.5	64.6	-0.8	65.3	1.1
1977	66.8	2.3	67.3	0.7	67.7	0.6	68.5	1.2	69.3	1.2	68.3	-1.4	68.5	0.3	68.6	0.1	68.4	-0.3	68.2	-0.3	68.5	0.4	69.1	0.9
1978	70.8	2.5	71.3	0.7	71.5	0.3	73.1	2.2	73.7	0.8	74.3	0.8	75.1	1.1	78.1	4.0	80.2	2.7	81.1	1.1	82.1	1.2	82.3	0.2
1979	85.1	3.4	88.4	3.9	96.5	9.2	98.6	2.2	102.6	4.1	102.0	-0.6	99.7	-2.3	98.2	-1.5	95.6	-2.6	96.7	1.2	94.8	-2.0	94.9	0.1
1980	97.3	2.5	95.5	-1.8	94.0	-1.6	92.7	-1.4	91.6	-1.2	91.7	0.1	93.3	1.7	95.7	2.6	94.3	-1.5	95.6	1.4	97.2	1.7	97.8	0.6
1981	98.3	0.5	98.1	-0.2	99.4	1.3	100.3	0.9	100.4	0.1	99.6	-0.8	99.4	-0.2	99.5	0.1	99.6	0.1	99.0	-0.6	98.9	-0.1	99.2	0.3
1982	99.7	0.5	99.6	-0.1	99.2	-0.4	100.3	1.1	100.2	-0.1	99.7	-0.5	100.2	0.5	99.8	-0.4	100.3	0.5	100.2	-0.1	100.2	0.0	100.6	0.4
1983	101.5	0.9	100.6	-0.9	100.9	0.3	101.8	0.9	102.6	0.8	103.3	0.7	103.7	0.4	104.6	0.9	104.5	-0.1	104.2	-0.3	105.5	1.2	105.6	0.1
1984	106.3	0.7	107.9	1.5	109.2	1.2	109.2	0.0	109.9	0.6	110.5	0.5	110.0	-0.5	109.9	-0.1	109.9	0.0	109.5	-0.4	108.1	-1.3	108.0	-0.1
1985	108.0	0.0	108.0	0.0	107.5	-0.5	108.4	0.8	108.2	-0.2	108.7	0.5	108.4	-0.3	109.0	0.6	109.3	0.3	109.9	0.5	110.4	0.5	111.3	0.8
1986	111.8	0.4	112.0	0.2	111.8	-0.2	112.3	0.4	112.9	0.5	113.4	0.4	113.2	-0.2	113.1	-0.1	112.9	-0.2	113.4	0.4	114.0	0.5	114.8	0.7
1987	114.9	0.1	115.0	0.1	116.5	1.3	118.3	1.5	120.7	2.0	120.2	-0.4	121.0	0.7	121.3	0.2	123.0	1.4	124.1	0.9	124.3	0.2	125.7	1.1
1988	128.4	2.1	129.1	0.5	132.6	2.7	134.2	1.2	134.6	0.3	131.2	-2.5	130.1	-0.8	131.6	1.2	132.5	0.7	131.9	-0.5	130.4	-1.1	130.1	-0.2
1989	131.2	0.8	133.2	1.5	136.8	2.7	136.1	-0.5	134.8	-1.0	135.2	0.3	136.9	1.3	137.2	0.2	138.0	0.6	138.2	0.1	138.0	-0.1	139.5	1.1
1990	138.9	-0.4	141.7	2.0	141.6	-0.1	142.9	0.9	143.7	0.6	143.0	-0.5	142.8	-0.1	142.2	-0.4	141.4	-0.6	140.9	-0.4	140.5	-0.3	140.6	0.1
1991	140.2	-0.3	140.0	-0.1	140.4	0.3	141.1	0.5	140.4	-0.5	140.0	-0.3	138.3	-1.2	138.1	-0.1	136.6	-1.1	136.3	-0.2	137.1	0.6	137.6	0.4
1992	138.6	0.7	139.0	0.3	139.8	0.6	139.9	0.1	140.7	0.6	140.8	0.1	140.1	-0.5	140.8	0.5	140.9	0.1	141.0	0.1	140.6	-0.3	142.0	1.0
1993	143.6	1.1	142.5	-0.8	142.9	0.3	143.6	0.5	143.8	0.1	143.7	-0.1	143.5	-0.1	143.9	0.3	144.1	0.1	143.7	-0.3	144.1	0.3	144.4	0.2
1994	145.1	0.5	143.8	-0.9	144.6	0.6	146.1	1.0	146.7	0.4	147.2	0.3	148.7	1.0	149.0	0.2	150.8	1.2	153.2	1.6	153.7	0.3	153.5	-0.1
1995	154.1	0.4	155.2	0.7	156.2	0.6	156.1	-0.1	157.8	1.1	155.0	-1.8	154.9	-0.1	153.2	-1.1	152.0	-0.8	150.6	-0.9	149.5	-0.7	149.5	0.0
1996	149.0	-0.3	149.3	0.2	149.7	0.3	148.4	-0.9	149.2	0.5	149.2	0.0	149.4	0.1	150.3	0.6	150.2	-0.1	153.1	1.9	153.6	0.3	154.4	0.5
1997	155.3	0.6	156.2	0.6	156.8	0.4	157.5	0.4	156.1	-0.9	153.6	-1.6	151.6	-1.3	152.2	0.4	151.5	-0.5	152.5	0.7	154.3	1.2	153.5	-0.5
1998	148.8	-3.1	148.4	-0.3	147.1	-0.9	147.5	0.3	147.8	0.2	150.8	2.0	149.2	-1.1	149.7	0.3	149.3	-0.3	146.4	-1.9	144.9	-1.0	146.6	1.2
1999	145.8	-0.5	144.1	-1.2	144.5	0.3	144.6	0.1	145.0	0.3	145.0	0.0	145.2	0.1	146.3	0.8	147.5	0.8	148.5	0.7	146.6	-1.3	149.1	1.7
2000	149.0	-0.1	148.9	-0.1	148.4	-0.3	149.2	0.5	149.7	0.3	149.6	-0.1	151.0	0.9	152.3	0.9	153.3	0.7	155.0	1.1	155.0	0.0	156.2	0.8
2001	156.7	0.3	157.9	0.8	159.5	1.0	163.9	2.8	166.0	1.3	163.4	-1.6	160.8	-1.6	156.1	-2.9	155.6	-0.3	153.4	-1.4	153.2	-0.1	151.8	-0.9

Source: U.S. Department of Labor, Bureau of Labor Statistics, Division of Industry Prices and Price Indexes. n.e.c. stands for not elsewhere classified. - indicates no data collected for period or unavailable.

Hides and Skins
Producer Price Index
Base 1982 = 100

For 1926-2001. Columns headed % show percentile change in the index from the previous period for which an index is available.

Year	Jan Index	%	Feb Index	%	Mar Index	%	Apr Index	%	May Index	%	Jun Index	%	Jul Index	%	Aug Index	%	Sep Index	%	Oct Index	%	Nov Index	%	Dec Index	%
1926	23.1	-	21.3	-7.8	20.0	-6.1	18.7	-6.5	19.4	3.7	19.3	-0.5	19.9	3.1	20.6	3.5	19.6	-4.9	21.7	10.7	21.1	-2.8	21.1	0.0
1927	21.5	1.9	20.8	-3.3	20.9	0.5	22.1	5.7	23.4	5.9	25.3	8.1	27.3	7.9	26.8	-1.8	26.3	-1.9	26.2	-0.4	26.9	2.7	27.9	3.7
1928	30.9	10.8	32.4	4.9	32.2	-0.6	34.2	6.2	33.6	-1.8	31.7	-5.7	31.8	0.3	28.8	-9.4	29.0	0.7	26.6	-8.3	26.6	0.0	26.8	0.8
1929	25.4	-5.2	21.7	-14.6	22.1	1.8	22.1	0.0	21.4	-3.2	22.6	5.6	23.4	3.5	24.0	2.6	24.8	3.3	24.1	-2.8	22.3	-7.5	22.0	-1.3
1930	21.3	-3.2	20.2	-5.2	19.6	-3.0	19.6	0.0	19.8	1.0	20.2	2.0	19.2	-5.0	18.6	-3.1	19.2	3.2	17.1	-10.9	15.4	-9.9	14.1	-8.4
1931	13.2	-6.4	11.8	-10.6	12.7	7.6	12.7	0.0	12.8	0.8	13.4	4.7	14.9	11.2	14.1	-5.4	12.0	-14.9	10.2	-15.0	10.0	-2.0	10.0	0.0
1932	10.0	0.0	9.5	-5.0	9.1	-4.2	8.3	-8.8	7.3	-12.0	6.6	-9.6	6.9	4.5	8.0	15.9	9.9	23.7	10.1	2.0	9.5	-5.9	8.5	-10.5
1933	8.8	3.5	8.4	-4.5	8.5	1.2	9.4	10.6	13.8	46.8	16.6	20.3	18.1	9.0	18.7	3.3	17.2	-8.0	14.5	-15.7	14.4	-0.7	15.2	5.6
1934	15.8	3.9	16.0	1.3	15.0	-6.3	15.7	4.7	15.0	-4.5	14.3	-4.7	13.6	-4.9	11.7	-14.0	12.3	5.1	12.2	-0.8	12.9	5.7	13.8	7.0
1935	14.5	5.1	14.2	-2.1	13.6	-4.2	14.5	6.6	15.6	7.6	16.0	2.6	16.3	1.9	16.4	0.6	17.1	4.3	19.0	11.1	19.7	3.7	19.7	0.0
1936	20.6	4.6	19.8	-3.9	18.6	-6.1	18.4	-1.1	17.8	-3.3	18.2	2.2	17.9	-1.6	18.4	2.8	19.1	3.8	19.8	3.7	20.7	4.5	22.6	9.2
1937	23.7	4.9	23.5	-0.8	24.2	3.0	24.8	2.5	24.0	-3.2	23.4	-2.5	23.8	1.7	24.9	4.6	24.6	-1.2	24.0	-2.4	19.3	-19.6	17.5	-9.3
1938	16.8	-4.0	15.3	-8.9	14.2	-7.2	12.8	-9.9	13.0	1.6	12.8	-1.5	14.5	13.3	15.4	6.2	15.5	0.6	16.8	8.4	17.5	4.2	16.1	-8.0
1939	16.0	-0.6	14.9	-6.9	15.1	1.3	14.0	-7.3	14.7	5.0	15.4	4.8	15.8	2.6	15.8	0.0	19.9	25.9	23.0	15.6	21.3	-7.4	21.5	0.9
1940	21.0	-2.3	19.8	-5.7	19.3	-2.5	19.4	0.5	18.8	-3.1	16.7	-11.2	17.3	3.6	15.8	-8.7	17.2	8.9	19.2	11.6	20.7	7.8	20.3	-1.9
1941	20.2	-0.5	19.4	-4.0	20.3	4.6	21.4	5.4	22.6	5.6	23.0	1.8	23.0	0.0	22.9	-0.4	22.9	0.0	23.1	0.9	23.3	0.9	23.7	1.7
1942	23.6	-0.4	23.6	0.0	23.8	0.8	25.3	6.3	24.8	-2.0	24.2	-2.4	24.2	0.0	24.3	0.4	24.1	-0.8	23.7	-1.7	23.7	0.0	23.7	0.0
1943	23.7	0.0	23.7	0.0	23.7	0.0	23.7	0.0	23.7	0.0	23.7	0.0	23.7	0.0	23.7	0.0	23.7	0.0	23.7	0.0	22.2	-6.3	22.8	2.7
1944	23.1	1.3	22.7	-1.7	22.7	0.0	22.7	0.0	22.9	0.9	22.2	-3.1	21.9	-1.4	21.6	-1.4	21.7	0.5	22.0	1.4	21.9	-0.5	23.3	6.4
1945	23.5	0.9	23.6	0.4	23.8	0.8	23.9	0.4	23.9	0.0	24.0	0.4	24.0	0.0	24.1	0.4	24.1	0.0	24.0	-0.4	24.0	0.0	24.0	0.0
1946	24.0	0.0	24.0	0.0	24.0	0.0	24.0	0.0	24.7	2.9	24.8	0.4	34.6	39.5	31.8	-8.1	31.0	-2.5	31.3	1.0	45.2	44.4	44.2	-2.2
1947	40.6	-8.1	42.7	5.2	43.8	2.6	41.4	-5.5	39.9	-3.6	41.7	4.5	46.1	10.6	49.6	7.6	50.4	1.6	55.6	10.3	60.5	8.8	58.7	-3.0
1948	53.7	-8.5	46.8	-12.8	39.3	-16.0	42.0	6.9	45.0	7.1	44.6	-0.9	46.6	4.5	44.4	-4.7	42.9	-3.4	41.3	-3.7	44.6	8.0	43.1	-3.4
1949	43.2	0.2	38.7	-10.4	37.0	-4.4	37.2	0.5	37.2	0.0	37.7	1.3	36.0	-4.5	38.0	5.6	40.0	5.3	40.8	2.0	40.5	-0.7	38.9	-4.0
1950	37.4	-3.9	37.0	-1.1	38.4	3.8	38.1	-0.8	39.0	2.4	41.2	5.6	45.1	9.5	46.6	3.3	52.6	12.9	52.5	-0.2	54.7	4.2	57.1	4.4
1951	61.5	7.7	58.8	-4.4	58.5	-0.5	57.0	-2.6	56.8	-0.4	56.5	-0.5	54.1	-4.2	49.5	-8.5	48.6	-1.8	47.8	-1.6	38.2	-20.1	35.7	-6.5
1952	30.4	-14.8	27.8	-8.6	26.0	-6.5	21.7	-16.5	25.4	17.1	26.0	2.4	27.0	3.8	28.1	4.1	28.1	0.0	28.4	1.1	30.2	6.3	30.8	2.0
1953	27.1	-12.0	29.0	7.0	28.3	-2.4	29.0	2.5	32.6	12.4	33.3	2.1	32.0	-3.9	32.6	1.9	32.4	-0.6	28.1	-13.3	28.0	-0.4	25.2	-10.0
1954	24.8	-1.6	24.2	-2.4	24.4	0.8	24.6	0.8	27.3	11.0	26.5	-2.9	25.4	-4.2	24.4	-3.9	22.5	-7.8	21.6	-4.0	23.0	6.5	20.7	-10.0
1955	21.6	4.3	22.5	4.2	22.1	-1.8	24.8	12.2	23.2	-6.5	24.3	4.7	25.4	4.5	25.7	1.2	26.6	3.5	27.2	2.3	26.3	-3.3	26.7	1.5
1956	24.7	-7.5	25.4	2.8	25.5	0.4	27.0	5.9	25.8	-4.4	26.7	3.5	26.4	-1.1	26.4	0.0	27.6	4.5	25.2	-8.7	25.8	2.4	23.5	-8.9
1957	22.7	-3.4	21.9	-3.5	22.2	1.4	22.6	1.8	24.4	8.0	25.9	6.1	27.1	4.6	26.8	-1.1	25.4	-5.2	24.8	-2.4	23.5	-5.2	22.0	-6.4
1958	22.1	0.5	22.3	0.9	22.3	0.0	23.2	4.0	24.2	4.3	24.9	2.9	25.4	2.0	26.4	3.9	25.8	-2.3	27.0	4.7	28.4	5.2	29.0	2.1
1959	30.0	3.4	31.8	6.0	38.3	20.4	47.4	23.8	43.0	-9.3	46.6	8.4	47.0	0.9	46.6	-0.9	44.7	-4.1	38.2	-14.5	29.3	-23.3	32.2	9.9
1960	32.2	0.0	30.4	-5.6	31.4	3.3	32.1	2.2	31.8	-0.9	29.3	-7.9	29.7	1.4	27.8	-6.4	27.2	-2.2	28.0	2.9	28.7	2.5	28.3	-1.4
1961	26.9	-4.9	26.4	-1.9	30.0	13.6	29.7	-1.0	31.0	4.4	29.7	-4.2	33.3	12.1	36.2	8.7	36.0	-0.6	35.9	-0.3	34.7	-3.3	33.3	-4.0
1962	32.6	-2.1	31.2	-4.3	30.7	-1.6	30.6	-0.3	31.2	2.0	32.1	2.9	30.8	-4.0	31.1	1.0	32.8	5.5	32.2	-1.8	31.7	-1.6	30.1	-5.0
1963	28.2	-6.3	25.4	-9.9	26.1	2.8	25.1	-3.8	25.9	3.2	25.4	-1.9	24.7	-2.8	23.8	-3.6	22.9	-3.8	23.8	3.9	24.5	2.9	22.6	-7.8
1964	22.5	-0.4	21.9	-2.7	22.4	2.3	26.1	16.5	25.4	-2.7	26.7	5.1	27.4	2.6	28.4	3.6	28.3	-0.4	28.2	-0.4	26.8	-5.0	26.7	-0.4
1965	25.6	-4.1	26.7	4.3	27.3	2.2	28.5	4.4	31.3	9.8	30.5	-2.6	34.7	13.8	39.5	13.8	37.0	-6.3	37.2	0.5	37.4	0.5	39.1	4.5
1966	41.4	5.9	45.2	9.2	43.7	-3.3	44.0	0.7	48.2	9.5	47.6	-1.2	46.3	-2.7	41.8	-9.7	39.7	-5.0	35.7	-10.1	33.8	-5.3	32.3	-4.4
1967	32.6	0.9	31.9	-2.1	29.3	-8.2	26.1	-10.9	25.8	-1.1	28.4	10.1	27.7	-2.5	25.7	-7.2	27.6	7.4	25.7	-6.9	26.9	4.7	26.8	-0.4
1968	26.1	-2.6	26.8	2.7	29.7	10.8	28.3	-4.7	29.0	2.5	28.2	-2.8	30.0	6.4	30.4	1.3	31.6	3.9	31.2	-1.3	31.7	1.6	31.6	-0.3
1969	32.3	2.2	31.4	-2.8	32.3	2.9	37.2	15.2	36.3	-2.4	34.7	-4.4	36.4	4.9	36.4	0.0	38.1	4.7	34.9	-8.4	32.7	-6.3	32.2	-1.5
1970	30.4	-5.6	29.9	-1.6	29.4	-1.7	31.6	7.5	30.1	-4.7	27.8	-7.6	26.9	-3.2	27.4	1.9	27.8	1.5	28.8	3.6	30.4	5.6	28.4	-6.6

[Continued]

Hides and Skins
Producer Price Index
Base 1982 = 100

[Continued]

For 1926-2001. Columns headed % show percentile change in the index from the previous period for which an index is available.

Year	Jan Index	%	Feb Index	%	Mar Index	%	Apr Index	%	May Index	%	Jun Index	%	Jul Index	%	Aug Index	%	Sep Index	%	Oct Index	%	Nov Index	%	Dec Index	%
1971	27.6	-2.8	29.3	6.2	29.4	0.3	33.8	15.0	33.9	0.3	31.8	-6.2	31.8	0.0	31.9	0.3	32.8	2.8	32.7	-0.3	34.3	4.9	35.8	4.4
1972	37.9	5.9	41.5	9.5	48.5	16.9	52.6	8.5	55.8	6.1	56.9	2.0	59.2	4.0	67.7	14.4	68.0	0.4	75.5	11.0	80.0	6.0	71.1	-11.1
1973	76.4	7.5	76.0	-0.5	68.7	-9.6	75.3	9.6	70.7	-6.1	67.3	-4.8	68.7	2.1	72.9	6.1	71.7	-1.6	71.4	-0.4	66.8	-6.4	63.4	-5.1
1974	61.6	-2.8	61.9	0.5	56.2	-9.2	58.9	4.8	60.9	3.4	57.7	-5.3	60.1	4.2	57.0	-5.2	54.3	-4.7	44.9	-17.3	43.6	-2.9	38.1	-12.6
1975	34.8	-8.7	34.1	-2.0	38.6	13.2	48.5	25.6	47.6	-1.9	50.9	6.9	52.1	2.4	52.0	-0.2	53.6	3.1	56.0	4.5	58.3	4.1	57.2	-1.9
1976	62.6	9.4	64.0	2.2	66.8	4.4	75.4	12.9	79.7	5.7	72.8	-8.7	77.7	6.7	79.4	2.2	81.4	2.5	70.1	-13.9	64.6	-7.8	70.0	8.4
1977	77.8	11.1	78.8	1.3	79.7	1.1	85.0	6.6	87.3	2.7	80.5	-7.8	81.3	1.0	80.4	-1.1	76.5	-4.9	74.3	-2.9	76.2	2.6	81.4	6.8
1978	83.7	2.8	83.1	-0.7	82.5	-0.7	89.4	8.4	89.7	0.3	96.6	7.7	100.5	4.0	111.7	11.1	121.4	8.7	119.3	-1.7	116.2	-2.6	111.9	-3.7
1979	126.2	12.8	138.8	10.0	178.3	28.5	179.0	0.4	185.9	3.9	170.3	-8.4	157.9	-7.3	142.7	-9.6	129.7	-9.1	133.5	2.9	124.8	-6.5	123.7	-0.9
1980	130.7	5.7	112.9	-13.6	97.2	-13.9	91.6	-5.8	80.8	-11.8	88.0	8.9	99.4	13.0	111.1	11.8	99.3	-10.6	106.4	7.2	114.0	7.1	109.5	-3.9
1981	105.2	-3.9	102.4	-2.7	-	-	-	-	107.4	4.9	102.6	-4.5	100.8	-1.8	102.0	1.2	103.5	1.5	103.5	0.0	103.0	-0.5	105.9	2.8
1982	107.7	1.7	107.5	-0.2	102.4	-4.7	104.5	2.1	104.7	0.2	103.2	-1.4	99.3	-3.8	96.7	-2.6	95.6	-1.1	92.7	-3.0	90.2	-2.7	95.4	5.8
1983	95.3	-0.1	94.3	-1.0	94.5	0.2	99.3	5.1	109.2	10.0	109.1	-0.1	110.8	1.6	116.9	5.5	116.4	-0.4	115.1	-1.1	127.1	10.4	130.0	2.3
1984	134.1	3.2	141.4	5.4	146.3	3.5	145.8	-0.3	150.0	2.9	150.9	0.6	150.2	-0.5	149.1	-0.7	150.6	1.0	145.0	-3.7	129.7	-10.6	133.0	2.5
1985	125.4	-5.7	119.3	-4.9	114.3	-4.2	125.6	9.9	126.4	0.6	123.6	-2.2	120.5	-2.5	124.8	3.6	124.8	0.0	129.6	3.8	133.7	3.2	144.8	8.3
1986	144.4	-0.3	145.0	0.4	143.4	-1.1	148.3	3.4	149.7	0.9	151.6	1.3	150.0	-1.1	144.5	-3.7	142.0	-1.7	146.6	3.2	151.7	3.5	154.7	2.0
1987	152.5	-1.4	153.6	0.7	160.7	4.6	171.8	6.9	189.2	10.1	185.4	-2.0	182.9	-1.3	183.3	0.2	188.0	2.6	195.2	3.8	196.4	0.6	199.9	1.8
1988	210.2	5.2	208.7	-0.7	225.6	8.1	234.2	3.8	234.6	0.2	208.6	-11.1	188.8	-9.5	199.5	5.7	205.0	2.8	193.9	-5.4	181.9	-6.2	178.0	-2.1
1989	181.2	1.8	190.3	5.0	228.1	19.9	222.3	-2.5	207.8	-6.5	211.2	1.6	221.3	4.8	214.3	-3.2	217.1	1.3	218.8	0.8	216.9	-0.9	225.8	4.1
1990	203.8	-9.7	227.4	11.6	220.1	-3.2	234.4	6.5	233.0	-0.6	227.8	-2.2	227.4	-0.2	217.2	-4.5	210.3	-3.2	207.2	-1.5	204.0	-1.5	202.6	-0.7
1991	196.8	-2.9	190.6	-3.2	188.1	-1.3	198.1	5.3	184.0	-7.1	174.2	-5.3	166.6	-4.4	161.4	-3.1	152.1	-5.8	154.4	1.5	160.1	3.7	163.9	2.4
1992	164.5	0.4	168.5	2.4	168.4	-0.1	175.3	4.1	180.2	2.8	174.8	-3.0	171.5	-1.9	171.7	0.1	176.8	3.0	178.2	0.8	175.2	-1.7	183.0	4.5
1993	188.1	2.8	178.1	-5.3	180.6	1.4	185.8	2.9	186.6	0.4	181.6	-2.7	185.1	1.9	178.9	-3.3	187.1	4.6	183.9	-1.7	186.3	1.3	188.1	1.0
1994	184.6	-1.9	180.3	-2.3	183.4	1.7	196.4	7.1	199.1	1.4	198.1	-0.5	207.8	4.9	210.0	1.1	217.2	3.4	235.9	8.6	234.1	-0.8	229.1	-2.1
1995	227.1	-0.9	229.6	1.1	238.1	3.7	229.7	-3.5	243.0	5.8	222.6	-8.4	223.3	0.3	212.4	-4.9	205.4	-3.3	191.0	-7.0	181.7	-4.9	182.4	0.4
1996	177.7	-2.6	180.7	1.7	182.1	0.8	180.7	-0.8	183.1	1.3	186.3	1.7	191.5	2.8	196.3	2.5	191.8	-2.3	210.5	9.7	210.1	-0.2	211.1	0.5
1997	213.2	1.0	215.2	0.9	217.5	1.1	217.7	0.1	214.8	-1.3	204.5	-4.8	185.6	-9.2	191.7	3.3	185.8	-3.1	188.4	1.4	196.6	4.4	192.8	-1.9
1998	161.0	-16.5	159.4	-1.0	150.4	-5.6	156.9	4.3	157.9	0.6	180.3	14.2	165.4	-8.3	169.1	2.2	166.6	-1.5	146.7	-11.9	137.2	-6.5	147.8	7.7
1999	147.5	-0.2	132.7	-10.0	136.7	3.0	136.9	0.1	141.4	3.3	140.2	-0.8	140.1	-0.1	147.1	5.0	155.2	5.5	161.0	3.7	147.1	-8.6	165.0	12.2
2000	161.0	-2.4	158.9	-1.3	156.4	-1.6	160.8	2.8	166.3	3.4	167.1	0.5	175.7	5.1	181.9	3.5	181.9	0.0	194.5	6.9	189.0	-2.8	195.0	3.2
2001	197.2	1.1	197.1	-0.1	200.2	1.6	219.2	9.5	231.0	5.4	218.4	-5.5	199.8	-8.5	163.1	-18.4	170.7	4.7	158.2	-7.3	165.1	4.4	156.8	-5.0

Source: U.S. Department of Labor, Bureau of Labor Statistics, Division of Industry Prices and Price Indexes. n.e.c. stands for not elsewhere classified. - indicates no data collected for period or unavailable.

Leather
Producer Price Index
Base 1982 = 100

For 1926-2001. Columns headed % show percentile change in the index from the previous period for which an index is available.

Year	Jan Index	%	Feb Index	%	Mar Index	%	Apr Index	%	May Index	%	Jun Index	%	Jul Index	%	Aug Index	%	Sep Index	%	Oct Index	%	Nov Index	%	Dec Index	%
1926	16.4	-	16.4	0.0	16.4	0.0	16.4	0.0	16.1	-1.8	16.1	0.0	16.0	-0.6	16.0	0.0	16.1	0.6	16.1	0.0	16.1	0.0	16.1	0.0
1927	16.1	0.0	16.1	0.0	16.2	0.6	16.2	0.0	16.7	3.1	17.4	4.2	18.3	5.2	18.5	1.1	18.7	1.1	18.9	1.1	18.9	0.0	19.8	4.8
1928	20.0	1.0	20.9	4.5	20.9	0.0	21.0	0.5	21.0	0.0	20.6	-1.9	20.8	1.0	20.8	0.0	20.4	-1.9	20.1	-1.5	19.2	-4.5	19.3	0.5
1929	19.5	1.0	18.9	-3.1	18.2	-3.7	18.0	-1.1	17.9	-0.6	17.9	0.0	18.1	1.1	18.0	-0.6	18.2	1.1	18.5	1.6	18.3	-1.1	17.9	-2.2
1930	17.5	-2.2	17.4	-0.6	17.4	0.0	17.0	-2.3	16.9	-0.6	16.6	-1.8	16.2	-2.4	16.2	0.0	15.9	-1.9	15.6	-1.9	15.1	-3.2	14.8	-2.0
1931	14.7	-0.7	14.4	-2.0	14.3	-0.7	14.3	0.0	14.2	-0.7	14.2	0.0	14.5	2.1	14.6	0.7	13.5	-7.5	13.0	-3.7	12.7	-2.3	12.7	0.0
1932	12.5	-1.6	12.4	-0.8	11.9	-4.0	10.9	-8.4	9.8	-10.1	9.5	-3.1	9.7	2.1	9.7	0.0	10.2	5.2	10.4	2.0	10.0	-3.8	9.5	-5.0
1933	9.2	-3.2	8.9	-3.3	9.0	1.1	9.2	2.2	11.0	19.6	12.0	9.1	12.6	5.0	13.3	5.6	13.8	3.8	13.5	-2.2	12.8	-5.2	12.9	0.8
1934	12.9	0.0	12.9	0.0	12.9	0.0	12.7	-1.6	12.3	-3.1	12.2	-0.8	12.1	-0.8	11.5	-5.0	11.4	-0.9	11.4	0.0	11.5	0.9	11.6	0.9
1935	12.0	3.4	12.0	0.0	12.0	0.0	12.1	0.8	12.9	6.6	13.0	0.8	13.0	0.0	13.0	0.0	13.4	3.1	14.0	4.5	14.2	1.4	14.2	0.0
1936	14.1	-0.7	13.9	-1.4	13.7	-1.4	13.6	-0.7	13.6	0.0	13.5	-0.7	13.4	-0.7	13.3	-0.7	13.6	2.3	13.8	1.5	14.3	3.6	15.0	4.9
1937	15.2	1.3	15.4	1.3	15.7	1.9	16.3	3.8	16.3	0.0	16.0	-1.8	16.0	0.0	16.2	1.3	16.0	-1.2	15.7	-1.9	15.0	-4.5	14.0	-6.7
1938	14.0	0.0	13.6	-2.9	13.5	-0.7	13.3	-1.5	13.3	0.0	13.2	-0.8	13.3	0.8	13.3	0.0	13.3	0.0	13.7	3.0	14.0	2.2	13.9	-0.7
1939	13.7	-1.4	13.6	-0.7	13.4	-1.5	13.4	0.0	13.4	0.0	13.6	1.5	13.6	0.0	13.6	0.0	14.9	9.6	15.8	6.0	15.8	0.0	15.4	-2.5
1940	15.5	0.6	15.2	-1.9	15.1	-0.7	15.1	0.0	15.1	0.0	14.9	-1.3	14.8	-0.7	14.3	-3.4	14.4	0.7	14.7	2.1	15.1	2.7	15.2	0.7
1941	15.3	0.7	15.3	0.0	15.3	0.0	15.4	0.7	15.7	1.9	15.8	0.6	15.9	0.6	15.9	0.0	16.2	1.9	16.3	0.6	16.4	0.6	16.4	0.0
1942	16.4	0.0	16.4	0.0	16.4	0.0	16.4	0.0	16.4	0.0	16.4	0.0	16.4	0.0	16.4	0.0	16.4	0.0	16.4	0.0	16.4	0.0	16.4	0.0
1943	16.4	0.0	16.4	0.0	16.4	0.0	16.4	0.0	16.4	0.0	16.4	0.0	16.4	0.0	16.4	0.0	16.4	0.0	16.4	0.0	16.4	0.0	16.4	0.0
1944	16.4	0.0	16.4	0.0	16.4	0.0	16.4	0.0	16.4	0.0	16.4	0.0	16.4	0.0	16.4	0.0	16.4	0.0	16.4	0.0	16.4	0.0	16.4	0.0
1945	16.4	0.0	16.4	0.0	16.4	0.0	16.4	0.0	16.4	0.0	16.4	0.0	16.4	0.0	16.4	0.0	16.8	2.4	16.8	0.0	16.8	0.0	16.8	0.0
1946	16.8	0.0	16.8	0.0	16.8	0.0	16.8	0.0	16.8	0.0	17.9	6.5	21.5	20.1	21.6	0.5	22.4	3.7	22.4	0.0	28.8	28.6	29.9	3.8
1947	29.2	-2.3	29.5	1.0	29.8	1.0	29.6	-0.7	29.2	-1.4	29.6	1.4	30.1	1.7	30.7	2.0	31.9	3.9	35.6	11.6	36.5	2.5	35.2	-3.6
1948	33.6	-4.5	30.5	-9.2	29.2	-4.3	29.7	1.7	30.3	2.0	30.4	0.3	30.4	0.0	29.1	-4.3	28.5	-2.1	28.5	0.0	29.8	4.6	29.2	-2.0
1949	29.2	0.0	27.9	-4.5	27.4	-1.8	27.1	-1.1	27.0	-0.4	27.1	0.4	26.7	-1.5	27.2	1.9	27.8	2.2	28.5	2.5	28.5	0.0	28.4	-0.4
1950	28.1	-1.1	27.9	-0.7	28.3	1.4	28.5	0.7	28.8	1.1	29.2	1.4	32.5	11.3	33.2	2.2	34.5	3.9	35.1	1.7	36.3	3.4	38.8	6.9
1951	40.8	5.2	40.9	0.2	40.9	0.0	40.9	0.0	40.8	-0.2	39.4	-3.4	37.9	-3.8	35.2	-7.1	35.7	1.4	32.7	-8.4	29.8	-8.9	29.3	-1.7
1952	28.8	-1.7	26.6	-7.6	26.0	-2.3	25.1	-3.5	25.1	0.0	26.4	5.2	26.5	0.4	26.5	0.0	26.5	0.0	26.7	0.8	26.8	0.4	27.6	3.0
1953	27.3	-1.1	27.3	0.0	27.7	1.5	27.5	-0.7	28.9	5.1	29.1	0.7	28.5	-2.1	28.2	-1.1	28.1	-0.4	26.8	-4.6	26.8	0.0	26.3	-1.9
1954	26.1	-0.8	26.0	-0.4	25.6	-1.5	25.5	-0.4	26.0	2.0	26.0	0.0	25.7	-1.2	25.1	-2.3	24.6	-2.0	24.4	-0.8	24.3	-0.4	24.2	-0.4
1955	24.1	-0.4	24.4	1.2	24.4	0.0	24.8	1.6	25.2	1.6	24.9	-1.2	25.3	1.6	25.2	-0.4	25.3	0.4	25.6	1.2	26.0	1.6	26.2	0.8
1956	26.6	1.5	26.7	0.4	27.0	1.1	28.1	4.1	27.6	-1.8	27.2	-1.4	27.2	0.0	27.0	-0.7	27.0	0.0	27.0	0.0	26.9	-0.4	27.0	0.4
1957	26.2	-3.0	26.0	-0.8	26.3	1.2	26.3	0.0	26.3	0.0	27.0	2.7	27.4	1.5	27.2	-0.7	27.2	0.0	27.1	-0.4	27.1	0.0	27.0	-0.4
1958	26.9	-0.4	26.9	0.0	27.0	0.4	27.0	0.0	27.0	0.0	27.3	1.1	27.2	-0.4	27.2	0.0	27.1	-0.4	27.6	1.8	28.1	1.8	29.5	5.0
1959	29.5	0.0	30.0	1.7	30.7	2.3	35.7	16.3	37.0	3.6	35.7	-3.5	35.2	-1.4	34.8	-1.1	34.8	0.0	33.3	-4.3	30.8	-7.5	30.7	-0.3
1960	31.3	2.0	31.1	-0.6	30.5	-1.9	31.1	2.0	30.7	-1.3	30.6	-0.3	30.4	-0.7	29.4	-3.3	28.9	-1.7	29.1	0.7	28.8	-1.0	29.5	2.4
1961	29.0	-1.7	28.9	-0.3	29.8	3.1	30.4	2.0	30.9	1.6	30.4	-1.6	30.4	0.0	31.6	3.9	32.0	1.3	32.5	1.6	32.2	-0.9	32.2	0.0
1962	32.3	0.3	32.2	-0.3	31.9	-0.9	31.9	0.0	32.2	0.9	32.0	-0.6	31.6	-1.2	31.1	-1.6	31.0	-0.3	31.0	0.0	31.1	0.3	30.9	-0.6
1963	30.6	-1.0	30.5	-0.3	30.2	-1.0	29.9	-1.0	30.1	0.7	29.8	-1.0	29.8	0.0	29.2	-2.0	29.0	-0.7	29.0	0.0	29.0	0.0	29.0	0.0
1964	29.0	0.0	29.0	0.0	29.0	0.0	29.7	2.4	30.4	2.4	30.1	-1.0	30.5	1.3	30.4	-0.3	30.3	-0.3	30.5	0.7	30.3	-0.7	30.3	0.0
1965	30.4	0.3	30.1	-1.0	30.8	2.3	30.2	-1.9	30.4	0.7	31.3	3.0	30.8	-1.6	32.8	6.5	32.3	-1.5	32.6	0.9	33.0	1.2	33.2	0.6
1966	33.9	2.1	34.4	1.5	35.9	4.4	35.6	-0.8	36.4	2.2	36.9	1.4	36.7	-0.5	36.4	-0.8	35.5	-2.5	34.2	-3.7	33.2	-2.9	33.8	1.8
1967	34.0	0.6	33.9	-0.3	33.4	-1.5	32.9	-1.5	32.3	-1.8	32.1	-0.6	31.9	-0.6	31.1	-2.5	30.7	-1.3	30.5	-0.7	31.0	1.6	31.8	2.6
1968	31.6	-0.6	31.7	0.3	32.1	1.3	32.5	1.2	32.8	0.9	32.9	0.3	33.1	0.6	33.1	0.0	33.2	0.3	33.5	0.9	33.1	-1.2	33.7	1.8
1969	34.0	0.9	33.9	-0.3	33.9	0.0	35.6	5.0	35.4	-0.6	35.4	0.0	35.3	-0.3	35.2	-0.3	35.4	0.6	35.0	-1.1	34.8	-0.6	34.8	0.0
1970	34.8	0.0	34.1	-2.0	34.4	0.9	35.1	2.0	35.1	0.0	34.9	-0.6	34.9	0.0	34.6	-0.9	34.0	-1.7	34.4	1.2	34.5	0.3	34.5	0.0

[Continued]

Leather
Producer Price Index
Base 1982 = 100

[Continued]

For 1926-2001. Columns headed % show percentile change in the index from the previous period for which an index is available.

Year	Jan Index	%	Feb Index	%	Mar Index	%	Apr Index	%	May Index	%	Jun Index	%	Jul Index	%	Aug Index	%	Sep Index	%	Oct Index	%	Nov Index	%	Dec Index	%
1971	34.8	0.9	34.9	0.3	34.9	0.0	35.6	2.0	36.3	2.0	36.7	1.1	36.7	0.0	36.7	0.0	36.6	-0.3	36.7	0.3	36.7	0.0	37.8	3.0
1972	38.5	1.9	38.7	0.5	41.3	6.7	44.4	7.5	44.3	-0.2	44.5	0.5	44.3	-0.4	45.1	1.8	46.1	2.2	49.2	6.7	52.2	6.1	52.1	-0.2
1973	52.3	0.4	52.3	0.0	52.8	1.0	51.8	-1.9	51.3	-1.0	50.2	-2.1	50.4	0.4	50.6	0.4	52.3	3.4	51.6	-1.3	51.5	-0.2	50.1	-2.7
1974	50.0	-0.2	49.8	-0.4	50.3	1.0	50.9	1.2	51.2	0.6	50.3	-1.8	49.9	-0.8	49.6	-0.6	49.9	0.6	48.7	-2.4	47.4	-2.7	46.7	-1.5
1975	45.3	-3.0	44.6	-1.5	45.5	2.0	48.7	7.0	49.2	1.0	49.2	0.0	49.0	-0.4	48.7	-0.6	49.5	1.6	49.8	0.6	52.2	4.8	52.3	0.2
1976	53.0	1.3	55.5	4.7	57.5	3.6	59.0	2.6	65.3	10.7	61.4	-6.0	61.7	0.5	63.1	2.3	63.4	0.5	62.0	-2.2	61.5	-0.8	61.6	0.2
1977	64.1	4.1	64.7	0.9	64.7	0.0	65.6	1.4	67.7	3.2	65.0	-4.0	63.8	-1.8	64.3	0.8	64.4	0.2	63.1	-2.0	63.2	0.2	64.4	1.9
1978	67.7	5.1	68.1	0.6	69.1	1.5	69.8	1.0	69.8	0.0	69.8	0.0	72.1	3.3	80.9	12.2	86.5	6.9	86.5	0.0	89.5	3.5	89.8	0.3
1979	94.0	4.7	99.3	5.6	119.4	20.2	126.4	5.9	137.9	9.1	133.2	-3.4	123.7	-7.1	117.5	-5.0	106.0	-9.8	110.3	4.1	102.7	-6.9	104.3	1.6
1980	111.6	7.0	109.3	-2.1	99.9	-8.6	95.6	-4.3	93.3	-2.4	91.3	-2.1	93.8	2.7	100.9	7.6	95.7	-5.2	97.0	1.4	101.9	5.1	106.8	4.8
1981	106.8	0.0	99.6	-6.7	103.6	4.0	108.5	4.7	106.0	-2.3	103.1	-2.7	102.4	-0.7	100.8	-1.6	100.6	-0.2	100.7	0.1	100.0	-0.7	100.3	0.3
1982	102.5	2.2	102.0	-0.5	100.6	-1.4	99.7	-0.9	99.5	-0.2	98.8	-0.7	98.7	-0.1	97.9	-0.8	99.3	1.4	99.4	0.1	100.5	1.1	101.0	0.5
1983	101.0	0.0	100.5	-0.5	101.6	1.1	102.9	1.3	104.9	1.9	107.9	2.9	108.5	0.6	110.3	1.7	109.0	-1.2	108.1	-0.8	109.4	1.2	110.5	1.0
1984	111.2	0.6	116.3	4.6	121.4	4.4	124.2	2.3	125.5	1.0	124.6	-0.7	123.1	-1.2	121.4	-1.4	119.3	-1.7	118.6	-0.6	115.5	-2.6	113.8	-1.5
1985	115.0	1.1	113.2	-1.6	111.9	-1.1	112.5	0.5	112.6	0.1	112.1	-0.4	112.0	-0.1	112.5	0.4	113.0	0.4	114.0	0.9	115.6	1.4	116.3	0.6
1986	118.4	1.8	118.4	0.0	118.5	0.1	118.9	0.3	123.2	3.6	126.6	2.8	125.4	-0.9	125.8	0.3	124.7	-0.9	122.7	-1.6	124.2	1.2	127.8	2.9
1987	128.1	0.2	129.4	1.0	131.9	1.9	137.5	4.2	140.5	2.2	143.1	1.9	142.3	-0.6	141.0	-0.9	145.6	3.3	148.6	2.1	149.6	0.7	153.0	2.3
1988	158.0	3.3	160.1	1.3	171.1	6.9	175.1	2.3	176.4	0.7	165.0	-6.5	165.7	0.4	168.2	1.5	168.8	0.4	170.7	1.1	166.0	-2.8	164.9	-0.7
1989	166.6	1.0	169.4	1.7	170.2	0.5	168.2	-1.2	166.7	-0.9	168.0	0.8	171.4	2.0	171.5	0.1	172.5	0.6	172.9	0.2	173.0	0.1	174.0	0.6
1990	176.6	1.5	178.0	0.8	177.7	-0.2	179.5	1.0	181.2	0.9	179.6	-0.9	179.0	-0.3	177.3	-0.9	176.5	-0.5	175.4	-0.6	174.9	-0.3	174.7	-0.1
1991	174.3	-0.2	173.7	-0.3	172.6	-0.6	172.1	-0.3	172.7	0.3	171.7	-0.6	167.7	-2.3	165.8	-1.1	163.4	-1.4	161.5	-1.2	162.4	0.6	162.8	0.2
1992	161.3	-0.9	161.8	0.3	163.4	1.0	162.8	-0.4	163.9	0.7	164.0	0.1	164.7	0.4	163.7	-0.6	164.8	0.7	165.1	0.2	164.0	-0.7	165.1	0.7
1993	166.6	0.9	169.0	1.4	169.0	0.0	168.3	-0.4	169.7	0.8	168.7	-0.6	167.2	-0.9	168.7	0.9	169.0	0.2	168.6	-0.2	168.9	0.2	169.1	0.1
1994	171.2	1.2	171.0	-0.1	172.9	1.1	173.6	0.4	174.9	0.7	178.5	2.1	180.7	1.2	181.2	0.3	184.4	1.8	186.8	1.3	189.4	1.4	190.4	0.5
1995	192.2	0.9	194.7	1.3	195.2	0.3	198.4	1.6	199.5	0.6	195.3	-2.1	193.9	-0.7	190.0	-2.0	186.5	-1.8	184.6	-1.0	183.5	-0.6	182.4	-0.6
1996	182.3	-0.1	181.0	-0.7	181.2	0.1	176.1	-2.8	178.1	1.1	175.2	-1.6	172.7	-1.4	173.4	0.4	176.0	1.5	177.4	0.8	179.4	1.1	182.5	1.7
1997	183.2	0.4	185.3	1.1	185.5	0.1	188.1	1.4	183.6	-2.4	180.2	-1.9	179.7	-0.3	178.0	-0.9	178.4	0.2	181.3	1.6	184.7	1.9	182.9	-1.0
1998	180.5	-1.3	179.3	-0.7	178.9	-0.2	176.6	-1.3	177.4	0.5	177.2	-0.1	179.7	1.4	179.5	-0.1	179.0	-0.3	178.0	-0.6	177.1	-0.5	177.9	0.5
1999	176.1	-1.0	176.0	-0.1	175.5	-0.3	175.9	0.2	175.1	-0.5	175.0	-0.1	175.6	0.3	176.1	0.3	176.7	0.3	177.8	0.6	177.8	0.0	177.9	0.1
2000	179.2	0.7	180.1	0.5	179.6	-0.3	180.5	0.5	178.9	-0.9	178.6	-0.2	179.2	0.3	181.0	1.0	184.8	2.1	185.1	0.2	189.0	2.1	190.7	0.9
2001	191.5	0.4	194.9	1.8	199.9	2.6	206.3	3.2	209.3	1.5	206.1	-1.5	205.0	-0.5	206.7	0.8	199.4	-3.5	197.3	-1.1	192.0	-2.7	191.0	-0.5

Source: U.S. Department of Labor, Bureau of Labor Statistics, Division of Industry Prices and Price Indexes. n.e.c. stands for not elsewhere classified. - indicates no data collected for period or unavailable.

Footwear

Producer Price Index
Base 1982 = 100

For 1926-2001. Columns headed % show percentile change in the index from the previous period for which an index is available.

Year	Jan Index	%	Feb Index	%	Mar Index	%	Apr Index	%	May Index	%	Jun Index	%	Jul Index	%	Aug Index	%	Sep Index	%	Oct Index	%	Nov Index	%	Dec Index	%
1926	14.7	-	14.7	0.0	14.7	0.0	14.7	0.0	14.7	0.0	14.7	0.0	14.5	-1.4	14.5	0.0	14.5	0.0	14.5	0.0	14.5	0.0	14.5	0.0
1927	14.5	0.0	14.5	0.0	14.5	0.0	14.5	0.0	14.6	0.7	14.7	0.7	15.0	2.0	15.1	0.7	15.4	2.0	15.4	0.0	15.5	0.6	15.6	0.6
1928	15.8	1.3	15.9	0.6	16.0	0.6	16.1	0.6	16.1	0.0	16.2	0.6	16.2	0.0	16.2	0.0	16.2	0.0	16.1	-0.6	15.9	-1.2	15.8	-0.6
1929	15.6	-1.3	15.6	0.0	15.6	0.0	15.6	0.0	15.5	-0.6	15.5	0.0	15.5	0.0	15.5	0.0	15.5	0.0	15.5	0.0	15.5	0.0	15.5	0.0
1930	15.1	-2.6	15.1	0.0	15.1	0.0	15.1	0.0	15.1	0.0	15.0	-0.7	15.0	0.0	14.7	-2.0	14.7	0.0	14.7	0.0	14.7	0.0	14.3	-2.7
1931	13.9	-2.8	13.8	-0.7	13.8	0.0	13.8	0.0	13.8	0.0	13.8	0.0	13.6	-1.4	13.6	0.0	13.6	0.0	13.6	0.0	13.5	-0.7	13.0	-3.7
1932	12.9	-0.8	12.9	0.0	12.9	0.0	12.9	0.0	12.9	0.0	12.7	-1.6	12.3	-3.1	12.3	0.0	12.3	0.0	12.3	0.0	12.3	0.0	12.2	-0.8
1933	12.2	0.0	12.1	-0.8	12.1	0.0	12.1	0.0	12.2	0.8	12.4	1.6	12.9	4.0	14.0	8.5	14.4	2.9	14.4	0.0	14.4	0.0	14.4	0.0
1934	14.4	0.0	14.4	0.0	14.4	0.0	14.4	0.0	14.4	0.0	14.4	0.0	14.3	-0.7	14.3	0.0	14.3	0.0	14.3	0.0	14.2	-0.7	14.2	0.0
1935	14.1	-0.7	14.2	0.7	14.2	0.0	14.2	0.0	14.2	0.0	14.2	0.0	14.3	0.7	14.3	0.0	14.3	0.0	14.4	0.7	14.5	0.7	14.6	0.7
1936	14.7	0.7	14.7	0.0	14.7	0.0	14.7	0.0	14.6	-0.7	14.5	-0.7	14.5	0.0	14.5	0.0	14.5	0.0	14.5	0.0	14.5	0.0	14.5	0.0
1937	14.5	0.0	14.8	2.1	14.9	0.7	15.1	1.3	15.5	2.6	15.7	1.3	15.6	-0.6	15.6	0.0	15.7	0.6	15.7	0.0	15.6	-0.6	15.4	-1.3
1938	15.3	-0.6	15.2	-0.7	15.2	0.0	15.2	0.0	14.9	-2.0	14.9	0.0	14.8	-0.7	14.7	-0.7	14.7	0.0	14.7	0.0	14.7	0.0	14.7	0.0
1939	14.8	0.7	14.7	-0.7	14.8	0.7	14.8	0.0	14.8	0.0	14.8	0.0	14.7	-0.7	14.7	0.0	14.9	1.4	15.4	3.4	15.6	1.3	15.7	0.6
1940	15.7	0.0	15.8	0.6	15.8	0.0	15.8	0.0	15.8	0.0	15.8	0.0	15.6	-1.3	15.6	0.0	15.6	0.0	15.6	0.0	15.6	0.0	15.6	0.0
1941	15.6	0.0	15.6	0.0	15.6	0.0	15.8	1.3	16.0	1.3	16.3	1.9	16.7	2.5	16.9	1.2	17.1	1.2	17.3	1.2	17.6	1.7	17.6	0.0
1942	17.7	0.6	17.8	0.6	18.1	1.7	18.5	2.2	18.5	0.0	18.4	-0.5	18.4	0.0	18.4	0.0	18.4	0.0	18.4	0.0	18.4	0.0	18.4	0.0
1943	18.4	0.0	18.4	0.0	18.4	0.0	18.4	0.0	18.4	0.0	18.4	0.0	18.4	0.0	18.4	0.0	18.4	0.0	18.4	0.0	18.4	0.0	18.4	0.0
1944	18.4	0.0	18.4	0.0	18.4	0.0	18.4	0.0	18.4	0.0	18.4	0.0	18.4	0.0	18.4	0.0	18.4	0.0	18.4	0.0	18.4	0.0	18.4	0.0
1945	18.4	0.0	18.4	0.0	18.4	0.0	18.4	0.0	18.4	0.0	18.4	0.0	18.4	0.0	18.4	0.0	18.4	0.0	18.4	0.0	18.5	0.5	18.5	0.0
1946	18.7	1.1	18.7	0.0	18.7	0.0	18.7	0.0	18.8	0.5	18.9	0.5	20.5	8.5	20.5	0.0	21.1	2.9	21.1	0.0	23.8	12.8	24.8	4.2
1947	25.3	2.0	25.3	0.0	25.3	0.0	25.4	0.4	25.6	0.8	25.6	0.0	25.7	0.4	26.0	1.2	25.8	-0.8	26.1	1.2	26.5	1.5	27.2	2.6
1948	27.4	0.7	27.4	0.0	27.6	0.7	27.8	0.7	27.6	-0.7	27.5	-0.4	27.6	0.4	27.8	0.7	27.9	0.4	27.8	-0.4	27.5	-1.1	27.5	0.0
1949	27.4	-0.4	27.4	0.0	27.4	0.0	27.3	-0.4	27.1	-0.7	27.1	0.0	27.1	0.0	27.1	0.0	27.1	0.0	27.1	0.0	27.3	0.7	27.5	0.7
1950	27.3	-0.7	27.3	0.0	27.4	0.4	27.4	0.0	27.6	0.7	27.6	0.0	27.8	0.7	28.7	3.2	29.1	1.4	30.1	3.4	31.2	3.7	32.2	3.2
1951	32.9	2.2	33.5	1.8	33.1	-1.2	33.1	0.0	33.1	0.0	33.0	-0.3	32.9	-0.3	32.8	-0.3	32.8	0.0	32.1	-2.1	31.8	-0.9	31.3	-1.6
1952	31.2	-0.3	31.2	0.0	31.2	0.0	30.4	-2.6	29.9	-1.6	29.8	-0.3	29.8	0.0	29.8	0.0	29.8	0.0	29.8	0.0	29.8	0.0	30.1	1.0
1953	30.1	0.0	30.2	0.3	30.2	0.0	30.0	-0.7	30.0	0.0	30.0	0.0	30.0	0.0	30.1	0.3	30.1	0.0	30.0	-0.3	30.1	0.3	30.1	0.0
1954	30.1	0.0	30.1	0.0	30.1	0.0	30.1	0.0	30.1	0.0	30.1	0.0	30.1	0.0	30.1	0.0	30.1	0.0	30.1	0.0	30.0	-0.3	30.0	0.0
1955	30.0	0.0	30.0	0.0	30.0	0.0	30.0	0.0	30.0	0.0	30.0	0.0	30.0	0.0	30.0	0.0	30.0	0.0	30.5	1.7	31.1	2.0	31.1	0.0
1956	31.1	0.0	31.1	0.0	31.3	0.6	32.2	2.9	32.3	0.3	32.4	0.3	32.4	0.0	32.4	0.0	32.4	0.0	32.5	0.3	32.5	0.0	32.5	0.0
1957	32.5	0.0	32.5	0.0	32.5	0.0	32.6	0.3	32.5	-0.3	32.5	0.0	32.6	0.3	32.6	0.0	32.6	0.0	32.8	0.6	32.9	0.3	32.7	-0.6
1958	32.8	0.3	32.8	0.0	32.8	0.0	32.7	-0.3	32.8	0.3	32.8	0.0	32.8	0.0	32.8	0.0	32.8	0.0	33.0	0.6	33.1	0.3	33.1	0.0
1959	33.1	0.0	33.1	0.0	33.3	0.6	34.5	3.6	34.8	0.9	35.0	0.6	35.1	0.3	35.6	1.4	35.6	0.0	35.9	0.8	36.0	0.3	36.1	0.3
1960	36.1	0.0	36.1	0.0	36.1	-1.2	35.9	-0.6	35.6	-0.8	35.6	0.0	35.6	0.0	35.6	0.0	35.6	0.0	35.6	0.0	35.6	0.0	35.6	0.0
1961	35.7	0.3	35.7	0.0	35.7	0.0	35.7	0.0	35.8	0.3	35.8	0.0	35.8	0.0	35.9	0.3	36.0	0.3	36.2	0.6	36.3	0.3	36.3	0.0
1962	36.3	0.0	36.3	0.0	36.3	0.0	36.3	0.0	36.3	0.0	36.3	0.0	36.4	0.3	36.4	0.0	36.4	0.0	36.2	-0.5	36.2	0.0	36.3	0.3
1963	36.2	-0.3	36.2	0.0	36.2	0.0	36.2	0.0	36.2	0.0	36.2	0.0	36.2	0.0	36.2	0.0	36.2	0.0	36.2	0.0	36.2	0.0	36.2	0.0
1964	36.2	0.0	36.2	0.0	36.2	0.0	36.2	0.0	36.2	0.0	36.2	0.0	36.2	0.0	36.2	0.0	36.2	0.0	36.5	0.8	36.5	0.0	36.5	0.0
1965	36.5	0.0	36.5	0.0	36.5	0.0	36.7	0.5	36.7	0.0	36.7	0.0	36.8	0.3	36.9	0.3	36.9	0.0	38.0	3.0	38.0	0.0	38.0	0.0
1966	38.3	0.8	38.5	0.5	38.6	0.3	39.5	2.3	39.8	0.8	39.8	0.0	39.8	0.0	39.8	0.0	39.8	0.0	40.2	1.0	40.2	0.0	40.2	0.0
1967	40.5	0.7	40.7	0.5	40.7	0.0	40.6	-0.2	40.6	0.0	40.6	0.0	40.6	0.0	40.5	-0.2	40.7	0.5	41.3	1.5	41.3	0.0	41.6	0.7
1968	42.0	1.0	42.0	0.0	42.0	0.0	42.3	0.7	42.5	0.5	42.5	0.0	42.6	0.2	42.5	-0.2	43.1	1.4	43.9	1.9	44.0	0.2	44.0	0.0
1969	44.2	0.5	44.2	0.0	44.0	-0.5	44.1	0.2	44.2	0.2	44.2	0.0	44.4	0.5	44.5	0.2	45.3	1.8	45.6	0.7	45.8	0.4	45.7	-0.2
1970	46.1	0.9	46.4	0.7	46.4	0.0	46.2	-0.4	46.1	-0.2	46.1	0.0	46.1	0.0	46.1	0.0	46.4	0.7	46.5	0.2	46.5	0.0	46.5	0.0

[Continued]

Footwear
Producer Price Index
Base 1982 = 100
[Continued]

For 1926-2001. Columns headed % show percentile change in the index from the previous period for which an index is available.

Year	Jan Index	%	Feb Index	%	Mar Index	%	Apr Index	%	May Index	%	Jun Index	%	Jul Index	%	Aug Index	%	Sep Index	%	Oct Index	%	Nov Index	%	Dec Index	%
1971	47.5	2.2	47.5	0.0	47.5	0.0	47.6	0.2	47.7	0.2	47.7	0.0	47.7	0.0	47.7	0.0	47.7	0.0	47.7	0.0	47.7	0.0	47.8	0.2
1972	48.2	0.8	48.4	0.4	49.0	1.2	50.0	2.0	50.9	1.8	51.4	1.0	51.6	0.4	51.6	0.0	51.7	0.2	51.8	0.2	52.4	1.2	52.5	0.2
1973	52.6	0.2	53.4	1.5	53.5	0.2	53.7	0.4	52.8	-1.7	52.8	0.0	52.9	0.2	52.9	0.0	53.2	0.6	53.5	0.6	53.8	0.6	54.1	0.6
1974	54.7	1.1	55.1	0.7	55.5	0.7	56.4	1.6	56.6	0.4	56.9	0.5	57.1	0.4	57.4	0.5	58.8	2.4	58.9	0.2	59.1	0.3	59.1	0.0
1975	59.3	0.3	59.6	0.5	59.6	0.0	59.9	0.5	59.9	0.0	60.0	0.2	60.1	0.2	60.2	0.2	61.0	1.3	61.3	0.5	61.3	0.0	61.4	0.2
1976	62.1	1.1	62.8	1.1	63.2	0.6	63.8	0.9	64.0	0.3	64.8	1.3	65.6	1.2	65.8	0.3	66.3	0.8	66.4	0.2	66.5	0.2	66.8	0.5
1977	67.1	0.4	67.5	0.6	67.9	0.6	68.2	0.4	68.6	0.6	68.6	0.0	69.3	1.0	69.4	0.1	69.4	0.0	69.9	0.7	70.0	0.1	70.1	0.1
1978	70.8	1.0	71.7	1.3	71.7	0.0	73.5	2.5	73.8	0.4	73.9	0.1	74.1	0.3	75.1	1.3	75.9	1.1	77.8	2.5	78.4	0.8	79.3	1.1
1979	80.2	1.1	82.8	3.2	85.7	3.5	86.6	1.1	88.3	2.0	90.3	2.3	90.5	0.2	92.0	1.7	92.6	0.7	92.9	0.3	93.0	0.1	93.0	0.0
1980	93.5	0.5	93.1	-0.4	94.6	1.6	94.7	0.1	94.7	0.0	94.7	0.0	95.0	0.3	95.4	0.4	96.1	0.7	96.6	0.5	97.0	0.4	96.7	-0.3
1981	97.3	0.6	98.2	0.9	98.1	-0.1	98.4	0.3	98.5	0.1	98.6	0.1	98.9	0.3	99.0	0.1	99.1	0.1	97.8	-1.3	97.9	0.1	98.0	0.1
1982	97.5	-0.5	97.4	-0.1	97.9	0.5	99.9	2.0	99.8	-0.1	99.7	-0.1	101.0	1.3	101.1	0.1	101.3	0.2	101.6	0.3	101.7	0.1	101.1	-0.6
1983	102.7	1.6	101.1	-1.6	101.3	0.2	102.1	0.8	101.5	-0.6	102.0	0.5	102.0	0.0	102.4	0.4	102.7	0.3	102.6	-0.1	102.6	0.0	102.2	-0.4
1984	102.4	0.2	103.1	0.7	103.5	0.4	102.7	-0.8	102.6	-0.1	102.3	-0.3	102.1	-0.2	102.4	0.3	102.8	0.4	102.9	0.1	103.0	0.1	103.1	0.1
1985	103.2	0.1	104.5	1.3	104.2	-0.3	104.1	-0.1	103.6	-0.5	104.9	1.3	104.9	0.0	105.3	0.4	105.7	0.4	105.7	0.0	105.5	-0.2	105.5	0.0
1986	105.9	0.4	106.3	0.4	106.8	0.5	107.1	0.3	106.8	-0.3	106.4	-0.4	106.5	0.1	106.8	0.3	107.0	0.2	107.5	0.5	107.5	0.0	107.8	0.3
1987	108.0	0.2	107.5	-0.5	108.4	0.8	108.2	-0.2	108.9	0.6	107.5	-1.3	109.7	2.0	110.3	0.5	111.0	0.6	110.9	-0.1	110.6	-0.3	111.4	0.7
1988	112.7	1.2	113.7	0.9	114.0	0.3	114.1	0.1	114.2	0.1	114.8	0.5	115.5	0.6	116.0	0.4	116.2	0.2	116.4	0.2	116.9	0.4	117.2	0.3
1989	118.1	0.8	119.5	1.2	119.8	0.3	120.0	0.2	119.9	-0.1	119.9	0.0	120.4	0.4	121.8	1.2	122.3	0.4	122.5	0.2	122.5	0.0	123.1	0.5
1990	124.2	0.9	125.3	0.9	125.5	0.2	125.4	-0.1	125.8	0.3	125.5	-0.2	125.6	0.1	126.0	0.3	126.1	0.1	126.2	0.1	125.9	-0.2	126.1	0.2
1991	126.3	0.2	127.1	0.6	128.0	0.7	128.3	0.2	128.7	0.3	128.8	0.1	129.2	0.3	129.3	0.1	129.5	0.2	129.1	-0.3	129.3	0.2	129.6	0.2
1992	130.6	0.8	131.8	0.9	131.4	-0.3	131.5	0.1	131.6	0.1	131.9	0.2	132.1	0.2	132.5	0.3	132.8	0.2	132.4	-0.3	132.4	0.0	133.3	0.7
1993	133.5	0.2	133.8	0.2	133.9	0.1	134.5	0.4	134.1	-0.3	134.2	0.1	134.8	0.4	134.8	0.0	134.9	0.1	134.7	-0.1	134.9	0.1	135.1	0.1
1994	135.5	0.3	135.1	-0.3	135.4	0.2	135.2	-0.1	135.4	0.1	135.2	-0.1	135.3	0.1	135.3	0.0	135.6	0.2	135.8	0.1	136.1	0.2	136.6	0.4
1995	137.5	0.7	138.6	0.8	138.7	0.1	138.8	0.1	138.9	0.1	139.0	0.1	139.2	0.1	139.3	0.1	139.3	0.0	140.1	0.6	140.4	0.2	140.5	0.1
1996	140.6	0.1	141.1	0.4	141.3	0.1	141.2	-0.1	141.2	0.0	141.6	0.3	141.7	0.1	142.0	0.2	142.0	0.0	142.2	0.1	142.2	0.0	142.3	0.1
1997	143.1	0.6	143.3	0.1	143.5	0.1	143.5	0.0	143.7	0.1	142.2	-1.0	144.1	1.3	144.3	0.1	144.4	0.1	144.4	0.0	144.2	-0.1	144.2	0.0
1998	144.5	0.2	144.7	0.1	144.7	0.0	144.7	0.0	144.6	-0.1	144.7	0.1	144.5	-0.1	144.6	0.1	144.7	0.1	144.7	0.0	144.7	0.0	144.9	0.1
1999	143.8	-0.8	144.6	0.6	144.6	0.0	144.6	0.0	144.4	-0.1	144.5	0.1	144.6	0.1	144.6	0.0	144.6	0.0	144.7	0.1	144.6	-0.1	144.5	-0.1
2000	144.8	0.2	144.8	0.0	144.8	0.0	144.9	0.1	145.0	0.1	144.8	-0.1	145.0	0.1	145.1	0.1	145.1	0.0	145.1	0.0	144.9	-0.1	144.9	0.0
2001	145.1	0.1	145.9	0.6	145.8	-0.1	146.7	0.6	146.0	-0.5	145.7	-0.2	145.7	0.0	145.6	-0.1	145.6	0.0	145.7	0.1	145.7	0.0	145.7	0.0

Source: U.S. Department of Labor, Bureau of Labor Statistics, Division of Industry Prices and Price Indexes. n.e.c. stands for not elsewhere classified. - indicates no data collected for period or unavailable.

Other Leather and Related Products
Producer Price Index
Base 1982 = 100

For 1947-2001. Columns headed % show percentile change in the index from the previous period for which an index is available.

Year	Jan Index	%	Feb Index	%	Mar Index	%	Apr Index	%	May Index	%	Jun Index	%	Jul Index	%	Aug Index	%	Sep Index	%	Oct Index	%	Nov Index	%	Dec Index	%
1947	35.0	-	34.4	-1.7	34.4	0.0	34.2	-0.6	33.6	-1.8	33.5	-0.3	34.5	3.0	35.0	1.4	35.4	1.1	36.0	1.7	37.6	4.4	37.8	0.5
1948	37.7	-0.3	37.2	-1.3	36.2	-2.7	35.7	-1.4	35.8	0.3	35.9	0.3	36.1	0.6	36.0	-0.3	35.5	-1.4	35.2	-0.8	35.3	0.3	35.6	0.8
1949	35.5	-0.3	35.4	-0.3	34.8	-1.7	34.3	-1.4	34.4	0.3	34.2	-0.6	34.0	-0.6	33.9	-0.3	33.8	-0.3	33.9	0.3	33.8	-0.3	34.0	0.6
1950	33.6	-1.2	33.6	0.0	33.6	0.0	33.6	0.0	33.7	0.3	33.5	-0.6	34.0	1.5	34.8	2.4	35.2	1.1	35.7	1.4	36.1	1.1	36.9	2.2
1951	40.0	8.4	40.6	1.5	40.6	0.0	40.9	0.7	40.7	-0.5	40.5	-0.5	40.1	-1.0	39.0	-2.7	39.0	0.0	37.6	-3.6	37.2	-1.1	37.2	0.0
1952	36.6	-1.6	36.3	-0.8	35.8	-1.4	35.2	-1.7	35.3	0.3	35.4	0.3	35.3	-0.3	35.2	-0.3	35.1	-0.3	34.8	-0.9	35.0	0.6	35.3	0.9
1953	34.8	-1.4	34.8	0.0	34.8	0.0	34.9	0.3	35.1	0.6	35.3	0.6	35.0	-0.8	35.0	0.0	34.8	-0.6	34.8	0.0	34.7	-0.3	34.5	-0.6
1954	34.5	0.0	34.4	-0.3	34.3	-0.3	34.2	-0.3	34.2	0.0	34.2	0.0	34.1	-0.3	34.0	-0.3	33.9	-0.3	33.8	-0.3	33.8	0.0	33.7	-0.3
1955	33.7	0.0	33.7	0.0	33.6	-0.3	33.7	0.3	33.4	-0.9	33.4	0.0	33.9	1.5	33.9	0.0	33.8	-0.3	33.8	0.0	33.8	0.0	34.0	0.6
1956	34.3	0.9	34.5	0.6	34.5	0.0	34.8	0.9	34.8	0.0	34.8	0.0	34.7	-0.3	34.8	0.3	34.6	-0.6	34.6	0.0	34.6	0.0	34.5	-0.3
1957	34.4	-0.3	34.2	-0.6	34.4	0.6	34.4	0.0	34.2	-0.6	34.2	0.0	34.6	1.2	34.5	-0.3	34.6	0.3	34.6	0.0	34.6	0.0	34.6	-0.3
1958	34.6	0.0	34.6	0.0	34.2	-1.2	34.3	0.3	34.2	-0.3	34.2	0.0	34.2	0.0	34.0	-0.6	34.0	0.0	34.2	0.6	34.2	0.0	34.5	0.9
1959	34.8	0.9	35.4	1.7	36.3	2.5	38.7	6.6	39.5	2.1	39.4	-0.3	40.0	1.5	40.1	0.2	40.0	-0.2	39.1	-2.3	38.4	-1.8	37.9	-1.3
1960	38.0	0.3	37.7	-0.8	37.7	0.0	37.7	0.0	37.5	-0.5	37.4	-0.3	37.1	-0.8	36.8	-0.8	36.5	-0.8	36.5	0.0	36.6	0.3	36.5	-0.3
1961	36.6	0.3	36.5	-0.3	36.4	-0.3	36.6	0.5	36.7	0.3	36.7	0.0	36.6	-0.3	36.9	0.8	37.0	0.3	36.9	-0.3	37.2	0.8	37.2	0.0
1962	37.4	0.5	37.3	-0.3	37.3	0.0	36.6	-1.9	36.3	-0.8	37.4	3.0	37.5	0.3	37.1	-1.1	37.1	0.0	37.4	0.8	37.5	0.3	37.6	0.3
1963	37.4	-0.5	37.4	0.0	37.4	0.0	37.3	-0.3	37.2	-0.3	37.2	0.0	37.1	-0.3	36.9	-0.5	36.9	0.0	36.9	0.0	36.8	-0.3	36.9	0.3
1964	36.3	-1.6	36.3	0.0	36.2	-0.3	37.0	2.2	36.9	-0.3	36.8	-0.3	37.1	0.8	37.0	-0.3	36.9	-0.3	36.9	0.0	37.1	0.5	37.1	0.0
1965	36.6	-1.3	36.7	0.3	36.7	0.0	37.2	1.4	37.4	0.5	37.4	0.0	37.6	0.5	38.8	3.2	39.0	0.5	38.9	-0.3	38.9	0.0	39.3	1.0
1966	39.4	0.3	39.8	1.0	40.1	0.8	40.8	1.7	41.2	1.0	41.3	0.2	41.6	0.7	41.4	-0.5	41.1	-0.7	41.2	0.2	41.1	-0.2	40.7	-1.0
1967	41.0	0.7	41.0	0.0	40.9	-0.2	40.9	0.0	40.8	-0.2	40.4	-1.0	40.3	-0.2	40.3	0.0	40.0	-0.7	39.9	-0.2	39.9	0.0	39.8	-0.3
1968	40.0	0.5	40.0	0.0	40.1	0.2	40.1	0.0	40.1	0.0	40.1	0.0	40.2	0.2	40.2	0.0	40.2	0.0	40.5	0.7	40.5	0.0	40.6	0.2
1969	41.0	1.0	41.0	0.0	41.2	0.5	41.5	0.7	41.7	0.5	41.8	0.2	42.0	0.5	41.9	-0.2	42.1	0.5	42.2	0.2	42.4	0.5	42.3	-0.2
1970	42.6	0.7	42.7	0.2	42.8	0.2	42.8	0.0	43.1	0.7	43.1	0.0	43.2	0.2	43.2	0.0	43.2	0.0	43.2	0.0	43.2	0.0	43.2	0.0
1971	43.4	0.5	43.5	0.2	43.5	0.0	43.5	0.0	43.6	0.2	43.7	0.2	43.8	0.2	44.0	0.5	44.1	0.2	44.1	0.0	44.1	0.0	44.4	0.7
1972	44.7	0.7	44.9	0.4	45.2	0.7	46.0	1.8	46.6	1.3	47.2	1.3	47.1	-0.2	48.0	1.9	48.7	1.5	50.0	2.7	51.4	2.8	51.9	1.0
1973	52.3	0.8	52.3	0.0	52.3	0.0	52.5	0.4	52.2	-0.6	52.1	-0.2	52.2	0.2	52.8	1.1	52.7	-0.2	52.8	0.2	52.6	-0.4	52.7	0.2
1974	53.3	1.1	53.8	0.9	54.8	1.9	54.7	-0.2	54.6	-0.2	55.3	1.3	55.4	0.2	55.4	0.0	56.3	1.6	56.0	-0.5	56.0	0.0	56.5	0.9
1975	56.6	0.2	56.4	-0.4	56.2	-0.4	56.2	0.0	56.4	0.4	56.8	0.7	57.0	0.4	57.2	0.4	57.3	0.2	57.4	0.2	58.0	1.0	58.3	0.5
1976	60.3	3.4	61.0	1.2	61.1	0.2	61.2	0.2	61.5	0.5	61.5	0.0	61.6	0.2	61.7	0.2	62.7	1.6	63.0	0.5	63.0	0.0	63.1	0.2
1977	64.5	2.2	65.3	1.2	65.7	0.6	66.0	0.5	66.2	0.3	66.2	0.0	66.2	0.0	66.4	0.3	66.5	0.2	66.5	0.0	66.6	0.2	66.6	0.0
1978	68.8	3.3	68.9	0.1	69.4	0.7	69.5	0.1	71.2	2.4	71.4	0.3	71.5	0.1	72.3	1.1	72.7	0.6	72.9	0.3	74.8	2.6	74.9	0.1
1979	77.1	2.9	77.7	0.8	79.2	1.9	81.2	2.5	84.5	4.1	85.8	1.5	85.7	-0.1	85.3	-0.5	84.9	-0.5	84.8	-0.1	84.3	-0.6	84.1	-0.2
1980	86.1	2.4	86.8	0.8	88.0	1.4	87.4	-0.7	87.9	0.6	87.3	-0.7	87.9	0.7	88.4	0.6	88.5	0.1	89.7	1.4	90.0	0.3	91.1	1.2
1981	93.0	2.1	95.8	3.0	96.4	0.6	96.4	0.0	98.7	2.4	98.8	0.1	98.2	-0.6	99.1	0.9	99.0	-0.1	99.0	0.0	99.2	0.2	99.2	0.0
1982	100.1	0.9	100.3	0.2	100.3	0.0	100.3	0.0	100.3	0.0	99.3	-1.0	99.8	0.5	99.0	-0.8	100.1	1.1	99.9	-0.2	99.9	0.0	100.7	0.8
1983	101.4	0.7	101.5	0.1	101.4	-0.1	101.5	0.1	101.7	0.2	101.7	0.0	102.5	0.8	102.6	0.1	102.5	-0.1	102.5	0.0	103.4	0.9	103.3	-0.1
1984	104.0	0.7	104.0	0.0	104.0	0.0	104.3	0.3	105.0	0.7	108.3	3.1	108.0	-0.3	108.2	0.2	108.2	0.0	108.4	0.2	108.3	-0.1	107.9	-0.4
1985	109.2	1.2	109.3	0.1	110.1	0.7	110.2	0.1	110.3	0.1	110.5	0.2	110.2	-0.3	110.2	0.0	110.6	0.4	110.8	0.2	111.3	0.5	111.3	0.0
1986	111.5	0.2	111.0	-0.4	109.7	-1.2	109.5	-0.2	109.5	0.0	109.9	0.4	109.9	0.0	110.0	0.1	110.2	0.2	111.0	0.7	111.0	0.0	111.1	0.1
1987	111.5	0.4	111.4	-0.1	111.6	0.2	111.6	0.0	112.2	0.5	112.5	0.3	112.9	0.4	113.4	0.4	114.2	0.7	114.4	0.2	114.8	0.3	115.2	0.3
1988	116.6	1.2	116.8	0.2	117.1	0.3	117.7	0.5	118.2	0.4	119.5	1.1	119.9	0.3	120.0	0.1	120.6	0.5	120.6	0.0	120.7	0.1	120.9	0.2
1989	121.4	0.4	121.9	0.4	122.2	0.2	122.4	0.2	123.2	0.7	122.9	-0.2	122.9	0.0	123.7	0.7	124.4	0.6	123.9	-0.4	123.7	-0.2	124.8	0.9
1990	126.0	1.0	126.3	0.2	127.9	1.3	127.6	-0.2	129.2	1.3	129.7	0.4	129.4	-0.2	130.6	0.9	130.1	-0.4	129.6	-0.4	130.0	0.3	130.8	0.6
1991	130.8	0.0	131.3	0.4	132.4	0.8	131.9	-0.4	132.7	0.6	134.4	1.3	132.4	-1.5	134.3	1.4	132.8	-1.1	132.8	0.0	132.9	0.1	133.0	0.1

[Continued]

Other Leather and Related Products
Producer Price Index
Base 1982 = 100

[Continued]

For 1947-2001. Columns headed % show percentile change in the index from the previous period for which an index is available.

Year	Jan Index	%	Feb Index	%	Mar Index	%	Apr Index	%	May Index	%	Jun Index	%	Jul Index	%	Aug Index	%	Sep Index	%	Oct Index	%	Nov Index	%	Dec Index	%
1992	135.7	2.0	133.7	-1.5	136.2	1.9	134.0	-1.6	134.4	0.3	136.2	1.3	134.2	-1.5	136.6	1.8	134.2	-1.8	134.3	0.1	134.6	0.2	134.6	0.0
1993	137.1	1.9	135.2	-1.4	135.3	0.1	135.7	0.3	135.8	0.1	137.8	1.5	135.9	-1.4	138.3	1.8	135.9	-1.7	136.1	0.1	136.1	0.0	136.1	0.0
1994	137.8	1.2	135.6	-1.6	135.8	0.1	136.0	0.1	136.2	0.1	136.3	0.1	136.4	0.1	136.5	0.1	137.5	0.7	137.6	0.1	137.8	0.1	137.6	-0.1
1995	138.2	0.4	138.0	-0.1	138.1	0.1	138.4	0.2	138.6	0.1	138.9	0.2	138.9	0.0	139.1	0.1	139.5	0.3	139.9	0.3	139.7	-0.1	140.1	0.3
1996	140.3	0.1	140.6	0.2	140.7	0.1	140.9	0.1	141.2	0.2	141.2	0.0	141.5	0.2	141.2	-0.2	141.2	0.0	141.2	0.0	141.3	0.1	141.3	0.0
1997	142.0	0.5	142.3	0.2	143.0	0.5	143.2	0.1	143.3	0.1	143.8	0.3	143.8	0.0	144.2	0.3	144.2	0.0	143.9	-0.2	144.0	0.1	144.5	0.3
1998	144.8	0.2	144.8	0.0	144.9	0.1	145.1	0.1	145.1	0.0	145.0	-0.1	144.7	-0.2	144.6	-0.1	144.7	0.1	144.7	0.0	144.8	0.1	144.7	-0.1
1999	144.9	0.1	145.0	0.1	145.1	0.1	145.1	0.0	145.0	-0.1	145.8	0.6	145.9	0.1	145.8	-0.1	145.8	0.0	145.7	-0.1	145.8	0.1	145.8	0.0
2000	146.2	0.3	146.0	-0.1	146.0	0.0	146.0	0.0	146.0	0.0	145.7	-0.2	146.0	0.2	146.2	0.1	146.4	0.1	146.2	-0.1	146.2	0.0	146.3	0.1
2001	146.1	-0.1	147.0	0.6	147.1	0.1	147.6	0.3	147.6	0.0	147.4	-0.1	148.1	0.5	148.1	0.0	148.0	-0.1	148.1	0.1	148.1	0.0	148.0	-0.1

Source: U.S. Department of Labor, Bureau of Labor Statistics, Division of Industry Prices and Price Indexes. n.e.c. stands for not elsewhere classified. - indicates no data collected for period or unavailable.

FUELS AND RELATED PRODUCTS AND POWER
Producer Price Index
Base 1982 = 100

For 1926-2001. Columns headed % show percentile change in the index from the previous period for which an index is available.

Year	Jan Index	%	Feb Index	%	Mar Index	%	Apr Index	%	May Index	%	Jun Index	%	Jul Index	%	Aug Index	%	Sep Index	%	Oct Index	%	Nov Index	%	Dec Index	%
1926	10.2	-	10.2	0.0	10.2	0.0	10.1	-1.0	10.4	3.0	10.4	0.0	10.3	-1.0	10.4	1.0	10.4	0.0	10.4	0.0	10.5	1.0	10.2	-2.9
1927	10.1	-1.0	10.0	-1.0	9.4	-6.0	9.0	-4.3	8.9	-1.1	8.9	0.0	8.9	0.0	8.9	0.0	8.9	0.0	8.9	0.0	8.8	-1.1	8.7	-1.1
1928	8.6	-1.1	8.6	0.0	8.5	-1.2	8.6	1.2	8.6	0.0	8.7	1.2	8.7	0.0	8.9	2.3	8.9	0.0	8.9	0.0	8.9	0.0	8.8	-1.1
1929	8.7	-1.1	8.6	-1.1	8.5	-1.2	8.5	0.0	8.5	0.0	8.7	2.4	8.6	-1.1	8.5	-1.2	8.5	0.0	8.6	1.2	8.6	0.0	8.6	0.0
1930	8.4	-2.3	8.4	0.0	8.2	-2.4	8.2	0.0	8.3	1.2	8.2	-1.2	8.1	-1.2	8.0	-1.2	8.2	2.5	8.0	-2.4	7.8	-2.5	7.6	-2.6
1931	7.6	0.0	7.5	-1.3	7.0	-6.7	6.8	-2.9	6.7	-1.5	6.5	-3.0	6.5	0.0	6.9	6.2	7.0	1.4	7.0	0.0	7.2	2.9	7.0	-2.8
1932	7.0	0.0	7.0	0.0	7.0	0.0	7.2	2.9	7.3	1.4	7.4	1.4	7.5	1.4	7.4	-1.3	7.3	-1.4	7.3	0.0	7.4	1.4	7.2	-2.7
1933	6.8	-5.6	6.6	-2.9	6.5	-1.5	6.3	-3.1	6.2	-1.6	6.3	1.6	6.7	6.3	6.8	1.5	7.3	7.4	7.6	4.1	7.6	0.0	7.6	0.0
1934	7.5	-1.3	7.5	0.0	7.4	-1.3	7.4	0.0	7.5	1.4	7.5	0.0	7.6	1.3	7.7	1.3	7.7	0.0	7.7	0.0	7.7	0.0	7.6	-1.3
1935	7.5	-1.3	7.5	0.0	7.5	0.0	7.5	0.0	7.5	0.0	7.7	2.7	7.7	0.0	7.6	-1.3	7.5	-1.3	7.6	1.3	7.7	1.3	7.7	0.0
1936	7.8	1.3	7.8	0.0	7.9	1.3	7.9	0.0	7.8	-1.3	7.8	0.0	7.9	1.3	7.9	0.0	7.8	-1.3	7.9	1.3	7.9	0.0	7.9	0.0
1937	7.9	0.0	7.9	0.0	7.9	0.0	7.9	0.0	8.0	1.3	8.0	0.0	8.1	1.3	8.1	0.0	8.1	0.0	8.1	0.0	8.1	0.0	8.1	0.0
1938	8.1	0.0	8.1	0.0	8.0	-1.2	7.9	-1.2	7.9	0.0	7.9	0.0	7.9	0.0	7.9	0.0	7.9	0.0	7.8	-1.3	7.6	-2.6	7.6	0.0
1939	7.5	-1.3	7.5	0.0	7.5	0.0	7.6	1.3	7.6	0.0	7.5	-1.3	7.5	0.0	7.5	0.0	7.5	0.0	7.6	1.3	7.6	0.0	7.5	-1.3
1940	7.5	0.0	7.5	0.0	7.4	-1.3	7.4	0.0	7.4	0.0	7.4	0.0	7.3	-1.4	7.3	0.0	7.3	0.0	7.4	1.4	7.4	0.0	7.4	0.0
1941	7.4	0.0	7.4	0.0	7.4	0.0	7.5	1.4	7.8	4.0	8.0	2.6	8.1	1.3	8.2	1.2	8.2	0.0	8.2	0.0	8.1	-1.2	8.1	0.0
1942	8.1	0.0	8.0	-1.2	8.0	0.0	8.0	0.0	8.0	0.0	8.1	1.3	8.2	1.2	8.2	0.0	8.2	0.0	8.2	0.0	8.2	0.0	8.2	0.0
1943	8.2	0.0	8.2	0.0	8.3	1.2	8.3	0.0	8.3	0.0	8.4	1.2	8.4	0.0	8.4	0.0	8.4	0.0	8.4	0.0	8.4	0.0	8.5	1.2
1944	8.5	0.0	8.6	1.2	8.6	0.0	8.6	0.0	8.6	0.0	8.6	0.0	8.6	0.0	8.6	0.0	8.6	0.0	8.6	0.0	8.6	0.0	8.6	0.0
1945	8.6	0.0	8.6	0.0	8.6	0.0	8.6	0.0	8.6	0.0	8.7	1.2	8.7	0.0	8.8	1.1	8.7	-1.1	8.7	0.0	8.7	0.0	8.7	0.0
1946	8.8	1.1	8.8	0.0	8.8	0.0	8.9	1.1	8.9	0.0	9.1	2.2	9.3	2.2	9.8	5.4	9.7	-1.0	9.7	0.0	9.8	1.0	9.9	1.0
1947	10.1	2.0	10.2	1.0	10.5	2.9	10.8	2.9	10.8	0.0	10.8	0.0	11.2	3.7	11.4	1.8	11.5	0.9	11.6	0.9	11.9	2.6	12.4	4.2
1948	12.9	4.0	13.0	0.8	13.0	0.0	13.0	0.0	13.0	0.0	13.0	0.0	13.2	1.5	13.1	-0.8	13.1	0.0	13.2	0.8	13.2	0.0	13.1	-0.8
1949	13.1	0.0	12.9	-1.5	12.7	-1.6	12.4	-2.4	12.3	-0.8	12.2	-0.8	12.2	0.0	12.2	0.0	12.2	0.0	12.3	0.8	12.3	0.0	12.3	0.0
1950	12.4	0.8	12.4	0.0	12.4	0.0	12.3	-0.8	12.4	0.8	12.5	0.8	12.6	0.8	12.7	0.8	12.7	0.0	12.8	0.8	12.9	0.8	12.8	-0.8
1951	13.0	1.6	13.1	0.8	13.1	0.0	13.0	-0.8	13.0	0.0	13.0	0.0	13.0	0.0	13.0	0.0	13.0	0.0	13.0	0.0	13.0	0.0	13.1	0.8
1952	13.1	0.0	13.1	0.0	13.1	0.0	13.0	-0.8	12.9	-0.8	12.9	0.0	12.9	0.0	12.9	0.0	13.0	0.8	13.0	0.0	13.0	0.0	13.1	0.8
1953	13.1	0.0	13.2	0.8	13.2	0.0	13.1	-0.8	13.1	0.0	13.2	0.8	13.5	2.3	13.5	0.0	13.5	0.0	13.6	0.7	13.6	0.0	13.5	-0.7
1954	13.5	0.0	13.5	0.0	13.3	-1.5	13.2	-0.8	13.2	0.0	13.1	-0.8	13.0	-0.8	13.0	0.0	13.0	0.0	13.0	0.0	13.1	0.8	13.1	0.0
1955	13.2	0.8	13.3	0.8	13.2	-0.8	13.1	-0.8	13.0	-0.8	13.0	0.0	13.0	0.0	13.1	0.8	13.2	0.8	13.2	0.0	13.2	0.0	13.3	0.8
1956	13.5	1.5	13.6	0.7	13.5	-0.7	13.5	0.0	13.5	0.0	13.5	0.0	13.5	0.0	13.5	0.0	13.5	0.0	13.6	0.7	13.6	0.0	13.9	2.2
1957	14.2	2.2	14.6	2.8	14.5	-0.7	14.6	0.7	14.5	-0.7	14.3	-1.4	14.2	-0.7	14.2	0.0	14.2	0.0	14.1	-0.7	14.1	0.0	14.2	0.7
1958	14.2	0.0	13.8	-2.8	13.7	-0.7	13.5	-1.5	13.4	-0.7	13.5	0.7	13.6	0.7	13.9	2.2	13.9	0.0	13.8	-0.7	13.7	-0.7	13.8	0.7
1959	13.9	0.7	14.0	0.7	14.0	0.0	13.9	-0.7	13.8	-0.7	13.6	-1.4	13.5	-0.7	13.7	1.5	13.6	-0.7	13.6	0.0	13.6	0.0	13.6	0.0
1960	13.6	0.0	13.7	0.7	13.7	0.0	13.7	0.0	13.5	-1.5	13.7	1.5	13.9	1.5	14.1	1.4	14.2	0.7	14.2	0.0	14.2	0.0	14.2	0.0
1961	14.3	0.7	14.4	0.7	14.3	-0.7	14.1	-1.4	13.8	-2.1	13.9	0.7	14.0	0.7	14.0	0.0	14.0	0.0	13.9	-0.7	13.8	-0.7	13.9	0.7	14.0	0.7
1962	14.1	0.7	14.0	-0.7	13.8	-1.4	14.0	1.4	13.9	-0.7	13.9	0.0	13.9	0.0	13.8	-0.7	14.0	1.4	14.0	0.0	14.0	0.0	14.0	0.0
1963	14.0	0.0	14.0	0.0	14.0	0.0	14.0	0.0	14.0	0.0	14.1	0.7	14.0	-0.7	13.8	-1.4	13.8	0.0	13.8	0.0	13.6	-1.4	13.8	1.5
1964	13.8	0.0	13.8	0.0	13.5	-2.2	13.4	-0.7	13.4	0.0	13.4	0.0	13.5	0.7	13.4	-0.7	13.3	-0.7	13.5	1.5	13.6	0.7	13.7	0.7
1965	13.7	0.0	13.6	-0.7	13.6	0.0	13.6	0.0	13.7	0.7	13.7	0.0	13.7	0.0	13.8	0.7	13.8	0.0	13.8	0.0	14.0	1.4	14.0	0.0
1966	14.0	0.0	14.0	0.0	13.9	-0.7	13.9	0.0	14.0	0.7	14.1	0.7	14.1	0.0	14.2	0.7	14.2	0.0	14.3	0.7	14.3	0.0	14.3	0.0
1967	14.3	0.0	14.4	0.7	14.4	0.0	14.4	0.0	14.5	0.7	14.5	0.0	14.5	0.0	14.6	0.7	14.6	0.0	14.4	-1.4	14.3	-0.7	14.3	0.0
1968	14.2	-0.7	14.3	0.7	14.2	-0.7	14.3	0.7	14.3	0.0	14.4	0.7	14.4	0.0	14.3	-0.7	14.3	0.0	14.2	-0.7	14.2	0.0	14.2	0.0
1969	14.2	0.0	14.3	0.7	14.5	1.4	14.5	0.0	14.5	0.0	14.6	0.7	14.6	0.0	14.6	0.0	14.6	0.0	14.7	0.7	14.7	0.0	14.8	0.7
1970	14.7	-0.7	14.8	0.7	14.8	0.0	15.0	1.4	15.1	0.7	15.1	0.0	15.2	0.7	15.3	0.7	15.6	2.0	15.8	1.3	15.9	0.6	16.4	3.1

[Continued]

FUELS AND RELATED PRODUCTS AND POWER
Producer Price Index
Base 1982 = 100
[Continued]

For 1926-2001. Columns headed % show percentile change in the index from the previous period for which an index is available.

Year	Jan Index	%	Feb Index	%	Mar Index	%	Apr Index	%	May Index	%	Jun Index	%	Jul Index	%	Aug Index	%	Sep Index	%	Oct Index	%	Nov Index	%	Dec Index	%
1971	16.5	0.6	16.5	0.0	16.4	-0.6	16.4	0.0	16.6	1.2	16.6	0.0	16.7	0.6	16.8	0.6	16.8	0.0	16.7	-0.6	16.7	0.0	16.9	1.2
1972	16.7	-1.2	16.7	0.0	16.8	0.6	16.9	0.6	16.9	0.0	17.0	0.6	17.1	0.6	17.3	1.2	17.4	0.6	17.4	0.0	17.5	0.6	17.6	0.6
1973	17.6	0.0	18.2	3.4	18.4	1.1	18.6	1.1	18.9	1.6	19.2	1.6	19.4	1.0	19.5	0.5	19.8	1.5	20.1	1.5	20.8	3.5	21.9	5.3
1974	23.4	6.8	25.6	9.4	27.3	6.6	28.5	4.4	29.5	3.5	30.4	3.1	32.0	5.3	32.6	1.9	32.5	-0.3	33.0	1.5	32.8	-0.6	33.0	0.6
1975	33.5	1.5	33.5	0.0	33.6	0.3	34.1	1.5	34.4	0.9	35.0	1.7	35.6	1.7	36.4	2.2	36.8	1.1	37.0	0.5	37.1	0.3	37.2	0.3
1976	37.1	-0.3	36.9	-0.5	36.9	0.0	37.1	0.5	37.1	0.0	37.6	1.3	38.3	1.9	38.8	1.3	39.1	0.8	40.0	2.3	40.6	1.5	40.3	-0.7
1977	40.2	-0.2	41.7	3.7	42.4	1.7	43.1	1.7	43.6	1.2	43.9	0.7	44.3	0.9	44.7	0.9	44.7	0.0	44.8	0.2	44.8	0.0	45.0	0.4
1978	45.1	0.2	45.1	0.0	45.5	0.9	45.8	0.7	46.1	0.7	46.6	1.1	46.8	0.4	46.9	0.2	47.1	0.4	47.4	0.6	47.6	0.4	48.2	1.3
1979	48.8	1.2	49.4	1.2	50.6	2.4	52.2	3.2	54.5	4.4	56.8	4.2	59.4	4.6	62.4	5.1	65.6	5.1	67.6	3.0	68.8	1.8	70.4	2.3
1980	73.3	4.1	76.8	4.8	79.9	4.0	81.7	2.3	82.5	1.0	83.2	0.8	84.5	1.6	85.2	0.8	85.6	0.5	85.5	-0.1	86.6	1.3	88.8	2.5
1981	91.5	3.0	96.3	5.2	100.5	4.4	102.0	1.5	102.3	0.3	102.1	-0.2	101.7	-0.4	101.6	-0.1	101.5	-0.1	100.7	-0.8	100.7	0.0	101.3	0.6
1982	101.7	0.4	100.7	-1.0	99.5	-1.2	96.7	-2.8	95.5	-1.2	97.7	2.3	101.1	3.5	101.8	0.7	101.0	-0.8	100.8	-0.2	101.9	1.1	101.5	-0.4
1983	98.6	-2.9	96.5	-2.1	94.9	-1.7	93.0	-2.0	94.0	1.1	96.0	2.1	96.5	0.5	96.9	0.4	97.0	0.1	96.6	-0.4	95.7	-0.9	94.9	-0.8
1984	94.1	-0.8	94.6	0.5	95.0	0.4	94.4	-0.6	95.3	1.0	96.1	0.8	95.9	-0.2	94.9	-1.0	94.1	-0.8	94.4	0.3	94.5	0.1	93.6	-1.0
1985	91.9	-1.8	90.2	-1.8	90.2	0.0	91.4	1.3	93.4	2.2	92.4	-1.1	91.7	-0.8	90.5	-1.3	90.7	0.2	90.6	-0.1	91.6	1.1	92.3	0.8
1986	89.5	-3.0	81.8	-8.6	73.9	-9.7	69.6	-5.8	69.8	0.3	69.9	0.1	64.1	-8.3	63.2	-1.4	65.3	3.3	63.3	-3.1	63.3	0.0	63.4	0.2
1987	66.6	5.0	68.0	2.1	68.3	0.4	69.1	1.2	69.7	0.9	71.1	2.0	72.6	2.1	73.8	1.7	72.2	-2.2	71.1	-1.5	70.8	-0.4	69.5	-1.8
1988	67.2	-3.3	66.7	-0.7	65.9	-1.2	67.6	2.6	68.4	1.2	68.6	0.3	68.0	-0.9	67.6	-0.6	66.1	-2.2	64.5	-2.4	64.4	-0.2	65.6	1.9
1989	68.1	3.8	68.9	1.2	69.9	1.5	74.2	6.2	76.0	2.4	75.8	-0.3	75.5	-0.4	72.0	-4.6	73.9	2.6	73.7	-0.3	72.8	-1.2	73.7	1.2
1990	79.8	8.3	77.0	-3.5	74.6	-3.1	73.4	-1.6	74.1	1.0	72.8	-1.8	72.7	-0.1	82.4	13.3	91.3	10.8	101.0	10.6	97.4	-3.6	90.5	-7.1
1991	90.1	-0.4	83.0	-7.9	78.5	-5.4	78.1	-0.5	80.2	2.7	80.3	0.1	80.1	-0.2	81.3	1.5	81.4	0.1	81.3	-0.1	81.2	-0.1	79.1	-2.6
1992	76.3	-3.5	76.8	0.7	75.8	-1.3	77.1	1.7	79.7	3.4	83.2	4.4	83.3	0.1	82.8	-0.6	84.4	1.9	83.2	-1.4	82.1	-1.3	79.7	-2.9
1993	79.4	-0.4	79.2	-0.3	79.7	0.6	80.3	0.8	81.9	2.0	83.2	1.6	81.0	-2.6	80.2	-1.0	80.9	0.9	81.2	0.4	78.3	-3.6	74.7	-4.6
1994	75.4	0.9	75.4	0.0	76.0	0.8	76.4	0.5	77.2	1.0	79.5	3.0	80.6	1.4	82.0	1.7	79.9	-2.6	77.4	-3.1	77.5	0.1	76.6	-1.2
1995	76.8	0.3	76.8	0.0	76.8	0.0	78.5	2.2	80.0	1.9	81.0	1.3	79.2	-2.2	78.3	-1.1	78.3	0.0	76.8	-1.9	75.9	-1.2	77.9	2.6
1996	80.6	3.5	80.9	0.4	82.0	1.4	86.2	5.1	86.6	0.5	85.2	-1.6	85.9	0.8	86.8	1.0	87.1	0.3	86.8	-0.3	88.5	2.0	93.3	5.4
1997	96.1	3.0	90.3	-6.0	83.4	-7.6	82.2	-1.4	83.4	1.5	84.5	1.3	83.9	-0.7	84.9	1.2	86.5	1.9	86.7	0.2	87.0	0.3	82.8	-4.8
1998	78.6	-5.1	76.6	-2.5	74.6	-2.6	75.8	1.6	77.0	1.6	76.4	-0.8	77.2	1.0	74.8	-3.1	74.3	-0.7	74.2	-0.1	73.2	-1.3	70.4	-3.8
1999	70.1	-0.4	68.6	-2.1	70.0	2.0	75.5	7.9	78.9	4.5	80.1	1.5	82.8	3.4	86.5	4.5	90.2	4.3	86.6	-4.0	89.4	3.2	87.0	-2.7
2000	88.4	1.6	93.1	5.3	96.1	3.2	93.7	-2.5	96.6	3.1	107.4	11.2	107.1	-0.3	105.1	-1.9	112.7	7.2	113.7	0.9	112.0	-1.5	116.5	4.0
2001	131.8	13.1	119.6	-9.3	111.3	-6.9	113.3	1.8	114.5	1.1	109.2	-4.6	100.7	-7.8	101.0	0.3	101.5	0.5	89.1	-12.2	91.1	2.2	82.4	-9.5

Source: U.S. Department of Labor, Bureau of Labor Statistics, Division of Industry Prices and Price Indexes. n.e.c. stands for not elsewhere classified. - indicates no data collected for period or unavailable.

Coal
Producer Price Index
Base 1982 = 100

For 1926-2001. Columns headed % show percentile change in the index from the previous period for which an index is available.

Year	Jan Index	%	Feb Index	%	Mar Index	%	Apr Index	%	May Index	%	Jun Index	%	Jul Index	%	Aug Index	%	Sep Index	%	Oct Index	%	Nov Index	%	Dec Index	%
1926	8.7	-	8.4	-3.4	8.3	-1.2	8.1	-2.4	8.1	0.0	8.1	0.0	8.1	0.0	8.2	1.2	8.3	1.2	8.7	4.8	9.4	8.0	8.9	-5.3
1927	8.7	-2.2	8.5	-2.3	8.4	-1.2	8.3	-1.2	8.3	0.0	8.3	0.0	8.3	0.0	8.4	1.2	8.5	1.2	8.3	-2.4	8.2	-1.2	8.2	0.0
1928	8.1	-1.2	8.1	0.0	8.0	-1.2	7.8	-2.5	7.7	-1.3	7.8	1.3	7.7	-1.3	7.8	1.3	7.8	0.0	7.9	1.3	7.9	0.0	7.8	-1.3
1929	7.9	1.3	7.9	0.0	7.8	-1.3	7.5	-3.8	7.5	0.0	7.5	0.0	7.6	1.3	7.6	0.0	7.7	1.3	7.7	0.0	7.7	0.0	7.8	1.3
1930	7.7	-1.3	7.7	0.0	7.6	-1.3	7.5	-1.3	7.4	-1.3	7.4	0.0	7.4	0.0	7.5	1.4	7.5	0.0	7.6	1.3	7.5	-1.3	7.5	0.0
1931	7.5	0.0	7.4	-1.3	7.3	-1.4	7.2	-1.4	7.2	0.0	7.2	0.0	7.2	0.0	7.3	1.4	7.3	0.0	7.3	0.0	7.3	0.0	7.3	0.0
1932	7.4	1.4	7.3	-1.4	7.2	-1.4	7.1	-1.4	7.0	-1.4	7.0	0.0	7.0	0.0	7.0	0.0	7.0	0.0	7.0	0.0	7.0	0.0	7.0	0.0
1933	7.0	0.0	6.9	-1.4	6.9	0.0	6.7	-2.9	6.6	-1.5	6.6	0.0	6.8	3.0	7.0	2.9	7.1	1.4	7.4	4.2	7.5	1.4	7.5	0.0
1934	7.5	0.0	7.5	0.0	7.5	0.0	7.6	1.3	7.6	0.0	7.6	0.0	7.7	1.3	7.8	1.3	7.8	0.0	7.8	0.0	7.8	0.0	7.8	0.0
1935	7.8	0.0	7.8	0.0	7.8	0.0	7.6	-2.6	7.6	0.0	7.6	0.0	7.7	1.3	7.7	0.0	7.8	1.3	7.9	1.3	8.0	1.3	8.0	0.0
1936	8.0	0.0	8.1	1.3	8.0	-1.2	7.8	-2.5	7.7	-1.3	7.7	0.0	7.7	0.0	7.8	1.3	7.8	0.0	7.9	1.3	7.9	0.0	7.9	0.0
1937	7.9	0.0	7.9	0.0	7.8	-1.3	7.7	-1.3	7.8	1.3	7.8	0.0	7.8	0.0	7.9	1.3	7.9	0.0	7.9	0.0	7.9	0.0	8.1	2.5
1938	8.2	1.2	8.2	0.0	7.9	-3.7	7.8	-1.3	7.7	-1.3	7.7	0.0	7.8	1.3	7.8	0.0	7.9	1.3	7.9	0.0	7.9	0.0	7.9	0.0
1939	7.9	0.0	7.9	0.0	7.9	0.0	7.8	-1.3	7.8	0.0	7.6	-2.6	7.6	0.0	7.6	0.0	7.6	0.0	7.8	2.6	7.8	0.0	7.8	0.0
1940	7.9	1.3	7.9	0.0	7.8	-1.3	7.7	-1.3	7.6	-1.3	7.7	1.3	7.7	0.0	7.7	0.0	7.8	1.3	8.0	2.6	8.0	0.0	8.1	1.3
1941	8.1	0.0	8.1	0.0	8.0	-1.2	8.0	0.0	8.2	2.5	8.3	1.2	8.4	1.2	8.5	1.2	8.6	1.2	8.6	0.0	8.6	0.0	8.6	0.0
1942	8.7	1.2	8.7	0.0	8.7	0.0	8.6	-1.1	8.7	1.2	8.7	0.0	8.7	0.0	8.8	1.1	8.8	0.0	8.8	0.0	8.8	0.0	8.9	1.1
1943	9.0	1.1	9.1	1.1	9.2	1.1	9.2	0.0	9.2	0.0	9.2	0.0	9.3	1.1	9.3	0.0	9.3	0.0	9.3	0.0	9.3	0.0	9.5	2.2
1944	9.6	1.1	9.6	0.0	9.6	0.0	9.6	0.0	9.6	0.0	9.6	0.0	9.6	0.0	9.6	0.0	9.6	0.0	9.6	0.0	9.6	0.0	9.6	0.0
1945	9.6	0.0	9.6	0.0	9.6	0.0	9.6	0.0	9.8	2.1	9.9	1.0	10.0	1.0	10.0	0.0	10.0	0.0	10.0	0.0	10.0	0.0	10.1	1.0
1946	10.1	0.0	10.1	0.0	10.1	0.0	10.1	0.0	10.1	0.0	10.6	5.0	11.0	3.8	11.1	0.9	11.1	0.0	11.1	0.0	11.1	0.0	11.2	0.9
1947	11.5	2.7	11.5	0.0	11.5	0.0	11.6	0.9	11.6	0.0	11.6	0.0	13.5	16.4	14.3	5.9	14.4	0.7	14.5	0.7	14.5	0.0	14.6	0.7
1948	14.7	0.7	14.7	0.0	14.7	0.0	14.8	0.7	15.0	1.4	15.1	0.7	16.3	7.9	16.4	0.6	16.4	0.0	16.3	-0.6	16.3	0.0	16.3	0.0
1949	16.3	0.0	16.2	-0.6	16.0	-1.2	15.4	-3.8	15.2	-1.3	15.2	0.0	15.3	0.7	15.3	0.0	15.3	0.0	15.3	0.0	15.5	1.3	15.6	0.6
1950	15.7	0.6	15.8	0.6	16.0	1.3	15.5	-3.1	15.4	-0.6	15.4	0.0	15.4	0.0	15.5	0.6	15.6	0.6	15.6	0.0	15.6	0.0	15.6	0.0
1951	15.6	0.0	16.2	3.8	16.2	0.0	15.9	-1.9	15.8	-0.6	15.9	0.6	15.7	-1.3	15.8	0.6	15.9	0.6	16.0	0.6	16.0	0.0	16.0	0.0
1952	16.0	0.0	16.0	0.0	16.0	0.0	15.4	-3.8	15.4	0.0	15.5	0.6	15.6	0.6	15.6	0.0	15.8	1.3	16.6	5.1	16.7	0.6	17.0	1.8
1953	17.1	0.6	17.0	-0.6	16.8	-1.2	16.3	-3.0	16.3	0.0	16.3	0.0	16.4	0.6	16.4	0.0	16.5	0.6	16.5	0.0	16.5	0.0	16.5	0.0
1954	16.4	-0.6	16.3	-0.6	15.8	-3.1	15.3	-3.2	15.4	0.7	15.4	0.0	15.4	0.0	15.4	0.0	15.5	0.6	15.4	-0.6	15.4	0.0	15.4	0.0
1955	15.4	0.0	15.4	0.0	15.4	0.0	15.0	-2.6	14.7	-2.0	14.8	0.7	14.9	0.7	15.0	0.7	15.9	6.0	16.0	0.6	16.0	0.0	16.1	0.6
1956	16.1	0.0	16.1	0.0	16.2	0.6	16.4	1.2	16.4	0.0	16.5	0.6	16.6	0.6	16.7	0.6	16.8	0.6	17.8	6.0	17.9	0.6	18.1	1.1
1957	18.2	0.6	18.2	0.0	18.1	-0.5	18.1	0.0	18.1	0.0	18.1	0.0	18.2	0.6	18.3	0.5	18.3	0.0	18.4	0.5	18.5	0.5	18.5	0.0
1958	18.5	0.0	18.5	0.0	18.5	0.0	17.6	-4.9	17.6	0.0	17.7	0.6	17.8	0.6	17.9	0.6	18.0	0.6	18.2	1.1	18.2	0.0	18.2	0.0
1959	18.4	1.1	18.5	0.5	18.3	-1.1	17.5	-4.4	17.4	-0.6	17.6	1.1	17.8	1.1	17.9	0.6	18.0	0.6	18.1	0.6	18.2	0.6	18.2	0.0
1960	18.2	0.0	18.2	0.0	18.2	0.0	17.5	-3.8	17.4	-0.6	17.5	0.6	17.7	1.1	17.8	0.6	18.0	1.1	18.0	0.0	18.0	0.0	18.1	0.6
1961	18.1	0.0	18.1	0.0	18.0	-0.6	17.6	-2.2	17.2	-2.3	17.3	0.6	17.4	0.6	17.5	0.6	17.6	0.6	17.7	0.6	17.8	0.6	17.9	0.6
1962	17.9	0.0	17.9	0.0	17.9	0.0	17.3	-3.4	17.1	-1.2	17.1	0.0	17.3	1.2	17.3	0.0	17.5	1.2	17.6	0.6	17.7	0.6	17.8	0.6
1963	17.8	0.0	17.8	0.0	17.8	0.0	17.2	-3.4	17.1	-0.6	17.2	0.6	17.3	0.6	17.4	0.6	17.6	1.1	17.7	0.6	17.8	0.6	17.8	0.0
1964	17.8	0.0	17.8	0.0	17.6	-1.1	17.2	-2.3	17.2	0.0	17.3	0.6	17.4	0.6	17.5	0.6	17.6	0.6	17.7	0.6	17.7	0.0	17.8	0.6
1965	17.8	0.0	17.8	0.0	17.6	-1.1	17.1	-2.8	17.1	0.0	17.1	0.0	17.2	0.6	17.3	0.6	17.5	1.2	17.6	0.6	17.7	0.6	17.7	0.0
1966	17.8	0.6	17.8	0.0	17.7	-0.6	17.2	-2.8	17.5	1.7	17.6	0.6	17.7	0.6	17.8	0.6	18.0	1.1	18.2	1.1	18.4	1.1	18.5	0.5
1967	18.5	0.0	18.5	0.0	18.5	0.0	18.6	0.5	18.6	0.0	18.6	0.0	18.6	0.0	18.8	1.1	18.8	0.0	18.9	0.5	19.0	0.5	19.0	0.0
1968	19.0	0.0	19.0	0.0	19.1	0.5	19.2	0.5	19.1	-0.5	19.1	0.0	19.2	0.5	19.2	0.0	19.2	0.0	19.9	3.6	20.2	1.5	20.4	1.0
1969	20.4	0.0	20.4	0.0	20.4	0.0	20.6	1.0	20.5	-0.5	20.7	1.0	20.9	1.0	20.9	0.0	21.0	0.5	22.0	4.8	22.4	1.8	22.5	0.4
1970	22.7	0.9	23.8	4.8	24.1	1.3	26.4	9.5	26.6	0.8	27.8	4.5	28.4	2.2	28.8	1.4	30.1	4.5	32.8	9.0	32.9	0.3	32.9	0.0

[Continued]

Coal
Producer Price Index
Base 1982 = 100

[Continued]

For 1926-2001. Columns headed % show percentile change in the index from the previous period for which an index is available.

Year	Jan Index	%	Feb Index	%	Mar Index	%	Apr Index	%	May Index	%	Jun Index	%	Jul Index	%	Aug Index	%	Sep Index	%	Oct Index	%	Nov Index	%	Dec Index	%
1971	32.9	0.0	32.9	0.0	32.9	0.0	34.4	4.6	34.2	-0.6	34.1	-0.3	34.2	0.3	34.2	0.0	34.2	0.0	34.2	0.0	34.2	0.0	36.0	5.3
1972	36.0	0.0	36.0	0.0	36.0	0.0	35.8	-0.6	35.8	0.0	35.8	0.0	35.8	0.0	35.8	0.0	35.9	0.3	36.0	0.3	37.6	4.4	38.4	2.1
1973	38.4	0.0	38.7	0.8	38.8	0.3	40.0	3.1	40.1	0.2	40.2	0.2	40.0	-0.5	40.1	0.2	41.6	3.7	41.9	0.7	44.7	6.7	45.0	0.7
1974	46.6	3.6	47.3	1.5	48.5	2.5	56.8	17.1	57.6	1.4	60.1	4.3	64.3	7.0	66.9	4.0	69.5	3.9	73.7	6.0	74.4	0.9	80.1	7.7
1975	80.2	0.1	76.6	-4.5	72.6	-5.2	72.4	-0.3	72.8	0.6	72.2	-0.8	71.5	-1.0	70.7	-1.1	69.8	-1.3	69.4	-0.6	68.2	-1.7	69.4	1.8
1976	69.2	-0.3	69.0	-0.3	68.8	-0.3	68.7	-0.1	68.7	0.0	68.6	-0.1	68.8	0.3	68.8	0.0	68.8	0.0	68.9	0.1	69.0	0.1	69.9	1.3
1977	70.3	0.6	70.6	0.4	70.8	0.3	71.0	0.3	72.3	1.8	73.0	1.0	73.5	0.7	73.7	0.3	73.9	0.3	74.5	0.8	74.9	0.5	75.2	0.4
1978	75.5	0.4	75.7	0.3	76.1	0.5	79.7	4.7	80.9	1.5	81.3	0.5	81.7	0.5	82.6	1.1	82.8	0.2	83.0	0.2	82.7	-0.4	83.0	0.4
1979	83.0	0.0	83.0	0.0	83.3	0.4	83.6	0.4	84.3	0.8	84.5	0.2	84.6	0.1	84.9	0.4	84.6	-0.4	85.0	0.5	85.1	0.1	85.8	0.8
1980	85.9	0.1	86.0	0.1	86.3	0.3	87.0	0.8	87.2	0.2	87.2	0.0	87.4	0.2	87.6	0.2	88.1	0.6	88.0	-0.1	88.9	1.0	88.9	0.0
1981	89.4	0.6	89.9	0.6	90.0	0.1	90.9	1.0	91.1	0.2	91.9	0.9	94.5	2.8	94.8	0.3	95.4	0.6	95.5	0.1	95.9	0.4	96.4	0.5
1982	98.2	1.9	99.1	0.9	99.0	-0.1	99.6	0.6	99.9	0.3	99.8	-0.1	100.6	0.8	100.8	0.2	100.7	-0.1	100.6	-0.1	100.9	0.3	100.7	-0.2
1983	100.2	-0.5	99.7	-0.5	100.7	1.0	100.6	-0.1	100.1	-0.5	99.9	-0.2	100.0	0.1	100.3	0.3	100.6	0.3	100.7	0.1	101.4	0.7	101.7	0.3
1984	101.2	-0.5	101.9	0.7	102.1	0.2	101.4	-0.7	102.4	1.0	101.8	-0.6	102.5	0.7	102.9	0.4	102.7	-0.2	102.7	0.0	102.6	-0.1	102.4	-0.2
1985	102.5	0.1	102.8	0.3	102.6	-0.2	102.4	-0.2	102.5	0.1	102.4	-0.1	102.8	0.4	102.9	0.1	102.6	-0.3	101.7	-0.9	100.6	-1.1	101.1	0.5
1986	101.3	0.2	100.9	-0.4	101.5	0.6	101.1	-0.4	100.9	-0.2	100.8	-0.1	100.9	0.1	100.7	-0.2	100.5	-0.2	100.5	0.0	100.1	-0.4	100.0	-0.1
1987	100.1	0.1	99.3	-0.8	99.0	-0.3	97.2	-1.8	96.8	-0.4	96.5	-0.3	96.1	-0.4	96.1	0.0	95.8	-0.3	96.0	0.2	96.4	0.4	95.9	-0.5
1988	95.6	-0.3	96.3	0.7	95.8	-0.5	95.5	-0.3	95.2	-0.3	95.2	0.0	95.7	0.5	95.1	-0.6	95.4	0.3	95.5	0.1	94.7	-0.8	94.6	-0.1
1989	94.1	-0.5	93.6	-0.5	93.6	0.0	94.2	0.6	94.6	0.4	94.9	0.3	96.2	1.4	96.6	0.4	96.5	-0.1	97.1	0.6	97.7	0.6	97.2	-0.5
1990	97.8	0.6	96.3	-1.5	96.4	0.1	96.7	0.3	97.7	1.0	97.9	0.2	98.0	0.1	96.9	-1.1	97.5	0.6	98.2	0.7	98.8	0.6	97.9	-0.9
1991	98.5	0.6	98.2	-0.3	97.4	-0.8	97.3	-0.1	97.1	-0.2	98.0	0.9	97.6	-0.4	96.6	-1.0	96.6	0.0	95.9	-0.7	97.1	1.3	96.3	-0.8
1992	93.7	-2.7	94.5	0.9	93.8	-0.7	94.8	1.1	95.0	0.2	96.0	1.1	95.3	-0.7	95.1	-0.2	95.1	0.0	95.7	0.6	94.8	-0.9	96.5	1.8
1993	95.6	-0.9	94.9	-0.7	94.9	0.0	94.6	-0.3	94.1	-0.5	94.1	0.0	94.4	0.3	95.5	1.2	97.8	2.4	100.3	2.6	99.5	-0.8	97.5	-2.0
1994	97.3	-0.2	96.1	-1.2	96.2	0.1	96.5	0.3	96.8	0.3	95.5	-1.3	95.6	0.1	96.2	0.6	97.8	1.7	98.4	0.6	98.3	-0.1	95.5	-2.8
1995	91.9	-3.8	94.6	2.9	96.9	2.4	95.9	-1.0	93.9	-2.1	94.3	0.4	96.0	1.8	95.3	-0.7	95.2	-0.1	96.4	1.3	94.8	-1.7	94.7	-0.1
1996	92.1	-2.7	95.3	3.5	95.7	0.4	94.3	-1.5	97.0	2.9	95.0	-2.1	93.3	-1.8	96.4	3.3	93.6	-2.9	93.3	-0.3	94.6	1.4	93.7	-1.0
1997	97.3	3.8	94.6	-2.8	96.7	2.2	100.3	3.7	95.2	-5.1	96.9	1.8	94.9	-2.1	95.4	0.5	96.2	0.8	95.0	-1.2	94.3	-0.7	96.2	2.0
1998	91.7	-4.7	94.5	3.1	93.5	-1.1	95.2	1.8	94.5	-0.7	94.7	0.2	94.3	-0.4	90.7	-3.8	90.1	-0.7	92.8	3.0	94.2	1.5	97.1	3.1
1999	88.2	-9.2	93.4	5.9	93.6	0.2	94.5	1.0	91.4	-3.3	92.2	0.9	90.4	-2.0	90.2	-0.2	88.6	-1.8	88.8	0.2	89.2	0.5	88.1	-1.2
2000	88.5	0.5	87.3	-1.4	87.9	0.7	90.0	2.4	90.0	0.0	88.8	-1.3	89.4	0.7	86.0	-3.8	86.3	0.3	86.3	0.0	86.8	0.6	88.1	1.5
2001	87.2	-1.0	95.6	9.6	94.7	-0.9	96.3	1.7	100.3	4.2	94.1	-6.2	98.0	4.1	96.4	-1.6	96.6	0.2	97.1	0.5	101.7	4.7	96.1	-5.5

Source: U.S. Department of Labor, Bureau of Labor Statistics, Division of Industry Prices and Price Indexes. n.e.c. stands for not elsewhere classified. - indicates no data collected for period or unavailable.

Coke Oven Products
Producer Price Index
Base 1982 = 100

For 1926-2001. Columns headed % show percentile change in the index from the previous period for which an index is available.

Year	Jan Index	%	Feb Index	%	Mar Index	%	Apr Index	%	May Index	%	Jun Index	%	Jul Index	%	Aug Index	%	Sep Index	%	Oct Index	%	Nov Index	%	Dec Index	%
1926	6.8	-	6.8	0.0	6.1	-10.3	5.6	-8.2	5.5	-1.8	5.6	1.8	5.6	0.0	5.6	0.0	5.7	1.8	5.7	0.0	6.3	10.5	6.1	-3.2
1927	5.8	-4.9	5.7	-1.7	5.7	0.0	5.7	0.0	5.6	-1.8	5.6	0.0	5.6	0.0	5.6	0.0	5.6	0.0	5.6	0.0	5.5	-1.8	5.5	0.0
1928	5.1	-7.3	5.0	-2.0	5.0	0.0	4.9	-2.0	5.0	2.0	5.0	0.0	5.0	0.0	5.0	0.0	5.0	0.0	5.0	0.0	5.0	0.0	5.0	0.0
1929	5.0	0.0	5.0	0.0	5.1	2.0	5.0	-2.0	5.0	0.0	5.0	0.0	5.0	0.0	5.0	0.0	5.0	0.0	5.0	0.0	5.0	0.0	5.0	0.0
1930	5.0	0.0	5.0	0.0	5.0	0.0	5.0	0.0	5.0	0.0	5.0	0.0	5.0	0.0	5.0	0.0	5.0	0.0	5.0	0.0	5.0	0.0	5.0	0.0
1931	5.0	0.0	5.0	0.0	5.0	0.0	5.0	0.0	5.0	0.0	4.9	-2.0	4.9	0.0	4.9	0.0	4.9	0.0	4.9	0.0	4.8	-2.0	4.8	0.0
1932	4.8	0.0	4.8	0.0	4.8	0.0	4.7	-2.1	4.6	-2.1	4.6	0.0	4.5	-2.2	4.6	2.2	4.6	0.0	4.6	0.0	4.5	-2.2	4.5	0.0
1933	4.5	0.0	4.5	0.0	4.5	0.0	4.5	0.0	4.5	0.0	4.5	0.0	4.5	0.0	4.6	2.2	4.7	2.2	4.9	4.3	5.0	2.0	5.0	0.0
1934	5.0	0.0	5.0	0.0	5.0	0.0	5.0	0.0	5.0	0.0	5.0	0.0	5.1	2.0	5.1	0.0	5.1	0.0	5.1	0.0	5.1	0.0	5.1	0.0
1935	5.1	0.0	5.3	3.9	5.3	0.0	5.3	0.0	5.3	0.0	5.3	0.0	5.3	0.0	5.3	0.0	5.3	0.0	5.3	0.0	5.3	0.0	5.3	0.0
1936	5.5	3.8	5.6	1.8	5.6	0.0	5.6	0.0	5.6	0.0	5.6	0.0	5.6	0.0	5.6	0.0	5.6	0.0	5.8	3.6	5.8	0.0	5.8	0.0
1937	5.8	0.0	5.8	0.0	5.8	0.0	6.1	5.2	6.2	1.6	6.2	0.0	6.2	0.0	6.2	0.0	6.2	0.0	6.2	0.0	6.3	1.6	6.3	0.0
1938	6.3	0.0	6.3	0.0	6.3	0.0	6.3	0.0	6.3	0.0	6.2	-1.6	6.2	0.0	6.2	0.0	6.2	0.0	6.2	0.0	6.2	0.0	6.2	0.0
1939	6.2	0.0	6.2	0.0	6.2	0.0	6.2	0.0	6.2	0.0	6.2	0.0	6.2	0.0	6.2	0.0	6.2	0.0	6.4	3.2	6.6	3.1	6.5	-1.5
1940	6.5	0.0	6.5	0.0	6.5	0.0	6.5	0.0	6.5	0.0	6.5	0.0	6.5	0.0	6.5	0.0	6.5	0.0	6.5	0.0	6.7	3.1	6.8	1.5
1941	6.8	0.0	6.8	0.0	6.8	0.0	6.8	0.0	7.1	4.4	7.3	2.8	7.3	0.0	7.3	0.0	7.3	0.0	7.3	0.0	7.3	0.0	7.3	0.0
1942	7.3	0.0	7.3	0.0	7.3	0.0	7.3	0.0	7.3	0.0	7.3	0.0	7.3	0.0	7.3	0.0	7.3	0.0	7.3	0.0	7.3	0.0	7.3	0.0
1943	7.3	0.0	7.3	0.0	7.3	0.0	7.3	0.0	7.3	0.0	7.3	0.0	7.3	0.0	7.3	0.0	7.3	0.0	7.3	0.0	7.4	1.4	7.4	0.0
1944	7.5	1.4	7.8	4.0	7.8	0.0	7.8	0.0	7.8	0.0	7.8	0.0	7.8	0.0	7.8	0.0	7.8	0.0	7.8	0.0	7.8	0.0	7.8	0.0
1945	7.8	0.0	7.8	0.0	7.8	0.0	7.8	0.0	7.8	0.0	7.8	0.0	7.8	0.0	8.0	2.6	8.0	0.0	8.0	0.0	8.0	0.0	8.0	0.0
1946	8.0	0.0	8.0	0.0	8.0	0.0	7.9	-1.2	7.9	0.0	7.9	0.0	8.8	11.4	8.8	0.0	8.8	0.0	8.8	0.0	8.8	0.0	8.8	0.0
1947	9.1	3.4	9.2	1.1	9.2	0.0	9.3	1.1	9.3	0.0	9.4	1.1	9.6	2.1	10.4	8.3	10.7	2.9	10.7	0.0	10.8	0.9	10.9	0.9
1948	11.3	3.7	11.4	0.9	11.4	0.0	11.5	0.9	12.1	5.2	12.4	2.5	12.6	1.6	12.9	2.4	12.9	0.0	12.9	0.0	12.9	0.0	12.9	0.0
1949	13.1	1.6	13.2	0.8	13.2	0.0	13.2	0.0	13.1	-0.8	13.1	0.0	13.1	0.0	13.1	0.0	13.1	0.0	13.1	0.0	13.1	0.0	13.1	0.0
1950	13.1	0.0	13.3	1.5	13.5	1.5	13.6	0.7	13.6	0.0	13.6	0.0	13.6	0.0	13.6	0.0	13.6	0.0	13.8	1.5	14.2	2.9	14.3	0.7
1951	14.5	1.4	14.5	0.0	14.5	0.0	14.6	0.7	14.6	0.0	14.6	0.0	14.6	0.0	14.6	0.0	14.6	0.0	14.6	0.0	14.6	0.0	14.6	0.0
1952	14.6	0.0	14.6	0.0	14.6	0.0	14.6	0.0	14.6	0.0	14.6	0.0	14.6	0.0	14.6	0.0	14.6	0.0	14.6	0.0	14.6	0.0	15.2	4.1
1953	15.5	2.0	15.5	0.0	15.5	0.0	15.5	0.0	15.5	0.0	15.5	0.0	15.5	0.0	15.5	0.0	15.5	0.0	15.6	0.6	15.6	0.0	15.6	0.0
1954	15.6	0.0	15.6	0.0	15.6	0.0	15.6	0.0	15.6	0.0	15.6	0.0	15.6	0.0	15.6	0.0	15.6	0.0	15.6	0.0	15.6	0.0	15.6	0.0
1955	15.6	0.0	15.6	0.0	15.6	0.0	15.7	0.6	15.7	0.0	15.7	0.0	15.7	0.0	16.2	3.2	16.1	-0.6	16.3	1.2	16.3	0.0	16.3	0.0
1956	17.1	4.9	17.1	0.0	17.1	0.0	17.1	0.0	17.1	0.0	17.1	0.0	17.1	0.0	18.0	5.3	18.4	2.2	18.4	0.0	18.4	0.0	18.4	0.0
1957	18.7	1.6	19.1	2.1	19.0	-0.5	19.0	0.0	19.0	0.0	19.0	0.0	19.0	0.0	19.0	0.0	19.0	0.0	19.0	0.0	19.0	0.0	19.0	0.0
1958	19.0	0.0	19.0	0.0	19.0	0.0	19.0	0.0	19.0	0.0	19.0	0.0	19.0	0.0	19.0	0.0	19.0	0.0	19.0	0.0	19.0	0.0	19.0	0.0
1959	19.2	1.1	20.0	4.2	20.0	0.0	20.0	0.0	20.0	0.0	20.0	0.0	20.0	0.0	20.0	0.0	20.0	0.0	20.0	0.0	20.0	0.0	20.0	0.0
1960	20.0	0.0	20.0	0.0	20.0	0.0	20.0	0.0	20.0	0.0	20.0	0.0	20.0	0.0	20.0	0.0	20.0	0.0	20.0	0.0	20.0	0.0	20.0	0.0
1961	20.0	0.0	20.0	0.0	20.0	0.0	20.0	0.0	20.0	0.0	20.0	0.0	20.0	0.0	20.0	0.0	20.0	0.0	20.0	0.0	20.0	0.0	20.0	0.0
1962	20.0	0.0	20.0	0.0	20.0	0.0	20.0	0.0	20.0	0.0	20.0	0.0	20.0	0.0	20.0	0.0	20.0	0.0	20.0	0.0	20.0	0.0	20.0	0.0
1963	20.0	0.0	20.0	0.0	20.0	0.0	20.0	0.0	20.0	0.0	20.0	0.0	20.0	0.0	20.0	0.0	20.0	0.0	20.0	0.0	20.0	0.0	20.0	0.0
1964	20.0	0.0	20.0	0.0	20.0	0.0	20.5	2.5	20.8	1.5	20.8	0.0	20.8	0.0	20.8	0.0	20.8	0.0	20.8	0.0	20.8	0.0	20.8	0.0
1965	20.8	0.0	20.8	0.0	20.8	0.0	20.8	0.0	20.8	0.0	20.8	0.0	20.8	0.0	20.8	0.0	20.8	0.0	20.8	0.0	20.8	0.0	20.8	0.0
1966	20.8	0.0	20.8	0.0	20.8	0.0	20.8	0.0	20.8	0.0	21.2	1.9	21.7	2.4	21.7	0.0	21.7	0.0	21.7	0.0	21.7	0.0	21.7	0.0
1967	21.7	0.0	21.7	0.0	21.7	0.0	21.7	0.0	21.7	0.0	21.7	0.0	21.7	0.0	21.7	0.0	21.7	0.0	21.7	0.0	21.7	0.0	21.7	0.0
1968	21.7	0.0	21.7	0.0	21.7	0.0	22.6	4.1	22.6	0.0	22.6	0.0	22.6	0.0	22.6	0.0	22.6	0.0	22.6	0.0	22.6	0.0	23.3	3.1
1969	23.3	0.0	23.3	0.0	23.3	0.0	23.3	0.0	23.3	0.0	23.3	0.0	23.3	0.0	23.3	0.0	23.3	0.0	24.5	5.2	24.5	0.0	24.5	0.0
1970	24.5	0.0	24.5	0.0	24.5	0.0	27.0	10.2	27.0	0.0	27.0	0.0	27.3	1.1	27.3	0.0	27.3	0.0	31.6	15.8	31.6	0.0	31.6	0.0

[Continued]

Coke Oven Products
Producer Price Index
Base 1982 = 100
[Continued]

For 1926-2001. Columns headed % show percentile change in the index from the previous period for which an index is available.

Year	Jan Index	%	Feb Index	%	Mar Index	%	Apr Index	%	May Index	%	Jun Index	%	Jul Index	%	Aug Index	%	Sep Index	%	Oct Index	%	Nov Index	%	Dec Index	%
1971	31.6	0.0	31.6	0.0	31.6	0.0	31.6	0.0	32.2	1.9	32.6	1.2	32.6	0.0	32.6	0.0	32.6	0.0	32.6	0.0	32.6	0.0	32.6	0.0
1972	32.6	0.0	33.6	3.1	33.6	0.0	33.6	0.0	33.6	0.0	33.6	0.0	33.6	0.0	33.6	0.0	33.6	0.0	34.0	1.2	34.0	0.0	34.6	1.8
1973	35.2	1.7	35.7	1.4	35.7	0.0	36.2	1.4	36.2	0.0	36.2	0.0	36.2	0.0	36.2	0.0	36.2	0.0	36.2	0.0	36.2	0.0	36.8	1.7
1974	37.7	2.4	37.6	-0.3	40.1	6.6	46.6	16.2	52.4	12.4	53.9	2.9	55.4	2.8	58.5	5.6	60.8	3.9	66.1	8.7	67.2	1.7	67.6	0.6
1975	71.6	5.9	71.6	0.0	71.6	0.0	72.0	0.6	72.0	0.0	72.0	0.0	71.4	-0.8	71.1	-0.4	71.7	0.8	71.7	0.0	71.7	0.0	71.7	0.0
1976	71.6	-0.1	74.9	4.6	75.0	0.1	75.0	0.0	75.0	0.0	75.0	0.0	75.0	0.0	75.0	0.0	75.0	0.0	75.8	1.1	75.8	0.0	78.7	3.8
1977	79.6	1.1	79.6	0.0	79.6	0.0	80.8	1.5	81.3	0.6	83.6	2.8	83.6	0.0	83.6	0.0	83.6	0.0	83.6	0.0	83.6	0.0	83.6	0.0
1978	84.1	0.6	86.8	3.2	86.8	0.0	86.8	0.0	90.7	4.5	90.7	0.0	90.7	0.0	90.7	0.0	90.7	0.0	90.7	0.0	90.7	0.0	90.7	0.0
1979	91.2	0.6	91.8	0.7	92.8	1.1	93.2	0.4	93.3	0.1	93.3	0.0	93.3	0.0	93.3	0.0	93.3	0.0	93.4	0.1	93.4	0.0	93.4	0.0
1980	93.3	-0.1	93.3	0.0	93.3	0.0	93.3	0.0	93.3	0.0	93.3	0.0	93.3	0.0	93.3	0.0	93.3	0.0	93.3	0.0	93.3	0.0	93.2	-0.1
1981	93.2	0.0	93.2	0.0	93.2	0.0	93.2	0.0	101.3	8.7	101.7	0.4	101.7	0.0	101.7	0.0	101.7	0.0	101.7	0.0	101.7	0.0	101.7	0.0
1982	101.7	0.0	101.7	0.0	101.3	-0.4	101.3	0.0	101.3	0.0	100.1	-1.2	99.7	-0.4	99.4	-0.3	99.6	0.2	98.0	-1.6	98.0	0.0	98.0	0.0
1983	97.7	-0.3	97.7	0.0	96.9	-0.8	96.9	0.0	95.0	-2.0	95.0	0.0	93.5	-1.6	98.3	5.1	98.3	0.0	98.1	-0.2	98.3	0.2	90.0	-8.4
1984	90.6	0.7	94.8	4.6	95.1	0.3	95.9	0.8	95.6	-0.3	95.8	0.2	95.7	-0.1	94.7	-1.0	94.4	-0.3	93.7	-0.7	93.7	0.0	94.2	0.5
1985	95.2	1.1	95.2	0.0	93.8	-1.5	93.2	-0.6	93.0	-0.2	93.0	0.0	92.8	-0.2	92.8	0.0	92.8	0.0	92.5	-0.3	92.5	0.0	91.8	-0.8
1986	90.2	-1.7	90.4	0.2	90.3	-0.1	89.1	-1.3	89.0	-0.1	88.1	-1.0	88.0	-0.1	87.9	-0.1	88.0	0.1	87.4	-0.7	84.0	-3.9	84.0	0.0
1987	81.9	-2.5	80.9	-1.2	82.3	1.7	83.2	1.1	84.0	1.0	82.5	-1.8	82.4	-0.1	82.5	0.1	82.3	-0.2	83.5	1.5	83.5	0.0	84.2	0.8
1988	84.3	0.1	84.6	0.4	85.0	0.5	85.0	0.0	85.0	0.0	85.0	0.0	85.0	0.0	85.0	0.0	85.0	0.0	85.0	0.0	85.0	0.0	85.0	0.0
1989	88.8	4.5	88.9	0.1	89.1	0.2	88.5	-0.7	90.5	2.3	90.4	-0.1	90.6	0.2	90.8	0.2	90.7	-0.1	91.0	0.3	89.8	-1.3	89.8	0.0
1990	90.4	0.7	94.1	4.1	91.1	-3.2	90.9	-0.2	90.7	-0.2	90.9	0.2	90.1	-0.9	91.2	1.2	91.0	-0.2	92.7	1.9	92.3	-0.4	91.7	-0.7
1991	90.7	-1.1	93.7	3.3	94.5	0.9	95.0	0.5	94.6	-0.4	94.6	0.0	94.6	0.0	93.1	-1.6	94.1	1.1	93.9	-0.2	94.2	0.3	93.8	-0.4
1992	94.4	0.6	94.3	-0.1	92.1	-2.3	91.8	-0.3	90.9	-1.0	89.5	-1.5	90.5	1.1	90.3	-0.2	90.1	-0.2	90.1	0.0	91.1	1.1	90.9	-0.2
1993	91.3	0.4	88.6	-3.0	88.7	0.1	88.8	0.1	88.2	-0.7	88.0	-0.2	88.7	0.8	89.8	1.2	90.7	1.0	89.7	-1.1	88.5	-1.3	88.9	0.5
1994	87.9	-1.1	88.3	0.5	88.7	0.5	90.4	1.9	90.1	-0.3	90.1	0.0	90.3	0.2	87.7	-2.9	87.5	-0.2	87.9	0.5	87.3	-0.7	87.0	-0.3
1995	87.9	1.0	91.7	4.3	91.7	0.0	91.5	-0.2	91.9	0.4	92.3	0.4	91.6	-0.8	91.8	0.2	93.0	1.3	93.5	0.5	93.5	0.0	93.8	0.3
1996	94.0	0.2	94.1	0.1	97.5	3.6	97.4	-0.1	97.4	0.0	97.3	-0.1	95.6	-1.7	95.7	0.1	95.4	-0.3	95.5	0.1	95.7	0.2	94.0	-1.8
1997	94.6	0.6	94.5	-0.1	94.8	0.3	94.5	-0.3	94.6	0.1	94.6	0.0	94.2	-0.4	94.6	0.4	94.9	0.3	94.8	-0.1	97.4	2.7	97.4	0.0
1998	97.5	0.1	97.2	-0.3	98.3	1.1	97.7	-0.6	99.3	1.6	99.1	-0.2	98.9	-0.2	99.2	0.3	97.0	-2.2	97.2	0.2	97.4	0.2	97.5	0.1
1999	96.2	-1.3	93.6	-2.7	95.6	2.1	96.2	0.6	96.3	0.1	96.2	-0.1	95.6	-0.6	92.8	-2.9	92.2	-0.6	92.3	0.1	92.4	0.1	92.2	-0.2
2000	88.0	-4.6	85.0	-3.4	84.7	-0.4	88.9	5.0	86.6	-2.6	87.2	0.7	87.2	0.0	87.9	0.8	89.3	1.6	89.2	-0.1	84.5	-5.3	84.3	-0.2
2001	87.8	4.2	86.8	-1.1	89.8	3.5	88.8	-1.1	88.5	-0.3	89.1	0.7	89.1	0.0	89.1	0.0	85.7	-3.8	-	-	85.6	-0.1	86.1	0.6

Source: U.S. Department of Labor, Bureau of Labor Statistics, Division of Industry Prices and Price Indexes. n.e.c. stands for not elsewhere classified. - indicates no data collected for period or unavailable.

Gas Fuels
Producer Price Index
Base 1982 = 100

For 1958-2001. Columns headed % show percentile change in the index from the previous period for which an index is available.

Year	Jan Index	%	Feb Index	%	Mar Index	%	Apr Index	%	May Index	%	Jun Index	%	Jul Index	%	Aug Index	%	Sep Index	%	Oct Index	%	Nov Index	%	Dec Index	%
1958	7.1	-	7.2	1.4	7.1	-1.4	6.9	-2.8	6.9	0.0	6.9	0.0	6.9	0.0	7.2	4.3	7.3	1.4	7.5	2.7	7.5	0.0	7.6	1.3
1959	7.9	3.9	7.9	0.0	8.0	1.3	7.7	-3.8	7.7	0.0	7.5	-2.6	7.5	0.0	7.7	2.7	8.0	3.9	7.8	-2.5	8.0	2.6	8.1	1.3
1960	8.2	1.2	8.1	-1.2	8.2	1.2	8.2	0.0	7.9	-3.7	7.9	0.0	8.1	2.5	8.2	1.2	8.5	3.7	8.5	0.0	8.5	0.0	8.5	0.0
1961	8.5	0.0	8.6	1.2	8.6	0.0	8.3	-3.5	8.4	1.2	8.1	-3.6	8.2	1.2	8.2	0.0	8.2	0.0	8.4	2.4	8.4	0.0	8.4	0.0
1962	8.3	-1.2	8.6	3.6	8.4	-2.3	8.1	-3.6	8.2	1.2	8.0	-2.4	8.4	5.0	8.3	-1.2	8.5	2.4	8.7	2.4	8.6	-1.1	8.7	1.2
1963	8.5	-2.3	9.0	5.9	9.0	0.0	8.7	-3.3	8.5	-2.3	8.5	0.0	8.5	0.0	8.5	0.0	8.6	1.2	8.6	0.0	8.6	0.0	8.8	2.3
1964	8.8	0.0	8.9	1.1	8.7	-2.2	8.5	-2.3	8.2	-3.5	8.2	0.0	8.5	3.7	8.5	0.0	8.4	-1.2	8.5	1.2	8.7	2.4	8.7	0.0
1965	8.6	-1.1	8.7	1.2	8.7	0.0	8.6	-1.1	8.6	0.0	8.7	1.2	8.6	-1.1	8.7	1.2	8.8	1.1	8.9	1.1	8.9	0.0	9.1	2.2
1966	9.0	-1.1	9.1	1.1	9.0	-1.1	9.1	1.1	9.0	-1.1	9.1	1.1	9.0	-1.1	9.1	1.1	9.1	0.0	9.2	1.1	9.2	0.0	9.3	1.1
1967	9.5	2.2	9.5	0.0	9.5	0.0	9.5	0.0	9.5	0.0	9.5	0.0	9.3	-2.1	9.4	1.1	9.4	0.0	9.4	0.0	9.4	0.0	9.4	0.0
1968	9.2	-2.1	9.4	2.2	8.9	-5.3	8.8	-1.1	8.7	-1.1	8.7	0.0	8.5	-2.3	8.5	0.0	8.5	0.0	8.5	0.0	8.5	0.0	8.6	1.2
1969	8.7	1.2	8.8	1.1	8.8	0.0	8.6	-2.3	8.6	0.0	8.6	0.0	8.6	0.0	8.7	1.2	8.7	0.0	9.1	4.6	9.1	0.0	9.3	2.2
1970	9.3	0.0	9.5	2.2	9.6	1.1	9.6	0.0	9.6	0.0	9.7	1.0	9.7	0.0	9.7	0.0	10.1	4.1	10.0	-1.0	10.1	1.0	10.3	2.0
1971	10.2	-1.0	10.3	1.0	10.4	1.0	10.1	-2.9	10.1	0.0	10.1	0.0	10.1	0.0	10.2	1.0	10.3	1.0	10.3	0.0	10.3	0.0	10.4	1.0
1972	10.4	0.0	10.4	0.0	10.5	1.0	10.6	1.0	10.7	0.9	10.6	-0.9	10.7	0.9	10.8	0.9	11.0	1.9	11.1	0.9	11.2	0.9	11.2	0.0
1973	11.2	0.0	11.2	0.0	11.2	0.0	11.3	0.9	11.4	0.9	12.1	6.1	12.1	0.0	12.3	1.7	12.5	1.6	12.6	0.8	12.5	-0.8	13.0	4.0
1974	12.9	-0.8	13.8	7.0	14.0	1.4	14.0	0.0	14.1	0.7	14.3	1.4	17.7	23.8	17.9	1.1	15.7	-12.3	15.8	0.6	16.5	4.4	16.7	1.2
1975	17.1	2.4	17.8	4.1	17.7	-0.6	19.5	10.2	20.6	5.6	20.7	0.5	21.3	2.9	21.4	0.5	21.8	1.9	21.8	0.0	22.2	1.8	23.1	4.1
1976	23.0	-0.4	23.3	1.3	24.0	3.0	25.1	4.6	25.2	0.4	26.0	3.2	26.1	0.4	27.0	3.4	27.3	1.1	31.2	14.3	34.4	10.3	31.8	-7.6
1977	30.4	-4.4	34.3	12.8	35.0	2.0	35.7	2.0	36.8	3.1	36.4	-1.1	36.9	1.4	37.8	2.4	38.2	1.1	38.3	0.3	39.0	1.8	39.8	2.1
1978	39.6	-0.5	39.4	-0.5	40.0	1.5	40.4	1.0	40.4	0.0	40.4	0.0	40.6	0.5	40.1	-1.2	40.7	1.5	40.5	-0.5	40.9	1.0	41.9	2.4
1979	42.4	1.2	43.2	1.9	44.4	2.8	45.0	1.4	47.8	6.2	49.2	2.9	51.7	5.1	54.0	4.4	56.9	5.4	58.4	2.6	60.0	2.7	62.4	4.0
1980	63.9	2.4	67.6	5.8	67.5	-0.1	68.8	1.9	70.2	2.0	70.6	0.6	71.8	1.7	72.8	1.4	74.1	1.8	75.6	2.0	77.8	2.9	79.6	2.3
1981	80.8	1.5	83.1	2.8	83.9	1.0	85.6	2.0	88.0	2.8	90.0	2.3	91.4	1.6	89.5	-2.1	92.1	2.9	91.0	-1.2	92.7	1.9	94.6	2.0
1982	93.1	-1.6	93.1	0.0	93.4	0.3	93.6	0.2	94.4	0.9	96.9	2.6	99.4	2.6	101.3	1.9	104.8	3.5	106.5	1.6	112.2	5.4	111.3	-0.8
1983	108.1	-2.9	108.8	0.6	111.2	2.2	109.0	-2.0	109.0	0.0	108.9	-0.1	108.3	-0.6	108.0	-0.3	108.1	0.1	106.4	-1.6	105.8	-0.6	105.6	-0.2
1984	105.9	0.3	105.4	-0.5	102.8	-2.5	103.9	1.1	104.1	0.2	104.6	0.5	104.7	0.1	105.3	0.6	104.1	-1.1	104.9	0.8	105.0	0.1	104.0	-1.0
1985	101.2	-2.7	100.6	-0.6	98.4	-2.2	98.9	0.5	101.7	2.8	99.7	-2.0	99.0	-0.7	96.7	-2.3	97.2	0.5	97.4	0.2	96.5	-0.9	97.1	0.6
1986	97.5	0.4	94.0	-3.6	94.2	0.2	88.6	-5.9	86.8	-2.0	85.2	-1.8	79.4	-6.8	76.3	-3.9	73.2	-4.1	74.4	1.6	74.9	0.7	73.6	-1.7
1987	73.6	0.0	73.0	-0.8	76.2	4.4	75.5	-0.9	74.4	-1.5	74.0	-0.5	74.1	0.1	74.8	0.9	75.4	0.9	73.1	-3.1	71.6	-2.1	73.8	3.1
1988	73.3	-0.7	71.7	-2.2	72.3	0.8	74.5	3.0	72.0	-3.4	69.8	-3.1	71.1	1.9	68.7	-3.4	69.0	0.4	71.7	3.9	70.5	-1.7	71.7	1.7
1989	75.2	4.9	77.3	2.8	74.0	-4.3	75.2	1.6	77.1	2.5	76.3	-1.0	76.2	-0.1	72.8	-4.5	75.4	3.6	73.7	-2.3	74.2	0.7	76.0	2.4
1990	82.5	8.6	81.8	-0.8	76.8	-6.1	74.3	-3.3	73.9	-0.5	71.8	-2.8	76.4	6.4	71.8	-6.0	76.5	6.5	80.7	5.5	85.9	6.4	88.4	2.9
1991	86.8	-1.8	80.5	-7.3	78.3	-2.7	74.6	-4.7	77.2	3.5	75.0	-2.8	73.2	-2.4	74.2	1.4	71.5	-3.6	74.3	3.9	78.4	5.5	80.6	2.8
1992	76.1	-5.6	73.7	-3.2	70.5	-4.3	70.1	-0.6	71.0	1.3	70.2	-1.1	75.9	8.1	75.3	-0.8	81.0	7.6	78.7	-2.8	86.2	9.5	82.5	-4.3
1993	82.2	-0.4	75.8	-7.8	74.0	-2.4	75.0	1.4	81.3	8.4	85.9	5.7	77.1	-10.2	75.7	-1.8	78.6	3.8	81.1	3.2	77.9	-3.9	77.5	-0.5
1994	82.7	6.7	75.6	-8.6	80.3	6.2	78.0	-2.9	72.7	-6.8	72.4	-0.4	69.1	-4.6	71.7	3.8	69.8	-2.6	66.1	-5.3	65.3	-1.2	70.3	7.7
1995	69.6	-1.0	66.0	-5.2	64.3	-2.6	65.2	1.4	66.0	1.2	67.8	2.7	65.5	-3.4	59.2	-9.6	60.3	1.9	62.7	4.0	65.6	4.6	70.7	7.8
1996	79.7	12.7	89.9	12.8	82.5	-8.2	88.5	7.3	83.8	-5.3	76.8	-8.4	83.2	8.3	85.1	2.3	78.7	-7.5	79.5	1.0	99.8	25.5	132.1	32.4
1997	145.8	10.4	113.9	-21.9	79.5	-30.2	75.7	-4.8	80.0	5.7	84.5	5.6	81.4	-3.7	83.0	2.0	91.3	10.0	102.3	12.0	111.7	9.2	94.2	-15.7
1998	85.5	-9.2	77.9	-8.9	80.0	2.7	81.8	2.3	82.3	0.6	74.9	-9.0	79.3	5.9	73.9	-6.8	64.4	-12.9	70.2	9.0	74.8	6.6	74.9	0.1
1999	66.6	-11.1	65.0	-2.4	61.7	-5.1	67.5	9.4	83.6	23.9	82.3	-1.6	84.8	3.0	97.2	14.6	108.3	11.4	101.7	-6.1	115.2	13.3	92.0	-20.1
2000	97.5	6.0	103.5	6.2	110.2	6.5	116.3	5.5	118.4	1.8	153.1	29.3	159.0	3.9	143.8	-9.6	162.8	13.2	184.5	13.3	172.8	-6.3	231.3	33.9
2001	329.4	42.4	236.1	-28.3	196.7	-16.7	196.5	-0.1	182.0	-7.4	145.3	-20.2	112.6	-22.5	114.1	1.3	98.4	-13.8	76.4	-22.4	114.1	49.3	87.2	-23.6

Source: U.S. Department of Labor, Bureau of Labor Statistics, Division of Industry Prices and Price Indexes. n.e.c. stands for not elsewhere classified. - indicates no data collected for period or unavailable.

Electric Power
Producer Price Index
Base 1982 = 100

For 1958-2001. Columns headed % show percentile change in the index from the previous period for which an index is available.

Year	Jan Index	%	Feb Index	%	Mar Index	%	Apr Index	%	May Index	%	Jun Index	%	Jul Index	%	Aug Index	%	Sep Index	%	Oct Index	%	Nov Index	%	Dec Index	%
1958	24.4	-	24.5	0.4	24.5	0.0	24.4	-0.4	24.4	0.0	24.5	0.4	24.5	0.0	24.6	0.4	24.6	0.0	24.6	0.0	24.6	0.0	24.6	0.0
1959	24.6	0.0	24.6	0.0	24.6	0.0	24.6	0.0	24.6	0.0	24.6	0.0	24.6	0.0	24.6	0.0	24.6	0.0	24.6	0.0	24.6	0.0	24.7	0.4
1960	24.7	0.0	24.9	0.8	24.9	0.0	24.9	0.0	24.8	-0.4	24.9	0.4	24.9	0.0	24.9	0.0	24.9	0.0	24.9	0.0	25.0	0.4	25.0	0.0
1961	25.0	0.0	25.0	0.0	25.0	0.0	25.0	0.0	25.0	0.0	25.0	0.0	25.0	0.0	25.0	0.0	25.0	0.0	25.0	0.0	25.1	0.4	25.0	-0.4
1962	25.0	0.0	25.2	0.8	25.2	0.0	25.2	0.0	25.1	-0.4	25.1	0.0	25.1	0.0	25.1	0.0	25.1	0.0	25.1	0.0	25.1	0.0	25.1	0.0
1963	25.0	-0.4	25.0	0.0	25.0	0.0	25.0	0.0	25.0	0.0	25.0	0.0	24.9	-0.4	24.9	0.0	24.9	0.0	24.8	-0.4	24.7	-0.4	24.7	0.0
1964	24.7	0.0	24.7	0.0	24.3	-1.6	24.7	1.6	24.7	0.0	24.6	-0.4	24.6	0.0	24.8	0.8	24.8	0.0	24.8	0.0	24.8	0.0	24.7	-0.4
1965	24.7	0.0	24.6	-0.4	24.6	0.0	24.6	0.0	24.6	0.0	24.6	0.0	24.6	0.0	24.6	0.0	24.6	0.0	24.6	0.0	24.6	0.0	24.6	0.0
1966	24.5	-0.4	24.5	0.0	24.5	0.0	24.5	0.0	24.5	0.0	24.5	0.0	24.5	0.0	24.5	0.0	24.5	0.0	24.5	0.0	24.5	0.0	24.6	0.4
1967	24.6	0.0	24.6	0.0	24.6	0.0	24.6	0.0	24.6	0.0	24.6	0.0	24.6	0.0	24.6	0.0	24.6	0.0	24.6	0.0	24.6	0.0	24.7	0.4
1968	24.7	0.0	24.7	0.0	24.7	0.0	24.7	0.0	24.7	0.0	24.7	0.0	24.9	0.8	24.9	0.0	24.9	0.0	24.9	0.0	24.9	0.0	24.9	0.0
1969	24.8	-0.4	24.8	0.0	24.9	0.4	24.9	0.0	24.9	0.0	24.9	0.0	24.9	0.0	25.1	0.8	25.3	0.8	25.3	0.0	25.3	0.0	25.3	0.0
1970	25.3	0.0	25.3	0.0	25.3	0.0	25.3	0.0	25.5	0.8	25.6	0.4	26.0	1.6	26.2	0.8	26.6	1.5	26.9	1.1	27.0	0.4	27.4	1.5
1971	27.5	0.4	27.8	1.1	28.1	1.1	28.1	0.0	28.2	0.4	28.4	0.7	28.8	1.4	29.1	1.0	29.1	0.0	29.0	-0.3	29.1	0.3	29.8	2.4
1972	29.2	-2.0	29.5	1.0	29.5	0.0	29.6	0.3	29.8	0.7	29.9	0.3	30.0	0.3	30.0	0.0	30.2	0.7	30.3	0.3	30.2	-0.3	30.2	0.0
1973	30.5	1.0	31.0	1.6	31.2	0.6	31.4	0.6	31.5	0.3	31.6	0.3	31.7	0.3	31.8	0.3	32.2	1.3	32.5	0.9	32.8	0.9	33.4	1.8
1974	33.8	1.2	35.0	3.6	36.6	4.6	37.7	3.0	39.3	4.2	40.5	3.1	41.2	1.7	42.0	1.9	42.8	1.9	43.9	2.6	44.2	0.7	44.4	0.5
1975	45.1	1.6	45.9	1.8	47.0	2.4	47.9	1.9	47.4	-1.0	46.9	-1.1	47.4	1.1	48.0	1.3	48.6	1.2	49.1	1.0	49.0	-0.2	48.6	-0.8
1976	48.8	0.4	49.0	0.4	49.6	1.2	50.3	1.4	50.4	0.2	50.8	0.8	51.7	1.8	52.5	1.5	52.8	0.6	52.4	-0.8	52.6	0.4	52.0	-1.1
1977	52.6	1.2	54.0	2.7	55.0	1.9	56.4	2.5	56.7	0.5	57.6	1.6	58.8	2.1	60.2	2.4	59.7	-0.8	59.6	-0.2	58.5	-1.8	58.3	-0.3
1978	58.9	1.0	59.7	1.4	61.5	3.0	61.7	0.3	62.2	0.8	63.2	1.6	62.7	-0.8	62.4	-0.5	62.1	-0.5	62.2	0.2	61.6	-1.0	61.7	0.2
1979	61.7	0.0	61.8	0.2	63.3	2.4	64.1	1.3	65.4	2.0	66.4	1.5	67.6	1.8	68.6	1.5	69.0	0.6	69.7	1.0	69.3	-0.6	70.6	1.9
1980	71.5	1.3	73.6	2.9	75.2	2.2	76.3	1.5	77.9	2.1	80.2	3.0	81.5	1.6	82.1	0.7	83.2	1.3	83.0	-0.2	82.1	-1.1	83.1	1.2
1981	84.0	1.1	85.2	1.4	86.4	1.4	87.4	1.2	88.7	1.5	90.2	1.7	92.2	2.2	94.9	2.9	94.4	-0.5	93.1	-1.4	93.1	0.0	94.5	1.5
1982	96.6	2.2	96.6	0.0	99.3	2.8	99.9	0.6	100.1	0.2	99.8	-0.3	102.3	2.5	102.1	-0.2	102.1	0.0	100.6	-1.5	99.6	-1.0	100.8	1.2
1983	101.1	0.3	101.1	0.0	101.2	0.1	100.7	-0.5	101.4	0.7	103.2	1.8	104.9	1.6	105.1	0.2	105.3	0.2	104.2	-1.0	103.0	-1.2	102.7	-0.3
1984	103.4	0.7	104.3	0.9	105.0	0.7	106.2	1.1	106.6	0.4	109.9	3.1	111.6	1.5	112.4	0.7	112.3	-0.1	109.6	-2.4	109.0	-0.5	108.4	-0.6
1985	109.7	1.2	109.7	0.0	110.1	0.4	110.5	0.4	110.2	-0.3	113.2	2.7	113.7	0.4	114.0	0.3	113.7	-0.3	112.0	-1.5	111.4	-0.5	111.0	-0.4
1986	112.3	1.2	113.2	0.8	112.7	-0.4	111.5	-1.1	112.1	0.5	114.0	1.7	114.8	0.7	114.8	0.0	114.8	0.0	111.0	-3.3	110.2	-0.7	109.9	-0.3
1987	108.4	-1.4	108.3	-0.1	108.7	0.4	108.0	-0.6	109.9	1.8	113.2	3.0	114.8	1.4	114.6	-0.2	114.1	-0.4	110.4	-3.2	108.1	-2.1	108.4	0.3
1988	107.8	-0.6	108.0	0.2	107.7	-0.3	107.6	-0.1	107.6	0.0	115.6	7.4	116.8	1.0	116.8	0.0	117.1	0.3	112.8	-3.7	107.8	-4.4	109.1	1.2
1989	110.6	1.4	110.8	0.2	110.9	0.1	111.1	0.2	112.6	1.4	119.3	6.0	120.8	1.3	120.7	-0.1	120.7	0.0	115.2	-4.6	111.8	-3.0	112.6	0.7
1990	113.1	0.4	113.6	0.4	113.8	0.2	113.7	-0.1	115.5	1.6	121.7	5.4	121.9	0.2	122.1	0.2	122.4	0.2	119.1	-2.7	117.6	-1.3	116.8	-0.7
1991	120.5	3.2	120.4	-0.1	120.2	-0.2	120.2	0.0	123.1	2.4	128.8	4.6	130.4	1.2	130.4	0.0	130.5	0.1	124.7	-4.4	120.2	-3.6	121.9	1.4
1992	122.2	0.2	121.8	-0.3	122.1	0.2	121.4	-0.6	124.5	2.6	131.7	5.8	132.7	0.8	132.4	-0.2	132.7	0.2	127.4	-4.0	122.8	-3.6	123.7	0.7
1993	124.2	0.4	123.9	-0.2	124.0	0.1	124.6	0.5	125.7	0.9	134.8	7.2	135.1	0.2	135.3	0.1	135.8	0.4	129.7	-4.5	125.3	-3.4	125.1	-0.2
1994	125.2	0.1	125.2	0.0	125.1	-0.1	124.8	-0.2	125.7	0.7	133.0	5.8	133.9	0.7	134.1	0.1	134.1	0.0	128.6	-4.1	127.0	-1.2	127.4	0.3
1995	127.5	0.1	127.7	0.2	127.9	0.2	126.3	-1.3	129.6	2.6	135.9	4.9	137.0	0.8	137.0	0.0	134.9	-1.5	131.2	-2.7	127.8	-2.6	127.9	0.1
1996	128.0	0.1	126.9	-0.9	127.7	0.6	128.1	0.3	131.4	2.6	137.2	4.4	137.0	-0.1	137.4	0.3	137.3	-0.1	131.9	-3.9	127.8	-3.1	128.2	0.3
1997	128.5	0.2	128.4	-0.1	128.4	0.0	127.9	-0.4	129.8	1.5	136.5	5.2	137.1	0.4	136.0	-0.8	137.2	0.9	131.7	-4.0	128.2	-2.7	128.5	0.2
1998	127.3	-0.9	127.0	-0.2	126.4	-0.5	126.3	-0.1	128.4	1.7	134.4	4.7	135.4	0.7	135.2	-0.1	135.2	0.0	130.2	-3.7	127.0	-2.5	125.8	-0.9
1999	125.5	-0.2	125.2	-0.2	125.2	0.0	124.9	-0.2	126.7	1.4	132.2	4.3	133.5	1.0	133.9	0.3	134.2	0.2	129.2	-3.7	126.4	-2.2	125.8	-0.5
2000	125.8	0.0	125.8	0.0	125.8	0.0	125.9	0.1	127.6	1.4	134.0	5.0	135.9	1.4	136.7	0.6	137.2	0.4	133.1	-3.0	129.7	-2.6	130.8	0.8
2001	133.4	2.0	133.7	0.2	134.3	0.4	133.5	-0.6	135.1	1.2	144.7	7.1	145.6	0.6	145.4	-0.1	145.2	-0.1	139.8	-3.7	136.7	-2.2	135.7	-0.7

Source: U.S. Department of Labor, Bureau of Labor Statistics, Division of Industry Prices and Price Indexes. n.e.c. stands for not elsewhere classified. - indicates no data collected for period or unavailable.

Utility Natural Gas
Producer Price Index
Base 1982 = 100

For 1990-2001. Columns headed % show percentile change in the index from the previous period for which an index is available.

Year	Jan Index	%	Feb Index	%	Mar Index	%	Apr Index	%	May Index	%	Jun Index	%	Jul Index	%	Aug Index	%	Sep Index	%	Oct Index	%	Nov Index	%	Dec Index	%
1990	-	-	-	-	-	-	-	-	-	-	-	-	-	-	-	-	-	-	-	-	-	-	100.0	-
1991	101.2	1.2	99.5	-1.7	97.7	-1.8	97.1	-0.6	96.2	-0.9	95.2	-1.0	95.0	-0.2	94.7	-0.3	95.1	0.4	96.2	1.2	98.6	2.5	99.8	1.2
1992	100.1	0.3	98.0	-2.1	96.9	-1.1	96.0	-0.9	95.5	-0.5	96.0	0.5	96.1	0.1	96.9	0.8	98.3	1.4	101.2	3.0	103.7	2.5	104.2	0.5
1993	104.0	-0.2	102.8	-1.2	102.2	-0.6	101.9	-0.3	103.9	2.0	103.5	-0.4	103.2	-0.3	104.0	0.8	105.0	1.0	104.9	-0.1	106.4	1.4	107.6	1.1
1994	107.6	0.0	107.7	0.1	108.1	0.4	106.7	-1.3	105.5	-1.1	103.0	-2.4	102.1	-0.9	102.2	0.1	101.9	-0.3	101.1	-0.8	103.1	2.0	103.7	0.6
1995	104.0	0.3	102.5	-1.4	101.2	-1.3	99.9	-1.3	97.5	-2.4	97.6	0.1	97.0	-0.6	96.2	-0.8	96.1	-0.1	95.8	-0.3	97.6	1.9	100.6	3.1
1996	102.5	1.9	103.6	1.1	104.9	1.3	104.4	-0.5	103.9	-0.5	104.1	0.2	104.5	0.4	105.6	1.1	103.5	-2.0	102.9	-0.6	108.4	5.3	114.3	5.4
1997	122.1	6.8	120.1	-1.6	111.8	-6.9	105.8	-5.4	105.4	-0.4	106.6	1.1	107.5	0.8	107.0	-0.5	108.4	1.3	112.9	4.2	119.8	6.1	116.3	-2.9
1998	113.3	-2.6	109.8	-3.1	109.4	-0.4	107.9	-1.4	107.9	0.0	105.4	-2.3	106.0	0.6	106.2	0.2	105.2	-0.9	106.6	1.3	108.6	1.9	111.2	2.4
1999	110.2	-0.9	106.7	-3.2	104.5	-2.1	103.2	-1.2	104.7	1.5	105.6	0.9	106.9	1.2	108.1	1.1	111.5	3.1	111.2	-0.3	117.7	5.8	114.6	-2.6
2000	114.9	0.3	115.3	0.3	114.9	-0.3	117.0	1.8	118.7	1.5	128.2	8.0	136.4	6.4	135.2	-0.9	142.6	5.5	152.9	7.2	155.8	1.9	176.5	13.3
2001	215.0	21.8	203.2	-5.5	184.3	-9.3	176.3	-4.3	175.2	-0.6	161.3	-7.9	154.9	-4.0	143.3	-7.5	136.0	-5.1	128.5	-5.5	128.9	0.3	126.3	-2.0

Source: U.S. Department of Labor, Bureau of Labor Statistics, Division of Industry Prices and Price Indexes. n.e.c. stands for not elsewhere classified. - indicates no data collected for period or unavailable.

Crude Petroleum (domestic production)
Producer Price Index
Base 1982 = 100

For 1991-2001. Columns headed % show percentile change in the index from the previous period for which an index is available.

Year	Jan Index	%	Feb Index	%	Mar Index	%	Apr Index	%	May Index	%	Jun Index	%	Jul Index	%	Aug Index	%	Sep Index	%	Oct Index	%	Nov Index	%	Dec Index	%
1991	-	-	-	-	-	-	-	-	-	-	-	-	59.3	-	60.4	1.9	60.4	0.0	66.3	9.8	64.0	-3.5	55.1	-13.9
1992	51.3	-6.9	53.5	4.3	51.0	-4.7	56.0	9.8	59.2	5.7	64.3	8.6	61.9	-3.7	60.5	-2.3	63.1	4.3	63.4	0.5	58.5	-7.7	53.8	-8.0
1993	52.0	-3.3	56.1	7.9	58.1	3.6	57.7	-0.7	57.9	0.3	52.9	-8.6	50.2	-5.1	48.3	-3.8	46.5	-3.7	51.8	11.4	46.0	-11.2	38.9	-15.4
1994	39.3	1.0	37.8	-3.8	39.6	4.8	42.7	7.8	48.9	14.5	52.9	8.2	56.2	6.2	54.4	-3.2	49.1	1.7	49.3	2.1	49.1	-0.4	47.1	-4.1
1995	48.4	2.8	51.0	5.4	50.6	-0.8	55.3	9.3	56.0	1.3	53.3	-4.8	48.3	-9.4	49.1	1.7	51.4	4.7	48.3	-6.0	49.0	1.4	52.2	6.5
1996	56.0	7.3	52.8	-5.7	57.7	9.3	66.0	14.4	61.0	-7.6	57.7	-5.4	59.9	3.8	62.0	3.5	67.2	8.4	72.0	7.1	68.5	-4.9	70.9	3.5
1997	73.4	3.5	64.5	-12.1	56.3	-12.7	56.1	-0.4	60.2	7.3	51.8	-14.0	54.9	6.0	54.9	0.0	53.3	-2.9	57.3	7.5	56.4	-1.6	50.8	-9.9
1998	43.4	-14.6	43.2	-0.5	35.8	-17.1	38.1	6.4	38.3	0.5	33.6	-12.3	35.9	6.8	30.4	-15.3	36.0	18.4	35.2	-2.2	32.7	-7.1	26.1	-20.2
1999	30.2	15.7	26.2	-13.2	33.3	27.1	42.4	27.3	47.2	11.3	48.8	3.4	53.7	10.0	57.2	6.5	65.5	14.5	60.9	-7.0	66.7	9.5	71.0	6.4
2000	72.2	1.7	83.5	15.7	86.9	4.1	69.6	-19.9	79.6	14.4	89.8	12.8	83.3	-7.2	89.3	7.2	97.4	9.1	93.1	-4.4	98.8	6.1	78.8	-20.2
2001	75.4	-4.3	80.7	7.0	73.1	-9.4	74.5	1.9	77.7	4.3	77.0	-0.9	72.8	-5.5	72.6	-0.3	73.9	1.8	59.4	-19.6	55.0	-7.4	43.1	-21.6

Source: U.S. Department of Labor, Bureau of Labor Statistics, Division of Industry Prices and Price Indexes. n.e.c. stands for not elsewhere classified. - indicates no data collected for period or unavailable.

Petroleum Products, Refined
Producer Price Index
Base 1982 = 100

For 1947-2001. Columns headed % show percentile change in the index from the previous period for which an index is available.

Year	Jan Index	%	Feb Index	%	Mar Index	%	Apr Index	%	May Index	%	Jun Index	%	Jul Index	%	Aug Index	%	Sep Index	%	Oct Index	%	Nov Index	%	Dec Index	%
1947	8.3	-	8.4	1.2	9.0	7.1	9.6	6.7	9.6	0.0	9.7	1.0	9.9	2.1	10.1	2.0	10.1	0.0	10.2	1.0	10.7	4.9	11.3	5.6
1948	12.1	7.1	12.3	1.7	12.3	0.0	12.3	0.0	12.3	0.0	12.3	0.0	12.3	0.0	12.2	-0.8	12.1	-0.8	12.2	0.8	12.1	-0.8	11.9	-1.7
1949	11.7	-1.7	11.2	-4.3	11.0	-1.8	10.7	-2.7	10.5	-1.9	10.4	-1.0	10.3	-1.0	10.4	1.0	10.5	1.0	10.6	1.0	10.4	-1.9	10.4	0.0
1950	10.5	1.0	10.5	0.0	10.5	0.0	10.6	1.0	10.9	2.8	11.1	1.8	11.3	1.8	11.6	2.7	11.7	0.9	11.8	0.9	11.8	0.0	11.8	0.0
1951	12.0	1.7	12.0	0.0	12.1	0.8	12.1	0.0	12.0	-0.8	12.1	0.8	12.1	0.0	12.1	0.0	12.1	0.0	12.1	0.0	12.1	0.0	12.1	0.0
1952	12.1	0.0	12.0	-0.8	12.1	0.8	11.9	-1.7	12.0	0.8	11.9	-0.8	11.9	0.0	11.8	-0.8	11.8	0.0	11.8	0.0	11.7	-0.8	11.7	0.0
1953	11.7	0.0	11.6	-0.9	11.8	1.7	11.8	0.0	11.9	0.8	11.9	0.0	12.6	5.9	12.6	0.0	12.6	0.0	12.6	0.0	12.6	0.0	12.4	-1.6
1954	12.3	-0.8	12.2	-0.8	11.9	-2.5	12.0	0.8	12.0	0.0	11.9	-0.8	11.5	-3.4	11.6	0.9	11.7	0.9	11.6	-0.9	11.7	0.9	11.8	0.9
1955	11.9	0.8	11.9	0.0	12.0	0.8	11.9	-0.8	11.9	0.0	11.9	0.0	11.9	0.0	12.1	1.7	12.2	0.8	12.3	0.8	12.3	0.0	12.4	0.8
1956	12.6	1.6	12.7	0.8	12.6	-0.8	12.7	0.8	12.8	0.8	12.8	0.0	12.8	0.0	12.8	0.0	12.8	0.0	12.8	0.0	12.7	-0.8	13.1	3.1
1957	13.5	3.1	14.2	5.2	14.1	-0.7	14.1	0.0	14.0	-0.7	13.8	-1.4	13.6	-1.4	13.5	-0.7	13.5	0.0	13.4	-0.7	13.2	-1.5	13.2	0.0
1958	13.1	-0.8	12.6	-3.8	12.4	-1.6	12.2	-1.6	12.1	-0.8	12.2	0.8	12.4	1.6	12.7	2.4	12.7	0.0	12.5	-1.6	12.4	-0.8	12.4	0.0
1959	12.6	1.6	12.8	1.6	12.8	0.0	12.8	0.0	12.6	-1.6	12.2	-3.2	12.2	0.0	12.3	0.8	12.2	-0.8	12.2	0.0	12.1	-0.8	12.1	0.0
1960	12.2	0.8	12.2	0.0	12.2	0.0	12.3	0.8	12.0	-2.4	12.3	2.5	12.6	2.4	12.8	1.6	13.0	1.6	13.0	0.0	12.9	-0.8	13.0	0.8
1961	13.2	1.5	13.3	0.8	13.2	-0.8	12.8	-3.0	12.5	-2.3	12.7	1.6	12.8	0.8	12.7	-0.8	12.5	-1.6	12.3	-1.6	12.5	1.6	12.7	1.6
1962	12.8	0.8	12.6	-1.6	12.2	-3.2	12.7	4.1	12.6	-0.8	12.6	0.0	12.6	0.0	12.5	-0.8	12.8	2.4	12.7	-0.8	12.7	0.0	12.7	0.0
1963	12.6	-0.8	12.5	-0.8	12.6	0.8	12.6	0.0	12.7	0.8	12.8	0.8	12.7	-0.8	12.3	-3.1	12.3	0.0	12.3	0.0	12.1	-1.6	12.3	1.7
1964	12.4	0.8	12.2	-1.6	11.9	-2.5	11.7	-1.7	11.8	0.9	11.9	0.8	11.9	0.0	11.7	-1.7	11.5	-1.7	11.8	2.6	12.0	1.7	12.1	0.8
1965	12.2	0.8	12.1	-0.8	12.1	0.0	12.1	0.0	12.3	1.7	12.3	0.0	12.3	0.0	12.4	0.8	12.4	0.0	12.4	0.0	12.6	1.6	12.7	0.8
1966	12.6	-0.8	12.6	0.0	12.5	-0.8	12.6	0.8	12.7	0.8	12.9	1.6	12.8	-0.8	12.9	0.8	13.0	0.8	13.0	0.0	13.0	0.0	12.9	-0.8
1967	12.9	0.0	13.1	1.6	13.2	0.8	13.1	-0.8	13.3	1.5	13.3	0.0	13.3	0.0	13.4	0.8	13.4	0.0	13.0	-3.0	12.9	-0.8	12.8	-0.8
1968	12.7	-0.8	12.8	0.8	12.8	0.0	12.9	0.8	12.9	0.0	13.3	3.1	13.2	-0.8	13.0	-1.5	13.0	0.0	12.8	-1.5	12.8	0.0	12.7	-0.8
1969	12.7	0.0	12.8	0.8	13.1	2.3	13.2	0.8	13.2	0.0	13.3	0.8	13.3	0.0	13.2	-0.8	13.1	-0.8	13.1	0.0	13.1	0.0	13.1	0.0
1970	13.0	-0.8	13.0	0.0	13.0	0.0	13.0	0.0	13.3	2.3	13.1	-1.5	13.2	0.8	13.3	0.8	13.3	0.0	13.3	0.0	13.5	1.5	14.2	5.2
1971	14.2	0.0	14.1	-0.7	14.0	-0.7	13.8	-1.4	14.1	2.2	14.1	0.0	14.2	0.7	14.2	0.0	14.2	0.0	14.1	-0.7	14.0	-0.7	14.0	0.0
1972	13.9	-0.7	13.9	0.0	14.0	0.7	14.0	0.0	14.1	0.7	14.3	1.4	14.3	0.0	14.5	1.4	14.6	0.7	14.6	0.0	14.7	0.7	14.7	0.0
1973	14.7	0.0	15.6	6.1	15.9	1.9	16.1	1.3	16.4	1.9	16.8	2.4	17.1	1.8	17.1	0.0	17.2	0.6	17.6	2.3	18.4	4.5	19.9	8.2
1974	21.9	10.1	24.7	12.8	27.1	9.7	28.3	4.4	29.5	4.2	30.5	3.4	31.5	3.3	32.0	1.6	31.9	-0.3	32.1	0.6	31.3	-2.5	31.3	0.0
1975	31.8	1.6	31.6	-0.6	31.8	0.6	32.0	0.6	32.3	0.9	33.1	2.5	34.0	2.7	35.3	3.8	35.7	1.1	36.0	0.8	36.1	0.3	36.1	0.0
1976	35.8	-0.8	35.8	0.0	35.4	-1.1	35.1	-0.8	35.1	0.0	35.5	1.1	36.4	2.5	36.9	1.4	37.3	1.1	37.4	0.3	37.5	0.3	37.8	0.8
1977	38.0	0.5	38.8	2.1	39.7	2.3	40.3	1.5	40.8	1.2	41.0	0.5	41.2	0.5	41.1	-0.2	41.1	0.0	41.3	0.5	41.2	-0.2	41.2	0.0
1978	41.3	0.2	41.1	-0.5	40.8	-0.7	40.9	0.2	41.3	1.0	41.8	1.2	42.2	1.0	42.5	0.7	42.8	0.7	43.3	1.2	43.6	0.7	44.4	1.8
1979	45.2	1.8	46.0	1.8	47.3	2.8	49.7	5.1	52.5	5.6	55.6	5.9	59.1	6.3	63.4	7.3	67.5	6.5	70.1	3.9	71.7	2.3	72.9	1.7
1980	76.6	5.1	81.5	6.4	86.6	6.3	89.1	2.9	89.4	0.3	89.5	0.1	91.1	1.8	91.6	0.5	91.5	-0.1	90.7	-0.9	91.6	1.0	94.2	2.8
1981	96.8	2.8	101.1	4.4	108.4	7.2	110.5	1.9	109.7	-0.7	108.8	-0.8	107.2	-1.5	106.9	-0.3	105.9	-0.9	105.4	-0.5	104.9	-0.5	104.9	0.0
1982	105.3	0.4	103.7	-1.5	101.2	-2.4	96.4	-4.7	93.7	-2.8	97.1	3.6	102.0	5.0	102.7	0.7	100.0	-2.6	99.1	-0.9	99.6	0.5	99.1	-0.5
1983	94.7	-4.4	91.0	-3.9	87.6	-3.7	84.8	-3.2	86.6	2.1	89.9	3.8	90.5	0.7	91.3	0.9	91.3	0.0	91.5	0.2	90.4	-1.2	89.1	-1.4
1984	87.1	-2.2	88.0	1.0	89.4	1.6	87.6	-2.0	89.0	1.6	89.3	0.3	88.4	-1.0	86.0	-2.7	84.9	-1.3	86.1	1.4	86.9	0.9	85.7	-1.4
1985	83.5	-2.6	80.9	-3.1	81.5	0.7	83.6	2.6	86.4	3.3	84.3	-2.4	82.8	-1.8	81.5	-1.6	81.7	0.2	82.1	0.5	84.3	2.7	85.4	1.3
1986	79.9	-6.4	68.9	-13.8	56.7	-17.7	52.0	-8.3	53.3	2.5	53.3	0.0	44.7	-16.1	44.3	-0.9	48.2	8.8	45.4	-5.8	45.5	0.2	46.4	2.0
1987	50.8	9.5	53.9	6.1	52.9	-1.9	55.4	4.7	56.1	1.3	57.7	2.9	59.3	2.8	61.5	3.7	58.9	-4.2	59.0	0.2	59.8	1.4	56.8	-5.0
1988	53.7	-5.5	52.9	-1.5	52.1	-1.5	54.4	4.4	56.4	3.7	55.4	-1.8	55.3	-0.2	55.8	0.9	52.9	-5.2	51.1	-3.4	53.5	4.7	52.9	-1.1
1989	54.4	2.8	55.0	1.1	57.1	3.8	64.9	13.7	67.7	4.3	65.6	-3.1	63.1	-3.8	58.9	-6.7	61.4	4.2	63.0	2.6	61.6	-2.2	61.9	0.5
1990	71.8	16.0	64.5	-10.2	63.3	-1.9	65.1	2.8	65.3	0.3	63.9	-2.1	62.3	-2.5	74.5	19.6	86.7	16.4	96.9	11.8	96.4	-0.5	87.0	-9.8
1991	79.1	-9.1	71.5	-9.6	64.0	-10.5	63.6	-0.6	66.4	4.4	65.4	-1.5	63.3	-3.2	66.4	4.9	67.9	2.3	66.9	-1.5	67.8	1.3	63.4	-6.5

[Continued]

Petroleum Products, Refined
Producer Price Index
Base 1982 = 100

[Continued]

For 1947-2001. Columns headed % show percentile change in the index from the previous period for which an index is available.

Year	Jan Index	%	Feb Index	%	Mar Index	%	Apr Index	%	May Index	%	Jun Index	%	Jul Index	%	Aug Index	%	Sep Index	%	Oct Index	%	Nov Index	%	Dec Index	%
1992	57.7	-9.0	59.7	3.5	59.2	-0.8	61.9	4.6	66.2	6.9	69.9	5.6	68.1	-2.6	67.5	-0.9	68.6	1.6	68.5	-0.1	67.0	-2.2	62.1	-7.3
1993	61.6	-0.8	62.5	1.5	63.9	2.2	65.1	1.9	66.5	2.2	64.5	-3.0	62.0	-3.9	60.3	-2.7	61.1	1.3	63.1	3.3	60.5	-4.1	52.9	-12.6
1994	52.9	0.0	56.4	6.6	55.8	-1.1	57.0	2.2	58.1	1.9	59.3	2.1	62.0	4.6	66.1	6.6	63.0	-4.7	60.0	-4.8	61.6	2.7	57.5	-6.7
1995	58.1	1.0	58.2	0.2	59.0	1.4	63.1	6.9	66.1	4.8	64.8	-2.0	61.4	-5.2	60.9	-0.8	61.1	0.3	59.3	-2.9	57.8	-2.5	59.8	3.5
1996	63.2	5.7	61.1	-3.3	65.3	6.9	73.2	12.1	75.1	2.6	69.9	-6.9	69.0	-1.3	69.4	0.6	72.1	3.9	74.2	2.9	74.6	0.5	74.5	-0.1
1997	74.3	-0.3	72.9	-1.9	69.5	-4.7	68.2	-1.9	67.9	-0.4	66.3	-2.4	64.3	-3.0	67.8	5.4	68.5	1.0	67.0	-2.2	66.3	-1.0	62.1	-6.3
1998	57.4	-7.6	54.4	-5.2	50.6	-7.0	52.7	4.2	54.9	4.2	53.2	-3.1	52.1	-2.1	49.1	-5.8	49.7	1.2	51.0	2.6	48.8	-4.3	42.2	-13.5
1999	44.9	6.4	42.6	-5.1	46.3	8.7	58.7	26.8	59.8	1.9	58.8	-1.7	63.6	8.2	68.6	7.9	72.5	5.7	69.5	-4.1	71.7	3.2	73.7	2.8
2000	75.2	2.0	84.0	11.7	89.7	6.8	84.6	-5.7	87.6	3.5	97.4	11.2	93.1	-4.4	90.6	-2.7	102.5	13.1	99.5	-2.9	99.6	0.1	91.6	-8.0
2001	91.4	-0.2	90.4	-1.1	85.9	-5.0	94.0	9.4	101.2	7.7	95.1	-6.0	82.4	-13.4	85.4	3.6	95.1	11.4	74.9	-21.2	69.1	-7.7	58.6	-15.2

Source: U.S. Department of Labor, Bureau of Labor Statistics, Division of Industry Prices and Price Indexes. n.e.c. stands for not elsewhere classified. - indicates no data collected for period or unavailable.

Petroleum and Coal Products, n.e.c.
Producer Price Index
Base 1982 = 100

For 1984-2001. Columns headed % show percentile change in the index from the previous period for which an index is available.

Year	Jan Index	%	Feb Index	%	Mar Index	%	Apr Index	%	May Index	%	Jun Index	%	Jul Index	%	Aug Index	%	Sep Index	%	Oct Index	%	Nov Index	%	Dec Index	%
1984	-	-	-	-	-	-	-	-	-	-	-	-	-	-	-	-	-	-	-	-	-	-	100.0	-
1985	100.0	0.0	99.9	-0.1	99.9	0.0	99.9	0.0	99.9	0.0	99.9	0.0	105.2	5.3	103.6	-1.5	103.1	-0.5	95.0	-7.9	100.2	5.5	99.2	-1.0
1986	95.2	-4.0	95.2	0.0	92.9	-2.4	90.8	-2.3	81.7	-10.0	78.7	-3.7	70.5	-10.4	70.8	0.4	63.4	-10.5	63.5	0.2	65.3	2.8	57.3	-12.3
1987	61.8	7.9	60.4	-2.3	63.7	5.5	63.6	-0.2	60.4	-5.0	62.4	3.3	62.8	0.6	63.7	1.4	64.6	1.4	65.6	1.5	66.0	0.6	69.9	5.9
1988	62.7	-10.3	70.8	12.9	62.6	-11.6	68.0	8.6	69.6	2.4	67.4	-3.2	69.4	3.0	69.9	0.7	68.1	-2.6	61.8	-9.3	63.7	3.1	62.7	-1.6
1989	59.1	-5.7	60.3	2.0	65.6	8.8	65.8	0.3	64.4	-2.1	63.5	-1.4	68.1	7.2	69.2	1.6	67.5	-2.5	67.1	-0.6	69.4	3.4	60.0	-13.5
1990	61.9	3.2	63.5	2.6	63.3	-0.3	64.2	1.4	67.6	5.3	68.3	1.0	66.6	-2.5	68.0	2.1	70.1	3.1	70.2	0.1	69.8	-0.6	74.2	6.3
1991	71.7	-3.4	76.3	6.4	67.0	-12.2	68.4	2.1	64.9	-5.1	68.4	5.4	61.4	-10.2	61.9	0.8	61.1	-1.3	61.9	1.3	55.9	-9.7	44.5	-20.4
1992	58.1	30.6	58.4	0.5	59.6	2.1	60.7	1.8	58.2	-4.1	54.7	-6.0	57.7	5.5	58.5	1.4	54.7	-6.5	61.1	11.7	63.1	3.3	60.5	-4.1
1993	67.0	10.7	66.8	-0.3	66.0	-1.2	69.3	5.0	68.0	-1.9	63.1	-7.2	69.0	9.4	65.8	-4.6	66.4	0.9	64.1	-3.5	67.3	5.0	64.0	-4.9
1994	65.0	1.6	65.2	0.3	61.6	-5.5	62.2	1.0	69.1	11.1	67.0	-3.0	68.4	2.1	65.3	-4.5	64.0	-2.0	66.5	3.9	68.1	2.4	66.9	-1.8
1995	67.5	0.9	67.9	0.6	68.1	0.3	76.7	12.6	71.8	-6.4	69.1	-3.8	69.5	0.6	70.9	2.0	73.9	4.2	72.1	-2.4	66.9	-7.2	63.5	-5.1
1996	67.4	6.1	68.9	2.2	66.9	-2.9	68.1	1.8	68.3	0.3	73.1	7.0	75.2	2.9	74.2	-1.3	73.0	-1.6	70.7	-3.2	70.6	-0.1	66.5	-5.8
1997	75.3	13.2	72.2	-4.1	71.4	-1.1	70.1	-1.8	73.1	4.3	73.1	0.0	70.5	-3.6	72.5	2.8	73.6	1.5	75.8	3.0	72.5	-4.4	69.6	-4.0
1998	68.7	-1.3	69.1	0.6	67.2	-2.7	71.0	5.7	69.9	-1.5	66.7	-4.6	68.6	2.8	68.2	-0.6	68.8	0.9	66.6	-3.2	66.3	-0.5	65.3	-1.5
1999	60.7	-7.0	60.2	-0.8	59.3	-1.5	64.3	8.4	64.4	0.2	65.3	1.4	65.7	0.6	65.3	-0.6	66.6	2.0	68.1	2.3	68.6	0.7	69.3	1.0
2000	72.6	4.8	75.0	3.3	79.0	5.3	83.3	5.4	84.5	1.4	85.8	1.5	86.7	1.0	88.9	2.5	87.8	-1.2	88.6	0.9	86.4	-2.5	82.4	-4.6
2001	79.4	-3.6	79.0	-0.5	77.3	-2.2	79.0	2.2	76.5	-3.2	73.9	-3.4	78.7	6.5	77.0	-2.2	77.0	0.0	76.8	-0.3	74.2	-3.4	73.4	-1.1

Source: U.S. Department of Labor, Bureau of Labor Statistics, Division of Industry Prices and Price Indexes. n.e.c. stands for not elsewhere classified. - indicates no data collected for period or unavailable.

CHEMICALS AND ALLIED PRODUCTS
Producer Price Index
Base 1982 = 100

For 1933-2001. Columns headed % show percentile change in the index from the previous period for which an index is available.

Year	Jan Index	%	Feb Index	%	Mar Index	%	Apr Index	%	May Index	%	Jun Index	%	Jul Index	%	Aug Index	%	Sep Index	%	Oct Index	%	Nov Index	%	Dec Index	%
1933	15.7	-	15.6	-0.6	15.7	0.6	15.7	0.0	16.0	1.9	16.2	1.3	16.6	2.5	16.7	0.6	16.6	-0.6	16.5	-0.6	16.5	0.0	16.6	0.6
1934	16.8	1.2	17.0	1.2	17.0	0.0	17.0	0.0	16.9	-0.6	16.9	0.0	16.9	0.0	16.9	0.0	17.0	0.6	17.1	0.6	17.0	-0.6	17.1	0.6
1935	17.2	0.6	17.3	0.6	17.6	1.7	17.6	0.0	17.7	0.6	17.8	0.6	17.6	-1.1	17.6	0.0	17.9	1.7	18.0	0.6	17.9	-0.6	17.9	0.0
1936	17.8	-0.6	17.7	-0.6	17.6	-0.6	17.6	0.0	17.4	-1.1	17.4	0.0	17.6	1.1	17.8	1.1	17.9	0.6	18.0	0.6	18.1	0.6	18.6	2.8
1937	18.9	1.6	19.0	0.5	19.0	0.0	19.0	0.0	18.7	-1.6	18.6	-0.5	18.7	0.5	18.6	-0.5	18.5	-0.5	18.4	-0.5	18.1	-1.6	17.9	-1.1
1938	18.1	1.1	18.1	0.0	18.0	-0.6	17.9	-0.6	17.7	-1.1	17.5	-1.1	17.5	0.0	17.6	0.6	17.6	0.0	17.6	0.0	17.6	0.0	17.5	-0.6
1939	17.5	0.0	17.4	-0.6	17.5	0.6	17.5	0.0	17.5	0.0	17.5	0.0	17.4	-0.6	17.3	-0.6	17.9	3.5	18.1	1.1	18.0	-0.6	18.1	0.6
1940	18.2	0.6	18.1	-0.5	18.1	0.0	18.3	1.1	17.9	-2.2	17.8	-0.6	17.8	0.0	17.7	-0.6	17.7	0.0	17.8	0.6	17.9	0.6	17.9	0.0
1941	18.1	1.1	18.1	0.0	18.4	1.7	18.8	2.2	19.2	2.1	19.4	1.0	19.7	1.5	19.9	1.0	20.3	2.0	20.6	1.5	20.6	0.0	20.8	1.0
1942	18.6	-10.6	21.9	17.7	22.1	0.9	22.1	0.0	22.1	0.0	22.0	-0.5	22.0	0.0	21.8	-0.9	21.9	0.5	21.9	0.0	21.8	-0.5	21.7	-0.5
1943	21.8	0.5	21.9	0.5	21.9	0.0	22.0	0.5	21.9	-0.5	21.9	0.0	21.9	0.0	22.0	0.5	22.0	0.0	22.0	0.0	22.0	0.0	22.0	0.0
1944	22.1	0.5	22.1	0.0	22.1	0.0	22.2	0.5	22.2	0.0	22.2	0.0	22.2	0.0	22.2	0.0	22.1	-0.5	22.2	0.5	22.2	0.0	22.2	0.0
1945	22.2	0.0	22.2	0.0	22.2	0.0	22.2	0.0	22.2	0.0	22.2	0.0	22.2	0.0	22.3	0.5	22.4	0.4	22.4	0.0	22.5	0.4	22.5	0.0
1946	22.5	0.0	22.5	0.0	22.5	0.0	22.5	0.0	22.6	0.4	22.6	0.0	23.5	4.0	23.3	-0.9	23.4	0.4	23.8	1.7	29.5	23.9	31.0	5.1
1947	32.1	3.5	32.4	0.9	32.9	1.5	32.8	-0.3	31.7	-3.4	31.2	-1.6	30.8	-1.3	30.5	-1.0	31.1	2.0	32.3	3.9	33.3	3.1	33.4	0.3
1948	33.8	1.2	33.3	-1.5	33.1	-0.6	33.0	-0.3	32.6	-1.2	32.8	0.6	32.9	0.3	32.7	-0.6	32.7	0.0	32.6	-0.3	32.4	-0.6	32.0	-1.2
1949	31.5	-1.6	31.1	-1.3	30.7	-1.3	30.1	-2.0	30.0	-0.3	29.9	-0.3	29.6	-1.0	29.6	0.0	29.5	-0.3	29.3	-0.7	29.3	0.0	29.2	-0.3
1950	29.2	0.0	29.1	-0.3	29.1	0.0	29.1	0.0	29.1	0.0	29.1	0.0	29.5	1.4	30.3	2.7	31.5	4.0	32.3	2.5	32.7	1.2	34.0	4.0
1951	35.2	3.5	35.6	1.1	35.4	-0.6	35.2	-0.6	35.2	0.0	34.8	-1.1	34.4	-1.1	34.3	-0.3	34.3	0.0	34.4	0.3	34.3	-0.3	34.3	0.0
1952	33.7	-1.7	33.5	-0.6	33.3	-0.6	33.1	-0.6	32.9	-0.6	32.9	0.0	32.9	0.0	32.9	0.0	32.9	0.0	32.8	-0.3	32.7	-0.3	32.6	-0.3
1953	32.7	0.3	32.7	0.0	32.9	0.6	33.4	1.5	33.4	0.0	33.4	0.0	33.6	0.6	33.6	0.0	33.7	0.3	33.7	0.0	33.9	0.6	33.9	0.0
1954	33.9	0.0	34.0	0.3	34.0	0.0	33.9	-0.3	33.9	0.0	33.8	-0.3	33.7	-0.3	33.8	0.3	33.8	0.0	33.8	0.0	33.8	0.0	33.8	0.0
1955	33.9	0.3	33.9	0.0	33.8	-0.3	33.9	0.3	33.8	-0.3	33.8	0.0	33.5	-0.9	33.5	0.0	33.5	0.0	33.7	0.6	33.7	0.0	33.7	0.0
1956	33.6	-0.3	33.6	0.0	33.7	0.3	33.8	0.3	33.8	0.0	33.9	0.3	33.9	0.0	33.9	0.0	33.9	0.0	34.0	0.3	34.2	0.6	34.2	0.0
1957	34.3	0.3	34.4	0.3	34.4	0.0	34.5	0.3	34.5	0.0	34.6	0.3	34.6	0.0	34.7	0.3	34.8	0.3	34.9	0.3	34.9	0.0	35.0	0.3
1958	35.0	0.0	35.0	0.0	35.0	0.0	35.1	0.3	35.0	-0.3	35.0	0.0	34.9	-0.3	34.8	-0.3	34.7	-0.3	34.8	0.3	34.8	0.0	34.8	0.0
1959	34.8	0.0	34.7	-0.2	34.7	0.0	34.8	0.3	34.8	0.0	34.8	0.0	34.7	-0.3	34.7	0.0	34.7	0.0	34.8	0.3	34.8	0.0	34.8	0.0
1960	34.7	-0.3	34.8	0.3	34.8	0.0	34.8	0.0	34.8	0.0	34.8	0.0	34.9	0.3	34.9	0.0	34.9	0.0	34.8	-0.3	34.8	0.0	34.8	0.0
1961	34.7	-0.3	34.8	0.3	34.8	0.0	34.8	0.0	34.7	-0.3	34.6	-0.3	34.4	-0.6	34.3	-0.3	34.2	-0.3	34.1	-0.3	34.1	0.0	34.1	0.0
1962	34.2	0.3	34.1	-0.3	34.1	0.0	34.0	-0.3	34.0	0.0	33.9	-0.3	33.8	-0.3	33.7	-0.3	33.7	0.0	33.8	0.3	33.7	-0.3	33.7	0.0
1963	33.7	0.0	33.6	-0.3	33.7	0.3	33.5	-0.6	33.5	0.0	33.5	0.0	33.4	-0.3	33.4	0.0	33.4	0.0	33.5	0.3	33.5	0.0	33.5	0.0
1964	33.5	0.0	33.5	0.0	33.6	0.3	33.6	0.0	33.6	0.0	33.6	0.0	33.6	0.0	33.6	0.0	33.6	0.0	33.7	0.3	33.8	0.3	33.8	0.0
1965	33.8	0.0	33.9	0.3	33.9	0.0	33.9	0.0	33.9	0.0	33.9	0.0	33.9	0.0	33.8	-0.3	33.8	0.0	33.9	0.3	33.9	0.0	33.9	0.0
1966	33.9	0.0	33.9	0.0	33.9	0.0	33.9	0.0	34.0	0.3	33.9	-0.3	34.0	0.3	34.0	0.0	34.1	0.3	34.0	-0.3	34.1	0.3	34.1	0.0
1967	34.2	0.3	34.2	0.0	34.2	0.0	34.3	0.3	34.3	0.0	34.2	-0.3	34.2	0.0	34.1	-0.3	34.0	-0.3	34.1	0.3	34.1	0.0	34.2	0.3
1968	34.1	-0.3	34.1	0.0	34.3	0.6	34.3	0.0	34.3	0.0	34.2	-0.3	34.1	-0.3	34.1	0.0	34.0	-0.3	34.0	0.0	34.0	0.0	34.0	0.0
1969	33.9	-0.3	34.0	0.3	34.1	0.3	34.0	-0.3	34.1	0.3	34.2	0.3	34.1	-0.3	34.3	0.6	34.4	0.3	34.3	-0.3	34.4	0.3	34.3	-0.3
1970	34.5	0.6	34.6	0.3	34.7	0.3	34.9	0.6	35.0	0.3	35.0	0.0	35.1	0.3	35.1	0.0	35.1	0.0	35.3	0.6	35.3	0.0	35.2	-0.3
1971	35.5	0.9	35.7	0.6	35.7	0.0	35.8	0.3	35.7	-0.3	35.7	0.0	35.7	0.0	35.6	-0.3	35.6	0.0	35.6	0.0	35.5	-0.3	35.4	-0.3
1972	35.4	0.0	35.4	0.0	35.4	0.0	35.6	0.6	35.7	0.3	35.7	0.0	35.6	-0.3	35.7	0.3	35.7	0.0	35.7	0.0	35.8	0.3	35.9	0.3
1973	36.0	0.3	36.1	0.3	36.5	1.1	36.8	0.8	37.4	1.6	37.8	1.1	37.9	0.3	38.0	0.3	38.1	0.3	38.6	1.3	38.8	0.5	39.6	2.1
1974	40.4	2.0	41.1	1.7	43.5	5.8	45.3	4.1	46.9	3.5	48.9	4.3	50.8	3.9	54.2	6.7	55.3	2.0	57.7	4.3	59.2	2.6	59.5	0.5
1975	60.2	1.2	60.9	1.2	62.2	2.1	62.4	0.3	62.3	-0.2	62.0	-0.5	62.1	0.2	62.3	0.3	62.3	0.0	62.4	0.2	62.6	0.3	62.7	0.2
1976	63.1	0.6	63.3	0.3	63.6	0.5	64.0	0.6	64.0	0.0	64.1	0.2	64.0	-0.2	64.3	0.5	64.5	0.3	64.5	0.0	64.5	0.0	64.4	-0.2
1977	64.6	0.3	65.0	0.6	65.4	0.6	66.0	0.9	66.4	0.6	66.4	0.0	66.2	-0.3	66.2	0.0	66.1	-0.2	66.3	0.3	66.4	0.2	66.4	0.0

[Continued]

CHEMICALS AND ALLIED PRODUCTS
Producer Price Index
Base 1982 = 100
[Continued]

For 1933-2001. Columns headed % show percentile change in the index from the previous period for which an index is available.

Year	Jan Index	%	Feb Index	%	Mar Index	%	Apr Index	%	May Index	%	Jun Index	%	Jul Index	%	Aug Index	%	Sep Index	%	Oct Index	%	Nov Index	%	Dec Index	%
1978	66.4	0.0	66.8	0.6	67.1	0.4	67.3	0.3	68.0	1.0	68.1	0.1	68.4	0.4	68.3	-0.1	68.5	0.3	69.0	0.7	69.2	0.3	69.2	0.0
1979	70.1	1.3	70.9	1.1	71.8	1.3	73.6	2.5	74.6	1.4	75.0	0.5	77.0	2.7	78.2	1.6	79.0	1.0	80.1	1.4	80.7	0.7	81.5	1.0
1980	84.2	3.3	85.1	1.1	86.5	1.6	88.9	2.8	89.8	1.0	89.9	0.1	90.1	0.2	90.5	0.4	90.1	-0.4	90.6	0.6	91.2	0.7	91.7	0.5
1981	93.9	2.4	95.0	1.2	95.9	0.9	97.8	2.0	98.7	0.9	99.4	0.7	99.7	0.3	100.3	0.6	100.4	0.1	100.1	-0.3	99.9	-0.2	99.8	-0.1
1982	100.2	0.4	100.5	0.3	100.8	0.3	100.7	-0.1	100.9	0.2	100.3	-0.6	99.7	-0.6	99.8	0.1	99.5	-0.3	99.2	-0.3	99.4	0.2	99.1	-0.3
1983	99.0	-0.1	99.4	0.4	99.2	-0.2	99.7	0.5	99.6	-0.1	99.5	-0.1	100.5	1.0	100.7	0.2	101.2	0.5	101.1	-0.1	101.4	0.3	101.9	0.5
1984	102.0	0.1	101.5	-0.5	102.7	1.2	103.3	0.6	103.6	0.3	103.4	-0.2	103.5	0.1	103.0	-0.5	103.0	0.0	103.1	0.1	103.2	0.1	102.9	-0.3
1985	103.2	0.3	103.4	0.2	103.5	0.1	103.8	0.3	103.7	-0.1	103.9	0.2	104.2	0.3	104.2	0.0	104.2	0.0	103.7	-0.5	103.5	-0.2	103.3	-0.2
1986	104.4	1.1	103.9	-0.5	104.0	0.1	102.7	-1.3	102.1	-0.6	102.1	0.0	102.1	0.0	101.6	-0.5	101.8	0.2	102.0	0.2	102.2	0.2	102.0	-0.2
1987	103.0	1.0	103.6	0.6	104.3	0.7	105.2	0.9	105.9	0.7	107.1	1.1	107.0	-0.1	107.1	0.1	107.5	0.4	108.2	0.7	108.8	0.6	109.1	0.3
1988	110.6	1.4	111.6	0.9	112.7	1.0	113.8	1.0	114.6	0.7	115.3	0.6	117.4	1.8	118.2	0.7	119.1	0.8	119.9	0.7	121.1	1.0	121.7	0.5
1989	123.7	1.6	124.3	0.5	124.5	0.2	124.9	0.3	124.9	0.0	124.1	-0.6	123.1	-0.8	121.9	-1.0	121.4	-0.4	121.4	0.0	121.0	-0.3	121.0	0.0
1990	121.2	0.2	121.7	0.4	121.8	0.1	121.9	0.1	122.3	0.3	122.2	-0.1	122.4	0.2	122.5	0.1	124.5	1.6	126.5	1.6	128.2	1.3	127.9	-0.2
1991	128.3	0.3	128.1	-0.2	126.0	-1.6	126.0	0.0	125.3	-0.6	125.0	-0.2	124.4	-0.5	124.5	0.1	124.5	0.0	124.9	0.3	124.9	0.0	125.0	0.1
1992	124.6	-0.3	124.5	-0.1	124.4	-0.1	124.8	0.3	125.2	0.3	126.0	0.6	126.4	0.3	126.7	0.2	127.0	0.2	127.1	0.1	127.5	0.3	127.0	-0.4
1993	127.6	0.5	128.1	0.4	127.8	-0.2	128.6	0.6	128.2	-0.3	128.5	0.2	128.2	-0.2	128.3	0.1	128.1	-0.2	128.2	0.1	128.5	0.2	127.9	-0.5
1994	128.3	0.3	128.2	-0.1	128.3	0.1	129.3	0.8	130.2	0.7	130.7	0.4	131.2	0.4	132.6	1.1	134.8	1.7	136.4	1.2	137.2	0.6	138.4	0.9
1995	140.4	1.4	141.8	1.0	142.5	0.5	144.1	1.1	144.4	0.2	143.8	-0.4	143.6	-0.1	142.9	-0.5	142.6	-0.2	141.8	-0.6	141.0	-0.6	140.7	-0.2
1996	140.8	0.1	140.9	0.1	141.1	0.1	141.4	0.2	142.2	0.6	142.2	0.0	142.0	-0.1	142.5	0.4	143.3	0.6	143.0	-0.2	142.8	-0.1	143.2	0.3
1997	143.6	0.3	143.8	0.1	143.7	-0.1	143.5	-0.1	143.5	0.0	143.4	-0.1	143.7	0.2	143.7	0.0	143.5	-0.1	144.0	0.3	143.9	-0.1	143.5	-0.3
1998	143.4	-0.1	143.0	-0.3	145.3	1.6	144.9	-0.3	144.9	0.0	144.8	-0.1	144.7	-0.1	144.1	-0.4	143.2	-0.6	143.3	0.1	143.0	-0.2	142.7	-0.2
1999	142.3	-0.3	141.8	-0.4	141.9	0.1	142.1	0.1	142.6	0.4	143.4	0.6	144.4	0.7	144.6	0.1	145.8	0.8	147.0	0.8	147.1	0.1	147.3	0.1
2000	147.7	0.3	148.9	0.8	149.9	0.7	150.7	0.5	151.3	0.4	151.7	0.3	152.6	0.6	152.0	-0.4	151.9	-0.1	151.9	0.0	151.3	-0.4	151.7	0.3
2001	153.9	1.5	155.2	0.8	155.4	0.1	154.8	-0.4	153.7	-0.7	153.2	-0.3	151.2	-1.3	149.9	-0.9	150.3	0.3	149.3	-0.7	148.5	-0.5	147.2	-0.9

Source: U.S. Department of Labor, Bureau of Labor Statistics, Division of Industry Prices and Price Indexes. n.e.c. stands for not elsewhere classified. - indicates no data collected for period or unavailable.

Industrial Chemicals
Producer Price Index
Base 1982 = 100

For 1926-2001. Columns headed % show percentile change in the index from the previous period for which an index is available.

Year	Jan Index	%	Feb Index	%	Mar Index	%	Apr Index	%	May Index	%	Jun Index	%	Jul Index	%	Aug Index	%	Sep Index	%	Oct Index	%	Nov Index	%	Dec Index	%
1926	-	-	-	-	-	-	-	-	-	-	-	-	-	-	-	-	-	-	-	-	-	-	-	-
1927	-	-	-	-	-	-	-	-	-	-	-	-	-	-	-	-	-	-	-	-	-	-	-	-
1928	-	-	-	-	-	-	-	-	-	-	-	-	-	-	-	-	-	-	-	-	-	-	-	-
1929	-	-	-	-	-	-	-	-	-	-	-	-	-	-	-	-	-	-	-	-	-	-	-	-
1930	-	-	-	-	-	-	-	-	-	-	-	-	-	-	-	-	-	-	-	-	-	-	-	-
1931	-	-	-	-	-	-	-	-	-	-	-	-	-	-	-	-	-	-	-	-	-	-	-	-
1932	-	-	-	-	-	-	-	-	-	-	-	-	-	-	-	-	-	-	-	-	-	-	-	-
1933	17.4	-	17.4	0.0	17.2	-1.1	17.2	0.0	17.3	0.6	17.3	0.0	17.2	-0.6	17.2	0.0	17.2	0.0	17.2	0.0	17.4	1.2	17.4	0.0
1934	17.4	0.0	17.4	0.0	17.4	0.0	17.3	-0.6	17.3	0.0	17.3	0.0	17.1	-1.2	17.2	0.6	17.2	0.0	17.2	0.0	17.2	0.0	17.3	0.6
1935	17.3	0.0	17.4	0.6	17.4	0.0	17.4	0.0	17.5	0.6	17.5	0.0	17.5	0.0	17.9	2.3	17.9	0.0	17.9	0.0	17.9	0.0	17.9	0.0
1936	17.8	-0.6	17.8	0.0	17.6	-1.1	17.6	0.0	17.5	-0.6	17.5	0.0	17.4	-0.6	17.3	-0.6	17.3	0.0	17.4	0.6	17.3	-0.6	17.4	0.6
1937	17.4	0.0	17.6	1.1	17.6	0.0	17.6	0.0	17.6	0.0	17.6	0.0	17.8	1.1	17.5	-1.7	17.5	0.0	17.4	-0.6	17.4	0.0	17.4	0.0
1938	17.4	0.0	17.4	0.0	17.3	-0.6	17.3	0.0	17.2	-0.6	17.2	0.0	17.2	0.0	17.1	-0.6	17.1	0.0	17.1	0.0	17.0	-0.6	17.0	0.0
1939	17.0	0.0	16.9	-0.6	16.8	-0.6	16.8	0.0	16.8	0.0	16.7	-0.6	16.7	0.0	16.7	0.0	16.8	0.6	17.0	1.2	17.0	0.0	17.0	0.0
1940	17.0	0.0	17.0	0.0	17.0	0.0	16.9	-0.6	17.0	0.6	17.0	0.0	16.9	-0.6	16.8	-0.6	16.8	0.0	16.9	0.6	17.0	0.6	17.0	0.0
1941	17.0	0.0	17.1	0.6	17.1	0.0	17.2	0.6	17.3	0.6	17.3	0.0	17.4	0.6	17.4	0.0	17.6	1.1	17.6	0.0	17.6	0.0	17.6	0.0
1942	18.9	7.4	19.2	1.6	19.2	0.0	19.2	0.0	19.2	0.0	19.2	0.0	19.2	0.0	19.2	0.0	19.2	0.0	19.2	0.0	19.2	0.0	19.1	-0.5
1943	19.3	1.0	19.3	0.0	19.2	-0.5	19.2	0.0	19.2	0.0	19.2	0.0	19.2	0.0	19.2	0.0	19.2	0.0	19.2	0.0	19.2	0.0	19.2	0.0
1944	19.2	0.0	19.2	0.0	19.2	0.0	19.2	0.0	19.2	0.0	19.2	0.0	19.2	0.0	19.2	0.0	19.1	-0.5	19.1	0.0	19.0	-0.5	19.0	0.0
1945	19.0	0.0	19.0	0.0	19.0	0.0	19.0	0.0	19.0	0.0	19.1	0.5	19.1	0.0	19.1	0.0	19.1	0.0	19.2	0.5	19.3	0.5	19.3	0.0
1946	19.3	0.0	19.3	0.0	19.3	0.0	19.3	0.0	19.5	1.0	19.5	0.0	19.6	0.5	19.6	0.0	19.6	0.0	19.7	0.5	21.2	7.6	22.2	4.7
1947	22.5	1.4	22.7	0.9	23.0	1.3	23.6	2.6	23.3	-1.3	23.4	0.4	23.2	-0.9	22.8	-1.7	23.0	0.9	23.6	2.6	24.1	2.1	24.2	0.4
1948	24.5	1.2	24.7	0.8	24.8	0.4	24.9	0.4	24.8	-0.4	24.8	0.0	25.2	1.6	24.9	-1.2	24.8	-0.4	24.9	0.4	24.4	-2.0	24.1	-1.2
1949	23.9	-0.8	23.3	-2.5	23.0	-1.3	22.6	-1.7	22.5	-0.4	22.4	-0.4	22.5	0.4	22.5	0.0	22.4	-0.4	22.3	-0.4	22.2	-0.4	22.2	0.0
1950	22.3	0.5	22.3	0.0	22.2	-0.4	22.4	0.9	22.4	0.0	22.7	1.3	23.1	1.8	23.7	2.6	24.8	4.6	26.1	5.2	26.3	0.8	27.5	4.6
1951	28.3	2.9	28.4	0.4	28.4	0.0	28.5	0.4	28.5	0.0	28.5	0.0	28.4	-0.4	28.4	0.0	28.4	0.0	28.5	0.4	28.5	0.0	28.4	-0.4
1952	27.8	-2.1	27.7	-0.4	27.5	-0.7	27.5	0.0	27.1	-1.5	27.1	0.0	27.0	-0.4	27.0	0.0	26.9	-0.4	26.8	-0.4	26.5	-1.1	26.4	-0.4
1953	26.5	0.4	26.6	0.4	26.8	0.8	27.5	2.6	27.8	1.1	28.1	1.1	28.3	0.7	28.3	0.0	28.3	0.0	28.2	-0.4	28.1	-0.4	27.9	-0.7
1954	27.9	0.0	27.9	0.0	27.8	-0.4	27.7	-0.4	27.6	-0.4	27.5	-0.4	27.6	0.4	27.7	0.4	27.7	0.0	27.7	0.0	27.7	0.0	27.7	0.0
1955	27.6	-0.4	27.7	0.4	27.7	0.0	27.8	0.4	27.7	-0.4	27.7	0.0	27.9	0.7	27.8	-0.4	27.9	0.4	28.0	0.4	28.1	0.4	28.1	0.0
1956	28.3	0.7	28.3	0.0	28.3	0.0	28.5	0.7	28.4	-0.4	28.5	0.4	28.8	1.1	28.8	0.0	28.7	-0.3	28.9	0.7	28.8	-0.3	28.8	0.0
1957	29.1	1.0	29.0	-0.3	29.0	0.0	29.1	0.3	29.1	0.0	29.2	0.3	29.1	-0.3	29.1	0.0	29.1	0.0	29.1	0.0	29.1	0.0	29.2	0.3
1958	29.2	0.0	29.1	-0.3	29.2	0.3	29.3	0.3	29.2	-0.3	29.1	-0.3	29.0	-0.3	28.9	-0.3	28.9	0.0	29.1	0.7	29.1	0.0	29.2	0.3
1959	29.2	0.0	29.2	0.0	29.1	-0.3	29.2	0.3	29.2	0.0	29.2	0.0	29.2	0.0	29.2	0.0	29.2	0.0	29.2	0.0	29.2	0.0	29.2	0.0
1960	29.2	0.0	29.3	0.3	29.3	0.0	29.3	0.0	29.4	0.3	29.4	0.0	29.4	0.0	29.4	0.0	29.3	-0.3	29.1	-0.7	29.1	0.0	29.1	0.0
1961	29.0	-0.3	29.0	0.0	29.0	0.0	29.0	0.0	28.9	-0.3	28.8	-0.3	28.5	-1.0	28.4	-0.4	28.4	0.0	28.3	-0.4	28.3	0.0	28.3	0.0
1962	28.3	0.0	28.2	-0.4	28.1	-0.4	28.1	0.0	28.1	0.0	28.0	-0.4	28.0	0.0	27.9	-0.4	27.9	0.0	28.0	0.4	27.9	-0.4	27.9	0.0
1963	28.0	0.4	27.7	-1.1	27.8	0.4	27.7	-0.4	27.7	0.0	27.7	0.0	27.6	-0.4	27.5	-0.4	27.5	0.0	27.4	-0.4	27.4	0.0	27.5	0.4
1964	27.5	0.0	27.4	-0.4	27.5	0.4	27.5	0.0	27.5	0.0	27.5	0.0	27.5	0.0	27.3	-0.7	27.3	0.0	27.5	0.7	27.4	-0.4	27.4	0.0
1965	27.5	0.4	27.6	0.4	27.5	-0.4	27.6	0.4	27.6	0.0	27.6	0.0	27.7	0.4	27.7	0.0	27.7	0.0	27.8	0.4	27.8	0.0	27.8	0.0
1966	27.7	-0.4	27.7	0.0	27.7	0.0	27.9	0.7	28.0	0.4	27.9	-0.4	27.9	0.0	27.9	0.0	27.9	0.0	27.9	0.0	28.0	0.4	28.1	0.4
1967	28.1	0.0	28.2	0.4	28.3	0.4	28.4	0.4	28.4	0.0	28.3	-0.4	28.3	0.0	28.3	0.0	28.3	0.0	28.6	1.1	28.6	0.0	28.6	0.0
1968	28.7	0.3	28.7	0.0	28.7	0.0	28.8	0.3	28.8	0.0	28.7	-0.3	28.6	-0.3	28.6	0.0	28.5	-0.3	28.5	0.0	28.5	0.0	28.5	0.0
1969	28.6	0.4	28.6	0.0	28.5	-0.3	28.2	-1.1	28.2	0.0	28.3	0.4	28.4	0.4	28.6	0.7	28.6	0.0	28.4	-0.7	28.5	0.4	28.5	0.0
1970	28.5	0.0	28.4	-0.4	28.3	-0.4	28.5	0.7	28.6	0.4	28.6	0.0	28.8	0.7	28.7	-0.3	28.7	0.0	28.8	0.3	28.8	0.0	28.7	-0.3

[Continued]

Industrial Chemicals
Producer Price Index
Base 1982 = 100
[Continued]

For 1926-2001. Columns headed % show percentile change in the index from the previous period for which an index is available.

Year	Jan Index	%	Feb Index	%	Mar Index	%	Apr Index	%	May Index	%	Jun Index	%	Jul Index	%	Aug Index	%	Sep Index	%	Oct Index	%	Nov Index	%	Dec Index	%
1971	28.9	0.7	28.9	0.0	29.0	0.3	28.9	-0.3	28.9	0.0	29.0	0.3	29.1	0.3	29.0	-0.3	29.1	0.3	29.1	0.0	28.8	-1.0	28.7	-0.3
1972	28.8	0.3	28.8	0.0	28.6	-0.7	28.8	0.7	28.8	0.0	28.8	0.0	28.8	0.0	28.7	-0.3	28.7	0.0	28.6	-0.3	28.6	0.0	28.6	0.0
1973	28.7	0.3	28.9	0.7	28.9	0.0	29.1	0.7	29.1	0.0	29.2	0.3	29.3	0.3	29.4	0.3	29.6	0.7	29.9	1.0	29.9	0.0	30.0	0.3
1974	30.7	2.3	31.3	2.0	34.6	10.5	37.1	7.2	39.2	5.7	41.7	6.4	44.1	5.8	47.6	7.9	49.5	4.0	51.6	4.2	53.9	4.5	55.2	2.4
1975	55.8	1.1	57.3	2.7	58.9	2.8	58.8	-0.2	59.2	0.7	58.7	-0.8	58.5	-0.3	58.8	0.5	59.1	0.5	59.3	0.3	59.7	0.7	59.9	0.3
1976	60.6	1.2	61.4	1.3	61.8	0.7	61.9	0.2	62.0	0.2	62.0	0.0	62.2	0.3	62.7	0.8	62.9	0.3	63.0	0.2	63.1	0.2	62.8	-0.5
1977	62.9	0.2	63.2	0.5	63.1	-0.2	63.4	0.5	63.6	0.3	63.6	0.0	63.7	0.2	63.7	0.0	63.6	-0.2	63.8	0.3	63.8	0.0	63.9	0.2
1978	63.6	-0.5	63.6	0.0	63.6	0.0	63.6	0.0	63.5	-0.2	63.5	0.0	63.8	0.5	64.2	0.6	64.2	0.0	64.7	0.8	64.5	-0.3	65.0	0.8
1979	66.4	2.2	67.3	1.4	68.0	1.0	70.4	3.5	72.5	3.0	73.5	1.4	76.7	4.4	78.6	2.5	79.4	1.0	81.0	2.0	81.8	1.0	82.9	1.3
1980	85.9	3.6	87.3	1.6	88.9	1.8	91.4	2.8	93.2	2.0	93.5	0.3	93.2	-0.3	93.6	0.4	92.9	-0.7	93.6	0.8	94.4	0.9	94.9	0.5
1981	97.7	3.0	99.9	2.3	100.5	0.6	102.8	2.3	104.5	1.7	104.9	0.4	105.1	0.2	105.4	0.3	105.5	0.1	104.3	-1.1	103.1	-1.2	102.9	-0.2
1982	102.9	0.0	102.7	-0.2	102.5	-0.2	101.5	-1.0	101.3	-0.2	99.6	-1.7	99.0	-0.6	99.0	0.0	98.3	-0.7	98.1	-0.2	97.9	-0.2	97.1	-0.8
1983	96.2	-0.9	96.5	0.3	96.1	-0.4	96.1	0.0	96.1	0.0	96.0	-0.1	98.4	2.5	98.6	0.2	98.0	-0.6	97.8	-0.2	98.2	0.4	99.1	0.9
1984	98.5	-0.6	95.8	-2.7	97.8	2.1	98.0	0.2	97.9	-0.1	98.0	0.1	98.0	0.0	96.7	-1.3	95.8	-0.9	95.3	-0.5	94.9	-0.4	95.0	0.1
1985	95.5	0.5	95.5	0.0	95.5	0.0	95.3	-0.2	95.5	0.2	96.3	0.8	96.4	0.1	97.5	1.1	97.1	-0.4	95.9	-1.2	95.4	-0.5	95.6	0.2
1986	96.9	1.4	95.0	-2.0	95.4	0.4	91.8	-3.8	90.2	-1.7	89.8	-0.4	89.7	-0.1	89.5	-0.2	89.9	0.4	90.2	0.3	89.8	-0.4	90.2	0.4
1987	92.0	2.0	92.8	0.9	93.7	1.0	94.1	0.4	95.2	1.2	97.8	2.7	96.3	-1.5	95.6	-0.7	95.5	-0.1	96.8	1.4	97.6	0.8	98.2	0.6
1988	99.4	1.2	100.3	0.9	102.1	1.8	103.3	1.2	104.3	1.0	105.8	1.4	108.6	2.6	109.4	0.7	110.0	0.5	111.4	1.3	112.8	1.3	114.2	1.2
1989	117.2	2.6	117.6	0.3	116.7	-0.8	117.5	0.7	117.8	0.3	115.6	-1.9	114.1	-1.3	113.4	-0.6	112.4	-0.9	112.5	0.1	111.7	-0.7	111.6	-0.1
1990	111.4	-0.2	111.3	-0.1	110.7	-0.5	110.4	-0.3	110.8	0.4	111.1	0.3	111.1	0.0	110.7	-0.4	114.9	3.8	118.4	3.0	120.1	1.4	117.8	-1.9
1991	117.5	-0.3	116.7	-0.7	113.2	-3.0	112.9	-0.3	111.9	-0.9	111.7	-0.2	109.7	-1.8	109.1	-0.5	109.7	0.5	109.7	0.0	109.7	0.0	109.9	0.2
1992	108.4	-1.4	107.3	-1.0	107.2	-0.1	107.5	0.3	107.7	0.2	109.9	2.0	110.2	0.3	110.5	0.3	111.0	0.5	110.7	-0.3	111.4	0.6	109.4	-1.8
1993	109.8	0.4	110.7	0.8	110.0	-0.6	111.9	1.7	111.1	-0.7	111.3	0.2	110.6	-0.6	110.4	-0.2	110.3	-0.1	110.2	-0.1	110.5	0.3	108.7	-1.6
1994	108.6	-0.1	108.1	-0.5	108.4	0.3	109.6	1.1	110.8	1.1	111.7	0.8	112.9	1.1	115.2	2.0	119.8	4.0	121.2	1.2	122.0	0.7	123.0	0.8
1995	125.6	2.1	127.9	1.8	128.5	0.5	131.5	2.3	132.0	0.4	130.3	-1.3	130.4	0.1	129.6	-0.6	128.8	-0.6	127.3	-1.2	124.6	-2.1	124.4	-0.2
1996	124.7	0.2	125.1	0.3	125.1	0.0	126.9	1.4	127.7	0.6	127.6	-0.1	126.8	-0.6	127.2	0.3	127.9	0.6	126.9	-0.8	127.1	0.2	127.5	0.3
1997	127.9	0.3	127.7	-0.2	126.7	-0.8	126.2	-0.4	125.8	-0.3	125.2	-0.5	125.8	0.5	126.7	0.7	126.8	0.1	127.2	0.3	127.3	0.1	127.0	-0.2
1998	125.8	-0.9	124.1	-1.4	123.1	-0.8	122.3	-0.6	121.9	-0.3	121.4	-0.4	121.1	-0.2	120.4	-0.6	119.5	-0.7	119.2	-0.3	119.4	0.2	118.9	-0.4
1999	118.3	-0.5	117.1	-1.0	116.4	-0.6	116.2	-0.2	117.0	0.7	117.6	0.5	118.1	0.4	118.2	0.1	119.6	1.2	121.8	1.8	122.8	0.8	123.8	0.8
2000	124.6	0.6	126.3	1.4	128.0	1.3	128.4	0.3	128.7	0.2	129.8	0.9	132.7	2.2	130.4	-1.7	130.4	0.0	130.5	0.1	129.3	-0.9	129.7	0.3
2001	132.9	2.5	134.7	1.4	134.6	-0.1	132.3	-1.7	131.9	-0.3	131.0	-0.7	126.9	-3.1	124.5	-1.9	126.8	1.8	123.4	-2.7	122.2	-1.0	120.1	-1.7

Source: U.S. Department of Labor, Bureau of Labor Statistics, Division of Industry Prices and Price Indexes. n.e.c. stands for not elsewhere classified. - indicates no data collected for period or unavailable.

Paints and Allied Products
Producer Price Index
Base 1982 = 100

For 1971-2001. Columns headed % show percentile change in the index from the previous period for which an index is available.

Year	Jan Index	%	Feb Index	%	Mar Index	%	Apr Index	%	May Index	%	Jun Index	%	Jul Index	%	Aug Index	%	Sep Index	%	Oct Index	%	Nov Index	%	Dec Index	%
1971	39.5	-	39.5	0.0	39.6	0.3	39.8	0.5	39.8	0.0	39.3	-1.3	39.4	0.3	39.4	0.0	39.4	0.0	39.4	0.0	39.4	0.0	39.6	0.5
1972	39.8	0.5	40.0	0.5	40.2	0.5	40.3	0.2	40.4	0.2	40.4	0.0	40.5	0.2	40.6	0.2	40.6	0.0	40.5	-0.2	40.5	0.0	40.7	0.5
1973	41.0	0.7	41.1	0.2	41.2	0.2	41.5	0.7	41.8	0.7	42.1	0.7	42.3	0.5	42.4	0.2	42.5	0.2	43.7	2.8	44.3	1.4	45.1	1.8
1974	46.1	2.2	46.5	0.9	47.9	3.0	49.3	2.9	49.6	0.6	52.2	5.2	53.9	3.3	54.5	1.1	55.3	1.5	56.8	2.7	59.2	4.2	59.2	0.0
1975	59.6	0.7	59.5	-0.2	60.4	1.5	60.3	-0.2	60.8	0.8	60.2	-1.0	60.4	0.3	60.3	-0.2	61.2	1.5	61.1	-0.2	61.0	-0.2	61.0	0.0
1976	60.8	-0.3	61.1	0.5	60.9	-0.3	64.1	5.3	64.2	0.2	64.3	0.2	65.0	1.1	65.5	0.8	66.1	0.9	66.2	0.2	66.6	0.6	66.6	0.0
1977	66.6	0.0	66.9	0.5	67.9	1.5	68.7	1.2	69.1	0.6	69.0	-0.1	68.9	-0.1	68.9	0.0	68.8	-0.1	68.6	-0.3	69.0	0.6	69.2	0.3
1978	69.0	-0.3	69.5	0.7	70.1	0.9	70.7	0.9	71.2	0.7	71.4	0.3	71.6	0.3	71.8	0.3	72.2	0.6	72.6	0.6	73.4	1.1	74.0	0.8
1979	74.3	0.4	75.2	1.2	75.7	0.7	76.7	1.3	77.1	0.5	77.7	0.8	79.6	2.4	79.8	0.3	80.6	1.0	81.0	0.5	82.0	1.2	82.3	0.4
1980	85.1	3.4	85.7	0.7	87.4	2.0	88.7	1.5	90.4	1.9	90.6	0.2	90.9	0.3	91.1	0.2	91.3	0.2	91.4	0.1	91.8	0.4	92.1	0.3
1981	92.9	0.9	94.0	1.2	94.6	0.6	95.7	1.2	96.9	1.3	-	-	-	-	-	-	-	-	98.4	1.5	99.1	0.7	99.0	-0.1
1982	99.6	0.6	99.6	0.0	99.7	0.1	99.6	-0.1	100.7	1.1	100.4	-0.3	100.3	-0.1	100.0	-0.3	100.1	0.1	100.1	0.0	100.0	-0.1	99.9	-0.1
1983	99.8	-0.1	99.5	-0.3	99.3	-0.2	99.6	0.3	99.6	0.0	99.5	-0.1	99.8	0.3	100.5	0.7	101.7	1.2	101.7	0.0	101.7	0.0	101.7	0.0
1984	102.0	0.3	102.6	0.6	102.5	-0.1	104.2	1.7	105.4	1.2	105.7	0.3	106.1	0.4	106.5	0.4	106.4	-0.1	106.6	0.2	106.6	0.0	106.8	0.2
1985	106.8	0.0	106.2	-0.6	106.4	0.2	106.7	0.3	107.0	0.3	107.2	0.2	107.1	-0.1	106.9	-0.2	106.5	-0.4	106.5	0.0	106.3	-0.2	106.6	0.3
1986	106.9	0.3	106.8	-0.1	107.0	0.2	105.4	-1.5	105.3	-0.1	105.3	0.0	105.9	0.6	105.5	-0.4	105.5	0.0	104.9	-0.6	105.0	0.1	105.1	0.1
1987	105.5	0.4	105.4	-0.1	105.7	0.3	106.8	1.0	106.9	0.1	107.9	0.9	108.1	0.2	108.7	0.6	108.8	0.1	108.8	0.0	107.6	-1.1	108.4	0.7
1988	109.6	1.1	109.8	0.2	110.6	0.7	111.2	0.5	111.5	0.3	112.2	0.6	113.7	1.3	114.1	0.4	114.7	0.5	115.4	0.6	117.0	1.4	117.2	0.2
1989	119.7	2.1	121.4	1.4	121.7	0.2	123.0	1.1	123.1	0.1	124.0	0.7	124.4	0.3	122.4	-1.6	123.0	0.5	123.3	0.2	122.2	-0.9	122.4	0.2
1990	122.8	0.3	125.3	2.0	125.5	0.2	126.1	0.5	126.4	0.2	127.0	0.5	127.3	0.2	127.5	0.2	131.8	3.4	132.3	0.4	134.7	1.8	134.7	0.0
1991	135.8	0.8	136.3	0.4	130.6	-4.2	130.7	0.1	130.7	0.0	131.3	0.5	131.4	0.1	131.3	-0.1	130.1	-0.9	130.1	0.0	130.5	0.3	130.4	-0.1
1992	130.3	-0.1	130.5	0.2	130.6	0.1	130.9	0.2	131.1	0.2	131.1	0.0	131.5	0.3	131.4	-0.1	131.2	-0.2	131.3	0.1	131.3	0.0	131.3	0.0
1993	131.7	0.3	132.0	0.2	131.9	-0.1	132.5	0.5	132.3	-0.2	132.2	-0.1	132.3	0.1	132.2	-0.1	132.2	0.0	132.1	-0.1	132.4	0.2	132.4	0.0
1994	132.6	0.2	133.0	0.3	133.1	0.1	133.1	0.0	133.3	0.2	133.5	0.2	133.8	0.2	134.1	0.2	134.4	0.2	134.7	0.2	135.3	0.4	135.8	0.4
1995	137.5	1.3	138.5	0.7	138.8	0.2	140.4	1.2	141.3	0.6	141.1	-0.1	141.5	0.3	142.1	0.4	142.2	0.1	142.5	0.2	143.1	0.4	142.8	-0.2
1996	143.5	0.5	143.6	0.1	144.4	0.6	144.6	0.1	144.5	-0.1	144.5	0.0	144.3	-0.1	145.7	1.0	145.5	-0.1	145.5	0.0	145.9	0.3	145.9	0.0
1997	146.2	0.2	146.9	0.5	147.0	0.1	148.2	0.8	148.1	-0.1	148.3	0.1	148.4	0.1	148.6	0.1	148.4	-0.1	148.9	0.3	148.7	-0.1	148.7	0.0
1998	149.0	0.2	149.7	0.5	150.5	0.5	150.7	0.1	150.8	0.1	150.8	0.0	151.2	0.3	151.0	-0.1	151.2	0.1	151.4	0.1	151.4	0.0	151.2	-0.1
1999	151.9	0.5	152.1	0.1	152.3	0.1	152.5	0.1	152.7	0.1	152.2	-0.3	152.6	0.3	152.6	0.0	152.7	0.1	152.9	0.1	152.6	-0.2	152.7	0.1
2000	154.2	1.0	155.1	0.6	155.8	0.5	156.0	0.1	157.2	0.8	157.2	0.0	156.5	-0.4	155.9	-0.4	156.5	0.4	156.8	0.2	157.2	0.3	157.0	-0.1
2001	158.1	0.7	159.7	1.0	159.5	-0.1	160.0	0.3	159.4	-0.4	160.0	0.4	160.1	0.1	159.8	-0.2	161.1	0.8	161.5	0.2	159.9	-1.0	159.6	-0.2

Source: U.S. Department of Labor, Bureau of Labor Statistics, Division of Industry Prices and Price Indexes. n.e.c. stands for not elsewhere classified. - indicates no data collected for period or unavailable.

Drugs and Pharmaceuticals
Producer Price Index
Base 1982 = 100

For 1947-2001. Columns headed % show percentile change in the index from the previous period for which an index is available.

Year	Jan Index	%	Feb Index	%	Mar Index	%	Apr Index	%	May Index	%	Jun Index	%	Jul Index	%	Aug Index	%	Sep Index	%	Oct Index	%	Nov Index	%	Dec Index	%
1947	59.3	-	59.3	0.0	58.7	-1.0	56.7	-3.4	56.8	0.2	56.5	-0.5	56.3	-0.4	55.6	-1.2	55.4	-0.4	55.6	0.4	56.5	1.6	57.5	1.8
1948	56.3	-2.1	56.3	0.0	55.4	-1.6	55.2	-0.4	55.0	-0.4	55.0	0.0	54.8	-0.4	55.3	0.9	54.6	-1.3	52.8	-3.3	52.9	0.2	52.9	0.0
1949	51.6	-2.5	51.9	0.6	51.5	-0.8	50.9	-1.2	50.9	0.0	50.9	0.0	50.5	-0.8	50.1	-0.8	50.1	0.0	50.1	0.0	50.0	-0.2	49.9	-0.2
1950	49.7	-0.4	49.5	-0.4	49.4	-0.2	49.4	0.0	49.4	0.0	49.4	0.0	49.5	0.2	50.2	1.4	50.5	0.6	50.8	0.6	51.3	1.0	51.7	0.8
1951	51.9	0.4	51.9	0.0	51.9	0.0	51.9	0.0	51.7	-0.4	51.8	0.2	51.7	-0.2	51.7	0.0	51.7	0.0	51.7	0.0	51.5	-0.4	51.6	0.2
1952	51.4	-0.4	50.6	-1.6	50.5	-0.2	50.2	-0.6	49.9	-0.6	49.9	0.0	49.9	0.0	49.9	0.0	49.9	0.0	49.8	-0.2	49.8	0.0	49.4	-0.8
1953	49.6	0.4	49.5	-0.2	49.6	0.2	50.4	1.6	50.5	0.2	50.5	0.0	50.7	0.4	50.6	-0.2	50.6	0.0	50.6	0.0	50.6	0.0	50.8	0.4
1954	50.8	0.0	50.8	0.0	50.8	0.0	50.9	0.2	50.9	0.0	50.9	0.0	50.9	0.0	50.9	0.0	50.9	0.0	50.7	-0.4	50.7	0.0	50.7	0.0
1955	50.7	0.0	50.6	-0.2	50.5	-0.2	50.5	0.0	50.5	0.0	50.4	-0.2	50.3	-0.2	50.0	-0.6	50.0	0.0	50.0	0.0	50.0	0.0	50.0	0.0
1956	50.1	0.2	49.8	-0.6	49.8	0.0	49.8	0.0	49.9	0.2	49.9	0.0	49.9	0.0	49.9	0.0	49.8	-0.2	49.8	0.0	50.0	0.4	50.1	0.2
1957	50.1	0.0	50.5	0.8	50.5	0.0	50.6	0.2	50.6	0.0	50.6	0.0	50.6	0.0	50.6	0.0	50.6	0.0	50.6	0.0	50.6	0.0	50.6	0.0
1958	50.7	0.2	50.7	0.0	50.9	0.4	50.9	0.0	51.1	0.4	51.2	0.2	51.1	-0.2	51.1	0.0	51.1	0.0	50.8	-0.6	50.5	-0.6	50.5	0.0
1959	50.5	0.0	50.5	0.0	50.3	-0.4	50.3	0.0	50.5	0.4	50.5	0.0	50.6	0.2	50.6	0.0	50.6	0.0	50.6	0.0	50.6	0.0	50.6	0.0
1960	50.6	0.0	50.6	0.0	50.6	0.0	50.7	0.2	50.9	0.4	51.1	0.4	51.1	0.0	51.1	0.0	50.7	-0.8	50.5	-0.4	50.3	-0.4	50.3	0.0
1961	50.2	-0.2	50.2	0.0	50.1	-0.2	50.1	0.0	50.0	-0.2	50.0	0.0	50.1	0.2	49.4	-1.4	49.1	-0.6	49.2	0.2	49.3	0.2	49.3	0.0
1962	49.2	-0.2	49.2	0.0	49.2	0.0	49.1	-0.2	49.1	0.0	49.1	0.0	48.2	-1.8	48.1	-0.2	48.1	0.0	48.2	0.2	48.2	0.0	48.0	-0.4
1963	48.2	0.4	48.2	0.0	48.2	0.0	48.2	0.0	48.2	0.0	48.2	0.0	48.2	0.0	48.1	-0.2	48.1	0.0	48.1	0.0	48.1	0.0	48.1	0.0
1964	48.3	0.4	48.3	0.0	48.2	-0.2	48.3	0.2	48.4	0.2	47.9	-1.0	48.0	0.2	47.9	-0.2	47.9	0.0	47.9	0.0	47.9	0.0	47.9	0.0
1965	47.8	-0.2	47.9	0.2	47.9	0.0	48.0	0.2	48.1	0.2	47.6	-1.0	47.6	0.0	47.6	0.0	47.6	0.0	47.6	0.0	47.9	0.6	47.9	0.0
1966	47.8	-0.2	47.8	0.0	47.8	0.0	47.6	-0.4	47.6	0.0	47.7	0.2	47.8	0.2	47.9	0.2	48.0	0.2	48.1	0.2	48.1	0.0	47.9	-0.4
1967	47.9	0.0	47.7	-0.4	47.8	0.2	47.6	-0.4	47.6	0.0	47.6	0.0	47.6	0.0	47.4	-0.4	47.4	0.0	47.4	0.0	47.5	0.2	47.5	0.0
1968	47.0	-1.1	47.1	0.2	47.3	0.4	47.3	0.0	47.3	0.0	47.4	0.2	47.3	-0.2	47.1	-0.4	47.0	-0.2	47.3	0.6	47.4	0.2	47.4	0.0
1969	47.4	0.0	47.4	0.0	47.4	0.0	47.5	0.2	47.6	0.2	47.5	-0.2	47.6	0.2	47.6	0.0	47.6	0.0	47.6	0.0	47.7	0.2	47.9	0.4
1970	47.8	-0.2	47.9	0.2	48.2	0.6	47.9	-0.6	48.0	0.2	48.1	0.2	48.2	0.2	48.4	0.4	48.1	-0.6	48.2	0.2	48.4	0.4	48.5	0.2
1971	48.5	0.0	48.7	0.4	48.8	0.2	48.6	-0.4	48.6	0.0	48.7	0.2	48.9	0.4	48.9	0.0	48.9	0.0	48.9	0.0	48.8	-0.2	48.8	0.0
1972	48.7	-0.2	48.7	0.0	48.8	0.2	48.8	0.0	48.9	0.2	49.1	0.4	49.1	0.0	49.2	0.2	49.1	-0.2	49.2	0.2	49.3	0.2	49.3	0.0
1973	49.3	0.0	49.3	0.0	49.4	0.2	49.4	0.0	49.5	0.2	49.7	0.4	49.7	0.0	49.7	0.0	49.8	0.2	49.8	0.0	49.9	0.2	50.0	0.2
1974	50.1	0.2	50.3	0.4	50.6	0.6	51.2	1.2	51.9	1.4	53.0	2.1	53.7	1.3	54.9	2.2	55.7	1.5	56.7	1.8	57.6	1.6	58.0	0.7
1975	58.9	1.6	59.1	0.3	59.3	0.3	59.9	1.0	59.9	0.0	60.2	0.5	60.7	0.8	60.7	0.0	60.6	-0.2	61.2	1.0	61.3	0.2	61.5	0.3
1976	62.3	1.3	62.7	0.6	62.9	0.3	63.3	0.6	63.4	0.2	64.0	0.9	64.1	0.2	64.3	0.3	64.5	0.3	64.5	0.0	64.7	0.3	64.9	0.3
1977	65.5	0.9	65.9	0.6	66.2	0.5	66.4	0.3	66.5	0.2	67.0	0.8	67.2	0.3	67.2	0.0	67.3	0.1	67.5	0.3	67.7	0.3	68.0	0.4
1978	68.6	0.9	69.0	0.6	69.2	0.3	69.6	0.6	69.8	0.3	70.3	0.7	70.7	0.6	70.9	0.3	71.2	0.4	71.5	0.4	72.4	1.3	72.9	0.7
1979	73.9	1.4	74.4	0.7	74.6	0.3	75.0	0.5	75.1	0.1	75.7	0.8	75.8	0.1	76.0	0.3	76.7	0.9	77.5	1.0	77.6	0.1	78.3	0.9
1980	79.3	1.3	79.8	0.6	80.4	0.8	82.2	2.2	82.3	0.1	83.0	0.9	83.6	0.7	83.8	0.2	84.2	0.5	84.9	0.8	86.2	1.5	86.9	0.8
1981	87.9	1.2	89.2	1.5	90.1	1.0	90.9	0.9	91.6	0.8	91.9	0.3	93.1	1.3	92.8	-0.3	94.2	1.5	94.5	0.3	94.3	-0.2	94.7	0.4
1982	96.2	1.6	97.3	1.1	98.0	0.7	99.4	1.4	99.9	0.5	99.8	-0.1	100.0	0.2	100.5	0.5	101.1	0.6	102.3	1.2	102.6	0.3	102.8	0.2
1983	104.1	1.3	105.7	1.5	106.1	0.4	107.2	1.0	107.2	0.0	107.2	0.0	108.3	1.0	108.2	-0.1	108.2	0.0	109.1	0.8	110.0	0.8	109.9	-0.1
1984	110.9	0.9	111.6	0.6	113.1	1.3	114.2	1.0	114.3	0.1	112.9	-1.2	114.5	1.4	114.6	0.1	114.1	-0.4	116.5	2.1	117.5	0.9	116.6	-0.8
1985	117.8	1.0	119.1	1.1	120.1	0.8	121.0	0.7	121.7	0.6	121.0	-0.6	123.6	2.1	122.9	-0.6	123.4	0.4	124.4	0.8	125.1	0.6	124.1	-0.8
1986	126.6	2.0	126.5	-0.1	128.0	1.2	129.2	0.9	129.6	0.3	129.8	0.2	130.3	0.4	130.7	0.3	131.5	0.6	132.5	0.8	133.2	0.5	133.2	0.0
1987	134.7	1.1	135.8	0.8	137.3	1.1	138.2	0.7	139.5	0.9	138.9	-0.4	139.2	0.2	139.5	0.2	141.0	1.1	140.0	-0.7	142.6	1.9	142.4	-0.1
1988	143.3	0.6	143.6	0.2	145.5	1.3	146.0	0.3	147.4	1.0	147.4	0.0	149.2	1.2	149.2	0.0	150.8	1.1	151.5	0.5	153.3	1.2	153.1	-0.1
1989	155.5	1.6	155.6	0.1	157.7	1.3	158.6	0.6	158.6	0.0	160.1	0.9	160.7	0.4	161.9	0.7	161.3	-0.4	162.3	0.6	163.6	0.8	164.3	0.4
1990	166.0	1.0	167.5	0.9	168.7	0.7	169.8	0.7	170.5	0.4	170.1	-0.2	171.0	0.5	171.7	0.4	171.6	-0.1	172.9	0.8	174.5	0.9	175.1	0.3
1991	176.3	0.7	178.0	1.0	178.3	0.2	181.1	1.6	181.7	0.3	182.6	0.5	184.7	1.2	185.5	0.4	184.0	-0.8	186.1	1.1	186.1	0.0	186.5	0.2

[Continued]

Drugs and Pharmaceuticals
Producer Price Index
Base 1982 = 100

[Continued]

For 1947-2001. Columns headed % show percentile change in the index from the previous period for which an index is available.

Year	Jan Index	%	Feb Index	%	Mar Index	%	Apr Index	%	May Index	%	Jun Index	%	Jul Index	%	Aug Index	%	Sep Index	%	Oct Index	%	Nov Index	%	Dec Index	%
1992	187.2	0.4	188.8	0.9	189.6	0.4	191.3	0.9	191.9	0.3	192.2	0.2	192.8	0.3	193.8	0.5	193.7	-0.1	194.8	0.6	194.6	-0.1	196.0	0.7
1993	197.9	1.0	199.1	0.6	199.2	0.1	200.5	0.7	200.3	-0.1	201.0	0.3	201.5	0.2	202.3	0.4	202.1	-0.1	202.6	0.2	202.2	-0.2	202.3	0.0
1994	204.6	1.1	204.5	-0.0	204.7	0.1	205.3	0.3	206.2	0.4	206.2	0.0	206.0	-0.1	206.3	0.1	206.6	0.1	206.4	-0.1	207.3	0.4	207.3	0.0
1995	207.8	0.2	208.9	0.5	208.9	0.0	210.4	0.7	210.4	0.0	210.2	-0.1	210.8	0.3	210.9	0.0	211.9	0.5	213.1	0.6	213.4	0.1	213.8	0.2
1996	213.5	-0.1	213.4	-0.0	214.4	0.5	214.1	-0.1	214.8	0.3	215.0	0.1	215.4	0.2	215.1	-0.1	215.1	0.0	215.4	0.1	214.8	-0.3	215.4	0.3
1997	217.4	0.9	218.2	0.4	218.6	0.2	217.7	-0.4	218.3	0.3	218.6	0.1	219.1	0.2	219.3	0.1	219.3	0.0	220.1	0.4	220.6	0.2	220.8	0.1
1998	221.6	0.4	224.5	1.3	243.3	8.4	243.4	0.0	244.1	0.3	245.9	0.7	247.7	0.7	247.2	-0.2	247.2	0.0	248.6	0.6	248.5	-0.0	249.1	0.2
1999	247.6	-0.6	248.0	0.2	249.0	0.4	249.4	0.2	249.8	0.2	251.6	0.7	252.9	0.5	252.7	-0.1	253.6	0.4	254.1	0.2	254.3	0.1	254.5	0.1
2000	255.5	0.4	256.2	0.3	256.5	0.1	257.2	0.3	256.8	-0.2	256.7	-0.0	257.5	0.3	258.4	0.3	258.5	0.0	258.4	-0.0	258.1	-0.1	259.1	0.4
2001	260.1	0.4	261.9	0.7	262.1	0.1	263.1	0.4	260.4	-1.0	262.5	0.8	260.6	-0.7	261.0	0.2	260.8	-0.1	260.7	-0.0	261.4	0.3	261.9	0.2

Source: U.S. Department of Labor, Bureau of Labor Statistics, Division of Industry Prices and Price Indexes. n.e.c. stands for not elsewhere classified. - indicates no data collected for period or unavailable.

Fats and Oils, Inedible
Producer Price Index
Base 1982 = 100

For 1926-2001. Columns headed % show percentile change in the index from the previous period for which an index is available.

Year	Jan Index	%	Feb Index	%	Mar Index	%	Apr Index	%	May Index	%	Jun Index	%	Jul Index	%	Aug Index	%	Sep Index	%	Oct Index	%	Nov Index	%	Dec Index	%
1926	-	-	-	-	-	-	-	-	-	-	-	-	-	-	-	-	-	-	-	-	-	-	-	-
1927	-	-	-	-	-	-	-	-	-	-	-	-	-	-	-	-	-	-	-	-	-	-	-	-
1928	-	-	-	-	-	-	-	-	-	-	-	-	-	-	-	-	-	-	-	-	-	-	-	-
1929	-	-	-	-	-	-	-	-	-	-	-	-	-	-	-	-	-	-	-	-	-	-	-	-
1930	-	-	-	-	-	-	-	-	-	-	-	-	-	-	-	-	-	-	-	-	-	-	-	-
1931	-	-	-	-	-	-	-	-	-	-	-	-	-	-	-	-	-	-	-	-	-	-	-	-
1932	-	-	-	-	-	-	-	-	-	-	-	-	-	-	-	-	-	-	-	-	-	-	-	-
1933	19.3	-	18.6	-3.6	18.8	1.1	19.1	1.6	22.2	16.2	23.4	5.4	23.0	-1.7	22.7	-1.3	21.0	-7.5	20.9	-0.5	21.1	1.0	20.3	-3.8
1934	19.5	-3.9	19.9	2.1	20.2	1.5	20.1	-0.5	20.4	1.5	19.8	-2.9	20.1	1.5	21.3	6.0	23.1	8.5	24.6	6.5	23.8	-3.3	25.4	6.7
1935	29.7	16.9	33.3	12.1	36.3	9.0	34.6	-4.7	35.3	2.0	33.0	-6.5	29.5	-10.6	29.4	-0.3	31.1	5.8	33.7	8.4	33.1	-1.8	32.8	-0.9
1936	32.8	0.0	31.8	-3.0	30.3	-4.7	29.4	-3.0	26.7	-9.2	27.4	2.6	30.8	12.4	32.6	5.8	36.8	12.9	37.6	2.2	39.8	5.9	45.7	14.8
1937	51.4	12.5	50.5	-1.8	50.1	-0.8	47.8	-4.6	42.8	-10.5	40.5	-5.4	39.4	-2.7	36.9	-6.3	34.4	-6.8	33.2	-3.5	31.2	-6.0	29.7	-4.8
1938	30.4	2.4	29.4	-3.3	28.5	-3.1	26.1	-8.4	25.2	-3.4	24.6	-2.4	26.1	6.1	25.6	-1.9	25.1	-2.0	25.0	-0.4	24.6	-1.6	24.5	-0.4
1939	24.6	0.4	24.3	-1.2	25.0	2.9	24.3	-2.8	24.7	1.6	24.5	-0.8	22.9	-6.5	21.5	-6.1	28.7	33.5	30.3	5.6	29.0	-4.3	28.2	-2.8
1940	27.8	-1.4	27.0	-2.9	25.4	-5.9	24.8	-2.4	24.4	-1.6	23.9	-2.0	22.8	-4.6	20.7	-9.2	21.1	1.9	21.0	-0.5	22.4	6.7	22.4	0.0
1941	24.5	9.4	24.8	1.2	29.5	19.0	36.7	24.4	42.7	16.3	42.7	0.0	44.4	4.0	46.2	4.1	48.4	4.8	49.4	2.1	49.2	-0.4	54.0	9.8
1942	56.3	4.3	57.3	1.8	57.6	0.5	57.7	0.2	57.5	-0.3	57.4	-0.2	55.2	-3.8	53.8	-2.5	53.8	0.0	53.8	0.0	53.8	0.0	53.8	0.0
1943	53.8	0.0	53.8	0.0	53.8	0.0	53.8	0.0	54.0	0.4	54.0	0.0	54.0	0.0	54.0	0.0	54.0	0.0	54.0	0.0	54.0	0.0	54.0	0.0
1944	54.0	0.0	54.0	0.0	54.0	0.0	54.0	0.0	54.0	0.0	54.0	0.0	54.0	0.0	54.0	0.0	54.0	0.0	54.0	0.0	54.0	0.0	54.0	0.0
1945	54.0	0.0	54.0	0.0	54.0	0.0	54.0	0.0	54.0	0.0	54.0	0.0	54.0	0.0	54.0	0.0	54.0	0.0	54.0	0.0	54.0	0.0	54.0	0.0
1946	53.8	-0.4	53.9	0.2	54.1	0.4	54.1	0.0	54.1	0.0	54.1	0.0	60.4	11.6	54.3	-10.1	54.7	0.7	58.8	7.5	101.1	71.9	107.5	6.3
1947	111.5	3.7	114.9	3.0	128.8	12.1	116.8	-9.3	86.3	-26.1	67.5	-21.8	64.5	-4.4	62.6	-2.9	82.4	31.6	103.6	25.7	121.2	17.0	111.0	-8.4
1948	120.6	8.6	96.0	-20.4	100.0	4.2	96.0	-4.0	85.6	-10.8	92.6	8.2	87.4	-5.6	77.9	-10.9	80.8	3.7	77.8	-3.7	79.0	1.5	70.2	-11.1
1949	56.2	-19.9	49.8	-11.4	44.8	-10.0	39.8	-11.2	42.0	5.5	40.1	-4.5	39.2	-2.2	46.1	17.6	41.7	-9.5	39.7	-4.8	39.7	0.0	39.9	0.5
1950	42.5	6.5	41.7	-1.9	43.4	4.1	43.3	-0.2	41.8	-3.5	37.3	-10.8	44.2	18.5	53.0	19.9	66.5	25.5	65.3	-1.8	71.5	9.5	80.1	12.0
1951	88.9	11.0	94.4	6.2	87.8	-7.0	82.3	-6.3	79.3	-3.6	67.7	-14.6	53.6	-20.8	53.8	0.4	55.8	3.7	54.9	-1.6	49.9	-9.1	47.0	-5.8
1952	43.4	-7.7	39.2	-9.7	36.2	-7.7	32.6	-9.9	36.1	10.7	39.8	10.2	38.1	-4.3	36.3	-4.7	37.4	3.0	39.0	4.3	40.6	4.1	40.4	-0.5
1953	40.9	1.2	40.3	-1.5	45.1	11.9	42.7	-5.3	38.2	-10.5	35.6	-6.8	35.7	0.3	35.9	0.6	39.1	8.9	40.8	4.3	44.4	8.8	44.8	0.9
1954	46.8	4.5	48.6	3.8	46.3	-4.7	45.7	-1.3	45.4	-0.7	42.6	-6.2	39.8	-6.6	40.9	2.8	41.3	1.0	43.2	4.6	44.2	2.3	45.4	2.7
1955	47.3	4.2	46.7	-1.3	42.4	-9.2	42.2	-0.5	40.7	-3.6	41.1	1.0	42.7	3.9	41.8	-2.1	42.7	2.2	44.5	4.2	44.1	-0.9	43.3	-1.8
1956	42.5	-1.8	41.6	-2.1	42.1	1.2	44.4	5.5	46.1	3.8	42.1	-8.7	41.1	-2.4	41.1	0.0	42.4	3.2	42.7	0.7	44.2	3.5	45.4	2.7
1957	44.9	-1.1	44.4	-1.1	44.3	-0.2	44.5	0.5	45.3	1.8	46.1	1.8	46.7	1.3	48.5	3.9	49.3	1.6	49.5	0.4	49.9	0.8	50.0	0.2
1958	48.3	-3.4	48.1	-0.4	49.1	2.1	47.6	-3.1	47.0	-1.3	47.3	0.6	47.8	1.1	47.8	0.0	47.2	-1.3	47.9	1.5	49.5	3.3	47.0	-5.1
1959	45.8	-2.6	45.0	-1.7	46.1	2.4	46.2	0.2	46.2	0.0	44.7	-3.2	42.3	-5.4	41.1	-2.8	42.1	2.4	41.7	-1.0	39.9	-4.3	38.9	-2.5
1960	37.6	-3.3	37.8	0.5	38.7	2.4	39.6	2.3	38.4	-3.0	36.6	-4.7	36.6	0.0	37.4	2.2	36.5	-2.4	36.6	0.3	37.4	2.2	37.1	-0.8
1961	38.4	3.5	41.8	8.9	44.1	5.5	47.5	7.7	47.0	-1.1	41.4	-11.9	39.9	-3.6	39.1	-2.0	37.3	-4.6	36.0	-3.5	35.2	-2.2	36.1	2.6
1962	38.2	5.8	35.5	-7.1	37.4	5.4	36.5	-2.4	35.5	-2.7	33.8	-4.8	33.9	0.3	33.6	-0.9	33.3	-0.9	35.3	6.0	35.0	-0.8	33.5	-4.3
1963	33.0	-1.5	33.5	1.5	34.3	2.4	35.8	4.4	36.2	1.1	37.1	2.5	37.5	1.1	37.6	0.3	37.4	-0.5	40.8	9.1	41.5	1.7	39.2	-5.5
1964	38.3	-2.3	38.3	0.0	39.5	3.1	40.2	1.8	40.8	1.5	42.9	5.1	44.2	3.0	46.7	5.7	48.9	4.7	49.6	1.4	51.9	4.6	53.8	3.7
1965	52.2	-3.0	54.5	4.4	54.7	0.4	55.8	2.0	53.7	-3.8	52.5	-2.2	50.8	-3.2	48.1	-5.3	49.9	3.7	50.7	1.6	49.1	-3.2	50.7	3.3
1966	52.1	2.8	50.7	-2.7	49.0	-3.4	47.9	-2.2	47.2	-1.5	46.8	-0.8	48.5	3.6	48.6	0.2	47.8	-1.6	43.5	-9.0	42.2	-3.0	43.8	3.8
1967	42.5	-3.0	41.0	-3.5	37.5	-8.5	39.3	4.8	38.2	-2.8	36.6	-4.2	35.5	-3.0	35.6	0.3	35.5	-0.3	36.2	2.0	35.9	-0.8	35.6	-0.8
1968	35.2	-1.1	35.3	0.3	36.8	4.2	37.2	1.1	36.1	-3.0	33.5	-7.2	31.8	-5.1	32.8	3.1	31.6	-3.7	32.2	1.9	33.8	5.0	32.2	-4.7
1969	33.3	3.4	33.9	1.8	37.0	9.1	38.6	4.3	38.4	-0.5	40.0	4.2	41.7	4.2	45.7	9.6	46.9	2.6	45.5	-3.0	46.3	1.8	42.7	-7.8
1970	43.8	2.6	43.4	-0.9	47.2	8.8	49.5	4.9	49.2	-0.6	49.8	1.2	49.6	-0.4	51.6	4.0	48.1	-6.8	54.1	12.5	56.7	4.8	53.8	-5.1

[Continued]

Fats and Oils, Inedible
Producer Price Index
Base 1982 = 100

[Continued]

For 1926-2001. Columns headed % show percentile change in the index from the previous period for which an index is available.

Year	Jan Index	%	Feb Index	%	Mar Index	%	Apr Index	%	May Index	%	Jun Index	%	Jul Index	%	Aug Index	%	Sep Index	%	Oct Index	%	Nov Index	%	Dec Index	%
1971	50.1	-6.9	53.4	6.6	54.0	1.1	53.6	-0.7	52.0	-3.0	49.4	-5.0	49.0	-0.8	50.2	2.4	49.8	-0.8	48.3	-3.0	46.9	-2.9	43.4	-7.5
1972	41.7	-3.9	41.4	-0.7	38.7	-6.5	42.0	8.5	43.4	3.3	43.4	0.0	42.4	-2.3	45.4	7.1	43.6	-4.0	43.9	0.7	46.1	5.0	48.0	4.1
1973	48.8	1.7	52.1	6.8	65.1	25.0	68.9	5.8	86.9	26.1	98.7	13.6	98.5	-0.2	102.3	3.9	104.7	2.3	102.2	-2.4	90.6	-11.4	107.1	18.2
1974	111.6	4.2	125.7	12.6	139.4	10.9	144.3	3.5	134.5	-6.8	135.3	0.6	130.1	-3.8	142.4	9.5	121.8	-14.5	122.9	0.9	112.8	-8.2	99.0	-12.2
1975	88.1	-11.0	86.7	-1.6	81.7	-5.8	97.9	19.8	93.8	-4.2	92.4	-1.5	97.5	5.5	107.0	9.7	108.5	1.4	99.0	-8.8	97.6	-1.4	96.3	-1.3
1976	92.3	-4.2	91.8	-0.5	95.9	4.5	91.2	-4.9	88.2	-3.3	91.2	3.4	97.0	6.4	93.4	-3.7	98.4	5.4	94.1	-4.4	94.1	0.0	95.3	1.3
1977	95.5	0.2	100.4	5.1	102.5	2.1	114.2	11.4	126.4	10.7	119.4	-5.5	105.6	-11.6	100.7	-4.6	92.4	-8.2	97.7	5.7	99.4	1.7	99.7	0.3
1978	98.6	-1.1	105.4	6.9	110.3	4.6	112.8	2.3	118.0	4.6	117.3	-0.6	125.7	7.2	117.2	-6.8	126.7	8.1	127.3	0.5	135.3	6.3	124.7	-7.8
1979	125.9	1.0	137.8	9.5	149.2	8.3	168.0	12.6	156.6	-6.8	140.1	-10.5	142.9	2.0	140.9	-1.4	142.3	1.0	137.4	-3.4	128.9	-6.2	122.5	-5.0
1980	121.9	-0.5	113.2	-7.1	112.3	-0.8	111.7	-0.5	110.4	-1.2	95.8	-13.2	97.4	1.7	115.2	18.3	114.0	-1.0	113.1	-0.8	115.4	2.0	118.8	2.9
1981	116.3	-2.1	108.5	-6.7	110.7	2.0	117.1	5.8	116.9	-0.2	113.5	-2.9	108.9	-4.1	114.4	5.1	106.9	-6.6	104.0	-2.7	105.8	1.7	105.0	-0.8
1982	102.1	-2.8	102.7	0.6	108.6	5.7	105.8	-2.6	108.0	2.1	107.6	-0.4	104.2	-3.2	95.2	-8.6	95.1	-0.1	90.7	-4.6	89.7	-1.1	90.2	0.6
1983	90.6	0.4	94.9	4.7	98.2	3.5	104.2	6.1	107.5	3.2	103.7	-3.5	97.7	-5.8	104.1	6.6	123.2	18.3	119.3	-3.2	120.4	0.9	119.4	-0.8
1984	125.2	4.9	130.7	4.4	137.3	5.0	143.5	4.5	149.5	4.2	155.1	3.7	141.8	-8.6	131.1	-7.5	134.6	2.7	136.7	1.6	142.3	4.1	141.1	-0.8
1985	129.7	-8.1	130.0	0.2	129.7	-0.2	130.7	0.8	124.0	-5.1	111.7	-9.9	104.8	-6.2	97.6	-6.9	92.6	-5.1	93.6	1.1	90.7	-3.1	91.9	1.3
1986	94.5	2.8	95.9	1.5	86.4	-9.9	81.6	-5.6	76.9	-5.8	71.5	-7.0	69.9	-2.2	71.2	1.9	72.2	1.4	76.9	6.5	80.2	4.3	84.1	4.9
1987	94.5	12.4	95.1	0.6	91.3	-4.0	83.0	-9.1	91.0	9.6	94.9	4.3	92.5	-2.5	93.0	0.5	95.5	2.7	94.8	-0.7	93.3	-1.6	93.4	0.1
1988	110.5	18.3	110.8	0.3	110.1	-0.6	109.6	-0.5	105.9	-3.4	115.1	8.7	123.0	6.9	122.0	-0.8	111.6	-8.5	107.2	-3.9	100.7	-6.1	103.7	3.0
1989	103.2	-0.5	102.4	-0.8	101.8	-0.6	99.1	-2.7	96.2	-2.9	99.2	3.1	94.5	-4.7	85.9	-9.1	86.8	1.0	93.9	8.2	92.2	-1.8	90.7	-1.6
1990	88.3	-2.6	94.2	6.7	90.6	-3.8	85.6	-5.5	86.8	1.4	88.5	2.0	88.4	-0.1	83.0	-6.1	82.4	-0.7	87.0	5.6	89.6	3.0	92.8	3.6
1991	96.6	4.1	89.5	-7.3	86.2	-3.7	86.5	0.3	83.5	-3.5	82.1	-1.7	80.5	-1.9	86.9	8.0	87.7	0.9	87.1	-0.7	88.3	1.4	87.0	-1.5
1992	88.9	2.2	86.5	-2.7	83.0	-4.0	84.6	1.9	87.2	3.1	91.7	5.2	94.7	3.3	98.1	3.6	99.4	1.3	98.8	-0.6	102.7	3.9	100.9	-1.8
1993	100.6	-0.3	97.5	-3.1	97.5	0.0	100.7	3.3	99.9	-0.8	96.5	-3.4	93.5	-3.1	94.7	1.3	91.2	-3.7	90.2	-1.1	90.1	-0.1	94.7	5.1
1994	99.9	5.5	102.8	2.9	101.7	-1.1	99.0	-2.7	99.3	0.3	105.0	5.7	106.6	1.5	112.6	5.6	116.1	3.1	118.4	2.0	125.2	5.7	140.2	12.0
1995	142.8	1.9	121.9	-14.6	124.1	1.8	122.0	-1.7	119.7	-1.9	121.8	1.8	125.7	3.2	124.8	-0.7	124.3	-0.4	125.5	1.0	135.0	7.6	134.8	-0.1
1996	132.3	-1.9	121.4	-8.2	115.8	-4.6	116.1	0.3	130.7	12.6	132.7	1.5	136.3	2.7	147.2	8.0	160.8	9.2	143.8	-10.6	125.3	-12.9	137.6	9.8
1997	150.3	9.2	146.4	-2.6	132.5	-9.5	115.8	-12.6	122.2	5.5	127.4	4.3	124.3	-2.4	121.7	-2.1	124.9	2.6	135.1	8.2	143.7	6.4	143.1	-0.4
1998	131.9	-7.8	111.7	-15.3	115.4	3.3	111.2	-3.6	125.0	12.4	128.6	2.9	114.6	-10.9	115.6	0.9	111.3	-3.7	113.8	2.2	111.0	-2.5	110.3	-0.6
1999	108.9	-1.3	97.2	-10.7	77.4	-20.4	81.8	5.7	79.2	-3.2	78.1	-1.4	79.5	1.8	78.9	-0.8	88.2	11.8	101.0	14.5	97.8	-3.2	92.7	-5.2
2000	87.2	-5.9	75.5	-13.4	74.3	-1.6	70.3	-5.4	71.4	1.6	72.5	1.5	66.3	-8.6	63.2	-4.7	63.9	1.1	65.5	2.5	63.9	-2.4	67.7	5.9
2001	78.7	16.2	69.3	-11.9	65.4	-5.6	63.5	-2.9	66.8	5.2	71.9	7.6	81.4	13.2	100.1	23.0	95.6	-4.5	80.4	-15.9	74.6	-7.2	82.0	9.9

Source: U.S. Department of Labor, Bureau of Labor Statistics, Division of Industry Prices and Price Indexes. n.e.c. stands for not elsewhere classified. - indicates no data collected for period or unavailable.

Agricultural Chemicals and Chemical Products
Producer Price Index
Base 1982 = 100

For 1947-2001. Columns headed % show percentile change in the index from the previous period for which an index is available.

Year	Jan Index	Jan %	Feb Index	Feb %	Mar Index	Mar %	Apr Index	Apr %	May Index	May %	Jun Index	Jun %	Jul Index	Jul %	Aug Index	Aug %	Sep Index	Sep %	Oct Index	Oct %	Nov Index	Nov %	Dec Index	Dec %
1947	28.3	-	28.3	0.0	28.9	2.1	29.0	0.3	29.0	0.0	28.8	-0.7	28.9	0.3	28.9	0.0	29.0	0.3	29.3	1.0	29.5	0.7	29.7	0.7
1948	29.9	0.7	29.8	-0.3	29.9	0.3	29.8	-0.3	29.7	-0.3	29.7	0.0	30.2	1.7	30.6	1.3	30.9	1.0	31.1	0.6	31.3	0.6	31.3	0.0
1949	31.6	1.0	31.5	-0.3	31.5	0.0	31.5	0.0	31.5	0.0	31.3	-0.6	31.5	0.6	31.4	-0.3	31.4	0.0	31.4	0.0	31.0	-1.3	30.9	-0.3
1950	30.8	-0.3	30.6	-0.6	30.7	0.3	30.8	0.3	30.8	0.0	30.1	-2.3	30.1	0.0	30.2	0.3	30.2	0.0	30.2	0.0	30.6	1.3	31.6	3.3
1951	32.1	1.6	32.1	0.0	32.1	0.0	32.1	0.0	32.1	0.0	31.9	-0.6	32.5	1.9	32.6	0.3	32.8	0.6	32.9	0.3	32.9	0.0	33.0	0.3
1952	33.0	0.0	33.1	0.3	33.3	0.6	33.3	0.0	33.5	0.6	32.9	-1.8	33.0	0.3	33.0	0.0	33.0	0.0	33.0	0.0	33.0	0.0	33.0	0.0
1953	32.9	-0.3	32.8	-0.3	32.8	0.0	32.9	0.3	33.0	0.3	32.7	-0.9	33.1	1.2	33.2	0.3	33.2	0.0	33.1	-0.3	33.3	0.6	33.4	0.3
1954	33.2	-0.6	33.4	0.6	33.4	0.0	33.4	0.0	33.4	0.0	33.1	-0.9	33.1	0.0	33.2	0.3	33.1	-0.3	33.0	-0.3	33.0	0.0	33.1	0.3
1955	33.2	0.3	33.2	0.0	33.2	0.0	33.1	-0.3	33.1	0.0	32.8	-0.9	32.9	0.3	33.0	0.3	32.9	-0.3	33.0	0.3	32.9	-0.3	32.9	0.0
1956	33.0	0.3	32.8	-0.6	32.8	0.0	32.8	0.0	32.3	-1.5	32.3	0.0	32.2	-0.3	32.3	0.3	32.2	-0.3	32.1	-0.3	32.3	0.6	32.3	0.0
1957	32.5	0.6	32.3	-0.6	32.3	0.0	32.5	0.6	32.4	-0.3	32.3	-0.3	32.3	0.0	32.5	0.6	32.7	0.6	32.8	0.3	32.8	0.0	33.1	0.9
1958	33.4	0.9	33.3	-0.3	33.4	0.3	33.6	0.6	33.6	0.0	33.6	0.0	33.6	0.0	33.4	-0.6	32.9	-1.5	32.8	-0.3	33.0	0.6	32.9	-0.3
1959	33.4	1.5	33.4	0.0	33.4	0.0	33.3	-0.3	33.2	-0.3	33.3	0.3	33.2	-0.3	33.0	-0.6	33.1	0.3	33.2	0.3	33.2	0.0	33.3	0.3
1960	33.4	0.3	33.5	0.3	33.5	0.0	33.5	0.0	33.5	0.0	33.5	0.0	33.7	0.6	33.7	0.0	33.8	0.3	34.0	0.6	34.0	0.0	33.9	-0.3
1961	34.0	0.3	34.0	0.0	34.0	0.0	34.0	0.0	34.0	0.0	33.8	-0.6	33.8	0.0	33.6	-0.6	33.8	0.6	33.4	-1.2	33.6	0.6	33.5	-0.3
1962	34.2	2.1	34.3	0.3	34.0	-0.9	34.0	0.0	33.9	-0.3	33.9	0.0	33.6	-0.9	33.2	-1.2	33.2	0.0	33.2	0.0	33.2	0.0	33.2	0.0
1963	33.4	0.6	33.2	-0.6	33.2	0.0	33.4	0.6	33.4	0.0	33.2	-0.6	33.1	-0.3	32.7	-1.2	32.8	0.3	32.8	0.0	32.9	0.3	32.7	-0.6
1964	32.8	0.3	32.9	0.3	32.9	0.0	32.9	0.0	32.9	0.0	32.9	0.0	33.0	0.3	32.8	-0.6	32.7	-0.3	32.8	0.3	33.0	0.6	33.0	0.0
1965	33.2	0.6	33.5	0.9	33.6	0.3	33.5	-0.3	33.5	0.0	33.6	0.3	33.7	0.3	33.6	-0.3	33.7	0.3	33.8	0.3	33.8	0.0	33.8	0.0
1966	33.8	0.0	33.9	0.3	33.9	0.0	34.1	0.6	34.2	0.3	34.0	-0.6	33.9	-0.3	33.6	-0.9	33.7	0.3	33.9	0.6	34.1	0.6	34.0	-0.3
1967	34.4	1.2	34.8	1.2	34.9	0.3	34.7	-0.6	34.7	0.0	34.7	0.0	34.2	-1.4	33.6	-1.8	33.4	-0.6	33.5	0.3	33.6	0.3	33.7	0.3
1968	32.8	-2.7	33.2	1.2	33.4	0.6	33.5	0.3	33.5	0.0	33.4	-0.3	33.4	0.0	32.7	-2.1	32.5	-0.6	32.3	-0.6	31.8	-1.5	31.8	0.0
1969	30.6	-3.8	30.4	-0.7	30.5	0.3	30.4	-0.3	30.4	0.0	30.4	0.0	29.2	-3.9	29.2	0.0	28.9	-1.0	28.5	-1.4	28.6	0.4	28.6	0.0
1970	28.9	1.0	30.2	4.5	30.4	0.7	30.5	0.3	30.3	-0.7	30.3	0.0	30.0	-1.0	30.2	0.7	30.4	0.7	30.6	0.7	30.6	0.0	30.6	0.0
1971	31.5	2.9	31.8	1.0	32.2	1.3	32.3	0.3	32.2	-0.3	32.2	0.0	31.5	-2.2	30.9	-1.9	30.9	0.0	30.9	0.0	30.9	0.0	30.9	0.0
1972	30.9	0.0	30.8	-0.3	31.0	0.6	31.5	1.6	31.5	0.0	31.6	0.3	31.4	-0.6	31.5	0.3	31.5	0.0	31.5	0.0	31.6	0.3	31.6	0.0
1973	31.8	0.6	31.8	0.0	32.0	0.6	32.3	0.9	32.4	0.3	32.5	0.3	33.1	1.8	32.8	-0.9	32.8	0.0	32.8	0.0	35.9	9.5	36.3	1.1
1974	38.4	5.8	38.7	0.8	40.4	4.4	40.4	0.0	40.4	0.0	41.1	1.7	44.8	9.0	48.6	8.5	49.7	2.3	58.3	17.3	61.9	6.2	62.3	0.6
1975	65.0	4.3	65.9	1.4	72.4	9.9	72.6	0.3	72.5	-0.1	72.2	-0.4	71.9	-0.4	70.6	-1.8	68.8	-2.5	68.4	-0.6	67.6	-1.2	67.7	0.1
1976	67.7	0.0	65.4	-3.4	65.1	-0.5	64.9	-0.3	64.9	0.0	64.3	-0.9	63.1	-1.9	63.7	1.0	63.9	0.3	63.9	0.0	63.0	-1.4	62.7	-0.5
1977	62.3	-0.6	62.9	1.0	64.0	1.7	64.6	0.9	64.5	-0.2	64.6	0.2	64.5	-0.2	64.8	0.5	65.0	0.3	65.0	0.0	64.4	-0.9	64.0	-0.6
1978	64.1	0.2	64.7	0.9	65.3	0.9	65.7	0.6	69.6	5.9	69.3	-0.4	69.1	-0.3	69.1	0.0	69.3	0.3	69.6	0.4	69.2	-0.6	69.1	-0.1
1979	69.0	-0.1	69.4	0.6	70.5	1.6	71.7	1.7	71.8	0.1	71.5	-0.4	72.2	1.0	73.6	1.9	75.0	1.9	76.7	2.3	78.5	2.3	79.6	1.4
1980	82.7	3.9	84.8	2.5	87.6	3.3	88.4	0.9	88.4	0.0	88.1	-0.3	88.5	0.5	88.9	0.5	89.1	0.2	89.1	0.0	89.3	0.2	90.0	0.8
1981	91.5	1.7	92.9	1.5	94.3	1.5	95.0	0.7	95.4	0.4	98.8	3.6	98.8	0.0	100.3	1.5	100.1	-0.2	100.2	0.1	101.1	0.9	100.8	-0.3
1982	101.5	0.7	101.9	0.4	101.6	-0.3	101.1	-0.5	100.8	-0.3	100.6	-0.2	99.7	-0.9	99.5	-0.2	99.1	-0.4	98.7	-0.4	98.0	-0.7	97.5	-0.5
1983	96.8	-0.7	96.9	0.1	97.2	0.3	96.7	-0.5	96.6	-0.1	96.0	-0.6	95.1	-0.9	94.8	-0.3	94.4	-0.4	94.5	0.1	95.9	1.5	96.4	0.5
1984	95.2	-1.2	97.7	2.6	98.5	0.8	98.6	0.1	98.1	-0.5	98.0	-0.1	97.4	-0.6	96.8	-0.6	97.4	0.6	97.6	0.2	96.6	-1.0	96.6	0.0
1985	96.7	0.1	96.3	-0.4	96.4	0.1	96.7	0.3	96.8	0.1	96.3	-0.5	96.4	0.1	96.5	0.1	96.4	-0.1	95.8	-0.6	95.7	-0.1	94.6	-1.1
1986	94.1	-0.5	95.1	1.1	95.6	0.5	95.5	-0.1	95.4	-0.1	95.7	0.3	95.1	-0.6	93.7	-1.5	93.5	-0.2	92.2	-1.4	92.4	0.2	92.2	-0.2
1987	92.1	-0.1	93.8	1.8	94.8	1.1	97.2	2.5	96.4	-0.8	96.5	0.1	96.8	0.3	97.3	0.5	97.8	0.5	97.7	-0.1	98.0	0.3	98.3	0.3
1988	101.1	2.8	103.1	2.0	104.3	1.2	104.5	0.2	103.9	-0.6	102.9	-1.0	103.4	0.5	103.8	0.4	104.4	0.6	105.5	1.1	107.6	2.0	109.2	1.5
1989	112.0	2.6	113.4	1.3	114.3	0.8	113.4	-0.8	112.2	-1.1	109.8	-2.1	106.5	-3.0	105.0	-1.4	104.7	-0.3	103.7	-1.0	104.4	0.7	104.5	0.1
1990	104.4	-0.1	105.8	1.3	105.7	-0.1	106.8	1.0	106.5	-0.3	105.3	-1.1	105.7	0.4	106.4	0.7	108.0	1.5	109.9	1.8	111.8	1.7	112.0	0.2
1991	112.0	0.0	112.3	0.3	112.3	0.0	112.2	-0.1	111.7	-0.4	111.2	-0.4	111.8	0.5	112.1	0.3	111.8	-0.3	111.5	-0.3	110.7	-0.7	110.9	0.2

[Continued]

Agricultural Chemicals and Chemical Products
Producer Price Index
Base 1982 = 100

[Continued]

For 1947-2001. Columns headed % show percentile change in the index from the previous period for which an index is available.

Year	Jan Index	%	Feb Index	%	Mar Index	%	Apr Index	%	May Index	%	Jun Index	%	Jul Index	%	Aug Index	%	Sep Index	%	Oct Index	%	Nov Index	%	Dec Index	%
1992	110.7	-0.2	110.9	0.2	111.2	0.3	111.3	0.1	111.7	0.4	111.6	-0.1	110.2	-1.3	109.3	-0.8	109.1	-0.2	109.3	0.2	109.4	0.1	109.3	-0.1
1993	110.6	1.2	110.2	-0.4	110.3	0.1	109.6	-0.6	109.3	-0.3	109.6	0.3	109.3	-0.3	107.7	-1.5	108.0	0.3	109.2	1.1	113.0	3.5	112.1	-0.8
1994	113.8	1.5	115.6	1.6	116.3	0.6	119.0	2.3	120.3	1.1	119.8	-0.4	120.5	0.6	120.1	-0.3	121.4	1.1	123.5	1.7	124.4	0.7	124.7	0.2
1995	126.9	1.8	129.6	2.1	131.5	1.5	132.5	0.8	132.1	-0.3	131.1	-0.8	129.4	-1.3	127.9	-1.2	128.2	0.2	128.7	0.4	130.7	1.6	132.7	1.5
1996	135.2	1.9	136.3	0.8	138.2	1.4	136.9	-0.9	134.9	-1.5	132.9	-1.5	129.9	-2.3	129.9	0.0	131.1	0.9	132.2	0.8	132.7	0.4	133.7	0.8
1997	134.1	0.3	133.8	-0.2	134.1	0.2	134.6	0.4	134.3	-0.2	132.7	-1.2	132.0	-0.5	132.0	0.0	131.7	-0.2	131.9	0.2	132.1	0.2	130.9	-0.9
1998	130.7	-0.2	129.9	-0.6	130.0	0.1	129.0	-0.8	129.7	0.5	129.8	0.1	129.1	-0.5	128.9	-0.2	126.2	-2.1	127.2	0.8	126.3	-0.7	125.5	-0.6
1999	125.4	-0.1	124.2	-1.0	125.0	0.6	125.3	0.2	123.0	-1.8	123.9	0.7	122.9	-0.8	123.3	0.3	123.2	-0.1	124.0	0.6	121.7	-1.9	121.8	0.1
2000	122.5	0.6	123.8	1.1	122.4	-1.1	122.8	0.3	123.2	0.3	121.7	-1.2	123.4	1.4	124.1	0.6	125.8	1.4	127.4	1.3	127.4	0.0	130.0	2.0
2001	139.2	7.1	140.7	1.1	140.7	0.0	138.0	-1.9	134.2	-2.8	130.5	-2.8	128.2	-1.8	125.7	-2.0	124.3	-1.1	123.4	-0.7	123.9	0.4	120.4	-2.8

Source: U.S. Department of Labor, Bureau of Labor Statistics, Division of Industry Prices and Price Indexes. n.e.c. stands for not elsewhere classified. - indicates no data collected for period or unavailable.

Plastic Resins and Materials
Producer Price Index
Base 1982 = 100

For 1947-2001. Columns headed % show percentile change in the index from the previous period for which an index is available.

Year	Jan Index	%	Feb Index	%	Mar Index	%	Apr Index	%	May Index	%	Jun Index	%	Jul Index	%	Aug Index	%	Sep Index	%	Oct Index	%	Nov Index	%	Dec Index	%
1947	37.3	-	37.3	0.0	37.3	0.0	37.3	0.0	37.5	0.5	37.5	0.0	37.5	0.0	37.5	0.0	37.5	0.0	37.5	0.0	37.2	-0.8	37.2	0.0
1948	37.6	1.1	37.2	-1.1	36.6	-1.6	36.6	0.0	36.6	0.0	36.6	0.0	37.5	2.5	37.4	-0.3	37.5	0.3	37.6	0.3	37.6	0.0	37.6	0.0
1949	38.1	1.3	38.1	0.0	37.6	-1.3	37.6	0.0	37.6	0.0	37.6	0.0	37.6	0.0	37.6	0.0	37.6	0.0	37.6	0.0	37.7	0.3	37.7	0.0
1950	37.5	-0.5	38.0	1.3	37.5	-1.3	37.5	0.0	37.3	-0.5	37.3	0.0	37.3	0.0	37.3	0.0	38.4	2.9	38.5	0.3	39.2	1.8	39.3	0.3
1951	45.9	16.8	46.9	2.2	47.4	1.1	47.4	0.0	47.4	0.0	47.4	0.0	47.4	0.0	47.4	0.0	47.6	0.4	47.6	0.0	47.7	0.2	47.7	0.0
1952	47.7	0.0	47.2	-1.0	47.0	-0.4	47.0	0.0	47.0	0.0	46.9	-0.2	46.9	0.0	46.9	0.0	46.9	0.0	46.9	0.0	46.9	0.0	47.0	0.2
1953	47.0	0.0	47.0	0.0	47.0	0.0	47.0	0.0	47.0	0.0	47.0	0.0	47.0	0.0	47.2	0.4	47.4	0.4	47.4	0.0	47.4	0.0	47.4	0.0
1954	47.0	-0.8	46.8	-0.4	46.8	0.0	46.8	0.0	46.8	0.0	46.8	0.0	46.8	0.0	46.8	0.0	46.8	0.0	46.8	0.0	46.5	-0.6	46.5	0.0
1955	46.3	-0.4	46.3	0.0	46.3	0.0	46.3	0.0	46.3	0.0	46.3	0.0	42.9	-7.3	42.9	0.0	42.9	0.0	42.9	0.0	42.9	0.0	42.9	0.0
1956	40.7	-5.1	40.7	0.0	40.7	0.0	40.6	-0.2	40.6	0.0	40.6	0.0	40.6	0.0	40.6	0.0	40.3	-0.7	40.3	0.0	40.3	0.0	40.4	0.2
1957	40.4	0.0	40.6	0.5	40.6	0.0	40.6	0.0	40.6	0.0	40.5	-0.2	40.5	0.0	40.7	0.5	40.7	0.0	40.7	0.0	40.5	-0.5	40.7	0.5
1958	40.7	0.0	40.7	0.0	40.5	-0.5	40.5	0.0	40.5	0.0	40.5	0.0	40.2	-0.7	39.4	-2.0	39.4	0.0	39.4	0.0	39.4	0.0	38.9	-1.3
1959	38.9	0.0	38.9	0.0	38.2	-1.8	38.2	0.0	38.2	0.0	38.2	0.0	38.2	0.0	38.2	0.0	38.2	0.0	38.2	0.0	38.2	0.0	38.2	0.0
1960	38.2	0.0	38.2	0.0	38.2	0.0	38.2	0.0	38.2	0.0	38.2	0.0	38.2	0.0	38.2	0.0	38.2	0.0	38.2	0.0	38.2	0.0	38.1	-0.3
1961	36.5	-4.2	36.5	0.0	36.5	0.0	36.5	0.0	36.5	0.0	36.5	0.0	36.4	-0.3	36.4	0.0	36.4	0.0	36.3	-0.3	36.3	0.0	36.3	0.0
1962	36.3	0.0	36.3	0.0	36.3	0.0	36.3	0.0	36.3	0.0	36.3	0.0	36.3	0.0	36.3	0.0	36.3	0.0	36.3	0.0	36.3	0.0	36.3	0.0
1963	36.3	0.0	36.3	0.0	36.3	0.0	35.3	-2.8	35.3	0.0	35.3	0.0	35.3	0.0	35.3	0.0	35.3	0.0	35.3	0.0	35.3	0.0	35.3	0.0
1964	35.3	0.0	35.3	0.0	35.3	0.0	35.3	0.0	35.3	0.0	35.3	0.0	35.3	0.0	35.3	0.0	35.3	0.0	35.3	0.0	35.0	-0.8	35.0	0.0
1965	35.0	0.0	35.0	0.0	35.0	0.0	35.0	0.0	35.0	0.0	35.0	0.0	35.0	0.0	35.0	0.0	35.0	0.0	35.0	0.0	35.0	0.0	35.0	0.0
1966	35.0	0.0	35.0	0.0	35.0	0.0	35.0	0.0	35.0	0.0	35.0	0.0	35.0	0.0	35.3	0.9	35.6	0.8	35.7	0.3	35.7	0.0	35.7	0.0
1967	35.7	0.0	35.8	0.3	35.8	0.0	35.8	0.0	36.0	0.6	35.7	-0.8	35.6	-0.3	35.5	-0.3	34.7	-2.3	34.0	-2.0	34.3	0.9	34.4	0.3
1968	34.0	-1.2	33.0	-2.9	32.8	-0.6	32.9	0.3	32.5	-1.2	32.2	-0.9	32.0	-0.6	31.9	-0.3	32.0	0.3	32.1	0.3	32.0	-0.3	31.9	-0.3
1969	31.9	0.0	32.1	0.6	32.1	0.0	32.0	-0.3	32.0	0.0	32.0	0.0	31.8	-0.6	32.0	0.6	32.1	0.3	31.7	-1.2	31.5	-0.6	31.7	0.6
1970	31.7	0.0	31.9	0.6	31.9	0.0	32.1	0.6	31.8	-0.9	31.7	-0.3	32.1	1.3	32.0	-0.3	32.1	0.3	32.3	0.6	32.0	-0.9	31.8	-0.6
1971	31.6	-0.6	31.4	-0.6	30.8	-1.9	31.1	1.0	31.1	0.0	31.0	-0.3	31.2	0.6	31.4	0.6	31.5	0.3	31.7	0.6	31.4	-0.9	31.4	0.0
1972	31.3	-0.3	31.5	0.6	31.4	-0.3	31.2	-0.6	31.3	0.3	31.0	-1.0	31.0	0.0	31.1	0.3	31.4	1.0	31.5	0.3	31.6	0.3	31.5	-0.3
1973	31.6	0.3	31.8	0.6	31.9	0.3	32.2	0.9	32.6	1.2	32.7	0.3	32.9	0.6	32.9	0.0	32.9	0.0	32.6	-0.9	32.8	0.6	32.8	0.0
1974	33.1	0.9	34.0	2.7	40.9	20.3	43.7	6.8	45.2	3.4	49.7	10.0	52.0	4.6	56.7	9.0	61.6	8.6	63.2	2.6	64.0	1.3	64.6	0.9
1975	64.6	0.0	64.3	-0.5	64.2	-0.2	64.3	0.2	62.2	-3.3	62.1	-0.2	62.5	0.6	62.6	0.2	63.2	1.0	64.9	2.7	65.2	0.5	65.8	0.9
1976	66.1	0.5	67.2	1.7	67.1	-0.1	68.4	1.9	68.5	0.1	68.9	0.6	69.7	1.2	69.6	-0.1	69.1	-0.7	69.0	-0.1	68.9	-0.1	68.8	-0.1
1977	68.3	-0.7	68.1	-0.3	68.7	0.9	69.1	0.6	69.4	0.4	69.7	0.4	70.6	1.3	70.6	0.0	70.6	0.0	70.5	-0.1	70.4	-0.1	70.1	-0.4
1978	70.1	0.0	70.0	-0.1	70.2	0.3	70.2	0.0	70.8	0.9	70.9	0.1	71.0	0.1	70.6	-0.6	70.6	0.0	70.4	-0.3	70.3	-0.1	71.0	1.0
1979	72.1	1.5	72.8	1.0	74.4	2.2	77.8	4.6	80.6	3.6	81.2	0.7	86.3	6.3	88.2	2.2	88.9	0.8	91.7	3.1	92.2	0.5	92.6	0.4
1980	95.4	3.0	96.0	0.6	96.8	0.8	101.5	4.9	101.8	0.3	101.5	-0.3	100.8	-0.7	99.3	-1.5	97.6	-1.7	97.4	-0.2	97.5	0.1	96.7	-0.8
1981	96.9	0.2	97.4	0.5	98.6	1.2	100.6	2.0	101.6	1.0	102.3	0.7	104.4	2.1	105.0	0.6	104.7	-0.3	105.7	1.0	103.4	-2.2	103.8	0.4
1982	100.9	-2.8	101.4	0.5	100.7	-0.7	100.9	0.2	99.9	-1.0	99.5	-0.4	99.1	-0.4	99.6	0.5	99.3	-0.3	99.3	0.0	99.6	0.3	99.7	0.1
1983	100.2	0.5	99.9	-0.3	99.5	-0.4	100.7	1.2	101.6	0.9	102.0	0.4	102.8	0.8	103.6	0.8	106.8	3.1	105.5	-1.2	105.1	-0.4	106.4	1.2
1984	107.7	1.2	107.6	-0.1	108.0	0.4	108.6	0.6	109.6	0.9	109.8	0.2	109.6	-0.2	109.5	-0.1	110.0	0.5	109.2	-0.7	109.0	-0.2	108.1	-0.8
1985	107.7	-0.4	108.3	0.6	108.1	-0.2	108.0	-0.1	107.8	-0.2	108.4	0.6	108.5	0.1	108.1	-0.4	107.7	-0.4	106.1	-1.5	106.0	-0.1	105.6	-0.4
1986	106.2	0.6	106.7	0.5	106.5	-0.2	104.7	-1.7	104.3	-0.4	104.2	-0.1	104.7	0.5	103.9	-0.8	102.4	-1.4	103.4	1.0	104.1	0.7	102.4	-1.6
1987	102.6	0.2	102.4	-0.2	103.2	0.8	106.3	3.0	107.0	0.7	109.7	2.5	112.8	2.8	113.1	0.3	114.2	1.0	116.8	2.3	117.4	0.5	117.7	0.3
1988	121.5	3.2	123.5	1.6	124.4	0.7	127.6	2.6	130.1	2.0	131.2	0.8	134.8	2.7	136.9	1.6	138.9	1.5	139.8	0.6	140.2	0.3	140.1	-0.1
1989	140.3	0.1	141.1	0.6	140.6	-0.4	140.7	0.1	139.8	-0.6	138.0	-1.3	135.3	-2.0	127.7	-5.6	126.1	-1.3	124.7	-1.1	123.7	-0.8	123.3	-0.3
1990	122.2	-0.9	121.6	-0.5	122.2	0.5	123.0	0.7	123.5	0.4	123.0	-0.4	122.3	-0.6	122.3	0.0	122.0	-0.2	125.9	3.2	129.1	2.5	132.1	2.3
1991	131.1	-0.8	128.7	-1.8	126.1	-2.0	122.9	-2.5	120.6	-1.9	117.0	-3.0	115.0	-1.7	114.9	-0.1	114.9	0.0	116.4	1.3	116.4	0.0	116.0	-0.3

[Continued]

Plastic Resins and Materials
Producer Price Index
Base 1982 = 100

[Continued]

For 1947-2001. Columns headed % show percentile change in the index from the previous period for which an index is available.

Year	Jan Index	%	Feb Index	%	Mar Index	%	Apr Index	%	May Index	%	Jun Index	%	Jul Index	%	Aug Index	%	Sep Index	%	Oct Index	%	Nov Index	%	Dec Index	%
1992	115.5	-0.4	115.6	0.1	114.2	-1.2	114.2	0.0	114.7	0.4	115.2	0.4	116.9	1.5	117.7	0.7	118.0	0.3	118.2	0.2	118.1	-0.1	118.1	0.0
1993	118.3	0.2	118.0	-0.3	117.6	-0.3	117.1	-0.4	116.3	-0.7	116.9	0.5	116.9	0.0	117.6	0.6	117.4	-0.2	116.9	-0.4	116.2	-0.6	116.2	0.0
1994	115.0	-1.0	114.7	-0.3	114.5	-0.2	116.5	1.7	117.7	1.0	119.1	1.2	119.6	0.4	121.5	1.6	126.3	4.0	131.9	4.4	134.1	1.7	138.1	3.0
1995	142.5	3.2	145.8	2.3	146.1	0.2	148.5	1.6	149.0	0.3	148.9	-0.1	147.0	-1.3	144.8	-1.5	142.7	-1.5	139.2	-2.5	135.8	-2.4	132.2	-2.7
1996	129.9	-1.7	128.4	-1.2	128.4	0.0	127.7	-0.5	130.6	2.3	132.1	1.1	133.2	0.8	135.2	1.5	137.9	2.0	138.0	0.1	138.0	0.0	137.7	-0.2
1997	137.0	-0.5	137.5	0.4	138.7	0.9	138.9	0.1	139.1	0.1	139.6	0.4	139.3	-0.2	137.4	-1.4	136.0	-1.0	136.7	0.5	134.3	-1.8	133.2	-0.8
1998	134.0	0.6	132.2	-1.3	131.0	-0.9	130.7	-0.2	128.8	-1.5	126.8	-1.6	125.0	-1.4	123.7	-1.0	119.6	-3.3	118.6	-0.8	117.1	-1.3	115.9	-1.0
1999	115.9	0.0	115.8	-0.1	117.3	1.3	118.6	1.1	122.1	3.0	123.1	0.8	127.9	3.9	130.0	1.6	133.8	2.9	135.6	1.3	135.8	0.1	134.3	-1.1
2000	133.2	-0.8	135.7	1.9	139.4	2.7	143.7	3.1	147.4	2.6	147.8	0.3	146.4	-0.9	146.3	-0.1	142.4	-2.7	140.7	-1.2	138.8	-1.4	137.3	-1.1
2001	137.8	0.4	139.3	1.1	141.4	1.5	141.9	0.4	139.9	-1.4	137.6	-1.6	135.1	-1.8	131.3	-2.8	129.1	-1.7	130.8	1.3	128.8	-1.5	125.2	-2.8

Source: U.S. Department of Labor, Bureau of Labor Statistics, Division of Industry Prices and Price Indexes. n.e.c. stands for not elsewhere classified. - indicates no data collected for period or unavailable.

Other Chemicals and Allied Products
Producer Price Index
Base 1982 = 100

For 1947-2001. Columns headed % show percentile change in the index from the previous period for which an index is available.

Year	Jan Index	%	Feb Index	%	Mar Index	%	Apr Index	%	May Index	%	Jun Index	%	Jul Index	%	Aug Index	%	Sep Index	%	Oct Index	%	Nov Index	%	Dec Index	%
1947	31.7	-	31.8	0.3	32.2	1.3	32.7	1.6	31.1	-4.9	30.8	-1.0	30.0	-2.6	30.0	0.0	30.1	0.3	32.1	6.6	33.4	4.0	34.2	2.4
1948	34.4	0.6	33.9	-1.5	33.2	-2.1	33.1	-0.3	32.2	-2.7	31.7	-1.6	32.1	1.3	32.2	0.3	32.1	-0.3	31.9	-0.6	31.8	-0.3	31.3	-1.6
1949	30.8	-1.6	30.0	-2.6	29.7	-1.0	29.0	-2.4	28.5	-1.7	28.5	0.0	28.0	-1.8	27.7	-1.1	27.8	0.4	27.8	0.0	27.8	0.0	27.7	-0.4
1950	27.3	-1.4	27.3	0.0	27.3	0.0	27.3	0.0	27.3	0.0	27.2	-0.4	27.2	0.0	28.5	4.8	29.7	4.2	30.2	1.7	30.7	1.7	32.0	4.2
1951	32.8	2.5	33.4	1.8	32.6	-2.4	32.4	-0.6	32.4	0.0	32.3	-0.3	31.7	-1.9	31.1	-1.9	30.7	-1.3	30.7	0.0	30.7	0.0	30.5	-0.7
1952	30.1	-1.3	30.1	0.0	30.1	0.0	29.7	-1.3	29.7	0.0	29.7	0.0	29.7	0.0	29.7	0.0	29.7	0.0	29.6	-0.3	29.5	-0.3	29.6	0.3
1953	29.6	0.0	29.5	-0.3	29.5	0.0	29.6	0.3	29.6	0.0	29.5	-0.3	29.5	0.0	29.4	-0.3	29.5	0.3	29.6	0.3	30.1	1.7	30.2	0.3
1954	30.4	0.7	31.0	2.0	31.4	1.3	31.4	0.0	31.4	0.0	31.3	-0.3	31.4	0.3	31.2	-0.6	31.3	0.3	31.4	0.3	31.4	0.0	31.5	0.3
1955	31.5	0.0	31.7	0.6	31.5	-0.6	31.4	-0.3	31.4	0.0	31.4	0.0	31.4	0.0	31.4	0.0	31.4	0.0	31.7	1.0	31.7	0.0	31.7	0.0
1956	31.8	0.3	31.8	0.0	31.7	-0.3	31.8	0.3	31.9	0.3	32.7	2.5	32.7	0.0	32.6	-0.3	32.6	0.0	32.8	0.6	33.0	0.6	33.0	0.0
1957	33.1	0.3	33.3	0.6	33.3	0.0	33.3	0.0	33.3	0.0	33.2	-0.3	33.5	0.9	33.5	0.0	34.1	1.8	34.1	0.0	34.1	0.0	34.2	0.3
1958	34.1	-0.3	34.1	0.0	34.1	0.0	34.4	0.9	34.4	0.0	34.4	0.0	34.4	0.0	34.4	0.0	34.5	0.3	34.4	-0.3	34.4	0.0	34.4	0.0
1959	34.6	0.6	34.5	-0.3	34.5	0.0	34.5	0.0	34.6	0.3	34.6	0.0	34.7	0.3	34.7	0.0	34.7	0.0	34.7	0.0	34.7	0.0	34.8	0.3
1960	34.6	-0.6	34.6	0.0	34.6	0.0	34.6	0.0	34.6	0.0	34.6	0.0	34.6	0.0	34.7	0.3	34.8	0.3	35.1	0.9	35.0	-0.3	35.0	0.0
1961	34.9	-0.3	35.0	0.3	35.0	0.0	35.0	0.0	35.1	0.3	35.1	0.0	35.1	0.0	34.9	-0.6	34.9	0.0	34.9	0.0	34.9	0.0	34.9	0.0
1962	34.9	0.0	34.8	-0.3	34.9	0.3	34.9	0.0	34.8	-0.3	34.9	0.3	34.9	0.0	34.8	-0.3	34.9	0.3	35.0	0.3	35.0	0.0	35.0	0.0
1963	35.1	0.3	35.1	0.0	35.2	0.3	35.3	0.3	35.3	0.0	35.3	0.0	35.3	0.0	35.4	0.3	35.4	0.0	35.5	0.3	35.5	0.0	35.5	0.0
1964	35.5	0.0	35.5	0.0	35.5	0.0	35.6	0.3	35.7	0.3	35.7	0.0	35.7	0.0	35.7	0.0	35.7	0.0	35.7	0.0	35.7	0.0	35.7	0.0
1965	35.8	0.3	35.9	0.3	35.9	0.0	35.9	0.0	35.9	0.0	35.9	0.0	35.9	0.0	36.0	0.3	36.1	0.3	36.2	0.3	36.3	0.3	36.2	-0.3
1966	36.4	0.6	36.4	0.0	36.4	0.0	36.4	0.0	36.4	0.0	36.3	-0.3	36.4	0.3	36.5	0.3	36.5	0.0	36.5	0.0	36.5	0.0	36.6	0.3
1967	36.8	0.5	36.8	0.0	36.8	0.0	37.1	0.8	37.1	0.0	37.1	0.0	37.1	0.0	37.2	0.3	37.1	-0.3	37.2	0.3	37.1	-0.3	37.1	0.0
1968	37.1	0.0	37.2	0.3	37.4	0.5	37.5	0.3	37.6	0.3	37.8	0.5	37.8	0.0	37.8	0.0	37.9	0.3	37.7	-0.5	37.7	0.0	37.7	0.0
1969	37.7	0.0	38.0	0.8	38.1	0.3	38.4	0.8	38.5	0.3	38.6	0.3	38.6	0.0	38.6	0.0	38.9	0.8	39.1	0.5	39.3	0.5	39.4	0.3
1970	39.5	0.3	39.5	0.0	39.8	0.8	39.9	0.3	40.2	0.8	40.3	0.2	40.5	0.5	40.5	0.0	40.5	0.0	40.5	0.0	40.5	0.0	40.4	-0.2
1971	41.1	1.7	41.2	0.2	41.3	0.2	41.3	0.0	41.5	0.5	41.6	0.2	41.6	0.0	41.6	0.0	41.6	0.0	41.6	0.0	41.6	0.0	41.6	0.0
1972	41.6	0.0	41.7	0.2	41.7	0.0	42.0	0.7	42.2	0.5	42.1	-0.2	41.9	-0.5	42.0	0.2	42.1	0.2	42.2	0.2	42.2	0.0	42.2	0.0
1973	42.2	0.0	42.3	0.2	42.6	0.7	43.1	1.2	43.6	1.2	43.7	0.2	43.7	0.0	43.8	0.2	43.8	0.0	44.9	2.5	45.2	0.7	46.1	2.0
1974	47.0	2.0	47.1	0.2	47.5	0.8	48.7	2.5	52.3	7.4	53.6	2.5	55.0	2.6	59.4	8.0	60.2	1.3	61.3	1.8	61.5	0.3	61.6	0.2
1975	62.8	1.9	63.1	0.5	63.1	0.0	62.2	-1.4	62.0	-0.3	62.0	0.0	61.9	-0.2	62.0	0.2	62.1	0.2	62.1	0.0	62.7	1.0	63.0	0.5
1976	63.5	0.8	63.4	-0.2	63.7	0.5	63.7	0.0	63.8	0.2	63.8	0.0	62.5	-2.0	62.6	0.2	62.7	0.2	62.9	0.3	62.9	0.0	62.7	-0.3
1977	63.8	1.8	64.2	0.6	64.6	0.6	64.9	0.5	65.1	0.3	65.2	0.2	65.1	-0.2	65.3	0.3	65.4	0.2	65.4	0.0	65.7	0.5	65.9	0.3
1978	66.1	0.3	66.8	1.1	67.1	0.4	67.2	0.1	67.3	0.1	67.5	0.3	67.6	0.1	67.1	-0.7	67.1	0.0	68.1	1.5	68.2	0.1	67.5	-1.0
1979	68.2	1.0	68.4	0.3	69.0	0.9	69.2	0.3	69.9	1.0	70.5	0.9	71.0	0.7	72.0	1.4	72.5	0.7	72.9	0.6	73.6	1.0	74.6	1.4
1980	77.5	3.9	78.2	0.9	79.6	1.8	82.6	3.8	83.2	0.7	84.0	1.0	84.6	0.7	84.8	0.2	84.8	0.0	85.5	0.8	86.0	0.6	86.7	0.8
1981	90.5	4.4	90.7	0.2	91.9	1.3	94.5	2.8	94.3	-0.2	94.9	0.6	94.3	-0.6	95.3	1.1	95.3	0.0	95.1	-0.2	96.2	1.2	96.2	0.0
1982	97.7	1.6	98.1	0.4	99.4	1.3	100.0	0.6	101.0	1.0	101.4	0.4	100.4	-1.0	100.8	0.4	100.4	-0.4	99.5	-0.9	100.8	1.3	100.7	-0.1
1983	101.0	0.3	101.6	0.6	100.7	-0.9	101.7	1.0	100.7	-1.0	100.9	0.2	101.5	0.6	101.5	0.0	101.6	0.1	101.6	0.0	101.4	-0.2	101.3	-0.1
1984	101.8	0.5	101.2	-0.6	101.9	0.7	102.6	0.7	102.6	0.0	102.1	-0.5	102.7	0.6	103.0	0.3	103.5	0.5	103.5	0.0	104.1	0.6	103.7	-0.4
1985	104.4	0.7	104.7	0.3	104.8	0.1	105.4	0.6	104.9	-0.5	105.4	0.5	105.5	0.1	105.1	-0.4	106.0	0.9	105.6	-0.4	105.5	-0.1	105.4	-0.1
1986	106.7	1.2	106.4	-0.3	105.5	-0.8	105.9	0.4	105.6	-0.3	106.0	0.4	105.8	-0.2	105.0	-0.8	105.5	0.5	105.8	0.3	105.8	0.0	105.3	-0.5
1987	105.9	0.6	106.0	0.1	106.2	0.2	106.1	-0.1	106.7	0.6	106.8	0.1	106.7	-0.1	107.4	0.7	107.7	0.3	107.9	0.2	108.2	0.3	108.1	-0.1
1988	108.6	0.5	109.3	0.6	109.4	0.1	110.1	0.6	110.6	0.5	111.0	0.4	112.5	1.4	113.4	0.8	114.2	0.7	114.1	-0.1	114.8	0.6	115.1	0.3
1989	115.7	0.5	116.1	0.3	116.8	0.6	117.1	0.3	117.3	0.2	117.6	0.3	117.7	0.1	118.0	0.3	118.0	0.0	118.1	0.1	117.6	-0.4	117.3	-0.3
1990	118.0	0.6	118.1	0.1	118.3	0.2	118.0	-0.3	118.1	0.1	118.1	0.0	118.5	0.3	118.8	0.3	119.6	0.7	119.7	0.1	120.4	0.6	120.6	0.2
1991	121.7	0.9	121.9	0.2	121.3	-0.5	121.4	0.1	121.1	-0.2	121.0	-0.1	120.9	-0.1	121.2	0.2	122.0	0.7	121.8	-0.2	122.1	0.2	122.1	0.0

[Continued]

Other Chemicals and Allied Products
Producer Price Index
Base 1982 = 100
[Continued]

For 1947-2001. Columns headed % show percentile change in the index from the previous period for which an index is available.

Year	Jan Index	%	Feb Index	%	Mar Index	%	Apr Index	%	May Index	%	Jun Index	%	Jul Index	%	Aug Index	%	Sep Index	%	Oct Index	%	Nov Index	%	Dec Index	%
1992	122.3	0.2	122.4	0.1	122.3	-0.1	122.7	0.3	123.0	0.2	123.1	0.1	123.3	0.2	123.4	0.1	123.8	0.3	124.0	0.2	124.4	0.3	124.3	-0.1
1993	124.9	0.5	125.3	0.3	125.1	-0.2	125.5	0.3	125.6	0.1	125.7	0.1	125.6	-0.1	125.6	0.0	125.5	-0.1	125.6	0.1	125.6	0.0	125.8	0.2
1994	126.0	0.2	126.1	0.1	125.9	-0.2	126.0	0.1	126.6	0.5	126.5	-0.1	126.6	0.1	127.9	1.0	127.6	-0.2	128.4	0.6	128.3	-0.1	129.1	0.6
1995	129.8	0.5	129.5	-0.2	130.6	0.8	130.5	-0.1	130.7	0.2	130.7	0.0	130.8	0.1	130.3	-0.4	130.8	0.4	130.6	-0.2	131.4	0.6	131.5	0.1
1996	132.1	0.5	132.5	0.3	132.1	-0.3	132.2	0.1	132.5	0.2	132.4	-0.1	132.5	0.1	132.3	-0.2	132.7	0.3	132.8	0.1	132.3	-0.4	132.3	0.0
1997	132.4	0.1	132.6	0.2	132.6	0.0	132.9	0.2	133.0	0.1	133.4	0.3	133.7	0.2	133.5	-0.1	133.6	0.1	133.7	0.1	134.1	0.3	133.8	-0.2
1998	133.9	0.1	134.2	0.2	134.1	-0.1	134.3	0.1	134.7	0.3	134.7	0.0	134.9	0.1	134.7	-0.1	135.3	0.4	135.1	-0.1	135.0	-0.1	135.0	0.0
1999	134.8	-0.1	134.7	-0.1	135.0	0.2	134.9	-0.1	134.6	-0.2	135.5	0.7	135.7	0.1	135.5	-0.1	135.5	0.0	135.8	0.2	135.8	0.0	135.7	-0.1
2000	135.9	0.1	136.6	0.5	136.5	-0.1	136.6	0.1	136.4	-0.1	136.8	0.3	136.9	0.1	137.2	0.2	137.9	0.5	138.1	0.1	138.4	0.2	138.6	0.1
2001	139.2	0.4	139.4	0.1	139.4	0.0	139.9	0.4	139.9	0.0	139.7	-0.1	139.6	-0.1	139.7	0.1	139.9	0.1	139.9	0.0	139.5	-0.3	139.4	-0.1

Source: U.S. Department of Labor, Bureau of Labor Statistics, Division of Industry Prices and Price Indexes. n.e.c. stands for not elsewhere classified. - indicates no data collected for period or unavailable.

RUBBER AND PLASTIC PRODUCTS
Producer Price Index
Base 1982 = 100

For 1926-2001. Columns headed % show percentile change in the index from the previous period for which an index is available.

Year	Jan Index	%	Feb Index	%	Mar Index	%	Apr Index	%	May Index	%	Jun Index	%	Jul Index	%	Aug Index	%	Sep Index	%	Oct Index	%	Nov Index	%	Dec Index	%
1926	59.1	-	53.7	-9.1	52.8	-1.7	51.0	-3.4	50.5	-1.0	49.4	-2.2	44.0	-10.9	42.7	-3.0	42.6	-0.2	43.0	0.9	39.1	-9.1	37.0	-5.4
1927	36.6	-1.1	36.3	-0.8	36.9	1.7	36.8	-0.3	36.9	0.3	36.0	-2.4	35.6	-1.1	35.5	-0.3	35.2	-0.8	34.3	-2.6	33.8	-1.5	34.5	2.1
1928	34.3	-0.6	32.5	-5.2	31.5	-3.1	30.1	-4.4	29.7	-1.3	27.2	-8.4	26.3	-3.3	26.3	0.0	26.1	-0.8	25.6	-1.9	25.0	-2.3	24.9	-0.4
1929	25.2	1.2	25.6	1.6	25.7	0.4	25.1	-2.3	24.9	-0.8	24.7	-0.8	24.8	0.4	24.6	-0.8	24.5	-0.4	24.2	-1.2	23.2	-4.1	23.1	-0.4
1930	22.9	-0.9	23.0	0.4	22.9	-0.4	22.8	-0.4	22.7	-0.4	21.3	-6.2	21.0	-1.4	20.6	-1.9	20.2	-1.9	20.2	0.0	20.5	1.5	20.4	-0.5
1931	19.2	-5.9	19.0	-1.0	19.0	0.0	18.7	-1.6	18.7	0.0	18.4	-1.6	18.4	0.0	18.1	-1.6	18.1	0.0	18.1	0.0	17.9	-1.1	16.1	-10.1
1932	15.7	-2.5	15.5	-1.3	15.2	-1.9	15.1	-0.7	15.1	0.0	15.2	0.7	15.4	1.3	15.6	1.3	16.5	5.8	17.1	3.6	17.1	0.0	17.1	0.0
1933	17.0	-0.6	16.2	-4.7	15.8	-2.5	14.5	-8.2	14.9	2.8	16.1	8.1	17.1	6.2	17.5	2.3	17.5	0.0	17.6	0.6	17.9	1.7	17.9	0.0
1934	18.0	0.6	18.4	2.2	18.9	2.7	19.1	1.1	19.5	2.1	19.5	0.0	19.7	1.0	20.0	1.5	19.9	-0.5	19.6	-1.5	20.3	3.6	20.3	0.0
1935	20.3	0.0	20.3	0.0	19.7	-3.0	19.6	-0.5	19.3	-1.5	19.4	0.5	19.3	-0.5	19.3	0.0	19.2	-0.5	19.5	1.6	19.6	0.5	19.6	0.0
1936	19.9	1.5	20.1	1.0	20.2	0.5	20.3	0.5	21.1	3.9	21.2	0.5	21.3	0.5	21.3	0.0	21.3	0.0	21.3	0.0	22.5	5.6	23.0	2.2
1937	23.9	3.9	24.4	2.1	25.8	5.7	26.1	1.2	25.6	-1.9	25.2	-1.6	25.0	-0.8	24.9	-0.4	24.9	0.0	24.3	-2.4	24.0	-1.2	24.0	0.0
1938	24.3	1.2	24.3	0.0	24.1	-0.8	23.7	-1.7	23.6	-0.4	23.9	1.3	24.4	2.1	24.6	0.8	24.6	0.0	24.9	1.2	25.2	1.2	25.2	0.0
1939	25.1	-0.4	25.3	0.8	25.5	0.8	25.4	-0.4	25.5	0.4	25.5	0.0	25.5	0.0	25.5	0.0	27.0	5.9	26.4	-2.2	23.5	-11.0	24.4	3.8
1940	24.2	-0.8	24.0	-0.8	24.0	0.0	23.0	-4.2	23.5	2.2	23.8	1.3	23.7	-0.4	23.3	-1.7	23.1	-0.9	23.4	1.3	23.6	0.9	24.3	3.0
1941	24.2	-0.4	24.3	0.4	24.6	1.2	24.7	0.4	24.7	0.0	24.2	-2.0	24.5	1.2	25.8	5.3	25.7	-0.4	27.3	6.2	27.9	2.2	27.9	0.0
1942	27.8	-0.4	27.8	0.0	27.8	0.0	28.4	2.2	30.5	7.4	30.5	0.0	30.5	0.0	30.5	0.0	30.5	0.0	30.5	0.0	30.5	0.0	30.5	0.0
1943	30.5	0.0	30.5	0.0	30.5	0.0	30.5	0.0	30.5	0.0	30.5	0.0	30.5	0.0	30.5	0.0	30.5	0.0	30.5	0.0	30.5	0.0	30.5	0.0
1944	30.5	0.0	30.6	0.3	30.6	0.0	30.6	0.0	29.8	-2.6	29.8	0.0	29.8	0.0	29.8	0.0	29.8	0.0	29.8	0.0	29.8	0.0	29.8	0.0
1945	29.9	0.3	29.9	0.0	29.9	0.0	29.4	-1.7	28.9	-1.7	28.9	0.0	28.9	0.0	28.9	0.0	28.9	0.0	28.9	0.0	28.9	0.0	28.9	0.0
1946	28.9	0.0	28.9	0.0	28.9	0.0	28.9	0.0	28.9	0.0	29.2	1.0	29.5	1.0	29.6	0.3	29.7	0.3	29.7	0.0	29.7	0.0	29.9	0.7
1947	30.4	1.7	30.5	0.3	30.5	0.0	30.4	-0.3	29.9	-1.6	28.4	-5.0	27.8	-2.1	27.8	0.0	28.0	0.7	28.5	1.8	29.0	1.8	29.4	1.4
1948	29.6	0.7	29.5	-0.3	29.5	0.0	29.7	0.7	29.8	0.3	29.8	0.0	30.7	3.0	30.7	0.0	30.7	0.0	30.7	0.0	30.5	-0.7	30.3	-0.7
1949	30.2	-0.3	30.0	-0.7	30.0	0.0	29.7	-1.0	29.6	-0.3	28.8	-2.7	28.4	-1.4	28.3	-0.4	28.4	0.4	28.3	-0.4	28.8	1.8	29.5	2.4
1950	29.7	0.7	29.9	0.7	29.9	0.0	30.6	2.3	31.5	2.9	32.3	2.5	34.1	5.6	38.2	12.0	39.9	4.5	41.5	4.0	44.0	6.0	44.9	2.0
1951	45.2	0.7	45.0	-0.4	45.0	0.0	44.7	-0.7	44.6	-0.2	43.8	-1.8	42.6	-2.7	42.6	0.0	42.7	0.2	42.7	0.0	42.7	0.0	42.6	-0.2
1952	42.5	-0.2	42.3	-0.5	41.9	-0.9	41.5	-1.0	41.4	-0.2	39.4	-4.8	38.4	-2.5	37.7	-1.8	37.3	-1.1	37.2	-0.3	37.3	0.3	37.7	1.1
1953	37.6	-0.3	37.2	-1.1	37.1	-0.3	36.8	-0.8	37.0	0.5	36.9	-0.3	36.8	-0.3	36.4	-1.1	36.6	0.5	36.6	0.0	36.7	0.3	36.8	0.3
1954	36.8	0.0	36.8	0.0	36.9	0.3	36.9	0.0	36.9	0.0	37.2	0.8	37.4	0.5	37.3	-0.3	37.5	0.5	37.9	1.1	38.8	2.4	38.9	0.3
1955	40.4	3.9	41.5	2.7	40.7	-1.9	40.8	0.2	40.7	-0.2	41.4	1.7	42.3	2.2	43.9	3.8	44.7	1.8	43.6	-2.5	44.4	1.8	44.5	0.2
1956	43.8	-1.6	43.4	-0.9	43.1	-0.7	42.8	-0.7	42.3	-1.2	42.2	-0.2	42.3	0.2	43.3	2.4	43.0	-0.7	43.0	0.0	43.3	0.7	43.7	0.9
1957	42.8	-2.1	42.5	-0.7	42.6	0.2	42.6	0.0	42.7	0.2	42.8	0.2	42.8	0.0	43.3	1.2	43.2	-0.2	43.1	-0.2	42.7	-0.9	43.0	0.7
1958	42.8	-0.5	42.7	-0.2	42.7	0.0	42.6	-0.2	42.4	-0.5	42.6	0.5	42.7	0.2	42.7	0.0	42.9	0.5	43.2	0.7	43.3	0.2	43.0	-0.7
1959	42.8	-0.5	42.9	0.2	43.1	0.5	43.3	0.5	43.7	0.9	43.1	-1.4	43.1	0.0	41.5	-3.7	41.8	0.7	41.8	0.0	42.6	1.9	41.9	-1.6
1960	42.3	1.0	42.7	0.9	42.7	0.0	42.7	0.0	43.2	1.2	43.3	0.2	43.3	0.0	42.9	-0.9	42.8	-0.2	42.7	-0.2	42.4	-0.7	41.6	-1.9
1961	41.2	-1.0	41.2	0.0	41.3	0.2	41.3	0.0	41.4	0.2	41.2	-0.5	41.0	-0.5	41.1	0.2	41.2	0.2	41.1	-0.2	40.9	-0.5	40.4	-1.2
1962	40.2	-0.5	40.0	-0.5	40.0	0.0	39.7	-0.7	39.9	0.5	39.8	-0.3	39.7	-0.3	39.7	0.0	39.7	0.0	39.8	0.3	40.1	0.8	40.4	0.7
1963	40.3	-0.2	40.3	0.0	40.2	-0.2	40.2	0.0	39.9	-0.7	39.8	-0.3	39.8	0.0	40.1	0.8	39.9	-0.5	40.3	1.0	40.3	0.0	40.1	-0.5
1964	40.1	0.0	40.0	-0.2	40.1	0.2	39.8	-0.7	39.6	-0.5	39.2	-1.0	39.2	0.0	39.2	0.0	39.3	0.3	39.4	0.3	39.4	0.0	39.4	0.0
1965	39.5	0.3	39.4	-0.3	39.4	0.0	39.5	0.3	39.7	0.5	39.8	0.3	39.8	0.0	39.9	0.3	39.9	0.0	39.9	0.0	40.0	0.3	40.0	0.0
1966	40.1	-0.2	40.2	0.2	40.3	0.2	40.8	1.2	40.8	0.0	40.8	0.0	40.6	-0.5	40.6	0.0	40.5	-0.2	40.4	-0.2	40.6	0.5	40.6	0.0
1967	40.9	0.7	41.0	0.2	41.0	0.0	41.0	0.0	40.9	-0.2	40.9	0.0	40.9	0.0	41.8	2.2	42.0	0.5	42.2	0.5	42.4	0.5	42.4	0.0
1968	42.4	0.0	42.5	0.2	42.5	0.0	42.5	0.0	42.6	0.2	42.7	0.2	42.9	0.5	43.1	0.5	43.1	0.0	43.2	0.2	43.2	0.0	43.3	0.2
1969	42.8	-1.2	43.0	0.5	43.1	0.2	43.3	0.5	43.2	-0.2	43.2	0.0	43.8	1.4	44.0	0.5	43.8	-0.5	44.2	0.9	44.5	0.7	44.5	0.0
1970	44.7	0.4	44.6	-0.2	44.6	0.0	44.5	-0.2	44.4	-0.2	44.4	0.0	45.0	1.4	45.2	0.4	45.2	0.0	45.2	0.0	45.2	0.0	45.2	0.0

[Continued]

RUBBER AND PLASTIC PRODUCTS
Producer Price Index
Base 1982 = 100
[Continued]

For 1926-2001. Columns headed % show percentile change in the index from the previous period for which an index is available.

Year	Jan Index	%	Feb Index	%	Mar Index	%	Apr Index	%	May Index	%	Jun Index	%	Jul Index	%	Aug Index	%	Sep Index	%	Oct Index	%	Nov Index	%	Dec Index	%
1971	44.9	-0.7	45.1	0.4	45.1	0.0	45.1	0.0	45.0	-0.2	45.0	0.0	45.3	0.7	45.5	0.4	45.4	-0.2	45.3	-0.2	45.3	0.0	45.3	0.0
1972	45.4	0.2	45.3	-0.2	45.1	-0.4	45.1	0.0	45.1	0.0	45.1	0.0	45.3	0.4	45.4	0.2	45.4	0.0	45.4	0.0	45.5	0.2	45.5	0.0
1973	45.6	0.2	45.6	0.0	45.7	0.2	45.8	0.2	46.2	0.9	46.6	0.9	46.8	0.4	46.9	0.2	46.7	-0.4	47.2	1.1	47.6	0.8	48.3	1.5
1974	48.8	1.0	49.6	1.6	51.3	3.4	53.6	4.5	55.4	3.4	56.2	1.4	57.8	2.8	59.4	2.8	60.3	1.5	61.1	1.3	61.5	0.7	61.9	0.7
1975	62.0	0.2	62.2	0.3	62.0	-0.3	61.9	-0.2	61.7	-0.3	61.6	-0.2	62.2	1.0	62.2	0.0	62.5	0.5	62.8	0.5	62.9	0.2	62.9	0.0
1976	63.1	0.3	63.9	1.3	64.4	0.8	64.9	0.8	65.1	0.3	65.1	0.0	65.6	0.8	66.7	1.7	67.9	1.8	68.2	0.4	68.3	0.1	68.2	-0.1
1977	68.2	0.0	68.0	-0.3	68.2	0.3	68.7	0.7	68.9	0.3	69.4	0.7	70.0	0.9	70.1	0.1	70.2	0.1	70.5	0.4	70.5	0.0	70.5	0.0
1978	70.5	0.0	70.5	0.0	71.0	0.7	71.6	0.8	72.0	0.6	72.3	0.4	72.5	0.3	72.8	0.4	73.2	0.5	73.8	0.8	74.3	0.7	74.4	0.1
1979	74.9	0.7	75.9	1.3	77.0	1.4	78.2	1.6	79.0	1.0	80.0	1.3	81.0	1.3	82.4	1.7	83.1	0.8	84.1	1.2	84.9	1.0	85.3	0.5
1980	86.1	0.9	87.3	1.4	88.1	0.9	88.7	0.7	89.1	0.5	90.0	1.0	90.7	0.8	91.3	0.7	92.0	0.8	92.3	0.3	92.6	0.3	92.5	-0.1
1981	93.2	0.8	93.8	0.6	94.6	0.9	95.6	1.1	96.1	0.5	96.7	0.6	96.2	-0.5	97.0	0.8	97.7	0.7	98.3	0.6	98.6	0.3	98.7	0.1
1982	98.3	-0.4	99.2	0.9	99.8	0.6	99.9	0.1	100.3	0.4	100.5	0.2	100.3	-0.2	100.5	0.2	100.5	0.0	100.4	-0.1	100.1	-0.3	100.3	0.2
1983	100.6	0.3	100.4	-0.2	100.2	-0.2	100.7	0.5	100.8	0.1	100.7	-0.1	100.8	0.1	101.0	0.2	100.8	-0.2	101.2	0.4	100.9	-0.3	101.0	0.1
1984	101.4	0.4	102.0	0.6	102.1	0.1	102.4	0.3	102.5	0.1	102.6	0.1	102.6	0.0	102.6	0.0	102.9	0.3	102.2	-0.7	102.0	-0.2	101.9	-0.1
1985	102.2	0.3	102.1	-0.1	102.1	0.0	102.2	0.1	102.1	-0.1	102.0	-0.1	101.9	-0.1	101.4	-0.5	101.5	0.1	101.6	0.1	101.7	0.1	101.9	0.2
1986	102.3	0.4	102.5	0.2	102.2	-0.3	102.2	0.0	102.0	-0.2	102.0	0.0	101.7	-0.3	102.0	0.3	101.8	-0.2	101.5	-0.3	101.3	-0.2	101.2	-0.1
1987	101.5	0.3	101.6	0.1	101.4	-0.2	101.8	0.4	102.0	0.2	102.3	0.3	102.9	0.6	103.2	0.3	103.7	0.5	104.4	0.7	105.1	0.7	105.5	0.4
1988	106.2	0.7	106.9	0.7	107.7	0.7	108.2	0.5	108.8	0.6	109.1	0.3	109.8	0.6	110.6	0.7	111.0	0.4	111.1	0.1	111.2	0.1	111.3	0.1
1989	111.9	0.5	112.2	0.3	112.7	0.4	113.0	0.3	113.0	0.0	112.8	-0.2	112.8	0.0	112.6	-0.2	112.7	0.1	112.5	-0.2	112.5	0.0	112.9	0.4
1990	113.2	0.3	112.9	-0.3	113.3	0.4	113.3	0.0	113.5	0.2	113.2	-0.3	113.1	-0.1	113.2	0.1	113.4	0.2	114.2	0.7	115.0	0.7	115.4	0.3
1991	116.0	0.5	116.0	0.0	115.8	-0.2	115.5	-0.3	115.2	-0.3	115.0	-0.2	114.8	-0.2	114.7	-0.1	114.6	-0.1	114.7	0.1	114.6	-0.1	114.7	0.1
1992	114.7	0.0	114.3	-0.3	114.3	0.0	114.6	0.3	114.9	0.3	115.0	0.1	115.2	0.2	115.3	0.1	115.5	0.2	115.7	0.2	115.8	0.1	115.7	-0.1
1993	115.7	0.0	115.7	0.0	115.6	-0.1	116.0	0.3	115.8	-0.2	115.9	0.1	115.9	0.0	116.0	0.1	116.4	0.3	116.5	0.1	116.4	-0.1	116.5	0.1
1994	116.2	-0.3	116.2	0.0	116.2	0.0	116.2	0.0	116.5	0.3	116.7	0.2	117.1	0.3	117.4	0.3	118.5	0.9	119.6	0.9	120.3	0.6	120.9	0.5
1995	122.1	1.0	122.7	0.5	123.4	0.6	124.1	0.6	124.7	0.5	125.1	0.3	125.2	0.1	125.3	0.1	125.3	0.0	125.1	-0.2	124.7	-0.3	124.3	-0.3
1996	123.9	-0.3	123.7	-0.2	123.6	-0.1	123.4	-0.2	123.7	0.2	123.8	0.1	123.9	0.1	124.2	0.2	124.1	-0.1	123.7	-0.3	123.7	0.0	123.7	0.0
1997	123.2	-0.4	123.1	-0.1	122.9	-0.2	123.2	0.2	123.3	0.1	123.2	-0.1	123.3	0.1	123.4	0.1	123.3	-0.1	123.2	-0.1	123.2	0.0	123.1	-0.1
1998	123.1	0.0	123.1	0.0	123.0	-0.1	122.9	-0.1	122.7	-0.2	122.5	-0.2	122.4	-0.1	122.3	-0.1	122.5	0.2	122.2	-0.2	122.2	0.0	122.3	0.1
1999	122.0	-0.2	121.7	-0.2	121.6	-0.1	121.9	0.2	122.0	0.1	122.1	0.1	122.4	0.2	122.8	0.3	123.1	0.2	123.1	0.0	123.5	0.3	123.6	0.1
2000	123.8	0.2	123.7	-0.1	123.9	0.2	124.3	0.3	124.4	0.1	125.2	0.6	125.8	0.5	125.7	-0.1	126.4	0.6	126.4	0.0	127.9	1.2	128.0	0.1
2001	127.5	-0.4	127.1	-0.3	127.5	0.3	127.6	0.1	127.9	0.2	127.7	-0.2	127.5	-0.2	127.1	-0.3	126.7	-0.3	126.9	0.2	126.7	-0.2	126.6	-0.1

Source: U.S. Department of Labor, Bureau of Labor Statistics, Division of Industry Prices and Price Indexes. n.e.c. stands for not elsewhere classified. - indicates no data collected for period or unavailable.

Rubber and Rubber Products
Producer Price Index
Base 1982 = 100

For 1967-2001. Columns headed % show percentile change in the index from the previous period for which an index is available.

Year	Jan Index	%	Feb Index	%	Mar Index	%	Apr Index	%	May Index	%	Jun Index	%	Jul Index	%	Aug Index	%	Sep Index	%	Oct Index	%	Nov Index	%	Dec Index	%
1967	36.9	-	36.9	0.0	37.0	0.3	37.0	0.0	36.9	-0.3	36.9	0.0	36.9	0.0	37.6	1.9	37.8	0.5	38.1	0.8	38.2	0.3	38.2	0.0
1968	38.2	0.0	38.3	0.3	38.3	0.0	38.3	0.0	38.4	0.3	38.5	0.3	38.7	0.5	38.8	0.3	38.8	0.0	38.9	0.3	38.9	0.0	39.0	0.3
1969	38.5	-1.3	38.8	0.8	38.9	0.3	39.0	0.3	38.9	-0.3	38.9	0.0	39.5	1.5	39.6	0.3	39.5	-0.3	39.8	0.8	40.1	0.8	40.1	0.0
1970	40.3	0.5	40.4	0.2	40.3	-0.2	40.4	0.2	40.4	0.0	40.4	0.0	41.3	2.2	41.7	1.0	41.9	0.5	42.0	0.2	42.0	0.0	42.0	0.0
1971	41.5	-1.2	41.5	0.0	41.5	0.0	41.4	-0.2	41.4	0.0	41.5	0.2	42.3	1.9	42.5	0.5	42.4	-0.2	42.3	-0.2	42.3	0.0	42.3	0.0
1972	42.4	0.2	42.2	-0.5	42.2	0.0	42.2	0.0	42.2	0.0	42.3	0.2	42.5	0.5	42.7	0.5	42.7	0.0	42.7	0.0	42.8	0.2	42.8	0.0
1973	42.9	0.2	43.0	0.2	43.1	0.2	43.2	0.2	43.7	1.2	44.1	0.9	44.3	0.5	44.4	0.2	44.2	-0.5	44.9	1.6	45.3	0.9	46.1	1.8
1974	46.6	1.1	47.4	1.7	49.1	3.6	49.7	1.2	50.7	2.0	51.1	0.8	52.4	2.5	53.5	2.1	53.8	0.6	54.4	1.1	54.6	0.4	55.2	1.1
1975	55.5	0.5	55.9	0.7	56.0	0.2	56.1	0.2	56.1	0.0	56.1	0.0	57.2	2.0	57.2	0.0	57.3	0.2	57.5	0.3	57.7	0.3	57.8	0.2
1976	58.0	0.3	58.4	0.7	59.2	1.4	59.3	0.2	59.4	0.2	59.5	0.2	59.9	0.7	62.1	3.7	63.4	2.1	64.0	0.9	64.0	0.0	64.0	0.0
1977	63.9	-0.2	63.0	-1.4	63.2	0.3	64.2	1.6	64.2	0.0	64.6	0.6	65.3	1.1	65.5	0.3	65.8	0.5	66.2	0.6	66.2	0.0	66.3	0.2
1978	66.5	0.3	66.5	0.0	66.9	0.6	68.0	1.6	68.9	1.3	69.3	0.6	69.5	0.3	69.8	0.4	70.2	0.6	71.1	1.3	71.9	1.1	72.0	0.1
1979	72.7	1.0	73.8	1.5	74.5	0.9	75.1	0.8	75.7	0.8	76.5	1.1	78.3	2.4	80.1	2.3	81.1	1.2	82.3	1.5	83.5	1.5	83.8	0.4
1980	84.5	0.8	86.4	2.2	86.5	0.1	87.1	0.7	87.6	0.6	88.4	0.9	89.3	1.0	89.7	0.4	90.6	1.0	91.3	0.8	91.5	0.2	91.5	0.0
1981	91.9	0.4	92.8	1.0	94.1	1.4	94.5	0.4	95.0	0.5	95.9	0.9	95.1	-0.8	95.9	0.8	97.2	1.4	98.2	1.0	98.7	0.5	98.8	0.1
1982	98.0	-0.8	99.3	1.3	99.6	0.3	99.6	0.0	100.5	0.9	100.6	0.1	100.4	-0.2	100.9	0.5	100.6	-0.3	100.4	-0.2	100.0	-0.4	100.2	0.2
1983	100.7	0.5	100.2	-0.5	99.8	-0.4	99.7	-0.1	99.7	0.0	99.2	-0.5	99.0	-0.2	99.0	0.0	98.5	-0.5	98.9	0.4	98.7	-0.2	98.8	0.1
1984	99.5	0.7	99.6	0.1	99.1	-0.5	99.8	0.7	99.4	-0.4	99.5	0.1	99.5	0.0	99.9	0.4	100.1	0.2	98.9	-1.2	98.5	-0.4	98.5	0.0
1985	98.7	0.2	99.1	0.4	99.0	-0.1	98.9	-0.1	99.0	0.1	98.7	-0.3	98.9	0.2	98.5	-0.4	98.6	0.1	98.5	-0.1	98.7	0.2	98.4	-0.3
1986	98.7	0.3	99.0	0.3	98.9	-0.1	98.8	-0.1	98.6	-0.2	98.5	-0.1	97.9	-0.6	97.8	-0.1	97.6	-0.2	97.6	0.0	97.0	-0.6	97.0	0.0
1987	97.5	0.5	97.5	0.0	97.4	-0.1	98.1	0.7	98.5	0.4	99.0	0.5	100.1	1.1	100.2	0.1	100.4	0.2	100.9	0.5	101.1	0.2	101.8	0.7
1988	102.3	0.5	102.5	0.2	102.6	0.1	102.9	0.3	102.6	-0.3	103.1	0.5	103.7	0.6	104.4	0.7	104.6	0.2	104.5	-0.1	104.5	0.0	104.9	0.4
1989	105.8	0.9	106.4	0.6	106.8	0.4	107.1	0.3	107.4	0.3	107.4	0.0	107.3	-0.1	107.1	-0.2	106.9	-0.2	107.2	0.3	107.4	0.2	107.7	0.3
1990	107.9	0.2	107.6	-0.3	108.5	0.8	108.1	-0.4	108.2	0.1	108.1	-0.1	108.1	0.0	108.5	0.4	108.6	0.1	109.2	0.6	110.1	0.8	110.4	0.3
1991	110.6	0.2	110.6	0.0	110.4	-0.2	109.9	-0.5	109.8	-0.1	109.7	-0.1	109.1	-0.5	108.8	-0.3	108.6	-0.2	109.1	0.5	109.1	0.0	109.0	-0.1
1992	109.2	0.2	109.1	-0.1	109.0	-0.1	108.9	-0.1	109.0	0.1	109.8	0.7	109.8	0.0	110.0	0.2	110.3	0.3	110.3	0.0	111.0	0.6	111.0	0.0
1993	110.4	-0.5	110.3	-0.1	110.4	0.1	110.9	0.5	110.9	0.0	111.0	0.1	111.0	0.0	110.9	-0.1	111.1	0.2	111.1	0.0	111.0	-0.1	111.0	0.0
1994	110.9	-0.1	110.8	-0.1	110.9	0.1	111.2	0.3	111.4	0.2	111.8	0.4	112.0	0.2	112.0	0.0	112.2	0.2	113.0	0.7	113.4	0.4	113.5	0.1
1995	114.5	0.9	115.1	0.5	116.1	0.9	116.5	0.3	116.9	0.3	117.7	0.7	118.2	0.4	118.3	0.1	118.3	0.0	118.3	0.0	118.2	-0.1	117.5	-0.6
1996	116.8	-0.6	116.4	-0.3	116.3	-0.1	116.5	0.2	116.6	0.1	116.0	-0.5	116.1	0.1	116.5	0.3	116.5	0.0	116.1	-0.3	115.9	-0.2	116.5	0.5
1997	116.5	0.0	116.1	-0.3	116.0	-0.1	116.3	0.3	116.2	-0.1	115.8	-0.3	115.4	-0.3	115.6	0.2	115.8	0.2	115.8	0.0	115.3	-0.4	115.3	0.0
1998	115.5	0.2	115.6	0.1	115.5	-0.1	115.4	-0.1	115.2	-0.2	115.2	0.0	115.1	-0.1	115.2	0.1	115.3	0.1	115.3	0.0	115.1	-0.2	114.9	-0.2
1999	114.4	-0.4	114.0	-0.3	113.9	-0.1	114.4	0.4	114.2	-0.2	114.2	0.0	113.7	-0.4	114.1	0.4	114.1	0.0	113.8	-0.3	114.6	0.7	114.6	0.0
2000	114.7	0.1	114.2	-0.4	114.3	0.1	114.9	0.5	114.6	-0.3	115.2	0.5	115.5	0.3	115.9	0.3	115.9	0.0	115.7	-0.2	116.1	0.3	116.4	0.3
2001	116.4	0.0	116.8	0.3	116.8	0.0	116.8	0.0	116.8	0.0	116.9	0.1	117.4	0.4	116.7	-0.6	116.9	0.2	116.6	-0.3	116.9	0.3	116.8	-0.1

Source: U.S. Department of Labor, Bureau of Labor Statistics, Division of Industry Prices and Price Indexes. n.e.c. stands for not elsewhere classified. - indicates no data collected for period or unavailable.

Plastic Products
Producer Price Index
Base 1982 = 100

For 1971-2001. Columns headed % show percentile change in the index from the previous period for which an index is available.

Year	Jan Index	%	Feb Index	%	Mar Index	%	Apr Index	%	May Index	%	Jun Index	%	Jul Index	%	Aug Index	%	Sep Index	%	Oct Index	%	Nov Index	%	Dec Index	%
1971	48.4	-	49.3	1.9	49.2	-0.2	49.2	0.0	48.9	-0.6	48.8	-0.2	48.2	-1.2	48.2	0.0	48.2	0.0	48.1	-0.2	48.1	0.0	48.0	-0.2
1972	48.1	0.2	48.1	0.0	47.7	-0.8	47.6	-0.2	47.6	0.0	47.4	-0.4	47.5	0.2	47.5	0.0	47.5	0.0	47.5	0.0	47.6	0.2	47.6	0.0
1973	47.6	0.0	47.6	0.0	47.6	0.0	47.7	0.2	47.8	0.2	48.5	1.5	48.4	-0.2	48.4	0.0	48.4	0.0	48.5	0.2	48.7	0.4	49.1	0.8
1974	49.7	1.2	50.5	1.6	52.0	3.0	57.4	10.4	60.7	5.7	62.1	2.3	64.2	3.4	66.7	3.9	68.8	3.1	70.0	1.7	70.8	1.1	70.6	-0.3
1975	70.3	-0.4	70.0	-0.4	69.4	-0.9	68.9	-0.7	68.4	-0.7	67.9	-0.7	67.6	-0.4	67.4	-0.3	68.2	1.2	68.6	0.6	68.7	0.1	68.6	-0.1
1976	68.7	0.1	69.9	1.7	70.1	0.3	71.1	1.4	71.4	0.4	71.2	-0.3	71.8	0.8	71.9	0.1	72.8	1.3	72.8	0.0	72.9	0.1	72.9	0.0
1977	72.9	0.0	73.6	1.0	73.7	0.1	73.6	-0.1	74.0	0.5	74.6	0.8	75.1	0.7	75.2	0.1	75.1	-0.1	75.3	0.3	75.2	-0.1	75.1	-0.1
1978	74.9	-0.3	75.0	0.1	75.5	0.7	75.6	0.1	75.4	-0.3	75.6	0.3	75.7	0.1	76.1	0.5	76.6	0.7	76.7	0.1	77.0	0.4	77.1	0.1
1979	77.3	0.3	78.2	1.2	79.9	2.2	81.6	2.1	82.7	1.3	83.9	1.5	84.0	0.1	84.8	1.0	85.4	0.7	86.1	0.8	86.4	0.3	87.0	0.7
1980	87.9	1.0	88.2	0.3	89.9	1.9	90.4	0.6	90.7	0.3	91.8	1.2	92.2	0.4	93.1	1.0	93.5	0.4	93.4	-0.1	93.7	0.3	93.6	-0.1
1981	94.5	1.0	94.9	0.4	95.2	0.3	96.9	1.8	97.2	0.3	97.6	0.4	97.3	-0.3	98.1	0.8	98.2	0.1	98.5	0.3	98.5	0.0	98.7	0.2
1982	98.6	-0.1	99.0	0.4	100.0	1.0	100.3	0.3	100.1	-0.2	100.4	0.3	100.1	-0.3	100.2	0.1	100.3	0.1	100.3	0.0	100.3	0.0	100.5	0.2
1983	100.6	0.1	100.6	0.0	100.7	0.1	101.7	1.0	101.9	0.2	102.4	0.5	102.8	0.4	103.1	0.3	103.2	0.1	103.8	0.6	103.3	-0.5	103.4	0.1
1984	103.5	0.1	104.6	1.1	105.4	0.8	105.4	0.0	106.0	0.6	105.9	-0.1	106.0	0.1	105.6	-0.4	105.9	0.3	105.9	0.0	105.8	-0.1	105.7	-0.1
1985	106.1	0.4	105.4	-0.7	105.6	0.2	105.9	0.3	105.6	-0.3	105.7	0.1	105.2	-0.5	104.7	-0.5	104.8	0.1	105.0	0.2	105.1	0.1	105.8	0.7
1986	106.3	0.5	106.5	0.2	106.0	-0.5	106.0	0.0	105.9	-0.1	105.9	0.0	105.9	0.0	106.7	0.8	106.5	-0.2	105.9	-0.6	106.0	0.1	105.8	-0.2
1987	106.1	0.3	106.1	0.0	106.0	-0.1	106.1	0.1	106.2	0.1	106.4	0.2	106.7	0.3	107.3	0.6	107.9	0.6	108.7	0.7	109.6	0.8	109.9	0.3
1988	110.8	0.8	111.7	0.8	112.9	1.1	113.5	0.5	114.6	1.0	114.9	0.3	115.6	0.6	116.5	0.8	117.0	0.4	117.3	0.3	117.4	0.1	117.4	0.0
1989	117.8	0.3	118.0	0.2	118.5	0.4	118.8	0.3	118.7	-0.1	118.4	-0.3	118.4	0.0	118.2	-0.2	118.5	0.3	117.9	-0.5	117.9	0.0	118.3	0.3
1990	118.7	0.3	118.4	-0.3	118.5	0.1	118.7	0.2	119.0	0.3	118.6	-0.3	118.4	-0.2	118.4	0.0	118.7	0.3	119.5	0.7	120.3	0.7	120.8	0.4
1991	121.6	0.7	121.6	0.0	121.5	-0.1	121.2	-0.2	120.8	-0.3	120.6	-0.2	120.6	0.0	120.6	0.0	120.6	0.0	120.3	-0.2	120.3	0.0	120.5	0.2
1992	120.4	-0.1	119.8	-0.5	119.9	0.1	120.4	0.4	120.7	0.2	120.5	-0.2	120.8	0.2	120.9	0.1	121.1	0.2	121.3	0.2	121.3	0.0	121.0	-0.2
1993	121.3	0.2	121.3	0.0	121.2	-0.1	121.5	0.2	121.3	-0.2	121.3	0.0	121.3	0.0	121.5	0.2	122.0	0.4	122.1	0.1	122.1	0.0	122.2	0.1
1994	121.8	-0.3	121.9	0.1	121.8	-0.1	121.8	0.0	122.0	0.2	122.2	0.2	122.6	0.3	123.1	0.4	124.6	1.2	125.9	1.0	126.8	0.7	127.5	0.6
1995	129.0	1.2	129.5	0.4	130.2	0.5	131.0	0.6	131.6	0.5	131.9	0.2	131.9	0.0	132.0	0.1	131.9	-0.1	131.7	-0.2	131.1	-0.5	130.8	-0.2
1996	130.5	-0.2	130.3	-0.2	130.3	0.0	129.9	-0.3	130.3	0.3	130.7	0.3	130.8	0.1	131.1	0.2	131.0	-0.1	130.5	-0.4	130.7	0.2	130.4	-0.2
1997	129.7	-0.5	129.7	0.0	129.5	-0.2	129.7	0.2	129.9	0.2	129.9	0.0	130.2	0.2	130.3	0.1	130.0	-0.2	130.0	0.0	130.1	0.1	130.0	-0.1
1998	130.0	0.0	129.8	-0.2	129.7	-0.1	129.7	0.0	129.5	-0.2	129.2	-0.2	129.1	-0.1	128.9	-0.2	129.1	0.2	128.7	-0.3	128.8	0.1	129.1	0.2
1999	128.7	-0.3	128.6	-0.1	128.5	-0.1	128.7	0.2	128.8	0.1	129.0	0.2	129.7	0.5	130.1	0.3	130.4	0.2	130.6	0.2	130.9	0.2	131.0	0.1
2000	131.3	0.2	131.3	0.0	131.5	0.2	131.9	0.3	132.1	0.2	133.0	0.7	133.8	0.6	133.5	-0.2	134.5	0.7	134.5	0.0	136.5	1.5	136.6	0.1
2001	135.8	-0.6	135.2	-0.4	135.7	0.4	135.9	0.1	136.3	0.3	136.0	-0.2	135.5	-0.4	135.1	-0.3	134.5	-0.4	135.0	0.4	134.5	-0.4	134.4	-0.1

Source: U.S. Department of Labor, Bureau of Labor Statistics, Division of Industry Prices and Price Indexes. n.e.c. stands for not elsewhere classified. - indicates no data collected for period or unavailable.

LUMBER AND WOOD PRODUCTS
Producer Price Index
Base 1982 = 100

For 1926-2001. Columns headed % show percentile change in the index from the previous period for which an index is available.

Year	Jan Index	%	Feb Index	%	Mar Index	%	Apr Index	%	May Index	%	Jun Index	%	Jul Index	%	Aug Index	%	Sep Index	%	Oct Index	%	Nov Index	%	Dec Index	%
1926	9.6	-	9.5	-1.0	9.5	0.0	9.4	-1.1	9.3	-1.1	9.2	-1.1	9.2	0.0	9.2	0.0	9.2	0.0	9.1	-1.1	9.3	2.2	9.2	-1.1
1927	9.0	-2.2	9.0	0.0	8.9	-1.1	8.9	0.0	8.9	0.0	8.9	0.0	8.8	-1.1	8.7	-1.1	8.6	-1.1	8.6	0.0	8.5	-1.2	8.4	-1.2
1928	8.4	0.0	8.4	0.0	8.4	0.0	8.3	-1.2	8.3	0.0	8.3	0.0	8.4	1.2	8.5	1.2	8.6	1.2	8.6	0.0	8.7	1.2	8.8	1.1
1929	8.7	-1.1	8.9	2.3	9.0	1.1	8.9	-1.1	8.8	-1.1	8.8	0.0	8.7	-1.1	8.8	1.1	8.9	1.1	8.9	0.0	8.6	-3.4	8.6	0.0
1930	8.6	0.0	8.6	0.0	8.6	0.0	8.6	0.0	8.4	-2.3	8.1	-3.6	7.8	-3.7	7.7	-1.3	7.7	0.0	7.5	-2.6	7.5	0.0	7.3	-2.7
1931	7.2	-1.4	6.9	-4.2	7.0	1.4	6.8	-2.9	6.6	-2.9	6.5	-1.5	6.4	-1.5	6.3	-1.6	6.3	0.0	6.1	-3.2	6.2	1.6	6.2	0.0
1932	6.2	0.0	6.0	-3.2	5.9	-1.7	5.8	-1.7	5.7	-1.7	5.5	-3.5	5.5	0.0	5.3	-3.6	5.4	1.9	5.4	0.0	5.4	0.0	5.4	0.0
1933	5.3	-1.9	5.4	1.9	5.5	1.9	5.5	0.0	5.7	3.6	6.4	12.3	7.1	10.9	7.4	4.2	7.7	4.1	7.9	2.6	8.1	2.5	8.1	0.0
1934	8.1	0.0	8.1	0.0	8.0	-1.2	8.1	1.3	8.0	-1.2	8.0	0.0	7.8	-2.5	7.6	-2.6	7.6	0.0	7.6	0.0	7.5	-1.3	7.5	0.0
1935	7.4	-1.3	7.5	1.4	7.4	-1.3	7.4	0.0	7.4	0.0	7.5	1.4	7.6	1.3	7.7	1.3	7.7	0.0	7.7	0.0	7.7	0.0	7.6	-1.3
1936	7.7	1.3	7.7	0.0	7.7	0.0	7.8	1.3	7.8	0.0	7.7	-1.3	7.8	1.3	7.8	0.0	8.0	2.6	8.0	0.0	8.1	1.3	8.4	3.7
1937	8.7	3.6	9.2	5.7	9.5	3.3	9.6	1.1	9.7	1.0	9.7	0.0	9.7	0.0	9.5	-2.1	9.4	-1.1	9.3	-1.1	9.2	-1.1	8.9	-3.3	8.9	0.0
1938	8.7	-2.2	8.6	-1.1	8.6	0.0	8.6	0.0	8.3	-3.5	8.3	0.0	8.3	0.0	8.4	1.2	8.5	1.2	8.4	-1.2	8.4	0.0	8.5	1.2
1939	8.6	1.2	8.6	0.0	8.6	0.0	8.5	-1.2	8.5	0.0	8.5	0.0	8.6	1.2	8.6	0.0	8.7	1.2	9.1	4.6	9.2	1.1	9.1	-1.1
1940	9.1	0.0	9.1	0.0	9.1	0.0	9.0	-1.1	9.0	0.0	9.0	0.0	9.0	0.0	9.3	3.3	10.1	8.6	10.7	5.9	11.0	2.8	11.1	0.9
1941	11.1	0.0	11.0	-0.9	11.0	0.0	11.0	0.0	11.0	0.0	11.0	0.0	11.4	3.6	11.9	4.4	12.0	0.8	12.2	1.7	12.1	-0.8	12.2	0.8
1942	12.4	1.6	12.5	0.8	12.5	0.0	12.4	-0.8	12.4	0.0	12.4	0.0	12.5	0.8	12.5	0.0	12.5	0.0	12.5	0.0	12.6	0.8	12.7	0.8
1943	12.7	0.0	12.8	0.8	12.8	0.0	12.8	0.0	12.9	0.8	13.0	0.8	13.1	0.8	13.5	3.1	13.7	1.5	13.7	0.0	13.8	0.7	13.8	0.0
1944	13.8	0.0	13.9	0.7	14.1	1.4	14.3	1.4	14.4	0.7	14.4	0.0	14.4	0.0	14.4	0.0	14.4	0.0	14.4	0.0	14.4	0.0	14.4	0.0
1945	14.4	0.0	14.4	0.0	14.4	0.0	14.4	0.0	14.4	0.0	14.4	0.0	14.5	0.7	14.5	0.0	14.5	0.0	14.5	0.0	14.5	0.0	14.6	0.7
1946	14.7	0.7	14.9	1.4	15.5	4.0	15.9	2.6	16.1	1.3	16.4	1.9	16.5	0.6	16.5	0.0	16.6	0.6	16.8	1.2	17.9	6.5	20.9	16.8
1947	23.4	12.0	23.9	2.1	24.7	3.3	25.4	2.8	25.5	0.4	25.4	-0.4	25.5	0.4	26.0	2.0	26.6	2.3	27.0	1.5	27.7	2.6	28.2	1.8
1948	28.7	1.8	28.9	0.7	29.2	1.0	29.3	0.3	29.6	1.0	29.8	0.7	30.0	0.7	30.2	0.7	30.1	-0.3	29.7	-1.3	29.5	-0.7	29.0	-1.7
1949	28.7	-1.0	28.3	-1.4	28.1	-0.7	27.8	-1.1	27.4	-1.4	27.0	-1.5	26.6	-1.5	26.3	-1.1	26.4	0.4	26.7	1.1	27.0	1.1	27.3	1.1
1950	27.7	1.5	28.3	2.2	28.9	2.1	29.3	1.4	30.3	3.4	30.9	2.0	31.7	2.6	33.1	4.4	34.3	3.6	34.0	-0.9	33.8	-0.6	33.9	0.3
1951	34.6	2.1	34.8	0.6	34.9	0.3	34.9	0.0	34.8	-0.3	34.3	-1.4	34.1	-0.6	33.7	-1.2	33.5	-0.6	33.5	0.0	33.4	-0.3	33.2	-0.6
1952	33.1	-0.3	33.2	0.3	33.2	0.0	33.3	0.3	33.3	0.0	33.1	-0.6	33.2	0.3	33.2	0.0	33.2	0.0	33.1	-0.3	33.0	-0.3	33.0	0.0
1953	33.2	0.6	33.4	0.6	33.5	0.3	33.7	0.6	33.6	-0.3	33.5	-0.3	33.4	-0.3	33.2	-0.6	32.8	-1.2	32.6	-0.6	32.3	-0.9	32.3	0.0
1954	32.2	-0.3	32.2	0.0	32.2	0.0	32.0	-0.6	32.0	0.0	32.1	0.3	32.8	2.2	32.8	0.0	32.9	0.3	33.0	0.3	33.0	0.0	33.1	0.3
1955	33.2	0.3	33.4	0.6	33.5	0.3	33.8	0.9	34.1	0.9	34.1	0.0	34.2	0.3	34.5	0.9	34.7	0.6	34.6	-0.3	34.5	-0.3	34.5	0.0
1956	34.8	0.9	34.9	0.3	35.3	1.1	35.4	0.3	35.3	-0.3	35.1	-0.6	34.9	-0.6	34.5	-1.1	34.1	-1.2	33.6	-1.5	33.5	-0.3	33.4	-0.3
1957	33.5	0.3	33.3	-0.6	33.1	-0.6	33.2	0.3	33.0	-0.6	33.0	0.0	32.9	-0.3	32.7	-0.6	32.5	-0.6	32.3	-0.6	32.2	-0.3	32.1	-0.3
1958	32.1	0.0	31.9	-0.6	31.8	-0.3	31.9	0.3	32.0	0.3	32.1	0.3	32.2	0.3	32.7	1.6	33.2	1.5	33.3	0.3	33.1	-0.6	33.0	-0.3
1959	33.2	0.6	33.8	1.8	34.2	1.2	34.8	1.8	35.3	1.4	35.5	0.6	35.4	-0.3	35.4	0.0	35.1	-0.8	34.8	-0.9	34.3	-1.4	34.4	0.3
1960	34.5	0.3	34.4	-0.3	34.3	-0.3	34.2	-0.3	34.1	-0.3	33.8	-0.9	33.5	-0.9	32.9	-1.8	32.8	-0.3	32.5	-0.9	32.2	-0.9	32.2	0.0
1961	31.9	-0.9	31.6	-0.9	31.8	0.6	32.5	2.2	32.4	-0.3	32.5	0.3	32.3	-0.6	32.0	-0.9	31.9	-0.3	31.6	-0.9	31.6	0.0	31.5	-0.3
1962	31.5	0.0	31.7	0.6	32.1	1.3	32.2	0.3	32.3	0.3	32.4	0.3	32.5	0.3	32.5	0.0	32.3	-0.6	32.2	-0.3	32.1	-0.3	31.9	-0.6
1963	32.0	0.3	32.0	0.0	32.2	0.6	32.3	0.3	32.5	0.6	32.8	0.9	33.9	3.4	34.2	0.9	33.3	-2.6	33.0	-0.9	33.0	0.0	33.0	0.0
1964	33.0	0.0	33.3	0.9	33.6	0.9	33.9	0.9	33.9	0.0	33.8	-0.3	33.7	-0.3	33.6	-0.3	33.5	-0.3	33.4	-0.3	33.2	-0.6	33.1	-0.3
1965	33.6	1.5	33.6	0.0	33.5	-0.3	33.5	0.0	33.5	0.0	33.4	-0.3	33.5	0.3	33.9	1.2	34.0	0.3	33.9	-0.3	33.9	0.0	34.0	0.3
1966	34.2	0.6	34.6	1.2	35.2	1.7	36.1	2.6	36.5	1.1	35.9	-1.6	35.5	-1.1	35.4	-0.3	35.3	-0.3	34.9	-1.1	34.3	-1.7	34.1	-0.6
1967	34.2	0.3	34.6	1.2	34.5	-0.3	34.7	0.6	34.7	0.0	34.9	0.6	35.1	0.6	35.4	0.9	36.2	2.3	35.7	-1.4	35.5	-0.6	35.9	1.1
1968	36.2	0.8	37.2	2.8	38.0	2.2	38.6	1.6	39.0	1.0	39.1	0.3	39.7	1.5	40.1	1.0	40.9	2.0	41.7	2.0	42.3	1.4	44.5	5.2
1969	45.9	3.1	48.2	5.0	49.8	3.3	47.8	-4.0	45.9	-4.0	43.3	-5.7	41.8	-3.5	41.3	-1.2	41.1	-0.5	40.9	-0.5	41.3	1.0	40.8	-1.2
1970	40.5	-0.7	40.0	-1.2	39.7	-0.7	40.0	0.8	40.3	0.7	40.0	-0.7	39.9	-0.2	40.1	0.5	40.1	0.0	39.7	-1.0	39.3	-1.0	39.0	-0.8

[Continued]

LUMBER AND WOOD PRODUCTS

Producer Price Index
Base 1982 = 100

[Continued]

For 1926-2001. Columns headed % show percentile change in the index from the previous period for which an index is available.

Year	Jan Index	%	Feb Index	%	Mar Index	%	Apr Index	%	May Index	%	Jun Index	%	Jul Index	%	Aug Index	%	Sep Index	%	Oct Index	%	Nov Index	%	Dec Index	%
1971	39.4	1.0	41.2	4.6	43.4	5.3	43.9	1.2	44.0	0.2	44.4	0.9	46.0	3.6	47.5	3.3	47.3	-0.4	46.4	-1.9	46.2	-0.4	46.7	1.1
1972	47.4	1.5	48.4	2.1	49.0	1.2	49.6	1.2	50.1	1.0	50.6	1.0	51.3	1.4	52.0	1.4	52.1	0.2	52.4	0.6	52.5	0.2	52.6	0.2
1973	53.0	0.8	56.5	6.6	60.8	7.6	63.9	5.1	65.6	2.7	64.3	-2.0	62.4	-3.0	62.8	0.6	63.9	1.8	63.3	-0.9	64.9	2.5	65.4	0.8
1974	64.5	-1.4	64.6	0.2	67.2	4.0	70.3	4.6	69.5	-1.1	67.5	-2.9	66.2	-1.9	64.5	-2.6	63.4	-1.7	59.5	-6.2	58.2	-2.2	58.1	-0.2
1975	57.9	-0.3	59.5	2.8	59.6	0.2	61.4	3.0	64.3	4.7	63.6	-1.1	63.1	-0.8	63.1	0.0	63.2	0.2	62.9	-0.5	62.6	-0.5	64.3	2.7
1976	67.0	4.2	68.9	2.8	71.1	3.2	71.4	0.4	71.1	-0.4	70.2	-1.3	71.5	1.9	72.9	2.0	74.7	2.5	75.0	0.4	75.3	0.4	77.3	2.7
1977	78.2	1.2	78.8	0.8	80.4	2.0	80.7	0.4	80.6	-0.1	80.3	-0.4	82.7	3.0	85.3	3.1	88.8	4.1	87.0	-2.0	85.5	-1.7	87.5	2.3
1978	90.0	2.9	92.6	2.9	93.5	1.0	94.7	1.3	96.0	1.4	97.8	1.9	97.4	-0.4	98.9	1.5	99.3	0.4	99.8	0.5	101.9	2.1	101.4	-0.5
1979	101.9	0.5	103.2	1.3	105.5	2.2	107.1	1.5	106.4	-0.7	105.3	-1.0	105.4	0.1	107.0	1.5	108.8	1.7	108.5	-0.3	105.0	-3.2	101.9	-3.0
1980	101.9	0.0	103.5	1.6	103.6	0.1	96.8	-6.6	95.5	-1.3	98.3	2.9	101.6	3.4	104.0	2.4	102.6	-1.3	101.5	-1.1	103.0	1.5	105.2	2.1
1981	104.1	-1.0	103.5	-0.6	103.4	-0.1	105.1	1.6	104.8	-0.3	104.7	-0.1	104.1	-0.6	103.4	-0.7	101.6	-1.7	99.8	-1.8	99.1	-0.7	100.2	1.1
1982	100.3	0.1	100.2	-0.1	100.2	0.0	100.6	0.4	99.9	-0.7	101.5	1.6	101.4	-0.1	99.8	-1.6	99.4	-0.4	98.1	-1.3	98.3	0.2	100.3	2.0
1983	103.0	2.7	106.4	3.3	107.4	0.9	107.9	0.5	108.2	0.3	110.6	2.2	110.5	-0.1	110.3	-0.2	107.3	-2.7	107.3	0.0	107.1	-0.2	108.4	1.2
1984	108.6	0.2	110.9	2.1	111.3	0.4	110.7	-0.5	108.3	-2.2	107.9	-0.4	106.9	-0.9	107.0	0.1	106.5	-0.5	105.5	-0.9	105.7	0.2	106.4	0.7
1985	106.9	0.5	106.5	-0.4	106.4	-0.1	105.9	-0.5	107.7	1.7	110.0	2.1	108.9	-1.0	107.3	-1.5	105.5	-1.7	105.2	-0.3	104.3	-0.9	104.7	0.4
1986	105.0	0.3	104.3	-0.7	105.8	1.4	108.4	2.5	108.2	-0.2	107.5	-0.6	107.8	0.3	107.9	0.1	108.4	0.5	107.9	-0.5	108.0	0.1	107.8	-0.2
1987	108.1	0.3	109.4	1.2	110.6	1.1	110.7	0.1	110.7	0.0	111.4	0.6	112.4	0.9	113.7	1.2	116.2	2.2	116.1	-0.1	116.9	0.7	117.1	0.2
1988	117.8	0.6	118.4	0.5	118.9	0.4	119.2	0.3	119.1	-0.1	119.3	0.2	120.0	0.6	118.8	-1.0	118.9	0.1	118.7	-0.2	118.8	0.1	119.0	0.2
1989	120.1	0.9	122.0	1.6	123.2	1.0	125.2	1.6	126.5	1.0	127.4	0.7	128.9	1.2	129.0	0.1	129.0	0.0	130.9	1.5	130.0	-0.7	128.5	-1.2
1990	129.0	0.4	129.7	0.5	130.5	0.6	132.4	1.5	132.0	-0.3	130.7	-1.0	131.3	0.5	130.2	-0.8	129.3	-0.7	127.5	-1.4	126.9	-0.5	126.8	-0.1
1991	127.6	0.6	127.2	-0.3	127.8	0.5	129.2	1.1	132.3	2.4	136.2	2.9	136.9	0.5	133.3	-2.6	133.4	0.1	133.2	-0.1	133.4	0.2	134.6	0.9
1992	137.6	2.2	142.9	3.9	145.7	2.0	147.5	1.2	147.6	0.1	146.3	-0.9	145.3	-0.7	145.4	0.1	148.7	2.3	148.7	0.0	149.5	0.5	154.4	3.3
1993	160.2	3.8	169.3	5.7	176.9	4.5	181.2	2.4	179.8	-0.8	174.1	-3.2	171.7	-1.4	171.1	-0.3	173.2	1.2	174.0	0.5	177.3	1.9	179.6	1.3
1994	184.6	2.8	183.3	-0.7	184.2	0.5	180.3	-2.1	178.2	-1.2	179.4	0.7	177.4	-1.1	177.7	0.2	178.3	0.3	177.8	-0.3	179.4	0.9	179.2	-0.1
1995	179.6	0.2	179.5	-0.1	180.6	0.6	180.4	-0.1	179.7	-0.4	178.0	-0.9	178.2	0.1	177.8	-0.2	178.9	0.6	177.2	-1.0	174.2	-1.7	173.5	-0.4
1996	172.9	-0.3	173.0	0.1	172.8	-0.1	171.9	-0.5	175.8	2.3	176.8	0.6	175.0	-1.0	177.0	1.1	180.2	1.8	177.8	-1.3	180.2	1.3	179.7	-0.3
1997	180.6	0.5	183.4	1.6	184.8	0.8	185.4	0.3	186.8	0.8	185.4	-0.7	185.9	0.3	185.0	-0.5	183.7	-0.7	180.8	-1.6	181.9	0.6	181.9	0.0
1998	181.1	-0.4	182.2	0.6	182.4	0.1	182.5	0.1	180.4	-1.2	177.5	-1.6	178.5	0.6	179.7	0.7	178.0	-0.9	175.5	-1.4	175.2	-0.2	175.9	0.4
1999	177.2	0.7	179.8	1.5	181.6	1.0	181.6	0.0	183.7	1.2	187.8	2.2	192.0	2.2	189.6	-1.2	184.9	-2.5	181.0	-2.1	181.6	0.3	182.7	0.6
2000	183.8	0.6	184.0	0.1	184.2	0.1	183.0	-0.7	179.3	-2.0	178.6	-0.4	177.0	-0.9	174.4	-1.5	174.1	-0.2	173.9	-0.1	173.2	-0.4	172.7	-0.3
2001	171.6	-0.6	171.5	-0.1	172.8	0.8	172.9	0.1	179.0	3.5	180.7	0.9	176.7	-2.2	176.8	0.1	175.6	-0.7	172.0	-2.1	171.4	-0.3	170.3	-0.6

Source: U.S. Department of Labor, Bureau of Labor Statistics, Division of Industry Prices and Price Indexes. n.e.c. stands for not elsewhere classified. - indicates no data collected for period or unavailable.

Lumber

Producer Price Index
Base 1982 = 100

For 1926-2001. Columns headed % show percentile change in the index from the previous period for which an index is available.

Year	Jan Index	%	Feb Index	%	Mar Index	%	Apr Index	%	May Index	%	Jun Index	%	Jul Index	%	Aug Index	%	Sep Index	%	Oct Index	%	Nov Index	%	Dec Index	%
1926	8.3	-	8.3	0.0	8.3	0.0	8.2	-1.2	8.1	-1.2	8.0	-1.2	8.0	0.0	7.9	-1.2	7.9	0.0	7.9	0.0	8.1	2.5	8.0	-1.2
1927	7.9	-1.2	7.8	-1.3	7.7	-1.3	7.7	0.0	7.7	0.0	7.7	0.0	7.6	-1.3	7.5	-1.3	7.4	-1.3	7.4	0.0	7.3	-1.4	7.2	-1.4
1928	7.2	0.0	7.2	0.0	7.2	0.0	7.1	-1.4	7.1	0.0	7.2	1.4	7.2	0.0	7.3	1.4	7.4	1.4	7.5	1.4	7.5	0.0	7.6	1.3
1929	7.5	-1.3	7.7	2.7	7.8	1.3	7.7	-1.3	7.6	-1.3	7.6	0.0	7.5	-1.3	7.5	0.0	7.7	2.7	7.8	1.3	7.4	-5.1	7.4	0.0
1930	7.5	1.4	7.4	-1.3	7.4	0.0	7.4	0.0	7.2	-2.7	6.9	-4.2	6.8	-1.4	6.6	-2.9	6.6	0.0	6.4	-3.0	6.5	1.6	6.3	-3.1
1931	6.2	-1.6	6.0	-3.2	6.0	0.0	6.0	0.0	5.6	-6.7	5.6	0.0	5.4	-3.6	5.4	0.0	5.4	0.0	5.3	-1.9	5.3	0.0	5.3	0.0
1932	5.3	0.0	5.1	-3.8	5.0	-2.0	4.8	-4.0	4.8	0.0	4.7	-2.1	4.6	-2.1	4.5	-2.2	4.5	0.0	4.6	2.2	4.6	0.0	4.6	0.0
1933	4.5	-2.2	4.5	0.0	4.7	4.4	4.7	0.0	4.8	2.1	5.5	14.6	6.1	10.9	6.4	4.9	6.6	3.1	6.8	3.0	7.0	2.9	7.1	1.4
1934	7.1	0.0	7.1	0.0	7.0	-1.4	7.1	1.4	7.0	-1.4	7.0	0.0	6.9	-1.4	6.6	-4.3	6.7	1.5	6.6	-1.5	6.6	0.0	6.6	0.0
1935	6.4	-3.0	6.4	0.0	6.3	-1.6	6.3	0.0	6.5	3.2	6.7	3.1	6.9	3.0	6.9	0.0	6.8	-1.4	6.7	-1.5	6.6	-1.5	6.7	1.5
1936	6.8	1.5	6.8	0.0	7.0	2.9	7.1	1.4	7.1	0.0	7.1	0.0	7.0	-1.4	7.0	0.0	7.0	0.0	7.1	1.4	7.1	0.0	7.4	4.2
1937	7.8	5.4	8.3	6.4	8.6	3.6	8.6	0.0	8.5	-1.2	8.3	-2.4	8.1	-2.4	8.0	-1.2	8.0	0.0	7.8	-2.5	7.5	-3.8	7.2	-4.0
1938	7.1	-1.4	7.1	0.0	7.1	0.0	7.0	-1.4	7.0	0.0	6.8	-2.9	6.8	0.0	7.0	2.9	7.1	1.4	7.1	0.0	7.2	1.4	7.4	2.8
1939	7.4	0.0	7.4	0.0	7.4	0.0	7.4	0.0	7.3	-1.4	7.2	-1.4	7.2	0.0	7.3	1.4	7.6	4.1	8.0	5.3	8.1	1.3	8.0	-1.2
1940	8.0	0.0	7.9	-1.2	7.9	0.0	7.8	-1.3	7.8	0.0	7.7	-1.3	7.7	0.0	7.9	2.6	8.7	10.1	9.3	6.9	9.5	2.2	9.6	1.1
1941	9.6	0.0	9.5	-1.0	9.4	-1.1	9.4	0.0	9.4	0.0	9.5	1.1	9.9	4.2	10.3	4.0	10.5	1.9	10.5	0.0	10.4	-1.0	10.5	1.0
1942	10.6	1.0	10.7	0.9	10.7	0.0	10.7	0.0	10.6	-0.9	10.6	0.0	10.7	0.9	10.7	0.0	10.7	0.0	10.5	-1.9	10.9	3.8	10.9	0.0
1943	10.9	0.0	11.0	0.9	11.0	0.0	11.0	0.0	11.2	1.8	11.2	0.0	11.3	0.9	11.7	3.5	11.8	0.9	11.9	0.8	12.0	0.8	12.0	0.0
1944	12.0	0.0	12.1	0.8	12.2	0.8	12.5	2.5	12.5	0.0	12.5	0.0	12.5	0.0	12.5	0.0	12.5	0.0	12.5	0.0	12.5	0.0	12.5	0.0
1945	12.5	0.0	12.5	0.0	12.5	0.0	12.5	0.0	12.5	0.0	12.5	0.0	12.5	0.0	12.5	0.0	12.5	0.0	12.5	0.0	12.5	0.0	12.8	2.4
1946	12.8	0.0	12.9	0.8	13.6	5.4	13.9	2.2	14.0	0.7	14.2	1.4	14.4	1.4	14.4	0.0	14.4	0.0	14.4	0.0	15.5	7.6	18.4	18.7
1947	20.6	12.0	21.1	2.4	22.0	4.3	22.7	3.2	22.7	0.0	22.6	-0.4	22.8	0.9	23.2	1.8	23.9	3.0	24.2	1.3	24.9	2.9	25.4	2.0
1948	25.6	0.8	25.8	0.8	26.0	0.8	26.0	0.0	26.4	1.5	26.4	0.0	26.5	0.4	26.7	0.8	26.5	-0.7	26.2	-1.1	25.8	-1.5	25.5	-1.2
1949	25.2	-1.2	24.9	-1.2	24.7	-0.8	24.4	-1.2	24.0	-1.6	23.6	-1.7	23.3	-1.3	22.9	-1.7	23.0	0.4	23.3	1.3	23.6	1.3	23.9	1.3
1950	24.3	1.7	24.9	2.5	25.5	2.4	25.9	1.6	27.0	4.2	27.6	2.2	28.4	2.9	29.6	4.2	30.7	3.7	30.2	-1.6	30.1	-0.3	30.2	0.3
1951	30.6	1.3	30.8	0.7	30.9	0.3	30.9	0.0	30.8	-0.3	30.3	-1.6	30.0	-1.0	29.7	-1.0	29.5	-0.7	29.5	0.0	29.5	0.0	29.4	-0.3
1952	29.3	-0.3	29.4	0.3	29.4	0.0	29.6	0.7	29.5	-0.3	29.3	-0.7	29.4	0.3	29.4	0.0	29.4	0.0	29.3	-0.3	29.3	0.0	29.2	-0.3
1953	29.3	0.3	29.3	0.0	29.5	0.7	29.7	0.7	29.5	-0.7	29.4	-0.3	29.3	-0.3	29.1	-0.7	28.9	-0.7	28.6	-1.0	28.4	-0.7	28.4	0.0
1954	28.3	-0.4	28.2	-0.4	28.2	0.0	28.1	-0.4	28.1	0.0	28.2	0.4	28.9	2.5	28.9	0.0	29.0	0.3	29.2	0.7	29.2	0.0	29.2	0.0
1955	29.3	0.3	29.6	1.0	29.7	0.3	30.0	1.0	30.3	1.0	30.4	0.3	30.5	0.3	30.9	1.3	31.0	0.3	31.0	0.0	30.9	-0.3	30.8	-0.3
1956	31.2	1.3	31.3	0.3	31.7	1.3	31.9	0.6	31.9	0.0	31.6	-0.9	31.4	-0.6	31.0	-1.3	30.6	-1.3	30.2	-1.3	30.1	-0.3	29.9	-0.7
1957	30.0	0.3	29.8	-0.7	29.6	-0.7	29.6	0.0	29.4	-0.7	29.4	0.0	29.3	-0.3	29.2	-0.3	28.9	-1.0	28.7	-0.7	28.6	-0.3	28.4	-0.7
1958	28.5	0.4	28.3	-0.7	28.3	0.0	28.3	0.0	28.5	0.7	28.5	0.0	28.5	0.0	29.1	2.1	29.5	1.4	29.5	0.0	29.3	-0.7	29.3	0.0
1959	29.5	0.7	30.1	2.0	30.6	1.7	30.9	1.0	31.5	1.9	31.8	1.0	31.7	-0.3	31.8	0.3	31.6	-0.6	31.2	-1.3	30.7	-1.6	30.8	0.3
1960	30.8	0.0	30.8	0.0	30.7	-0.3	30.7	0.0	30.5	-0.7	30.1	-1.3	29.7	-1.3	29.1	-2.0	28.8	-1.0	28.4	-1.4	28.1	-1.1	28.1	0.0
1961	27.9	-0.7	27.7	-0.7	27.9	0.7	28.4	1.8	28.5	0.4	28.5	0.0	28.5	0.0	28.2	-1.1	28.1	-0.4	27.9	-0.7	27.8	-0.4	27.8	0.0
1962	27.9	0.4	28.2	1.1	28.4	0.7	28.7	1.1	28.9	0.7	29.0	0.3	29.1	0.3	29.0	-0.3	28.9	-0.3	28.7	-0.7	28.6	-0.3	28.4	-0.7
1963	28.5	0.4	28.5	0.0	28.7	0.7	29.0	1.0	29.2	0.7	29.4	0.7	30.3	3.1	30.5	0.7	29.9	-2.0	29.5	-1.3	29.5	0.0	29.4	-0.3
1964	29.4	0.0	29.8	1.4	30.1	1.0	30.3	0.7	30.3	0.0	30.2	-0.3	30.1	-0.3	30.0	-0.3	29.9	-0.3	29.8	-0.3	29.4	-1.3	29.4	0.0
1965	29.9	1.7	30.1	0.7	30.1	0.0	30.0	-0.3	30.0	0.0	30.0	0.0	30.1	0.3	30.4	1.0	30.6	0.7	30.6	0.0	30.6	0.0	30.7	0.3
1966	31.0	1.0	31.3	1.0	31.8	1.6	32.9	3.5	33.6	2.1	33.2	-1.2	32.8	-1.2	32.7	-0.3	32.5	-0.6	32.0	-1.5	31.3	-2.2	31.0	-1.0
1967	31.0	0.0	31.3	1.0	31.5	0.6	31.6	0.3	31.8	0.6	32.0	0.6	32.1	0.3	32.6	1.6	33.3	2.1	33.0	-0.9	32.8	-0.6	33.2	1.2
1968	33.9	2.1	34.8	2.7	35.7	2.6	36.7	2.8	37.2	1.4	37.1	-0.3	37.9	2.2	38.5	1.6	39.0	1.3	39.6	1.5	40.4	2.0	42.2	4.5
1969	43.9	4.0	46.3	5.5	48.9	5.6	49.0	0.2	46.3	-5.5	42.3	-8.6	39.6	-6.4	38.9	-1.8	38.5	-1.0	38.0	-1.3	38.4	1.1	38.1	-0.8
1970	37.7	-1.0	36.9	-2.1	36.5	-1.1	36.7	0.5	36.9	0.5	36.5	-1.1	36.2	-0.8	36.5	0.8	36.8	0.8	36.6	-0.5	36.1	-1.4	35.7	-1.1

[Continued]

Lumber
Producer Price Index
Base 1982 = 100
[Continued]

For 1926-2001. Columns headed % show percentile change in the index from the previous period for which an index is available.

Year	Jan Index	%	Feb Index	%	Mar Index	%	Apr Index	%	May Index	%	Jun Index	%	Jul Index	%	Aug Index	%	Sep Index	%	Oct Index	%	Nov Index	%	Dec Index	%
1971	36.4	2.0	38.7	6.3	41.5	7.2	42.5	2.4	42.9	0.9	43.5	1.4	46.1	6.0	47.6	3.3	47.5	-0.2	46.1	-2.9	45.8	-0.7	46.4	1.3
1972	47.3	1.9	48.4	2.3	49.0	1.2	49.9	1.8	50.5	1.2	51.2	1.4	52.0	1.6	52.8	1.5	53.1	0.6	53.5	0.8	53.7	0.4	54.0	0.6
1973	54.4	0.7	58.7	7.9	63.0	7.3	66.7	5.9	69.3	3.9	69.1	-0.3	67.4	-2.5	67.8	0.6	69.8	2.9	69.0	-1.1	67.9	-1.6	69.1	1.8
1974	68.6	-0.7	68.4	-0.3	71.2	4.1	74.3	4.4	73.1	-1.6	70.9	-3.0	68.9	-2.8	66.5	-3.5	64.2	-3.5	59.1	-7.9	57.3	-3.0	57.0	-0.5
1975	56.8	-0.4	58.3	2.6	58.7	0.7	60.9	3.7	64.6	6.1	64.2	-0.6	63.3	-1.4	63.7	0.6	63.3	-0.6	63.1	-0.3	62.1	-1.6	64.4	3.7
1976	67.6	5.0	70.7	4.6	74.1	4.8	74.2	0.1	73.1	-1.5	72.2	-1.2	74.4	3.0	76.0	2.2	78.6	3.4	79.0	0.5	78.6	-0.5	81.1	3.2
1977	83.0	2.3	83.5	0.6	85.7	2.6	86.5	0.9	86.3	-0.2	85.2	-1.3	88.8	4.2	92.1	3.7	97.1	5.4	94.1	-3.1	91.6	-2.7	93.6	2.2
1978	96.7	3.3	99.3	2.7	100.5	1.2	101.9	1.4	101.8	-0.1	103.2	1.4	102.7	-0.5	105.1	2.3	106.9	1.7	107.6	0.7	110.0	2.2	109.1	-0.8
1979	108.3	-0.7	109.4	1.0	112.8	3.1	114.3	1.3	114.2	-0.1	114.2	0.0	114.2	0.0	117.5	2.9	120.3	2.4	119.2	-0.9	114.4	-4.0	109.2	-4.5
1980	108.2	-0.9	109.9	1.6	109.6	-0.3	99.8	-8.9	97.0	-2.8	100.7	3.8	105.3	4.6	107.4	2.0	105.6	-1.7	103.2	-2.3	104.6	1.4	107.1	2.4
1981	106.6	-0.5	105.2	-1.3	104.9	-0.3	107.4	2.4	108.2	0.7	108.0	-0.2	107.0	-0.9	106.2	-0.7	103.0	-3.0	100.3	-2.6	98.7	-1.6	99.7	1.0
1982	99.7	0.0	99.1	-0.6	99.2	0.1	100.5	1.3	99.9	-0.6	101.6	1.7	102.7	1.1	100.3	-2.3	99.8	-0.5	98.3	-1.5	98.2	-0.1	100.6	2.4
1983	105.2	4.6	110.9	5.4	112.4	1.4	114.0	1.4	115.4	1.2	120.0	4.0	120.1	0.1	118.0	-1.7	111.5	-5.5	110.9	-0.5	110.3	-0.5	113.0	2.4
1984	113.5	0.4	117.4	3.4	119.2	1.5	118.9	-0.3	114.4	-3.8	112.8	-1.4	110.2	-2.3	110.1	-0.1	108.8	-1.2	107.6	-1.1	108.3	0.7	109.2	0.8
1985	110.4	1.1	110.4	0.0	110.7	0.3	109.4	-1.2	112.4	2.7	116.8	3.9	114.1	-2.3	110.0	-3.6	107.0	-2.7	105.3	-1.6	103.8	-1.4	104.8	1.0
1986	106.0	1.1	105.7	-0.3	108.3	2.5	113.3	4.6	113.0	-0.3	110.4	-2.3	111.1	0.6	111.3	0.2	112.9	1.4	111.1	-1.6	112.0	0.8	111.3	-0.6
1987	111.9	0.5	114.4	2.2	116.0	1.4	116.8	0.7	116.9	0.1	117.9	0.9	119.7	1.5	120.2	0.4	123.3	2.6	120.5	-2.3	120.4	-0.1	120.3	-0.1
1988	120.8	0.4	121.5	0.6	123.0	1.2	123.9	0.7	123.8	-0.1	124.4	0.5	125.1	0.6	123.2	-1.5	120.9	-1.9	120.0	-0.7	119.9	-0.1	118.8	-0.9
1989	119.8	0.8	122.3	2.1	123.4	0.9	126.5	2.5	128.5	1.6	128.7	0.2	130.0	1.0	128.8	-0.9	127.0	-1.4	127.3	0.2	123.2	-3.2	123.1	-0.1
1990	124.5	1.1	125.8	1.0	127.4	1.3	129.3	1.5	128.0	-1.0	125.9	-1.6	126.5	0.5	124.8	-1.3	123.5	-1.0	120.5	-2.4	119.4	-0.9	119.3	-0.1
1991	120.0	0.6	118.8	-1.0	119.6	0.7	121.6	1.7	125.2	3.0	132.7	6.0	133.2	0.4	125.1	-6.1	125.0	-0.1	124.5	-0.4	125.4	0.7	128.2	2.2
1992	132.3	3.2	140.9	6.5	146.4	3.9	148.6	1.5	148.7	0.1	144.1	-3.1	142.8	-0.9	142.0	-0.6	144.8	2.0	143.8	-0.7	146.9	2.2	155.5	5.9
1993	164.6	5.9	181.1	10.0	196.4	8.4	197.3	0.5	189.0	-4.2	178.7	-5.4	172.9	-3.2	175.9	1.7	179.0	1.8	181.5	1.4	188.6	3.9	195.9	3.9
1994	202.0	3.1	196.6	-2.7	197.4	0.4	188.2	-4.7	185.7	-1.3	189.7	2.2	184.4	-2.8	185.5	0.6	184.7	-0.4	181.4	-1.8	183.4	1.1	181.7	-0.9
1995	182.1	0.2	177.8	-2.4	179.3	0.8	175.7	-2.0	173.4	-1.3	169.9	-2.0	173.0	1.8	172.2	-0.5	174.1	1.1	171.0	-1.8	167.0	-2.3	165.7	-0.8
1996	165.7	0.0	166.8	0.7	169.6	1.7	172.2	1.5	181.3	5.3	184.7	1.9	181.0	-2.0	184.4	1.9	189.6	2.8	182.8	-3.6	190.3	4.1	189.3	-0.5
1997	190.2	0.5	195.3	2.7	196.4	0.6	199.9	1.8	203.3	1.7	197.9	-2.7	199.0	0.6	196.8	-1.1	192.2	-2.3	186.5	-3.0	189.0	1.3	189.1	0.1
1998	185.3	-2.0	186.9	0.9	187.4	0.3	187.2	-0.1	182.7	-2.4	175.9	-3.7	178.9	1.7	180.0	0.6	174.2	-3.2	171.7	-1.4	170.4	-0.8	173.5	1.8
1999	177.4	2.2	181.6	2.4	186.0	2.4	185.5	-0.3	188.9	1.8	194.9	3.2	202.8	4.1	195.6	-3.6	189.2	-3.3	183.6	-3.0	185.6	1.1	187.6	1.1
2000	189.1	0.8	189.2	0.1	188.5	-0.4	186.3	-1.2	180.3	-3.2	179.6	-0.4	176.1	-1.9	173.2	-1.6	171.4	-1.0	171.6	0.1	170.4	-0.7	169.6	-0.5
2001	166.6	-1.8	168.2	1.0	169.5	0.8	170.0	0.3	181.1	6.5	183.2	1.2	175.4	-4.3	174.5	-0.5	172.2	-1.3	166.8	-3.1	166.3	-0.3	163.3	-1.8

Source: U.S. Department of Labor, Bureau of Labor Statistics, Division of Industry Prices and Price Indexes. n.e.c. stands for not elsewhere classified. - indicates no data collected for period or unavailable.

Millwork

Producer Price Index
Base 1982 = 100

For 1926-2001. Columns headed % show percentile change in the index from the previous period for which an index is available.

Year	Jan Index	%	Feb Index	%	Mar Index	%	Apr Index	%	May Index	%	Jun Index	%	Jul Index	%	Aug Index	%	Sep Index	%	Oct Index	%	Nov Index	%	Dec Index	%
1926	10.7	-	10.7	0.0	10.7	0.0	10.7	0.0	10.7	0.0	10.7	0.0	10.7	0.0	10.7	0.0	10.7	0.0	10.7	0.0	10.7	0.0	10.7	0.0
1927	10.7	0.0	10.7	0.0	10.7	0.0	10.7	0.0	10.7	0.0	10.7	0.0	10.7	0.0	10.7	0.0	10.7	0.0	10.7	0.0	10.7	0.0	10.7	0.0
1928	10.7	0.0	10.7	0.0	10.7	0.0	10.7	0.0	10.7	0.0	10.7	0.0	10.7	0.0	10.7	0.0	10.7	0.0	10.7	0.0	10.7	0.0	10.7	0.0
1929	10.8	0.9	10.8	0.0	10.8	0.0	10.8	0.0	10.8	0.0	10.8	0.0	10.7	-0.9	10.7	0.0	10.7	0.0	10.7	0.0	10.7	0.0	10.7	0.0
1930	10.7	0.0	10.7	0.0	10.7	0.0	10.7	0.0	10.6	-0.9	10.6	0.0	9.9	-6.6	9.9	0.0	9.9	0.0	9.4	-5.1	9.4	0.0	9.1	-3.2
1931	8.9	-2.2	8.7	-2.2	8.7	0.0	8.7	0.0	8.7	0.0	8.7	0.0	8.7	0.0	8.7	0.0	8.4	-3.4	8.1	-3.6	8.1	0.0	8.1	0.0
1932	8.7	7.4	8.7	0.0	8.7	0.0	8.7	0.0	8.7	0.0	8.7	0.0	8.3	-4.6	8.3	0.0	8.3	0.0	7.8	-6.0	7.8	0.0	7.8	0.0
1933	7.8	0.0	7.8	0.0	8.3	6.4	8.3	0.0	8.3	0.0	8.4	1.2	8.9	6.0	9.7	9.0	9.7	0.0	9.7	0.0	9.7	0.0	9.5	-2.1
1934	9.5	0.0	9.5	0.0	9.5	0.0	9.6	1.1	9.7	1.0	9.7	0.0	9.2	-5.2	8.7	-5.4	8.7	0.0	8.7	0.0	8.7	0.0	8.7	0.0
1935	8.7	0.0	8.7	0.0	8.7	0.0	8.7	0.0	8.7	0.0	8.7	0.0	8.9	2.3	9.6	7.9	9.6	0.0	9.6	0.0	9.6	0.0	9.6	0.0
1936	9.6	0.0	9.6	0.0	9.6	0.0	9.6	0.0	9.6	0.0	9.8	2.1	9.8	0.0	9.8	0.0	9.8	0.0	9.8	0.0	9.8	0.0	10.1	3.1
1937	10.2	1.0	10.7	4.9	10.7	0.0	10.7	0.0	12.7	18.7	12.7	0.0	12.3	-3.1	12.1	-1.6	12.1	0.0	12.1	0.0	12.0	-0.8	11.9	-0.8
1938	11.1	-6.7	11.1	0.0	11.1	0.0	11.1	0.0	10.2	-8.1	10.2	0.0	10.1	-1.0	10.1	0.0	10.1	0.0	10.2	1.0	10.2	0.0	10.2	0.0
1939	10.2	0.0	10.2	0.0	10.2	0.0	10.2	0.0	10.2	0.0	10.2	0.0	10.2	0.0	10.2	0.0	10.2	0.0	10.2	0.0	10.7	4.9	10.7	0.0
1940	10.7	0.0	10.7	0.0	10.7	0.0	10.7	0.0	10.7	0.0	11.3	5.6	11.5	1.8	11.5	0.0	11.5	0.0	11.5	0.0	12.1	5.2	12.1	0.0
1941	12.1	0.0	12.1	0.0	12.2	0.8	12.3	0.8	12.5	1.6	12.5	0.0	12.6	0.8	12.8	1.6	12.8	0.0	13.9	8.6	14.0	0.7	14.0	0.0
1942	14.0	0.0	14.0	0.0	14.0	0.0	14.0	0.0	14.0	0.0	14.0	0.0	14.0	0.0	14.0	0.0	14.0	0.0	14.0	0.0	14.0	0.0	14.0	0.0
1943	14.0	0.0	14.0	0.0	14.0	0.0	14.0	0.0	14.0	0.0	14.0	0.0	14.0	0.0	14.0	0.0	14.0	0.0	14.4	2.9	14.4	0.0	14.4	0.0
1944	14.4	0.0	14.4	0.0	14.4	0.0	14.4	0.0	14.7	2.1	14.7	0.0	14.7	0.0	14.7	0.0	14.7	0.0	14.7	0.0	14.7	0.0	14.7	0.0
1945	14.7	0.0	14.7	0.0	14.7	0.0	14.7	0.0	14.7	0.0	14.7	0.0	14.7	0.0	14.7	0.0	14.7	0.0	14.7	0.0	14.7	0.0	14.7	0.0
1946	14.7	0.0	14.7	0.0	14.7	0.0	14.7	0.0	17.0	15.6	17.0	0.0	17.0	0.0	17.0	0.0	17.5	2.9	18.3	4.6	18.4	0.5	18.4	0.0
1947	19.5	6.0	19.9	2.1	20.1	1.0	20.3	1.0	20.6	1.5	21.0	1.9	21.4	1.9	21.6	0.9	22.2	2.8	22.8	2.7	23.0	0.9	23.0	0.0
1948	23.7	3.0	23.9	0.8	24.7	3.3	24.8	0.4	24.8	0.0	25.5	2.8	26.4	3.5	26.7	1.1	26.8	0.4	26.8	0.0	26.8	0.0	26.8	0.0
1949	26.6	-0.7	26.6	0.0	26.5	-0.4	26.4	-0.4	26.4	0.0	26.3	-0.4	26.2	-0.4	26.1	-0.4	26.0	-0.4	26.0	0.0	26.0	0.0	26.1	0.4
1950	26.4	1.1	26.6	0.8	26.6	0.0	26.8	0.8	26.9	0.4	27.1	0.7	27.6	1.8	28.4	2.9	29.5	3.9	29.8	1.0	29.9	0.3	29.9	0.0
1951	31.5	5.4	32.0	1.6	31.9	-0.3	32.0	0.3	32.0	0.0	31.9	-0.3	31.8	-0.3	31.6	-0.6	31.6	0.0	31.6	0.0	31.5	-0.3	31.4	-0.3
1952	31.0	-1.3	30.8	-0.6	30.9	0.3	30.8	-0.3	30.8	0.0	30.8	0.0	30.9	0.3	31.0	0.3	31.0	0.0	31.1	0.3	31.1	0.0	31.3	0.6
1953	31.5	0.6	32.1	1.9	32.1	0.0	32.2	0.3	32.2	0.0	32.2	0.0	32.1	-0.3	32.1	0.0	32.1	0.0	32.0	-0.3	32.0	0.0	32.0	0.0
1954	32.0	0.0	32.0	0.0	32.0	0.0	31.9	-0.3	31.9	0.0	31.9	0.0	31.9	0.0	31.6	-0.9	31.7	0.3	31.7	0.0	31.7	0.0	31.8	0.3
1955	31.8	0.0	31.5	-0.9	31.4	-0.3	31.5	0.3	31.5	0.0	31.3	-0.6	31.3	0.0	31.3	0.0	31.2	-0.3	31.2	0.0	31.2	0.0	31.4	0.6
1956	31.5	0.3	31.5	0.0	31.5	0.0	31.5	0.0	31.5	0.0	31.6	0.3	31.6	0.0	31.6	0.0	31.5	-0.3	31.4	-0.3	31.3	-0.3	31.3	0.0
1957	31.4	0.3	31.4	0.0	31.4	0.0	31.3	-0.3	31.3	0.0	31.3	0.0	31.3	0.0	31.3	0.0	31.3	0.0	31.3	0.0	31.2	-0.3	31.1	-0.3
1958	31.1	0.0	31.1	0.0	31.1	0.0	31.1	0.0	31.0	-0.3	31.0	0.0	31.0	0.0	30.9	-0.3	31.1	0.6	31.8	2.3	31.8	0.0	31.8	0.0
1959	31.7	-0.3	31.7	0.0	31.7	0.0	33.0	4.1	33.5	1.5	33.5	0.0	33.6	0.3	33.8	0.6	33.8	0.0	33.8	0.0	33.7	-0.3	33.6	-0.3
1960	33.6	0.0	33.6	0.0	33.6	0.0	33.4	-0.6	33.4	0.0	33.4	0.0	33.5	0.3	33.3	-0.6	33.0	-0.9	33.0	0.0	33.1	0.3	33.0	-0.3
1961	33.1	0.3	32.9	-0.6	32.9	0.0	32.9	0.0	32.5	-1.2	32.7	0.6	32.2	-1.5	31.9	-0.9	32.3	1.3	32.3	0.0	32.2	-0.3	32.2	0.0
1962	32.2	0.0	32.1	-0.3	32.2	0.3	32.3	0.3	32.5	0.6	32.5	0.0	32.6	0.3	32.7	0.3	32.6	-0.3	32.6	0.0	32.6	0.0	32.6	0.0
1963	32.6	0.0	32.6	0.0	32.7	0.3	32.7	0.0	32.7	0.0	32.9	0.6	33.2	0.9	33.5	0.9	33.7	0.6	33.9	0.6	33.9	0.0	33.9	0.0
1964	34.0	0.3	34.1	0.3	34.2	0.3	34.7	1.5	34.8	0.3	34.8	0.0	34.8	0.0	34.8	0.0	34.8	0.0	34.8	0.0	34.8	0.0	34.8	0.0
1965	34.4	-1.1	34.3	-0.3	34.3	0.0	34.3	0.0	34.4	0.3	34.4	0.0	34.4	0.0	34.4	0.0	34.4	0.0	34.4	0.0	34.4	0.0	34.4	0.0
1966	34.4	0.0	34.6	0.6	34.9	0.9	35.0	0.3	35.2	0.6	35.3	0.3	35.3	0.0	35.4	0.3	35.4	0.0	35.4	0.0	35.2	-0.6	35.2	0.0
1967	35.2	0.0	35.5	0.9	35.5	0.0	35.6	0.3	35.6	0.0	35.6	0.0	35.8	0.6	35.9	0.3	36.1	0.6	36.2	0.3	36.2	0.0	36.3	0.3
1968	36.4	0.3	36.6	0.5	36.9	0.8	37.2	0.8	37.6	1.1	37.8	0.5	37.8	0.0	38.0	0.5	38.5	1.3	38.8	0.8	39.2	1.0	39.5	0.8
1969	39.9	1.0	40.5	1.5	41.1	1.5	42.2	2.7	42.6	0.9	43.4	1.9	43.3	-0.2	43.1	-0.5	42.9	-0.5	42.7	-0.5	42.5	-0.5	42.0	-1.2
1970	41.9	-0.2	41.7	-0.5	41.7	0.0	41.7	0.0	41.8	0.2	41.8	0.0	41.8	0.0	41.8	0.0	41.4	-1.0	40.9	-1.2	40.9	0.0	40.8	-0.2

[Continued]

Millwork
Producer Price Index
Base 1982 = 100
[Continued]

For 1926-2001. Columns headed % show percentile change in the index from the previous period for which an index is available.

Year	Jan Index	%	Feb Index	%	Mar Index	%	Apr Index	%	May Index	%	Jun Index	%	Jul Index	%	Aug Index	%	Sep Index	%	Oct Index	%	Nov Index	%	Dec Index	%
1971	40.9	0.2	41.3	1.0	41.6	0.7	42.5	2.2	43.1	1.4	43.7	1.4	44.0	0.7	44.4	0.9	44.3	-0.2	44.3	0.0	44.3	0.0	44.5	0.5
1972	44.7	0.4	44.9	0.4	45.0	0.2	45.3	0.7	45.7	0.9	46.0	0.7	46.4	0.9	46.5	0.2	46.6	0.2	46.8	0.4	46.8	0.0	46.8	0.0
1973	47.0	0.4	47.7	1.5	48.3	1.3	50.5	4.6	52.4	3.8	52.9	1.0	53.1	0.4	53.1	0.0	53.3	0.4	53.5	0.4	53.5	0.0	53.8	0.6
1974	54.2	0.7	54.3	0.2	54.9	1.1	56.1	2.2	57.5	2.5	58.4	1.6	57.9	-0.9	57.7	-0.3	57.5	-0.3	56.2	-2.3	55.0	-2.1	54.9	-0.2
1975	55.1	0.4	55.5	0.7	55.5	0.0	56.0	0.9	57.4	2.5	57.9	0.9	58.3	0.7	58.4	0.2	58.5	0.2	58.7	0.3	58.7	0.0	59.0	0.5
1976	59.8	1.4	60.5	1.2	61.7	2.0	62.7	1.6	63.6	1.4	63.7	0.2	63.5	-0.3	63.8	0.5	64.5	1.1	65.0	0.8	65.5	0.8	65.5	0.0
1977	65.7	0.3	66.6	1.4	67.4	1.2	68.2	1.2	68.5	0.4	68.9	0.6	68.8	-0.1	69.7	1.3	70.8	1.6	71.8	1.4	72.5	1.0	73.1	0.8
1978	74.9	2.5	78.5	4.8	80.8	2.9	83.7	3.6	86.1	2.9	87.7	1.9	88.3	0.7	86.5	-2.0	86.0	-0.6	85.8	-0.2	86.4	0.7	86.5	0.1
1979	87.5	1.2	90.0	2.9	92.3	2.6	95.2	3.1	93.6	-1.7	92.7	-1.0	90.4	-2.5	89.3	-1.2	89.8	0.6	91.5	1.9	90.3	-1.3	89.6	-0.8
1980	90.9	1.5	92.3	1.5	93.8	1.6	92.2	-1.7	90.1	-2.3	90.5	0.4	91.6	1.2	93.2	1.7	94.6	1.5	94.7	0.1	96.6	2.0	97.8	1.2
1981	97.9	0.1	98.0	0.1	98.7	0.7	99.0	0.3	98.4	-0.6	97.4	-1.0	97.9	0.5	97.5	-0.4	97.1	-0.4	97.1	0.0	97.3	0.2	97.9	0.6
1982	99.2	1.3	99.7	0.5	98.9	-0.8	99.0	0.1	98.9	-0.1	100.4	1.5	101.0	0.6	100.3	-0.7	100.0	-0.3	99.7	-0.3	100.3	0.6	102.5	2.2
1983	105.1	2.5	107.5	2.3	108.8	1.2	108.4	-0.4	107.0	-1.3	105.5	-1.4	106.0	0.5	109.7	3.5	109.5	-0.2	110.0	0.5	110.2	0.2	110.4	0.2
1984	110.4	0.0	110.5	0.1	110.9	0.4	109.9	-0.9	108.9	-0.9	109.2	0.3	109.8	0.5	109.9	0.1	110.0	0.1	109.9	-0.1	110.8	0.8	111.5	0.6
1985	111.9	0.4	111.5	-0.4	111.0	-0.4	110.8	-0.2	111.1	0.3	111.6	0.5	112.2	0.5	112.3	0.1	112.3	0.0	112.0	-0.3	111.9	-0.1	111.8	-0.1
1986	111.6	-0.2	111.7	0.1	112.1	0.4	112.8	0.6	113.3	0.4	114.4	1.0	114.8	0.3	115.1	0.3	115.1	0.0	114.5	-0.5	114.2	-0.3	114.2	0.0
1987	114.7	0.4	115.0	0.3	116.1	1.0	116.9	0.7	117.4	0.4	118.1	0.6	118.5	0.3	118.8	0.3	118.9	0.1	119.3	0.3	119.4	0.1	119.5	0.1
1988	119.7	0.2	120.3	0.5	120.8	0.4	121.2	0.3	121.6	0.3	121.9	0.2	122.4	0.4	122.5	0.1	122.7	0.2	123.3	0.5	122.9	-0.3	123.0	0.1
1989	123.5	0.4	125.1	1.3	126.3	1.0	127.4	0.9	128.0	0.5	128.3	0.2	127.9	-0.3	128.0	0.1	127.9	-0.1	128.2	0.2	128.3	0.1	128.7	0.3
1990	128.9	0.2	129.5	0.5	130.0	0.4	130.6	0.5	130.9	0.2	130.4	-0.4	130.5	0.1	130.5	0.0	130.6	0.1	130.5	-0.1	130.8	0.2	131.0	0.2
1991	131.5	0.4	131.6	0.1	131.9	0.2	133.6	1.3	134.3	0.5	135.8	1.1	136.9	0.8	137.6	0.5	137.6	0.0	138.0	0.3	138.1	0.1	139.3	0.9
1992	140.3	0.7	142.2	1.4	142.9	0.5	144.0	0.8	144.0	0.0	144.0	0.0	143.3	-0.5	142.3	-0.7	143.3	0.7	143.6	0.2	143.7	0.1	145.7	1.4
1993	148.0	1.6	151.8	2.6	155.9	2.7	158.8	1.9	158.2	-0.4	156.6	-1.0	155.7	-0.6	156.1	0.3	158.7	1.7	159.1	0.3	159.9	0.5	160.7	0.5
1994	162.8	1.3	163.4	0.4	163.2	-0.1	162.4	-0.5	161.5	-0.6	161.7	0.1	161.5	-0.1	161.3	-0.1	161.6	0.2	162.6	0.6	163.3	0.4	163.3	0.0
1995	163.9	0.4	163.4	-0.3	163.8	0.2	163.8	0.0	163.7	-0.1	163.7	0.0	163.9	0.1	164.0	0.1	164.2	0.1	164.0	-0.1	163.4	-0.4	163.6	0.1
1996	163.6	0.0	163.8	0.1	164.1	0.2	164.6	0.3	165.8	0.7	166.7	0.5	167.0	0.2	167.9	0.5	168.7	0.5	168.7	0.0	169.3	0.4	169.3	0.0
1997	170.1	0.5	170.3	0.1	170.4	0.1	170.8	0.2	171.2	0.2	171.4	0.1	171.5	0.1	171.4	-0.1	171.3	-0.1	171.0	-0.2	170.6	-0.2	170.8	0.1
1998	170.9	0.1	170.8	-0.1	170.9	0.1	171.0	0.1	171.2	0.1	171.1	-0.1	170.9	-0.1	170.8	-0.1	171.5	0.4	171.7	0.1	171.5	-0.1	171.4	-0.1
1999	171.5	0.1	171.6	0.1	172.3	0.4	173.3	0.6	174.1	0.5	175.6	0.9	176.7	0.6	177.3	0.3	177.0	-0.2	175.9	-0.6	175.5	-0.2	175.5	0.0
2000	175.8	0.2	175.6	-0.1	176.7	0.6	176.9	0.1	176.7	-0.1	176.7	0.0	176.9	0.1	176.4	-0.3	176.2	-0.1	176.2	0.0	176.4	0.1	176.4	0.0
2001	176.8	0.2	177.1	0.2	177.7	0.3	178.1	0.2	179.3	0.7	180.6	0.7	180.6	0.0	180.6	0.0	179.9	-0.4	180.1	0.1	179.4	-0.4	179.2	-0.1

Source: U.S. Department of Labor, Bureau of Labor Statistics, Division of Industry Prices and Price Indexes. n.e.c. stands for not elsewhere classified. - indicates no data collected for period or unavailable.

Plywood
Producer Price Index
Base 1982 = 100

For 1947-2001. Columns headed % show percentile change in the index from the previous period for which an index is available.

Year	Jan Index	%	Feb Index	%	Mar Index	%	Apr Index	%	May Index	%	Jun Index	%	Jul Index	%	Aug Index	%	Sep Index	%	Oct Index	%	Nov Index	%	Dec Index	%
1947	47.9	-	48.2	0.6	48.2	0.0	48.6	0.8	48.7	0.2	48.7	0.0	45.7	-6.2	45.7	0.0	45.7	0.0	45.7	0.0	45.8	0.2	46.9	2.4
1948	51.8	10.4	51.8	0.0	52.1	0.6	52.2	0.2	53.0	1.5	53.9	1.7	54.6	1.3	54.8	0.4	54.8	0.0	54.8	0.0	54.8	0.0	54.3	-0.9
1949	49.6	-8.7	49.0	-1.2	49.0	0.0	48.7	-0.6	47.0	-3.5	45.1	-4.0	44.5	-1.3	45.2	1.6	45.0	-0.4	45.5	1.1	46.1	1.3	47.0	2.0
1950	48.3	2.8	49.2	1.9	49.5	0.6	49.5	0.0	49.6	0.2	50.0	0.8	51.1	2.2	54.3	6.3	56.0	3.1	56.7	1.3	56.7	0.0	57.4	1.2
1951	57.7	0.5	57.9	0.3	57.9	0.0	57.9	0.0	57.9	0.0	57.9	0.0	57.5	-0.7	57.5	0.0	56.5	-1.7	56.2	-0.5	53.8	-4.3	50.5	-6.1
1952	51.2	1.4	51.5	0.6	51.9	0.8	51.9	0.0	51.9	0.0	52.0	0.2	52.0	0.0	52.1	0.2	52.1	0.0	52.2	0.2	50.3	-3.6	50.3	0.0
1953	53.4	6.2	54.5	2.1	55.1	1.1	55.1	0.0	55.3	0.4	55.3	0.0	55.4	0.2	55.3	-0.2	52.5	-5.1	51.5	-1.9	50.7	-1.6	51.1	0.8
1954	50.9	-0.4	51.6	1.4	50.6	-1.9	49.5	-2.2	49.8	0.6	49.0	-1.6	50.7	3.5	51.8	2.2	50.7	-2.1	51.3	1.2	51.3	0.0	51.3	0.0
1955	51.5	0.4	51.5	0.0	51.5	0.0	51.5	0.0	51.9	0.8	51.9	0.0	52.0	0.2	52.0	0.0	52.2	0.4	52.2	0.0	52.1	-0.2	52.0	-0.2
1956	52.8	1.5	52.8	0.0	52.8	0.0	52.6	-0.4	50.5	-4.0	49.6	-1.8	50.8	2.4	48.8	-3.9	48.8	0.0	47.2	-3.3	46.6	-1.3	46.5	-0.2
1957	47.7	2.6	47.4	-0.6	47.3	-0.2	47.5	0.4	47.6	0.2	48.0	0.8	47.6	-0.8	46.8	-1.7	46.6	-0.4	47.6	2.1	47.4	-0.4	47.0	-0.8
1958	47.0	0.0	46.0	-2.1	45.7	-0.7	46.4	1.5	45.4	-2.2	46.7	2.9	48.3	3.4	49.2	1.9	50.1	1.8	50.5	0.8	49.2	-2.6	48.7	-1.0
1959	49.0	0.6	51.0	4.1	51.1	0.2	52.4	2.5	52.4	0.0	51.7	-1.3	50.3	-2.7	49.6	-1.4	47.5	-4.2	47.4	-0.2	46.4	-2.1	47.8	3.0
1960	48.3	1.0	47.7	-1.2	47.1	-1.3	47.2	0.2	47.0	-0.4	47.0	0.0	47.0	0.0	46.6	-0.9	47.4	1.7	47.7	0.6	47.2	-1.0	46.7	-1.1
1961	45.1	-3.4	44.6	-1.1	45.2	1.3	48.7	7.7	47.8	-1.8	47.8	0.0	47.8	0.0	46.8	-2.1	46.1	-1.5	44.7	-3.0	45.0	0.7	44.8	-0.4
1962	44.5	-0.7	44.8	0.7	45.5	1.6	45.5	0.0	44.5	-2.2	44.8	0.7	44.6	-0.4	44.5	-0.2	44.5	0.0	44.4	-0.2	44.2	-0.5	43.6	-1.4
1963	43.7	0.2	43.7	0.0	44.0	0.7	43.9	-0.2	43.9	0.0	44.7	1.8	48.7	8.9	50.3	3.3	44.7	-11.1	44.6	-0.2	44.7	0.2	44.6	-0.2
1964	44.0	-1.3	44.5	1.1	45.7	2.7	45.8	0.2	45.5	-0.7	44.7	-1.8	44.6	-0.2	44.3	-0.7	44.3	0.0	44.0	-0.7	43.8	-0.5	43.6	-0.5
1965	45.6	4.6	44.9	-1.5	44.5	-0.9	44.4	-0.2	44.1	-0.7	43.7	-0.9	43.9	0.5	45.7	4.1	45.1	-1.3	44.2	-2.0	44.3	0.2	44.5	0.5
1966	45.4	2.0	45.4	0.0	47.2	4.0	49.5	4.9	48.4	-2.2	44.5	-8.1	44.2	-0.7	43.5	-1.6	43.1	-0.9	42.6	-1.2	42.0	-1.4	42.2	0.5
1967	42.2	0.0	43.1	2.1	42.3	-1.9	42.4	0.2	42.3	-0.2	42.3	0.0	43.2	2.1	43.9	1.6	46.2	5.2	43.4	-6.1	42.4	-2.3	43.6	2.8
1968	43.4	-0.5	45.7	5.3	47.0	2.8	47.0	0.0	47.0	0.0	47.4	0.9	48.9	3.2	49.2	0.6	51.5	4.7	54.0	4.9	54.4	0.7	62.3	14.5
1969	65.2	4.7	70.7	8.4	71.0	0.4	53.6	-24.5	50.0	-6.7	45.5	-9.0	45.4	-0.2	45.2	-0.4	45.6	0.9	46.4	1.8	48.1	3.7	46.8	-2.7
1970	45.9	-1.9	46.4	1.1	45.5	-1.9	47.0	3.3	47.9	1.9	47.4	-1.0	47.6	0.4	48.0	0.8	47.7	-0.6	46.5	-2.5	45.5	-2.2	45.1	-0.9
1971	45.2	0.2	48.4	7.1	51.8	7.0	49.9	-3.7	47.6	-4.6	47.5	-0.2	48.1	1.3	51.9	7.9	51.2	-1.3	49.9	-2.5	50.0	0.2	50.8	1.6
1972	51.8	2.0	53.9	4.1	55.5	3.0	55.5	0.0	56.1	1.1	56.7	1.1	57.3	1.1	58.5	2.1	58.0	-0.9	58.0	0.0	57.4	-1.0	57.0	-0.7
1973	57.8	1.4	64.4	11.4	76.2	18.3	78.6	3.1	76.6	-2.5	66.7	-12.9	59.4	-10.9	60.3	1.5	59.5	-1.3	58.0	-2.5	73.2	26.2	71.5	-2.3
1974	66.7	-6.7	68.0	1.9	73.6	8.2	81.5	10.7	77.3	-5.2	70.2	-9.2	69.4	-1.1	66.9	-3.6	68.1	1.8	63.4	-6.9	63.7	0.5	64.2	0.8
1975	63.1	-1.7	67.9	7.6	67.5	-0.6	71.1	5.3	74.4	4.6	69.9	-6.0	69.4	-0.7	68.3	-1.6	69.8	2.2	68.6	-1.7	70.2	2.3	73.1	4.1
1976	77.9	6.6	79.2	1.7	79.8	0.8	79.7	-0.1	78.8	-1.1	76.1	-3.4	78.0	2.5	80.8	3.6	82.5	2.1	82.0	-0.6	83.8	2.2	88.4	5.5
1977	88.2	-0.2	88.2	0.0	89.6	1.6	87.3	-2.6	86.2	-1.3	87.3	1.3	91.3	4.6	94.7	3.7	99.3	4.9	95.5	-3.8	92.0	-3.7	97.3	5.8
1978	99.9	2.7	100.5	0.6	97.5	-3.0	94.9	-2.7	98.4	3.7	101.7	3.4	99.7	-2.0	104.5	4.8	102.6	-1.8	103.5	0.9	107.7	4.1	107.3	-0.4
1979	110.9	3.4	110.8	-0.1	109.7	-1.0	108.7	-0.9	107.4	-1.2	102.8	-4.3	107.6	4.7	109.6	1.9	111.1	1.4	109.4	-1.5	104.3	-4.7	102.5	-1.7
1980	102.6	0.1	104.9	2.2	103.4	-1.4	94.7	-8.4	99.4	5.0	104.1	4.7	108.9	4.6	114.6	5.2	108.8	-5.1	109.0	0.2	110.6	1.5	113.5	2.6
1981	108.2	-4.7	108.2	0.0	107.2	-0.9	110.3	2.9	107.0	-3.0	108.4	1.3	106.7	-1.6	105.8	-0.8	103.8	-1.9	100.9	-2.8	100.6	-0.3	103.3	2.7
1982	102.3	-1.0	101.3	-1.0	101.9	0.6	100.8	-1.1	99.3	-1.5	103.0	3.7	100.1	-2.8	98.7	-1.4	98.4	-0.3	96.5	-1.9	98.2	1.8	99.6	1.4
1983	101.4	1.8	103.2	1.8	102.9	-0.3	103.1	0.2	103.9	0.8	110.1	6.0	108.8	-1.2	106.1	-2.5	104.3	-1.7	106.2	1.8	105.4	-0.8	106.5	1.0
1984	106.9	0.4	107.5	0.6	107.1	-0.4	104.9	-2.1	101.4	-3.3	101.8	0.4	102.2	0.4	106.0	3.7	104.9	-1.0	103.4	-1.4	101.2	-2.1	101.6	0.4
1985	100.9	-0.7	97.6	-3.3	96.3	-1.3	96.0	-0.3	100.1	4.3	102.2	2.1	102.0	-0.2	102.4	0.4	99.2	-3.1	100.8	1.6	99.0	-1.8	99.4	0.4
1986	98.9	-0.5	98.5	-0.4	100.6	2.1	105.3	4.7	103.3	-1.9	101.5	-1.7	101.6	0.1	101.3	-0.3	101.6	0.3	101.9	0.3	101.3	-0.6	100.6	-0.7
1987	100.5	-0.1	102.3	1.8	103.4	1.1	101.1	-2.2	99.3	-1.8	98.8	-0.5	100.3	1.5	102.8	2.5	107.4	4.5	104.6	-2.6	105.9	1.2	104.2	-1.6
1988	105.3	1.1	104.4	-0.9	103.4	-1.0	102.1	-1.3	100.3	-1.8	102.2	1.9	105.3	3.0	100.3	-4.7	106.3	6.0	103.1	-3.0	103.6	0.5	104.7	1.1
1989	105.9	1.1	109.9	3.8	111.1	1.1	111.3	0.2	113.4	1.9	113.4	0.0	118.4	4.4	115.2	-2.7	118.5	2.9	127.6	7.7	128.7	0.9	116.9	-9.2
1990	114.3	-2.2	115.8	1.3	116.1	0.3	125.3	7.9	122.7	-2.1	115.8	-5.6	117.6	1.6	112.6	-4.3	111.3	-1.2	106.8	-4.0	105.7	-1.0	106.7	0.9
1991	104.0	-2.5	102.7	-1.3	105.4	2.6	106.9	1.4	118.9	11.2	129.3	8.7	130.0	0.5	114.4	-12.0	116.2	1.6	112.6	-3.1	114.3	1.5	116.4	1.8

[Continued]

Plywood
Producer Price Index
Base 1982 = 100
[Continued]

For 1947-2001. Columns headed % show percentile change in the index from the previous period for which an index is available.

Year	Jan Index	%	Feb Index	%	Mar Index	%	Apr Index	%	May Index	%	Jun Index	%	Jul Index	%	Aug Index	%	Sep Index	%	Oct Index	%	Nov Index	%	Dec Index	%
1992	119.5	2.7	132.2	10.6	135.3	2.3	132.2	-2.3	130.1	-1.6	128.8	-1.0	125.2	-2.8	128.8	2.9	143.5	11.4	140.3	-2.2	138.0	-1.6	145.8	5.7
1993	154.9	6.2	164.8	6.4	168.9	2.5	158.7	-6.0	148.5	-6.4	144.0	-3.0	143.3	-0.5	146.4	2.2	149.6	2.2	147.9	-1.1	150.8	2.0	155.5	3.1
1994	159.7	2.7	153.8	-3.7	152.5	-0.8	147.8	-3.1	149.2	0.9	153.8	3.1	153.7	-0.1	157.6	2.5	165.7	5.1	164.6	-0.7	172.5	4.8	172.0	-0.3
1995	166.0	-3.5	162.8	-1.9	164.5	1.0	164.0	-0.3	165.2	0.7	159.3	-3.6	167.6	5.2	171.1	2.1	173.4	1.3	169.9	-2.0	161.7	-4.8	157.4	-2.7
1996	154.0	-2.2	154.2	0.1	152.1	-1.4	151.6	-0.3	158.3	4.4	155.8	-1.6	154.0	-1.2	157.4	2.2	166.7	5.9	160.1	-4.0	157.9	-1.4	155.3	-1.6
1997	154.5	-0.5	158.8	2.8	163.6	3.0	159.1	-2.8	158.2	-0.6	162.7	2.8	162.6	-0.1	161.6	-0.6	162.6	0.6	156.0	-4.1	157.9	1.2	153.9	-2.5
1998	152.9	-0.6	153.3	0.3	151.3	-1.3	152.4	0.7	151.4	-0.7	151.1	-0.2	159.1	5.3	167.6	5.3	170.0	1.4	156.7	-7.8	160.9	2.7	161.1	0.1
1999	161.6	0.3	169.3	4.8	173.0	2.2	170.2	-1.6	179.1	5.2	196.9	9.9	208.3	5.8	202.1	-3.0	177.8	-12.0	158.7	-10.7	159.5	0.5	160.8	0.8
2000	162.0	0.7	162.2	0.1	166.0	2.3	167.2	0.7	156.6	-6.3	155.3	-0.8	154.0	-0.8	152.6	-0.9	156.4	2.5	155.1	-0.8	152.6	-1.6	150.9	-1.1
2001	147.0	-2.6	145.6	-1.0	148.0	1.6	147.1	-0.6	165.1	12.2	166.5	0.8	156.8	-5.8	163.8	4.5	160.7	-1.9	150.5	-6.3	150.3	-0.1	148.1	-1.5

Source: U.S. Department of Labor, Bureau of Labor Statistics, Division of Industry Prices and Price Indexes. n.e.c. stands for not elsewhere classified. - indicates no data collected for period or unavailable.

Other Wood Products
Producer Price Index
Base 1982 = 100

For 1966-2001. Columns headed % show percentile change in the index from the previous period for which an index is available.

Year	Jan Index	%	Feb Index	%	Mar Index	%	Apr Index	%	May Index	%	Jun Index	%	Jul Index	%	Aug Index	%	Sep Index	%	Oct Index	%	Nov Index	%	Dec Index	%
1966	-	-	-	-	-	-	-	-	-	-	-	-	-	-	-	-	-	-	-	-	-	-	41.6	-
1967	42.4	1.9	42.4	0.0	42.4	0.0	42.4	0.0	42.4	0.0	42.4	0.0	42.4	0.0	42.3	-0.2	42.1	-0.5	42.2	0.2	42.2	0.0	42.2	0.0
1968	42.5	0.7	44.0	3.5	44.0	0.0	44.1	0.2	44.2	0.2	44.2	0.0	44.3	0.2	44.3	0.0	44.7	0.9	44.8	0.2	45.4	1.3	45.9	1.1
1969	46.0	0.2	46.2	0.4	46.7	1.1	46.8	0.2	47.6	1.7	47.8	0.4	48.0	0.4	48.5	1.0	48.4	-0.2	48.5	0.2	48.5	0.0	49.2	1.4
1970	49.7	1.0	49.7	0.0	49.7	0.0	49.6	-0.2	49.6	0.0	49.6	0.0	49.7	0.2	49.7	0.0	49.6	-0.2	49.6	0.0	49.6	0.0	49.9	0.6
1971	49.9	0.0	50.0	0.2	50.1	0.2	50.5	0.8	50.5	0.0	50.4	-0.2	50.4	0.0	50.4	0.0	50.4	0.0	50.4	0.0	50.4	0.0	50.4	0.0
1972	50.6	0.4	50.8	0.4	50.9	0.2	51.3	0.8	51.9	1.2	52.2	0.6	53.2	1.9	53.7	0.9	54.0	0.6	54.3	0.6	55.1	1.5	55.2	0.2
1973	56.4	2.2	57.2	1.4	59.7	4.4	62.4	4.5	63.4	1.6	64.3	1.4	64.7	0.6	64.9	0.3	66.0	1.7	67.0	1.5	67.3	0.4	67.4	0.1
1974	67.4	0.0	68.5	1.6	69.2	1.0	69.5	0.4	70.8	1.9	71.3	0.7	71.6	0.4	71.8	0.3	72.1	0.4	71.7	-0.6	71.3	-0.6	71.1	-0.3
1975	70.4	-1.0	70.2	-0.3	69.5	-1.0	68.9	-0.9	68.7	-0.3	68.4	-0.4	68.0	-0.6	68.1	0.1	68.0	-0.1	67.8	-0.3	67.7	-0.1	66.9	-1.2
1976	67.8	1.3	68.7	1.3	68.9	0.3	69.2	0.4	69.3	0.1	70.0	1.0	70.3	0.4	70.4	0.1	71.9	2.1	72.1	0.3	72.5	0.6	73.0	0.7
1977	73.4	0.5	74.7	1.8	75.8	1.5	76.7	1.2	78.1	1.8	78.5	0.5	78.6	0.1	79.0	0.5	80.3	1.6	80.3	0.0	80.4	0.1	80.9	0.6
1978	82.4	1.9	84.3	2.3	85.6	1.5	86.7	1.3	88.4	2.0	90.6	2.5	92.0	1.5	92.0	0.0	92.8	0.9	93.4	0.6	93.8	0.4	94.0	0.2
1979	94.5	0.5	95.8	1.4	98.3	2.6	99.7	1.4	100.9	1.2	101.0	0.1	100.6	-0.4	100.5	-0.1	100.8	0.3	100.7	-0.1	101.6	0.9	101.8	0.2
1980	102.6	0.8	103.0	0.4	102.9	-0.1	102.3	-0.6	101.9	-0.4	101.1	-0.8	100.3	-0.8	100.0	-0.3	100.3	0.3	100.2	-0.1	100.2	0.0	100.0	-0.2
1981	101.0	1.0	100.8	-0.2	100.3	-0.5	100.9	0.6	100.9	0.0	101.5	0.6	101.9	0.4	101.5	-0.4	101.8	0.3	101.6	-0.2	101.3	-0.3	101.4	0.1
1982	100.9	-0.5	101.1	0.2	101.0	-0.1	100.7	-0.3	100.5	-0.2	99.9	-0.6	99.9	0.0	99.8	-0.1	99.8	0.0	99.8	0.0	98.7	-1.1	97.9	-0.8
1983	98.2	0.3	98.7	0.5	98.1	-0.6	97.7	-0.4	97.9	0.2	97.2	-0.7	97.3	0.1	97.1	-0.2	97.1	0.0	97.2	0.1	97.3	0.1	97.6	0.3
1984	97.4	-0.2	97.7	0.3	98.2	0.5	98.8	0.6	99.4	0.6	99.5	0.1	99.6	0.1	100.1	0.5	99.9	-0.2	100.2	0.3	100.2	0.0	100.8	0.6
1985	100.7	-0.1	100.7	0.0	101.0	0.3	101.2	0.2	100.1	-1.1	99.9	-0.2	99.9	0.0	99.7	-0.2	99.6	-0.1	99.7	0.1	99.5	-0.2	99.5	0.0
1986	99.7	0.2	99.6	-0.1	99.6	0.0	99.6	0.0	99.8	0.2	100.8	1.0	101.4	0.6	101.0	-0.4	101.1	0.1	102.0	0.9	102.7	0.7	102.9	0.2
1987	103.0	0.1	102.9	-0.1	103.0	0.1	103.2	0.2	103.3	0.1	103.5	0.2	103.5	0.0	103.8	0.3	104.1	0.3	104.6	0.5	104.6	0.0	105.0	0.4
1988	105.4	0.4	105.8	0.4	106.2	0.4	106.5	0.3	106.5	0.0	107.1	0.6	107.5	0.4	107.7	0.2	107.9	0.2	108.3	0.4	108.6	0.3	108.3	-0.3
1989	108.5	0.2	109.4	0.8	110.2	0.7	111.4	1.1	112.4	0.9	113.7	1.2	114.2	0.4	115.6	1.2	116.2	0.5	115.1	-0.9	115.2	0.1	114.9	-0.3
1990	114.6	-0.3	114.4	-0.2	114.1	-0.3	114.4	0.3	114.5	0.1	114.9	0.3	114.8	-0.1	115.1	0.3	115.0	-0.1	115.3	0.3	114.9	-0.3	114.8	-0.1
1991	115.4	0.5	116.1	0.6	117.0	0.8	117.9	0.8	118.3	0.3	119.1	0.7	120.4	1.1	119.3	-0.9	120.5	1.0	119.7	-0.7	119.9	0.2	119.9	0.0
1992	119.9	0.0	119.8	-0.1	121.7	1.6	122.4	0.6	125.1	2.2	125.6	0.4	125.4	-0.2	125.4	0.0	126.0	0.5	126.8	0.6	127.7	0.7	127.6	-0.1
1993	129.7	1.6	131.4	1.3	133.6	1.7	135.1	1.1	137.1	1.5	136.2	-0.7	136.4	0.1	135.6	-0.6	136.9	1.0	136.4	-0.4	136.4	0.0	138.1	1.2
1994	137.2	-0.7	137.7	0.4	137.6	-0.1	138.4	0.6	138.9	0.4	137.4	-1.1	137.8	0.3	137.5	-0.2	137.1	-0.3	137.8	0.5	138.0	0.1	137.5	-0.4
1995	139.0	1.1	141.5	1.8	141.6	0.1	141.8	0.1	144.0	1.6	142.8	-0.8	143.5	0.5	145.2	1.2	148.5	2.3	147.6	-0.6	144.9	-1.8	144.2	-0.5
1996	137.8	-4.4	135.8	-1.5	133.8	-1.5	130.7	-2.3	126.6	-3.1	126.1	-0.4	122.5	-2.9	122.7	0.2	123.2	0.4	123.4	0.2	123.7	0.2	123.6	-0.1
1997	123.3	-0.2	123.4	0.1	127.1	3.0	127.1	0.0	127.1	0.0	127.3	0.2	128.2	0.7	128.7	0.4	129.2	0.4	131.2	1.5	132.8	1.2	134.3	1.1
1998	135.0	0.5	136.6	1.2	136.8	0.1	136.0	-0.6	136.0	0.0	136.1	0.1	135.0	-0.8	135.1	0.1	134.8	-0.2	134.2	-0.4	133.6	-0.4	133.6	0.0
1999	132.1	-1.1	132.0	-0.1	131.2	-0.6	131.3	0.1	130.3	-0.8	130.0	-0.2	130.1	0.1	130.8	0.5	130.9	0.1	130.8	-0.1	131.6	0.6	131.7	0.1
2000	131.7	0.0	131.7	0.0	131.8	0.1	129.8	-1.5	129.8	0.0	129.7	-0.1	129.9	0.2	129.9	0.0	129.9	0.0	130.5	0.5	130.7	0.2	130.7	0.0
2001	131.2	0.4	131.8	0.5	131.7	-0.1	131.2	-0.4	131.2	0.0	131.1	-0.1	130.2	-0.7	130.0	-0.2	130.1	0.1	129.6	-0.4	128.9	-0.5	128.6	-0.2

Source: U.S. Department of Labor, Bureau of Labor Statistics, Division of Industry Prices and Price Indexes. n.e.c. stands for not elsewhere classified. - indicates no data collected for period or unavailable.

Logs, Bolts, Timber and Pulpwood
Producer Price Index
Base 1982 = 100

For 1981-2001. Columns headed % show percentile change in the index from the previous period for which an index is available.

Year	Jan Index	%	Feb Index	%	Mar Index	%	Apr Index	%	May Index	%	Jun Index	%	Jul Index	%	Aug Index	%	Sep Index	%	Oct Index	%	Nov Index	%	Dec Index	%
1981	-	-	-	-	-	-	-	-	-	-	-	-	-	-	-	-	-	-	-	-	-	-	103.1	-
1982	102.0	-1.1	103.3	1.3	104.4	1.1	104.8	0.4	103.3	-1.4	102.7	-0.6	99.8	-2.8	98.6	-1.2	97.1	-1.5	94.4	-2.8	93.7	-0.7	95.9	2.3
1983	94.8	-1.1	96.0	1.3	96.9	0.9	96.6	-0.3	96.2	-0.4	96.9	0.7	96.5	-0.4	97.3	0.8	97.9	0.6	96.2	-1.7	97.1	0.9	96.5	-0.6
1984	95.9	-0.6	100.8	5.1	96.9	-3.9	97.9	1.0	100.2	2.3	100.5	0.3	99.1	-1.4	94.7	-4.4	96.5	1.9	93.4	-3.2	93.7	0.3	93.8	0.1
1985	94.4	0.6	96.5	2.2	96.8	0.3	97.3	0.5	97.2	-0.1	97.5	0.3	96.5	-1.0	95.5	-1.0	94.4	-1.2	95.4	1.1	95.3	-0.1	95.3	0.0
1986	94.5	-0.8	90.6	-4.1	91.6	1.1	91.9	0.3	92.4	0.5	92.9	0.5	91.8	-1.2	92.3	0.5	92.0	-0.3	92.4	0.4	92.2	-0.2	92.6	0.4
1987	93.2	0.6	94.8	1.7	96.2	1.5	95.9	-0.3	96.0	0.1	97.3	1.4	98.5	1.2	102.1	3.7	107.2	5.0	111.0	3.5	114.0	2.7	115.6	1.4
1988	117.3	1.5	118.2	0.8	118.6	0.3	119.1	0.4	118.9	-0.2	117.5	-1.2	117.3	-0.2	116.6	-0.6	116.4	-0.2	116.8	0.3	117.4	0.5	118.7	1.1
1989	120.8	1.8	122.2	1.2	123.6	1.1	127.2	2.9	128.2	0.8	131.1	2.3	133.7	2.0	137.2	2.6	137.3	0.1	140.7	2.5	140.8	0.1	140.4	-0.3
1990	142.1	1.2	142.1	0.0	143.3	0.8	143.7	0.3	144.2	0.3	144.8	0.4	146.1	0.9	145.2	-0.6	143.3	-1.3	140.9	-1.7	139.5	-1.0	138.6	-0.6
1991	141.9	2.4	142.1	0.1	141.0	-0.8	141.6	0.4	144.3	1.9	144.0	-0.2	144.4	0.3	146.3	1.3	145.4	-0.6	147.5	1.4	145.8	-1.2	145.4	-0.3
1992	151.6	4.3	155.8	2.8	158.8	1.9	164.1	3.3	164.9	0.5	165.1	0.1	165.1	0.0	165.9	0.5	168.1	1.3	170.7	1.5	171.4	0.4	176.4	2.9
1993	183.2	3.9	193.8	5.8	200.9	3.7	222.6	10.8	233.5	4.9	224.9	-3.7	222.5	-1.1	212.6	-4.4	212.6	0.0	212.9	0.1	215.6	1.3	212.4	-1.5
1994	223.7	5.3	226.5	1.3	230.7	1.9	227.2	-1.5	220.7	-2.9	218.1	-1.2	215.5	-1.2	213.5	-0.9	212.6	-0.4	213.3	0.3	212.8	-0.2	214.5	0.8
1995	218.1	1.7	224.5	2.9	225.9	0.6	229.3	1.5	228.4	-0.4	228.8	0.2	219.9	-3.9	216.0	-1.8	216.0	0.0	214.6	-0.6	211.5	-1.4	212.3	0.4
1996	214.5	1.0	214.0	-0.2	209.3	-2.2	200.2	-4.3	202.8	1.3	201.5	-0.6	201.7	0.1	203.6	0.9	206.0	1.2	208.8	1.4	209.8	0.5	209.5	-0.1
1997	213.0	1.7	215.9	1.4	216.2	0.1	215.7	-0.2	216.6	0.4	215.2	-0.6	215.4	0.1	214.8	-0.3	214.7	-0.0	211.5	-1.5	212.0	0.2	212.5	0.2
1998	214.3	0.8	216.4	1.0	217.0	0.3	217.3	0.1	213.3	-1.8	209.0	-2.0	204.2	-2.3	204.7	0.2	202.9	-0.9	201.0	-0.9	199.4	-0.8	197.9	-0.8
1999	198.6	0.4	200.6	1.0	200.4	-0.1	201.1	0.3	201.2	0.0	200.4	-0.4	201.0	0.3	202.2	0.6	202.9	0.3	204.5	0.8	205.6	0.5	205.9	0.1
2000	208.8	1.4	209.8	0.5	207.5	-1.1	204.8	-1.3	200.6	-2.1	198.1	-1.2	194.9	-1.6	187.2	-4.0	187.4	0.1	186.8	-0.3	186.1	-0.4	185.2	-0.5
2001	186.1	0.5	182.0	-2.2	184.0	1.1	183.7	-0.2	184.0	0.2	185.7	0.9	184.8	-0.5	182.7	-1.1	182.8	0.1	179.2	-2.0	178.5	-0.4	179.0	0.3

Source: U.S. Department of Labor, Bureau of Labor Statistics, Division of Industry Prices and Price Indexes. n.e.c. stands for not elsewhere classified. - indicates no data collected for period or unavailable.

Prefabricated Wood Buildings & Components
Producer Price Index
Base 1982 = 100

For 1984-2001. Columns headed % show percentile change in the index from the previous period for which an index is available.

Year	Jan Index	%	Feb Index	%	Mar Index	%	Apr Index	%	May Index	%	Jun Index	%	Jul Index	%	Aug Index	%	Sep Index	%	Oct Index	%	Nov Index	%	Dec Index	%
1984	-	-	-	-	-	-	-	-	-	-	-	-	-	-	-	-	-	-	-	-	-	-	100.0	-
1985	100.4	0.4	100.2	-0.2	100.6	0.4	100.7	0.1	101.1	0.4	101.6	0.5	101.9	0.3	102.1	0.2	102.2	0.1	102.2	0.0	102.1	-0.1	102.1	0.0
1986	102.7	0.6	103.1	0.4	103.3	0.2	104.1	0.8	104.4	0.3	104.4	0.0	104.3	-0.1	104.4	0.1	104.7	0.3	104.7	0.0	104.7	0.0	104.8	0.1
1987	104.8	0.0	104.9	0.1	104.5	-0.4	105.4	0.9	105.5	0.1	105.2	-0.3	105.7	0.5	105.8	0.1	105.8	0.0	105.8	0.0	106.1	0.3	106.1	0.0
1988	106.2	0.1	107.3	1.0	107.8	0.5	107.9	0.1	107.6	-0.3	108.1	0.5	108.5	0.4	108.5	0.0	108.5	0.0	109.2	0.6	109.2	0.0	109.2	0.0
1989	109.8	0.5	109.8	0.0	110.5	0.6	110.7	0.2	110.7	0.0	110.7	0.0	111.0	0.3	111.0	0.0	111.0	0.0	111.0	0.0	110.8	-0.2	111.0	0.2
1990	111.3	0.3	111.8	0.4	111.6	-0.2	111.9	0.3	112.8	0.8	113.1	0.3	113.2	0.1	113.8	0.5	113.9	0.1	114.7	0.7	114.7	0.0	114.7	0.0
1991	115.7	0.9	115.7	0.0	115.9	0.2	117.2	1.1	117.5	0.3	119.6	1.8	119.7	0.1	120.1	0.3	120.2	0.1	119.0	-1.0	118.9	-0.1	118.9	0.0
1992	119.3	0.3	120.3	0.8	120.6	0.2	122.8	1.8	122.9	0.1	123.0	0.1	122.9	-0.1	123.1	0.2	123.2	0.1	124.5	1.1	125.2	0.6	125.4	0.2
1993	125.7	0.2	128.3	2.1	130.1	1.4	132.1	1.5	134.7	2.0	134.4	-0.2	134.0	-0.3	133.2	-0.6	132.9	-0.2	133.6	0.5	134.5	0.7	136.3	1.3
1994	135.3	-0.7	138.5	2.4	139.6	0.8	141.8	1.6	141.9	0.1	142.4	0.4	142.5	0.1	142.7	0.1	143.1	0.3	144.0	0.6	143.9	-0.1	144.0	0.1
1995	145.3	0.9	146.1	0.6	146.5	0.3	148.2	1.2	148.5	0.2	148.8	0.2	148.4	-0.3	148.4	0.0	148.4	0.0	148.2	-0.1	148.2	0.0	148.2	0.0
1996	148.9	0.5	149.2	0.2	149.7	0.3	150.0	0.2	150.6	0.4	150.7	0.1	151.3	0.4	150.8	-0.3	151.1	0.2	151.5	0.3	151.6	0.1	153.3	1.1
1997	153.5	0.1	153.8	0.2	154.3	0.3	155.1	0.5	157.1	1.3	157.2	0.1	157.2	0.0	157.1	-0.1	157.9	0.5	158.0	0.1	158.0	0.0	157.8	-0.1
1998	157.7	-0.1	157.9	0.1	158.0	0.1	158.9	0.6	160.6	1.1	160.6	0.0	160.9	0.2	161.5	0.4	161.1	-0.2	160.6	-0.3	160.8	0.1	161.5	0.4
1999	161.6	0.1	162.6	0.6	163.5	0.6	164.7	0.7	165.3	0.4	166.7	0.8	167.7	0.6	168.2	0.3	167.5	-0.4	167.9	0.2	167.3	-0.4	167.7	0.2
2000	167.6	-0.1	167.7	0.1	169.7	1.2	171.0	0.8	172.8	1.1	172.8	0.0	172.4	-0.2	172.3	-0.1	172.3	0.0	172.5	0.1	171.8	-0.4	172.2	0.2
2001	171.5	-0.4	171.6	0.1	173.0	0.8	174.5	0.9	176.8	1.3	177.3	0.3	176.2	-0.6	175.9	-0.2	177.3	0.8	176.6	-0.4	176.2	-0.2	176.3	0.1

Source: U.S. Department of Labor, Bureau of Labor Statistics, Division of Industry Prices and Price Indexes. n.e.c. stands for not elsewhere classified. - indicates no data collected for period or unavailable.

Treated Wood and Contract Wood Preserving
Producer Price Index
Base 1982 = 100

For 1985-2001. Columns headed % show percentile change in the index from the previous period for which an index is available.

Year	Jan Index	%	Feb Index	%	Mar Index	%	Apr Index	%	May Index	%	Jun Index	%	Jul Index	%	Aug Index	%	Sep Index	%	Oct Index	%	Nov Index	%	Dec Index	%
1985	-	-	-	-	-	-	-	-	-	-	100.0	-	99.5	-0.5	99.0	-0.5	99.0	0.0	98.9	-0.1	98.9	0.0	98.8	-0.1
1986	98.8	0.0	98.3	-0.5	98.9	0.6	98.1	-0.8	98.2	0.1	98.0	-0.2	97.7	-0.3	97.8	0.1	97.6	-0.2	97.7	0.1	97.3	-0.4	97.4	0.1
1987	97.0	-0.4	97.7	0.7	98.0	0.3	98.5	0.5	98.9	0.4	100.0	1.1	99.4	-0.6	99.5	0.1	99.4	-0.1	98.9	-0.5	98.9	0.0	99.1	0.2
1988	100.0	0.9	100.9	0.9	100.9	0.0	101.0	0.1	101.4	0.4	102.2	0.8	102.6	0.4	102.1	-0.5	101.8	-0.3	103.9	2.1	104.6	0.7	104.8	0.2
1989	106.6	1.7	107.9	1.2	108.3	0.4	108.9	0.6	110.6	1.6	110.9	0.3	111.2	0.3	111.1	-0.1	110.9	-0.2	110.1	-0.7	109.9	-0.2	110.0	0.1
1990	110.3	0.3	111.7	1.3	111.9	0.2	112.3	0.4	113.3	0.9	113.2	-0.1	113.5	0.3	113.6	0.1	112.7	-0.8	112.0	-0.6	113.3	1.2	113.3	0.0
1991	113.5	0.2	113.4	-0.1	114.4	0.9	114.8	0.3	114.6	-0.2	118.9	3.8	119.6	0.6	115.5	-3.4	115.3	-0.2	115.0	-0.3	115.9	0.8	116.7	0.7
1992	118.9	1.9	122.6	3.1	123.2	0.5	123.4	0.2	124.0	0.5	122.4	-1.3	122.2	-0.2	123.2	0.8	125.5	1.9	124.3	-1.0	124.4	0.1	127.6	2.6
1993	131.1	2.7	135.9	3.7	141.7	4.3	142.4	0.5	138.3	-2.9	132.4	-4.3	132.1	-0.2	134.3	1.7	136.7	1.8	139.2	1.8	146.1	5.0	147.3	0.8
1994	152.0	3.2	149.8	-1.4	151.4	1.1	148.2	-2.1	145.6	-1.8	149.2	2.5	148.4	-0.5	149.3	0.6	148.4	-0.6	147.0	-0.9	149.6	1.8	148.7	-0.6
1995	148.9	0.1	151.3	1.6	151.9	0.4	152.9	0.7	149.7	-2.1	147.5	-1.5	148.9	0.9	149.2	0.2	148.7	-0.3	147.6	-0.7	146.7	-0.6	147.3	0.4
1996	147.1	-0.1	147.0	-0.1	148.8	1.2	151.0	1.5	157.4	4.2	162.7	3.4	156.8	-3.6	158.4	1.0	159.7	0.8	154.8	-3.1	157.6	1.8	157.1	-0.3
1997	157.2	0.1	163.4	3.9	165.7	1.4	168.5	1.7	171.3	1.7	167.4	-2.3	166.9	-0.3	165.5	-0.8	162.3	-1.9	159.0	-2.0	159.1	0.1	162.6	2.2
1998	162.5	-0.1	164.7	1.4	167.6	1.8	167.6	0.0	164.9	-1.6	159.1	-3.5	163.5	2.8	161.5	-1.2	158.1	-2.1	158.1	0.0	158.0	-0.1	159.0	0.6
1999	161.5	1.6	165.9	2.7	168.0	1.3	166.0	-1.2	167.3	0.8	171.4	2.5	176.7	3.1	174.6	-1.2	166.0	-4.9	162.9	-1.9	159.5	-2.1	164.9	3.4
2000	165.1	0.1	164.8	-0.2	164.1	-0.4	162.5	-1.0	156.7	-3.6	159.6	1.9	159.4	-0.1	153.2	-3.9	150.1	-2.0	149.0	-0.7	146.9	-1.4	148.3	1.0
2001	145.4	-2.0	148.1	1.9	149.5	0.9	151.5	1.3	163.2	7.7	169.9	4.1	160.6	-5.5	157.8	-1.7	155.7	-1.3	148.2	-4.8	147.7	-0.3	148.6	0.6

Source: U.S. Department of Labor, Bureau of Labor Statistics, Division of Industry Prices and Price Indexes. n.e.c. stands for not elsewhere classified. - indicates no data collected for period or unavailable.

PULP, PAPER, AND ALLIED PRODUCTS
Producer Price Index
Base 1982 = 100

For 1947-2001. Columns headed % show percentile change in the index from the previous period for which an index is available.

Year	Jan Index	%	Feb Index	%	Mar Index	%	Apr Index	%	May Index	%	Jun Index	%	Jul Index	%	Aug Index	%	Sep Index	%	Oct Index	%	Nov Index	%	Dec Index	%
1947	24.5	-	24.7	0.8	24.8	0.4	25.1	1.2	25.1	0.0	25.1	0.0	25.1	0.0	25.2	0.4	25.3	0.4	25.5	0.8	25.5	0.0	25.8	1.2
1948	26.0	0.8	26.3	1.2	26.2	-0.4	26.1	-0.4	26.1	0.0	26.1	0.0	26.2	0.4	26.3	0.4	26.4	0.4	26.4	0.0	26.3	-0.4	26.3	0.0
1949	26.3	0.0	26.2	-0.4	26.0	-0.8	25.7	-1.2	25.3	-1.6	24.8	-2.0	24.5	-1.2	24.4	-0.4	24.5	0.4	24.5	0.0	24.6	0.4	24.6	0.0
1950	24.6	0.0	24.5	-0.4	24.5	0.0	24.5	0.0	24.4	-0.4	24.5	0.4	24.9	1.6	25.9	4.0	26.4	1.9	27.4	3.8	28.0	2.2	29.2	4.3
1951	30.6	4.8	30.7	0.3	30.7	0.0	30.5	-0.7	30.5	0.0	30.6	0.3	30.6	0.0	30.5	-0.3	30.4	-0.3	30.3	-0.3	30.2	-0.3	30.2	0.0
1952	30.1	-0.3	30.2	0.3	30.0	-0.7	29.9	-0.3	29.8	-0.3	29.7	-0.3	29.4	-1.0	29.5	0.3	29.5	0.0	29.4	-0.3	29.4	0.0	29.5	0.3
1953	29.5	0.0	29.4	-0.3	29.3	-0.3	29.4	0.3	29.4	0.0	29.5	0.3	29.5	0.0	29.6	0.3	29.8	0.7	30.0	0.7	29.9	-0.3	29.8	-0.3
1954	29.8	0.0	29.8	0.0	29.7	-0.3	29.6	-0.3	29.5	-0.3	29.5	0.0	29.6	0.3	29.6	0.0	29.6	0.0	29.6	0.0	29.6	0.0	29.5	-0.3
1955	29.6	0.3	29.7	0.3	29.8	0.3	29.9	0.3	30.0	0.3	30.2	0.7	30.3	0.3	30.5	0.7	30.7	0.7	31.3	2.0	31.4	0.3	31.5	0.3
1956	31.8	1.0	32.0	0.6	32.3	0.9	32.5	0.6	32.4	-0.3	32.5	0.3	32.5	0.0	32.6	0.3	32.6	0.0	32.7	0.3	32.6	-0.3	32.6	0.0
1957	32.8	0.6	32.8	0.0	32.8	0.0	32.8	0.0	32.9	0.3	32.9	0.0	33.0	0.3	33.1	0.3	33.2	0.3	33.4	0.6	33.4	0.0	33.4	0.0
1958	33.3	-0.3	33.3	0.0	33.3	0.0	33.3	0.0	33.3	0.0	33.3	0.0	33.4	0.3	33.4	0.0	33.6	0.6	33.6	0.0	33.6	0.0	33.5	-0.3
1959	33.5	0.0	33.6	0.3	33.6	0.0	33.7	0.3	33.6	-0.3	33.7	0.3	33.7	0.0	33.7	0.0	33.7	0.0	33.8	0.3	33.7	-0.3	33.7	0.0
1960	34.1	1.2	33.9	-0.6	33.9	0.0	33.9	0.0	34.0	0.3	34.0	0.0	34.0	0.0	33.9	-0.3	33.9	0.0	34.0	0.3	33.9	-0.3	33.7	-0.6
1961	33.7	0.0	33.7	0.0	33.5	-0.6	33.4	-0.3	32.1	-3.9	32.2	0.3	32.2	0.0	32.2	0.0	33.0	2.5	33.3	0.9	33.1	-0.6	33.3	0.6
1962	33.3	0.0	33.3	0.0	33.7	1.2	33.8	0.3	33.6	-0.6	33.5	-0.3	33.4	-0.3	33.3	-0.3	33.2	-0.3	33.1	-0.3	33.1	0.0	33.0	-0.3
1963	33.0	0.0	33.1	0.3	33.0	-0.3	33.0	0.0	33.1	0.3	33.2	0.3	33.0	-0.6	33.1	0.3	33.1	0.0	33.2	0.3	33.2	0.0	33.2	0.0
1964	33.3	0.3	33.3	0.0	33.1	-0.6	33.1	0.0	32.9	-0.6	32.9	0.0	32.9	0.0	32.9	0.0	32.9	0.0	33.1	0.6	33.0	-0.3	33.0	0.0
1965	33.0	0.0	33.0	0.0	33.2	0.6	33.3	0.3	33.4	0.3	33.4	0.0	33.3	-0.3	33.3	0.0	33.4	0.3	33.5	0.3	33.6	0.3	33.7	0.3
1966	33.8	0.3	33.8	0.0	34.0	0.6	34.2	0.6	34.3	0.3	34.4	0.3	34.4	0.0	34.4	0.0	34.4	0.0	34.4	0.0	34.4	0.0	34.4	0.0
1967	34.4	0.0	34.4	0.0	34.5	0.3	34.6	0.3	34.6	0.0	34.6	0.0	34.7	0.3	34.6	-0.3	34.6	0.0	34.7	0.3	34.8	0.3	34.9	0.3
1968	34.9	0.0	35.1	0.6	35.1	0.0	35.1	0.0	35.1	0.0	35.1	0.0	34.9	-0.6	35.0	0.3	34.9	-0.3	35.0	0.3	35.1	0.3	35.1	0.0	35.1	0.0
1969	35.4	0.9	35.6	0.6	35.8	0.6	35.9	0.3	36.0	0.3	36.0	0.0	36.0	0.0	36.0	0.0	36.2	0.6	36.3	0.3	36.4	0.3	36.5	0.3	36.6	0.3
1970	37.2	1.6	37.3	0.3	37.4	0.3	37.5	0.3	37.4	-0.3	37.4	0.0	37.5	0.3	37.4	-0.3	37.5	0.3	37.7	0.5	37.7	0.0	37.6	-0.3
1971	37.8	0.5	37.8	0.0	37.9	0.3	38.0	0.3	38.1	0.3	38.2	0.3	38.3	0.3	38.3	0.0	38.3	0.0	38.3	0.0	38.3	0.0	38.4	0.3
1972	38.4	0.0	38.7	0.8	38.9	0.5	39.1	0.5	39.2	0.3	39.3	0.3	39.4	0.3	39.5	0.3	39.6	0.3	39.7	0.3	39.8	0.3	39.9	0.3
1973	40.1	0.5	40.4	0.7	41.0	1.5	41.5	1.2	41.8	0.7	42.3	1.2	42.4	0.2	42.7	0.7	43.1	0.9	43.6	1.2	44.2	1.4	44.6	0.9
1974	45.6	2.2	46.0	0.9	47.5	3.3	50.0	5.3	50.8	1.6	51.1	0.6	53.1	3.9	56.4	6.2	56.9	0.9	57.5	1.1	57.8	0.5	57.9	0.2
1975	58.8	1.6	58.8	0.0	58.9	0.2	58.8	-0.2	58.8	0.0	58.8	0.0	58.9	0.2	58.9	0.0	59.0	0.2	59.2	0.3	59.3	0.2	59.9	1.0
1976	60.5	1.0	60.9	0.7	61.3	0.7	61.9	1.0	62.1	0.3	62.2	0.2	62.5	0.5	62.7	0.3	62.9	0.2	62.9	0.0	62.9	0.0	63.0	0.2
1977	63.4	0.6	63.4	0.0	63.6	0.3	64.2	0.9	64.5	0.5	64.9	0.6	65.0	0.2	65.1	0.2	65.2	0.2	65.3	0.2	65.2	-0.2	65.0	-0.3
1978	65.1	0.2	65.3	0.3	65.7	0.6	66.5	1.2	66.9	0.6	67.0	0.1	67.7	1.0	67.8	0.1	68.9	1.6	70.1	1.7	70.6	0.7	71.1	0.7
1979	71.7	0.8	72.3	0.8	73.5	1.7	74.5	1.4	74.9	0.5	75.0	0.1	75.6	0.8	77.0	1.9	77.2	0.3	78.8	2.1	79.5	0.9	80.3	1.0
1980	82.2	2.4	82.8	0.7	84.0	1.4	85.8	2.1	86.3	0.6	87.0	0.8	87.2	0.2	87.4	0.2	87.5	0.1	88.1	0.7	88.3	0.2	88.9	0.7
1981	91.6	3.0	92.5	1.0	93.2	0.8	94.0	0.9	94.3	0.3	94.5	0.2	95.2	0.7	95.6	0.4	96.2	0.6	96.7	0.5	97.1	0.4	97.3	0.2
1982	98.9	1.6	99.2	0.3	99.5	0.3	99.9	0.4	100.3	0.4	100.3	0.0	100.1	-0.2	100.2	0.1	100.2	0.0	100.4	0.2	100.4	0.0	100.6	0.2
1983	101.7	1.1	101.9	0.2	102.1	0.2	102.3	0.2	102.5	0.2	102.9	0.4	103.2	0.3	103.5	0.3	103.9	0.4	104.7	0.8	105.2	0.5	105.3	0.1
1984	107.0	1.6	108.1	1.0	108.8	0.6	109.5	0.6	110.1	0.5	110.3	0.2	110.8	0.5	111.3	0.5	111.5	0.2	111.9	0.4	112.2	0.3	112.3	0.1
1985	113.3	0.9	113.5	0.2	113.5	0.0	113.5	0.0	113.4	-0.1	113.3	-0.1	113.2	-0.1	113.2	0.0	113.1	-0.1	113.3	0.2	113.4	0.1	113.4	0.0
1986	114.5	1.0	114.7	0.2	114.7	0.0	115.3	0.5	115.6	0.3	115.8	0.2	116.1	0.3	116.5	0.3	117.0	0.4	117.6	0.5	117.9	0.3	118.1	0.2
1987	119.5	1.2	120.3	0.7	120.6	0.2	120.9	0.2	121.0	0.1	121.2	0.2	121.6	0.3	122.2	0.5	122.9	0.6	123.8	0.7	123.9	0.1	124.2	0.2
1988	126.6	1.9	127.3	0.6	128.0	0.5	128.9	0.7	129.6	0.5	130.0	0.3	131.0	0.8	131.3	0.2	132.1	0.6	132.8	0.5	133.1	0.2	133.5	0.3
1989	135.1	1.2	136.3	0.9	136.9	0.4	137.4	0.4	137.8	0.3	137.9	0.1	138.0	0.1	138.4	0.3	138.6	0.1	139.1	0.4	139.3	0.1	139.2	-0.1
1990	140.3	0.8	140.5	0.1	140.7	0.1	140.9	0.1	141.1	0.1	141.0	-0.1	141.1	0.1	141.1	0.0	141.3	0.1	142.0	0.5	142.3	0.2	142.3	0.0
1991	143.6	0.9	143.8	0.1	143.7	-0.1	143.2	-0.3	143.0	-0.1	142.7	-0.2	142.3	-0.3	142.2	-0.1	142.3	0.1	142.6	0.2	142.8	0.1	142.7	-0.1

[Continued]

PULP, PAPER, AND ALLIED PRODUCTS
Producer Price Index
Base 1982 = 100
[Continued]

For 1947-2001. Columns headed % show percentile change in the index from the previous period for which an index is available.

Year	Jan Index	%	Feb Index	%	Mar Index	%	Apr Index	%	May Index	%	Jun Index	%	Jul Index	%	Aug Index	%	Sep Index	%	Oct Index	%	Nov Index	%	Dec Index	%
1992	144.1	1.0	144.2	0.1	144.4	0.1	144.9	0.3	145.2	0.2	145.1	-0.1	145.2	0.1	145.4	0.1	145.8	0.3	146.1	0.2	145.9	-0.1	145.9	0.0
1993	147.0	0.8	147.1	0.1	147.3	0.1	147.7	0.3	147.7	0.0	147.1	-0.4	147.1	0.0	147.1	0.0	147.1	0.0	147.6	0.3	147.6	0.0	147.8	0.1
1994	148.6	0.5	148.8	0.1	149.2	0.3	149.4	0.1	150.1	0.5	151.0	0.6	152.0	0.7	153.1	0.7	154.5	0.9	156.2	1.1	158.0	1.2	159.5	0.9
1995	163.2	2.3	165.9	1.7	168.1	1.3	170.6	1.5	172.7	1.2	174.5	1.0	175.4	0.5	175.6	0.1	175.4	-0.1	175.4	0.0	175.2	-0.1	174.7	-0.3
1996	174.1	-0.3	173.2	-0.5	171.1	-1.2	169.2	-1.1	168.0	-0.7	167.5	-0.3	167.0	-0.3	166.6	-0.2	166.9	0.2	166.9	0.0	166.9	0.0	167.2	0.2
1997	167.6	0.2	167.1	-0.3	166.5	-0.4	166.3	-0.1	166.1	-0.1	166.4	0.2	166.9	0.3	167.8	0.5	168.7	0.5	169.5	0.5	170.4	0.5	171.2	0.5
1998	172.3	0.6	172.2	-0.1	172.1	-0.1	172.2	0.1	172.2	0.0	171.8	-0.2	171.9	0.1	171.8	-0.1	171.5	-0.2	171.1	-0.2	170.6	-0.3	170.4	-0.1
1999	170.7	0.2	170.7	0.0	171.6	0.5	172.0	0.2	172.6	0.3	173.4	0.5	174.4	0.6	175.2	0.5	176.0	0.5	177.0	0.6	177.7	0.4	177.9	0.1
2000	179.3	0.8	180.0	0.4	181.7	0.9	183.8	1.2	184.9	0.6	185.5	0.3	185.1	-0.2	184.5	-0.3	184.4	-0.1	185.1	0.4	185.0	-0.1	184.8	-0.1
2001	185.4	0.3	185.3	-0.1	185.5	0.1	185.6	0.1	185.3	-0.2	185.0	-0.2	184.8	-0.1	184.2	-0.3	184.2	0.0	183.8	-0.2	183.7	-0.1	183.9	0.1

Source: U.S. Department of Labor, Bureau of Labor Statistics, Division of Industry Prices and Price Indexes. n.e.c. stands for not elsewhere classified. - indicates no data collected for period or unavailable.

Pulp, Paper, and Products, ex. Building Paper
Producer Price Index
Base 1982 = 100

For 1947-2001. Columns headed % show percentile change in the index from the previous period for which an index is available.

Year	Jan Index	%	Feb Index	%	Mar Index	%	Apr Index	%	May Index	%	Jun Index	%	Jul Index	%	Aug Index	%	Sep Index	%	Oct Index	%	Nov Index	%	Dec Index	%
1947	25.8	-	26.0	0.8	26.2	0.8	26.6	1.5	26.5	-0.4	26.5	0.0	26.5	0.0	26.7	0.8	26.8	0.4	26.9	0.4	26.9	0.0	27.3	1.5
1948	27.5	0.7	27.7	0.7	27.7	0.0	27.6	-0.4	27.6	0.0	27.6	0.0	27.7	0.4	27.8	0.4	27.8	0.0	27.8	0.0	27.8	0.0	27.7	-0.4
1949	27.7	0.0	27.6	-0.4	27.5	-0.4	27.1	-1.5	26.6	-1.8	26.1	-1.9	25.8	-1.1	25.7	-0.4	25.8	0.4	25.8	0.0	25.9	0.4	25.9	0.0
1950	25.9	0.0	25.8	-0.4	25.8	0.0	25.8	0.0	25.7	-0.4	25.7	0.0	26.2	1.9	27.3	4.2	27.8	1.8	28.8	3.6	29.6	2.8	30.8	4.1
1951	32.4	5.2	32.5	0.3	32.4	-0.3	32.2	-0.6	32.2	0.0	32.4	0.6	32.4	0.0	32.2	-0.6	32.1	-0.3	32.0	-0.3	31.9	-0.3	31.9	0.0
1952	31.8	-0.3	31.8	0.0	31.7	-0.3	31.6	-0.3	31.5	-0.3	31.4	-0.3	31.0	-1.3	31.1	0.3	31.1	0.0	31.1	0.0	31.0	-0.3	31.1	0.3
1953	31.1	0.0	31.0	-0.3	30.9	-0.3	31.0	0.3	31.0	0.0	31.1	0.3	31.1	0.0	31.2	0.3	31.4	0.6	31.6	0.6	31.5	-0.3	31.4	-0.3
1954	31.4	0.0	31.4	0.0	31.3	-0.3	31.2	-0.3	31.1	-0.3	31.1	0.0	31.2	0.3	31.2	0.0	31.2	0.0	31.2	0.0	31.1	-0.3	31.1	0.0
1955	31.2	0.3	31.3	0.3	31.3	0.0	31.5	0.6	31.6	0.3	31.8	0.6	32.0	0.6	32.1	0.3	32.4	0.9	32.9	1.5	33.1	0.6	33.2	0.3
1956	33.5	0.9	33.7	0.6	34.1	1.2	34.2	0.3	34.2	0.0	34.2	0.0	34.3	0.3	34.4	0.3	34.3	-0.3	34.4	0.3	34.3	-0.3	34.4	0.3
1957	34.5	0.3	34.5	0.0	34.6	0.3	34.5	-0.3	34.6	0.3	34.6	0.0	34.7	0.3	34.9	0.6	35.0	0.3	35.1	0.3	35.2	0.3	35.2	0.0
1958	35.1	-0.3	35.1	0.0	35.0	-0.3	35.0	0.0	35.0	0.0	35.0	0.0	35.1	0.3	35.2	0.3	35.3	0.3	35.4	0.3	35.4	0.0	35.0	-1.1
1959	35.3	0.9	35.3	0.0	35.4	0.3	35.5	0.3	35.4	-0.3	35.5	0.3	35.5	0.0	35.5	0.0	35.5	0.0	35.5	0.0	35.5	0.0	35.5	0.0
1960	35.9	1.1	35.7	-0.6	35.7	0.0	35.7	0.0	35.8	0.3	35.8	0.0	35.9	0.3	35.7	-0.6	35.7	0.0	35.8	0.3	35.7	-0.3	35.5	-0.6
1961	35.5	0.0	35.4	-0.3	35.3	-0.3	35.1	-0.6	33.8	-3.7	33.9	0.3	33.8	-0.3	33.8	0.0	34.7	2.7	35.0	0.9	34.8	-0.6	35.0	0.6
1962	35.1	0.3	35.1	0.0	35.5	1.1	35.7	0.6	35.5	-0.6	35.4	-0.3	35.2	-0.6	35.1	-0.3	35.0	-0.3	34.9	-0.3	34.8	-0.3	34.8	0.0
1963	34.8	0.0	34.9	0.3	34.8	-0.3	34.8	0.0	34.8	0.0	35.0	0.6	34.8	-0.6	34.8	0.0	34.8	0.0	35.0	0.6	35.0	0.0	35.0	0.0
1964	35.1	0.3	35.2	0.3	35.0	-0.6	34.9	-0.3	34.7	-0.6	34.7	0.0	34.7	0.0	34.7	0.0	34.7	0.0	34.9	0.6	34.8	-0.3	34.8	0.0
1965	34.8	0.0	34.9	0.3	35.1	0.6	35.2	0.3	35.2	0.0	35.2	0.0	35.2	0.0	35.2	0.0	35.2	0.0	35.4	0.6	35.5	0.3	35.5	0.0
1966	35.7	0.6	35.7	0.0	35.9	0.6	36.1	0.6	36.2	0.3	36.3	0.3	36.4	0.3	36.4	0.0	36.4	0.0	36.3	-0.3	36.3	0.0	36.3	0.0
1967	36.3	0.0	36.4	0.3	36.5	0.3	36.6	0.3	36.6	0.0	36.6	0.0	36.7	0.3	36.6	-0.3	36.6	0.0	36.7	0.3	36.9	0.5	36.9	0.0
1968	37.0	0.3	37.1	0.3	37.0	-0.3	37.0	0.0	37.1	0.3	36.9	-0.5	37.0	0.3	36.9	-0.3	37.0	0.3	37.0	0.0	37.0	0.0	37.0	0.0
1969	37.4	1.1	37.6	0.5	37.8	0.5	37.9	0.3	37.9	0.0	38.0	0.3	38.1	0.3	38.3	0.5	38.4	0.3	38.5	0.3	38.7	0.5	38.7	0.0
1970	39.4	1.8	39.5	0.3	39.6	0.3	39.7	0.3	39.6	-0.3	39.6	0.0	39.7	0.3	39.7	0.0	39.7	0.0	39.9	0.5	39.9	0.0	39.9	0.0
1971	40.1	0.5	40.0	-0.2	40.1	0.2	40.2	0.2	40.3	0.2	40.5	0.5	40.6	0.2	40.6	0.0	40.6	0.0	40.6	0.0	40.6	0.0	40.6	0.0
1972	40.7	0.2	41.0	0.7	41.2	0.5	41.4	0.5	41.5	0.2	41.6	0.2	41.7	0.2	41.9	0.5	41.9	0.0	42.1	0.5	42.2	0.2	42.3	0.2
1973	42.5	0.5	42.8	0.7	43.4	1.4	44.0	1.4	44.3	0.7	44.8	1.1	44.9	0.2	45.3	0.9	45.7	0.9	46.2	1.1	46.8	1.3	47.2	0.9
1974	48.4	2.5	48.8	0.8	50.4	3.3	53.1	5.4	53.9	1.5	54.3	0.7	56.5	4.1	60.1	6.4	60.6	0.8	61.3	1.2	61.7	0.7	61.8	0.2
1975	62.7	1.5	62.8	0.2	62.8	0.0	62.7	-0.2	62.7	0.0	62.7	0.0	62.8	0.2	62.8	0.0	62.9	0.2	63.1	0.3	63.2	0.2	63.9	1.1
1976	64.6	1.1	64.9	0.5	65.3	0.6	65.9	0.9	66.2	0.5	66.2	0.0	66.6	0.6	66.7	0.2	67.0	0.4	67.0	0.0	66.9	-0.1	67.0	0.1
1977	67.4	0.6	67.5	0.1	67.7	0.3	68.3	0.9	68.6	0.4	69.0	0.6	69.1	0.1	69.0	-0.1	69.1	0.1	69.2	0.1	69.1	-0.1	68.8	-0.4
1978	68.9	0.1	69.0	0.1	69.3	0.4	70.2	1.3	70.6	0.6	70.7	0.1	71.5	1.1	71.7	0.3	72.9	1.7	74.2	1.8	74.8	0.8	75.3	0.7
1979	76.0	0.9	76.7	0.9	78.0	1.7	79.0	1.3	79.5	0.6	79.7	0.3	80.4	0.9	81.9	1.9	82.1	0.2	83.8	2.1	84.6	1.0	85.4	0.9
1980	87.5	2.5	88.1	0.7	89.3	1.4	91.3	2.2	91.7	0.4	92.4	0.8	92.6	0.2	92.9	0.3	93.0	0.1	93.6	0.6	93.8	0.2	94.4	0.6
1981	95.5	1.2	96.8	1.4	97.7	0.9	98.3	0.6	98.8	0.5	99.3	0.5	99.6	0.3	100.2	0.6	100.6	0.4	100.9	0.3	100.9	0.0	100.9	0.0
1982	101.0	0.1	101.3	0.3	101.3	0.0	100.8	-0.5	100.6	-0.2	100.3	-0.3	99.8	-0.5	99.6	-0.2	99.4	-0.2	98.9	-0.5	98.6	-0.3	98.4	-0.2
1983	98.4	0.0	98.4	0.0	98.4	0.0	98.3	-0.1	98.3	0.0	98.5	0.2	98.9	0.4	99.2	0.3	100.0	0.8	100.7	0.7	101.4	0.7	101.5	0.1
1984	102.8	1.3	104.3	1.5	105.5	1.2	106.7	1.1	107.1	0.4	107.4	0.3	108.2	0.7	108.5	0.3	108.9	0.4	109.6	0.6	109.7	0.1	109.4	-0.3
1985	109.1	-0.3	108.7	-0.4	108.2	-0.5	107.8	-0.4	107.4	-0.4	107.0	-0.4	106.3	-0.7	106.0	-0.3	105.7	-0.3	105.6	-0.1	105.4	-0.2	105.4	0.0
1986	105.4	0.0	105.5	0.1	105.9	0.4	106.3	0.4	106.7	0.4	106.9	0.2	107.6	0.7	108.2	0.6	108.7	0.5	109.3	0.6	109.8	0.5	110.0	0.2
1987	111.3	1.2	112.4	1.0	112.6	0.2	113.2	0.5	113.1	-0.1	113.4	0.3	114.0	0.5	114.8	0.7	115.7	0.8	116.7	0.9	117.1	0.3	117.6	0.4
1988	119.9	2.0	120.5	0.5	121.6	0.9	123.1	1.2	124.1	0.8	124.6	0.4	125.8	1.0	126.4	0.5	127.6	0.9	128.1	0.4	128.3	0.2	128.5	0.2
1989	129.5	0.8	131.1	1.2	131.8	0.5	132.4	0.5	132.9	0.4	132.8	-0.1	132.5	-0.2	132.8	0.2	132.8	0.0	133.6	0.6	133.6	0.0	133.4	-0.1
1990	133.4	0.0	133.3	-0.1	133.2	-0.1	133.4	0.2	133.1	-0.2	132.8	-0.2	132.6	-0.2	132.5	-0.1	132.3	-0.2	132.7	0.3	132.8	0.1	132.8	0.0
1991	132.6	-0.2	132.4	-0.2	131.8	-0.5	130.8	-0.8	129.8	-0.8	129.1	-0.5	128.6	-0.4	128.1	-0.4	128.5	0.3	128.4	-0.1	128.6	0.2	128.5	-0.1

[Continued]

Pulp, Paper, and Products, ex. Building Paper
Producer Price Index
Base 1982 = 100
[Continued]

For 1947-2001. Columns headed % show percentile change in the index from the previous period for which an index is available.

Year	Jan Index	%	Feb Index	%	Mar Index	%	Apr Index	%	May Index	%	Jun Index	%	Jul Index	%	Aug Index	%	Sep Index	%	Oct Index	%	Nov Index	%	Dec Index	%
1992	128.5	0.0	128.6	0.1	128.6	0.0	129.4	0.6	129.5	0.1	129.4	-0.1	129.4	0.0	129.4	0.0	129.9	0.4	129.6	-0.2	129.2	-0.3	128.8	-0.3
1993	128.3	-0.4	128.0	-0.2	128.2	0.2	128.3	0.1	128.2	-0.1	128.0	-0.2	127.5	-0.4	127.0	-0.4	126.6	-0.3	126.9	0.2	126.9	0.0	126.9	0.0
1994	126.7	-0.2	127.0	0.2	127.3	0.2	127.9	0.5	128.6	0.5	130.5	1.5	132.3	1.4	134.2	1.4	136.3	1.6	139.5	2.3	142.0	1.8	144.4	1.7
1995	149.2	3.3	154.0	3.2	157.8	2.5	162.2	2.8	165.8	2.2	168.4	1.6	169.1	0.4	169.2	0.1	168.3	-0.5	166.9	-0.8	165.4	-0.9	164.2	-0.7
1996	161.6	-1.6	159.4	-1.4	155.1	-2.7	151.2	-2.5	148.4	-1.9	147.4	-0.7	146.6	-0.5	145.4	-0.8	145.2	-0.1	145.2	0.0	145.0	-0.1	145.4	0.3
1997	145.1	-0.2	144.1	-0.7	143.1	-0.7	142.1	-0.7	142.1	0.0	142.5	0.3	143.2	0.5	144.8	1.1	146.2	1.0	146.7	0.3	147.7	0.7	148.9	0.8
1998	149.5	0.4	149.5	0.0	149.1	-0.3	148.1	-0.7	148.0	-0.1	147.7	-0.2	147.7	0.0	147.2	-0.3	146.1	-0.7	144.8	-0.9	143.6	-0.8	143.2	-0.3
1999	142.7	-0.3	142.6	-0.1	143.5	0.6	144.3	0.6	145.2	0.6	146.8	1.1	148.5	1.2	149.7	0.8	151.2	1.0	152.8	1.1	153.5	0.5	153.9	0.3
2000	155.5	1.0	156.3	0.5	159.2	1.9	162.4	2.0	164.6	1.4	164.7	0.1	163.8	-0.5	162.4	-0.9	162.4	0.0	162.4	0.0	162.0	-0.2	161.3	-0.4
2001	160.5	-0.5	159.9	-0.4	159.6	-0.2	159.4	-0.1	158.3	-0.7	158.1	-0.1	157.5	-0.4	156.3	-0.8	156.3	0.0	155.5	-0.5	154.9	-0.4	155.2	0.2

Source: U.S. Department of Labor, Bureau of Labor Statistics, Division of Industry Prices and Price Indexes. n.e.c. stands for not elsewhere classified. - indicates no data collected for period or unavailable.

Building Paper & Building Board Mill Products
Producer Price Index
Base 1982 = 100

For 1947-2001. Columns headed % show percentile change in the index from the previous period for which an index is available.

Year	Jan Index	%	Feb Index	%	Mar Index	%	Apr Index	%	May Index	%	Jun Index	%	Jul Index	%	Aug Index	%	Sep Index	%	Oct Index	%	Nov Index	%	Dec Index	%
1947	29.0	-	29.0	0.0	29.1	0.3	29.1	0.0	29.1	0.0	29.1	0.0	29.1	0.0	29.0	-0.3	29.0	0.0	29.5	1.7	30.9	4.7	30.9	0.0
1948	31.1	0.6	31.4	1.0	31.4	0.0	31.4	0.0	31.8	1.3	33.1	4.1	33.4	0.9	33.4	0.0	33.4	0.0	33.4	0.0	33.4	0.0	33.4	0.0
1949	33.3	-0.3	33.2	-0.3	33.2	0.0	33.2	0.0	32.9	-0.9	32.8	-0.3	32.8	0.0	32.8	0.0	32.8	0.0	32.8	0.0	32.8	0.0	32.8	0.0
1950	32.8	0.0	32.8	0.0	32.8	0.0	32.8	0.0	32.8	0.0	33.6	2.4	34.4	2.4	34.4	0.0	34.7	0.9	35.6	2.6	35.6	0.0	35.9	0.8
1951	35.9	0.0	35.9	0.0	35.9	0.0	35.9	0.0	35.9	0.0	35.9	0.0	35.9	0.0	35.9	0.0	35.9	0.0	35.9	0.0	35.9	0.0	35.9	0.0
1952	35.9	0.0	35.9	0.0	35.9	0.0	36.0	0.3	36.6	1.7	36.6	0.0	36.6	0.0	36.6	0.0	36.6	0.0	36.6	0.0	37.3	1.9	37.3	0.0
1953	37.3	0.0	37.3	0.0	37.3	0.0	37.3	0.0	38.9	4.3	38.9	0.0	38.9	0.0	38.9	0.0	38.9	0.0	38.9	0.0	38.9	0.0	38.9	0.0
1954	40.4	3.9	40.4	0.0	40.4	0.0	40.4	0.0	40.4	0.0	40.4	0.0	40.4	0.0	40.3	-0.2	40.3	0.0	40.3	0.0	40.3	0.0	40.3	0.0
1955	40.3	0.0	40.9	1.5	41.0	0.2	41.0	0.0	41.0	0.0	41.0	0.0	41.0	0.0	41.9	2.2	41.9	0.0	42.2	0.7	42.2	0.0	42.2	0.0
1956	42.2	0.0	42.2	0.0	42.2	0.0	43.7	3.6	43.7	0.0	43.7	0.0	43.7	0.0	43.7	0.0	43.7	0.0	43.7	0.0	43.7	0.0	43.7	0.0
1957	44.6	2.1	44.6	0.0	44.6	0.0	44.8	0.4	44.8	0.0	44.8	0.0	44.8	0.0	44.8	0.0	44.8	0.0	44.8	0.0	44.8	0.0	44.8	0.0
1958	44.8	0.0	44.8	0.0	45.1	0.7	45.6	1.1	45.6	0.0	45.6	0.0	45.3	-0.7	45.3	0.0	45.3	0.0	45.3	0.0	45.3	0.0	45.4	0.2
1959	45.5	0.2	45.6	0.2	45.6	0.0	45.8	0.4	46.4	1.3	46.4	0.0	46.6	0.4	46.7	0.2	46.7	0.0	46.7	0.0	46.7	0.0	46.7	0.0
1960	46.7	0.0	46.7	0.0	46.3	-0.9	45.9	-0.9	45.9	0.0	45.9	0.0	45.6	-0.7	46.0	0.9	45.9	-0.2	46.1	0.4	46.0	-0.2	46.0	0.0
1961	46.0	0.0	46.2	0.4	46.1	-0.2	45.9	-0.4	45.7	-0.4	45.8	0.2	45.8	0.0	45.8	0.0	45.8	0.0	45.8	0.0	45.5	-0.7	45.3	-0.4
1962	44.8	-1.1	44.7	-0.2	44.6	-0.2	44.5	-0.2	44.4	-0.2	43.4	-2.3	43.8	0.9	44.1	0.7	44.1	0.0	43.7	-0.9	43.8	0.2	43.6	-0.5
1963	43.3	-0.7	43.3	0.0	42.7	-1.4	43.3	1.4	43.6	0.7	44.2	1.4	44.2	0.0	44.2	0.0	44.3	0.2	43.9	-0.9	43.1	-1.8	43.2	0.2
1964	43.2	0.0	43.0	-0.5	42.5	-1.2	42.4	-0.2	42.8	0.9	42.8	0.0	42.8	0.0	42.7	-0.2	42.8	0.2	42.8	0.0	42.6	-0.5	42.3	-0.7
1965	42.3	0.0	41.8	-1.2	41.8	0.0	41.8	0.0	42.0	0.5	42.0	0.0	42.3	0.7	42.3	0.0	42.3	0.0	42.5	0.5	42.3	-0.5	42.0	-0.7
1966	42.0	0.0	42.0	0.0	42.0	0.0	42.0	0.0	42.0	0.0	42.0	0.0	42.1	0.2	42.2	0.2	42.1	-0.2	42.3	0.5	42.3	0.0	42.1	-0.5
1967	42.0	-0.2	42.2	0.5	41.9	-0.7	41.9	0.0	41.7	-0.5	41.5	-0.5	41.5	0.0	41.3	-0.5	41.5	0.5	41.8	0.7	41.8	0.0	41.7	-0.2
1968	41.7	0.0	41.6	-0.2	41.7	0.2	41.8	0.2	41.9	0.2	41.8	-0.2	41.8	0.0	42.3	1.2	42.4	0.2	42.5	0.2	42.6	0.2	43.0	0.9
1969	44.2	2.8	44.6	0.9	45.2	1.3	45.6	0.9	45.8	0.4	45.1	-1.5	43.5	-3.5	43.2	-0.7	43.2	0.0	42.9	-0.7	42.9	0.0	42.7	-0.5
1970	42.3	-0.9	42.2	-0.2	42.1	-0.2	42.4	0.7	42.3	-0.2	42.3	0.0	42.2	-0.2	42.1	-0.2	42.0	-0.2	42.0	0.0	42.0	0.0	41.8	-0.5
1971	41.7	-0.2	41.7	0.0	42.2	1.2	42.5	0.7	42.9	0.9	43.2	0.7	43.2	0.0	43.5	0.7	43.5	0.0	43.6	0.2	43.6	0.0	43.6	0.0
1972	43.7	0.2	43.7	0.0	44.1	0.9	44.3	0.5	44.5	0.5	44.5	0.0	44.6	0.2	44.7	0.2	44.8	0.2	44.8	0.0	44.8	0.0	44.8	0.0
1973	44.7	-0.2	45.1	0.9	45.3	0.4	45.6	0.7	46.3	1.5	46.7	0.9	46.8	0.2	47.1	0.6	48.4	2.8	49.2	1.7	49.6	0.8	50.2	1.2
1974	50.8	1.2	50.9	0.2	51.5	1.2	51.6	0.2	52.4	1.6	52.2	-0.4	51.9	-0.6	52.2	0.6	52.3	0.2	51.8	-1.0	50.5	-2.5	50.6	0.2
1975	51.8	2.4	51.9	0.2	51.6	-0.6	51.5	-0.2	52.5	1.9	52.7	0.4	53.2	0.9	53.3	0.2	53.8	0.9	54.8	1.9	54.9	0.2	55.0	0.2
1976	54.8	-0.4	55.6	1.5	57.2	2.9	56.9	-0.5	56.9	0.0	58.3	2.5	59.0	1.2	58.7	-0.5	59.2	0.9	58.9	-0.5	59.4	0.8	60.2	1.3
1977	60.6	0.7	60.3	-0.5	60.9	1.0	62.1	2.0	63.2	1.8	64.2	1.6	65.9	2.6	67.8	2.9	69.6	2.7	70.5	1.3	70.3	-0.3	71.3	1.4
1978	73.1	2.5	75.2	2.9	77.9	3.6	78.8	1.2	79.7	1.1	80.3	0.8	80.6	0.4	79.3	-1.6	78.1	-1.5	79.1	1.3	78.8	-0.4	77.9	-1.1
1979	76.9	-1.3	76.7	-0.3	76.2	-0.7	76.6	0.5	76.5	-0.1	75.5	-1.3	74.3	-1.6	74.8	0.7	76.3	2.0	76.6	0.4	76.7	0.1	77.1	0.5
1980	77.7	0.8	80.0	3.0	83.0	3.8	84.0	1.2	86.4	2.9	87.2	0.9	88.4	1.4	87.8	-0.7	87.8	0.0	88.8	1.1	90.4	1.8	91.7	1.4
1981	91.7	0.0	94.3	2.8	95.2	1.0	97.1	2.0	99.1	2.1	99.1	0.0	98.3	-0.8	97.8	-0.5	97.8	0.0	97.4	-0.4	96.9	-0.5	96.2	-0.7
1982	97.6	1.5	96.6	-1.0	100.1	3.6	98.7	-1.4	100.3	1.6	100.2	-0.1	100.1	-0.1	102.1	2.0	101.6	-0.5	101.1	-0.5	100.6	-0.5	101.1	0.5
1983	100.7	-0.4	100.8	0.1	102.0	1.2	103.1	1.1	104.1	1.0	106.8	2.6	107.0	0.2	105.3	-1.6	105.5	0.2	106.3	0.8	106.4	0.1	104.6	-1.7
1984	105.2	0.6	106.5	1.2	108.0	1.4	111.0	2.8	110.7	-0.3	110.7	0.0	109.8	-0.8	108.5	-1.2	108.3	-0.2	107.6	-0.6	105.9	-1.6	105.8	-0.1
1985	106.6	0.8	107.0	0.4	107.0	0.0	107.5	0.5	108.0	0.5	108.5	0.5	108.5	0.0	108.0	-0.5	108.6	0.6	106.5	-1.9	106.4	-0.1	105.9	-0.5
1986	105.8	-0.1	106.4	0.6	107.4	0.9	108.9	1.4	109.6	0.6	109.6	0.0	109.5	-0.1	109.5	0.0	109.7	0.2	110.7	0.9	109.7	-0.9	109.4	-0.3
1987	109.6	0.2	109.3	-0.3	109.2	-0.1	109.1	-0.1	109.8	0.6	110.2	0.4	111.1	0.8	112.2	1.0	113.2	0.9	113.8	0.5	113.4	-0.4	113.7	0.3
1988	113.7	0.0	114.0	0.3	113.1	-0.8	113.3	0.2	113.4	0.1	114.2	0.7	113.9	-0.3	112.7	-1.1	112.5	-0.2	112.5	0.0	112.7	0.2	113.3	0.5
1989	112.9	-0.4	113.8	0.8	114.2	0.4	115.1	0.8	115.5	0.3	115.8	0.3	116.4	0.5	116.2	-0.2	116.3	0.1	116.6	0.3	117.0	0.3	116.9	-0.1
1990	116.6	-0.3	116.0	-0.5	115.5	-0.4	113.7	-1.6	113.4	-0.3	111.9	-1.3	111.2	-0.6	110.3	-0.8	109.8	-0.5	109.4	-0.4	109.1	-0.3	108.9	-0.2
1991	109.3	0.4	109.8	0.5	111.3	1.4	112.7	1.3	113.5	0.7	113.4	-0.1	114.6	1.1	112.8	-1.6	112.2	-0.5	110.9	-1.2	110.6	-0.3	110.9	0.3

[Continued]

Building Paper & Building Board Mill Products
Producer Price Index
Base 1982 = 100
[Continued]

For 1947-2001. Columns headed % show percentile change in the index from the previous period for which an index is available.

Year	Jan Index	%	Feb Index	%	Mar Index	%	Apr Index	%	May Index	%	Jun Index	%	Jul Index	%	Aug Index	%	Sep Index	%	Oct Index	%	Nov Index	%	Dec Index	%
1992	112.5	1.4	117.1	4.1	119.2	1.8	118.5	-0.6	119.1	0.5	118.9	-0.2	118.8	-0.1	120.0	1.0	123.7	3.1	123.5	-0.2	121.8	-1.4	121.7	-0.1
1993	124.9	2.6	129.0	3.3	133.9	3.8	135.4	1.1	133.8	-1.2	132.0	-1.3	131.2	-0.6	131.6	0.3	134.7	2.4	133.8	-0.7	135.1	1.0	137.5	1.8
1994	138.7	0.9	139.2	0.4	140.4	0.9	140.9	0.4	142.3	1.0	142.9	0.4	143.2	0.2	146.0	2.0	148.6	1.8	146.9	-1.1	149.8	2.0	149.6	-0.1
1995	147.3	-1.5	148.0	0.5	147.3	-0.5	146.6	-0.5	145.4	-0.8	141.3	-2.8	141.4	0.1	142.3	0.6	145.8	2.5	146.3	0.3	145.5	-0.5	141.9	-2.5
1996	138.5	-2.4	138.2	-0.2	136.3	-1.4	136.2	-0.1	137.9	1.2	135.9	-1.5	137.4	1.1	137.3	-0.1	140.5	2.3	138.7	-1.3	136.2	-1.8	133.7	-1.8
1997	132.4	-1.0	130.9	-1.1	130.9	0.0	129.1	-1.4	128.1	-0.8	128.7	0.5	127.4	-1.0	127.0	-0.3	128.4	1.1	127.1	-1.0	135.2	6.4	134.6	-0.4
1998	127.3	-5.4	128.6	1.0	128.2	-0.3	131.0	2.2	132.0	0.8	131.6	-0.3	136.2	3.5	141.9	4.2	142.8	0.6	134.6	-5.7	131.3	-2.5	129.3	-1.5
1999	131.5	1.7	131.1	-0.3	137.8	5.1	138.3	0.4	141.6	2.4	145.9	3.0	149.6	2.5	150.5	0.6	146.5	-2.7	142.7	-2.6	141.2	-1.1	142.6	1.0
2000	142.7	0.1	144.3	1.1	147.0	1.9	148.7	1.2	144.7	-2.7	142.0	-1.9	137.9	-2.9	133.6	-3.1	132.3	-1.0	131.5	-0.6	131.3	-0.2	129.3	-1.5
2001	126.6	-2.1	126.4	-0.2	127.1	0.6	127.5	0.3	135.9	6.6	136.6	0.5	132.5	-3.0	131.6	-0.7	129.4	-1.7	125.5	-3.0	122.3	-2.5	125.5	2.6

Source: U.S. Department of Labor, Bureau of Labor Statistics, Division of Industry Prices and Price Indexes. n.e.c. stands for not elsewhere classified. - indicates no data collected for period or unavailable.

Publications, Printed Matter & Printing Materials
Producer Price Index
Base 1982 = 100

For 1980-2001. Columns headed % show percentile change in the index from the previous period for which an index is available.

Year	Jan Index	%	Feb Index	%	Mar Index	%	Apr Index	%	May Index	%	Jun Index	%	Jul Index	%	Aug Index	%	Sep Index	%	Oct Index	%	Nov Index	%	Dec Index	%
1980	-	-	-	-	-	-	-	-	-	-	-	-	-	-	-	-	-	-	-	-	-	-	84.5	-
1981	88.5	4.7	89.1	0.7	89.5	0.4	90.5	1.1	90.5	0.0	90.6	0.1	91.6	1.1	91.8	0.2	92.7	1.0	93.3	0.6	94.1	0.9	94.5	0.4
1982	97.2	2.9	97.5	0.3	98.2	0.7	99.3	1.1	100.1	0.8	100.2	0.1	100.4	0.2	100.6	0.2	100.9	0.3	101.5	0.6	101.7	0.2	102.4	0.7
1983	104.4	2.0	104.7	0.3	105.1	0.4	105.5	0.4	105.8	0.3	106.2	0.4	106.4	0.2	106.8	0.4	106.9	0.1	107.8	0.8	108.1	0.3	108.3	0.2
1984	110.5	2.0	111.1	0.5	111.4	0.3	111.8	0.4	112.3	0.4	112.6	0.3	112.8	0.2	113.6	0.7	113.7	0.1	113.9	0.2	114.4	0.4	114.7	0.3
1985	116.8	1.8	117.4	0.5	118.0	0.5	118.2	0.2	118.3	0.1	118.5	0.2	118.8	0.3	119.2	0.3	119.2	0.0	119.8	0.5	120.0	0.2	120.0	0.0
1986	122.0	1.7	122.2	0.2	122.1	-0.1	122.7	0.5	122.9	0.2	123.0	0.1	123.2	0.2	123.4	0.2	123.9	0.4	124.4	0.4	124.7	0.2	124.8	0.1
1987	126.4	1.3	127.0	0.5	127.3	0.2	127.4	0.1	127.6	0.2	127.8	0.2	128.0	0.2	128.4	0.3	128.8	0.3	129.5	0.5	129.4	-0.1	129.6	0.2
1988	132.2	2.0	132.8	0.5	133.3	0.4	133.6	0.2	134.0	0.3	134.3	0.2	135.1	0.6	135.2	0.1	135.6	0.3	136.5	0.7	136.9	0.3	137.3	0.3
1989	139.7	1.7	140.5	0.6	140.9	0.3	141.3	0.3	141.5	0.1	142.0	0.4	142.4	0.3	142.9	0.4	143.3	0.3	143.5	0.1	143.8	0.2	143.9	0.1
1990	146.0	1.5	146.6	0.4	147.0	0.3	147.4	0.3	148.0	0.4	148.0	0.0	148.4	0.3	148.7	0.2	149.3	0.4	150.2	0.6	150.7	0.3	150.9	0.1
1991	153.5	1.7	154.1	0.4	154.5	0.3	154.4	-0.1	154.9	0.3	155.0	0.1	154.7	-0.2	155.0	0.2	154.9	-0.1	155.5	0.4	155.8	0.2	155.7	-0.1
1992	158.4	1.7	158.3	-0.1	158.7	0.3	159.0	0.2	159.4	0.3	159.2	-0.1	159.5	0.2	159.8	0.2	160.1	0.2	161.0	0.6	161.0	0.0	161.3	0.2
1993	163.8	1.5	164.3	0.3	164.3	0.0	164.8	0.3	164.9	0.1	164.2	-0.4	164.5	0.2	165.1	0.4	165.2	0.1	166.0	0.5	165.9	-0.1	166.3	0.2
1994	168.0	1.0	168.1	0.1	168.5	0.2	168.5	0.0	169.0	0.3	169.1	0.1	169.3	0.1	169.6	0.2	170.3	0.4	170.8	0.3	171.8	0.6	172.6	0.5
1995	175.3	1.6	176.3	0.6	177.0	0.4	177.9	0.5	178.6	0.4	179.8	0.7	180.8	0.6	181.1	0.2	181.6	0.3	182.7	0.6	183.8	0.6	184.0	0.1
1996	185.7	0.9	186.1	0.2	186.1	0.0	186.4	0.2	186.7	0.2	186.8	0.1	186.5	-0.2	186.8	0.2	187.5	0.4	187.7	0.1	188.1	0.2	188.3	0.1
1997	189.5	0.6	189.5	0.0	189.3	-0.1	189.9	0.3	189.6	-0.2	189.8	0.1	190.1	0.2	190.3	0.1	190.7	0.2	192.0	0.7	192.4	0.2	192.9	0.3
1998	194.9	1.0	194.6	-0.2	194.7	0.1	195.8	0.6	195.8	0.0	195.5	-0.2	195.6	0.1	195.6	0.0	196.1	0.3	196.8	0.4	197.1	0.2	197.3	0.1
1999	198.3	0.5	198.5	0.1	199.0	0.3	199.1	0.1	199.3	0.1	199.2	-0.1	199.3	0.1	199.6	0.2	200.0	0.2	200.5	0.3	201.1	0.3	201.2	0.0
2000	202.4	0.6	202.9	0.2	203.3	0.2	204.3	0.5	204.3	0.0	205.6	0.6	205.8	0.1	206.3	0.2	206.2	-0.0	207.6	0.7	207.8	0.1	208.2	0.2
2001	210.2	1.0	210.7	0.2	211.3	0.3	211.9	0.3	212.0	0.0	211.7	-0.1	211.8	0.0	212.0	0.1	212.0	0.0	212.2	0.1	212.7	0.2	212.6	-0.0

Source: U.S. Department of Labor, Bureau of Labor Statistics, Division of Industry Prices and Price Indexes. n.e.c. stands for not elsewhere classified. - indicates no data collected for period or unavailable.

METALS AND METAL PRODUCTS
Producer Price Index
Base 1982 = 100

For 1926-2001. Columns headed % show percentile change in the index from the previous period for which an index is available.

Year	Jan Index	%	Feb Index	%	Mar Index	%	Apr Index	%	May Index	%	Jun Index	%	Jul Index	%	Aug Index	%	Sep Index	%	Oct Index	%	Nov Index	%	Dec Index	%
1926	13.9	-	13.8	-0.7	13.8	0.0	13.7	-0.7	13.6	-0.7	13.6	0.0	13.6	0.0	13.7	0.7	13.8	0.7	13.8	0.0	13.7	-0.7	13.7	0.0
1927	13.2	-3.6	13.0	-1.5	13.0	0.0	13.0	0.0	12.9	-0.8	12.8	-0.8	12.8	0.0	12.9	0.8	12.8	-0.8	12.7	-0.8	12.7	0.0	12.7	0.0
1928	12.7	0.0	12.8	0.8	12.8	0.0	12.8	0.0	12.8	0.0	12.8	0.0	12.8	0.0	12.8	0.0	12.9	0.8	13.0	0.8	13.1	0.8	13.1	0.0
1929	13.2	0.8	13.3	0.8	13.7	3.0	13.6	-0.7	13.4	-1.5	13.4	0.0	13.3	-0.7	13.3	0.0	13.3	0.0	13.3	0.0	13.2	-0.8	13.1	-0.8
1930	12.9	-1.5	12.8	-0.8	12.8	0.0	12.5	-2.3	12.2	-2.4	11.9	-2.5	11.7	-1.7	11.6	-0.9	11.6	0.0	11.4	-1.7	11.4	0.0	11.4	0.0
1931	11.2	-1.8	11.2	0.0	11.2	0.0	11.1	-0.9	10.9	-1.8	10.8	-0.9	10.7	-0.9	10.6	-0.9	10.6	0.0	10.4	-1.9	10.4	0.0	10.3	-1.0
1932	10.2	-1.0	10.0	-2.0	9.9	-1.0	9.9	0.0	9.9	0.0	9.9	0.0	9.6	-3.0	9.8	2.1	10.0	2.0	10.1	1.0	9.9	-2.0	9.8	-1.0
1933	9.7	-1.0	9.5	-2.1	9.5	0.0	9.5	0.0	9.7	2.1	10.0	3.1	10.3	3.0	10.4	1.0	10.6	1.9	10.8	1.9	10.7	-0.9	10.9	1.9
1934	10.9	0.0	11.1	1.8	11.2	0.9	11.3	0.9	11.6	2.7	11.4	-1.7	11.2	-1.8	11.2	0.0	11.2	0.0	11.1	-0.9	11.1	0.0	11.1	0.0
1935	11.1	0.0	11.1	0.0	11.1	0.0	11.1	0.0	11.2	0.9	11.2	0.0	11.2	0.0	11.2	0.0	11.2	0.0	11.3	0.9	11.3	0.0	11.3	0.0
1936	11.3	0.0	11.3	0.0	11.2	-0.9	11.2	0.0	11.2	0.0	11.2	0.0	11.4	1.8	11.4	0.0	11.5	0.9	11.6	0.9	11.7	0.9	12.0	2.6
1937	12.3	2.5	12.4	0.8	13.4	8.1	13.5	0.7	13.3	-1.5	13.3	0.0	13.3	0.0	13.4	0.8	13.3	-0.7	13.1	-1.5	12.8	-2.3	12.7	-0.8
1938	12.8	0.8	12.6	-1.6	12.6	0.0	12.7	0.8	12.8	0.8	12.6	-1.6	12.4	-1.6	12.5	0.8	12.5	0.0	12.5	0.0	12.6	0.8	12.5	-0.8
1939	12.5	0.0	12.5	0.0	12.5	0.0	12.4	-0.8	12.3	-0.8	12.3	0.0	12.3	0.0	12.3	0.0	12.6	2.4	12.7	0.8	12.7	0.0	12.7	0.0
1940	12.7	0.0	12.6	-0.8	12.6	0.0	12.4	-1.6	12.4	0.0	12.4	0.0	12.4	0.0	12.4	0.0	12.5	0.8	12.6	0.8	12.6	0.0	12.6	0.0
1941	12.6	0.0	12.6	0.0	12.7	0.8	12.7	0.0	12.7	0.0	12.8	0.8	12.8	0.0	12.8	0.0	12.8	0.0	12.8	0.0	12.9	0.8	12.9	0.0
1942	12.9	0.0	12.9	0.0	13.0	0.8	13.0	0.0	13.0	0.0	13.0	0.0	12.9	-0.8	12.9	0.0	13.0	0.8	13.0	0.0	13.0	0.0	12.9	-0.8
1943	12.9	0.0	12.9	0.0	12.9	0.0	12.9	0.0	12.9	0.0	13.0	0.8	12.9	-0.8	12.9	0.0	12.9	0.0	12.9	0.0	12.9	0.0	12.9	0.0
1944	12.9	0.0	12.9	0.0	13.0	0.8	13.0	0.0	12.9	-0.8	12.9	0.0	12.9	0.0	12.9	0.0	12.9	0.0	12.9	0.0	12.9	0.0	12.9	0.0
1945	13.0	0.8	13.0	0.0	13.0	0.0	13.0	0.0	13.0	0.0	13.1	0.8	13.1	0.0	13.1	0.0	13.2	0.8	13.2	0.0	13.3	0.8	13.3	0.0
1946	13.3	0.0	13.5	1.5	13.9	3.0	14.0	0.7	14.1	0.7	14.7	4.3	15.0	2.0	15.1	0.7	15.1	0.0	15.2	0.7	15.7	3.3	16.4	4.5
1947	17.5	6.7	17.6	0.6	17.9	1.7	18.0	0.6	17.8	-1.1	17.9	0.6	18.1	1.1	18.5	2.2	18.6	0.5	18.7	0.5	18.8	0.5	18.9	0.5
1948	19.3	2.1	19.5	1.0	19.7	1.0	20.1	2.0	20.0	-0.5	20.1	0.5	20.5	2.0	21.6	5.4	21.8	0.9	21.9	0.5	22.0	0.5	22.1	0.5
1949	22.2	0.5	21.9	-1.4	21.7	-0.9	21.1	-2.8	20.6	-2.4	20.3	-1.5	20.3	0.0	20.4	0.5	20.5	0.5	20.5	0.0	20.6	0.5	20.6	0.0
1950	20.8	1.0	20.9	0.5	20.9	0.0	21.0	0.5	21.3	1.4	21.7	1.9	21.8	0.5	22.1	1.4	22.6	2.3	23.1	2.2	23.5	1.7	24.3	3.4
1951	24.7	1.6	24.7	0.0	24.6	-0.4	24.6	0.0	24.6	0.0	24.4	-0.8	24.4	0.0	24.3	-0.4	24.3	0.0	24.4	0.4	24.4	0.0	24.4	0.0
1952	24.4	0.0	24.4	0.0	24.4	0.0	24.4	0.0	24.3	-0.4	24.1	-0.8	24.3	0.8	24.7	1.6	24.8	0.4	24.7	-0.4	24.7	0.0	24.7	0.0
1953	24.7	0.0	24.8	0.4	25.0	0.8	24.9	-0.4	25.0	0.4	25.3	1.2	25.8	2.0	25.8	0.0	25.6	-0.8	25.5	-0.4	25.5	0.0	25.4	-0.4
1954	25.4	0.0	25.2	-0.8	25.2	0.0	25.3	0.4	25.3	0.0	25.3	0.0	25.5	0.8	25.6	0.4	25.7	0.4	25.9	0.8	25.9	0.0	25.9	0.0
1955	25.9	0.0	26.2	1.2	26.3	0.4	26.5	0.8	26.4	-0.4	26.4	0.0	27.3	3.4	27.8	1.8	28.3	1.8	28.4	0.4	28.5	0.4	28.7	0.7
1956	28.9	0.7	28.9	0.0	29.2	1.0	29.4	0.7	29.2	-0.7	29.1	-0.3	28.9	-0.7	29.9	3.5	30.3	1.3	30.3	0.0	30.3	0.0	30.4	0.3
1957	30.3	-0.3	30.2	-0.3	30.1	-0.3	29.9	-0.7	29.9	0.0	30.0	0.3	30.4	1.3	30.5	0.3	30.3	-0.7	30.1	-0.7	30.0	-0.3	30.0	0.0
1958	29.9	-0.3	29.9	0.0	29.9	0.0	29.6	-1.0	29.6	0.0	29.6	0.0	29.6	0.0	30.1	1.7	30.2	0.3	30.3	0.3	30.5	0.7	30.5	0.0
1959	30.5	0.0	30.6	0.3	30.6	0.0	30.5	-0.3	30.5	0.0	30.6	0.3	30.4	-0.7	30.5	0.3	30.6	0.3	30.8	0.7	31.1	1.0	30.9	-0.6
1960	31.0	0.3	30.9	-0.3	30.8	-0.3	30.8	0.0	30.7	-0.3	30.6	-0.3	30.6	0.0	30.6	0.0	30.6	0.0	30.5	-0.3	30.4	-0.3	30.3	-0.3
1961	30.3	0.0	30.4	0.3	30.4	0.0	30.4	0.0	30.5	0.3	30.5	0.0	30.5	0.0	30.6	0.3	30.6	0.0	30.5	-0.3	30.4	-0.3	30.4	0.0
1962	30.5	0.3	30.4	-0.3	30.4	0.0	30.3	-0.3	30.3	0.0	30.2	-0.3	30.2	0.0	30.2	0.0	30.2	0.0	30.1	-0.3	30.0	-0.3	30.0	0.0
1963	30.1	0.3	30.1	0.0	30.1	0.0	30.1	0.0	30.2	0.3	30.2	0.0	30.2	0.0	30.3	0.3	30.3	0.0	30.5	0.7	30.6	0.3	30.6	0.0
1964	30.8	0.7	30.8	0.0	30.9	0.3	30.9	0.0	30.9	0.0	30.9	0.0	31.0	0.3	31.2	0.6	31.2	0.0	31.4	0.6	31.6	0.6	31.7	0.3
1965	31.6	-0.3	31.6	0.0	31.7	0.3	31.8	0.3	32.0	0.6	32.0	0.0	32.0	0.0	32.1	0.3	32.1	0.0	32.2	0.3	32.3	0.3	32.3	0.0
1966	32.4	0.3	32.5	0.3	32.7	0.6	32.7	0.0	32.8	0.3	32.9	0.3	32.9	0.0	32.8	-0.3	32.8	0.0	32.9	0.3	33.0	0.3	33.0	0.0
1967	33.1	0.3	33.2	0.3	33.1	-0.3	33.0	-0.3	33.0	0.0	33.0	0.0	33.0	0.0	33.0	0.0	33.2	0.6	33.3	0.3	33.6	0.9	33.7	0.3
1968	34.0	0.9	34.3	0.9	34.4	0.3	34.2	-0.6	33.8	-1.2	33.8	0.0	33.7	-0.3	33.7	0.0	33.9	0.6	34.0	0.3	34.0	0.0	34.1	0.3
1969	34.6	1.5	34.8	0.6	35.0	0.6	35.2	0.6	35.5	0.9	35.7	0.6	35.9	0.6	36.4	1.4	36.8	1.1	37.0	0.5	37.1	0.3	37.5	1.1
1970	37.8	0.8	38.2	1.1	38.4	0.5	38.7	0.8	38.9	0.5	39.1	0.5	39.0	-0.3	38.9	-0.3	38.9	0.0	39.0	0.3	38.7	-0.8	38.5	-0.5

[Continued]

METALS AND METAL PRODUCTS
Producer Price Index
Base 1982 = 100

[Continued]

For 1926-2001. Columns headed % show percentile change in the index from the previous period for which an index is available.

Year	Jan Index	%	Feb Index	%	Mar Index	%	Apr Index	%	May Index	%	Jun Index	%	Jul Index	%	Aug Index	%	Sep Index	%	Oct Index	%	Nov Index	%	Dec Index	%
1971	38.6	0.3	38.5	-0.3	38.5	0.0	38.9	1.0	39.1	0.5	39.2	0.3	39.5	0.8	40.1	1.5	40.1	0.0	40.0	-0.2	40.0	0.0	39.9	-0.2
1972	40.3	1.0	40.6	0.7	40.9	0.7	40.9	0.0	41.0	0.2	41.0	0.0	40.9	-0.2	41.0	0.2	41.1	0.2	41.1	0.0	41.2	0.2	41.2	0.0
1973	41.6	1.0	42.1	1.2	42.8	1.7	43.3	1.2	43.7	0.9	43.9	0.5	44.0	0.2	44.3	0.7	44.5	0.5	45.1	1.3	45.9	1.8	47.0	2.4
1974	48.1	2.3	49.1	2.1	51.3	4.5	53.4	4.1	55.9	4.7	57.7	3.2	59.8	3.6	61.5	2.8	62.0	0.8	62.0	0.0	61.9	-0.2	61.2	-1.1
1975	61.5	0.5	61.8	0.5	61.7	-0.2	61.6	-0.2	61.4	-0.3	61.2	-0.3	60.8	-0.7	61.1	0.5	61.5	0.7	62.1	1.0	62.0	-0.2	62.0	0.0
1976	62.3	0.5	62.7	0.6	63.2	0.8	64.0	1.3	64.4	0.6	65.2	1.2	65.9	1.1	66.2	0.5	66.3	0.2	66.3	0.0	66.3	0.0	66.6	0.5
1977	67.0	0.6	67.4	0.6	68.5	1.6	69.0	0.7	69.1	0.1	68.9	-0.3	69.8	1.3	70.2	0.6	70.5	0.4	70.2	-0.4	70.3	0.1	70.7	0.6
1978	71.4	1.0	72.6	1.7	73.3	1.0	74.2	1.2	74.5	0.4	74.9	0.5	75.4	0.7	76.6	1.6	76.7	0.1	77.6	1.2	78.1	0.6	78.5	0.5
1979	80.2	2.2	82.0	2.2	83.5	1.8	84.9	1.7	84.9	0.0	85.6	0.8	86.5	1.1	86.8	0.3	87.4	0.7	89.4	2.3	89.9	0.6	90.7	0.9
1980	94.3	4.0	95.8	1.6	95.1	-0.7	94.3	-0.8	93.4	-1.0	93.5	0.1	93.7	0.2	94.5	0.9	95.3	0.8	96.8	1.6	96.5	-0.3	96.4	-0.1
1981	97.5	1.1	97.5	0.0	98.3	0.8	99.1	0.8	99.2	0.1	98.9	-0.3	100.1	1.2	100.8	0.7	101.1	0.3	101.2	0.1	100.9	-0.3	100.5	-0.4
1982	101.0	0.5	100.9	-0.1	100.4	-0.5	100.5	0.1	100.4	-0.1	99.2	-1.2	99.3	0.1	99.2	-0.1	100.0	0.8	100.0	0.0	99.6	-0.4	99.4	-0.2
1983	99.6	0.2	101.0	1.4	100.9	-0.1	101.0	0.1	101.5	0.5	101.5	0.0	101.9	0.4	102.2	0.3	103.0	0.8	103.1	0.1	103.1	0.0	103.4	0.3
1984	103.7	0.3	104.4	0.7	105.0	0.6	105.4	0.4	105.2	-0.2	105.2	0.0	104.8	-0.4	104.8	0.0	104.7	-0.1	104.8	0.1	104.9	0.1	104.6	-0.3
1985	104.4	-0.2	104.6	0.2	104.6	0.0	105.0	0.4	104.9	-0.1	104.4	-0.5	104.3	-0.1	104.3	0.0	104.2	-0.1	104.2	0.0	103.9	-0.3	103.9	0.0
1986	103.1	-0.8	103.2	0.1	103.2	0.0	103.1	-0.1	103.0	-0.1	103.0	0.0	102.9	-0.1	103.1	0.2	103.3	0.2	103.4	0.1	103.4	0.0	103.3	-0.1
1987	103.7	0.4	103.8	0.1	104.0	0.2	104.4	0.4	105.2	0.8	105.8	0.6	106.7	0.9	107.7	0.9	108.8	1.0	110.8	1.8	111.7	0.8	112.9	1.1
1988	114.4	1.3	114.7	0.3	115.4	0.6	116.9	1.3	117.4	0.4	118.0	0.5	119.2	1.0	119.8	0.5	120.2	0.3	121.4	1.0	122.8	1.2	124.0	1.0
1989	125.3	1.0	125.1	-0.2	125.6	0.4	125.6	0.0	125.2	-0.3	124.0	-1.0	123.0	-0.8	123.0	0.0	123.7	0.6	123.9	0.2	122.8	-0.9	121.7	-0.9
1990	121.7	0.0	120.9	-0.7	122.0	0.9	122.9	0.7	123.1	0.2	122.6	-0.4	122.9	0.2	124.2	1.1	124.6	0.3	124.5	-0.1	123.3	-1.0	122.4	-0.7
1991	122.4	0.0	121.9	-0.4	121.5	-0.3	121.3	-0.2	120.5	-0.7	119.7	-0.7	119.6	-0.1	119.5	-0.1	119.5	0.0	119.3	-0.2	118.9	-0.3	118.7	-0.2
1992	118.2	-0.4	118.9	0.6	119.4	0.4	119.6	0.2	119.5	-0.1	119.6	0.1	120.0	0.3	120.2	0.2	119.6	-0.5	118.8	-0.7	118.2	-0.5	118.5	0.3
1993	118.9	0.3	119.2	0.3	119.0	-0.2	118.7	-0.3	118.4	-0.3	118.9	0.4	119.5	0.5	119.5	0.0	119.5	0.0	119.4	-0.1	119.6	0.2	120.2	0.5
1994	120.7	0.4	121.7	0.8	122.3	0.5	122.5	0.2	122.7	0.2	123.5	0.7	124.7	1.0	125.5	0.6	126.5	0.8	127.3	0.6	129.4	1.6	130.6	0.9
1995	133.4	2.1	134.6	0.9	134.7	0.1	135.2	0.4	134.7	-0.4	134.8	0.1	135.2	0.3	135.5	0.2	135.0	-0.4	134.1	-0.7	133.7	-0.3	133.4	-0.2
1996	132.8	-0.4	131.8	-0.8	131.8	0.0	132.0	0.2	132.4	0.3	131.9	-0.4	130.4	-1.1	130.0	-0.3	130.0	0.0	129.4	-0.5	129.4	0.0	129.9	0.4
1997	131.0	0.8	131.6	0.5	132.2	0.5	131.8	-0.3	132.2	0.3	132.5	0.2	132.0	-0.4	132.2	0.2	132.0	-0.2	131.9	-0.1	131.3	-0.5	130.6	-0.5
1998	130.1	-0.4	130.0	-0.1	129.5	-0.4	129.6	0.1	129.2	-0.3	128.7	-0.4	127.9	-0.6	127.2	-0.5	126.7	-0.4	125.5	-0.9	124.8	-0.6	124.0	-0.6
1999	123.5	-0.4	123.4	-0.1	122.9	-0.4	123.1	0.2	123.8	0.6	123.8	0.0	124.4	0.5	124.9	0.4	125.5	0.5	126.3	0.6	126.6	0.2	127.3	0.6
2000	128.3	0.8	128.8	0.4	128.7	-0.1	128.6	-0.1	128.2	-0.3	127.9	-0.2	128.0	0.1	128.0	0.0	128.4	0.3	127.9	-0.4	126.8	-0.9	126.9	0.1
2001	126.9	0.0	126.6	-0.2	126.6	0.0	126.0	-0.5	126.1	0.1	125.8	-0.2	125.5	-0.2	125.0	-0.4	124.8	-0.2	124.2	-0.5	123.6	-0.5	123.5	-0.1

Source: U.S. Department of Labor, Bureau of Labor Statistics, Division of Industry Prices and Price Indexes. n.e.c. stands for not elsewhere classified. - indicates no data collected for period or unavailable.

Iron and Steel
Producer Price Index
Base 1982 = 100

For 1926-2001. Columns headed % show percentile change in the index from the previous period for which an index is available.

Year	Jan Index	%	Feb Index	%	Mar Index	%	Apr Index	%	May Index	%	Jun Index	%	Jul Index	%	Aug Index	%	Sep Index	%	Oct Index	%	Nov Index	%	Dec Index	%
1926	11.4	-	11.4	0.0	11.4	0.0	11.3	-0.9	11.3	0.0	11.2	-0.9	11.2	0.0	11.2	0.0	11.3	0.9	11.3	0.0	11.3	0.0	11.2	-0.9
1927	10.9	-2.7	10.7	-1.8	10.7	0.0	10.7	0.0	10.7	0.0	10.7	0.0	10.6	-0.9	10.6	0.0	10.6	0.0	10.5	-0.9	10.5	0.0	10.4	-1.0
1928	10.5	1.0	10.6	1.0	10.6	0.0	10.6	0.0	10.6	0.0	10.5	-0.9	10.5	0.0	10.5	0.0	10.5	0.0	10.6	1.0	10.6	0.0	10.7	0.9
1929	10.7	0.0	10.7	0.0	10.7	0.0	10.8	0.9	10.8	0.0	10.8	0.0	10.8	0.0	10.7	-0.9	10.7	0.0	10.7	0.0	10.6	-0.9	10.6	0.0
1930	10.4	-1.9	10.3	-1.0	10.3	0.0	10.2	-1.0	10.2	0.0	10.1	-1.0	10.0	-1.0	9.9	-1.0	9.9	0.0	9.9	0.0	9.8	-1.0	9.8	0.0
1931	9.6	-2.0	9.7	1.0	9.6	-1.0	9.5	-1.0	9.5	0.0	9.4	-1.1	9.4	0.0	9.3	-1.1	9.3	0.0	9.2	-1.1	9.2	0.0	9.1	-1.1
1932	9.0	-1.1	9.0	0.0	9.0	0.0	9.1	1.1	9.0	-1.1	9.0	0.0	8.7	-3.3	8.9	2.3	9.0	1.1	9.1	1.1	9.0	-1.1	8.9	-1.1
1933	8.8	-1.1	8.7	-1.1	8.6	-1.1	8.6	0.0	8.5	-1.2	8.6	1.2	8.8	2.3	8.9	1.1	9.1	2.2	9.3	2.2	9.2	-1.1	9.4	2.2
1934	9.4	0.0	9.7	3.2	9.8	1.0	9.9	1.0	10.2	3.0	10.0	-2.0	9.8	-2.0	9.8	0.0	9.8	0.0	9.7	-1.0	9.7	0.0	9.7	0.0
1935	9.7	0.0	9.7	0.0	9.7	0.0	9.7	0.0	9.8	1.0	9.9	1.0	9.8	-1.0	9.9	1.0	9.8	-1.0	9.8	0.0	9.8	0.0	9.8	0.0
1936	9.9	1.0	9.8	-1.0	9.8	0.0	9.8	0.0	9.7	-1.0	9.7	0.0	9.9	2.1	9.9	0.0	10.0	1.0	10.1	1.0	10.1	0.0	10.2	1.0
1937	10.4	2.0	10.4	0.0	11.0	5.8	11.2	1.8	11.2	0.0	11.2	0.0	11.3	0.9	11.3	0.0	11.3	0.0	11.2	-0.9	11.2	0.0	11.2	0.0
1938	11.2	0.0	11.2	0.0	11.2	0.0	11.3	0.9	11.5	1.8	11.4	-0.9	11.0	-3.5	11.0	0.0	11.0	0.0	10.9	-0.9	11.0	0.9	10.9	-0.9
1939	10.9	0.0	10.9	0.0	10.9	0.0	10.9	0.0	10.8	-0.9	10.7	-0.9	10.7	0.0	10.7	0.0	10.8	0.9	10.9	0.9	10.9	0.0	10.9	0.0
1940	10.9	0.0	10.9	0.0	10.9	0.0	10.6	-2.8	10.6	0.0	10.6	0.0	10.7	0.9	10.7	0.0	10.7	0.0	10.7	0.0	10.8	0.9	10.8	0.0
1941	10.8	0.0	10.8	0.0	10.8	0.0	10.8	0.0	10.9	0.9	10.9	0.0	10.9	0.0	11.0	0.9	11.0	0.0	11.0	0.0	11.0	0.0	11.0	0.0
1942	11.0	0.0	11.0	0.0	11.0	0.0	11.0	0.0	11.0	0.0	11.0	0.0	11.0	0.0	11.0	0.0	11.0	0.0	11.0	0.0	11.0	0.0	11.0	0.0
1943	11.0	0.0	11.0	0.0	11.0	0.0	11.0	0.0	11.0	0.0	11.0	0.0	11.0	0.0	11.0	0.0	11.0	0.0	11.0	0.0	11.0	0.0	11.0	0.0
1944	11.0	0.0	11.0	0.0	11.0	0.0	11.0	0.0	11.0	0.0	11.0	0.0	11.0	0.0	11.0	0.0	11.0	0.0	11.0	0.0	11.0	0.0	11.0	0.0
1945	11.1	0.9	11.1	0.0	11.1	0.0	11.1	0.0	11.1	0.0	11.2	0.9	11.2	0.0	11.2	0.0	11.2	0.0	11.3	0.9	11.3	0.0	11.4	0.9
1946	11.4	0.0	11.7	2.6	12.1	3.4	12.1	0.0	12.2	0.8	12.4	1.6	12.6	1.6	12.8	1.6	12.8	0.0	12.8	0.0	12.9	0.8	13.3	3.1
1947	14.4	8.3	14.5	0.7	14.7	1.4	14.7	0.0	14.4	-2.0	14.5	0.7	14.9	2.8	15.8	6.0	15.7	-0.6	15.9	1.3	15.9	0.0	16.0	0.6
1948	16.5	3.1	16.7	1.2	16.8	0.6	16.9	0.6	16.8	-0.6	16.8	0.0	17.2	2.4	18.5	7.6	18.5	0.0	18.6	0.5	18.7	0.5	18.8	0.5
1949	18.8	0.0	18.4	-2.1	18.3	-0.5	17.7	-3.3	17.4	-1.7	17.4	0.0	17.3	-0.6	17.4	0.6	17.7	1.7	17.8	0.6	17.9	0.6	18.1	1.1
1950	18.3	1.1	18.5	1.1	18.5	0.0	18.5	0.0	18.7	1.1	19.1	2.1	19.0	-0.5	19.2	1.1	19.3	0.5	19.4	0.5	19.6	1.0	20.6	5.1
1951	21.0	1.9	20.8	-1.0	20.7	-0.5	20.7	0.0	20.7	0.0	20.7	0.0	20.7	0.0	20.7	0.0	20.7	0.0	20.7	0.0	20.7	0.0	20.7	0.0
1952	20.7	0.0	20.8	0.5	20.8	0.0	20.7	-0.5	20.7	0.0	20.6	-0.5	20.6	0.0	21.4	3.9	21.5	0.5	21.4	-0.5	21.4	0.0	21.4	0.0
1953	21.4	0.0	21.5	0.5	21.5	0.0	21.5	0.0	21.7	0.9	22.0	1.4	22.9	4.1	22.9	0.0	22.7	-0.9	22.5	-0.9	22.5	0.0	22.4	-0.4
1954	22.2	-0.9	22.1	-0.5	22.0	-0.5	22.1	0.5	22.2	0.5	22.2	0.0	22.5	1.4	22.5	0.0	22.6	0.4	22.7	0.4	22.8	0.4	22.7	-0.4
1955	22.9	0.9	22.9	0.0	22.9	0.0	23.0	0.4	22.8	-0.9	22.9	0.4	24.1	5.2	24.4	1.2	24.4	0.0	24.5	0.4	24.6	0.4	24.8	0.8
1956	25.2	1.6	25.1	-0.4	25.2	0.4	25.4	0.8	25.4	0.0	25.2	-0.8	25.2	0.0	26.8	6.3	27.2	1.5	27.1	-0.4	27.4	1.1	27.5	0.4
1957	27.7	0.7	27.6	-0.4	27.6	0.0	27.3	-1.1	27.5	0.7	27.9	1.5	28.7	2.9	28.8	0.3	28.7	-0.3	28.3	-1.4	28.1	-0.7	28.1	0.0
1958	28.1	0.0	28.3	0.7	28.2	-0.4	28.1	-0.4	28.0	-0.4	28.1	0.4	28.1	0.0	28.9	2.8	28.9	0.0	28.9	0.0	29.0	0.3	28.9	-0.3
1959	29.0	0.3	29.1	0.3	29.0	-0.3	28.8	-0.7	28.7	-0.3	28.9	0.7	28.9	0.0	29.0	0.3	29.1	0.3	29.1	0.0	29.2	0.3	29.0	-0.7
1960	29.1	0.3	28.9	-0.7	28.7	-0.7	28.7	0.0	28.7	0.0	28.6	-0.3	28.6	0.0	28.6	0.0	28.6	0.0	28.4	-0.7	28.4	0.0	28.4	0.0
1961	28.5	0.4	28.6	0.4	28.7	0.3	28.8	0.3	28.7	-0.3	28.7	0.0	28.6	-0.3	28.7	0.3	28.8	0.3	28.7	-0.3	28.5	-0.7	28.5	0.0
1962	28.6	0.4	28.6	0.0	28.4	-0.7	28.3	-0.4	28.3	0.0	28.2	-0.4	28.2	0.0	28.2	0.0	28.2	0.0	28.1	-0.4	28.0	-0.4	28.1	0.4
1963	28.1	0.0	28.1	0.0	28.0	-0.4	28.1	0.4	28.3	0.7	28.2	-0.4	28.2	0.0	28.2	0.0	28.2	0.0	28.4	0.7	28.4	0.0	28.5	0.4
1964	28.5	0.0	28.5	0.0	28.5	0.0	28.5	0.0	28.6	0.4	28.6	0.0	28.7	0.3	28.8	0.3	28.6	-0.7	28.7	0.3	28.7	0.0	28.8	0.3
1965	28.9	0.3	28.8	-0.3	28.8	0.0	28.9	0.3	28.9	0.0	28.8	-0.3	28.9	0.3	28.9	0.0	28.8	-0.3	28.8	0.0	28.8	0.0	29.0	0.7
1966	29.1	0.3	29.1	0.0	29.1	0.0	29.1	0.0	29.0	-0.3	29.1	0.3	29.1	0.0	29.2	0.3	29.2	0.0	29.2	0.0	29.3	0.3	29.3	0.0
1967	29.4	0.3	29.4	0.0	29.5	0.3	29.4	-0.3	29.4	0.0	29.4	0.0	29.4	0.0	29.4	0.0	29.6	0.7	29.6	0.0	29.7	0.3	29.8	0.3
1968	30.1	1.0	30.1	0.0	30.0	-0.3	29.9	-0.3	29.9	0.0	29.9	0.0	29.9	0.0	29.9	0.0	30.4	1.7	30.4	0.0	30.2	-0.7	30.2	0.0
1969	30.6	1.3	30.7	0.3	30.9	0.7	31.0	0.3	31.3	1.0	31.4	0.3	31.6	0.6	32.1	1.6	32.2	0.3	32.4	0.6	32.4	0.0	32.5	0.3
1970	32.7	0.6	33.3	1.8	33.5	0.6	33.4	-0.3	33.9	1.5	34.3	1.2	34.3	0.0	34.2	-0.3	34.4	0.6	34.6	0.6	34.3	-0.9	34.3	0.0

[Continued]

Iron and Steel

Producer Price Index
Base 1982 = 100

[Continued]

For 1926-2001. Columns headed % show percentile change in the index from the previous period for which an index is available.

Year	Jan Index	%	Feb Index	%	Mar Index	%	Apr Index	%	May Index	%	Jun Index	%	Jul Index	%	Aug Index	%	Sep Index	%	Oct Index	%	Nov Index	%	Dec Index	%
1971	34.6	0.9	34.8	0.6	34.8	0.0	34.9	0.3	35.4	1.4	35.5	0.3	36.0	1.4	37.0	2.8	37.1	0.3	37.1	0.0	37.0	-0.3	37.0	0.0
1972	37.4	1.1	37.8	1.1	37.9	0.3	37.8	-0.3	37.8	0.0	37.8	0.0	37.8	0.0	37.9	0.3	38.0	0.3	38.0	0.0	38.1	0.3	38.2	0.3
1973	38.9	1.8	39.2	0.8	39.3	0.3	39.5	0.5	39.9	1.0	40.1	0.5	40.1	0.0	40.1	0.0	40.3	0.5	40.9	1.5	41.8	2.2	42.0	0.5
1974	42.7	1.7	43.9	2.8	46.5	5.9	48.6	4.5	49.9	2.7	52.5	5.2	56.2	7.0	57.7	2.7	58.4	1.2	58.7	0.5	58.9	0.3	58.0	-1.5
1975	58.8	1.4	59.1	0.5	59.2	0.2	59.3	0.2	59.2	-0.2	58.8	-0.7	58.2	-1.0	58.5	0.5	59.1	1.0	60.4	2.2	60.2	-0.3	60.3	0.2
1976	60.8	0.8	61.8	1.6	62.4	1.0	62.9	0.8	62.9	0.0	64.4	2.4	64.9	0.8	64.9	0.0	64.5	-0.6	64.5	0.0	64.6	0.2	65.7	1.7
1977	66.1	0.6	66.3	0.3	67.1	1.2	67.3	0.3	67.2	-0.1	66.9	-0.4	68.5	2.4	68.8	0.4	69.6	1.2	69.1	-0.7	68.9	-0.3	69.5	0.9
1978	70.2	1.0	72.2	2.8	73.0	1.1	74.3	1.8	74.3	0.0	74.5	0.3	74.9	0.5	76.3	1.9	76.3	0.0	76.7	0.5	77.2	0.7	77.6	0.5
1979	80.3	3.5	81.1	1.0	82.6	1.8	82.6	0.0	82.4	-0.2	83.5	1.3	84.6	1.3	84.4	-0.2	84.2	-0.2	85.3	1.3	86.1	0.9	86.4	0.3
1980	87.7	1.5	88.6	1.0	89.0	0.5	90.6	1.8	89.9	-0.8	89.5	-0.4	88.7	-0.9	89.3	0.7	89.8	0.6	91.6	2.0	92.2	0.7	93.3	1.2
1981	95.3	2.1	95.3	0.0	96.8	1.6	97.6	0.8	97.5	-0.1	97.4	-0.1	99.9	2.6	100.3	0.4	100.2	-0.1	100.7	0.5	100.3	-0.4	100.3	0.0
1982	101.2	0.9	101.1	-0.1	101.0	-0.1	101.1	0.1	100.7	-0.4	99.8	-0.9	99.5	-0.3	99.4	-0.1	99.3	-0.1	99.6	0.3	99.1	-0.5	98.2	-0.9
1983	98.3	0.1	100.3	2.0	100.8	0.5	100.7	-0.1	100.6	-0.1	100.7	0.1	100.9	0.2	101.2	0.3	102.7	1.5	102.8	0.1	103.1	0.3	103.5	0.4
1984	104.4	0.9	105.1	0.7	105.1	0.0	105.1	0.0	105.4	0.3	105.3	-0.1	105.4	0.1	105.4	0.0	105.6	0.2	105.7	0.1	105.5	-0.2	105.3	-0.2
1985	105.3	0.0	105.4	0.1	105.5	0.1	105.4	-0.1	105.0	-0.4	104.6	-0.4	104.5	-0.1	104.6	0.1	104.6	0.0	104.5	-0.1	104.1	-0.4	104.1	0.0
1986	101.0	-3.0	101.1	0.1	100.8	-0.3	101.0	0.2	101.2	0.2	101.1	-0.1	101.1	0.0	101.2	0.1	101.4	0.2	101.4	0.0	101.3	-0.1	101.3	0.0
1987	102.0	0.7	102.3	0.3	101.9	-0.4	101.9	0.0	102.2	0.3	102.5	0.3	103.1	0.6	103.7	0.6	105.4	1.6	109.5	3.9	110.4	0.8	109.9	-0.5
1988	110.9	0.9	113.0	1.9	113.6	0.5	114.8	1.1	115.0	0.2	114.9	-0.1	117.0	1.8	118.0	0.9	117.4	-0.5	118.3	0.8	117.6	-0.6	117.6	0.0
1989	119.7	1.8	120.6	0.8	120.7	0.1	120.8	0.1	120.6	-0.2	119.8	-0.7	119.0	-0.7	118.4	-0.5	118.1	-0.3	117.8	-0.3	116.9	-0.8	116.5	-0.3
1990	116.7	0.2	116.2	-0.4	116.5	0.3	117.1	0.5	117.9	0.7	117.4	-0.4	117.5	0.1	118.2	0.6	117.9	-0.3	117.5	-0.3	116.9	-0.5	116.8	-0.1
1991	117.0	0.2	116.6	-0.3	115.8	-0.7	115.4	-0.3	114.5	-0.8	113.5	-0.9	113.3	-0.2	113.0	-0.3	112.8	-0.2	112.4	-0.4	112.3	-0.1	112.3	0.0
1992	112.1	-0.2	112.3	0.2	112.7	0.4	112.3	-0.4	112.2	-0.1	111.4	-0.7	111.4	0.0	111.2	-0.2	111.0	-0.2	110.3	-0.6	110.1	-0.2	110.6	0.5
1993	111.9	1.2	113.1	1.1	113.4	0.3	113.5	0.1	114.2	0.6	115.6	1.2	116.5	0.8	116.7	0.2	117.3	0.5	119.0	1.4	119.9	0.8	120.8	0.8
1994	121.3	0.4	122.0	0.6	121.8	-0.2	121.4	-0.3	120.6	-0.7	118.8	-1.5	120.4	1.3	122.3	1.6	123.1	0.7	123.1	0.0	124.1	0.8	124.7	0.5
1995	127.2	2.0	128.4	0.9	129.1	0.5	129.8	0.5	129.9	0.1	129.7	-0.2	129.9	0.2	130.4	0.4	129.4	-0.8	128.4	-0.8	126.9	-1.2	126.6	-0.2
1996	127.0	0.3	126.3	-0.6	125.7	-0.5	125.9	0.2	126.3	0.3	126.2	-0.1	125.8	-0.3	126.2	0.3	126.4	0.2	125.5	-0.7	124.3	-1.0	124.2	-0.1
1997	125.5	1.0	126.6	0.9	126.2	-0.3	125.8	-0.3	126.0	0.2	126.1	0.1	126.7	0.5	126.8	0.1	126.8	0.0	127.1	0.2	127.6	0.4	127.1	-0.4
1998	127.0	-0.1	126.6	-0.3	125.7	-0.7	125.5	-0.2	125.3	-0.2	125.0	-0.2	124.2	-0.6	122.6	-1.3	120.5	-1.7	117.6	-2.4	115.6	-1.7	114.5	-1.0
1999	113.9	-0.5	113.8	-0.1	112.9	-0.8	112.8	-0.1	113.1	0.3	113.8	0.6	113.4	-0.4	114.0	0.5	113.9	-0.1	114.3	0.4	115.5	1.0	117.1	1.4
2000	118.3	1.0	118.2	-0.1	118.4	0.2	119.0	0.5	118.4	-0.5	117.6	-0.7	117.1	-0.4	116.2	-0.8	116.1	-0.1	114.7	-1.2	112.8	-1.7	112.4	-0.4
2001	112.1	-0.3	110.6	-1.3	110.6	0.0	110.2	-0.4	109.9	-0.3	109.7	-0.2	110.0	0.3	109.9	-0.1	109.9	0.0	108.6	-1.2	107.8	-0.7	106.8	-0.9

Source: U.S. Department of Labor, Bureau of Labor Statistics, Division of Industry Prices and Price Indexes. n.e.c. stands for not elsewhere classified. - indicates no data collected for period or unavailable.

Nonferrous Metals
Producer Price Index
Base 1982 = 100

For 1926-2001. Columns headed % show percentile change in the index from the previous period for which an index is available.

Year	Jan Index	%	Feb Index	%	Mar Index	%	Apr Index	%	May Index	%	Jun Index	%	Jul Index	%	Aug Index	%	Sep Index	%	Oct Index	%	Nov Index	%	Dec Index	%
1926	16.8	-	16.8	0.0	16.6	-1.2	16.2	-2.4	16.0	-1.2	16.1	0.6	16.5	2.5	16.8	1.8	16.8	0.0	16.6	-1.2	16.4	-1.2	16.0	-2.4
1927	15.7	-1.9	15.5	-1.3	15.8	1.9	15.5	-1.9	15.2	-1.9	15.0	-1.3	14.9	-0.7	15.4	3.4	15.1	-1.9	15.0	-0.7	15.1	0.7	15.4	2.0
1928	15.3	-0.6	15.1	-1.3	15.0	-0.7	15.2	1.3	15.3	0.7	15.4	0.7	15.4	0.0	15.4	0.0	15.6	1.3	15.9	1.9	16.2	1.9	16.2	0.0
1929	16.7	3.1	17.4	4.2	19.3	10.9	18.6	-3.6	17.4	-6.5	17.4	0.0	17.4	0.0	17.4	0.0	17.3	-0.6	17.3	0.0	17.0	-1.7	16.8	-1.2
1930	16.7	-0.6	16.7	0.0	16.4	-1.8	15.1	-7.9	13.5	-10.6	13.2	-2.2	12.4	-6.1	12.3	-0.8	12.1	-1.6	11.5	-5.0	11.6	0.9	11.8	1.7
1931	11.5	-2.5	11.3	-1.7	11.4	0.9	11.1	-2.6	10.4	-6.3	10.1	-2.9	10.1	0.0	9.9	-2.0	9.7	-2.0	9.1	-6.2	9.0	-1.1	8.9	-1.1
1932	9.1	2.2	8.7	-4.4	8.3	-4.6	8.1	-2.4	7.9	-2.5	7.9	0.0	7.7	-2.5	8.0	3.9	8.5	6.3	8.3	-2.4	8.1	-2.4	7.9	-2.5
1933	7.7	-2.5	7.6	-1.3	7.9	3.9	8.1	2.5	9.3	14.8	10.4	11.8	11.2	7.7	11.2	0.0	11.3	0.9	11.0	-2.7	11.2	1.8	11.0	-1.8
1934	10.9	-0.9	10.8	-0.9	10.9	0.9	11.2	2.8	11.2	0.0	11.3	0.9	11.3	0.0	11.3	0.0	11.3	0.0	11.2	-0.9	11.2	0.0	11.1	-0.9
1935	11.2	0.9	11.1	-0.9	11.1	0.0	11.2	0.9	11.4	1.8	11.4	0.0	10.9	-4.4	11.0	0.9	11.3	2.7	11.7	3.5	11.8	0.9	11.6	-1.7
1936	11.5	-0.9	11.5	0.0	11.5	0.0	11.6	0.9	11.7	0.9	11.5	-1.7	11.6	0.9	11.7	0.9	11.8	0.9	11.8	0.0	12.4	5.1	13.0	4.8
1937	14.0	7.7	14.8	5.7	16.7	12.8	16.0	-4.2	15.1	-5.6	15.1	0.0	15.3	1.3	15.4	0.7	15.3	-0.6	14.1	-7.8	12.9	-8.5	12.4	-3.9
1938	12.4	0.0	11.9	-4.0	11.8	-0.8	11.7	-0.8	11.3	-3.4	11.1	-1.8	11.8	6.3	12.0	1.7	12.1	0.8	12.6	4.1	12.8	1.6	12.7	-0.8
1939	12.6	-0.8	12.6	0.0	12.6	0.0	12.3	-2.4	12.1	-1.6	12.0	-0.8	12.1	0.8	12.3	1.7	14.0	13.8	14.1	0.7	14.0	-0.7	13.9	-0.7
1940	13.6	-2.2	13.0	-4.4	13.2	1.5	13.0	-1.5	13.2	1.5	13.4	1.5	13.4	0.0	13.0	-3.0	13.3	2.3	13.8	3.8	13.8	0.0	13.7	-0.7
1941	13.8	0.7	13.8	0.0	13.9	0.7	13.9	0.0	13.9	0.0	13.9	0.6	14.0	0.7	13.9	-0.7	13.9	0.0	13.9	0.0	14.0	0.7	14.0	0.0
1942	14.1	0.7	14.1	0.0	14.1	0.0	14.1	0.0	14.1	0.0	14.1	0.0	14.1	0.0	14.1	0.0	14.2	0.7	14.2	0.0	14.2	0.0	14.2	0.0
1943	14.2	0.0	14.2	0.0	14.2	0.0	14.2	0.0	14.2	0.0	14.2	0.0	14.2	0.0	14.2	0.0	14.2	0.0	14.2	0.0	14.2	0.0	14.2	0.0
1944	14.1	-0.7	14.1	0.0	14.1	0.0	14.1	0.0	14.1	0.0	14.1	0.0	14.1	0.0	14.1	0.0	14.1	0.0	14.1	0.0	14.1	0.0	14.1	0.0
1945	14.1	0.0	14.2	0.7	14.1	-0.7	14.1	0.0	14.1	0.0	14.1	0.0	14.1	0.0	14.1	0.0	14.1	0.0	14.1	0.0	14.1	0.0	14.1	0.0
1946	14.1	0.0	14.1	0.0	14.2	0.7	14.4	1.4	14.6	1.4	16.4	12.3	16.9	3.0	16.7	-1.2	16.7	0.0	16.8	0.6	19.5	16.1	21.3	9.2
1947	21.5	0.9	21.7	0.9	22.6	4.1	22.8	0.9	22.8	0.0	22.7	-0.4	22.5	-0.9	22.5	0.0	22.5	0.0	22.5	0.0	22.5	0.0	22.8	1.3
1948	23.0	0.9	23.2	0.9	23.2	0.0	23.6	1.7	23.6	0.0	23.9	1.3	24.6	2.9	26.1	6.1	26.1	0.0	26.3	0.8	27.0	2.7	27.1	0.4
1949	27.0	-0.4	26.8	-0.7	26.1	-2.6	24.4	-6.5	22.4	-8.2	21.2	-5.4	21.4	0.9	21.9	2.3	21.9	0.0	21.5	-1.8	21.7	0.9	21.4	-1.4
1950	21.4	0.0	21.3	-0.5	21.2	-0.5	21.4	0.9	22.4	4.7	23.9	6.7	24.1	0.8	24.9	3.3	26.4	6.0	27.9	5.7	28.9	3.6	29.1	0.7
1951	29.6	1.7	29.7	0.3	29.4	-1.0	29.5	0.3	29.4	-0.3	28.9	-1.7	28.5	-1.4	28.5	0.0	28.6	0.4	29.1	1.7	29.1	0.0	29.1	0.0
1952	29.1	0.0	29.3	0.7	29.3	0.0	29.3	0.0	28.6	-2.4	28.1	-1.7	29.1	3.6	29.2	0.3	29.2	0.0	28.8	-1.4	28.8	0.0	28.7	-0.3
1953	28.8	0.3	29.2	1.4	30.8	5.5	30.1	-2.3	29.7	-1.3	29.9	0.7	29.7	-0.7	29.2	-1.7	28.8	-1.4	28.6	-0.7	28.7	0.3	28.6	-0.3
1954	28.5	-0.3	28.1	-1.4	28.4	1.1	28.9	1.8	29.0	0.3	29.0	0.0	29.1	0.3	29.3	0.7	29.6	1.0	29.9	1.0	29.9	0.0	29.9	0.0
1955	30.0	0.3	31.4	4.7	31.5	0.3	32.4	2.9	32.3	-0.3	32.3	0.0	32.7	1.2	34.0	4.0	36.2	6.5	36.1	-0.3	36.1	0.0	36.6	1.4
1956	36.8	0.5	36.9	0.3	38.0	3.0	38.3	0.8	37.5	-2.1	37.1	-1.1	35.8	-3.5	36.5	2.0	36.3	-0.5	36.2	-0.3	35.1	-3.0	35.1	0.0
1957	34.9	-0.6	34.1	-2.3	33.6	-1.5	33.4	-0.6	32.8	-1.8	32.4	-1.2	31.5	-2.8	31.6	0.3	30.9	-2.2	30.5	-1.3	30.7	0.7	30.6	-0.3
1958	30.2	-1.3	30.0	-0.7	29.8	-0.7	29.1	-2.3	29.1	0.0	29.3	0.7	29.3	0.0	29.6	1.0	29.9	1.0	30.7	2.7	31.4	2.3	31.3	-0.3
1959	31.3	0.0	31.5	0.6	31.9	1.3	31.6	-0.9	31.9	0.9	31.9	0.0	31.4	-1.6	31.4	0.0	31.9	1.6	32.2	0.9	33.1	2.8	33.0	-0.3
1960	33.5	1.5	33.5	0.0	33.0	-1.5	32.9	-0.3	32.9	0.0	32.6	-0.9	32.5	-0.3	32.5	0.0	32.5	0.0	32.2	-0.9	31.8	-1.2	31.4	-1.3
1961	31.0	-1.3	31.0	0.0	31.0	0.0	31.1	0.3	31.5	1.3	31.7	0.6	31.9	0.6	31.9	0.0	32.0	0.3	31.7	-0.9	31.4	-0.9	31.6	0.6
1962	31.5	-0.3	31.5	0.0	31.4	-0.3	31.3	-0.3	31.3	0.0	31.1	-0.6	31.1	0.0	31.1	0.0	31.0	-0.3	30.7	-1.0	30.8	0.3	30.7	-0.3
1963	30.8	0.3	30.8	0.0	30.8	0.0	30.8	0.0	31.0	0.6	31.0	0.0	31.1	0.3	31.2	0.3	31.3	0.3	31.3	0.0	31.4	0.3	31.7	1.0
1964	31.8	0.3	31.9	0.3	32.2	0.9	32.6	1.2	32.6	0.0	32.6	0.0	32.8	0.6	33.2	1.2	33.6	1.2	34.6	3.0	35.1	1.4	35.5	1.1
1965	35.0	-1.4	35.1	0.3	35.2	0.3	35.6	1.1	36.2	1.7	36.5	0.8	36.2	-0.8	36.6	1.1	36.7	0.3	36.8	0.3	37.3	1.4	36.8	-1.3
1966	37.1	0.8	37.5	1.1	37.9	1.1	38.3	1.1	38.4	0.3	38.7	0.8	38.6	-0.3	37.8	-2.1	37.6	-0.5	37.7	0.3	38.0	0.8	37.8	-0.5
1967	38.2	1.1	38.4	0.5	38.0	-1.0	37.7	-0.8	37.3	-1.1	37.3	0.0	37.2	-0.3	37.3	0.3	37.5	0.5	38.0	1.3	39.0	2.6	39.5	1.3
1968	40.0	1.3	41.1	2.8	41.8	1.7	40.9	-2.2	38.8	-5.1	38.7	-0.3	38.3	-1.0	38.1	-0.5	38.0	-0.3	38.2	0.5	38.3	0.3	38.7	1.0
1969	39.8	2.8	40.4	1.5	40.7	0.7	41.5	2.0	42.0	1.2	42.5	1.2	42.6	0.2	43.7	2.6	45.0	3.0	45.4	0.9	45.9	1.1	47.0	2.4
1970	48.0	2.1	48.0	0.0	48.2	0.4	49.3	2.3	49.3	0.0	48.6	-1.4	47.8	-1.6	47.2	-1.3	46.4	-1.7	46.1	-0.6	45.0	-2.4	44.0	-2.2

[Continued]

Nonferrous Metals
Producer Price Index
Base 1982 = 100
[Continued]

For 1926-2001. Columns headed % show percentile change in the index from the previous period for which an index is available.

Year	Jan Index	%	Feb Index	%	Mar Index	%	Apr Index	%	May Index	%	Jun Index	%	Jul Index	%	Aug Index	%	Sep Index	%	Oct Index	%	Nov Index	%	Dec Index	%
1971	43.3	-1.6	42.8	-1.2	42.6	-0.5	44.0	3.3	43.9	-0.2	43.6	-0.7	43.7	0.2	43.9	0.5	43.7	-0.5	43.6	-0.2	43.5	-0.2	43.1	-0.9
1972	43.4	0.7	43.6	0.5	44.5	2.1	44.6	0.2	44.7	0.2	44.6	-0.2	44.3	-0.7	44.3	0.0	44.5	0.5	44.5	0.0	44.5	0.0	44.5	0.0
1973	44.7	0.4	45.9	2.7	48.7	6.1	49.8	2.3	50.5	1.4	51.2	1.4	51.5	0.6	52.3	1.6	52.6	0.6	53.4	1.5	55.0	3.0	59.0	7.3
1974	61.1	3.6	62.6	2.5	66.9	6.9	70.8	5.8	76.0	7.3	76.0	0.0	75.3	-0.9	76.0	0.9	74.7	-1.7	72.4	-3.1	71.0	-1.9	69.0	-2.8
1975	67.8	-1.7	66.8	-1.5	66.0	-1.2	65.3	-1.1	64.9	-0.6	64.2	-1.1	63.6	-0.9	64.2	0.9	64.8	0.9	64.8	0.0	64.5	-0.5	64.3	-0.3
1976	64.1	-0.3	64.4	0.5	65.2	1.2	67.4	3.4	68.9	2.2	69.5	0.9	71.0	2.2	71.3	0.4	72.0	1.0	71.5	-0.7	71.1	-0.6	70.2	-1.3
1977	70.7	0.7	71.9	1.7	74.3	3.3	75.9	2.2	76.2	0.4	74.8	-1.8	75.1	0.4	75.3	0.3	74.0	-1.7	73.4	-0.8	73.7	0.4	74.0	0.4
1978	75.1	1.5	75.8	0.9	76.3	0.7	77.0	0.9	77.1	0.1	77.9	1.0	78.1	0.3	80.1	2.6	80.2	0.1	82.4	2.7	82.8	0.5	83.1	0.4
1979	84.8	2.0	90.7	7.0	93.6	3.2	98.5	5.2	98.0	-0.5	98.5	0.5	99.5	1.0	99.8	0.3	102.2	2.4	107.4	5.1	107.8	0.4	110.7	2.7
1980	123.8	11.8	128.1	3.5	121.9	-4.8	113.2	-7.1	109.9	-2.9	109.6	-0.3	111.0	1.3	113.2	2.0	114.6	1.2	117.4	2.4	114.6	-2.4	111.3	-2.9
1981	110.8	-0.4	109.0	-1.6	108.7	-0.3	109.4	0.6	109.1	-0.3	107.9	-1.1	107.3	-0.6	109.0	1.6	109.8	0.7	108.3	-1.4	106.6	-1.6	105.1	-1.4
1982	104.1	-1.0	103.8	-0.3	101.4	-2.3	100.9	-0.5	100.0	-0.9	96.1	-3.9	97.3	1.2	97.0	-0.3	100.6	3.7	99.7	-0.9	99.3	-0.4	99.8	0.5
1983	101.3	1.5	104.6	3.3	102.6	-1.9	103.1	0.5	105.3	2.1	104.6	-0.7	105.6	1.0	106.1	0.5	107.0	0.8	106.0	-0.9	104.9	-1.0	105.5	0.6
1984	105.0	-0.5	106.3	1.2	108.6	2.2	109.7	1.0	107.8	-1.7	107.3	-0.5	105.1	-2.1	104.4	-0.7	103.1	-1.2	101.2	-1.8	102.2	1.0	100.9	-1.3
1985	99.9	-1.0	100.5	0.6	99.6	-0.9	101.8	2.2	101.7	-0.1	100.0	-1.7	99.2	-0.8	99.2	0.0	98.9	-0.3	98.6	-0.3	97.8	-0.8	97.6	-0.2
1986	98.5	0.9	98.6	0.1	99.3	0.7	98.5	-0.8	97.9	-0.6	98.2	0.3	97.6	-0.6	98.2	0.6	98.7	0.5	99.0	0.3	98.9	-0.1	98.5	-0.4
1987	99.1	0.6	99.1	0.0	100.2	1.1	101.8	1.6	104.6	2.8	106.0	1.3	109.1	2.9	112.0	2.7	114.2	2.0	116.7	2.2	118.5	1.5	124.1	4.7
1988	127.5	2.7	124.8	-2.1	125.7	0.7	128.9	2.5	129.3	0.3	131.7	1.9	132.8	0.8	132.9	0.1	134.8	1.4	137.8	2.2	144.0	4.5	148.3	3.0
1989	149.9	1.1	147.1	-1.9	148.2	0.7	147.2	-0.7	144.6	-1.8	140.1	-3.1	136.3	-2.7	136.9	0.4	139.5	1.9	140.2	0.5	136.5	-2.6	131.9	-3.4
1990	130.9	-0.8	127.9	-2.3	131.8	3.0	134.5	2.0	134.0	-0.4	132.1	-1.4	133.2	0.8	137.3	3.1	139.0	1.2	139.2	0.1	134.8	-3.2	130.6	-3.1
1991	129.6	-0.8	128.1	-1.2	127.2	-0.7	126.5	-0.6	124.2	-1.8	121.6	-2.1	120.9	-0.6	121.2	0.2	121.3	0.1	121.1	-0.2	120.2	-0.7	118.9	-1.1
1992	117.1	-1.5	119.4	2.0	121.0	1.3	121.5	0.4	121.6	0.1	122.8	1.0	124.0	1.0	125.2	1.0	122.9	-1.8	120.0	-2.4	117.6	-2.0	117.9	0.3
1993	119.1	1.0	118.8	-0.3	117.5	-1.1	115.7	-1.5	113.2	-2.2	113.5	0.3	114.6	1.0	114.7	0.1	113.4	-1.1	111.1	-2.0	110.2	-0.8	111.5	1.2
1994	112.8	1.2	116.2	3.0	118.5	2.0	119.1	0.5	120.5	1.2	125.2	3.9	128.1	2.3	128.8	0.5	131.2	1.9	134.0	2.1	140.5	4.9	144.5	2.8
1995	151.2	4.6	152.8	1.1	151.5	-0.9	152.1	0.4	149.1	-2.0	149.4	0.2	150.3	0.6	150.8	0.3	149.3	-1.0	146.6	-1.8	146.4	-0.1	145.4	-0.7
1996	142.7	-1.9	140.3	-1.7	140.5	0.1	140.5	0.0	141.8	0.9	139.8	-1.4	133.9	-4.2	131.8	-1.6	131.3	-0.4	130.1	-0.9	131.4	1.0	133.4	1.5
1997	136.0	1.9	137.0	0.7	139.7	2.0	138.2	-1.1	139.1	0.7	139.7	0.4	136.9	-2.0	137.4	0.4	136.4	-0.7	135.4	-0.7	132.7	-2.0	130.4	-1.7
1998	128.0	-1.8	127.9	-0.1	126.8	-0.9	127.2	0.3	125.6	-1.3	123.4	-1.8	121.6	-1.5	120.5	-0.9	120.7	0.2	119.3	-1.2	118.1	-1.0	116.4	-1.4
1999	115.3	-0.9	115.1	-0.2	114.2	-0.8	114.9	0.6	117.1	1.9	116.2	-0.8	119.0	2.4	120.2	1.0	122.4	1.8	124.8	2.0	124.2	-0.5	125.2	0.8
2000	127.8	2.1	129.9	1.6	128.9	-0.8	127.5	-1.1	126.8	-0.5	126.5	-0.2	127.4	0.7	128.3	0.7	129.8	1.2	129.4	-0.3	127.0	-1.9	127.7	0.6
2001	127.2	-0.4	127.5	0.2	127.5	0.0	125.3	-1.7	126.0	0.6	125.0	-0.8	123.4	-1.3	121.7	-1.4	120.8	-0.7	120.0	-0.7	118.5	-1.2	119.3	0.7

Source: U.S. Department of Labor, Bureau of Labor Statistics, Division of Industry Prices and Price Indexes. n.e.c. stands for not elsewhere classified. - indicates no data collected for period or unavailable.

Metal Containers
Producer Price Index
Base 1982 = 100

For 1926-2001. Columns headed % show percentile change in the index from the previous period for which an index is available.

Year	Jan Index	%	Feb Index	%	Mar Index	%	Apr Index	%	May Index	%	Jun Index	%	Jul Index	%	Aug Index	%	Sep Index	%	Oct Index	%	Nov Index	%	Dec Index	%
1926	15.2	-	15.2	0.0	15.2	0.0	15.2	0.0	15.2	0.0	15.2	0.0	15.2	0.0	15.2	0.0	15.2	0.0	15.2	0.0	15.2	0.0	15.2	0.0
1927	15.2	0.0	15.2	0.0	15.2	0.0	15.2	0.0	15.2	0.0	15.2	0.0	15.2	0.0	15.2	0.0	15.2	0.0	15.2	0.0	15.2	0.0	15.2	0.0
1928	14.7	-3.3	14.7	0.0	14.7	0.0	14.7	0.0	14.7	0.0	14.7	0.0	14.7	0.0	14.7	0.0	14.7	0.0	14.7	0.0	14.7	0.0	14.7	0.0
1929	14.9	1.4	14.9	0.0	14.9	0.0	14.9	0.0	14.9	0.0	14.9	0.0	14.9	0.0	14.9	0.0	14.9	0.0	14.9	0.0	14.9	0.0	14.9	0.0
1930	14.7	-1.3	14.7	0.0	14.7	0.0	14.7	0.0	14.7	0.0	14.7	0.0	14.7	0.0	14.7	0.0	14.6	-0.7	14.6	0.0	14.6	0.0	14.6	0.0
1931	14.2	-2.7	14.2	0.0	14.1	-0.7	14.1	0.0	14.1	0.0	14.1	0.0	14.0	-0.7	14.0	0.0	14.0	0.0	14.0	0.0	14.0	0.0	14.0	0.0
1932	13.5	-3.6	13.5	0.0	13.5	0.0	13.5	0.0	13.5	0.0	13.5	0.0	13.5	0.0	13.5	0.0	13.5	0.0	13.5	0.0	13.5	0.0	13.5	0.0
1933	12.6	-6.7	12.6	0.0	12.6	0.0	12.6	0.0	12.6	0.0	12.6	0.0	12.6	0.0	12.6	0.0	12.6	0.0	12.7	0.8	12.7	0.0	12.7	0.0
1934	14.4	13.4	14.4	0.0	14.4	0.0	14.5	0.7	14.5	0.0	14.5	0.0	14.5	0.0	14.5	0.0	14.5	0.0	14.5	0.0	14.5	0.0	14.5	0.0
1935	14.4	-0.7	14.4	0.0	14.4	0.0	14.4	0.0	14.4	0.0	14.4	0.0	14.4	0.0	14.4	0.0	14.4	0.0	14.4	0.0	14.4	0.0	14.4	0.0
1936	14.4	0.0	14.4	0.0	14.4	0.0	14.4	0.0	14.4	0.0	14.4	0.0	14.4	0.0	14.4	0.0	14.4	0.0	14.6	1.4	14.6	0.0	14.6	0.0
1937	13.4	-8.2	13.4	0.0	13.4	0.0	13.5	0.7	13.5	0.0	13.5	0.0	13.5	0.0	13.5	0.0	13.5	0.0	13.5	0.0	13.5	0.0	13.5	0.0
1938	14.4	6.7	14.4	0.0	14.4	0.0	14.4	0.0	14.4	0.0	14.4	0.0	14.4	0.0	14.4	0.0	14.4	0.0	14.4	0.0	14.4	0.0	14.4	0.0
1939	13.8	-4.2	13.8	0.0	13.8	0.0	13.8	0.0	13.8	0.0	13.8	0.0	13.8	0.0	13.8	0.0	13.8	0.0	13.8	0.0	13.8	0.0	13.8	0.0
1940	13.5	-2.2	13.5	0.0	13.5	0.0	13.5	0.0	13.5	0.0	13.5	0.0	13.5	0.0	13.5	0.0	13.5	0.0	13.5	0.0	13.5	0.0	13.5	0.0
1941	13.5	0.0	13.5	0.0	13.5	0.0	13.5	0.0	13.5	0.0	13.5	0.0	13.6	0.7	13.6	0.0	13.6	0.0	13.6	0.0	13.6	0.0	13.6	0.0
1942	13.8	1.5	13.8	0.0	13.8	0.0	13.8	0.0	13.8	0.0	13.8	0.0	13.8	0.0	13.8	0.0	13.8	0.0	13.8	0.0	13.8	0.0	13.8	0.0
1943	13.8	0.0	13.8	0.0	13.8	0.0	13.8	0.0	13.8	0.0	13.8	0.0	13.8	0.0	13.8	0.0	13.8	0.0	13.8	0.0	13.8	0.0	13.8	0.0
1944	13.8	0.0	13.8	0.0	13.8	0.0	13.8	0.0	13.8	0.0	13.8	0.0	13.8	0.0	13.8	0.0	13.8	0.0	13.8	0.0	13.8	0.0	13.8	0.0
1945	13.8	0.0	13.8	0.0	13.8	0.0	13.8	0.0	13.8	0.0	13.8	0.0	13.8	0.0	13.8	0.0	13.8	0.0	13.8	0.0	13.8	0.0	13.8	0.0
1946	13.8	0.0	13.8	0.0	13.8	0.0	13.8	0.0	14.3	3.6	14.3	0.0	14.3	0.0	14.3	0.0	14.3	0.0	14.3	0.0	14.3	0.0	14.3	0.0
1947	15.9	11.2	15.9	0.0	15.9	0.0	15.9	0.0	15.9	0.0	15.9	0.0	15.9	0.0	16.3	2.5	16.3	0.0	16.3	0.0	16.3	0.0	16.3	0.0
1948	17.8	9.2	17.8	0.0	17.8	0.0	17.8	0.0	17.7	-0.6	17.7	0.0	17.8	0.6	17.9	0.6	17.9	0.0	17.9	0.0	17.9	0.0	17.9	0.0
1949	19.3	7.8	19.3	0.0	19.3	0.0	19.3	0.0	19.3	0.0	19.3	0.0	19.3	0.0	19.3	0.0	19.3	0.0	19.3	0.0	19.3	0.0	19.3	0.0
1950	19.4	0.5	19.4	0.0	19.3	-0.5	19.3	0.0	19.3	0.0	19.3	0.0	19.3	0.0	19.3	0.0	19.3	0.0	19.3	0.0	19.3	0.0	19.6	1.6
1951	21.5	9.7	21.5	0.0	21.5	0.0	21.5	0.0	21.5	0.0	21.5	0.0	21.5	0.0	21.5	0.0	21.5	0.0	21.5	0.0	21.5	0.0	21.5	0.0
1952	21.4	-0.5	21.4	0.0	21.4	0.0	21.4	0.0	21.4	0.0	21.4	0.0	21.4	0.0	21.4	0.0	22.0	2.8	22.2	0.9	22.2	0.0	22.2	0.0
1953	22.2	0.0	22.2	0.0	22.2	0.0	22.4	0.9	22.4	0.0	22.4	0.0	22.8	1.8	22.8	0.0	22.8	0.0	22.8	0.0	22.8	0.0	22.8	0.0
1954	23.0	0.9	23.0	0.0	23.0	0.0	23.0	0.0	23.0	0.0	23.0	0.0	23.1	0.4	23.2	0.4	23.2	0.0	23.2	0.0	23.3	0.4	23.3	0.0
1955	23.3	0.0	23.3	0.0	23.3	0.0	23.3	0.0	23.3	0.0	23.3	0.0	23.3	0.0	23.5	0.9	23.5	0.0	23.5	0.0	24.4	3.8	24.4	0.0
1956	24.4	0.0	24.4	0.0	24.4	0.0	24.4	0.0	25.0	2.5	25.0	0.0	25.0	0.0	25.1	0.4	25.4	1.2	25.4	0.0	26.1	2.8	26.1	0.0
1957	26.1	0.0	26.1	0.0	26.2	0.4	26.2	0.0	27.0	3.1	27.0	0.0	27.1	0.4	27.1	0.0	27.1	0.0	27.1	0.0	27.1	0.0	27.1	0.0
1958	27.1	0.0	27.1	0.0	27.6	1.8	27.6	0.0	27.6	0.0	27.6	0.0	27.6	0.0	27.6	0.0	27.7	0.4	27.7	0.0	27.7	0.0	28.3	2.2
1959	27.7	-2.1	27.7	0.0	27.7	0.0	27.1	-2.2	27.1	0.0	27.1	0.0	27.1	0.0	27.1	0.0	27.1	0.0	27.1	0.0	27.1	0.0	27.1	0.0
1960	27.1	0.0	27.4	1.1	27.4	0.0	27.4	0.0	27.4	0.0	27.2	-0.7	27.2	0.0	27.2	0.0	27.2	0.0	27.2	0.0	27.2	0.0	27.2	0.0
1961	27.8	2.2	27.8	0.0	27.8	0.0	27.8	0.0	27.8	0.0	27.8	0.0	27.8	0.0	27.8	0.0	27.8	0.0	27.8	0.0	27.8	0.0	27.8	0.0
1962	28.2	1.4	28.2	0.0	28.2	0.0	28.2	0.0	28.2	0.0	28.2	0.0	28.2	0.0	28.2	0.0	28.2	0.0	28.2	0.0	28.2	0.0	28.2	0.0
1963	28.4	0.7	28.4	0.0	28.4	0.0	28.4	0.0	28.5	0.4	28.5	0.0	28.6	0.4	28.6	0.0	28.5	-0.3	28.5	0.0	28.5	0.0	28.5	0.0
1964	28.5	0.0	28.7	0.7	28.7	0.0	28.7	0.0	28.7	0.0	28.7	0.0	28.7	0.0	28.7	0.0	28.7	0.0	28.7	0.0	28.7	0.0	28.7	0.0
1965	28.8	0.3	28.8	0.0	28.8	0.0	28.8	0.0	29.5	2.4	29.5	0.0	29.5	0.0	29.5	0.0	29.5	0.0	29.5	0.0	29.5	0.0	29.9	1.4
1966	29.9	0.0	29.9	0.0	29.9	0.0	29.9	0.0	30.0	0.3	30.0	0.0	30.0	0.0	30.0	0.0	30.0	0.0	30.0	0.0	30.0	0.0	30.0	0.0
1967	30.3	1.0	30.3	0.0	30.3	0.0	30.4	0.3	30.4	0.0	30.4	0.0	30.4	0.0	30.4	0.0	30.4	0.0	30.4	0.0	30.7	1.0	30.7	0.0
1968	30.7	0.0	30.8	0.3	30.8	0.0	31.8	3.2	31.8	0.0	31.8	0.0	31.8	0.0	31.8	0.0	31.8	0.0	31.9	0.3	31.9	0.0	31.8	-0.3
1969	31.8	0.0	32.4	1.9	32.4	0.0	32.5	0.3	32.5	0.0	32.5	0.0	32.5	0.0	32.5	0.0	32.7	0.6	32.8	0.3	32.8	0.0	32.8	0.0
1970	32.8	0.0	34.0	3.7	34.0	0.0	34.0	0.0	34.0	0.0	34.0	0.0	34.3	0.9	34.3	0.0	34.3	0.0	35.2	2.6	35.2	0.0	35.2	0.0

[Continued]

Metal Containers

Producer Price Index
Base 1982 = 100

[Continued]

For 1926-2001. Columns headed % show percentile change in the index from the previous period for which an index is available.

Year	Jan Index	%	Feb Index	%	Mar Index	%	Apr Index	%	May Index	%	Jun Index	%	Jul Index	%	Aug Index	%	Sep Index	%	Oct Index	%	Nov Index	%	Dec Index	%
1971	35.2	0.0	35.2	0.0	35.2	0.0	37.5	6.5	37.5	0.0	37.5	0.0	37.5	0.0	37.8	0.8	37.8	0.0	37.8	0.0	37.8	0.0	37.8	0.0
1972	37.8	0.0	38.7	2.4	38.7	0.0	38.7	0.0	38.8	0.3	39.2	1.0	39.5	0.8	39.8	0.8	39.9	0.3	39.9	0.0	39.9	0.0	39.9	0.0
1973	39.9	0.0	39.8	-0.3	41.3	3.8	41.3	0.0	41.3	0.0	41.3	0.0	41.3	0.0	41.3	0.0	41.3	0.0	41.0	-0.7	41.0	0.0	41.0	0.0
1974	42.2	2.9	42.3	0.2	42.5	0.5	44.7	5.2	46.3	3.6	50.3	8.6	52.0	3.4	56.1	7.9	56.2	0.2	56.4	0.4	56.4	0.0	56.4	0.0
1975	56.4	0.0	60.0	6.4	59.6	-0.7	59.6	0.0	58.2	-2.3	58.2	0.0	58.2	0.0	58.1	-0.2	58.2	0.2	58.2	0.0	58.4	0.3	58.7	0.5
1976	58.6	-0.2	58.7	0.2	61.9	5.5	61.9	0.0	61.9	0.0	61.9	0.0	62.3	0.6	62.2	-0.2	62.2	0.0	62.2	0.0	62.3	0.2	62.3	0.0
1977	62.3	0.0	62.3	0.0	66.0	5.9	66.1	0.2	66.0	-0.2	66.0	0.0	66.2	0.3	66.4	0.3	68.5	3.2	69.0	0.7	69.1	0.1	69.1	0.0
1978	69.2	0.1	71.1	2.7	72.1	1.4	72.1	0.0	73.9	2.5	74.0	0.1	74.3	0.4	75.0	0.9	74.9	-0.1	77.5	3.5	77.5	0.0	77.4	-0.1
1979	78.2	1.0	78.2	0.0	80.5	2.9	82.2	2.1	81.7	-0.6	81.4	-0.4	81.3	-0.1	81.7	0.5	81.8	0.1	85.2	4.2	85.5	0.4	85.5	0.0
1980	86.2	0.8	86.6	0.5	87.8	1.4	91.6	4.3	92.1	0.5	92.1	0.0	92.2	0.1	92.3	0.1	92.3	0.0	92.7	0.4	92.3	-0.4	92.3	0.0
1981	94.8	2.7	95.5	0.7	95.6	0.1	95.6	0.0	95.6	0.0	95.6	0.0	96.0	0.4	97.0	1.0	97.0	0.0	96.9	-0.1	96.8	-0.1	96.4	-0.4
1982	98.7	2.4	99.3	0.6	99.6	0.3	100.5	0.9	100.5	0.0	100.4	-0.1	100.5	0.1	100.1	-0.4	100.1	0.0	100.3	0.2	100.1	-0.2	99.9	-0.2
1983	99.8	-0.1	100.8	1.0	100.9	0.1	101.0	0.1	102.6	1.6	102.7	0.1	102.4	-0.3	102.5	0.1	103.0	0.5	103.0	0.0	102.9	-0.1	103.6	0.7
1984	104.7	1.1	104.9	0.2	105.1	0.2	105.1	0.0	105.9	0.8	105.9	0.0	105.9	0.0	107.2	1.2	107.2	0.0	108.8	1.5	108.8	0.0	108.7	-0.1
1985	108.8	0.1	109.0	0.2	108.9	-0.1	108.9	0.0	109.0	0.1	109.0	0.0	109.0	0.0	108.9	-0.1	108.9	0.0	108.9	0.0	109.0	0.1	109.9	0.8
1986	110.2	0.3	110.1	-0.1	110.2	0.1	110.1	-0.1	110.0	-0.1	110.0	0.0	110.3	0.3	110.4	0.1	110.4	0.0	110.4	0.0	110.4	0.0	110.4	0.0
1987	109.9	-0.5	110.0	0.1	109.8	-0.2	109.8	0.0	109.6	-0.2	109.7	0.1	109.0	-0.6	109.1	0.1	109.8	0.6	109.6	-0.2	109.8	0.2	108.0	-1.6
1988	108.3	0.3	108.9	0.6	109.5	0.6	110.1	0.5	110.4	0.3	110.3	-0.1	110.1	-0.2	110.9	0.7	111.3	0.4	111.1	-0.2	111.0	-0.1	110.1	-0.8
1989	110.1	0.0	109.7	-0.4	109.7	0.0	110.3	0.5	111.3	0.9	111.5	0.2	112.5	0.9	112.0	-0.4	112.2	0.2	113.0	0.7	113.1	0.1	112.6	-0.4
1990	113.6	0.9	113.5	-0.1	113.8	0.3	113.8	0.0	114.2	0.4	114.1	-0.1	114.2	0.1	114.1	-0.1	114.2	0.1	114.1	-0.1	114.1	0.0	113.9	-0.2
1991	114.7	0.7	114.9	0.2	114.6	-0.3	114.7	0.1	114.9	0.2	114.9	0.0	116.1	1.0	116.3	0.2	116.2	-0.1	116.4	0.2	116.3	-0.1	116.2	-0.1
1992	113.8	-2.1	114.3	0.4	113.9	-0.3	114.0	0.1	113.8	-0.2	114.0	0.2	113.9	-0.1	113.7	-0.2	113.9	0.2	113.9	0.0	113.9	0.0	114.0	0.1
1993	109.9	-3.6	110.2	0.3	109.5	-0.6	109.2	-0.3	109.1	-0.1	109.1	0.0	109.2	0.1	108.8	-0.4	109.8	0.9	110.1	0.3	111.0	0.8	110.1	-0.8
1994	109.0	-1.0	108.5	-0.5	107.7	-0.7	108.0	0.3	108.0	0.0	106.6	-1.3	106.9	0.3	108.1	1.1	108.2	0.1	108.6	0.4	108.8	0.2	108.9	0.1
1995	109.6	0.6	117.8	7.5	117.8	0.0	118.1	0.3	118.1	0.0	118.3	0.2	118.0	-0.3	118.0	0.0	117.8	-0.2	117.9	0.1	117.7	-0.2	117.8	0.1
1996	115.1	-2.3	110.5	-4.0	110.5	0.0	110.5	0.0	109.7	-0.7	109.5	-0.2	109.6	0.1	109.6	0.0	109.5	-0.1	108.5	-0.9	108.4	-0.1	109.1	0.6
1997	108.0	-1.0	108.0	0.0	108.2	0.2	107.9	-0.3	107.9	0.0	107.8	-0.1	107.6	-0.2	107.8	0.2	107.7	-0.1	107.8	0.1	107.7	-0.1	107.7	0.0
1998	109.1	1.3	109.2	0.1	109.3	0.1	108.6	-0.6	108.6	0.0	108.5	-0.1	108.5	0.0	108.5	0.0	108.5	0.0	107.1	-1.3	107.2	0.1	107.1	-0.1
1999	107.1	0.0	107.0	-0.1	107.0	0.0	106.3	-0.7	106.3	0.0	106.0	-0.3	106.0	0.0	105.9	-0.1	106.0	0.1	106.5	0.5	106.5	0.0	106.5	0.0
2000	105.9	-0.6	106.0	0.1	106.1	0.1	107.2	1.0	107.2	0.0	107.2	0.0	107.3	0.1	107.3	0.0	107.4	0.1	107.4	0.0	106.0	-1.3	106.1	0.1
2001	105.5	-0.6	105.6	0.1	105.7	0.1	106.7	0.9	106.6	-0.1	106.6	0.0	106.8	0.2	106.6	-0.2	106.6	0.0	106.1	-0.5	106.0	-0.1	106.3	0.3

Source: U.S. Department of Labor, Bureau of Labor Statistics, Division of Industry Prices and Price Indexes. n.e.c. stands for not elsewhere classified. - indicates no data collected for period or unavailable.

Hardware
Producer Price Index
Base 1982 = 100

For 1947-2001. Columns headed % show percentile change in the index from the previous period for which an index is available.

Year	Jan Index	%	Feb Index	%	Mar Index	%	Apr Index	%	May Index	%	Jun Index	%	Jul Index	%	Aug Index	%	Sep Index	%	Oct Index	%	Nov Index	%	Dec Index	%
1947	16.7	-	16.9	1.2	16.9	0.0	16.9	0.0	17.0	0.6	17.0	0.0	17.1	0.6	17.2	0.6	17.4	1.2	17.6	1.1	17.7	0.6	17.7	0.0
1948	17.7	0.0	17.8	0.6	17.9	0.6	17.9	0.0	18.2	1.7	18.3	0.5	18.3	0.0	19.1	4.4	19.7	3.1	19.8	0.5	19.9	0.5	19.9	0.0
1949	19.9	0.0	19.9	0.0	19.9	0.0	19.7	-1.0	19.7	0.0	19.7	0.0	19.7	0.0	19.7	0.0	19.5	-1.0	19.2	-1.5	19.2	0.0	19.2	0.0
1950	19.6	2.1	20.1	2.6	20.2	0.5	20.3	0.5	20.5	1.0	20.6	0.5	20.9	1.5	21.4	2.4	21.8	1.9	22.2	1.8	22.9	3.2	23.2	1.3
1951	23.3	0.4	23.3	0.0	23.3	0.0	23.3	0.0	23.3	0.0	23.3	0.0	23.3	0.0	23.3	0.0	23.3	0.0	23.3	0.0	23.3	0.0	23.3	0.0
1952	23.3	0.0	23.3	0.0	23.4	0.4	23.4	0.0	23.4	0.0	22.9	-2.1	22.9	0.0	22.9	0.0	22.9	0.0	23.2	1.3	23.2	0.0	23.3	0.4
1953	23.3	0.0	23.3	0.0	23.3	0.0	23.7	1.7	24.7	4.2	24.9	0.8	24.9	0.0	25.1	0.8	25.3	0.8	25.4	0.4	25.4	0.0	25.4	0.0
1954	25.4	0.0	25.5	0.4	25.5	0.0	25.6	0.4	25.5	-0.4	25.5	0.0	25.5	0.0	25.7	0.8	26.0	1.2	26.2	0.8	26.3	0.4	26.3	0.0
1955	26.4	0.4	26.5	0.4	26.7	0.8	26.7	0.0	26.7	0.0	26.7	0.0	26.8	0.4	27.0	0.7	27.3	1.1	28.0	2.6	28.0	0.0	28.0	0.0
1956	28.0	0.0	28.0	0.0	28.3	1.1	28.5	0.7	28.5	0.0	28.6	0.4	28.7	0.3	29.3	2.1	29.3	0.0	29.5	0.7	29.6	0.3	29.6	0.0
1957	29.9	1.0	29.9	0.0	30.0	0.3	30.2	0.7	30.4	0.7	30.4	0.0	30.4	0.0	30.7	1.0	30.9	0.7	30.9	0.0	30.9	0.0	31.1	0.6
1958	31.2	0.3	31.2	0.0	31.2	0.0	31.3	0.3	31.6	1.0	31.8	0.6	31.8	0.0	31.8	0.0	31.8	0.0	31.8	0.0	31.9	0.3	31.9	0.0
1959	31.9	0.0	32.0	0.3	32.0	0.0	32.0	0.0	32.0	0.0	32.0	0.0	32.0	0.0	32.0	0.0	32.0	0.0	32.0	0.0	32.0	0.0	32.0	0.0
1960	32.1	0.3	32.1	0.0	32.1	0.0	32.2	0.3	32.2	0.0	32.3	0.3	32.3	0.0	32.3	0.0	32.3	0.0	32.3	0.0	32.3	0.0	32.3	0.0
1961	32.3	0.0	32.4	0.3	32.4	0.0	32.4	0.0	32.6	0.6	32.6	0.0	32.6	0.0	32.6	0.0	32.7	0.3	32.7	0.0	32.7	0.0	32.7	0.0
1962	32.8	0.3	32.7	-0.3	32.7	0.0	32.6	-0.3	32.6	0.0	32.7	0.3	32.5	-0.6	32.5	0.0	32.5	0.0	32.5	0.0	32.5	0.0	32.5	0.0
1963	32.5	0.0	32.6	0.3	32.6	0.0	32.6	0.0	32.6	0.0	32.6	0.0	32.6	0.0	32.6	0.0	32.7	0.3	32.7	0.0	32.7	0.0	32.7	0.0
1964	32.8	0.3	32.8	0.0	32.9	0.3	32.9	0.0	32.9	0.0	32.9	0.0	32.9	0.0	32.9	0.0	32.9	0.0	32.9	0.0	32.9	0.0	32.9	0.0
1965	32.9	0.0	32.9	0.0	33.0	0.3	33.0	0.0	33.2	0.6	33.2	0.0	33.3	0.3	33.4	0.3	33.4	0.0	33.5	0.3	33.5	0.0	33.6	0.3
1966	33.6	0.0	33.7	0.3	34.0	0.9	34.0	0.0	34.4	1.2	34.4	0.0	34.4	0.0	34.5	0.3	34.6	0.3	34.8	0.6	35.0	0.6	35.1	0.3
1967	35.0	-0.3	35.0	0.0	35.3	0.9	35.3	0.0	35.4	0.3	35.4	0.0	35.7	0.8	36.1	1.1	36.1	0.0	36.2	0.3	36.3	0.3	36.4	0.3
1968	36.4	0.0	36.6	0.5	36.5	-0.3	36.5	0.0	36.6	0.3	36.6	0.0	36.6	0.0	36.6	0.0	36.7	0.3	36.8	0.3	36.8	0.0	37.1	0.8
1969	37.3	0.5	37.4	0.3	37.5	0.3	37.5	0.0	37.6	0.3	37.6	0.0	37.8	0.5	37.8	0.0	37.9	0.3	38.4	1.3	38.6	0.5	38.6	0.0
1970	39.0	1.0	39.1	0.3	39.2	0.3	39.3	0.3	39.4	0.3	39.5	0.3	39.7	0.5	39.9	0.5	40.1	0.5	40.3	0.5	41.0	1.7	41.1	0.2
1971	41.2	0.2	41.3	0.2	41.3	0.0	41.3	0.0	41.3	0.0	41.4	0.2	41.7	0.7	42.0	0.7	42.0	0.0	42.0	0.0	42.1	0.2	42.2	0.2
1972	42.3	0.2	42.5	0.5	42.5	0.0	42.7	0.5	42.9	0.5	43.0	0.2	43.0	0.0	43.1	0.2	43.1	0.0	43.2	0.2	43.3	0.2	43.3	0.0
1973	43.4	0.2	43.5	0.2	43.6	0.2	43.8	0.5	44.0	0.5	44.3	0.7	44.4	0.2	44.4	0.0	45.2	1.8	45.6	0.9	45.7	0.2	46.1	0.9
1974	46.5	0.9	46.7	0.4	46.9	0.4	47.1	0.4	48.4	2.8	49.3	1.9	49.9	1.2	51.0	2.2	52.5	2.9	53.9	2.7	55.0	2.0	55.5	0.9
1975	56.0	0.9	56.5	0.9	57.7	2.1	57.7	0.0	58.1	0.7	58.2	0.2	58.3	0.2	58.4	0.2	58.6	0.3	59.3	1.2	59.5	0.3	59.6	0.2
1976	60.2	1.0	60.5	0.5	60.7	0.3	60.9	0.3	61.5	1.0	61.7	0.3	61.8	0.2	61.9	0.2	62.2	0.5	62.6	0.6	63.2	1.0	63.9	1.1
1977	64.8	1.4	65.1	0.5	65.4	0.5	65.5	0.2	65.6	0.2	65.9	0.5	66.7	1.2	66.7	0.0	66.9	0.3	66.7	-0.3	67.1	0.6	67.6	0.7
1978	69.0	2.1	69.2	0.3	69.4	0.3	70.2	1.2	70.7	0.7	70.8	0.1	71.5	1.0	71.9	0.6	72.2	0.4	73.5	1.8	74.4	1.2	75.2	1.1
1979	75.5	0.4	76.1	0.8	76.4	0.4	77.0	0.8	77.4	0.5	77.5	0.1	78.0	0.6	78.5	0.6	79.0	0.6	79.9	1.1	80.5	0.8	80.7	0.2
1980	81.4	0.9	82.2	1.0	82.6	0.5	84.7	2.5	85.1	0.5	85.8	0.8	86.6	0.9	86.8	0.2	87.7	1.0	88.0	0.3	89.1	1.2	89.8	0.8
1981	90.8	1.1	92.1	1.4	92.3	0.2	92.2	-0.1	92.6	0.4	92.6	0.0	94.1	1.6	94.7	0.6	95.6	1.0	96.2	0.6	96.9	0.7	97.1	0.2
1982	97.8	0.7	98.0	0.2	99.3	1.3	99.4	0.1	99.5	0.1	100.0	0.5	100.3	0.3	100.8	0.5	100.9	0.1	101.0	0.1	101.0	0.0	102.0	1.0
1983	102.5	0.5	102.7	0.2	102.8	0.1	103.0	0.2	103.0	0.0	104.0	1.0	104.2	0.2	104.3	0.1	104.4	0.1	104.5	0.1	104.6	0.1	104.7	0.1
1984	104.7	0.0	104.9	0.2	105.1	0.2	105.1	0.0	105.4	0.3	105.7	0.3	106.0	0.3	106.3	0.3	106.7	0.4	107.0	0.3	107.0	0.0	107.4	0.4
1985	108.0	0.6	108.2	0.2	108.8	0.6	109.1	0.3	109.1	0.0	109.1	0.0	109.2	0.1	109.4	0.2	109.4	0.0	109.6	0.2	109.7	0.1	109.9	0.2
1986	110.8	0.8	110.9	0.1	109.1	-1.6	109.2	0.1	109.3	0.1	109.3	0.0	109.4	0.1	109.5	0.1	109.2	-0.3	109.4	0.2	108.7	-0.6	108.9	0.2
1987	108.5	-0.4	108.9	0.4	109.0	0.1	109.2	0.2	109.6	0.4	109.8	0.2	109.6	-0.2	109.7	0.1	109.8	0.1	110.1	0.3	110.2	0.1	111.0	0.7
1988	111.5	0.5	111.9	0.4	112.2	0.3	112.8	0.5	113.0	0.2	112.9	-0.1	113.6	0.6	114.0	0.4	114.3	0.3	115.6	1.1	116.1	0.4	116.7	0.5
1989	117.3	0.5	118.4	0.9	119.1	0.6	119.2	0.1	119.7	0.4	119.9	0.2	120.5	0.5	120.7	0.2	121.2	0.4	122.3	0.9	122.8	0.4	123.2	0.3
1990	124.0	0.6	124.8	0.6	125.0	0.2	125.5	0.4	125.6	0.1	125.7	0.1	126.0	0.2	126.2	0.2	126.5	0.2	126.9	0.3	127.0	0.1	127.7	0.6
1991	129.4	1.3	129.7	0.2	129.9	0.2	129.9	0.0	130.0	0.1	130.1	0.1	130.1	0.0	130.2	0.1	130.3	0.1	130.7	0.3	130.6	-0.1	131.2	0.5

[Continued]

Hardware
Producer Price Index
Base 1982 = 100
[Continued]

For 1947-2001. Columns headed % show percentile change in the index from the previous period for which an index is available.

Year	Jan Index	%	Feb Index	%	Mar Index	%	Apr Index	%	May Index	%	Jun Index	%	Jul Index	%	Aug Index	%	Sep Index	%	Oct Index	%	Nov Index	%	Dec Index	%
1992	131.6	0.3	132.0	0.3	132.2	0.2	132.5	0.2	132.6	0.1	132.6	0.0	132.8	0.2	133.0	0.2	133.1	0.1	133.2	0.1	133.5	0.2	133.8	0.2
1993	134.1	0.2	134.3	0.1	134.6	0.2	134.8	0.1	134.8	0.0	135.2	0.3	135.3	0.1	135.5	0.1	135.6	0.1	135.7	0.1	135.9	0.1	136.2	0.2
1994	136.4	0.1	136.5	0.1	136.7	0.1	137.2	0.4	137.4	0.1	137.5	0.1	137.6	0.1	137.8	0.1	138.0	0.1	138.1	0.1	138.5	0.3	138.6	0.1
1995	139.4	0.6	139.7	0.2	140.4	0.5	140.8	0.3	140.9	0.1	141.4	0.4	141.5	0.1	141.6	0.1	141.7	0.1	141.7	0.0	141.9	0.1	142.2	0.2
1996	142.8	0.4	143.1	0.2	143.5	0.3	143.5	0.0	143.6	0.1	143.7	0.1	143.7	0.0	144.2	0.3	144.2	0.0	144.6	0.3	144.1	-0.3	144.2	0.1
1997	144.9	0.5	144.7	-0.1	145.2	0.3	145.4	0.1	145.5	0.1	145.7	0.1	145.2	-0.3	145.9	0.5	145.9	0.0	146.4	0.3	145.9	-0.3	146.1	0.1
1998	146.5	0.3	147.2	0.5	146.8	-0.3	146.9	0.1	146.9	0.0	147.1	0.1	147.3	0.1	147.1	-0.1	147.1	0.0	147.2	0.1	147.2	0.0	147.2	0.0
1999	147.4	0.1	147.2	-0.1	147.4	0.1	147.8	0.3	147.9	0.1	149.1	0.8	149.1	0.0	149.7	0.4	149.7	0.0	149.8	0.1	149.8	0.0	150.0	0.1
2000	150.0	0.0	150.6	0.4	150.8	0.1	151.1	0.2	150.8	-0.2	151.3	0.3	151.3	0.0	151.4	0.1	151.6	0.1	151.7	0.1	151.7	0.0	151.9	0.1
2001	152.3	0.3	152.8	0.3	153.1	0.2	153.2	0.1	154.9	1.1	154.9	0.0	155.0	0.1	155.0	0.0	155.5	0.3	155.4	-0.1	155.3	-0.1	155.7	0.3

Source: U.S. Department of Labor, Bureau of Labor Statistics, Division of Industry Prices and Price Indexes. n.e.c. stands for not elsewhere classified. - indicates no data collected for period or unavailable.

Plumbing Fixtures and Brass Fittings
Producer Price Index
Base 1982 = 100

For 1926-2001. Columns headed % show percentile change in the index from the previous period for which an index is available.

Year	Jan Index	%	Feb Index	%	Mar Index	%	Apr Index	%	May Index	%	Jun Index	%	Jul Index	%	Aug Index	%	Sep Index	%	Oct Index	%	Nov Index	%	Dec Index	%
1926	26.4	-	26.4	0.0	26.4	0.0	26.4	0.0	26.3	-0.4	25.9	-1.5	25.8	-0.4	26.0	0.8	26.2	0.8	26.2	0.0	26.1	-0.4	26.2	0.4
1927	26.2	0.0	25.5	-2.7	23.5	-7.8	23.5	0.0	23.1	-1.7	22.8	-1.3	22.8	0.0	22.8	0.0	22.9	0.4	22.9	0.0	22.9	0.0	22.7	-0.9
1928	22.7	0.0	22.7	0.0	23.4	3.1	23.5	0.4	23.6	0.4	24.3	3.0	24.3	0.0	24.3	0.0	24.3	0.0	24.3	0.0	24.4	0.4	24.4	0.0
1929	24.1	-1.2	22.4	-7.1	22.4	0.0	22.6	0.9	22.6	0.0	22.6	0.0	22.1	-2.2	22.5	1.8	22.5	0.0	22.1	-1.8	22.1	0.0	22.1	0.0
1930	22.1	0.0	22.7	2.7	23.0	1.3	24.1	4.8	24.1	0.0	20.8	-13.7	19.9	-4.3	19.9	0.0	19.8	-0.5	19.8	0.0	19.7	-0.5	20.5	4.1
1931	20.6	0.5	20.2	-1.9	20.2	0.0	20.2	0.0	20.2	0.0	20.2	0.0	20.2	0.0	20.2	0.0	20.0	-1.0	20.1	0.5	20.0	-0.5	19.3	-3.5
1932	16.4	-15.0	16.2	-1.2	15.6	-3.7	15.6	0.0	15.6	0.0	16.6	6.4	16.8	1.2	16.8	0.0	16.8	0.0	16.8	0.0	16.8	0.0	16.8	0.0
1933	14.5	-13.7	12.8	-11.7	12.8	0.0	12.8	0.0	13.8	7.8	16.2	17.4	16.7	3.1	16.9	1.2	19.1	13.0	19.1	0.0	19.1	0.0	19.0	-0.5
1934	19.0	0.0	18.8	-1.1	18.8	0.0	18.8	0.0	17.9	-4.8	16.9	-5.6	16.9	0.0	17.0	0.6	15.5	-8.8	14.0	-9.7	13.9	-0.7	13.9	0.0
1935	13.9	0.0	14.0	0.7	14.1	0.7	14.0	-0.7	14.0	0.0	14.0	0.0	14.9	6.4	15.5	4.0	15.5	0.0	15.5	0.0	15.5	0.0	15.5	0.0
1936	15.8	1.9	16.9	7.0	16.9	0.0	16.9	0.0	16.9	0.0	16.9	0.0	16.9	0.0	16.9	0.0	16.9	0.0	16.9	0.0	16.9	0.0	16.9	0.0
1937	16.9	0.0	16.9	0.0	17.0	0.6	17.2	1.2	17.2	0.0	17.2	0.0	17.2	0.0	17.2	0.0	17.2	0.0	17.2	0.0	17.2	0.0	17.2	0.0
1938	17.1	-0.6	17.1	0.0	17.0	-0.6	17.0	0.0	17.0	0.0	17.0	0.0	17.0	0.0	17.0	0.0	16.6	-2.4	16.6	0.0	16.6	0.0	16.6	0.0
1939	16.6	0.0	16.9	1.8	16.9	0.0	16.9	0.0	16.9	0.0	16.9	0.0	16.9	0.0	16.9	0.0	16.9	0.0	16.9	0.0	16.9	0.0	16.9	0.0
1940	17.0	0.6	17.2	1.2	18.1	5.2	18.1	0.0	18.1	0.0	18.1	0.0	18.1	0.0	18.1	0.0	18.1	0.0	18.1	0.0	18.1	0.0	18.1	0.0
1941	18.1	0.0	18.1	0.0	18.0	-0.6	18.0	0.0	18.0	0.0	18.0	0.0	18.1	0.6	18.3	1.1	18.5	1.1	18.6	0.5	18.7	0.5	19.2	2.7
1942	21.2	10.4	21.1	-0.5	20.5	-2.8	20.6	0.5	20.6	0.0	20.6	0.0	19.8	-3.9	19.8	0.0	19.8	0.0	19.8	0.0	19.8	0.0	19.8	0.0
1943	19.8	0.0	19.8	0.0	19.8	0.0	19.8	0.0	19.8	0.0	19.8	0.0	19.8	0.0	19.8	0.0	19.7	-0.5	19.7	0.0	19.7	0.0	19.7	0.0
1944	19.7	0.0	19.7	0.0	19.7	0.0	19.7	0.0	18.6	-5.6	18.6	0.0	18.6	0.0	18.6	0.0	18.6	0.0	18.6	0.0	18.6	0.0	18.6	0.0
1945	18.6	0.0	18.6	0.0	18.6	0.0	18.7	0.5	18.7	0.0	18.7	0.0	18.7	0.0	18.9	1.1	19.1	1.1	19.1	0.0	19.1	0.0	19.1	0.0
1946	19.1	0.0	19.1	0.0	19.6	2.6	19.9	1.5	19.9	0.0	19.8	-0.5	19.8	0.0	20.0	1.0	20.4	2.0	20.4	0.0	20.4	0.0	22.8	11.8
1947	22.9	0.4	23.6	3.1	23.8	0.8	23.8	0.0	23.8	0.0	23.8	0.0	23.8	0.0	23.9	0.4	24.1	0.8	24.6	2.1	24.6	0.0	24.7	0.4	24.7	0.0
1948	25.2	2.0	25.7	2.0	25.7	0.0	25.7	0.0	25.7	0.0	25.7	0.0	25.7	0.0	25.8	0.4	26.6	3.1	26.7	0.4	26.7	0.0	26.7	0.0	26.6	-0.4
1949	26.5	-0.4	26.3	-0.8	26.2	-0.4	26.2	0.0	25.9	-1.1	25.9	0.0	25.9	0.0	25.9	0.0	25.9	0.0	25.9	0.0	25.9	0.0	25.8	-0.4
1950	25.8	0.0	25.8	0.0	25.8	0.0	25.9	0.4	26.2	1.2	26.2	0.0	26.2	0.0	27.8	6.1	28.1	1.1	29.6	5.3	30.8	4.1	31.3	1.6
1951	31.3	0.0	31.3	0.0	31.3	0.0	31.3	0.0	31.3	0.0	31.2	-0.3	31.1	-0.3	31.0	-0.3	30.9	-0.3	30.8	-0.3	30.8	0.0	30.7	-0.3
1952	29.6	-3.6	29.6	0.0	29.6	0.0	29.5	-0.3	29.4	-0.3	29.9	1.7	30.0	0.3	30.0	0.0	30.0	0.0	30.0	0.0	30.0	0.0	30.0	0.0
1953	28.8	-4.0	29.0	0.7	29.0	0.0	28.9	-0.3	28.9	0.0	28.8	-0.3	29.5	2.4	30.1	2.0	30.1	0.0	30.0	-0.3	30.0	0.0	30.0	0.0
1954	30.0	0.0	30.0	0.0	30.0	0.0	30.0	0.0	30.0	0.0	30.1	0.3	30.1	0.0	30.1	0.0	30.1	0.0	30.1	0.0	30.1	0.0	30.1	0.0
1955	30.1	0.0	30.1	0.0	31.2	3.7	31.3	0.3	31.3	0.0	31.3	0.0	31.3	0.0	32.5	3.8	32.5	0.0	32.8	0.9	33.8	3.0	33.8	0.0
1956	33.8	0.0	33.8	0.0	33.8	0.0	34.0	0.6	34.3	0.9	34.0	-0.9	34.0	0.0	34.0	0.0	34.0	0.0	34.0	0.0	34.0	0.0	34.0	0.0
1957	33.8	-0.6	33.8	0.0	33.5	-0.9	33.4	-0.3	33.0	-1.2	32.8	-0.6	32.8	0.0	32.7	-0.3	32.7	0.0	32.6	-0.3	32.6	0.0	32.6	0.0
1958	32.3	-0.9	31.9	-1.2	31.6	-0.9	31.4	-0.6	31.1	-1.0	31.1	0.0	30.4	-2.3	30.4	0.0	31.4	3.3	31.6	0.6	31.6	0.0	31.6	0.0
1959	31.7	0.3	31.9	0.6	32.8	2.8	32.9	0.3	33.2	0.9	33.2	0.0	33.2	0.0	33.2	0.0	33.2	0.0	33.2	0.0	33.6	1.2	33.8	0.6
1960	34.0	0.6	34.0	0.0	34.0	0.0	33.5	-1.5	33.7	0.6	33.3	-1.2	33.3	0.0	33.3	0.0	33.3	0.0	33.1	-0.6	33.1	0.0	33.1	0.0
1961	33.2	0.3	33.2	0.0	33.2	0.0	33.2	0.0	33.3	0.3	33.5	0.6	33.6	0.3	33.8	0.6	33.8	0.0	33.9	0.3	33.9	0.0	33.8	-0.3
1962	33.8	0.0	33.8	0.0	33.7	-0.3	33.7	0.0	33.7	0.0	32.0	-5.0	31.5	-1.6	31.4	-0.3	31.4	0.0	31.5	0.3	31.6	0.3	31.6	0.0
1963	31.6	0.0	32.8	3.8	32.8	0.0	32.7	-0.3	32.7	0.0	32.6	-0.3	32.5	-0.3	32.5	0.0	32.5	0.0	32.5	0.0	32.5	0.0	32.5	0.0
1964	32.4	-0.3	32.4	0.0	32.3	-0.3	32.3	0.0	32.3	0.0	32.3	0.0	32.6	0.9	33.1	1.5	33.1	0.0	33.4	0.9	33.4	0.0	33.4	0.0
1965	33.3	-0.3	33.3	0.0	33.3	0.0	33.3	0.0	33.3	0.0	33.3	0.0	33.3	0.0	33.6	0.9	33.6	0.0	33.6	0.0	33.7	0.3	34.1	1.2
1966	34.0	-0.3	34.1	0.3	34.3	0.6	34.8	1.5	35.0	0.6	35.2	0.6	35.7	1.4	35.7	0.0	35.9	0.6	35.9	0.0	35.9	0.0	35.9	0.0
1967	35.9	0.0	36.0	0.3	36.0	0.0	36.0	0.0	36.0	0.0	36.0	0.0	35.7	-0.8	35.7	0.0	35.7	0.0	35.7	0.0	35.7	0.0	35.9	0.6
1968	36.0	0.3	37.0	2.8	37.1	0.3	37.2	0.3	37.2	0.0	37.0	-0.5	37.0	0.0	37.1	0.3	37.1	0.0	37.2	0.3	37.4	0.5	37.4	0.0
1969	37.6	0.5	37.7	0.3	37.8	0.3	37.8	0.0	38.0	0.5	38.3	0.8	38.8	1.3	38.8	0.0	39.1	0.8	39.2	0.3	39.6	1.0	39.4	-0.5
1970	39.2	-0.5	39.2	0.0	39.2	0.0	40.0	2.0	39.6	-1.0	39.8	0.5	40.0	0.5	39.8	-0.5	40.6	2.0	40.5	-0.2	40.4	-0.2	40.6	0.5

[Continued]

Plumbing Fixtures and Brass Fittings
Producer Price Index
Base 1982 = 100
[Continued]

For 1926-2001. Columns headed % show percentile change in the index from the previous period for which an index is available.

Year	Jan Index	%	Feb Index	%	Mar Index	%	Apr Index	%	May Index	%	Jun Index	%	Jul Index	%	Aug Index	%	Sep Index	%	Oct Index	%	Nov Index	%	Dec Index	%
1971	40.7	0.2	40.7	0.0	40.7	0.0	41.3	1.5	41.6	0.7	42.0	1.0	42.3	0.7	42.4	0.2	42.4	0.0	42.4	0.0	42.4	0.0	42.5	0.2
1972	42.4	-0.2	42.6	0.5	42.6	0.0	42.7	0.2	42.7	0.0	42.9	0.5	43.0	0.2	43.1	0.2	43.2	0.2	43.3	0.2	43.3	0.0	43.3	0.0
1973	43.4	0.2	43.6	0.5	44.2	1.4	44.8	1.4	45.1	0.7	45.3	0.4	45.3	0.0	45.4	0.2	45.6	0.4	45.8	0.4	46.3	1.1	46.7	0.9
1974	47.9	2.6	48.3	0.8	48.8	1.0	50.5	3.5	52.2	3.4	53.1	1.7	54.6	2.8	56.6	3.7	57.2	1.1	57.4	0.3	57.7	0.5	57.9	0.3
1975	58.3	0.7	58.4	0.2	58.7	0.5	58.3	-0.7	58.1	-0.3	58.0	-0.2	57.7	-0.5	57.6	-0.2	57.8	0.3	58.6	1.4	58.7	0.2	58.7	0.0
1976	59.0	0.5	60.4	2.4	60.5	0.2	60.9	0.7	61.4	0.8	62.8	2.3	63.8	1.6	63.8	0.0	64.2	0.6	64.2	0.0	64.3	0.2	64.3	0.0
1977	64.4	0.2	64.5	0.2	65.4	1.4	65.6	0.3	66.4	1.2	66.8	0.6	67.9	1.6	68.1	0.3	68.5	0.6	68.5	0.0	68.6	0.1	68.9	0.4
1978	69.0	0.1	69.9	1.3	70.3	0.6	70.9	0.9	71.1	0.3	71.4	0.4	71.7	0.4	72.2	0.7	72.4	0.3	72.6	0.3	72.6	0.0	73.1	0.7
1979	73.3	0.3	74.6	1.8	75.2	0.8	76.1	1.2	76.7	0.8	77.8	1.4	78.8	1.3	79.8	1.3	80.0	0.3	80.2	0.2	80.9	0.9	81.3	0.5
1980	83.5	2.7	84.9	1.7	87.0	2.5	87.5	0.6	88.8	1.5	89.2	0.5	89.6	0.4	89.9	0.3	89.9	0.0	89.9	0.0	90.5	0.7	91.5	1.1
1981	92.1	0.7	93.0	1.0	93.1	0.1	95.2	2.3	95.5	0.3	96.5	1.0	97.2	0.7	97.3	0.1	97.4	0.1	97.9	0.5	98.0	0.1	98.3	0.3
1982	98.5	0.2	99.2	0.7	100.2	1.0	100.6	0.4	100.8	0.2	101.4	0.6	101.6	0.2	98.5	-3.1	99.4	0.9	99.7	0.3	99.9	0.2	100.2	0.3
1983	100.7	0.5	101.7	1.0	102.5	0.8	103.2	0.7	103.7	0.5	104.3	0.6	104.2	-0.1	104.1	-0.1	104.9	0.8	105.0	0.1	105.5	0.5	105.5	0.0
1984	105.5	0.0	106.3	0.8	107.6	1.2	108.2	0.6	108.2	0.0	108.5	0.3	108.6	0.1	109.3	0.6	109.2	-0.1	109.9	0.6	110.9	0.9	111.0	0.1
1985	109.9	-1.0	110.1	0.2	110.4	0.3	111.7	1.2	112.1	0.4	112.3	0.2	112.3	0.0	112.4	0.1	112.6	0.2	113.0	0.4	113.0	0.0	112.9	-0.1
1986	113.0	0.1	113.5	0.4	115.7	1.9	115.8	0.1	115.9	0.1	116.3	0.3	116.2	-0.1	115.9	-0.3	116.1	0.2	115.9	-0.2	115.8	-0.1	115.6	-0.2
1987	116.2	0.5	118.4	1.9	118.3	-0.1	118.7	0.3	120.0	1.1	120.1	0.1	120.2	0.1	120.5	0.2	120.6	0.1	120.9	0.2	121.2	0.2	121.7	0.4
1988	121.9	0.2	123.6	1.4	127.6	3.2	127.9	0.2	128.4	0.4	128.7	0.2	129.0	0.2	130.6	1.2	130.8	0.2	131.6	0.6	131.8	0.2	132.2	0.3
1989	133.8	1.2	135.6	1.3	135.8	0.1	136.7	0.7	137.5	0.6	137.7	0.1	138.0	0.2	138.7	0.5	139.5	0.6	139.5	0.0	139.9	0.3	139.9	0.0
1990	141.2	0.9	141.9	0.5	142.7	0.6	143.5	0.6	144.0	0.3	144.1	0.1	144.3	0.1	144.5	0.1	145.9	1.0	146.3	0.3	146.5	0.1	146.6	0.1
1991	146.5	-0.1	149.0	1.7	149.4	0.3	150.0	0.4	150.1	0.1	150.1	0.0	150.3	0.1	150.3	0.0	150.0	-0.2	150.2	0.1	150.3	0.1	150.5	0.1
1992	150.7	0.1	151.0	0.2	152.1	0.7	153.4	0.9	153.7	0.2	153.9	0.1	154.1	0.1	154.2	0.1	152.9	-0.8	153.8	0.6	153.5	-0.2	153.8	0.2
1993	153.7	-0.1	153.3	-0.3	155.2	1.2	156.2	0.6	156.3	0.1	156.5	0.1	155.9	-0.4	156.5	0.4	156.5	0.0	156.8	0.2	156.9	0.1	156.8	-0.1
1994	157.4	0.4	157.8	0.3	158.6	0.5	159.2	0.4	159.3	0.1	160.3	0.6	159.7	-0.4	160.3	0.4	160.3	0.0	160.5	0.1	161.1	0.4	161.1	0.0
1995	161.7	0.4	164.8	1.9	165.7	0.5	165.9	0.1	166.5	0.4	166.5	0.0	166.5	0.0	166.7	0.1	166.8	0.1	167.2	0.2	166.7	-0.3	166.6	-0.1
1996	167.6	0.6	170.2	1.6	170.9	0.4	171.0	0.1	171.5	0.3	171.8	0.2	171.6	-0.1	171.5	-0.1	171.6	0.1	171.6	0.0	171.8	0.1	171.4	-0.2
1997	171.9	0.3	174.3	1.4	174.5	0.1	174.7	0.1	175.0	0.2	175.1	0.1	174.8	-0.2	174.9	0.1	174.6	-0.2	175.2	0.3	175.0	-0.1	174.7	-0.2
1998	174.2	-0.3	175.6	0.8	175.7	0.1	175.8	0.1	176.1	0.2	175.7	-0.2	175.4	-0.2	175.2	-0.1	174.6	-0.3	174.4	-0.1	174.5	0.1	174.0	-0.3
1999	175.3	0.7	175.7	0.2	176.2	0.3	176.7	0.3	176.1	-0.3	177.0	0.5	176.8	-0.1	176.7	-0.1	176.9	0.1	177.0	0.1	177.4	0.2	178.3	0.5
2000	178.5	0.1	179.8	0.7	180.1	0.2	180.3	0.1	180.0	-0.2	180.7	0.4	181.6	0.5	182.1	0.3	180.7	-0.8	180.7	0.0	180.1	-0.3	179.7	-0.2
2001	179.8	0.1	182.6	1.6	181.8	-0.4	180.5	-0.7	180.2	-0.2	180.7	0.3	180.3	-0.2	180.7	0.2	180.2	-0.3	180.7	0.3	180.9	0.1	180.3	-0.3

Source: U.S. Department of Labor, Bureau of Labor Statistics, Division of Industry Prices and Price Indexes. n.e.c. stands for not elsewhere classified. - indicates no data collected for period or unavailable.

Heating Equipment
Producer Price Index
Base 1982 = 100

For 1947-2001. Columns headed % show percentile change in the index from the previous period for which an index is available.

Year	Jan Index	%	Feb Index	%	Mar Index	%	Apr Index	%	May Index	%	Jun Index	%	Jul Index	%	Aug Index	%	Sep Index	%	Oct Index	%	Nov Index	%	Dec Index	%
1947	35.3	-	35.3	0.0	35.3	0.0	35.3	0.0	35.4	0.3	35.2	-0.6	35.5	0.9	35.7	0.6	36.3	1.7	36.5	0.6	36.6	0.3	36.7	0.3
1948	36.6	-0.3	36.8	0.5	36.8	0.0	37.0	0.5	37.1	0.3	37.1	0.0	37.2	0.3	38.6	3.8	39.7	2.8	39.7	0.0	39.7	0.0	39.7	0.0
1949	39.7	0.0	39.7	0.0	39.4	-0.8	39.3	-0.3	39.2	-0.3	38.9	-0.8	38.6	-0.8	38.5	-0.3	38.4	-0.3	38.4	0.0	38.3	-0.3	38.3	0.0
1950	38.2	-0.3	38.3	0.3	38.3	0.0	38.3	0.0	38.4	0.3	38.3	-0.3	38.6	0.8	39.6	2.6	40.3	1.8	41.2	2.2	41.5	0.7	42.4	2.2
1951	43.0	1.4	43.1	0.2	43.1	0.0	43.1	0.0	43.1	0.0	43.0	-0.2	42.9	-0.2	43.0	0.2	43.0	0.0	43.0	0.0	42.9	-0.2	43.0	0.2
1952	42.8	-0.5	42.8	0.0	42.8	0.0	42.7	-0.2	42.7	0.0	42.6	-0.2	42.7	0.2	42.7	0.0	42.7	0.0	42.7	0.0	42.7	0.0	42.7	0.0
1953	42.7	0.0	42.7	0.0	42.7	0.0	42.7	0.0	42.9	0.5	43.0	0.2	43.2	0.5	43.4	0.5	43.5	0.2	43.5	0.0	43.5	0.0	43.4	-0.2
1954	43.3	-0.2	43.1	-0.5	42.9	-0.5	43.0	0.2	42.7	-0.7	42.7	0.0	42.8	0.2	42.8	0.0	42.8	0.0	42.9	0.2	42.9	0.0	42.9	0.0
1955	42.7	-0.5	42.7	0.0	42.7	0.0	42.7	0.0	42.6	-0.2	42.6	0.0	42.7	0.2	43.5	1.9	44.0	1.1	44.0	0.0	44.1	0.2	44.0	-0.2
1956	44.0	0.0	44.0	0.0	44.0	0.0	44.0	0.0	44.0	0.0	44.1	0.2	44.3	0.5	44.7	0.9	45.4	1.6	45.7	0.7	45.8	0.2	45.8	0.0
1957	46.0	0.4	46.0	0.0	45.5	-1.1	45.5	0.0	45.4	-0.2	45.6	0.4	46.0	0.9	45.7	-0.7	45.7	0.0	45.7	0.0	45.7	0.0	45.5	-0.4
1958	45.4	-0.2	45.3	-0.2	45.1	-0.4	45.1	0.0	45.1	0.0	45.2	0.2	45.3	0.2	45.3	0.0	45.4	0.2	45.4	0.0	45.4	0.0	45.5	0.2
1959	45.5	0.0	45.6	0.2	45.5	-0.2	45.5	0.0	45.5	0.0	45.5	0.0	45.5	0.0	45.4	-0.2	45.4	0.0	45.4	0.0	45.4	0.0	45.4	0.0
1960	45.2	-0.4	44.9	-0.7	44.9	0.0	44.9	0.0	44.9	0.0	44.9	0.0	44.3	-1.3	44.4	0.2	44.6	0.5	44.6	0.0	44.3	-0.7	43.6	-1.6
1961	42.9	-1.6	42.9	0.0	42.7	-0.5	43.0	0.7	43.1	0.2	43.1	0.0	43.1	0.0	43.2	0.2	43.0	-0.5	42.9	-0.2	42.7	-0.5	42.9	0.5
1962	42.7	-0.5	42.7	0.0	42.6	-0.2	42.6	0.0	42.3	-0.7	42.2	-0.2	42.2	0.0	42.2	0.0	42.1	-0.2	42.2	0.2	42.2	0.0	42.4	0.5
1963	42.1	-0.7	42.0	-0.2	42.1	0.2	42.2	0.2	42.3	0.2	42.4	0.2	42.4	0.0	42.3	-0.2	42.3	0.0	42.3	0.0	42.2	-0.2	42.2	0.0
1964	41.8	-0.9	41.7	-0.2	41.9	0.5	41.9	0.0	41.8	-0.2	42.0	0.5	41.8	-0.5	41.7	-0.2	41.7	0.0	41.7	0.0	41.8	0.2	41.9	0.2
1965	41.5	-1.0	41.6	0.2	41.7	0.2	41.8	0.2	41.7	-0.2	41.8	0.2	41.7	-0.2	41.8	0.2	41.8	0.0	41.8	0.0	41.7	-0.2	41.7	0.0
1966	41.6	-0.2	41.7	0.2	41.7	0.0	41.9	0.5	41.9	0.0	42.1	0.5	42.2	0.2	42.1	-0.2	42.2	0.2	42.4	0.5	42.5	0.2	42.5	0.0
1967	42.1	-0.9	41.8	-0.7	41.9	0.2	41.9	0.0	41.9	0.0	42.2	0.7	42.2	0.0	42.1	-0.2	42.2	0.2	42.3	0.2	42.5	0.5	42.6	0.2
1968	42.5	-0.2	42.7	0.5	42.9	0.5	43.1	0.5	43.3	0.5	43.4	0.2	43.5	0.2	43.5	0.0	43.5	0.0	43.5	0.0	43.6	0.2	43.8	0.5
1969	43.7	-0.2	43.8	0.2	43.9	0.2	44.1	0.5	44.1	0.0	44.3	0.5	44.4	0.2	44.5	0.2	44.6	0.2	44.9	0.7	45.4	1.1	45.4	0.0
1970	45.4	0.0	45.5	0.2	45.7	0.4	46.1	0.9	46.2	0.2	46.6	0.9	47.0	0.9	47.0	0.0	47.1	0.2	47.4	0.6	47.6	0.4	47.7	0.2
1971	47.8	0.2	48.1	0.6	48.1	0.0	48.3	0.4	48.6	0.6	48.5	-0.2	48.8	0.6	49.0	0.4	49.0	0.0	49.0	0.0	49.0	0.0	49.0	0.0
1972	48.9	-0.2	49.0	0.2	49.3	0.6	49.7	0.8	49.8	0.2	50.0	0.4	50.2	0.4	50.2	0.0	50.3	0.2	50.2	-0.2	50.3	0.2	50.2	-0.2
1973	50.1	-0.2	50.3	0.4	50.4	0.2	50.8	0.8	50.7	-0.2	50.9	0.4	51.0	0.2	50.9	-0.2	50.9	0.0	50.9	0.0	51.0	0.2	51.3	0.6
1974	51.8	1.0	52.1	0.6	52.5	0.8	53.8	2.5	54.8	1.9	56.0	2.2	57.8	3.2	59.0	2.1	59.6	1.0	61.1	2.5	62.0	1.5	62.6	1.0
1975	62.5	-0.2	62.8	0.5	63.0	0.3	63.1	0.2	63.3	0.3	63.5	0.3	63.3	-0.3	63.4	0.2	63.4	0.0	64.1	1.1	64.5	0.6	65.4	1.4
1976	65.5	0.2	65.5	0.0	65.4	-0.2	65.7	0.5	66.1	0.6	66.2	0.2	66.8	0.9	67.2	0.6	67.6	0.6	67.5	-0.1	67.8	0.4	68.2	0.6
1977	68.7	0.7	68.8	0.1	69.0	0.3	68.9	-0.1	69.1	0.3	69.4	0.4	69.7	0.4	70.0	0.4	70.3	0.4	70.8	0.7	70.9	0.1	71.4	0.7
1978	72.2	1.1	72.0	-0.3	72.2	0.3	72.8	0.8	73.1	0.4	73.3	0.3	73.5	0.3	74.3	1.1	74.2	-0.1	74.6	0.5	74.7	0.1	75.5	1.1
1979	75.9	0.5	76.3	0.5	77.3	1.3	77.5	0.3	78.3	1.0	78.1	-0.3	78.4	0.4	79.3	1.1	80.7	1.8	81.0	0.4	81.4	0.5	82.4	1.2
1980	84.1	2.1	85.4	1.5	85.4	0.0	86.1	0.8	86.0	-0.1	86.4	0.5	86.9	0.6	87.7	0.9	88.0	0.3	88.8	0.9	89.4	0.7	90.2	0.9
1981	91.3	1.2	91.7	0.4	92.5	0.9	92.7	0.2	93.7	1.1	94.2	0.5	95.4	1.3	96.1	0.7	96.3	0.2	96.5	0.2	96.5	0.0	96.9	0.4
1982	98.4	1.5	98.3	-0.1	99.3	1.0	99.5	0.2	100.0	0.5	100.5	0.5	100.7	0.2	100.5	-0.2	100.8	0.3	100.5	-0.3	100.7	0.2	100.9	0.2
1983	101.5	0.6	101.5	0.0	101.6	0.1	102.2	0.6	102.3	0.1	102.4	0.1	103.2	0.8	103.3	0.1	104.0	0.7	103.4	-0.6	103.5	0.1	103.6	0.1
1984	104.2	0.6	104.6	0.4	104.8	0.2	105.5	0.7	106.4	0.9	106.5	0.1	107.6	1.0	107.7	0.1	107.8	0.1	107.9	0.1	107.9	0.0	108.1	0.2
1985	108.0	-0.1	108.5	0.5	108.6	0.1	108.7	0.1	109.4	0.6	109.5	0.1	109.6	0.1	110.0	0.4	110.3	0.3	110.2	-0.1	110.3	0.1	110.5	0.2
1986	111.6	1.0	111.7	0.1	111.6	-0.1	112.5	0.8	112.3	-0.2	113.0	0.6	113.1	0.1	113.5	0.4	113.4	-0.1	114.3	0.8	114.4	0.1	114.5	0.1
1987	115.3	0.7	115.4	0.1	115.7	0.3	115.6	-0.1	115.6	0.0	115.1	-0.4	115.5	0.3	115.6	0.1	115.5	-0.1	115.7	0.2	117.1	1.2	114.1	-2.6
1988	115.9	1.6	118.4	2.2	118.4	0.0	118.5	0.1	118.8	0.3	118.5	-0.3	119.9	1.2	120.1	0.2	120.0	-0.1	120.5	0.4	120.8	0.2	121.0	0.2
1989	121.8	0.7	123.2	1.1	123.7	0.4	124.6	0.7	124.7	0.1	124.3	-0.3	124.8	0.4	125.1	0.2	126.9	1.4	126.9	0.0	127.3	0.3	127.6	0.2
1990	129.9	1.8	130.8	0.7	130.9	0.1	130.7	-0.2	130.7	0.0	130.6	-0.1	131.7	0.8	131.8	0.1	132.0	0.2	133.3	1.0	133.3	0.0	133.3	0.0
1991	134.0	0.5	134.3	0.2	134.1	-0.1	133.2	-0.7	133.5	0.2	133.5	0.0	134.1	0.4	134.4	0.2	134.0	-0.3	134.8	0.6	134.8	0.0	134.6	-0.1

[Continued]

Heating Equipment
Producer Price Index
Base 1982 = 100
[Continued]

For 1947-2001. Columns headed % show percentile change in the index from the previous period for which an index is available.

Year	Jan Index	%	Feb Index	%	Mar Index	%	Apr Index	%	May Index	%	Jun Index	%	Jul Index	%	Aug Index	%	Sep Index	%	Oct Index	%	Nov Index	%	Dec Index	%
1992	136.2	1.2	136.6	0.3	137.2	0.4	137.1	-0.1	137.6	0.4	137.4	-0.1	137.6	0.1	137.4	-0.1	137.3	-0.1	137.6	0.2	137.0	-0.4	138.1	0.8
1993	139.2	0.8	139.3	0.1	139.4	0.1	140.6	0.9	140.7	0.1	141.2	0.4	140.9	-0.2	140.7	-0.1	140.4	-0.2	140.6	0.1	140.7	0.1	140.7	0.0
1994	141.2	0.4	141.8	0.4	142.1	0.2	142.4	0.2	142.6	0.1	142.4	-0.1	142.6	0.1	142.9	0.2	143.0	0.1	143.0	0.0	143.1	0.1	143.3	0.1
1995	145.3	1.4	146.5	0.8	147.0	0.3	147.2	0.1	147.4	0.1	147.6	0.1	147.7	0.1	148.1	0.3	148.2	0.1	148.4	0.1	148.4	0.0	148.5	0.1
1996	150.1	1.1	150.5	0.3	150.5	0.0	150.6	0.1	150.8	0.1	151.1	0.2	151.5	0.3	151.8	0.2	151.8	0.0	151.8	0.0	151.8	0.0	151.9	0.1
1997	152.0	0.1	152.0	0.0	152.0	0.0	152.2	0.1	151.7	-0.3	152.1	0.3	152.7	0.4	152.8	0.1	152.9	0.1	153.0	0.1	153.3	0.2	153.9	0.4
1998	152.8	-0.7	153.2	0.3	153.1	-0.1	153.4	0.2	153.4	0.0	153.0	-0.3	153.2	0.1	153.2	0.0	153.2	0.0	153.5	0.2	153.5	0.0	154.0	0.3
1999	153.9	-0.1	153.4	-0.3	153.6	0.1	153.6	0.0	154.0	0.3	153.8	-0.1	154.2	0.3	154.3	0.1	154.5	0.1	154.4	-0.1	154.2	-0.1	154.1	-0.1
2000	154.1	0.0	154.1	0.0	154.4	0.2	155.5	0.7	155.8	0.2	155.9	0.1	156.0	0.1	156.1	0.1	156.1	0.0	156.3	0.1	156.1	-0.1	156.4	0.2
2001	157.9	1.0	157.8	-0.1	156.6	-0.8	156.8	0.1	156.7	-0.1	157.1	0.3	156.9	-0.1	156.7	-0.1	157.0	0.2	157.0	0.0	157.3	0.2	157.6	0.2

Source: U.S. Department of Labor, Bureau of Labor Statistics, Division of Industry Prices and Price Indexes. n.e.c. stands for not elsewhere classified. - indicates no data collected for period or unavailable.

Fabricated Structural Metal Products
Producer Price Index
Base 1982 = 100

For 1947-2001. Columns headed % show percentile change in the index from the previous period for which an index is available.

Year	Jan Index	%	Feb Index	%	Mar Index	%	Apr Index	%	May Index	%	Jun Index	%	Jul Index	%	Aug Index	%	Sep Index	%	Oct Index	%	Nov Index	%	Dec Index	%
1947	22.2	-	22.2	0.0	22.4	0.9	22.4	0.0	22.3	-0.4	22.3	0.0	22.3	0.0	22.3	0.0	22.9	2.7	23.0	0.4	23.1	0.4	23.1	0.0
1948	23.2	0.4	23.2	0.0	23.3	0.4	23.4	0.4	23.2	-0.9	23.2	0.0	23.4	0.9	24.5	4.7	24.7	0.8	24.7	0.0	24.7	0.0	24.7	0.0
1949	24.6	-0.4	24.5	-0.4	24.4	-0.4	24.0	-1.6	23.7	-1.2	23.4	-1.3	23.4	0.0	22.8	-2.6	22.7	-0.4	22.7	0.0	22.8	0.4	22.9	0.4
1950	23.0	0.4	23.4	1.7	23.4	0.0	23.3	-0.4	23.3	0.0	23.3	0.0	23.9	2.6	24.2	1.3	24.6	1.7	25.7	4.5	26.0	1.2	27.2	4.6
1951	27.6	1.5	27.8	0.7	27.7	-0.4	27.7	0.0	27.7	0.0	27.7	0.0	27.3	-1.4	27.1	-0.7	27.1	0.0	27.0	-0.4	27.0	0.0	27.0	0.0
1952	27.0	0.0	26.9	-0.4	26.9	0.0	26.9	0.0	26.9	0.0	26.9	0.0	26.9	0.0	26.9	0.0	26.9	0.0	26.6	-1.1	26.6	0.0	26.5	-0.4
1953	26.5	0.0	26.5	0.0	26.5	0.0	26.5	0.0	26.5	0.0	26.7	0.8	27.4	2.6	27.5	0.4	27.5	0.0	27.4	-0.4	27.4	0.0	27.3	-0.4
1954	27.4	0.4	27.2	-0.7	27.2	0.0	27.2	0.0	27.1	-0.4	27.0	-0.4	27.0	0.0	27.4	1.5	27.5	0.4	27.5	0.0	27.4	-0.4	27.5	0.4
1955	27.5	0.0	27.5	0.0	27.5	0.0	27.6	0.4	27.7	0.4	27.7	0.0	28.8	4.0	29.5	2.4	29.6	0.3	29.7	0.3	29.7	0.0	29.8	0.3
1956	30.0	0.7	30.0	0.0	30.2	0.7	30.6	1.3	30.1	-1.6	30.1	0.0	30.2	0.3	31.3	3.6	31.9	1.9	31.9	0.0	32.0	0.3	32.0	0.0
1957	31.2	-2.5	31.1	-0.3	31.1	0.0	30.9	-0.6	30.8	-0.3	30.7	-0.3	31.3	2.0	31.6	1.0	31.4	-0.6	31.4	0.0	31.4	0.0	31.4	0.0
1958	31.4	0.0	31.4	0.0	31.3	-0.3	31.3	0.0	31.3	0.0	31.2	-0.3	31.0	-0.6	31.1	0.3	31.0	-0.3	31.1	0.3	31.2	0.3	31.2	0.0
1959	31.2	0.0	31.2	0.0	30.8	-1.3	30.8	0.0	30.8	0.0	30.8	0.0	30.8	0.0	30.8	0.0	31.3	1.6	31.3	0.0	31.6	1.0	31.6	0.0
1960	31.6	0.0	31.6	0.0	31.7	0.3	31.5	-0.6	31.4	-0.3	31.4	0.0	31.4	0.0	31.4	0.0	31.3	-0.3	31.2	-0.3	31.2	0.0	31.2	0.0
1961	31.1	-0.3	31.1	0.0	30.9	-0.6	30.9	0.0	30.8	-0.3	30.8	0.0	30.8	0.0	30.8	0.0	30.7	-0.3	30.7	0.0	30.7	0.0	30.7	0.0
1962	30.6	-0.3	30.6	0.0	30.6	0.0	30.6	0.0	30.6	0.0	30.6	0.0	30.6	0.0	30.6	0.0	30.6	0.0	30.6	0.0	30.6	0.0	30.6	0.0
1963	30.6	0.0	30.5	-0.3	30.5	0.0	30.4	-0.3	30.5	0.3	30.6	0.3	30.6	0.0	30.6	0.0	30.7	0.3	30.7	0.0	30.8	0.3	30.8	0.0
1964	30.8	0.0	30.9	0.3	30.7	-0.6	30.8	0.3	30.7	-0.3	30.9	0.7	30.9	0.0	31.0	0.3	31.0	0.0	31.0	0.0	31.1	0.3	31.2	0.3
1965	31.3	0.3	31.2	-0.3	31.3	0.3	31.4	0.3	31.5	0.3	31.5	0.0	31.6	0.3	31.7	0.3	31.7	0.0	31.7	0.0	31.8	0.3	31.8	0.0
1966	31.9	0.3	32.0	0.3	32.1	0.3	32.3	0.6	32.3	0.0	32.4	0.3	32.5	0.3	32.5	0.0	32.5	0.0	32.6	0.3	32.6	0.0	32.7	0.3
1967	32.6	-0.3	32.6	0.0	32.6	0.0	32.7	0.3	32.7	0.0	32.7	0.0	32.8	0.3	32.9	0.3	32.9	0.0	33.0	0.3	33.0	0.0	33.0	0.0
1968	33.1	0.3	33.1	0.0	33.3	0.6	33.3	0.0	33.2	-0.3	33.5	0.9	33.5	0.0	33.7	0.6	33.8	0.3	33.9	0.3	33.9	0.0	34.0	0.3
1969	34.0	0.0	34.1	0.3	34.1	0.0	34.3	0.6	34.5	0.6	34.8	0.9	34.9	0.3	35.1	0.6	35.2	0.3	35.3	0.3	35.4	0.3	35.4	0.0
1970	35.6	0.6	35.8	0.6	36.2	1.1	36.3	0.3	36.5	0.6	36.8	0.8	37.1	0.8	37.2	0.3	37.3	0.3	37.3	0.0	37.3	0.0	37.5	0.5
1971	37.7	0.5	37.9	0.5	38.2	0.8	38.3	0.3	38.4	0.3	38.6	0.5	38.8	0.5	39.5	1.8	39.4	-0.3	39.4	0.0	39.4	0.0	39.4	0.0
1972	39.9	1.3	40.0	0.3	40.1	0.2	40.1	0.0	40.0	-0.2	40.1	0.2	40.1	0.0	40.2	0.2	40.2	0.0	40.4	0.5	40.4	0.0	40.5	0.2
1973	40.8	0.7	40.9	0.2	41.0	0.2	41.2	0.5	41.6	1.0	41.6	0.0	41.7	0.2	41.9	0.5	42.2	0.7	42.5	0.7	42.9	0.9	43.2	0.7
1974	44.4	2.8	44.9	1.1	46.0	2.4	47.2	2.6	49.8	5.5	52.1	4.6	54.2	4.0	57.5	6.1	59.0	2.6	59.7	1.2	59.9	0.3	60.0	0.2
1975	60.8	1.3	62.2	2.3	62.3	0.2	61.8	-0.8	61.9	0.2	61.9	0.0	61.8	-0.2	62.0	0.3	62.1	0.2	62.4	0.5	62.3	-0.2	62.6	0.5
1976	62.5	-0.2	62.4	-0.2	62.6	0.3	62.5	-0.2	62.6	0.2	63.0	0.6	63.5	0.8	64.1	0.9	64.6	0.8	64.8	0.3	65.0	0.3	65.3	0.5
1977	65.4	0.2	65.7	0.5	66.2	0.8	66.6	0.6	67.0	0.6	67.2	0.3	68.2	1.5	68.9	1.0	69.5	0.9	69.5	0.0	69.6	0.1	70.0	0.6
1978	70.4	0.6	71.8	2.0	72.6	1.1	73.7	1.5	73.9	0.3	74.1	0.3	74.8	0.9	75.5	0.9	75.7	0.3	76.0	0.4	76.2	0.3	76.6	0.5
1979	78.2	2.1	78.9	0.9	79.2	0.4	80.0	1.0	81.0	1.3	81.4	0.5	82.2	1.0	82.7	0.6	83.2	0.6	84.1	1.1	84.2	0.1	84.5	0.4
1980	84.9	0.5	85.2	0.4	87.0	2.1	88.3	1.5	88.5	0.2	88.6	0.1	89.3	0.8	89.6	0.3	89.9	0.3	90.9	1.1	91.2	0.3	91.6	0.4
1981	92.9	1.4	93.6	0.8	95.0	1.5	96.1	1.2	96.4	0.3	96.8	0.4	97.7	0.9	98.2	0.5	98.4	0.2	99.3	0.9	99.5	0.2	99.4	-0.1
1982	99.6	0.2	99.7	0.1	99.9	0.2	100.1	0.2	100.0	-0.1	100.2	0.2	99.7	-0.5	99.8	0.1	100.5	0.7	100.4	-0.1	100.2	-0.2	100.0	-0.2
1983	99.6	-0.4	99.4	-0.2	99.6	0.2	99.2	-0.4	99.1	-0.1	99.1	0.0	99.2	0.1	99.4	0.2	99.8	0.4	99.8	0.0	100.2	0.4	100.4	0.2
1984	100.6	0.2	100.7	0.1	101.2	0.5	101.5	0.3	101.9	0.4	102.1	0.2	102.3	0.2	102.4	0.1	102.4	0.0	102.9	0.5	102.6	-0.3	102.8	0.2
1985	102.9	0.1	102.9	0.0	103.2	0.3	103.2	0.0	103.2	0.0	103.2	0.0	103.2	0.0	103.4	0.2	103.3	-0.1	103.5	0.2	103.3	-0.2	103.3	0.0
1986	103.3	0.0	103.5	0.2	103.4	-0.1	103.4	0.0	103.3	-0.1	103.5	0.2	103.5	0.0	103.7	0.2	103.7	0.0	103.6	-0.1	104.1	0.5	103.8	-0.3
1987	103.6	-0.2	103.8	0.2	104.0	0.2	104.2	0.2	104.4	0.2	104.9	0.5	105.2	0.3	105.6	0.4	106.1	0.5	107.0	0.8	107.8	0.7	108.6	0.7
1988	110.2	1.5	110.8	0.5	111.7	0.8	112.9	1.1	113.8	0.8	114.4	0.5	115.4	0.9	115.8	0.3	116.2	0.3	116.5	0.3	116.8	0.3	117.4	0.5
1989	118.2	0.7	118.9	0.6	119.4	0.4	119.8	0.3	120.5	0.6	120.5	0.0	120.7	0.2	120.8	0.1	120.9	0.1	121.0	0.1	121.2	0.2	121.1	-0.1
1990	121.1	0.0	121.2	0.1	121.3	0.1	121.4	0.1	121.9	0.4	122.0	0.1	122.0	0.0	122.1	0.1	122.1	0.0	122.2	0.1	122.1	-0.1	122.4	0.2
1991	122.7	0.2	122.5	-0.2	122.5	0.0	122.9	0.3	122.7	-0.2	122.6	-0.1	122.5	-0.1	122.6	0.1	122.5	-0.1	122.0	-0.4	121.7	-0.2	121.7	0.0

[Continued]

Fabricated Structural Metal Products
Producer Price Index
Base 1982 = 100
[Continued]

For 1947-2001. Columns headed % show percentile change in the index from the previous period for which an index is available.

Year	Jan Index	%	Feb Index	%	Mar Index	%	Apr Index	%	May Index	%	Jun Index	%	Jul Index	%	Aug Index	%	Sep Index	%	Oct Index	%	Nov Index	%	Dec Index	%
1992	122.0	0.2	121.8	-0.2	122.0	0.2	122.2	0.2	122.0	-0.2	122.0	0.0	122.2	0.2	122.3	0.1	122.1	-0.2	122.2	0.1	122.2	0.0	122.2	0.0
1993	121.8	-0.3	122.1	0.2	122.4	0.2	122.7	0.2	122.9	0.2	123.1	0.2	123.4	0.2	123.6	0.2	123.8	0.2	124.1	0.2	124.4	0.2	124.6	0.2
1994	124.9	0.2	125.0	0.1	125.2	0.2	125.7	0.4	126.3	0.5	127.1	0.6	127.4	0.2	128.0	0.5	128.7	0.5	129.2	0.4	130.1	0.7	130.4	0.2
1995	131.9	1.2	132.5	0.5	133.6	0.8	134.4	0.6	134.6	0.1	135.2	0.4	135.8	0.4	136.0	0.1	136.5	0.4	136.6	0.1	136.7	0.1	136.7	0.0
1996	136.8	0.1	136.9	0.1	137.1	0.1	137.2	0.1	137.5	0.2	138.0	0.4	138.0	0.0	138.2	0.1	138.4	0.1	138.6	0.1	138.6	0.0	138.6	0.0
1997	139.0	0.3	139.1	0.1	139.2	0.1	139.8	0.4	140.2	0.3	140.4	0.1	140.6	0.1	140.8	0.1	141.0	0.1	141.1	0.1	141.5	0.3	141.3	-0.1
1998	141.4	0.1	141.4	0.0	141.6	0.1	141.9	0.2	142.6	0.5	143.1	0.4	143.0	-0.1	142.9	-0.1	143.2	0.2	143.2	0.0	143.1	-0.1	142.8	-0.2
1999	142.7	-0.1	142.6	-0.1	142.8	0.1	142.8	0.0	142.9	0.1	143.0	0.1	143.1	0.1	143.2	0.1	143.4	0.1	143.7	0.2	144.3	0.4	144.4	0.1
2000	144.9	0.3	145.0	0.1	145.4	0.3	145.6	0.1	144.7	-0.6	144.8	0.1	144.5	-0.2	144.5	0.0	144.8	0.2	145.0	0.1	145.0	0.0	144.9	-0.1
2001	144.9	0.0	145.0	0.1	145.1	0.1	144.9	-0.1	144.8	-0.1	144.5	-0.2	144.6	0.1	144.5	-0.1	144.6	0.1	144.2	-0.3	144.2	0.0	144.2	0.0

Source: U.S. Department of Labor, Bureau of Labor Statistics, Division of Industry Prices and Price Indexes. n.e.c. stands for not elsewhere classified. - indicates no data collected for period or unavailable.

Miscellaneous Metal Products
Producer Price Index
Base 1982 = 100

For 1947-2001. Columns headed % show percentile change in the index from the previous period for which an index is available.

Year	Jan Index	%	Feb Index	%	Mar Index	%	Apr Index	%	May Index	%	Jun Index	%	Jul Index	%	Aug Index	%	Sep Index	%	Oct Index	%	Nov Index	%	Dec Index	%
1947	17.4	-	17.4	0.0	17.7	1.7	17.9	1.1	17.9	0.0	18.0	0.6	18.1	0.6	18.2	0.6	18.2	0.0	18.5	1.6	18.6	0.5	18.6	0.0
1948	18.6	0.0	18.9	1.6	20.0	5.8	22.5	12.5	22.5	0.0	22.6	0.4	22.6	0.0	23.6	4.4	23.8	0.8	23.8	0.0	23.9	0.4	23.9	0.0
1949	23.9	0.0	23.9	0.0	23.9	0.0	24.0	0.4	24.0	0.0	23.9	-0.4	23.9	0.0	23.8	-0.4	23.8	0.0	23.8	0.0	23.7	-0.4	23.6	-0.4
1950	24.0	1.7	24.1	0.4	24.2	0.4	24.2	0.0	24.2	0.0	24.2	0.0	24.3	0.4	24.4	0.4	25.1	2.9	25.7	2.4	25.8	0.4	26.4	2.3
1951	26.9	1.9	26.9	0.0	26.9	0.0	26.9	0.0	26.9	0.0	26.9	0.0	26.9	0.0	26.8	-0.4	26.6	-0.7	26.6	0.0	26.6	0.0	26.6	0.0
1952	26.6	0.0	26.6	0.0	26.6	0.0	26.6	0.0	26.6	0.0	26.6	0.0	26.6	0.0	26.6	0.0	26.8	0.8	26.9	0.4	26.9	0.0	27.0	0.4
1953	27.0	0.0	27.1	0.4	26.1	-3.7	26.2	0.4	26.5	1.1	26.5	0.0	26.8	1.1	27.0	0.7	27.1	0.4	27.2	0.4	27.2	0.0	27.2	0.0
1954	27.2	0.0	27.0	-0.7	27.0	0.0	26.8	-0.7	26.8	0.0	26.8	0.0	26.8	0.0	26.9	0.4	26.9	0.0	26.9	0.0	27.0	0.4	26.9	-0.4
1955	26.9	0.0	26.9	0.0	26.9	0.0	26.9	0.0	26.9	0.0	26.9	0.0	27.1	0.7	27.7	2.2	27.9	0.7	28.1	0.7	28.2	0.4	28.3	0.4
1956	28.3	0.0	28.3	0.0	28.4	0.4	28.3	-0.4	28.3	0.0	28.3	0.0	28.3	0.0	28.5	0.7	29.3	2.8	30.2	3.1	30.2	0.0	30.2	0.0
1957	30.2	0.0	30.4	0.7	30.5	0.3	30.6	0.3	30.6	0.0	30.6	0.0	31.1	1.6	31.3	0.6	31.5	0.6	31.5	0.0	31.4	-0.3	31.6	0.6
1958	31.4	-0.6	31.3	-0.3	31.3	0.0	31.2	-0.3	31.2	0.0	31.0	-0.6	31.0	0.0	31.1	0.3	31.1	0.0	31.1	0.0	31.0	-0.3	31.0	0.0
1959	31.1	0.3	31.2	0.3	31.2	0.0	31.2	0.0	31.2	0.0	31.2	0.0	31.1	-0.3	31.0	-0.3	31.2	0.6	31.3	0.3	31.5	0.6	31.3	-0.6
1960	31.3	0.0	31.3	0.0	31.2	-0.3	31.2	0.0	31.2	0.0	31.2	0.0	31.2	0.0	31.2	0.0	31.2	0.0	31.2	0.0	31.3	0.3	31.7	1.3
1961	32.0	0.9	32.0	0.0	32.0	0.0	32.1	0.3	32.1	0.0	32.0	-0.3	31.9	-0.3	32.2	0.9	32.2	0.0	32.2	0.0	32.1	-0.3	32.1	0.0
1962	32.1	0.0	32.1	0.0	32.4	0.9	32.5	0.3	32.4	-0.3	32.3	-0.3	32.3	0.0	32.3	0.0	32.3	0.0	32.3	0.0	32.3	0.0	32.3	0.0
1963	32.2	-0.3	32.2	0.0	32.2	0.0	32.3	0.3	32.3	0.0	32.6	0.9	32.7	0.3	32.7	0.0	32.7	0.0	33.3	1.8	33.3	0.0	33.6	0.9
1964	34.0	1.2	34.0	0.0	33.9	-0.3	33.9	0.0	33.6	-0.9	33.7	0.3	33.6	-0.3	33.6	0.0	33.6	0.0	33.6	0.0	33.6	0.0	33.7	0.3
1965	33.7	0.0	33.9	0.6	33.9	0.0	34.0	0.3	34.0	0.0	34.0	0.0	33.9	-0.3	34.2	0.9	34.2	0.0	34.1	-0.3	34.1	0.0	34.1	0.0
1966	34.2	0.3	34.4	0.6	34.5	0.3	34.5	0.0	34.5	0.0	34.6	0.3	34.6	0.0	34.9	0.9	35.0	0.3	35.0	0.0	35.2	0.6	35.2	0.0
1967	35.3	0.3	35.3	0.0	35.3	0.0	35.3	0.0	35.3	0.0	35.3	0.0	35.4	0.3	35.5	0.3	35.5	0.0	35.5	0.0	35.5	0.0	35.6	0.3
1968	35.7	0.3	35.9	0.6	35.9	0.0	35.9	0.0	35.9	0.0	35.9	0.0	36.0	0.3	36.0	0.0	36.3	0.8	36.6	0.8	36.6	0.0	36.8	0.5
1969	37.2	1.1	37.4	0.5	37.5	0.3	37.5	0.0	37.5	0.0	37.6	0.3	38.0	1.1	38.5	1.3	38.7	0.5	38.7	0.0	38.7	0.0	38.8	0.3
1970	38.9	0.3	39.0	0.3	39.6	1.5	39.6	0.0	39.9	0.8	40.6	1.8	40.8	0.5	40.9	0.2	41.5	1.5	41.6	0.2	41.7	0.2	41.7	0.0
1971	41.6	-0.2	41.7	0.2	41.7	0.0	41.8	0.2	41.8	0.0	42.0	0.5	42.3	0.7	42.4	0.2	42.4	0.0	42.3	-0.2	42.3	0.0	42.8	1.2
1972	43.0	0.5	43.6	1.4	44.0	0.9	44.0	0.0	44.0	0.0	44.1	0.2	44.0	-0.2	44.2	0.5	44.2	0.0	44.2	0.0	44.2	0.0	44.2	0.0
1973	44.4	0.5	44.5	0.2	44.8	0.7	45.1	0.7	45.4	0.7	45.6	0.4	45.7	0.2	46.4	1.5	46.5	0.2	46.8	0.6	47.4	1.3	47.7	0.6
1974	48.5	1.7	49.1	1.2	49.5	0.8	50.7	2.4	53.2	4.9	54.6	2.6	57.1	4.6	59.0	3.3	60.5	2.5	61.7	2.0	62.2	0.8	62.6	0.6
1975	63.1	0.8	63.3	0.3	63.7	0.6	63.8	0.2	63.5	-0.5	64.3	1.3	64.5	0.3	64.5	0.0	64.5	0.0	64.6	0.2	64.7	0.2	64.7	0.0
1976	65.0	0.5	65.0	0.0	64.9	-0.2	65.2	0.5	65.5	0.5	65.7	0.3	66.3	0.9	67.0	1.1	67.2	0.3	67.4	0.3	67.7	0.4	67.5	-0.3
1977	67.8	0.4	68.0	0.3	68.1	0.1	68.1	0.0	68.3	0.3	68.9	0.9	69.7	1.2	70.2	0.7	70.8	0.9	71.0	0.3	71.4	0.6	71.6	0.3
1978	71.8	0.3	72.2	0.6	72.8	0.8	73.3	0.7	73.9	0.8	74.8	1.2	75.6	1.1	76.4	1.1	77.0	0.8	77.3	0.4	77.9	0.8	78.2	0.4
1979	78.6	0.5	79.1	0.6	79.8	0.9	80.4	0.8	80.9	0.6	81.5	0.7	82.1	0.7	83.4	1.6	83.8	0.5	84.5	0.8	84.5	0.0	84.7	0.2
1980	85.2	0.6	85.6	0.5	86.5	1.1	87.2	0.8	87.4	0.2	88.7	1.5	88.9	0.2	89.7	0.9	90.3	0.7	90.8	0.6	91.0	0.2	91.2	0.2
1981	92.3	1.2	93.2	1.0	93.8	0.6	94.6	0.9	95.5	1.0	95.4	-0.1	96.3	0.9	96.7	0.4	96.9	0.2	97.8	0.9	98.5	0.7	98.6	0.1
1982	99.6	1.0	98.7	-0.9	98.8	0.1	99.1	0.3	100.8	1.7	100.6	-0.2	100.3	-0.3	100.4	0.1	100.5	0.1	100.6	0.1	100.4	-0.2	100.3	-0.1
1983	98.9	-1.4	98.8	-0.1	99.3	0.5	99.4	0.1	99.5	0.1	100.4	0.9	100.5	0.1	100.6	0.1	100.7	0.1	102.3	1.6	102.6	0.3	102.6	0.0
1984	102.8	0.2	103.1	0.3	103.5	0.4	103.8	0.3	103.9	0.1	104.2	0.3	104.2	0.0	104.5	0.3	104.8	0.3	106.8	1.9	106.8	0.0	106.9	0.1
1985	106.9	0.0	107.0	0.1	107.0	0.0	107.0	0.0	107.0	0.0	107.2	0.2	107.3	0.1	107.2	-0.1	107.1	-0.1	107.0	-0.1	107.1	0.1	107.0	-0.1
1986	107.1	0.1	107.2	0.1	107.2	0.0	107.2	0.0	106.8	-0.4	106.8	0.0	106.6	-0.2	106.7	0.1	106.9	0.2	107.1	0.2	107.2	0.1	107.3	0.1
1987	107.5	0.2	107.6	0.1	107.6	0.0	107.5	-0.1	107.5	0.0	107.6	0.1	107.8	0.2	107.7	-0.1	107.7	0.0	108.2	0.5	108.4	0.2	108.8	0.4
1988	109.2	0.4	109.7	0.5	110.3	0.5	111.3	0.9	112.0	0.6	111.9	-0.1	112.3	0.4	113.1	0.7	113.4	0.3	113.8	0.4	114.2	0.4	114.5	0.3
1989	115.3	0.7	115.7	0.3	115.9	0.2	116.5	0.5	116.9	0.3	117.0	0.1	117.1	0.1	117.6	0.4	117.7	0.1	117.8	0.1	118.0	0.2	118.3	0.3
1990	118.6	0.3	118.8	0.2	118.9	0.1	119.1	0.2	119.2	0.1	119.4	0.2	119.3	-0.1	119.6	0.3	119.9	0.3	119.8	-0.1	119.9	0.1	119.8	-0.1
1991	120.1	0.3	120.1	0.0	120.2	0.1	120.1	-0.1	120.4	0.2	120.6	0.2	120.9	0.2	120.7	-0.2	120.7	0.0	120.6	-0.1	120.4	-0.2	120.6	0.2

[Continued]

Miscellaneous Metal Products
Producer Price Index
Base 1982 = 100
[Continued]

For 1947-2001. Columns headed % show percentile change in the index from the previous period for which an index is available.

Year	Jan Index	%	Feb Index	%	Mar Index	%	Apr Index	%	May Index	%	Jun Index	%	Jul Index	%	Aug Index	%	Sep Index	%	Oct Index	%	Nov Index	%	Dec Index	%
1992	120.9	0.2	121.0	0.1	121.1	0.1	121.2	0.1	121.2	0.0	121.2	0.0	121.3	0.1	121.3	0.0	121.5	0.2	121.9	0.3	121.9	0.0	121.9	0.0
1993	121.8	-0.1	122.0	0.2	122.0	0.0	122.2	0.2	122.3	0.1	122.3	0.0	122.5	0.2	122.3	-0.2	122.4	0.1	122.4	0.0	122.7	0.2	122.8	0.1
1994	123.0	0.2	123.0	0.0	123.2	0.2	123.3	0.1	123.4	0.1	123.5	0.1	123.5	0.0	123.6	0.1	123.8	0.2	124.0	0.2	124.2	0.2	124.4	0.2
1995	125.0	0.5	125.3	0.2	125.4	0.1	125.5	0.1	125.8	0.2	125.9	0.1	126.0	0.1	126.3	0.2	126.4	0.1	126.3	-0.1	126.4	0.1	126.3	-0.1
1996	126.5	0.2	126.5	0.0	126.7	0.2	126.8	0.1	127.0	0.2	126.9	-0.1	127.0	0.1	127.0	0.0	127.1	0.1	127.1	0.0	127.0	-0.1	127.1	0.1
1997	127.3	0.2	127.4	0.1	127.4	0.0	127.3	-0.1	127.6	0.2	127.6	0.0	127.8	0.2	127.8	0.0	127.8	0.0	127.9	0.1	127.9	0.0	128.0	0.1
1998	128.0	0.0	128.0	0.0	128.2	0.2	128.2	0.0	128.2	0.0	128.2	0.0	128.0	-0.2	128.0	0.0	127.9	-0.1	127.7	-0.2	127.8	0.1	127.7	-0.1
1999	127.7	0.0	127.5	-0.2	127.4	-0.1	127.7	0.2	127.6	-0.1	127.8	0.2	127.7	-0.1	127.6	-0.1	127.7	0.1	127.9	0.2	127.8	-0.1	127.8	0.0
2000	127.9	0.1	127.9	0.0	127.9	0.0	128.0	0.1	128.0	0.0	128.1	0.1	128.1	0.0	128.1	0.0	128.2	0.1	128.0	-0.2	128.0	0.0	128.0	0.0
2001	128.6	0.5	128.5	-0.1	128.5	0.0	128.8	0.2	128.8	0.0	128.7	-0.1	128.7	0.0	128.7	0.0	128.6	-0.1	128.6	0.0	128.6	0.0	128.7	0.1

Source: U.S. Department of Labor, Bureau of Labor Statistics, Division of Industry Prices and Price Indexes. n.e.c. stands for not elsewhere classified. - indicates no data collected for period or unavailable.

Metal Treatment Services
Producer Price Index
Base 1982 = 100

For 1984-2001. Columns headed % show percentile change in the index from the previous period for which an index is available.

Year	Jan Index	%	Feb Index	%	Mar Index	%	Apr Index	%	May Index	%	Jun Index	%	Jul Index	%	Aug Index	%	Sep Index	%	Oct Index	%	Nov Index	%	Dec Index	%
1984	-	-	-	-	-	-	-	-	-	-	-	-	-	-	-	-	-	-	-	-	-	-	100.0	-
1985	100.4	0.4	100.9	0.5	100.8	-0.1	101.4	0.6	102.2	0.8	102.2	0.0	102.7	0.5	103.4	0.7	103.4	0.0	103.4	0.0	103.8	0.4	104.0	0.2
1986	104.5	0.5	104.2	-0.3	104.3	0.1	104.4	0.1	104.4	0.0	104.5	0.1	104.7	0.2	104.9	0.2	105.0	0.1	105.1	0.1	105.2	0.1	105.1	-0.1
1987	105.5	0.4	105.6	0.1	105.7	0.1	105.8	0.1	106.1	0.3	106.1	0.0	106.0	-0.1	106.5	0.5	106.2	-0.3	106.7	0.5	106.8	0.1	107.4	0.6
1988	107.5	0.1	107.7	0.2	107.8	0.1	108.7	0.8	108.3	-0.4	109.1	0.7	110.0	0.8	110.3	0.3	111.8	1.4	112.1	0.3	112.2	0.1	112.6	0.4
1989	113.3	0.6	113.6	0.3	114.0	0.4	114.6	0.5	114.6	0.0	114.7	0.1	114.6	-0.1	114.7	0.1	114.9	0.2	115.0	0.1	115.0	0.0	115.2	0.2
1990	115.5	0.3	115.6	0.1	115.7	0.1	115.7	0.0	115.8	0.1	115.9	0.1	116.7	0.7	116.8	0.1	116.9	0.1	117.1	0.2	116.9	-0.2	116.9	0.0
1991	117.5	0.5	117.6	0.1	117.5	-0.1	117.4	-0.1	117.3	-0.1	117.3	0.0	117.3	0.0	117.3	0.0	117.3	0.0	117.7	0.3	117.7	0.0	117.5	-0.2
1992	117.7	0.2	117.8	0.1	117.9	0.1	118.0	0.1	118.1	0.1	118.1	0.0	118.3	0.2	118.4	0.1	118.5	0.1	118.5	0.0	118.5	0.0	118.7	0.2
1993	119.1	0.3	119.3	0.2	119.4	0.1	119.6	0.2	119.6	0.0	119.7	0.1	119.9	0.2	120.1	0.2	120.1	0.0	120.3	0.2	120.3	0.0	120.3	0.0
1994	120.6	0.2	121.0	0.3	121.0	0.0	121.1	0.1	121.2	0.1	121.3	0.1	121.5	0.2	121.7	0.2	121.6	-0.1	121.6	0.0	122.2	0.5	122.2	0.0
1995	122.5	0.2	122.7	0.2	123.1	0.3	123.2	0.1	123.3	0.1	123.1	-0.2	123.6	0.4	123.6	0.0	124.1	0.4	124.3	0.2	124.3	0.0	124.3	0.0
1996	124.4	0.1	124.6	0.2	124.6	0.0	124.7	0.1	124.7	0.0	124.8	0.1	124.9	0.1	125.0	0.1	125.0	0.0	125.1	0.1	125.2	0.1	125.1	-0.1
1997	125.2	0.1	125.3	0.1	125.5	0.2	125.7	0.2	125.7	0.0	125.9	0.2	126.1	0.2	126.7	0.5	126.9	0.2	126.8	-0.1	126.3	-0.4	126.4	0.1
1998	126.3	-0.1	126.4	0.1	126.3	-0.1	126.5	0.2	126.5	0.0	126.7	0.2	126.4	-0.2	126.5	0.1	126.5	0.0	126.5	0.0	129.6	2.5	129.5	-0.1
1999	129.4	-0.1	129.5	0.1	129.4	-0.1	129.6	0.2	129.7	0.1	129.3	-0.3	129.3	0.0	129.4	0.1	129.5	0.1	129.5	0.0	129.5	0.0	129.4	-0.1
2000	129.7	0.2	129.5	-0.2	129.3	-0.2	129.3	0.0	129.3	0.0	129.3	0.0	129.4	0.1	129.6	0.2	130.2	0.5	130.2	0.0	130.5	0.2	130.9	0.3
2001	132.8	1.5	132.7	-0.1	132.8	0.1	133.1	0.2	133.2	0.1	133.1	-0.1	133.3	0.2	133.5	0.2	133.5	0.0	133.6	0.1	133.6	0.0	133.5	-0.1

Source: U.S. Department of Labor, Bureau of Labor Statistics, Division of Industry Prices and Price Indexes. n.e.c. stands for not elsewhere classified. - indicates no data collected for period or unavailable.

MACHINERY AND EQUIPMENT
Producer Price Index
Base 1982 = 100

For 1939-2001. Columns headed % show percentile change in the index from the previous period for which an index is available.

Year	Jan Index	%	Feb Index	%	Mar Index	%	Apr Index	%	May Index	%	Jun Index	%	Jul Index	%	Aug Index	%	Sep Index	%	Oct Index	%	Nov Index	%	Dec Index	%
1939	14.9	-	14.9	0.0	14.9	0.0	14.8	-0.7	14.8	0.0	14.8	0.0	14.8	0.0	14.8	0.0	14.8	0.0	14.8	0.0	14.8	0.0	14.8	0.0
1940	14.9	0.7	14.9	0.0	14.9	0.0	14.9	0.0	14.8	-0.7	14.9	0.7	14.9	0.0	14.9	0.0	14.9	0.0	14.9	0.0	14.9	0.0	14.9	0.0
1941	14.9	0.0	15.0	0.7	15.0	0.0	15.0	0.0	15.0	0.0	15.1	0.7	15.1	0.0	15.1	0.0	15.2	0.7	15.2	0.0	15.4	1.3	15.4	0.0
1942	15.4	0.0	15.4	0.0	15.4	0.0	15.4	0.0	15.4	0.0	15.4	0.0	15.4	0.0	15.3	-0.6	15.2	-0.7	15.2	0.0	15.2	0.0	15.2	0.0
1943	15.2	0.0	15.2	0.0	15.2	0.0	15.2	0.0	15.2	0.0	15.2	0.0	15.2	0.0	15.2	0.0	15.2	0.0	15.2	0.0	15.2	0.0	15.1	-0.7
1944	15.2	0.7	15.2	0.0	15.2	0.0	15.2	0.0	15.2	0.0	15.1	-0.7	15.1	0.0	15.1	0.0	15.1	0.0	15.1	0.0	15.1	0.0	15.1	0.0
1945	15.1	0.0	15.1	0.0	15.1	0.0	15.1	0.0	15.1	0.0	15.2	0.7	15.2	0.0	15.2	0.0	15.2	0.0	15.2	0.0	15.2	0.0	15.2	0.0
1946	15.3	0.7	15.4	0.7	15.4	0.0	15.6	1.3	16.3	4.5	16.6	1.8	16.9	1.8	17.1	1.2	17.4	1.8	17.5	0.6	17.9	2.3	18.4	2.8
1947	18.6	1.1	18.7	0.5	18.7	0.0	18.8	0.5	19.2	2.1	19.3	0.5	19.3	0.0	19.4	0.5	19.6	1.0	19.7	0.5	19.9	1.0	19.9	0.0
1948	20.1	1.0	20.1	0.0	20.2	0.5	20.2	0.0	20.2	0.0	20.4	1.0	20.7	1.5	21.2	2.4	21.6	1.9	21.8	0.9	21.9	0.5	22.0	0.5
1949	22.0	0.0	22.1	0.5	22.0	-0.5	22.0	0.0	21.9	-0.5	21.8	-0.5	21.8	0.0	21.8	0.0	21.8	0.0	21.7	-0.5	21.7	0.0	21.7	0.0
1950	21.7	0.0	21.7	0.0	21.7	0.0	21.8	0.5	21.8	0.0	22.0	0.9	22.2	0.9	22.8	2.7	23.2	1.8	23.6	1.7	23.9	1.3	24.8	3.8
1951	25.2	1.6	25.3	0.4	25.3	0.0	25.3	0.0	25.3	0.0	25.3	0.0	25.3	0.0	25.3	0.0	25.3	0.0	25.4	0.4	25.4	0.0	25.4	0.0
1952	25.4	0.0	25.4	0.0	25.4	0.0	25.4	0.0	25.4	0.0	25.3	-0.4	25.3	0.0	25.3	0.0	25.3	0.0	25.3	0.0	25.3	0.0	25.3	0.0
1953	25.3	0.0	25.3	0.0	25.4	0.4	25.6	0.8	25.7	0.4	25.9	0.8	26.0	0.4	26.2	0.8	26.3	0.4	26.3	0.0	26.3	0.0	26.3	0.0
1954	26.3	0.0	26.4	0.4	26.4	0.0	26.3	-0.4	26.3	0.0	26.3	0.0	26.3	0.0	26.3	0.0	26.3	0.0	26.3	0.0	26.4	0.4	26.4	0.0
1955	26.5	0.4	26.6	0.4	26.6	0.0	26.6	0.0	26.7	0.4	26.8	0.4	27.0	0.7	27.3	1.1	27.8	1.8	27.9	0.4	28.1	0.7	28.2	0.4
1956	28.3	0.4	28.4	0.4	28.5	0.4	28.8	1.1	29.1	1.0	29.1	0.0	29.2	0.3	29.4	0.7	30.0	2.0	30.3	1.0	30.6	1.0	30.7	0.3
1957	30.9	0.7	31.0	0.3	31.1	0.3	31.1	0.0	31.2	0.3	31.2	0.0	31.4	0.6	31.5	0.3	31.7	0.6	31.9	0.6	32.0	0.3	32.0	0.0
1958	32.1	0.3	32.0	-0.3	32.0	0.0	32.1	0.3	32.1	0.0	32.1	0.0	32.1	0.0	32.1	0.0	32.1	0.0	32.1	0.0	32.2	0.3	32.3	0.3
1959	32.4	0.3	32.4	0.0	32.5	0.3	32.5	0.0	32.6	0.3	32.7	0.3	32.9	0.6	33.0	0.3	33.0	0.0	33.0	0.0	33.1	0.3	33.1	0.0
1960	33.1	0.0	33.1	0.0	33.1	0.0	33.1	0.0	33.0	-0.3	33.0	0.0	33.0	0.0	33.0	0.0	33.0	0.0	33.0	0.0	33.0	0.0	33.0	0.0
1961	33.1	0.3	33.1	0.0	33.1	0.0	33.0	-0.3	33.0	0.0	33.0	0.0	33.0	0.0	32.9	-0.3	32.9	0.0	33.0	0.3	33.0	0.0	33.0	0.0
1962	33.0	0.0	33.0	0.0	33.1	0.3	33.1	0.0	33.1	0.0	33.0	-0.3	33.0	0.0	33.0	0.0	33.0	0.0	33.0	0.0	33.0	0.0	33.0	0.0
1963	33.0	0.0	33.0	0.0	32.9	-0.3	33.0	0.3	33.0	0.3	33.1	0.3	33.0	-0.3	33.0	0.0	33.1	0.3	33.1	0.0	33.2	0.3	33.3	0.3
1964	33.2	-0.3	33.3	0.3	33.3	0.0	33.4	0.3	33.4	0.0	33.3	-0.3	33.3	0.0	33.3	0.0	33.3	0.0	33.3	0.0	33.4	0.3	33.4	0.0
1965	33.5	0.3	33.5	0.0	33.5	0.0	33.6	0.3	33.6	0.0	33.7	0.3	33.6	-0.3	33.7	0.3	33.7	0.0	33.8	0.3	33.9	0.3	33.9	0.0
1966	34.0	0.3	34.2	0.6	34.3	0.3	34.4	0.3	34.6	0.6	34.7	0.3	34.8	0.3	34.8	0.0	34.9	0.3	35.1	0.6	35.4	0.9	35.5	0.3
1967	35.7	0.6	35.7	0.0	35.7	0.0	35.8	0.3	35.8	0.0	35.8	0.0	35.8	0.0	35.9	0.3	35.9	0.0	36.0	0.3	36.2	0.6	36.3	0.3
1968	36.6	0.8	36.7	0.3	36.7	0.0	36.9	0.5	37.0	0.3	37.0	0.0	37.1	0.3	37.1	0.0	37.2	0.3	37.3	0.3	37.4	0.3	37.5	0.3
1969	37.6	0.3	37.7	0.3	37.8	0.3	37.9	0.3	38.0	0.3	38.1	0.3	38.2	0.3	38.2	0.0	38.5	0.8	38.7	0.5	38.9	0.5	39.1	0.5
1970	39.4	0.8	39.4	0.0	39.5	0.3	39.6	0.3	39.7	0.3	39.8	0.3	40.0	0.5	40.0	0.0	40.2	0.5	40.4	0.5	40.6	0.5	40.8	0.5
1971	41.0	0.5	41.1	0.2	41.2	0.2	41.3	0.2	41.4	0.2	41.4	0.0	41.6	0.5	41.7	0.2	41.6	-0.2	41.6	0.0	41.6	0.0	41.7	0.2
1972	41.8	0.2	42.0	0.5	42.1	0.2	42.2	0.2	42.3	0.2	42.4	0.2	42.4	0.0	42.4	0.0	42.4	0.0	42.5	0.2	42.5	0.0	42.5	0.0
1973	42.6	0.2	42.8	0.5	43.0	0.5	43.3	0.7	43.6	0.7	43.7	0.2	43.8	0.2	43.9	0.2	44.0	0.2	44.2	0.5	44.4	0.5	44.7	0.7
1974	45.2	1.1	45.6	0.9	46.3	1.5	46.9	1.3	48.1	2.6	49.2	2.3	50.3	2.2	51.8	3.0	52.7	1.7	53.8	2.1	54.8	1.9	55.2	0.7
1975	56.2	1.8	56.6	0.7	57.0	0.7	57.3	0.5	57.5	0.3	57.7	0.3	58.0	0.5	58.2	0.3	58.5	0.5	58.9	0.7	59.3	0.7	59.5	0.3
1976	60.0	0.8	60.2	0.3	60.4	0.3	60.7	0.5	60.9	0.3	61.1	0.3	61.4	0.5	61.6	0.3	62.0	0.6	62.4	0.6	62.6	0.3	62.9	0.5
1977	63.4	0.8	63.7	0.5	63.9	0.3	64.2	0.5	64.6	0.6	64.8	0.3	65.2	0.6	65.6	0.6	65.9	0.5	66.6	1.1	67.0	0.6	67.3	0.4
1978	67.9	0.9	68.3	0.6	68.7	0.6	69.1	0.6	69.6	0.7	70.1	0.7	70.5	0.6	70.9	0.6	71.3	0.6	71.9	0.8	72.7	1.1	73.1	0.6
1979	73.6	0.7	74.1	0.7	74.6	0.7	75.2	0.8	75.8	0.8	76.2	0.5	77.0	1.0	77.5	0.6	78.1	0.8	78.9	1.0	79.4	0.6	80.1	0.9
1980	81.6	1.9	82.6	1.2	83.4	1.0	84.8	1.7	85.2	0.5	85.8	0.7	86.6	0.9	87.0	0.5	87.8	0.9	88.5	0.8	89.1	0.7	89.6	0.6
1981	90.9	1.5	91.6	0.8	92.4	0.9	93.1	0.8	93.5	0.4	94.0	0.5	95.0	1.1	95.5	0.5	96.2	0.7	96.6	0.4	97.0	0.4	97.6	0.6
1982	98.3	0.7	98.8	0.5	99.1	0.3	99.6	0.5	99.8	0.2	99.9	0.1	100.3	0.4	100.4	0.1	100.5	0.1	100.8	0.3	101.1	0.3	101.3	0.2
1983	101.6	0.3	102.0	0.4	102.1	0.1	102.4	0.3	102.6	0.2	102.7	0.1	103.1	0.4	103.1	0.0	103.3	0.2	103.2	-0.1	103.3	0.1	103.6	0.3

[Continued]

MACHINERY AND EQUIPMENT
Producer Price Index
Base 1982 = 100
[Continued]

For 1939-2001. Columns headed % show percentile change in the index from the previous period for which an index is available.

Year	Jan Index	%	Feb Index	%	Mar Index	%	Apr Index	%	May Index	%	Jun Index	%	Jul Index	%	Aug Index	%	Sep Index	%	Oct Index	%	Nov Index	%	Dec Index	%
1984	103.9	0.3	104.1	0.2	104.4	0.3	104.8	0.4	105.0	0.2	105.2	0.2	105.5	0.3	105.5	0.0	105.6	0.1	105.8	0.2	105.9	0.1	106.0	0.1
1985	106.5	0.5	106.8	0.3	106.8	0.0	106.9	0.1	107.1	0.2	107.2	0.1	107.3	0.1	107.5	0.2	107.6	0.1	107.6	0.0	107.7	0.1	107.8	0.1
1986	108.0	0.2	108.2	0.2	108.3	0.1	108.6	0.3	108.6	0.0	108.7	0.1	109.0	0.3	109.1	0.1	109.1	0.0	109.2	0.1	109.4	0.2	109.5	0.1
1987	109.8	0.3	109.9	0.1	110.0	0.1	110.0	0.0	110.2	0.2	110.1	-0.1	110.4	0.3	110.6	0.2	110.6	0.0	110.9	0.3	111.0	0.1	111.3	0.3
1988	111.9	0.5	112.2	0.3	112.3	0.1	112.5	0.2	112.9	0.4	112.9	0.0	113.2	0.3	113.6	0.4	113.9	0.3	114.2	0.3	114.5	0.3	114.8	0.3
1989	115.6	0.7	116.0	0.3	116.3	0.3	116.5	0.2	116.9	0.3	117.3	0.3	117.8	0.4	118.0	0.2	118.2	0.2	118.5	0.3	118.7	0.2	118.9	0.2
1990	119.6	0.6	119.7	0.1	120.0	0.3	120.2	0.2	120.4	0.2	120.5	0.1	120.8	0.2	120.9	0.1	121.2	0.2	121.4	0.2	121.7	0.2	122.0	0.2
1991	122.6	0.5	122.9	0.2	123.0	0.1	123.1	0.1	123.1	0.0	123.1	0.0	123.0	-0.1	123.0	0.0	123.0	0.0	123.0	0.0	123.1	0.1	123.2	0.1
1992	123.3	0.1	123.5	0.2	123.6	0.1	123.4	-0.2	123.4	0.0	123.2	-0.2	123.1	-0.1	123.2	0.1	123.2	0.0	123.3	0.1	123.4	0.1	123.5	0.1
1993	123.9	0.3	123.9	0.0	123.9	0.0	124.0	0.1	123.9	-0.1	124.0	0.1	124.0	0.0	124.0	0.0	124.1	0.1	124.2	0.1	124.2	0.0	124.2	0.0
1994	124.6	0.3	124.7	0.1	124.9	0.2	125.1	0.2	125.2	0.1	125.2	0.0	125.3	0.1	125.2	-0.1	125.2	0.0	125.2	0.0	125.3	-0.1	125.4	0.1
1995	125.9	0.4	126.2	0.2	126.2	0.0	126.4	0.2	126.5	0.1	126.5	0.0	126.6	0.1	126.5	-0.1	126.7	0.2	127.0	0.2	127.2	0.2	127.0	-0.2
1996	127.3	0.2	127.3	0.0	127.0	-0.2	126.6	-0.3	126.4	-0.2	126.2	-0.2	126.3	0.1	126.4	0.1	126.3	-0.1	126.2	-0.1	126.2	0.0	126.2	0.0
1997	126.4	0.2	126.3	-0.1	126.3	0.0	126.2	-0.1	125.9	-0.2	125.9	0.0	126.0	0.1	125.7	-0.2	125.6	-0.1	125.6	0.0	125.6	0.0	125.4	-0.2
1998	125.5	0.1	125.3	-0.2	125.3	0.0	125.1	-0.2	124.9	-0.2	125.0	0.1	124.8	-0.2	124.7	-0.1	124.7	0.0	124.6	-0.1	124.6	0.0	124.5	-0.1
1999	124.7	0.2	124.7	0.0	124.6	-0.1	124.5	-0.1	124.3	-0.2	124.2	-0.1	124.1	-0.1	124.0	-0.1	123.9	-0.1	124.0	0.1	124.0	0.0	124.0	0.0
2000	124.0	0.0	123.9	-0.1	123.9	0.0	123.9	0.0	123.9	0.0	124.0	0.1	124.2	0.2	124.1	-0.1	124.1	0.0	124.1	0.0	124.1	0.0	123.8	-0.2
2001	124.0	0.2	123.9	-0.1	123.9	0.0	123.9	0.0	123.9	0.0	123.8	-0.1	123.6	-0.2	123.4	-0.2	123.2	-0.2	123.1	-0.1	123.2	0.1	123.3	0.1

Source: U.S. Department of Labor, Bureau of Labor Statistics, Division of Industry Prices and Price Indexes. n.e.c. stands for not elsewhere classified. - indicates no data collected for period or unavailable.

Agricultural Machinery and Equipment
Producer Price Index
Base 1982 = 100

For 1926-2001. Columns headed % show percentile change in the index from the previous period for which an index is available.

Year	Jan Index	%	Feb Index	%	Mar Index	%	Apr Index	%	May Index	%	Jun Index	%	Jul Index	%	Aug Index	%	Sep Index	%	Oct Index	%	Nov Index	%	Dec Index	%
1926	14.1	-	14.1	0.0	14.1	0.0	14.1	0.0	14.1	0.0	14.1	0.0	14.1	0.0	14.1	0.0	14.1	0.0	14.1	0.0	14.1	0.0	14.1	0.0
1927	14.1	0.0	14.1	0.0	14.1	0.0	14.1	0.0	14.1	0.0	14.1	0.0	14.1	0.0	14.1	0.0	14.1	0.0	14.0	-0.7	14.0	0.0	14.0	0.0
1928	14.0	0.0	14.0	0.0	14.0	0.0	14.0	0.0	14.0	0.0	14.0	0.0	14.0	0.0	14.0	0.0	14.0	0.0	14.0	0.0	14.0	0.0	14.0	0.0
1929	14.0	0.0	14.0	0.0	14.0	0.0	14.0	0.0	14.0	0.0	14.0	0.0	14.0	0.0	14.0	0.0	14.0	0.0	13.8	-1.4	13.8	0.0	13.7	-0.7
1930	13.7	0.0	13.7	0.0	13.5	-1.5	13.3	-1.5	13.3	0.0	13.3	0.0	13.3	0.0	13.3	0.0	13.3	0.0	13.3	0.0	13.3	0.0	13.3	0.0
1931	13.3	0.0	13.3	0.0	13.3	0.0	13.3	0.0	13.3	0.0	13.3	0.0	13.3	0.0	13.3	0.0	13.3	0.0	12.1	-9.0	12.1	0.0	12.1	0.0
1932	12.1	0.0	12.0	-0.8	12.0	0.0	12.0	0.0	12.0	0.0	12.0	0.0	12.0	0.0	12.0	0.0	12.0	0.0	12.0	0.0	12.0	0.0	11.9	-0.8
1933	11.9	0.0	11.7	-1.7	11.7	0.0	11.7	0.0	11.7	0.0	11.7	0.0	11.7	0.0	11.7	0.0	11.7	0.0	11.8	0.9	11.8	0.0	12.0	1.7
1934	12.0	0.0	12.0	0.0	12.0	0.0	12.0	0.0	12.9	7.5	12.9	0.0	13.0	0.8	13.0	0.0	13.0	0.0	13.0	0.0	13.0	0.0	13.1	0.8
1935	13.1	0.0	13.2	0.8	13.2	0.0	13.2	0.0	13.2	0.0	13.2	0.0	13.2	0.0	13.2	0.0	13.2	0.0	13.2	0.0	13.3	0.8	13.3	0.0
1936	13.3	0.0	13.4	0.8	13.3	-0.7	13.3	0.0	13.3	0.0	13.3	0.0	13.3	0.0	13.3	0.0	13.3	0.0	13.3	0.0	13.1	-1.5	13.1	0.0
1937	13.1	0.0	13.1	0.0	13.1	0.0	13.0	-0.8	13.2	1.5	13.3	0.8	13.3	0.0	13.3	0.0	13.3	0.0	13.3	0.0	13.6	2.3	13.6	0.0
1938	13.6	0.0	13.6	0.0	13.6	0.0	13.6	0.0	13.6	0.0	13.6	0.0	13.6	0.0	13.5	-0.7	13.5	0.0	13.5	0.0	13.2	-2.2	13.2	0.0
1939	13.2	0.0	13.1	-0.8	13.1	0.0	13.2	0.8	13.2	0.0	13.2	0.0	13.2	0.0	13.2	0.0	13.2	0.0	13.2	0.0	13.2	0.0	13.2	0.0
1940	13.2	0.0	13.2	0.0	13.2	0.0	13.2	0.0	13.1	-0.8	13.1	0.0	13.0	-0.8	13.0	0.0	13.1	0.8	13.1	0.0	13.1	0.0	13.1	0.0
1941	13.1	0.0	13.1	0.0	13.1	0.0	13.0	-0.8	13.1	0.8	13.1	0.0	13.1	0.0	13.1	0.0	13.2	0.8	13.2	0.0	13.6	3.0	13.6	0.0
1942	13.6	0.0	13.7	0.7	13.7	0.0	13.7	0.0	13.7	0.0	13.7	0.0	13.7	0.0	13.7	0.0	13.7	0.0	13.7	0.0	13.7	0.0	13.7	0.0
1943	13.7	0.0	13.7	0.0	13.7	0.0	13.7	0.0	13.7	0.0	13.7	0.0	13.7	0.0	13.7	0.0	13.7	0.0	13.7	0.0	13.7	0.0	13.7	0.0
1944	13.7	0.0	13.7	0.0	13.7	0.0	13.7	0.0	13.7	0.0	13.7	0.0	13.7	0.0	13.8	0.7	13.8	0.0	13.8	0.0	13.8	0.0	13.8	0.0
1945	13.8	0.0	13.8	0.0	13.8	0.0	13.8	0.0	13.8	0.0	13.8	0.0	13.8	0.0	13.8	0.0	13.8	0.0	13.8	0.0	13.9	0.7	13.9	0.0
1946	13.8	-0.7	13.8	0.0	13.8	0.0	13.9	0.7	14.4	3.6	14.8	2.8	14.8	0.0	15.2	2.7	15.3	0.7	15.3	0.0	15.8	3.3	16.7	5.7
1947	16.8	0.6	16.8	0.0	16.8	0.0	16.8	0.0	16.9	0.6	16.9	0.0	16.9	0.0	17.0	0.6	17.1	0.6	17.3	1.2	17.7	2.3	18.1	2.3
1948	18.2	0.6	18.3	0.5	18.4	0.5	18.5	0.5	18.6	0.5	18.8	1.1	19.1	1.6	19.3	1.0	20.0	3.6	20.3	1.5	20.5	1.0	20.5	0.0
1949	20.5	0.0	20.5	0.0	20.5	0.0	20.5	0.0	20.5	0.0	20.5	0.0	20.5	0.0	20.5	0.0	20.5	0.0	20.5	0.0	20.4	-0.5	20.4	0.0
1950	20.4	0.0	20.4	0.0	20.4	0.0	20.5	0.5	20.5	0.0	20.5	0.0	20.5	0.0	20.8	1.5	21.4	2.9	21.7	1.4	21.9	0.9	22.4	2.3
1951	22.4	0.0	22.8	1.8	22.8	0.0	22.8	0.0	22.8	0.0	22.8	0.0	22.8	0.0	22.8	0.0	22.8	0.0	22.8	0.0	22.8	0.0	22.8	0.0
1952	23.0	0.9	23.0	0.0	23.0	0.0	23.0	0.0	23.0	0.0	23.0	0.0	23.0	0.0	23.0	0.0	23.0	0.0	23.0	0.0	23.0	0.0	23.0	0.0
1953	23.0	0.0	23.0	0.0	23.1	0.4	23.2	0.4	23.2	0.0	23.2	0.0	23.2	0.0	23.2	0.0	23.2	0.0	23.2	0.0	23.2	0.0	23.2	0.0
1954	23.2	0.0	23.3	0.4	23.2	-0.4	23.2	0.0	23.2	0.0	23.2	0.0	23.2	0.0	23.1	-0.4	23.1	0.0	23.1	0.0	23.0	-0.4	23.0	0.0
1955	23.0	0.0	23.0	0.0	23.0	0.0	23.0	0.0	23.0	0.0	23.0	0.0	23.0	0.0	23.2	0.9	23.9	3.0	24.0	0.4	23.9	-0.4	23.9	0.0
1956	24.0	0.4	24.0	0.0	23.9	-0.4	23.9	0.0	23.9	0.0	24.0	0.4	24.0	0.0	24.0	0.0	24.1	0.4	24.5	1.7	24.8	1.2	24.8	0.0
1957	24.9	0.4	25.0	0.4	25.0	0.0	25.0	0.0	25.0	0.0	25.0	0.0	25.0	0.0	25.1	0.4	25.3	0.8	25.8	2.0	26.0	0.8	26.2	0.8
1958	26.2	0.0	26.2	0.0	26.2	0.0	26.2	0.0	26.2	0.0	26.2	0.0	26.2	0.0	26.1	-0.4	26.3	0.8	26.4	0.4	26.9	1.9	27.1	0.7
1959	27.1	0.0	27.1	0.0	27.1	0.0	27.1	0.0	27.2	0.4	27.2	0.0	27.2	0.0	27.2	0.0	27.2	0.0	27.2	0.0	27.3	0.4	27.3	0.0
1960	27.3	0.0	27.5	0.7	27.5	0.0	27.6	0.4	27.6	0.0	27.6	0.0	27.6	0.0	27.7	0.4	27.7	0.0	27.8	0.4	28.1	1.1	28.0	-0.4
1961	28.1	0.4	28.1	0.0	28.1	0.0	28.2	0.4	28.2	0.0	28.2	0.0	28.2	0.0	28.2	0.0	28.2	0.0	28.2	0.0	28.3	0.4	28.5	0.7
1962	28.6	0.4	28.7	0.3	28.7	0.0	28.7	0.0	28.7	0.0	28.8	0.3	28.8	0.0	28.7	-0.3	28.7	0.0	28.8	0.3	28.8	0.0	28.9	0.3
1963	29.1	0.7	29.1	0.0	29.2	0.3	29.1	-0.3	29.1	0.0	29.2	0.3	29.1	-0.3	29.1	0.0	29.1	0.0	29.2	0.3	29.3	0.3	29.4	0.3
1964	29.4	0.0	29.5	0.3	29.6	0.3	29.6	0.0	29.6	0.0	29.6	0.0	29.6	0.0	29.7	0.3	29.7	0.0	29.6	-0.3	29.9	1.0	30.0	0.3
1965	30.0	0.0	30.1	0.3	30.1	0.0	30.1	0.0	30.1	0.0	30.1	0.0	30.2	0.3	30.2	0.0	30.2	0.0	30.2	0.0	30.7	1.7	30.7	0.0
1966	30.8	0.3	30.9	0.3	31.0	0.3	31.0	0.0	31.1	0.3	31.1	0.0	31.1	0.0	31.1	0.0	31.1	0.0	31.1	0.0	31.6	1.6	31.7	0.3
1967	31.9	0.6	32.0	0.3	32.0	0.0	32.0	0.0	32.0	0.0	32.0	0.0	32.1	0.3	32.1	0.0	32.1	0.0	32.1	0.0	32.7	1.9	32.9	0.6
1968	33.0	0.3	33.1	0.3	33.1	0.0	33.1	0.0	33.1	0.0	33.2	0.3	33.3	0.3	33.4	0.3	33.5	0.3	33.7	0.6	34.0	0.9	34.2	0.6
1969	34.5	0.9	34.6	0.3	34.6	0.0	34.6	0.0	34.6	0.0	34.7	0.3	34.8	0.3	34.8	0.0	34.9	0.3	35.1	0.6	35.6	1.4	35.8	0.6
1970	35.9	0.3	36.1	0.6	36.1	0.0	36.1	0.0	36.2	0.3	36.1	-0.3	36.2	0.3	36.2	0.0	36.4	0.6	36.6	0.5	37.4	2.2	37.5	0.3

[Continued]

Agricultural Machinery and Equipment
Producer Price Index
Base 1982 = 100
[Continued]

For 1926-2001. Columns headed % show percentile change in the index from the previous period for which an index is available.

Year	Jan Index	%	Feb Index	%	Mar Index	%	Apr Index	%	May Index	%	Jun Index	%	Jul Index	%	Aug Index	%	Sep Index	%	Oct Index	%	Nov Index	%	Dec Index	%
1971	37.5	0.0	37.5	0.0	37.5	0.0	37.6	0.3	37.6	0.0	37.7	0.3	37.8	0.3	37.9	0.3	37.9	0.0	37.9	0.0	37.9	0.0	38.2	0.8
1972	38.5	0.8	39.1	1.6	39.2	0.3	39.3	0.3	39.3	0.0	39.4	0.3	39.4	0.0	39.5	0.3	39.4	-0.3	39.4	0.0	39.5	0.3	39.5	0.0
1973	39.7	0.5	40.0	0.8	40.1	0.2	40.1	0.0	40.2	0.2	40.3	0.2	40.3	0.0	40.4	0.2	40.4	0.0	41.0	1.5	41.4	1.0	41.6	0.5
1974	42.1	1.2	42.2	0.2	42.6	0.9	42.9	0.7	44.3	3.3	45.3	2.3	46.3	2.2	47.6	2.8	48.9	2.7	49.8	1.8	51.3	3.0	51.5	0.4
1975	52.6	2.1	52.8	0.4	53.4	1.1	53.6	0.4	53.8	0.4	53.9	0.2	54.2	0.6	54.3	0.2	54.4	0.2	55.1	1.3	56.0	1.6	56.3	0.5
1976	56.9	1.1	57.2	0.5	57.6	0.7	57.8	0.3	58.2	0.7	58.5	0.5	58.8	0.5	59.1	0.5	59.7	1.0	59.9	0.3	60.7	1.3	61.3	1.0
1977	61.8	0.8	62.2	0.6	62.5	0.5	62.6	0.2	62.8	0.3	63.0	0.3	63.2	0.3	63.8	0.9	64.4	0.9	64.7	0.5	66.0	2.0	66.3	0.5
1978	66.4	0.2	66.8	0.6	66.9	0.1	67.2	0.4	67.4	0.3	67.8	0.6	68.2	0.6	68.8	0.9	70.0	1.7	70.3	0.4	70.9	0.9	71.3	0.6
1979	71.6	0.4	72.0	0.6	72.3	0.4	72.8	0.7	73.4	0.8	73.7	0.4	74.3	0.8	75.0	0.9	76.3	1.7	77.1	1.0	78.2	1.4	78.5	0.4
1980	79.8	1.7	80.3	0.6	81.0	0.9	81.8	1.0	82.4	0.7	82.7	0.4	83.1	0.5	83.5	0.5	84.8	1.6	85.3	0.6	87.3	2.3	87.7	0.5
1981	88.8	1.3	89.5	0.8	90.0	0.6	90.8	0.9	91.8	1.1	92.2	0.4	92.6	0.4	93.3	0.8	94.1	0.9	95.0	1.0	96.7	1.8	97.3	0.6
1982	97.4	0.1	97.9	0.5	98.5	0.6	98.6	0.1	99.1	0.5	99.6	0.5	100.0	0.4	100.4	0.4	101.0	0.6	102.1	1.1	102.5	0.4	103.1	0.6
1983	103.6	0.5	103.9	0.3	104.0	0.1	104.1	0.1	104.9	0.8	104.9	0.0	105.1	0.2	105.2	0.1	105.6	0.4	105.4	-0.2	105.6	0.2	106.1	0.5
1984	106.4	0.3	106.5	0.1	107.0	0.5	107.9	0.8	108.7	0.7	108.6	-0.1	108.9	0.3	108.9	0.0	108.4	-0.5	108.4	0.0	108.3	-0.1	108.5	0.2
1985	108.8	0.3	108.7	-0.1	108.8	0.1	108.7	-0.1	108.8	0.1	108.9	0.1	108.9	0.0	108.7	-0.2	108.4	-0.3	108.5	0.1	108.6	0.1	108.7	0.1
1986	108.8	0.1	108.8	0.0	109.0	0.2	109.1	0.1	109.1	0.0	109.2	0.1	109.3	0.1	109.4	0.1	109.3	-0.1	109.6	0.3	109.7	0.1	109.6	-0.1
1987	108.9	-0.6	109.0	0.1	109.1	0.1	109.6	0.5	109.9	0.3	109.9	0.0	110.0	0.1	109.8	-0.2	109.7	-0.1	109.8	0.1	109.9	0.1	109.9	0.0
1988	111.4	1.4	111.5	0.1	112.2	0.6	112.3	0.1	112.5	0.2	111.8	-0.6	112.4	0.5	113.2	0.7	113.3	0.1	113.3	0.0	114.0	0.6	114.2	0.2
1989	114.2	0.0	116.5	2.0	116.5	0.0	116.9	0.3	117.7	0.7	117.6	-0.1	117.9	0.3	118.3	0.3	118.7	0.3	118.5	-0.2	119.5	0.8	120.1	0.5
1990	120.4	0.2	120.5	0.1	120.7	0.2	121.2	0.4	121.3	0.1	121.4	0.1	121.5	0.1	122.3	0.7	122.6	0.2	122.3	-0.2	122.8	0.4	123.4	0.5
1991	123.7	0.2	124.4	0.6	124.7	0.2	124.9	0.2	125.1	0.2	125.4	0.2	125.6	0.2	126.2	0.5	126.5	0.2	126.6	0.1	127.7	0.9	127.7	0.0
1992	127.9	0.2	128.3	0.3	128.5	0.2	128.7	0.2	128.7	0.0	128.8	0.1	128.9	0.1	129.1	0.2	131.3	1.7	131.4	0.1	131.4	0.0	131.5	0.1
1993	131.7	0.2	132.1	0.3	132.3	0.2	133.1	0.6	133.5	0.3	133.6	0.1	133.6	0.0	133.7	0.1	134.5	0.6	134.7	0.1	134.9	0.1	135.3	0.3
1994	135.8	0.4	136.0	0.1	136.1	0.1	136.4	0.2	136.5	0.1	136.6	0.1	136.7	0.1	136.8	0.1	137.5	0.5	138.2	0.5	138.4	0.1	139.0	0.4
1995	140.3	0.9	140.4	0.1	140.7	0.2	141.1	0.3	143.0	1.3	143.2	0.1	143.3	0.1	143.5	0.1	144.0	0.3	144.6	0.4	145.5	0.6	145.6	0.1
1996	146.0	0.3	146.7	0.5	147.0	0.2	147.4	0.3	146.1	-0.9	146.1	0.0	146.3	0.1	146.7	0.3	147.0	0.2	147.4	0.3	147.7	0.2	147.7	0.0
1997	148.2	0.3	148.5	0.2	148.9	0.3	149.1	0.1	148.8	-0.2	148.5	-0.2	148.9	0.3	149.1	0.1	149.2	0.1	148.3	-0.6	148.4	0.1	148.3	-0.1
1998	149.7	0.9	150.1	0.3	150.4	0.2	150.5	0.1	149.7	-0.5	150.0	0.2	150.0	0.0	150.4	0.3	150.7	0.2	151.2	0.3	150.8	-0.3	150.8	0.0
1999	151.2	0.3	151.1	-0.1	151.2	0.1	152.1	0.6	152.3	0.1	152.1	-0.1	152.2	0.1	152.2	0.0	152.5	0.2	152.6	0.1	152.8	0.1	152.7	-0.1
2000	152.8	0.1	153.0	0.1	153.2	0.1	153.4	0.1	153.7	0.2	153.6	-0.1	153.5	-0.1	153.7	0.1	154.0	0.2	154.1	0.1	154.4	0.2	154.5	0.1
2001	154.5	0.0	154.8	0.2	155.3	0.3	155.8	0.3	156.1	0.2	156.0	-0.1	156.0	0.0	156.4	0.3	155.2	-0.8	155.6	0.3	156.5	0.6	156.4	-0.1

Source: U.S. Department of Labor, Bureau of Labor Statistics, Division of Industry Prices and Price Indexes. n.e.c. stands for not elsewhere classified. - indicates no data collected for period or unavailable.

Construction Machinery and Equipment
Producer Price Index
Base 1982 = 100

For 1939-2001. Columns headed % show percentile change in the index from the previous period for which an index is available.

Year	Jan Index	%	Feb Index	%	Mar Index	%	Apr Index	%	May Index	%	Jun Index	%	Jul Index	%	Aug Index	%	Sep Index	%	Oct Index	%	Nov Index	%	Dec Index	%
1939	-	-	-	-	-	-	-	-	-	-	-	-	-	-	9.3	-	9.3	0.0	9.3	0.0	9.4	1.1	9.4	0.0
1940	9.4	0.0	9.4	0.0	9.4	0.0	9.4	0.0	9.4	0.0	9.4	0.0	9.5	1.1	9.5	0.0	9.5	0.0	9.5	0.0	9.5	0.0	9.5	0.0
1941	9.6	1.1	9.7	1.0	9.7	0.0	9.8	1.0	9.8	0.0	9.9	1.0	9.9	0.0	10.1	2.0	10.2	1.0	10.3	1.0	10.3	0.0	10.3	0.0
1942	10.3	0.0	10.3	0.0	10.3	0.0	10.3	0.0	10.3	0.0	10.3	0.0	10.3	0.0	10.3	0.0	10.3	0.0	10.3	0.0	10.3	0.0	10.3	0.0
1943	10.3	0.0	10.3	0.0	10.3	0.0	10.3	0.0	10.3	0.0	10.3	0.0	10.3	0.0	10.3	0.0	10.3	0.0	10.3	0.0	10.3	0.0	10.3	0.0
1944	10.3	0.0	10.3	0.0	10.3	0.0	10.3	0.0	10.3	0.0	10.3	0.0	10.3	0.0	10.3	0.0	10.3	0.0	10.3	0.0	10.3	0.0	10.4	1.0
1945	10.4	0.0	10.4	0.0	10.4	0.0	10.4	0.0	10.4	0.0	10.4	0.0	10.4	0.0	10.4	0.0	10.4	0.0	10.5	1.0	10.6	1.0	10.6	0.0
1946	10.6	0.0	10.7	0.9	10.7	0.0	11.0	2.8	11.2	1.8	11.4	1.8	11.4	0.0	11.4	0.0	11.5	0.9	11.7	1.7	11.7	0.0	12.0	2.6
1947	12.3	2.5	12.4	0.8	12.4	0.0	12.4	0.0	12.6	1.6	12.7	0.8	12.9	1.6	12.9	0.0	13.0	0.8	13.1	0.8	13.3	1.5	13.5	1.5
1948	13.6	0.7	13.7	0.7	13.8	0.7	13.9	0.7	13.9	0.0	14.2	2.2	14.4	1.4	14.8	2.8	15.2	2.7	15.4	1.3	15.4	0.0	15.5	0.6
1949	15.5	0.0	15.5	0.0	15.4	-0.6	15.4	0.0	15.4	0.0	15.4	0.0	15.4	0.0	15.4	0.0	15.4	0.0	15.4	0.0	15.4	0.0	15.4	0.0
1950	15.4	0.0	15.4	0.0	15.4	0.0	15.4	0.0	15.4	0.0	15.4	0.0	15.5	0.6	16.0	3.2	16.3	1.9	16.5	1.2	16.5	0.0	17.3	4.8
1951	17.5	1.2	17.6	0.6	17.6	0.0	17.6	0.0	17.6	0.0	17.6	0.0	17.6	0.0	17.6	0.0	17.6	0.0	17.6	0.0	17.6	0.0	17.6	0.0
1952	17.7	0.6	17.8	0.6	17.8	0.0	17.8	0.0	17.8	0.0	17.9	0.6	17.9	0.0	17.8	-0.6	17.9	0.6	17.9	0.0	18.0	0.6	18.0	0.0
1953	18.0	0.0	18.0	0.0	18.1	0.6	18.3	1.1	18.3	0.0	18.4	0.5	18.6	1.1	18.6	0.0	18.6	0.0	18.6	0.0	18.6	0.0	18.6	0.0
1954	18.7	0.5	18.7	0.0	18.7	0.0	18.7	0.0	18.7	0.0	18.7	0.0	18.7	0.0	18.7	0.0	18.7	0.0	18.7	0.0	18.7	0.0	18.9	1.1
1955	19.0	0.5	19.0	0.0	19.0	0.0	19.1	0.5	19.1	0.0	19.2	0.5	19.2	0.0	19.7	2.6	20.0	1.5	20.2	1.0	20.2	0.0	20.3	0.5
1956	20.4	0.5	20.4	0.0	20.4	0.0	20.6	1.0	20.8	1.0	20.8	0.0	21.0	1.0	21.3	1.4	21.5	0.9	22.0	2.3	22.1	0.5	22.2	0.5
1957	22.2	0.0	22.2	0.0	22.2	0.0	22.4	0.9	22.4	0.0	22.4	0.0	22.4	0.0	22.9	2.2	23.1	0.9	23.4	1.3	23.5	0.4	23.5	0.0
1958	23.5	0.0	23.5	0.0	23.5	0.0	23.5	0.0	23.5	0.0	23.5	0.0	23.5	0.0	23.5	0.0	23.6	0.4	23.7	0.4	23.9	0.8	24.2	1.3
1959	24.3	0.4	24.4	0.4	24.4	0.0	24.4	0.0	24.4	0.0	24.4	0.0	24.4	0.0	24.4	0.0	24.5	0.4	24.5	0.0	24.5	0.0	24.6	0.4	24.6	0.0
1960	24.7	0.4	24.7	0.0	24.8	0.4	24.9	0.4	24.9	0.0	24.9	0.0	25.0	0.4	25.1	0.4	25.1	0.0	25.1	0.0	25.2	0.4	25.2	0.0
1961	25.3	0.4	25.4	0.4	25.4	0.0	25.4	0.0	25.4	0.0	25.4	0.0	25.4	0.0	25.4	0.0	25.4	0.0	25.4	0.0	25.4	0.0	25.4	0.0
1962	25.4	0.0	25.4	0.0	25.4	0.0	25.4	0.0	25.4	0.0	25.4	0.0	25.4	0.0	25.4	0.0	25.4	0.0	25.5	0.4	25.5	0.0	25.6	0.4
1963	25.6	0.0	25.6	0.0	25.7	0.4	25.7	0.0	25.8	0.4	25.9	0.4	25.9	0.0	26.0	0.4	26.0	0.0	26.1	0.4	26.2	0.4	26.3	0.4
1964	26.4	0.4	26.4	0.0	26.4	0.0	26.5	0.4	26.5	0.0	26.5	0.0	26.5	0.0	26.5	0.0	26.5	0.0	26.5	0.0	26.8	1.1	26.8	0.0
1965	26.9	0.4	27.0	0.4	27.0	0.0	27.1	0.4	27.2	0.4	27.2	0.0	27.2	0.0	27.3	0.4	27.3	0.0	27.3	0.0	27.5	0.7	27.5	0.0
1966	27.6	0.4	27.7	0.4	27.8	0.4	28.0	0.7	28.1	0.4	28.1	0.0	28.1	0.0	28.1	0.0	28.2	0.4	28.3	0.4	28.5	0.7	28.6	0.4
1967	28.6	0.0	28.7	0.3	28.8	0.3	28.8	0.0	28.9	0.3	28.9	0.0	29.0	0.3	29.0	0.0	29.0	0.0	29.4	1.4	29.7	1.0	29.9	0.7
1968	30.2	1.0	30.3	0.3	30.4	0.3	30.5	0.3	30.6	0.3	30.6	0.0	30.6	0.0	30.6	0.0	30.9	1.0	31.1	0.6	31.4	1.0	31.4	0.0
1969	31.6	0.6	31.7	0.3	31.8	0.3	31.8	0.0	31.8	0.0	31.9	0.3	32.0	0.3	32.0	0.0	32.3	0.9	32.7	1.2	32.9	0.6	33.1	0.6
1970	33.1	0.0	33.2	0.3	33.2	0.0	33.2	0.0	33.4	0.6	33.4	0.0	33.4	0.0	33.6	0.6	33.7	0.3	34.4	2.1	34.7	0.9	35.0	0.9
1971	35.1	0.3	35.2	0.3	35.2	0.0	35.3	0.3	35.3	0.0	35.3	0.0	35.5	0.6	35.5	0.0	35.5	0.0	35.5	0.0	35.5	0.0	35.9	1.1
1972	36.1	0.6	36.3	0.6	36.3	0.0	36.5	0.6	36.5	0.0	36.6	0.3	36.6	0.0	36.7	0.3	36.7	0.0	36.7	0.0	36.7	0.0	36.7	0.0
1973	36.8	0.3	37.0	0.5	37.4	1.1	37.9	1.3	38.1	0.5	38.2	0.3	38.2	0.0	38.2	0.0	38.2	0.0	38.5	0.8	38.6	0.3	39.0	1.0
1974	39.4	1.0	39.8	1.0	40.3	1.3	40.7	1.0	42.2	3.7	43.3	2.6	44.0	1.6	46.9	6.6	47.5	1.3	48.6	2.3	49.1	1.0	49.4	0.6
1975	51.6	4.5	52.4	1.6	52.9	1.0	53.5	1.1	53.5	0.0	53.6	0.2	53.8	0.4	53.9	0.2	54.5	1.1	54.8	0.6	55.6	1.5	56.0	0.7
1976	56.2	0.4	56.6	0.7	56.7	0.2	56.8	0.2	57.1	0.5	57.5	0.7	58.1	1.0	58.3	0.3	58.4	0.2	58.9	0.9	59.5	1.0	59.9	0.7
1977	60.2	0.5	60.5	0.5	60.6	0.2	61.1	0.8	61.6	0.8	61.7	0.2	62.2	0.8	62.6	0.6	62.4	-0.3	63.2	1.3	64.2	1.6	64.9	1.1
1978	65.0	0.2	65.4	0.6	65.6	0.3	66.4	1.2	67.0	0.9	67.2	0.3	67.7	0.7	68.2	0.7	68.9	1.0	69.9	1.5	70.5	0.9	70.9	0.6
1979	71.4	0.7	72.1	1.0	72.3	0.3	73.2	1.2	73.8	0.8	73.9	0.1	74.7	1.1	75.2	0.7	75.3	0.1	76.7	1.9	77.2	0.7	78.2	1.3
1980	80.3	2.7	80.9	0.7	81.3	0.5	82.6	1.6	83.1	0.6	83.6	0.6	84.8	1.4	85.3	0.6	86.0	0.8	87.0	1.2	87.3	0.3	87.6	0.3
1981	88.9	1.5	90.1	1.3	90.9	0.9	92.2	1.4	92.6	0.4	93.1	0.5	94.2	1.2	94.5	0.3	94.9	0.4	95.5	0.6	95.9	0.4	96.5	0.6
1982	98.0	1.6	98.3	0.3	98.6	0.3	99.3	0.7	99.9	0.6	100.0	0.1	100.6	0.6	100.8	0.2	101.1	0.3	101.1	0.0	101.2	0.1	101.2	0.0
1983	101.3	0.1	101.6	0.3	101.7	0.1	102.0	0.3	102.4	0.4	102.5	0.1	102.6	0.1	102.6	0.0	102.8	0.2	102.8	0.0	102.9	0.1	102.8	-0.1

[Continued]

Construction Machinery and Equipment
Producer Price Index
Base 1982 = 100
[Continued]

For 1939-2001. Columns headed % show percentile change in the index from the previous period for which an index is available.

Year	Jan Index	%	Feb Index	%	Mar Index	%	Apr Index	%	May Index	%	Jun Index	%	Jul Index	%	Aug Index	%	Sep Index	%	Oct Index	%	Nov Index	%	Dec Index	%
1984	103.0	0.2	103.5	0.5	103.3	-0.2	104.0	0.7	104.0	0.0	104.1	0.1	104.2	0.1	103.8	-0.4	103.9	0.1	104.0	0.1	104.0	0.0	104.0	0.0
1985	105.3	1.3	105.6	0.3	105.4	-0.2	105.2	-0.2	105.2	0.0	105.3	0.1	105.3	0.0	105.4	0.1	105.5	0.1	105.6	0.1	105.7	0.1	105.7	0.0
1986	106.2	0.5	106.3	0.1	106.3	0.0	106.4	0.1	106.5	0.1	106.7	0.2	106.7	0.0	106.7	0.0	106.7	0.0	106.7	0.0	107.5	0.7	107.5	0.0
1987	107.7	0.2	107.9	0.2	108.4	0.5	108.5	0.1	109.2	0.6	109.2	0.0	109.1	-0.1	109.2	0.1	109.3	0.1	109.4	0.1	109.5	0.1	109.7	0.2
1988	110.6	0.8	111.0	0.4	111.0	0.0	111.1	0.1	111.1	0.0	111.2	0.1	111.9	0.6	112.3	0.4	112.3	0.0	112.3	0.0	113.0	0.6	113.2	0.2
1989	115.1	1.7	115.3	0.2	115.8	0.4	116.1	0.3	116.3	0.2	117.6	1.1	117.9	0.3	118.2	0.3	118.3	0.1	118.2	-0.1	118.5	0.3	118.6	0.1
1990	119.7	0.9	120.5	0.7	120.5	0.0	120.5	0.0	120.8	0.2	121.3	0.4	122.4	0.9	122.7	0.2	122.5	-0.2	122.6	0.1	122.8	0.2	123.1	0.2
1991	123.7	0.5	124.2	0.4	124.4	0.2	124.5	0.1	124.6	0.1	124.7	0.1	125.7	0.8	125.8	0.1	125.8	0.0	125.8	0.0	126.3	0.4	126.6	0.2
1992	126.8	0.2	127.3	0.4	127.4	0.1	127.7	0.2	127.7	0.0	128.2	0.4	129.4	0.9	129.6	0.2	129.7	0.1	129.8	0.1	130.2	0.3	130.5	0.2
1993	131.6	0.8	132.3	0.5	132.3	0.0	132.0	-0.2	132.1	0.1	132.2	0.1	132.2	0.0	132.3	0.1	131.4	-0.7	131.7	0.2	131.9	0.2	132.0	0.1
1994	133.4	1.1	133.4	0.0	133.3	-0.1	133.4	0.1	133.5	0.1	133.3	-0.1	133.6	0.2	133.6	0.0	133.8	0.1	134.1	0.2	134.3	0.1	134.6	0.2
1995	135.6	0.7	136.0	0.3	136.1	0.1	136.2	0.1	136.6	0.3	136.6	0.0	136.7	0.1	136.7	0.0	137.1	0.3	137.3	0.1	137.3	0.0	137.9	0.4
1996	138.8	0.7	139.4	0.4	139.4	0.0	139.5	0.1	139.7	0.1	139.9	0.1	140.0	0.1	140.1	0.1	140.1	0.0	140.3	0.1	140.5	0.1	140.4	-0.1
1997	142.0	1.1	142.0	0.0	141.9	-0.1	142.0	0.1	142.0	0.0	142.0	0.0	142.0	0.0	142.1	0.1	142.2	0.1	142.9	0.5	142.8	-0.1	142.8	0.0
1998	144.8	1.4	144.9	0.1	145.0	0.1	145.0	0.0	145.2	0.1	145.3	0.1	145.3	0.0	145.4	0.1	145.3	-0.1	145.2	-0.1	145.3	0.1	145.5	0.1
1999	146.2	0.5	146.6	0.3	146.6	0.0	147.3	0.5	147.3	0.0	147.3	0.0	147.4	0.1	147.4	0.0	147.4	0.0	147.7	0.2	147.6	-0.1	147.6	0.0
2000	148.2	0.4	148.3	0.1	148.3	0.0	148.6	0.2	148.5	-0.1	148.6	0.1	148.7	0.1	148.8	0.1	148.9	0.1	148.9	0.0	148.9	0.0	148.9	0.0
2001	149.0	0.1	148.9	-0.1	149.0	0.1	149.1	0.1	149.1	0.0	149.1	0.0	149.1	0.0	149.1	0.0	149.2	0.1	149.1	-0.1	149.3	0.1	148.7	-0.4

Source: U.S. Department of Labor, Bureau of Labor Statistics, Division of Industry Prices and Price Indexes. n.e.c. stands for not elsewhere classified. - indicates no data collected for period or unavailable.

Metalworking Machinery and Equipment
Producer Price Index
Base 1982 = 100

For 1947-2001. Columns headed % show percentile change in the index from the previous period for which an index is available.

Year	Jan Index	%	Feb Index	%	Mar Index	%	Apr Index	%	May Index	%	Jun Index	%	Jul Index	%	Aug Index	%	Sep Index	%	Oct Index	%	Nov Index	%	Dec Index	%
1947	13.9	-	13.9	0.0	13.9	0.0	14.0	0.7	14.2	1.4	14.3	0.7	14.3	0.0	14.5	1.4	14.5	0.0	14.7	1.4	14.8	0.7	14.8	0.0
1948	15.0	1.4	15.0	0.0	15.0	0.0	15.1	0.7	15.1	0.0	15.1	0.0	15.2	0.7	15.6	2.6	15.9	1.9	16.0	0.6	16.0	0.0	16.1	0.6
1949	16.2	0.6	16.2	0.0	16.2	0.0	16.2	0.0	16.2	0.0	16.2	0.0	16.2	0.0	16.1	-0.6	16.1	0.0	16.1	0.0	16.1	0.0	16.1	0.0
1950	16.3	1.2	16.3	0.0	16.3	0.0	16.6	1.8	16.7	0.6	16.7	0.0	16.9	1.2	17.4	3.0	17.7	1.7	17.9	1.1	18.2	1.7	18.8	3.3
1951	19.1	1.6	19.1	0.0	19.1	0.0	19.1	0.0	19.1	0.0	19.0	-0.5	19.0	0.0	19.0	0.0	19.2	1.1	19.4	1.0	19.5	0.5	19.6	0.5
1952	19.5	-0.5	19.5	0.0	19.5	0.0	19.5	0.0	19.5	0.0	19.5	0.0	19.5	0.0	19.5	0.0	19.5	0.0	19.5	0.0	19.5	0.0	19.5	0.0
1953	19.5	0.0	19.5	0.0	19.5	0.0	19.6	0.5	19.7	0.5	19.8	0.5	19.9	0.5	19.9	0.0	20.0	0.5	20.0	0.0	20.0	0.0	20.0	0.0
1954	20.0	0.0	20.1	0.5	20.1	0.0	20.0	-0.5	20.0	0.0	20.0	0.0	20.0	0.0	20.1	0.5	20.1	0.0	20.2	0.5	20.2	0.0	20.2	0.0
1955	20.3	0.5	20.4	0.5	20.4	0.0	20.5	0.5	20.8	1.5	21.2	1.9	21.5	1.4	21.6	0.5	21.7	0.5	21.8	0.5	21.9	0.5	22.0	0.5
1956	22.2	0.9	22.3	0.5	22.6	1.3	22.8	0.9	22.9	0.4	23.0	0.4	23.0	0.0	23.2	0.9	23.7	2.2	24.0	1.3	24.0	0.0	24.1	0.4
1957	24.1	0.0	24.2	0.4	24.3	0.4	24.3	0.0	24.3	0.0	24.3	0.0	24.5	0.8	24.6	0.4	24.8	0.8	25.1	1.2	25.2	0.4	25.2	0.0
1958	25.2	0.0	25.2	0.0	25.2	0.0	25.2	0.0	25.1	-0.4	25.1	0.0	25.1	0.0	25.1	0.0	25.1	0.0	25.2	0.4	25.2	0.0	25.2	0.0
1959	25.3	0.4	25.4	0.4	25.6	0.8	25.6	0.0	25.6	0.0	25.7	0.4	25.7	0.0	26.0	1.2	26.1	0.4	26.1	0.0	26.1	0.0	26.1	0.0
1960	26.1	0.0	26.2	0.4	26.3	0.4	26.3	0.0	26.4	0.4	26.5	0.4	26.5	0.0	26.5	0.0	26.6	0.4	26.7	0.4	26.8	0.4	26.8	0.0
1961	26.8	0.0	26.8	0.0	26.8	0.0	26.6	-0.7	26.6	0.0	26.6	0.0	26.6	0.0	26.6	0.0	26.7	0.4	26.8	0.4	26.9	0.4	27.0	0.4
1962	27.1	0.4	27.1	0.0	27.2	0.4	27.2	0.0	27.2	0.0	27.3	0.4	27.3	0.0	27.3	0.0	27.3	0.0	27.3	0.0	27.3	0.0	27.2	-0.4
1963	27.2	0.0	27.2	0.0	27.2	0.0	27.2	0.0	27.2	0.0	27.3	0.4	27.3	0.0	27.4	0.4	27.4	0.0	27.4	0.0	27.4	0.0	27.5	0.4
1964	27.5	0.0	27.5	0.0	27.5	0.0	27.6	0.4	27.7	0.4	27.8	0.4	28.0	0.7	28.0	0.0	28.0	0.0	28.1	0.4	28.1	0.0	28.1	0.0
1965	28.3	0.7	28.4	0.4	28.4	0.0	28.4	0.0	28.5	0.4	28.5	0.0	28.5	0.0	28.7	0.7	28.8	0.3	28.9	0.3	28.9	0.0	29.0	0.3
1966	29.1	0.3	29.3	0.7	29.4	0.3	29.4	0.0	29.7	1.0	29.9	0.7	29.9	0.0	30.1	0.7	30.3	0.7	30.5	0.7	30.6	0.3	30.7	0.3
1967	30.7	0.0	30.8	0.3	30.9	0.3	30.9	0.0	31.1	0.6	31.1	0.0	31.2	0.3	31.3	0.3	31.3	0.0	31.4	0.3	31.6	0.6	31.7	0.3
1968	31.8	0.3	31.9	0.3	32.0	0.3	32.2	0.6	32.3	0.3	32.3	0.0	32.5	0.6	32.6	0.3	32.7	0.3	32.7	0.0	32.8	0.3	32.9	0.3
1969	33.0	0.3	33.1	0.3	33.1	0.0	33.2	0.3	33.3	0.3	33.3	0.0	33.6	0.9	33.7	0.3	33.9	0.6	34.1	0.6	34.5	1.2	34.8	0.9
1970	35.1	0.9	35.2	0.3	35.3	0.3	35.3	0.0	35.7	1.1	35.8	0.3	35.9	0.3	35.5	-1.1	35.6	0.3	35.7	0.3	35.8	0.3	35.9	0.3
1971	36.0	0.3	36.2	0.6	36.2	0.0	36.4	0.6	36.6	0.5	36.8	0.5	36.9	0.3	37.0	0.3	37.0	0.0	37.0	0.0	37.0	0.0	37.0	0.0
1972	36.9	-0.3	37.1	0.5	37.2	0.3	37.3	0.3	37.4	0.3	37.4	0.0	37.5	0.3	37.6	0.3	37.7	0.3	37.8	0.3	37.8	0.0	37.8	0.0
1973	38.0	0.5	38.1	0.3	38.5	1.0	38.8	0.8	39.0	0.5	39.2	0.5	39.2	0.0	39.2	0.0	39.5	0.8	39.7	0.5	39.9	0.5	40.2	0.8
1974	40.9	1.7	41.2	0.7	41.8	1.5	42.6	1.9	43.9	3.1	45.1	2.7	46.5	3.1	47.6	2.4	48.6	2.1	49.8	2.5	50.4	1.2	50.8	0.8
1975	51.4	1.2	52.1	1.4	52.6	1.0	52.9	0.6	53.0	0.2	53.6	1.1	53.8	0.4	53.9	0.2	53.9	0.0	54.6	1.3	54.9	0.5	55.1	0.4
1976	55.5	0.7	55.7	0.4	55.9	0.4	56.3	0.7	56.5	0.4	56.7	0.4	56.9	0.4	57.2	0.5	57.5	0.5	57.9	0.7	58.4	0.9	58.8	0.7
1977	59.5	1.2	60.0	0.8	60.4	0.7	60.7	0.5	61.0	0.5	61.7	1.1	62.1	0.6	62.6	0.8	62.9	0.5	63.4	0.8	63.9	0.8	64.2	0.5
1978	64.9	1.1	65.3	0.6	65.7	0.6	66.1	0.6	66.7	0.9	67.2	0.7	67.5	0.4	68.0	0.7	68.7	1.0	69.7	1.5	70.5	1.1	71.1	0.9
1979	71.8	1.0	72.3	0.7	72.6	0.4	73.3	1.0	74.1	1.1	74.5	0.5	75.2	0.9	75.9	0.9	76.8	1.2	77.8	1.3	78.6	1.0	79.3	0.9
1980	80.7	1.8	81.6	1.1	82.3	0.9	84.2	2.3	85.0	1.0	85.8	0.9	86.6	0.9	86.9	0.3	87.3	0.5	88.0	0.8	88.5	0.6	89.0	0.6
1981	90.3	1.5	90.9	0.7	91.9	1.1	93.1	1.3	93.5	0.4	93.9	0.4	94.4	0.5	94.6	0.2	95.1	0.5	95.5	0.4	95.9	0.4	97.5	1.7
1982	98.4	0.9	98.9	0.5	99.0	0.1	99.6	0.6	99.9	0.3	100.1	0.2	100.5	0.4	100.6	0.1	100.7	0.1	100.7	0.0	100.8	0.1	100.8	0.0
1983	101.0	0.2	101.3	0.3	101.4	0.1	101.7	0.3	101.8	0.1	101.9	0.1	101.8	-0.1	101.7	-0.1	101.8	0.1	101.9	0.1	102.0	0.1	102.4	0.4
1984	102.6	0.2	102.9	0.3	103.0	0.1	103.6	0.6	103.9	0.3	103.9	0.0	104.1	0.2	104.3	0.2	104.6	0.3	105.0	0.4	105.4	0.4	105.5	0.1
1985	105.5	0.0	105.8	0.3	106.0	0.2	106.2	0.2	106.3	0.1	106.5	0.2	106.6	0.1	107.1	0.5	107.1	0.0	107.2	0.1	107.2	0.0	107.2	0.0
1986	107.6	0.4	107.8	0.2	107.9	0.1	108.1	0.2	108.2	0.1	108.5	0.3	108.7	0.2	108.7	0.0	108.7	0.0	108.9	0.2	109.0	0.1	109.2	0.2
1987	109.3	0.1	109.4	0.1	109.6	0.2	109.8	0.2	109.9	0.1	109.8	-0.1	110.3	0.5	110.3	0.0	110.5	0.2	110.6	0.1	110.8	0.2	111.0	0.2
1988	111.4	0.4	111.7	0.3	112.4	0.6	112.7	0.3	113.0	0.3	113.2	0.2	113.6	0.4	114.2	0.5	114.5	0.3	114.7	0.2	115.0	0.3	115.3	0.3
1989	116.0	0.6	116.4	0.3	116.9	0.4	117.4	0.4	117.8	0.3	118.1	0.3	118.5	0.3	118.8	0.3	119.0	0.2	119.3	0.3	119.9	0.5	120.1	0.2
1990	120.7	0.5	121.4	0.6	122.2	0.7	122.4	0.2	122.7	0.2	122.8	0.1	122.9	0.1	123.1	0.2	123.6	0.4	124.3	0.6	124.6	0.2	124.8	0.2
1991	126.4	1.3	126.7	0.2	127.1	0.3	127.2	0.1	127.3	0.1	127.8	0.4	128.0	0.2	128.0	0.0	128.1	0.1	128.2	0.1	128.4	0.2	128.5	0.1

[Continued]

Metalworking Machinery and Equipment
Producer Price Index
Base 1982 = 100

[Continued]

For 1947-2001. Columns headed % show percentile change in the index from the previous period for which an index is available.

Year	Jan Index	%	Feb Index	%	Mar Index	%	Apr Index	%	May Index	%	Jun Index	%	Jul Index	%	Aug Index	%	Sep Index	%	Oct Index	%	Nov Index	%	Dec Index	%
1992	129.4	0.7	129.7	0.2	130.2	0.4	130.6	0.3	130.8	0.2	130.8	0.0	131.0	0.2	131.5	0.4	131.6	0.1	131.7	0.1	131.6	-0.1	131.7	0.1
1993	132.4	0.5	132.5	0.1	133.0	0.4	132.8	-0.2	133.0	0.2	133.3	0.2	133.7	0.3	133.8	0.1	134.3	0.4	134.4	0.1	134.5	0.1	134.6	0.1
1994	134.8	0.1	135.0	0.1	135.4	0.3	136.5	0.8	136.7	0.1	136.5	-0.1	136.7	0.1	136.8	0.1	137.0	0.1	137.1	0.1	137.4	0.2	137.4	0.0
1995	137.9	0.4	138.6	0.5	138.9	0.2	139.2	0.2	139.7	0.4	139.8	0.1	140.4	0.4	140.5	0.1	140.5	0.0	140.6	0.1	140.8	0.1	140.9	0.1
1996	142.0	0.8	142.2	0.1	142.5	0.2	142.7	0.1	143.1	0.3	143.3	0.1	143.3	0.0	143.4	0.1	143.5	0.1	143.6	0.1	144.0	0.3	144.1	0.1
1997	144.3	0.1	144.6	0.2	144.7	0.1	145.0	0.2	145.3	0.2	145.4	0.1	145.5	0.1	145.7	0.1	145.8	0.1	146.0	0.1	145.9	-0.1	145.9	0.0
1998	146.5	0.4	146.9	0.3	147.2	0.2	147.2	0.0	147.3	0.1	147.1	-0.1	147.2	0.1	147.3	0.1	147.3	0.0	147.5	0.1	147.5	0.0	147.5	0.0
1999	147.5	0.0	147.6	0.1	147.7	0.1	148.0	0.2	148.1	0.1	148.2	0.1	148.2	0.0	148.3	0.1	148.3	0.0	148.4	0.1	148.5	0.1	148.5	0.0
2000	148.7	0.1	149.0	0.2	149.2	0.1	149.3	0.1	149.4	0.1	149.7	0.2	149.7	0.0	149.9	0.1	149.9	0.0	149.9	0.0	150.1	0.1	150.2	0.1
2001	150.6	0.3	150.6	0.0	150.4	-0.1	150.6	0.1	150.7	0.1	151.6	0.6	150.7	-0.6	150.7	0.0	150.6	-0.1	150.4	-0.1	150.4	0.0	150.4	0.0

Source: U.S. Department of Labor, Bureau of Labor Statistics, Division of Industry Prices and Price Indexes. n.e.c. stands for not elsewhere classified. - indicates no data collected for period or unavailable.

General Purpose Machinery and Equipment
Producer Price Index
Base 1982 = 100

For 1939-2001. Columns headed % show percentile change in the index from the previous period for which an index is available.

Year	Jan		Feb		Mar		Apr		May		Jun		Jul		Aug		Sep		Oct		Nov		Dec	
	Index	%	Index	%	Index	%	Index	%	Index	%	Index	%	Index	%	Index	%	Index	%	Index	%	Index	%	Index	%
1939	13.4	-	13.3	-0.7	13.3	0.0	13.3	0.0	13.3	0.0	13.3	0.0	13.3	0.0	13.3	0.0	13.3	0.0	13.3	0.0	13.3	0.0	13.3	0.0
1940	13.3	0.0	13.3	0.0	13.3	0.0	13.3	0.0	13.3	0.0	13.3	0.0	13.3	0.0	13.3	0.0	13.3	0.0	13.3	0.0	13.3	0.0	13.3	0.0
1941	13.4	0.8	13.4	0.0	13.4	0.0	13.4	0.0	13.4	0.0	13.6	1.5	13.6	0.0	13.7	0.7	13.7	0.0	13.7	0.0	13.7	0.0	13.8	0.7
1942	13.9	0.7	13.8	-0.7	13.8	0.0	13.8	0.0	13.8	0.0	13.8	0.0	13.8	0.0	13.6	-1.4	13.6	0.0	13.6	0.0	13.5	-0.7	13.5	0.0
1943	13.5	0.0	13.5	0.0	13.5	0.0	13.5	0.0	13.4	-0.7	13.4	0.0	13.4	0.0	13.4	0.0	13.4	0.0	13.4	0.0	13.4	0.0	13.4	0.0
1944	13.4	0.0	13.4	0.0	13.4	0.0	13.4	0.0	13.4	0.0	13.4	0.0	13.4	0.0	13.4	0.0	13.4	0.0	13.4	0.0	13.4	0.0	13.4	0.0
1945	13.4	0.0	13.4	0.0	13.4	0.0	13.4	0.0	13.4	0.0	13.4	0.0	13.4	0.0	13.4	0.0	13.4	0.0	13.4	0.0	13.4	0.0	13.4	0.0
1946	13.4	0.0	13.5	0.7	13.5	0.0	13.5	0.0	13.8	2.2	14.0	1.4	14.4	2.9	14.7	2.1	15.2	3.4	15.3	0.7	15.6	2.0	16.0	2.6
1947	16.2	1.3	16.3	0.6	16.3	0.0	16.3	0.0	16.4	0.6	16.6	1.2	16.6	0.0	16.7	0.6	17.0	1.8	17.2	1.2	17.2	0.0	17.3	0.6
1948	17.4	0.6	17.4	0.0	17.5	0.6	17.5	0.0	17.6	0.6	17.6	0.0	17.9	1.7	18.5	3.4	18.8	1.6	19.1	1.6	19.1	0.0	19.1	0.0
1949	19.2	0.5	19.3	0.5	19.2	-0.5	19.2	0.0	19.2	0.0	19.2	0.0	19.1	-0.5	19.1	0.0	19.1	0.0	19.1	0.0	19.1	0.0	19.1	0.0
1950	19.0	-0.5	19.1	0.5	19.1	0.0	19.2	0.5	19.2	0.0	19.2	0.0	19.5	1.6	20.0	2.6	20.4	2.0	20.7	1.5	21.0	1.4	21.9	4.3
1951	22.2	1.4	22.2	0.0	22.2	0.0	22.2	0.0	22.2	0.0	22.2	0.0	22.2	0.0	22.2	0.0	22.2	0.0	22.3	0.5	22.3	0.0	22.2	-0.4
1952	22.2	0.0	22.2	0.0	22.1	-0.5	22.1	0.0	22.1	0.0	22.0	-0.5	22.0	0.0	22.0	0.0	22.0	0.0	21.9	-0.5	21.9	0.0	21.9	0.0
1953	21.9	0.0	21.9	0.0	22.0	0.5	22.2	0.9	22.3	0.5	22.5	0.9	22.6	0.4	22.8	0.9	23.0	0.9	23.1	0.4	23.1	0.0	23.1	0.0
1954	23.1	0.0	23.1	0.0	23.1	0.0	23.1	0.0	23.1	0.0	23.1	0.0	23.0	-0.4	23.0	0.0	23.1	0.4	23.1	0.0	23.1	0.0	23.1	0.0
1955	23.1	0.0	23.5	1.7	23.5	0.0	23.6	0.4	23.6	0.0	23.7	0.4	23.8	0.4	24.2	1.7	24.6	1.7	24.9	1.2	25.3	1.6	25.5	0.8
1956	25.5	0.0	25.5	0.0	25.7	0.8	25.9	0.8	26.3	1.5	26.2	-0.4	26.3	0.4	26.8	1.9	27.3	1.9	27.5	0.7	27.7	0.7	27.8	0.4
1957	28.0	0.7	28.0	0.0	28.1	0.4	28.1	0.0	28.1	0.0	28.2	0.4	28.3	0.4	28.4	0.4	28.5	0.4	28.7	0.7	28.9	0.7	28.9	0.0
1958	28.9	0.0	28.7	-0.7	28.7	0.0	28.7	0.0	28.7	0.0	28.8	0.3	28.7	-0.3	28.6	-0.3	28.7	0.3	28.8	0.3	29.1	1.0	29.2	0.3
1959	29.3	0.3	29.5	0.7	29.4	-0.3	29.3	-0.3	29.3	0.0	29.8	1.7	29.9	0.3	29.9	0.0	30.0	0.3	30.1	0.3	30.1	0.0	30.2	0.3
1960	30.1	-0.3	30.2	0.3	30.1	-0.3	30.2	0.3	30.1	-0.3	29.9	-0.7	29.9	0.0	29.9	0.0	30.0	0.3	29.9	-0.3	29.9	0.0	29.9	0.0
1961	29.9	0.0	29.9	0.0	29.9	0.0	29.8	-0.3	29.8	0.0	29.9	0.3	29.8	-0.3	29.7	-0.3	29.7	0.0	29.6	-0.3	29.7	0.3	29.7	0.0
1962	29.8	0.3	29.8	0.0	29.9	0.3	29.9	0.0	29.9	0.0	29.9	0.0	29.8	-0.3	29.9	0.3	30.0	0.3	30.0	0.0	30.0	0.0	30.1	0.3
1963	30.1	0.0	30.0	-0.3	29.9	-0.3	29.9	0.0	29.9	0.0	30.0	0.3	30.0	0.0	30.0	0.0	30.1	0.3	30.2	0.3	30.2	0.0	30.3	0.3
1964	30.3	0.0	30.3	0.0	30.4	0.3	30.3	-0.3	30.4	0.3	30.3	-0.3	30.2	-0.3	30.0	-0.7	30.0	0.0	30.3	1.0	30.3	0.0	30.4	0.3
1965	30.1	-1.0	30.2	0.3	30.2	0.0	30.2	0.0	30.3	0.3	30.3	0.0	30.3	0.0	30.5	0.7	30.6	0.3	30.8	0.7	30.9	0.3	30.9	0.0
1966	30.9	0.0	30.9	0.0	31.1	0.6	31.4	1.0	31.6	0.6	31.8	0.6	31.8	0.0	32.0	0.6	32.2	0.6	32.4	0.6	32.5	0.3	32.5	0.0
1967	32.7	0.6	32.8	0.3	32.8	0.0	32.8	0.0	32.8	0.0	32.7	-0.3	32.8	0.3	32.9	0.3	33.0	0.3	33.1	0.3	33.2	0.3	33.3	0.3
1968	33.4	0.3	33.6	0.6	33.7	0.3	33.8	0.3	33.9	0.3	34.0	0.3	34.0	0.0	34.1	0.3	34.2	0.3	34.3	0.3	34.2	-0.3	34.3	0.3
1969	34.4	0.3	34.5	0.3	34.7	0.6	34.8	0.3	34.9	0.3	35.1	0.6	35.2	0.3	35.3	0.3	35.6	0.8	35.8	0.6	35.9	0.3	36.2	0.8
1970	36.6	1.1	36.6	0.0	36.8	0.5	36.9	0.3	37.1	0.5	37.1	0.0	37.5	1.1	37.6	0.3	37.8	0.5	38.1	0.8	38.2	0.3	38.5	0.8
1971	38.5	0.0	38.6	0.3	38.8	0.5	39.0	0.5	39.2	0.5	39.3	0.3	39.5	0.5	39.6	0.3	39.6	0.0	39.6	0.0	39.6	0.0	39.7	0.3
1972	39.7	0.0	39.9	0.5	40.0	0.3	40.1	0.2	40.2	0.2	40.4	0.5	40.4	0.0	40.4	0.0	40.5	0.2	40.5	0.0	40.6	0.2	40.6	0.0
1973	40.7	0.2	40.9	0.5	41.1	0.5	41.3	0.5	41.6	0.7	41.8	0.5	41.9	0.2	41.9	0.0	42.0	0.2	42.2	0.5	42.9	1.7	43.0	0.2
1974	43.6	1.4	44.0	0.9	44.7	1.6	45.9	2.7	47.5	3.5	49.1	3.4	50.5	2.9	52.0	3.0	53.2	2.3	54.7	2.8	55.6	1.6	56.2	1.1
1975	56.8	1.1	57.2	0.7	57.5	0.5	57.9	0.7	58.4	0.9	58.6	0.3	59.1	0.9	59.3	0.3	59.6	0.5	59.8	0.3	60.1	0.5	60.4	0.5
1976	60.7	0.5	61.0	0.5	61.2	0.3	61.6	0.7	62.0	0.6	62.5	0.8	62.6	0.2	62.8	0.3	63.3	0.8	63.7	0.6	63.7	0.0	64.0	0.5
1977	64.4	0.6	64.7	0.5	65.0	0.5	65.2	0.3	65.9	1.1	66.4	0.8	66.7	0.5	67.0	0.4	67.3	0.4	67.6	0.4	68.0	0.6	68.2	0.3
1978	68.7	0.7	69.1	0.6	69.5	0.6	69.9	0.6	70.5	0.9	71.0	0.7	71.5	0.7	71.8	0.4	72.3	0.7	72.9	0.8	73.6	1.0	74.0	0.5
1979	74.5	0.7	74.9	0.5	75.8	1.2	76.5	0.9	77.0	0.7	77.3	0.4	78.0	0.9	78.4	0.5	79.0	0.8	79.9	1.1	80.3	0.5	81.4	1.4
1980	82.6	1.5	83.3	0.8	84.4	1.3	85.9	1.8	86.4	0.6	87.1	0.8	87.5	0.5	87.8	0.3	88.8	1.1	89.6	0.9	90.2	0.7	90.7	0.6
1981	91.6	1.0	92.2	0.7	92.9	0.8	93.5	0.6	94.1	0.6	94.4	0.3	95.6	1.3	96.1	0.5	96.7	0.6	97.1	0.4	97.4	0.3	98.0	0.6
1982	98.7	0.7	99.1	0.4	99.3	0.2	99.8	0.5	99.9	0.1	99.8	-0.1	100.3	0.5	100.3	0.0	100.3	0.0	100.6	0.3	100.8	0.2	101.0	0.2
1983	101.1	0.1	101.3	0.2	101.2	-0.1	101.4	0.2	101.5	0.1	101.5	0.0	101.5	0.0	101.3	-0.2	101.4	0.1	101.3	-0.1	101.5	0.2	101.9	0.4

[Continued]

General Purpose Machinery and Equipment
Producer Price Index
Base 1982 = 100
[Continued]

For 1939-2001. Columns headed % show percentile change in the index from the previous period for which an index is available.

Year	Jan Index	%	Feb Index	%	Mar Index	%	Apr Index	%	May Index	%	Jun Index	%	Jul Index	%	Aug Index	%	Sep Index	%	Oct Index	%	Nov Index	%	Dec Index	%
1984	102.2	0.3	102.3	0.1	102.5	0.2	103.0	0.5	103.0	0.0	103.3	0.3	103.7	0.4	103.8	0.1	103.9	0.1	103.9	0.0	104.1	0.2	104.2	0.1
1985	104.7	0.5	104.9	0.2	105.2	0.3	105.4	0.2	105.7	0.3	105.8	0.1	106.0	0.2	106.1	0.1	106.0	-0.1	106.1	0.1	106.2	0.1	106.2	0.0
1986	106.4	0.2	106.7	0.3	106.9	0.2	107.2	0.3	107.2	0.0	107.2	0.0	107.3	0.1	107.4	0.1	107.4	0.0	107.5	0.1	107.5	0.0	107.6	0.1
1987	107.8	0.2	107.8	0.0	107.9	0.1	107.9	0.0	108.0	0.1	108.1	0.1	108.2	0.1	108.3	0.1	108.6	0.3	108.6	0.0	108.9	0.3	109.4	0.5
1988	110.2	0.7	110.7	0.5	111.3	0.5	111.7	0.4	112.0	0.3	112.3	0.3	112.9	0.5	113.3	0.4	113.9	0.5	114.3	0.4	115.1	0.7	115.8	0.6
1989	116.6	0.7	117.0	0.3	117.7	0.6	118.0	0.3	118.6	0.5	119.1	0.4	119.3	0.2	119.6	0.3	120.2	0.5	120.5	0.2	120.7	0.2	121.0	0.2
1990	121.8	0.7	122.3	0.4	122.9	0.5	123.0	0.1	123.3	0.2	123.5	0.2	123.8	0.2	124.1	0.2	124.3	0.2	124.7	0.3	124.8	0.1	125.4	0.5
1991	126.3	0.7	126.9	0.5	127.2	0.2	127.3	0.1	127.7	0.3	128.0	0.2	128.0	0.0	128.1	0.1	128.2	0.1	128.4	0.2	128.5	0.1	128.6	0.1
1992	129.2	0.5	129.4	0.2	129.7	0.2	130.0	0.2	130.1	0.1	129.5	-0.5	129.8	0.2	130.0	0.2	130.2	0.2	130.2	0.0	130.3	0.1	130.3	0.0
1993	131.2	0.7	131.4	0.2	131.5	0.1	131.7	0.2	131.8	0.1	132.1	0.2	132.3	0.2	132.6	0.2	132.7	0.1	132.8	0.1	133.0	0.2	133.2	0.2
1994	133.6	0.3	133.7	0.1	134.1	0.3	134.2	0.1	134.3	0.1	134.6	0.2	134.9	0.2	135.1	0.1	135.2	0.1	135.7	0.4	135.9	0.1	136.1	0.1
1995	136.9	0.6	137.7	0.6	138.1	0.3	138.5	0.3	138.7	0.1	138.9	0.1	139.3	0.3	139.5	0.1	139.7	0.1	140.0	0.2	140.5	0.4	140.8	0.2
1996	141.6	0.6	141.9	0.2	142.2	0.2	142.3	0.1	142.3	0.0	142.4	0.1	142.6	0.1	142.7	0.1	142.7	0.0	143.0	0.2	143.3	0.2	143.4	0.1
1997	143.8	0.3	144.0	0.1	144.5	0.3	144.9	0.3	144.9	0.0	145.0	0.1	145.2	0.1	145.3	0.1	145.4	0.1	145.5	0.1	145.5	0.0	145.6	0.1
1998	146.1	0.3	146.3	0.1	146.5	0.1	146.7	0.1	146.8	0.1	147.1	0.2	147.5	0.3	147.5	0.0	147.9	0.3	147.9	0.0	148.1	0.1	148.3	0.1
1999	148.8	0.3	148.9	0.1	149.0	0.1	149.4	0.3	149.3	-0.1	149.5	0.1	149.6	0.1	149.6	0.0	149.3	-0.2	149.3	0.0	149.4	0.1	149.6	0.1
2000	149.9	0.2	150.2	0.2	150.4	0.1	150.5	0.1	150.6	0.1	150.7	0.1	151.0	0.2	151.0	0.0	151.0	0.0	151.1	0.1	151.2	0.1	151.4	0.1
2001	151.8	0.3	151.9	0.1	152.1	0.1	152.7	0.4	152.8	0.1	152.8	0.0	153.0	0.1	153.1	0.1	153.2	0.1	153.1	-0.1	153.0	-0.1	153.2	0.1

Source: U.S. Department of Labor, Bureau of Labor Statistics, Division of Industry Prices and Price Indexes. n.e.c. stands for not elsewhere classified. - indicates no data collected for period or unavailable.

Electronic Computers and Computer Equipment
Producer Price Index
Base 1982 = 100

For 1990-2001. Columns headed % show percentile change in the index from the previous period for which an index is available.

Year	Jan Index	%	Feb Index	%	Mar Index	%	Apr Index	%	May Index	%	Jun Index	%	Jul Index	%	Aug Index	%	Sep Index	%	Oct Index	%	Nov Index	%	Dec Index	%
1990	-	-	-	-	-	-	-	-	-	-	-	-	-	-	-	-	-	-	-	-	-	-	100.0	-
1991	97.9	-2.1	97.2	-0.7	96.2	-1.0	95.7	-0.5	93.1	-2.7	89.7	-3.7	86.1	-4.0	83.5	-3.0	83.2	-0.4	82.0	-1.4	81.6	-0.5	80.6	-1.2
1992	79.7	-1.1	78.9	-1.0	77.7	-1.5	75.7	-2.6	75.0	-0.9	73.1	-2.5	71.1	-2.7	70.8	-0.4	69.7	-1.6	68.9	-1.1	68.8	-0.1	68.6	-0.3
1993	67.6	-1.5	66.1	-2.2	64.9	-1.8	63.5	-2.2	62.9	-0.9	62.0	-1.4	61.3	-1.1	60.3	-1.6	60.3	0.0	59.2	-1.8	59.2	0.0	58.9	-0.5
1994	58.4	-0.8	57.8	-1.0	58.1	0.5	57.8	-0.5	57.5	-0.5	57.4	-0.2	57.0	-0.7	56.6	-0.7	56.7	0.2	55.8	-1.6	55.2	-1.1	55.2	0.0
1995	54.7	-0.9	53.8	-1.6	53.4	-0.7	53.5	0.2	53.2	-0.6	52.6	-1.1	52.2	-0.8	51.4	-1.5	50.9	-1.0	50.6	-0.6	50.2	-0.8	50.0	-0.4
1996	49.2	-1.6	48.1	-2.2	47.5	-1.2	46.3	-2.5	45.9	-0.9	45.4	-1.1	44.9	-1.1	44.7	-0.4	44.3	-0.9	43.7	-1.4	43.1	-1.4	42.5	-1.4
1997	42.1	-0.9	41.7	-1.0	41.3	-1.0	40.8	-1.2	39.5	-3.2	39.0	-1.3	38.6	-1.0	38.1	-1.3	37.7	-1.0	37.5	-0.5	37.0	-1.3	36.8	-0.5
1998	118.9	223.1	116.1	-2.4	113.8	-2.0	110.9	-2.5	109.4	-1.4	108.6	-0.7	107.3	-1.2	105.0	-2.1	104.4	-0.6	102.4	-1.9	101.8	-0.6	100.0	-1.8
1999	97.9	-2.1	97.3	-0.6	96.7	-0.6	95.0	-1.8	94.5	-0.5	94.0	-0.5	92.9	-1.2	91.6	-1.4	91.3	-0.3	90.8	-0.5	90.4	-0.4	89.9	-0.6
2000	88.8	-1.2	88.4	-0.5	87.7	-0.8	87.1	-0.7	86.2	-1.0	85.9	-0.3	86.0	0.1	85.3	-0.8	85.1	-0.2	85.2	0.1	85.0	-0.2	84.2	-0.9
2001	82.9	-1.5	81.7	-1.4	80.5	-1.5	80.4	-0.1	80.0	-0.5	79.1	-1.1	78.6	-0.6	76.1	-3.2	75.0	-1.4	73.7	-1.7	74.8	1.5	74.3	-0.7

Source: U.S. Department of Labor, Bureau of Labor Statistics, Division of Industry Prices and Price Indexes. n.e.c. stands for not elsewhere classified. - indicates no data collected for period or unavailable.

1061

Special Industry Machinery and Equipment
Producer Price Index
Base 1982 = 100

For 1961-2001. Columns headed % show percentile change in the index from the previous period for which an index is available.

Year	Jan Index	%	Feb Index	%	Mar Index	%	Apr Index	%	May Index	%	Jun Index	%	Jul Index	%	Aug Index	%	Sep Index	%	Oct Index	%	Nov Index	%	Dec Index	%
1961	26.4	-	26.4	0.0	26.4	0.0	26.4	0.0	26.5	0.4	26.5	0.0	26.5	0.0	26.5	0.0	26.5	0.0	26.5	0.0	26.5	0.0	26.6	0.4
1962	26.7	0.4	26.8	0.4	26.8	0.0	26.8	0.0	26.8	0.0	26.8	0.0	26.9	0.4	26.9	0.0	26.9	0.0	26.9	0.0	27.0	0.4	27.1	0.4
1963	27.1	0.0	27.2	0.4	27.2	0.0	27.4	0.7	27.4	0.0	27.4	0.0	27.4	0.0	27.5	0.4	27.6	0.4	27.6	0.0	27.6	0.0	27.7	0.4
1964	27.7	0.0	27.7	0.0	27.9	0.7	27.9	0.0	27.9	0.0	27.9	0.0	27.9	0.0	27.9	0.0	27.9	0.0	27.9	0.0	28.1	0.7	28.1	0.0
1965	28.3	0.7	28.3	0.0	28.4	0.4	28.4	0.0	28.4	0.0	28.4	0.0	28.4	0.0	28.4	0.0	28.5	0.4	28.5	0.0	28.7	0.7	28.7	0.0
1966	28.8	0.3	28.8	0.0	29.0	0.7	29.0	0.0	29.2	0.7	29.5	1.0	29.6	0.3	29.7	0.3	29.8	0.3	30.0	0.7	30.1	0.3	30.1	0.0
1967	30.4	1.0	30.5	0.3	30.5	0.0	30.5	0.0	30.7	0.7	30.7	0.0	30.7	0.0	30.8	0.3	30.8	0.0	31.2	1.3	31.2	0.0	31.4	0.6
1968	31.8	1.3	31.8	0.0	31.8	0.0	32.2	1.3	32.3	0.3	32.4	0.3	32.5	0.3	32.5	0.0	32.6	0.3	32.7	0.3	32.9	0.6	32.9	0.0
1969	33.0	0.3	33.3	0.9	33.4	0.3	33.5	0.3	33.6	0.3	33.7	0.3	34.0	0.9	34.0	0.0	34.1	0.3	34.2	0.3	34.4	0.6	34.9	1.5
1970	35.1	0.6	35.1	0.0	35.2	0.3	35.2	0.0	35.3	0.3	35.4	0.3	35.6	0.6	35.6	0.0	35.8	0.6	36.1	0.8	36.1	0.0	36.4	0.8
1971	36.7	0.8	36.8	0.3	36.8	0.0	36.9	0.3	37.0	0.3	37.2	0.5	37.4	0.5	37.4	0.0	37.5	0.3	37.5	0.0	37.5		37.5	
1972	37.7	0.5	37.9	0.5	37.8	-0.3	37.9	0.3	38.0	0.3	38.1	0.3	38.1	0.0	38.1	0.0	38.1	0.0	38.2	0.3	38.3	0.3	38.3	0.0
1973	38.4	0.3	38.9	1.3	39.1	0.5	39.5	1.0	39.7	0.5	40.0	0.8	40.0	0.0	40.5	1.3	40.8	0.7	40.9	0.2	41.0	0.2	41.5	1.2
1974	41.8	0.7	42.5	1.7	43.6	2.6	44.1	1.1	45.2	2.5	45.8	1.3	46.2	0.9	48.0	3.9	48.8	1.7	49.8	2.0	50.4	1.2	51.0	1.2
1975	51.8	1.6	52.2	0.8	53.1	1.7	53.3	0.4	53.3	0.0	53.6	0.6	54.0	0.7	54.3	0.6	54.3	0.0	54.9	1.1	55.2	0.5	55.7	0.9
1976	56.3	1.1	56.5	0.4	56.8	0.5	57.5	1.2	57.5	0.0	57.8	0.5	58.3	0.9	58.4	0.2	58.7	0.5	59.0	0.5	59.0	0.0	59.6	1.0
1977	60.1	0.8	60.4	0.5	60.7	0.5	61.2	0.8	61.7	0.8	62.1	0.6	62.4	0.5	62.7	0.5	62.8	0.2	64.4	2.5	64.6	0.3	65.1	0.8
1978	65.7	0.9	65.9	0.3	66.6	1.1	67.1	0.8	67.4	0.4	68.3	1.3	68.7	0.6	69.2	0.7	69.8	0.9	70.8	1.4	71.6	1.1	71.9	0.4
1979	72.7	1.1	72.9	0.3	73.5	0.8	74.9	1.9	75.4	0.7	75.7	0.4	76.8	1.5	77.2	0.5	77.2	0.0	78.1	1.2	78.4	0.4	78.8	0.5
1980	80.1	1.6	80.9	1.0	81.6	0.9	83.6	2.5	84.0	0.5	84.4	0.5	85.1	0.8	85.2	0.1	87.0	2.1	88.0	1.1	88.5	0.6	89.5	1.1
1981	90.9	1.6	92.0	1.2	92.6	0.7	93.3	0.8	94.5	1.3	95.0	0.5	95.6	0.6	95.4	-0.2	96.2	0.8	96.8	0.6	96.9	0.1	97.3	0.4
1982	98.6	1.3	98.6	0.0	98.8	0.2	99.3	0.5	99.6	0.3	100.0	0.4	100.6	0.6	100.5	-0.1	100.5	0.0	100.8	0.3	101.2	0.4	101.5	0.3
1983	102.1	0.6	102.3	0.2	102.6	0.3	102.9	0.3	103.3	0.4	103.5	0.2	103.9	0.4	104.3	0.4	104.5	0.2	104.7	0.2	104.9	0.2	105.2	0.3
1984	105.2	0.0	105.5	0.3	106.0	0.5	106.7	0.7	107.1	0.4	107.2	0.1	108.2	0.9	108.5	0.3	108.0	-0.5	108.1	0.1	108.2	0.1	108.4	0.2
1985	109.4	0.9	109.8	0.4	110.0	0.2	110.2	0.2	110.4	0.2	110.7	0.3	111.0	0.3	111.2	0.2	111.4	0.2	111.5	0.1	111.8	0.3	112.2	0.4
1986	112.6	0.4	112.9	0.3	113.0	0.1	113.3	0.3	113.6	0.3	114.2	0.5	114.4	0.2	114.8	0.3	115.2	0.3	115.2	0.0	115.4	0.2	115.8	0.3
1987	116.2	0.3	116.6	0.3	116.7	0.1	116.8	0.1	117.0	0.2	117.0	0.0	117.3	0.3	117.3	0.0	117.5	0.2	118.1	0.5	118.4	0.3	118.8	0.3
1988	119.3	0.4	119.8	0.4	120.1	0.3	120.7	0.5	121.0	0.2	121.5	0.4	122.0	0.4	122.3	0.2	122.6	0.2	123.2	0.5	123.9	0.6	124.1	0.2
1989	124.7	0.5	125.4	0.6	125.7	0.2	126.2	0.4	126.7	0.4	127.1	0.3	127.3	0.2	127.6	0.2	127.9	0.2	128.1	0.2	128.3	0.2	128.6	0.2
1990	129.2	0.5	129.8	0.5	130.1	0.2	131.0	0.7	131.2	0.2	131.5	0.2	131.8	0.2	131.9	0.1	132.4	0.4	132.7	0.2	133.1	0.3	133.4	0.2
1991	134.7	1.0	134.9	0.1	135.2	0.2	135.6	0.3	136.0	0.3	136.1	0.1	136.1	0.0	136.1	0.0	136.4	0.2	136.7	0.2	136.8	0.1	136.9	0.1
1992	137.6	0.5	138.1	0.4	138.3	0.1	138.8	0.4	139.2	0.3	139.3	0.1	139.4	0.1	139.5	0.1	140.5	0.7	140.7	0.1	141.0	0.2	141.2	0.1
1993	141.9	0.5	142.6	0.5	143.0	0.3	143.3	0.2	143.4	0.1	143.7	0.2	143.9	0.1	143.9	0.0	144.1	0.1	144.5	0.3	144.7	0.1	144.7	0.0
1994	145.1	0.3	145.5	0.3	145.7	0.1	145.9	0.1	146.0	0.1	146.2	0.1	146.4	0.1	146.4	0.0	146.5	0.1	146.6	0.1	146.8	0.1	147.0	0.1
1995	148.1	0.7	148.6	0.3	149.0	0.3	149.3	0.2	149.7	0.3	150.0	0.2	150.2	0.1	150.3	0.1	150.5	0.1	150.7	0.1	150.8	0.1	151.0	0.1
1996	152.0	0.7	152.4	0.3	152.7	0.2	152.9	0.1	153.0	0.1	153.2	0.1	153.4	0.1	153.8	0.3	153.9	0.1	154.0	0.1	154.4	0.3	154.4	0.0
1997	155.3	0.6	156.1	0.5	156.3	0.1	156.4	0.1	156.4	0.0	156.5	0.1	156.7	0.1	157.1	0.3	157.2	0.1	157.1	-0.1	157.4	0.2	157.5	0.1
1998	158.0	0.3	158.2	0.1	158.4	0.1	158.7	0.2	159.0	0.2	159.2	0.2	159.3	0.0	159.3	0.0	159.4	0.1	159.3	-0.1	160.0	0.4	160.0	0.0
1999	160.5	0.3	160.8	0.2	161.0	0.1	161.2	0.1	161.3	0.1	161.3	0.0	161.4	0.1	161.5	0.1	161.6	0.1	161.7	0.1	161.7	0.0	161.9	0.1
2000	162.4	0.3	162.7	0.2	162.8	0.1	162.8	0.0	162.9	0.1	163.2	0.2	163.1	-0.1	163.4	0.2	163.5	0.1	163.3	-0.1	163.3	0.0	163.6	0.2
2001	164.1	0.3	164.4	0.2	164.9	0.3	165.1	0.1	165.2	0.1	165.2	0.0	165.4	0.1	165.4	0.0	165.0	-0.2	164.2	-0.5	164.6	0.2	164.8	0.1

Source: U.S. Department of Labor, Bureau of Labor Statistics, Division of Industry Prices and Price Indexes. n.e.c. stands for not elsewhere classified. - indicates no data collected for period or unavailable.

Electrical Machinery and Equipment
Producer Price Index
Base 1982 = 100

For 1939-2001. Columns headed % show percentile change in the index from the previous period for which an index is available.

Year	Jan Index	%	Feb Index	%	Mar Index	%	Apr Index	%	May Index	%	Jun Index	%	Jul Index	%	Aug Index	%	Sep Index	%	Oct Index	%	Nov Index	%	Dec Index	%
1939	19.6	-	19.6	0.0	19.6	0.0	19.6	0.0	19.6	0.0	19.6	0.0	19.5	-0.5	19.5	0.0	19.5	0.0	19.5	0.0	19.5	0.0	19.5	0.0
1940	19.5	0.0	19.5	0.0	19.5	0.0	19.5	0.0	19.5	0.0	19.5	0.0	19.5	0.0	19.5	0.0	19.5	0.0	19.5	0.0	19.5	0.0	19.5	0.0
1941	19.5	0.0	19.5	0.0	19.5	0.0	19.5	0.0	19.5	0.0	19.5	0.0	19.5	0.0	19.6	0.5	19.7	0.5	19.7	0.0	19.8	0.5	19.8	0.0
1942	19.8	0.0	19.8	0.0	19.7	-0.5	19.6	-0.5	19.6	0.0	19.6	0.0	19.6	0.0	19.6	0.0	19.6	0.0	19.6	0.0	19.5	-0.5	19.5	0.0
1943	19.5	0.0	19.5	0.0	19.5	0.0	19.5	0.0	19.5	0.0	19.5	0.0	19.5	0.0	19.4	-0.5	19.4	0.0	19.4	0.0	19.4	0.0	19.4	0.0
1944	19.4	0.0	19.4	0.0	19.4	0.0	19.4	0.0	19.4	0.0	19.1	-1.5	19.0	-0.5	19.0	0.0	19.0	0.0	19.0	0.0	19.0	0.0	19.0	0.0
1945	19.0	0.0	19.0	0.0	19.0	0.0	19.0	0.0	19.2	1.1	19.3	0.5	19.3	0.0	19.3	0.0	19.4	0.5	19.5	0.5	19.5	0.0		
1946	19.6	0.5	19.6	0.0	19.6	0.0	20.5	4.6	21.9	6.8	22.3	1.8	22.5	0.9	22.6	0.4	22.8	0.9	23.3	2.2	24.4	4.7	25.3	3.7
1947	25.5	0.8	25.6	0.4	25.7	0.4	26.0	1.2	27.3	5.0	27.5	0.7	27.4	-0.4	27.5	0.4	27.6	0.4	27.5	-0.4	27.5	0.0	27.6	0.4
1948	27.4	-0.7	27.3	-0.4	27.3	0.0	27.3	0.0	27.2	-0.4	27.3	0.4	27.9	2.2	28.8	3.2	29.1	1.0	29.2	0.3	29.4	0.7	29.5	0.3
1949	29.7	0.7	29.8	0.3	29.8	0.0	29.2	-2.0	28.8	-1.4	28.5	-1.0	28.4	-0.4	28.4	0.0	28.4	0.0	28.4	0.0	28.4	0.0	28.4	0.0
1950	28.2	-0.7	28.0	-0.7	28.1	0.4	28.1	0.0	28.1	0.0	28.5	1.4	29.1	2.1	30.4	4.5	30.9	1.6	31.9	3.2	32.0	0.3	33.5	4.7
1951	34.0	1.5	34.0	0.0	34.0	0.0	34.0	0.0	34.0	0.0	34.0	0.0	34.2	0.6	34.1	-0.3	34.1	0.0	34.0	-0.3	34.1	0.3	34.0	-0.3
1952	33.9	-0.3	34.0	0.3	33.9	-0.3	33.8	-0.3	33.8	0.0	33.5	-0.9	33.5	0.0	33.5	0.0	33.4	-0.3	33.3	-0.3	33.4	0.3	33.4	0.0
1953	33.4	0.0	33.4	0.0	33.5	0.3	33.9	1.2	34.2	0.9	34.7	1.5	34.9	0.6	35.1	0.6	35.2	0.3	35.3	0.3	35.4	0.3	35.4	0.0
1954	35.4	0.0	35.4	0.0	35.4	0.0	35.3	-0.3	35.2	-0.3	35.2	0.0	35.2	0.0	35.1	-0.3	35.1	0.0	35.0	-0.3	35.4	1.1	35.4	0.0
1955	35.4	0.0	35.4	0.0	35.3	-0.3	35.3	0.0	35.3	0.0	35.3	0.0	35.3	0.0	35.4	0.3	35.7	0.8	36.5	2.2	36.5	0.0	36.7	0.5
1956	37.0	0.3	37.2	0.5	37.3	0.3	37.9	1.6	38.3	1.1	38.4	0.3	38.4	0.0	38.6	0.5	39.6	2.6	40.0	1.0	40.6	1.5	40.6	0.0
1957	40.8	0.5	41.1	0.7	41.2	0.2	41.3	0.2	41.4	0.2	41.4	0.0	41.8	1.0	41.8	0.0	42.2	1.0	42.1	-0.2	42.2	0.2	42.2	0.0
1958	42.2	0.0	42.2	0.0	42.2	0.0	42.4	0.5	42.5	0.2	42.6	0.2	42.6	0.0	42.7	0.2	42.7	0.0	42.7	0.0	42.5	-0.5	42.5	0.0
1959	42.5	0.0	42.5	0.0	42.7	0.5	42.7	0.0	43.0	0.7	43.0	0.0	43.5	1.2	43.4	-0.2	43.5	0.2	43.6	0.2	43.6	0.0	43.4	-0.5
1960	43.5	0.2	43.5	0.0	43.5	0.0	43.3	-0.5	42.8	-1.2	42.8	0.0	42.9	0.2	42.8	-0.2	42.7	-0.2	42.6	-0.2	42.6	0.0	42.6	0.0
1961	42.9	0.7	42.9	0.0	42.9	0.0	42.4	-1.2	42.4	0.0	42.4	0.0	42.4	0.0	42.0	-0.9	42.0	0.0	42.2	0.5	42.2	0.0	42.1	-0.2
1962	41.9	-0.5	41.9	0.0	41.9	0.0	41.8	-0.2	41.8	0.0	41.8	0.0	41.6	-0.5	41.6	0.0	41.8	0.5	41.8	0.0	41.6	-0.5	41.6	0.0
1963	41.5	-0.2	41.5	0.0	41.1	-1.0	41.2	0.2	41.4	0.5	41.5	0.2	41.2	-0.7	41.2	0.0	41.2	0.0	41.3	0.2	41.4	0.2	41.5	0.2
1964	41.0	-1.2	41.1	0.2	41.2	0.2	41.5	0.7	41.5	0.0	40.9	-1.4	40.9	0.0	41.0	0.2	40.9	-0.2	40.9	0.0	40.9	0.0	40.9	0.0
1965	41.0	0.2	41.1	0.2	41.1	0.0	41.2	0.2	41.2	0.0	41.1	-0.2	41.2	0.2	41.0	-0.5	41.0	0.0	41.0	0.0	40.9	-0.2	41.0	0.2
1966	41.2	0.5	41.5	0.7	41.7	0.5	41.8	0.2	42.0	0.5	41.9	-0.2	42.0	0.2	42.0	0.0	42.1	0.2	42.2	0.2	42.7	1.2	43.1	0.9
1967	43.2	0.2	43.2	0.0	43.2	0.0	43.2	0.0	43.2	0.0	43.2	0.0	43.2	0.0	43.1	-0.2	43.1	0.0	43.0	-0.2	43.1	0.2	43.4	0.7
1968	43.5	0.2	43.6	0.2	43.6	0.0	43.6	0.0	43.7	0.2	43.7	0.0	43.7	0.0	43.7	0.0	43.9	0.5	43.9	0.0	44.0	0.2	43.9	-0.2
1969	43.9	0.0	44.2	0.7	44.2	0.0	44.2	0.0	44.3	0.2	44.4	0.2	44.4	0.0	44.4	0.0	44.7	0.7	44.8	0.2	45.0	0.4	45.1	0.2
1970	45.3	0.4	45.2	-0.2	45.4	0.4	45.5	0.2	45.6	0.2	45.9	0.7	46.1	0.4	46.2	0.2	46.4	0.4	46.4	0.0	46.6	0.4	46.7	0.2
1971	46.9	0.4	47.1	0.4	47.2	0.2	47.1	-0.2	47.1	0.0	47.1	0.0	47.2	0.2	47.3	0.2	47.2	-0.2	47.2	0.0	47.1	-0.2	47.1	0.0
1972	47.3	0.4	47.5	0.4	47.6	0.2	47.6	0.0	47.7	0.2	47.8	0.2	47.8	0.0	47.8	0.0	47.7	-0.2	47.7	0.0	47.8	0.2	47.8	0.0
1973	47.9	0.2	47.9	0.0	48.1	0.4	48.2	0.2	48.5	0.6	48.7	0.4	48.7	0.0	48.7	0.0	48.7	0.0	48.8	0.2	48.9	0.2	49.2	0.6
1974	49.7	1.0	50.0	0.6	50.5	1.0	51.2	1.4	52.1	1.8	53.3	2.3	54.5	2.3	55.5	1.8	56.3	1.4	57.2	1.6	58.5	2.3	59.0	0.9
1975	59.6	1.0	59.9	0.5	60.1	0.3	60.2	0.2	60.5	0.5	60.6	0.2	60.8	0.3	60.9	0.2	61.2	0.5	61.5	0.5	61.8	0.5	61.8	0.0
1976	62.3	0.8	62.5	0.3	62.6	0.2	62.7	0.2	62.8	0.2	63.1	0.5	63.2	0.2	63.3	0.2	64.0	1.1	64.4	0.6	64.6	0.3	64.8	0.3
1977	65.1	0.5	65.4	0.5	65.6	0.3	65.7	0.2	66.0	0.5	66.1	0.2	66.5	0.6	66.7	0.3	67.2	0.7	67.9	1.0	68.2	0.4	68.2	0.0
1978	69.1	1.3	69.4	0.4	69.9	0.7	70.3	0.6	70.6	0.4	71.1	0.7	71.4	0.4	71.6	0.3	71.9	0.4	72.3	0.6	73.2	1.2	73.6	0.5
1979	73.9	0.4	74.6	0.9	75.1	0.7	75.6	0.7	76.2	0.8	76.7	0.7	77.7	1.3	78.2	0.6	78.8	0.8	79.6	1.0	79.8	0.3	80.6	1.0
1980	82.3	2.1	83.9	1.9	84.9	1.2	85.9	1.2	86.3	0.5	87.1	0.9	88.0	1.0	88.5	0.6	89.0	0.6	89.4	0.4	89.6	0.2	90.2	0.7
1981	91.5	1.4	92.3	0.9	93.3	1.1	93.9	0.6	93.9	0.0	94.7	0.9	95.5	0.8	96.2	0.7	96.8	0.6	97.3	0.5	97.6	0.3	98.0	0.4
1982	98.8	0.8	99.1	0.3	99.5	0.4	100.0	0.5	99.9	-0.1	100.0	0.1	100.0	0.0	100.1	0.1	100.1	0.0	100.5	0.4	100.9	0.4	101.2	0.3
1983	101.6	0.4	102.4	0.8	102.6	0.2	102.9	0.3	103.0	0.1	103.1	0.1	104.4	1.3	104.4	0.0	104.9	0.5	104.8	-0.1	104.9	0.1	105.3	0.4

[Continued]

Electrical Machinery and Equipment

Producer Price Index
Base 1982 = 100

[Continued]

For 1939-2001. Columns headed % show percentile change in the index from the previous period for which an index is available.

Year	Jan Index	%	Feb Index	%	Mar Index	%	Apr Index	%	May Index	%	Jun Index	%	Jul Index	%	Aug Index	%	Sep Index	%	Oct Index	%	Nov Index	%	Dec Index	%
1984	105.7	0.4	106.1	0.4	106.5	0.4	107.0	0.5	107.1	0.1	107.6	0.5	107.7	0.1	107.7	0.0	107.9	0.2	108.3	0.4	108.6	0.3	108.7	0.1
1985	109.3	0.6	109.6	0.3	109.6	0.0	109.3	-0.3	109.5	0.2	109.4	-0.1	109.6	0.2	109.7	0.1	109.8	0.1	109.9	0.1	109.8	-0.1	110.0	0.2
1986	110.3	0.3	110.6	0.3	110.8	0.2	111.0	0.2	111.0	0.0	110.9	-0.1	111.5	0.5	111.5	0.0	111.7	0.2	111.7	0.0	111.8	0.1	111.9	0.1
1987	112.3	0.4	112.4	0.1	112.3	-0.1	112.2	-0.1	112.3	0.1	112.2	-0.1	112.7	0.4	112.9	0.2	112.7	-0.2	113.1	0.4	113.2	0.1	113.4	0.2
1988	113.7	0.3	114.1	0.4	113.7	-0.4	113.8	0.1	114.4	0.5	114.2	-0.2	114.4	0.2	114.7	0.3	114.8	0.1	115.1	0.3	115.2	0.1	115.4	0.2
1989	116.2	0.7	116.6	0.3	116.7	0.1	116.8	0.1	117.0	0.2	117.5	0.4	117.9	0.3	118.0	0.1	117.9	-0.1	118.4	0.4	118.3	-0.1	118.4	0.1
1990	118.9	0.4	118.6	-0.3	118.9	0.3	119.0	0.1	119.0	0.0	119.2	0.2	119.5	0.3	119.4	-0.1	119.5	0.1	119.6	0.1	119.8	0.2	119.9	0.1
1991	120.5	0.5	120.6	0.1	120.7	0.1	120.9	0.2	120.7	-0.2	120.8	0.1	120.9	0.1	120.9	0.0	120.8	-0.1	120.8	0.0	120.9	0.1	120.9	0.0
1992	120.9	0.0	121.2	0.2	121.4	0.2	121.2	-0.2	121.3	0.1	121.2	-0.1	121.2	0.0	121.2	0.0	121.2	0.0	121.4	0.2	121.6	0.2	121.7	0.1
1993	122.0	0.2	122.2	0.2	122.2	0.0	122.6	0.3	122.4	-0.2	122.4	0.0	122.4	0.0	122.5	0.1	122.6	0.1	122.7	0.1	122.8	0.1	122.7	-0.1
1994	123.1	0.3	123.2	0.1	123.3	0.1	123.6	0.2	123.7	0.1	123.7	0.0	123.8	0.1	123.5	-0.2	123.4	-0.1	123.2	-0.2	123.4	0.2	123.4	0.0
1995	123.9	0.4	124.2	0.2	124.1	-0.1	124.2	0.1	124.2	0.0	124.1	-0.1	124.0	-0.1	124.0	0.0	124.2	0.2	124.8	0.5	124.9	0.1	124.3	-0.5
1996	124.6	0.2	124.6	0.0	124.1	-0.4	123.6	-0.4	123.2	-0.3	122.9	-0.2	123.1	0.2	123.2	0.1	123.2	0.0	122.9	-0.2	122.9	0.0	123.2	0.2
1997	123.0	-0.2	122.9	-0.1	122.7	-0.2	122.6	-0.1	122.4	-0.2	122.4	0.0	122.6	0.2	122.1	-0.4	122.0	-0.1	121.9	-0.1	122.1	0.2	121.8	-0.2
1998	121.8	0.0	121.6	-0.2	121.5	-0.1	121.2	-0.2	121.1	-0.1	121.1	0.0	120.8	-0.2	120.7	-0.1	120.6	-0.1	120.6	0.0	120.6	0.0	120.4	-0.2
1999	120.6	0.2	120.6	0.0	120.5	-0.1	120.3	-0.2	119.8	-0.4	119.6	-0.2	119.5	-0.1	119.4	-0.1	119.2	-0.2	119.3	0.1	119.3	0.0	119.3	0.0
2000	119.0	-0.3	118.8	-0.2	118.6	-0.2	118.7	0.1	118.8	0.1	118.8	0.0	119.0	0.2	118.9	-0.1	118.9	0.0	118.7	-0.2	118.6	-0.1	118.1	-0.4
2001	118.2	0.1	118.0	-0.2	118.1	0.1	117.8	-0.3	117.7	-0.1	117.4	-0.3	117.1	-0.3	116.9	-0.2	116.5	-0.3	116.5	0.0	116.5	0.0	116.7	0.2

Source: U.S. Department of Labor, Bureau of Labor Statistics, Division of Industry Prices and Price Indexes. n.e.c. stands for not elsewhere classified. - indicates no data collected for period or unavailable.

Miscellaneous Instruments
Producer Price Index
Base 1982 = 100

For 1980-2001. Columns headed % show percentile change in the index from the previous period for which an index is available.

Year	Jan Index	%	Feb Index	%	Mar Index	%	Apr Index	%	May Index	%	Jun Index	%	Jul Index	%	Aug Index	%	Sep Index	%	Oct Index	%	Nov Index	%	Dec Index	%
1980	-	-	-	-	-	-	-	-	-	-	86.1	-	86.4	0.3	86.3	-0.1	87.4	1.3	89.1	1.9	90.3	1.3	91.6	1.4
1981	89.9	-1.9	89.1	-0.9	88.5	-0.7	88.8	0.3	88.9	0.1	89.8	1.0	91.0	1.3	94.4	3.7	95.8	1.5	95.2	-0.6	95.8	0.6	95.8	0.0
1982	96.2	0.4	98.7	2.6	98.2	-0.5	99.3	1.1	99.4	0.1	99.3	-0.1	99.6	0.3	98.0	-1.6	100.8	2.9	103.1	2.3	101.9	-1.2	105.4	3.4
1983	106.1	0.7	107.1	0.9	106.9	-0.2	106.3	-0.6	105.9	-0.4	104.7	-1.1	104.6	-0.1	104.7	0.1	105.0	0.3	105.1	0.1	104.9	-0.2	104.6	-0.3
1984	104.9	0.3	105.4	0.5	105.6	0.2	105.0	-0.6	105.2	0.2	105.7	0.5	106.5	0.8	108.1	1.5	108.4	0.3	108.3	-0.1	108.0	-0.3	108.8	0.7
1985	109.4	0.6	109.5	0.1	109.0	-0.5	108.3	-0.6	108.8	0.5	109.6	0.7	110.5	0.8	110.1	-0.4	110.4	0.3	110.6	0.2	110.9	0.3	110.8	-0.1
1986	111.4	0.5	111.7	0.3	111.4	-0.3	111.7	0.3	111.9	0.2	112.3	0.4	113.2	0.8	113.7	0.4	113.7	0.0	113.9	0.2	114.0	0.1	114.2	0.2
1987	114.8	0.5	115.3	0.4	115.3	0.0	115.4	0.1	115.5	0.1	115.1	-0.3	115.7	0.5	115.9	0.2	116.1	0.2	116.3	0.2	116.4	0.1	116.8	0.3
1988	117.6	0.7	118.2	0.5	118.9	0.6	118.6	-0.3	118.6	0.0	118.6	0.0	118.9	0.3	119.2	0.3	119.2	0.0	119.3	0.1	119.9	0.5	119.9	0.0
1989	121.0	0.9	121.4	0.3	121.5	0.1	121.9	0.3	122.1	0.2	122.4	0.2	122.8	0.3	123.1	0.2	123.2	0.1	123.1	-0.1	123.4	0.2	123.9	0.4
1990	125.0	0.9	125.5	0.4	125.9	0.3	126.1	0.2	126.5	0.3	126.2	-0.2	126.9	0.6	127.1	0.2	127.2	0.1	127.5	0.2	128.1	0.5	128.3	0.2
1991	129.1	0.6	129.5	0.3	129.5	0.0	129.8	0.2	129.7	-0.1	129.9	0.2	130.5	0.5	130.6	0.1	130.8	0.2	131.4	0.5	131.3	-0.1	131.5	0.2
1992	132.4	0.7	132.6	0.2	132.6	0.0	132.9	0.2	132.9	0.0	133.4	0.4	134.0	0.4	134.2	0.1	134.4	0.1	135.0	0.4	135.1	0.1	135.2	0.1
1993	136.7	1.1	136.8	0.1	136.9	0.1	137.5	0.4	137.5	0.0	137.8	0.2	138.2	0.3	138.3	0.1	138.3	0.0	138.4	0.1	138.3	-0.1	138.5	0.1
1994	138.9	0.3	139.1	0.1	139.2	0.1	139.4	0.1	139.5	0.1	139.6	0.1	139.8	0.1	140.0	0.1	139.8	-0.1	139.8	0.0	140.1	0.2	139.6	-0.4
1995	139.9	0.2	140.2	0.2	140.2	0.0	140.4	0.1	140.6	0.1	140.9	0.2	141.6	0.5	141.3	-0.2	141.5	0.1	141.7	0.1	142.0	0.2	141.9	-0.1
1996	142.7	0.6	142.9	0.1	142.9	0.0	142.8	-0.1	143.1	0.2	143.3	0.1	143.5	0.1	143.6	0.1	143.4	-0.1	143.4	0.0	143.6	0.1	144.0	0.3
1997	145.3	0.9	145.4	0.1	145.6	0.1	146.0	0.3	146.0	0.0	146.0	0.0	146.3	0.2	146.5	0.1	146.6	0.1	145.8	-0.5	146.2	0.3	145.9	-0.2
1998	147.0	0.8	146.9	-0.1	147.1	0.1	147.5	0.3	147.7	0.1	147.7	0.0	147.8	0.1	147.9	0.1	148.0	0.1	148.1	0.1	148.2	0.1	148.2	0.0
1999	148.9	0.5	148.9	0.0	148.4	-0.3	148.5	0.1	148.5	0.0	148.2	-0.2	147.8	-0.3	148.4	0.4	148.5	0.1	148.8	0.2	148.9	0.1	149.1	0.1
2000	150.1	0.7	150.3	0.1	150.2	-0.1	150.3	0.1	150.4	0.1	150.2	-0.1	150.1	-0.1	150.0	-0.1	150.3	0.2	150.4	0.1	150.5	0.1	150.7	0.1
2001	151.3	0.4	151.6	0.2	151.7	0.1	151.9	0.1	151.9	0.0	152.0	0.1	152.0	0.0	151.9	-0.1	152.2	0.2	152.3	0.1	153.3	0.7	153.2	-0.1

Source: U.S. Department of Labor, Bureau of Labor Statistics, Division of Industry Prices and Price Indexes. n.e.c. stands for not elsewhere classified. - indicates no data collected for period or unavailable.

Miscellaneous Machinery
Producer Price Index
Base 1982 = 100

For 1947-2001. Columns headed % show percentile change in the index from the previous period for which an index is available.

Year	Jan Index	%	Feb Index	%	Mar Index	%	Apr Index	%	May Index	%	Jun Index	%	Jul Index	%	Aug Index	%	Sep Index	%	Oct Index	%	Nov Index	%	Dec Index	%
1947	21.2	-	21.3	0.5	21.4	0.5	21.4	0.0	21.5	0.5	21.6	0.5	21.6	0.0	21.7	0.5	21.8	0.5	22.0	0.9	22.2	0.9	22.4	0.9
1948	22.5	0.4	22.6	0.4	22.7	0.4	22.8	0.4	22.8	0.0	22.9	0.4	23.4	2.2	23.8	1.7	24.0	0.8	24.2	0.8	24.3	0.4	24.3	0.0
1949	24.3	0.0	24.3	0.0	24.3	0.0	24.3	0.0	24.3	0.0	24.3	0.0	24.3	0.0	24.3	0.0	24.3	0.0	24.3	0.0	24.3	0.0	24.2	-0.4
1950	24.2	0.0	24.3	0.4	24.3	0.0	24.3	0.0	24.3	0.0	24.3	0.0	24.4	0.4	24.9	2.0	25.2	1.2	25.5	1.2	25.8	1.2	26.5	2.7
1951	27.5	3.8	27.5	0.0	27.5	0.0	27.5	0.0	27.5	0.0	27.5	0.0	27.6	0.4	27.6	0.0	27.6	0.0	27.6	0.0	27.6	0.0	27.8	0.7
1952	27.8	0.0	27.8	0.0	27.6	-0.7	27.6	0.0	27.5	-0.4	27.5	0.0	27.5	0.0	27.5	0.0	27.5	0.0	27.6	0.4	27.6	0.0	27.6	0.0
1953	27.6	0.0	27.8	0.7	27.8	0.0	27.8	0.0	28.2	1.4	28.3	0.4	28.5	0.7	28.7	0.7	28.7	0.0	28.7	0.0	28.7	0.0	28.8	0.3
1954	28.8	0.0	28.8	0.0	28.9	0.3	28.9	0.0	28.9	0.0	29.0	0.3	29.0	0.0	29.0	0.0	29.1	0.3	29.1	0.0	29.1	0.0	29.1	0.0
1955	29.2	0.3	29.2	0.0	29.3	0.3	29.3	0.0	29.4	0.3	29.4	0.0	29.4	0.0	30.1	2.4	30.5	1.3	30.7	0.7	30.8	0.3	30.8	0.0
1956	30.8	0.0	30.9	0.3	31.0	0.3	31.0	0.0	31.2	0.6	31.3	0.3	31.6	1.0	31.7	0.3	32.1	1.3	32.5	1.2	32.8	0.9	32.9	0.3
1957	32.9	0.0	33.0	0.3	33.1	0.3	33.2	0.3	33.2	0.0	33.2	0.0	33.4	0.6	33.8	1.2	34.0	0.6	34.1	0.3	34.2	0.3	34.3	0.3
1958	34.4	0.3	34.4	0.0	34.4	0.0	34.4	0.0	34.1	-0.9	34.1	0.0	34.1	0.0	34.1	0.0	34.1	0.0	34.1	0.0	34.2	0.3	34.3	0.3
1959	34.3	0.0	34.4	0.3	34.5	0.3	34.5	0.0	34.5	0.0	34.5	0.0	34.5	0.0	34.6	0.3	34.5	-0.3	34.6	0.3	34.6	0.0	34.6	0.0
1960	34.6	0.0	34.6	0.0	34.7	0.3	34.7	0.0	34.7	0.0	34.7	0.0	34.7	0.0	34.7	0.0	34.7	0.0	34.7	0.0	34.8	0.3	34.9	0.3
1961	34.9	0.0	34.9	0.0	34.9	0.0	35.0	0.3	35.0	0.0	35.0	0.0	35.1	0.3	35.1	0.0	35.1	0.0	35.0	-0.3	35.0	0.0	35.1	0.3
1962	35.1	0.0	35.1	0.0	35.2	0.3	35.1	-0.3	35.1	0.0	35.2	0.3	35.2	0.0	35.3	0.3	35.2	-0.3	35.2	0.0	35.2	0.0	35.2	0.0
1963	35.2	0.0	35.2	0.0	35.4	0.6	35.2	-0.6	35.2	0.0	35.2	0.0	35.2	0.0	35.2	0.0	35.3	0.3	35.3	0.0	35.4	0.3	35.4	0.0
1964	35.5	0.3	35.5	0.0	35.6	0.3	35.6	0.0	35.6	0.0	35.6	0.0	35.7	0.3	35.7	0.0	35.8	0.3	35.8	0.0	35.8	0.0	35.5	-0.8
1965	35.8	0.8	35.8	0.0	35.8	0.0	35.9	0.3	35.9	0.0	36.0	0.3	35.8	-0.6	35.8	0.0	35.8	0.0	35.8	0.0	35.9	0.3	35.9	0.0
1966	35.9	0.0	36.0	0.3	36.1	0.3	36.0	-0.3	36.1	0.3	36.1	0.0	36.3	0.6	36.3	0.0	36.4	0.3	36.6	0.5	36.7	0.3	36.8	0.3
1967	37.0	0.5	37.1	0.3	37.1	0.0	37.1	0.0	37.1	0.0	37.2	0.3	37.2	0.0	37.2	0.0	37.3	0.3	37.4	0.3	37.6	0.5	37.7	0.3
1968	38.2	1.3	38.4	0.5	38.5	0.3	38.6	0.3	38.9	0.8	38.9	0.0	38.9	0.0	38.9	0.0	39.0	0.3	39.3	0.8	39.3	0.0	39.4	0.3
1969	39.5	0.3	39.6	0.3	39.7	0.3	39.9	0.5	40.1	0.5	40.1	0.0	40.3	0.5	40.4	0.2	40.6	0.5	40.8	0.5	41.0	0.5	41.2	0.5
1970	41.3	0.2	41.4	0.2	41.6	0.5	41.9	0.7	41.8	-0.2	41.9	0.2	41.9	0.0	41.9	0.0	42.3	1.0	42.5	0.5	42.7	0.5	43.1	0.9
1971	43.3	0.5	43.3	0.0	43.4	0.2	43.7	0.7	43.8	0.2	43.7	-0.2	43.8	0.2	44.0	0.5	43.9	-0.2	43.9	0.0	43.9	0.0	44.0	0.2
1972	44.1	0.2	44.3	0.5	44.3	0.0	44.6	0.7	44.8	0.4	45.0	0.4	45.0	0.0	45.0	0.0	45.0	0.0	45.1	0.2	45.0	-0.2	45.1	0.2
1973	45.1	0.0	45.3	0.4	45.6	0.7	45.9	0.7	46.4	1.1	46.4	0.0	46.4	0.0	46.5	0.2	46.6	0.2	46.6	0.0	46.8	0.4	47.0	0.4
1974	47.6	1.3	47.9	0.6	48.7	1.7	49.3	1.2	50.0	1.4	51.0	2.0	52.0	2.0	53.5	2.9	54.0	0.9	55.7	3.1	56.9	2.2	57.1	0.4
1975	58.9	3.2	59.1	0.3	59.0	-0.2	59.7	1.2	60.2	0.8	60.2	0.0	60.3	0.2	60.8	0.8	61.5	1.2	61.8	0.5	62.1	0.5	62.2	0.2
1976	62.9	1.1	63.2	0.5	63.5	0.5	63.7	0.3	63.7	0.0	63.8	0.2	64.2	0.6	64.1	-0.2	64.4	0.5	65.0	0.9	65.0	0.0	65.2	0.3
1977	65.6	0.6	65.9	0.5	66.1	0.3	66.3	0.3	66.8	0.8	67.0	0.3	67.3	0.4	67.8	0.7	68.3	0.7	68.6	0.4	69.0	0.6	69.3	0.4
1978	70.1	1.2	70.5	0.6	71.2	1.0	71.4	0.3	71.8	0.6	72.3	0.7	72.9	0.8	73.3	0.5	73.6	0.4	73.9	0.4	74.6	0.9	74.7	0.1
1979	75.5	1.1	75.8	0.4	76.0	0.3	76.5	0.7	77.1	0.8	77.3	0.3	78.1	1.0	78.1	0.0	79.0	1.2	79.6	0.8	80.1	0.6	80.6	0.6
1980	82.1	1.9	82.4	0.4	83.2	1.0	84.7	1.8	84.7	0.0	85.0	0.4	86.1	1.3	86.5	0.5	87.0	0.6	88.1	1.3	88.9	0.9	89.3	0.4
1981	90.7	1.6	91.3	0.7	92.0	0.8	92.6	0.7	92.7	0.1	93.2	0.5	94.7	1.6	95.4	0.7	96.3	0.9	96.5	0.2	96.8	0.3	97.0	0.2
1982	97.4	0.4	98.4	1.0	98.7	0.3	99.2	0.5	99.8	0.6	100.1	0.3	100.4	0.3	100.9	0.5	101.1	0.2	101.2	0.1	101.4	0.2	101.5	0.1
1983	101.7	0.2	101.6	-0.1	102.0	0.4	102.1	0.1	102.6	0.5	102.5	-0.1	102.5	0.0	102.6	0.1	102.3	-0.3	101.8	-0.5	102.0	0.2	102.0	0.0
1984	102.7	0.7	102.2	-0.5	102.3	0.1	102.3	0.0	102.0	-0.3	102.1	0.1	102.2	0.1	102.1	-0.1	102.3	0.2	102.2	-0.1	102.4	0.2	102.3	-0.1
1985	102.5	0.2	102.6	0.1	102.6	0.0	103.1	0.5	103.0	-0.1	103.5	0.5	103.5	0.0	103.6	0.1	103.7	0.1	103.6	-0.1	103.7	0.1	103.7	0.0
1986	103.8	0.1	103.7	-0.1	103.8	0.1	104.2	0.4	104.3	0.1	104.3	0.0	104.3	0.0	104.3	0.0	104.0	-0.3	104.2	0.2	104.3	0.1	104.6	0.3
1987	105.1	0.5	105.2	0.1	105.4	0.2	105.5	0.1	105.6	0.1	105.4	-0.2	105.3	-0.1	105.9	0.6	105.9	0.0	106.1	0.2	106.6	0.5	106.9	0.3
1988	107.5	0.6	107.5	0.0	107.7	0.2	107.9	0.2	108.0	0.1	108.1	0.1	108.5	0.4	109.1	0.6	109.5	0.4	109.5	0.0	109.7	0.2	110.2	0.5
1989	110.7	0.5	110.8	0.1	111.1	0.3	111.3	0.2	111.7	0.4	112.2	0.4	113.1	0.8	113.5	0.4	114.2	0.6	114.4	0.2	114.6	0.2	114.7	0.1
1990	115.7	0.9	115.7	0.0	115.9	0.2	116.0	0.1	116.1	0.1	116.2	0.1	116.3	0.1	116.8	0.4	117.5	0.6	117.6	0.1	118.4	0.7	118.3	-0.1
1991	119.1	0.7	119.4	0.3	119.8	0.3	119.8	0.0	120.0	0.2	120.1	0.1	120.4	0.2	120.8	0.3	121.0	0.2	120.9	-0.1	121.0	0.1	121.2	0.2

[Continued]

Miscellaneous Machinery

Producer Price Index
Base 1982 = 100

[Continued]

For 1947-2001. Columns headed % show percentile change in the index from the previous period for which an index is available.

Year	Jan Index	%	Feb Index	%	Mar Index	%	Apr Index	%	May Index	%	Jun Index	%	Jul Index	%	Aug Index	%	Sep Index	%	Oct Index	%	Nov Index	%	Dec Index	%
1992	121.5	0.2	121.5	0.0	121.4	-0.1	121.3	-0.1	121.5	0.2	121.6	0.1	121.7	0.1	121.9	0.2	121.9	0.0	121.9	0.0	122.0	0.1	122.0	0.0
1993	122.3	0.2	122.4	0.1	122.5	0.1	122.4	-0.1	122.5	0.1	122.4	-0.1	122.6	0.2	122.9	0.2	123.0	0.1	123.2	0.2	123.1	-0.1	123.3	0.2
1994	123.9	0.5	124.2	0.2	124.2	0.0	124.2	0.0	124.2	0.0	124.4	0.2	124.5	0.1	124.7	0.2	125.2	0.4	125.5	0.2	125.6	0.1	125.7	0.1
1995	126.2	0.4	126.4	0.2	126.4	0.0	126.6	0.2	126.7	0.1	126.8	0.1	127.2	0.3	127.2	0.0	127.3	0.1	127.4	0.1	127.6	0.2	127.7	0.1
1996	128.2	0.4	128.6	0.3	128.7	0.1	128.8	0.1	128.8	0.0	128.9	0.1	129.5	0.5	129.5	0.0	129.8	0.2	129.8	0.0	129.9	0.1	130.1	0.2
1997	130.4	0.2	130.3	-0.1	130.6	0.2	130.7	0.1	130.7	0.0	130.7	0.0	131.0	0.2	131.1	0.1	131.1	0.0	131.1	0.0	131.3	0.2	131.3	0.0
1998	131.4	0.1	131.5	0.1	131.6	0.1	131.7	0.1	131.7	0.0	131.9	0.2	132.1	0.2	132.0	-0.1	132.1	0.1	132.2	0.1	132.3	0.1	132.4	0.1
1999	132.9	0.4	132.9	0.0	133.0	0.1	133.0	0.0	133.1	0.1	133.2	0.1	133.3	0.1	133.2	-0.1	133.2	0.0	133.2	0.0	133.4	0.2	133.2	-0.1
2000	133.4	0.2	133.6	0.1	133.7	0.1	133.7	0.0	133.8	0.1	134.0	0.1	134.4	0.3	134.5	0.1	134.6	0.1	134.8	0.1	134.9	0.1	135.0	0.1
2001	135.3	0.2	135.4	0.1	135.4	0.0	135.4	0.0	135.6	0.1	135.7	0.1	136.1	0.3	136.2	0.1	136.3	0.1	136.3	0.0	136.1	-0.1	136.2	0.1

Source: U.S. Department of Labor, Bureau of Labor Statistics, Division of Industry Prices and Price Indexes. n.e.c. stands for not elsewhere classified. - indicates no data collected for period or unavailable.

FURNITURE AND HOUSEHOLD DURABLES

Producer Price Index
Base 1982 = 100

For 1926-2001. Columns headed % show percentile change in the index from the previous period for which an index is available.

Year	Jan Index	%	Feb Index	%	Mar Index	%	Apr Index	%	May Index	%	Jun Index	%	Jul Index	%	Aug Index	%	Sep Index	%	Oct Index	%	Nov Index	%	Dec Index	%
1926	28.8	-	28.8	0.0	28.8	0.0	28.7	-0.3	28.6	-0.3	28.6	0.0	28.6	0.0	28.6	0.0	28.5	-0.3	28.5	0.0	28.5	0.0	28.2	-1.1
1927	28.0	-0.7	28.0	0.0	27.9	-0.4	27.9	0.0	27.9	0.0	28.0	0.4	27.9	-0.4	27.9	0.0	27.6	-1.1	27.8	0.7	27.9	0.4	27.9	0.0
1928	27.6	-1.1	27.6	0.0	27.4	-0.7	27.3	-0.4	27.4	0.4	27.1	-1.1	27.1	0.0	27.1	0.0	27.1	0.0	26.9	-0.7	26.9	0.0	26.9	0.0
1929	26.9	0.0	26.8	-0.4	26.8	0.0	26.9	0.4	26.9	0.0	27.1	0.7	27.0	-0.4	27.0	0.0	27.0	0.0	27.1	0.4	27.1	0.0	27.1	0.0
1930	26.8	-1.1	26.8	0.0	26.8	0.0	26.8	0.0	26.8	0.0	26.8	0.0	26.6	-0.7	26.6	0.0	26.4	-0.8	26.4	0.0	26.2	-0.8	25.4	-3.1
1931	25.4	0.0	25.4	0.0	25.3	-0.4	25.3	0.0	24.9	-1.6	24.8	-0.4	24.6	-0.8	24.4	-0.8	23.7	-2.9	23.2	-2.1	23.2	0.0	22.5	-3.0
1932	22.3	-0.9	22.2	-0.4	22.1	-0.5	21.9	-0.9	21.4	-2.3	21.4	0.0	21.2	-0.9	21.2	0.0	21.1	-0.5	21.2	0.5	21.2	0.0	21.2	0.0
1933	20.8	-1.9	20.6	-1.0	20.6	0.0	20.5	-0.5	20.6	0.5	21.0	1.9	21.4	1.9	21.8	1.9	22.3	2.3	23.0	3.1	23.0	0.0	23.0	0.0
1934	23.1	0.4	23.2	0.4	23.3	0.4	23.4	0.4	23.6	0.9	23.6	0.0	23.5	-0.4	23.5	0.0	23.6	0.4	23.5	-0.4	23.4	-0.4	23.4	0.0
1935	23.2	-0.9	23.2	0.0	23.3	0.4	23.2	-0.4	23.3	0.4	23.2	-0.4	23.2	0.0	23.2	0.0	23.2	0.0	23.2	0.0	23.2	0.0	23.2	0.0
1936	23.5	1.3	23.5	0.0	23.5	0.0	23.5	0.0	23.5	0.0	23.5	0.0	23.4	-0.4	23.5	0.4	23.6	0.4	23.7	0.4	23.8	0.4	24.1	1.3
1937	25.4	5.4	25.7	1.2	25.8	0.4	25.9	0.4	26.1	0.8	26.1	0.0	26.4	1.1	26.6	0.8	26.6	0.0	26.6	0.0	26.4	-0.8	26.2	-0.8
1938	25.8	-1.5	25.8	0.0	25.8	0.0	25.7	-0.4	25.7	0.0	25.7	0.0	25.4	-1.2	25.4	0.0	25.3	-0.4	25.2	-0.4	25.2	0.0	25.3	0.4
1939	25.2	-0.4	25.2	0.0	25.2	0.0	25.2	0.0	25.2	0.0	25.3	0.4	25.3	0.0	25.3	0.0	25.5	0.8	25.9	1.6	25.9	0.0	25.9	0.0
1940	25.8	-0.4	25.9	0.4	25.9	0.0	26.0	0.4	26.0	0.0	26.0	0.0	26.0	0.0	26.0	0.0	26.0	0.0	26.0	0.0	26.0	0.0	26.1	0.4
1941	26.1	0.0	26.1	0.0	26.4	1.1	26.6	0.8	26.8	0.8	27.4	2.2	27.8	1.5	28.0	0.7	28.5	1.8	29.1	2.1	29.3	0.7	29.6	1.0
1942	29.8	0.7	29.8	0.0	29.8	0.0	29.9	0.3	29.9	0.0	29.9	0.0	29.9	0.0	29.9	0.0	29.9	0.0	29.9	0.0	29.9	0.0	29.9	0.0
1943	29.7	-0.7	29.7	0.0	29.7	0.0	29.7	0.0	29.7	0.0	29.7	0.0	29.7	0.0	29.7	0.0	29.7	0.0	29.7	0.0	29.7	0.0	29.7	0.0
1944	30.5	2.7	30.4	-0.3	30.4	0.0	30.4	0.0	30.4	0.0	30.4	0.0	30.4	0.0	30.5	0.3	30.5	0.0	30.5	0.0	30.5	0.0	30.5	0.0
1945	30.5	0.0	30.5	0.0	30.5	0.0	30.5	0.0	30.5	0.0	30.5	0.0	30.5	0.0	30.5	0.0	30.5	0.0	30.5	0.0	30.5	0.0	30.5	0.0
1946	30.8	1.0	30.9	0.3	31.0	0.3	31.2	0.6	31.6	1.3	32.2	1.9	32.4	0.6	32.5	0.3	32.9	1.2	33.2	0.9	34.2	3.0	35.9	5.0
1947	36.5	1.7	36.6	0.3	36.6	0.0	36.8	0.5	36.8	0.0	36.9	0.3	37.2	0.8	37.3	0.3	37.5	0.5	37.8	0.8	37.9	0.3	38.1	0.5
1948	38.4	0.8	38.4	0.0	38.5	0.3	38.8	0.8	38.8	0.0	38.9	0.3	39.2	0.8	39.5	0.8	40.0	1.3	40.8	2.0	40.9	0.2	40.9	0.0
1949	40.7	-0.5	40.7	0.0	40.6	-0.2	40.5	-0.2	40.3	-0.5	40.2	-0.2	39.8	-1.0	39.7	-0.3	39.6	-0.3	39.5	-0.3	39.6	0.3	39.7	0.3
1950	39.7	0.0	39.8	0.3	39.8	0.0	39.9	0.3	40.1	0.5	40.1	0.0	40.3	0.5	40.8	1.2	41.6	2.0	42.6	2.4	43.1	1.2	43.6	1.2
1951	44.4	1.8	44.6	0.5	44.7	0.2	44.9	0.4	44.8	-0.2	44.7	-0.2	44.5	-0.4	44.1	-0.9	44.0	-0.2	43.9	-0.2	43.8	-0.2	43.8	0.0
1952	43.7	-0.2	43.7	0.0	43.5	-0.5	43.6	0.2	43.4	-0.5	43.4	0.0	43.4	0.0	43.3	-0.2	43.5	0.5	43.5	0.0	43.6	0.2	43.7	0.2
1953	43.8	0.2	43.9	0.2	44.0	0.2	44.3	0.7	44.4	0.2	44.5	0.2	44.6	0.2	44.6	0.0	44.7	0.2	44.6	-0.2	44.7	0.2	44.7	0.0
1954	44.8	0.2	44.7	-0.2	44.7	0.0	44.9	0.4	44.9	0.0	44.9	0.0	44.8	-0.2	44.8	0.0	44.8	0.0	44.9	0.2	44.9	0.0	45.0	0.2
1955	44.9	-0.2	44.9	0.0	44.7	-0.4	44.7	0.0	44.7	0.0	44.8	0.2	44.9	0.2	45.1	0.4	45.3	0.4	45.5	0.4	45.6	0.2	45.6	0.0
1956	45.9	0.7	46.0	0.2	46.0	0.0	45.9	-0.2	45.9	0.0	46.0	0.2	46.0	0.0	46.3	0.7	46.5	0.4	47.0	1.1	47.1	0.2	47.1	0.0
1957	47.4	0.6	47.4	0.0	47.4	0.0	47.2	-0.4	47.3	0.2	47.3	0.0	47.5	0.4	47.6	0.2	47.5	-0.2	47.6	0.2	47.7	0.2	48.0	0.6
1958	48.1	0.2	48.0	-0.2	48.0	0.0	48.0	0.0	47.9	-0.2	47.8	-0.2	47.9	0.2	47.8	-0.2	47.8	0.0	47.8	0.0	47.7	-0.2	47.7	0.0
1959	47.9	0.4	47.9	0.0	48.0	0.2	48.0	0.0	48.0	0.0	48.0	0.0	48.0	0.0	48.1	0.2	48.0	-0.2	48.0	0.0	47.9	-0.2	47.9	0.0	47.9	0.0
1960	48.0	0.2	48.0	0.0	48.1	0.2	48.0	-0.2	47.9	-0.2	47.8	-0.2	47.8	0.0	47.8	0.0	47.7	-0.2	47.7	0.0	47.6	-0.2	47.6	0.0
1961	47.5	-0.2	47.5	0.0	47.5	0.0	47.6	0.2	47.6	0.0	47.6	0.0	47.5	-0.2	47.5	0.0	47.5	0.0	47.5	0.0	47.5	0.0	47.5	0.0
1962	47.5	0.0	47.4	-0.2	47.3	-0.2	47.3	0.0	47.3	0.0	47.3	0.0	47.2	-0.2	47.2	0.0	47.1	-0.2	47.1	0.0	47.1	0.0	47.0	-0.2
1963	47.0	0.0	46.9	-0.2	46.9	0.0	46.9	0.0	46.8	-0.2	46.9	0.2	46.8	-0.2	46.9	0.2	46.9	0.0	46.9	0.0	46.9	0.0	46.8	-0.2
1964	47.0	0.4	47.1	0.2	47.1	0.0	47.1	0.0	47.1	0.0	47.1	0.0	47.1	0.0	47.1	0.0	47.1	0.0	47.1	0.0	47.1	0.0	47.0	-0.2
1965	47.0	0.0	46.9	-0.2	47.0	0.2	46.8	-0.4	46.8	0.0	46.8	0.0	46.7	-0.2	46.7	0.0	46.7	0.0	46.7	0.0	46.8	0.2	46.9	0.2
1966	47.0	0.2	47.0	0.0	47.0	0.0	47.1	0.2	47.3	0.4	47.3	0.0	47.3	0.0	47.4	0.2	47.4	0.0	47.6	0.4	47.9	0.6	48.0	0.2
1967	48.0	0.0	48.0	0.0	48.0	0.0	48.1	0.2	48.2	0.2	48.2	0.0	48.2	0.0	48.3	0.2	48.4	0.2	48.6	0.4	48.8	0.4	48.9	0.2
1968	49.2	0.6	49.4	0.4	49.5	0.2	49.6	0.2	49.7	0.2	49.6	-0.2	49.7	0.2	49.8	0.2	49.8	0.0	49.9	0.2	49.9	0.0	50.1	0.4
1969	50.4	0.6	50.4	0.0	50.5	0.2	50.5	0.0	50.5	0.0	50.5	0.0	50.6	0.2	50.7	0.2	50.8	0.2	50.9	0.2	51.0	0.2	51.2	0.4
1970	51.4	0.4	51.6	0.4	51.6	0.0	51.8	0.4	51.7	-0.2	51.8	0.2	52.0	0.4	52.0	0.0	52.1	0.2	52.2	0.2	52.4	0.4	52.5	0.2

[Continued]

FURNITURE AND HOUSEHOLD DURABLES
Producer Price Index
Base 1982 = 100
[Continued]

For 1926-2001. Columns headed % show percentile change in the index from the previous period for which an index is available.

Year	Jan Index	%	Feb Index	%	Mar Index	%	Apr Index	%	May Index	%	Jun Index	%	Jul Index	%	Aug Index	%	Sep Index	%	Oct Index	%	Nov Index	%	Dec Index	%
1971	52.8	0.6	53.0	0.4	53.0	0.0	53.0	0.0	53.1	0.2	53.1	0.0	53.3	0.4	53.3	0.0	53.3	0.0	53.3	0.0	53.2	-0.2	53.2	0.0
1972	53.3	0.2	53.5	0.4	53.6	0.2	53.6	0.0	53.7	0.2	53.7	0.0	53.8	0.2	54.0	0.4	54.1	0.2	54.1	0.0	54.3	0.4	54.3	0.0
1973	54.4	0.2	54.6	0.4	54.8	0.4	55.1	0.5	55.6	0.9	55.7	0.2	55.7	0.0	56.0	0.5	56.1	0.2	56.3	0.4	56.6	0.5	56.8	0.4
1974	57.5	1.2	58.1	1.0	58.6	0.9	59.4	1.4	60.2	1.3	60.9	1.2	62.0	1.8	62.7	1.1	64.2	2.4	65.5	2.0	66.2	1.1	66.5	0.5
1975	67.1	0.9	67.2	0.1	66.9	-0.4	66.9	0.0	67.0	0.1	67.2	0.3	67.3	0.1	67.6	0.4	67.7	0.1	68.2	0.7	68.4	0.3	68.6	0.3
1976	69.3	1.0	69.4	0.1	69.6	0.3	69.8	0.3	70.0	0.3	70.2	0.3	70.4	0.3	70.6	0.3	70.9	0.4	71.1	0.3	71.3	0.3	71.5	0.3
1977	71.9	0.6	72.1	0.3	72.3	0.3	72.5	0.3	72.8	0.4	73.2	0.5	73.2	0.0	73.7	0.7	73.8	0.1	74.0	0.3	74.3	0.4	74.5	0.3
1978	75.6	1.5	75.7	0.1	76.2	0.7	76.5	0.4	76.9	0.5	77.1	0.3	78.0	1.2	78.2	0.3	78.3	0.1	78.7	0.5	79.0	0.4	79.5	0.6
1979	80.5	1.3	81.1	0.7	81.3	0.2	81.5	0.2	82.0	0.6	82.2	0.2	82.5	0.4	82.9	0.5	83.5	0.7	84.6	1.3	85.2	0.7	86.0	0.9
1980	88.6	3.0	89.7	1.2	89.7	0.0	89.1	-0.7	89.6	0.6	90.1	0.6	90.8	0.8	91.3	0.6	91.6	0.3	92.2	0.7	92.5	0.3	93.3	0.9
1981	93.7	0.4	94.3	0.6	94.6	0.3	94.9	0.3	95.4	0.5	95.3	-0.1	96.4	1.2	96.4	0.0	97.1	0.7	97.3	0.2	97.6	0.3	98.1	0.5
1982	98.3	0.2	98.9	0.6	99.3	0.4	99.6	0.3	99.8	0.2	100.0	0.2	100.0	0.0	100.5	0.5	100.7	0.2	101.0	0.3	100.9	-0.1	101.1	0.2
1983	101.8	0.7	102.7	0.9	102.6	-0.1	102.8	0.2	103.2	0.4	103.4	0.2	103.8	0.4	103.9	0.1	104.1	0.2	104.0	-0.1	104.2	0.2	104.2	0.0
1984	104.7	0.5	105.0	0.3	105.1	0.1	105.4	0.3	105.9	0.5	105.9	0.0	105.9	0.0	105.9	0.0	105.8	-0.1	105.9	0.1	106.3	0.4	106.3	0.0
1985	106.4	0.1	106.7	0.3	106.8	0.1	107.1	0.3	107.1	0.0	107.1	0.0	107.3	0.2	107.3	0.0	107.2	-0.1	107.2	0.0	107.4	0.2	107.5	0.1
1986	107.6	0.1	107.7	0.1	107.9	0.2	108.1	0.2	108.3	0.2	108.4	0.1	108.3	-0.1	108.4	0.1	108.3	-0.1	108.5	0.2	108.7	0.2	108.7	0.0
1987	109.0	0.3	109.1	0.1	109.2	0.1	109.6	0.4	109.8	0.2	109.9	0.1	110.0	0.1	110.3	0.3	110.3	0.0	110.5	0.2	110.7	0.2	110.9	0.2
1988	111.6	0.6	111.9	0.3	112.3	0.4	112.5	0.2	112.8	0.3	112.7	-0.1	113.1	0.4	113.4	0.3	113.7	0.3	113.9	0.2	114.3	0.4	114.5	0.2
1989	115.0	0.4	115.3	0.3	115.7	0.3	116.2	0.4	116.5	0.3	117.0	0.4	117.5	0.4	117.9	0.3	117.9	0.0	117.7	-0.2	117.8	0.1	117.9	0.1
1990	118.4	0.4	118.7	0.3	118.7	0.0	119.0	0.3	119.0	0.0	119.2	0.2	119.1	-0.1	119.2	0.1	119.3	0.1	119.5	0.2	119.8	0.3	120.0	0.2
1991	120.6	0.5	120.9	0.2	121.0	0.1	121.2	0.2	121.2	0.0	121.2	0.0	121.2	0.0	121.2	0.0	121.2	0.0	121.4	0.2	121.4	0.0	121.5	0.1
1992	121.8	0.2	121.8	0.0	121.9	0.1	122.0	0.1	122.1	0.1	122.2	0.1	122.2	0.0	122.2	0.0	122.4	0.2	122.3	-0.1	122.6	0.2	122.6	0.0
1993	122.6	0.0	122.9	0.2	123.0	0.1	123.2	0.2	123.4	0.2	123.6	0.2	123.8	0.2	124.0	0.2	124.0	0.0	124.5	0.4	124.8	0.2	124.8	0.0
1994	125.2	0.3	125.4	0.2	125.5	0.1	125.8	0.2	126.1	0.2	126.2	0.1	126.4	0.2	126.3	-0.1	126.2	-0.1	126.4	0.2	126.7	0.2	126.7	0.0
1995	127.2	0.4	127.5	0.2	127.5	0.0	127.8	0.2	128.0	0.2	128.1	0.1	128.2	0.1	128.4	0.2	128.5	0.1	128.9	0.3	129.3	0.3	129.3	0.0
1996	129.6	0.2	129.9	0.2	129.9	0.0	130.0	0.1	130.3	0.2	130.2	-0.1	130.6	0.3	130.5	-0.1	130.6	0.1	130.9	0.2	130.9	0.0	130.9	0.0
1997	130.9	0.0	130.9	0.0	131.0	0.1	130.7	-0.2	130.9	0.2	130.9	0.0	130.9	0.0	130.7	-0.2	130.7	0.0	130.9	0.2	130.6	-0.2	130.7	0.1
1998	130.8	0.1	131.1	0.2	131.2	0.1	131.2	0.0	131.5	0.2	131.5	0.0	131.5	0.0	131.3	-0.2	131.2	-0.1	131.3	0.1	131.3	0.0	131.4	0.1
1999	131.4	0.0	131.3	-0.1	131.4	0.1	131.5	0.1	131.5	0.0	131.8	0.2	131.7	-0.1	131.8	0.1	131.7	-0.1	131.8	0.1	131.9	0.1	132.0	0.1
2000	132.1	0.1	132.3	0.2	132.5	0.2	132.6	0.1	132.6	0.0	132.9	0.2	132.7	-0.2	132.6	-0.1	132.6	0.0	133.0	0.3	132.9	-0.1	133.2	0.2
2001	133.2	0.0	133.4	0.2	133.1	-0.2	133.4	0.2	133.2	-0.1	133.1	-0.1	133.2	0.1	132.9	-0.2	132.8	-0.1	133.0	0.2	133.1	0.1	133.0	-0.1

Source: U.S. Department of Labor, Bureau of Labor Statistics, Division of Industry Prices and Price Indexes. n.e.c. stands for not elsewhere classified. - indicates no data collected for period or unavailable.

Household Furniture
Producer Price Index
Base 1982 = 100

For 1926-2001. Columns headed % show percentile change in the index from the previous period for which an index is available.

Year	Jan Index	%	Feb Index	%	Mar Index	%	Apr Index	%	May Index	%	Jun Index	%	Jul Index	%	Aug Index	%	Sep Index	%	Oct Index	%	Nov Index	%	Dec Index	%
1926	23.2	-	23.1	-0.4	23.1	0.0	23.0	-0.4	22.9	-0.4	22.8	-0.4	22.8	0.0	22.8	0.0	22.8	0.0	22.8	0.0	22.8	0.0	22.8	0.0
1927	22.4	-1.8	22.4	0.0	22.4	0.0	22.4	0.0	22.4	0.0	22.4	0.0	22.4	0.0	22.4	0.0	22.4	0.0	22.2	-0.9	22.3	0.5	22.2	-0.4
1928	22.3	0.5	22.3	0.0	22.2	-0.4	22.2	0.0	22.2	0.0	22.2	0.0	22.2	0.0	22.2	0.0	22.2	0.0	21.8	-1.8	21.8	0.0	21.8	0.0
1929	21.6	-0.9	21.6	0.0	21.6	0.0	21.6	0.0	21.6	0.0	21.8	0.9	21.8	0.0	21.8	0.0	21.8	0.0	21.5	-1.4	21.8	1.4	21.8	0.0
1930	21.7	-0.5	21.7	0.0	21.7	0.0	21.7	0.0	21.7	0.0	21.6	-0.5	21.5	-0.5	21.5	0.0	21.4	-0.5	21.4	0.0	21.4	0.0	21.1	-1.4
1931	21.1	0.0	21.1	0.0	21.1	0.0	21.1	0.0	20.7	-1.9	20.5	-1.0	20.4	-0.5	20.3	-0.5	19.4	-4.4	18.8	-3.1	18.8	0.0	18.4	-2.1
1932	18.2	-1.1	18.2	0.0	18.1	-0.5	17.7	-2.2	17.0	-4.0	16.9	-0.6	16.7	-1.2	16.6	-0.6	16.7	0.6	16.7	0.0	16.7	0.0	16.6	-0.6
1933	16.5	-0.6	16.4	-0.6	16.4	0.0	16.4	0.0	16.4	0.0	16.8	2.4	17.1	1.8	17.5	2.3	17.9	2.3	18.2	1.7	18.2	0.0	18.1	-0.5
1934	18.1	0.0	18.1	0.0	18.2	0.6	18.3	0.5	18.3	0.0	18.1	-1.1	18.0	-0.6	18.1	0.6	18.1	0.0	18.1	0.0	18.0	-0.6	17.9	-0.6
1935	17.9	0.0	17.7	-1.1	17.7	0.0	17.7	0.0	17.7	0.0	17.7	0.0	17.6	-0.6	17.6	0.0	17.6	0.0	17.6	0.0	17.7	0.6	17.7	0.0
1936	17.8	0.6	17.8	0.0	17.8	0.0	17.8	0.0	17.8	0.0	17.7	-0.6	17.7	0.0	17.7	0.0	17.8	0.6	17.9	0.6	18.1	1.1	18.2	0.6
1937	19.2	5.5	19.4	1.0	19.4	0.0	19.6	1.0	19.7	0.5	19.8	0.5	19.8	0.0	19.9	0.5	19.9	0.0	19.9	0.0	19.7	-1.0	19.7	0.0
1938	19.1	-3.0	19.1	0.0	19.1	0.0	19.1	0.0	19.1	0.0	19.1	0.0	18.8	-1.6	18.8	0.0	18.8	0.0	18.8	0.0	18.7	-0.5	18.7	0.0
1939	18.4	-1.6	18.4	0.0	18.4	0.0	18.5	0.5	18.5	0.0	18.5	0.0	18.5	0.0	18.5	0.0	18.6	0.5	18.7	0.5	18.8	0.5	18.8	0.0
1940	18.7	-0.5	18.7	0.0	18.7	0.0	18.7	0.0	18.7	0.0	18.7	0.0	18.7	0.0	18.7	0.0	18.7	0.0	18.7	0.0	18.7	0.0	18.8	0.5
1941	18.9	0.5	18.9	0.0	19.0	0.5	19.1	0.5	19.3	1.0	19.9	3.1	20.4	2.5	20.5	0.5	21.1	2.9	21.6	2.4	21.9	1.4	22.1	0.9
1942	22.3	0.9	22.3	0.0	22.3	0.0	22.3	0.0	22.3	0.0	22.3	0.0	22.3	0.0	22.3	0.0	22.3	0.0	22.3	0.0	22.3	0.0	22.3	0.0
1943	22.4	0.4	22.4	0.0	22.4	0.0	22.4	0.0	22.4	0.0	22.4	0.0	22.4	0.0	22.4	0.0	22.4	0.0	22.4	0.0	22.4	0.0	22.6	0.9
1944	22.9	1.3	23.1	0.9	23.1	0.0	23.1	0.0	23.1	0.0	23.1	0.0	23.1	0.0	23.1	0.0	23.1	0.0	23.1	0.0	23.2	0.4	23.2	0.0
1945	23.2	0.0	23.2	0.0	23.2	0.0	23.2	0.0	23.2	0.0	23.5	1.3	23.5	0.0	23.5	0.0	23.5	0.0	23.5	0.0	23.5	0.0	23.5	0.0
1946	23.9	1.7	24.0	0.4	24.0	0.0	24.1	0.4	24.5	1.7	24.8	1.2	24.9	0.4	25.2	1.2	25.4	0.8	25.8	1.6	26.3	1.9	26.9	2.3
1947	29.4	9.3	29.4	0.0	29.4	0.0	29.5	0.3	29.5	0.0	29.5	0.0	29.7	0.7	29.9	0.7	30.3	1.3	30.7	1.3	30.8	0.3	31.1	1.0
1948	31.9	2.6	31.9	0.0	31.9	0.0	32.0	0.3	31.9	-0.3	32.0	0.3	32.0	0.0	32.3	0.9	32.5	0.6	32.5	0.0	32.5	0.0	32.5	0.0
1949	32.3	-0.6	32.3	0.0	32.3	0.0	32.3	0.0	32.0	-0.9	31.9	-0.3	31.2	-2.2	31.3	0.3	31.3	0.0	31.3	0.0	31.3	0.0	31.4	0.3
1950	31.5	0.3	31.5	0.0	31.5	0.0	31.6	0.3	31.6	0.0	31.8	0.6	32.2	1.3	33.2	3.1	34.2	3.0	34.8	1.8	35.2	1.1	35.9	2.0
1951	36.7	2.2	36.8	0.3	36.8	0.0	36.8	0.0	36.7	-0.3	36.5	-0.5	36.2	-0.8	36.2	0.0	36.2	0.0	36.1	-0.3	36.2	0.3	36.0	-0.6
1952	35.5	-1.4	35.5	0.0	35.5	0.0	35.5	0.0	35.4	-0.3	35.2	-0.6	35.2	0.0	35.2	0.0	35.2	0.0	35.2	0.0	35.3	0.3	35.3	0.0
1953	35.4	0.3	35.5	0.3	35.5	0.0	35.6	0.3	35.6	0.0	35.7	0.3	35.6	-0.3	35.6	0.0	35.7	0.3	35.7	0.0	35.7	0.0	35.7	0.0
1954	35.7	0.0	35.6	-0.3	35.6	0.0	35.5	-0.3	35.5	0.0	35.4	-0.3	35.3	-0.3	35.3	0.0	35.3	0.0	35.3	0.0	35.3	0.0	35.3	0.0
1955	35.2	-0.3	35.2	0.0	35.2	0.0	35.3	0.3	35.4	0.3	35.3	-0.3	35.4	0.3	35.8	1.1	36.0	0.6	36.2	0.6	36.4	0.6	36.5	0.3
1956	36.7	0.5	36.7	0.0	36.8	0.3	36.9	0.3	36.9	0.0	36.9	0.0	37.3	1.1	37.4	0.3	37.6	0.5	37.8	0.5	37.9	0.3	37.9	0.0
1957	38.2	0.8	38.2	0.0	38.2	0.0	38.3	0.3	38.3	0.0	38.3	0.0	38.4	0.3	38.5	0.3	38.3	-0.5	38.3	0.0	38.4	0.3	38.4	0.0
1958	38.5	0.3	38.6	0.3	38.4	-0.5	38.4	0.0	38.4	0.0	38.3	-0.3	38.3	0.0	38.3	0.0	38.4	0.3	38.5	0.3	38.7	0.5	38.8	0.3
1959	38.8	0.0	38.8	0.0	38.8	0.0	38.6	-0.5	38.7	0.3	38.8	0.3	38.9	0.3	38.9	0.0	38.8	-0.3	38.9	0.3	38.9	0.0	38.9	0.0
1960	39.0	0.3	39.1	0.3	39.1	0.0	39.1	0.0	39.1	0.0	39.1	0.0	39.1	0.0	39.1	0.0	39.1	0.0	39.3	0.5	39.3	0.0	39.3	0.0
1961	39.5	0.5	39.5	0.0	39.5	0.0	39.5	0.0	39.6	0.3	39.6	0.0	39.6	0.0	39.6	0.0	39.6	0.0	39.7	0.3	39.9	0.5	39.8	-0.3
1962	39.9	0.3	39.9	0.0	39.9	0.0	39.9	0.0	40.0	0.3	40.0	0.0	40.1	0.2	40.1	0.0	40.0	-0.2	40.1	0.2	40.1	0.0	40.2	0.2
1963	40.3	0.2	40.3	0.0	40.3	0.0	40.2	-0.2	40.2	0.0	40.3	0.2	40.3	0.0	40.3	0.0	40.4	0.2	40.4	0.0	40.4	0.0	40.3	-0.2
1964	40.5	0.5	40.5	0.0	40.5	0.0	40.6	0.2	40.6	0.0	40.5	-0.2	40.6	0.2	40.6	0.0	40.6	0.0	40.6	0.0	40.7	0.2	40.7	0.0
1965	40.9	0.5	40.9	0.0	40.9	0.0	40.9	0.0	40.9	0.0	40.8	-0.2	40.8	0.0	40.9	0.2	40.9	0.0	41.0	0.2	41.1	0.2	41.1	0.0
1966	41.2	0.2	41.3	0.2	41.3	0.0	41.7	1.0	42.0	0.7	42.0	0.0	42.0	0.0	42.2	0.5	42.3	0.2	42.5	0.5	43.0	1.2	43.1	0.2
1967	43.1	0.0	43.2	0.2	43.3	0.2	43.3	0.0	43.3	0.0	43.3	0.0	43.4	0.2	43.6	0.5	43.6	0.0	43.7	0.2	44.0	0.7	44.0	0.0
1968	44.4	0.9	44.6	0.5	44.7	0.2	44.8	0.2	45.1	0.7	45.2	0.2	45.3	0.2	45.3	0.0	45.4	0.2	45.7	0.7	45.9	0.4	46.0	0.2
1969	46.6	1.3	46.7	0.2	46.8	0.2	46.8	0.0	47.0	0.4	47.1	0.2	47.4	0.6	47.4	0.0	47.5	0.2	47.6	0.2	47.7	0.2	47.6	-0.2
1970	47.9	0.6	48.3	0.8	48.4	0.2	48.4	0.0	48.6	0.4	48.6	0.0	48.7	0.2	48.8	0.2	48.8	0.0	48.8	0.0	48.9	0.2	49.0	0.2

[Continued]

Household Furniture
Producer Price Index
Base 1982 = 100
[Continued]

For 1926-2001. Columns headed % show percentile change in the index from the previous period for which an index is available.

Year	Jan Index	%	Feb Index	%	Mar Index	%	Apr Index	%	May Index	%	Jun Index	%	Jul Index	%	Aug Index	%	Sep Index	%	Oct Index	%	Nov Index	%	Dec Index	%
1971	49.2	0.4	49.7	1.0	49.7	0.0	49.7	0.0	50.1	0.8	50.1	0.0	50.2	0.2	50.3	0.2	50.3	0.0	50.3	0.0	50.0	-0.6	50.0	0.0
1972	50.5	1.0	50.8	0.6	50.8	0.0	50.9	0.2	51.0	0.2	51.0	0.0	51.1	0.2	51.3	0.4	51.2	-0.2	51.2	0.0	51.4	0.4	51.6	0.4
1973	51.8	0.4	51.9	0.2	52.2	0.6	53.0	1.5	53.2	0.4	53.6	0.8	53.6	0.0	53.8	0.4	54.1	0.6	54.5	0.7	55.1	1.1	55.3	0.4
1974	56.1	1.4	56.5	0.7	56.7	0.4	57.8	1.9	58.7	1.6	58.9	0.3	59.5	1.0	60.0	0.8	60.9	1.5	62.1	2.0	62.9	1.3	62.9	0.0
1975	63.3	0.6	63.3	0.0	63.2	-0.2	63.3	0.2	63.2	-0.2	63.2	0.0	63.3	0.2	63.3	0.0	63.6	0.5	64.3	1.1	64.6	0.5	65.1	0.8
1976	65.6	0.8	65.5	-0.2	65.6	0.2	65.8	0.3	66.1	0.5	66.6	0.8	66.8	0.3	66.9	0.1	67.4	0.7	68.1	1.0	68.5	0.6	69.0	0.7
1977	69.1	0.1	69.1	0.0	69.5	0.6	69.9	0.6	70.1	0.3	70.6	0.7	70.9	0.4	71.0	0.1	71.1	0.1	71.4	0.4	71.8	0.6	72.4	0.8
1978	73.2	1.1	73.4	0.3	73.7	0.4	73.9	0.3	74.3	0.5	75.0	0.9	76.0	1.3	76.4	0.5	76.6	0.3	77.4	1.0	77.8	0.5	78.0	0.3
1979	78.8	1.0	78.9	0.1	79.1	0.3	79.5	0.5	80.4	1.1	80.6	0.2	80.8	0.2	81.0	0.2	82.0	1.2	82.7	0.9	84.0	1.6	84.8	1.0
1980	85.9	1.3	86.4	0.6	86.6	0.2	87.2	0.7	88.3	1.3	88.8	0.6	89.8	1.1	90.5	0.8	90.7	0.2	91.3	0.7	91.8	0.5	92.3	0.5
1981	92.6	0.3	93.0	0.4	93.3	0.3	94.2	1.0	94.1	-0.1	95.1	1.1	95.7	0.6	96.0	0.3	96.7	0.7	96.9	0.2	97.9	1.0	98.6	0.7
1982	99.0	0.4	98.9	-0.1	99.0	0.1	99.9	0.9	100.1	0.2	100.2	0.1	100.1	-0.1	100.2	0.1	100.4	0.2	100.6	0.2	100.7	0.1	100.9	0.2
1983	100.9	0.0	101.2	0.3	100.6	-0.6	100.8	0.2	102.0	1.2	102.2	0.2	102.4	0.2	102.8	0.4	102.9	0.1	103.1	0.2	103.3	0.2	103.2	-0.1
1984	103.5	0.3	104.0	0.5	104.4	0.4	104.8	0.4	105.1	0.3	105.4	0.3	105.4	0.0	105.6	0.2	105.9	0.3	106.3	0.4	106.6	0.3	106.8	0.2
1985	107.4	0.6	107.7	0.3	107.7	0.0	108.3	0.6	108.8	0.5	109.0	0.2	108.7	-0.3	108.8	0.1	108.8	0.0	108.7	-0.1	108.9	0.2	109.0	0.1
1986	109.3	0.3	109.8	0.5	110.0	0.2	109.8	-0.2	110.3	0.5	110.2	-0.1	110.1	-0.1	110.6	0.5	110.4	-0.2	110.7	0.3	110.8	0.1	111.0	0.2
1987	111.2	0.2	111.7	0.4	112.0	0.3	112.5	0.4	112.8	0.3	112.8	0.0	112.8	0.0	113.1	0.3	113.6	0.4	113.6	0.0	114.2	0.5	115.2	0.9
1988	115.8	0.5	116.2	0.3	116.8	0.5	117.0	0.2	117.2	0.2	117.4	0.2	117.8	0.3	118.1	0.3	118.1	0.0	118.6	0.4	119.0	0.3	119.5	0.4
1989	119.6	0.1	120.2	0.5	120.7	0.4	121.3	0.5	121.6	0.2	121.7	0.1	121.9	0.2	122.3	0.3	122.5	0.2	123.1	0.5	123.4	0.2	123.5	0.1
1990	123.6	0.1	123.9	0.2	124.0	0.1	124.4	0.3	124.9	0.4	125.1	0.2	125.2	0.1	125.3	0.1	125.5	0.2	126.0	0.4	126.5	0.4	126.6	0.1
1991	126.9	0.2	127.3	0.3	127.7	0.3	127.8	0.1	127.9	0.1	127.9	0.0	128.0	0.1	128.1	0.1	128.3	0.2	128.7	0.3	128.9	0.2	128.9	0.0
1992	129.2	0.2	129.4	0.2	129.6	0.2	129.7	0.1	129.7	0.0	129.9	0.2	130.0	0.1	130.1	0.1	130.4	0.2	130.5	0.1	130.9	0.3	131.0	0.1
1993	131.2	0.2	131.6	0.3	131.7	0.1	132.2	0.4	132.6	0.3	133.0	0.3	133.2	0.2	133.3	0.1	133.6	0.2	135.8	1.6	136.4	0.4	135.8	-0.4
1994	136.1	0.2	136.9	0.6	137.2	0.2	137.4	0.1	137.8	0.3	138.0	0.1	138.1	0.1	138.1	0.0	138.6	0.4	138.9	0.2	139.2	0.2	139.4	0.1
1995	140.0	0.4	140.4	0.3	140.7	0.2	141.0	0.2	141.6	0.4	141.8	0.1	142.0	0.1	142.2	0.1	142.5	0.2	142.7	0.1	143.2	0.4	143.2	0.0
1996	143.6	0.3	143.8	0.1	144.1	0.2	144.2	0.1	144.4	0.1	144.5	0.1	144.6	0.1	144.5	-0.1	144.7	0.1	144.9	0.1	145.2	0.2	145.2	0.0
1997	145.4	0.1	145.7	0.2	145.9	0.1	146.0	0.1	146.0	0.0	146.1	0.1	146.4	0.2	146.3	-0.1	146.6	0.2	146.5	-0.1	146.8	0.2	146.8	0.0
1998	147.4	0.4	147.6	0.1	147.8	0.1	147.9	0.1	148.2	0.2	148.2	0.0	148.4	0.1	148.5	0.1	148.6	0.1	149.2	0.4	149.2	0.0	149.6	0.3
1999	149.8	0.1	150.0	0.1	150.1	0.1	150.1	0.0	150.1	0.0	150.2	0.1	150.4	0.1	150.5	0.1	150.8	0.2	151.3	0.3	151.2	-0.1	151.4	0.1
2000	151.5	0.1	151.7	0.1	152.1	0.3	152.4	0.2	152.5	0.1	152.7	0.1	152.8	0.1	152.9	0.1	153.1	0.1	153.5	0.3	153.6	0.1	153.8	0.1
2001	153.8	0.0	153.9	0.1	154.4	0.3	154.7	0.2	155.1	0.3	155.1	0.0	155.2	0.1	154.9	-0.2	155.1	0.1	155.3	0.1	155.5	0.1	155.7	0.1

Source: U.S. Department of Labor, Bureau of Labor Statistics, Division of Industry Prices and Price Indexes. n.e.c. stands for not elsewhere classified. - indicates no data collected for period or unavailable.

Commercial Furniture

Producer Price Index
Base 1982 = 100

For 1947-2001. Columns headed % show percentile change in the index from the previous period for which an index is available.

Year	Jan		Feb		Mar		Apr		May		Jun		Jul		Aug		Sep		Oct		Nov		Dec	
	Index	%	Index	%	Index	%	Index	%	Index	%	Index	%	Index	%	Index	%	Index	%	Index	%	Index	%	Index	%
1947	19.5	-	19.5	0.0	19.6	0.5	20.1	2.6	20.3	1.0	20.3	0.0	20.3	0.0	20.3	0.0	20.4	0.5	20.5	0.5	20.5	0.0	20.7	1.0
1948	20.9	1.0	21.0	0.5	21.1	0.5	21.1	0.0	21.1	0.0	21.1	0.0	21.2	0.5	21.9	3.3	22.0	0.5	22.3	1.4	22.3	0.0	22.3	0.0
1949	22.3	0.0	22.3	0.0	22.3	0.0	22.3	0.0	22.2	-0.4	22.2	0.0	22.2	0.0	22.2	0.0	22.2	0.0	22.2	0.0	22.2	0.0	22.2	0.0
1950	22.2	0.0	22.2	0.0	22.2	0.0	22.2	0.0	22.5	1.4	22.6	0.4	23.0	1.8	23.7	3.0	23.8	0.4	24.5	2.9	25.4	3.7	26.0	2.4
1951	26.6	2.3	26.6	0.0	26.6	0.0	26.6	0.0	26.6	0.0	26.6	0.0	26.6	0.0	26.6	0.0	26.6	0.0	26.4	-0.8	26.1	-1.1	26.1	0.0
1952	26.1	0.0	26.1	0.0	26.2	0.4	26.2	0.0	26.2	0.0	26.2	0.0	26.2	0.0	26.1	-0.4	26.1	0.0	26.2	0.4	26.2	0.0	26.2	0.0
1953	26.2	0.0	26.2	0.0	26.2	0.0	26.2	0.0	26.5	1.1	26.8	1.1	26.8	0.0	26.8	0.0	26.8	0.0	26.8	0.0	26.9	0.4	26.9	0.0
1954	26.9	0.0	26.9	0.0	26.9	0.0	26.9	0.0	26.9	0.0	26.9	0.0	26.9	0.0	26.9	0.0	26.9	0.0	27.1	0.7	27.4	1.1	27.4	0.0
1955	27.4	0.0	27.4	0.0	27.4	0.0	27.4	0.0	27.4	0.0	27.6	0.7	27.7	0.4	28.6	3.2	29.0	1.4	29.2	0.7	29.2	0.0	29.2	0.0
1956	29.3	0.3	29.5	0.7	29.5	0.0	29.5	0.0	29.5	0.0	29.5	0.0	29.6	0.3	31.1	5.1	31.3	0.6	31.3	0.0	31.3	0.0	31.3	0.0
1957	31.3	0.0	31.3	0.0	31.3	0.0	31.4	0.3	31.4	0.0	31.4	0.0	32.7	4.1	32.7	0.0	32.7	0.0	32.7	0.0	32.8	0.3	32.8	0.0
1958	32.8	0.0	32.8	0.0	32.8	0.0	32.8	0.0	32.8	0.0	32.8	0.0	33.0	0.6	33.0	0.0	33.0	0.0	33.0	0.0	33.0	0.0	33.0	0.0
1959	33.0	0.0	33.0	0.0	33.0	0.0	33.0	0.0	33.0	0.0	33.0	0.0	33.1	0.3	33.1	0.0	33.1	0.0	33.1	0.0	33.1	0.0	33.1	0.0
1960	33.2	0.3	33.2	0.0	33.4	0.6	33.4	0.0	33.4	0.0	33.4	0.0	33.5	0.3	33.5	0.0	33.5	0.0	33.5	0.0	33.5	0.0	33.5	0.0
1961	33.2	-0.9	33.2	0.0	33.2	0.0	33.2	0.0	33.2	0.0	33.2	0.0	33.2	0.0	33.2	0.0	33.4	0.6	33.4	0.0	33.4	0.0	33.4	0.0
1962	33.4	0.0	33.4	0.0	33.4	0.0	33.4	0.0	33.4	0.0	33.4	0.0	33.5	0.3	33.5	0.0	33.5	0.0	33.5	0.0	33.5	0.0	33.4	-0.3
1963	33.4	0.0	33.4	0.0	33.4	0.0	33.4	0.0	33.4	0.0	33.6	0.6	33.6	0.0	33.7	0.3	33.7	0.0	33.7	0.0	33.7	0.0	33.7	0.0
1964	33.7	0.0	33.7	0.0	33.7	0.0	33.7	0.0	33.7	0.0	33.7	0.0	33.7	0.0	33.7	0.0	33.7	0.0	33.7	0.0	33.7	0.0	33.8	0.3
1965	33.8	0.0	33.8	0.0	33.8	0.0	33.8	0.0	33.9	0.3	33.9	0.0	33.9	0.0	33.9	0.0	33.9	0.0	33.9	0.0	34.0	0.3	34.0	0.0
1966	34.0	0.0	34.0	0.0	34.0	-0.0	34.0	0.0	34.4	1.2	34.4	0.0	34.6	0.6	34.6	0.0	34.6	0.0	35.1	1.4	35.3	0.6	35.5	0.6
1967	35.5	0.0	35.7	0.6	35.7	0.0	35.7	0.0	36.6	2.5	36.6	0.0	36.6	0.0	36.6	0.0	36.6	0.0	36.6	0.0	36.7	0.3	36.8	0.3
1968	37.1	0.8	37.1	0.0	37.2	0.3	37.4	0.5	37.6	0.5	37.8	0.5	37.9	0.3	37.9	0.0	37.9	0.0	38.1	0.5	38.1	0.0	38.2	0.3
1969	38.2	0.0	38.3	0.3	38.5	0.5	38.5	0.0	38.9	1.0	39.0	0.3	39.1	0.3	39.1	0.0	39.8	1.8	40.0	0.5	40.5	1.3	40.5	0.0
1970	40.7	0.5	40.7	0.0	40.9	0.5	40.9	0.0	40.9	0.0	41.7	2.0	41.7	0.0	42.0	0.7	42.0	0.0	42.1	0.2	42.7	1.4	42.7	0.0
1971	42.7	0.0	42.9	0.5	42.9	0.0	42.9	0.0	42.9	0.0	42.9	0.0	42.9	0.0	42.9	0.0	42.9	0.0	42.9	0.0	42.9	0.0	42.9	0.0
1972	42.9	0.0	42.9	0.0	43.1	0.5	43.3	0.5	43.3	0.0	43.4	0.2	43.5	0.2	43.5	0.0	44.0	1.1	44.2	0.5	44.8	1.4	44.8	0.0
1973	44.9	0.2	44.9	0.0	44.9	0.0	44.9	0.0	47.4	5.6	47.4	0.0	47.4	0.0	48.0	1.3	48.2	0.4	48.5	0.6	48.6	0.2	48.6	0.0
1974	49.5	1.9	50.5	2.0	51.0	1.0	51.4	0.8	52.3	1.8	53.5	2.3	55.5	3.7	56.7	2.2	60.4	6.5	60.6	0.3	61.3	1.2	61.3	0.0
1975	60.5	-1.3	60.4	-0.2	60.3	-0.2	60.3	0.0	60.3	0.0	60.3	0.0	60.3	0.0	60.8	0.8	60.8	0.0	61.3	0.8	60.6	-1.1	60.6	0.0
1976	60.9	0.5	61.5	1.0	61.6	0.2	62.5	1.5	63.0	0.8	63.3	0.5	63.5	0.3	63.7	0.3	63.7	0.0	64.0	0.5	64.0	0.0	64.0	0.0
1977	64.3	0.5	64.7	0.6	64.9	0.3	66.5	2.5	67.1	0.9	67.8	1.0	66.9	-1.3	69.3	3.6	69.2	-0.1	69.2	0.0	69.8	0.9	69.8	0.0
1978	70.7	1.3	70.8	0.1	72.2	2.0	72.8	0.8	72.8	0.0	72.8	0.0	73.7	1.2	74.0	0.4	73.9	-0.1	74.2	0.4	74.4	0.3	75.2	1.1
1979	77.8	3.5	80.3	3.2	80.3	0.0	80.5	0.2	80.5	0.0	80.5	0.0	80.8	0.4	80.8	0.0	80.8	0.0	81.1	0.4	81.1	0.0	81.7	0.7
1980	82.4	0.9	84.0	1.9	84.5	0.6	84.8	0.4	84.9	0.1	85.5	0.7	86.1	0.7	86.1	0.0	86.3	0.2	87.6	1.5	87.9	0.3	88.0	0.1
1981	89.6	1.8	91.3	1.9	92.0	0.8	92.4	0.4	93.5	1.2	93.6	0.1	93.9	0.3	94.1	0.2	94.9	0.9	95.2	0.3	95.6	0.4	95.8	0.2
1982	96.8	1.0	98.4	1.7	99.3	0.9	99.5	0.2	99.9	0.4	100.2	0.3	100.7	0.5	100.9	0.2	101.0	0.1	101.0	0.0	101.1	0.1	101.1	0.0
1983	102.0	0.9	102.4	0.4	103.5	1.1	103.9	0.4	103.8	-0.1	104.1	0.3	104.3	0.2	104.0	-0.3	104.3	0.3	104.3	0.0	105.2	0.9	105.1	-0.1
1984	106.5	1.3	107.0	0.5	107.0	0.0	107.5	0.5	107.9	0.4	107.8	-0.1	108.2	0.4	108.3	0.1	108.0	-0.3	107.9	-0.1	109.1	1.1	108.8	-0.3
1985	109.0	0.2	109.9	0.8	110.2	0.3	111.2	0.9	111.4	0.2	111.7	0.3	112.5	0.7	112.9	0.4	113.1	0.2	112.9	-0.2	113.9	0.9	113.9	0.0
1986	114.2	0.3	114.2	0.0	114.2	0.0	114.9	0.6	114.9	0.0	115.3	0.3	115.5	0.2	115.4	-0.1	115.5	0.1	116.2	0.6	116.7	0.4	116.5	-0.2
1987	116.9	0.3	117.1	0.2	117.5	0.3	118.2	0.6	118.4	0.2	118.6	0.2	118.6	0.0	118.9	0.3	119.1	0.2	119.7	0.5	119.9	0.2	120.0	0.1
1988	121.2	1.0	121.4	0.2	122.7	1.1	123.5	0.7	123.8	0.2	123.8	0.0	125.0	1.0	125.2	0.2	125.8	0.5	125.7	-0.1	125.9	0.2	126.5	0.5
1989	126.9	0.3	126.9	0.0	127.4	0.4	127.7	0.2	128.2	0.4	128.6	0.3	129.3	0.5	130.1	0.6	130.8	0.5	130.6	-0.2	130.8	0.2	130.8	0.0
1990	131.8	0.8	132.4	0.5	132.4	0.0	132.7	0.2	133.2	0.4	133.4	0.2	133.5	0.1	133.7	0.1	133.9	0.1	134.3	0.3	134.6	0.2	135.4	0.6
1991	135.9	0.4	136.4	0.4	135.9	-0.4	135.8	-0.1	136.1	0.2	136.1	0.0	136.2	0.1	136.2	0.0	136.3	0.1	136.5	0.1	136.6	0.1	136.6	0.0

[Continued]

Commercial Furniture
Producer Price Index
Base 1982 = 100
[Continued]

For 1947-2001. Columns headed % show percentile change in the index from the previous period for which an index is available.

Year	Jan		Feb		Mar		Apr		May		Jun		Jul		Aug		Sep		Oct		Nov		Dec	
	Index	%	Index	%	Index	%	Index	%	Index	%	Index	%	Index	%	Index	%	Index	%	Index	%	Index	%	Index	%
1992	137.0	0.3	137.2	0.1	137.3	0.1	137.9	0.4	138.0	0.1	138.1	0.1	137.8	-0.2	138.2	0.3	138.5	0.2	138.5	0.0	139.1	0.4	139.3	0.1
1993	139.2	-0.1	139.8	0.4	139.6	-0.1	140.1	0.4	140.3	0.1	140.5	0.1	140.8	0.2	141.0	0.1	140.7	-0.2	140.8	0.1	141.0	0.1	141.8	0.6
1994	143.2	1.0	143.5	0.2	143.6	0.1	144.5	0.6	145.3	0.6	145.2	-0.1	145.6	0.3	145.3	-0.2	144.8	-0.3	144.5	-0.2	145.2	0.5	145.4	0.1
1995	146.2	0.6	146.6	0.3	146.6	0.0	147.8	0.8	147.4	-0.3	148.1	0.5	148.0	-0.1	148.9	0.6	148.5	-0.3	149.6	0.7	150.2	0.4	150.4	0.1
1996	150.6	0.1	151.4	0.5	150.9	-0.3	151.3	0.3	150.7	-0.4	151.1	0.3	151.8	0.5	151.5	-0.2	151.8	0.2	153.0	0.8	153.2	0.1	153.4	0.1
1997	153.6	0.1	153.4	-0.1	153.2	-0.1	153.9	0.5	154.3	0.3	154.2	-0.1	154.7	0.3	154.3	-0.3	154.7	0.0	154.4	-0.2	155.0	0.4	155.1	0.1
1998	154.7	-0.3	155.2	0.3	155.2	0.0	155.0	-0.1	155.6	0.4	155.3	-0.2	155.2	-0.1	155.2	0.0	155.2	0.0	155.5	0.2	155.4	-0.1	155.4	0.0
1999	155.8	0.3	155.8	0.0	155.9	0.1	155.9	0.0	156.2	0.2	156.7	0.3	156.7	0.0	157.0	0.2	157.1	0.1	157.2	0.1	157.2	0.0	157.2	0.0
2000	157.5	0.2	157.6	0.1	158.0	0.3	158.2	0.1	158.3	0.1	158.5	0.1	158.4	-0.1	158.6	0.1	158.7	0.1	158.7	0.0	158.9	0.1	158.9	0.0
2001	159.5	0.4	159.7	0.1	160.1	0.3	160.2	0.1	160.2	0.0	160.4	0.1	160.6	0.1	160.5	-0.1	160.4	-0.1	160.9	0.3	160.7	-0.1	160.4	-0.2

Source: U.S. Department of Labor, Bureau of Labor Statistics, Division of Industry Prices and Price Indexes. n.e.c. stands for not elsewhere classified. - indicates no data collected for period or unavailable.

Floor Coverings
Producer Price Index
Base 1982 = 100

For 1926-2001. Columns headed % show percentile change in the index from the previous period for which an index is available.

Year	Jan Index	%	Feb Index	%	Mar Index	%	Apr Index	%	May Index	%	Jun Index	%	Jul Index	%	Aug Index	%	Sep Index	%	Oct Index	%	Nov Index	%	Dec Index	%
1926	31.9	-	31.9	0.0	31.9	0.0	31.9	0.0	31.9	0.0	31.7	-0.6	31.7	0.0	31.7	0.0	31.7	0.0	31.7	0.0	31.7	0.0	30.3	-4.4
1927	30.3	0.0	30.3	0.0	30.1	-0.7	30.1	0.0	30.1	0.0	30.3	0.7	30.3	0.0	30.3	0.0	30.3	0.0	30.3	0.0	30.3	0.0	30.4	0.3
1928	30.4	0.0	30.4	0.0	30.4	0.0	30.4	0.0	30.4	0.0	29.1	-4.3	29.1	0.0	29.1	0.0	29.1	0.0	29.1	0.0	29.4	1.0	29.4	0.0
1929	29.4	0.0	29.4	0.0	29.4	0.0	29.4	0.0	29.4	0.0	29.4	0.0	29.7	1.0	29.7	0.0	29.7	0.0	30.2	1.7	30.2	0.0	30.3	0.3
1930	30.6	1.0	30.6	0.0	30.6	0.0	30.6	0.0	30.6	0.0	30.6	0.0	30.6	0.0	30.6	0.0	29.9	-2.3	29.9	0.0	29.9	0.0	25.6	-14.4
1931	25.6	0.0	25.6	0.0	25.6	0.0	25.6	0.0	25.6	0.0	25.6	0.0	25.6	0.0	25.6	0.0	25.6	0.0	25.6	0.0	25.6	0.0	22.7	-11.3
1932	22.7	0.0	22.7	0.0	22.7	0.0	22.7	0.0	22.9	0.9	23.0	0.4	22.8	-0.9	22.7	-0.4	22.7	0.0	22.7	0.0	22.7	0.0	22.7	0.0
1933	22.7	0.0	22.7	0.0	22.7	0.0	22.7	0.0	22.7	0.0	23.2	2.2	23.5	1.3	24.0	2.1	24.3	1.2	24.7	1.6	24.7	0.0	24.7	0.0
1934	24.7	0.0	24.7	0.0	24.7	0.0	24.7	0.0	25.4	2.8	26.7	5.1	26.7	0.0	26.7	0.0	26.7	0.0	26.1	-2.2	26.1	0.0	26.1	0.0
1935	26.2	0.4	26.2	0.0	26.2	0.0	26.2	0.0	26.2	0.0	26.2	0.0	26.2	0.0	26.2	0.0	26.2	0.0	26.2	0.0	26.2	0.0	26.2	0.0
1936	26.3	0.4	26.3	0.0	26.3	0.0	26.3	0.0	26.3	0.0	26.4	0.4	26.0	-1.5	26.0	0.0	26.1	0.4	26.3	0.8	26.3	0.0	27.1	3.0
1937	27.4	1.1	28.9	5.5	28.9	0.0	28.9	0.0	28.9	0.0	28.9	0.0	29.8	3.1	30.7	3.0	30.7	0.0	30.7	0.0	30.7	0.0	29.6	-3.6
1938	29.1	-1.7	29.1	0.0	28.7	-1.4	28.4	-1.0	28.4	0.0	28.4	0.0	28.2	-0.7	28.2	0.0	27.9	-1.1	27.0	-3.2	27.3	1.1	27.9	2.2
1939	28.1	0.7	28.1	0.0	28.1	0.0	28.1	0.0	28.1	0.0	28.1	0.0	28.0	-0.4	28.0	0.0	29.5	5.4	30.9	4.7	31.1	0.6	31.1	0.0
1940	30.8	-1.0	30.8	0.0	30.8	0.0	31.2	1.3	31.3	0.3	31.3	0.0	31.3	0.0	31.3	0.0	31.3	0.0	31.3	0.0	31.3	0.0	31.3	0.0
1941	31.3	0.0	31.3	0.0	31.5	0.6	32.0	1.6	32.2	0.6	32.5	0.9	32.5	0.0	32.5	0.0	32.5	0.0	32.5	0.0	32.5	0.0	32.5	0.0
1942	33.1	1.8	33.2	0.3	33.2	0.0	33.2	0.0	33.2	0.0	33.2	0.0	33.2	0.0	33.2	0.0	33.2	0.0	33.2	0.0	33.2	0.0	33.2	0.0
1943	33.2	0.0	33.2	0.0	33.2	0.0	33.2	0.0	33.2	0.0	33.2	0.0	33.2	0.0	33.2	0.0	33.2	0.0	33.2	0.0	33.2	0.0	33.2	0.0
1944	33.2	0.0	33.2	0.0	33.2	0.0	33.2	0.0	33.2	0.0	33.2	0.0	33.2	0.0	33.2	0.0	33.2	0.0	33.2	0.0	33.2	0.0	33.2	0.0
1945	33.1	-0.3	33.1	0.0	33.1	0.0	33.1	0.0	33.1	0.0	33.1	0.0	33.1	0.0	33.1	0.0	33.1	0.0	33.1	0.0	33.1	0.0	33.1	0.0
1946	34.3	3.6	34.8	1.5	35.3	1.4	36.3	2.8	37.0	1.9	37.0	0.0	37.0	0.0	37.0	0.0	37.3	0.8	37.4	0.3	39.0	4.3	39.9	2.3
1947	42.7	7.0	42.7	0.0	42.8	0.2	42.9	0.2	42.9	0.0	43.1	0.5	44.0	2.1	44.0	0.0	44.1	0.2	44.1	0.0	44.1	0.0	45.3	2.7
1948	45.5	0.4	45.6	0.2	45.6	0.0	45.6	0.0	45.6	0.0	46.2	1.3	46.5	0.6	46.6	0.2	47.2	1.3	47.4	0.4	47.4	0.0	47.4	0.0
1949	47.8	0.8	47.9	0.2	48.0	0.2	47.3	-1.5	47.3	0.0	46.5	-1.7	45.6	-1.9	45.6	0.0	45.5	-0.2	45.6	0.2	46.0	0.9	46.8	1.7
1950	47.4	1.3	48.2	1.7	48.4	0.4	48.5	0.2	49.6	2.3	49.6	0.0	50.4	1.6	53.9	6.9	55.3	2.6	57.9	4.7	58.3	0.7	60.3	3.4
1951	63.0	4.5	64.0	1.6	66.6	4.1	68.0	2.1	68.0	0.0	66.9	-1.6	64.8	-3.1	60.8	-6.2	58.4	-3.9	57.7	-1.2	57.1	-1.0	57.5	0.7
1952	57.5	0.0	57.6	0.2	57.4	-0.3	57.7	0.5	55.0	-4.7	54.2	-1.5	54.2	0.0	54.1	-0.2	55.7	3.0	55.7	0.0	55.7	0.0	55.9	0.4
1953	56.5	1.1	56.5	0.0	56.5	0.0	56.5	0.0	56.9	0.7	56.8	-0.2	57.0	0.4	57.0	0.0	57.0	0.0	57.0	0.0	56.9	-0.2	56.8	-0.2
1954	55.8	-1.8	55.7	-0.2	55.8	0.2	55.8	0.0	55.8	0.0	55.8	0.0	55.9	0.2	56.2	0.5	56.6	0.7	56.4	-0.4	56.4	0.0	56.4	0.0
1955	56.5	0.2	56.6	0.2	56.6	0.0	56.9	0.5	56.9	0.0	57.5	1.1	57.7	0.3	57.7	0.0	58.3	1.0	58.6	0.5	58.6	0.0	58.8	0.3
1956	59.4	1.0	59.4	0.0	59.4	0.0	59.4	0.0	59.4	0.0	59.4	0.0	59.8	0.7	59.8	0.0	60.1	0.5	60.0	-0.2	60.1	0.2	60.1	0.0
1957	61.4	2.2	61.1	-0.5	61.1	0.0	60.9	-0.3	60.9	0.0	60.9	0.0	60.3	-1.0	60.3	0.0	60.3	0.0	60.3	0.0	60.3	0.0	60.3	0.0
1958	59.8	-0.8	59.1	-1.2	58.8	-0.5	58.5	-0.5	58.5	0.0	58.2	-0.5	57.7	-0.9	57.7	0.0	57.5	-0.3	57.4	-0.2	57.4	0.0	57.4	0.0
1959	57.4	0.0	57.5	-0.2	57.9	0.7	58.1	0.3	58.1	0.0	58.3	0.3	58.5	0.3	58.5	0.0	58.7	0.3	58.8	0.2	58.8	0.0	58.7	-0.2
1960	59.0	0.5	59.0	0.0	59.5	0.8	59.5	0.0	59.5	0.0	59.5	0.0	59.5	0.0	59.5	0.0	59.4	-0.2	59.4	0.0	59.3	-0.2	59.3	0.0
1961	58.6	-1.2	58.5	-0.2	58.5	0.0	58.5	0.0	58.5	0.0	58.5	0.0	58.8	0.5	58.8	0.0	58.8	0.0	58.7	-0.2	58.7	0.0	58.6	-0.2
1962	58.4	-0.3	57.2	-2.1	57.2	0.0	57.2	0.0	57.2	0.0	57.2	0.0	57.1	-0.2	57.1	0.0	57.1	0.0	57.1	0.0	57.1	0.0	56.9	-0.4
1963	56.8	-0.2	56.6	-0.4	56.7	0.2	56.6	-0.2	56.5	-0.2	56.6	0.2	57.0	0.7	57.0	0.0	57.1	0.2	57.5	0.7	57.8	0.5	57.9	0.2
1964	59.1	2.1	59.1	0.0	59.1	0.0	59.1	0.0	58.9	-0.3	58.2	-1.2	58.5	0.5	58.5	0.0	58.5	0.0	58.5	0.0	58.5	0.0	58.5	0.0
1965	57.9	-1.0	57.9	0.0	57.8	-0.2	57.7	-0.2	57.7	0.0	57.7	0.0	57.7	0.0	57.6	-0.2	57.6	0.0	57.5	-0.2	57.5	0.0	57.6	0.2
1966	57.7	0.2	57.7	0.0	57.6	-0.2	57.6	0.0	57.6	0.0	57.4	-0.3	57.1	-0.5	57.0	-0.2	57.0	0.0	57.0	0.0	57.0	0.0	56.8	-0.4
1967	55.5	-2.3	55.0	-0.9	55.2	0.4	54.9	-0.5	54.9	0.0	54.9	0.0	54.5	-0.7	54.5	0.0	55.0	0.9	55.9	1.6	55.9	0.0	56.1	0.4
1968	56.1	0.0	56.0	-0.2	56.0	0.0	56.0	0.0	56.0	0.0	55.7	-0.5	55.8	0.2	56.0	0.4	55.9	-0.2	55.9	0.0	55.9	1.0	55.9	0.0
1969	56.3	0.7	56.4	0.2	56.3	-0.2	56.0	-0.5	55.8	-0.4	55.3	-0.9	54.9	-0.7	54.9	0.0	54.9	0.0	54.9	0.0	54.9	0.0	54.9	0.0
1970	55.1	0.4	55.1	0.0	55.0	-0.2	55.0	0.0	54.7	-0.5	54.5	-0.4	54.9	0.7	54.7	-0.4	54.7	0.0	54.9	0.4	54.9	0.0	55.0	0.2

[Continued]

Floor Coverings
Producer Price Index
Base 1982 = 100
[Continued]

For 1926-2001. Columns headed % show percentile change in the index from the previous period for which an index is available.

Year	Jan Index	%	Feb Index	%	Mar Index	%	Apr Index	%	May Index	%	Jun Index	%	Jul Index	%	Aug Index	%	Sep Index	%	Oct Index	%	Nov Index	%	Dec Index	%
1971	55.7	1.3	55.5	-0.4	55.4	-0.2	55.2	-0.4	55.2	0.0	54.2	-1.8	54.2	0.0	53.9	-0.6	53.9	0.0	53.9	0.0	53.9	0.0	54.1	0.4
1972	54.2	0.2	54.2	0.0	54.2	0.0	54.2	0.0	54.2	0.0	54.4	0.4	54.5	0.2	54.5	0.0	54.7	0.4	54.7	0.0	54.7	0.0	54.7	0.0
1973	55.0	0.5	55.7	1.3	55.8	0.2	56.1	0.5	56.6	0.9	56.7	0.2	56.7	0.0	56.7	0.0	56.6	-0.2	57.1	0.9	57.1	0.0	57.2	0.2
1974	58.6	2.4	59.0	0.7	59.4	0.7	61.0	2.7	61.4	0.7	63.2	2.9	64.0	1.3	65.8	2.8	67.6	2.7	68.1	0.7	68.2	0.1	68.6	0.6
1975	68.4	-0.3	68.2	-0.3	68.2	0.0	68.1	-0.1	67.9	-0.3	67.9	0.0	68.4	0.7	69.9	2.2	70.0	0.1	70.0	0.0	70.0	0.0	70.2	0.3
1976	72.1	2.7	72.4	0.4	72.4	0.0	72.4	0.0	72.4	0.0	72.5	0.1	72.5	0.0	72.6	0.1	72.6	0.0	72.6	0.0	72.6	0.0	72.8	0.3
1977	74.8	2.7	74.8	0.0	74.8	0.0	74.8	0.0	74.8	0.0	75.0	0.3	75.2	0.3	75.4	0.3	75.4	0.0	75.7	0.4	76.3	0.8	76.4	0.1
1978	77.2	1.0	77.2	0.0	77.3	0.1	78.2	1.2	78.3	0.1	78.6	0.4	78.7	0.1	78.7	0.0	78.6	-0.1	78.4	-0.3	78.4	0.0	78.5	0.1
1979	79.1	0.8	79.3	0.3	79.5	0.3	79.7	0.3	80.6	1.1	80.9	0.4	82.3	1.7	82.8	0.6	83.0	0.2	84.0	1.2	84.4	0.5	84.4	0.0
1980	87.8	4.0	87.5	-0.3	88.8	1.5	89.5	0.8	89.4	-0.1	89.5	0.1	90.1	0.7	90.4	0.3	90.5	0.1	90.7	0.2	91.4	0.8	94.2	3.1
1981	95.1	1.0	94.9	-0.2	96.1	1.3	96.8	0.7	99.1	2.4	99.8	0.7	100.9	1.1	100.4	-0.5	100.3	-0.1	99.9	-0.4	100.6	0.7	100.2	-0.4
1982	99.5	-0.7	99.7	0.2	99.7	0.0	100.0	0.3	100.1	0.1	100.4	0.3	100.0	-0.4	99.9	-0.1	100.2	0.3	100.2	0.0	100.1	-0.1	100.2	0.1
1983	100.6	0.4	100.5	-0.1	100.4	-0.1	100.6	0.2	100.5	-0.1	100.2	-0.3	103.0	2.8	104.3	1.3	104.6	0.3	104.6	0.0	104.5	-0.1	104.5	0.0
1984	103.9	-0.6	104.0	0.1	103.9	-0.1	103.9	0.0	105.8	1.8	106.4	0.6	106.4	0.0	106.3	-0.1	106.3	0.0	106.5	0.2	106.5	0.0	106.7	0.2
1985	106.9	0.2	106.2	-0.7	106.4	0.2	106.5	0.1	105.7	-0.8	104.8	-0.9	105.2	0.4	104.9	-0.3	105.2	0.3	104.9	-0.3	105.2	0.3	105.3	0.1
1986	107.4	2.0	107.7	0.3	107.7	0.0	107.8	0.1	108.1	0.3	108.6	0.5	108.1	-0.5	108.3	0.2	108.4	0.1	109.0	0.6	109.3	0.3	109.2	-0.1
1987	109.9	0.6	109.8	-0.1	109.2	-0.5	109.4	0.2	109.9	0.5	110.2	0.3	111.1	0.8	111.5	0.4	111.6	0.1	112.0	0.4	111.9	-0.1	111.6	-0.3
1988	112.7	1.0	113.1	0.4	112.9	-0.2	113.6	0.6	114.0	0.4	113.8	-0.2	114.7	0.8	115.4	0.6	116.0	0.5	116.5	0.4	117.1	0.5	117.0	-0.1
1989	117.5	0.4	116.7	-0.7	117.3	0.5	117.3	0.0	116.9	-0.3	117.9	0.9	118.6	0.6	119.0	0.3	117.5	-1.3	117.0	-0.4	117.4	0.3	117.7	0.3
1990	117.7	0.0	118.3	0.5	119.3	0.8	119.5	0.2	119.6	0.1	119.4	-0.2	119.4	0.0	119.2	-0.2	118.8	-0.3	118.6	-0.2	119.1	0.4	119.5	0.3
1991	120.3	0.7	121.4	0.9	120.9	-0.4	120.7	-0.2	120.5	-0.2	120.1	-0.3	120.1	0.0	120.1	0.0	119.9	-0.2	120.2	0.3	120.4	0.2	120.3	-0.1
1992	120.1	-0.2	120.1	0.0	119.5	-0.5	119.7	0.2	120.4	0.6	120.8	0.3	121.0	0.2	120.7	-0.2	120.5	-0.2	120.5	0.0	120.2	-0.2	120.2	0.0
1993	119.4	-0.7	119.5	0.1	119.5	0.0	119.4	-0.1	119.2	-0.2	119.1	-0.1	120.0	0.8	120.8	0.7	121.2	0.3	121.3	0.1	121.4	0.1	121.2	-0.2
1994	121.4	0.2	121.3	-0.1	120.9	-0.3	121.1	0.2	121.0	-0.1	121.3	0.2	121.9	0.5	121.8	-0.1	121.2	-0.5	121.7	0.4	122.4	0.6	122.2	-0.2
1995	122.6	0.3	122.9	0.2	122.7	-0.2	123.1	0.3	123.8	0.6	123.3	-0.4	123.5	0.2	123.6	0.1	124.0	0.3	125.1	0.9	124.8	-0.2	125.0	0.2
1996	124.9	-0.1	125.2	0.2	125.8	0.5	124.8	-0.8	126.4	1.3	125.6	-0.6	126.8	1.0	127.3	0.4	128.0	0.5	128.1	0.1	128.2	0.1	127.8	-0.3
1997	127.8	0.0	128.8	0.8	129.0	0.2	125.8	-2.5	126.7	0.7	126.9	0.2	128.5	1.3	128.5	0.0	128.4	-0.1	127.9	-0.4	127.2	-0.5	127.6	0.3
1998	128.0	0.3	128.6	0.5	128.6	0.0	128.2	-0.3	128.3	0.1	128.7	0.3	128.3	-0.3	128.6	0.2	128.0	-0.5	127.9	-0.1	128.3	0.3	127.9	-0.3
1999	126.7	-0.9	126.6	-0.1	127.4	0.6	126.9	-0.4	126.7	-0.2	127.9	0.9	126.8	-0.9	126.9	0.1	126.8	-0.1	127.7	0.7	127.7	0.0	127.8	0.1
2000	127.1	-0.5	128.1	0.8	129.0	0.7	128.7	-0.2	128.8	0.1	130.3	1.2	129.3	-0.8	130.2	0.7	129.4	-0.6	131.1	1.3	130.6	-0.4	132.2	1.2
2001	131.8	-0.3	132.3	0.4	129.9	-1.8	131.5	1.2	130.3	-0.9	129.8	-0.4	131.3	1.2	129.6	-1.3	128.1	-1.2	128.2	0.1	129.1	0.7	128.7	-0.3

Source: U.S. Department of Labor, Bureau of Labor Statistics, Division of Industry Prices and Price Indexes. n.e.c. stands for not elsewhere classified. - indicates no data collected for period or unavailable.

Household Appliances
Producer Price Index
Base 1982 = 100

For 1947-2001. Columns headed % show percentile change in the index from the previous period for which an index is available.

Year	Jan Index	%	Feb Index	%	Mar Index	%	Apr Index	%	May Index	%	Jun Index	%	Jul Index	%	Aug Index	%	Sep Index	%	Oct Index	%	Nov Index	%	Dec Index	%
1947	50.3	-	50.4	0.2	50.5	0.2	50.6	0.2	50.8	0.4	51.1	0.6	51.5	0.8	51.7	0.4	52.3	1.2	52.7	0.8	52.9	0.4	53.2	0.6
1948	53.1	-0.2	53.1	0.0	53.1	0.0	53.2	0.2	53.0	-0.4	53.1	0.2	54.0	1.7	54.3	0.6	54.7	0.7	55.4	1.3	55.5	0.2	55.5	0.0
1949	54.6	-1.6	54.6	0.0	54.4	-0.4	54.1	-0.6	53.7	-0.7	53.5	-0.4	53.4	-0.2	53.2	-0.4	53.2	0.0	53.1	-0.2	53.1	0.0	53.1	0.0
1950	53.1	0.0	53.0	-0.2	53.0	0.0	53.2	0.4	53.2	0.0	53.1	-0.2	53.2	0.2	53.8	1.1	54.7	1.7	55.5	1.5	56.0	0.9	56.7	1.3
1951	57.1	0.7	57.3	0.4	57.3	0.0	57.3	0.0	57.3	0.0	57.4	0.2	57.1	-0.5	57.1	0.0	57.3	0.4	57.3	0.0	57.3	0.0	57.4	0.2
1952	57.3	-0.2	57.3	0.0	57.0	-0.5	57.2	0.4	56.9	-0.5	56.7	-0.4	56.7	0.0	56.7	0.0	56.9	0.4	56.9	0.0	56.9	0.0	57.0	0.2
1953	57.0	0.0	57.0	0.0	57.3	0.5	57.3	0.0	57.4	0.2	57.4	0.0	57.8	0.7	57.8	0.0	57.9	0.2	57.9	0.0	57.9	0.0	57.9	0.0
1954	58.1	0.3	58.2	0.2	58.1	-0.2	58.3	0.3	58.3	0.0	58.3	0.0	58.2	-0.2	58.2	0.0	58.0	-0.3	58.1	0.2	57.9	-0.3	58.0	0.2
1955	57.7	-0.5	57.6	-0.2	56.9	-1.2	56.9	0.0	56.5	-0.7	56.5	0.0	56.5	0.0	56.6	0.2	56.4	-0.4	56.3	-0.2	56.4	0.2	56.2	-0.4
1956	56.0	-0.4	56.1	0.2	55.9	-0.4	55.8	-0.2	55.8	0.0	55.8	0.0	55.4	-0.7	55.8	0.7	56.0	0.4	56.5	0.9	56.5	0.0	56.2	-0.5
1957	56.5	0.5	56.7	0.4	56.7	0.0	55.9	-1.4	55.8	-0.2	55.8	0.0	55.7	-0.2	55.6	-0.2	55.5	-0.2	55.9	0.7	55.8	-0.2	55.9	0.2
1958	55.9	0.0	55.9	0.0	55.9	0.0	55.9	0.0	55.7	-0.4	55.7	0.0	55.7	0.0	55.6	-0.2	55.2	-0.7	55.3	0.2	55.1	-0.4	55.1	0.0
1959	55.8	1.3	55.8	0.0	55.8	0.0	55.8	0.0	55.8	0.0	55.8	0.0	55.4	-0.7	55.4	0.0	55.4	0.0	55.2	-0.4	55.3	0.2	55.0	-0.5
1960	54.8	-0.4	54.8	0.0	54.7	-0.2	54.7	0.0	54.2	-0.9	53.9	-0.6	53.9	0.0	53.6	-0.6	53.5	-0.2	53.5	0.0	53.4	-0.2	53.3	-0.2
1961	53.2	-0.2	53.2	0.0	53.1	-0.2	53.1	0.0	53.0	-0.2	52.9	-0.2	52.9	0.0	52.9	0.0	52.9	0.0	53.0	0.2	52.9	-0.2	52.8	-0.2
1962	52.9	0.2	52.9	0.0	52.8	-0.2	52.7	-0.2	52.5	-0.4	52.5	0.0	52.3	-0.4	52.0	-0.6	51.9	-0.2	51.8	-0.2	51.8	0.0	51.8	0.0
1963	51.4	-0.8	51.4	0.0	51.4	0.0	51.3	-0.2	51.2	-0.2	51.2	0.0	51.1	-0.2	51.1	0.0	50.9	-0.4	50.8	-0.2	50.8	0.0	50.7	-0.2
1964	50.9	0.4	51.1	0.4	51.1	0.0	51.0	-0.2	51.0	0.0	50.8	-0.4	50.8	0.0	50.8	0.0	50.7	-0.2	50.8	0.2	50.5	-0.6	50.4	-0.2
1965	50.2	-0.4	50.1	-0.2	50.1	0.0	49.8	-0.6	49.7	-0.2	49.8	0.2	49.7	-0.2	49.3	-0.8	49.3	0.0	49.3	0.0	49.3	0.0	49.4	0.2
1966	49.6	0.4	49.6	0.0	49.6	0.0	49.7	0.2	49.8	0.2	49.8	0.0	49.6	-0.4	49.4	-0.4	49.4	0.0	49.5	0.2	49.7	0.4	49.7	0.0
1967	49.9	0.4	50.0	0.2	50.0	0.0	50.1	0.2	50.0	-0.2	50.2	0.4	50.3	0.2	50.2	-0.2	50.3	0.2	50.4	0.2	50.6	0.4	50.6	0.0
1968	50.7	0.2	50.9	0.4	51.1	0.4	51.2	0.2	51.1	-0.2	51.0	-0.2	51.2	0.4	51.3	0.2	51.3	0.0	51.4	0.2	51.2	-0.4	51.3	0.2
1969	51.4	0.2	51.6	0.4	51.6	0.0	51.6	0.0	51.6	0.0	51.6	0.0	51.6	0.0	51.6	0.0	51.8	0.4	51.9	0.2	51.9	0.0	52.1	0.4
1970	52.7	1.2	52.6	-0.2	52.6	0.0	52.8	0.4	52.7	-0.2	52.7	0.0	52.8	0.2	52.9	0.2	52.9	0.0	53.2	0.6	53.3	0.2	53.3	0.0
1971	53.8	0.9	53.9	0.2	54.0	0.2	53.9	-0.2	53.9	0.0	53.9	0.0	54.1	0.4	54.2	0.2	54.2	0.0	54.2	0.0	54.1	-0.2	54.1	0.0
1972	53.7	-0.7	54.0	0.6	53.9	-0.2	54.0	0.2	53.9	-0.2	53.8	-0.2	53.9	0.2	54.1	0.4	54.3	0.4	54.2	-0.2	54.2	0.0	54.2	0.0
1973	54.1	-0.2	54.3	0.4	54.4	0.2	54.4	0.0	54.2	-0.4	53.9	-0.6	54.1	0.4	54.7	1.1	54.7	0.0	54.8	0.2	55.0	0.4	55.2	0.4
1974	55.9	1.3	56.1	0.4	56.5	0.7	56.9	0.7	57.3	0.7	58.0	1.2	58.6	1.0	59.4	1.4	60.7	2.2	62.8	3.5	63.7	1.4	64.6	1.4
1975	65.3	1.1	65.6	0.5	65.3	-0.5	65.6	0.5	65.8	0.3	66.4	0.9	66.4	0.0	66.5	0.2	67.1	0.9	67.4	0.4	68.0	0.9	68.2	0.3
1976	68.5	0.4	69.0	0.7	69.5	0.7	69.7	0.3	69.7	0.0	69.9	0.3	70.2	0.4	70.3	0.1	70.4	0.1	70.5	0.1	70.6	0.1	70.8	0.3
1977	71.0	0.3	71.4	0.6	71.8	0.6	72.0	0.3	72.0	0.0	72.7	1.0	73.2	0.7	73.6	0.5	74.1	0.7	74.2	0.1	74.3	0.1	74.3	0.0
1978	75.1	1.1	75.2	0.1	75.9	0.9	76.5	0.8	76.6	0.1	76.7	0.1	77.1	0.5	77.4	0.4	77.4	0.0	77.6	0.3	78.2	0.8	78.2	0.0
1979	78.9	0.9	79.5	0.8	79.8	0.4	79.7	-0.1	80.0	0.4	80.4	0.5	80.9	0.6	81.5	0.7	81.7	0.2	82.0	0.4	82.6	0.7	83.0	0.5
1980	83.6	0.7	84.8	1.4	85.3	0.6	85.9	0.7	87.0	1.3	88.1	1.3	88.3	0.2	88.5	0.2	89.0	0.6	89.2	0.2	89.6	0.4	90.1	0.6
1981	91.5	1.6	92.2	0.8	92.5	0.3	93.0	0.5	93.2	0.2	93.5	0.3	94.8	1.4	95.0	0.2	95.5	0.5	95.8	0.3	95.9	0.1	96.1	0.2
1982	97.1	1.0	98.1	1.0	99.1	1.0	99.3	0.2	99.9	0.6	100.2	0.3	100.6	0.4	101.0	0.4	101.1	0.1	101.1	0.0	101.1	0.0	101.3	0.2
1983	102.4	1.1	102.9	0.5	103.0	0.1	103.6	0.6	104.2	0.6	104.2	0.0	104.4	0.2	104.3	-0.1	104.5	0.2	104.3	-0.2	104.5	0.2	104.7	0.2
1984	105.4	0.7	105.8	0.4	106.0	0.2	105.9	-0.1	105.9	0.0	106.1	0.2	106.2	0.1	106.5	0.3	106.3	-0.2	106.0	-0.3	106.0	0.0	106.1	0.1
1985	106.1	0.0	106.1	0.0	106.3	0.2	106.5	0.2	106.7	0.2	106.8	0.1	107.1	0.3	107.2	0.1	107.0	-0.2	107.0	0.0	106.9	-0.1	106.6	-0.3
1986	105.5	-1.0	105.6	0.1	105.8	0.2	106.1	0.3	106.4	0.3	105.9	-0.5	105.9	0.0	105.6	-0.3	105.5	-0.1	105.4	-0.1	105.2	-0.2	105.0	-0.2
1987	105.2	0.2	105.3	0.1	105.6	0.3	105.7	0.1	105.8	0.1	105.8	0.0	106.0	0.2	105.8	-0.2	105.5	-0.3	105.4	-0.1	105.7	0.3	105.2	-0.5
1988	105.5	0.3	106.0	0.5	106.2	0.2	106.2	0.0	106.3	0.1	106.1	-0.2	105.6	-0.5	105.6	0.0	105.8	0.2	106.0	0.2	106.5	0.5	106.2	-0.3
1989	107.0	0.8	107.3	0.3	107.6	0.3	107.7	0.1	108.1	0.4	108.5	0.4	109.2	0.6	109.3	0.1	109.7	0.4	110.0	0.3	110.0	0.0	110.1	0.1
1990	110.5	0.4	110.6	0.1	110.7	0.1	110.9	0.2	110.4	-0.5	111.0	0.5	110.7	-0.3	110.8	0.1	110.9	0.1	110.9	0.0	111.0	0.1	110.9	-0.1
1991	111.6	0.6	111.3	-0.3	111.3	0.0	111.4	0.1	111.5	0.1	111.3	-0.2	111.3	0.0	111.4	0.1	111.3	-0.1	111.3	0.0	111.2	-0.1	111.0	-0.2

[Continued]

Household Appliances
Producer Price Index
Base 1982 = 100
[Continued]

For 1947-2001. Columns headed % show percentile change in the index from the previous period for which an index is available.

Year	Jan Index	%	Feb Index	%	Mar Index	%	Apr Index	%	May Index	%	Jun Index	%	Jul Index	%	Aug Index	%	Sep Index	%	Oct Index	%	Nov Index	%	Dec Index	%
1992	111.2	0.2	111.1	-0.1	111.1	0.0	111.4	0.3	111.3	-0.1	111.2	-0.1	111.2	0.0	111.2	0.0	111.3	0.1	111.6	0.3	112.3	0.6	111.8	-0.4
1993	112.0	0.2	112.3	0.3	112.5	0.2	112.8	0.3	113.0	0.2	113.4	0.4	113.4	0.0	113.4	0.0	113.4	0.0	113.0	-0.4	113.0	0.0	112.7	-0.3
1994	112.8	0.1	112.8	0.0	113.0	0.2	113.1	0.1	113.2	0.1	112.9	-0.3	112.9	0.0	112.7	-0.2	112.7	0.0	112.9	0.2	112.7	-0.2	112.4	-0.3
1995	112.3	-0.1	112.3	0.0	112.1	-0.2	112.4	0.3	112.4	0.0	112.2	-0.2	112.3	-0.1	112.2	-0.1	112.6	0.4	112.6	0.0	112.7	0.1	112.5	-0.2
1996	112.4	-0.1	112.5	0.1	112.6	0.1	113.0	0.4	113.1	0.1	113.1	0.0	113.0	-0.1	113.0	0.0	112.5	-0.4	112.4	-0.1	112.4	0.0	111.9	-0.4
1997	111.5	-0.4	111.0	-0.4	111.1	0.1	110.4	-0.6	110.5	0.1	110.4	-0.1	110.0	-0.4	109.7	-0.3	109.4	-0.3	109.4	0.0	109.3	-0.1	109.0	-0.3
1998	108.3	-0.6	108.5	0.2	108.8	0.3	108.7	-0.1	109.1	0.4	109.3	0.2	109.2	-0.1	109.1	-0.1	109.0	-0.1	109.0	0.0	108.8	-0.2	108.8	0.0
1999	108.8	0.0	108.5	-0.3	108.4	-0.1	108.7	0.3	108.7	0.0	108.6	-0.1	108.6	0.0	108.7	0.1	108.4	-0.3	108.1	-0.3	108.2	0.1	108.2	0.0
2000	108.1	-0.1	108.2	0.1	108.0	-0.2	108.1	0.1	107.8	-0.3	107.9	0.1	107.6	-0.3	106.5	-1.0	106.3	-0.2	106.7	0.4	106.5	-0.2	106.4	-0.1
2001	106.4	0.0	106.3	-0.1	105.6	-0.7	105.4	-0.2	105.4	0.0	105.3	-0.1	104.8	-0.5	104.6	-0.2	104.6	0.0	104.9	0.3	105.1	0.2	105.1	0.0

Source: U.S. Department of Labor, Bureau of Labor Statistics, Division of Industry Prices and Price Indexes. n.e.c. stands for not elsewhere classified. - indicates no data collected for period or unavailable.

Home Electronic Equipment
Producer Price Index
Base 1982 = 100

For 1947-2001. Columns headed % show percentile change in the index from the previous period for which an index is available.

Year	Jan Index	%	Feb Index	%	Mar Index	%	Apr Index	%	May Index	%	Jun Index	%	Jul Index	%	Aug Index	%	Sep Index	%	Oct Index	%	Nov Index	%	Dec Index	%
1947	140.1	-	140.5	0.3	140.5	0.0	140.5	0.0	140.5	0.0	140.5	0.0	140.5	0.0	140.8	0.2	142.3	1.1	142.3	0.0	142.3	0.0	142.3	0.0
1948	142.1	-0.1	142.1	0.0	142.1	0.0	141.6	-0.4	141.6	0.0	143.8	1.6	143.8	0.0	143.8	0.0	152.6	6.1	155.5	1.9	155.5	0.0	155.3	-0.1
1949	154.6	-0.5	154.6	0.0	154.6	0.0	154.4	-0.1	154.4	0.0	154.2	-0.1	153.5	-0.5	149.9	-2.3	149.9	0.0	146.9	-2.0	146.9	0.0	146.7	-0.1
1950	146.2	-0.3	146.7	0.3	146.7	0.0	146.7	0.0	146.7	0.0	146.4	-0.2	141.8	-3.1	131.4	-7.3	134.9	2.7	139.1	3.1	139.0	-0.1	136.4	-1.9
1951	135.7	-0.5	135.7	0.0	135.7	0.0	135.7	0.0	135.7	0.0	135.7	0.0	137.1	1.0	136.5	-0.4	136.2	-0.2	136.3	0.1	136.3	0.0	136.3	0.0
1952	136.4	0.1	136.4	0.0	132.8	-2.6	132.8	0.0	132.8	0.0	137.3	3.4	137.3	0.0	137.2	-0.1	137.2	0.0	137.2	0.0	137.3	0.1	137.3	0.0
1953	-	-	-		-		-		-		-		-		-		-		-		-		-	
1954	-	-	-		-		-		-		-		-		-		-		-		-		-	
1955	137.0	-0.2	136.5	-0.4	136.4	-0.1	136.4	0.0	136.6	0.1	136.5	-0.1	136.4	-0.1	134.9	-1.1	135.7	0.6	135.8	0.1	135.9	0.1	136.4	0.4
1956	136.4	0.0	136.6	0.1	136.6	0.0	135.9	-0.5	135.7	-0.1	135.2	-0.4	136.2	0.7	136.5	0.2	137.2	0.5	137.0	-0.1	137.0	0.0	136.6	-0.3
1957	137.0	0.3	137.0	0.0	136.4	-0.4	136.4	0.0	136.4	0.0	136.8	0.3	138.9	1.5	140.1	0.9	140.1	0.0	140.1	0.0	140.1	0.0	140.4	0.2
1958	139.7	-0.5	138.8	-0.6	138.8	0.0	138.8	0.0	138.2	-0.4	137.2	-0.7	139.1	1.4	139.0	-0.1	139.0	0.0	139.0	0.0	135.8	-2.3	135.6	-0.1
1959	136.5	0.7	136.5	0.0	135.9	-0.4	135.9	0.0	135.9	0.0	136.2	0.2	138.2	1.5	136.6	-1.2	135.8	-0.6	134.9	-0.7	134.5	-0.3	134.6	0.1
1960	134.3	-0.2	134.5	0.1	134.5	0.0	134.3	-0.1	134.3	0.0	133.9	-0.3	133.9	0.0	133.5	-0.3	133.5	0.0	132.5	-0.7	132.5	0.0	133.7	0.9
1961	133.1	-0.4	132.5	-0.5	132.8	0.2	132.8	0.0	131.6	-0.9	131.8	0.2	131.8	0.0	129.9	-1.4	129.3	-0.5	128.8	-0.4	129.0	0.2	129.0	0.0
1962	127.1	-1.5	126.1	-0.8	125.7	-0.3	125.4	-0.2	126.8	1.1	124.9	-1.5	124.8	-0.1	124.8	0.0	124.7	-0.1	124.7	0.0	124.2	-0.4	124.2	0.0
1963	123.9	-0.2	123.9	0.0	122.9	-0.8	122.9	0.0	122.2	-0.6	122.2	0.0	120.6	-1.3	120.6	0.0	120.7	0.1	120.7	0.0	120.7	0.0	120.0	-0.6
1964	119.9	-0.1	119.9	0.0	119.9	0.0	120.0	0.1	120.0	0.0	120.0	0.0	120.0	0.0	120.0	0.0	120.0	0.0	120.0	0.0	119.9	-0.1	119.0	-0.8
1965	118.8	-0.2	118.1	-0.6	118.1	0.0	118.1	0.0	118.1	0.0	118.1	0.0	116.3	-1.5	116.1	-0.2	116.1	0.0	116.2	0.1	116.2	0.0	116.2	0.0
1966	115.4	-0.7	115.3	-0.1	114.8	-0.4	114.8	0.0	114.8	0.0	114.8	0.0	114.8	0.0	114.2	-0.5	114.5	0.3	115.3	0.7	115.3	0.0	115.3	0.0
1967	114.9	-0.3	114.5	-0.3	114.5	0.0	114.5	0.0	114.0	-0.4	112.8	-1.1	112.4	-0.4	112.4	0.0	112.2	-0.2	113.4	1.1	113.6	0.2	112.9	-0.6
1968	112.9	0.0	113.0	0.1	112.7	-0.3	112.3	-0.4	112.4	0.1	111.2	-1.1	110.9	-0.3	110.9	0.0	110.8	-0.1	110.3	-0.5	109.7	-0.5	109.7	0.0
1969	108.2	-1.4	108.2	0.0	108.1	-0.1	107.8	-0.3	107.2	-0.6	107.0	-0.2	107.0	0.0	107.0	0.0	107.0	0.0	107.0	0.0	106.6	-0.4	106.6	0.0
1970	105.8	-0.8	105.8	0.0	105.8	0.0	105.8	0.0	105.6	-0.2	105.5	-0.1	105.8	0.3	106.0	0.2	106.2	0.2	106.4	0.2	107.0	0.6	106.5	-0.5
1971	106.6	0.1	106.3	-0.3	106.2	-0.1	106.1	-0.1	106.1	0.0	106.2	0.1	106.3	0.1	105.9	-0.4	105.8	-0.1	105.8	0.0	105.8	0.0	105.8	0.0
1972	105.9	0.1	105.5	-0.4	105.6	0.1	105.4	-0.2	105.5	0.1	105.2	-0.3	104.9	-0.3	104.9	0.0	105.5	0.6	105.5	0.0	105.0	-0.5	104.8	-0.2
1973	104.9	0.1	104.9	0.0	104.7	-0.2	104.7	0.0	104.7	0.0	104.0	-0.7	104.0	0.0	104.4	0.4	103.9	-0.5	103.9	0.0	103.9	0.0	103.4	-0.5
1974	103.7	0.3	103.8	0.1	104.7	0.9	104.7	0.0	105.0	0.3	105.7	0.7	106.3	0.6	106.3	0.0	106.8	0.5	106.8	0.0	107.3	0.5	107.5	0.2
1975	108.3	0.7	108.6	0.3	108.4	-0.2	104.4	-3.7	104.4	0.0	105.6	1.1	105.9	0.3	107.4	1.4	105.4	-1.9	105.4	0.0	105.4	0.0	105.4	0.0
1976	104.8	-0.6	104.1	-0.7	103.7	-0.4	103.7	0.0	103.7	0.0	103.6	-0.1	103.6	0.0	103.6	0.0	103.6	0.0	103.6	0.0	103.3	-0.3	103.2	-0.1
1977	101.8	-1.4	101.5	-0.3	101.5	0.0	100.2	-1.3	100.3	0.1	100.4	0.1	98.6	-1.8	98.6	0.0	98.1	-0.5	97.9	-0.2	98.3	0.4	98.2	-0.1
1978	101.0	2.9	100.7	-0.3	101.1	0.4	100.7	-0.4	102.2	1.5	100.5	-1.7	103.2	2.7	103.1	-0.1	104.0	0.9	103.7	-0.3	103.9	0.2	104.9	1.0
1979	104.7	-0.2	104.8	0.1	104.8	0.0	104.8	0.0	105.0	0.2	105.4	0.4	102.4	-2.8	102.4	0.0	102.5	0.1	102.5	0.0	102.6	0.1	102.8	0.2
1980	103.3	0.5	103.5	0.2	103.6	0.1	103.8	0.2	104.5	0.7	104.3	-0.2	104.1	-0.2	103.7	-0.4	104.1	0.4	103.9	-0.2	103.6	-0.3	103.4	-0.2
1981	103.4	0.0	103.7	0.3	103.7	0.0	103.3	-0.4	103.1	-0.2	98.4	-4.6	99.3	0.9	99.4	0.1	99.7	0.3	100.0	0.3	99.9	-0.1	101.8	1.9
1982	101.4	-0.4	101.7	0.3	101.2	-0.5	99.8	-1.4	100.0	0.2	100.4	0.4	99.1	-1.3	99.9	0.8	99.2	-0.7	99.7	0.5	98.8	-0.9	98.9	0.1
1983	99.2	0.3	98.8	-0.4	98.8	0.0	98.3	-0.5	98.1	-0.2	98.2	0.1	97.6	-0.6	97.1	-0.5	97.4	0.3	97.4	0.0	96.7	-0.7	95.9	-0.8
1984	95.9	0.0	95.5	-0.4	95.4	-0.1	96.4	1.0	96.0	-0.4	95.3	-0.7	95.6	0.3	95.2	-0.4	94.3	-0.9	94.4	0.1	94.3	-0.1	93.9	-0.4
1985	91.8	-2.2	93.0	1.3	92.0	-1.1	91.8	-0.2	90.8	-1.1	90.1	-0.8	90.9	0.9	90.4	-0.6	89.7	-0.8	89.4	-0.3	89.4	0.0	90.3	1.0
1986	89.8	-0.6	89.8	0.0	89.8	0.0	89.8	0.0	89.8	0.0	90.5	0.8	90.1	-0.4	89.9	-0.2	89.9	0.0	89.9	0.0	89.9	0.0	89.9	0.0
1987	89.1	-0.9	88.5	-0.7	88.9	0.5	89.1	0.2	88.9	-0.2	88.8	-0.1	88.7	-0.1	89.0	0.3	88.9	-0.1	88.7	-0.2	88.7	0.0	88.7	0.0
1988	88.5	-0.2	89.0	0.6	88.2	-0.9	87.1	-1.2	87.2	0.1	86.3	-1.0	86.7	0.5	86.6	-0.1	86.7	0.1	86.6	-0.1	86.8	0.2	86.7	-0.1
1989	88.0	1.5	88.0	0.0	88.0	0.0	88.3	0.3	88.3	0.0	88.4	0.1	88.4	0.0	88.0	-0.5	87.5	-0.6	83.2	-4.9	83.2	0.0	83.0	-0.2
1990	83.0	0.0	82.9	-0.1	82.8	-0.1	82.7	-0.1	82.6	-0.1	82.6	0.0	82.6	0.0	82.6	0.0	82.6	0.0	82.6	0.0	82.7	0.1	82.8	0.1	82.8	0.0
1991	82.9	0.1	83.1	0.2	83.1	0.0	83.1	0.0	83.5	0.5	83.6	0.1	83.5	-0.1	83.0	-0.6	83.0	0.0	83.1	0.1	83.0	-0.1	83.0	0.0

[Continued]

Home Electronic Equipment
Producer Price Index
Base 1982 = 100
[Continued]

For 1947-2001. Columns headed % show percentile change in the index from the previous period for which an index is available.

Year	Jan Index	%	Feb Index	%	Mar Index	%	Apr Index	%	May Index	%	Jun Index	%	Jul Index	%	Aug Index	%	Sep Index	%	Oct Index	%	Nov Index	%	Dec Index	%
1992	83.0	0.0	82.8	-0.2	82.8	0.0	82.6	-0.2	82.3	-0.4	81.9	-0.5	81.9	0.0	81.9	0.0	81.6	-0.4	81.0	-0.7	80.8	-0.2	80.8	0.0
1993	80.6	-0.2	80.7	0.1	80.5	-0.2	80.4	-0.1	80.2	-0.2	79.9	-0.4	80.0	0.1	79.8	-0.2	79.4	-0.5	79.6	0.3	80.8	1.5	80.7	-0.1
1994	80.7	0.0	80.7	0.0	80.6	-0.1	80.7	0.1	80.1	-0.7	80.0	-0.1	80.0	0.0	80.0	0.0	79.9	-0.1	80.2	0.4	80.1	-0.1	80.1	0.0
1995	80.2	0.1	80.2	0.0	79.5	-0.9	79.1	-0.5	78.3	-1.0	78.3	0.0	78.4	0.1	78.4	0.0	77.9	-0.6	77.9	0.0	79.4	1.9	79.3	-0.1
1996	79.4	0.1	79.3	-0.1	79.0	-0.4	79.0	0.0	79.1	0.1	79.0	-0.1	79.2	0.3	79.0	-0.3	79.0	0.0	78.7	-0.4	78.3	-0.5	78.3	0.0
1997	78.2	-0.1	78.3	0.1	78.2	-0.1	78.3	0.1	78.3	0.0	78.3	0.0	76.0	-2.9	76.1	0.1	76.1	0.0	78.3	2.9	76.0	-2.9	76.0	0.0
1998	76.9	1.2	76.9	0.0	76.8	-0.1	76.8	0.0	76.8	0.0	76.8	0.0	76.8	0.0	74.9	-2.5	74.7	-0.3	74.5	-0.3	74.5	0.0	74.5	0.0
1999	74.4	-0.1	74.4	0.0	74.2	-0.3	74.2	0.0	74.0	-0.3	74.0	0.0	74.0	0.0	73.9	-0.1	73.1	-1.1	72.7	-0.5	72.7	0.0	72.8	0.1
2000	72.7	-0.1	72.4	-0.4	72.0	-0.6	72.3	0.4	72.3	0.0	72.3	0.0	71.7	-0.8	71.4	-0.4	71.2	-0.3	71.2	0.0	71.2	0.0	71.2	0.0
2001	71.1	-0.1	71.2	0.1	71.2	0.0	71.3	0.1	70.7	-0.8	70.1	-0.8	70.0	-0.1	69.8	-0.3	70.0	0.3	69.8	-0.3	69.8	0.0	69.7	-0.1

Source: U.S. Department of Labor, Bureau of Labor Statistics, Division of Industry Prices and Price Indexes. n.e.c. stands for not elsewhere classified. - indicates no data collected for period or unavailable.

Other Household Durable Goods
Producer Price Index
Base 1982 = 100

For 1947-2001. Columns headed % show percentile change in the index from the previous period for which an index is available.

Year	Jan Index	%	Feb Index	%	Mar Index	%	Apr Index	%	May Index	%	Jun Index	%	Jul Index	%	Aug Index	%	Sep Index	%	Oct Index	%	Nov Index	%	Dec Index	%
1947	19.5	-	19.4	-0.5	19.5	0.5	19.5	0.0	19.5	0.0	19.5	0.0	19.4	-0.5	19.4	0.0	19.5	0.5	19.5	0.0	19.5	0.0	19.6	0.5
1948	19.5	-0.5	19.5	0.0	19.5	0.0	19.5	0.0	19.6	0.5	19.6	0.0	19.9	1.5	20.2	1.5	20.2	0.0	20.5	1.5	20.8	1.5	21.0	1.0
1949	21.1	0.5	21.1	0.0	21.1	0.0	21.1	0.0	21.0	-0.5	21.0	0.0	20.9	-0.5	20.9	0.0	20.8	-0.5	20.8	0.0	20.8	0.0	20.8	0.0
1950	21.0	1.0	21.0	0.0	21.0	0.0	21.0	0.0	21.0	0.0	21.0	0.0	21.1	0.5	21.2	0.5	21.4	0.9	21.7	1.4	22.0	1.4	22.3	1.4	22.7	1.8
1951	23.0	1.3	23.1	0.4	23.1	0.0	23.1	0.0	23.1	0.0	23.1	0.0	23.1	0.0	23.1	0.0	23.2	0.4	23.2	0.0	23.2	0.0	23.2	0.0
1952	23.2	0.0	23.2	0.0	23.2	0.0	23.3	0.4	23.2	-0.4	23.2	0.0	23.3	0.4	23.3	0.0	23.3	0.0	23.3	0.0	23.3	0.0	23.4	0.4
1953	23.8	1.7	24.0	0.8	24.0	0.0	24.0	0.0	24.0	0.0	24.0	0.0	24.4	1.7	24.4	0.0	24.4	0.0	24.5	0.4	24.7	0.8	24.8	0.4
1954	24.9	0.4	24.9	0.0	24.9	0.0	25.0	0.4	25.0	0.0	25.0	0.0	25.0	0.0	25.0	0.0	25.0	0.0	25.2	0.8	25.3	0.4	25.3	0.0
1955	25.4	0.4	25.4	0.0	25.4	0.0	25.4	0.0	25.4	0.0	25.5	0.4	25.8	1.2	26.1	1.2	26.1	0.0	26.4	1.1	26.5	0.4	26.7	0.8
1956	26.9	0.7	27.1	0.7	27.1	0.0	27.0	-0.4	27.1	0.4	27.1	0.0	27.1	0.0	27.2	0.4	27.3	0.4	27.8	1.8	27.8	0.0	28.3	1.8
1957	28.3	0.0	28.4	0.4	28.4	0.0	28.4	0.0	28.6	0.7	28.7	0.3	28.7	0.0	28.7	0.0	28.8	0.3	28.9	0.3	29.0	0.3	29.3	1.0
1958	29.8	1.7	29.8	0.0	29.8	0.0	29.8	0.0	29.8	0.0	29.9	0.3	29.8	-0.3	29.7	-0.3	29.8	0.3	29.8	0.0	29.8	0.0	30.0	0.7
1959	30.0	0.0	30.1	0.3	30.1	0.0	30.1	0.0	30.2	0.3	30.2	0.0	30.3	0.3	30.2	-0.3	30.2	0.0	30.2	0.0	30.2	0.0	30.2	0.0
1960	30.7	1.7	30.8	0.3	30.8	0.0	30.8	0.0	30.8	0.0	30.8	0.0	30.9	0.3	30.9	0.0	30.9	0.0	30.9	0.0	30.9	0.0	30.9	0.0
1961	30.8	-0.3	30.7	-0.3	30.7	0.0	30.7	0.0	30.8	0.3	30.8	0.0	30.8	0.0	30.8	0.0	30.8	0.0	30.8	0.0	30.9	0.3	31.0	0.3
1962	31.3	1.0	31.2	-0.3	31.4	0.6	31.4	0.0	31.4	0.0	31.4	0.0	31.3	-0.3	31.2	-0.3	31.4	0.6	31.2	-0.6	31.2	0.0	31.2	0.0
1963	31.2	0.0	31.2	0.0	31.2	0.0	31.4	0.6	31.3	-0.3	31.5	0.6	31.6	0.3	31.5	-0.3	31.6	0.3	31.6	0.0	31.6	0.0	31.5	-0.3
1964	31.7	0.6	31.7	0.0	31.7	0.0	31.7	0.0	31.8	0.3	31.8	0.0	31.8	0.0	31.8	0.0	31.8	0.0	31.8	0.0	31.8	0.0	32.0	0.6
1965	32.2	0.6	32.2	0.0	32.2	0.0	32.2	0.0	32.2	0.0	32.2	0.0	32.2	0.0	32.1	-0.3	32.2	0.3	32.2	0.0	32.2	0.0	32.2	0.0
1966	32.5	0.9	32.6	0.3	32.6	0.0	32.6	0.0	32.6	0.0	32.6	0.0	33.1	1.5	33.1	0.0	33.3	0.6	33.6	0.9	33.6	0.0	33.7	0.3
1967	33.9	0.6	33.9	0.0	34.0	0.3	34.2	0.6	34.3	0.3	34.3	0.0	34.5	0.6	34.9	1.2	35.0	0.3	35.2	0.6	35.2	0.0	35.3	0.3
1968	36.5	3.4	36.6	0.3	36.7	0.3	36.8	0.3	36.7	-0.3	36.7	0.0	36.9	0.5	37.0	0.3	37.1	0.3	37.1	0.0	37.2	0.3	37.9	1.9
1969	38.1	0.5	38.2	0.3	38.3	0.3	38.4	0.3	38.4	0.0	38.5	0.3	38.7	0.5	38.7	0.0	38.8	0.3	38.9	0.3	38.8	-0.3	39.5	1.8
1970	39.5	0.0	39.9	1.0	39.8	-0.3	40.1	0.8	40.0	-0.2	40.1	0.2	40.1	0.0	40.1	0.0	40.4	0.7	40.3	-0.2	40.4	0.2	40.6	0.5
1971	41.2	1.5	41.4	0.5	41.4	0.0	41.5	0.2	41.5	0.0	41.5	0.0	42.1	1.4	42.2	0.2	42.2	0.0	42.1	-0.2	42.1	0.0	42.2	0.2
1972	42.3	0.2	42.9	1.4	43.0	0.2	43.0	0.0	43.2	0.5	43.4	0.5	43.7	0.7	43.8	0.2	43.9	0.2	43.9	0.0	43.9	0.0	43.9	0.0
1973	43.9	0.0	44.3	0.9	44.6	0.7	45.0	0.9	45.2	0.4	45.3	0.2	45.2	-0.2	45.2	0.0	45.1	-0.2	45.4	0.7	45.6	0.4	45.9	0.7
1974	46.3	0.9	47.2	1.9	48.1	1.9	49.2	2.3	50.2	2.0	50.8	1.2	52.3	3.0	52.6	0.6	53.3	1.3	55.1	3.4	55.5	0.7	56.1	1.1
1975	57.7	2.9	58.1	0.7	57.4	-1.2	58.1	1.2	58.1	0.0	58.1	0.0	58.1	0.0	58.0	-0.2	58.1	0.2	58.7	1.0	59.1	0.7	59.4	0.5
1976	60.6	2.0	60.9	0.5	61.0	0.2	61.1	0.2	61.4	0.5	61.4	0.0	61.7	0.5	62.1	0.6	62.9	1.3	62.9	0.0	63.2	0.5	63.4	0.3
1977	64.8	2.2	65.0	0.3	65.1	0.2	64.9	-0.3	65.5	0.9	65.6	0.2	65.9	0.5	66.1	0.3	66.1	0.0	66.3	0.3	66.5	0.3	66.9	0.6
1978	68.5	2.4	68.5	0.0	68.4	-0.1	68.4	0.0	69.3	1.3	69.9	0.9	70.9	1.4	70.7	-0.3	70.7	0.0	71.9	1.7	72.1	0.3	73.4	1.8
1979	74.7	1.8	74.9	0.3	75.3	0.5	75.6	0.4	75.9	0.4	76.3	0.5	77.3	1.3	78.3	1.3	79.8	1.9	84.9	6.4	85.8	1.1	87.9	2.4
1980	99.3	13.0	102.1	2.8	99.6	-2.4	92.4	-7.2	91.8	-0.6	92.1	0.3	93.8	1.8	95.4	1.7	95.5	0.1	97.4	2.0	97.2	-0.2	98.7	1.5
1981	96.4	-2.3	97.0	0.6	96.1	-0.9	95.2	-0.9	95.6	0.4	95.5	-0.1	97.5	2.1	97.1	-0.4	98.8	1.8	98.8	0.0	98.6	-0.2	98.9	0.3
1982	98.0	-0.9	98.1	0.1	98.5	0.4	98.8	0.3	98.7	-0.1	98.9	0.2	98.6	-0.3	100.9	2.3	101.4	0.5	102.5	1.1	102.7	0.2	103.1	0.4
1983	104.7	1.6	108.8	3.9	108.1	-0.6	107.8	-0.3	108.1	0.3	108.6	0.5	108.8	0.2	108.5	-0.3	108.7	0.2	108.5	-0.2	108.9	0.4	108.9	0.0
1984	109.9	0.9	109.5	-0.4	109.5	0.0	110.3	0.7	111.2	0.8	110.6	-0.5	110.1	-0.5	109.5	-0.5	109.5	0.0	109.8	0.3	110.8	0.9	110.8	0.0
1985	111.5	0.6	111.5	0.0	112.0	0.4	111.9	-0.1	111.7	-0.2	111.9	0.2	111.5	-0.4	111.4	-0.1	111.2	-0.2	111.9	0.6	111.8	-0.1	112.0	0.2
1986	112.6	0.5	112.1	-0.4	112.3	0.2	112.6	0.3	112.6	0.0	112.9	0.3	113.0	0.1	112.9	-0.1	113.1	0.2	113.1	0.0	113.3	0.2	113.6	0.3
1987	114.6	0.9	114.5	-0.1	114.7	0.2	114.7	0.0	115.2	0.4	115.3	0.1	115.6	0.3	115.8	0.2	115.8	0.0	116.2	0.3	116.3	0.1	116.6	0.3
1988	117.8	1.0	118.1	0.3	118.4	0.3	118.8	0.3	119.4	0.5	119.3	-0.1	119.8	0.4	120.5	0.6	120.9	0.3	121.2	0.2	121.4	0.2	121.8	0.3
1989	122.7	0.7	123.5	0.7	124.1	0.5	126.2	1.7	126.7	0.4	127.9	0.9	128.5	0.5	129.0	0.4	129.2	0.2	129.7	0.4	129.6	-0.1	129.7	0.1
1990	130.9	0.9	131.5	0.5	130.5	-0.8	131.1	0.5	130.7	-0.3	130.9	0.2	130.0	-0.7	130.4	0.3	130.7	0.2	130.8	0.1	130.7	-0.1	130.7	0.0
1991	132.1	1.1	132.6	0.4	133.5	0.7	134.6	0.8	134.5	-0.1	134.6	0.1	134.8	0.1	134.8	0.0	134.7	-0.1	134.7	0.0	134.8	0.1	135.2	0.3

[Continued]

Other Household Durable Goods
Producer Price Index
Base 1982 = 100
[Continued]

For 1947-2001. Columns headed % show percentile change in the index from the previous period for which an index is available.

Year	Jan		Feb		Mar		Apr		May		Jun		Jul		Aug		Sep		Oct		Nov		Dec	
	Index	%	Index	%	Index	%	Index	%	Index	%	Index	%	Index	%	Index	%	Index	%	Index	%	Index	%	Index	%
1992	136.1	0.7	136.6	0.4	137.2	0.4	136.1	-0.8	136.2	0.1	136.5	0.2	136.5	0.0	136.7	0.1	136.9	0.1	136.6	-0.2	136.5	-0.1	136.7	0.1
1993	137.3	0.4	137.4	0.1	137.8	0.3	137.9	0.1	137.8	-0.1	137.8	0.0	137.8	0.0	138.0	0.1	138.2	0.1	138.5	0.2	138.6	0.1	138.7	0.1
1994	139.4	0.5	139.4	0.0	139.7	0.2	139.6	-0.1	140.0	0.3	140.9	0.6	141.1	0.1	141.5	0.3	141.5	0.0	141.9	0.3	142.2	0.2	142.4	0.1
1995	143.4	0.7	144.1	0.5	144.5	0.3	144.5	0.0	144.8	0.2	144.8	0.0	145.0	0.1	145.1	0.1	145.2	0.1	145.3	0.1	145.6	0.2	145.7	0.1
1996	146.9	0.8	147.3	0.3	147.6	0.2	147.7	0.1	148.3	0.4	148.4	0.1	148.4	0.0	148.4	0.0	148.4	0.0	148.4	0.0	148.5	0.1	148.9	0.3
1997	149.2	0.2	149.3	0.1	149.7	0.3	150.0	0.2	150.2	0.1	150.2	0.0	149.9	-0.2	150.1	0.1	149.4	-0.5	149.3	-0.1	149.4	0.1	149.6	0.1
1998	150.4	0.5	150.6	0.1	151.0	0.3	151.0	0.0	151.2	0.1	151.3	0.1	151.2	-0.1	151.4	0.1	151.6	0.1	151.6	0.0	151.7	0.1	151.8	0.1
1999	152.1	0.2	152.0	-0.1	152.1	0.1	152.4	0.2	152.8	0.3	152.6	-0.1	152.9	0.2	153.0	0.1	153.0	0.0	153.1	0.1	153.2	0.1	153.4	0.1
2000	154.6	0.8	154.7	0.1	154.9	0.1	155.0	0.1	155.1	0.1	155.1	0.0	155.5	0.3	155.9	0.3	156.1	0.1	156.4	0.2	156.5	0.1	156.5	0.0
2001	156.9	0.3	157.1	0.1	157.1	0.0	157.1	0.0	157.3	0.1	157.3	0.0	157.2	-0.1	157.4	0.1	157.6	0.1	157.5	-0.1	157.6	0.1	157.3	-0.2

Source: U.S. Department of Labor, Bureau of Labor Statistics, Division of Industry Prices and Price Indexes. n.e.c. stands for not elsewhere classified. - indicates no data collected for period or unavailable.

NONMETALLIC MINERAL PRODUCTS
Producer Price Index
Base 1982 = 100

For 1926-2001. Columns headed % show percentile change in the index from the previous period for which an index is available.

Year	Jan Index	%	Feb Index	%	Mar Index	%	Apr Index	%	May Index	%	Jun Index	%	Jul Index	%	Aug Index	%	Sep Index	%	Oct Index	%	Nov Index	%	Dec Index	%
1926	16.4	-	16.4	0.0	16.5	0.6	16.5	0.0	16.4	-0.6	16.4	0.0	16.4	0.0	16.3	-0.6	16.2	-0.6	16.4	1.2	16.4	0.0	16.4	0.0
1927	16.1	-1.8	15.9	-1.2	15.8	-0.6	15.8	0.0	15.8	0.0	15.8	0.0	15.8	0.0	15.7	-0.6	15.6	-0.6	15.6	0.0	15.3	-1.9	15.4	0.7
1928	15.5	0.6	15.4	-0.6	15.2	-1.3	16.0	5.3	16.3	1.9	16.6	1.8	16.6	0.0	16.6	0.0	16.6	0.0	16.6	0.0	16.6	0.0	16.3	-1.8
1929	16.1	-1.2	16.1	0.0	16.0	-0.6	16.1	0.6	16.1	0.0	16.0	-0.6	16.1	0.6	16.0	-0.6	15.8	-1.2	15.7	-0.6	15.8	0.6	16.1	1.9
1930	16.1	0.0	16.1	0.0	16.1	0.0	16.1	0.0	16.0	-0.6	15.7	-1.9	15.8	0.6	15.8	0.0	15.8	0.0	15.9	0.6	16.0	0.6	15.8	-1.2
1931	15.6	-1.3	15.6	0.0	15.3	-1.9	15.1	-1.3	15.0	-0.7	14.9	-0.7	14.5	-2.7	14.6	0.7	14.6	0.0	14.6	0.0	14.5	-0.7	14.3	-1.4
1932	14.1	-1.4	14.0	-0.7	14.0	0.0	13.9	-0.7	13.5	-2.9	13.4	-0.7	13.7	2.2	13.8	0.7	14.1	2.2	14.1	0.0	14.2	0.7	14.3	0.7
1933	14.2	-0.7	14.1	-0.7	14.1	0.0	14.1	0.0	14.2	0.7	14.4	1.4	14.8	2.8	15.1	2.0	15.2	0.7	15.5	2.0	15.6	0.6	15.6	0.0
1934	15.8	1.3	15.8	0.0	15.7	-0.6	15.6	-0.6	15.6	0.0	15.8	1.3	15.8	0.0	15.7	-0.6	15.7	0.0	15.7	0.0	15.7	0.0	15.7	0.0
1935	15.8	0.6	15.7	-0.6	15.7	0.0	15.7	0.0	15.8	0.6	15.8	0.0	15.8	0.0	15.7	-0.6	15.7	0.0	15.7	0.0	15.7	0.0	15.6	-0.6
1936	15.6	0.0	15.6	0.0	15.6	0.0	15.7	0.6	15.8	0.6	15.8	0.0	15.8	0.0	15.8	0.0	15.8	0.0	15.8	0.0	15.9	0.6	16.0	0.6
1937	16.0	0.0	16.1	0.6	16.1	0.0	16.2	0.6	16.3	0.6	16.2	-0.6	16.3	0.6	16.3	0.0	16.1	-1.2	16.1	0.0	16.0	-0.6	15.8	-1.2
1938	15.8	0.0	15.8	0.0	15.6	-1.3	15.6	0.0	15.6	0.0	15.6	0.0	15.7	0.6	15.6	-0.6	15.6	0.0	15.7	0.6	15.3	-2.5	15.4	0.7
1939	15.3	-0.6	15.3	0.0	15.3	0.0	15.4	0.7	15.3	-0.6	15.3	0.0	15.3	0.0	15.2	-0.7	15.3	0.7	15.3	0.0	15.3	0.0	15.4	0.7
1940	15.4	0.0	15.4	0.0	15.4	0.0	15.3	-0.6	15.3	0.0	15.3	0.0	15.3	0.0	15.3	0.0	15.3	0.0	15.3	0.0	15.3	0.0	15.3	0.0
1941	15.4	0.7	15.4	0.0	15.4	0.0	15.4	0.0	15.5	0.6	15.6	0.6	15.6	0.0	15.8	1.3	15.8	0.0	16.0	1.3	16.3	1.9	16.2	-0.6
1942	16.2	0.0	16.2	0.0	16.3	0.6	16.3	0.0	16.3	0.0	16.3	0.0	16.3	0.0	16.3	0.0	16.3	0.0	16.3	0.0	16.3	0.0	16.3	0.0
1943	16.3	0.0	16.3	0.0	16.3	0.0	16.3	0.0	16.3	0.0	16.3	0.0	16.3	0.0	16.3	0.0	16.5	1.2	16.5	0.0	16.5	0.0	16.5	0.0
1944	16.5	0.0	16.5	0.0	16.5	0.0	16.5	0.0	16.6	0.6	16.6	0.0	16.7	0.6	16.7	0.0	16.8	0.6	17.0	1.2	17.0	0.0	17.0	0.0
1945	17.2	1.2	17.3	0.6	17.3	0.0	17.3	0.0	17.3	0.0	17.3	0.0	17.4	0.6	17.4	0.0	17.5	0.6	17.6	0.6	17.7	0.6	17.7	0.0
1946	17.9	1.1	17.9	0.0	18.0	0.6	18.1	0.6	18.2	0.6	18.3	0.5	18.5	1.1	18.8	1.6	18.9	0.5	19.0	0.5	19.2	1.1	19.5	1.6
1947	20.0	2.6	20.1	0.5	20.4	1.5	20.6	1.0	20.6	0.0	20.6	0.0	20.7	0.5	20.7	0.0	20.8	0.5	21.0	1.0	21.2	1.0	21.4	0.9
1948	21.8	1.9	21.9	0.5	21.9	0.0	22.0	0.5	22.0	0.0	22.1	0.5	22.6	2.3	22.8	0.9	22.8	0.0	22.9	0.4	22.9	0.0	22.9	0.0
1949	23.0	0.4	23.0	0.0	23.0	0.0	23.0	0.0	23.0	0.0	23.0	0.0	22.9	-0.4	23.0	0.4	23.0	0.0	23.0	0.0	23.0	0.0	23.0	0.0
1950	23.1	0.4	23.1	0.0	23.2	0.4	23.2	0.0	23.1	-0.4	23.2	0.4	23.2	0.0	23.4	0.9	23.6	0.9	24.1	2.1	24.4	1.2	24.6	0.8
1951	25.0	1.6	25.0	0.0	25.0	0.0	25.0	0.0	25.0	0.0	25.0	0.0	25.0	0.0	25.0	0.0	25.0	0.0	25.0	0.0	25.0	0.0	24.8	-0.8
1952	24.9	0.4	24.9	0.0	24.9	0.0	24.8	-0.4	24.9	0.4	25.0	0.4	25.0	0.0	25.0	0.0	25.0	0.0	25.2	0.8	25.2	0.0	25.2	0.0
1953	25.2	0.0	25.2	0.0	25.3	0.4	25.7	1.6	25.8	0.4	26.0	0.8	26.3	1.2	26.3	0.0	26.5	0.8	26.5	0.0	26.6	0.4	26.6	0.0
1954	26.6	0.0	26.6	0.0	26.6	0.0	26.6	0.0	26.3	-1.1	26.2	-0.4	26.5	1.1	26.5	0.0	26.8	1.1	26.8	0.0	26.8	0.0	26.8	0.0
1955	26.9	0.4	26.8	-0.4	26.8	0.0	26.9	0.4	27.1	0.7	27.2	0.4	27.6	1.5	27.8	0.7	27.8	0.0	27.9	0.4	27.5	-1.4	27.6	0.4
1956	28.0	1.4	28.0	0.0	28.1	0.4	28.3	0.7	28.3	0.0	28.4	0.4	28.7	1.1	28.8	0.3	28.9	0.3	28.9	0.0	28.9	0.0	28.9	0.0
1957	29.0	0.3	29.2	0.7	29.3	0.3	29.6	1.0	29.7	0.3	29.7	0.0	29.8	0.3	29.8	0.0	29.8	0.0	29.8	0.0	29.8	0.0	29.9	0.3
1958	30.0	0.3	30.0	0.0	29.8	-0.7	29.8	0.0	29.8	0.0	29.8	0.0	29.8	0.0	29.8	0.0	30.1	1.0	30.1	0.0	30.1	0.0	30.1	0.0
1959	30.2	0.3	30.3	0.3	30.3	0.0	30.4	0.3	30.4	0.0	30.2	-0.7	30.3	0.3	30.2	-0.3	30.3	0.3	30.3	0.0	30.3	0.0	30.3	0.0
1960	30.4	0.3	30.4	0.0	30.4	0.0	30.4	0.0	30.3	-0.3	30.3	0.0	30.3	0.0	30.3	0.0	30.4	0.3	30.4	0.0	30.3	-0.3	30.3	0.0
1961	30.5	0.7	30.4	-0.3	30.5	0.3	30.5	0.0	30.5	0.0	30.4	-0.3	30.4	0.0	30.5	0.3	30.5	0.0	30.6	0.3	30.5	-0.3	30.4	-0.3
1962	30.5	0.3	30.6	0.3	30.6	0.0	30.7	0.3	30.6	-0.3	30.5	-0.3	30.4	-0.3	30.4	0.0	30.4	0.0	30.4	0.0	30.4	0.0	30.4	0.0
1963	30.4	0.0	30.4	0.0	30.4	0.0	30.4	0.0	30.3	-0.3	30.3	0.0	30.2	-0.3	30.2	0.0	30.3	0.3	30.3	0.0	30.3	0.0	30.3	0.0
1964	30.3	0.0	30.3	0.0	30.3	0.0	30.3	0.0	30.3	0.0	30.4	0.3	30.4	0.0	30.4	0.0	30.5	0.3	30.5	0.0	30.5	0.0	30.4	-0.3
1965	30.4	0.0	30.5	0.3	30.5	0.0	30.5	0.0	30.5	0.0	30.5	0.0	30.4	-0.3	30.4	0.0	30.4	0.0	30.4	0.0	30.4	0.0	30.4	0.0
1966	30.5	0.3	30.6	0.3	30.6	0.0	30.6	0.0	30.7	0.3	30.7	0.0	30.8	0.3	30.8	0.0	30.9	0.3	30.9	0.0	30.9	0.0	30.9	0.0
1967	31.1	0.6	31.1	0.0	31.1	0.0	31.2	0.3	31.0	-0.6	31.1	0.3	31.2	0.3	31.3	0.3	31.3	0.0	31.4	0.3	31.5	0.3	31.6	0.3
1968	31.9	0.9	32.0	0.3	32.2	0.6	32.2	0.0	32.3	0.3	32.4	0.3	32.5	0.3	32.5	0.0	32.5	0.0	32.6	0.3	32.7	0.3	32.7	0.0
1969	33.1	1.2	33.3	0.6	33.3	0.0	33.5	0.6	33.6	0.3	33.6	0.0	33.7	0.3	33.7	0.0	33.8	0.3	33.9	0.3	33.9	0.0	34.1	0.6
1970	34.8	2.1	34.9	0.3	34.9	0.0	35.3	1.1	35.1	-0.6	35.1	0.0	35.2	0.3	35.3	0.3	35.3	0.0	35.5	0.6	35.8	0.8	36.0	0.6

[Continued]

NONMETALLIC MINERAL PRODUCTS
Producer Price Index
Base 1982 = 100
[Continued]

For 1926-2001. Columns headed % show percentile change in the index from the previous period for which an index is available.

Year	Jan Index	%	Feb Index	%	Mar Index	%	Apr Index	%	May Index	%	Jun Index	%	Jul Index	%	Aug Index	%	Sep Index	%	Oct Index	%	Nov Index	%	Dec Index	%
1971	37.1	3.1	37.2	0.3	37.8	1.6	38.0	0.5	38.1	0.3	38.3	0.5	38.5	0.5	38.7	0.5	38.7	0.0	38.7	0.0	38.7	0.0	38.8	0.3
1972	38.8	0.0	38.9	0.3	39.0	0.3	39.2	0.5	39.3	0.3	39.3	0.0	39.4	0.3	39.6	0.5	39.6	0.0	39.7	0.3	39.8	0.3	39.8	0.0
1973	40.0	0.5	40.1	0.2	40.3	0.5	40.6	0.7	40.7	0.2	40.9	0.5	40.6	-0.7	40.6	0.0	40.6	0.0	40.9	0.7	41.1	0.5	41.4	0.7
1974	43.3	4.6	44.4	2.5	45.0	1.4	45.8	1.8	47.1	2.8	47.6	1.1	48.8	2.5	49.2	0.8	49.9	1.4	50.7	1.6	51.0	0.6	51.3	0.6
1975	52.6	2.5	53.2	1.1	53.4	0.4	54.0	1.1	54.1	0.2	54.1	0.0	54.6	0.9	54.9	0.5	55.0	0.2	55.3	0.5	55.5	0.4	55.6	0.2
1976	56.6	1.8	56.7	0.2	57.1	0.7	57.9	1.4	58.1	0.3	58.2	0.2	58.5	0.5	58.7	0.3	58.9	0.3	59.1	0.3	59.2	0.2	59.2	0.0
1977	60.1	1.5	60.5	0.7	60.9	0.7	62.0	1.8	62.2	0.3	62.6	0.6	63.0	0.6	63.3	0.5	63.8	0.8	64.1	0.5	64.2	0.2	64.5	0.5
1978	66.5	3.1	67.2	1.1	67.4	0.3	68.2	1.2	68.5	0.4	69.3	1.2	70.2	1.3	71.0	1.1	71.3	0.4	71.6	0.4	71.8	0.3	72.2	0.6
1979	74.4	3.0	75.1	0.9	75.2	0.1	76.0	1.1	76.7	0.9	77.1	0.5	77.9	1.0	78.1	0.3	79.5	1.8	80.0	0.6	80.4	0.5	81.1	0.9
1980	83.8	3.3	85.6	2.1	86.4	0.9	88.6	2.5	88.7	0.1	88.5	-0.2	88.9	0.5	89.3	0.4	89.6	0.3	90.1	0.6	90.2	0.1	90.9	0.8
1981	92.6	1.9	93.1	0.5	94.0	1.0	97.0	3.2	97.4	0.4	97.9	0.5	98.2	0.3	98.1	-0.1	97.8	-0.3	97.8	0.0	98.0	0.2	97.9	-0.1
1982	98.6	0.7	99.6	1.0	99.9	0.3	100.0	0.1	100.3	0.3	100.2	-0.1	100.3	0.1	100.1	-0.2	100.3	0.2	100.3	0.0	100.3	0.0	100.1	-0.2
1983	100.4	0.3	100.7	0.3	100.6	-0.1	101.2	0.6	101.2	0.0	101.4	0.2	101.5	0.1	101.9	0.4	102.2	0.3	102.4	0.2	102.7	0.3	102.7	0.0
1984	103.1	0.4	103.7	0.6	104.1	0.4	104.9	0.8	105.4	0.5	105.6	0.2	106.1	0.5	106.4	0.3	106.3	-0.1	106.2	-0.1	106.0	-0.2	106.2	0.2
1985	106.7	0.5	107.0	0.3	107.4	0.4	107.9	0.5	108.7	0.7	109.1	0.4	109.2	0.1	109.4	0.2	109.3	-0.1	109.5	0.2	109.5	0.0	109.6	0.1
1986	110.1	0.5	110.0	-0.1	110.1	0.1	110.2	0.1	110.4	0.2	110.2	-0.2	110.2	0.0	109.9	-0.3	109.7	-0.2	109.7	0.0	109.7	0.0	109.3	-0.4
1987	109.3	0.0	109.6	0.3	109.7	0.1	109.9	0.2	109.9	0.0	110.1	0.2	110.1	0.0	109.9	-0.2	110.0	0.1	110.4	0.4	110.5	0.1	110.4	-0.1
1988	110.8	0.4	110.9	0.1	110.9	0.0	111.0	-0.1	111.2	0.2	111.3	0.1	111.1	-0.2	111.1	0.0	111.3	0.2	111.4	0.1	111.5	0.1	111.7	0.2
1989	111.8	0.1	111.8	0.0	112.0	0.2	112.6	0.5	112.7	0.1	112.8	0.1	112.8	0.0	112.8	0.0	112.9	0.1	113.0	0.1	113.1	0.1	113.2	0.1
1990	113.8	0.5	113.9	0.1	114.2	0.3	114.3	0.1	114.5	0.2	114.6	0.1	114.6	0.0	114.7	0.1	115.0	0.3	115.3	0.3	115.8	0.4	115.8	0.0
1991	116.9	0.9	117.2	0.3	117.4	0.2	117.3	-0.1	117.3	0.0	117.3	0.0	117.2	-0.1	117.1	-0.1	117.2	0.1	117.4	0.2	117.2	-0.2	117.1	-0.1
1992	117.2	0.1	117.1	-0.1	117.3	0.2	116.9	-0.3	116.9	0.0	117.0	0.1	117.1	0.1	117.4	0.3	117.4	0.0	117.4	0.0	117.7	0.3	117.8	0.1
1993	118.4	0.5	118.6	0.2	118.9	0.3	119.6	0.6	119.7	0.1	120.0	0.3	120.2	0.2	120.5	0.2	120.8	0.2	121.0	0.2	121.2	0.2	121.4	0.2
1994	121.8	0.3	122.2	0.3	122.9	0.6	123.4	0.4	123.7	0.2	124.3	0.5	124.5	0.2	124.8	0.2	125.1	0.2	125.5	0.3	125.8	0.2	126.0	0.2
1995	126.9	0.7	127.5	0.5	128.2	0.5	129.3	0.9	129.4	0.1	129.3	-0.1	129.3	0.0	129.4	0.1	129.6	0.2	129.5	-0.1	129.8	0.2	129.7	-0.1
1996	130.0	0.2	130.2	0.2	130.2	0.0	130.5	0.2	130.8	0.2	130.9	0.1	131.2	0.2	131.2	0.0	131.6	0.3	131.7	0.1	132.0	0.2	131.9	-0.1
1997	132.3	0.3	132.5	0.2	132.6	0.1	133.3	-0.5	133.3	0.0	133.4	0.1	133.4	0.0	133.5	0.1	133.5	0.0	133.6	0.1	133.7	0.1	133.7	0.0
1998	133.6	-0.1	133.8	0.1	133.9	0.1	134.9	0.7	135.2	0.2	135.6	0.3	136.0	0.3	136.2	0.1	136.4	0.1	136.6	0.1	136.5	-0.1	136.6	0.1
1999	136.9	0.2	137.6	0.5	137.8	0.1	138.3	0.4	138.5	0.1	138.8	0.2	138.9	0.1	139.5	0.4	139.6	0.1	140.0	0.3	140.3	0.2	140.5	0.1
2000	141.5	0.7	141.7	0.1	142.1	0.3	142.7	0.4	143.0	0.2	143.1	0.1	142.9	-0.1	142.7	-0.1	142.8	0.1	142.6	-0.1	142.4	-0.1	142.3	-0.1
2001	142.8	0.4	143.6	0.6	143.6	0.0	144.0	0.3	144.0	0.0	143.8	-0.1	144.3	0.3	144.5	0.1	144.8	0.2	145.1	0.2	145.7	0.4	145.3	-0.3

Source: U.S. Department of Labor, Bureau of Labor Statistics, Division of Industry Prices and Price Indexes. n.e.c. stands for not elsewhere classified. - indicates no data collected for period or unavailable.

Glass
Producer Price Index
Base 1982 = 100

For 1947-2001. Columns headed % show percentile change in the index from the previous period for which an index is available.

Year	Jan Index	%	Feb Index	%	Mar Index	%	Apr Index	%	May Index	%	Jun Index	%	Jul Index	%	Aug Index	%	Sep Index	%	Oct Index	%	Nov Index	%	Dec Index	%
1947	28.9	-	28.9	0.0	30.0	3.8	30.5	1.7	30.5	0.0	30.5	0.0	30.5	0.0	30.5	0.0	30.5	0.0	30.5	0.0	30.5	0.0	30.5	0.0
1948	30.7	0.7	30.5	-0.7	30.5	0.0	30.7	0.7	30.5	-0.7	30.5	0.0	31.8	4.3	33.1	4.1	33.1	0.0	33.3	0.6	33.5	0.6	33.5	0.0
1949	33.5	0.0	33.5	0.0	33.4	-0.3	33.3	-0.3	33.3	0.0	33.3	0.0	33.3	0.0	33.3	0.0	33.3	0.0	33.3	0.0	33.3	0.0	33.3	0.0
1950	33.3	0.0	33.1	-0.6	33.9	2.4	34.0	0.3	33.6	-1.2	33.6	0.0	33.6	0.0	33.6	0.0	33.6	0.0	35.0	4.2	36.3	3.7	36.3	0.0
1951	36.3	0.0	36.3	0.0	36.3	0.0	36.3	0.0	36.3	0.0	36.3	0.0	36.3	0.0	36.3	0.0	36.3	0.0	36.3	0.0	36.3	0.0	36.3	0.0
1952	36.3	0.0	36.3	0.0	36.3	0.0	36.3	0.0	36.3	0.0	36.3	0.0	36.3	0.0	36.3	0.0	36.3	0.0	36.3	0.0	36.3	0.0	36.3	0.0
1953	36.3	0.0	36.3	0.0	37.0	1.9	37.0	0.0	37.0	0.0	39.1	5.7	39.6	1.3	39.6	0.0	39.6	0.0	39.6	0.0	39.6	0.0	39.6	0.0
1954	39.6	0.0	39.6	0.0	39.6	0.0	39.6	0.0	39.6	0.0	39.6	0.0	39.6	0.0	39.6	0.0	39.4	-0.5	39.4	0.0	39.4	0.0	39.4	0.0
1955	39.4	0.0	39.4	0.0	39.4	0.0	39.7	0.8	39.7	0.0	40.1	1.0	41.7	4.0	41.7	0.0	41.7	0.0	42.3	1.4	41.7	-1.4	41.7	0.0
1956	41.7	0.0	41.7	0.0	41.7	0.0	41.7	0.0	41.7	0.0	41.9	0.5	42.9	2.4	43.1	0.5	43.1	0.0	43.1	0.0	43.1	0.0	43.1	0.0
1957	43.1	0.0	43.1	0.0	43.1	0.0	43.1	0.0	43.1	0.0	43.1	0.0	43.1	0.0	43.1	0.0	43.1	0.0	43.1	0.0	43.1	0.0	43.1	0.0
1958	43.1	0.0	43.1	0.0	43.1	0.0	43.1	0.0	43.1	0.0	43.1	0.0	43.1	0.0	43.0	-0.2	42.9	-0.2	42.9	0.0	42.9	0.0	42.9	0.0
1959	42.9	0.0	42.9	0.0	42.9	0.0	42.9	0.0	42.9	0.0	43.0	0.2	43.0	0.0	43.0	0.0	43.0	0.0	43.0	0.0	43.0	0.0	43.0	0.0
1960	43.0	0.0	43.0	0.0	43.0	0.0	43.0	0.0	41.4	-3.7	41.4	0.0	41.4	0.0	41.4	0.0	42.0	1.4	42.0	0.0	42.0	0.0	42.0	0.0
1961	42.0	0.0	42.0	0.0	42.0	0.0	42.0	0.0	42.0	0.0	41.4	-1.4	41.4	0.0	41.4	0.0	41.4	0.0	41.4	0.0	41.4	0.0	41.4	0.0
1962	41.4	0.0	41.4	0.0	41.4	0.0	42.1	1.7	42.2	0.2	42.2	0.0	42.2	0.0	41.6	-1.4	41.6	0.0	41.6	0.0	41.6	0.0	41.6	0.0
1963	41.6	0.0	41.6	0.0	41.6	0.0	41.6	0.0	41.6	0.0	41.6	0.0	41.6	0.0	42.6	2.4	43.0	0.9	43.8	1.9	43.5	-0.7	43.5	0.0
1964	43.5	0.0	43.5	0.0	43.8	0.7	44.2	0.9	44.1	-0.2	44.1	0.0	44.1	0.0	44.4	0.7	44.4	0.0	44.4	0.0	44.4	0.0	43.9	-1.1
1965	43.9	0.0	43.8	-0.2	43.8	0.0	43.8	0.0	43.8	0.0	43.8	0.0	43.1	-1.6	43.1	0.0	43.0	-0.2	43.0	0.0	43.0	0.0	43.0	0.0
1966	43.0	0.0	43.0	0.0	42.7	-0.7	42.9	0.5	43.1	0.5	43.1	0.0	43.2	0.2	42.9	-0.7	43.3	0.9	43.9	1.4	44.5	1.4	44.5	0.0
1967	-	-	-	-	-	-	-	-	-	-	-	-	-	-	-	-	-	-	-	-	-	-	-	-
1968	-	-	-	-	-	-	-	-	-	-	-	-	-	-	-	-	-	-	-	-	-	-	-	-
1969	-	-	-	-	-	-	-	-	-	-	-	-	-	-	-	-	-	-	-	-	-	-	-	-
1970	-	-	-	-	-	-	-	-	-	-	-	-	-	-	-	-	-	-	-	-	-	-	-	-
1971	55.6	24.9	55.6	0.0	56.6	1.8	57.0	0.7	55.3	-3.0	55.3	0.0	55.3	0.0	55.3	0.0	55.3	0.0	55.3	0.0	55.3	0.0	55.4	0.2
1972	55.8	0.7	55.8	0.0	55.3	-0.9	54.7	-1.1	54.9	0.4	54.7	-0.4	55.0	0.5	55.5	0.9	55.5	0.0	55.3	-0.4	55.3	0.0	55.3	0.0
1973	55.3	0.0	55.3	0.0	56.0	1.3	56.0	0.0	56.2	0.4	55.2	-1.8	53.2	-3.6	53.2	0.0	53.4	0.4	53.4	0.0	54.5	2.1	55.8	2.4
1974	56.3	0.9	56.3	0.0	56.3	0.0	56.3	0.0	56.6	0.5	57.8	2.1	58.1	0.5	58.1	0.0	60.1	3.4	60.6	0.8	60.5	-0.2	60.9	0.7
1975	60.9	0.0	60.9	0.0	60.9	0.0	62.5	2.6	62.3	-0.3	61.4	-1.4	63.3	3.1	63.8	0.8	63.8	0.0	64.8	1.6	64.7	-0.2	64.7	0.0
1976	64.7	0.0	64.7	0.0	65.7	1.5	67.6	2.9	67.6	0.0	68.3	1.0	69.0	1.0	69.0	0.0	69.0	0.0	69.0	0.0	68.9	-0.1	68.9	0.0
1977	69.1	0.3	72.0	4.2	72.0	0.0	72.0	0.0	72.2	0.3	73.0	1.1	72.3	-1.0	72.8	0.7	72.8	0.0	73.4	0.8	74.1	1.0	76.0	2.6
1978	76.0	0.0	76.9	1.2	76.9	0.0	78.0	1.4	78.0	0.0	78.0	0.0	78.2	0.3	78.4	0.3	78.4	0.0	78.4	0.0	78.5	0.1	80.8	2.9
1979	81.8	1.2	82.7	1.1	82.7	0.0	82.7	0.0	82.7	0.0	83.1	0.5	83.1	0.0	83.1	0.0	83.3	0.2	83.4	0.1	83.7	0.4	84.2	0.6
1980	86.3	2.5	86.3	0.0	86.4	0.1	88.2	2.1	88.2	0.0	87.4	-0.9	87.7	0.3	90.1	2.7	90.2	0.1	90.6	0.4	91.7	1.2	91.7	0.0
1981	92.1	0.4	92.3	0.2	92.5	0.2	94.9	2.6	94.9	0.0	94.9	0.0	98.6	3.9	98.6	0.0	98.6	0.0	98.6	0.0	98.6	0.0	97.6	-1.0
1982	97.6	0.0	97.6	0.0	97.6	0.0	97.6	0.0	102.2	4.7	102.2	0.0	102.1	-0.1	99.8	-2.3	99.8	0.0	99.8	0.0	101.7	1.9	101.7	0.0
1983	103.7	2.0	103.7	0.0	103.7	0.0	103.7	0.0	103.7	0.0	103.7	0.0	103.7	0.0	103.7	0.0	103.8	0.1	104.5	0.7	104.8	0.3	104.7	-0.1
1984	107.0	2.2	107.1	0.1	106.8	-0.3	107.1	0.3	105.9	-1.1	106.0	0.1	106.0	0.0	103.9	-2.0	104.2	0.3	104.3	0.1	104.1	-0.2	104.2	0.1
1985	103.4	-0.8	103.3	-0.1	103.3	0.0	103.8	0.5	104.6	0.8	104.5	-0.1	105.1	0.6	105.4	0.3	105.2	-0.2	105.8	0.6	106.0	0.2	106.2	0.2
1986	106.8	0.6	106.8	0.0	106.8	0.0	107.0	0.2	106.9	-0.1	106.9	0.0	108.1	1.1	107.8	-0.3	107.8	0.0	107.8	0.0	108.1	0.3	108.2	0.1
1987	108.2	0.0	108.3	0.1	109.1	0.7	109.2	0.1	109.0	-0.2	109.5	0.5	109.7	0.2	109.8	0.1	109.6	-0.2	110.1	0.5	110.0	-0.1	110.7	0.6
1988	110.8	0.1	111.2	0.4	111.7	0.4	111.9	0.2	112.3	0.4	111.9	-0.4	112.3	0.4	112.7	0.4	113.1	0.4	113.0	-0.1	113.2	0.2	113.9	0.6
1989	113.4	-0.4	113.1	-0.3	112.6	-0.4	112.8	0.2	113.7	0.8	113.2	-0.4	113.3	0.1	113.0	-0.3	113.2	0.2	113.5	0.3	113.2	-0.3	113.7	0.4
1990	114.8	1.0	114.5	-0.3	114.3	-0.2	114.0	-0.3	114.1	0.1	113.9	-0.2	113.6	-0.3	113.2	-0.4	113.3	0.1	113.4	0.1	113.4	0.0	113.3	-0.1
1991	113.9	0.5	113.9	0.0	114.4	0.4	114.2	-0.2	114.3	0.1	113.7	-0.5	113.4	-0.3	114.0	0.5	115.0	0.9	115.8	0.7	115.2	-0.5	115.1	-0.1

[Continued]

Glass
Producer Price Index
Base 1982 = 100
[Continued]

For 1947-2001. Columns headed % show percentile change in the index from the previous period for which an index is available.

Year	Jan		Feb		Mar		Apr		May		Jun		Jul		Aug		Sep		Oct		Nov		Dec	
	Index	%	Index	%	Index	%	Index	%	Index	%	Index	%	Index	%	Index	%	Index	%	Index	%	Index	%	Index	%
1992	115.4	0.3	114.8	-0.5	114.9	0.1	115.3	0.3	115.3	0.0	115.2	-0.1	115.2	0.0	116.6	1.2	116.4	-0.2	116.0	-0.3	116.1	0.1	117.1	0.9
1993	116.3	-0.7	116.8	0.4	116.6	-0.2	116.9	0.3	117.0	0.1	117.1	0.1	117.0	-0.1	117.4	0.3	117.2	-0.2	116.5	-0.6	117.1	0.5	117.2	0.1
1994	117.6	0.3	118.2	0.5	118.6	0.3	118.7	0.1	119.7	0.8	120.5	0.7	120.7	0.2	121.1	0.3	120.8	-0.2	121.3	0.4	122.6	1.1	121.4	-1.0
1995	122.4	0.8	123.2	0.7	123.8	0.5	124.7	0.7	124.7	0.0	122.4	-1.8	122.6	0.2	122.3	-0.2	122.3	0.0	122.2	-0.1	122.0	-0.2	121.7	-0.2
1996	122.1	0.3	122.1	0.0	121.3	-0.7	120.9	-0.3	120.4	-0.4	120.4	0.0	120.5	0.1	120.4	-0.1	120.3	-0.1	120.3	0.0	120.6	0.2	120.9	0.2
1997	120.6	-0.2	120.4	-0.2	120.1	-0.2	120.2	0.1	120.1	-0.1	120.2	0.1	120.3	0.1	120.5	0.2	120.3	-0.2	120.6	0.2	120.7	0.1	120.6	-0.1
1998	119.1	-1.2	118.6	-0.4	118.3	-0.3	118.3	0.0	118.7	0.3	118.6	-0.1	119.1	0.4	118.2	-0.8	118.3	0.1	118.5	0.2	118.4	-0.1	118.3	-0.1
1999	116.1	-1.9	117.9	1.6	116.7	-1.0	117.0	0.3	117.2	0.2	117.4	0.2	117.9	0.4	117.9	0.0	117.6	-0.3	118.3	0.6	117.7	-0.5	117.8	0.1
2000	118.9	0.9	118.8	-0.1	118.7	-0.1	119.7	0.8	120.1	0.3	119.7	-0.3	120.5	0.7	120.3	-0.2	121.1	0.7	121.2	0.1	121.4	0.2	120.7	-0.6
2001	121.2	0.4	121.1	-0.1	121.1	0.0	121.5	0.3	121.5	0.0	121.7	0.2	121.7	0.0	122.1	0.3	121.5	-0.5	121.5	0.0	121.7	0.2	121.2	-0.4

Source: U.S. Department of Labor, Bureau of Labor Statistics, Division of Industry Prices and Price Indexes. n.e.c. stands for not elsewhere classified. - indicates no data collected for period or unavailable.

Concrete Ingredients and Related Products
Producer Price Index
Base 1982 = 100

For 1926-2001. Columns headed % show percentile change in the index from the previous period for which an index is available.

Year	Jan Index	%	Feb Index	%	Mar Index	%	Apr Index	%	May Index	%	Jun Index	%	Jul Index	%	Aug Index	%	Sep Index	%	Oct Index	%	Nov Index	%	Dec Index	%
1926	15.0	-	15.0	0.0	15.0	0.0	14.9	-0.7	14.9	0.0	14.9	0.0	14.9	0.0	14.8	-0.7	14.8	0.0	14.9	0.7	14.9	0.0	15.0	0.7
1927	14.9	-0.7	14.6	-2.0	14.6	0.0	14.6	0.0	14.6	0.0	14.6	0.0	14.6	0.0	14.4	-1.4	14.4	0.0	14.4	0.0	14.4	0.0	14.5	0.7
1928	14.6	0.7	14.6	0.0	14.5	-0.7	16.5	13.8	17.1	3.6	17.1	0.0	17.0	-0.6	17.1	0.6	16.9	-1.2	16.8	-0.6	16.9	0.6	17.0	0.6
1929	17.0	0.0	17.0	0.0	16.7	-1.8	16.6	-0.6	16.6	0.0	16.6	0.0	16.6	0.0	16.4	-1.2	15.8	-3.7	15.7	-0.6	15.9	1.3	16.4	3.1
1930	16.5	0.6	16.7	1.2	16.6	-0.6	16.6	0.0	16.6	0.0	16.2	-2.4	16.6	2.5	16.6	0.0	16.6	0.0	16.6	0.0	16.6	0.0	16.5	-0.6
1931	16.5	0.0	16.2	-1.8	15.9	-1.9	15.6	-1.9	15.4	-1.3	15.2	-1.3	14.4	-5.3	14.6	1.4	14.6	0.0	14.5	-0.7	14.5	0.0	14.2	-2.1
1932	13.9	-2.1	13.9	0.0	13.9	0.0	13.7	-1.4	13.6	-0.7	13.8	1.5	14.7	6.5	14.8	0.7	14.8	0.0	14.8	0.0	14.9	0.7	15.1	1.3
1933	15.1	0.0	15.2	0.7	15.2	0.0	15.2	0.0	15.2	0.0	15.2	0.0	15.8	3.9	16.1	1.9	16.1	0.0	16.2	0.6	16.2	0.0	16.3	0.6
1934	16.6	1.8	16.7	0.6	16.6	-0.6	16.2	-2.4	16.2	0.0	16.6	2.5	16.6	0.0	16.6	0.0	16.6	0.0	16.6	0.0	16.6	0.0	16.6	0.0
1935	16.6	0.0	16.6	0.0	16.6	0.0	16.7	0.6	16.6	-0.6	16.6	0.0	16.6	0.0	16.6	0.0	16.6	0.0	16.6	0.0	16.7	0.6	16.7	0.0
1936	16.6	-0.6	16.7	0.6	16.6	-0.6	16.6	0.0	16.7	0.6	16.7	0.0	16.7	0.0	16.7	0.0	16.7	0.0	16.7	0.0	16.7	0.0	16.7	0.0
1937	16.7	0.0	16.6	-0.6	16.6	0.0	16.6	0.0	16.6	0.0	16.6	0.0	16.7	0.6	16.7	0.0	16.3	-2.4	16.7	2.5	16.7	0.0	16.7	0.0
1938	16.7	0.0	16.7	0.0	16.7	0.0	16.7	0.0	16.7	0.0	16.6	-0.6	16.8	1.2	16.7	-0.6	16.6	-0.6	16.7	0.6	16.9	1.2	16.9	0.0
1939	16.7	-1.2	16.7	0.0	16.7	0.0	16.7	0.0	16.7	0.0	16.7	0.0	16.7	0.0	16.7	0.0	16.7	0.0	16.7	0.0	16.7	0.0	16.7	0.0
1940	16.7	0.0	16.7	0.0	16.7	0.0	16.6	-0.6	16.6	0.0	16.6	0.0	16.6	0.0	16.6	0.0	16.6	0.0	16.6	0.0	16.6	0.0	16.6	0.0
1941	16.6	0.0	16.6	0.0	16.6	0.0	16.6	0.0	16.7	0.6	16.7	0.0	16.8	0.6	16.8	0.0	16.9	0.6	16.9	0.0	17.0	0.6	17.1	0.6
1942	17.1	0.0	17.2	0.6	17.2	0.0	17.3	0.6	17.3	0.0	17.3	0.0	17.3	0.0	17.3	0.0	17.3	0.0	17.3	0.0	17.3	0.0	17.3	0.0
1943	17.3	0.0	17.3	0.0	17.3	0.0	17.3	0.0	17.3	0.0	17.2	-0.6	17.2	0.0	17.3	0.6	17.3	0.0	17.2	-0.6	17.2	0.0	17.2	0.0
1944	17.2	0.0	17.2	0.0	17.2	0.0	17.3	0.6	17.6	1.7	17.6	0.0	17.6	0.0	17.6	0.0	17.6	0.0	17.7	0.6	17.7	0.0	17.7	0.0
1945	17.7	0.0	17.9	1.1	17.9	0.0	17.9	0.0	17.9	0.0	17.9	0.0	17.9	0.0	17.9	0.0	18.0	0.6	18.1	0.6	18.1	0.0	18.1	0.0
1946	18.4	1.7	18.4	0.0	18.5	0.5	18.5	0.0	18.5	0.0	18.6	0.5	18.7	0.5	18.9	1.1	19.0	0.5	19.0	0.0	19.1	0.5	19.2	0.5
1947	19.6	2.1	19.9	1.5	20.0	0.5	20.2	1.0	20.2	0.0	20.3	0.5	20.4	0.5	20.7	1.5	20.9	1.0	21.0	0.5	21.1	0.5	21.1	0.0
1948	21.7	2.8	21.9	0.9	22.0	0.5	22.1	0.5	22.1	0.0	22.2	0.5	22.7	2.3	22.7	0.0	22.8	0.4	22.8	0.0	22.9	0.4	23.0	0.4
1949	23.1	0.4	23.2	0.4	23.2	0.0	23.2	0.0	23.2	0.0	23.2	0.0	23.1	-0.4	23.1	0.0	23.1	0.0	23.2	0.4	23.2	0.0	23.2	0.0
1950	23.3	0.4	23.3	0.0	23.3	0.0	23.3	0.0	23.3	0.0	23.3	0.0	23.3	0.0	23.4	0.4	23.5	0.4	23.9	1.7	24.0	0.4	24.1	0.4
1951	24.9	3.3	24.9	0.0	24.9	0.0	24.9	0.0	24.9	0.0	24.9	0.0	24.9	0.0	24.9	0.0	24.9	0.0	24.9	0.0	24.9	0.0	24.9	0.0
1952	24.9	0.0	24.9	0.0	24.9	0.0	24.9	0.0	24.9	0.0	24.9	0.0	24.9	0.0	24.9	0.0	24.9	0.0	24.9	0.0	24.9	0.0	24.9	0.0
1953	24.9	0.0	24.9	0.0	25.0	0.4	25.9	3.6	26.0	0.4	26.0	0.0	26.0	0.0	26.1	0.4	26.3	0.8	26.3	0.0	26.3	0.0	26.3	0.0
1954	26.4	0.4	26.4	0.0	26.4	0.0	26.4	0.0	26.4	0.0	26.5	0.4	26.9	1.5	26.9	0.0	26.9	0.0	26.9	0.0	26.9	0.0	26.9	0.0
1955	27.1	0.7	27.3	0.7	27.3	0.0	27.5	0.7	27.5	0.0	27.5	0.0	27.5	0.0	27.6	0.4	27.6	0.0	27.6	0.0	27.6	0.0	27.7	0.4
1956	28.6	3.2	28.6	0.0	28.6	0.0	28.6	0.0	28.6	0.0	28.7	0.3	28.7	0.0	28.7	0.0	28.7	0.0	29.0	1.0	29.0	0.0	29.0	0.0
1957	29.6	2.1	29.7	0.3	29.7	0.0	29.8	0.3	29.8	0.0	29.9	0.3	30.0	0.3	30.0	0.0	30.1	0.3	30.1	0.0	30.1	0.0	30.1	0.0
1958	30.6	1.7	30.6	0.0	30.5	-0.3	30.6	0.3	30.6	0.0	30.6	0.0	30.6	0.0	30.6	0.0	30.6	0.0	30.6	0.0	30.6	0.0	30.6	0.0
1959	30.9	1.0	30.9	0.0	30.9	0.0	30.9	0.0	30.9	0.0	30.8	-0.3	30.9	0.3	30.9	0.0	30.9	0.0	30.9	0.0	30.9	0.0	30.9	0.0
1960	31.3	1.3	31.3	0.0	31.3	0.0	31.3	0.0	31.3	0.0	31.3	0.0	31.3	0.0	31.3	0.0	31.3	0.0	31.3	0.0	31.3	0.0	31.3	0.0
1961	31.3	0.0	31.3	0.0	31.4	0.3	31.4	0.0	31.4	0.0	31.4	0.0	31.4	0.0	31.4	0.0	31.4	0.0	31.4	0.0	31.2	-0.6	31.0	-0.6
1962	31.3	1.0	31.4	0.3	31.4	0.0	31.4	0.0	31.5	0.3	31.5	0.0	31.5	0.0	31.5	0.0	31.5	0.0	31.5	0.0	31.5	0.0	31.5	0.0
1963	31.3	-0.6	31.4	0.3	31.4	0.0	31.4	0.0	31.4	0.0	31.5	0.3	31.5	0.0	31.4	-0.3	31.4	0.0	31.4	0.0	31.4	0.0	31.4	0.0
1964	31.3	-0.3	31.3	0.0	31.3	0.0	31.3	0.0	31.3	0.0	31.3	0.0	31.3	0.0	31.3	0.0	31.3	0.0	31.3	0.0	31.4	0.3	31.4	0.0
1965	31.5	0.3	31.5	0.0	31.5	0.0	31.5	0.0	31.5	0.0	31.4	-0.3	31.4	0.0	31.5	0.3	31.5	0.0	31.5	0.0	31.5	0.0	31.5	0.0
1966	31.6	0.3	31.6	0.0	31.6	0.0	31.6	0.0	31.6	0.0	31.6	0.0	31.6	0.0	31.6	0.0	31.6	0.0	31.8	0.6	31.7	-0.3	31.8	0.3
1967	32.2	1.3	32.2	0.0	32.2	0.0	32.3	0.3	32.2	-0.3	32.2	0.0	32.2	0.0	32.3	0.3	32.3	0.0	32.4	0.3	32.4	0.0	32.5	0.3
1968	32.9	1.2	33.1	0.6	33.1	0.0	33.2	0.3	33.2	0.0	33.3	0.3	33.4	0.3	33.4	0.0	33.4	0.0	33.4	0.0	33.6	0.6	33.6	0.0
1969	34.3	2.1	34.2	-0.3	34.3	0.3	34.3	0.0	34.3	0.0	34.4	0.3	34.5	0.3	34.5	0.0	34.6	0.3	34.6	0.0	34.6	0.0	34.6	0.0
1970	35.9	3.8	36.1	0.6	36.1	0.0	37.1	2.8	36.2	-2.4	36.3	0.3	36.3	0.0	36.3	0.0	36.4	0.3	36.4	0.0	36.4	0.0	36.4	0.0

[Continued]

Concrete Ingredients and Related Products

Producer Price Index
Base 1982 = 100

[Continued]

For 1926-2001. Columns headed % show percentile change in the index from the previous period for which an index is available.

Year	Jan Index	%	Feb Index	%	Mar Index	%	Apr Index	%	May Index	%	Jun Index	%	Jul Index	%	Aug Index	%	Sep Index	%	Oct Index	%	Nov Index	%	Dec Index	%
1971	37.7	3.6	37.8	0.3	38.9	2.9	39.0	0.3	39.1	0.3	39.2	0.3	39.8	1.5	40.0	0.5	40.1	0.2	40.1	0.0	40.1	0.0	40.1	0.0
1972	40.1	0.0	40.2	0.2	40.2	0.0	40.8	1.5	40.9	0.2	40.9	0.0	40.9	0.0	41.3	1.0	41.4	0.2	41.4	0.0	41.4	0.0	41.4	0.0
1973	41.6	0.5	41.7	0.2	41.9	0.5	42.5	1.4	42.4	-0.2	42.5	0.2	42.5	0.0	42.5	0.0	42.5	0.0	42.6	0.2	42.6	0.0	42.6	0.0
1974	44.8	5.2	45.1	0.7	45.3	0.4	46.2	2.0	46.9	1.5	47.1	0.4	49.5	5.1	49.7	0.4	49.8	0.2	50.2	0.8	50.4	0.4	50.5	0.2
1975	53.9	6.7	54.4	0.9	54.7	0.6	55.3	1.1	55.5	0.4	55.6	0.2	56.1	0.9	56.1	0.0	56.5	0.7	56.4	-0.2	56.4	0.0	56.4	0.0
1976	58.2	3.2	58.4	0.3	58.6	0.3	60.3	2.9	60.4	0.2	60.5	0.2	60.9	0.7	60.9	0.0	61.0	0.2	61.1	0.2	61.0	-0.2	61.1	0.2
1977	62.6	2.5	62.7	0.2	63.0	0.5	64.0	1.6	64.4	0.6	64.5	0.2	64.7	0.3	64.8	0.2	64.9	0.2	64.9	0.0	65.0	0.2	65.0	0.0
1978	67.7	4.2	68.0	0.4	68.4	0.6	69.9	2.2	70.0	0.1	70.2	0.3	70.7	0.7	71.0	0.4	71.3	0.4	71.6	0.4	72.1	0.7	72.1	0.0
1979	76.1	5.5	76.9	1.1	77.4	0.7	78.1	0.9	78.2	0.1	78.5	0.4	79.1	0.8	79.3	0.3	79.6	0.4	80.1	0.6	80.5	0.5	81.0	0.6
1980	85.5	5.6	86.0	0.6	86.3	0.3	87.7	1.6	87.9	0.2	88.1	0.2	89.0	1.0	89.9	1.0	90.0	0.1	90.0	0.0	90.1	0.1	90.2	0.1
1981	93.5	3.7	94.0	0.5	94.4	0.4	96.0	1.7	96.0	0.0	96.0	0.0	96.1	0.1	96.1	0.0	96.3	0.2	96.3	0.0	96.3	0.0	96.4	0.1
1982	98.8	2.5	99.5	0.7	99.9	0.4	99.8	-0.1	100.8	1.0	100.9	0.1	100.6	-0.3	100.4	-0.2	100.3	-0.1	100.0	-0.3	100.0	0.0	98.9	-1.1
1983	99.1	0.2	100.0	0.9	99.5	-0.5	100.9	1.4	101.2	0.3	101.4	0.2	101.3	-0.1	102.1	0.8	102.3	0.2	102.2	-0.1	101.6	-0.6	101.5	-0.1
1984	101.8	0.3	103.2	1.4	104.6	1.4	104.6	0.0	105.8	1.1	105.4	-0.4	105.5	0.1	106.0	0.5	105.9	-0.1	105.7	-0.2	106.0	0.3	106.3	0.3
1985	106.8	0.5	107.6	0.7	108.2	0.6	108.5	0.3	109.3	0.7	109.3	0.0	108.9	-0.4	109.1	0.2	108.7	-0.4	108.6	-0.1	108.1	-0.5	108.4	0.3
1986	109.4	0.9	109.4	0.0	109.7	0.3	110.1	0.4	109.7	-0.4	109.5	-0.2	109.4	-0.1	109.3	-0.1	109.4	0.1	109.5	0.1	109.5	0.0	108.2	-1.2
1987	109.1	0.8	109.6	0.5	110.1	0.5	110.4	0.3	110.7	0.3	110.8	0.1	110.8	0.0	110.8	0.0	110.8	0.0	110.8	0.0	110.8	0.0	110.6	-0.2
1988	111.3	0.6	111.6	0.3	111.6	0.0	112.3	0.6	112.6	0.3	112.3	-0.3	112.1	-0.2	112.2	0.1	112.0	-0.2	111.9	-0.1	111.9	0.0	111.9	0.0
1989	112.3	0.4	112.3	0.0	112.3	0.0	113.1	0.7	113.3	0.2	113.3	0.0	113.3	0.0	113.2	-0.1	113.7	0.4	113.8	0.1	113.6	-0.2	113.6	0.0
1990	113.9	0.3	114.3	0.4	114.8	0.4	115.2	0.3	115.5	0.3	115.5	0.0	115.3	-0.2	115.5	0.2	115.8	0.3	115.8	0.0	116.0	0.2	115.9	-0.1
1991	117.1	1.0	118.3	1.0	118.3	0.0	118.6	0.3	118.8	0.2	118.9	0.1	118.7	-0.2	118.8	0.1	118.5	-0.3	118.5	0.0	118.3	-0.2	118.2	-0.1
1992	118.8	0.5	118.8	0.0	119.4	0.5	119.3	-0.1	119.4	0.1	119.4	0.0	119.4	0.0	119.5	0.1	119.4	-0.1	119.6	0.2	119.7	0.1	119.9	0.2
1993	120.9	0.8	121.1	0.2	121.4	0.2	123.2	1.5	123.2	0.0	123.5	0.2	123.7	0.2	123.8	0.1	124.5	0.6	125.5	0.8	125.2	-0.2	125.3	0.1
1994	126.2	0.7	126.6	0.3	127.0	0.3	128.4	1.1	128.4	0.0	129.0	0.5	129.2	0.2	129.7	0.4	129.8	0.1	130.2	0.3	130.2	0.0	130.2	0.0
1995	131.6	1.1	132.1	0.4	132.4	0.2	134.5	1.6	134.8	0.2	135.2	0.3	135.7	0.4	135.7	0.0	135.9	0.1	135.8	-0.1	136.0	0.1	135.9	-0.1
1996	136.5	0.4	136.7	0.1	137.0	0.2	138.6	1.2	139.2	0.4	139.2	0.0	139.4	0.1	139.3	-0.1	140.0	0.5	140.0	0.0	140.2	0.1	140.0	-0.1
1997	140.7	0.5	140.7	0.0	140.8	0.1	142.3	1.1	142.7	0.3	143.0	0.2	143.2	0.1	143.3	0.1	143.2	-0.1	143.2	0.0	143.2	0.0	143.4	0.1
1998	144.2	0.6	144.6	0.3	145.0	0.3	147.3	1.6	147.6	0.2	148.4	0.5	148.8	0.3	148.9	0.1	149.0	0.1	149.0	0.0	149.0	0.0	149.3	0.2
1999	150.4	0.7	150.7	0.2	151.0	0.2	151.7	0.5	152.1	0.3	152.4	0.2	152.6	0.1	152.8	0.1	153.0	0.1	153.0	0.0	153.2	0.1	153.0	-0.1
2000	153.8	0.5	153.9	0.1	154.3	0.3	155.3	0.6	156.0	0.5	156.2	0.1	156.3	0.1	156.3	0.0	156.4	0.1	156.3	-0.1	156.3	0.0	155.8	-0.3
2001	157.2	0.9	157.9	0.4	157.9	0.0	158.9	0.6	159.2	0.2	159.3	0.1	159.6	0.2	159.8	0.1	159.8	0.0	159.8	0.0	160.0	0.1	159.9	-0.1

Source: U.S. Department of Labor, Bureau of Labor Statistics, Division of Industry Prices and Price Indexes. n.e.c. stands for not elsewhere classified. - indicates no data collected for period or unavailable.

Concrete Products
Producer Price Index
Base 1982 = 100

For 1926-2001. Columns headed % show percentile change in the index from the previous period for which an index is available.

Year	Jan Index	%	Feb Index	%	Mar Index	%	Apr Index	%	May Index	%	Jun Index	%	Jul Index	%	Aug Index	%	Sep Index	%	Oct Index	%	Nov Index	%	Dec Index	%
1926	23.7	-	23.7	0.0	23.7	0.0	23.7	0.0	23.7	0.0	23.7	0.0	23.7	0.0	23.7	0.0	23.7	0.0	23.7	0.0	23.7	0.0	23.7	0.0
1927	23.7	0.0	23.7	0.0	23.7	0.0	23.7	0.0	23.7	0.0	23.7	0.0	23.7	0.0	23.7	0.0	23.7	0.0	23.7	0.0	23.7	0.0	23.7	0.0
1928	23.7	0.0	23.7	0.0	23.7	0.0	23.7	0.0	23.7	0.0	23.7	0.0	23.7	0.0	23.7	0.0	23.7	0.0	23.7	0.0	23.7	0.0	23.7	0.0
1929	23.7	0.0	23.7	0.0	23.7	0.0	23.7	0.0	23.7	0.0	23.7	0.0	23.0	-3.0	23.0	0.0	23.0	0.0	23.0	0.0	23.0	0.0	23.0	0.0
1930	23.0	0.0	23.0	0.0	23.0	0.0	23.0	0.0	22.6	-1.7	22.6	0.0	23.0	1.8	23.7	3.0	25.0	5.5	25.0	0.0	25.0	0.0	25.0	0.0
1931	24.6	-1.6	23.2	-5.7	22.6	-2.6	22.6	0.0	22.6	0.0	22.6	0.0	22.5	-0.4	21.3	-5.3	21.3	0.0	21.3	0.0	21.3	0.0	21.3	0.0
1932	21.3	0.0	21.2	-0.5	21.2	0.0	20.0	-5.7	20.0	0.0	20.0	0.0	20.0	0.0	20.0	0.0	20.0	0.0	20.9	4.5	20.9	0.0	20.9	0.0
1933	20.9	0.0	20.9	0.0	20.9	0.0	20.9	0.0	20.9	0.0	20.9	0.0	20.9	0.0	20.9	0.0	20.9	0.0	20.9	0.0	20.9	0.0	20.9	0.0
1934	20.9	0.0	20.9	0.0	20.9	0.0	20.9	0.0	20.9	0.0	20.9	0.0	20.9	0.0	20.9	0.0	20.9	0.0	20.9	0.0	20.9	0.0	20.9	0.0
1935	20.9	0.0	20.9	0.0	19.7	-5.7	18.6	-5.6	18.6	0.0	18.6	0.0	18.6	0.0	18.6	0.0	18.6	0.0	18.6	0.0	18.6	0.0	18.6	0.0
1936	20.9	12.4	20.9	0.0	20.9	0.0	20.9	0.0	20.9	0.0	20.9	0.0	20.9	0.0	20.9	0.0	20.4	-2.4	18.6	-8.8	18.6	0.0	18.6	0.0
1937	18.6	0.0	18.6	0.0	18.6	0.0	21.2	14.0	21.2	0.0	21.2	0.0	21.2	0.0	21.2	0.0	21.2	0.0	21.2	0.0	21.2	0.0	19.2	-9.4
1938	18.6	-3.1	18.6	0.0	18.6	0.0	18.6	0.0	18.6	0.0	18.6	0.0	18.6	0.0	18.6	0.0	18.6	0.0	18.6	0.0	18.6	0.0	19.9	7.0
1939	21.2	6.5	21.2	0.0	21.2	0.0	21.2	0.0	18.0	-15.1	15.9	-11.7	15.9	0.0	15.9	0.0	17.2	8.2	18.6	8.1	18.6	0.0	18.6	0.0
1940	18.6	0.0	18.6	0.0	16.6	-10.8	15.9	-4.2	15.9	0.0	15.9	0.0	15.9	0.0	15.9	0.0	15.9	0.0	15.9	0.0	15.9	0.0	18.0	13.2
1941	18.6	3.3	18.6	0.0	18.6	0.0	18.6	0.0	18.6	0.0	18.9	1.6	19.9	5.3	19.9	0.0	19.9	0.0	19.9	0.0	19.9	0.0	19.9	0.0
1942	19.9	0.0	19.9	0.0	19.9	0.0	19.9	0.0	19.9	0.0	19.9	0.0	19.9	0.0	19.9	0.0	19.9	0.0	19.9	0.0	19.9	0.0	19.9	0.0
1943	19.9	0.0	19.9	0.0	19.9	0.0	19.9	0.0	19.9	0.0	19.9	0.0	19.9	0.0	19.9	0.0	19.9	0.0	19.9	0.0	19.9	0.0	19.9	0.0
1944	19.9	0.0	19.9	0.0	19.9	0.0	19.9	0.0	19.9	0.0	19.9	0.0	19.9	0.0	19.9	0.0	19.9	0.0	19.9	0.0	19.9	0.0	19.9	0.0
1945	19.9	0.0	19.9	0.0	19.9	0.0	19.9	0.0	19.9	0.0	19.9	0.0	19.9	0.0	19.9	0.0	19.9	0.0	19.9	0.0	19.9	0.0	19.9	0.0
1946	19.9	0.0	19.9	0.0	19.9	0.0	19.9	0.0	20.2	1.5	21.2	5.0	22.0	3.8	21.2	-3.6	21.2	0.0	21.2	0.0	22.5	6.1	23.9	6.2
1947	23.9	0.0	23.9	0.0	23.9	0.0	23.9	0.0	23.9	0.0	23.9	0.0	24.0	0.4	23.8	-0.8	23.6	-0.8	24.0	1.7	24.2	0.8	24.2	0.0
1948	24.7	2.1	24.8	0.4	24.8	0.0	24.8	0.0	24.8	0.0	24.8	0.0	25.0	0.8	25.4	1.6	25.4	0.0	25.4	0.0	25.4	0.0	25.4	0.0
1949	25.4	0.0	25.4	0.0	25.6	0.8	25.6	0.0	25.6	0.0	25.6	0.0	25.6	0.0	25.8	0.8	25.8	0.0	25.8	0.0	25.8	0.0	25.8	0.0
1950	25.8	0.0	25.8	0.0	25.8	0.0	25.8	0.0	25.9	0.4	26.0	0.4	26.0	0.0	26.2	0.8	26.6	1.5	27.0	1.5	27.0	0.0	27.2	0.7
1951	27.9	2.6	28.0	0.4	28.0	0.0	28.0	0.0	28.0	0.0	28.0	0.0	28.0	0.0	28.0	0.0	28.0	0.0	28.0	0.0	28.0	0.0	28.0	0.0
1952	28.0	0.0	28.0	0.0	28.0	0.0	28.0	0.0	28.0	0.0	28.0	0.0	28.0	0.0	28.0	0.0	28.0	0.0	28.0	0.0	28.0	0.0	28.0	0.0
1953	28.1	0.4	28.1	0.0	28.1	0.0	28.4	1.1	28.7	1.1	28.7	0.0	28.8	0.3	28.9	0.3	29.2	1.0	29.2	0.0	29.2	0.0	29.1	-0.3
1954	29.1	0.0	29.2	0.3	29.2	0.0	29.2	0.0	29.2	0.0	29.2	0.0	29.3	0.3	29.3	0.0	29.3	0.0	29.3	0.0	29.2	-0.3	29.2	0.0
1955	29.0	-0.7	29.1	0.3	29.4	1.0	29.4	0.0	29.4	0.0	29.4	0.0	29.4	0.0	29.5	0.3	29.8	1.0	29.9	0.3	29.9	0.0	29.9	0.0
1956	30.2	1.0	30.2	0.0	30.2	0.0	30.3	0.3	30.3	0.0	30.3	0.0	30.6	1.0	30.7	0.3	31.1	1.3	31.1	0.0	31.2	0.3	31.2	0.0
1957	31.3	0.3	31.3	0.0	31.3	0.0	31.5	0.6	31.5	0.0	31.5	0.0	31.4	-0.3	31.4	0.0	31.4	0.0	31.5	0.3	31.5	0.0	31.6	0.3
1958	31.8	0.6	31.8	0.0	31.8	0.0	31.8	0.0	31.9	0.3	31.9	0.0	32.0	0.3	31.9	-0.3	31.8	-0.3	31.9	0.3	31.9	0.0	32.0	0.3
1959	32.0	0.0	32.1	0.3	32.2	0.3	32.2	0.0	32.3	0.3	32.3	0.0	32.3	0.0	32.3	0.0	32.3	0.0	32.4	0.3	32.4	0.0	32.4	0.0
1960	32.5	0.3	32.6	0.3	32.6	0.0	32.6	0.0	32.7	0.3	32.6	-0.3	32.6	0.0	32.6	0.0	32.6	0.0	32.6	0.0	32.6	0.0	32.6	0.0
1961	32.6	0.0	32.6	0.0	32.6	0.0	32.6	0.0	32.6	0.0	32.6	0.0	32.6	0.0	32.6	0.0	32.7	0.3	32.7	0.0	32.6	-0.3	32.6	0.0
1962	32.6	0.0	32.7	0.3	32.7	0.0	32.7	0.0	32.6	-0.3	32.6	0.0	32.7	0.3	32.7	0.0	32.7	0.0	32.7	0.0	32.7	0.0	32.6	-0.3
1963	32.6	0.0	32.6	0.0	32.6	0.0	32.6	0.0	32.5	-0.3	32.5	0.0	32.2	-0.9	32.2	0.0	32.3	0.3	32.3	0.0	32.3	0.0	32.3	0.0
1964	32.2	-0.3	32.2	0.0	32.1	-0.3	32.0	-0.3	32.0	0.0	32.1	0.3	32.1	0.0	32.1	0.0	32.2	0.3	32.2	0.0	32.2	0.0	32.2	0.0
1965	32.3	0.3	32.2	-0.3	32.2	0.0	32.3	0.3	32.3	0.0	32.4	0.3	32.4	0.0	32.3	-0.3	32.4	0.3	32.4	0.0	32.4	0.0	32.4	0.0
1966	32.5	0.3	32.5	0.0	32.6	0.3	32.7	0.3	32.7	0.0	32.8	0.3	32.8	0.0	32.9	0.3	33.0	0.3	33.0	0.0	33.0	0.0	33.1	0.3
1967	33.3	0.6	33.4	0.3	33.4	0.0	33.5	0.3	33.5	0.0	33.6	0.3	33.6	0.0	33.7	0.3	33.7	0.0	33.7	0.0	33.7	0.0	33.7	0.0
1968	33.9	0.6	34.0	0.3	34.1	0.3	34.3	0.6	34.3	0.0	34.5	0.6	34.5	0.0	34.6	0.3	34.6	0.0	34.8	0.6	34.8	0.0	34.9	0.3
1969	35.3	1.1	35.4	0.3	35.5	0.3	35.6	0.3	35.6	0.0	35.6	0.0	35.8	0.6	35.9	0.3	36.1	0.6	36.2	0.3	36.2	0.0	36.4	0.6
1970	37.0	1.6	37.1	0.3	37.3	0.5	37.3	0.0	37.4	0.3	37.6	0.5	37.7	0.3	37.8	0.3	38.1	0.8	38.1	0.0	38.2	0.3	38.4	0.5

[Continued]

Concrete Products
Producer Price Index
Base 1982 = 100
[Continued]

For 1926-2001. Columns headed % show percentile change in the index from the previous period for which an index is available.

Year	Jan Index	%	Feb Index	%	Mar Index	%	Apr Index	%	May Index	%	Jun Index	%	Jul Index	%	Aug Index	%	Sep Index	%	Oct Index	%	Nov Index	%	Dec Index	%
1971	39.3	2.3	39.5	0.5	39.8	0.8	40.1	0.8	40.1	0.0	40.3	0.5	40.8	1.2	41.2	1.0	41.1	-0.2	41.1	0.0	41.1	0.0	41.3	0.5
1972	41.4	0.2	41.6	0.5	41.8	0.5	42.0	0.5	42.0	0.0	42.1	0.2	42.3	0.5	42.3	0.0	42.4	0.2	42.7	0.7	42.7	0.0	42.8	0.2
1973	43.1	0.7	43.3	0.5	43.5	0.5	43.9	0.9	44.1	0.5	44.4	0.7	44.4	0.0	44.4	0.0	44.5	0.2	44.9	0.9	45.0	0.2	45.2	0.4
1974	47.0	4.0	47.8	1.7	48.6	1.7	48.8	0.4	49.6	1.6	50.3	1.4	52.1	3.6	52.5	0.8	52.8	0.6	53.6	1.5	53.9	0.6	54.3	0.7
1975	56.1	3.3	56.4	0.5	56.8	0.7	57.0	0.4	57.1	0.2	57.2	0.2	57.5	0.5	57.5	0.0	57.5	0.0	57.8	0.5	57.9	0.2	58.1	0.3
1976	59.6	2.6	59.8	0.3	59.8	0.0	59.9	0.2	60.2	0.5	60.3	0.2	60.8	0.8	60.9	0.2	60.9	0.0	60.9	0.0	61.2	0.5	61.5	0.5
1977	62.9	2.3	63.1	0.3	63.2	0.2	63.8	0.9	64.0	0.3	64.1	0.2	64.7	0.9	65.0	0.5	65.1	0.2	65.5	0.6	65.6	0.2	65.7	0.2
1978	68.1	3.7	68.9	1.2	69.2	0.4	69.8	0.9	70.4	0.9	71.1	1.0	72.0	1.3	73.8	2.5	74.4	0.8	74.6	0.3	74.8	0.3	75.3	0.7
1979	79.1	5.0	79.4	0.4	79.8	0.5	80.7	1.1	81.1	0.5	81.8	0.9	82.3	0.6	82.7	0.5	83.5	1.0	84.0	0.6	84.1	0.1	85.0	1.1
1980	89.1	4.8	89.6	0.6	90.3	0.8	91.6	1.4	92.4	0.9	92.6	0.2	92.6	0.0	92.7	0.1	93.1	0.4	93.2	0.1	93.3	0.1	93.2	-0.1
1981	96.1	3.1	96.2	0.1	96.3	0.1	97.3	1.0	97.8	0.5	98.5	0.7	98.5	0.0	98.5	0.0	98.4	-0.1	98.5	0.1	98.5	0.0	98.6	0.1
1982	99.2	0.6	99.3	0.1	99.5	0.2	100.0	0.5	100.1	0.1	100.2	0.1	100.3	0.1	100.4	0.1	100.3	-0.1	100.3	0.0	100.1	-0.2	100.2	0.1
1983	100.5	0.3	100.8	0.3	100.9	0.1	101.1	0.2	101.1	0.0	101.3	0.2	101.5	0.2	101.7	0.2	101.9	0.2	101.9	0.0	102.1	0.2	102.2	0.1
1984	102.4	0.2	102.7	0.3	102.8	0.1	103.7	0.9	103.9	0.2	104.1	0.2	104.3	0.2	104.5	0.2	104.7	0.2	104.8	0.1	104.7	-0.1	104.8	0.1
1985	105.6	0.8	105.6	0.0	106.0	0.4	106.3	0.3	107.5	1.1	107.9	0.4	107.9	0.0	108.4	0.5	108.5	0.1	108.4	-0.1	108.6	0.2	108.8	0.2
1986	109.1	0.3	109.1	0.0	109.1	0.0	109.6	0.5	109.6	0.0	109.3	-0.3	109.4	0.1	109.2	-0.2	109.1	-0.1	108.9	-0.2	108.9	0.0	109.1	0.2
1987	109.4	0.3	109.4	0.0	109.2	-0.2	109.3	0.1	109.4	0.1	109.3	-0.1	109.4	0.1	109.3	-0.1	109.4	0.1	109.4	0.0	109.6	0.2	109.4	-0.2
1988	109.7	0.3	109.8	0.1	109.8	0.0	109.7	-0.1	109.9	0.2	110.1	0.2	110.1	0.0	110.1	0.0	109.9	-0.2	109.9	0.0	110.2	0.3	110.3	0.1
1989	110.4	0.1	110.7	0.3	110.7	0.0	110.7	0.0	110.8	0.1	111.2	0.4	111.4	0.2	111.7	0.3	111.6	-0.1	111.6	0.0	111.6	0.0	111.9	0.3
1990	112.1	0.2	112.2	0.1	112.8	0.5	112.6	-0.2	113.1	0.4	113.3	0.2	113.7	0.4	113.9	0.2	114.2	0.3	114.2	0.0	114.8	0.5	115.0	0.2
1991	116.0	0.9	116.2	0.2	116.5	0.3	116.3	-0.2	116.5	0.2	116.9	0.3	117.0	0.1	116.9	-0.1	116.7	-0.2	116.7	0.0	116.7	0.0	116.9	0.2
1992	117.1	0.2	117.2	0.1	117.2	0.0	116.9	-0.3	117.1	0.2	117.0	-0.1	117.1	0.1	117.3	0.2	117.1	-0.2	117.2	0.1	117.7	0.4	118.0	0.3
1993	118.7	0.6	118.9	0.2	119.2	0.3	119.5	0.3	119.7	0.2	120.0	0.3	120.2	0.2	120.3	0.1	120.7	0.3	121.0	0.2	121.7	0.6	122.1	0.3
1994	122.5	0.3	122.7	0.2	123.4	0.6	123.7	0.2	124.0	0.2	124.2	0.2	124.7	0.4	125.1	0.3	125.3	0.2	125.8	0.4	126.5	0.6	127.0	0.4
1995	127.8	0.6	128.1	0.2	128.5	0.3	129.1	0.5	129.3	0.2	129.3	0.0	129.6	0.2	129.7	0.1	130.0	0.2	130.2	0.2	130.8	0.5	131.0	0.2
1996	131.5	0.4	132.0	0.4	132.4	0.3	132.8	0.3	133.0	0.2	133.2	0.2	133.6	0.3	133.5	-0.1	133.8	0.2	133.8	0.0	134.5	0.5	134.7	0.1
1997	135.0	0.2	135.2	0.1	135.4	0.1	135.9	0.4	136.1	0.1	135.8	-0.2	136.2	0.3	136.1	-0.1	136.1	0.0	136.4	0.2	136.8	0.3	136.8	0.0
1998	136.9	0.1	137.4	0.4	137.6	0.1	139.5	1.4	139.9	0.3	140.7	0.6	141.3	0.4	141.3	0.0	141.4	0.1	141.3	-0.1	141.4	0.1	141.4	0.0
1999	142.2	0.6	142.6	0.3	142.8	0.1	143.5	0.5	144.1	0.4	143.9	-0.1	143.8	-0.1	143.8	0.0	144.2	0.3	144.4	0.1	144.5	0.1	144.3	-0.1
2000	145.8	1.0	145.7	-0.1	146.3	0.4	147.2	0.6	147.6	0.3	148.1	0.3	148.0	-0.1	148.1	0.1	149.4	0.9	149.4	0.0	149.1	-0.2	149.3	0.1
2001	149.2	-0.1	150.7	1.0	150.7	0.0	151.3	0.4	152.1	0.5	150.7	-0.9	152.0	0.9	152.2	0.1	152.7	0.3	152.7	0.0	152.9	0.1	152.9	0.0

Source: U.S. Department of Labor, Bureau of Labor Statistics, Division of Industry Prices and Price Indexes. n.e.c. stands for not elsewhere classified. - indicates no data collected for period or unavailable.

Clay Construction Products ex. Refractories
Producer Price Index
Base 1982 = 100

For 1947-2001. Columns headed % show percentile change in the index from the previous period for which an index is available.

Year	Jan Index	%	Feb Index	%	Mar Index	%	Apr Index	%	May Index	%	Jun Index	%	Jul Index	%	Aug Index	%	Sep Index	%	Oct Index	%	Nov Index	%	Dec Index	%
1947	23.5	-	23.5	0.0	23.6	0.4	23.6	0.0	23.7	0.4	23.7	0.0	23.7	0.0	24.0	1.3	24.2	0.8	24.3	0.4	24.5	0.8	24.5	0.0
1948	24.9	1.6	25.1	0.8	25.2	0.4	25.3	0.4	25.5	0.8	25.7	0.8	25.9	0.8	26.0	0.4	26.1	0.4	26.3	0.8	26.3	0.0	26.3	0.0
1949	26.5	0.8	26.5	0.0	26.5	0.0	26.5	0.0	26.5	0.0	26.5	0.0	26.5	0.0	26.4	-0.4	26.3	-0.4	26.3	0.0	26.4	0.4	26.4	0.0
1950	26.5	0.4	26.6	0.4	26.7	0.4	26.7	0.0	27.0	1.1	27.2	0.7	27.6	1.5	28.1	1.8	28.4	1.1	28.7	1.1	28.9	0.7	29.4	1.7
1951	29.8	1.4	29.9	0.3	29.9	0.0	29.9	0.0	29.9	0.0	29.9	0.0	29.9	0.0	29.9	0.0	29.9	0.0	29.9	0.0	29.9	0.0	29.9	0.0
1952	29.9	0.0	29.9	0.0	29.9	0.0	29.8	-0.3	29.9	0.3	29.9	0.0	29.8	-0.3	29.8	0.0	29.8	0.0	29.8	0.0	29.8	0.0	29.8	0.0
1953	29.8	0.0	29.8	0.0	29.9	0.3	30.1	0.7	30.1	0.0	30.3	0.7	30.4	0.3	30.6	0.7	30.8	0.7	30.8	0.0	30.8	0.0	30.8	0.0
1954	30.8	0.0	30.8	0.0	30.8	0.0	30.8	0.0	30.8	0.0	30.8	0.0	30.8	0.0	30.9	0.3	31.0	0.3	31.0	0.0	31.0	0.0	31.0	0.0
1955	31.2	0.6	31.3	0.3	31.5	0.6	31.6	0.3	31.7	0.3	31.9	0.6	32.0	0.3	32.3	0.9	32.8	1.5	33.0	0.6	33.0	0.0	33.1	0.3
1956	33.4	0.9	33.5	0.3	33.6	0.3	33.7	0.3	33.7	0.0	33.9	0.6	33.9	0.0	33.9	0.0	33.9	0.0	33.9	0.0	34.1	0.6	34.1	0.0
1957	34.2	0.3	34.2	0.0	34.3	0.3	34.3	0.0	34.3	0.0	34.4	0.3	34.4	0.0	34.3	-0.3	34.3	0.0	34.3	0.0	34.3	0.0	34.4	0.3
1958	34.5	0.3	34.5	0.0	34.5	0.0	34.5	0.0	34.5	0.0	34.5	0.0	34.5	0.0	34.5	0.0	34.6	0.3	34.6	0.0	34.7	0.3	34.9	0.6
1959	35.0	0.3	35.2	0.6	35.2	0.0	35.2	0.0	35.3	0.3	35.4	0.3	35.5	0.3	35.5	0.0	35.5	0.0	35.5	0.0	35.5	0.0	35.6	0.3
1960	35.8	0.6	35.9	0.3	35.9	0.0	35.9	0.0	35.9	0.0	35.9	0.0	35.9	0.0	36.0	0.3	36.1	0.3	36.1	0.0	36.1	0.0	36.1	0.0
1961	36.0	-0.3	36.0	0.0	36.0	0.0	36.0	0.0	36.1	0.3	36.1	0.0	36.1	0.0	36.2	0.3	36.2	0.0	36.3	0.3	36.3	0.0	36.3	0.0
1962	36.3	0.0	36.4	0.3	36.4	0.0	36.5	0.3	36.5	0.0	36.5	0.0	36.5	0.0	36.5	0.0	36.5	0.0	36.4	-0.3	36.4	0.0	36.4	0.0
1963	36.5	0.3	36.5	0.0	36.5	0.0	36.6	0.3	36.7	0.3	36.7	0.0	36.7	0.0	36.7	0.0	36.6	-0.3	36.6	0.0	36.7	0.3	36.7	0.0
1964	36.5	-0.5	36.7	0.5	36.7	0.0	36.8	0.3	36.8	0.0	36.7	-0.3	36.7	0.0	36.7	0.0	36.8	0.3	36.8	0.0	36.8	0.0	36.9	0.3
1965	36.9	0.0	36.9	0.0	36.9	0.0	36.9	0.0	36.9	0.0	36.9	0.0	36.9	0.0	37.1	0.5	37.2	0.3	37.2	0.0	37.2	0.0	37.3	0.3
1966	37.3	0.0	37.4	0.3	37.5	0.3	37.5	0.0	37.5	0.0	37.7	0.5	37.7	0.0	37.8	0.3	37.8	0.0	37.8	0.0	38.0	0.5	37.9	-0.3
1967	38.0	0.3	38.0	0.0	38.1	0.3	38.1	0.0	38.2	0.3	38.2	0.0	38.5	0.8	38.5	0.0	38.6	0.3	38.6	0.0	38.6	0.0	38.8	0.5
1968	38.9	0.3	38.9	0.0	39.0	0.3	39.0	0.0	39.2	0.5	39.0	-0.5	39.1	0.3	39.6	1.3	39.6	0.0	39.7	0.3	40.1	1.0	40.1	0.0
1969	40.3	0.5	40.3	0.0	40.3	0.0	40.6	0.7	40.6	0.0	40.6	0.0	40.6	0.0	40.7	0.2	40.9	0.5	41.0	0.2	41.2	0.5	41.2	0.0
1970	41.5	0.7	41.5	0.0	41.7	0.5	42.0	0.7	42.1	0.2	42.1	0.0	42.2	0.2	42.2	0.0	42.4	0.5	42.5	0.2	42.5	0.0	42.6	0.2
1971	43.0	0.9	43.5	1.2	43.8	0.7	44.0	0.5	44.0	0.0	44.1	0.2	44.1	0.0	44.3	0.5	44.0	-0.7	44.0	0.0	44.0	0.0	44.3	0.7
1972	44.0	-0.7	44.5	1.1	44.6	0.2	44.9	0.7	45.0	0.2	45.0	0.0	45.1	0.2	45.1	0.0	45.1	0.0	45.4	0.7	45.5	0.2	45.6	0.2
1973	46.1	1.1	46.6	1.1	46.9	0.6	47.2	0.6	47.4	0.4	47.5	0.2	47.5	0.0	47.5	0.0	47.5	0.0	47.8	0.6	47.8	0.0	47.9	0.2
1974	48.8	1.9	49.2	0.8	50.1	1.8	50.4	0.6	50.9	1.0	51.4	1.0	51.9	1.0	52.6	1.3	53.4	1.5	54.2	1.5	54.2	0.0	54.9	1.3
1975	55.7	1.5	56.3	1.1	56.3	0.0	57.0	1.2	57.2	0.4	57.9	1.2	58.0	0.2	58.4	0.7	59.1	1.2	59.7	1.0	59.9	0.3	59.9	0.0
1976	61.0	1.8	61.4	0.7	61.6	0.3	61.9	0.5	62.0	0.2	62.2	0.3	62.5	0.5	63.2	1.1	63.7	0.8	63.7	0.0	64.5	1.3	64.7	0.3
1977	65.2	0.8	64.6	-0.9	65.4	1.2	68.1	4.1	68.5	0.6	69.1	0.9	70.5	2.0	70.8	0.4	71.2	0.6	72.0	1.1	71.0	-1.4	71.2	0.3
1978	72.7	2.1	73.0	0.4	73.9	1.2	74.3	0.5	74.5	0.3	75.0	0.7	75.4	0.5	75.8	0.5	77.6	2.4	77.6	0.0	78.4	1.0	79.2	1.0
1979	80.4	1.5	80.8	0.5	81.6	1.0	82.4	1.0	82.7	0.4	83.0	0.4	84.5	1.8	85.3	0.9	85.8	0.6	84.8	-1.2	84.8	0.0	86.9	2.5
1980	88.0	1.3	88.6	0.7	88.7	0.1	90.1	1.6	88.2	-2.1	88.2	0.0	88.2	0.0	88.1	-0.1	88.2	0.1	89.5	1.5	89.6	0.1	89.6	0.0
1981	91.8	2.5	92.0	0.2	93.8	2.0	94.3	0.5	95.9	1.7	96.1	0.2	96.2	0.1	96.2	0.0	97.9	1.8	98.2	0.3	98.4	0.2	98.7	0.3
1982	98.7	0.0	98.8	0.1	98.8	0.0	99.0	0.2	99.2	0.2	99.3	0.1	99.4	0.1	101.2	1.8	101.2	0.0	101.2	0.0	101.5	0.3	101.5	0.0
1983	101.6	0.1	101.3	-0.3	103.8	2.5	105.7	1.8	106.5	0.8	107.9	1.3	108.3	0.4	108.3	0.0	108.3	0.0	108.7	0.4	108.9	0.2	109.0	0.1
1984	109.0	0.0	108.8	-0.2	109.0	0.2	109.3	0.3	109.5	0.2	109.8	0.3	109.8	0.0	110.5	0.6	111.0	0.5	111.0	0.0	111.0	0.0	111.1	0.1
1985	111.7	0.5	111.8	0.1	111.9	0.1	112.1	0.2	112.3	0.2	113.9	1.4	113.8	-0.1	114.2	0.4	114.5	0.3	114.7	0.2	114.9	0.2	115.8	0.8
1986	116.8	0.9	115.5	-1.1	116.8	1.1	117.6	0.7	117.7	0.1	118.3	0.5	119.2	0.8	119.0	-0.2	118.9	-0.1	119.6	0.6	118.6	-0.8	118.3	-0.3
1987	119.6	1.1	119.5	-0.1	119.8	0.3	120.9	0.9	121.4	0.4	121.8	0.3	121.5	-0.2	122.4	0.7	122.2	-0.2	122.5	0.2	122.7	0.2	122.7	0.0
1988	123.1	0.3	124.0	0.7	124.0	0.0	123.7	-0.2	124.4	0.6	125.4	0.8	125.9	0.4	125.1	-0.6	125.2	0.1	125.5	0.2	125.7	0.2	126.2	0.4
1989	126.1	-0.1	125.6	-0.4	126.3	0.6	126.5	0.2	125.7	-0.6	126.9	1.0	126.8	-0.1	127.5	0.6	127.7	0.2	127.9	0.2	128.2	0.2	128.6	0.3
1990	128.5	-0.1	128.6	0.1	129.4	0.6	129.4	0.0	129.6	0.2	130.0	0.3	130.5	0.4	130.4	-0.1	130.4	0.0	130.5	0.1	130.2	-0.2	130.7	0.4
1991	129.5	-0.9	129.7	0.2	129.9	0.2	130.4	0.4	130.6	0.2	130.2	-0.3	130.1	-0.1	130.0	-0.1	130.3	0.2	130.4	0.1	130.3	-0.1	130.4	0.1

[Continued]

Clay Construction Products ex. Refractories
Producer Price Index
Base 1982 = 100
[Continued]

For 1947-2001. Columns headed % show percentile change in the index from the previous period for which an index is available.

Year	Jan Index	%	Feb Index	%	Mar Index	%	Apr Index	%	May Index	%	Jun Index	%	Jul Index	%	Aug Index	%	Sep Index	%	Oct Index	%	Nov Index	%	Dec Index	%
1992	130.3	-0.1	130.7	0.3	131.2	0.4	131.0	-0.2	132.0	0.8	132.4	0.3	132.5	0.1	132.7	0.2	132.6	-0.1	132.8	0.2	132.9	0.1	132.8	-0.1
1993	133.4	0.5	134.1	0.5	134.0	-0.1	134.7	0.5	134.9	0.1	135.3	0.3	135.5	0.1	135.8	0.2	135.9	0.1	136.1	0.1	136.1	0.0	135.7	-0.3
1994	135.9	0.1	136.7	0.6	138.2	1.1	138.1	-0.1	138.5	0.3	138.7	0.1	138.8	0.1	138.8	0.0	138.8	0.0	138.9	0.1	138.8	-0.1	138.9	0.1
1995	139.3	0.3	139.7	0.3	140.6	0.6	141.2	0.4	141.4	0.1	141.8	0.3	141.9	0.1	142.0	0.1	142.0	0.0	142.0	0.0	142.0	0.0	142.1	0.1
1996	142.3	0.1	141.9	-0.3	141.9	0.0	142.0	0.1	142.0	0.0	142.4	0.3	142.6	0.1	142.6	0.0	142.6	0.0	142.7	0.1	142.7	0.0	142.6	-0.1
1997	142.4	-0.1	142.4	0.0	142.9	0.4	143.3	0.3	143.3	0.0	143.2	-0.1	143.3	0.1	143.9	0.4	144.1	0.1	144.1	0.0	144.1	0.0	144.1	0.0
1998	144.0	-0.1	144.8	0.6	144.8	0.0	144.7	-0.1	144.6	-0.1	144.6	0.0	144.7	0.1	145.1	0.3	145.3	0.1	145.3	0.0	145.3	0.0	145.5	0.1
1999	146.7	0.8	147.6	0.6	148.2	0.4	147.8	-0.3	147.9	0.1	147.9	0.0	148.5	0.4	148.9	0.3	148.9	0.0	148.8	-0.1	149.5	0.5	149.4	-0.1
2000	151.7	1.5	152.2	0.3	153.3	0.7	152.7	-0.4	152.8	0.1	152.8	0.0	153.1	0.2	153.0	-0.1	152.8	-0.1	152.8	0.0	153.0	0.1	153.7	0.5
2001	156.6	1.9	156.8	0.1	157.5	0.4	158.7	0.8	158.9	0.1	159.0	0.1	159.1	0.1	158.9	-0.1	158.9	0.0	157.0	-1.2	157.3	0.2	157.3	0.0

Source: U.S. Department of Labor, Bureau of Labor Statistics, Division of Industry Prices and Price Indexes. n.e.c. stands for not elsewhere classified. - indicates no data collected for period or unavailable.

Refractories
Producer Price Index
Base 1982 = 100

For 1947-2001. Columns headed % show percentile change in the index from the previous period for which an index is available.

Year	Jan Index	%	Feb Index	%	Mar Index	%	Apr Index	%	May Index	%	Jun Index	%	Jul Index	%	Aug Index	%	Sep Index	%	Oct Index	%	Nov Index	%	Dec Index	%
1947	13.4	-	13.4	0.0	13.4	0.0	14.5	8.2	14.5	0.0	14.5	0.0	14.5	0.0	14.5	0.0	14.5	0.0	14.5	0.0	15.0	3.4	15.1	0.7
1948	15.1	0.0	15.1	0.0	15.1	0.0	15.1	0.0	15.1	0.0	15.1	0.0	16.1	6.6	16.5	2.5	16.5	0.0	16.5	0.0	16.5	0.0	16.5	0.0
1949	16.5	0.0	16.5	0.0	16.5	0.0	16.5	0.0	16.5	0.0	16.5	0.0	16.5	0.0	16.5	0.0	16.5	0.0	16.5	0.0	16.5	0.0	16.5	0.0
1950	17.6	6.7	17.8	1.1	17.8	0.0	17.8	0.0	17.8	0.0	17.8	0.0	17.8	0.0	17.8	0.0	17.8	0.0	19.1	7.3	19.6	2.6	19.6	0.0
1951	19.6	0.0	19.6	0.0	19.6	0.0	19.6	0.0	19.6	0.0	19.6	0.0	19.6	0.0	19.6	0.0	19.6	0.0	19.6	0.0	19.6	0.0	19.6	0.0
1952	19.6	0.0	19.6	0.0	19.6	0.0	19.6	0.0	19.6	0.0	19.6	0.0	19.6	0.0	19.6	0.0	19.6	0.0	20.5	4.6	20.5	0.0	20.5	0.0
1953	20.5	0.0	20.5	0.0	20.5	0.0	20.5	0.0	20.5	0.0	20.5	0.0	22.5	9.8	22.5	0.0	22.5	0.0	22.5	0.0	22.5	0.0	22.5	0.0
1954	22.5	0.0	22.5	0.0	22.5	0.0	22.5	0.0	22.5	0.0	22.5	0.0	22.5	0.0	22.5	0.0	23.6	4.9	23.6	0.0	23.6	0.0	23.6	0.0
1955	23.6	0.0	23.6	0.0	23.6	0.0	23.6	0.0	23.6	0.0	23.6	0.0	24.9	5.5	25.2	1.2	25.2	0.0	25.2	0.0	25.2	0.0	25.2	0.0
1956	25.2	0.0	25.2	0.0	25.2	0.0	25.2	0.0	25.2	0.0	25.2	0.0	26.2	4.0	26.5	1.1	26.5	0.0	26.5	0.0	26.5	0.0	26.5	0.0
1957	26.5	0.0	26.5	0.0	26.5	0.0	27.9	5.3	27.9	0.0	27.9	0.0	27.9	0.0	27.9	0.0	27.9	0.0	27.9	0.0	27.9	0.0	27.9	0.0
1958	27.9	0.0	27.9	0.0	27.9	0.0	27.9	0.0	27.9	0.0	27.9	0.0	27.9	0.0	27.9	0.0	29.0	3.9	29.0	0.0	29.0	0.0	29.0	0.0
1959	29.0	0.0	29.0	0.0	29.0	0.0	29.0	0.0	29.0	0.0	29.0	0.0	29.0	0.0	29.0	0.0	29.0	0.0	29.0	0.0	29.0	0.0	29.0	0.0
1960	29.0	0.0	29.0	0.0	29.0	0.0	29.0	0.0	29.0	0.0	29.0	0.0	29.0	0.0	29.0	0.0	29.0	0.0	29.0	0.0	29.0	0.0	29.0	0.0
1961	29.0	0.0	29.0	0.0	29.0	0.0	29.0	0.0	28.7	-1.0	28.7	0.0	28.7	0.0	28.7	0.0	28.7	0.0	28.7	0.0	28.7	0.0	28.7	0.0
1962	28.7	0.0	28.7	0.0	28.7	0.0	28.7	0.0	28.7	0.0	28.7	0.0	28.7	0.0	28.7	0.0	28.7	0.0	28.7	0.0	28.7	0.0	28.7	0.0
1963	28.7	0.0	28.7	0.0	28.7	0.0	28.7	0.0	28.7	0.0	28.7	0.0	28.4	-1.0	28.4	0.0	28.4	0.0	28.4	0.0	28.4	0.0	28.4	0.0
1964	28.4	0.0	28.4	0.0	28.4	0.0	28.9	1.8	28.9	0.0	28.9	0.0	28.9	0.0	28.9	0.0	28.9	0.0	29.0	0.3	29.1	0.3	29.1	0.0
1965	29.1	0.0	29.1	0.0	29.1	0.0	29.1	0.0	29.1	0.0	29.1	0.0	29.1	0.0	29.1	0.0	29.1	0.0	29.1	0.0	29.1	0.0	29.1	0.0
1966	29.1	0.0	29.1	0.0	29.1	0.0	29.2	0.3	29.4	0.7	29.4	0.0	29.4	0.0	29.4	0.0	29.4	0.0	29.4	0.0	29.4	0.0	29.4	0.0
1967	29.6	0.7	29.6	0.0	29.6	0.0	29.6	0.0	29.6	0.0	29.6	0.0	29.6	0.0	29.6	0.0	29.6	0.0	29.6	0.0	29.9	1.0	29.9	0.0
1968	30.1	0.7	31.7	5.3	31.8	0.3	31.8	0.0	31.8	0.0	31.8	0.0	31.8	0.0	31.8	0.0	31.8	0.0	31.8	0.0	31.8	0.0	31.8	0.0
1969	31.8	0.0	31.8	0.0	31.8	0.0	32.1	0.9	32.1	0.0	32.1	0.0	32.1	0.0	33.0	2.8	33.1	0.3	33.1	0.0	33.1	0.0	34.1	3.0
1970	34.9	2.3	35.3	1.1	35.4	0.3	35.6	0.6	35.6	0.0	35.5	-0.3	35.6	0.3	35.6	0.0	35.6	0.0	35.6	0.0	37.6	5.6	37.6	0.0
1971	37.6	0.0	37.6	0.0	37.6	0.0	37.6	0.0	37.6	0.0	37.7	0.3	37.7	0.0	37.7	0.0	37.7	0.0	37.7	0.0	37.7	0.0	37.7	0.0
1972	37.7	0.0	37.7	0.0	37.7	0.0	37.7	0.0	37.7	0.0	37.7	0.0	37.7	0.0	38.5	2.1	39.2	1.8	39.2	0.0	39.2	0.0	39.2	0.0
1973	40.4	3.1	40.4	0.0	40.4	0.0	40.4	0.0	40.4	0.0	40.4	0.0	40.4	0.0	40.4	0.0	40.4	0.0	40.4	0.0	40.4	0.0	40.4	0.0
1974	40.4	0.0	40.4	0.0	40.4	0.0	40.4	0.0	40.4	0.0	40.4	0.0	40.9	1.2	40.9	0.0	45.5	11.2	46.6	2.4	46.8	0.4	47.6	1.7
1975	47.8	0.4	48.4	1.3	48.5	0.2	48.5	0.0	48.6	0.2	48.6	0.0	48.6	0.0	48.6	0.0	48.7	0.2	48.7	0.0	52.5	7.8	53.3	1.5
1976	53.3	0.0	53.3	0.0	53.4	0.2	53.5	0.2	53.5	0.0	53.5	0.0	53.6	0.2	53.8	0.4	56.0	4.1	56.7	1.3	57.2	0.9	57.2	0.0
1977	57.3	0.2	57.3	0.0	57.3	0.0	57.3	0.0	57.6	0.5	58.3	1.2	58.5	0.3	58.9	0.7	61.4	4.2	61.8	0.7	62.1	0.5	62.1	0.0
1978	62.2	0.2	62.3	0.2	62.3	0.0	62.4	0.2	62.5	0.2	62.5	0.0	63.2	1.1	66.0	4.4	66.4	0.6	66.9	0.8	67.1	0.3	67.1	0.0
1979	67.5	0.6	67.6	0.1	67.7	0.1	67.8	0.1	67.8	0.0	69.0	1.8	71.4	3.5	71.7	0.4	71.9	0.3	72.6	1.0	73.4	1.1	73.6	0.3
1980	73.7	0.1	74.5	1.1	75.3	1.1	77.6	3.1	78.4	1.0	78.9	0.6	79.7	1.0	80.3	0.8	80.3	0.0	81.1	1.0	81.1	0.0	81.1	0.0
1981	83.8	3.3	87.1	3.9	87.9	0.9	87.9	0.0	90.2	2.6	91.1	1.0	91.1	0.0	91.1	0.0	91.1	0.0	91.3	0.2	91.6	0.3	92.4	0.9
1982	94.0	1.7	99.4	5.7	100.1	0.7	100.5	0.4	100.7	0.2	101.0	0.3	101.0	0.0	101.1	0.1	101.1	0.0	101.1	0.0	100.0	-1.1	100.0	0.0
1983	100.2	0.2	100.2	0.0	100.2	0.0	100.3	0.1	100.3	0.0	99.9	-0.4	100.3	0.4	100.7	0.4	100.9	0.2	102.3	1.4	104.8	2.4	104.8	0.0
1984	105.0	0.2	105.6	0.6	107.1	1.4	107.3	0.2	107.3	0.0	107.3	0.0	107.3	0.0	107.3	0.0	107.3	0.0	107.3	0.0	108.4	1.0	108.4	0.0
1985	108.6	0.2	108.6	0.0	108.9	0.3	109.5	0.6	110.1	0.5	110.1	0.0	110.1	0.0	110.1	0.0	110.1	0.0	110.1	0.0	110.1	0.0	110.2	0.1
1986	110.2	0.0	110.2	0.0	110.2	0.0	110.3	0.1	110.5	0.2	110.5	0.0	110.5	0.0	110.5	0.0	110.4	-0.1	109.9	-0.5	109.3	-0.5	109.7	0.4
1987	109.9	0.2	109.9	0.0	109.9	0.0	110.0	0.1	110.0	0.0	110.4	0.4	110.6	0.2	110.8	0.2	110.9	0.1	110.9	0.0	111.1	0.2	111.9	0.7
1988	112.6	0.6	112.6	0.0	112.5	-0.1	113.5	0.9	113.7	0.2	113.8	0.1	113.8	0.0	113.8	0.0	114.1	0.3	115.1	0.9	115.2	0.1	115.4	0.2
1989	118.1	2.3	119.0	0.8	119.2	0.2	119.6	0.3	119.6	0.0	119.6	0.0	119.8	0.2	119.3	-0.4	119.4	0.1	119.6	0.2	119.6	0.0	119.6	0.0
1990	120.3	0.6	120.9	0.5	121.5	0.5	122.0	0.4	122.1	0.1	122.8	0.6	122.8	0.0	122.9	0.1	122.7	-0.2	122.8	0.1	123.4	0.5	123.4	0.0
1991	124.7	1.1	125.1	0.3	125.3	0.2	125.4	0.1	125.8	0.3	125.3	-0.4	125.3	0.0	125.4	0.1	125.5	0.1	125.5	0.0	125.5	0.0	125.9	0.3

[Continued]

Refractories
Producer Price Index
Base 1982 = 100
[Continued]

For 1947-2001. Columns headed % show percentile change in the index from the previous period for which an index is available.

Year	Jan Index	%	Feb Index	%	Mar Index	%	Apr Index	%	May Index	%	Jun Index	%	Jul Index	%	Aug Index	%	Sep Index	%	Oct Index	%	Nov Index	%	Dec Index	%
1992	126.1	0.2	125.6	-0.4	126.8	1.0	126.7	-0.1	126.7	0.0	126.8	0.1	126.3	-0.4	127.6	1.0	126.3	-1.0	126.3	0.0	125.2	-0.9	125.8	0.5
1993	126.1	0.2	126.1	0.0	126.5	0.3	126.5	0.0	127.2	0.6	127.4	0.2	127.7	0.2	127.9	0.2	127.6	-0.2	127.9	0.2	127.5	-0.3	127.4	-0.1
1994	128.5	0.9	128.0	-0.4	127.7	-0.2	127.8	0.1	127.7	-0.1	127.9	0.2	128.3	0.3	127.8	-0.4	128.4	0.5	128.4	0.0	128.9	0.4	128.9	0.0
1995	128.8	-0.1	129.8	0.8	131.5	1.3	132.4	0.7	132.4	0.0	132.5	0.1	132.5	0.0	132.3	-0.2	133.0	0.5	132.9	-0.1	132.9	0.0	133.9	0.8
1996	134.2	0.2	136.0	1.3	136.4	0.3	136.9	0.4	136.8	-0.1	137.0	0.1	137.5	0.4	137.3	-0.1	137.7	0.3	137.3	-0.3	137.3	0.0	137.2	-0.1
1997	137.4	0.1	138.3	0.7	138.2	-0.1	138.8	0.4	138.6	-0.1	137.8	-0.6	138.1	0.2	139.3	0.9	139.4	0.1	139.5	0.1	139.6	0.1	139.7	0.1
1998	140.3	0.4	141.3	0.7	141.7	0.3	141.0	-0.5	141.4	0.3	141.4	0.0	140.8	-0.4	141.1	0.2	141.2	0.1	141.3	0.1	140.8	-0.4	141.2	0.3
1999	141.0	-0.1	142.2	0.9	142.5	0.2	143.2	0.5	142.1	-0.8	142.5	0.3	142.1	-0.3	142.9	0.6	142.4	-0.3	142.3	-0.1	142.1	-0.1	141.9	-0.1
2000	142.0	0.1	141.8	-0.1	142.6	0.6	142.4	-0.1	142.8	0.3	144.3	1.1	145.0	0.5	145.0	0.0	145.2	0.1	145.8	0.4	145.4	-0.3	145.5	0.1
2001	149.0	2.4	149.1	0.1	150.2	0.7	151.1	0.6	150.8	-0.2	151.3	0.3	151.1	-0.1	151.6	0.3	151.1	-0.3	151.6	0.3	151.1	-0.3	151.8	0.5

Source: U.S. Department of Labor, Bureau of Labor Statistics, Division of Industry Prices and Price Indexes. n.e.c. stands for not elsewhere classified. - indicates no data collected for period or unavailable.

Asphalt Felts and Coatings
Producer Price Index
Base 1982 = 100

For 1926-2001. Columns headed % show percentile change in the index from the previous period for which an index is available.

Year	Jan Index	%	Feb Index	%	Mar Index	%	Apr Index	%	May Index	%	Jun Index	%	Jul Index	%	Aug Index	%	Sep Index	%	Oct Index	%	Nov Index	%	Dec Index	%
1926	20.6	-	20.5	-0.5	20.8	1.5	21.0	1.0	21.2	1.0	21.3	0.5	21.4	0.5	21.4	0.0	21.4	0.0	21.4	0.0	21.4	0.0	21.3	-0.5
1927	20.8	-2.3	20.8	0.0	20.5	-1.4	20.1	-2.0	20.3	1.0	20.3	0.0	20.2	-0.5	20.3	0.5	20.3	0.0	20.3	0.0	17.7	-12.8	17.8	0.6
1928	18.0	1.1	17.6	-2.2	15.6	-11.4	15.8	1.3	15.8	0.0	18.9	19.6	19.2	1.6	19.2	0.0	19.3	0.5	19.4	0.5	19.4	0.0	15.9	-18.0
1929	14.4	-9.4	14.3	-0.7	14.3	0.0	15.4	7.7	16.1	4.5	16.2	0.6	16.4	1.2	16.4	0.0	16.4	0.0	16.4	0.0	16.4	0.0	16.4	0.0
1930	15.6	-4.9	15.6	0.0	15.6	0.0	15.6	0.0	15.6	0.0	15.6	0.0	15.6	0.0	15.8	1.3	16.4	3.8	17.3	5.5	17.3	0.0	17.3	0.0
1931	16.7	-3.5	16.7	0.0	16.7	0.0	16.7	0.0	16.7	0.0	16.7	0.0	16.7	0.0	16.7	0.0	16.7	0.0	16.7	0.0	16.7	0.0	16.7	0.0
1932	15.8	-5.4	15.3	-3.2	15.5	1.3	15.6	0.6	15.3	-1.9	14.3	-6.5	13.2	-7.7	13.6	3.0	15.1	11.0	16.1	6.6	17.0	5.6	16.9	-0.6
1933	15.7	-7.1	13.7	-12.7	13.8	0.7	13.9	0.7	15.1	8.6	15.8	4.6	16.0	1.3	16.4	2.5	16.5	0.6	16.9	2.4	17.1	1.2	17.1	0.0
1934	17.2	0.6	16.2	-5.8	15.2	-6.2	15.4	1.3	16.2	5.2	16.6	2.5	17.0	2.4	17.5	2.9	17.7	1.1	17.7	0.0	17.8	0.0	17.8	0.6
1935	17.9	0.6	17.8	-0.6	17.7	-0.6	17.7	0.0	18.0	1.7	18.1	0.6	18.0	-0.6	17.5	-2.8	17.5	0.0	17.7	1.1	17.8	0.6	16.7	-6.2
1936	16.5	-1.2	16.4	-0.6	16.4	0.0	17.2	4.9	17.5	1.7	17.5	0.0	17.5	0.0	17.6	0.6	17.7	0.6	18.3	3.4	18.4	0.5	18.4	0.0
1937	18.5	0.5	18.7	1.1	19.3	3.2	19.3	0.0	19.8	2.6	20.0	1.0	20.0	0.0	20.0	0.0	19.6	-2.0	19.1	-2.6	18.3	-4.2	16.3	-10.9
1938	16.1	-1.2	15.9	-1.2	15.0	-5.7	15.2	1.3	15.3	0.7	15.3	0.0	15.3	0.0	15.3	0.0	15.3	0.0	15.3	0.0	15.3	0.0	15.3	-0.0
1939	15.5	1.3	15.5	0.0	15.5	0.0	15.6	0.6	15.9	1.9	15.9	0.0	15.9	0.0	16.0	0.6	16.2	1.3	16.3	0.6	16.3	0.0	16.6	1.8
1940	17.0	2.4	17.0	0.0	17.5	2.9	17.8	1.7	17.8	0.0	17.8	0.0	17.7	-0.6	17.4	-1.7	17.3	-0.6	17.1	-1.2	17.1	0.0	17.1	0.0
1941	17.2	0.6	17.2	0.0	16.9	-1.7	16.7	-1.2	17.0	1.8	17.5	2.9	18.0	2.9	18.5	2.8	18.8	1.6	19.5	3.7	19.5	0.0	18.3	-6.2
1942	17.5	-4.4	17.5	0.0	17.5	0.0	17.5	0.0	17.5	0.0	17.5	0.0	17.5	0.0	17.5	0.0	17.5	0.0	17.5	0.0	17.5	0.0	17.5	0.0
1943	17.5	0.0	17.5	0.0	17.5	0.0	17.5	0.0	17.5	0.0	17.5	0.0	17.5	0.0	17.5	0.0	17.5	0.0	17.5	0.0	17.5	0.0	17.5	0.0
1944	17.5	0.0	17.5	0.0	17.5	0.0	17.5	0.0	17.5	0.0	17.5	0.0	17.5	0.0	17.6	0.6	17.9	1.7	18.0	0.6	18.0	0.0	18.0	0.0
1945	18.0	0.0	18.0	0.0	18.0	0.0	18.0	0.0	18.0	0.0	18.0	0.0	18.0	0.0	18.0	0.0	18.0	0.0	18.0	0.0	18.0	0.0	18.0	0.0
1946	18.0	0.0	18.0	0.0	18.0	0.0	18.0	0.0	18.5	2.8	18.9	2.2	19.0	0.5	19.1	0.5	19.1	0.0	19.2	0.5	19.3	0.5	20.7	7.3
1947	20.5	-1.0	20.6	0.5	21.4	3.9	21.6	0.9	21.6	0.0	21.6	0.0	21.6	0.0	21.5	-0.5	21.5	0.0	21.5	0.0	21.5	0.0	22.6	5.1
1948	23.2	2.7	23.2	0.0	23.2	0.0	23.2	0.0	23.2	0.0	23.6	1.7	24.2	2.5	23.6	-2.5	23.6	0.0	23.6	0.0	23.6	0.0	23.6	0.0
1949	23.6	0.0	23.6	0.0	23.6	0.0	23.6	0.0	23.6	0.0	23.6	0.0	23.4	-0.8	23.4	0.0	23.4	0.0	23.2	-0.9	23.2	0.0	23.2	0.0
1950	23.2	0.0	23.2	0.0	23.2	0.0	22.9	-1.3	22.5	-1.7	22.5	0.0	22.5	0.0	22.9	1.8	22.9	0.0	23.2	1.3	24.0	3.4	24.0	0.0
1951	24.0	0.0	24.0	0.0	24.0	0.0	24.0	0.0	24.0	0.0	24.0	0.0	24.0	0.0	24.0	0.0	24.0	0.0	24.0	0.0	24.0	0.0	22.5	-6.3
1952	22.5	0.0	22.5	0.0	22.5	0.0	22.5	0.0	22.5	0.0	24.2	7.6	24.2	0.0	24.2	0.0	24.2	0.0	24.2	0.0	24.2	0.0	24.2	0.0
1953	24.2	0.0	24.2	0.0	24.2	0.0	24.2	0.0	24.2	0.0	24.2	0.0	24.1	-0.4	24.1	0.0	25.0	3.7	25.1	0.4	25.1	0.0	25.1	0.0
1954	25.1	0.0	25.1	0.0	25.1	0.0	24.7	-1.6	21.9	-11.3	21.5	-1.8	22.5	4.7	22.5	0.0	23.7	5.3	24.2	2.1	24.2	0.0	24.2	0.0
1955	24.2	0.0	22.9	-5.4	22.5	-1.7	22.5	0.0	24.1	7.1	24.3	0.8	25.3	4.1	26.1	3.2	26.1	0.0	26.1	0.0	23.0	-11.9	23.0	0.0
1956	22.7	-1.3	22.7	0.0	24.3	7.0	25.5	4.9	25.5	0.0	25.5	0.0	26.9	5.5	26.8	-0.4	26.8	0.0	26.8	0.0	26.1	-2.6	26.1	0.0
1957	25.4	-2.7	26.3	3.5	26.9	2.3	27.7	3.0	28.7	3.6	28.7	0.0	28.7	0.0	28.7	0.0	28.4	-1.0	28.4	0.0	28.4	0.0	28.4	0.0
1958	28.4	0.0	28.4	0.0	24.4	-14.1	24.4	0.0	24.2	-0.8	23.5	-2.9	23.5	0.0	23.5	0.0	27.0	14.9	27.0	0.0	27.0	0.0	27.0	0.0
1959	27.0	0.0	27.3	1.1	27.2	-0.4	28.8	5.9	28.8	0.0	25.9	-10.1	25.5	-1.5	25.5	0.0	25.3	-0.8	25.3	0.0	25.9	2.4	25.9	0.0
1960	25.9	0.0	24.5	-5.4	24.5	0.0	24.3	-0.8	24.3	0.0	24.3	0.0	24.3	0.0	24.3	0.0	24.3	0.0	24.3	0.0	24.3	0.0	24.3	0.0
1961	26.0	7.0	26.0	0.0	26.0	0.0	26.0	0.0	25.8	-0.8	25.8	0.0	26.0	0.8	26.0	0.0	26.0	0.0	27.5	5.8	27.5	0.0	27.5	0.0
1962	27.3	-0.7	27.1	-0.7	27.1	0.0	27.1	0.0	26.4	-2.6	25.5	-3.4	23.9	-6.3	23.9	0.0	23.9	0.0	23.9	0.0	23.9	0.0	23.9	0.0
1963	23.9	0.0	25.1	5.0	25.1	0.0	25.1	0.0	24.7	-1.6	23.8	-3.6	23.5	-1.3	23.5	0.0	23.5	0.0	23.3	-0.9	23.3	0.0	23.3	0.0
1964	23.3	0.0	23.3	0.0	23.1	-0.9	23.1	0.0	23.1	0.0	23.1	0.0	23.7	2.6	24.3	2.5	24.3	0.0	24.3	0.0	24.3	0.0	24.3	0.0
1965	24.3	0.0	24.3	0.0	24.5	0.8	24.6	0.4	24.6	0.0	24.6	0.0	24.6	0.0	24.6	0.0	25.4	3.3	25.3	-0.4	25.3	0.0	25.3	0.0
1966	25.3	0.0	25.3	0.0	25.3	0.0	25.3	0.0	25.2	-0.4	25.2	0.0	26.1	3.6	26.1	0.0	26.1	0.0	26.1	0.0	26.1	0.0	25.6	-1.9
1967	25.6	0.0	25.3	-1.2	25.3	0.0	25.3	0.0	23.6	-6.7	23.6	0.0	24.4	3.4	24.4	0.0	25.3	3.7	25.3	0.0	26.5	4.7	26.5	0.0
1968	26.6	0.4	26.2	-1.5	26.2	0.0	26.1	-0.4	26.1	0.0	25.8	-1.1	26.1	1.2	26.1	0.0	25.4	-2.7	25.4	0.0	25.4	0.0	25.4	0.0
1969	25.4	0.0	26.1	2.8	26.0	-0.4	26.0	0.0	25.6	-1.5	26.3	2.7	26.6	1.1	25.1	-5.6	25.1	0.0	25.1	0.0	25.1	0.0	27.1	8.0
1970	27.2	0.4	26.9	-1.1	26.1	-3.0	25.4	-2.7	25.4	0.0	24.5	-3.5	24.3	-0.8	24.9	2.5	25.4	2.0	25.6	0.8	26.5	3.5	26.9	1.5

[Continued]

Asphalt Felts and Coatings
Producer Price Index
Base 1982 = 100
[Continued]

For 1926-2001. Columns headed % show percentile change in the index from the previous period for which an index is available.

Year	Jan Index	%	Feb Index	%	Mar Index	%	Apr Index	%	May Index	%	Jun Index	%	Jul Index	%	Aug Index	%	Sep Index	%	Oct Index	%	Nov Index	%	Dec Index	%
1971	27.3	1.5	27.3	0.0	31.0	13.6	31.0	0.0	31.0	0.0	32.8	5.8	32.9	0.3	32.9	0.0	32.9	0.0	32.9	0.0	32.9	0.0	32.9	0.0
1972	32.9	0.0	32.9	0.0	32.9	0.0	32.9	0.0	32.9	0.0	32.9	0.0	32.9	0.0	32.9	0.0	32.9	0.0	32.9	0.0	32.9	0.0	32.9	0.0
1973	32.9	0.0	32.9	0.0	32.9	0.0	33.7	2.4	34.3	1.8	34.3	0.0	34.2	-0.3	34.2	0.0	34.2	0.0	34.3	0.3	35.1	2.3	35.1	0.0
1974	37.7	7.4	40.1	6.4	43.0	7.2	48.2	12.1	50.2	4.1	50.8	1.2	51.8	2.0	52.9	2.1	52.9	0.0	54.1	2.3	54.3	0.4	54.3	0.0
1975	54.3	0.0	54.7	0.7	54.7	0.0	57.2	4.6	57.2	0.0	57.2	0.0	57.5	0.5	56.9	-1.0	57.4	0.9	58.1	1.2	57.5	-1.0	57.5	0.0
1976	57.5	0.0	57.6	0.2	59.3	3.0	60.1	1.3	59.6	-0.8	59.6	0.0	59.6	0.0	62.1	4.2	61.6	-0.8	61.7	0.2	60.1	-2.6	58.9	-2.0
1977	57.9	-1.7	57.9	0.0	61.0	5.4	61.0	0.0	61.0	0.0	61.8	1.3	63.6	2.9	63.6	0.0	67.0	5.3	69.1	3.1	69.1	0.0	69.1	0.0
1978	69.6	0.7	69.6	0.0	69.7	0.1	72.2	3.6	72.2	0.0	72.6	0.6	74.2	2.2	74.7	0.7	74.8	0.1	76.6	2.4	76.6	0.0	76.6	0.0
1979	77.0	0.5	79.8	3.6	76.1	-4.6	79.4	4.3	79.8	0.5	81.1	1.6	82.4	1.6	81.8	-0.7	83.6	2.2	84.7	1.3	87.2	3.0	87.0	-0.2
1980	89.5	2.9	93.5	4.5	97.6	4.4	102.6	5.1	100.7	-1.9	100.6	-0.1	103.9	3.3	103.2	-0.7	102.4	-0.8	102.5	0.1	99.7	-2.7	99.1	-0.6
1981	99.1	0.0	97.8	-1.3	98.0	0.2	104.4	6.5	102.3	-2.0	107.6	5.2	105.9	-1.6	105.6	-0.3	100.8	-4.5	101.1	0.3	103.0	1.9	101.8	-1.2
1982	100.7	-1.1	100.5	-0.2	99.0	-1.5	97.1	-1.9	96.8	-0.3	99.5	2.8	100.4	0.9	100.4	0.0	103.8	3.4	102.1	-1.6	100.2	-1.9	99.6	-0.6
1983	98.8	-0.8	95.5	-3.3	94.0	-1.6	96.4	2.6	95.4	-1.0	95.3	-0.1	96.7	1.5	96.2	-0.5	97.2	1.0	97.4	0.2	97.3	-0.1	96.4	-0.9
1984	96.6	0.2	98.5	2.0	96.8	-1.7	99.4	2.7	100.1	0.7	99.0	-1.1	99.0	0.0	102.5	3.5	102.4	-0.1	102.7	0.3	102.9	0.2	103.4	0.5
1985	102.8	-0.6	102.3	-0.5	101.9	-0.4	103.4	1.5	103.6	0.2	103.0	-0.6	103.0	0.0	102.5	-0.5	102.1	-0.4	101.7	-0.4	102.7	1.0	102.2	-0.5
1986	101.8	-0.4	101.8	0.0	100.6	-1.2	99.3	-1.3	99.3	0.0	97.3	-2.0	97.1	-0.2	97.3	0.2	96.6	-0.7	95.6	-1.0	94.6	-1.0	94.0	-0.6
1987	91.8	-2.3	91.5	-0.3	90.8	-0.8	91.4	0.7	91.3	-0.1	90.9	-0.4	90.6	-0.3	92.8	2.4	93.4	0.6	94.4	1.1	94.9	0.5	94.8	-0.1
1988	93.8	-1.1	92.7	-1.2	93.4	0.8	92.7	-0.7	93.1	0.4	94.6	1.6	95.8	1.3	95.6	-0.2	96.3	0.7	97.1	0.8	96.0	-1.1	95.4	-0.6
1989	95.0	-0.4	94.9	-0.1	94.2	-0.7	96.0	1.9	95.7	-0.3	95.9	0.2	95.8	-0.1	95.7	-0.1	96.2	0.5	96.6	0.4	96.7	0.1	97.1	0.4
1990	97.1	0.0	95.8	-1.3	95.7	-0.1	96.0	0.3	95.6	-0.4	94.9	-0.7	94.3	-0.6	95.9	1.7	96.5	0.6	100.4	4.0	101.5	1.1	101.7	0.2
1991	100.5	-1.2	100.0	-0.5	100.4	0.4	99.3	-1.1	97.9	-1.4	98.4	0.5	98.4	0.0	97.0	-1.4	97.2	0.2	97.1	-0.1	96.5	-0.6	96.0	-0.5
1992	96.0	0.0	95.6	-0.4	95.4	-0.2	95.1	-0.3	95.6	0.5	95.9	0.3	96.3	0.4	96.2	-0.1	96.0	-0.2	97.1	1.1	98.1	1.0	97.8	-0.3
1993	98.2	0.4	97.3	-0.9	97.6	0.3	96.9	-0.7	96.7	-0.2	96.8	0.1	97.0	0.2	97.1	0.1	96.5	-0.6	96.1	-0.4	95.6	-0.5	95.8	0.2
1994	95.8	0.0	94.9	-0.9	94.5	-0.4	94.6	0.1	94.9	0.3	95.2	0.3	95.2	0.0	95.8	0.6	95.6	-0.2	95.7	0.1	95.8	0.1	95.8	0.0
1995	96.1	0.3	96.6	0.5	97.7	1.1	99.8	2.1	100.9	1.1	101.4	0.5	101.6	0.2	101.1	-0.5	101.1	0.0	101.3	0.2	101.1	-0.2	100.8	-0.3
1996	100.8	0.0	100.4	-0.4	100.3	-0.1	99.9	-0.4	100.2	0.3	99.3	-0.9	99.7	0.4	99.8	0.1	100.1	0.3	100.1	0.0	100.4	0.3	99.7	-0.7
1997	99.6	-0.1	99.9	0.3	99.4	-0.5	100.3	0.9	100.2	-0.1	100.6	0.4	100.3	-0.3	100.4	0.1	100.2	-0.2	99.3	-0.9	99.2	-0.1	98.8	-0.4
1998	98.7	-0.1	98.5	-0.2	98.4	-0.1	99.0	0.6	99.5	0.5	99.4	-0.1	99.7	0.3	100.1	0.4	100.3	0.2	100.5	0.2	100.1	-0.4	99.3	-0.8
1999	99.0	-0.3	99.0	0.0	98.4	-0.6	99.5	1.1	98.7	-0.8	98.1	-0.6	98.6	0.5	99.1	0.5	99.7	0.6	99.7	0.0	100.5	0.8	100.7	0.2
2000	100.7	0.0	99.8	-0.9	101.0	1.2	103.6	2.6	104.7	1.1	105.5	0.8	106.3	0.8	106.5	0.2	104.6	-1.8	105.6	1.0	104.9	-0.7	105.4	0.5
2001	104.8	-0.6	104.5	-0.3	104.6	0.1	105.8	1.1	106.0	0.2	107.1	1.0	108.2	1.0	108.6	0.4	109.6	0.9	109.6	0.0	110.5	0.8	110.3	-0.2

Source: U.S. Department of Labor, Bureau of Labor Statistics, Division of Industry Prices and Price Indexes. n.e.c. stands for not elsewhere classified. - indicates no data collected for period or unavailable.

Gypsum Products
Producer Price Index
Base 1982 = 100

For 1947-2001. Columns headed % show percentile change in the index from the previous period for which an index is available.

Year	Jan Index	%	Feb Index	%	Mar Index	%	Apr Index	%	May Index	%	Jun Index	%	Jul Index	%	Aug Index	%	Sep Index	%	Oct Index	%	Nov Index	%	Dec Index	%
1947	26.9	-	26.9	0.0	26.9	0.0	26.9	0.0	26.9	0.0	26.9	0.0	26.9	0.0	26.9	0.0	26.9	0.0	28.6	6.3	29.4	2.8	29.4	0.0
1948	29.4	0.0	29.4	0.0	29.4	0.0	29.6	0.7	30.2	2.0	30.2	0.0	30.2	0.0	30.2	0.0	30.2	0.0	30.2	0.0	30.2	0.0	30.1	-0.3
1949	29.8	-1.0	29.7	-0.3	29.7	0.0	29.7	0.0	29.7	0.0	29.7	0.0	29.7	0.0	29.7	0.0	29.7	0.0	29.7	0.0	29.7	0.0	29.7	0.0
1950	29.7	0.0	29.7	0.0	29.7	0.0	29.7	0.0	29.7	0.0	29.7	0.0	29.7	0.0	30.4	2.4	31.1	2.3	31.1	0.0	31.1	0.0	32.9	5.8
1951	34.1	3.6	34.1	0.0	34.1	0.0	34.1	0.0	34.1	0.0	34.1	0.0	34.1	0.0	34.1	0.0	34.1	0.0	34.1	0.0	34.2	0.3	34.2	0.0
1952	34.2	0.0	34.2	0.0	34.2	0.0	34.2	0.0	34.2	0.0	34.2	0.0	34.2	0.0	34.2	0.0	34.2	0.0	34.2	0.0	34.2	0.0	34.2	0.0
1953	34.2	0.0	34.2	0.0	34.4	0.6	35.5	3.2	35.5	0.0	35.5	0.0	35.5	0.0	35.5	0.0	35.5	0.0	35.5	0.0	35.5	0.0	35.5	0.0
1954	35.5	0.0	35.5	0.0	35.5	0.0	35.5	0.0	35.5	0.0	35.5	0.0	35.5	0.0	35.5	0.0	35.5	0.0	35.5	0.0	35.5	0.0	35.5	0.0
1955	35.5	0.0	35.5	0.0	35.5	0.0	35.5	0.0	35.5	0.0	35.5	0.0	35.5	0.0	35.5	0.0	35.5	0.0	35.5	0.0	35.5	0.0	35.5	0.0
1956	36.9	3.9	36.9	0.0	36.9	0.0	36.9	0.0	36.9	0.0	36.9	0.0	36.9	0.0	36.9	0.0	36.9	0.0	36.9	0.0	36.9	0.0	36.9	0.0
1957	36.9	0.0	36.9	0.0	36.9	0.0	36.9	0.0	36.9	0.0	36.9	0.0	36.9	0.0	36.9	0.0	36.9	0.0	36.9	0.0	36.9	0.0	36.9	0.0
1958	36.9	0.0	36.9	0.0	38.7	4.9	38.7	0.0	38.7	0.0	38.7	0.0	38.7	0.0	38.7	0.0	38.7	0.0	38.7	0.0	38.7	0.0	38.7	0.0
1959	38.7	0.0	38.7	0.0	38.7	0.0	38.7	0.0	38.7	0.0	38.7	0.0	38.7	0.0	38.7	0.0	38.7	0.0	38.7	0.0	38.7	0.0	38.7	0.0
1960	38.7	0.0	38.7	0.0	38.7	0.0	38.7	0.0	38.7	0.0	38.7	0.0	38.7	0.0	38.7	0.0	38.7	0.0	38.7	0.0	38.7	0.0	38.7	0.0
1961	39.1	1.0	39.1	0.0	39.1	0.0	39.1	0.0	39.1	0.0	39.1	0.0	39.1	0.0	39.9	2.0	39.9	0.0	39.9	0.0	39.9	0.0	39.9	0.0
1962	39.9	0.0	39.9	0.0	39.9	0.0	39.9	0.0	39.9	0.0	39.9	0.0	39.9	0.0	39.9	0.0	39.9	0.0	39.9	0.0	39.9	0.0	39.9	0.0
1963	39.9	0.0	39.9	0.0	39.9	0.0	39.9	0.0	39.9	0.0	39.9	0.0	39.9	0.0	40.2	0.8	40.3	0.2	40.3	0.0	40.3	0.0	40.3	0.0
1964	40.3	0.0	41.2	2.2	41.2	0.0	41.2	0.0	41.2	0.0	41.2	0.0	41.2	0.0	41.2	0.0	41.2	0.0	41.2	0.0	41.2	0.0	40.5	-1.7
1965	40.5	0.0	40.9	1.0	41.2	0.7	41.1	-0.2	41.1	0.0	40.9	-0.5	40.1	-2.0	38.2	-4.7	38.0	-0.5	37.6	-1.1	37.5	-0.3	37.0	-1.3
1966	38.5	4.1	38.5	0.0	38.5	0.0	38.5	0.0	38.8	0.8	39.0	0.5	39.0	0.0	39.0	0.0	39.0	0.0	39.0	0.0	39.3	0.8	39.3	0.0
1967	39.4	0.3	39.4	0.0	38.9	-1.3	38.9	0.0	38.9	0.0	38.4	-1.3	38.3	-0.3	38.3	0.0	38.3	0.0	40.1	4.7	40.1	0.0	40.1	0.0
1968	40.1	0.0	40.5	1.0	40.5	0.0	40.5	0.0	40.5	0.0	40.5	0.0	40.5	0.0	40.5	0.0	40.5	0.0	40.3	-0.5	40.3	0.0	40.3	0.0
1969	40.3	0.0	40.3	0.0	40.3	0.0	40.3	0.0	41.7	3.5	40.2	-3.6	40.2	0.0	39.6	-1.5	40.2	1.5	40.9	1.7	41.6	1.7	39.5	-5.0
1970	40.7	3.0	41.2	1.2	40.6	-1.5	40.1	-1.2	39.5	-1.5	38.3	-3.0	38.1	-0.5	38.7	1.6	37.7	-2.6	37.9	0.5	37.5	-1.1	37.1	-1.1
1971	38.0	2.4	39.4	3.7	40.4	2.5	41.4	2.5	42.6	2.9	43.4	1.9	44.0	1.4	44.7	1.6	45.0	0.7	44.7	-0.7	44.1	-1.3	44.8	1.6
1972	44.3	-1.1	44.1	-0.5	45.0	2.0	44.9	-0.2	44.3	-1.3	44.5	0.5	45.2	1.6	45.4	0.4	45.0	-0.9	45.1	0.2	44.9	-0.4	44.9	0.0
1973	45.8	2.0	45.2	-1.3	46.1	2.0	46.7	1.3	47.0	0.6	48.5	3.2	48.0	-1.0	47.8	-0.4	47.6	-0.4	47.8	0.4	47.7	-0.2	48.1	0.8
1974	49.9	3.7	50.8	1.8	50.6	-0.4	51.8	2.4	52.1	0.6	53.7	3.1	54.2	0.9	55.8	3.0	56.9	2.0	56.5	-0.7	56.2	-0.5	56.4	0.4
1975	56.1	-0.5	56.1	0.0	56.9	1.4	56.2	-1.2	56.0	-0.4	56.0	0.0	55.0	-1.8	55.9	1.6	56.2	0.5	56.7	0.9	57.4	1.2	56.4	-1.7
1976	58.7	4.1	58.0	-1.2	58.7	1.2	58.9	0.3	60.0	1.9	59.9	-0.2	59.9	0.0	60.6	1.2	61.6	1.7	62.1	0.8	62.5	0.6	62.5	0.0
1977	62.8	0.5	63.5	1.1	64.1	0.9	67.2	4.8	68.7	2.2	73.1	6.4	72.9	-0.3	74.1	1.6	75.6	2.0	78.7	4.1	79.4	0.9	80.0	0.8
1978	81.9	2.4	84.3	2.9	84.8	0.6	86.4	1.9	89.1	3.1	89.9	0.9	91.4	1.7	92.1	0.8	92.2	0.1	92.5	0.3	94.5	2.2	94.8	0.3
1979	96.7	2.0	97.9	1.2	98.0	0.1	98.5	0.5	97.2	-1.3	98.2	1.0	98.3	0.1	98.5	0.2	99.6	1.1	99.7	0.1	100.1	0.4	99.6	-0.5
1980	99.7	0.1	102.4	2.7	104.5	2.1	103.1	-1.3	100.2	-2.8	100.4	0.2	98.9	-1.5	98.4	-0.5	98.3	-0.1	97.5	-0.8	98.9	1.4	98.7	-0.2
1981	101.4	2.7	100.5	-0.9	100.6	0.1	100.3	-0.3	102.0	1.7	101.8	-0.2	101.4	-0.4	99.7	-1.7	98.8	-0.9	98.6	-0.2	98.2	-0.4	97.5	-0.7
1982	97.8	0.3	99.6	1.8	101.8	2.2	102.8	1.0	101.3	-1.5	100.1	-1.2	99.9	-0.2	99.2	-0.7	99.2	0.0	99.6	0.4	99.6	0.0	99.2	-0.4
1983	102.7	3.5	104.4	1.7	103.9	-0.5	106.2	2.2	107.7	1.4	106.9	-0.7	107.8	0.8	113.0	4.8	116.3	2.9	122.2	5.1	123.1	0.7	126.0	2.4
1984	128.3	1.8	132.6	3.4	132.6	0.0	137.9	4.0	140.9	2.2	140.7	-0.1	140.5	-0.1	140.4	-0.1	138.8	-1.1	132.4	-4.6	130.6	-1.4	129.1	-1.1
1985	128.3	-0.6	134.5	4.8	131.4	-2.3	130.2	-0.9	130.1	-0.1	132.0	1.5	132.2	0.2	132.1	-0.1	129.4	-2.0	132.7	2.6	135.9	2.4	139.2	2.4
1986	140.7	1.1	141.4	0.5	137.4	-2.8	135.2	-1.6	140.7	4.1	138.3	-1.7	136.5	-1.3	134.3	-1.6	133.2	-0.8	134.0	0.6	137.0	2.2	135.7	-0.9
1987	133.9	-1.3	131.8	-1.6	127.1	-3.6	127.2	0.1	129.5	1.8	128.0	-1.2	124.0	-3.1	119.5	-3.6	118.8	-0.6	119.8	0.8	120.8	0.8	121.5	0.6
1988	120.9	-0.5	116.7	-3.5	113.3	-2.9	111.7	-1.4	112.7	0.9	110.4	-2.0	108.6	-1.6	108.0	-0.6	110.6	2.4	113.6	2.7	114.6	0.9	113.9	-0.6
1989	111.3	-2.3	110.8	-0.4	110.1	-0.6	110.3	0.2	110.6	0.3	110.4	-0.2	109.8	-0.5	107.9	-1.7	108.9	0.9	109.5	0.6	111.5	1.8	109.4	-1.9
1990	106.9	-2.3	106.0	-0.8	106.3	0.3	106.8	0.5	107.0	0.2	106.2	-0.7	105.4	-0.8	102.4	-2.8	104.0	1.6	103.4	-0.6	104.5	1.1	103.3	-1.1
1991	102.8	-0.5	105.4	2.5	104.8	-0.6	101.4	-3.2	100.3	-1.1	97.0	-3.3	96.0	-1.0	95.0	-1.0	97.5	2.6	98.2	0.7	96.8	-1.4	96.9	0.1

[Continued]

Gypsum Products
Producer Price Index
Base 1982 = 100
[Continued]

For 1947-2001. Columns headed % show percentile change in the index from the previous period for which an index is available.

Year	Jan Index	%	Feb Index	%	Mar Index	%	Apr Index	%	May Index	%	Jun Index	%	Jul Index	%	Aug Index	%	Sep Index	%	Oct Index	%	Nov Index	%	Dec Index	%
1992	94.8	-2.2	92.8	-2.1	96.0	3.4	96.6	0.6	100.5	4.0	100.4	-0.1	100.4	0.0	103.0	2.6	105.4	2.3	104.1	-1.2	104.0	-0.1	101.2	-2.7
1993	99.4	-1.8	102.0	2.6	103.4	1.4	108.8	5.2	108.2	-0.6	107.6	-0.6	106.7	-0.8	110.2	3.3	112.5	2.1	112.6	0.1	114.2	1.4	114.2	0.0
1994	113.0	-1.1	117.9	4.3	128.8	9.2	130.7	1.5	131.3	0.5	139.5	6.2	139.8	0.2	140.7	0.6	146.2	3.9	149.0	1.9	146.3	-1.8	149.4	2.1
1995	148.4	-0.7	151.9	2.4	157.6	3.8	161.2	2.3	159.9	-0.8	158.7	-0.8	154.8	-2.5	153.5	-0.8	152.7	-0.5	152.5	-0.1	151.5	-0.7	150.9	-0.4
1996	149.8	-0.7	149.5	-0.2	146.4	-2.1	145.3	-0.8	148.0	1.9	152.3	2.9	152.5	0.1	157.4	3.2	159.3	1.2	162.2	1.8	165.0	1.7	160.8	-2.5
1997	169.0	5.1	168.3	-0.4	168.2	-0.1	171.3	1.8	173.6	1.3	172.0	-0.9	169.4	-1.5	168.9	-0.3	169.6	0.4	173.8	2.5	172.8	-0.6	172.0	-0.5
1998	172.0	0.0	172.2	0.1	173.3	0.6	172.0	-0.8	172.6	0.3	176.6	2.3	179.1	1.4	179.6	0.3	181.6	1.1	184.2	1.4	182.9	-0.7	184.7	1.0
1999	190.0	2.9	194.7	2.5	198.1	1.7	199.0	0.5	202.3	1.7	209.1	3.4	207.1	-1.0	214.1	3.4	212.6	-0.7	218.0	2.5	223.2	2.4	227.3	1.8
2000	227.6	0.1	229.2	0.7	221.6	-3.3	218.2	-1.5	214.9	-1.5	209.8	-2.4	200.9	-4.2	194.2	-3.3	187.2	-3.6	177.8	-5.0	170.2	-4.3	165.6	-2.7
2001	158.2	-4.5	166.4	5.2	160.1	-3.8	155.8	-2.7	146.8	-5.8	145.5	-0.9	145.3	-0.1	145.7	0.3	153.1	5.1	157.7	3.0	172.0	9.1	166.3	-3.3

Source: U.S. Department of Labor, Bureau of Labor Statistics, Division of Industry Prices and Price Indexes. n.e.c. stands for not elsewhere classified. - indicates no data collected for period or unavailable.

Glass Containers
Producer Price Index
Base 1982 = 100

For 1947-2001. Columns headed % show percentile change in the index from the previous period for which an index is available.

Year	Jan Index	%	Feb Index	%	Mar Index	%	Apr Index	%	May Index	%	Jun Index	%	Jul Index	%	Aug Index	%	Sep Index	%	Oct Index	%	Nov Index	%	Dec Index	%
1947	14.1	-	14.5	2.8	14.5	0.0	14.5	0.0	14.5	0.0	14.5	0.0	14.9	2.8	14.9	0.0	14.9	0.0	14.9	0.0	14.9	0.0	14.9	0.0
1948	14.9	0.0	14.9	0.0	14.9	0.0	16.9	13.4	16.9	0.0	16.9	0.0	16.9	0.0	16.9	0.0	16.9	0.0	19.2	13.6	19.2	0.0	19.2	0.0
1949	19.2	0.0	19.2	0.0	19.2	0.0	19.2	0.0	19.2	0.0	19.0	-1.0	19.0	0.0	19.0	0.0	19.0	0.0	19.0	0.0	19.0	0.0	19.0	0.0
1950	18.7	-1.6	18.7	0.0	18.7	0.0	18.7	0.0	18.7	0.0	18.7	0.0	18.7	0.0	18.7	0.0	18.7	0.0	20.0	7.0	20.0	0.0	20.0	0.0
1951	20.6	3.0	20.6	0.0	20.6	0.0	20.6	0.0	20.6	0.0	20.6	0.0	20.6	0.0	20.6	0.0	20.6	0.0	20.6	0.0	20.6	0.0	20.6	0.0
1952	20.6	0.0	20.6	0.0	20.6	0.0	20.6	0.0	21.4	3.9	21.4	0.0	21.4	0.0	21.4	0.0	21.4	0.0	21.4	0.0	21.4	0.0	21.4	0.0
1953	21.4	0.0	21.4	0.0	21.4	0.0	23.2	8.4	23.2	0.0	23.2	0.0	23.2	0.0	23.2	0.0	23.2	0.0	23.0	-0.9	23.0	0.0	23.0	0.0
1954	23.0	0.0	23.0	0.0	23.0	0.0	24.1	4.8	24.1	0.0	24.1	0.0	24.1	0.0	24.1	0.0	24.1	0.0	24.1	0.0	24.1	0.0	24.1	0.0
1955	24.1	0.0	24.1	0.0	24.1	0.0	24.1	0.0	24.1	0.0	24.1	0.0	24.1	0.0	24.1	0.0	24.1	0.0	24.3	0.8	24.3	0.0	24.3	0.0
1956	24.9	2.5	24.9	0.0	24.9	0.0	24.9	0.0	24.9	0.0	24.9	0.0	24.9	0.0	24.9	0.0	24.9	0.0	26.7	7.2	26.7	0.0	26.7	0.0
1957	26.7	0.0	26.7	0.0	26.7	0.0	26.7	0.0	26.7	0.0	26.7	0.0	26.7	0.0	26.7	0.0	26.7	0.0	26.7	0.0	26.9	0.7	28.3	5.2
1958	28.3	0.0	28.3	0.0	28.3	0.0	28.3	0.0	28.3	0.0	28.3	0.0	28.3	0.0	28.3	0.0	28.3	0.0	28.3	0.0	28.3	0.0	28.3	0.0
1959	28.3	0.0	28.3	0.0	28.3	0.0	28.3	0.0	28.3	0.0	28.3	0.0	28.3	0.0	28.3	0.0	28.3	0.0	28.3	0.0	28.3	0.0	28.3	0.0
1960	28.2	-0.4	28.2	0.0	28.2	0.0	27.5	-2.5	27.5	0.0	27.5	0.0	27.5	0.0	27.5	0.0	27.5	0.0	27.0	-1.8	27.0	0.0	27.0	0.0
1961	27.0	0.0	27.0	0.0	27.0	0.0	27.8	3.0	27.8	0.0	27.8	0.0	27.4	-1.4	27.4	0.0	27.4	0.0	27.4	0.0	27.4	0.0	26.9	-1.8
1962	26.9	0.0	26.9	0.0	26.9	0.0	26.9	0.0	26.9	0.0	26.9	0.0	26.9	0.0	26.9	0.0	26.9	0.0	26.9	0.0	26.9	0.0	26.9	0.0
1963	26.9	0.0	26.9	0.0	26.9	0.0	26.9	0.0	26.9	0.0	26.8	-0.4	26.8	0.0	26.8	0.0	26.8	0.0	26.8	0.0	26.8	0.0	26.8	0.0
1964	26.8	0.0	26.8	0.0	26.8	0.0	27.1	1.1	27.1	0.0	27.1	0.0	27.1	0.0	27.1	0.0	27.1	0.0	27.1	0.0	27.1	0.0	27.1	0.0
1965	27.1	0.0	27.1	0.0	27.1	0.0	27.1	0.0	27.1	0.0	27.2	0.4	27.2	0.0	27.3	0.4	27.3	0.0	27.3	0.0	27.8	1.8	27.8	0.0
1966	27.8	0.0	27.9	0.4	27.8	-0.4	27.6	-0.7	27.6	0.0	27.6	0.0	27.6	0.0	27.6	0.0	27.6	0.0	28.1	1.8	28.1	0.0	28.1	0.0
1967	28.1	0.0	28.1	0.0	28.1	0.0	28.1	0.0	28.1	0.0	28.1	0.0	28.1	0.0	28.1	0.0	28.1	0.0	28.1	0.0	28.1	0.0	28.1	0.0
1968	29.3	4.3	29.6	1.0	29.6	0.0	29.6	0.0	30.5	3.0	30.5	0.0	30.5	0.0	30.5	0.0	30.5	0.0	30.7	0.7	30.7	0.0	30.7	0.0
1969	32.3	5.2	32.3	0.0	32.3	0.0	32.3	0.0	32.3	0.0	32.3	0.0	32.3	0.0	32.3	0.0	32.3	0.0	32.3	0.0	32.3	0.0	32.3	0.0
1970	33.6	4.0	33.6	0.0	33.6	0.0	33.6	0.0	33.6	0.0	33.6	0.0	33.6	0.0	33.6	0.0	33.6	0.0	33.6	0.0	35.0	4.2	35.0	0.0
1971	37.1	6.0	37.0	-0.3	37.0	0.0	37.0	0.0	37.0	0.0	37.0	0.0	37.0	0.0	37.0	0.0	37.0	0.0	37.0	0.0	37.0	0.0	37.0	0.0
1972	37.0	0.0	37.0	0.0	37.0	0.0	38.3	3.5	38.3	0.0	38.3	0.0	38.4	0.3	38.4	0.0	38.4	0.0	38.4	0.0	38.4	0.0	38.4	0.0
1973	38.4	0.0	38.4	0.0	38.4	0.0	38.5	0.3	38.5	0.0	39.8	3.4	38.6	-3.0	38.6	0.0	38.6	0.0	40.4	4.7	40.4	0.0	40.4	0.0
1974	40.4	0.0	40.4	0.0	41.0	1.5	41.3	0.7	44.2	7.0	44.3	0.2	44.3	0.0	44.3	0.0	44.3	0.0	46.7	5.4	46.7	0.0	46.7	0.0
1975	46.7	0.0	49.8	6.6	49.8	0.0	49.8	0.0	49.8	0.0	49.8	0.0	49.8	0.0	52.3	5.0	52.2	-0.2	52.2	0.0	52.2	0.0	52.2	0.0
1976	52.1	-0.2	52.1	0.0	52.1	0.0	55.3	6.1	55.5	0.4	55.5	0.0	55.5	0.0	55.5	0.0	55.5	0.0	56.8	2.3	56.8	0.0	56.8	0.0
1977	56.8	0.0	56.8	0.0	56.8	0.0	61.3	7.9	61.3	0.0	61.3	0.0	61.3	0.0	61.3	0.0	61.3	0.0	61.5	0.3	61.5	0.0	61.5	0.0
1978	66.5	8.1	66.5	0.0	66.5	0.0	66.5	0.0	66.5	0.0	70.0	5.3	70.0	0.0	70.5	0.7	70.5	0.0	70.5	0.0	70.5	0.0	70.5	0.0
1979	70.5	0.0	70.5	0.0	70.5	0.0	70.5	0.0	74.6	5.8	74.6	0.0	74.6	0.0	74.6	0.0	74.6	0.0	74.6	0.0	74.6	0.0	77.1	3.4
1980	77.1	0.0	77.1	0.0	77.1	0.0	82.8	7.4	82.8	0.0	82.8	0.0	82.8	0.0	82.8	0.0	82.8	0.0	86.1	4.0	86.1	0.0	87.6	1.7
1981	87.6	0.0	87.6	0.0	87.6	0.0	91.9	4.9	94.3	2.6	94.3	0.0	94.4	0.1	94.4	0.0	94.4	0.0	94.4	0.0	94.4	0.0	94.4	0.0
1982	94.3	-0.1	99.1	5.1	100.1	1.0	100.7	0.6	100.7	0.0	100.7	0.0	100.7	0.0	100.7	0.0	100.9	0.2	100.8	-0.1	100.6	-0.2	100.6	0.0
1983	100.3	-0.3	100.1	-0.2	99.6	-0.5	99.4	-0.2	99.0	-0.4	98.9	-0.1	98.9	0.0	98.8	-0.1	98.8	0.0	98.5	-0.3	98.5	0.0	98.6	0.1
1984	98.6	0.0	98.6	0.0	98.9	0.3	100.7	1.8	101.8	1.1	102.7	0.9	103.0	0.3	103.0	0.0	102.5	-0.5	102.6	0.1	102.4	-0.2	102.4	0.0
1985	102.3	-0.1	102.5	0.2	105.2	2.6	105.3	0.1	105.9	0.6	107.4	1.4	108.8	1.3	108.9	0.1	108.8	-0.1	109.2	0.4	108.8	-0.4	108.8	0.0
1986	109.5	0.6	109.5	0.0	111.0	1.4	111.1	0.1	112.2	1.0	112.6	0.4	112.8	0.2	113.1	0.3	113.1	0.0	112.7	-0.4	112.7	0.0	112.5	-0.2
1987	112.5	0.0	113.4	0.8	113.7	0.3	113.8	0.1	113.2	-0.5	113.3	0.1	113.0	-0.3	112.9	-0.1	112.9	0.0	112.7	-0.2	112.5	-0.2	112.5	0.0
1988	112.3	-0.2	112.2	-0.1	112.2	0.0	112.1	-0.1	112.1	0.0	112.2	0.1	112.2	0.0	112.5	0.3	112.3	-0.2	112.3	3.6	112.3	0.0	112.3	0.0
1989	112.3	0.0	112.3	0.0	113.8	1.3	116.9	2.7	116.4	-0.4	115.9	-0.4	115.9	0.0	115.9	0.0	115.7	-0.2	115.7	0.0	115.7	0.0	115.7	0.0
1990	118.9	2.8	119.5	0.5	120.0	0.4	120.2	0.2	120.4	0.2	120.7	0.2	120.7	0.0	120.7	0.0	121.0	0.2	121.0	0.0	121.0	0.0	121.0	0.0
1991	124.8	3.1	124.9	0.1	125.0	0.1	125.3	0.2	125.6	0.2	125.6	0.0	125.6	0.0	125.5	-0.1	125.7	0.2	125.7	0.0	125.7	0.0	125.7	0.0

[Continued]

Glass Containers
Producer Price Index
Base 1982 = 100
[Continued]

For 1947-2001. Columns headed % show percentile change in the index from the previous period for which an index is available.

Year	Jan Index	%	Feb Index	%	Mar Index	%	Apr Index	%	May Index	%	Jun Index	%	Jul Index	%	Aug Index	%	Sep Index	%	Oct Index	%	Nov Index	%	Dec Index	%
1992	125.5	-0.2	125.5	0.0	125.4	-0.1	125.3	-0.1	125.0	-0.2	125.1	0.1	125.1	0.0	125.0	-0.1	124.9	-0.1	124.9	0.0	124.7	-0.2	124.7	0.0
1993	124.5	-0.2	124.9	0.3	125.0	0.1	124.9	-0.1	125.4	0.4	126.0	0.5	126.4	0.3	126.5	0.1	126.7	0.2	126.7	0.0	126.6	-0.1	126.5	-0.1
1994	126.6	0.1	126.4	-0.2	126.4	0.0	126.4	0.0	127.9	1.2	127.9	0.0	127.9	0.0	127.9	0.0	128.2	0.2	128.2	0.0	128.2	0.0	128.3	0.1
1995	128.7	0.3	128.6	-0.1	130.1	1.2	129.9	-0.2	130.7	0.6	130.7	0.0	131.0	0.2	131.0	0.0	131.2	0.2	131.2	0.0	131.2	0.0	131.2	0.0
1996	130.2	-0.8	130.2	0.0	129.2	-0.8	129.7	0.4	129.6	-0.1	129.6	0.0	129.6	0.0	129.6	0.0	129.3	-0.2	127.4	-1.5	127.4	0.0	127.4	0.0
1997	126.0	-1.1	126.0	0.0	125.9	-0.1	125.9	0.0	125.5	-0.3	125.5	0.0	125.5	0.0	125.5	0.0	125.7	0.2	125.7	0.0	125.9	0.2	125.9	0.0
1998	125.9	0.0	125.9	0.0	125.9	0.0	125.9	0.0	125.9	0.0	125.5	-0.3	125.5	0.0	126.2	0.6	126.0	-0.2	126.0	0.0	126.0	0.0	126.0	0.0
1999	125.9	-0.1	125.9	0.0	125.9	0.0	126.0	0.1	126.0	0.0	126.3	0.2	126.1	-0.2	125.9	-0.2	125.7	-0.2	125.7	0.0	125.7	0.0	125.7	0.0
2000	127.3	1.3	127.3	0.0	127.3	0.0	127.3	0.0	127.5	0.2	127.5	0.0	127.5	0.0	127.5	0.0	127.5	0.0	127.6	0.1	127.4	-0.2	127.4	0.0
2001	131.2	3.0	130.9	-0.2	132.4	1.1	133.3	0.7	133.9	0.5	133.9	0.0	133.1	-0.6	133.0	-0.1	133.8	0.6	132.7	-0.8	132.8	0.1	133.0	0.2

Source: U.S. Department of Labor, Bureau of Labor Statistics, Division of Industry Prices and Price Indexes. n.e.c. stands for not elsewhere classified. - indicates no data collected for period or unavailable.

Other Nonmetallic Minerals
Producer Price Index
Base 1982 = 100

For 1947-2001. Columns headed % show percentile change in the index from the previous period for which an index is available.

Year	Jan Index	%	Feb Index	%	Mar Index	%	Apr Index	%	May Index	%	Jun Index	%	Jul Index	%	Aug Index	%	Sep Index	%	Oct Index	%	Nov Index	%	Dec Index	%
1947	14.4	-	14.6	1.4	14.7	0.7	14.8	0.7	14.9	0.7	14.9	0.0	14.9	0.0	14.9	0.0	15.0	0.7	15.0	0.0	15.5	3.3	15.7	1.3
1948	15.9	1.3	16.0	0.6	16.0	0.0	16.1	0.6	16.1	0.0	16.3	1.2	16.6	1.8	16.6	0.0	16.6	0.0	16.6	0.0	16.5	-0.6	16.7	1.2
1949	16.6	-0.6	16.6	0.0	16.6	0.0	16.6	0.0	16.6	0.0	16.6	0.0	16.5	-0.6	16.4	-0.6	16.4	0.0	16.3	-0.6	16.3	0.0	16.3	0.0
1950	16.3	0.0	16.7	2.5	16.8	0.6	16.8	0.0	16.8	0.0	16.8	0.0	16.9	0.6	17.1	1.2	17.3	1.2	17.3	0.0	17.4	0.6	17.7	1.7
1951	17.7	0.0	17.7	0.0	17.7	0.0	17.7	0.0	17.7	0.0	17.7	0.0	17.7	0.0	17.7	0.0	17.7	0.0	17.7	0.0	17.7	0.0	17.7	0.0
1952	17.7	0.0	17.7	0.0	17.7	0.0	17.8	0.6	17.8	0.0	17.8	0.0	17.8	0.0	17.8	0.0	17.8	0.0	17.9	0.6	18.3	2.2	18.4	0.5
1953	18.4	0.0	18.4	0.0	18.4	0.0	18.4	0.0	18.4	0.0	18.5	0.5	18.7	1.1	18.8	0.5	18.8	0.0	18.8	0.0	18.9	0.5	18.9	0.0
1954	19.1	1.1	19.1	0.0	19.1	0.0	19.1	0.0	19.1	0.0	19.1	0.0	19.1	0.0	19.2	0.5	19.2	0.0	19.2	0.0	19.0	-1.0	19.0	0.0
1955	19.0	0.0	19.0	0.0	19.0	0.0	19.0	0.0	19.3	1.6	19.5	1.0	19.5	0.0	19.5	0.0	19.6	0.5	19.6	0.0	19.4	-1.0	19.4	0.0
1956	19.4	0.0	19.6	1.0	19.5	-0.5	19.6	0.5	19.6	0.0	19.6	0.0	19.7	0.5	19.7	0.0	19.7	0.0	19.8	0.5	19.8	0.0	19.8	0.0
1957	19.8	0.0	20.1	1.5	20.3	1.0	20.4	0.5	20.4	0.0	20.4	0.0	20.4	0.0	20.5	0.5	20.5	0.0	20.5	0.0	20.5	0.0	20.9	2.0
1958	20.9	0.0	20.9	0.0	20.9	0.0	20.9	0.0	20.9	0.0	20.9	0.0	20.9	0.0	20.9	0.0	20.9	0.0	20.9	0.0	20.9	0.0	20.9	0.0
1959	20.9	0.0	21.0	0.5	21.1	0.5	21.1	0.0	21.1	0.0	21.1	0.0	21.1	0.0	21.1	0.0	21.1	0.0	21.1	0.0	21.1	0.0	21.1	0.0
1960	21.1	0.0	21.3	0.9	21.3	0.0	21.4	0.5	21.4	0.0	21.4	0.0	21.4	0.0	21.4	0.0	21.4	0.0	21.5	0.5	21.3	-0.9	21.3	0.0
1961	21.3	0.0	21.2	-0.5	21.3	0.5	21.3	0.0	21.3	0.0	21.3	0.0	21.3	0.0	21.3	0.0	21.2	-0.5	21.2	0.0	21.2	0.0	21.1	-0.5
1962	21.1	0.0	21.4	1.4	21.4	0.0	21.4	0.0	21.2	-0.9	21.2	0.0	21.1	-0.5	21.1	0.0	21.1	0.0	21.2	0.5	21.3	0.5	21.3	0.0
1963	21.2	-0.5	21.1	-0.5	21.1	0.0	21.1	0.0	21.1	0.0	21.0	-0.5	21.0	0.0	20.9	-0.5	21.0	0.5	21.1	0.5	21.1	0.0	21.1	0.0
1964	21.0	-0.5	21.0	0.0	21.0	0.0	21.0	0.0	21.0	0.0	21.1	0.5	21.2	0.5	21.2	0.0	21.1	-0.5	21.1	0.0	21.1	0.0	21.0	-0.5
1965	21.0	0.0	21.0	0.0	21.1	0.5	21.1	0.0	21.1	0.0	21.1	0.0	21.1	0.0	21.1	0.0	21.0	-0.5	21.0	0.0	21.0	0.0	21.0	0.0
1966	21.2	1.0	21.1	-0.5	21.2	0.5	21.2	0.0	21.1	-0.5	21.0	-0.5	21.1	0.5	21.2	0.5	21.2	0.0	21.2	0.0	21.0	-0.9	21.0	0.0
1967	21.1	0.5	21.1	0.0	21.3	0.9	21.2	-0.5	21.2	0.0	21.2	0.0	21.2	0.0	21.2	0.0	21.1	-0.5	21.2	0.5	21.2	0.0	21.3	0.5
1968	21.6	1.4	21.6	0.0	21.6	0.0	21.6	0.0	21.6	0.0	21.9	1.4	22.0	0.5	22.0	0.0	22.0	0.0	22.2	0.9	22.2	0.0	22.2	0.0
1969	22.3	0.5	22.4	0.4	22.4	0.0	22.7	1.3	22.7	0.0	22.7	0.0	22.7	0.0	22.7	0.0	22.8	0.4	23.0	0.9	23.0	0.0	23.0	0.0
1970	23.0	0.0	23.1	0.4	23.4	1.3	23.6	0.9	23.6	0.0	23.6	0.0	23.7	0.4	23.8	0.4	23.8	0.0	24.4	2.5	24.4	0.0	24.9	2.0
1971	25.6	2.8	25.7	0.4	25.7	0.0	25.9	0.8	26.5	2.3	26.5	0.0	26.6	0.4	26.6	0.0	26.6	0.0	26.6	0.0	26.6	0.0	26.6	0.0
1972	26.6	0.0	26.7	0.4	26.8	0.4	26.8	0.0	27.2	1.5	27.0	-0.7	26.9	-0.4	26.9	0.0	27.0	0.4	27.0	0.0	27.0	0.0	27.0	0.0
1973	27.1	0.4	27.1	0.0	27.2	0.4	27.2	0.0	27.4	0.7	27.5	0.4	27.1	-1.5	27.1	0.0	27.0	-0.4	27.0	0.0	27.1	0.4	27.9	3.0
1974	31.9	14.3	35.4	11.0	36.2	2.3	37.5	3.6	40.1	6.9	40.4	0.7	41.4	2.5	42.0	1.4	42.8	1.9	43.1	0.7	44.4	3.0	44.5	0.2
1975	45.2	1.6	45.3	0.2	45.3	0.0	46.4	2.4	46.4	0.0	46.6	0.4	47.3	1.5	47.4	0.2	47.3	-0.2	47.7	0.8	47.6	-0.2	47.7	0.2
1976	48.5	1.7	48.5	0.0	49.3	1.6	49.0	-0.6	49.2	0.4	49.2	0.0	49.3	0.2	49.2	-0.2	49.7	1.0	49.8	0.2	49.8	0.0	49.8	0.0
1977	51.0	2.4	51.2	0.4	52.0	1.6	52.5	1.0	52.5	0.0	53.1	1.1	53.3	0.4	53.8	0.9	54.6	1.5	54.3	-0.5	54.3	0.0	54.5	0.4
1978	55.3	1.5	56.7	2.5	56.9	0.4	57.0	0.2	57.2	0.4	58.1	1.6	59.9	3.1	59.8	-0.2	59.8	0.0	60.0	0.3	60.1	0.2	60.1	0.0
1979	61.2	1.8	62.3	1.8	62.4	0.2	63.6	1.9	64.2	0.9	64.0	-0.3	65.8	2.8	65.7	-0.2	71.2	8.4	72.3	1.5	72.5	0.3	72.5	0.0
1980	74.6	2.9	80.9	8.4	82.0	1.4	84.7	3.3	84.9	0.2	83.7	-1.4	84.1	0.5	84.2	0.1	84.9	0.8	85.4	0.6	85.5	0.1	88.8	3.9
1981	88.7	-0.1	90.0	1.5	93.6	4.0	101.5	8.4	101.2	-0.3	101.1	-0.1	100.9	-0.2	100.7	-0.2	100.5	-0.2	100.3	-0.2	100.4	0.1	100.6	0.2
1982	100.6	0.0	101.5	0.9	101.6	0.1	101.5	-0.1	99.9	-1.6	98.6	-1.3	98.9	0.3	98.8	-0.1	99.1	0.3	99.7	0.6	99.9	0.2	99.8	-0.1
1983	99.9	0.1	100.9	1.0	101.0	0.1	101.5	0.5	101.4	-0.1	101.6	0.2	101.7	0.1	102.1	0.4	102.3	0.2	102.4	0.1	103.3	0.9	103.2	-0.1
1984	103.1	-0.1	103.4	0.3	104.0	0.6	104.1	0.1	104.9	0.8	105.8	0.9	107.5	1.6	108.4	0.8	108.0	-0.4	107.9	-0.1	107.2	-0.6	107.5	0.3
1985	109.0	1.4	109.0	0.0	109.0	0.0	110.0	0.9	110.9	0.8	111.0	0.1	111.0	0.0	111.1	0.1	111.1	0.0	111.5	0.4	111.0	-0.4	110.9	-0.1
1986	111.1	0.2	110.9	-0.2	110.8	-0.1	110.6	-0.2	111.0	0.4	111.0	0.0	110.4	-0.5	109.5	-0.8	109.3	-0.2	109.6	0.3	109.4	-0.2	109.0	-0.4
1987	108.6	-0.4	109.1	0.5	109.6	0.5	109.8	0.2	109.6	-0.2	110.3	0.6	110.9	0.5	110.1	-0.7	110.6	0.5	111.8	1.1	111.9	0.1	111.3	-0.5
1988	112.5	1.1	112.8	0.3	112.9	0.1	113.1	0.2	113.2	0.1	113.4	0.2	112.4	-0.9	112.3	-0.1	112.7	0.4	112.8	0.1	113.0	0.2	113.2	0.2
1989	113.6	0.4	113.5	-0.1	113.9	0.4	114.3	0.4	114.1	-0.2	114.2	0.1	114.5	0.3	114.4	-0.1	114.4	0.0	114.3	-0.1	114.5	0.2	114.7	0.2
1990	115.2	0.4	115.4	0.2	115.4	0.0	115.5	0.1	115.5	0.0	115.6	0.1	115.6	0.0	115.8	0.2	116.5	0.6	116.6	0.1	117.6	0.9	117.7	0.1
1991	118.5	0.7	118.4	-0.1	118.3	-0.1	118.5	0.2	118.6	0.1	118.5	-0.1	118.4	-0.1	118.4	0.0	118.4	0.0	118.5	0.1	118.5	0.0	118.1	-0.3

[Continued]

Other Nonmetallic Minerals
Producer Price Index
Base 1982 = 100
[Continued]

For 1947-2001. Columns headed % show percentile change in the index from the previous period for which an index is available.

Year	Jan Index	%	Feb Index	%	Mar Index	%	Apr Index	%	May Index	%	Jun Index	%	Jul Index	%	Aug Index	%	Sep Index	%	Oct Index	%	Nov Index	%	Dec Index	%
1992	117.8	-0.3	118.0	0.2	117.8	-0.2	116.1	-1.4	115.0	-0.9	115.5	0.4	115.8	0.3	116.0	0.2	116.0	0.0	116.0	0.0	116.2	0.2	116.3	0.1
1993	117.6	1.1	117.8	0.2	118.0	0.2	118.5	0.4	118.7	0.2	119.2	0.4	119.7	0.4	119.8	0.1	120.1	0.3	120.2	0.1	120.0	-0.2	120.3	0.3
1994	120.7	0.3	121.3	0.5	121.4	0.1	121.5	0.1	121.5	0.0	121.5	0.0	121.5	0.0	121.7	0.2	121.7	0.0	121.9	0.2	122.0	0.1	122.3	0.2
1995	123.6	1.1	124.3	0.6	124.7	0.3	125.4	0.6	125.1	-0.2	125.6	0.4	125.2	-0.3	125.9	0.6	126.3	0.3	126.0	-0.2	126.3	0.2	126.3	0.0
1996	126.7	0.3	126.7	0.0	127.3	0.5	127.0	-0.2	127.7	0.6	127.4	-0.2	127.9	0.4	127.5	-0.3	128.4	0.7	128.6	0.2	128.6	0.0	128.5	-0.1
1997	128.9	0.3	129.8	0.7	130.2	0.3	130.5	0.2	130.2	-0.2	130.6	0.3	130.5	-0.1	130.8	0.2	130.5	-0.2	130.3	-0.2	130.2	-0.1	130.2	0.0
1998	130.2	0.0	130.2	0.0	130.4	0.2	130.7	0.2	130.7	0.0	130.6	-0.1	131.1	0.4	131.8	0.5	132.2	0.3	132.5	0.2	132.6	0.1	132.5	-0.1
1999	132.8	0.2	133.5	0.5	134.1	0.4	134.2	0.1	134.0	-0.1	134.1	0.1	134.2	0.1	135.6	1.0	136.1	0.4	136.3	0.1	136.5	0.1	137.5	0.7
2000	138.0	0.4	139.1	0.8	140.2	0.8	140.2	0.0	140.4	0.1	140.8	0.3	140.6	-0.1	140.3	-0.2	140.3	0.0	140.5	0.1	141.2	0.5	141.6	0.3
2001	142.2	0.4	142.6	0.3	142.6	0.0	142.5	-0.1	142.5	0.0	143.1	0.4	143.3	0.1	143.2	-0.1	143.2	0.0	144.2	0.7	143.7	-0.3	143.4	-0.2

Source: U.S. Department of Labor, Bureau of Labor Statistics, Division of Industry Prices and Price Indexes. n.e.c. stands for not elsewhere classified. - indicates no data collected for period or unavailable.

TRANSPORTATION EQUIPMENT
Producer Price Index
Base 1982 = 100

For 1969-2001. Columns headed % show percentile change in the index from the previous period for which an index is available.

Year	Jan Index	%	Feb Index	%	Mar Index	%	Apr Index	%	May Index	%	Jun Index	%	Jul Index	%	Aug Index	%	Sep Index	%	Oct Index	%	Nov Index	%	Dec Index	%
1969	40.1	-	40.1	0.0	40.1	0.0	40.1	0.0	40.1	0.0	40.2	0.2	40.2	0.0	40.1	-0.2	40.1	0.0	41.0	2.2	41.2	0.5	41.2	0.0
1970	41.3	0.2	41.2	-0.2	41.4	0.5	41.3	-0.2	41.4	0.2	41.4	0.0	41.4	0.0	41.5	0.2	41.5	0.0	43.3	4.3	43.5	0.5	43.5	0.0
1971	43.7	0.5	43.9	0.5	44.0	0.2	44.0	0.0	44.1	0.2	44.1	0.0	44.3	0.5	44.3	0.0	43.9	-0.9	44.4	1.1	44.4	0.0	45.2	1.8
1972	45.4	0.4	45.5	0.2	45.5	0.0	45.6	0.2	45.6	0.0	45.7	0.2	45.7	0.0	45.7	0.0	45.7	0.0	45.2	-1.1	45.3	0.2	45.7	0.9
1973	45.7	0.0	45.7	0.0	45.9	0.4	46.0	0.2	46.1	0.2	46.0	-0.2	46.1	0.2	46.1	0.0	45.9	-0.4	46.4	1.1	46.5	0.2	47.0	1.1
1974	47.5	1.1	47.6	0.2	47.7	0.2	47.8	0.2	48.6	1.7	49.2	1.2	50.1	1.8	50.8	1.4	51.1	0.6	53.8	5.3	54.1	0.6	54.9	1.5
1975	54.9	0.0	55.4	0.9	55.9	0.9	56.0	0.2	56.0	0.0	56.1	0.2	56.1	0.0	56.3	0.4	56.5	0.4	58.7	3.9	59.0	0.5	59.1	0.2
1976	59.6	0.8	59.6	0.0	59.7	0.2	59.7	0.0	59.7	0.0	59.8	0.2	59.8	0.0	60.2	0.7	60.5	0.5	62.5	3.3	62.6	0.2	62.9	0.5
1977	62.9	0.0	63.0	0.2	63.4	0.6	63.6	0.3	63.7	0.2	63.9	0.3	63.9	0.0	64.4	0.8	64.7	0.5	67.2	3.9	67.3	0.1	67.4	0.1
1978	67.7	0.4	67.9	0.3	67.9	0.0	68.3	0.6	68.9	0.9	69.1	0.3	69.2	0.1	69.3	0.1	69.5	0.3	71.8	3.3	72.1	0.4	72.3	0.3
1979	73.2	1.2	73.5	0.4	73.6	0.1	74.8	1.6	75.0	0.3	75.1	0.1	75.4	0.4	74.5	-1.2	74.8	0.4	77.8	4.0	78.0	0.3	78.3	0.4
1980	79.6	1.7	79.4	-0.3	79.6	0.3	81.4	2.3	81.1	-0.4	81.4	0.4	82.6	1.5	83.6	1.2	81.9	-2.0	87.1	6.3	87.2	0.1	89.8	3.0
1981	91.1	1.4	91.8	0.8	91.4	-0.4	92.9	1.6	93.6	0.8	93.8	0.2	94.1	0.3	94.5	0.4	92.8	-1.8	97.9	5.5	98.7	0.8	98.9	0.2
1982	99.6	0.7	98.2	-1.4	98.2	0.0	98.4	0.2	99.1	0.7	99.8	0.7	100.1	0.3	100.4	0.3	97.9	-2.5	102.5	4.7	102.6	0.1	103.1	0.5
1983	102.7	-0.4	102.5	-0.2	102.2	-0.3	102.4	0.2	102.5	0.1	102.6	0.1	102.6	0.0	102.9	0.3	100.3	-2.5	104.4	4.1	104.4	0.0	104.4	0.0
1984	104.8	0.4	105.0	0.2	105.1	0.1	105.2	0.1	105.1	-0.1	105.0	-0.1	105.1	0.1	105.0	-0.1	103.2	-1.7	106.1	2.8	106.4	0.3	106.2	-0.2
1985	106.9	0.7	107.4	0.5	107.2	-0.2	107.4	0.2	107.8	0.4	107.9	0.1	108.1	0.2	108.1	0.0	104.1	-3.7	110.2	5.9	110.2	0.0	109.8	-0.4
1986	109.5	-0.3	109.7	0.2	109.5	-0.2	110.3	0.7	110.2	-0.1	110.3	0.1	110.4	0.1	110.0	-0.4	107.5	-2.3	113.2	5.3	113.1	-0.1	112.8	-0.3
1987	113.1	0.3	112.1	-0.9	112.4	0.3	113.0	0.5	112.4	-0.5	112.3	-0.1	112.2	-0.1	111.9	-0.3	110.9	-0.9	113.8	2.6	113.5	-0.3	112.5	-0.9
1988	113.2	0.6	113.2	0.0	113.1	-0.1	113.5	0.4	113.7	0.2	114.0	0.3	113.9	-0.1	114.0	0.1	113.2	-0.7	116.6	3.0	116.3	-0.3	116.3	0.0
1989	116.8	0.4	117.1	0.3	116.8	-0.3	116.4	-0.3	117.2	0.7	117.6	0.3	116.9	-0.6	117.1	0.2	116.6	-0.4	120.0	2.9	120.0	0.0	119.8	-0.2
1990	119.7	-0.1	120.2	0.4	120.3	0.1	120.5	0.2	120.4	-0.1	121.0	0.5	121.2	0.2	121.1	-0.1	121.0	-0.1	124.0	2.5	124.2	0.2	124.2	0.0
1991	125.2	0.8	125.7	0.4	125.7	0.0	125.5	-0.2	125.6	0.1	125.6	0.0	125.7	0.1	126.0	0.2	125.2	-0.6	129.1	3.1	128.9	-0.2	129.0	0.1
1992	129.8	0.6	129.7	-0.1	130.0	0.2	130.2	0.2	130.2	0.0	130.1	-0.1	130.2	0.1	130.0	-0.2	128.5	-1.2	132.3	3.0	132.2	-0.1	132.1	-0.1
1993	132.7	0.5	133.1	0.3	133.3	0.2	133.4	0.1	133.3	-0.1	133.3	0.0	133.6	0.2	133.5	-0.1	131.7	-1.3	135.2	2.7	135.5	0.2	135.6	0.1
1994	136.5	0.7	136.6	0.1	136.6	0.0	136.7	0.1	137.1	0.3	137.0	-0.1	137.2	0.1	137.2	0.0	135.6	-1.2	138.5	2.1	138.3	-0.1	138.7	0.3
1995	139.6	0.6	139.6	0.0	139.4	-0.1	139.3	-0.1	139.3	0.0	139.0	-0.2	139.0	0.0	138.9	-0.1	137.1	-1.3	141.1	2.9	141.7	0.4	141.7	0.0
1996	141.7	0.0	141.7	0.0	141.8	0.1	141.6	-0.1	141.6	0.0	141.7	0.1	141.3	-0.3	141.4	0.1	140.0	-1.0	142.9	2.1	142.7	-0.1	142.6	-0.1
1997	142.9	0.2	142.8	-0.1	142.7	-0.1	142.3	-0.3	141.5	-0.6	141.4	-0.1	140.5	-0.6	140.5	0.0	139.5	-0.7	142.5	2.2	142.0	-0.4	141.5	-0.4
1998	141.4	-0.1	141.5	0.1	141.5	0.0	141.3	-0.1	140.7	-0.4	140.2	-0.4	140.4	0.1	140.0	-0.3	139.6	-0.3	142.9	2.4	142.8	-0.1	142.3	-0.4
1999	142.0	-0.2	142.3	0.2	141.8	-0.4	141.9	0.1	141.5	-0.3	141.1	-0.3	140.5	-0.4	140.4	-0.1	140.1	-0.2	143.7	2.6	143.3	-0.3	143.3	0.0
2000	143.5	0.1	143.4	-0.1	143.4	0.0	143.5	0.1	143.5	0.0	143.1	-0.3	143.1	0.0	142.9	-0.1	142.9	0.0	145.4	1.7	145.6	0.1	145.5	-0.1
2001	145.7	0.1	144.9	-0.5	145.1	0.1	145.5	0.3	144.8	-0.5	144.5	-0.2	144.9	0.3	144.8	-0.1	144.6	-0.1	145.7	0.8	145.7	0.0	145.1	-0.4

Source: U.S. Department of Labor, Bureau of Labor Statistics, Division of Industry Prices and Price Indexes. n.e.c. stands for not elsewhere classified. - indicates no data collected for period or unavailable.

Motor Vehicles and Equipment
Producer Price Index
Base 1982 = 100

For 1926-2001. Columns headed % show percentile change in the index from the previous period for which an index is available.

Year	Jan Index	%	Feb Index	%	Mar Index	%	Apr Index	%	May Index	%	Jun Index	%	Jul Index	%	Aug Index	%	Sep Index	%	Oct Index	%	Nov Index	%	Dec Index	%
1926	-	-	-	-	-	-	-	-	-	-	-	-	-	-	-	-	-	-	-	-	-	-	-	-
1927	-	-	-	-	-	-	-	-	-	-	-	-	-	-	-	-	-	-	-	-	-	-	-	-
1928	-	-	-	-	-	-	-	-	-	-	-	-	-	-	-	-	-	-	-	-	-	-	-	-
1929	-	-	-	-	-	-	-	-	-	-	-	-	-	-	-	-	-	-	-	-	-	-	-	-
1930	-	-	-	-	-	-	-	-	-	-	-	-	-	-	-	-	-	-	-	-	-	-	-	-
1931	-	-	-	-	-	-	-	-	-	-	-	-	-	-	-	-	-	-	-	-	-	-	-	-
1932	-	-	-	-	-	-	-	-	-	-	-	-	-	-	-	-	-	-	-	-	-	-	-	-
1933	-	-	-	-	-	-	-	-	-	-	-	-	-	-	-	-	-	-	-	-	-	-	-	-
1934	-	-	-	-	-	-	-	-	-	-	-	-	-	-	-	-	-	-	-	-	-	-	-	-
1935	-	-	-	-	-	-	-	-	-	-	-	-	-	-	-	-	-	-	-	-	-	-	-	-
1936	-	-	-	-	-	-	-	-	-	-	-	-	-	-	-	-	-	-	-	-	-	-	-	-
1937	14.4	-	14.4	0.0	14.4	0.0	14.5	0.7	14.5	0.0	14.5	0.0	14.5	0.0	15.0	3.4	15.2	1.3	15.4	1.3	15.9	3.2	15.9	0.0
1938	15.9	0.0	15.9	0.0	15.9	0.0	15.9	0.0	16.0	0.6	16.0	0.0	16.0	0.0	16.0	0.0	16.0	0.0	15.8	-1.2	15.6	-1.3	15.6	0.0
1939	15.6	0.0	15.6	0.0	15.6	0.0	15.6	0.0	15.5	-0.6	15.5	0.0	15.5	0.0	15.4	-0.6	15.4	0.0	15.6	1.3	15.8	1.3	15.8	0.0
1940	15.8	0.0	15.8	0.0	15.8	0.0	15.8	0.0	15.8	0.0	15.8	0.0	15.9	0.6	15.9	0.0	16.0	0.6	16.7	4.4	16.7	0.0	16.7	0.0
1941	16.7	0.0	16.6	-0.6	16.6	0.0	16.7	0.6	16.7	0.0	16.7	0.0	16.8	0.6	16.8	0.0	16.8	0.0	18.7	11.3	18.7	0.0	18.7	0.0
1942	18.7	0.0	18.7	0.0	18.8	0.5	18.8	0.0	18.8	0.0	18.8	0.0	18.8	0.0	18.8	0.0	18.8	0.0	18.8	0.0	18.8	0.0	18.8	0.0
1943	18.8	0.0	18.8	0.0	18.8	0.0	18.8	0.0	18.8	0.0	18.8	0.0	18.8	0.0	18.8	0.0	18.8	0.0	18.8	0.0	18.8	0.0	18.8	0.0
1944	18.8	0.0	18.8	0.0	18.8	0.0	18.8	0.0	18.8	0.0	18.9	0.5	18.9	0.0	18.9	0.0	18.9	0.0	18.9	0.0	19.0	0.5	19.0	0.0
1945	19.0	0.0	19.0	0.0	19.1	0.5	19.1	0.0	19.2	0.5	19.3	0.5	19.3	0.0	19.3	0.0	19.3	0.0	19.3	0.0	19.5	1.0	19.5	0.0
1946	19.7	1.0	20.1	2.0	20.4	1.5	20.9	2.5	21.9	4.8	22.6	3.2	22.6	0.0	23.1	2.2	23.4	1.3	23.6	0.9	24.3	3.0	24.8	2.1
1947	24.9	0.4	24.9	0.0	24.9	0.0	24.8	-0.4	24.9	0.4	25.0	0.4	25.0	0.0	25.9	3.6	26.4	1.9	26.4	0.0	26.5	0.4	26.6	0.4
1948	26.8	0.8	26.7	-0.4	26.7	0.0	26.7	0.0	26.8	0.4	27.8	3.7	28.5	2.5	29.4	3.2	29.6	0.7	29.6	0.0	29.7	0.3	29.9	0.7
1949	30.0	0.3	30.3	1.0	30.4	0.3	30.2	-0.7	30.1	-0.3	30.0	-0.3	30.1	0.3	30.1	0.0	30.1	0.0	30.1	0.0	30.1	0.0	30.1	0.0
1950	30.0	-0.3	29.9	-0.3	29.8	-0.3	29.8	0.0	29.9	0.3	29.9	0.0	29.9	0.0	29.9	0.0	30.1	0.7	30.1	0.0	30.1	0.0	30.4	1.0
1951	30.5	0.3	30.6	0.3	31.4	2.6	31.4	0.0	31.4	0.0	31.4	0.0	31.4	0.0	31.6	0.6	31.9	0.9	32.4	1.6	32.5	0.3	32.6	0.3
1952	32.7	0.3	33.5	2.4	33.5	0.0	33.5	0.0	33.5	0.0	33.5	0.0	33.5	0.0	33.5	0.0	33.5	0.0	33.5	0.0	33.5	0.0	33.5	0.0
1953	33.5	0.0	33.5	0.0	33.5	0.0	33.2	-0.9	33.2	0.0	33.2	0.0	33.2	0.0	33.2	0.0	33.2	0.0	33.2	0.0	33.2	0.0	33.2	0.0
1954	33.2	0.0	33.2	0.0	33.2	0.0	33.2	0.0	33.2	0.0	33.2	0.0	33.2	0.0	33.2	0.0	33.2	0.0	33.2	0.0	33.8	1.8	34.0	0.6
1955	34.0	0.0	34.0	0.0	34.0	0.0	34.1	0.3	34.1	0.0	34.1	0.0	34.1	0.0	34.1	0.0	34.1	0.0	34.9	2.3	35.3	1.1	35.4	0.3
1956	35.4	0.0	35.6	0.6	36.1	1.4	36.1	0.0	36.1	0.0	36.1	0.0	36.1	0.0	36.1	0.0	36.2	0.3	36.6	1.1	37.5	2.5	37.5	0.0
1957	37.5	0.0	37.6	0.3	37.6	0.0	37.7	0.3	37.7	0.0	37.7	0.0	37.7	0.0	37.7	0.0	37.7	0.0	37.9	0.5	38.8	2.4	38.9	0.3
1958	38.9	0.0	38.9	0.0	38.9	0.0	38.9	0.0	38.9	0.0	38.9	0.0	38.9	0.0	38.9	0.0	38.9	0.0	39.0	0.3	39.9	2.3	40.0	0.3
1959	40.0	0.0	40.0	0.0	40.0	0.0	40.0	0.0	40.0	0.0	40.0	0.0	40.0	0.0	40.0	0.0	40.0	0.0	39.6	-1.0	39.6	0.0	39.6	0.0
1960	39.6	0.0	39.6	0.0	39.6	0.0	39.6	0.0	39.6	0.0	39.6	0.0	39.6	0.0	39.6	0.0	37.9	-4.3	39.2	3.4	39.2	0.0	39.3	0.3
1961	39.4	0.3	39.2	-0.5	39.2	0.0	39.2	0.0	39.2	0.0	39.2	0.0	39.2	0.0	39.2	0.0	39.2	0.0	39.2	0.0	39.2	0.0	39.2	0.0
1962	39.2	0.0	39.1	-0.3	39.1	0.0	39.1	0.0	39.1	0.0	39.4	0.8	39.4	0.0	39.4	0.0	39.4	0.0	39.2	-0.5	39.2	0.0	39.2	0.0
1963	39.2	0.0	39.2	0.0	39.2	0.0	39.0	-0.5	38.9	-0.3	38.7	-0.5	38.9	0.5	38.8	-0.3	38.7	-0.3	38.9	0.5	38.9	0.0	38.9	0.0
1964	38.9	0.0	38.9	0.0	38.9	0.0	38.9	0.0	39.4	1.3	39.3	-0.3	39.3	0.0	39.2	-0.3	39.1	-0.3	39.2	0.3	39.2	0.0	39.2	0.0
1965	39.2	0.0	39.3	0.3	39.2	-0.3	39.2	0.0	39.2	0.0	39.2	0.0	39.2	0.0	39.2	0.0	39.2	0.0	39.1	-0.3	39.1	0.0	39.1	0.0
1966	39.1	0.0	39.1	0.0	39.0	-0.3	39.0	0.0	39.3	0.8	39.2	-0.3	39.2	0.0	39.1	-0.3	39.0	-0.3	39.6	1.5	39.6	0.0	39.6	0.0
1967	39.6	0.0	39.6	0.0	39.6	0.0	39.6	0.0	39.4	-0.5	39.5	0.3	39.4	-0.3	39.6	0.5	39.6	0.0	40.6	2.5	40.6	0.0	40.6	0.0
1968	40.7	0.2	40.7	0.0	40.7	0.0	40.7	0.0	40.6	-0.2	40.8	0.5	40.7	-0.2	40.7	0.0	40.7	0.0	41.6	2.2	41.6	0.0	41.6	0.0
1969	41.5	-0.2	41.5	0.0	41.4	-0.2	41.5	0.2	41.5	0.0	41.6	0.2	41.5	-0.2	41.4	-0.2	41.4	0.0	42.3	2.2	42.5	0.5	42.5	0.0
1970	42.5	0.0	42.5	0.0	42.7	0.5	42.5	-0.5	42.7	0.5	42.7	0.0	42.7	0.0	42.7	0.0	42.8	0.2	44.9	4.9	45.0	0.2	45.0	0.0

[Continued]

Motor Vehicles and Equipment
Producer Price Index
Base 1982 = 100
[Continued]

For 1926-2001. Columns headed % show percentile change in the index from the previous period for which an index is available.

Year	Jan Index	%	Feb Index	%	Mar Index	%	Apr Index	%	May Index	%	Jun Index	%	Jul Index	%	Aug Index	%	Sep Index	%	Oct Index	%	Nov Index	%	Dec Index	%
1971	45.2	0.4	45.4	0.4	45.5	0.2	45.6	0.2	45.6	0.0	45.7	0.2	45.8	0.2	45.8	0.0	45.3	-1.1	46.0	1.5	46.0	0.0	46.9	2.0
1972	46.9	0.0	47.0	0.2	46.9	-0.2	47.0	0.2	47.0	0.0	47.2	0.4	47.1	-0.2	47.1	0.0	47.1	0.0	46.5	-1.3	46.6	0.2	47.1	1.1
1973	47.0	-0.2	47.1	0.2	47.2	0.2	47.4	0.4	47.4	0.0	47.3	-0.2	47.4	0.2	47.4	0.0	47.1	-0.6	47.7	1.3	47.8	0.2	48.3	1.0
1974	48.9	1.2	49.0	0.2	49.0	0.0	49.1	0.2	49.7	1.2	50.2	1.0	51.1	1.8	51.8	1.4	52.0	0.4	55.0	5.8	55.3	0.5	56.0	1.3
1975	55.8	-0.4	56.3	0.9	56.9	1.1	56.9	0.0	56.9	0.0	57.0	0.2	56.9	-0.2	57.1	0.4	57.3	0.4	59.7	4.2	59.9	0.3	60.0	0.2
1976	60.2	0.3	60.2	0.0	60.4	0.3	60.4	0.0	60.3	-0.2	60.4	0.2	60.4	0.0	60.8	0.7	61.1	0.5	63.3	3.6	63.4	0.2	63.5	0.2
1977	63.4	-0.2	63.5	0.2	64.0	0.8	64.1	0.2	64.3	0.3	64.4	0.2	64.4	0.0	64.9	0.8	65.2	0.5	68.0	4.3	67.9	-0.1	68.0	0.1
1978	68.2	0.3	68.4	0.3	68.4	0.0	68.8	0.6	69.5	1.0	69.7	0.3	69.8	0.1	70.0	0.3	70.0	0.0	72.4	3.4	72.6	0.3	72.8	0.3
1979	73.6	1.1	74.0	0.5	74.1	0.1	75.4	1.8	75.6	0.3	75.7	0.1	76.0	0.4	74.7	-1.7	75.0	0.4	78.4	4.5	78.6	0.3	78.9	0.4
1980	79.9	1.3	79.6	-0.4	79.9	0.4	81.8	2.4	81.4	-0.5	81.7	0.4	83.0	1.6	84.2	1.4	81.8	-2.9	86.9	6.2	87.0	0.1	90.0	3.4
1981	91.1	1.2	91.9	0.9	91.4	-0.5	93.1	1.9	93.9	0.9	94.2	0.3	94.5	0.3	94.9	0.4	92.7	-2.3	98.6	6.4	99.1	0.5	99.3	0.2
1982	99.8	0.5	98.2	-1.6	98.2	0.0	98.4	0.2	99.2	0.8	99.9	0.7	100.3	0.4	100.6	0.3	97.4	-3.2	102.6	5.3	102.6	0.0	102.7	0.1
1983	102.3	-0.4	102.0	-0.3	101.7	-0.3	101.8	0.1	102.0	0.2	102.1	0.1	102.1	0.0	102.2	0.1	99.2	-2.9	103.7	4.5	103.7	0.0	103.7	0.0
1984	103.9	0.2	104.0	0.1	104.1	0.1	104.2	0.1	104.1	-0.1	103.9	-0.2	104.0	0.1	103.9	-0.1	101.6	-2.2	105.0	3.3	105.2	0.2	104.9	-0.3
1985	105.5	0.6	106.1	0.6	105.9	-0.2	106.0	0.1	106.4	0.4	106.5	0.1	106.5	0.0	106.5	0.0	101.4	-4.8	108.8	7.3	108.8	0.0	108.2	-0.6
1986	107.6	-0.6	107.8	0.2	107.5	-0.3	108.6	1.0	108.5	-0.1	108.7	0.2	108.8	0.1	108.3	-0.5	105.2	-2.9	113.1	7.5	113.0	-0.1	112.5	-0.4
1987	112.6	0.1	110.9	-1.5	111.1	0.2	112.3	1.1	111.8	-0.4	111.5	-0.3	111.4	-0.1	110.8	-0.5	108.9	-1.7	114.2	4.9	113.3	-0.8	111.8	-1.3
1988	112.0	0.2	111.9	-0.1	111.8	-0.1	112.0	0.2	112.3	0.3	112.4	0.1	112.6	0.2	112.8	0.2	110.9	-1.7	116.9	5.4	116.1	-0.7	116.0	-0.1
1989	116.2	0.2	116.5	0.3	115.5	-0.9	114.8	-0.6	115.6	0.7	115.9	0.3	114.5	-1.2	114.5	0.0	113.8	-0.6	119.6	5.1	118.8	-0.7	118.6	-0.2
1990	117.2	-1.2	117.3	0.1	117.0	-0.3	116.9	-0.1	116.6	-0.3	117.6	0.9	117.8	0.2	117.2	-0.5	116.7	-0.4	121.6	4.2	121.5	-0.1	121.5	0.0
1991	121.9	0.3	122.4	0.4	122.2	-0.2	121.5	-0.6	120.7	-0.7	120.6	-0.1	120.5	-0.1	120.6	0.1	119.2	-1.2	125.8	5.5	125.4	-0.3	124.9	-0.4
1992	124.8	-0.1	124.6	-0.2	124.9	0.2	124.8	-0.1	124.7	-0.1	124.3	-0.3	124.4	0.1	123.9	-0.4	121.3	-2.1	127.1	4.8	127.1	0.0	126.9	-0.2
1993	127.1	0.2	127.8	0.6	127.8	0.0	127.7	-0.1	127.6	-0.1	127.7	0.1	127.8	0.1	127.7	-0.1	124.9	-2.2	129.7	3.8	129.9	0.2	130.0	0.1
1994	130.7	0.5	130.9	0.2	130.8	-0.1	130.8	0.0	131.4	0.5	131.3	-0.1	131.5	0.2	131.6	0.1	129.0	-2.0	132.8	2.9	132.5	-0.2	133.0	0.4
1995	133.4	0.3	133.3	-0.1	133.1	-0.2	132.9	-0.2	132.7	-0.2	132.2	-0.4	132.2	0.0	131.9	-0.2	129.1	-2.1	134.8	4.4	135.5	0.5	135.4	-0.1
1996	134.5	-0.7	134.5	0.0	134.5	0.0	134.1	-0.3	134.1	0.0	134.2	0.1	133.5	-0.5	133.3	-0.1	131.0	-1.7	135.2	3.2	134.9	-0.2	134.8	-0.1
1997	134.6	-0.1	134.5	-0.1	134.3	-0.1	133.7	-0.4	132.5	-0.9	132.3	-0.2	131.0	-1.0	131.0	0.0	129.6	-1.1	134.3	3.6	133.5	-0.6	132.6	-0.7
1998	132.0	-0.5	132.1	0.1	132.0	-0.1	131.7	-0.2	130.6	-0.8	129.9	-0.5	130.2	0.2	129.6	-0.5	128.8	-0.6	133.7	3.8	133.6	-0.1	132.9	-0.5
1999	132.0	-0.7	132.4	0.3	131.7	-0.5	131.9	0.2	131.4	-0.4	130.6	-0.6	129.8	-0.6	129.7	-0.1	129.1	-0.5	134.5	4.2	133.7	-0.6	133.5	-0.1
2000	133.1	-0.3	132.7	-0.3	132.5	-0.2	132.4	-0.1	132.4	0.0	131.4	-0.8	131.0	-0.3	130.5	-0.4	130.2	-0.2	133.8	2.8	133.9	0.1	133.7	-0.1
2001	133.2	-0.4	131.7	-1.1	131.9	0.2	132.5	0.5	131.2	-1.0	130.5	-0.5	130.9	0.3	130.5	-0.3	130.3	-0.2	132.0	1.3	132.1	0.1	131.2	-0.7

Source: U.S. Department of Labor, Bureau of Labor Statistics, Division of Industry Prices and Price Indexes. n.e.c. stands for not elsewhere classified. - indicates no data collected for period or unavailable.

Aircraft and Aircraft Equipment
Producer Price Index
Base 1982 = 100

For 1971-2001. Columns headed % show percentile change in the index from the previous period for which an index is available.

Year	Jan Index	%	Feb Index	%	Mar Index	%	Apr Index	%	May Index	%	Jun Index	%	Jul Index	%	Aug Index	%	Sep Index	%	Oct Index	%	Nov Index	%	Dec Index	%
1971	36.7	-	36.7	0.0	36.7	0.0	36.7	0.0	36.7	0.0	36.7	0.0	36.7	0.0	36.7	0.0	36.7	0.0	36.1	-1.6	36.1	0.0	37.0	2.5
1972	38.4	3.8	38.4	0.0	38.4	0.0	38.4	0.0	38.4	0.0	38.4	0.0	38.4	0.0	38.4	0.0	38.4	0.0	38.6	0.5	38.6	0.0	38.6	0.0
1973	38.6	0.0	38.8	0.5	39.0	0.5	39.0	0.0	39.0	0.0	39.0	0.0	39.0	0.0	39.0	0.0	39.0	0.0	39.0	0.0	39.1	0.3	39.2	0.3
1974	39.2	0.0	39.2	0.0	39.2	0.0	39.7	1.3	41.8	5.3	41.8	0.0	42.0	0.5	42.0	0.0	43.3	3.1	43.9	1.4	44.3	0.9	45.1	1.8
1975	46.1	2.2	46.1	0.0	46.3	0.4	48.2	4.1	48.2	0.0	48.2	0.0	48.2	0.0	48.2	0.0	49.4	2.5	50.9	3.0	50.9	0.0	50.9	0.0
1976	53.9	5.9	53.8	-0.2	53.8	0.0	53.8	0.0	53.8	0.0	53.8	0.0	53.8	0.0	53.8	0.0	54.7	1.7	55.7	1.8	55.7	0.0	57.6	3.4
1977	58.3	1.2	58.3	0.0	58.3	0.0	58.4	0.2	58.4	0.0	58.4	0.0	58.4	0.0	58.4	0.0	59.2	1.4	60.8	2.7	62.0	2.0	62.0	0.0
1978	63.1	1.8	63.1	0.0	63.1	0.0	63.1	0.0	63.1	0.0	63.1	0.0	63.1	0.0	63.1	0.0	64.3	1.9	65.9	2.5	67.3	2.1	67.4	0.1
1979	68.4	1.5	68.4	0.0	68.8	0.6	69.0	0.3	69.2	0.3	69.3	0.1	69.5	0.3	70.3	1.2	70.3	0.0	71.0	1.0	71.8	1.1	72.3	0.7
1980	75.3	4.1	75.3	0.0	75.3	0.0	75.9	0.8	75.9	0.0	75.9	0.0	76.1	0.3	76.1	0.0	78.9	3.7	87.0	10.3	87.0	0.0	87.4	0.5
1981	89.4	2.3	89.4	0.0	89.9	0.6	90.0	0.1	90.0	0.0	90.3	0.3	90.3	0.0	90.3	0.0	92.7	2.7	92.4	-0.3	95.5	3.4	95.5	0.0
1982	97.3	1.9	97.3	0.0	97.3	0.0	98.6	1.3	98.6	0.0	98.6	0.0	98.6	0.0	98.6	0.0	101.5	2.9	102.5	1.0	103.6	1.1	107.4	3.7
1983	106.3	-1.0	106.7	0.4	107.1	0.4	107.1	0.0	107.1	0.0	107.1	0.0	107.1	0.0	108.7	1.5	108.7	0.0	111.1	2.2	111.1	0.0	111.1	0.0
1984	112.5	1.3	114.4	1.7	114.4	0.0	114.4	0.0	114.4	0.0	114.4	0.0	114.6	0.2	114.6	0.0	116.1	1.3	116.2	0.1	117.2	0.9	117.2	0.0
1985	118.2	0.9	118.2	0.0	118.2	0.0	119.9	1.4	120.0	0.1	120.0	0.0	121.4	1.2	121.5	0.1	-	-	-	-	-	-	-	-
1986	124.1	2.1	124.4	0.2	124.4	0.0	124.6	0.2	124.3	-0.2	124.3	0.0	124.5	0.2	124.6	0.1	122.6	-1.6	122.8	0.2	122.8	0.0	122.7	-0.1
1987	123.5	0.7	123.5	0.0	123.9	0.3	123.9	0.0	122.8	-0.9	122.9	0.1	122.9	0.0	122.9	0.0	123.1	0.2	123.1	0.0	123.4	0.2	123.3	-0.1
1988	125.1	1.5	125.2	0.1	125.3	0.1	126.2	0.7	126.0	-0.2	126.7	0.6	125.8	-0.7	126.0	0.2	126.4	0.3	126.3	-0.1	126.6	0.2	126.7	0.1
1989	127.9	0.9	128.1	0.2	128.9	0.6	129.3	0.3	129.4	0.1	129.6	0.2	129.9	0.2	130.4	0.4	130.4	0.0	130.7	0.2	132.0	1.0	132.2	0.2
1990	134.3	1.6	134.9	0.4	135.4	0.4	136.1	0.5	136.3	0.1	136.4	0.1	136.7	0.2	137.5	0.6	137.6	0.1	138.4	0.6	138.9	0.4	139.1	0.1
1991	141.7	1.9	142.0	0.2	142.3	0.2	142.8	0.4	144.2	1.0	144.3	0.1	144.7	0.3	145.5	0.6	145.6	0.1	146.0	0.3	146.2	0.1	146.4	0.1
1992	149.5	2.1	149.7	0.1	149.9	0.1	150.6	0.5	150.9	0.2	151.4	0.3	151.4	0.0	152.0	0.4	152.5	0.3	152.8	0.2	152.5	-0.2	152.6	0.1
1993	153.5	0.6	153.5	0.0	153.9	0.3	154.6	0.5	154.7	0.1	154.0	-0.5	154.7	0.5	155.1	0.3	154.8	-0.2	156.4	1.0	156.8	0.3	156.9	0.1
1994	158.4	1.0	158.6	0.1	158.5	-0.1	158.7	0.1	158.7	0.0	158.7	0.0	158.8	0.1	158.9	0.1	159.0	0.1	160.5	0.9	160.8	0.2	160.8	0.0
1995	163.1	1.4	163.1	0.0	162.9	-0.1	162.8	-0.1	163.0	0.1	163.3	0.2	163.4	0.1	163.5	0.1	163.5	0.0	164.8	0.8	165.2	0.2	165.3	0.1
1996	167.0	1.0	167.1	0.1	167.3	0.1	167.1	-0.1	167.3	0.1	167.6	0.2	167.7	0.1	168.1	0.2	168.4	0.2	168.6	0.1	168.8	0.1	169.0	0.1
1997	170.1	0.7	170.0	-0.1	170.3	0.2	169.8	-0.3	170.0	0.1	170.1	0.1	169.9	-0.1	169.7	-0.1	169.4	-0.2	169.4	0.0	169.1	-0.2	169.4	0.2
1998	170.3	0.5	170.4	0.1	170.7	0.2	170.8	0.1	170.9	0.1	171.0	0.1	170.7	-0.2	170.6	-0.1	171.0	0.2	171.6	0.4	171.7	0.1	171.5	-0.1
1999	172.3	0.5	172.4	0.1	172.2	-0.1	172.2	0.0	172.0	-0.1	172.0	0.0	172.0	0.0	171.8	-0.1	172.0	0.1	172.5	0.3	173.0	0.3	173.5	0.3
2000	175.0	0.9	175.4	0.2	175.7	0.2	176.2	0.3	176.3	0.1	177.2	0.5	177.8	0.3	178.3	0.3	178.8	0.3	179.4	0.3	179.8	0.2	180.0	0.1
2001	181.7	0.9	182.2	0.3	182.4	0.1	182.8	0.2	183.0	0.1	183.7	0.4	184.2	0.3	184.6	0.2	184.2	-0.2	184.2	0.0	184.2	0.0	184.4	0.1

Source: U.S. Department of Labor, Bureau of Labor Statistics, Division of Industry Prices and Price Indexes. n.e.c. stands for not elsewhere classified. - indicates no data collected for period or unavailable.

Ships and Boats
Producer Price Index
Base 1982 = 100

For 1981-2001. Columns headed % show percentile change in the index from the previous period for which an index is available.

Year	Jan Index	%	Feb Index	%	Mar Index	%	Apr Index	%	May Index	%	Jun Index	%	Jul Index	%	Aug Index	%	Sep Index	%	Oct Index	%	Nov Index	%	Dec Index	%
1981	-	-	-	-	-	-	-	-	-	-	-	-	-	-	-	-	-	-	-	-	-	-	97.5	-
1982	98.1	0.6	98.9	0.8	99.2	0.3	99.7	0.5	99.8	0.1	100.3	0.5	100.1	-0.2	100.4	0.3	100.6	0.2	100.9	0.3	101.0	0.1	100.9	-0.1
1983	101.0	0.1	101.4	0.4	101.5	0.1	102.4	0.9	102.7	0.3	102.9	0.2	103.1	0.2	103.2	0.1	104.1	0.9	104.5	0.4	104.4	-0.1	105.2	0.8
1984	106.1	0.9	106.3	0.2	106.5	0.2	106.6	0.1	108.1	1.4	108.0	-0.1	108.6	0.6	108.0	-0.6	107.0	-0.9	107.3	0.3	107.6	0.3	108.1	0.5
1985	108.6	0.5	109.0	0.4	109.1	0.1	110.0	0.8	110.0	0.0	110.0	0.0	109.7	-0.3	110.4	0.6	110.5	0.1	111.6	1.0	112.0	0.4	112.4	0.4
1986	113.2	0.7	113.2	0.0	113.3	0.1	113.4	0.1	113.6	0.2	113.6	0.0	113.5	-0.1	113.4	-0.1	113.4	0.0	113.6	0.2	113.6	0.0	113.6	0.0
1987	113.8	0.2	113.9	0.1	114.0	0.1	114.1	0.1	114.1	0.0	114.1	0.0	114.1	0.0	114.1	0.0	114.2	0.1	114.2	0.0	114.2	0.0	114.3	0.1
1988	114.4	0.1	114.5	0.1	114.1	-0.3	114.1	0.0	114.2	0.1	114.2	0.0	114.5	0.3	114.6	0.1	116.5	1.7	116.3	-0.2	116.8	0.4	116.7	-0.1
1989	116.9	0.2	117.2	0.3	117.2	0.0	114.8	-2.0	119.9	4.4	122.1	1.8	122.4	0.2	124.0	1.3	122.1	-1.5	122.0	-0.1	122.1	0.1	120.6	-1.2
1990	120.9	0.2	123.5	2.2	125.0	1.2	125.1	0.1	125.1	0.0	125.2	0.1	125.3	0.1	125.9	0.5	127.0	0.9	127.4	0.3	127.2	-0.2	127.3	0.1
1991	127.5	0.2	127.7	0.2	128.7	0.8	128.7	0.0	130.6	1.5	130.6	0.0	130.8	0.2	130.8	0.0	130.8	0.0	131.3	0.4	131.3	0.0	134.9	2.7
1992	135.0	0.1	135.2	0.1	137.2	1.5	137.8	0.4	137.9	0.1	137.9	0.0	137.9	0.0	137.6	-0.2	137.9	0.2	137.9	0.0	138.0	0.1	138.1	0.1
1993	142.5	3.2	142.9	0.3	143.1	0.1	143.5	0.3	143.5	0.0	143.5	0.0	143.5	0.0	143.1	-0.3	143.4	0.2	143.5	0.1	143.5	0.0	143.5	0.0
1994	144.6	0.8	144.8	0.1	145.6	0.6	145.8	0.1	145.8	0.0	145.8	0.0	145.0	-0.5	145.1	0.1	145.3	0.1	145.5	0.1	145.5	0.0	145.6	0.1
1995	146.4	0.5	147.7	0.9	147.7	0.0	147.9	0.1	147.9	0.0	148.0	0.1	147.7	-0.2	147.8	0.1	148.1	0.2	148.2	0.1	148.3	0.1	148.4	0.1
1996	150.5	1.4	150.7	0.1	150.7	0.0	153.7	2.0	153.3	-0.3	153.5	0.1	153.9	0.3	155.1	0.8	155.0	-0.1	159.5	2.9	156.3	-2.0	156.6	0.2
1997	158.2	1.0	158.2	0.0	158.4	0.1	160.8	1.5	157.5	-2.1	157.5	0.0	158.9	0.9	160.4	0.9	160.5	0.1	160.2	-0.2	161.1	0.6	161.1	0.0
1998	161.2	0.1	161.4	0.1	161.5	0.1	161.8	0.2	161.8	0.0	161.8	0.0	162.1	0.2	162.1	0.0	162.1	0.0	162.1	0.0	162.2	0.1	162.2	0.0
1999	162.7	0.3	162.7	0.0	162.7	0.0	162.8	0.1	162.9	0.1	162.9	0.0	163.4	0.3	163.5	0.1	163.3	-0.1	163.5	0.1	163.5	0.0	163.6	0.1
2000	163.9	0.2	164.0	0.1	164.6	0.4	164.7	0.1	164.7	0.0	165.1	0.2	166.2	0.7	166.3	0.1	166.4	0.1	168.1	1.0	168.2	0.1	168.2	0.0
2001	168.7	0.3	168.8	0.1	168.8	0.0	168.9	0.1	169.3	0.2	169.2	-0.1	169.6	0.2	169.8	0.1	169.8	0.0	169.7	-0.1	169.5	-0.1	169.7	0.1

Source: U.S. Department of Labor, Bureau of Labor Statistics, Division of Industry Prices and Price Indexes. n.e.c. stands for not elsewhere classified. - indicates no data collected for period or unavailable.

Railroad Equipment
Producer Price Index
Base 1982 = 100

For 1961-2001. Columns headed % show percentile change in the index from the previous period for which an index is available.

Year	Jan Index	%	Feb Index	%	Mar Index	%	Apr Index	%	May Index	%	Jun Index	%	Jul Index	%	Aug Index	%	Sep Index	%	Oct Index	%	Nov Index	%	Dec Index	%
1961	27.9	-	27.9	0.0	27.9	0.0	27.9	0.0	27.9	0.0	27.9	0.0	27.9	0.0	27.9	0.0	27.9	0.0	28.0	0.4	28.0	0.0	28.0	0.0
1962	28.0	0.0	28.0	0.0	28.0	0.0	28.0	0.0	28.0	0.0	28.0	0.0	28.0	0.0	28.0	0.0	28.0	0.0	28.0	0.0	28.0	0.0	28.0	0.0
1963	28.0	0.0	28.0	0.0	28.0	0.0	28.0	0.0	28.0	0.0	28.0	0.0	28.0	0.0	28.0	0.0	28.0	0.0	28.0	0.0	28.0	0.0	28.0	0.0
1964	28.0	0.0	28.0	0.0	28.0	0.0	27.9	-0.4	27.9	0.0	27.9	0.0	28.0	0.4	28.0	0.0	28.0	0.0	28.0	0.0	28.0	0.0	28.0	0.0
1965	28.0	0.0	28.0	0.0	28.0	0.0	28.0	0.0	28.0	0.0	28.1	0.4	28.1	0.0	28.1	0.0	28.1	0.0	28.1	0.0	28.1	0.0	28.1	0.0
1966	28.1	0.0	28.1	0.0	28.1	0.0	28.1	0.0	28.1	0.0	28.1	0.0	28.1	0.0	28.1	0.0	28.1	0.0	28.1	0.0	28.1	0.0	28.6	1.8
1967	28.7	0.3	28.7	0.0	28.7	0.0	28.7	0.0	28.7	0.0	28.7	0.0	28.7	0.0	28.7	0.0	28.7	0.0	29.2	1.7	29.3	0.3	29.3	0.0
1968	29.4	0.3	29.4	0.0	29.4	0.0	29.4	0.0	29.4	0.0	29.4	0.0	29.8	1.4	29.9	0.3	29.9	0.0	30.3	1.3	30.3	0.0	30.3	0.0
1969	30.3	0.0	30.3	0.0	30.8	1.7	30.8	0.0	31.0	0.6	31.2	0.6	31.9	2.2	32.0	0.3	32.0	0.0	32.2	0.6	32.2	0.0	32.3	0.3
1970	32.7	1.2	32.8	0.3	33.0	0.6	33.1	0.3	33.1	0.0	33.2	0.3	33.2	0.0	33.2	0.0	33.3	0.3	33.5	0.6	33.5	0.0	33.7	0.6
1971	34.3	1.8	34.3	0.0	34.5	0.6	34.5	0.0	34.7	0.6	34.8	0.3	35.2	1.1	35.3	0.3	35.3	0.0	35.3	0.0	35.3	0.0	35.3	0.0
1972	35.7	1.1	35.8	0.3	36.7	2.5	37.1	1.1	37.4	0.8	37.4	0.0	37.6	0.5	37.6	0.0	37.6	0.0	37.6	0.0	37.6	0.0	37.8	0.5
1973	38.0	0.5	38.2	0.5	38.3	0.3	38.5	0.5	38.8	0.8	38.9	0.3	38.9	0.0	39.0	0.3	39.3	0.8	39.3	0.0	39.4	0.3	40.0	1.5
1974	40.5	1.3	40.7	0.5	41.8	2.7	42.9	2.6	44.4	3.5	47.2	6.3	48.5	2.8	50.4	3.9	51.4	2.0	52.2	1.6	53.1	1.7	54.2	2.1
1975	56.7	4.6	56.9	0.4	57.2	0.5	57.2	0.0	57.6	0.7	57.5	-0.2	58.4	1.6	58.2	-0.3	58.4	0.3	59.1	1.2	59.7	1.0	60.0	0.5
1976	60.4	0.7	61.2	1.3	61.2	0.0	61.7	0.8	61.7	0.0	62.2	0.8	62.6	0.6	63.2	1.0	63.2	0.0	64.3	1.7	64.3	0.0	64.4	0.2
1977	65.8	2.2	65.8	0.0	66.4	0.9	66.7	0.5	66.7	0.0	66.9	0.3	67.6	1.0	67.9	0.4	67.9	0.0	68.9	1.5	68.9	0.0	69.2	0.4
1978	70.3	1.6	70.6	0.4	70.6	0.0	72.2	2.3	72.4	0.3	72.4	0.0	73.2	1.1	73.4	0.3	74.1	1.0	75.1	1.3	75.5	0.5	75.6	0.1
1979	76.9	1.7	77.4	0.7	77.6	0.3	78.4	1.0	78.4	0.0	79.3	1.1	81.0	2.1	81.1	0.1	81.3	0.2	82.6	1.6	83.2	0.7	83.4	0.2
1980	85.9	3.0	86.4	0.6	87.2	0.9	89.4	2.5	89.6	0.2	90.1	0.6	91.3	1.3	91.8	0.5	92.4	0.7	93.3	1.0	93.4	0.1	93.5	0.1
1981	96.0	2.7	96.0	0.0	96.4	0.4	96.9	0.5	95.6	-1.3	95.7	0.1	97.6	2.0	97.8	0.2	97.8	0.0	97.8	0.0	98.5	0.7	98.2	-0.3
1982	99.8	1.6	99.8	0.0	99.9	0.1	99.1	-0.8	98.9	-0.2	98.9	0.0	98.9	0.0	100.4	1.5	100.4	0.0	101.2	0.8	101.2	0.0	101.2	0.0
1983	101.3	0.1	101.2	-0.1	101.1	-0.1	101.0	-0.1	101.1	0.1	101.0	-0.1	101.4	0.4	101.3	-0.1	101.2	-0.1	100.6	-0.6	100.6	0.0	101.2	0.6
1984	101.5	0.3	101.5	0.0	101.6	0.1	102.3	0.7	102.3	0.0	102.3	0.0	102.9	0.6	103.2	0.3	103.2	0.0	103.6	0.4	103.6	0.0	103.6	0.0
1985	103.9	0.3	104.4	0.5	104.7	0.3	104.8	0.1	104.6	-0.2	105.0	0.4	105.1	0.1	105.2	0.1	105.2	0.0	105.2	0.0	105.1	-0.1	105.2	0.1
1986	105.9	0.7	105.5	-0.4	105.6	0.1	105.6	0.0	105.3	-0.3	105.3	0.0	106.1	0.8	104.9	-1.1	105.2	0.3	105.2	0.0	105.2	0.0	105.3	0.1
1987	105.2	-0.1	104.6	-0.6	104.7	0.1	104.6	-0.1	104.5	-0.1	104.4	-0.1	104.7	0.3	104.8	0.1	104.8	0.0	104.6	-0.2	105.0	0.4	105.0	0.0
1988	105.3	0.3	104.8	-0.5	105.5	0.7	106.2	0.7	107.0	0.8	108.1	1.0	108.2	0.1	108.6	0.4	108.8	0.2	108.8	0.0	109.0	0.2	110.2	1.1
1989	111.8	1.5	112.2	0.4	112.2	0.0	114.2	1.8	114.2	0.0	114.3	0.1	114.6	0.3	114.6	0.0	114.7	0.1	114.8	0.1	114.9	0.1	115.6	0.6
1990	116.3	0.6	117.5	1.0	117.4	-0.1	117.6	0.2	117.7	0.1	118.5	0.7	118.5	0.0	118.5	0.0	119.9	1.2	119.9	0.0	120.9	0.8	120.9	0.0
1991	122.0	0.9	121.9	-0.1	122.2	0.2	122.1	-0.1	122.2	0.1	122.2	0.0	122.6	0.3	122.8	0.2	122.8	0.0	122.3	-0.4	121.9	-0.3	121.8	-0.1
1992	122.5	0.6	123.2	0.6	123.6	0.3	123.6	0.0	123.7	0.1	123.9	0.2	124.0	0.1	123.9	-0.1	124.2	0.2	124.2	0.0	123.8	-0.3	123.3	-0.4
1993	123.6	0.2	124.2	0.5	124.3	0.1	124.5	0.2	124.5	0.0	124.6	0.1	125.0	0.3	125.8	0.6	126.1	0.2	125.7	-0.3	125.7	0.0	127.6	1.5
1994	127.9	0.2	128.1	0.2	128.5	0.3	128.5	0.0	128.7	0.2	129.0	0.2	129.1	0.1	129.8	0.5	129.9	0.1	130.0	0.1	130.1	0.1	130.2	0.1
1995	130.9	0.5	132.7	1.4	133.2	0.4	134.2	0.8	134.7	0.4	135.2	0.4	135.5	0.2	135.7	0.1	135.6	-0.1	136.1	0.4	136.6	0.4	136.9	0.2
1996	136.7	-0.1	137.7	0.7	137.6	-0.1	137.8	0.1	137.7	-0.1	137.3	-0.3	137.3	0.0	137.2	-0.1	137.0	-0.1	137.0	0.0	136.5	-0.4	136.3	-0.1
1997	142.4	4.5	136.6	-4.1	132.2	-3.2	131.6	-0.5	134.2	2.0	134.3	0.1	133.8	-0.4	133.5	-0.2	134.2	0.5	134.8	0.4	135.6	0.6	134.7	-0.7
1998	134.6	-0.1	134.5	-0.1	134.5	0.0	135.5	0.7	135.3	-0.1	135.6	0.2	135.2	-0.3	135.3	0.1	135.3	0.0	134.5	-0.6	134.3	-0.1	135.2	0.7
1999	134.6	-0.4	134.6	0.0	134.6	0.0	134.5	-0.1	134.5	0.0	135.8	1.0	135.9	0.1	135.9	0.0	135.8	-0.1	135.7	-0.1	135.3	-0.3	135.5	0.1
2000	135.3	-0.1	135.3	0.0	135.6	0.2	135.8	0.1	135.7	-0.1	135.8	0.1	135.8	0.0	135.7	-0.1	135.9	0.1	135.8	-0.1	135.8	0.0	135.8	0.0
2001	135.9	0.1	135.9	0.0	135.4	-0.4	135.5	0.1	135.6	0.1	135.7	0.1	135.1	-0.4	135.1	0.0	135.6	0.4	135.8	0.1	134.7	-0.8	134.5	-0.1

Source: U.S. Department of Labor, Bureau of Labor Statistics, Division of Industry Prices and Price Indexes. n.e.c. stands for not elsewhere classified. - indicates no data collected for period or unavailable.

Transportation Equipment, n.e.c.
Producer Price Index
Base 1982 = 100

For 1985-2001. Columns headed % show percentile change in the index from the previous period for which an index is available.

Year	Jan Index	%	Feb Index	%	Mar Index	%	Apr Index	%	May Index	%	Jun Index	%	Jul Index	%	Aug Index	%	Sep Index	%	Oct Index	%	Nov Index	%	Dec Index	%
1985	-	-	-	-	-	-	-	-	-	-	100.0	-	100.0	0.0	99.5	-0.5	99.3	-0.2	99.3	0.0	99.3	0.0	99.3	0.0
1986	99.0	-0.3	99.4	0.4	100.1	0.7	100.0	-0.1	99.9	-0.1	100.0	0.1	100.1	0.1	100.6	0.5	100.2	-0.4	100.3	0.1	101.1	0.8	101.1	0.0
1987	101.1	0.0	101.2	0.1	101.2	0.0	101.2	0.0	101.6	0.4	101.8	0.2	102.0	0.2	102.1	0.1	102.8	0.7	103.2	0.4	103.1	-0.1	103.1	0.0
1988	103.3	0.2	103.9	0.6	104.0	0.1	105.4	1.3	105.4	0.0	105.3	-0.1	106.5	1.1	106.6	0.1	108.0	1.3	108.0	0.0	108.3	0.3	108.2	-0.1
1989	108.7	0.5	109.0	0.3	109.1	0.1	109.4	0.3	109.4	0.0	109.2	-0.2	109.4	0.2	109.7	0.3	110.3	0.5	110.9	0.5	111.1	0.2	111.2	0.1
1990	111.2	0.0	111.2	0.0	111.0	-0.2	111.7	0.6	111.7	0.0	111.7	0.0	111.8	0.1	111.8	0.0	111.8	0.0	111.7	-0.1	112.0	0.3	111.8	-0.2
1991	112.4	0.5	112.6	0.2	113.1	0.4	113.3	0.2	113.7	0.4	113.8	0.1	113.8	0.0	113.9	0.1	114.3	0.4	114.2	-0.1	114.2	0.0	114.2	0.0
1992	114.8	0.5	114.9	0.1	114.7	-0.2	114.7	0.0	114.7	0.0	114.8	0.1	114.6	-0.2	114.6	0.0	114.6	0.0	114.8	0.2	114.8	0.0	114.8	0.0
1993	115.0	0.2	115.5	0.4	115.4	-0.1	115.5	0.1	115.5	0.0	115.5	0.0	115.6	0.1	115.8	0.2	116.0	0.2	115.8	-0.2	116.3	0.4	116.3	0.0
1994	116.4	0.1	116.6	0.2	116.6	0.0	116.8	0.2	117.1	0.3	117.4	0.3	117.5	0.1	117.5	0.0	117.8	0.3	118.3	0.4	118.4	0.1	119.0	0.5
1995	119.9	0.8	120.5	0.5	121.1	0.5	121.2	0.1	121.1	-0.1	121.3	0.2	121.2	-0.1	121.6	0.3	122.2	0.5	122.6	0.3	122.9	0.2	122.9	0.0
1996	123.1	0.2	124.3	1.0	124.7	0.3	125.0	0.2	124.9	-0.1	125.2	0.2	125.1	-0.1	124.9	-0.2	124.9	0.0	124.9	0.0	125.4	0.4	126.0	0.5
1997	126.1	0.1	126.2	0.1	126.8	0.5	126.9	0.1	126.9	0.0	126.9	0.0	126.8	-0.1	126.9	0.1	127.1	0.2	126.8	-0.2	128.9	1.7	128.9	0.0
1998	129.4	0.4	129.4	0.0	129.3	-0.1	129.8	0.4	129.8	0.0	130.3	0.4	130.9	0.5	130.3	-0.5	130.6	0.2	130.2	-0.3	129.0	-0.9	129.4	0.3
1999	129.9	0.4	129.9	0.0	130.2	0.2	130.2	0.0	130.2	0.0	130.6	0.3	130.7	0.1	130.7	0.0	131.1	0.3	131.2	0.1	131.3	0.1	131.3	0.0
2000	131.7	0.3	133.3	1.2	133.4	0.1	133.4	0.0	133.4	0.0	133.4	0.0	133.5	0.1	133.3	-0.1	134.8	1.1	134.8	0.0	134.9	0.1	134.9	0.0
2001	135.7	0.6	135.7	0.0	136.3	0.4	136.5	0.1	136.3	-0.1	136.3	0.0	136.6	0.2	136.8	0.1	136.6	-0.1	137.8	0.9	136.9	-0.7	136.7	-0.1

Source: U.S. Department of Labor, Bureau of Labor Statistics, Division of Industry Prices and Price Indexes. n.e.c. stands for not elsewhere classified. - indicates no data collected for period or unavailable.

MISCELLANEOUS PRODUCTS
Producer Price Index
Base 1982 = 100

For 1947-2001. Columns headed % show percentile change in the index from the previous period for which an index is available.

Year	Jan Index	%	Feb Index	%	Mar Index	%	Apr Index	%	May Index	%	Jun Index	%	Jul Index	%	Aug Index	%	Sep Index	%	Oct Index	%	Nov Index	%	Dec Index	%
1947	26.5	-	26.5	0.0	26.5	0.0	26.6	0.4	26.7	0.4	26.6	-0.4	26.4	-0.8	26.6	0.8	26.6	0.0	26.6	0.0	26.8	0.8	26.8	0.0
1948	27.0	0.7	27.1	0.4	27.2	0.4	27.2	0.0	27.3	0.4	27.3	0.0	27.3	0.0	28.2	3.3	28.3	0.4	28.3	0.0	28.4	0.4	28.5	0.4
1949	28.5	0.0	28.5	0.0	28.5	0.0	28.2	-1.1	28.2	0.0	28.1	-0.4	28.1	0.0	28.0	-0.4	28.0	0.0	28.0	0.0	28.1	0.4	28.2	0.4
1950	28.1	-0.4	28.1	0.0	28.1	0.0	28.1	0.0	28.1	0.0	28.1	0.0	28.2	0.4	29.0	2.8	29.2	0.7	29.4	0.7	29.6	0.7	29.9	1.0
1951	30.3	1.3	30.3	0.0	30.3	0.0	30.4	0.3	30.4	0.0	30.3	-0.3	30.4	0.3	30.4	0.0	30.4	0.0	30.4	0.0	30.3	-0.3	30.3	0.0
1952	30.3	0.0	30.3	0.0	30.2	-0.3	30.2	0.0	30.2	0.0	30.1	-0.3	30.1	0.0	30.1	0.0	30.1	0.0	30.1	0.0	30.1	0.0	30.1	0.0
1953	30.1	0.0	30.1	0.0	31.1	3.3	31.1	0.0	31.1	0.0	31.1	0.0	31.1	0.0	31.1	0.0	31.1	0.0	31.1	0.0	31.1	0.0	31.1	0.0
1954	31.1	0.0	31.1	0.0	31.1	0.0	31.3	0.6	31.2	-0.3	31.3	0.3	31.3	0.0	31.3	0.0	31.3	0.0	31.3	0.0	31.3	0.0	31.3	0.0
1955	31.2	-0.3	31.1	-0.3	31.1	0.0	31.2	0.3	31.2	0.0	31.2	0.0	31.2	0.0	31.3	0.3	31.3	0.0	31.3	0.0	31.4	0.3	31.5	0.3
1956	31.6	0.3	31.6	0.0	31.6	0.0	31.7	0.3	31.7	0.0	31.7	0.0	31.7	0.0	31.7	0.0	31.8	0.3	31.8	0.0	31.9	0.3	31.9	0.0
1957	32.1	0.6	32.2	0.3	32.2	0.0	32.2	0.0	32.2	0.0	32.2	0.0	33.0	2.5	33.0	0.0	33.1	0.3	33.1	0.0	33.2	0.3	33.2	0.0
1958	33.2	0.0	33.2	0.0	33.2	0.0	33.2	0.0	33.2	0.0	33.4	0.6	33.3	-0.3	33.4	0.3	33.3	-0.3	33.3	0.0	33.3	0.0	33.3	0.0
1959	33.3	0.0	33.3	0.0	33.4	0.3	33.4	0.0	33.4	0.0	33.4	0.0	33.4	0.0	33.4	0.0	33.4	0.0	33.4	0.0	33.4	0.0	33.5	0.3
1960	33.6	0.3	33.6	0.0	33.6	0.0	33.6	0.0	33.6	0.0	33.6	0.0	33.6	0.0	33.6	0.0	33.7	0.3	33.7	0.0	33.7	0.0	33.7	0.0
1961	33.7	0.0	33.7	0.0	33.7	0.0	33.7	0.0	33.7	0.0	33.7	0.0	33.7	0.0	33.8	0.3	33.8	0.0	33.9	0.3	33.9	0.0	33.9	0.0
1962	33.8	-0.3	33.9	0.3	33.9	0.0	33.9	0.0	33.9	0.0	33.9	0.0	33.9	0.0	33.9	0.0	33.9	0.0	34.0	0.3	34.0	0.0	34.0	0.0
1963	34.0	0.0	34.0	0.0	33.9	-0.3	33.9	0.0	34.1	0.6	34.3	0.6	34.3	0.0	34.3	0.0	34.3	0.0	34.4	0.3	34.4	0.0	34.4	0.0
1964	34.4	0.0	34.4	0.0	34.4	0.0	34.4	0.0	34.4	0.0	34.4	0.0	34.4	0.0	34.5	0.3	34.5	0.0	34.5	0.0	34.5	0.0	34.5	0.0
1965	34.5	0.0	34.5	0.0	34.5	0.0	34.7	0.6	34.8	0.3	34.6	-0.6	34.8	0.6	34.8	0.0	34.8	0.0	34.8	0.0	34.8	0.0	34.8	0.0
1966	34.9	0.3	34.9	0.0	35.2	0.9	35.3	0.3	35.3	0.0	35.4	0.3	35.4	0.0	35.4	0.0	35.4	0.0	35.5	0.3	35.6	0.3	35.6	0.0
1967	35.7	0.3	35.7	0.0	35.7	0.0	35.7	0.0	35.8	0.3	36.3	1.4	36.4	0.3	36.4	0.0	36.5	0.3	36.6	0.3	36.6	0.0	36.7	0.3
1968	36.7	0.0	36.8	0.3	36.8	0.0	36.9	0.3	36.9	0.0	36.9	0.0	36.9	0.0	37.0	0.3	37.0	0.0	37.1	0.3	37.3	0.5	37.3	0.0
1969	37.3	0.0	37.3	0.0	37.3	0.0	37.4	0.3	37.4	0.0	38.2	2.1	38.4	0.5	38.5	0.3	38.6	0.3	38.7	0.3	38.7	0.0	38.7	0.0
1970	38.9	0.5	39.0	0.3	39.1	0.3	39.0	-0.3	39.2	0.5	40.1	2.3	40.2	0.2	40.2	0.0	40.3	0.2	40.3	0.0	40.3	0.0	40.4	0.2
1971	40.6	0.5	40.7	0.2	40.7	0.0	40.7	0.0	40.8	0.2	40.8	0.0	40.9	0.2	41.0	0.2	41.0	0.0	41.0	0.0	41.0	0.0	41.0	0.0
1972	41.1	0.2	41.2	0.2	41.3	0.2	41.3	0.0	41.3	0.0	41.3	0.0	41.6	0.7	41.6	0.0	41.7	0.2	41.6	-0.2	41.6	0.0	41.6	0.0
1973	41.9	0.7	42.4	1.2	42.7	0.7	42.9	0.5	43.2	0.7	43.5	0.7	43.7	0.5	43.8	0.2	43.8	0.0	43.8	0.0	43.9	0.2	44.0	0.2
1974	44.7	1.6	45.1	0.9	45.5	0.9	46.4	2.0	48.2	3.9	48.6	0.8	48.9	0.6	49.0	0.2	49.3	0.6	49.6	0.6	50.9	2.6	51.5	1.2
1975	52.6	2.1	52.9	0.6	53.1	0.4	53.3	0.4	53.3	0.0	53.4	0.2	53.4	0.0	53.4	0.0	53.6	0.4	53.4	-0.4	53.8	0.7	54.7	1.7
1976	54.9	0.4	55.1	0.4	55.2	0.2	55.2	0.0	55.2	0.0	55.8	1.1	55.6	-0.4	55.5	-0.2	55.7	0.4	55.7	0.0	56.4	1.3	56.8	0.7
1977	57.9	1.9	58.1	0.3	58.2	0.2	58.8	1.0	59.0	0.3	59.1	0.2	59.3	0.3	59.4	0.2	60.1	1.2	60.9	1.3	61.1	0.3	61.4	0.5
1978	62.1	1.1	62.0	-0.2	62.4	0.6	65.6	5.1	66.1	0.8	66.7	0.9	68.6	2.8	69.2	0.9	69.8	0.9	69.0	-1.1	68.4	-0.9	70.0	2.3
1979	71.5	2.1	72.3	1.1	72.6	0.4	72.9	0.4	73.6	1.0	74.2	0.8	74.9	0.9	75.6	0.9	77.1	2.0	79.2	2.7	80.1	1.1	82.3	2.7
1980	87.9	6.8	95.1	8.2	92.6	-2.6	91.4	-1.3	91.0	-0.4	93.3	2.5	94.6	1.4	94.1	-0.5	95.9	1.9	96.2	0.3	95.4	-0.8	96.0	0.6
1981	95.6	-0.4	95.8	0.2	95.5	-0.3	96.2	0.7	96.5	0.3	96.3	-0.2	95.2	-1.1	95.0	-0.2	96.6	1.7	97.1	0.5	96.8	-0.3	96.8	0.0
1982	97.1	0.3	98.9	1.9	98.7	-0.2	98.8	0.1	98.5	-0.3	98.2	-0.3	98.9	0.7	98.4	-0.5	101.1	2.7	103.3	2.2	103.1	-0.2	105.0	1.8
1983	103.3	-1.6	104.4	1.1	104.0	-0.4	104.0	0.0	103.8	-0.2	104.2	0.4	105.5	1.2	105.6	0.1	105.4	-0.2	105.5	0.1	105.5	0.0	105.9	0.4
1984	106.5	0.6	106.7	0.2	106.7	0.0	106.6	-0.1	106.4	-0.2	107.0	0.6	107.5	0.5	107.9	0.4	107.3	-0.6	107.2	-0.1	107.2	0.0	107.3	0.1
1985	108.2	0.8	108.8	0.6	108.7	-0.1	109.1	0.4	109.0	-0.1	109.0	0.0	109.8	0.7	109.8	0.0	109.9	0.1	110.0	0.1	110.1	0.1	109.9	-0.2
1986	111.2	1.2	111.0	-0.2	111.1	0.1	111.2	0.1	111.1	-0.1	111.0	-0.1	111.9	0.8	112.0	0.1	112.1	0.1	112.3	0.2	112.4	0.1	112.2	-0.2
1987	113.1	0.8	113.1	0.0	113.3	0.2	113.9	0.5	114.0	0.1	114.0	0.0	115.1	1.0	115.5	0.3	115.8	0.3	116.2	0.3	116.7	0.4	117.7	0.9
1988	118.7	0.8	119.2	0.4	119.1	-0.1	119.4	0.3	119.4	0.0	119.4	0.0	120.9	1.3	120.7	-0.2	120.7	0.0	121.1	0.3	121.2	0.1	122.6	1.2
1989	124.0	1.1	124.2	0.2	124.5	0.2	124.6	0.1	125.2	0.5	126.7	1.2	127.2	0.4	127.4	0.2	127.6	0.2	128.2	0.5	128.4	0.2	130.0	1.2
1990	131.2	0.9	131.9	0.5	132.0	0.1	132.3	0.2	133.2	0.7	134.4	0.9	134.6	0.1	134.9	0.2	135.3	0.3	135.9	0.4	136.9	0.7	138.2	0.9
1991	139.1	0.7	138.9	-0.1	139.4	0.4	140.0	0.4	140.1	0.1	140.9	0.6	141.8	0.6	141.7	-0.1	141.5	-0.1	141.4	-0.1	141.8	0.3	143.4	1.1

[Continued]

MISCELLANEOUS PRODUCTS
Producer Price Index
Base 1982 = 100
[Continued]

For 1947-2001. Columns headed % show percentile change in the index from the previous period for which an index is available.

Year	Jan Index	%	Feb Index	%	Mar Index	%	Apr Index	%	May Index	%	Jun Index	%	Jul Index	%	Aug Index	%	Sep Index	%	Oct Index	%	Nov Index	%	Dec Index	%
1992	143.9	0.3	143.9	0.0	144.0	0.1	144.8	0.6	146.4	1.1	146.2	-0.1	146.3	0.1	143.8	-1.7	145.3	1.0	145.5	0.1	145.8	0.2	147.3	1.0
1993	148.6	0.9	149.4	0.5	149.4	0.0	150.4	0.7	150.7	0.2	149.6	-0.7	149.6	0.0	138.9	-7.2	138.9	0.0	138.8	-0.1	139.1	0.2	140.9	1.3
1994	141.9	0.7	141.8	-0.1	141.6	-0.1	141.7	0.1	141.5	-0.1	141.6	0.1	141.8	0.1	141.8	0.0	141.8	0.0	142.0	0.1	142.4	0.3	142.4	0.0
1995	143.0	0.4	143.6	0.4	143.8	0.1	144.3	0.3	145.2	0.6	145.3	0.1	145.7	0.3	146.6	0.6	146.6	0.0	147.0	0.3	147.0	0.0	146.9	-0.1
1996	147.7	0.5	146.6	-0.7	146.4	-0.1	146.4	0.0	147.8	1.0	147.8	0.0	148.3	0.3	148.1	-0.1	147.9	-0.1	148.3	0.3	148.4	0.1	148.5	0.1
1997	148.7	0.1	148.9	0.1	149.5	0.4	150.6	0.7	150.9	0.2	150.9	0.0	151.0	0.1	151.0	0.0	152.2	0.8	152.3	0.1	152.3	0.0	152.7	0.3
1998	152.3	-0.3	153.2	0.6	153.5	0.2	154.7	0.8	155.6	0.6	155.6	0.0	155.4	-0.1	156.3	0.6	156.3	0.0	156.3	0.0	156.4	0.1	166.0	6.1
1999	166.0	0.0	165.7	-0.2	165.4	-0.2	165.4	0.0	165.4	0.0	165.0	-0.2	164.8	-0.1	164.8	0.0	168.6	2.3	169.1	0.3	169.6	0.3	169.5	-0.1
2000	167.2	-1.4	170.4	1.9	170.1	-0.2	169.6	-0.3	169.4	-0.1	169.9	0.3	170.5	0.4	171.5	0.6	172.3	0.5	172.6	0.2	173.1	0.3	173.5	0.2
2001	177.1	2.1	177.9	0.5	178.3	0.2	179.2	0.5	182.4	1.8	182.8	0.2	182.7	-0.1	183.0	0.2	183.2	0.1	182.8	-0.2	183.3	0.3	183.4	0.1

Source: U.S. Department of Labor, Bureau of Labor Statistics, Division of Industry Prices and Price Indexes. n.e.c. stands for not elsewhere classified. - indicates no data collected for period or unavailable.

Toys, Sporting Goods, Small Arms, etc.
Producer Price Index
Base 1982 = 100

For 1947-2001. Columns headed % show percentile change in the index from the previous period for which an index is available.

Year	Jan Index	%	Feb Index	%	Mar Index	%	Apr Index	%	May Index	%	Jun Index	%	Jul Index	%	Aug Index	%	Sep Index	%	Oct Index	%	Nov Index	%	Dec Index	%
1947	34.8	-	34.8	0.0	34.9	0.3	35.1	0.6	35.1	0.0	35.1	0.0	35.3	0.6	35.3	0.0	35.1	-0.6	35.1	0.0	35.1	0.0	35.3	0.6
1948	36.0	2.0	36.1	0.3	36.3	0.6	36.5	0.6	36.6	0.3	36.6	0.0	36.6	0.0	37.0	1.1	37.0	0.0	37.0	0.0	37.1	0.3	37.1	0.0
1949	36.6	-1.3	36.8	0.5	36.9	0.3	36.9	0.0	36.8	-0.3	36.8	0.0	36.6	-0.5	36.5	-0.3	36.4	-0.3	36.5	0.3	36.9	1.1	36.9	0.0
1950	37.6	1.9	37.7	0.3	37.7	0.0	37.8	0.3	37.8	0.0	37.9	0.3	38.2	0.8	38.5	0.8	39.6	2.9	40.1	1.3	40.2	0.2	41.0	2.0
1951	41.8	2.0	42.0	0.5	42.2	0.5	42.2	0.0	42.2	0.0	42.2	0.0	42.1	-0.2	42.1	0.0	42.0	-0.2	42.0	0.0	41.7	-0.7	41.7	0.0
1952	41.5	-0.5	41.4	-0.2	41.1	-0.7	41.0	-0.2	41.0	0.0	41.0	0.0	41.0	0.0	40.9	-0.2	40.9	0.0	40.9	0.0	40.9	0.0	40.9	0.0
1953	40.8	-0.2	40.8	0.0	40.8	0.0	41.1	0.7	41.3	0.5	41.2	-0.2	41.2	0.0	41.2	0.0	41.2	0.0	41.2	0.0	41.2	0.0	40.9	-0.7
1954	40.9	0.0	40.9	0.0	40.9	0.0	41.0	0.2	41.0	0.0	41.0	0.0	41.0	0.0	41.0	0.0	40.8	-0.5	40.8	0.0	40.8	0.0	40.8	0.0
1955	40.9	0.2	40.9	0.0	40.9	0.0	40.9	0.0	40.9	0.0	40.9	0.0	40.9	0.0	41.0	0.2	41.0	0.0	41.1	0.2	41.3	0.5	41.6	0.7
1956	41.9	0.7	41.9	0.0	41.8	-0.2	41.9	0.2	41.9	0.0	41.9	0.0	41.9	0.0	41.8	-0.2	42.0	0.5	42.2	0.5	42.2	0.0	42.3	0.2
1957	42.4	0.2	42.4	0.0	42.4	0.0	42.4	0.0	42.4	0.0	42.4	0.0	42.4	0.0	42.6	0.5	42.7	0.2	42.6	-0.2	42.6	0.0	42.6	0.0
1958	43.2	1.4	43.2	0.0	43.1	-0.2	43.1	0.0	43.1	0.0	43.1	0.0	43.1	0.0	43.1	0.0	42.9	-0.5	42.9	0.0	42.9	0.0	42.9	0.0
1959	42.6	-0.7	42.6	0.0	42.4	-0.5	42.3	-0.2	42.3	0.0	42.3	0.0	42.4	0.2	42.5	0.2	42.5	0.0	42.5	0.0	42.5	0.0	42.6	0.2
1960	42.5	-0.2	42.6	0.2	42.6	0.0	42.8	0.5	42.8	0.0	42.8	0.0	42.9	0.2	42.9	0.0	42.9	0.0	42.9	0.0	42.9	0.0	42.9	0.0
1961	42.8	-0.2	42.8	0.0	43.0	0.5	43.0	0.0	43.0	0.0	43.0	0.0	43.0	0.0	43.3	0.7	43.2	-0.2	43.4	0.5	43.4	0.0	43.1	-0.7
1962	42.9	-0.5	42.8	-0.2	42.9	0.2	42.9	0.0	42.9	0.0	42.9	0.0	43.0	0.2	43.1	0.2	43.1	0.0	43.2	0.2	43.2	0.0	43.2	0.0
1963	43.2	0.0	43.2	0.0	42.9	-0.7	43.0	0.2	43.0	0.0	43.0	0.0	43.1	0.2	43.2	0.2	43.2	0.0	43.2	0.0	43.1	-0.2	43.2	0.2
1964	43.1	-0.2	43.1	0.0	43.2	0.2	43.0	-0.5	43.0	0.0	43.1	0.2	43.1	0.0	43.1	0.0	43.2	0.2	43.2	0.0	43.2	0.0	43.2	0.0
1965	43.6	0.9	43.6	0.0	43.6	0.0	43.7	0.2	43.8	0.2	43.8	0.0	43.9	0.2	43.8	-0.2	44.0	0.5	44.0	0.0	44.0	0.0	44.0	0.0
1966	44.0	0.0	44.1	0.2	44.1	0.0	44.3	0.5	44.3	0.0	44.3	0.0	44.6	0.7	44.8	0.4	44.8	0.0	44.8	0.0	44.8	0.0	44.8	0.0
1967	45.0	0.4	45.0	0.0	44.9	-0.2	45.0	0.2	45.0	0.0	45.1	0.2	45.2	0.2	45.2	0.0	45.3	0.2	45.4	0.2	45.4	0.0	45.4	0.0
1968	45.6	0.4	45.5	-0.2	46.1	1.3	46.1	0.0	46.2	0.2	46.2	0.0	46.3	0.2	46.4	0.2	46.5	0.2	46.5	0.0	46.6	0.2	46.6	0.0
1969	47.1	1.1	47.1	0.0	47.2	0.2	47.2	0.0	47.3	0.2	47.3	0.0	47.5	0.4	47.8	0.6	47.9	0.2	48.0	0.2	48.1	0.2	48.2	0.2
1970	48.9	1.5	49.0	0.2	49.6	1.2	49.1	-1.0	49.4	0.6	49.4	0.0	49.5	0.2	49.6	0.2	49.9	0.6	49.9	0.0	49.9	0.0	50.0	0.2
1971	50.8	1.6	50.8	0.0	51.0	0.4	50.8	-0.4	50.8	0.0	51.0	0.4	51.0	0.0	50.9	-0.2	50.9	0.0	50.9	0.0	51.0	0.2	51.0	0.0
1972	51.3	0.6	51.5	0.4	51.7	0.4	51.5	-0.4	51.5	0.0	51.6	0.2	51.7	0.2	51.7	0.0	51.8	0.2	51.9	0.2	51.9	0.0	52.0	0.2
1973	52.5	1.0	52.6	0.2	52.9	0.6	52.9	0.0	53.0	0.2	53.1	0.2	53.1	0.0	53.2	0.2	53.4	0.4	53.8	0.7	54.1	0.6	54.2	0.2
1974	56.2	3.7	57.0	1.4	57.5	0.9	57.8	0.5	58.4	1.0	59.0	1.0	59.6	1.0	61.3	2.9	61.8	0.8	62.4	1.0	63.0	1.0	63.0	0.0
1975	65.4	3.8	65.9	0.8	66.0	0.2	65.8	-0.3	65.8	0.0	65.9	0.2	65.9	0.0	65.9	0.0	65.9	0.0	66.1	0.3	66.3	0.3	66.3	0.0
1976	66.9	0.9	67.1	0.3	67.5	0.6	67.4	-0.1	67.6	0.3	67.9	0.4	68.0	0.1	67.9	-0.1	68.1	0.3	68.1	0.0	68.2	0.1	68.2	0.0
1977	69.4	1.8	69.6	0.3	69.8	0.3	69.7	-0.1	69.8	0.1	69.9	0.1	70.1	0.3	70.3	0.3	70.2	-0.1	70.7	0.7	70.8	0.1	70.9	0.1
1978	72.1	1.7	72.9	1.1	73.3	0.5	73.5	0.3	73.3	-0.3	73.7	0.5	73.7	0.0	74.0	0.4	74.1	0.1	74.5	0.5	74.6	0.1	74.4	-0.3
1979	76.9	3.4	77.2	0.4	77.5	0.4	78.2	0.9	78.7	0.6	78.9	0.3	79.9	1.3	80.2	0.4	81.2	1.2	81.8	0.7	81.8	0.0	82.6	1.0
1980	86.2	4.4	87.4	1.4	87.8	0.5	88.2	0.5	88.5	0.3	89.2	0.8	90.4	1.3	90.9	0.6	91.4	0.6	91.5	0.1	91.6	0.1	92.9	1.4
1981	94.1	1.3	95.1	1.1	95.3	0.2	95.4	0.1	95.4	0.0	95.4	0.0	96.3	0.9	96.0	-0.3	96.5	0.5	96.2	-0.3	96.1	-0.1	96.3	0.2
1982	98.6	2.4	99.4	0.8	99.6	0.2	99.8	0.2	100.2	0.4	100.2	0.0	100.3	0.1	100.9	0.6	100.1	-0.8	99.9	-0.2	100.0	0.1	101.0	1.0
1983	100.6	-0.4	101.7	1.1	101.9	0.2	102.2	0.3	102.1	-0.1	102.0	-0.1	101.3	-0.7	101.4	0.1	101.5	0.1	102.0	0.5	101.7	-0.3	101.7	0.0
1984	102.7	1.0	102.9	0.2	102.8	-0.1	102.3	-0.5	102.4	0.1	102.3	-0.1	102.3	0.0	102.3	0.0	102.5	0.2	102.7	0.2	102.8	0.1	102.8	0.0
1985	103.0	0.2	104.3	1.3	104.5	0.2	104.4	-0.1	104.4	0.0	104.3	-0.1	104.2	-0.1	104.2	0.0	104.4	0.2	105.7	1.2	105.9	0.2	105.2	-0.7
1986	105.7	0.5	106.1	0.4	106.3	0.2	106.4	0.1	106.5	0.1	106.6	0.1	106.8	0.2	106.9	0.1	106.8	-0.1	107.1	0.3	107.1	0.0	106.6	-0.5
1987	106.5	-0.1	107.3	0.8	107.1	-0.2	107.4	0.3	107.4	0.0	107.6	0.2	107.7	0.1	107.7	0.0	108.3	0.6	108.6	0.3	108.8	0.2	109.0	0.2
1988	110.1	1.0	110.9	0.7	111.0	0.1	111.1	0.1	111.2	0.1	111.5	0.3	112.0	0.4	112.2	0.2	112.3	0.1	112.7	0.4	112.9	0.2	113.2	0.3
1989	114.7	1.3	115.5	0.7	115.9	0.3	116.0	0.1	116.2	0.2	116.7	0.4	116.9	0.2	117.4	0.4	117.6	0.2	118.0	0.3	117.7	-0.3	118.1	0.3
1990	118.5	0.3	119.1	0.5	119.1	0.0	119.2	0.1	119.3	0.1	119.4	0.1	119.3	-0.1	119.6	0.3	119.5	-0.1	120.8	1.1	120.6	-0.2	120.8	0.2
1991	121.3	0.4	121.6	0.2	121.9	0.2	122.0	0.1	122.2	0.2	122.6	0.3	122.7	0.1	123.1	0.3	123.2	0.1	123.6	0.3	123.3	-0.2	123.2	-0.1

[Continued]

Toys, Sporting Goods, Small Arms, etc.
Producer Price Index
Base 1982 = 100

[Continued]

For 1947-2001. Columns headed % show percentile change in the index from the previous period for which an index is available.

Year	Jan Index	%	Feb Index	%	Mar Index	%	Apr Index	%	May Index	%	Jun Index	%	Jul Index	%	Aug Index	%	Sep Index	%	Oct Index	%	Nov Index	%	Dec Index	%
1992	123.8	0.5	124.1	0.2	123.9	-0.2	124.0	0.1	124.4	0.3	124.6	0.2	124.6	0.0	124.7	0.1	125.9	1.0	125.9	0.0	124.6	-1.0	124.2	-0.3
1993	125.0	0.6	125.2	0.2	125.1	-0.1	125.2	0.1	125.3	0.1	125.3	0.0	125.3	0.0	125.9	0.5	125.8	-0.1	126.0	0.2	125.9	-0.1	126.0	0.1
1994	126.5	0.4	126.5	0.0	126.4	-0.1	126.5	0.1	126.7	0.2	126.8	0.1	127.4	0.5	127.3	-0.1	127.3	0.0	127.2	-0.1	127.5	0.2	127.7	0.2
1995	128.1	0.3	128.5	0.3	128.7	0.2	129.0	0.2	128.8	-0.2	128.9	0.1	129.4	0.4	129.3	-0.1	129.4	0.1	129.5	0.1	129.5	0.0	129.6	0.1
1996	129.7	0.1	130.2	0.4	130.2	0.0	130.3	0.1	130.4	0.1	130.5	0.1	130.5	0.0	130.7	0.2	130.8	0.1	130.8	0.0	130.6	-0.2	130.3	-0.2
1997	130.7	0.3	130.9	0.2	131.5	0.5	131.7	0.2	131.6	-0.1	131.3	-0.2	131.4	0.1	131.8	0.3	131.9	0.1	132.1	0.2	131.8	-0.2	131.7	-0.1
1998	132.4	0.5	132.3	-0.1	132.3	0.0	132.4	0.1	132.4	0.0	132.5	0.1	132.4	-0.1	132.6	0.2	132.4	-0.2	132.2	-0.2	132.4	0.2	132.4	0.0
1999	132.5	0.1	132.7	0.2	132.5	-0.2	132.5	0.0	132.5	0.0	132.6	0.1	132.6	0.0	132.3	-0.2	132.2	-0.1	132.3	0.1	132.0	-0.2	132.0	0.0
2000	132.3	0.2	132.7	0.3	132.6	-0.1	133.0	0.3	132.2	-0.6	132.4	0.2	132.6	0.2	132.4	-0.2	132.4	0.0	132.3	-0.1	132.4	0.1	132.8	0.3
2001	132.9	0.1	133.0	0.1	133.2	0.2	133.4	0.2	133.4	0.0	133.4	0.0	133.4	0.0	133.5	0.1	133.1	-0.3	133.2	0.1	132.0	-0.9	132.2	0.2

Source: U.S. Department of Labor, Bureau of Labor Statistics, Division of Industry Prices and Price Indexes. n.e.c. stands for not elsewhere classified. - indicates no data collected for period or unavailable.

Tobacco Products, incl. Stemmed & Redried
Producer Price Index
Base 1982 = 100

For 1947-2001. Columns headed % show percentile change in the index from the previous period for which an index is available.

Year	Jan Index	%	Feb Index	%	Mar Index	%	Apr Index	%	May Index	%	Jun Index	%	Jul Index	%	Aug Index	%	Sep Index	%	Oct Index	%	Nov Index	%	Dec Index	%
1947	20.4	-	20.4	0.0	20.4	0.0	20.5	0.5	20.5	0.0	20.5	0.0	20.5	0.0	20.5	0.0	20.5	0.0	20.5	0.0	20.5	0.0	20.5	0.0
1948	20.5	0.0	20.5	0.0	20.5	0.0	20.5	0.0	20.5	0.0	20.5	0.0	20.6	0.5	22.3	8.3	22.3	0.0	22.3	0.0	22.3	0.0	22.3	0.0
1949	22.3	0.0	22.3	0.0	22.3	0.0	22.3	0.0	22.3	0.0	22.3	0.0	22.3	0.0	22.4	0.4	22.4	0.0	22.4	0.0	22.4	0.0	22.4	0.0
1950	22.4	0.0	22.4	0.0	22.4	0.0	22.4	0.0	22.4	0.0	22.4	0.0	22.4	0.0	23.3	4.0	23.3	0.0	23.4	0.4	23.4	0.0	23.4	0.0
1951	23.4	0.0	23.4	0.0	23.4	0.0	23.4	0.0	23.4	0.0	23.4	0.0	23.4	0.0	23.4	0.0	23.4	0.0	23.4	0.0	23.6	0.9	23.6	0.0
1952	23.6	0.0	23.6	0.0	23.6	0.0	23.6	0.0	23.6	0.0	23.6	0.0	23.6	0.0	23.6	0.0	23.6	0.0	23.6	0.0	23.6	0.0	23.6	0.0
1953	23.7	0.4	23.7	0.0	25.6	8.0	25.6	0.0	25.6	0.0	25.6	0.0	25.6	0.0	25.6	0.0	25.6	0.0	25.6	0.0	25.6	0.0	25.6	0.0
1954	25.6	0.0	25.6	0.0	25.6	0.0	25.6	0.0	25.6	0.0	25.6	0.0	25.6	0.0	25.6	0.0	25.6	0.0	25.6	0.0	25.6	0.0	25.6	0.0
1955	25.6	0.0	25.6	0.0	25.6	0.0	25.6	0.0	25.6	0.0	25.6	0.0	25.6	0.0	25.6	0.0	25.6	0.0	25.6	0.0	25.6	0.0	25.6	0.0
1956	25.6	0.0	25.6	0.0	25.6	0.0	25.6	0.0	25.6	0.0	25.6	0.0	25.6	0.0	25.6	0.0	25.6	0.0	25.6	0.0	25.6	0.0	25.7	0.4
1957	25.7	0.0	25.7	0.0	25.7	0.0	25.7	0.0	25.8	0.4	25.8	0.0	27.7	7.4	27.7	0.0	27.7	0.0	27.7	0.0	27.7	0.0	27.7	0.0
1958	27.7	0.0	27.7	0.0	27.7	0.0	27.7	0.0	27.7	0.0	27.7	0.0	27.7	0.0	27.7	0.0	27.7	0.0	27.7	0.0	27.7	0.0	27.7	0.0
1959	27.7	0.0	27.8	0.4	27.9	0.4	27.9	0.0	27.9	0.0	27.9	0.0	27.9	0.0	27.9	0.0	27.9	0.0	27.9	0.0	27.9	0.0	27.9	0.0
1960	27.9	0.0	27.9	0.0	27.9	0.0	27.9	0.0	27.9	0.0	27.9	0.0	27.9	0.0	27.9	0.0	27.9	0.0	27.9	0.0	27.9	0.0	27.9	0.0
1961	27.9	0.0	27.9	0.0	27.9	0.0	27.9	0.0	27.9	0.0	27.9	0.0	27.9	0.0	27.9	0.0	27.9	0.0	27.9	0.0	27.9	0.0	27.9	0.0
1962	27.9	0.0	27.9	0.0	27.9	0.0	27.9	0.0	27.9	0.0	27.9	0.0	27.9	0.0	27.9	0.0	27.9	0.0	28.0	0.4	28.0	0.0	28.0	0.0
1963	28.0	0.0	28.0	0.0	28.0	0.0	28.0	0.0	28.7	2.5	29.0	1.0	29.0	0.0	29.0	0.0	29.0	0.0	29.0	0.0	29.0	0.0	29.0	0.0
1964	29.0	0.0	29.0	0.0	29.1	0.3	29.1	0.0	29.1	0.0	29.1	0.0	29.1	0.0	29.1	0.0	29.1	0.0	29.1	0.0	29.1	0.0	29.1	0.0
1965	29.1	0.0	29.1	0.0	29.1	0.0	29.2	0.3	29.4	0.7	29.1	-1.0	29.1	0.0	29.1	0.0	29.1	0.0	29.1	0.0	29.1	0.0	29.1	0.0
1966	29.2	0.3	29.2	0.0	30.1	3.1	30.2	0.3	30.2	0.0	30.2	0.0	30.2	0.0	30.2	0.0	30.2	0.0	30.2	0.0	30.2	0.0	30.2	0.0
1967	30.2	0.0	30.2	0.0	30.2	0.0	30.2	0.0	30.2	0.0	31.5	4.3	31.5	0.0	31.5	0.0	31.5	0.0	31.5	0.0	31.5	0.0	31.5	0.0
1968	31.5	0.0	31.5	0.0	31.5	0.0	31.5	0.0	31.5	0.0	31.5	0.0	31.5	0.0	31.5	0.0	31.5	0.0	31.6	0.3	32.0	1.3	32.0	0.0
1969	32.0	0.0	32.0	0.0	32.0	0.0	32.1	0.3	32.1	0.0	33.8	5.3	33.9	0.3	33.9	0.0	34.0	0.3	34.0	0.0	34.0	0.0	34.0	0.0
1970	34.0	0.0	34.0	0.0	34.0	0.0	34.0	0.0	34.0	0.0	36.3	6.8	36.0	-0.8	35.9	-0.3	35.9	0.0	35.9	0.0	35.9	0.0	35.9	0.0
1971	36.0	0.3	36.1	0.3	36.1	0.0	36.1	0.0	36.1	0.0	36.1	0.0	36.1	0.0	36.1	0.0	36.1	0.0	36.1	0.0	36.1	0.0	36.1	0.0
1972	36.3	0.6	36.3	0.0	36.3	0.0	36.3	0.0	36.4	0.3	36.4	0.0	36.4	0.0	36.4	0.0	36.4	0.0	36.4	0.0	36.4	0.0	36.4	0.0
1973	36.4	0.0	37.5	3.0	37.7	0.5	37.7	0.0	37.9	0.5	37.9	0.0	37.9	0.0	37.9	0.0	37.9	0.0	38.0	0.3	38.0	0.0	38.1	0.3
1974	38.1	0.0	38.2	0.3	38.2	0.0	38.3	0.3	41.2	7.6	41.7	1.2	41.7	0.0	41.9	0.5	41.9	0.0	41.9	0.0	44.8	6.9	45.4	1.3
1975	45.6	0.4	45.8	0.4	45.9	0.2	46.0	0.2	46.0	0.0	46.0	0.0	46.0	0.0	46.0	0.0	46.1	0.2	46.2	0.2	46.8	1.3	49.2	5.1
1976	49.2	0.0	49.2	0.0	49.3	0.2	50.2	1.8	50.1	-0.2	50.1	0.0	50.1	0.0	50.1	0.0	50.2	0.2	50.3	0.2	53.3	6.0	53.3	0.0
1977	54.1	1.5	54.1	0.0	54.1	0.0	54.2	0.2	54.2	0.0	54.3	0.2	54.4	0.2	54.4	0.0	57.8	6.3	58.7	1.6	58.7	0.0	58.8	0.2
1978	59.0	0.3	59.2	0.3	59.2	0.0	59.3	0.2	59.3	0.0	61.3	3.4	63.6	3.8	63.6	0.0	63.6	0.0	63.1	-0.8	63.1	0.0	63.1	0.0
1979	66.1	4.8	66.1	0.0	66.2	0.2	66.4	0.3	66.4	0.0	66.4	0.0	66.5	0.2	68.5	3.0	68.7	0.3	68.8	0.1	68.8	0.0	70.1	1.9
1980	73.2	4.4	73.4	0.3	73.5	0.1	73.7	0.3	76.7	4.1	76.8	0.1	76.8	0.0	76.8	0.0	76.8	0.0	77.2	0.5	78.8	2.1	78.9	0.1
1981	78.9	0.0	79.3	0.5	79.3	0.0	83.2	4.9	83.2	0.0	83.2	0.0	83.2	0.0	83.2	0.0	85.0	2.2	86.1	1.3	86.1	0.0	86.1	0.0
1982	86.1	0.0	94.9	10.2	94.9	0.0	94.9	0.0	95.0	0.1	95.0	0.0	96.4	1.5	96.4	0.0	101.9	5.7	113.1	11.0	112.8	-0.3	118.5	5.1
1983	110.2	-7.0	110.3	0.1	109.5	-0.7	109.6	0.1	109.5	-0.1	109.0	-0.5	115.6	6.1	116.6	0.9	116.6	0.0	116.6	-0.0	116.7	0.1	116.7	0.0
1984	120.5	3.3	120.8	0.2	120.8	0.0	120.8	0.0	120.9	0.1	123.9	2.5	126.5	2.1	125.9	-0.5	125.9	0.0	124.5	-1.1	124.6	0.1	124.7	0.1
1985	130.0	4.3	130.2	0.2	130.2	0.0	130.2	0.0	130.2	0.0	130.2	0.0	134.9	3.6	134.9	0.0	134.9	0.0	134.7	-0.1	134.8	0.1	134.8	0.0
1986	139.6	3.6	139.7	0.1	139.8	0.1	139.7	-0.1	139.8	0.1	139.8	0.0	145.2	3.9	145.2	0.0	145.2	0.0	145.2	0.0	145.2	0.0	145.2	0.0
1987	150.8	3.9	150.8	0.0	150.8	0.0	150.9	0.1	150.9	0.0	150.9	0.0	157.5	4.4	157.6	0.1	157.6	0.0	157.5	-0.1	157.6	0.1	163.3	3.6
1988	166.6	2.0	166.7	0.1	166.7	0.0	166.8	0.1	166.8	0.0	166.8	0.0	175.4	5.2	175.4	0.0	175.4	0.0	175.6	0.1	175.5	-0.1	184.7	5.2
1989	187.2	1.4	187.3	0.1	187.3	0.0	187.3	0.0	187.4	0.1	196.8	5.0	197.9	0.6	198.1	0.1	198.1	0.0	200.4	1.2	200.4	0.0	209.6	4.6
1990	212.3	1.3	212.8	0.2	212.8	0.0	212.8	0.0	217.4	2.2	224.1	3.1	224.3	0.1	224.3	0.0	225.0	0.3	224.9	-0.0	230.4	2.4	236.1	2.5
1991	237.4	0.6	237.4	0.0	239.6	0.9	243.3	1.5	243.4	0.0	249.1	2.3	254.4	2.1	255.0	0.2	254.9	-0.0	255.0	0.0	259.8	1.9	267.2	2.8

[Continued]

Tobacco Products, incl. Stemmed & Redried
Producer Price Index
Base 1982 = 100

[Continued]

For 1947-2001. Columns headed % show percentile change in the index from the previous period for which an index is available.

Year	Jan Index	%	Feb Index	%	Mar Index	%	Apr Index	%	May Index	%	Jun Index	%	Jul Index	%	Aug Index	%	Sep Index	%	Oct Index	%	Nov Index	%	Dec Index	%
1992	268.1	0.3	268.2	0.0	268.2	0.0	273.7	2.1	283.2	3.5	283.2	0.0	283.4	0.1	265.9	-6.2	274.1	3.1	274.2	0.0	276.5	0.8	285.1	3.1
1993	291.8	2.4	292.2	0.1	292.2	0.0	296.2	1.4	296.9	0.2	289.2	-2.6	287.2	-0.7	213.3	-25.7	213.2	-0.0	213.5	0.1	213.6	0.0	224.2	5.0
1994	224.7	0.2	224.7	0.0	224.7	0.0	224.7	0.0	224.7	0.0	224.7	0.0	224.7	0.0	224.1	-0.3	224.9	0.4	224.6	-0.1	225.1	0.2	225.2	0.0
1995	225.4	0.1	226.0	0.3	228.1	0.9	228.5	0.2	233.7	2.3	233.6	-0.0	233.5	-0.0	233.6	0.0	233.4	-0.1	233.5	0.0	233.5	0.0	233.2	-0.1
1996	233.2	0.0	233.2	0.0	233.2	0.0	233.3	0.0	240.0	2.9	239.9	-0.0	240.1	0.1	240.4	0.1	238.2	-0.9	239.1	0.4	238.8	-0.1	239.2	0.2
1997	239.4	0.1	239.2	-0.1	241.4	0.9	247.2	2.4	248.2	0.4	248.5	0.1	248.4	-0.0	247.8	-0.2	256.4	3.5	255.7	-0.3	256.0	0.1	257.9	0.7
1998	257.5	-0.2	261.9	1.7	262.0	0.0	271.0	3.4	278.4	2.7	278.7	0.1	278.7	0.0	286.4	2.8	287.4	0.3	288.0	0.2	288.8	0.3	364.1	26.1
1999	363.4	-0.2	363.9	0.1	363.5	-0.1	363.4	-0.0	363.5	0.0	363.6	0.0	363.5	-0.0	363.9	0.1	394.6	8.4	394.6	0.0	394.7	0.0	395.2	0.1
2000	378.5	-4.2	400.0	5.7	398.9	-0.3	392.7	-1.6	392.6	-0.0	393.2	0.2	393.4	0.1	402.3	2.3	402.9	0.1	403.8	0.2	403.9	0.0	404.3	0.1
2001	426.7	5.5	426.9	0.0	426.8	-0.0	426.6	-0.0	447.3	4.9	447.8	0.1	447.4	-0.1	447.4	0.0	447.6	0.0	447.6	0.0	455.5	1.8	455.5	0.0

Source: U.S. Department of Labor, Bureau of Labor Statistics, Division of Industry Prices and Price Indexes. n.e.c. stands for not elsewhere classified. - indicates no data collected for period or unavailable.

Notions
Producer Price Index
Base 1982 = 100

For 1947-2001. Columns headed % show percentile change in the index from the previous period for which an index is available.

Year	Jan Index	%	Feb Index	%	Mar Index	%	Apr Index	%	May Index	%	Jun Index	%	Jul Index	%	Aug Index	%	Sep Index	%	Oct Index	%	Nov Index	%	Dec Index	%
1947	37.9	-	37.9	0.0	37.9	0.0	37.9	0.0	37.9	0.0	37.9	0.0	37.9	0.0	37.9	0.0	37.6	-0.8	37.5	-0.3	37.5	0.0	37.5	0.0
1948	37.9	1.1	37.9	0.0	37.9	0.0	37.9	0.0	37.9	0.0	37.9	0.0	38.0	0.3	38.0	0.0	38.3	0.8	37.8	-1.3	37.8	0.0	37.5	-0.8
1949	37.5	0.0	37.5	0.0	37.1	-1.1	33.4	-10.0	33.0	-1.2	33.0	0.0	33.0	0.0	33.0	0.0	33.0	0.0	33.0	0.0	33.0	0.0	33.0	0.0
1950	33.0	0.0	33.0	0.0	33.0	0.0	33.0	0.0	32.5	-1.5	32.5	0.0	32.3	-0.6	33.6	4.0	34.6	3.0	34.9	0.9	35.8	2.6	36.1	0.8
1951	36.4	0.8	37.1	1.9	37.1	0.0	37.1	0.0	37.1	0.0	37.1	0.0	37.1	0.0	37.1	0.0	37.1	0.0	37.1	0.0	37.1	0.0	37.1	0.0
1952	36.7	-1.1	36.7	0.0	36.0	-1.9	35.2	-2.2	33.5	-4.8	33.5	0.0	33.5	0.0	33.2	-0.9	33.2	0.0	33.3	0.3	33.4	0.3	34.0	1.8
1953	34.0	0.0	34.0	0.0	34.5	1.5	34.1	-1.2	34.1	0.0	34.1	0.0	34.1	0.0	34.2	0.3	34.2	0.0	34.2	0.0	34.2	0.0	34.2	0.0
1954	34.2	0.0	34.2	0.0	34.2	0.0	34.2	0.0	34.2	0.0	35.2	2.9	35.2	0.0	35.2	0.0	35.1	-0.3	35.1	0.0	35.1	0.0	35.1	0.0
1955	35.1	0.0	33.8	-3.7	33.8	0.0	33.8	0.0	34.0	0.6	34.0	0.0	33.3	-2.1	33.3	0.0	33.3	0.0	33.3	0.0	33.3	0.0	33.3	0.0
1956	33.9	1.8	33.9	0.0	34.4	1.5	34.9	1.5	35.0	0.3	35.0	0.0	35.0	0.0	35.1	0.3	35.3	0.6	35.3	0.0	35.3	0.0	35.3	0.0
1957	35.4	0.3	35.4	0.0	35.4	0.0	35.6	0.6	35.6	0.0	35.6	0.0	35.6	0.0	35.6	0.0	35.6	0.0	35.6	0.0	35.8	0.6	36.0	0.6
1958	35.6	-1.1	35.7	0.3	35.7	0.0	35.7	0.0	35.7	0.0	35.7	0.0	35.7	0.0	35.7	0.0	35.7	0.0	35.7	0.0	35.7	0.0	35.7	0.0
1959	35.7	0.0	35.7	0.0	35.7	0.0	35.7	0.0	35.7	0.0	35.7	0.0	35.7	0.0	35.2	-1.4	35.2	0.0	35.7	1.4	35.7	0.0	35.7	0.0
1960	35.7	0.0	35.7	0.0	35.7	0.0	35.6	-0.3	35.3	-0.8	35.3	0.0	35.6	0.8	35.6	0.0	35.3	-0.8	35.3	0.0	35.3	0.0	35.3	0.0
1961	35.3	0.0	35.3	0.0	35.3	0.0	35.3	0.0	35.2	-0.3	35.2	0.0	35.2	0.0	35.2	0.0	35.2	0.0	35.2	0.0	35.2	0.0	35.2	0.0
1962	35.2	0.0	35.2	0.0	35.2	0.0	35.2	0.0	35.2	0.0	35.2	0.0	35.2	0.0	35.2	0.0	35.2	0.0	35.2	0.0	35.2	0.0	35.2	0.0
1963	35.2	0.0	35.2	0.0	35.2	0.0	35.2	0.0	35.2	0.0	35.2	0.0	35.2	0.0	35.2	0.0	35.3	0.3	35.3	0.0	35.3	0.0	35.3	0.0
1964	35.3	0.0	35.3	0.0	35.3	0.0	35.3	0.0	35.3	0.0	35.3	0.0	35.3	0.0	35.3	0.0	35.3	0.0	35.3	0.0	35.3	0.0	35.3	0.0
1965	35.3	0.0	35.3	0.0	35.3	0.0	35.3	0.0	35.3	0.0	35.3	0.0	35.3	0.0	35.3	0.0	35.3	0.0	35.3	0.0	35.3	0.0	35.3	0.0
1966	35.3	0.0	35.6	0.8	35.6	0.0	35.6	0.0	35.9	0.8	36.3	1.1	35.9	-1.1	35.9	0.0	35.9	0.0	35.9	0.0	35.9	0.0	35.9	0.0
1967	35.9	0.0	35.9	0.0	35.9	0.0	35.9	0.0	35.9	0.0	35.9	0.0	35.9	0.0	35.9	0.0	35.9	0.0	35.7	-0.6	37.0	3.6	37.0	0.0
1968	37.0	0.0	38.2	3.2	35.7	-6.5	35.7	0.0	35.7	0.0	35.7	0.0	35.7	0.0	35.8	0.3	35.8	0.0	36.0	0.6	36.0	0.0	36.0	0.0
1969	36.0	0.0	36.0	0.0	36.0	0.0	36.0	0.0	36.5	1.4	36.7	0.5	36.7	0.0	38.3	4.4	38.3	0.0	38.3	0.0	38.3	0.0	38.3	0.0
1970	38.3	0.0	39.0	1.8	39.0	0.0	38.8	-0.5	39.0	0.5	39.1	0.3	39.2	0.3	39.2	0.0	39.5	0.8	39.5	0.0	39.5	0.0	39.7	0.5
1971	40.4	1.8	40.4	0.0	40.4	0.0	40.4	0.0	40.4	0.0	40.4	0.0	40.4	0.0	40.4	0.0	40.4	0.0	40.4	0.0	40.4	0.0	40.4	0.0
1972	40.3	-0.2	40.3	0.0	40.3	0.0	40.3	0.0	40.3	0.0	40.3	0.0	40.3	0.0	40.3	0.0	40.8	1.2	40.8	0.0	40.8	0.0	40.8	0.0
1973	40.8	0.0	40.8	0.0	40.8	0.0	40.8	0.0	41.4	1.5	41.4	0.0	40.8	-1.4	41.0	0.5	41.0	0.0	41.7	1.7	42.3	1.4	42.6	0.7
1974	42.9	0.7	42.9	0.0	44.0	2.6	45.5	3.4	49.5	8.8	50.9	2.8	51.9	2.0	52.5	1.2	53.8	2.5	53.8	0.0	53.8	0.0	53.8	0.0
1975	54.2	0.7	54.2	0.0	54.2	0.0	54.2	0.0	54.2	0.0	54.2	0.0	54.2	0.0	54.2	0.0	54.2	0.0	54.7	0.9	55.7	1.8	56.5	1.4
1976	56.5	0.0	56.5	0.0	57.1	1.1	57.4	0.5	58.4	1.7	59.4	1.7	59.4	0.0	59.7	0.5	59.7	0.0	59.7	0.0	59.7	0.0	59.8	0.2
1977	61.3	2.5	62.3	1.6	62.3	0.0	62.3	0.0	62.3	0.0	62.3	0.0	62.3	0.0	62.4	0.2	62.4	0.0	62.4	0.0	62.4	0.0	62.4	0.0
1978	65.3	4.6	65.3	0.0	65.5	0.3	65.5	0.0	65.5	0.0	65.5	0.0	65.5	0.0	65.6	0.2	66.2	0.9	66.2	0.0	66.2	0.0	66.2	0.0
1979	67.9	2.6	67.9	0.0	68.7	1.2	68.7	0.0	68.8	0.1	68.8	0.0	69.3	0.7	69.3	0.0	69.3	0.0	70.6	1.9	70.7	0.1	71.0	0.4
1980	73.3	3.2	73.4	0.1	74.8	1.9	78.3	4.7	78.4	0.1	78.4	0.0	78.4	0.0	80.0	2.0	80.8	1.0	80.8	0.0	80.9	0.1	81.2	0.4
1981	82.0	1.0	89.3	8.9	89.3	0.0	89.7	0.4	96.7	7.8	96.7	0.0	96.6	-0.1	96.7	0.1	96.7	0.0	97.4	0.7	97.4	0.0	97.4	0.0
1982	97.6	0.2	97.6	0.0	98.0	0.4	98.0	0.0	101.1	3.2	101.1	0.0	101.1	0.0	101.1	0.0	101.1	0.0	101.1	0.0	101.0	-0.1	101.0	0.0
1983	101.3	0.3	101.3	0.0	101.3	0.0	101.2	-0.1	101.2	0.0	101.2	0.0	101.2	0.0	101.0	-0.2	101.0	0.0	101.0	0.0	100.9	-0.1	101.1	0.2
1984	101.6	0.5	101.9	0.3	101.9	0.0	102.2	0.3	102.5	0.3	102.5	0.0	102.5	0.0	102.5	0.0	102.5	0.0	102.3	-0.2	102.3	0.0	102.4	0.1
1985	102.4	0.0	102.6	0.2	102.6	0.0	103.1	0.5	103.1	0.0	103.1	0.0	103.1	0.0	103.0	-0.1	103.0	0.0	103.0	0.0	103.0	0.0	102.9	-0.1
1986	103.0	0.1	103.8	0.8	103.6	-0.2	103.8	0.2	103.9	0.1	103.8	-0.1	103.8	0.0	103.8	0.0	103.7	-0.1	103.7	0.0	103.9	0.2	103.9	0.0
1987	103.6	-0.3	104.8	1.2	105.0	0.2	105.0	0.0	105.1	0.1	105.2	0.1	105.5	0.3	105.7	0.2	105.7	0.0	105.8	0.1	105.5	-0.3	105.9	0.4
1988	106.3	0.4	106.6	0.3	106.5	-0.1	107.4	0.8	107.4	0.0	108.1	0.7	108.2	0.1	108.5	0.3	108.9	0.4	108.9	0.0	109.1	0.2	109.2	0.1
1989	109.9	0.6	110.6	0.6	111.1	0.5	111.5	0.4	112.0	0.4	112.2	0.2	112.1	-0.1	112.1	0.0	113.8	1.5	114.7	0.8	114.6	-0.1	114.7	0.1
1990	114.9	0.2	115.2	0.3	115.3	0.1	115.4	0.1	115.3	-0.1	115.7	0.3	115.7	0.0	115.7	0.0	115.9	0.2	116.5	0.5	116.5	0.0	116.9	0.3
1991	117.0	0.1	116.8	-0.2	116.9	0.1	116.9	0.0	117.5	0.5	118.2	0.6	118.4	0.2	118.7	0.3	118.5	-0.2	118.1	-0.3	118.2	0.1	119.1	0.8

[Continued]

Notions
Producer Price Index
Base 1982 = 100
[Continued]

For 1947-2001. Columns headed % show percentile change in the index from the previous period for which an index is available.

Year	Jan Index	%	Feb Index	%	Mar Index	%	Apr Index	%	May Index	%	Jun Index	%	Jul Index	%	Aug Index	%	Sep Index	%	Oct Index	%	Nov Index	%	Dec Index	%
1992	119.1	0.0	119.1	0.0	119.1	0.0	119.0	-0.1	119.3	0.3	119.4	0.1	119.6	0.2	119.0	-0.5	118.7	-0.3	119.4	0.6	120.1	0.6	119.3	-0.7
1993	119.6	0.3	120.4	0.7	119.8	-0.5	120.1	0.3	120.4	0.2	120.6	0.2	120.5	-0.1	120.4	-0.1	120.9	0.4	120.9	0.0	121.1	0.2	121.1	0.0
1994	121.0	-0.1	121.8	0.7	121.5	-0.2	121.6	0.1	121.9	0.2	121.9	0.0	121.5	-0.3	121.8	0.2	122.0	0.2	121.7	-0.2	122.1	0.3	122.4	0.2
1995	122.7	0.2	123.4	0.6	124.0	0.5	123.6	-0.3	123.6	0.0	123.3	-0.2	123.8	0.4	123.7	-0.1	123.8	0.1	124.3	0.4	124.7	0.3	125.4	0.6
1996	125.6	0.2	125.7	0.1	126.0	0.2	125.8	-0.2	124.9	-0.7	125.2	0.2	125.2	0.0	125.4	0.2	125.3	-0.1	126.6	1.0	126.6	0.0	126.6	0.0
1997	126.8	0.2	127.0	0.2	126.5	-0.4	125.2	-1.0	125.5	0.2	125.7	0.2	125.7	0.0	125.2	-0.4	125.2	0.0	125.3	0.1	125.6	0.2	125.4	-0.2
1998	125.7	0.2	125.0	-0.6	125.7	0.6	125.4	-0.2	125.0	-0.3	125.6	0.5	126.6	0.8	127.0	0.3	125.9	-0.9	125.8	-0.1	126.3	0.4	126.3	0.0
1999	127.2	0.7	127.0	-0.2	126.4	-0.5	126.1	-0.2	127.4	1.0	128.4	0.8	129.2	0.6	129.6	0.3	129.4	-0.2	129.4	0.0	129.7	0.2	129.7	0.0
2000	129.1	-0.5	129.1	0.0	129.1	0.0	129.1	0.0	129.0	-0.1	129.2	0.2	129.2	0.0	130.7	1.2	130.7	0.0	130.9	0.2	130.9	0.0	130.9	0.0
2001	130.9	0.0	130.4	-0.4	130.4	0.0	129.7	-0.5	129.9	0.2	129.9	0.0	129.9	0.0	129.9	0.0	129.9	0.0	129.9	0.0	129.5	-0.3	129.7	0.2

Source: U.S. Department of Labor, Bureau of Labor Statistics, Division of Industry Prices and Price Indexes. n.e.c. stands for not elsewhere classified. - indicates no data collected for period or unavailable.

Photographic Equipment and Supplies
Producer Price Index
Base 1982 = 100

For 1947-2001. Columns headed % show percentile change in the index from the previous period for which an index is available.

Year	Jan Index	%	Feb Index	%	Mar Index	%	Apr Index	%	May Index	%	Jun Index	%	Jul Index	%	Aug Index	%	Sep Index	%	Oct Index	%	Nov Index	%	Dec Index	%
1947	31.5	-	31.5	0.0	31.6	0.3	31.6	0.0	31.8	0.6	31.9	0.3	31.9	0.0	32.9	3.1	32.9	0.0	32.9	0.0	33.0	0.3	33.4	1.2
1948	34.4	3.0	34.6	0.6	34.7	0.3	34.8	0.3	34.9	0.3	35.0	0.3	35.0	0.0	35.3	0.9	35.5	0.6	35.8	0.8	36.4	1.7	36.7	0.8
1949	36.7	0.0	37.5	2.2	37.1	-1.1	37.0	-0.3	36.7	-0.8	36.5	-0.5	36.5	0.0	36.5	0.0	36.5	0.0	36.3	-0.5	36.3	0.0	36.3	0.0
1950	36.3	0.0	36.2	-0.3	35.9	-0.8	35.9	0.0	36.0	0.3	36.0	0.0	36.0	0.0	36.0	0.0	36.0	0.0	36.4	1.1	36.9	1.4	36.9	0.0	37.1	0.5
1951	37.2	0.3	37.2	0.0	37.2	0.0	37.2	0.0	37.2	0.0	37.2	0.0	37.8	1.6	37.8	0.0	37.8	0.0	37.8	0.0	37.9	0.3	37.9	0.0
1952	37.7	-0.5	38.0	0.8	38.0	0.0	38.0	0.0	38.0	0.0	38.0	0.0	38.0	0.0	38.0	0.0	38.0	0.0	38.0	0.0	38.0	0.0	38.0	0.0
1953	38.0	0.0	38.0	0.0	38.1	0.3	38.1	0.0	38.2	0.3	38.4	0.5	38.4	0.0	38.3	-0.3	38.5	0.5	38.5	0.0	38.5	0.0	38.5	0.0
1954	38.5	0.0	38.5	0.0	38.5	0.0	38.7	0.5	38.7	0.0	38.7	0.0	38.8	0.3	38.7	-0.3	38.7	0.0	38.7	0.0	38.7	0.0	38.7	0.0
1955	38.6	-0.3	38.6	0.0	38.7	0.3	39.0	0.8	39.0	0.0	39.0	0.0	39.2	0.5	39.3	0.3	39.3	0.0	39.4	0.3	39.5	0.3	39.5	0.0
1956	39.6	0.3	39.7	0.3	39.7	0.0	39.6	-0.3	39.6	0.0	39.8	0.5	39.8	0.0	39.8	0.0	39.8	0.0	39.8	0.0	40.5	1.8	40.5	0.0
1957	41.1	1.5	41.1	0.0	41.2	0.2	41.3	0.2	41.3	0.0	41.3	0.0	41.3	0.0	41.8	1.2	42.2	1.0	42.2	0.0	42.2	0.0	42.3	0.2
1958	42.3	0.0	42.4	0.2	42.4	0.0	42.4	0.0	42.4	0.0	42.8	0.9	42.8	0.0	42.7	-0.2	42.7	0.0	42.7	0.0	42.8	0.2	42.8	0.0
1959	43.3	1.2	43.3	0.0	44.0	1.6	44.1	0.2	44.1	0.0	44.1	0.0	44.1	0.0	44.2	0.2	44.3	0.2	44.3	0.0	44.3	0.0	44.3	0.0
1960	44.2	-0.2	44.2	0.0	44.2	0.0	44.2	0.0	44.2	0.0	44.2	0.0	44.2	0.0	44.4	0.5	44.4	0.0	44.6	0.5	44.9	0.7	44.9	0.0
1961	44.8	-0.2	44.9	0.2	44.8	-0.2	44.8	0.0	44.5	-0.7	44.4	-0.2	44.5	0.2	45.0	1.1	45.2	0.4	45.4	0.4	45.5	0.2	45.7	0.4
1962	45.7	0.0	46.0	0.7	46.0	0.0	45.9	-0.2	46.0	0.2	46.1	0.2	46.1	0.0	46.2	0.2	46.1	-0.2	46.1	0.0	46.1	0.0	46.1	0.0
1963	46.2	0.2	46.2	0.0	45.9	-0.6	45.9	0.0	46.0	0.2	46.1	0.2	46.2	0.2	45.9	-0.6	45.8	-0.2	45.9	0.2	45.9	0.0	46.1	0.4
1964	46.2	0.2	46.2	0.0	46.2	0.0	46.2	0.0	46.2	0.0	46.2	0.0	46.2	0.0	46.3	0.0	46.3	0.0	46.3	0.0	46.5	0.4	46.5	0.0	46.5	0.0
1965	46.5	0.0	46.5	0.0	46.6	0.2	46.8	0.4	46.8	0.0	46.7	-0.2	46.7	0.0	46.7	0.0	46.7	0.0	46.7	0.0	46.7	0.0	46.7	0.0
1966	46.6	-0.2	46.6	0.0	46.6	0.0	46.5	-0.2	46.5	0.0	46.5	0.0	46.5	0.0	46.4	-0.2	46.3	-0.2	46.3	0.0	46.9	1.3	47.0	0.2
1967	47.1	0.2	47.1	0.0	47.1	0.0	47.1	0.0	47.1	0.0	47.1	0.0	47.1	0.0	47.6	1.1	47.7	0.2	48.6	1.9	48.6	0.0	48.6	0.0
1968	48.0	-1.2	48.6	1.2	48.6	0.0	48.6	0.0	49.0	0.8	49.0	0.0	48.5	-1.0	48.5	0.0	48.5	0.0	48.6	0.2	48.6	0.0	48.6	0.0
1969	48.4	-0.4	48.4	0.0	48.1	-0.6	48.2	0.2	48.4	0.4	48.4	0.0	48.7	0.6	48.7	0.0	49.0	0.6	49.1	0.2	49.2	0.2	49.3	0.2
1970	49.4	0.2	49.5	0.2	49.5	0.0	49.7	0.4	49.7	0.0	49.5	-0.4	50.1	1.2	50.2	0.2	50.1	-0.2	50.1	0.0	50.2	0.2	50.2	0.0
1971	50.3	0.2	50.4	0.2	50.4	0.0	50.4	0.0	50.4	0.0	50.5	0.2	50.6	0.2	50.6	0.0	50.6	0.0	50.6	0.0	50.6	0.0	50.6	0.0
1972	50.6	0.0	50.7	0.2	50.8	0.2	50.5	-0.6	50.5	0.0	50.5	0.0	50.5	0.0	50.8	0.6	50.8	0.0	50.8	0.0	50.8	0.0	50.8	0.0
1973	51.0	0.4	51.1	0.2	51.6	1.0	51.5	-0.2	51.4	-0.2	51.5	0.2	51.6	0.2	51.6	0.0	51.6	0.0	51.6	0.0	51.7	0.2	51.9	0.4
1974	51.9	0.0	52.3	0.8	52.5	0.4	52.6	0.2	55.6	5.7	55.6	0.0	56.4	1.4	56.4	0.0	57.4	1.8	57.6	0.3	58.0	0.7	59.9	3.3
1975	60.3	0.7	60.5	0.3	61.1	1.0	61.8	1.1	61.9	0.2	62.2	0.5	62.3	0.2	62.4	0.2	62.8	0.6	63.4	1.0	63.5	0.2	62.7	-1.3
1976	63.2	0.8	64.0	1.3	64.1	0.2	64.2	0.2	64.2	0.0	65.2	1.6	65.1	-0.2	65.1	0.0	65.1	0.0	65.1	0.0	65.2	0.2	66.2	1.5
1977	65.7	-0.8	65.8	0.2	65.8	0.0	65.6	-0.3	66.5	1.4	66.7	0.3	67.1	0.6	67.0	-0.1	66.8	-0.3	66.9	0.1	66.9	0.0	67.2	0.4
1978	67.6	0.6	67.8	0.3	67.8	0.0	68.7	1.3	68.8	0.1	69.4	0.9	69.4	0.0	69.6	0.3	70.2	0.9	70.7	0.7	70.7	0.0	70.7	0.0
1979	71.4	1.0	71.4	0.0	71.4	0.0	71.3	-0.1	71.6	0.4	72.1	0.7	72.2	0.1	72.3	0.1	73.3	1.4	74.8	2.0	76.6	2.4	78.1	2.0
1980	78.9	1.0	103.9	31.7	104.1	0.2	100.9	-3.1	94.9	-5.9	95.9	1.1	95.8	-0.1	95.5	-0.3	95.5	0.0	95.4	-0.1	98.2	2.9	98.2	0.0
1981	98.6	0.4	99.6	1.0	100.4	0.8	100.9	0.5	101.0	0.1	101.0	0.0	100.5	-0.5	98.4	-2.1	99.2	0.8	99.3	0.1	99.4	0.1	99.4	0.0
1982	99.8	0.4	100.0	0.2	100.8	0.8	101.8	1.0	100.1	-1.7	100.0	-0.1	99.3	-0.7	99.3	0.0	99.8	0.5	99.7	-0.1	99.7	0.0	99.8	0.1
1983	99.8	0.0	100.7	0.9	102.9	2.2	103.0	0.1	103.0	0.0	102.9	-0.1	102.9	0.0	102.9	0.0	102.9	0.0	103.0	0.1	103.0	0.0	103.0	0.0
1984	103.1	0.1	103.6	0.5	101.1	-2.4	101.5	0.4	101.5	0.0	101.5	0.0	101.6	0.1	102.4	0.8	102.4	0.0	102.5	0.1	101.2	-1.3	101.3	0.1
1985	101.5	0.2	101.6	0.1	102.6	1.0	102.6	0.0	102.5	-0.1	102.6	0.1	102.5	-0.1	102.5	0.0	103.0	0.5	103.0	0.0	103.1	0.1	103.2	0.1
1986	103.2	0.0	103.2	0.0	103.9	0.7	103.8	-0.1	104.7	0.9	104.1	-0.6	104.1	0.0	104.1	0.0	104.1	0.0	104.2	0.1	104.2	0.0	104.1	-0.1
1987	104.2	0.1	104.4	0.2	104.3	-0.1	105.4	1.1	105.6	0.2	105.7	0.1	105.7	0.0	105.7	0.0	105.9	0.2	106.1	0.2	106.1	0.0	105.8	-0.3
1988	105.8	0.0	105.8	0.0	105.8	0.0	106.5	0.7	106.5	0.0	107.1	0.6	107.1	0.0	107.3	0.2	107.3	0.0	108.9	1.5	109.1	0.2	108.7	-0.4
1989	111.8	2.9	111.9	0.1	112.7	0.7	113.1	0.4	114.4	1.1	114.4	0.0	114.4	0.0	114.5	0.1	115.8	1.1	116.2	0.3	116.2	0.0	116.2	0.0
1990	117.5	1.1	117.8	0.3	117.8	0.0	117.8	0.0	117.9	0.1	117.9	0.0	118.9	0.8	118.8	-0.1	119.0	0.2	118.9	-0.1	118.9	0.0	119.5	0.5
1991	119.6	0.1	117.6	-1.7	117.7	0.1	118.0	0.3	117.9	-0.1	117.9	0.0	117.9	0.0	117.9	0.0	117.9	0.0	118.3	0.3	118.4	0.1	118.5	0.1

[Continued]

Photographic Equipment and Supplies
Producer Price Index
Base 1982 = 100
[Continued]

For 1947-2001. Columns headed % show percentile change in the index from the previous period for which an index is available.

Year	Jan Index	%	Feb Index	%	Mar Index	%	Apr Index	%	May Index	%	Jun Index	%	Jul Index	%	Aug Index	%	Sep Index	%	Oct Index	%	Nov Index	%	Dec Index	%
1992	118.6	0.1	118.7	0.1	118.2	-0.4	118.2	0.0	118.4	0.2	118.7	0.3	118.7	0.0	118.7	0.0	118.9	0.2	118.8	-0.1	118.9	0.1	118.9	0.0
1993	117.7	-1.0	117.8	0.1	117.8	0.0	117.9	0.1	117.9	0.0	117.9	0.0	118.3	0.3	118.8	0.4	118.6	-0.2	117.1	-1.3	118.0	0.8	117.1	-0.8
1994	120.3	2.7	119.1	-1.0	118.0	-0.9	118.2	0.2	116.9	-1.1	116.2	-0.6	116.4	0.2	116.2	-0.2	114.5	-1.5	115.4	0.8	115.6	0.2	115.6	0.0
1995	116.6	0.9	117.9	1.1	117.6	-0.3	118.5	0.8	118.4	-0.1	118.5	0.1	119.5	0.8	120.0	0.4	117.9	-1.7	119.6	1.4	118.4	-1.0	118.3	-0.1
1996	120.3	1.7	120.8	0.4	120.1	-0.6	119.4	-0.6	120.3	0.8	119.8	-0.4	119.9	0.1	119.5	-0.3	119.7	0.2	120.4	0.6	119.6	-0.7	118.9	-0.6
1997	118.6	-0.3	118.6	0.0	119.6	0.8	119.6	0.0	119.8	0.2	118.0	-1.5	118.0	0.0	118.0	0.0	118.6	0.5	118.1	-0.4	118.0	-0.1	118.5	0.4
1998	113.5	-4.2	114.3	0.7	115.5	1.0	116.3	0.7	115.3	-0.9	115.3	0.0	114.4	-0.8	114.7	0.3	114.3	-0.3	113.3	-0.9	114.3	0.9	113.3	-0.9
1999	113.7	0.4	113.5	-0.2	112.2	-1.1	111.8	-0.4	112.4	0.5	110.6	-1.6	110.9	0.3	110.9	0.0	110.6	-0.3	110.3	-0.3	110.7	0.4	110.7	0.0
2000	108.4	-2.1	108.9	0.5	108.5	-0.4	108.9	0.4	108.4	-0.5	108.8	0.4	109.1	0.3	109.1	0.0	109.5	0.4	109.9	0.4	109.8	-0.1	109.8	0.0
2001	109.8	0.0	109.6	-0.2	109.6	0.0	111.8	2.0	111.8	0.0	111.8	0.0	111.8	0.0	111.8	0.0	111.8	0.0	111.8	0.0	111.6	-0.2	111.6	0.0

Source: U.S. Department of Labor, Bureau of Labor Statistics, Division of Industry Prices and Price Indexes. n.e.c. stands for not elsewhere classified. - indicates no data collected for period or unavailable.

Mobile Homes
Producer Price Index
Base 1982 = 100

For 1981-2001. Columns headed % show percentile change in the index from the previous period for which an index is available.

Year	Jan Index	%	Feb Index	%	Mar Index	%	Apr Index	%	May Index	%	Jun Index	%	Jul Index	%	Aug Index	%	Sep Index	%	Oct Index	%	Nov Index	%	Dec Index	%
1981	94.5	-	94.6	0.1	95.8	1.3	96.2	0.4	96.3	0.1	96.4	0.1	97.7	1.3	97.8	0.1	98.0	0.2	98.3	0.3	98.4	0.1	98.4	0.0
1982	98.5	0.1	98.6	0.1	100.0	1.4	100.2	0.2	100.4	0.2	100.3	-0.1	100.5	0.2	100.6	0.1	100.6	0.0	100.5	-0.1	99.9	-0.6	99.9	0.0
1983	100.0	0.1	99.9	-0.1	100.6	0.7	100.3	-0.3	100.3	0.0	100.8	0.5	101.0	0.2	101.2	0.2	101.5	0.3	101.8	0.3	101.9	0.1	102.0	0.1
1984	100.1	-1.9	100.3	0.2	100.4	0.1	101.2	0.8	101.1	-0.1	100.5	-0.6	100.7	0.2	100.8	0.1	101.1	0.3	101.1	0.0	101.6	0.5	101.5	-0.1
1985	101.5	0.0	101.6	0.1	101.5	-0.1	101.5	0.0	101.5	0.0	101.8	0.3	101.7	-0.1	101.8	0.1	102.0	0.2	101.8	-0.2	101.9	0.1	101.9	0.0
1986	102.2	0.3	100.9	-1.3	101.1	0.2	102.8	1.7	102.9	0.1	103.1	0.2	103.1	0.0	103.2	0.1	103.2	0.0	103.3	0.1	103.5	0.2	103.6	0.1
1987	103.7	0.1	103.7	0.0	103.7	0.0	103.5	-0.2	104.0	0.5	104.0	0.0	104.4	0.4	103.9	-0.5	104.7	0.8	105.0	0.3	105.1	0.1	106.2	1.0
1988	106.5	0.3	107.0	0.5	107.7	0.7	108.2	0.5	108.9	0.6	109.3	0.4	109.8	0.5	109.9	0.1	110.4	0.5	110.7	0.3	111.6	0.8	111.4	-0.2
1989	111.6	0.2	111.9	0.3	112.1	0.2	112.5	0.4	113.9	1.2	113.9	0.0	114.3	0.4	114.8	0.4	115.2	0.3	115.5	0.3	115.8	0.3	115.9	0.1
1990	115.9	0.0	116.2	0.3	116.2	0.0	116.4	0.2	116.9	0.4	117.5	0.5	117.7	0.2	118.0	0.3	118.2	0.2	118.4	0.2	119.3	0.8	119.3	0.0
1991	119.3	0.0	119.5	0.2	119.5	0.0	119.6	0.1	120.1	0.4	120.4	0.2	120.8	0.3	121.1	0.2	121.0	-0.1	121.0	0.0	121.2	0.2	121.2	0.0
1992	120.4	-0.7	120.4	0.0	120.4	0.0	120.9	0.4	121.3	0.3	121.4	0.1	121.7	0.2	122.0	0.2	122.1	0.1	123.0	0.7	123.5	0.4	123.5	0.0
1993	123.5	0.0	124.6	0.9	125.5	0.7	126.6	0.9	127.3	0.6	127.6	0.2	129.2	1.3	129.2	0.0	129.1	-0.1	129.3	0.2	130.7	1.1	131.1	0.3
1994	132.6	1.1	132.6	0.0	135.7	2.3	135.8	0.1	135.8	0.0	137.0	0.9	137.2	0.1	137.3	0.1	138.0	0.5	139.1	0.8	141.0	1.4	142.0	0.7
1995	143.9	1.3	144.7	0.6	144.7	0.0	144.9	0.1	144.9	0.0	145.9	0.7	146.1	0.1	144.9	-0.8	145.2	0.2	145.6	0.3	148.6	2.1	148.5	-0.1
1996	148.5	0.0	148.6	0.1	148.8	0.1	148.9	0.1	149.3	0.3	149.9	0.4	150.2	0.2	150.2	0.0	150.4	0.1	150.5	0.1	150.8	0.2	151.4	0.4
1997	151.1	-0.2	151.1	0.0	151.3	0.1	152.1	0.5	152.1	0.0	152.2	0.1	152.7	0.3	152.7	0.0	152.5	-0.1	152.6	0.1	153.1	0.3	152.8	-0.2
1998	153.0	0.1	153.2	0.1	153.1	-0.1	153.4	0.2	153.9	0.3	154.2	0.2	154.3	0.1	154.5	0.1	155.0	0.3	155.1	0.1	155.7	0.4	155.7	0.0
1999	156.3	0.4	156.3	0.0	156.5	0.1	157.8	0.8	158.3	0.3	158.6	0.2	159.3	0.4	158.6	-0.4	159.6	0.6	159.9	0.2	160.0	0.1	159.7	-0.2
2000	160.2	0.3	160.0	-0.1	160.2	0.1	160.7	0.3	160.8	0.1	161.6	0.5	161.5	-0.1	161.8	0.2	162.0	0.1	162.1	0.1	162.5	0.2	162.1	-0.2
2001	162.2	0.1	162.2	0.0	162.2	0.0	162.7	0.3	163.0	0.2	164.2	0.7	164.7	0.3	164.9	0.1	164.9	0.0	166.3	0.8	166.2	-0.1	166.4	0.1

Source: U.S. Department of Labor, Bureau of Labor Statistics, Division of Industry Prices and Price Indexes. n.e.c. stands for not elsewhere classified. - indicates no data collected for period or unavailable.

Medical, Surgical & Personal Aid Devices
Producer Price Index
Base 1982 = 100

For 1978-2001. Columns headed % show percentile change in the index from the previous period for which an index is available.

Year	Jan Index	%	Feb Index	%	Mar Index	%	Apr Index	%	May Index	%	Jun Index	%	Jul Index	%	Aug Index	%	Sep Index	%	Oct Index	%	Nov Index	%	Dec Index	%
1978	-	-	-	-	-	-	-	-	-	-	86.5	-	86.4	-0.1	86.9	0.6	86.9	0.0	87.4	0.6	87.4	0.0	88.3	1.0
1979	88.6	0.3	88.6	0.0	88.6	0.0	88.6	0.0	89.1	0.6	89.6	0.6	89.8	0.2	90.2	0.4	90.2	0.0	90.2	0.0	90.3	0.1	90.3	0.0
1980	90.1	-0.2	90.5	0.4	92.9	2.7	92.9	0.0	94.2	1.4	94.2	0.0	94.2	0.0	94.2	0.0	94.7	0.5	93.8	-1.0	93.8	0.0	93.8	0.0
1981	93.8	0.0	94.0	0.2	94.9	1.0	97.4	2.6	98.2	0.8	98.2	0.0	98.2	0.0	98.2	0.0	98.2	0.0	98.2	0.0	98.2	0.0	98.2	0.0
1982	98.7	0.5	98.7	0.0	98.7	0.0	98.7	0.0	99.0	0.3	99.0	0.0	100.5	1.5	100.5	0.0	101.4	0.9	101.6	0.2	101.6	0.0	101.6	0.0
1983	102.7	1.1	101.7	-1.0	102.6	0.9	102.4	-0.2	102.6	0.2	102.8	0.2	104.4	1.6	104.7	0.3	104.5	-0.2	105.2	0.7	105.9	0.7	105.9	0.0
1984	107.6	1.6	107.7	0.1	107.8	0.1	108.3	0.5	108.2	-0.1	108.2	0.0	108.4	0.2	108.9	0.5	108.4	-0.5	108.6	0.2	108.7	0.1	108.7	0.0
1985	109.4	0.6	109.2	-0.2	109.3	0.1	109.2	-0.1	109.2	0.0	109.2	0.0	108.7	-0.5	108.7	0.0	108.7	0.0	108.9	0.2	108.9	0.0	109.0	0.1
1986	110.4	1.3	110.5	0.1	110.8	0.3	111.0	0.2	111.0	0.0	111.2	0.2	111.5	0.3	111.6	0.1	111.8	0.2	112.4	0.5	114.7	2.0	114.3	-0.3
1987	114.1	-0.2	114.2	0.1	114.6	0.4	117.8	2.8	117.6	-0.2	117.8	0.2	117.6	-0.2	117.9	0.3	117.7	-0.2	117.8	0.1	118.4	0.5	118.2	-0.2
1988	119.1	0.8	119.2	0.1	119.4	0.2	119.5	0.1	119.8	0.3	117.8	-1.7	118.0	0.2	118.1	0.1	118.1	0.0	119.3	1.0	119.4	0.1	119.4	0.0
1989	121.2	1.5	121.5	0.2	121.8	0.2	122.1	0.2	123.1	0.8	123.1	0.0	122.9	-0.2	123.0	0.1	123.8	0.7	124.4	0.5	124.5	0.1	124.8	0.2
1990	125.9	0.9	126.0	0.1	126.3	0.2	126.9	0.5	127.2	0.2	127.3	0.1	127.4	0.1	127.8	0.3	128.0	0.2	128.4	0.3	128.3	-0.1	128.5	0.2
1991	129.3	0.6	129.5	0.2	129.7	0.2	130.0	0.2	130.0	0.0	130.2	0.2	130.4	0.2	130.6	0.2	131.2	0.5	130.9	-0.2	131.1	0.2	130.9	-0.2
1992	132.4	1.1	132.8	0.3	133.5	0.5	133.6	0.1	133.8	0.1	133.9	0.1	133.5	-0.3	134.4	0.7	134.3	-0.1	134.8	0.4	134.7	-0.1	134.6	-0.1
1993	136.0	1.0	137.5	1.1	137.9	0.3	137.8	-0.1	138.5	0.5	137.9	-0.4	137.5	-0.3	138.3	0.6	137.7	-0.4	138.0	0.2	138.1	0.1	138.7	0.4
1994	139.3	0.4	140.3	0.7	140.6	0.2	140.4	-0.1	140.1	-0.2	140.3	0.1	140.7	0.3	140.5	-0.1	140.7	0.1	140.7	0.0	140.7	0.0	140.1	-0.4
1995	140.2	0.1	141.0	0.6	140.9	-0.1	140.6	-0.2	140.9	0.2	141.0	0.1	141.3	0.2	141.1	-0.1	142.0	0.6	142.2	0.1	142.0	-0.1	142.2	0.1
1996	143.5	0.9	143.4	-0.1	143.6	0.1	143.4	-0.1	143.5	0.1	143.4	-0.1	143.6	0.1	142.2	-1.0	142.1	-0.1	142.4	0.2	142.7	0.2	142.9	0.1
1997	142.9	0.0	142.9	0.0	142.8	-0.1	143.1	0.2	143.1	0.0	143.3	0.1	143.4	0.1	143.2	-0.1	143.1	-0.1	143.0	-0.1	142.8	-0.1	142.8	0.0
1998	143.1	0.2	143.5	0.3	143.4	-0.1	143.0	-0.3	143.0	0.0	142.9	-0.1	143.2	0.2	143.2	0.0	143.5	0.2	143.9	0.3	144.0	0.1	144.0	0.0
1999	144.2	0.1	144.1	-0.1	144.4	0.2	145.1	0.5	144.9	-0.1	144.5	-0.3	144.5	0.0	144.8	0.2	144.5	-0.2	145.0	0.3	145.0	0.0	144.8	-0.1
2000	145.4	0.4	145.7	0.2	145.7	0.0	145.6	-0.1	145.7	0.1	145.7	0.0	145.8	0.1	145.9	0.1	146.2	0.2	146.5	0.2	146.5	0.0	146.9	0.3
2001	147.6	0.5	147.8	0.1	147.6	-0.1	147.7	0.1	148.0	0.2	148.0	0.0	148.2	0.1	148.3	0.1	149.0	0.5	148.8	-0.1	149.3	0.3	149.7	0.3

Source: U.S. Department of Labor, Bureau of Labor Statistics, Division of Industry Prices and Price Indexes. n.e.c. stands for not elsewhere classified. - indicates no data collected for period or unavailable.

Industrial Safety Equipment
Producer Price Index
Base 1982 = 100

For 1978-2001. Columns headed % show percentile change in the index from the previous period for which an index is available.

Year	Jan Index	%	Feb Index	%	Mar Index	%	Apr Index	%	May Index	%	Jun Index	%	Jul Index	%	Aug Index	%	Sep Index	%	Oct Index	%	Nov Index	%	Dec Index	%
1978	-	-	-	-	-	-	-	-	-	-	77.3	-	77.5	0.3	77.5	0.0	77.8	0.4	78.5	0.9	79.0	0.6	79.6	0.8
1979	80.2	0.8	81.0	1.0	81.6	0.7	82.5	1.1	82.9	0.5	83.1	0.2	83.7	0.7	83.9	0.2	84.2	0.4	84.5	0.4	86.3	2.1	86.1	-0.2
1980	87.4	1.5	88.2	0.9	88.6	0.5	89.0	0.5	89.5	0.6	89.9	0.4	90.2	0.3	90.2	0.0	90.2	0.0	90.5	0.3	90.5	0.0	91.1	0.7
1981	93.0	2.1	94.4	1.5	94.7	0.3	95.0	0.3	94.9	-0.1	94.9	0.0	95.7	0.8	96.1	0.4	96.1	0.0	96.3	0.2	96.4	0.1	96.6	0.2
1982	98.1	1.6	99.2	1.1	99.6	0.4	99.6	0.0	99.8	0.2	100.2	0.4	100.2	0.0	100.6	0.4	100.5	-0.1	100.7	0.2	100.7	0.0	100.7	0.0
1983	101.9	1.2	102.0	0.1	102.5	0.5	102.9	0.4	102.9	0.0	103.0	0.1	103.6	0.6	103.6	0.0	103.6	0.0	103.2	-0.4	103.2	0.0	104.2	1.0
1984	103.6	-0.6	103.6	0.0	103.6	0.0	103.6	0.0	103.8	0.2	109.5	5.5	108.1	-1.3	110.1	1.9	109.2	-0.8	109.2	0.0	109.0	-0.2	109.8	0.7
1985	111.1	1.2	111.2	0.1	111.0	-0.2	111.2	0.2	111.1	-0.1	110.9	-0.2	110.9	0.0	110.7	-0.2	111.1	0.4	111.1	0.0	112.1	0.9	113.4	1.2
1986	117.5	3.6	117.6	0.1	118.1	0.4	120.8	2.3	120.7	-0.1	120.7	0.0	120.8	0.1	121.7	0.7	121.9	0.2	123.2	1.1	124.4	1.0	125.0	0.5
1987	125.1	0.1	128.0	2.3	128.0	0.0	128.4	0.3	127.9	-0.4	128.7	0.6	129.3	0.5	130.0	0.5	130.2	0.2	130.9	0.5	131.0	0.1	131.1	0.1
1988	132.0	0.7	132.1	0.1	133.8	1.3	136.5	2.0	136.5	0.0	136.7	0.1	137.6	0.7	137.7	0.1	137.7	0.0	137.8	0.1	140.9	2.2	140.9	0.0
1989	140.9	0.0	140.9	0.0	142.0	0.8	144.6	1.8	144.6	0.0	144.8	0.1	144.9	0.1	144.9	0.0	144.8	-0.1	146.1	0.9	145.9	-0.1	146.0	0.1
1990	146.1	0.1	146.1	0.0	146.1	0.0	149.5	2.3	150.2	0.5	150.7	0.3	150.4	-0.2	150.4	0.0	151.0	0.4	151.5	0.3	151.2	-0.2	152.7	1.0
1991	154.6	1.2	153.7	-0.6	156.4	1.8	157.0	0.4	156.7	-0.2	156.9	0.1	158.5	1.0	159.9	0.9	159.8	-0.1	161.1	0.8	158.8	-1.4	159.5	0.4
1992	159.7	0.1	159.8	0.1	160.0	0.1	163.1	1.9	163.7	0.4	163.6	-0.1	166.3	1.7	166.3	0.0	165.5	-0.5	165.5	0.0	164.8	-0.4	164.7	-0.1
1993	165.0	0.2	166.0	0.6	165.3	-0.4	165.0	-0.2	165.5	0.3	166.0	0.3	166.1	0.1	166.7	0.4	166.6	-0.1	166.9	0.2	169.5	1.6	169.9	0.2
1994	169.9	0.0	172.1	1.3	172.2	0.1	172.2	0.0	172.4	0.1	172.6	0.1	173.2	0.3	173.2	0.0	173.2	0.0	173.7	0.3	173.7	0.0	172.9	-0.5
1995	173.6	0.4	173.7	0.1	179.6	3.4	179.7	0.1	179.7	0.0	180.4	0.4	180.4	0.0	180.3	-0.1	180.0	-0.2	177.8	-1.2	178.2	0.2	178.3	0.1
1996	178.4	0.1	182.7	2.4	183.3	0.3	182.1	-0.7	180.2	-1.0	184.7	2.5	183.4	-0.7	183.4	0.0	183.4	0.0	183.8	0.2	183.5	-0.2	183.9	0.2
1997	184.0	0.1	184.6	0.3	186.3	0.9	186.3	0.0	186.4	0.1	186.6	0.1	186.6	0.0	186.8	0.1	186.8	0.0	186.4	-0.2	186.4	0.0	186.5	0.1
1998	186.9	0.2	186.9	0.0	187.1	0.1	191.1	2.1	192.0	0.5	190.0	-1.0	190.8	0.4	190.8	0.0	190.8	0.0	190.9	0.1	191.0	0.1	191.0	0.0
1999	191.0	0.0	191.6	0.3	193.3	0.9	194.7	0.7	194.7	0.0	193.4	-0.7	193.4	0.0	193.4	0.0	193.8	0.2	193.8	0.0	193.8	0.0	193.8	0.0
2000	195.4	0.8	197.6	1.1	197.6	0.0	197.7	0.1	197.8	0.1	197.8	0.0	197.5	-0.2	197.5	0.0	197.5	0.0	197.5	0.0	197.5	0.0	199.9	1.2
2001	202.6	1.4	202.7	0.0	202.7	0.0	202.9	0.1	202.9	0.0	202.8	-0.0	203.1	0.1	203.3	0.1	203.1	-0.1	203.0	-0.0	203.5	0.2	203.5	0.0

Source: U.S. Department of Labor, Bureau of Labor Statistics, Division of Industry Prices and Price Indexes. n.e.c. stands for not elsewhere classified. - indicates no data collected for period or unavailable.

Mining Services
Producer Price Index
Base 1982 = 100

For 1985-2001. Columns headed % show percentile change in the index from the previous period for which an index is available.

Year	Jan Index	%	Feb Index	%	Mar Index	%	Apr Index	%	May Index	%	Jun Index	%	Jul Index	%	Aug Index	%	Sep Index	%	Oct Index	%	Nov Index	%	Dec Index	%
1985	-	-	-	-	-	-	-	-	-	-	100.0	-	99.6	-0.4	99.6	0.0	99.6	0.0	99.5	-0.1	99.2	-0.3	99.0	-0.2
1986	98.8	-0.2	97.0	-1.8	95.9	-1.1	93.7	-2.3	91.7	-2.1	90.7	-1.1	89.6	-1.2	88.8	-0.9	88.7	-0.1	87.6	-1.2	86.9	-0.8	86.7	-0.2
1987	86.5	-0.2	86.2	-0.3	86.4	0.2	86.5	0.1	86.5	0.0	86.3	-0.2	86.5	0.2	87.2	0.8	87.8	0.7	88.5	0.8	89.5	1.1	90.0	0.6
1988	90.6	0.7	91.6	1.1	91.1	-0.5	91.2	0.1	91.0	-0.2	91.0	0.0	90.9	-0.1	90.0	-1.0	89.9	-0.1	89.8	-0.1	89.8	0.0	89.8	0.0
1989	90.4	0.7	90.3	-0.1	90.3	0.0	90.0	-0.3	90.5	0.6	90.7	0.2	91.3	0.7	91.6	0.3	91.2	-0.4	91.4	0.2	91.7	0.3	91.9	0.2
1990	92.8	1.0	93.8	1.1	93.8	0.0	94.4	0.6	94.7	0.3	95.0	0.3	95.0	0.0	95.7	0.7	96.4	0.7	97.4	1.0	97.8	0.4	98.7	0.9
1991	99.6	0.9	99.6	0.0	99.8	0.2	99.5	-0.3	99.6	0.1	99.2	-0.4	99.0	-0.2	98.3	-0.7	97.9	-0.4	97.0	-0.9	96.3	-0.7	97.5	1.2
1992	97.0	-0.5	96.6	-0.4	96.8	0.2	95.6	-1.2	95.7	0.1	93.7	-2.1	94.2	0.5	93.3	-1.0	94.0	0.8	94.3	0.3	94.7	0.4	95.8	1.2
1993	96.3	0.5	98.4	2.2	98.3	-0.1	99.2	0.9	99.2	0.0	99.8	0.6	100.4	0.6	100.5	0.1	101.6	1.1	101.6	0.0	101.7	0.1	102.6	0.9
1994	103.3	0.7	103.3	0.0	102.2	-1.1	101.9	-0.3	101.7	-0.2	102.3	0.6	102.3	0.0	103.1	0.8	103.6	0.5	103.4	-0.2	104.1	0.7	103.9	-0.2
1995	103.6	-0.3	103.5	-0.1	102.7	-0.8	103.0	0.3	103.0	0.0	102.9	-0.1	103.1	0.2	109.0	5.7	110.2	1.1	110.5	0.3	110.5	0.0	110.7	0.2
1996	111.2	0.5	101.9	-8.4	101.9	0.0	103.0	1.1	105.4	2.3	105.6	0.2	108.7	2.9	109.4	0.6	110.0	0.5	110.6	0.5	111.5	0.8	112.2	0.6
1997	113.7	1.3	114.5	0.7	115.3	0.7	116.6	1.1	118.2	1.4	119.5	1.1	120.0	0.4	120.5	0.4	120.8	0.2	121.9	0.9	122.5	0.5	123.3	0.7
1998	124.0	0.6	124.3	0.2	125.1	0.6	125.1	0.0	124.9	-0.2	125.5	0.5	124.4	-0.9	123.6	-0.6	122.2	-1.1	121.7	-0.4	120.8	-0.7	120.4	-0.3
1999	119.5	-0.7	117.3	-1.8	116.5	-0.7	115.0	-1.3	114.7	-0.3	114.1	-0.5	112.7	-1.2	112.5	-0.2	111.0	-1.3	113.8	2.5	116.3	2.2	115.0	-1.1
2000	115.5	0.4	116.3	0.7	116.4	0.1	117.4	0.9	117.3	-0.1	118.6	1.1	121.5	2.4	121.1	-0.3	124.9	3.1	125.4	0.4	128.0	2.1	128.7	0.5
2001	132.2	2.7	137.2	3.8	140.0	2.0	142.7	1.9	144.8	1.5	147.2	1.7	146.9	-0.2	148.4	1.0	148.1	-0.2	145.5	-1.8	142.1	-2.3	142.2	0.1

Source: U.S. Department of Labor, Bureau of Labor Statistics, Division of Industry Prices and Price Indexes. n.e.c. stands for not elsewhere classified. - indicates no data collected for period or unavailable.

Other Miscellaneous Products
Producer Price Index
Base 1982 = 100

For 1947-2001. Columns headed % show percentile change in the index from the previous period for which an index is available.

Year	Jan Index	%	Feb Index	%	Mar Index	%	Apr Index	%	May Index	%	Jun Index	%	Jul Index	%	Aug Index	%	Sep Index	%	Oct Index	%	Nov Index	%	Dec Index	%
1947	23.2	-	23.2	0.0	23.2	0.0	23.4	0.9	23.4	0.0	23.1	-1.3	22.9	-0.9	22.9	0.0	23.0	0.4	23.2	0.9	23.4	0.9	23.4	0.0
1948	23.5	0.4	23.7	0.9	23.7	0.0	23.7	0.0	23.7	0.0	23.8	0.4	23.8	0.0	23.9	0.4	23.9	0.0	23.9	0.0	24.0	0.4	24.2	0.8
1949	24.2	0.0	24.2	0.0	24.2	0.0	23.8	-1.7	23.9	0.4	23.9	0.0	23.7	-0.8	23.7	0.0	23.7	0.0	23.7	0.0	23.9	0.8	23.9	0.0
1950	23.6	-1.3	23.6	0.0	23.6	0.0	23.7	0.4	23.7	0.0	23.6	-0.4	23.7	0.4	24.3	2.5	24.2	-0.4	24.6	1.7	24.7	0.4	25.2	2.0
1951	25.7	2.0	25.7	0.0	25.7	0.0	25.7	0.0	25.7	0.0	25.7	0.0	25.7	0.0	25.7	0.0	25.7	0.0	25.7	0.0	25.7	0.0	25.7	0.0
1952	25.7	0.0	25.7	0.0	25.7	0.0	25.7	0.0	25.7	0.0	25.7	0.0	25.7	0.0	25.7	0.0	25.7	0.0	25.7	0.0	25.7	0.0	25.7	0.0
1953	25.7	0.0	25.7	0.0	25.8	0.4	25.8	0.0	25.7	-0.4	25.7	0.0	25.7	0.0	25.7	0.0	25.7	0.0	25.7	0.0	25.7	0.0	25.7	0.0
1954	25.7	0.0	25.8	0.4	25.9	0.4	26.0	0.4	25.9	-0.4	26.0	0.4	26.0	0.0	26.0	0.0	26.0	0.0	26.1	0.4	26.1	0.0	26.1	0.0
1955	26.0	-0.4	26.0	0.0	26.0	0.0	26.0	0.0	26.0	0.0	26.0	0.0	26.1	0.4	26.2	0.4	26.2	0.0	26.2	0.0	26.3	0.4	26.4	0.4
1956	26.4	0.0	26.4	0.0	26.4	0.0	26.5	0.4	26.5	0.0	26.5	0.0	26.5	0.0	26.5	0.0	26.6	0.4	26.6	0.0	26.7	0.4	26.7	0.0
1957	27.0	1.1	27.1	0.4	27.1	0.0	27.1	0.0	27.1	0.0	27.0	-0.4	27.1	0.4	27.1	0.0	27.2	0.4	27.3	0.4	27.3	0.0	27.3	0.0
1958	27.2	-0.4	27.3	0.4	27.3	0.0	27.3	0.0	27.3	0.0	27.5	0.7	27.4	-0.4	27.4	0.0	27.4	0.0	27.4	0.0	27.4	0.0	27.5	0.4
1959	27.5	0.0	27.5	0.0	27.5	0.0	27.5	0.0	27.5	0.0	27.4	-0.4	27.4	0.0	27.5	0.4	27.5	0.0	27.5	0.0	27.5	0.0	27.7	0.7
1960	27.9	0.7	27.9	0.0	27.9	0.0	27.9	0.0	28.0	0.4	27.9	-0.4	28.0	0.4	28.0	0.0	28.0	0.0	28.0	0.0	27.9	-0.4	28.0	0.4
1961	28.1	0.4	28.1	0.0	28.0	-0.4	27.9	-0.4	28.0	0.4	28.0	0.0	28.0	0.0	28.1	0.4	28.1	0.0	28.1	0.0	28.1	0.0	28.1	0.0
1962	28.0	-0.4	28.0	0.0	28.0	0.0	28.1	0.4	28.1	0.0	28.1	0.0	28.1	0.0	28.1	0.0	28.1	0.0	28.1	0.0	28.2	0.4	28.1	-0.4
1963	28.1	0.0	28.1	0.0	28.1	0.0	28.0	-0.4	28.0	0.0	28.0	0.0	28.0	0.0	28.0	0.0	28.0	0.0	28.0	0.0	28.0	0.0	28.0	0.0
1964	28.1	0.4	28.0	-0.4	28.1	0.4	28.1	0.0	28.1	0.0	28.0	-0.4	28.2	0.7	28.2	0.0	28.2	0.0	28.2	0.0	28.2	0.0	28.2	0.0
1965	28.1	-0.4	28.1	0.0	28.1	0.0	28.1	0.0	28.1	0.0	28.3	0.7	28.6	1.1	28.6	0.0	28.6	0.0	28.6	0.0	28.6	0.0	28.6	0.0
1966	28.7	0.3	28.7	0.0	28.6	-0.3	28.7	0.3	28.7	0.0	28.7	0.0	28.8	0.3	28.9	0.3	28.9	0.0	28.9	0.0	29.0	0.3	29.0	0.0
1967	29.3	1.0	29.3	0.0	29.4	0.3	29.4	0.0	29.5	0.3	29.6	0.3	29.7	0.3	29.7	0.0	29.7	0.0	29.7	0.0	29.8	0.3	29.9	0.3
1968	30.1	0.7	30.1	0.0	30.1	0.0	30.2	0.3	30.2	0.0	30.2	0.0	30.3	0.3	30.4	0.3	30.5	0.3	30.6	0.3	30.6	0.0	30.6	0.0
1969	30.4	-0.7	30.4	0.0	30.5	0.3	30.5	0.0	30.6	0.3	30.9	1.0	31.2	1.0	31.2	0.0	31.3	0.3	31.4	0.3	31.4	0.0	31.4	0.0
1970	31.5	0.3	31.5	0.0	31.5	0.0	31.5	0.0	32.0	1.6	32.1	0.3	32.5	1.2	32.5	0.0	32.6	0.3	32.6	0.0	32.7	0.3	32.7	0.0
1971	32.9	0.6	33.0	0.3	32.9	-0.3	33.1	0.6	33.2	0.3	33.3	0.3	33.5	0.6	33.5	0.0	33.5	0.0	33.5	0.0	33.5	0.0	33.5	0.0
1972	33.7	0.6	33.8	0.3	33.8	0.0	34.0	0.6	34.0	0.0	34.1	0.3	34.7	1.8	34.8	0.3	34.8	0.0	34.6	-0.6	34.5	-0.3	34.6	0.3
1973	35.1	1.4	35.2	0.3	35.4	0.6	36.1	2.0	36.9	2.2	37.6	1.9	38.3	1.9	38.3	0.0	38.3	0.0	37.8	-1.3	37.9	0.3	38.0	0.3
1974	39.0	2.6	39.4	1.0	40.3	2.3	42.4	5.2	42.7	0.7	42.9	0.5	43.1	0.5	42.2	-2.1	42.5	0.7	42.9	0.9	43.1	0.5	43.6	1.2
1975	45.3	3.9	45.8	1.1	46.0	0.4	46.1	0.2	46.2	0.2	46.2	0.0	46.3	0.2	46.3	0.0	46.6	0.6	45.5	-2.4	45.5	0.0	45.8	0.7
1976	46.0	0.4	45.9	-0.2	45.9	0.0	45.0	-2.0	45.0	0.0	45.7	1.6	45.0	-1.5	44.6	-0.9	44.7	0.2	44.8	0.2	44.8	0.0	45.1	0.7
1977	47.4	5.1	47.6	0.4	47.9	0.6	49.4	3.1	49.4	0.0	49.4	0.0	49.4	0.0	49.5	0.2	49.6	0.2	51.2	3.2	51.5	0.6	51.7	0.4
1978	52.5	1.5	51.5	-1.9	52.5	1.9	61.0	16.2	62.3	2.1	62.4	0.2	66.9	7.2	68.1	1.8	69.3	1.8	66.6	-3.9	64.6	-3.0	69.4	7.4
1979	70.3	1.3	72.1	2.6	72.6	0.7	72.7	0.1	74.1	1.9	75.6	2.0	76.8	1.6	77.3	0.7	80.5	4.1	85.2	5.8	86.7	1.8	91.3	5.3
1980	103.9	13.8	111.8	7.6	103.8	-7.2	100.8	-2.9	100.6	-0.2	106.5	5.9	109.6	2.9	107.8	-1.6	112.9	4.7	113.3	0.4	108.5	-4.2	109.5	0.9
1981	107.4	-1.9	105.9	-1.4	103.8	-2.0	103.2	-0.6	103.3	0.1	102.6	-0.7	98.5	-4.0	98.9	0.4	102.1	3.2	103.0	0.9	101.9	-1.1	101.8	-0.1
1982	101.2	-0.6	100.8	-0.4	98.9	-1.9	98.7	-0.2	97.9	-0.8	97.1	-0.8	98.6	1.5	96.7	-1.9	102.0	5.5	102.0	0.0	102.0	0.0	103.9	1.9
1983	103.7	-0.2	106.4	2.6	103.6	-2.6	103.6	0.0	103.2	-0.4	104.5	1.3	104.5	0.0	104.3	-0.2	103.3	-1.0	103.2	-0.1	103.2	0.0	104.4	1.2
1984	103.7	-0.7	103.6	-0.1	104.7	1.1	104.0	-0.7	103.6	-0.4	103.5	-0.1	103.5	0.0	104.4	0.9	102.6	-1.7	103.0	0.4	103.4	0.4	103.5	0.1
1985	102.6	-0.9	103.7	1.1	103.0	-0.7	104.2	1.2	103.9	-0.3	103.7	-0.2	103.5	-0.2	103.4	-0.1	103.3	-0.1	103.4	0.1	103.5	0.1	103.1	-0.4
1986	103.7	0.6	103.9	0.2	104.2	0.3	104.4	0.2	104.5	0.1	104.5	0.0	104.6	0.1	105.1	0.5	105.5	0.4	106.1	0.6	106.0	-0.1	105.8	-0.2
1987	106.4	0.6	106.5	0.1	106.8	0.3	107.2	0.4	107.6	0.4	107.9	0.3	108.1	0.2	108.5	0.4	108.5	0.0	109.0	0.5	109.4	0.4	109.5	0.1
1988	110.0	0.5	109.8	-0.2	109.9	0.1	110.3	0.4	110.6	0.3	110.9	0.3	111.4	0.5	111.6	0.2	111.7	0.1	111.6	-0.1	111.9	0.3	112.1	0.2
1989	112.6	0.4	112.9	0.3	113.3	0.4	113.6	0.3	113.8	0.2	113.9	0.1	114.2	0.3	114.5	0.3	114.6	0.1	114.7	0.1	115.0	0.3	115.4	0.3
1990	116.5	1.0	117.0	0.4	117.4	0.3	117.2	-0.2	117.3	0.1	117.6	0.3	117.6	0.0	118.1	0.4	118.1	0.0	118.5	0.3	118.6	0.1	118.5	-0.1
1991	119.7	1.0	119.8	0.1	120.2	0.3	120.4	0.2	120.5	0.1	120.8	0.2	120.9	0.1	120.6	-0.2	120.4	-0.2	120.6	0.2	120.7	0.1	120.9	0.2

[Continued]

Other Miscellaneous Products
Producer Price Index
Base 1982 = 100

[Continued]

For 1947-2001. Columns headed % show percentile change in the index from the previous period for which an index is available.

Year	Jan Index	%	Feb Index	%	Mar Index	%	Apr Index	%	May Index	%	Jun Index	%	Jul Index	%	Aug Index	%	Sep Index	%	Oct Index	%	Nov Index	%	Dec Index	%
1992	121.6	0.6	121.6	0.0	121.7	0.1	122.2	0.4	122.3	0.1	122.4	0.1	122.5	0.1	122.7	0.2	122.6	-0.1	122.8	0.2	123.1	0.2	123.5	0.3
1993	123.9	0.3	124.2	0.2	124.2	0.0	124.9	0.6	125.3	0.3	125.3	0.0	125.8	0.4	126.0	0.2	125.8	-0.2	125.9	0.1	126.1	0.2	126.6	0.4
1994	126.8	0.2	126.6	-0.2	126.5	-0.1	127.0	0.4	127.3	0.2	127.4	0.1	127.7	0.2	127.7	0.0	127.8	0.1	128.0	0.2	128.4	0.3	128.9	0.4
1995	129.8	0.7	130.3	0.4	130.6	0.2	131.4	0.6	132.0	0.5	132.3	0.2	132.5	0.2	132.6	0.1	132.6	0.0	132.7	0.1	133.1	0.3	132.9	-0.2
1996	133.4	0.4	133.3	-0.1	132.6	-0.5	132.6	0.0	132.5	-0.1	132.7	0.2	132.7	0.0	132.9	0.2	132.6	-0.2	132.8	0.2	132.8	0.0	133.1	0.2
1997	133.3	0.2	133.2	-0.1	133.4	0.2	133.7	0.2	133.4	-0.2	133.5	0.1	133.2	-0.2	133.3	0.1	133.3	0.0	133.8	0.4	133.8	0.0	133.7	-0.1
1998	134.4	0.5	134.7	0.2	134.9	0.1	134.6	-0.2	134.9	0.2	134.5	-0.3	134.6	0.1	134.5	-0.1	134.8	0.2	134.9	0.1	134.6	-0.2	134.5	-0.1
1999	135.0	0.4	135.0	0.0	135.1	0.1	135.0	-0.1	134.9	-0.1	135.1	0.1	135.1	0.0	134.7	-0.3	134.9	0.1	135.4	0.4	135.7	0.2	135.9	0.1
2000	136.3	0.3	136.3	0.0	136.0	-0.2	136.2	0.1	136.4	0.1	136.8	0.3	136.8	0.0	136.6	-0.1	136.6	0.0	136.9	0.2	137.3	0.3	137.4	0.1
2001	137.8	0.3	137.9	0.1	137.9	0.0	138.4	0.4	139.1	0.5	139.1	0.0	138.8	-0.2	139.1	0.2	139.4	0.2	139.1	-0.2	139.1	0.0	139.2	0.1

Source: U.S. Department of Labor, Bureau of Labor Statistics, Division of Industry Prices and Price Indexes. n.e.c. stands for not elsewhere classified. - indicates no data collected for period or unavailable.

CHAPTER 8

SELECTED STOCK MARKET
PRICE INDEXES

SELECTED STOCK MARKET PRICE INDEXES

This chapter presents stock market index data for the American Stock Exchange, the NASDAQ Stock Market, and the New York Stock Exchange. The Standard & Poors composite index, used by the Conference Board as a component of the composite index of leading indicators, is shown in Chapter 3.

General Concepts

Stock indexes measure the value of stocks traded on exchanges or in the over-the-counter (OTC) market.

Index Weightings. All the indexes presented here are so-called "market-value weighted" indexes, also called "capitalization-weighted" indexes. This means that the contribution of any one stock to the index is weighted by the stock's overall value—its price multiplied by the number of its shares outstanding.

A stock (Stock A) with a price of $100 per share and 50,000 shares outstanding has a capitalization of $5 million; another stock (Stock B), with a price of $50 and 30,000 shares outstanding has a capitalization of $1.5 million. If only these two stocks were present in a market, the total market would be valued at $6.5 million. Stock A's contribution to index changes would be 77% ($5 million as a percent of $6.5 million); Stock B's contribution would be 23%. Since prices and the number of shares outstanding are constantly changing—and the number of stocks traded is large—any one stock's contribution to an index is continuously in flux and relatively small.

Indexes are calculated so that the distorting effect of stock splits, mergers, and similar changes in corporate capitalization are eliminated.

Alternatives to the market-value weighted indexes are price-weighted indexes (none is shown in *EIH*). In these indexes, for example, in the American Stock Exchange's Major Market Index and the Dow Jones Industrial Average, high-priced stocks have a greater influence on the index than low-priced issues.

Market-value weighted indexes reflect overall market performance; price-weighted indexes tend to reflect the performance of important, leading stocks.

Index Basing. Index values are expressed in relation to a base—the value of the market on a given date. The *base index* may be any value but is 50, 100, or 550 for the data shown here. Index values are calculated using the following formula:

(Market Today / Base Period Market) x Base Index

We can apply this formula to a situation where the base period market was $1,000, today's market is $1,050, and the base index is 100. The new index will be 105 (1,050 / 1,000 x 100). If a different base index is used, 50, for example, the same formula and values would yield a new index of 52.5.

The total market values ("market today" and "base period market") are obtained by adding, for each period, the capital value of all stocks: each stock's price multiplied by the number of shares of that stock outstanding. This, in effect, produces a market-value weighting of each stock.

Analytical Uses

The most common use of stock market indexes is to measure the performance of a given market or, by combining various indexes, measuring the performance of stocks as a whole. Investors can use stock market indexes to measure how well their portfolios are doing. The indexes included in this chapter are all broad composites; therefore, portfolios that under-perform these indexes may be overdue for review. Stock markets are sensitive indicators of anticipated economic conditions; the sustained rise or fall of composite indexes, therefore, can be used to forecast the future—the future as it is seen by all those buying and selling stocks.

Presentation

The composite indexes for the NASDAQ, New York, and American stock exchanges are presented in the first table. The AMEX Composite Index begins in December 1995 (see below), the others begin in 1984. All other tables in this chapter are specific to one of these three markets.

American Stock Exchange. The AMEX Market Value Index was replaced, in early 1996, by a new AMEX Composite Index with a base of 550 on December 1995. The revision was made to bring the AMEX Composite more in line with other stock indexes. The old Market Value Index included the value of stock dividends paid. The new index is a market capitalization-weighed, price appreciation index. A single table highlights the new AMEX Composite. The table shows highs and lows of the index for the 1995 through 2001 period and the annual close. A monthly presentation of this index is shown alongside the NASD and NYSE indexes in the first table.

The American Stock Exchange is the second largest floor-based exchange in the United States. On November 2, 1998, the exchange became a subsidiary of the National Association of Securities Dealers, Inc. (NASD). AMEX and NASDAQ are operated by the Nasdaq-Amex Market Group, Inc., which is a subsidiary of the NASD.

NASDAQ Stock Market. NASDAQ stands for the National Association of Security Dealers Automated Quotation System; NASDAQ reports the prices of more than 5,000 stocks traded over-the-counter (OTC); this is a relatively small subset of the more than 40 million OTC stock issues traded. The base period for the NASDAQ Price Index is February 5, 1971; the base index is 100. Two tables are included for the NASDAQ index; the first shows high, low, and close data for the 1971 to 1995 period; the second shows quarterly data for 1980 through 1999. In addition to the composite index, data for six sub-indices are also included.

New York Stock Exchange. The New York Stock Exchange (NYSE) is the largest U.S. stock exchange, and the NYSE Composite Index reflects the share prices of more than 1,600 stocks traded on the exchange. The index base period is December 31, 1965 and the base index is 50. Two tables are included to summarize the NYSE's performance. The first shows the index from 1990 to 1999 by quarters. Sub-indices are included. The second shows annual high, low, and close data from 1966 through 1999.

Bibliography

1. Berlin, Howard M. *The Handbook of Financial Market Indexes, Averages, and Indicators*. Dow Jones-Irwin, Homewood, IL, 1990.

2. Downes, John and Jordan Elliot Goodman. *Dictionary of Finance and Investment Terms*. Barron's, New York, 1991.

3. *1997 Amex Fact Book*. American Stock Exchange, New York, 1997 and the AMEX web page, accessed January 25, 2002, www.amex.com.

AMEX, NASD, and NYSE Indexes
1984-2001

For 1984-2001. Index is the closing value at month end. Columns headed % show percentile change in each index from the previous period. The acronyms AMEX, NASD, and NYSE stand for American Stock Exchange, National Association of Securities Dealers (over the counter market), and New York Stock Exchange. The American Stock Exchanged introduced a new index in 1996. The old Market Value Index is not shown. For an explanation of the index and related matters, please see the text.

Year	Month	AMEX		NASD		NYSE	
		Index	%	Index	%	Index	%
1984	JAN		-	268.43	-3.7	94.32	-0.9
	FEB		-	252.57	-5.9	90.44	-4.1
	MAR		-	250.78	-0.7	91.67	1.4
	APR		-	247.44	-1.3	91.98	0.3
	MAY		-	232.82	-5.9	86.71	-5.7
	JUN		-	239.65	2.9	88.38	1.9
	JUL		-	229.70	-4.2	86.73	-1.9
	AUG		-	254.64	10.9	95.86	10.5
	SEP		-	249.94	-1.8	95.77	-0.1
	OCT		-	247.03	-1.2	95.74	-0.0
	NOV		-	242.53	-1.8	94.30	-1.5
	DEC		-	247.35	2.0	96.38	2.2
1985	JAN		-	278.70	12.7	103.75	7.6
	FEB		-	284.17	2.0	104.93	1.1
	MAR		-	279.20	-1.7	104.60	-0.3
	APR		-	280.56	0.5	104.12	-0.5
	MAY		-	290.80	3.6	109.63	5.3
	JUN		-	296.20	1.9	111.11	1.3
	JUL		-	301.29	1.7	110.47	-0.6
	AUG		-	297.31	-1.3	109.47	-0.9
	SEP		-	280.33	-5.7	105.19	-3.9
	OCT		-	292.54	4.4	109.65	4.2
	NOV		-	313.95	7.3	116.55	6.3
	DEC		-	324.93	3.5	121.58	4.3
1986	JAN		-	335.77	3.3	122.13	0.5
	FEB		-	359.53	7.1	130.74	7.0
	MAR		-	374.72	4.2	137.71	5.3
	APR		-	383.24	2.3	135.75	-1.4
	MAY		-	400.16	4.4	142.06	4.6
	JUN		-	405.51	1.3	143.96	1.3
	JUL		-	371.37	-8.4	135.89	-5.6
	AUG		-	382.86	3.1	145.32	6.9
	SEP		-	350.67	-8.4	133.44	-8.2
	OCT		-	360.77	2.9	140.42	5.2
	NOV		-	359.57	-0.3	142.57	1.5
	DEC		-	348.83	-3.0	138.58	-2.8
1987	JAN		-	392.06	12.4	156.11	12.6
	FEB		-	424.97	8.4	162.01	3.8
	MAR		-	430.05	1.2	165.89	2.4
	APR		-	417.81	-2.8	162.86	-1.8
	MAY		-	416.54	-0.3	163.48	0.4
	JUN		-	424.67	2.0	171.07	4.6
	JUL		-	434.93	2.4	178.63	4.4
	AUG		-	454.97	4.6	184.45	3.3
	SEP		-	444.29	-2.3	180.24	-2.3
	OCT		-	323.30	-27.2	140.80	-21.9
	NOV		-	305.16	-5.6	129.69	-7.9
	DEC		-	330.47	8.3	138.23	6.6

[Continued]

AMEX, NASD, and NYSE Indexes
1984-2001

[Continued]

Year	Month	AMEX		NASD		NYSE	
		Index	%	Index	%	Index	%
1988	JAN		-	344.66	4.3	144.13	4.3
	FEB		-	366.94	6.5	150.46	4.4
	MAR		-	374.64	2.1	146.60	-2.6
	APR		-	379.23	1.2	147.87	0.9
	MAY		-	370.34	-2.3	148.04	0.1
	JUN		-	394.66	6.6	154.47	4.3
	JUL		-	387.33	-1.9	153.35	-0.7
	AUG		-	376.55	-2.8	148.29	-3.3
	SEP		-	387.71	3.0	153.57	3.6
	OCT		-	382.46	-1.4	156.94	2.2
	NOV		-	371.45	-2.9	153.90	-1.9
	DEC		-	381.38	2.7	156.26	1.5
1989	JAN		-	401.30	5.2	166.63	6.6
	FEB		-	399.71	-0.4	162.49	-2.5
	MAR		-	406.73	1.8	165.63	1.9
	APR		-	427.55	5.1	173.13	4.5
	MAY		-	446.17	4.4	178.85	3.3
	JUN		-	435.29	-2.4	177.90	-0.5
	JUL		-	453.84	4.3	192.41	8.2
	AUG		-	469.33	3.4	195.27	1.5
	SEP		-	472.92	0.8	193.97	-0.7
	OCT		-	455.63	-3.7	188.24	-3.0
	NOV		-	456.09	0.1	191.30	1.6
	DEC		-	454.82	-0.3	195.04	2.0
1990	JAN		-	415.81	-8.6	181.50	-6.9
	FEB		-	425.83	2.4	183.07	0.9
	MAR		-	435.54	2.3	186.84	2.1
	APR		-	420.07	-3.6	181.49	-2.9
	MAY		-	458.97	9.3	196.94	8.5
	JUN		-	462.29	0.7	195.48	-0.7
	JUL		-	438.24	-5.2	194.60	-0.5
	AUG		-	381.21	-13.0	176.97	-9.1
	SEP		-	344.51	-9.6	167.85	-5.2
	OCT		-	329.84	-4.3	166.17	-1.0
	NOV		-	359.06	8.9	176.06	6.0
	DEC		-	373.84	4.1	180.49	2.5
1991	JAN		-	414.20	10.8	187.59	3.9
	FEB		-	453.05	9.4	200.70	7.0
	MAR		-	482.30	6.5	205.30	2.3
	APR		-	484.72	0.5	205.37	0.0
	MAY		-	506.11	4.4	212.99	3.7
	JUN		-	475.92	-6.0	203.47	-4.5
	JUL		-	502.04	5.5	212.34	4.4
	AUG		-	525.68	4.7	216.69	2.0
	SEP		-	526.88	0.2	213.34	-1.5
	OCT		-	542.98	3.1	216.54	1.5
	NOV		-	523.90	-3.5	207.75	-4.1
	DEC		-	586.34	11.9	229.44	10.4

[Continued]

AMEX, NASD, and NYSE Indexes
1984-2001
[Continued]

Year	Month	AMEX		NASD		NYSE	
		Index	%	Index	%	Index	%
1992	JAN		-	620.21	5.8	226.20	-1.4
	FEB		-	633.47	2.1	228.21	0.9
	MAR		-	603.77	-4.7	223.25	-2.2
	APR		-	578.68	-4.2	228.30	2.3
	MAY		-	585.31	1.1	228.87	0.2
	JUN		-	563.60	-3.7	224.33	-2.0
	JUL		-	580.83	3.1	233.15	3.9
	AUG		-	563.12	-3.0	228.03	-2.2
	SEP		-	583.27	3.6	229.46	0.6
	OCT		-	605.17	3.8	230.57	0.5
	NOV		-	652.73	7.9	237.45	3.0
	DEC		-	676.95	3.7	240.21	1.2
1993	JAN		-	696.34	2.9	241.92	0.7
	FEB		-	670.77	-3.7	244.08	0.9
	MAR		-	690.13	2.9	249.42	2.2
	APR		-	661.42	-4.2	243.46	-2.4
	MAY		-	700.53	5.9	248.60	2.1
	JUN		-	703.95	0.5	249.10	0.2
	JUL		-	704.70	0.1	248.49	-0.2
	AUG		-	742.84	5.4	256.88	3.4
	SEP		-	762.78	2.7	255.23	-0.6
	OCT		-	779.26	2.2	259.38	1.6
	NOV		-	754.39	-3.2	254.79	-1.8
	DEC		-	776.80	3.0	259.08	1.7
1994	JAN		-	800.47	3.0	267.10	3.1
	FEB		-	792.50	-1.0	259.23	-2.9
	MAR		-	743.46	-6.2	247.06	-4.7
	APR		-	733.84	-1.3	250.36	1.3
	MAY		-	735.19	0.2	252.24	0.8
	JUN		-	705.96	-4.0	245.15	-2.8
	JUL		-	722.16	2.3	252.62	3.0
	AUG		-	765.62	6.0	261.99	3.7
	SEP		-	764.29	-0.2	255.52	-2.5
	OCT		-	777.49	1.7	258.61	1.2
	NOV		-	750.32	-3.5	248.41	-3.9
	DEC		-	751.96	0.2	250.94	1.0
1995	JAN		-	755.20	0.4	255.93	2.0
	FEB		-	793.73	5.1	264.65	3.4
	MAR		-	817.21	3.0	271.04	2.4
	APR		-	843.98	3.3	277.31	2.3
	MAY		-	864.58	2.4	286.44	3.3
	JUN		-	933.45	8.0	291.84	1.9
	JUL		-	1001.21	7.3	301.32	3.2
	AUG		-	1020.11	1.9	302.00	0.2
	SEP		-	1043.54	2.3	313.26	3.7
	OCT		-	1036.06	-0.7	309.61	-1.2
	NOV		-	1059.20	2.2	323.59	4.5
	DEC	550.00	-	1052.13	-0.7	329.51	1.8

[Continued]

AMEX, NASD, and NYSE Indexes
1984-2001

[Continued]

Year	Month	AMEX		NASD		NYSE	
		Index	%	Index	%	Index	%
1996	JAN	554.51	0.8	1059.79	0.7	340.03	3.2
	FEB	564.61	1.8	1100.05	3.8	342.80	0.8
	MAR	573.76	1.6	1101.40	0.1	346.92	1.2
	APR	592.94	3.3	1190.52	8.1	351.24	1.2
	MAY	613.15	3.4	1243.43	4.4	358.83	2.2
	JUN	576.28	-6.0	1185.02	-4.7	359.20	0.1
	JUL	537.15	-6.8	1080.59	-8.8	342.70	-4.6
	AUG	556.88	3.7	1141.50	5.6	350.99	2.4
	SEP	568.17	2.0	1226.92	7.5	367.33	4.7
	OCT	561.56	-1.2	1221.51	-0.4	374.50	2.0
	NOV	582.73	3.8	1292.61	5.8	398.43	6.4
	DEC	572.34	-1.8	1291.03	-0.1	392.30	-1.5
1997	JAN	588.77	2.9	1379.85	6.9	411.98	5.0
	FEB	594.24	0.9	1309.00	-5.1	415.51	0.9
	MAR	568.71	-4.3	1221.70	-6.7	398.55	-4.1
	APR	552.91	-2.8	1260.76	3.2	416.94	4.6
	MAY	605.38	9.5	1400.32	11.1	441.78	6.0
	JUN	622.57	2.8	1442.07	3.0	462.44	4.7
	JUL	646.30	3.8	1593.81	10.5	494.50	6.9
	AUG	650.16	0.6	1587.32	-0.4	470.48	-4.9
	SEP	699.26	7.6	1685.69	6.2	497.23	5.7
	OCT	675.75	-3.4	1593.61	-5.5	481.14	-3.2
	NOV	662.11	-2.0	1600.55	0.4	499.10	3.7
	DEC	684.61	3.4	1570.35	-1.9	511.19	2.4
1998	JAN	668.42	-2.4	1619.36	3.1	510.63	-0.1
	FEB	706.23	5.7	1770.51	9.3	544.26	6.6
	MAR	741.63	5.0	1835.68	3.7	572.78	5.2
	APR	746.52	0.7	1868.41	1.8	577.37	0.8
	MAY	714.60	-4.3	1778.87	-4.8	565.28	-2.1
	JUN	721.28	0.9	1894.74	6.5	578.73	2.4
	JUL	706.26	-2.1	1872.39	-1.2	565.27	-2.3
	AUG	565.07	-20.0	1499.25	-19.9	480.60	-15.0
	SEP	621.00	9.9	1693.84	13.0	504.47	5.0
	OCT	645.41	3.9	1771.39	4.6	543.35	7.7
	NOV	663.58	2.8	1949.54	10.1	571.50	5.2
	DEC	688.99	3.8	2192.69	12.5	595.81	4.3
1999	JAN	714.86	3.8	2505.89	14.3	600.44	0.8
	FEB	698.29	-2.3	2288.03	-8.7	586.46	-2.3
	MAR	710.30	1.7	2461.40	7.6	603.59	2.9
	APR	776.97	9.4	2542.85	3.3	634.30	5.1
	MAY	778.74	0.2	2470.52	-2.8	622.26	-1.9
	JUN	797.93	2.5	2686.12	8.7	648.13	4.2
	JUL	788.23	-1.2	2638.49	-1.8	626.07	-3.4
	AUG	775.41	-1.6	2739.35	3.8	612.33	-2.2
	SEP	788.23	1.7	2746.16	0.2	592.79	-3.2
	OCT	800.80	1.6	2966.43	8.0	625.47	5.5
	NOV	823.81	2.9	3336.16	12.5	631.18	0.9
	DEC	876.97	6.5	4069.31	22.0	650.30	3.0

[Continued]

AMEX, NASD, and NYSE Indexes

1984-2001

[Continued]

Year	Month	AMEX Index	AMEX %	NASD Index	NASD %	NYSE Index	NYSE %
2000	JAN	860.25	-1.9	3940.35	-3.2	621.73	-4.4
	FEB	973.23	13.1	4696.69	19.2	592.64	-4.7
	MAR	1005.03	3.3	4572.83	-2.6	647.70	9.3
	APR	922.45	-8.2	3860.66	-15.6	644.16	-0.5
	MAY	904.97	-1.9	3400.91	-11.9	643.60	-0.1
	JUN	935.89	3.4	3966.11	16.6	642.93	-0.1
	JUL	906.44	-3.1	3766.99	-5.0	640.63	-0.4
	AUG	943.48	4.1	4206.35	11.7	674.53	5.3
	SEP	954.31	1.1	3672.82	-12.7	663.04	-1.7
	OCT	909.30	-4.7	3369.63	-8.3	666.02	0.4
	NOV	846.59	-6.9	2597.93	-22.9	629.78	-5.4
	DEC	897.75	6.0	2470.52	-4.9	656.87	4.3
2001	JAN	930.12	3.6	2772.73	12.2	663.64	1.0
	FEB	907.72	-2.4	2151.83	-22.4	626.94	-5.5
	MAR	877.04	-3.4	1840.26	-14.5	595.66	-5.0
	APR	951.78	8.5	2116.24	15.0	634.83	6.6
	MAY	939.63	-1.3	2110.49	-0.3	641.67	1.1
	JUN	917.80	-2.3	2161.24	2.4	621.76	-3.1
	JUL	896.21	-2.4	2027.13	-6.2	616.94	-0.8
	AUG	873.40	-2.5	1805.43	-10.9	587.84	-4.7
	SEP	808.77	-7.4	1498.80	-17.0	543.84	-7.5
	OCT	827.69	2.3	1690.20	12.8	546.34	0.5
	NOV	816.00	-1.4	1930.58	14.2	579.27	6.0
	DEC	847.61	3.9	1950.40	1.0	589.80	1.8

Source: Data obtained from each of the exchanges shown.

American Stock Exchange Composite Index
Yearly High, Low, and Close
1995-2001

For 1995 through December 2001. Dates indicate the date of high and low values reached in the year. Close is the last day of the year. Percent change is from previous year-end.

Year	High		Low		Close	% Change
	Index	Date	Index	Date	Index	
1995	553.58	9/12	433.54	1/30	548.23	-
1996	614.99	5/22	526.60	7/16	572.34	4.4
1997	721.90	10/7	541.20	4/28	684.61	19.6
1998	753.67	4/22	563.75	10/8	699.99	6.4
1999	876.97	12/31	683.61	1/4	876.97	27.3
2000	1036.40	3/23	846.59	11/30	897.75	2.4
2001	958.75	5/18	780.46	9/25	847.61	-5.5

Source: American Stock Exchange.

NASDAQ Composite Index
Yearly High, Low, and Close
1971-2001

For 1971 through 2001. Dates indicate the date of high and low values reached in the year. Close is the last day of the year. Percent change is from previous year-end. The NASDAQ index began on February 5, 1971. Dates shown are in month/day format.

Year	High Index	High Date	Low Index	Low Date	Close Index	% Change
1971	114.12	12/31	99.68	2/22	114.12	-
1972	135.15	12/8	113.65	1/3	133.73	17.2
1973	136.84	1/11	88.67	12/24	92.19	-31.1
1974	96.53	3/15	54.87	10/3	59.82	-35.1
1975	88.00	7/15	60.70	1/2	77.62	29.8
1976	97.88	12/31	78.06	1/2	97.88	26.1
1977	105.05	12/30	93.66	4/5	105.05	7.3
1978	139.25	9/13	99.09	1/11	117.98	12.3
1979	152.29	10/5	117.84	1/2	151.14	28.1
1980	208.15	11/28	124.09	3/27	202.34	33.9
1981	223.47	5/29	175.03	9/28	195.84	-3.2
1982	240.70	12/8	159.14	8/13	232.41	18.7
1983	328.91	6/24	230.59	1/3	278.60	19.9
1984	287.90	1/6	225.30	7/25	247.35	-11.2
1985	325.22	12/31	245.91	1/2	325.22	31.5
1986	411.16	7/3	323.01	1/9	348.83	7.3
1987	455.26	8/26	291.88	10/28	330.47	-5.3
1988	396.11	7/5	331.97	1/12	381.38	15.4
1989	485.73	10/9	378.56	1/3	454.82	19.3
1990	469.60	7/16	325.44	10/16	373.84	-17.8
1991	586.34	12/31	355.75	1/14	586.34	56.8
1992	676.95	12/31	547.84	6/26	676.95	15.5
1993	787.42	10/15	645.87	4/26	776.80	14.7
1994	803.93	3/18	693.79	6/24	751.96	-3.2
1995	1069.79	12/4	743.58	1/3	1052.13	40.0
1996	1316.27	12/9	988.57	1/15	1291.03	22.7
1997	1745.85	10/9	1201.00	4/2	1570.35	21.6
1998	2192.69	12/31	1419.12	10/8	2192.69	39.6
1999	4069.31	12/31	2208.05	1/4	4069.31	85.6
2000	5048.62	3/10	2332.78	12/20	2470.52	-39.7
2001	2859.15	1/24	1423.19	9/21	1950.40	-21.1

Source: The NASDAQ Stock Market, Historical Data Services.

NASDAQ Stock Market Index
Quarterly Index and Sub-Indices

For 1980-1999 by Quarters. Data show closing index for each period.

QTR	Year	Composite Index	Industrials	Banks	Insurance	Financials	Trans-portation	Computers
1	1980	131.00	155.70	93.29	133.26	109.84	105.28	-
2		157.78	185.74	108.34	158.94	136.35	125.10	-
3		187.76	233.90	114.87	176.90	148.74	160.17	-
4		202.34	261.36	118.39	166.81	154.07	164.19	-
1	1981	210.18	264.85	126.96	184.80	168.44	171.81	-
2		215.75	265.68	138.92	198.44	178.53	193.04	-
3		180.03	212.22	128.86	177.56	160.41	166.15	-
4		195.84	229.29	143.13	194.31	176.20	167.77	-
1	1982	175.65	199.05	136.66	188.09	165.00	148.10	-
2		171.30	196.33	130.61	172.49	158.52	151.46	-
3		187.65	213.35	134.16	201.84	177.31	172.50	-
4		232.41	273.58	156.37	226.40	207.50	195.48	-
1	1983	270.80	323.52	169.58	259.19	235.16	230.82	-
2		318.70	392.90	186.70	268.63	269.96	259.46	-
3		296.65	353.52	201.06	262.89	280.58	277.99	-
4		278.60	323.68	203.75	257.63	277.53	280.80	-
1	1984	250.78	283.34	204.09	254.19	270.20	228.19	-
2		239.65	270.65	194.48	244.26	258.28	203.71	-
3		249.94	275.16	209.23	271.59	281.23	224.99	-
4		247.35	260.73	229.77	283.11	298.62	239.29	-
1	1985	279.20	297.37	253.43	326.29	330.37	255.54	-
2		296.20	303.82	290.49	350.14	377.06	261.79	-
3		280.33	284.39	296.10	329.77	365.53	256.52	-
4		325.22	330.17	349.36	382.07	423.49	291.59	-
1	1986	374.72	375.91	403.25	455.06	499.73	340.56	-
2		405.51	409.96	450.45	452.72	543.95	362.92	-
3		350.67	344.16	403.70	425.20	482.84	322.95	-
4		348.83	349.33	412.53	404.14	460.64	348.84	-
1	1987	430.05	454.21	506.19	446.17	527.82	398.87	-
2		424.67	450.71	475.48	433.04	511.97	406.13	-
3		444.29	475.25	489.82	457.39	520.74	418.38	-
4		330.47	338.94	390.66	351.06	406.96	319.21	-
1	1988	374.64	383.67	448.77	397.65	456.39	373.51	-
2		394.66	411.48	455.91	398.36	468.43	374.07	-
3		387.71	388.19	456.94	435.45	473.20	390.74	-
4		381.38	378.95	435.31	429.14	459.34	395.81	-
1	1989	406.73	398.63	458.57	470.56	487.75	412.84	-
2		435.29	421.71	466.03	505.05	513.14	421.25	-
3		472.92	458.97	478.84	533.63	559.54	476.97	-
4		454.82	447.99	391.02	546.01	505.64	498.20	-
1	1990	435.54	450.51	366.25	502.65	466.36	476.70	-
2		462.29	499.01	335.71	506.31	446.61	488.28	-
3		344.51	368.46	249.25	406.56	340.34	389.31	-
4		373.84	406.05	254.91	451.84	359.13	417.07	-
1	1991	482.30	545.03	310.15	548.98	437.31	509.21	-
2		475.92	527.10	327.30	534.39	472.42	513.80	-
3		526.88	590.19	343.52	534.10	521.94	530.73	-
4		586.34	668.95	350.56	601.09	560.79	571.39	-

[Continued]

NASDAQ Stock Market Index
Quarterly Index and Sub-Indices
[Continued]

QTR	Year	Composite Index	Industrials	Banks	Insurance	Financials	Trans-portation	Computers
1	1992	603.77	676.05	396.32	617.46	621.85	604.09	-
2		563.60	601.65	442.93	623.26	666.02	551.92	-
3		583.27	620.85	462.50	705.60	687.31	567.47	-
4		676.95	724.94	532.93	803.91	788.81	634.10	-
1	1993	690.13	713.55	627.47	861.30	860.92	672.01	-
2		703.95	729.52	607.88	853.02	834.96	673.48	-
3		762.78	780.13	698.81	946.00	907.00	701.78	-
4		776.80	805.84	689.43	920.59	892.64	746.26	-
1	1994	727.41	760.80	662.57	864.59	860.68	734.19	201.48
2		706.85	715.83	761.83	880.94	931.59	690.03	188.43
3		760.88	773.25	767.81	942.65	931.93	706.39	212.27
4		743.58	743.47	702.95	921.12	861.99	657.00	229.99
1	1995	818.05	801.44	769.10	1021.77	944.26	701.26	269.10
2		934.53	886.49	849.88	1057.38	1033.25	777.65	336.69
3		1027.57	966.32	962.09	1171.88	1166.12	795.36	360.03
4		1052.13	964.68	1009.41	1292.64	1240.87	816.36	366.13
1	1996	1106.57	1029.59	1056.39	1295.38	1296.98	882.14	382.40
2		1197.45	1119.92	1079.18	1319.56	1306.18	892.01	438.37
3		1221.51	1099.02	1150.46	1340.68	1434.97	844.62	465.99
4		1291.03	1109.63	1273.46	1465.43	1595.10	907.43	518.79
1	1997	1216.93	1010.52	1371.10	1425.24	1661.43	848.54	484.98
2		1438.25	1181.41	1629.86	1655.45	1917.56	969.70	589.21
3		1690.30	1376.36	1903.18	1822.97	2256.92	1118.17	702.79
4		1570.35	1221.03	2083.22	1797.95	2503.68	1064.77	618.66
1	1998	1835.68	1361.76	2216.54	1902.96	2642.44	1220.48	772.99
2		1894.74	1333.96	2122.90	1782.79	2590.67	1154.68	849.07
3		1693.84	1031.72	1731.78	1486.05	2143.61	823.87	853.49
4		2192.69	1304.25	1838.00	1796.79	2601.30	981.21	1134.19
1	1999	2461.40	1386.65	1750.46	2035.09	3045.39	925.99	1305.01
2		2686.12	1631.13	1867.30	2359.46	3800.14	1029.09	1386.34
3		2746.16	1609.39	1683.15	2033.00	2784.23	939.37	1503.79
4		4069.31	2238.97	1691.29	1896.28	3380.35	999.11	2325.40
1	2000	4572.83	4606.48	4381.38	2420.17	1530.54	1928.43	3282.30
2		3966.11	3967.49	3877.23	2106.56	1497.35	1700.16	2518.51
3		3672.82	3778.32	3670.31	2046.65	1779.01	1881.24	2926.95
4		2470.52	2577.02	2456.54	1482.99	1939.45	2193.37	2437.00
1	2001	1840.26	1855.58	1794.30	1230.11	1883.23	2066.26	2230.40
2		2161.24	2180.11	2118.11	1516.34	2105.97	2280.55	2590.69
3		1498.80	1526.38	1460.71	1090.51	2059.82	2285.26	2048.51
4		1950.40	1989.17	1950.40	1389.19	2134.89	2349.04	2386.00

Source: The NASDAQ Stock Market, Historical Data Services.

New York Stock Exchange Composite Index
Yearly High, Low, and Close
1966-2001

For 1966 through 2001. Dates indicate the date of high and low values reached in the year in month/day format. Close is the last day of the year. Percent change is from previous year-end.

Year	High		Low		Close	% Change
	Index	Date	Index	Date	Index	
1966	51.06	2/9	39.37	10/7	43.72	-12.6
1967	54.16	10/9	43.74	1/3	53.83	23.1
1968	61.27	11/29	48.70	3/5	58.90	9.4
1969	59.32	5/14	49.31	7/29	51.53	-12.5
1970	52.36	1/5	37.69	5/26	50.23	-2.5
1971	57.76	4/28	49.60	11/23	56.43	12.3
1972	65.14	12/11	56.23	1/3	64.48	14.3
1973	65.48	1/11	49.05	12/5	51.82	-19.6
1974	53.37	3/13	32.89	10/3	36.13	-30.3
1975	51.24	7/15	37.06	1/2	47.64	31.9
1976	57.88	12/31	48.04	1/2	57.88	21.5
1977	57.69	1/3	49.78	11/2	52.50	-9.3
1978	60.38	9/11	48.37	3/6	53.62	2.1
1979	63.39	10/5	53.88	2/27	61.95	15.5
1980	81.02	11/28	55.30	3/27	77.86	25.7
1981	79.14	1/6	64.96	9/25	71.11	-8.7
1982	82.35	11/9	58.80	8/12	81.03	14.0
1983	99.63	10/10	79.79	1/3	95.18	17.5
1984	98.12	11/6	85.13	7/24	96.38	1.3
1985	121.90	12/16	94.60	1/4	121.58	26.1
1986	145.75	9/4	117.75	1/22	138.58	14.0
1987	187.99	8/25	125.91	12/4	138.23	-0.3
1988	159.42	10/21	136.72	1/20	156.26	13.0
1989	199.34	10/9	154.98	1/3	195.04	24.8
1990	201.13	7/16	162.20	10/11	180.49	-7.5
1991	229.44	12/31	170.97	1/9	229.44	27.1
1992	242.08	12/18	217.92	4/8	240.21	4.7
1993	260.67	12/29	236.21	1/8	259.08	7.9
1994	267.71	2/2	243.14	4/4	250.94	-3.1
1995	331.17	13/12	250.73	3/1	329.51	31.3
1996	398.86	25/11	321.41	10/1	392.30	19.1
1997	514.31	5/12	389.47	11/4	511.19	30.3
1998	600.75	7/17	477.20	10/8	595.81	16.6
1999	663.12	7/16	576.17	10/15	650.30	9.1
2000	677.58	1/9	576.42	25/2	656.87	1.0
2001	666.57	1/2	504.21	21/9	589.80	-10.2

Source: New York Stock Exchange Data Services.

New York Stock Exchange Index
Quarterly Index and Sub-Indices

Data show closing values for the New York Stock Exchange composite index and sub-indices for 1990-2001 by quarters.

Quarter	Year	Composite	Industrial	Transportation	Utility	Finance
1	1990	186.85	227.42	177.41	93.48	140.75
2		195.48	242.35	172.56	91.87	144.75
3		167.85	209.19	130.38	84.41	110.78
4		180.49	223.60	141.49	91.30	122.07
1	1991	205.30	256.82	164.05	93.53	148.94
2		203.47	256.02	169.75	89.19	147.69
3		213.34	266.08	179.93	95.50	159.54
4		229.44	285.82	201.87	102.13	172.68
1	1992	223.25	279.66	200.93	93.70	172.33
2		224.33	277.98	199.68	97.31	178.36
3		229.46	283.52	190.86	102.89	180.96
4		240.21	294.39	214.72	104.83	200.83
1	1993	249.42	299.62	232.00	114.30	218.31
2		249.10	298.44	238.08	231.03	217.33
3		255.23	301.11	251.75	242.72	231.56
4		259.08	315.26	270.48	229.92	216.82
1	1994	247.06	304.56	252.48	208.35	204.19
2		245.16	301.49	242.06	202.68	208.91
3		255.52	320.63	231.66	205.26	205.94
4		250.94	318.10	222.46	198.41	195.80
1	1995	271.04	344.26	252.43	205.07	215.33
2		291.84	370.63	262.99	216.94	235.86
3		313.26	392.66	294.59	234.90	264.89
4		329.51	413.29	301.96	252.90	274.25
1	1996	346.92	439.26	323.40	245.68	292.39
2		359.20	457.35	329.80	254.55	295.83
3		367.33	467.90	327.90	244.28	315.08
4		392.30	494.38	352.30	259.91	351.17
1	1997	398.55	502.88	358.40	257.21	360.32
2		462.44	586.33	414.70	284.53	421.02
3		497.23	626.04	459.79	297.35	469.59
4		511.19	630.38	466.25	335.19	495.96
1	1998	572.78	706.92	525.11	383.00	547.77
2		578.73	714.34	505.02	381.00	560.16
3		504.47	625.42	406.50	384.50	446.80
4		595.81	743.65	482.38	445.94	521.42
1	1999	603.59	755.05	502.47	428.16	540.27
2		648.13	806.64	527.84	498.89	563.16
3		592.79	746.31	448.62	481.98	478.94
4		650.30	828.21	466.70	511.15	516.61
1	2000	647.70	820.42	407.27	509.35	529.09
2		642.93	823.83	384.68	479.57	520.11
3		663.04	818.64	406.35	467.29	624.78
4		656.87	803.29	462.76	440.54	646.95
1	2001	595.66	729.20	454.83	394.69	585.48
2		621.76	765.92	469.65	376.61	626.65
3		543.84	667.82	366.02	340.74	549.41
4		589.80	735.71	438.81	329.84	593.69

Source: New York Stock Exchange. Obtained from the NYSE Web page at www.nyse.com in January 2002.

KEYWORD INDEX

The *Keyword Index* is an alphabetical arrangement of the topics covered in the text and tables of *Economic Indicators Handbook*, 6th edition. The table of contents (page v) provides an alternative means of locating tables. The primary reference numbers that follow subject index terms are page numbers. Cities cited in this index are metropolitan statistical areas (MSAs). The abbreviation 'n.e.c.' stands for 'not elsewhere classified.'

Numbers following p. or pp. are page references.

Numbers following p. or pp. are page references.

Numbers following p. or pp. are page references.

Numbers following p. or pp. are page references.

Numbers following p. or pp. are page references.

Keyword Index

Numbers following p. or pp. are page references.

Numbers following p. or pp. are page references.

Numbers following p. or pp. are page references.

Numbers following p. or pp. are page references.

Numbers following p. or pp. are page references.

Numbers following p. or pp. are page references.

Numbers following p. or pp. are page references.